INTRODUCTION

Historically identified by various terms, the "Developing World" has always existed, but it came into vogue as a concept immediately after the close of World War II in 1945. For the next generation, the "Third World" was the most commonly used term, followed for the next two decades by the "Underdeveloped World." Influenced by trade liberalization, globalization, and the policy agenda known as the Washington Consensus, the term "Developing World" came into prominence in the 1980s. In response, at least one professional organization, the Association of Third World Studies, briefly considered changing its name.

The most commonly asked questions about the "Developing World" focus upon the countries and residents that comprise it, the status of its economy, its political and social characteristics, and its cultural components. At the end of World War II, analysts identified Africa, Asia, and Latin America as the most underdeveloped global regions. Within each were numerous sub-regions, such as South Asia, sub-Saharan Africa, and Latin America's Southern Cone. Over time, the Middle East was added to the mix and the regions were further subdivided. Although the Soviet Union and its East European Bloc often demonstrated advances in scientific achievement, industrial output, or military hardware, it remained an underdeveloped area in terms of the low quality of life for its inhabitants and the lack of civil and human rights, factors that became glaringly apparent with the end of the Cold War in 1991.

Today's conventional wisdom suggests that all but the Group of Seven, or G-7, nations and their periphery fall into the so-called "Developing World." The G-7 is comprised of the world's seven largest industrial nations: United States, Japan, Great Britain, France, Germany, Italy, and Canada, though the industrialized world also includes the other Western European nations, Australia, and New Zealand. By the 1990s Singapore, South Korea, and Taiwan became prosperous nations. The inclusion of the latter three countries suggests that an economic definition of the "Developing World" remains too simplified.

Beyond economic development, analysts came to consider the extent of public participation in the political process. How democratic and representative of its people is any given government? Are human and civil rights secured and protected? What is the availability of basic human services such as education and health care? Are there environmental protections? The assumption is that developed nations are representative democracies where the rights of people are guaranteed, basic human needs are satisfied, and the environment secured from various forms of pollution. Although several of the developed nations fall short in some of these categories, the absence of most is a characteristic of the "Developing World."

The logo map used in the publications of the Association of Third World Studies substantiates the given economic, political, and social definitions of the "Developing World." The G-7 nations and their periphery are absent from that map.

The assistance programs sponsored by the developed world since 1945 reflect the changing definition of the "Developing World." Immediately after World War II, assistance focused upon improvement in infrastructure—roads, ports, electricity, water supplies, and the like—to provide for increased opportunities to export primary products, including raw materials. By the late 1950s and into the early 1960s, assistance programs shifted direction. The end of colonialism, the independence of India and Indonesia, the emergence of new and independent nations in Africa, and Fidel Castro's Revolution in Cuba brought an awareness of the need to focus upon economic opportunities for the general population, improvement in quality of life, and the right of a nation's people to political participation and civil and human rights. These goals remained the objectives of programs sponsored by government and non-government organizations that continued into the 1980s when world politics again shifted. Identified best by the Washington Consensus, a set of suggested reforms set forth for Latin America by the economist John Williamson in 1989, this change in policy by developed nations cut back on their international assistance programs and, instead, called upon the nations of the "Developing World" to remove their protective barriers against foreign investment, provide for the privatization of state owned industries and for increased exports, particularly of so-called niche products. As they invited developing nations to enter the global arena, developed nations increased their pressure on developing nations to

democratize the political process, protect civil and human rights, and encourage environmentalism. International agreements since the 1980s often contain provisons for the implementation of plans to address these human needs.

Despite the good intentions, the "Developing World" persists. Poverty, with its concomitant shortcomings in education, health care, housing, and other basic human needs, remains a reality for a disproportionate number of the world's inhabitants. Political democracy and civil and human rights are not universally guaranteed. Environmental pollution continues to go unchecked, taking its most devastating toll upon the "Developing World."

As the twenty-first century dawned, many analysts queried the advisability of imposing the developed world's criteria for modernization upon the "Developing World." The histories of the world's regions varied with their own political experiences, their own ethnic and religious conflicts, and their political, religious, and social traditions that resist and in some cases, outright defy modernization as envisioned by the developed world.

The *Encyclopedia of the Developing World* provides a ready reference work for understanding the issues that affect approximately three quarters of the globe's residents. The *Encyclopedia* is unique because of its focus upon the post 1945 period when the old colonial structures in Africa, Asia, and the Middle East crumbled and elsewhere, as in China, Japan, and Latin America the traditional elite structure has been replaced by something new. During the same time period, the "Developing World" began to demand a greater share of the world's economy and an improvement in quality of life, along with social justice, political participation, and individual liberties.

How to Use This Book

The *Encyclopedia of the Developing World* is composed of almost 800 free-standing entries of 500 to 5000 words in length. They range from factual narratives, such as country descriptions and biographies, to thematic interpretations and analytical discussions of timely topics like global trading patterns, and a combination of all three, such as overview articles on the history and economic development of a particular region. As much as possible, the encyclopedia covers the history, economic development, and politics of the developing world from 1945 to the present, providing the reader with a reliable, up-to-date view of the current state of scholarship on the developing world.

Perhaps the most significant feature of the encyclopedia is the easily accessible **A to Z format**. Cross-referencing in the form of **See Alsos** at the end of most entries refers the reader to other related entries. Each article contains a list of **References and Further Reading**, including sources used by the writer and editor as well as additional items that may be of interest to the reader. Most books or articles cited are easily available through interlibrary loan services in libraries. **Blind Entries** direct readers to essays listed under another title. For example, the blind entry "World Bank" refers the reader to the article entitled with that institution's official name, "International Bank for Reconstruction and Development." A thorough, analytical **index** complements the accessibility of the entries, easing the reader's entry into the wealth of information provided. A **thematic list of entries** is also included to assist readers with research in particular subjects.

Each country has a stand-alone entry, but also is included in larger regional studies. For example, discussion of Chile can be found under the country's entry, but its place in regional matters can be found in "Southern Cone (Latin America): History and Economic Development"; "Southern Cone (Latin America): International Relations"; and "Ethnic Conflicts: Southern Cone (Latin America)." There are stand-alone entries for important individuals, like Jomo Kenyatta, but for context readers should also refer to the country entry on Kenya and the topical entries, such as "Colonialism: History" and "Colonialism: Legacies," to more fully understand Kenyatta's philosophy and objectives. The discussion of "Development History and Theory" is augmented by the entry "Development, Measures of." Both are enhanced by the discussions of the various economic models: capitalist, communist, socialist, and so on. The cross-references will lead readers from stop to stop on such paths throughout the encyclopedia, and the index is another good starting place to find the connected discussions.

A total of 251 authors have contributed the entries to this encyclopedia. They are based around the world, in both developing and developed nations, including Argentina, Australia, Austria, Belgium, Bulgaria, Cameroon, Canada, China, Egypt, France, Germany, Hungary, India, Israel, Japan, Kenya, Malaysia, Mexico, the Netherlands, New Zealand, the Philippines, Poland, Romania, Singapore, South Africa, Sweden, Switzerland, Thailand, the United Arab Emirates, the United Kingdom, the United States, and Zimbabwe. In keeping with the global and interdisciplinary nature of this encyclopedia, contributors represent a variety of fields, among them finance, religion, anthropology, geography, environmental science, and law, with

subspecialties such as global business, human rights, ethics, and refugee studies. The expertise of a wide-ranging and diverse group of contributors will provide the reader with a broad-based overview of issues, events, and theories of the developing world.

Acknowledgments

Several people helped to bring this work to its completion. A special thanks goes to Lorraine Murray of Fitzroy Dearborn Publishers, who kindly provided me the opportunity to undertake this project and to Mark L. Georgiev at the Taylor and Francis imprint of Routledge, for directing its completion following Routledge's acquisition of the project from Fitzroy Dearborn. The guidance offered by the Board of Advisors—Ade Adefuye, Akwasi B. Assensoh, Nader Entessar, Stephen Fischer-Galati, Alexander Gungov, Harold Isaacs, Gary Kline, Paul J. Magnarella, John Mukum Mbaku, Alojzy Z. Nowak, Philip Oxhorn, Paul A. Rodell, Houman A. Sadri, Barbara Tenenbaum and Pamela A. Zeiser—ensured the *Encyclopedia's* comprehensiveness. The expertise of each author made possible the accuracy and completeness of the 762 entries. The editorial efforts by Mark O'Malley and particularly Rachel Granfield made this a more readable work. As always, Yvonne offered the encouragement, support, and understanding that only a wife could. This work is dedicated to her.

Thomas M. Leonard

O

OCEANIA: HISTORY AND ECONOMIC DEVELOPMENT

Most people take "Oceania" to mean the Pacific basin, comprising the geographical areas of Micronesia, Polynesia, and Melanesia (originally proposed by the French explorer and writer Jules-Sébastien-César Dumont d'Urville in 1832). For many researchers, Oceania also includes the large island-continent of Australia. Australia, however, is treated separately in most sources, except when dealing with its Aboriginal, pre-1788 inhabitants. Papua New Guinea (Melanesia) and Aotearoa/New Zealand (Polynesia) are prominent places in Oceania; these places are often excluded from the region because Papua New Guinea is large and Aotearoa/New Zealand, like Australia, has mainly a European settler population.

The mainly Austronesian-speaking discoverers and settlers of this vast region (excluding the much older arrival of humans to Australia) have their origins in southern China and Taiwan. For more than five thousand years, these voyaging peoples spread their language and culture from Madagascar in the west to Hawaii and Rapanui (Easter Island) in the east in what was the most extensive geographical coverage of any language group, until the epoch of European colonialism, commencing a little more than five hundred years ago.

Particularly in the first millennium of the Common Era, it is likely that extensive trading but not territorial empires existed; trading linked all these dispersed peoples in networks of commercial and social interaction. Evidence of this can be found in the distribution of natural resources, such as obsidian (a volcanic product), much-valued red bird feathers, and hard basalt, throughout the region. Older Oceanic genealogies show, for example, that Fiji, Tonga, and Samoa share a number of ancestors with spouses who traded extensively. The firmest evidence of this region-wide trade is found in the distribution of Lapita pottery, which is found on nearly every island that people had settled, even after its manufacture had ceased. This epic voyaging and contact diminished with the radical climate change of the "1300 Event," so-called because it can be detected in the archaeology of Oceania (and the rest of the planet, of course) at around 1300 AD and is frequently termed The Little Ice Age. This age broke long-distance contacts, reducing trade to local archipelagos, and the trade eventually became curtailed with the intrusion and imposition of European webs of alliance and control.

There have been speculations that Chinese and South Asian navigators may have explored Oceania extensively during this yearly period. These speculations are largely based on inference from early European sources, but nothing substantial has been found to date of any expeditions that may have come from those places.

The first European explorers in Oceania were Spanish, Dutch, and Portuguese who were seeking new wealth and fields of exploitation. Apart from settlements on the rim, these ventures used Oceania as a pathway for shipping their riches between New World and Asian ports for two centuries, with imprecise maps and occasional reports of new peoples (and

possibilities) found. For that early time, shipping and piracy were the main forms of economic development; only Guam had a foreign settlement as an outfitting and repair station for the Spanish galleons plying the waters between the Philippines and the Americas.

The eighteenth century saw new Europeans seeking to replace old empires in the Americas, often bringing their home rivalries with them to battle in distant colonial lands. France and Britain were the superpowers of the eighteenth and nineteenth centuries, and both countries sponsored complex and well-provisioned expeditions for scientific, economic, and, as always, military advantages. James Cook and the Comte de La Pérouse charted new lands (to Europeans) to be sure, but they also developed strategically important ways of finding such places that soon became part of naval armaments in recurring conflicts in Europe and around the world. European explorers and military investigators of this era are often erroneously called in the older literature "discoverers" of various places; some cases document Europeans arriving on uninhabited (when they arrived) places, but mostly Europeans mapped places already discovered and settled by indigenous peoples for centuries.

Whaling and exotic commodities, such as Béche-de-Mer (a sea slug valued in Asia for medicinal properties) and sandalwood, were early exploitations in Oceania, with colonial settlement following soon after. Whaling not only provided wealth for German, English, and American whalers, it gave the peoples of Oceania a way to escape their own islands and to seek advantage as crew and missionary assistants on a larger stage. Crews were multiethnic, with Asians and Europeans jostling Oceanians from north and south. The major whaling ports of Lahaina (on Maui in the Hawaiian chain), Bay of Plenty (New Zealand), and Sydney were cosmopolitan capitals with Oceanians from all over the region, many meeting one another for the first time in centuries. Such crews also brought back to their islands cash capital and new goods, often weaponry, altering local power balances forever.

Even the visits of these whaling expeditions changed power structures as one side of an island provided safe harbour and acquired European gunnery, whilst another side languished in outsider material neglect. Although not the case everywhere, on the whole islanders favoured shallow lagoons, rich in easily exploited shore life, with abundant rainfall for crops. The outsider navigators sought deep harbours, safe from disturbing storms, that before had been the less affluent areas for islander settlement.

The great early impulse in the economic development of Oceania was the quest for the Great South Land, where fabulous peoples and wealth were meant to exist. After it was shown that such a place did not exist, the next obsession was for a northwest passage that could connect the European Atlantic with the rich pickings of the Asian Pacific. That, too, proved to be a forlorn hope.

The products of the whale, from its blubber to features of its body, provided the world with many products that in more recent times have been replaced by petroleum-based fuels and plastics. Sea voyages of three and four years were common in nineteenth-century Oceania, and small places with new ports developed from remote communities were becoming part of a vibrant network of trade, resource exploitation, migration, and communications. People in Honolulu were in regular contact and exchange with family and associates in Auckland, New Zealand. Sydney, Australia, and Levuka (later removed to Suva), Fiji, exchanged goods, letters, and news with Santiago, Chile, and San Francisco, California, part of the growing northern Pacific power, the United States of America (San Francisco was once in northern Mexico).

The peoples of the Pacific Islands, with new belief systems through missionaries and new nationalities through colonial conquest, also learned new skills in manufacture, trade, and habit that profoundly altered their societies. Most notably, islanders who lived inland were encouraged to gather around the trader's outpost, then the church, and later the administrative centre. Cities became a dominant form of living; in the twenty-first century, Oceania, including Australia, is one of the most urbanised regions on the planet.

Although never as much a scourge as in Africa, there were episodes of forced labour in Oceania by Europeans of the relatively small populations of the Pacific islands. Rim countries sought labourers. Agricultural and domestic workers were dragooned into a short-lived trade from Eastern Oceania into Peru in 1862–1863; similarly, field hands were imported into Australia to solve a sugar industry labour shortage. "Blackbirding," an Australian term signifying the historic practice of separating out and discriminating against aborigines, as well as discriminating against people of non-European origins through immigration policies, was a general and single entrepreneurial enterprise that was condemned by authorities but welcomed quietly by plantation owners.

Blackbirding came about in various forms after the abolition and general condemnation of slavery, early in the emerging republics of Latin America, later by half a century in the United States. Blackbirding, whether by force, deceit, or lures of wealth, supplied a good part of agricultural labour in Fiji (until South Asian immigration schemes developed from 1879) and, especially, in Australia. So-called "Kanaks" (from the Hawaiian word for "human" or "person") were the

foundation of plantation development in Australia's tropical north until the practice was ended in 1901 by the first Act of the New Commonwealth of Australia: the "White Australia" policy called for residues of those former migrants to be forcibly repatriated, and only a handful of descendants of those tens of thousands remaining in the country today.

Whaling waned, and sun-dried coconut meat ("copra") as well as sugar became less important economic activities, with military colonialism taking over in the twentieth century as the dominant mode of production. Troop installations, weapons testing by various powers, and two major conflicts (World Wars I and II) brought economic development to Oceania, often at a very high cost in lives and the destruction of fragile environments.

As the twentieth century's most extensive wars closed, military testing and the construction of military bases slowed down, and tourism came to prevail as the prime mode of economic development for Oceania. No state or territory of Oceania today lacks its tourism development plan, with islanders pinning their hopes and skills on people from the developed world coming to spend their leisure time (and much larger wealth) in resorts and on beaches throughout the region. Whilst there are various devices for telling one "brand" of island tourism from another, the image continuity in beach, sun, and languid days is pervasive; most brochures show a poolside/beach-front folding lounge chair with a waving palm. An occasional Oceanic face or body may be added for decoration.

The exploitation of primary resources remains a watery feature of Oceanic economic development, with fisheries being a major industry at present. Terrestrial resource development is a feature of the larger Melanesian lands of Papua New Guinea, New Caledonia (still the largest nickel mine in the world), and the Solomon Islands; there is even a small but thriving gold industry in Fiji.

Table 1: 2004 Pacific island populations, areas, and densities

Country, state, or territory	Population estimate in mid-2004	Land area (km^2)	Exclusive economic zones (EEZ) (000s km^2)	Population density (land)
American Samoa	62,600	200	390	313
Cook Islands	14,000	237	1,830	59
Easter Island (Rapanui)*	4,446	166	2,930	27
Federated States of Micronesia	112,700	701	2,978	161
Fiji	836,000	18,272	1,290	46
French Polynesia	250,500	3,521	5,030	71
Guam	166,100	541	218	307
Kiribati	93,100	811	3,550	89
Marshall Islands	55,400	181	2,131	306
Nauru	10,100	21	320	481
New Caledonia (Kanaky)	236,900	18,576	1,740	13
Niue	1,600	259	390	6
Northern Mariana Islands	78,000	471	1,823	166
Palau (Belau)	20,700	488	629	42
Papua New Guinea	5,695,300	462,840	3,120	12
Pitcairn	47	39	800	1
Samoa (formerly Western Samoa)	182,700	2,935	120	62
Solomon Islands	460,100	28,370	1,340	16
Tokelau	1,500	12	290	125
Tonga	98,300	650	700	151
Tuvalu	9,600	26	900	369
Vanuatu	215,800	12,190	680	18
Wallis and Futuna	14,900	142	300	105
South Pacific	8,620,393	551,649	33,499	128
South Pacific (excluding Papua New Guinea)	2,925,093	88,809	30,379	139

Note: All data from Secretariat, Pacific Community (http://www.spc.org.nc/demog/) published July 2004.
* Rapanui (Easter Island) population is based on genealogical fieldwork of Grant McCall, carried out in 2001–2002 and projected at an approximate growth of fifty persons per year. EEZ is based on the Chilean Navy for Rapanui alone with a 12-mile limit. With a 350-nautical mile limit ("continental shelf"), the figure is 1,934,433 square kilometers including neighbouring and uninhabited Salas y Gomez, part of the Chilean Province of Easter Island.

A major source of economic development for some of the island Pacific is through remittances sent from rim states to relatives in home villages. This has led to the famous concept of MIRAB by Bertram and Watters, whereby some dependent economies are analysed as consisting of **MI**gration, **R**emittances, **A**id, and **B**ureaucracy, to form the sometimes contested MIRAB acronym. MIRAB is not solely an Oceanic mode of economic development, but the conception derives from that part of the world.

The future of Oceania lies in the development of its potential in human and natural resources. Given the rate of exploitation, fish stocks already are declining at the beginning of the twenty-first century. Marine exploitation has discovered rich caches of mineral resources in Oceania that are still too costly to exploit: the area around Pitcairn Island, for example, may contain one of the largest diamond deposits in the world. Similar deep-sea mining has already been imagined in the ministries and boardrooms of Pacific rim nations, a kind of twenty-first century version of the fabled "Great South Land" sought so eagerly centuries before but submerged under costly megalitres of ocean water.

The people of Oceania as a group are amongst the most literate in the developing world and speak some of the most important world languages for the present and future, such as Chinese (Mandarin and Cantonese), English, French, Hindi, and Spanish, along with their own nearly one thousand indigenous tongues. Oceanic governments through the Forum and the Secretariat of the Pacific Community are moving rapidly to increase cooperation and the development of their people's potential to face the challenges for inhabitants of one-third of the Earth's surface, Oceania!

GRANT MCCALL

References and Further Reading

Borofsky, Robert, ed. *Remembrance of Pacific Pasts*. Honolulu: University of Hawaii Press, 2000.

Campbell, I. C. *Worlds Apart: A History of the Pacific Islands*. Christchurch, New Zealand: Canterbury University Press, 2003.

Crocombe, Ron. *The South Pacific*. Suva: Institute of Pacific Studies, The University of the South Pacific, 2001.

Foucrier, Annick, ed. *The French and the Pacific World*. Aldershot, United Kingdom: Achgate Variorum 2000, 2003.

Hau'ofa, Epeli, *et al*. *A New Oceania. Rediscovering Our Sea of Islands*. Suva: Pearson School of Social and Economic Development, the University of the South Pacific, 1993.

Howe, K. R. *Where the Waves Fall*. Honolulu: University of Hawaii Press, 1989.

Lockwood, Victoria, ed. *Globalization and Culture Change in the Pacific Islands*. Upper Saddle River, NJ: Pearson Education, 2004.

Nunn, Patrick. *Oceanic Islands: The Natural Environment*. Oxford: Blackwells, 1994.

Sand, Christophe, ed. *Pacific Archaeology*. Nouméa, New Caledonia: Departement Archéologie, Service des Musées et du Patrimoine, 2003.

Spate, O. H. K. *Paradise Found and Lost*. Canberra: Australian National University Press, 1988.

Tcherkezoff, Serge. "'First contacts' in Polynesia: The Samoan Case (1722–1843)." *Western Misunderstandings About Sexuality and Divinity, Canberra, & Christchurch: The Journal of Pacific History*. The Macmillan Brown Centre for Pacific Studies, 2004.

OCEANIA: INTERNATIONAL RELATIONS

Few geographic areas in the world are as diverse in terms of peoples, environments, and cultures as Oceania. The vast region contains thousands of contrasting islands, more than six million inhabitants, and hundreds of languages. Composed of Micronesia, Melanesia, and Polynesia, it stretches north from Australia and New Zealand to Alaska and west from the South American coast to the Philippines. Population centres within this expanse range from large urban hubs to isolated atolls whose only outside contact is an occasional freighter entering the port.

Oceania is as culturally as it is geographically heterogeneous. Anthropologists have described Micronesia and Polynesia as retaining a relatively high degree of social stratification and centralised political authority. Melanesia has been perceived as different; traditionally, there was greater egalitarianism and more decentralised politics through multiple clans; an array of chiefs and little chiefs; and familial, adoption, and marriage processes that were primarily group affairs.

Although Oceania was one of the last areas to be "discovered" by European explorers, Pacific islanders have coped with varying levels of Western contact since the early sixteenth century. The cultural divergence found within Oceania is important but less so for contemporary peoples than the region's rapid entry into the development processes engendered by globalising capitalist societies. The historic domination of colonial powers restructured indigenous societies, and Oceania was one of the last areas to enter the post-World War II period of decolonisation and development. Its contemporary societies are experiencing similar transformations in their respective adaptations to neocolonial and postcolonial forces of change. Consequently, most island societies can now be understood within a postcolonial framework that clarifies the political narratives, authorities, and loyalties of colonial repercussions.

Commentators note that once independence in most island-states in the region had been gained, the fundamental opposition between indigenous people and colonial powers was displaced by a more disparate array of local divisions. Differences between diverse indigenous populations, the exacerbation of conflict and suppression of warfare during the colonial period, uneven development, and corruption have found their expression in many conflicts, the most obvious that of the Bougainville war. Because Bougainville's copper was a major source of income for Papua New Guinea (45% of national export earnings), its people's aspirations for self-determination were met with violent repression. Resentment over the loss of control of hereditary lands, the transfer of mining revenues to the central government, and concern for environmental damage led to a separatist rebellion that forced the mine to close in mid-1989.

Its astonishing diversity of cultures ensure that Oceania as a region, an imagined world, and a conglomeration of island-states whose peoples are constantly evolving within an increasingly globalising economic and political environment, is never static. Anthropologists claim that, occasionally, the scenarios they study become history before their observations are printed, particularly when tribal societies encounter the modern world and then change rapidly. What continues, what has been modified, and what is discarded can be noted, but how does one describe a society in which some practices change while others continue? The Massim region is used as an example to show how people continue to participate in *kula* exchange but in contexts radically different from those first reported. Whereas people once traveled by outrigger canoe and communicated by conch shell, they now use outboard launches and telephones.

Despite Oceania's cultural variety and the diffusion of a cash economy, commentators note that certain classes of objects remain important in the maintenance of interisland and local international relations. Objects vary greatly from one place to another. They range from strings of button-sized seashell discs arranged in tyre-like coils to ochre crescents cut from pearl-shell valves and from elaborate ornaments of dogs' teeth to enormous decorated yam tubers, but the contexts in which people transact their goods and the principles underlying their exchange are similar. Oceanic peoples use objects as culturally evocative and powerful symbols to construct new identities and relationships in and through "traditional" celebrations. They create new realities through ongoing and vital ideas and practices that are used to provide continuity with, and contrast to, their indigenous views of the past.

Observers also propose that the larger ethnic categories that have resonance for contemporary Oceanic peoples are not the new concepts of nation-state but are of the older geographic, ethnological, and cultural divisions of Melanesia and Polynesia, an important understanding for development planners and theorists of international relations. It is argued that Melanesia, Polynesia, and present archipelago nations such as Vanuatu are historical categories that evolved in the nineteenth century from the discoveries of peoples and places and have been legitimated by use and further research in the region. Although, as categories, they consist of linguistic, biological, and cultural affinities that create a sense of sameness, this does not mean there is cultural uniformity. Nonetheless, cultural uniformity can be constructed for political purposes. In Papua New Guinea, for example, Bernard Narokobi aimed to define "a Melanesian way" to support his ideology for postindependence rule, as did Jean-Marie Tjibaou in his appeal during the 1980s to Kanak people to agitate for New Caledonian independence from France. Indigenous leaders' appeals to commonality frequently do not correspond with contemporary island-state borders but with wider cultural regions that bear European names and were formed by precolonial trading relationships.

Oceania and International Powers

The myth of Oceania has been part of the French imagination since the eighteenth century, and, in the twenty-first, it continues to influence both the Fifth Republic and development policies for Oceanic islanders. For many French artists and writers, however, it was the Polynesian islands rather than Oceania *en masse* that crystallised their dreams and fueled their sexualised desires. Historians write that Bougainville's reports of his voyage to Polynesia were so compelling that his perceptions shaped metropolitan imaginings for more than 200 years. From a more pragmatic perspective, Britain rivaled France throughout the nineteenth century for commercial supremacy in Oceania. Captain Cook aimed to bring commerce and civilisation to the known world via *pax britannica*. In contrast to Polynesia, Melanesia has generated less interest, even though French colonies were established in the archipelagos of New Caledonia and Vanuatu. In contemporary times, many islanders identify strongly with their own island or region, but sharp contrasts remain between the dynamism and mineral wealth of Melanesian countries and the picturesque Pacific atolls that lack basic resources.

Late to be colonised, except for the Spanish intervention in Micronesia, Oceania was among the last of the world's regions to enter the cycle of decolonisation. Decolonisation began in 1962 when Western Samoa achieved independence from New Zealand and continued throughout the 1980s and 1990s, with the political independence of French Polynesia and New Caledonia still unresolved in the twenty-first century. Since the end of World War II, the international movements toward decolonisation and the recognition of the rights of indigenous peoples have framed the questions Oceanic communities have posed about their future in relation to sovereignty, self-determination, and indigenous rights. In American Samoa and the Northern Mariana Islands, for example, decolonisation movements have influenced the United States perceptions of its obligations as an administering power, and indigenous rights have fueled political and legal moves in Hawaii for the peoples to gain recognition as original islanders.

Following World War II, the 1947 Canberra Agreement led to the creation of the South Pacific Commission and provided a focus for Australia and New Zealand to offer technical assistance to Oceanic island-states. In contrast, US policies have been erratic; from 1962 to 1976, the United States was not attentive to Oceanic peoples' needs. The United States altered its treatment of Oceania in 1977 when the Carter administration reacted to Soviet initiatives and to accelerating socioeconomic change in the region. Consequently, the first comprehensive Pacific policies were generated. But once again, US awareness vanished in 1981 and throughout the Reagan administration until 1987. During this period, the US image was damaged through perceived and actual neglect of Oceania's island-states and continuous disputes over fishing rights. Concerns remain about the adequacy of US involvement and goodwill in Oceania.

Most development in relation to French power in Oceania since World War II has been driven by nuclear testing. When the war in Algeria ended, France had to reduce its program in the Algerian hinterland. The establishment of the nuclear testing centre in French Polynesia introduced profound economic and social changes, not just to the atolls of Moruroa and Fangataufa, as significant financial aid was introduced to the whole territory. When the test sites were closed in 1996, French Polynesia laboured to reintegrate with the broader Oceanic region.

New Caledonia, an archipelago and French overseas territory, has endured a more erratic development process. During the events of the mid-1980s, when indigenous Kanak peoples barricaded roads to and from the capital Nouméa and agitated for political independence, France developed a policy for New Caledonia that began to focus on the islanders' needs. Critics now argue that New Caledonians suffer from political neglect as policy has since fluctuated, is dominated by short-term interests, is heavily dependent on the whims of succeeding waves of French politicians, and is usually treated as a low priority.

New Caledonians, like many Oceanic peoples, are experiencing rapid social change generated by globalisation processes. There has been an increase in the number of indigenous Kanak people who squat in makeshift cabins on the outskirts of Nouméa, and there have been changes to the way Kanak people dress. In addition, many young people listen to Radio Kanaky, a station that informs them of events taking place in their rural communities and that plays an array of Pacific island music. Many Kanak people also discuss their aspirations for items considered desirable in the West, such as a car and a home with modern conveniences, and they express a need for leisure time, such as watching television or engaging in sports such as volleyball or windsurfing.

Although rapid local development has been anchored in a history of colonisation that was racist and denigrating to Kanak peoples, the peoples have nonetheless appropriated the foreign and the new. Their ways of being have been shaped by their recognition of their location in international and regional relations, such as Japan's use of New Caledonia's waters for tuna fishing and France's appropriation of the main island's nickel reserves. They have adapted and acted within the changing social relations wrought by industry and tourist development. Some social commentators argue that the serious problem New Caledonia has faced over the final two decades of the twentieth century, and that has also worked toward political and administrative independence, is rooted in two opposing conceptions of life. The conceptions of progress and development, in contrast to that of tradition and custom, go beyond the ethnic cleavage of the French settler and Kanak indigenous person.

Social change is a concomitant to development in Oceania as is also true elsewhere. Researchers show how the rhetoric and the structure of relations concerned with marriage have been transformed under the direct influences of colonialism and are now being changed by urbanisation, Western-style education, and the introduction of a cash economy.

Yet, as occurred in many Oceanic islands, traders, settlers, ex-convicts, and rural police often cohabited with island women. The resulting children were assimilated into the indigenous or the settler communities. In contemporary Oceania, people of mixed heritage now work to provoke a different awareness, that of the

opportunities and problems that challenge Pacific peoples through their contribution to global *and* local communities. Researchers trace the historical process whereby a specific marriage system is being converted into another, changing in relation to its context. In addition, mixed heritage people discuss the ways they traffic between urban, European-educated ways of being and indigenous community customs, of changing relationships between women and men, of intergenerational differences, and of people's need for space for individual creativity while retaining links with their community.

Oceanic Elites

In comparison to the growing numbers and potential influence of mixed heritage, Oceanic peoples' Tongan writer Epeli Hau'ofa refers to the evolution of transnational Pacific rulers. These are described as elite groups that are locked together through their privileged access to and control of resources in the region and through the resources moving between Oceania and other regions of the world. Commentators note that Oceania's ruling classes are increasingly interdependent and culturally homogenous, as many have studied together at prestigious universities in Fiji, Hawaii, Australia, and New Zealand. Other privileged people work in administration, technical, or bureaucratic branches of government and the private sector. In addition, intermarriage amongst educated islanders from different countries has provoked a pan-Pacific awareness and culture that links with music, literature, song, video, and mass media communications to generate a growing sense of Oceania as a coherent region.

It is argued that many contemporary young New Zealanders also strongly self-identify as members of Aotearo, a Pacific nation. This is in contrast to Australians who have experienced a different history, culture, and geopolitical relations. The large Maori population has prompted demands for recognition of indigenous rights and culture in New Zealand's parliament, legislation, and consciousness, and many Maori have continued to ally themselves with their fellow Polynesians in French Polynesia.

The armed forces of France, New Zealand, and Australia cooperate on maritime surveillance of the small island states of the region, with a May 1993 joint agreement of aerial surveillance flights of Exclusive Economic Zones. Yet Australians tend not to self-identify as Oceanic people. Older residents speak with nostalgia of their sense of Australia as a British

enclave. Younger residents identify more closely with being citizens of a multicultural country that should develop by engaging more profoundly with the dynamic economies of Asian nations. Furthermore, development processes in Australia have largely ignored the social construction and constraints of racism, through Australian colonisation practices that were driven by a fear and ignorance of the intricate logic of Australia's indigenous peoples and through assimilation policies that negated ethnic and cultural differences until the 1970s.

As Australia and New Zealand have operated with conservative governments in the mid-1990s, support for indigenous rights and self-determination has fluctuated. Just as significant is that development practices that are generated by Western perceptions of social good have introduced little positive change in indigenous Australian communities. Anthropologists describe how the worldviews of indigenous Australians are shaped by embodied and intangible realities—bodies and places are perceived as defining indicators of social identity. Their countries are sung into tangible present reality through mnemonic song lines. Landscape maps social relations that are recreated through sand designs, body paintings, dance, and story to recall places people have walked, hunted, and visited.

Local "big men," chiefs, and the rise of women's groups offer a noteworthy contrast to pan-Pacific elites. Those who make attempts to redress the deterioration of processes of tribal decision making can face problems in that most indigenous Oceanic peoples, like other members of diverse communities, have been acutely affected by processes of modernisation. Questions now arise about how traditional authority is accepted by those who have moved beyond its present reach and how it can be adapted to meet the new needs of local administration in a globalising world. Monetisation of island economies and decreasing reliance on subsistence agriculture are driving social change within Oceanic communities and internationally, as is the increasing importance of trade unions in labour-management relationships and as a political force.

The ongoing conflict between modernisation and traditional authority is potentially greatest in Tonga, where all political power and most wealth has been customarily reserved to the king and a few nobles. Despite some reforms, the local ruling class effectively restricts commoners' potential political, economic, or social advancement, except through out-migration. Fiji offers a subtle contrast. A gradual return to the path of constitutional rule following several coups based on indigenous Fijian rights is showing that a commitment to living in harmony is being only

reluctantly implemented by those in power. Despite generations of occupation and commitment to the country, the exclusion of people not ethnically Fijian continues.

Oceanic Nationalisms

The tenuous character and embryonic evolution of national cultures in Oceania mark the region as being of interest..The societies and cultures of Oceanic island-states are vital because of the will and energy of their populations. Oceanic peoples are not cultural objects but are active actors in an unceasingly moving and dynamic reality. They are frequently denied the power to direct their future because of their feeble numbers and the constraints of their living space. But these perceptions are those of a continental rather than an islander vision. It has not stopped them from being and from thinking in their own ways and of reclaiming their value in the twenty-first century.

Researchers argue that nationality or national consciousness is becoming more significant in comparison to what is more readily recognised as "nationalism." People perceive themselves as members of a nation and as similar to other nationals, without necessarily possessing the loyal or civic consciousness considered desirable by Western theorists of nationalism. For example, the growth of tourism in the Cook Islands has led to culture and national identity becoming a commodity. Rather than constructions of nationhood being generated by citizens, new representations are born as a result of tourist presentations for foreign consumers. These, it is argued, may produce a more explicit sense of being a member of a collective group than one emerging from an identification with the common use of betelnut, drinking local brands of beer, or using currencies with national signatures.

Nonetheless, the contradictory character of island-state formation is amplified in postcolonial countries where political elites are pursuing Western goals of emancipation and nation building while intentionally maintaining an anti-Western stance by founding their project on local traditions. Commentators have noted how this ambivalent discourse poses special problems and challenges to women. The language of a nation based on "custom" has adopted a masculine character in spite of constant references to the traditional worth of women. It is argued that women's best strategy is to adopt, adapt, and indigenise the language of human rights while asserting their "traditional" power as women of the land.

Oceanic Women

In many island-states, constructions of gender and identity are entwined with concepts of development and progress. The South Pacific Commission, for example, published a Pacific Women's Directory in 1993 and 1997 to provide details about women's organisations and their activities to aid local interventions in the twenty-two island countries and territories that are part of the Commission.

Health care is one arena in which Oceanic peoples create meaningful interpretations of development processes. Massive outbreaks of diseases, such as dysentery that was prevalent until the 1950s, have been curtailed. Dispensaries conduct basic medical care, and hospitals offer surgery for many villagers of outlying islands. Local people cite telephones, helicopters, aircraft, and European medication as some of the benefits of modernisation in relation to health care. In French territories, the state provision of welfare benefits and sophisticated forms of inter-island transport are appreciated as aspects of modern life that enhance well-being.

The transfer of technology and knowledge that often characterises "development," however, is a cultural and political action that can reinforce international and local inequalities. Wider economic and historical changes can produce local cultural and political consequences that are different from the benefits assumed to flow from development. Although many researchers describe how Oceanic women discuss their ownership, access to, and use of property; their strengths in household and small business management; and their affirmation of regional women, it is important to acknowledge women's added economic responsibility for children. Many Pacific islander women are active agents in shaping their social identities, and their move into creating income is an important social change. They manage their households through local perceptions of women's power that are anchored in their labour on their land or in their garden, on their ability to sell the varied produce of their labour, or on their broader commercial skills. Village women frequently manage the markets where they sell their horticultural produce, distributing the profits at the end of the morning's trading.

Critics suggest it is necessary to include Oceanic women's use of property in development planning. Gender should be used as an analytical prism that recognises changes to local practices and shows how women actively invoke and manipulate notions of development and progress to their benefit. Research by female scholars clarifies women's different yet socially important roles as producers and distributors

of wealth. Interpretations of women's power, ritual importance, and social status contingent on a specific event or celebration add local context and complexity to analyses of the ways that gender is socially constructed and enacted in different Oceanic societies.

Land and local concepts of property are important signifiers of elaborate and varied social relations such as reciprocal duty. Through reciprocal duty, the complex dynamics of women's roles in exchanges of produce and property can be analysed. Women have a productive role in providing yams that are distributed through male status ceremonies. Their role needs to be acknowledged and celebrated as an essential component of, rather than mere support for, male festivities. Although some researchers have noted that the role of producer is less prestigious than that of transactor in many Melanesian societies in particular, Oceanic women are generally energetically involved in both types of activities. As the *Wok Meri* organisations developed by women in Papua New Guinea to redress their economic grievances also exemplify, women's skills and diligence are socially respected.

Women's land ownership, their ability to sell their surplus produce, and their authority as household managers illustrate their social power. Many decide how household money should be spent and enact power within family and clan contexts through a range of social interactions. Their practices show how women control some cultural resources defined as their own and therefore enact social power that differs from male social power. This recognition should be used to contest simplistic Western perceptions of a single structure of hierarchic domination operating in all Oceanic societies, to identify the equal value of women and men when it occurs, as well as to acknowledge how social inequalities can be constructed. Because many Oceanic peoples entwine gender with judgments of youth and elder status, concepts about the use of property, and social interactions shaped by evaluations of power, the peoples show how concepts of "global development" can misinterpret the nuances of local ways of being.

As the preceding discussion illustrates, there is a subtle yet damaging irony in theoretical frames that portray Oceanic societies as passive victims or receivers of globalising social and technological changes, rather than as constituted by people who actively negotiate social change, local and international relations, and development processes. Too frequently Oceanic peoples are perceived to be an homogeneous group of subsistence-oriented victims, with physical survival their most demanding issue, a view that discounts the diversity of their lived experiences and their proactive engagement with their societies and environments.

HELEN JOHNSON

See also Fiji; Marshall Islands, Republic of; Micronesia, Federated States of; Papua New Guinea; Solomon Islands; Tonga; Tuvalu; Vanuatu

References and Further Reading

Alley, Roderic. *The Domestic Politics of International Relations: Cases from Australia, New Zealand, and Oceania.* Aldershot, United Kingdom: Ashgate Publishing Company, 2000.

De Deckker, Paul, and Laurence Kuntz. *La Bataille de la Coutume et ses Enjeux pour le Pacifique Sud.* Paris and Montréal: L'Harmattan, 1998.

Dorrance, John. *The United States and the Pacific Islands.* Westport, CT: Praeger, 1992.

Friedman, Jonathan, and James Carrier, eds. *Melanesian Modernities.* Sweden: Lund University Press, 1996.

Gelber, Marilyn. *Gender and Society in the New Guinea Highlands: An Anthropological Perspective on Antagonism Toward Women.* Boulder, CO; London: Westview Press, 1986.

Maclellan, Nic, and Jean Chesneaux. *After Mororua, France in the South Pacific.* Melbourne, NY: Ocean Press, 1998.

Marksbury, Richard, ed. *The Business of Marriage: Transformations in Oceanic Matrimony.* Pittsburgh, PA; London: University of Pittsburgh Press, 1993.

Otto, Ton, and Ad Borsboom, eds. *Cultural Dynamics of Religious Change in Oceania.* Leiden, Netherlands: KITLV Press, 1997.

Otto, Ton, and Nicholas Thomas, eds. *Narratives of Nation in the South Pacific.* The Netherlands: Harwood Academic Publishers, 1997.

Renwick, William, ed. *Sovereignty and Indigenous Rights: The Treaty of Waitangi in International Contexts.* Melbourne, Australia: Victoria University Press, 1991.

Sexton, Lyn. *Mothers of Money, Daughters of Coffee: The Wok Meri Movement.* Ann Arbor, MI: UMI Research Press, 1986.

Sillitoe, Paul. *An Introduction to the Anthropology of Melanesia.* Cambridge: Cambridge University Press, 1998.

Weiner, Annette. *Women of Value, Men of Reknown: New Perspectives in Trobriand Exchange.* Brisbane, Australia: University of Queensland Press, 1977.

OKELLO, JOHN

John Okello was born on October 6, 1937, in Lango district, Uganda. He was reputedly the mastermind behind the Zanzibar Revolution in 1964. He arrived on Pemba Island (the second largest island of the Zanzibari isles) in 1959 as a migrant clove picker. On Pemba, Okello worked various jobs (clove picking, brick making) while becoming involved in nationalist politics. He remained on Pemba, working for the Afro-Shirazi Party (ASP) until 1963. When the

Zanzibar Nationalist Party (ZNP) won the 1963 election over the ASP, Okello moved to Zanzibar Island. The British granted the islands independence in December of 1963, leaving the ZNP in charge.

When the ZNP came to power, it fired many of the police officers who originally were from the mainland of Tanganyika and who the ZNP perceived to be ASP supporters. Whether these police officers were ASP or not, they were unhappy about losing their jobs. Okello secretly recruited members from the ASP's youth wing and among the newly laid-off police force. These two groups were already trained in firearm usage, and the former police officers were knowledgeable about the interiors of the police barracks and armory in the capital city of Zanzibar.

There has been considerable debate about whether John Okello informed the ASP leadership before he conducted the attacks on the police barracks and armory. Most scholarship points to Okello having acted alone. Around 3:00 AM on January 12, 1964, Okello and three hundred men attacked the police facilities. Within a few hours, they had captured all of the weapon caches in the capital Zanzibar and had taken control of the radio broadcasting system. Okello declared the ASP the party of the revolution and christened himself Field Marshal Okello. He formed the Revolutionary Council, which consisted of members of the ASP and the Umma Parties. Okello decided which leaders should be ministers and chose Abeid Karume as president of the new nation.

Okello's glory was short-lived. Within months of the revolution, ASP leaders, concerned about the chaos that followed Okello and his brutal lieutenants, tricked Okello into visiting mainland Tanganyika. There he was imprisoned by President Julius Nyerere for several months until he was declared an unwanted person and put onto a plane for Nairobi. In Kenya, the government watched him with suspicion and soon required that Okello leave the country. Over the next decade, he bounced between African countries and was variously imprisoned by the governments of Malawi, Tanzania, and Kenya for illegal entry as well as by his home country of Uganda. He published his memoir *Revolution in Zanzibar* in 1967.

Okello was eventually killed in the Lango district of Uganda during the reign of Idi Amin, probably out of concern that he would lead a revolt against Amin. Throughout the early postcolonial years, Okello was feared by East African leaders because of the ease with which he had led the Zanzibar Revolution. Even after his death, rebel leaders in Uganda used the pseudonym "John Okello" as a rebel moniker.

ELISABETH MCMAHON

See also Tanzania

References and Further Reading

Lofchie, Michael F. *Zanzibar: Background to Revolution.* Princeton, NJ: Princeton University Press, 1965.

Martin, Esmond Bradley. *Zanzibar: Tradition and Revolution.* London: Hamish Hamilton, 1978.

Oakeshott, Robert. "An Embroiderer's Licence?" *The Spectator.* June 23, 2001.

Okello, John. *Revolution in Zanzibar.* Nairobi: East African Publishing House, 1967.

OMAN

The Sultanate of Oman is located in the southeast corner of Arabia. It emerged over the last two hundred years and incorporates parts of ancient Oman and Dhofar in the south. Until 1970, the Sultanate of Oman was justifiably regarded as the "Tibet of Arabia" so complete was its isolation from the rest of the world. Its population, however, was markedly heterogeneous and included an elite merchant class with pronounced cultural and trade links with India and the coast of East Africa. Along the coast, subsistence fishing settlements prevailed, and in the valleys and mountains parallel to the coastline, terraced farming communities were common. A few towns of the interior of the country were the centers of local and regional trade and some religious learning. These communities were a reflection of Oman's once large and successful colonial empire that incorporated Baluchi, Persian, and East African elements into the dominant culture. In the central desert of the country were a number of nomadic pastoral tribes with cultural and social links that were derived from the Arabian Peninsula.

Prior to 1970, it was reported that only 3.1 miles (five kilometres) of tarmacadam roads existed within the country. Schooling was limited to three modern units that took in a total of one hundred boys, who were personally selected by the sultan. Many families resorted to smuggling their young men out of the country to be educated in Bahrain, Bombay, Cairo, Kuwait, or Mombassa. Whole families went into exile and raised a generation of Omanis in East African Indian and even British contexts. After Sultan Qabus bin Sa'id came to power in 1970 by overthrowing his father, the state moved rapidly to make up for lost time. Whereas the previous ruler had been wary of "modernization" and progress, preferring to carry out only those developments he could actually pay for in cash, his son, Qabus, set about commissioning schools, clinics, and hospitals and laying down the infrastructure of a modern state.

The sultan is the head of state and head of government. His position is hereditary. There are few checks

on his power, and his decrees form the basis of law. He appoints a council of ministers and can dismiss ministers without explanation. There is no prime minister. Senior members of the sultan's family routinely receive important government positions. More distant members of the family serve as ministers, other government officials, and the equivalent of governors throughout the country. Other ministers and senior government officials are chosen by merit and family or tribal connections. There are no political parties, and a limited electorate chooses candidates for the *Majlis al-Shura*, a consultative council that deals with social issues.

Omani culture, furthermore, remains based on a hierarchy built on family connections (tribal ties), relative wealth, and religious education. At the top is the sultan and his immediate family, the Al-Sa'id. This top level is followed by a large tribal group, the Al-Bu Sa'id. Prior to the discovery of oil in the country, the wealthiest sector of the population was arguably made up of the merchant families, many of them Indian in origin, language, and culture. Certain families and tribes had built reputations for religious learning and mediation skills, and they often represented the government in the interior of the country. In the late twentieth century, wealth spread somewhat, and a few more Omani families joined the ranks of the extremely wealthy. Oman has a small but growing middle class, and, while the vast majority of its population outside of the capital area is engaged in subsistence agriculture, fishing, or animal husbandry, the population drift from the countryside to the capital is growing. Out of a population of approximately 2 million (1993 Omani National Census), only a quarter are expatriates mainly from the Indian subcontinent.

Oman is an oil-producing nation, and revenues from petroleum products have been the backbone of Oman's dramatic development during the last three decades of the twentieth century. But oil resources are not extensive, and natural gas reserves are becoming more prominent, with liquefied natural gas exports expected to provide significant new income in the early twenty-first century. Agriculture and fishing, however, are the traditional economic activities in Oman. Fish and shellfish exports create a steady income of roughly US $40 million.

A large percentage of Omanis live in rural areas, and many others own land and property in the countryside even though they live and work in the towns. Many of those in the countryside are self-sufficient farmers and fishermen. Both men and women engage in agricultural activities: men work the date gardens, while women tend to the fields of wheat, barley, and alfalfa. Men fish, while women often mend fishing nets. Children as young as eight or nine years old take on domestic agricultural and fishing tasks. The elderly are greatly respected and are often relieved from any physical work, but their opinions and ideas are eagerly sought by the middle-aged and young.

Gender roles are shaped by the demands of the economic realities of peoples' lives. In the desert interior of the country, women contribute very actively to work associated with raising livestock and have significant social and political power. In the agricultural oasis settlements, the economic role of women is not as conspicuous, and this is reflected in reduced social and political power. In urban centers and towns, however, many women teach in formal schools and in religious preschools (*kuttaib*) as well as work in the private sector. From the early 1990s, the government has made great efforts to include women in government. Women were nominated to run for election to the consultative council in 1997, and several speeches of the sultan emphasized the importance of integrating women into public life. Two women were elected to the consultative council in 2000.

Education has been a major focus of government activity. Primary education for both boys and girls is encouraged. In the later intermediary and high school years, however, attendance by girls, particularly in rural areas, declines, largely due to a persistent pattern of early marriage. Many boys also leave school before the end of their secondary education to seek jobs, thus contributing to a large low-skill sector of the workforce. In 1986, Oman opened its first university modeled on an Anglo-American vision of higher education. The first colleges were of medicine, engineering, science, Islamic studies and education, and agriculture. In the 1990s, several more colleges were opened including a faculty of commerce and economics and a faculty of law. Enrollment in the university is nearly equally split between male and female students.

DAWN CHATTY AND J. E. PETERSON

See also Middle East: History and Economic Development; Middle East: International Relations

References and Further Reading

Allen, Calvin H. Jr., and W. Lynn Rigsbee II. *Oman under Qaboos: From Coup to Constitution, 1970–1996.*

Chatty, Dawn. *Mobile Pastoralists: Development Planning and Social Change in Oman.* New York: Columbia University Press, 1996.

———. "Women and Work in Oman: Cultural Constraints and Individual Choice." *International Journal of Middle East Studies* 32, no. 2 (2000): 241–254.

Peterson, J. E. *Oman in the Twentieth Century: Political Foundations of an Emerging State.* New York: Barnes and Noble, 1978.

———. "Legitimacy and Political Change in Yemen and Oman." *Orbis* 27, no. 4 (1984): 971–998.

Skeet, Ian. *Oman: Politics and Development*. London: Macmillan, 1992.

Townsend, John. *Oman: The Making of the Modern State*. London: Croom Helm, 1977.

OPERATION BOOTSTRAP

Operation Bootstrap attempted to shift the Puerto Rican economy from dependence on low-paying agricultural jobs to dependence on high-paying industrial jobs. From its beginning in 1947, the program took advantage of Puerto Rico's freedom from federal taxes and stable political climate to attract a range of industries. Upon its demise in 1996, Operation Bootstrap had succeeded in industrializing the island and increasing its standard of living.

American Governance

Long a colony of Spain, Puerto Rico became an American possession following the victory of the United States in the Spanish-American War of 1898. Congress made the island the first unincorporated territory in United States history. As a consequence, it was not eligible for American statehood yet it remained part of the United States. On April 2, 1900, President William McKinley approved the Organic Act of Porto Rico (amended to "Puerto Rico" in 1932), which established civil government on the island. It provided that all the laws of the United States would have the same force and effect in Puerto Rico except for the internal revenue laws.

The aftermath of the Spanish-American War left the Puerto Rican economy in shambles. The replacement of the peso by the dollar had reduced the net worth of many Puerto Ricans, and a heavy tax on coffee made it unprofitable to grow what had once been the main export crop. Americans, seeing an opportunity to acquire cheap land, bought coffee plantations and converted them to producing sugar. The result of this shift was the marginalization of a substantial part of the Puerto Rican workforce since sugar growing is only a six-month long job. While sugar workers had historically spent the non-growing period in the manufacture of sugar, Congress had mandated that sugar production would only occur on the mainland United States.

In 1921, Congress attempted to assist the Puerto Rican economy by passing a law that eliminated federal taxes for businesses operating in the island.

The legislation permitted Puerto Rico to offer a 100% tax exemption to industries, unlike any state in the Union. Essentially, Puerto Rico now had all the political benefits associated with the United States but not the financial obligations.

Puerto Rican Control

A succession of governors, all Americans from the mainland, saw Puerto Rico as an overpopulated mess that would forever be mired in poverty. The Chardon Sugar Plan of 1934 identified the economic problems of Puerto Rico as landlessness, chronic unemployment, and steady population growth. The Plan proposed that the US government buy the most productive sugar lands and redistribute them to small Puerto Rican growers. Congress refused to endorse anything that would threaten private property rights and, instead, added to the Puerto Rican troubles by restricting the amount of sugar that could be exported into the United States.

In 1941, Rexford Tugwell became governor of Puerto Rico. An economist and former member of President Franklin D. Roosevelt's brain trust, Tugwell was a New Yorker known for his progressive views on economic recovery. Between 1941 and 1946, Tugwell worked closely with Luis Muñoz Marín and the Popular Democratic Party to change the political and economic structure of Puerto Rico. Tugwell's and Muñoz's efforts led to the changes in the Foraker Act permitting Puerto Rico to elect its own governor as well as the establishment of a Puerto Rican Planning Board. Muñoz believed that the economic transformation of the Puerto Rican economy would result in political independence.

Industrialization as a Cure

Muñoz became the first Puerto Rican-born governor of the island, winning the election in 1948. He believed Puerto Rico's problems could not be halted without addressing population growth. He aimed to bring up the minimum family income to $700–$800 annually, which was the economic level in the 1940s when the birth rate decreased and the population stabilized. Since agricultural businesses could not provide the money needed, Muñoz argued for industrialization as the only way to raise living standards.

Muñoz appointed Teodoro Moscoso to oversee the industrial development of Puerto Rico. A University

of Michigan graduate who had returned to Puerto Rico to run the family pharmacy, Moscoso knew well both the United States and Puerto Rico. He created and ran Fomento, Puerto Rico's Economic Development Administration; but the agency had been in the plans of the Popular Democratic Party since 1940. Muñoz gave the agency the nickname of Operation Bootstrap when speaking before a US congressional committee in July 1949.

Moscoso had no specific job description other than to improve the island. Like Muñoz, he saw industrialization as the only solution to the problems of underemployment and low wages, but Moscoso differed from his mentor in his belief that political independence was economically impossible. Muñoz would subsequently decide in 1952 to abandon hopes of independence and join Puerto Rico to the US commonwealth as a means of ensuring the continued success of industrialization.

To industrialize Puerto Rico, Moscoso had to change a deeply ingrained view held by Puerto Rican leaders that industrialization was impossible in such a small area of 2 million consumers and producers. He also broke with established thought by conceiving industrialization as more than simply an extension of agricultural production through such industries as rum and sugar. Moscoso believed that he had to transform every part of Puerto Rico to make industrialization succeed.

Historically, the standards of living and education in Latin American countries had been serious limitations to the expansion of a producing market and a consuming market. Broken-down shacks, a lack of clean water, and sewage running in the streets did not entice skilled Americans to move to the island. A skilled base of Puerto Ricans did not exist. The island lacked the trained engineers to run factories and the technicians to fix broken equipment. Moscoso persuaded the Puerto Rican government to improve living conditions, but had less success with raising educational standards.

To bring about industrialization, Puerto Rico needed free access to the US market. This market was the largest and richest in the world at the midpoint of the twentieth century, as well as one protected against Puerto Rico's competitors. Without free access to the American market, Puerto Rico could not accumulate the capital through exports that was needed for industrialization. It received such access from Congress. Puerto Rico's export-led economy industrialization program began much earlier than similar programs in other Caribbean nations because of the stimulation of this free access to the US market.

Promoting Puerto Rico

Yet free trade in itself would not bring industry to Puerto Rico. The island needed a powerful magnet, and both Muñoz and Moscoso suggested full tax exemption. On May 13, 1948, the Puerto Rican legislature approved Act No. 184 granting tax exemption on income, property, excise, and municipal taxes to new industries for a period of ten years, with an additional three years of partial exemption. Any new industry was eligible for this tax benefit as long as it manufactured a product not being produced on the island as of January 2, 1947. Forty-two specific industries then in existence were also eligible.

Moscoso began to promote Puerto Rico through a public relations campaign. Many American businesses did not realize that the island enjoyed political stability and honesty in government. One businessman came to the island prepared to offer bribes to legislators, as he believed was standard practice in Third World countries. Moscoso consistently stressed that Puerto Rico was the only part of the United States where industry could operate with 100% tax exemption.

In 1948, Textron became the first company to take advantage of Operation Bootstrap. Eager to use the textile company to give credibility to the program, Moscoso required that it make only a relatively small investment. He gave it a lease and a loan with extremely generous terms. Unfortunately, Textron came from New England as part of the flight of textile companies to low-wage areas in the south. New England legislators accused Puerto Rico of using unfair tactics to lure "runaway" industries away from the United States. Moscoso was charged with robbing U.S. workers of their jobs by means of the federal tax exemption. Muñoz was forced by the threat of a loss of the exemption to declare that Puerto Rico would not grant such benefits to runaway companies. No other business would again receive such advantageous terms.

Textron had proposed to build six mills in Puerto Rico. It only built two by 1951. In that year, Textron management publicly announced that the move to the island had been a mistake. The company complained that Puerto Rican workers took too many holidays, lacked technical skills, and that women had too many children which caused associated increases in child care demands. Textron shifted production to the southeastern United States by the mid-1950s. Moscoso acknowledged these problems by telling companies that they had to send their best people and latest technology to Puerto Rico.

Success and Termination

Designed in an era in which policymakers did not see women as breadwinners, the industrialization program was initially designed to provide employment solely to men. However, the labor intensive industries attracted to Puerto Rico, such as textiles and food processing, traditionally employed more women than men. In the first stage of Operation Bootstrap, women were the main beneficiaries of the program. Growing male unemployment, higher wages, and the increasing cost of transportation were factors that prompted the inauguration in the mid-1960s of the second stage of industrialization. This stage focused on capital intensive industries, such as petrochemicals and pharmaceuticals, which tended to employ more men than women. In the third stage in the 1970s, Puerto Rico welcomed high-tech and electronics industries that employed younger workers of both sexes.

Moscoso had no long-term strategy for industrialization. He simply sought good paying jobs. He brought over 631 industries to Puerto Rico, as well as such companies as General Electric and the Hilton hotel chain. Much of the industry centered in San Juan and other heavily populated cities. The hope of good paying jobs enticed many people to migrate from the country into the exploding city. The resulting slums prompted heavy migration into the United States, especially New York City.

In the 1980s, Operation Bootstrap began to collapse. Puerto Rico lost its competitive advantage to countries that offered tax incentives and even lower wages. Mexico and other Caribbean countries took much industry away from the island. When the island lost its labor and other cost advantages, it became increasingly difficult to promote Fomento. Operation Bootstrap ended in 1996 when Congress terminated the tax exemption.

By most measures, Operation Bootstrap was a resounding success. It transformed Puerto Rico from an agrarian to an urban, industrial economy with a ten-fold increase in per capita Gross National Product (GNP) between 1950 and 1980. In practically all economic and social indices, from per capita income to life expectancy, Puerto Rico joined the ranks of the developed countries of the world. Yet even with massive migration to the United States mixing with industrial achievement, Puerto Rico failed to provide sufficient income or jobs to sustain continued heavy population growth. Sharp inequalities in income remain in existence on the island.

CARYN E. NEUMANN

See also Puerto Rico

References and Further Reading

Maldonado, A. W. *Teodoro Moscoso and Puerto Rico's Operation Bootstrap.* Gainesville, FL: University Press of Florida, 1997.

McElheny, John Richard. *Industrial Education in Puerto Rico: An Evaluation of the Program in "Operation Bootstrap" from 1948 to 1958.* Ph.D. diss. The Ohio State University, 1960.

Pérez, Gina M. *The Near Northwest Side Story: Migration, Displacement, and Puerto Rican Families.* Berkeley, CA: University of California Press, 2004.

Safa, Helen I. *The Myth of the Male Breadwinner: Women and Industrialization in the Caribbean.* Boulder, CO: Westview Press, 1995.

ORGANIZATION OF AFRICAN UNITY (OAU)

Established on May 25, 1963, in Addis Ababa, Ethiopia, by thirty-two independent African nations, the Organization of African Unity (OAU) was Africa's premier body for political and economic cooperation. The organization grew gradually over the years—to a total membership of fifty-three in 1994, when South Africa joined—until it was formally disbanded and replaced by the African Union (AU) in July 2002. Founded at the time when African leaders were experiencing their first taste of freedom from colonialism and were understandably anxious to consolidate their leadership, the OAU aimed to promote the unity and solidarity of African states; coordinate and intensify their cooperation and efforts to achieve a better life for the peoples of Africa; defend their sovereignty, territorial integrity, and independence; eradicate all forms of colonialism and neocolonialism in Africa; and promote international cooperation, with due regard to the Charter of the United Nations and the Universal Declaration of Human Rights (OAU Charter Article II).

The signing of the OAU Charter was quite an achievement at a time when Africa was sharply split into three rival blocs—the Casablanca group, spearheaded by radicals such as Ghana's Kwame Nkrumah and Morocco's King Mohammed V, who favored the political integration of Africa; the Monrovia group, led by President Tubman of Liberia, who opposed the union of African states for fear of it being dominated by some overambitious leaders; and the Brazzaville Twelve, made up of mostly French-speaking nations that usually found themselves sandwiched (ideologically) between the other two groups.

In pursuance of its objectives, the founding nations pledged to coordinate their policies in such areas as international politics and diplomacy; economic development; education, and culture; health sanitation and

nutrition; science and technology; and defence and security. The underlying principles of OAU, as contained in Article III of its Charter, included adherence to noninterference in the international affairs of states; respect for the sovereign equality of all member states; respect for the sovereignty and territorial integrity of each state; peaceful settlement of dispute; unreserved condemnation of political assassination and subversion; dedication to the total emancipation of Africa; and affirmation of a policy of nonalignment in international affairs.

Institutions

The leading institutions of the OAU were the Assembly of Heads of States and Governments, which met annually, and had all the decision-making powers of the organization; the Council of Ministers, which included a foreign minister (or any other minister designated by member states) and was charged with the responsibility of implementing the decisions of the assembly; and the General Secretariat, which was the main administrative organ of the organization, with the responsibility of serving and coordinating the meetings of all other OAU institutions and drawing up OAU programs and budget.

The General Secretariat, located at the headquarters in Addis Ababa, was headed by the secretary general, who was elected by the assembly for a term of four years. In addition to these institutions, the OAU had a number of specialized commissions, the most notable of which were the Economic and Social Commission; Defence Commission; Educational, Scientific, Cultural and Health Commission; the Commission of Fifteen on Refugees; and the Mediation, Conciliation, and Arbitration Commission. These commissions generally met irregularly, depending on the issue at hand, and their meetings were subjected to a quorum of two-thirds majority. Although not provided for in the charter, the OAU Coordinating Committee for the Liberation of Africa, created by a 1963 resolution on decolonization, understandably became a powerful institution of the organization, as the liberation struggle and the fight against apartheid heated up over the years. In addition to these commissions, several specialized agencies in Africa operated under the auspices of the OAU; these included the Pan-African Telecommunications Union (PATU); Pan-African Postal Union (PAPU); Pan-African News Agency (PANA); Union of African Railways (UAR); Organization of African Trade Unions Unity (OATUU); and the Supreme Council for Sports in Africa. In recognition of the polyglot

character of Africa, the OAU conducted its official activities in four languages: Arabic, English, French, and Portuguese.

Contribution to Africa's Development

There are many Africans, both on the continent and in the diaspora, who candidly feel that the OAU did not accomplished much, given the persistence of geopolitical conflicts, ethnic cleansing, poverty, famine, HIV/AIDS afflictions, and other daunting development problems on the continent. However, it must be said that despite its many weaknesses, the OAU deserves some acclaim, especially in the settlement of interstate conflicts and the fight against colonialism and apartheid.

Armed with Article Two of its charter, which sought to eliminate all forms of colonialism from the continent, and working through its Coordination Committee for the Liberation of Africa, the OAU organized diplomatic support and channeled financial, military, and logistical aid to the liberation movements in such places as Angola, Namibia, South Africa, Mozambique, Guinea Bissau, and Rhodesia. Arguably, no other issue received the same unreserved attention, devotion, and unanimity of OAU members than that of decolonization and the fight against apartheid and international racism. The OAU managed to have the United Nations (UN) legitimize its liberation struggle, including the recourse to violence by Africans and other native people, and to obtain the rights proclaimed in the UN Charter and the Declaration of Human Rights. Hence, Salim A. Salim, the former secretary general of the OAU, once noted that "By all accounts, it [decolonization] is a monumental achievement of which the OAU is justifiably proud" (Salim 1996, 230).

For decades, the OAU waged a relentless fight against the apartheid system in South Africa. With the help of like-minded nations and international organizations, the OAU compelled the United Nations to condemn the apartheid system as a crime against humanity, years before its demise in 1994. With this condemnation, South Africa was forced out of many international organization and sporting activities. In as early as June 17, 1963, less than a month of its inception, the OAU initiated a protest against South Africa at the International Labour Organization (ILO) that culminated in the withdrawal of South Africa from that body in March 1964. Similarly, on September 1963, intense protest by African and Asian delegates prevented South African delegates from speaking at the UN General Assembly; similar action, with

homologous result, was taken by the African group at the International Association of Tourism Agency in Rome and at the International Atomic Energy Agency Conference in Vienna the same year. The barring of South Africa from the Olympic Games and from the International Tennis Tournaments owed much to the efforts of the OAU and its sympathizers in the international scene. Following the dismantling of the apartheid regime in South Africa, the OAU offered its services for the smooth transition of political power in that country by sending observer missions to oversee South Africa's first democratic elections in April 27, 1994.

The unity that the OAU managed to garner, through its fight against apartheid, decolonization, and international racism, gave it a moral standing that no African regional bloc or single country could possibly match (Cervenka 1977). With this moral clout, the OAU often provided the necessary mechanism for the peaceful settlement of disputes amongst its members. For instance, when the Biafra civil war flared up in the 1960s and threatened the Nigerian federation, it was the OAU's unequivocal stand for a solution that preserved the territorial integrity of Nigeria by preventing any big power from siding with the Biafra insurgents. Indeed, there is hardly any African conflict regarding the OAU in which it did not play a major mediating role in its resolution. Using certain African leaders as emissaries and agents of arbitration and pacification, the OAU helped settle many geopolitical disputes across the continent. Notable examples in this regard include the mediatory roles played by Emperor Haile Selassie of Ethiopia and President Modibo Keita of Mali in the Moroccan-Algerian conflict of 1963; by President Ibrahim Abboud of Sudan in the Ethiopian-Somali conflict of 1964; by President Nyerere of Tanzania in the Kenya-Somali conflict of 1965; and by President Eyadema of Togo in the 1974 border dispute between Mali and Upper Volta (now Burkina Faso). The OAU was also instrumental in the settlement of the Liberian civil war through its support for the Economic Community of West African States Cease-Fire Monitoring Group (ECOMOG) of the Economic Community of West African States (ECOWAS).

In 1980, with the liberation struggle almost over, the OAU turned much of its collective attention to economic development problems facing Africa, with the adoption of the Lagos Plan of Action that served as the organization's blueprint for Africa's development at its Economic Summit. Among other things, the Lagos Plan sought to provide Africa with rapid, self-sufficient economic development. With poverty, famine, and ethnic violence still ravaging the continent a decade later, the OAU, in yet another historic session in 1990, revisited the Lagos Plan of Action and reaffirmed its resolve to play an active role in finding lasting solutions to the internal conflicts and socioeconomic problems of Africa. This move, culminating in the 1991 signing of the Abuja Treaty, called for the establishment of the African Economic Community (AEC). Following the ratification of the Abuja Treaty in May 1994, the OAU operated on the basis of two legal instruments and changed its official name to OAU/AEC, until July 2002 when it was disbanded and replaced by the African Union (AU) at the Durban Summit.

The formation of the AU was first proposed by Muammar Qaddafi at the Fourth Extraordinary Summit of the OAU/AEC held in Sirte, Libya, in September 1999. The Sirte Declarations, which emerged out of this summit, aimed at effectively addressing the new social, political, and economic realities in Africa and the world; fulfilling the African peoples' aspirations for greater unity; eliminating the scourge of conflicts; and harnessing the human and natural resources of the continent to improve the living conditions of its people. With the establishment of the AU, the African leaders hope to ascertain the political and economic integration of the continent, with initiatives that are different from and, arguably, far more ambitious than those pursued under the erstwhile OAU/AEC. The AU asserts an explicit shift from the pursuit of mere unity among African nations to that of a political union and asserts an equality explicit acceptance of the tenet of the New Partnership for Africa's Development (NEPAD), which was launched concurrently with the AU at the OAU/AEC Summit in Lusaka, Zambia, in July 2001.

As the main socioeconomic program of the AU, NEPAD's objective is to eradicate poverty in Africa by establishing the necessary conditions for peace and security, promoting sustainable economic growth and development, and enhancing Africa's participation in global political and economic issues. Unlike the OAU/AEC (which focused mostly on decolonization and interstate conflicts and keenly respected the political boundaries of Africa), inherited from colonialism, the AU is primarily aimed at the elimination of Africa's colonial borders, with an eye toward the political integration of the continent. The AU's integration process is anchored in democracy, popular participation, and a conscious effort to mobilize all African regional economic blocs and people, including those in the diaspora. The AU hopes to create, by the year 2030, a prosperous United States of Africa, "driven by its own citizens and representing a dynamic force in the international arena" (African Union Commission, 2004: 26).

JOSEPH MENSAH

See also Apartheid; Economic Community of West African States (ECOWAS); Nkrumah, Kwame; Selassie, Emperor Haile; Pan-Africanism

References and Further Reading

Andemicael, Berhanykun. *Peaceful Settlement among African States: Roles of the United Nations and the Organization of African Unity.* New York: United Nations Institute for Training and Research, 1972.

Amnesty International. *Organization of African Unity: Making Human Rights a Reality for Africans.* New York: Amnesty International USA, 1998.

African Union Commission. *Strategic Plan of the African Union Commission (Volume 1: Vision and Mission of the African Union).* Addis Ababa, Ethiopia: The African Union Commission, (May) 2004.

Cervenka, Zdenek. *The Unfinished Quest for Unity: Africa and the OAU,* New York: Africana Publishing Company, 1977.

El-Ayouty, Yassin, ed. *The Organization of African Unity after Thirty Years.* Westport, CT; London: Praeger, 1994.

El-Ayouty, Yassin, and I. William Zartman. *The OAU: Twenty Years.* Westport, CT; London: Praeger, 1984.

Esedebe, Olisanwuche P. *Pan-Africanism: The Idea and Movement 1776–1991.* Washington, DC: Howard University Press, 1994.

Naldi, Gino J. *The Organization of African Unity: An Analysis of Its Role.* London and New York: Mansell, 1999.

Nyangoni, Wellington Winter. *Africa in the United Nations System.* Rutherford, NJ: Fairleigh Dickinson University Press, 1985.

Salim, Salim A. "The OAU and the Future." *Pan Africanism: Politics, Economy, and Social Change in the Twenty-First Century,* Tajudee Abdul-Raheem, ed. New York: New York University Press, 1996.

Wolfers, Michael. *Politics in the Organization of African Unity.* London: Metheun, 1976.

ORGANIZATION OF AMERICAN STATES (OAS)

A regional security organization was created at the conclusion of the Ninth Pan-American Conference held in Bogotá in 1948 to replace the Pan American Union. The Organization of American States (OAS) was founded as a continuation of the idea that the nations of the Western hemisphere share a unique identity, historically expressed as Pan-Americanism, Bolivarianism, or the Western Hemisphere Idea. More immediate factors included inter-American cooperation that had developed during World War II coupled with global tensions due to the advent of the Cold War. The original charter listed five purposes: (i) to provide peace and security of the Western Hemisphere; (ii) to prevent possible causes of difficulties that may arise and ensure a peaceful settlement among the member states; (iii) to provide for common action on the part of member states in the event of aggression; (iv) to seek the solution of political, juridical, and economic problems that may arise among the member states; and (v) to promote by cooperative action their economic, social, and cultural development. Twenty-one nations signed the original charter (Argentina, Bolivia, Brazil, Chile, Colombia, Costa Rica, Cuba, Dominican Republic, Ecuador, El Salvador, Guatemala, Haiti, Honduras, Mexico, Nicaragua, Panama, Paraguay, Peru, United States, Uruguay, and Venezuela). As of 2004, there are fourteen additional members: Barbados, Trinidad and Tobago (1967); Jamaica (1969); Grenada (1977); Suriname (1977); Dominica, Saint Lucia (1979); Antigua and Barbuda (1981); Saint Vincent and the Grenadines (1981); Bahamas (1982); St. Kitts and Nevis (1982); Canada (1990); Belize (1991); and Guyana (1991).

The charter was later revised by protocols signed at Buenos Aires (1967) and went into effect in February 1970. For Cartagena (1985), it was effective in November 1988; for Managua (1993), it was ratified in March 1996; and for Washington (1992), it took effect in September 1997. The annual General Assembly was created by the Buenos Aires Protocol. The Permanent Council, the Economic and Social Council, and the Council for Education Science and Culture were given equal status within the organization. The Cartegena and Managua Protocols greatly strengthened the role of the secretary general and provided procedures for the peaceful resolution of disputes as well as called for greater economic and social development throughout the hemisphere. The Managua Protocol also created the Inter-American Council for Integral Development (CIDI) to replace the Economic and Social Council and the Council for Education, Science, and Culture. The main goals of CIDI are to promote development activities, to strengthen hemispheric partnership, and to assist in the elimination of extreme poverty in the Americas. The Washington Protocol established the OAS as the first regional political organization to provide for the suspension of a member-state whose democratically elected government is overthrown by force.

The OAS attempts to achieve its objectives through seven subunits, including the General Secretariat, the Meeting of Consultation of Ministers of Foreign Affairs, the General Assembly, the Permanent Council, the Inter-American Council for Integral Development; the Inter-American Juridical Committee, and the Inter-American Commission of Human Rights. In addition, there are specialized committees and commissions established by the General Assembly.

The permanent organ of the OAS is the General Secretariat that is headquartered in Washington, DC. The secretary general, the executive for the

organization, is elected by the General Assembly to a five-year term. The Meeting of Consultation is the arm of OAS tasked with handling security crises as provided for by the Inter-American Treaty of Reciprocal Assistance (Rio Treaty) and also is the unit responsible for a joint response to military aggression against a member state by a non-American state power. The General Assembly meets annually but can also be called into special session to consider urgent matters. The Permanent Council, composed of an ambassador from each member state, implements decisions and resolutions assigned by the General Assembly, the Meeting of Consultation, and the secretary general. Its most notable function includes a role in the peaceful settlement of disputes through the Organ of Consultation as provided for in the Rio Treaty. The remaining councils and committees promote cooperation among the Latin American states in their respective areas of expertise and hold annual meetings as mandated by the OAS charter.

One early achievement of OAS members was the establishment of the Inter-American Development Bank in 1959. The Inter-American Development Bank was created out of concern that the World Bank was not meeting the needs of Latin American members for social lending and was overly concentrated on infrastructure improvements. The creation of the bank was followed by the Act of Bogota in 1960 that called for members to commit to economic and social development. This was followed by OAS endorsement of the Alliance for Progress.

Before 1990, the Cold War cast a long shadow over the cooperative ideals of the Organization of American States and resulted in different visions of regional security between the United States and some members, most notably Cuba and Mexico. However, in the aftermath of the Cold War, the OAS initiated conventions against corruption, illegal drug and arms trafficking, and violence against women. These missions were largely formulated at the 1994 Summit of the Americas in Miami when the organization was challenged by the Western Hemisphere's heads of state to strengthen democratic values and institutions.

The promotion of peace and democracy is the responsibility of the OAS Unit for Promotion of Democracy (UPD), which acts under the authority of Resolution 1080. Resolution 1080 was passed by the 1991 General Assembly to deter threats to legitimate democratically elected governments. The resolution calls for the general secretary to convene the Permanent Council followed by a meeting of the hemisphere's foreign ministers within ten days of a *coup d'état* or other actions against an elected government. The resolution has been enacted four times: in Haiti in 1991, Peru in 1992, Guatemala in 1993, and Paraguay in 1996.

The OAS was instrumental in seeking a peaceful resolution after the *coup* that removed Haitian President Jean Baptiste Aristide from power in September 1991. OAS foreign ministers met as required and sought economic and political sanctions against the illegitimate government. In cooperation with the UN, the joint International Civilian Mission (ICM) was founded to monitor human rights abuses. These measure in part led to the restoration of the Aristide government in 1994.

On April 5, 1992, President Alberto Fujimori of Peru declared an auto *coup* and suspended the constitution. The OAS Permanent Council condemned the *coup* and called for an immediate restoration of the democratic process. At the request of the hemisphere's foreign ministers, the secretary general headed a mission of foreign ministers to start a dialog between the government and other political forces in Peru. As a result of OAS interest, Fujimori agreed to call elections for a new Congress to draft a new constitution. The OAS sent two hundred observers to monitor the elections. In this instance, OAS actions proved only marginally effective as Fujimori used the new constitution to extend his power in Peru.

A more successful example of OAS promotion of democracy occurred in Guatemala when President Jorge Serrano suspended constitutional democracy on May 25, 1993. Resolution 1080 was invoked, and Secretary General Baena Soares was dispatched to Guatemala. The condemnation of Serrano's auto *coup* helped lead to his removal and Guatemalan Congress's constitutional election of Ramiro de Leon Carpio as president.

The fourth instance of the use of Resolution 1080 involved an attempt to force the resignation of Paraguay's President Juan Carlos Wasmosy by the Paraguayan Army Commander in April 1996. After the OAS Permanent Council called for a meeting of foreign ministers, Secretary General Gavaria traveled to Paraguay in support of Wasmosy. Buoyed by OAS, other international support, and the Paraguayan people, Wasmosy remained in office.

Another aspect of promoting democracy is monitoring of elections. The first instance of election monitoring occurred in Nicaragua in 1990. In the following years, OAS teams have expanded the mission of observing elections. The most recent example was in the August 2004 recall election in Venezuela. OAS certification of the electoral process has helped to boost public confidence in the electoral process throughout the Western Hemisphere. In addition, the UPD conducts education programs, exchanges, and conferences on the democratic process. It has developed peacebuilding programs and has supervised the eradication of land mines in the Western Hemisphere.

In 1993, the OAS created the Committee on Hemispheric Security to assist in the peaceful resolution of disputes between member nations. The purpose of the committee and other conferences is to decrease historic rivalries and suspicions and create an environment of mutual trust. In 1997, OAS members negotiated the Inter-American Convention Against the Illicit Manufacturing of and Trafficking in Firearms, Ammunition, Explosives, and other Related Materials—the first legally binding regional agreement on illicit firearms trafficking. In October 1999, the Counterterrorism Committee (CTC) was established to promote cooperation on counterterrorism issues.

The OAS has played a key role in monitoring elections to ensure they are fair and open. This includes initiating educational programs at the local and regional level to foster democratic ideals. The organization has sent special teams to support the peace process in Guatemala, Nicaragua, Haiti, and Suriname and has been a key participant in clearing land mines in Central America. The Washington, DC-based Inter-American Commission on Human Rights and the Inter-American Court of Human Rights, located in San José, Costa Rica, monitor the status of human rights in member countries and also provide a legal recourse to individuals and groups that have suffered abuses. Special attention is given to the rights of indigenous peoples and women. The OAS is supporting the Free Trade Area of the Americas by providing technical support and working closely with the Inter-American Development Bank and the United Nations Economic Commission for Latin America and the Caribbean. The Inter-American Drug Abuse Control Commission was established to curb the illegal trafficking in narcotics that has resulted in violence and instability in a number of member states. The commission's objectives include assisting countries in strengthening laws, improving law enforcement, and encouraging the cultivation of alternative crops. It also evaluates each country's progress in meeting its antidrug goals. The OAS is committed to promoting sustainable development and administers a variety of programs in this area, including river basin management, conservation, dealing with climatic changes, and assistance during natural disasters.

The Organization of American States has continued to promote cultural programs, and this, perhaps, is its most enduring achievement. The OAS headquarters in Washington houses the Art Museum of the Americas as well as the Columbus Memorial Library. In addition, *Américas*, a fully illustrated popular magazine, depicts the rich mosaic of the peoples and cultures of the Western Hemisphere. Other specialized organizations managed by the OAS include the Inter-American Children's Institute, the Inter-American Commission on Women, the Pan American Institute on Geography and History, the Inter-American Indian Institute, the Inter-American Institute for Cooperation on Agriculture, and the Pan American Health Organization.

GEORGE M. LAUDERBAUGH

References and Further Reading

Rosenberg, Robin L. "*The OAS and the Summit of the Americas: Coexistence, or Integration of Forces for Multilateralism?*" Latin American Politics and Society 43, no. 1 (Spring 2001).

Slater, Jerome. *The OAS and United States Foreign Policy.* Columbus, OH: Ohio State University Press, 1967.

Stoetzer, O. Carlos. *The Organization of American States,* 2d. ed. Westport, CT: Praeger, 1993.

Thomas, Ann Van Wynen, and A. J. Thomas Jr. *The Organization American States.* Dallas, TX: Southern Methodist University Press, 1963.

ORGANIZATION OF ARAB PETROLEUM EXPORTING COUNTRIES (OAPEC)

Arab states had a fourth of the world's 160 trillion cubic meters of gas in 2001, but they supplied only 13% of the world's demand. The states also produced two-thirds of the world's 653 billion barrels of oil, with new discoveries exceeding increased production. In 2004, OAPEC planned an $84.5 billion expansion, with $43 billion of that committed to natural gas.

Structure

In 1968, the Organization of Arab Petroleum Exporting Countries (OAPEC) came into being with headquarters in Kuwait. It serves to support the Arab oil industry through cooperation by member producers. It is a regional, intergovernmental development agency. Only Arab countries with significant gross domestic product (GDP) from petroleum are allowed to join. The OAPEC meets with the Arab League every four years on energy matters. Its operating assumption is that the cornerstone of future economic development in the Arab countries is petroleum. Thus, the use of the resource must be effective, including joint ventures. OAPEC also wants equity in the market and a favorable climate for investment in petroleum. It works to make the policies and laws of the members compatible and to train and employ citizens of members. OAPEC activities take place cooperatively

because OAPEC coordinates those activities, promotes exchange of information, and hosts seminars with both regional and international participation. The seminars allow dissemination of the latest technological news and problems of member countries. The OAPEC information exchange program also includes the Arab Energy Conference.

Initial signatories to the January 9, 1968, agreement were Kuwait, Libya, and Saudi Arabia. In Beirut, Lebanon, the three established OAPEC and headquartered it in Kuwait. By 1982, the organization had eleven member exporters, an agreement that established the OAPEC. The three founding members agreed that the organization would be located in the State of Kuwait. Subsequently, other states joined OAPEC: Algeria (1970), Bahrain (1970), Qatar (1970), Iraq (1972), Syria (1972), Egypt (1973), United Arab Emirates (1970), and Tunisia (1982). In 1986, when Tunisia requested to withdraw, the Ministerial Council decided that Tunisia would be suspended from the rights and obligations of membership until such time as Tunisia chose to resume active participation.

Oversight lies with the Ministerial Council, composed of the oil ministers or comparable officials from each of the member countries. Providing budget and regulation and other inputs to the council agenda is the Executive Bureau. Administering the policies and programs is the General Secretariat, which accepts staff from all Arab countries, not just the producing ones. The Secretariat includes the Arab Center for Energy Studies. The enforcement component is the Judicial Tribunal, which arbitrates disputes with oil companies as well as between members. Judgments are binding and final.

The OAPEC publishes annual reports in Arabic and English; the quarterly *Oil and Arab Cooperation* in Arabic with English abstracts; the *Arabic Energy Resources Monitor* (an annual statistical report in Arabic and English); and various papers, proceedings, and studies.

The Council of Ministers reviewed the OAPEC General Secretariat's performance in 1987 and established ideas for improved efficiency and rationalization of expenditure. It urged maximum use of its companies, particularly APICORP. It transferred projects previously under the General Secretariat to APICORP. It also decided that at least three interested members should approve any project and that each of the three should bear 10% of the costs of the study.

Under OAPEC are four independent companies and a training institute:

- The Arab Maritime Petroleum Company (AMPTC) was established in January 1973 after members signed the formal agreement on May 6, 1972. The AMPTC had a fully subscribed capital of $500 million. It was to be involved in all operations pertaining to marine transport of petroleum and its products. Shareholders in the company included Algeria, Bahrain, Egypt, Iraq, Kuwait, Libya, Qatar, Saudi Arabia, and the United Arab Emirates. Tanker demand shrank, however, and the company took losses until its authorized capital was $200 million, subscribed at $150 million.

- The Arab Shipbuilding and Repair Yard Company (ASRY), agreed to on December 8, 1973, is headquartered in Bahrain and counts as shareholders Bahrain, Iraq, Kuwait, Libya, Qatar, Saudi Arabia, and the United Arab Emirates. In December 1974, ASRY incorporated with capital of $100 million. This increased to $300 million in 1976 and $340 million 1977. ASRY was to build, repair, and maintain the various vessels of the petroleum fleet. It established a dry dock in Bahrain in 1977 to service and repair tankers. It also added two floating docks and related facilities. The three docks allowed ASRY to take care of medium and supersized tankers and ships. Its level of productivity made it competitive with other dock facilities.

- The Arab Petroleum Investments Corporation (APICORP) was formed in Dammam, Saudi Arabia, in November 1975. All OAPEC members had shares. Authorized capital was $1.2 billion, but only $400 million was subscribed. The subscription was increased to $460 million in 1996 by tapping APICORP's general reserve. APICORP helps members to finance industry-related projects, most of which require substantial investment. The corporation's twelve projects were in Bahrain, Egypt, Iraq, Jordan, Libya, Saudi Arabia, and Tunisia. APICORP partners with the OAPEC-sponsored Arab Petroleum Services Company in two subsidiaries: the Arab Drilling and Workover Company (ADWOC) and the Arab Geophysical Exploration Services Company (AGESCO). APICORP has equities of 20% and 10% in the respective companies as well as a 32% equity in the Arab Company for Detergent Chemicals (ARADET), capitalized in Baghdad, Iraq, on March 12, 1981, at $72 million ID. The company worked from its Linear Alkyl Benzene Complex, but sanctions and then war hampered its activity severely.

- The Arab Petroleum Services Company (APSCO) was founded in Tripoli, Libya, in

January 1977 by all member states. Capital was $100 million Libyan dinars. The company provides petroleum services through subsidiaries specialized by type of service. The company has three subsidiaries, one of which is the Arab Drilling and Workover Company (ADWOC), established in Tripoli in February 1980 to deal with onshore and offshore drilling operations, water well drilling, well maintenance, and other technical operations associated with member and other countries. The company's fourteen rigs operate in Jordan, Syria, and Libya. ADWOC has workshops and storage facilities for maintenance and testing of equipment and production of oxygen and nitrogen. Another wholly owned subsidiary is the Arab Well Logging Company (AWLC) established in Baghdad in March 1983, which logs, perforates, and does the other technical things necessary to discover and develop. The AWLC was largely dormant during the sanctions and war, but Iraq attempted to revitalize it in 2003. The Arab Geophysical Exploration Services Company (AGESCO) is in Tripoli. APSC has 40% of this company, chartered in 1984. Halliburton Geophysical Services Company also owns 40%. AGESCO performs geophysical surveys.

- The Arab Petroleum Training Institute (APTI), established in Baghdad in May 1978, was to research and publish studies on industrial organization and training theory. APTI performs research and studies concerning modern industrial organization and training theory. It also provides a central information and documentation resource. The 1990–1991 crisis in the gulf precluded APTI's handling of its mission, and not until 2003 did Iraq request a reopening of the institute.

Impact

Oil is the world's primary energy source. It is a commodity, and as a commodity its price is volatile. Developed and undeveloped nations share the world's wealth unequally. Undeveloped nations get the highly variable price of the raw commodity, a price determined largely by the buyer rather than the seller. The developed ones get the more stable income from transport, manufacture, packaging, and the other processes—and jobs—that make a finished product. Developing nations want greater control over the processes that occur once their raw material—petroleum, for instance—leaves the ground. Developing nations recognize that they have to move into industrialization

and manufacturing and control of the entire life of their product if they are ever to achieve reasonable economic development and stability.

Before the 1950s, the Middle East was of interest for a potential location of strategic military bases just as much as for its petroleum. Much of the region remained predominantly agricultural. Then, in the 1950s, multinational petroleum companies began exploration and development of Arabian Gulf oil resources under leases, contracts, or concessions by the local governments.

In 1959 and 1960, the petroleum companies unilaterally decided to lower prices. The Arabian producers protested. At the Baghdad Conference of September 10–14, 1960, Saudi Arabia, Iraq, and Kuwait—supported by Venezuela and Iran—founded the Organization of Petroleum Exporting Countries (OPEC). Prices stabilized until the end of the 1960s. In the late 1960s, the third Arab-Israeli War took place. One reaction to this war was the creation of the Organization of Arab Petroleum Exporting Countries (OAPEC).

Initially, the member countries were predominantly agricultural, but the rising oil revenues of the 1960s allowed governments to invest heavily in industry and infrastructure. Economic growth was marked, and members of OAPEC raised prices and taxes. In 1971, some went so far as to nationalize majority shares of Western oil concessions. Then, the fourth Arab-Israeli War began on October 6, 1973. With OPEC support, Arab petroleum exporters embargoed oil shipments to Western countries that had supported Israel. At this point, the OPEC countries, not the oil companies, controlled price shifts. As supplies shrank, prices rose 400% over six months. Shortly after the embargo, Henry Kissinger of the United States established the International Energy Agency (IEA), composed of just about all of the Western industrial nations. IEA was to establish ways to ensure that an OAPEC embargo could not happen again. The IEA established a formula for sharing in the event of a supply disruption. It was the Emergency Sharing System, which obligated members to buy and sell oil at fixed prices for a set amount. The United States began filling its Strategic Petroleum Reserve, the salt mines of Texas and Louisiana. In 1976, oil was on average 74.4% of GDP in the OAPEC countries. Qatar and the United Arab Emirates. hit 100%. GDP per capita increased from $433 US dollars (USD) in 1970 to $1,916 (USD) in 1976. The range among countries was from $424 in Egypt to $15,323 in the United Arab Emirates in 1975.

The increased revenues allowed the OAPEC countries to repay foreign debt, increase foreign exchange reserves and financial stability, and continue investing in internal improvements and social programs. In the late 1970s, the Arab petroleum producers began

shifting from merely producing crude oil to producing and exporting refined oil products, petrochemicals, and gas. Libya opened a methanol plant, Saudi Arabia opened a lube-oil plant, and Qatar opened a steel mill. Iran began smelting copper, producing fertilizer, and expanding its refining capability. Other ventures produced steel and aluminum and fertilizer in Iran, Iraq, Dubai, Qatar, Algeria, and Egypt. The OAPEC oversaw this attempt to overcome the area's colonial history.

Numbers (1970–1995)

The increase in income during the booms was due to increased output rather than more efficient production. In addition, the types of infrastructure projects that the states spent their money on were large-scale mass employment projects that encouraged low productivity instead of efficiency. When the boom faded, the social welfare costs were difficult to bear.

In the mid-1980s, oil prices declined. OAPEC countries were slow to adjust their economies to the reduced income. Growth was weak between 1984 and 1995. The Seventh Arab Energy Conference took place in Cairo on May 11–14, 2002. Arab energy conferences take place every four years. The first came from a 1977 agreement between the OAPEC ministerial council and the Arab Fund for Economic and Social Development. After the first, the OAPEC incorporated the Arab League's Arab Petroleum Conference, held since 1959. Another sponsor was the Arab Industrial Development and Mining Organization.

At Cairo, the members discussed ways to raise the $84 billion anticipated for 2002–2006 energy projects. Members indicated an increased willingness to let the private sector join their national companies in these ventures. The inclusion of international oil companies was anticipated to increase chances for funding from international banks rather than from regional sources, historically small and undercapitalized compared to the international banks. Still, more than 40% of the money was from regional sources. At the time of the seventh conference, the globalizing world was moving increasingly toward regional economic organizations, and the Greater Arab Free Trade Area was six years old. A 2004 estimate was that a $1 million increase in exports increased GDP by $4 million, and a $10-a-barrel increase raised the European fuel bill by 4 million euros.

JOHN H. BARNHILL

See also Energy: Impact on Development; Extractive Industries; Organization of Petroleum Exporting Countries (OPEC); Petrodollars

References and Further Reading

International Monetary Fund. 2003. "Organization of Arab Petroleum Exporting Countries (OAPEC)." *Directory of Economic Commodity and Development Organizations.* http://www.imf.org/external/np/sec/decdo/oapec.htm

Maachou, Abdelkader. *Organization of Arab Petroleum Exporting Countries.* New York: St. Martin's Press, 1982.

Middle East Economic Survey. "Apicorp Reviews Prospects for Financing Arab Energy Projects." *Energy Finance* XLV, o 223 (June 2002). http://www.mees.com/postedarticles/finance/energy/a45n22b04.htm

Middle East North Africa Financial Network. "Arab Oil Wealth up by over 10b Barrels/U.A.E." *The Daily Star.* September 17, 2003. http://www.menafn.com/qn_news_story_s.asp?StoryId=29186

———. "OAPEC: Regional Energy Needs $84.5b to Expand" *The Daily Star.* August 21, 2004. http://www.menafn.com/qn_news_story_s.asp?storyid=61060

OAPEC. "Editorial: Arab Energy Conference: An All-Embracing Framework for Arab Energy Issues." *Monthly Bulletin.* April 2002. http://www.oapecorg.org/Editorial%20April%202002.htm

OAPEC. 2005. Home Page. http://www.oapecorg.org/

Saleh, Obadi, and Obadi Mothana. "Impact of Oil Sector for the Economic Development of the Middle East and North Africa Countries Targeted for OAPEC Member Countries." *Ekonomický Časopis* 47, no. 4 (1999). http://www.sav.sk/journals/ekoncas/ekon499.htm

Tetreault, Mary Ann. *The Organization of Arab Petroleum Exporting Countries: History, Policies, and Prospects.* Westport, CT: Greenwood Press, 1981.

World Energy Council. 1998. *Potential Supply of Hydrocarbons in OAPEC Member Countries.* Retrieved December 2004: http://www.worldenergy.org/wec-geis/publications/default/tech_papers/17th_congress/1_2_03.asp#Heading1

ORGANIZATION OF EASTERN CARIBBEAN STATES (OECS)

On June 18, 1981, representatives of seven English-speaking states in the Leeward and Windward Islands—Antigua and Barbuda, Dominica, Grenada, Montserrat, St. Christopher (St. Kitts) and Nevis, St. Lucia, and St. Vincent and the Grenadines—signed the Treaty of Basseterre to promote unity and solidarity. The Treaty of Basseterre, named in honor of the capital of St. Kitts and Nevis, where the treaty was signed, created the Organization of Eastern Caribbean States (OECS). The treaty was signed by Deputy Prime Minister Lester Bird (b. 1938) of Antigua and Barbuda, who became the first chairman of the OECS; Prime Minister Mary Eugenia Charles (b. 1919) of Dominica; Prime Minister Maurice Bishop (1944–1983) of Grenada; Minister of Education Franklyn Margetson of Montserrat; Premier Kennedy Simmonds (b. 1936) of St. Kitts and Nevis; Prime Minister Winston Cenac (1925–2004) of St. Lucia; and Deputy Prime Minister Hudson Tannis (1928–1986) of St. Vincent and the Grenadines. Anguilla and the

British Virgin Islands became associate members of the OECS in 1995 and 1994, respectively. The headquarters of the OECS are located in Castries, St. Lucia.

In 1947, the groundwork for an association of English-speaking Caribbean colonies was laid by British authorities at a regional conference held at Montego Bay, Jamaica. The British suggested that the creation of a political federation of British colonies in the Caribbean would eventually culminate in the political independence of the region. The West Indies Federation (1957–1962) united ten island territories: Jamaica, Trinidad and Tobago, Barbados, Grenada, St. Kitts-Nevis-Anguilla, Antigua and Barbuda, St. Lucia, St. Vincent and the Grenadines, Dominica, and Montserrat. In 1961, Jamaica, the most economically significant of the member states, withdrew from the West Indies Federation following a dispute over the implementation of a customs union. In 1962, the West Indies Federation collapsed when Trinidad and Tobago withdrew from the group. Simultaneously, in 1962, Jamaica and Trinidad and Tobago became the first Anglophone Caribbean countries to achieve independence. Barbados achieved its independence in 1966. In 1966, the remaining nonindependent members of the defunct West Indies Federation formed the West Indies States Association (WISA). Designed to give greater autonomy to the British colonies in the Windward and Leeward Islands, the creation of WISA resulted in the independence of Grenada in 1974; Dominica in 1978; St. Lucia and St. Vincent and the Grenadines in 1979; Antigua and Barbuda in 1981; and St. Kitts and Nevis in 1983. Led by Premier Paul Southwell of St. Kitts and Nevis, representatives of WISA met in St. Lucia in May 1979 to discuss the need for greater regional cooperation. The result was the Treaty of Basseterre and the creation of the OECS.

The OECS has sought to promote cooperation among the members at the regional and international level; defend their sovereignty, territorial integrity, and independence; adopt common positions on international issues; arrange for joint overseas representation; and promote economic integration among the members. The OECS is charged with assisting member states to maximize the benefits of their limited resources to achieve sustainable development. The OECS's four major advisory and regulatory activities are the Eastern Caribbean Telecommunications Authority (ECTEL), which regulates the telecommunications sector; the Directorate of Civil Aviation (DCA), which provides guidance and direction on airport development and adequacy of air services; the Eastern Caribbean Central Bank (ECCB), which monitors the common currency of the member states; and the Eastern Caribbean Supreme Court. In 2002, the OECS, in an effort to facilitate travel within the region, declared that all OECS citizens could travel in the region with a valid photo identification card, such as a driver's license. There are plans for the creation of a common passport.

Notwithstanding the high literacy rates of the member states, the potential to expand tourism, and valid efforts at economic diversification, there are significant challenges to development in the region. The small population of the OECS states (less than 1 million people collectively); the high rate of HIV/AIDS that poses a serious health challenge; vulnerability to natural disasters that disrupt agriculture and tourism (such as hurricanes); the decline in access to preferential markets, especially for bananas, during the 1990s; increased competition in the tourism industry from other Caribbean states, especially the Dominican Republic that has offered all-inclusive vacation packages at greatly reduced rates; and the impact of the events of September 11, 2001, on global tourism continue to inhibit development. Moreover, foreign debt increased dramatically during the 1990s.

The leaders of the OECS also sought to insulate their region from the vagaries of the Cold War during the 1980s. In October 1982, the governments of Antigua and Barbuda, Barbados, Dominica, St. Lucia, and St. Vincent and the Grenadines signed a regional security accord—the Regional Security System (RSS)—that allowed for the coordination of defense efforts and the establishment of paramilitary units drawn from the islands' police forces. On October 19, 1983, Prime Minister Bishop of Grenada was murdered by a faction of Grenada's government that wanted to implement a more rigorous policy of Marxist-Leninism. The OECS supported the US invasion of Grenada on October 25, 1983. National defense forces from Antigua and Barbuda, Dominica, St. Lucia, and St. Vincent and the Grenadines assisted in the US-orchestrated event. After the end of the Cold War, the primary security concern of the OECS was no longer socialism. The new threat was drug trafficking. The United States provided training, two C-26 Metros (decommissioned U.S. Air Force jets), and spare parts to help the OECS monitor the region against drug traffickers.

Notwithstanding attempts at greater regional integration, it is conceivable that one or more of the multiple-island states, such as St. Kitts and Nevis or St. Vincent and the Grenadines, might split into separate entities in the future.

MICHAEL R. HALL

See also Anguilla; Antigua and Barbuda; Bishop, Maurice; Caribbean: History and Economic Development; Caribbean: International Relations; Dominica;

Grenada; Montserrat; St. Christopher (St. Kitts) and Nevis; St. Lucia; St. Vincent and the Grenadines

References and Further Reading

Anthony, Kenny. *The Legal Framework of Education in the Organization of Eastern Caribbean States.* Washington, DC: Organization of American States, 1997.

Bolland, O. Nigel. *The Politics of Labour in the British Caribbean: The Origins of Authoritarianism and Democracy in the Labour Movement.* Kingston, Jamaica: Ian Randle Publishers, 2001.

Ferguson, James. *Eastern Caribbean in Focus: A Guide to the People, Politics, and Culture.* Northampton, MA: Interlink Publishing, 1997.

Sheridan, Richard B., *et al. West Indies Accounts: Essays on the History of the British Caribbean and the Atlantic Economy.* Kingston, Jamaica: University of the West Indies Press, 2002.

Van Beck, Fritz, *et al. The Eastern Caribbean Currency Union—Performance, Progress, and Policy Issues.* Washington, DC: International Monetary Fund, 2000.

Williams, Eric. *From Columbus to Castro: The History of the Caribbean, 1492–1969.* New York: Vintage, 1984.

ORGANIZATION OF PETROLEUM EXPORTING COUNTRIES (OPEC)

The Organization of Petroleum Exporting Countries (OPEC) officially came into existence as a result of a conference held in Baghdad, Iraq, on September 14–19, 1960. OPEC's founding members, five of the principal oil exporting countries, were Saudi Arabia, Iran, Kuwait, Iraq, and Venezuela. The five founding members were later joined by eight other countries: Qatar (1961), Indonesia (1962), Libya (1962), United Arab Emirates (1967), Algeria (1969), Nigeria (1971), Ecuador (1973–1982), and Gabon (1975–1994). OPEC had its headquarters in Geneva, Switzerland, during the first five years of its existence. The headquarters were moved to Vienna, Austria, on September 1, 1965.

The founding members have veto power over admission of new members, but otherwise all full members have equal rights within the organization. Any country that is a "substantial net exporter" and whose petroleum interests are "fundamentally similar" to those of member countries is eligible to join. Trinidad and Tobago, Syria, and Congo have applied for membership but have not been accepted.

OPEC's objective is to coordinate and unify petroleum policies among member countries to secure fair and stable prices for petroleum producers; to provide an efficient, economic, and regular supply of petroleum to consuming nations; and to enable fair return on capital to those investing in the industry.

OPEC derives its power from the fact that its members own two-thirds of known petroleum reserves and that their extraction costs are minimal. Members of OPEC export 40% of all oil moving in international trade, primarily because their reserves are large and extraction costs are low. However, OPEC is not a perfect cartel because there are inherent conflicts of interest among its members. OPEC is not an Arab organization, as is sometimes mistakenly believed. Only three founding and four new members are Arab. In all, they are geographically dispersed over three continents and an island and vary considerably both in population and land area. It is not even true that all member countries are wealthy; per capita output and petroleum reserves vary enormously.

Brief History of OPEC

Long before OPEC was formed, the international oil industry was dominated by seven major companies (Exxon Corporation, Mobil Oil Corporation, Texaco, Standard Oil Company of California, Gulf Oil Corporation, British Petroleum Company, and Shell Petroleum Company), that controlled more than 90% of the world oil production outside the United States and the Soviet Union in addition to owning most transportation, refining, and marketing facilities. The US majors also controlled the sizable part of the US oil industry. As early as 1928, representatives of Exxon, Royal Dutch Shell, and British Petroleum met at the Achnacarry Castle in Scotland to form an "as-is" agreement. The agreement established principles to correct overproduction, reduce competition, and freeze individual market shares of their 1928 levels. They also agreed to sell crude oil and products at a fixed price regardless of source or production cost. Prices in the US Gulf (of Mexico) Coast terminals constituted the basis for price quotations throughout the world.

The oil companies persuaded oil-producing states to adopt a series of regulations controlling oil production by prorating the estimated demand for crude oil among all producing fields and wells. Demand was estimated on the basis of current prices so that additional production would not undermine the existing price structure. It should be noted here that because of this control system, consumers in Iraq were charged prices based on quotations at the US Gulf Coast, despite that (i) the crude oil was produced in Iraq, (ii) it was produced at low cost, (iii) it was refined in a nearby refinery, and (iv) the products were marketed by a local company.

The oil companies, whose goal was an orderly development of oil production through market allocation and price stabilization, were able to solidify

their control through the utilization of two important strategies. The first was the joint ownership of oil-producing companies in the Middle East and Venezuela. This strategy helped major oil companies to coordinate and direct output to meet corporate oil requirements and avoid excessive output. Second, to allow new oil to enter the world market through the major's integrated channel, long-term contracts were concluded between certain majors. The provisions of these contacts, which specified where crude oil was to be marketed and the terms of its sale, had the effect of tightening the joint control of the majors over the international oil industry.

As World War II was coming to an end, it became clear that the United States would no longer continue to be a major exporter of oil and that the Middle East would be called upon to meet the rising needs of the world. The United States and the United Kingdom signed an agreement in 1944 to enable U.S. oil companies to have access to Middle East oil and to have virtual control over international petroleum trade. In 1848, the Arabian American Oil Company (ARAMCO) was formed by Esso (now Exxon), Texaco, Socal, and Mobil to develop Saudi concession. Huge deposits of oil were soon discovered, and the US companies reaped profits from supplying low-cost oil to Europe and Japan and later to the United States. Other American companies gained access to concession in Kuwait, Iran, and other important Middle East oil producers.

Although the short-lived Iranian nationalization of Anglo-Iranian Oil Company in 1951 presented a temporary challenge to the majors' authority, by 1954 the majors had almost total control over the oil produced in Iran, Kuwait, and Saudi Arabia. As a result, the majors held enormous power over the political and economic destinies of these countries.

The oil-producing countries resented the fact that the foreign oil companies were given a free hand to exploit the oil reserves under concessions granted by the local rulers. Those agreements required the companies to pay only a nominal royalty, an average of twenty-one cents a barrel, to oil-producing countries. In return, the oil companies were exempted from taxes and were given a blank check to determine production and pricing policy.

The oil-producing countries were satisfied with these arrangements prior to World War II, when demand was low, prices were fluctuating or dropping, and prospect for discovering oil was uncertain. These oil-producing countries eventually decided to get their share of the oil being produced in their countries. Venezuela was one of the first countries to challenge these arrangements, when in 1945 the government demanded and received an even split in oil profits with companies. The Venezuela oil minister, Juan Pablo Perez Alfonzo, later a founder of OPEC, formulated the new rules and tax system.

In subsequent years, the oil-producing countries of the Middle East, which had been getting royalties of 12.5% of oil profits, adopted the Venezuela sharing plan. By the early 1950s, all the oil-producing countries had negotiated agreements providing for a 50/50 split of the profits with the oil company or consortium producing the oil.

The entry into the oil-production business in the 1950s of many new and independent companies put downward pressure on prices. The seven major corporations (the so-called Seven Sisters) discovered that smaller, more aggressive companies were eager to produce at high levels. The Seven Sisters had in the past reduced overseas production when the world oil market was saturated, thus preventing a drop in price.

By the end of 1957, prices were dropping. US producers felt turmoil when sales of oil from domestic wells were undercut by cheaper foreign oil. In an attempt to protect US oil producers, President Dwight D. Eisenhower asked the suppliers of foreign oil to limit their imports voluntarily to about 12% of US production. The effort failed, however, and President Eisenhower decided in 1959 to impose mandatory oil import quotas. Venezuela and Arab producers suddenly found themselves unable to expand their share of the world's biggest oil market.

Producing countries were also angered by a price cut in August 1960 by Esso and other companies. In September 1960, Iraq called a meeting of oil-producing governments to discuss the situation. Saudi Arabia, Iran, Kuwait, and Venezuela responded quickly and favorably. Leaders of the group were Perez Alfonzo of Venezuela, whose country was then the top world producer, and Sheik Abdullah Tariki, the oil minister of Saudi Arabia. The participation at the Baghdad Conference of September 10–14 decided to establish OPEC. The initial goal of OPEC was to return oil prices to their earlier levels and to gain the right to consult with oil companies on future pricing decisions. In June 1968, OPEC held a conference at its Vienna headquarters that produced a declaration of principles asserting the right of member nations to control world oil production and prices—a goal that at that time seemed unlikely to be realized. The 1969 revolution in Libya tilted the balance of power toward the producing countries, making it possible for OPEC to press for further authority. In September 1969, a group of officers headed by Muammar Qaddafi seized control of the Libyan government. He successfully pressured OPEC to cut oil production and to demand higher oil prices and a greater percentage of profits in the form of taxes.

In the early 1970s, OPEC countries were able to band together so effectively that the United States and other major industrial powers were forced to pay almost whatever OPEC decided to charge for oil. OPEC countries were able to control most of the supply and hence the price of one or more products. In February 1971, the Persian Gulf States of Abu Dhabi, Iran, Iraq, Kuwait, Qatar, and Saudi Arabia met in Tehran with oil company officials. Following the precedent set by Libya, they demanded and won what was considered at the time a major price increase of thirty to fifty cents a barrel. The Tehran agreement also raised the minimum tax rate on oil profits from 50% to 55%.

As a result of OPEC's controlling power, two so-called oil shocks hit the world in the 1970s. The first oil shock concerned Arab oil embargoes that were imposed against United States and Western Europe as a result of the 1973 Arab-Israeli conflict. The embargoes sent oil prices skyrocketing from three to twelve US dollars per barrel. The embargo was said to have cost the United States about 2 million barrels of oil a day. A 1974 Federal Energy Administration report estimated that the five-month embargo cost half a million American jobs and a gross national product loss between $10 billion and $20 billion. Hardest hit were Japan and Western Europe, areas most dependent on foreign oil. Most of northern Europe suffered from the embargo against the Netherlands because the Dutch port of Rotterdam was Europe's largest oil-refining and transshipment center. The second oil shock was caused by the Iranian revolution of 1979. The Iranian Revolution of February 1979 reduced Iran's crude exports to a trickle. Revolutionary turmoil, strikes in the oil fields, and other disturbances caused oil output to decline from a peak of 6.1 million barrels a day in September 1978 to virtually nothing in December and to an only partial recovery in March 1979. Even though Saudi Arabia and others increased production, there still was not enough oil to meet the strong world demand. The upward pressure on prices prompted OPEC to decide in March to move at once to a price of $14.54 a barrel, the level originally scheduled for October. The organization also agreed to allow countries to add surcharges to the official price. This was the first time OPEC had authorized members to set prices individually. Meanwhile, global oil markets fell into total disarray. Despite Saudi Arabia's 2 million barrels a day, extra output to compensate for the Iranian shortfall, spot crude prices escalated upward to $40 a barrel. Panic buying was largely to blame. The outbreak of the Iran/Iraq war on September 22, 1980, and a sudden loss of almost 4 million barrels a day, pushed up spot prices once again beyond $41 a barrel. In December 1980, the official price of the market crude was set at $32 a barrel, with a maximum of $36 a barrel for the same quality oil. The maximum price of any OPEC crude was fixed at $42 a barrel.

Oversupply and OPEC

Many observers predicted that OPEC would remain powerful forever or that the world would run out of oil by the early 2000s. These predictions did not materialize for several reasons. First, the global demand for oil plummeted to 53.5 million barrels a day in 1982 from 62.9 million barrels a day in 1979. OPEC's output, however, fell to about 18.7 million barrels a day, down from 30.5 million barrels a day—a drop of 40%. A large percentage of this drastic fall was generally believed to be due to the recession itself, a decrease in commercial energy consumption through conservation and use of oil substitutes. Second, after the 1970s, new oil was discovered in several parts of the world. In addition, non-OPEC countries helped push global supply levels to the point when prices started to drop. For example, oil production in Mexico, China, Egypt, Malaysia, Britain, Norway, and other countries all helped increase global supply. In the early twenty-first century, even more oil is expected to be pumped from wells in the Caspian Sea and other locations around the world, including Eastern Siberia, the Gulf of Mexico, Canada's tar sands deposits, and Venezuela's Orinoco Belt. Second, by the 1990s, most OPEC members were pumping out more oil than they were supposed to. This occurred in part because most of the world's oil-rich countries were struggling economically. The economies of the OPEC countries relied—and continue to rely—almost exclusively on oil; for many, oil accounts for about 75% of their national incomes. In the case of Kuwait, more than 90% of its revenues were coming from oil. Even Saudi Arabia, the leading oil producer in the world and the political leader of OPEC, faced debt problems and economic recession. In 1997, for example, Saudi Arabia earned about $45 billion from oil exports. In 1998, it earned only $30 billion. This helped put the Saudi budget of $13 billion in debt. As a result of the economic difficulty in oil-producing states, each individual OPEC member had an incentive to sell more oil. According to the dynamics of supply and demand, if countries produce more oil, then world oil prices should drop. This is exactly what happened in the 1980s and especially in the 1990s. In short, many OPEC countries simply could not afford not to pump more oil. Due to excessive production by both OPEC and non-OPEC producers throughout the 1990s, prices remained weak. Oil prices in the summer of 2000 were still

about one-third below what they were in 1990 and half of 1981 prices.

Future of OPEC

In the 1990s, many observers concluded that oil prices will stay, on average, at less than $20 per barrel for the next decade and that supplies will be maintained beyond 2020. This, however, changed as a result of the US invasion of Iraq. The price of oil shot up to almost $55 per barrel in October 2004. By their military action in the Gulf War and invasion of Iraq, the United States and its allies demonstrated that they consider Middle Eastern oil vital to their national security and economic interests. The United States and many other nations of the world sorely need access to Middle Eastern oil. US reliance on foreign oil imports had been increasing and seems likely to keep increasing. The main threat to energy security now seems to come from internal strife among Middle Eastern nations themselves. Both the Iran-Iraq War and Persian Gulf War emphasized this lesson.

Although Saudi domination of OPEC and of the world market was almost as strong in 2004 as it had ever been, there are no guarantees it will continue. It seems possible that other nations such as Iran, or former Soviet republics, could gain or regain status as major producers. Despite price fluctuation and rivalry among Middle Eastern nations, the importance of OPEC and the Middle Eastern oil remains unquestioned. The three biggest Persian Gulf countries—Saudi Arabia, Iran, and Iraq—could potentially supply 50% of oil in world trade. If they cooperate with each other, as they have in the past, they could dominate the world oil market. However, what is certain is that world oil prices and supplies will continue to fluctuate.

NASSER MOMAYEZI

See also Cartels; Energy: Alternative Development; Energy: Impact on Development; Middle East: History and Economic Development; Middle East: International Relations; Organization of Arab Petroleum Exporting Countries (OAPEC); Petrodollars

References and Further Reading

Alnasrawi, Abbas. *OPEC in a Changing World Economy.* Baltimore, MD: The Johns Hopkins University Press, 1985.

Amuzegar, Jahangir. *Managing the Oil Wealth: OPEC's Windfalls and Pitfalls.* New York: I.B. Tauris, 1999.

Carnoy, Martin, Manuel Castells, Stephen S. Cohen, and Fernando H. Cardoso. *The Global Economy in the Information Age: Reflections on Our Changing World.* University Park, PA: The Pennsylvania State University Press, 1993.

Danielsen, Albert L. *The Evolution of OPEC.* New York: Harcourt Brace Jovanovich, 1982.

Economides, Michael, and Ronald Oligney. *The Color of Oil: The History, the Money, and the Politics of the World's Biggest Business.* Katy, TX: Round Oak Publishing, 2000.

Evans, John. *OPEC and the World Energy Market: A Comprehensive Reference Guide.* 2d ed. United Kingdom: Longman Current Affairs, 1992.

Mabro, Robert, ed. *OPEC and the World Oil Market: The Genesis of the 1986 Price Crisis.* Oxford, : Oxford University Press, 1986.

Moran, Theodore H. *Oil Prices and the Future of OPEC: The Political Economy of Tension and Stability in the Organization of Petroleum Exporting Countries.* Washington, DC: Resources for the Future, 1978.

OPEC Annual Statistical Bulletin 1998. Vienna, Austria: The Secretariat Organization of the Petroleum Exporting Countries, 1999.

Tehranian, Majid. *Global Communication and World Politics: Domination, Development, and Discourse.* Boulder, CO: Lynne Rienner Publishers, 1999.

Skeet, Ian. *OPEC: Twenty-five Years of Prices and Politics.* Cambridge, UK: Cambridge University Press, 1988.

ORGANIZATION OF THE ISLAMIC CONFERENCE (OIC)

After World War I, the idea of the Organization of the Islamic Conference (OIC) was born and aimed at establishing a pan-Islamic organization to defend Islamic interests in the international arena and to enhance the inter-Islamic countries relations as well. The first step of formalizing the OIC was in 1969 in the aftermath the Zionist assault on Al-Aqsa Mosque. The leaders of Muslim states met in the Moroccan capital of Rabat to discuss a reasonable strategy. They decided to lay the foundation of an organization that would coordinate their relations in the future. In 1972, the Organization of Islamic Conference was formally established after approving the charter, which became a legally binding document. The membership was thirty countries in 1972 and increased to fifty-seven countries in 2004. In conflict management, OIC played a crucial role in some conflicts concerning Muslim countries, such as the Arab-Israeli issue and the Bosnia-Herzegovina war.

The headquarters of OIC were supposed to be Jerusalem, but due to the Israeli policies and occupation of the city, the leaders decided to locate the headquarters in Jeddah temporarily. Under the charter, the organization has three main aims. First, it must strengthen Islamic solidarity among member states and support the struggle of all Muslim people to safeguard their dignity, independence, and national rights. Second, the OIC must coordinate action to

safeguard the holy places as well as support the struggle of the Palestinian people and assist them in recovering their rights and liberating their occupied territories. Third, the OIC must work to eliminate racial discrimination and all forms of colonialism.

Five principles of the OIC were also enumerated by the charter: full equality among member states; observation of the right to self-determination and noninterference in the internal affairs of member states; observation of the sovereignty, independence, and territorial integrity of each state; the settlement of any dispute that might arise among member states by peaceful means; and a pledge to refrain, in relations among member states, from resorting to force or threatening to resort to use force against the unity and territorial integrity or the political independence of any state.

In addition to secondary organs and institutions, the Conference of Kings and Heads of State and Government, The Conference of Foreign Ministers, and The General Secretariat are the three main bodies that compose the OIC.

NILLY KAMAL EL-AMIR

References and Further Reading

Nafaa, Hassan. *Studies of International Organizations: From the Holy Alliance to the United Nations.* Cairo, Egypt: Cairo University Press, 1996.

Shalabi, Ibrahim. *International Organization: The International Regional and Specialized Organization.* Beirut, Lebanon: El-Dar El-Gamia, 1992.

OVERSEAS PRIVATE INVESTMENT CORPORATION (OPIC)

In 1971, the US government established the Overseas Private Investment Corporation (OPIC) to help US businesses invest overseas. OPIC, an independent agency in the executive branch of the federal government, attempts to foster economic development in new and emerging markets in the developing world, assist the US private sector in managing the risks associated with foreign direct investment, and support the basic tenets of US foreign policy. OPIC officials evaluate project proposals on the basis of their contribution to economic development and their potential for success. OPIC provides qualified investors with project financing, investment insurance, and a variety of investor services in some 150 developing nations and emerging economies throughout the world.

OPEC-supported projects have the potential to generate political and economic stability in the developing world, while simultaneously creating jobs in the US market. OPIC, which is based in Washington, DC, and has a staff of about two hundred employees, charges user fees for its services and operates on a self-sustaining basis at no cost to US taxpayers. OPIC clients are US companies. Unlike other governmental development agencies, OPIC does not provide direct aid or grants to foreign governments. In 2004, OPIC had about four hundred active clients, including small, medium, and large US businesses. In the post-Cold War world, demand for OPIC services has rapidly increased due to the demand for large-scale private sector infrastructure projects in the developing world. US companies engaging in infrastructure projects in the developing world have the potential to increase US exports to those nations.

OPIC can offer up to $400 million US dollars in total project support for any one project. Project support can come in two forms: project finance and political risk insurance. No more than $250 million can be spent in any one of these two areas. Although direct loans for any single project cannot exceed $250 million, most development projects receive between $2 million and $30 million. OPIC political risk insurance protects U.S. companies against currency inconvertibility, expropriation, and loss of assets or income due to war, revolution, insurrection, or politically motivated civil strife, terrorism, or sabotage. Rather than relying on foreign government guaranties, OPIC looks for repayment from revenues generated by the OPIC-funded development project. Thus, OPIC can finance infrastructure projects in countries where traditional financial institutions are reluctant to lend.

The OPIC Investor's Information Gateway Country Link Database allows potential investors to search the World Wide Web (WWW) for economic, political, and social data about all of the countries where OPIC operates. OPIC operates in virtually all countries in the developing world, with the noticeable exceptions of Cuba, the People's Republic of China (PRC), North Korea, Burma, Libya, and Sudan.

OPIC supports development projects in virtually every industrial and economic sector, including agriculture, energy, construction, natural resources, telecommunications, and transportation. Since 1971, OPIC has supported more than three thousand projects throughout the developing world, and the organization has funded almost $150 billion worth of investments that have helped developing countries generate over $11 billion in host-government revenues and create over seven hundred thousand host-country jobs.

OPIC supported transportation infrastructure improvements in Ecuador and Brazil that will update Ecuador's main airport and Brazil's railway system, setting the stage for economic growth in each country. OPIC granted $200 million in OPIC financing to a US

corporation for the construction of a new international airport in Quito, enabling Ecuador to move the Mariscal Sucre airport out of the center of Quito and thereby accommodate greater commercial air traffic and improve safety. OPIC provided a $2 million loan to a US corporation for the purchase of used railway cars from US suppliers. These used railway cars will be leased to users of the Brazilian railroad system, helping the country meet growing transportation needs. OPIC also provided $50 million to a US corporation to expand a wireless telecommunications network, which has expanded Bolivia's telecommunications infrastructure.

MICHAEL R. HALL

See also Brazil; Bolivia; Canadian International Development Agency (CIDA); Development History and Theory; Ecuador; Industrialization; Modernization; Technology: Impact on Development; United Nations Development Program (UNDP); United States Agency for International Development (USAID)

References and Further Reading

Brennglass, Alan C. *The Overseas Private Investment Corporation: A Study in Political Risk*. New York: Praeger Publishers, 1983.

Burnham, Jeffrey B. *The Overseas Private Investment Guaranty Program: From the Marshall Plan to the Overseas Private Investment Corporation*. Claremont, CA: Claremont Graduate School, 1978.

International Business Publications. *Overseas Private Investment Corporation Handbook*. Washington, DC: International Business Publications, 2000.

Overseas Private Investment Corporation. *Latin America and the Caribbean: A Special Report on the Activities of the Overseas Private Investment Corporation*. Washington, DC: Overseas Private Investment Corporation, 1995.

OXFAM

Oxfam is a nongovernmental development organisation that began in England in 1942 as the Oxford Committee for Famine Relief to support civilian populations in Europe during World War II. After the war, Oxfam's attention shifted to the needs of people in developing countries. Oxfam also spread to Canada (1963), Belgium (1964), the United States (1970), and Hong Kong (1976). Secular, welfare-oriented aid agencies were independently established in other countries with similar objectives; for example, Community Aid Abroad in Australia (1953), NOVIB in the Netherlands (1956), and Intermon in Spain (1956) were established. In 1994, this loose network of Oxfams and like-minded organisations decided to formally establish a confederation for greater impact

in cooperatively addressing the global causes of suffering and injustice. Oxfam International is an international group of independent nongovernmental organizations whose mission is fighting poverty and related injustice around the world. In 2004, the confederation was composed of twelve affiliates working in more than one hundred countries.

Oxfam affiliates collectively govern Oxfam International, set policy, and create plans that align their work. However, affiliates take independent responsibility for managing their work, and they retain autonomy and distinctiveness. The affiliates vary considerably in size, budget, geographical focus, thematic emphasis and proportions of long-term development, and humanitarian and advocacy work. Over the years, the approach of each organisation has evolved, reflecting a maturing understanding of the development challenge. The initial emphasis on relief shifted to long-term development working through local non-government organisations as partners and operating in a tradition of innovation and solidarity.

Recognising "development" as involving social and political as well as economic and technical obstacles, Oxfam has led a campaign on behalf of the people they work with overseas. The organization attempts to influence the larger forces that perpetuate poverty and to shape government, private sector, and multilateral policies on a range of relevant issues. An abiding challenge for developing countries is the need for greater trade and export opportunities. Besides lobbying for a fairer world trade regime, many of the Oxfam organisations have established alternative trading operations that sell goods handmade by producer organisations and fairly traded commodities.

Several things distinguish the Oxfam approach. These are the commitment to addressing the structural causes of poverty and related injustice; a focus on oppressed and marginalised people, especially women and indigenous people; the principles of "partnership" (working as equals with democratic, accountable local organisations) and investing in local organisational capacity; making interconnections between the local and the global; and also making links between networked organisations. Beyond their own work and the way it enhances the impact of partners' efforts, Oxfam organisations attempt to leverage wider change by building people's movements through advocacy based on (i) experience and closeness to poor and dispossessed communities and (ii) a broad constituency of supporters in their own communities.

Each Oxfam has a rights-based approach to development, seeking to enable people to exercise their rights and manage their own lives. Their work is integrated around five aims: the right to livelihood,

the right to basic services, the right to life, the right to be heard, and the right to identity.

JO-ANNE EVERINGHAM

See also Humanitarian Relief Projects; Non-Governmental organisations (NGOs)

References and Further Reading

Blackburn, Susan. *Practical Visionaries: A Study of Community Aid Abroad*. Carlton, Victoria: Melbourne University Press, 1993.

Eade, Deborah. *Development Methods and Approaches. Critical Reflections*. Oxford, UK: Oxfam, 2003.

Lindenberg, Marc, and Coralie Bryant. *Going Global. Transforming Relief and Development NGOs*. Bloomfield, CT: Kumarian Press, 2001.

Valk, Minke, Sarah Cummings, and Henk van Dam. *Gender, Citizenship, and Governance. A Global Source Book*. Oxford, UK: Oxfam, 2004.

Watkins, Kevin, and Penny Fowler. Rigged Rules and Double Standards. Trade, Globalisation, and the Fight Against Poverty. Oxford, UK: Oxfam, 2003.

P

PACIFIC ISLANDS FORUM

The Pacific Islands Forum has a membership of sixteen countries of the region: Australia, Cook Islands, Federated States of Micronesia, Fiji, Kiribati, Nauru, New Zealand, Niue, Palau, Papua New Guinea, Republic of the Marshall Islands, Samoa, Solomon Islands, Tonga, Tuvalu, and Vanuatu.

The Forum is similar to the Secretariat of the Pacific Community (SPC; formerly, the "South Pacific Commission"), but differs in important respects in terms of its history and composition. In 1972, the Forum was founded as the Trade Bureau, and it continues to act as a bureau in the twenty-first century with representative offices in Auckland, Beijing, Sydney, and Tokyo. Many people still refer to this Suva, Fiji-based organisation as the South Pacific Forum, this original title being approved by member governments only in 1988. The current name, Pacific Forum, was established in 2000 and reflects the projection of the organisation into the region, both north and south of the equator.

Most commentators will say that the South Pacific Forum began as a more closed organisation than the much older (founded in 1949) South Pacific Commission, itself renamed in 1999 as the Secretariat of the Pacific Community. One of the prime movers of the project, the late Ratu Sir Kamisese Mara, was explicit with his colleague Sir Michael Somare that emerging and about-to-be independent nations wanted an organisation where they could be free to speak about regional matters, away from the eyes of the withdrawing colonial powers that they believed dominated the older institution.

Australia and New Zealand are prominent members and financial supporters of both the Forum and the SPC. In contrast to the sixteen-member Forum, the SPC has a total of twenty-seven members. They are divided into two groups: the five founding members of Australia, France, New Zealand, United Kingdom, and United States of America, and the countries where the SPC programs take place. These countries are American Samoa, Cook Islands, Federated States of Micronesia (FSM), Fiji Islands, French Polynesia, Guam, Kiribati, Marshall Islands, Nauru, New Caledonia, Niue, Commonwealth of Northern Mariana Islands (CNMI), Palau, Papua New Guinea (PNG), Pitcairn Islands, Samoa, Solomon Islands, Tokelau, Tonga, Tuvalu, Vanuatu, and Wallis and Futuna.

Apart from their different membership and history, the two organisations differ in terms of what they do in the Pacific. Broadly speaking, the forum is conceived as a place for political and economic debate, whilst the SPC is known for its role advising on aspects of development, such as health and education. There are abiding overlaps.

There are four divisions of the Forum Secretariat in Suva, which is located near the University of the South Pacific. These four divisions are Development and Economic Policy, Trade and Investment, Political International Legal Affairs, and Corporate Services. The Pacific Islands Forum also chairs another regional organisation called the Council of Regional Organisations in the Pacific (CROP), consisting of ten institutions: Fiji School of Medicine (FShM), Forum Fisheries Agency (FFA), Pacific Islands Development Programme (PIDP), South Pacific Board

for Educational Assessment (SPBEA), South Pacific Regional Environmental Programme (SPREP), South Pacific Applied Geoscience Commission (SOPAC), Secretariat of the Pacific Community (SPC), South Pacific Tourism Organisation (SPTO), the University of the South Pacific (USP), and itself.

It is likely that in line with other name changes over the last few years, many of these organisations will drop the "south" part of their name since they all, just like the Forum and SPC, have activities in both the North and South Pacific.

All of the CROP institutions are autonomous and have governing bodies, funding sources, and programs of their own. It is for cooperation, sharing resources, and convenience that CROP exists under a Forum meeting structure. Two of the CROP organisations, FFA and SOPAC, though, grew directly out of the Pacific Islands Forum in earlier years, and one, SPREP, began its life as an arm of the SPC. SPREP is located in Samoa, just outside Apia, the capital city of that island country.

Notable in the CROP group is the Pacific Islands Development Programme (PIDP), which with its head Tongan-born Dr. Sitiveni Halapua is part of the East-West Center, a US State Department funded educational and advisory institution adjacent to the Manoa campus of the University of Hawaii. Like the Forum, the PIDP is meant to be a meeting of heads of government. A quite likely heading for a new name is the Pacific Islands Conference; the PIDP meets every three years, convening the heads of twenty states and territories, including the US state of Hawaii.

The Forum Fisheries Agency (FFA) is located in the Solomon Islands. Its headquarters were damaged during the civil turmoil in the Solomons in 2000, but it soon after began operating once again. Given the crucial importance of fisheries to the Pacific Islands countries, it is not surprising that the FFA occupies a central role in the Pacific Islands Forum's expenditure and activities. SOPAC is located in Suva and takes as its role the need to keep up on "nonliving" resource development by which minerals and especially future seabed mining prospects can be understood.

One of the most sensitive matters in the early twenty-first century has been the growing Australian insistence for the country to have a greater role in the actual running of regional institutions to which it is a substantial contributor. A fraught meeting in 2003, followed by another in 2004, reluctantly led to the appointment of Australian-born, career diplomat Gregory Urwin as the Secretary-General of the SPC.

For the future is the prospect of old colonial-established borders breaking down. After all, could not Japan and the Philippines be called the "Pacific Islands"? And, if Pacific Rim countries, such as the United States and New Zealand, hold membership in Pacific regional bodies, why could Latin American states bordering on the Pacific Ocean not hold membership as well? In fact, Chile has been gaining observer status progressively, first at the SPC and more recently at the Forum. The first instance was made possible by virtue of Rapanui (Easter Island), its province of 2,237 miles (3,600 kilometers) from the Chilean coast claimed in 1888; the early twenty-first century has brought with it interest in the island.

GRANT MCCALL

References and Further Reading

Crocombe, Ron. *The South Pacific*. Suva: Institute of Pacific Studies, The University of the South Pacific, 2001.

Hoadley, Steve. *The South Pacific Foreign Affairs Handbook*. Sydney: Allen and Unwin, 1992.

Pacific Islands Forum. 2005. Home Page. http://www.forum sec.org.fj/.

PAHLAVI, SHAH MUHAMMED REZA

Known as "The Shah of Iran," Muhammad Reza Pahlavi (1919–1980) was the last leader of Iran before the fall of the monarchy and the establishment of an Islamic republic under the Ayatollah Ruhollah Khomeini.

The Shah's father, Reza Shah (1878–1944), was a military officer who overthrew the Qajar Dynasty in 1921 and established his own, which he named Pahlavi, in 1925. The name was significant: Pahlavi was the language of Iran's pre-Islamic religion, Zoroastrianism. Reza Shah was a secular modernizer whose policies were anathema to the clerical establishment.

Muhammad Reza was five years old when he became Crown Prince. In 1931, he was sent to a finishing school in Switzerland after which he spent three years (1935–1938) in a military school in Tehran. In 1939, he married a sister of King Farouk I of Egypt. They had a daughter (b. 1940) but no heir to the throne. Reza Shah had wrested partial control of Iran's lucrative oil industry from the British, introduced modern schooling, and begun construction of Iran's first railroad. He had also leaned toward Germany in its looming confrontation with Britain and Russia. However, British and Russian forces invaded Iran in August 1941, deposed Reza Shah, and placed Muhammad Reza, then twenty-one years old, on the throne. The two allied powers occupied Iran for the remainder of the war.

The confrontation between the Shah and Ayatollah Ruhollah Khomeini began immediately. Khomeini

denounced the Shah's "dictatorial regime" and called on the nation to "rise up for God." The Shah became dependent on US support, which grew stronger as the Cold War developed. Stalin withdrew Soviet troops from northern Iran in May 1946 only under severe pressure from Washington, DC. The main threat to the Pahlavi Dynasty now seemed to come from the Tudeh (Communist) Party, not from the clerics. After a February 1949 assassination attempt, the Shah imposed martial law and banned the Tudeh Party.

A power struggle between the Majlis (parliament) and the Shah became entangled with Cold War politics. In March 1951, Prime Minister Muhammad Mossadeq passed a bill nationalizing the Anglo-Iranian Oil Company. The Shah tried to remove Mossadeq from power but was forced to flee Iran on August 16, 1953. The US Central Intelligence Agency (CIA) financed street riots against Mossadeq, and three days later the Shah was back on his throne but with the stigma of foreign sponsorship. Mossadeq was imprisoned, and the nationalization of oil industry was reversed. In 1954, the Shah rigged parliamentary elections, and in 1955 he joined the Baghdad Pact. The United States greatly increased foreign aid to Iran while urging internal reform. The Shah's secret police received training from the Israeli Mossad.

In 1959, the Shah married his third wife Farah Diba, who bore a son in 1960. The dynasty now appeared secure. The 1960s was a decade of progressive reform in Iran. Secular education was greatly expanded, and voting rights were extended to women. These innovations offended the ultraconservative Shi'a religious establishment, and the Shah's land reform program, begun in 1961, threatened their financial base. Ayatollah Khomeini denounced the government in such vitriolic terms that the Shah's men arrested him in 1963 and jailed him for three months. Ayatollah resumed his verbal attacks immediately upon his release. By now the Shah had disbanded parliament and was ruling by decree. Khomeini was forced into exile. All political opposition was now channeled through the clergy. The Shah pushed ahead with his economic reforms, which he called his "White Revolution." The reforms included building roads, initiating irrigation projects, and establishing public health programs.

His throne seemingly secure, the Shah's megalomania grew. He staged a royal ceremony in 1967 that included dropping 17,532 roses from air force planes, one rose for every day of his life. His wife was designated Empress. The anger of the clerics simmered. In 1971, the royal couple spent hundreds of millions of dollars on a lavish festival in Persepolis, commemorating 2,500 years of monarchy (traced back to the Persian king Cyrus). The deliberate emphasis on Iran's pre-Islamic past enraged the clerics.

In 1973, the Organization of Petroleum Exporting Countries (OPEC) quadrupled the price of crude oil. In response, the Nixon Administration sought to repatriate capital by selling a panoply of advanced weapons systems to Iran, with the understanding that the Shah would protect the Persian Gulf from Soviet threats.

The Shah was at the height of his power in 1974 when he was diagnosed with lymphatic leukemia and began secretly to undergo medical treatment. Corruption was rampant within his government. Political opponents could only be held in check by the secret police, who routinely resorted to torture. American President Jimmy Carter, inaugurated in January 1977, urged respect for human rights on the Shah, who, as he grew sicker, wavered between liberalism and repression. Students in Tehran rioted in December 1977, demanding Khomeini's return from exile. The Ayatollah was living outside of Paris, dictating fiery sermons into a tape recorder. His messages, reproduced by the hundreds, were played over loudspeakers in mosques throughout Iran.

On January 16, 1979, the Shah, now very ill, left Iran, never to return. Khomeini arrived on February 1, and declared Iran an Islamic republic two months later. The US government pressured other countries to provide the Shah with refuge. His final *hegira* took him to Egypt, Morocco, the Bahamas, and Mexico before finally being admitted to the United States for medical treatment. Muhammad Reza Pahlavi died on July 27, 1980, in Cairo, Egypt.

ROSS MARLAY

See also Iran; Islamic Fundamentalism; Khomeini, Ayatollah Ruhollah; Mossaddeq, Muhammed

References and Further Reading

Cockcroft, James D. *Muhammad Reza Pahlavi, Shah of Iran.* New York: Chelsea House, 1989.
Mackey, Sandra. *The Iranians: Persia, Islam and the Soul of a Nation.* New York: Plume, 1996.
Shawcross, William. *The Shah's Last Ride.* New York: Simon & Schuster, 1989.

PAKISTAN

The present Islamic Republic of Pakistan is bounded by Afghanistan on much of its western border and by Iran on the southwest portion of it. Its entire eastern border is bounded by India. On the south, the country opens to the Arabian Sea, and in the extreme north it abuts China. Roughly twice the size of California,

much of its land is a hot, dry desert. A more temperate climate is found where the northern piedmont begins its rise toward some of the world's highest mountains in the Hindu Kush and Karakorum ranges. All five rivers that give the Punjab its name feed into the Indus, making it one of the world's great rivers and providing irrigation waters to support Pakistan's agriculture, which centers on wheat and cotton.

However, when the country gained independence in 1947 as a homeland for the Muslims of the Indian subcontinent, it included East Bengal, bounded on three sides by India and by the Bay of Bengal on the fourth, which caused the two "wings" of Pakistan to be separated by about 1,500 miles of land or 2,500 miles of sea. The two regions were utterly different in most physical aspects. East Pakistan (which broke away in 1971 to become Bangladesh) consists largely of a fertile alluvial plain laid down by the revered Ganges and the broad Brahmaputra rivers, both of which originate in the Himalayan Mountains. East Pakistan, which is now Bangladesh, was only about one-sixth the size of West Pakistan, but it contained far more people. Its hot and humid climate favors a riot of subtropical vegetation where agriculture emphasizes rice and jute. Lacking stone, its roads have been made from burnt bricks laboriously broken by hand to make artificial gravel, and many of its rural houses have been sited on human-made earthen plinths to raise them above the expected crests of annual floods.

At Independence, only Lahore in West Pakistan and Dacca in East Pakistan were major cities; Karachi, chosen as the first capital, was a small port city that had served as an *entrepôt* for the produce of the Punjab during the British colonial period. Later, as government buildings for the new capital, Islamabad, were being constructed on the Potwar Plateau during Ayub Khan's rule, so were new capital buildings being erected in Dacca in the expectation that meetings of the National Assembly would alternate between the two cities. Such double expenditures in the interest of maintaining parity between the two wings continued to drain the resources of this poor country until 1971. Then, with the intervention of India in what had started as a civil war resulting from a disputed election, East Pakistan became the sovereign nation of Bangladesh. Painful as the separation was, in the view of many observers since, the dissociation has been a positive benefit for both.

Chronic political instability underlies most of Pakistan's development problems. In fifty years, the country has had fifteen different prime ministers, and for more than half of its brief history it has been under military rule. Such turmoil has also made it difficult to root out endemic corruption and put in place a just system of taxation. It is believed that taxes collected represent less than 50% of taxes owed; kickbacks are customary in most business transactions, whether with the government or with private firms. One finance minister estimated that illegal payments extracted by government officials amounted to about 60% of the total the government was able to collect in taxes. As a consequence of such practices, Pakistan ranks among the most corrupt nations in the developing world.

Mohammed Ali Jinnah, founder of Pakistan who was given the honorary title Quaid-i-Azam (Great Leader), served as governor general along lines derived from British rule, but he died in 1948 after barely a year in office. His Prime Minister Liaquat Ali Khan was assassinated in 1951, and the tenures of those prime ministers who followed him were of short duration. During this first decade of independence, the *Mohajir* immigrants from India, who dominated the government, largely maintained the secular, democratic state envisioned by the Quaid-i-Azam and favored industry over agriculture in their development investments. But by the mid-1950s, the economy was stagnant, and the country was unable to feed its population, increasing at the rate of more than 3% each year.

General Mohammed Ayub Khan's martial law regime (1958–1969) brought political stability and enabled the country to embark on a planned economy that made real progress, resulting in an average 5.5% growth rate, but it was also during this period that wealth became concentrated in twenty-two families of industrialists and bankers. Meanwhile, as a result of the Green Revolution, Pakistan approached self-sufficiency in food and fibers, but productive agricultural lands also became concentrated in the holdings of a few "feudal" landlords.

After the brief rule of General Agha Mohammed Yahya Khan (1968–1971), which ended with the creation of Bangladesh, Zulfikar Ali Bhutto was elected to power on a populist platform that promised an *Awami raj* (people's rule). Even though a large landowner himself and the scion of an aristocratic Sindhi family, Bhutto promised land reform (which proved to be ineffective) and did nationalize ten basic industries as well as the banks and insurance companies. Then, as the inefficient state-owned enterprises created budget deficits, the Bhutto government (1971–1977) became more and more dependent on foreign loans and the remittances of overseas Pakistani workers, an economic situation further exacerbated by the perceived need to counter the threat posed when India detonated a nuclear device in 1974.

Following a bitterly contested election in 1977, Bhutto was ousted by his own appointee to the top

military post, General Mohammed Zia ul-Haq, and eventually was hanged by Zia as the outcome of flimsy criminal charges. Longest lasting of the Pakistani governments, the government of Zia (1977–1988) brought back martial law, did little to tamper with the status quo of the economy, but did introduce a program of austere Islamization. Of special interest to the Zia government was an attempt to free the financial system of *riba* (variously defined either as usury or interest). "Interest-free banking" has been a chimera pursued ever since by successor governments, while the bankers themselves have dragged their heels about implementing so-called profit sharing to replace interest. It has never been clear how a country that depends so heavily on external interest-bearing loans can meet its obligations should the desired financial utopia ever be achieved.

After the violent end of Zia in the explosion of his airplane that also killed the US ambassador, Benazir Bhutto, the daughter of Zia's nemesis, came to power as prime minister in an ineffectual coalition government. As the first woman to hold such a lofty position in a Muslim country, Bhutto was never able to carry out the ambitious reform measures she had campaigned for. Caught between the demands of the ever-powerful military leaders and the cunning self-serving interests of officials of the provincial government of the Punjab, Pakistan's most populous province, she was unable even to quell spreading social unrest and the growing ethnic violence in Sindh, her home province. Mian Nawaz Sharif, Governor of the Punjab, succeeded in persuading the president in 1990 to dissolve the National Assembly and to dismiss Benazir Bhutto for failing to maintain law and order. She and her husband also were under a cloud of unspecified charges of corruption.

From 1990 until 1999, the government seesawed between Nawaz Sharif and Benazir Bhutto, with four different caretaker prime ministers serving as the powerless fulcrum between them. As had now become traditional, Bhutto and Sharif took turns getting each other dismissed on charges of corruption. Despite their disparate backgrounds—Bhutto from a Sindhi "feudal" family and Sharif a Punjabi industrialist—both managed to continue the process of privatizing the industries that the elder Bhutto had nationalized. During this period, investment in development decreased while military costs increased, and the country was unable to meet the fiscal targets demanded by the International Monetary Fund (IMF). When Pakistan removed all doubt that it had attained nuclear capability by testing a nuclear device on May 28, 1998, in the Chaghi hills in Balochistan, it incurred the punishment of economic sanctions that left it in an even worse financial condition. Once again, the

military became involved, this time in a bloodless *coup d'état* on October 12, 1999, that resulted in Nawaz Sharif being sent into exile in Saudi Arabia and General Pervez Musharraf taking over as chief executive, a title he exchanged in less than a year to that of president.

At great hazard to his own continued tenure, since so large and so vocal a portion of the population opposed the policy, Musharraf sided with the United States and its allies in the military strike against Afghanistan in the War on Terrorism. The reward for this decision was the lifting of economic sanctions on his country and a renewed generosity on the part of Pakistan's creditors to pump fresh money into the economy.

During all this hectic period of political instability, there has been a steady increase in life expectancy and a decline in infant death rates. Encouraging as these trends are, they nevertheless have exacerbated the population problem. As more and more people crowd into the cities, whose infrastructure cannot keep pace, public health has suffered and social unrest has increased.

Public safety, both in urban and rural areas, has declined for a number of reasons, principal among them being increased ethnic and sectarian disputes that end in greater violence as a result of guns diverted from armaments funneled through Pakistan during the 1980s to assist the Afghan *Mujahedin* fighting the Soviet occupation army. Adding to Pakistan's problems were some 2 million Afghans who crossed the border seeking refuge and either have remained in squalid camps or migrated to little less squalid slums in the cities. At this time, too, Pakistan became a major pipeline for hard drugs to the West. Just as thousands of AK-47s were diverted from their intended destination in Afghanistan, much of the heroin was diverted and remained in Pakistan. No known heroin addicts were reported for Pakistan in 1980, but eight years later there were 1.2 million.

Public education has never received adequate funding, but from 1960 to 1990, it did increase from 1.1% of the gross national product (GNP) to 3.4%, yet even the latter figure must be contrasted with at least 30% of the GNP that went into defense. There has been a tendency, too, to build the educational system from the top down. Having inherited only one university from undivided India—Punjab University—Pakistan rushed to erect universities, first in every province, then to accommodate demands in every large city, while neglecting primary and secondary schools. To some extent, this lack was met by the organization of private schools at all levels, including colleges for undergraduates. As a result of the thrust of Islamization of the Zia administration, *deeni madaris*,

religious schools, sprang up all over the country to give free primary education to poor students, especially orphan boys, who otherwise would have had none. These schools later became breeding grounds for the fanatical Taliban.

For a country where once the attitude prevailed of "let government do it," it is heartening to see that since the 1990s there has been a proliferation of nongovernmental agencies (NGOs) devoted to various sectors of social and human betterment, human rights, democratization, women's empowerment, and low-income housing. One of the earliest of these was the Fauji Foundation, established to help the more than 9 million ex-military personnel and their dependents lead satisfactory lives in civil society. Under the direction of retired officers, the foundation funds educational institutions and awards scholarships and manages hospitals and dispensaries; it carries out these activities with income it generates by its own industrial operations ranging from the manufacture of corn flakes to cement and fertilizer. Looking to the future, the foundation has pioneered in training young people to write software for computers.

Equally inspiring is the Edhi Foundation that began as a one-man affair when a peddler in Karachi named Abdul Sattar Edhi saved up enough from his earnings to open a modest dispensary to serve the poor. When others contributed money to help in his work, the foundation he then established grew to the point that it fields more than four hundred ambulances (and can even provide air ambulance service), has two hundred welfare centers scattered throughout the country, operates a blood bank, provides maternal and child welfare services, supplements the scanty food provided to prisoners in jails, and arranges a decent burial for indigents who die on the street. Combining the compassionate virtues of Mahatma Gandhi and Mother Teresa, Edhi himself drives his ambulances and helps to prepare the dead for burial.

CHARLES BOEWE

See also Ayub Khan, Mohammed; Bangladesh; Bhutto, Benazir; Mujahedin; Taliban; Yahya Khan, Agha Mohammed; Zia ul-Haq, Mohammed

References and Further Reading

Baxter, Craig, and Charles H. Kennedy, eds. *Pakistan 2000.* Lanham, MD: Oxford, England: Lexington Books, 2000.

Blood, Peter R., ed. *Pakistan: A Country Study.* 6th ed. Washington, DC: Library of Congress, 1995.

Burki, Shahid Javed. *Pakistan: The Continuing Search for Nationhood.* Boulder, CO: Westview Press, 1991.

Central Intelligence Agency. "Pakistan." *The World Fact Book.* Washington, DC: Government Printing Office, 2000.

Harrison, Selig S., Paul H. Kreisberg, and Dennis Kux, eds. *India and Pakistan, the First Fifty Years.* Washington, DC: Woodrow Wilson Center Press, 1999.

Malik, Hafeez, ed. *Pakistan: Founders' Aspirations and Today's Realities.* Karachi: Oxford University Press, 2001.

Mahmood, Safdar. *Pakistan: Political Roots and Development, 1947–1999.* Karachi: Oxford University Press, 2000.

Schofield, Victoria, ed. *Old Roads, New Highways: Fifty Years of Pakistan.* Karachi and New York: Oxford University Press, 1997.

Weiss, Anita M. *Culture, Class, and Development in Pakistan: The Emergence of an Industrial Bourgeoisie in Punjab.* Boulder, CO: Westview Press, 1991.

PALAU, REPUBLIC OF

The Republic of Palau, a nation of more than 250 islands (7° 30′ N latitude, 134° 30′ E longitude) in the western Pacific, lies 650 kilometers southeast of the Philippines. The islands (land area 458 square kilometers or 177 square miles), mostly fringed by coral reefs, vary from low-lying coral atolls to islands with mountains of high altitudes; Mount Ngerchelchuus reaches the highest altitude at 242 meters (790 feet) above sea level. The regional climate is tropical, hot, and humid throughout the year with a wetter season from May to November. Typhoons, although rare, may occur over the islands from June to December. Tropical forests cover most of the islands, and littoral zones have mangroves interspersed with white, sandy beaches. On Babeldaob (also referred to as Babelthaup) there are extensive areas of savanna and grasslands. The capital is Oreor (formerly Koror), but a new site is under construction twenty kilometers to the northeast.

Migrants, probably from Indonesia, first settled the islands of Palau around 3,500 years ago. The Spanish explorer Ruy López de Villalobos visited the islands in 1543, but the islands, although notionally belonging to Spain, were not colonized until late in the nineteenth century. Spain sold the islands to Germany in 1899, and the German colonists established coconut plantations and phosphate mining. The islands were seized by Japan during World War I. The League of Nations mandated the islands to Japan in 1920. During this period, the Japanese population grew to more than twenty-five thousand and significant development occurred in Oreor with paved roads, water supplies, and schools established. However, Palauans lost much of their traditional lifestyle and inheritance patterns as their lands were confiscated by Japanese colonists. In the late 1930s, the Japanese closed Palau to the outside world and began building military bases and fortifications.

During World War II, fighting between the United States and Japan occurred on the islands of Peleliu and Angaur. The United States took control of the islands in 1944, and in 1947, the islands became a part of the United Nations Trust Territory of the Pacific Islands administered by the United States. Palauans voted in 1979 not to become part of the Federated States of Micronesia, and a new constitution was adopted in 1980; Palau became self-governing in 1981. In a transitional period, marked by the violent deaths of Presidents Haruo Remeliik (assassinated in 1985) and Lazarus Salii (committed suicide in 1988), Palauans negotiated terms of the Free Association Compact with the United States that was finally approved in 1993. On October 1, 1994, Palau became an independent nation and was admitted to the United Nations on December 15, 1994.

Under the Free Association Compact, Palau is a sovereign nation, conducting its own foreign relations, but the United States is responsible for its defense. Palau is a democratic republic with directly elected executive and legislative branches. The president and vice president are elected every four years, and the bicameral legislature consists of a house of delegates (one member for each of the sixteen states) and a Senate with nine members. Each state government has an elected governor and state legislature. A council of chiefs advises the president on traditional customs. Tommy Esang Remengesau, Jr., was elected president in 2001.

In 2004, the population of twenty thousand had a growth rate of 1.46% and a life expectancy of 66.6 years (males) and 73.2 years (females). The population is dominated by Micronesians (70%), with Asians (28%, mainly Filipinos, Chinese, Taiwanese, and Vietnamese) and white people (2%). English and Palauan are the official languages, but other official languages are recognized in certain states: Sonsorol (Sonsoralese and English), Tobi (Tobi and English), and Angaur (Angaur, Japanese, and English). Most Palauans are Christians (Roman Catholics, Seventh Day Adventists, Jehovah's Witnesses, and Assembly of God parishioners). Approximately one-third of the population follows the indigenous religion known as *Modekngei*.

The economy is based on tourism, subsistence agriculture, and fishing. Tourism is focused on scuba diving and snorkeling over pristine coral reefs and war wrecks, and this sector accounts for more than half of the country's gross domestic product. Major tourist attractions are the Rock Islands, forest-clad limestone pinnacles that seem to rise out of the sea; Jellyfish Lake (a marine lake with dense jellyfish populations); and limestone caves with stalactites and rock art. The majority of tourists come from Japan, Taiwan, and the United States. The principal crops are coconuts, cassava, sweet potatoes, taro, and bananas. Industrial activities include garment making and production of tourist artifacts from shells, wood, and pearls. Major exports are shellfish, tuna, and copra.

Environmental problems include inadequate disposal sites for solid waste and threats to marine systems from sand and coral mining, illegal fishing practices (with use of dynamite), and overfishing in areas with high human population densities.

The service sector employs 75% of the workforce, with the government providing over one-quarter of all jobs. Per capita income is high for the region, being approximately double that of the Philippines and much of Micronesia. Economic aid, largely from the United States but also from Japan, Australia, and New Zealand, provides significant budgetary support, and a major challenge for the country is reducing its reliance on this foreign assistance.

PATRICK L. OSBORNE

See also Oceania: History and Economic Development; Oceania: International Relations

Further Reading

Leibowitz, A.H. *Embattled Island: Palau's Struggle for Independence*. Westport, CT: Praeger Publishers, 1996.

PALESTINE

Palestine has never been and is not yet a state. It has never been governed fully and completely by Palestinian-Arab leadership. Yet, for decades, it has existed, if only in the hearts and minds of the Palestinian people and others who sympathize with their cause.

The Arabs moved from the Arabian Peninsula into the region of *Filistin*, the land of the biblical Philistines, in the middle of the seventh century AD. Under Umayyad and then Abbasid control, Palestine was but one of several provinces of the Islamic caliphate, located on the eastern shores of the Mediterranean Sea. The region held limited importance within these empires; its capital, Jerusalem, held Islamic religious significance but was never a city of political strength or economic power.

In the eighteenth and nineteenth centuries, Great Britain began to establish a sphere of influence in the Palestinian region as Ottoman strength in the Middle East began to wane. For the British and other Europeans, including the French and the Russians, Palestine was attractive for two primary reasons. First, it was strategically located at the crossroads of Africa and Asia and offered potential land and sea access to other major interests in the Far East, including India and China. Second, the region held Christian religious

value. The biblical cities of Jerusalem, Bethlehem, and Nazareth were home to numerous holy sites. Palestine also included the Galilee region and other areas of Christian interest, all of which attracted Christian pilgrims and others hailing back to the Crusades.

The fall of the Ottoman Empire at the end of World War I saw the dissection of the Middle East and a redistribution of sections of the region to the Great Powers. Arrangements between the French and the British, such as the Sykes-Picot Agreement of 1916, allotted parts of the former empire to the victorious Europeans. Britain was awarded Palestine, which was placed under British Mandate in 1917.

The purported purpose of the Mandate was to serve as an interim governing authority. The British would remain in Palestine only until a Palestinian leadership could develop and was capable of running its own affairs of state.

While governing Palestine, the British allowed Jewish immigration from Europe on a large scale. The November 1917 Balfour Declaration stated unequivocally that the British supported the creation of a Jewish national home in Palestine and that they would abet its development. Yet the indigenous Palestinian community feared the immigration of Jews, who identified with the Zionist movement that sought to create a Jewish homeland in their historic Jewish home. Increasingly, it became clear that the Jews were coming to stay and that their intention was indeed to take a part, or all, of Palestine as their own for the purpose of creating a separate Jewish state on Palestinian soil.

From 1936 to 1939, the indigenous Palestinian community rose up against the Jewish immigration. This period, known as the Arab Revolt, was similar to later uprisings (*intifada*). The revolt represented indigenous Palestinian efforts to stave off Jewish immigration and to press the British to rein in the flows of Jewish immigrants from abroad. The 1939 White Paper, issued by the British Mandatory authorities, resulted, with the goal of limiting and further restricting Jewish immigration to Palestine. While immigration was largely stymied, however, Jewish efforts to come to Palestine from Europe continued unabated.

The Creation of Israel and the Destruction of Arab Palestine

With the end of World War II, war-torn Britain saw the need to divest itself of many parts of its empire, including Palestine. The departure from Palestine was no simple task, however; two leaderships with two conflicting sets of interests and both with compelling historical and cultural connections to the same land now sat poised ready to take control of Palestinian governance. The answer, the United Nations (UN) determined, was to partition Palestine into two states, one Jewish, the other Arab.

The UN Palestine Partition Plan of 1947 sought to equitably resolve the problem of Palestine. Palestine was to be divided into seven parts; three for the Arabs and three for the Jews, with Jerusalem remaining in a unique state separate from the rest, given that it was the home to Jewish, Muslim, and Christian holy sites and therefore held international interest.

While the Jews saw the Plan as an opportunity to legitimize their land claim and provide the basis for the future Jewish state, Arab Palestinians saw the plan as a capitulation to illegitimate foreign colonial interests. World guilt resulting from the European Jewish Holocaust was, the Arabs feared, playing a role in the invalidation of their own long-held historic claim to the land of Palestine. Thus, their response was clear: not an inch of Palestine could be sacrificed to Jewish national interests.

Yet throughout this period (1946–1948), Jewish interests had already begun to mobilize militarily and otherwise conquer Palestine, pushing Arab residents out in the process whenever and however possible. Through land purchases, paramilitary activity, and the fostering of an atmosphere of fear, the *Yishuv* (the Jewish settlement governance structure) slowly succeeded in methodically overtaking Arab Palestine and replacing it with what would soon be a Jewish state. The development of a huge Palestinian Diaspora resulted, part of the larger catastrophe (*al-Nakba*) that befell the Palestinians as a result of Israel's creation.

The State of Israel was declared in Tel Aviv on May 15, 1948. Immediately thereafter, surrounding Arab states attacked the new state. The goal of these Arab states was presumably to push the Jews out to reassert the authority that was due to the indigenous Palestinian-Arab leadership. Yet, upon the conclusion of the war, a war won by the Israelis, most of the regions of Palestine that had been designated by the UN Partition Plan as the territory of Arab Palestine were now under Jordanian and Egyptian control. Arab Palestine had been destroyed, divided into three parts by three countries: Israel, Egypt, and Jordan.

The Role of Terror/Freedom Fighting in Palestine's Independence Struggle

The struggle to reassert sovereignty over all of Arab Palestine was not initially fought by the Palestinians themselves. From 1948 until 1964, the Palestinian

Arabs were in a state of chaos and disarray. While some efforts to attack Jewish interests in the new Israeli state were made, the outside Arab states (primarily Egypt and later Syria) played the most significant military role in seeking to destroy Israel. But of course, in every instance, they failed.

It was in this context that a liberation movement created by the Palestinians themselves began to emerge in 1964. The purpose of the Palestine Liberation Organization, the most significant group to arise at this time, was to liberate Palestine from Israeli control. When Israel conquered and then occupied the West Bank, East Jerusalem, and Gaza from the Jordanians and Egyptians in 1967 (that is, the parts of Palestine that these countries had taken during the 1948 war), the whole of historic western Palestine became the center of Palestinian-Arab liberation activity.

The primary mode of operation utilized was terror—that is, the use of surprise attacks on civilians in nonmilitary locations in an effort to instill fear in the enemy while at the same time attract global media attention to the Palestinian plight. While many such attacks occurred within Israel, others were carried out against Israeli interests in Europe and elsewhere. El Al Airline flights became a regular hijacking target.

Perhaps the most notorious Palestinian terrorist attack, however, was the capture and eventual murder of eleven Israeli athletes and coaches during the 1972 Olympic Games in Munich, West Germany. The attack was carried out by a group calling itself Black September, in reference to the many Palestinian deaths that had occurred in Jordan in September 1970 as a result of civil conflict between the Jordanian military and the Palestinian refugees who had fled there in 1948 and 1967. Covered by the media internationally, the Munich attack put a new and terrifying face on the Arab-Israeli conflict, although it did little to change world public opinion in favor of the Palestinian people. This face of terror dominated world public opinion for years and only began to soften following the outbreak of the Palestinian *intifada* (uprising) in 1987.

The Two-State Solution Revisited

In September 1988, at the height of the Palestinian *intifada*, Yasser Arafat ,as chairman of the Palestine Liberation Organization renounced terror and accepted, pending further discussions and negotiation, a two-state solution in which Israel would be accepted alongside a State of Palestine. Arafat's statement essentially redefined the meaning of the word "Palestine"; from that moment forward, Palestine

meant the West Bank, Gaza, and East Jerusalem. After four decades of war, terror, and bloodshed, Palestine had effectively been divided, bearing an intended outcome that would not differ that greatly from the UN Partition Plan of 1947.

This change paved the way for negotiations between the George H. W. Bush Administration and the Palestine Liberation Organization. Soon thereafter, Israel began negotiations with the Palestinians as well. Secret meetings between the Palestinians and the Israelis in Oslo, Norway, led to the signing of a Declaration of Principles on September 13, 1993. The Declaration called for a ceasing of hostilities between the two sides, and discussed ways in which the Israeli occupation of the West Bank and Gaza would be phased out to make way for Palestinian Authority control of Palestinian Arab land. This would be the first time that the Palestinian people would be able to run their own affairs, govern their own citizens, and protect their own domestic and international interests.

And yet, the slow implementation of Oslo and the obvious oversights in moving toward complete Palestinian sovereignty led to its breakdown and, eventually, the al-Aqsa Intifada, which began at the end of September 2000. This uprising in many ways mirrored previous Palestinian terror activities carried out between the late 1960s and the late 1980s although its primary terror tactic, suicide bombings, was an innovation in Palestinian liberation activity.

Although the al-Aqsa Intifada served to slow the progress of a movement toward Palestinian self-rule, the Palestinian people are unlikely to give up on their goal of some day achieving a fully independent sovereign state in at least part of historic Palestine. Indeed, the death of Palestinian Authority President Yasser Arafat in late 2004 only served to catalyze Palestinian resolve to finally achieve the creation of a reconstituted Palestine, revitalizing what was, to that point, a moribund peace process between Palestinians and Israelis. Thus, the question to be asked when referring to the creation of the State of Palestine is not *if* it will eventually occur but *when*.

STEVEN C. DINERO

See also Arab–Israeli Wars (1948, 1956, 1967, 1973); Arafat, Yasser; Hezbollah; Intifada; Israel; Palestine Liberation Organization (PLO); Palestinian Diaspora; Zionism

References and Further Reading

Brown, Nathan J. *Palestinian Politics After the Oslo Accords: Resuming Arab Palestine.* Berkeley, CA: University of California Press, 2003.

Farsoun, Samih K., and Christina E. Zacharia. *Palestine and the Palestinians*. Reading, MA: Perseus Books, 1997.

Gerner, Deborah J. *One Land, Two Peoples: The Conflict over Palestine (Dilemmas in World Politics Series)*, 3rd ed. Reading, MA: Perseus Books, 2004.

Hadawi, Sami. *Bitter Harvest: A Modern History of Palestine*. 4th ed. Northampton, MA: Interlink Publishing Group, 1998.

Idinopulos, Thomas A. *Weathered by Miracles: A History of Palestine from Bonaparte and Muhammad Ali to Ben-Gurion and the Mufti*. Chicago: Ivan R. Dee Publisher, 1998.

Jung, Dietrich, ed. *The Middle East and Palestine: Global Politics and Regional Conflict*. New York: Palgrave Macmillan, 2004.

Khan, Mushtaq H. *State Formation in Palestine: Viability and Governance During a Social Transformation (Political Economy of the Middle East and North Africa, 2)*. New York: Routledge/Curzon, 2004.

Said, Edward W. *The Question of Palestine*. New York: Vintage Books, 1992.

———. *From Oslo to Iraq and the Road Map: Essays*. New York: Pantheon, 2004.

Shepherd, Naomi. *Ploughing Sand: British Rule in Palestine, 1917–1948*. Piscataway, NJ: Rutgers University Press, 1999.

PALESTINE LIBERATION ORGANIZATION (PLO)

The Palestine Liberation Organization (PLO) has served as a key actor in the Palestinian-Israeli conflict since its founding at the first Arab Summit in Cairo in 1964. From its creation, it has presented itself as the soul legitimate representative of the Palestinian people. Global recognition of this role, however, and of the PLO's ability to pursue the true interests of the Palestinian people took decades to be achieved. Indeed, some would argue that this status never was attained and that in the end, the PLO only served to pursue its own interests and not those of the Palestinian community it claimed to represent.

The PLO was created initially as an umbrella organization of *fedayeen* guerilla groups committed to the liberation of Palestine from Israeli control. Its stated goal in its early years of existence was the destruction of Israel as a state and people. The illegitimate and illegal creation of Israel was, from the PLO's perspective, more than adequate justification for its elimination at any cost.

Although the PLO consisted of several factions, al-Fatah, directed by Palestinian activist Yasser Arafat, was the core group of the PLO from the outset. In 1969, Arafat was elected as the PLO's chairman due to the significant role he played in the al-Fatah movement.

Throughout the late 1960s, the PLO operated out of Jordan, where its leadership coordinated *fedayeen* raids across the border into Israel. Jordan was a natural staging ground of Palestinian operations against Israel, both due to its geographic proximity and to the demographic makeup of the country, which became a majority Palestinian following the Arab-Israeli War of June 1967.

The PLO carried out its operations from Jordan until September 1970, a key turning point in the history of the PLO. At that time, a civil war took place as King Hussein moved against the Palestinian leadership in the belief that a continued PLO presence in Jordan was proving too destabilizing for the future of his regime. The PLO leadership fled, taking up residence in southern Lebanon.

Throughout the early 1970s, the PLO became increasingly infamous for its use of international terror as a mode of fighting for the liberation of Palestine from Zionist control. While many attacks were carried out within Israel itself, many also took place outside of the Middle East, primarily in Europe, in the belief that such acts would garner greater media coverage and would draw the West into the conflict in the hopes that these powers, in turn, would be motivated to press for Israeli concessions.

In many instances, some of the most heinous acts were carried out by leftist groups and other factions within the PLO and not by al-Fatah. The Popular Front for the Liberation of Palestine, the Democratic Front for the Liberation of Palestine, and the Popular Front for the Liberation of Palestine-General Command each became known for the bombings of European airports, hijackings of El Al Airline flights, and similar acts. In 1970, three planes were hijacked to Jordan, emptied, and blown up. It is the contention of some that this incident served as the final impetus that precipitated the expulsion of the PLO from Jordan in September of that year.

One of the most well-known attacks occurred during the 1972 Olympic Games in Munich, West Germany, where eleven Israeli athletes and coaches were captured and eventually murdered. The attack was carried out by a PLO splinter group calling itself Black September, in reference to the many Palestinian deaths that had occurred in Jordan during the PLO expulsion.

In another well-known attack in 1974, twenty-one Israeli schoolchildren were killed in the Israeli town of Ma'alot. That same year, the United Nations recognized the PLO for the first time as the rightful representative of the Palestinian people. Yasser Arafat was allowed to speak before the United Nations (UN) in New York on behalf of his people's plight. The speech allowed the PLO the final global recognition it had long sought although a holstered pistol at Arafat's side throughout the speech did little to

counter the PLO's reputation for violence and acts of terror.

By the early 1980s, the PLO had again begun to strengthen and finally recover from the blow dealt by its expulsion from Jordan. From an Israeli perspective, however, the existence of a mini-state of *"Fatahland"* within southern Lebanon and just north of its border (which, like Jordan before it, was regularly used as a staging ground for terrorist attacks against Israel) became increasingly intolerable. In June 1982, the Israeli army under then-Defense Minister Ariel Sharon's direction moved into southern Lebanon, destroying the PLO infrastructure there and eventually pressing the Palestinian leadership to flee once again, this time out of the region altogether to Tunisia, the only state willing to take them in at the time.

The PLO leadership was greatly weakened as a result of its expulsion from Lebanon. At the same time, an indigenous Palestinian grassroots movement in the West Bank and Gaza Strip, embodied in the *intifada* (uprising) that erupted in 1987, began to develop, revealing that the PLO was no longer the soul legitimate representative of the Palestinian people. It also became evident that the interests of those residing in these territories under Israeli occupation differed greatly from those who, like the PLO leadership, had resided outside of Palestine for some decades.

Thus, in 1988, the PLO declared Palestinian independence but only in the West Bank and Gaza, effectively surrendering the remainder of historic Palestine to Israeli sovereignty. In 1993, as a result of the Oslo negotiations with Israel, the Palestine National Charter's clauses calling for the destruction of Israel were finally abrogated although no replacement for this document with these clauses removed was ever disseminated thereafter by the PLO leadership.

In 1996, soon after the signing of Oslo Accords and the creation of the Palestinian Authority (PA) to rule over the West Bank and Gaza, elections were held in which Arafat was chosen as Palestine's first President. The Palestinian Council has eighty-eight members, and twenty ministers oversee twenty-three ministries.

Although the PA, in theory, should have replaced the PLO as a representative mechanism for the Palestinian people, most PA governmental positions created by agreements made at Oslo, as well as the Prime Minister's position itself, were held by ministers who were al-Fatah members or who had strong commitments to Yasser Arafat and his movement. Indeed, until the day he died, Yasser Arafat's al-Fatah faction continued to strongly influence and dominate virtually every aspect of the Palestinians' political aspirations.

That said, it remains to be seen how and to what extent Arafat's death will impact the PLO as well as how it will affect future hopes of Palestine achieving self-rule and, ultimately, independent statehood that the PLO has long sought to achieve.

STEVEN C. DINERO

See also Arab–Israeli Wars (1948, 1956, 1967, 1973); Arafat, Yasser; Hezbollah; Intifada; Israel; Palestine; Palestinian Diaspora

References and Further Reading

Aburish, Said K. *Arafat: From Defender to Dictator*. New York: Bloomsbury Publishing, 1998.

Becker, Jillian. *The PLO: The Rise and Fall of the Palestine Liberation Organization*. London: Weidenfeld and Nicolson, 1984.

Cobban, Helena, Roger Owen, Edmund Burke, Michael C. Hudson, Walid Kazziha, Rashid Khalidi, and Serif Mardin, eds. *The Palestinian Liberation Organisation: People, Power, and Politics (Cambridge Middle East Library)*. Cambridge, UK: University Press, 1984.

Gowers, Andrew, and Tony Walker. *Behind the Myth: Yasser Arafat and the Palestinian Revolution*. 1st American ed. Northampton, MA: Interlink Pub Group, 1991.

Nasser, Jamal R. *The Palestine Liberation Organization: From Armed Struggle to the Declaration of Independence*. New York: Praeger Publishers, 1991.

Rudenberg, Cheryl. *Palestine Liberation Organization: Its Institutional Infrastructure*. Northampton, MA: Interlink Pub Group, 1983.

Rubin, Barry. *Revolution Until Victory? The Politics and History of the PLO (Political Science/Middle Eastern Studies)*. Cambridge, MA: Harvard University Press, 1994.

PALESTINIAN DIASPORA

The term of "Palestinian Diaspora" refers to the major displacement of refugees that occurred during the Arab-Israeli war of 1948, known today as the *naqba* (the catastrophe). An estimated 600,000 to 760,000 persons fled or were forced to flee in four waves (Morris 1987), confronted with fierce battles between Jews and Palestinians, Israelis, and Arabs. While the educated and middle class managed to settle in Beirut, Naplouse, Damascus, or Amman, the peasants found their ways to more than fifty camps in the surrounding Arab countries. In 1949, the United Nations (UN) created the UN Relief and Works Agency for Palestine (UNRWA) with the purpose of rehabilitating the refugees. Since then, what were meant to be temporary refugee camps became permanent. The UNRWA administers close to 4 million registered refugees of whom approximately two hundred thousand are original refugees. While 15% of the Palestinians remained on the land of Israel, nearly 60% ended up on the West Bank and in Gaza, under the trusteeship of Jordan and Egypt.

Jordan: Civil Integration and Diaspora in the Making

The Jordanian Kingdom opened its doors to the refugees in 1948 and did so again in 1950 after the annexation of the West Bank and East Jerusalem. Close to 450,000 refugees were under the hospices of the UNRWA. With the occupation of these territories by Israel in 1967, approximately 210,000 Palestinians were displaced to the East Bank (Kodmany-Darwish 1997). Today, the monarchy is home to 1.5 million Palestinians, to whom all rights have been extended, including citizenship. Although the camps' residents considered integration (*tawteen*) a taboo and dreamed of *awda* (return), many found their way into the market place, education, the private sector, and civil services. The relative openness of the Jordanian society is due to a nationalizing state, which tried to create a new nationality by absorbing the Palestinians in a modernizing society. These efforts have indeed alleviated the destitution of the refugees leaving the camps and starting a process of rehabilitation, without forgetting the trauma of their uprooting (in the early twenty-first century, only 20% of the refugees remain in thirteen camps). An estimated one hundred thousand refugees from Gaza, however, encounter deprivation and hardship as they detain Egyptian travel documents (Lindholm Schulz 2003).

Symbolic settling in Jordan is still a matter of contention according to political allegiances, social class, and networks. Many Palestinians are represented in parliament and running the state, while others constitute the backbone of the educated middle class in a society in which Palestinians are an absolute majority. Until the defeat of the PLO in 1970, they were excluded from the army, but they were admitted in 1973. Jordan tried to speak out on behalf of the Palestinian people but has relinquished any assimilation scheme after the signing of the peace accords with Israel in 1994.

The territorialization of the Palestinian Authority has closed the circle in many ways. The middle class experienced the "condition of diaspora," while maintaining its language, family ties, and social mobility and would be at peace with a double citizenship. The poorest in the camps or in the cities wish to reenact their right of return to villages that no longer exist. They prefer their estrangement and "Jordanian-ness" until the crux of the refugee problem is solved between the state of Israel, their nation, and their host country.

Lebanon: A Reluctant Diaspora

Lebanon admitted 104,000 Palestinians in 1948 (Sayigh 1994) who constituted at the time one-tenth of the country's population. Particularly the Maronite community depicted them with distrust. Most of them had fled coastal cities and Galilee and settled in the southern regions until they were displaced to the Bekaa valley and the suburbs of Beirut. According to the UNRWA in 1949, 380,000 persons were recognized refugees, living in twelve camps. In most fields, this population experienced exclusion and marginalization. They could not work without permits, own a property, or have free access to education and social security. Their quasi-majority was barred from citizenship. A happy few managed to become Lebanese through marriage or being wealthy Christians. The sectarian divisions within Lebanon have reinforced the hopelessness and humiliation of the refugees and led later to their radicalization by the PLO. Indeed, the headquarters of their national organization were hosted in Beirut in 1970, after being rejected by Jordan. The PLO rapidly established a quasi-state in the camps where it delivered, in cooperation with UNRWA, education, work, and social services. The peasant refugees became proletarianized and socialized to be revolutionaries, *fedais* (fighters), for the redemption of the land of a romanticized Palestine. They were intent on resisting assimilation, which in practice was almost impossible in Lebanon (Peteer 1996).

The rivalry between confessional and/or political groups exploded in the civil war of 1975. Camp battles turned into messy alliances between Palestinians and other religious groups. Christians but also poor Shiites resented the role played by the PLO in Lebanese politics until the conflict was crushed by the Israeli invasion in 1982. With the ruled departure of the leadership of the organization to Tunisia, the subeconomy it had installed declined. The refugees became powerless, unstable, and unemployed. The economic and political insecurity prompted the wealthy and educated to migrate to Europe, the Americas, and Kuwait. In the twenty-first century, the population is estimated to have dropped to two hundred thousand. These refugees are the most destitute (together with those of the Gaza Strip).

Syria: A Quiet Social and Economic Integration

Syria has had uncertainties about its borders, as reflected in its relationships with Israel and Lebanon or with the Palestinians. While supporting the Palestinian struggle, the state tried to integrate the one hudred thousand refugees of 1948 and to watch closely their political activities. The refugees who fled the north of Palestine are estimated to total 280,000, and

part of them live in ten camps. About 70% of them left the camps to settle in towns, and their positions in the social and economic spheres are proof that they have been able to take advantage of the same opportunities as the overall population. They remain hosts and foreigners, however, waiting for their resettlement. With time passing, a relative "Syrianization" has occurred. Their future is tied to the conclusion of a peace treaty with Israel and the recognition of the new Palestinian state by Syria. Many refugees will then have to face a dilemma: to live in a Palestinian state that no longer resembles their home or to stay in Syria, without giving up their moral right of return or their memories of a lost home.

Egypt: A Small and Silent Diaspora

The settlement of Palestinians in Egypt has been limited from the outset and has counted both migrants and refugees. As a community of seventy-five thousand persons, they have been closely monitored under the different regimes. Afforded with more rights in education and the labor market under the aegis of Nasser, they have experienced restrictions and rights according to regional politics and the reasons of the state under the Sadat and Mubarak presidencies. Any end of the conflict could lead to a more secure position of these refugees or resettlement in the Palestinian state, notably in Gaza from where many among them originate.

The Gulf and Kuwait: From Migrants to Refugees

Until the first Gulf war, this diaspora was the third in importance of the disseminated Palestinian people. In 1990, they numbered around 450,000 persons. Most of them had migrated from Jordan and other Arab countries to seek work and education during the expansion of the oil economy.

Peasants became unskilled laborers and servants. Many professionals were in great demand for the state machinery. A member of the educated middle class with capital, knowledge, and social cohesion would be easily integrated in the service of this annuity-economy. Cautious in their allegiance, they maintained a distant relation to the PLO. Prosperity was viewed as a venture every Palestinian could seek, though for many purposes the migrants remained foreigners with no chance to become part of the citizenry. Their aspirations were shattered in two phases. The first was the drive of the monarchy to "nationalize" the Kuwait economy and to put aside the feared Palestinian rebels, notably in unions. Second, with Arafat's blessing of the annexation of Kuwait by Saddam Hussein, the rulers reacted with a clear-cut revenge: the *manu miltari* mass expulsion of three hundred thousand Palestinians, without any complaints from the UN or other human rights advocates. Most of them found refuge, for a second time, in Jordan and a minority in the West Bank. Those who disposed of cultural and economic capital pursued their journey to Europe and the Americas. In this case, an analogy is depicted with the tribulations of the Jewish diaspora, who knows more than any other group what "scapegoating" means: to be on the move, uncertain about place and state, in perpetual exile.

Israel: Exile in the Homeland

Approximately 150,000 Palestinians stayed within the borders acquired by Israel at the end of the war. Many were internally displaced, while others were dispossessed of their land for security reasons or to make place for the settlement of new Jewish refugees and migrants from the Arab world—nine hundred thousand Arab Jews were forced or induced to seek refuge in Israel following the Israeli–Arab wars. While recognized as citizens and allocated the right to vote since 1950, these Palestinians were closely watched by a military regime until 1966. Their quality of life has been reduced, as compared to Jewish citizens, due to expropriations, discrimination, and lack of higher education. They have assisted the renaming of villages and the transformation of the landscape (Benvenisti 2000). For some time, however, they stayed voiceless, separated from their brethren, and were regarded as a submissive remnant by those outside. Their process of integration into civil society and later into politics was gradual and hectic, with the emergence of a new generation of leaders asserting their right to the land with "the day land" in 1976 (Ghanem 2001). Furthermore, from the first *intifada* to the Oslo Agreements, their Palestinization became open and vocal. Since the beginning of the second *intifada*, they have manifested outbursts of solidarity with the struggle within the occupied territories. They have formed new political parties and are conscious of the power of demographics: at 1.2 million, they constitute 18% of Israeli society and have reasons to believe they will change the contours of the state. Their future struggle for equal rights is epitomized in the transformation of Israel into a state for all its citizens. Its practical meaning remains to be seen in terms of rights, obligations (conscription), and meaningful alterations of the

symbolic emblems of the Jewish-Israeli nation. Here lies a formidable challenge to Israel in the best-case scenario of lasting peace with the nascent Palestinian state.

West Bank and Gaza: From Occupation to State-Building

West Bank and Gaza have 2.4 and 1.25 million Palestinians of whom respectively 608,000 and 853,000 are registered refugees. Each society still carries the influences that marked their domination by Jordan and Egypt.

The West Bank has been characterized by a diversified economy and a vibrant civil society, with deeply divided elites from 1967 until the first *intifada*. After 1967, many Palestinians became rotating migrants, both in the settlements and in Israel, securing employment and being confronted with Israel's democracy and repressive state measures, such as the confiscation of land for ideological and security purposes. Repressive actions addressed the attitude of the *sumud* (resistance) against expropriation, expressing the West Bank's national identity. While increased confinement, closures, and checkpoints became the means to curb the rebellion, a new generation of leaders emerged, ready to use limited violence and civil disobedience to deadlock the expansion of the settlement policy. The community feared that the time was running against its hope to achieve an independent state. This may explain why the PLO, encumbered by its disastrous collusion with Saddam Hussein, had to find a way to hijack the peace process following the Madrid international conference and to supplant the "insiders" with the "outsiders" from Tunisia to conclude the Oslo Agreements.

Gaza is a densely populated and impoverished strip of land with refugees from Lydda, Ramla, and Ashkelon. The Egyptians envisioned no real development. The Israelis opened their labor market to rotating migrant workers and exchanged services and goods. The high unemployment rate of this fast growing population, their isolation from the West Bank, and the dispossession of land have led many to frustration and alienation. It is no coincidence that the first *intifada* was ignited there in 1987. Arafat's 1994 actions and the pouring of international aid encouraged investments by wealthy Palestinians from the diaspora, and many residents felt an improvement of their socioeconomic condition that would not last (Roy). The community's disillusion had to do with sheer patronage by the Authority and "internal closures" by the Israelis following attacks on its

settlements and even more so with the rampage of suicide bombers within Israel. The Authority did not supplement the gradual and permanent loss of employment in Israel. The result is that after four years of deadly *intifada*, 64% of the population (57% in the West Bank) live below the poverty line and find solace and services with Hamas and Islamic Jihad. The eschatological millenarism of these two terrorist groups has deepened after the collapse of the Camp David negotiations in 2000. More than ever, the refugees supported the militarization of the al-Aqsa Intifada that has shattered their dreams, created more repressive measures, and brought an electronic fence by the Israelis.

In both occupied territories, however, a turning point could be witnessed, from resistance to erotization of death by the *shaheed*, the martyrs who die to liberate the land. Blood and land are the mystification needed to create an "imagined community" where the 1967 borders are not considered an end to the conflict.

Palestinians' Many Diasporas: The Americas and Western Europe

Palestinian migration to Latin America and the United States began at the turn of the last century, notably by Christians. Headed to many countries in 1936, and from 1948 to 1967, the migrants left behind them Bettleheim, Ramallah, and Haifa. They formed close-knitted communities in Chile, Argentina, Uruguay, and Honduras. Economic success made them a "wealthy diaspora" that was well integrated in their host societies. In the United States, there are about two hundred thousand Palestinians who are more politicized than their southern counterparts. Many are former students or exiles from the civil war in Lebanon, and the *ghurba* or the collective memory of strangeness is present in their minds. The most Americanized among them have no desire to return to an undeveloped state and economy. They would rather lobby in favor of a more impartial US position to ground the path to a just peace between Israel and Palestine.

In Western Europe, the settlement of migrants has occurred since the 1980s, and no reliable data are available. According to some authors, there could be two hundred thousand Palestinian expatriates, most of them having first arrived as students or liberal professionals. Later, with the collapse of the PLO in Jordan and Lebanon and the mass expulsion of Palestinians from Kuwait, more found their way through family networks to Europe. The most populous community has settled in Germany (approximately eighty thousand, a few thousand coming from Socialist countries

after 1989). There is also a professional and business community in Great Britain, while twenty thousand Palestinians have found a home in Sweden (Lindholm Schulz 2003).

These many diasporas have one of the most learned intelligentsias of the Arab world and could constitute a formidable engine for the new Palestinian state. For some of those who have returned to the occupied territories since 1994, the experience was inconclusive; the refugees who had suffered viewed them as "others."

The Right of Return, Nation-Building, and the Conditions of Exile

The PLO has initiated institutions of nation-building in exile. It has been the architect of a memory and the inventor of an identity through many icons: the peasant (the land), the refugee (the victim), the *fedai'* (the fighter), the *sumud* (the resistant), the *shaheed* (the human bomb, the martyr), and the returnee (the subject). On the long march toward recognizing the state of Israel, the PLO has in fact substituted state to land without stating clearly the consequences of this transition in its mythological rhetoric.

The PLO had from its inception inscribed the "right of return" as the pillar of its charter, ideology, and politics. In doing so, it designed the refugees to be the vessel of the liberation of the land for the Palestinian nation. With the Oslo Accords and later the Clinton parameters, it became clear that the stumbling block of the "right of return" was not only a matter of principle but of rewriting the imagined community. The negotiations in Taba in 2001 were implicitly based on the fact that most of the refugees would be resettled or rehabilitated. Moreover, the Palestinian Authority was not willing to absorb massive waves of refugees. Loss and bitterness afflicted many individuals and communities who in Lebanon or in many other camps resented the PLO's compromising stance, while others understood that the failure of the Arafat-Barak negotiations was tied up with the solution of the refugee problem. The upsurge of the al-Aqsa Intifada was the symbol of the agonizing stress to build a state that would not be the home to all refugees and a reminder that the Palestinians' collective identity is an undesirable pilgrimage in other settings. For many refugees, the loss has been internalized. For others, "returning" to the West Bank and Gaza is not experienced as coming home but arriving in a "non-place." Many prefer to wait "until the last sky" (Said 1995) or to embrace the Hamas rhetoric.

Many Palestinian individuals and communities are now on the move in the cities of the West—Athens, London, New York, and Paris—but also of the Arab world: Dubai and Amman today, Beirut and Kuwait yesterday. As Jews before them, but still in the diaspora, they feel how important it is to maintain religious, linguistic, and family ties together with the landscape of memory.

MIKHAEL ELBAZ AND RUTH MURBACH

See also Arab–Israeli Wars (1948, 1956, 1967, 1973); Arafat, Yasser; HAMAS; Intifada; Israel; Palestine; Palestine Liberation Organization (PLO); United Nations Relief and Works Agency for Palestine (UNRWA)

References and Further Reading

Arzt, D. *Refugees into Citizens: Palestinians and the End of the Arab-Israeli Conflict.* U.S. Council of Foreign Relations Press, 1997.
Benvenisti, M. *Sacred Landscape: The Buried History of the Holy Land since 1948.* Berkeley, CA: University of California Press, 2000.
Ghanem, A. *The Palestinian-Arab Minority in Israel, 1948–2000.* New York: State University of New York Press, 2001.
Haddad, S. 2000. "Palestinians in Lebanon: Towards Integration or Conflict?" http://www.arts.mcgill.ca/MEPP/PRRN/papers/haddad.html.
Karmi, G., and Cotran, E., eds. *The Palestinian Exodus, 1948–1998.* New York: Ithaca Press, 1999.
Khalidi, R. *Palestinian Identity: The Construction of Modern National Consciousness.* New York: Columbia University Press, 1997.
Kimmerling, G. B., and Migdal, J. S. *Palestinians: The Making of a People.* New York: The Free Press, 2000.
Kodmany-Darwish, B. *La Diaspora Palestinienne.* Paris: Presses Universitaires de France, 1997.
Lindholm Schulz, M. *The Palestinian Diaspora.* New York: Routledge, 2003.
Morris, B. *The Birth of the Palestinian Refugee Problem, 1947–1949.* Cambridge, UK: Cambridge University Press, 1987.
Peteer, J. "From Refugees to Minority: Palestinians in Post-War Lebanon." *Middle East Report* 200 (July-September 1996).
Roy, S. "Palestinian Society and Economy: The Continued Denial of Possibility." *Journal of Palestine Studies* 30, no. 4: 5–20.
Said, E. *Peace and its Discontents.* London: Vintage, 1995.
———. *Out of Place: A Memoir.* London: Vintage, 1999.
Sayigh, R. *Too Many Enemies: The Palestinian Experience in Lebanon.* London: Zed Press, 1994.

PAN-AFRICANISM

The Pan-African movement is subject to many claims of precisely what it is. The movement is related to anticolonial movements in the former European colonies in Africa, but it is also seen as a sense of unity of all persons of African descent. The first organized descriptions of Pan-Africanism had their emphasis

on Americans of African descent; the early leaders of this movement were W.E.B. Du Bois, Marcus Garvey, and Booker T. Washington, each of whom had his own ideas on what Pan-Africanism was.

The original focus of Pan-Africanism was one on race or color as a unifying factor, much as the Hindu Nationalist movement in India sought the unifying factor of religion in attempting to determine what it meant to be Indian. In both cases the vast diversity (of being African, or Indian) made identity complex. In the case of Pan-Africanism, racial identity was seen as a unifying factor and not one that divided people of African descent from others.

However, in Africa, black Americans were not considered to be African. This division would become more complex as persons of African descent in Europe and the Caribbean became involved in the Pan-African movement, particularly in the attempts of some American interests to encourage migration of African-Americans back to Africa in the late nineteenth and early twentieth centuries. Marcus Garvey, one of the original American supporters and definers of Pan-Africanism, created a "Back to Africa" movement that failed; Garvey himself never went to Africa, but instead died in Europe.

In addition to the attempts to unify people of African descent and to bring Western political ideals of freedom to Africa, a literary genre called *négritude* developed in Europe. This was also an expression of unity between Africans in Africa and those who had been taken from their continent.

The African Diaspora, as the forced migration of Africans to other continents is known, was equated to the Jewish Diaspora, with the difference that Africans had no single unifying religious identity. The US intellectual efforts to establish an African identity attempted to provide this missing basis for unification. However, another difference was that throughout history, Jews had been cast out of their homeland and of most other countries where they had settled; Africans were taken away from their homelands.

Initial efforts to develop and define this African identity were held in Europe and the United States. The First Pan-African Congress was held in London in 1900, organized by H. Sylvester Williams, a lawyer from Trinidad. In 1912, Booker T. Washington organized an International Conference on the Negro at Tuskegee University. Although the conference was supposed to examine the common ties between persons of African descent, most attendees at this conference were black America missionaries concerned about how to spread Christianity to Africa.

A Second Pan-African Congress was held in Paris in 1919. This meeting washeaded by W.E.B. Du Bois, and the focus of the conference was on the prevention of further exploitation of Africans in Africa by the former colonial powers. A Third Pan-African Congress in London and Brussels in 1921, also headed by Du Bois, placed its emphasis on self-government by Africans and the spread of democracy.

Two years later, a Fourth Pan-African Congress in London and Lisbon addressed a continued emphasis on self-government, and also expressed a desire for black people to be treated as equal to whites.

The Fifth Pan-African Congress in New York in 1927 was a major break from these earlier meetings, and recognized that the growing Communist movement in the world was not necessarily a source of support for Pan-Africanism. It was recognized at this conference that Communists saw Pan-Africanism as nationalism, which was contrary to the internationalist view of the Communists. In addition, white Communists were not seen as a source of support for Pan-African efforts.

By the mid-1930s, with the global difficulties of the economic depression and reduced focus on internationalism in the United States, enthusiasm for Pan-Africanism had declined there. However, Italian intervention in Ethiopia in the 1930s, followed by World War II (which was seen by some as a "white people's war"), brought about renewed attention to Pan-Africanism.

A Sixth Pan-African Congress was held in Manchester, England, in 1945. This conference raised demands for political autonomy in Black Africa, and its speakers suggested an acceptance of socialism as an economic model for Africa. Equally as significant, a new generation of leaders was more influential than the aging leaders like Du Bois. These new leaders included Dr. Kwame Nkrumah of Ghana, Jomo Kenyatta of Kenya, H.O. Davies of Nigeria, and others.

In the early 1950s, after the end of World War II, the newly freed colonies of the European powers and Japan met in Bandung, Indonesia, to form what would become known as the Non-Aligned Movement (NAM). While not directly associated with the Pan-African movement, the NAM countries rejected colonialism much as the formerly colonized African countries had and sought to avoid postcolonial exploitation and ties to either side in the Cold War. Later that decade, an attempt was made to combine the postcolonial movements of Africa, some Arab countries, and Asia through the Afro-Asian Solidarity Movement. However, the reluctance of some countries, notably Egypt, from joining what might be seen as an alternative international bloc to the East and West kept this association from prospering. In April 1958, the First Conference of Independent African States (which excluded South Africa) met in Accra, Ghana. This conference included countries

from black Africa (Liberia, Ghana, and Ethiopia) and from the Arab Muslim states of Tunisia, Egypt, Sudan, Libya, and Morocco. This meeting showed that color was not the only factor on which unity in the postcolonial world could be based.

Later that year, a similar meeting was held in Accra, and this first conference of the All-Africa Peoples Organisation (AAPO) was followed by others in Tunis in 1960 and Cairo in 1961. At the first and second AAPO conferences, whites from South Africa attended, but they were excluded from the conference at Cairo, as were people of Indian descent. The motto of "Africa for the Africans" adopted by the organization at its first meeting (taken from the title of Joseph Booth's book by the same name) was nevertheless intended to be anticolonialist, not a statement of racial exclusion.

In 1960, the Second Conference of Independent African States was also held in Addis Ababa, Ethiopia. This conference was divided between those countries that sought to build a Pan-Africanist consensus (led by Nigeria) and those that sought to lead African countries to power (led by Ghana). Kwame Nkrumah, of Ghana, did not want to wait for incremental change.

That same year in the United States, a conference organized by the American Society of African Culture (AMSAC) met to discuss Pan-Africanism. This conference primarily included participants from the United States (many of African descent) as well as participants from West Africa and the Caribbean. The primary division at this conference was between the academics (who were not from Africa) who encouraged a unified Africa (and who saw nationalist movements as "Balkanization," a reference to the traditional trouble spot in eastern Europe) and the Africans who recognized that the first step in independence was the establishment of nation-states in Africa. This latter view was expressed best by George Padmore, who had years before been an advisor to Kwame Nkrumah. His Padmore Dictum, which called for nationalist movements in Africa, was seen as a necessary step before a broader African unity could be established.

The conflicting forces of nationalism (based on the many artificial boundaries drawn up by the European colonial powers) and Pan-Africanism (which was the result of the common colonial and postcolonial experiences of the African peoples, both black and Arab) resulted in the establishment of the Organization of African Unity (OAU). The OAU, like the NAM, sought to avoid association with the major sides in the Cold War.

Colin Legum described the nine points of the Pan-African Movement of the mid-twentieth century as:

1. "**Africa for the Africans**" refers to a complete independence of the whole of Africa and a total rejection of colonialism in all its forms, including white domination.

2. **United States of Africa** is the ideal of a wholly unified continent through a series of interlinking regional federations where there would have been a limitation on national sovereignty.

3. **African renaissance of morale and culture** means a quest for the "African personality," a determination to recast African society into its own forms, drawing from its past what is valuable and desirable and marrying it to modern ideas. Modernism is heavily accentuated.

4. **African nationalism** replaces the tribalism of the past: a concept of African loyalty wider than "the nation" to transcend tribal and regional affiliations.

5. **African regeneration of economic enterprise** replaces colonial economic methods: the belief in a nonexploiting Socialist or *communalistic* type of socialism. International Communism is rejected outright.

6. **Belief in democracy** at the most desirable method of government is based on the principle of "one man, one vote."

7. **Rejection of violence** is a method of struggle, unless peaceful methods of struggle—*positive action*—are met with military repression.

8. **Solidarity of black peoples everywhere** and a fraternal alliance of coloured peoples are based on a mutual history of struggle against white domination and colonialism.

9. **Positive neutrality** (as it was then called) refers to noninvolvement of partisans in power politics but "neutral in nothing that affects African interests."

In examining Pan-Africanism in the modern context, Ali Mazrui distinguishes several branches: sub-Saharan (black Africans in the nations south of the Sahara Desert), trans-Saharan (black Africans as well as Arabs in the north), and transatlantic (Africans, Caribbean people of African descent, as well as African-Americans). Mazrui noted that the Pan-Africanism thought developed not in Africa but among those Americans and Caribbean people of African descent, the "Black Diaspora."

The negative effects of Pan-Africanism in the modern world are the breakdown of national identities in African countries, leading to a rejection of "nationalism" and a resurgence in tribal identities. This is shown through the breakdown of civil order in Somalia (where tribal conflict led to the dissolution of effective governmental order in the 1900s), genocide

between Hutus and Tutsis in Rwanda at the same time, and the ethnic conflicts in Nigeria and the Congo.

THOMAS P. DOLAN

See also African Diaspora; Colonialism: Legacies; Kenyatta, Jomo; Nkrumah, Kwame

References and Further Reading

American Society of African Culture. *Pan-Africanism Reconsidered*. Berkeley: University of California Press, 1962.

Esedebe, P. Olisanwuche. *Pan-Africanism: The Idea and Movement, 1776–1963*. Washington, DC: Howard University Press, 1982.

Gailey, Harry A. *History of Africa from 1800 to Present*. New York: Holt, Rinehart, and Winston, 1972.

Langley, J. Ayodele. *Pan-Africanism and Nationalism in West Africa, 1900–1945: A Study in Ideology and Social Classes*. Oxford, UK: Clarendon Press, 1973.

Legum, Colin. *Pan-Africanism: A Short Political Guide*. New York: Frederick A. Praeger, 1965.

Ostergard, Jr., Robert L., Ricardo Rene Laremont, and Fouad Kalouche, eds. *Power, Politics, and the African Condition: Collected Essays of Ali A. Mazrui*. Vol III. Trenton, NJ: Africa World Press.

Sagay, J. O., and D.A. Wilson. *Africa—A Modern History (1800–1975)*. New York: Africana Publishing Company, 1978.

PANAMA

Panama is a Central American republic that occupies the southeastern end of the isthmus that connects North and South America. Panama encompasses 77,381 square kilometers (29,762 square miles); the terrain is mountainous (highest elevation is 3,475 meters or 11,468 feet) with a tropical wet/dry climate that produces more than one hundred inches of annual rainfall. The population in 2001 was estimated to be 2.9 million with an ethnic composition of Mestizo 70%, West Indian 14%, Caucasian 10%, and Indian 8%. Panama compares favorably with most of Central America with a per capita gross domestic product (GDP) of $3,699 and an overall GDP of $12.3 billion; the life expectancy is seventy-five years and infant mortality rate is 20 per 1,000. The economy centers on services that account for 78% of GDP and includes banking, insurance, health and medicine, transportation, telecommunications, tourism, and the Panama Canal with related maritime services.

Panama's geography has been the key element in its development. As a long slender country that would stretch from New York City to Cleveland in the United States, Panama is the narrowest point between the Caribbean Sea and the Pacific Ocean and forms the land bridge that links North America to South America. Panama's modern history has been shaped by its famous canal. In 1903, with assistance from the United States, Panama gained independence from Colombia and signed the Hay Bunau-Varilla Treaty with the United States. The treaty enabled the United States to build the Panama Canal, which was completed in 1914. The treaty granted the United States rights "as if it were sovereign" in the Canal Zone, an area approximately ten miles wide and fifty miles long that bifurcated Panama. While Panama benefited from the commerce generated by the canal and received rent payments from the United States, the issue of US sovereignty over what Panamanians considered their greatest resource was contentious. Successive Panamanian governments, however, sought more favorable terms with the United States without challenging its control over the Canal Zone.

In 1968, a *coup d'état* staged by Panama's National Guard eventually established Colonel Omar Torrijos Herrera as Panama's dictator. Torrijos was determined to gain full sovereignty of the Canal and its zone that he saw as the key to Panama's future development. Torrijos was more assertive than previous leaders, but for nine years, the United States would not consider relinquishing its control over the strategic waterway. In 1977, President Jimmy Carter ordered that talks be resumed, and the Panama Canal Treaties were signed on September 7. Panama ratified the treaties in a plebiscite, and the US Senate approved the treaties by a vote of sixty-eight to thirty-two. The treaties provided for a twenty-year phased withdrawal of US military forces and the turnover of all territory and facilities to Panama by December 31, 1999.

Torrijos also promoted a new offshore banking industry in an attempt to make Panama the Switzerland of Latin America. His efforts brought much needed cash deposits, and international banks built gleaming skyscrapers to house their operations in Panama City. Panama's lax banking laws also made it a haven for money laundering and other illegal activities. Torrijos won over the urban poor by establishing schools and clinics in slum areas. Torrijos died in a 1982 plane crash. By 1982, real power in Panama was in the hands of General Manuel Noriega. Noriega was a venal and corrupt dictator who used repression to maintain his power and to cover his involvement in narcotics trafficking. In May 1989, Noriega annulled the election of opposition candidate, Guillermo Endara, and assumed complete control of the country. He was removed from power in 1989 when the United States invaded Panama, arrested Noriega, and brought him to the United States to stand trial on charges of drug trafficking. Noriega was found guilty and sentenced to forty years in prison.

Panama has functioned under democratic governments since Noriega's removal. President Guillermo Endara took office promising economic recovery, civilian control of the military, and stronger democratic institutions. A civilian "public force" replaced the military and consisted of four branches, with the Panamanian National Police being the largest. The new police force proved a welcome replacement for the thugs of the Noriega era but was unable to curb a raising crime rate. The Endara government proved to be a disappointment; in 1994, Ernesto Pérez Balladares of the *Partido Revolucionario Democrático* (PRD), translated as the Democratic Revolutionary Party, the political arm of the former military regimes, won the presidency. Pérez Balladares proved to be a moderate who governed with the support of other parties. He carried out economic reforms and worked with the United States to implement the Panama Canal treaties. His quest to seek a second consecutive term was denied in a referendum.

On May 2, 1999, Mireya Moscoso was elected in a close election as the first female president of Panama. Moscoso, the widow of Arnulfo Arias Madrid, a former president and perennial candidate, was from the opposition *Partido Arnulfista* (PA), or Party Arnulfista, and seemed to solidify Panama's emerging democratic course.

The United States honored its agreements under the Panama Canal Treaties and turned over assets valued at $15 billion on December 31, 1999. Panama has made a number of improvements since gaining full control of the Panama Canal assets. Some of the former canal and defense sites have been converted to tourist accommodations, including golf courses and luxury hotels. One former US Army post is being refurbished as a city of knowledge and houses offices for companies that research tropical diseases or are engaged in bioprospecting. The Panama Railroad had been upgraded and offers expanded freight and passenger services. Panama is also studying plans to expand canal operations through the construction of larger locks. Panama's newfound political tranquility has enabled expansion of tourism, which now generates more revenue than the Panama Canal. In 2004, Martin Torrijos, son of the late dictator, won the presidential election as the candidate of the PRD.

GEORGE M. LAUDERBAUGH

References and Further Reading

Buckley, Kevin. *Panama*. New York: Simon & Schuster, 1989.

Howarth, David. *Panama: Four Hundred Years of Dreams and Cruelty*. New York: McGraw Hill, 1966.

Koster, R. M., and Guillermo Sánchez. *In the Time of Tyrants: Panama 1903–1990*. New York: W.W. Norton & Co., 1990.

McCullough, David. *The Path Between the Seas*. New York: Simon and Schuster, 1977.

PANAMA CANAL TREATIES, 1977

Also known as the Carter Torrijos Treaties, the Panama Canal Treaties, signed in 1977 and ratified in 1979, provided for the turnover of the Panama Canal by the United States to Panama on December 31, 1999. The relationship between Panama and the United States began on November 3, 1903, when the United States supported the Panamanian Revolution against Colombia. On November 18, the two countries signed the Hay-Bunau-Varilla Treaty, which gave the United States a ten-mile wide zone in the middle of Panama for the purpose of constructing an interoceanic canal in exchange for a payment of $10 million, $250,000 annual rent, and a guarantee of Panamanian independence. The treaty also granted the United States the right of eminent domain in the cities of Panama and Colon to make sanitary improvements necessary for the construction and maintenance of the canal. Construction of the Canal began in 1904, and the waterway was opened in August 1914.

The Panama Canal proved to be a mixed blessing to Panama's economic development. The greatest early benefit was the eradication of tropical diseases and other sanitary improvements made under the direction of Dr. William Crawford Gorgas. The Panama Canal was the greatest engineering feat of the era, and the United States built modern port and industrial facilities, defense sites, schools, and housing areas. Lake Gatun, at the time the largest human-made lake in the world, provided the country with an abundant supply of fresh water and electricity. The United States upgraded Panama's firefighting capability and introduced the automobile. However, the Canal Zone bifurcated Panama, inhibiting the development of a countrywide transportation system and isolated the western interior from the capital. Moreover, few Panamanians were employed in the construction of the canal or its later operation. The vast majority of the construction workers were imported from the West Indies, and many remained and settled in the Canal Zone. The West Indian immigrants spoke English, largely practiced the Anglican faith, and considered themselves part of the Canal Zone rather than Panama. The Canal Zone became a self-sufficient US government enterprise with all proceeds from Panama Canal tolls being reinvested in maintaining the Zone and the Canal. Other than the $250,000 annual rent, Panama's economic benefit was minimal.

The Canal became an issue to Panamanian nationalists who felt that Panama was not receiving its fair share of the revenue generated by the waterway. In 1932, Harmodio Arias, Panama's president, sought concessions from the United States. The result was a 1936 treaty that eliminated Panama's protectorate status, increased the annual rent on the canal to $430,000, ended the right to the arbitrary acquisition of land, placed limitations on the use of military and zone stores by non-US personnel, permitted the operation of radio stations, and promised equal treatment of US and Panamanian canal employees.

Panamanian President José Remón presented new demands during a visit with President Dwight D. Eisenhower in 1953. Subsequent negotiations resulted in the Treaty of 1955 that granted further economic concessions, including the right to tax non-US canal employees, an increase in the annual annuity to $1.93 million, the construction of a bridge over the canal to link western Panama to Panama City, equal pay rates for all employees, and an extension on the lease of the air base at Rio Hato. Under this treaty, the United States retained sovereign rights over the Canal Zone.

The central disagreement between the United States and Panama centered on the issue of sovereignty in the Canal Zone. This issue erupted in the January 1964 flag riots that left twenty-four Panamanians and six US soldiers dead. In 1962, the United States agreed to fly the Panamanian Flag side by side with the US flag at fifteen sites in the Canal Zone; however, implementation of the agreement was delayed by lawsuits. When tensions mounted over the flag issue, the Canal Zone governor ordered that no flags be raised at certain sites including the US Balboa High School, which was not far from Panama City. On January 7, 1964, US students defied this restriction and raised the US flag on school grounds. On January 9, Panamanian students marched to the school to protest and demand that Panama's flag also be raised. During the confrontation, the Panamanian flag was torn, and several students were roughed up. News of this event led to larger demonstrations on the open border between the Canal Zone and the Republic. Canal Zone and Panamanian police were unable to control the crowd, and the commander of the US Southern Command took over and called in troops. The incident resulted in Panama breaking diplomatic relations with the United States. In the aftermath of the flag riots, President Lyndon Johnson agreed to begin negotiations to revise the 1903 Treaty including the issue of sovereignty.

In 1968, a *coup d'état* staged by Panama's National Guard eventually established Colonel Omar Torrijos Herrera as Panama's dictator. Torrijos was determined to gain full sovereignty of the Canal and its zone, and in 1973, he skillfully arranged a meeting of the United Nations Security Council in Panama. The Council voted thirteen to one for a resolution that recognized Panama's right to eventually have sovereignty. The United States vetoed the resolution, but this tactic backfired as Panama appeared more and more to be a victim of imperialism. Panama sought three outcomes from the treaties. First was the establishment of sovereignty over the Canal Zone, an area that it had always considered part of its national domain. Second was the removal of US military forces from Panama so that the chances of intervention by the United States in Panama's internal affairs would be lessened. Third was to gain the full economic benefit of the Canal, which was viewed as the key to improving Panama's economy.

In 1977, President Jimmy Carter ordered that talks be resumed, and treaties were signed on September 7. Panama ratified the treaties in a plebiscite. After a difficult ratification process, the US Senate approved the treaty by a vote of sixty-eight to thirty-two. The main treaty provided for a phased withdrawal of the United States to be completed by December 31, 1999. In the interim, the Panama Canal Commission was established to replace the Panama Canal Company. The United States agreed to train Panamanian employees to replace US employees at all levels of canal operations. A second treaty established the neutrality of the canal as an international waterway and assigned defensive responsibilities to both Panama and the United States, with Panama accepting full responsibility by the year 2000. Drafted by Arizona Senator, Dennis De Concini, an amendment to the second treaty extended the right of the United States to defend the canal if Panama proved incapable. The treaties were fully complied with on December 31, 1999, when all US military forces were withdrawn and all territories and facilities were relinquished to Panama.

Panama has made a number of improvements since gaining full control of Canal assets. Some of the former canal and defense sites have been converted to tourist accommodations, including golf courses and luxury hotels. One former US Army post is being refurbished as a city of knowledge and houses offices for companies that research tropical diseases or are engaged in bioprospecting. The Panama Railroad had been upgraded and offers expanded freight and passenger services. Panama is also studying plans to expand canal operations through the construction of larger locks. The Panama Canal Treaties have proven to be a very positive factor in Panama's recent economic and social development.

GEORGE M. LAUDERBAUGH

See also Central America: History and Economic Development; Central America: International Relations; Panama; Torrijos Herrera, Omar

References and Further Reading

Conniff, Michael L. *Panama and the United States*, 2d ed. Athens, GA: University of Georgia Press, 2001.

Farnsworth, David N., and James W. McKenney. *U.S.-Panama Relations, 1903–1978 A Study in Linkage Politics*. Boulder, CO: Westview Press, 1983.

Jorden, William J. *Panama Odyssey*. Austin: University of Texas Press, 1984.

PAPUA NEW GUINEA

Papua New Guinea comprises the eastern half of the island of New Guinea; the large islands of Manus, New Britain, New Ireland, and Bougainville; and some six hundred other small islands. The country (6° S, 146° E) lies to the north of Australia, east of the Solomon Islands, and south of the Philippines. The land area is 463,000 square kilometers (179,000 square miles). The Indonesian province of Papua (formerly Irian Jaya) fills the western half of New Guinea. The population in 2003 was estimated at 5,295,000. Major cities and their populations are the capital, Port Moresby (200,000), Lae (90,000), Madang (28,000), Wewak (25,000), and Goroka (18,000). The population growth rate in 2003 was 2.3%, and 39% of the population was between zero and fourteen years old. Birth and death rates are 31 per 1,000 and 7.6 per 1,000, respectively, and life expectancy is sixty-two years (males) and sixty-six years (females). Major causes of morbidity and mortality are infectious diseases: pneumonia, malaria, and tuberculosis. Infant mortality is high. Diseases related to changes in diet and lifestyle are increasing and include HIV/AIDS, cardiovascular disease, diabetes, strokes, and cancers (from smoking and betel nut chewing). The population is made up of 5% Anglican, 58% Protestant sects, and 33% Roman Catholic; the remainder follow local tribal beliefs and customs.

The main island is dominated by a central cordillera rising (in Papua New Guinea) reaching more than 4,000 meters (the highest peak is Mt. Wilhelm at 4,509 meters or 14,790 feet above sea level). Broad, deep upland valleys covered in rainforest or grassland dominate the highlands. The Sepik, Ramu, and Markham Rivers drain the highlands to the north and the Fly, Strickland, Kikori, and Purari Rivers are the principal rivers flowing south into the Coral Sea. The lower Sepik and Fly Rivers flow through extensive, low-lying floodplains with numerous oxbow and tributary lakes. These rivers are navigable by shallow-draft vessels for some distance inland. The southern coastline is dominated by mangrove swamps lining the estuaries of the major rivers and by coral reefs in areas away from rivers with heavy sediment loads. The northern coastline is undergoing significant geological uplift, and this is reflected in the rugged, coastal terrain. The coral reefs in Papua New Guinea are amongst the most diverse in the world, and scuba diving is a major tourist attraction.

The islands are tectonically unstable, and earthquakes and volcanic eruptions are common. The Matupit Volcano erupted in September 1994 and destroyed the town of Rabaul; in July 1998, an earthquake-triggered tsunami off the north coast killed around 1,500 people and left thousands injured and homeless.

The climate is tropical and in the coastal lowlands is hot and humid throughout the year. Along the southern coastal region near Port Moresby, the climate has a long dry season from April to November (southeast monsoon) and a wet season from December to March (northwest monsoon). Annual rainfall elsewhere exceeds 39.37 inches (1,000 millimeters) and in the highlands generally varies between 2,500 to 3,500 millimeters, but some areas of the country receive as much as 10,000 millimeters per year. Seasonality in rainfall is generally muted. Average lowland temperatures throughout the year range from 26°C–32°C. Temperatures decline with altitude. Frosts may occur in the highlands, and snow occasionally falls on the higher peaks. High temperatures and rainfall lead to generally high humidity and cloudiness with only moderate rates of evaporation.

It is estimated that 85% of the population lives as subsistence farmers, with sweet potato, taro, sago, bananas, and leafy vegetables being the main food crops. Pigs and chickens are kept as livestock. Agricultural exports (copra, rubber, coffee, cocoa, tea, palm oil, and minor high value products such as vanilla and cardamom) are increasing, but mining of silver, copper, and gold accounts for over two-thirds of export earnings. Oil production began in 1992, and natural gas reserves are being tapped. Tropical hardwood timbers are harvested for export, and timber is also harvested for plywood and wood chip production. Tuna, crayfish, prawn, and other fisheries are minor components of the economy. The gross domestic product (GDP) was estimated at $10.86 billion in 2002, and the country receives approximately $400 million in annual aid (most for Australia). Major trading partners are Australia, Japan, China, Singapore, and New Zealand.

The government is a constitutional monarchy with a governor-general representing the British Crown. The country has a Westminster-style democracy with a prime minister, cabinet, and an elected, unicameral

parliament with 109 members. Politically, the country is divided into nineteen provinces and the National Capital District. English is the official language, but Tok Pisin (Pidgin) and Motu (trade language of the southern coast) are *lingua francas* in a country with more than 700 distinct languages.

Humans colonized New Guinea more than forty thousand years ago, and the early inhabitants, isolated by the dissected terrain and tribal conflicts, developed enormous cultural and linguistic diversity. Archaeological evidence suggests that the early inhabitants developed agricultural techniques some ten thousand years ago and did so independently from the rest of the world. The eastern half of New Guinea was explored in the sixteenth century by the Spanish and Portuguese. In 1828, the Netherlands annexed the western half of the island (now the Indonesian province, Papua). In 1884, Germany annexed the northern coast and offshore islands, and Britain took control of the southern sector of Papua New Guinea. In 1906, British New Guinea was transferred to Australia, and the area became the Territory of Papua. Australian troops invaded German New Guinea (called Kaiser-Wilhelmsland) at the start of World War I and gained control of the territory under a League of Nations mandate. The highlands were considered by European settlers to be too inhospitable for habitation; but in the 1930s, explorers in search of gold discovered more than 1 million people, with Stone Age cultures, inhabiting the fertile valleys of the central highlands.

The Japanese invaded New Guinea in 1942, and following their defeat by US and Australian forces in 1945, the Territory of Papua New Guinea became a United Nations trusteeship administered by Australia. The country was granted limited self-governing powers in 1951, autonomy in internal affairs in 1960, and full independence as Papua New Guinea on September 16, 1975. Michael Somare was the first Prime Minister. In 1976, ethnic secessionist threats led to the establishment of decentralized provincial governments. Papua New Guinean politics are characterized by frequent changes in leadership through parliamentary maneuvers and fluid loyalties to political parties. Julius Chan succeeded Somare as Prime Minister in 1980, only to be replaced by him in 1982. Somare led the government until 1987.

In 1988, ethnic unrest in Bougainville resulted in fighting between government forces and the Bougainville Revolutionary Army (BRA). This led, in 1989, to the closure of the Bougainville Copper Mine and significant reduction in export earnings. In 1991, the government signed a peace treaty with the Bougainville rebels that established a South Bougainville Interim Authority although unrest continued. In 1992, the government launched an offensive on Bougainville

that resulted in the capture of Arawa, the provincial capital.

In April 1988, Prime Minister Paias Wingti suspended Parliament in an attempt to halt a pending vote of no confidence; however, in the July election, he was deposed. Wingti was replaced by Rabbie Namaliu who initiated political and economic reforms. In July 1991, legislation was passed that limited the number of no-confidence motions against an incoming government for its first twelve months in office. In June 1992, Prime Minister Namaliu was defeated in general elections and was succeeded by Wingti. In September 1993, Wingti resigned but was reelected almost immediately, thereby outmaneuvering his opposition and minimizing the possibility of a vote of no-confidence. Chan led the government from 1994 to 1997.

In July 1999, Prime Minister Bill Skate resigned following repercussions from his recognition of Taiwan as a separate political entity from mainland China. Mekere Morauta became prime minister, and in 2002, after an election marred by violence and alleged vote rigging, Michael Somare became prime minister for the third time.

The country is home to an impressive variety of birds, including most of the known species of birds of paradise. Other animals include marsupials (opossum, wallaby, tree kangaroo, and echidna), two species of crocodiles, monitor lizards, flying foxes and bats. Insect diversity is enormous and includes the world's largest butterflies (birdwings). Plant diversity is also high with probably more kinds of orchids than any other country. Major environmental challenges include deforestation to satisfy demand for tropical hardwoods and to provide land for agriculture. Water pollution with waste rock and tailings from mining projects is a problem in many parts of the country but particularly in the Fly and Strickland River catchments with wastes from the Ok Tedi and Porgera mines.

PATRICK L. OSBORNE

See also Oceania: History and Economic Development; Oceania: International Relations

References and Further Reading

Connell, J. *Papua New Guinea: The Struggle for Development*. Routledge, New York, 1977.

Löffler, E. *Geomorphology of Papua New Guinea*. Cranberra: ANU Press, 1977.

McAlpine, J.R., G. Keig, and R. Falls. *Climate of Papua New Guinea*. Cranberra: CSIRO and ANU Press, 1983.

Zimmer-Tamakoshi, L. *Modern Papua New Guinea*. Kirksville, MO: Truman State University Press, 1998.

World Health Organization. 1998. *Country Situation and Trends: Papua New Guinea*. http://www.wpro.who.int/chip/png.htm.

PARACEL AND SPRATLY ISLANDS

The South China Sea region has become a hot spot of conflicting historical and legal claims over the sovereignty of islands and areas of maritime jurisdiction among its neighbouring states, mainly on account of their potential oil and gas riches. Not surprisingly, China has described the South China Sea as "the second Persian Gulf," estimated to have possessed 130 billion barrels of oil and natural gas and a proven 7 billion barrels of oil. Given this, the Paracel and Spratly Islands, located in the South China Sea, have emerged as a focal point of fierce contest among rival states to bolster their claims to sovereignty either by occupying the islands or reinforcing their military presence there by stationing garrisons on a small scale. There are six major parties—Brunei, China, Philippines, Malaysia, Vietnam, and Taiwan—staking their claims over the Spratly Islands either fully or partly. With respect to the Paracel Islands, the parties interlocked in the dispute are Vietnam, China, and Taiwan.

The Paracel Islands lie 300 nautical miles south of Hong Kong and 145 nautical miles east of the Vietnamese port of Danang. China has been claiming the Paracel Islands as part of its tropical island province of Hainan since ancient times, while Vietnam claims its sovereignty on the legal and inheritance grounds. In 1932, the islands were annexed by French Indochina. During World War II, they were occupied by Japan and, after its defeat in the War, Japan renounced its sovereignty under the San Francisco Peace Treaty of September 1951. On the other hand, the Chinese claim to the islands was rejected at the 1951 San Francisco Conference. Despite this decision, China ignored all the principles and norms of international behaviour and annexed the Paracel Islands from Vietnam in 1974 by using military force. Since the 1970s, they have been in China's complete control. Going one step further, China announced its plan in 1997 to open the islands for a tourist centre on Yongxing Island, the largest of the Paracel Islands. In July 2003, China stationed its troops in the Paracel Islands although protested vehemently by Vietnam and Taiwan but to no avail.

The Spratly Islands, consisting of 100–230 islets and coral reefs, possess less than five square miles as landmass. They are scattered 215 nautical miles south of the Paracels and in the middle of the South China Sea. The Spratlys have strategic significance since they are located close to the main supply lanes in the central South China Sea. Of the six disputant nations, China, Vietnam, and Taiwan are claiming an exclusive sovereignty to the islands, while Malaysia, Philippines, and Brunei are claiming control over some of their parts on the basis of the continental shelf under the Law of the Sea Convention. China's claim over the Spratly Islands, which it terms the Nansha islands, is based on historical and archeological grounds arguing that it had undertaken naval expeditions during the Han Dynasty in 110 AD, and the Ming Dynasty (1403–1433). Vietnam stakes its claim to the Spratlys as the natural inheritor of the French who withdrew from Indochina in 1956, and Vietnam declared the islands as part of its Phuoc Tuy province in 1973. Taiwan's claim is similarly based on China's historical argument. The Philippines has been developing oil between the Spratly Islands and the island of Palawan since 1976 and had stationed its troops on seven of the islands in 1978. Malaysia, interlocked in the territorial dispute since 1979, has claimed three of the islands. Brunei is claiming the territory and resources in the southern part of the Spratly chain. It established an exclusive fishing zone in 1984 in the southern Spratly Islands. Claimant states have stationed their forces in about forty-five islands, such as China (about 450 soldiers), Malaysia (70 to 90), the Philippines (about 100), and Vietnam (about 1,500).

Given the mutually conflicting claims, China demonstrated its military offensive when its naval vessels entered the islands and sunk Vietnam's two naval ships in February 1988, killing more than seventy Vietnamese sailors. Another instance of China's "military intimidation" became manifest when it occupied the Philippine's Mischief Reef in 1995. However, this occupation was due to the mounting US pressure that China agree to resolve the Spratly Islands dispute with the Philippines and Vietnam peacefully. But the Chinese government did not commit to return the Mischief Reef to the Philippines. Besides, China has been conducting naval exercises in the South China Sea to project its military power projection vis-á-vis its Southeast Asian neighbours.

The continuing impasse over the Paracel and Spratly Islands has caused serious security concerns to the member countries of Association of Southeast Asian Nations (ASEAN), given China's overwhelming military capabilities as well as its dominant position in the South China Sea that might threaten peace and stability in the region. To resolve the territorial disputes in a peaceful manner, ASEAN had issued a declaration at Manila in 1992 "urging all parties concerned to exercise restraint in order to create a positive climate for the eventual resolution of all disputes." Moreover, ASEAN's Regional Forum, since its inaugural meeting in Bangkok in July 1994, has undertaken several diplomatic initiatives to promote confidence building as well as to work out preventive measures to conflicts among disputant states. Because of ASEAN's initiative at its ministerial meetings in

1996 and 1999, the member nations had agreed to a "regional code of conduct" for the South China Sea to resolve disputes through peaceful dialogue. China had also agreed to a draft code of conduct laying down principles and norms of "state-to-state-relations."

The Declaration of the Conduct of Parties in the South China Sea was signed by the Foreign Ministers of ASEAN and China at the ASEAN-China Summit in Phnom Penh in November 2002, pledging "to resolve their territorial and jurisdictional disputes by peaceful means." However, ASEAN members refused to include any "code of conduct" with regard to the Paracel Islands since the dispute is considered a bilateral one between China and Vietnam. Be that as it may, with the easing of tension between Beijing and Hanoi, both the countries are engaged in finding a political solution to the lingering dispute. This apart, ASEAN's collective approach to resolve the territorial disputes through peaceful dialogue might help restrain China from establishing its "hegemony" over the Spratlys and the South China Sea.

B. M. JAIN

See also Southeast Asia: History and Economic Development; Southeast Asia: International Relations

References and Further Reading

Acharya, Amitav. *Constructing a Security Community in Southeast Asia: ASEAN and the Problem of Regional Order*. London and New York: Routledge, 2001.

Borje, Adolf. *The Spratly Islands: A Brewing Flashpoint in Asia*. Monterey, CA: Naval Postgraduate School, 1994.

Catley, Robert, and Keliat, Makmur. *Spratlys: The Dispute in the South China Sea*. Brookfield, VT: Ashgate, 1997.

Kang, Tong H. *Vietnam and the Spratly Islands Dispute Since 1992*. Monterey, CA: Naval Postgraduate School, June 2000.

Lu, Tzu-chien. *China's Policy towards Territorial Disputes: The Case of the South China Sea Islands*. New York: Routledge, 1989.

Samuels, Marwyn S. *Contest for the South China Sea*. New York: Methuen, 1982.

Valencia, Mark J. *China and the South China Sea Disputes: Conflicting Claims and Potential Solutions in the South China Sea*. Adelphi papers, no. 298. New York: Oxford University Press for the International Institute for Strategic Studies, 1995.

PARAGUAY

Paraguay is a land-locked country located on the upper reaches of the Plate River system in South America's Southern Cone. It is divided into two distinct regions by the Paraguay River. The vast majority of the population lives in the region to the east of the river. Mixed forests, swampy pasturelands, and low ridges are typical of this part of the country. The climate is subtropical, with hot and humid summers, mild winters, and regular rainfall. To the west of the river lies the Chaco, which is increasingly arid and inhospitable as one moves west toward the Bolivian border. This territory was won in a brutal war with Bolivia from 1932 to 1935. In spite of its small population and lack of resources, the Chaco figures importantly in Paraguayans' aspirations for national development and as a symbol of the national struggle to survive.

Paraguay's history has been structured by the country's relationship to Argentina and Brazil. Although Paraguay gained its independence in 1811, Argentina did not formally recognize Paraguay's sovereignty until 1856. Paraguay's defeat at the hands of the Brazilians, Argentines, and Uruguayans in the War of the Triple Alliance (1864–1870) left it as a buffer state between Argentina and Brazil. Paraguay's foreign policy ever since has been characterized by the "pendulum politics" of balancing Brazilian and Argentine ambitions. Paraguay's political history is one of authoritarianism, marked by alternating periods of long-lived dictatorships and extreme instability. Political and economic development through authoritarianism has been a nearly permanent feature of Paraguayan politics since independence.

In the twenty-first century, the World Bank classifies Paraguay as a middle-income developing country. Its major exports are soy, cotton, and electricity. Textile production and food processing are the most important local industries. Transborder trade, much of it unregistered, is an important source of income, especially in Ciudad del Este on the Brazilian border.

At the end of World War II, Paraguay was a predominately rural society. The state's presence in the countryside was limited. Economic activity centered on agriculture and forestry. Trade was primarily conducted by river through Argentina. After a civil war in 1947, the regime became highly unstable because of intense partisan and intraparty factional conflict. Ultimately, General Alfredo Stroessner came to power in 1954. By the early 1960s, Stroessner had pacified the country through clientelism and repression.

The United States contributed much in the 1950s and 1960s to the development of state institutions capable of directing development strategies. Stroessner proved a reliable Cold War ally for the United States although the United States began to pressure the regime to implement political reform in the mid-1980s. While Paraguay under Stroessner could not be considered a bureaucratic-authoritarian regime, Stroessner did preside over a growing bureaucratic structure in which professionals worked to implement

the state's development priorities. Nevertheless, corruption and cronyism channeled through the Colorado Party remained important features of the regime. The regime extolled the "granite-like unity" of the military, the party, and the strongman that served as the basis for authority.

In the rural sector, development after 1963 focused on frontier settlement through colonization, directed by the Institute of Rural Welfare. Tens of thousands of peasants were encouraged to settle in official colonies in the eastern region along the borders with Brazil and Argentina. Tens of thousands more joined this migration without official government support. From the east came some three hundred thousand Brazilian settlers who capitalized on the sale of lands in Brazil and purchased cheap land and machinery in Paraguay. This policy failed to relieve the problem of landlessness or pressures for land reform.

The Stroessner regime promoted "outward directed development" *(desarrollo hacia afuera)* in which foreign investment and export agriculture were encouraged. Production of agricultural commodities boomed, beginning first with cotton in the 1970s. Cotton is a crop usually grown by peasants, who benefited for a time from high international prices. However, thanks to government policies, the primary beneficiaries of the cotton boom were intermediaries and currency speculators, including Colorado Party members and high-ranking military officers. As the cotton boom subsided in the 1980s, soy became the primary commodity export earner. Soy is generally produced on mechanized farms often owned by Brazilians or managed according to foreign agribusiness concerns.

Stroessner also employed pendulum politics to decrease dependence on Argentina and strengthen ties with Brazil. Transportation routes were opened across the Brazilian border, which became the primary route for commodity exports. Brazil and Argentina competed for influence in Paraguay, especially for agreements to build huge hydroelectric complexes on the Parana River. Although treaties were signed with both neighbors in 1973, the Brazilian-Paraguayan project at Itaipú came on line only in 1983 and the construction of the Yacyretá Dam, built in condominium with Argentina, began only in 1985. Paraguay exports almost its entire share of the electricity, with the Itaipú production sold by treaty arrangement only to Brazil and at below-market prices. In 1991, Paraguay joined the regional economic integration organization, MERCOSUR, along with Argentina, Brazil, and Uruguay.

Since 1989, when Stroessner was overthrown in a military *coup d'etat*, Paraguay has struggled to establish functioning democratic institutions and reverse a long-term economic decline. While the 1992 constitution describes a democratic regime in which legitimate authority is established through direct elections, power is often obtained through bitter and often violent intra-elite extraconstitutional struggles. This was seen in the Colorado presidential primary elections of 1992 and again in 1998, the civil-military conflict of 1996, and the assassination of the vice president and removal of the president in 1999. Civil society has been a positive actor in these crises, but the country has not seen the development of stable institutional channels for demand making by society and positive response by government. Presidential elections in 2003, won again by the Colorado Party, were considerably more orderly and the freest and fairest in the country's history.

Paraguay's economy has been stagnant since 1989, and contracted between 1997 and 2002. The per capita annual growth rate for the 1990s was −5.4%, making Paraguay the third worst performer in Latin America for the decade, after Ecuador and Venezuela. At the same time, inequality in the distribution of income, always marked, has increased. The economy continues to suffer from distortions caused by high levels of corruption and unregistered trade, including drug transshipment and money laundering.

BRIAN TURNER

See also Argentina; Brazil; Stroessner, Alfredo

References and Further Reading

Borda, Dionisio, and Fernando Masi. *Los Límites de la Transición: Economía y Estado en el Paraguay en los Años 90*, Asuncion: CIDSEP, 1998.
———, eds. *Economías Regionales y Desarrollo Territorial*. Asuncion: CADEP, 2002.
Flecha, Víctor-jacinto, and Carlos Martini. *Historia de la Transición: Pasado y Futuro de la Democracia en el Paraguay*. Asuncion: Última Hora, 1994.
Fogel, Ramón. *Pobreza y Políticas Sociales en el Paraguay*. Asuncion: El Lector, 1996.
Hicks, Frederic. "Interpersonal Relationships and Caudillismo in Paraguay." *Journal of Interamerican Studies and World Affairs* 13, no. 1 (1971).
Kleinpenning, J. M. G. *Man and Land in Paraguay*. Amsterdam: Centrum voor Studie en Documentatie van Latijns Amerika, 1987.
Lambert, Peter, and Andrew Nickson, eds. *The Transition to Democracy in Paraguay*. New York: St. Martin's, 1997.
Lewis, Paul H. *Paraguay Under Stroessner*. Chapel Hill: The University of North Carolina Press, 1980.
Nagel, Beverly Y. "'Unleashing the Fury': The Cultural Discourse of Rural Violence and Land Rights in Paraguay." *Comparative Studies in Society and History* 41, no. 1 (1999).
Richards, Donald G. "Booming-Sector Economic Activity in Paraguay 1973–86: A Case of Dutch Disease?" *The Journal of Development Studies* 31, no. 2 (1994).

Turner, Brian. *Community Politics and Peasant-State Relations in Paraguay*, Lanham, MD: University Press of America, 1993.

Vial, Alejandro, ed. *Cultura Política, Sociedad Civil y Participación Ciudadana: El Caso Paraguayo*. Asuncion: CIRD, 2003.

Zoomers, E. B. *Rural Development and Survival Strategies in Central Paraguay*. Amsterdam: Centrum voor Studie en Documentatie van Latijns Amerika, 1988.

PARK SYSTEMS, NATIONAL

As the industrial society expanded throughout the world during the nineteenth century, urban areas were growing more and more. The demand for natural resources like coal and wood was crucial for the development of the factories that powered the growth of the new society. Although the human pressure over the resources was still fairly low, the quick pace at which industries expanded was a potential danger for many natural areas. Out of concern about the possible destruction of wilderness for the benefit of industrialization and urbanization, the idea of establishing a protection on green areas was born. The first protected areas were created with this objective: the preservation of the natural resources by forbidding all kinds of commercial exploitations in those areas.

The first national park in history was created in the United States (US). Yellowstone National Park was founded in 1872 in the states of Wyoming and Montana to preserve the hot springs and geysers. From then on, the concept of National Parks spread to other countries: Canada created its first in 1885, then New Zealand in 1894, and Australia and South Africa followed; Mexico established its first El Chico Forest Reserve in 1898, Argentina established in 1922 the South National Park (now the Nahuel Huapi National Park), and Chile created in 1926 the Vicente Pérez Rosales National Park. Ecuador established the Galapagos National Park in 1936, and Brazil and other Latin American and African countries created their own national parks soon after.

National Parks were set up primarily to preserve vast areas of natural beauty and resources from industrial exploitation. First, the idea was to preserve the areas by isolating them from any contact with the civilization, that is, by leaving the area on its own without any human intervention whatsoever. In 1933, the Convention on the Conservation of Flora and Fauna, at a meeting in London, defined National Parks as the following:

1. Areas reserved for the protection and conservation of animal and vegetal life, the conservation of objects with an geological, historical, archaeological, or scientific interest and the benefit and recreation of general public
2. Areas under the control of the government and whose limits cannot be altered
3. Areas where hunting and destruction of fauna or flora are prohibited

As years went by, it became impossible to keep these areas isolated from the activity in their surroundings, and the vision had to change. From a perspective of *preservation,* environmentalists changed to a perspective of *conservationism.* This new approach implies that National Parks and all kinds of protected areas should not be isolated from their contexts. With this idea came the concept of "zoning," which means creating different areas within the reserves and parks to allow visitors and activities that are not so harmful for the environment.

Therefore, in the last decades of the twentieth century, the functions of the National Parks became wider. National Parks have the following functions in the twenty-first century: (i) to conserve the natural environment on a dynamic basis; (ii) to promote the ecotourism in the parks and allow sustainable development in the areas where the parks are located; (iii) to educate visitors with an environmentalist perspective that teaches them the complexity and beauty of the ecosystems; (iv) to preserve the biodiversity; (v) to protect endangered species, either animal or vegetal, from becoming extinct; and (vi) to protect the ecosystems.

As stated, the maintenance of national parks is very important because they do not only conserve a beautiful landscape but are a vital part of the world's environment. Deforestation, the permanent extinction of species, and the consequent reduction of biodiversity are all global problems that affect all mankind. In this way, National Parks are like a refugee camp that should be supported to help mankind itself.

The International Parks System and the Quest for Sustainable Development

After World War II, capitalist economies went through an unprecedented growth process with industry as the leading sector. This meant the destruction of habitats at an unknown scale that troubled specialists in the field. Therefore, an international organisation was created to keep surveillance and to coordinate efforts to conserve areas. In 1948, the International Union for the Protection of Nature (IUPN) was created, which changed its name to its present one in 1956: the Union for the Conservation of Nature and Natural

Resources (IUCN). This organisation pointed out that conservation was not a rival of production but that industry and environmental groups could work together.

The creation of the IUCN provided the states with international support, but much earlier, many developing countries had already established national parks. For instance, in Africa, a most important continent with great needs of protection, the Addo Elephants National Park was created in 1931, and in Kenya the Marsabit Federal Reserve was established in 1940.

Although some parks were established during the early decades of the twentieth century, most of the National Parks systems worldwide, in both developing and developed nations, were set up during the 1960s and 1970s. Botswana established in 1968 the National Parks Act, and in Namibia the Nature Conservation Ordinance was declared in 1975; in South Africa the National Pars Act dates back to 1976, in Tanzania the Wildlife Conservation Act dates from 1974, and so on. In northern Eurasia, although natural reserves date back to the early beginnings of the twentieth century, national parks were established only during the 1970s.

In general, this period brought an increased awareness of ecology, and international environmental organizations such as Greenpeace and the World Wildlife Fund (WWF) were founded. The latter organization, the WWF, was fundamental in the creation of national parks and reserves worldwide by using a powerful weapon: education through publicity. The WWF became famous for their panda bear logo. One of the major accomplishments of the WWF was the organization of the *Project Tiger* in 1973 to help the Indian government protect the tiger and its natural habitats. Just as important was the WWF's role in the creation of the Cross River National Park in Nigeria in 1991, whose aim is to establish an area where gorillas are protected. The WWF, often in partnership with the IUCN, has played an important role in Pakistan, Indonesia, Nepal, and Malaysia.

The establishment of the national parks systems in most developing countries occurred in times of relative economic welfare. However, the global crisis inaugurated in the mid-1970s resulted in budget cuts that affected the parks' budgets as well. The economic crisis also had a severe impact on the population, which became poorer in many cases. The worsening of the social conditions of people who lived near protected areas resulted in the use of the parks for hunting or otherwise use of the resources. These problems are common in African or Asian National Parks, especially in the poorest countries like India or Kenya. The parks located in those countries often suffer from poachers who hunt endangered species like the India tiger or the black rhino to get its horn and export it. Hunters capture live animals to trade them in the black market and sell them as pets or as animals for a circus. The poaching business moves around $5 billion annually worldwide.

However, the existence of poachers is not the only major threat to the national parks. Unlike national parks in developed countries, illegal deforestation, mining activities, and pasturage are activities that can be seen in many national parks in developing countries. These are large-scale activities that cause serious and irreversible damage to the protected areas. South America provides excellent examples. For instance, the Amazon Rain Forest contains enormous biodiversity as well as species of plants whose medicinal properties are valuable to fight conditions such as cancer and heart disease. The rain forests are also important in the conversion of atmospheric carbon dioxide to oxygen. However, deforestation continues to be rampant in the Amazon.

Another example is provided by the Selva de las Yungas (Yungas Rain Forest) Biosphere Reserve in the north of Argentina. This rain forest is the home of the *yaguarete,* a family member of the tigers that is suffering from the effects of deforestation caused by the encroachment of the agricultural frontier by multinational agribusinesses; the felled trees are also used to produce paper.

The Future of National Parks and Some Recommendations

Since the creation of the first national parks, there has been an increasing conscience of supporting and promoting protected areas. In the international arena, the first international organization was founded on October 5, 1948, as the International Union for the Protection of Nature (IUPN). This organization later on changed its name to the International Union for Conservation of Nature and Natural Resources (IUCN) in 1956. In 1990, it was shortened to the World Conservation Union (though retaining the IUCN acronym). This organization's aim is "to influence, encourage, and assist societies throughout the world to conserve the integrity and diversity of nature and to ensure that any use of natural resources is equitable and ecologically sustainable." The IUCN also organizes the World Congress on National Parks and Protected Areas where specialists from all over the world meet to exchange information and to produce documents and recommendations useful for governments.

Eleven years after the World Congress was held in Caracas (Venezuela), the most recent World Congress took place in the city of Durban, South Africa, in September 2003. As a result, the Closing Plenary of the Congress delivered the Durban Accord and an Action Plan consisting of thirty-two specific recommendations, spurring conservation in Africa. However, the alarming levels of poverty, HIV/AIDS, diseases, and civil wars that destroy the African continent make it very hard for the ecosystems and the national parks to achieve the goals of sustainable development. To help the conservation of national parks in developing countries, it is also necessary to fight against poverty, unemployment, and the lack of education.

DIEGO I. MURGUÍA

See also Biodiversity Conservation; Deforestation; Ecotourism; Environment: Government Policies; Environmentalism; Rain Forest, Destruction of; Sustainable Development; Wildlife Preservation

References and Further Reading

Igoe, Jim. *Conservation and Globalization: A Study of National Parks and Indigenous Communities from East Africa to South Dakota*. Belmont, CA: Thomson/Wadsworth, 2004.
International Union for the Conservation of Nature and Natural Resources (IUCN). *World Conservation Strategy: Living Resource Conservation for Sustainable Development*. Gland, Switzerland: IUCN-UNEP-WWF, 1980.
———. *Protected Areas of the World: A Review of National Systems*. Gland Switzerland and Cambridge, UK: IUCN, 1992.
———. *Regional Reviews*. Gland Switzerland and Cambridge, United Kingdom: IUCN, January 1992.
———. *Parks for Life: Report of the IVth World Congress on National Parks and Protected Areas (the Caracas Action Plan)*. Gland, Switzerland: IUCN, 1993.

PARTY OF THE INSTITUTIONALIZED REVOLUTION (PRI)

The Party of the Institutionalized Revolution (*Partido Revolucionario Institucional*, PRI) constituted the most influential political force in the evolution of modern Mexico, governing the country uninterruptedly from 1929 to 2000. Emerging from the instability and violence of the Mexican Revolution, the PRI initially functioned as a mechanism of compromise that absorbed the various conflicting factions contesting power to create a "revolutionary family" where interests could be balanced out equitably and disputes could be settled through political means. The PRI was initially successful in integrating the voices of the dispossessed classes into its official ideology, especially through the enactment of laws that favored the peasant

and urban working classes. Yet, the PRI's overall vision for Mexico's development underlined a fundamentally capitalist project that favored both national and international economic elites and eventually made them key partners of the PRI's mode of governance. As the PRI consolidated its power in the aftermath of civil war and bloodshed, it gradually transformed itself into an all-encompassing force in Mexican politics and often resorted to authoritarian means to retain power and undermine potential opposition.

The Origins of the PRI: Compromise, Nationalism, and Authoritarian Rule

The civil conflict that erupted in Mexico in 1910 involved several players that opposed the long-standing dictatorship of Porfirio Díaz, most notably middle class reformers led by Francisco Madero and populist forces led by Emiliano Zapata and Francisco "Pancho" Villa. Not only were those leaders disposed of in the bloodshed and confusion that eventually engulfed the Mexican Revolution, but also the lack of assertive political leadership and the constant recreation of unresolved conflicts between the main revolutionary factions submerged Mexico into a cycle of violence that lasted until 1928. The leadership of Plutarco Calles was successful in advancing a systematic "elite settlement" based on compromise and power-sharing, convincing all the major surviving factions that endless uncertainty was inevitable without a centralized authority that could settle ongoing disputes through peaceful means. Calles founded the National Revolutionary Party (*Partido Nacional Revolucionario*, PNR, the predecessor of the PRI) as the vehicle to achieve that compromise.

The Mexican masses were subsequently incorporated into the PNR by Calles' succesor, Lázaro Cárdenas, a progressive-minded politician who served as Mexico's president from 1934 to 1940. Cárdenas encouraged the formation of worker and peasant organizations as a way to advance the underlying populist and reformist ideals of the Mexican Revolution and the Constitution of 1917. Cárdenas implemented a package of sweeping reforms that promoted socioeconomic development among the lower classes, awarded them official representation by creating peasant and labor sectors within the party, and nationalized key industries, including oil. Within this context, the crucial dichotomy for a successful national compromise occurred: Calles gained the cooperation of the elites, and Cárdenas galvanized the support of the masses behind the regime.

In 1938, Cárdenas renamed the PNR as the Party of the Mexican Revolution (*Partido de la Revolución*

Mexicana, PRM). One of the most significant achievements of the Cárdenas presidency was the implementation of a comprehensive program of land reform. More than fifty million acres of large-estate land holdings were transferred to Mexican peasants through a system of communally owned lands known as *ejidos*. This was the first major agrarian reform in Latin American history and was instrumental in destroying Mexico's semi-feudal landholding system. Moreover, a series of labor and socially progressive laws were introduced by Cárdenas to further consolidate the support of the working class, including higher wages, social housing, and subsidized credit. Popular organizations were fostered and supported by the party leadership, such as the Confederation of Mexican Workers (*Confederación de Trabajadores Mexicanos*, CTC) and the National Peasant Confederation (*Confederación Nacional de Campesinos*, CNC). The establishment of these organizations gave a voice to popular classes, but they also allowed the PRM to control its organizational and ideological structures. Cárdenas also established a state oil monopoly, PEMEX (*Petróleos Mexicanos*), after the assets of Western oil companies were expropriated. By the early 1940s, the PRM had consolidated its national political leadership by relying on the support of four key sectors of Mexican society: labor, the peasantry, the middle classes, and the military.

In 1946, the PRM was renamed the Party of the Institutionalized Revolution (*Partido Revolucionario Institucional*, PRI). The idea that a revolution could be "institutionalized" signified a fundamental shift in the PRI's ideology and practice. In theory, the interests of the lower classes were to be guaranteed through the election of representatives to all levels of party and government structures, but in practice, the post-Cárdenas PRI leadership gradually abandoned this inclusive character in favor of probusiness and elitist modes of governance. An increasingly entrenched alliance between the party elite and the economically powerful classes eventually appropriated the party's decision-making apparatus. This new emphasis on business allowed the PRI to achieve sustained economic growth during the 1950s and 1960s but at the cost of reversing many of the early achievements of the post-1928 period.

Increased Repression and Economic Slowdown

By the 1960s, the PRI had become the only and unchallenged force in Mexican politics at the levels of government. Elections were periodically held, but very few or no opposition candidates were to be found on the ballots. Moreover, the tight control that PRI officials exercised over the electoral processes and the leadership of popular organizations guaranteed a generalized consent whereby the regime's candidates would get easily elected. As the PRI's supremacy began to decline, the party resorted to more coercive methods, including electoral fraud and explicit intimidation tactics, to preserve its grip on power. From the 1940s to the mid-1980s, only one other party, namely the National Action Party (*Partido de Acción Nacional*, PAN) was allowed to participate in national or local elections, never posing a clear challenge to the hegemony of the PRI.

One political feature that characterized the PRI's governing style was that of a very powerful and overriding president. All major decisions and conflict mediation revolved around the judgment of the president, who had virtually unrestricted power and was generally insulated from any form of democratic scrutiny. Even if the Constitution theoretically provided for a formal separation of powers within the state, both the legislative and judicial branches were controlled by the directives coming from the president. It became a tradition for the president to appoint his successor (a process colloquially called *dedazo*, or finger-pointing) without resorting to any process of internal consultation. At the same time, it is important to note that within the PRI there is a degree of heterogeneity whereby *camarillas* (political groups of factions) engage in intraparty competition and diverge on ideological and policy matters. Although these internal rivalries do not threaten the unity of the party, every presidential term was initially judged on the basis of what *camarilla* was represented or who had more influence.

A turning point in the PRI relationship with Mexican society came on October 2, 1968. On that tragic day, a rally of students protesting against government corruption and the rather wasteful organization of that year's summer Olympic Games was met by military authorities with brutal force. An order to disperse was allegedly ignored, and the police began shooting directly at the crowd, killing hundreds of protesters in the process. The Massacre of *Tlatelolco*, named after the main square where the students had congregated, shed light on the moral and political bankruptcy of the PRI, but it also sent the chilling message that challenges to the PRI's political dominance would be answered with merciless repression.

Even in the face of increasing political decadence, Mexico under the PRI managed to register an impressive economic record in the post–World War II period. Adding to the nationalistic policies that laid a socioeconomic foundation for further growth, the

strategy of import substitution industrialization (ISI) enabled Mexico to increase its overall economic output, diversify the employment base, and boost purchasing power for the masses. A favorable currency rate resulted in considerable levels of foreign direct investment, tourism flourished, and balance of payments deficits were substantially reduced. Between the early 1950s and the late 1960s, Mexico's annual growth rate averaged 6%. However, by the early 1970s, the economic boom began to dissipate mainly due to spiraling inflation, dependence on expensive technological imports, and decreasing productivity. The PRI leadership tried to go back to the nationalist style that had characterized the party in its early years, but changing times, both domestically and internationally, left little maneuvering room for allegedly outdated strategies. As the 1980s approached, the Mexico that the PRI had built was heading toward crisis and significant multifaceted transformations.

Neoliberalism, Technocrats, and Political Decline

In 1982, Mexico declared its inability to service its foreign debt, paving the road for a radical transformation of socioeconomic direction. As Mexico had to comply with structural adjustment programs imposed by foreign creditors to reschedule old debts, the PRI turned to its increasingly influential technocratic *camarilla* to lead the way toward a painful reconfiguration of national development strategies. It was Miguel de la Madrid, governing the country from 1982 to 1988, who oversaw the shift from a largely protectionist economy to one espousing free-market and export-oriented principles. Miguel de la Madrid substantially reduced the size of the public service, began the systematic privatization of state enterprises, and implemented significant cuts in the national budgets for food subsidies and social services.

As the economy changed course, so did the unchallenged stand of the PRI in national politics. In the presidential elections of 1988, a PRI breakaway faction led by Cuáuhtemoc Cárdenas, son of former president Lázaro Cárdenas, posed a serious threat to the PRI's electoral domination. Despite largely substantiated accusations of massive fraud, the PRI candidate, Carlos Salinas de Gortari, was declared the winner with 50.3% of the votes. The systematic use of fraudulent methods by the PRI to retain power, coupled with a growing discontent of an electorate that supported opposition candidates with half of the votes, signified the beginning of the end of the PRI-led one-party rule in Mexico. The PRI also lost power in state and municipal elections as well as seats in the Chamber of Deputies and the Senate.

Salinas de Gortari consolidated Mexico's shift toward market economics, expanding deregulation and privatization policies and negotiating the entry of Mexico into the North American Free Trade Agreement (NAFTA) with the United States and Canada. To facilitate Mexico's membership in NAFTA, Salinas amended Article 27 of the Constitution, whereby state protection of the *ejido* was removed and the door was opened for multinational corporations to buy *ejido* land to expand agrobusiness ventures. As the *ejidos* lost official support and small producers failed to compete with cheaper grain coming from the United States, a deep crisis in the Mexican countryside ensued. On January 1, 1994, the day when NAFTA entered into force, an indigenous uprising in the southern state of Chiapas, led by the Zapatista National Liberation Army (Ejército Zapatista de Liberación Nacional, EZLN), erupted as a stunning manifestation of protest from those left behind by the neoliberal transition.

The PRI survived the 1994 elections, but not without controversy. Salinas de Gortari's handpicked successor, Luis Donaldo Colosio, was assassinated during a campaign stop in Tijuana, an event that revealed the ferocious internal power struggled within the PRI. Ernesto Zedillo was chosen to replace Colosio, winning comfortably due to the implosion of the opposition's campaigns. Zedillo refused to continue with the old-style politics of the PRI, introducing important measures to democratize the party and the political system as a whole. Zedillo dropped the *dedazo* tradition and allowed party primaries to choose the PRI's candidate for the 2000 elections, electoral reform policies were put forward to make elections more transparent, and the executive stopped using extraconstitutional means to impose the president's desires. In July 2000, and as a result of a general atmosphere of awakening democracy combined with the ripe mood for change among the electorate, the PAN's Vicente Fox won the first-ever presidential elections by an opposition party in seventy-one years. Despite losing control of the executive branch in 2000, the PRI remains an extremely powerful and influential force in Mexico's state, legislative, and municipal politics.

CARLOS VELÁSQUEZ CARRILLO

See also Mexico: History and Economic Development; North American Free Trade Agreement (NAFTA);

Salinas de Gortari, Carlos; Zapatista National Revolutionary Army (EZLN)

References and Further Reading

Brenner, Anita. *The Wind That Swept Mexico: The History of the Mexican Revolution of 1910–1942*. Austin, TX: University of Texas Press, 1971.

Dogan, Mattei, and John Higley. *Elites, Crises, and the Origins of Regimes*. Lanham, MD: Rowman and Littlefield, 1998.

Dominguez, Jorge, and James McCann. *Democratizing Mexico: Public Opinion and Electoral Choices*. Baltimore, MD: John Hopkins University Press, 1996.

Hamilton, Nora. *The Limits of State Autonomy: Post-Revolutionary Mexico*. Princeton, NJ: Princeton University Press, 1982.

Harvey, Neil, ed. *Mexico: Dilemmas of Transition*. New York: St. Martin's Press, 1993.

Joseph, Gilbert, and Daniel Nugent, eds. *Everyday Forms of State Formation: Revolution and the Negotiation of Rule in Modern Mexico*. Durham, NC: Duke University Press, 1994.

Levy, Daniel, and Kathleen Bruhn. *Mexico: The Struggle for Democratic Development*. Berkeley, CA: Berkeley University Press, 2001.

Pempel, T. J. *Uncommon Democracies: The One Party Dominant Regime*. Ithaca, NY: Cornell University Press, 1990.

Rodriguez, Victoria E., and Peter Ward, eds. *Opposition Government in Mexico*. Albuquerque, NM: University of New Mexico Press, 1995.

Smith, Peter H. *Labyrinths of Power: Political Recruitment in Twentieth-Century Mexico*. Princeton, NJ: Princeton University Press, 1979.

Teichman, Judith. *Privatization and Political Change in Mexico*. Pittsburgh, PA: University of Pittsburgh Press, 1995.

PATHET LAO

Pathet Lao (PL) means "Lao Nation" or "Land of the Lao." It was the name given to a clandestine, nationalist, anti-French organization created in August 1950 by Prince Souphanouvong (1909–1995), a French-educated member of the Lao royal family and Kaysone Phomvihane of the Indochina Communist Party (ICP). The PL was inspired by Prince Phetsarath's formation of the nationalist *Lao Seri* (Free Lao) group and later the underground *Lao Issara* (Independent Lao) quasi-government cell in the late 1940s. The PL was based on Marxist-Leninist principles.

During the final years of French rule in Indochina, PL cadres were formed nationwide. They were supplied and trained by the Vietminh. After the French withdrew from Indochina, PL leaders met at Sam Neua on March 22, 1955, and formed the Lao People's Revolutionary Party (LPRP), also known as the People's Party of Laos or *Phak Pasason Pativat Lao*. In January 1956, supported by the Democratic Republic of Vietnam (DRV), the PL created a covert branch called the Lao Patriotic Front or *Neo Lao Hak Sat* and the Lao People's Liberation Army (LPLA). Copying the Vietminh model, PL cadres moved into the countryside, forming party cells and people's action committees. Like the Vietminh, their programs focused on social change, land reform, curbing the power of business elites, and expelling Westerners.

In 1957, Souphanouvong and his half-brother Prince Souvanna Phouma (1901–1984) tried to create a coalition government with a national election. Initially, it seemed the PL had won thirteen of the twenty-one contested seats. Widespread fraud and ballot-box stuffing on all sides further clouded the results. Conservative Prime Minister Phoui Sanaikone contested the election by having some PL leaders in the Laotian capital of Vientiane arrested and by attempting to disarm LPLA. They fled to hideouts in the jungles.

US leaders provided Souvanna Phouma with material support to fight the PL, but he was unable to hold the diverse coalition government together. In 1959, the United States turned its support to Lao/Thai forces led by General Phoumi Nosavan (1920–1985) who captured Vientiane, forcing Phouma's neutralist government to the Plain of Jars. Soon, Souphonouvang and Phouma joined forces against Nosavan, leading to the Laotian Crisis of 1961.

President John F. Kennedy, seeking a diplomatic settlement, approved the Convention of 1962, which restored Phouma to power and, in theory, gave the PL a lesser role in the new coalition government. However, the tenuous nature of the settlement led US intelligence agencies to expand covert operations against PL forces. In hindsight, it is easy to see how this action eventually drew Laos into the expanding conflict in Indochina and provided future sanctuaries for communist forces. Instead of defeating the PL, US policy drove the PL deeper into the arms of its mentors, the People's Army of Vietnam (PAVN).

The LPLA was a gathering of various ethnic, political, and racial groups with one thing in mind: rid Laos of US influence. By 1970, this once rag-tag force of the early 1960s, numbered over fifty thousand well-trained and intensely dedicated troops.

Among those fighting this formidable foe was the Royal Lao Army (RLA), an ineffectual force with an overabundance of often-corrupt officers. It is worth noting that the marshal arts had never been part of Buddhist Laotian cultural traditions. However, with PAVN leadership and supplies, the LPLA proved adequate guerilla fighters, most often supporting the PAVN within Laos or near the border. Given the rugged mountain-jungle terrain, LPLA units most often operated in units of one hundred and no larger than five hundred.

Beginning in 1964, the LPLA's primary role became the construction and maintenance of the ever-expanding labyrinth of truck parks, supply centers, hospitals, paved roads, foot paths, streamlets, and raging rivers known as the Ho Chi Minh Trail. In 1965, in an effort to close this massive resupply route into South Vietnam, the United States began an extensive covert bombing campaign sponsored by the Central Intelligence Agency (CIA) and dubbed the operation "Barrell Roll." In the meantime, with the RLA avoiding confrontation with the LPLA and PAVN, the United States decided to support a forty thousand-man force of ethnic Hmong peoples led by General Vang Pao. They enjoyed periodic success, especially during the dry season when they could count on air cover. However, the covert nature of the war and the fits and start of US involvement meant that US supplies were not always available when needed. This coupled with concerted PAVN offensives against the Hmong during the rainy season meant that by the early 1970s, the Hmong were in a tenuous position.

Many writers have argued that much of Vang Pao's motivation for supporting the CIA had to do with his desire to maintain the profitable flow of raw opium out of the Laotian part of the Golden Triangle to Saigon via Air America, the CIA's airline. Some of these authors claim that the money from the sale of this opium was used to fund the "Secret War." Most of these authors base their claims on anecdotal evidence that does not convincingly link the CIA to such activities. Indeed, there is very hard evidence to suggest that the DRV and PL were the "godfathers" of the opium trade in this area.

In February 1973, only days after the Paris Peace Accords were signed, a cease-fire was signed in Laos. Even so, the war continued until the US abandoned Laos in April 1975. By this time, the PL dominated the government. All anti-PL forces soon collapsed without US support. Several hundred Hmong, including Vang Pao, were relocated to the US state of Montana. During the succeeding twenty-five years, many thousand Hmong and other minorities suffered severe persecutions and even death at the hands of the PL. Phouma fled Laos in April 1975, and the last commander of the RLA, General Oudone Sananikone, formerly surrendered on May 8, 1975.

On December 2, 1975, PL leaders established the Lao People's Democratic Republic. Souphanouvang became the president, while Kaysone Phomvidane became Prime Minister and Secretary of the ruling LPRP. In 1986, Souphanouvang died of a stroke. He was succeeded by Phoumi Vonguichit. In 1991, Phomvihone took control of the government only to die a year later. He was succeeded by Nouhak Phoumsavane.

Less doctrinaire than their counterparts in Kampuchea, the PL leaders had greater success in restoring order to Laos after 1975. Even so, their international isolation and lack of economic skills left them much dependent on the Vietnamese. Their economy languished until the late 1980s when they began to open their doors to foreign, even US, tourists and investors. While many conservationists fear the uncontrolled exploitation of their natural resources, clearly these moves have made Laos more prosperous. Still, the country's woeful human rights record, especially the continued persecution of its minorities, have kept Laos from the socioeconomic renaissance enjoyed by the more democratic states of Southeast Asia.

WILLIAM P. HEAD

See also Laos; Southeast Asia: History and Economic Development; Southeast Asia: International Relations

References and Further Reading

Adams, Nina S., and Alfred W. McCoy, eds. *Laos: War and Revolution.* New York: Random House, 1970.
Castle, Timothy. *At War in the Shadow of Vietnam: United States Military Aid to the Royal Lao Government, 1955–1975.* New York: Columbia University Press, 1993.
Conboy, Kenneth, and James Morrison. *Shadow War: The CIA's Secret War in Laos.* Boulder, CO: Paladin Press, 1995.
Dommen, Arthur J. *Conflict in Laos: The Politics of Neutralization.* New York: Paeger, 1971.
———. *Laos: Keystone of Indochina.* Boulder, CO: Westview, 1985.
Hamilton-Merritt, Jane. *Tragic Mountains: The Hmong, The Americans, and the Secret Wars for Laos, 1942–1992.* Bloomington, IN: Indiana University Press, 1993.
McCoy, Alfred W. *The Politics of Heroin: CIA Complicity in the Global Drug Trade.* Brooklyn, NY: Lawrence Hill Books, 1991.
Zarloff, Joseph J., and McAlister Brown. *Apprentice Revolutionaries: The Communist Movement in Laos, 1930–1985.* Stanford, CA: Hoover Institution Press, 1986.

PEACEKEEPING OPERATIONS, REGIONAL AND INTERNATIONAL

Peacekeeping responds to a practical necessity of stabilizing violent conflict situations, either interstate or internal. Traditionally, peacekeeping has been introduced when the belligerent parties are willing to accept a cease-fire and agree to the separation of forces with a shared interest in at least limited settlement. Military deployment can be made to prevent renewed violence or to stop further escalation of violence where conflict is in progress. A multinational military and police force under the authority of the United Nations (UN) or a regional organization can intervene

between the warring parties in a conflict. Prior consent of the belligerent parties is normally essential for peacekeeping operations other than humanitarian intervention. In general, the mandates are related to the enforcement of the terms of a negotiated cease-fire and the advancement of peaceful resolution of conflict.

Between its inception in 1948 and 2001, the UN has undertaken 54 operations, and two-thirds of these operations have been established since 1991. A growing demand for UN peacekeeping operations surged with the increase in the number of internal conflicts and their negotiated settlement since the end of the Cold War. Peacekeeping activities have been extended geographically from the Middle East and other traditionally recognized hot spots in Southeast Asia, Southern and Eastern Africa, Central America, and Southeastern Europe. The wide use of peacekeeping, ranging from small-scale observation to enforcement, reflects the necessity to intervene in an increasing number of civil wars.

Most peacekeeping efforts adopt diverse approaches to their respective tasks with an *ad hoc* nature of operations in a unique environment (illustrated by Somalia, Cambodia, and Liberia).

Objectives

Traditionally, peacekeepers have served as neutral observers in conflict zones, but the function of peacekeeping can be adaptable to different situations. The control or stabilization of violent conflicts has been known as the most classic function of peacekeeping. Lightly armed forces position themselves to help manage relations between hostile forces without being part of the conflict. The deployment of neutral troops with the consent of the conflicting parties is regarded as a confidence-building measure, as it decreases tensions and allows time for negotiated settlement. Dispatch of peacekeepers most commonly follows a cessation of active violence. In addition to maintaining a cease-fire, peacekeeping also means verifying the withdrawal of troops. Through observing and reporting any cease-fire violations, peacekeeping can be used for reduction in tensions and mistrust rather than imposition of its own conceptions of peace on the warring parties.

As neutral parties, peacekeepers are not supposed to be allies of any participants in the conflict. While serving as a buffer zone, peacekeeping troops police truce lines and prevent recurring violence through the observation of any violations of a cease-fire or truce

lines. The peacekeeping can also be used to maintain order in the establishment of a new government in post-conflict situations. Force as self-defence or to maintain law and order is used only when the peacekeepers are attacked. The presence of peacekeeping is based on consent or at least tolerance of the disputing parties.

Given that peaceful resolution of conflict is not possible without the cessation of hostilities, the cycle of hostilities ought to be neutralized. Peacekeeping can buy time for building trust between belligerents for negotiated settlement by containing violent conflict. However, durable solutions to conflicts should be sought by direct negotiation between the adversaries or through mediation involving a third-party facilitation.

Since the operations by themselves do not provide solutions to hostile relationships, they are seen as temporary measures and are intended to be provisional.

Evolution of Operations

There are different international circumstances under which peacekeeping has been introduced. The majority of peacekeeping during the Cold War period was limited to separating national armies in ending hostilities between belligerent states. Since then, the roles of peacekeepers have been diverse with the rise of demand for new functions of the international military forces in response to hostilities among ethnic groups. If any enforcement actions are necessary in internal conflict situations, the rules of engagement and use of force need to be flexibly adjusted to humanitarian needs and protect civilians. Civilian police and the military observers monitor human rights abuses as well as protection of relief workers and distribution of aid. Peacekeeping operations in internal conflicts promote confidence building by being involved in logistical support as well as maintaining law and order.

The majority of conflicts in the last decade are characterized by physical and psychological abuses involving heavy civilian causalities. Internal conflicts in many ethnically divided societies have destroyed social and economic infrastructure, and overcoming deep divisions is a paramount task. Military forces are expected to provide support for the implementation of conflict settlement agreements. As peacekeeping in post-conflict settings is oriented toward rebuilding war-torn societies, the troops have to assist and support displaced people and other victims of war as well as provide security for them. To perform these functions better, social-psychological skills and other skills

for the management of communal relationships need to be incorporated into military missions.

Traditional Peacekeeping Roles

Most peacekeeping operations during the Cold War period were limited to monitoring truces following intrastate wars. Peacekeeping initially started with small-scale unarmed observation units dispatched to Palestine (1948), Kashmir (1949), Lebanon (1958), and Yemen (1963–1964). The United Nations Mission in Ethiopia and Eritrea was organized to monitor the cessation of armed hostilities following the civil war in 2000.

Examples of regional intervention (the Organization of African Unity) exist in the Chadian civil conflict of the early 1980s. Although it was designed to enforce the cease-fire, its success was limited to establishing a security zone, temporarily giving a reprieve from destruction and violence, but the intervention failed to establish peace throughout the country. The three thousand peacekeeping forces were outnumbered by more than ten militia groups with thousands of combatants who refused to cooperate.

The first large military peacekeeping forces were organized during the Suez War to contain the escalation of the crisis in November 1956. The six thousand troops under the United Nations Emergency Force (UNEF) I created buffer zones around the Suez Canal and facilitated the withdrawal of Israeli, French, and British armies that invaded Egypt. Whereas UNEF I was terminated by the request of Egypt, resulting in the Six Day War, the second United Nations Emergency Force II was deployed in Sinai following a cease-fire. UNEF II sustained the cease-fire long enough to allow negotiated settlements at Camp David in 1979. The two operations are viewed as classic peacekeeping examples of supporting interstate conflict management by stabilizing the situation in the region. The UNEF II, in particular, successfully forestalled the competitive intrusion of the United States and the Soviet Union into the Middle East, thus managing an explosive global confrontation.

One of the longest armed peacekeeping operations is the UN Force in Cyprus (UNFICYP), which was placed in 1964 and still remains to manage explosive conflict on the island. Although the immediate dispatch of UN peacekeeping forces prohibited the direct intervention of Turkish and Greek governments and created stable conditions, their sustained mission has not accomplished peace due to the continuing hostilities between the Turkish and Greek communities. The unintended adverse effect of the operations

has been the maintenance of the status quo without resolving the underlying causes. Political accord has become an elusive goal despite the presence of peacekeepers in Cyprus for over thirty years.

The UN Interim Force in Lebanon (UNIFIL) was given a mandate that could not be fulfilled since it was deployed in early 1978 following the Israeli invasion of Lebanon. It was not able to stop the powerful Israelis from attacking the territory and failed to restore the authority of the disintegrating Lebanese government. The continuing presence represents the maintenance of status quo because of the fear that withdrawal would precipitate further chaos.

Even during the early period of the UN's peacekeeping efforts, there were variations in peacekeeping operations adjusted to different local conflict dynamics. The UN's peacekeeping mission in the Congo (1960–1964), known as *Opération des Nations Unies au Congo* (ONUC), was sent to control a major secessionist movement in the country's civil war, distancing from the traditional neutral roles of international peacekeeping. To achieve its goal, the Congo operation had twenty thousand troops from twenty-nine countries, the largest unit before 1992. The troops were involved in heavy fighting, including the use of air strikes against the secessionist forces. The change in the nature of UN operations within the Congo is characterized by enforcement actions with the goal of achieving stability and preservation of the unity, but any serious peace-building work was not introduced, leaving the prewar situation almost the same.

Before the end of the Cold War, peacekeeping made a contribution to preventing further escalation of regional war into a major crisis between the two superpowers. On the other hand, peacekeeping can become controversial if impartiality is questioned by an international community. UN Operation within the Congo was seen as an attempt to install a Western-supported government by the Soviet Union and some African states.

Post-Cold War Operations

Controlling unpredictable conflict situations between hostile communities within a state requires different operational imperatives. With the rise of civil wars and ethnic rivalries (replacing geostrategic conflict between the Socialist and Western countries around the globe during the Cold War period), the functions and scopes of peacekeeping have been redefined. Peacekeeping serves a variety of purposes, ranging from conflict prevention, humanitarian intervention, to peace building.

Preventive Deployment

A preventive military response includes positioning military observers, troops, and related personnel before the actual breakout of a violent conflict. Its goal is to control the escalation of an emerging threat of conflict into armed conflict. The intervention is designed to prevent the imminent escalation of violence where there is an emerging threat. Observers may prepare reports on development that undermine stability and confidence in the vicinity of conflict zones. Other activities include monitoring local authorities in the protection of minorities and other vulnerable populations by maintaining law and order. Early warning signs can be developed based on an insufficient supply of essential services, such as water and power, as well as human rights violations.

The North Atlantic Treaty Organization's (NATO's) quick response to escalation of violence in Kosovo in the spring of 2004 included strong pressure on the community leaders and politicians to control their ethnic constituents. The United States, Canada, and France sent troops to Haiti to control chaos following the overthrow of the government that spring. French intervention was made in the Ivory Coast (Cote d'Ivoire) in 2003 to control further escalation of violent conflict, bringing about a peace agreement. The most noticeable and successful examples of peacekeeping for preventive purposes were the operations in Macedonia devoted to curbing violent civil war between Albanian militia forces and the Macedonian government in the late 1990s.

The Organization for Security and Cooperation in Europe (OSCE) promotes early warning and confidence building as a strategy for prevention. The OSCE used fact-finding missions in Estonia and Latvia as tension arose between Estonian and Latvian governments and the Russian speaking populations. OSCE observer missions were also sent to Moldova, Georgia, and Nagorno-Karabakh to explore strategies to effectively deal with conflict over minorities. Other regional organizations, including the Organization of American States (OAS) along with the UN, were actively involved in the negotiations of ending violent conflicts in Central America.

Quasi-Enforcement

The quasi-enforcement functions are oriented toward the relief of suffering among the civilian population and restoring order. Forces can be used to protect the convoys of humanitarian aids and the movements of refugees. The UN peacekeeping force in Somalia (UNOSOM) II was involved in disarming the militias

and maintaining order needed to deliver humanitarian aid. The moral imperatives are often related to reducing human sufferings with the protection of human rights of unarmed civilians under attack.

A response to an act of aggression or campaign of genocide may involve a costly and difficult option of forceful intervention. Some missions failed to provide security (such as in Rwanda) in the mid 1990s and, in fact, even reduced their strength in the face of escalating violence. The early NATO operations in Kosovo failed to protect minority populations, such as Gypsies and Serbs, due to the refusal of some national contingents to directly intervene in arson and killings by Albanians. Political realities combined with the difficulty of formulating objective criteria to be applied on a case-by-case basis may deter timely intervention in violent armed struggles. In the absence of well-organized military preparation, peacekeeping operations may invite disastrous outcomes, as we saw in the failure of UN troops to protect "safe havens" in Bosnia and to prevent genocide in Rwanda. It is more appropriate for better-armed regional forces to intervene to control violent situations. Humanitarian intervention is largely involved in internal conflict and differs from collective security actions that aim to punish an aggressor state. The use of force is a stop-gap measure to induce diplomatic negotiations rather than deterrence of aggression.

In its long involvement in the bloody internal wars of Liberia during the early and mid-1990s, the Economic Community of West African States Cease-Fire Monitoring Group (ECOMOG) had to take military enforcement actions, especially following a chaos created by the failure of warring factions to implement peace agreements. Especially in internal wars, it is not easy to find blurred boundaries between different types of military operations. ECOMOG chose the course of aggressive intervention with a vague and open mandate. ECOMOG tried to revive the communication and transportation infrastructure that broke down as well as tried to transport refugees and protect relief supplies. The capital city of Monrovia has to be secured to support an interim government. ECOMOG oscillates between traditional peacekeeping and peace enforcement to be adaptable to the prevailing political and military situations in Liberia.

Peace Building

When peacekeeping is introduced as part of political settlement following a civil war, troops may get engaged in weapons collection, resettlement of refugees, disarmament and demobilization of combatants, and creation of logistical support for elections.

Multidimensional operations are designed to support comprehensive settlements following lengthy periods of civil wars in such countries as Cambodia, El Salvador, Mozambique, and Namibia.

Whereas overseeing the withdrawal of hostile forces was a major focus of the UN verification mission in Angola, it became a critical task in Mozambique and El Salvador to arrange for the return of refugees as well as disarming rebels. A monitoring operation sent to the Iraq-Kuwait border at the end of the Gulf War became engaged in the policing and relief activities for the Kurdish populations in northern Iraq. International Commission for Support and Verification, the first UN-authorized mission in the Western Hemisphere, successfully disarmed the Nicaraguan Contras with demobilization of twenty-two thousand combatants during April and June 1990 and enabled the reintegration of former combatants and their family members with social and economic support.

For a lasting peace settlement, facilitating transitions to a stable government has become an important priority. In conjunction with UN civilian personnel, transitional authority was set up in Bosnia-Herzegovina and Cambodia to temporarily run the government preceding popular elections. The implementation of a comprehensive settlement is also made possible by the reconstruction of governmental functions and rehabilitation of a civil society assisted by civic education as well as military and police retraining programs.

Deployment Procedures

In the UN-mandated operations, various missions are generally set up by the UN Security Council that consists of the United States, Russia, France, Britain, and other major powers. UNEF I was a unique exception to this latter rule since the Security Council was inactive due to the involvement of two Security Council Permanent Members in the armed conflict. The management of UN activities was authorized by the UN General Assembly, whose resolution required the invading forces, including France and Britain, to withdraw from the Egyptian territory.

In general, based on the guidance of the UN Security Council, the Secretary-General can mobilize troops with contributions from UN member states on a voluntary basis. The Secretary-General has the authority for the appointment of the force commander and selection of national contingents and other activities related to assembling troops, while he is required by the Council to provide regular reports. The power of the Secretary-General in directing UN peacekeeping forces was curtailed following a more dominant role played by Dag Hammarskjöld in the management of a crisis in the Congo in July 1960. Since then, the Security Council began to have more control over such aspects of operations, such as setting time limits on the deployment of forces. In integrated peace settlement missions, which have become important in the recent decade, the Secretary-General's authority has been broadened again to instigate and direct force activities within the overall framework of the UN Security Council's mandate.

In a response to tenuous cease-fire situations characterized by a lack of trust between parties, the contingents are organized in a hurry, often without much preparation and briefing. While the military personnel were mostly offered by small neutral states during the early period of peacekeeping, the contributing countries have become diverse with the involvement of regional organizations with the end of the Cold War. NATO troops to the Balkans include the United States, Britain, Germany, the Netherlands, and Denmark. Regional powers such as Nigeria led ECO-MOG operations in Liberia, and troops sent to Sierra Leone were dominated by other African countries. Difficult logistic issues created by a lack of coordination with soldiers from different countries can be more easily solved by the troops that belong to a regional alliance.

Regional organizations such as the Organization of American States (OAS), the Economic Community of West African States, or a group of allied states can execute a military operation with international authorization by the UN Security Council. The quasi-enforcement operations in Haiti and Somalia were commanded, both politically and militarily, by an *ad hoc* coalition, under a loose UN Security Council mandate. In Haiti, the regional intervention led by the United States was approved by the OAS, and the removal of the military dictatorship and control of violence allowed the initiation of United Nations work for reconstruction of the country. The OAS had also made a serious contribution to the disarmament and demobilization of the rebel forces following the Contra War in Nicaragua. A Western alliance carried out a mission to provide humanitarian assistance to Kurds in northern Iraq at the end of the Gulf War with the authorization of the UN Security Council. On another occasion, the Nigeria dominated quasi-enforcement peacekeeping operation in Liberia was retrospectively endorsed by the UN Security Council in 1992.

Subcontracting with regional organizations is a new phenomenon to meet with the operational needs to back up, or replace, traditional peacekeeping. On the other hand, variations exist in the cooperative

arrangements between regional organizations and the UN, given that different types of forces are available under regional and UN commands. In the earlier Bosnian operation, NATO provided air support for the UN ground troops and later replaced the UN forces with stronger contingents following the peace agreement, while the UN's contribution remains with the provision of civilian police forces.

In Liberia and Georgia, regional forces conducted military operations although the civilian aspects of the missions belonged to the responsibility of UN observers. The Contonou Peace Agreement of July 1993 for Liberia contained provisions for the involvement of UN observers in the disarmament and elections process. Because the presence of the United Nations Observer Mission (UNOMIL) in Liberia did not help bring about a peaceful solution, the UN Security Council requested in September 1994 that ECOMOG protect UNOMIL personnel.

Challenges and Future Directions

Although peacekeeping is considered a tool for active conflict containment and management in an era of growing communal violence, it has limitations without full international support. Because the UN capacity has been outstripped by the demand for peacekeeping, a lack of a sound financial basis poses a particularly serious challenge for large operations that involve more than ten thousand troops. The rising costs of several big operations are well illustrated by the following examples: peacekeeping operations in Cambodia cost US$1.65 billion; Mozambique required US$541.7 million; and the annual cost of UNPROFOR in the former Yugoslavia was US$1.1 billion.

UN resources were exhausted with the two largest missions (overseeing the rebuilding of war-torn Cambodia and monitoring the cease-fire in former Yugoslavia) simultaneously organized in early 1990s. While the successful mission for Mozambique is attributed to the devotion of Western donors, the failure of a peace process and a renewed war in Angola, to a great extent, are explained by a lack of enough commitment from the international community. Sometimes the interest in avoiding instability motivates regional or neighboring countries to get involved in peace operations to control chaos, which can generate refugees. While Australia led the operations in East Timor, Japan played a major role in Cambodia.

With respect to internal operations of peacekeeping, as some national contingents were criticized for being corrupt and abusive, concerns have been raised about a lack of ethics. The Economic Community of West African States' intervention in Liberia (with 66% of the force being made up of Nigerian soldiers) served as the Nigerian military regime's foreign policy tool to assert its regional influence and promote commercial interests. Some Nigerian commanders even took part in clandestine economic activities, such as trade of goods obtained by looters and exploitation of rubber resources. Military operations, in particular, by regional alliances need more international scrutiny and supervision so that peacekeeping will not serve to legitimize the political interests of the intervening states.

Success or failure of peacekeeping should be judged within a given mandate, such as halting a recurrence of hostilities. Coordination often proves vital to success of multilateral military operations. The UN Department of Peacekeeping Operations developed Civilian Unit and Deming Unit in a response to emerging needs. In addition, task forces were created to respond to field operations. Further reform may need to be made to include more improved coordination between regional and UN-sponsored operations.

HO-WON JEONG

See also Balkan Wars of the 1990s; Central America: International Relations; Central and Eastern Europe: International Relations; Congo, Democratic Republic of the; Congo, Republic of the; East Africa: International Relations; Kashmir Dispute; Middle East: International Relations; West Africa: International Relations

References and Further Reading

Boulden, Jane. *Peace Enforcement: The United Nations Experience in Congo, Somalia, and Bosnia.* Westport, CT: Praeger, 2001.
Connaughton, Richard M. *Military Intervention and Peacekeeping: The Reality.* Aldershot, UK: Ashgate, 2001.
Docking, Tim. *Peacekeeping in Africa.* Washington, DC: US. Institute of Peace, 2001.
Gordon, D. Stuart, and F. H. Toase, eds. *Aspects of Peacekeeping.* London: Frank Cass, 2001.
Holm, Tor Tanke, and Espen Barth Eide, eds. *Peacebuilding and Police Reform.* London: Frank Cass, 2000.
Jett, Dennis C. *Why Peacekeeping Fails.* New York: St. Martin's Press, 2000.
Manwaring, Max G., and Anthony James Joes, eds. *Beyond Declaring Victory and Coming Home: The Challenges of Peace and Stability Operations.* Westport, CT: Praeger, 2000.
McRae, Robert Grant, and Don Hubert, eds. *Human Security and the New Diplomacy: Protecting People, Promoting Peace.* Montreal: McGill-Queen's University Press, 2001.
Rotberg, Robert I., et al. *Peacekeeping and Peace Enforcement in Africa: Methods of Conflict Prevention.* Washington, DC: Brookings Institution Press, 2000.

Schmidl, Erwin A., ed. *Peace Operations between War and Peace.* London: Frank Cass, 2000.

Stockholm International Peace Research Institute. *Armaments, Disarmament and International Security.* New York: Oxford University Press, 2003.

Woodhouse, Tom, and Oliver Ramsbotham, eds. *Peacekeeping and Conflict Resolution.* London: Frank Cass, 2000.

PEASANTS, IMPACT OF DEVELOPMENT ON

Peasants are smallholder farmers who have been incorporated into the polities and economies of large-scale societies. Found throughout Latin America, Asia, Africa, and in parts of Europe, peasants are oriented toward villages rather than cities and towns. Though most commonly associated with Europe of the Middle Ages, peasants have been around for thousands of years, since the origins of the state. It may be safe to assert that a majority of the world's peoples could still, in some way, be considered peasants.

Compared to the capital-intensive, highly mechanized operations of large-scale farming in industrial societies, peasants utilize relatively simple technology and labor-intensive production methods. The family is the basic unit of production and consumption. Saul and Woods (1987) state that peasants are "those whose ultimate security and subsistence lies in their having certain rights in land and in the labour of family members on the land, but who are involved, through rights and obligations, in a wider system which includes the participation of non-peasants."

The terms of their incorporation into this wider system are mostly disadvantageous. Peasants grow food that supports urban dwellers, and their taxes sustain the government; however, they usually do not receive commensurate rewards in return. Generally, peasants have not benefited from development efforts thrust upon them by governments, multinational corporations, and international agencies (Barker 1989; Richards 1985). In the 1960s, the Green Revolution, which began decades earlier with the discovery of new, higher yielding varieties of grains (wheat, rice, and maize), was heralded as the chance to solve the developing world's food-related problems. Tremendous success occurred initially on experimental agricultural stations in Mexico and the Philippines, followed by their dissemination to parts of India, Pakistan, and Indonesia. Although overall yields doubled and in some cases tripled, it was not long before skeptics began questioning the value of the Green Revolution for peasants. Major criticisms of the Green Revolution included that (i) it is

dependent on the use of chemical fertilizers and pesticides, irrigation, and other inputs that poor peasant farmers cannot afford, thereby exacerbating inequality; (ii) it may be ecologically harmful (e.g., chemical contamination of groundwater); and it promotes monocultures and hence contributes to a loss of genetic diversity. Franke (1974) examined the Green Revolution's effects in central Java and found that, despite potential yield increases of up to 70%, only 20% of farming households in the village joined the program. The chief beneficiaries tended to be farmers who were already better off, who owned most of the land, and who had adequate water supplies. The poorest families did not adopt the new miracle seeds. Instead, they made do by working part-time for the well-off farmers who lent them money to buy food. Furthermore, because they were afraid of losing their supply of cheap labor, richer farmers prevented their part-time workers from adopting the new seeds. For their part, poor farmers feared that if they cut themselves off from their patrons, they would have no one to turn to in cases of sickness or drought. Franke concluded that the theories behind the Green Revolution were really rationalizations for elites who were to achieve economic development without engaging in the social and political transformation their societies needed.

Structural adjustment policies, multifaceted programs designed to correct decades of mismanaged centralized economies and mandated by the International Monetary Fund and World Bank as conditions for continued loans, have taken a high toll on peasants. Their effects have been especially devastating on women (Gladwin 1991). As both producers and consumers, peasants suffer doubly—the minimal producer prices once assured by grain/cereal boards have disappeared, as have price caps on purchased staple consumer goods such as flour and cooking oil.

Among urban elites, even in the developing nations in which they are encapsulated, derogatory stereotypes about peasants abound (peasants are inordinately conservative, are bound by tradition and superstition, and are lazy and stupid). An alternative view is that peasants, by virtue of their relative lack of power, are forced to adapt to risky circumstances, most of which are out of their control. As such, they behave in ways that are very different from people who hold greater degrees of political and economic power.

As a result of the unfavorable terms through which they have been incorporated into state systems, peasant communities often chose to bind together, in what Eric Wolf (1966) has termed *closed corporate communities.* These groups emphasize community identity and discourage outsiders from settling within by

restricting land–use to village members and prohibiting the sale or lease of property to outsiders. Often the community, not the individual, has ultimate control of land. Parts of the Valley of Oaxaca in southern Mexico exemplify closed, corporate peasant communities. Peasants there are often seen as economically conservative, suspicious of change, and pessimistic about the future. George Foster (1967), who studied the village of Tzintzuntzan, called this view the *image of the limited good*. This position sees all good things in the world as existing in limited supply, and an individual's success occurs only at the expense of others who soon become envious. Even those who are moderately successful experience social pressures to share the wealth. This comes in the form of sponsoring lavish *fiestas* to honor the patron saint of each village. Fiesta sponsorship rotates among the people of the village, and individuals take great pride in doing a good job of sponsorship. These fiestas, sometimes referred to as the *cargo system*, along with exchanges of labor and goods across households, act as *levelling mechanisms* and function to lessen wealth differentials. Rather than see these kinds of practices as inhibiting progress, anthropologists like Foster and Wolf have generally concluded that, given their lack of capital and lack of political power, these types of customs are adaptive practices that help to enhance group solidarity and ensure cooperation in the face of uncertainty.

In certain historical contexts, most conspicuously twentieth century examples such as Mexico, Russia, China, Vietnam, Algeria, and Cuba, peasants have openly rebelled (Hobsbawm 1963; Wolf 1969), leading to massive social upheaval, if not genuine social change. However, perhaps more commonly exhibited are what James Scott (1985) called *weapons of the weak*, everyday forms of resistance that are manifested by individual social actors in both symbolic and material ways, such as feigning confusion, slowing down work, pilfering, performing shabby work, tampering, lampooning, performing sarcastic mimicry, or evading work.

Peasants produce primarily for subsistence and household maintenance rather than for profit. This *subsistence first economic orientation* is not necessarily the product of an inherent antimarket bias; rather, it derives from the reality that in most cases, peasants are fortunate simply to break even. Peasants must use part of what they produce to feed themselves, but there are other uses to which any surplus must be put. Eric Wolf (1966) identified these as: (i) *the ceremonial fund*—that portion of the budget that is allocated to social and religious activities; (ii) *the replacement fund*—that portion of the household budget that is allocated for repair or replacement of

materials depleted by wear and tear; and (iii) *the rent fund*—that portion of the budget that must be allocated for payment of rent for the use of land and/or equipment. Hence, in general by the time all of these expenses are met, the peasant household has little left over to invest in profit-making enterprises.

Johnson (1971) found that Brazilian sharecropper peasants face *multiple sources of risk* emanating from both the physical environment (for example, rainfall variation, pests, illness) and economic environments (such as uncertain land tenure, or externally controlled market prices). In response, they engage in a number of practices that may help reduce this uncertainty, such as accumulation of subsistence needs first; tilling of multiple small, scattered plots rather than one larger consolidated field; careful experimentation with new crops and methods; creation and maintenance of interhousehold dyadic relations between equals and with patrons; and further diversification through off-farm sources of employment (Johnson 1971; Ortiz 1973; Barlett 1980). Entrepreneurs, business people who are able and willing to take risks in new economic ventures, do not fare well among the sharecroppers Johnson studied. In Zinacantan, Mexico, Frank Cancian (1972) found a curvilinear relation between rank and risk taking, with the middle class being especially conservative during the early stages of change, when uncertainty is greatest. On the other hand, those at the top and at the bottom were more willing to endure the risk associated with adopting changes. In Nigeria, Sara Berry (1985) found that, among Yoruba farmers, the tendency to diversify was very strong and that people engage in a number of activities besides farming to generate income. Trained as an economist, Berry goes on to claim that there is no inherent conflict between safety-first orientation and profit maximization. It seems imperative, therefore, to try and understand peasant economic systems on their own terms first before implementing changes.

After decades of studying peasants firsthand in Europe (Switzerland) and West Africa (Nigeria), Netting suggested that there are clear reasons why the smallholder peasant farming mode of production, and the various social formations that accompany it, persist across space and time.

Smallholders are not as rich as landed aristocrats, the higher officialdom of government, the commercial elite, or urban professionals. What they do have is their experience, their fertile land, their livestock, and their diversified production strategies as a set of defenses against the uncontrollable vagaries of weather, prices, and war. Smallholders may not always live well, but they are seasoned survivors. They may moonlight as craftsmen, petty traders, field hands,

or factory workers, but they do not keep one foot on the farm out of sentiment or stupidity. And the society that dispossesses smallholders in favor of factory farms, plantations, or socialistic communes simultaneously risks a decline in agricultural production, increase in rural unemployment, and an ecological deterioration (Netting 1993).

The course of the twentieth century saw the deleterious consequences resulting from the dispossession of smallholders by large-scale plantation agriculture in Latin America and the Caribbean and socialist/communal farms in Europe and Asia. In the twenty-first century, the dispossession of smallholders by factory farms proceeds around the world, even in North American with agribusiness. What long-term repercussions will ensue from these processes, and how will governments deal with them?

BRUCE D. ROBERTS

See also Green Revolution; Structural Adjustment Programs (SAPs); Subsistence Living; Sustainable Development

References and Further Reading

Barker, Jonathan. *Rural Communities Under Stress: Peasant Farmers and the State in Africa.* New York: Cambridge University Press, 1989.

Berry, Sara. *Fathers Work for Their Sons: Accumulation, Mobility, and Class Formation in an Extended Yoruba Community.* Berkeley, CA: University of California Press, 1985.

Cancian, Frank. *Change and Uncertainty in a Peasant Economy: The Maya Corn Farmers of Zinacantan.* Stanford, CA: Stanford University Press, 1972.

Gladwin, Chistina H. *Structural Adjustment and African Women Farmers.* Gainesville, FL: University of Florida Press, 1991.

Hobsbawm, Eric J. *Primitive Rebels: Studies in Archaic Forms of Social Movement in the 19th and 20th Centuries.* New York: Norton, 1963.

Johnson, Allen. "Security and Risk Taking Among Poor Peasants." *Studies in Economic Anthropology*, George Dalton, ed. Washington, DC: American Anthropological Association, 1971.

Netting, Robert. *Smallholders, Householders: Farm Families and the Ecology of Intensive, Sustainable Agriculture.* Stanford, CA: Stanford University Press, 1993.

Ortiz, Sutti. *Uncertainties in Peasant Farming.* London: Athlone Press, 1973.

Richards, Paul. *Indigenous Agricultural Revolution: Ecology and Food Production in West Africa.* London: Hutchinson, 1985.

Saul, J. S., and R. Woods. "African Peasantries." *Peasants and African Societies*, Teodor Shanin, ed. Oxford: Basil Blackwell, 1987.

Scott, James C. *Weapons of The Weak: Everyday Forms of Peasant Resistance.* New Haven, CT: Yale University Press, 1985.

Wolf, Eric R. *Peasant Wars of the Twentieth Century.* New York: Harper & Row, 1969.

PEOPLE'S LIBERATION ARMED FORCES (PLAF)

The People's Liberation Armed Forces (PLAF) was the military arm of the National Front for the Liberation of South Vietnam (NFLSV), better known to US citizens as the National Liberation Front (NLF). Most of the world knew the PLAF as the "Viet Cong" (VC), a contraction of the Vietnamese term *Viet Nam Cong San*, or Vietnamese Communist. It was slang term of derision conjured by Ngo Dinh Diem, who used the term to describe his political opponents, many of whom were not Communists, starting after the 1954 partition of Vietnam between the Republic of Vietnam (RVN) in the south and the Democratic Republic of Vietnam (DRV) in the north. The NLF and the PLAF never referred to themselves as VC and always asserted that they were a national front of all anti-RVN forces, Communist or not. US and allied soldiers in Vietnam used the term and even added to the jargon the term "Charlie."

The leaders of the NFLSV formally established the PLAF at a meeting of insurgent leaders in early 1961, based on a decision by North Vietnamese communists to escalate the level of armed struggle in South Vietnam. Like its predecessor, the Vietminh, which had fought successfully against the Japanese in 1941–1946 and French in 1946–1954, organized the PLAF on three levels: fully trained and equipped regular forces ("main force") ostensibly operating under the command of the southern leadership, primarily the Central Office for South Vietnam (COSVN); full-time guerrillas organized in companies and serving under provincial or district leaders; and part-time self-defense militia, composed of units organized in squads and platoons and used mostly for village defense. In truth, at times, they resorted to intimidation to gain their ends.

Throughout the early 1960s, the PLAF grew rapidly in strength and numbers, reaching an estimated thirty thousand by August 1964, around the time the North began the full-scale infiltration of regular People's Army of Vietnam (PAVN) troops into the South; only a few months before, the United States, based on the Gulf of Tokin Resolution, began to build up its forces in earnest. While a few leading PLAF cadres and officers infiltrated from the North to the South along the Ho Chi Minh Trail, the vast majority came from villages, towns, or cities in South Vietnam.

Especially in the beginning, the PLAF used classic guerilla tactics and initiated a series of hit-and-run attacks on government installations, military outposts, convoys, strategic hamlets, and even district towns throughout the RVN. Its most noteworthy victory occurred in the village of Ap Bac in early

January 1963, when Viet Cong guerrillas engaged the Army of the Republic of Vietnam (ARVN) regular forces flown in by US helicopters. The day-long battle resulted in heavy casualties for ARVN units. Most experts reported it as a PLAF victory.

Between March 1965 and January 1968, as the role of US combat troops increased, the role of PLAF units was gradually superseded by regular PAVN forces. Whereas the PAVN bore the brunt of the fighting with US troops, in such major battles as the Ia Drang Valley in November 1965, Communist leaders most often assigned PLAF units to combat against less well-armed ARVN units.

The PLAF, however, assumed the primary role in the Tet Offensive, launched in January through February 1968. PLAF troops attacked villages, towns, and cities throughout the RVN. The offensive began at 3:00 AM on January 31, 1968, when VC sappers entered the US Embassy compound in Saigon, which had seemed to be a safe haven. US television accounts of the devastation and carnage throughout the RVN, especially in places like the old imperial capital of Hue, shocked and disheartened most US citizens. While the attackers suffered heavy casualties— between twenty-five thousand and forty thousand depending on your source—and it was a tactical Allied victory, Tet eventually had the strategic impact of leading to the end of direct US involvement.

Many historians have argued, and certainly the military did at the time, that as a result of Tet Offensive, the PLAF, which totaled between 150,000 and 200,000 on the eve of Tet, declined as a major battlefield factor after Tet. Some have speculated that the communist leadership in the North deliberately ordered PLAF units into the fighting to reduce southern influence within the movement, but there is no absolute evidence to support this assertion.

Others, especially ethnic Vietnamese scholars, have argued that the PLAF was not as damaged as first believed and that they suffered more casualties in the follow-up campaigns of late 1968 and in the Allied Pacification Programs of 1969–1970 and eventually recovered to pre-Tet strength by the Spring Offensive of 1972. In 1969, the NFLSV formed the Provisional Revolutionary Government (PRG) of South Vietnam that technically assumed power briefly after the fall of Saigon in 1975.

However, the viewpoint expressed in the latter paragraph is not held by the majority of scholars who believe PLAF was badly hurt by the Tet defeats and subsequent set-backs. In any case, the final reunification struggles were led by Northern Communists, and PLAF played a lesser role in the 1975 offensive that led to the fall of South Vietnam. After the war, PLAF units were disbanded or integrated with the PAVN in a nation dominated by Northern Communists.

Cecil B. Currey and William P. Head

References and Further Reading

Currey, Cecil B. *Victory at Any Cost: The Genius of Viet Nam's Gen. Vo Nguyen Giap.* Washington, DC: Brassey's, 1997.

Duiker, William J. *Historical Dictionary of Vietnam.* Lanham, MD: Scarecrow Press, 1995.

Gilbert, Marc Jason, and William Head, eds. *The Tet Offensive.* Westport, CT: Praeger Press, 1996.

Pike, Douglas. *Viet Cong: The Organization and Techniques of the National Liberation Front of South Vietnam.* Cambridge, MA: MIT University Press, 1966.

Truong Nhu Tang. *A Viet Cong Memoir: An Inside Account of the Vietnam War and Its Aftermath.* New York: Vintage Books, 1985.

PÉREZ JIMÉNEZ, MARCOS

Marcos Pérez Jiménez (1914–2001), a career soldier who joined the army at age seventeen, was the military dictator of Venezuela from 1952 to 1958. The death of military dictator Juan Vicente Gómez in 1935 unleashed a wave of democratic outpouring in Venezuela. *Acción Democrática* (AD), a middle-class reformist party formed in 1941, repeatedly called for a transition to electoral democracy. On October 19, 1945, a coalition of AD political supporters and young military officers that included Pérez Jiménez overthrew the military dictatorship of Isaías Medina Angarita. Although initially supportive of AD's political agenda, the young military officers began to criticize the increasingly leftist rhetoric of AD politicians Rómulo Gallegos and Rómulo Betancourt. In 1948, the military overthrew Gallegos's AD government and implemented a three-man military junta. Although the United States had initially supported the transition to civilian democracy in Venezuela, the advent of the Cold War convinced the US government that the reckless statements issued by Venezuelan politicians could provide an opening for communism in Venezuela. By 1952, Pérez Jiménez, who had been part of the military *junta*, had eliminated the other members of the *junta* and proclaimed himself the military dictator of Venezuela. The Eisenhower administration, which actively supported the Pérez Jiménez dictatorship, awarded the dictator the Legion of Merit medal.

Pérez Jiménez implemented a brutal, corrupt authoritarian regime. He maintained power by suppressing internal dissent by unleashing his security forces on Venezuelan dissidents. Once in power, he rapidly increased Venezuela's infrastructure. Pérez Jiménez's

massive construction projects, funded by a greatly expanded petroleum industry controlled by foreign capital, were responsible for building roads, expanding tourism, and appeasing the military. The construction of an extravagant Military's Officers Club was designed to appease the Venezuelan Armed Forces. These extravagant construction projects, plus rampant corruption, fostered rapid inflation that facilitated his overthrow in 1958. Pérez Jiménez fled to the United States.

Pérez Jiménez, however, had left behind a briefcase full of documents that detailed his illegal activities. In 1963, he was extradited to Venezuela and sentenced to four years in prison. After his release in 1968, he moved to Generalissimo Francisco Franco's Spain. Pérez Jiménez, however, still maintained a base of support in Venezuela. Although elected to the Venezuelan Congress, the AD government never allowed him to take his seat. His attempt to run for the Venezuelan presidency in absentia was also foiled by the AD government. Although invited to attend the inauguration of Hugo Chavez in 1999, Pérez Jiménez declined. He died of a heart attack on September 20, 2001, in Madrid, Spain.

LAZARUS F. O'SAKO

See also Betancourt, Rómulo; Northern South America: History and Economic Development; Venezuela

References and Further Reading

Ewell, Judith. *Indictment of a Dictator: The Extradition of Marcos Pérez Jiménez*. College Station, TX: Texas A & M University Press, 1981.

Kelly, Janet, and Carlos A. Romero. *The United States and Venezuela: Rethinking a Relationship*. New York: Routledge, 2002.

Rivas, Darlene. *Missionary Capitalist: Nelson Rockefeller in Venezuela*. Chapel Hill, NC: University of North Carolina Press, 2002.

PERÓN, JUAN DOMINGO

From the fertile pampas to the rugged Andes Mountains, no figure dominated twentieth century Argentine political life as that of Juan Domingo Perón (1943–1974). On June 4, 1943, a cadre of nationalist armed forces officers known as the United Officers' Group overthrew the corrupt government of President Ramón Castillo. Among these officers was the former military attaché to Italy and Mussolini admirer, Colonel Juan Domingo Perón. As a clever manipulator, Perón, who was appointed as head of Secretariat of Labor, would use his post to launch his political career by granting workers innumerable rights and siding with them in labor disputes.

Concern over his political ambitions as well as with the rising popularity of his companion, Eva Duarte, prompted his fellow officers to remove him from his post on October 9, 1945, and confine him to the island of Martín García. Eight days later, massive workers' demonstrations on his behalf resulted in his release.

After his return, Perón was unstoppable. In the presidential election of 1946, Perón, aided by the vote of the *descamisados* (working-class supporters) scored a decisive victory over a coalition of different political groups. Immediately, he set out to fulfill his promise of social justice, economic independence, and national sovereignty.

A believer in the corporate state, Perón used this philosophy to transform Argentina's politics, economics, and society. Through the government-controlled Argentine Institute for the Promotion of Trade, Perón used revenues from Argentine agricultural exports to materially benefit the workers. Laws expanding minimum wages, workmen's compensation, health insurance, paid vacations, and social security were promulgated. Peronist-controlled labor unions gained unprecedented power as Perón expanded the national civil service.

In 1946, Perón's five-year plan for development, based on the creation of state-owned enterprises, was initiated. Perón addressed his promise of economic independence by nationalizing the public utilities in 1946 and the British-owned railways a year later. Since Perón viewed industrialization as an important ingredient of economic independence, projects ranging from power plants to steel mills were given top priority in the plan. Ironically, Perón would finance his grandiose industrialization scheme through Argentine grain and beef sales.

The *descamisados* were not the only ones who benefited from Perón's policies. Women were given the right to vote in 1947 and the right to hold public office in 1949. The military also saw its budget increased, while the Catholic Church exerted its influence in public education.

In terms of foreign relations, Perón's "Third Position," a policy of nonalignment between the Cold War superpowers, brought Argentina prestige throughout the Third World. His economic and diplomatic support for Generalissimo Francisco Franco's Spanish regime was proof of Argentine defiance of both the Soviet Union and the Western powers.

Under the emblem of *justicialismo,* Perón won another presidential term in 1951. His second term, however, proved to be a stormy one. Although he enjoyed unlimited popularity among the *descamisados,* Perón's second five-year plan would collapse amid a devastating drought, exorbitant inflation, dismal industrial productivity, and bureaucratic inefficiency.

Moreover, he never recovered from the devastating impact of losing the charismatic Evita to cancer on July 26, 1952.

Dissatisfaction with Peronist policies among landowners, business leaders, intellectuals, and a portion of armed forces officers galvanized in 1955 when Perón struck at the Catholic Church. Angered at Perón's legalization of divorce and proposed legislation to end the Church's involvement in public education, the hierarchy began to criticize the regime through pastoral letters. Overzealous Peronists responded by burning churches. On September 16, 1955, armed forces officers staged a revolt that culminated in Perón's departure three days later.

In spite of "de-Peronization" campaigns on the part of subsequent military and civilian governments, Peronism remained a major factor in Argentine politics. Unable to stop the rising tide of discontent, the military government of General Alejandro Lanuse allowed free elections in 1973, which were won by Héctor Cámpora, an avowed Peronist. Cámpora, however, resigned; on September 23, 1973, the aging Juan Perón, who had returned from his exile in Madrid in 1973, won another presidential election with his third wife Maria Estela "Isabelita" as his running mate.

For this occasion, Perón had no time to implement another five-year plan. His heart condition worsened throughout his brief presidential term and on July 1, 1974, he died at seventy-eight. Perón has been dead for years, but Peronism is still alive in Argentina.

JOSÉ B. FERNÁNDEZ

See also Argentina

References and Further Reading

Crassweller, Robert D. *Perón and the Enigmas of Argentina*. New York: Norton, 1987.
Fraser, Nicolás, and Marysa Navarro. *Eva Perón*. New York: Norton, 1985.
Hodges, Donald C., *Argentina, 1943–1987*. Albuquerque: University of New Mexico Press, 1988.
James, Daniel. "October 17th and 18th, 1945: Mass Protest, Peronism and the Argentine Working Class." *Journal of Social History* 22, no.2 (Spring 1988): 441–61.
McGuire, James W. *Peronism Without Perón: Union, Parties and Democracy in Argentina*. Stanford, CA: Stanford University Press, 1997.
Page, Joseph A. *Perón: A Biography*. New York: Random House, 1983.

PERSIAN GULF WAR, 1991

The Persian Gulf conflict of 1991 began at 1:00 AM on August 2, 1990, with the movement of 120,000 Iraqi troops and 1,800 tanks over the Kuwaiti border. Within thirty-six hours, Iraqi forces had succeeded in overcoming Kuwait's military defences and driving its leadership into exile. The occupation of Kuwait was to last 210 days and ended with the overwhelming defeat of Iraq by a US-led United Nations (UN) coalition force on February 27, 1991.

The Causes of War

The invasion and annexation of Kuwait took many states by surprise, including Kuwait and those in the United States. However, with hindsight, there were a number of factors that in combination provided motives for the invasion. First, there is evidence to suggest that the invasion was partly motivated by the desire to improve Iraq's economic position through the appropriation of Kuwait's vast financial resources and its oil wealth. The Iran-Iraq war of the 1980s had left the Iraqi economy close to collapse. At the end of the war, Iraq faced reconstruction costs estimated at around $60 billion and a foreign debt of $70 billion, the latter being owed mostly to the Gulf States, including Kuwait, which had been eager to counter the revolutionary threat posed by Iran. The war had also resulted in high inflation and a substantial drop in living standards, which reversed a twelve-year positive trend. As 50% of the population was in some way employed by the state, the inability of the Ba'ath regime to raise or at least maintain living standards for the general population and to provide economic benefits to the party elite threatened its very survival. With four military *coup* attempts against the regime between 1988 and 1990, finding a solution to this problem became essential for the Hussein regime.

Second, at such a time of economic crisis, the Iraqi government was particularly dependent on generating as much income as possible from its oil revenues. In 1990, oil prices fell from $22 per barrel in January to $16 per barrel in June, with every $1 drop in the price of oil costing Iraq $1 billion in revenue. This was due in part to the general trend toward using alternative fuels in demand countries; the discovery of new sources of oil in Alaska, the North Sea, and the former Soviet Union; and to overproduction by Organization of Petroleum Exporting Countries (OPEC) countries such as Kuwait and the United Arab Emirates. The actions of Kuwait in disregarding oil production quotas set by OPEC and refusing demands by Iraq to forgive Iraq's war debts provided the proximate causes of the war. From February to July 1990, Iraq declared that Kuwait was waging economic warfare against it, issued a series of verbal threats, and began to move troops toward the Kuwaiti border in mid-July 1990.

Third, the invasion of Kuwait can be seen as part of a long-standing territorial dispute in which Iraq has claimed that Kuwait's territory should have formed part of Iraq. Its claim reached back to the days of the Ottoman Empire, when Kuwait had formed part of the province of Basra in 1971. Whilst Iraq's 1963 regime formally recognised Kuwait as an independent sovereign nation, its government and its people have continued to hold a historical grievance.

Fourth, on a personal level, President Hussein had for many years expressed an ambition to lead the Arab world. His pursuit of a nuclear weapons capability formed part of the broader goal to challenge Israeli power in the region. The invasion of Kuwait would allow Iraq to dominate the oil wealth of the Persian Gulf and possibly the Arab world by giving it control of more than 22% of the world's known oil reserves, second only to Saudi Arabia's with 28%. With a large military capability and significant oil resources, Iraq would have been able to exert significant influence within OPEC and therefore on global oil prices. With the dependence of industrialised countries on OPEC oil, and the experience of the oil-price shocks of the 1970s still in memory, this situation was unlikely to be allowed to continue.

The International Response

The invasion of Kuwait by Iraqi forces was immediately condemned internationally. On August 2, 1990, the UN Security Council unanimously passed Resolution 660 (UN Security Council Resolution or UNSCR) that declared the invasion and occupation of Kuwait a threat to international peace and security and demanded an immediate Iraqi withdrawal. With no withdrawal being forthcoming, on August 6, economic sanctions were imposed under UNSCR 661 encompassing a ban on the import and export of goods, financial resources, and arms to Iraq or Kuwait. The United States and United Kingdom set up a naval blockade of the Persian Gulf to enforce the sanctions, as a form of collective-self defence under article 51 of the UN Charter and later authorised under Chapter VII by the UN Security Council on August 25.

The international military response initially took a defensive form known as Operation Desert Shield. In response to the fear that an invasion of Saudi Arabia could be next, the Saudis were easily persuaded to allow US forces to be deployed onto Saudi territory from August 8. Operation Desert Shield was to become one of the largest military deployments ever made. It included an alliance of twenty-eight member nations, which grew to thirty-seven by the end of the war and included more than half a million soldiers, with a ten thousand-soldier brigade from the Arab Gulf states, seven thousand Kuwaiti soldiers, fifteen thousand Syrian troops, forty-three thousand British, and sixteen thousand French.

Despite the international response, President Hussein made his intent to hold onto Kuwait clear, announcing the annexation of Kuwait as part of Iraq's nineteenth province on August 8. On August 18, Iraq added to its outlaw status by taking sixty American, British, German, and French citizens from Kuwait as hostages to be used as human shields who would be released on the withdrawal of US forces from Saudi Arabia and the lifting of sanctions. Hussein threatened to deliver the "mother of all battles" to any attacking coalition force, to destroy Kuwait's and Saudi Arabia's oil infrastructure, and to draw Israel into the conflict.

Preparations for military action intensified in November, with US Secretary of State James Baker traveling to Bahrain, Saudi Arabia, Egypt, Turkey, the Soviet Union, Japan, Germany, and France to maintain the resolve of the coalition states to pursue the matter until Kuwait was liberated. On November 29, UNSCR 678 was passed by unanimous vote, authorising the use of "all necessary means" to force Iraq to withdraw from Kuwait if it did not withdraw by January 15, an ultimatum that was not met.

Operation Desert Storm

On the night of January 16, 1991, the US-led coalition began Operation Desert Storm with an intense air bombardment targeting Iraq's known weapons of mass destruction (WMD) and arms production facilities, troop formations, defensive fortifications, supply lines, air defences, command and control network, bridges, railroads, major roads, and much of Iraq's electricity, water, and oil production facilities. This attack was to last for thirty-nine days. The hitherto unseen technological superiority of the US air force, with its stealth fighter jets, Tomahawk cruise missiles, and advanced "surgical strike" capabilities ensured that the coalition air forces achieved air supremacy with relative ease. Iraq responded on January 18 by firing al-Hussein Scud missiles at Israel and Saudi Arabia to test the resolve of Arab nations within the coalition and to sabotage world oil supplies. Israel, however, was persuaded not to respond by the United States.

With Iraq's air force effectively suppressed within one week, Iraq was given a further chance to withdraw unconditionally from Kuwait. On February 22, Iraqi

forces set more than six hundred Kuwaiti oil wells alight. With the passing of the deadline for acceptance of the cease-fire conditions on February 23, the US-led ground war commenced on February 24, 1990. In the first stage of the attack, Iraqi troops were targeted with by bombs and artillery to create confusion and undermine morale. The second stage of the attack consisted of a diversionary amphibious assault off the coast of Kuwait by eighteen thousand US marines who succeeded in drawing Iraqi divisions away from a surprise attack to the west. Under the cover of the allied air attack, 240,000 coalition troops engaged in a major flanking maneuver three hundred miles west of the Iraq-Kuwait border, which was undetected. On February 24, the third stage of the attack began with US marines and Saudi troops attacking across the Kuwaiti-Saudi border toward Kuwait City. Both the attack from the West and that from Saudi Arabia proved to be highly successful. Thousands of Iraqi troops chose to surrender rather than be killed by the clearly better trained, equipped, and rested coalition forces. Within two days, the Iraqi defensive position had been broken, and on February 25, Baghdad announced the withdrawal of Iraqi troops from Kuwait. On the evening of the same day, large numbers of Iraqi troops attempted to escape from Kuwait with their equipment and stolen goods, coming under attack from the air. Whilst it was possible to continue the attack against Iraqi forces, particularly against its elite Republican Guard divisions, President Bush chose to call a cease-fire. The following day, Iraqi Foreign Minister Azziz announced his country's willingness to rescind its official annexation of Kuwait, release all prisoners of war, and pay war reparations in exchange. Finally, on February 27, Iraq announced that it would comply with all 12 UN Security Council resolutions that had been passed.

The decision not to march on Baghdad to depose President Hussein was one that was regretted by future US administrations in the 1990s. However, the mandate given to the coalition forces was limited to the goal of liberating Kuwait, rather than that of regime change, a policy that was unlikely to have mustered support within the Arab world. The decision was based also on the assumption that Iraq's WMD capabilities and conventional armed forces had been significantly degraded and that it was highly unlikely that Saddam Hussein could remain in power after suffering such a comprehensive and humiliating defeat. Lastly, the United States was unprepared for the difficulty and expense of undertaking a nation-building exercise in Iraq, a country already split among three disparate ethnic and religious groups that had not experienced democracy in recent times.

The terms of the cease-fire set out in UNSCR 687 sought to ensure Iraq was unable to threaten its neighbours again. Under these terms, Iraq agreed not to acquire or develop a nuclear weapons capability; to declare and destroy its nuclear, chemical, and biological weapons arsenal and any ballistic missiles with a range greater than 150 kilometers; and to compensate Kuwait for any loss or damage suffered at a set percentage of its petroleum exports. A comprehensive weapons inspection regime was set up to verify Iraq's disarmament with economic sanctions to be lifted on compliance with all terms of the cease-fire. The disarmament of Iraq was expected to take less than a year. However, in the period between 1991 and 1998, the Hussein regime proved to be resilient and defiant amidst the breaking down of consensus in the UN Security Council concerning the threat the regime posed to the international world community.

The Significance of the War

The Gulf War of 1991 is primarily remembered as the first real demonstration of the proper working of the UN collective security mechanism. With the end of the Cold War, the UN Security Council was able to function as intended with nations from all around the world joining together to defend a weak state against an aggressor. The broad-based support for military action as well as military, financial, and political terms demonstrated the resounding legitimacy with which the core principles of nonintervention, sovereignty, and the peaceful resolution of disputes were viewed by a majority of states. Here, the world saw a brief glimpse of a possible "new world order" in which states would demonstrate their shared commitment to these principles and their intolerance for blatant aggression. The level of cooperation reached within the UN Security Council was to set a high benchmark for future collective action to restore international peace and security that unfortunately has not been replicated. The action is also remembered as the benchmark for US leadership internationally, creating the expectation that US leadership in security matters would be exercised multilaterally through the UN Security Council. These expectations continued during the 1990s, whilst US foreign policy increasingly began to display unilateralist tendencies.

LAVINA LEE

See also Arab Nationalism; Hussein, Saddam; Iran-Iraq War 1980–1988; Iraq; Kuwait; Middle East: International Relations; Organization of Petroleum Exporting Countries (OPEC); Persian Gulf War, 2003

References and Further Reading

Bin, Alberto, Richard Hill, and Archer Jones. *Desert Storm: A Forgotten War*. Westport, CT: London: Praeger Publishers, 1998.

Cronin, Bruce. "The Paradox of Hegemon: America's Ambiguous Relationship with the United Nations." *European Journal of International Relations* 7, no. 1 (2001): 103–130.

Danchev, Alex, and Keohane, Dan. *International Perspectives on the Gulf Conflict 1990–91*. London: The MacMillan Press, 1994.

Freedman, Lawrence, and Karsh, Efraim. *The Gulf Conflict 1990–1991: Diplomacy and War in the New World Order*. London: Faber and Faber, 1993.

Gow, James, ed. *Iraq, The Gulf Conflict and the World Community*. London and New York: Brasseys 1993.

Matthews, Ken. *The Gulf Conflict and International Relations*. London and New York: Routledge, 1993.

Woodward, Bob. *Plan of Attack: The Road to War*. London: Simon & Schuster, 2004.

Yetiv, Steve A. *The Persian Gulf Crisis*. Westport, CT: London: Greenwood Press, 1997.

PERSIAN GULF WAR, 2003

Background to the Conflict

The seeds of a further conflict in the Persian Gulf were sown in the years following the 1991 Persian Gulf War. Following Iraq's comprehensive defeat in this war, the United Nations (UN) Security Council imposed a range of disarmament obligations on the country as a condition of cease-fire set out in UN Security Council Resolution (UNSCR) 687. This resolution provided that Iraq agree not to acquire or develop a nuclear weapons capability, destroy its chemical and biological weapons arsenal and any ballistic missiles with a range greater than 150 kilometers, as well as compensate Kuwait for any loss or damage it had suffered. To verify Iraq's agreement to disarm a UN weapons inspection team was created, known as the UN Special Commission for the Disarmament of Iraq (UNSCOM), which together with the International Atomic Energy Agency (IAEA) were to conduct inspections on Iraqi territory. Economic sanctions and restrictions on Iraq's ability to sell oil and to use the proceeds were to be lifted should Iraq comply with these terms.

It is now believed that UNSCOM and the IAEA made good progress in uncovering and destroying a substantial portion of Iraq's WMD stockpiles and ballistic missiles, despite the efforts of the Iraqi regime to obstruct and deceive them. However, from 1993 to 1998, Iraq began a sustained and largely successful campaign to impede disarmament by the UN. During the same time period, consensus among the permanent members of the UN Security Council began to unravel in relation to whether Iraq continued to pose a grave threat to international peace and security. A split emerged, with the United Kingdom and the United States believing the threat to be real and continuing, sufficient to warrant military action in response to Iraq's determined policy to obstruct, restrict, and finally to refuse to allow weapons inspections to continue. France and Russia, on the other hand, pushed for a relaxation of the sanctions regime, which was causing great suffering among the Iraqi people and opposed the use of force to punish the Iraqi regime when a crisis was reached in 1997 and 1998. By the end of 1998, despite an unauthorised punitive bombing raid by the United Kingdom and the United States (Operation Desert Fox), Iraq succeeded in expelling UN weapons inspectors from its territory and gaining a significant relaxation of economic sanctions, a state of affairs which continued until 2002.

The US Push for Iraqi Disarmament

The Bush Administration indicated its intention to put Iraq back on the agenda internationally in January 2002 with the deployment of approximately eighty-six thousand troops, military aircraft, and warships to Kuwait and the Persian Gulf. Whilst at the start of his administration, President Bush took an anti-interventionist line, the terrorist attacks of September 11, 2001 on the Twin Towers and the Pentagon, convinced the administration that the United States could not afford to be disengaged with the world. Whilst al-Qaeda was clearly America's most immediate threat, the possibility that Saddam Hussein's Iraq could join forces with fundamentalist Islamic terrorist groups was thought to be an extremely dangerous prospect that required preventive action.

In his January 29, 2002, State of the Union Address to Congress, President Bush declared Iraq, Iran, and North Korea as members of the "axis of evil" and threatened preventive action against them. During the next few months, in a series of speeches and interviews, the president explained why Iraq was a threat like no other and how September 11 had demonstrated a more urgent need to confront it. In September 2002, President Bush made his case to the UN General Assembly that Iraq continued to pose a serious danger to international peace and security, detailing evidence of Saddam Hussein's aggression, his attempts to acquire and develop weapons of mass

destruction, his use of chemical weapons against segments of the Iraqi people, his defiance of the UN itself, and finally his support for terrorism.

On November 8, 2002, on the initiative of the United States and the United Kingdom, the UN Security Council unanimously passed Resolution 1441, which proclaimed Iraq to be in "material breach" of its cease-fire obligations under Resolution 678 of 1990; offered Iraq "a final opportunity to comply with its disarmament obligations"; demanded Iraq prove that it no longer possessed weapons of mass destruction; provided for weapons inspections to resume by the UN Monitoring and Verification Commission (UNMOVIC) and the IAEA; provided that it cooperate fully with the inspectors; required the UN Security Council to convene immediately if Iraq failed to comply fully; and warned of "serious consequences" should it not do so. All permanent members reiterated that the resolution did not automatically authorise the use of force should Iraq be found to have breached its obligations. However, in its post-vote statement, the United States made clear its intentions to act alone if necessary.

On November 25, 2002, the inspection teams began their difficult task. On December 7, Iraq delivered a large number of documents to the UN as proof that it held no weapons of mass destruction (WMD). The United States analysed the documents and announced that they contained no new information than was already known through previous inspections. On December 19, 2002, President Bush declared Iraq to be in "material breach" of Resolution 1441. Whilst the United States did not believe that a further resolution was necessary to support military action, Tony Blair's labour government was coming under direct popular pressure to return to the UN for further authorisation.

On March 7, the head of the UNMOVIC inspection team, Hans Blix, stated that the Iraqis were cooperating more fully with UNMOVIC but not to the point of full disclosure as required under Resolution 1441. Whilst the UN Security Council was in agreement that Iraq needed to be disarmed, Russia, Germany, and France argued that the inspectors should be given more time. In justifying the planned use of force against Iraq, the United States and the United Kingdom stated that military action was authorised by the UN Security Council through a revived authority to use force under resolution 678, the resolution that authorised the use of force against Iraq in the 1991 Persian Gulf War. Under this argument, Iraq's repeated failure to prove it no longer had WMD or missile delivery capability represented a material breach of its cease-fire obligations under Resolution 687. Resolution 1441 reaffirmed that

Iraq was in material breach of its obligations under Resolution 687 and gave it one last chance to comply. With its failure to do so, the basis of the cease-fire was removed, which revived authority to use force under Resolution 678, making a further resolution unnecessary.

This legal argument was largely not accepted by a number of other members of the UN Security Council. Within Europe, a rough split between old and new Europe emerged, with France and Germany opposed to military action and with newer members such as Spain, Poland, Hungary, Bulgaria, and Romania in support of military action. Large antiwar protests were held in France, Germany, and even in the United Kingdom, where it is estimated that one million people took to the streets. In the open UN Security Council debate on Iraq held on March 26–27, 2003, the broad majority of state representatives who spoke (sixty-eight in total) emphasised that the war was a violation of international law and the UN Charter and was thus found to be illegitimate both in terms of its goals as well as the mode of its prosecution. The lack of support for military action was also evidenced by the small number of states that took an active role with the United States, United Kingdom, and Australia.

Operation Iraqi Freedom

On March 20, 2003, coalition troops launched Operation Iraqi Freedom with US and UK forces invading Iraq from positions in Kuwait. Within two days, combined forces had taken control of the Rumaila oil fields, the second richest oil field in Iraq (located in Southern Iraq), with little resistance. On March 22, the main bulk of US forces moved north, with a mixture of US and British forces moving up the Fao peninsula and taking the port of Umm Qasr and the Iraqi naval base of Zubayr. On March 23, the forces split, with British forces laying siege to the Shi'ite city of Basra. A full-scale assault was launched on April 6, with British troops taking control of the city the same day and having suffered few casualties. In the northern regions, a coalition of Kurdish *peshmerga* fighters, a coalition of Special Forces, and conventional US troops easily took control of the countryside and major northern cities.

The US forces began their advance on Baghdad with the First Marine Expeditionary Force (MEF) advancing along major roads via Jalibal, Nasiriyah, and Kut before heading to Baghdad from the southeast. A second force, the Third Infantry Division, traveled up the Euphrates valley over the desert

before swinging back onto main roads for an advance on Baghdad via Karbala from the southwest. US forces met strong resistance in Nasiriyah from Iraqi *fedayeen fighters, a* mixture of Ba'ath Party militias and Muslim extremists from other Arab countries, but took control of the city by the end of March. Separate coalition forces assaulted and took control of Najaf on April 1 and Samawah on April 4, sites on-route to Baghdad. Further north, the Iraqi Republican Guard put up fierce fighting to defend the city of Hillah, being defeated after eight days on April 10. Up to this point, the US forces had achieved a speed of advance never seen before with the loss of little equipment and few soldiers. Unexpectedly, the invasion had met little strong resistance, with most regular soldiers deserting their positions.

The final objective was the assault on Baghdad, where a fierce defence by Iraq's elite Republican Guard divisions was expected. On April 3, after two days of heavy fighting, US troops took control of Karbala and secured the necessary bridge crossings to allow them into Baghdad. After overcoming attacks by a mix of *fedayeen fighters*, the Republican Guard, and regular army troops, US troops gained control on April 5 of the Baghdad (Saddam) International Airport, an objective of strong logistical and psychological value. The attack then pressed on toward central Baghdad through the southern suburbs, with US forces taking control of the "regime district" of ministries and residential palaces by April 7. From the southeast, marines crossed the Diyala River into Baghdad on April 7–8 and succeeded in securing important targets, such as the Atomic Energy Commission, the Ministry of Defence, *fedayeen* headquarters, and one presidential palace with little difficulty. On April 9, the marines reached Firdos (Paradise) Square, and here they famously assisted a group of Iraqis in pulling down a statue of Saddam Hussein, an image which became symbolic of the fall of the regime.

Occupation and Reconstruction

The defeat of Saddam Hussein's regime was achieved with a surprisingly low level of coalition fatalities— 122 US and 33 British soldiers, and some were killed by accident or by "friendly fire." It has been harder to estimate the number of casualties on the Iraqi side, but with the desertion of most conscripts and the avoidance of heavy combat by the Republican Guard, the most serious fighting and death affected the *fedayeen*, Saddam loyalists, supporters of the Ba'ath Party, as well as foreign Islamic fighters from Syria, Algeria, and other Muslim countries.

Whilst the coalition's victory over the regime proved to have been relatively easy, the reconstruction of Iraq as a multiethnic democratic state has proved far more difficult and complex. Internationally, the illegitimacy with which military action was viewed has led few states to offer to substantially share the financial and military costs of occupation and reconstruction, despite UN endorsement of a temporary occupation and the setting up of a peacekeeping force. Domestically, the failure of weapons inspectors to find WMD stockpiles in Iraq has led to damaging political inquiries in the United States, United Kingdom, and Australia about the use of intelligence prior to the war. Within Iraq, the United States has been unable to shift its image as a foreign occupier. Throughout 2003 and 2004, an insurgency against the occupying forces has gathered intensity that has hindered the ability of US forces and interim Iraqi governments from maintaining security, a prerequisite for political and physical reconstruction. Insurgent groups have ranged from ex-Saddam militiamen and Ba'ath Party members, foreign terrorist organisations including al-Qaeda (in the Sunni areas), and followers of the radical Shi'ite cleric, Moqtadr al-Sadr in the South. Since the occupation, terrorist acts have occurred with regularity, targeting individuals and groups seen to be assisting the United States to restore order, including the occupying forces themselves, new army and police recruits, interim Iraqi government leaders, the United Nations, and foreign workers, and sabotaging oil pipelines and essential services has also occurred with regularity. With nationwide elections held in for January 2005, it remains to be seen whether the United States's nation-building experiment can succeed in replacing Saddam Hussein's dictatorial regime with a stable, multiethnic democracy.

LAVINA LEE

See also Arab Nationalism; Ba'ath Party; Hussein, Saddam; International Atomic Energy Agency (IAEA); Iran–Iraq War 1980–1988; Iraq; Jihad; Middle East: International Relations; Persian Gulf War, 1991; Sanctions, Economic

References and Further Reading

Keegan, John. *The Iraq War*. New York: Alfred A. Knopf, 2004.
Ramesh Randeep. *The War We Could Not Stop: The Real Story of the Battle for Iraq*. Kent, England: Faber and Faber, 2003.
Israeli, Raphael. *The Iraq War: The Regional Impact on Shiites, Kurds, Sunnis and Arabs*. Brighton, United Kingdom: Sussex Academic Press, 2004.

Murray, Williamson, and Scales, Robert H. *The Iraq War: A Military History*. Boston, MA: Harvard University Press, 2004.

Woodward, Bob. *Plan of Attack: The Road to War*. London: Simon & Schuster, 2004.

Sifry, Michah L., and Cerf, Christopher, eds. *The Iraq War Reader: History, Documents and Opinions*. New York: Simon & Schuster, 2003.

Roberts, Adam. "Law and the Use of Force after Iraq." *Survival* 45, no. 2 (2003): 31–56.

Kagan, Robert. Of *Paradise and Power: America and Europe in the New World Order*. New York: Knopf, 2003.

PERU

Peru is a large country (1,285,216 square kilometers) located on the west central part of South America, bordered by Ecuador and Colombia in the north, Brazil in the east, and Bolivia and Chile in the south. Its long coastal area, on the west, is on the Pacific Ocean. Peru's population is over 26.8 million with an estimated rate of annual population growth of 1.48%. Close to seven million live in the capital, Lima, located on the coast; the port of entry, however, is Callao. Three main regions with different climatic conditions can be found in Peru: the semidesert coastal plain; the Andes, also called Andean highlands, which run north to south; and the Amazon jungle in the east with its tropical rainforests.

In this ethnically diverse country, more than 45% of the population identifies as Indigenous (Quechua, Aymara, Ashaninka, and others), 37% as Mestizo (mixed white/Native American blood), 15% as White (of European descent), and the rest as Black, Asian, or other minorities. If religiously speaking, the country is still predominantly Catholic (90% of the population); both Spanish and Quechua are official languages, with other indigenous languages such as Aymara, Campa, and Aguaruno also being used in some regions. Ethnicity is still, unfortunately, a high predictor of socioeconomic status, with indigenous Peruvians forming the majority of the poor in Peru.

Historical Background

The Inca Empire occupied an important part of what is now contemporary Peru at the time when the Spanish conquered the territory in the 1500s. After three centuries of colonial rule, Peru became an independent nation in 1824 after the Battle of Ayacucho was won over Spanish troops. A constitutional republic since 1860, Peru's postcolonial economy was structured early on around large agroindustrial plantations in the coastal area, some mining enclaves in the highlands, and survival agriculture in most of the country. Sugar, cotton, fish, and fish products as well as silver, gold, copper, zinc, and petroleum have historically been the main country exports. In the twenty-first century, coffee and other food crops have also joined the list of primary exports, while sugar has declined. The coca leaf is one of Peru's most important export crops although mostly produced and sold illegally for drug trafficking.

From a "Republican Aristocracy" in the early part of the twentieth century, where a limited democratic system ensured the domination of the Peruvian oligarchy and the continuing exclusion of the majority of the population, the country entered into a phase of mass-based party politics through the formation of the *Alianza Popular Revolucionaria Americana* party (American Revolutionary Popular Alliance, or the APRA) in 1924. The latter, seeking the inclusion of lower and middle classes in national politics, was a central political actor throughout the rest of the century but only won state power in 1985, through the election of Alan García as President. In the meantime, the often-banned APRA challenged a closed political system that only held free and fair democratic elections with universal suffrage in 1980. By then, however, the APRA had already been legalized for some decades and had gradually moved away from its original platform, choosing to ally with elite groups at different points in time. A number of left-wing parties emerging in the 1960s replaced the APRA as the representative of labour and popular classes.

The military regime, which took power in 1968 through a *coup d'état*, was the breaking point of the old oligarchic order that had remained deeply entrenched in politics and in the economy even if importantly challenged since the mid-1920s. President General Juan Velasco Alvarado implemented a number of key social and economic reforms and led the first serious attempt at building a state-led model of development supported by new state institutions. Mounting social protest and rising economic difficulties, however, led the military to return power to civilians in 1980. This coincided with the launching of an armed insurrection by a Maoist guerrilla organization, *Sendero Luminoso* (Shining Path), which managed to sustain a war against state security forces until the early 1990s. The conflict caused a massive death toll, with close to seventy thousand deaths or forced disappearances and numerous human rights violations committed by the state as well as by insurgents.

Alberto Fujimori, a political unknown who won the 1990 presidential elections, completely reshaped

the Peruvian political, economic, and social landscape during his ten-year rule. After applying one of the harshest structural adjustment programs of Latin America, Fujimori perpetrated a "self-*coup*" in 1992 in alliance with the military. Following his shutting down the Congress and the Judiciary, Fujimori reconfigured entirely the country's institutions. A new Constitution was drafted in 1993 where powers were further concentrated in the hands of the President and that allowed him to run for a second term; the bicameral Congress was transformed into a single house, and many social and economic rights protected by the 1979 Constitution were abolished to facilitate the implementation of Fujimori's trade liberalization agenda.

New elections were held in 1995 and won easily by Fujimori, who had managed to redress the economy and put the leader of the Shining Path under arrest. The second term of Fujimori, however, was marked by increasing encroachments on civil liberties, executive control over the Judiciary and Electoral Bodies, and the President's intent on running for a third term. After intense opposition from civil society and stronger scrutiny by the international community, the 2000 elections were decisive in revealing the Fujimori regime's corrupt and repressive nature. Soon after these highly questioned elections, the regime broke down, and Fujimori went into self-exile in Japan, where he was granted protection due to his Japanese citizenship. Vladimiro Montesinos, the Head of Intelligence Services who is said to have been the real power figure in the regime, was arrested and put in jail.

After a transitional regime led by Valentín Paniagua (2000–2001), Alejandro Toledo was elected President in 2001. Toledo, an economist trained in the United States, was the first President of indigenous origins to assume power in Peru. His party, *Perú Posible* (Possible Peru), faced important difficulties in governing the country due in part to the many different political tendencies of its leading members. Low presidential popularity and numerous accusations of corruption dominated Toledo's term.

Economic Situation

Peru has been slowly recovering since the early 1990s from the worst economic crisis of its history, which built up in the 1970s and was at its peak in 1990, with hyperinflation ranging as high as 7,482%. From a negative gross domestic product (GDP) annual growth rate of –7% in 1990, the country's economy was growing at a rate of 6.39% in 1995, before coming down again to 1.33% in 2000 with a slight increase to 2.44% in 2003. Its GDP per capita was 5,010 purchasing power parity (PPP) US dollars in 2002.

The more stable macroeconomic framework since the 1990s has not been successful in addressing Peru's socioeconomic ills from the point of view of sustainable employment and social development. Informal sector employment has continued to grow, from 52.7% of the economically active population in metropolitan Lima in 1991 to 59.2% in 2000. Meanwhile, the unemployment rate was 7.4% of the total labour force in 2000. The share of national income of the lowest 20% population was 2.9%, while the share of the highest 20% was 53.2% in 2000. It is estimated that 54% of the population is poor, while 14.8% is extremely poor, and 20% of the population still does not have access to an improved water source. Life expectancy at birth was 69.7 years in 2002. Only 59% of births are attended by skilled attendants (compared to the average of 83% in Latin America and the Caribbean), and 410 Peruvian women die for every 100,000 live births (compared to 190 on average in the region). An estimated 85% of the population above the age of fifteen was said to be literate, with around 95% of young females and 94% of young males attending primary schools.

Peru's Development in the Post-World War II Period

In comparison to the other main South American countries, Peru can be described as a late "industrializer," with the predominance of the primary-export sector being explained as both a function of the diversity of natural resource exports and a greater penetration of US foreign investment from the late nineteenth century up to the late 1960s.

From the years of post-World War I to the end of the 1960s, with the brief exception of a failed attempt at adopting import-substitution policies during the government of President Bustamante in the mid-1940s, state intervention was confined to investing in infrastructure and promoting foreign investment and loans to support the primary-export sector. After a decade of growth and economic expansion in the 1950s, the 1960s were dominated by the need to undertake major structural changes to accommodate a growing middle class, a vibrant labour movement, and increasing mobilization by peasants seeking access to land and credit. An important process of migration to cities had also created a new sector among Peru's major cities, mainly Lima, calling for

state intervention at the local level to organize the new settlements.

From the 1960s onward, a new model of state-led development took hold, with the promotion of import-substituting industrialization being implemented in response to the exhaustion of the export-based model. This late shift to an inward-looking industrialization strategy in the 1960s was a daunting task in light of the fact that Peru had remained one of the more open Latin American economies for foreign investment up to then. Moreover, state institutions had no previous experience of development planning and there was no central financial institution managing the economy. Only in 1963 was the *Banco de la Nación* (National Bank) created as a revenue collector and treasurer for the state.

The process of building state institutions that would manage the economy began under the government of Fernando Belaúnde Terry (1963–1968), head of the center-Right party *Acción Popular* (Popular Action), who installed a set of measures seeking to bring Peru more in line with the Latin American industrialization level. Yet, Belaúnde's policies remained at the level of developing the first stage of import-substituting industrialization, that of consumer-durable industries. State policy making in general was still very weak as a result of extensive patronage and corruption within the bureaucracy.

More fundamental macroeconomic change and institutional reform was brought about by the reformist military regime in 1968–1980. Long overdue reforms that involved the state in major redistributing schemes were implemented for the first time in Peruvian history. This included one of the most generous land reforms of Latin America, with land redistribution as well as the formation of agricultural cooperatives. In total, about 30% of all peasants and agrarian producers were allocated 9,672,017 hectares of land out of a total of 23 million. Even if the land reform can be credited for having ended the domination of the landed oligarchy, the overall policy framework favoring cheap food prices for urban consumption was not positive for agricultural development.

Other important reforms included the nationalization of petroleum and mining industries, worker participation in industrial ownership, and the creation of numerous state agencies and programs seeking to foster greater participation and reduce social inequalities. On the side of civil society, that period is also recalled as one of extensive popular mobilizations with the rise of new left-wing parties, increased labour mobilization, and the formation of local community organizations, some of which were originally founded by the state.

On the side of economic policy, the same fundamental defects that had marked Belaúnde's first government were reproduced under the military regime: an over-reliance on external borrowing and a lack of adequate fiscal and tax policies to ensure that expanding state spending could be financed on a sustainable level by domestic resources. The second half of the military regime was marked by its more conservative orientations with the replacement of General Velasco by General Francisco Morales Bermúdez in 1975. A growing popular and labour unrest was met with repression, and the military was soon forced to proceed to a transition to democratic civilian rule, which was initiated in 1978. The 1980 democratic elections saw the return of Fernando Belaúnde Terry as the new president.

The "lost decade" of the 1980s was marked by deep economic crisis and rising political violence, and ended with a debt crisis, hyperinflation, and political chaos. As an indication of the transformation of Peruvians' living conditions, in 1984 the minimum wage in Peru was 46% of what people had received ten years earlier. By 1990, real incomes had fallen to 20% of the levels achieved ten years earlier. These losses were accompanied by a dramatic drop of state social spending, which only started to resume in the early 1990s, together with the shift towards a new export-based model of development. These were founded on a new openness to foreign investment and compliance with international financial institutions' macroeconomic policy prescriptions.

STÉPHANIE ROUSSEAU

See also Andean South America: History and Economic Development; Andean South America: International Relations; Aprismo; Fujimori, Alberto; Haya de la Torre, Víctor Raúl; Shining Path/*Sendero Luminoso*

References and Further Reading

Cameron, Maxwell, and Philip Mauceri, eds. *The Peruvian Labyrinth. Polity, Society, Economy.* University Park, PA: The Pennsylvania State University Press, 1997.

Comisión de la Verdad y Reconciliación (Truth and Reconciliation Commission). 2003. *Final Report.* http://www.cverdad.org.pe/ingles/ifinal/index.php.

Contreras, Carlos, and Marcos Cuetos. *Historia del Perú contemporáneo.* Lima: Red Para el Desarrollo de las Ciencias Sociales en el Perú, 1999.

Crabtree, John, and Jim Thomas, eds. *Fujimori's Peru: The Political Economy.* London: Institute of Latin American Studies, 1998.

Lowenthal, Abraham, and Cynthia McClintock, eds. *The Peruvian Experiment Reconsidered.* Princeton, NJ: Princeton University Press, 1983.

Matos Mar, José. *Desborde Popular y Crisis del Estado. Veinte Años Después.* Lima: Fondo Editorial del Congreso del Perú, 2004.

Sheahan, John. *Searching for a Better Society. The Peruvian Economy from 1950.* University Park, PA: The Pennsylvania State University Press, 1999.

Stepan, Alfred. *The State and Society. Peru in Comparative Perspective*. Princeton, NJ: Princeton University Press, 1978.

Stern, Steve, ed. *Shining and Other Paths: War and Society in Peru, 1980–1995*. Durham, NC: Duke University Press, 1998.

Wise, Carol. *Reinventing the State. Economic Strategy and Institutional Change in Peru*. Ann Arbor, MI: The University of Michigan Press, 2003.

PETRODOLLARS

Petrodollars commonly refer to US dollars earned from the sale of oil. The term originates from the worldwide custom of quoting oil prices and clearing oil transactions in US dollars. Therefore, the term "petrodollars" can also be used synonymously with the oil revenues of members of the oil producers' cartel Organization of Petroleum Exporting Countries (OPEC) and non-OPEC oil producers' countries.

Petrodollars Surpluses

In October 1973, following the fourth Arab-Israeli conflict, the Organization of Arab Petroleum Exporting Countries (OAPEC) declared an oil embargo against the United States and the Netherlands–countries judged too friendly with Israel. The embargo caused severe energy shortages during the winter of 1973–1974 and a sudden and sharp rise in oil prices. At the same time, OPEC, which includes OAPEC plus Algeria, Indonesia, Ecuador, and Venezuela, sharply increased the price of crude oil. OPEC's decision was dictated by economic considerations. During the early 1970s, the value of petrodollars had fallen because of the devaluation and depreciation of the US dollar. Oil prices had not kept up with other commodities' prices. From 1960 to 1973, the price of oil had increased a mere 25%, much less than prices of other commodities. OPEC was also convinced that underpricing had caused oil to be wasted. To protect resources from depletion, price increases and production cuts were necessary.

From October 1973 to January 1974, the price of crude oil shot up 300%. The sudden surge in petroleum prices generated trade imbalances between oil importing and exporting countries. Because of the sudden and exceptional higher prices, oil-importing countries had no time to adjust to the new prices and accumulated huge trade deficits, and import expenditure greatly outstripped export revenues. Oil exporters faced the opposite phenomenon: oil export revenues soared while imports remained unchanged; this phenomenon generated vast current accounts surpluses. The additional petrodollars produced by the 1973–1974 price hike became to be known as petrodollar surpluses.

Petrodollars Recycling

While oil importers faced a cash shortage because they accumulated huge import bills that they could not honor, oil-exporting countries had to deal with cash surpluses, as they were unable to spend all the extra petrodollars generated by the price rise. The best solution to this imbalance would have been for oil-producing countries to increase their imports from oil-importing countries, mostly industrialized Western countries. However, this was unfeasible because several OPEC members had small populations, and many were still at early stages of industrialization. They simply could not import enough products to keep from accumulating enormous petrodollars surpluses.

The most serious consequence of these imbalances was the short- to long-term impact on the world economy. If petrodollars surpluses were not spent or loaned to someone else to be spent, there would be a serious shortage of liquidity, and the world economy would contract. It was apparent that while oil exporters needed investment outlets for their petrodollars, oil importers needed to borrow money to keep importing oil. The economic mechanisms used to match these two monetary flows became known as petrodollars recycling.

"Petrodollars recycling" can be defined as the economic process through which the excessive dollar inflows (surpluses) of the current account of the balance of payments of oil-producing countries are reversed with dollar outflows from the capital account. These dollar outflows are used to finance the current account deficits of oil-importing countries. The mechanism is described as the following. OPEC countries deposited their petrodollars surpluses into a foreign Western bank. The bank then loaned the money to governments in need of financing their balance of payments deficits. These countries used the borrowed money to buy more oil and other imports, keeping the economy flowing.

Petrodollars recycling also took place through the International Money Fund via an *ad hoc* lending mechanism: the Oil Facility. The fund was created using money from oil-exporting countries and other lenders and was used by countries with balance of payments problems caused by the oil price rise.

Petrodollars Recycling Problems

Recycling petrodollars through the banking system alleviated the contraction of world economy. Large sections of petrodollars surpluses were invested in the stock market in industrialized countries and therefore sustained Western economies. However, the recycling created vast repayment problems, especially in developing countries, which kept accumulating vast debts to meet their energy imports demand. From 1973 to 1977, the foreign debt of one hundred developing countries (excluding oil exporting countries) increased 150%.

From the mid-1970s, higher oil prices led to mounting inflationary pressure placed on debtor countries, while soaring debts inevitably slowed down growth. By 1979, this unprecedented combination had a new name: "stagflation."

New Patterns of Petrodollars Recycling

The 2004 oil price increases have recreated a sudden surge in dollars earned by oil-producing countries. Since the first oil crisis, oil-importing countries have successfully introduced energy-saving schemes to reduce the impact of sudden oil price increases, yet the problem of petrodollars surpluses persists, especially in Arab oil-exporting countries. New patterns of recycling have emerged, however. Petrodollars surpluses are not any longer exclusively invested in the West or used to fund current account deficits of oil-importing countries but are invested in the Arab world. Gulf investors are pouring additional liquidity generated by higher oil prices into equities and stocks of Arab public companies. By the end of 2005, it is estimated that $9 billion will be raised through several public offerings in the six Gulf Cooperation Council states (Saudi Arabia, Kuwait, Bahrain, Oman, Qatar, and the United Arab Emirates).

Record corporate performance of Arab stocks coupled with psychological fear of investing abroad are at the root of the new phenomenon. Post-September 11 fears persist, and Persian Gulf investors now prefer to invest at home rather than in the United States or other Western countries.

Petrocurrencies

The depreciation of the dollar also contributes to the reluctance of several oil-producing countries to recycle their petrodollars in dollar-denominated investment. In addition, the weakening of the dollar is reducing oil revenues net revenues and increasing the net cost of European imports for oil-exporting countries. At the same time, the strengthening of the euro is appealing to commodity traders who see the new common European currency as the future reserve currency. Commodity trading to and from Europe has increasingly been conducted in euros and not dollars. Against this background, oil-exporting countries that trade with European countries may decide to denominate their oil sales in euros, ending the custom of quoting and trading oil in US dollars and paving the way to the advent of petrocurrencies, that is, more than one currency to clear oil transactions.

LORETTA NAPOLEONI

See also Organization of Arab Petroleum Exporting Countries (OAPEC); Organization of Petroleum Exporting Countries (OPEC)

References and Further Reading

Field, Michael. *A Hundred Million Dollars a Day, Inside the World of Middle East Money*. New York: Praeger Publishers, 1976.
Napoleoni, Loretta. *Terror Inc.* London: Penguin, 2004.
Shapiro, David. *The Hidden Hand of American Hegemony: Petrodollar Recycling and International Markets* (Cornell Studies in Political Economy). Cornell, NY: Cornell University, 1999.
"Dollar vs. Euro—Hegemony." *Pressure Point.* January 1, 2003.

PHILIPPINES

The Republic of the Philippines, an archipelago situated between the Philippine Sea and the South China Sea, east of Vietnam, comprises approximately 7,100 islands; Luzon, Mindanao, and Visayas are the largest islands. With a total landmass of 115,831 square miles (300,000 square kilometers), the republic is roughly the size of Arizona. The terrain is largely mountainous, creating narrow coastal plains and interior valleys and plains. The climate is tropical with two distinct seasons: a northeast monsoon season (December to February) and a southwest monsoon season (May to October). Annual rainfall varies significantly by region. Mountainous regions receive approximately 195 inches of rain annually, whereas the more sheltered inland regions receive as little as 39 inches. The population is estimated at 76.5 million with an estimated growth rate of 2.36% annually.

The Negritos were the first peoples to inhabit the Philippines. They are believed to have come to the islands thirty thousand years ago from Borneo and

Sumatra, utilizing then-existing land bridges. Subsequently, people of Malay ancestry migrated to the islands from the South, utilizing then-existing land bridges and boats called "baranguays." The Malays settled in scattered communities, also known as "baranguays." Baranguys were ruled by local chieftains, called "datus." In the ninth century, the Chinese merchants and traders arrived. In the fourteenth century, Arabs migrated from Indonesia, thus introducing Islam in the South and to a lesser extent to Luzon in the North. The Malays were the dominant group until the arrival of the Spanish in the sixteenth century.

The first European-recorded sighting of the Philippines occurred on March 16, 1521, during Ferdinand Magellan's circumnavigation of the globe. He landed on the island of Cebu and claimed it for King Charles I of Spain. Eager to display his supremacy, Magellan initiated the Battle of Mactan in which he was struck and killed by a poison arrow. The islands were given their present name in honor of Philip II of Spain, who ruled from 1556 to 1598.

Filipinos were restive under Spanish rule, and there were numerous uprisings. The revolutionary leader, Emilo Aguinaldo, who proclaimed Philippine independence on June 12, 1898, headed the most important uprising. Aguinaldo was able to unify historically disparate groups into one national voice. The revolution against Spain was increasingly successful by the time the Americans arrived. Their arrival, however, culminated in the defeat of Spain. Soon thereafter, Spain ceded the islands to the United States pursuant to the terms of the Treaty of Paris (December 10, 1898).

On July 4, 1946, the Philippine Islands became the independent Republic of the Philippines. In 1962, the official Independence Day was changed to June 12 to commemorate Aguinaldo's original declaration of independence from Spain in 1898.

Ramon Magsaysay was the first post-independence president of the Philippines. His first success was the suppression of the communist-inspired Huk Rebellion (1945–1953) that had complicated recovery efforts. Magsaysay died in an airplane crash in March of 1957. His vice president, Carlos P. Garcia, who was elected to office shortly thereafter, succeeded him. Garcia was instrumental in negotiating the relinquishment of large areas of land initially reserved for American military forces and that were no longer needed. As a result, the United States turned over to the Philippines the town of Olongapo on Subic Bay, which was previously under the jurisdiction of the United States Navy. Diosdado Macapagal (1961–1965) was elected president in 1961. He sought to expand Philippine ties with its neighbors. In 1963, he convened a summit meeting in Manila consisting of Malaysia,

Indonesia, and the Philippines (MAPHILINDO). The goal of MAPHILINDO was to bring together the Malay peoples. However, continuing disputes between Malaysia and Indonesia and the Philippines's controversial claim to Subah, a territory in the northeastern Borneo that had become a Malaysian state in 1961, ended the summit. In the election of 1965, Ferdinand E. Marcos (1917–1990) defeated Macapagal. Marcos was in office for the next two decades, winning the presidential election again in 1969. His first term in office was ambitious and marked by numerous public works projects designed to improve the Filipino quality of life. He also lobbied vigorously for US military and economic aid. His second term in office was less idyllic. Economic growth slowed, and quality of living deteriorated, especially in the urban areas. The Communist Party, formerly the Huks, reestablished a visible communist presence. Crime rates and random violence were spiraling out of control. On August 21, 1971, nine people were killed, and grenade explosions wounded one hundred during a Liberal Party rally. Marcos blamed leftist guerillas and suspended *habeas corpus*. However, evidence eventually surfaced that implicated the administration as having some involvement in the attacks. Marcos declared martial law on September 21, 1972.

The martial law period persisted from 1972 to 1981. Under Marcos's command, the military arrested opposition figures, including Benigno Aquino, journalists, student and labor activists, and criminal elements. Approximately thirty thousand people were incarcerated at various military compounds run by the army and the Philippine Constabulary. Weapons were confiscated, and individuals connected with opposition politicians and other figures were broken up. Newspapers were shut down, and the mass media were severely restricted. Moreover, Marcos closed the Philippine Congress and assumed its legislative responsibilities. During the martial law period, Marcos issued hundreds of presidential decrees; few of these were ever published. On January 17, 1981, Marcos issued the Proclamation 2045, which formally ended the period of martial law. While some controls were loosened, Marcos's New Society was a liberalized version of the crony capitalism that defined his administration.

One of the first arrested was long-time Marcos opposition figure, Benigno Aquino. Aquino was found guilty of subversion and sentenced to death by a military court in November 1977. While in prison, he led the *Lakas Ng Bayan* (LABAN) or "Strength of the Nation" Party campaign to win seats in the 1978 legislative election. Despite being unsuccessful at gaining seats, he managed to get 40% of the metro Manila vote. In 1980, Aquino was allowed to travel to the

United States for medical treatment. Accompanied by his wife, he remained in the United States for three years. Aquino feared the Philippines were headed toward civil war. Despite warning from Imelda Marcos about the dangers of returning to the Philippines, Aquino's love of country was more powerful. On August 23, 1983, Aquino was shot in the head when he was escorted off an airplane at Manila International Airport. The soldiers of the Aviation Security Command (ASC) shot him. The government claimed he was killed by a lone gunman named Rolando Galman, who was conveniently killed by the ASC immediately after he shot Aquino. Finally, on September 28, 1990, the courts convicted General Luther Custodio and fifteen members of the ASC of murdering Aquino and Galman.

Aquino's assassination would be the downfall of Marcos. His public credibility and support were waning, as was support from the United States. The United States was becoming increasingly uncomfortable with the Marcos regime. Finally, on February 22, Enrile and General Fidel Ramos, commander of the Philippine Constabulary, issued a joint statement demanding Marcos's resignation. They established their rebel headquarters inside Camp Aguinaldo and the adjoining Camp Crame in Metro Manila, which was guarded by several hundred troops. In response, Marcos ordered units to suppress the uprising, but Cardinal Sin, broadcasting over the Catholic-run Radio Veritas (which became the voice of the revolution), appealed to the people to bring food and supplies for the rebels and to use nonviolence to block pro-Marcos troops. On the evening of February 25, 1986, Marcos was forced from office in a bloodless revolution.

Corazon Aquino became the seventh president of the Philippines. Aquino's presidency was armed with a mandate to undertake a new direction in the country's economic policy. Her initial cabinet contained was diverse. It contained individuals from across the political spectrum. Over time, however, the cabinet became increasingly homogeneous, particularly with respect to the economic perspective, reflecting the strong influence of the powerful business community and international creditors. The businesspeople that directed the Central Bank and headed the departments of finance and trade and industry became the dominating voices in the economic decision-making process. Foreign policy also reflected this power relationship, focusing on attracting more foreign loans, aid, trade, investment, and tourists.

Aquino's immediate concern was to get the economy moving, and a turnaround was achieved in 1986. Economic growth was 1.9%. It was minimal but positive. For the next two years, growth was at 5.9% and

6.7%. In 1986 and 1987, consumption led the growth process, but then investment began to increase. In 1985, industrial growth was at 40%. By mid-1988, however, industries were working at near full capacity. Investment in durable goods grew almost 30% in both 1988 and 1989. Moreover, the international community was supportive. Foreign investment did not respond immediately after Aquino took office. In 1987, however, it began to pick up. The economy also was helped by foreign aid. The 1989 and 1991 meetings of the Multilateral Aid Initiative, also known as the Philippine Assistance Plan, a multinational initiative to provide assistance to the Philippines, pledged a total of US$6.7 billion. The Aquino administration was successful at restoring respect of civil liberties and revitalizing democratic institutions. However, many viewed the administration as weak and fractious. During Aquino's tenure, there were numerous coup attempts by disaffected members of the Philippine military. This affected the overall return to full political stability.

Fidel Ramos succeeded Corazon Aquino as president of the Philippines on June 30, 1992. He won a 23.6% plurality in the May 11, 1992, general election. Ramos' victory was based on his platform for stability as well as his commitment to the Aquino administration policies. Ramos was instrumental in reconciling with his opponents, most notably the Communists. He legalized the Communist Party and created the National Unification Commission, which laid the groundwork for peaceful talks with communist insurgents, Muslim separatists, and military rebels.

Joseph Estrada, a well-known film star, was elected in May of 1998. He was elected with overwhelming popular support based on his promises to alleviate the suffering of the poor. Despite his promises, his administration was among the most corrupt. During his tenure in office, Estrada illegally amassed an excess of $80 million, mostly from bribes from illegal gambling operations and skimming taxes. He was removed from office on January 20, 2001. Estrada was succeeded by his Vice President, Gloria Macapagal-Arroyo.

The Philippine economy has progressed slowly over time. Prior to the 1970s, agricultural and mineral products were the primary export. The agricultural sector employed approximately 60% of the workforce. In the 1970s, however, manufactured commodities (garment and electronic products) began to take increasingly larger shares of the export market. By the mid-1980s, manufactured commodities equaled 75% of the total value of all exports. The economy has evolved, such that by 1990 agriculture only employed 45% of the workforce, while the manufacturing

sector employed 12%. The service sector, which employed 25% of the workforce in 1960, became the residual employer and by the late 1980s employed 40% of the workforce. In 2002, the services sector employed 47% of the workforce; agriculture 37%; and industry 16%. Per capita gross domestic product (GDP) was $962 in 2002, and 52% of the population lived at or below the poverty line. In 2002, the infant mortality rate was 25.7 per 1000. The life expectancy was 66.9 years for males and 72.2 years for females.

The Philippine economy suffers from poor infrastructure. While there is a vibrant industrial production sector of the economy (for products of food, beverages, tobacco, and pharmaceuticals), it is concentrated primarily in the urban areas. Poor transportation and communications infrastructure hinder any significant linkages to the provinces. The Philippines are rich in agricultural potential as well. However, inadequate infrastructure, lack of financing, and government policies have hindered growth. Moreover, the Philippines are endowed with vast mineral and thermal energy resources. High production costs, low metal prices, and a lack of infrastructure investment have caused the industry to decline in growth.

Despite a slow maturing economy and relatively high unemployment rates, the Philippines have a literacy rate of 92%. One of the most serious problems in the Philippines in the 1980s and early 1990s concerned the large number of students who completed college but then could not find a job. If properly utilized, these new graduates could spur economic development. However, when left idle or forced to take jobs beneath their qualifications, this group could be a major source of discontent.

W. JOHN HANSEN

See also Aquino, Benigno, and Corazón; Marcos, Ferdinand

References and Further Reading

Blitz, Amy. *The Contested State: American Foreign Policy and Regime Change in the Philippines.* Oxford, UK: Rowman & Littlefield Publishers, 2000.

"Brief Overview of Philippine History." *Heritage* 9, no. 4 (Winter 1995): 18–20.

Calit, Harry. *The Philippines: Current Issues and Historical Background.* Hauppauge, NY: Nova Science Publishers, 2003.

Greenberg, Lawrence. *The Hukbalahap Insurrection: A Case Study of a Successful Anti-Insurgency Operation in the Philippines, 1946–1955.* Washington, DC: US Army Center of Military History, 1987.

Linn, Brian McAllister. *The Philippine War.* Lawrence, KS: University of Kansas Press, 2000.

Rodell, Paul. "Culture and Customs of The Philippines." Westport, CT: Greenwood Press, 2002.

PINOCHET UGARTE, AUGUSTO

On September 11, 1973, the Chilean armed forces overthrew the democratically elected Marxist president Salvador Allende Gossens in a bloody coup *d'état* that ended Allende's life. The coup signaled the end of Chile's democratic tradition and the beginning of General Augusto Pinochet Ugarte's seventeen-year authoritarian rule.

General Pinochet (b. 1915) is probably the most controversial figure in Chilean political history. His enemies have portrayed him as a repressive dictator and violator of human rights, responsible for the murders of his political opponents. His advocates, on the other hand, have depicted him as the crusader who rescued Chile from communism and the visionary who paved the way for Chile's economic recovery.

The son of middle class parents, Augusto Pinochet Ugarte was born on November 25, 1915, in the port city of Valparaíso and entered Chile's Army Academy in 1933. After his graduation in 1937, he rose through the ranks, and on August 23, 1973, President Allende appointed him as Army Commander.

Since being elected president by the Chilean Congress—no candidate received a majority of the vote in the September 1970 elections—Allende began a radical program for Chilean development consisting of land reform, nationalization of the banking and copper mining industries, and social welfare programs. Allende's program ran into difficulty as copper prices plummeted in the world market, inflation skyrocketed, import prices rose, and food shortages were common. Lacking a clear majority in Congress, Allende angered the Christian Democratic Party majority in the Chilean Congress when he threatened to replace the said body with a Popular Assembly. In response, the Christian Democrats sponsored a resolution in the Chamber of Deputies on August 22, 1973, calling for the military to establish law and order.

An exasperated Allende appointed General Pinochet as Army Commander. Presumed to be apolitical, Pinochet, as Army Chief of Staff, had put down a short-lived coup against Allende carried out by disgruntled military officers on June 29, 1973.

When public discontent against the Allende regime increased, the military decided to act and on September 11, 1973, staged a blood coup that toppled the Allende government. The coup's principal architects were Navy Commander, Admiral José Toribio Merino Castro, and Air Force Commander, General Gustavo Leigh Guzmán. Yet Pinochet, soon emerged as the leader of the military *junta* that was to rule Chile, for he commanded the Chilean armed forces' most numerous and powerful branch.

Pinochet's assumption of power marked the beginning of what he termed as "Authoritarian Democracy." Under this system, Congress was dismissed, the *junta* assumed control of all legislative and executive powers, press censorship was established, and labor union activity was curtailed.

Pinochet's seventeen-year rule was a repressive one. Chileans and foreigners presumed to be leftist sympathizers were arrested, exiled, or physically eliminated. In addition, political activism was banned. When in 1978, for example, fellow *junta* member General Leigh Guzmán declared in a newspaper interview his hopes for the return of democracy, Pinochet dismissed him from the *junta* and replaced him with General Fernando Matthei.

'While the Pinochet regime was characterized by political repression, economic liberalization became its trademark. Pinochet's economic plan conducted by the Chicago Boys—disciples of American economist Milton Friedman's supply-side economics theory—consisted of anti-inflationary measures, reduced state spending, privatization of state-owned enterprises, and economic diversification. An example of this economic liberalization was Law 600 that placed no limits on foreign investments and allowed for immediate repatriation of profits. The program brought such positive results that Chile became the most economically sound nation in Latin America.

Pinochet's political philosophy was best revealed in the 1980 Chilean Constitution, parts which remain in effect today. Holding to his firm belief that political factionalism was responsible for Allende's advent to power and that political pluralism was an obstacle to progress, Pinochet's 1980 Constitution granted the executive branch numerous powers while reducing Congress's traditional legislative role. Furthermore, the constitution granted the military an unprecedented role in Chilean politics by denying the president the right to remove military commanders and by granting the military budgetary autonomy.

In terms of international relations, the Pinochet regime was often cited as a frequent violator of human rights by organizations such as the United Nations General Assembly, the Organization of American States, and Amnesty International. Furthermore, relations with the United States deteriorated during Jimmy Carter's presidency because of the latter's insistence on human rights. Trade with the United States, however, grew during the Reagan administration—Reagan, like Pinochet, was a firm believer in supply-side economics—to the point that the United States became Chile's largest trading partner and primary investor.

During Pinochet's regime, a major diplomatic crisis occurred, ironically, with the right-wing Argentine military *junta*. Both nations almost went to war over sovereignty of the Beagle Channel in 1978. Only the mediation of Pope John Paul II prevented war between the two Southern Cone neighbors.

An interesting feature of the 1980 Chilean Constitution was its provision for a plebiscite, whereby voters could choose between the continuance of the governing *junta* for another eight years or a plebiscite that elections be held for a new government. In October 1988, seventeen parties known as the *Concertación* rallied Chilean voters for a 54.7% vote against eight more years of *junta* rule. To his credit, Pinochet respected the plebiscite vote and even chose not to become a presidential candidate in the December 14, 1989, elections, which were won by Christian Democrat Patricio Aylwin, a *Concertación* candidate.

On March 11, 1990, Pinochet handed power to the civilian president. The end of his presidency, however, did not mean an end to his involvement in Chilean politics. Due to a 1980 constitutional provision, he remained Commander of the Armed Forces until 1998, and as a former president, he retained the right to appoint nine of the thirty-eight senators in Congress as well as to remain a senator for life.

In October 1998, while undergoing medical treatment in London, Pinochet was arrested under a warrant issued by the Spanish judge Baltasar Garzón. The judge demanded Pinochet's extradition to Spain on grounds of human rights violations against Spanish citizens in Chile during his regime. After tense negotiations between Chile and Great Britain, the British allowed Pinochet to return to Chile on humanitarian grounds. In March 2000, Pinochet received a warm welcome from the Chilean military, and thousands of his supporters lined the streets from the airport to his home. A few months later, however, Pinochet was ordered to stand trial for human rights violations. In 2003, the Chilean Supreme Court ruled that the aging general was mentally unfit to stand trial.

In May 2004, a Chilean appellate court opened hearings for Pinochet to stand trial for his role in Operation Condor, a plan implemented by Latin American right-wing regimes to eliminate leftist sympathizers during the 1970s and 1980s. While arguments persist regarding his ability to stand trial, there is no doubt that Augusto Pinochet Ugarte has left an indelible mark in Chilean history.

JOSÉ B. FERNÁNDEZ

See also Allende Gossens, Salvador; Chile; Southern Cone (Latin America): History and Economic Development

Further Reading

Arriagada, Genaro. *Pinochet: The Politics of Power*. Boulder, CO: Westview Press, 1988.

Constable, Pamela, and Arturo Valenzuela. *A Nation of Enemies*. New York: Norton, 1991.

Nunn, Frederick M. *The Military in Chilean History: Essays on Civil Military Relations 1810–1973*. Albuquerque, NM: University of New Mexico Press, 1976.

Pinochet Ugarte, Augusto. *Camino Recorrido*. 3 vols. Santiago: Instituto Geográfico Militar de Chile, 1990–1994.

Remmer, Karen L. "Chile: The Breakdown of Democracy." *Latin America: Its Problems and Its Promise*, Jan Knippers Black, ed. Boulder, CO: Westview Press, 1984.

Siavelis, Paul M. *The President and Congress in Post-Authoritarian Chile: Institutional Constraints to Democratic Consolidation*. University Park, PA: The Pennsylvania State University Press, 2000.

Sigmund, Paul. *The Overthrow of Allende and the Politics of Chile*. Pittsburgh, PA: University of Pittsburgh Press, 1977.

Valenzuela, Arturo. "The Military in Power: The Consolidation of One-Man Rule." *The Struggle for Democracy in Chile*, Paul W. Drake and Iván Jaksic, eds. Lincoln, NE: University of Nebraska Press, 1995.

———. "Party Politics and the Crisis of Presidentialism in Chile." *The Failure of Presidential Democracy* Juan Ling and Arturo Valenzuela, eds. Vol. II. Baltimore, MD: Johns Hopkins University Press, 1994.

Vergara, Pilar. "Changes in the Economic Structure of the Chilean State Under the Military Regime." *Military Rule in Chile: Dictatorship and Oppositions*, J. Samuel Valenzuela and Arturo Valenzuela, eds. Baltimore, MD: Johns Hopkins University Press, 1986.

PLAN COLOMBIA

Plan Colombia was formally unveiled in 1999 and implemented in 2000 by the United States, under the administration of President Bill Clinton, and by the Colombian government, under the administration of President Andrés Pastrana Arango. There is some dispute over Plan Colombia's authorship and whether it is primarily Colombia's or Washington's plan. Over the years, there have been several versions of the plan, and even the English and Spanish texts of the final 1999 document differ. Despite variations in the official rhetoric, in effect the plan's central goal has been to combat drug trafficking, narcoterrorism, and drug-fueled guerrilla insurgencies in Colombia. It has since developed into an ambitious multiyear foreign aid and antidrug program.

The lengthy 1999 Colombian document, entitled *Plan Colombia: A Plan for Peace, Prosperity, and the Strengthening of the State*, detailed a comprehensive, ten-point strategy to demonstrate Colombia's commitment to achieving "lasting peace," to securing extensive international economic assistance to rebuild the country, and to increasing military support to fight the "war on drugs." In order of funding priority, however, the plan had several specific targets that it sought to realize over a five-to-six-year period: curb overall drug trafficking; reduce coca cultivation by 50%; restore the Colombian government's control over its territory; strengthen democracy; promote economic development; protect human rights; and provide humanitarian assistance. The Colombian government, despite the greater resources that were dedicated to the military components of the plan, preferred to emphasize its social and political aspects, especially when seeking contributions from the European Union (EU).

As announced by the Colombian government in September 1999, Plan Colombia optimistically projected an overall budget of $7.5 billion for antinarcotics control and development assistance over five years. President Pastrana pledged more than half or $4 billion from Colombian resources, and the remaining $3.5 billion was to be raised in loans and credits from the United States and the international community, including the EU, Canada, Japan, the International Monetary Fund (IMF), the World Bank, Inter-American Development Bank, and the Andean Development Corporation. Despite three donor's conferences by 2004, the actual commitments have fallen far short of the amount initially hoped for by the United States' and Colombian governments.

In June 2000, the US Congress made good on the US pledge and approved a one-time, emergency supplemental $1.3 billion aid package to Colombia (in addition to funds of more than $330 million approved earlier). A tiny portion of these funds was meant for counternarcotics programs in the Andean region as well. Most of the funds, however, were earmarked for military and intelligence support in Colombia during the next two years with around a quarter of a billion dollars dedicated to social development programs. This funding package represented the largest military aid to Latin America to date (making Colombia the third highest recipient of US aid worldwide in 2001 and the fourth highest in 2004). Specifically, the military assistance bought fourteen Blackhawk and thirty Huey helicopters and provided advanced training for Colombia's counter-narcotics battalions, and it paid for stepped-up forcible eradication and extensive aerial glyphosate fumigation of coca leaf and opium poppy crops. At the time, Colombia was supplying 90% of the cocaine that entered the United States, as well as most of the heroin.

Critics of this militarization blamed US influence for shifts in the Plan Colombia's priorities. Earlier versions of the plan had placed greater emphasis on economic and alternative development and

nonmilitary support for the peace process. And a review of the 1999 plan's ten strategies reveals economic activation and fiscal reorganization at the top of the list and counternarcotics and international drug control strategies listed sixth and last, respectively. Especially by 2001, Plan Colombia also marked a distinct shift away from counternarcotics enforcement to an emphasis on counterinsurgency and antiterrorism. This redefinition of the enemy was partly a result of the September 11 terrorist attack on the United States, but it was also a consequence of the escalation in terrorist and criminal activities by Colombia's largest Marxist guerrilla group, *Fuerzas Armadas Revolucionarias de Colombia* (Revolutionary Armed Forces of Colombia, FARC). Most of Colombia's coca and poppy crops were being grown in the so-called "liberated" or "demilitarized" zones under the control of Marxist guerrillas, primarily the FARC, but also under the control of the smaller *Ejercito de Liberación Nacional* (ELN) or the National Liberation Army.

By 2003, the US State Department described Colombia as "home to three of the four US-designated foreign terrorist organizations" in the hemisphere. Intelligence evidence had been mounting, according to US and Colombian military sources, that the FARC had strengthened or established connections with other terrorist groups from the Irish Republican Army (IRA) to the Islamic fundamentalists such as the Taliban in Afghanistan, Osama bin Laden, and Al Qaeda. Also, after the September 11 attacks, the Colombian Army routinely replaced "narcoguerrillas," their term for the rebel force, with that of "narcoterrorists," and the definition of the threat both in Colombia and in the United States shifted from one of insurgency to one of terrorism. Critics of US policy, however, tended to discount these global terrorist connections and viewed the linkage of drugs and terror as a way to "sell" to the US public and Congress the unprecedented military funding and more aggressive US role in Colombia and the Andes region.

Moreover, the Colombian military was linked to rightist paramilitary forces—the United Self-Defense Forces of Colombia or the AUC—and has been complicit in human rights violations. Human Rights organizations and progressive foreign policy lobbies, such as the Washington Office on Latin America, described the Colombian army as "one of the most abusive in the hemisphere." Critics feared that Plan Colombia, by training and arming thousands of Colombian troops against guerrillas, would further enmesh the United States in Colombia's intractable forty-year civil war and undermine peace initiatives by the Pastrana and (since August 2002) Alvaro Uribe

governments. The Colombian document itself ignores the compromised role of the security forces. It limits the armed conflict to three protagonists: the guerrillas, with roots in an agrarian and Marxist movement; the self-defense groups that want an armed solution to the leftist insurgency; and the majority of Colombians, who have been forcibly displaced and victimized by the violence, kidnapping, and extortion of both groups.

Officially, the US support for Plan Colombia emphasized five components: human rights and judicial reform; expansion of counternarcotics operations; alternative economic development; increased interdiction; and assistance for Colombian National Police. In theory and sometimes in practice, US policy provided for human rights protections in implementing Plan Colombia. Under US law, the Leahy Amendment provided that no aid could be given to any Colombian police or military units involved in gross human rights violations, unless the Secretary of State certified that the Colombian government had taken significant measures to improve human rights. Nevertheless, the critics countered that the aid package was inconsistent and did not do enough to curb military collusion with the paramilitaries. The plan entrenched military control over civil society, and aerial fumigation increased the forcible displacement of the population deeper into the country's jungle. As a result, Colombia has over a million internally displaced persons, one of the largest such populations in the world.

In spring 2001, the incoming administration of President George W. Bush announced a new Andean Regional Initiative that attempted to defuse some of the criticism of Plan Colombia and also to address the plan's spillover effects in neighboring countries. To some extent, the Andean Initiative represented a more regional and balanced approach to counternarcotics control. Funding increased to Peru, Bolivia, and Ecuador, and more than $730 million was requested for 2002 to support social and economic assistance. These are only supplementary, and Plan Colombia programs and funding, however, have continued.

After five years of implementation, Plan Colombia's achievements are mixed. The plan remains, primarily, a bilateral rather than multilateral approach. The United States provided more than 90% of the military funding and $4 billion in aid to Colombia during 2000 to 2005, while much of the promised European commitments (even "soft-side," nonmilitary aid) have not materialized. And 80% of this US aid has been for military, police, and aerial eradication programs. Despite a 30% decrease in coca acreage and less poppy production, the plan has not reduced drug trafficking or the price of drugs. With

hundreds of thousands of acres of production fumigated and eradicated annually since 2000, environmental and health concerns have also increased proportionately. And alternative development programs have not kept apace, pushing desperate farmers who have lost their livelihoods to restart illegal cultivations in more inaccessible regions of Colombia and continue the cycle of poverty and drug activity.

There has been a significant increase in the size and capabilities of Colombia's armed forces but at a price. Despite drops in violence levels and greater security in Colombia's cities and towns, a majority of the countryside remains a no-man's land in the hands of guerrillas and paramilitaries, who are more squeezed but also more desperate and violent. Civilians bear the brunt of this "sociopolitical violence" by both state and antistate groups. In the uneven balance of forces, the paramilitaries now hold greater power and continue to traffic in drugs, assassinate labor leaders and human rights workers, and kill peasants. Out of a total population of 36 million in Colombia, two million are internal refugees, many of these children. These children flood into the cities, and without hope or education become fodder for drug gangs. The humanitarian costs, therefore, have also been excessive. There have been rumors of widespread corruption and alleged drug trade connections at the top levels of the Colombian government. Repeated identification of Colombia with the "global war on terror," for example, when President Uribe called the military the "defenders of terrorism," has further polarized the country.

As Plan Colombia completes its term, critics fear that a new "Plan Colombia 2" could be approved in 2006. They warn that defense contractors and companies that profit from Plan Colombia have a stake in continuing military assistance to Colombia. The multinational oil industry, especially, hopes to benefit by greater security for pipelines and civilian contractors. The expectation is that these corporations will lobby US Congress and the president to renew Plan Colombia when it ends in 2005. In October 2004, Congress approved the Bush administration's request to raise the cap on troops and private US contractors present in country under Plan Colombia. Given the controversial history of Plan Colombia, there are real concerns that the military and eradication gains that have been achieved cannot be solidified as long as most social and developmental needs remain unmet.

WALTRAUD Q. MORALES

See also Colombia; Drug Trade; Drug Use; United Nations International Drug Control Program (UNDCP)

References and Further Reading

Berquist, Charles, Ricardo Peñaranda, and Gonzalo Sánchez G., ed.. *Violence in Colombia, 1999–2000: Waging War and Negotiating Peace*. Wilmington, DE: Scholarly Resources, 2001.

Colombia, President. *Plan Colombia: Plan for Peace, Prosperity, and the Strengthening of the State*. Bogota, Colombia: Presidency of the Republic, United States Institute of Peace Library, 1999. Retrieved October 31, 2004: http://www.usip.org/library/pa/colombia/adddoc/plan_colombia_101999.html.

Cooper, Marc. "Plan Colombia." *The Nation*. March 19, 2001. Retrieved October 31, 2001: http://www.thenation.com/doc.mhtml?i=20010319&s=cooper.

Isacson, Adam, Ingrid Vaicius, and CIP Colombia Program. "President Bush's Visit to Colombia." Retrieved November 19, 2004: http://ciponline.org/colombia/041119bush.htm.

Isikoff, Michael, Gregory Vistica, and Steven Ambrus. "The Other Drug War: Is a $1.3 Billion Colombia Aid Package Smart Policy, Dirty Politics, Good Business or a Costly Mistake?" *Newsweek Magazine*. April 3, 2000, p. 38.

Lennard, Jeremy. "UN Warns Colombia Mired in 'Grave Crisis.'" *The Guardian*. May 11, 2004.

"Plan Colombia, U.S. Anti-Drug Aid Fueling Brutal Civil War." *Washington Office on Latin America*. News Sheet, no date.

Simons, Paul E. "U.S. Narcotics Control Initiatives in Colombia." Acting Assistant Secretary of State for International Narcotics and Law Enforcement Affairs. *Testimony before the Senate Drug Caucus*. Washington, DC. June 3, 2003.

Thoumi, Francisco E. *Illegal Drugs, Economy, and Society in the Andes*. Washington, DC: Woodrow Wilson Center Press, 2003.

U.S. Department of State. "Plan Colombia." *Fact Sheet, Bureau of Western Hemisphere Affairs*. Washington, DC. March 14, 2001. Retrieved September 13, 2001: http://www.state.gov/g/inl/rls/fs/2001.

———. "U.S. Narcotics Control Initiatives in Colombia." Paul E. Simons, Acting Assistant Secretary of State for International Narcotics and Law Enforcement Affairs. *Testimony before the Senate Drug Caucus*. Washington, DC. June 3, 2003.

———. "Why Americans Should Care about Plan Colombia." *Fact Sheet, Bureau of Western Hemisphere Affairs*. Washington, DC. February 21, 2001.

POLAND

Poland is a medium-sized European country with a total surface area of 120,728 square miles (312,685 square kilometers). The population is estimated at 38,626,439 (CIA July 2004). It is divided into sixteen provinces (*voivodeships*). For more than 98% of the citizens, Polish is a mother tongue. Ethnically, Poland is 97% Polish, with small Belorussian, Ukrainian, and German minorities. About 95% of population is Catholic, with about 75% practicing. Beyond them, 1.5% is Orthodox and about 1% is Protestant. The economic centres are Warsaw (the capital, with

almost 2 million of citizens); Lodz (with approximately 1 million citizens); and Cracow, Poznan, and the Silesian with an agglomeration of Katowice, Wroclaw, Gdansk (with Gdynia), and Szczecin. The most important Polish universities are Warsaw University founded in 1816 (the largest in the country) founded in, Jagellonian University founded in 1364 (the oldest one), Warsaw Technical University, Academy of Mining and Metallurgy–Technical University in Cracow, Agricultural University in Warsaw, and the Military Technical University.

Poland borders on Russia, Lithuania, Belarus, Ukraine, Slovakia, the Czech Republic, and Germany. The gross domestic product (GDP) per capita according to the power purchase parity is about $11,100 US dollars (2003 estimate). The level of the economic development is average. The sector of services produces more than 65% GDP, with industry at 31% and agriculture at 4%. The main Polish export goods are average and low-processed industrial articles, such as chemicals and mineral materials (copper, pit-coal), and agricultural products. Poland exports highly processed goods to its developing Eastern European neighbours and mostly low-processed products and raw materials to markets of well-developed countries. Recently, the level of processing and the technological advancement of the exports to markets of the Western countries have grown. Similarly, types of goods imported by Poland depend on the same geographical criteria. The import of raw materials from Russia and Ukraine predominates, mainly energetic ones, such as petroleum and earth gas or iron ore. Highly processed products with large technical advancement are imported from the Western Europe countries. Poland is a member of the European Union (EU, since 2004), the North Atlantic Treaty Organization (NATO, since 1999), the West European Union, the Organization for Economic Cooperation and Development (OECD), the Council of Europe, and other organizations. It is a long-standing member of the United Nations (UN).

The political-economic situation of Poland has been heavily influenced by geopolitical issues, primarily its position in the central part of the Europe between Russia and Germany. Poland became its own region in the tenth century as a result of the connection of Slavic tribes between the Oder, the Vistula, and the San (the largest Polish rivers). The first historical ruler of Poland, Mieszko (Dagobert), converted to Christianity in 966 AD. The first "modernization" of Poland was initiated by Kazimierz (the Great) in the 1300s. He improved the Polish defense system, reformed the country's economy and money turnover, and ensured solid treasury incomes. Moreover, he introduced the uniform legislation and the transparent

political system. In addition, he founded the University in Cracow in 1364.

Under Jadwiga Andegaweńskiej, the female ruler of Poland who in 1386 married the ruler of Lithuania, Jagiello Wladyslaw, to form a union with Lithuania, a parliamentary democracy (albeit limited to the noble classes) was founded. The Polish Seym (the lower chamber) and the Senate (the upper chamber) created legal binding solutions for the King who, together with his own ministers (foreign affairs, the chancellor) and internal administration (the marshal, the treasurer), performed the executive power. Following the last ruler of the Jagiellonian dynasty, the Polish Congress also chose the king.

Traditionally, the Polish army was professional. However, in the beginning of the eighteenth century, this approach was replaced by the "levy of mass," meaning every gentleman had a duty of defense. Twenty-first century Poland retains a period of mandatory military service for all males at the age of eighteen.

In 1772, Russia, Austria, and Prussia took under occupation parts of Polish grounds (about 30% of Polish territory). In 1791, the new Polish Constitution was announced. This caused immediate Russian military intervention and, in consequence, further territorial changes. About half of the territories were occupied by Russia and Prussia. The national uprising led by General Tadeusz Kosciuszko also ended with defeat, and in 1795, Poland ceased to exist.

During the Napoleonic period, Poland appeared again on a European map (1807). After the fall of Napoleon and the Viennese Congress in 1815, Poland became dynastically joint with Russia. However, unlike Russia, its political system was the constitutional monarchy with a liberal character. In 1831, after a period of significant economic development, Poland was released from Russia. Uprisings in 1830–1831 and 1863–1864 began encroachments on Poland's independence, and the Polish state was reabsorbed by Russia in 1865.

Large firms and banks were established in Poland, and soon, they were able to operate at a very strong position on Russian markets. In the part of Poland under German administration, local societies tried to defend against "Germanization" pressure. The self-organization of Polish communities grew up as a reply of German actions; similar events took place in the Austrian-controlled areas. That process took place with the strong cooperative movement and founding of the first Polish cooperative banks. In 1866, Polish representatives took official seats in the Viennese Parliament.

The Austrian part of Poland was one of the most neglected economically (comparably only with the Russian part). Situations improved after the

development of the petroleum industry. At the end of nineteenth century, this part of Poland provided circa 10% of world oil production.

Poland regained its independence in 1918 and was accepted by the United States, France, and England. After the Polish army's victory in 1920 over the Red Army, a truce with Russia was established until 1939. Though Poland suffered great destruction during World War I, the interwar years were a period of standardizing and modernization; women were given suffrage and a number of modern social policies were introduced. In 1939, Poland was one of the most developed countries in the world with a stable and modern legal system, a stable financial system and a stable currency, and a large industrial sector, including then-modern aircrafts and an electronic industry.

The political situation, however, was less stable. There was a great deal of fragmentation of political parties, leading to a military revolution in 1926. Until 1939, the military played a large role in the Polish government.

The international situation was also unstable. Germany was encroaching on the western border. On the other hand, Soviet Russia did not acknowledge Poland as a stable state. In addition, Poland had border conflicts with Czechoslovakia and Lithuania. In September 1939, World War II exploded.

The Polish nation went to war both abroad and within the country against Germany and Russian hegemony and suffered persecution and terror both on the part of Russia and Germany. On the Polish territory in Nazi death camps, Germans perpetrated the Holocaust of the European Jewish population.

In Poland grew an armed resistance movement with approximately four hundred thousand members. On both European fronts more than five hundred thousand soldiers fought (not to count members of the resistance movement) on the side of the Allies. After the war, the agreement of the Western Powers and counterfeit elections (1947) began a Polish period of forty-five years under a Communist regime and dependence on Russia. The economic system was an essential modification of the Soviet system. Many legal solutions, characteristic of free market economies, were kept; these included stock companies law, drafts, promissory notes, and Bills of Lading (documents used in the transportation industry). Unfortunately, they were seldom used. Private property existed in agriculture (where it predominated) and in microindustry or crafts. Many cooperatives operated. Metallurgical and machine industry as well as mining predominated. The inventory of consumptive goods was quite weakly developed. The technological gap, little diversity of enterprises, and cost of foreign debt had driven the economy to fall in 1980s.

The Communist regime was not popular, and social protests exploded in 1956, 1968, 1970, 1976, and 1980. However, the Communist period did bring many social changes. Basic education for all eight years of primary school was made obligatory. This caused the practical elimination of illiteracy. Unfortunately, until 1989, only 10% to 15% of the young population attended secondary school, and in consequence, only about half of them went onto higher education. The political and economic systems gave a minimal amount of encouragement to continue education on an average or higher level.

In the Communist period, previously existing social structures were violated by the higher material position of members of the Communist Party. Simultaneously, with a bad economic situation, violations were also caused by social anxieties.

In 1980, worker strikes brought the beginning of the organized social movement Solidarity. The short carnival of freedom ended with the martial law in December 1981. However, a falling economic position, a high external debt, and the lack of the support of the society for Communist authorities forced Poland into negotiations with the opposition. On the basis of negotiations in 1989, partly free and democratic Parliamentary elections took place. The break-up of the Soviet Union (1991) accelerated the process of the democratization, and the next elections (1991) were fully democratic. In 1990 began the difficult Balcerowicz-Sachs Plan of economic reforms. These led to privatization of the economy and to quick economic development in the second half of 1990s. In 1999, Poland joined NATO, and the country joined the European Union in 2004.

WALDEMAR KOZIOL

See also Central and Eastern Europe: History and Economic Development; Central and Eastern Europe: International Relations; Ethnic Conflicts: Central and Eastern Europe; Jaruzelski, Wojciech; Solidarity Union; Walesa, Lech

References and Further Reading

Biskupski, Mieczysław B. *The History of Poland.* Westport, CT: Greenwood Press, 2000.
Davies N. *God's Playground. A History of Poland.* Vol. I. New York: Columbia University Press, 1982.
———. *God's Playground. A History of Poland.* Vol. II. Oxford: Oxford University Press, 1981.
Jędruch J. *Constitutions, Elections and Legislatures of Poland 1493–1977.* Washington, DC: University Press of America, 1982.
Johnson, Simon. *Starting Over in Eastern Europe: Entrepreneurship and Economic Renewal.* Boston: Harvard Business School Press, 1995.

Kenney, Padraic. *Rebuilding Poland: Workers and Communists, 1945–1950*. Ithaca, NY: Cornell University Press, 1997.

Kirby D. *The Baltic World 1772–1993, Europe's Northern Periphery in an Age of Change*. London: Longman, 1995.

Lukowski J., and H. Zawadzki. *A Concise History of Poland*. Cambridge: Cambridge University Press, 2001.

Michta, Andrew A. *America's New Allies: Poland, Hungary, and the Czech Republic in NATO*. Seattle: University of Washington Press, 1999.

———. *The Red Eagle: The Army in Polish Politics, 1944–1988*. Stanford, CA: Hoover Institution Press, 1990.

Rachwald, Arthur R. *In Search of Poland: The Superpowers' Response to Solidarity, 1980–1989*. Stanford, CA: Hoover Institution Press, 1990.

POLITICAL CULTURE

The Term Political Culture

The term "Political Culture" is particularly used in political science but is also employed in the analysis of problems in sociology, psychology, history, philosophy, anthropology, and other such subjects. This term appears in academic writing in the 18th century. However, scientific research into political culture truly flourished after World War II.

Some authors define it as basic *characteristic of a nation's character*. Others define it as a specific *trait of individual political behavior*. Still others emphasize on its *moral aspect* and so on. Regardless of the diversity of opinions, the idea that political culture is people's *way of political life* and at the same time it is a *product of their political behavior* is a prevailing opinion. It represents a complexity of *beliefs, values, habits, and behavior regarding political matters* existing in society.

Political culture may be classified in accordance with a variety of indicators. So, for instance, some authors define two types of political culture—integrated culture, which builds upon trust and consensus among members of society, and fragmented culture, which is defined by a lack of agreement and trust among the stakeholders in the political process. According to one of the most popular political classifications, political culture falls into three categories: (i) patriarchal or local political culture, manifestly centered on specific local values, local patriotism, and familial loyalty; (ii) the political culture of the subjects, characterized by respect and recognition of political institutions but in combination with a passive attitude to political change; (iii) participative political culture typified by the proactive behaviour of the populace in political life and a high level of political awareness.

Most authors share the opinion that there are subcultures within the frames of the political culture. Thus, they distinguish between two types of political culture. The first type is called "General Political Culture," and is related to the beliefs, values, habits, and political behavior of the prevailing entity of people. The other type is "Elite Political Culture," and is related to the political behavior, beliefs, and values of the authorities and of influential individuals and groups.

Each country is characterized with its typical (national) political culture, and in this sense, in scientific literature one can talk about American political culture, British political culture, Japanese political culture, French political culture, and others. Some authors tend to differentiate the political cultures even by geographical and other features.

Changes of Political Culture

Culture is dynamic and constantly changing due to a couple of factors. The **first source** of change is related to *the level of general economic development*: the advanced economy of a given country sets up the economic conditions necessary for the development of common culture and political culture in particular. The **second factor** for cultural change is related to *the technical progress and the development of new technologies*. The **third source** of the change must be looked for in *the nature of culture itself*: just like authors of genius whose work can accelerate the development of culture, the appearance of great political leaders can bring forward political culture in much the same way. The constant collision and *conflicts* between the different social groups and countries represent the **fourth factor** for the changes in the political culture in a given society. A **fifth factor** can be pointed out: the "pressure from the outside" due to different types of *pressure* from outside forces; a given country can change its political structures, which can lead to a change of the existing political culture. Usually, the change in the master cultural model is an evolutionary process, but it can be accomplished through revolution. With regard to this, revolution can be classified as the **sixth factor** for the change in political culture.

The process of changing the old political culture with a new one in Eastern Europe during 1989 was done in different manners due to the different factors that existed. First, each country had its typical cultural model, which included its specific national psychology, traditions, mentality, and other such factors. Second, each Eastern European country had reached its own level of economic development. Third, some of those countries had tried to change their political

situation in the past (The Hungarian revolution of 1956, The Prague Spring in Czechoslovakia of 1968, and other such revolutions). Fourth, in some Eastern European countries, some political structures had already started trying to change the existing political system (the nonformal movements of the "Greens" and "Solidarnost" in Poland). Fifth, in some Eastern European countries, dissident leaders (such as L. Valensa, V. Havel) appeared on the political scene. Sixth, the Eastern European countries had different historical commitments with the former USSR. These and some other reasons have helped make the change in the cultural model and encourage the development of the political culture to take on different paths in the different countries. For example, in some countries, the process was accompanied with a modification of their government model: the previously existing USSR, Czechoslovakia, and Yugoslavia fell apart and new states were formed instead. The German Democratic Republic (GDR) and the Federal Republic of Germany (FRG) united into one state. In some countries, the change of the old political culture with a new one was accompanied with wars and ethnic conflicts, while in others it took place in a peaceful manner.

Similarities and Differences in Political Cultures of Developing Countries

There are similarities as well as differences in the political cultures of the developing countries. The similarities between the countries are as follows. First, there is a common tendency for change of both the political culture of the masses and the political culture of the elite. Second, the political culture of the ruling elite changes more intensively than the general political culture. Third, at the beginning of the twenty-first century, the so-called "image of the enemy" present in the political cultures of the developing countries have changed. After the terrorist acts in New York on September 11, 2001, the political culture in the developing countries is forming a uniform image, and this is the image of terrorism.

Along with these common tendencies in the political culture of each developing country, there are specifics that differentiate each country's culture from the others. For example, due to the specific characteristics of their historical development, the political cultures of most countries from Latin America are characterized with the so-called *paternalism*. *Authoritarianism* is another characteristic of the political culture of the developing world. "*Machoism*" is a valid characteristic for the political culture in most Latin American countries. It is related to the idea that the political leader has to be a man ("*macho*"), who has to be distinguished, strong, and handsome, and women should like him. A significant characteristic of the political cultures of the developing countries is the *tolerance of corruption*. Corruption among the political elite in the Latin American countries is taken for granted. This is due to the fact that during the Spanish colonization of South America, the administrative positions in the newly formed Latin American countries were not earned, but bought by the rich representatives of the Spanish upper class. In that sense, the common people have seen the position of a high government official as an investment, from which dividends will be gained in the future. Such mechanism is the basis for understanding corruption as something natural for the political elite.

Peculiarities of Political Culture in Asian and African Countries

The political cultures of Asian countries are dominated, in varying degrees, by the great civilizations of China and India, which explains some similarities therein. Individual regions on the continent have been directly influenced by the cultural traditions of Confucianism, Islam, and Buddhism, creating a complex miscellany of political cultures. So for example, Confucian cultural tradition dominates in China, Japan, South Korea, Vietnam, Singapore, and Taiwan; Islamic cultural tradition dominates in Indonesia, Malaysia, and Brunei; and Buddhist cultural tradition dominates in Thailand and Cambodia. In the Philippines and Burma, there is a mixture of all these traditional influences.

By and large, Asia is far too diverse economically, socially, and politically, which determines the diversity of political cultures in the different countries. Although there are differences in the political cultures among countries on other continents, these differences are particularly striking in Asia. For instance, Asia is home to four of the world's five remaining Communist countries: China, North Korea, Vietnam, and Laos. Whilst there has been an encouraging rise of democracy at the end of twentieth century in South Korea, Taiwan, Thailand, and the Philippines; authoritarian regimes are firmly in power in Pakistan and Burma; and the governments in Malaysia and Singapore practice forms of "soft authoritarianism." The Asian version of a political culture is distinguished by the dominance of local tradition. India

may serve as a case in point, having inherited a sufficiently advanced political system, parliamentary institutions, and much else from Great Britain's colonial rule. Nevertheless, the political behaviour of voters in this country is determined by the opinions of chieftains in the villages, heads of the clan aristocracy, and by religious leaders and others rather than by the election platforms of the relevant political parties.

One of the salient features of the region is the change in political culture. With the exception of North Korea, where Communist ideology has remained firmly embedded for decades, all other Asian countries exhibit a trend favoring change in political culture in the positive direction. Major political reform has taken place in the 1980s and 1990s in various countries; some has been carried out in the Philippines, there were constitutional changes in Thailand in the late 1990s, and there was the introduction of political pluralism in Mongolia in the 1990s.

Political culture in African countries is similarly multifaceted. Typically, it is defined by the dominance of a variety of symbols, beliefs, images, and ideologies, some clearly traditional and others European in origin. Pride of place is allotted to the following factors: partiality for the values of the traditional community—the family, the commune, the tribe, and the clan; mythology-based vision, combined with the view that man is intricately linked to animals and plants; the immense polyethnicity of societies; dependence on traditional values; and Afrocentricity associated with attaching superior value to African culture. Three countries, Nigeria, Ethiopia, and the Republic of South Africa (RSA), are representative of this region and may serve as illustrations of the state-of-affairs and developmental trends in political culture in Africa.

The political culture of twenty-first century Nigeria is characterized by a peculiar blend of traditional/ collective and modern individualist precepts. This is a political culture that reflects the political behaviour of a population of 110 million, consisting of more than two hundred ethnic groups. Although lack of economic growth, underdevelopment, and illiteracy prevail among the population, the country is experiencing a positive tendency in political culture development. In the late twentieth century, Nigeria saw a resurgence in the election process: elections were held for the position of Governor, for Parliament, and for President.

The ethnic factor plays an important role in Ethiopia, and all attempts to accomplish some political reform lead to the emergence of a distinctive "ethnic democracy" that is totally dependent on the interests of the relevant ethnic group. Until 1991, the country was dominated by an artificial political culture model imposed by the extant communist regime. Following

that year, however, and in the aftermath of the regime's ousting a distinctive "ethnic democracy," a "broad ethnic federalism" was enforced, supported by political forces with a conspicuously regional practicability.

RSA is a typical example of the fundamental change in political culture. Following the decades-long struggle to abolish apartheid, elections were held in that country in 1994. For the first time ever, the representatives of all races and ethnic communities participated on an equal footing. These elections were won with a sweeping majority by the African National Congress (ANC)—the party that represents the broad popular masses. For the first time in its history, the country democratically elected its president: President Nelson Mandela had spent twenty-seven years in prison for participating in the liberation struggle. At the subsequent elections in 1999, the election victory of the ANC was even more pronounced, opening the gate for positive socioeconomic reform that fundamentally changed political culture in that country.

KRUM KRUMOV

See also Andean South America: History and Economic Development; Central and Eastern Europe: History and Economic Development; Central America: History and Economic Development; East Africa: History and Economic Development; East Asia: History and Economic Development; North Africa: History and Economic Development; Northern South America: History and Economic Development; Southeast Asia: History and Economic Development; Southern Africa: History and Economic Development; Southern Cone (Latin America): History and Economic Development; West Africa: History and Economic Development

References and Further Reading

Abramson P. R., and R. Inglehart. *Value Change in Global Perspective.* Ann Arbor, MI: University of Michigan Press, 1995.
Almond G., and S. Verba. *The Civic Culture. Political Attitudes and Democracy in Five Nations.* Princeton, NJ, 1963.
Diamond, L. *Political Culture & Democracy in Developing Countries.* Boulder, CO: Lynne Rienner Publishers, 1994.
Fitzgibbon, R. H., and J. A. Fernando. *Latin America: Political culture and Development.* Englewood Cliffs, NJ: Prentice-Hall, 1981.
Greenstein, F. I., and N. W. Polsby, eds. *Handbook of Political Science.* Reading, MA: Addison-Wesley, 1975.
Lane, R. "Political Culture: Residual Category or General Theory." *Comparative Political Studies* 5, 1992: 362–387.
Pye, L. W., and S. Verba, eds. *Political Culture and Political Development.* Princeton, NJ: Princeton University Press, 1965.

Rosenbaum, W. *Political Culture: Basic Concepts in Political Science.* New York, 1975.

Wilson, R. W. *Compliance Ideologies: Rethinking Political Culture.* New York: Cambridge University Press, 1993.

POLLUTION, AGRICULTURAL

Types of Agricultural Pollution

Agricultural activities are strongly connected with the environment. Throughout the history of humankind these activities have resulted in changes in the environment, although until the twentieth century, there were few cases of negative effects on nature and wildlife caused by agricultural activities. Farms were small, and agriculture was based on natural processes. Livestock farming and soil cultivation were integrated in a single farm, which supported stability and sustainability in farming activities.

Heavily industrialized agriculture appeared after the Second World War when new applications of science and technology were introduced in agricultural activities. This has resulted in the mechanization of farms, which became larger, fewer in number, and reliant on the use of chemicals and inorganic fertilizers. Farms started to be more specialized either in crops or livestock. As a result, crop residues and animal manure that were natural fertilizers in the past have brought new problems of waste disposal to agricultural activities (Conway and Pretty 1991).

The intensification of agriculture was accompanied by an increase in environmental pollution. This is true both for point and nonpoint source or diffuse source pollution. According to the definition of the United Nations Environmental Program (UNEP), point source pollution is "any pollution from a confined and discrete conveyance" (UNEP 1996). Examples of point source pollution could be the leakage of chemicals from containers, banana washing activities, and waste from sugar processing factories.

The same source also defines nonpoint source (or diffuse) pollution as that which "emanates from unconfined sources, including agricultural runoff, drainage or seepage, and atmospheric deposition" (UNEP 1996). This kind of pollution could be the result of the use of pesticides and fertilizers, of soil erosion due to intensive cultivation practices and livestock production, or of the inappropriate disposal of waste from agricultural activities. The introduction of Genetically Modified Organisms (GMOs) may also cause pollution if their possible crossbreeding with natural varieties is considered.

The main environmental problems caused by agricultural activities reviewed in this article are the following:

- Water pollution
- Air pollution
- Soil degradation
- Loss of biodiversity and degradation of natural habitats
- Impact on human health

Although environmental pollution from agriculture is a global problem, its effects in the developing world are even worse. The lack of appropriate regulations and control over the listed environmental issues, the absence of knowledge and information about the proper use and disposal of pesticides and fertilizers that are being introduced to the agricultural lands, and finally the improper management of both agricultural and nonagricultural lands have resulted in the presence of significant agricultural pollution in the environment. Thus, the joint statement of the World Health Organization (WHO) and the Food and Agriculture Organization (FAO) of the United Nations (UN) says that the "amount of poor quality pesticides sold in developing countries is alarmingly high" (WHO/FAO 2001). According to the same statement, around 30% of pesticides marketed in developing countries do not meet internationally accepted quality standards. This percentage is counted without taking into account the quality of labeling and packaging, which are often the only source of product information for consumers and the only guarantee of the safe and proper use of chemicals in the field.

Agricultural production, and especially the export of so-called "cash crops," is the key component of economies in many developing countries. As a result, large quantities of fertilizers and pesticides are being introduced to secure the expected yield of such crops as sugar cane, coffee, cocoa, pineapple, oil palm, rice, cotton, bananas, and many other economically important crops. Moreover, in almost all countries of the developing world, agricultural pollution takes place also because of inadequate education and ignorance of potential hazards. Farmers in these countries identify pesticides and synthetic fertilizers with modern agriculture. For example, in the Philippines, the frequent application of synthetic pesticides by rice farmers was believed to guarantee higher yield (Conway and Pretty 1991).

There are several internationally approved conventions, treaties, and protocols relating to the reduction of the pressure from agricultural and related activities to the environment; these include the Stockholm Convention on Persistent Organic Pollutants, the

Rotterdam Convention on the Prior Informed Consent Procedure for Certain Hazardous Chemicals and Pesticides in International Trade, and the Cartagena Protocol on Biosafety to the Convention on Biological Diversity. Despite international attention to the issues of agricultural pollution, projections suggest that due to the increase of food demand and, consequently, the further intensification of agricultural activities, the pressure on the environment will continue to increase in developing countries. For example, by 2030, emissions of ammonia and methane from the livestock sector of developing countries could be at least 60% higher than at present (FAO 2002).

Water Pollution

Agricultural water pollution mainly arises from the introduction of nutrients in the form of fertilizers and farm wastes, containing both nitrate and phosphate, that enter waters and cause changes to the ecology by enrichment known as "eutrophication." The main sources of phosphorus are raw sewage from livestock and fish farms and from arable lands. These discharges also include nitrogen. Nitrogen is mostly introduced to water bodies from cultivated lands through fertilization activities and soil disturbance. It may also come from the atmosphere if biomass burning took place (Moss 1998).

Although the eutrophication of surface waters can be the result of various natural and anthropogenic activities, agriculture remains one of the key contributors to this kind of water pollution. Eutrophication can lead to algal blooms, some of which may even be toxic, when they cover the surface of the water. After the blooms' death, the bacteria that decompose them require so much oxygen from the water that the conditions created are anaerobic, causing organisms that cannot tolerate the environment to die. Eutrophication of surface waters due to inputs from agricultural activities is not so well documented in the developing world as it is in developed countries, but it is a serious environmental problem in many tropical and subtropical rivers and lakes, where the load of nutrients is accompanied by favorable weather conditions. Eutrophication may also occur on a smaller scale when paddy fields are flooded (Conway and Pretty 1991).

Agriculture is the largest user of freshwater resources. It uses around 70% of all surface water supplies (Ongley 1996). This issue becomes even more significant for developing countries when considering the shortage in fresh water resources and the fact that most irrigated lands are situated near those

areas. Since the increase in world population is taking place mostly in developing countries and there is a need to produce more food, more and more land is being used for agricultural activities with a consequent increase in irrigational projects and fertilization. The irrigation water is returned to the water bodies, is heavily eutrophicated, and there are also significant losses in evaporation. The shortage in freshwater supply has already caused many serious conflict situations not only at community level but also between nations. For example, Israel and its Arab neighbors have had disputes over the Jordan; Ethiopia, Sudan, and Egypt have struggled over the Nile; and Turkey, Syria, and Iraq have argued over the headwaters of the Tigris and the Euphrates (Moss 1998).

Agricultural water pollution also results from the introduction of pesticides to waters from leaching, runoff, or direct introduction to the water bodies and from soil losses that may carry pesticides and fertilizers absorbed in soil particles. In general, the application of pesticides in large quantities can directly or indirectly pollute water resources, affecting water quality. Pesticides may be carried to surface waters through spreading, settling, and rainfall, causing pollution (Li 1991). Water pollution from pesticides in developing countries varies from region to region. While in large parts of Africa there is almost no water pollution from pesticides, in some intensive agricultural areas in Brazil and Central America, extremely heavy contamination is taking place (Ongley 1996). Groundwater is being polluted also by nitrates and heavy metals from fertilizer use and direct discharges of wastes from intensive livestock units. The issue of groundwater pollution is of great importance in many developing countries where groundwater is the major source of drinking water.

Air Pollution

Air pollution largely arises from suspended particles of pesticide from spraying or dusting of crops and vegetables as well as from insect vectors of medical importance. Pollution also comes from the vaporization of pesticides from crops in soil and water (Richardson 1991).

Another source of air pollution is intensive livestock production. Some gases such as carbon dioxide, methane, ozone, nitrous oxide, and other trace gases produced by livestock waste serve as a basis for the formation of greenhouse gases and contribute to global climate change. Although the concentration of intensive livestock units is not widespread in developing countries, there is a trend for their number to

increase. For example, in some South American countries, industrial-scale chicken farms are becoming more and more common, with a corresponding increase in the negative impact on the environment (Sustainable Agri-Food Production and Consumption Forum 2002).

Some of the polluting gases are also being generated by other intensive agricultural practices. For example, rice paddies are one of the key contributors of methane emissions to the atmosphere. The introduction of nitrogen fertilizers or the conversion of forests to agricultural land may cause an immediate increase in atmospheric emissions of nitrous oxide. However, the major source of air pollution from agricultural activities is biomass burning (Convay and Pretty 1991).

Biomass burning is in common use in almost all the developing world to clear land for cultivation, to convert nonagricultural land into land suitable for cultivation, or increase productivity of lands by removing other plants. It is probably the quickest and most economic way of dealing with the disposal problem. These activities are widespread especially on the African continent, in the Amazon basin, and in Southeast Asia. The result of biomass burning is the release of aerosols that are an important source of trace gases and atmospheric particulate matter that have a negative impact on air quality and human health (Seong *et al.* 2004). Practices of burning farm wastes in developing countries are most common in sugar cane and pineapple plantations although as already mentioned, burning rice straw is also a big problem in the lowland regions of Asia (Convay and Pretty 1991).

Thus, agricultural activities are the major source of air pollution. Paddy fields, livestock wastes, and biomass burning together produce gases that affect atmospheric processes, causing a direct negative impact on human health and the environment as well as contributing to global climate change.

Soil Degradation

Although soil erosion is a natural process driven by the displacement of soil particles through rainfall, flowing water, or wind, agricultural activities increase the rate of erosion by irrigation, improper use of land for cultivation or grazing, and by deforestation (UNEP 1998). The reasons for soil degradation and their significance vary from country to country. Summarizing these reasons by continent reveals that soil degradation in Africa results from overgrazing, water, and wind-borne erosion; in Asia and South America,

degradation is caused mostly by deforestation, combined with water and wind-borne erosion (in Asia) and chemical deterioration (mainly in South America) (Varallyay 2004). Soil pollution due to pesticides results mainly from the application of pesticides to control pests and weeds, which in turn leads to direct soil pollution. Pesticides that are not lost by volatilization or in runoff enter the soil. This kind of pollution is associated with intensive agricultural activities; therefore, its contribution is significant in intensively cultivated areas of Asia, South America, and Africa.

Irrigation projects are commonly used in arid and semiarid regions of the developing world to increase food production. For all its benefits, irrigated agriculture also has a negative impact on the environment due to the development of soil salinity and accumulation of salts in soils and shallow groundwater. An example of such degradation could be the Aral Sea disaster in Central Asia. The Aral Sea basin includes Southern Russia, Uzbekistan, and Tajikistan and partly Kazakhstan, Kyrgyzstan, Turkmenistan, Afghanistan, and Iran. Almost all cultivated lands in those areas are irrigated. The increase in irrigation areas and water withdrawals due to extensive monoculture and the increase in the use of pesticides and fertilizers have led to degradation of land that was productive before the introduction of intensive agricultural activities. Although there are many other impacts on water quality, the main cause of the Aral Sea disaster was poor management and planning of agricultural activities in the region (Ongley 1996).

Loss of Biodiversity and Degradation of Natural Habitats

The use of pesticides is essential for maintaining food supplies. But the concern is that they affect not only targets, such as insects, fungi, bacteria, weed, or other unwanted organisms, but they also kill nontarget organisms that are similar to the target pest organisms, thus contributing to the degradation of natural habitats and loss of biodiversity. Moreover, after this immediate effect, pesticides remain in the environment and continue to degrade for a long time, as very few pesticides break down into nonharmful constituents after being introduced to the field. This is especially true in the case of Persistent Organic Pollutants (POPs), such as dichlorodiphenyltrichloroethane (DDT) and chlordane. These are chemicals that are "extremely toxic, resistant to degradation, characterized by their ability of bioaccumulation, and can be transported through air, water, migratory

species and accumulated in terrestrial and aquatic ecosystems" (Stockholm Convention 2001).

This kind of contamination often includes the entire food chain. In many developing countries, the pesticides that are banned by international regulations are being introduced for agricultural purposes but more often for securing human health from epidemics such as malaria and other vector-borne diseases. These chemicals affect not only organisms and food chains but also directly damage the habitats and resources on which other organisms rely. For example, in Malaysia, rats treated with rodenticides have caused owl deaths; in Surinam, spraying pesticides on an intensive rice-growing region near the coast caused extensive bird and fish deaths (Conway and Pretty 1991).

Due to lack of knowledge and appropriate information in developing countries, some pesticide users do not apply pesticides according to manufacturers' instructions. Incorrect dosages could result in increasing resistance in the target organisms, destruction of nontarget organisms, contamination of soil, and accumulation in other species that provide an opportunity for movements of hazardous residues through the food chain, thus having a negative impact on wildlife in general.

Fertilizers are believed to be less dangerous for wildlife than pesticides. Although fertilizers have no direct toxic impact on wildlife, they can also damage natural habitats, and especially plants, by causing excessive growth. The most serious problem is associated with eutrophication, as described previously. The increase in phytoplankton crops results in the development of anaerobic conditions in water bodies with an increase in sulphide concentrations. These kinds of waters are not suitable for some fish groups, such as salmonids. By contrast, the fish groups tolerant of lower oxygen concentrations may increase in number as other groups disappear. This unbalance may be further developed by intensive algal growth that may cause changes in marginal aquatic plant beds and, therefore, result in loss of structure in the ecosystem. These changes can result in a decline of fish-eating and plant-eating bird populations, leading to the degradation of the entire habitat (Moss 1998). Another source of water pollution that affects biodiversity is the use of antibiotics or hormones in intensive livestock units, which causes the emergence of drug-resistant strains of bacteria and, in some cases, also anomalies in water fauna.

Conversion of wetlands into cultivated lands, deforestation, introduction of pesticides and fertilizers, inappropriate disposal of farm wastes, and inadequate soil management techniques are serious threats to biodiversity and natural habitats. It can be concluded that intensification of agriculture causes losses in many species and entire habitats through fragmentation and reduction as well as through the decline in plant species populations. Loss of forests takes place notably in the Amazon Rain Forest in South America; the forests of Columbia (one of the richest countries in biodiversity); the Gir Forest in India; and the forests of the Philippines, Ethiopia, Costa Rica, Madagascar, and many other places in the developing world. These areas are marked by poverty and inadequate management in natural resources, resulting in a loss of biodiversity and degradation of natural habitats (Tuba et al. 2004).

Impact on Human Health

Modern agricultural activities have a direct impact on human health. The biggest health problems in developing countries are caused by pesticides, both occupationally and through food and polluted drinking water. Although water pollution can arise from different sources, agriculture remains one of its main contributors due to the introduction of pesticides, fertilizers, and farm wastes. Moreover, many pesticides that are banned internationally or severely restricted in developed countries are freely available in many developing countries, causing serious health problems. Some developed countries continue to produce them not for internal use but for export to developing countries (Gore 2000).

In many developing countries, a major hazard to human health comes also from locally marketed food. Pesticide poisoning is more common than in developed countries because of ignorance, inappropriate control, poverty, and poor living conditions (Conway and Pretty 1991).

Although fertilizers are not designed to kill organisms and are not directly toxic to the environment and humans, they can serve as components for chemical reactions that cause significant pollution. If fertilizers are properly applied and absorbed by target crops, there may be no contamination. But farmers usually apply more than the optimum quantity to secure their yield and maximize the profit (Conway and Pretty 1991). The contamination arises from redundant use of fertilizers, taking place mainly due to rainfall or irrigation. Both avenues of pollution are very typical of developing countries because most irrigated lands are situated there and rainfalls are crucial in tropical regions. Fertilizers can leach to surface waters, causing eutrophication, and to groundwater, contributing to the contamination of drinking waters in many developing countries.

The increase in the use of inorganic nitrogen fertilizers is the major source of rising nitrate levels in many water supply sources. There is a risk that nitrates may cause methemoglobinemia in infants and even some forms of human cancer through the formation of N-nitroso compounds (Conway and Pretty 1991).

The other threat to human health comes from improper disposal of farm wastes. Runoff from livestock production may lead not only to the water problems described earlier but could also transmit animal diseases to humans. A number of pathogenic bacteria that cause many dangerous diseases can be found in untreated wastewater (UNEP 1998).

There are also many serious accidents during pesticide and chemical fertilizer production, distribution, and disposal activities that affect human health and the environment. One of the catastrophic examples is the gas leak from a pesticide plant in Bhopal, India, in 1984. Around half a million people were exposed to toxic chemicals during the accident. More than seven thousand people died within days and another fifteen thousand died in the following years (Amnesty International 2004).

ARMAN MANUKYAN

See also Biodiversity Conservation; Environment: Government Policies; Environmentalism; Pollution, Industrial; Waste Management

References and Further Reading

Convay, Gordon R., and Jules N. Pretty. *Unwelcome Harvest: Agriculture and Pollution*. London: Earthscan Publications, 1991.

FAO. *World agriculture: Towards 2015/2030*. Summary Report. Rome: Food and Agriculture Organization of the United Nations, 2002.

FAO/WHO. 2001. "FAO/WHO: Amount of Poor-Quality Pesticides sold in Developing countries Alarmingly High." Press Release. http://www.who.int/inf-pr-2001/en/pr2001-04.html.

Gore, Al. Introduction to *Silent Spring* by Rachel Carson. New York: Houghton Mifflin Company, 1994.

Lang, Marton Jolankai, and Tamas Komives, eds. Budapest: Akaprint Publishers, 2004.

Li, S. "Pesticides, Environmental Pollution and Human Health in China." *Chemistry, Agriculture and the Environment*, Mervyn L. Richardson, ed. Cambridge: Royal Society of Chemistry, 1991.

Moss, Brian. *Ecology of Fresh Waters: Man and Medium, Past and Future*. Oxford: Blackwell Science, 1998.

Ongley, Edwin, D. *Control of Water Pollution from Agriculture—FAO Irrigation and Drainage Paper 55*. Rome: Food and Agriculture Organization of the United Nations, 1996.

Seong, Ryu Y., Kim E. Jeong, H. Zhuanshi, Kim J. Young, and Kang U. Gong. "Chemical Composition of Post Harvest Biomass Burning Aerosols in Gwangju, Korea." *Air and Waste Management Association* 54 (2004): 1124–1137.

Stockholm Convention on Persistent Organic Pollutants. 2000. http://www.pops.int/documents/convtext/convtext_en.pdf.

Sustainable Agri-Food Production and Consumption Forum, 2002. "Good Practices, Sectors: Livestock Farms." http://www.agrifood-forum.net/practices/sector/livestock/22pollution.asp.

Tuba, Zoltan, Gabor Bakonyi, and Mahesh Kumar Singh. "Impacts on Biodiversity." *Pollution Processes in Agri-Environment: A New Approach*, Istvan Lang, Marton Jolankai, and Tamas Komives, eds. Budapest: Akaprint Publishers, 2004.

UNEP. *Guidelines for Integrated Planning and Management of Coastal and Marine Areas in the Wider Caribbean*. Kingston: United Nations Environment Programme, Caribbean Environment Programme, 1996. Cited in UNEP, 1998.

———. 1998. *Best Management Practices from Agricultural Non-Point Sources of Pollution*. Caribbean Environment Programme Technical Report #41. http://www.cep.unep.org/pubs/Techreports/tr41en.

Varallyay, Gyorgy. "Degradation Processes of Soils—A Global Overview." *Pollution Processes in Agri-Environment: A New Approach*, Istvan.

POLLUTION, INDUSTRIAL

Introduction

Since the beginning of time, humankind has transformed raw materials and produced all kinds of useful goods and tools. The massive production of weapons to equip the primitive armies, the manufacturing of clothes or uniforms, and even the manipulation of minerals to produce jewelry or bullets are all different and ancient ways of the industry. The early stages of industry began during the Stone Age, and followed during the Copper Age (6000 BC) and Bronze Age (2500 BC), when technology was still very elementary. Industrial activities were rudimentary, relatively small scale, and handmade. First, the wheel was invented, and then many industrial fittings were invented that helped humans to make products, such as clothes or weapons, on a larger scale.

It was not until the Industrial Revolution during the eighteenth century that the manufacturing sector went through a major quality change. This revolution turned upside down most of the traditional ways in which people produced most goods. It introduced the assistance of machines powered by coal and the extended division of labour as Adam Smith described it. These new methods of production revolutionized the prices of products, changed the scales of production, increased productivity enormously, enhanced largely the benefits of capitalists, and changed the landscapes of towns and turned them into cities.

But one of the most important changes was the appearance of *industrial pollution*. The massive industrial processes carried out in factories create large amounts of waste that contaminate the resources of the environment in different measures. If not properly treated, these wastes can contaminate all of biosphere's elements: water, air, and soil, sometimes in an irreversible way.

The twentieth century has been one of the most environmentally conflictive centuries due to the boom of the industrial sector. During and after World War II, industrialization took place around the world on a larger scale than ever before. Large factories following Henry Ford's assembly-line model were built to supply the increasing demand, mainly in the Western developed countries but also in the developing ones.

As a consequence, during this period, the industrial pollution reached new levels. It remains a severe issue today. For instance, air pollution is one of the most crucial topics in the international agenda. The release of industrial gases into the atmosphere for many years has provoked two major global environmental issues: *global warming* and the *greenhouse effect*. Both effects are said to be provoking the rise of the world's temperature at a worrying pace, which could cause the rising of the sea level, floods, and heat waves, among other disastrous consequences.

The pollution generated by the industrial sector is a global problem. However, responsibilities are not the same. Industrialized countries like the United States, China, Russia, Japan, and Great Britain have been responsible for the release of most industrial pollutants. The amounts of pollutants released by nondeveloped and nonindustrialized countries are minimal compared to those of developed ones. The worldwide list of the most carbon dioxide-emitting countries shows that the superpowers contaminate the most. The list reads as follows, with the most polluting nation as number one: (1) United States, (2) Russia, (3) Japan, (4) Germany, and (5) Great Britain.

Pollution not only affects the atmosphere but also the water and the soil. All this information raises the question whether sustainable development is a sound and reasonable option for humankind and what should be done to stop industrial pollution from endangering the next generation's future.

Industrial Pollution and Effects on the Environment

In the twenty-first century, industrial activity is one of the most important sources of pollution worldwide, causing damage to water, air, and soil.

Water Pollution

Together with untreated sewage waters and agricultural chemicals such as fertilizers and pesticides, industrial wastes are the main cause of *water pollution*. Pollutants from industrial sources many times pour out directly from the outfall pipes of factories or may leak from pipelines and underground storage tanks. Polluted water may also flow from mines where the water has leached through mineral-rich rocks or has been contaminated by the chemicals used in the process. All around the world, the pollution of water implies contamination of streams, underground water, lakes, or oceans by substances harmful to living things. This turns into a major global problem when considering that only 3% of the world's water is fresh, and only half of that percentage is drinkable. Therefore, the pollution of fresh water is not only a contemporary threat to the living creatures that consume it but is also a potential source of future conflicts and wars.

The major water pollutants are chemical, biological, or physical materials that degrade water quality. Among the most common are *thermal pollutants* and *industrial pollutants,* such as petroleum products, heavy metals, and hazardous wastes. All these can cause serious damage to the health of living beings and to humans. For instance, heavy metals, such as copper, lead, mercury, and selenium, get into water from many sources, including industries, automobile exhaust, and mines. In this way, these metals reach animals or plants that drink or take in water and finally reach humans who eat those plants and animals. The regular introduction of these toxic nondegradable chemicals released by industries in large amounts provokes the killing of large numbers of fish, birds, microorganisms, and the ecosystem where all creatures live. When they reach high levels in the human body, heavy metals can be immediately poisonous or can result in long-term health problems similar to those caused by pesticides and herbicides. Consequently, people who ingest polluted water can become ill and, with prolonged exposure, may develop cancers or bear children with birth defects.

Until the Minamata Bay incident during the 1950s and 1960s, the dreadful effects of chemicals on water pollution were not known, and most hazardous wastes were legally dumped in solid waste landfills, buried, or dumped into water. As effects were not known, toxic chemicals freely contaminated surface and underground waters, which were later consumed by people. However, during those decades, more than four hundred residents living near Minamata Bay in Japan died before authorities discovered that a local

industry had carelessly released mercury into the bay's waters. This highly toxic element had accumulated in the bodies of local fish and eventually in the bodies of people who had consumed the fish; the people developed nervous disorders, tremors, and paralysis, which caused many to die. Scientific research has revealed that many chemical pollutants, such as dichlorodiphenyltrichloroethane (DDT) and polychlorinated biphenyls (PCBs) interfere with the human body's reproductive and developmental functions. These substances are known as *endocrine disrupters*; when they reach high levels in the human body, they can cause death.

In the twenty-first century, legal regulations restrict how such materials may be used or disposed, and many corporations publicize their support of environmental efforts and compliance with environmental laws. However, such laws are difficult to enforce and are often contested by industry. Many multinational companies have decided to move their factories to nondeveloped countries where the regulations are flexible and full enforcement may not be possible.

Air Pollution

The US Environmental Protection Agency (EPA) defines an air pollutant as "any substance in the air that can cause harm to humans or the environment. Pollutants may be natural or man-made and may take the form of solid particles, liquid droplets or gases." Industrial activity generates a lot of gases that are released into the atmosphere through chimneys, some with filters and others without them. These gases are usually a mixture of chemical compounds, with carbon dioxide and different sulphur dioxides being the most common. Together with the gases released by automobiles (motorbikes and buses to some extent, but mostly privately owned cars), planes, and the construction industry, the industrial-related gases contribute to the formation of the *smog* that is a peril for citizens' health in modern cities like Mexico City, Beijing, Cairo, Jakarta, Los Angeles, Sao Paulo, and Moscow, the most contaminated cities in the world.

The emission of large amounts of carbon dioxide, however, not only directly affects human health but causes a more important and harmful effect: *the greenhouse effect*. The greenhouse effect is a warming of the Earth's surface and lower atmosphere because certain gases (for instance, water vapour, carbon dioxide, nitrous oxide, and methane) trap energy within the atmosphere.

In the natural process, the energy that the sun emits travels through space and through the Earth's atmosphere until it reaches the Earth's surface and heats it. Then, a part of it is reradiated by the Earth's surface in the form of long-wave infrared radiation, much of which is absorbed by molecules of carbon dioxide and water vapour in the atmosphere, and the rest escapes back into the space. However, the excess and concentration of these so-called "greenhouse gases," like carbon dioxide, in the upper layer of the atmosphere create a barrier that refrains the reradiated energy from escaping and provokes the overheating of the Earth's surface. The permanent industrial activities and the incineration of wastes together with the reduction of the forests and rain forests in the world have contributed to the increasing concentration of carbon dioxide in the atmosphere that creates this effect.

Although the topic is controversial, most experts and laypeople accept that emission of these greenhouse gases have a great deal of responsibility in the increasing of the global temperature, a phenomenon known as *global warming*. This has occurred mainly in the last thirty years with different effects worldwide. For instance, the change in seasonal temperatures has caused an increase in the frequency and quantities of rainfall in South American countries like Argentina.

Global temperature is expected to increase from 2°F–10°F in the twenty-first century. This is likely to provoke serious catastrophes, among them the flooding of lower parts of the planet and many coastal cities. Again, the primary responsible countries for releasing excessive emissions are the most industrialized ones: the United States, those of the European Union, and Russia.

Another effect provoked by industries is *acid precipitation*, or acid rain. Acid precipitation is rain, snow, or fog that is polluted by acid in the atmosphere and damages the environment. Two common air pollutants, sulphur dioxide (SO_2) and nitrogen oxide (NOX), are the primary causes of acid rain. When these substances are released into the atmosphere regularly and in large amounts, they can be carried over long distances by prevailing winds before returning to earth in acid rain, snow, fog, or dust. Acid rain occurs when these gases react in the atmosphere with water, oxygen, and other chemicals to form various acidic compounds. This type of rain has a variety of effects, including damage to forests and soils, to fish and other living things, structures, and also to human health. Acid rain is mainly caused by the indiscriminate emission of acid gases by industries. For instance, in the United States, about two-thirds of all sulfur dioxide (SO_2) and one-fourth of all

nitrogen oxide (NOX) come from electric power generation that relies on burning fossil fuels like coal.

Other Types of Industrial Pollution: Soil and Water Bodies

Industrial activities create other types of pollution: the pollution of soil and water bodies due to hazardous wastes and the thermal pollution.

As industrialized society generates more hazardous wastes, there is an increased need to find a way to dispose of them. Prior to the 1970s, the industrialized countries disposed of these wastes within their own countries, often with little regard to the environmental impact of disposal. Incidents of improperly disposed of waste, such as the Love Canal affair in the United States, in which a fifteen-acre working-class neighborhood (including over one thousand residences and three schools) was built over the site of a toxic-waste landfill near Niagara Falls, began to create serious health and ecological problems. Public awareness of the consequences of improper disposal increased. Eventually, this awareness led to people in industrialized countries expressing an increasing unwillingness to have waste disposed of at home. This new awareness led to an increase in the export of hazardous wastes to developing nations. Many of these countries had neither the technical expertise nor the facilities to dispose of the waste in an environmentally sound manner. Often, these wastes were simply dumped on properties in leaking barrels, with environmentally devastating results. Ultimately, the waste would leach into the soil and water table, causing health and environmental problems for the local areas. This *waste trade* is not well observed by the general public, but many times governments will agree to accept hazardous materials for disposal because of money or other benefits offered by the exporting country.

Thermal pollution is another effect derived from the industrial activity. This type of pollution is a rise in the temperature of rivers or lakes that is injurious to water-dwelling life and is caused by the disposal of heated industrial wastewater or water from the cooling towers of nuclear power plants. Even small temperature changes in a body of water can drive away the fish and other wildlife that were originally present. Thermal pollution can accelerate biological processes in plants and animals or deplete oxygen levels in water. The result may be fish and other wildlife deaths near the discharge source. Thermal pollution can also be caused by the removal of trees and vegetation that shade and cool streams. Obviously, this type of industrial pollution occurs in those countries that are most dependent on nuclear energy:

France, Lithuania, Belgium, Slovakia, Ukraine, and Sweden, among others.

International Agreements and Sustainable Development

Concern has grown around the world regarding the pollution of the Earth's resources, the deforestation processes, the permanent emissions of carbon dioxide, and global heating effects. In 1992, the United States and other nations met at the United Nations Earth Summit in Rio de Janeiro, Brazil, to agree on policies on how to fight against the greenhouse effect. In that year, they agreed to voluntarily reduce greenhouse gas emissions to 1990 levels by the year 2000, among other proposals in the quest of a *sustainable development*. Ten years later, in the Johannesburg Summit 2002 (Rio plus 10), the results were not very encouraging as many institutions, such as the World Watch Institute, showed that the destruction of forests, the emission of greenhouse gases, the reduction of the biodiversity, and the expansion of transgenic crops were still issues; global warming was still a factor. Because the Rio Treaty was not legally binding and because reducing emissions would likely cause great economic damage, most nations did not meet the goals.

Another attempt to gather forces with the aim of reducing the air pollution occurred in December 1997, when representatives from around the world met at a conference in Kyoto (Japan), the Third Session of the Conference of the Parties (COP 3), to sign an agreement that legally bound signing countries to reduce the emissions of six gases, the main one being carbon dioxide. The aim was to stop the global warming. The Kyoto Protocol was signed by most industrialized countries. However, the United States, a country that in 1997 emitted about one-fifth of total global greenhouse gases, decided to quit the protocol in 2001. In December 2004, the Tenth Session of the Conference of the Parties (COP 10) took place in Buenos Aires (Argentina), and most industrialized countries, including Russia and the European Union nations, confirmed their adherence to the protocol. Once again, the United States did not ratify its commitment to reduce the emissions of gases.

All these controversies and problems created by industrial pollution worldwide prove that a *sustainable development* is not an easy option. In spite of the international attempts to reach agreements to reduce the emission of greenhouse effects or other conventions to prevent the pollution of water or soil,

industrial pollution is still contaminating the planet's resources. In times when the fossil-fuel era is entering its sunset years, the use of alternative, clean, and renewable energies, like wind energy or hydrogen energy, is very little developed. Many critics believe that a key factor in the minimal use and the underdevelopment of clean energy is the reduction in profits it would mean for oil companies. It is cheaper for developed countries to export hazardous nuclear wastes to the Third World than to build disposal sites in their own territories or stop using nuclear energy.

DIEGO I. MURGUÍA

See also Acid Precipitation; Biodiversity Conservation; Deforestation; Environment: Government Policies; Environmentalism; Global Climate Change; Pollution, Agricultural; Rain Forest, Destruction of; Waste Management; Water Resources and Distribution; Wildlife Preservation

References and Further Reading

Andersen, Mikael Skou. *Governance by Green Taxes: Making Pollution Prevention Pay*. Manchester, UK: Manchester University Press, 1994.

Andersson, Thomas. "Multinational Firms and Pollution in Developing Countries." *Linking The Natural Environment and The Economy: Essays From The Eco-Eco Group*, C. Folke and T. Kaberger, eds. Boston, MA: Kluwer Academic Publishers, 1991.

Boubel, R. W., D. L. Fox, D. B. Turner, and A.C. Stern. *Fundamentals of Air Pollution*. San Diego, CA: Academic Press, 1994.

Carlin, Alan. *The United States Experience With Economic Incentives To Control Environmental Pollution*. Report No. Epa-230-R-92-001. Washington, DC: US Environmental Protection Agency, 1992.

Crandall, Robert W. *Controlling Industrial Pollution*. Washington, DC: Brookings Institution, 1983.

Gale Research. *Environmental Encyclopedia*. Detroit: Gale Research, 1994.

Hirschhorn, Joel S., and Kirsten U. Oldenburg. *Prosperity Without Pollution: The Prevention Strategy for Industry and Consumers*. New York: Van Nostrand Reinhold, 1991.

Klaassen, G., and F. R. Forsund, eds. *Economic Instruments For Air Pollution Control*. Boston: Kluwer Academic Publishers, 1994.

Markowitz, Gerald E., and David Rosner. *Deceit and Denial: The Deadly Politics of Industrial Pollution*. Berkeley, CA: University of California Press, 2002.

Miller, G. Tyler, Jr. *Living in the Environment*. Belmont: Wadsworth Publishing Company, 1987.

Rifkin, Jeremy. *The Hydrogen Economy: The Creation of the World-Wide Energy Web and the Redistribution of Power on Earth*. New York: Jeremy P. Tarcher/Putnam, 2002.

Steger, Will, and Jon Bowermaster. *Saving the Earth*. New York: Bryon Press, 1990.

Theodore, Louis, and Young C. McGuinn. *Pollution Prevention*. New York: Van Nostrand Reinhold, 1992.

World Health Organization and United Nations Environment Programme. *Urban Air Pollution in Megacities of the World: Earthwatch: Global Monitoring System*. Oxford; Cambridge, MA: 1992.

POPULAR MOVEMENT FOR THE LIBERATION OF ANGOLA (MPLA)

The *Movimiento Popular de Libertaçãp de Angola* (MPLA), or the Popular Movement for the Liberation of Angola, was the main liberation movement opposing the Portuguese in Angola. It took power at independence in November 1975 and eventually won the long civil war that followed. It remains the ruling party in Angola today.

The MPLA was founded in December 1956 when, under the influence of students in Portugal, two small Nationalist coalitions merged in Luanda, capital of the Portuguese overseas territory of Angola. An urban-based movement, the MPLA attracted support from the small native elite that was assimilated to Portuguese culture (*assimilados*), people of mixed race (mestico or Afro-Portuguese), intellectuals who had studied abroad, and Marxists in Portugal itself. It was hard-hit by the Portuguese secret police in 1959 and 1960, when many of its leaders were arrested and imprisoned. MPLA militants urged peasants and workers to take up the armed struggle in response, and February 4, 1961, is commemorated as the beginning of the national liberation struggle against the Portuguese. The MPLA opened exile offices in Conakry, Guinea, in 1960, in Kinshasa in the former Belgian Congo in 1961, and in Brazzaville, Congo, in 1963. Its first national conference, held in Kinshasa in 1962, elected Agostinho Neto as president; he was a poet, medical doctor, and Marxist who had been a political activist against the Portuguese in Luanda from the 1940s, and he succeeded Mario de Andrade as president. Neto was to remain president until his death in 1979, when he was succeeded by José Eduardo dos Santos, still president in 2005.

From 1966, the MPLA faced competition from the rival *Uniao Nacional de Independencia Total de Angola* (UNITA), or the National Union for the Total Independence of Angola, under Jonas Savimbi. The MPLA denounced UNITA as an ethnic (*Ovimbundu*) and regional (southern) organisation, as antinational and nonrevolutionary. UNITA in turn accused the MPLA of being sectional (Kimbundu) and wedded to an alien ideology. For a time, the MPLA claimed support in the South, where Daniel Chipenda worked for it in Lobito, but in 1973, Chipenda was accused of plotting take over Neto's position, and he soon broke away.

Factionalism almost destroyed the MPLA, but it retained the support of the Organisation of African Unity Liberation Committee, which recognised it as the legitimate national movement, and of Cuba and other Socialist countries. When the struggle between the rival Angolan Nationalist movements reached a head in 1975 and the South Africans sent in a military force to try to prevent the MPLA from coming to power, Cuban forces, arriving in large numbers, saved the day for the MPLA, which took over the institutions of the state on November 11, 1975, and raised the red, yellow, and black flag of an independent Angola. Later that month, Nigeria recognised the new government, and other states followed but not the United States. There was to be no election for another seventeen years. A large Cuban military force was to remain in the country for more than fifteen of those years to help ensure the MPLA remained in power. For most of that period, the MPLA had effective control over the western and northern parts of the country only. But though the MPLA took over the state, it never became a national party and remained dominated by Kimbundu and Afro-Portuguese. When in 1977 the Nito Alves faction came out in favor of a more African-centred focus for the party, the faction was purged from the MPLA central committee and the armed forces. At its congress held in December that year, the central committee of the MPLA voted to transform the movement into a Marxist-Leninist party of militants, and it now called itself MPLA-Partido dos Trabalhadores (MPLA-PT), the party of workers.

The MPLA was sympathetic to the struggle being waged by the South West Africa People's Organisation (SWAPO) against the South African occupation regime in Namibia, and SWAPO was allowed to operate from bases in southern Angola. This led the South African Defence Force to raid into southern Angola from the late 1970s, and for much of the 1980s, the South Africans occupied the most southernmost part of Angola and gave massive support to UNITA, which launched an economic sabotage campaign against the MPLA-PT government as well as military attacks. Under pressure, the party's second congress, held in December 1985, began the move away from strong support for the Soviet Union. In 1988, the MPLA government agreed to a settlement of the Namibian issue, which involved the total withdrawal of the Cuban forces and the independence of Namibia.

After the Cubans left, an election was held in 1992 under the auspices of the United Nations. By then, the MPLA had gotten rid of much of its Marxism-Leninism and had come out in favour of a multiparty system. But when the MPLA was declared the winner

with 53.74% of the vote, UNITA refused to accept the result, and the civil war began again, this time at even greater intensity than before; UNITA-held cities such as Huambo and Cuito were reduced to ruins. In the long fight against UNITA, the revenues from the oil being pumped off the coast at Cabinda in the north was indispensable to the MPLA. It was not until 2002 that, with the death of Savimbi, the war came to an end, and the MPLA was able to further consolidate itself in power in the new era of peace. There was talk of an election being held in 2006, but problems such as the resettlement of hundreds of thousands of refugees and the removal of millions of landmines hampered preparations for such an election. Meanwhile, the MPLA remains in power, its leadership having enriched itself by siphoning off much of the oil revenues, and most of Angola's population continues to be mired in poverty despite the wealth of the country.

CHRISTOPHER SAUNDERS

See also Angola

References and Further Reading

Gleijeses, P. *Conflicting Missions.* Chapel Hill, NC: University of North Carolina Press, 2002.
Heywood, L. *Contested Power in Angola.* Rochester: University of Rochester Press, 2000.
Somerville, K. *Angola.* London: Pinter, 1986.

POPULAR SECTORS

In the developing world, popular sectors are identical with *meaningful participation,* a distinctly cultural proposition, observable within the creative aims of representative organizations.

Conventional working definitions are interested in how activities in the popular sectors occur outside the spheres of the state and the market. This focus proves inadequate for the developing world for the following reasons. It overstates sectoral independence and masks complementarities across the three social sectors. It inaccurately implies internal homogeneity as opposed to the *array* of groups—often with antagonistic aims—that characterizes the popular sectors. It also relies on a veiled hypothesis that popular sectors are a democratic power-balancing agency, which was central to the thought of Talcott Parsons (1902–1979), who saw ties between social sectors as a "moving equilibrium," based on a disprovable premise of evenness and symmetry of power.

For the developing world, an adequate working definition needs to characterize the *functional* role of popular sectors as power relationships with the state and the market. Interdependency is characteristic, but

the state and market play dominant roles. Second, the definition needs to identify the relationship between sectors as based on conflict and on inherent differences between the aims of individuals and society. Third, there needs to be acknowledgment of the diversity of aims *within* the popular sector. The sector is a pluralized concept encompassing an array of agencies that include such organizations as church groups, universities, environmental organizations, volunteerism advocates, and women's crisis groups. Fourth, its causal principle transmits cultural achievements: as history is the collective memory of society, and literature and arts its popular imagination, the popular sectors enact collective vision. This description points to a distinctive cultural value and the crucial role of *meaningful* participation. Ultimately, it substantiates the proposition that the causal principle of popular sectors is a creative, constructive force.

Three particular social thinkers expound on these systemic qualities of popular sectors. The first, Ibn Khaldun (1332–1395 CE), born in Tunisia, is celebrated for producing social science four centuries before its start in the "North." Viewed as *the systematic study of society encompassing human experiences,* social science began in the North in the eighteenth century. Elsewhere, it was in the fourteenth century that Khaldun wrote on the factors contributing to the rise and fall of successful societies in the Arab world. He remains an exemplary figure for Egypt's embryonic popular sectors, where a research centre bears his name with a mission to develop democracy through popular sector organisations. Characteristically, in Egypt and across the developing world, the relationship between the state and popular sectors is vitreous. This is illustrated by long jail terms that the director and other staff of the Khaldun Centre have served more than once for advocating universal suffrage.

During the time of his work, Khaldun encountered a crisis in creative participation. He observed how urbanisation alienated nomads as it increasingly drew them in. Khaldun was concerned that *asabiyah* (group feeling demonstrated by participation) noticeably declined, when compared with prestate communities. Khaldun arrived at the view that participation is the problem of power centralised and tilted against the popular sectors.

The second writer of note is Antonio Gramsci (1891–1937). From Sardinia, his work undertook to clarify the social consequences of an overabundance of popular sector organizations. Previously, G.W.F. Hegel (1770–1831) saw this as reason for more state power to navigate social ethos in the absence of the popular sectors, which were inattentive due to infighting. On the other hand, Gramsci saw differentiation as an inevitable attribute of the buffer against autocratic civic norms and traditions. This struck a chord during the 1970s and 1980s with resistance movements in Latin America and with others in this millennium, particularly in Chile and the Philippines. They favoured Gramsci's thinking above the "liberal" notions that underpin contemporary constructions of "social capital" propounded by Alexis de Tocqueville (1820–1840). They preferred Gramsci's understanding of conflict. Whereas de Tocqueville wanted to eliminate conflict by protecting the popular sector against state domination, Gramsci saw conflict as an inextricable part of the social contract.

Criticism of Gramsci surrounds his idea that the popular sectors are independent of changing power relationships. This is seen as underestimating the creative force and inherent fragility of the sector. Since power relations are the primary concern in the developing world, at issue are the contemporary uses of the popular sectors. Whereas the struggle against totalitarianism defined their former role, they now implement policy indifferent to social transformation within a market system unresponsive to their ethical mission. Since popular sectors grew and flourished in the developing world as sovereign agencies effective at transforming oppression, any decline in meaningful participation is deeply troubling for democratic societies of every kind and at every stage of development.

The next thinker, Mikhail Bakhtin (1895–1975) from central European Russia, took up the challenge of clarifying the social necessity of meaningful participation. He undertook to locate typical sites of meaningful participation and how to observe participation. Bakhtin found that popular sectors sustain themselves through practices of belief that are in marked conflict with official interpretations of reality. He saw this as observable in activities within situations of cultural friction between official and unofficial codes. This signaled a major shift in theoretical understanding, overturning the long-standing belief of Emile Durkheim (1858–1917) who argued that cultural conflict indicates the *loss* of group feeling. Bakhtin showed how individuals express social experience in symbol systems that meaningful participation generates. He pointed out the irreconcilable differences between personal and social aims, explaining that the collision of interests operates as the causal principle in social identification. Bakhtin's findings affirm the social necessity of meaningful participation by the popular sectors.

The discussion now turns to an example of an emergent popular sector, with its members (youths) remaining relatively unorganized. The example involves musical expressiveness in contemporary Melanesia against a backdrop of twenty-first century urbanization.

From the perspective of official urban culture, contemporary music in Melanesia is "noisy music." While elders are mostly content with traditional themes and styles from their respective ethnic groups, contemporary youths have a more adventurous, free, and culturally diverse taste in music. This is expressed in a blend of locally traditional and borrowed Western themes, lyrics, instruments, and styles. The music most heard, and most played by youths, represents their response to official codes.

What constitutes these unofficial symbols, which their more patriotic, conservative elders perceive as "noise" rather than music with aesthetics and poetry? The range of instruments is diverse. They can be divided into two main categories, local and imported. Most are imported and adapted, that is not official. Local instruments include wooden gongs (garamut), wooden drums with reptile skins on either end (kundu), panpipes (flutes), shell rattles, conch shells, and nutshell rattles. Imported instruments include guitar, ukulele, piano, keyboards, flutes, horns, trumpets and trombones, and other innovations. Nearly all these instruments feature in the music of the region. Diversity is also a key characteristic of the range of songs. (Readers may recall the Hegel/Gramsci debate about how to deal with diversity when ethical irresponsibility results).

Regarding musical preferences, Melanesian elders prefer locally traditional sounds. These include the archetypal Pacific dance hula hula (tamure), specifically among coastal Motuan and Central Province villages of Papua New Guinea. These performances allude to closer historical links with Polynesian ethnicity and demarcation from neighboring Melanesian traditions of the Western Pacific. Other themes of romance, adventure, deceit, ambush, and robbery have a significant place in official prestate community codes. Similarly, songs that tell the tale of colonialism and those that attest to the increasing prevalence of Christianity, which overlay unmistakable Melanesian variations on original Western sounds, also have a significant place in the society.

Contrasting vividly with the official sounds of prestate and urban societies is the more recent music of youths. The predominant sounds are a mix of reggae and heavy metal blended with local tunes in vogue. Rap also has an integral role, with its "ugly, blunt" sounds about poverty, destitution, and deprivation in a harsh urban environment. The songs belt out a message on marginalization by waves of state and market forces. An undercurrent of alienation focuses on rejection by partners, parents, and/or the state.

The artists themselves are role models. They show youths that despite being deprived and pushed to the margins, they can survive in their own world within their own confines and rules. Their attire shows rebellion against mainstream expectations, helping shape a lean but frail and fragile human frame moving precariously across the neighborhood, smoking local tobacco and sometimes marijuana, faces unkempt, bearded, dreadlocks, balaclavas, caps with hoods twisted to the sides or the back, torn jeans, and slack belts pulled well below the accepted waist line level almost exposing pubic hair.

It is the voiced codes that predominate, though noisy, expressing a right to be heard. Indicative of an emergent popular sector, Melanesian youths see themselves as a group. Their code is meaningful to them and amplifies their belief they are a potential political force, despite rejection and marginalization by state and society. Unlike dissenting middle-class youths in the developed world who reject society rather than being rejected by it, mainstream urban environments reject Melanesian youths. This is shown by unemployment statistics and how they fall out of the mainstream education process. And they view the state as paying lip service under the rubric of youth groups.

In Papua New Guinea, the informal economic sector has become a haven for some urban youths, where unemployed women and men till vacant lands and sell vegetable produce to city markets. Most lack the enthusiasm to do this work and spend much of their time idling along the streets, blasting music boxes as they drift into social oblivion. These are the "Street Boys" or "Home Boys." The labels identify their preoccupation with home-brewed alcohol. Abuse of alcohol, marijuana, and local tobacco is enmeshed with daily petty criminal activities, which destines them for confrontation with the official law. Youths are adamant there is no other way to alleviate their ever-deteriorating social condition. They perceive the efforts of elders, media commentators, donors, and personnel from nongovernmental organizations (NGOs), who engage in isolated media articles and workshops, as well intended but misguided. They are skeptical of NGOs and church groups that are seen as swooping down on opportunities to promote the lost cause of youths whilst gaining publicity from their charitable intentions.

Contemporary music is a source of solace for many Melanesian youths. They quickly identify with songs that realize their daily predicaments and lack of opportunities, which promote their rejected lives, and that alienate elders and the state by mirroring the experience of rejection. Discotheques and clubs provide a safety net with music loud enough to shut out the world and to induce illusions of outer acceptance. It is important not to overgeneralize, since youths do not all believe and behave alike. But

many share the need to say these things to the world, and music is the way they want to say it. It is their code, and it constructively transfers the threat of being marginalized by rapid urbanization. It enables unofficial voices to be counted and recognized against a backdrop of meager economic promise.

Most youths are economically impoverished. But this does not exhaust the significance of music as an indicator of meaningful participation and of broader sectoral participation because also included in this social grouping are significant numbers of youths from well-off families. They not only share the same taste for *reggae, rap,* heavy metal, and rock and roll, but they also often take the lead in the construction of the unofficial code, which encompasses attire, gestures, moves, tempo, and volume. The music is noisy. It draws attention and portends power. It mirrors marginalization, blending frustration, and inspiration in a demonstration of strength. It is offensive, and heralds change while transferring estrangement. It is creative, consistent with the origins of a popular sector.

The example of Melanesian societies enables several propositions to be examined: first, it further explains Bakhtin's hypothesis that transformed the idea that cultural conflict implies the *loss* of group feeling. It clarifies how popular sectors nourish themselves through practices of belief that conflict with official construal of reality. It shows how conflicting values generate unofficial symbols, which reject but also express felt rejection, while beginning the longer task of building social identity. And, by focusing on the creative principle in the popular sectors, it highlights the social necessity for meaningful participation. Equally, it shows that when the constructive element of participation collides with rather than promotes the social good, alienation can be traced. Khaldun explained this more than seven centuries ago with his finding that urbanizing society marginalizes individuals who leave prestate society. While the Melanesian example shows participation persists, it also demonstrates that constructive quality depends on interdependency between social sectors and, consequently, on decentralization of power.

JAMES CHALMERS AND LINUS DIGIM'RINA

References and Further Reading

Baali, Fuad. *Society, State and Urbanism. Ibn Khaldun's Sociological Thought.* Albany, NY: State University of New York Press, 1988.

Bakhtin, Mikhail. *Rabelais and His World.* Cambridge, MA: MIT Press, 1968.

———. *The Dialogic Imagination,* ed. Michael Holquist. Austin, TX: University of Texas Press, 1981.

Black, Sandra E., and Elizabeth Brainerd. "Importing Equality?: The Impact of Globalization on Gender Discrimination." Cambridge, MA: National Bureau of Economic Research, 2002.

Chalmers, Jim. "Ethical Questions Raised by the Industrialization of an Indigenous Community." *Journal of Contemporary Asia, Manila/Sydney* 26, no. 2 (1996).

Frers, Lars. 2004. "Ibn Khaldun and Comte. Discontinuity or progress?" http://userpage.fu-berlin.de/~frers/ibn_khaldun.html#References.

Gewertz, Deborah, and Frederick Errington. *Twisted Histories, Altered Contexts. Representing the Chambri in a World System.* Cambridge, UK: Cambridge University Press, 1991.

Gramsci, Antonio. *The Modern Prince, and Other Writings.* London: Lawrence and Wishart, 1957.

———, and David Forgacs. *Gramsci Reader: Selected Writings, 1916–1935.* London: Lawrence and Wishart, c1988.

Held, David, and Anthony G. McGrew. *Governing Globalization: Power, Authority and Global Governance.* Cambridge, UK: Blackwell, 2002.

Jones, Robert Alun. *Emile Durkheim: An Introduction to Four Major Works.* Beverly Hills, CA: Sage Publications, 1986.

Jussila, Heikki, Roser Majoral i Moliné, and Fernanda Delgado Cravidão. *Globalization and Marginality in Geographical Space: Political, Economic and Social Issues of Development in the New Millennium.* Aldershot, UK: Ashgate, 2001.

Khaldun, Ibn. *The Muqaddimah: An Introduction to History.* 3 vols. Translated by Franz Rosenthal. Princeton, NJ: Princeton University Press, 1980.

Miller, Berna, and James D. Torr. *Developing Nations.* San Diego, CA: Greenhaven Press, 2003.

Mozaffari, Mehdi. *Globalization and Civilizations.* London: Routledge, 2002.

Perlas, Nicanor. *Shaping Globalization: Civil Society, Cultural Power, and Threefolding.* Quezon City, Philippines: Center for Alternative Development Initiatives, 1999.

Parsons, Talcott. "Action Systems and Social Systems." *The System of Modern Societies.* Englewood Cliffs, NJ: Prentice-Hall, 1971.

POPULATION GROWTH: IMPACT ON DEVELOPMENT

Human Resources

Population is a key variable in any discussion of development. When assessing human resources within a country, the demographics of the population under study provide indicators of the probable level of its development. Larger populations, with high concentrations of the very young and the elderly, tend to be concentrated in less developed countries. During the initial years of the twenty-first century, the developing

world accounted for approximately 80% of the total world population. According to Coast in "Population Trends in Developing Countries," the population growth rate in these countries has slowed down since reaching its peak of 2.04% in the late 1960s. In the 1990s, the growth rate was at 2.0% for low-income countries while only 0.6% for high-income countries. Between 2000 and 2005, the World Bank projected a 2 billion person increase in the world population, with 97% of it occurring in developing countries. A large percentage of that population will be young, the consequences of low-life expectancy rates and high fertility rates in many parts of the world. The British Department for International Development (DFID) research indicates that as of the first few years of the twenty-first century, 44% of the world's poverty is concentrated in South Asia, 24% in Sub-Saharan Africa, and 23% in East Asia and the Pacific. These statistics provide a picture of some of the challenges and status of development in certain regions.

A key component of development is the human factor, that is the availability of human resources. As the term implies, "human resources" refers to the population and both its potential and actual contributions to development. Selected scholars and researchers describe three components to the human side of development: life sustenance, self-esteem (self-respect and independence), and freedom. Using this paradigm for analysis, a country cannot be considered fully developed if all of its people are not provided with such basic needs as housing, clothing, food, and minimal education. Poverty directly impacts nourishment, which in turn impacts survival rates of a people and that people's capacity to engage in initiatives that foster sustainable development. In Africa, for example, high rates of poverty and hunger are directly related to low per capita agricultural income, consequently forming a vicious, recurring cycle that results in what the United States Agency for International Development (USAID) describes as "a low-growth trap." Approximately one-third of all the world's undernourished people reside in sub-Saharan Africa. Poverty limits people's ability to purchase food. The lack of food results in malnutrition and poor health. The poor health limits their ability to earn income. The inability to earn income leads to still deeper poverty, and what emerges is a never-ending cycle that inhibits development and sometimes dissipates a people.

Continuing with this paradigm, a country cannot be considered fully developed if it is being exploited by other countries and/or cannot conduct economic relations on equal terms. There must be independence, freedom, and the ability of a people to determine its own destiny.

Population Size

Population size is critical in the level and direction of development. The larger the population, the more limited the resources available for development and the more limited the development in that society. According to *demographic transition theory*, societies move from high birth and death rates to relatively low birth and death rates as a result of technological development. There are four stages in this evolution. In the preindustrial stage, there is little population growth. High death rates (mortality rate) offset high birth rates (fertility rate). The transitional stage, also known as early industrial stage, is characterized by the continued high birth rate but a decline in the death rate because of technological advances.

In the advanced industrialization/urbanization stage, the birth rates decline because fertility is controlled through various contraceptive methods, and death rates decline because of advances in health care technology. These advances help control disease, provide cures, and control chronic and acute disease. The fourth stage is the postindustrial stage in which there is a decreasing birth rate coupled with a stabilized death rate. Using this theory for analyses, the developing world is in the second stage of development. The fertility rates remain very high while the mortality rates are decreasing. As a result, more resources are necessary to meet the basic survival needs and age-specific demands of the society.

In terms of the cause-effect relationship between population, development, and social conditions, such as poverty, there are varying views. One popular view is the "survival and assurance of continuity" perspective. When life expectancy is low and mortality and morbidity are high, there is a tendency to have large families with a larger young population. Families choose to have a higher number of children so that they can be assured that at least a few of the children will survive to adulthood. In addition, agrarian-based economies need the larger populations to maintain a reasonable labor force. On the other hand, some scholars have chosen a different viewpoint. They suggest that poor people are not poor because they have large families, but rather they have large families because they are poor. In countries where there is limited or no viable welfare or social security/pension program for the elderly, the larger families ensure that there will be relatives who can care for the elderly. In addition, males tend to have a higher mortality rate and a lower life expectancy rate than women. This causes widowhood to be high. In patriarchal societies with gender inequality, opportunities for females to do well are extremely

limited, if existent at all. The consequence of the higher male mortality rate is the destined poverty of the widow.

Population Movement

Population movement is another important variable in development. In developing countries, there are four major motivations for the movement, be it internal (migration) or international (emigration). Examining the movement in the context of a "push-pull" relationship, the push is what makes the persons leave, the pull is what encourages them into a particular direction and encourages them to remain. The first motivational category for population movement has an economic base. It arises from the need for certain members of the family, primarily males, to seek employment outside of the community. Limited employment opportunities (the "push" factor) inhibit those seeking economic security and advancement at home and encourage movement to more urban areas since there is broader job availability (the "pull" factor). Those who are able will follow employment to other countries where even more opportunities for economic advancement exist. One example is found in the seasonal West Indian sugar cane workers who, for more than a half-century, have come to Florida regularly during certain times of the year; a second example is found in the seasonal migrant workers from both the Caribbean and Latin America who follow the agricultural growing seasons in the United States. Income is generated, and improved familial economic status occurs; however, major hardships are placed on many of those workers. There is the need to maintain two households, and there is the minimal or absence of family interactions during major parts of each year. This seasonal emigration also impacts the workforce population within the home country because it reduces the total number of available labors. One positive outcome of this arrangement is the system of return remittances; that is, paychecks are sent home to support the family back home. The seasonal workers and temporary imported workers improve the conditions of the family and sometimes the economy of the region from which the workers come. From an economic perspective, another positive outcome is temporary emigration influences the direction of foreign direct investments. This encourages the flow of enterprise, ideas, and knowledge across borders.

The emigration, however, is not always legal. Sometimes estimated to be as large as one-third, a number of temporary immigrants engage in immigration through illegal channels. The destination country sometimes tacitly tolerates this illegal immigration because it meets that country's labor needs. Indirectly, this illegal immigration also induces petty corruption, encourages profitable smuggling opportunities for criminal networks, and perpetuates unfair treatment of the immigrants. Illegal trafficking of human cargo is a lucrative and an established profession in many parts of the world. The number of cases is rapidly increasing in both the developing and the developed worlds. Some people die en route or soon after arrival to the destination country. If they survive the smuggling phase, they are vulnerable to exploitation, intimidation, and abuse (physical, emotional, and sexual) since they are usually isolated and have no one advocating for or protecting them. They tend to have limited (or no) education, a limited capacity to speak and understand the predominant language of the destination country, and cannot go to authorities when exploited or abused because they will be discovered to be illegal. The status of "illegal" also discourages their effective integration into the fabric of the host country. They frequently live in fear of discovery and will attempt to remain invisible in this foreign setting. From the perspective of the developing country, the potential negative outcome of this migration is the increasing economic dependency of the country, and its inhabitants, on those remittances.

The second motivational category of population movement is a combination of economic needs and the need for personal development. This combination is manifested in youth flight from rural areas to urban areas because of the lack or limitations of economic opportunities and the desire to advance socially and economically. In general, there is a large economic gap between the rural and urban populations. The economic base in rural areas is often very fragile, with residents dependent on nature for products and younger generations to provide the labor. Often the youth do not want to follow the paths of their parents. Since opportunities for professional and personal growth are very minimal (the "push") and the social and professional outlets as well as the "glamour" of the urban areas are tempting (the "pull"), youth flight and minimal return to the area is common. Rural areas are left with a smaller and limited labor force that cannot provide the economic stability necessary for development. The depletion of the labor pool results in reduced production of goods that would generate income. The lack of income results in limited availability of services and resources because resources are not there to pay for the services. New initiatives and opportunities are not forthcoming, so there are virtually no professional and personal growth opportunities for the younger generations.

The third category of population movement involves migration and, more often, emigration to acquire education (the "push"). When the citizens are sent to more developed countries for education, the tendency is for them, when possible, to remain in the host country after the completion of their education. Reasons for this vary from opportunities for economic advancement that often result in remittances to home to the acquisition of knowledge and skills inappropriate or not viable in the home country (the "pull"). For example, a highly skilled advanced computer programmer would have difficulty finding employment in rural Thailand where electricity, if available, would be limited and sporadic, and phone lines may not exist. The longer these original students stay away from their home countries, the more likely they will establish permanent residency in the host country. The result is what is commonly known as "brain drain." The developing country loses its citizens who could contribute significantly to the development of that country. This problem became rampant in the mid-twentieth century. Developing countries were voicing serious concern and, at times, opposition to the practice of permitting their residents to come to the more developed countries for education and training. It took a period of time for aid donors to effectively address this problem related to educating individuals from the developing countries. The most effective approach was the creation of a training model that emphasized in-country training and/or "training trainers" rather than removing large numbers of citizens from their home country to acquire training and education.

A fourth category of population movement involves infrastructures that enfranchise some and disenfranchise others. Rural residents are forced to leave the area because of overpopulation, lack of empowerment, and limited space. In various parts of Central America, for example, poorer migrants who move from the rural areas to the urban areas are sometimes driven from the lands they once owned for many generations because of the expansion of land estates or the redistribution of lands. Frequently, the redistribution of the land results in a division of plots into such small sizes that subsistence farming is impossible. In El Salvador, this situation has been rampant for a while. The country has the most intense population pressure on the land. The majority of the country's land is privately owned and devoted to export crops. Since 2003, El Salvador was classified as the country with the highest population growth rate in the world, and there is no unpopulated land left in the country. Many people migrate to the cities, and overpopulation occurs there. Others choose to cross the borders into Honduras in hordes that

ultimately resulted in restrictions on immigration and wars at the border between the two countries.

In deeply depressed rural areas where emmigration is large, those people who remain either do not want to leave their birthplace and heritage, despite the insurmountable obstacles, or cannot move to town. The absolute poorest of the poor are often bound to the rural areas and are destined to a life of abject poverty because, by law or custom, they have to work off old family debts that they cannot pay off. They usually have limited or no education and cannot compete with those more educated town dwellers. They also do not have a support system that could sustain them in the town until they could earn enough to be self-sufficient. They have limited or no access to health care, sanitary environments, or infrastructures that enhance or encourage development.

Measures are being introduced to encourage the retention of rural residents. A number of donor organizations are providing fiscal and technical assistance to the rural areas with the intent of improving the living conditions, increasing life chances, and refining (or developing) their entrepreneurial skills and resources.

Ethnicity and Cultural Heritage as Factors in Development

A frequently overlooked aspect of development is ethnicity, with its corresponding cultural heritage and traditions. The beliefs and values of the people directly influence the level of acceptance of new and different approaches to development. Since culture is generally dynamic, there is room for the inclusion of new and innovative approaches to development. The nature and form of the introduction to the people, however, is critical to ultimate acceptance. Vignettes of "lessons learned" and "what not to do" can be cited by most scholars and development agencies. Very often, the connecting thread in these vignettes is the lack of understanding of, and sensitivity to, the cultural heritages of peoples receiving the development initiatives. Without that understanding, initiatives fail, are misinterpreted, or are ineffective. The people do not benefit, the resources are often wasted, and the donors are frustrated.

The culture and demographic characteristics of the population influence the nature, level, and direction of the development. For example, Max Weber, in his seminal work *The Protestant Ethic and the Spirit of Capitalism*, suggested that there is a direct relationship between the religion of a society and the level of

development that society achieves. According to his analysis, Western Protestant societies are more technologically advanced because of their national religion. Unlike some of the other major religions, the Protestant religions placed emphasis on smaller families; a work ethic that encouraged tireless effort, self-sacrifice, and deferred gratification; and a separation of religion and work. With the emphasis on work, accumulation of wealth, and deferred gratification, the larger families become obstacles to development because more resources must be provided for human development, that is for the survival of the people. Fewer resources are available for technological development.

Cultural heritage and traditions also affect the view of birth control. While the expansive need to have a larger family to ensure that some of the members reach adulthood may no longer exist in many developing countries, religious and cultural beliefs often mitigate against effective birth control, thus population control. Numerous religions view fertility as a gift from a deity, and thus something that should not have interference. Families with many children are considered blessed, and efforts to limit the number of children are in direct conflict with religious beliefs and practices. Scholars such as Paul and Anne Ehrlich point out that population increases will occur, and they are determined directly by cultural factors.

Natural Resources

An obvious outcome of population size, population needs, and development is the impact on natural resources. The larger the population, the more natural resources consumed and the greater the demand on the natural environment and resources. Often the infrastructure must be so concentrated on meeting the basic needs for survival and maintaining order. Throughout the developing world, numerous instances can be cited where the excessive use, and at times exploitation, of the natural resources have resulted in natural disasters. Rapid deforestation in some areas causes the depletion of the necessary topsoil to maintain fertile lands. Extensive soil erosion, sometimes resulting in massive landslides, sometimes follows. The deforestation is often more the result of basic survival than wanton disregard for the environment. In Haiti, for example, where the population is large, the primary source for cooking is charcoal. For the poor, few alternative methods exist for cooking. In the wealthier areas, people are able to buy cooking fuel or use electric/gas stoves; however, the majority of the people in many parts of Haiti do not have

access to these alternative methods. There are areas without electricity, and the people cannot afford cooking fuel. Coupled with the exploitation and destruction of the natural environment is the rapid consumption of endangered resources for basic survival. All of these situations combine to facilitate a rapid decrease in the level and speed of development in the region. An observer needs only to examine countries such as Bangladesh and Haiti for examples. The land is intensively cultivated and, as it becomes depleted, agricultural employment decreases and unemployment increases.

Summary

There is a clear relationship between development and the characteristics of the population. This relationship is affected by the size as well as the ethnic and cultural characteristics. The three are intertwined. They determine the direction of the development of the economic, natural (environment), and physical resources. Scholars have studied, and continue to study, the variables that impact development. They examine cause-and-effect relationships and provide strategies for altering the existing paths of development. Critical in all of those strategies must be consideration and incorporation of the human factor in all development. It is the human factor, meaning the population with its characteristics and patterns of growth, that determines the rate and level of development because, after all, without people there is no need for or possibility of development.

E. VALERIE SMITH

See also Children and Development; Family Planning and Structure; Food and Nutrition; Infant Mortality; International Organization for Migration (IOM); International Planned Parenthood Federation; Migration; Poverty: Definition and Trends; Poverty: Impact on Development; Refugees

References and Further Reading

ActionAid. "Reducing Poverty in a World of Plenty." *Impact of Rich Countries' Policies on Poor Countries*, Robert Picciotti and Rachel Weaving, eds. New Brunswick, NJ: Transactions Books, 2004.

Coast, Ernestina. "Population Trends in Developing Counties." *The Companion to Development Studies*, Vandana Desai and Robert B. Potter, eds. London: Arnold Publishing Company, 2002.

Corbridge, Stuart. "How Poor People Survive: The Weapons of the Week, Editor's Introduction." Stuart Corbridge, ed. *Development Studies: A Reader*. London: Arnold Publishing Company, 1995.

Ehrlich, Paul, and Anne Ehrlich. *The Population Explosion.* New York: Simon and Schuster, 1990.

Goodwin, Paul B. *Global Studies: Latin America.* 10th ed. Guilford, CT: McGraw-Hill/Dushkin Publishers, 2004.

Harf, James E., and Mark Owen Lombardi. *Taking Sides.* Guilford, CT: McGraw-Hill/Dushkin Publishers, 2003.

Harrison, Neil E. *Constructing Sustainable Development.* Albany, NY: State University of New York Press, 2000.

Picciotti, Robert. "Overview." *Impact of Rich Countries' Policies on Poor Countries*, Robert Picciotti and Rachel Weaving, eds. New Brunswick, NJ: Transactions Books, 2004.

Thirwall, A. P. "Development as Economic Growth." *The Companion to Development Studies*, Vandana Desai and Robert B. Potter, eds. London: Arnold Publishing Company, 2002.

Weber, Max. *The Protestant Ethic and the Spirit of Capitalism.* New York: Routledge, 1992.

World Bank. *World Development Report 2000/2001: Attacking Poverty.* Oxford: Oxford University Press, 2001.

POPULISM

Populism Defined

Populism as an ideology and movement arises in transitional societies experiencing rapid expansion of industrialization and urbanization. Industrialization induces social differentiation, increasing the gap between the rich and the poor, migration of peasants to the cities, and the permeation of urban culture and values. On the one hand, these developments usher in increasing rates of literacy, social awakening, politicization, and mobilization of the masses; on the other hand, they invite the centralization and bureaucratization of power. The destruction of feudal and semifeudal political and social structures engenders decline of communal bonds and traditional sources of identity. Hence, the increasing integration of global economy and commercialization of culture and its export as a commodity by the countries of the global North induce the loss of autonomy and cultural alienation. Thus, populism with different variations emerges to respond to the popular aspirations for increased political participation and the empowerment of the powerless as well as to provide a resolution to the identity crisis and the affirmation of perceived national "authenticity."

Populism as a movement and an ideology is a multiclass as well as a cross-class phenomenon. In so far as its base of support is drawn from different strata (although the lower classes often constitute the broader and the more solid core of this base), and in so far as it purports to speak on behalf of "the people" as a whole rather than a distinct class (Marxism), Populist appeal cuts across class lines.

Accompanying this multiple base of support is a monist and Unitarian ideological thrust. In response to the fragmentation and alienation in modern life, the Populists call for a unifying vision that would make the creation of an organic society possible. Populist ideologies tend to glorify the common people and advocate supremacy of the masses over the elite. They also call for the revival of traditional values, defying foreign economic and cultural domination. These salient characteristics of populism are complemented by its eclectic sources of ideological inspiration.

Populists consider the ordinary people and their collective tradition as the source of virtue. Hence, the power that stems from "the people" is perceived to be the only legitimate source of authority. Populists represent a moral outlook rather than a systematic ideology or program. They tend to be antiintellectual, antiestablishment, and aspire to revive the traditional culture. As such, Populists are intensely nationalistic. They oppose foreign domination and "alien" cultural influences. They often promote the revival of folk culture, traditional art forms, and conservative social values. They also romanticize the lower classes as the social groups that personify the authentic national culture and embody superior moral virtues. For example, the Russian Populists, the *Narodniks*, developed a romantic image of the peasantry, envisioning them as pure and the true agents of national salvation and the cornerstone of the future utopia. Similarly, US Populists glorified the farmers and their traditions as the true representatives of unspoiled moral values of an earlier age, uncontaminated by the dross of modernity and urban life. Mexican Populists took a strong interest in Indian culture, glorifying it as the true heir to Mexican national culture and identity. Idealization of traditional culture and celebration of purported superior moral virtues of the poor grounds populism in history and lends Populists legitimacy and a popular following.

Populist ideologies in the Third World are partially evoked by the economic and cultural impact of the West, thus engendering reactive Nationalist response. One of the major manifestations of the Nationalist thrust of Populist movements is demonstrated by the affinity toward traditional cultural values. As a common cultural denominator and the source of primordial loyalties, evocation of such values (including religion) is particularly helpful in unifying the masses, thus, enhancing their mobilization.

The mythical glorification of "the people" as the repository of the noble virtues lends Populist ideologies a messianic aura. Populists promise a new utopia in which the alienated and the oppressed would find a new heaven in the organic and egalitarian society of the future. No longer living a fragmented existence, the individual can become whole again by embracing the new creed, "the political religion," that would make deliverance and salvation possible. While Williams Jennings Bryan in the United States, Perón in Argentina, Echeverría in Mexico, and Vargas in Brazil (each to a different extent) all drew from Christianity to legitimize their political message, Nasser in Egypt, Ben Bella and Bomedien in Algeria, Qaddafi in Libya, and Khomeini in Iran utilized Islam (again to different extent) to mobilize the masses and wrap themselves in the flag of cultural authenticity.

In order to solidify their base of support, the Populist leaders thrive on patron-client relationships found between the landlord and peasants in agrarian societies. By implementing reforms that would benefit their client groups and political constituency, they establish a dependent paternalistic relationship that ensures them a continued base of support. Perón's dependence on trade unions' unconditional support, Qaddafi's dependence on "people's committees" to keep his political opponents at bay, and Khomeni's support of *Mostazafeen* (dispossessed) all are indicative of this cliental relationship. Thus, Populist leaders' rhetoric abounds with calls for economic reform, equality, and social justice to ensure the mobilization of their base of support.

Another characteristic of Populism is its purported third path of development between and beyond Capitalism and Communism. The Narodniki's Peasant Commune of Russia in the 1870s, Perón's *Justicialismo* in Argentina in the 1940s and 1950s, Nasser's Arab Socialism in the 1950s and 1960s, Qaddafi's Third Universal Theory and his People's *Jamahiria* in the 1970s and 1980s, and Khomeini's Neither East Nor West policy in the 1980s all attest to this common ideological attribute.

Economically, Populist leaders are opposed to laissez-faire policies. They favor nationalization of major industries and opt for interventionist, regulatory, and egalitarian policies to benefit the poor. This includes land reform, imposition of high tariffs on the imports, bolstering of the domestic industries, state guided growth, protectionism, provision of subsidies, public work programs to cope with unemployment, low-income housing, and other welfare policies. While they borrow from some Socialist principles, they do not favor abolishing of private property (with the exception of Russian Populists).

Their economic policies attempt to soften some of the harsher impacts of Capitalist development rather than abolishing it.

While populism could be economically progressive and forward looking in so far as it promotes economic reform and some measure of equality and protection for the poor, culturally it could be backward looking and reactionary in so far as it gets its source of inspirations from the past and its archaic values.

While ideologically populism advocates rule of the masses over the elite, in reality democratic representation of the people is not necessarily an attribute or a function of Populist movements. The mass mobilization and rule by the majority vote, the two characteristics of populism, is no guarantee for implementation of democratic principles. Indeed, many Populist leaders of the past have been authoritarian demagogues who are masterful in the art of manipulation of the masses. They often replace mass mobilization, initiated and controlled from above, for genuine democratic political participation from below. But in so far as they need to validate their leadership through popular vote, they allow formal political participation, and they favor electoral politics.

What abounds in Populist movements is the emergence of charismatic leaders. Perón, Echeverría, Vargas, Nasser, Ben Bella and Bomedien, Qaddafi, and Khomeini are a few examples. Charismatic leaders often emerge in a crisis milieu, and they are perceived by their followers to have answers to national problems. Their ability to articulate national frustrations as well as suppress mass aspirations and portray an alluring image of a future utopia is the key to their popular appeal. The messianic aura surrounding them and their message, and the use of mass mobilization to intimidate the political opponents, all serve to insulate Populist leaders from the vulnerabilities of mundane politics and keep their charisma intact.

Populism in Comparative Perspective

Populism as an ideology and movement has had different forms and manifestations in different parts of the world. The discussion that follows attempts to present a selective survey of some of the more prominent Populist movements to date. Russian and American populism emerged in the latter half of the nineteenth century in reaction to dislocations caused by accelerated pace of industrialization and urbanization. In Latin America in contrast, where the process of industrial development occurred later, Populist movements did not appear until the early twentieth

century. In the Middle East, where gaining independence and industrial development came later, populism is a post-World War II phenomenon.

In Russia, the term "populism" referred to the movement of the *Narodniks* in the 1870s. Populism in Russia was closely related to an idealized vision of the peasantry in general, and the peasant commune in particular. In its quest for a uniquely Russian path of development, the Russian intelligentsia romanticized the peasantry as the class that represented superior and pure Russian national virtues. Liberation of peasants from the oppression and exploitation of the Czarist absolutism would put Russia on the path of peasant socialism. Peasant socialism would usher in a third path of development separate from Capitalism and classical socialism. It would overcome Russia's backwardness without succumbing to the individualism, materialism, and pervasive corruption found in Western societies. The peasant commune would give birth to equality, social justice, harmony, and spiritual wholeness.

As they became aware that their leisure and education had become possible by the toil of impoverished masses, many Russian intellectuals were filled with the feelings of guilt and a sense of moral responsibility and obligation. Many students, for example, left their schools and went to the villages to "join the masses," experience their sufferings, and shed their "decadent" middle-class values. By joining the masses and arousing their political consciousness, Russian Populists sought to fulfill their moral obligation. By arousing the masses to political action, they aspired to overthrow czarism and to liberate society from the stifling grip of absolutism, thus emancipating themselves as a persecuted minority as well.

The major paradox of Russian populism was that it was not a movement of "the people," that is of the peasantry that constituted the vast majority of Russian population. Rather, it was a movement of radicalized and alienated intellectuals who projected their hopes and dreams unto a perceived revolutionary potential of peasantry.

Populism in the nineteenth- and early twentieth-century United States was the ideological banner of a declining peasantry whose prominence and livelihood as a class was threatened by the insurgent forces of industrial capitalism. It was the ideological banner of farmers and small producers. The main base of support for the Populists was in the South and the Midwest. The two antecedents of American populism were centralization of power in the commercial and political centers of the northeast and the domination of the South by the North. On the cultural level, the old values were disappearing, yet the new ones were still alien. This identity crisis and cultural alienation induced a longing for the past folk traditions among farmers and more traditional social layers. US populism expressed the agrarian sentiment for a return to social wholeness, self-government, and public authority. Industrialization and centralization of power in the Northeast meant that the agrarians, who were extolled as the backbone of the United States by its founders, romanticized by Jefferson, and glorified by Jackson, now faced the danger of economic ruin and political decline.

Although Russian and US populism were two entirely different movements—one a populism of the intelligentsia and primarily an urban movement and the other an agrarian movement—both can be regarded as agrarian populism. Russian populism was inspired by the image of peasantry, and the majority of recruits to US populism came from the ranks of farmers. One major difference between these two diverse forms of agrarian populism was that the US Populists, unlike their Russian counterparts, were not socialistic in their view of private property. Furthermore, the religious nature of populism in the United States was far stronger than its Russian counterpart.

William Jennings Bryan, the most distinguished leader of the Populist Movement in the United States, was deeply religious. Bryan's message was always moral, and his followers were primarily "the bible people." Biblical metaphors abounded in his writings, and he often accused his political opponents of being "sinners." But beyond its religious form, US populism combined agrarian radicalism, a tradition of Jeffersonian grassroots democracy and Jacksonian faith in the common man.

Although US populism as an organized movement did not last more than fifteen years, many regard the legacy of US populism to be the source of reforms enacted later by the Progressives during the period of 1901 through 1914. Hence, the watering down and the adaptation of the platform of the people's party (1892–1900), the major Populist Party in the United States, by the Democratic Party did not hinder the assimilation of many of its programs and agenda as the major fixture of US politics for years to come. Neither did it prevent the emergence of such a local strong man as Huey Long, the Populist senator and the governor of Louisiana who emerged as the powerful leader of the South in 1930s. Long attacked the big corporations and promised to distribute their wealth among the poor. He was intolerant of criticism and had a strong contempt for the constitutional and judicial processes.

Latin America also has a rich tradition of Populist politics. Latin American history from the 1920s through the 1960s has been deeply influenced by Populist movements and ideologies. Among the most

renowned Populist leaders of Latin America are Perón from Argentina, Vargas from Brazil, Echeverría from Mexico, Haya de la Tore from Peru, Ibarra from Ecuador, and Estensorro from Bolivia; these men and their policies are a few examples of the rich Populist tradition of the region.

Latin American populism was induced by the economic prosperity of the 1920s, which led to the acceleration of the metropolitan revolution throughout the region from the end of the nineteenth century onward. Urbanization and the expansion of literacy heightened the level of interest in politics and ushered in the entrance of the lower classes in the political arena.

There are two distinct periods in Latin American populism. First is the period between World Wars I and II. Second is the post-World War II period. In the first phase, Populist movements were concerned with legitimate representation, thus characterized by reformist politics. In the next phase, the Populist movements became more radicalized, addressing issues such as distribution of wealth, economic growth, and political development. Hence, policies that would promote aid for the poor, social integration in the face of differentiation in modern societies, equality, social justice, and democracy became widely popular.

Vargas, the Populist leader of Brazil from 1930 to 1945, launched a campaign that encouraged mobilization of workers and peasants and introduced a welfare program to benefit them. Vargas was highly authoritarian and strongly opposed the Communists as well as Western influence. He revived traditional values and encouraged patriotism and nationalism. Having suppressed his liberal and left-wing domestic foes successfully, he developed an elaborate network of patron-client based relationships on the local and state levels. The beneficiaries of this new cliental system guaranteed his regime a solid base of support. Consequently, the consolidation of power in this way made the use of force less necessary.

Perón, the president of Argentina from 1946 to 1955, drew his base of support primarily from the workers and peasants. His political opponents, for the most part, came from the ranks of the middle and the upper classes. He enacted several reforms that benefited the urban and rural poor and campaigned against big business and foreign imperialists. Perón termed his philosophy *Justicialismo*, or the "third position," between capitalism and communism that favored neither the Yankees nor Soviets. *Justicialismo* not only grounded Perónism in Argentine nationalism but also distinguished it from fascism.

Middle Eastern populism is primarily a post-World War II phenomenon. While the region had experienced Islamic Revivalist, Constitutionalist, and Nationalist movements in the late nineteenth and early twentieth centuries, only with the postindependence political and cultural awakenings and the acceleration of the urban revolution does one witness the systematic emergence and popularity of Populist ideologies since the 1950s.

Middle Eastern populism synthesized nationalism, anti-imperialism, elements of socialism, and Islam (to varying degrees). As such, it provided a nativist ideology, a third path of development that would distinguish the region from the Eastern (Communist) and Western (Capitalist) ideological and political hegemony.

Nasser, the charismatic Populist leader of Egypt in the 1950s and 1960s, came from peasant origins and was passionately committed to improving the condition of the poor. His ideology synthesized anti-Imperialism, Nationalism, Pan-Arabism, and "Arab Socialism." Although he was a secular leader, when necessary, he used Islamic symbolism to wrap his political message in the flag of cultural authenticity. For example, after the Egyptian defeat in the 1967 war against Israel, Nasser chose to address the crowd from the pulpit of the al-Azhar Mosque in Cairo.

Domestically, Nasser nationalized the major industries and collectivized some of the land of the richest landowners. While not opposed to private property, he was against "exploitative ownership." While he opposed the sector of the Capitalist class that was dependent on foreign capital, he supported the gains of the domestic Capitalists.

Internationally, Nasser promoted the idea of positive neutralism and nonalignment. He negotiated with the British to gain Egypt's independence in 1954, and in 1956 after nationalizing the Suez Canal, he fought the combined armies of the British, the French, and the Israelis in which he lost the battle but won the hearts and minds of the popular masses throughout the Arab World. Consequently, Nasser emerged as the strong advocate of Pan-Arabism. He wanted to restore the Arab pride and national identity as well as foster Pan-Arab unity. His firebrand Nationalist rhetoric evoked an overwhelmingly positive response throughout the Arab World. It provided a remedy for the sense of wounded dignity that many Arabs had experienced due to a history of colonial and semicolonial domination.

His immense popularity notwithstanding, Nasser was intolerant of his political opponents on the Right (Muslim Brotherhood) and the Left (the Communists). He had several leaders of both parties executed and many of their members imprisoned and tortured. He was the prototype of Arab Populist charismatic authoritarian leaders who followed him. Indeed, "Nasser's Revolution" inspired other movements in

the Arab world, such as the Algerian Revolution of 1954 and the Libyan Revolution of 1969.

The Algerian revolution of 1954–1962 was a Nationalist movement against French Colonial rule. On assuming power, Ben Bella, the first Populist leader of the revolution, implemented a system known as "Autogestion," a system of workers' management through popularly elected representation. Autogestion was designed to transform the colonial economy into a "socialist economy." The new leaders declared compatibility of Islam, nationalism, and Marxism.

Ben Bella like his predecessor, Nasser in Egypt, banned all political parties. In 1963, he drafted a new constitution that gave him enormous powers as the head of state, the commander in chief of the armed forces, and the General Secretary of the National Liberation Front or the *Frente de Liberacion Naciónal* (FLN), the party that led the Algerian Revolution. Ben Bella's attempt to consolidate all the power in his own hands and curb the influence of the army, led to a *coup d'état* in 1965 by Minister of Defense Houari Boumédiènne.

Boumédiènne dissolved the national assembly and suspended the constitution. The eleven years of rule by decree that followed effectively began the era of authoritarian populism in Algerian politics. From 1965 until the election of the national popular assembly in 1977 and the creation of FLN political bureau in 1979, all executive and legislative powers were concentrated in the Algerian Council of Revolution and the Council of Ministers, both headed by Boumédiènne. Hence, it was only in 1976 that a new constitution was approved by a referendum; Boumédiènne, as the sole candidate of the only legitimate party, the FLN, was formally elected as president for six years. Boumédiènne began an extensive campaign, nationalizing the major industries and banks. To expand the state penetration of the civil society, in 1967 Boumédiènne established communal (township) assemblies. These institutions were complemented by Waliya (provincial) assemblies in 1969. In 1971, he initiated extensive land reform, silencing the land owners' resistance in the process. These reforms were designed to improve the lot of the impoverished masses.

Internationally, Boumédiènne opted for nonalignment and Third World solidarity, supporting the movements of national liberation. In an attempt to give Third World nations better control over their resources, Algeria played an active role in creating the Organization of Petroleum Exporting Countries (OPEC) and developing its policies. Algeria also took a leading role in the North–South dialogue, calling for a new international economic order.

In 1969, a young army officer named Muammar Qaddafi led a revolt of "free officers" that overthrew King Idris and abolished the monarchy, replacing it with the People's Republic. Qaddafi's political philosophy, referred to as the Third Universal Theory, is articulated in his Green Book. The Green Book criticizes Capitalism and Socialism and presents an alternative path.

Qaddafi's Populist message has endeared him particularly among the lower classes. Qaddafi's charisma is rooted in his humble origins and his strong identification with Islamic and Arab identity. He mingles freely with the masses, often resides in a tent, and drives his own car. He admires the virtues of rural Libya and is a champion of Arab unity and solidarity.

Once in power, Qaddafi banned all political parties and created a single monopolistic political party called the Arab Socialist Union. To mobilize his base of support, he created People's Committees and their armed detachments, People's Militias, as instruments of "Direct Democracy." But, in reality, these organizations came under the direct control of Qaddafi and his supporters. When these committees became organs of independent power, they were dissolved.

Economically, Qaddafi implemented extensive nationalization of major industries and imposed state control and regulation. Private property was tolerated as long as it remained "nonexploitative." He proposed abolishing the wage system in favor of granting workers a share of production proportionate to their contribution to the production effort. He also promoted workers' control and self-management of many industries and created state-controlled supermarkets in an attempt to prevent the escalation in rising food prices. Qaddafi's other reforms included reducing rents, providing affordable mass housing, doubling the minimum wage, and converting foreign banks into Libyan joint stock companies.

In 1973, he launched his Cultural Revolution. He declared the Islamic law, the Shari'a, to be the only source of law and himself as the sole arbiter and interpreter of religious issues, thus elevating himself as the political as well as the spiritual leader of his people. By closing the nightclubs, banning alcohol, and restricting the non-Muslim religious institutions, he gained the critical support of the clergy. Qaddafi, however, has proven to be highly intolerant of both secular and Islamic opposition, and he does not hesitate to use repression to silence them.

When the Islamic Revolution of 1979 brought the clergy to power, they drafted a new constitution that defined the goal of the revolution as a movement aimed at the triumph of all "the oppressed over the oppressors." This Populist tone not only reflected the

composition of the movement that overthrew the monarchy but also the ideology of its leadership led by Ayatolah Khomeini. After the revolution, the new regime confiscated the property of those who fled the country and nationalized major industries, including banks, factories, insurance companies, foreign trade, and undeveloped land. Hence, a housing foundation was created to build affordable accommodations for the poor. Some of the shanty town residents were allowed to take over the luxurious houses of the prominent members of the former regime.

The new regime also built a wide array of institutions to buttress its support among the popular masses. Among such institutions were revolutionary committees (*komitehs*) that were spontaneous mass-based organizations that sprang up throughout the country right after the revolution. Another important institution was the revolutionary guards. They became the main alternative to the regular army, which was mistrusted by the regime. If the revolutionary guards provided the regime with a military arm, *bonyAd-e mostaza'fan* (the foundation of the dispossessed) became the financial arm of the regime. This organization confiscated and administered the property of the royal family and other officials of the Shah's regime on behalf of the downtrodden and provided many financial services for the poor. Hence, the institution of Friday Prayer (*Imam Jom'aeh*) allowed Ayatollah Khomeini to appoint his relatives, former students, and associates to key positions of power. They in turn informed him of mass sentiment in the provinces and took his messages directly to the people in an attempt to expand and consolidate his base of support.

Ayatollah Khomeini's charismatic authority and his credentials as the spiritual and political leader of the revolution legitimized these institutions as the organs of people-clergy power. His effective use of Shi'ite mythology and sacred traditions rendered his message communicable to the ordinary people. For the laity, he personified the link of historical continuity with their past and resolved their cultural anxiety and identity crisis in a rapidly changing world. Many of them identified with his simple lifestyle, religious vision, and traditional values. His politicized interpretation of Shi'ite Islam proved to be a potent political force. As a common cultural denominator, it could be used to unify and mobilize the people. Hence, his forceful personality kept the heterogeneous clerical coalition together. His depiction of the descending utopia as a "unitarian classless Islamic society," in which justice and virtue reign, and worldly and heavenly salvation can be attained, created hope in the midst of a hopeless situation. He repeatedly referred to the "dispossessed" as the people who have

sacrificed the most for the revolution and are its true heirs. By championing their cause, Khomeini developed a sense of mutual identification between himself and the popular masses. Khomeini's populism, however, was decidedly authoritarian, as he consolidated much of the power in his own hand. He was the ultimate interpreter and implementer of the Islamic law, the commander in chief of the armed forces, and the ultimate authority on all religious and policy matters. Under his theocratic rule, political opponents were suppressed, and civil and democratic rights were restricted.

In the realm of foreign affairs, Khomini's Neither East, Nor West policy grounded him in nationalism and nonalignment. Whereas Iran's relation with the West deteriorated, its economic and political relations with the Third World nations in general and Islamic nations in particular expanded considerably. Khomeini also promoted Pan-Islamism in an attempt to export Islamic revolution elsewhere in the region. These policies changed considerably in the post-Khomeini era.

MANOCHEHR DORRAJ

See also Boumédiènne, Houari; Khomeini, Ayatollah Ruhollah; Nasser, Gamal Abdel; Perón, Juan Domingo; Vargas, Getúlio

References and Further Reading

Blanksten, George L. *Peron's Argentina*. New York: Russell and Russell, 1953.

Canovan, Margaret. *Populism*. New York: Harcourt Brace Jovanovich, 1981.

Connif, Michael L., ed. *Latin American Populism in Comparative Perspective*. Albuquerque, NM: University of New Mexico Press, 1982.

Entelis, John, P. *Algeria: The Revolution Institutionalized*. Boulder, CO: Westview Press, 1986.

Germani, Gino. *Authoritarianism, Fascism and National Populism*. New Brunswick, NJ: Transaction Books, 1978.

Goodwyne, Lawrence. *The Populist Movement: Short History of the Agrarian Revolt in America*. New York: Oxford University Press, 1978.

Harris, Lillian. C. *Libya: Qadaffi's Revolution and the Modern State*. Boulder, CO: Westview Press, 1986.

Levine, Robert, L. *The Vargas Regime: The Critical Years, 1934–1938*. New York: Columbia University Press, 1970.

McKenna, George, ed. *American Populism*. New York: G.P. Putnam's Sons, 1974.

Ramazani, Ruhollah, K. *Revolutionary Iran*. Baltimore, MD: John Hopkins University Press, 1986.

Rejwan, Nissim. *Nasserist Ideology: Its Exponents and Critics*. New York: Halsted Press, 1974.

Walicki, Andrzej. *Controversy over Capitalism: Studies in the Social Philosophy of the Russian Populists*. Oxford, UK: Clarendon Press, 1969.

POVERTY: DEFINITION AND TRENDS

Conceptualizing Poverty

The concept of poverty has many interpretations. The diversity of interpretations is caused by time and space factors, culture, and conventions of the society (Hobsbawm 1972) and philosophical worldviews. "Poverty" expresses many connotations and has always had a relevance to notions like deprivation, insufficiency, deficiency, and the like. It is viewed as an age-old social malaise, a complex socioeconomic state that characterizes any particular individual or families in a given society. Poverty takes different forms in different societies and varies over time and across cultures. Since all societies are, more or less, stratified according to some criteria, the consequence is that somebody always has to be at the bottom; whether this bottom layer is an expression of poverty and the people inhabiting this bottom layer are considered poor, depends on indigenous definition of poverty (Oyen 2003). However, the understanding of poverty and its measurement and analysis is crucially important for a number of purposes. The main purposes are to understand the situation of poverty, to find the factors that determine that situation, to design interventions best adapted to the issue, and to assess the effectiveness of current policies and determine whether the situation is changing (World Bank 2002).

Worldview of Poverty

Poverty is seen from different worldviews. In one worldview, poverty is seen as lack of distribution of income with equity. This is mostly the case with developed countries where poverty occurs due to problem of distribution of income or resources rather than total amount of national income. In an opposite worldview, poverty in poor or developing countries is seen as lack of creation of income coupled with economic underdevelopment. Another worldview of poverty involves "moneylessness" and "powerlessness." Moneylessness means not merely an insufficiency of cash but a chronic inadequacy of all types of resources to satisfy such basic human needs as nutrition, rest, warmth, and bodily care. Powerlessness, however, means a lack of opportunities and choices open to the poor whose lives seem to be governed by forces and persons outside their control, such as by people in position of authority (Tussing).

However, the dominant worldview of poverty that has attained much attention in poverty literature regards "absolute" and "relative" poverty. Absolute poverty means absolute deprivation or starvation. It illustrates a people or family who simply does not have enough to eat and sustain itself. People living in absolute poverty are usually characterized as undernourished, illiterate, and prone to diseases and have high infant mortality and low life expectancy. Absolute poverty is common in the poorer Third World countries. Relative poverty, on the other hand, refers to a low standard of living compared to the average standard. In industrial countries, relative poverty is essentially a measure of inequality. Thus, relative poverty varies from country to country and from time to time.

A different worldview of poverty is moral poverty. It goes beyond material well-being and emphasizes the holding of a value system for equal access to opportunities and egalitarianism. It means the abolition of social inequalities along with the universal elevation of a standard of material life attained by the upper strata of the society.

Definition of Poverty

Based on different worldviews, the definition of poverty may vary. Interestingly, however, sociologists, economists, and philosophers also might not come under a common umbrella in defining the concept of poverty. The problem in defining poverty has further been aggravated with widened ideas attached to it.

Before attempting to define poverty, it is necessary to distinguish those who are poor from those who are not poor. The common method is to classify an individual as poor based on a set of consumption norms that he or she cannot meet. However, it is not simple either conceptually or empirically to specify a set of such norms. Even if there were the agreement that the minimum amount of food, clothing, and shelter needed to sustain life should constitute a universal set of norms, these minimal requirements could not be either unambiguously defined or easily quantified. Besides, the minimum energy from food needed to sustain the basic bodily functions of an individual of a given age, sex, height, weight, and activity is not a constant (ADB 1992). This inability to identify a constant is the reason why it is often argued that universal poverty norms are not feasible to develop and, rather, that they are very time, space, and culture specific.

Still scholars have attempted to define poverty with a universalistic approach. One such universally

accepted notion is that poverty is "a matter of deprivation" (Sen 1981). The deprivation is premised on social norms and varies substantially as noted earlier through time and space. With this view in mind, poverty in developing countries can indicate absolute deprivation, infringing on basic sustenance of life, whereas poverty in developed countries can indicate relative deprivation, meaning a lack of ability to afford a standard of living enjoyed by a reference group with higher incomes (Quibria 1991).

The concept of deprivation, however, has evolved through time. With rapid industrial growth and advancement in communication and technology, the global economy has changed remarkably. This increased global economy has given birth to the notion of deprivation in its relative sense. At the beginning of the twentieth century, the prevailing notion in today's developed countries was one of failure to meet basic nutritional and biological requirements for the sustenance of life. Rowntree (1901) noted that "primary poverty . . . [means] earnings insufficient to obtain the minimum necessities for the maintenance of merely physical efficiency." This definition of poverty relates to a concept of absolute poverty as it is employed in developing countries today. In developed countries, with increasing material wealth, this definition has lost a good deal of its significance. The specter of hunger and poverty has been, more or less, banished from most of these economies. Poverty, in most advanced industrial nations, is now a matter of deviation from social and economic norms. In other words, as the threat of starvation has receded from the scene, poverty is being interpreted in advanced countries in relative terms.

Some contemporary scholars have also attempted to redefine poverty as incorporating the issues of gender, environment, and easy access to private and public goods. Lipton and Maxwell write that the concept of poverty has:

> Been broadened, beyond the notions of inadequate private income or consumption, toward a more comprehensive perspective: absence of a secure and sustainable livelihood ... [which] allows us to measure and evaluate the level and vulnerability—and freedom from bias by gender and age—of individuals' access to privately and publicly provided goods and services and to common property. (1992: 10)

However, in a different light, poverty is also viewed as a politically sensitive theme while compared to the concept of inequality. Inequality is a relatively safe theme, for after all there are many positions, philosophical and political, in relation to inequality. It may be viewed as necessary, inevitable, or even beneficial in relation to a particular mode of progress.

According to a classic liberal view, inequality of outcomes may be acceptable as long as there is equality of opportunity. Poverty, on the other hand, is politically sensitive and challenging, for it undermines social cohesion; hence, the conceptualization and measurement of poverty are matters of political dispute (Wilson 1996).

Measuring Poverty and the Poverty Line

There are many standards available to measure poverty both at country and global levels. Measurement of poverty in a systematic fashion was pioneered by Booth and Rowntree in the late nineteenth century. Later on, some other scholars like Galbraith (1958), Harrington (1960), Orshansky (1965), and A.K. Sen (1973) as well as various international organizations like International Labour Organization (ILO), World Bank, and United Nations Development Programme (UNDP) have done much research to devise more appropriate measures for accurate and scientific quantification of poverty.

At first, obtaining a measurement requires drawing a poverty line. The poverty line is defined as the minimum acceptable standard of living for the society. It is essentially a cut-off point that separates those in poverty from the rest of the population. A poverty line generally comprises two elements: (i) the expenditure necessary to buy a minimum standard of nutrition and other basic necessities and (ii) a further amount that varies from country to country, reflecting the cost of participating in the everyday life of society. The first element can be calculated in a straightforward manner. The cost of minimum adequate caloric intakes and other necessities is estimated from the prices of the goods that constitute the consumption bundles of the poor. The second element, however, is subjective and varies with per capita income—that is, the richer a country, the higher is its poverty line (Nixon 1996). For example, in the United States, since the 1960s, the federal government has established a poverty line to designate people officially regarded as poor. The line is fixed by calculating the average cost of food that average-sized families need for minimum nutrition. This figure is then tripled to cover the minimum cost of clothing, housing, medical care, and other necessities. The official poverty line for a family of four in 1996 was set at $16,036. By that measure, in that year, about 14% of the population—about 36.5 million people—were defined as living in poverty (US Bureau of the Census, 1998).

However, to measure poverty at the global level, the same reference poverty line is used, expressed in a common unit across countries. Therefore, for the purpose of global aggregation and comparison, the World Bank uses reference lines set at $1 and $2 per day, more precisely at $1.08 and $2.15 in the 1993 Purchasing Power Parity [PPP] terms (World Bank 2005). The most common measure of poverty is the head-count measure, often expressed at H, given by the proportion of the total population that happens to be identified as poor and as falling below the specified poverty line income. If q is the number of people who are identified as being poor and n the total number of people in the community, then the head-count measure H is simply q/n (Sen 1999). The H ratio makes a nondiscriminatory, "gross-category" approach in measuring the number of people who are below the poverty line (Ghosh 1994). In view of the shortcomings of the H ratio, Sen uses the P index to measure poverty. Sen examines the income shortfall of each person from the poverty line. A weighted norm of the income shortfalls of the poor can be viewed as a measure of poverty. Sen uses a simple method in which he takes the rank values of the poor in the income ranking as the weights to be put on the income shortfalls of different persons within the category of the poor. It is an absolute measure of poverty using "rank order weights" on the basis of gaps in the income of the poor, where more weight per unit is attached to lower incomes (Sen 1973). Another frequently used measure of poverty is the Gini coefficient that basically measures the level of inequality within societies and applies on a global scale as well.

Trends of Poverty

Poverty has always been associated with humanity throughout many civilizations. With the advance of time, industrial growth, and scientific and technological innovations, the trends of poverty have shifted their routes with many ups and downs in different epochs of human history. "Poor," as is considered of some people in society, is perhaps the result of stratified societies where upper and lower strata coexist and have direct contact with each other. In medieval legal terminology, poverty is seen as lower strata, and people belonging to those strata are regarded as *arme liute* (poor people). Before the turn of twentieth century, the changes in trends of poverty were basically conceptual. For example, in preindustrial societies, poverty (more specifically pauperism) was seen as abnormal and called for remedial action. In fact, the traditional "policy of provision" that imposed on the public authorities the duty to provide regular food supplies at reasonable prices, rather than the "poor law," is the ancestor of modern welfare policies (Hobsbawm 1972). This perception was slightly changed in the industrial era, during which the lower and upper strata of the society were recognized as socioeconomic classes. In this time, the poor, often recognized as the working class (proletariat) who were employed for wages, developed a specific form of supralocal organization that called for the protection and advancement of living standards insofar as these depended on employment. The early phases of industrialism saw an unusual crisis of extreme poverty. The trend in perception of poverty in this period was that the actual needs of the poor lied in the formulation of public policy. Before this time, no criterion of poverty was usually recognized other than destitution and positively asking for relief.

Beginning in the late nineteenth century, a socialistic approach slowly took its roots with an emphasis on pro-poor policy formulation that abandoned self-regulated capitalist economy. Due to growing political influence of the poor and the appearance of planned Socialist economies, the problem of extreme poverty in that period was considered a wider social problem, which gave emphasis to providing all citizens with a minimum standard of living at all levels. Thus, special "poor laws" that existed in that time disappeared, as in Britain in 1929 (Hobsbawm 1972). However, quantification of "poor" or inquiring into the "state of the poor" was started in Britain in the late eighteenth century and has received impetus with a firmer statistical base since the 1830s. From the late nineteenth century, the trends of poverty started to be identified with a statistical quantification, and poverty measure and the official poverty line began to take shape.

The trends of poverty in the twentieth century are characterized by rapid industrial growth and speedy technological advancement yet a huge gap between the lower and upper strata of the society. The basic factors responsible for such gaps or global inequality in the second half of the twentieth century were, according to UNDP, (i) rapid economic growth in already rich countries in Western Europe, North America, and Oceania relative to most of the rest of the world; and (ii) slow growth on the Indian subcontinent until the late twentieth century and consistently slow growth in Africa (UNDP 2002). Poverty during this period was reduced in an accelerated pace, and the per capita income jumped to a high status compared to any other time in history, but the status of inequality did not lessen but rather increased with big strides.

Summarizing the findings of an econometric study for the World Bank, Pritchett notes "the ratio of per capita income in the richest versus the poorest country (between 1870 and 1989) has increased by a factor of six and the standard deviation of GDP per capita has increased between 60% and 100%. (Pritchett, 1995)." If the distribution of wealth between countries continues to diverge, Castells observes, the average living conditions of the world's population, as measured by the United Nations Human Development Index, overall have improved steadily over the past three decades since 1970s (Castells 2000). This improvement is due, primarily, to better educational opportunities and improved health standards, which translate into a dramatic increase in life expectancy that in developing countries went up from 46 years in the 1960s to 62 years in 1993 and 64.4 years in 1997, particularly for women (UNDP 1996). But the evolution of the income gap presents a different picture from a global perspective as well as from a comparative perspective when looking at specific countries.

The first major overall gap in human inequality emerges in the wake of the Industrial Revolution and has been widening ever since. Estimates of income gap between the fifth of the world's people living in the richest country and the fifth in the poorest are as follows: 1820: three to one; 1870: seven to one; 1913: eleven to one; 1960: thirty to one; 1990: sixty to one; 1997: seventy-four to one (UNDP 1999). Since 1970s, globally speaking, there has been inequality and polarization in the distribution of wealth at a very fast rate. According to UNDP's 1996/1999 Human Development Reports, in 1993 only $5 trillion of the $23 trillion (US dollars, USD) global gross domestic product (GDP) were from the developing countries even if they accounted for nearly 80% of total population. The poorest 20% of the world's people have seen their share of global income decline from 2.3% to 1.4% in the past thirty years. Meanwhile, the share of the richest 20% of people in the world has risen from 70% to 85%. In 1994, the assets of the world's 358 billionaires (USD) exceeded the combined annual incomes of countries with 45% of the world's population. The concentration of wealth at the very top accelerated in the second half of the 1990s: the net worth of the world's two hundred richest people increased from $440 billion to more than $1 trillion (USD) between 1994 and 1998.

Thus, in 1998, the assets of the three richest people in the world were more than the combined gross national product (GNP) of the forty-eight least developed countries, including 600 million people (UNDP 1999). The gap in per capita income between the industrial and the developing worlds tripled, from $5,700 in 1960 to $15,000 (USD) in 1993 (UNDP

1996). Between 1960 and 1991, all but the richest quintile (of the world's people) saw their income share fall, so that by 1991, more than 85% of the world's population received only 15% of its income—yet another indication of an even more polarized world (UNDP 1996). This polarization and the trend of inequality continue to increase even after the world reached a new millennium. Milanovic finds some startling statistics, taking into account inequality within countries and using PPP exchange rates. The most recent available estimates are for 1993, but stagnation in the poorest countries and robust growth in many of the richest countries imply that these are unlikely to have improved. Milanovic estimated that the world's richest 1% receive as much income as the poorest 57%. The richest 10% of the US population has an income equal to that of the poorest 43% of the world. Put differently, the income of the richest 25 million US citizens is equal to that of almost 2 billion people. His calculation also estimates that the income of the world's richest 5% is 114 times that of the poorest 5% (Milanovic 2001).

However, the statistics of intracountry inequality also show considerable disparity in different areas of the world. Since the 1980s, income inequality has increased in the United States (Fischer et al. 1996), United Kingdom (Townsend 1993), Brazil, Argentina, Venezuela, Bolivia, Peru, Thailand, Russia (UNDP 1996), Japan (Bauer and Mason 1992), Canada, Sweden, Australia, Germany (Green et al. 1992), and Mexico (Skezely 1995), just to cite a few relevant countries. But income inequality decreased in the 1960–1990 period in India, Malaysia, Hong Kong, Singapore, Taiwan, and South Korea (UNDP 1996). In addition, according to data elaborated by Deininger and Squire, the level of income inequality can be compared, measured by the Gini coefficient, among the major regions of the world between the 1990s and the 1970s; in 1990, it was much higher in Eastern Europe, somewhat higher in Latin America, but lower in all other regions when analyzed at a highly aggregate level (Deininger and Squire 1996). The Gini coefficient remained for Latin America as a whole at about 0.58 throughout the 1990s, thus reflecting the highest level of inequality among major regions in the world (Castells 2000).

Yet, while allowing for a certain range of trend variations in different countries, a predominant trend toward increasing inequality has been shown between the late 1970s and the mid-1990s. In examining the level of inequality, Castells observes the United Kingdom to be the fastest growing. But what is particularly striking is that the two other countries with rapidly increasing inequality are Sweden and Denmark, which were until recently egalitarian

societies. If Japan is added to the same category of fast-growing inequality in societies with low levels of inequality, this observation would suggest the hypothesis of a structural trend toward increasing inequality in the network society. On the other hand, Finland, a very advanced network society, did not follow the trend of its Scandinavian neighbors, and Italy significantly reduced inequality. If Spanish and Portuguese data were included in the table, they would show a pattern of stable, moderate inequality. Transition economies in Eastern Europe and the Commonwealth of Independent States (CIS) experienced, in the 1990s, the fastest rise in inequality ever. By the end of the twentieth century, the income share of the richer 20% was 11 times that of the poorer 20% in Russia (UNDP 1999).

In the mid-1990s, taking as the extreme poverty line a consumption equivalent of $1 a day, 1.3 billion people, accounting for 33% of the developing world's population, were in misery. Of these poor people, 550 million lived in South Asia, 215 million in sub-Saharan Africa, and 150 million in Latin America (UNDP 1996). In a similar estimate, using a $1 per day dividing line for extreme poverty, the ILO estimated that the percentage of the population below this line increased from 53.05% in 1985 to 54.4% in 1990 in sub-Saharan Africa and from 23 to 27.8% in Latin America; the percentage decreased from 61.1 to 59% in South Asia and from 15.7 to 14.7% in East/Southeast Asia (not including China). According to the UNDP, between 1987 and 1993, the number of people with incomes of less than $1 (USD)a day increased by 100 million to reach 1.3 billion. If the level of income of less than $2 a day is considered, another 1 billion people should be added to this list. Thus, at the turn of the millennium, well over one-third of humankind was living at subsistence or below subsistence level.

In addition to income poverty, other dimensions of poverty are even more striking: in the mid-1990s, about 840 million people were illiterate, more than 1.2 billion lacked access to safe water, 800 million lacked access to health services, and more than 800 million suffered hunger. Nearly one-third of the people in the least developed countries—mainly in sub-Saharan Africa—were not expected to survive to the age of forty. Women and children suffer most from poverty: 160 million children under five were malnourished, and the maternal mortality rate was about five hundred women per one hundred thousand live births (ILO 1995). The largest concentration of poverty was, by far, in the rural areas: in 1990, the proportion of the poor among the rural population was 66% in Brazil, 72% in Peru, 43% in Mexico, 49% in India, and 54% in the Philippines (ILO, 1994). As for Russia, the CIS countries, and Eastern Europe, a report issued by the World Bank in April 1999 calculated that there were 147 million people living below the poverty line of $4 (USD) a day; the equivalent figure for 1989 was 14 million.

Thus, overall, the ascent of informational, global capitalism is indeed characterized by simultaneous economic development and underdevelopment as well as social inclusion and social exclusion, in a process very roughly reflected in comparative statistics. There is polarization in the distribution of wealth at the global level and differential evolution of intra-country income inequality, albeit with a predominantly upward trend toward increasing inequality and substantial growth of poverty and misery in the world at large and in most—but not all—countries, both developed and developing. However, the patterns of social exclusion, and the factors accounting for them, require a qualitative analysis of the processes by which they are induced.

MOHAMMAD EHSAN AND MUHAMMAD MUINUL ISLAM

See also Basic Human Needs; Income Distribution; Peasants, Impact of Development on; Poverty: Impact on Development; Quality of Life: Definition; Subsistence Living

References and Further Reading

Bauer, John, and Andrew Mason, "The Distribution of Income and Wealth in Japan." *Review of Income and Wealth* 38, no. 4 (1992): 403–428.

Booth, C. *Life and Labour of the People in London.* London, 1889.

Castells, Manuel. *End of Millennium.* United Kingdom: Blackwell Publishers, 2000.

Deininger, Klaus, and Lyn Squire. "A New Dataset Measuring Income Inequality." *The World Bank Economic Review* 10, no. 3 (1996): 565–591.

Fischer, Claude et al., *Inequality by Design.* Princeton, NJ: Princeton University Press, 1996.

Galbraith, J. K. *The Affluent Society.* Boston: Houghton Miffin, 1958.

Ghosh, Alak. *Indian Economy.* Calcutta: World Press, 1994.

Green, Gordon et al., "International Comparisons of Earnings Inequality for Men in the 1980s." *Review of Income and Wealth* 38, no. 1 (1992): 1–15.

Harrington, M. *The Other America.* New York: MacMillan Company, 1960.

Hobsbawm, E. J. "Poverty." *International Encyclopedia of Social Sciences.* Vol. XII. New York: MacMillan Company and The Free Press, 1972.

Lipton, M., and S. Maxwell. The New Poverty Agenda: An Overview. Discussion Paper 306. Brighton, Sussex: Institute of Development Studies, 1992.

Milanovic, Branko. Correspondence on Income, Inequality, and Poverty During the Transition from Planned to Market Economy. Washington, DC: World Bank, March 2002.

Orshansky, M. "Who's Who Among the Poor: A Demographic View of Poverty." *Social Security Bulletin* 28, no. 7 (1965).

Oyen, Else. *Poverty Production: A Different Approach to Poverty Understanding*. Norway: Center for International Poverty Research, 1965.

Pritchett, Lant. *Divergence, Big Time. Policy Research Working Paper, no. 1522*. Washington, DC: The World Bank, 1995.

Quibria, M.G. "Understanding Poverty: An Introduction to Conceptual and Measurement Issues." *Asian Development Review* 9, no. 2 (1991).

Rowntree, S. *Poverty: A Study of Town Life*. London: MacMillan Company, 1901.

Sen, A. K. "Poverty, Inequality, and Unemployment." *Economic and Political Weekly. Special Number*. August 1973.

————. *Poverty and Famines*. Oxford: Clarendon Press, 1982.

————. *Poverty and Famines: An Essay on Entitlement and Deprivation*. New York: Oxford University Press, 1999.

Skezely, Miguel. "Poverty in Mexico During Adjustment." *Review of Income and Wealth* 41, no. 3: 331–348.

Townsend, Peter. *The International Analysis of Poverty*. London: Harvester/Wheatsheaf, 1993.

Tussing, Dale A. "Poverty." *Encyclopedia Americana*.

United Nations Development Programme (UNDP). *Human Development Report 2004*. New York: Oxford University Press, 2004.

————. 2002. *Human Development Report 2002*. New York: Oxford University Press, 2002.

————. 1996. *Human Development Report 1996*. New York: Oxford University Press, 1996.

————.1999. *Human Development Report 1999*. New York: Oxford University Press, 1999.

US Bureau of the Census. *Statistical Abstract of the United States*. Washington, DC: Government Printing Office, 1998.

Wilson, F. "Drawing Together Some Regional Perspectives on Poverty." *Poverty: A Global Review*, E. Oyen, S. M. Miller, and S. A. Samad, eds. Oslo, Norway: Scandinavian University Press, 1996.

World Bank. 2005. *Poverty: Overview*. URI:http://web. worldbank.org/. WBSITE/EXTERNAL/TOPICS/EXTPOVERTY/0,,content MDK:20153855~menuPK 373757~pagePK:148956~piPK: 216618~theSitePK:336992,00.html.

————. "Core Technique and Cross-cutting Issues." *A Sourcebook for Poverty Reduction Strategies*, Jeni Klugman, ed. Vol. I. Washington, DC: World Bank.

POVERTY: IMPACT ON DEVELOPMENT

The term "poverty" can be used in relation to a wide range of phenomena that relate to a lack or deficiency. In relation to development issues, the meaning of "poverty" is most often confined to material poverty in respect of money, goods, and services (such as education or health care). In everyday usage, the term "poverty" is used to mean a shortage of income.

More accurately, one could say that poverty is a condition where an individual is unable to secure the things that he or she needs to survive. Development literature stresses the multidimensionality of poverty; in addition to material consumption, the aspects of health, education, social life, environmental quality, and spiritual and political freedom all make up human well-being. In other words, poverty is pronounced deprivation in human well-being: to be poor is to be hungry, to lack shelter and clothing, to be sick and not cared for, to be illiterate and not schooled, and to be socially excluded. Poor people are also more vulnerable to adverse events outside their control. In most cases, poor people are unable to plan for the future with any degree of certainty, and they are often mistreated by the institutions of state and society and excluded from voice and power in those institutions. In some sense, poverty could then be seen as the contrast to development, though development and poverty are not opposites. Poverty is a condition, while development is a process or, rather, a set of processes; and "development" refers often to processes that aim to reduce "poverty."

Nevertheless, the processes of economic development (such as the development of industries, the creation of new jobs and forms of employment, the extension of global trade, and the transition from rural to urban life) have not been able to overcome the global inequalities between the world's rich and poor. Poverty still remains a problem of huge proportions: of the world's 6 billion people, 2.8. billion live on less than $2 (USD) a day and 1.3 billion live below the World Bank's poverty line, that is, on less than $1 a day. Each year, some 18 million of them die prematurely from poverty-related causes. About eight out of every one hundred infants do not see their first birthday. This is one-third of all human death, about fifty thousand every day. It is estimated that nine of every one hundred boys and fourteen of every one hundred girls who reach school age do not attend school. Nearly 900 million adults still cannot read or write. Poverty is also evident in poor people's social exclusion and in their extreme vulnerability to ill health, economic dislocation, personal violence, and natural disasters. The scourge of HIV/AIDS, the frequency and brutality of civil conflicts, and rising disparities between affluent countries and the developing appear to further widen the gap between the rich and the poor.

Absolute and Relative Poverty

The question remains of how such severe and extensive poverty can exist while there is great and rising

affluence elsewhere. The average income of the citizens of affluent countries is about fifty times greater in purchasing power than that of the global poor. The latter 2.8 billion people together have about 1.2% of aggregate global income, while the 903 million people of the "high income economies" together have 80%. Shifting merely 1% of aggregate global income, $312 billion annually, from the first group to the second could eradicate severe poverty worldwide. Instead, developed countries spend $600 billion a year on defense and $300 billion in direct and indirect agricultural subsidies, while official development assistance from all nations of the Organization for Economic cooperation and Development (OECD) during 2002 represented only $56 billion (about 0.22% of total gross domestic product or GDP of those nations).

The paradox of wealth and poverty leads us to the question concerning the relativity of poverty. Poverty can be understood both in absolute as well as in relative terms. "Relative poverty" is the comparison of one person's wealth with another. When poverty in affluent and developed nations (though not all) the concern is relative poverty. People might be, or at least regard themselves, as poor in comparison to their more affluent neighbors who may own more material assets. They might have low self-esteem and feel they do not meet the expectations of their communities, despite the fact that their income may be well beyond the minimum needed to survive and their material wealth is ten times greater than that of the world's poorest people. Most citizens of the industrialized countries in comparison to people in the developing world are very wealthy. For example, gross national product (GNP) per capita in the United Kingdom is around $8,460 (USD), while in Ethiopia the amount is closer to $110. This would make the average person in the United Kingdom around seventy-six times wealthier than the average Ethiopian.

While people live in absolute poverty in every country of the world, the numbers and proportions are far greater in the developing world. In the global context, and particularly in relation to the development of poor nations, a discussion of poverty means "absolute poverty." If the focus is on the poorest quarter of humanity (including very few indeed in Europe or North America), then the poverty is one of an absolute sense of severe deprivation of, for example, food, shelter, education, and health care; these people are living on the verge of survival. Absolute poverty prevents people from meeting their most basic biological needs for food, clothing, and shelter. This type of poverty and lack of purchasing power can threaten an individual's very existence.

Multidimensional Poverty and Human Well-Being

Poverty means having insufficient money and other resources when these are needed; it also refers to standards of consumption that are below those judged by the community at large to be acceptable or adequate to sustain a full and meaningful life. This definition of poverty shows the multidimensional nature of poverty and its direct relation to the concept of "human welfare" as well as "human well-being." Taking into account the multidimensionality of poverty enables an understanding of the complex nature of poverty and allows the appreciation of "the poor" as a heterogeneous group. However, arguments against this approach of "multidimensional poverty" and in favor of emphasizing income poverty (i.e., lack of material well-being) as the "correct" definition of poverty first claim that there is high correlation between income and other measures of well-being, such as health and education status. Second, these arguments claim that governments and other organizations can implement effective poverty reduction programs by supporting economic growth, providing social services, and controlling markets and taxing systems, hence improving levels of income; however, it is less desirable for government or external agencies to interfere with, for instance, people's spiritual well-being.

Recognizing the multidimensionality of poverty also reflects the viewpoints of the poor, who often rank other dimensions besides income as important to the quality of life. In the World Bank 2000 study on world poverty, for instance, people in poor countries were asked to define what "well-being" and "ill-being" meant for them. Well-being was in general described as "happiness," "harmony," "peace," "freedom from anxiety," and "peace of mind." Ill-being was seen as a "lack of material things," as "bad experiences," and as "bad feeling about oneself." The interpretations of well-being and ill-being often vary between people and cultures and conditions. A 1988 study in India showed that the well-being of the poor in India had risen by measures they considered important, such as wearing shoes and having a separate accommodation for people and livestock, even in cases where the surveys showed their actual income had fallen.

The concepts of "well-being," "quality of life," and "standards of living" have a direct relation to the concept of "development." While two of the main principles in various development programs (United Nations Development Program [UNDP], United Nations Children's Fund [UNICEF], and United Nations Education, Science, and Cultural Organization

[UNESCO]) are cultural integrity and multiculturalism, human well-being is still the programs' main goal. However, if participatory approaches to poverty measurement rely merely on individual views of poverty or well-being, there is a danger of relativism that can justify vast global inequality. While it is essential to plan what people can do with particular goods and commodities, rather than giving material wealth intrinsic value, it is also important not to let the idea that humans' needs are relative to their environment, culture, or existing resources lead to the acceptance of global imbalance in resources distribution. Nobel Prize economist and development ethicist Amartya Sen has pointed out that in the attempt to measure and compare human well-being in various cultural and geographical contexts, one should pay more attention to the actual capabilities of people in different environments and situations gained from their resources. The material resources and commodities should then be seen as means to well-being rather than as a goal in themselves (Sen 1984).

As Daniel Little has noted, in previous years economists did not feel a need to formulate a particular theory of poverty because it was possible to address issues of poverty from perspectives arising out of other theories that explain demand management, production economics, fiscal policy, the gains for trade and exchange, or the cause of the wealth of nations. Poverty was then dealt with in a manner that by implication depicts it as the result of failure, a consequence of circumstances that are deficient in the essential requirements for economic progress. Poverty in economics was largely associated with an absence of growth and an absence of wealth creation. As a result, since 1945, countries of the nonindustrialized world have made major efforts at stimulating modern economic growth. Economic development processes have resulted from a number of forces, including the domestic government's economic policy, the private activities of national and multinational corporations, the influence of industrialized-nation governments, and a variety of bilateral and multilateral development agencies. The outcomes of economic development strategies are at least as varied as the strategies themselves; some parts of the less developed world have experienced tremendous economic growth since the 1960s. For instance, South Asia's growth has been slightly lower than 2% per capita per year since 1965, but East Asia has grown at a much faster rate. During this period, per capita in India has grown 1.8% and in China 5.1%. Portions of sub-Saharan Africa, for their part, have witnessed falling per capita GDP since the early 1980s.

How has economic growth affected the poor in the developing world? Have the benefits of economic growth been broadly distributed over all income levels? The geographical and gender divisions in poverty give a partial answer to these questions. The profits of economic development are unequally divided between the rich Northern Hemisphere and the poor Southern Hemisphere. The northern industrialized countries, located mostly in Europe and North America but also including Australia and New Zealand, live in abundance while the southern countries, mainly in Asia and Africa, remain deprived. In addition, currently more than 70% of people living below the poverty line live in rural areas. Asia has the highest proportion of the rural poor with some 633 million, followed by 204 million in sub-Saharan Africa, and 76 million in Latin America and the Caribbean, with the balance in the Near East and North Africa. Finally, of all the poor, the rural women tend to be the poorest, most marginalized and most vulnerable.

Thus, in spite of more than fifty years of growth in many of the economies of the less developed world, problems of poverty are as severe as ever. The inequitable distribution of income has direct effects on the well-being of the poor: malnutrition, disease, inadequate water, low educational levels, high infant and child morality rates, and depressed longevity statistics. Environments are suffering severe degradation throughout the world, and conditions of poverty and rapid economic development alike intensify pressure on the environment. Extreme and moderate poverty creates one set of pressures on environment, as poor people seek out ways of satisfying their needs that have harmful environmental effects (firewood harvesting, over cultivation, destruction of forests). Governments in developing countries may take "shortcuts" with respect to the environment. If securing foreign currency to pay foreign debts or if securing imports from foreign markets take priority, environmental side effects of industry or agriculture may be ignored. Moreover, poor countries may be exploited by rich countries: they may be more willing to receive pollutants from wealthier ones to receive financial benefits, and the governments of developing nations may ignore environmentally suspect practices by foreign-owned corporations and industries. At the same time, a child born in rich, industrialized countries will consume, waste, and pollute more in a lifetime than that of fifty children in developing nations. All in all, intensive processes of economic growth can pose even greater risks for environmental quality through rising rates of fossil fuel usage (and the subsequent production of greenhouse gases), intensive nonsustainable agriculture (and the pesticides and herbicides that this requires), and the exhaustion of nonrenewable natural resources.

How Is Poverty Measured?

Current attempts to measure deprivation take the multidimensional nature of poverty into account in an attempt to relate poverty to development and permit an overview of poverty that goes beyond individual experiences. Reliable ways to measure poverty present an aggregate view of poverty over time. This enables a government, or the international community, to set measurable targets for judging actions and policies in relation to the realization of the international development goals.

At the time when poverty was seen merely as an economic problem, the most commonly reported development statistic was a country's GNP per capita. While a case may be made for using GNP as an overall measure of development, it is not a fine measure of poverty for two reasons. First, as an average, the statistic takes no account of distribution. Hence, two countries can have the same level of GNP per capita, but in one of the two, a far greater proportion of the population will fall below the poverty line if income is less equally distributed. Second, GNP is of course an income measure, which ignores other dimensions of poverty.

The World Bank has been estimating global income poverty since 1990. It measures consumption and income data through household surveys. Consumption is conventionally viewed as the preferred welfare indicator because consumption is thought to better capture long-run welfare levels and current income. To compare consumption levels across countries, however, requires an estimate of price levels. Calculations referring to $1 (USD) per day refer to the purchasing power of $1 a day in terms of domestic goods. Interpreting the information on income and consumption as a measure of well-being requires many assumptions, such as allowing for measurement errors and accounting for household size and composition in converting household data into measures for individuals. Moreover, income or consumption data collected at the household level have a basic shortcoming: they cannot reveal inequality within the household, so they can understate overall inequality and poverty. In particular, the conventional household survey approach does not allow direct measurement of income or consumption poverty among women. Thus, data on education and health, which can be collected at the individual level, are valuable since the data allow a gender-disaggregated perspective on key dimensions of poverty.

Over the years, a number of composite measures of development and poverty have been proposed. The previously used Physical Quality of Life Index (PQLI) has been superseded by the Human Development Index (HDI) of the United Nations Development Program (UNDP). The HDI is a composite of statistics regarding GDP per capita, life expectancy, and education attainments (which are an average of literacy and mean years of schooling). UNDP has also proposed a Human Poverty Index (HPI) that focuses on deprivations. Specifically, the HPI is calculated as the average of the percentage of the population not expected to live to forty, the percentage who are illiterate, and what is called the "deprivation in living standard" (the average of those without access to water and healthcare and the percentage of children under five years of age who are underweight) (White 2002; World Bank 2004a).

Taking health and education dimensions into account in poverty measurement can be traced back to classic economists such as Malthus, Ricardo, and Marx. And while these dimensions are currently well reflected in international development goals, collecting data on these nonincome indicators is problematic. For instance, infant and children under-five mortality rates derived mostly from census and survey information are available in the majority of countries only at periodic intervals, and life expectancy is not often measured directly. In data on education, the most commonly available indicator, the gross primary enrollment rate, suffers from serious conceptual shortcomings, particularly since school enrollment is only a proxy for actual school attendance. Social exclusion (voicelessness and powerlessness) is usually measured using a combination of participatory methods, polls, and national surveys on qualitative variables, such as the extent of civil and political liberties. Measuring "vulnerability" is especially difficult because the concept of "vulnerability" does not only indicate the risk of a household or individual experiencing an episode of income and health poverty over time, but it also refers to being exposed to a number of other risks, such as violence, crime, natural disasters, being pulled out of school, as well as social exclusion. Thus, the concept is dynamic, and it cannot be measured merely by observing households once and needs panel data in the form of surveys that follow the same households over several years.

Multidimensionality of poverty has also raised the question on how to measure overall poverty in comparison to achievements in the different dimensions of well-being. One dimension might move in a different direction from another; for example, health could improve while income worsens. Or one country might show greater improvement in education than in vulnerability, while another shows the converse. This brings to the forefront the relative values of the different dimensions: how much income are people

willing to give up for, say, a unit of improvement in health or in voice? In other words, what weights can be assigned to the different dimensions to allow comparisons across countries, households, or individuals over time? According to World Bank, one approach to addressing comparability is to define a multidimensional welfare function or a composite index. An alternative is either to define as poor anyone who is poor in any one of the dimensions—without attempting to estimate tradeoffs among dimensions—or anybody who is poor in all dimensions and to measure the intensity of poverty accordingly.

Moral Dimensions of Poverty and Poverty Reduction

While poverty undoubtedly is a phenomenon that has existed through human existence in one form or another, a central developmental question is the persistence of poverty and the increasing mass-poverty in certain parts of the world in the twenty-first century despite technological, scientific, and economic advancements. While one single cause for the persistence of poverty cannot be named, continuing issues include justice, equality, and moral responsibility. While environmental problems contribute partially to poverty, the geographical location of countries; their respective levels of economic, scientific, and political development; the relationships of global and local power structures to colonial history; and various problems of a globalized economy (unfair trade relations, foreign investments that do not benefit poor countries, the overwhelming foreign debt from which many developing nations suffer) leading to economic dependence are to a large extent to blame. And simultaneously, while the physical environment of most poverty-stricken regions is highly relevant (especially to agricultural productivity as well as conditions of disease and hardship), there are many other components that are particular to each region's culture and its political structures and social hierarchies.

To alleviate persistent poverty in the year 2000, the World Bank committed more than $6.8 billion (USD) in concessionary loans targeted directly at facilitating economic development in the world's poorest countries. Nongovernmental organizations (NGOs) provided another $6.9 billion in grants to developing countries. Despite this funding, the gap between rich and poor is not diminishing. The already affluent are getting even richer, and the poor remain at or below the subsistence minimum. This gap is partly a result of the developing world's debt, and for many poor developing countries, the repayment of their debt may involve around 8% of the country's GNP each year. This means that the poor countries have to devote much of their production to the export market and set their emphasis on "cash crop" production instead of crop production to meet the needs of the country's own population. This is one reason why even in many developing countries with abundant natural resources, people are not benefiting from production but live in poverty, and their citizens are suffering from hunger and malnutrition.

Hunger, for its part, is both a cause and consequence of poverty. World hunger is not merely an issue of supply and demand; the problem lies in distribution and access. Imbalanced distribution means that increases in food production do not prevent people from dying of starvation and malnutrition. In addition, while during the next twenty-five years 50 million people will be added to the population of rich countries, over the same period, about 1.5 billion people will be added to the population of poor countries.

Many countries, on principles of justice and equality, have adopted strategies to deal with poverty, and there has been a reduction in poverty in various parts of the world. However, great inequities still exist throughout the globe. There are three particularly persistent assumptions given to explain this phenomenon.

The first argument claims that preventing poverty deaths is counterproductive because it will lead to overpopulation and hence to more poverty deaths in the futures. However, there is abundant evidence that birth rates tend to fall dramatically when poverty is alleviated, and women gain better economic opportunities, more control within their households and communities, and better access to reproductive information and technologies. Accelerated progress against poverty and the subordination of women may actually be the best strategy against overpopulation and toward an early leveling-off of the human population at around 10 billion.

Second, world poverty has often been seen as so massive a problem that it simply cannot be eradicated in a few years, at least not at a cost that would be bearable for the rich societies. One main doubt against the eradication of world poverty has been that helping the global poor would require extreme sacrifices from the rich. Redistribution of world prosperity and wealth may require those who are well-off to lower their standards of living considerably (to reduce their access to material commodities: fashion, entertainment, hobbies, and latest technology) and thus to radically lessen their "quality of life." This presumption ignores, however, the enormous extent of global inequality. The aggregate shortfall of all the people living under the $2 (USD) per day poverty line

amounts to some $300 billion annually, which is just 1.2% of the aggregate annual gross national incomes of the high-income economies. In other words, eradication of severe income poverty worldwide would require those who are well-off to accept only a 1.2% reduction in their annual incomes.

The third argument made is that world poverty cannot be eradicated merely by throwing money at the problem. The official Overseas Development Assistance (ODA) appears to have done little to overcome persistent poverty and even less for increasing equality and social justice. This, however, could be based on an unjust distribution of aid. Politicians from the wealthy donor countries focus often on strategically important developing states rather than on the poorest ones. They also tend to use aid—or loans—as forms of investments that are expected later on to profit the affluent donor countries and that are given with strict conditions. While the complaints about local corruption are often justified, the problem could be more efficiently dealt with in the example of more transparent and just global economies. Altogether, if global order and markets were instead restructured to be more hospitable to a democratic government, economic justice, and growth in developing countries, poverty could be significantly alleviated across the globe.

Poverty Reduction Strategies

Despite its vast scope and persistence, until very recently, poverty reduction had not been the main goal of global development policies and of "economic development" in particular. Development as "modernization" has relegated poverty reduction to a lower priority. While sustained economic growth has been a constant priority in the development plans of developing countries, poverty reduction driven by policies for equitably distributed economic growth has not been the main aim in contemporary development programs. Only since the early 1990s has mainstream thinking stressed the importance of pro-poor growth in local development policies as well as in global economy. "Pro-poor growth" is growth that is the result of poverty-reducing economic activities, and it is taken into account in such development programs as Heavily Indebted Poor Countries Initiative (HIPC), which promises to cancel debts of poor countries that commit themselves to reduce poverty locally by preparing national poverty reduction strategies in the form of Poverty Reduction Strategy Papers (PRSP). Rich countries, however, have been slow in granting debt relief under the HIPC initiative.

Other international steps in poverty alleviation have been taken in the twenty-first century; for instance, the United Nations and donor countries have agreed to a set of international Millennium Development Goals (MDGs) to reduce poverty by half by 2015. The social development targets aim toward universal primary education for all, eliminating gender disparities in primary and secondary education, reducing infant mortality and maternal mortality by two-thirds, and enabling access to reproductive health services for all, among other such goals. These goals have established not only benchmarks against which progress can be measured, but they also acknowledge an unequivocal link between development and poverty reduction.

When the multidimensional nature of poverty is taken into account, it becomes evident that policies in combating poverty have to be integrated and their influence on each other recognized; improving health outcomes not only improves well-being but also increases income-earning potential. Increasing education not only improves well-being, but it also leads to better health outcomes, to more active social and political participation, and to higher incomes. Providing protection for poor people (reducing vulnerability in dealing with risk) not only makes people feel less vulnerable, but it also allows them to take advantage of higher risk opportunities with a higher return. Increasing people's voices and participation not only addresses their sense of exclusion, but it also leads to better targeting of health and education services to their needs.

Conclusion

Poverty causes individual suffering and death, but from a wider perspective, it can also have harmful environmental impacts, which can be a source for further poverty, disease, and death. Poverty may also lead to social unrest, civil strife, and wars, especially where poverty is so abject that people feel they have nothing to lose.

Due to imbalanced power relations, the course of social and political development is important in order for resources and economic development to benefit the poor. Lack of access to education as well as obstacles in the way of democratic participation prevent equal shares of the profits of economic development. The patterns of gender disparity and severe limitation of opportunities and freedom of women found throughout the world have marginalized women to be "the poorest of the poor" in many developing countries.

Alleviating poverty and avoiding its negative impact on development requires direct action and serious political commitment to sharing resources. Markets must be accessible to poor countries, state institutions must be more responsive to poor people, and social barriers must be removed that exclude a vast number of people from participation (on grounds of gender, ethnicity, race, and other such factors). To help those living in poverty there is also a need to enhance security by providing mechanisms to reduce the sources of vulnerability that most poor people face and by providing them opportunities for self-help. These initiatives must be set in a global context. Global actions need to complement national and local initiatives to achieve alleviation of poverty and maximize benefit for poor people across the globe.

SIRKKU K. HELLSTEN

See also Basic Human Needs; Children and Development; Infant Mortality; Poverty: Definition and Trends; Quality of Life: Definition; Sustainable Development; Women: Role in Development

References and Further Reading

IMF. *Global Poverty Report, A Better World for All*. G8 Okinawa Summit, July 2004: http://www.paris21.org/betterworld.

Little, Daniel. *The Paradox of Wealth and Poverty. Mapping the Ethical Dilemmas of Global Development*. Boulder, Colo; Oxford, United Kingdom: Westview/Perseus Books Group, 2003.

Mullen, Joe. "Rural Poverty." *The Companion to Development Studies*, Vandana Desai and Robert B. Potter, eds. New York: Arnold/Hodder Headline Group, 2002.

Remenyi, Joe. "Poverty and Development." *Key Issue in Development*, Damien Kingsbury, Joe Remenyi, John MacKay, and Janet Hunt, eds. New York: Palgrave Macmillan, 2004.

O'Connor, Anthony. "Poverty in Global Terms. The Measurement of Poverty." *The Companion to Development Studies*, Vandana Desai and Robert B. Potter, eds. New York: Arnold/Hodder Headline Group, 2002.

Pogge, Thomas. *World Poverty and Human Rights*. Cambridge: Polity Press, 2002.

Sen, Amartya. *Poverty and Famines*. Oxford: Clarendon Press, 1984.

UNDP. *UNDP Human Development Report 2000*. New York: UOP, 2000.

United Nations Statistic Division. 2004. *Millennium Indicators. Monitoring progress Towards the Achievement of Millennium Development Goals*. http://milleniumindicators.un.org/unsd/mi/mi_highlights.asp.

UNICEF. *State of the World's Children 2000*. New York: Author, 2000.

Walker, Joe. *Environmental Ethics*. London: Hodder and Stoughton, 2000.

White, Howard. "The Measurement of Poverty." *The Companion to Development Studies*, Vandana Desai and Robert B. Potter, eds. New York: Arnold/Hodder Headline Group, 2002.

World Bank. 2004a. *World Bank Development Report 2000/2001: Attacking Poverty*. http://www.worldbank.org/poverty/wdrpoverty/index.htm.
———. 2004b. *Partnership in Development. Progress in the Fight Against Poverty*. Washington, DC: The World Bank Group, 2004.

PRAGUE SPRING, 1968

The political situation of Czechoslovakia was quite different from other Central and Eastern European countries under Soviet rule. This was a result of a special connection between the Czechoslovakian government and Stalin. During World War II, the Czechoslovakian president Eduard Benes had good relations with the Stalinist regime and could count on special treatment by the Kremlin. The Czechoslovakians accepted the Red Army with goodwill, in anticipation of future benefits.

The immediate period after World War II made these expectations seem realistic. Benes came back to Czechoslovakia in March 1945. His first step was to form a coalition government, including the Communist, National Socialist (with himself as leader), Catholic-folk, and Social Democratic parties, with Zdenek Fierlinger as prime minister. At the same time, two other main parties, the Agrarian Party and Slovak Folk Party, were declared illegal. The official programof the new government, a parliamentary democracy, promoted alliance with the USSR, agricultural reforms, and nationalization of industry.

In the elections of May 1946, the Communists won with a 38% plurality and went on to play a crucial role in the new government. They took control over positions of the Prime Minister and the Ministry of Internal Affairs (the key element of administration because of the control over the secret police). The ministry of defense also gave them great influence on the army. It was after the elections that a process of limiting the number and political strength of Democratic parties began. With the cooperation of President Benes, the Communists declared the Slovak Democratic Party as illegal. Finally on February 20, 1948, Communists executed a *coup d'état* supported by the army. The non-Communists ministers were excluded from the government. In May 1948, the Communists dissolved all independent social organizations and political parties. On May 9, they resolved a new Constitution, and Czechoslovakia became a Communist state.

After unsuccessful attempts at resistance, President Benes accepted the political changes and retired. Czechoslovakian democracy was liquidated. In 1949, approximately thirteen thousand people were imprisoned for political reasons. The new President, Klement Gottwald, became a symbol of Stalinism.

Even after Stalin and Gottwald's deaths in the same year, the policies of the Czechoslovakian Communist Party did not change. The new party leader was Antonin Novotny, and Antonin Zapotocky was nominated as the new President. Curtailment of civil liberties continued. In May 1956, authorities suppressed student's revolts. In November of that year, after Zapotocky's death, Novotny became President. Student protests of October 1967 did not have any significance either.

Nevertheless, the liberal faction within the Communist Party became stronger. In January of 1968, Alexander Dubcek became the leader of the Communist Party. The idea of "Socialism with a human face" appeared, and the country seemed to be taking steps towards democratization, despite the disfavor of the Russian Communist Party. In March 1968, Ludwik Svoboda, a popular leader famous for the Slovak Uprising, became president. In March 1968, the censorship was limited. Two months later, the government set free all political prisoners. The political police was reorganized, foreign travel was permitted, and new economic reforms were proposed. In April, the ban on independent Democratic political parties was lifted. The government prepared for deeper economic reform, though within the framework of the current system, and established bases for future sound relations with the Catholic Church. A Communist Party convention was planned for the following September to execute these changes.

The Liberal activists within the Communist Party announced the changes in a manifesto known as Two Thousand Worlds. This manifesto was criticized by Moscow, which then formulated its policy in relation to dependent countries in a doctrine known as the Brezhnev Doctrine after the Soviet leader at that time. It stated that "we can not be inactive on the fate of the socialism in a different country" and threatened direct military intervention within the Soviet bloc. In the policy, the Kremlin had many allies, such as leaders of the dependent states that were afraid of changes. This anxiety had become sharper. From May to July on the terrain of southern Poland, Czechoslovakia, and Eastern Germany, Warsaw Pact armies gathered. Because of the pressures of other Communist countries and their own fears, Russians began military intervention. On August 21, 1968, the armies of the countries of the Warsaw Pact crossed the borders of Czechoslovakia. The forces were made up of 170,000 Soviet troops, 40,000 Polish, 15,000 German, 10,000 Hungarian, and 5,000 Bulgarian. The Soviet armies occupied the key points of Prague very quickly. Afraid of extensive civilian casualties, the Czechoslovakian army did not offer resistance. The military action was completed with a full occupation

of the country. Dubeck and other key leaders were arrested and brought to Moscow.

This did not solve the Kremlin's problem. The Liberal's position was still strong. Within the general population, outbursts of vandalism, defacement, and derision of the occupiers signified the opposition to the invading forces. In January 1969, as a sign of protest, a student named Jan Palach committed suicide by self-immolation in a public square and became a national hero. Dubcek returned to Prague from Moscow after agreeing to resign from the party leadership.

However, changes slowly occurred in the direction desired by Kremlin. Gustaw Husak became the new leader of the Communist Party. The purges and the persecution of leaders of the Prague Spring began. In 1970, the prime minister was replaced. In 1969 and 1970, five hundred thousand Communist Party members were removed. Most of the students and academics involved in the Prague Spring were sentenced to hard labor. More than 280,000 lost their jobs, and 150,000 were forced to emigrate. The development of democratic opposition was made nearly impossible. The formulation of the Brezhnev Doctrine intimidated dissidents from engaging in direct and open confrontation with local powers.

WALDEMAR KOZIOL

See also Central and Eastern Europe: History and Economic Development; Soviet Bloc

References and Further Reading

Fodor, N. *The Warsaw Treaty Organization*. London: Macmillan, 1990.

Golan G. *Reform Rule in Czechoslovakia. The Dubcek Era 1968–1969*. Cambridge, UK: Cambridge University Press, 1973.

Korbel J. *The Communist Subversion of Czechoslovakia*. Princeton, NJ: Princeton University Press, 1959.

Loebl E. *Stalinism in Prague*. New York: Grove Press, 1969.

Szulc T. *Czechoslovakia since World War II*. New York: Viking Press, 1971.

Wandycz, P. S. *The Price of Freedom: A History of East Central Europe from the Middle Ages to the Present*. New York: Columbia University Press, 1993.

PREBISCH, RAÚL

Argentinian economist Raúl Prebisch (1901–1986) played a significant role in outlining and spreading the once influential ideas of Dependency Theory and the Latin American Structuralist School of Development. Prebisch served as executive secretary from 1948 to 1962 for the Economic Commission for Latin America (ECLA, renamed ECLAC in the

early 1980s), a United Nations agency established in 1947. Prebisch's work concentrated on the analysis of the main obstacles that hindered Latin American development and on the formulation of alternate polices to overcome them. During the 1960s and 1970s, the ideas coming out of ECLA were widely studied in Latin American academic circles and influenced the economic and developmental policies of national states in the continent.

The contributions of Prebisch to the Structuralist School can be encapsulated in three major ideas. First, Prebisch introduced the centre-periphery paradigm, which describes the economic relation between prosperous, self-sufficient industrialized countries and those that are backward, isolated, and dependent. In essence, this paradigm formulates the idea that inequalities between centre and peripheral countries emerge from the dynamics of international trade, in which the former's command of technological and economic power facilitates development in all areas of the economy, whereas the latter must depend on primary exports and the imports from the centre, creating in the process systematic relations of dependence. Moreover, Multinational Corporations (MNCs) from centre countries penetrate peripheral economies under extremely favorable conditions, enabling them to extract surplus from nature and labor and to repatriate the profits back to the center countries, reinforcing unequal exchange and dependence.

Second, and to remedy the aforementioned disparities, Prebisch argued that peripheral countries had to promote Import Substitution Industrialization (ISI) to curb the gradual deterioration of their terms of trade in relation to centre countries. Unfavorable terms of trade referred to the tendency of primary exports to lose value in international markets in comparison to the increasing value of centre-based finished products. For Prebisch, ISI would allow periphery countries to create an economic base to manufacture those finished products locally, not only reducing dependence but also decreasing unemployment through a diversified industrial labor market and boosting purchasing power at home through higher wages. Furthermore, national states had to establish protective tariffs to shield local infant industries from foreign competition.

Finally, Prebisch's model also called for Latin American states to invest heavily in social programs to empower their population and prepare them for the challenges of domestic industrialization. These three sets of ideas influenced many countries in Latin America and Africa; however, inflation and technological dependence on centre countries, coupled with the sweeping consequences of the debt crisis

of the 1980s, diminished the viability of Prebisch ideas as long-term developmental alternatives.

Prebisch also headed the United Nations Conference on Trade and Development (UNCTAD) from 1964 to 1969. With the return of democracy to Argentina in 1984, Prebisch was appointed personal advisor to president Raúl Alfonsín. Prebisch remained closely associated with ECLA's work in Santiago, Chile, where he died in 1986.

CARLOS VELÁSQUEZ CARRILLO

See also Import Substitution Industrialization; United Nations Economic Commission for Latin America and the Caribbean (ECLAC)

References and Further Reading

Di Marco, Luis Eugenio, ed. *International Economies and Development: Essays in Honor of Raul Prebisch*. New York: Academic Press, 1972.
Grossman, G., ed. *Essays in Development, Vol. I: Wealth and Poverty*. Oxford: Basil Blackwell, 1985.
Kay, Cristóbal. *Latin American Theories of Development and Underdevelopment*. New York: Routledge, 1989.
Meier, G. M., and D. Seers, eds. *Pioneers in Development*. New York: Oxford University Press, 1984.

PRIVATE PROPERTY RIGHTS

Private property rights refer to the acquisition of goods from nature, the creation of material things, and the willful definition of objective ownership. These classic philosophical notions informed Western political thought about democracy that underscored the transition from feudalism to capitalism. Modern democratic revolutions broke the power of aristocratic privilege and royal lineage and eroded the basis for despotic rule in Western European societies. The development of individual rights forged a link between private property and democratic citizenship.

The English philosopher John Locke believed that the right of private property stemmed from individuals' daily labor to extract from their natural surroundings that which they need to survive. Individual entitlement rested on the common consent of all citizens that shaped the relationship between society and authority. Therefore, the creation of private property promoted the welfare of the community at large. The French scholar Alexis de Tocqueville viewed the widespread private ownership of land as a pillar of democracy in the United States. The relative egalitarian structure of property rights reflected republican practices and equality before the law. Of course, Karl Marx insisted that private property motivated the owners of capital to use forceful and fraudulent

means to exploit the working classes (Rosen and Wolff 1999).

Western ideas about development after World War II identified the right to property as a fundamental human right. Article 17 of the Universal Declaration of Human Rights (General Assembly 1948) states that "everyone has the right to own property alone as well as in association with others" and "no one shall be arbitrarily deprived of his property." However, most areas of the developing world had not experienced fundamental changes in the exercise of power and the control of wealth determined by kinship, class, race, and ethnicity. European colonial rule and settler communities introduced private landed property into sub-Saharan Africa where customary land tenure once prevailed. The struggle for independence and liberation (by Nationalist liberation movements) lacked the progressive force of indigenous Capitalist interests (Kiamba 1989; Herbst 2001). The property clause of the Constitution of post-Apartheid South Africa contemplates a legal balance between individual freedom and collective justice (Constitutional Assembly 1997).

In Latin America, the vagaries of the Cold War and conservative resistance from plantation owners and peasants foiled the genuine attempts of revolutionary and radical Nationalist parties to execute comprehensive agrarian reform. Peace accords and democratic elections in Central America brought longstanding disputes over property rights into full relief. The uncertainty surrounding legitimate ownership of land became particularly complex in Nicaragua and Guatemala in the 1990s after decades of repressive dictatorship and social violence (Everingham 2001; Sieder 1998). The Second Summit of the Americas, held in Santiago de Chile in 1998, emphasized the regularization of registration and titling to ensure that all valid property rights are formally recognized in accordance with national legislation. The General Assembly of the Organization of American States, held in Windsor, Canada, in 2000, proposed the Inter-American Declaration on the Rights of Indigenous Populations that supports the legal challenges of indigenous communities to mining concessions and land claims that date as far back as the Spanish conquests (Summit of the Americas 2001).

The dominant neoliberal ethos assumes that the protection of private property rights is essential for economic growth. Gwartney and Lawson assert that "individuals have economic freedom when ... their property acquired without the use of force, fraud, or theft is protected from physical invasion by other [s] and they are free to use, exchange, or give their property to another as long as their rights do not violate the identical rights of others" (2001). Yet, the definition of property rights has a complex political dimension. The importance placed on individual rationality in the marketplace often does not acknowledge the imperative of collective demands expressed by working-class urban groups, the rural poor, and other economic actors who seek to defend their precarious rights to property.

Debates over public policy intended to modify the rules that govern property rights are contingent on interaction among organized political interests and bureaucratic agencies. The transition to democracy from various forms of authoritarian rule shaped the institution of private property across the developing world in the late twentieth century. Bargaining over the privatization of assets in the former Soviet republics and Communist countries of Eastern Europe gave rise to legal ambiguity that hampered economic growth (Comisso 1991; Weimer 1996). Furthermore, Communist regimes in China, Vietnam, and Cuba continue to resist international pressures toward the restitution of prerevolutionary rights to private property.

MARK EVERINGHAM

References and Further Reading

Adelman, Jeremy. "Institutions, Property, and Economic Development in Latin America." *The Other Mirror: Grand Theory through the Lens of Latin America*, Miguel Angel Centeno and Fernando López-Alves, eds. Princeton: Princeton University Press, 2001.

Comisso, Ellen. "Property Rights, Liberalism, and the Transition from Actually Existing Socialism." *East European Politics and Societies* 5, no. 1 (1991).

Everingham, Mark. "Agricultural Property Rights and Political Change in Nicaragua." *Latin American Politics and Society* 43, no. 3 (2001).

Gwartney, James, and Roberty Lawson. *Economic Freedom of the World, 2001 Annual Report*. Vancouver, British Columbia: The Fraser Institute, 2001.

Herbst, Jeffrey. "Political Liberalization in Africa after Ten Years." *Comparative Politics*, 33, no. 3 (2001).

Kiamba, Makau. "The Introduction and Evolution of Private Landed Property in Kenya." *Development and Change* 20, no. 1 (1989).

Rosen, Michael, and Jonathan Wolff, eds. *Political Thought*. New York: Oxford University Press, 1999.

Sieder, Rachel, ed. *Guatemala after the Peace Accords*. London: Institute of Latin American Studies, 1998.

Weimer, David, ed. *The Political Economy of Property Rights: Institutional Change and Credibility in Centrally Planned Economies*. Cambridge: Cambridge University Press, 1996.

PRIVATIZATION

Driven by a combination of factors, such as the scarcity of financial resources in private hands, a sense of social welfarism, a surge in economic nationalism,

and a strong belief that the state should serve as the primary "engine" of growth, many countries around the world invested very heavily in public enterprises. They invested in a plethora of manufacturing and service enterprises ranging from pencil, furniture, and automobile factories to water, hotel, and transport and telephone companies. In many countries, roads and buses, rail lines and trains, as well as airports and airlines either attracted substantial state investments or were the exclusive preserve of the state.

Often set up with lofty developmental goals and viewed as integral parts of the nation's drive for true independence, national self-sufficiency, technological advancement, and rapid industrialize growth, such enterprises were often forced to operate according to political and social imperatives rather than sound economic and financial management principles. Governments often ran them down as they used them to perpetuate themselves in office by dispensing favors and privileges to supporters and families. In addition, the enterprises suffered from bloated payrolls as well as rampant inefficiency in their management and productivity. The net result was that by the 1980s, it had become very clear that, generally, most of such enterprises were not only performing poorly but also had become major drains to national financial coffers as they required annual state subsidies just to stay afloat.

Privatization: Definition and Meaning

Typically, the word "privatization" is used to denote one of two ideas: (i) the shifting of a company's ownership structure from being publicly traded in the open market because of the repurchasing of the company's entire stocks by its employees or a private investor and (ii) the process of moving government-owned or government-controlled enterprises to privately owned or run firms. The task of this discussion is limited to the second definition. Specifically, this review seeks to examine some of the critical issues around public enterprise reform programs that achieved the level of orthodoxy during the 1980s.

The intent and principal impetus for privatization derives from reactions in the West against the growing role and perceived interventionist inefficiency of government and the public sector. Privatization means different things to people in different parts of the world and countries. This is because each country's position within the global economy often helps in determining the likely buyers of the privatized assets. Whereas for citizens of the more advanced economies privatization of state-owned enterprises is seen as falling primarily under the gambit of domestic policy (because the likely buyers are predominantly nationals of those countries), for people of the developing world, privatization signifies something vastly different because it often means the actual or possible transfer of state-owned assets to foreign investors and managers. Therefore, for citizens of countries in the developing world, privatization programs are seen not only as the denationalization of state assets but also are often shrouded in deep suspicion, controversy, resentment, and recrimination. This emotive reaction may be better understood within the context of the original intention of state ownership of the assets, which was usually driven by national self-assertion, concern for public access and welfare, and a commitment to equitable distribution of economic benefits. As such, the decision to privatize such assets by selling them to foreigners or without due regard to whom would get them locally is often seen as a betrayal of national interests and economic policy due to external coercion.

Such a response should neither be surprising nor understood as different from Western responses to the perceived excessive role of foreigners in their political economies. The negative reactions are worse when a country's growing dependence on foreign investment creates concerns or Nationalist passions about erosions of its sovereign independence and authority. Beyond the foreign angle, privatization also triggers similar emotional responses frequently in countries that are experiencing severe societal cleavages. Race, ethnicity, class, religion, and region have also served as bases for challenging national privatization programs around the world. Due to these factors—collectively and singularly—privatization policies are repeatedly challenged, blocked, or delayed until the needs of citizens, domestic firms, and significant sectional interests are addressed. Specifically, this often means the setting aside or delineation of special rights to assets or shares of publicly offered companies for citizens and sectional interests.

The Logic and Scope of Privatization Programs

During the past two and a half decades, the idea of privatization has taken center stage in domestic and international political economic circles as many governments (particularly in developing countries) struggled to make their policies and macroeconomic performance effective. Since 1980, more than fifteen thousand state-owned enterprises have been privatized in more than one hundred countries from Argentina

and the Czech Republic to Indonesia and Zambia. As already noted, privatization often followed decades of miserable economic results, which, despite some differences across a wide-range of states, were marked by a number of common characteristics. They include the following:

- Pervasive government participation in the domestic economy not only through widespread ownership of land, infrastructure, and industry but also through extensive regulatory frameworks that monitor day-to-day economic activity;
- Poorly developed and often disarticulated financial institutions and services;
- The use of money creation by government to finance activities rather the use of taxes and domestic borrowing;
- Government reliance on and use of fixed exchange rates and capital controls or direct controls of foreign exchange transactions; and
- The recourse to extensive foreign borrowing to finance current account deficits.

In examining the characteristics in the bulleted list, international financial institutions such as the International Monetary Fund (IMF) and the World Bank concluded that economic inefficiency, rampant protectionism, extensive government subsidies, and public ownership of key industries were crucial contributory factors to the pervasive economic underdevelopment and underperformance. As such, they advocated economic restructuring or an adjustment strategy in which the government would disentangle itself from direct interventions in the market. In its place, the invisible hand of the market would take sway and reallocate resources rationally and more efficiently. The net result would be economic growth and development.

Generally without other viable alternatives, affected governments found themselves needing refinancing and the good graces of the creditor community to avoid costly default. However, since refinancing and technical assistance involves not only the provision of external resources but also the monitoring and restructuring of the debtor's macroeconomic affairs, this meant that the countries found themselves accepting the policy influences of either the IMF or the World Bank. Although the lines of focus have become less rigid, the IMF provides the premier institutional framework for debt management—new credits, demands for austerity measures, and a two-phase debt renegotiation function. Anchored on an ideological rejection of the activist state, the reform policies compel states to adopt minimalist and noninterventionist postures that encourage economic

stabilization, liberalization, and the privatization of state-owned assets.

Typically, the IMF and World Bank economic recovery packages have three component parts: (i) stabilization, which is a monetarist instrument that seeks to prevent chronic inflation by checking demand through the control of fiscal spending and money growth; (ii) structural adjustment, which seeks to effect a positive shift in the supply curve by enhancing market and trade incentives and eliminating gross productive inefficiencies; and (iii) growth conditionality, which seeks to free market forces by attracting investments and improving access to productive technology. The classic conditionality program focuses on the cutting of public and private spending, general public sector reforms, devaluation of the national currency, deregulation of financial sectors and interest rates, agricultural sector reforms, liberalization of trade and payments regimes, removal of subsidies, and the privatization of public enterprises.

In many ways, privatization represents one of the principal focus areas of a typical structural adjustment program. It is also one of the most politically sensitive issues that faces a reforming government in the developing world. Its requirement that national assets and icons be sold to individuals or companies who will then run such enterprises on the basis of market principles and the profit motive, however, runs counter to preferred and often-stated national social and economic objectives, which is one of the reasons it is such a sensitive issue. Furthermore, the effects of privatization are often not neutral because they touch quite directly on matters of who benefits or who loses from the reforms. Quite aside from the possibility that the sale of such enterprises may have politically sensitive ethnic, religious, or regional implications, there is also the possibility of class sensitivities as labor groups worry about potential job losses and price increases in the company's products or services as the new owners make critical decisions such as what and how much to produce, which suppliers must be abandoned or retained, whether to mechanize or use a labor-intensive production system, and whom to lay off or retain.

The sensitivities surrounding privatization may explain the general political controversies, conflicting attitudes, and half-hearted implementation of the program in different countries and regions around the world. In the Middle East, the implementation of privatization programs has been very slow in countries such as Iraq, Iran, Syria, and Saudi Arabia. In Eastern Europe and Central Asia, the privatization experience has been generally controversial and mixed; there has been very slow progress in Azerbaijan, Belarus,

Tajikistan, and Turkmenistan, while very rapid progress has been made in much of the rest of the region, including in Armenia, Bulgaria, Croatia, Czech Republic, Estonia, Georgia, Hungary, Lithuania, Russia, and Slovak Republic.

In East, Southeast, and South Asia, privatization has been implemented with variable enthusiasm in a number of countries, such as Malaysia, Singapore, and Thailand. In a number of other countries, such as in India, Indonesia, Philippines, South Korea, and Taiwan, the implementation of the program has been far more controversial and tumultuous. In India, for instance, protests against privatization reportedly attracted more than 50 million protesters on May 21, 2003. By contrast, and despite being a relatively closed economy, China has shown a strong desire to push its capitalist reform agenda very vigorously. With more than one hundred thousand state-owned enterprises, the Chinese government has moved aggressively to open up a wide range of firms for privatization. China Telecom and China Unicom, two of the country's biggest telecommunications companies, are among the companies slated for divestiture. This directly bucks the trend around the world toward protecting large state-owned firms. Furthermore, while many privatization programs around the world are weakened by lack of political resolve, the Chinese government has dismissed millions of workers since the late 1990s as part of its preparation to streamline state enterprises to make them easier to sell to foreign investors.

In Latin America and the Caribbean, privatization programs have often proven to be more political landmines than visionary initiatives for governments. In Haiti, Prime Minister Smarck Michel was forced to resign in September of 1995 after popular demonstrations and parliamentary opposition dogged his privatization and economic reform program. In other countries such as Argentina, Bolivia, Brazil, Chile, Colombia, Cuba, Peru, and Venezuela, privatization programs have also faced stiff public opposition. Although historically more open and diverse than other developing regions and perhaps driven by stiff opposition, several Latin American governments have sometimes taken backward steps from the global trend toward privatization. Forced by the failures of some important privatization efforts, many Latin American countries have attempted to make amends by actually establishing new state-owned firms or retaking control of previously privatized enterprises. For instance, for the first time since 1967, Argentina created a state-owned firm in 2004. The government also took over a troubled mail company and an airline; Uruguay not only conducted a plebiscite that reversed the privatization of the country's water

services but also amended its constitution to mandate permanent state-ownership of water companies; and Bolivia and Venezuela have both moved to reimpose strong public interest and to oversee rights over their respective oil and gas companies.

In Africa, whereas some of the privatizing countries embarked on the program with considerable excitement (Togo, Guinea, and the Ivory Coast or Cote d'Ivoire), many others did so with huge public outcries and recriminations (Kenya, Nigeria, South Africa, Tanzania, and Zambia). The reason for the variation was simple. Although many supporters of privatization in Africa are attracted by the efficiency logic for the disorganized and highly unproductive parastatal (owned or controlled at least partly by the government) companies, the political support for privatization has been very weak in most countries due to deep fears about the makeup of the likely beneficiaries. In other words, a privatization policy has been severely hampered by a widespread belief that the process would lead to a great concentration of economic power in the "wrong hands."

Specific national outcomes or the outlook toward privatization can be accounted for by a number of internal factors. They include ethnic, racial, and regional considerations; social structure and class factors; and state capacity and ideological propensity. It is hard to generalize about the continent or subregions as a whole; nevertheless, all three of these sets of variables are relatively similar within the main subregions. For instance, the social structures in East Africa consist of small indigenous business classes and comparatively large non-African commercial groups (Indians, Pakistanis, and Greeks). Similar patterns can be detected in the social structures of Central Africa and much of Southern Africa, where the economic power of ethnic and racial minorities (Indians, Pakistanis, and Europeans) has served sometimes to inflame emotions and seriously complicate privatization exercises. Because of fears about these groups becoming more deeply entrenched, official state doctrines in the subregions have tended toward interventionism. Not surprisingly, privatization has received lukewarm support or outright opposition in many of those countries.

By contrast, the situation in West Africa is somewhat different despite Indian and Lebanese presence. Though the non-African commercial groups are significant in some countries within the area, the indigenous commercial class is much larger and more confident than its East, Central, and Southern African counterparts. Moreover, a stronger tradition of probusiness ideologies is prevalent among many significant ethnic groups in West Africa despite the entrenchment of non-African elements by deliberate colonial policy. The conditions for privatization also

have been more propitious because of the prevalent promarket state doctrines in the subregion. Pressured by local groups to privatize, many West African governments have embraced the policy with greater enthusiasm than their counterparts in other regions. This is with the notable exception of Nigeria, where ethnic political competition has served to create a highly sensitive and politicized privatization environment.

In essence, in countries where there are differences in the racial or ethnic composition of the bureaucratic and entrepreneurial classes, privatization tends to be resisted because of perceptions that it serves either to transfer national wealth and power from one group to another or that it helps to entrench or exacerbate group inequalities. In this sense, privatization is not neutral for social groups since the exercise results in winners and losers. Thus, governments are often unable to implement privatization programs without significant attention to potential beneficiaries as well as the social and economic consequences of the program.

The Case for Privatization

Basically, the case for privatization pivots around six specific arguments as described here:

- **The Efficiency/Profitability Argument** maintains that overwhelming evidence in both developed and developing countries demonstrate that ownership is a crucial determinant of company performance. As in developed countries such as Britain, Japan and New Zealand, privatization has produced strong results during the end of the twentieth and beginning of the twenty-first centuries in developing countries such as Argentina, Chile, Cote d'Ivoiri, Jamaica, Mexico, Niger, and Singapore. According to proponents, the reason for this improved performance is the role individual incentives play in human use of scarce resources. Private ownership entails several inducement rights, such as the rights to use an asset; to change its form, substance, and location; and to transfer it in whole or in parts. Therefore, any restrictions to such rights would have a tranquilizing effect on activities that seek to maximize the utilization of an asset. In other words, individuals will work harder to grow and nurture their properties the more they stand to gain by doing so. On the other hand, individuals are less motivated to use their assets productively when they are faced with regulatory frameworks that severely restrict or weaken their property rights. As such, whereas private ownership clusters rights and economic rewards, public ownership actually weakens them. Although modern firms often operate without the direct involvement of their owners, managers are often controlled through the workings of the market and the mobility of shareholders who may sell their shares as a signal of their unhappiness with management performance and inability to produce adequate returns on investment. The fear of losing their jobs due to poor performance will stimulate management into working harder to produce satisfactory results. By contrast, with no real checks on their dissipation of value, public enterprises lack a similar incentive system and, as such, are prone to underperformance.

- **The Political Interference Argument** contends that even when governments have good intentions and work hard to restructure poor performing state enterprises, the efforts frequently come to naught soon after things appear to have turned a positive corner due largely to endemic political interference. Lawrence Summers notes the following concerning the subject:

While it may be true in theory that a properly managed public enterprise can be as productive and efficient as a private one, the reality is that politics, usually of a virulent nature, intrudes, and efficiency is sacrificed. Public enterprise managers are rarely permitted to shed labor to produce at minimum cost. Moreover, procurement is often treated as a way of enriching contractors and procurement officers. (1992: 8)

- **The Deregulation as Panacea Argument** insists that privatization contributes toward macroeconomic stabilization by getting rid of losses and the need for subsidies to keep the enterprises afloat. Privatization also enables governments to reduce budget deficits and economic monetary overhang as individuals use accumulated cash to purchase shares in the enterprises being sold. Beyond those, it also serves as a useful mechanism for weaning governments of developing countries from serving as the locus for primitive capitalist accumulation for those either in state office or with access to the corridors of power. In countries such as Nigeria, Romania, and Russia, where proximity to state officeholders often is critical for the accumulation of wealth, the resultant struggle or associated corruption can impose destabilizing influences on the polity. In such countries, privatization can serve as a panacea to the productive incompetence of the elite clusters.

- **The Growth of the Private Sector Argument** holds that privatization of state assets will help grow and nurture not only the private sector but also a robust and competitive environment for the productive sectors of the economy. This will serve to ensure the creation of job opportunities as well as the direct involvement of citizens in economic activities of the country.
- **The Expansion of Foreign Partnership and Participation Argument** maintains that privatization can be very instrumental in attracting not only highly needed foreign and domestic financial investments but also cutting-edge managerial and technical know-how. This will have the positive effect of creating an atmosphere of confidence for actors in the domestic economy while also boosting opportunities for export trade due to more efficient and competitive production processes.
- **The Reduction or Elimination of Costly Government Role in the Economy Argument** sees privatization as an important mechanism for ensuring a more efficient government by pruning its role in the economy and its expenditures and budget deficits as well as by improving its budgetary structure, the allocation of resources, and the taxation and revenue collection system.

The Case Against Privatization

The case against privatization is centered on six primary arguments:

- **The Efficiency/Profitability Argument** is frequently discussed by opponents of privatization who contend that economic efficiency has little to do with the ownership of the factors of production since there can be huge inefficiencies in the allocation of resources in both the public and private sectors. It all depends on the institutional checks and balances that are put in place to thwart or control potential problems such as graft, corruption, and abuses of public trust that can occur in both private and state-owned firms. Just as officials of state-owned enterprises have been known to run government firms for private ends—not for public good—officials of private companies have been known to engage in scandalous behaviors in pursuit of personal gains (at the expense of their shareholders). Indeed, empirical evidence from some studies across dozens of countries on the singular relevance of change in ownership as a decisive factor

in achieving positive gains in economic performance seem to demonstrate that other factors are very important. Factors such as market competitiveness, regulatory framework, and institutions to address agency issues are indispensable if privatization is to result in positive economic performance.
- **Fear of Renewed Foreign Domination Argument** represents one bitter source of unhappiness about privatization, that is the belief that it would result in the sale of national assets to foreign individuals and businesses and that it would result in entrenched neocolonial relationships. A corollary to this is often the belief that the program is an externally dictated imposition by the IMF, the World Bank, or Western governments.
- **Fear of Ethnic or Racial Domination Argument** is described by the fear that privatization would open or encrust economic domination by a rival ethnic or racial group. This may also serve to open the door for political domination by the now privileged group.
- **Social Justice Argument** describes the battle against the policy as literally a battle between good and evil, a fight between ill-gotten wealth and abject poverty. To these opponents, privatization represents another economic channel used by the Capitalist class to deny other citizens of their national patrimony by taking over ventures, often with resources earned largely by dubious means. Some proponents maintain that rather than sell off state assets at heavily discounted prices to a few wealthy persons or groups, it would be preferable to open up the terrain to competition. This would not only allow the would-be-buyers of the state assets to use their finances to build new and more efficient companies, but it would boost the economy by creating jobs and a more competitive and efficient economic environment.
- **Protection of Jobs Argument** is yet another argument of opponents of privatization. Although divestiture programs have an overarching aim of improving the efficiency of state-owned enterprises to free up scarce resources for social services and for economic expansion and national modernization, governments have been severely challenged by the impact of privatization on labor. Usually, there are fears that privatization will cause a massive amount of job losses as the state readies the target companies for privatization and as the new owners look to rationalize their payrolls to improve efficiency by shedding excess labor. The

potential of devastated lives due not only to unemployment and the loss of benefits but also to the absence of social safety nets for jobless workers have the regular effect of galvanizing workers and trade unions into rabid opponents of privatization.

- **Consumer Welfare Argument** refers to the critique that the benefits many state-owned enterprises often provide through their socially conscious pricing policies really seek to ensure that their products and services are accessible to broader segment of the citizenry; proponents of privatization point to poor service records and substandard goods often provided by these state-owned enterprises. Many such benefits, such as access to potable water, health care, and better nutrition, are so fundamental to improved human existence and economic productivity that their value cannot be properly factored into simple calculations. In a privatized economic environment grounded on simple profit calculations, many people will not only lose access to such basic services and jobs but also will be ravaged by a sense of hopelessness and inhumanity.

Conclusion

In much of the developing world, privatization has come under severe domestic and external attacks for a variety of reasons, ranging from corrupt deals to unacceptable levels of social welfare losses and punitive impact on the poor. Yet, the reform of state-owned firms is often necessary—regardless of the decision on whether to privatize them—given the encumbering effects that loss-making and inefficient firms impose on the political economies of many developing states, which must divert scarce financial resources as subsidies to such ventures. Studies point to several areas of beneficial results for the privatized enterprises, such as improvements in operating efficiency and output, capital spending, state revenues, choices and prosperity for both consumers and employees, access to private finances, and profitability. Nevertheless, the net evidence on performance after privatization suggests mixed results depending on a variety of factors around the context of state capacity and the reform exercise. Among the key national variables are per capita income levels, the level of capital market development, government and foreign investors' shares in the privatized companies, and the timing and size of the issue.

UFO OKEKE UZODIKE

See also Agriculture: Impact of Privatization; Capitalist Economic Model; Free Market Economy; Industrialization; Modernization; Private Property Rights; State-Directed Economy

Bibliography

Anderson, Robert E. *Just Get out of the Way: How Government Can Help Business in Poor Countries*. Washington, DC: Cato Institute, 2004.

Boubakri, Narjess, and Jean-Claude Cosset. "Does Privatization Meet the Expectations? Evidence from African Countries." *African Economic Research Consortium*, 1999.

Brune, Nancy, Geoffrey Garrett, and Bruce Kogut. "The International Monetary Fund and the Global Spread of Privatization." *IMF Staff Papers* 51 (2004).

Cowan, L. Gray. *Privatization in the Developing World*. Westport, CT: Greenwood Press, 1990.

Hodge, Graeme A. *Privatization: An International Review of Performance*. Boulder, CO: Westview Press, 2000.

Hopps, June Gary, and Demetrius S. Iatridis, eds. *Privatization in Central and Eastern Europe: Perspectives and Approaches*. Westport, CT: Praeger Publishers, 1998.

Mitsuhiro Kagami, and Tsuji Masatsugu. *Privatization, Deregulation and Economic Efficiency: A Comparative Analysis of Asia, Europe, and the Americas*. Cheltenham, United Kingdom; Northampton, MA: Edward Elgar, c2000.

Kayizzi-Mugerwa, Steve. *Reforming Africa's Institutions: Ownership, Incentives, and Capabilities*. New York: United Nations University Press, 2003.

Kohli, Atul, Chung-In Moon, and George Sørensen. *States, Markets, and Just Growth: Development in the Twenty-First Century*. New York: United Nations University Press, 2003.

McCollum, James K., and Niles C. Schoening. "Romania: A Case Study in Delayed Privatization." *International Journal of Public Administration* 68 (2002).

Puffer, Sheila M. *The Russian Capitalist Experiment: From State-Owned Organizations to Entrepreneurships*. Cheltenham, United Kingdom; Northampton, MA: Edward Elgar, c2000.

Sanger, M. Byrna. "The Welfare Marketplace: Privatization and Welfare Reform." *Journal of Sociology & Social Welfare* 31 (2004).

Wertheim, Stephen. "State for Sale: The Privatization of Iraq." *Harvard International Review* 25 (2004).

Yelkina, Anna. "Privatization in Russia: Its Past, Present, and Future." *SAM Advanced Management Journal* 68 (2003).

Yergin, Daniel. *The Commanding Heights: The Battle Between Government and the Marketplace That Is Remaking the Modern World*. New York: Simon and Schuster, 1998.

PUBLIC HEALTH

While developing countries have seen improvements in overall health and well-being, public health in most developing countries is problematic. This is due in large part to the very issues that challenge development

itself: economic difficulties, demographic changes, the environment, education, infrastructure, and food security. Together, these overlapping issues magnify common public health difficulties and create new difficulties in developing countries.

Just as development is a broad concept, so are the concepts of health and public health. In its definition of "health," the World Health Organization (WHO) emphasizes not only the absence of disease but also the positive health of well-being. Public health is part of this, but it is not synonymous with health care or curative medicine. Public health focuses on the health of communities rather than individuals. As Garrett (2000) explains, public health fights "on behalf of the community, placing special attention on the poorest, least advantaged elements of that community, for it [is] amid conditions of poverty that disease usually arose." In countries like the United States, public health has come to also mean, at least popularly, health care for the poor. This misperception carries over into the developing world and into the literature on health and development. The two are related, obviously, but not the same. When poverty-stricken populations experience difficulty in gaining access to health care and appropriate curative treatment, individual illness may create community health issues.

As a broad term, public health concentrates on the general well-being of a community and the means to that end. Because of the focus on society as whole, public health systems, like defense or roadway systems, become the responsibility of governments. Public health activities include the keeping of vital statistics; community prevention of and responses to infectious disease outbreaks; societywide prevention and education programs for chronic diseases; standard settings and regulations regarding water, food safety, and injuries; and assessment of environmental hazards and their effects on community health.

In developed and developing countries alike, public health systems face a number of challenges: limited financial resources, lack of political will, tension between community and individual rights, and moral or cultural obstacles. In developing countries, these challenges are magnified, and additional challenges are present. The magnified challenge of limited financial resources is obvious, particularly in the poorest of countries where governments can spend only a few dollars per person per year on health. Leaders of developing countries face many opportunity-cost choices for the revenue they do have; public health and health more generally are all too often at the bottom of the list.

For young democracies, governmental support for individual rights is often weak; public health measures may complicate efforts to strengthen these rights and indeed may present a threat to individual rights during situations such as quarantines. In nondemocratic societies, where oppression is present, individual rights are often severely limited. This can, ironically, allow for effective public health interventions such as immunization campaigns. However, the lasting effects of associations between public health and oppression can be extremely detrimental to public health. The overall well-being of the Russian population, as a transitioning country, has dropped drastically since the break up of the Soviet Union due in part to its public health legacy.

In the immediate post-World War II period, the Soviet public health system was effective at reducing incidence of infectious diseases and other community health hazards. The public health system was one arm, albeit a successful one, of the repressive state. As time moved forward, however, the situation deteriorated. After 1991, Russians and Westerners alike learned that the Soviet Union's mortality and life expectancy rates had worsened. Societal well-being suffered even more as the Soviet Union broke up and the Russian Federation faced serious economic problems. Russian citizens were suspicious of immunizations and other public health programs because of the negative associations with Soviet repression. Governmental funding for health care and public health has all but disappeared. Patients have become responsible for providing their own pharmaceuticals, if medicines are available at all. Hospitals lack basic infection-control tools, such as gloves and clean needles. Rates of infectious diseases, including drug-resistant tuberculosis or TB in prisons, have soared. With incredibly steep inflation, access to proper nutrition has become limited; estimates range widely but suggest as many as three-quarters of all Russian children may be malnourished. By the mid-1990s, Russia was in the unique position of having seen its male life expectancy drop by nearly ten years, due in part to alcoholism, drug use, and violent crime.

Moral and cultural challenges to public health exist as well. With the emergence of HIV/AIDS and the presence of other behavior-related diseases, communities face prevention methods that could collide with moral and cultural values. Campaigns promoting condom use to prevent HIV/AIDS remain controversial in the United States; they could hardly be less so in developing countries, particularly those with strong religious influences. Successful public health practices, imported from elsewhere in the world, can also disrupt traditional cultures or be ineffective in the face of cultural values. Again with regard to HIV/AIDS prevention, the cultures of many developing countries limit women's rights and thus their ability to insist on condom use by their spouses or partners.

In addition to the problems they have in common with industrialized countries, developing countries face challenges that make public health problematic. Conflict, political instability, and governmental corruption all have deleterious effects on public health. Conflict damages what public health systems do exist. For example, Kim *et al.* (2000) write that in early 1990s Haiti, the *coup d'état* overthrowing Aristide disrupted measles vaccinations. Despite WHO and UNICEF intervention, immunization rates were already low, at about 40 percent. Rates dropped to 24% overall, and as low as 4% in some regions. Consequently, a major measles epidemic occurred. Kim *et al.* (2000) also write about conflict in El Salvador and document that one region, isolated by fighting, went without government health services for thirteen years. Through battlefields and existence of refugees, conflict also creates the potential for public health crises, such as infectious disease outbreaks.

It is important to note that a reciprocal relationship exists: public health crises can lead to conflict as well as be caused by them. As Price-Smith (2002) argues, severe infectious disease outbreaks and other public health situations can lead to internal conflict through the placement of blame on ethnic or socio-economic groups or even to external conflict if a government seeks to turn society's focus outward, away from societal weaknesses due to a health crisis.

Even short of outright conflict, political instability limits the often already debatable political will for attention to public health. Government corruption leads to misappropriated funds and poorly regulated medical, water, environment, and public safety standards. Through poor regulation or overt corruption, patients in developing countries may find themselves in possession of counterfeit drugs—little more than vials of water, in some instances. Pharmaceutical companies may take advantage of poor governmental regulation to "dump" in developing countries drugs banned by industrialized countries (Phillips and Verhasselt 1994).

Developing countries lack support networks to mitigate the impact of not only conflict and instability but also other human-made or natural public health crises. As development begins, urbanization increases. Hundreds of thousands of people may live in inadequate housing with no safe water or sanitation—the very breeding ground of disease that led to the development of public health in late nineteenth and early twentieth centuries in cities like New York or London. Earthquakes, floods, mudslides, or typhoons only further magnify these conditions that are so damaging to public health. Moreover, as development occurs, populations encroach more and more into undisturbed environments. The emergence of new infectious diseases is a public health crisis that can result from expanding communities and deforestation. Remote areas may lack medical personnel and surveillance mechanisms, thus allowing disease to spread.

Weak economies mean weak infrastructure. Lack of health infrastructure limits health services and the number of clinics, which in turn limit surveillance and data gathering. Vital statistics, such as birth and death rates, in developing countries have been difficult to obtain and frequently unreliable. The absence of electricity complicates primary health care and public health efforts, such as vaccination campaigns reliant upon cold storage. Lack of physical infrastructure, such as roads and railways, and lack of communication infrastructure limit individuals' access to health care as well as to public health information and immunization campaigns. Media reports present images of health care workers and volunteers traveling on foot or mule as they seek to immunize children house-to-house in remote regions of developing countries.

Garrett (2000) also argues that, given globalization, *community health* applies not only to localities but also to the nation-state and the world as a whole. In this world of rapid air travel and trade, the problematic public health of developing countries impacts the entire world. For this reason, international organizations such as WHO are active in addressing the public health of developing countries. WHO services to developing countries include information gathering and dissemination, surveillance, technical assistance, and emergency response. Other international organizations such as United Nations Children's Fund (UNICEF), Joint United Nations Programme on HIV/AIDS (UNAIDS), and the World Bank as well as national agencies, such as the United States Centers for Disease Control and Prevention (CDC), give attention to public health crises and campaigns throughout the developing world. Nongovernmental organizations (NGOs) are also quite active in the areas of health services and public health in developing countries.

International efforts to eradicate poliomyelitis from the planet serve as an example of a global public health campaign. Following the example of successful eradication of smallpox, various international public health partners seek to eradicate polio by 2005. Begun in 1985, the campaign involves Rotary International, WHO, UNICEF, CDC, and numerous governments as key partners. In addition to arranging massive vaccination efforts, the campaign raises money and supplies, provides education and communication regarding immunizations, and has developed new techniques and tools for vaccine delivery. Volunteers are

crucial to the success of the global public health campaign, as illustrated in 1999 when more than 1 million Indian Rotary members and their families joined the government of India in immunizing more than 130 million children in one day, signaling the largest public health event ever in the world." The campaign has so far succeeded in reducing the number of countries experiencing polio infections from 125 (1985) to 20 (2001). Incredibly, the global partners have succeeded in arranging for cease-fires in war-torn countries, such as the Democratic Republic of the Congo and Afghanistan, to hold National Immunization Days. The campaign is currently on track but faces continued challenges to vaccinating children in countries experiencing conflict and in the poorest of nations (Rotary International 2002).

Global and local public health campaigns throughout developing countries have engendered some success. Indicators of public health in developing countries include overall societal well-being, as measured by statistics such as life expectancy or infant mortality. These statistics are problematic due to data availability and methodological questions but are nonetheless commonly presented. The world, developed and developing, has seen significant improvements in life expectancy and decreases in infant and adult mortality during the twentieth century. WHO's *World Health Report 1999* provides the example of life expectancy improvements in Chile: a woman born in 1910 could expect to live to the age of thirty-three; a Chilean woman born in 1998 could expect to live to the age of seventy-eight. WHO data suggests that similar improvements in life expectancy have or soon will occur in most developing countries.

Though undeniably positive, these global improvements in life expectancy as well as decreases in mortality disguise considerable disparities between and within countries. In its 1999 report, WHO notes that the increases in life expectancy are being reversed in Africa, where HIV/AIDS is taking its terrible toll. Due to various factors, including alcohol and crime, the former Soviet-bloc countries have experienced drops in male life expectancies as they undergo transitions to democracy. Despite general global progress, developing countries as a group still experience higher proportions of infant and adult mortality rates than industrialized countries. As infant and under-five mortality decreases, more people live into adulthood but then die at a relatively young adult age due to a combination of poor nutrition as well as communicable and noncommunicable diseases.

Just as there are differences between countries, however, there are also differences within countries. The wealthy people of a society are better able to avoid weakened health because they have access to good nutrition, adequate sanitation, and health care to prevent and/or treat infectious and noninfectious disease. What the history of public health teaches, however, is that wealth is an imperfect barrier to disease. Interactions between the upper classes and lower classes occur through domestic servants, for example, and so infectious diseases can affect all segments of society. However large the rich-poor gap is within a country, it is simply not broad enough to provide health safety to the rich. Public health should thus be the concern of all segments of society.

As measured by statistics such as life expectancy, the overall health of many developing societies is improved relative to their own history. Studies of these improvements suggest policies for further progress in societal well-being. Increases in life expectancy came from improved nutrition, water safety, and sanitation resulting from the industrial revolution and related emphasis on infrastructure improvements. Income and education levels also affect mortality, as does access to medical knowledge and technology. "Because ill-health traps people in poverty, sustained investment in the health of the poor could provide a policy lever for alleviating persistent poverty" (WHO 1999) and, thus, a policy lever for improving public health.

Other measures of overall societal well-being include a community's or country's ability to respond to public health emergencies. The capacity of developing countries to respond to infectious disease, for example, remains inadequate for both ever-present problems such as malaria and for more urgent outbreaks. This inadequacy is due to the various challenges to public health listed previously. International actors have proven vital to dealing with outbreaks of the Ebolavirus in Zaire/Democratic Republic of Congo, Uganda, and Gabon. The public health systems of these developing countries were wholly unable to deal with the emergencies. The WHO and US CDC were especially vital to primary care, epidemiology, and prevention of further infection. Here, also, is seen a reciprocal relationship between health and development; lack of development has limited public health care and required international intervention in these infectious disease emergences. But, as quarantines affected local trade and thus local development in Gabon, citizens blamed and turned against the foreigners in their midst. International public health teams had to withdraw, for a time, for their own safety.

In addition to infectious disease, developing countries face chronic, noninfectious diseases as well. The term "epidemiological transition" developed to explain the shift, in industrialized countries, from prevalence of infectious to chronic, noninfectious problems, such as cardiovascular diseases, cancers, and diabetes.

As their economies prospered, industrialized countries no longer faced widespread malnutrition or poor sanitation and could afford public health interventions, such as immunizing their populations against infectious diseases. They moved beyond general concern for communicable diseases and turned their focus to noncommunicable diseases. Developing countries, however, face what WHO (1999) calls the "double burden of emerging epidemics and persistent problems." Developing societies still face the persistent problems of poor nutrition, lack of water safety and sanitation, and infectious diseases. At the same time, however, the process of development itself and even increased life expectancy open the doors to the chronic diseases and age-related mental illnesses associated with industrialized countries.

Tobacco-related illnesses provide a clear example of an "emerging epidemic" of chronic and preventable diseases. Production of tobacco products is a big business globally and, thus, the related illnesses form a global public health crisis. WHO (1999) estimates that roughly 4 million people worldwide died from tobacco use in 1998. One-third of the world's smokers are Chinese, and China has the highest rate of smoking-related deaths in the world. More men than women smoke worldwide, but tobacco-use rates among women in developing countries are increasing. Public health campaigns against tobacco and smoking are commonplace and effective in industrialized countries. WHO (1999) reports that the percentages of US adults using tobacco products declined by not quite half between 1964 and 1997. This trend is visible in other industrialized countries as well. Tobacco control programs in industrialized countries include taxes, government regulation of tobacco sales and advertising, and antismoking public health campaigns focusing on health hazards.

While tobacco use in industrialized countries decreases, it increases by 3% to 4% per year in developing countries; among men in developing countries, tobacco use is at about 40% (WHO 1999). As the tobacco industry loses consumers in industrialized countries, it becomes more aggressive at marketing its product in developing countries, where tobacco control efforts are limited or nonexistent. In Africa, for example, the health consequences of smoking are little known (Elder 2001). Among developing country governments, misperceptions exist about the potential negative economic consequences of tobacco control measures, such as taxes and regulations. Many governments fear a reduction of revenue due to increased taxes as well as unemployment if cigarette makers go out of business. Tobacco companies, which make huge profits and wield considerable influence, often reinforce these misperceptions.

The WHO has instituted its "Tobacco-Free Initiative" to encourage tobacco control mechanisms such as taxes and regulations and increase public education campaigns throughout the developing world. Thailand is one success story. It banned smoking in many public venues, banned cigarette advertising, and engaged in antismoking public health campaigns. Smoking rates have dropped by about 4% in Thailand. Many Latin American countries now regulate advertising, and Brazil and Mexico both have national tobacco control programs (WHO 1999). The political will to engage in tobacco control is, however, lacking in many developing countries, which further demonstrates the challenges to improving public health worldwide.

Challenges to public health systems—limited financial resources, lack of political will, tension between community and individual rights, and moral or cultural obstacles—that are present in industrialized countries are even more difficult for developing countries to manage. In addition, developing countries must contend with conflict, political instability, lack of infrastructure, and other obstacles to public health. While there has been progress toward overall societal well-being in developing countries, the situation is still extremely serious in many areas. HIV/AIDS is reversing progress in life expectancies, infectious diseases continue to take their toll, and developing countries must now also contend with chronic, noncommunicable diseases. Global public health efforts and the involvement of international actors in developing countries support these countries' public health. The development of strong public health systems in these countries requires just that: development. The level of development of a country complicates public health through simple economics, political stability, distribution of resources as reflected in the rich-poor gap, and conditions such as water safety and nutrition. The very issues that challenge development also challenge public health; bringing about successful development in developing countries will also bring about overall societal well-being and the means to protect public health.

PAMELA A. ZEISER

See also Health Care; HIV/AIDS; Infant Mortality; Infectious Diseases; Mental Health; Nongovernmental Organizations (NGOs); United Nations Children's Fund (UNICEF); World Health Organization (WHO)

References and Further Reading

Elder, John P. *Behavior Change & Public Health in the Developing World.* Thousand Oaks, CA: Sage Publications, 2001.

Feachem, Richard G. A., Tord Kjellstrom, Chrisopher J.L. Murray, Mead Over, and Margaret A. Phillips. *The Health of Adults in the Developing World*. New York: Oxford University Press, 1992.

Garrett, Laurie. *Betrayal of Trust: The Collapse of Global Public Health*. New York: Hyperion, 2000.

Kim, Jim Yong, Joyce V. Millen, Alec Irwin, and John Gershman. *Dying for Growth: Global Inequality and the Health of the Poor*. Monroe, ME: Common Courage Press, 2000.

Leon, David, and Gill Walt. *Poverty, Inequality, and Health: An International Perspective*. New York: Oxford University Press, 2001.

Phillips, David R., and Yola Verhasselt. *Health and Development*. London: Routledge, 1994.

Price-Smith, Andrew. *The Health of Nations: Infectious Disease, Environmental Change, and Their Effects on National Security and Development*. Cambridge, MA: The MIT Press, 2002.

Rotary International. *PolioPlus*. Retrieved March 16, 2002: http://www.rotary.org/foundation/polioplus.

Weil, D. E., A. P. Cooper, J. F. Alicbusan, M. R. Reich Wilson, and D. J. Bradley. *The Impact of Development Policies on Health: A Review of the Literature*. Geneva: World Health Organization, 1990.

World Health Organization. *The World Health Report 1999—Making a Difference*. Geneva: Author, 1999.

PUBLIC SECTOR REFORM

Determining how states should be organized and structured is the most common and intractable problem in politics. It is especially vexing in the formative years of states. New polities, even when supported by well-established political cultures, often find the difficulties in ensuring that state organizations are reliable agents hard to overcome. The problem is further aggravated when, as is the case in many developing countries, political identity is fragmented and the state's capacity to meet demands is limited. Since the middle of the twentieth century, however, the general recognition of popular sovereignty and steadily increasing demands for accountable, transparent governments has placed reform of the public sector at the apex of public policy in the developing world.

Ideally, state organizations are agents of politically relevant populations. Controlling the actions of states requires, at a minimum, an elite consensus concerning the goals of state policy and structural designs calculated to direct the actions of both institutions and governments to achieve those goals (Posner 1999). It is just these conditions, however, that have proven problematic in developing countries. Elite consensus has proven hard to maintain as the goals of state policy have changed over time due to difficulties in building state capacity, demands for increased political participation, and pressures from an increasingly integrated global capitalist economy. This, in turn,

has led to cyclical efforts to reform states to meet these changing priorities and concomitant dangers of structural instability.

There have been two waves of public sector reform in the developing world since the middle of the twentieth century. The first occurred with the achievement of independence by the remaining colonial dependencies after World War II. The newly independent nations of Africa and Asia inherited governmental structures ill-suited for tasks of nation-building and promoting self-sufficient economic growth. Indeed, colonial institutions, both public and private, had been specifically created to nip independent political and economic action by the "native" population in the bud. Further, governments in the new states found themselves under considerable international pressure to adopt regimes compliant with existing international political blocs.

There was a general consensus concerning needed changes in the inherited public sector. First, state institutions needed to be reformed to ensure that they could take steps to promote self-sufficient and rapid economic growth. Faced with dependent economies, dominated by foreign firms, financed by foreign banks, and tied to foreign markets, public sector reforms were undertaken to provide organizations capable of accumulating capital and planning its investment for economic growth. Building on earlier examples of import substitution strategies, public sector institutions were restructured to increase the regulatory, planning, and extractive capacities of governments (Lewis 1955).

Second, there was a concerted effort made to increase popular participation in government. New election laws, more truly representative legislatures, stronger local presence by central governments, and reformed civil services were all put into place. Party organizations established in the colonial period were expanded and dedicated to political agitation in favor of government development policy. Bold attempts were made to tie increased government capacity to increased electoral participation as well (Weiner 1967).

Unhappily, many of these initiatives fell afoul of the legacy of economic underdevelopment and authoritarian politics left by the colonial era. As participation increased, the capacity of governments to deflect demands that would siphon off development capital for more immediate benefits became harder to resist. Directing economic development programs proved, in many cases, beyond the talents and means available. In response, governing elites often took refuge in the bureaucratic traditions of colonial times (Seidman 1972; Fitch and Oppenheimer 1966). Party regimes, ostensibly established to quell "tribalism,"

began the slow decay of the relevance of representative institutions and, finally, of parties themselves (Torres 1967). The reform efforts accompanying independence began to collapse into debt-ridden kleptocracy in much of the developing world (Andreski 1969).

A second wave of public sector reform in developing countries began to gain momentum in the final decades of the twentieth century. Paradoxically, the impetus for this new reform effort has been the indebtedness caused by the first. As desperate governments turned to the International Monetary Fund (IMF) and the World Bank for financial assistance, they found a new round of public sector reform being forced on them in return. Here the focus was on actions that would enable governments in developing countries to meet their international debt obligations.

The international agencies recommended reversing the initial reforms that followed independence. In place of planning and regulation, governments were counseled to unleash market forces by decreasing regulation of financial transactions and foreign trade, abandoning domestic control of investment, and retreating from planning. Economic subsidies of all sorts were to be cut drastically or eliminated. Infrastructural projects were to be scaled back to more reasonable goals. Finally, services and benefits providing a "social wage" were to be severely restricted and the remaining funds were to be focused on education and provision of basic services (World Bank 1991).

In addition to these steps, the international organizations expressed strong support for political liberalization, including the establishment of multiparty regimes and regular elections. Anticorruption efforts were recommended and tied to stabilization of state finances. Independent court systems and police organizations supporting effective protection of property rights and the rule of law were also promoted (World Bank 1992). While no developing country has fully adopted this "Washington consensus" on public sector reform, enough measures have been instituted by various governments for this to be considered a second wave of public sector reform.

States adopting the new reforms have become more adept at obtaining foreign investment and have generally improved on their capacity to deliver services. The promised spurt in economic growth, however, has failed to materialize (Easterly 2001). Further, while corruption and organizational decay have been reduced, no one would assert that the second wave of public sector reform has ended these problems.

What is missing from both reform prescriptions is a commitment to the participatory imperative in economic development. Both reform efforts were erected at the expense of popular mobilization; post-independence reforms smothered it under top-down planning and one-party regimes, "neoliberal" reforms under economic dependency, and constitutional restrictions on public policy. Unless public sector institutions can provide substantial communication concerning development laws and regulations between mass publics and legislatures and administrators, reform efforts are unlikely to bear full fruit (Ferguson 1994; Seidman 1978). With the encouraging purchase of democratic institutions in developing countries, future efforts may be more likely to succeed at this task.

TRACY L. R. LIGHTCAP

References and Further Reading

Andreski, Stanislav. *The African Predictment: A Study in the Pathology of Modernization.* London: Michael Joseph, 1989.

Easterly, William. "The Lost Decades: Developing Countries' Stagnation in Spite of Policy Reform 1980–1998." *Journal of Economic Growth* 6, no. 2 (2001): 135–157.

Ferguson, James. *The Anti-Politics Machine: "Development," Depoliticization, and Bureaucratic Power in Lesotho.* Minneapolis: University of Minnesota, 1994.

Fitch, Bob, and Mary Oppenheimer. *Ghana: End of an Illusion.* New York: Monthly Review, 1966.

Lewis, W. A. *The Theory of Economic Growth.* London: Allen and Unwin, 1955.

Posner, Eric. "Agency Models in Law and Economics." *Chicago Lectures in Law and Economics*, Eric Posner, ed. New York: Foundation Press, 1999.

Seidman, Robert. *The State, Law, and Development.* New York: St. Martin's, 1978.

Torres, Jose. "The Political Ideology of Guided Democracy." *Political Modernization*, Claud Welch, ed. Belmont: Wadsworth, 1967.

Weiner, Myron. "Political Integration and Political Development." *Political Modernization*, Claud Welch, ed. Belmont, CA: Wadsworth, 1967.

World Bank. *Governance and Development.* Washington, DC: Author, 1992.

———. *World Development Report 1991: The Challenge of Development.* Washington, DC: Author, 1991.

PUERTO RICO

The Commonwealth of Puerto Rico sits at the easternmost part of the island chain that forms the Greater Antilles in the Caribbean Sea. It is the smallest of these islands with a size of about thirty-five miles by one hundred miles and an area of 3,435 square miles. The Commonwealth consists of the island of Puerto Rico plus the adjacent islets of Vieques, Culebra, and Mona. Generally viewed as a colony of the United States, Puerto Rico is one thousand miles from

Miami, and it is part of the eastern gateway to the Panama Canal. Puerto Rico has a tropical ecosystem with coastal flatlands and mountainous central highlands. Small deposits of copper and nickel are its only mineral resources although there is the potential of onshore and offshore oil drilling. Spanish and English are the official languages of Puerto Rico, but English is a compulsory second language in schools, and it is widely used in business, industry, research, and education. The capital, San Juan, has an estimated population of 433,412, while the entire Commonwealth is home to about 3,897,960 people. More than 90% of the population is of Spanish ancestry.

Christopher Columbus claimed Puerto Rico for the Spanish upon his arrival in 1493. The Spanish chiefly regarded Puerto Rico as a military bastion, and they never concerned themselves much with agricultural or industrial development. Puerto Rico remained economically undeveloped until 1830, when sugarcane, coffee, and tobacco plantations were gradually developed. After Puerto Ricans began to press for independence, Spain granted the island broad powers of self-government in 1897. But during the Spanish-American War of 1898, American troops invaded the island, and Spain ceded it to the United States as part of the resulting peace treaty. Puerto Rico has remained an unincorporated US territory. Its people were granted US citizenship under the Jones Act in 1917 but essentially remain as the last colonists in the world. United States laws apply to the Puerto Rican people without their consent, and the US government contends that sovereignty over Puerto Rico resides solely in the United States and not in the people of Puerto Rico. In the Caribbean, Latin America, and the United Nations, Puerto Rico is widely regarded as a colony of the United States.

In 1940, industrialization was almost nonexistent. The tourism industry had not yet developed, with San Juan possessing only one adequate hotel. Government services were deficient. Few towns had sewer service, while running water and electricity were absent from most of the countryside. Puerto Rico, however, had all the stability of the US government as well as an exemption from federal taxation. The tax policy had developed in 1921 when US investors in the Philippines requested that Congress grant them a tax exemption for the Philippine business investments. Congress did not want to discriminate against its colonial investors, so it gave both the Philippines and Puerto Rico an exemption. Puerto Rico's tax laws, political stability, and supply of cheap labor led to a burst in industrialization in the late 1940s through the 1970s.

When World War II ended, Puerto Ricans began to press for independence from the United States.

Luis Muñoz Marín and his Popular Democratic Party, after pushing for independence, decided in 1946 to accept a Commonwealth status that essentially changed nothing in the relationship between Puerto Rico and the United States. Under the commonwealth formula, residents of Puerto Rico lack voting representation in Congress and do not participate in presidential elections. As US citizens, Puerto Ricans are subject to military service and most federal laws. Residents of the Commonwealth pay no federal income tax on locally generated earnings, but Puerto Rico government income tax rates are set at a level that closely parallels federal-plus-state levies on the mainland.

Muñoz became Puerto Rico's first elected governor in 1948 and remained in the position until 1964. Puerto Rico's governor is elected directly for a four-year term. A bicameral legislature consists of a twenty-seven-member Senate and a fifty-one-member House of Representatives, all elected for four-year terms. The enormous power entrusted to Muñoz and his party made possible a long-range program of economic and social change in the form of Operation Bootstrap.

Under the control of Teodoro Moscoso, Operation Bootstrap attempted to improve the lot of the Puerto Rican people by industrializing the economy. From the 1940s to the 1960s, Puerto Rico was transformed, largely by local initiative, from a rural to an industrialized society. Moscoso brought every type of industry that showed any interest in Puerto Rico to the island. He brought pharmaceutical, electronic, apparel, food product, and tourism industries. Such employment would provide better paying jobs and a steadier income than agricultural work. Puerto Rico continued to produce agricultural products, chiefly sugarcane, coffee, pineapples, plantains, and bananas; the country also offered livestock products and chickens, but people flocked to the cities to take advantage of industrial employment. Operation Bootstrap succeeded to the extent that by 1957, the United States boasted that Puerto Rico had become the showpiece of the Caribbean and a model of how free enterprise could transform a nation once thoroughly rooted in agriculture. While still poor by US standards, Puerto Rico stood ahead of the rest of Latin America and the Caribbean.

Moscoso could not provide enough jobs for the people who wanted them. Unemployment actually increased during the 1948 to 1963 heyday of Operation Bootstrap. It remains at the level of 12% among the 1.3 million-person labor force. Moscoso did succeed in creating one of the best educated labor forces in Latin America, but an estimated 2.5 million Puerto Ricans have moved to the shores of the United States in search of better opportunities.

The Puerto Rican rate of growth is now well behind that of many other developing countries. The school dropout rate before the twelfth grade is 30%. The homicide rate is three times that of the United States. The island has also been designated by the United States Justice Department as having particularly severe problems with drug trafficking and is considered the prime point of entry for the South American drug cartels. Puerto Rico remains a major hub of Caribbean commerce, finance, tourism, and communications, but its future is unclear.

CARYN E. NEUMANN

See also Operation Bootstrap, Puerto Rico

References and Further Reading

Fernandez, Ronald, Serafín Méndez Méndez, and Gail Cueto. *Puerto Rico Past and Present: An Encyclopedia.* Westport, CT: Greenwood Press, 1998.

Monge, José Trías. *Puerto Rico: The Trials of the Oldest Colony in the World.* New Haven, CT: Yale University Press, 1997.

Wagenheim, Kal, and Olga Jiménez de Wagenheim. *The Puerto Ricans: A Documentary History.* Princeton, NJ: Markus Wiener Publishers, 2002.

Q

QADDAFI, MUAMMAR

Qaddafi was born in 1942 (the exact date is uncertain) in a tent in the Libyan desert. His nomadic Bedouin family belonged to the Qadhdhafa tribe. The boy was tutored privately and then sent to an elementary (Koranic) school in the coastal town of Surt from 1953 to 1955. Qaddafi absorbed passionate Libyan nationalism from his father, who had once been jailed by the Italian colonial authorities. Qaddafi was fourteen years old at the time of the 1956 Suez crisis when Egyptian President Gamal Abdel Nasser electrified radio listeners across the Arab world with fiery speeches. He attended the Sebha Preparatory School in the Fezzan region for five years but was expelled in 1961 for pan-Arab political agitation. After two years of high school in Misrata, he entered the Royal Libyan Military Academy at Benghazi in October 1963. There he organized a secretive Free Unionist Officers Movement. After graduating in 1965, the young officer was sent to Beaconsfield Military Academy in England for a nine-month training course.

Qaddafi organized revolutionary cells among fellow officers in the Royal Libyan Army. These plotters overthrew King Muhammad Idris al-Sanusi in a bloodless coup on September 1, 1969, and proclaimed a Libyan Arab Republic. The previously unknown Qaddafi emerged as president of the Revolutionary Command Council. He expelled Italians and Jews from Libya and forced the United States and Great Britain to vacate air bases in the country.

Qaddafi's idiosyncratic ideology is codified in his *Green Book*. He admired some aspects of Maoism and called for a Libyan "Cultural Revolution" to eliminate foreign influence, but he rejected both atheistic Marxism and Western representative democracy. Qaddafi proclaimed his "Third Universal Theory," which embraced pan-Arab nationalism, "true Islam," and "natural socialism." Islam is Libya's state religion, but Qaddafi forbids politicized sermons in Libyan mosques.

The official name for Libya is the Great Socialist People's Libyan Arab Jamahiriyya. Its unique political system is, in theory, a populist "government by the masses." No regional or class interests are recognized, and there is no role for traditional tribal leaders or modern urban entrepreneurs. The people are involved directly, indeed compulsorily: When elections are held for "Revolutionary Committees," all schools, shops, and factories close. The committees elect three thousand delegates to a national "People's Congress" that meets for only one week every year.

All real political power emanates from Qaddafi himself, who long ago renounced official titles and simply styles himself "Brother Leader." The government controls the media. There are no political parties or labor unions. Qaddafi has survived at least eight coup attempts, and he dispatches hit squads to assassinate exiled political opponents. Public administration is chaotic, especially since Qaddafi forced all government ministries to move their headquarters

from Tripoli to Surt and then replaced them with "people's communities." More confusing still is Qaddafi's unique Libyan calendar, which counts the years from the Prophet's birth, or sometimes from his death. The months July and August, named after Julius and Augustus Caesar, are now Nasser and Hannibal, respectively.

Qaddafi's economic policies are intended to create "true socialism." Rent is considered exploitative. Finance, commerce, and industry are largely nationalized, but in 2003, Qaddafi proposed privatization of the public sector. In fact, almost everyone is on the government payroll. Living standards are fairly high, thanks to oil revenues, which Qaddafi tries to distribute equitably. The government has built many schools, clinics, and public housing projects.

Colonel Qaddafi's most ambitious development scheme is his Great Man-Made River Project, begun in 1984. The plan is to irrigate 185,000 acres of farmland along the Mediterranean coast with water drawn from underground aquifers in the southern desert and pumped through 2,500 miles of concrete pipe thirteen feet in diameter. Phase I was completed 1991 at a cost of $3 billion. Tripoli began receiving water in 1996. The cost reached $12 billion by 2000. American military analysts note that the pipe is large enough to accommodate military vehicles, and that it runs through a mountain where Qaddafi is thought to have built an underground chemical weapons factory.

Qaddafi's foreign policy is quirky and dangerous, but not without its own principles of anti-imperialism and nonalignment. He refuses all contact with Israel. Qaddafi has attempted to merge Libya with Egypt, Syria, Tunisia, Chad, and Morocco, but these initiatives foundered, perhaps because other leaders feared Qaddafi's penchant for military adventurism. He supported rebels in Chad for twelve years (1975–1987) and has encouraged coup plotters in Egypt and Sudan.

Since 1998, Qaddafi has directed his attention southward. The Libyan radio service was renamed the Voice of Africa. Qaddafi sent economic aid to Ghana, Zimbabwe, and Kenya and opened Libya's borders to Africans, who came in great numbers to take even the most menial jobs. This policy proved highly unpopular among the citizenry, and race riots ensued.

In 2001, Colonel Qaddafi condemned the World Trade Center attacks and declared his opposition to terrorism, a surprising reversal for a man whose record includes support for the IRA, Basque separatists, Filipino secessionists, the Black Panthers, and various Palestinian factions. President Reagan claimed that Qaddafi tried to assassinate him, and after a 1986 Libyan-sponsored bombing of a West Berlin nightclub that killed two US soldiers, Reagan

sent jet fighters to bomb Qaddafi's tent. The bombs missed Qaddafi but killed his five-year-old adopted daughter. The British Secret Service allegedly tried to assassinate Qaddafi in 1996 by using members of the Libyan Islamic Fighting Group, an organization linked to Osama bin Laden.

In 2003, Qaddafi seemed on his way to rehabilitation in the eyes of Western countries eager for normal trading relations with oil-rich Libya. Blame for the 1988 bombing of Pan American Flight 103 over Lockerbie, Scotland, which killed all 270 people aboard, settled on a lower-level operative. Blame for the 1989 bombing of UTA Flight 772 over Niger, which killed all 170 people aboard, was pinned on Libyan intelligence chief Abdullah al-Sanusi, Qaddafi's brother-in-law. Libya paid compensation to survivors but stipulated that this was not an admission of guilt.

The Libyan population will double in the next twenty-five years, and the government needs to create thirty thousand new jobs annually. Qaddafi recognizes the need for foreign investment. United Nations trade sanctions, which had seriously damaged the Libyan economy, were lifted in 1999.

There currently appears to be no viable domestic political opposition to Muammar Qaddafi. Muslim fundamentalists linked to Osama bin Laden operate from caves in eastern Libya but pose no serious threat to his continuation in power. The leader would like to bequeath power to his four sons.

Ross Marlay

See also Libya; North Africa: History and Economic Development; North Africa: International Relations

References and Further Reading

Blundy, D. and A. Lycett. *Qaddafi and the Libyan Revolution.* London, 1987.
Cooley, J. K. *Libyan Sandstorm.* 1982.
Davis, J. *Libyan Politics: Tribe and Revolution.* London, 1988.
Gottfried, Ted. *Muammar El-Qaddafi.* Chelsea House, 1987.
Harris, Lillian C. *Libya: Qaddafi's Revolution and the Modern State.* Boulder, CO: Westview, 1986.
Sicker, Martin. *The Making of a Pariah State: The Adventurist Politics of Muammar Qaddafi.* Greenwood, 1987.
Tremlett, George. *Gadaffi: The Desert Mystic.* Carroll & Graff, 1993.

QATAR

Qatar is a small peninsular state in the Persian Gulf, covering 4,427 square miles. Its only land border is with Saudi Arabia. Almost entirely desert, a mere 1.27% of its land is arable. Rain is rare, and temperatures in the summer average 48°C. Qatar underwent a

long-running dispute with Bahrain over the Hawar Islands, which they ended by referring the case to the International Court of Justice (ICJ). The ICJ ruling in 2001 gave the main island to Bahrain, with Qatar receiving significant maritime areas and resources.

Roughly 750,000 people live in Qatar, over 90% of them in urban areas. A sizeable proportion of the citizenry is part of the ruling al-Thani family. Four-fifths of the population are foreign workers, and immigrants must be residents for a minimum of twenty years (for Arabs) or thirty years (for non-Arabs) before being eligible for citizenship. Arabs comprise 40% of the population, Indians and Pakistanis each comprise 18%, Iranians comprise 10%, and the remaining 14% are other nationalities. Sunni Islam is the dominant faith, and Qataris subscribe to the strict Wahhabi sect also practiced in Saudi Arabia.

The area has been inhabited for several millennia, although its harsh conditions kept the population to a minimum. The Ottoman Empire ruled the territory for four centuries, beginning in 1538 when it wrested control from the Portuguese. During the nineteenth century, the al-Khalifa family—now the ruling family in Bahrain—dominated Qatar, until the British helped negotiate an end to tribute payments in 1872. The British replaced the Ottomans as the governing power, signing a treaty in 1916 that traded British protection for Qatar's pledge not to surrender territory or enter into relationships with foreign governments without British consent. The al-Thani family assumed absolute political control.

Britain's decision to withdraw east of the Suez Canal initially led Qatar to seek federation with Bahrain and the seven trucial states (now the United Arab Emirates). When such plans showed little progress, Qatar proclaimed its independence on September 3, 1971. Within six months, Shaykh Khalifa bin Hamad al-Thani, the kingdom's de facto ruler since the 1950s, replaced his cousin Shaykh Ahmad bin Ali al-Thani, who had formally assumed power in 1960. Ahmad's lax attitude toward governance and extravagant spending—his personal allowance represented 25% of Qatar's annual oil revenues—both contributed to Khalifa's decision to seize power. Khalifa immediately clamped down on the spending of the royal family, which often failed to draw a distinction between their personal finances and those of the state.

In 1995, Hamad bin Khalifa al-Thani overthrew his father in a bloodless coup and embarked on an ambitious program of political and economic liberalization. Qatar became the first Gulf state to adopt universal suffrage in 1999, and despite its conservative and traditional society, women are playing a more visible role. In 2003, Hamad appointed a woman as Cabinet minister—the first woman to serve in a ministerial capacity in the Gulf; a woman was elected to the Central Municipal Council; and a woman is president of the University of Qatar. Elections were held in 1999 and 2003 for the Central Municipal Council, which aims to improve the provision of municipal services; the twenty-nine-member body has consultative powers. A new constitution was overwhelmingly approved in an April 2003 public referendum. It grants some legislative powers to and increases the membership in the Advisory Council; thirty of the Council's forty-five members will be elected, and the emir will appoint the remainder. Hamad abolished official censorship in 1995, leading to the creation two years later of al-Jazeera, the outspoken and influential satellite news outlet. However, al-Jazeera rarely criticizes the al-Thani family or covers local news. Political parties are still not permitted.

Until oil was discovered in 1940, the economy was traditionally based on pearling, fishing, and herding. Commercial exports began in 1949. Oil revenues brought dramatic social improvements to Qatar. Health care, education, utilities, and housing are free to Qatari citizens. The formal school system opened in 1956, and the education budget grew 31% per year over the next decade. By 1970, eighty-eight schools had been established, including forty for girls, and the university opened in 1973. The literacy rate in 2002 was 84.2%. Women have fared well in the educational system, enjoying a literacy rate roughly equal to that of men, and markedly higher enrollments in tertiary educational institutions. Education and the workplace are segregated. The private Qatar Foundation has developed branch campuses of several leading American universities, including Carnegie-Mellon, Cornell, Texas A & M, and Virginia Commonwealth University, allowing students to study a Western curriculum in Qatar. The health system also has shown marked improvements. The first state hospital opened in 1959, and by 1970, Qatar led the Arab Middle East in terms of availability of services. Life expectancy rates increased from 62.1 to 72.2 years between 1970 and 2000, as infant and child mortality rates fell substantially.

Qatar's economy is dominated by the oil and gas sectors, which account for 55% of gross domestic product (GDP), 70% of government revenues, and 85% of export earnings. As its oil fields are expected to run dry by 2023, Qatar has begun to shift its economy from reliance on exports of oil to natural gas. It boasts the world's third largest natural gas reserves, and its North Field is the world's largest unassociated field. Qatar is participating in the multi-billion-dollar Dolphin Project, which will interconnect the natural gas grids of Qatar, the United Arab Emirates, and Oman, providing gas for both export

and domestic use. Hamad borrowed billions of dollars in the 1990s and restricted government spending so that he could devote resources to upgrading the oil and gas sectors. Qatar was rewarded with robust growth, a 9.9% average annual GDP growth between 1992 and 2002, driven by a sharp increase in exports of natural gas, increased oil production capacity, and increased refinery capacity. It produced between eight hundred thousand and nine hundred thousand barrels per day in 2002 and 2003.

BETH K. DOUGHERTY

See also Middle East: History and Economic Development; Middle East: International Relations

References and Further Reading

Anthony, John Duke. *The Arab States of the Lower Gulf: People, Politics, Petroleum.* Washington, DC: Middle East Institute, 1975.

Crystal, Jill. *Oil and Politics in the Gulf: Rulers and Merchants in Kuwait and Qatar.* New York: Cambridge University Press, 1995.

Mallakh, Ragaei el-, *Qatar: Energy and Development.* London: Croom Helm, 1985.

Metz, Helen Chapin, ed. *Persian Gulf States: Country Studies.* Washington, DC: Library of Congress, 1994.

Nafi, Zuhair Ahmed. *Economic and Social Development in Qatar.* London: F. Pinter, 1983.

Zahlan, Rosemarie Said. *The Creation of Qatar.* London: Croom Helm, 1979.

———. *The Making of the Modern Gulf States: Kuwait, Bahrain, Qatar, the United Arab Emirates, and Oman.* New York: Routledge, 1989.

QUALITY OF LIFE: DEFINITION

Quality of life is not a term that can be simply defined. This is because quality of life is to be able to determine for oneself what quality of life actually means.

Development ethicists have argued that development theory should have at its core a concern to make assessments and devise a theoretical framework for how quality of life can be achieved for and by everyone. At its basis, there is a concern with equality as the principal constituent element of justice; the Nobel Laureate Amartya Sen states, for example, that "every normative theory of social arrangement that has stood the test of time seems to demand equality of something—something that is regarded as particularly important in that theory." Therefore, the question becomes what equality should consist of and how this can be brought about in practice. Sen's proposal is that this equality lies in the equal freedom to pursue a life that "we have reason to value" (Sen 1992). The philosopher and public intellectual Martha Nussbaum takes this one step further and states that it is necessary to ground this in more concrete notions of human quality of life. Nussbaum and Sen's work in this area has fostered the development of the capability approach, which uses the language of functionings and capabilities to designate a theoretical framework from which to develop policies to improve the quality of life of individuals in developing countries. A functioning is an activity or state of being; a capability is the capacity or ability to exercise a certain functioning. For example, a person has the capability to eat healthfully if they have the capability to exercise the functioning of taking up and digesting food, coupled with the capability to exercise the functioning of accessing food that is nutritious.

Going beyond measurements of a state's Gross Domestic Product, other factors such as distributive measurements of wealth (such as per capita income), the purchasing power of a currency, and a person's access to goods and services are deemed absolutely central for any serious analysis of quality of life of the individual. The individual is the core unit of analysis of the assessment of quality of life. Yet a person's access to political power, emotional health, and spiritual well-being are equally important components of this approach.

This necessitates a theory that can make prescriptions about procedures and desired outcomes, as well as criteria for measurement and evaluation. To do this, one needs to address the existence of different and supposedly irreconcilable value systems in the world today, an issue that has become more acute due to the ever-increasing interdependence of human beings worldwide. People from different backgrounds are more likely to interact with each other, which, in turn, is more likely to bring conflict (but also similarities) to the fore. Any list of what a human being requires to live a life that is said to have quality needs to be sensitive to this.

Key theorists tackling quality-of-life questions have sought to resolve these tensions in different ways. Some have started from a deliberation about "human needs"(see, for example, Goodin); others, such as Sen, have tried to develop approaches that do not necessitate agreement in the absolute but allow for unfinished agreement and overlap where synthesis in certain elements, known as capability sets, can be found; this method is more suited to making assessments of existing structures, rather than designating ideals to strive for. On the other hand, Nussbaum, for example, has opted for a more prescriptive approach with a more definite list of functionings that people must be able to exercise as capabilities. She holds these out as ideals that secure power for each person to pursue their own interpretation of the "good life" and has devised a list of capabilities of which all components are deemed of equal importance: life;

bodily integrity; bodily health; senses, imagination and health; emotions; practical reason; affiliation; symbiosis with other species; and control over one's own environment, political and material.

One critique of this is that even the basic premises of this approach—their starting points, such as equality, freedom, and autonomy—cannot be regarded as universally justifiable, and their roles might vary quite substantially in different societies. This makes it difficult to determine concrete impediments to freedom and choice, to determine where oppression occurs, and to make a moral case for injustice, if one wishes to respect cultural life in the forms that it is currently expressed. Related to this is the concern about when preferences have been adapted and capabilities compensated for (i.e., a determination of when a person has real freedom and real choice or when a person is constrained and socialized by factors that could be designated as wrong or alleviable). This has a bearing on the methodology of detecting what people really want and need and how this is to be measured. Questions posed relate to whether people's own personal preferences are to be the measure for capabilities and what a preference should be based on: desire and overall happiness of people taken together to form a society, justice, stability, or need. Likewise, going beyond autonomy and taking into consideration the affiliative aspect of human life, one needs to define what the relationship between individual freedom and societal duties is, and lastly, it needs to be ascertained what all of this means for the socioeconomic structure of societies, local and global.

For these reasons, quality of life is not a straightforward concept. However, it is a crucial one in improving development policies beyond a one-dimensional economic assessment of a country's productivity.

EMMA DOWLING

See also Basic Human Needs; Children and Development; Women: Role in Development

References and Further Reading

Cohen, G. "Equality of What? On Welfare, Goods and Capabilities," in *The Quality of Life*. Nussbaum, M. and Sen, A., eds. Oxford: Clarendon Press, 1993.

Goodin, R. "Relative Needs," in *Needs and Welfare*. Ware, A. and Goodin, R., eds. London: Sage, 1990.

Nussbaum, M. C. *Women and Human Development: The Capabilities Approach*. Cambridge: Cambridge University Press, 2000.

Sen, A. *Inequality Reexamined*. Oxford: Clarendon Press, 1992.

———. *Development as Freedom*. Oxford: Oxford University Press, 2001.

Sen, A. and M. Nussbaum. *The Quality of Life*. Oxford: Clarendon Press, 1993.

R

RAFSANJANI, ALI AKBAR

Born in the town of Rafsanjan, province of Kerman in 1934, Ali Akbar Rafsanjani has been, and remains, one of the most influential figures in postrevolutionary Iranian politics. He studied Islamic jurisprudence under Ayatollah Ruhollah Khomeini beginning in 1951. He was active in the anti-Shah forces prior to the revolution and was jailed for his association with the Mujahedin e-Khalq. In 1979, the year the Shah was deposed, Rafsanjani formed the Islamic Republican Party. In 1980, he was elected to parliament, and since then has filled every major political position in the government since the revolution, including Speaker of the Parliament (1980–1989), Commander-in-Chief of the Iranian Armed Forces (1988–1989), and president (two terms, 1989–1993, 1993–1997).

He has been characterised as a pragmatic conservative, and his efforts towards reform in Iran should be seen in this light. During his time as speaker and his two terms as president, he sought a rapprochement with the West. As a result, Iran renewed diplomatic relations with France and Canada in 1988, the Soviet Union in 1989, and the United Kingdom in 1990. He was also instrumental in brokering the release of Western hostages from Lebanon during the same period. This reestablishment of links was part of an attempt to engage with the West as a necessary requirement to alleviate economic pressures felt by the Republic.

Rafsanjani has been closely aligned with both Supreme Leaders, and many of his appointments have grown out of this close link. This was the case with his appointment by Ayatollah Khomeini as his representative on the war committee during the Iran-Iraq war, and subsequently as the Commander-in-Chief. This was also the case when Khomeini appointed him to the position of Chairman of the Expediency Council. He has been a proponent of reform within Iran, although this has been nearly exclusively applied to economic, rather than political, matters. On becoming president, Rafsanjani needed to address issues that were causing significant economic hardship to the people. A war-ravaged economy resulting from years of fighting Iraq, economic sanctions from the West, and a burgeoning, increasingly urbanised population put pressure on the system. Rafsanjani instituted successive five-year plans designed to revive the moribund economy. The emphasis was on a move towards a market economy, seeking both foreign and private investment, reducing government subsidies, and an increase in private ownership of economic assets. The first of the five-year plans put particular emphasis on the privatisation of state-controlled enterprises.

The economic reforms were only partially successful, given allegations of corruption over the privatisation of some enterprises, and the emergence of differences between the political factions within the parliament who were ultimately responsible for the passage of the reforms. On the positive side, agricultural output was increased, and a growth in privatised industrial production geared to exports was developed. These attempts at economic reform, however, have not been matched by any similar move towards political reform. While he has been characterised as a

pragmatist, willing to ally himself with conservatives or technocrats, depending on the issue he was confronting, he has generally been considered an opponent of political liberalisation. During the 1999 student riots against the nature of clerical rule, for example, Rafsanjani sided with the Supreme Leader and the conservatives, condemning the students for providing encouragement to what he claimed were United States efforts to regain influence in Iran.

RODGER SHANAHAN

See also Middle East: History and Economic Development; Pahlavi, Shah Muhammed Reza

References and Further Reading

Keddie, Nikki R. *Modern Iran: Roots and Results of Revolution.* New Haven, CT: Yale University Press, 2003.
Menashri, David. *Post-Revolutionary Politics in Iran: Religion, Society, and Power.* London: Frank Cass, 2001.

RAHMAN, TUNKU ABDUL

Known by his honorific title *Tunku*, Abdul Rahman (1903–1990) was Prime Minister (PM) of the Federation of Malaya (1957–1963) and Malaysia (1963–1970). The *Bapa Kemerdekaan* ("Father of Independence") was born Abdul Rahman Putra Al-Haj, prince of the Sultan of Kedah. Educated in England, he claimed that racial discrimination there motivated his Malayan nationalism. He joined the civil service before returning to England for further studies, but was interrupted by World War II. Like many nationalists, Rahman saw the war as a definitive turning point. Malaya came under Japanese occupation in early 1942. Some Malays heralded this as the end of British imperialism. Most, however, realized Japanese brutality, and by 1945, accepted gradual independence under reinstated British rule. Britain's "Alliance Plan" organized Malayan territories into an ethnically diverse union—formally cast as the Federation of Malaya in 1948.

Rahman became Chair of the nationalist United Malay National Organization (UMNO) in 1949, and its President in 1951. Malaya avoided the divisive nationalism endured elsewhere in Southeast Asia but was not without problems. There were secessionist movements, and between 1948 and 1960, the "Emergency"—a communist insurrection led by ethnic Chinese. Rahman worked with the British to suppress the insurgency. He also forged the multi-ethnic anti-communist Alliance Party with Chinese and Indian leaders. Emphasizing cooperation, he guaranteed minority rights in exchange for support backing Malay-led independence.

Some Malays opposed Rahman. They regarded UMNO as an elitist organization, or insufficiently Muslim. They also resented Chinese economic power. However, Rahman's alliance worked, and on August 31, 1957, Malaya declared independence. Rahman was its first leader. He won additional elections in 1959, 1964, and 1969.

In September 1963, Rahman negotiated British-held Sarawak and Singapore into the Federation of Malaysia. Indonesia, and Philippines opposed the move. Clashes with Indonesian troops followed, but Rahman avoided war. He did the same when Singapore declared independence in 1965. As PM, Rahman also gained Malaysia an elected seat on the United Nations Security Council (1965) and helped form the Association of Southeast Asian Nations (ASEAN) (1967).

Critics see Rahman as dictatorial in ignoring his party and Parliament. They also believe that he exacerbated ethnic tensions, culminating with violent race riots following May 1969 elections. The riots seriously divided UMNO. Future PM Mahatir Mohammed and others were expelled for denouncing Rahman as pro-Chinese. Some members defected to PAS—the opposition *Parti Islam se Tanah Malaya* (Pan-Malayan Islamic Party). Under pressure, Rahman resigned as PM in September 1970 and as UMNO President in June 1971. His multi-ethnic alliance collapsed.

Rahman later chaired the Organization of Islamic Conference (OIC), and headed *The Star* newspaper, often criticizing the government. PM Mahatir banned the newspaper in 1987. Rahman tried dividing UMNO to oppose Mahatir, backing the splinter group *Parti Melayu Semangat 46* (Spirit of '46 Malaysian Party) in 1990 general elections.

Some argue that Rahman spent too much time focusing on racial harmony and not enough time developing the economy. However, others note that without his attempts to unify ethnicities, economic prosperity could never have been achieved.

ARNE KISLENKO

See also Association of Southeast Asian Nations (ASEAN); Colonialism: History; Commonwealth (British); Counterinsurgency; Ethnic Conflicts: Southeast Asia; Indonesia; Inter-Religious Relations; Islam; Malaysia; Organization of the Islamic Conference (OIC); Southeast Asia: History and Economic Development; Southeast Asia: International Relations; Sukarno; United Malays National Organization (UMNO)

References and Further Reading

Ahmad, Zakaria Haji, ed. *Government and Politics of Malaysia.* Singapore: Oxford University Press, 1987.

Andaya, Barbara Watson and Leonard Y. Andaya. *A History of Malaysia*, 2nd ed. Houndmills, UK: Palgrave, 2001.

Cheah, Boon Kheng. *Malaysia: The Making of a Nation.* Singapore: Institute of Southeast Asian Studies, 2002.

Heryanto, Ariel and Sumit K. Mandal. *Challenging Authoritarianism in Southeast Asia: Comparing Indonesia and Malaysia.* London: RoutledgeCurzon, 2003.

Shome, Anthony S. K. *Malay Political Leadership.* London: Routledge, 2002.

Tarling, Nicholas, ed. *The Cambridge History of Southeast Asia* (Vol. 4: From World War II to the Present). Cambridge: Cambridge University Press, 1992.

RAIN FOREST, DESTRUCTION OF

Rain forests constitute the richest, most productive, and complex ecosystems on earth.

Tropical rain forests can be found in the Amazonian basin, South Asia, Australia, and Africa; Australia also has temperate rain forests, which can be found on the northwest coast of North America, New Zealand, Ireland, Scotland, and Norway as well.

Rain Forest: Definition and Status

Rain forests cover less than 2% of the earth's surface; (or 6% of its land mass) they originally covered twice the current area. As some of the earth's richest natural reserves, the tropics contain the oldest living ecosystems of our planet. Southeast Asian forests can be traced back for 70 million to 100 million years. Rain forests receive four to eight meters of rain per year (Myers, Norman, The Primary Source). Without a dry or cold season, the tropical forests absorb as much as five times more rain than forests in a moderate climate. (Myers, Norman, The Primary Source)

Despite the small land area they cover, rain forests are home for about half of all life forms on our planet—as many as 30 million species of plants, animals, and insects. A typical four-square-mile patch of rain forest hosts as many as 125 mammal species, 400 species of birds, 100 of reptiles, 60 of amphibians, and 150 different species of butterflies, as well as 1,500 species of flowering plants and 750 species of trees. Rain forest species do not spread easily beyond their native habitats, and hence are found nowhere else in the world.

The Extent of Destruction

The global rate of tropical deforestation has increased rapidly by more than 50% over the past decade. Many scientists believe that nearly all tropical rain forest ecosystems will be gone by the year 2030.

Southeast Asian countries such as Indonesia, Thailand, Laos, and the Philippines lost 88% of natural forests. Nearly all the primary rain forests in India, Bangladesh, and Sri Lanka have been ruined. The rain forest in Ivory Coast has been almost completely logged; however, the Congo, Cote D'Ivoire and other African countries have gone through the most severe rain forest destruction. More than 60% of Mexico's woodlands have fallen while Haiti rain forests have been completely destroyed. In contrast with other regions, South America still maintains a relatively high percentage of natural ecosystems, particularly in the Amazon and the southern tip of the continent. Unfortunately, however, these pristine areas are being degraded at an alarming rate due to disturbance by human activities.

The Amazon

South America contains some of the world's largest remaining blocks of tropical rain forests, blanketing millions of square miles with the Amazon, Orinoco, and Paraguay Rivers (considered among the largest freshwater systems on earth). A vast expanse of the Amazon River Basin covers an area nearly the size of Europe (stretching over 2 million square miles). The Amazon River Basin retains the most extensive system of flooded forests on earth covering nearly 116,000 square miles. As the world's largest river basin, its streams and rivers supply 20% of the earth's fresh water. A dynamic ecosystem is maintained by yearly patterns of water levels creating and demolishing land along with the constant erosion of riverbanks. Annual fertilization comes from the deposited soil eroded from the Andes carried by annual flooding.

The Amazon is endowed with a variety of ecosystems containing an astonishing array of wildlife. One-third of the world's tropical woods (2,500 tree species) are known to exist only in the Amazon. The forests and freshwater ecosystems of the Amazon Basin host an extraordinary seasonal migration of aquatic and terrestrial animals in and out of the flooded forests. Animals and plants (found nowhere else in the world) thrive along the slopes of the Andes and Guayanan mountains. Rich aquatic and wildlife colonies abound along much of its coastlines.

The Southwestern Amazonian forests of western Brazil, northern Bolivia, and southeastern Peru (covering more than two hundred thousand square miles) form part of the world's largest intact rain forest ecoregion (with its distinctive oxbow lakes), cooled by

winds sweeping down from the Andes and warmed by a jungle blanket. The eco-region's forest types (considered to be among the earth's most biologically rich) are comprised of lowland tropical moist forests, unique flooded savannas dotted with palm trees, as well as an extensive area of bamboo-dominated forests (covering more than sixty-nine thousand square miles—an area the size of England) (World Wildlife Fund 2002). This extraordinary eco-region is maintained by high rainfall, complex topography and soils, and the meandering river systems that create habitat mosaics.

The region has an incredible array of freshwater fish, birds, and butterflies, many of which are found nowhere else. As many as 1,200 species of butterflies have been recorded. In addition, the Southwestern Amazonian forests remain one of the last refuges of the highly threatened jaguar, howler monkeys, pumas, ocelots, bush dogs, the harpy eagle, pink freshwater dolphins, the giant river otter, tapirs, and black caimans.

Many plant species (giant kapok trees, the forests' symbols, and the virola) in these flooded forests face extinction from exploitation due to the region's tripled human population since 1950. Logging the kapok tree and virola is accelerating deforestation over vast regions for biodiversity conservation in flooded forest ecosystem. The open floodplains are threatened by conversion to cattle ranches and the widespread introduction of water buffalo, which are not native to the region and cause damage to the shoreline vegetation and fish nursery areas. Overfishing, to supply the region's growing urban centers, could result in the localized extinction of prized species and the consequent loss of subsistence fishing for traditional river dwellers. Hydroelectric dams for the region disrupt such ecological processes as the migration of catfish, which travels from the estuary at the mouth of the Amazon upstream to Colombia and Peru to spawn.

The Effects of Rain Forest Destruction

Human capacity for meeting material needs is seriously undermined by the elimination of diverse rain forest systems. Natural ecosystems provide genetic resources for improving human well-being. The supply from the rain forests includes a wide assortment of edible fruits and nuts as well as numerous plant products. Many of our favorite foods (avocado, banana, eggplant, fig, lemon, orange, peanut, pineapple, tomato, and countless others) were originally found in the rain forests. Many plants contain genetic materials essential to fortify our existing agricultural stock.

Medicinal plants from tropical rain forests were long used by native tribes. According to the National Cancer Institute, 70% of the plants useful for developing cancer treatment medicines are available only in the rain forests. Many medicines for other serious conditions such as heart ailments, arthritis, and Hodgkin's disease come from rain forest plants. The chemical compounds of fewer than 1% of tropical forest species have been thoroughly studied. We still do not know completely which plant species may contain the properties for curing various human diseases.

Many of the world's most biologically diverse regions are affected by rain forest destruction with the loss of rare species (tree, birds, fish, reptiles, amphibians, and mammals). Rapid lumbering has devastated native tribes. Timber-cutting and the building of dams and other industrial infrastructure has infringed upon or destroyed indigenous villages; overdevelopment of rain forest areas has also contributed to loss of food resources, contamination of drinking water, the spread of disease and loss or damage to archeological sites. Six to nine million indigenous people inhabited the Brazilian rain forest in 1500, but less than two hundred thousand remained by the end of the last century. Several uncontacted indigenous tribes living in biologically rich areas were exposed to a whooping cough and influenza epidemic that killed an estimated 50% of their population.

Forests fulfill human needs by performing ecologically balancing roles or functions, including the protection of soils, preservation of water, and provision of timber. The disappearance of forest (deforestation) causes various environmental consequences such as soil erosion, flooding, and climate changes. Forests control soil erosion by reducing flooding and replenishing groundwater supplies. The soils experience erosion within a few years after rain forest clearance and become unproductive without the nutrients provided by the vegetation.

Photosynthesis of plants within rain forest ecosystems plays a critical role in maintaining the earth's atmosphere: 50% of all oxygen comes from rain forests. By converting carbon into cellulose and releasing oxygen through photosynthesis, forests keep increases in carbon dioxide in check. Throughout past millennia, this has maintained a balance between oxygen and carbon dioxide levels in the air.

However, the consequences of human activities in the rain forests have interrelated and cumulative effects in the environment. Loss of the forests undermines the long-term ability of the earth's atmosphere to neutralize greenhouse gases. Tropical deforestation eliminates our planet's ability to absorb excessive atmospheric carbon since forests absorb and store

atmospheric carbon through photosynthesis. Rain forest loss, and hence increased levels of atmospheric carbon dioxide which contribute to global warming, has an impact on global climate patterns: the warmer temperatures cause melting of the polar ice caps and a rise in sea levels.

More carbon is being released into the atmosphere than ever, but fewer forests exist to remove it. About half the world's forests were removed over a thousand years ago; the concentration of carbon dioxide in the atmosphere has been increasing steadily since 1850 with changes in the composition of the atmosphere caused by human activities.

In addition to coal, oil, and gas (which emits the most carbon dioxide into the atmosphere), the burning of vegetation in deforestation is the second largest contributing factor to the greenhouse effect with the release of huge amounts of carbon into the atmosphere (including carbon dioxide, methane, ozone, and nitrous oxide) through burning and decaying trees. According to some estimates, 23%–30% of all carbon dioxide in the atmosphere comes from deforestation taking place in Brazil, Indonesia, Burma, Mexico, Thailand, and other tropical countries.

Causes of Destruction

The economic pressure on the developing world is difficult to reverse, and thus it is difficult to prevent the exploitation of rain forests for economic purposes. Timber extraction by clear-cutting results in wholesale environmental destruction. Destruction of rain forests is mainly attributed to various human activities, including logging, mineral exploration, and setting up plantations of rubber, coffee, and other crops.

Logging and clearing land for farming have proved the biggest causes of deforestation in places like Cameroon, which experienced the fastest deforestation rate in Africa in the late 1990s. Most tropical timber (teak, mahogany, rosewood, ebony, and iroko) consumed in the United States comes from in Indonesia, Malaysia, and other Southeast Asian countries that dominate world trade in tropical hardwoods. A growing timber trade encourages logging, and the majority of the globe's forests do not receive much protection.

Political corruption often feeds the destruction of rain forests, with bribery leading to lucrative logging concessions that generate exceptional profits for private contractors. Government policies have even contributed to excessive forest depletion with tax and credit subsidies for wood-processing industries.

A direct and immediate process of depredations involves slash-and-burn farming, expansion of ranchland, and unsustainable logging of hardwoods. The uneven distribution of wealth and land is one major factor in the destruction of tropical forests; in the Amazon region, for example, people living on infertile land have traveled to the Amazon basin to practice slash-and-burn agriculture. With the arable land concentrated in the hands of a small, wealthy class, the Brazilian government has encouraged landless peasants to convert the Amazonian forest into small farms and ranches. Rapid population growth often is linked to forest destruction through pressure on new land by small farmers.

Large tracts of rain forest are in danger of being replaced by monocultural plantations of fast-growing, nonindigenous trees for paper-pulp production. Brazil may become one of the world's largest paper-pulp producers at the expense of rain forests. In addition, expansion of ranch land for beef production is responsible for rapid forest conversion, especially in the Amazon and Central America.

Agricultural expansion is not planned in a sustainable fashion, and economic gains have mostly been short-term and concentrated in a few hands. Land development and settlement schemes create monocultures of cash crops. The activities of multinational corporations, engaged in logging, mineral extraction, and agribusiness, emphasize use of chemical fertilizers and specialization in a few crops.

In addition, oil drilling, gas explorations, and mining, large-scale development projects also take their toll on the Amazon's wealth of forests. Exploration and production of oil represents one of the greatest threats to large areas of rain forest in Papua New Guinea, Africa, and the Amazon Basin. Forests are also depleted by the infrastructure, such as dams and highways, which must be built to support these enterprises. Critics have accused multinational corporations and international aid-lending institutions of contributing directly and indirectly to the destruction of the rain forests and indigenous peoples through unregulated investments and tax incentives for projects that contribute to deforestation.

Unmanageable debt, lending policies of international financial institutions, fiscal incentives, and consumerism in affluent societies in Europe and the United States in particular all contribute to rapid deforestation and conversion of tropical land to other purposes. Large-scale, export-oriented commodity production for foreign exchange are driven by the need to service huge debt burdens.

Efforts to Mitigate Deforestation

The forest supports many communities of indigenous people whose livelihood depends on the sustainability of the forest. Many indigenous systems of knowledge recognize the relationship between the forest and its human inhabitants. Sustainable use of resources for indigenous communities is dictated by religious teachings and sheer necessity and derives from an intimate familiarity with the workings of their habitat. Although the concept of sustainable development has been adopted by some national governments and nongovernmental conservation organizations, it is an ancient way of life for most traditional cultures. Indigenous populations make use of everything they harvest in the forest for food, clothing, medicine, and construction materials, and hence are able to take advantage of their resources without depleting them.

Advocates of rain forest preservation argue that income from extractive reserves set aside for use by their original inhabitants actually exceeds revenues generated from lumber and grazing on the same land. When harvested properly, these reserves will produce sustainable supplies of rubber, nuts, fruits, and other products. While maintaining a sustainable income, the reserves also are used to maintain native species. This system has been successfully implemented with the establishment of forest and lake reserves in Brazil, Peru, and Guatemala. Rubber tappers have been strong advocates for conservation and are helping prevent conversion of forest to pasture and agriculture. Local movements led by internationally known activist Chico Mendes and others attempted to save the Amazonian forests by helping inhabitants make a sustainable living. The oppression of the groups drew strong opposition from human rights, environmental, and indigenous groups around the world.

Forest Management Programs

Sustainable use can generate a synergy between environment and development. Farmers can be more productive on smaller portions of land by using more effective agro-forestry methods. A variety of crop species and trees produce higher yields with organic farming than the usual methods of commercial agriculture. Though this small-scale farming is not yet widely practiced, it provides a hope for easing pressure on the rain forests. Logged land can be reclaimed to grow plants that support the subsistence of local people and help reduce the pressure on nearby primary forests.

Additionally, lifestyle changes by consumers can reduce demands on rain forest resources. Conserving energy reduces the need to for petroleum drilling. Recycling reduces waste of paper, aluminum, and tin products that, in many cases, come from the rain forests.

International Efforts

A number of NGOs have engaged in various methods of preserving the rainforest. Some, including the Nature Conservancy and the Rainforest Preservation Foundation, have simply purchased large tracts of rain forest in order to keep them untouched. The Rainforest Preservation Foundation drew international attention by establishing the Mamiraua Sustainable Development Reserve, the largest Brazilian protected area for the conservation of flooded forests. Additionally, nonprofit organizations in Brazil and elsewhere have been established to help the indigenous populations manage the land.

International efforts also include support of the establishment of public preserves of rainforest land. For example, in return for financial assistance, Brazil agreed to preserve 10% of its remaining forest. However, this agreement was undermined by loosening of legal controls on the development of other parts of the Amazon by the Brazilian Congress. Additionally, the positions taken by Western governments and corporations have not been consistent. While the European Union supports rain forest conservation in Brazil, it also has funded the construction and rehabilitation of roads into the forests. The International Tropical Timber Organization also took some initiatives to slow deforestation in Malaysia and other countries, but without cooperation of member states, the measures have not been effective.

HO-WON JEONG

See also Biodiversity Conservation; Environmentalism; Sustainable Development

References and Further Reading

Aiken, S. Robert and Colin Leigh. *Vanishing Rain Forests: The Ecological Transition in Malaysia.* Oxford: Clarendon Press, 1992.

Bevis, William W. *Borneo Log: The Struggle for Sarawak's Forests.* Seattle: University of Washington Press, 1995.

Caufield, Catherine. *In the Rainforest.* Chicago: University of Chicago Press, 1991.

Coffee, Russell G. *The Truth about Rainforest Destruction.* Austin, TX: Better Planet Press, 1996.

Colfer, Carol J. and Yvonne Byron, eds. "A Conservation Ethic in Forest Management" in *People Managing*

Forests: The Links between Human Well-Being and Sustainability. Washington, DC: Resources for the Future, 2001.

Dalton, Stephen. *Vanishing Paradise: The Tropical Rainforest*. Woodstock: Overlook Press, 1990.

Gay, Kathlyn. *Rainforests of the World: A Reference Handbook*. Santa Barbara, CA: ABC-CLIO, 2001.

Head, Suzanne and Robert Heinzman. *Lessons of the Rainforest*. San Francisco: Sierra Club Books, 1990.

Johnson, Darv. *The Amazon Rain Forest*. San Diego: Lucent Books, 1999.

Maloney, Bernard K. *Human Activities and the Tropical Rainforest: Past, Present, and Possible Future*. Boston: Kluwer Academic Publishers, 1998.

Monaghan, Paul Francis. *Peasants, the State, and Deforestation in Haiti's Last Rainforest*, 2000.

Newman, Arnold. *Tropical Rainforest: Our Most Valuable and Endangered Habitat with a Blueprint for Its Survival into the Third Millennium*. New York: Checkmark, 2002.

Nichol, John. *The Mighty Rainforest*. Newton Abbot: David and Charles Press, 1994.

Tucker, Richard P. *Insatiable Appetite: The United States and the Ecological Degradation of the Tropical World*. Berkeley, CA: University of California Press, 2000.

Weber, William, ed. *African Rain Forest Ecology and Conservation: An Interdisciplinary Perspective*. New Haven, CT: Yale University Press, 2001.

RAMOS, FIDEL

Fidel Valdez Ramos, the twelfth president of the Republic of the Philippines, was the first military professional to be president of the country.

Born on March 18, 1928, to Narciso and Angela Ramos in Lingayen, Pangasinan, Ramos joined the military on 1951, where he was Second Lieutenant. He then served in the Philippine Expeditionary Force to Korea in 1952 and in the Philippine Civic Action Group to Vietnam from 1966 to 1968.

During the Marcos era, he headed the Philippine Constabulary, now known as the Philippine National Police, and served as Vice-Chief of Staff of the Armed Forces of the Philippines. From February 22, 1986, Ramos, together with Defense Minister Juan Ponce Enrile, led the People Power movement that lasted for four days. The movement was successful and Corazon Aquino became president of the country. She at once promoted Ramos to full General and Chief of Staff. When Ramos retired after having served thirty years in the military, Aquino then appointed him as her Secretary of National Defense. In 1991, Ramos declared his candidacy for the presidency.

Endorsed by Aquino, he won the election and was sworn in as president on June 20, 1992. As president, his leadership of the country has been guided by his five planks. These five points are as follows: (1) peace and stability, (2) economic growth and sustainable development, (3) energy and power generation, (4) environmental protection, and (5) streamlined democracy.

Ramos addressed the problem of the power shortage in 1992 and 1993 by building power plants. Known as Mr. Fix-It, he later built and renovated roads and infrastructure, knowing that this is one of the basic components of development. He also has liberated telecommunications and built the Light Rail Transit (LRT). Because of these renovations, investors have increased their presence in the nation. These developments helped the country's economy recover dramatically; the gross national product grew 5.5% in 1994. *Newsweek* magazine then hailed the Philippines as the world's first "green tiger" country.

But Ramos's crowning achievement was the signing of the peace agreement between the government and the Moro National Liberation Front (MNLF), which was led by Nur Misuari. After four years of careful negotiations, the peace agreement was finally signed on September 2, 1996. This treaty finally ended a longstanding uprising in Mindanao.

Toward the end of his term, Ramos wanted to amend the Constitution to allow him a second term. Public protests forced him to drop the demand. He stepped down from office after the end of his term in 1998.

Ramos became the country's third president of Ilocano descent and the first Protestant. He is married to Amelita and has five daughters.

ARVEE S. SALAZAR

References and Further Reading

Cal, Ben. *FVR Through the Years*. Quezon City: Philippine Academy for Continuing Education and Research, 1997.

Crisostomo, Isabelo. *Resident Fidel V. Ramos, Builder, Reformer, Peacemaker*. Quezon City: J. Kriz Publication Enterprises, 1997.

Ramos, Fidel. *Break Not the Peace: The Story of the GRP-MNLF Peace Negotiations, 1992–1996*. Quezon City: Capitol Bookstore, 1996.

RASTAFARIANISM

Rastafarianism is a social movement that arose among poor Jamaicans in 1930 during British colonial rule. As a revitalization movement with religious aspects, it brought hope to the poor people who adopted it and served as both protest and resistance to colonial rule, racism, and class differences that characterized the society at that time. From its inception it has served as an alternative to mainstream Jamaican society, politics, and religion. It became a repository of African values and practices in Jamaican culture. Later, it emerged as a broad cultural

movement that spread beyond Jamaica to the rest of the Caribbean, Canada, England, the United States, and Africa.

The name of the movement derives from Ras Tafari, which means "Duke Tafari," the title and given name of the Ethiopian Emperor, Haile Selassie I (often referred to as Jah Ras Tafari). Central to the development and meaning of the movement is the belief that Ras Tafari is the black messiah or even the incarnation of *Jah* (God). Rastafarians believe that black people are the descendants of King Solomon and the Queen of Sheba, and therefore the modern incarnation of ancient Israel.

Rastafarians place an emphasis on Pan-African values, and the movement can be seen as a means of retaining important Jamaican cultural elements devalued by the larger society. They see establishment Jamaica and other parts of the world as Babylon, places of oppression, and Ethiopia or Africa as the Promised Land, or even as heaven, to which blacks should return. The idea of repatriation has been a strong sentiment within Rastafarianism from its beginnings. Most scholars acknowledge that the movement is patriarchal in its sentiments and treatment of women. Although some Rasta men have embraced the equality of women, others cite biblical sources for their subordination.

Typical of the Rastafarian way of life are a number of customs and rituals. Rastafarians tend to work and live communally; they wear dreadlocks, long and matted coils of hair; they employ the ritual use of *ganja* (marijuana); they use a special language/dialect as a marker of identity; many Rastas are vegetarians; and they prize self-reliance. Reggae music and its messages of protest and resistance are emblematic of the role that Rastafarianism has always played in the developing world. The lion, which symbolizes Ras Tafari, is a common symbol, along with the symbolic colors of red (blood of martyrs), black (the people), and green (the plant life).

Colonial Origins of Rastafarianism

In 1930, Jamaica, like the rest of the world, was experiencing the Great Depression, which came in the wake of great changes in the world of Jamaican peasants: the shift from agriculture to wage labor with the coming of industrialization and the shift from rural to urban life. In addition, Jamaica was racially stratified with black peasants at the bottom of the social order and mostly living in poverty. All of these conditions led to the formation of the new movement,

making it nativistic in many of its elements, recapturing traditional practices and values of the Jamaican peasantry that were disrupted with the coming of industry.

Some scholars suggest that Rastafarianism can trace its roots back to the Maroon tradition of Jamaican slavery in which escaped slaves set up autonomous communal enclaves, which served as havens for other escaped slaves and repositories of African culture. And while there is certainly historical continuity in the maintenance of their African heritage and the use of religion as a means of unity, most scholars of the Rastafarian movement see a more direct connection between Rastafarianism and Garveyism, an earlier movement that arose around charismatic leader Marcus Mosiah Garvey (1887–1940) in the 1920s. Although Garvey had more followers in the United States, his movement began in Jamaica.

Garvey formed the Universal Negro Improvement Association (UNIA) in 1914. Central to the goals of the UNIA was the unity of blacks everywhere, the reclaiming of the African heritage and repatriation to an African homeland. The flag of the UNIA was red, black, and green, the colors that would later become symbols of the Rastafarians. Ethiopia also was central to Garveyism as was the African homeland. Marcus Garvey has endured as a key figure in Rastafarian thought and is seen by some as a prophet of Ras Tafari.

Rastafarianism had its inception with the crowning of Haile Selassie I in 1930, and the recognition and celebration of this event by ministers who worked in the poorest parts of Kingston constitute the actual beginnings of Rastafarianism. Some believed that he should replace the British monarch as the head of Jamaica. Early leaders of Rastafarianism, such as Leonard Howell, Joseph Hibbert, Archibald Dunkley, and Robert Hinds were all ministers and probable followers of Marcus Garvey. Of these, Leonard Howell may have had the most impact on the movement and its development.

The Development of Rastafarianism

From the beginning, Rastafarianism posed a threat to the established political, religious, and social order in colonial Jamaica, so much so that its leaders were arrested and jailed with relative frequency. In 1940, Howell purchased land in rural Jamaica and started a commune called The Pinnacle. It was there, living much as the Maroons had, that many of the characteristics of the Rastafarian movement emerged and became fixed.

The 500–1,600 people in Howell's group lived communally, engaging in the growing and sale of a variety of crops. The Pinnacle allowed Rastafarians to recapture part of their lost affection for the land through this small-scale agriculture. It was also during this time that men began letting their hair grow long and began smoking *ganja*. This rural stage of Rastafarianism ended in 1954, when a final raid on the Pinnacle closed it down permanently.

The suppression of the Rastafarians forced them back into urban life, but they maintained many of the characteristics that they had developed in the country. Intensely anti-establishment and anti-authoritarian, they constituted a steady voice of protest against the conditions of colonialism under which they lived and generally refused to become involved with its politics. The movement entered a period during which it took firm root among the poor of Kingston, manifested itself in continual clashes with the establishment, and experienced a couple of abortive attempts at repatriation to Africa. However, changes in both the understanding of Rastafarianism by outsiders and increased activism on the part of Rastas themselves began after Jamaican independence came on August 6, 1962.

Post-Colonial Resurgence of Rastafarianism

In the 1960s and 1970s Rastafarianism grew and branched out into formal associations, became linked to reggae music, and transformed itself from a local movement to an international one, largely due to its persistent voice against oppression and the state powers that be. The movement was also galvanized by a visit from Emperor Haile Selassie in 1966 and by his later offer of five hundred acres of land in Ethiopia for the repatriation of people of African descent.

After Jamaican independence, Rastas became embroiled in the political machinations of the competing political parties and in the political violence that ensued. These parties adopted Rasta symbolism as a connection to the poorer classes and, in so doing, legitimized Rastafarianism to a certain extent. Some formal religious associations emerged, each embodying a slightly different approach or ideology, such as the Ethiopian Orthodox Church; the Ethiopian Zion Coptic Church; and the Twelve Tribes of Israel.

Much of the controversy that continued to surround Rastafarianism centered on the use of *ganja* and the widespread sale and distribution throughout the Caribbean, whether or not the Rastas were directly involved. The Ethiopian Zion Coptic Church became known for its attempt to establish the legal use of marijuana in the United States. Perhaps the most

important element in the spread of Rastafarianism came from its association with reggae music, which became an internationally recognized form of protest. Its best-known practitioner, Bob Marley (1945–1981) engaged in political activism, much of it on behalf of African causes.

Because of its roots in protest and resistance, Rastafarianism grew from a local to an international phenomenon that took hold in parts of the world where people of African descent struggled to not only maintain their identities and values but to end the racial oppression to which they had been subjugated.

Susan Love Brown

See also Caribbean: History and Economic Development; Coptic Church (Copts); Ethiopia; Jamaica; Pan-Africanism; Peasants, Impact of Development on; Selassie, Emperor Haile; Social Revolution

References and Further Reading

Barrett, Leonard E. *The Rastafarians: Sounds of Cultural Dissonance*. Boston: Beacon Press, 1997.

Campbell, Horace. *Rasta and Resistance: From Marcus Garvey to Walter Rodney*. Trenton, NJ: Africa World Press, 1987.

Chevannes, Barry. *Rastafari: Roots and Ideology*. Syracuse, NY: Syracuse University Press, 1994.

Edmonds, Ennis Barrington. *Rastafari: From Outcasts to Culture Bearers*. New York: Oxford University Press, 2003.

Hamid, Ansley. *The Ganja Complex: Rastafari ad Marijuana*. Lanham, MD: Lexington Books, 2002.

King, Stephen A. *Reggae, Rastafari, and the Rhetoric of Social Control*. Jackson, MS: University Press of Mississippi, 2002.

Lewis, William F. *Soul Rebels: The Rastafari*. Prospect Heights, IL: Waveland Press, 1993.

Mulvaney, Rebekah Michele. *Rastafari and Reggae: A Dictionary and Sourcebook*. New York: Greenwood Press, 1990.

Murrell, Nathaniel Samuel, William David Spencer, and Adrian Anthony, eds. *Chanting Down Babylon: The Rastafari Reader*. Philadelphia: Temple University Press, 1998.

Owens, Joseph. *Dread: The Rastafarians of Jamaica*. Kingston, Jamaica: Sangster, 1976.

Pollard, Velma. *Dread Talk: The Language of Rastafari*. Montreal: McGill-Queen's University Press, 2000.

Van Dijk, Frank Jan. *Jahmaica: Rastafari and Jamaican Society, 1930–1990*. Utrecht: ISOR, 1993.

REFUGEES

Defining Refugees

The flight of people from situations of danger to places of safety and refuge has been a constant feature

of human history. All world religions contain some notions of asylum and protection, and churches and other religious institutions have frequently provided refuge for people in flight. Throughout history, people have fled either individually, as a family, or as part of a group to escape persecution and acts of violence. In the first half of the twentieth century, however, the large-scale movements of people across international borders within Europe as a result of war and the persecution of minorities, meant that refugees became matters of international politics for the first time.

In the aftermath of World War II, and in an attempt to control the flow of some four hundred thousand mainly Jewish European refugees fleeing the Third Reich and Fascism, the 1951 Geneva Convention Relating to the Status of Refugees came into force. While initially concerned with the post-war European refugee crisis, the Refugee Convention provides the global definition of a refugee and sets out the responsibility of states in an international legal framework that is current today. That framework places an obligation on states and governments to guarantee people fleeing violence and persecution the right to asylum, and the right not to be returned to a country where his or her life or freedom would be threatened (non-refoulement). The United Nations (UN), through its specialised refugee agency, the UN High Commission for Refugees (UNHCR), is tasked with assisting governments to meet their Refugee Convention obligations, and provide international protection and assistance to people in flight.

The Refugee Convention defines a "refugee" as any person who:

> Owing to a well-founded fear of being persecuted for reason of race, religion, nationality, membership of a particular social group or political opinion, is outside the country of his nationality and is unable, or owing to such fear, unwilling to avail himself of the protection of that country. (Article 1A)

The diplomats who drafted the Refugee Convention anticipated the limitations of their work and by urging states to "apply the Convention beyond its strictly contractual scope, to other refugees in their territory" recognised that the definition adopted was restrictive and would not cover every refugee (Goodwin-Gill 1996:19). In recognition of this, and in response to changed circumstances, the scope of the Refugee Convention was broadened beyond events in pre-1950 Europe by the 1967 Protocol Relating to the Status of Refugees to include refugees anywhere in the world. However, the definition of a refugee has remained unchanged and has been incorporated into most states' municipal laws. It is on the basis of this definition that the international community decides which people should be entitled to protection and assistance from the UN, and which should be granted refugee status and the benefits of citizenship in a country of asylum; and conversely, which people should be excluded.

Recent Refugee History

The postwar response to the refugees in Europe was relatively successful. Most who fled or were forcibly removed from Nazi Germany and other refugees from Fascism, were able to integrate into the refugee receiving countries of Western Europe and North America, and in an era of postwar reconstruction, these new populations found their skills in demand. Beyond Europe, however, following World War II and throughout the period of the Cold War, the refugee situation became far larger and more complex politically, institutionally and practically.

Decolonisation, which brought an end to British, French, and other European empires in the 1950s and 1960s, was associated with a series of national liberation wars. Particularly in Africa with conflicts in Zambia, Zaire, and Guinea-Bissau in the 1960s, but also civil war in Latin America, triggered large exoduses of people within countries and across borders into neighbouring states. These large, unplanned and chaotic movements of people brought about unprecedented political, economic, and humanitarian challenges for countries receiving refugees, and for the international system responding to those crises.

Further conflicts in the 1970s in Mozambique, Ethiopia, Sudan, Afghanistan, and Indo-China, generated even larger movements of people and demanded a proportionate international humanitarian response meeting immediate needs for food, shelter, medical care, and clothing. Solutions also had to be found for refugees in the medium and long-term. Camps created in countries of first asylum provided short-term protection and permitted the provision of assistance, but did not offer a long-term solution. The UN and refugee-receiving governments evolved three main strategies: (1) refugees returning home once conditions had improved, (2) local integration in the country of asylum, and (3) resettlement in another country prepared to take refugees on a permanent basis. The majority of refugees do return home once conflict has ended, and only around 1% find permanent resettlement in Europe, Australia, or North America.

The legal status of refugees fleeing liberation wars and other Cold War era conflicts was unclear. The

majority of refugees was not fleeing individual persecution at the hands of a state, but rather was fleeing generalised violence, insecurity, and poverty. Conflicts in the 1970s and 1980s were complex, involving many parties within states, but also with regional and international involvement. The nature of those conflicts meant that refugees found it increasingly difficult to meet the Refugee Convention requirement to prove individual persecution.

Protracted refugee emergencies in Africa in the 1980s and in Central America resulted in new regional approaches to improve the situation of refugees and to make clear the obligations of states and the international community. The 1984 Cartagena Declaration, for example, signed by Central American governments meeting in Colombia, accepted a broadened definition of refugees to reflect the more complex situation. The new refugee definition included people who fled their country, because their lives, safety, or freedom were threatened by generalised violence, foreign aggression, internal conflicts, massive violation of human rights, or other circumstances seriously disturbing public order. The Declaration, building on the earlier 1969 Organisation of African Unity Convention on Refugees, was a response to the new phenomena of the sudden mass influx of refugees, and the prolonged nature of conflicts. The new regional approaches also took into account the evolution of international human rights law throughout the 1960s and 1970s, and the relevance of human rights for the refugee response.

Despite expectations to the contrary, the end of the Cold War brought about greater political instability and a sharp increase in internal conflicts. Cross-border refugee influxes and internal displacement as a result of conflict in Northern Iraq, the Great Lakes region of Central Africa, Chechnya, and in Sri Lanka increased refugee numbers from a few million in the 1970s to more than 25 million in the 1990s. Human rights abuses, most notably through "ethnic cleansing" in Bosnia and Kosovo, became a deliberate strategy of conflict and the creation of refugees a deliberate war goal. Added to the cross-border population were a fluctuating number (but generally exceeding 7 million) of Internally Displaced Persons (IDPs). The UN, and in particular the UNHCR, recognised that IDPs were people in "refugee-like situations" and UNHCR practice extended its mandate to include IDPs as "people of concern to the organisation."

The contemporary refugee challenge remains unchanged—how best to respond to sudden movements of people against a backdrop of complex conflicts in a manner that guarantees refugee protection, provides short-term assistance, and offers a durable solution to their plight. The challenge is made more difficult, however, as refugee receiving countries in Europe, North America, and Australia apply ever more restrictive asylum policies, sometimes blocking asylum seekers access to territory, reducing welfare rights, and making more stringent the determination of asylum requests. Countries of asylum are concerned about the increasing number of people on the move globally, the costs of hosting refugees, the perceived misuse of asylum procedures by "economic migrants," and security threats. Proposed solutions to improve the management of refugees and general forced migration emergencies, include greater sharing of the "refugee burden" between states, increased funding for UNHCR and other agencies, the addressing of root causes of refugee flight, and the adoption of new legal instruments.

However, the main responsibility for responding to refugee needs and the main burden of costs is borne by countries in the Developing World that host refugee populations for long periods of time. More than 70% of people of concern who fall under the mandate of UNHCR and, therefore, are in need of protection and assistance are in Asia and Africa. Over the past ten years, the quality of asylum for refugees in those countries of first asylum has deteriorated. Wars have spilled over into camps, which have become recruiting grounds for new soldiers, and a resource for the continuation of war. Assistance in camps is in decline, and access across borders between developing countries is increasingly denied. The so-called "CNN effect" has tended to mean that international attention on refugee situations is short-term, resulting in funding shortfalls. Refugee movements, the creation and maintenance of camps, repatriation, and reintegration, pose a range of challenges for security and development in the Developing World.

Explaining Refugee Movements

In seeking to explain the causes of refugee flight, there is a tendency to over-generalise, and it is often the case in such analysis that cause and effect are confused. While it is typically the case, as UN High Commissioner for Refugees, Mrs. Ogata stated in 1995, that "refugees are a direct result of conflict, which is often aggravated by poverty and social inequities" (Olaf Palme Memorial Lecture, June 14, Stockholm), academics have sought to uncover the underlying processes that result in poverty and conflict in any given situation.

It is clear that the immediate factors that precipitate refugee flight are diverse. For example, in the

1990s they ranged from violent struggles over the control of the illegal diamond market in Sierra Leone, the forced resettlement of villages with the intent of ethnically realigning populations, famine and drought, or what appears to be ethnic conflict between rival groups in a situation of resource scarcity. A number of theories have been advanced to explain forced migration episodes by making linkages between identified underlying processes and forced migration.

Aristide Zolberg (Zolberg 1983; Zolberg, Suhrke and Aguaio 1989) contends that mass refugee flows are a likely result of nation-state formation, which is frequently accompanied by political crises, the generation of victimised groups, and interstate wars. Together, Zolberg argues, these processes lead to persecution and the creation of three "types" of refugee. The *targeted* refugees who are singled out for violent treatment because of their membership in a particular group; *activists* who are the dissenters and rebels forced to flee the regimes to which they are opposed; and the *victims* who are accidentally caught in a violent situation.

Anthony Richmond, however, believes that this categorisation is insufficient to account for different behaviour under similar violent conditions, or for the compelling circumstances inducing migration which are not necessarily "violent" in the physical sense, but which are nonetheless extremely coercive (1993:9). Richmond has developed a "multivariate typology of reactive migration," and a "systems model" that seek to explain the relationship between predisposing factors, structural constraints, precipitating events, and enabling circumstances in a given refugee movement.

In Richmond's model, predisposing factors increasing the probability of "reactive migration" (refugee flight) are similar to those identified by Zolberg, and include extreme inequalities in wealth, new state formation, decolonisation and ethnic nationalism, the global military-industrial complex, and processes of economic, political and cultural globalisation. Structural factors constraining the movement of refugees include border enforcement and immigration control. Precipitating events include sudden changes in the economic, political, social, or environmental situation through for example genocidal programmes or internal revolution. Finally, enabling circumstances may include government policies that facilitate migration, and access to resources to organise flight.

Richmond's multivariate model goes some way to identifying the multiple events and factors that combine at any given time to create conditions in which refugee movements are likely. However, refugee flight continues to be sporadic and unpredictable. Not all situations of violent social change, extreme poverty, and repressive government generate refugee flows—South Africa, for example, was noticeable in the 1980s and early 1990s for the very low levels of cross-border refugee movement despite the considerable instability. Sri Lanka, on the other hand, during the same period generated more than five hundred thousand refugees, mainly Tamils from the North and East of the island who sought asylum in Europe and North America.

A number of authors and international organisations such as the World Bank make causal linkages between processes of underdevelopment, poverty, and refugees. J.K Galbraith, for example, argues that the more widespread occurrence of political oppression and persecution in developing countries is part and parcel of the vicious cycle of poverty. It is certainly the case that the majority of refugees in transit or in camps in developing countries are drawn from the poorest segments of society. It also is the case that countries generating the largest number of refugees are those with the lowest per capita gross domestic product, most notably Ethiopia, Sudan, Eritrea, Somalia, and Afghanistan. Poverty alone, however, does not generate refugees, it is generally thought that only when other factors combine with poverty, for example, drought and famine, conflict, repressive government, and human rights violations, that large-scale refugee movements are likely to occur.

Refugees: Development and Humanitarianism

The current international response to refugee crises is sometimes criticised for addressing the symptoms and ignoring the root causes of forced population displacement. The main components of the humanitarian response to forced migration emergencies include, temporary protection in refugee camps, the meeting of basic needs through provision of food, water, sanitation, health care and shelter, resettlement in third countries, and the repatriation of refugees to their countries of origin. These strategies, however, are frequently ameliorative measures that provide no long-term solutions to the problems of refugees or for the countries that generate refugees. In extreme cases, international assistance, for example, through the creation of insecure camps, the providing of food aid to combatants, repatriation programmes without safeguards for protection and livelihood re-establishment, may even exacerbate the conditions that precipitated flight in the first place. Others argue that that politically-driven humanitarian assistance "does harm" by delaying the resolution of conflicts, and commonly cite the role of aid in "sustaining a genocidal leadership

and its supporters in the refugee camps of Eastern Zaire" (in 1994) and by so doing dramatically increase the vulnerability of refugees.

In a bid to improve the response to refugee crises, there have been calls for a substantial increase in development aid to countries with refugee populations. Both to assist countries of origin and countries playing host to refugees, particularly in areas of poverty alleviation, education, good governance, and respect for human rights, and health care. Correlations are drawn between the reduction in official development assistance (aid from Western nations to poorer less developed nations) over the past ten years, and the increase in refugee numbers during the same period. However, others are more skeptical, arguing that "pro-poor growth" strategies pursued by donor governments in partnership with less developed countries since the late-1980s have failed to break the cycle of poverty and are unlikely to impact positively on the conditions that create forced migrants.

Elsewhere, it is argued that processes of globalisation, particularly through international trading arrangements that benefit advanced industrialised nations driven by the telecommunications revolution, have actively disadvantaged less developed countries, excluding them from the advantages of the global market and worsening the conditions that lead to oppressive government, poverty, and conflict. Lobbyists from the nongovernmental sector tend to argue that too much globalisation is the cause of deepening underdevelopment. While organisations such as the World Trade Organisation and the World Bank argue conversely that greater integration and inclusion of less developed economies in the global economy is the solution to poverty and good governance, and will lead to a reduction in refugee flows.

Agencies engaged in humanitarian assistance to refugees initiated a number of reforms in the 1990s to improve the situation of refugees. These included improved coordination between the main players leading to a speedier and more relevant response, targets for the quantity and quality of material assistance were agreed upon, and the increased involvement of displaced people in assistance operations was promoted.

A more significant development, however, since the end of the Cold War that has significantly shaped the response to forced migration emergencies has been the readiness of UN Security Council member states and other states to undertake humanitarian operations in ongoing civil wars for substantially humanitarian objectives. The first of these operations took place in April 1991 to create Safe Havens for displaced and persecuted Kurds in Northern Iraq, later interventions included the January 1992 creation of UNPROFOR in the former Yugoslavia and the December 1992

deployment of US troops in Somalia as part of the United Task Force operation. However, the success of these operations was extremely limited, and the beneficial impacts on refugees and IDPs minimal.

Post-Cold War humanitarian intervention, however, has proven to be selective, marked by a reluctance to intervene to halt human rights abuses in certain countries (for example, in Indonesia or Chechnya), and preferring a policy of refugee containment (that is, maintaining refugee populations close to the country of origin). In addition, poor countries perceive the international community as failing to share the burden imposed by refugees, whether in the form of compensation for impacts on the host areas or in ensuring that refugee camps include only bonafide refugees. The principle of voluntary repatriation is also being increasingly overridden: twenty countries expelled refugees from their territory during 1996. The starkest case was the repatriation of 1.2 million Rwandan refugees from Zaire and Tanzania in late 1996. The consequence according to the Overseas Development Institute in London, is that civilians fleeing conflict are now much more likely to remain within their own country than to cross the border as refugees. The September 11 attacks on the United States, and US-led military action in Afghanistan in 2001 and 2002, and the changed World Order will once again reshape "conflict management" and the "conditional approach" to intervention. The implications for forced migrants, however, are unclear.

Refugees and Human Rights

Over the past decade, there has been an attempt, initiated in part by the UN, to strengthen the international legal framework for the protection of refugees. One initiative seeks to integrate international human rights law, refugee law, and humanitarian law into a comprehensive single body of law. Proponents point to the commonalities between the three historical streams, notably the shared roots in the aftermath of World War II and a determination that the Holocaust should not happen again; and common values reflected in a commitment to the inalienability of rights, the dignity and worth of the individual, and freedom and equality. It is argued that such integration would strengthen refugee policy and practice by making clear states legal obligations to refugees, and the rights to which refugees are entitled. Others are concerned, however, that in the absence of a fully-functioning, trusted, and independent judicial system in many developing countries, a rights-based approach would not be effective.

The Refugee Experience

As refugee numbers have grown in the 1980s and 1990s, so academic and literary interest also has grown. Studies of the refugee experience have tended to focus on the impact on individuals and families or being uprooted from one's home and familiar surroundings, the risks and dangers of flight, and the difficult transitions involved in creating a new home. The refugee experience has provided a source of inspiration for authors, poets, and artists.

Academic work has focused on the success or otherwise in the "adaptation" of refugees and refugee communities in their place of resettlement. Adaptation relates mainly to refugees' participation in the economic, political, and social life of their host communities. It includes questions about social identity in the new setting, the retaining of language, and the continuation or discontinuation of values, traditions, and social habits characteristic of their culture. Particular attention has been paid to understanding the social worlds of refugees, which comprise the dense networks of social relationships in which they are enmeshed, the social forces that impinge on them, and the changes to these worlds brought about by displacement and resettlement.

For anthropologists in particular, the experiences of refugees have contributed to knowledge and understanding of the impact of rapid change, culture clash, the social construction of boundaries, conflicts between generations, and livelihood concerns in both the developing and developed world. A less developed area of research examines the psychological costs associated with forced uprooting. This includes attempts to better understand the significance of trauma arising from the direct experience of violence where refugees are either witnesses or participants to violence and the effects of such exposure on women and children, and the development of new approaches to psychological support.

Refugees: Burden or Benefit?

The environmental impact of some refugee camps, reception centres and settlement schemes impose serious costs on developing countries playing host to refugee populations and have resulted in opposition to refugee influxes from certain countries and host communities. Camps with extremely high population density are frequently located in marginal or ecologically sensitive areas, and without environmental management, they rapidly become depleted as a result of tree clearing for firewood and shelter construction. Whole lakes have been drained for camp consumption, and other water sources permanently contaminated. As attitudes towards the environment changed in the 1990s, so efforts were made to minimise the negative impact of refugee populations. Particular attention is now paid to the improved management of shelter construction, water and sanitation provision, and the development of new cooking stoves and fuel types.

Concerns also have been expressed by populations and states playing host to refugees about the socioeconomic impact of sudden and large-scale refugee influxes. Host communities frequently contend that refugee populations are temporary and unstable and do not share the indigenous population's commitment to the land and its natural resources. There is fear that refugee populations pursue short-term livelihood strategies and unsustainable resource use methods that degrade the land. It is feared that foreign aid used to establish and maintain camps inflates prices for all goods, and introduces a reliance on expensive imported produce. Development country governments are concerned that international aid is insufficient to cover recurrent costs of providing for refugee populations, and there is a danger that the sudden introduction of foreign NGOs creates alternative structures of government. Security concerns arise when refugee camps become a site for the continuation of a conflict and a recruiting ground for combatants—particularly where this leads to instability among the host society.

However, there also are examples where refugees have been able to play a more positive role in the local development process. The UNHCR cites the case during the 1980s, for example, where the large number of Ugandan refugees who fled to southern Sudan were able to contribute to a massive expansion in the area of land under cultivation. As a result, a number of refugee settlements that had initially been dependent on international assistance were soon able to provide the commodities which the World Food Programme needed for its projects in other parts of the country. More recently, the UNHCR claims, the presence of Mozambican refugees in southeastern Zambia also had many positive consequences for the local economy.

Other Forced Migrants

"Development Refugees"

In academic analysis, and less so in policy discussions, there are attempts to consider the whole range of circumstances that create different types of forced

population displacement, interconnections between them, and how best to respond to them. This recognition of different domains of forced displacement has generated new categories of refugees, "environmental refugees," "disaster refugees," and "development refugees."

The second largest group of forcibly displaced people in the world behind Refugee Convention defined refugees comprises people uprooted to make way for planned infrastructure development projects in developing countries. In 1994, the World Bank, following a review of World Bank-funded projects that involved the involuntary resettlement of populations, estimated that between 9 million and 10 million people are displaced each year as a direct result of hydro schemes (dams, reservoirs, and so forth) and road and other transport construction. The actual number is far greater when one adds to that total the numbers of people displaced by urban projects (such as slum clearance programmes and industrial developments), conservation programmes (for example, game parks and forestry initiatives), and schemes to promote the commercialisation of agriculture. Many more are indirectly displaced by planned development initiatives (for example, fisherfolk living downstream of a newly created dam which diverts rivers and removes livelihood opportunities).

While "development refugees" have not crossed an international border and are not considered "people of concern" to the UN, evidence suggests that the majority of people displaced and involuntarily resettled by planned development share many similarities with refugees and IDPs. Michael M. Cernea (2000) argues that the experience of involuntary resettlement is cumulated deprivation leading to multifaceted and persistent poverty. Cernea's Impoverishment Risks and Reconstruction model suggests that the key impoverishment risks confronting development displacees are associated with the loss of land, jobs, housing, food security, and common property resources, and these losses are exacerbated by morbidity and mortality, social disarticulation, and marginalisation.

Further seminal longitudinal research by Thayer Scudder (1993) and Elizabeth Colson among people displaced by the construction of the Kariba Dam on the border between Zambia and Zimbabwe, reveals negative psychological, physiological, and sociocultural impacts over a number of generations. These include the undermining of community institutions and leaders, trauma, grief and anxiety, and declining health.

The numbers of people displaced by planned development is likely to increase dramatically over the coming decades as the need grows for irrigation, electricity, and infrastructure necessary to satisfy the demands of growing and increasingly urbanising populations. At the same time, there is likely to be increased organised opposition to large projects on the grounds of environmental damage. As water scarcity becomes an issue of political tension between a number of countries (that is, Ethiopia, Sudan and Egypt; Turkey and neighbouring countries who share the Euphrates River) and directly affecting minority populations in sensitive border areas, future hydro-schemes will be highly contested.

'Environmental Refugees'

Since the early 1980s, evidence has been accumulating to suggest that environmental change leading to natural resource depletion, particularly land degradation, is creating conditions in certain areas of developing countries that are hazardous for human habitation. As a result, people are leaving these areas and without alternative land for resettlement, enter a refugee-like situation and require assistance. The number of people who could be categorised as "environmental refugees" is difficult to estimate. Some reports predict there will be as many as 25 million environmentally induced forced migrants by 2020. Kibreab, however, argues that while environmental change may be one of the reasons for mass displacement, particularly in arid and semi-arid areas, displacement is more often a result of deliberate political actions that remove the capacity of people to manage predictable periods of environmental change, than the degraded conditions alone.

Recent scientific understanding has shown that emissions of greenhouse gases from developed countries have risen steeply over the past three decades, and international action, such as the 1997 Kyoto Protocol, have sought to reduce emissions and halt global warming. It is thought that global warming is contributing to the creation of environmental refugees as a result of more and increasingly erratic rainfall, and an increase in the frequency and severity of tropical storms. Such changed conditions directly threaten tens of millions of people who live in low-lying coastal areas and are dependent on coastal resources for their livelihoods.

CHRISTOPHER MCDOWELL

See also Migration; United Nations High Commissioner for Refugees (UNHCR)

References and Further Reading

Cernea, Michael M. "Risks, Safeguards, and Reconstruction: A Model Displacement and Resettlement," in *Risks and Reconstruction: Experiences of Resettlers and Refugees*. Michael M. Cernea and Christopher McDowell, eds. Washington, DC: World Bank, 2000.

Galbraith, J. K. *The Nature of Mass Poverty*. Cambridge, MA: Harvard University Press, 1979.

Goodwin-Gill, Guy S. *The Refugee in International Law*. Oxford: Clarendon Paperbacks, 2nd ed., 1996.

Kibreab, Gaim. *People on the Edge in the Horn: Displacement, Land Use, and the Environment in the Gedaref Region*. Sudan, Oxford: James Curry, 1996.

Ogata, Sagata. "Olaf Palme Memorial Lecture," June 14, Stockholm, 1995.

Overseas Development Institute. *The State of the International Humanitarian System*. Briefing Paper, London, March 1998.

Richmond, Anthony. "Reactive Migration: Sociological Perspectives on Refugee Movements," *Journal of Refugee Studies*. 6:4, 1993.

Scudder, Thayer. "Development-Induced Relocation and Refugee Studies: 37 Years of Change and Continuity among Zambia's Ovenbe Tonga," *Journal of Refugee Studies*. 6:2 (1994).

Skran, Claudena. *Refugees in Inter-War Europe: The Emergence of a Regime*. Oxford: Oxford University Press, 1995.

United Nations General Assembly, 1951 Convention Relating to the Status of Refugees, Geneva.

———, 1967 Protocol Relating to the Status of Refugees, Geneva.

World Bank. *Resettlement and Development: The Bankwide Review of Projects Involving Involuntary Resettlement, 1996-1993*, Environment Department Paper no. 32, Washington, DC: World Bank, 1994.

Zolberg, Aristide R. "The Formation of New States as a Refugee Generating Process," *Annals*, 467, 1983.

———, Suhrke Astri, and Ahuaio, Sergio. *Escape from Violence: Conflict and Refugee Crisis in the Developing World*. New York: Oxford University Press, 1989.

RELIGION

Religion has had a significant and profound effect on development since the end of World War II. Consequently, churches have been key players within developing nations and civil society in a Western context, and accordingly made efforts to further their religious intentions. As political regimes changed, democracies emerged, and development occurred, the churches throughout the world have responded to meet the challenges faced in the new societies. Development occurs, and democracies arise out of any number of historical and cultural contexts that pose a unique set of circumstances for every developing nation and thus for the responding religious establishments. While some religious movements and churches have sought the betterment of their communities through peace, justice, and equality, others have done their fair share of contributing to, legitimating, and sustaining authoritarian and repressive political regimes. What is important is the commonality of responses by the churches and religious organizations, not the specifics of the processes of democratization and development, since every country that is developing does so

in different ways and under different political, economic and social conditions that cannot transcend the contexts in which change is occurring.

Religion and the churches have been involved in the political arena and in situations of change throughout the ages. The examples are numerous and continue into the modern era. Some churches have been prominent in liberation struggles throughout the world, responding to the political reality, from the Civil Rights Movement in the United States to liberation movements against authoritarianism in Latin America, communism in Eastern Europe, and the Soviet Union, and colonialism and despotism in Africa.

Religion and a Developing Society

From a religious perspective, church leaders throughout the world have argued for the necessity of churches' involvement in politics. Kyril, the Archbishop of Smolensk and Kaliningrad as a representative of world church leader believes that the churches must not refrain from participating in lawmaking and the political process. They must formulate positions on issues that affect society, including: individual and social morality, politics, economics, ecology, culture, education, international relations, the rearing of children, marriage, and much more.

Churches are important actors in transitioning societies and can be effective in responding to newly emerging democratic civil societies. They have a unique access to the grassroots and can help in building a political culture of tolerance, reconciliation, and democratic values.

During periods of transition, the churches redefine their missions in response to the change occurring in the political, social, and economic contexts. This redefinition of mission and the dilemmas that arise from change have been prevalent among churches and religious ideologies throughout the world as they find themselves in changing and developing political situations. While transitioning political realities, historically, have not always led to democratization, emerging democracies (either liberal or popular, with varying degrees of success) are the order of the second half of the twentieth century. Within this democratization context, distinct according to a nation's history and cultures, some common global responses from the churches can be discerned.

As realities change, churches tend to experience a "crisis of identity," in which they are compelled to respond to a new situation with innovative political, social, and economic analysis, at the same time considering the appropriateness of their own pastoral

functions. With democratization, there often is an increase in secularization. With this, churches are confronted with a weakening of their influence and must address issues that accompany a more open, free, and competitive society, all the while preserving their constituencies. Interconnected with the churches' "crisis of identity" and an increase in secularization is their concern for the "common good." As the rich/poor, North/South divide increases, as ethnic wars continue, the environment is dissipated, and the poor struggle to be heard, churches are looked upon to provide a moral voice and sense of social responsibility. Further, they provide a civil society venue for debate and resources as democracies emerge and societies require reconstructing and reconciliation from a destructive past.

Latin America

The majority of the literature dealing with the role of religion and church change in development comes from Latin American analyses of the relationship between religion and politics. One predominate theme emerges from Latin America. As the churches have responded, specifically to democratization, they strive to maintain their position in society and their influence among their members. They do this, however, in a variety of ways that are contingent upon and intricately interwoven with the historical and cultural context in with the churches function.

For example, as democracies emerged in Venezuela and Colombia in the early 1960s, the Catholic Church in these two countries responded differently because of the position and influence it held within each society. Venezuela is one of the more secular societies in Latin America. Here, the Church, historically poor and weak, consequently has had less influence on the populace than the Church in neighboring countries. It has been reluctant to alienate potential members by engaging in the political debates that are prevalent in a democracy, thus remaining focused on its internal spiritual and pastoral functions. The Catholic Church in Colombia, on the other hand, traditionally very powerful with a broad network of organizations and a great tradition of leadership had been at the forefront of innovative change in relation to the democratic political reality. It has acted in partnership with the government to further democratic values. The churches in both countries, however, work to build better communities as reflects their social and cultural contexts through pastoral activities. This has meant everything from striving for the consolidation of democracy, unifying the structures of the churches, and

working to alleviate the pressures of the poor and oppressed, all the while dealing with the questions of its identity, secularization and the common good.

Throughout Latin America a number of divergent responses with the churches have occurred due to democratization and development. One such response, expressed by the most conservative and corporatist social and political elements of various Latin American populations and supported by similar elements within the Catholic Church, has sought to establish a social and political order suffused with Christian principles in the name of Christendom. An alternative response to the conservatism of the Christendom advocates is that of Neo-Christendom, manifested by the Christian Democratic political parties. This element within the churches seeks to reform the world while giving more autonomy to the laity, relying on the laity to help the churches fulfill their missions, as opposed to relying on the sole authority of the priesthood.

A more radical response within the churches as they struggle for democracy is found in Liberation Theology, which brings together human and salvation history with the temporal and spiritual dimension of life. This response emphasizes the need for participation, involvement, and action in the here and now, while revealing the social and political implication of the gospel to the oppressed. It is a response to authoritarianism, springing from the churches' efforts to bring about a just and democratic society. Finally, those churches that hold the Evangelical-Pastoral position, in the "center" between the Christendom/Neo-Christendom and Liberation Theology emphasize the unity of the churches, building community and fraternity, revitalizing the message of the gospel, and disengaging from partisan politics in favor of a more general denunciation of injustice. The churches in Latin America have responded to democratization or the move towards democracy away from authoritarianism in all of these ways. In essence, these responses are manifested in the churches' pastoral actions, which strive for a community in the interest of the common good.

Europe

Shifting focus from the Catholic Church in Latin America to a mixture of Protestant and Catholic churches in Europe, from countries that are highly religious to those that are more secular, similar patterns of change can be found. The power and influence of mainline churches fluctuates as the political and social reality of a nation changes. In Germany, for

example, the mainline churches held prominent and influential positions in the first decade after World War II as democracy emerged and developed after the fall of fascism. In the 1960s and 1970s, value changes in the people's priorities toward personal and social development left the influence of the churches in decline, especially in the political arena. The churches have responded to the increased secularization inherent in a democracy by going into a self-preservation mode while maintaining their influence in the traditional rites of passage (baptism, marriage, and death).

Contrary to the churches' limited position in West Germany, the churches in the former East Germany are held in high esteem by the citizens, in part due to their contribution to the opposition movement leading up to and during the 1989 revolution, which resulted in democratic transition. Nevertheless, these churches have experienced a period of disillusionment and a subsequent reorientation of their mission. This redefinition of mission, in a period of democratic transition, includes the acknowledgement that the churches have a continuing responsibility to be a witness in the public dimension (political, social and economic) and strive for reconciliation of the victims of the changing reality.

Other examples from Europe provide insight into the role that religions and churches can have when faced with changing political and social realities. In the Netherlands after World War II, with the ravages of fascism and the rebuilding of society, the value of democracy was strongly asserted in the churches. Later, as the society became more secularized and church membership declined, the importance of the laity in shaping religious life was emphasized. In Italy, reconstruction was a priority after World War II. The Catholic Church struggled between endorsing modernization and maintaining traditional religious values, while placing a moral expectation on society that economic and cultural opportunities would be promoted, along with a guarantee of democracy. Yet the church in Italy has been caught between taking definitive stands on social issues and losing political support. It has responded to the political reality by compromising itself on political problems and by adopting an attitude of moderation regarding development. As a result, it has isolated itself and is judged more for its actions than its statement of morals and beliefs.

While these individual cases provide examples within specific democratic contexts, they do not address religious and church responses to the changing reality in contemporary Europe: as the Common Market and the European Community become consolidated; as democratic structures are extended to the international arena; and as the nations in the former Eastern bloc struggle to become more developed and democratized. From meetings held by the European Ecumenical Assembly in May 1989 (the first time since the Reformation that delegates from all the Christian churches on the continent met to examine the contemporary reality of their position within society), and the Central Committee of the World Council of Churches in August 1992, a number of themes emerge as the churches respond to the changing political reality in Europe.

Functioning within a secular social context where the churches suffer from weak influence and the non-involvement of the population, there is the recognition for continuing conversion efforts—maintaining and increasing church memberships. In an effort to accomplish this, the churches realize they must continue in social, economic, political and cultural analysis, developing positions on economic justice, peace and security, ecology and the environment, and immigrants and refugees. They must be a voice of brotherly love and justice for the "other"—the Third World and oppressed whom Europe continues to tower above. They must examine themselves while defining the terms of the public debate on issues of democracy and social morality, acknowledging that what is good for civil society is also good for the churches.

Africa

As with Latin America and Europe, the churches and religious movements throughout Africa have responded to political change and development, as independence movements succeeded, colonialism ended, and democracies emerged, in specific ways that are unique to their historical and cultural experiences. Generally speaking, churches throughout Africa responded to the oppressive political reality and the hopes for democratic justice with the theological doctrines of inculturation (African cultural rejuvenation) and liberation (freedom from oppression). While emphasizing different things, these are simply two names for the same process—mainly the empowerment of the black African in the face of oppression and domination, calling on spiritual and cultural aspects of the past and looking with hope toward the future. These religious movements, being affected by and contributing to the political reality, have been manifested within society in a number of different ways.

The first manifestation of church participation within civil and political society is dependent on the degree to which a religious movement or organization seeks ideological purity. In other words, high levels

of ideological purity and focus on sectarian customs and rituals will lead to a low degree of political involvement. Whereas religious groups that are multifaceted and open to diversity are more inclined to be activist and politically involved. Those religious groups with a greater commitment to ideological purity, with charismatic leaders, with closed recruitment patterns and which place a heavy emphasis on one particular issue or custom, will be less likely to become involved in political activity.

A second manifestation of African church involvement in society, responding to the political reality while striving for democracy, is one of accommodation. Succumbing to the White-dominant colonial regime in the hopes that eventually it would fall in the face of pleas for Christian morality. This describes the mainline English-speaking churches, yet the tendency toward accommodation had been embarked upon with considerable ambivalence, especially in the church environments that were predominately African, as opposed to European. In such churches, the Africans have struggled to maintain their equality in the face of White domination, claiming that all men are created equal before God. They have consistently refused to accommodate the political regime in their own oppression. Unfortunately, African accommodation and pleas for Christian morality and democratic justice, repeatedly fell upon deaf ears, often meeting with increased repression.

A third manifestation is seen in considering the differences between institutional (established) and independent and indigenous churches and how they engaged in political action in response to political change. Institutional churches, those arising from the European missions, are thought to be more accommodationist, working for change within the established power structure. Independent churches, those that have severed ties with the European mission churches and exist independently from the establishment, are thought to be more revolutionary and liberationist in their beliefs. The African indigenous churches, those with primarily traditional African religious elements but exhibiting many characteristics of Christianity, tend to be isolationist in their behavior—not engaging in the secular realm, but nevertheless political by being pastorally active.

Religion's Involvement in Change

These examples show that religion, as embodied by churches have effected and are affected by development and political, social, and economic change in a variety of ways depending on the context in which they function. A society that is developing and transitioning to democracy will experience more freedoms and, consequently, more forces competing for a voice, a condition inherent to democracy. In changing political contexts, churches either choose to continue to have a political voice or retreat into a purely spiritual realm, or function somewhere in between, as they grapple with the myriad of social issues that arise in a more open, modern, developing and democratic society. Some religions and their corresponding churches, as seen here, have positively contributed to development through the advocation of peace, equality, and liberation. However, it is important to remember that others have often failed to live up to the ideals of justice and peace, while acting as coconspirators with the political elite to maintain authoritarian power structures.

DEE F. MATREYEK

See also Buddhism; Christianity; Christians in the Middle East; Coptic Church (Copts); Evangelical Protestantism; Hinduism; Islam; Islamic Fundamentalism; Judaism; Khomeini, Ayatollah Ruhollah; Liberation Theology; Roman Catholic Church; Sufism; Tutu, Bishop Desmond; World Council of Churches; Wojtyła, Karol (Pope John Paul II); Wyszyński, Cardinal Stefan; Zionism

References and Further Reading

De Gruchy, John W. *Christianity and Democracy*. Cape Town: David Philip, 1995.
Johnston, Douglas and Cynthia Sampson, eds. *Religion: The Missing Dimension of Statecraft*. New York: Oxford University Press, 1994.
Levine, David H. ed. *Religion and Political Conflict in Latin America*. Chapel Hill, NC: The University of North Carolina Press, 1986.
Pérez-Diaz, Victor. "The Possibility of Civil Society: Traditions, Character and Challenges," in *Civil Society: Theory, History, Comparison*. John Hall, ed. Cambridge: Polity Press, 1995.
Rieger, Joerg, ed. *Liberating the Future: God, Mammon, and Theology*. Minneapolis: Fortress Press, 1998.
Roberts, Richard H., ed. *Religion and the Transformations of Capitalism: Comparative Approaches*. London and New York: Routledge, 1995.
Robertson, Roland and William R. Garrett, eds. *Religion and the Global Order*. New York: Paragon House, 1991.
Roof, Wade Clark, Jackson W. Carroll, and David A. Roozen, eds. *The Post-War Generation and Establishment Religion: Cross-Cultural Perspective*. Boulder, CO: Westview Press, 1995.
Sahliyeh, Emile, ed. *Religious Resurgence and Politics in the Contemporary World*. Albany, NY: State University of New York Press, 1990.
Villa-Vicencio, Charles. *A Theology of Reconstruction*. Cambridge, MA: Cambridge University Press, 1992.
Weigel, George. *The Final Revolution: The Resistance Church and the Collapse of Communism*. New York: Oxford University Press, 1992.

REVOLUTIONARY ARMED FORCES OF COLOMBIA (FARC)

The Revolutionary Armed Forces of Colombia (known by its Spanish acronym, FARC) traces its origins to a power-sharing compromise between Colombia's two main political parties in the early 1960s. Although the agreement ended more than a decade of political violence, Fidel Castro's nationalist revolution in Cuba inspired the formation of the FARC in 1964, and its intellectual founders were loyal followers of the Colombian Communist Party. Communists and dissident liberals originally constituted the organization, but the leadership now insists that it represents the rural poor against the influence of wealthy landowners and the United States over natural resources and national politics. The FARC is governed by a secretariat, led by Manuel Marulanda, and several senior military commanders. It consists of about eighteen thousand armed members. In FARC's early years, its guerrilla founders concentrated on expanding their bases of support in rural areas where centuries of colonization, exploitation and forced migration had impoverished the peasant population. Its main areas of operation were the southern provinces of Caquetá, Putumayo, Huila, Cauca, and Tolima, in the central regions of Magdalena Medio and Santander, and along the Antioquia-Córdoba northern border. FARC presently operates mostly in the jungles of the southeast and the plains at the base of the Andes mountain range, though it now includes several urban fronts.

During the late 1960s and early 1970s, the FARC was one of several guerrilla groups that included the National Liberation Army, the Popular Liberation Army, and the M-19. Though torn by internal disputes in the late 1970s, resulting in a diminished military capacity, the FARC received funding from the Soviet Union and support from Cuba during the Cold War and now maintains offices in Cuba, Mexico, and various European capitals. Experts blame FARC for 10%–15% of the approximately 3,500 civilian deaths that occur yearly in Colombia's civil war, which has killed some two hundred thousand people since 1964.

From 1982 to 1984, the government of conservative Belisario Betancur negotiated a ceasefire with the FARC and two other guerilla groups. Hundreds of political prisoners, including many guerrilla leaders, received amnesty. In March 1984, the FARC signed a peace accord with the National Peace Commission and renounced the armed struggle. However, a paramilitary movement formed to break the ceasefire while Betancur took action against drug traffickers. These factors ended the peace process in 1986 when the guerrillas retreated to withstand the force unleashed against them by the drug traffickers and right-wing paramilitary groups. By the mid 1990s, paramilitaries and drug traffickers had penetrated FARC-controlled areas of coca cultivation in the south, buying land, recruiting peasants, and organizing campaigns of terror and massacres against the civilian population.

Over the course of the 1990s, the civil war shifted from an ideological battle against a Marxist insurgency to a major conflict over control of territory and the drug market. In 1998, just before his inauguration as president, Conservative Andrés Pastrana visited FARC leader Manuel Marulanda to explore the possibility of peace talks. Pastrana agreed to withdraw army troops from five towns in guerrilla-controlled territory ceding an area twice the size of New Jersey. However, in February 2002, Pastrana ended peace negotiations after a plane hijacking and kidnapping of a Colombian senator from the aircraft and ordered the military to retake FARC-controlled zones. Alvaro Uribe Vélez won a landslide victory in Colombia's May 2002 presidential election by promising to crack down on the FARC. In August 2002, the FARC launched a mortar attack on the Presidential Palace where the new president was being inaugurated.

With the fall of the notorious Medellín and Cali cartels, the FARC gained greater access to lucrative sources of income in coca and heroin. The FARC generates income of $200 million to $400 million annually from the illegal drug trade, in addition to profits from kidnappings, extortion schemes, and unofficial taxes that it collects in the countryside for protection against government raids and right-wing paramilitary forces and the provision of social services. Poor farmers began to grow coca in neglected areas of the country under the protection of the FARC. However, some peasants complained of being ordered by local guerrilla commanders to grow coca and sell their harvests to a guerrilla-controlled monopoly. Colombian traffickers eclipsed their competitors in Peru and Bolivia but also captured part of the heroin market from interests in Southeast Asia and Afghanistan who deal in the United States market.

The Clinton administration proposed a $1.6 billion military aid package for Colombia in January 2000 to eradicate the cultivation of the coca plant and eliminate the alliance between the FARC leadership and the producers of cocaine and heroin. In response, the FARC launched armed resistance in the southern department of Putumayo where the US anti-drug offensive was centered and demanded a halt to the so-called Plan Colombia's military component. The FARC has carried out dramatic ransom kidnappings of wealthy landowners, foreign tourists, and

prominent international and domestic officials. For example, the FARC kidnapped a presidential candidate, Ingrid Betancourt, who was traveling in guerrilla territory in February 2002. In March 1999, the FARC killed three American missionaries working in Colombia. The US State Department placed the FARC on its list of foreign terrorist organizations during this period.

MARK EVERINGHAM

See also Guerilla Warfare; Northern South America: History and Economic Development

Further Reading

Arson, Cynthia, ed. *Comparative Peace Processes in Latin America*. Stanford, CA: Stanford University Press, 1999.
Cala, Andres. "The Enigmatic Guerrilla: FARC's Manuel Marulanda," *Current History* 99 (February 2000).
Pearce, Jenny. *Colombia: Inside the labyrinth*. London: Latin America Bureau, 1990.
Rohter, Larry. "Cocaine War: Weave of Drugs and Strife in Colombia," *New York Times* 21 (April 2000).
Shifter, Michael. "The United States and Colombia: Partners in Ambiguity," *Current History* 99 (February 2000).
Vargas Meza, Ricardo. *The Revolutionary Armed Forces of Colombia (FARC) and the Illicit Drug Trade*, Washington, DC: Washington Office on Latin America (WOLA), 1999.

REVOLUTIONARY ARMY OF THE PEOPLE

The Argentinian Revolutionary Army of the People, or the *Ejercito Revolucionario del Pueblo* (ERP) was the militant arm of the Revolutionary Workers' Party, or the *Partido Revolucionario del Trabajo* (PRT), and the most active guerrilla group in Argentina in the early 1970s. Inspired by the success of the Cuban Revolution, Latin American guerrilla movements of this period grew in response to the instability of their governments and the effects of their faltering economies. From the late 1960s through the 1970s, there were more than a dozen guerrilla groups operating in Argentina alone.

The PRT-ERP shared in the belief that violent armed struggle could bring socialism to state power, envisioning a government responsive to working-class needs and liberated from North American imperialism. Yet the ERP distinguished itself from other guerilla organizations by the level of its military development, by maintaining a separate political party that directed its armed struggle, and by its specific revolutionary principles, manifest in the organization's slogan: For the working class, Latin American and socialist revolution.

The PRT was founded in 1965 through a union of the IndoAmerican Popular Revolutionary Front, a socialist organization that both supported local indigenous sugar workers' protests and was influenced by a vision of Latin American revolutionary unity, and the Worker's Word, a Trostkyist organization with ties to the Peronist Resistance. In 1968, PRT leader Mário Roberto Santucho cited the need to move from theoretical discussions to more concrete practices and formed the branch of PRT that later organized the ERP as a "popular army." These early influences on the PRT-ERP marked its most salient characteristics: a Marxist focus on and incorporation of the working class, an internationalism that led to continent-wide collaboration (concretized in the Latin American Revolutionary Coordinating Council), an anti-intellectual tendency and emphasis on militant action, and a conviction in the need for armed struggle to replace capitalist structures with socialism.

Created in 1970, the ERP began its armed tactics with small actions for provisioning and "propaganda actions" meant to popularize its cause. In 1973, it changed its strategy and began attacking Argentinian Army bases and in 1975 fought in the largest military-guerrilla battle in Argentina at Mount Chingolo. With this armed activity, the ERP became more popularly recognizable than its political party, the PRT. The ERP's guerrilla actions, combined with the organizing work of the PRT, led to the height of the organization's membership in 1975, when the PRT-ERP counted five thousand to six thousand militants.

The PRT-ERP provided dispossessed and working-class Argentinians with a revolutionary and international alternative to the widespread populist Peronism. But military response to guerilla groups led to the annihilation of the ERP's armed ranks by 1976. Mário Roberto Santucho and other PRT-ERP directors were killed by the army in July 1976. Yet despite the virtual elimination of the militant left by the time of the 1976 coup, the military *junta* in power used the threat of rebel groups as a pretext for the brutal violence and ruthless repression that lasted from 1976 to 1983 and became known as the Dirty War.

CRISTINA CIELO

See also Argentina; Guerrilla Warfare; Marxism; Montoneros; Perón, Juan Domingo

References and Further Reading

Mattini, Luis. *Hombres y Mujeres del PRT-ERP*. Buenos Aires: Editorial Contrapunto, 1990.
Petras, James. "Questions to a Militant of the PRT-ERP." In *Urban Guerrilla Warfare in Latin America*, James Kohl and John Litt, eds., (Cambridge, MA, 1974), pp. 387–393.

Pozzi, Pablo. *"Por las sendas argentinas..."*: *El PRT-ERP: La Guerrilla Marxista.* Buenos Aires: Editorial Universitaria de Buenos Aires, 2001.

Seoane, María. *Todo o Nada: La Historia Secreta y la Historia Pública del Jefe Guerrillero Mário Roberto Santucho.* Buenos Aires: Planeta, 1991.

REVOLUTIONARY DEMOCRATIC FRONT (FDR)

The Revolutionary Democratic Front (Frente Democratico Revolucionario, FDR) was the largest group representing the political left in El Salvador during the 1980s. On April 1, 1980, the FDR was established by the Revolutionary Coordinator of the Masses (Coordinadora Revolucionaria de las Masas, CRM), an umbrella group representing a plethora of leftist political groups that included the social democrats. Until the presidential elections of 1988, however, political groups were excluded from the electoral process. Leftist political parties had been repressed since the late 1970s by right-wing paramilitary groups supporting the military dictatorship. By the mid-1980s, political violence had declined considerably, which allowed for greater political mobilization on the left.

In October 1980, the FDR joined the Farabundo Marti National Liberation Front (Frente Farabundo Marti de Liberacion Nacional–FMLN), a militant leftist guerilla group. The new political/military alliance, the FMLN-FDR, represented five guerilla groups: the People's Revolutionary Army (Ejercito Revolucionario del Pueblo, ERP), the Popular Liberation Forces (Fuerzas Populares de Liberacion, FPL), the Armed Forces of National Resistance (Fuerzas Armadas de Resistencia Nacional, FARN), the Communist Party of El Salvador (Partido Comunista de El Salvador, PCES), and the Revolutionary Party of Central American Workers (Partido Revolucionario de Trabajadores Centroamericanos, PRTC).

The FMLN-FDR was a Marxist-Leninist movement with a pro-Soviet and pro-Cuban orientation. They committed themselves to seizing power through a two-pronged military strategy of economic sabotage and a prolonged guerilla war of attrition based on a combination of Maoist, Vietnamese, and Guevarist principles. The FMLN-FDR sought to entrench its rural guerrilla forces, while simultaneously developing urban support bases in preparation for overthrowing the Salvadoran government. From 1980 to 1982, politically-related violence in El Salvador increased dramatically as the FMLN-FDR increased its activities. The FMLN-FDR used kidnapping, torture, and murder to achieve its agenda. The guerilla groups armed their forces with US-made weapons captured from the Salvadoran army.

The FMLN-FDR focused international attention on El Salvador and became a formidable force both politically and militarily. In August 1981, the governments of France and Mexico recognized the FDR as a representative political force and called for a negotiated settlement between the rebels, and the government. FDR representatives carried on a political campaign abroad, while the FMLN forces continued their organizational and operational efforts in the field.

As the FMLN-FDR began to grow in strength and size, with the assistance of Nicaragua and Cuba, the Salvadoran army became less able to control the guerilla groups. The FMLN-FDR, however, was put on the defensive in 1984 when the United States sent substantial military aid to support the Salvadoran Army. On January 16, 1992, the administration of President Alfredo Cristiani (of ARENA, the right-wing Nationalist Republican Alliance) signed a peace treaty with the FMLN-FDR, formally ending the twelve-year civil war that killed seventy-five thousand Salvadorans.

CHARLENE T. OVERTURF

See also Central America: History and Economic Development; El Salvador; Guerilla Warfare

References and Further Reading

Armstrong, Robert. *El Salvador: The Face of Revolution.* Cambridge, MA: South End Press, 1982.

Montgomery, Tommy Sue. *Revolution in El Salvador: From Civil Strife to Civil Peace.* Philadelphia, PA: Westview Press, 1995.

O'Neill, Bard E. *Insurgency and Terrorism: Inside Modern Revolutionary Warfare.* Dulles, VA: Brassey's Inc., 2001.

Wood, Elisabeth Jean, *et al. Insurgent Collection Action and Civil War in El Salvador.* Cambridge, MA: Cambridge University Press, 2003.

RHEE, SYNGMAN

As the first president (1948–1961) of the Republic of Korea (South Korea), Syngman Rhee is considered the "Father of Korea" and is credited with transforming South Korea from agricultural society to an industrial power. Politically, Rhee parlayed South Korea's status as a victim of Communist aggression into financial and military support from the United States that secured the transformation of the South Korean economy. Eventually his authoritarian rule, mismanagement of the Korean economy and his obvious rigging of the 1960 presidential election led to mass demonstrations that led to his forced resignation in April 1960 and subsequent exile to Hawaii.

He was born April 26, 1875, in Kaesong, Hwanghai Province, Korea. He entered the American

missionary Paejae High School in 1894, and worked as a reporter for the newspaper *Hyopsung* in 1896. During his teens, he became an ardent nationalist, advocating the independence of Korea. He was imprisoned in 1897 for leading demonstrations against the Korean monarchy. He was released from prison and moved to the United States in November 1904, where he studied at both Harvard and Princeton Universities, eventually earning a Ph.D. In 1911, Rhee returned to Korea as a YMCA teacher-evangelist. Forced into exile in 1904, Rhee was educated in the United States and was elected president of the Korean Government in Exile in 1919. He lived in Hawaii from 1913 to 1940, where he was principal of a Korean school and the leader of a Korean expatriate faction called *Tongjihoe* (Comrades' Society).

In 1919, Rhee was elected president of the Korean Provisional Government in exile. He served as president of the provisional government in 1921 and waged an independent movement for Korean independence in the United States.

Rhee returned to Korea on October 16, 1945, and became president of the Central Independence Promotion Council. Upon his return, Rhee called for the immediate independence of Korea. Following highly disputed elections in the south, Rhee was installed as the first President of the Republic of Korea in 1948. Rhee continually called for the reunification of the Korean Peninsula, by force if necessary. Shortly thereafter, the outbreak of the Korean War divided the Korean Peninsula into the capitalist South and communist North. For the duration of the Korean War, Rhee continually tried to sabotage armistice negotiations hoping to reunify the Korean Peninsula by force under his rule.

Faced with the task of building a nation that had been torn apart by a brutal civil war that divided the Korean Peninsula, Rhee succumbed to the temptation faced by leaders of emerging democracies: the centralization and consolidation of power. Rhee centralized his control over the state through the perpetuation of the buildup of the armed forces and control of the government apparatus. In order to consolidate power over government apparatus, Rhee aligned himself with the business and land-owning classes and oversaw the suppression of political dissent. He promulgated laws meant to intimidate and imprison political opponents.

Politically, Rhee parlayed Korea's status as a victim of Communist aggression into support from the United States. In 1953, Rhee signed the *United States–Republic of Korea Mutual Security Treaty* that secured long-term economic and military aid meant to rebuild South Korea's economy and military. Economically, Rhee mismanaged the development aid meant to kick-start the South Korean economy. Instead of channeling foreign aid into industry, money went to the armed forces. Rhee also subsidized the import of various consumer goods such as food and beverages, clothing, and footwear. He also gave government protection to huge conglomerates (*chaebols*) that continue to dominate the Korean economy today.

Eventually, Rhee's heavy-handed centralization of power, political corruption, and continued military expansion alienated him from the Korean populace. Rhee was forced from power on April 26, 1960, largely in part to student-led demonstrations.

Syngman Rhee died in Honolulu, Hawaii, on July 19, 1965, at age ninety.

KEITH A. LEITICH

References and Further Reading

Principal Writings

Japan Inside Out, New York, 1940.
Korea Flaming High; Excerpts from Statements by President Syngman Rhee.
The Syngman Rhee Telegrams, Seoul, Korea: Joong Ang Ilbo: Institute for Modern Korean Studies, Yonsei University, 2000.
Tongnip chongsin, 1945 as *The Spirit of Independence: A Primer of Korean Modernization and Reform*, translated, annotated, and with an introduction by Han-Kyo Kim, 2001.

Further Reading

Allen, Richard C. *Korea's Syngman Rhee: An Unauthorized Portrait*. Tokyo, Rutland, VT: Tuttle, 1960.
Hong, Yong-pyo. *State Security and Regime Security: President Syngman Rhee and the Insecurity Dilemma in South Korea, 1953–1960*. New York: St. Martin's Press, 1999.
Kim, Quee–Young. *The Fall of Syngman Rhee*. Berkeley, CA: Institute of East Asian Studies, University of California, Berkeley, Center for Korean Studies, 1983.
———, Stephen Jin-woo. *Master of Manipulation: Syngman Rhee and the Seoul–Washington Alliance, 1953–1960*, Seoul: Yonsei University Press.
Lee, Chong-sik. *Syngman Rhee: The Prison Years of a Young Radical*. Seoul: Yonsei University Press, 2001.
Oliver, Robert T. *Syngman Rhee and American Involvement in Korea, 1942–1960: A Personal Narrative*. Seoul: Panmun Book Co., 1978.
———. *Syngman Rhee, The Man Behind the Myth*. New York: Dodd, Mead, 1954.

ROCKEFELLER FOUNDATION

The Rockefeller Foundation (RF) is a philanthropic institution established by John D. Rockefeller, a North American industrialist, one of the so-called

robber barons of the late nineteenth and early twentieth centuries. In June 1909, Mr Rockefeller donated seventy-three thousand shares of the Standard Oil Company (at that time it represented a sum of $50 million) to the creation of the Foundation. His son, John D. Rockefeller, Jr., his son-in-law Harold Mac Cormick, and his usual partner Frederick Gates received the funds and started the organization. However, only in May 14, 1913, New York Governor William Sulzer approved the charter for the foundation, and soon that same year, it began operations, because of which many people claim that it was created in 1913.

Since its beginnings the Foundation set clearly its objectives: it was destined to promote the well-being and progress of the United States (US) and foreign citizens, to acquire and diffuse knowledge, and to promote the prevention and relief of all kind of human suffering. Its motto has since then stated: "To promote the well-being of mankind throughout the world." Its slogan ran: "We Are a Partner, Not a Patron."

In 1913, the Rockefeller Foundation was endowed in several installments that totaled about $250 million. But by the end of 2001, the market value of the Rockefeller Foundation's endowment was $3.1 billion. It has given more than $1.8 billion to thousands of grantees worldwide and has assisted directly in the training of nearly thirteen thousand Rockefeller Fellows.

Its headquarters were established in New York City, but the Foundation has had an increasingly global presence with the establishment of regional offices in Bangkok (Thailand), Nairobi (Kenya), San Francisco (US), and a also conference and study centre in Bellagio (Italy).

Through the years the Foundation has given assistance to all the aspects that encompass the concept of development. Therefore, it has financed projects related to the public health, medical education, increasing food production (agricultural and natural sciences division), scientific advancement, social research, the arts and humanities, international relations, and other fields formerly more focused on the US but then also all over the world.

During its early years the Foundation focused its actions on Public Health issues. Therefore, it participated in a worldwide campaign against the hookworm (a parasitical disease acquired by walking barefoot on polluted ground) until 1954. As a means to fight against the disease, the people were educated to change their environment and their habits so as to suppress the fatal animal agent. For that they used public health workers. The cure for hookworm, besides wearing shoes, consisted of capsules of thymol and salts. The RF acted through illustrated lectures and pamphlets to create the necessity among the

people to maintain sanitary conditions and defeat the illness. The main efforts were conducted in the rural areas of the southern US led by Dr. Wickliffe Rose but also important campaigns were carried out in India, Puerto Rico, and Colombia. Having recognized the success of the Rockefeller Sanitary Commission for the Eradication of Hookworm Disease in the US, the Foundation formed the International Health Board (IHB) to extend its public health work overseas in 1913.

A similar campaign was held by the RF against the yellow fever in 1935. That year, a breakthrough was achieved when Dr. Max Theiler and his associates in the International Health Division (IHD), under the supervision of Dr. Sawyer, managed to develop a successful yellow fever vaccine. Although it was a team work, Dr. Theiler himself was honored in 1951 by receiving the Nobel Prize in medicine for this discovery.

Another accomplishment of the RF in the health medicine was the formation of nurses and the establishment of the first Public Health Schools. To accomplish that, the Foundation financed the creation of Public Health Nursing Schools in more than fifty countries besides the US. From 1921 on, Public Health Schools were installed in Prague, Toronto, London, Budapest, Copenhagen, Ankara, Madrid, Rome, Tokyo, Stockholm, Athens, and other cities. Also important was the Foundation's role in organizing the Public Health system in the postrevolutionary Mexico with, first, the campaign against the yellow fever and then with the establishment of Permanent Sanitary Units and the award of scholarships that allowed the training of Mexican professionals in the US.

The Foundation also established the China Medical Board (CMB) in its first years (1911) to develop a system of modern western medical education in China. In 1919, a formal Medical Education Eivision was established to carry out a program of medical education outside the US. The General Education Board (GEB), a separate Rockefeller philanthropy, was responsible for US medical education. Within this program, grants were made to related fields such as nursing and hospital and dispensary development. Fellowships in physics and chemistry through the National Research Council became a continuing interest in 1919. From 1919 to 1923, a Division of Studies within the RF was responsible for projects not covered by the IHB, CMB, or Medical Education Division.

The Foundation also financed scientists who fought battles against the Kyanasur disease (Kyanasur Forest Fever) in India in 1957, mainly in the Indian state of Mysore and against the Influenza virus. Besides, the Foundation played an important role in the development of medicine to fight malaria. In 1915, it

supported Sir Ronald Ross' experiments in the US to find a cure for malaria until he found a way to control it. By 1944, malaria had been eradicated from the US. Besides infectious diseases, the Foundation also supported research and advances in psychiatry, such as in the field of Biology of Behaviour at the University of Cambridge, the study of physiological psychology at the Polish Academy of Sciences, and the establishment of a department of Psychiatry at the University of Ibadan.

The RF carried the programs overseas. It favoured, together with the Brazilian government, the installment of the Belem Laboratory in Brazil, devoted to the study of viruses transmitted by mosquitoes, ticks, and other arthropods. The Foundation also created the Peking Union Medical College in China in the 1920s.

The Foundation also supported research in the genetics field mainly in the US but also in universities in Japan, Sweden, and Italy.

All this was part of the RF's early interests. In its early years, the Foundation's interest was concentrated on medicine and public health, as the hookworm and yellow fever campaigns prove. Later on, the Foundation's interest was more concerned with the development of agriculture and the agricultural sciences, in the US and overseas.

In 1951, the International Health Division was merged with the medical sciences program, and public health activity was deemphasized. Population studies, international relations, legal and political philosophy, institutional support of the arts, historical research, and agriculture were the main areas of grants during the 1950s.

During the 1960s, a formal population program was established. Grants were made to various institutions for the purpose of improving race relations. In 1968, the RF convened US and foreign experts at an international symposium, "Strategy for the Conquest of Hunger," to develop a plan to eradicate world hunger. Significant contributions were made by the Foundation to the modernization of agriculture in the developing countries, a fact known as the "Green Revolution."

During that decade, the Foundation began supporting research activities in Chile as part of Chile's Ten-Year Plan of Economic Development. The aim was to increase agricultural production by a more efficient use of existing farmlands. Therefore, the RF supported the building of two experimental stations, one near Santiago (Chile's capital) and the other near Temuco.

The Foundation also was present in Colombia in a project to increase the agricultural production. The main objective was to carry out laboratory and field work so as to train skilled Colombian personnel to develop the programs. Also, in Mexico (University of Nuevo Leon in Monterrey) and Colombia (University of Andes), the Foundation has provided grants and funds. In Mexico, the scientists who worked under the Foundation's support developed the so-called "Green Revolution" in the country, which helped to increase the production of corn, the main alimentary Mexican resource, reducing the imports of this product.

Also, in India, the RF sponsored studies in native agricultural research, specially with the creation of the postgraduate school of the Indian Agriculture Research Institute in New Delhi, which the RF has helped with funds and by providing advisors and visiting professors. In 1959, it also established the International Rice Research Institute in Philippines.

In Africa, the Foundation has aided universities to deal with critical food and disease problems in the continent, and also in order to train personnel to staff governments and institutions.

Besides the agricultural sector, the Foundation also devoted resources to the promotion of the social sciences. For instance, in 1962, it provided a large amount of dollars to create the Institute of African Studies at the University of Ibadan and also to the University of Karthoum (Sudan) with library assistance in all disciplines.

The Foundation has helped developing countries by supporting the building of centers of academic excellence, such as the University of Ibadan (Nigeria); the University of East Africa, a complex of three separate growing colleges in Uganda, Kenya, and Tanganyika; and the University of Valle in Cali (Colombia).

In the field of Social Sciences and Humanities, the RF contributed to the archaeological digs and excavations in the Agora zone, Greece. The Foundation also has supported the works of significant authors who were winners of the Nobel Prize, such as Ralph Bunche (winner in 1950), T. S. Eliot (1948 Nobel in literature). Other great achievements of the RF were providing a grant for the building of Oxford's world-famous Bodleian Library and the making of photographic copies of the complete card catalogues of the Library of Congress.

In the field of Arts and Culture, a remarkable work was the construction of the Art Conservation Centre of the Institute of Fine Arts in New York University, whose purpose is to explore and arrive at standards of conservation that can be disseminated to museums and other repertories. The Foundation also helped in the establishment of the Lincoln Centre in New York City and the Berkshire Music Festival at Tanglewood in Western Massachusetts.

During the 1970s, cooperative efforts with the Ford Foundation included the Consultative Group on International Agricultural Research (CGIAR), and regional research programs to improve understanding of population development links in Third World countries. Social history, including women's history, family history, and the use of oral history and film to document America's cultural heritage, was another new area in which the RF made grants. Grants in the humanities continued, including a fellowship program.

More recently, the Foundation has kept on contributing to the development of many countries by sponsoring the African Agricultural Technology Foundation to help farmers in sub-Saharan Africa gain access to hunger-reducing agricultural technologies. The Foundation also has financed the Public Sector Intellectual Property Resource for Agriculture (PIPRA) to make agricultural technologies more easily available for humanitarian purposes in the developing world.

One of the most valuable contributions was, during the 1990s, the resources spent on the International AIDS Vaccine Initiative, a research project destined to speed the search for a vaccine to prevent HIV/AIDS all over the world. In relation to that research, the International Partnership for Microbicides Program was established to accelerate the discovery, development, and accessibility of microbicides to prevent transmission of HIV and other sexually transmitted infections.

Within the medicine research field, the Foundation is currently financing the Global Alliance for Tuberculosis Drug Development, which seeks to accelerate the discovery and development of faster-acting and affordable drugs to fight tuberculosis.

Among the 170 Nobel Prize winners who developed their work under the Foundation's support (more recently also working in the Rockefeller University), we could name Werner Heisenberg (1932, Physics), Enrico Fermi (1938, Physics), Sir Hans Kreb (1953, Medicine), Edward L. Tatum (1958, Medicine), Emilio Segré (1959, Physics), Christian De Duve (1974, Medicine), John Harsanyi (1994, Economics, together with John Nash), Günter Blobel (1999, Physiology or Medicine), Paul Greengard (2000, Physiology or Medicine), and Roderick MacKinnon (2003, Chemistry).

DIEGO I. MURGUÍA

See also Non-Governmental Organizations (NGOs)

References and Further Reading

Abrams, Sarah E. *Dreams and Awakenings: The Rockefeller Foundation and Public Health Nursing Education, 1913–1930*. Ph.D. dissertation., University of California, San Francisco, 1992.

Bullock, Mary Brown. *An American Transplant: The Rockefeller Foundation and Peking Union Medical College*. Berkeley, CA: University of California Press, 1980.

Coleman, James S. and Court, David. *University Development in the Third World: The Rockefeller Foundation Experience*. New York: Pergamon Press, 1993.

Cueto, Marcos, ed. *Missionaries of Science: The Rockefeller Foundation and Latin America*. Bloomington, IN: Indiana University Press, 1994.

Fosdick, Raymond B. *The Story of The Rockefeller Foundation*. New York: Harper & Brothers, 1952.

Harrar, George. *The Agricultural Program of the Rockefeller Foundation*. New York: The Rockefeller Foundation, 1956.

Kay, Lily. *The Molecular Vision of Life: Caltech, the Rockefeller Foundation, and the Rise of the New Biology*. New York: Oxford University Press, 1993.

Shaplen, Robert. *Toward the Well-Being of Mankind: 50 Years of the Rockefeller Foundation*. New York: Doubleday, 1964.

ROMAN CATHOLIC CHURCH

Throughout its long history of two millennia, the Catholic Church, in addition to carrying out its religious mission, has served as a builder of basic institutions that have been fundamental to the development of Western civilization and many prosperous societies. Institutions of law, local governance, education, and economic and social welfare were established and maintained by bishops within the diocesan structure of the Church, by individuals pursuing their own apostolic endeavors, and by religious orders that established semi-independent monastic foundations. As the largest single religious organization in the world today, the Church continues to call its membership to action. It has developed many relief and social welfare arms.

Some Historical Considerations

The Catholic Church has served as a primary mechanism for institution building, first in the history of Western Europe and then in more recent centuries throughout the entire world. Christians of the first centuries established hospitals for the sick, hospices for weary travelers, and orphanages for abandoned children as part of the call to good works. As the Roman Empire collapsed under the weight of successive incursions by the competing tribes of Northern Europe, the Church, which was organized along ancient Roman territorial lines into diocese governed by bishops, served as the means through which law and civil organization was preserved. Bishops throughout

Europe established schools in association with their cathedrals to educate priests, and from these emerged eventually the first universities of Europe, which began forming in the eleventh and twelfth centuries. These centuries also saw the rise of the guilds, medieval precursors to unions, in which various trades and industries were organized to protect the interests of various groups of artisans and to encourage spiritual awareness in the context of labor and production.

Another influence on the development of Europe during the early Middle Ages commenced as early as the sixth century, when Western monasticism took firm hold in Italy and Ireland. From these two centers of monasticism, monks radiated out into the furthest reaches of Europe to establish monasteries, which became institutions not only of prayer, but also islands of settled economic activity, centers of agricultural industry, and hives of education and preservation of scholarship. Monks invented books, kept libraries, set up schools, pharmacies, and hospitals. In the Benedictine tradition, monks worked in the fields, promoting settled agricultural industry in areas previously inhabited by nomadic tribes. Various monastic reform movements, including notably the Cluniac and Cistercian reforms in the tenth, eleventh, and twelfth centuries, served as engines of commerce, trade, and economic development. The wealth generated by these monastic establishments garnered the attention and often the jealousy of local leaders, princes and kings, thus provoking conflict and contest over control of these important centers of learning and prosperity. During these times, the Roman Catholic Church served as a kind of transnational organization that knit various budding nations into an overarching cultural unit known as Christendom. However, under the pressure of growing nationalism and the Protestant Reformation, the Church's influence declined in Europe as nation-states emerged to claim control over activities once dominated by churchmen and religious orders. However, even as the Church lost its luster as a political actor on the European stage, its missionaries continued to practice evangelism throughout the world. This missionary activity followed the older familiar pattern not only of preaching and church-building, but also establishing Western-style schools, hospitals, orphanages, and social welfare organizations.

Throughout much of human history, charity and concern for the poor was the work of churches and private action, and only rarely as the primary work of national governments. Only in recent centuries, and most particularly in the last half of the twentieth century, did governments establish what are today called economic development or social welfare programs. While the governmental role in these activities has increased substantially in modern times, a large part of the charitable work done in the world still remains in the hands of private bodies, chiefly religious institutions.

Contemporary Activities

Through the Church's diocesan and parish structures and its hundreds of religious orders for men and women, bishops, pastors, and religious workers in every corner of the world continue to raise revenues for charitable redistribution, supporting religious schools and universities, food banks, orphanages, battered women's shelters, homes for unwed mothers, hospitals, health clinics, community development centers, AIDS hospices, emergency relief centers, and refugee assistance programs, among many other activities. One example is the St. Vincent De Paul Societies, active in distribution of food to the poor. These organizations were a product of action by Catholic laymen in honor of the founder of the Vincentians and the Sisters of Charity, St. Vincent de Paul, who in the seventeenth century founded the first Catholic religious orders to be free of cloister rules, so that they could work directly with the poor and orphaned children. A more recent example is the work of Mother Teresa of Calcutta, whose work among the poor in the slums of India has become legendary, and whose establishments now exist throughout the world offering care to millions of desperately poor and sick individuals. During the recent war in Kosovo, the principal agent of support to displaced persons and refugees, whether Serbs or Kosovar Albanian Muslims, was the local Mother Teresa Society.

Catholic action on behalf of the poor has spawned a growing number of private assistance agencies, which are motivated by Church teaching and serve as relief arms of national bishops conferences. The largest of these is Catholic Relief Services (CRS), which is the international relief arm of the US Catholic Conference of Bishops, with ties to other national Catholic bodies through Caritas Internationalis. CRS budgets for development and humanitarian assistance programs in nearly seventy countries typically exceed $300 million annually. On the development programming side, its programs emphasize community development, agriculture, and water development programs and nutrition projects. CRS also serves as one of the main NGO collaborators with the US government in distribution of food aid throughout the world in famine emergencies. Caritas Internationalis, established in 1951 as the umbrella organization

for Roman Catholic national relief and development agencies in more than 150 countries, which include such bodies as the Catholic Fund for Overseas Development (CAFOD), which was founded by the Catholic bishops of England and Wales in 1962. This work is truly global in nature, and contributes handsomely to the resource base available globally for work in humanitarian relief and development efforts. Catholic NGOs are among the largest, most numerous, influential, and reliable NGOs participating in the global development arena, many enjoying consultative status with the United Nations.

The Holy See also is engaged in activities related to the relief and development needs of the poor. There emerged as early as the eighth century in England a tradition of collecting and sending Alms to Rome for the special charitable intentions of the poor. This tradition rapidly spread throughout the European Church, and today is known as the "Peter's Pence" collection, which in modern times is undertaken throughout the universal church. Revenues collected in this global effort are redistributed to the most needy diocese and to emergency relief efforts. The Holy See also is a regular participant in international conferences dealing with international relief and development activities.

Church Social Teaching

The modern papacy as well as modern materialist ideologies have contributed substantially to modern thinking about social and economic development. The nineteenth century saw the rise of two competing materialist conceptions of human economic development: capitalism and communism. In his landmark encyclical of 1891, *Rerum Novarum (On the Condition of the Working Classes)*, Pope Leo XIII offered a vision of human development emphasizing the spiritual nature of the human being in contrast to the view that human beings were but a factor in the processes of production and consumption of material goods. The rich and poor were seen by Leo as being bound by mutual obligations of respect and dignity. The worker was obliged to give a fair day's labor, the employer a fair day's wage. Workers were not to be exploited, worked beyond their capacity, exposed to corrupt influences, deprived of savings, or denied periods of rest and recreation. At the same time, Leo called on governments to recognize the rights of individuals to organize into associations, including not only unions, but also religious associations for mutual aid. He decried attempts by government to invade the

primary and natural rights of families, churches, and local associations to function at the local level for the benefit of persons.

Pope Pius XI, writing forty years later, at a time when fascist and communist systems of government were well-entrenched, reiterated many of the principles laid out by Leo XIII, attempting to advance a humane and just conception of human and economic development. In more recent times, Pope John Paul II, in his encyclical *On the Hundredth Anniversary of Rerum Novarum*, reflected on the themes treated by his predecessors in light of the then recent collapse of the Communist system. These and many additional papal encyclicals asserted the principles of solidarity and subsidiarity. The principle of solidarity calls human institutions to bring people together at various levels of cooperation to support peace and prosperity. The principle of subsidiarity demands that each level of cooperative endeavor respect and support the rights of the more immediate, intimate, particular, and local levels of cooperation to their independent spheres of action. No local government should usurp the proper role of families and local religious bodies to supply mutual aid and assistance, but rather local government should facilitate and complement such activity. Similarly, national government and international bodies should support the capacity of local governments to tend to their local activities, by complementing and facilitating such action through stimulating cooperation to help when local institutions and bodies require aid.

ROBERT F. GORMAN

See also Christianity; Liberation Theology; Religion

References and Further Reading

Eberhardt, Newman C. *A Summary of Catholic History.* New York: B. Herder Book Co., 1961.
Hastings, Adrian. *African Catholicism: Essays in Discovery.* London: SCM Press & Philadelphia: Trinity Press International, 1989.
Henriot, Peter J., *et al. Catholic Social Teaching.* Maryknoll, NY: Orbis Books, 1995. (Contains useful summaries of papal encyclicals and bishop's statements.)
McKenna, Kevin. *A Concise Guide to Catholic Social Teaching.* Ann Arbor, MI: Ave Maria Press, 2002.
Pope John Paul II. *On the Hundredth Anniversary of Rerum Novarum.* Boston: St. Paul Books and Media, 1991.
Pope Leo XIII. *On the Condition of the Working Classes.* Boston: St. Paul Editions, 1942.
Pope Pius XI. *On Social Reconstruction.* Boston: St. Paul Editions, n.d.
Ruether, Rosemary. *Contemporary Roman Catholicism: Crises and Challenges.* Kansas City: Sheed & Ward, 1987.
Sobrino, Jon. *The True Church and the Poor.* Maryknoll, NY: Orbis, 1984.

ROMANIA

Romania is located in southeastern Europe, bordering with Moldova in the east, with Ukraine in the north, Hungary and Serbia in the west, Bulgaria in the south, and bounded on the southeast by the Black Sea. The country has a land area of 237,500 square kilometers, comparatively its territory slightly smaller than the state of Oregon in the United States.

The population of Romania was estimated at 22,356,000 in 2004. It is a moderately urbanized country with about 52% of the people living in cities and towns. The country's capital city, Bucharest, is home to 2.4 million people (2004 est.) or 12% of the population. Romania has a negative population growth rate of –0.6%, and the population steadily declines due to a low birth rate and emigration. Its official language is Romanian; Hungarian and German also are widely spoken. The population is 87% Eastern Orthodox Christianity, with 6.8% other types of Protestant, 5.6% Catholic, and a small 0.4% Muslim population.

For centuries, the territory of present-day Romania was contested by the Ottoman Empire, Hungary and Poland. In the eighteenth century, the Russian Empire stepped into the political arena in an attempt to establish its influence in the region. Romania entered the nineteenth century as a backward, feudal country with most of the population engaged in subsistence economy. The local elite waged a war for independence from foreign powers, and in 1857, the councils of the two major regions—Moldavia and Walachia—were united under the name of Romania. However, Romania was not recognized as a fully independent kingdom by the Congress of Berlin until 1878.

The most major economic and social changes arrived in the late nineteenth and early twentieth centuries, when the rulers of the country introduced limited economic reforms, including the land reform that broke up large estates. During World War I, Romania joined the Allies and acquired Transylvania and some other areas from Hungary, Bukovina from Austria, and Bessarabia from Russia. In the 1930s, however, the country moved away from the Allies and came under the influence of Nazi Germany. It entered World War II as a Nazi ally, but in 1944, the country surrendered to the Soviet Army and declared war on the Nazis. In 1947, the monarchy was abolished and the communist government came to power.

The communist government introduced a number of radical political and economic changes, and established the state control over all types of economic activities and a central state planning. In the 1950s and 1960s, the government introduced the program of collectivization and nationalized most of the industrial enterprises. During the post–World War II period, the government emphasized the state-led industrialization that focused on building of heavy industry, light industries, mining, extraction of oil, and large-scale agriculture. However, unlike most of the socialist countries, Romania asserted some degree of economic and political independence from the Soviet Union and Soviet dominated economic block. Until the 1990s, Romania remained one of the poorest countries in Eastern Europe due to the economic mismanagement, distortions in economic planning, and authoritarian policies of the Romanian leadership.

Major changes came in 1989 as the regime of Nicolae Ceauşescu, the Romanian authoritarian leader, collapsed and a new leadership came to power. The new government relinquished the centrally-planned economy and introduced limited democratization and economic reforms. The economic changes were inconsistent, however, and the country experienced a severe economic decline in the early 1990s. Many industrial enterprises and mines lost state subsidies and were gradually closed. The unemployment rate skyrocketed, and many people moved to western Europe in search of jobs and a better life.

Recent Development

Romania introduced its new democratic constitution in 1991, and the Romanian government promised to conduct major political and economic changes. Several factors, however, undermined the post-communist development in the country. One was the inconsistency of the economic reforms and privatization. Inflation remained high throughout the 1990s. Many enterprises and newly created private farms remained inefficient, and a significant proportion of the population expressed its anger and disapproval of the government's policies. The other problem was the ethnic tensions between the Romanians and some ethnic minorities, such as Hungarians, Roma, and Germans. There also was a deep disagreement within the ruling political coalition. All together, this led to political instability and consequently made the country less attractive for foreign direct investments.

Agriculture, industries, and services are the three main pillars of Romanian economy, contributing 13.0%, 37.9%, and 49.1%, respectively to the gross domestic product (World Bank estimate 2003). The county exports raw materials, textile, metals, and some manufactured products to international markets. Romania imports machinery, fuel, industrial

consumer goods, and food products. Due to the transitional recession and the loss of traditional markets for Romanian goods, the country's economy increasingly relies on foreign assistance and credits. Total external debt has reached about $20 billion (World Bank estimate 2003).

In the early 2000s the country achieved macroeconomic stability and stabilized the living standards among the population. The government continued to negotiate full membership in the NATO and European Union. Yet, Romania remains one of the poorest countries of the southeastern Europe, with about 25% of the population living below the poverty line (World Bank estimate 2004) and a sizeable number of people leaving for other countries in search of jobs. In 2004, the United Nations Development Programme's Human Development Index put Romania in sixty-ninth place out of 177, behind neighboring Bulgaria and Hungary but ahead of Moldova and the Ukraine.

RAFIS ABAZOV

See also Ceausescu, Nicolae; Central and Eastern Europe: History and Economic Development; Central and Eastern Europe: International Relations; Ethnic Conflicts: Central and Eastern Europe

References and Further Reading

Carey, Henry and Norman Manea. *Romania Since 1989: Politics, Economics, and Society*. Lexington Books, 2004.
International Monetary Fund. *Romania: Selected Issues and Statistical Appendix*. Washington, DC, International Monetary Fund, 2004.
———. *Interest Rate Pass-Through in Romania and Other Central European Economies*. Washington, DC, International Monetary Fund, 2004.
Shen, Raphael. *The Restructuring of Romania's Economy: A Paradigm of Flexibility and Adaptability*. New York: Praeger Publishers, 1997.
World Bank. *Romania: Human Resources and the Transition to a Market Economy (World Bank Country Study)*. Washington, DC: World Bank, 1992.

RUSSIA

Historically, economic development in Russia has faced major natural handicaps: isolation from world markets, vast distances, and a harsh climate (in northern regions, the soil is poor, while in the fertile black-earth belt, the short growing season and inadequate precipitation make harvests uncertain). Until the 1860s, peasant cultivators toiled under serf-like conditions that restricted entrepreneurial initiative, while the urban merchant class was relatively weak. An industrial spurt, aided by foreign capital, in the 1890s was interrupted by war and revolution (1904–1906); thereafter the economy revived on a broader base but collapsed under the immense strains of World War I. This touched off another violent revolution and three years of civil war, famine, and disease that cost 10 million lives. Reconstruction under the Bolshevik (Communist) regime was rapid but marred by tension between the favored industrial workers and supposedly "backward" peasant smallholders. The town–country divide deepened after 1929, when Joseph Stalin imposed the Socialist Economic Model involving brutal agricultural collectivization and centralized planning (what Westerners call a "command economy"). Emphasis on the expansion of heavy industry (including armaments) engendered an endemic shortage of consumer goods; 5 million died in the catastrophic famine of 1932–1933; millions more Gulag convicts toiled until they dropped. Stalinist totalitarianism left no place for autonomous civic organizations or human rights; the individual was just a cog in a faceless administrative machine. Even so, ordinary folk did manage to express their preferences indirectly, for example, by resisting imposition of higher work norms and distrusting exaggerated claims by regime propagandists. They appreciated improved provision of health and educational facilities. In many scientific and technological fields, expertise reached a high level. The "Soviet intelligentsia," officially categorized as a social stratum distinct from the working classes, lacked physical security yet was granted material advantages to keep it loyal. Its aspirations posed an implicit long-term threat to the viability of the dictatorship.

In 1941–1945, the command economy proved its worth as the State Defense Council mobilized human and material resources on a massive scale to boost the war effort. In threatened areas, factories were evacuated for reassembly in the rear. By 1944, output of aircraft was four, and output of tanks was ten times 1940 levels. In 1945, the USSR had 11.6 million men and women under arms; 60% of the labor force was female. Agricultural production plummeted, because much land was lost to the enemy and able-bodied workers were scarce; peasant women sometimes pulled the ploughs themselves. State controls were somewhat relaxed, and private allotments informally allowed to expand. Most people went hungry. The rationing system, which operated erratically, entitled nonessential workers to only 400 grams of bread a day (1944). Food also was received, along with arms and equipment, from the Western allies and made a significant contribution to victory. The war cost the USSR dearly: casualties were enormous (9.1 million troops, ca. 27 million overall), among them, over 2 million people, mainly Jews, massacred by the Nazis and some 3 million prisoners of war who died in German captivity. More than 1,700 towns, seventy thousand

villages, thirty thousand factories and 65,000 kilometers of railroad track were reduced to rubble.

In the postwar years, Stalin reasserted traditional controls and priorities. During the Fourth Five-Year plan (1946–1950), heavy industrial output more than doubled, while that of consumer goods grew by less than a quarter. The urban labor force was swollen by the resumed influx from the countryside, where in 1946, drought and infrastructural damage led to another serious famine. By 1953, the Gulag population topped 5 million (including "settlers," mostly deported non-Russians, but excluding Axis POW). The abrupt cessation of Lend-Lease (August 1945) dashed hopes of obtaining Western capital, but some was derived by looting resources in Germany and eastern Europe, where "joint-stock companies" provided the USSR with raw materials, machinery, and manufactures at nominal prices. More important were the funds squeezed from the peasantry. Private plots were scaled down and confiscatory taxes levied on the revenue they generated; quotas for compulsory delivery of farm produce were raised. These impositions helped to bring about the famine. In 1952, the actual grain harvest (kept secret!) was lower than in 1940, when there had been fewer mouths to feed. Another source of state funds was a currency reform (1947) which wiped out nine-tenths of people's wartime savings—a means of reducing inflation while goods were scarce—and the practice of deducting state loan contributions from workers' pay packets. Ceaseless campaigns of "socialist emulation" helped to keep wage-earners compliant. At first, many willingly bore sacrifices for the common good, but this mood evaporated.

The post-Stalin leaders realized the need for economic reform yet wanted to keep the Stalinist command economy fundamentally unchanged. G.M. Malenkov, identified with a shift of effort towards consumer goods production, was worsted by N.S. Khrushchev, who claimed expertise on agricultural problems. Collective farmers received higher prices, while quotas and taxes were reduced; yet no encouragement was offered to the private sector, with which 3% of the sown area provided nearly half the country's meat and milk (1958–1965). Instead of increasing incentives for producers in the European heartland, the regime launched a bold campaign to sow grain on "virgin and idle land" (actually used by natives as pasture) in Kazakhstan and elsewhere. Hundreds of thousands of "volunteers" went east, but the authorities underestimated the operation's costs and disregarded scientists' warnings of the high ecological risks. Another campaign, which later had to be abandoned, fostered the cultivation of corn (maize) as fodder, even in unsuitable areas. Artificial

fertilizer output rose from 7 million tons in 1953 to 31 million in 1965 and 112 million in 1985, but here, too, careless application resulted in environmental damage. Food output increased under Khrushchev (cereals from an annual average of 82 million tons in 1949–1952 to 132 million in 1961–1964, milk from 36 million to 63 million tons), but the main beneficiaries of constant meddling were not farmers but omnipotent local officials in the party *nomenklatura*.

Leonid Brezhnev (1964–1982) and his immediate successors pursued a more consistent long-term agricultural strategy, boosting investment, which in the 1970s ran at 26% of total state outlays, over twice the proportion under Stalin. Despite these subsidies, which the state could ill afford, many weaker farms ran into debt, notably because managers had too little power or incentive to think in terms of profitability: livestock raising, for example, was uneconomic at official prices, and by international comparison, Soviet cattle were skinny beasts. Even so, annual per capita consumption of dairy products rose from 251 to 323 kg. (1962–1985); for eggs the corresponding figures were 124 and 260 units, while bread and flour consumption declined (156 to 133 kg.), signifying a shift to a more wholesome diet. But in the 1970s, statisticians were told to stop publishing data on cereal output, as harvests were embarrassingly low, and in the worst years, grain had to be imported from the West.

Khrushchev tried to devolve the cumbersome system of industrial management but ran into bureaucratic obstruction, so that after his fall in 1964, power was again concentrated in Gosplan and central (all-Union) ministries for various branches (including "medium machine-building," the code word for nuclear weapons manufacture). In the late 1960s, A.I. Kosygin's name was associated with another administrative reform that gave managers and workers bonuses if their enterprise made a profit. But since prices were still fixed centrally, it was hard to establish profit levels, and the bonus system lent itself to abuse. The output of staple producer goods grew exponentially: steel from 45 million tons (1953) to 91 million in 1965 and 155 million twenty years later; iron ore rose from 72 to 153 and then 248 million tons. The figures for cotton fabrics, characteristically, were less spectacular: 4.2, 5.5, and 7.7 million square metres; for footwear 271, 486, and 787 million pairs. Most significant was the shift in the fuel balance from coal to oil, and especially natural gas, vast reserves of which were discovered and exploited in western Siberia. By 1985, this source contributed 35.5% of total energy consumption. Nuclear power, a relatively "late developer," stood at 10.8%. Soviet reactors had serious design flaws, which were one factor in the Chernobyl disaster (April 26, 1986). Nuclear waste often was

disposed of casually, and serious environmental pollution also occurred from leaky oil pipelines, chemical factory emissions, and the like: Arctic regions, the Aral Sea, Lake Baikal, and the Kazakh steppe were among the hardest hit areas. An informal "Green" movement emerged in the 1970s but made little impact on the thinking of industrial officials concerned with fulfilling their plan targets for physical output, cost what it may.

Road transport and automobile production were relatively neglected, but the railroad system expanded, and by 1985, one-third of the network had been electrified. Much effort went into constructing an alternative to the Trans-Siberian route, the 3,500-kilometer Baikal-Amur line through the eastern Siberian taiga, where permafrost posed tough problems. Civilian air transport became an important means of communication over long distances and in more remote regions. By 1980, the state enterprise Aeroflot carried 100 million passengers; fares were uneconomically cheap, so that Armenian fruit-growers, for instance, could fly to Moscow to market their wares.

Soviet town dwellers enjoyed inexpensive subsidized housing, although average apartment size ("living space") was only nine square metres per capita. From the 1950s onward, rows of standardized apartment blocks, built of prefabricated materials by modern techniques, appeared in city suburbs. Though aesthetically unappealing, they represented a pragmatic solution to the acute accommodation shortage among the burgeoning urban population—a factor that strained family cohesion. The divorce rate grew alarmingly. Most wives had to combine jobs with household chores, including endless queuing for scarce commodities. Women usually earned lower wages and held positions with lesser status than men, who enjoyed more leisure—and drink. Statistically, alcoholism cost fifty thousand lives (probably an underestimate) in 1980; five years later, 4.5 million addicts were receiving medical treatment. Young people preferred Western-style "pop" culture to unimaginative officially sponsored offerings; their parents' political views, at least in private, were often unorthodox. Cynicism became widespread, behind a mask of conformity; people with means shopped on the black market ("second economy"), which the regime had to tolerate *faute de mieux*. Workers sometimes grumbled about wages or conditions or even the lack of independent trade unions, but most were reconciled to a system that provided full employment, "free" health care, and the prospect of social promotion for those who regularly fulfilled their norms. Peasant earnings were at last catching up on those of urban workers.

Benefits also accrued to elites in developing countries that Moscow sought to wean away from "imperialism." Initially, policy was liberal: loans were repayable in locally produced goods or soft currency at low interest rates, but from the 1960s, as debts mounted, there was a shift towards greater discrimination (and the supply of military hardware). According to US estimates, from 1954 to 1985 the USSR supplied $97.9 billion in aid. About half went to Cuba and Vietnam; smaller amounts reached India, Turkey, Ethiopia, Iran, Angola, and Syria; the last-named country received mostly arms transfers. Soviet "third world" aid was much smaller than that from Western sources, but its political and psychological impact was often greater. These foreign investments had to be unceremoniously abandoned once priorities changed after 1985.

Mikhail S. Gorbachev (1985–1991) was the first Soviet leader to tackle the economic "stagnation" (his term) resulting from long-standing neglect of vital problems, notably the decline in growth and productivity rates. The drying up of the labor supply as rural overpopulation eased made it essential to use manpower less wastefully. Behind these dilemmas lay disenchantment among the Soviet intelligentsia, which now formed a sizeable "middle class," at the ruling party's ideological dogmatism and at bureaucratic incompetence. Gorbachev's "acceleration" drive encouraged managers to modernize equipment and adopt information technology while simultaneously boosting output and improving the quality of goods. This overambitious campaign engendered inflationary pressures and budgetary deficits. The extra currency put into circulation rose from 4% (1985–1986) to 11.8% in 1988 and 28% two years later; by 1989, the state debt reached 42.8% of gross national product (GNP). "Restructuring" (*perestroika*) was broadened in scope to endorse the formation of producers' cooperatives and, more generally, the emancipation of civil society from ideological constraints. From 1987, stimulated by the new "openness" (*glasnost*), thousands of informal organizations appeared, some of which adopted political goals. Pressure from below—it was mainly a "middle-class" phenomenon—forced Gorbachev to adjust his thinking further and come out in favor of market socialism and (quasi-) constitutional government, thereby reluctantly yielding the party's monopoly on state power. National minority leaders vociferously sought control over regional resources, which undermined economic relationships across the Union. The elected Russian president, Boris Yeltsin, and several teams of professional advisers recommended rapid transition to free-enterprise capitalism, with extensive privatization, but Gorbachev held back. He knew that such radical ideas were unpopular; the general public associated them with profiteering, criminality, and vast income

differentials that offended entrenched egalitarian sentiments.

Initially, the Soviet collapse (1991) held out the prospect of a flourishing market economy based on extensive foreign investment in Russia's immense natural resources and skilled labor force. However, "transition" turned out to be a slow, painful process, and a depression ensued; one can even speak of "demodernization." In 1992, Egor Gaidar's "shock therapy" led to a sudden twenty-six fold increase in prices. Hyper-inflation wiped out people's savings and devalued wages and pensions. Privatization made little headway in agriculture, but industrial assets were given away to insiders (managers and other employees) under a voucher system which, although designed to empower ordinary people, ended up enriching a new class of "oligarchs," as they pejoratively came to be called. In later years, privatization was handled more discreetly by selling state enterprises via the new commercial banks. These financial institutions mushroomed but remained under-capitalized, since ordinary Russian savers distrusted them and preferred to keep their money under the mattress (or in the state savings bank), as they had done before, while businessmen transferred their profits to safe offshore locations, taking advantage of lax exchange controls, instead of investing them productively at home; meanwhile foreign investors were deterred by the prevalent corruption and red tape. Irresponsible banking practices, e.g. loans with inadequate security, were factors in the August 1998 crash, when the government declared a moratorium on its payments and the twenty largest banks were wiped out. Many new entrepreneurs faced ruin; fortunately, less damage was done at lower levels, and after a few months, the economy began to revive. Yet market reform had been badly discredited, not least because it went hand in hand with rampant crime. Mafia bosses built villas with high-security installations and indulged in other forms of conspicuous consumption, while one fifth—and after the crash one third—of the population was reduced to subsistence level. They survived by petty barter trade and transactions on the margin of the law that went unrecorded in official statistics. In 1999, average life expectancy sank to 65.5 years (men 59.9, women 72), one year lower than in 1998. Health spending per capita was minimal, and the population shrank by 5%–6% per annum.

Still more ominous was the decline in manufacturing. Numerous large Soviet-era plants, no longer economic, fell idle. In 1996, total employment stood at 4.2 million (1985; 8.3 million); output of trucks and tractors amounted to 134,000 and 14,000, respectively (1985; 688,000 and 261,000). Spending on research and development all but collapsed. The Russian economy was living largely on its Soviet inheritance. Oil and gas output, much of it exported—Gasprom, the giant consortium, became a major player in international markets—held up relatively well, but here, too, the industry's capital stock was not renewed, storing up problems for the future.

In 2000, a new president, V.V. Putin, set out to overcome the unplanned attrition of state power and prestige. This entailed *inter alia* reforming the notoriously inefficient system of tax collection, which imposed a heavy burden even on privileged large enterprises. Harsh police measures had proved ineffective in the face of a "fiscal evasion culture". Another problem was the competition for resources between the center and the regions. Faint signs appeared of a possible turnaround. In 2000, GNP grew unprecedentedly by 8.3%. In May 2001, the Duma approved a legislative package, long advocated by the IMF, strengthening the Central Bank's powers over insolvent financial institutions and providing incentives for the repatriation of fugitive capital (estimated at $24 billion in 2000 alone). The stock exchange rallied, and optimists hoped that Russia might yet find a middle way between the Scylla of the Stalinist command economy and the Charybdis of Yeltsin's "market bolshevism."

JOHN KEEP

See also Communist Economic Model; De-Stalinization (1953–1956); Khrushchev, Nikita; Socialist Economic Model; Stalin, Joseph

References and Further Reading

Aslund, Anders. *Gorbachev's Struggle for Economic Reform*. London: Pinter, 1991.

Cohen, Stephen F. *Failed Crusade: America and the Tragedy of Post-Communist Russia*. New York: W.W. Norton, 2000.

Gustafson, Thane. *Capitalism Russian-Style*. Cambridge: Cambridge University Press, 1999.

Hough, Jerry. *The Logic of Economic Reform in Russia*. Washington DC: Brookings Institution Press, 2001.

Lane, David. *The Transition from Communism to Capitalism: Ruling Elites from Gorbachev to Yeltsin*. Basingstoke: Macmillan, 1999.

McCauley, Martin. *Bandits, Gangsters, and the Mafia: Russia, the Baltic States, and the CIS Since 1991*. London: Longmans, 2001.

Nove, Alec. *An Economic History of the USSR, 1917–1991*, 3rd ed. London and New York: Penguin, 1992.

Reddaway, Peter and Glinski, Dmitri. *The Tragedy of Russia's Reforms: Market Bolshevism Against Democracy*. Herndon, VA: US Institute of Peace Press, 2001.

Shevtsova, Lilia. *Yeltsin's Russia: Myths and Reality*. Washington, DC: Carnegie Endowment for International Peace, 1999.

Wegren, Stephen K. *Agriculture and the State in Soviet and Post-Soviet Russia*. Pittsburgh, PA: University of Pittsburgh Press, 1998.

RUSSIAN ORTHODOX CHURCH

The Eastern Slavs were converted to Christianity at the end of the tenth century of our era. The Church was organized on the Greek pattern, being under the canonical authority of the Patriarch of Constantinople. The Russian patriarchate did not establish its autonomy, i.e. its separation from Constantinople, until 1589.

Peter the Great abolished the patriarchate in 1721 and established a synod composed of prelates and presided over by a layman. The Holy Synod was housed with other lay ministries in the new capital Peter built, St. Petersburg. Ordinary Russians, however, continued to see Moscow as their spiritual home.

The Church and 1917

The February Revolution of 1917 undermined the Orthodox Church, but the Provisional Government did not try to crush it by force. Rather, they illegitimated all church rituals and adopted the Gregorian calendar used in the West. The government also interfered with the old Cyrillic alphabet by dispensing with some of the familiar letters.

What affected it most in the new era proclaimed after the October Revolution was the separation of church and state on February 5, 1918. Among other things, schools still under the Church's administration were taken away; however, the Church, for a brief period, was no longer under the state's control, enabling it to summon a council and re-establish the Patriarchate.

Vladimir Lenin (1917–1925) considered the Orthodox Church a contemptible form of "fideism." However, more tolerant Marxists argued that socialism would naturally undermine the "superstructure," and religion would peter out by itself. But the revolutionary regime did not hesitate to seize Church property.

During the Civil War, most of the clergy took sides against the Bolsheviks. A Temporary Ecclesiastical Administration emerged in southern Russia, then controlled by the Whites. When the Red Army forced their retreat, this body moved to Sremski Karlovci in Serbia. Calling itself the Church in Exile, it refused to recognize the Moscow patriarchate which appointed Evlogii (Vasilii Georgievsky, 1868–1948) as the Metropolitan of the Russian Church in Western Europe. Russians abroad had to choose between the Karlovci Synod, which refused to recognize the Soviet controlled Moscow patriarchate, and Evlogii's metropolitanate, which did. In the United States, despite the breakdown of the USSR, authority still remains divided between the Church in Exile and the Orthodox Church of America (OCA).

The Soviet regime also backed a movement called the "Living Church," which had been set up by liberals and enjoyed the support of parish priests who wished to curb the power of monks and bishops. With the help of the secret police, which infiltrated it, the "Living Church" was able to take over close to a third of the Orthodox churches in Russia.

In 1925, a gathering of bishops nominated Metropolitan Sergei to lead the "Patriarchal" Church, which was recognized in 1927 by a regime no longer interested in the "Living Church." By then, it has been estimated that, despite the church's setbacks, it was functioning on a scale not much smaller than in 1917.

The Church in Stalin's Shadow

The census of 1937, which included a question about religious belief, was suppressed—in part because of the population deficiency they recorded following collectivization and the purges. Another rumored reason for the suppression was that no less than 40% of the population had declared their religious conviction. But the leadership of the Orthodox Church had by now been cowed, and the coming of the war further complicated its position.

In a dramatic reversal of Soviet policy, Stalin promulgated a truce with the Church. Churches were reopened, and in return, Metropolitan Sergei publicly announced in 1942 that Stalin was "the divinely anointed leader of our armed and cultural forces leading us to victory over the barbarian invasion." Stalin reciprocated by restoring the patriarchate, to which the wily Sergei was duly nominated. Along with this official resumption of relations between Church and State, the government retained strict control over ecclesiastical property and personnel.

During the war, the leadership of the Orthodox Church of Georgia, the Armenian Church, the Baptists and Evangelical Christians, and the Moslems accepted a similar status to the Orthodox Church, although some clergymen—such as the Roman Catholics and the imprisoned prelates of Solovetsk—refused to accept it. Jews suffered more than any other religious group.

During the de-Stalinization campaign that began three years after Stalin's death, convicted clergymen were—like political prisoners—released from the camps. But Nikita Khrushchev (1953–1964), for all his compassion, is said to have been responsible for the closing down of more than ten thousand churches.

Dissent and Freedom of Worship

Leonid Brezhnev (1964–1982), who led a plot to oust Khrushchev from power in 1964, was more tolerant than his predecessor on matters of religion and permitted about five hundred Orthodox churches to be reopened. The convergence that occurred in the Brezhnev years between literary dissidence and religious protest was not surprising, although it seemed so at the time. The dissidents did not call for the overthrow of the Soviet system, but for the elimination of abuses, "socialist legality," and enforcement of the provisions of the Constitution and of other laws dealing with freedom of conscience, speech and press.

By its cynicism and lack of conviction either in Communism or in any viable alternative, the worn-out *apparatchiks* around Brezhnev paved the way for the surprising revival of the Orthodox faith, which came with Mikhail Gorbachev (1985–1991). *Perestroika* and *glasnost*, the twin policies of renewal and openness which he advocated, did not at first include the Church as such, but its authority was brought in to lend Gorbachev's reforms legitimacy. Under the present post-Soviet constitution, Orthodoxy shares its recognition as an official religion of state together with Islam and Judaism.

Whether the external revival of Orthodoxy, as manifested in the building of hundreds of churches and ecclesiastical foundations of various sorts and the generous publication of Christian literature, represents a genuine religious revival with deeper roots, it is perhaps still too early to tell. Urban and educated Russia is, for obvious reasons today, a largely secular society, but Orthodoxy appears to have become a part of the cultural identity even of citizens whose attendance at church is limited to Easter and Christmas (newly restored as public holidays, and now nationally celebrated under the old Julian calendar).

Numbers

In 1996, the overall number of Orthodox worshippers was estimated at 182 million. Of these, 70 million to 80 million are to be found in the Russian Federation. Of Ukraine's population, close to 30 million are Orthodox. Next in size is Rumania with 20 million and Greece with 9.5 million. The United States has close to 7 million Orthodox citizens, which is about the same number as the Orthodox population of Serbia and Monte Negro. Poland has 800,000; Finland, 56,000; Estonia, 300,000; Latvia, 400,000; Lithuania, 150,000; Georgia, 2.8 million; Kazakhstan, 4 million; Uzbekistan, 900,000; Belarus, around 5 million; Bulgaria, 6 million; Moldavia, around 3 million; Macedonia, 1.2 million; Germany, 550,000; United Kingdom, 440,000; France, 260,000; Austria and Switzerland, about 70,000 each; and Australia, 480,000.

VALENTIN BOSS

See also Russia

Bibliography

Batalden, Stephen K. *Seeking God: The Recovery of Religious Identity in Orthodox Russia, Ukraine, and Georgia.* DeKalb, IL: Northern Illinois University Press, 1993.

Bourdeaux, Michael. *The Politics of Religion in Russia and the New States of Eurasia.* Armonk, NY: M.E. Sharpe, 1995.

Brumfield, William Craft and Milos Velimirovic. *Christianity and the Arts in Russia.* Cambridge, UK, and New York: Cambridge University Press, 1991.

Conquest, Robert, ed. *Religion in the USSR.* London, Bodley Head, 1968.

Fennell, John Lister Illingworth. A History of the Russian Church to 1448. London and New York: Longman, 1995.

Fireside, Harvey *Icon and Swastika: The Russian Orthodox Church under Nazi and Soviet Control.* Cambridge, MA, Harvard University Press, 1971.

Florovsky, Georges. *Ways of Russian Theology.* Belmont, MA: Nordland Pub. Co., 1979.

Kaz'mina, O. E. "Pravoslavie," in V. A. Tishkov (chief ed.), Narody i religii mira, Nauchnoe izdatel'stvo Bol'shaia Rossiiskaia Entsiklopediia, Moscow, 1998, pp. 795–803.

Kivelson, Valerie A. and Robert H. Greene. *Orthodox Russia: Belief and Practice Under the Tsars.* University Park, PA: Pennsylvania State University Press, 2003.

Kornblatt, Judith Deutsch. *Doubly chosen: Jewish Identity, the Soviet Intelligentsia, and the Russian Orthodox Church.* Madison, WI: University of Wisconsin Press, 2004.

Shevzov, Vera. *Russian Orthodoxy on the Eve of Revolution.* Oxford and New York: Oxford University Press, 2004.

RWANDA

The "Land of a Thousand Hills" is situated in East Central Africa, bordering to the North with Uganda, with Tanzania to the East, Burundi to the South, and the Democratic Republic of the Congo to the West. The total territory is 26,338 square kilometers (24,948 square kilometers land area). The country is landlocked. Most of the country is savanna grassland, mostly grassy uplands and hills, with declining altitude from west to east. Climate is mild, with frost and snow possible in mountains; there are rainy seasons between November and April. Rwanda is the most densely populated African country with an estimated 8.24 million residents (2004), comprised of the dominating ethnicity Hutu (84%), minority Tutsi (15%), and pygmoid Twa (1%). The capital is Kigali, founded in 1907 (with a population close to four hundred thousand).

In the fourteenth century, Tutsis settled massively into what is now Rwanda and, under King Ruganzu Ndori, removed the indigenous Twa and Hutu peoples. About the end of eighteenth century, Tutsi King Kigeri Rwabugiri established a centralized military state. In 1890, Rwanda became part of German East Africa, but in 1916, Belgian forces occupied it. After the World War I, League of Nations granted Belgium mandate to govern Rouanda-Urundi—transferred in 1946 by the United Nations (UN) as trust territory, ruled indirectly by Tutsi. In 1957, Hutus called for a change in Rwanda's power structure to give them a voice, and formed political parties. In 1959, they overthrew the Tutsi King Kigeri V, forcing him with tens of thousands of Tutsis into exile in Uganda. Within the next years, thousands of Tutsis were killed, and some 150,000 were driven into exile.

In 1961, Rwanda separated with Urundi, later Burundi, and was proclaimed a republic. The next year, it became independent with a Hutu president, Gregoire Kayibanda; another Tutsi exodus. Following an incursion by Tutsi rebels from Burundi, in 1963, twenty thousand Hutus were killed. In 1973, Kayibanda was ousted in military coup led by Juvenal Habyarimana. He was elected president in 1978, and a new constitution was ratified. In 1988, some fifty thousand Hutu refugees fled from Burundi following ethnic violence there. The Tutsi exiles formed a rebel group, the Rwandan Patriotic Front (RPF), to invade from Uganda in 1990. In the next year, new multiparty constitution was promulgated. In 1993, President Habyarimana signed in Arusha, Tanzania a power-sharing agreement with the Tutsis. In April 1994, Habyarimana and his Burundian homologue were killed after their plane was shot down near Kigali. RPF launched a major offensive; extremist Hutu militia and elements of the Rwandan military began massacre of Tutsis. Within one hundred days, around eight hundred thousand Tutsis and moderate Hutus were slaughtered.

Fearing Tutsi retaliation, Hutu militias fled to neighboring countries, taking with them around 2 million Hutu refugees. Later, most of them returned home, but about ten thousand remaining formed an extremist insurgency in the neighboring Zaire. In 1995, UN-appointed international tribunal began charging and sentencing those responsible for the atrocities. In 1996, Rwandan troops assaulted Hutu militia in Zaire. In 1997, Rwandan- and Ugandan-backed Zaire rebels deposed president Mobutu; Laurent Kabila replaced him and renamed the country the Democratic Republic of Congo. Next year, however, Rwanda switched to support rebel forces against Kabila for failing to expel Hutu militias. In March 2000, Rwandan President Pasteur Bizimungu, a Hutu, resigned after a feud regarding the cabinet composition and after parliament began anti-corruption investigations against Hutu politicians. Vice President Paul Kagame became the new president. In October, traditional *gacaca* courts started to clear the 1994 genocide cases. A new flag and national anthem were unveiled to promote national unity and reconciliation. In April 2002, former president Bizimungu was arrested and charged with illegal political activity and threats to state security. In July, Rwanda and the Democratic Republic of Congo signed a peace deal. In May 2003, a draft constitution designed to prevent another genocide, banning the incitement of ethnic hatred, was adopted. In August, Paul Kagame claimed a landslide victory in the first presidential elections since the 1994 genocide, and his Rwandan Patriotic Front won absolute majority in the first multiparty parliamentary elections, marred by irregularities and fraud. In March, French reports accused President Kagame of ordering an attack on the president's plane in 1994, which sparked genocide. In June, Bizimungu was sentenced to fifteen years in jail for embezzlement, inciting violence and associating with criminals.

Increasing power centralization, intolerance of dissent, the rigid Hutu extremist insurgency across the border, and involvement in two wars in the neighboring Democratic Republic of Congo continue to hinder Rwanda's efforts to escape the violence. Despite UN peacekeeping and political leaders' efforts to end hostilities, localized clashes persist. Tutsi, Hutu, Hema, Lendu, and other adverse ethnic groups, guerrilla fighters, armed gangs, and various government forces continue fighting in the Great Lakes region, transgressing the boundaries.

Rwanda is a poor rural country, with about 90% of the population engaged in mainly subsistence agriculture. Tea and coffee are main export commodities. The 1994 genocide practically wiped out Rwanda's fragile economic base, gravely impoverishing the population. Rwanda succeeded in stabilizing and recovering economically to prewar levels, although poverty persists. World prices' decline deprived Rwanda of desperately needed hard currency. A fertile ecosystem fails to meet the needs of the fast population growth. Imports exceed about three times export revenues. Rwanda qualified for debt relief in 2000, but high defense expenditures make international donors limit the program. Strife restricts prospects for tourism.

The economic infrastructure of Rwanda is extremely inadequate. There are less than one thousand kilometers of paved roads from a total of about eleven thousand kilometers. Only one airport is capable of hosting contemporary aircrafts. There are no railroads. The adult literacy rate is 70.4% (2003). According to the World Health Organization data,

there are approximately twenty-one nurses and 1.9 physicians per one hundred thousand persons. Life expectancy is slightly less than forty years for males and about year and half more for females (2004 estimate). The population growth rate is of 1.82% (2004 estimate), while infant mortality (101.68 deaths per 1,000 live births) is among the highest in Africa. Rwanda began economic reforms in 1995, focusing on trade, privatization, improvement of public administration, the budget, and financial management, as well as private-sector development.

STEPHAN E. NIKOLOV

See also African Development Bank (ADB); African Monetary Fund (AfMF); Burundi; Congo, Democratic Republic of the; East Africa: History and Economic Development; East Africa: International Relations; East African Community; Ethnic Conflicts: East Africa; Ethnicity: Impact on Politics and Society; Organization of African Unity (OAU)

References and Further Reading

Adelman, Howard and Suhrke, Astri. *The Path of a Genocide: The Rwanda Crisis from Uganda to Zaire.* New York: Transaction Publishers, 1999.

Barnett, Michael. *Eyewitness to a Genocide: The United Nations and Rwanda.* Ithaca, NY: Cornell University Press, 2003.

Berkeley, Bill. *The Graves Are Not Yet Full: Race, Tribe, and Power in the Heart of Africa.* New York: Basic Books, 2002.

Dallaire, Romeo. *Shake Hands with the Devil: The Failure of Humanity in Rwanda.* New York: Carrol and Graf, 2004.

Eltringham, N. *Accounting for Horror: Genocide Debate in Rwanda.* London: Pluto Press, 2004.

Harell, P. *Rwanda's Gamble: Gacaca and a New Model of Traditional Justice.* New York: Writer's Club Press, 2003.

Melvera, Linda. *Conspiracy to Murder: The Rwanda Genocide and the International Community.* New York: Verso, 2004.

Prunier, Gerard. *The Rwanda Crisis.* New York: Columbia University, 1997.

S

SADAT, ANWAR

Muhammad Anwar al-Sadat (1918–1981) became the president of Egypt in 1970, succeeding Gamal Abdel Nasser. During the eleven years of his presidency, until his assassination, Sadat was involved with war and then peace with Israel, for which he was a joint winner of the Nobel Prize, as well as negotiating with the Soviet Union and other Arab states for support of the economic development of his country.

Born into modest circumstances, Sadat entered a country ruled as a colony by the British. A new constitution was adopted in 1922 which set in place a monarchy and a parliament. However, the British found themselves required to make accommodations with the nationally popular Wafd party for the sake of order. One such accommodation was the creation of a military school and it was here that Sadat received crucial formative education. He graduated in 1938 and, during World War II, plotted with fellow officers to drive the British out of Egypt. He was captured and imprisoned but subsequently escaped and went on to join Nasser's Free Officers group. In the revolution of 1952, Sadat was an active participant and the status he gained led to his enjoying high office under Nasser, although it was far from clear that he would emerge as the designated successor.

Under Nasser, pan-Arab socialist policies were favoured which led to an import-substitution growth model which featured significant levels of trade protection. Sadat's administration faced the problems caused by this model, which failed in Egypt because of the inability to develop sufficient exports and export markets, as well as improving the level of human capital. Facing problems of internal unrest and sporadic violence, Sadat introduced a new *intifah* (openness) policy which led to progressively higher levels of foreign trade and which was continued by his successor Hosni Mubarak. These policies have struggled to overcome the problems of embedded interests benefiting from existing barriers, together with persistent failures to develop the labour market, partly resulting from cultural and religious factors. The ability of Middle East Muslim states to establish suitable methods for economic cooperation.

However, Sadat is better known for his foreign policy actions than his very limited amount of domestic success. During the Cold War period, Egypt had accepted Soviet support to counter American backing for the state of Israel. However, Sadat felt the thousands of Soviet technicians present in the country were insufficiently productive and a drag on his foreign policy freedom. Consequently, they were all expelled shortly after he became president. In the following year, a joint invasion of Israel with Syria led to the 1973 Arab–Israeli War, which was a limited success in that Sadat became the first Arab leader to reclaim territory lost to the Israelis—in the Sinai Peninsula in this case. After this war, Sadat changed his policy and worked instead for peace, despite the great unpopularity of such a change in Egypt. He visited Israel in 1977, traveling to the Knesset in Jerusalem to outline his plans for peace. This subsequently gave rise to the 1978 Camp David Accords between Sadat and Israeli Prime Minister Menachem Begin which

were mediated by the US President, Jimmy Carter. The fruits of the Accords included the first treaty between an Arab country and Israel and, in 1978, the joint award of the Nobel Peace Prize for Sadat and Begin. Sadat's actions were in part motivated by the desire to secure badly needed US aid for the Egyptian economy. This began in 1975 and had reached flows of more than $1 billion US per year by the 1980s. Sadat was also concerned by the slow progress of negotiations with the Israelis: two agreements about the Sinai Peninsula had been signed in 1974 and 1975 but many problems remained unresolved. The Palestinian issue was prominent among these but so too were the status of the West Bank and the Gaza Strip. Popular belief in Egypt that Sadat had failed to do enough to promote Palestinian interests fuelled economic protests and, early in 1977, riots throughout the country led to nearly one hundred dead and thousands wounded or else arrested.

The inflows of economic assistance only slowly provided assistance to the Egyptian people, since a great deal was inefficiently used in trying to promote uncompetitive industries. At the same time, there has been something of a brain drain of Egyptian intellectuals to many of the oil-producing states of the Middle East.

However, continued inability to provide sustained growth in the domestic economy coupled with unrest among religious groups arising from the peace process made Egypt an increasingly dangerous place for Sadat. His attempts to suppress dissent were only partly successful and, reviewing the troops in 1981 on the anniversary of the Arab–Israeli War, he was assassinated by members of the armed forces.

Anwar Sadat was a transitional political figure on a road to the future that has not yet, five years into the twenty-first century, arrived for the Egyptian people. He demonstrated some fleeting Arab military success against the US-backed Israeli military and he opened the economy to development methods more suitable for the time but without being able to ensure that these were sufficient or sufficiently well sustained. His pan-Arab internationalist brothers and cousins failed him and failed to follow the vision he was able to enounce.

JOHN WALSH

See also Arab–Israeli Wars (1948, 1956, 1967, 1973); Egypt

References and Further Reading

Beattie, Kirk J. *Egypt During the Sadat Years*. New York: Palgrave Macmillan, 2000.
Madani, Dorsati, and Marcelo Olarreaga. "Politically Optimal Tariffs: An Application to Egypt," *World Bank Policy Research Paper No. 2882* (September, 2002), downloaded from: http://econ.worldbank.org/files/18102_wps 2882.pdf.
Sadat, Anwar-El. *Anwar El-Sadat: In Search of Identity, An Autobiography*. HarperCollins, 1978.

SALINAS DE GORTARI, CARLOS

President of Mexico from 1988 to 1994, Carlos Salinas de Gortari's administration carried out major transformations in the social and economic structures of the country by opening its once-protectionist borders to international markets and transnational forces. By embracing the neoliberal recipes of privatization, liberalized trade, and deregulating economic governance, Salinas de Gortari increased Mexico's international competitiveness; however, social polarization, inequalities, and political conflicts also increased. Controversy and corruption also plagued his presidency, making him and several of his closest collaborators the targets of various criminal investigations.

Salinas de Gortari was born in 1948 and grew up in a family closely associated with Mexico's Institutionalized Revolutionary Party (PRI for its acronym in Spanish) at that time the unchallenged centre of national political rule. Salinas de Gortari received a doctoral degree in political economy from Harvard University in 1978, and using his active militancy in the PRI as a springboard managed to occupy high-ranking positions in key financial and planning departments of the public service. Capitalizing on a growing reputation as an efficient and assertive public servant, Salinas de Gortari played an important role in Miguel de la Madrid's presidency (1982–1988), especially in the drafting and implementation of drastic austerity measures and structural adjustment that followed Mexico's almost catastrophic period of foreign debt repayment crises (1982–1984).

Salinas de Gortari's technocratic character and unwavering party loyalty earned him the PRI's presidential nomination for the 1988 general elections. His main opponent was Cuauhtémoc Cárdenas Solórzano, the charismatic son of former PRI revered leader Lázaro Cárdenas, who had broken ranks with the PRI after unsuccessfully leading a campaign for democratic reform within the party. On election day controversy ensued: as early results projected favorable results for Cárdenas, the electronic system that tallied the votes suffered a sudden technical breakdown. At the end of the impasse, Salinas de Gortari was declared the winner with barely 50% of the votes. Cárdenas and his followers accused the PRI of perpetrating an electoral fraud of massive proportions, and although the evidence supported their claims, the country's electoral authorities validated the results.

These accusations of fraud and corruption would taint Salinas de Gortari's administration, while shedding light on the growing political decadence of the PRI and fueling the development of a national multi-dimensional movement pushing for nationwide political reform.

Salinas de Gortari was determined to transform Mexico from a largely protectionist country to one espousing market-oriented principles that embraced international capital and dealt on the basis of free trade. Three sets of reforms constituted the basis of this ambitious project. First, Salinas de Gortari set out to privatize the country's entire banking system. In essence, the administration claimed that this campaign of privatization would eliminate inefficiency and provide the state with funds to finance pressing socioeconomic needs. Eventually, the drive to privatize went beyond the banking sector and touched all publicly owned corporations and institutions, from telecommunications to drinking water facilities. By the end of Salinas de Gortari's presidency, more than 90% of the country's formerly public enterprises were totally or partially owned by private hands.

Second, Salinas de Gortari amended Article 27 of the 1917 Constitution, one of the pillars of socioeconomic justice that resulted from the Mexican Revolution. Article 27 guaranteed state protection and assistance for small agricultural cooperative communities, or ejidos, that were established during the comprehensive land reform campaigns of the 1930s and 1940s and played a major role in securing the country's supply of staple foods. Salinas de Gortari claimed that these protectionist agricultural measures curtailed the competitiveness and productivity of the Mexican countryside given the allegedly large percentage of land used for "unproductive purposes." The reform of Article 27 allowed private capital to buy and/or rent ejido land, while eliminating all public programs that assisted ejidos in the attainment of inputs, credit, and market access. Moreover, this constitutional amendment was seen as a prerequisite for Mexico to successfully negotiate its entry into the North American Free Trade Agreement (NAFTA) in order to enable multinational corporations (MNCs) to buy previously protected land for the development of agribusiness ventures.

Finally, Salinas de Gortari intensified the outward-oriented, export-based model of economic development by multiplying Mexico's free trade agreements. The most important of these was NAFTA, which entered into force in 1994. Moreover, Salinas de Gortari also signed free trade agreements with most Central American countries, Colombia, Venezuela, Chile, and Bolivia, and managed to obtain membership in transnational economic organizations, such as

Asia-Pacific Economic Cooperation (APEC) and the Organization for Economic Cooperation and Development (OECD).

Undoubtedly, the substantial changes undertaken during Salinas de Gortari's administration enabled Mexico to diversify its economic base, increase its exports, receive more foreign direct investment (FDI), and create jobs in key sectors of the economy, such as the manufacturing and auto assembling industries. However, these market reforms also provoked major disruptions for millions of Mexicans at the middle and lower strata, especially for the small producer agricultural sector given its inability to compete with cheap grain coming from the United States, the impacts of the rise in prices for basic services due to privatization, and the fall in real wages due to recurring monetary crises that neoliberal policies allegedly helped to trigger. In December 1994, just a few days after Salinas de Gortari had left power, the national currency, the peso, lost 60% of its value. All fingers pointed to Salinas de Gortari's economic policies as the main cause of the crisis. Furthermore, the growing displacement and poverty in the Mexican countryside due to the liberal agricultural policies implemented by Salinas de Gortari have been identified as the elements that catalyzed the 1994 indigenous uprising in the southern state of Chiapas, which was led by the Zapatista National Liberation Army (EZLN).

Since leaving office Salinas de Gortari has been burdened by several criminal charges that range from murder to embezzlement of public funds. Taking advantage of Ireland's lack of an extradition treaty with Mexico, Salinas de Gortari has resided in Dublin since 1996 and has managed to avoid prosecution.

CARLOS VELÁSQUEZ CARRILLO

See also Mexico: History and Economic Development; Party of the Institutionalized Revolution (PRI); North American Free Trade Agreement (NAFTA); Zapatista National Liberation Army (EZLN)

References and Further Reading

Barkin, David. *Distorted Development: Mexico in the World Economy.* Boulder, CO: Westview, 1990.

Barry, Tom. *Zapata's Revenge: Free Trade and the Farm Crisis in Mexico.* Boston: South End Press, 1995.

Centeno, Miguel. *Democracy Within Reason: Technocratic Revolution in Mexico.* University Park, PA: Pennsylvania State University Press, 1994.

Harvey, Neil. *The Chiapas Rebellion: The Struggle for Land and Democracy.* Durham, NC: Duke University Press, 1998.

Lustig, Nora. *Mexico: The Remaking of an Economy.* Washington DC: Brookings Institute, 1992.

Teichman, Judith. *Privatization and Political Change in Mexico*. Pittsburgh: University of Pittsburgh Press, 1995.

Russell, Philip. *Mexico Under Salinas*. Austin: Mexico Resource Centre, 1994.

SALVATION ARMY

The Salvation Army traces its origins as a Protestant home mission begun by the Reverend William Booth in London's East End in 1865. But its post–World War II growth has occurred mainly in the developing world. When his mission's growth faltered in the 1878, Booth developed strategies to save it: a military system of command; employment of women ministers (officers); and by 1890, social services to appeal to the poor and urban ethnic minorities. And he opened overseas missions in Asia, Africa, and Latin America.

Before 1945, the Salvation Army followed Britain's Union Jack into British colonies, and after the colonizer's retreat, it turned over most leadership to nationals. Booth's commissioner Frederick St. George de Lautour Tucker, a third generation member of the Indian Civil Service, arrived in Bombay in 1882. As Fakir Singh (prince of religious mendicants) he tried to convert Indians to evangelical Christianity by dressing as a wandering fakir. But he found few to join his Army. Other Christian missions had already partitioned India, and Tucker only enrolled malcontents from other missions.

Finally he found that the Army appealed to India's outcasts and "criminal tribes." Starting with these poor "soldiers" and farm colonies, schools, hospitals, and other social services, his Army grew. By January 2000, India had 227,133 soldiers. In Asia, the Army had 357,057 soldiers, 35% of its international membership. In Africa it had 422,721 soldiers, 41.5% of its membership. In Latin America there were 17,492 soldiers. Thus 797,270 (77.5%) of all 1,019,137 Salvationists live in developing nations, with its largest membership in India, Kenya-Uganda, and Zimbabwe. However, it is unclear how accurate these statistics are. According to a Salvation Army leader, they vary by national culture. An Indian born into a religion may be inactive, but s/he may not be removed from the register even upon death. What is clear is that most Salvationists live in the developing world of the Army's 108 countries and territories. (Membership statistics are from *The Salvation Army 2004 Yearbook* [London: The Salvation Army International Headquarters, 2004]).

In each country the Army's churches are largely self-supporting, but schools, hospitals, and other social services receive financial support from funds the Army raises from governments and public contributions in the developed world. Prior to 1947, nearly all Salvation Army leaders were Europeans, North Americas, or from Australia–New Zealand. By 2001, most in Africa and South Asia are native-born. The transition came as African and Asian Salvationists insisted on leading their post-colonial countries, and developing world governments refused to accept foreign leaders. No longer would the leaders speak only English, nor would Salvationists pray, as one Indian officer put it, to "our father who art in London."

Salvation Army history in the developing world is written or edited by officers in the West. And the Army has not yet elected a General, its sole international commander, from a developing country. But there are now new voices in the Army's high councils who represent the developing nations.

NORMAN H. MURDOCH

See also Christianity; Non-Governmental Organizations (NGOs)

References and Further Reading

Murdoch, Norman H. "The World Council of Churches and The Salvation Army: 1978–1985 Debate over Zimbabwe's Liberation Movement," Jacksonville, Florida: Assn. of Third World Studies, 1995.

Pavez, Oscar Cornejo. *El Ejercito de Salvacion en la Costa del Pacifico Sudamericano, 1909–1989*. Santiago de Chile: Ejercito de Salvacion, 1989.

Tuck, Brian. *Salvation Safari: The Salvation Army in Southern Africa, 1883–1993*, 2nd edn. Johannesburg, The Salvation Army, 1993.

Williams, Harry. *Booth-Tucker: William Booth's First Gentleman*. London: Hodder and Stoughton, 1980.

SAMOA

The Samoan archipelago, which stretches across more than three hundred miles of the South Pacific Ocean, is divided into two political entities, the Independent State of Samoa (formerly Western Samoa, now known generally as "Samoa") and American Samoa. The people of both countries are linked by extended familial ties, owing to the two countries' long-standing but now discarded reciprocal free immigration policies, but political and economic distinctions still divide the two countries.

Samoa consists chiefly of the two large islands of Savai'I (656 square miles) and Upolu (430 square miles), the latter including the capital city of Apia. American Samoa occupies the archipelago's seven eastern islands, the largest of which, Tutuila (fifty-six square miles), hosts the country's capital, Pago Pago. The island chain lies on the South Pacific's primary

hurricane corridor, with major storms regularly forming each year between November and April, and devastating cyclones regularly destroy crops, damage infrastructure, and disrupt economic activity. The larger islands have high mountain peaks that drop off sharply to the sea, with few plains and little cultivable land area. The population of Samoa is 160,000, while American Samoa has approximately 68,000 citizens. Both countries have an average annual population growth rate of 2%.

In the late nineteenth century, the Samoan islands were the focus of intense competition among the Great Powers, which needed Pacific coaling stations for their fleets. In 1899, the archipelago was partitioned at the 171st meridian. Germany took possession of the larger western sector, while the United States obtained the smaller eastern islands. After Germany's defeat in World War I, its Pacific possessions were placed under a League of Nations mandate administered by New Zealand. Wellington enforced its authority against an independence movement in 1920s, but after World War II it promoted measured progress toward autonomy for Western Samoa. The country became independent in January 1962.

The economy of Western Samoa, traditionally dependent upon intensive plantation-style cultivation of coconuts and copra, has remained heavily oriented toward agricultural exports. As a result, domestic budgets are vulnerable to commodity price fluctuations, a fact that inhibits long-term economic development planning. Since the mid-1980s, a relatively new industry has emerged, that of tropical hardwood harvesting, processing, and export. Although profitable, the industry has caused widespread environmental damage, including the deforestation of 40% of the country's total land area. With United Nations aid money, the Samoan government has designated several zones as "conservation areas" where tree harvesting is banned. A small environmental movement is growing, and both the government and commercial entrepreneurs are beginning to promote eco-tourism as a new source of hard currency revenues.

To curb its welfare expenses and as a mechanism to reduce overcrowding, the Samoan government encourages emigration, and Samoan youth regularly leave the country in search of employment. New Zealand accepts 1,100 Samoan immigrants annually, and during periods of prosperity many times this number are allowed in on "guest" visas, on the assumption that young Samoans will accept unattractive low-wage jobs. Hundreds more Samoans are believed to enter New Zealand and Australia illegally each year, merging into the underground economies of the host countries. Samoans regularly move to American Samoa, attracted by relatively high-wage cannery jobs. Remittances

from family members working abroad support many Samoan households. The government also relies upon international development aid, particularly for financing large infrastructure projects.

After the 1899 partition, the American sector of Samoa was administered by the US Navy, which established coaling facilities at the deep water harbor of Pago Pago. During World War II, Tutuila island saw the construction of air fields, storage depots, and training facilities to support Navy and Marine forces in the Pacific. Nonetheless, central features of traditional Samoan political culture remained intact, including communal land ownership and the relaxed administration of social affairs by local familial chiefs, known as "matai." In 1951, the Navy transferred its authority over the territory to the US Department of the Interior, and consultations began on the introduction of a constitution. The new document, introduced in 1960, provided for a bicameral legislative body with special roles for senior matai, but all foreign affairs issues remained under the control of Washington, DC. In 1980, American Samoa elected its first non-voting delegate to the US House of Representatives.

During the early 1960s, President John F. Kennedy ordered that federal educational, welfare, and infrastructure development programs be implemented in American Samoa. Roads, schools, harbor and airport facilities, electricity production plants, and medical clinics were built, welfare and educational benefits were introduced, and new jobs were created in the construction and operation of large tuna canneries near Pago Pago. Funding cuts in the 1970s and 1980s reduced benefits paid to individuals supported by federal programs, and public facilities went without regular maintenance or improvements. In the early 2000s, more than half the government's revenue was supplied by direct grants from the United States.

As a US territory, American Samoa has absorbed American popular culture through radio, television, music, and films. Traditionalists and nationalists pointed to these influences to explain the rising incidence of juvenile delinquency, alcoholism, and illegal drug usage during the 1990s, stimulating a movement for a return to "fa'a Samoa," or traditional Samoan folkways. Local legislative initiatives placed restrictions on foreign investment and land purchases by non-Samoans.

Over 90% of American Samoa's populace resides on Tutuila, concentrated around the harbor at Pago Pago. Unemployment regularly exceeds 10%, and it is estimated that each year, half of the country's high school graduates move to the United States, particularly to Hawaii and the West Coast, in search of better educational and employment opportunities.

Most make permanent homes in the United States and regularly remit cash to family members remaining in American Samoa.

Tuna canning and fish processing are the largest industries in American Samoa, with agricultural products a distant second. The largest market for all exports is the United States. The canneries at Pago Pago attract migrants from Western Samoa and Tonga. For many, moving to American Samoa presents the possibility of obtaining permanent resident status in the territory, and thereby eventually gaining the right to legally enter the United States.

LAURA M. CALKINS

See also Oceania: History and Economic Development; Oceania: International Relations

References and Further Reading

Davidson, James W. *Samoa mo Samoa: The Emergence of the Independent State of Western Samoa.* New York: Oxford University Press, 1967.

Field, Michael. *Mau: Samoa's Struggle for Freedom.* Auckland: Polynesia Press, 1991.

Lawson, Stephanie. *Tradition versus Democracy in the South Pacific: Fiji, Tongo, and Western Samoa.* New York: Cambridge University Press, 1996.

Linkels, Ad. *Faa Samoa/The Samoan Way: Between Conch Shell and Disco: A Portrait of Western Samoa at the End of the Twentieth Century.* Tilburg: Mudo Etnico Foundation, 1995.

Maiava, Susas. *A Clash of Paradigms: Intervention, Response, and Development in the South Pacific.* Burlington, VT: Ashgate, 2001.

Meleisea, Malama. *Change and Adaptation in Western Samoa.* Christchurch: Macmillan Brown Centre, 1992.

———. *The Making of Modern Samoa: Traditional Authority and Colonial Administration in the History of Western Samoa.* Suva: University of the Pacific, 1987.

O'Meara, Tim. *Samoa Planters: Tradition and Economic Development in Polynesia.* Fort Worth, TX: Holt, Rinehart, & Winston, 1990.

SANCTIONS, ECONOMIC

In recent decades, economic sanctions have become a household phrase as they have been imposed more frequently on a number of countries—Cuba, Iraq, Libya, Haiti (1991–1994), Iran, North Korea, and South Africa (before it abandoned apartheid) to name a few—although some of these date back 40 years. Economic sanctions involve one or more countries, referred to as *sender(s)*, who inflict or threaten to inflict on another country, the *target*, economic and financial costs in order to change that country's behavior. The action by the sender consists of but is not restricted to boycott, restriction of access to financial resources, denial of trade, and blocking of assets. The offending behavior of the target country could be in the sphere of military (occupation of Kuwait by Iraq), human rights (South Africa during apartheid, Poland in 1981, China), hostage taking (Iran), support for terrorism (Libya), the economy (countries who restrict their markets), or environmental concerns. Sanctions are unilateral when there is only one sender and multilateral when there are a number of senders or are even imposed by the United Nations. The target is usually a single country although there have been cases where several countries were targets of economic sanctions. As a result of sanctions both the sender and target incur costs, and the costs to the sender may be even greater in absolute magnitude. Yet because usually the sender is a powerful country and the target a smaller nation, the relative costs to the target are more pronounced. Sanctions are usually applied to the government, companies, and citizens of the target country or to companies and citizens of the sender country who trade with or invest in the target country. Cases exist, however, where sanctions acquire extraterritorial character and are imposed on third-country companies who deal with the target.

Sanctions have a long history and date back to 432 BC when Athens imposed a trade embargo on Megara. In their modern reincarnation during the twentieth and twenty-first centuries, economic sanctions have been imposed close to 170 times on different countries. What is interesting is the proliferation of economic sanctions in the past two decades. Between 1914 and 1990, the number of sanctions is estimated at 115, but since 1990 more than fifty sanctions have been imposed.

The rate of success of sanctions in achieving their publicly stated goals—that is, to change the offending countries political behavior—is low. The best estimates put it at 25% to 30%. One has only to look at four decades of sanctions on Cuba and more than ten years on Iraq for the confirmation of their ineffectiveness. Sanctions are more effective when multilateral and when third parties—countries or blocks of countries which are neither senders nor targets—do not thwart them. It is not unusual for the neighbors of the target country or nations with which it has had trade and investment relations to continue their dealings clandestinely or even openly and reap financial benefits. Nevertheless, these considerations should not be taken to mean that economic sanctions do not inflict economic costs on the countries under sanctions. Indeed, such costs can be quite substantial and cripple an economy. Therefore, some have argued that economic sanctions have a broader purpose, that they send a signal to the world as to the resolve and power of the sanction-imposing country. Others have sought

to explain the rationale for sanctions and the recent surge in their number by the actions of interest groups and by public choice theory. We present three rationales for imposing economic sanctions. None of these explanations are applicable to all cases. Nevertheless, individually or in combination, they account for the majority if not all instances of economic sanctions. Empirical work on the study of sanctions and their impact has just begun. Work on econometric models specifically designed to quantify the effect of sanctions on both sender and target countries would be a desirable avenue of research.

One explanation for the proliferation of economic sanctions observes that sanctions are something between war and no action at all. Faced with an international situation that is morally objectionable or politically unacceptable—for instance, apartheid in South Africa, ethnic conflict in Yugoslavia, human rights violations in Haiti, Iraq's intentions toward its neighbors, and state-sponsored terrorism of Libya—other countries have a number of choices. Warfare is costly in human and financial terms and may not be popular at home. Passivity, on the other hand, could be politically damaging and morally unacceptable both at home and abroad. Economic sanctions are a happy medium. But this does not explain why in the face of the lackluster performance of sanctions, governments still resort to them. The problem is that this view does not consider the signal or expressive value of sanctions.

A second explanation may be that in reality sanctions have been more successful than raw statistics show. First, there have been many successful episodes, albeit small ones, while a few prominent unsuccessful cases have grabbed headlines. Second, sanctions prevent the recurrence of the offending behavior by other countries. For example, it has been noted that by imposing an embargo on Cuba, the United States discouraged other Latin American countries from becoming communist. Thus, a country facing a situation where its principles are trampled upon has to make a stand. Failure to do so or follow through with economic sanctions (even if the stated goals of the sanctions are not achieved) would be to invite further encroachments. It also may earn the sender a reputation of being a paper tiger, and serve as a signal to other countries that they too need not take warnings seriously. The target on its part may refuse to budge because to submit once may invite blackmail. The sender may demand more and more concessions. Thus, regardless of the costs, the target may refuse to change its behavior. Furthermore, it may turn the sanctions into a national cause and try to rally the populace around the flag. The upshot of all these reactions would be two countries in a locked-horn position and with no end in sight. Such episodes of sanctions could be considered successful in achieving their aims, because their prolonged histories stand as a reminder to other nations and relieve the sender of the need to impose further sanctions.

While the previous view seems sound and has explanatory value, it requires econometric validation. We cannot believe in a theory based on an event not happening, unless we clearly specify what might have happened and show evidence as to its likely occurrence. This may be a tall order in the case of sanctions, but it should be possible to specify a behavioral model along the lines of models dealing with self-selection in labor economics, and subject it to empirical testing.

A third view of economic sanctions is based on the observation that a nation consists of many interest groups with different and sometimes opposing objectives. Thus, for simplicity, we can divide voters in the sender country into three interest groups; one group may benefit from or be in favor of sanctions, another may be harmed by or oppose them, and the third be neutral or unaffected. The same division could be applied to people in the target country. Now each of the first two groups in the sender country would try to advance their own agenda through influencing the elected officials. Each group would try to elect candidates sympathetic to their cause and find allies among the neutral group. Elected officials, in turn, would try to curry favor with influential interest groups. When the group in favor of economic sanctions gets the upper hand, sanctions will be instituted against the target country, and when those opposed to it muster the necessary votes, they will prevent them from going into effect or if they are already in place remove them. For its part the interest group in the target country which benefits from sanctions will do its utmost to prevent any softening on the part of its own government that could lead to the removal of the sanctions. Hence, members of the group rally around the flag and organize demonstrations against foreign meddling in the internal affairs of the homeland. In this game, third parties—that is, governments, companies, and citizens of the countries that are neither senders nor target—will try to maximize their own gains. This may entail trying to circumvent or even remove the sanctions, or to make lucrative deals with the target country.

As an example, observe that groups concerned about terrorism in the Middle East and the proliferation of weapons of mass destruction as well as supporters of Israel work hard to keep the Iran-Libya Sanctions Act (ILSA) in place. While as a result of the prohibition of trade with and investment in Iran many businesses and particularly oil companies stand

to lose. On their part, Iranian people and their elected representatives have sought rapprochement with the United States while the unelected conservative officials have spurned even dialogue with America. Conservatives have both financial and political vested interests in confronting the United States. Third parties have also been at work. When the American company Conoco had to withdraw from a deal with Iran, the French company Total took its place. Similarly, European countries and Russia have tried to benefit from trade with Iran.

A parallel situation exists regarding Cuba. The large Cuban community in the United States is against any dealing with the Castro regime, while many businesses would like to trade with that country. European firms, on the other hand, are against the provision of the Cuban Liberty and Democratic Solidarity (LIBERTAD) Act of 1996 that imposes sanctions on companies who benefit from the use of properties of Americans, including naturalized citizens, confiscated by the Cuban government.

This theory too helps us to better understand the reasons for imposing sanctions through an analysis of the political process. Nevertheless, the model should not be taken too literally. The two co-sponsors of the LIBERTAD Act, Helmes of North Carolina and Burton of Indiana, could not be said to have been influenced by the Cuban community in America, as neither state has a large presence of Cuban-Americans. Their motives may have been ideological opposition to communism and promotion of international recognition of and respect for private property rights. One may surmise that it is more likely for an interest group to succeed in enacting its legislation when its goal is in line with a broader consensus. Also one has to be skeptical of the rallying-around-the-flag argument if it is based only on demonstrations in the target country. Petty dictators run many target countries and the populace may have no choice but to participate in these public shows of support for the government.

The communications revolution has brought people around the globe ever closer to each other. Any conflict, civil rights violation, or terrorist act immediately attains the character of an international problem. The global village calls for the observance of rules of civil society by all, and since this is not going to be the case, the need and calls for sanctions will increase. In the absence of an international body to enforce human rights and the rules of civil society, powerful countries individually or in coalitions will find it necessary to enforce compliance. The use of military force will not always be desirable or even possible. Therefore, sanctions will become the weapon of choice on many occasions. Moreover, globalization has resulted in the growing interdependence of markets and economies. This, in turn, requires that all participants submit to the discipline of the market and play the game fairly or, at the least, refrain from flagrant violations. It is unlikely that in the foreseeable future all nations will give up on export subsidies and protectionist policies, the World Trade Organization (WTO) and its rules notwithstanding. Economic disputes too will add to the cases of sanctions. On the other hand, many in the business community consider sanctions an interference with free trade. Fearful of their abuse by interest groups, a trend to oppose sanctions as frivolous acts has taken shape. Thus, for the foreseeable future, economic sanctions will remain an important issue of our time. A rigorous theoretical and empirical analysis of this subject is vitally needed.

KAMRAN M. DADKHAH

See also Private Property Rights

References and Further Reading

Bayard, Thomas O., Joseph Pelzman, and Jorge Perez-Lopez. "Stakes and Risks in Economic Sanctions," *The World Economy*, 6, 1983, pp. 73–87.

Chan, Steve, and A. Cooper Drury, eds. *Sanctions as Economic Statecraft, Theory and Practice*. New York: St. Martin's Press, 2000.

Elliott, Kimberly Ann, and Gary Clyde Hufbauer. "Same Song, Same Refrain? Economic Sanctions in the 1990's," *American Economic Review* (Papers and Proceedings), 89, 1999, pp. 403–408.

Eaton, Jonathan, and Maxim Engers. "Sanctions: Some Simple Analytics," *American Economic Review* (Papers and Proceedings), 89, 1999, pp. 409–414.

———. "Sanctions," *Journal of Political Economy*, 100, 1992, pp. 899–928.

Hufbauer, Gary Clyde, Jeffrey J. Schott, and Kimberly Ann Elliott. *Economic Sanctions Reconsidered, History and Current Policy*. Washington, DC: 2nd Institute for International Economics, 1990.

Kaempfer, William H., and Anton D. Lowenberg. "The Theory of International Economic Sanctions: A Public Choice Approach," *American Economic Review*, 78, 1988, pp. 786–793.

Levy, Philip P. "Sanctions on South Africa: What Did They Do?" *American Economic Review* (Papers and Proceedings), 89, 1999, pp. 415–420.

Lundborg, Per. *The Economics of Export Embargoes: The Case of the U.S.-Soviet Grain Suspension*. London: Groom Helm, 1987.

Manby, Bronwen. "South Africa: The Impact of Sanctions," *Journal of International Affairs*, 46, 1992, pp. 193–217.

Niblock, Tim. *Pariah States and Sanctions in the Middle East: Iraq, Libya, Sudan*. Boulder, CO: Lynne Rienner, 2001.

Preeg, Ernest H. *Feeling Good or Doing Good with Sanctions*. Washington, DC: Center for Strategic and International Studies, 1999.

SANDINISTA NATIONAL LIBERATION FRONT (FSLN)

The Sandinista National Liberation Front (FSLN) led a successful insurgency that ousted Nicaraguan dictator Anastasio Somoza Debayle on July 19, 1979, then ruled the impoverished Central American country until 1990, when it was defeated in democratic elections. It remains the main opposition political party in the country, winning nearly half of the seats in the National Assembly in the 2001 elections. Since 1990, its support has been fairly constant at about 30%–40% of the vote, despite the defection of certain key leaders such as former Vice President Sergio Ramirez.

Origins and History

The FSLN takes its name from Nicaraguan hero Augusto César Sandino, a Liberal reformer who held US forces at bay for six years, leading to their departure in 1933, following a relatively fair election won by fellow Liberal Juan Sacasa. Sandino's philosophy was, above all, nationalistic, and he even broke ties with Augustín Farabundo Martí—who led a failed rebellion in El Salvador in 1932—because of the latter's adherence to communism. Sandino was double-crossed and killed in 1934 by then head of the newly created National Guard, Anastasio Somoza García, who later became president and founded the familial dictatorship overthrown by the self-declared heirs to Sandino's nationalist cause in 1979.

The FSLN, according to the sole surviving founder Tomás Borge, was an historical response to this dictatorship and its ties to the United States. Its primary goal was to defeat the Somoza dictatorship via armed struggle, and to take political power in order to achieve democratization and progress in Nicaragua. It drew not only upon the nationalism of Sandino but on certain aspects of Marxism-Leninism and Christian humanism, borrowing the latter from Liberation Theology, which resonated throughout Latin America. Founded in 1961, the FSLN was an obscure guerrilla movement that took its inspiration from the successful insurgency led by Fidel Castro in Cuba. Its principal leader until his death in 1976 was Carlos Fonseca, whose writings continue to inspire the movement. The Sandinistas resisted, however, the temptation to build a cult of personality around any one leader, relying instead on a nine-man National Directorate that represented equally the three "tendencies" within the movement—the Prolonged Popular War tendency, the Terceristas (of which Daniel and brother Humberto Ortega were leading members), and the Proletarian tendency. In theory, as well as in practice, these nine men made decisions based upon discussion and consensus.

The Sandinista Revolution

When the Sandinistas triumphed over the National Guard and Somoza in 1979, they had built a broad opposition coalition that included twenty existing political parties and groups in Nicaragua. At first, a five-person junta was named to govern the country, including Ortega, Ramirez, Alfonso Robelo, Violeta de Chamorro, and Moisés Hassan. But the FSLN moved quickly to strengthen its own base of support by creating a number of affiliated organizations, including the Sandinista Workers Central (CST) labor union, the Association of Rural Workers (ATC), and the Sandinista Defense Committees (CDS), the latter of which were neighborhood groups criticized for allegedly silencing dissent, though their primary purpose was to attend to peoples' immediate needs. Despite the defection of several of its coalition members, the Sandinistas continued to tolerate a political opposition, even after evidence of US influence emerged. The Reagan administration, upon taking office in early 1981, was openly hostile to the FSLN-dominated government and financed a covert war to overthrow it. Undeterred, the Sandinistas carried out sweeping economic and land reforms, aimed primarily at the country's impoverished population. Private investment was tolerated and even encouraged in what was declared to be a mixed economy.

The Sandinistas held their first elections in November 1984, despite the ongoing proxy war. Six political parties to both the left and the right of the FSLN agreed to participate, while four others opted to boycott, claiming the conditions did not meet their demands. The United States used that boycott to contend that the elections were a sham, but most observers present concluded that, given the circumstances, the voting was as free and fair as could be expected. Daniel Ortega was elected president with 67% of the popular vote, while the FSLN captured sixty-one of the ninety-six seats in the new National Assembly. By 1987, Nicaragua had a new constitution, but its economic situation was deteriorating rapidly in the face of the US embargo and covert war. By the late 1980s, inflation had reached 675% and more than two-thirds of the government's budget was being devoted to defense.

It was under these trying conditions that the Sandinistas submitted to another election in 1990, facing off against former junta member Chamorro and the United Nicaraguan Opposition (UNO), which

enjoyed US backing. Ortega lost to Chamorro, 55% to 41%, and the FSLN agreed to hand over power. But they captured thirty-nine of the ninety-two National Assembly seats and, with the dissolution of UNO soon after the election, the Sandinistas continued to exercise considerable influence and power. They worked to minimize the impact of neoliberal reforms (neo-liberalism) on workers while defending other aspects of their revolution, such as land redistribution and education. In the most recent elections, on November 4, 2001, Ortega again ran for president and again lost, this time to Enrique Bolaños of the Constitutionalist Liberal Party (PLC). But the FSLN won forty-three of the ninety assembly seats and claimed victory in that regard.

LAWRENCE BOUDON

See also Central America: History and Economic Development; Central America: International Relations

References and Further Reading

Brentlinger, John. *The Best of What We Are: Reflections on the Nicaraguan Revolution.* Amherst, MA: University of Massachusetts Press, 1995.

Hoyt, Katherine. *The Many Faces of Sandinista Democracy.* Athens, OH: Ohio University Center for International Studies, 1997.

Luciak, Ilja A. *The Sandinista Legacy: Lessons from a Political Economy in Transition.* Gainesville, FL: University Press of Florida, 1995.

Merrill, Tim, ed. *Nicaragua: A Country Study.* 3rd Edition. Washington, DC: Federal Research Division, Library of Congress, 1994.

Prevost, Gary, and Harry E. Vanden, eds. *The Undermining of the Sandinista Revolution.* New York: St. Martin's Press, 1997.

Spalding, Rose J. *Capitalists and Revolution in Nicaragua: Opposition and Accomodation, 1979-1993.* Chapel Hill, NC: University of North Carolina Press, 1994.

Vanden, Harry E., and Gary Prevost. *Democracy and Socialism in Sandinista Nicaragua.* Boulder, CO: Lynn Rienner, 1993.

Walker, Thomas W., ed. *Nicaragua Without Illusions: Regime Transition and Structural Adjustment in the 1990s.* Wilmington, DE: SR Books, 1997.

SAUDI ARABIA

The Kingdom of Saudi Arabia extends from the Red Sea in the west to the Arabian Gulf in the east; bordered on the north by Jordan, Iraq and Kuwait, on the south, by Yemen and Oman, and on the east by the United Arab Emirates (UAE), Qatar and Bahrain. Almost all of Saudi Arabia consists of semi-desert and desert with oases, where half of the total surface is uninhabitable desert. The two major desert regions are, in the north, the An Nefud Desert, and in the south, the great Rub al-Khali desert also called the Empty Quarter due to its lack of inhabitants. Between those lie the Nejd massif central plateau and the plain of El Hasa, the country's only fertile region.

Most of the western parts of Saudi Arabia are plateau; the east is lowland, with a very hot climate. With the exception of the province of Asir with its towns of Jizan on the western coast and Najran, Saudi Arabia has a desert climate characterized by extreme heat during the day, a sudden drop in temperature at night and erratic rainfall. The two main extremes in climate are felt between the coastal lands and the interior. Along the coastal regions of the Red Sea and the Persian Gulf temperatures seldom rise above 100°F, but the relative humidity is usually more than 85% and frequently 100% for extended periods.

The inner part of the country includes the Nejd, and the great deserts. The average summer temperature is 113°F, but readings of up to 129°F are common. The heat becomes intense shortly after sunrise and lasts until sunset, followed by comparatively cool nights. During winter, the temperature seldom drops below 32°F, but the almost total absence of humidity and the high wind factor create a cold atmosphere. In the spring and autumn, temperatures average 84°F. All over the country there is very little rain. There are no permanent rivers and lakes. Although the average rainfall is four inches per year, whole regions may not experience rainfall for several years. When such droughts occur affected areas may not be able to sustain either livestock or agriculture with great losses as happened in the 1957 droughts.

The population is currently estimated at 25.1 million and has a growth rate of 3% annually. The total area of the country is estimated at 829,995 square miles with a population density of 30.3 persons per square mile. The boundaries of the Kingdom are not clearly determined in desert areas, especially the border with the Sultanate of Oman and the UAE. The city of Riyadh, located in the Nejd plateau, is the capitol and largest city with an estimated population of 3.5 million, which accounts for 14% of the total population.

Besides the capitol, major cities are located in the west side of the country. They include Jedda, the religious centres of Makah al-Mukarama (Mecca) and Medina. On the east coast, are located the cities of Dhamman, Al-Khubar and Dhahran, the oil industry capitol. In a similar way to other countries that posses lots of desert land (for example, Libya), most of the population lives in the cities, making 86% of the population urban. The geographical concentration of the population in the cities is the result of the disappearance of the Bedouin way of life as the Kingdom was united in 1932.

The Muslim tradition in the Arabia peninsula originated with Muhammad, the prophet of Islam, who was born in Mecca around 570 CE. He started the Islamic traditions when the Qur'an (or Koran) was revealed to him, which later was written and considered the holy book of the Muslims. After conquering the Mecca in 630 CE, Muhammad died two years later but left behind him an Islamic Community ruled by caliphs as political leaders who spread the Islam. However in the year 661 CE the caliphs moved the political centre of the Islam to Damascus (Syria). The Muslims wouldn't gain a total control of the country until the eighteenth century. The Kingdom's origins lay in the eighteenth century with the ancient Wahhabi movement, which gained the allegiance of the powerful and traditional Saud family of the Nejd, in central Arabia. Supported by a large Bedouin following, the Sauds brought most of the peninsula under their control. It was Abdulaziz bin Abdelrahman Al-Saud (also known as Abd al-Aziz ibn Saud or more simply as Ibn Saud) who laid the basis of the present Saudi Arabian state. After facing some conflicts, Ibn Saud took Riyadh in 1902 to become master of the Nejd by 1906. He later conquered the Al-Hasa region from the Ottoman Turks and soon extended his control over other areas.

Finally on September 23, 1932, that region was combined with the Nejd to establish the *Kingdom of Saudi Arabia*, an absolute and united monarchy, ruled under Islamic law. The Holy Qur'an was established as the constitution and Ibn Saud became the king and prime minister. Saudi Arabia became a hereditary monarchy. It was then when King Ibn Saud compelled most of the Bedouins to abandon traditional ways and encouraged their settlement as farmers. During his time, Ibn Saud initiated the real process of nation building as he began the development of the country's infrastructure by first establishing roads, basic communications systems, improving education, national health care and agriculture.

His three sons continued his work: Saud, Faisal, and Khalid. The eldest son of King Ibn Saud, Saud acceded to the throne upon his father's death in 1953. He instituted the Council of Ministers and established the Ministries of Health, Education and Commerce. A large number of schools and the Kingdom's first institute of higher education, King Saud University, were opened in Riyadh in 1957. In 1960, the Organization of Petroleum Exporting Countries (OPEC) was formed and Saudi Arabia became a stable and strong member until the present days. Faisal bin Abdulaziz became king in 1964. While his father had shaped the Kingdom, Faisal built and consolidated the country. Following the assassination of Faisal in 1975, King Khalid's reign (1975–1982) began.

Stressing Islamic orthodoxy and conservatism while expanding the country's economy, Khalid continued developing social programs and educational structures. Later on, due to an illness Khalid died in June 1982 and King Fahd bin Abdulaziz took over the government.

For thousands of years, the economy of the Arabian Peninsula had been determined by autonomous clusters of people living near wells and oases, under the Bedouin way of life. Until the middle of the 1930s, the recently united Kingdom's economical structure was based on agriculture, including nomads who raised livestock by moving their animals to the limited forage produced by infrequent rains. Production was limited to serve very small markets and existed essentially on a subsistence level. Trade was limited primarily to camel caravans. As cities formed, the main sources of income were trade and fishing on the Red Sea coast, the annual influxes of income derived from pilgrims who visited the holy places and the growing of products mainly on the eastern coast. Imports on several alimentary products were necessary to satisfy the demand.

However, in 1938, the discovery of huge reserves of oil by a United States company provoked the most structural change for the economy of Saudi Arabia. Initially, the newly established oil industry had only an indirect impact on this primitive economy. The establishment of the Arabian American Oil Company (Aramco, predecessor of Saudi Aramco) triggered major changes in the economy of the kingdom, especially in the Eastern Province. Development of the oil fields required ancillary construction of modern ports, roads, housing, power plants, and water systems.

The discovery of oil ended the kingdom's isolation and introduced new ways to organize the production and distribution of goods and services. Nowadays, the oil industry located in the northeast along the Persian Gulf dominates the Kingdom's economy: the petroleum sector accounts for roughly 75% of budget revenues, 45% of the gross domestic product (GDP), and 90% of export earnings. In 2004, Saudi Arabia's GDP was estimated at $287.8 billion with a per capita income of about $11,800. Major trading partners are the United States, Japan, Great Britain, and other European Union countries. Saudi Arabia contains about one quarter of the world's known reserves. The dynamics of the oil industry encouraged the development of other sectors in the Kingdom. Since 1962, Saudi Arabia has increasingly been producing natural gas liquids along with the exploitation of petroleum. Also some minerals are extracted and exported such as limestone, gypsum, marble, clay, iron ore, copper, gold, bauxite, and uranium. Agriculture only represents 4% of the GDP and consists mainly

of wheat, barley, dates, citrus fruit, vegetables, and livestock products. Agriculture is a growing economic sector and the country is approaching food self-sufficiency.

Due to the large incomes provided by the oil sector, the country has gone through considerable social development. During the last four decades the health standards have improved significantly with the establishment of a network of public primary health care centres and clinics throughout the country, which provide preventive, prenatal, emergency, and basic health services. The number of health centres and clinics rose from 591 in 1970 to over 3,300 by 2000.

This is complemented by a network of hospitals and specialized treatment facilities, located strategically in major urban areas such as Riyahd or Makkah. The results of the program have been to lower the infant mortality rate from 105 per 1,000 births in 1975 to 25 per 1,000 live births in 2000. Consequently, the life expectancy at birth rose from fifty-four years in 1975 to seventy-two in 2002. Also the mortality of children under age five has significantly been lowered from 141 per 1,000 births in 1975 to 30 per 1,000 in 2000. However, despite having increased the number of hospitals and beds, Saudi Arabia's ratio of one hospital bed per 440 people is among the lowest in the world.

The Saudi government also cares for social welfare having instituted during the 1980s some programs that provide social security pensions, benefits, and relief assistance to the disabled, the elderly, orphans, and widows without income. The government has also been active in housing policies by financing construction and building the infrastructure to enable housing development. Substantial housing has been built for low-income Saudis, public employees, and students. An important government policy has been to provide interest-free, easy-term loans for home construction. For this purpose, the Real Estate Development Fund was established in 1975 to provide financing to individuals and private companies. However, despite the large number of foreign workers within Saudi Arabia, only Saudi citizens are allowed to own property.

As for education, the formal primary education began in Saudi Arabia in the 1930s. By 1945, King Ibn Saud had initiated an extensive program to establish schools in the Kingdom. By 1951, the country had 226 schools with 29,887 students. Today, Saudi Arabia's nationwide public educational system comprises eight universities, more than twenty-four thousand schools, and a large number of colleges and other educational and training institutions. The first university, now known as King Saud University, was founded in Riyadh in 1957. Other universities such as the Islamic University of Imam Muhammad Ibn Saud in Riyadh, the Islamic University at Medina or the King Fahd University of Petroleum and Minerals were later founded.

Since the government extended public education to girls in 1960, the public educational system is open to every citizen and provides students with free education, books and health services. Although school is not compulsory, 59% of children were attending primary school in 2002 and the secondary school enrollment ratio reached 53% in 2002. A noticeable increase in literacy over the last decades of the twentieth century is one indicator of the success of the government's efforts. According to 1970 data, the Saudis had one of the lowest literacy rates in the Middle East: 15% for men and 3% for women. In 1990, 66% of the adult population was literate while in 2002 it reached 78% for both men and women.

DIEGO I. MURGUÍA

See also Arabian American Oil Company (ARAMCO); Arab–Israeli Wars (1948, 1956, 1967, 1973); Ethnic Conflicts: Middle East; Middle East: History and Economic Development; Middle East: International Relations; Organization of Exporting Petroleum Countries (OPEC); Palestinian Diaspora

References and Further Reading

Al-Farsy, Fouad. *Saudi Arabia: A Case Study in Development*. London: Kegan Paul International, 1982.
Beling, Willard A., ed. *King Faisal and the Modernisation of Saudi Arabia*. Boulder, CO: Westview Press, 1980.
Economist Intelligence Unit. *Country Profile: Saudi Arabia, 1991–92*. London: 1991.
El Mallakh, Ragaei. *Saudi Arabia. Rush to Development: Profile of an Energy Economy and Development*. Baltimore, MD: Johns Hopkins University Press, 1982.
Lindsey, Gene. *Saudi Arabia*. New York: Hippocrene Books, 1991.
Long, David E. *The Kingdom of Saudi Arabia*. Gainesville, FL: University Press of Florida, 1997.
Looney, Robert E. *Economic Development in Saudi Arabia: Consequences of the Oil Price Decline*. Greenwich, CT: Jai Press, 1990.
Madawi, Al-Rasheed. *A History of Saudi Arabia*. New York: Cambridge University Press, 2002.

SELASSIE, EMPEROR HAILE

Haile Selassie (1892–1975), Conquering Lion of Judah, Elect of God, King of Kings, and 225th emperor of the Ethiopian dynasty was born on July 23, 1892. Until his official coronation at age thirty-eight he was known by his birth name, Tafari Makonnen. His father was a cousin of the progressive Emperor Menelik II. He received a modern education from French missionary tutors. In Tafari's youth, Ethiopia used a feudal system of land tenure. Speakers of the Amhara

language controlled the economy, the established Coptic church and the political system. Most administrators were large landowners. Peasant farmers were taxed up to 90% of their harvest.

By age twenty, Tafari had married Woizero Menen (with whom he eventually had six children). In 1913, Menelik II died and was succeeded by his grandson, Lij Yasu. Yasu sided with Ottoman Turks in World War I, and converted to Islam. Tafari deposed Yasu in 1916. Menelik's daughter Zawditu was named Empress, and Tafari became her regent, and heir apparent, with the title *Ras* (prince). For the next decade Ras Tafari built up his own military force while maneuvering between conservatives and reformers. His heart lay entirely with the latter faction, especially after he returned from his first visit to Europe in 1924. In 1928, he forced Zawditu to crown him as *Negus* (king) and two years later, after Zawditu mysteriously died, he became Emperor with the throne name Haile Selassie I.

Ethiopia, with very few roads across its mountainous terrain and with more than eighty local languages, was nearly ungovernable. Haile Selassie promulgated a constitution in 1931, but this was hardly a move toward democracy, as it provided that "the person of the Emperor is sacred, his dignity inviolable, and his power indisputable." The real purpose was to centralize power. That meant installing relatives as provincial governors and rotating them frequently.

Haile Selassie wanted Ethiopia to have modern schools, clinics, and banks, but his reforms were halted by the Italian invasion of October 1935. He is best remembered for his eloquent but futile appeal to the League of Nations to resist Fascist aggression. He spent five years in London before returning to Addis Ababa with British troops in May 1941.

In the postwar period, Haile Selassie continued, but at a slower pace, his cautious program of modernization. He abolished slavery but was unable to implement land reform. He steered effectively through the shoals of international politics, granted base rights to the United States Air Force, and annexed Eritrea. He held elections for the lower house of parliament in 1957, but continued to rule as an absolute monarch.

From 1960 onward, the Emperor's life grew increasingly difficult. In that year, one of his sons was implicated in a coup attempt. In 1962, his wife died. The seventy-year-old man sought respite from his loneliness by frequent foreign travel (including a visit to Jamaica, where members of the Rastafarian sect greeted him as Jesus Christ) but his government ground to a halt when he was gone. By 1970, he had become isolated, and seemed oblivious to the coming storm. A terrible famine in 1973 and 1974 took the lives of an estimated two hundred thousand people. In February 1974, a general strike called to protest unchecked inflation spread to all sectors of the population, including teachers, taxi drivers, Coptic priests, and even prostitutes. The aged emperor's response was to hand out cash from the window of his limousine.

Haile Selassie was deposed in a military coup on September 12, 1974. He lived out his days under house arrest, still believing, or pretending, that he was in power. The new military government announced on August 27, 1975, that he had died in his sleep, but they hid his remains under a toilet in the palace, where they were discovered in 1992. In November 2000, the emperor was reburied alongside his wife in Addis Ababa's Trinity Cathedral.

Ross Marlay

See also Ethiopia; Rastafarianism

References and Further Reading

Kapuscinski, Ryszard. *The Emperor*. New York: Vintage, 1984.
Schwab, Peter. *Haile Selassie I: Ethiopia's Lion of Judah*. Chicago: Nelson-Hall, 1979.

SELF-DETERMINATION

Self-determination consists of the political and legal processes and structures through which a people gain and maintain control over their own destinies. With the creation of the United Nations (UN), self-determination of peoples became an established principle of international law. The principle is embodied in the Charter of the United Nations and in both the International Covenant on Civil and Political Rights and the International Covenant on Economic, Social and Cultural Rights. Common Article 1(1) of these Covenants provides that: "All peoples have the right of self-determination. By virtue of that right they freely determine their political status and freely pursue their economic, social and cultural development."

The UN General Assembly invoked this principle in its 1960 Declaration on the Granting of Independence to Colonial Countries and Peoples, in which it stated that subjection of peoples to alien domination constitutes a denial of fundamental human rights and violates the peoples' right to freely determine their political status and pursue their economic, social, and cultural development. In accordance with the principle of self-determination, the UN supported the independence of colonies in Africa, Asia, and elsewhere.

Although there is no international legal definition of "peoples," who are entitled to the right of self-determination, the term is generally used to describe

a population who shares the following characteristics: (1) a common historical tradition; (2) self-identity as a distinctive cultural or ethnic group; (3) cultural homogeneity; (4) a shared language; (5) a shared religion; and (6) a traditional territorial connection. In practice, however, the United Nations and its member states have been reluctant to extend the right of self-determination of peoples beyond overseas colonized territories. Even the former colonies (now independent states) are reluctant to recognize their own ethnically distinct citizens' full right to self-determination, fearing it might lead to demands for separation and secession.

Today, many indigenous communities throughout the world are claiming the right to self-determination. These are peoples, such as American Indians and Australian Aborigines, who constitute a "first people," with a prior history of territorial occupation and an ancestral attachment to their land before it was conquered and occupied by others. They now live within existing states as subordinate peoples. They are determined, however, to preserve and transmit to future generations their ancestral territories and their ethnic identity, as the bases of their continued existence as peoples with their own cultural patterns, social institutions, and legal systems.

Indigenous peoples see their situations as being identical to those of colonized peoples who have been conquered and then ruled by others. They argue that the so-called "salt water test" (which limits the rights of self-determination to colonized lands that exist across the oceans from the colonizing country) should not apply to them. Other conquered peoples claiming the right to self-determination include the Chechens, who are dominated by Russia; the Palestinians, whose land is occupied by Israel; the Kurds, living in Turkey, Iraq and Iran; and the Catholics of Northern Ireland. The first three of these peoples want to establish their own independent states, while the Northern Irish Catholics want to become part of Ireland.

The right of self-determination conflicts with the principle of preserving the territorial integrity of sovereign states—a principle also found in the UN Charter. Although the exercise of self-determination can include secession from an existing state and the creation of a new one, it also includes other less dramatic choices. The UN General Assembly's 1970 Declaration on Principles of International Law concerning Friendly Relations and Cooperation among States explains that implementation of the right to self-determination need not conflict with the territorial sovereignty or political unity of a state. The Declaration provides that a people exercising their right of self-determination may choose to form a federation with an existing state, integration into an existing state as an autonomous region, or "any other political status freely determined by a people" short of secession.

The Declaration goes on to explain the conditions under which peoples are not justified in seeking secession and independence from a sovereign state. It states that independent countries possessing a government that effectively represent the whole of their population (ethnic minorities included) are considered to be conducting themselves in conformity with the principle of equal rights and self-determination of peoples. For example, if an indigenous people or ethnic minority reside in a democratic state that enables them to participate effectively in the political process and economy and to practice their religion and culture, then they are exercising their right of self-determination and have no cause to secede. When this is not the case, however, peoples have the right to act to control their own destinies.

The right to secede is an option of last resort, justified by serious government violations of human rights, persistent discrimination, and other grave injustices. Self-determination examples of succession in recent decades include the dissolution of the Soviet Union and Yugoslavia, the separation of East Pakistan from West Pakistan to form Bangladesh, and the separation of East Timor from Indonesia. In each of these cases, distinct peoples created independent states and thereby shattered the federations or unitary state of which they had been a part.

Examples of self-determination within an existing state include Italy's five special autonomous regions with extensive local powers defined by the constitution: Trentino–Alto Adige (containing the German-speaking people of the South Tyrol), Friuli–Venezia Giulia (containing Slovene and Friulian speakers), Val d'Aosta (containing French speakers), as well as the islands of Sardinia and Sicily. Each of these regions has unique, "non-Italian" cultural, linguistic, and historical characteristics that have justified extensive delegations of powers from Rome to the regional authorities to permit decision-making on local educational, economic, cultural, and budgetary issues.

Some other autonomy arrangements include the Sami Parliaments in the Nordic countries, the Nunavut territory in Canada, and the ancestral territory of indigenous people in Panama.

The trend in world politics has been for enlightened states to attempt sincerely to accommodate the self-determination aspirations of their ethnic minorities, while other states continue to suppress and deny their minorities or subjugated peoples this fundamental right.

PAUL J. MAGNARELLA

See also Political Culture

References and Further Reading

Anaya, S. James. *Indigenous Peoples in International Law.* New York: Oxford University Press, 1996.

Burger, Julian. *The Gaia Atlas of First Peoples.* New York: Anchor Books, 1990.

Cassese, Antonio. *Self-Determination of Peoples.* Cambridge: Cambridge University Pres, 1995.

Lam, Maivan Clech. *At the Edge of the State: Indigenous Peoples and the Right of Self-Determination.* Ardsley, NY: Transnational Publishers, 2000.

Moody, Roger, editor. *The Indigenous Voice.* London: Zed Books, 1988.

Musgrave, Thomas D. *Self-Determination and National Minorities.* Oxford: Clarendon Press, 1997.

Thornberry, Patrick. *International Law and the Rights of Minorities.* Oxford: Clarendon Press, 1991.

SENEGAL

The Republic of Senegal is a coastal West African country just south of the Sahara Desert, bordered by Mauritania, Mali, Guinea, and Guinea-Bissau. The country has about 310 miles of Atlantic coastline. The Gambia constitutes a sliver of territory about twenty miles wide and two hundred miles long that extends from the coast eastward along the Gambia River, separating the southern region of the Casamance from the rest of Senegal. The climate is predominantly tropical, with a rainy season, lasting from June through October, followed by a cool dry season. The greatest amount of rainfall occurs in the south, which receives about seventy inches annually, compared to twenty inches in the far north along the Senegal River. The nation is drained by the Senegal, Sine, Saloum, Gambia and Casamance Rivers. Flat, rolling plains and sandy soil characterize much of Senegal except in the Casamance region which has some forest areas. The population is estimated at approximately 10 million, with an estimated growth rate of 3.3% annually. The capital, Dakar, situated on the Atlantic coast, has a population of about 1.7 million.

Prior to French occupation and the consolidation of colonial rule in the middle to late nineteenth century, the Senegal region was dominated by a series of Muslim Wolof and Fulbe kingdoms and some non-Muslim Serer states. Wars among the various states produced significant numbers of slaves for the trans-Atlantic trade. With abolition of slavery in the early nineteenth century, the French shifted their emphasis to the production and export of peanuts, creating a monocrop colony. Throughout the colonial period, Senegal occupied a special place in the Federation of West Africa. In 1960, the country achieved independence under the leadership of Leopold Sedar Senghor, a prominent intellectual as well as politician.

Senghor maintained close ties with France, which continued to supply considerable technical, financial, and military assistance to the country. He also courted the powerful Muslim brotherhoods whose support was critical to his electoral victories and the dominance of his Socialist Party. The country was often hailed as one of the few democracies in Africa with an enviable record of religious toleration and ethnic cooperation. The military was kept in check and did not interfere in politics. However, the monocrop economy, centered on peanut production, was vulnerable to world market fluctuations and the severe Sahelian droughts of the 1970s. The state intervened directly in the economy, with poor results. When Senghor voluntarily handed over power in 1980 to his chosen successor, Abdou Diouf, the country faced a serious economic crisis. Diouf continued his predecessor's policies of strong ties to France and close cooperation with the Muslim leadership. Diouf attempted to diversify the economy by promoting fishing and tourism. He also announced a plan to privatize state-owned firms, but economic progress was minimal. Falling export values, rising costs of living, periodic droughts, and growing unemployment, especially among secondary school and university graduates, led to some unrest among students and the urban population in Dakar, most notably in widespread riots in 1988. Diouf also faced a mounting secessionist movement in the largely non-Muslim and non-Wolof southern region of the Casamance. In 1989, ethnic tensions with Mauritania erupted into massacres and mass repatriation between the two countries. Despite these problems, Diouf and the Socialist party continued to dominate national politics throughout the 1980s and 1990s.

In 1994, the devaluation of Senegal's currency, which is tied to the French franc, caused serious economic disruption, especially in the urban areas. Inflation, falling living standards, rapid urbanization and population growth, and a decline in agricultural production led to increased discontent with the regime. In the late 1990s, Senegalese intervention in a coup d'etat in neighboring Guinea-Bissau and a harsh crackdown on Casamance separatists further eroded popular support for the regime. In the elections of 2000, Abdoulaye Wade, a long-time leader of the Senegalese Democratic Party and the candidate of a coalition of opposition parties, defeated Diouf who retired from politics. Wade has promised economic reform and privatization, political liberalization, and a peaceful resolution to the secessionist crisis in the Casamance. Progress in all these areas has been slow. The secessionist movement in the Casamance has continued with mounting casualties on both sides. Much of the nation's trade is dominated by Lebanese and French merchants who deposit their profits overseas. While

some peace talks have been initiated with Casamance rebels, violence has dramatically curtailed the tourism industry, one of the region's few economic prospects.

Senegal's economic infrastructure, which at independence was relatively advanced for the region, has deteriorated somewhat since the 1970s. Some roads have been constructed but the railroads, built during colonial rule, are antiquated and unreliable. Plans for a bridge across the Gambia River to link the northern and southern regions remain at a standstill. The port at Dakar needs modernization to accommodate larger vessels, and the fisheries industry has not been actively developed. Senegal has some phosphate deposits but advances have been slow in exploiting the resource. The country does have two universities, one in Dakar and one in Saint-Louis, and numerous secondary schools. During the Senghor and Diouf years, the schools were periodically closed to prevent unrest. The adult literacy rate averages less than 50%, and is markedly lower in the rural areas. Modern health care is accessible to only a small, urban elite group. France continues to provide large amounts of aid, as do some oil-rich Muslim states. Another important source of income is remittances from Senegalese living in Europe and the United States. Migration from the rural areas to Dakar, and out-migration to other countries, pose serious problems for the country. Although over 90% of the population is Muslim, there is no militant Islamic movement of note in the country. Lack of noticeable improvement in the nation's economy may lead to serious political and social disruption in the future.

ANDREW F. CLARK

References and Further Reading

Behrman, Lucy. *Muslim Brotherhoods and Politics in Senegal*. Cambridge, MA: Harvard University Press, 1970.

Boone, Catherine. *Merchant Capital and the Roots of State Power in Senegal, 1930–1985*. Cambridge, UK: Cambridge University Press, 1992.

Clark, Andrew F. "Imperialism, Independence and Islam in Senegal and Mali," *Africa Today* 46, no. 3/4, 1999.

—— and Lucie C. Phillips. *Historical Dictionary of Senegal*. Metuchen, NJ: Scarecrow Press, 1994.

Cruise O'Brien, Donal B. *Saints and Politicians: Essays in the Organization of a Senegalese Peasant Society*. Cambridge, UK: Cambridge University Press, 1975.

Curtin, Philip. *Economic Change in Precolonial Africa: Senegambia in the Era of the Slave Trade*. Madison, WI: University of Wisconsin Press, 1975.

Gellar, Sheldon. *Senegal: An African Nation Between Islam and the West*. Boulder, CO: Westview Press, 1995.

Vengroff, Richard and Lucy Creevey. "Senegal: The Evolution of a Quasi Democracy," in *Political Reform in Francophone Africa*, edited by John F. Clark and David E. Gardiner, Boulder, CO: Westview Press, 1997.

Villalon, Leonardo. *Islamic Society and State Power in Senegal*. Cambridge, UK: Cambridge University Press, 1995.

SÉNGHOR, LEOPOLD

The founding father and first president of the Republic of Senegal in West Africa from 1960 to 1980, Leopold Sedar Senghor is one of Africa's outstanding intellectual and political figures. A Roman Catholic and member of the Serer ethnic group, he led a predominantly Muslim and Wolof nation. Although an intellectual, his greatest appeal was to the peasants. He is also a renowned poet and the main promoter of the concept of *negritude*. In 1983, he was the first African elected to the prestigious *Academie Francaise*. He retired to France in the 1980s.

Lepold Sedar Sénghor was born October 9, 1906, in Joal, a coastal town in central Senegal. His father was a Serer Catholic and his mother a Fulani Muslim, but Senghor was raised as a Catholic in predominantly Muslim Senegal. The country is also dominated by the Wolof ethnic group, making Senghor a "double minority." He was also the major political figure not to come from the "Four Communes" where Africans could get French citizenship and special privileges. He attended the Ngasobil Catholic Mission School and prepared for the priesthood at Libermann Seminary in Dakar but he transferred to the Public Secondary School in Dakar (later Lycee Van Vollenhoven). By all accounts, he was an exceptional pupil. In 1928, he went to France to study at the Lycee Louis le Grand where one of his classmates was Georges Pompidou, later president of France. They remained lifelong friends.

In France in the 1930s, inspired by the romantic vision of Africa in Harlem Renaissance authors and early European ethnographers, Senghor began to produce poetry that helped launch the concept of *negritude*. He contrasted African ways with all that he considered wrong with the West—rationalism, mechanization, capitalism, materialism, bourgeois values, individualism, competition, and a stiff, cold ugliness. He became one of the first Africans to express discontent with the French colonial policy of assimilation. He retained an intense and lifelong admiration for French culture, especially in the fields of language, literature, and philosophy. He married a Frenchwoman and always spent considerable time in France.

In 1931, Senghor received his *licence es lettres*. In 1935, he became the first African to pass the *Agregation* competitive examination, but only after he had become a naturalized French citizen. The following year he was drafted into the French army. After military service, he taught in Tours and outside of Paris. At the start of World War II, he was again called up. After being captured and nearly killed by German troops, he spent two years as a prisoner of war and upon his release in 1942, he returned to teaching near Paris and worked with the French resistance.

With the end of the war, his literary career reached fruition with the publication of his first volume of poetry, *Chants d'Ombre*. In 1945, he entered politics and was elected a deputy to the French Assembly with the support of the French Socialist Party. In 1948, Senghor formed the *Bloc Democratie Senegalais* which promoted a type of "African socialism," based on traditional village cooperation, religious faith, and a new nationalism. That same year, he and Alioune Diop launched *Presence Africaine*, a Paris magazine devoted to the promotion of African culture and *negritude*. He was also appointed professor at the *Ecole nationale d'Outre-Mer*.

When given the choice in 1958 to vote for autonomy or continued association with France, Senghor argued strongly for autonomy and continued close ties with France. But in 1960, as the French ended colonial rule in West Africa, Senghor negotiated independence for the Mali Federation (Senegal and French Soudan, later Mali) which became independent in June. The federation quickly fell apart and Senghor declared Senegal an independent republic. He was elected president and he appointed Mamadou Dia prime minister. Senghor quickly nationalized peanut marketing, initiated rural cooperatives, and instituted a national system of agricultural credit, extension services, and cooperative administration. He also carefully courted powerful Muslim leaders.

In 1962, a constitutional crisis erupted and Mamadou Dia and his top allies were arrested and imprisoned for treason. The constitution was rewritten to provide for a single, strong executive, and Senghor ruled with an iron hand for the next eight years. Opposition parties were eliminated through banning or absorption, and freedom of the press and association were severely limited. Senghor overcame political unrest in 1963 and student riots in 1968 by force. He was reelected president unopposed in 1963, 1968, and 1973. His strong political position allowed him free reign to promote African culture. The Festival of Negro Arts in Dakar in 1966 crowned his promotion of *negritude*. He helped set up various regional development associations, winning him respect as an elder statesman. However, Senegal's economic base did not expand, the national debt increased and infrastructure deteriorated. The Senegalese peasants, however, never wavered in their admiration for Senghor.

In 1970, Senghor felt confident enough to reintroduce the position of prime minister and appointed Abdou Diouf, an obscure young technocrat. Two opposition parties were legalized in the 1970s but Senghor still won the 1978 election in a landslide. He changed the name of his political party from the *Union Progressiste Senegalaise* to the *Parti Socialiste* (PS). The 1970s were a particularly difficult period for

the Senegalese economy with a major drought in the mid-1970s and declining prices and demand for peanuts, the country's only real export. Many of the socialist policies promoted by Senghor were clearly not working. Even large amounts of international assistance, especially from France, did not improve economic conditions. Senghor appeared increasingly distant and aloof from politics, with Abou Diouf taking over the running of the daily government and international affairs. Senghor continued to write poetry. In 1974, he won the Apollonaire Prize for Poetry and he published volumes of poetry in 1979 and 1980. On December 31, 1980, Senghor resigned in favor of Diouf who ruled the country for the next twenty years. Senghor thus became the first African leader installed at independence to resign voluntarily.

In 1983, he was the first African elected to the *Acadamie Francaise*. He continued to pursue his career as one of Africa's most respected statesmen, remaining on the international scene for many years being involved with the Socialist International and the Palestine Liberation Organization. In 1988, he published a philosophical memoir, *Ce que je crois* (What I Believe). He also published some poetry in the 1990s. He now lives in Verson, France, the home of his wife, and is rarely seen in public.

ANDREW F. CLARK

See also Ethnic Conflicts: West Africa; Senegal; West Africa: History and Economic Development; West Africa: International Relations

References and Further Reading

Ba, Sylvia. *The Concept of Negritude in the Poetry of Leopold Senghor*. Princeton, NJ: University Press, 1973.

Collins, Grace. *Trumpet for His People: Leopold Sedar Senghor of Senegal*. New York: Sights Productions, 1995.

Klubach, William. *Leopold Sedar Senghor: From Politics to Poetry*. New York: Peter Lang, 1997.

Markovitz, Irving. *Leopold Sedar Senghor and the Politics of Negritude*., New York: Atheneum, 1969.

Spleth, Janice. *Leopold Sedar Senghor*. New York: Macmillan, 1985.

Vaillant, Janet. *Black, French and African: A Life of Leopold Sedar Senghor*. Cambridge, MA: Harvard University Press, 1990.

SERBIA

The largest of former Yugoslavia's republics, and currently a partner with Montenegro in a loose union known as Serbia and Montenegro, Serbia is located in the heart of Southeastern Europe. Its location plays an important role as a traffic corridor between Western Europe and Asia. In terms of physical geography,

the country has an ideal combination of Panonian and Kosovo lowlands in the north and south, separated by uplands that reach elevations exceeding seven thousand feet. Although technically landlocked, Serbia has a direct connection with the global sea through the Danube River. The climate is continental with cold, occasionally harsh, winters and hot summers. The population is 7.5 million, without Kosovo and Metohija province. If this province is included, the population is estimated to be approximately 10 million. The capital, Belgrade (1.57 million), is a modern city that grew from an ancient settlement. It is situated at the juncture of the Sava and Danube rivers.

Serbia's ethnic and religious composition is rather complex. Serbs, people of South Slavic origin and generally practitioners of Eastern Orthodox Christian religion, constitute two thirds of the population. Ethnic Albanians, who are overwhelmingly Muslim, and for political reasons boycott the census, are the largest minority group. They number approximately 16% to 17% of the population and are found primarily in Kosovo and Metohija. Hungarians are a Roman Catholic minority with significant numbers in the province of Vojvodina.

As is true of its neighboring states, Serbia's history began during medieval times when it emerged as a kingdom under the rule of the Nemanjić dynasty. Before falling under control of the advancing Ottoman Empire, the Serbian kingdom reached its greatest extent during the period of Dušan Nemanjić's reign (1331–1355). Although he built a strong empire, it crumbled soon after Dušan's death. For the next four centuries, Serbia was a province of the Ottoman Empire. It often became a war torn area during the endless conflicts between Ottomans and Habsburgs over their quest for domination of Southeastern Europe. This conflict, in fact, slowed the pace of development that was occurring in other parts of Europe at the time. When it finally achieved independence from the Turks in 1878, Serbia lagged far behind much of the remainder of Europe in terms of both political and economic development. It was primarily an agricultural country with a dominantly peasant population and with very little urban industrial development. In addition to its historical lack of development, economic growth was further hindered by the country's involvement in several wars. After World War I, the South Slavs joined the new country known since 1929 as Yugoslavia. The Serbian dynasty, Karaorević, ruled the country.

Until World War II, agriculture remained the leading economic activity. Yet in the war's aftermath, the situation gradually began changing with the implementation of new economic policies in the late 1940s and early 1950s. Communist revolutionaries gained power and abolished the kingdom. They promoted rapid urbanization and industrialization wherever possible. A Socialist self-management economic policy, involving worker-managed enterprises, was implemented. It proved to be both different and more effective than the Soviet-style management and was largely responsible for the improved economic growth and living conditions experienced during the 1950s, improved the conditions and growth during the 1950s. Unfortunately, additional reforms that could have reduced inflation and limited the mounting external debt were blocked in the 1960s, because of fear that reforms might undermine communist ideology and weaken communism's strength and importance. Serbia suffered limited economic growth under the burden of communist control, while both the rate of inflation and unemployment increased during the following decade. Many citizens, rather than being unemployed at home, emigrated westward to more developed republics, or elsewhere in Europe.

At the time of President Tito's death in 1980, Serbia and other former Yugoslav republics were suffering severe economic difficulties, including high foreign debt. As a country that relied on imports for its energy, Serbia was further crippled economically by soaring oil prices. Internal ethnic problems were at the same time fueling the rise of nationalism and separatism in Kosovo and Metohija province, Serbia's least developed region. A great majority of the province's residents were ethnic Albanians who believed that their rights were endangered. Poor economic conditions, high unemployment, exploding population growth, and sharp cultural differences increased antagonisms between Serbs and ethnic Albanians who agitated for Kosovo and Metohija's elevation to the status of a republic independent from Serbia. In 1987, by riding the wave of reactionary Serb nationalism, Slobodan Milošević became a leading figure in Serbia's governing body, the League of Communists. Immediately, he began to implement hard measures on Kosovo and Metohija. Two years later he was elected president of Serbia which, in the aftermath of former Yugoslavia's 1991 breakup, formed a union (also called Yugoslavia) with Montenegro in 1992. Because of direct involvement in ethnic conflicts in Croatia and Bosnia and Herzegovina, Serbia suffered both politically and economically from the sanctions implemented by the international community. Inflation, measured in thousands of percent, skyrocketed to some of the highest rates ever recorded. International trade relations almost disintegrated and the local economy underwent restructuring. Yet the country continued to fall into an ever deeper crisis.

By the end of the twentieth century, the gross domestic product (GDP) had plummeted more than

50% below the 1990 level. In addition to the already existing crisis, NATO's attack against Serbia in 1999 destroyed much of its still functioning infrastructure. An air campaign conducted to prevent hostilities in Kosovo and Metohija targeted communications, factories, bridges, power plants, and administration buildings throughout the country. In the years that followed, Serbians ousted Milošević—who ruled as president of Serbia and Yugoslavia for over a decade—elected a new government, and was able to finally remove the long-standing economic sanctions. Even though the military conflict is now over, economic hardship continues. Inflation is under control, but the unemployment rate is close to 30%, with the underemployment rate standing much higher. Drastic budget cuts that were necessary to manage fiscal deficits allow hardly any additional spending. The government continues to rely on foreign assistance in order to prevent yet another crisis, a situation hardly conducive to the development of a stable, long-term economic policy.

ZORAN PAVLOVIĆ

See also Balkan Wars of the 1990s; Tito, Josip Broz (Marshall Tito); Yugoslavia

References and Further Reading

Ćirkovic, Sima. *Serbs*. Malden, MA: Blackwell Publishing, 2004.
Country Watch Incorporated. *Serbia and Montenegro Country Review*. Houston, 2004.
Silber, Laura, and Little Allan. *Yugoslavia: Death of a Nation*. New York: Penguin Books, 1997.
Thomas, Robert. *The Politics of Serbia in the 1990s*. New York: Columbia University Press, 1999.

SEX TRADE/TRAFFICKING

Descriptions of how the bodies of women and children can become sexual commodities to be traded and trafficked range from compassionate elucidations of Geisha values and practices to examinations of the socioeconomic basis for using children for sex. Understanding how people's bodies become sexual commodities through development processes can be gained by focusing on Asia and Eastern Europe. Although different geographic regions they are enmeshed in similar global relations of power.

Many texts examine how clients from First World countries, who use impoverished people's bodies for sex, frame their social values in terms of racial and economic dominance. And, within economically disadvantaged countries, sex trade workers can experience profoundly different work encounters due to social prejudice, unequal privilege, and class difference.

Many poor Asian countries, for example, are shaped by ambiguous yet powerful notions of economic 'development' that are predicated on the use of women and children's bodies in particular. Since World War II, Asian peoples' exposure to military bases, the unequal distribution of wealth and employment opportunities, and social perceptions of women's family role, have placed acute pressures on women to earn an income. Despite their gains towards social, political, and legal equality, impoverished Asian and Eastern European women and children also remain the targets of sexual violence. Class and caste-based prejudices are forged by perceptions of their social and sexual inferiority in societies that are intensely patriarchal in structures, relations, and ideologies.

Sex trade workers should not, however, be conceived solely as "victims." Researchers note the real physical dangers of sexually transmitted diseases among sex workers but many also show how sex workers negotiate their daily experience. It is important to acknowledge the diversity of people who work in the global sex trade, their differing motivations, and the variation in how they may be coerced. A singular notion of the prostitute is reductive for "the prostitute" does not exist. Rather, there are different women, men, and children whose bodies are marketed as commodities within an assorted range of circumstances and for a variety of purposes. Examining the difficulties of their lives within the context of the social, economic, and political constraints of class and country enables a more complex and compassionate understanding of their experiences to be portrayed.

The Sex Trade and Sex Tourism

In the past twenty-five years, there has been a substantial rise in mass tourism, particularly to "developing" countries. Immediately after the 1940–1945 war, most travel trafficked between North America and Western Europe. A change then occurred in the mid-1970s: from 8% of tourists who travelled to third world countries, the figure rose to 17% in the mid-1980s. Mass tourism was promoted by international power brokers such as the World Bank and the International Monetary Fund as an integral part of modernisation and development processes. To promote growth and social transformation, tourism was marketed as an industry that would metamorphose poor countries' poverty into an unspoilt paradise that would draw desirable foreign currency.

Tourism now provides a conduit for foreign currency that Third World countries require in order to operate in the global marketplace. Yet the ways that

tourism is organised can range from benign indifference to deliberate economic and political exploitation. Critics argue that media images, tourist brochures, and airline advertising have exhorted the yielding promise of the "Singapore girl," Thailand as the "Land of Smiles," or Lauda Air's offer to "Fly Your Dreams" through the naked body of a woman of color. Images of women as uni-dimensional objects are associated with corporate male adventure and domesticated female availability, selling Third World tourism while simultaneously constructing women and young children as unspoiled and powerless resources, ready to be acquired.

Acquisitive economic power relations are linked with women and children's impoverishment as key factors that shape the sex trade, for destitution affects women and men differently. Researchers argue that the social myths that women do not acquire financial responsibilities during their lifetimes are simplistic, given that more than a third of the world's households are headed by women who are solely responsible for all their household production and needs. Women are further disadvantaged when life circumstances dictate they become head of household, because they lack the necessary social support and training.

Inequalities in development become clear when recognising that women and children from poorer countries are trafficked to wealthier. Thai women have increasingly been trafficked to Japan since the 1970s. The trade peaked during the early 1990s, with estimations that there were about one hundred thousand Filipino and Thai sex workers in Japan. It is important to recognise also that trafficking is not limited to impoverished Third World countries. A Belgian court has sentenced eight people for participating in a criminal ring that trafficked pre-pubescent girls from Hungary and Romania to Belgium for forced sex work. The example shows that there are multiple suppliers and many destinations for women and children drawn into the global sex trade and how raw relations of economic, physical, and gendered power have shaped "sex" into an international industry.

The international and gendered nature of sex trafficking is also manifested in rich nation-state men crossing borders to purchase the use of other's bodies. Eighty-five percent of tourists into the Philippines are male. Further, the growing trade in Eastern European women to destinations such as Germany, the United States, Switzerland, Japan, and Macau supports substantial criminal involvement, with most trafficking businesses owned or protected by criminal groups. Inhabitants from European Union affiliated countries are legally able to start businesses in the Netherlands, so that criminal groups may use lawful opportunities to enter the sex trade.

The Sex Trade and Free Choice

The common structural factors to the sex trade and trafficking as connections to development are the impoverishment of women, social, and cultural perceptions of women and children's bodies as profitable commodities, and the increased acceptance of capitalism as the primary economic and political frame. So why do perceptions of sex work as profitable enterprise and protestations that women and children assert free choice when entering the industry exist? Critics argue that "choice" encompasses negotiating and enforcing contracts on terms that also suit the sex worker. But there are reports that some clients use impoverished children *because* they are seen to eroticise extreme powerlessness. The reports suggest there is little public recognition that conditions of work can constitute modern slavery and provide opportunities for sadistic practices.

Critics allege that the sex trade mirrors relations of domination, subordination and exploitation between First and Third Worlds. Men travel from bordering countries, such as Malaysia with Thailand, and Middle Eastern countries where religious censure restricts sexual practices. Consumers in countries such as Thailand or Sri Lanka exploit the permissive attitude towards sex with children. They are individuals, small groups of friends, and larger groups of men travelling as a company bonus. They enjoy the novelty of a different experience and an escape from the constraints of the social codes and customs of home. Although many travel specifically to use impoverished women and children's bodies for sex governments maintain an ambiguous standpoint, arguing that any tourist is welcome due to their expenditure of foreign currency.

Significantly however, and in contrast to Westerners' profession of an ideology that favours and protects children until their late teenage years, research has exposed the conflicting reality of indigent children. Undercover agents have been offered children of four, five, or six years of age for sexual use. Rather than discussing sex work as consensual acts of sexuality between adults, researchers have analysed how well-bred squeamishness and crosscultural blindness to behaviour outside First World countries means that the global criminalisation of the use of children for sex is resisted. Prejudices of race, age, class, and gender intersect to culturally sanction sex with children that do not safeguard their psyches and bodies. Such work shows how the notion of worker control is a conceptual delusion for impoverished children who have nothing other than their bodies to sell in order to survive, and who are enmeshed in relations where powerlessness has sexual value.

There is a "need" that drives a consumer-oriented society that works on the principle of supply and demand, in which the growth of child prostitution can occur only because there are people who want such services. Indeed, estimates suggest that 1,380,000 children are presently working in the commercial sex trade in Asia and the Pacific Islands, more than 702,000 in Latin America, in the United States one hundred thousand to three hundred thouand. Global profits from trafficking in children for sexual exploitation reach approximately $5 billion per year.

Pragmatists argue that while community responses must be examined and enacted, there are strong arguments for global society to guarantee the safety and interests of its most vulnerable members. They propose a deeper political awareness of the problem in terms of creating relevant legislation, effective implementation of the law, and adequate penalties such as mandatory jail sentences rather than fines of a few hundred dollars. However, because legislation is rarely written with a consideration for children it can conflict with customary law that maintains patriarchal control. Community organisations consequently need to develop educational programs aimed at children, parents, and community leaders, particularly stressing the strong social bonds of rural communities so that children are not merely exchanged for consumer goods.

It is proposed that parliamentarians must also recognise that: (1) rising gross national product in many third world countries is produced through the bodies of women and children as merchandise in the sex trade; (2) tourists are not above a host country's law and that traffic in children is as malignant as traffic in drugs; and (3) countries that are targeted as destinations for paedophiles should not bear the educative burden of local communities alone. Social commentators argue that an international effort to make the child sex trade a crime against humanity must be conducted and, as is the case in Australia, internationalising the crime would ensure that nationals are tried in their home country.

Researchers' analyses of the sex trade in the impoverished countries of Eastern Europe and Asia argue that development processes, travel, and sex trafficking are profoundly gendered. Male capacity to control women and children's sense of security and self-worth is at the heart of the sex trade's power relations. Yet women and children's personal and physical lives cannot be separated from the increasingly complex, globalised, and commodified relations of power generated within development processes. Authors argue that sex workers should not be judged but that ethical boundaries should be imposed upon the use of sexual labour.

HELEN JOHNSON

See also Children and Development; Women: Role in Development

References and Further Reading

Allison, Anne. *Nightwork: Sexuality, Pleasure, and Corporate Masculinity in a Tokyo Hostess Club.* Chicago and London: The University of Chicago Press, 1994.

Atlink, Sietske. *Stolen Lives: Trading Women into Sex and Slavery.* London and New York: Scarlet Press and Harrington Park Press, 1995.

Brock, Rita and Susan Thistlethwaite. *Casting Stones: Prostitution and Liberation in Asia and the United States.* Minneapolis: Fortress Press, 1996.

Dalby, Liza. *Geisha.* Berkeley, Los Angeles, London: University of California Press, 1998.

Davidson, Julia. *Prostitution, Power and Freedom.* Cambridge, Oxford: Polity Press, 1998.

Enloe, Cynthia. *Bananas, Beaches, and Bases.* London: Pandora, 1989.

Odzer, Cleo. *Patpong Sisters: An American Woman's View of the Bangkok Sex World.* New York: Arcade Publishing, 1994.

O'Grady, Ron. *The Child and the Tourist: The Story Behind the Escalation of Child Prostitution in Asia.* The Campaign to End Child Prostitution in Asian Tourism (ECPAT), Bangkok: Thailand, 1992.

Pettman, Jan J. *Worlding Women: A Feminist International Politics.* Sydney: Allen & Unwin, 1996.

Sleightholme, Carolyn, and Indrani Sinha. *Guilty Without Trial: Women in the Sex Trade in Calcutta.* New Brunswick, NJ: Rutgers University Press, 1997.

Vanwesenbeeck, Ina. *Prostitutes Well-being and Risk.* Amsterdam: VU Uitgeverij, 1994.

Williams, Phil, editor. *Illegal Immigration and Commercial Sex: The New Slave Trade.* London: Frank Cass, 1999.

Wood, Carl, editor. *Sexual Positions: An Australian View.* Melbourne: Hill of Content, 2001.

SEYCHELLES

The Republic of Seychelles is an archipelago in the Indian Ocean off the East-African coast north of Madagascar. Consisting of 115 islands—partly granitic, partly coralline—Seychelles are scattered over 1.3 million square kilometers of ocean. The total landmass adds up to 454 square kilometers. Only thirty-three islands are inhabited. The main island, Mahé, has an area of 154 square kilometers and rises to over nine hundred meters at its highest point. Of the approximately eighty-one thousand inhabitants about 80% live on Mahé, most of them in the capital, Victoria. Being located outside the cyclone belt, Seychelles have a most favorable tropical climate with average maximum temperatures around 30°C and average minimum temperatures around 24°C.

Originally uninhabited, Seychelles were claimed by the French in 1756 and named after the influential French family de Séchelles. The first settlement was

established in 1770 and some rather unsuccessful efforts were taken to cultivate rice and maize based on slave labor. When a British Naval squadron took possession of Mahé in 1794 total population was less than two thousand. In spite of the British claim French administration continued, the status of the islands being uncertain for two decades. In 1810, the British invaded the Île de France, and in 1814 British sovereignty over the islands in the south-west Indian Ocean, including Seychelles, was established by the Treaty of Paris. Britain's interest in the southwest Indian Ocean Islands rather followed strategic considerations than developmental concerns. Hence Seychelles, administered from Mauritius, comprised a rather neglected part of the British Empire throughout the nineteenth century. When Seychelles took up copra production in the late nineteenth century living conditions improved, however, with the opening of the Suez Canal the route around Africa became less important and Seychelles lost their strategic position and were virtually cut off from shipping routes. In 1903, Seychelles was separated from Mauritius becoming a colony of its own. Colonial legacy is reflected in the official languages of modern Seychelles, English, French, and Seselwa. Seselwa—or simply Kreol—a French based creole-language is spoken by over 95% of Seychelois.

First elections for four of the twelve seats in the Legislative Counsel were held in 1948; however, franchise was restricted to literacy and property. Universal adult franchise was introduced only in 1967, when two newly established parties, the *Seychelles Democratic Party* (SDP), led by James Mancham, and the *Seychelles People's United Party* (SPUP), led by France-Albert René, won four respectively three of the eight elected seats. Subsequently a new constitution was adopted, widening the government's responsibilities. New elections in 1970 resulted in a victory of the SDP and Mancham became chief minister, a position he held until independence in 1976. Following independence Mancham became the first elected president of the newly formed Republic of Seychelles, with René being prime minister in a coalition government. In 1977, Mancham was overthrown in a coup d'etat, when Tanzanian trained Seychelois rebels took over power and made René president. It is hardly disputed that the coup was engineered by René and Tanzanian president Julius Nyerere. However, while René's personal ambitions must not be neglected, Marcus Franda points to the possibility that Mancham's international reputation as a playboy, spending more time abroad than governing his country while his duties were left to information minister David Jaubert, a notorious man-about-town, may have furthered events (Franda 1982:49 ff.). As of 1978 Seychelles

was declared a single-party state governed according to "socialist" principles. However, the government managed to avoid any deeper involvement in the east-west conflict. At the same time the SPUP merged with other, smaller parties and was renamed *Seychelles People's Progressive Front* (SPPF). In 1979 and successive elections, René was confirmed in office by more than 90% of the votes in each case. A failed coup in 1981 lead to prosecution and imprisonment of the alleged mercenaries in Seychelles and South Africa. According to their leader, Michael Hoare, the mercenaries were supported by South African military and intelligence officials; however, this involvement was not officially confirmed. In 1991, the SPPF declared an end to the one-party state and drafting of a new constitution was initiated. After rejection by the electorate in 1992, a revised constitution was approved in a 1993 referendum. Accordingly the president is both head of state and head of government. The cabinet is appointed by the president and has to be approved by the parliament. In subsequent presidential elections René was reelected president with 59.5% of the votes. Parliamentary elections held at the same time yielded twenty-eight seats for the SPPF, four seats for Mancham's reestablished SDP, and one seat for the newly founded *Parti Seselwi*, later renamed *Seychelles National Party* (SNP), originally founded as an underground movement by the Anglican priest Wavel Ramkalavan. Freedom of press and independence of the national broadcasting corporation were granted in 1992 and at the same time the state of emergency, declared after the 1981 coup attempt, was abolished. In the latest presidential elections in 2001, René was reelected with 54.19% while Ramkalavan gained 44.95% of the votes. In April 2004, René stepped down in favor of vice-president James Michel. The latest parliamentary elections in 2002 yielded 54.3% and twenty-three seats for the SPPF and 42.6% and eleven seats for the SNP.

Regarding economical and social development, major improvements have been achieved only within the last thirty years. Despite governor Percy Selwyn-Clarke's attempts in the late 1940s to improve public schooling, housing, and health service which were quickly canceled when Selwyn-Clarke was removed from office in 1952, no progress worth mentioning was gained during the last colonial decades. With construction of the international airport on Mahé in 1971, however, the foundation of the country's most important economical resource—tourism—was laid. Following the 1977 coup, measures were taken to develop fishing industry and agriculture in order to diversify the economic basis. For this purpose a number of parastatal companies were founded. Most important trading partner is the EU. As of 2002, the per capita gross domestic product was $18,232 PPP— the

highest rate in sub-Saharan Africa while life expectancy is estimated at seventy-one years. Medical care is free for all citizens. While in colonial times primary education was provided either privately or by the church, following independence the educational system was nationalized, improved and a polytechnic and several training centers for post-secondary education were established. As of 2002, 99.1% of citizens between fifteen and twenty-four years of age are literate. The tsunami of 2004 is reported to have caused relatively minor damage.

LARS V. KARSTEDT

See also Nyerere, Julius

References and Further Reading

Bennett, George. *Seychelles*. Oxford etc.: Clio, 1993.
Franda, Marcus. *The Seychelles: Unquiet Islands*. Boulder and Hampshire: Westview and Gower, 1982.
Ostheimer, John M. "Independence Politics in the Seychelles" In *The Politics of the Western Indian Ocean Islands*, edited by John M. Ostheimer, pp. 161–192, New York: Praeger, 1975.
Tartter, Jean R. "Seychelles" In *Indian Ocean: Five Island Countries*, edited by Helen Chapin Metz, pp. 199–248, Washington: US Government Printing Office, 1995.
UNDP. "Human Development Reports: Seychelles," http://hdr.undp.org/statistics/data/cty/cty_f_SYC.html (2004).

SHINING PATH/*SENDERO LUMINOSO*

The Shining Path was founded in the 1968 as a splinter group of the Communist party of Peru, headed by Abimael Guzmán Raynoso ("Presidente Gonzalo"), a professor of philosophy at the Universidad Nacional San Cristóbal de Huamanga in Ayacucho. It has been described as one of the most effective, terrifying, and elusive armed organizations in Latin America. Because of its indiscriminate use of violence, it has been compared with Pol Pot's Khmer Rouge. But Sendero is a unique phenomenon. Unlike most revolutionary movements in Latin America, it managed to be virtually independent of foreign support. It was also the first military organization to gain a broad following among the urban, marginalized poor, while attracting sections of the upper classes and significant numbers of women militants, thus penetrating all walks of Peruvian life.

Brief Chronology of the Movement

From its beginnings through the late 1970s, Sendero confined its activities to Ayacucho and the neighboring provinces of Huancavelica and Apurímac, and remained a university based, unarmed movement. In April 1980, on the eve of the first democratic elections in seventeen years, Sendero began pursuing the armed struggle to overthrow the Peruvian government and its institutions. It also began its geographic expansion. By the mid-1980s, it controlled about two thirds of the highlands and had spread out to Lima and to other areas of the Peruvian hinterland, mainly the Upper Huallaga Valley and Amazonia. In 1983, the Peruvian army entered the conflict. The "dirty war" escalated plunging Peru into a cycle of brutal repression, increasing violence, killings, and disappearances. It is estimated that as a consequence of the conflict between Sendero and the army, approximately thirty thousand people, mostly civilians, died and six hundred thousand became internal refugees. After Alberto Fujimori came to power in 1990, local officials and peasants, angered by some of Sendero's tactics, shifted their allegiance back to the government. Rural paramilitary units, created and armed by the army to defend the countryside against Sendero, greatly weakened the movement. Support decreased even further following Guzman's capture in 1992, arrests of Shining Path leaders in 1995, defections, and Fujimori's amnesty program for repentant terrorists which saw more than six thousand Sendero members surrendered to the authorities. In 1993, when Guzmán declared an end to the armed struggle, a Sendero faction continued armed opposition conducting sporadic attacks. The movement seems to have settled in for a long period of low-level conflict.

Goals, Ideology, and Strategies

Sendero's stated goal is to destroy existing Peruvian institutions and establish the "People's Republic of Peru," a united front based on the alliance of the working classes and the peasantry and led by the Communist Party. Its ideology, known as "Gonzalo Thought" is an adaptation of Marxism-Leninism-Maoism to the concrete conditions of Peruvian reality. It is particularly influenced by the doctrines of Mao Zedong and José Carlos Mariátegui. From Maoism it embraced the strategy of a protracted "people's war," that envisaged developing base areas in the countryside to eventually take control of the cities by combining attacks from the outside with insurrections from within. From Mariátegui, it adopted the analysis of Peru as a semi-feudal society. Mariátegui, the founder of Peru's first communist party, believed that Marxism would open "a shining path to revolution." It is from this line that the name of the movement derives.

Social Appeal

A number of factors contributed to create a fertile ground for revolutionary change in Ayacucho during the 1960s and 1970s. One important factor was the extreme poverty of the region. Among Peru's most underdeveloped provinces, plagued by continuing economic problems, with little commerce and scarce resources, the Ayacucho people lived in pre-industrial conditions. Another factor is the dramatic growth of Huamanga University in Ayacucho, a result of the educational efforts that Peruvian governments carried out during that period. In 1977, the university population constituted more than a quarter of the overall population of Ayacucho, and at its peak half of the students were actively involved with the movement. Thus Sendero appealed initially to peasants and students, angered by Peru's racial and class division and by the region's economic depression. Sendero is not an indigenous organization. Although it made inroads into many of the Indian communities of the area, it did not identify with the struggles of the indigenous populations. It is rather a mestizo organization in a nation where mestizos are a majority discriminated upon and excluded from status and power. In the cities, Sendero was active in developing a broad base, which included impoverished shantytown dwellers, different sectors of the working class and some sectors of the middle class.

Revolutionary Activities

Once the armed struggle began, Sendero employed mainly guerrilla tactics, including the blowing up of bridges and power lines, bombing campaigns, selective assassinations, terrorist actions against state officers, army and police personnel, foreign interests, and groups accused of cooperating with neocolonialists, such as NGOs, peasant and labor leaders and community organizers. It is widely believed that these activities were financed by Sendero's links with the drug trade, allegedly developed following its expansion into the Upper Huallaga Valley, the most important coca leaf growing region in the world. According to many sources, Sendero charged drug runners and coca growers for protection and taxed producers, thus gaining a multi-million dollar source of revenue, used to finance arms and training programs. Sendero has strenuously denied this accusation.

In 1985, Sendero began developing "base areas" in the countryside, controlled by "people's committees." In these areas, Sendero performed all government functions, including collecting taxes, distributing land, setting production targets and prices, running schools, dispensing justice, and providing welfare for the elderly. Women were given ownership of land and were equally represented by the local people's committees. Abuses against women, such as rape and domestic violence, were not tolerated. In some of these areas, peasants noted a marked improvement in public services and safety. But Sendero eventually alienated initial supporters with its attempts to institute collective farms, forced recruitment, and "popular trials" of local officials.

Similar attempts to organise all aspects of social life at the neighbourhood level were carried out in the impoverished urban areas, either by infiltrating existing local associations or by destroying them and replacing them with front organisations. Thus, Sendero tried to dominate every aspect of social activity in both countryside and cities. The aim was to create a shadow state led by Guzmán, which would emerge openly in due time and replace the Peruvian government. Sendero's decline brought an end to this plan. Whether the movement will ever recover is doubtful, particularly given present events in the world focussed on terrorism as the major enemy of civilised people.

SUSANA A. EISENCHLAS

References and Further Reading

Bennett, J.M., & L. Hallewell. *Sendero Luminoso in Context: An Annotated Bibliography.* Lanham, Md.: Scarecrow Press, 1998.

Gorriti Ellenbogen, G. *The Shining Path: A History of the Millenarian War in Peru.* Chapel Hill: University of North Carolina Press, 1999.

Stern, S., ed., *Shining and Other Paths: War and Society in Peru, 1980–1995.* Durham: Duke University Press, 1998.

McClintock, C. "Peru's Sendero Luminoso Rebellion: Origins and Trajectory", in *Power and Popular Protest: Latin American Social Movements*, edited by S. Eckstein. Berkeley: University of California Press, 1989.

———. *Revolutionary Movements in Latin America: El Salvador's Fmln & Peru's Shining Path.* London: Hurst, 1998.

Scott Palmer, D., editor. *The Shining Path of Peru.* New York: St. Martin's Press, 1992.

Strong, S. *Shining Path: The World's Deadliest Revolutionary Force.* London: Harper Collins, 1992.

———. *Shining Path: Terror and Revolution in Peru.* New York: Times Books, 1992.

SIAD BARRE, MOHAMMED

Mohammad Siad Barre ruled Somalia from 1969–1991, and presided over the country's economic and political disintegration. His rule was marked by repression, civil and international wars, an intensification of divisive clan loyalties, and economic crisis.

Born in 1919, Siad Barre belonged to the Mareehaan and Ogadeni clans. He joined the police in 1941 and rose through the ranks of the Somali National Army (SNA) to become commander-in-chief in 1965. After the army took power in October 1969, Siad Barre became president of the ruling Supreme Revolutionary Council (SRC). One year later, he declared Somalia a socialist state. His pursuit of socialism was more pragmatic than ideological, and was heavily influenced by Islam. He employed the feared National Security Services to stifle dissent and instituted a cult of personality, styling himself the "Victorious Leader."

The SRC initiated a sweeping program of economic and social development. It promised to attack corruption and diminish the strength of clan loyalties; resettled 140,000 nomads in agricultural settlements; promoted the rights of women; restructured local government; introduced a script for written Somali; and launched a crash literacy campaign. Somalia's literacy rate rose from an estimated 5% to a reported 55% in the mid-1970s, but had slid back to 24% by 1990. The SRC emphasized state control of the economy and central planning, and its program produced some modest success. However, by the late 1970s, massive military spending, corruption, and drought were dragging the economy down.

The Somali army nearly quintupled in size from 1969–1977, as the Soviet Union and its allies poured military aid into Somalia. In 1977, Siad Barre ordered an invasion of Ethiopia aimed at seizing the Ogaden region. Viewing Ethiopia as the more strategic state, the Soviets switched sides, and cut off arms supplies to Somalia. Siad Barre expelled all Soviet bloc personnel in November and turned instead to the United States for assistance. The SNA suffered devastating losses before withdrawing in March 1978, and the war brought exports to a halt. Forced to borrow to cover the military's losses and the cost of food imports, Somalia labored under an enormous debt burden. Throughout the 1980s, real gross domestic product (GDP) declined at 1.7% a year.

The humiliating Ogaden defeat sharpened clan conflicts, which in turn intensified the regime's repression. As a result of an unsuccessful coup in 1978 and the emergence of armed opposition led by the Majeerteen, the government took severe reprisals against the clan. The settlement of 250,000 Ogadeni refugees in the Isaaq-dominated northwest helped spur the creation the Somali National Movement (SNM), which also took up arms against the regime. Siad Barre's government waged a ruthless scorched earth campaign against its enemies; in addition to murder, rape, and torture, it destroyed water sources and grazing grounds, and looted and killed animals. Full-scale civil war erupted in 1988 when the SNM tried to capture

Hargeisa and Burao. The regime responded with ferocity, leveling the two mainly Isaaq cities. The regime's brutality alienated the Hawiye, which dominated the Mogdishu area, and the clan joined the struggle against Siad Barre in 1989. Siad Barre fled Mogadishu for Nigeria in January 1991, and the Somali state collapsed. Siad Barre died in Nigeria on January 2, 1995.

BETH K. DOUGHERTY

See also East Africa: History and Economic Development; East Africa: International Relations; Ethnic Conflicts: East Africa; Somalia

References and Further Reading

Laitin, David D. and Said S. Samatar. *Somalia: Nation in Search of State*. Boulder, CO: Westview Press, 1987.
Metz, Helen Chapin. *Somalia: A Country Study*. Washington, DC: Library of Congress, 1993.
Samatar, Abdi Ismail. "Destruction of State and Society in Somalia: Beyond the Tribal Convention," *Journal of Modern African Studies*, 30, no. 4 (1992).
Samatar, Said S. *Somalia: A Nation in Turmoil*. London: Minority Rights Group, 1991.

SIERRA LEONE

Sierra Leone was founded in 1787, by British abolitionists as a refuge for freed slaves from London, Jamaica, and the United States. The number of so-called "Poor Blacks" had increased dramatically following the American Revolution, leading to clashes with White unemployed. The Sierra Leone settlement was to be a self-governing agrarian commune, modelled on a romantic vision of ancient Israel. The initial settlers consisted of four hundred freed slaves, mainly male, and sixty White prostitutes, to be reformed through marriage.

The enterprise was reorganised as the Sierra Leone Company in 1791, and the settlement replenished in 1792 by Nova Scotian "Black Loyalists." Former slaves who fled their American revolutionary masters, they were evacuated with other "loyalists" to Canada, where they pioneered homesteads in Nova Scotia. Swindled out of their farms by unscrupulous Canadian land speculators, they sent a delegation of England, where they were persuaded to move in Sierra Leone.

Exactions by the Company led to a Nova Scotian rebellion in 1800. The uprising was put down by the unexpected arrival of a British squadron bringing Maroon ex-slaves, transported to Sierra Leone following a protracted rebellion in Jamaica.

Following the British abolition of the slave trade in 1807, the bankrupt Sierra Leone Company sold the settlement, now called Freetown, to the Crown as an

anti-slave trade naval station. During the following decades, thousands of recaptives from slaving ships were liberated and settled in rural villages around Freetown, under the supervision of missionaries. The humanitarian vision was of Christian, Western-educated peasant communities under the authority of the vicar and supplying produce to Freetown.

In 1827, the Church Missionary Society established Fourah Bay College to train African clergy to evangelise "heathen" Africa. By 1854, Fourah Bay College was offering Durham University degrees: ex-slaves rose to become doctors, lawyers and even an Anglican bishop—Bishop Samuel Ajayi Crowther, a Yoruba recaptive. The settlers and recaptives gradually intermarried to form a Creole elite. However by the 1880s, racism was undermining Creole opportunities: excluded from the colonial senior service and unable to compete against powerful European trading companies.

In 1896, the hinterland was incorporated as a British protectorate but imposition of a hut-tax sparked a bloody rebellion by indigenous peoples two years later. The need to raise revenue to pay for British colonisation was a problem as Sierra Leone had limited resources. Diamonds were then discovered in 1930.

In 1933, Sierra Leone Selection Trust (SLST), linked to De Beers, was granted ninety-nine-year exclusive prospecting and marketing rights, with a percentage of profits going to the colonial government. By 1937, SLST was exporting over £1 million in diamonds, however the real expansion came after World War II.

From the start, SLST had problems of protecting its monopoly. Alluvial diamonds could be recovered by simple technology. The 1936 Diamond Industry Protection Ordinance prohibited strangers from entering diamond areas but was difficult to enforce.

By the mid-1950s, illicit diamond dealing was a major problem. Sierra Leone nationalists denounced the SLST monopoly, the local Kono people resented received little from the diamond wealth, and the colonial authorities found it politically difficult to move against illicitly diamond-mining peasants. Illicit diamonds were sold to unauthorised Lebanese merchants, who smuggled them to the growing Middle Eastern cutting and polishing industry. In 1955, territory and lease-time held by SLST were greatly reduced but by then independence for Sierra Leone was rapidly advancing.

Milton Margai's Sierra Leone People's Party (SLPP), an alliance of southern Mende and the Creole elite, formed the first government, in 1961. When Milton died in 1964, his half-brother Albert Margai took power but alienated the Creole civil servants by his Africanisation policies. The opposition All-People's Congress (APC) of Siaka Stevens, a trade union leader supported by northern Temne, won the 1967 elections. The army staged a coup but civilian rule was restored in 1968, with Siaka Stevens as prime minister.

In 1970, the government acquired a 51% stake in SLST, restructured as the National Diamond Mining Company (DIMINCO). Official exports of Sierra Leone diamonds fell dramatically, from over 2 million carats in 1970 to less than six hundred thousand carats in 1980 to less than fifty thousand carats by the end of the 1980s, with an escalation of illicit diamond dealing. Stevens exploited popular resentment against Lebanese traders, while doing deals with Jamil Mohammed, one of the leading illicit diamond traders.

Another attempted coup in 1971 led to Stevens declaring Sierra Leone a republic, however discontent mounted as the economic situation deteriorated. The peasant majority survived on a subsistence economy, supplemented by sale of vegetable oil-seed (peanuts and palm oil) for exports, produce such as rice for the domestic market or meagre wages in mining—in addition to diamonds, there was the development of iron mining and rutile—one of the world largest suppliers of titanium oxide used on non-stick frying pans and heat shields on space craft. However, Sierra Leone suffered from declining terms of trade and corruption.

Stevens retired in 1985 and was succeeded by the incompetent General Joseph Momoh. Plagued by conspiracies and strikes, he ruled under a state of emergency until overthrown in 1992 by Captain Valentine Strasser.

Meanwhile, popular discontent coalesced around the militant Revolutionary United Front (RUF) under Foday Sankoh, allied with the Liberian rebel Charles Taylor. RUF degenerated into banditry and illicit diamond dealing. In 1993, Strasser, with the support of peasant *Kamajor* militia trained by Executive Outcomes mercenaries, launched a campaign against RUF. However, the Sierra Leone army fragmented and Strasser was overthrown in a bloody coup in 1996, by Brig. Maada-Bio, a Mende with links to RUF.

Under international pressure, Maada-Bio held a presidential election, won by Ahmad Tejan Kabba of a revised SLPP. When the army attempted another coup in 1996, President Kabba sought protection from the Nigerian ECOMOG forces, based in Freetown for operations in Liberia. RUF, under pressure from the Nigerians and the *Kamajor*, signed a peace accord.

In May 1997, Major Johnny-Paul Koroma, with the support of RUF, staged a coup and sought to drive the Nigerian-led ECOMOG forces out of Freetown. President Kabba fled to Guinea.

In February 1998, ECOWAS forces, supported by the *Kamajor*, defeated the Koroma junta. By mid-1998, President Kabbah was back in Freetown and

RUF forced back to negotiations. The Lome Accord of 1999 imposed a fragile "government of national unity," including RUF, who began demanding the withdrawal of the United Nations peacekeepers (UNAMSIL). RUF attacks on UNAMSIL led to British military intervention.

On July 5, 2000, United Nations Security Council passed Resolution 1306, prohibiting "the direct or indirect import of all rough diamonds from Sierra Leone," except diamonds certified by the Sierra Leone government. Tejan Kabba was elected president in 2002; SLPP won 83 of 112 Parliamentary seats. The UN established a Special Court for crimes against humanity; however, Foday Sankoh died in a hospital in 2003.

DAVID DORWARD

See also West Africa: History and Economic Development; West Africa: International Relations

References and Further Reading

Braidwood, Stephen J. *Black Poor and White Philanthropists: London's Blacks and the Foundation of the Sierra Leone Settlement, 1786–1791*, Liverpool: Liverpool University Press, 1994.

Fyle, Christopher Magbaily. *The History of Sierra Leone: A Concise Introduction.* London: Evans, 1981.

Ibrahim Abdullah, and Patrick Muana. "The Revolutionary United Front of Sierra Leone," in *African Guerrillas*, ed. Christopher Clapham, London, James Currey, 1998.

Mukonoweshuro, Eliphas G. *Colonialism, Class Formation, and Underdevelopment in Sierra Leone.* Lanham: University Press of America, 1993.

Peterson, John. *Province of Freedom: A History of Sierra Leone, 1787–1870*, Evanston: Northwestern University Press, 1969.

Richards, Paul. *Fighting for the Rain Forest: War, Youth and Resources in Sierra Leone.* Portsmouth: Heinemann, 1996.

van der Laan, H.L. *The Sierra Leone Diamonds: An Economic Study Covering the Years 1952–1961.* Oxford: Oxford University Press, 1965.

———. *The Lebanese Traders in Sierra Leone.* The Hague: Mouton, 1975.

Walker, James W. St. G. *The Black Loyalist: The Search for a Promised Land in Nova Scotia and Sierra Leone, 1783–1870.* London: Longman, 1976.

SIHANOUK, NORODOM

Preah Bat Samdeeh Prea, better known by his royal name of Norodom Sihanouk (b. 1922), was born in Phnom Penh on October 31, 1922. Between 1930 and 1940 he received his primary schooling at Francois Baudin School in that city, and then traveled south to Saigon for his secondary training at Chasseloupe-Laubat School.

He assumed the throne of Cambodia at age nineteen in April 1941 when he was elected king by the Council of the Crown. Throughout the rest of his years his actions have often caused him to be portrayed in the West as erratic and flighty. However, the intent behind his frequent reversals of policy was to keep his nation neutral and to avoid the power struggles of larger and stronger countries.

He has been a man of wide-ranging interests, trying his hand at writing, producing, directing, and acting in movies. He wrote songs and was a sufficiently competent musician to play clarinet and saxophone. He dabbled at cooking, promoted sports for his people, and was a fair horseman. He wrote books, one of which was *My War with the CIA: Memoirs of Norodom Sihanouk* (New York: Pantheon, 1973). He is the father of fourteen children.

His political efforts were often fruitful. As a result of his lobbying in 1952 and 1953, Cambodia won its complete independence from France without a shot fired. Shortly afterward, in April 1955, he abdicated the throne in honor of his father, Norodom Suramarit. He then founded the People's Socialist Community, a political party that received 82% of the vote in the next election. Thus Sihanouk—no longer king—became prime minister and was again at the helm of Cambodia. In the 1950s and 1960s, he was the dominant figure in Cambodian affairs, giving rise to the saying that "Sihanouk is Cambodia."

In 1956, along with Josip Broz Tito, Gamal Abdul Nasser, President Sukarno of Indonesia, and Jawaharlal Nehru, Sihanouk—always desirous of neutrality in world affairs—became one of the founders of the Movement of Nonaligned Nations. In 1960, upon the death of his father, the Parliament elected Sihanouk as Head of State.

In the years of the Vietnam conflict, Sihanouk's greatest concern was to keep his country out of the violence engulfing his eastern neighbor. The two countries had long been enemies in a contest that went centuries into the past. Already Vietnamese troops and settlers were in eastern Cambodia, even moving boundary markers. Sihanouk came to believe that if he helped the Vietnamese revolutionaries, they might be more willing to respect Cambodian independence after their victory. Thus he allowed them to set up bases on Cambodian soil and to bring supplies into the region through the port city of Sihanoukville. Sihanouk also did not object when troops of the Viet Cong and the northern People's Army used the eastern portion of Cambodia as a sanctuary, safe from US bombings. Such actions, however, infuriated the government of the United States. For Cambodia the consequences were severe.

From March 18, 1969, to May 26, 1970, the United States pursued a top secret bombing campaign in Cambodia known as MENU, supposedly to deny

sanctuary to enemy forces in the eastern portion of the country. Try as he might, there was little Sihanouk could do about it, and even after the secrecy was lifted the bombing continued.

As the MENU bombing came to an end, with the country in turmoil, Sihanouk chose an army officer, General Lon Nol, to head a new right-wing Government of National Salvation. For a time he and Sihanouk were able to work together but Nol became increasingly agitated when Sihanouk objected to some of his policies. On March 18, 1970, while on a visit to the USSR, Sihanouk became a victim of a *coup d'etat.* Lon Nol established the short-lived Khmer Republic (1972–1975). Despite massive injections of advisers, equipment, and financial aid from the United States, however, Lon Nol was unable to quiet the unrest rampant in Cambodia. Warring factions continued to clash and the communists began to emerge as the strongest political force in the land.

Following the coup d'etat that had unseated him, Sihanouk joined forces with the communists (Khmer Rouge) who had become increasingly active and powerful, and he soon headed their National United Front.

Civil war continued to engulf the land, ending only with Pol Pot's emergence as leader of the Cambodian communist National United Front, headed by the Sihanouk government in exile that sought to overthrow the Lon Nol government. On April 17, 1975, Pol Pot's regime decreed a new constitution providing that the old kingdom be abolished in favor of the Democratic State of Kampuchea, a communist experiment in which Pol Pot wanted to destroy Cambodian culture so that he and his party could start from year zero to build a resilient communist state. The communists murdered about one-third of the Cambodian people. Sihanouk resigned as president of Pol Pot's Democratic State of Kampuchea after a year's service. He did, however, still retain his royal title. The troubles that beset his country so preyed upon Sihanouk's mind that on August 11, 1997, he offered to abdicate (again) and objected to the Khmer Rouge government's recent ouster of his son as prime minister in a bloody coup, calling it an illegal act. Pol Pot was not influenced by such behavior. His devastating rule lasted until the Vietnamese invaded in 1978 after months of escalating quarrels. The Vietnamese entered Phnom Penh in January 1979, forcing Pol Pot to flee, and they remained there as occupiers for ten years. Sihanouk also departed that year, flying out of Phnom Penh into self-imposed exile just ahead of the Vietnamese Army.

In 1982 he again became president of his nation for a short time before once again leaving office. In 1991, returning from thirteen years in exile, and convinced he could play a part in healing the wounds caused by

years of civil war and societal unrest, Sihanouk returned to Cambodia as "head of state" to govern until elections could be held in 1993. That year, at the head of a new party, the United Front for an Independent, Neutral, Peaceful, and Cooperative Cambodia, Sihanouk won a narrow electoral victory. Shortly thereafter, a new constitution restored the monarchy with Sihanouk as king, a position he had abdicated thirty-eight years earlier. This time, however, his kingship became a constitutional monarchy in which Sihanouk reigned but did not rule.

The turmoil of the Cambodian government and people continued in the following years. Still, as of the date of this writing (2004) Sihanouk, aged eighty-one and in fragile health, continued his efforts to serve his people. Royalty for six decades and living in a palatial guesthouse in Beijing, the mercurial Sihanouk announced that he would (again) abdicate.

CECIL B. CURREY

See also Cambodia; Southeast Asia: History and Economic Development

References and Further Reading

Kuckreja, Madhavi. *Prince Norodom Sihanouk*. New York: Chelsea House, 1990.
Osborne, Milton E. *Sihanouk: Prince of Light, Prince of Dark*. Honolulu: University of Hawaii Press, 1994.
Sihanouk, Norodom. *My War with the CIA*. New York: Pantheon Books, 1973.

SIKHISM (SIKHS)

A striking feature of Sikhism is that its development can be traced closely with historical events. The roots of Sikhism can be traced to the fifteenth century, to its founding by Guru Nanak (1469–1539 CE). Nanak hailed from the Punjab, which before the partition of India and Pakistan in 1947, belonged to a single region.

The word "Sikh" derives from Sanskrit, from the word *sisya*, meaning "disciple." The Sikhs are the followers of the ten Gurus whose teachings are compiled in the *Adi Granth* later known as the *Guru Granth Sahib*. It is a composition of hymns of which 974 hymns have been composed by Guru Nanak. His compositions resonate with the teachings of spiritual Gurus of the *Bhakti* tradition of the time such as Kabir (1440–1518 CE), Ravidas (1500 CE) and other *Bhakti* reformers. Nanak communicated his divine revelations through songs and poems. His message to his followers included: faith in one true God; worship of *satnam* (true name), which was synonymous with the nature and being of God; importance of the Guru's instruction in the realization of God;

faith in *karma* (good deeds); attainment of *moksha* by serving others and on the Guru's grace. In the words of Guru Nanak, "Words do not the saint or sinner make, Actions alone are written in the book of fate." He condemned the caste system of Hinduism as folly and irrelevant in the attainment of *moksha*, and disapproved of the practice of asceticism and renunciation of family life. According to him only in community life could one practice righteous living in a meaningful way. His *Janam Sakhis* (life stories) tells us how he was called into God's presence.

The institution of what can be termed Guruship, founded by Guru Nanak, was continued under the succeeding nine Gurus, whose contributions preserved and enhanced the Sikh faith. The fifth Guru, Arjun Dev completed the construction of the Golden temple at Amritsar and installed in it the holy scripture known as *Adi Granth*. His martyrdom in 1606 by the Mughal Emperor Jahangir, marked the militarization of the Sikhs. The sixth Guru, Hargobind established the *Akal Takht* (Timeless Throne) from which he issued edicts in his role as the spiritual and military leader. The Sikhs fought several battles to preserve their faith. The ninth Guru, Tegh Bahadur was executed in 1675 by the orders of the Mughal Emperor Aurangzeb. The tenth Guru, Gobind Singh established the brotherhood of all Sikhs through their commitment to the *Khalsa*, which was intended to protect the Sikh faith. Members of the *Khalsa* were required to adopt *panj kakke* (the five Ks): *kesh* (uncut hair), *kangha* (comb), *kirpan* (sword), *kachha* (cotton breeches), and *kara* (bangle). After Guru Gobind Singh the authority of the Sikh faith was vested in the Sikh community and on the scriptures which were placed in the *Gurdwara*, the sacred sanctuary of the Sikh community.

The disintegration of the Mughal empire at the end of the eighteenth century, led to the creation of a Sikh kingdom in the Punjab under Ranjit Singh (1780–1839). Though successful in building a large army, his successors were unable to withstand British pressure and in 1850, Punjab was annexed to British India. The Sikhs earned a distinction as outstanding soldiers in the British army. However, the Jallianwala Bagh massacre in 1919 was a major turning point in the relation between Sikhs and the British. By the orders of General E H Dyer ten thousand people who were holding a protest meeting were fired on. This massacre fueled anti-British sentiments and added strength to the freedom movement.

Throughout its history the Sikh community has been struggling to maintain a distinct identity from the dominant Hindus. In 1909, the *Anand Marriage Act* recognized distinctive Sikh rites in order to distinguish it from Hindu practice. Between the years 1920–1925, the Sikh movement was led by a Sikh leadership known as the *Akali Dal*. By the *Sikh Gurdwara Act* of 1925, control of *gurdwaras* was conferred on the *Shiromani Gurdwara Parbandhak Committee* (SGPC) which continues to be the most powerful elected body of the Sikhs. The independence of India from British rule and the consequent partition in 1947 divided the Sikh homeland of Punjab between India and the new state of Pakistan. Most Sikhs and Hindus fled to the Indian side of the border.

The Sikhs in the Indian Punjab campaigned for a new state of Punjabi speakers to be created from the existing Punjab. The state boundaries were redrawn in 1966 and Punjab became the majority Sikh state. In 1973, the *Anandpur Sahib* resolution was issued. However, the Indian Government did not accept the *Akali's* religious and economic demands as put forth by the resolution. Frustrated with the situation the followers of a militant Sikh preacher Jarnail Singh Bhindrawala (1947–1989) espoused violence as the path for Sikh autonomy. Their demands for greater political autonomy culminated in "Operation Bluestar" in June 1984, when Indian troops attacked the Golden Temple complex in order to flush out the militants from within the confines of the holy temple. Sikhs saw this attack as a persecution of their faith. This was followed by the assassination of Prime Minister Indira Gandhi by her Sikh bodyguards on October 31, 1984. Anti-Sikh rioting followed in India for four days. Sikh politics was dominated by anger and frustration until the mid-1990s. Indira Gandhi's son and successor Rajiv Gandhi reached an agreement with the moderate Sikh leader Sant Harchand Singh Longowal and conceded much of what the Akalis had all along been demanding. In 1999, Sikhs worldwide celebrated the three hundredth anniversary of the Sikh *Khalsa*, the community of saint-soldiers. Currently the Punjab is peaceful. However, the rise of Hindu nationalism have given Sikhs cause for alarm as they continue to be vigilant about maintaining their distinct identity.

YOSAY WANGDI

See also India; Kashmir Dispute

References and Further Reading

Kapur, Rajiv. *Sikh Separatism: The Politics of Faith*. London; Boston: Allen & Unwin, 1986.

McLeod, W.H. *Exploring Sikhism: Aspects of Sikh Identity, Culture and Thought*. New Delhi: Oxford University Press, 2000.

———. *The Sikhs: History, Religion and Society*. New York: Columbia University Press, 1989.

———. *Guru Nanak and the Sikh Religion*. Oxford: Clarendon Press, 1968.

Singh, Patwant. *The Sikhs*. New York: Knopf, 1999.

SILVA, LUIZ INÁCIO "LULA" DA

Born in the Northeast Brazilian city of Garanhuns, interior of the state of Pernambuco, on the October 27, 1945, Luis Inácio "Lula" da Silva, nicknamed "the son of Brazil," was one of eight children. The family was not well off, and "Lula" da Silva began working at age seven as a vendor of peanuts and oranges on the streets of Santos, São Paulo, while attending primary school. At the age of fourteen he landed a new job with Armazéns Gerais Columbia. Afterwards, "Lula" da Silva transferred to the Fábrica de Parafusos Marte and at the age of fifteen, he was admitted to the Senai—Serviço Nacional da Indústria (National Industry Service) where he studied for the next three year and graduated as a metal worker.

During the 1960s at the height of the Brazilian authoritarian government, "Lula" da Silva landed a new job in the city of São Bernardo do Campo, part of the ABC *paulista* (formed by the cities of Santo Andre, São Bernardo do Campo, and São Caetano located in the State of São Paulo), where he began his involvement with politics. "Lula" da Silva's involvement in politics was a matter of coincidence rather than aspirations. His brother, José Ferreira da Silva, better known as Frei Chico, had been invited to run for office for the worker's union but he declined passing that responsibility to "Lula" da Silva who gladly accepted.

In April 1980, "Lula" da Silva and the worker's union led a worker's strike that paralyzed the industrial heart of Brazil: São Paulo. The military regime in power along with the industrial elite retaliated against the workers. Several union workers were detained under Brazil's National Security Law. Among the detainees was da Silva, who was sentenced to three years and six months in prison. But, the following year the Brazilian Supreme Court overturned the conviction. Convinced that the workers needed their own representation in Congress, da Silva on February 10, 1980, founded the *Partido dos Trabalhadores* (Workers Party or PT) together with other union workers, Brazilian intellectuals, politicians, and members of Brazil's social movements.

The following year, in August 1983, da Silva founded the *Central Unica dos Trabalhadores* (CUT), an organization to advance the rights of workers without the tutelage of the state, as it was commonly practiced in Brazil. In 1984, da Silva participated in one of the most important events in the history of Brazil: the movement for *"diretas-já"* [*direct elections now*]. The movement, which took millions of Brazilians to the street, demanded that the military step down and return democracy to Brazil, after twenty-one years of military dictatorship. "Lula" da Silva ran

for governor of São Paulo in 1982 but lost; in 1986 he ran for senator (federal deputy) and became the most voted senator in the history of Brazil with 651,763 votes.

In 1989, the PT launched "Lula" da Silva as their presidential candidate. "Lula" da Silva ran against the unknown candidate Fernando Collor de Mello from the state of Alagoas. "Lula" da Silva lost in his first attempt to win the presidency, receiving 47% of the votes. In 1993, "Lula" da Silva began his campaign for human rights and citizenship for all Brazilians regardless of their socio-economic status or ethnicity, which would later became the cornerstone of his presidency (Programa Fome Zero or Program Hunger Zero). "Lula" da Silva attempted again the office of the presidency running in 1994 against Senator Fernando Henrique Cardoso. Cardoso received 44% of the vote against da Silva's 22%. In 1998, da Silva made another attempt for the presidency against Cardoso, who had modified the Constitution to allow him to run a second term. The results were almost identical to 1994. However, in 2002, da Silva was elected president, defeating José Serra, the government candidate, in a run-off election.

The Brazilian government under "Lula" da Silva has been pressing for enhanced international cooperation to combat international terrorism; da Silva was, however, fiercely opposed to the 2003 invasion of Iraq led by the United States. Brazil is also arguing for an expansion of the United Nations' Security Council, to which it desires addition as a permanent member.

President "Lula" da Silva's administration has given priority to strengthening of the scientific and technological infrastructure. However, the *Bolsa Família* (Family Assistance Program) is perhaps its most ambitious program. The *Bolsa Família* provides up to R$100 ($50 US) per family per month in addition to health care, education, and other social programs. Another program started by the "Lula" da Silva government was *Programa Fome Zero* (Zero Hunger Program) which has as its main objectives the total eradication of hunger and social exclusion in Brazil. The program's initial efforts were geared towards emergency relief, but the program's long-term goal is to create long-term food security throughout Brazil via agrarian form and support of family farms, with the aim of making Brazil self-sufficient for its food supplies. Vouchers for poor families are also part of the program, along with food banks, school meals programs, and programs aimed at pregnant women and mothers with infants.

The da Silva administration has faced criticism regarding its environmental policies. Despite da Silva's reputation as a supporter of environmental causes,

deforestation in Brazil continues to increase. He has also expressed support for a bill that will lift Brazil's ban on genetically modified crops. There have also been allegations of corruption within both the Worker's Party and da Silva's inner circle; nevertheless, da Silva's popularity remains high.

JOSE DA CRUZ

See also Brazil; Cardoso, Fernando Henrique

References and Further Reading

Alves, Brito. *A História de Lula: O Operário Presidente* [The History of Lula: Factory Worker President]. Rio de Janeiro: Espaço e Tempo, 2003.
Cavalcanti, Luiz Otávio. *O Que é o Governo Lula* [What is the Lula Government]. São Paulo: Landy Editora, 2003.
Paraná, Denise. Lula, *O Filho do Brasil* [*Lula, the Son of Brazil*]. São Paulo: Editora Fundação Perseu Abramo, 2002.
Thomas E. Skidmore and Peter H. Smith. *Modern Latin America* 6th ed. New York: Oxford University Press.

SINGAPORE

Singapore's Early Era: The Challenge of Poverty and Insecurity

The Republic of Singapore is an island located in the middle of Southeast Asia at geographical coordinates 1°17′N 103°51′E, its land area of 648 square kilometers. It is home to 4,185,000 people, of whom 3,437,000 are Singapore citizens. Foreign guest workers and their families, who occupy 25% of the country's jobs—mainly in low productive sectors such as services and construction and high productivity sectors such as high tech manufacturing and information technology— comprise the remainder of the population. The island is at sea level and its climate features hot, humid monsoon rainy periods without pronounced rainy or dry seasons. Singapore's diverse ethnic composition is 77% Chinese, 15% Malay, 6% Indian, and 2% persons of mixed ethnicity. Four official languages exist: English, Chinese, Malay and Tamil. The population's religious composition includes persons who practice Buddhism, Islam, Christianity, Hinduism, Sikhism, Taoism, and Confucianism.

The small but complex city-state achieved its independence from Britain in 1963 as part of the Federation of Malaysia, an arrangement doomed not to last because of ethnic tensions involving Chinese dominated Singapore and the remainder of Malaysia. It was expelled from the Federation in 1965, a time when Singapore's economy was in shambles and its national and regional security was tenuous.

Early Singapore's Poverty and Insecurity

Singapore's maritime infrastructure had barely been able to sustain the island's fragile and one-dimensional economy, which was stagnating from wartime damages. The island's once pre-eminent role in Britain's Asian defense strategy had come to an inglorious end due to its defeat at the hands of the Japanese. Singapore's ethnically diverse population was segregated throughout the island. A severe housing shortage went unabated. The existing housing stock was decaying, and the concentrated and fragmented nature of land ownership inhibited housing development. A rapidly growing population was putting increasing pressures on the economy's dwindling capacity to satisfy housing requirements and other basic needs, particularly for education and health care. Only one in five housing units had a sewage connection and consequently water-borne communicable diseases were epidemic. Malaria and tuberculosis were rampant and cholera was part of everyday life throughout the island. Rat infestation plagued schools, health clinics and opium houses alike. Medical facilities were woefully inadequate to deal with the widespread public health problems that these conditions produced.

Unemployment and underemployment abounded and poverty was widespread. Education, civic participation, and business and employment opportunities were reserved mainly for the Chinese elite—this was a legacy of British colonial rule. Ethnic chauvinism persisted throughout the island pitting Chinese against Malay against Indian, and eventually leading to interracial rioting—a phenomenon that ultimately separated Singapore from Malaysia. Ethnic antagonism produced student militancy and gave rise to a climate of bitter antagonism among the young of Singapore. The ethnic conflict, combined with ideological dogmatism and inflexibility, exacerbated the chaos and ultimately caused Singapore's expulsion from the Federation. It was up to the country's leadership both in the Government and within the People's Action Party to find Singapore's "own way" to pursue economic development and maintain national sovereignty.

Singapore's Pursuit of Development and Sovereignty

In 1965, the government began to design and to apply policies aimed at eradicating poverty by promoting

economic growth that would provide the basis for social development and security. The government's key objective was to maintain social order within the country's multi-racial society. It pursued its objectives via policies that collectively had a three-fold focus: educating and training people, maintaining peace with Singapore's regional neighbors (particularly Malaysia and Indonesia) and gaining the confidence of investors from developed market economy countries. The systematically applied policies and administrative practices sought to create internal social order, more educated and productive workers, regional security, and a positive investment climate.

Specific policies and practices centered on developing a sound saving and investment system, an outward looking free market orientation, a superb education and training system, a substantial commitment to invest in research and development, and above all, an honest and efficient government and bureaucracy. Government operated on the conviction that policies and practices need to be combined in a way that formed an organic whole where the key to success would always be a capable, non-corruptible, development-oriented government and bureaucracy.

From the onset of nationhood, Singapore's relatively small national economy has been highly open to trade and foreign investment and its growth export-led. Monetary and fiscal policies continue to face constraints in the form of financial leaks into the global economy. As a consequence, macroeconomic stability has always been pursued via a combination of handling imports and re-exports efficiently and promoting exports of domestic origin effectively through exchange rate policies and wage and salary controls that have kept the country's prices competitive in global markets.

In its committed pursuit of material progress, internal stability, and national sovereignty, the government gave lower priority to other goals such as equity in the distribution of economic benefits. Virtually no public attention was paid to promoting non-economic values such as individual freedom, intellectual, and artistic creativity and political competition. The road chosen by Prime Minister Lee Kuan Yew and the authoritarian leadership of the People's Action Party and the government has been widely criticized as harsh and careless when it comes to paying attention to the non-economic costs of Singapore's material progress. Despite the criticism coming from abroad and from some citizens at home, Lee Kwan Yew and his associates have been unquestionably successful in furthering Singapore's economic development. From 1965 onward, almost miraculous material progress began to take place. Throughout the four decades that followed independence, Singapore was one of the world's fastest growing economies.

A Modern, Developed Market Economy

Progress took place because the aforementioned policies were put into place effectively and efficiently. The result was an economy that was transformed from a trading entrepot to a balanced, multi-segment economic structure. The new structure featured a basic transportation and financial infrastructure to support the economy's growing external sector and a manufacturing sector that shifted from low value added, basic labor intensive items to higher value added items that were more sophisticated and consequently were more capital and highly skilled labor intensive.

Material progress was not the result of a "miracle." It came about through a combination of human effort and public policies based up this important recognition: Singapore has a small domestic demand and attempts to improve macroeconomic performance through monetary and fiscal policies have little domestic impact because the "foreign leakage" is too large. Instead, the government has employed micro economic policies in the form of wage and salary controls that have a direct impact on the cost of exports. Flexible wages and salaries keep employment levels high, assure that export prices remain competitive, and when price regulation is introduced into the policy mix, the domestic consumption of basic need items is sustained.

Production has been continually aimed at progressively higher value added exports destined for markets in North America, Europe, and Asia. Production processes continue to combine foreign capital and technology and domestic investment with a continually improving domestic human resource base augmented by critically important expatriate labor. Efforts to continue gaining and maintaining access to markets abroad has always been a key feature of the country's foreign economic policy mix. Singapore became a member of the Association of Southeast Asian Nations (ASEAN), the Asia Pacific Economic Cooperation (APEC) group, the Pacific Economic Cooperation Council (PECC) and, at the global level, the World Trade Organization (WTO).

Singapore's sustained material progress was so pronounced that by the late 1990s its capita income was among the highest in the world and it is now classified as a "developed market economy country." In addition to Singapore's high per capita income, the indices measuring the personal quality of material life and the state of human development place contemporary Singapore within the higher echelon of the world's economies. From 1976 to the onset of the Asian financial crisis of 1999–2000, the country's gross domestic product (GDP) grew by an average

7.8% in real terms while the annual rate of inflation was only 1.6%. The growth and price stability that the economy experienced during the period was based on exports that on average made accounted for 51.6% of Singapore's GDP during the period.

By the year 2000, per capita national income in Singapore grew to $25,000 US annually. The infant mortality rate dropped to four per one thousand births and life expectancy rose to seventy-eight years. Primary and secondary school participation rates for male and female students reached 92% while the literacy rate exceeded 95%. The United Nation's human development index (HDI) that measures a nation's progress based on the above factors rose to 0.876 placing Singapore among the top fifteen high performing countries based on this measure. The financial crisis temporarily put a stop to Singapore's progress but by 2002 economic growth and social development resumed their upward swings.

Other evidences of domestic progress include a superb international airline, a "state-of-the art" convention center and a clean and safe environment that attracts millions of professional visitors and tourists to the island republic each year. On the professional front, not only was the first Ministerial Meeting of the World Trade Organization held in Singapore, but also it is home to the Secretariats of both APEC and PECC. The country's infrastructure is strong. The Port of Singapore ranks along side the ports of Hong Kong and Rotterdam as the world's largest in terms of dockings, tonnage, and values handled. The Singapore Monetary Authority, operating on the bases of both prudential financial practices and the principle of transparency, oversees a finance and banking system that provides financial services to countries throughout the region. Because of its sound financial system, Singapore was less seriously affected by the recent Asian financial crisis. Because of this, the International Monetary Fund uses Singapore as a base for training bankers and financial service personnel from other countries.

Consequences Arising from Singapore's Road to Progress

The road to progress chosen by Singapore's founding and current leaders not only produced domestic economic progress and national sovereignty but it contributed to regional stability. Home ownership is at 80%–85%, homelessness is rare, and high-quality basic health care is universally accessible. The educational system is superb. Singapore's Central Providence Fund (CPF) provides support for older Singaporeans. It is also the financial means via which people purchase housing. The CPF continues to grow and it is managed in a sound and prudential fashion so that it continues to provide the people of Singapore with a superb social-financial system. In 1997, the CPF was modified to add an important new feature—the CPF Investment Scheme that permitted individuals more opportunities to choose patterns of individual investments within a set of government approved companies.

The firm guiding hand of government that propelled Singapore's economic development process has not been highly successful in furthering other social values such as open competitive politics and individual freedom. There has arisen a clear and profound dichotomy between Singapore's material and social progress and its authoritative government and non-competitive political system: along the road to material success, official Singapore became suspicious of real and perceived threats both external and internal.

The seeds of suspicion were sown during the period 1963 to 1965 when the government responded to an external environment that was perceived to be hostile, unstable, and threatening. At that time Singapore's leadership chose a social and political governance structure that was based upon three principles. First, it created a climate of political and social discipline that was to become the cornerstone to government policies and practices. The intent was to assure that no internal threat would develop in a way that permitted outside influences to challenge the leadership and the government. Second, it spawned a willing group of followers who would acquiesce to being governed tightly regardless of any inequities and unfairness associated with the government's actions. Third, it fostered an environment wherein authoritarian social engineering was practiced in an effort to assure social and political stability.

The key question facing contemporary Singapore is whether a government and political system based upon suspicion has outlived its usefulness. Even with broadly based acquiescence and support, during future elections the ruling People's Action Party (PAP) will have to confront this basic issue as well as others including the gaps in income distribution and wealth. The wealth and income distribution gaps are serious and widening. From the government's perspective this is a natural consequence of globalization. However, a growing number of citizens see distribution inequities as the result of reliance on expatriate labor and favoritism among the local economic elite. While the PAP continues to receive some 65% of the vote, one out of every three citizens voted for a minority party candidate, which could cause the ruling party's magnitude of control over the Parliament to dissipate.

ROBERT L. CURRY, JR.

See also Export-Oriented Economies; Foreign Residents in Developing Countries; Southeast Asia: History and Economic Development; Southeast Asia: International Relations

References and Further Reading

Chee, Soon Juan. *Dare to Change: An Alternative Vision for Singapore*. Singapore: Singapore Democratic Party, 1994.

Chew, Ernest C.T. and Edwin Lee, editors. *A History of Singapore*. Singapore and New York: Oxford University Press, 1991.

da Cunha, Derek, editor. *Debating Singapore: Reflective Essays*. Singapore: Institute of Southeast Asian Studies, 1994.

———. *Singapore in the New Millenium: Challenges Facing the City State*. Singapore: Institute of Southeast Asian Studies, 2000.

Hock, Saw Swee. *The Population of Singapore*. Singapore: Institute of Southeast Asian Studies, 1999.

Lee, Edwin. *The British as Rulers: Governing Multiracial Singapore*. Singapore: Singapore University Press, 1991.

Seow, Francis. *To Catch a Tartar: A Dissident in Lee Kwan Yew's Prison*. New Haven, CT: Yale Center for Southeast Asian Studies, 1995.

Vasil, Raj. *Governing Singapore: A History of National Development and Policy*. New York: Allen and Unwin, 2000.

SINGLE-PARTY STATES

Single-party states are those in which one political party, which goes largely unchallenged, enjoys a monopoly on power within the state structures. The ruling party has a wider variety of functions than is usually the case in a multi-party competitive democracy. The ruling party may serve as the primary mechanism for determining access to decision-making authority, staffing the bureaucracy, distributing political goods, articulating and channeling interests, maintaining security, and articulating state ideology, as well as organizing and contesting elections. These elections may not offer real choices to voters, but serve important legitimizing functions for the regime.

Such a party may still have competitors for control of government functions. These competitors might include the military, the bureaucracy, and the authoritarian leader. The party is generally independent from these non-party actors. For instance, the Brazilian military regime (1964–1985) did not permit any real autonomy to the Alliance for National Renovation (ARENA), its political party vehicle, and would therefore not be considered an example of a single-party state. Likewise, a system such as Iraq under Saddam Hussein, in which the party serves primarily as a vehicle for a personalistic leader, is not properly considered a single-party state.

Within the category of single-party states there is considerable variation in regime characteristics. Some regimes have a constitutionally mandated role for the party, often describing the party as the leading force in society and prohibiting all other political parties. These are typically Communist party-states, but this was also true of many African regimes. Other states, including Communist Poland, permitted the existence of other parties, but only those that were supporters of the ruling party's right to govern. Still others, such as Mexico and Senegal (except from 1966–1976), permitted various parties to contest elections but did not permit any but the ruling party to win them. This differentiates the single-party state from a dominant party in a democratic system, as found in Japan and Sweden throughout much of the same period. In these last two cases, the governing party had no guarantee of continued political dominance, opposition parties could expect to form a legitimate opposition in the legislature, and the party system's primary role was to legitimize government through elections.

The historic origins of the single-party state lie in Marxism-Leninism, although fascist parties in Europe in the twentieth century also employed the party-state regime model. Marxism calls for the dictatorship of the proletariat to govern the state until the state itself withers away. V. I. Lenin articulated a model for the exercise of this dictatorship based on a centralized political party made up of cadres acting as the vanguard of the proletariat. Many single-party states adopted the Leninist model, including non-Marxist regimes. The Kuomintang in the Republic of China is a particularly interesting example of a non-Marxist party organized along Leninist principles. Many of Asia's nationalist movements did adopt Marxist ideology along with Leninist organizational principles as they successfully fought their way to power, as in China, North Korea, and Indochina.

For much of the post–World War II period, the single-party state was the most widespread regime type in the developing world. Communist party-states were established in Central and Eastern Europe, China and North Korea in the late 1940s, and North Vietnam in 1954, joining the two pre-war Communist party-states, the Soviet Union and Mongolia. Non-communist hegemonic party-states were established in Mexico in 1938 and Paraguay in 1947. Depending on how one classifies different cases, some eighteen single-party states were established in the 1960s, mostly in Africa. The only new Communist party-state established in the 1960s was in Cuba. Numerous other African states moved effectively towards single-party status, although formal establishment of such a regime may not have taken place until the 1970s. By 1988, some fifty-seven countries had single-party

regimes. These included the Soviet Union and the eight Communist states in Central Europe and the Balkans; fifteen of the seventeen countries in East and Central Africa; seven countries each in Southern Africa and in West Africa; five Arab countries; ten countries in Central, East, and Southeast Asia; and four countries in Latin America.

Lenin's theories of imperialism were compelling to many of the leaders of the newly independent states of the 1950s and 1960s, who articulated justifications for the adoption of the single-party model to overcome the legacies of colonialism. Kwame Nkrumah in Ghana and Sékou Touré in Guinea, for example, sought to nationalize their nations' economies in order to prevent the repatriation of profits to Europe, to promote industrialization, and to allow for the distribution of wealth. The movement of all the people, represented in the single mass party and led by the vanguard elite, was needed to break the power of particular interests that enjoyed special links to the metropolitan state and benefited from neo-colonial relationships. The Chinese referred to these local agents of the metropolitan bourgeoisie as the comprador class, whose interests were inherently anti-national.

However, relatively few single-party regimes adopted a fully developed class analysis as part of their ideology. In Africa and the Arab world, various versions of African and Arab Socialism became official regime ideology. Sékou Touré argued that African class structure did not resemble that of Europe, and as parties represent class interests, the Democratic Party of Guinea (PDG) was not in fact a party because it represented the nation, not any single set of class interests. Arab or African Socialism took on even more flexible ideological shapes in the hands of Gamal Abdel Nasser in Egypt and Kenneth Kaunda in Zambia. While Sékou Touré denied the existence of classes and internal class conflict, Nasser saw the creation of a single-party as a means to contain the potential for class conflict in Egyptian society. Similarly, Zambia's United National Independence Party (UNIP) promoted Kaunda's official ideology of "Humanism" rather than a more rigorously socialist ideology. African Socialism was usually conceived to be a revalorization of pre-colonial communitarian norms, modernized by the activity of the Party. The local committees of the PDG in the early period after independence in Guinea may not have behaved much differently from traditional village councils.

In many African states, the mass-based independence movement led by a Western-educated elite became the base for the post-independence single-party. The goals of this party were to provide national unity, political stability, and social and economic development. The concern for national unity was not unfounded, as multiparty systems in Africa have tended to reflect ethnic divisions, with tragic consequences in several cases, such as in Nigeria and more recently the Republic of Congo. As Nkrumah said, "A multi-party system introduced into Africa results in the perpetuation of feudalism, tribalism and regionalism, and in inordinate power struggle and rivalry." Many parties in single-party regimes adopted national symbols as their own and denied the use of these symbols to others. Indeed, the possibility of loyal opposition is denied to other parties, for in the nationalist formulation of the single-party ideology, to oppose the ruling party is to oppose the nation itself. On the other hand, single-party systems have also provided political cover for ethnic-based interests that have sought to dominate the state, as in Kenya and Malawi.

The Leninist model was particularly well suited to the developmentalist state that characterized the developing world from the 1950s to the 1970s. Mobilizing resources for what was envisioned as a rapid, dramatic, and revolutionary change in society required institutions capable of communicating directly with the masses and subordinating opposition embedded in either neo-colonialist or traditionalist structures to the general will of the new nation. Tanzanian president Julius Nyerere argued that:

> The Party has to help the people to understand what the government is doing and why; it has to help the people to co-operate with their government... But the Party has also to ensure that the government stays in close touch with the feelings, the difficulties and the aspirations of the people. It has to speak for the people. And it has to educate the people and help them to see what the government's actions mean in terms of their own future security and their own future opportunities.

The role of the party in actual implementation of development policies varies greatly among single-party states. The strong role of the Tanganyika African National Union (TANU) in Tanzania contrasts markedly with the role of the Kenya African National Union (KANU) in Kenya, which played almost no part in policy implementation. As states adopted extensive economic planning, including cooperativization and in several cases collectivization of agriculture, party militants became essential promoters of state goals on the ground. In some cases the party acted as the state bureaucracy, while in others it served as a check on the bureaucrats who actually implemented policy. In Syria, for example, the Baath party under Hafiz al-Asad had the power to review and influence the formulation of policies as they were developed through regular institutions of government. Many single-party states found that administration through the party was often inefficient, and sought eventually

to separate the party from the bureaucracy and administration. This was particularly characteristic of the Communist-party states in the late 1970s, including Cuba, China, and Vietnam.

Single-parties also played more non-ideological roles in many states. Party membership was often essential for participation in distributional alliances controlled by the party or the national leader. States that permitted opposition parties, such as Mexico, Paraguay, and Senegal, used elections as a means to determine access to divisible goods among competitive patron-client networks. However, this was also true in Côte d'Ivoire and Kenya during periods when opposition parties were prohibited and competing networks operated as factions within the party. The relatively prosaic distribution of largesse has had at least as great of an impact on patterns of development, for good and for ill, as have great schemes based on central state planning.

The overall impact of the single-party state on political and economic development has often been negative. While these regimes have arguably contributed to national unity and have created periods of political stability, most of them have fallen well short of the goals they set for themselves. The single-party model has suffered several problems. These include personalism, corruption, inflexibility, irrationality, authoritarianism, and human rights violations. In short, these regimes suffer from the ills of dictatorship, and while some have been less abusive than others the tendency for abuse is inherent in the regime design itself.

Few single-party regimes were able to overcome the tendency towards personalistic decision-making. While some, such as Mexico and Vietnam, were able to achieve a degree of rotation of elites and avoid cults of personality, personalistic and capricious decision-making is still found in regimes without external checks. While competitive multi-party systems may be as corrupt, the combination of unchecked corruption and inflexibility in an authoritarian state is more likely to lead to disasters, as Amartya Sen has famously observed. Likewise, while single-party regimes are not alone in authoritarianism and human rights abuses, they have generally not been good performers on these measures, contrasting notably on these grounds with competitive multi-party systems.

The economic crises and adoption of neoliberal ideology in the 1980s accompanied the abandonment of both Marxist political economy and Leninist political organization in much of the world. Between 1989 and 1992, twenty-nine single-party regimes were replaced by either multi-party democracies, military regimes, or, in several cases, anarchy. By the end of 2001, only fourteen of these regimes survived, and of these, only five, all Communist party-states, retained the constitutional mandate for single-party hegemony. The commitment to single-party rule as the means for national development has been completely abandoned, except in Cuba and North Korea. In virtually no part of the world is the single-party model today celebrated as the appropriate means for the developing world to achieve development.

BRIAN TURNER

See also Authoritarianism; Bureaucratic-Authoritarian Regimes; Central and Eastern Europe, History and Economic Development; China; Cuba; Dictatorships; Egypt; Ghana; Guinea; Kenya; Paraguay; Senegal; Taiwan; Vietnam

References and Further Reading

Arhin, Kwame, ed. *The Life and Work of Kwame Nkrumah.* Trenton, NJ: Africa World Press, Inc., 1993.

Barkan, Joel D. *Politics and Public Policy in Kenya and Tanzania.* Revised Edition. New York: Praeger, 1984.

Brooker, Paul. *Twentieth-Century Dictatorships: The Ideological One-Party States.* New York: New York University Press, 1995.

Carter, Gwendolen M., ed. *African One-Party States.* Ithaca, NY: Cornell University Press, 1962.

Hermet, Guy, Richard Rose, and Alain Rouquié, eds. *Elections Without Choice.* New York: John Wiley & Sons, 1978.

Huntington, Samuel P., and Clement H. Moore, eds. *Authoritarian Politics in Modern Society: The Dynamics of Established One-Party Systems.* New York: Basic Books, Inc., 1970.

Lenin, V. I. *Selected Works.* New York: International Publishers, 1943.

Nohlen, Dieter, Michael Krennerich, and Barbara Thibaut, eds. *Elections in Africa: A Data Handbook.* New York: Oxford University Press, 1999.

Nyerere, Julius K. *Freedom and Development.* New York: Oxford University Press, 1973.

Sen, Amartya. *Poverty and Famines: An Essay on Entitlement and Deprivation.* Oxford, UK: Oxford University Press, 1981.

Waterbury, John. *The Egypt of Nasser and Sadat: The Political Economy of Two Regimes.* Princeton, NJ: Princeton University Press, 1983.

Zolberg, Aristide R. *One-Party Government in the Ivory Coast.* Revised Edition. Princeton, NJ: Princeton University Press, 1969.

SLOVAKIA

A new, land-locked Central European nation of approximately 5.3 million, Slovakia, or the Slovak Republic, is bordered by Poland to the north, the Ukraine to the east, Hungary to the south, and Austria and the Czech Republic to the west. Thirty percent of its 18,922 square miles is mountainous in the north; 20% of Slovakia is forested. The Danube is the nation's major river. Slovakia's two largest

cities—Bratislava, the capital in the southwest, and Kosice, in the southeast—dominate the otherwise agricultural lowlands. One-third of the country's land is under cultivation. Slovakia has a continental climate with cold, dry winters and hot, humid summers. Temperatures in the capital range from 30°F in the winter to 70°F in the summer; rainfall averages 25.5 inches annually.

Political History

For centuries, Slovakia was a small part of much larger empires. It first was part of the Great Moravian Empire (830–907), then under Hungarian rule from the eleventh until the early twentieth centuries. Under the Hapsburgs, Slovakia was called Upper Hungary. As part of the Austro-Hungarian Empire, Slovaks were pressured to relinquish their national identity. Despite these efforts to eradicate the Slovakian identity, a nationalist revival occurred in the late eighteenth and nineteenth centuries.

Partial sovereignty was realized after World War I under the leadership of Thomas G. Masaryk, the founding first president of the Republic of Czechoslovakia (1918–1935). Despite his democratic leadership, some Slovaks were frustrated by a unitary state directed from Prague. The dissatisfaction of Sudeten Germans within the newly created state, as well as its noted industrial capacity, provided Adolf Hitler with a pretext for occupying Czechoslovakia after the Munich Agreement of 1938. A puppet fascist Slovak state was established in March 1939 under the national cleric, Monsignor Josef Tiso. In contrast to the passive resistance of the Czechs, the Slovak National Uprising began in August 1944 and continued for several months before it was quashed.

Czechoslovakia was restored after the end of World War II, with some concessions to Slovak demands for autonomy by means of a regional legislature and an executive. The Communists seized power in 1947–1948, ending this federal experiment for twenty years. Alexander Dubcek (1921–1992), a Slovak, was made head of the Communist party of Czechoslovakia in January 1968. His immediate reform movement, known as the Prague Spring—in part a delayed de-Stalinization program—was crushed on August 21, 1968. Czechoslovakia, however, continued one of the reforms that led to the country's federalization in 1969, again giving Slovaks some national institutions that enjoyed limited autonomy. Ironically, both fascism and communism contributed to Slovak nationalism.

Dubcek's replacement was his early supporter and fellow Slovak, Gustav Husak (1913–1991). Husak was jailed from 1940–1943 by the Nazi-backed Slovak puppet government and afterward played a role in the 1944 Slovak uprising. In 1951, he was purged from the Communist party on charges of "nationalism." While serving a subsequent six-year sentence, Husak wrote a history of the 1944 revolt. His prison sentence was declared illegal in 1963 when he was politically rehabilitated.

Historically an agricultural region, Slovakia began to industrialize after the 1948 communist takeover. Enormous heavy industry and armament plants were constructed, creating dependence on the Soviet Union as a customer for the products. Husak's government was one of the sternest in east Central Europe, but it helped to improve the Slovak standard of living.

Independence

Communist Czechoslovakia unraveled within the twenty-three days of the "Velvet Revolution" of late 1989, leaving opposition forces unprepared for the sudden transition to parliamentary democracy. Economic, political, and ethnic tensions between the Czechs and the Slovaks overwhelmed the new leadership, and the seventy-four-year-old union crumbled, despite public-opinion polls that suggested that a majority of both Czechs and Slovaks were against independence. The Slovak Republic gained its independence on January 1, 1993, largely because of Vaclav Klaus and Vladimir Meciar. Klaus, Czechoslovakia's ideological prime minister with a Ph.D. in economics, saw himself as the Margaret Thatcher of Central Europe. Meciar, Slovakia's first prime minister, is sometimes referred to as the Huey Long of the Danube. Political inexperience coupled with ideological inclinations in both leaders led to the split.

A former amateur boxer, corporate lawyer, and an authoritarian populist, Meciar slowed the pace of privatization of the economy. He dominated foreign policy and aggravated tensions with Hungary. His demagogic methods—exploiting ethnic fears, efforts to control the media and corrupt political practices—led to his public rejection in the fall of 1998.

The Anti-Meciar Coalition

For the past three years, opposition political parties to Meciar's Movement for a Democratic Slovakia (HZDS) have provided stability for the nation and moved it in a progressive direction. In 2000, The Organization for Economic Cooperation and

Development (OECD) for the first time classified Slovakia as having a functioning market economy. A majority of the population favors entry into the European Union (EU). Also in 2000, Slovakia received more foreign investment than in the previous seven years combined. And in late 2001, the governing coalition initiated the process to decentralize state authority, a goal popular among Slovaks and urged by the EU. Public administration reform is scheduled to be completed in 2004, the date by which Slovaks hope to be eligible for EU entry. The European Union is Slovakia's largest trading partner; more than 60% of its exports go to the EU.

Despite many reforms, the unemployment rate hovers near 19%, the highest in Europe. Polls show that Meciar's HZDS with 28.1% of the public remains the single most popular party. National elections are scheduled for fall 2002, creating a challenge for the smaller opposition parties to stay united against Meciar. All parties, however, lack leaders of the stature of the late Dubcek. Even Meciar has been forced to favor integration with the EU and NATO, supported by nearly half of the Slovakian public and which the Czechs joined in 1999.

WILLIAM D. PEDERSON

See also Central and Eastern Europe: History and Economic Development; Central and Eastern Europe: International Relations; Czech Republic; Dubcek, Alexander; Soviet Bloc

References and Further Reading

Batt, Judy. *Czecho-Slovakia in Transition: From Federation to Separation*. London: Royal Institute of International Affairs, 1993.

Cottey, Andrew. *East-Central Europe After the Cold War*. New York: St. Martin's Press, 1996.

Felak, James R. "At the Price of the Republic": *Hlinka's Slovak People's Party, 1929–1938*. Pittsburgh: University of Pittsburgh Press, 1996.

Goldman, Minton F. *Slovakia Since Independence. A Struggle for Democracy*. Westport, CT: Praeger Publishers, 1999.

Kirschbaum, Stanislav J. *A History of Slovakia. The Struggle for Survival*. New York: St. Martin's Press, 1995.

Leff, Carol S. *The Czech and Slovak Republics. Nation versus State*. Boulder, CO: Westview Press, 1997.

Pynsent, Robert B. *Questions of Identity: Czech and Slovak Ideas of Nationality and Personality*. New York: Oxford University Press, 1994.

SLOVENIA

The Republic of Slovenia lies at the crossroads called the Balkans—sandwiched between the remnants of the Hapsburg Empire to the north, the Ottoman Empire to the south and east, and the Venetian Republic to the west. The small nation, of about 7,800 square miles in area, has long been known for its alpine vistas and pleasant climate. Ninety percent of the nation—lined by the Karawanken Mountains along its northern border with Austria and the Julian Alps and Kras (Karst) Plateau along its western border with Italy—lies above one thousand feet elevation, with a range of above nine thousand feet in the mountains to sea level along the Adriatic coast. More than 60% of the landscape is forested; 30% is classified as agricultural land, according to Slovenia government statistics. Climate is mild and humid—no dry season. Temperatures in the capitol city of Ljubljana, for example, typically range from 24°F in the winter to 80°F in the summer. Precipitation—snow in the winter and rain at other times of the year—is plentiful year-round. Slovenia has approximately 2 million residents—the largest cities are Ljubljana (250,000 residents) and Maribor (ninety-five thousand residents).

The Slovene people first settled in the Danube Valley and eastern Alps in the sixth century CE. Shortly afterward, Germanic rulers, the Carolingians in the eighth century, assumed control of what is now Slovenia. Rule then passed to another line of Germanic rulers, the Holy Roman Emperors in, the ninth century, and to the Hapsburgs in turn in the fifteenth century. The Hapsburgs retained control of Slovenia for most of the next four centuries—with a brief interruption during the Napoleonic Wars. The Hapsburg Empire began to fragment in the nineteenth century, with subject peoples—including the Slovenes—clamoring for more autonomy. The empire collapsed following its defeat in World War I, and the Slovenes in 1919 joined the Kingdom of Serbs, Croats and Slovenes—which was later named the Kingdom of Yugoslavia in 1928. Shortly after the start of World War II, Axis powers (Italy and subsequently Germany) invaded and ruled the region from 1941 to 1945. A Soviet satellite state, the Federative People's Republic of Yugoslavia (later the Socialist Federal Republic of Yugoslavia), was established following the end of World War II.

While Soviet strongman Joseph Stalin intended Yugoslavia to be a subservient, vassal state, Yugoslav strongman Josip Broz Tito, who was elected president of the republic in 1953, had other intentions and managed to keep Yugoslavia free of Soviet dominance. Tito also managed to suppress separatist movements throughout Yugoslavia, and the disparate peoples—including the Slovenes—managed to get along reasonably peacefully until Tito's death in 1980.

Following Tito's death, Serb politicians began to assert more control over the affairs of the other peoples that comprised Yugoslavia. Nationalist

rhetoric by Serb strongman Slobodan Milošević did little to encourage most of the other peoples to remain a part of Yugoslavia. Despite pressure from the United States and the many European nations that Yugoslavia should remain united, the General Assembly of the Yugoslav Republic of Slovenia declared the right to secede from Yugoslavia. Eighty-eight percent of the Slovene people voted to do so on December 23, 1990. The republic then declared its independence on June 25, 1991, and won that independence in a ten-day war in which the Yugoslav army withdrew in the face of stiff resistance from the Slovenes. The Slovenes escaped Yugoslavia at relatively little cost.

The Vatican was the first to recognize Slovenia, which has a majority Roman Catholic population. Germany likewise recognized the new nation, and the European Economic Community and the United States followed suit early in 1992. The new Slovene republic then joined the United Nations on May 22, 1992. Slovenia was determined to be an active member of the European and world communities, and, after years of preparation, joined both the North Atlantic Treaty Organization (NATO) and the European Union in 2004.

The Slovenes quickly established a stable democracy after declaring independence in 1991. Milan Kučan was elected its first president on December 6, 1992. Kučan was reelected in 1997. Janez Drnovšek was elected Slovenia's second president on December 1, 2002.

Slovenia was one of the former Yugoslavia's most advanced and prosperous republics. As a result of its nearly bloodless war of independence, its democratic government, and its close ties to the West, Slovenia has been able to remain relatively prosperous. Its economy has kept growing, even though many other nations in transition from communist or socialist economist have experienced slowdowns. In March 2004, Slovenia's prosperity allowed it to change roles from a borrower nation to a donor nation at the World Bank.

Slovenia's estimated gross domestic product in 2003 was $37 billion, which amounts to about $19,000 GDP per capita. The nation boasts of abundant natural resources, such as forest products, hydropower, coal, and metals. (It likewise suffers from environmental problems as a result of developing these resources, but is making more progress than similar states in mitigating those problems.) Despite Slovenia's natural wealth, the biggest sector of its economy is the service sector, which comprises 57% of Slovenia's GDP. The industrial sector is second at 40%. Both inflation and unemployment are something of a problem, with the inflation rate in 2003 estimated Inflation (in consumer prices) was estimated to be a little more than 5% in 2003. According to government statistics, unemployment was estimated to be about 6.6% in 2003, with the highest rate for adults being among those aged between twenty and twenty-four (14.8%). Slovenia enjoys a slight trade surplus with other nations.

The population is fairly stable, with the growth rate essentially at 0%. Fourteen percent of the population is younger than fifteen years of age. Fifteen percent is older than sixty-five. The median age is about forty. Average life expectancy at birth is seventy-six years (seventy-two for males; eighty for females). Death rates per one thousand population slightly exceed birth rates (10.15 to 8.9).

Slovenia was much more fortunate than its sister nations in escaping the bloodshed visited upon its sister nations following the breakup of Yugoslavia. It enjoys many advantages—in terms of human, economic, and natural resources—that bode well for the republic's future.

DAVID M. LAWRENCE

See also Albania; Balkan Wars of the 1990s; Bosnia and Herzegovina; Croatia; Ethnic Conflicts: Central and Eastern Europe; Macedonia; Milošević, Slobodan; Montenegro; Serbia; Nationalism, Definition; North Atlantic Treaty Organization (NATO); Self-Determination; Tito, Josip Broz (Marshall Tito); Tudzhman, Franio; Yugoslavia

References and Further Reading

Benderly, Jill, and Evan Kraft. *Independent Slovenia: Origins, Movements, Prospects.* New York: St. Martin's Press, 1996.

Mrak, Mojmir, Matija Rojec, and Carlos Silva-Jauregui. *Slovenia: From Yugoslavia to the European Union.* Washington, DC: World Bank Publications, 2004.

Prunk, Janko. *A Brief History of Slovenia: Historical Background of the Republic of Slovenia.* Ljubljana, Slovenia: Zalozba Mihelac.

Silber, Laura, and Allan Little. *Yugoslavia: Death of a Nation.* New York: Penguin Books, 1997.

Woodward, Susan L. *Balkan Tragedy: Chaos and Dissolution After the Cold War.* Washington, DC: Brookings Institution Press, 1995.

SMAZE

Smaze or smoke haze is defined as a heavy atmospheric condition that offers reduced visibility because of the presence of suspended particles. Air pollution is placed in two general categories: indoor and outdoor. Indoor air pollution is created by cooking and heating inside, while outdoor air pollution results from the combustion of fossil fuels for human consumption. Smaze is a type of outdoor pollution that causes public health problems, such as respiratory

infections, and increases the burden of disease within a country.

In the developing world, since 1945, a rapidly increasing birth rate, coupled with a decreasing death rate, has caused a population boom that has resulted in rapid urbanization and exacerbated the phenomena of smaze. For example, Mexico City has a population of 22 million people and approximately 3.5 million automobiles. Automobiles are a primary cause of smaze in Mexico City and throughout the developing world. The World Health Organization (WHO) recommends that cities have ninety milligrams or less per cubic meter of suspended particles in the air. The WHO estimates that the air of Mexico City has double the recommended number of suspended particles. These suspended particles cause respiratory conditions, increased disease prevalence, and contribute to higher infant mortality rates. Smaze also causes adverse environmental problems, such as acid rain and corrosion.

The Mexican government has responded to this crisis by implementing legislation during the late 1980s to combat the problem. The General Law of Ecological Balance and Environmental Protection (LGEEPA) of 1988 aimed to reduce all environmental pollution. In 1996, the LGEEPA was amended to include sustainable development projects. These projects included the creation of the Center for Sustainable Transport in Mexico City (CSTMC), which aimed to create sustainable transportation infrastructure, such as a rapid transit bus system and retrofitting older diesel engines on vehicles and trucks to reduce air pollutants. In addition, the Mexican government enacted a five-year National Environmental Program (1996–2000), which invested over $10 million to reduce air pollution in Mexico City. This program included tax incentives to purchase pollution control equipment and alternative fuels, while requiring catalytic converters on all automobiles.

Another reason for smaze was increased deforestation caused by slash and burn agriculture and increased logging activities. Throughout the developing world, agricultural expansion, exasperated by food insecurity issues of the rural Third World poor, has decreased the size of the rain forests as peasants move deeper into the rain forests. The rain forests, however, have traditionally served as natural filters to eliminate pollutants from the air. As the size of tropical rain forests decreases, smaze levels increase. In addition, deforestation leads to increased drought conditions, which makes forests more susceptible to fire, which also increases smaze.

LAZARUS F. O'SAKO

See also Acid Precipitation; Deforestation; Environment: Government Policies; Mexico; Rain Forest, Destruction of; Sustainable Development; Urbanization: Impact on Environment

References and Further Reading

Lewis, A. *Clean Air Fighting Smoke, Smog, and Smaze*. New York: McGraw Hill, 1965.
Pezzoli, Keith. *Human Settlements and Planning for Ecological Sustainability: The Case of Mexico City*. Cambridge, MA: The MIT Press, 1998.
Wark, Kenneth. *Air Pollution: Its Origin and Control*. Upper Saddle River, NJ: Pearson Education, 1997.

SOCIAL REVOLUTION

Social Revolution is a complex phenomenon and an elusive term. Generally the concept is subsumed within the sociological literature under the category of collective behavior, or that group behavior which is less predictable, less formal, and less subject to routine human activity. Social revolution represents the "extreme situations" in human behavior when the relatively stable social order has been disrupted and even irreparably shattered. As a phenomenon, social revolution incorporates many aspects of societal change including the political, the economic, the cultural, and the social structural. As *social* revolution rather than simply revolution, the phenomenon may incorporate uprisings, rebellions, and insurrections but is never limited to these violent events alone.

There are many competing definitions of social revolution and of revolution in general. Key disputes include the following: the kind, extent, and persistence of social change; the means of effecting change, that is, whether violence and the threat of force are essential components of social revolution; and the ideological direction of that societal change. Social revolution in contrast to simple revolution implies broad and fundamental change in all or most aspects of societal life from values to institutions. Also, social revolution is considered more than an attempted change; the revolutionary process and subsequent societal change must succeed or persist—how long remains in dispute. Thus, a revolutionary uprising that fails or a process of social change that is not consolidated cannot be a true revolution or a social revolution.

Most theorists of revolution, such as the sociologist, Chalmers Johnson, also tend to agree that such widespread societal change can only be effected by the threat or use of force and violence, so that a nonviolent social revolution is not only a contradiction in terms but impossible in the real world. Nevertheless, briefly in the 1960s, the idea of a non-violent, cultural revolution, or "revolution in the minds of men" represented a popular alternative to this view.

Although, there have been no historical cases of a non-violent, cultural revolution, some theorists of revolution, such as Dale Yoder and Rex Hopper, focused on normative and cultural change, however effected. They described revolution as "the change in the social attitudes and values basic to the traditional institutional order."

Finally, some theorists, such as Hannah Arendt, insisted that all revolutions must be progressive ideologically and/or incorporate "the struggle for freedom" and "the sense of a new beginning." This last "democratic" revolution theory posed some difficulties in meshing the theoretical literature with the historical cases of social revolution in the twentieth century. Major social revolutions of the twentieth century, such as the Russian Revolution of 1917, the Chinese Revolution of 1949, and the Cuban Revolution of 1959 were Marxist revolutions. In one sense, these revolutions used violence, in Arendt's words, to institute a "different form of government." However, most scholars of revolution would agree that these historical cases did not meet Arendt's test to create a "new body politic, where the liberation from oppression aims at least at the constitution of freedom."

Despite the debate over the exact components of social revolution, and the means by which an astute observer can determine if it has indeed occurred, several definitions of revolution and of social revolution are especially helpful. Chalmers Johnson views revolution as expanding concentric circles of violent change "in government, and/or regime, and/or society." Although this broad definition does not distinguish between societal revolution and mere insurrections, Johnson notes that "total" revolution, in contrast with "simple" revolution, recasts a society's entire structure of values and division of labor, or society's norms and institutions.

The most comprehensive description of social revolution is that of Samuel P. Huntington. "A revolution," he writes, "is a rapid, fundamental, and violence domestic change in the dominant values and myths of a society, in its political institutions, social structure, leadership, government activity and policies." His definition clearly distinguishes among lower-level, and perhaps unsuccessful coup d'etats, rebellions and insurrections, and "social" or "great" revolutions. In the latter category Huntington includes the French, Mexican, Chinese, Russian, and Cuban revolutions, but notably excludes from his list of historical cases the American Revolution of 1776. Huntington insists on the distinction between wars of independence, or "a struggle of one community against rule by an alien community," and a social revolution which necessitates major changes to the social structure.

As important as determining *what* constitutes social revolution, is explaining the *why* or the causality of social revolution. In the literature of revolution theories of revolutionary change abound with little distinction between the "simple" revolution and the "total," or "great," or "social" revolutions. A shared, central assumption of theorists is that causality of human rebellion remains operative in all types of revolution. Some theorists, however, accord this dimension greater importance than others. For example, in the view of leading political theorist, Ted Robert Gurr, revolution can be best understood as but one of many expressions of civil strife and collective violence.

Theories of revolutionary causality can be grouped into four main categories: psychological and social psychological; social systemic and structural; power-conflict; and international systemic. Gurr is an exponent of the psychological explanation of civil violence, which includes simple revolution and great or social revolutions. Another related theorist is James Davies who incorporates a social and historical dimension. The psychological and social psychological explanation for revolution focuses on "the minds of men" or states of mind of individuals and groups. The psychological theory which triggers individual and group rebellion is that of frustration-aggression activated by perceptions or feelings of relative deprivation. It is important to note that relative deprivation is distinct from absolute deprivation, which describes the actual conditions of poverty, inequality, repression, or injustice, as opposed to perceptions of these conditions. When individuals become frustrated by relative deprivation, which is a perceived and comparative sense of discrepancy between their expectations and capabilities to achieve "the goods and conditions of life' to which they believe they are rightfully entitled," they respond with aggression. If the government is blamed for this frustration, then aggression is most likely to take the form of civil or political violence against the government and its political leaders. The degree of politicized discontent, therefore, influences the magnitude and forms that political violence can take, ranging from turmoil to full-scale social revolution.

James Davies relies upon this relative deprivation model to propose the J-curve theory of rising expectations. In his words, "revolution is most likely to take place when a prolonged period of rising expectations and rising gratifications is followed by a short period of sharp reversal." It is the suddenness of the reversal in social conditions after a prolonged period of improvement that triggers insecurity, fear, and discontent. Davies terms this period of sharp reversal the "intolerable gap" between a person's expectations and gratifications. This gap provokes individual and

societal-wide frustrations, and when it becomes intolerable may explode into violent action or revolution. The Davies theory of revolutionary causality ostensibly places a greater emphasis on collective behavior and societal factors as induced by economic downturns and tragic historical events. Both the Gurr and Davies' psychological explanations of revolution, however, have been difficult to test or verify empirically, in large part, because neither theory has successfully measured, as opposed to inferred, qualitative factors, and individual or collective states of mind.

A number of the social systemic and structural explanations of revolution focus on either or both the "lag" and "disharmony" effects believed to exist in the complex process of social change. Theories in this category generally assume that extensive and rapid social change is disruptive and breeds discontent and strain which feed social turmoil. To some degree these theories imply a type of "systemic frustration" or systemic failure as the necessary preconditions for social revolution. Although reminiscent of the relative deprivation and J-curve effects of the psychological theories, certain social systemic explanations (for example, Ivo and Rosalind Feierabend and Betty Nesvold) rely more on structural conditions and their wider impact in creating "the revolutionary state of mind."

Modernization and the conflict between traditional societies and transitional and modernizing ones, especially the tensions between the values and structures of an old or receding social order and a new and emergent one are often identified to be at fault. A classic in this genre is Barrington Moore's the *Social Origins of Dictatorship and Democracy*, which describes social revolution as one outcome of the challenge of modernization and the process of capitalist economic development. Employing the Marxian historical dialectic, Moore argues that the transformation of traditional agrarian and pre-capitalist societies into a new capitalist and industrialized economic order unleashed class conflict and social revolution. Democracy resulted out of this struggle, either peacefully or via social revolution, when the bourgeoisie or capitalists emerged as the dominant class in the modernization process. Social revolution of the peasant type, however, led to an authoritarian or totalitarian outcome.

The anthropologist, Eric Wolf, proposes a similar theory linking social revolution and the diffusion of "North Atlantic capitalism." Historically, the process of capitalist development inflicted an alien cultural and economic system on wide geographical regions of the world which precipitated internal strife and social revolution. This diffusion of capitalist values and structures of economic organization reduced the value of man into that of an economic actor and alienated him from the production and creative process and eroded his social and communal ties. The insidious process of societal subversion in the transition from and old to new social order created social conflict and intolerable strain, which was ultimately expressed in social revolution.

Perhaps the culmination of this social subversion explanation for revolution is found in the social systemic theory of revolutionary change of Chalmers Johnson. In the sociological literature, Johnson is a structural-functionalist, or one who views the social system as analogous to a living, adaptive organism with established structures, processes, goals, and functions. The main purpose or goal of all these structures and processes is to preserve and maintain vital functions and the viability of the social system. Society as a system must maintain itself in a steady state or adaptive equilibrium. Social revolution occurs when the components of society are unable to "preserve system structure in the face of changing environmental conditions." In short, society can no longer adapt to the forces of change, so that, in his terms, the social system falls into disequilibrium. Social revolution, therefore, represents the complete breakdown of a "disequilibrated social system."

Despite the jargon, Johnson's schema of social revolution is an elegant process model that moves from longer term environmental and social causes to medium-term political and more immediate strategic causes of revolution. "There are two clusters of mutually-influencing necessary ... causes of any revolution," he explains. "First there are the pressures created by a disequilibrated social system—a society which is changing and which is in need of further change if it is to continue to exist." Then a "second cluster of necessary causes revolves around the quality of the purposeful change being undertaken while a system is disequilibrated." And lastly, he writes, "the final, or sufficient, cause of a revolution is some ingredient, usually contributed by fortune, which deprives the elite of its chief weapon for enforcing social behavior (accelerator)." Terms, such as "power-deflation" in the decision-making arena and "status protestors" describe attempts by policy elites to correct or rebalance the system and to control polarization of pro-and anti-system interest groups. Finally an "accelerator" or an event that provides hope to the insurgents and undermines and prevents authorities from using force to reestablish order, leads to the loss of authority of the elites and a revolutionary insurrection.

The Johnson model serves as an effective organizing device to explain the key elements of major social revolutions. The theory explains revolution within a holistic framework, emphasizing the important relationship between values and structures and between

objective conditions and evaluations of these. Nevertheless, Johnson's model of social revolution has not served as a predictive theory. Moreover, some critics argue that the theory distorts social reality and exaggerates the degree of social stability that generally exists in most societies.

The competing explanation of social revolution by Charles Tilly, in contrast to Johnson's assumptions of social stability, holds that the norm in social and political behavior is power struggle and conflict. Ultimately revolution can only succeed because of supportive political conditions and power relationships. Developed in reaction to the complex conditions for revolution imposed by the social systemic theorists, the power-conflict approach redefined revolution as primarily a political phenomenon and an endemic struggle over scarce resources, power and influence. Thus the focus is not on social revolution but on revolution generally and challenges to the established political order and its monopoly of coercive force.

Conflict is endemic because not all groups enjoy access to power and influence, and political actors must compete constantly for access to the state. Government is defined as the organizational structure which controls the principal means of coercion. The non-governmental actors are the contenders in the struggle for power and influence. These include the polity, or the groups which interact with the government and are generally successful in realizing their political demands; and the challengers which are excluded from the polity and compete unsuccessfully in the political struggle. A third group, the non-contenders, are not active participants in the political system. The patterns of interaction among these actors, much like competing interest groups, create potentially conflictive political behavior that can readily escalate into revolution. Indeed revolution occurs when the government controlled by a single polity becomes the object of struggle by contending groups. Because threat and conflict are constant features of political participation, no special psychological or motivational factors of rage or deprivation are necessary to explain revolution. In a sense, this "realist" theory reduces revolution to an innate, instinctual struggle for power, comparable to realism in the international relations theory of Hans Morgenthau.

Although within this conflict tradition, Marxist-Leninist explanations of social revolution focus on another set of key actors: classes, the state, and the international system. Karl Marx's classic theory describes social revolutions as "the locomotives of history" or as the product of inevitable historical forces driven by the mode of production within any given society and the violent clash between the owners and non-owners of the means of production or property.

In the capitalist stage of production these opposing classes are the capitalists or bourgeoisie and the workers or the proletariat, respectively. As the relations of production in capitalism deteriorate and workers misery intensifies, workers develop class consciousness and launch a "national struggle," which spontaneously "breaks out into open revolution" against the bourgeoisie.

Lenin, the famous Russian revolutionary, internationalized the Marxist theory of social revolution and adapted it to the particular reality of medieval Czarist Russia. Through the creation of a Marxist-Leninist party and a broad class alliance of workers and peasants, Lenin defied classic Marxism and proved that social revolution could also engulf Russia, a backward, pre-capitalist, and pre-industrial society. His greatest contribution to social revolution, however, was his theory of imperialism as "the highest stage of capitalism." Mature capitalism, Lenin argued, had extended its lease on life by exporting its system abroad to colonies, opening up new markets and new sources of cheap raw materials. In the process, the world capitalist revolution which Marx predicted to begin in the most highly developed and industrialized countries instead shifted to the underdeveloped, Third World countries. The Russian Revolution became the vanguard in this chain of international social revolution. Joseph Stalin extended this Leninist theory: "Formerly, it was the accepted thing to speak of the existence or absence of objective conditions for the proletarian revolution in individual countries.... Now we must speak of the existence of objective conditions for the revolution in the entire system of world imperialist economy as an integral unit." Thus, revolution will begin "where the chain of imperialism is weakest."

In *States and Social Revolution*, Theda Skocpol adapts both the class struggle and internationalizing dimensions of the Marxist-Leninist theories of revolution by redefining and emphasizing the role of the state as a central autonomous actor. "Social revolutions," she argues, "should be analyzed from a structural perspective, with special attention devoted to international contexts and to developments at home and abroad that affect the breakdown of the state organizations." Skocpol views the state as a power broker between dominant and subject classes in society, sometimes reflecting dominant class interests, but fundamentally independent of class and motivated by the goals of internal order, efficient governance and resource extraction, and survival in the competitive international system.

In the final analysis, social revolution is caused by a crisis of state that is both domestically and internationally induced. Social revolution involves

the "intersection between international conditions and pressures ... and class-structured economies, and politically organized interests." In other words, a powerful and effective state and a supportive international system translate into the absence of social revolution. Skocpol's explanation of the causes of social revolution clearly exemplifies an international systemic theory. Her theory departs from the traditional view of revolution as an exclusively internal or sub-national phenomenon, and demonstrates the correctness of Lenin's logic that social revolution remains internationally conditioned.

Indeed, the most significant trend in theories of social revolution in the twentieth and twenty-first centuries has been in the international dimension. Skocpol's focus on the international environment of the state and on its structural properties represents a necessary conceptual shift, long implied, but never as explicitly and convincingly elaborated. Social revolution exclusively conceptualized as "internal war," the innovative term of Harold Eckstein, no longer resonates in this era of globalization when the theoretical and actual boundaries between revolution and war are less defined. In the twentieth century, the term revolutionary war favored by Mao Zedong and Ho Chi Minh in their Marxist social revolutions in China and Vietnam, respectively, exemplified this growing elision of revolution and war. Today, for example, global terrorism operates extraterritorially and serves both the ends of internal and external war.

Nevertheless, an essential lesson learned in the most recent historical cases of social revolution in Nicaragua and Iran is that causality is fundamentally internal. National societies and people make social revolutions because the causes are rooted in internal, domestic conditions. External influences and intervention may temporarily tip the scales in revolutionary strategy, but have been unsuccessful in promoting lasting reform or stability. Internationalization or globalization of social revolution through intervention has confounded local and regional problems with global power conflicts—earlier East-West tensions, today North-South tensions. Global terrorism, to the extent that it may have become an instrument of social revolution within countries, as well as within specific world regions, or the world system as a whole, appears to have fallen into a similar trap. Perhaps this meshing of internal and external war has become the face of social revolution today.

WALTRAUD Q. MORALES

References and Further Reading

Arendt, Hannah. *On Revolution.* New York: Viking Press, 1963.

Brinton, Crane. *Anatomy of Revolution.* Englewood, NJ: Prentice-Hall, 1965.

Davies, James C., Ed. *When Men Revolt and Why.* New York: Free Press, 1971.

Eckstein, Harry, Ed. *Internal War: Problems and Approaches.* New York: Free Press, 1964.

Foran, John, Ed. *Theorizing Revolutions.* New York: Routledge, 1997.

Huntington, Samuel P. *Political Order in Changing Societies.* New Haven, CT: Yale University Press, 1968.

Katz, Mark N., Ed. *Revolution: International Dimensions.* Washington, DC: Congressional Quarterly, 2001.

Gurr, Ted R. *Why Men Rebel.* Princeton, NJ: Princeton University Press, 1970.

Johnson, Chalmers. *Revolutionary Change.* Boston: Little, Brown, 1966.

Moore, Barrington, Jr. *Social Origins of Dictatorship and Democracy.* Boston: Beacon Press, 1966.

Morales, Waltraud Q. *Social Revolution: Theory and Historical Application.* University of Denver, The Social Science Foundation and Graduate School of International Studies Monograph Series in World Affairs, Vol. II, Monograph No. 1, 1973–1974. University of Denver: Denver, CO.

Skocpol, Theda. *Social Revolutions in the Modern World.* Cambridge: Cambridge University Press, 1994.

———. *States and Social Revolutions: A Comparative Analysis of France, Russia, and China.* Cambridge: Cambridge University Press, 1979.

Tilly, Charles. *From Mobilization to Revolution.* Reading, MA: Addison-Wesley, 1978.

Wolf, Eric. *Peasant Wars of the Twentieth Century.* New York: Harper and Row, 1969.

SOCIALISM

In Marxist doctrine, Socialism is the stage of society that comes between the capitalist stage and the communist stage, in which private ownership of the means of production and distribution has been eliminated. Socialism established itself worldwide to the extent of receiving global acceptance in the twentieth century not so much because it was built into a system by such profound thinkers as Marx and Engels; nor even because it was espoused by a devoted and brilliant activist like Lenin, who applied the theory, with such variations as were necessary, to a concrete situation. Those were certainly important, but the main reason for the spread of socialism was that it answered some specific needs. It was only because the prevailing social order, capitalism, was unable to meet these needs, or the contradictions, to use the Marxian jargon, which it had generated, that an alternative system was conceived, and, that is why, most importantly, it was widely accepted.

Two consequences follow from this. First, socialism as a social order which seeks to supplant capitalism can succeed only as long as it needs, or resolves the contradictions of capitalism, to the satisfaction of the people, specifically the articulate section thereof,

and does not itself generate contradictions which alienate the people. Second, socialism can retain its competitive advantage over capitalism, which continues to exist as a parallel order, as long as the latter does not, by suitable modifications of its system, resolve by itself the grosser forms of contradiction it had earlier generated.

Karl Marx is sometimes criticised for having built his system round the basic conflict between the owners of the means of production, the industrial bourgeoisie, and the industrial workers, the proletariat. On this basis, he foresaw socialist revolutions taking place in the highly industrialised countries where the proletariat was or could be well organised. This did not happen. The criticism of the Marxian thesis is, therefore, legitimate. The system that Marx built was, however, not vitiated, because the contradiction which he had identified did exist in reality between the owners of the means of production and the private profit motive which inspired them, on the one hand and the interests of the property-less masses on the other. In fact, where Marx erred was to take a narrow view of the contradiction and emphasize the conflict between the industrial bourgeoisie and the workers only.

Another illusion that early communists cherished was that of a world revolution. Trotsky, for instance, regarded socialism in only one country as an anomaly. As a consequence, an element of competition was introduced which led to the ruinous Cold War. The Cold War exhausted both sides, the United States and the Union of Soviet Socialist Republics (USSR). It converted the former into the biggest debtor country in the world. The United States also lost some of its competitive edge to its allies, and industrial rivals like Japan and Germany. It, however, not only survived, but with the help of the entire capitalist bloc, was able to inflict a mortal blow on the Soviet Union and the then socialist countries of Eastern Europe. Engaged in a financially exhausting arms race with the United States and concentrating all its energies on such areas as space research, missile technology, *et al.*, the socialist group lagged behind in industries and manufactures.

The contradictions of capitalism, which were the *raison d'etre* of socialism were indeed to an extent resolved by the socialist regimes. The health and education services were superior to any in the capitalist world. As a consequence, there was a certain amount of leveling down. The glittering shop windows catering for the rich, the luxuries of five-star existence in the developed capitalist countries were markedly absent in the socialist states. This was not inconsistent with the socialist philosophy and would have presented no insuperable contradiction if the cardinal

mistake had not been made of denying democracy to the masses. In fact, not only was democracy denied, but the state resorted to violence and terror in enforcing its diktat. This certainly reached its height under Stalin in the Soviet Union, but was accepted as a principle of state policy by all communist regimes, even in the post-Stalin Soviet Union and in all Eastern European states.

Two consequences followed from this. First, the masses, denied all participation in governance of the country and often forced to accept decisions handed down from above, developed no understanding of the socialist system. They regarded the benefits they received in social affairs as gratuitous, while they not only resented such high-handed measures as forced collectivisation, but nursed grievances against some of the development measures of the five year plans that were handed down to them without consultation. In these circumstances, socialist consciousness did not develop and when socialism was in peril, there was no mass upsurge to defend it.

Second, a more serious contradiction developed from the denial of democracy. In the name of the vanguard role of the Party, power was appropriated by Party cadres, and shared by them with the government bureaucracy which grew in strength with the implementation of centralised plan. A new class thus developed in what should have been a classless society, which exercised the immense powers of the state. And it was here that the time-tested dictum, that power corrupts and absolute power corrupts absolutely, operated. The Party and government bosses lived in luxurious dachas, moved about in limousines and generally threw their weight about. This not only alienated the masses, but what was perhaps worse, distorted the vision of the young aspiring Party cadres and government bureaucracy who, with no allegiance to the concept of socialistic equality, were lured by the luxuries of the developed capitalist countries. It was this class of people, executives in state undertakings, Party and government officials, who started the drift, some by physical migration to the West.

Stalin is generally blamed for having introduced dictatorial and terrorist methods in state administration. The blame is not undeserved except that these practices were not introduced, but only carried to an excess by him. The seeds of Stalinism were sown when pleas for democracy by leaders like Rosa Luxemburg were not heeded and concepts of democratic centralism and dictatorship of the proletariat were sponsored by Lenin himself, the architect of the Revolution of 1917. It is possible that the circumstances immediately following the Revolution compelled him to do so, and that had Lenin lived longer, he would have introduced real democracy. This is, however, a matter

of speculation. The fact remains that the humanistic aspect of socialism which was not only the reason for its emergence as a social system, but its basic strength is replacing the then unjust social order, was overlooked in the popular mind, and socialism came to be identified with denial of democracy, dictatorial methods and even violence.

The second factor, namely, readjustment of mature capitalism to meet the contradictions generated in the earlier phase, also operated. With technological advancement, the needs for exploitation of local labour as in nineteenth century Britain, or of slave labour as in the United States, or even of the colonial masses as practised by several of the West European countries for primary accumulation of capital, ceased to exist. Enough was produced for the employers to share a part of it with the workers. This was reflected not only in better conditions of service, but in welfare measures and social security systems. Roosevelt's New Deal in the United States during the Great Depression of the 1930s, and the Beveridge Plan in Britain, as also Welfareism in the Nordic countries during the post World War II period, represented this changing face of capitalism.

These measures undoubtedly lacked stability. They depended on the decisions of capitalists of what could be spared after providing the necessary incentives to risk capital and attracting managerial talent. An industrial recession, as at present, has witnessed such measures being slashed. Social security has suffered with the rise of unemployment, again as at present. With "jobless growth" on account of technological advances, the future holds little prospects of improvement.

Nevertheless, the improvements offered to the standard of living of the workers in the developed capitalist countries have lured them to demand more out of the present system rather than change it. Economism has taken the place of revolutionary fervour in these countries.

It is not within the purview of this essay to undertake a detailed analysis of the immediate circumstances that led to the collapse of socialism in the erstwhile Soviet Union and the East European combines. Obviously, no leader firmly rooted in socialist values appeared who had sufficient stature to make the much-needed changes in the prevailing regimes. In retrospect, Khrushchev who exposed excesses of Stalin at the Twentieth Congress showed no understanding of the basic malaise. The system continued, though the excesses were avoided. The last attempt to change the system was by Mikhail Gorbachev with his *perestroika* and *glasnost*. They were ill-conceived, and ended in disaster, throwing doubts about his credentials as a devoted socialist. The collapse was complete both in the heartland of the erstwhile Soviet Union and in East Europe. Socialism was replaced by the primordial instincts of ethnicity, regionalism, and religious fundamentalism. But socialism is not dead beyond revival.

P. GODFREY OKOTH

References and Further Reading

Bogolyubov, Kalenski. *Development of the Agrarian Sector in the U.S.S.R*, Moscow: Novosti Press, 1983.

Bunce, Valerie. "Domestic Reforms and International change: The Gorbachev Reform in Historical Perspective". *International Organization*, 47(1), Winter 1993.

Degras, Jirus. *The Communist International, 1919–1943 Documents Vol. I*. London: Arnold, 1956.

Dupee, Franklin W. *The Russian Revolution: The Overthrow of Tzarism and the Triumph of the Soviets*. New York: Doubleday, 1959.

Fukuyama, Francis. "The End of History?" *The National Interest* Summer 1989.

Gorbachev, Mikhail. *Perestroika – New Thinking for Our Country and the World*. New York: Harper and Row, 1987.

Hyland, William G. *The Cold War is Over*, New York: Times Books, Random House, 1990.

Lenin, Vladim I. *Imperialism: The Highest Stage of Capitalism*. Moscow: Progress Publishers, Twentieth Printing, 1986.

Marx, Karl. *Capital*, 3 Volumes. New York: Verso, 1967.

SOCIALIST ECONOMIC MODEL

There are many types of socialist economic models; however, all share the key principles of collective ownership of the means of production, egalitarianism, and public provision of social services.

The oldest and most widespread type is the Marxist one, based on the philosophies of German radical philosopher Karl Marx. He considered communist society, an association of free men acting as one collective, yielding a great social workforce which is used consciously and in a planned manner to achieve the society's common goals.

The Marxist theory is based on the classical economic theory of labor value adjusted to modern capitalist production methods. The only source of value is the work itself, the value of each demanded good is directly proportional only with the amount of labor used to produce that good. In capitalism the workers sell their labor as a commodity. The capitalists, who own the means of production, sell goods at higher prices than they have paid for the labor. This extra value enriches the capitalist, who profits without working, just by owning the means of production which are also the result of previous exploitation.

Capitalists can better exploit their workers if they put them to work on machines, hence producing more goods for the same labor costs. The "relative surplus

value" of each good grows. The hopes of higher profits will result in competition, which can increase to that extent when too much is produced, exceeding demand. This extra production capacity, leads to crises, which lead to massive layoffs and bankruptcy of smaller firms. This subsequently fosters the concentration of capital as the large firms survive. These firms, taking advantage of the large pool of available labor versus the small number of jobs, can drive down the wage level. The reduction of labor costs and the reduced competition, paralleled with the crisis, cause the devaluation of capital goods which in turn favors the increase of the production until the process repeats itself ending into a new depression, after a shorter cycle by this time. As the main ideology of capitalism is the struggle for permanent, unlimited growth, the system draws itself into collapse by its inherent nature, since unlimited growth cannot be sustained. Thus wages become smaller and smaller to increase profits. Classical Marxism affirms that this decadence is continuous, the process can be delayed but the final collapse cannot be avoided. Therefore the "inherently rotten" capitalism is speeding its way towards self-destruction. The socialist revolution wipes out the roots of the establishment—the private ownership, the capitalist class—but maintains at the same time its achievements: the high productivity, educated worker class, and the economies of scale. Thus according to Marx, the order of achieving perfection looks as it follows: capitalism as the thesis, socialism as the antithesis and communism as the synthesis.

In Lenin's vision of this accelerated process of self-combustion, capitalism cannot be satisfied with the existing resources; therefore, in the highest stage of its evolution, it turns into imperialism. The continuing growth can be maintained only through conquests and other ways of extended control and domination. This will result in leading capitalist countries trying to control the world's resources, causing large scale wars. Because wars destroy production factors, there is need for another successful war to repair or complete the depleted resources. In this case, war prospects eliminate competition and gearing up production, causing growth and excess supply of goods. However, this will cause price levels to plummet, and therefore yet another war will be needed to create proper demand. The resulting high prices yielded by the shortage will increase revenue levels to satisfy the ever growing capitalist hunger for profits. So capitalist states will destroy each other in the end—a vision Stalin firmly believed.

Stalin continued the societal transformation started by Lenin, but in a radical style Marx or Lenin couldn't have imagined. The Stalinist model meant the total nationalization of all the means of production, including land, services, and commercial activity. Thus the state became the one and only capitalist, having a complete monopoly not only in the economy but in the society as well, in the form of totalitarianism.

The economy operated according to the will of its central planners. In five-year plans, bureaucrats forecast the needs of the economy and population for five years ahead. The price system was determined by the state, by planners who made forecasts regarding production targets and consumption patterns. This socialist model involved a huge bureaucratic apparatus without feedback from the markets. This in turn avoided the influence of business cycles; thus the model would ideally achieve macroeconomic stability mostly due to its closed character. Since markets and the price mechanism were nonexistent or could not play their regulatory role, planners created a rigid system based on dirigisme. This resulted in an economy of shortages due to forced savings and industrialization.

The ownership and control structure of the socialist enterprise has three pillars: the paternalist leader (the party), the state bureaucracy, and the corporate management. In the Stalinist model, the greatest role was played by the paternalist leader; in the central European model, by the corporate management. The state paternalism was expressed by the securing of markets for the products.

When socialism was first introduced, it was beneficial to the poorer strata of society, as it leveled incomes and wealth through reallocation of the existing resources. Countries who adopted it virtually put an end to unemployment, although at the costs of giving up competition as well as productivity requirements. As the surplus value and previously seized capital stock vanished, accompanied by fading enthusiasm on the part of workers, most of the socialist companies stayed in a situation of permanent bankruptcy governed by the state. Due to central planning an economy of shortages followed, certain categories of consumer goods, especially basic ones like food and energy had to be rationed leading to severe malnutrition (Stalinist Soviet Union, Ceausescu's Romania) and famine (Ukraine after WWI and currently North Korea).

After de-Stalinization, market socialism emerged. Market socialism, as with all socialist models, relies on public ownership of the means of production, but the decision-making and information structure are decentralized and the economy is coordinated by the market forces. Labor incentives are pecuniary. In the event of shortage or surplus, prices are adjusted to reach macroeconomic equilibrium. This control of pricing can be used to correct market failures like

externalities or to lessen the impact of business cycles. The income of the economy can be viewed as "social dividend" and is used to finance investment to achieve growth and distributional goals.

The cooperative version of market socialism differs from the prototype (Lange) model in that that decisions at the enterprise level are taken by the workers, which in turn leads to an equitable income distribution. This resembles more a market system as the prices are set by markets, not by the planners, and the labor market is liberalized. Cooperative market socialism eliminates capitalist dichotomy between management and labor and achieves greater social justice, but can lead to misallocation of labor and resources, resulting in unemployment.

Some leaders of Central European countries tried to turn the socialist model into "socialism with human face." The Hungarian model of welfare communism, "goulash communism," adopted in compensation after the crushing of the anti–Soviet Hungarian revolution in 1956, aborted partially the forced industrialization path. The economy became more open, allowing private entrepreneurship in form of small cooperatives or economic workgroups. The quasi-socialist model couldn't overcome the inherent difficulties of the system; growth and the standards of living were maintained at the heavy cost of foreign debt.

In the former Yugoslavia, Marshall Tito introduced a cooperative type of socialism, based on worker ownership and open economy where foreign trade wasn't used only to correct planning failures. The Yugoslav model inspired neighboring socialist countries. The country replacing central planning with bottom-up and informational indicative planning. The economy became open and integrated into the world economy, with non binding macroeconomic targets. Fiscal or monetary policy was used at a minimum level to stabilize economy. Ongoing decentralization led to enterprise autonomy, allowing workers to control the use of their profits. Private entrepreneurship was allowed as in Hungary, but if a workforce exceeded five people, it must be organized as a workers' cooperative. In cooperatives, workers elected the workers' council which acted as a board of directors. Governance structures resembled that of a capitalist firm. In spite of worker management of the enterprises, however, investment remained highly centralized and saving was forced especially through high taxes. The government would over invest and routinely bail out failing enterprises.

Fidel Castro remained faithful to total isolation. The Cuban model was inspired also by pre Colombian cooperative labor and was based on a combination of national pride with social dignity, augmented by strong fears of total social and economic annihilation by the United States. The paternalistic regime has survived, and has gradually opened its markets without changing its ideology.

The isolationist stance was followed by Ceausescu, who turned Romania into a model Stalinist economy mixed with nationalist socialist ideology. National-communist Romania adopted an almost complete autarky compensated by a state fueled aggressive nationalism—denying the key principle of communism, the brotherhood of the nations.

All these routes to communist socialism converged to a common and nearly simultaneous end—the mostly peaceful collapse of the Soviet Union, its European satellite regimes, and most of its third world allies. This was the consequence of the adoption of the human-face socialism in the Soviet Union under party leader and president Mikhail Gorbachev. As the Soviet Union's status as a superpower vanished, the forces of international solidarity were proven too weak to withhold the system from economic and political collapse.

One reason for the failure of the socialist economic model was the political ideology that promised better standards of living than in capitalism, but which failed to deliver. The other reason was purely political and mostly cultural: former communist societies in Europe and Eurasia were fed up with dictatorship and longed for democracy, which was seen as inextricably linked to capitalism. Some nations, such as China, maintained their communist political establishment but loosened their markets, leading to a state-controlled capitalist development path.

Vietnam abandoned its mixture of national ideological unity and orthodox socialism and has adopted market economy with socialistic orientation. After twenty years of reforms, or "doi moi," Vietnam has accepted market mechanisms and international economic integration as the means to build-up socialism. In spite of the successes, the necessary market—economy institutions are not fully established and lack transparency. The economy does not provide a level playing field for private enterprises and is largely dominated by big state-owned monopolies.

The Chinese model of socialism evolved on Marxist foundations, settling on extreme uniformization and canceling individual initiative. Mao Zedong envisioned development based on agriculture, given the rural nature of most of the country, but the Cultural Revolution tried to wipe out every traditional value and thus make way for rootless modernity. Witnessing the reform process and the downfall of socialism in the Soviet bloc, China developed a socialist market economy, becoming more of a developmental economy without much social concern. The Chinese socialist market economy model maintained the classical

planned economy structure allowing for privatization, small private enterprise creation and foreign direct investment, while heavily subsidizing large state companies in order to develop successful Chinese multinational corporations in strategic sectors. The economy is controlled from the top; leading enterprises are founded or owned by important party officials, while the general population is given small investment and entrepreneurship opportunities. The country has embarked on a breakneck pace of industrialization, transforming the mainly rural society into the factory of the world. Although producing outstanding growth and posing serious economic challenges to other market leaders, the Chinese production is mainly low-tech assembly-line output of components, while the developed world's companies own the intellectual property rights. This situation may change soon as China tries to follow a similar technological development path like Japan and the earlier "tigers." On the other hand the uneven income distribution affects the masses heavily and lack of democratic freedom makes the foundations of this third way quite fragile.

A noncommunist socialist economic model was developed by Sweden which preserved private ownership and markets but leveled the inefficiencies of the resulting income distribution by differentiated taxation, regulating the labor market, and providing a social security net for every employee, creating a successful welfare state.

LASZLO KOCSIS

See also China; Communist Economic Model; Cuba; Free Market Economy; Marxism; Mixed Economy; Soviet Bloc; State-Directed Economy

References and Further Reading

Bardhan, Pranab and Roemer, John Market. *Socialism: The Current Debate*. Oxford: Oxford University Press, 1993.

Bottomore, T. B. The Socialist Economy: Theory and Practice. New York: Harvester Wheatsheaf, 1990.

Craig, P. R. *Alienation and the Soviet Economy: The Collapse of the Socialist Era*. New York: Holmes & Meier, 1990.

Ellen Comiso, L. and D' Andre Tyson, Eds. *Power, Purpose and Collective Choice: Economic Strategy in Socialist States*. Ithaca, NY: Cornell University Press, 1986.

Kornai, J. *Growth, Shortage and Efficiency—A Macrodynamic Model of the Socialist Economy*. Oxford: Blackwell, 1982.

———. *Contradictions and Dilemmas. Studies in the Socialist Economy and Society*. Budapest: Corvina, 1985.

———. *The Socialist System: The Political Economy of Communism*. Oxford: Clarendon Press, 1992.

Lange, Oscar and Taylor, Fred. "On the Economic Theory of Socialism" in A. Nove and I. Thatcher (eds.) *Markets and Socialism*, 1994.

Roemer, John. "Can There Be Socialism after Communism?" in P. Bardhan and J. Roemer (eds.) *Market Socialism: The Current Debate*. Oxford: Oxford University Press, 1993.

Socialist Union: Twentieth Century Socialism: The Economy of Tomorrow. Penguin Books, 1956.

SOLIDARITY UNION

Solidarity (*Solidarnosc* in Polish), Polish trade union that initiated the beginning of political reform in communist Poland. Founded in Gdansk in September 1980 as a coalition of trade unions, Solidarity's original goals were to protest sharp inflationary pressures in the 1970s, particularly of high price increases for food.

Like much of the industrialized world in the 1970s, increased energy and material costs imposed inflationary pressures that damaged the Polish economy. Furthermore, contractual agreements with the Soviet Union favored supplying Moscow with raw materials and food at lower than any reasonable market rate. Poland and other countries within the Warsaw Pact essentially subsidized some of the Soviet Union's costs. Though the system was packaged differently, it economically resembled some of the unfair trading practices that Britain and France had imposed on their colonies during their imperial eras. Moscow routinely issued demands with regard to trade, production, and distribution on its satellite countries. Locals had virtually no input and national governments in many ways performed as provincial or state governments. This Soviet command economy system was inefficient and resulted in tremendous shortages in essential products such as food, toilet paper, and soap.

Economists frequently blame the lack of a market mechanism in determining price and value for the collapse of the communist system. Black markets, which inevitably benefit the wealthy and the well-connected, flourished under such conditions. It is an economic paradox in that a government-controlled price system would create black markets that would benefit the elite. Solidarity emerged as a movement that sought to correct such injustices. The government-controlled market adjusted prices upward to reflect the growing costs endured by the state agricultural board. By the mid-1970s, serious protests emerged from workers who endured increasingly difficult conditions. After a food strike in 1976 that resulted in the arrest of thousands of workers, a group of intellectuals decided to form the Workers' Defense Committee (*Komitet Obrony Robotnikow*; KOR). The KOR provided assistance to the families of those that were imprisoned.

Gdansk, a large industrial port city, was the geographic center of the Solidarity movement. Lech Walesa, an electrician by trade, became one of the leaders of the effort to improve living conditions for workers. By the summer of 1980, Walesa was widely perceived as a "moderate" leader who sought to negotiate better pay and lower prices for workers. As protesters grew in size (from the thousands to tens of thousands) and in scope (they began to spread throughout Poland), Walesa obtained stronger bargaining powers with the government. On August 30, 1980, the Polish government signed an accord that allowed unions to be free and independent from the national communist party, gave them the right to strike, and allowed limited freedoms of religious and political expression. These reforms were substantial for the time in Eastern Europe. In many ways, these reflected the efforts of the Czechoslovakian government in spring 1968 and in Hungary during 1956 to develop a more democratic version of communism.

On September 22, 1980, a delegation of thirty-six regional trade unions met and Solidarity was formally founded as a national political entity. The formalization disbanded the KOR as members became part of a legitimately recognized group. After viewing heavy industry's success, a group of over a thousand farmers met in Warsaw on December 14, 1980, to form Rural Solidarity (*Wiejska Solidarnosc*) to assist the agricultural sector in voicing opposition to national communist production and pricing policies.

The Polish government under the leadership of Premier General Wojciech Jaruzelski played a difficult balancing act in trying to keep Polish workers satisfied and maintaining the confidence of the Soviet government. Throughout 1981, the Solidarity efforts increased. Walesa and other moderates continued to struggle between the militant wing of their movement and continual negotiations with Jaruzelski's regime. The Soviet government openly and covertly interfered with Solidarity's negotiations. Jaruzelski was constantly reminded by the Soviets of the consequences (a Soviet invasion such as in Czechoslovakia in 1968 and in Hungary in 1956) of his inability to restrict the Solidarity movement. The pressures increased too much for Jaruzelski. Fearing military intervention by the Soviets, martial law was imposed on December 13, 1981. For over nineteen months, the Polish military ran the daily affairs of the government. Walesa and most of the leadership were imprisoned during this crackdown. Polish martial law continued until after the political climate in Moscow softened (with the deaths of Soviet leader Brezhnev in November 1982 and the terminal illness of longtime KGB director and succeeding Soviet leader Andropov). By the summer of 1983, conditions slowly became normalized. Throughout the remainder of the 1980s Solidarity functioned as the voice of opposition to the national communist party. In 1989, political reforms due in part to Soviet leader Gorbachev's increasing tolerance, allowed open elections. Walesa became the first democratically elected leader of Poland by the end of 1989.

Solidarity's chief contribution to development was that it functioned as a type of evolution within the communist system. The organization also underscored the paradox of the communist system established under Stalin after WWII. The political system was supposed to represent the interests of the workers and yet when the workers expressed an opinion different from the establishment, they were suppressed. Solidarity serves as a reminder of the non-democratic nature of Polish communism. Ideologically, the movement was compromised of many types. The organization's power was based in its opposition to tyrannical conditions. The movement functioned more as a social democratic movement. However, there were other minor coalitions or special interest groups within (such as Catholics, small farmers who sought privatization, and intellectuals seeking more freedom of speech) Solidarity that gave it national and international appeal.

The martial law crisis of 1981–1983 reminded the world of the essential communist imperialism that Stalin and his agents had established. This coincided with Ronald Reagan's rise to the US presidency with his accusations of the Soviet Union as "an evil empire." The martial law and other suppressive actions used against Solidarity played right into President Reagan's portrayal of the immoral Soviet Union. Many authors cite Solidarity's civil disobedience as the beginning of the end of Soviet control of Eastern Europe. However, it was new Soviet leadership under Gorbachev (not within Poland) that allowed significant reform to occur. Solidarity can be viewed as a product of the elitist form of communism constructed during the Cold War. The workers sought better living conditions against a government that claimed to guarantee them.

JOSIAH R. BAKER

See also Central and Eastern Europe: History and Economic Development; Central and Eastern Europe: International Relations; Jaruzelski, Wojciech; Poland; Soviet Bloc; Stalin, Joseph; Walesa, Lech

References and Further Reading

Eringer, Robert. *Strike for Freedom: The Story of Lech Walesa and Polish Solidarity*. New York: Dodd, Mead, c1982.

Goodwyn, Lawrence. *Breaking the Barrier: The Rise of Solidarity in Poland.* New York: Oxford University Press, 1991.

Kubik, Jan. *The Power of Symbols against the Symbols of Power: The Rise of Solidarity and the Fall of State Socialism in Poland.* University Park, PA: Pennsylvania State University Press, c1994.

Laba, Roman. *The Roots of Solidarity: A Political Sociology of Poland's Working-Class Democratization.* Princeton, NJ: Princeton University Press, c1991.

Moses, John Anthony. *Trade Union Theory rom Marx to Walesa.* New York: Berg: Distributed exclusively in the United States and Canada by St. Martin's Press, 1990.

Perdue, William D. *Paradox of Change: The Rise and Fall of Solidarity in the New Poland.* Westport, CT: Praeger, 1995.

Stefoff, Rebecca. *Lech Walesa: The Road to Democracy.* Rebecca Stefoff. Edition: 1st ed. New York: Fawcett Columbine, 1992.

SOLOMON ISLANDS

The Solomon Islands are a constitutional monarchy with the English monarch as Head of State, represented by a Governor General appointed by the Parliament for five years. The National Parliament comprises fifty members elected by first past the post vote for a four-year term. The Prime Minister, elected by the Members of Parliament for a four-year term, selects a Ministry who are officially appointed by the Governor General. The country is divided into nine provinces, each with a local Assembly elected by popular vote and a Premier. The Provincial Assemblies have local responsibilities in the fields of health, education and communications.

In late 1998 a violent conflict erupted between the inhabitants of the island of Guadalcanal and thousands of migrant-settlers, mainly from the neighbouring island of Malaita, who were attracted to the economic opportunities offered by the capital, Honiara. A *coup* by the Malaita Eagle Force in June 2000 ousted Prime Minister Ulufa'alu. A peace agreement signed in Townsville in October 2000, failed to end the violence and armed groups are still active in Honiara and elsewhere in Guadalcanal. In late August 2002, a Cabinet Minister was assassinated on the Weathercoast of Guadalcanal for which rebel leader, Harold Keke claimed responsibility. The Solomon Islands cabinet has been criticised by donor countries for failing to curb militia members and Cabinet Ministers themselves have been responsible for attacks on a local newspaper office and threats to kill. Many of the police are reported to be running illegal businesses and have refused to hand in weapons stolen from police armouries. A ceasefire was signed between warring ethnic groups on August 5, 2000, followed by the Townsville Peace Agreement on October 15, 2000,

and the Marau Peace Agreement on February 7, 2001, which was facilitated by Australia and New Zealand. An International Peace Monitoring Team was forced by ex-combatants to withdraw from most of its outposts, illustrating the failure of the agreements to bring about sustainable peace.

The social, economic, and political complexities of resource extraction are common to conflicts about development in the Solomon Islands, to which must be added the difficulties generated by in-migration. The conflict resolution process that was used to diminish the 1998–2000 conflict in the Solomon Islands was critiqued for failing to address underlying governance related problems that were focused on decentralisation and internal migration. The central government failed to respond effectively to demands for better distribution of resources to the different provinces; failed to address problems that had arisen from internal migrations, in particular the settlement of Malaitans on Guadalcanal Island; and failed to ameliorate confusion regarding the applicability of the traditional practice of compensation payments, which meant that the people of Guadalcanal did not have access to clear channels to seek redress for their grievances.

The Solomon Islands Alliance for Change party's *kastom* feast in Honiara, held to try to settle the conflict, was also deemed ineffective because opposition party members were not present, and issues raised by people from Guadalcanal were not addressed. However, the government did establish a committee to review the existing government system, and the Honiara Peace Accord called for an investigation into land that had allegedly been illegally acquired by Malaitan settlers. Nevertheless, as the conflict escalated, resolution efforts were concentrated on stopping the violence, attention to underlying issues dissipated, and progress towards the implementation of constitutional reform and discussion of internal migration was slowed. Hence, it is likely that conflict about development will continue in the Solomon Islands due to the problems generated by an incapable and failing state, young male unemployment, in-migration, and patriarchal attitudes towards women, combined with ineffective internationally based conflict resolution processes that do not respect local concerns.

Indeed, Australia perceives the Solomon Islands' inherent political instability as providing a potential site for terrorist activities. But inequitable distribution of resource extraction benefits link to ethnic tensions, the subordination of women, and youth unemployment and warrior constructions of masculinity to limit potential benefits from development.

Solomon Islands women, in particular, have faced the many challenges of ethnic conflict and then

lawlessness as armed gangs held sway before 2003's Australian-led intervention. Solomon Islands men, used to the status gained from war and weapons, had difficulty reintegrating into fragile postwar societies, which offered few employment opportunities. As frustration led to battering of wives and children, violence and lack of respect for girls and women are now considered key human rights issues throughout Pacific countries.

Significantly, the capacities of Solomon Islands women are also unrecognised. Women interposed themselves between the two militias in the capital Honiara for weeks in an effort to end conflict, and formed the Bougainville Women for Peace and Freedom (BWPF) group, which worked with militia groups, the government and others to promote peace in 2000. Recent publications recount the stories of women who fled their homes for the jungle to escape violence, living on the run, giving birth in leaf shelters and caring for the frail and the elderly, and using customary knowledge and self-reliance to rebuild community structures in their bushland.

Also unrecognised by development project designers and practitioners in the Solomon Islands is the social significance of the Christian church. The organisation is a key to effective policy implementation and potential political stability in many south Pacific nations where significant proportions of the population self-identify as Christian. Church institutions play both positive and negative roles, sometimes generating strong connections between peoples and a constructive sense of nationhood, at others denominations become sources of division and members mobilise around their ethnic and religious identities. Another important oversight is that women's groups created by churches which are active in townships and rural areas, conduct important group activities, and serve their community's needs, are barely acknowledged.

Currently a mosaic of post-conflict societies, Solomon Islanders have significant work ahead to ensure all citizens receive the benefits of development.

HELEN JOHNSON

See also Globalization: Impact on Development; Oceania: History and Economic Development; Oceania: International Relations; Women: Role in Development

References and Further Reading

Bennett, J. "Roots of Conflict in Solomon Islands - though much is taken, much abides: legacies of tradition and colonialism" in *State, Society and Governance in Melanesia Project Discussion Paper*, No. 5. 2002.

Dinnen, S. "Winners and Losers: Politics and Disorder in the Solomon Islands 2000–2002, (Political Chronicles)" in *The Journal of Pacific History*, Vol 36, No.3, December 2002.

Forman, C. "'Sing to the Lord a New Song: Women in the Churches of Oceania" in *Rethinking Women's Roles Perspectives from the Pacific*, D. O'Brien and S. Tiffany (Eds.) Berkeley, Los Angeles, London: University of California Press, 1984.

Fry, G. "Political Legitimacy and the Post-colonial State in the Pacific: Reflections on Some Common Threads in the Fiji and Solomon Islands *Coups*" in *Pacifica Review*, Vol.12, No.3, 2000.

Howley, P. *Breaking Spears and Mending Hearts: Peacemakers and Restorative Justice in Bougainville*, London, Annandale NSW: Zed Books, The Federation Press, 2002.

Jourdan, C. "Where Have All the Cultures Gone?: Sociocultural Creolisation in the Solomon Islands" in *Melanesian Modernities*, J. Friedman and J. Carrier (Eds.), Sweden: Lund University Press, 1996.

Kabutaulaka, T. "'Failed State' and the War on Terrorism: Intervention in Solomon Islands" in *Asia Pacific Issues*, Honolulu: East-West Center—University of Hawaii, No. 72, March, 2004.

Naitoro, John. "Solomon Islands Conflict: Demands for Historical Recitification and Restorative Justice" in *Asia Pacific School of Economics and Management*, Asia Pacific Press: ANU, 2000.

Takunani Sirivi, J. and Marilyn Taleo Havini, eds. *As Mothers of the Land: The Birth of the Bougainville Women for Peace and Freedom*. Canberra, ACT: Pandanus Books, 2004.

Wielders, I. *Conflict Resolution and Governance in Solomon Islands*. Sydney, NSW: Centre for Peace and Conflict Studies, University of Sydney, 2003.

SOMALIA

Somalia is an arid country in the northeast Horn of Africa. The plains between the Jubba and Shebelle rivers, south of the capital of Mogadishu, are the only significant farming areas. Most Somalis were traditionally nomadic camel and goat herders, organised around clan and lineage ties. The limits of clan territory were that which they could successfully defend amidst constantly shifting clan alliances. Somali perceived no boundaries in the Western sense of tenure or fixed territory. There are Somali communities in Djibouti, Kenya, and the Ogaden region of Ethiopia, as well as Somalia.

Today many educated Somali have moved to the towns seeking employment. The main export trade is livestock through the northern ports of Berbera and Bossaso to the Middle East market and across the southern border into Kenya. However, the main sources of income for many are remittances, some $1 billion US per year, from relatives in the Somalia diaspora. In November 2001, many Somalis suffered when the United States froze the assets of al-Barakaat, the main international exchange institution

in Somalia, on the grounds of possible links to al Qaida.

Arab traders established coastal towns, which came under Omani rule in the sixteenth century, though pastoral Somali nomads of the interior were little affected. Egypt claimed northern Somalia in 1875, but withdraw in 1884. In 1885, Britain declared a protectorate over northern Somaliland to safeguard access to the Red Sea and the Suez Canal but largely ignored it. Italy claimed the southern Indian Ocean coastline in 1889 and established cotton, sugar, and banana plantations in the Jubba.

After Italy's defeat in 1941, southern Somalia was briefly occupied by British forces but returned to Italy as a United Nations (UN) trusteeship in 1950, in preparation for independence. The nationalist Somali Youth League (SYL) won the election in Italian Somaliland in 1956. Elections in British Somaliland in 1960 were won by the Somali National League (SNL), which advocated reunification and independence, achieved on July 1, 1960.

Somali reunification proved difficult. The new republic was built on two quite different colonial experiences and lacked a national infrastructure. There were irredentist claims against Ethiopia, French Somaliland (became Djibouti in 1977), and the Somali-populated Northern Frontier District of Kenya, as well as internal clan rivalries reflected in the proliferation of political parties. An unsuccessful war with Ethiopia in 1964, over the irredentist claims to the Somali region of Ogaden in Ethiopia, exacerbated internal tension, culminating in the assassination of Pres. Shermakhe. A week later on October 21, 1969, a military coup brought Maj.-Gen. Mohammed Siyad Barre to power.

The Revolutionary Council under Siyad Barre adopted a policy of "scientific socialism," close ties with the Soviet Union, and nationalism through the use of Somali as a written language. Yet the country remained desperately poor. Barre sought to rally popularity by launching an attack on Ethiopia over the Ogaden in 1977. The Soviets changed sides and Cuban-backed Ethiopian forces routed the Somali army, leading to an attempted coup. The autocratic one-party government held elections in August 1979, in an attempt at legitimacy against the clandestine opposition Somalia Salvation Democratic Front (SSDF), founded in 1979. In 1981, the Issaq-separatist Somali National Movement (SNM) began demanding regional autonomy for former British Somaliland. When Ethiopia and Somalia signed an accord in 1987, alienated Ogadenis formed the rebel Somali Patriotic Movement (SPM).

In August 1990, the SPM, SNM and Hawiye-based United Somali Congress (USC) formed a loose alliance against Barre, who fled to Kenya in January 1991. A short-lived government of national reconciliation ruptured when Ali Mahdi Mohamed was named interim president, reigniting clan rivalries. Ali Mahdi was forced to flee Mogadishu in November 1991, after an assault by USC forced under Gen. Mohammed Farrah Aydid, who proclaimed himself head of state.

The Issaq separatists formed a breakaway Somaliland Republic under SNM leader Abduraham Ahmed Ali, who was ousted as president by SNM rival Mohamed Ibrahim Egal in May 1993. Egal died in 2002, succeeded as president by Dahir Riyale Kahin.

Civil war raged, infrastructure collapsed and drought hit, putting 1.5 million at risk. UN Secretary General Boutros Boutros Ghali berated the UN Security Council for inaction. Ali Mahdi pleaded for UN intervention, opposed by Aydid. The airlifts of food aid sparked fresh clan violence, forcing the withdrawal of aid workers.

In December 1992, some twenty-eight thousand US troops, plus contingents of the French Foreign Legion, Italy, Canada, Australia, Nigeria, Zimbabwe, and a host of other countries, arrived in Somalia, though their mission was unclear. While the US administration insisted they were there simply to secure humanitarian aid, the UN Secretary-General pushed for a more interventionist disarming of hostile factions and pacification. Short-term military and aid objectives took precedence over any Somali political resolution.

The US-led military and UN failed to understand the shifting alliances of Somali clan politics. Many Somalis saw US policy of blaming Aydid as anti-Hawiye clan and pro-Majerteen/Darod. When the US helicopter attacked an alleged Aydid munitions base, killing numerous Somali clan leaders who had gathered for negotiations, opposition to the US/UN presence broadened, leading to a military withdrawal in 1995, amidst mutual accusations and self-justifications.

In June 1995, Aydid was ousted as head of the United Somali Congress-Somali National Alliance (USC-SNA) by rival kinsmen Osman Ali Ato, though Aydid's son, US-educated former Marine, Hussien 'Aydid,' eventually assumed control of the USC.

In January 1997, leaders of 26 Somali factions met at Sodere in Ethiopia to form a National Salvation Council, boycotted by Hussien Aydid. In December 1997, another peace accord based on a federal structure was formulated in Cairo. A third Somali National Salvation Council meeting in Addis Ababa, Ethiopia, in January 1998, but few were prepared to surrender parochial power. An interim Somali government of national unity under Abdulkassim Salat Hassan was proclaimed at Arta, Djibouti, in August 2000, only to be challenged by a coalition of southern Somali warlords backed by Ethiopia.

Failure of the Cairo accord led to the creation of a Harti/Darod clan-based state of 'Puntland' in 1998, under strongman Abdullahi Yusuf Ahmed of the Somali Salvation Democratic-Front. In 1992, Yusuf had thwarted an incursion from the south by Aydid's Hawiye-based United Somali Congress and crushed the Islamic fundamentalist in the northern port of Bosasso, thereby earning to support of the Americans, channeled through their ally, Ethiopia.

In 2004, a new federal government of national unity was negotiated in Nairobi. The parliament was based on clan allegiances, the four major clans—Digil-Mirifle, Darod, Hawiya, and Dir, with sixty-one seats each, with thirty-one seats divided amongst the lesser clans. Abdullahi Yusuf of Puntland, a Harti-Darod, became president. The speaker of the Parliament went to Shariff Hassan Sheikh Adan, of the Digil-Mirifle clan, with a Hawiye as Prime Minister. Somaliland has refused to join the new government. While the international community has tended to cautiously welcome the new government, to many educated Somalis it merely rewards the warlords.

DAVID DORWARD

See also East Africa: History and Economic Development; East Africa: International Relations

References and Further Reading

Africa Watch. *Somalia: A Government at War with its Own People: Testimonies about the Killings and the Conflict in the North.* New York: Africa Watch, Jan 1990.

Doornbos, M., and Markakis, J. "Society and state in crisis: What went wrong in Somalia?", in *Crisis Management and the Politics of Reconciliation in Somalia.* M.A. Mohamed & Lennart Wohlgemuth, eds. Uppsala: Nordiska Africainstitutet, 1994.

Laitin, David, and Samatar, Abdi Ismail. *Somalia: Nation in Search of a State.* Boulder, CO: Westview, 1987.

Lewis, I. M. *The Modern History of Somaliland: From Nation to State.* London: Weidenfeld & Nicolson, 1965.

Loughran, K. S., et al. *Somalia in Word and Image.* Bloomington, IN: University Press, 1986.

Markaki, J. *National and Class Conflict in the Horn of Africa* 2 ed. London: Zed, 1990.

Samatar, Abdi Ismail. *The State and Rural Transformation in Northern Somalia, 1884–1986.* Madison, WI: University Press, 1989.

Samatar, Ahmed. *Socialist Somalia: Rhetoric and Reality.* London: Zed, 1988.

SOMOZA DEBAYLE, ANASTASIO

Anastasio Somoza Debayle, the second son of Nicaraguan dictator Anastasio Somoza Garcia, was born on December 5, 1925. He was educated at Saint Leo Preparatory College in Florida (at present Saint Leo University), and on Long Island before graduating West Point Military Academy in 1946. The following year his father appointed him as a head of the National Guard. At this position, he was able effectively to hold enormous power.

Following Somoza Senior's murder in 1956, Anastasio's elder brother, Luis, accepted the presidency, according to a special provision in the constitution for the possible sudden death of the president. He was politically-oriented, educated at Louisiana State University, the University of California, and the University of Maryland. Luis wanted to promote modernization of Nicaragua. He tried to keep lower family profile, and to bring new leaders to rise in the Liberal party. He created new jobs, but they failed to help the poor. This provoked mutinies that were strongly suppressed by the National Guard under Anastasio. Luis despised the idea of his younger brother becoming president, even kept him from running in 1963. After Luis died from a heart attack, just few months later in a rigged election Anastasio won the presidency. Anastasio stepped down from the presidency in 1972, due to the legal provision that barred immediate re-election.

One of the most notorious incidents of corruption in Somoza's regime occurred in 1972 after an earthquake that killed and wounded hundreds of thousands of Nicaraguans. By imposing the martial law, Somoza—as head of the National Guard—became again the country's leader. Thirty million dollars in international relief supplies were seized and sold to the highest bidder.

These circumstances did not prevent Somoza from re-election as a president in the following elections in 1974—even after the powerful Catholic church joined opposition against him. By the late 1970s, human rights groups were reproving the sad record of human rights violations by Somoza's government. Support for the opposition Sandinista National Liberation Front (FSLN) was growing all over the country, and resistance reached the point of a rebellion. This forced Somoza to escape on July 17, 1979, and to fly off initially to Miami, Florida, and later to Asunción, Paraguay, where he was assassinated by Sandinista agents on September 17, 1980.

STEPHAN E. NIKOLOV

See also Central America: History and Economic Development; Nicaragua; Nicaraguan Revolution; Sandinista National Liberation Front (FSLN); Somoza García, Anastasio

References and Further Reading

Donahue, John M. *The Nicaraguan Revolution in Health: From Somoza to the Sandinistas.* South Hadley, MA: Bergin and Garvey, 1986.

Kagan, R. *A Twilight Struggle: American Power and Nicaragua, 1977—1990.* 1996.

Pezzullo, Lawrence, and Ralph Pezzullo. *At the fall of Somoza.* Pittsburgh, PA: University of Pittsburgh Press, 1993.

Sklar, Holly. *Washington's War on Nicaragua.* Boston: South End Press, 1988.

Stimson, Henry Lewis. *American Policy in Nicaragua: The Lasting Legacy.* New York: Markus Wiener, 1991.

SOMOZA GARCÍA, ANASTASIO

Anastasio Somoza García (1896–1956) was born in 1896 to a relatively well-off coffee grower in San Marcos. He was educated at the National Institute of Oriental Studies to earn his degree from the Pierce School of Business Administration in Philadelphia. He married Salvadora Debayle to enter one of the country's most important aristocratic families. In 1933, he was appointed as the first Nicaraguan commander of National Guard, he skillfully used it to seize power. On February 21, 1934, he induced the popular hero, Augusto Sandino—who had earlier signed a truce and put down his arms, ending years of armed battle that caused an US intervention, to attend a special dinner, where he was executed.

Three years later, following the assasination of President Juan Bautista Sacasa, Somoza seized control of the country to initiate a dynasty of dictators that ruled country with US support for forty-three years.

Somoza managed to stay in power by applying a triple rule. The first element of the Somoza strategy was keeping the National Guard sated, pleased, and loyal. With Somoza's encouragement the guardsmen ran gambling houses, prostitution and smuggling rings in order to bring in profits. The next element, keeping the United States happy, involved as first priority backing the US policy, at least nominally. During World War II, Nicaragua allowed the United States to use national territory as a staging ground for international operations. After eliminating the Sandino threat, Somoza began to give out political appointments to his more powerful opponents in exchange for making them silent. Somoza was the authentic ruling power all over his career; even while sometimes he yielded others take the presidency as puppet leaders for an appearance of legitimacy. He maintained this system for twenty years, that turned Nicaragua in a family venture, and his sons continued it after him. Although Somoza succeeded in enormously increasing his personal wealth while in office, he also encouraged certain economic policies that strengthened the national infrastructure and wealth of the nation to a certain extent.

Somoza García had many political enemies, and coups against him were attempted periodically, even within the National Guard. For protection, he constructed a secure compound within his residence and kept private bodyguards. Nevertheless, on September 21, 1956, while attending a PLN party in Leon to celebrate his nomination for the presidency, Somoza García was fatally wounded by Rigoberto Lopez Pérez, a twenty-seven-year-old poet. The dictator was flown to the Panama Canal Zone, where he died eight days later.

STEPHAN E. NIKOLOV

See also Central America: History and Economic Development; Nicaragua; Nicaraguan Revolution; Sandinista National Liberation Front (FSLN); Somoza DeBayle, Anastasio

References and Further Reading

Diederich, Bernard. *Somoza and the Legacy of U.S. Involvement in Central America.* New York: Dutton, 1981.

Gambone, Michael D. *Eisenhower, Somoza, and the Cold War in Nicaragua, 1953–1961,* 1997.

Kamman, W. *A Search for Stability: United States Diplomacy Nicaragua, 1925–1933.* 1968.

Nogales y Méndez, R. de *The Looting of Nicaragua.* 1928, repr. 1970.

SOROS FOUNDATIONS NETWORK

Soros Foundations Network (SFN) is a group of autonomous foundations established by the Hungarian American philanthropist, George Soros. The Network is committed to promote open society throughout the Central and Eastern European countries, the Commonwealth of Independent States, and a number of developing countries in Africa and South East Asia, as well as to strengthen the existing open society in the United States.

The Idea of Open Society

The term "open society" was coined by the Austrian British philosopher Sir Karl Popper in his monumental study *Open Society and its Enemies.* Being Popper's disciple George Soros has adopted this concept, provided it with further meanings, and began working on its implementation into practice. According to Soros, open society recognizes all positive aspects of democracy. Open society is opposed to the closed societies of various dictatorial types. Closed society preaches unjustified optimism and "offers certainty and permanence but denies individual freedom" (Soros 2000). On the other hand, individual freedom is the highest value of open society but the later does

not promise certainty and permanence to its citizens. Soros builds his whole conception upon the notion of fallibility meaning that there is no guarantee any of human projects will succeed. Criticism is the main characteristic of open society, that is, individual expectations are constantly corrected by criticism forming a near-equilibrium relationship with reality. While dogmatism belongs to closed society characterized by far from equilibrium relationship between individual expectations and reality. At present, the most serious threat to open society is not closeness but disintegration featuring dynamic disequilibrium of chaos and disorientation due to rapid change of economic and social reality entirely out of government and citizen control.

The core principal of open society is social justice as a matter of international concern. It is viewed not as equality but in Rawlsian terms holding that the increasing wealth must also benefit the disadvantaged in the developing countries, as well as those in the industrialized ones. This principle and the principles of individual freedom and human rights constitute the seven conditions of an open society:

- Regular, free, and fair elections;
- Free and pluralistic media;
- The rule of law upheld by an independent judiciary;
- Constitutional protection of minority rights;
- A market economy that respects property rights and provides opportunities and a safety net for the disadvantaged;
- A commitment to the peaceful resolution of conflicts; and
- Laws that are enforced to curb corruption (Aryeh Neier as cited by Soros 2000).

Soros Foundations

The first Soros foundation, Open Society Fund began in South Africa in 1979 and then continued in Hungary in 1985. A number of foundations were established in Central and Eastern Europe and former Soviet Union after the Communist Parties started loosing power there in 1989. At the end of 2000, Soros foundations included twenty-eight national foundations, two sub-national foundation in Yugoslavian province of Kosovo and in Yugoslavian Republic of Montenegro, and two regional foundations—one for Southern Africa, another for West Africa. They all share the common mission to promote the development of open society but they are autonomous institutions and structure their activities according to the specific conditions in the given country or region.

The foundations in the ten Central and Eastern European countries that are candidates for European Union membership shifted their focus in 1999 from developmental approach to public policy. They promote membership criteria that are also essential for the open society mission: (1) protection of the rights of Roma and other minorities, (2) criminal justice reform, (3) the reduction of corruption, and (4) strengthening civil society participation in policy-making.

Another part of Europe that is covered by the Soros foundations is the Balkans, recently named South East Europe. Immediately after the 1999 NATO's humanitarian military operation in Yugoslavia, the European Union countries, the United States, Canada, and Russia decided to establish a Stability Pact (SP) for South East Europe aiming at coping with the war destruction in Montenegro and Serbia, including Kosovo, as well as creating conditions for democratization of the Yugoslavian nation. The SP was designed with the wider scope to support the economic development and foster civil society in the entire region of South East Europe. Along these lines, Soros foundations are working to enhance "European integration through the development of peaceful, lawful, tolerant, and democratic states" (*Building Open Societies* 2001).

Activities of the foundations in Russia are directed to "facilitate the country's political, economic, and social development" (*Building Open Societies* 2001). An issue of special urgent actions is public health deteriorated significantly after the collapse of the Soviet Union. In the other nations of the Commonwealth of Independent States the foundations "are attempting to persuade the governments and institutions to adopt the international standards of good governance, human rights, and economic policy" (*Building Open Societies* 2001).

Open society has being promoted in Africa by two regional foundations—for Southern Africa and Western Africa and one national foundation—for South Africa. All three of them are "working for peace and stability, human rights, fair elections, independent media, and the rule of law" (*Building Open Societies* 2001). They support public radio as a powerful means for education about issues of public health and reconciliation. Another topical issue here is crime prevention in South Africa.

Network Programs and Other Initiatives

There are a number of issues across the countries where Soros foundations operate, which are

addressed by the network programs. Each particular foundation participates in these programs on its own discretion. The activities of the programs are divided into three categories: those that provide assistance to foundations' initiatives, others that provide services outside a specific foundation operation area, and scholarship and fellowship competition programs. Network programs are administered by the Open Society Institute (OSI), a private operating and grant making foundation, with offices in New York City, Budapest, Brussels, Paris, and Washington, DC (closed in June 2001). The offices in New York and Budapest also secure administrative, financial, and technical support to the network foundations (the New York office administrates the US programs, which are not discussed in this entry). The Budapest office organizes certain programs throughout Central and Eastern Europe and the Commonwealth of Independent States centered on human rights, ethnic and minority issues, civil society, and women's issues. The Brussels office maintains relations between Soros Foundation Network (SFN) and the European Union (EU) and the Paris office is involved in bilateral cooperation with France and other West European countries.

Network programs include among others Arts and Culture Program, Constitutional and Legal Policy Institute, Economic and Business Development Program, International Higher Education Support Program, Local Government and Public Service Reform Program, and Public Health Programs. The Art and Culture Program is committed to work for autonomous and innovative arts sector, to support international cooperation in the field of art and culture, and to encourage structural changes in cultural policy. Constitutional and Legal Policy Institute operates in Central and Eastern Europe, Central Asia, and Mongolia. It assists developing the rule of law, respect for human rights, and democratic institutions. Its activities deal with criminal justice, anticorruption, juvenile justice, access to justice and legal aid, judicial reform, media legislation, and legal education. Economic and Business Development Program aims at helping to introduce market economy and create more jobs. It concentrates on small businesses development, microfinance, retraining the former military staff, and business education. International Higher Education Support Program has as its strategic goal institution building and faculty development. It also creates new opportunities for students from Central and Eastern Europe and the Commonwealth of Independent States. The objective of the Local Government and Public Service Reform Program is to enhance effective and democratic local governments and public administration,

as well as to assist public policy research in the all countries where the SFN is active. Public Health Programs are developed in Central and Eastern Europe. Before 1999, the Programs were attempting to improve the individual health care but later they began dealing with the relationship between the development of society and the health level of its citizens. Now, the programs center on new approaches in medical service delivery, development of nongovernmental organizations (NGOs) working on health care issues, and training medical and social care professionals.

Other initiatives of the SFN treat topics or regions of common importance beyond the reach of its national or regional foundations. They consist of Belarusian Initiative, the Burma Project/Southeast Asia Initiative, Central Eurasia Project, Landmines Project, Project Syndicate, and Roma Program. Belarusian Initiative encourages various grassroots activities aiming foremost at empowering the NGOs. Here preparation of a new generation of leaders, training programs, and projects promoting rights of women are included. The Burma Project provides scholarships and internships for Burmese students worldwide. It also helps creating electronic newspapers and web sites in several local languages. The principal nation to benefit from the Southeast Asia Initiative is Indonesia. In this case, OSI does not build its own structures but tries to work with local organizations that share its mission and commitment. The Central Eurasia Project attempts to increase the respect for the rule of law, the free exchange of ideas and information, and tolerance for different cultures. This Project extends over Turkey and Iran. Fostering civil society is the core objective in Turkey and in Iran; the goal is building closer relations between Iran and the United States through exchange of scholars, writers, journalists, and publishers.

SFN established an institution of higher learning, the Central European University (CEU) in 1991. Now, CEU has campuses in Budapest and Warsaw. It is committed to advance open society in the former Soviet block countries through outstanding level of graduate studies in fields of social sciences, humanities, and comparative and international law.

The Open Society Alliance

Soros foundations have been working for promotion of civil society and other elements of democracy as an alternative to the totalitarian societies. Within ten years, they became a substantial factor in building open society throughout the post-totalitarian

countries of Europe and Eurasia and in other places that have suffered of dictatorial regimes. In late 1990s, George Soros concluded that the main enemy of the open society is not the dogmatism of closed societies anymore but the dogmatism of market fundamentalism. According to the later, common good can be described in the terms of market values and all social and political problems can be resolved by the free market. In fact, market values constitute only one part of common good; another very important part of it is sustained by social values. NGOs on behalf of civil society and governments can be very useful in developing market and social values all over the globe. Nevertheless, they are not sufficient to strive for the common good since more often than not they are run "like businesses, generating revenues by advocating a case" (Soros 2000). A new international organization is needed to be committed solely to working for common good through developing open society worldwide. It is described as the global alliance for open society and ought to be led by the most developed democracies.

The goal of the Alliance would be to coordinate the activities of member countries in promoting a global open society. There are two distinct but interconnected objectives to be accomplished: One is to help evolution of open societies within individual countries; the other is to foster the development of international law and international standards of behavior (Soros 2000).

The first step forming this Alliance was founding an intergovernmental body, Community for Democracies (CD) in Warsaw, Poland in June 2000. Foreign ministers and other high officials from about 100 countries were the founders of this organization. The funding for CD is expected to come from the governments to support the intergovernmental activities and from OSI for NGO's that would enhance CD in its mission to develop open society. Many of the CD countries participate in the Stability Pact for the South East Europe. The fate of the Stability Pact will be a test for CD and the development of global open society. SFN participates in the Pact's Working Tables on Democratization and Human Rights and on Security Issues.

SFN have planed both the foundations and the global alliance to become self-sustainable by 2010 when Soros support will cease.

ALEXANDER GUNGOV

See also Central and Eastern Europe: History and Economic Development; Commonwealth of Independent States: History and Economic Development; Commonwealth of Independent States: International Relations

References and Further Reading

Building Open Societies: Soros Foundations Network 2000 Report. New York: Open Society Institute, 2001.
Building Open Societies: Soros Foundations Network 1999 Report. New York: Open Society Institute, 2000.
Germino, Dante, and Beyme, Klaus von, editors. *The Open Society in Theory and Practice.* The Hague: Martinus Nijhoff, 1974.
Popper, Karl Raimund, Sir. *The Open Society and Its Enemies.* Princeton, NJ: Princeton University Press, 1971.
Smit, Marbel Wisse. "Fostering Peace and Democracy in a Volatile Region," *Open Society News,* no. 3, (2000).
Soros, George. *Open Society: Reforming Global Capitalism.* New York: BBS/Public Affairs, 2000.
———. *The Crisis of Global Capitalism: Open Society Endangered.* New York: BBS/Public Affairs, 1998.
———, Byron Wien, and Krisztina Koenen. *Soros on Soros: Staying Ahead of the Curve.* New York: John Wiley, 1995.

SOUTH AFRICA

South Africa is the southernmost country in Africa. On its western, southern, and eastern sides, it has a long coastline bordering the South Atlantic and Indian Oceans. It is bordered on the northwest by Namibia, to the north by Botswana, and to the northeast by Zimbabwe, Mozambique, and Swaziland. The nation of Lesotho is enclosed entirely by South Africa, situated in South Africa's eastern central plain.

South Africa's climate varies throughout its regions, which include mountains to the west, east, and south; grasslands on the central plateau; and coastal regions along the ocean. However, temperatures remain temperate to tropical most of the year, though the mountainous regions and parts of the plains experience cold weather during the winters. The dry season is from May to August. The population is estimated at 42,718,530, with an negative growth rate of -0.25% annually due to AIDS and emigration. The administrative capital, Pretoria, is located in the northeastern part of the country, and has a population of about 2 million. Cape Town, located on the southwestern coast on the Cape of Good Hope, with a population of about 3 million, is the legislative center, and Bloemfontein, in the middle of the central plain, with a population of about 750,000, is the judicial center.

South Africa is divided into nine provinces: Eastern Cape, Northern Cape and Western Cape in the west and south; Free State in the central region; Limpopo and North West in the north and northwest; KwaZulu-Natal in the eastern region; Gauteng and Mpumalanga in the northeast. There are eleven languages spoken in the country. The major categories of indigenous inhabitants of the region are the Nguni,

including various Ndebele (Western Cape and North-West), Swazi, Xhosa (in the Eastern Cape), and Zulu (KwaZulu-Natal) peoples, the Sotho-Tswana (Free State), and the *Venda* (North).

Beginning in the seventeenth century, streams of immigrants began to arrive to the country. Many were either seeking economic advancement or fleeing persecution. Key groups were the Dutch, the British, the Hugeunots, and East Indian. Currently there are four major ethnic categories. Traditionally the most powerful group was the Whites, which could be sub-divided into Afrikaner (highest ranked) and the British. Next are the Coloureds, the South African term for multiracial people. Third are the Indians. Fourth are the indigenous Black African Tribes. The Cape (especially Cape Town) is considered the locus for the Coloured and Natal is the locus for the Indians.

The History of South Africa

Cape Town was the first European settlement in South Africa. The British initially decided not to settle in the Cape area. The Dutch, on the other hand, recognized the strategic value of the area and began emigrating there in 1652. The Dutch East India Trading Company, which commissioned the first settlement in the area, was instrumental in the development of the Cape region. More Dutch immigrants, commonly called as the Boers and Afrikaners, settled in the area. As the port city developed, the need for labor rapidly became intense. Initially slaves and exiled Indonesians were imported.

In 1671, the first Huguenot refugee, Francois Villion (later known with the last name Viljoen), arrived to the Cape. The major stream of Huguenots, fleeing France to escape religious persecution, arrived between 1688 and 1689. The Dutch East India Company encouraged emigration because it would provide needed labor. It preferred Dutch immigrants because they possessed desired qualities, common religious beliefs, and weretrained as craftsmen or farmers. As the Dutch settlement expanded, the Huguenots found themselves being forced to recede from their original lands. In 1695, they rose up against the Dutch, but were defeated. They retreated to the northern part of the country.

With the increasing presence of abolitionist missionaries and the emancipation of the slaves in 1834, approximately twelve thousand Afrikaner farmers (known as the Trek Boers) began to expand their territories toward the north and the east into lands occupied by the indigenous populations and

Huguenots, seeking grazing lands for their cattle. The Huguenots resisted the attempted conquest, so the Trekkers then attempted to conquer the indigenous Xhosa people living in the east. The Xhosa engaged in skirmishes against the Trekkers and finally, in 1779, wars erupted.

The Colonial government was weak, and two short-lived Dutch republics were established. The power struggle continued until the arrival of the British to the area and the resulting annexation of the colony into the United Kingdom in 1795. Battles occurred between the Whites (both British and Afrikaners) and the indigenous peoples. Two key Zulu leaders in some of these battles were King Shaka and military leader Mzilikazi. The Boers initially attempted to settle in Natal, occupied by the British, but moved on to establish the Free Orange State and the South Africa Republic (Transvaal or ZAR: Zuid-Afrikaansche Republiek) to the north.

The Cape colony, still a British territory, was evolving. Tacit steps had been taken to develop a system of political equality among races. In theory it was to be based upon economic qualifications, but in practice it excluded the majority of Africans and multiracial people. This was due, in part because of the discovery of diamonds. The Natal region was more conducive to sugar production and as the crop prospered the need labor needs increased. Indian laborers were imported to work in the fields.

In 1877, the Transvaal was taken over by the British, however, soon after there was a major rebellion. Several years later, pro-Afrikaner Paul Kruger had been elected as president of the republic. In 1886, gold was discovered in Witwaterstrand. Two wars were fought for possession of key territories. The first Anglo-Boer War was fought from 1880 to1881. The second Anglo-Boer War, also known as the South African War, started on October 11, 1899. After ultimate defeat of the British, the Union of South Africa was established on May 31, 1910.

The Apartheid System

Introduction of the Apartheid System

In 1910, the policy of consistent racial separation was introduced via a group of laws that seriously curtailed the rights of the Black majority. The "Mines and Works Act"of 1911 limited black workers to only menial work. In the "Native Land Act"of 1913, approximately 7.3% of South African territories were designated as reservations for Blacks. They were barred from purchasing any lands outside these

areas. The only province with a non-racial franchise was the Cape, and there Blacks were barred from being members of parliament. At the establishment of the Union, there was an estimated 6 million inhabitants with 67% being Black African, 9% Coloured, and 2.5% Asian (Indian). Under General Louis Botha, the Afrikaners maintained power as a result of the merger of two Afrikaner parties into the South African Party. Soon thereafter, White supremacy became permanently entrenched as a result of the passage of the Masters and Servants Act, the restriction of skilled work to Whites only, the implementation of the pass laws, the institution of the Native Poll Tax and the 1913 Land Act that ensured white ownership of 90% of the country.

Independence was achieved in 1934 by South Africa. Soon thereafter, in 1936, Blacks were further disenfranchised when they were removed from the common voters roll in the Cape. During 1937, laws were passed to stem Black urbanization and municipalities were compelled to segregate black African and white residents. In 1946, Jan Smuts introduced a bill that limited the movement, property ownership, residence, and empowerment of Indians.

As of 1948, the apartheid (literally "aparthood" in Afrikaans) system became the official policy of the country with the election of the Nationalist Party. D.F. Malan coined the concept of "apartheid"and consistently enforced the policy. The separation of the "races" was not limited to the economic sector. Marriage or any conjugal relationship between members of different racial groups were strictly forbidden. Racial segregation was introduced in all public institutions and offices, in public transport, and on public toilets. Until the 1980s, Blacks were expected to step off of the sidewalk when a White person approached. Under this Party, such laws as the Group Areas Act which rigidly specified the racial division of land and the Populations Registration Act classifying people based upon race were passed in 1950. What is commonly referred to as the "petty apartheid" practice on buses and in post offices was introduced with the passage of the *Separate Amenities Act* of 1953.

After members of the ANC ratified the Freedom Charter which endorsed non-racialism and human rights in 1955, 156 leaders were arrested and charged with high treason. Their trial continued until 1961 when they were acquitted. In 1958, the foundation for the establishment of homelands was laid with *The Promotion of Black Self-Government Act*s. The homelands, or "bantustans," established in the harshest, driest, and least fertile areas in the country, were designed to alienate the indigenous African Blacks from their traditional lands. The National Party and its policies remained in power until 1994.

Resistance to Apartheid

The resistance to apartheid occurred both internally and globally. In the 1940s, the government of India seized many opportunities to bring attention to the disenfranchisement of Indians in the General Assembly of the United Nations. The Defiance Campaign began in 1952 and took a non-violent approach. Yet the outcome was the imprisonment of thousands of participants.

During the 1960s and 1970s, anti-apartheid protests occurred both within South Africa and in other countries. The 1960s ushered in massive resistance to apartheid and even greater repressive measures imposed by the South African government. On March 21, 1960, a peaceful demonstration in Sharpesville changed to a massacre when police killed sixty-nine and injured 160 unarmed demonstrators. A State of Emergency was declared giving the government the opportunity to introduce the new "right to detain without trial." The African National Congress (ANC) and the Pan–African Congress (PAC) and other empowerment organizations were declared illegal.

The indigenous peoples organized grassroots organizations and widespread resistance, but the worldwide outcry against the massive violation of human rights did not occur until the Soweto Massacre occurred on June 16, 1976. Children who were peacefully protesting the imposition of Afrikaans as the official language for instruction were struck down. In response, groups around the world mounted major anti-apartheid initiatives. Marches, demonstrations, and boycotts against corporations that did business with and/or had investments in South Africa organized worldwide. Embassies were picketed and ships headed to South Africa were physically blocked by demonstrators. Some demonstrations were peaceful and others became violent. The United Nations constituencies began to call for economic sanctions against South Africa. Resolution 1761 was passed in November 1962, and subsequent resolutions at the World Conference Against Racism in 1978 and 1982 were also passed.

The Demise of the Formal Apartheid System

During earlier periods in the twentieth century, various countries contributed to the South Africa's development through financial assistance and donor aid. From an economic perspective, the various countries benefited from the South African system, and an intricate system of interdependence developed. For example, South Africa has traditionally been the

primary source for diamonds worldwide. As technology evolved, the need for diamonds increased. In addition to the traditional use of diamonds as a luxury item, industries began to design tools and equipment using diamonds because of its strength. Countries found themselves in a dilemma. While they may not have supported the apartheid system, overt pressure and interference could result in the denial of critically needed minerals found in abundance in South Africa. Thus, for a long time South Africa had the leverage to prevent major interference with the social structure. As time passed however, the constituency pressures within many countries, including the United States, became too great and national governments were pressured into taking stances against the continuation of the apartheid system. In the 1980s, the apartheid system began to crumble and a movement to end strengthened.

On February 2, 1990, South African president F.W. de Klerk lifted the ban on thirty-three major activist human rights groups including ANC and PAC. After 27 years of imprisonment, Nelson Mandela, the leader of ANC, was released on February 11, 1990. The first democratic election was held April 26–29, 1994, with Nelson Mandela being inaugurated as the first indigenous South African president on May 10, 1994. Both F.W. de Klerk and ANC's Thabo Mbeki were inaugurated as deputy presidents. The country's second democratic election on June 2, 1999, brought Thabo Mbeki to the office of president.

Education

After the dismantling of the apartheid system, a new educational system was established that permits intermingling between the various ethnic groups, although the major institutions continue to have the ethnic specific concentrations of past eras.

The major education spans approximately thirteen years (grades). Of those, grades 10–12 and the reception year (grade 0) are not compulsory. Students have access to higher education, but the vast majority of the minority groups cannot afford it. There are twenty-two universities/colleges, sixteen technikons, and an evolving community college system.

Concluding Comments

Since established as a colony, South Africa has had a deeply divisive and destructive legacy of inequality and severe human rights violations. Yet, its oppressed peoples have shared their cultures with the world through their music, traditional dress, food, and artwork, making the world richer. With the transition from an all white apartheid system to an inclusive pluralist democracy, the world will follow its evolution with anticipation. In its new configuration, it is a young country with tremendous potential. As it evolves, it could become a model for inclusiveness, or it could return to its old path. The leadership, attitudes, and commitment of the people will determine this beautiful and unique country's fate.

E. VALERIE SMITH

See also Apartheid; Botha, P.W.; Buthelezi, Mangosuthu Gatsha; De Klerk, Frederik W.; Ethnic Conflicts: Southern Africa; Mandela, Nelson; Mbeki, Thabo; Minorities/Discrimination; Southern Africa: History and Economic Development; Southern Africa: International Relations; Tutu, Bishop Desmond; Verwoerd, Hendrik

References and Further Reading

Davenport, Rodney, and Christopher Saunders. *South Africa: A Modern History*, 5th edition. New York: St. Martin's Press, 2000.

Davidson, Basil. *The Black Man's Burden: Africa & the Curse of the Nation State*. New York: Three Rivers Press, 1992.

Gay, Phillip T. *Modern South Africa*. Boston: McGraw-Hill, 2001.

Mudimbe, V. Y. *The Idea of Africa*. Bloomington, IN: Indiana University Press, 1994.

Parker, Franklin. "Separate Schools and Separate People of South Africa." The Journal of Negro Education 41, no. 3 The Education of Disadvantaged People in International Perspective (Summer, 1972): 266–275.

Seidman, Ann. *The Roots of Crisis in Southern Africa*. Trenton, NJ: Africa World Press, 1985.

Seidman, Gary. "Is South Africa Different? A Sociological Comparison and Theoretical Contributions from the Land of Apartheid." Annual Review of Sociology, vol 25 (1999); 419–440.

Simon, David, ed. *South Africa in Southern Africa*. Oxford: James Currey, 1998.

Thompson, Leonard. *A History of South Africa*, 3rd edn. New Haven, CT: Yale University Press, 2000.

Williams, John A. *From the South African Past: Narratives, Documents, & Debates*. Boston: Houghton Mifflin, 1997.

World Statesmen. "Black South African Homelands." http://www.worldstatesmen.org/South_African_homelands.html (2002–2005).

SOUTH ASIAN ASSOCIATION FOR REGIONAL COOPERATION (SAARC)

The South Asian Association for Regional Cooperation (SAARC) was established on December 5, 1985, by the leaders of seven South Asian countries—Bangladesh, Bhutan, India, Maldives, Nepal, Pakistan,

and Sri Lanka—to address the issues of regional peace and development in South Asia. The first concrete proposal for establishing a framework for regional cooperation in South Asia came from the late president of Bangladesh, Ziaur Rahman on May 2, 1980. Prior to this, the idea of regional cooperation in South Asia was discussed in at least three conferences: the Asian Relations Conference in New Delhi in April 1947, the Baguio Conference in the Philippines in May 1950, and the Colombo Powers Conference in April 1954. During his visit to India in December 1977, the Bangladesh President Ziaur Rahman discussed the need for a framework of regional cooperation with the newly elected Indian Prime Minister, Morarji Desai. At the same time, in his inaugural speech to the Colombo Plan Consultative Committee, which met in Kathmandu in December 1977, King Birendra of Nepal called for close regional cooperation among the South Asian countries in sharing river waters. Welcoming the King's call, President Ziaur Rahman further pursued the discussion of regional cooperation informally with the leaders of the South Asian countries during the Commonwealth Summit meeting in Lusaka in 1979 and the Non-Aligned Summit meeting in Havana in 1979. After his visit to Sri Lanka and discussion with the Sri Lankan President J.R. Jayawardene in November 1979, the Bangladesh president finalized a proposal of regional cooperation among the South Asian countries.

President Ziaur Rahman's initiative to establish a regional organization in South Asia during 1975–1979 was shaped by the following factors: (1) Ziaur Rahman's need for Indian support to legitimize his coup d'etat regime after the assassination of Bangladesh's first and most popular President Mujibur Rahman in 1975; (2) change in the political leadership in the South Asian countries and the new leaders' willingness to embrace accommodative diplomacy; (3) the second oil crisis in 1979 and its adverse impact on the balance of payment situations of all the South Asian countries; (4) assurance of economic assistance for multilateral cooperative projects on sharing water resources of Ganga and Brahmaputra by the US President Jimmy Carter and British Prime Minister James Callaghan during their visit to India, Pakistan and Bangladesh in January 1978; (5) the rapid deterioration of the South Asian security environment as a result of the Soviet military intervention in Afghanistan in December 1979; and (6) the publication of a background report by the Committee on Studies for Cooperation in Development in South Asia (CSCD), identifying many feasible areas of cooperation.

The Bangladesh proposal was promptly endorsed by the smaller states of South Asia—Nepal, Sri Lanka, the Maldives, and Bhutan. Initially, India and Pakistan expressed skepticism for the proposal. India's main concern was the proposal's reference to the security matters in South Asia and the inclusion of all bilateral disputes with India on the SAARC agenda for discussion. Indian policy makers were strongly opposed to such an idea because of their fear that discussions on bilateral conflicts in a multilateral forum will eventually lead to India's isolation, and will provide an opportunity for South Asian neighbors to "gang up" against India. Pakistan assumed that it might be an Indian strategy to create a regional organization that would ensure India's economic and military dominance in the region. After a series of quiet diplomatic consultations at the United Nations headquarters in New York from August to September 1980, the South Asian foreign ministers agreed to ask Bangladesh to prepare the draft of a working paper for discussion among the foreign secretaries of the South Asian countries. After intense discussion on the issue of security provision with the foreign secretaries of India and Pakistan, the new Bangladesh draft paper dropped all references to security matters and suggested only noncontroversial areas for cooperation. After three years of preparatory discussion at the foreign secretaries level, the first South Asian foreign ministers' conference was held in Delhi from August 1–3, 1983, where a formal declaration on regional cooperation was adopted establishing an organization known as the South Asian Regional Cooperation (SARC). Following the New Delhi meeting, three more meetings of the foreign ministers were held at Male (July 10–11, 1984), Thimpu (May 13–14, 1985), and Dhaka (December 5, 1985) to finalize the details of the areas of cooperation. At the Dhaka meeting, the South Asian foreign ministers decided to change the name of the organization from South Asian Regional Cooperation (SARC) to South Asian Association for Regional Cooperation (SAARC). The change in the acronym was based on the thinking that while SARC refers to the process of South Asian regional cooperation, SAARC marks the establishment of an organization to promote and develop such cooperation. Following this change in the name, the first SAARC summit meeting of the heads of state or government of the seven South Asian member countries was held at Dhaka from December 7–8, 1985.

Since 1985, SAARC has evolved slowly in terms of institutions and programs. In 1987, a permanent SAARC Secretariat was established in Kathmandu, Nepal. Four SAARC regional institutions have been established so far: SAARC Agricultural Information Center (Dhaka/ Bangladesh); SAARC Tuberculosis Center (Baktapur/Nepal); SAARC

Meteorological Center (Dhaka/Bangladesh); and SAARC Documentation Center (New Delhi/India). Four regional conventions/agreements have been signed: Agreement on Establishing SAARC Food Security Reserve (Third SAARC Summit, Kathmandu, 1987); SAARC Regional Convention on Suppression of Terrorism (Third SAARC Summit, Kathmandu, 1987); SAARC Convention on Narcotic Drugs and Psychotropic Substances (Fifth SAARC Summit, Male, 1990); Agreement on SAARC Preferential Trading Arrangement (Seventh SAARC Summit, Dhaka 1993). Three SAARC Funds have also been established: SAARC Fund for Regional Projects (1991); SAARC-Japan Special Fund (1993); and South Asian Development Fund (1995).

SAARC's slow growth can be attributed to the following factors. First, the Indo-Pakistan tension remains the most important reason for SAARC's modest growth since 1990s. The root of Indo-Pakistan tension lies in the Kashmir issue and India's overwhelming military and economic domination in the region and Pakistan's continuing challenge to achieve military power parity with India. With the acquisition of nuclear bombs in May 1998 by both India and Pakistan, the latter's objective of balancing India's military power may have been partially fulfilled. But the strategic military balance of power achieved by Pakistan does not alleviate South Asia's so called "security complex" and does not guarantee peace or growth of cooperative activities in the region. The unresolved Kashmir issue and an increase in cross-border terrorism have further deepened the political divide between India and Pakistan, limiting the growth of multilateral cooperation in South Asia. One discernible consequence of Indo-Pakistan tension is the frequent cancellation of SAARC annual summits since 1998. It is important to note that one of the critical objectives of the SAARC annual summits is to facilitate the so called "courtesy call" meeting between the political leaders of South Asian countries. This informal courtesy call meeting allows the leaders to carry on dialog outside the SAARC forums in order to deepen their mutual understanding of each other's problems. But since SAARC's inception in 1985, only twelve summits have been held, limiting the opportunity for the leaders to meet at frequent intervals and engage in multilateral cooperation. In fact, while the first six SAARC Summits were held annually, the rest six Summits were held without any regular annual interval. The eleventh SAARC Summit, which was scheduled to be held in 1999, was cancelled many times due to Indo-Pak tension, triggered by a regime change in Pakistan in 1999, when General Pervez Musharraf deposed prime minister Nawaz Sharif in a military coup. The Indian

initiative, led by the former prime minister A.B.Vajpayee, to improve relations with Pakistan did not produce any positive result due to the failure of Agra Summit in 2001, where Pakistan raised the Kashmir issue much to the disliking of India. Eventually, after four years of the tenth summit, the eleventh summit was held in Kathmandu in 2002. Similarly, the twelfth SAARC Summit at Islamabad was eventually held after two postponements caused by India's refusal to confirm Pakistan's earlier proposed dates of Summit on January 11–13, 2003.

Second, South Asian countries do not share a common external threat perception, which makes it difficult for the leaders of these countries to work toward common regional security strategies. Most South Asian countries perceive their main threat to be India. India, on the other hand, perceives an external threat to her regional security concerns by Pakistan's military challenge with the support of external powers. The narrow political base of the South Asian ruling elites provides few opportunities for them to ignore regional security threats or to transcend the necessity of support from their dominant domestic groups. Thus, scapegoating has become a preferred policy choice for the South Asian ruling elites, making regional accommodation a difficult goal. It is not surprising, therefore, that SAARC-related policies and programs have received low priorities by the South Asian ruling elites over the past decade.

Third, SAARC's progress has remained limited during the past decade due to the emergence of two types of mutually competing ruling coalitions, i.e., a weak liberalizing coalitions in India and a nationalist-fundamentalist coalitions in Pakistan. India's weak liberalizing coalitions since early 1990s have come under greater pressure to accommodate the varying demands and interests of their coalition partners to ensure their political survival. It has becomes difficult for weak liberalizing coalitions to downplay regional security threat and to ignore scapegoating (blaming external enemy) as an instrument of their national policies. Thus, India's weak liberalizing coalitions remain tentative about regional cooperative initiatives, although they do not demonstrate the same degree of antipathy toward regional cooperation policies as the nationalist-fundamentalist coalitions.

The nationalist-fundamentalist ruling coalitions in Pakistan since 1990s and the military regime after 1999 have often shown more preference for domestic-oriented and extra-regional-oriented policies than policies with a regional thrust in order to ensure Pakistan's strategic significance to extra-regional powers and maintain their political clout in domestic politics. Needless to say, such policies of externalization and external mediation of bilateral problems have

prevented close and continuous regional interactions between India and Pakistan, making regional cooperation goals difficult to achieve.

Fourth, intra-regional trade among SAARC countries is quite modest, which has contributed to a limited interdependence among the South Asian countries. India's trade with SAARC members amount to only 2% of its total global trade, while Pakistan's trade with the region is less than 5% of its total trade. The low level of intra-regional imports and exports of India and Pakistan indicate how little these two relatively developed economies in South Asia depend on the region's markets. On the other hand, the industrialized countries remain the major trading partners for the SAARC countries. Also, the SAARC countries' trade with the developing countries and other Asian countries far outweigh the trade among themselves.

One major reason for this limited intra-regional trade is that SAARC countries, with the exception of India and Pakistan, do not have a diversified product base. Being primary producers, they tend to export similar items and thus compete with each other. The existence of a high rate of tariff and nontariff barriers in South Asian countries, with some modest exception of Sri Lanka, has become an important constraining factor for the expansion of intra-regional trade. Second, the fear of Indian goods dominating regional market has prevented South Asian countries, and most notably Pakistan, to increase the volume of intra-regional trade. Third, the lack of adequate transport and information links among the South Asian countries poses serious problems for the expansion of intra-regional trade. Finally, although most SAARC members have pursued economic liberalization policies after the early 1990s, these paths have not led to an increase in intra-regional trade because of political differences and a lack of willingness to create trade complementarities among the leaders of the South Asian countries.

Following the example of ASEAN (Association of Southeast Asian Nations), the SAARC member countries signed a framework pact for the creation of South Asian Free Trade Area (SAFTA) on January 6, 2004, in order to reduce or eliminate tariffs among the SAARC member countries. The SAFTA is scheduled to come into force at the start of 2006. Besides contributing to an increase in the volume of trade among the South Asian countries, the SAFTA would also enable SAARC member countries to obtain production inputs from each other at lower costs. The savings on logistics due to shorter distances and storage times would result in huge savings for South Asian manufacturers and consumers. Despite the potential of substantial economic benefits, the success of SAFTA will depend largely on the rapprochement between India and Pakistan.

KISHORE C. DASH

See also Association of Southeast Asian Nations (ASEAN); Central Asia: History and Economic Development; Central Asia: International Relations; Ethnic Conflicts: Central Asia; Indian–Pakistani Wars; Kashmir Dispute

References and Further Reading

Dash, Kishore. "The Political Economy of Regional Cooperation in South Asia." *Pacific Affairs*, Vol. 69, no. 2 (Summer 1996).
———. "The Challenge of Regionalism in South Asia." *International Politics*. Vol. 38, June 2001.
Haas, Michael. *The Asian Way to Peace*. New York: Praeger, 1989.
Muni, S.D. and Muni, Anuradha. *Regional Cooperation in South Asia*. New Delhi: National Publishing House, 1984.
Sen Gupta, Bhavani. *South Asian Perspectives: Seven Nations in Conflict and Cooperation*. Delhi: B. R. Publishing Corporation, 1988.

SOUTH WEST AFRICA PEOPLE'S ORGANIZATION (SWAPO)

The South West Africa People's Organization (SWAPO) was the leading liberation movement in Namibia's long struggle for independence from South African rule. It has been Namibia's ruling party since 1990.

SWAPO traces its origins to the Ovamboland People's Congress, founded in Cape Town, South Africa, in 1958 by Toivo ya-Toivo and others, as a body to resist the system of contract labour introduced into the north of Namibia by the South African rulers. At about the same time, the young Sam Nujoma tried to organise workers in Namibia itself, and was one of those responsible for the founding of the Ovamboland People's Organisation (OPO) in 1959. It was the Windhoek massacre of December 1959, in which the police killed twelve unarmed protesters in the territory's capital, that persuaded Nujoma and others of the need for a broad-based liberation movement that would, if necessary, take up arms to resist the South African occupation regime. In the aftermath of the massacre, Nujoma and other leading activists fled from Namibia to raise the cause of their country's independence from South African rule at the United Nations (UN), which recognised the special status of the territory as a former mandate of the League of Nations.

In April 1960, the OPO changed its name to SWAPO, the new name reflecting the desire on the part of Nujoma and others to bring together all the people of the territory to oust the South Africans. Though SWAPO did always have supporters from other ethnic groups, its dominant support has always come from the Ovambo-speaking people of the north, who make up over half of the country's population. Nujoma became president of the organization, a position which he has retained since its founding. Though the UN adopted the name "Namibia" for the country in the late 1960s, in place of the colonial "South West Africa," used by the South Africans, by then the name SWAPO was so well known that the organization decided to retain it. Though its leadership was based first at Dar es Salaam, then Lusaka and then Luanda in Angola, SWAPO always retained a significant presence inside Namibia. Though never banned by the South Africans, SWAPO was treated very harshly by the South African authorities, and most of the internal leadership was detained at one time or another. For much of the 1970s and early 1980s it was hardly able to operate above ground in Namibia, and with mass mobilisation within the country virtually impossible, it was the external leadership that drove the struggle, both militarily and diplomatically.

In the early 1960s, SWAPO competed for support both within Namibia and internationally with the South West African National Union (SWANU), which drew most of its support from the Herero people and developed links with the Chinese. Though SWANU was regarded as more radical than SWAPO at that time, it was SWAPO that was able to gain the crucial support of the Organisation of African Unity's liberation committee. SWAPO was recognised as the sole and authentic representative of the Namibian people, first by the OAU and then by the General Assembly of the United Nations.

SWAPO gained this recognition largely through armed struggle. Until mid-1966, the SWAPO leadership hoped that the International Court of Justice in The Hague would rule that South Africa's rule of Namibia was illegal. When it did not, SWAPO announced that it was launching its armed struggle, and in August 1966 the first clash took place in northern Namibia between SWAPO guerrillas and the South African police. By the end of the liberation war twenty-three years later, SWAPO had lost over ten thousand fighters in a conflict that over time began to resemble a conventional war rather than a guerilla conflict and was fought mainly in southern Angola rather than in Namibia itself. In the single bloodiest encounter, over six hundred SWAPO supporters were killed when the South African Defence Force raided the SWAPO settlement at Cassinga in southern Angola on May 4, 1978.

In the achievement of Namibia's liberation, SWAPO's diplomatic activity was as important as its armed struggle. Through constant lobbying at the UN and in other fora, SWAPO forced the Namibian issue onto the international agenda. In 1977, the key Western powers negotiated with SWAPO and the South Africans to compromise on a plan providing for UN involvement in the transition to independence. The compromise was not popular within SWAPO, but it accepted the agreement in July 1978, only to find that the South Africans would then not implement the plan for a UN-led transition to independence. There followed a decade of waiting for that plan to be implemented, years in which SWAPO was traumatised by a so-called spy scandal, in which those alleged to be spies were detained and tortured, sometimes to death, in southern Angola. Finally, as a result of negotiations for the withdrawal of the Cuban forces from Angola, the transition plan was implemented from April 1, 1989. In early April 1989, over three hundred SWAPO fighters were killed by the South Africans in northern Namibia before the UN arrived, but after the UN's arrival, the country was able to engage in peaceful preparations for an election in November.

In the November election, SWAPO gained 57% of the vote for the Constituent Assembly (CA) to draw up a constitution for the new country. By then SWAPO had dropped much of its earlier socialist rhetoric, initially adopted in part because of the support it obtained from the Soviet Union, and had accepted that the economy would remain mixed and there should be a multi-party democracy. The CA chose Nujoma to be the country's first president, and after a liberal democratic constitution was adopted, Namibia became independent in March 1990 and the first SWAPO government was sworn in. In subsequent elections, SWAPO increased its support to over two-thirds of the electorate, and it changed the constitution to allow Nujoma to run for a third term as president, on the grounds that he had first become the country's president as a result of the wishes of the CA rather than the people. In 2004, he was persuaded not to run for a fourth term. He then in effect chose his successor, Hifikepunye Pohamba, who was elected the new president of the country in the November 2004 election.

CHRISTOPHER SAUNDERS

See also Namibia; South Africa; Southern Africa: History and Economic Development; Southern Africa: International Relations

References and Further Reading

Dobel, L. *SWAPO's Struggle for Namibia*. Basel: Schlettwein Publishing, 1999.

Leys, C. and J. Saul. *Namibia's Liberation Struggle*. London: James Currey, 1995.

Nujoma, S. *Where Others Wavered*. London: Panaf Books, 2001.

SOUTHEAST ASIA: HISTORY AND ECONOMIC DEVELOPMENT

To refer to Southeast Asia as a single region is a relatively recent phenomenon stemming from its new-found strategic importance during World War II. Research has identified historical links between the countries and commonalities in traditions such as the governance of kingdoms and the rise and fall of empires. However, in general Southeast Asia is regarded more as a political and geographical concept than a region defined by cultural similarities. From Myanmar (formerly Burma) in the west, to the Philippines and Indonesia on its eastern side, with Thailand, Cambodia, Laos, Vietnam, Malaysia, Singapore, and Brunei in between, the area is marked by diverse histories, religions, languages, ethnicity, geography, political, and economic systems.

For example, Indonesia is the fourth most populated country in the world (2004), with 219 million people living on six thousand of the more than seventeen thousand islands that make up this archipelago. It is also the country with the largest Muslim population (82%) in the world. In contrast to Indonesia, Laos' 5.6 million people are predominantly Buddhist. This landlocked country is the lowest ranked in the region on the UNDP's Human Development Index (2004, ranked 135/177). Political systems in the region range from the authoritarian regime of Myanmar, to centralised socialist states such as Vietnam, the absolute monarchy of Brunei, to the constitutional monarchy of Thailand and the presidential democracy of the Philippines. Countries such as Indonesia, Malaysia, and Laos are relatively modern states with their borders determined by colonial occupation in the nineteenth century and in the case of Malaysia, a federation formed after WWII.

Over 8% of the world's population (548 million in 2004) live within Southeast Asia's 1,735,448 square miles. Thirty-one percent of that population is under the age of fifteen years and 38% live in urban areas. Four of the world's major religions, Islam, Buddhism (both Mahayana and Theravada), Hinduism, and Christianity are widely practiced. Generational change, population growth, urbanisation and subsequent environmental challenges, ethnic and communal conflict and health concerns such as AIDS and the outbreaks of new diseases such as Severe Acute Respiratory Syndrome (SARS) are increasingly important issues in the region, impacting on its economic development.

Climatically, Southeast Asia is predominantly a tropical zone, affected by two monsoons that bring heavy rains during October to February in the east, and between April and August in the western parts of the region. Monsoons can bring with them devastating storms, but when the rains are weak, the area is subject to drought and declining agricultural production. In recent years, dry conditions have also led to massive bush fires (in Malaysia and Indonesia in 1998, for example). The region's geography ranges from mountain ranges to forested hillsides, flat river valleys and coastal plains. One of the world's major rivers, the Mekong, runs from Tibet through the heart of Southeast Asia, crossing Myanmar, Thailand, Laos, Cambodia, and Vietnam.

Despite their diversity the countries of Southeast Asia have been linked for centuries by trade and the movement of people. Stories of colonialism, struggles for independence, and the economic and social challenges within the region post-World War II continue to thread the countries together. The following sections will briefly overview the history and economic development of the region, beginning with the decline of European colonialism. Southeast Asia's colonial past still influences the economic, political, and social structures in the region today.

Colonialism in Southeast Asia

Southeast Asia's strategic position on the trade routes between Europe and China, and its own production of attractive commodities such as spice, led to increasing contact with European traders. By the eighteenth century, the region consisted of some forty states, principalities and kingdoms with European control of various regional maritime trading posts (Osbourne 1997). But by the nineteenth century new international boundaries became established and new political institutions were created as European states exerted their power. All of the countries of present day Southeast Asia were under the control of a European state, with the exception of Thailand: the Dutch in Indonesia, the Portuguese in what is now Timor L'este, the French in Cambodia, Laos and Vietnam, the British in Brunei, Malaya, Myanmar, and Singapore, and Spain and the United States in the Philippines. While Thailand was the only country to escape direct rule, its royal family did make diplomatic concessions

and lost control of parts of their territory to the French and British.

The impact of colonialism was uneven. Writers such as Osbourne (1997) argue that the Dutch were of little importance to the majority of the Indonesian population until the mid-eighteenth century. The Spanish on the other hand, in the Philippines from the seventeenth century, embedded Christianity into the country and created strong links between church and state. Europeans were not the first foreign influences in Southeast Asia. India and China had for hundreds of years impinged on the region, from outright Chinese incursion into Vietnam, to the spread of India's Buddhism across Myanmar. Contact with traders from the Arab states led to the relocation of Islam throughout the Malay peninsula, Indonesia, and the Philippines by the thirteenth and fourteenth centuries. However, European colonisation coincided with the industrial revolution which created rapid changes in economic organisation.

The transformation of the economies of the region, and the establishment of a new economic relationship with Europe began in earnest in the nineteenth and twentieth centuries. New industries such as rubber production were established, and traditional ones such as rice, sugar, and copra were expanded to meet European demands. Agribusiness in the form of plantation farming was introduced and economies reoriented towards producing exports. These changes disrupted economic patterns and at times impoverished local, rural populations. The result was at times rural unrest, for example, in Cambodia in 1915 and 1916, as many as one hundred thousand farmers protested against economic change (Osbourne 1997).

Some of the adjustments included the introduction of a cash economy as opposed to former practices of bartering; wage labour as opposed to feudal labour and subsistence farming; the availability of consumer goods for those now with disposable incomes; the growth of retail businesses; and the expansion of infrastructure and communications such as road and rail. New institutions such as banking were introduced. New taxes were imposed in some areas, and new authorities inserted into village structures. At the same time, a process of urbanisation was taking place and the major trading cities of the colonial period became cosmopolitan centres with a mix of European, local, Indian, and Chinese communities.

While rapid economic transition was taking place between the latter half of the nineteenth century and up to WWII, it was also at this time that the colonial regimes began to feel the impact of the growing nationalist independence movements. Nationalism was fuelled by an awareness of political domination and the accrual of the economic benefits of development to European countries rather than to nationals within Southeast Asia itself.

The Rise of Nationalism

There were many incidents of resistance and rebellion against the colonial powers (the wars fought against the Dutch as they expanded their control over Indonesia, for example, and the British "pacification" of Myanmar). However, following WWI, these struggles began to develop new approaches, based not only on the idea of removing European control, but also instituting new forms of government once they had gone. The period between the World Wars saw the coming to prominence of some of the most well-known Southeast Asian leaders, such as Sukarno in Indonesia and Ho Chi Minh in Vietnam.

Ideas relating to socialism, communism, and localised variants of democracy were proposed, stemming from a new class of intelligentsia. The Japanese defeat of Russia in 1905 and the Chinese Revolution of 1911 provided inspiration. Religions such as Islam in Malaysia and Indonesia, and Buddhism in Myanmar were also rallying points for ideas of national unity. At times these movements were designed to differentiate 'nationals' from immigrants who were a source of economic competition, such as the Chinese community in Indonesia and the Indian community in Myanmar.

The independence movements in each country found themselves facing different challenges and developing diverse responses as a result. In Cambodia and Laos, the French had retained the traditional ruling class under their administration and, according to Osbourne (1997), there was therefore less nationalist sentiment than in neighbouring Vietnam. In the Philippines, the United States, who had seized control from the Spanish in 1898, found themselves in another conflict with forces of the new Philippine Republic that had declared independence. In 1901, most hostilities ceased when America stated they would grant independence, although it wasn't until 1935 that internal self-government was granted, and full independence came in 1946. The response of the French and the Dutch towards resistance in Vietnam and Indonesia was repression, exile, and imprisonment of leaders. Even Thailand, so far untouched by large scale effects of colonialism, underwent something of a revolution in 1932, when it was declared that the King would be a constitutional monarch rather than an absolute ruler.

World War II was a turning point in the history of Southeast Asia. There was both collaboration and

resistance by existing colonial rulers, local elites, and nationalist movements. The French brokered a deal with the Japanese where they would retain nominal control in return for Japanese use of Indochina as a training, supply and staging area. This agreement lasted until 1945 when the Japanese finally took control. The British and Dutch were defeated and lost Malaya, Singapore, Myanmar, and Indonesia in 1942. The Philippines fell a few months later. Only Thailand, again, escaped occupation by brokering a deal with the Japanese, allowing troops to move across its territory in return for maintaining its independence.

At the end of the war, Thailand was relatively unscathed but the same could not be said for the former colonial powers. Britain was counting the cost of keeping its empire and one by one its former colonies achieved independence. Myanmar (1948), Malaya, and Singapore had relatively smooth transitions to independence over the next twenty years. Malaya gained its independence in 1957 and formed the Federation of Malaysia in 1963, incorporating the last of the British empire's Southeast Asian outposts (Singapore, Sarawak, and Sabah). Singapore separated and formed its own state in 1965 primarily as a result of communal tensions and unresolved administrative issues.

The transfer of power, however, was not without a degree of conflict. There was factional fighting and dissidence in Myanmar. In Malaya, an Emergency was imposed by the British between 1948 and 1960 as a communist inspired insurgency threatened the state. In the Philippines, Huk insurgents, another Communist-led group that had fought against the Japanese, began a rebellion post-1946 independence, after elected representatives were refused their seats in parliament. The insurgency was defeated by the 1950s. In Brunei, a revolt following the only elections to ever be held in the country in 1962 (won by a party who opposed the monarchy but whose demands were rejected by the ruling elite) was quickly overcome by British troops. Brunei became self-governing in 1959 but remained a British protectorate until its independence in 1984.

Two major conflicts in particular marked the post-World War II period. From 1946, the Dutch fought a loose coalition of anti-colonial forces for control over Indonesia, eventually relinquishing power in 1949. Vietnam's conflict lasted much longer. While France granted independence to Cambodia and Laos in 1953, attempts to reassert their authority in Vietnam were met by resistance and war from 1945 until 1954, when the country was eventually partitioned at the 17th parallel. In the following decade United States military involvement in the region increased until an overt war was being fought with communist forces in the south that lasted until 1975. This conflict spilled over into neighbouring Cambodia and Laos.

Post-Independence Development

During the immediate post-World War II period, agriculture still dominated the economies of Southeast Asia, however there were changes taking place that would see a new phase of economic and social reorganisation. The countries in the region faced similar challenges post-Independence: the transfer of control over resources and commerce to new governments; poverty alleviation; increasing population growth that was threatening to erode economic gains; the need for social infrastructure such as education and health care; maintaining national unity and the management of immigrant and minority ethnic communities (particularly in those countries which prior to annexation by colonial forces or prior to independence did not exist, such as Indonesia, Malaysia, and Laos); and in the case of Indochina, ongoing conflict and civil war.

To address these challenges, according to Hussey (1996), there were four key elements of the dominant development model of the 1950s and 1960s that were applied to Southeast Asia: the need to promote savings and investment; the need to support agriculture as a resource for the generation of capital to invest in industrialisation; the need to promote domestic production and nascent industries through adopting policies of import substitution and tariff protection; and the need to encourage national governments to direct development to prevent market failure. However, different countries again took different paths, with varying degrees of success.

In terms of governance, three dominant political systems were adopted in the region: first, institutions influenced by British– or United States–style democracy with a preference for more market oriented economies; second, the instituting of centralised, authoritarian government with a preference for command economies; and third, the installation of a military regime or a form of government with close ties to the military, also with a more centralised economic framework. An inherent uncertainty in some countries saw nascent democracies overthrown by military coups. This degree of insecurity was not surprising. Old orders were threatened by new ideas, and deep inequalities and disparities in wealth and power still existed throughout Southeast Asia despite the promise of a better future once independence was gained.

Ferdinand Marcos, leader of the Philippines from 1965 to 1986, adopted a policy of 'constitutional

authoritarianism' after he declared martial law in 1972. Myanmar, following a coup in 1962, ushered in a new totalitarian regime that remains one of the most repressive in the region. Until the 1990s, Myanmar continued to prefer to look inwards, developing policies of self-reliance and shunning foreign alliances. In 1965 in Indonesia, after a failed coup attempt involving the Communist party, the army installed General Suharto as President and massacres of suspected communist and communist sympathisers followed. It is conservatively estimated that at least 250,000 people were killed at this time (Osbourne 1997). South Vietnam's American sponsored President, Ngo Dinh Diem, was overthrown in a coup in 1963. In the 1970s and 1980s, Thailand had a succession of military and authoritarian governments.

The former monarchies of Southeast Asia provided a sense of continuity although in less powerful formats in Malaysia, Thailand, and Indochina. The monarchy in Brunei, however, has maintained a more absolute authority. The former king of Cambodia, Norodom Sihanouk, who abdicated to form his own political party and rule the country as a politician from 1955, espoused a form of "Buddhist Socialism" (Church 1999). He was later overthrown in a right-wing coup in 1970. A civil war ensued, with United States military involvement. Vietnamese communist forces assisted the newly formed Khmer Rouge in their fight with Cambodia's new government. In 1975, the Khmer Rouge, under the leadership of Pol Pot, gained control and began their return to "year zero," a policy that removed technological development and intellectual life from Cambodia in the name of removing foreign and capitalist influences. The country was forcibly returned to an agrarian society. It is believed that up to 1 million people were executed and a million more died as a result of the Khmer Rouge's policies between 1975 and 1979. The regime only came to an end when Vietnam retaliated over Khmer incursions into their territory, invading the country in 1978 and installing a new regime. China in turn attacked the northern borders of Vietnam in 1979. Vietnam had undergone its own process of agrarian collectivisation following the 1975 fall of Saigon and the instigation of the Socialist Republic of Vietnam. Its economy declined, exacerbated by natural disasters (in particular, floods in 1977–1978), and a United States trade embargo. Industrial and agricultural output fell and food rations were instituted.

Indochina, that is, Laos, Vietnam, and Cambodia, was shattered by its regional and civil wars. As a result, by the 1970s there was a clear division between these countries and Myanmar, still languishing in terms of social and economic indicators, and those

with stable government and increasing economic growth; countries such as Malaysia and Singapore, led by the iconic figures of Dr. Mahathir Mohamad (1981–2003) and Lee Kwan Yew (1965–1990) respectively. Mahathir and Lee at times espoused the idea of an "Asian Values" approach to development, based on traditions of elite governance and bureaucratic administration, in opposition to western ideas of "liberal democracy." While regular elections are held in both Malaysia and Singapore, there are tight restrictions on media, freedom of speech, political opposition and the management of communal diversity. Whether there is a link between this more authoritarian approach to governance and economic growth is debatable but certainly by the 1990s, there was considerable development in these countries; Singapore, in particular, which is the only Southeast Asian country regarded as industrialised.

Reform and Economic Growth

Economic development has been uneven in Southeast Asia, not only between countries but also within them, between urban and rural areas in particular and between ethnic communities. Lubeck (1998) argues that differing combinations of social class, ethnicity, and gender contributed to the varying experiences of economic development, but the impact of wars, internal strife, and political ideology that ravaged Southeast Asian states cannot be discounted either.

In 1967, the Association of South East Asian Nations (ASEAN) was formed to promote economic cooperation among its members (at that time, Indonesia, Malaysia, the Philippines, Singapore, and Thailand). As is evident from the inaugural membership, the ASEAN was originally a grouping of countries opposed to communist expansion in the region. Its expanding membership however, reflects the changing status of those communist states. Indochina, while still heavily dependent on subsistence farming and international aid, has moved towards hybrid models including private production. Laos, as with Cambodia, had begun a policy of agricultural co-operatisation in 1978 that was ended in 1979 after resistance from local farmers. It began a 'New Economic Management' program in 1986, but development has been hindered by its landlocked geography and lack of resources for industrialisation. Cambodia emphasised private sector development in its 1986–1990 Five Year Plan, introducing foreign investment laws in 1989. Since 1993, market-based economic practices began to dominate but political unrest and uncertainty

throughout the 1990s has hampered growth and reconstruction. As with Laos in particular and Vietnam to some extent, the economy is supported by foreign aid and loans, and hindered by inadequate infrastructure and opaque governance.

The end of Cold War support from the former Soviet Union helped to drive economic reform in Vietnam. Thirty percent of Vietnam's state budget had been aid from the former Union of Soviet Socialist Republics (USSR) (Church 1999). Vietnam's centralised economy began to waver in 1986, when, in line with the reforms taking place in Russia, a policy of *doi moi* or 'renovation' began. By the mid to late 1990s, relations were re-established with regional neighbours, and the United States lifted its trade embargo. Contemporary Vietnam has free market enterprises alongside state owned ones, although there are some concerns that prosperity, concentrated in the south, is again dividing the country.

Myanmar also announced a new economic regime, an "Open Door" policy, in 1988, but as with all aspects of life in this country, the economy remains under tight state control. Various countries have called for a boycott of trade with Myanmar, to add to embargos on arms sales, visa bans and asset freezing, as a result of the state's repression of the democracy movement. However, data in 2003 would indicate that there is a still a willingness on the part of international companies, particularly from the Asia region, to develop trade relations with this resource rich country. Myanmar maintained its non-aligned stance until 1997 when it too joined ASEAN, following on from Brunei (1987), Vietnam (1995), Laos (1997), and Cambodia (1999).

In 2003, agriculture was still the largest sector of gross domestic product for the Indochina countries and Myanmar although Vietnam's manufacturing sector was almost equal to that of its agricultural production. On the other economic side of Southeast Asia, Malaysia, Indonesia, Singapore, and Thailand were racing ahead in terms of economic development, with rapid growth and diversification during the 1970s and 1980s, and measurable declines in poverty. By the 1990s, they were experiencing booming economies with manufacturing the largest sector of their gross domestic product (2003 data). Capital cities such as Bangkok and Kuala Lumpur became major global financial and trade centres. Reorienting their economies towards exports and foreign direct investment (FDI) played an important role in accelerating growth rates (Hussey 1996). Thompson (1998) argues that the region also benefited from the international trade and investment regime established by such bodies as the IMF, the World Bank, and the World Trade Organisation.

New technologies, including high yield varieties of rice, revolutionised agricultural production. Indonesia, for example, by 1983 had its first rice surplus in a hundred years (Church 1999). As with the industrial revolution that came with European colonialism, the impact of post-independence agrarian reform was not always positive, creating social dislocation for often the poorest, most vulnerable sectors of Southeast Asian society and driving rural migration to cities (Scott 1985). Promised land redistribution after Independence was not as wide spread as had been hoped by many farmers who had become landless under colonial rule (Mackerras 1995). However, it can be argued that the agricultural reforms did provide a basis for contemporary economic development. The Indonesian economy was subject to continuous financial growth from the 1960s. Agricultural development was followed by industrialisation, then international investment and export oriented manufacturing, particularly in consumer goods.

Malaysia's New Economic Policy (NEP) was instigated in 1971, motivated by Malaysia's new leaders and the idea that economic and social disparity fuelled ethnic and communal tensions. The policy saw a massive increase in government intervention in the Malaysian business sector. Between the 1970s and 1990s, the economy grew on average 6.8% per year (Church 1999). The privatisation of public enterprises began in the 1980s and exports were diversified from primary products such as rubber and tin to include manufactured goods (electronics, chemicals, foods, textiles) and increasingly the services sector.

By the late nineteenth century Singapore was an important warehousing, distribution and shipping centre for British companies operating in Southeast Asia. By 1960, at least 70% of its workforce was employed in the services sector (Church 1999). Under Lee Kwan Yew, the next thirty years were spent building Singapore's manufacturing base and establishing massive government owned enterprises. The city-state has subsequently transformed itself from a fishing village to a financial and services sector hub for Asia with one of the highest rates of per capita income in the region. It is, in the twentieth century, positioning itself as a centre for research and development and the export of high- and bio-technology.

Thailand, having avoided colonial rule and contemporary war, and having had only an occasional political crisis, maintained high growth rates throughout the 1980s, fuelled by foreign investment from Asian powerhouses such as Japan and also from the United States. Japan has had an influential role in the development of Southeast Asia viewing the region as both a source of raw materials and a market for Japanese goods. Thailand's economy, once based on

rice growing, now included diversified agricultural and manufacturing products, and Bangkok had become another important financial centre in the region.

The Philippines on the other hand saw its economic development stagnate. According to Church (1999), in the 1960s the Philippines was one of the most successful and prosperous manufacturing countries in Southeast Asia. Major family controlled conglomerates grew but as a whole the country's economic growth was not sustainable. According to Hussey (1996), declining growth rates were largely due to unwillingness within the Marcos government to create social and economic reform. After Marcos' exile in 1986, and the return of democracy, the economy has again improved but the country still faces serious social and economic challenges. Manufacturing is the dominant sector of its gross domestic product but the economy is supported by remittances from foreign nationals working in other parts of Asia, the Middle East, and North America (approximately 7% of gross national product, 2003). A rural-urban divide has underpinned unrest in the country and Islamic insurgents continue to clash sporadically with government forces.

Collectively, the countries of Southeast Asia have maintained a commitment to promote cooperation in the region. Apart from ASEAN, another economic grouping, Asia Pacific Economic Cooperation (APEC), was established in 1989, to further support economic growth and cooperation in the region by lobbying to reduce tariffs and trade barriers. It has twenty-one members, including all ASEAN states except Cambodia, Laos, and Myanmar. ASEAN itself is expanding to incorporate cooperation with China, Japan, and South Korea (becoming ASEAN + 3). Since 1992, six of the ASEAN countries have signed a Free Trade Agreement, incorporating almost 96% of ASEAN trade, reducing and eliminating tariff and non-tariff barriers within the region in an attempt to create a trading bloc. Vietnam, Laos, Myanmar and Cambodia are yet to be in a position to sign on to the agreement but are expected to do so by 2010.

By the 1990s, Indonesia, Malaysia, Singapore, and Thailand had maintained extremely high levels of growth over several decades. Even the Philippines and Vietnam were showing signs of recuperation. The speed of economic development, however, brought with it inevitable stresses: an overburdened infrastructure (particular in mega-cities such as Manila or Bangkok); deforestation and environmental degradation; depopulation of rural centres; and questions around labour rights were prominent issues. The rapid pace of change also created tensions within the economic system itself. As a result newly industrialising Southeast Asia's growth was to come to a shuddering halt in 1997.

The Asian Economic Crisis and Beyond

In 1997, the Thai government, in the face of market-driven pressure on the currency, floated the Baht, which had previously been fixed to the US dollar. The economy was already showing signs of strain as a result of high rates of borrowing and a large current account deficit. The financial sector had been liberalised during the 1990s but safeguards had failed to keep pace, and weaknesses in the banking system were exposed. The combination sent the currency into free-fall, halving its value and causing the stockmarket to lose three quarters of its worth. The impact on the economy resulted in estimated job losses of over a million initially and more followed when the International Monetary Fund imposed strict conditions on its 'bailout' package (Church 1999).

The crisis in Thailand triggered similar events in neighbouring countries and as far away as Korea and Japan, sending Southeast Asia region into recession. The impact of the crisis varied from country to country but Indonesia was worse affected with its currency at one point just one-sixth of its pre-crisis value (Arndt and Hill 1999), inflation increasing and its gross domestic product severely declining. In Malaysia, the Ringgit's value was halved· and the share market decimated. Unemployment and poverty rose throughout the region, particularly among urban poor. The agricultural sector was less affected, being less exposed to the financial system and export crops benefiting from currency devaluations.

Vietnam, Singapore, and the Philippines were the least affected countries but the crisis in general augured the need for reform. Structural problems were highlighted, in particular a lack of good governance and investment in unproductive infrastructure and speculation. The crisis also led to a questioning of the international financial system as foreign speculators profited from the falling markets in Asia.

In Indonesia, the economic downturn impacted on the legitimacy of the Suharto government. Ruling for over thirty years, corruption and lack of transparency had been tolerated while the economy was stable but as increasing numbers of people suffered they looked to the government for accountability. Public protests led to Suharto's resignation in 1998. This is generally regarded as the beginning of the introduction of wider political reform in Indonesia.

While it could be argued that the crisis of 1997–1998 resulted in stronger economic accountability, there are still issues that need to be addressed that will impact on development in the region in the future. The environment is a particularly contentious issue as regional leaders have argued that they be

allowed to develop as industrialised nations in the West have done, without restrictions due to environmental factors. Environmental groups continue to lobby for greater implementation of sustainable development strategies, control of green house gas emissions and an end to logging of rainforests. A related issue is that of energy security. Countries whose natural resources are the mainstay of their economies, for example, Brunei's oil and gas supplies, are beginning to look for alternative means of productivity. Brunei's investments in other countries will no doubt assist in maintaining its high standard of living. On the other hand, Indonesia, a major supplier of petroleum, has not been able to translate the wealth from this resource into the wider well being of its population. It is argued by writers such as Hussey that this is because the benefits are dissipated by Indonesia's population growth.

Population growth is another issue for the region. Indonesia had a population of 8.5 million in 1800 but 219 million today. The population of Thailand has increased by almost 50% in the thirty years since 1975. The demographic composition of the region is also shifting. The youth population (fifteen to twenty-five years) has become the largest segment, driving changing consumption patterns and social attitudes. The population is increasingly urbanised, educated, and middle class, increasing the impetus for political change.

The likelihood of conflict increases as populations grow and pressure is placed on arable land and urban centres. There are deep divisions still between rural poor and urban affluence that also feeds into black markets such as "the Golden Triangle," one of the world's major narcotics producing areas, linking Myanmar, Laos, and Thailand. Issues of national unity have become particularly pertinent post-September 11, 2001. There has been a resurgence of Islamic fundamentalism in the Philippines and Thailand, and bombings of western tourist sites and embassies in Indonesia (2002–2004). Indonesia finally relinquished Timor-L'este in 2002, but is still attempting to overcome communal violence in another of its provinces, Aceh. Countries such as Myanmar have outstanding unresolved conflicts with their indigenous ethnic minorities. Internationally, there is also a degree of underlying tension between China and its smaller neighbours over the Spratly Islands (South China Sea), claimed by Malaysia, the Phillipines, Brunei, Vietnam, Taiwan, and China.

Health issues, such as AIDS, are likely to impact on future development in particular areas. Almost 1% of people between the ages of fifteen and forty-nine (some 5 million) are living with HIV/AIDS in Southeast Asia (2004). A new deadly virus, SARS (Severe Acute Respiratory Syndrome), spread from China in 2003 to other parts of the region including Hong Kong and Singapore (and as far away as Canada). The disease impacted heavily on tourism, one of the region's growing economic sectors.

In terms of economic development, the newly industrialising countries of Southeast Asia continue to adapt to changing global conditions. The region has been a supplier of raw materials for European markets, then a manufacturer of materials for export, and in the future economies could be restructured yet again as the services sector, including tourism and business process outsourcing (call centres, for example), becomes dominant. The Philippines and Malaysia have already established outsourcing as a viable sector of the economy, although it is still a small industry compared with India. While trade ties with India and China have existed for over 2,500 years this relationship is also taking on a new form. The growth of the Indian and Chinese economies is drawing in resources from Southeast Asia and creating competition particularly in the manufacturing of cheaper consumer goods. However, transformation is a hallmark of post-World War II economic development in Southeast Asia. Enmeshed in increasing interconnections of trade and the movement of people, the region will maintain its historical position as a central point of global contact and change.

MELISSA BUTCHER

See also Brunei; Cambodia; Cultural Perceptions; Ethnic Conflicts: Southeast Asia; Green Revolution; Indonesia; Laos; Malaysia; Myanmar; Philippines; Singapore; Southeast Asia: International Relations; Thailand; Vietnam

References and Further Reading

Arndt, H.W. & H. Hill (eds). *Southeast Asia's Economic Crisis: Origins, Lessons and the Way Forward*. Singapore: Institute of Southeast Asian Studies, 1999.

Church, P. *A Short History of South East Asia*, 2nd edition. Sydney: ASEAN Focus Group, 1999.

Dutt, A. K. *Southeast Asia: A Ten Nation Region*. Dordrecht/Boston/London: Kluwer Academic Publishers, 1996.

Hewison, K., R. Robinson, and G. Rodan, eds. *Southeast Asia in the 1990s: Authoritarianism, Democracy and Capitalism*. Sydney, Allen & Unwin, 1993.

Hussey, A. 'The Agro-Economic Setting,' in A. K. Dutt (ed.), *Southeast Asia: A Ten Nation Region*. Dordrecht/Boston/London: Kluwer Academic Publishers, 1996.

Knight, N. *Understanding Australia's Neighbours: an Introduction to East and Southeast Asia*, 2nd ed. Cambridge/New York: Cambridge University Press, 2004.

Lubeck, P. 'Winners and Losers in the Asia-Pacific,' in G. Thompson (ed.), *Economic Dynamism in the Asia-Pacific*. London/Canada/US: Routledge, 1998.

Mackerras, C., ed. *East and Southeast Asia: A Multidisciplinary Survey*. USA: Lynne Rienner Publishers, 1995.

Mills, L. *Southeast Asia*. Minneapolis, MN: University of Minnesota Press, 1964.

Osbourne, M. *South East Asia: An Introductory History*, 7th edition. Sydney: Allen and Unwin, 1997.

Scott, J. C. *Weapons of the Weak: Everyday Forms of Peasant Resistance*. USA: Yale University Press, 1985.

Siegel, J. T. and A. R. Kahin, eds. *Southeast Asia over Three Generations: Essays Presented to Benedict Anderson*. New York: Southeast Asia Program Publications, 2003.

Thompson, G., ed. *Economic Dynamism in the Asia-Pacific*. London/Canada/USA: Routledge, 1998.

SOUTHEAST ASIA: INTERNATIONAL RELATIONS

Southeast Asia is one of the most politically and ethnically diverse regions of the world. As a result, international relations within the region and with countries from outside the region are particularly complex and intricate. Few of the ten countries considered have such a dominant political constituency that there is not widespread opinion about relations with almost any external actor.

In the past, critical external relations were with China and with trading representatives of India, Persian, and the Arab states. Subsequently, European and then American involvement became increasingly important as trading gave way to colonisation. International relations then became subject to international geostrategic concerns, such as World War II, the spread of communism and forces such as international terrorism. States within Southeast Asia have also increasingly become important actors in their own right, moving from passive to active participants on the international stage.

Historical Background

State formation in Southeast Asia has historically concerned the creation of loose networks of small, often city-based states. Population density has always been low and there have been insufficient people to fill up the whole of the landscape. Kings and rulers throughout history, therefore, have treated people (including people of other states) as valuable resources to be maintained or acquired from elsewhere, by force if necessary. Consequently, the long history of warfare between states within the region has been characterized not by the desire to gain territory—for there have never been enough people available to hold on to large swathes of land for more than a few years but, rather, the desire to obtain slaves and to destroy the works of rival states. Slaves as well as domestic labour were used to build monuments and religious works to demonstrate the vigour and merit of rulers.

Most states, therefore, consisted of comparatively small areas of land surrounding a central city, with a few villages acting as a network to the next small state. In archipelago Southeast Asia, states would mostly be based on coastal sites and be linked together with other islands by convenient shipping lanes. Alliances to counter the threat of external aggressors were possible (for example the famous three way alliance established in northern Thailand to resist the Mongol advance) but these were limited in scale and in time.

At one stage or another, almost every state in the region accepted the nominal or actual suzerainty of the Chinese emperor. This was advantageous in that it permitted access to trade networks with China—often conducted under the guise of providing tribute to the emperor—and connecting the states with those as far away as the Mediterranean and even the Americas. The spice trade linking locations as remote as the Moluccas Islands has a history of thousands of years and involved numerous intermediaries at different stages to make it feasible. Consequently, most states had a more or less permanent contingent of international merchants to help organise trade and in some cases these foreigners were permitted to achieve high office. Relations were more or less friendly over the long-term, therefore, although local incidences of xenophobia and racial tension have erupted from time to time. The smooth organisation of a cosmopolitan population was assisted by the general practice of allowing foreigners to cohabit with local women on a formal, contracted basis (in addition to the numerous informal occasions) in a social system in which the woman concerned did not lose any status after the end of the arrangement and, indeed, may have gained some by access to material goods provided by the foreigner.

Southeast Asian states were originally passive providers of accommodation for international traders but, eventually, goods produced in the region did obtain popularity and Southeast Asian nations took more active roles in commerce. However, this active role ceased when the arrival of European traders to participate in the system changed into colonizers who sought to dominate the political and economic systems completely. Prior to colonisation, accounts of Southeast Asia depict a healthy, wealthy population equal in stature to Europeans. After several generations of colonisation, most Southeast Asians have become known as short of stature, short-lived and short of money.

The Legacy of Colonisation

The Philippines were colonised by the Spanish and subsequently by the United States; Vietnam, Laos, and Cambodia were colonised by the French; Indonesia was colonized by the Dutch, with some continuing Portuguese enclaves, such as East Timor (now Timor Leste); Malaysia, Singapore and Burma (now Myanmar) were colonised by the British. Only Thailand (previously known as Siam) was able to avoid formal colonisation and even then this was achieved through lengthy bouts of diplomacy and provision of concessions, willingly or unwillingly provided.

Just as there were various colonizers, so too were there various colonial experiences. Former French and Dutch possessions, for example, consider the experience to be wholly negative and destructive and people in those countries still harbour a significant amount of resentment and ill-will towards the colonisers. The attitudes of former British colonies, on the other hand, are more complex because of the British policy of divide and rule, which set one class or ethnicity within a country to rule or administer others and, as a result, some local people certainly gained as a result of colonisation. Nevertheless, every country was involved in its own struggle for independence and self-determination which intensified during the twentieth century as first communism provided a different ideology offering ostensible freedom and secondly the victories of Japan in World War II demonstrated that Europeans were not invincible after all. While the British ceded their empire at the conclusion of WWII, the French and Dutch were more reluctant to do so and attempted to re-establish their dominance in Indochina and in Indonesia—both of which actions led to bloody wars and the eventual expulsion of the Europeans, in the case of Vietnam, the expulsion of the French opened the way for communism and the subsequent American War.

The Communist Threat

In the early years of its manifestation, Communism was seen as an immensely attractive form of ideology which demonstrated a logic for the operations of colonisation but also showed how it would ultimately wither and be defeated. The eventual victory of the Chinese Communist Party in expelling Chiang Kai-Shek's foreign backed Nationalists and the Japanese invaders alike through purely local efforts, particularly through the efforts of apparently disempowered

rural people such as were to be found throughout Southeast Asia, only hardened the resolve. As a result, it attracted adherents in nearly every country of the region. In most cases, a fierce struggle ensued as the nationalist governments sought to eliminate an ideology that they believed would result in their countries again being dominated by a foreign power. Most notably, the northern part of Vietnam turned to Communism and this sparked the invasion of the United States and allied troops, which only resulted amidst terrible casualties and destruction in the fall of the west-looking South Vietnamese government and massive outflows of refugees and migrants. Subsequent international relations were hugely affected by this war, which resulted in the imposition of sanctions upon the country by the United States and the locking of Vietnam into the Communist world, where aid and assistance could be most commonly obtained either from the Soviet Union or China, which introduced a new twist into a long and generally problematic relationship.

The US War in Vietnam had many other consequences. The presence of large numbers of US and allied troops in the region stimulated the industrial level development of bar and sex industries in friendly local cities such as Bangkok, Taipei, and Singapore. It also brought alliances with various ethnic minorities who had been encouraged to make common cause with the Americans in return for future autonomy that the Americans were not able to grant. This subsequently led to the large-scale relocation of the Hmong people from their homes in upland Laos and Thailand into the United States in a process that has so far lasted decades.

Communism was also victorious in Laos, which was dragged into the conflict in Vietnam and has the dubious distinction of having the most heavily bombed population per capita in the world. Domination of Laos by Vietnamese subsequently ensured that almost all of the former's relations with the outside world were mediated on the official level by Vietnamese trained sensibilities. This even extended to having a significant impact on cross-Mekong contacts between the Laotians and the millions of ethnic Lao living in the northeastern part of Thailand. The situation was even more extreme in Cambodia, where the Communist-inspired Khmer Rouge swept to power and launched a campaign of ideological purification that led to the deaths of millions and the almost complete absence of contact with the outside world. Refugees on the Thai border, for example, were sent back to Cambodia. The Vietnamese invasion of 1979 that ended the Khmer Rouge reign led to further sanctions against Vietnam and a brief border war with China. The frozen atmosphere with China

followed by the collapse of the Soviet system led to the almost complete absence of badly needed overseas assistance and effectively drove the return to a market-based system.

The struggle against Communism in Malaya, Singapore, and Thailand, was ultimately successful and helped to cement relations with western powers. However, measures taken were often extreme and, in Malaysia, involved an extensive internal war (labelled an "emergency" by the British state prosecuting it for insurance reasons). These actions further distanced the pro- and anti-communist positions of states and actors within the region and led to further disunity.

Irredentism and Autonomous Movements

Southeast Asian states have in common, therefore, multiethnic populations distributed unevenly across their territories. State borders have been arbitrarily drawn in many cases by colonial powers and in others borders are not yet fully demarcated. Low levels of population in most parts of the region have reduced the need to maximize geographical territory and this has meant that disputes over ownership of some remote areas have emerged with the discovery of important resources located near them. One example of this is the Spratly Islands, which are a chain of almost uninhabitable island tops spread over a wide expanse of ocean but which are nevertheless claimed and partly occupied by forces from China, Vietnam, and Taiwan in full and Malaysia, the Philippines and Brunei in part. Establishing a diplomatic process to determine ownership has required a difficult and lengthy effort that is not yet complete. However, it has offered some guidelines for future negotiations.

Irredentism is the desire of fragmented communities to reintegrate into their own state. It is related to the desire for autonomy, which involves the desire of a community wholly administered by a state of which it is part to rule itself with a greater degree of independence. Many states fear these phenomena because of the danger to stability to security and indeed to access to resources. In recent years, the former Portuguese colony of Timor Leste (East Timor) has managed to gain independence from Indonesia in the face of determined opposition and at the cost of the almost complete physical destruction of its infrastructure. The presence of offshore reserves of oil and gas are partly responsible for the bitterness of much of the opposition to independence. Other areas within Indonesia also wishing to

obtain independence include Aceh on Sumatra, which has been the result of years of revolt suppression by central state forces and which has continued despite the recent devastation following the earthquake and tsunami disaster of December 26, 2004. Other areas in which these movements are of importance include the Moros islands in the Philippines, the southern provinces of Thailand that were once Pattani and the Shan states of Myanmar. In each of these cases, acts of terrorism by insurgents and government reprisals in response have become an almost daily phenomenon.

These movements have had numerous impacts on international relations. Firstly, cross-border conflict or the use of border regions as hiding places divides neighbouring states. Secondly, other regions may be drawn into the conflict; both from within or without the region and this can lead to intensification of disputes, especially if the all-important loss of face becomes a reality. Dealing with these actual and potential issues was an important spurring force for the creation of the Association of Southeast Asian Nations (ASEAN), which has become the main forum for international discussion.

ASEAN

International relations within the Southeast Asian region have been dominated by the creation of the Association of South-East Asian Nations (ASEAN), which provided a forum for debate that was previously lacking. Despite the numerous apparent problems with the debates produced, which frequently appear to be greatly abstracted from real life, the importance of ASEAN has been to provide a place where Southeast Asian leaders can communicate with each other informally and, at the beginning of the twenty-first century, sufficient commonality of purpose has been established for ASEAN to undertake negotiations on a bilateral and multilateral basis with economic partners such as China, South Korea, Japan, and Australia.

In a region lacking political forums and much commonality of purpose, it was both essential and highly problematic that an association of nations be formed to create a space in which issues of mutual importance may be discussed, even if public discourse necessarily remained drenched in rhetoric. The first incarnation of the Big 5 that constituted the early ASEAN were, in 1967, a disparate group united by a few common concerns. Singapore, Malaysia, Thailand, Indonesia, and the Philippines were a collection of largely post-colonial societies fearing the spread of

Communism and the outbreak of ethnically based violence. As autocratic societies, they were unwilling to participate in international discussions in which their own undemocratic nature could be criticised. Hence, a *modus operandi* was developed in which no public discussion of what were considered to be each other's internal affairs was considered acceptable. Deals, when possible, were done strictly behind doors. Those numerous technocrats and diplomats who devoted years to negotiating agreements could find their efforts apparently cast aside by the effects of a grandstanding speech. Yet, nevertheless, the scope of agreements between ASEAN members has both broadened and deepened.

In subsequent years, the five remaining Southeast Asian states have also joined ASEAN: Brunei joined in 1984, Vietnam in 1995, Laos and Myanmar in 1997 and, finally, Cambodia in 1998. Only tiny new East Timor remains outside the fold. There are few if any other organisations in the world in which military autocracies can rub shoulders with communist states, absolute monarchies, and democracies. While ASEAN is far from perfect, it is a great deal better than the alternative. The original declaration of association read in part that:

> The Association represents the collective will of the nations of to bind themselves together in friendship and cooperation and, through joint efforts and sacrifices, secure for their peoples and for posterity the blessings of peace, freedom, and prosperity.

This was restated slightly in 1995 in the following terms: "Cooperative peace and shared prosperity shall be the fundamental goals of ASEAN." It is true that no large scale warfare between ASEAN members has broken out since its inception, although genuine peace has always been and remains a fragile vision. Areas of considerable tension include the *konfrontasi* between Indonesia and Malaysia, rivalry between Malaysia and Singapore and access to water resources, the destruction of East Timor by Indonesian forces, the sporadic outbreaks of violence on the Thai-Myanmar border as Myanmar forces battle against various ethnic groups seeking autonomy and, perhaps most significant of all, the Vietnamese invasion of Cambodia in 1979 intended to rid that benighted country of the scourge of the Khmer Rouge.

Ethnic Vietnamese suffered greatly during the Khmer Rouge domination of Cambodia and the fact that the two states can now co-exist in ASEAN without either publicly demanding reparations or trials points to a possibly sustainable model of international relations in one of the more problematic areas of the world.

Within the ASEAN region, a number of specific issues exist which have particular impact upon international relations and these will now be dealt with individually.

Migration Issues

The most important migration issue in Southeast Asia has been the presence of Chinese migrants within the region. Chinese have been present in almost every part of the region since at least the sixth century CE. While most may never throughout history have been to mainland China or know anyone there individually, nevertheless the link to the antecedent village or province has remained strong. The claim of the central state upon the loyalties of emigrants has also, of course, historically been of great importance. This has led to a variety of implications of a more or less positive nature. On the positive side, the remittances of money and trading relationships established with ancestral villages and regions has been economically beneficial, while the practice of exporting Chinese women for marriage to migrants has in some case prevented integration into local societies. Resentment against ethnic Chinese has been easy to foster in times of economic or political distress and, during the 1997 financial crisis, for example, ethnic Chinese were attacked with particular savagery in Indonesia.

The low level of public and political discourse throughout most of the region has meant that it has become very easy for ethnic violence to flare very quickly. For the sake of rumours and gossip, there were intense although short-lived riots against Thais and Thai interests in Cambodia, for example, while Burmese migrant workers have been persecuted by Thai citizens and authorities, as too have Indonesian migrant workers been persecuted in Malaysia. Migrant workers, central figures in most modern economies, have proved themselves to be vulnerable to various types of abuse across border and negotiations concerning their fair treatment has constituted an important issue in some state relations.

The Role (Post-War) of Japan

Having been part of the lengthy struggle for independence, many sections of Southeast Asian society were reluctant to welcome the large scale arrival of Japanese corporations investing in their economies. While governments welcomed the prospect of employment

opportunities and possible technology transfer, they were also wary of possibly giving away economic sovereignty to organisations that seemed unwilling to accept local people among the management structure. The Japanese government was slow to accept a political leadership role and, partly as a result, overseas development assistance (international aid) was often considered to have an ulterior motive. This coloured relationship between Southeast Asian nations and Japan that is only in the twenty-first century that Japanese government agencies began meaningfully to take a leadership role in economic reform and integration within the area, leading to more openness about the intentions of the Japanese state.

The globalisation of popular media and of many consumer goods markets has meant that aspects of Japanese culture (as well as those from various other countries) have become much more prevalent in Southeast Asia and this too has assisted in promoting friendly relations, as have also various exchange schemes.

Religious Issues

State relations in the premodern world were often influenced by religion and their legacy has continued until the current day. The Islamisation of many of the island regions of Southeast Asia has meant that states in those areas frequently look west to their Islamic brothers in the Arab world rater than north to their rather closer neighbours in mainland Southeast Asia. This has become more important in recent years as the internationalisation of religious teaching in Malaysia, the south of Thailand and Indonesia, as well as southern regions of the Philippines, has been associated with the rise of fundamentalist beliefs and a possible link with terrorism. Certainly, movements seeking autonomy from a non-Islamic state government have taken on a more violent nature which has included targeting western people and interests.

Development Implications

The concept of statehood came late to most Southeast Asian nations and so the practice of conducting international state relations that are binding on all actors within a state was also only lately developed. Centuries of treating with other states from a position of often supine weakness further influenced the nature of the discourse and intention of state leaders.

Cultural factors have also played a part. The result has been a frequent degree of defensiveness and obfuscation when dealing with the world. State leaders neither wish to reveal facts about their home countries nor accept criticism of their policies or state of development. As previous de facto spokesperson for ASEAN, Malaysia's Dr. Mahathir Mohammed was not averse to bringing up the ills of the colonial past caused by western powers both to explain present imperfections and to turn the tables of criticism.

Generally, therefore, the level of political discourse in public, together with the low level of meaningful public participation in policy formation, has meant that not only has international dialogue been of an inefficient manner but also that decisions taken at governmental level have little or no ownership at lower levels and hence are difficult to implement.

The use of minority peoples as proxies by external states as also increased internal fragmentation and led to some punitive policies taken against them. In the case of international development assistance, the additional agenda issues brought to negotiations by international partners has led to a short term approach to development priorities and unevenness in application.

ASEAN has proved successful within the very limited remit that it has provided for itself. While cooperation has slowly evolved, a more open and wide-ranging discourse would have provided more development opportunities for the people of the region. In any case, greater openness to cultural influences within the region should have helped to promote understanding and tolerance an would have saved a great deal of misery for put upon minorities.

JOHN WALSH

See also Ethnic Conflicts: Southeast Asia; Southeast Asia: History and Economic Development

References and Further Reading

Acharya, Amitav. *The Quest for Identity: International Relations of Southeast Asia*. Oxford: Oxford University Press, 2001.

Aspinall, Edward and Mark T Berger. "The Break-up of Indonesia? Nationalisms after Decolonisation and the Limits of the Nation-State in Post-Cold War Southeast Asia," *Third World Quarterly*, Vol. 22, No. 6 (December, 2001), pp. 1003–1024.

Christie, Clive J. *A Modern History of Southeast Asia: Decolonization, Nationalism and Separatism*. London and New York: Tauris Academic Publishers, 1996.

Karnow, Stanley. *In Our Image: America's Empire in the Philippines*. New York: Ballantine Books, 1990.

Lee Kan Yew. *From Third World to First: The Singapore Story: From 1965–2000*. Harper Collins, 2000.

Myint, U. *The Making of Modern Burma*. Cambridge: Cambridge University Press, 2001.

Neher, Clark D. *Southeast Asia in the New International Era*, fourth edition. Westview Press, 2002.

Skeldon, Robert. "Emigration Pressure and Structural Change in Southeast and East Asia," *ILO Unpublished Report* (1997), downloaded from: http://www.ilo.org/public/english/region/asro/bangkok/paper/se_asia.htm.

The official ASEAN website is available at: http://www.aseansec.org/

SOUTHEAST ASIA TREATY ORGANIZATION (SEATO)

The Southeast Asia Treaty Organization (SEATO) was inspired by President Dwight D. Eisenhower and forged by Secretary of State John Foster Dulles in 1954. In that year, following the Geneva Conference, the United States (US), led by Dulles, who feared communist advances in Southeast Asia, began negotiations with indigenous states and colonial powers in the region in an effort to form a regional defense system. On September 8, 1954, eight signed the SEATO treaty as part of the Manila Pact. The organization, which ostensibly paralleled the North Atlantic Treaty Organization (NATO), officially began operations on February 19, 1955, following ratification of the treaty by the US Senate.

The founding members included Australia, New Zealand, Pakistan, the Philippines, Thailand, the US, Great Britain, and France. Of note were those nations not included: Taiwan, because the treaty did not accept countries north of 21'300 North latitude; neutral states such as India, Burma, and Indonesia, which refused membership; and Cambodia, Laos, and South Viet Nam, which were denied membership by the tenets of the Geneva Accords. Indeed, France, still smarting from its humiliating defeat at Dien Bien Phu and its resulting loss of Indochina, opposed full membership for her former colonies–Cambodia, Laos, and South Viet Nam.

While the agreement created a council to provide for consultation and it allowed "for the common defense" of all the treaty partners, promising action "to meet the common danger," unlike NATO, it did not form a unified military command. At the same time, the SEATO Treaty contained a separate protocol that designated Cambodia, Laos, and South Viet Nam as "vital" to regional security. As such, SEATO nations were obligated to place a "security umbrella" over these states. In spite of the questionable legality of this protocol, which essentially countered the tenets of the Geneva Accords, Dulles insisted that it was essential to assure the "tranquility and safety" of the treaty signers.

Following the Gulf of Tonkin Incident in mid-1964, President Lyndon Baines Johnson cited this protocol as the basis for the Gulf of Tonkin Resolution and the expansion of America's military commitment to what became the Second Indochina War. In fact, he never consulted his SEATO partners in this matter. Ironically, by March 1969, his successor, President Richard M. Nixon had reinterpreted this very same protocol, declaring that it did not justify or require the commitment of US military forces to the region. This led to the initiation of Nixon's "Vietnamization" policy.

By 1971, many SEATO nations, especially France and Thailand, had become very uncomfortable with America's handling of the war in Viet Nam, Cambodia, and Laos. These escalating tensions reached a climax with the fall of Sai Gon in 1975. With the advent of detente and the beginning of US policies that would eventually end the Cold War, most SEATO states no longer saw a need for the organization. On June 30, 1977, the alliance was formally dissolved during laconic ceremonies in Bangkok, Thailand.

Clearly, SEATO did little for the development of states in Southeast Asia since it was a Cold War political creation, mostly designed to protect US interests in its broader struggle against the Soviet Union and China. One could argue that SEATO retarded the growth of nations such as Kampuchea, Laos, and Viet Nam. One thing it did contribute was to inspire indigenous leaders to seek an alternative organization made up of regional states. Indeed, over the past thirty years, the Association of Southeast Asian Nations (ASEAN), comprised of, and led by regional nations, has successfully facilitated significant economic growth and social stability in Southeast Asia.

WILLIAM P. HEAD

References and Further Reading

Arnold, James R. *The First Domino: Eisenhower, the Military and America's Intervention in Vietnam*. New York: William Morrow, Inc., 1991.

Hess, Gary R. *Vietnam and the United States*. Boston: Twayne, Inc., 1990.

LaFaber, Walter F. *America, Russia, and the Cold War, 1945–1990*. 5th Edition. New York: John Wiley and Sons, 1991.

Marks, Frederick W., III. *Power and Peace: The Diplomacy of John Foster Dulles*. Westport, CT: Praeger, 1993.

Moss, George D. *Vietnam: An American Ordeal*. Englewood Cliffs, NJ: Prentice-Hall, 1994.

Williams, William Appleman, Thomas McCormick, Lloyd Gardner, and Walter LaFaber, eds. *America In Vietnam: A Documentary History*. 1985.

SOUTHERN AFRICA: HISTORY AND ECONOMIC DEVELOPMENT

The Region Defined

The Southern Africa region has been defined as including as few as nine nations and as many as fourteen. The principal organizing group since 1979 has been the Southern African Development Community (SADC). The SADC deals with political and economic development, but it is also concerned with social and cultural issues. When the SADC first organized it included nine states, but in 1992 it expanded to fourteen: Angola; Botswana; the Democratic Republic of the Congo; Lesotho; Malawi; Mauritius; Mozambique; Namibia; Seychelles; South Africa; Swaziland; Tanzania; Zambia; and Zimbabwe. This essay will discuss the joint historical and economic development of the fourteen state region.

Early Residents

Southern African history began with the arrival of the San and Khoikhoi who inhabited each of the fourteen nations. The Khoisan (Khoikoi and San) arrived long before other African migrants and Europeans. For the pre-historic period archaeologists and anthropologists have uncovered fossil remains that show that Homo sapiens had arrived in Southern Africa from the North around 50,000 BCE, long before San hunter-gatherers and Khoikhoi herdsmen. The Khoisan, later termed "Bushmen" and "Hottentots" by Europeans, came from the North around 14,000 BCE. Bantu followed in the first century CE and gradually displaced most of the Khoisan by intermarriage or force. Africans at this juncture were multi-ethnic as was apparent in the numerous languages they spoke.

The region's history and economy were influenced by its semi-tropical/temperate climate and its location in the Southern half of the African continent. By the fifteenth century the Cape of Good Hope, at Africa's southern tip, became a port on a route that tied Europe to East Africa and Asia until the completion of the Suez Canal in 1869. The climate on the Atlantic and Indian Ocean coasts made the Cape an ideal market for Portuguese, Dutch, French, Spanish, Belgian, and British ships to restock food and fuel stores en route to valued Asian and East African spices, cloths, exotic foods, and slaves. In the fifteenth to nineteenth centuries European immigrants began to arrive in Southern Africa where they established spheres of influence and political hegemony.

European migration and economic interest in Southern Africa began when Portugal's Bartholomew Dias rounded the Cape of Good Hope in 1488 after navigating the southwestern Atlantic coast. Vasco da Gama's 1497 expedition sailed up Africa's east coast to present-day Kenya where he established a port at Melinda before he continued on to Arabia, then eastward to India. Portugal dominated the trade route to Asia throughout the sixteenth century and built forts in what are now the Southern African states of Angola and Mozambique. Most of Southern Africa had direct or indirect trade with the Portuguese.

At the end of the sixteenth century English and Dutch merchant-sailors challenged Portugal's economic monopoly in Southern Africa and bartered with Africans of the Cape to replenish their ships with meat, water, and timber for the ships' broken masts. English trade with the Khoisan continued until 1652, when they decided not to build a permanent fort at the Cape. In place of the English, the Dutch East India Company set up a supply station at Table Bay and encouraged trade with the Khoisan and Dutch settlers. At the same time as the Dutch increased their presence during the seventeenth century, Bantu-speaking Africans were moving south and French Huguenot (Reformed Protestants) arrived to escape religious persecution in France and melted into the Dutch Protestant Afrikaner community. Germany colonized Namibia and Tanganyika (Tanzania) in 1884. The Asian influence in southern Africa was most pronounced in Madagascar and Zanzibar and began 2,000 years ago. Madagascar's population is primarily Malayo-Indonesian, but its official languages are French and Malagasi. It became independent of France in 1960.

Southern Africa was thus distinguished by a mix of people who gathered there. By the twentieth century southern Africans spoke eleven official languages and many local dialects. After 1945, this polyglot of people threw off the European yoke and formed democratic states. Events that abolished apartheid (racial separation) marked the region's greatest success as it rejected laws and customs that marked a brutal political, economic, social, and cultural history in the pre– and post–World War II era.

Precursors of Post-1945 Economic Development

The post-1945 Southern African economies evolved out of early nineteenth century clashes between rival

Bantu-speaking communities due to increasing population and decreasing water supply that depleted grain and hunting resources. The African population increase that began at the end of the eighteenth century came as a result of the introduction of corn (maize), a crop that the Portuguese brought from America where native people grew it. Because corn was less drought-resistant than indigenous grains it caused periods of famine that paralleled what happened in Ireland as a result of the failure of another Native American crop, the potato, in the 1840s. The Portuguese ivory trade drew Africans to Mozambique and increased the need for food and water.

Economic conditions led to political tensions, with large tribes fighting to dominate the land and food supply. The arrival of Dutch Afrikaans-speakers, French Huguenot, British, Portuguese, Belgian, German, and Bantu, further disrupted the lives of the generally peaceful Khoisan. When Africans refused to work for Europeans on the land and in mines, the whites imported slaves from West and East Africa, as well as India and China. Wars between Africans and Europeans, and African and African, were over land with scarce water resources, but also over valuable mineral resources.

European states in the nineteenth century drew boundaries that did not take into consideration religious, cultural, and language differences. African states with no cultural core found it difficult to resist service to European economic interests. Therefore Southern African wars fought since 1945 over land, mineral wealth, and ethnic dominance were ignited by a European scramble for Southern Africa's land and wealth. As a result, post-1945 African independence movements were complicated by internal and external ethnic struggles for dominance. Southern Africa, as much as any African region, provides historical insight into problems of balkanization, ethnic tensions, and control of land and wealth that have elevated the grasping for power. To discuss wars and treaties in Southern Africa is beyond the scope of this essay. More specific information is covered in essays on the fourteen nations in the region. This essay deals with the regional history and economies.

South Africa, Zimbabwe, Zambia, Namibia, Malawi, Lesotho, Swaziland, Mauritius, Seychelles, Tanzania, and Namibia

Eleven of the fourteen nations in the South African Development Community are former British colonies. They are sufficiently similar to discuss them together.

The dominant nation in 2005 in terms of economic and political leadership, size, and population, is the Republic of South Africa. South Africa was the base from which Britain launched its expansion in Southern Africa and Asia. From South Africa it conquered the territories of present-day Zimbabwe, Zambia, Malawi, Botswana, and Indian Ocean islands of Madagascar, Mauritius, and the Seychelles. Britain received former German colonies of Tanzania and Namibia after World War I as League of Nations mandates. Two states within the borders of South Africa, Lesotho and Swaziland, were Native Reserves, later Homelands. These states became members of the British Commonwealth in the post-1945 period. South Africa continued to dominate the region after 1945 in spite of the fact that it was the last to gain African majority rule (1994).

In 1890, the British South Africa Company (BSAC), a commercial enterprise headed by diamond czar Cecil John Rhodes, moved to conquer what are today Zimbabwe, Zambia in 1890, and Malawi (Nyasaland Protectorate) in 1891. Rhodes' dream was to create a Cape to Cairo British economic corridor—to take minerals from Africa and such other wealth as his BSAC could develop. Missionaries, mainly Protestant evangelicals, followed the union jack in the name of Western Christian civilization. Zimbabwe was under imperial rule till 1880; Zambia and Malawi gained independence in 1964. European political rule was supported by white settler economic, social-cultural domination. Malawi, visited by the Scottish missionary David Livingston in 1859, became a British Protectorate in 1891. The BSAC ruled Zimbabwe (Southern Rhodesia) until 1923, when it turned the government over to white settler regimes.

South Africa has 1,219,912 square kilometers of land (about twice the size of the American state of Texas). The Republic, composed after 1984 of four provinces: Cape, Natal, Transvaal, and the Orange Free State, includes in its territory several islands in the Atlantic and Indian Oceans. It borders on six independent nations: Botswana; Lesotho; Swaziland; Mozambique; Namibia; and Zimbabwe. Like most Southern African nations, 12% of South Africa's land is arable and even that land is susceptible to prolonged droughts. Its interior is a large plateau (veldt) surrounded by rugged hills and a thin coastal plain along the Atlantic and Indian Oceans. A new multi-ethnic African-led federal democracy took over in 1996 under President Nelson Mandela. Its 42,718,530 citizens wrestle with criminal and ethnic violence in their quest for peace, justice, and prosperity. The struggle is reflected in books by Nobel Prize winner Nadine Gordimer and Booker Prize

winner J. M. Coetzee. While South Africans are not alone in working out economic, racial, and language differences, they are doing so with people from three continents—Africa, Europe, and Asia, another phenomena they share with the other Southern African states.

Modern South Africa's economic history began with a discovery of rich mineral deposits in 1860–1880. In 1867 prospectors found diamonds and by 1869–70 the claims produced a rush of prospectors. The British annexed the fields and denied the claims of Dutch Afrikaners in the area. By the 1880s, Cecil Rhodes' DeBeers Consolidated Mines had bought the original mines and most small claims. Diamonds, South Africa's largest export, provided employment and subsidiary industries that fueled economic growth. By 1900, exports grew to £15 million; £4 million came from diamonds. A growing economy spurred immigration and produced a lust for more diamonds and gold, and attacks on African tribes in Shona and Ndebele territories to the north where there were more mineral deposits, but not the large gold and diamond deposits that Rhodes BSAC sought.

Africans had mined gold in southern Africa for centuries and traded it with the Portuguese and Arabs. After Afrikaners discovered gold in South Africa about fifty thousand Africans migrated each year to mines around Kimberley and Johannesburg. African farmers in Basutoland (Lesotho), the Cape and Natal, supplied growing populations around mines, interior cities and coastal ports. "Coloureds" (mixed African and white) and Indians prospered as skilled tradesmen and shopkeepers. When there was a gold strike near Johannesburg in Witwatersrand (the Rand) in 1886, English businessmen, enriched by diamond mining, bought the claims. Gold output increased to almost £8 million in 1895, 20% of the world's production. By 1900, Europeans had invested more in South African diamond and gold mines than in all the rest of Africa. Gold mines employed one hundred thousand Africans; diamond mines about twenty thousand.

In 1945, diamond and gold still dominated the mining industry. In 2005, South Africa maintained its position as the world's largest producer of platinum, gold, chromium. Minerals dominated its combined exports of $33.8 billion. Its major trading partners were the European Union, United States, and Japan. Its gross domestic product (GDP) was $456.7 billion, an estimated $10,700 per capita. The 12% of its land that was arable produced corn (the staple food of its African population), wheat, sugarcane, fruits, and vegetables. Meat products included beef, poultry, mutton, wool, and

dairy products. Of its 17 million workers, 45% worked in service industries, 30% in agriculture, 25% in industry and commerce, but 37 % were unemployed. Service industries in Southern Africa include many low paid domestic servants from villages who are seeking cash income for school fees and other necessities.

Six of the countries in the former British colonies of Southern Africa are landlocked: Zimbabwe, Zambia, Malawi, Botswana, Swaziland, and Lesotho. They are therefore dependent on neighbors, particularly South Africa, for access to markets. In 2004, the estimated populations were: Zimbabwe, 12,671,860; Malawi, 11,906,855; Zambia, 10,462,436; Botswana, 1,561,973; Lesotho, 1,864,040, and Swaziland, 1,167,241. In the area approximately 98% of the people are African; the other 2% are European and Asian. Between one and 11% of the land was arable and produced maize, tobacco, sugarcane, tea, coffee, cotton, chocolate, rice, and peanuts (ground nuts). While the principal livestock was cattle, which had a social value in bargaining for brides for sons (bride price), they also grew sheep, goats, and pigs. Zimbabwe, Zambia, and Botswana are rich in mineral resources: copper; chromium; nickel; there were deposits of gold, diamonds, coal, asbestos, cobalt, zinc, and lead in the six countries. In each country, approximately 86% of the population is at least partially employed, but most rural farmers are operating on subsistence basis of virtually no cash income. A primary concern, most notably in Zimbawe and South Africa, was the uneven distribution of land between the majority African farmers, and the minority of white commercial farmers. Options facing the governments are: compensation to white farmers and redistribution to Africans; and confiscation without compensation based on the taking of the land in the nineteenth century by Europeans with no compensation to Africans. Funds for compensation would to come from outside the region, mainly Europe and America.

Lesotho and Swaziland, former African Homelands (and before that Native Reserves), are surrounded by South Africa. They gained independence from Britain in 1966 and 1968. Apart from a few diamond deposits in Lesotho they have few minerals. Lesotho's GDP was estimated at $5.5 billion, $3,000 per capita in 2003. Seventy percent of its trade was with the United States; 24% with South Africa. Eighty-six percent of its workers were subsistence farmers, many of whom also worked in South Africa. Swaziland had an estimated GDP of $5.7 billion in 2003; $4,900 per capita. Its principal industries were asbestos and coal mining. Seventy-two percent of its exports went to South Africa.

The island nations of Madagascar, Mauritius, and Seychelles, located in the Indian Ocean, have characteristics that differ from the six former British mainland colonies. Madagascar has an area of just 226,656 square miles, but a three thousand mile coastline. On the 4% of its land that is arable, it grows coffee, vanilla, sugarcane, and cloves. Its 17,501,871 people are of mixed ethnicity: Malayo-Indonesian, African, Arab, French, Indian, Creole, and Comoran. In 1964, it received independence from Britain. It had a 2003 estimated GDP of $13 billion, $800 per person and few natural resources. Mauritius has an area of just 718 square miles, and a 110 mile coastline. But 49% of its land is arable. Its population of 1,220,481 is 68% Indo-Mauritian, and 27% Creole. The official language is English, but the largest religious groups are Hindu (52%), Christian (28%), and Muslim (16.6%), where most nations in the region have a majority Christian population and a significant number of indigenous religions. It gained independence from Britain in 1968. The Seychelles area is 27,699 square miles, with 250 miles of coastline. Seven percent of its land is arable. Its population was 5,883,889 by a 2003 estimate and its people were a mix of Asians, Africans, and Europeans. English and French are both official languages. The GDP was $626 million, $7,800 per person, in a 2002 estimate. Tourism was its largest industry. Seventy-one percent of its workers were employed in service industries; only 10% in agriculture. Ninety-four percent of its people were Christian.

The former Portuguese colonies of Angola on the Atlantic Ocean and Mozambique on the Indian Ocean received their independence in 1975, due to turmoil in the Portuguese government. Angola has a territory of 481,352 square miles (nearly twice the size of Texas) and a coastline of 994 miles. Only 2% of its land is arable. Its 2004 population estimate was 10,978,552. Ninety-seven percent came from African ethnic groups, 2% mestizo, and 1% European. Eighty-five percent of the population was engaged in subsistence agriculture; 15% in industry. Agriculture includes sheep grazing, bananas, sugarcane, coffee, sisal, corn, cotton, tapioca, and vegetables. It is rich in natural resources, including petroleum, diamonds, iron, phosphates, and copper. Its GDP in 2003 was $20.5 billion, $1,900 per capita, with 41% of its exports going to the US and 14% to China. Mozambique had a population estimated at 18,811,731 in 2003, 99% of whom were African. Only 4% of its 309,494 sq. miles of land are arable. Its crops are cotton, cashew nuts, sugar, tea, and its natural resources are coal, natural gas, and titanium. Forty-one percent of its imports come from South Africa.

Post–World War II: Apartheid Laws (1948–1976) and the Freedom Struggle (1948–2005) in Southern Africa

In 1913, the Union of South Africa passed a Natives Land Act, limiting Africans to Native Reserves (the United States called their restricted areas "Indian Reservations"). This was the first of many apartheid (separation) laws of the 1913–1948 period. The dominant political parties were Afrikaner coalitions, with little British interference. Africans organized the African National Congress. These policies increased after World War II throughout southern Africa.

From 1948 to 2005, Southern Africa moved from white-run minority governments, many of whom opposed racial mingling, to one-person-one-vote rule majority-run democracies. The change was accompanied by both physical violence and heroic gestures of line-crossing on the part of Africans and whites to accommodate the interests of all parties. The 1910–1948 apartheid laws in Southern Africa rested on assumptions that placed race above class, religion, education, or other distinctions. By 1948, the Afrikaner South African National Party had gained the support of both Afrikaans and English-speakers and retained political and economic dominance for four decades. (For the history of separation in other thirteen Southern African states see the entries on each state).

South Africa's Population Registration Act (1950) separated races into white, coloured, and native (Bantu). Identity cards insured apartheid's enforcement. A 1950 Group Areas Act updated the Natives Land Acts, in spite of the 1954 Tomlinson Commission finding that African areas could support only two-thirds of their populations. Rather than provide more land in Native Reserves, the government removed more Africans from white areas. A Prohibition of Mixed Marriages Act (1949) disallowed interracial marriages; and an Immorality Act (1950) banned interracial sexual relations. Under a 1951 Bantu Authorities Act, the government appointed chiefs and headmen as tribal, regional, and territorial authorities and abolished elected Natives Representative Councils.

There was little opposition to apartheid in South Africa. The Afrikaner National Party won reelection in 1953 and 1958 with increasing majorities. In 1958, Hendrik F. Verwoerd, the leading exponent of apartheid, became Prime Minister, and in 1961, based on a referendum, declared South Africa to be a republic, independent of Britain. In 1965, when independent African nations of the British Commonwealth, supported by Canada and India, attacked South Africa's

ethnic agenda, the National Party withdrew South Africa from the British Commonwealth. On September 6, 1966, an attendant stabbed Verwoerd to death, but his successor, B. J. Vorster, carried the apartheid legacy from 1966 to 1978.

The Birth of Democracy in Southern Africa, 1961–2005

Apartheid died a slow death in the 1970s and 1980s. Black South Africans, the international community of nations, and a few South African whites led the way. The freedom struggle, begun in the 1950s in Britain's southern African territories, was encouraged by the independence of Gwame Nkrumah's Ghana in 1957. It grew in the 1960s as the African National Congress (ANC), Pan-African Congress (PAC), and South African Communist Party (SACP), turned in frustration to violent means to overcome apartheid. Strategic targets included power plants, police stations, and chiefs and headmen who collaborated with the government. By 1964, many black leaders were arrested, including Walter Sisulu and Nelson Mandela, who went to prison for life. Oliver Tambo escaped capture and led the resistance from Zambia. African leaders in other southern African colonies were suffering the same fate. But Tanzania gained independence in 1961 and united with Zanzibar in 1964, the year Zambia and Malawi won independence.

Several forces pressured white regimes while black leaders were in prison. African Trades Unions led strikes for better working conditions and pay. Workers racial consciousness was partly due to economic growth and international support. In 1973, the United Nations (UN) declared apartheid to be a "crime against humanity." In 1976, thousands of South Africa's black school children revolted against teaching in Afrikaans, the language of their oppressor. In 1977, police killings of black civilians climaxed with the death of student leader Steve Bilko while in police custody. Other blacks went to neighboring African states for military training. In 1975, Mozambique and Angola gained independence from Portugal, and in 1979 Rhodesia's white government was on the verge of yielding power to Robert Mugabe's Patriotic Front that led to Zimbabwe's independence in 1980.

In the 1980s, economic problems caused white government and business leaders to reevaluate South Africa's isolation. Following boom years in the 1960s and 1970s, GDP was declining. Many whites were becoming poorer and skilled labor was leaving the country. Apartheid had become expensive to administer and

the black population was growing much faster than the white. In 1977, the UN embargoed the sale of arms to South Africa and the American civil rights movement made significant progress. In 1978, Prime Minister Vorster resigned under corruption charges and P.W. Botha replaced him.

Two forces nudged South Africa away from apartheid. Black trades unions grew to over 1 million members and demanded accommodation. Prime Minister Botha, in a 1994 constitution, reached out to Coloureds (those of mixed African-white ancestry) and Indians, by setting up a tricameral legislature: a 178 member white House of Assembly; eighty-five member coloured House of Representatives; forty-five member Indian House of Delegates; all democratically elected. Africans, 75% of the population, remained unrepresented. But in 1986 Botha gave in to demands to rescind pass laws and repeal bans on multiracial political parties and interracial sex and marriage, but he stopped short of desegregating schools, closing disparities in health and welfare services, and allowing Africans to own property outside "homelands" (formerly Native Reserves). In 1985, British Prime Minister Margaret Thatcher of Britain and US President Ronald Reagan opposed sanctions, but in 1986 the US Congress passed an Anti-Apartheid Act over Reagan's veto, as other nations put pressure on the South African government.

In 1989, F.W. de Klerk succeeded Botha as National Party head and State President, and in 1990 de Klerk unbanned three African parties, the ANC, PAC, and SACP, and released Nelson Mandela and other political prisoners. In 1991, after the de Klerk government repealed most apartheid laws, white voters supported a resolution to negotiate with African leaders. In 1992, South Africa joined the Southern African Development Community (SADC) with Angola, Botswana, Lesotho, Malawi, Mozambique, Namibia, Tanzania, Zambia, and Zimbabwe. In 1993, de Klerk and Mandela, with eighteen other party leaders, endorsed an interim constitution under which South Africa would be ruled pending a permanent constitution. In 1994, the African National Congress (ANC) won South Africa's first democratic, nonracial election under an interim constitution. Nelson Mandela became president on May 10.

Foreign governments lifted economic sanctions. South Africa rejoined the British Commonwealth and negotiated cooperative agreements with Southern African states of the SADC. In the 1999 election, the ANC won 66% of the vote and the Democratic Party replaced the National Party as the official opposition. Mandela had retired after his five-year term and Thabo Mbeki, his Deputy President, became President. This completed the transition from white

colonial-era governments to fourteen majority-led democratic states. Not all of the states are stable, nor are all of the economies viable. An HIV/AIDS pandemic is producing huge death tolls and millions of orphans. Much of the Southern African economy is in subsistence farming as Africans are farming minimally productive arid land prone to devastating droughts. White commercial farmers are on the best land, which their families inherited from white colonial government grants in the nineteenth century. Land reform and health are the obsessions of Southern African governments in 2005.

NORMAN H. MURDOCH

See also Ethnic Conflicts: Southern Africa; Southern Africa: International Relations

References and Further Reading

Davenport, Rodney and Christopher Saunders. *South Africa: A Modern History*, 5th edition. New York: St. Martin's Press, 2000.
Gay, Philip T. *Modern South Africa*. Boston: McGraw-Hill, 2001.
Seidman, Ann. *The Roots of Crisis in Southern Africa*. Trenton, NJ: Africa World Press, 1985.
Simon, David, ed. *South Africa in Southern Africa*. Oxford: James Currey, 1998.
Thompson, Leonard. *A History of South Africa*, 3rd edition. New Haven, CT: Yale University Press, 2000.
Wright, John, ed. *The New York Times Almanac, 2005*. New York: New York Times Co., 2005.

SOUTHERN AFRICA: INTERNATIONAL RELATIONS

Brief History and Background

Arguably, contemporary Southern Africa is Africa's most diverse subregion in terms not only of geography but also of the people who populate it. Sandwiched between the Indian and the Atlantic oceans and spotting great landmarks in the Drakensburg Mountains and the Kalahari Desert, the subregion includes Angola, Botswana, Lesotho, Madagascar, Malawi, Mauritius, Mozambique, Namibia, South Africa, Swaziland, Zambia, and Zimbabwe. Although other countries such as Burundi, Democratic Republic of Congo, Seychelles, and Tanzania are sometimes included in some scholarly definitions of the subregion, they are perhaps more properly located in other continental subregions. This is despite their economic links to the subregion through membership (previous

in the case of Seychelles) in the Southern African Development Community (SADC). Madagascar and Mauritius are included despite their comparatively more distinct contexts. With a population of approximately 127.5 million people and over 6.5 million square kilometers of territory, Southern Africa is a vast region.

Although their broad areas of differences can easily separate Southern African states, they are linked and united by their common historical experiences, cultures, and challenges. Artificial creations of former colonial powers—Britain, France, Germany, and Portugal—they show remarkable similarity in the diversity of their peoples who include the numerically dominant Bantu groups as well as the variously significant Khoisan, European, South Asian, and Malay-Polynesian communities. In many ways, this diversity has helped to define and give shape to the internal and external relations of virtually all member states of the subregion.

The human similarities notwithstanding, it is the differentiating characteristics that punctuate the nature and contours of Southern African intra-regional and non-regional relations. Southern African states vary widely in terms of size, ranging from Lesotho and Swaziland at less than thirty-one thousand and eighteen thousand square kilometers respectively to Angola and South Africa, which are far larger with more than 1.2 million square kilometers each of total land area. At between 1.1 million and 2 million people, Swaziland, Botswana, Lesotho, and Namibia are considerably much smaller than Mozambique with 19 million people or South Africa with more than 42 million people.

In many ways, Southern Africa's unique historical and cultural contexts as well as its recent colonial and post-colonial political and economic activities have coalesced to transform the subregion from Africa's most conflict-ridden and troubled area before the 1990s to one of the continent's most stable and prosperous subregions (along with North Africa). It is also probably the most integrated and harmonized subregion in Africa not only in terms of the linkages between the national economies but also in terms of the transport and communications infrastructure, and the human migration patterns centering on the mining of one of the world's most resource-laden areas.

Attracted by the resources of the subregion as well as more congenial (European friendly) climatic conditions, Southern Africa was completely colonized by European states before the beginning of the twentieth century—thus culminating a process that began during the fifteenth century. Unlike West Africa, with its less friendly climatic conditions, Southern Africa

experienced a significant demographic transformation that saw the entrance and resettlement of significant numbers of Europeans and South Asians in the area. The resultant white minority rule, which followed or coupled European colonialism, shaped not only the political and cultural experiences of much of the subregion but also the nature and development of its economies. By the middle of the twentieth century, European presence and rule had created severely segmented societies in much of Southern Africa in which whites were given special privileges and rights. By contrast, Africans were explicitly denied extensive array of rights—including that of citizenship in extreme cases. Although European colonialism was often harsh everywhere, it was especially so in many parts of Southern Africa. Africans lost their land, cattle, and human dignity more extensively and with far greater intensity and purpose than occurred anywhere else in Africa or Asia. Although European colonial and minority rule brought certain benefits to Southern Africa, particularly in the form of technology, technical know-how, and capital, the racism and highly exploitative labor system which characterized the use of Africans in both the mining and agricultural sectors combined to trigger violent eruptions and resistance to white domination. Although military progress and complete success were forestalled for decades due to the vast superiority of European military technology, the last bastions of white minority rule in Angola, Mozambique, Namibia, South Africa, and Zimbabwe finally gave way to majoritarian rule by the mid-1990s.

Nevertheless, the period of European minority domination also coincided with both the linking and deepening of Southern African incorporation—rather than integration—into the global political economy as a peripheral producer of raw minerals and unprocessed agricultural products. With the solitary exception of South Africa, spared because of its vast mineral resources and white control, the rest of Southern Africa states also became reservoirs of cheap migrant labor and effectively (more or less) indirect outposts of South African economic hegemony. For its part, South Africa—riding on its mineral wealth and designated semi-periphery status—developed a significant industrial capacity, which is not only crucial for the Southern African subregion but also has become increasingly important for the rest of Africa and the world. As the premier mineral producing subregion of Africa, Southern Africa produces and exports a wide variety of mineral resources such as coal, chrome, diamonds, gold, petroleum, platinum, and uranium to Europe, North America, and Asia. The subregion receives value-added consumer goods and capital equipment.

Intra-Southern African Relations

In many ways, South Africa is the one country whose activities in the subregion serve to define and shape regional relations. Without a doubt, South Africa is by far the pivotal state in Southern Africa. In no other subregion of Africa is one country's fate so closely woven to the prospects of its regional partners. With superior transport and communications infrastructure, educational and research institutions, modern manufacturing, mining and agricultural sectors, and an overall economy that dwarfs the combined output of its subregional neighbors, South Africa dominates Southern African economic relations. With a gross domestic product (GDP) that is 60% larger than the combined GDP of the other subregional states, large trade surpluses with every Southern African state, and with widening import and export trade ratios with the subregion, post-apartheid South Africa is a reluctant hegemon in Southern Africa.

However, with a checkered apartheid history that was marked by aggressive and hostile attitudes towards its neighbors, post-apartheid South Africa is still grappling to find its non-economic niche in Southern Africa. Although other states within the subregion need South Africa's industrial output, economic strength, and technology, they remain deeply weary of its intentions and commitment to mutually beneficial and cooperative relations. Chastened by the apartheid-era policy and vision of subjecting the subregion to serving South African interests through ambitious cooperation proposals that envisaged South Africa at the center of a constellation of states. This was not only Pretoria's brazen response to the breaching of the formerly impervious white buffer zone around apartheid South Africa due to Angolan and Mozambican independence from Portugal but also a desperate attempt to woo neighboring states away from Soviet influence and from giving support and sanctuary to both the African National Congress (ANC) and the South West African People's Organization (SWAPO).

The Southern African subregion was not only caught in the crossfire of the anti-apartheid struggle but also was deeply affected and devastated by the political, economic, and military destabilization policies that constituted South Africa's "total onslaught" strategy against them. Southern Africa shouldered the bulk of the burdens associated with apartheid South Africa's desperate attempts to maintain white minority rule. As such, Southern African subregional relations were particularly marked and blighted by apartheid. This legacy, along with negative perceptions about post apartheid South Africa's aggressive

economic expansion in the subregion and political arrogance, has continued to inform and shape Southern Africa relations. This is despite Pretoria's deliberate efforts to allay concerns through policy pronouncements and indications about its benign intentions, and about shared regional destiny and the imperative of integration. To drive the point home, South Africa's ruling ANC party has been forced to explicitly reject any hegemonic ambitions for South Africa.

Top government leaders have reaffirmed this position as has the Department of Foreign Affairs with its outline of government's new priorities in Southern Africa: promotion of peace and security; promotion of intra-regional trade and investment; promotion of regional tourism; poverty alleviation; promotion of health; promotion of all people to people contacts between South Africa and its neighbors; human resource development; promotion of human rights; inter-regional co-operation aimed at combating crime.

Despite such efforts at reassurance, the rapid expansion into other parts of Southern Africa by South African corporate capital has awakened new concerns about the country's evolving status as an economic hegemon. This is not helped by the historical asymmetry between South Africa and the rest of the subregion in terms not only of population size, technical knowhow and technology, economic and financial capacity, transport and communications infrastructure, and energy-production capacity. Furthermore, South Africa's domestic imperatives, which have contributed to its reluctance to concede commercial terrain to its neighbors in their areas of comparative advantage as well as her slowness to actively adopt unfavorable SADC policies, have fuelled suspicions and perceptions that it continues to harbor hegemonic ambitions in Southern Africa.

Also facilitating Southern African relations are a number of institutions and organizations including Common Monetary Area (Lesotho, Namibia, South Africa, and Swaziland), Southern African Customs Union (Botswana, Lesotho, Namibia, South Africa, and Swaziland), and SADC. Of these, SADC is the largest and potentially most important for each of the member states. However, both the Common Monetary Area (CMA) and Southern African Customs Union (SACU) provide vital services for the member states. For instance, the CMA not only links and places at par the currencies of Lesotho, Namibia, and Swaziland to the South African rand but also allows the rand to circulate freely within the other countries. The net effects of the arrangement include the following for the affiliated countries: access to the South African capital markets, fully convertible currencies, and greater and easier trading links with South Africa.

The peoples of Southern Africa have been interacting for hundreds of years. Relations in the modern era have been defined by both the anti-colonial struggles and the war against the white minority rule in Namibia, South Africa, and Zimbabwe as well as the civil wars in Angola and Mozambique. As noted previously, the anti-apartheid conflict imposed huge costs on the entire subregion in terms of damaged and lost lives and property.

Relations with Other African States

Contemporary relations between Southern Africa and other parts of the continent were defined primarily over the past fifty years by the struggle to rid the continent of white minority rule in the subregion. Variously, other African countries assisted in a number of ways; they contributed scarce financial resources, provided travel documents and used their diplomatic offices, extended educational grants and scholarships, provided arms and military training to Southern African resistance fighters, and took the causes to other governments and internal forums for external political, financial, diplomatic, and military support. These efforts were necessary because Southern Africa was the last region to be liberated politically from European domination.

Although post-liberation relations have centered on economic linkages, particularly the New Partnership for Africa's Development (NEPAD), important relationships have also evolved around the civil wars, political struggles and instability, and issues of human rights violations around the continent. NEPAD has contributed towards building a general understanding that the subregional and regional integration is vital if Africa is to deal successfully with the long-term challenges facing the continent. This has reinforced the Abuja treaty of 1991, which envisioned subregional integration as crucial parts of the puzzle for the development of the African Economic Community. Through the various activities of NEPAD, Africa is gradually moving closer to articulating fully the goal of an integrated and complementary subregional infrastructure, with skills development and exchange, import substitution, and diversified production and markets.

Amongst the major contestations have been the land reform controversy in Zimbabwe; human rights violations in Nigeria's Niger Delta; coups attempts in Equatorial Guinea, Sao Tome and Principe, and Togo; and conflicts in Angola, Burundi, Cote d'Ivoire,

DRC, Rwanda, Somalia, Sudan, and Western Sahara. Through the good offices of the African Union, ECOWAS, SADC and other regional and subregional organizations and institutions, Southern African countries have been interacting with other African countries on issues of mutual interest. Together, they have also worked to address continental relations with other parts of the world. With the leadership of President Thabo Mbeki (South Africa) and his colleagues Presidents Olusegun Obasabnjo (Nigeria), Abdelaziz Bouteflika (Algeria) and Abdoulaye Wade, (Senegal), through their articulation and work on NEPAD, Africa's developmental challenges have received and stimulated global attention and growing commitment. The commitment to address common economic and political issues, including sticky problems around conflict management and resolution as well as good governance, transparency, and accountability have served not only to transform public and intellectual discourse about the nature of African leadership but also elevated issues about external links and responsibility for many African problems.

Relations with Global Powers and Beyond the Continent

Given its large number of Europeans and persons of South Asian and Southeast Asian background, it is not surprising that Southern Africa states generally have strong links with Europe and Asia. France, Germany, Greece, India, Indonesia, Netherlands, Pakistan, Portugal, United Kingdom, United States, and the Scandinavian states are some of the states with which Southern Africa states have built strong ties economic, political, and cultural ties. These ties have also been reinforced by the historical links between the various countries. While some of the ties, especially the South-South links, have been largely fraternal, the relationships with members of the OECD tend to reflect the realities of interactions between unequal partners. In the main, Southern African states (including South Africa) are very dependent on external transaction flows to maintain their economic viability. Furthermore, with the exception of a few counties such as Botswana, Mauritius, and South Africa, the member states of the subregion require (and attract) substantial levels of concessional aid flows, particularly from the OECD states, to tackle serious developmental challenges. Unfortunately, such flows fall way short of actual needs. For instance, Angola, Mozambique, Zambia, and Zimbabwe have struggled to deal with problems inherited from preceding colonial governments without the necessary support from relevant or other Western aid donors. Indeed, the little amount of aid flows that came through could be subjected to the policy preferences of the donor states. As Zimbabwe discovered with its controversial land reforms, aid flows can be interrupted abruptly when national policies run afoul of donor imperatives.

Indeed, as with other African countries, Southern African countries not only inherited unfavorable social, political, and economic circumstances from their colonial rulers but also they lack the capacity to restructure their future. A postcolonial international environment that is dominated by the West exacerbates this situation. The net result is that collectively, they are finding it extremely difficult to have relevance in a fast changing and globalizing international environment.

Southern African International Relations: Prospects for the Future

Southern Africa is a subregion on the mend despite a series of very serious challenges, particularly the world's highest incidence of HIV/AIDS infection. With serious conflict now contained in Angola, Mozambique, Namibia, South Africa, and Zimbabwe, the subregion has gone from Africa's problem area in 1980 to one of its most stable subregions in 2005. There is now a need to move forward and build on the gains from the resolution of some of the world's more sticky conflicts. Addressing and winning the battle against the HIV/AIDS pandemic and subregional integration should be high on the list. Although the battle against HIV/AIDS seems to be on, the failure to tackle the problems aggressively has not only retarded many of the gains made within the health fields over the past two or three generations as life expectancy has crashed within the southern African subregion but also threatens to impinge on other efforts aimed at fostering transformative processes of development.

In regard to subregional integration, there is a bit of a lull in the struggle to wrestle with the challenge. Perhaps, at the base of the problem is South African inability to develop a stable and mutually acceptable relationship with other SADC and Southern African partners. Lingering problems have persisted on a number of issue-areas: immigration policies, differing views on armed conflicts, the question of land reforms in Zimbabwe, and South African role as a subregional economic power. South Africa's decision to sign a separate agreement with the European Union as well as its foot dragging on liberalizing its trade regimes

within SADC stipulations have caused serious consternation and protests among other SADC members.

These problems notwithstanding, Southern Africa is well placed to further build and consolidate the historical lines of interactions of the communities and peoples of the subregion. For this to happen, however, South Africa would have to play a more positive role of engaging its subregional partners in a way that builds confidence in its leadership. As the most capable and the country with the most to gain from subregional cooperation, South Africa must assume the burden of effective leadership, which may entail commitment of resources and willingness to forego certain short-term gains. The positive political roles that South Africa is now playing through its active mediation efforts in Burundi and Cote d'Ivoire are positive signals, which must be sustained and extended to concrete economic activities in Southern Africa and the entire continent.

UFO OKEKE UZODIKE

See also Ethnic Conflicts: Southern Africa; Southern Africa: History and Economic Development

References and Further Reading

Ahwireng-Obeng, F. and P. J McGowan. "Partner or Hegemon? South Africa in Africa," *Journal of Contemporary African Studies*, (Part 1), 16, 1, (Part 2), 16, 2, 1998.
ANC. "Foreign Policy Perspective in a Democratic South Africa," African *National Congress*, Johannesburg: Department of International Affairs, 1994.
Cilliers, J. 'An Emerging South African Foreign Policy Identity," *Institute for Security Studies*, Occasional Paper, 39, 1999.
Daniel, J., V. Naidoo and S. Naidu. "The South Africans Have Arrived: Post-apartheid corporate expansion into Africa" Daniel, J., A. Habib and R. Southall (eds.), State of the Nation, South Africa 2003–2004, Cape Town: HSRC Press, 2003.
Gibb, R. "Southern Africa in Transition: Prospects and Problems Facing Regional Integration," *Journal of Modern African Studies*, 36, 2, 1998.
Kalenga, P. "Trade and Industrial Integration in Southern Africa: Pitfalls and Challenges," *Global Dialogue*, 4, 3, 1999.
Makoa, F. "South Africa's Foreign Policy Towards the Rest of Africa," *African Foreign Policies in the Twenty-First Century*, Working Papers, Pretoria: Africa Institute of South Africa, 2001.
Malewezi, J. "Regional Integration: The Path to Prosperity?" Clapham, C., G. Mills, A. Morner, and E. Sidiropoulos (eds.), *Regional Integration in Southern Africa: Comparative International Perspectives*, Johannesburg: SAIIA, 2001.
McGowan, Patrick J. and Philip Nel *Power, Wealth and Global Equity: An International Relations Textbook for Africa*, Second Edition Lansdowne, SA: UCT Press, 2002.
Mills, G. and E. Sidiropoulos. "Trends, Problems and Projections in Southern African Integration," Clapham, C.,
G. Mills, A. Morner, and E. Sidiropoulos (eds.), *Regional Integration in Southern Africa: Comparative International Perspectives*. Johannesburg: SAIIA, 2001.
Mlambo, A.S. "Partner or Hegemon? South Africa and its Neighbours," *South African Yearbook of International Affairs 2000/01*. Johannesburg: The South African Institute of International Affairs, 2000.

SOUTHERN AFRICAN CUSTOMS UNION (SACU)

SACU being the oldest Customs Union in the world came into existence in 1910 through a multilateral union agreement between South Africa, Botswana, Lesotho and Swaziland. On December 11, 1969, following the independence of the later countries in the 1960s, a new agreement was entered into between the four contracting parties which amongst others reformed the revenue sharing arrangements. Namibia became part of the agreement formally in 1990 after her political independence. Before independence, Namibia was regarded as a de facto member of SACU even though BLN never recognised this de facto membership.

The aim of SACU is to establish free trading area in goods among the member countries and to impose a common tariff on imports from non-member countries. In this regard the customs union is therefore intended to provide wider and unhindered market access to members. The BLNS countries are believed to not have fully maximised this benefit of expanded market access both in terms of population and income. South Africa is believed to have been utilising this advantaged offered by the Customs union. The situation of the BLNS inability to compete with the South Africa can be explained by the following factors:

- *South African predominance in terms of economic size and industrial development driven at times by strong nationally pursued industrial development schemes;*
- *South Africa's and consequently, SACU isolation from foreign trade due to sanctions being applied to South Africa during the apartheid era;*
- *South Africa's unilateral use of tariff rebates to certain domestic industry (notably the monitor vehicle assembly and textile industries) giving it a one-sided advantage vis-à-vis BLNS;*
- *BLNS limited use of infant industry concessions in the 1969 agreement due to stringent and onerous provisions;*
- *However, it can be equally stated that the BLNS have rarely and seriously attempted to penetrate the South Africa and each other's markets, despite the protected trade environment by the customs union.*

Apart from the fact that SACU provides a common excise tariff (CET), which are at the moment set unilaterally by South Africa, South Africa also remained the custodian of the SACU revenue pool. Therefore all customs and excise duties collected are paid into the South African national revenue fund. The revenue is shared among the member states according to the formula as stipulated in the 1969 agreement. Each member state's share was therefore calculated accordingly, except for South Africa, which received the residual.

For the BLNS countries, SACU revenue constituted a greater share of their state revenue and therefore that is why SACU is viewed by the member states especially the BLNS to be of such an utmost important to them.

Against this backdrop, with South Africa receiving the residual and setting the common external tariff amongst others, the 1969 agreement was viewed to be undemocratic and non-transparent as the concentration of all discretionary powers was given to South Africa. In addition, it was established that BLNS have not been fairly compensated. Another shortcoming within the 1969 was the fact that there were no formal structures established except for the SACU commission. This situation called for the renegotiation of the agreement. The renegotiation started off in 1994, following the political independence of South Africa, with the objectives of democratising the governance of SACU, setting new institutional arrangements, setting of a new revenue formula amongst others. After a length and protracted renegotiation process, the new SACU agreement was finally signed in October 2002.

The 2002 agreement ensured that each member country has equal powers in terms of trade policy formulations, tariffs determination, duties, and rebates determination. In this light the following institutions are provided for:

Council of Ministers: It is a supreme decision making authority made up of member states' ministers responsible for SACU affairs. It is responsible for the overall policy direction and functioning of SACU institutions.

SACU Commission: Consists of permanent secretaries of departments/ministries responsible for SACU affairs. It is responsible for the implementation of the new agreement, ensuring that decisions taken by the council are implemented and in addition oversee the management of common revenue pool and supervises the work of the Secretariat.

The Secretariat: It is located in Windhoek, Namibia and it is responsible for the day-to-day administration of the SACU.

The Tariff Board: An independent institution made up of experts from member countries, it makes recommendations to the Council with regard to tariffs and customs.

Technical Liaison Committees: These are sector specific committees responsible to advice the Commission on sector specific issues. They are Agricultural Liaison Committee, Customs Technical Liaison Committee, Trade and Industry Liaison Committee, and Transport Liaison Committee.

The Tribunal: Settles disputes arising from the applications of the agreement.

Apart from the above institutions as specified in the new agreement, another notable development is the introduction of the new SACU revenue sharing formula. The new formula dictates that the share accruing to each member state will be calculated from the following three components:

The Customs Component: Each country share is derived from the proportion of the country's Cost-Insurance-Freight (CIF) intra-SACU imports to the total intra-SACU imports of Common Customs Area.

The Excise Component: It is set at 85% of total excise duties and each member's share shall be calculated from the value of its GDP in a specific calendar year as a percentage of total SACU GDP in that specific calendar year.

The Development Component: It is set at 15% of excise duties, however this rate is subject to change from time to time. The share accruing to each member country is calculated based on the country's GDP per capita compared to the average of SACU's GDP per capita. The development component ensured that poorer countries, that is countries whose GDP per capita falls below per capita SACU average, are compensated by the other relatively well do member states.

In the era of globalisation, SACU is also involved in several free trade talks with MERCOSOUR, EFTA, and the United States. Whereas it is expected that upon finalisation of these negotiations, SACU will be able to extend its own markets and have improved access to the world's largest markets such as United States, China, and South American states. The challenge that is facing SACU at the moment is the capacity of being able to negotiate with the other parties, for an agreement that would be able to accommodate the wider interests of all the SACU member countries. In addition, upon completion of the FTAs is the anticipated fall in the revenue accrued to SACU countries as a result of trade liberalisation. This should raise a concern to SACU countries in particular the BLNS, as SACU receipts contribute considerable amount to their fiscal revenue.

In the midst of these however, it is hoped that with the introduction of the new agreement and the free

trade agreements that SACU is involved in will enhance trade promotion both within SACU and without SACU so as to increase standard of living, economic growth, and poverty alleviation for the SACU states.

SYLVANUS IKHIDE

See also Botswana; Lesotho; South Africa; Southern Africa: History and Economic Development; Southern Africa: International Relations; Swaziland

References and Further Reading

Bank of Namibia. *Annual Report.* Windhoek, Namibia, 2003.
———. *Challenges and Implications of the 2002 SACU Agreement.* Windhoek, Namibia, 2003.
———. *Forecasting SACU Revenue using the New Revenue Sharing Formula.* Windhoek, Namibia, 2003.
Bradshaw, York and Stephen N. Ndegwa. *The Uncertain Promise of Southern Africa.* Bloomington, IN: Indiana University Press, 2000.
Harmon, Daniel E. *Southeast Africa: 1880 to the Present: Reclaiming a Region of Natural Wealth.* Philadelphia: Chelsea House Publishers, 2002.
Mazur, Robert E.. *Breaking the Links: Development Theory and Practice in Southern Africa.* Trenton, NJ: Africa World Press, c1990.
Minter, William. *King Solomon's Mines Revisited: Western Interests and the Burdened History of Southern Africa.* New York: Basic Books, 1986.

SOUTHERN AFRICAN DEVELOPMENT COMMUNITY (SADC)

Established in 1992 to replace the Southern African Development Coordination Conference (SADCC), which had been in existence since 1980, SADC is now one of the major regional economic blocs in Africa. Its forerunner, SADCC, was founded by the Frontline States, to foster economic development and political solidarity among members, and to reduce their dependence on apartheid South Africa. Accordingly, SADCC's integrative strategy deliberately avoided competition and duplication, and favored the coordination of economic projects among member states. The transformation from SADCC into SADC was prompted by several factors, including the release of Nelson Mandela (in 1990) and the ensuing negotiations within South Africa to end apartheid; the proliferation of trading blocs; and the intensification of global economic competition. By the early 1990s, the leaders had realized that while SADCC had served them well, there was the need to shift their focus from mere coordination of development projects and opposition to South Africa to the more complex task of integrating their economies, hence the signing of the SADC Treaty at Windhoek, Namibia, in August 1992. In 2005, SADC had fourteen members: Angola, Botswana, Democratic Republic of Congo (DRC), Lesotho, Malawi, Mauritius, Mozambique, Namibia, Seychelles, South Africa, Swaziland, Tanzania, Zambia, and Zimbabwe.

Objectives

SADC's objectives, as contained in Article Five of its Treaty, are to

... achieve development and economic growth, alleviate poverty, enhance the standard and quality of life of the people of Southern Africa and support the socially disadvantaged through regional integration; evolve common political values, systems and institutions; promote and defend peace and security; promote self-sustaining development on the basis of collective self-reliance, and the interdependent of Members States. (SADC 1992)

Other expressed goals are to achieve complementarity between national and regional programs; promote productive use of the region's resources; foster environmental sustainability; and strengthen the cultural ties among people in the region (SADC 1992). In 2000, SADC added the explicit aim of combating HIV/AIDS to its objectives, in cognizance of the devastation wreaked by this disease in Southern Africa. In pursuance of these objectives, SADC proposed to harmonize political, social, and economic policies of members; mobilize people of the region to take initiatives to enhance their socio-economic and cultural ties; to promote the free movement of capital, labour, goods and service across the region. The guiding principles of SADC, according to its Treaty, entail a respect for the sovereign equality of all members; the promotion of peace and security in the region; and adherence to democratic principles such as rule of law and respect for human rights.

Institutional Structure

SADC started with a decentralized institutional framework, with which all members were given responsibility to coordinate projects in specific sectors throughout the regions. This structure was to avoid the pitfalls of many regional blocs in Africa, by which centralized bureaucracies alienated some members. However, by the late 1990s, it was clear that this decentralized system was not working, due to the lack of staffing and resources in some member states

to handle their coordinating responsibilities and the differences in administrative procedures, qualifications, and performance criteria for staffs involved in the management of regional programs. Consequently, at an Extraordinary Summit in Windhoek, in 2001, a centralized structure was adopted, and the exiting Co-coordinating Units were grouped into four clusters (or Directorates)—Trade Industry, Finance and Investment; Infrastructure and Services; Food, Agriculture and Natural Resources; Social and Human Development and Special Programs. The main institutions, following this restructuring, are the Summit, which is the ultimate policy-making body, made up of Heads of States and Governments; the Secretariat, which is headed by the Executive Secretary at the headquarters in Gaborone, Botswana; the Troika, which consists of the Chair, Incoming Chair, and Outgoing Chair; and the Organ, which is responsible for politics, defense, and security. Others are the Council of Ministers, which oversees the implementation of SADC programmes; and the Tribunal, which settles SADC-related disputes.

Contributions to Development

To help meet the challenges and economic competition engendered by globalization, SADC has focused much of its attention on its regional economic integration initiatives, with a major thrust of its activities dealing with the development of infrastructure to facilitate factor mobility across member states. More specifically, SADC has upgraded and developed regional roads and airports in several cities in the region (for example, Gaborone, Lilongwe and Mastapa), and developed direct air travel and satellite telecommunication links between all capitals. In March 2004, SADC launched a Strategic Plan, setting out specific measures and timeframes for bringing down trade barriers: these include the elimination of exchange controls on intra-SADC transactions by 2006; the creation of a Free Trade Area by 2008; and the establishment of a Custom Union by 2010. Also, SADC launched its Regional Indicative Strategic Development Plan (RISPD) in 2004 to intensify its efforts toward the alleviation of poverty and hunger; democratic governance; conflict prevention and resolution; and the fight against HIV/AIDS. Other RISPD initiatives relate to the development of science and technology; the creation of effective disaster preparedness mechanisms; and the consolidation of international cooperation with other regional blocs. The Summit has also signed a Declaration on Gender and Development, calling for the equitable representation and involvement of men and women in all SADC operations.

Despites its accomplishments, SADC still needs to grapple with several difficult problems in Southern Africa if it is to bring its current initiative to fruition. These include the huge disparity in economic development among its members; the dominance of South Africa; the biting poverty and HIV/AIDS pandemic in the region; and the political crisis in countries such as Zimbabwe, Angola, and DRC. There is also the need to expedite land reforms in Namibia and South Africa to prevent Zimbabwe-style land invasion; to resolve the dialectical tensions and overlaps between SADC and other blocs in the region (for example, Southern African Custom Union and the Common Market for Eastern and Southern Africa); and, to build alliances with such pan-African organizations and initiatives as the African Union and the New Partnership for Africa's Development.

JOSEPH MENSAH

See also Southern African Custom Union (SACU); Common Market for Eastern and Southern Africa (COMESA); South Africa; Southern Africa: History and Economic Development; Southern Africa: International Relations.

References and Further Reading

Amin, S., Chitala, D., and Mandaza I. *SDCC: Prospects for Disengagement and Development in Southern Africa.* London: Zed Books, 1987.
Asante, S.K.B. *Regionalism and Africa's Development: Expectations, Reality, and Challenges.* Houndmills, Basingstoke, Hampshire: Macmillan Press; New York: St. Martin's Press, 1997.
Hansohm, Dirk, Willie Breytenbach, and Trudi Hartzenberg, editors. *Monitoring Regional Integration in Southern Africa.* Windhoek, Namibia: Gamsberg Macmillan Publishers Ltd., 2003.
Lemon, Anthony and Christian M. Rogerson, editors. *Geography and Economy in South Africa and its Neighbours.* Aldershot, Hampshire, England and Burlington, VT: Ashgate, 2002.
Lee, Margaret C. *The Political Economy of Regionalism in Southern Africa.* Boulder and London: Lynne Rienner Publishers, Inc. and Cape Town: University of Cape Town Press, 2003.
Jenkins, Carolyn, Jonathan Leape, and Lynn Thomas. *Gaining from Trade in Southern Africa.* Basingstoke, Hampshire: Macmillan Press Ltd., and New York: St. Martin's Press, 2000.
Poku, Nana. *Regionalization and Security in Southern Africa.* Basingstoke, Hampshire: Palgrave, 2001.
Southern African Development Community (SADC). *Treaty of the Southern African Development Community.* Gaborone: SADC, 1992.
South African Development Community. *Regional Human Development Report.* Gaborone: SADC, 2000.

SOUTHERN CONE COMMON MARKET (MERCOSUR)

Introduction

MERCOSUR (MERCOSUL in Portuguese), or Common Market of the South, is the name used for the free trade agreement among the countries of the Southern Cone of South America, namely, Argentina, Bolivia, Brazil, Chile, Paraguay, and Uruguay. Bolivia and Chile are associate members. MERCOSUR is designed to increase the levels and range of products traded amongst these neighboring countries. Indeed, the MERCOSUR includes approximately 44% of Latin America's territory, and 59% of its gross domestic product (GDP).

As we discuss later, the MERCOSUR should also be seen in a strategic context, as a means of bolstering the negotiating strength of the region vis-à-vis the United States, the European Union and Japan in international trade talks. In that regard, the timing of the MERCOSUR is clearly tied to the development of the North American Free Trade Agreement in 1992, from which every Latin American country except for Mexico was excluded. MERCOSUR countries still constitute a small amount of the overall international economic activity, with a combined GDP of approximately $1.9 trillion as of 2002 versus $10.4 for the US, $5.7 for China, and $3.6 for Japan alone. Still, the common market fulfills a long-standing dream within Latin America to create greater intra-regional connections, particularly in terms of economic ties. In this sense, MERCOSUR is a bold experiment both in Latin America, given a long history of trade integration failures in the region, and globally, in the sense of being only one of a few trade integration regimes among developing countries. Indeed, a basic calculation of intra- vs. extra-regional trade from 1994–2000 shows significant increases in the share of intra-MERCOSUR trade, with the lone exception of Uruguay. However, much of the trade has involved bilateral increases in trade with Brazil and Argentina and between those two countries.

Origins of MERCOSUR

The development of MERCOSUR must be understood in the context of the transition of military to civilian rule which took place through most of the region in the early 1980s. Significant military expenditures had been created on the premise of national security risks from neighboring countries. Indeed, the sub-region has historically been convulsed with high international tensions, including devastating wars between Peru, Bolivia, and Chile; Paraguay and Uruguay, Brazil, and Argentina; and Bolivia and Paraguay.

In 1985, Jose Sarney became the first civilian Brazilian president in over two decades. Meanwhile, his Argentine counterpart Raul Alfonsin had taken over as the first civilian President since a 1976 coup. These two Presidents met in 1985 to sign the *Foz de Iguazu* Declaration establishing the High-level Joint Commission spur on binational integration. In July 1986, Argentina and Brazil signed the Integration and Economic Cooperation Program and 12 protocols were approved. Special importance was given in the agreement to the capital assets sector, wheat, foods, the iron and steel industry, and the automobile industry. In 1988, the Integration, Cooperation, and Development Agreement was created. The Agreement aimed at creating a common market between Argentina and Brazil over a ten-year period. The Agreement focused on tariff reductions, and was signed in 1990 by both parties, with an expected date of implementation of December 1994.

On March 26, 1991, Paraguay and Uruguay joined the Agreement under the Treaty of Asunción, with the idea of creating a regional common mkt. The preamble to the agreement states that the purpose of MERCOSUR is the expansion of domestic markets, through integration, in order to achieve economic development and social justice. The Treaty mentions the integration of other regions in the world as a motivating factor. It also states that integration is an important way to improve economic efficiency, environmental preservation, infrastructure linking the countries, and macroeconomic coordination. It also emphasizes gradualism, flexibility, and balance, as guiding principles, and these help to explain the nature of MERCOSUR's historical development, as described below.

There are several important amendments to the MERCOSUR. The Brasilia Protocol was signed in 1992 to set up a dispute settlement mechanism. On December 17, 1994, the Ouro Preto Protocol was signed, creating a common external tariffs and some basic institutional architecture, both set to take effect in January 1995.

While MERCOSUR has an elaborate formal structure, in practice, much of the MERCOSUR's activity appears to operate through informal negotiations and meetings, through "Grupos de Trabajo," or working groups that focus on particular issues. As of 2003, there were working groups in the following areas: commercial issues; customs issues; technical

standards; fiscal and monetary policies relating to trade; coordination of macroeconomic policies; inland transport; maritime transport; industrial and technological policy; agricultural policy; and energy policy. For example, the Brasilia Protocol has yet to be fully enforced. In practice, the Trade Commission has negotiated solutions for emerging problems, rather than relying upon the formal dispute resolution mechanism.

Similarly, the main focus of MERCOSUR in substantive terms has been on tariff reduction, and the transition period of the agreement should have led to a progressive liberalization. In practice, however, an "Adaptation System" was established for cases in which tariff reductions were not completed by August 1994 or where appeals were made for protection clauses. Through this system, countries obtained an additional time to for tariff reductions and significant exemptions for sensitive sectors have been continued.

Problems Within MERCOSUR

It is important to note that, historically speaking, the MERCOSUR economies have had limited internal trade owing to a number of differences within the region. As Spanish colonies, the countries of the Southern Cone generally developed with a limited number of products and a heavy reliance on commodity exports. Moreover, geographic obstacles, including the Amazon jungle and the Andes have created major obstacles to the creation of dense internal infrastructure that would allow for trade within and amongst the various trade partners. The political regimes in the region are also at different stages of development. While democracies seem stable in Argentina, Brazil, and Uruguay, there is more volatility and military presence in Bolivia and Paraguay.

MERCOSUR also has serious internal differences in the size and nature of the different economies. Brazil has the tenth largest economy in the world. Argentina's economy is about one quarter the size of Brazil's and Chile about 10% of Brazil's. Uruguay, Paraguay, and Bolivia are each only about 2% the size of Brazil's economy. Moreover, while Brazil, Argentina, and Chile have diversified economies, Uruguay and Paraguay's are concentrated in services and agriculture, and Bolivia in mining. This has naturally led to tensions along two axes: between Brazil and Argentina on the one hand, and between these big two and the smaller economies of the MERCOSUR on the other. In a sense, we can surmise that the enticement of the Brazilian market, with its population of approximately 180 million, and a rapidly growing middle class, is the main attraction for other partners to the agreement.

Unlike the rest of the countries of South America, MERCOSUR has not been as dominated in its trade relations with the United States. Instead, MERCOSUR countries have historically traded equally with the European Union. However, because Chile's neoliberal economic policies, including a recently signed free trade agreement with the United States, have set it apart from the rest of the members in the sense that it has a more liberalized economy and a number of separate free trade agreements with other parties. Therefore, Chile has remained an associate and not integral member. Bolivia is also an associate member as it is also a part of the Andean Pact free trade association, with a different set of rules and interests.

In fact, the MERCOSUR countries still have a strong dependency on outside investment, technology, and markets. MERCOSUR countries, particularly Argentina, Brazil, Bolivia, and Uruguay have huge external debts, so that they are continually in negotiations with the International Monetary Fund and private lenders to ensure the continuing flow of external investment. Major differences and ongoing crises in fiscal policy make the next logical step, a move towards monetary union, highly unlikely for the foreseeable future. Furthermore, given the economic crisis in Argentina and Uruguay, it is even unlikely that further tariff reductions in sensitive sectors will take place.

On the other hand, Brazil also has needs for its growing economy. For example, Brazil has recently developed a multimillion dollar gas pipeline to move natural gas from Bolivia to meet the growing energy demands of its population centers. It is noteworthy that Bolivia and Chile have had increasing tensions over Bolivia's desire for access rights to Chile's northern ports, dating back to the nineteenth century when the territory was seized by Chile from Bolivia. Brazil, like Argentina, also shares hydroelectric dams with Paraguay and Uruguay.

On an external level, Brazil has become an important player in terms of international trade negotiations. As noted previously, a rapprochement between Brazil and Argentina occurred in 2003, following the Argentine devaluation. The new Argentine government, after the nadir of the crisis, seems attuned towards a foreign policy more independent of the United States and more pro-active towards further developing MERCOSUR. A vibrant and coordinated MERCOSUR can strengthen each of the members' bargaining positions, which is crucial to the outcomes of negotiations for subsequent multilateral trade rounds and for a Free Trade Agreement of the Americas in particular. Ongoing negotiations on a free trade agreement with the European Union remain a possibility, however, the

large potential agricultural exports from MERCO-SUR have been a stumbling block. Indeed, there are continuing discussions of the possibility of extending MERCOSUR to other countries in the region, however, the level of liberalization, geographic boundaries (the Amazon), and even lower levels of trade across the continent have historically inhibited trade across the continent.

The MERCOSUR has wider implications for development. MERCOSUR seeks to increase internal trade amongst developing countries, creating a method of development that allows some time for the member countries to reach international levels of competitiveness while continuing to grow. MERCO-SUR is one of the few global examples of successful "horizontal" or "South-South" trade. In sum, MER-COSUR is an important step forward not only for creating internal solidarity, but also for reducing, if not replacing, external dependency.

ANIL HIRA

See also Southern Cone (Latin America): History and Economic Development; Southern Cone (Latin America): International Relations

References and Further Reading

Coffey, P., ed. *Latin America—MERCOSUR*. Boston: Kluwer, 1998.
Hira, Anil. *The Political Economy of Energy in the Southern Cone*. Greenwood, Westport, 2003.
Inter-American Development Bank, INTAL program, http://www.iadb.org/intal/
Roett, R., ed. *MERCOSUR: Regional Integration, World Markets*. Boulder, CO: Lynne Rienner, 1999.
Sanchez Bajo, Claudio. "The European Union and Mercosur: a case of inter-regionalism," *Third World Quarterly*, Special Issue, 20(5): 927–942, 1999.

SOUTHERN CONE (LATIN AMERICA): HISTORY AND ECONOMIC DEVELOPMENT

History and Economic Development

The Southern Cone refers to the countries of Argentina, Brazil, Chile, Paraguay, and Uruguay, which are located in the southern half of South America and resembles a cone shape, with the tip pointing towards Antarctica. The Southern Cone has had quite a distinctive development trajectory from other Latin American regions. To begin with, because it is located much farther away from the United States, there has been less interference from the superpower to the north. Moreover, while encompassing a wide variety of geographical regions, a large part of the Cone has a very temperate climate and extremely fertile plains growing areas, where massive amounts of wheat, cattle, and coffee are produced for export. Equally important is the fact that most of the indigenous population of the region was wiped out by war and disease, so the development dynamics are quite distinct from the rest of Latin America. With the exception of Paraguay and parts of Brazil, the Southern Cone is largely a region of European immigrants. The military has been a ubiquitous actor in the region, with frequent coups and takeovers of governments. Similarly, the economic development of the region has been highly volatile. Both of these factors have roots in both geography and historical developments. Unfortunately, the periodic economic spurts have not led to any equitable growth in the region. Despite these commonalties, we should also note that Brazil has quite distinct characteristics and a different development trajectory within the region.

In terms of geography, we must discuss Brazil separately from the rest of the region. Brazil covers a vast amount of territory, some 3.3 million square miles, and has a population of around 159.7 million. This dwarfs the size of other members of the region. Argentina has a population of only 35.4 million and 1.1 million square miles. The territory of Chile, Uruguay, and Paraguay is considerably smaller in each case. Chile has 14.6 million people; Paraguay 5.1 million, and Uruguay just 3.2 million. Brazil also has an incredible variety of geographic features and biodiversity. Brazil is famous as the home of most of the Amazon rainforest, which is considered an international treasure for its biodiversity and the significant contribution to oxygen in the Earth's atmosphere. The Amazon river itself is one of the longest in the world. However, much of the Amazon so far remains underdeveloped. Because of the difficulty of the terrain and the tropical climate, as the Brazilian government paves roads in the rainforest, there is the spread of slash-and-burn agricultural techniques. By these practices, the rainforest is burned down, and cattle or other agricultural crops are grown in the soil. Experience has shown that the rainforest soil tends to leach its nutrients rather quickly, so that the rancher is forced to move on to another stretch of the rainforest. Unfortunately, once the rainforest is burned down, in many cases, it is lost forever. International organizations, the Brazilian government, and non-governmental organizations are all trying to preserve portions of the Amazon, but they seem to be fighting an uphill battle, since Brazil's poverty so overwhelmingly motivates new waves of migration and forest development.

Because of the inhospitableness of the Amazon area, there is a feeling that Brazil is still a frontier country, slowly expanding into the unknown territory of the jungle. The southwest area of the country includes the pantanal, an area of swamps, and the Brazilian highlands, where the capital, Brasilia, is located. Brasilia was created as a planned city in 1960 to try to redirect Brazilians' attention towards the vast untapped interior of the country. The majority of the country's population and activity have traditionally been concentrated close to the Atlantic coast, in the cities of Rio de Janeiro and São Paulo, which dominate Brazil's economy and politics. The Northeast, which contains rich agricultural land as well, producing much of the world's oranges and sugar, has in modern times lagged behind the rest of the country for a variety of historical and political reasons.

As we move south from Brazil in the region, the climate and topography change considerably. Paraguay is, geographically speaking, a country with two regions. The northwestern part, called the Chaco, is part steppe and part desert. The southeastern part is an area of rich agricultural and cattle-raising land, and the home to the majority of the population. Paraguay's population is somewhat unique in that a large majority have some Guarani blood, from the indigenous groups that inhabited the region. Guarani is still the major language spoken in Paraguay, along with Spanish. The capital of Paraguay, Asunción, is a major port. The two major rivers of the region, the Paraná and the Paraguay, pass from Brazil past Paraguay and then form the incredibly rich soils of the Río de la Plata river basin, which empties into the Atlantic Ocean between Argentina and Uruguay. The areas around the rivers in each of the countries are home to a significant portion of the world's wheat and cattle production. Much of Uruguay's economy has been based upon the export of meat from cattle raising, and its capital city, Montevideo, is an important port. Uruguay is largely a flat plains area, but its coast line boasts fantastic beaches.

Argentina's capital city, Buenos Aires, is the main port city for the Río de la Plata and home to about half the country's population. Buenos Aires has dominated the country's political and economic decision making. The other main pole of development in Argentina has been northward along the river in the cattle-producing and industrialized cities of Santa Fé, Rosario, and Cordobá. To the west is the wine-producing area of Mendoza, which is on the eastern side of the towering Andes mountain chain. The Argentine national symbol, the gaucho, represents the cowboy rancher from before the nineteenth century, who worked in the vast pampas, or plains, moving cattle along to new grazing spots. Argentina has newfound

wealth in this area in terms of rich sources of natural gas, as well as in the area farther south called Patagonia. Along with Bolivia, Argentina has become the main fuels supplier to the Southern Cone. Patagonia in the south is a cold but generally dry area that ends with the famous Straits of Magellan area and then Antarctica.

Across the Andes mountains to the west is Chile. Because of the quite formidable obstacle of the Andes, and the sparsely populated Atacama desert to the north, where it borders Peru and Bolivia, Chile has had an isolated historical development. Chile occupies a narrow area of land from the Andes to the Pacific ocean. Being on the fault line means that Chile suffers from occasional earthquakes, some of which have been quite devastating. The northern part of the country provides much of the copper and other mining that has been the backbone of the Chilean economy. The central valleys around Santiago are the home to a large proportion of the population as well as the wine making industry and cattle and agricultural producers. Santiago has been the center of political and economic decision-making and is the home to much of the country's manufacturing and service industries. Farther south is the Swiss-like lake district where much of the important fruit industry is located. The South also hosts the important port cities of Concepción, Temuco, Valdivia, and Puerto Montt. These ports serve as an important conduit for the vast quantities of timber, some of it grown in the largely undeveloped areas to the south, that Chile exports each year. Chile's main outpost close to Antarctica is Punta Arenas. Though most of Chile's indigenous population was wiped out, there are important remaining concentrations in the South, mostly of the Araucanian group. In sum, in Chile, as elsewhere in the Southern Cone, significant geographic obstacles exist to both national and regional economic development.

Brazil's historical roots also put it apart from its neighbors. First, Brazil was a Portuguese, not a Spanish colony, and Portuguese remains the official language. Second, Brazil passed through a largely peaceful transition from colony to independent country, unlike its neighbors who fought for their freedom from Spain. Third, Brazil has a large population of African descendants who were an important part of the sugar cane boom of the eighteenth century in the northeast and the coffee boom of the nineteenth and early twentieth centuries. Slavery was abolished in Brazil in 1888, but the legacy of slavery continues to haunt Brazil. Fourth, Brazil has been a much more centralized country in terms of economic and political decision-making with a high level of government planning.

From the turn of the twentieth century, there is some convergence between Brazil's history and the rest of the Southern Cone. In Brazil, Argentina, Chile, and Uruguay, (but not Paraguay) there were massive waves of European immigration. Some estimates have increases of more than 500% in the population of the major cities from the 1890s to the 1920s. These waves of immigration changed the politics, economics, and identity of the nations. The new wave of immigrants included vast numbers from central and southern Europe, including Germany and Italy. The new immigrants brought new ideas, including socialism, anarchism, communism, and fascism. With the new wave of immigration, labor unionization really took off. The unions provided a backbone for a long historical struggle between leftist adherents of a socialist vision and more conservative elements who wanted a limited democracy and economic growth without major redistribution of income or wealth.

The new politics of the 1920s in the region was one of a transition from a landed agricultural oligarchy, whose power was based on control of the primary agricultural exports, including mining, cattle, and wheat, to a broader-based political and economic structure. It is quite ironic to note that it was the success of the agricultural boom in exports, along with the new immigration wave, that created the new economic base for the middle class. The new middle class consisted of businessmen, state bureaucrats, and skilled laborers who worked in mining and in new infrastructure. While the military has been a long-standing feature of the region as a bulwark of conservative oligarchy, in the 1920s it was "progressive" military officers who carried out coups on behalf of "radical" political leaders who promised the growing middle class new access to political decision making through increasing voting and other rights. These reforms faced significant resistance to them by the agricultural elite. Thus, in Argentina, Brazil, and Chile, the 1920s were marked by great uncertainty as the radical parties attempted to consolidate a new political order, but conservative elements, backed by other parts of the military, launched operations, including coups, to stop these changes.

In Paraguay, by contrast, the agricultural oligarchy was never effectively challenged. In good part, this is because Paraguay remains a largely agriculturally-based economy. Thus, the industrialization process and the large waves of immigration never really hit Paraguay as it did in the neighboring states. Moreover, the Paraguayan military was effectively united for long stretches under a series of iron fist dictatorships, culminating in the Stroessner regime from 1954 to 1989. During this time the Colorado Party of Stroessner allowed token elections, but the press and dissent were tightly controlled. In 1989, Paraguay joined the democratic transition of its neighbors but its problems remain somewhat idiosyncratic.

Uruguay also had a unique historical feature in the rise of José Batlle y Ordóñez (or Batlle for short). As in Argentina, Uruguay's gaucho base had undergone a severe transformation in the end of the nineteenth century, moving from free-range cattle to the forceful fencing in of ranches. After a series of civil wars involving the military between rival Blanco and Colorado factions in good part related to these changes, Batlle, a Colorado leader, was elected in 1905. Batlle then presided over a long period in which he was able to utilize the political stability and economic boom of Uruguay's growing cattle and wool exports to create an extremely unusual socioeconomic experiment in the history of development. Batlle presided over a period in which, with moderate exaggeration, Uruguay became known as "the Switzerland" of Latin America. This term referred to the highly developed social legislation and state direction of Batlle's government. Batlle enacted strong labor protection laws, initiated basic social welfare programs, and began a legacy of state led corporations that continue today, albeit in a more fragile state.

The export boom as well as Batlle's experiment were brought to an abrupt halt with the onset of the Great Depression in 1929. Since colonial times, like other developing countries, Southern Cone countries' economies have been centered around primary product exports. When the prices and/or demand of those exports (see entry for Trade Policies and Development) decline, every economy falls into a tailspin. With the Great Depression, Southern Cone exports faltered initially but recovered when demand during World War II resumed. However, the economies remained cut off from new imports of manufactured and industrial goods. This started a necessary transformation of the Cone economies that would lead to a new set of political and economic relationships.

The 1930s and 1940s in Argentina and Brazil were marked by the rise of a new kind of dictatorship—one based on popular support. While in Chile and Uruguay the period of new middle class participation was carried out democratically, Argentina and Brazil were dominated by the personal rule of Juan Perón and Getulio Vargas. Peron and Vargas shared the unusual role of both organizing the middle class and then limiting its participation through channels they established in the state. Both used the military to achieve power and to repress enemies. Both initiated a strong program of state-led domestic industrialization through a policy now called import substituting industrialization (ISI, see entry for Trade Policies and Development). As a result, Vargas and Perón can be seen as the key

figures that consolidate the transition from an agricultural oligarchy to a centralized and industrialized state. In order to consolidate this transition, both set up strong state bureaucracies that planned and managed their economies. In political terms, both dictators also set up strong political parties that were linked to state-created unions. In effect, both had the ingenious idea of undercutting union support for Marxist parties by creating their own. However, centralization of power has its costs. In the case of Vargas and Perón, both were overthrown by the same military that had supported their initial efforts.

While both dictators consolidated power and changed the political and economic trajectories of their countries, there have been important differences in their legacies. The Peronist political party, linked initially to the dictator, but with its base in the labor unions, continues to be a major force in Argentine politics. Peronists were able to attract most disaffected sectors of Argentina's middle class, thus usurping and consolidating support away from Marxist parties. Because of the blocking power of the Peronist party, Argentina has had a hard time carrying through on neoliberal (see entry entitled "Neoliberalism") economic reforms. In Brazil, meanwhile, though there are a number of important unions, after Vargas, the unions never really coalesced into a major political force. It is interesting to note that in both Argentina and Brazil, the agricultural oligarchy, though defeated for control, continues to play a major role in decisions.

Throughout the Southern Cone, with the exception of Paraguay, the 1960s and 1970s was a period of civil war. While some countries, such as Chile, managed to maintain democracy at least initially, the outcome of the political polarization of the times was military dictatorship. We should remember that the key event in Latin America was the Cuban Revolution in 1959, which symbolized and inspired Marxist parties throughout the region to move decisively from attempts to gain power through elections to guerrilla actions. The 1960s was a period of polarization between Left (Marxist) and Right (Conservatives) throughout the world. The leftist guerrillas seem in hindsight to have been quite naïve about the difficulties and levels of resistance that they would face in attempting to institute a socialist revolution. Unlike the inept and corrupt Bautista regime in Cuba, there was not the same level of popular anger at existing regimes. Moreover, once the Cuban Revolution had occurred, the military in Latin America became more vigilant to prevent the surprise turn to Marxism and the Soviet Union that Castro had pulled off. The Soviet Union also became reluctant to put forward the substantial resources needed for successful military campaigns to counter the vastly increased training and funding that the United States began to provide to Latin American militaries.

The military governments that took over in the 1960s and 1970s were authoritarian, but of a different nature than the previous regimes. Guillermo O'Donnel, an Argentine, coined the term "bureaucratic authoritarianism" to describe these regimes. Rather than relying solely upon a personalistic dictatorship, they built up bureaucracies. While the initial motivation of these regimes was to wipe out leftist guerrillas, their purpose came to include leading the economic development process. O'Donnel explained that these two purposes were relate through repression of labor in order to keep wages down during the import-substituting industrialization phase of development (see Trade and Development entry). Thus, some parts of the bureaucracy were designed towards repression, such as the secret policy, and others towards economic planning. The Southern Cone's experience roughly fits O'Donnel's description, but with some important caveats. First, in both Paraguay and Chile, there was more of a military dictatorship. Second, the military showed that it was not necessarily wedded to the planning model, since, in Chile and Argentina in the 1970s and the rest of the region in the 1980s, the military began to endorse Neo-Liberal (see entry) ideas, involving the removal of the state from economic planning.

In Chile, the Left took a unique step in actually winning an election, albeit by a small fraction, and then attempting to institute socialism, at times extraconstitutionally. Salvador Allende, the Socialist elected President of Chile in 1970, seemed to move back and forth with the multiparty factions of his coalition. As in other countries, the Chilean Left was highly fragmented among those who wanted an immediate revolution, and those who thought it was important to work more gradually. Once in power, Allende was not able to follow through on the sketchy economic plans he had for Chile. While expropriating the US-dominated copper interests was a huge popular success, the dispute over compensation solidified US enmity towards the Allende regime. After a good first year, a major decline in copper prices, uncertainty about which other companies would be taken over by the state, and hyper-inflation, led to a period of economic chaos. Ironically, it was middle class workers and unions' actions, such as a trucker's strike, that landed the decisive blow to the regime. The chaos was ended by a military coup led by Augusto Pinochet in 1973, who then instituted one of the most severe repressions in the region's history.

In Uruguay and Argentina, the urban guerrilla warfare of the Left brutalized the population. While the guerrillas were able to gain an occasional big

victory, for the most part, in hindsight clear victory seems unlikely against a well-organized and fortified foe such as the military. Moreover, the chaos that the guerrillas brought to both the economic and political situation wore on the general population, some of whom eventually openly supported military intervention. We should remember that the classic guerrilla campaigns of Mao in China and Castro in Cuba involved rural areas, where there was popular support, continual cover in the topography and foliage, and outside support in the form of funding and arms from the Soviet Union.

The military victory in Chile was eventually repeated in Brazil, Argentina, and Uruguay. However, the brutality of both the guerrillas and the military, and the ensuing economic chaos left a deep scar on the region. The generation who grew up amidst the chaos are still dealing with the fact their families were divided in the civil wars, that loved ones "disappeared," and the brutality of both sides. Much of the activist portion of the Left went into exile, often in Europe, an experience which moderated their view on revolutionary change and the desirability of socialism à la the Soviet Union.

The military governments' economic legacies are decidedly more mixed. While Chile's neoliberal policies have been hailed as an economic miracle and a model for the rest of the region, Chile has had some very rough economic periods. Chile experienced a major recession from 1975–1977 and another as well as a series of bank failures in 1982. Nonetheless, Chile's macroeconomic stability is remarkable among developing countries and some of its economic reforms, such as the privatization of pension funds, have attracted international attention. In Argentina, the Argentine military's inability to control inflation led initially to a handover of power to former archrivals, the Peronists in 1973. The military took over again in 1976, this time half-heartedly following macroeconomic reforms similar to those in Chile. Paul Lewis, among others, described this as the "cyclical crisis of Argentine capitalism." The cycle describes the attempt to set up economic pacts across the important labor and industrial groups in society when a new government takes over. At some point, one of the members of this coalition is unable or unwilling to keep their end of the bargain, and the attempt to maintain economic reform falls apart, leading to another crisis. This model seemed to describe well the inflationary cycles in Argentina for the past three decades until democratic President Carlos Menem took power (see entries for Argentina and Menem, Carlos) in 1989. A Peronist, Menem turned his back on the labor and domestic industry base of the party in a turn towards neoliberalism. The Argentine

economy went through an almost decade-long growth spurt with low inflation, albeit with continuing unemployment, and seemed poised to break out of the cycle. Unfortunately, amidst severe pressure on the fixed exchange rate and with the collapse of the Brazilian currency in 1999, the Argentine economy went into a tail-spin from which it has yet to recover.

Paraguay, under Stroessner, experienced economic stability, but much of the country remains backwards in terms of basic indicators of the quality of life, such as access to education and health care. Besides basic agricultural exports, the Paraguayan government depends on the large Itaipú and Yacyretá dam projects by which they sell most of their share of the hydroelectricity to Brazil and Argentina respectively. In Uruguay, the military was able to restore some confidence to the economy following the civil war, and Montevideo became an international financial and trade services center. However, economic growth never approached the glory days of Batlle. Brazil's military, by contrast, prides itself on the bureaucratic planning of industrialization. In the early years of the dictatorship in the 1960s, Brazil was being hailed as a "miracle" growth economy among developing nations. During this decade the Brazil managed to build a strong industrial base which allowed it to diversify its exports away from agriculture, a feat Argentina never came close to matching to the same degree. Today, Brazil is a world-leading exporter of armaments, airplanes, steel, and a leading assembly site of automobiles. Thus, there remains some lingering nostalgia today for the economic achievements of the military government as well as the high growth rates of that era. In 1994, Brazilian democracy seemed consolidated with the victory of former dependency theorist Fernando Henrique Cardoso (see Brazil entry). A former socialist, Cardoso was elected on the basis of his successful fight against inflation as Finance Minister in the former Administration. Cardoso's successful management of Brazilian macroeconomics, controlling inflation for the first time in decades, earned him re-election in 1998. By the Constitution, Cardoso could not run again. Moreover, by the time of the next election in 2002, there was a growing desire by many Brazilians for a change in direction. Not only did the middle and upper classes feel that their opportunities had stagnated, but representatives of marginalized groups, such as the MST (*Movimento sem Terra*, or Movement of the Landless) had become more active in their demands. The result was the election of Luis Ignacio "Lula" da Silva, who promised a new era in Brazilian politics. Coming from humble origins, Lula had worked his way up the union and Workers' Party (PT) hierarchy in Brazil. After several unsuccessful campaigns, Lula finally

succeeded through moving towards the political center, in particular promising financial stability. However, this promise seemed to become a greater priority to some than his efforts to reduce poverty, including a "War on Hunger."

These economic developments have had major effects on the politics of the region. In every case, economic growth was accompanied by increasing inequality of distribution. Moreover, a lot of the growth of the 1970s, with the partial exception of Chile, was based upon international borrowing. A good portion of the borrowing in the region went to pay for increased oil prices, as every country in the region at the time was heavily dependent upon oil imports. With the exception of Argentina and Paraguay, that remains the case today. Therefore, when international interest rates were raised by double digits in the early 1980s by US monetary policy, the debt crisis hit the region hard. With the exception of Chile, every country in the region experienced major inflationary pressures and a recession. A combination of the consolidation of the civilian opposition towards a centrist coalition and the ongoing inability of the military to get their economies jump-started led to an overwhelming pressure for the return of democracy by the mid-1980s.

However, the circumstances of the transition varied greatly from one country to another. With the exception of Argentina, the military seems to lurk in the shadows of the new democratic governments. In every case but Argentina, the military was able to guarantee itself amnesty for its human rights abuses. In Uruguay, the population, fearing further military intervention as well as social polarization, passed a plebiscite granting the amnesty. As a result, Uruguay seems to be moving back towards a more stable democratic base. In Argentina, the resounding failure of the military in economic affairs as well as the Malvinas War (see later) led to a much clearer renunciation of their role. Brazil had an unusual transition to democracy as the military went through a series of attempts at creating a stable but "responsible" two party system to be slowly introduced that it called "abertura," or opening. The military government's attempts seem to have failed, as Brazil's political parties remain highly fragmented. Brazil's attempts to create a more stable democracy resulted in a new Constitution in 1988, but the new political rules, including a partly proportional representation voting system, seems to have even further exacerbated the situation. In Chile, Pinochet and the constitutional restrictions he placed upon democracy remain in place. The famous attempt at bringing Pinochet to trial for war crimes in London during a visit in 1999 seems to have failed to bring any closure to the dark period of military rule. In Paraguay, the democracy remains equally fragile, with the military interfering directly and indirectly in political decision making. Lacking any history of democratic rule, Paraguay seems to be struggling in its transition.

In general, the greatest threat to the new centrist democracies of the Southern Cone continues to be slow economic growth. Even Chile, the star pupil of neoliberal policies, slowed down by the late 1990s. The ongoing monetary crises in Brazil (1998–1999) and Argentina (beginning in 2000) equally wreaked havoc in Paraguay and Uruguay, whose economies are so dependent upon their larger neighbors. In sum, it remains to be seen whether the current economic malaise will create a serious problem for the continuation of neoliberal policies. With staggering levels of external debt on one side and domestic economic disquiet on the other, Southern Cone governments find themselves in exceedingly difficult positions regarding development strategies.

International Relations

Unlike other developing regions, the Southern Cone has a limited history of international warfare. Almost all the most significant wars took place before the twentieth century. The War of the Triple Alliance (1864–1870), in which a dispute between Paraguay and Uruguay resulted in Brazil and Argentina joining Uruguay, reportedly wiped out half the Paraguayan population and more than 80% of the males. Among them were Chile's seizure of Bolivia's only seaport and occupation of Lima, Peru, in the War of the Pacific (1879–1883) centered around control of the then booming nitrate resources located in that region. The only significant recent war was the Chaco War (1932–1935) in which Paraguay defeated Bolivia for control of a disputed desert territory which supposedly contains large petroleum reserves. While there have been ongoing border disputes among many of the countries in the region, these disputes seem to have died down considerably with the democratic transition and the strengthening of regional economic ties in MERCOSUR (discussed below).

The major international war that involved outside powers was the Malvinas War (1982), in which the Argentine military invaded the Falkland Islands (called the Malvinas by Argentina), which had been controlled for some time by the United Kingdom. Given the naval superiority of Britain and the help of the United States, the result was predictable. The invasion was a spectacular failure, with the main result being the complete loss of face of the Argentine military at home.

While Argentina and Uruguay had achieved virtual First World economic levels early in the twentieth century, the period after World War II has been one of steady decline. By contrast, Brazil's territorial size and immense relative population, coupled with high economic growth rates and successful industrialization over the same period have placed it in a position of regional superpower, eclipsing its one-time regional rival in Argentina. With the consummation of the North American Free Trade Agreement (NAFTA) in 1992, in which Mexico gained unencumbered access to the US market, the economic dynamics of the Southern Cone shifted towards Brazilian economic leadership.

While every country in the region has traditionally looked to Europe and to a lesser extent, the United States as the main trading partner, there was a growing fear that the successful integration experiments in both the European Union and the NAFTA would leave the Southern Cone left without competitive access to its main markets. Moreover, when US President George Bush began raising the ideas of a Free Trade Agreement of the Americas (FTAA), the traditionally protectionist Southern Cone countries began to consider banding together in order to improve their bargaining position with the United States. The result is a free trade agreement for the Southern Cone, called the MERCOSUR (Common Market of the South) which began in 1994. MERCOSUR revolves around free trade between Brazil and Argentina, but Paraguay and Uruguay are also partners. Bolivia and Chile are associate members. Though intra-regional trade increases have been spectacular, there have been important limits to the MERCOSUR process. First, there are several key sectors, such as autos and footwear, that have exceptions to open trade. Second, unlike NAFTA, MERCOSUR does not have a clear dispute mechanism settlement. Third, MERCOSUR is really just a forum for national-level negotiations. There are working groups who attempt to negotiate new agreements in MERCOSUR, but they can not be considered part of a regional institution. With ongoing currency crises in Brazil (1999) and Argentina (2001), the prospects for further agreements in the MERCOSUR seem unlikely, at least for the short-term. Given domestic US opposition, the FTAA process seems equally stalled. In the long-run, however, the ongoing increases in trade and investment among the MERCOSUR countries, such as those in energy, may revive progress.

ANIL HIRA

See also Allende Gossens, Salvador; Argentina; Brazil; Chile; Ethnic Conflicts: Southern Cone (Latin America); Paraguay; Perón, Juan Domingo; Pinochet Ugarte, Augusto; Southern Cone (Latin America): International Relations; Uruguay

References and Further Reading

Bradford, Burns E. *A History of Brazil.* New York: Columbia University Press, 3rd Edition, 1993.

Busey, James L. *Latin American Political Guide.* Manitou Springs, CO: Juniper Editions, 1995.

Caviedes, Cesar. *The Southern Cone: Realities of the Authoritarian State in South America.* Totowa, NJ: Rowman and Allanheld, c1984.

Collier, Simon and William F. Sater. *A History of Chile, 1808–2002.* New York: Cambridge University Press, 2004.

Davis, William Columbus. *Warnings From the Far South: Democracy versus Dictatorship in Uruguay, Argentina, and Chile.* Westport, CT: Praeger, 1995.

Drake, Paul. *Labor Movements and Dictatorships: The Southern Cone in Comparative Perspective.* Baltimore, MD: The Johns Hopkins University Press, 1996.

Jelin, Elizabeth, and Hershberg, Eric. *Constructing Democracy: Human Rights, Citizenship, and Society in Latin America.* Boulder, CO: Westview Press, 1996.

Kelly, Philip, and Child, Jack. *Geopolitics of the Southern Cone and Antarctica.* Boulder: Lynne Rienner, 1988.

Lewis, Paul. *The Crisis of Argentine Capitalism.* Chapel Hill, NC: University of North Carolina Press, 1990.

O'Brien, Philip, and Cammack, Paul. *Generals in Retreat: The Crisis of Military Rule in Latin America.* Manchester: Manchester University Press, 1985.

Roniger, Luis, and Sznajder, Mario. *The Legacy of Human-Rights Violations in the Southern Cone: Argentina, Chile, and Uruguay.* New York: Oxford University Press, 1999.

Stepan, Alfred C. *Rethinking military Politics: Brazil and the Southern Cone.* Princeton, NJ: Princeton University Press, 1988.

SOUTHERN CONE (LATIN AMERICA): INTERNATIONAL RELATIONS

Latin America's southern cone is composed of the independent nations of Argentina, Brazil, Chile, Paraguay, and Uruguay. Prior to 1945, foreign relations were primarily dominated by relationships with the United Kingdom. It was not until after 1945, however, that the United States became significant economically or politically in the region. The military governments that ruled the southern cone nations during the Cold War were vehemently anti-communist and received generous US economic and military aid packages. The southern cone nations, because of their distance from the United States and their European outlook, however, have often pursued foreign policies independent of US policy goals and objectives. The most important foreign policy initiatives in the post-Cold War period revolve around economic issues. The formation of MERCOSUR—a regional program of economic integration and cooperation

between Argentina, Brazil, Paraguay, and Uruguay—
in the early 1990s is an essential component of the
foreign relations of those nations.

Argentina

After achieving independence from Spain in 1816,
Argentina was marked by a bitter struggle for national self-determination between two contending elite
factions: the Liberal elites in the Buenos Aires region,
who wanted a strong central government, and the
Conservative elites, who wanted a federal government
based on regional control. The ensuing political confusion allowed Paraguay and Uruguay, once part of
the Viceroyalty of La Plata, to achieve their independence. In addition, the British and French were able
to take advantage of Argentina politically and economically. For example, in 1833, the British occupied
the Falkland Islands.

The Liberal elites were able to implement a stable
political and economic system in 1862. They attempted to create a national identity and a foreign
policy based on Argentinian exceptionalism and European civilization. They also implemented an export-
led economy based on beef and wheat exports. During the last quarter of the nineteenth century, the
Argentinian government promoted the immigration
of millions of Europeans, especially from Italy, to
help develop the beef and wheat industry. These Europeans, known as Inquilinos, were promised land in
return for clearing the pampas grass from the large
estates of the elites. The Inquilinos, however, were
denied their land and Argentina lost its chance to
develop a large rural middle class. Nevertheless, the
Argentinians created a viable economic system, based
on beef and wheat exports to the British, that thrived
until the Great Depression. During the first three decades of the twentieth century, Argentina accounted for
30% of British foreign investment. The entire meat
packing industry was dominated by US and British
investors.

During the 1930s, the Conservative elites and their
supporters in the military eliminated democracy, repressed labor, and led the nation out of the Great
Depression by reinforcing economic ties to the British.
The 1933 Roca-Runciman Treaty secured a market in
England for Argentinian exports while maintaining
Argentina's dependent relationship on the British. In
1943, reacting to elite domination, labor unrest, and
Argentina's economic dependence on England, a
group of middle level military officers, who called the
elites *vendepatrias* (country sellers), led a military coup
that demanded a new domestic and foreign policy

geared to restore Argentinian pride and prosperity.
The new government, composed of officers who were
members of the Group of United Officers (GOU) and
favorable towards Fascism, declared neutrality in
World War II. In response, the United States froze
Argentinian gold reserves in the United States, recalled the US ambassador, and restricted trade with
Argentina. US pressure convinced the Argentinian
government to break diplomatic relations with the
Axis powers in 1944. Nevertheless, although Argentina eventually declared war on Germany, after the
war Argentina became a refuge for Nazi war criminals.

In 1946, Juan Perón, a member of the military
government since 1943 who had been openly sympathetic to the Nazis, ran for president of Argentina. On
the eve of Argentina's 1946 presidential elections, US
Assistant Secretary of State for Latin American
Affairs Spruille Braden spearheaded an anti-Perón
campaign. The US government published a "Blue
Book" charging Perón with pro-Nazi activities.
Perón responded by charging the US with imperialism
and easily won the elections. An ardent anti-communist, Perón initiated a government based on economic
nationalism. He nationalized most foreign companies
in Argentina and established state-run industries. Because of his export earnings, he was able to offer
economic advantages to the workers. Perón's popularity with labor was enhanced by his wife, Eva "Evita"
Duarte. Declining export prices in the early 1950s
meant, however, that his concessions to labor could
not be sustained. In 1955, the Argentinian industrialists, supported by the military, ousted Perón, who
went into exile.

From 1955 to 1973, Argentina abandoned its nationalistic economic and foreign policy. The civilian-
military administrations, which were vehemently anti-
communist, de-nationalized Argentinian companies
and encouraged foreign investment. By 1968, the US
had over $1 billion invested in Argentina. Argentina's
economy, however, failed to recover and the foreign
debt, all but eliminated by Perón, rose to over $3
billion during the 1960s. Disgruntled workers, however, continued to clamor for Perón's return from exile.
Economic and political chaos, enhanced by increased
left-wing revolutionary activity, convinced the military to allow Perón to return from exile in 1973 and
assume the presidency. Returning with his third wife,
Isabel Martínez, Perón was unable to address Argentina's economic and political woes. In 1974, he died
and Isabel took over, but chaos ensued and she was
deposed by a military coup in 1976.

The new military dictatorship instituted a reign of
terror, the so-called Dirty War, against all leftist
forces. Thousands of people disappeared, which
placed Argentina in the international spotlight of

human rights agencies such as Amnesty International. The military, inept at running the economy, attempted to divert attention by invading the Falkland Islands in 1982. Argentina's military generals, believing that the British would not resort to force to regain islands that were militarily and strategically unimportant, miscalculated the determination of British Prime Minister Margaret Thatcher. To compound the situation, the Argentinian military government, which was ill-prepared to fight a war, lied to the Argentinian people that they were winning the war. Argentina's defeat led to the return of civilian government in 1983.

Since 1983, US–Argentinian foreign relations have been excellent. Argentina was the only Latin American nation to participate in the 1990–1991 Gulf War and all phases of the 1994 Haiti operation. Argentina, however, was reluctant to contribute troops to the coalition forces in Iraq in 2003. Eager for closer ties to industrialized nations, Argentina abandoned the non-aligned movement in the early 1990s. In 1999, Argentina and the United Kingdom agreed to normalize travel between Argentina and the Falkland Islands. A strong proponent of enhanced regional stability in South America, Argentina has revitalized its relationship with Brazil and settled border disputes with Chile. Argentina's most important trading partners are the MERCOSUR members and the European Union (EU).

Brazil

Brazilian independence in 1822 was bloodless and much less turbulent than the destructive wars of independence in the rest of South America. Whereas the former Spanish colonies in South America splintered into numerous nations and spent decades searching for a form of government that would have legitimacy in the eyes of its populace, the Brazilians, who remained united, had the Portuguese royal family, the Braganzas. In 1821, when Portugal's João VI returned to Lisbon to quell a rebellion, he left his son Pedro I in Brazil to lead the Brazilian independence movement. Although the constitutional monarchy served the Brazilians well and the nation grew economically and geographically during the nineteenth century, in 1889, after Emperor Pedro II became debilitated by diabetes, the military, and the elites, who viewed the monarchy as an archaic institution, sent the Braganzas into exile and established a republic. During the twentieth century, because of its size—the seventh largest economy and the fifth largest nation in the world—Brazil has played an important role in

hemispheric relations. Although critics of US foreign policy frequently refer to the United States as the Colossus of the North, many Brazilians approvingly refer to their nation as the Colossus of the South.

In 1808, when the Braganzas first arrived in Rio de Janeiro, the United States was the first nation to establish a consulate in Brazil. It was, however, not until after World War II that the United States became Brazil's primary trading partner and foreign investor. In addition, the US has consistently supported Brazil's impressive attempts at industrialization. In 1941, the United States, fearful of expanding German economic activity in South America, facilitated the construction of Latin America's largest steel mill at Volta Redonda, which became the cornerstone of Brazil's import substitution industrialization strategy. The US has also sought Brazilian support for US foreign policy initiatives. Although the Brazilians have frequently pursued an independent foreign policy, US-Brazilian relations have, for the most part, been close.

During the presidency of Enrico Dutra, which maintained very friendly relations with the United States, Brazil outlawed the Brazilian Communist Party (PCB) and broke off diplomatic relations with the Soviet Union. In 1947, Brazil hosted the conference that established the Inter-American Treaty of Reciprocal Assistance, the so-called Rio Treaty. When Getúlio Vargas returned to power in 1951, relations with the United States cooled. Vargas, who blamed the United States for his removal from power in 1945, pushed for a more independent foreign policy and supported nationalistic policies such as the creation of Petrobrás, Brazil's state-run oil company. After Vargas's suicide in 1954, however, friendly relations with the United States were resumed.

During Juscelino Kubitschek's administration, the Brazilians lured US investors to Brazil with very favorable terms. By 1960, US investments in Brazil were over $1.5 billion. Relations with the US cooled after Jânio Quadros took office in 1961. Quadros renewed relations with the Soviet Union and criticized Kennedy's failed Bay of Pigs invasion. Citing his inability to deal with Brazil's elite-dominated congress, Quadros resigned in 1961 and was replaced by his vice president, João Goulart. Goulart's populist rhetoric and attempt at centrist politics alienated the increasingly vocal forces of the left and right wings of the political spectrum. In 1962, the Brazilian government passed a law that severely restricted profit remittances from foreign investment in Brazil, which caused new foreign investment in Brazil to disappear by 1964. In late 1963, to show its disfavor, the US reduced foreign aid to Brazil. Although the US was not directly involved in the overthrow of Goulart on March 31, 1964, it

immediately recognized the military dictatorship established by Humberto Castello Branco.

Castello Branco, the first of a series of military presidents, received generous economic and military aid packages from the United States. Between 1964 and 1970, Brazil received over $2 billion is US aid. In return, the Brazilian government adopted a policy of total alignment with the United States. Brazil broke diplomatic relations with Cuba, sent Brazilian communists into exile, and compensated foreign investors who had their investments expropriated. In 1965, the Brazilian army contributed two thousand troops to the OAS force sent to the Dominican Republic to end that nation's civil war. Subsequent military presidents, although maintaining friendly relations with the United States, pursued a more independent course in foreign policy, especially in the aftermath of the failure of the United States to contain communism in Vietnam. For example, the Brazilians refused to sign a nuclear non-proliferation treaty. Relations chilled when the Carter administration published a report citing human rights violations in Brazil. Relations were further strained during the early 1980s by Brazil's $5 billion trade surplus with the United States.

Following Brazil's return to civilian government in 1985, the Brazilians have opened their economy to increased international participation through privatization of state-run industries and neo-liberal economic reforms. Since the nineteenth century, Brazil's greatest rival in Latin America has been Argentina. In 1991, however, Brazil and Argentina, along with Uruguay and Paraguay, signed the Treaty of Asunción, which resulted in the formation of MERCOSUR, a regional economic integration program in the southern cone. Plans are under negotiation to also incorporate Chile and Bolivia.

Trade between the EU and Brazil is also extensive. By 1995, German investments in Brazil were second only to the United States. In December 1995, the EU signed an important free-trade protocol with MER-COSUR, the first protocol ever between two regional trading blocs. Since 1995, Brazil has used the potential to expand trade with the EU to pressure the United States to grant more favorable trade relations with Brazil. Since the EU members do not require visas from Brazilians, the Brazilians do not require visas from EU members. The US, however, requires Brazilians to have a visa to enter the United States. As such, the Brazilians, citing reciprocity, insist that US citizens purchase visas before entering Brazil.

Brazil attaches great importance to its foreign relations with Japan. Since Brazil established diplomatic relations with Japan in 1897, there has been a large influx of Japanese immigrants to Brazil. Brazilians of Japanese descent constitute one of the largest ethnic segments of Brazil's population. Brazil is also home to Japan's largest expatriate community. Beginning in the 1960s, Japan began to invest heavily in Brazil's mining, steel, aluminum, telecommunications, manufacturing, and agricultural sectors. As a result, mineral and agricultural exports to Japan increased dramatically. Currently, 250,000 Brazilians of Japanese descent work in Japan. Their remittances to family members in Brazil comprise a significant component of the Brazilian economy.

Chile

During the nineteenth century, Chile's foreign policy was characterized by close economic ties with the British and territorial expansion against the Mapuche Indians in the south and the Bolivians and Peruvians in the north. Since independence, Chilean elites had invested in the vast nitrate fields of the Atacama Desert, then belonging to Bolivia and Peru. The Atacama Desert had the world's largest deposit of nitrates, which were used by the Europeans as a fertilizer to increase food production. The British were the largest importers of nitrates from Chile and the largest supplier of manufactured goods to Chile. During the 1870s, Bolivia increased taxation on the Chilean mine owners operating in Bolivia, while the Peruvian government nationalized the Chilean-owned nitrate mines in Peru. Although the mine owners were compensated with Peruvian government bonds, the Chilean government launched the War of the Pacific (1879–1883) against Bolivia and Peru. The superior Chilean forces, which defeated Bolivia and Peru, conquered the Atacama Desert for Chile. Bolivia became a landlocked nation and Valparaíso, Chile replaced Callao, Peru as the main port on South America's Pacific coast. During the war, however, British speculators, such as John Thomas North, purchased the virtually worthless Peruvian government bonds. At the end of the war, therefore, the Chilean government decided that the British speculators were the legal owners of the nitrate mines. The result was a Chilean economy dependent on exports and imports to and from England.

The Chilean nitrate boom, however, was short-lived. During World War I, the Germans discovered a way to produce nitrates by fixing nitrogen from the air, which signaled the end of Chile's Liberal export-led economy based on nitrates. Although Chile had limited foreign relations with the United States during the nineteenth century, after World War I copper became Chile's leading export and the United States replaced England as the dominant economic power in Chile. Chilean copper was a strategic metal used

in airplanes and bullets by the Allied powers during World War II. Despite strong internal pressure in Chile to support the Axis powers, the Chilean government eventually broke diplomatic relations with Germany.

During the early post–World War II years, the Chilean government supported the US struggle against international communism. The growing influence of the Marxist left in Chilean politics, however, led to an increase of anti-US public sentiment in Chile. This resentment was exacerbated by the decline of international copper prices after the Korean War, opposition to US intervention in Vietnam, and US meddling in domestic Chilean politics. As part of President John F. Kennedy's agenda of presenting Latin American nations as models of democratic development to counteract the popularity of Fidel Castro's Cuban Revolution in the Third World, in 1964 the US CIA financially supported the candidacy of political centrist Eduardo Frei Montalva. The CIA funding, which amounted to over $20 million, facilitated Frei's victory over Marxist presidential candidate Salvador Allende. During the 1960s, Chile received more US aid per capita than any other Latin American nation.

The US government viewed Allende's 1970 presidential victory as detrimental to the struggle against international communism. US National Security Adviser Henry Kissinger was especially concerned about the implications for European politics following the democratic election of a Marxist in Chile. The US government, failing to keep Allende from taking office, initiated a covert campaign to destabilize his government after Allende's inauguration. Allende's government nationalized the Chilean holdings of International Telephone and Telegraph (ITT) and copper giants Anaconda and Kennecott. In 1971, Castro toured Chile, often accompanied by Allende. Much of Chile's press, controlled by the elites, condemned Allende's actions and called for his overthrow. Although the United States did not directly overthrow the Allende regime, it welcomed Augusto Pinochet's 1973 military coup and provided extensive economic and military aid to Pinochet's military regime. Pinochet's dictatorship was responsible for the disappearance of almost 3,000 Chileans. Although this number pales in comparison to the number of disappeared people in Argentina at the same time, human rights activists labeled Pinochet's regime a brutal authoritarian dictatorship. Nevertheless, Pinochet introduced neo-liberal economic reforms that revived Chile's economy.

Although relations between the US and Chile were strained during Jimmy Carter's presidential administration, Ronald Reagan's 1980 election restored amicable US-Chilean relations. During Reagan's first administration, US officials argued that anti-communist authoritarian regimes, such as Pinochet's government, were needed to stop the spread of international communism. By 1984, however, facing increased criticism for US actions against Nicaragua's Sandinistas, US officials, cognizant of human rights abuses in Chile, began to worry that Pinochet was no longer a solution to a potential threat from the radical left, but part of the problem. The US and Western European nations welcomed the October 5, 1988, plebiscite by Chilean voters that rejected the continuation of Pinochet's government into the 1990s. The 1989 election of Christian Democrat Patricio Aylwin to the presidency once again restored the amicability of US-Chilean relations. The US welcomed Chile's commitment to free-market economic policies while praising the Chilean government's commitment to democracy. The US has indicated a willingness to sign a free-trade agreement with Chile in the aftermath of the successful implementation of the North American Free Trade Agreement (NAFTA) with Mexico and Canada. Although the US continues to be an important trading partner for Chile, in the post-Cold War period Japan has replaced the United States as Chile's largest trading partner.

Paraguay

Since independence in 1812, Paraguay has been a buffer state between Brazil and Argentina, the two largest nations in South America. As such, Paraguayan foreign relations have been conditioned by its relations with its larger neighbors. Being one of Latin America's two landlocked nations has caused Paraguayan foreign relations to oscillate between periods of isolationism and expansionism. Paraguay's first leader, José Gaspar Rodríguez de Francia, established a strong, centralized state that attempted to develop independently of its stronger neighbors. In 1864, however, Paraguayan leader Francisco Solano López, in an attempt to expand and reinforce Paraguay's northern frontier, declared war on Brazil. The War of the Triple Alliance (1864–1870), fought against Brazil, Argentina, and Uruguay, resulted in the death of over half of Paraguay's population and the loss of over 25% of Paraguay's territory to Brazil and Argentina. Subsequent Paraguayan leaders sought to strike a balance between the influence of its two larger neighbors. Nevertheless, since the port of Buenos Aires provided the only access to external markets, Paraguay depended heavily on Argentina for trade, which caused many Paraguayans to resent their dependence on Argentina.

During the Chaco War (1932–1935), Paraguay expanded westward into Bolivian territory. In the aftermath of the conflict, war hero Colonel Rafael Franco attempted to establish a democratic regime, but Liberal elites overthrew his government in 1937. The Liberal government, facing mounting pressure from the US government, surrendered the oil-rich land that it had won during the war with Bolivia. During World War II, the military government of Higinio Morínigo, although favoring German economic interests, supported the Allied cause in return for generous US loans and military hardware. After World War II, liberal forces launched a civil war in 1947 that resulted in economic and political pandemonium. Alfredo Stroessner, a veteran of the Chaco War, established a military dictatorship in 1954 that lasted until 1989.

Stroessner's foreign policy was based on two principles: nonintervention in the affairs of other countries and no relations with nations ruled by Marxists. In 1959, Stroessner severed relations with Cuba after Fidel Castro's revolution. In 1980, Stroessner broke diplomatic relations with Nicaragua after the Sandinistas came to power. Like most Paraguayans, Stroessner resented Paraguay's dependence on Argentina. In an attempt to lessen Paraguayan dependence on Argentina, Stroessner encouraged increased ties with Brazil. During the 1950s, Brazil granted Paraguay free-port privileges on the Brazilian coast at Paranagua and built the Friendship Bridge over the Río Paraná, which linked Asunción, Paraguay's capital, to the Paranagua coast. The signing of the Treaty of Itaipú in 1973, which eventually resulted in the construction of the world's largest hydroelectric dam, epitomized the growing relationship between Paraguay and Brazil.

Stroessner benefitted politically and economically from his new relationship with Brazil. The infusion of money and jobs associated with the Itaipú dam project caused the Paraguayan economy to grow rapidly during the 1970s. During the 1980s, Brazil provided most of Paraguay's military equipment and training and Brazilian banks financed much of Paraguay's foreign debt. Since Paraguayan energy consumption was limited, the Treaty of Itaipú authorized Paraguayan sales of excess electricity to Brazil. Although the electricity was sold at discounted prices, it generated millions of dollars for the Paraguayan government. Notwithstanding Brazil's transition to civilian government in 1985, Paraguayan-Brazilian relations remained friendly. The Brazilian government, content with the stability that Stroessner provided, refrained from criticizing the aging dictator. In 1986, however, Brazil's president met with Argentina's president to discuss increased economic cooperation in the southern cone. The Brazilian and Argentinian leaders

insisted that only democratic nations could participate in the proposed regional economic integration program. Although participation in the proposed program could have helped the Paraguayan economy, Stroessner refused to consider the democratization of the Paraguayan political system.

During the 1980s, diplomatic relations between Paraguay and Argentina were increasingly strained. During the 1983 Argentine presidential elections, Paraguayan civilian opposition leader Domingo Laíno campaigned for Radical Civic Union (UCR) candidate Raúl Alfonsín among the thousands of Argentine citizens of Paraguayan descent. After Alfonsín's election, the Argentinian president allowed Laíno to stage anti-Stroessner rallies in Argentina. Stroessner also refused to respond to Argentina's requests for the extradition of former Argentinian military officers accused of human rights violations during the so-called Dirty War of the late 1970s.

From 1945 to the late 1970s, foreign relations between Paraguay and the United States were conditioned by the Cold War. The US was concerned about anti-communism and security interests, while the Stroessner government desired economic aid. As such, Stroessner was one of the staunchest supporters of US security policies in the hemisphere. In the OAS and the UN, when security issues were raised, Paraguay voted with the United States more consistently than did any other South American country. Paraguay was rewarded with generous economic aid packages and one of the largest Peace Corps contingents in Latin America. The human rights agenda of Jimmy Carter's presidential administration, however, signaled an end to overtly friendly US-Paraguayan relations. US concern over continued human rights abuses in Paraguay continued after the election of Ronald Reagan. US-Paraguayan relations were also strained by the involvement of some members of Stroessner's government in narcotics trafficking, especially the participation of certain sectors of the Paraguayan military in the operation of cocaine laboratories. Critics claimed that Stroessner's sons Gustavo and Alfredo, Jr. were heavily involved in the narcotics trade. Nevertheless, in 1988, the Reagan administration certified to the US Congress that the Paraguayan government was cooperating with US drug enforcement officials.

In 1988, when Chilean voters rejected Augusto Pinochet's attempt to extend the Chilean military dictatorship into the 1990s, the possibility of implementing a democratic government in Chile in 1990 served to further isolate Stroessner from the democratic tide sweeping through South America. In 1989, Stroessner's youngest son Alfredo's father-in-law, General Andrés Rodríguez, overthrew the aging dictator. Stroessner retired to a fortified home in Brazil,

safe from possible extradition attempts in the future. Rodríguez initiated the transition to democracy in Paraguay. As a result, Paraguay was admitted to MERCOSUR, the regional common market phasing out tariffs between Argentina, Brazil, Uruguay, and Paraguay. In addition, the US rewarded Paraguay with preferential trade arrangements and increased amounts of foreign aid.

Uruguay

Uruguay's foreign policy has been shaped by its status as the second smallest country in South America, its location between Argentina and Brazil, its history of being a victim of foreign intervention, and its long democratic tradition. Although traditionally a part of the Spanish empire in the New World, Uruguay was seized by Portuguese forces from Brazil in 1817. Uruguayan revolutionaries, supported by Argentina, launched an invasion of Uruguay in 1825, defeated the army of newly-independent Brazil, and declared independence in 1828. The British government, eager to preserve Uruguay as a buffer state between Argentina and Brazil, convinced Uruguay's neighbors to accept Uruguayan independence. Nevertheless, England, France, Italy, Argentina, and Brazil frequently intervened in Uruguayan politics during the nineteenth century.

Beginning with José Batlle y Ordóñez's government in 1903, Uruguay has actively pursued democratic government and been active in international and regional organizations. US–Uruguayan relations have been based on a common dedication to democratic ideals. Although Uruguay initially attempted neutrality in both world wars, it ultimately sided with the Allied powers. In World War I, Uruguay broke diplomatic relations with Germany in October 1917. In 1941, Uruguay allowed the United States to build naval and air bases in Uruguay. US military training and supplies helped the Uruguayan military deter Argentina's expansionist agenda during the 1940s. In January 1942, Uruguay broke diplomatic relations with the Axis powers. The US responded with increased loans. In February 1945, Uruguay declared war on the Axis powers. Uruguay joined the UN in 1945 and has been a member of most UN specialized agencies. In 1947, Uruguay signed the Rio Treaty, a regional alliance that established a mutual defense system in the Americas.

During the post–World War II period Uruguay underwent rapid industrialization and urbanization. Although the government made great advances in social welfare reform, the elites, allied with foreign investors, continued to dominate the political economy. During the 1960s, however, industrial production dropped by 50% and agricultural production stagnated. At the same time, increased left-wing guerrilla activity exacerbated the ensuing political and economic chaos. The violent Tupamaro urban guerrillas—middle class Marxists, for the most part—attacked businesses, government buildings, and foreign embassies. Although the Tupamaros wreaked havoc on the national economy and committed numerous atrocities, during their raids the guerrillas uncovered numerous documents that revealed excessive corruption at national and international levels.

The Tupamaros, attempting to change the political system democratically, called for a cease-fire in 1971. Meanwhile, the Brazilian military plotted a military coup with the Uruguayan military in the event of a leftist victory in the 1971 presidential elections. The election of ultra-conservative Juan María Bordaberry, however, shelved the Brazilian plan while simultaneously increasing the radicalization of the Tupamaros. In 1973, with the support of the Brazilian military and President Bordaberry, the Uruguayan military, opposed to communist insurgency and liberal democracy, established a military dictatorship that lasted until 1985. During the military dictatorship, US economic and military aid increased dramatically. At the same time, the Uruguayan government, in an attempt to reestablish economic stability, signed a series of economic agreements with Brazil and Argentina designed to increase Uruguayan trade with its larger neighbors.

In 1985, following the return to civilian rule with the presidential election of Julio María Sanguinetti, Uruguay's foreign policy underwent an abrupt change. Although disagreeing with their political systems, Sanguinetti renewed foreign relations with Cuba, Nicaragua, the People's Republic of China, and the Soviet Union. Despite Uruguay's criticism of US military interventionism in Nicaragua, Libya, and Panama, US-Uruguayan relations after 1985 were excellent. In 1986, Sanguinetti received a warm welcome at the White House during an official visit to the United States.

The key to Uruguay's new foreign policy, however, was Sanguinetti's desire for regional integration in the Río de la Plata basin. Sanguinetti's efforts at promoting regional integration, built on the protocols signed by the military government during the 1970s, were facilitated in the late 1980s by the demise of military dictatorships in Argentina, Bolivia, Brazil, Chile, Peru, and Paraguay. Sanguinetti was especially eager to establish a closer economic relationship with Argentina, Brazil, and Paraguay. The presidents of Argentina, Brazil, and Uruguay met in 1985 to advance their

integration process, which resulted in the creation of MERCOSUR, a regional economic association that was eventually joined by Paraguay when the four nations signed the Treaty of Asunción in 1991.

MICHAEL R. HALL

See also Allende Gossens, Salvador; Amnesty International; Argentina; Authoritarianism; Bolivia; Brazil; Bureaucratic Authoritarianism; Cardoso, Fernando Henrique; Central Intelligence Agency; Chile; Import Substitution Industrialization; Itaipú; Dam; Kubitschek, Juscelino; Menem, Carlos; North American Free Trade Agreement (NAFTA); Paraguay; Perón, Juan Domingo; Pinochet Ugarte, Augusto; Southern Cone (Latin America): History and Economic Development; Southern Cone Common Market (MERCOSUR); Stroessner, Alfredo; Uruguay; Vargas, Getúlio

References and Further Reading

Armony, Ariel C. *Argentina, the United States, and the Anti-Communist Crusade in Central America, 1977–1984.* Athens, OH: Ohio University Center for International Studies, 1997.

Gallo, Klaus. *Great Britain and Argentina: From Invasion to Recognition, 1806–26.* New York, NY: Palgrave Macmillan, 2002.

Hollerman, Leon. *Japan's Economic Strategy in Brazil: Challenge for the United States.* Lanham, MD: Lexington Books, 1988.

Leuchars, Chris. *To the Bitter End: Paraguay and the War of the Triple Alliance.* Westport, CT: Greenwood Press, 2002.

Mares, David R. and Francisco Rojas Aravena. *United States and Chile: Coming in from the Cold.* New York, NY: Routledge, 2001.

Morris, Michael A. *Great Power Relations in Argentina, Chile, and Antarctic.* Boston, MA: St. Martin's Press, 1990.

Norden, Deborah L. and Roberto Russell. *The United States and Argentina: Changing Relations in a Changing World.* New York, NY: Routledge, 2002.

Petras, James F. *The United States and Chile: Imperialism and the Overthrow of the Allende Government.* New York, NY: Monthly Review Press, 1975.

Sater, William F. *Chile and the United States: Empires in Conflict.* Athens: University of Georgia Press, 1990.

Selcher, Wayne S. *The Afro-Asian Dimension of Brazilian Foreign Policy, 1956–1972.* Gainesville, FL: University Press of Florida, 1974.

Sigmund, Paul E. *The United States and Democracy in Chile.* Baltimore, MD: Johns Hopkins University Press, 1993.

Tulchin, Joseph S. *Argentina and the United States: A Conflicted Relationship.* New York, NY: Macmillan Publishing Company, 1990.

Weis, W. Michael. *Cold Warriors & Coups D'Etat: Brazilian-American Relations, 1945–1964.* Albuquerque, NM: University of New Mexico Press, 1993.

Weyland, Kurt. *The Politics of Market Reform in Fragile Democracies: Argentina, Brazil, Peru, and Venezuela.* Princeton, NJ: Princeton University Press, 2004.

Whitagke, Arthur Preston. *The United States and the Southern Cone: Argentina, Chile, and Uruguay.* Cambridge, MA: Harvard University Press, 1977.

SOVIET BLOC

The Soviet Bloc was an affiliation of Eastern and Central European nations, led by the Union of Soviet Socialist Republics (USSR) that emerged from the destruction and chaos of World War II. The core nations included the Soviet Union, Poland, East Germany, Czechoslovakia, Hungary, Bulgaria, Romania, and, for nearly fifteen years, Albania.

Following the end of WWII, the Soviet Red Army found itself in a dominant position in most of Eastern and Central Europe with the exceptions of Yugoslavia and Albania. The Soviets aimed to transform East-Central Europe into a buffer zone that would impede any future aggression from Western Europe. In addition, significant ideological differences worsened relations between the Western nations (Western Europe and the United States) and the emerging Soviet Bloc.

Following the partition of Germany into military zones of occupation by the Allies, which was ratified at the Yalta and Potsdam Conferences in 1945, the Soviet Union pursued a policy of political intervention that began with the formation of East Germany in 1948. Encouraged by the power vacuum created by the defeat of Nazi Germany, Soviet forces moved into much of East-Central Europe. The leaders of Romania, for example, had expected the Western Allies to fill the void in Eastern Europe after WWII and did not anticipate the arrival of the Red Army. The Soviets helped to transform East-Central Europe into a series of pro-Soviet regimes that would take their cues from Moscow.

Outside this immediate core of the Soviet Bloc were two ideologically allied states—Yugoslavia and Albania. In Albania, under the leadership of Enver Hoxha, a highly repressive Stalinist regime was established and an initially close relationship with the Soviet Bloc was reversed in favor of increased isolationism and a tacit alliance with China by 1960. Marshall Tito of Yugoslavia had initially expected Yugoslavia to be directly integrated into a greater Soviet Union and yet, because he had come to power without Soviet aid, Tito turned Yugoslavia into the only neutral and independent Communist state in Eastern Europe that remained outside of the orbit of the Soviet Bloc. The core Soviet Bloc survived these peripheral events, and the member states cemented their relations economically and politically through the formation of Comecon (Council for Mutual Economic Assistance) in 1949 and the Warsaw Pact in 1955.

The Soviet Bloc found itself the main rival of an alliance of nations led by the United States. During a period of hostile relations referred to as the Cold War, the US-led Western Allies and the Soviet Bloc vied for power in post-war Europe and came close to war on a number of occasions such as with the crisis caused by the Soviet blockade of Berlin in 1948 to 1949. This act resulted in the Berlin airlift that prompted the USSR to back down from a direct confrontation with the Western Allies. The USSR installed a socialist post-war government in neighboring Austria, but Austria evolved (with covert US assistance) into an officially neutral state outside the Soviet Bloc.

The US and its allies formed a defence pact in 1949 called the North Atlantic Treaty Organization (NATO). President Truman's Marshall Plan (initiated between 1949 and 1951) helped to rebuild and revitalize Western Europe in order to maintain a prodigious front against the Soviet Bloc. The US remained the economic and industrial superpower and initially was the sole nation with the atomic bomb, until the Soviets also developed nuclear weapons in 1949. This situation developed into a nuclear arms race between the two superpowers of the United States and USSR that resulted in a military standoff, as both sides feared mutual nuclear annihilation. This also kept the two sides divided along what came to be referred to as the Iron Curtain, which separated the Soviet Bloc states from Western Europe.

The nations of the Soviet Bloc did not always exist in a harmonious and unified manner and periods of internal unrest often required Soviet Bloc military intervention (or threats) in order to maintain governments favorable to Moscow. The 1956 Hungarian Revolution was a direct challenge to the Soviet Bloc and in particular its ideology of totalitarianism. The Soviet army moved against the Hungarian uprising and forcibly brought Hungary back into the Soviet Bloc. This challenge to Soviet Bloc unity was repeated with the Prague Spring of 1968. Most of the countries of the Warsaw Pact participated in an invasion of Czechoslovakia in order to insure that the Soviet Bloc would remain intact. The USSR justified its intervention with a policy that came to be known as the Brezhnev Doctrine, following a speech by Leonid Brezhnev that specified that any nations that sought to reverse the "socialist" ideology of communist states would become a concern for all communist states (and thus be subject to military intervention).

The intervention by the Soviet Bloc was not universally praised even by its own member states. The most pronounced opposition to this incursion was Romanian President Nicolai Ceausesu who refused to support the invasion of Czechoslovakia, but stopped short of attempting to leave the Soviet Bloc.

Romania did in fact pursue a semi-independent course that included renewing relations with Albania and China even though both states were no longer amicable towards the Soviet Bloc as a whole. Despite his defiance, Ceausescu's brutally repressive policies appear to have placated Soviet leaders.

Another serious challenge to the unity of the Soviet Bloc came in the early 1980s, when Poland saw the ascension of the Solidarity Movement led by Lech Walesa. The Solidarity Movement agitated against the Soviet-backed Polish puppet regime, but was quelled in 1980 by the invocation of martial law and fears by the Polish government that the build-up of Soviet Bloc troops, along the Polish border, signified a possible military intervention. By contrast, Bulgaria and East Germany maintained stable pro-Soviet regimes and remained unwavering members of the Soviet Bloc.

The Soviet Bloc began to disintegrate in 1989 following the reforms of Mikhail Gorbachev in the USSR. With the USSR transforming itself from a totalitarian nation to a more democratic one, the Soviet Bloc states of East-Central Europe instituted rapid reforms and began to move away from communism. Many of the Soviet Bloc nations have since joined the West through such organizations as the European Union and even NATO.

ALI AHMED

References and Further Reading

Bialer, Seweryn. *The Soviet Paradox: External Expansion, Internal Decline*. New York: Knopf, 1986.

Holmes, Leslie. *Politics in the Communist World*. Oxford: Clarendon Press, 1986.

Janos, Andrew C. *East Central Europe in the Modern World: the Politics of the Borderlands from Pre to Postcommunism*. Stanford, CA: Stanford University Press, 2000.

Laird, Robbin F. (ed.). *Soviet Foreign Policy*. Montpelier, VT: Capital City Press for Academy of Political Science, 1987.

Mitrovich, Gregory. *Undermining the Kremlin: America's Strategy to Subvert the Soviet Bloc, 1947-1956*. Ithaca, NY: Cornell University Press, 2000.

Riasanovsky, Nicolas V. *A History of Russia*. Oxford: Oxford University Press, 6th edition, 1999.

SRI LANKA

Sri Lanka is a relatively small developing nation in South Asia with a land area of 65,610 square kilometers. Sri Lanka is located between latitudes 5°55′–9°51′ N and longitudes 79°41′–81°53′ E, 880 kilometers north of equator, in the Indian ocean to the south of India but separated from the Indian subcontinent by a strip of sea which, at its narrowest, is

about 40 kilometers. Sri Lanka possesses a pleasant tropical climate with average temperature of 25–30°C in the low lands. The temperature goes down with rising altitude. The highest point is Mt. Pidurutalagala (2,524 meters).

Sri Lanka's 19 million (2000) population is diverse both in ethnicity (Sinhalese 74%, Tamils 18.1%, and Moors 7.5%) and religion (Buddhists 69.3%, Hindus 15.5%, Christians 7.6%, and Muslims 7.5%). Sri Lanka is the home of Theravada Buddhism and her Pali chronicles, the Dipavamsa (Chronicle of the Island) and Mahavamsa (The Great Chronicle) composed in the fourth and fifth centuries CE, the only historical records that prevail in South Asia, give extensive descriptions of the history of Buddhism and its expansion and success in the island and record a history which traces the first Sinhala inhabitants in the island in the fifth century BCE and mentions the first formal introduction of Buddhism to Sri Lanka with the auspicious of the Indian Emperor Asoka in the third century BCE.

Sri Lanka has a complex colonial history extending over four hundred years. The Portuguese colonized some coastal areas from 1505; then the Dutch succeeded in controlling those areas from the mid-seventeenth century and finally, the British ruled the entire country from 1815 until 1948 when Sri Lanka became an independent nation. With the introduction of a new constitution in 1972, the name of the country changed from Ceylon to Sri Lanka.

Natural resources of Sri Lanka are limestone, graphite, mineral sands, gems, phosphates, clay, and hydropower. Arable lands are 14%. Current environmental issues are deforestation, soil erosion, endangered wildlife due to urbanization and increased pollution and threats to freshwater due to industrial waste and sewage runoff. With a strategic location in the Indian Ocean, Sri Lanka has the potential to become an industrialized nation. In 1978, Sri Lanka implemented an "open market" economic policy, which had significant impact in changing the shape of the economy. Though plantation crops were 93% of exports in 1970, they decreased to 20% in 1996; in that year, textiles and garments accounted for 63% of exports. Thus, Sri Lanka's most dynamic industries are food processing, textiles and apparel, food and beverages, telecommunications, and insurance and banking.

While gross domestic product (GDP) grew at an annual rate of 5.5% in the early 1990s due to drought and deteriorating security condition, it declined to 3.8% in 1996. Economy comprises of agriculture 21%, industries 19%, and services 60% (1998). Population below poverty line is 22% (1997). Unemployment rate is 9.5% (1998). As a developing nation, Sri Lanka's per capita GDP is $856 US (2000). Five to six percent of GDP goes for military expenses. The economic conditions in Sri Lanka deteriorated rapidly during the last five decades after Independence on February 4, 1948. Before the current ethnic conflict, for many years, Sri Lanka was regarded as a model for development. In 1977, the United Nations (UN) development report scored Sri Lanka as a seven out of ten.

During the last two decades, in particular, Sri Lanka has been struggling hard to survive by facing one of the most feared separatist movements in history costing both human lives and material resources which can be efficiently used for Sri Lanka's economic development. The ethnic conflict between Sinhalese and Tamils has drawn the country backward economically and damaged all aspects of human life threatening to destroy civil society, social structures and harmony on local, regional, and national scales. The most serious hurdle for Sri Lanka's development today is the worst natural disaster, the Tsunami Tidal Waves of December 26, 2004. The tsunami killed nearly forty thousand people, displacing another two hundred thousand and seriously damaging over five hundred miles in coastal areas. This brutal destruction of the livelihood of an already impoverished nation will slow down the development in the years to come.

However, Sri Lanka has some important human resources that are not adequately used for effective development. Literacy rate is 90.2% (male 93.4% and female 87.2%), one of the highest in Asia, second only to Japan, Korea, and Singapore; school enrollment rate is 90% for elementary, 70% for secondary. Sri Lanka has a nationalized higher education system with more than seven national universities where education is free of charge. Three languages—Sinhala, Tamil, and English—are widely used in daily transactions in official business and language of instruction in schools and universities are Sinhala and Tamil. Ten percent of the population speaks English competently. Sri Lanka's life expectancy is seventy-two years; infant mortality rate is 16.5 persons per 1,000. As a social welfare state, Sri Lanka provides basic healthcare for 93% of the population.

In terms of female participation in politics, economic development, and social welfare, Sri Lanka has made a remarkable progress. Women have been active in politics and made a mark in world politics. In July 1960, Mrs. Sirimavo R.D. Bandaranaike (1916–2000), widow of Mr. S.W.R.D. Bandaranaike (1899–1959), became the Prime Minister of Sri Lanka becoming the first female to hold such as post. In terms of rural development, Sarvodaya Sramadana Movement (f. 1958) of A.T. Ariyaratne, inspired by Buddhist values, has made a remarkable success. Also the Gam Udava (Village Awakening) Project of

President R. Premadasa (d. 1993) has made a significant contribution for village development.

Important changes that occurred in Sri Lankan politics after 1956 had serious implications on the development of the country. The "Sinhala only" language policy of Mr. Bandaranaike's government in the late 1950s devastated national harmony, alienating moderate Tamils from the political process by encouraging them to seek alternative solutions to their problems. Party politics with limited vision abused national sensibilities of Sinhalese, Tamils, and Muslims, feeding into a great sense of insecurity, unrest, and distrust towards each other. The decline of the economy had severe impact in intensifying growing distrust among ethnic groups leading to violent and militant armed groups. Growing unrest among the youth expressed by Janatha Vimukti Peramuna in 1971 and later by Tamil youth groups demonstrate that economic conditions are roots of the current civil strife in Sri Lanka. Complicating the unforeseen consequences of ethnic unrest, Sri Lanka has failed to foster harmony among various ethnic and religious minorities who consider Sri Lanka as their home.

In achieving Sri Lanka's economic objectives for development, Sri Lanka's burden is seeking resources and strategies in building trust and respect towards each ethnic and religious minorities who live in the island and encouraging them to share country's resources on an egalitarian basis.

MAHINDA DEEGALLE

See also Central Asia: History and Economic Development; Central Asia: International Relations

References and Further Reading

De Silva, Chandra R. *Sri Lanka: A History*. New Delhi: Vikas Publishing House, 1992.
De Silva, K. M. *Religion, Nationalism and the State in Modern Sri Lanka*. Tampa, FL: University of South Florida, 1986.
Manor, James (ed.). *Sri Lanka in Change and Crisis*. New York: St. Martin's Press, 1984.
Roberts, Michael. *Sri Lanka: Collective Identities Revisited*. 2 vols. Colombo: Marga Institute, 1997.
Spencer, Jonathan. *Sri Lanka: History and the Roots of Conflict*. London: Routledge, 1990.
Tambiah, Stanley J. *Sri Lanka: Ethnic Fratricide and the Dismantling of Democracy*. Chicago: University of Chicago Press, 1986.
Wickremeratne, Ananda. *Buddhism and Ethnicity in Sri Lanka: A Historical Analysis*. New Delhi: Vikas Publishing House, 1995.

ST. CHRISTOPHER AND NEVIS

The islands of St. Christopher (also known as St. Kitts) and Nevis, which are part of the Leeward Islands, are geographically mountainous and volcanic in origin. They are separated by a narrow strait 3.2 kilometers wide. St. Kitts, the larger of the two islands, is 168 square kilometers. It is oval-shaped with a small peninsula at its southeastern end. Mountains extend through the central part of the island. Mount Liamuiga, a dormant volcano with an elevation of 1,156 meters, is the highest point on the island. Nevis, which lies to the south of St. Kitts, is cone-shaped, ten kilometers wide and thirteen kilometers long, and has a total land area of ninety-three square kilometers. Nevis Peak is the highest point on the island at 965 meters. Nevis's soil is less fertile than St. Kitts's soil and has experienced much worse erosion. St. Kitts and Nevis was a founding member of the Organization of Eastern Caribbean States (OECS) in 1983. The Eastern Caribbean Central Bank is located in St. Kitts.

St. Kitts was the first English colony in the Caribbean. Although Christopher Columbus discovered the island in 1493, it was not settled by Europeans until 1623, when a party of Englishmen established a colony at Sandy Bay. In 1624, the French established a colony on the other side of the island. The French founded Basseterre, the capital, in 1627. Nevis was colonized in 1628 by a group of English colonists from St. Kitts. In 1713, the Treaty of Utrecht granted the entire island to the British. After furtive attempts at tobacco cultivation, sugar was introduced on both islands during the mid-seventeenth century. Slaves were imported from Africa to expand the sugar industry. The majority of the forty-five thousand people in St. Kitts and Nevis are descended from Africans.

Soil erosion caused by extensive sugar cultivation on Nevis convinced the British to replace large-scale sugar cultivation with small-scale subsistence agriculture on that island. During the colonial period, to simplify administrative tasks, the British attached the somewhat distant Anguilla to the colony of St. Kitts and Nevis. In 1958, the three-island group of St. Kitts-Nevis-Anguilla entered the West Indies Federation, which was dismantled in 1962. In 1967, the British government, which continued to control foreign affairs and national defense, granted St. Kitts-Nevis-Anguilla local autonomy. Anguilla immediately opted out of the association. St. Kitts and Nevis became independent on September 19, 1983. St. Kitts and Nevis supported the October 1983 US intervention in Grenada and dispatched a small force of police to participate in the Caribbean Peace Force on the island.

St. Lucia is a parliamentary democracy based on the British model. The head of state, Queen Elizabeth II, is represented by a governor–Cuthbert Sebastian–who is appointed by the British government. Since the governor's power is primarily advisory and

ceremonial, real power is vested in the prime minister, who is usually the leader of the majority party in the National Assembly. The National Assembly is composed of eleven elected members (representatives) and three appointed members (senators). Two of the senators are appointed by the governor general on the advice of the prime minister. The other is named on the advice of the leader of the opposition.

The uniqueness of the 1983 Constitution derives from the provisions for the autonomy of the island of Nevis and the establishment of the separate Nevis Island Assembly. The island of Nevis elects representatives both to the National Assembly and to its own Nevis Island Assembly, a body of five elected and three appointed representatives. The Nevis Island Assembly may amend or revoke legislation passed by the National Assembly. At the time of independence, Nevis was also granted the right of secession. Secession from the nation requires a two-thirds vote in the Nevis Island Assembly and the approval of two-thirds of the voters in an island-wide referendum. The Nevis Island Assembly is led by a premier, a position analogous to a prime minister.

The Labour Party, organized by Robert Bradshaw in 1932, dominated the political system until 1979. By 1979, political opposition to the Labour Party had coalesced into two party groupings, the People's Action Movement (PAM) on St. Kitts, which supported economic diversification away from sugar and toward tourism, increased domestic food production, and increased autonomy for Nevis, and the Nevis Reformation Party (NRP) on Nevis. PAM and NRP, who had formed a coalition led by Kennedy Simmonds (b. 1936), came to power in 1979. The PAM/NRP coalition cleared the way for the independence of St. Kitts and Nevis as a two-island federation. The Labour Party, led by Denzil Douglas (b. 1953), returned to power in 1995.

In the mid-1980s, the government envisioned the economic future of St. Kitts and Nevis as dependent on tourism, light manufacturing, and a scaled-down sugar industry. To create a workforce to manage the country's tourist industry, the government invested heavily in the economic and social infrastructure of the nation. The result was an extensive road network, the Golden Rock International Airport that allowed for direct flights from the United States and Canada, and a deep-water port in Basseterre that allowed for an increase in the number of cruise ship calls. The government also encouraged labor-intensive export light manufacturing. Although the potential seemed great, the economy did not keep pace with the rapidly expanding population. As a result, nearly 20% of the population has left in search of employment. Remittances to family members at home became a

substantial portion of the national economy. In addition, natural disasters, such as hurricanes, and man-made disasters, such as the events of September 11, 2001, have impeded the growth of the tourist industry.

MICHAEL R. HALL

See also Caribbean: History and Economic Development; Caribbean: International Relations; Organization of Eastern Caribbean States (OECS)

References and Further Reading

Grossman, Lawrence S. *The Political Ecology of Bananas: Contract Farming, Peasants, and Agrarian Change in the Eastern Caribbean*. Chapel Hill, NC: University of North Carolina Press, 1998.

Ferguson, James. *Eastern Caribbean in Focus: A Guide to the People, Politics, and Culture*. Northampton, MA: Interlink Publishing, 1997.

Hackett, Kieran J. *Of Nevis Lighters and Lightermen: The Sailing Lighters of St. Kitts and Nevis*. Cranston, RI: Writers Collective, 2003.

Richardson, Bonham. *Caribbean Migrants: Environment and Human Survival on St. Kitts and Nevis*. Knoxville, TN: University of Tennessee Press, 1983.

ST. HELENA

St. Helena is one of the United Kingdom's few remaining overseas territories and one of the world's most isolated island settlements. A lone mid-ocean island, volcanic in origin, and a mere 122 square kilometers in size, St. Helena is situated at Latitude 15°55′ S and Longitude 5°45′ W, 1,930 kilometers west of Angola, its nearest mainland. The nearest land is Ascension Island, 1,125 kilometers away. St. Helena is surrounded by steep cliffs and has a central ridge which reaches 818 meters above sea level. The only inland waters are small streams which are fed by springs in the central hills. Two-thirds of the island is now barren. The vegetation below four hundred meters is very scanty and consists largely of cactus. Above that level, the island consists mostly of pasture, introduced pine forests, and now disused plantations of New Zealand flax. There is little arable land.

St. Helena was uninhabited when it was discovered by the Portuguese in about 1502 and was only settled and fortified by the London East India Company in 1659. The Company's proprietorship of the island continued until April 1834, when St. Helena was vested in the Crown by the Government of India Act 1833. The island has been a British territory ever since. St. Helena's present day community, which is wholly British in character, has its origins in the East India Company's seventeenth century settlement, which consisted of English settlers and an increasing number of slaves, from West Africa initially, but

predominantly from the Indian subcontinent and from Madagascar. By 1718, the island's population amounted to 542 whites (including a garrison of 128) and 411 slaves. The population continued to increase gradually, although the importation of slaves was made illegal in 1792, and slavery was finally abolished in 1832. Immigration to St. Helena had largely come to an end by the 1830s, a period followed by the gradual and by now complete integration of the island's various ethnic groups. The island's population peaked at 5,838 in 1871, but economic depression led to the emigration of more than two thousand St. Helenians to the Cape and to Natal. By 1901, St. Helena's population had sunk to 3,342. At the last census in 1998, St. Helena's resident population numbered 4,916 (including expatriates), of whom over eight hundred lived in the capital Jamestown. In 2004, the population was estimated to have declined to around four thousand, emigration having been boosted by the islander's re-acquisition of the right to full UK passports, as provided for by the British Overseas Territories Act 2002 (the automatic right of entry into the United Kingdom had been lost by St. Helenians under the Commonwealth Immigrants Act 1962).

Under the proprietorship of the East India Company, St. Helena was administered by a governor and council appointed by the Company, a system continued after St. Helena came under the control of Her Majesty's (HM) Government. The first non-official members were introduced onto the council in 1878, and a separate advisory council was formed in 1939. This new council allowed for a small element of popular representation, a measure which was enlarged by reforms in 1956. In 1963, the island's first general elections to a newly constituted advisory council took place. This council was reconstituted as a legislative council in 1966. The island's 1988 constitution enhanced the responsibilities of the legislative council and today both the legislative and the executive council have a majority of non-official members. Island politics is marked by personalities, rather than parties; and there are no unions. Authority over the island is ultimately vested in Her Majesty, while the island's executive authority rests with the governor in council, the latter composed of ex-officio members as well as the elected heads of legislative council committees. A new constitution introducing a ministerial system of government is currently being considered. The governor retains a number of reserved powers, primarily with respect to defence, external affairs, internal security, justice, finance, and shipping. There have certainly never been any moves towards independence from the United Kingdom and if anything, there has been a desire for a closer integration with "the mother country."

St. Helena had originally been intended to serve as a maritime base, rather than as a colony, and its economy was never geared towards self-sufficiency. During the proprietorship of the East India Company and during most of the nineteenth century, the island's economy revolved around the provision of supplies for shipping and for the local garrison. In 1802, a total of 169 ships called at the island, and this figure had risen to 1,044 ships in 1860. Partly due to the advent of steam, the number of visiting ships began to decline in the decade prior to the opening of the Suez Canal (850 ships in 1865), which lead to the eventual collapse in shipping by 1910, when a mere fifty-one ships called at the island. This also resulted in the collapse of the island's economy. The establishment of a flax industry, started in earnest in 1907, went a considerable way towards easing unemployment and increasing local revenue in the early half of the twentieth century. But this new industry in turn declined and its last mills closed during the 1960s. Since then the island has had virtually no industry of its own, and is nowadays largely dependent on aid from the United Kingdom. In 2004/2005 this amounted to a grant-in-aid of £5.66 million out of an expenditure of £18.56 million. In addition the island received a shipping subsidy (£2.45 million), development aid (£1.9 million), and technical cooperation (£2.53 million), accounting for a total of £12.56 million in aid. The island's gross domestic product (GDP) for 2002–2003 amounted to £3,076 per capita. In the same period, exports of goods and services amounted to a 7% of GDP, while imports amounted to 76% of GDP. The island's only major export is fish, although a promising new industry is coffee, which has been exported in small quantities since 1989. While the majority of St. Helena's labour force (62% in 1998) are employed by government and its agencies on the island itself, over 1,200 islanders work off-shore, primarily on Ascension Island and the Falkland Islands. 12.7% of the labour force were unemployed in 2001–2002. Educational provision is well developed on St. Helena, which in 1998 had a literacy rate of 98% (population twelve years and older), although there is no local provision for higher/further education. For islanders with overseas qualifications, local wages (especially when compared to wages paid to expatriates) provide little incentive to return to the island. The average life expectancy is seventy-five years, with infant mortality (under five years) a low 0.3%.

Improvements in transport links are now seen as they key to improvements in St. Helena's economy, which suffers, as in the sixteenth century, from the fact that the island's only transport link with the outside world is by ship. The island's London registered RMS

St. Helena, a purpose built cargo/passenger vessel of 6,767 tonnes, travels at regular intervals between St. Helena and South Africa (via Namibia). There has never been an airstrip on the island, but plans to construct one have been under serious consideration since the 1990s. It is hoped that an airport will solve some of the difficulties of access which have prevented the development of a larger scale tourist industry, in turn providing local employment and reducing emigration, while providing a more efficient link with the island for those St. Helenians who do work off-shore.

ALEXANDER HUGO SCHULENBURG

References and Further Reading

Ashmole, Philip and Myrtle Ashmole. *The Natural History of St. Helena and Ascension Island*, Oswestry: Anthony Nelson, 2000.

Cross, Tony. *St. Helena, Including Ascension Island and Tristan da Cunha*, London: David & Charles, 1980.

Foreign and Commonwealth Office. *Partnership for Progress and Prosperity: Britain and the Overseas Territories*, London: Foreign and Commonwealth Office, 1999.

Gosse, Philip. *St. Helena, 1502–1938*, Oswestry: Anthony Nelson, 1990; orig. 1938.

St. Helena: The Official Government Website, http://www.sainthelena.gov.sh (2004 -).

St. Helena Government, *The 1998 Population Census of St. Helena*, St. Helena: St. Helena Government, 1999.

Steiner, Sue. *St. Helena, Ascension Island, Tristan da Cunha*. Chalfont St Peter: Bradt Travel Guides, 2002.

United Nations Development Programme, *Human Development Report for St. Helena 1999*. New York: United Nations Development Programme, 1999.

ST. LUCIA

St. Lucia, which is located roughly in the center of the Windward Islands, lies between Martinique to the north and St. Vincent and the Grenadines to the south. The pear-shaped island is 616 square kilometers and is a typical Windward Island formation of volcanic rock. The island is dominated by high peaks and rain forests in the interior and has a 158 kilometer coastline of sandy beaches. The highest point on the island is Mount Gimie, which is 950 meters above sea level. St. Lucia is also known for its natural deep-water harbors. Castries, the capital city where about one-third of the population lives, is located on the northwest coast and has an excellent natural harbor. The island is named in honor of St. Lucy, the patron saint of blindness and one of the major saints in the Catholic canon. St. Lucia was a founding member of the Organization of Eastern Caribbean States (OECS) in 1983. St. Lucia is also the headquarters of the Eastern Caribbean Telecommunications Authority.

The Carib Indians inhabited the island when it was first sighted by Spanish explorers during the early sixteenth century. The Indians resisted British, French, and Dutch attempts at colonization until the seventeenth century. The French, however, were able to establish the first permanent settlement on the island in 1660. Nevertheless, during the seventeenth and eighteenth centuries, the British and French fought over control of St. Lucia. Since the island's deep-water harbors afforded protection for naval vessels, control of St. Lucia changed hands fourteen different times during the eighteenth and early nineteenth centuries.

The British established absolute control in 1814 after they defeated Napoleon's armies in Europe. The majority of the island's inhabitants, however, were pro-French and the British government experienced decades of internal conflict before the people of St. Lucia accepted British rule. Although English is the official language and spoken by 80% of the population, the cultural footprint of the early French presence on the island is still evident. Many of St. Lucia's 160,000 people, especially those in rural areas, speak a French patois. In addition, over 90% of the people are Roman Catholics. In 1958, St. Lucia joined the West Indies Federation, which was dissolved in 1962 after Jamaica and Trinidad and Tobago withdrew from the association. In 1967, the British government, which continued to control foreign affairs and national defense, granted St. Lucia local autonomy. St. Lucia became independent on February 22, 1979. In 1983, St. Lucia sent members of its Special Services Unit into active duty in the 1983 US-sponsored invasion of Grenada.

St. Lucia is a parliamentary democracy based on the British model. The head of state, Queen Elizabeth II, is represented by a governor—Pearlette Louisy since 1997—who is appointed by the British government. Since the governor's power is primarily advisory and ceremonial, real power is vested in the prime minister, who is usually the leader of the majority party in the House of Assembly. The bicameral legislature in St. Lucia consists of the House of Assembly, whose seventeen members are elected for five year terms, and a Senate, whose eleven members are appointed by the governor after consultation with political, economic, and religious figures in society. Politics has been dominated by competition between the United Workers Party (UWP) and the St. Lucia Labor Party (SLP). John Compton, the former leader of the UWP, was premier of St. Lucia from 1964 until independence in 1979, when he became prime minister. Shortly after independence, the SLP took control of the House of Assembly. Compton returned to power in 1982 and remained the prime minister until his resignation in 1996. The SLP won an overwhelming majority in the House of Assembly in 1997 and

Kenny Anthony became the prime minister. Anthony and the SLP won subsequent elections in 2001.

During the colonial period, St. Lucia's economy was dominated by sugar production. The importation of African slaves stimulated sugar production and transformed the ethnic composition of the island. Over 90% of St. Lucia's people are descendants of African slaves. During the 1960s, the economy was dramatically transformed from a sugar-based economy to one dedicated to banana production. This transformation initially improved the economic situation of small farmers because banana crops could be produced on small plots. During the 1990s, however, as the Europeans implemented more restrictive trade policies, St. Lucia, faced with declining revenues from banana exports, began to implement a long-term economic development program based on a diversified economy. Particularly ominous for the people of St. Lucia was the European Union's plan to end preferential access to its markets by St. Lucia's bananas by 2006.

Although agriculture is still an important component of the national economy, St. Lucia has made significant gains in developing the manufacturing sector and attracting a greater portion of the West Indies' tourist trade. As of 2004, St. Lucia's manufacturing sector is the most diverse in the Eastern Caribbean. Small-scale manufacturing has benefitted from improvements in roads, sewage, communications, schools, and port facilities. The largest economic transformation has been the construction of a Caribbean Development Bank-funded petroleum storage and transshipment center. Despite a series of devastating hurricanes, the tourist industry continued to grow until the terrorist attacks of September 11, 2001.

MICHAEL R. HALL

See also Caribbean Development Bank; Caribbean: History and Economic Development; Caribbean: International Relations; Grenada; Organization of Eastern Caribbean States (OECS)

References and Further Reading

Brownlie, Alison. *The Heart of the Caribbean: People of St. Lucia.* London: Hodder & Stoughton, 2001.

Grossman, Lawrence S. *The Political Ecology of Bananas: Contract Farming, Peasants, and Agrarian Change in the Eastern Caribbean.* Chapel Hill, NC: University of North Carolina Press, 1998.

Ferguson, James. *Eastern Caribbean in Focus: A Guide to the People, Politics, and Culture.* Northampton, MA: Interlink Publishing, 1997.

Showker, Kay. *Caribbean Ports of Call: Eastern and Southern Regions.* Guilford, CT: Globe Pequot, 2004.

Taylor, Jeremy, ed. *The Caribbean Handbook.* St. John's, Antigua and Barbuda: FT Caribbean, 1986.

ST. VINCENT AND THE GRENADINES

St. Vincent and the Grenadines, a federation of thirty-two islands in the Windward Islands, lies between St. Lucia to the north and Grenada to the south. St. Vincent occupies 344 square kilometers of the nation's total territory. The Grenadines, a collection of islands between St. Vincent and Grenada, comprise the remaining forty-five square kilometers of the nation's territory. The most notable islands in the Grenadines are Bequia, Baliceaux, Mustique, Petit Mustique, Savan, Petit Canouan, Canouan, Mayreau, Tobago Cays, Union Island, and Petit St. Vincent. Kingston, the capital, is located on St. Vincent. St. Vincent and the Grenadines were founding members of the Organization of Eastern Caribbean States (OECS) in 1983.

The Carib Indians on St. Vincent resisted European conquest until the eighteenth century. Runaway African slaves from St. Lucia and Grenada frequently sought refuge on St. Vincent. The Carib Indians not only gave the runaway slaves shelter, they also intermarried with the blacks, which created a large population of zambos known in St. Vincent as the Black Caribs. Nevertheless, by the 1720s, the French had established settlements on St. Vincent and were using slave labor to grow sugar, cotton, and tobacco. After France lost the French and Indian War in 1763, St. Vincent was ceded to the British. Although St. Vincent was returned to France in 1779, the British resumed authority in 1783.

Whereas the French had been conciliatory towards the Black Caribs, the British were intent on crushing dissent. Following a Black Carib revolt in 1796, the British deported five thousand Black Caribs to Roatan Island off the coast of Honduras. Nevertheless, the French colonial footprint is still evident. Although the country's official language is English and most of the people speak English, a French patois is still spoken in the rural areas of some of the Grenadine Islands. The British abolished slavery in St. Vincent in 1834. To address the resulting labor shortage, the British encouraged the immigration of Portuguese and East Indians during the nineteenth century. In an attempt to establish a unified administration in the eastern Caribbean, in 1958, the British placed St. Vincent and the Grenadines in the West Indies Federation, which was dissolved in 1962 after Jamaica and Trinidad and Tobago withdrew from the association. In 1967, the British government, which continued to control foreign affairs and national defense, granted St. Vincent and the Grenadines local autonomy. St. Vincent and the Grenadines became independent on October 27, 1979, the last of the Windward Islands to gain independence from the United Kingdom.

St. Vincent and the Grenadines is a parliamentary democracy based on the British model. The head of state, Queen Elizabeth II, is represented by a governor—Fredrick Ballantyne—who is appointed by the British government. Since the governor's power is primarily advisory and ceremonial, real power is vested in the prime minister, who is usually the leader of the majority party in the House of Assembly. The legislature in St. Vincent and the Grenadines consists of fifteen elected representatives and six appointed senators. The six senators are appointed by the governor, four on the advice of the prime minister, and two on the advice of the leader of the opposition. The parliamentary term in office is five years, although the prime minister can call elections earlier.

Politics has been dominated by competition between the St. Vincent Labour Party (SVLP) and the New Democratic Party (NDP). SVLP Prime Minister R. Milton Cato led the nation to independence and held power until 1984. In September 1979, militant Rastafarians led by Lennox Charles seized Union Island. Cato requested military assistance from Barbados, which sent detachments of the Barbados Defense Force to capture the insurgents and restore order. NDP Prime Minister James Mitchell held power from 1984 until 2001. In 2001, a revised labor party called the United Labour Party (ULP) took power under Ralph Gonsalves (b. 1945).

St. Vincent's economy is heavily dependent on agriculture. Bananas account for over 50% of the nation's exports. In April 1979, La Soufriere volcano erupted and there was extensive agricultural damage. Hurricanes have also devastated banana plantations. Dependence on a single crop export-led economy has made the nation's economy vulnerable to external factors. Particularly ominous for the people of St. Vincent and the Grenadines is the European Union's plan to end preferential access to its markets by 2006. During the 1980s, therefore, the government encouraged the development of the tourist industry. During the 1990s, tourism replaced banana exports as the chief source of foreign exchange. The Grenadines have become especially popular with yachtsmen. Affordable boat trips within the Grenadines have also increased the number of visitors per year. New cruise ship berths helped to increase the number of tourists to over two hundred thousand annually by 2000. Nevertheless, because of a high birth rate, unemployment, and the negative impact of the events of September 11, 2001, on the tourist industry, thousands of people have emigrated in search of employment.

MICHAEL R. HALL

See also Barbados; Caribbean: History and Economic Development; Caribbean: International Relations; Grenada; Organization of Eastern Caribbean States (OECS); St. Lucia

References and Further Reading

Bobrow, Jill and Dana Jinkins. *St. Vincent and the Grenadines–Bequia, Mustique, Canoouan, Mayreau, Tobago Cays, Palm, Union, PSV: A Plural Country*. New York: W. W. Norton, 1985.

Grossman, Lawrence S. *The Political Ecology of Bananas: Contract Farming, Peasants, and Agrarian Change in the Eastern Caribbean*. Chapel Hill, NC: University of North Carolina Press, 1998.

Ferguson, James. *Eastern Caribbean in Focus: A Guide to the People, Politics, and Culture*. Northampton, MA: Interlink Publishing, 1997.

Sutty, Lesley. *St. Vincent and the Grenadines*. London: MacMillan Caribbean, 2002.

STALIN, JOSEPH

"Joseph Stalin" was the byname of Josef Vissarionovich Dzhugashvili (born December 21 [9 December, old style], 1879, Gori, Georgia, Russia). Born into poverty, Stalin trained to become an Orthodox priest. In 1900, after leaving the priesthood training due to his communist/atheist beliefs, he joined the Russian revolutionar and earned his name, Stalin ("man of steel" in Russian), by supervising and committing violent acts against the Czarist government.

In 1922, with the support of Vladimir Lenin, he became the secretary general of the communist party. By 1924, Stalin with Bukharin's assistance had contaminated most state documents with fraudulent and revisionist information. After Lenin's death, Stalin formed an unofficial "triumvirate" (himself, Zinoviev, and Kamenev) to control the fledgling communist state. Throughout the mid-1920s, he struggled with numerous political rivals but emerged as the Soviet Union's undisputed leader by 1928. He controlled the population through fear, repressing any dissent through systematic purges, which included imprisonment and executions. His harsh regime and cult of personality soon made communism synonymous with totalitarianism.

Stalin's approach to foreign policy was largely influenced by Zinoviev and Kamenev who advocated "one-state socialism." Under this theory, the Soviet Union would serve as a successful global model of socialism, helping to covertly promote and control satellite regimes. Instead of launching outright revolutionary activities, internal workers' movements were promoted with the assistance of Stalin's secret police and KGB global network. This tactic spurred revolutions against capitalism in Latin America, Africa, and Asia.

The 1939 Molotov-Ribbontrop Non-Aggression Pact briefly allied Stalin with Hitler until the 1941 German invasion. Stalin then switched alliances and awkwardly cooperated with the United States and Great Britain until the defeat of Germany and Japan in 1945. After the war, Stalin's determination to control all occupied lands with communist governments created the Cold War struggle.

Considered the father of the Soviet Union, of which he declared himself General Secretary in 1941, Stalin's greatest achievement, other than defeating Nazi Germany, was rapid industrialization and the construction of an elaborate infrastructure. However, Stalin's impact on the Soviet Union was often profoundly negative: disastrous agricultural reforms that resulted in the starvation of millions; highly mechanized five-year plans that created massive shortages and surpluses of goods; and an enormous network of military, paramilitary, police and secret police networks that eventually consumed over half of the country's gross domestic product..

Though Stalin claimed to be a devout communist, he consistently ignored ideology in his operational concerns. He shifted alliances within the party based on the advantage they would give him. While his rivals were consumed with debate and theories, Stalin focused on the practical matters of expanding and accumulating power. Stalin's quest for power fueled his paranoia, which caused numerous disruptions in the Soviet hierarchy. This included the expulsion, forced exile, and eventual assassination of arch-rival Trotsky in 1940, who was writing a book to expose Stalin as a fraud of communism.

Whether in peace or war, civil liberties were few. During Stalin's roughly thirty years of control, 40–50 million Soviets died due to war and political purges in the 1930s and again in the early 1950s.

Though more Russians died in World War II than any other nationality, the country emerged as the world's second strongest power. Stalin exhibited shrewd diplomatic skills in the allied conferences (Tehran, Yalta, and Potsdam) which resulted in substantial territorial concessions in Eastern Europe and North Korea.

Stalin died in Moscow on March 5, 1953.

JOSIAH R. BAKER

See also De-Stalinization (1953–1956); Khrushchev, Nikita; Russia; Soviet Bloc

References and Further Reading

Dolot, Miron. *Execution by Hunger: The Hidden Holocaust.* 1st ed. New York: W.W. Norton, 1985.

Pomper, Philip. *Lenin, Trotsky, and Stalin: The Intelligentsia and Power.* New York: Columbia University Press, c1990.

Trotsky, Leon, translated by John G. Wright. *The Stalin School of Falsification.* New York: Pioneer Publishers, 1937.

Tucker, Robert C. *The Soviet Political Mind; Stalinism and Post-Stalin Change.* Rev. ed.: New York: Norton, 1971.

Von Laue, Theodore Hermann. *Why Lenin? Why Stalin? A Reappraisal of the Russian Revolution, 1900–1930.* Edition: 2d ed. Philadelphia: Lippincott [c1971].

Wolfe, Bertram David. *Three Who Made a Revolution: A Biographical History.* Edition: 1st Stein and Day ed. New York: Stein and Day, 1984, c1964.

STATE-DIRECTED ECONOMY

Mainly characteristic of the socialist Marxist model, a state-directed economy signifies an economy where production—distribution of the products, prices, output, export-import structure and volume, wages, allocation of resources—are determined by the state, an administrative body through its government, commissions, and public bodies. In almost every country there is some government intervention in the economy—voluntarily or involuntarily—through the tax system, tariffs and non tariff barriers to international trade, credit rationing, subsidies, and separate fiscal and economic regimes for state and private companies.

In its purest form, a state directed economy is the opposite of a free market economy. Production is determined through comprehensive countrywide sectoral and synthetic plans, both for the short term (one to five years) and for the long term in the form of general directives forming a kind of "strategy." Thus the supply of each product or at least the significant commodities are planned; however, the statistics upon which the planning is based can be unreliable, since there is a tendency to inflate results for the sake of producing growth at the forecasted rate. The central planners also fix the wages and the prices and thus determine the demand for each product, though this is usually not done via any sort of market analysis. By fixing the price of consumer necessities and all other commodities produced by the state, the standards of living can be determined and maintained for long time if shortages do not occur. But it is difficult to plan accurate with so many variables and unknown data.

While consumption of individuals can be forecasted with a margin of error, the consumption of state enterprises is much more difficult to foresee. For an economy to function smoothly, all companies must meet the planned output, costs, and revenues. If the economy is not closed, the fluctuations of supply and demand and prices on the world market will wreak havoc in the raw material and energy supply of the production.

Shortages occurring in a chain can be alleviated by fixing prices of high-demand commodities at high levels, since there are no markets to serve as alternate suppliers. Rationing is done via regulating the delivery of the commodity in question or imposition of administrative barriers for the purchase of that commodity.

The labor market can also be planned: the state will determine how many specialists the work force needs in various sectors, and thus the composition and education level of the work force is determined in advance, according to the economy's needs. This makes a rigid labor force structure which cannot adapt easily to new plans or circumstances.

Changing demands of the world market require readjusting the qualifications structure, including provisions for retraining adults in different fields to keep the economy competitive. Of course, this planning policy creates shortages in certain professions and produces excess number of graduates from others. On the other hand, the employees benefit when education costs are supported by the state; in market economies, such training puts a heavy burden on the individuals' financial and time budgets.

By fixing wages, the state establishes a job hierarchy which reflects the social cost of producing a certain professional and the social importance of his activity. This isn't much reflected in income level differences due to egalitarian policies. Similar salary levels achieve a equitable income distribution, since the basic needs of most people are the same. The central planner may efficiently use the human resources of the society by practically eliminating unemployment and securing everybody a source of income. Thus the use of resources becomes more efficient on a social scale than it would be under purely market considerations. For increasing productivity, more flexible approaches allow for performance-related wage systems and the functioning of market mechanisms in the nonessential goods markets, keeping fixed prices at least for necessities such as food, housing, and energy.

Most of the state directed economies of the developing world have relied on the Solow model of economic growth, favoring accumulation of physical capital, namely industrialization, and using a high savings ratio necessary for large-scale industrial, social, and transportation infrastructure. These planners generally favored the primary and secondary sector, neglecting the tertiary, and became less competitive entering the actual post-industrial phase. Low levels of consumption led to the neglecting of the domestic markets' demand, while the countries found themselves with superfluous industrial capacities both in mining and processing. In spite of their decade-long efforts these economies couldn't reach their steady state with optimal consumption because of over-investment on one hand and under-consumption on the other.

Another consequence of the fixed price system and non profit orientation of the companies was that even high-performing companies were not allowed to retain their profits and begin the necessary microeconomic investment for increasing productivity and competivity. Profits were redistributed among companies with net losses, regardless of whether the loss occurred because the nature of the company's activity was unprofitable, or because the company was mismanaged. Thus, funds were often regularly given to institutions that did not manage them well, and hence lowered productivity even further. In the early 1990s, privatization of the enterprises seemed to be the only solution for the sake of increasing efficiency, productivity inside the firms and competivity on the markets.

LASZLO KOCSIS

See also Communist Economic Model; Free Market Economy; Marxism; Mixed Economy; Socialist Economic Model

References and Further Reading

Bosworth, B. and Ofer, G. Reforming Planned Economy in an Integrating World Economy. Washington, D.C.: Brookings Institution Press, 1995.

Carr, E. H. and Davies, R. W. *Foundations of a Planned Economy, 1926–1929.* London: Macmillan, 1971-1978, 6 volumes.

Dembinski, P. H. *The Logic of the Planned Economy: The Seeds of Collapse.* Oxford: Clarendon Press, 1991.

Eatwel, J and Murray, H., eds. The New Palgrave: Problems of the Planned Economy. London: Macmillan, 1990.

Kaser, M. C. and E.A. Radice. The Economic History of Eastern Europe: 1919—1975. Oxford: Oxford University Press, 1985, 1986.

Lavique, M. *The Economics of Transition: From Socialist Economy to Market Economy.* Houndmills, UK: Macmillan, 1995.

Xavier, R. *The Hungarian Model: Markets and Planning in a Socialist Economy.* Cambridge University Press, 1989.

STROESSNER, ALFREDO

Alfredo Stroessner, president of Paraguay from 1954–1989, was born to German immigrant parents in Encarnación, Paraguay on November 3, 1912. He entered the Paraguayan military academy in 1929 and fought in the Chaco War from 1932–1935. He was promoted to major and studied in Brazil in 1940 and then given command of a main artillery unit followed by an assignment to army staff headquarters. He defended Paraguay's capital, Asunción, during the 1947 civil war and became the head of the army in

1951. In 1954, he ousted the sitting president and assumed the office himself. He was re-elected seven times between 1954–1989.

Stroessner presided over one of the longest military dictatorships in Latin American history. Other than rhetorical attention, no effective emphasis was given to social or economic development.

The regime managed the country via the force of the military and the network of the historic, conservative party, the Colorado. Military brutality and political repression were justified based on allegations of threats to national security from communist and leftist subversion.

Paraguay has always been among the poorest countries of the world, with vast social divides between rich and poor. A small elite of Spanish, or other European, descent has held most of the property and assets of the country. It continued to do so under Stroessner with an economy of export agriculture and nascent, elementary industry. The majority of the population, as today, was Guarani Indian or *mestizo*, people of mixed native and European blood. Even though the majority of Paraguayans spoke Guarani as their native or first language, this population was marginalized. Any expression of dissatisfaction or criticism by the native or *mestizo* population or by an opposition politician was brutally repressed, the country kept under a stage of siege. Seven presidential elections were staged that dutifully returned Stroessner to power.

Stroessner's power was initially based on his reputation as a military hero beginning in the Chaco War, between Paraguay and Bolivia during the 1930s. He built upon that base, once in the presidency, by regularly purging disloyal officers. He strengthened his hold over the Colorado Party by allowing its many bickering factions to fight among themselves. They progressively eliminated each other and he remained the dominant, stable power. Dominance of the party gave him a massive organization for control of civilian and political life.

The Stroessner regime did not aim to destroy the existing political and/or socioeconomic power structure. Rather, it sought to reinforce it under the control of one man. The fervid anti-Communism of the regime at a time when Marxists such as Cheddi Jagan in British Guyana and Fidel Castro in Cuba were emerging in the region earned Stroessner the support of the United States. Stroessner tolerated widespread illegal activities by military and political leaders and encouraged foreign investment.

He obtained some significant rural support by enticing peasants to move to the northeast of the country with the promise of free public land. These agricultural settlements considerably increased the country's agricultural production and exports yet at the same time subjected settlers to the uncertainties of world commodities markets.

The highpoint of the Stroessner regime occurred in 1982 with the inauguration of the Itaipú Dam. Built in conjunction with Brazil on the Paraná River, the boundary between the two countries, the mammoth dam was able to supply electricity to all of Paraguay. However, the country was too underdeveloped to use so much energy. The Stroessner regime profited by selling most of it back to the dynamic industrial sector in southern Brazil.

The stagnation of the Paraguayan economy, accompanied by inflation and unemployment, and relentless repression, prompted the military to remove from office in 1989. He was exiled to Brazil, and resides in Brasília.

EDWARD A. RIEDINGER

See also Paraguay; Southern Cone (Latin America): History and Economic Development; Southern Cone (Latin America): International Relations

References and Further Reading

Abente Brun, Diego. *Stronismo, Post-stronismo, and the Prospects for Democratization in Paraguay*. Notre Dame, IN: Kellogg Institute for International Studies, 1989.

Bouvier, Virginia Marie. *Decline of the Dictator: Paraguay at a Crossroads*. Washington, DC: Washington Office on Latin America, 1988.

Chamber, Kevin Conrad. *Rural Transformation of Paraguay under General Alfredo Stroessner, 1954–89*. Dissertation, University of California, Santa Barbara, 1999.

Lambert, Peter and Andrew Nickson, eds. *The Transition to Democracy in Paraguay*. Houndmills, UK: Macmillan Press, 1997.

Lewis, Paul. *Paraguay under Stroessner*. Chapel Hill, NC: University of North Carolina Press, 1980.

Miranda, Carlos. *The Stroessner Era*. Boulder, CO: Westview Press, 1990.

Sondrol, Paul C. *Power Play in Paraguay: The Rise and Fall of General Stroessner*. Washington, DC: Institute for the Study of Diplomacy, School of Foreign Service, Georgetown University, 1996.

STRUCTURAL ADJUSTMENT PROGRAMS (SAPS)

Developing or emerging market economies may be faced with economic instability in the form of either or both external and internal imbalance. The former is manifested in a balance of payments crisis, a falling currency and unsustainable foreign debt obligations. The latter may involve a stagnant or declining economy, high inflation, and large government budget deficits. In these circumstances, member countries may look for financial support from the world's two

main multilateral aid and financial institutions, the World Bank and the International Monetary Fund.

The World Bank consults and lends money for a range of sectoral activities including agriculture, energy, transportation, education, health and nutrition, and urban development. It also focuses on improving economic policies within individual countries. A significant part of its lending is for structural adjustment: to support reforms rather than specific investments. The International Monetary Fund allows member countries to borrow, subject to agreed-upon conditions regarding their economic policies. Adherence to these conditions and reforms is in many cases a prerequisite to obtaining other larger public and private loans.

A SAP provides loans to countries on the condition that they undertake a combination of economic policy reforms measures aimed to improve long-term economic growth outcomes. These programs links disbursements of funds to the meeting of specified conditions (performance criteria) negotiated with the government of the member country. While these programs are often negotiated in the context of economic crisis, and attempt to restore balance of payments viability and macroeconomic stability, they are geared to increasing international competitiveness and improved economic efficiency in the use of domestic resources. Recently, these programs, which frequently involve some combination of higher interest rates, government spending cuts and higher taxes, and the abolition of various subsidies on consumption items have provoked criticism as having negative effects on populations who are already economically and socially disadvantaged. Additionally, environmentalists have objected to the conditions in which natural resources are exploited to meet the productivity and export quotas.

The SAPs often include trade liberalization measures that require fewer restrictions on foreign trade. These include reducing or abolishing tariffs and quotas on imports, a less restrictive stance towards foreign investment, an adjusted exchange rate, and capital account liberalization that reduces controls on any form of capital flows across national boundaries. The internal market-oriented structural reforms promote deregulation of domestic markets and the privatization of government enterprises.

The Effectiveness of Structural Adjustment Programs

The effectiveness of SAPs is a hotly debated issue. One issue relates to the speed of the structural adjustment required. Should all of these policies be implemented immediately or only gradually? Many economists argue that what is needed are gradual reforms to minimise short-term costs, such as business failure and unemployment. Others argue that the most serious problem with a market liberalisation program is the political resistance that it generates, as the long-term benefits can be difficult to perceive while the short-term costs are all too apparent. Hence the longer the delay, the greater the political opposition to further reform that will arise. In addition, many of the structural reforms implemented may be reversed once the program is over. If the liberalisation measures are expected to be reversed in time, then the government or the public may actually take steps that will undermine the effectiveness of the reform program.

A second issue relates to the sequencing of structural reforms. Many commentators point to the crucial role of foreign capital inflow during the structural reform period to reduce the frictions that will emerge during the transition. However, it may be preferable that controls on foreign capital only be relaxed after trade and other industrial sector distortions have been dismantled. The reason for this is that capital inflow will result in a real exchange rate appreciation that disadvantages exporters. Meanwhile, the tariff reductions will disadvantage domestic producers facing lower-priced imports.

There is also considerable disagreement on the benefits of trade liberalization policies. Have trade liberalisation packages played an important role in the strong performance of outward-oriented economies? A number of countries, such as Japan, Korea, Singapore, and Taiwan have promoted exports but in an environment where imports had not been fully liberalised. The success of the East Asian countries with export-led growth suggests that some selectively determined degree of government intervention played a key role.

Privatization strategies have also been questioned, particularly in the transitional economies of Eastern Europe. Public assets may be sold off below their real value in order to find a buyer and to generate quick cash flow, with a loss of public accountability. Privatization might then mean that income-generating assets are sold, leaving behind all the residual 'unproductive' activities, plus a new layer of watchdog agencies to regulate the newly privatized activities.

Many of these issues have been examined empirically but the results are mixed on the SAPs overall effectiveness. Often the results depend on the characteristics of the specific country concerned. Countries have generated a variety of responses to basically similar SAPs. This seems to reflect the importance of

differences in institutional, social, and historical conditions between countries. In the context of the 1997 Asian Crisis further debate has escalated on the effectiveness of SAPs, particularly the financial deregulation requirements. The impacts of SAPs on social sectors and the poor have been particularly troublesome and the IMF and World Bank are attempting to incorporate social safety nets into their programs.

JOHN LODEWIJKS

References and Further Reading

Cornea, G., R. Jolly, and F. Stewart (eds.) *Adjustment with a Human Face*, Oxford: Clarendon Press, 1987.

Edwards, S. "Structural Adjustment Policies in Highly Indebted Countries" in J.D. Sachs (ed.) *Developing Country Debt and Economic Performance*. Chicago: University of Chicago Press, Vol. I. 1989.

Sheahan, John. *Patterns of Development in Latin America: Poverty, Repression and Economic Strategy*. Princeton, NJ: Princeton University Press, 1987.

Standing, Guy and Victor Tokman (ed.) *Towards Social Adjustment*. Geneva: International Labour Office, 1991.

Stewart, Frances. *Adjustment and Poverty*. London: Routledge, 1995.

Tarp, Finn. *Stabilization and Structural Adjustment*. London: Routledge, 1993.

Taylor, Lance. *Varieties of Stabilization Experience: Towards Sensible Macroeconomics in the Third World*. Oxford: Clarendon Press, 1988.

SUBSISTENCE LIVING

The seemingly infinite *ways by which human beings could make a living,* especially food acquisition and satisfaction of basic needs such as clothing and shelter, can actually be narrowed down to four basic types: *foraging, horticulture, pastoralism,* and *agriculture.* It is important to recognize that variation exists within each of these subsistence patterns; thus, the characteristics that are identified for each should be regarded as tendencies, not absolutes.

Foraging

Foragers rely entirely on *wild food sources*—plants, animals, and fish. Contemporary (and presumably prehistoric) foragers live(d) in small, kin-based nomadic groups called *bands.* Social organization tends toward fluidity and flexibility, as the band size, location and composition are adjusted to both variation in food sources and also social factors such as interpersonal tensions. Resources are freely shared with other group members, an exchange pattern known as *generalized reciprocity* (Sahlins 1972). While

not completely equal, nonetheless foraging groups tend to be the most *egalitarian* societies known cross-culturally (Friedl 1978; Kent 1993).

Division of labor is minimal and usually based loosely upon gender, with men usually doing most of the hunting and women performing the bulk of the gathering. Valued though meat is, it is gathering of plant foods (especially among tropical foragers) that usually provide a larger portion of the diet than hunting (Lee 1992). This is one of the reasons why today the alternative term, *hunting and gathering,* is little used to describe this mode of subsistence.

Long presumed to be an excessively harsh lifestyle, in recent decades foraging has been reassessed by anthropologists (Lee and DeVore 1968). It appears that members of many foraging groups work fewer hours per day/week and have greater amounts of leisure time persons living in agricultural and/or industrial societies. Foragers today are usually found in areas of marginal agricultural potential, e.g., deserts and semi-deserts, arctic regions, and tropical rainforests, often as a result of having been pushed there over time by larger, more powerful societies. A corollary is that contemporary foragers, such as the *San* of Southern Africa, are *not* Stone Age relics; rather, they are modern humans who have been interacting with members of other societies for long periods of time (Gordon 1992).

The coming of the *Neolithic* ("New Stone Age") roughly ten thousand years ago saw humans gradually domesticate certain wild plant and animal species. This seemingly modest development eventually triggered massive changes in human settlement patterns, division of labor, social stratification, as well as political and religious organization (Diamond 1987). The production of surplus permitted some individuals to specialize in non-food producing tasks, including religious and political leadership (Harris 1989).

Pastoralism

Pastoralism entails subsistence reliance on *domesticated herd animals,* with variation in the species kept depending upon environment. Normally herds will be comprised of mixed species, as different varieties of animals contribute different products and often utilize different sources of forage. Although pastoralism is frequently combined with small-scale cultivation, ideologically animal husbandry is considered to be preferable. If pastoralists do not themselves cultivate crops, then invariably they trade animal products for foodstuffs such as cereals, as well as non-food necessities such as domestic goods or clothing. The Middle

Eastern *Bedouin* and East African *Maasai* are prime examples. Like foraging, pastoralism normally involves a high degree of *mobility* and it too is usually found in areas of marginal agricultural potential, that is, those which are too dry or too high for farming, such as deserts and mountainous areas of the Middle East, savannas of Eastern and Southern Africa, and parts of the Himalayas. In mountainous areas, such as major portions of Iran and Iraq, it usually consists of seasonal vertical migrations, a pattern designated as *transhumance*.

Horticulture

Though in popular usage it usually connotes flower gardening, in terms of subsistence patterns this term refers to *non-intensive crop production* without the use of animal or chemical fertilizers, irrigation, draft animals, or mechanization. Tools are relatively simple (for example, digging sticks, hoes, machetes) and the primary goal is *food production for self sufficiency.* Horticulture usually relies on the use of *slash and burn techniques*, both to clear land of natural vegetation and enhance soil fertility in the form of ash. Plots are typically intercropped, as multiple species are planted in the same field, for variable lengths of time, depending upon local conditions. These fields are then abandoned and this fallowing allows rejuvenation of natural vegetation. Horticulturalists have excellent knowledge of their environments, often making more taxonomic distinctions than scientists (Conklin 1954). Most often found in tropical forests, given the proper set of conditions—especially abundant land and relatively small populations—horticultural systems *can* be infinitely sustainable, contrary to their prevalent image as wasteful, destructive, and "primitive" practices (Reed 1997). Only recently, with disruption of traditional land-use practices and population controls among horticultural groups, in tandem with exogenous pressures (for example, the influx of urban settlers, cattle ranchers, loggers, and gold miners), have areas such as the Amazon Basin faced such dire threats as exist today.

Agriculture

Agriculture involves *intensive, continuous use of land* for crop production, at least some of which is marketed. Agricultural intensification has been an ongoing process for thousands of years (Boserup 1965) and today a huge continuum of agricultural production

exists—from the smallholder peasant farms of Latin America, Africa, and Asia to the large, industrialized and commercial farms of Europe and North America. Since they are under almost continuous use, *agricultural fields must be fertilized*. While peasant farmers still tend to utilize animal fertilizer, commercial farmers depend heavily upon petroleum based chemicals for their fertilizers, as well as for pesticides and herbicides. Contrary to the intercropping typical of horticultural systems, with agricultural intensification, especially mechanized production, there is a distinct tendency toward *monocropping*. This is true even in time-tested systems such as the traditional wet-rice cultivation of Southeast Asia (for example, Vietnam and Thailand) and the Indonesian archipelago (Geertz 1963).

BRUCE D. ROBERTS

See also Bedouins; Peasants, Impact of Development on

References and Further Reading

Boserup, Ester. *The Conditions of Agricultural Growth.* Chicago: Aldine Publishing Company, 1965.
Geertz, Clifford. *Agricultural Involution: The Processes of Ecological Change in Indonesia.* Berkeley, CA: University of California Press, 1963.
Gordon, Robert. *The Bushman Myth: The Making of a Namibian Underclass.* Boulder, CO: Westview Press, 1992.
Kent, Susan. "Sharing in an Egalitarian Kalahari Community," *Man,* 28, No. 3 (1993).
Lee, Richard B. *The Dobe.* New York: Harcourt Brace, 1993.
Lee, Richard B. and Irven DeVore, editors. *Man The Hunter.* Chicago: Aldine, 1968.
Reed, Richard. *Forest Dwellers, Forest Protectors: Indigenous Models for International Development.* Boston: Allyn and Bacon, 1997.
Sahlins, Marshall. *Stone Age Economics.* Chicago: Aldine, 1972.

SUDAN

Al-Jumhurriya as-Sudan—the Republic of Sudan—is one of the poorest countries of the world and is rife with ethnic and religious warfare, while social problems such as slavery and disease seriously restrict life expectancy and the possibilities for social and economic development. Life expectancy is low, at fifty-four for men and fifty-seven for women, while per capita gross national income (GNI) was estimated to be $460 US in 2003.

Geography and Climate

Sudan is located in north eastern Africa, at approximately 15° N and 30° E. It lies to the south of Egypt,

the west of Eritrea and Ethiopia, the north of Uganda and the east of Chad, among other neighbours. Sudan has a port on the Red Sea at Port Sudan and a large part of inhabited Sudan is located on the valley drained by the River Nile. There are few large settlements apart from the three cities of the capital of Khartoum, North Khartoum, and Omdurman. Regional cities are little more than towns and generally suffer from poor communications and infrastructure.

Sudan is a very large country, approximately the same size as western Europe, occupying some 2.5 million square kilometers. It links the Sahara Desert with the tropical rainforest far to the south. This area includes a wide variety of different types of terrain. Transportation and communications are very difficult on such a scale.

The population was estimated to be around 34 million in 1999, approximately 30% of whom live in urban areas.

History

The first people to live in Sudan were Africans centred on what is now modern Khartoum, where contact was made with Egypt and other states. Sudanese created the Nubian empire in the north of the country and, with the introduction of the camel around 300 CE, navigation of the desert became possible and trade between African and Mediterranean states was greatly facilitated. In the sixth century, Christian missionaries entered the region and made conversions and built churches among the Nobatae and Beja people living in the north and east.

The Arab Conquest period saw a powerful Arab army invade the country to as far south as Dongola. However, the Arabs could not conquer the land and an arrangement was made to fix the border with Arab-controlled Egypt at its current location and a barrier posted to prevent cross-border movements. This arrangement enabled stability until the invasion of Sudan by Ottoman Egypt in 1820, which resulted in the conquest of a large tranche of the country. The successful occupation was repressive but succeeded in modernizing the country. Western pressure added to local Egyptian control ended some corruption and banned but did not stop the centuries' old practice of slavery.

Resentment of external control, especially the presence of Christian merchants and their importance, led to the emergence of the Mahdi, Muhammad Ahmed, who led a rebellion of religious nature aimed at sweeping away everything considered to be corrupt.

This rebellion led to the defeat of Anglo-Egyptian forces and the independence of Sudan. This did not last long before Anglo-Egyptian forces reconquered the country, ruling it according to a subsequently established Anglo-Egyptian Condominium. This regime aimed at suppressing rebellion and maintaining a light tax burden to avoid arousing more unrest. Nevertheless, nationalism erupted into a fresh revolt in 1924 which was crushed by the British who also took the occasion to expel Egyptian interests from the country, albeit temporarily. It was not until after WWII that British rule over Sudan was finally ended.

The early years of independent Sudan proved to be something of a disappointment to the people as parliamentary rule was insufficient to rid the country of entrenched interests or corruption. In 1958, a military coup brought a new administration that favoured the promotion of Islam and Arabic interests and the rejection of western ideals and indeed missionaries. This was deeply unpopular among the Christian and animist peoples of the south who have spent much of the time subsequently in revolt against government forces. Prosecuting military activities at a distance has proved very difficult for the government and the Sudan People's Liberation Army (SPLA) were able to achieve a number of important successes. However, ethnic differences remain of critical importance to many Sudanese and arming tribes with modern firearms has led to hugely increased loss of life.

Government and Politics

The parliamentary democracy instituted by the British has fallen into disrepute as a result of military coup and autocratic control of government. Democracy and free speech throughout the country are severely curtailed by government censoring of all media. Poverty and poor communications mean few people have access to alternative sources of news and information. Parliament itself was suspended by presidential decree at the end of 1999. No elections have been held since 1996.

Sharia Law was imposed in 1989 after the military coup that brought Lieutenant-General Umar Hasan Ahmed al-Bashir to power. It calls for strong penalties for offences such as drinking alcohol, fornication, or criticizing Muslim institutions. This law is supported by the Arabic people of the north but alien to the traditions of many other people. As poverty and crime are deeply correlated, many poor people have fallen foul of the amputations required for theft and similar penalties that hugely reduce their future economic and social opportunities.

Resistance to government control in the south has been led by the Sudan People's Liberation Army (SPLA) under the leadership of John Garang, formerly a member of the national military force. The SPLA has received covert material support from the United States, which considers Sudan to be a supporter of terrorism, as the cruise missile strikes against the Al-Shifa pharmaceutical plant in 1998 demonstrated. There have been persistent attempts to link Sudan with the Osama Bin Laden–inspired al Qaeda network.

Economy and Industry

Sudan has very little industry and much of its economy is based on subsistence agriculture, with some 80% of the labour force involved in agriculture. The lack of natural resources, especially potable water, and the harshness of much of the terrain mean that any form of production for exports is very difficult. One of the few exceptions is the breeding of camels which are sent to Arabia for use in racing. Other exports include basic agricultural commodities such as cotton. Philanthropic and charitable giving by Islamic societies and states has replaced the inflows of aid and investment that, in the 1970s, led to a large number of failed projects. A noticeable brain drain was stimulated by the demand for skilled labour in the oil-producing countries of the Persian Gulf and, until 1999, the reliance on imports of oil and many other basic commodities left the country at the mercy of market forces. However, the discovery of oil and the creation of an oil pipeline for exports, together with a program of structural adjustment have stabilized the economy to some extent. Nevertheless, national indebtedness remains a significant problem. So too is a general skilled labour shortage and low levels of literacy and education, especially among women.

Health Issues

Most of the health problems associated with poverty and warfare affect Sudan. In addition, female health is significantly negatively affected by the practice of female circumcision among some peoples. This practice is disastrous for women's health and has a serious impact on reproduction. Cultural practices are instrumental in withholding health treatment for some categories of people, including some with mental health problems. For people living in the desert or jungles of the south, access to health care of any sort is problematic. Government priorities for healthcare usually do not include older people.

Approximately 2.6% of the population is estimated to be HIV positive while other diseases include Ebola haemorrhagic fever, hepatitis E, shigellosis, and yellow fever. Many forms of foodborne and waterborne disease are considered to be endemic and chloroquine-resistant malaria is prevalent throughout the country.

Mental health is particularly poorly catered for and many healthcare professionals have left the country. Trauma and stress needs caused by warfare and slavery are not currently catered for and government intervention in non-governmental organization (NGO) work is reducing such development aid as reaches Sudan.

Ethnic Diversity

The country is sharply divided between the Arabic people of the north, who are strongly Muslim in faith and mostly derive from nomadic tribes such as the Hadendowa and related Beja peoples, and the African peoples from mostly the south and the west. Fifty-two percent of the population are black, 39% are Arabs, and 6% Beja peoples. Some black African people are Muslims but dislike the Sharia laws, while many are Christians or animists. A wide range of diverse peoples has been placed in the same country for the purposes of administrative convenience on behalf of previously colonizing British. The diversity of peoples and beliefs make nation-building particularly difficult as few have a coherent image of Sudan as a unitary state or even any desire to belong to a larger social structure. The state itself appears to be predatory to many and, at the end of 2004, more evidence is emerging of state attacks on refugee camps inhabited by ethnic minority peoples.

Slavery

Sudan suffers from a slavery trade that is one of the most persistent and pernicious in the world. Evidence suggests that the government itself colludes with slave raiders who capture people during attacks on communities of black Christians or animists or Muslims whose devotion is questioned. It is said that some seventy thousand people have been trafficked into forced labour and sex slavery by these means. The result has been to clear areas considered to be problematic, either because of resistance to the government

or because of proximity to the construction sites of the Greater Nile Oil Project.

Darfur

The Region of Darfur in the west of Sudan has witnessed tensions for many years between the nomadic Arabs and the sedentary African farmers of the Massaleet, Zagawa, and Fur tribes. These have escalated in recent years and armed conflict was initiated by some who claimed the government was supporting the Arab people to the detriment of the black Sudanese. This has been followed by the emergence of the Janjaweed militia force, which has taken reprisals on the black peoples, riding into villages and towns on horses, camels, and vehicles, and engaging in rape, pillage, and slave-taking. It is argued by some that the Janjaweed are supported by members of the government. In any case, some seventy thousand people are believed to have been killed as a result of fighting in the region as of October 2004 and around 1.5 million have fled their homes, leading to a major humanitarian crisis. Aid efforts are being hampered by political considerations as the Sudanese government contends with the allegation made against it by NGOs of genocide.

Prospects

The Sudanese government is being placed under continuing aggressive scrutiny as a result of its possible support of militia such as the Janjaweed in Darfur, its alleged support of or links with terrorism and its role in promoting slavery in the country. Until transparency is enforced on government actions, it seems unlikely that much progress will be made on developmental goals.

As the US-led "War on Terror" seems set to continue, Sudan would need to distance itself firmly from supposed support for terrorism in order to benefit fully from the international support it so badly needs.

JOHN WALSH

See also East Africa: History and Economic Development; East Africa: International Relations; Ethnic Conflicts: East Africa

References and Further Reading

Beaumont, Peter. "US 'Hyping' Darfur Genocide Fears," *The Observer* (October 3, 2004), downloaded from: http://observer.guardian.co.uk/international/story/0,6903,1318628,00.html.

Holt, P.M., and M.W. Daly. *A History of the Sudan: From the Coming of Islam to the Present Day*, fifth edition. Longman, 2000.

International Monetary Fund (IMF). "Sudan: Recent Economic Developments," *IMF Staff Country Report No.99/53* (June 1999), downloaded from: http://www.imf.org/external/pubs/ft/scr/1999/cr9953.pdf.

Metelits, Claire. "Reformed Rebels? Democratization, Global Norms, and the Sudan People's Liberation Army," *Africa Today*, Vol. 51, No. 1 (2004), pp. 65–82.

Re, Richard. "A Persisting Evil: The Global Problem of Slavery," *Harvard International Review*, Vol. 23, No. 4 (Winter, 2002), pp. 32–35.

SUFISM

Sufism is the mystical and esoteric practice of the religion of Islam. It refers to a broad set of various different movements, some founded in antiquity, others of more modern vintage, but all of which trace their roots to the early establishment of the Islamic faith. Sufi orders are found throughout the Islamic world, representing all of the traditions of Islam, and have also been established among Muslims in Western nations.

The most likely origin of the term is in the Arabic word *suf*, meaning "wool," describing the woolen cloak worn by Muslim mystics during the seventh century. Sufis understand Muhammed to be to the originator of the tradition of Islamic mysticism, which was handed down directly and indirectly to several Sufi orders. The early successors Abu Bakr and Ali are said to have been Sufis, and their leadership led to the emergence of several important early Sufi practices laid down by Hasan al-Basri and his students in the eighth century. The movement declined as a result of opposition from religious authorities in the tenth and eleventh centuries by virtue of its perceived heterodoxy and openness to strong drink. It was reinvigorated in the works of Muhammed al-Ghazali (1059–1111), an Iranian scholar living in Baghdad, and Muhyi al-Din ibn al-Arabi (1165–1240), a Spanish scholar who completed his work in the city of Damascus. While these two are among the greatest authorities in the Sufi tradition, neither established his own unique order.

Since the twelfth century, Sufis have been loosely organized into orders called *turuq,* (paths, s. *tariqa*) founded by eminent leaders known as *walis* (saints) or *shaykhs* (leaders). The largest and most significant of these include the Qadiriya, the Rifa'iya, the Shadhiliya, the Mevleviya, the Naqshbandiya, and the Chishtiya. More modern *tariqas* include the Tijaniya, the Ahmadiya, the Sanusiya, and the Khatmiya.

Sufi theology begins with an endeavor to be "drowned," or to become "extinct" in the Eternal, an attempt to lose one's finite existence in an experience of divine unity. To this end, individual Sufis consider themselves to be strongly directed: central figures are said to be travelers on their way back to God. It shares many features in common with the mystical traditions of other faiths, including the desire to move beyond mere righteousness toward a closer union with the deity. Sufis argue that their movement is universal in that it is reflective of the general search for God in spirit, and therefore can be informed by other religious viewpoints in its general search for the divine. This has led many to understand Sufi theology and practice to be syncretistic, reflecting a mixture of beliefs to be found in the monastic and mystical life of other religions.

In addition to the usual Islamic strictures placed on Muslims, Sufi practices include direct emulation of the leaders of the order, fasting and prayer, incantation and repetition of the names of God, (*dhikr Allah*), veneration of saints at community celebrations (*mawlids*) and tombs, attendance at instructional sessions with the head of the order (*dars*), and the practice of retreat or isolation (*khalwa*). The Sufi tradition is one that seeks to emulate spiritual over temporal enrichment, and as a result they are often called by Arabic *faqir* and Turkish *dervish* (meaning "poor"). Some don inexpensive robes known as *khalwa* and use simple wooden rosaries known as *sibha*. One group, the Mevleviya, is particularly noted for the practice of dancing in circular motion, earning them the name "whirling dervishes."

While most Sufi orders are predominantly male, women have long had an important role to play as Sufis. One woman, Rabi'a al-Adawiya (717–801) was among the earliest and most revered of the Sufis. Many Sufi orders permit women to lead female orders and to participate equally in Sufi rituals and ceremonies.

Sufism was integral to the spread of Islam in many parts of Asia and Africa, particularly in areas beyond the spread of Muslim empires. Given their strict discipline and organization, Sufi orders became natural poles of opposition to colonial powers in many of these areas in the nineteenth and twentieth centuries. In China, leaders of the Naqshbandi order began a revolt against Chinese domination in the late eighteenth century. Shamil (1796–1871), from a Chechen branch of the Naqshbandi order, led a war against the Russian Empire from 1834 to 1859. Muhammed Ahmad (1844–1885), founder of the Sudanese *ansar* Sufi order, known by his followers as the Mahdi, led an independence movement against British authorities in the 1880s. Sufi orders remain important sources of political authority in Sudan, where the Umma Party remains closely associated the *ansar* and the Democratic Unionist Party is dominated by the *khatmiya* Sufi order. In Libya, the Sanusiya order presented a significant challenge to French and Italian colonial authorities during the early twentieth century.

As a result of opposition coming from orthodox Islamic elements beginning with the Salafist movement of the early nineteenth century, Sufis have been marginalized as representatives of backward and overly syncretistic "folk religion" in some areas of the Middle East. Urbanization and modernization both presented major challenges to the largely rural Sufi movements. However, Sufi orders continue to be significant to social and political life in places such as South Asia, Indonesia, Sudan, and the Sahel, where their tombs and shrines remain important centers of ritual devotion. For example, in the West African states of Senegal and Gambia, the Tijaniya order directs social services such as shelters for the homeless, medical supports, and educational initiatives for poor farmers. Likewise among Pashtuns in Afghanistan, sufis of the Naqshbandi Qadiriya order take on the role of mediators and arbitrators in many local settings, also being prominent local educators.

Sufi orders often create communal and commercial opportunities for their members, including agricultural collectives and businesses. Sufi meeting houses (*zawiya*) serve as important social centers in small communities and neighborhoods. The magical power attributed to Sufis—they are commonly held to possess the ability to convey a special blessing (*baraka*)—means that they are often approached for healing and spiritual advice. In many locales, Sufi orders have tended to become involved in social development and service projects, such as health care, orphanages, and educational facilities. All of this gives Sufi orders a natural political resonance, and has led to increased regulation and control over their leadership and practices through governing bodies. For example, in Syria, a policy of co-optation by the state has provided room for pro-regime orders such as the Kuftariya while restricting and silencing orders more critical of the state through repression. The increasing politicization and polarization of Islam in the developing world has contributed to the diversification of Sufi orders. They have adapted both by supporting the more radicalized elements in locations such as Iraq and Afghanistan, and in seeking to present a more moderate and popular face to Western audiences.

PAUL S. ROWE

See also Islam

References and Further Reading

James Fadiman and Robert Frager. *Essential Sufism*. San Francisco: Harper San Francisco, 1997.

Julian Johansen. *Sufism and Islamic Reform in Egypt*. Oxford: Clarendon Press, 1996.

Mark J. Sedgwick. *Sufism: the Essentials*. Cairo: American University in Cairo Press, 2000.

Martin Lings. *What is Sufism?* London: George Allen & Unwin, 1975.

Michael Gilsenan. *Saint and Sufi in Modern Egypt*. Oxford: Clarendon Press, 1973.

J. Spencer Trimingham. *The Sufi Orders in Islam*. Oxford: Clarendon Press, 1971.

SUKARNO

Achmed Sukarno (1901–1970) was the most respected, admired, charismatic, and remembered leader of Indonesia.

After graduating from High School, he studied in his country engineering and architecture at the Bandung Technical College where he first became involved in nationalist activity. In 1927, Sukarno established the Indonesian Nationalist Union, which was later known as the Indonesian Nationalist Party (PNI). This new party's aim was to achieve independence for Indonesia through popular struggle against the Dutch, who had been controlling Indonesia as a colony since the beginning of the seventeenth century.

As years passed, Sukarno managed to gather large crowds who followed him because of his persuasive oratory skills and his ideas of liberation from secular colonialism. He was imprisoned some times during Dutch occupation and then, in 1942, after the Japanese invaded the country, he collaborated with them but only as an opportunity to gain popularity. After World War II and, with the defeat of the Japanese, on August 17, 1945, Sukarno and Mohamad Hatta declared the long-waited Indonesian independence, and became, respectively, Indonesia's first president and vice-president. He also established the first Constitution which constituted a very important progress for national unity, a long data trouble since Indonesia's territory is composed by hundred of separated islands.

A year later, in 1946, began the *Independence War*, when Dutch and British forces invaded the country; and during those years armed conflicts between the Dutch and Indonesian guerrilla persisted. Due to international pressure, in 1949 the war finished when Netherlands agreed to transfer sovereignty over almost all Indonesia to the federal Republic of the United States of Indonesia (RUSI). On July 5, 1959, President Sukarno decided to put an end to current liberal democracy regime and started what he called *Guided Democracy,* a coalition of very dissimilar groups in the government. Sukarno had always tried to balance the three primary social forces in Indonesia: the revolutionary nationalistic Army; the popular mass-based Islamic organizations; and the Indonesian Communist Party (PKI), and Guided Democracy was an attempt to do so. It was a delicate balance between Nationalism (NAS), Religion or *Agama* (A), and Communism (KOM) (NASAKOM). Then Sukarno carried out several measures to unify and help develop the Archipelago as a country and a nation.

One of his most important achievements was to adopt Bahasa Indonesia as the national language. This was very important as most of the people who lived on the different islands had developed greatly different dialects and there wasn't a common language for all that created a common identity.

So as to solve his many economical difficulties, several established Dutch banks were nationalized during the 1950s, including the Bank of Java, which became the central bank of Indonesia, in 1953. The five state banks were merged into a single conglomerate, and private banking virtually ceased.

Another of his contributions to development was the installation of democracy as the political regime for excellence. Outside of a small number of urban areas, the people still lived in a cultural milieu that stressed status hierarchies and obedience to authority. Therefore, although his regime was forced to add some dictatorial features, he promoted democracy as the best political regime for the country. Independent Indonesia's first general election took place on September 29, 1955, and Sukarno's PNI won a slim plurality with the largest number of votes, 22.3%.

In spite of all this encouraging measures, Sukarno has often come in for a lot of criticism for not setting economical growth as a priority in the country's development strategy. However, this point is controversial because his attempts to improve the economical situation were often blocked. For instance, he tried to implement a vast land reform but his efforts were blocked by landowners and Sukarno's own bureaucrats.

Notwithstanding the bad economical situation, Sukarno retained enormous popularity among ordinary Indonesians, awakening in them a great sense of pride in being Indonesian. In 1963, having Sukarno proclaimed himself president for life, the PKI announced a policy of direct action and began dispossessing landlords and distributing the land to poor Javanese, northern Sumatrans, and Balinese peasants.

Regarding his foreign policy, he was the president who initiated the historic Asia-Africa Conference at Bandung (Indonesia) in 1955, which encouraged the spread of the *Non-Aligned Movement*. He also turned away from the West by rejecting their financial aid and came closer towards the People's Republic of

China and the Soviet Union for development assistance. Later on in 1965, owing to the creation of the Malaysian Federation, he separated his country from the United Nations and its affiliated organizations, the International Monetary Fund and the World Bank He argued that the British-supported state (Malaysia) would function as a base from which "neocolonial" forces could exert influence in the region.

This challenging foreign policy was opposed to the United States and other Western countries, which saw his regime as an obstacle for the free exploitation of Indonesia's valuable natural resources (mainly oil and minerals). Indonesia had also a great value as a strategic position in the South East of Asia. All this reasons account for the permanent interest of the superpowers for the Archipelago, known as the Asian Jewel.

All his inner and foreign policy were resented by the Western countries that considered him as a rival. The weight of superpowers would be very important to disrupt the delicate balance of power he had formed. The end of Sukarno's regime was suddenly prompted on September 30, 1965, when an alleged communist coup by the so-called September 30 Movement killed six generals and one lieutenant. The next day Maj-Gen. Suharto, seized the situation, including the army's control and blamed the Indonesian Communist Party as the coup-plotter. Although controversial, many researchers sustain that this incident had been organized and financially supported by the United States Central Intelligence Agency (CIA) in order to end with Sukarno's communist and hostile regime. In 1967, the Parliament named Suharto acting president and installed him as president a year later. Sukarno's power over the nation had already been fully diminished until his formal deposition on March 27, 1968. Sukarno finally retired to the island of Jakarta where he died in June 21, 1970.

DIEGO I. MURGUÍA

See also Bandung Conference (1955); Ethnic Conflicts: Southeast Asia; Indonesia; Islam; Nonaligned Movement

References and Further Reading

Adams, Cindy. *Sukarno: an Autobiography as told by Cindy Adams*. New York: Bobbs-Merril Co. 1965.
Brands, H. W. "The Limits of Manipulation: How the United States Didn't Topple Sukarno", *Journal of American History* Vol. 76 (December 1989).
Dahm, Bernard. *Sukarno and the Struggle for Indonesian Independence*. Ithaca, NY: Cornell University Press, 1969.
Hughes, John. *The end of Sukarno*. London: Angus and Robertson, 1978.
Legge, John D. *Sukarno: A Political Biography*. New York: Praeger, 1972.
Masashi, Nishihara. *The Japanese and Sukarno's Indonesia*. Honolulu: University Press of Hawaii, 1976.
Vittachi, Tarzie. *The fall of Sukarno*. New York: Praeger, 1967.
Weinstein, Franklin B. *Indonesian Foreign Policy and the Dilemma of Dependence: from Sukarno to Soeharto*. Ithaca, NY: Cornell University Press, 1976.

SURINAME

Suriname (former Dutch Guiana) is located on the northeast coast of South America between Guyana (former British Guiana) and French Guiana. Brazil lies to the south and the Atlantic Ocean to the north. The land area is about sixty-three thousand square miles.

Suriname's coastline consists largely of mangrove swamps rooted in alluvial mud from the Amazon River deposited by coastal currents. A strip of low land running along the coast and averaging thirty miles in width contains most of the nation's agricultural land and population. Inland lies a narrow savannah zone. The interior (80% of the land area) consists of very sparsely populated, largely roadless, upland rain forest. Lying just north of the equator, Suriname is hot year round. There are two rainy seasons, a short one in December and a longer one from March to July.

The population of Suriname (only 430,000 by 2003 estimate) is very diverse. Using official census categories, the largest group (37% of the population) is "Hindustanis," whose ancestors came from India. The second largest group (31%) is Creoles, Christian of African descent. The Muslim Javanese (15%) are mostly employed in rice agriculture. Maroons (also called Bush Negroes) constitute 10% of the population. They are descended from slaves who escaped and created independent African societies in the jungle. Six Bush Negro tribes are recognized today: the Aluku, Ndjuka, Kwinti, Matawai, Paramaka, and Saramaka. Amerindians (Arawaks, Caribs, Tirios, Akoerio, and Wajana) are only 2.5% of the population. Their traditional way is little affected by the modern world. There are small numbers of Chinese and Europeans. Not counted in any census are illegal Brazilian immigrants, mostly gold miners. There may be as many as thirty-five thousand of these. The religious breakdown of Suriname's population is Hindu (27%), Muslim (20%), Roman Catholic (23%), Protestant (25%), and animists (5%).

The Guiana coast was sparsely populated when first sighted by Spanish explorers in 1498. British settlers failed to establish viable plantations and by the terms of the Treaty of Breda (1667) the Netherlands

acquired Suriname in exchange for New Amsterdam (New York) and Suriname remained a Dutch colony for the next three centuries. Dutch plantation owners were notoriously cruel to their slaves, many of whom fled upriver. Suriname's rivers are navigable by shallow-draft boats only up to the first fall line; thereafter frequent portages are required. Due to their isolation, the Bush Negroes preserve their synoptic African culture in relatively undisturbed form. This may change, as some now work in Paramaribo and in the Netherlands.

Plantation crops grown for export (coffee, indigo, cacao, cotton, and especially sugar) were by the nineteenth century mostly replaced by food crops grown for internal consumption: rice, plantain, and bananas. Britain re-occupied Suriname in 1804 and banned the slave trade in 1808. The Dutch regained control in 1816. The Dutch abolished slavery in 1863 but bound slaves to their plantations at low wages for another ten years. Almost all slaves left the plantations at the first chance. They were replaced by indentured laborers from India (a total of thirty-seven thousand between 1873 and 1916) and from Java (a total of thirty-three thousand between 1890 and 1940).

Bauxite, the ore from which aluminum is refined, was discovered in Suriname in 1915. During World War II, Suriname supplied the allies with this strategic metal, essential for the manufacture of airplanes. After the war the Dutch granted Suriname progressively greater autonomy, despite the absence of strong pro-independence sentiment among the people. Elections in November 1973 brought to power an alliance of Creole and Javanese parties advocating independence. Suriname became a sovereign nation on November 25, 1975, with Henk Arron, a Creole, as Prime Minister. Approximately forty thousand people of Asian descent emigrated to the Netherlands.

Prime Minister Arron was deposed in a military coup on February 25, 1980. Sergeant-Major Désiré Bouterse emerged as leader of the ruling National Military Council. Bouterse closed newspapers, banned political parties, dissolved parliament, suspended the constitution, and promoted himself to Lieutenant-Colonel. A period of extreme political chaos ensued, including six attempted coups over the next three years. After fifteen prominent opposition leaders were tortured and killed in December 1982 the United States and the Netherlands suspended economic aid. Government social services went into decline. Bush Negro insurgents, led by Bouterse's ex-bodyguard Ronnie Brunswijk, shut down the mining industry around the eastern town of Moengo. In 1987, the military agreed to elections. Bouterse's party won only two of fifty-one seats in the National Assembly but he continued in power,

having by now promoted himself to commander-in-chief. Bouterse "resigned" in 1990 but influenced policy from behind the scenes for the rest of the decade. In July 1999, a Dutch court convicted Bouterse *in absentia* of smuggling nearly two tons of cocaine.

Civil society in Suriname is highly concentrated in Paramaribo. Political parties tend to represent ethnic groups rather than ideological positions. The National Party of Suriname represents Creoles and the Progressive Reform Party represents Hindustanis. The Javanese and Maroons are represented by smaller parties.

Government mismanagement of the economy has brought inflation and unemployment. Nearly half the workforce is employed by the government itself. Agriculture accounts for another 20% of the labor force. Rice is the food staple and the main crop. Food exports include bananas, coconuts, and shrimp. A dam on the Surinam River at Afobaka, paid for by the aluminum companies, creates one of the largest reservoirs in the world and produces electricity needed for aluminum production. Gold mining is carried on illegally and therefore contributes little to the official national budget while generating toxic runoff. Oil production is controlled by the state oil company. There are potentially exploitable deposits of iron ore, copper, nickel, platinum, and manganese. The rainforest contains much valuable timber, but decision-makers must balance receipts from the forestry industry, which it controls, against potential income from eco-tourism. Suriname's rich bio-diversity is now recognized as an economic asset and the government has designated a large area of the highlands as the Central Suriname Nature Reserve.

Health and nutrition are good, with life expectancy at sixty-nine years. Suriname has achieved a 93% literacy rate despite its linguistic diversity. Dutch is the official language but the *lingua franca* is Sranan Tongo, a pidgin consisting of words derived from English, Dutch, and other European and African languages. Hindi, Javanese, and various tribal languages are also spoken. Education is compulsory for ages six to twelve.

Suriname's foreign policy is constrained by the need for economic aid from the Netherlands and the United States. Assistance has been conditionally resumed now that the military has relinquished some of its power and the Bush Negro insurgents have been integrated into the national police force. Territorial claims against Guyana and French Guiana remain active, but neither neighbor is likely to concede territory, as the Armed Forces of Suriname number less than two thousand men.

In elections held in May 2000, the fifty-one-member National Assembly elected Ronald

Venetiaan president. The next elections are scheduled for May 2005. In January 2004, Suriname changed the name of its national currency from the guilder to the dollar.

Ross Marlay

References and Further Reading

Chin, Henk E. and Hans Buddingh. *Surinam: Politics, Economics and Society.* London and New York: Frances Pinter, 1987.

Dew, Edward,. *The Difficult Flowering of Surinam: Ethnicity and Politics in a Plural Society.* The Hague: Martinus Nijhoff, 1978.

Price, Richard. *The Guiana Maroons: A Historical and Bibliographical Introduction.* Baltimore, MD, and London: Johns Hopkins University Press, 1976.

Van Lier, R.A.J. *Frontier Society: A Social Analysis of the History of Surinam.* The Hague: Martinus Nijhoff, 1971.

SUSTAINABLE DEVELOPMENT

As defined by the United Nations-sponsored Brundtland Report, the objective of sustainable development is to meet the demands of the current generation without compromising the needs of future generations. It is an attempt to be both environmentally conscious and economically productive, two ideals which have traditionally clashed with one another, both in the developing and developed world. This debate is probably most pronounced in the developing world where the rate of increase in environmental change and pollution is highest. While blame for the vast majority of the greenhouse gas emissions to date lies at the feet of the developed world, carbon dioxide emissions from developing countries are expected to pass those from the developed states of the Organization of Economic Cooperation and Development by the year 2025. The differences in the Northern and Southern hemisphere, the developed and developing world, are central to understanding the debate about sustainable development. Yet before broaching this subject and the neocolonial and green imperialism arguments it introduces, it is important to consider some of the fundamental definitional issues that remain in contention regarding sustainable development.

Sustainable development is about development as opposed to growth. The distinction between development and growth is a critical point. While direct tension between these two interests can at times exist (that is, choosing to allow ivory trade by states such as Botswana, South Africa, and Namibia in 1997 and 2002 as those states have viable elephant populations despite the overall threatened status of African elephants and the resulting international ban on African elephant ivory trade in place since 1989), the two are more accurately described as complimentary. Any viable long term economic development must directly incorporate ecological health. Just precisely how this is done politically, however, remains a highly contentious issue. Short and long term interests often clash. No consensus exists when it comes to implementing the ideas of sustainable development.

Too often, discussion of economic development is wrongly used interchangeably with that of economic growth. Yet the two terms are decidedly not synonymous. Growth is a quantitative measure; development is qualitative. There is a point where growth comes too fast, or there is simply too much of it. Unsustainable development is development without a plan—which, depending on the definition may not be development at all, but instead simply uncontrolled growth. It is a cancer that ultimately hurts the economy as well as the ecological base on which this economy is built.

To avoid this pitfall, scholars such as former World Bank economist Herman Daly and theologian John Cobb advocate restructuring economies so that they live off the interest of the earth without encroaching upon its capital. Again, what is most notable about this definition is the fact that it incorporates both an inter-generational and intra-generational equity dimension. Future generations are left the resources and ecologically viable environment they will need, and the environmental costs and benefits of today are distributed equitably among those living in the current generation. One generation does not shoulder a disproportionate share of burden. And one region or class within the generation does not shoulder more than its share either. This approach shifts emphasis to maintenance of the earth and its resources, encouraging societies to limit the degree to which they borrow from their children's future. Stewardship becomes the modus operandi instead of exploitation.

Looking past this theoretical introduction to the diplomatic history of sustainable development offers additional insight here. The term became part of the global discourse in 1980 with the publication of *World Conservation Strategy* by the hybrid non-governmental organization (NGO) and international organization (IO) known popularly as the World Conservation Union and more formerly as the International Union for Conservation of Nature and Natural Resources (IUCN), a serendipitous source considering the central role NGOs play in the sustainable development debate today. By 1987, the earlier mentioned Brundtland Commission, led by Norwegian Prime Minister Gro Brundtland, popularized the term outright with its publication, *Our Common Future.* Often referred to as the Brundtland Report this work sought to establish a foundation for the 1992 Earth Summit in Rio de

Janeiro, Brazil. Officially referred to as the United Nations Conference on Environment and Development (UNCED), this was the largest gathering of state leaders at the time. Held twenty years after the 1972 ground-breaking United Nations Conference on the Human Environment in Stockholm, Sweden, the Earth Summit sought to achieve multilateral agreements in five key areas. These were the Rio Declaration, Agenda 21, Statement of Forest Principles, Climate Convention, and Biodiversity Convention. Despite high prioritization in a number of state delegations and vast press coverage worldwide, delegates came away with little more than non-binding recommendations. Development interests, particularly within the constraints of an overarching Northern-Southern hemisphere conflict, prevented any tangible results from emerging. Thus some charge that nothing more than hot air emerged out of Rio, that the primary legacy of the Earth Summit has been the extent to which the term sustainable development is now a contested political terrain. This continued even in the aftermath of the progressive World Summit on Sustainable Development (WSSD) in Johannesburg, South Africa, in 2002.

Part of the blame here must still fall on a continuing fundamental deficiency in traditional economic thinking. More than just two measures are needed to describe profit. To truly measure development, economists and diplomats alike need more categories than merely net and gross profit. To consider sustainable development, decision-makers require a more elaborate system, one that better incorporates environmental accounting. Proposals on the table include basic measures of environmental "goods" and environmental "bads," to add and subtract respectively from the gross national product (GNP). Of course, application of such practices raises critical complications in terms of cost-benefit analysis. How does one determine what is good and what is bad? And perhaps just as controversial, precisely who makes this determination? Several genuine efforts to meet this demand do exist. Perhaps the most universally accepted new measure to date is the United Nations' Human Development Index (HDI). Developed in 1990 by the Pakistani economist Mahbub ul Haq, it has been an integral component of the annual report for the United Nations Development Program since 1993. The HDI incorporates life expectancy, literacy, poverty, and education, in addition to per capita gross domestic product adjusted for purchasing power parity (PPP).

Much of what makes sustainable development complicated today is its truly global nature, that is, the problems of climate change, ozone depletion, and species extinction all rest in unsustainable practices. Globalization shapes this, particularly as the technological advances in communication and transportation have brought even the most physically distant markets ever closer together. Still other impacts are somewhat more localized yet not region specific, appearing in both developed and developing world communities, for example, hazardous waste disposal, transportation pollution, and urban or suburban sprawl. And some such as over-consumption and rampant population growth are generally considered most problematic in either one region of the world or the other, that is, they are symbolic of the North-South divide. For example, in the North, in the developed world, the major sustainable development issues revolve around consumption and waste—and the impact of these activities on the so-called "green agenda" which targets depletion of water and forest resources. More precisely there is a systemic problem with over-consumption in the developed world, where some 20% of the world's population consumes roughly 80% of the world's resources. This, in turn, is tied to a problem with waste, specifically the packaging from the products of this consumption. One should also acknowledge that our original definition of the term sustainable development used the phrase development needs, not wants. Much of the consumption in the developed world fits the latter category instead of the former.

Looking towards the South, in the developing world, local communities deal with a somewhat different subset of sustainable development difficulties, one more often described in the context of the "brown agenda." These are the "pollution of poverty" issues such as sanitation, soil erosion, and drinking water quality. In essence, this type of unsustainable development is tied to two phenomena. One such phenomenon is burgeoning population in areas ill-equipped to handle this rapid growth, that is, the Sudan's estimated population growth rate in 2004 was 2.64%. Another phenomenon at work is the simple fact that the developing world is trying to catch up economically to the rest of the world—and to do so quickly in much the same manner as the developed world did. Being relatively late comers to the industrial revolution, the developing world is at a disadvantage in the global trading market. Herein lays partial validity in the charges of neo-colonialism or green imperialism that are, at times, levied against the Northern hemisphere. Those from the rich developed world essentially insist that the developing states not to make the same mistakes the developed states did, that the developing world should be more patient in pursuing the benefits of economic development. One could easily label such advice as hypocritical—unless developed states put their money where their mouth is so to speak and provide the necessary financial assistance

to offset any economic sacrifices made by the developing world. Furthermore, there can be the perception that developed states might not always be offering well intentioned advice. Some developing states fear their sovereignty may be compromised to the benefit of more advanced powers just as during the late nineteenth and early twentieth century heyday of imperialism and its extraction of natural resources for the mother country. But these fears notwithstanding, developing states best interests are indeed served by pursuing a carefully planned development path. The advice to consider long term as well as short term development interests is highly advantageous to both the developing and developed world. Yes the developed world can make a common heritage of humankind argument when it comes to protecting species diversity or the lungs of the planet in the Amazonian rainforests. But this is not a zero-sum game where one player's gain is another's loss. All parties, both developing and developed states alike can benefit here—and all can lose.

It is with this understanding that a handful of international agreements have come into force during the last two to three decades, each seeking to address common interests in fostering global sustainable development. Some examples of these range from the 1997 Kyoto Protocol on climate change to the 1987 Montreal Protocol on Substances that Deplete the Ozone Layer to the 1973 Convention on International Trade in Endangered Species (CITES). Within the United Nations (UN) family, a number of organs often aid in developing both specific international treaties such as these and the larger, more amorphous regimes they foster. Two agencies of particular note are the United Nations Development Program (UNDP) and United Nations Environment Program (UNEP), the latter of which is the only UN agency headquartered in the developing world. Over the last decade, moreover, The Global Environment Facility (GEF) is still another UN-affiliated institution that supports more sustainable development. In short, the GEF helps developing countries with projects by granting funds to decrease environmental impacts of these projects. Managed by the three implementing agencies of UNEP, UNDP, and the World Bank, this institution targets the six environmental issues of biodiversity, climate change, land degradation, international waters, ozone depletion, and persistent organic pollutants (POPs).

From this broad overview a few final concluding comments can be made. First, while some natural resources are renewable, others are certainly finite—and even renewable resources such as water, trees, or fish can be harvested in ways that make their replacement impossible. This means fundamental limits to the carrying capacity of the earth do exist. Second, most parties agree that communities need to incorporate such limits into the economic, environmental, and social goals they establish. The interdependence of these issues must be fully recognized. Third, thanks largely to the eloquent and concise wording of the Brundtland Report, general agreement on the need for both inter-generational and intra-generational equity now exists. Together these three components represent the common denominator in effective sustainable development programs around the globe. Of course, identifying these characteristics is not meant to suggest that there is one correct path towards sustainable development. While planning ahead is critical, the blueprint model, a one size fits all mentality, will not work when it comes to sustainable development.

MICHAEL M. GUNTER, JR.

See also Biodiversity Conservation; Development History and Theory; Development, Measures of; Ecotourism; Environmentalism; Global Climate Change; International Bank for Reconstruction and Development (IBRD) (World Bank); Population Growth: Impact on Development; Third World; United Nations Development Program (UNDP)

References and Further Reading

Brown, Lester R. *Eco-Economy: Building an Economy for the Earth*. New York: W.W. Norton & Company, 2001.

Daily, Gretchen, ed. *Nature's Services: Societal Dependence on Natural Ecosystems*. Washington, DC: Island Press, 1997.

Daly, Herman E. *Beyond Growth: The Economics of Sustainable Development*. Boston: Beacon Press, 1996.

Daly, Herman and John Cobb, Jr. *For the Common Good: Redirecting the Economy Toward Community, the Environment and a Sustainable Future*. Boston: Beacon Press, 1989.

Hardin, Garret. "The Tragedy of the Commons," *Science*, 162, 1243–1248 (1968).

Hawken, Paul. *The Ecology of Commerce: A Declaration of Sustainability*. New York: HarperCollins Publishers, 1993.

Hawken, Paul, Amory Lovins and L. Hunter Lovins. *Natural Capitalism: Creating the Next Industrial Revolution*. Boston: Little, Brown, 1999.

IUCN with UNEP and WWF. *World Conservation Strategy: Living Resources Conservation for Sustainable Development*. Gland, Switzerland: IUCN, 1980.

Meadows, Donella H., Dennis L. Meadows and Jorgen Randers. *The Limits to Growth: A Report for the Club of Rome's Project on the Predicament of Mankind*. New York: Universe Books, 1972.

Rich, Bruce. *Mortgaging the Earth: The World Bank, Environmental Impoverishment and the Crisis of Development*. Boston: Beacon Press, 1994.

Schumacher, E. F. *Small is Beautiful: A Study of Economics as if People Mattered*. London: Blond & Briggs, 1973.

United Nations Development Program. http://www.undp.org/.

UN Division for Sustainable Development. http://www.un. org/esa/sustdev/index.html.

World Commission on Environment and Development. *Our Common Future*. Oxford: Oxford University Press, 1987.

The Worldwatch Institute. *State of the World 2005: A Worldwatch Institute Report on Progress Toward a Sustainable Society*. New York: W.W. Norton & Company, 2005.

SWAZILAND

The Kingdom of Swaziland is a small landlocked country in southeast Africa, bounded by South Africa on the north, west, and south, and Mozambique to the East. This eastern border coincides with the Lebombo Mountains, a traditional limit to the Swazi. Prior to the arrival of Europeans in the region the various tribes which make up the Swazi people were not bound but national borders but by geography and the presence of competing tribes, particularly the Zulu.

The tribes which make up the Swazi are the Nguni, the Sotho, and the Tonga. Tongaland, part of what is now South Africa, was the home of these tribes until they were forced to the north in the eighteenth century. The earliest recognized ruler of these tribes which make up the Swazi was Ngwane, who led the tribes westward through the Lebombo Mountains to what is now Swaziland. Further definition of the borders was made by his great-grandson, Mswati, who became king in 1840. The Swazi name is derived from King Mswati's.

Mswati attempted to avoid conflict with the arriving Europeans (British and Boers) as well as with the Zulu. He granted lands to the Europeans, and the British helped to remove the threat of the Zulu. Following his death in 1858, a struggle for power within the royal family resulted in the appointment of one of Mswati's sons, Mbandzeni, as king to rule alongside the mother of Mswati's other son Ludonga, who had been killed; because Swazi tradition calls for the king to rule alongside the queen mother and Mbandzeni's mother had died, Mswati's other wife took the post. Mbandzeni reaffirmed the concessions which Mswati had made to the Boers.

The presence of white Europeans caused difficulty for the Swazi rulers, because these foreigners did not respect the traditions and territories of the native population. In addition, the foreigners saw value in such things as minerals (including gold) which would require development for extraction. In exchange for territorial concessions, the Europeans offered relatively cheap trade goods (including firearms) and animals.

Great Britain acquired control over Swaziland as a result of its victory in the Anglo Boer War of 1899.

Under British rule, modern institutions such as money, schools, political redistricting, and taxes were introduced. One of the princes of the royal family, Sobhuza II, was eventually sent to school in the Union of South Africa and would become the first "modern" ruler of Swaziland.

During the first half of the twentieth century, Swaziland was a largely underdeveloped country, with its people torn between traditional ways and the Western ways brought in by the Europeans. During the 1930s, the first efforts were made by Hilda Kuper to document Swazi culture, and her writings provide the basis for much of what is known of Swazi history in the West.

Swaziland's location (nearly surrounded by South Africa) put Swaziland at a disadvantage in trade. Because the country is landlocked it must export through either South Africa or Mozambique, and South Africa was able to effectively control its trade policies. In World War II, some of these restrictions were lifted, and following the war the economic status of the Swazi improved somewhat, since the mining industry made employment opportunities available.

By the 1950s, highways were being built, and even traditional activities like agriculture were being modernized leading to greater productivity.

In 1963, Great Britain imposed the Swaziland Independence Constitution on the nation, establishing legislative and executive councils. While this was in keeping with European institutions of government, it was very much at odds with traditional forms of government in Swaziland. Nevertheless in 1964 elections were held for the Legislative Council, and subsequently the council proposed changes to the constitution leading to the establishment of a Senate and House of Assembly. This constitution took effect in 1967. Swaziland declared independence from Great Britain on September 6, 1968, and a new Independence Constitution took effect; this constitution was suspended in 1973. Other changes were made, and Swaziland currently operates under a constitution put in place in November 2003.

Between the 1950s and 1990s, the population of Swaziland nearly quadrupled, and by 1995 over 1 million people lived in the country. Population growth is expected to moderate in the first decade of the twenty-first century, then drop slightly before the middle of this century.

Swaziland is still a functioning monarchy, although it also has many Western political institutions. One of King Sobhuza II's wives gave birth to the present king, in 1968. The prince was named Makhosetive ("King of All Nations"), and like his father was educated in South Africa. Upon the death of his father in 1982, King Sobhuza II's primary wife

became the Queen Regent. Makhosetive took the title of King Mswati III, and with his own mother began to rule the country.

King Mswati III came under criticism in 2002 over an incident which reveals the degree to which the nation has developed. Traditionally the Swazi king has selected his wives at an annual event, the Reed Dance, at which young women dance for him. In October 2002, one such woman was chosen and taken by the king's agents to one of the palaces, from which she was not permitted communication with her mother. The girl's mother sued the king, and King Mswati III threatened to dismiss the judges hearing the case.

The demand for human rights, particularly women's rights, in Swaziland is very much a modern development in Africa's last monarchy and the king has shown no willingness to change. However, advocates for human rights point out the king's behavior might encourage other men to kidnap their own brides, a procedure unacceptable anywhere but especially in Swaziland, which has a rate of infection with HIV/ AIDS which became the highest in the world in 2004.

THOMAS P. DOLAN

See also Ethnic Conflicts: Southern Africa; Southern Africa: History and Economic Development; Southern Africa: International Relations

References and Further Reading

Kuper, Hilda. *Sobhuza II: Ngwenyama and King of Swaziland*. New York: Africana Publishing Company, 1978.
———. *The Swazi: A South African Kingdom*. New York: Holt, Rinehart and Winston, 1963.
———. *The Uniform of Colour*. New York: Negro Universities Press, 1969.
Ottenberg, Simon, and Phoebe Ottenberg, eds. *Culture and Societies of Africa*. New York: Random House, 1960.
Stevens, Richard P. *Lesotho, Botswana, & Swaziland: The Former High CommissionTerritories in Southern Africa*. New York: Frederick A. Praeger, Publishers, 1967.

SYRIA

Syria had a gross domestic product (GDP) of $17 billion and a population of 16 million in 2000. About 80% of the population are Arab speaking and about 70% Sunni Moslems. The main sectors of the economy are agriculture and oil. Syria is one of the few economies in the Middle East not to have experienced significant liberalization, privatization, and freer foreign trade. President Bashar el-Assad was appointed after the death of his father, Hafez el-Assad in 2000. They are both from the minority Alawite community. The later took power in a military coup in 1971.

In the 1970s, gross domestic product increased by an annual average of 10% in real terms. Although the 1970s were years of growth, the economy did not experience structural change. In 1970, agriculture accounted for 20% of GDP, industry 25%, and services 48%, in 1980 and in 1990 the shares were virtually unchanged. The increase in the share of industry was due to the development of the oil sector rather than to the industrialization of the economy: the share of manufacturing in the economy hardly changed.

In the early 1970s, the Syrian economy experienced nationalization; import protection; large-scale state investment; expansion of the public sector, restrictions on the private sector; subsidization of many goods and services, a multiple exchange rate system and tight controls over the movement of capital. The banking system was totally controlled by the government.

Economic policy in the 1970s aimed at increasing industrial employment, expanding the role of the public sector, while at the same time, private sector activity was permitted within strict limits. The aim was to transform the country within the ideological framework of Arab socialism, from an agriculturally based economy to an industrial one.

Syria benefited from foreign aid from both the Union of Soviet Socialist Republics (USSR) and the Arab Gulf States. Private remittances also increased as Syrians joined other Arab emigrants to work in the Gulf after the 1973–1974 rise in oil prices. As a result of the decline in Gulf oil revenues in the mid-1980s and disputes with the Syrian and Gulf Cooperation Council (GCC), capital inflows declined. The fall in the oil revenues of Gulf States also reduced the demand for Syrian labor there and remittances consequently declined. These factors, accompanied by bad harvests, due to drought in 1982–1984, led to a near zero economic growth rate between 1982 and 1985. This deterioration led to a series of changes in economic policies, at first in the direction of austerity and later towards liberalization.

Given the country's backward technological state, turnkey projects were imported; whole plants were bought from foreign firms and they supplied personnel to set them up. Syria lacked the skilled manpower to operate many of these plants and the heavily politicized and centralized management systems employed failed to make optimal use of the investments after they were completed. Most economic activity was carried out within the framework of a series of five year plans which were inspired by the Soviet Union's experience. The main aim was to generate fast economic growth through public sector investment. The emphasis of the plans varied, with a larger share of

funds being allocated to industry in the 1970s and 1980s than in the 1960s.

In the 1970s and 1980s, the public sector was dominant. However, the actual amount invested in the public sector was always much lower than planned. This was due to the failure of the government to obtain finance for projects in the plan and its inability to undertake all that it hoped to because of administrative failings. On the other hand the private sector exceeded its share in every plan, suggesting that a more decentralized approach would have been more successful.

The 1980s were much more problematic. Between 1980 and 1990, the economy grew more slowly than the population. Capital inflows from the Arab world declined. It was against this background that Syria began to reform its economy in the late 1980s. This was done on an ad hoc basis designed to cope with increasing internal pressures rather than on the basis of a comprehensive program.

Some of the problems that affected the economy in the 1970s and 1980s continued in the early 1990s. These included rapid population growth; reliance on rental incomes such as workers' remittances and foreign aid; a very small manufacturing sector; formidable bureaucracy and politicization of the public sector; high defense spending and a large military establishment; economic isolation, water and electricity shortages. The government subsidized prices through a complex budgetary system and administered other controls with distorting effects throughout the economy.

The period 1990–1994 was one of fast economic growth, with GDP increasing by an annual average of 7.5%. In 1995–1996, it was 6.5% and in 1997–1999 it was estimated at –3%. The deceleration was due to a number of factors. The manufacturing sector suffered from increased competition from imports that resulted from the partial liberalization of foreign trade. The adoption of more stringent financial policies by the government squeezed demand and thus helped to slow the rate of growth. Crude oil production and refining output declined in 1996. A draught that had severe effects on agricultural production in 1999 reinforced these trends.

In recent years, oil exports revenues have also played an important role. Changes in aid and remittance as well as oil revenues have had significant effects on the economy, but their levels were largely outside the control of the government. Since 1994 there has also been a significant inflow of capital from Syrian residents abroad who have invested in new projects under Law Number 10 of 1991.

Economic reforms have had ideological significance in that the regime now wants the private sector to play a major role, especially in investment. Private capital has been invested in sectors of the economy that were previously closed to it.

Structural change takes time and it is therefore necessary to measure development over a period of five to ten years. Between 1980 and 1994, agriculture's share in the economy declined by 4.1%; the mining and quarrying sector's share tripled as a result of the expansion of the oil sector. Although, manufacturing increased in absolute terms, it was very significant that its share in the economy declined. In 1998, it accounted for only 7% of GDP, less than in 1985.

PAUL RIVLIN

See also Ethnic Conflicts: Middle East; Middle East: History and Economic Development; Middle East: International Relations

References and Further Reading

Hinnebusch, Raymond. *Authoritarian Power and State Formation in Ba'athist Syria. Army, Party and Peasant.* Boulder, CO: Westview, 1990.

Maoz, Moshe. *Asad The Sphinx of Damascus.* London: Weidenfeld and Nicolson, 1988.

Perthes, Volker. *The Political Economy of Syria under Asad.* London: I.B. Tauris, 1995.

Rivlin, Paul. *Economic Policy and Performance in the Arab World.* Boulder, CO: Lynne Rienner, 2001.

Seale, Patrick. *Asad of Syria: The Struggle for the Middle East.* London: I.B. Tauris, 1988.

Van Dam, Nicholas. *Struggle for Power in Syria.* London: I. B. Tauris, 1996.

T

TAIWAN

Background Information

Taiwan, officially known as the Republic of China (ROC), is an island of thirty-six thousand square kilometres in the Western Pacific and has a population of 22,749,838. The island is located north of the Philippines, south of Japan, and to the southeast of China. Most of Taiwan is composed of rugged mountain terrain, leaving the alluvial plains of the western coast as the major areas of population and urban settlement. The east coast of the island, with the exception of a rift valley extending from Hualien to Taitung, is largely unsuitable for agriculture and is sparsely settled. The Central Mountain Range runs down the centre of the island from north to south. Jade Mountain (Yushan), at 13,113 feet (3,997 meters), is the tallest mountain peak in East Asia. Straddling the Tropic of Cancer, Taiwan has long, hot summers and cool winters. Winters are cold and rainy in the north, but generally remain warm and sunny in the south. Typhoon season lasts from July to September, which can bring violent storms and dangerous floods to Taiwan.

From 1895 to 1945, Taiwan was a Japanese colony. During that time, its economy was based primarily on agricultural exports and industrial processing of agricultural by-products. Major infrastructure projects, including railroads, ports, and hydroelectric dams, were constructed at that time and served as the base for later development. The island's development under the subsequent rule of the Chinese Nationalist Party (*Kuomintang*, KMT) has thus appeared as nothing short of phenomenal. In 1962, Taiwan had a per capita gross national product (GNP) of $170 USD, placing its economy between those of Zaire and Congo. In 1999, Taiwan calculated its Human Development Index as twenty-third in the world, including a per capita gross domestic product (GDP) of $19,197 USD, showing that its economy had reached the standards of Southern Europe. This economic feat has been treated in academic literature as a paradigmatic example of growth with equity.

The Political Context of Taiwan's Postwar Development

Taiwan's rapid economic development is closely related to the exigencies of the Cold War. At the conclusion of World War II in 1945, the Allies "returned" Taiwan to the Republic of China (ROC) under the leadership of Generalissimo Chiang Kai-shek (1887–1975) and his party, the KMT. The first two years of KMT rule were marked by high inflation, widespread unemployment, and rampant corruption in forms ranging from KMT soldiers stealing from the local population to the government moving entire factories to China.

When local Taiwanese people protested against corruption and undemocratic rule in February 1947,

the KMT state responded by sending troops to Taiwan and killing more than twenty thousand people in the massacre, which is now known as the 2:28 Incident. After the Chinese Communist Party (CCP) established the People's Republic of China (PRC) in 1949, the KMT retreated to Taiwan. The KMT ruled the island—under martial law for forty years—with the claims that only they remained the legitimate government of China and that they would eventually push back the Communists.

Due to its experience in the Korean War, the United States perceived the importance of KMT-ruled Taiwan as an "unsinkable battleship" in the Cold War against Communism and began full support of Chiang Kai-shek. Faced with the spectre of potential domestic opposition and/or invasion from the Communist mainland, the KMT was willing to cooperate with the US government and build Taiwan into a model of successful Asian capitalism.

Agricultural Development

With US encouragement, Taiwan began implementing "Land-to-the-Tiller" agricultural reforms in agriculture in 1953. Members of the landlord class, still cowered by the violent events of February 28, 1947, offered no resistance and accepted stock holdings in nascent state industrial enterprises as compensation for their lands. The state also invested heavily in rural infrastructure and irrigation. From 1954 to 1967, agricultural production maintained an annual rate of 4.4%, a growth that helped check discontentment in the countryside. Overvaluation of the New Taiwan (NT) dollar on world markets, combined with agricultural taxes and policies (such as compulsory procurement of rice at below-market prices), made it possible for the government to transfer resources from agriculture to industry.

Industrial Development

Taiwan began its postwar industrial development with import substitution policies by establishing public enterprises in fields such as steel, petroleum refineries, and shipbuilding; the island also started protecting and nurturing private investment in textiles, plastics, and synthetic fibres. With US financial support and expert advice, as well as preferential access to US markets, Taiwan by the 1960s was able to begin selective policies of export substitution. The initial thrust was primarily focused on labour-intensive production of textiles, footwear, plastic goods, and bicycles.

Taiwan soon developed an industrial structure combining large, often state-owned, industries in the upstream sectors with dense subcontracting networks of private Small and Medium Enterprises (SMEs) in the downstream sectors. "Mainlanders," the Mandarin-speaking people who came with Chiang Kai-shek from China in 1949, held most of the key positions in government and large industry. The "native Taiwanese," who had already lived in Taiwan for generations, were mostly left with positions in labour and in the riskier SME sector.

State campaigns played an instrumental role in the development of these industries. The KMT government, for example, launched a "Living Rooms as Factories" Movement in the 1970s to channel the surplus labour of mothers into subcontracting production in family-owned SMEs. In the larger firms, strong social control, including the placement of security forces in all large factories, ensured a docile workforce with little opposition and no autonomous labour movement.

Economic and Political Shock Waves

In the mid-1970s through the late 1970s, Taiwan was hit by a number of economic and political shocks. Taiwan responded to the Oil Crisis of 1973–1974 and subsequent inflationary pressures by shifting the emphasis of industrial policies to non-energy-intensive, less polluting, and technology-intensive fields such as machine tools, semiconductors, computers, telecommunications, and biotechnology. In 1980, the Hsinchu Science-based Industry was opened to facilitate cooperation between research units of universities and government institutions as well as between domestic and foreign high-tech firms.

At approximately the same time, as the world began to recognize the existence of the People's Republic of China, the KMT's "Republic of China" of Taiwan lost international recognition. The United Nations (UN) ceased recognition of the ROC in 1971, giving the Chinese seat in the UN Security Council to the PRC. Japan and Canada both shifted diplomatic recognition to the PRC in 1972. The United States followed suit in 1979. Chiang Kai-shek died in 1975. His son, Chiang Ching-kuo (1909–1988), replaced him as chairman of the KMT in 1975 and as president of the ROC in 1978. Throughout these political changes, a democratic opposition arose demanding the end of martial law and independence of Taiwan from the KMT-imposed Republic of China.

In December 1979, a Human Rights Day celebration in the southern city of Kaohsiung ended in chaos after pro-government instigators incited violence, and

police used tear gas against the crowd. The KMT used the incident, known as the Kaohsiung Incident, as an excuse to arrest leading members of the opposition. Many of those arrested, including Annette Lu (Lu Hsiu-lien), continued to build up an opposition movement and the opposition Democratic Progressive Party (DPP) in the years to come.

Political and Economic Restructuring

In response to demands of a renewed opposition movement, martial law was finally abolished in 1987. Chiang Ching-kuo died in 1988, to be replaced by his handpicked successor Vice President Lee Teng-hui (b. 1923). In 1996, Lee Teng-hui was the first democratically elected and the first native Taiwanese president in the history of the ROC. In 2000, the opposition DPP candidate Chen Shui-bian was elected president with feminist opposition leader Annette Lu as his chosen vice president.

In the 1990s, due to a rise in the value of the NT dollar and correspondingly high cost of Taiwanese labour, Taiwan underwent further industrial restructuring with a shift from labour-intensive to capital-intensive production. Labour-intensive manufacturing processes, such as for shoes and electronic goods, largely shifted production to mainland China and Southeast Asia, with domestic production shifting to high-tech, capital-intensive industries. Those labour-intensive firms that remained in Taiwan began hiring foreign workers from Thailand, the Philippines, and other Southeast Asian countries to cut labour costs. Taiwan thus became a net exporter of capital in the region.

Rise and Decline of the Information Technology Sector

With economic restructuring, the Taiwanese economy became increasingly dependent on computers and related industries. In 1997, the hardware information technology industry yielded a total production value of $30 billion USD, making it Taiwan's most important foreign exchange earner. Since 1995, Taiwan has been the world's third largest computer hardware supplier, trailing only behind the United States and Japan. In 2000 to 2001, this dependency brought relative economic hardship to Taiwan as the result of a world downturn in the information technology industries. In the second quarter of 2001, the economy contracted by 2.35%, after more than two decades of more than 6% annual growth. In September 2001,

unemployment rose to 5.32%, bringing hardship and economic insecurity to a population that had enjoyed unemployment rates of around 2% since the 1970s. This negative economic condition was surely exacerbated by rapid movement of industrial production from Taiwan to China.

Development of Civil Society

Economic development and prosperity in Taiwan have also led to the creation of a vibrant civil society. Women, formerly urged to follow Confucian virtues of submission to men during the "Living Rooms as Factories" campaign, began lobbying for equal rights through feminist groups such as the Women's Awakening Foundation. Independent labour unions, such as the Taiwan Labour Front, were formed to lobby for workers' rights and began holding an annual march on Labour Day. Environmental groups, including the Taiwan Environmental Protection Union, the Green Party, and local chapters of Greenpeace, started working on issues ranging from nuclear waste to the protection of endangered migratory birds. In 2000, the planned construction of the controversial fourth nuclear power plant became one of the main issues in the presidential election. Some Taiwanese industrialists began claiming that vocal labour and environmental lobbies make Taiwan an unattractive place for investment.

An indigenous rights movement emerged to defend the 3% of Taiwan's population who are of Austronesian ethnicity. Systematically marginalized culturally and economically under both Japanese and KMT rule, these First Nations of Formosa are arguably the main losers in Taiwan's economic development. Many of the issues raised by the movement are thus directly related to development. The Tao people of Orchid Island, for example, lobbied for the removal of nuclear waste from their island and limited self-rule. The Taroko people of Hualien County demanded that Asia Cement return land plots that had been illegally transferred from aboriginal farmers. Indigenous rights received institutional recognition through the establishment of a cabinet-level Council of Aboriginal Affairs in 1996 and the inclusion of indigenous rights in a 1997 amendment to the ROC Constitution.

Relations with China

As many Taiwanese-owned firms transfer industrial production to low-wage China, the economies of

Taiwan and China have became more closely inter-related than ever in history. China, which claims Taiwan as part of its own territory, has isolated the island state diplomatically. China's actions towards Taiwan in recent years have wavered between promises of economic cooperation and threats of military invasion, which have even escalated to a missile crisis during Taiwan's presidential election of 1996. Some Taiwanese people, especially those who came over from China with Chiang Kai-shek in 1949, see in the Chinese economic reform hopes for reviving a united, democratic, and prosperous Republic of China that encompasses both China and Taiwan. The possibility of economic and political union with China has thus become one of the main development debates in Taiwan.

Pro-unification forces argue that only full integration of the two economies will protect Taiwan's high standard of living by making it easier for Taiwanese entrepreneurs to invest in the mainland. Those who argue for the status quo or legal independence argue that it is precisely mainland investment and the related loss of production in Taiwan that have precipitated economic crisis. Surveys conducted by the Mainland Affairs Council in July 2001 showed that 20% of the Taiwanese populace lean toward unification, 16.6% toward legal independence, and the remaining majority prefer to maintain the status quo of *de facto* independence. However, President Chen Shui-bian has been a supporter of Taiwanese independence, and many (including China) think that he will eventually attempt to officially separate Taiwan, which was granted full UN membership in 2001 from mainland China. In early 2005, China passed an anti-secession law, permitting the use of military force should Taiwan attempt to break away. This law has caused great consternation not just for Taiwan but internationally, as the United States has its own legal requirement to assist Taiwan in the event of military action against it, in order to maintain democracy.

SCOTT E. SIMON

References and Further Reading

Amsden, Alice. "Taiwan's Economic History: A Case of Etatisme and a Challenge to Dependency Theory." *Modern China* 5, no. 3 (1979).

Arrigo, Linda Gail. "Economic and Political Control of Women Workers in Multinational Electronics Factories in Taiwan: Martial Law Coercion and World Market Uncertainty." *Contemporary Marxism* no. 11 (1985).

Clark, Cal. *Taiwan's Development: Implications for Contending Political Economy Paradigms*. New York: Greenwood Press, 1989.

Gold, Thomas. *State and Society in the Taiwanese Miracle*. Armonk, NY: M.E. Sharpe, 1986.

Ho, Sam. *Economic Development of Taiwan, 1860–1970*. New Haven, CT: Yale University Press, 1978.

Hsiung, Ping-chun. *Living Rooms as Factories: Class, Gender and the Satellite Factory System in Taiwan*. Philadelphia, PA: Temple University Press, 1996.

Kuo, Shirley W.Y. *The Taiwan Success Story: Rapid Growth with Improved Distribution in the Republic of China*. Boulder, CO: Westview Press, 1981.

Rubinstein, Murray, ed. *The Other Taiwan: 1945 to the Present*. Armonk, NY: M.E. Sharpe, 1994.

———. *Taiwan: A New History*, Armonk, NY: M.E. Sharpe, 1999.

Shieh, Gwo-Shyong. *"Boss" Island: The Subcontracting Network and Micro-Entrepreneurship in Taiwan's Development*. New York: Peter Lang, 1992.

Wade, Robert. *Governing the Market: Economic Theory and the Role of Government in East Asian Industrialization*. Princeton, NJ: Princeton University Press, 1990.

Winkler, Edwin, and Susan Greenhalgh, eds. *Contending Approaches to the Political Economy of Taiwan*. Armonk, NY: M.E. Sharpe, 1990.

TAJIKISTAN

The Republic of Tajikistan is located in Central Asia, bordering with China in the east, with Kyrgyzstan in the northeast, with Uzbekistan in the northwest and west, and with Afghanistan in the south. This land-locked mountainous country has a land area of 143,100 square kilometers (55,250 square miles) and is the smallest in the Central Asian region.

The population of Tajikistan was estimated at about 6,578,680 in 2001. It is one of the least urbanized countries in the Commonwealth of Independent States (CIS) with around 72% of its people living in rural areas (CIA estimate). The country's capital city, Dushanbe (known as Stalinabad between 1929 and 1961), is home to 550,000 people (estimated in 2001) or 8% of the population. Tajikistan has one of the fastest growing populations in the CIS with the growth rate of 2.12% (33.23 births per 1,000 people estimated in 2001), and its population could double within the next twenty to twenty-five years. The official language is Tajik; Russian is widely used in government and business; and Uzbek is also widely spoken. Sunni Muslims make up 85% of the population, with a 5% Shi'a minority, and 10% of the population follows other religions, such as Eastern Orthodox Christianity, Lutheranism, and Evangelical Lutheranism.

Since ancient times, the Persian-speaking Tajiks were engaged in labor-intensive agriculture, crafts, and servicing trade on the Great Silk Road. They established flourishing city-states in Central Asia and developed sophisticated architectural and irrigation skills. However, these city-states suffered considerably from the thirteenth century onward because of the devastating Genghis Khan invasion and numerous incursions led by various Turkic-speaking khans.

Consequently, the Tajik society entered the nineteenth century as a backward, feudal country with most of the population engaged in subsistence economy. The Great Game—the competition between Great Britain and Russia—established a line of control between the great empires, when one part of Tajik-populated land was given to Afghanistan and the other part was annexed to a Turkistan governor-generalship that was controlled by Russia.

Major economic and social changes were brought to the Tajik society after the Russian Revolution of 1917. The territory of Tajikistan was the last area in Central Asia where the Bolsheviks had established their control after suppressing British-sponsored resistance. In 1924, with Soviet assistance, Tajikistan became a Soviet Autonomous Republic (province), a constituent part of the Uzbekistan Republic. Only in 1929 was it granted the status of the union republic, a constituent part of the USSR, when it was established within its present borders plus an additional territory of Leninabad region. The Communist Party of Tajikistan (CPT) came to power, to remain the single ruling party for the next seventy years.

After establishing full control over the territory of Tajikistan, the Soviet government has made consistent attempts to overcome both the patriarchal nature of the society and the backwardness of the national economy that was mainly based on subsistence agriculture. Although informally the government tolerated some degree of entrepreneurship, it established tight state control over most of the enterprises and directed economic development through central planning. In the 1930s, the government forced all farmers to join *kolkhozy*, or the state-controlled cooperatives (specializing in cotton, silk, and crop cultivation). During World War II, the Soviet government relocated a number of factories from the Nazi-occupied territories and established new industries, including defense, heavy industry (such as agricultural machinery), light industry (such as food processing and textile and garment manufacturing), and mining of nonferrous metals. It also invested in construction of huge hydroelectric power stations, one of the most expensive schemes in the USSR. According to official statistics, Tajikistan's economy grew twenty-one-fold between 1940 and 1984; however, in the 1970s and 1980s, the economy grew at a considerably slower rate due to rising structural and other difficulties in the Soviet-planned economy. The state-led rapid economic development and intensive agriculture led to environmental degradation and erosion of the fragile soil of mountainous oases and valleys.

In the middle of the 1980s, Gorbachev launched his *perestroika* policy that aimed at the stimulation of economic growth through economic decentralization.

This policy split the ranks of the CPT and led to a popular unrest in Dushanbe in 1990. Although the CPT won parliamentary elections in 1990 and its representative, Rahmon Nabyev, won presidential elections, the opposition refused to recognize the results. On the eve of its independence, Tajikistan was sliding into a civil war.

Late Twentieth and Early Twenty-First Century Developments

Tajikistan declared its independence from the USSR on September 9, 1991. The conservative government resisted any kind of radical political and economic reforms and stuck to the Soviet era policies and ideology. In 1992, the civil war, fueled by a regional rivalry and growing Islamic radicalism, broke out in Tajikistan and led to the ousting of President Nabyev. After numerous clashes in which both sides——the government and the opposition——destroyed infrastructure, properties, and irrigation systems, a coalition of regional elites installed Imomali Rakhmonov as the head of the parliament. In 1994, he won the presidential elections. In 1997, with Russian assistance, he managed to end the war after signing a peace accord with the United Tajik Opposition (UTO). The agreement granted the UTO several governmental positions. In the bitter contested presidential elections of 1999, the UTO candidate lost to President Rakhmonov.

Since 1997, the Tajikistan's government has adopted a program of postwar economic reconstruction focusing on restoration of major sectors of the economy and achieving food self-efficiency. The government welcomes private initiatives, promotes liberalization of its trade, and has opened up the national economy to international investment. It was among the last CIS states to introduce its national currency, the somoni, in October 2000. According to the World Bank, Tajikistan's economy declined at an average annual rate of 10% between 1990 and 2000 due to devastating effects of the civil war. The country increasingly relies on the export of raw materials to the international market, especially aluminum, cotton, and fruits. The country needs considerable foreign direct investments and international assistance to modernize existing technologies and to conduct major economic changes.

Agriculture, industries, and services are the three main pillars of the modern Tajikistan's economy, contributing 19.4, 25.7, and 54.9%, respectively, to the gross domestic product (GDP) (World Bank, 2001 estimate). The country depends heavily on imports of

machinery, fuel, industrial consumer goods, and food products. In 1999 and 2000, the national government appealed to the international community for food assistance, as its population faced hunger and starvation from the devastating drought. Total external debt reached $922 million (USD) in 2001, and it is expected to grow in the near future.

Due to the civil war and difficulties of postwar reconciliation, there was a steady decline in living standards among all groups of the population, especially women and children. The country remains the poorest country in the former Soviet Union, with average monthly wages equal to $12 to $15 USD and with 83% of the population living below the poverty line (World Bank 2001 estimate). At least fifty thousand people per annum leave for other countries in a search for jobs and better standards of living. In 2001, the United Nations Development Programme's (UNDP's) Human Development Index (HDI) put Tajikistan in 103rd place out of 162, behind all the former Soviet countries.

ALFIA ABAZOVA AND RAFIS ABAZOV

See also Commonwealth of Independent States: History and Economic Development; Commonwealth of Independent States: International Relations

References and Further Reading

Allworth, Edward. *Central Asia: 130 Years of Russian Dominance. A Historical Overview*. London: Duke University Press, 1994.

Djalili, Mohammad-Reza, Frédéric Grare, and Shirin Akiner, eds. *Tajikistan: The Trials of Independence*. New York: St. Martin's Press, 1997.

International Monetary Fund. *Tajikistan*. Washington, DC: 1992.

———.*Tajikistan: Second Review Under the Third Annual Arrangement. Country Report, No. 01/115*. Washington, DC: 2001.

Pomfret, R. *The Economies of Central Asia*. Princeton, NJ: Princeton University Press, 1995.

World Bank. *Tajikistan*, Washington, DC: 1994.

UNDP. *Tajikistan. National Human Development Report*. Bishkek: 2000.

TALIBAN

The Taliban is a fundamentalist Islamic movement that came to power in the chaos of Afghanistan in the years after the Soviet occupation (1979–1989). The group's most notorious act was to have provided safe havens for Osama bin Laden and his al-Qaeda terrorist organization after the attacks of September 11, 2001 against the United States' World Trade Center in New York and Pentagon in Washington, DC.

Background

In the 1970s, Afghanistan was a client state of the Soviet Union. Unsatisfied with the leadership of its client, the Soviets staged an invasion on Christmas Eve 1979 and put in place a more compliant government. This brutal invasion inspired a widespread revolt against the Soviet presence. A guerilla war against the Soviets went on for ten years. The guerillas were supported by Islamic states around the world (as well as by the United States, which provided covert aid to the anti-Soviet fighters). The fighters in this war, many of them volunteers from the Islamic world, called themselves *mujahideen* (holy warriors). The war did immense damage to Afghanistan, killing hundreds of thousands and leaving millions homeless. The war also radicalized Islamic extremists who saw the guerilla wars in Afghanistan as part of a larger war between Islamic values and corrupt foreign ideologies.

By the late 1980s, the Soviets had decided that the war in Afghanistan could not be won. In 1989, they pulled out their troops. The Soviet defeat, however, did not end the fighting in Afghanistan. The *mujahideen* spent three more years fighting against the pro-Soviet government that remained in place, finally defeating it in 1992. They then fought amongst themselves as different factions of the *mujahideen*, each backing a different leader and fighting over control of the country. It was in this context of more than a dozen years of turmoil that the Taliban rose to power.

The word Taliban comes from the Arabic word for student, "talib," combined with the Persian plural suffix "-an." This name is appropriate because the Taliban began as a student movement. The roots of the Taliban's ideology are in India. In the nineteenth century, a conservative Islamic movement arose called the Deobandi Movement, named after the Indian town of Deoband, in which its most famous learning center was located. Deobandi *madrassas* (religious schools) taught a very traditional interpretation of Islam in which modern education was disparaged and women were placed in a strongly subservient role. Deobandi-style *madrassas* spread across South Asia but were particularly prominent and influential in Pakistan, a country to which many Afghanis had fled during the ongoing wars in their country. Many Afghani returned to their country after spending time in these *madrassas* and were strongly committed to bringing about a traditional Islamic state in their homeland. Starting in 1994 in the southern province of Kandahar, a group of these Deobandi-inspired Afghan students began the Taliban movement.

The students' attempt to retake the country received broad support from many people in Afghanistan who

were tired of the constant fighting between various *mujahideen* warlords. The Taliban was also aided in its rise to power by early financial support from Osama bin Laden, a wealthy Saudi who had dedicated his life to Islamic holy war. From a small group of men, the Taliban quickly expanded into a nationwide movement and spread across the country, defeating most of the Afghan warlords (many of whose troops deserted wholesale to the Taliban forces). By 1999, the group controlled 95% of the country (a small area remained under the control of the opposition warlord named Ahmad Shah Massoud). Afghanistan's civil war was largely over, and the country's new rulers were the Taliban forces.

Afghanistan Under the Taliban

Following ideological roots, the Taliban set about imposing its interpretation of Islam on Afghanistan. Under the leadership of Mullah Muhammad Omar, the Taliban forces attacked anything they interpreted as not in accord with traditional Islamic values. They banned television, ordered men to grow traditionally long beards, and attacked non-Muslim religious symbols. The most infamous of these attacks was the March 2001 destruction of the Bamiyan Buddhas, giant statues carved into a mountainside that were at least 1,500 years old.

The Taliban also targeted the producers of opium and heroin in Afghanistan (both drugs are derived from the poppy plant, which is easily grown in Afghanistan's climate). The Taliban's strict adherence to the Koran, and the group's ruthless methods, led it to successfully ban the opium and heroin trade in Afghanistan. Although this was supported by some foreign anti-drug organizations, it had a negative effect on many Afghanis because heroin export was one of their main sources of income.

A key group victimized by Taliban orthodoxy was Afghan women. The Taliban decreed that women be covered from head to toe in a traditional black robe called a chador. Women who wore high heels under their robes were beaten. Most damagingly, women were forced to quit their jobs. In a poor country where many men were dead after the years of fighting and where women were therefore often the primary income earners, this decree was economically devastating. The Taliban's restrictions also extended to young girls who were forbidden from attending school (Deoband orthodoxy argued that girls needed no education after the age of eight).

The Taliban's narrow-minded religious attitudes hampered efforts of international aid organizations

that were making efforts to rebuild the war-shattered country. Female aid workers were often harassed, and some organizations responded by withdrawing their employees. Even those organizations that stayed found it difficult to raise funds for a country that had such anti-Western beliefs.

The Taliban also allied itself with forces hostile to the United States, most notoriously Osama bin Laden. Bin Laden was a close confidant of Afghan leader Mullah Omar and was allowed to establish bases and training camps for his al-Qaeda organization in Afghanistan. By 2001, Afghanistan had become the primary base of bin Laden and al-Qaeda.

Many Afghans were unhappy with the Taliban. Its extremist polices did not suit Afghanistan's relatively more relaxed attitudes toward Islam. Afghanistan's many ethnic minorities also were disturbed by the Taliban's tendency to favor the Pashtun over other ethnic groups. Kandahar, where the Taliban gained their first foothold, was dominated by ethnic Pashtun. The inability of the Taliban to relieve Afghanistan's desperate poverty also alienated many people. Nevertheless, the Taliban had many supporters among conservative Muslims and Pashtun chauvinists.

The United States Intervention

The Taliban's support for bin Laden and al-Qaeda became fatally important after the September 11, 2001, terrorist attacks against the United States. President George Bush, with widespread international support, held the Taliban government partially responsible for the attacks because of its support for Bin Laden. The Taliban refused US demands that bin Laden be extradited for his responsibility in the September 11 attacks. President Bush responded by ordering US forces to overthrow the Taliban. The United States was aided in its efforts by Ahmad Shah Massoud and his Northern Alliance, which had never given up in its war against the Taliban. Backed by heavy US air power and a small numbers of elite US troops, the Northern Alliance was able to come down out of its strongholds and retake the country in a few months. US bombing began in early October, and by December 7, the Taliban had lost their final base in Kandahar.

Although the US-aided attack was able to overthrow the Taliban, it did not succeed in capturing bin Laden, who was believed to have escaped into the mountainous regions of neighboring Pakistan. Pakistan's government had been one of the Taliban's few international supporters (along with Saudi Arabia). After September 11, Pakistan became officially hostile

to the Taliban, but many Pakistanis, including some government officials, were still sympathetic to both the Taliban and Osama bin Laden.

Under US supervision, but also with extensive help from the rest of the international community, a coalition of Afghan groups met in Bonn, Germany, and agreed to the creation of a coalition government. Hamid Karzai was elected president of the first post-Taliban government by representatives from around the country. Karzai was reelected in October 2004 in the new Afghanistan's first national elections (in contrast with the Taliban's attitudes toward women, Karzai's government included three women ministers).

The new Afghan government faced significant challenges, including a country still devastated by war, regional warlords who were reluctant to share power with the central government, and a Taliban force that still had not completely admitted defeat. Thousands of US and other foreign troops continued to operate in Afghanistan, helping Karzai's government to maintain order and track down still active bands of Taliban guerillas. The Talibans period of rule had left impoverished the country, but some Afghanis, particularly in the southern areas, remained sympathetic to its conservative Islamic ideology. The hostility to the presence of foreigners on Afghan soil also helped to give Taliban insurgents some popular support. Even after the 2004 elections, Taliban attacks, particularly in hard-to-reach rural areas, remained a serious problem.

Most Afghanis, however, seemed to be generally relieved to be free from the Taliban's onerous restrictions and religious rulings. Taliban government bodies, like the Department to Prevent Vice, were replaced by schools and hospitals (funded, in part, by more than $2 billion of international aid). A dark lining to this silver cloud is the resurgence of the heroin trade. In 2004, freed from the Taliban's antidrug policies, Afghanistan again became the world's number one exporter of heroin.

CARL SKUTSCH

See also Afghanistan; Women: Legal Status; Women Living under Muslim Laws (WLUML); Women: Role in Development

References and Further Reading

Ewans, Martin. *Afghanistan: A Short History of Its People and Politics.* New York: HarperCollins Perennial, 2002.
Griffin, Michael. *Reaping the Whirlwind: Al Qa'ida and the Holy War.* London: Pluto Press, 2003.
Marsden, Peter Richard Valentine. *The Taliban: War, Religion and the New Order in Afghanistan.* London; New York: Oxford University; Zed Books, 1998.
Matinuddin, Kamal. *The Taliban Phenomenon: Afghanistan 1994–1997.* Karachi: Oxford University Press, 1999.
Rashid, Ahmed. *Taliban: Militant Islam, Oil and Fundamentalism.* New Haven, CT: Yale Nota Bene, 2001.

TANZANIA

Geography, Topography, and Climate

Tanzania consists of Tanganyika, on the African mainland, and the offshore islands of Zanzibar and Pemba. The country is situated in East Africa, bordered by the Indian Ocean to the east and by Lake Tanganyika to the west, and comprises 945,087 square kilometres. From the coast, it rises to high plateaus and mountainous regions. The climate is heavily influenced by the monsoon seasons. The coast has a tropical climate with an annual rainfall of approximately one thousand millimetres, while the highlands have a moderate climate with an annual rainfall of approximately two thousand millimetres. Ecological conditions limit agriculture to a relatively small section of the country.

Historic Past and Economic Situation

Tanzania is inhabited by the Bantu peoples, with Indian and Arab minorities on the coast. From the first century CE onward, the coast and the islands have had commercial contacts with the Middle East. In part, this has led to the near total Islamization of the coast and islands. Main export goods were raw materials, such as ivory. The coast was occupied by the Portuguese from the beginning of the sixteenth to the middle of the eighteenth centuries and thereafter by the Omanis, many of whom settled on Zanzibar. In 1884, the Germans claimed formal possession of Tanganiyka, and in 1890, the British became the hegemonial power in the Omani Sultanate of Zanzibar. After the First World War, Britain received a League of Nations mandate for Tanganyika.

In the 1920s Africans founded local welfare societies to help those whose livelihoods suffered under the colonial economy. One of these societies, the Tanganyika African Association (TAA), gained influence throughout the whole territory. In April 1953, the teacher Julius K. Nyerere was elected president of the TAA. Together with other young Nationalists, he founded the Tanganyika African National Union (TANU) in 1954. The focus of TANU's program was the fight for independence and the establishment of a

democratic state. TANU grew rapidly and became influential in the entire country. Pressure on the colonial government grew; in September 1958 and February 1959, TANU had to concede elections for African members for the Legislative Council, which were overwhelmingly won by TANU. The first free, common and equal elections in 1962 were also won by TANU with an absolute majority.

Tanganyika became independent in 1961 and Zanzibar in 1963; in 1964, Tanganyika and Zanzibar merged into the United Republic of Tanzania. The republic was ruled as a one-party state by Julius Nyerere and TANU. In 1977, TANU and the Afro-Shirazi Party (ASP), which had ruled Zanzibar under the auspices of TANU, formed the Revolutionary Party or *Chama cha Mapinduzi* (CCM). Nyerere surrendered office to his Vice President Hassan Ali Mwinyi in 1985, who ruled Tanzania until 1995. In 1990, the government officially sanctioned political debate on multiparty democracy as an alternative to continued one-party rule by the CCM. This one-party rule had led to a bureaucratic paralysis, though the population largely accepted this. In 1992, Tanzania changed its constitution and introduced a multiparty system. This transition was executed in an orderly fashion. In October 1995, multiparty legislative elections were held for the first time. The CCM achieved a significant majority, particularly because of their omnipresence in the political and social sectors and because the new political parties and their candidates remained weak. Benjamin Mkapa of the CCM was elected President and was easily reelected in October 2000.

Tanzania's economy is still predominantly dependent on agriculture. Main export goods are coffee, cotton, tobacco, and sisal. Main trading partners are the United Kingdom, France, Japan, and India. The government seeks to maintain macroeconomic stability and has received good marks from the donor community for its economic and administrative reform efforts. Foreign direct investment into the industrial sector is relatively high. Significant efforts are being made to develop tourism. However, the disastrous economic and social situations of vast parts of the population have not improved and continue to show a downward tendency. Many people earn their living in the informal sector. The situation has been aggravated by the privatisation of state enterprises, which has resulted in job losses. In addition, occasional droughts have reduced agricultural production and have served to aggravate the already precarious situation. As such, Tanzania is still one of the poorest countries in the world.

The gross domestic product (GDP) per capita was estimated at $600 (USD) in 2003; the labor force occupation in 2002 included agriculture (80%) and industry and services (20%). The infant mortality rate was estimated at 102.13 deaths per 1,000 live births in 2004. Life expectancy of the total population amounts to 44.39 years (2004). The HIV/AIDS rate in the country is high: the prevalence of the disease amongst adults was 7.8% (1.5 million people in 2001). In 2001, approximately 140,000 Tanzanians died of AIDS. The *CIA Fact Book* (2003) estimates that 78.2% of the total population aged fifteen and over can read and write English, Swahili, or Arabic.

Economic and Civil Development Since 1945

In 1945, Africans were nominated for the first time to the Legislative Council in Tanganyika, through which the British administration maintained political control. The number of African members was subsequently increased from two to four, with three unofficial Asian members and four European members. During the second half of the 1950s, the influence of TANU in the council increased considerably, partially through effective co-optation of the Asian minority. In September 1960, a predominantly TANU government took office.

On Zanzibar, only the Europeans and Arabs were represented in the Legislative Council. Though a reform of the Council took place in the mid-1950s, the unrest among local African and Arab political circles increased and was channeled into the formation of political parties. The first was the mostly Arab Zanzibar Nationalist Party (ZNP) created in 1955, whose political program was modeled on the Marxist/Pan-Arabist regime in Egypt. In 1957, the more moderate Afro-Shirazi Party (ASP) was founded. Subsequently, the Zanzibar and Pemba Peoples' Party (ZPPP) splintered off from the ASP. The British finally agreed to allow free elections for six of the seats in the Legislative Council. The elections took place in July 1957; the ASP won five seats, and the small Muslim League won the sixth seat. The ethnic and political hostility among the parties continued to grow, however, and manifested itself especially in the form of the mutual boycotting of the one party by the other. The elections of January 1961 produced a deadlock because of the twenty-two seats; the ASP and ZNP each occupied eleven. New elections took place in June, with the ZNP and ZPPP forming an election coalition. Favoured by the majority voting system, the coalition won thirteen seats and the ASP only ten, though the ASP had the most votes. The ASP smelled electoral fraud; fighting broke out, leaving sixty-eight people dead. The last preindependence elections, which took place in June 1963, confirmed the results of 1961, even

though the ASP again topped the list. In December 1963, Zanzibar became independent under a ZNP/ZPPP government, which, however, was swept away by a "revolution" in January 1964. This revolution was mainly pursued by the ASP under Sheikh Karume, who expelled the Sultan and many Arabs and Indians from the island. TANU and ASP, which had maintained friendly relations since the struggle for independence, formed Tanganyika and Zanzibar into a union on April 26, 1964. However, Zanzibar remained relatively autonomous in respect to its domestic affairs.

Immediately following Tanganyika's independence, efforts were made to implement a program that depended on foreign investment to support massive, capital-intensive industrialization and agricultural development projects. From 1961 to 1965, the number of manufacturing establishments employing ten people or more increased by almost 160%. However, Tanzania's economy was mainly governed by the still-existing colonial-style economic structures, namely large tea, sisal, and cotton plantations producing for the European markets. These structures supported a pattern of investment and income distribution that favoured a small number of farmers and foreign entrepreneurs. On the other hand, Tanzania completely neglected its own national food requirements and the diversification of export products.

By the middle of the 1960s, it became apparent that the ambitious plans were not yielding anticipated results and that Tanzania's economy had to rely mainly on foreign donors. Income differentials increased dramatically, rural-based development was ignored, and local expertise remained inadequate. Facing these imbalances, President Nyerere launched a Socialist development agenda in 1967, outlined in the so-called Arusha Declaration. Priority was now given to the state-controlled development of the agricultural sector through *Ujamaa Vijijini* (Socialism in the Villages). Peasants were moved to newly constructed settlements to promote efficient agricultural production; foreign investment was discouraged to limit the dependence on outside help. These policies of self-reliance, however, provoked a long-term economic downswing and macroeconomic imbalances: since every domestic demand was to be fulfilled by domestic production, Tanzania forced its withdrawal from international markets. Outside factors like severe price fluctuations for coffee on the world market and two oil-price shocks (1973–1974 and 1979) worsened the situation. When the *Ujamaa* policies failed to produce the desired results, Tanzania found itself in a serious economic crisis in the early 1980s. However, by leveling the potentially divisive array of social groups and by promoting Swahili as a national language, *Ujamaa* made Tanzania one of the few African countries that remained relatively undisturbed by ethnic, racial, and religious conflicts.

In 1986, the newly appointed CCM government under President Mwinyi embarked on a broad-based Economic Recovery Programme supported by the International Monetary Fund (IMF) and the World Bank. The statist *Ujamaa* orientation was gradually abandoned in favour of a market-oriented approach, and the government started to sell off some of its many parastatals.

Once Tanzania changed its constitution and introduced a multiparty system in 1992, the first multiparty elections were held in 1995, first on the islands of Zanzibar and Pemba and then on the mainland. To a high degree, the elections on Zanzibar revolved around the issue of future relations between the islands and the mainland. The ruling party, the CCM, stood for the continuation of the Union status quo, while the Zanzibarian Civic United Front (CUF) wanted greater independence for Zanzibar within the Union. CCM won twenty-six seats in Zanzibar's Parliament against CUF's twenty-four. Subsequently, the CCM was accused by CUF of electoral fraud, and foreign observers reported irregularities. For example, in some constituencies, the numbers of votes were counted higher than the number of registered voters. The elections on the mainland were clearly won by the CCM.

The new President, Benjamin Mkapa, represented a break with the past. In accordance with the IMF, he launched reforms aiming at increasing the effectiveness of fiscal policy, promoting the private sector by deregulating investments, divesting parastatals, and paying more attention to basic health care and infrastructure. In 1996, the IMF approved a three-year credit. Though Tanzania still enjoys political stability, the steady growth of the private economical sector and successive job losses endanger the social cohesion of the country. Moreover, in the wake of the formation of political parties, ethnic and religious tensions have increased. In particular, Indians have been under frequent verbal attack by opposition parties on the mainland. For example, in January 1993, the leader of the Democratic Party (DP), Christopher Mtikila, utilizing African resentments against the Asian residents, stirred up aggression against the Asian Tanzanians by accusing them of economically exploiting the African majority. Violence immediately followed Mtikila's campaign, and Indian Tanzanians were physically attacked by DP supporters.

The Muslim-Christian divide within the Union shows signs of widening because of Zanzibar's strife for more independence from the Christian-dominated mainland. There exists growing dissatisfaction of African Muslims on the mainland in regard to their continuing discrimination in many sectors of life, and

there are a latent mixture of social problems and religious animosities. The general elections in October 2000 brought a convincing victory for Mkapa and the CCM on the mainland, while the CCM victory on Zanzibar was again suspected by the CUF and foreign observers to have been doctored by the election committee. Subsequent outbreaks of violence by CUF supporters and bomb threats create a tense atmosphere on both the islands and the mainland.

REINHARD KLEIN-ARENDT

Further Reading

Iliffe, John. *A Modern History of Tanganyika.* Cambridge: Cambridge University Press, 1979.

Kaiser, Paul J. "Structural Adjustment and the Fragile Nation: The Demise of Social Unity in Tanzania." *The Journal of Modern African Studies* 34, no. 2 (1996).

Kebede, John Admassu. *The Changing Face of Rural Policy in Tanzania.* London: Minerva Press, 2000.

Kurtz, Laura S. *Historical Dictionary of Tanzania.* Metuchen and London: Scarecrow Press, 1979.

McHenry, Dean E. *Limited Choices. The Political Struggle for Socialism in Tanzania.* Boulder, CO: Lynne Rienner Publishers, 1994.

Ofcansky, Thomas P., and Rodger Yeager. *Historical Dictionary of Tanzania.* 2nd ed. Lanham, MD: Scarecrow Press, 1997.

Rugumamu, Severine M. *Lethal Aid: The Illusion of Socialism and Self-Reliance in Tanzania.* Trenton, NJ: African World Press, 1996.

Voigt-Graf, Carmen. *Asian Communities in Tanzania: A Journey Through Past and Present Times.* Hamburg: Institute of African Affairs, 1998.

TECHNOLOGY: IMPACT ON DEVELOPMENT

The Premises of Transferring Technology and Economic Development

J. Schumpeter (1939), who states that the main cause of the 1929 Depression was too-sudden economic growth, was inspired by the ideas of the economist C. Juglar (1862). As a matter of fact, the rapid increase of entrepreneurs led to the decrease of profits, and when the export markets were overloaded, incentives for innovation dramatically declined; then depression set in. The new phase of economic expansion would begin only with the emergence of new markets, followed by innovations. J. Schumpeter (1954) considers that profit seeking is the heart of the capitalistic system's growth. Profit is the reward of the dynamic and innovative entrepreneur. Profit seeking is thus the

motivator of technological progress, which is the engine of growth. Irregularities in technological progress explain the irregularities in economic growth. Then, innovation develops best in clusters, where complementary innovations bring the dynamic of economic growth. For R. Solow (1956), technological progress comes about with the increase of population, which then increases the work factor; thus, technological progress sustains the rhythm of economic growth. Solow states that these two factors are exogenous: (i) technological progress and (ii) increase in population.

Technological Progress and Technological Learning for Development

For his work on the Indian Economic Plan in the 1960s, A. Sen (1982) made technological choices, and these choices were represented by the intermediary choice of techniques in terms of capital intensity and were stated to maximize capital and labor strengths.

In general, the question of choice of technology led the economy in a specific direction that is called dualism, with its own distinction between technological progress in the traditional sector and technology in the modern sector. The modern sector has the capacity to attract capital and is characterized by a fixed coefficient of substitution between various sectors with more or fewer techniques incorporated according to the sector. These techniques are determined by the greater or lesser necessity of combining capital and labor resources; technological progress in this modern sector increases the capital-intensive sector. However, in the traditional sector, the production methods are more flexible. There can be substitutions between capital and labor resources. The dominant vision in the 1960s gave preference to technological progress that maximized the capital intensity of the product. This technological progress resulted in accelerating economic growth.

The economist F. Perroux (1961) in his book, *The Economy of the Twentieth Century,* explains that economic growth must not be confused with economic progress. According to the author, the evolution of society does not depend on the increase in the real revenue of the population but rather on living and social conditions, especially health, education, security, and freedom. Economic progress is linked to social progress and technological progress.

In the 1970s, the economic debate on technological progress was centered on the question of intermediate technologies, a question analyzed by I. Sachs (1980) in his book on ecodevelopment. Arguments continued with A. Emmanuel (1981); he analyzed

ecodevelopment with the use of appropriated technologies, mentioning the saving of nature and local technological capacity, enabling the selection of intermediate technologies. For both economists, ecodevelopment signifies respect toward the environment and traditions in an idyllic vision of village organization. Local and imported technology could act as a bridge between traditional and modern techniques and could result in appropriately adapted technology. These adapted technologies formed the pattern used in Southeast Asian countries at the end of the 1970s. But J. Galtung (1978), in is research paper for UNCTAD which became the highlight point for the researchers at the United Nations University, developed a new approach to economics in mentioning the necessary step toward an autonomous technology for developing countries that can lead to development and ecological balance.

Up to the 1980s, technological progress was considered to be an exogenous production factor, which means not being influenced by the behavior of economic agents, or resulted from economic activity. In the following decade, a neoclassical economic current suggests that technological progress and innovation are endogenous variables. Paul Romer (1986), in his article "Increasing Returns and Long-Run Growth," clearly stipulates that technological progress is a decisive factor of growth. In his article "Increasing Returns and New Development in the Theory of Growth," P. Romer (1991) mentions that technological progress is naturally endogenous because it is the result of the behavior of economic agents and especially the behavior of enterprises. As a result, state intervention is also considered to be more legitimate. Governments then support research and development, and technological progress is accepted as endogenous to the enterprise. Government has gained a new legitimacy in its intervention in business affairs, especially in the Newly Industrialized Economies; this new theory of growth comes with technological change and the right institutions. The New Theory of Growth tends to promote knowledge economy as the base to sustain economic growth.

Some economists mention that innovation is often the source of efficient specialization. When top companies are the only ones to master microchip production, they are the ones that particularly benefit because of their specialization and because of the strong demand for data-processing products. In the beginning of the 2000, this industry of high-added value, because of its great innovative capacity, could contribute to effective specialization in the home country and in the producing country.

If governments are to sustain technological progress, the question is: How can governments best support technological progress? Technological progress is often the condition for the enterprise to maintain its quality competitiveness vis-à-vis its competitors in new promising markets, especially in East Asian countries.

The economic and technological interdependence in East Asia was an important background for the development of the New Industrialized Economies. Innovation was the most important point for the development of these economies, and each country was linked to the "dynamic regional system of innovation and technological learning" (Hobday, 1995). Direct investment and trade linkage to the technological system were the crucial points of the development of these economies. In East Asian countries, high technology start-up companies were the mainstay of frontier innovation. Governments of the East Asian countries were able to foster modern infrastructures to respond to companies that were involved in innovation.

The latecomers have passed through different stages of technological development. At the beginning, firms were producing labor-intensive products by means of joint ventures and subcontracting, and these arrangements were made mainly by Japanese companies and in a lesser degree by US and European firms. However, transnational companies were also attracted to East Asian countries for the reason of low labor costs. These latter companies supplied training and taught manufacturing processes to local engineers, who in turn trained local technicians.

Later, the same companies were set up to produce consumer electrical goods and electronic products. Some local companies at that time set up their own subsidiaries, becoming thus the supplier of transnational companies by upgrading their production process. Then, to meet more complex export demands, these firms were forced to acquire higher technological know-how. They learned to design products under Original Equipment Manufacture (OEM) arrangements. These new companies benefited from the improvement of transportation and communication infrastructures. Furthermore, they took advantage of a well-educated labor force.

Industrial and technological innovations were set up to further new opportunities. New suppliers for local companies learned new skills and responded positively to foreign investment. Technological advance and automation were improved particularly in Singapore; but as labor costs increased, companies relocated to technological parks, such as Batamin.

Industrial structures, especially in the electronics industry, comprising transnational companies as well as smaller ones emerged. The vision of technological integration in East Asia was devised in Hong Kong through the interplay of technological learning and

practice by which firms acquired technological excellence. Firms, by this process, could increase their knowledge and improve the skills of their labor force.

The Hobday (2000) thesis was meant to show that the latecomer. countries were able to upgrade their way of managing their economies by technological learning. This model consisted in bringing together industry, research, and technological learning to better their production system in stages. This model of the 1980s had to confront and replace the rigid traditional stages of development. In order to bring latecomer countries up to leader country standards, it was imperative to invent new products and simultaneously to combine innovative capacities, low-cost production facilities, and high-range niche markets.

The originality of East Asian subsidiaries was to link technology and export markets in such a way as to avoid technological bottlenecks in some export markets. Thus, the linkage of technological learning and market capabilities had so increased profit margins and markets that new products needed to be introduced through long-term investments in research and development.

This unique system of technological development through innovation in East Asian countries took center stage in development and research. Through the electronics industry, manufacturing technology could be mastered, thereby improving the process of technological production. This pattern of technological innovation is responsible for the dominant development of East Asian countries, through progressively updating the innovative capacities to take advantage of market opportunities.

Global Production Networking and Technological Change

After the financial crisis of 1997, which badly disrupted the Asian and global economies, the process of technological advance and production networking started again under World Trade Organization (WTO) impetus. Furthermore, China's entry in the WTO was also an overriding factor for regional development and the setting up of international networks.

Firms that had developed the OEM have now risen to Original Design Manufacture (ODM) codes and even to Original Brand Manufacture status, which extend to global production networks.

These networks were implemented to level trade barriers; to consolidate such industries as electronics, engineering, and automotive; and to bring geographic proximity to markets. For instance, the production of trucks and passenger cars for East Asian markets has shifted to Thailand, and now leading automotive companies are choosing China and to some extent Korea as the competitive hub for regional networking. Companies have favored China and Thailand because of lower costs and the better-educated labor force.

East Asian firms are responding to the changes in their market environment by using global production networks, the competitiveness of their technological capacities, and the increase in foreign direct investment.

The export-led growth of development in East Asian countries in the 1960s, spurred by the "Dragons," was followed by other newly industrialized countries (Yusuf, Altaf, and Nabeshima 2004a).

Japanese foreign direct investment and technology have largely stimulated an upward movement of Asian economies (Androuais 2003). Japanese international companies have, starting in the 1960s, built a regional division of labor that has consistently emphasized technology-intensive production in Asia to serve Japanese markets. The East Asian countries won the reputation of a politically stable region with an industrial performance coupled with export competitiveness, all of which has attracted foreign direct investment, especially from Japanese companies but also from US and European firms. By the 1980s, East Asian countries were drawn into an interregional network of trade and direct foreign investment.

Market deregulation and WTO rulings sustaining trade liberalization have favored high-range markets to improve the competitive level of technological changes. The integration of East Asian countries, including China, will extend the dynamics of trade liberalization both for exports and FDI, which in turn will aid the Asian firms to become a part of the global network of competitiveness and technological development.

If the newly industrialized Asian countries have already found the way to rapid industrialization, China is gaining technological capacities even more quickly than her neighbors. The increase of technological capacity is becoming urgent for the East Asian countries because they have to avoid the trap of low-level growth associated with light commodity production.

In the middle of the 1990s, a new element of information technology used in all transactions appeared in production networks, especially in the multinational firms. The assimilation of this new element has been particularly rapid because of the desire to dispatch new technology and establish technological mechanisms in the new markets. Information technology has reinforced competitiveness in the regional and global markets.

Some governments, such as in East Asian countries, have set up policies for the support of technological advance. The major condition required is an educated

labor force; labor migration of educated human capital is a factor in technological advance. In addition, private and public research institutions financed by subsidies, grants, and tax incentives are needed; and finally, technology transfer through foreign direct investment is required. Liberalization of economies is a necessary step for the increase of Research and Development (R&D) capacity (Yusuf, Altaf, and Nabeshima 2004b).

To innovate, sufficient capacity to assimilate and absorb new technology is a requisite. In an analytical framework for understanding the evolution of an innovation, it is essential to have a broad perspective on the economy (Tigre and O'Connor 2003). Then, to consider the innovation, three questions should be asked: (1) What difference will the innovation bring to economy at the national level? (2) What impact will the innovation have on the increase of income distribution and the reduction of poverty? (3) What measures are needed to implement the innovation?

In order to boost research and development, governments usually orient their efforts toward state-of-the-art technology. In technological change and innovation, it is important to work at the macroeconomic level concerning long-term economic development and the internationalization of an economy as well as at the microeconomic level within the firm. Different authors in the 1990s gave a definition of the new technology of knowledge (Kagami, Humphery, and Piore 1998) by singling out five main paths of technological acquisition for developing countries:

1. **Transfer of technology through foreign direct investment**: A multinational company establishes a branch in the developing country to produce, for example, electronic goods by assembling parts and components. Local industries provide the workforce that learns the new production methods, and then these local industries supply standardized parts and components. The multinational companies give on-the-job training to local workers for the assembling process, and the local technicians learn the production process and are aided by foreign technicians. With the new technology information, new forms of capital appear. Joint ventures employ this new technology, reduce costs, and bring up the level of technology in production know-how.

2. **Purchasing new technology**: Technology has a cost, and R&D workshops have to be organized. New technologies must be registered under local patent laws.

3. **Acquisition of new machines embodying new technology**: New machinery produces new products in which are embedded innovative technologies. Moreover, developing countries disassemble new products and produce new copies equal to the original; this phenomenon is called "reverse engineering." As shown earlier, appropriate products were devised to facilitate the adaptation to local conditions; this process was hotly criticized by developed countries because of violation of industrial property rights and also criticized in developing countries because consumers wanted the upgraded products immediately.

4. **Catching-up efforts on the part of developing countries**: Domestic efforts can be divided into two forms, private sector initiatives and government support. In the private sector, new products are mainly the result of a combination of various factors, such as quality control, design and materials innovations, and management know-how. Foreign direct investment usually provides the major capital needed. As for government support, it is primarily in the form of R&D for the development and dissemination of technology through national institutions by direct financial support and subsidies.

5. **Technological cooperation through Official Development Assistance (ODA)**: Other paths for technology transfer are provided by a multinational or binational cooperation. Governmental assistance in technology development takes different forms, such as constructing training centers, dispatching experts, providing financial assistance, and offering information services dealing with technology.

The new strategies for transferring technology in developing countries have had positive results. In the local subsidiaries, the level of skills and knowledge in the production process improved through the transfer of technology. Technology fostered small and medium enterprises to create supporting industries. Many governments in Southeast Asian countries have assisted these enterprises through various programs: (i) financial and fiscal support for new innovative businesses; (ii) assistance in basic technological development; (iii) horizontal networking among small and medium enterprises; and (iv) upgrading of skills.

The Innovation Cluster Process

The cyclical characteristics of economic activity result from the fact that entrepreneurs tend to associate in new combinations called "innovation clusters,"

grouped around a major innovation or an important new niche. In the beginning of the twenty-first century, in the context of globalization, economists paid great attention to the impact of innovation on economic competitiveness. When state-of-the-art production is reached, innovation and a competitive quality-price ratio are conditions of survival for the company at the global level. Innovation also impacts quality competitiveness by improving product performance.

Spatial networks have been organized to accomplish different forms of clusters. It is possible to identify these clusters through different patterns of activity or innovative capacities. The major clusters benefit from the reduction of distance-related costs and from internalizing the stationary external savings. New forms of clusters are taking place that favor interchanges between local firms and universities.

Another type of effective cluster involves the export-processing zones that exist in developing countries; but these clusters cannot be fully integrated into the local economy because they are merely enclaves and are not linked to the rest of the region. The last type of cluster takes form in science and technology parks; its infrastructure and technological orientation have to generate human resources, knowledge, and capital. This type of cluster is engaged in resource, market, and investment seeking. The best examples are the technological Batamin Park in the Riau archipelago of the transboundary experiment of Singapore and Johor as well as the software cluster in Bangalore.

The first growth triangle was established in the Singapore-Johor-Riau archipelago in 1989, combining three competitive areas to attract regional and international investors to the subregion. Three geographic points formed this joint development: Singapore because of its technological and industrial infrastructure that attracted multinational companies; Johor because of its water resources and its proximity to and traditional links with Singapore; and Batam (Riau) because of its ability to profit from the new liberalization of India and attract foreign investments (Chia Siow Yue 1997).

A few years later, the Indonesia-Malaysia-Singapore (IMS) growth triangle (GT) was formed. It was a new form of subregional economic cooperation in the Association of Southeast Asian Nations (ASEAN) countries. This form of cooperation was set up to establish industrial cooperation programs and to enhance their economic clout. The IMS-GT has strengthened the economic complementarities and geographical proximity. This form of subregional process has developed factor endowments, competitive advantages, research allocation, and reduction of costs, all at different levels. The system has enhanced the clustering effect in the region and has developed

infrastructures in commerce, finance, transportation, and telecommunications. It has also, because of the participating governments, organized the education and training of a high quality labor force.

These joint ventures brought about greater cooperation between Indian and foreign software companies. The main elements promoting hi-tech clusters (Saxenian 1983) have been identified by regional economists (Krugman 1992). In the case of Bangalore, engineers came to live in the city next to the university and established links with companies in the software and computer industry. At the same time, state-owned companies in the communications, machine tools, and electronics industries set up research institutions. These combinations have fostered the growth of hi-tech software clusters. High technology parks have also been set up in Bangalore, benefiting from fiscal incentives to attract the most highly reputed firms, which, in turn, attract the best-educated engineers.

Transport cost reduction is also an important element of the cluster concept. Concentration in a specific location gives advantages in cost reduction. Information is transferred globally in real time by satellite between Bangalore enterprises and client companies (Dunning 2002). This software cluster in the city of Bangalore was able to attract a number of knowledge-related industries and succeeded in becoming less isolated because of its networking and the development of its computer software industry that broke into the global economy. The software cluster is designed for human-resource-intensive and knowledge-oriented industry. In Bangalore, clusters consist mainly of the electronics industry, small and medium companies, subsidiaries of larger companies, and joint ventures that were set up in the mid-1990s.

Another example of a knowledge-based economy is in Hong Kong, which has developed a finance and information center for both local and multinational firms. Moreover, Hong Kong has forged linkage with other Asian economies. Its cluster economy, knowledge intensive and research centered, has developed in spite of lack of clear governmental policies. This form of cluster is able to intensify competitive advantage and link the globalization-localization characteristics in the economy.

Because of its cluster economy, beginning in 1995, Hong Kong has surpassed its small-scale geographic situation and has become a motor in the regional economy. Hong Kong's cluster economy has served as a magnet for foreign firms. Although Hong Kong is an enclave, its competitive clusters have evolved from its knowledge-based economy.

In most clusters, cross-border labor flow has contributed to the success of the enterprises. In their field work for the Japan Bank for International

Cooperation, M. Hafiz M., A. Giroud, and K. Koster wrote in 2001 that "the multinational firms have been useful routes for transferring knowledge to East Asian and Southeast Asian workers and companies." However, this transfer was not done in an automatic way because on the one hand, the multinational firms were not delivering enough technology, and on the other hand, the local companies were not absorbing the transferred technology, meaning that more significant efforts have to be made for improving the transfer of knowledge. Furthermore, recently specific recommendations associated with the transfer of technology through foreign direct investments have been set up to improve mechanisms and find ways for reducing poverty in poor countries in such a way that they can learn from the experience of the new industrialized economies (NIES). Other studies have been started in the form of questionnaire surveys and used to complete research work on the transfer of technology affected by multinational firms. For instance, the surveys conducted in multinational firms in ASEAN countries point out that they need an incentive to establish good-quality support industries for creating an enabling environment for foreign direct investment (FDI). ASEAN countries request the support of multinational institutions especially because of the competitive companies from China in the region. The knowledge-technology base of the ASEAN firms need quite a boost, and multinational firms are able to assist in the transfer of technology.

Case studies, made in Brazil and South Korea, show that innovative products and cluster processes were competitive in the domestic and export markets (Mytelka 1999). But in the two countries, the reasons for innovation linked to competitiveness are different, especially regarding telecommunication products. Mytelka presents five factors to explain the differences between the two countries: (i) opportunities and constraints imposed by the evolution of world technology; (ii) evolution of the characteristics of international competitiveness in the telecommunications sector; (iii) structure of the telecommunications supply sector and enterprises that form the national telecommunications network; (iv) traditional practice of local enterprises in terms of competitiveness and innovation; and (v) impact of governmental actions.

Concluding Remarks: Competitive Environment for Technology and Challenges

Even in highly protected national markets, the new digital technology has rapidly spread in spite of high R&D costs. This new technology encouraged numerous start-ups in the 1980s and has contributed to modifying production, leading to other advanced techniques and giving developing countries access to these techniques. A competitive environment accelerated the phenomena although national telecommunications monopolies initially constituted an obstacle for the start-ups. Investment in telecommunications equipment, special rules for bidding, and protective practices stimulated local efforts for R&D.

Although technology has a central place in Asian and Pacific economies, poverty has not yet been completely eradicated and remains one of the biggest challenges for these economies (Braga and Chino, 2002). Technological impetus has improved nutrition, health, and livelihood, but some regions and various social groups remain excluded from this promise and progress. Their needs are better addressed because of the diffusion of information technology, and in the twenty-first century, they will hopefully be able to get access to this form of technology.

ANNE ANDROUAIS

References and Further Reading

Androuais, Anne. "Japon: Le Pays de la Technologie." *Japan: Country of Technology*. Emission de radio des Fréquences Protestantes. Paris: Janvier 18, 2003.

Braga de Macedo, Jorge, and Tadao Chino. *Technology and Poverty Reduction in Asia and the Pacific*. Paris: OCDE & Asian Development Bank, 2002.

Chia Siow Yue. "Singapore: Advanced Production Base and Smart Hub of the Electronics Industry." *Multinationals and East Asian Integration*, W. Dobson and Chia Siow Yue, eds. Ottawa, Singapore: IDRC, ISEAS, 1997.

Dunning, John H. *Regions, Globalization, and the Knowledge-Based Economy*. Oxford: Oxford University Press, 2002.

Emmanuel, Arghiri. *Technologie Appropriée ou Technologie Sous-Développée? (Appropriated Technology or Underdeveloped Technology*. Paris: PUF/IRM, 1980.

Galtung, Johan. *Development, Environment, and Technology, Towards an Autonomous Technology*. United Nations on Trade and Development (UNCTAD), td/b/c.6/23, June 1978.

Hafiz, Mirza, Axèle Giroud, and Kathrin Koster. "Transnational Corporations and the Upgrading of Technological Competencies of ASEAN Economies." *Financing Southeast Asia's Economic Development*, Nick J. Freeman, ed. Singapore: ISEAS, 2001.

Hobday, Michael. *Innovation in East Asia. The Challenge to Japan*. Cheltenham: Edward Elgar, 1995.

———. "East versus Southeast Asian Innovation Systems: Comparing OEM and TNC-led Growth in Electronics." *Technological Learning & Innovation, Experiences of Newly Industrializing Countries*, Linsu Kim and Richard R. Nelson, eds. Cambridge, United Kingdom: Cambridge University Press, 2000.

Juglar, Clément. *Des Crises Commerciales Périodiques en France, en Angleterre & aux Etats-Unis (Periodical Commercial Crisis in France, in England & in the United-States)*. Paris: Guillaume & Cie, 1862. (Reprint: Bibliothèque Nationale de France, Gallica).

Kagami, Mitsuhiro, John Humphery, Michael Piore. *Learning,Liberalization, and Economic Adjustment.* Tokyo: Institute of Developing Economies (IDE), 1998.

Krugman, Paul. *Geography and Trade.* Leuven, Cambridge: University Press, MIT Press, 1992.

Mytelka, Lynn K., ed. *Concurrence, Innovation et Compétitivité dans les Pays en Dévelopement (Competition, Innovation and Competitiveness in Developing Countries).* Paris: OECD, Development Centre, 1999.

Perroux, Francois. *L'Economie du XXe Siècle (XX Century Economics).* Paris: PUF, 1961.

Romer, Paul. "Increasing Returns and Long-Run Growth." *Journal of Political Economy* no. 94 (1986).

———. "Increasing Returns and New Development in the Theory of Growth." *Equilibrium Theory and Applications: Proceedings of the 6th International Symposium in Economic Theory and Econometrics*, William Barnett *et al.*, eds., 1991.

Sachs, Ignacy. *Stratégie de l'Éco-éveloppement (Strategy of Eco-development).* Paris: Editions Ouvrières, 1980.

Saxenian, AnnaLee. "The Genesis of Silicon Valley." *Built Environ* 9(1983): 7–17,.

Schumpeter, Joseph. *Business Cycle: A Theoretical, Historical, & Statistical Analysis of Capitalist Process.* Cambridge, MA: Harvard University Press, 1939.

———. *Capitalism. Socialism & Democracy.* London: Allen & Unwin, 1954.

Sen, Armathya. *Choice, Welfare and Measurement.* Oxford: Basil Blackwell, 1982.

Solow, Robert. "A Contribution to the Theory of Economic Growth." *Quarterly Journal of Economy* 70 (February 1956).

Tigre, Paulo B., and David O'Connor. *Policies & Institutions for E-Commerce Readiness: What Can Developing Countries learn from OECD Experience?* Working Paper no. 189. OECD Development Centre, 2003.

Yusuf, Shahid, Anjum M. Altaf, and Kaoru Nabeshima. *Global Production Networking and Technological Change in East Asia.* Manila: Asian Development Bank, 2004a.

———. *Global Change and East Asian Policy Initiatives.* Washington, DC; Oxford: World Bank; Oxford University Press, 2004b.

TERRITORIAL DISPUTES

Territorial disputes can be defined as conflicting claims over a territory between states or groups being on opposite footing, often recognized as warring parties. The parties are usually states recognized by each other, but frequently one of them is a national community or regional population that had prior statehood on the disputed land (such as Tibet) that is no longer recognized by the occupying power (such as by China). In other cases, the dispute is between a state (Sri Lanka) and a secessionist group that can have or even not have some of the disputed territory under control (such as the group of Tamil Tigers). In other cases, both parties claim exclusive rights on the territory that they posses or control partially (the Koreas). The material object of this political and legal dispute is a territory consisting either exclusively of land or

sea, or the territory has both, such as islands and their surrounding sea (Falklands). Otherwise, the territory's composition may include fresh water surfaces on border lakes and rivers (the Aral Sea or the Danube).

The legal object is the possession or control of such territories for geostrategic, economic, historical, or purely political reasons. Strategic reasons include the right of passage and therefore the right to levy taxes on through traffic (Suez canal, Panama Canal, airspace over the territory), to extend the territorial waters for defense purposes, to extend exclusive mining rights over the continental shelf by the coastal country, or to exert exclusive fishing rights or control of the fishing activities of other countries in the disputed sea area.

Exclusive economic reasons explain the disputes over regions with huge natural resources like fertile farmland, oil, gas, timber, or fresh water (such as from the rivers Tigris, Euphrates, Jordan, Danube, or Ganges). Mixed reasons include the existence of the same or similar ethnicity population (Russians, Slavs, or Kurds), the presence of those with the same religion (Muslims of Kashmir), or the prior statehood over that land (Turkey, Hungary, Greece, or Ecuador). Claims may be open (Palestine) or hidden where the parties try to avoid open confrontation because they fear direct war or negative international reactions (Europe), leading to isolation and subsequently imposed political and economic sanctions. The latter are used many times to deter a party to abandon its claims (such as South Africa in the case of Namibia, Yugoslavia and Serbia in case of Croatia, or Bosnia).

Religion was a major cause of territory disputes during the history leading to crusades, with the *Dzihads* aiming at control of the Holy Land, Palestine, which is considered the birthplace of many religions. In other cases, the extension of that religion served as a political justification for conquering large territories (Spain for Latin-America, Russia for Eastern Europe and Siberia, or the Arabs for the Middle-East and North Africa). After the nineteenth- and twentieth-century emergence of nationalism, religion became the driving force behind the claims of new territories (Romania, Serbia, and Bulgaria due to Arab and Jewish nationalism) or reclaiming previously lost territories (Germany, Ethiopia, Bolivia, and Japan). The drive for asserting previously lost independence was also a factor in claiming territories (such as in Poland, Ukraine, India, or Vietnam). This claim might have been directed toward one state (Ottoman, Russian, British, French, or Spanish empires) or more states at the same time. In many cases, territorial disputes arouse from contractual ambiguity (the main stream of the river, which changes over time, such as the Danube) concerning boundaries drawn only on the

map a very long time ago whose exact location is disputed (Persian Gulf states, Latin America countries) or concerning borders through uninhabited and uniform areas, like plains, deserts, jungles, seas, where there are no natural demarcation objects (such as Arabia, Amazonas basin, sea boundaries). Territorial disputes are the most frequent causes of modern day wars (Falklands), and if direct confrontation is too risky for one of the parties because of a lack of adequate military power, terrorism may replace usual military actions (Basque country, Palestine, Chechnya). With terrorism, usually nonstate entities try to influence the leading politicians of the decisive powers (United States, former colonial powers within the European Union (EU), Russia, China, India, or Australia); to influence states having military might (United States, France, or United Kingdom) to withdraw troops (from Iraq, Algeria, Northern Ireland); or to exert pressure on another state to withdraw its troops (Israel, Indonesia). By invasion, a party in a territorial dispute asserts its imagined or real sovereignty over that territory (Irianjaya, Falklands, Cyprus, Aksai-Chin, West Bank of the Jordan River, Golan Heights) in spite of the fact that international law in general and the United Nations charter condemns such actions or threats with the use of force. For the great powers, condemnation is almost absolute for annexations of territories and crushing of political independence of a sovereign country, principles largely ignored.

Europe

Europe is full of hidden claims—irrespective to the developmental stage of the parties involved. These are based on ethnic, historical, and cultural identity reasons and on nationalism, but nonetheless many have great economic implications. Among the less developed countries, the most virulent disputes arose after the breakup of the Socialist Yugoslavia. The Serbian-Croatian and Bosnian wars served also to define the territorial extent of the newly independent nations as well as to gain as much territory and hence economic power as possible to the detriment of the others. Finally, the administrative boundaries of the former federation have survived, but the disputes have remained.

The most active one concerns the 90% ethnic-Albanian province of Kosovo, which is ardently disputed between Serbia and the local Albanian community. Albanian majority areas neighboring the Albanian border are looking for independence and possibly a later union with the fatherland. Greece and Bulgaria and Serbia are disputing over Macedonia. Greece also fears possible future territorial claims from an independent Slavic Macedonia on the neighboring Greek province of lower or maritime Macedonia.

Morocco continues to dispute existing Spanish sovereignty over strategic harbors situated on the African (Moroccan) mainland—Ceuta and Melilla, occupied by Spain during the reconquista from the Muslims—and also a small uninhabited rock called Isla Perejil near the Gibraltar strait. Finland has a hidden claim on eastern Karelia, while the ethnic Swedish Alands islands look for more autonomy or even independence from Finland. Border and water management disputes arose between Slovakia and Hungary, Romania, and Ukraine on the Danube. Slovakia unilaterally diverted the Danube in the 1990s for hydroelectric power-generation purposes, and the Ukraine has challenged the Romanian monopoly over Danubian access routes to the Black Sea; in 2004, the Ukraine started to deepen the Chilia border branch of the river.

Turkey has many disputed areas along or inside its borders. It has an inactive claim over minority ethnic Turkish areas of Bulgaria near Istanbul as well as a longstanding dispute concerning the Aegean continental shelf and the pertaining territorial waters, disputes that have twice almost led to war with Greece. After 1923, the Turkish–Greek territorial dispute was focused on Cyprus, which sought union with Greece in a Pan-Hellenic upheaval of the 1970s. To protect its 28% Turkish community, Turkey had invaded Northern Cyprus in 1974, which led to the creation of two puppet states that have been unrecognized mutually. Due to Greek intrigue and Turkish reluctance, the reunification of Cyprus as a federal state was aborted; thus, only the bigger, internationally recognized Greek part joined the EU in 2004, leaving the Turkish part on the sidewalk of the European development.

In eastern Europe after the collapse of the Soviet Union, disputes flared up between and among the successor and former satellite states. The most recent one, between Romania and Ukraine, concerns the Black Sea border and the ownership of the Snake Island, adding to the existing conflict regarding Ukrainian border areas: Northern Bucowina and the small Hertza regions. These and the state of Moldavia are secretly claimed by Romania more or less on ethnic, nationalistic, and historical grounds. Although made artificially part of Moldavia, the secessionist region of Transnistria with its 60% Slavic majority is also claimed by Moldavia and subsequently by Romania. The self-proclaimed Republic of Transnistria is an ideal strategic area for Russia, and in case of annexation attempts coming from the West, the region will surely join Ukraine or choose independence. A bitter and longstanding but now inactive dispute exists over

Transylvania, or at least parts of it, between Hungary and Romania on historical, economic, and ethnic grounds. Hidden claims have also been made for the ethnic Hungarian majority regions along the newly Serbian, Ukrainian, and Slovakian, and former Hungarian territories until 1945. Similar inactive claims also concern former Polish territories in the Ukraine and Belarus.

Ukraine and Byelorussia is entirely and secretly claimed by Russia on historical, economic, and Slavic kinship or "brotherhood" grounds. Russia alternatively looks to form a confederation with these core elements of the former Soviet empire, including the 40% Russian-populated Kazakhstan, to form a "Russian" or "Eurasian" economic union. Thus, almost every valuable region of the former USSR would have been saved, including the nuclear testing facility of Semipalatinsk and the cosmic launch center of Baikonur, both on rent from Kazakhstan. Russia would eventually leave Ukraine to break off and subsequently seize the pro-Russian part of the country. Especially disputed seems to be the Russian-majority Donetsk coal-mining region and the Crimea, where an autonomous Russian republic exists. The countrywide 19% Russian minority forms in Crimea an 80% settler majority, which is a strategic peninsula for international trade and military control of the Black Sea. Sevastopol is the location of the Russian Black Sea Fleet's naval base, now on rent from Ukraine, and this nearly 3 million person republic asserts openly its Russian legacy and allegiance, leaving almost hopeless the 10% Crimean Tatar community's claim for resettlement and eventual establishment of an autonomous Tatar Crimea as successor of the historic Crimean Khaganate. The quest for independence in the early 1990s of the middle Volga region oil-rich Tatar Republic of nearly 6 million inhabitants around Kazan had a relatively happy ending, reaching greater autonomy under president Yeltsin but avoiding the bloody fate of Chechnya.

The Caucasus

The Caucasus itself is a unique region of ethnic and cultural mix and a region full of resources, such as mainly oil, natural gas, fresh water, timber, and agricultural land. The borders were drawn according to Russian imperialist interests, and later, the Georgian Communists led by Stalin carved out a greater Georgia, creating "the small empire" in the big (Soviet) empire. Some of its provinces, however, questioned their status beginning with the dismantling of the Soviet Union in 1991.

Thus, Abkhazia, the tiny former autonomous republic of Georgia, consisting of only 3,320 square miles (8,600 square kilometers), declared its independence in 1992 as a move against the "Georgianisation" of the province. In spite of missing international recognition, it fought a successful war against Tbilisi, with the backing of other Caucasian nations' solidarity troops and Russian weaponry. The ethically motivated dispute serves also Russian strategic interests at the "backyard borders" of the centuries-old great regional rival of Turkey.

South Ossethia, also *de facto* independent from 1992, is another flashpoint between Moscow and Tbilisi. This tiny republic, with only 1,506 square miles (3,900 square kilometers) and a mixed population, sought union with bordering North Ossethia under Russian rule.

The most long-standing dispute exists over Chechnya, between the Separatist population and the Russian federal government. After 1945, Joseph Stalin ordered the deportation of the whole Chechen population to Asia on charges of Nazi German collaborationism during World War II. Chechnya first declared its independence in the region, but the Russians did not allow for this tiny oil-rich republic of 7,452 square miles (19,300 square kilometers) and 1 million people to break away. More than 250,000 civilians, including 42,000 children, have died so far in this ongoing partisan-style war, leading to the total destruction of the country and setback the development of the whole region.

The enclave of Nagorno-Karabakh is another disputed territory between Armenia and Azerbaijan, with a 75% Armenian majority seeking union with neighboring Armenia. The Armenians had won the war occupying 20% of Azerbaijani territory. Thus, Armenian Nationalist forces tried to redraw the hastily sketched borders by the Soviet commissars in the 1920s and establish a greater national state. In such political circumstances, the overall development of the Caucasus region is vitiated, and a new international order should be set up in this far away "Balkans" of Eurasia.

The Middle East and Asia

Much of southeastern Turkey or Turkish Kurdistan has been the center of disputes for decades by the secessionist organization *Partiya Karkeren Kurdistan* (PKK), or the Kurdistan's worker party, which tries to create an independent Kurd state on ethnic, nationalistic, and economic grounds. That state would include the rest of Kurdistan, namely the northern

border zone of Syria, northern Iraq, and Iran, encompassing the whole 20 million people in the stateless Kurdish nation. None of these states wants to yield, even for Kurdish autonomy, for geopolitical and economic reasons: Kurdistan has plenty of natural resources like oil, timber, and fresh water. Turkey has water management disputes with Syria and Iraq over the Tigris and Euphrates, while Israel disputes the use of the Jordan River and the Sea of Galilee with Syria and Jordan.

The territorial disputes between the Palestine nation and Israel concern survival on a small patch of land where a 10% Jewish minority is gradually being squeezed out by the majority Arab population through immigration and state formation. Both of the parties want the whole of the territory (Palestine) on both historical as well as religious grounds. Israel spends annually 40% of its gross domestic product (GDP) on defense and could not survive without the serious military and financial backing of the United States, which provokes fierce Arab resistance all over the Middle East. Syria has open claims on the geostrategic Golan Heights occupied by Israel during in the 1967 Arab-Israeli War and hidden claims on the Iskenderun coastal region of Turkey on the basis of a local Arab majority and its proper climate. The Iraqi-Iranian war of the 1980s was fought for the control of the other side's Kurdistan and for the annexation of a wider access area to the Persian Gulf for Iraq. Iraq claimed repeatedly the whole of Kuwait, based on former Ottoman boundaries, and unsuccessfully annexed it in 1961 and again in 1991. Iraq has maintained its claims over this oil-rich area, which holds one-third of the most easily exploitable oil resources on the Earth, by constant military pressure or by demanding long-term lease of the strategically located Bubiyan and Warbah islands.

In the Arabian Peninsula, before the coming of the oil era in the 1930s, official boundaries had little significance as was the case elsewhere in the uninhabited desert areas, and organized authority was confined to ports and oases. Arab pastoral tribes felt loyalty to their tribal leaders only and roamed across the sands according to their grazing needs. British-drawn international boundaries were not properly demarcated, so with the coming of the oil era, the exact definition of the ownership rights became inevitable. Thus, after the British colonial withdrawal in 1971, old and suppressed territorial claims became actual again: Iran has claimed Bahrain, on historical and religion grounds, dropping and reiterating it periodically. Iran also claimed and occupied in 1971 three smaller islands named Abu Musa, Greater Tumb, and Lesser Tumb in the Hormuz straits; Iran

reached an agreement with the United Arab Emirates (UAE) over one of them in 1992.

Formal tribal settlement areas and dynastic struggle are at the heart of the often militarized and internationalized disputes between Bahrain and Qatar. The Bahraini claim the Az Zubarah Island on the northwest coast of Qatar, while Qatar claims Bahraini-occupied Hawar situated about twenty-five miles (forty kilometers) off the coast but situated just at its shorelines. After 1955, Saudi Arabia recognized the claims of Abu Dhabi and Oman to the Al Burayami Oasis, and in return Saudi Arabia was granted a land corridor to the gulf and a share of a disputed oil field, ending the long dispute among local pastoral tribes. The border between Oman and Yemen remained only partially defined, leading to border skirmishes, but relations improved after Yemeni unification. Earlier, the southern borders of Oman caused friction with the UAE on the Musandam Peninsula.

In Asia proper, a hotspot is the location of the frontier line across the Aral Sea between Kazakhstan and Uzbekistan. The line also crosses the disputed Vozrojdenie Island, highly polluted as the dying sea itself. The once 26,255-square mile (68,000-square kilometer) Aral Lake (Sea) has been separated into two parts: the northern (mainly Kazakh) lake can be saved if proper dams are built in the seabed, but this would stop the overflow of the feeding river to the southern lake, which falls mostly inside Uzbek territory.

Further south there is a border dispute on the Caspian between Azerbaijan, Iran, Russia (Dagestan), and Turkmenistan over oil mining rights on the continental shelf and over caviar-producing sites. Independent Azerbaijan is too weak to claim openly two-thirds of the national territory outside international boundaries, mainly in Iran, home to 20 million Irani Azerbaijanis who hope that the creation of a Turkic state confederation would solve the dispute. A confederation has been long sought by Turkey to assert its leading role and somehow reestablish the Ottoman Empire, but this goal is now more or less based on ethnical kinship grounds. This Turkic world called "Kipchakia" would stretch from Hungary, the Carpathians, and across the great steppes to Uyghuria in the Altays. This Sinkiang region or Eastern Turkestan claims its independence from China on ethnic, geographic, and historical grounds.

In the southern mountainous ridge, in the Himalayas, a set of territorial disputes exists. The northern Turkmen, Tadzhik tribes who have liberated Afghanistan from the Taliban rule, seek a greater role for themselves or a federal status and otherwise wish to join their territories with their motherland.

Afghanistan claims a corridor-like territory called Pakuristan, which reaches down to the Indus River.

In the north, the region of Dzhammu and Kashmir is disputed between India and Pakistan, having a *de facto* borderline traced after cease-fire agreements. The two states fought three wars over the territory in the late twentieth century and are even threatening each other with the use of nuclear weapons. Pakistan claims the area on the grounds of Muslim majority, and this claim is refused by India, stating that the ruler (*maharaja*) of this province decided to stay Indian in 1947. In fact, both countries want to acquire a mountainous wetland, with forest vegetation and fresh water reservoirs, which is so badly needed by these mostly dry tropical countries. In addition, India is involved in two main disputes with China. Aksai-Chin was seized by China after the annexation of Tibet in 1950, and the seizure was not recognized by India or by the Tibetan Government in Exile, led by the Dalai Lama. On the other hand, China claims the border zone of the Indian-Aruntshal-Pradesh province and massively colonized Tibet, leading to the local minority status of the oppressed Tibetans.

China and Taiwan (officially the People's Republic of China and the Republic of China) form a pair of claimants for exclusive control of the other's territory, each considering itself to be the sole and real leader of a unitary nation. A similar debate exists between communist North Korea and capitalist South Korea. These disputes are mainly ideological, but the strategic location of Taiwan could boost Chinese economic development in the South China Sea region. China's imperialist ambitions increased significantly after the reannexing Hong Kong and Macao, in parallel with its spectacular economic growth, and looks also farther south to the Paracel and Spratly Islands. In both cases, China is the main claimant alongside Vietnam with whom it had fought and lost a war in the 1980s; the Spratly Islands are also claimed by the Philippines. Vietnam also has ongoing disputes concerning Kokinchina, the Mekong Delta region, with Cambodia.

In addition, China has longstanding territorial disputes with the Soviet Union and some of its successor states, which at the union's height targeted an area totaling 386,102 square miles (1 million square kilometers). The most active concerns the Ussuri–Amur confluence area in the Habarovsk region of Russia. China contests the existence of (outer) independent Mongolia, considering it a Chinese province. China also looks for eventual Siberian independence, which could be its natural resource pool hinterland of its booming economy, a prospect much feared by Europe and especially Russia. In the case of Korea, not only is the legitimacy of the governments and regimes disputed, but the economic future of the peninsula is also in question. Divided actually by

tightest border in the world, North and South Koreas have experienced a halted economic development, with prosperous South Korea having no area of extensive development and with the separated Communist North starving to death. Farther east, the Take Shima (Lioncurt Rocks) are disputed between the Koreas and Japan because of their strategic significance.

The Indian peninsula is also full of such disputes. The wealthy but divided state of the Sikhs, Punjab, seeks independence from India and eventually a union with Pakistani Punjab. Although this objective seems difficult to achieve, two Indian prime ministers have already fallen as victims of their stance against it. In the east after Bhutan and East Pakistan/Bangladesh went independent, a fragile and volatile situation has developed as neighboring regions may want to follow suit. In the southern areas, there is a strong drive toward an independent and greater Tamil state and perhaps a Dravida confederation. In its quest for independence and union with mainland Tamilnadu, the local Tamil majority of the neighboring big island, named Ceylon, has fought a long guerilla war against the Singhaleze government of Sri Lanka.

In Indochina, besides territorial disputes between Cambodia, Laos, and Vietnam following the collapse of the colonial rule, four minority and mostly tribal nations (the Katshin, the Shan, the Kaya, and the Kotuley) have tried to establish their own states in the border regions of Burma, while the Malaysian province of Sabah is claimed by the neighboring Philippines. Indonesia has annexed Western New Guinea, a former Dutch colony that became independent in 1961 and was renamed Irianjaya. Both the native Papuan population's government in exile and the Papuan Liberation Organization (PMO) claim sovereignty over this rich territory of 162,163 square miles (420,000 square kilometers). Indonesia has also annexed East Timor, which could hardly obtain independence at the turn of the twentieth century; other Indonesian provinces, like the Moluccas and tsunami-struck Aceh, are also on a secessionist footing.

In the north, much of Mongolia (inner Mongolia) with its 6 million inhabitants was annexed by China followed by the annexation of Manchuria in 1945; these annexations revealed hidden claims to the territories from Russian, Mongolian, Japanese, and Manchurian organizations. Japan hotly disputes the four largest (lower) Kurili islands, insignificant territories for Russia, occupied by the Soviet Union after the end of World War II. Japan looks not only at the renewed possession of some small islands but is trying to extend its territorial waters to boost its national pride left in ruins after the shock of losing World War II as well as its Pacific-rim empire.

Africa

The continent as well the whole world entered into an era of territorial integrity after World War II, as claiming territories became the key principle in guaranteeing the status quo of the new division of the world between the great powers. Newly independent countries accepted this principle worldwide due to their weaknesses, fearing external attack or internal secessionist drives. Therefore, after decolonization, the continent of Africa experienced only few border disputes in spite of the fact that hastily drawn colonial borders had little if any concern for tribal, language, or ethnic unity. Independent sub-Saharan Africa's boundaries changed remarkably little; changes had occurred only following the independence of Eritrea from Ethiopia, that of Namibia from South Africa, and the separation of Guinea-Bissau and Cape Verde.

A long-lasting territorial dispute between Morocco and the Polisario liberation organization of the native Berber tribes concerns the former Spanish Sahara of 100,386 square miles (260,000 square kilometers). Morocco annexed it after colonial withdrawal in 1976, but the Polisario resisted Moroccan troops; the Sahrawi nationality nomads wanted to establish the Sahrawi/Saharan Arab Democratic Republic. At present, the area is largely occupied and entirely claimed by Morocco, without broad universal recognition. Another long-lasting and bloody dispute involved France and Algeria between 1945 and 1962. France has only bitterly accepted defeat and loss of its main overseas territory, which has caused a refugee wave of 1.5 million "black-legs" to continental France.

Similar guerilla-type fights were carried out, with Cuban help however in the former Portuguese colonies of Angola and Mozambique. Sudan is home to the continent's longest lasting bloody civil war, in which the Muslim-Arab North fights against self-determination of the Animist and Christian black South. The civil war broke out in 1962, leading to the South's autonomy in 1972, but the discovery of oil resources in 1983 again fueled the secessionist drive. The rebels joined under the Sudan People's Liberation Army (SPLA) and have achieved an internationally mediated peace deal addressing power and wealth sharing. In the meantime, the western, mainly black region of Darfur also rose against the government and suffered ethnic cleansing transformed into genocide in 2004 by the government-backed Arab *Janjaweed* militias.

Egypt disputes the Hala'ib triangle with Sudan, an area extending to the north and south of the 1899 Treaty boundary, along the Twenty-Second Parallel. In the nonmilitarized conflict, Egypt is effectively administering the northern part of the triangle, north of the Treaty Line. Sudan has border disputes with Kenya, whose administration still extends into Sudan, in the Ilemi Triangle; Sudan also has disputes with the Central African Republic over water and grazing rights along the border and with Eritrea on border demarcation issues, accusing it with supporting Sudanese rebel groups. Left landlocked after the secession of 1991, Ethiopia claims its former coastal province Eritrea (and Tigre), which actually won its independence in a bloody war after being united with Ethiopia in 1961. Ethiopia has unresolved territorial disputes with its eastern neighbor of Somalia, which has openly claimed Ethiopia's border of the Ogaden plateau region. The standoff resulted in a bloody war in 1977 and 1978 and caused a huge refugee wave and a subsequent crisis, but the territorial status quo was preserved in the end.

Somalia on its own has suffered secessionist drives from its breakaway Somaliland region. Somaliland, the former British colony on the coast of the Gulf of Aden, was united in 1960 with the former Italian colony of Somalia, forming actual Somalia. The province declared its independence in 1991, following a bloody secessionist struggle after the overthrow of the Somali military dictatorship. Somaliland has a *de facto* but unrecognized independence, with a working political system and economy but is also involved in a border dispute with the neighboring autonomous Somali region of Puntland over the Sanaag and Sool areas.

In former Belgian Congo or Zaire, the religious and tribal leaders demanded federalism after the country declared its independence in 1960. The mineral-rich southeastern province of Katanga had seceded successfully for three years, and riots were still flashing in the 1980s, leaving Zaire's future uncertain. White-led South Africa emerged as the regional power and had annexed Namibia from 1979 until 1990, fighting against the Southwest Africa People's Organization (SWAPO) and later against the Communist Popular Movement for the Liberation of Angola (MPLA) in the Angolan civil war. The end of the Cold War led to regime changes that put an end to or stopped many African conflicts, to give birth later to new ones emerging from regional and tribal animosities (such as in Uganda, Rwanda, Malawi).

Latin America

As did their African counterparts, Latin American states have been formed respecting the legal principle of *uti-possidenti juris*, meaning that states' right to keep what its predecessor colony had possessed.

Land boundary disputes remained mostly inactive for long periods of time due to poor cartography, remote locations, and inaccessibility of the jungle or high mountainous border areas. Population growth, subsequent development pressures, and the use of new technology facilitated penetration into unpopulated areas, triggering sovereignty claims.

The other source of territorial disputes lie in modern international law evolution that allowed for the extension of territorial waters to two hundred nanometers and secured priority for the exploration of the real or imagined rich resources of the underlying seabed and its marine life. As a consequence, most of the sea boundaries between the Caribbean island states have not been established, provoking fresh disputes. Thus, countries ending their territorial disputes like Colombia and Venezuela in the 1940s ended up with disputes over maritime boundaries in the 1960s, as oil was discovered in the Gulf of Venezuela.

The third source of the disputes is the legacy of the British colonial advance after Spanish-American independence. These disputes since 1966 between Venezuela and Guyana concern more than half of British Guyana's territory; Guatemala and Belize have had disputes since 1981 over the latter's very independence. These disputes are the by-products of decolonization between the Spanish-speaking older and English-speaking newer states.

In spite of these tensions, South America is relatively free of major disputes thanks to the balance of power that developed in the late nineteenth century. South American countries also have a shared identity, and most Spanish-American elites have accepted the idea of being part of a larger cultural and possibly political entity. International hatred was mostly absent from the political ideology due also to common Spanish ancestry and language, which do not provide room for the general idea of "my country's neighbor is my enemy."

The existence of the regional effective conflict resolution system successfully deters territorial pretenders and defuses interstate conflicts. Interstate war remained rare also because both South and Central American countries were relatively insulated from the wider international system. The Cold War also contributed to this regional stability because the United States did not want to have any quarrel in its "backyard" and intervened militarily when necessary. In spite of the US management of such disputes, the Central American subsystem remained unstable because many underlying disputes were not addressed.

Paradoxically, the existence of this collective security system is also a cause for disputes. Aggressor states may refuse to compromise, certain that the inter-American system will not intervene before the aggressed state would retaliate. Thus, they can achieve concessions from the victimized country without risking high costs and huge military efforts. Conflict generation is thus part of a strategy of coercive bargaining, during which the aggressor state may maintain otherwise normal nonmilitary relations. On the other hand, long-lasting militarized disputes are partly due to their existing domestic political support, fueled by political leaders who want to gather electoral capital and see such nationalistic rhetoric as a cost-effective means of communicating. Nonetheless, existing conflicts can have high opportunity or direct costs due to the uncertainty of long-lasting militarized disputes or threatening intervention by the stronger neighboring state (such as Venezuela), as the case of a high-tech military project's fate showed in 2000.

Colombia's central government has fought for more than half a century, a bloody civil war claiming more than two hundred thousand lives. The war is directed against left-wing guerilla organizations: The Armed Revolutionary Forces of Colombia (FARC) and the National Liberation Army (ELN). The guerillas control a *de facto* independent territory of the size of Switzerland.

Peru also has had wars with most of its neighbors. The century-old dispute with Chile over the mining region of Tarapacas was solved finally in 1999, by securing Peru's access to the Pacific port of Africa. Peru's disputes over the Letitia and Zarumilla regions with Colombia and Ecuador, respectively, ended in war, however.

Peru's dispute with Ecuador clearly shows that if sovereignty and border issues are given higher priority than developmental objectives, then territorial disputes will linger and perhaps worsen. Ecuador lost much of its territory in its 1870s wars with Colombia and during wars in1939 through 1941 with Peru. The last one has ended with a peace treaty in 1942 (the Rio Protocol) guaranteed by the United States, Argentina, Brazil, and Chile, which institutionalized the role of outsiders in the dispute. Despite these changes, the territorial dispute continues, with Ecuador claiming the Maynas region in the Amazon basin. In addition, a border dispute in the Cordillera del Cóndor ridge region flared up due to its insufficient demarcation. The repeated Ecuadorian challenges ended in a short but violent war in 1995. Finally, the dispute was solved through international mediation in 1998.

Bolivia still claims an access area to the Pacific Coast in the Atacama desert region of Chile, incurring high economic opportunity costs because of its landlocked status as a consequence of previously losing its Antofagasta coastal region to Chile in the War of the Pacific in the 1870s. The longest and bloodiest war of Latin America, claiming 350,000

lives, is the war caused by the Bolivian claims over the Gran Chaco region, lost in the 1930s to Paraguay.

El Salvador and Honduras went to a bloody war in 1969 over disputed boundaries and related cross-border migration issues, following a riot at a binational soccer game. The war caused the collapse of the Central American Common Market; after international mediation and jurisdiction, 80% of the disputed territory was awarded to Honduras in 1992. In spite of this, militarized disputes recurred later due to factual boundary demarcation disputes, and international jurisdiction resumed in 1999.

Nicaragua has militarized all its borders that are dispute, and this became part of the repertoire of international tactics in spite of political changes. Later, as the Nicaragua-Honduras dispute over small islands, cays, and reefs started, the country turned to international jurisdiction.

Chile and Argentina have had twenty-four territorial and boundary disputes; the longest lasting one concerned the Beagle Channel and the southern glaciers. Argentina tried to solve all of these disputes after Chile's democratization cycles, but a long-term history of past conflicts rallied domestic support for diplomatic and military confrontation. In 1971, the two political and ideological adversaries sought British arbitration for the Beagle Channel, but this brought the parties to the brink of war in 1978, which was avoided only by a later Papal mediation, leading to a treaty in 1984. The Laguna del Desierto dispute was settled by international jurisdiction in the 1990s, while the most controversial dispute concerning the delimitation of the boundary through the southern cone glaciers required ratification from the parliaments. Argentina was exacerbating nationalistic feelings amidst its severe economic recession years, claiming the Islas Malvinas/Falklands. Argentina occupied them in 1982, triggering a swift response from the United Kingdom that retook possession after a short war, but Argentina did not abandon its century-long claim.

Brazil used common economic and social development projects in its strategy of solving territorial disputes. Thus, during the last two centuries, Brazil has won almost all territorial disputes peacefully and expanded its territory greatly (the third most successful country in the world to do so) without relying on military force or triggering an encircling coalition of its neighbors. In 1979, Brazil defused existing tensions with Argentina by initiating the joint exploitation of the hydroelectric potential of the Paraná River system, but an inactive dispute with Uruguay remained. The cooperation process culminated in 1991 in the establishment of the Southern Cone Common Market (MERCOSUR).

It is widely believed that democratization is a panacea for solving territorial issues, but the Latin American experience shows almost no evidence for any positive correlation in between. Territorial disputes are permanent, and some vanish while others commence in the ever-changing world, shaping history and the destiny of the peoples and nations forever.

LASZLO KOCSIS

See also Azerbaijan; Balkan Wars of the 1990s; China, People's Republic of; Kashmir Dispute; Milošević, Slobodan; Russia; Taiwan

References and Further Reading

Allock, J. *Border and Territorial Disputes*. Essex: Longman, 1992.

Anderson, E. W. *Global Geopolitical Flashpoints: An Atlas of Conflicts*. London: HMSO, 2000.

Harvey, Starr, and Benjamin Most. "The Substance and Study of Borders in International Relations Research." *International Studies Quarterly* 20, no. 44 (December 1976).

Hirschleifer, J. *The Dark Side of the Force: Economic Foundations of Conflict Theory*. Cambridge: Cambridge University Press, 2001.

Huth, Paul K. *Standing Your Ground: Territorial Disputes and International Conflict*. Ann Arbor, MI: University of Michigan Press, 1996.

———. "Enduring Rivalries and Territorial Disputes, 1950–1990." *Conflict Management and Peace Science* 15, no. 1.

Klare, M. *Resource Wars: The New Landscape of Global Conflict*. New York: New York Metropolitan Books, 2001.

Lalonde, S. *Determining Boundaries in a Conflicted World: The Role of Uti Possidentis*. Montreal; Ithaca, NY: McGill University Press, 2002.

Szajkowski, B. Encyclopedia of conflicting disputes and flashpoints in Eastern Europe, Russia and the successor states, Longman, Essex, 1993.

Valencia, M. *China and the Sea of China Disputes*. London: Oxford University Press, 1995.

TERRORISM

The word "terror" is derived from Latin and means "fear." Thus, terrorizing civilians creates fear. "State-sponsored terror" is government by intimidation, as in the French Revolution's Reign of Terror (1793–1794). States employ terror to undermine other states, and internal and international groups use terror to attack hated political, economic, and cultural symbols. Since 1945, the use of terror in the developing world has aimed to achieve political, social, economic, and cultural goals. Since the dawn of history, people have used terror to intimidate civilians through such means as genocide, torture, and incineration.

Legal Definitions

After World War II, the developed world started developing an international law of terrorism. The United Nations' International Convention for the Suppression of the Financing of Terrorism, 1999, defined "terrorist acts" as "intended to cause death or serious bodily injury to a civilian, or to any other person not taking an active part in the hostilities in a situation of armed conflict;" these are acts that are meant to "intimidate a population, or to compel a government or an international organization to do or to abstain from doing any act." Britain's Terrorism Act 2000 defines "terrorism" as acts "to influence the government or to intimidate the public... for the purpose of advancing a political, religious or ideological cause." In the United States Code Title 22, " 'terrorism' means premeditated, politically motivated violence perpetrated against noncombatant targets by subnational groups or clandestine agents, usually intended to influence an audience." In addition, " 'international terrorism' means terrorism involving the territory or the citizens of more than one country." The code adds that a " 'terrorist group' means any group that practices, or has significant subgroups that practice, international terrorism."

The developed world has defined terrorism for its own protection. In 1946, international tribunals judged war crimes committed by Germany and Japan but not crimes committed by the winners. After the Vietnam conflict, American atrocities did not bring US commanders to justice in the manner the United States had prosecuted Japan's World War II commanders. Under international protocols, developing nations may not possess chemical or biological weapons but developed nations can.

Terrorism's Tools

The military, police, and courts have tools to defend citizens and institutions. Unpopular regimes employ force to subdue those who oppose their rule. Rogue states terrorize rebels by suppressing civil liberties by illegal searches, arrests, and detentions. Ian Smith's illegal minority Rhodesian regime (1965–1979) and South Africa's apartheid governments silenced the majority through terror. When those out of power cannot defeat such regimes through legal means, they often overthrow them by using crude weapons of terror. This may be done with support from sympathizers outside the country. When Western states did not support African uprisings in the 1950s through the

1990s, Rhodesia's Patriotic Front and South Africa's African National Congress sought aid in African states that had ousted colonial rulers. They received training and weapons from Marxist states in Asia and Eastern Europe that were engaged in a Cold War against what they termed Western "imperialism." They also received aid from the World Council of Churches and other humanitarian organizations. Africans finally gained access to international media that put them on an equal footing with colonial regimes that had termed them "terrorists." With access to media, Africans termed their own soldiers "freedom fighters" and named their enemies "terrorists." International opinion slowly accepted an African claim to one-person-one-vote, economic equity, and equal justice. The United Nations (UN) placed sanctions on the oppressive white regimes. Power to persuade through political and economic appeals, and the use of "terror," turned the tide.

Terrorism's goal is not rational discussion. Its power comes from inducing fear among civilians. Terrorists lack the means to defeat regular military forces. They define "the other" negatively so as to motivate their agents to risk all for a cause. Targets may be political structures, or economic and cultural symbols, that bear the stigma of the hated "other."

Motives

Why do terrorists do what they do when they do it? The motives test goes beyond the law to political and moral values. When civilizations clash, historians compare and contrast them. In "just" or "holy" wars, religious/cultural terrorists strike at targets with symbolic value. Yahweh commanded Hebrews to invade Palestine in the thirteenth century BCE, often demanding *herem* annihilation of people and property as a *ban* (sacrifice). Medieval Christians limited war, prohibiting attacks on Christian lands and persons (Peace of God) and seasons (Truce of God). But they exempted non-Christians from these protections. Islam initiated *jihad*, holy war carried out under a mufti's decree, to target "evil" places and infidels for destruction.

In 1996, Osama bin Laden offered an Islamic rationale for *jihad* against America. A 1930s Sunni fundamentalist, Sayyid Qutb, had found a way around prohibitions against overthrowing Muslim rulers by declaring them "infidel." Osama bin Laden made the United States an infidel for defending a Jewish state in Palestine and placing military bases in Saudi Arabia, the site of Islam's major shrines. The United States's secular culture profaned God, and it refused to share its wealth with poor developing nations. His ideas

resonated with developing world Muslims who compared their poverty to the United States' riches. Osama bin Laden also condemned wealthy Muslims whose greed and secularism made them targets.

International Terrorism

International terrorism is not new, but since 1945 a shift has occurred as African, Asian, and Latin American voices have joined the UN to redefined terror. The developing world's political, economic, cultural, and political interests finally had to be acknowledged. Some saw access to oil as a prime motivator for acts of terror, but religious and political motives also had to be discussed. Motives, tactics, and law will be the focus of the twenty-first century. Terrorism studies will no longer ignore the developing world.

NORMAN H. MURDOCH

References and Further Reading

Ensalco, Mark. *Chile Under Pinochet: Recovering the Truth.* Philadelphia: University of Pennsylvania Press, 2000.

Gearty, Conor, ed. *Terrorism.* Aldershot, England: Dartmouth, 1996.

Lobban, Michael. *White Man's Justice: South African Political Trials in the Black Consciousness Era.* Oxford; New York: Clarendon Press; Oxford University Press, 1996.

Rashid, Ahmed. *Taliban: Militant Islam, Oil & Fundamentalism in Central Asia.* New Haven, CT, London: Yale Nota Bene/Yale University Press, 2001.

Safferling, Christoph Johannes Maria. *Towards an International Criminal Procedure.* New York: Oxford University Press, 2001.

Yonah, Alexander, ed. *International Terrorism: Political & Legal Documents.* The Hague, Netherlands: Martinus Nijhoff, 1992.

THAILAND

Thailand, formerly Siam, is in the heart of mainland Southeast Asia, with its southern tip extending into the Malay Peninsula. The Chao Phraya River and its fertile rice plain runs north to south through the country, and there is just over three thousand kilometers of coastline on the Gulf of Thailand and the Andaman Sea. Thailand's climate is tropical, with a warm and wet monsoon from May through September and a cool and dry monsoon from November to March. The southern tip, stretching into the Malay Peninsula and including the Isthmus of Kra, is generally hot and dry.

Thailand's population is around 64 million and is ethnically homogeneous, with approximately 75% of the population ethnic Tais, followed by approximately 15% ethnic Chinese, with the remainder of the population being ethnic minorities, including Hmong, Akha, White Tai, and Black Tai. A significant Malay minority exists in the southern part of Thailand. Thailand is also religiously homogeneous, with approximately 95% of the population practicing some form of Buddhism (mostly Theravada Buddhism). The large ethnic Chinese minority in Thailand is well integrated, the royal bloodline is said to have Chinese blood, and conflicts between Chinese and the majority Tais are infrequent and minor compared to some of Thailand's neighbors (Indonesia and Malaysia, for example). The national language is Thai, based on the Bangkok Thai dialect, and literacy is approximately 92%.

Thailand is exceptional among its Southeast Asian neighbors in that it was never formally colonized by a European power, a continuing source of pride for Thais (although it was heavily influenced by both France, from Indochina to the east, and Great Britain, from Burma to the west and Malaya to the south). Thailand's avoidance of colonialism is generally attributed to its strategic location as a buffer between French and British colonies and to the shrewdness of its rulers, beginning with Rama IV of the Chakri Dynasty, King Mongkut (reign: 1851–1868), and his son, Rama V, King Chulalongkorn (reign: 1868–1910). Both kings are attributed with modernizing Siam, including introducing European education, abolishing debt bondage and slavery, forging links to European countries, rationalizing taxes, bureaucratizing the government, and mapping the country. These policies, along with the introduction of cash crops and the increase in rice production, allowed Siam to thrive, and subsequent rulers began to focus on the consolidation of the state through nationalism and centralization.

In 1932, the absolute monarchy came to an end through a relatively peaceful *coup d'état* led by Western-educated elites. The country was given the name Thailand in 1939 as a way to embrace a Thai version of modernity. The monarchy itself was not a target of the coup, and so it retained its prestige. King Rama IX, Bhumibol Adulyadej, was born in Massachusetts, educated in Switzerland, and assumed the throne in 1946. Still in power at the beginning of the twenty-first century, he became the longest ruling monarch in the world. King Rama IX has been generally loved and respected by the people of Thailand for his kingly virtues, his patronage of the Sangha (Buddhist monkhood), and his support of various royal development projects. Disrespecting the king in any way is a crime not tolerated. Despite his lack of formal powers, Bhumibol was the catalyst for the resolution of a *coup d'état* in 1991. By the following year, demonstrations against the *coup* plotter, General Suchinda

Kraprayoon, had become widespread, and the military reacted with violence, killing student protesters. The king convened a meeting between Suchinda and his opponent, Chamlong Srimuang, on national television and ordered them to resolve their conflict, a strategy that proved successful and paved the way for elections and the restoration of democracy.

Thailand's history since World War II has been fraught with several *coups d'état* and periods of military rule interrupted by periods of open democracy. Thailand is considered one of the most established democracies in Southeast Asia, and the king remains an import figure and patron of Buddhism; however, certain policies, such as the unofficial assassinations of suspected drug users and sellers, have called into question Thailand's commitment to democracy. Thailand is also one of the more economically prosperous countries of the region, despite the effects of the 1997–1998 East Asian economic crisis, which had its roots in the devaluation of the Thai currency, the baht. Its recovery from the crisis was led by its export-oriented economy and driven by external demand for its products. The United States is Thailand's largest export market and second largest supplier (Japan is the first).

The roots for Thailand's strong economic development were established in the late nineteenth century, as aforementioned. The military's strong hand in the economy was consolidated following World War II under the influence of Plaek Phibunsongkhram, a former field marshall, who was involved in various *coups* since 1932. The military's discipline and organization, coupled with its system of patronage, has allowed it to be a major player in the Thai economy, in both legal and illegal enterprises. Many of these "vice" oriented ventures, such as bars staying open late, host prostituting, and catering to tourists (often viewed as holdovers from the America-Vietnam conflict), have become targets for current Prime Minister Thaksin Shinawatra; it appears, however, as though little is being done about the corrupt business practices of the military in other sectors.

One of the most striking features of Thailand's postwar economy concerns the timber industry. Positioning itself as anti-communist country, Thailand welcomed foreign investment and participated wholeheartedly in trade with the West. Its forests were some of the victims of these policies; by the time the Thai government instituted a moratorium on logging in 1989, Thailand's forest cover had dropped from 50% to less than 30% of its total land mass (approximately 193,051 square miles or five hundred thousand square kilometers). Rampant corruption betrayed the overall effectiveness of the plan, as evinced in occasional well-publicized scandals. Following the ban,

Thai companies immediately began seeking concessions in neighboring countries such as Burma, Laos, and Cambodia, all of which have laws that are much more lax, weaker law enforcement, and widespread corruption that enables black market business on a large scale.

An increase in manufacturing centered around big cities has also greatly affected Thailand's development. Thailand's cities are swelling at an enormous rate, just as are those of its neighbors, and the swelling is followed by the attendant crime, poverty, and pollution that accompany this change. Traffic congestion, for example, in Bangkok has increased dramatically, leading to production losses estimated in the billions of baht. An increase in the middle class since the 1960s, however, has produced a large segment of society that supports a vast network of nongovernmental organizations (NGOs) with environmental, gender equity, economic, and developmental goals and that subscribes to democratic ideals (although there remain questions about the overall distribution of the benefits of Thailand's economic growth).

Thailand's relatively free press allows for the open debate of ideas, but Thailand's labor organizations and unions remain relatively small and weak. In 2000, the Thai government passed the State Enterprise Labor Relations Act, which allowed public sector employees the same rights as private sector employees, including the right to organize. The East Asian economic crisis has led to the abandonment or postponement of many of the projects that accompanied the early 1990s construction boom in Bangkok although the economy as a whole is well on the way to recovery. The year 2000 brought the opening of Bangkok's above ground rail system, the Sky Rail. The gross domestic product (GDP) of 2002 grew by 6.3%. Under Thaksin, foreign investment has resumed, and exports such as textiles, footwear, rice, fish and marine products, rubber, appliances, and computers continue to fuel the economy. Services, as well as goods, have become a strong point for the Thai economy, and were the highest contributor by sector to the GDP in 2003 (46.3%) although agriculture still employs by far the highest percentage of the population (49%). Tourism is a significant contributor to the Thai economy (about 4%), and mining continues to be another significant contributor.

These shifts in the economy, from manufacturing to high technology and services, present a problem for Thailand. As its traditionally strong manufacturing sector begins to shrink due to competition from its neighbors (most notably Vietnam and China), the demand for a highly skilled labor force increases, but at this time it appears as though the educational system in Thailand is lagging. The illegal production

and transit of drugs, mostly opium, heroin, and marijuana mostly originating in Laos and Burma, have been decreasing due to stepped up enforcement. Amphetamine distribution and use, however, has become increasingly widespread and problematic and has become a major law enforcement target. HIV/AIDS is also a serious problem for Thailand, especially given the widespread nature of and tolerance for prostitution and given Thailand's role as a destination for sex tourism. The government has aggressively instituted HIV/AIDS education programs and counseling and has been relatively effective in preventing a huge rise in the number of infections (especially when compared to Thailand's neighbors, many of whom ignored or refused to address the problem in its initial stages).

Perhaps the most glaring security problem facing Thailand is the Separatists in the southernmost provinces of Songkhla, Pattani, Yala, and Narathiwat; this group is predominantly ethnically and linguistically Malay and Muslim, and its history of inclusion within Thailand is debated. Exacerbating any claims to sovereignty based on ethnicity or religion is the fact that Buddhist Thais have been relocated to the region, most of the civil service and police are ethnically Thai, and the provinces are among the poorest and least developed in Thailand. As a rubber-producing region, the global downturn in rubber prices in the 1950s worsened the Malays' lot (although rubber prices are going up more recently), and the response to the plight of the Southerners by the Thai central government has generally been apathy or antagonism. Although there are several organized groups with varying goals, violence in the region has been on the increase, and Thailand has been moving to shore up the porous border shared with Malaysia. Although not marked by the violence of the South, various hill tribes echo to some degree their complaints of Thai/Buddhist chauvinism and inequitable development. Moreover, ethnic rebels from neighboring Burma/Myanmar have caused security and diplomatic concerns, some quite serious.

CHRISTOPHER LUNDRY

References and Further Reading

Amara Pongsapich. "Non-Governmental Organizations in Thailand." *Emerging Civil Society in the Asia Pacific Community*, Tadashi Yamamoto, ed. Singapore: Institute of Southeast Asian Studies, 1995.

Central Intelligence Agency. 2005. *The World Factbook.* http://www.cia.gov/cia/publications/factbook/geos/th.html.

Hunsaker, Bryan *et al.*, eds. *Loggers, Monks, Students and Entrepreneurs: Four Essays on Thailand.* Occasional Paper No.18. DeKalb, IL: Northern Illinois University, Southeast Asia Publications.

Pasuk Phongpaichit, Sungsidh Piriyarangsan, and Nualnoi Treerat. *Guns, Girls, Gambling, Ganja: Thailand's Illegal Economy and Public Policy.* Chiang Mai: Silkworm Books, 1998.

Rush, James. *The Last Tree: Reclaiming the Environment in Tropical Asia.* Boulder, CO: Westview Press, 1991.

Steinberg, David Joel, ed. *In Search of Southeast Asia: A Modern History.* Honolulu: University of Hawaii Press, 1987 (1971).

Yegar, Moshe. *Between Integration and Secession: The Muslim Communities of the Southern Philippines, Southern Thailand, and Western Burma/Myanmar.* Boulder, CO: Lexington Books, 2002.

THIRD WORLD

Definition of "Third World"

The "Third World" is a catch-all term referring to countries with diverse histories, peoples, and geographic locations—yet they share certain attributes in relation to the countries defined as part of the First World and the Second World. The countries of Third World share a non-Western heritage, have higher population growth rates and infant mortality rates, are generally economically poor, and therefore have a lower standard of living as compared to the countries of the First World and the Second World. Most of the Third World countries share a history of colonial domination at the hands of Western powers. As a rough conceptual category, the Third World consists of all the nations in Asia (except Japan), Africa (except South Africa), Latin America, the Caribbean, and some states of Oceania.

The Origin of the Term and Its Alternates

The French economist Alfred Sauvy coined the concept Third World—"*tiers monde*" in French—in a newspaper article penned for the August 14, 1952, issue of *L'Observateur*. The initial usage of the word in French referred to the three-tiered social classification used in the pre-Revolutionary French society, where the third estate was composed of commoners as opposed to the nobility of the first estate and priests of the second estate. The Third World for Sauvy is made up two ideas. First, much as the commoners were exploited in pre-Revolutionary France, the Third World today is exploited. And second, much as the commoners adopted a different kind of political program demanding social justice, the Third

World needed a different political approach for achieving a just global order.

Alfred Sauvy's conception of the Third World came to stand for a group of exploited countries that were economically not in the same league as those in either the First World or the Second World. The First World in this conceptual scheme stood for mostly Western countries (except Japan) that had tried from 1492 to colonize the rest of the world. These countries were focused on a European-centered imperial project, which then passed on to a United States-centered system post-1945. The Second World was composed of countries that espoused state socialism and were oriented to the Soviet Union as their center. The Third World consisted of countries that had been colonized by Europeans to get natural resources for building a world economy that benefited the peoples of Europe.

The industrial revolution first happened in the First World around the 1750s. The industrial development in the Second World was also advanced by the time the countries in the Third World began getting their freedom from European domination. The idea of the Third World is then an idea of countries that were not economically developed and that on the political scale had been exploited by the First World via colonization. In economic sense, this meant that the Third World was made up of countries that lacked industrial infrastructure, had to depend on supplying raw material to the First World, and were therefore poor. On social terms, it meant that these countries because of their poverty had fast-growing populations that suffered from higher infant mortality rates, were less educated in general, and suffered from numerous social problems.

Deployed as a term in public discourse, the concept of the Third World carries negative connotations; indeed, in the common discourse in the First World, the Third World connotes poverty and backwardness. But in more intellectual discussions, since mostly those sympathetic to the Third World used the word, the term became preferred over a number of competing options. One of the competing notions is the notion of "underdeveloped countries." But the concept of underdeveloped countries implies that Third World countries lack development—and that development is measured in reference to the Western model of development. This idea is ethnocentric because it takes the Western model as the eventual goal for everyone on this planet. A number of scholars, such as Ivan Illich, who belong to antidevelopment school have criticized the very definition of development—as measured by an increase in the growth domestic product (GDP) growth—as in fact a form of social regression rather than development.

The countries of the Third World are also sometimes referred to as countries of the South. This derives from the division of world into North and South. The northern countries are mostly white, industrialized, and have higher standards of living, while the southern countries are mostly non-white, are not industrialized, and have lower standard of living. This strategy of dividing the world, however, is criticized because Japan, a non-white country, is in the Northern Hemisphere, while Australia and New Zealand, both industrialized, white countries, are in the Southern Hemisphere. Another alternate term that approximates the concept of Third World is "postcolonial." The concept of "postcolonial," which is another competing term for Third World, suggests that the countries of the Third World were formerly colonized and therefore share a certain uniform experience of history. But the idea of postcolonialism is not accurate because countries such as Canada and Australia, though they were colonized by Europeans and thus fit the definition, differ vastly in almost any social and economic indicator from Third World countries.

Cold War and the Rise of Development

In the Cold War context, with competition between Capitalism and Communism, the Third World came to be playground on which the United States and Soviet Union played out their global conflict. While the Soviet Union supported the decolonization movement in many countries in the Third World, the United States—with its own relative lack of colonial history—took over from the British in establishing hegemony in the Third World. In the case of the United States, the idea of development and foreign aid was proposed for fighting off the increasing appeal of Communism in Third World countries. Supported by big foundations, the United States government undertook a program to economically targets areas in the Third World that were pure and were thought to be more prone to going Communist. For the Soviet Union, its own model of economic and social organization was the best for development, and therefore, it encouraged and pressured Third World countries to follow its model.

The countries of Third World themselves were interested in development as a mechanism for solving myriad social and economic problems. They adopted the language of development marked by a modernistic outlook. This adoption of a narrative of development meant that to develop the Third World, countries had to adopt the ways and means of the First or Second

World. This essentially meant the choice between Capitalist or Communist modes of organizing economies. Out of this jostling between the first and second worlds came the idea of official development, with each one providing aid and technology transfers to countries in the Third World. This concern with alleviating poverty in the Third World gave rise to the academic field of development studies.

The first school examining the reasons for the Third World's lack of development proposed a cultural theory. The modernization theory school suggested that the Third World countries are poor because their cultures do not encourage modernistic thinking, and therefore, they are not able to give rise to wealth. But the dependency school criticized this school of thought. The dependency school theorists suggested that the reason for the poverty in Third World countries lies not in the cultural mores of populations but in external factors. According to the dependency theory, developed countries—the First World—dictated the condition for exchange in the international markets; hence, the Third World countries were not competitive because the colonial structuring of their economies during European domination left them as just suppliers of raw materials.

The world-system theory, which built upon the dependency theory, continued the dependency theory's stress on external factors, but it did not take the nation-state as a basic system of analysis. The world-system approach looks at the world as a whole unit containing three different levels of countries in it: core, semiperiphery, and periphery. Both the proponents of dependency and world-systems approaches predicted that, given the inability to sustain capitalism, with the passage of time, the contradictions of the present economic order will make it possible for the transition to socialism. Yet another theory to address the question of development of the Third World is that of globalization.

The globalization approach stresses that the Third World is not wealthy because it is not participating in the transnational movements of goods and services. The Third World countries keep their domestic economies protected, and therefore, they suffer from poor governance. The best way to encourage development in the Third World is to follow the model of open economies, an approach named as the Washington Consensus. The other way of conceptualizing this is captured in the idea of neoliberalism, which is the argument for the least intervention of governments in the actions of economic actors nationally. The globalization approach argues that the best way for Third World countries to develop involves the least intervention possible from national governments and the most empowered entrepreneurs.

The debate about the development of the Third World is about whether the international system provides possibilities for upward mobility to the Third World countries. The modernization theory has argued that if people in the Third World change their cultural mores to reflect the mores of northern European Protestant ethics, they will develop. The dependency and world-system approaches argue that there is not much space for the development of Third World countries under capitalism and that only an end of capitalism will ensure development of the Third World. While this debate is to a certain extent still ongoing, the rise of foreign aid agencies and of government agencies concerned with overseas development has made the Third World their target. Most of these programs, however, are dependent on the idea of security for First World countries. The First World countries take part in foreign aid because any instability in the Third World will likely be felt in other parts of the world.

Politics of the Third World

The establishment of the United Nations (UN) in the aftermath of World War II gave a station to the countries in the Third World to demand independence and decolonization. As the increasing number of countries gained independence in the 1940s and 1950s, the Third World issue became prominent. The French desire for continuing colonial control in Vietnam and Algeria gave rise to wars in both countries, and the United States got involved in Vietnam and other conflicts in the Third World to counteract the rising tide of socialism. The passing of the hegemonic torch in the international system from the waning European colonial powers to the rising power of the United States led to the involvement of United States in the Third World—and because of its rising interventionism, the United States became the new hegemony in Third World countries. The military defeats of France in Algeria in 1962 and of the United States in the Vietnam War were prominent events in Third World history.

The movements and leaders in the Third World against neocolonial and imperial policies of the First World also became prominent during these times. The Cuban Revolution in 1959 brought forth Fidel Castro and Ernesto "Che" Guevara, who as a figure of youthful rebellion is still admired and emulated in the youth culture the world over. The anticolonial war in Algeria led to independence in 1962, with Ahmed Ben Bella as the leader. Franz Fanon, originally from Martinique but active in the Algerian anticolonial

movement, wrote the most definitive Third World manifesto in his *Wretched of the Earth*, arguing that for the colonized to overcome the colonizer, an absolute revolution was needed, even if it required violence. In Africa, the newly independent countries of Ghana and Congo were led by Kwame Nkrumah and Patrice Lumumba, respectively, both who defended their peoples' freedom while risking great harm to their own selves. A number of African and Caribbean intellectuals—Leopold Senghor and Aime Ceasire, among others—began the Negritude Movement to restore the dignity of Africa after centuries of subjugation. The victory of Ho Chi Minh's Vietcong in Vietnam over the United States, the most advanced First World country, inspired peoples in the Third World.

Politically, the idea of the "third world" was adopted by a number of countries that had been formerly colonized, and it was used as an emblem of a distinctive political orientation in the international arena: nonalignment with either of the two poles, the Communists and the Capitalists. This movement came to be known as Non-Alignment Movement (NAM). While the term "nonalignment" was used first by the Indian Prime Minister Jawaharlal Nehru during a speech in Colombo, Sri Lanka, in 1955, it was in Bandung, Indonesia, where the leaders of newly independent leaders from Asian and African countries met, that the foundation for the NAM was laid. Organized by India, Pakistan, Indonesia, Ceylon (Sri Lanka), and Burma (Myanmar), the conference was attended by twenty-nine Afro-Asian countries that announced cultural and economic cooperation in order to oppose colonialism and neocolonialism by both the United States and the Soviet Union.

The Bandung conference set in motion the process that resulted in the formation of NAM at a conference organized by Yugoslavian President Josip Broz Tito in Belgrade in 1961. The NAM—which has 116 members—has never found much of a cohesive identity, but a summit is held every three years to discuss issues relevant to member nations. The initial unity among Third World countries was also exhibited via the formation of the Group of 77 by the UN. The Group of 77 is a loose coalition of Third World nations that intends to defend members' interests and to create an enhanced negotiating capacity. Founded on June 15, 1964, by seventy-seven charter members, the group has expanded at present to include 133 countries.

The End of Third World?

As a concept and idea of unity, Third World has always existed with tension. While the intellectual

vision of writers and activists in the Third World was one of unity, the political and economic tensions contradicted this vision. India and China, two of the biggest members of Third World, signed an agreement on April 29, 1954, in Beijing that enunciated the Panchsheel Principles, the five principles that stressed noninterference and mutual respect in reciprocal relations and opposition to colonialism and neocolonialism. These principles were incorporated into ten principles of Bandung and were signed by India, China, and Pakistan, among others. But the efforts at formation of a unified policy against Cold War polarities were a failure as a number of countries were incorporated into either the United States-lead North American Treaty Organization (NATO) alliance or the Soviet-led Warsaw Pact. Thus, Pakistan came under the US umbrella, and India sided informally with the Soviet Union. In their mutual affairs, tensions began to corrode the outward unity expressed at the Bandung Conference.

The rising number of conflicts and wars among members of the Third World led to the decline of initial enthusiasm and solidarity that existed among peoples in Asia and Africa. India and China fought a war in 1962, and India and Pakistan fought two wars in 1965 and 1971. In Africa, Cold War conflicts broke out in Angola, Congo, Ghana, Kenya, Sudan, and Nigeria as well as among others. The decades following highlighted the tensions among members of the Third World with wars and festering conflicts between Ethiopia-Eritrea, India-Pakistan, Egypt-Yemen, Algeria-Morocco, Rwanda-Burundi, China-Vietnam, Iran-Iraq, and others. And even oil-rich countries—especially those in the Persian Gulf—that had been counted as Third World members became rich overnight after the oil shock of 1973, and they laid claim to a different kind of status. With the rise of per capita in these countries, outstripping those of even European countries, the Third World appellation did not mean anything in economic terms. But in political terms, these nations remained under the imperial ambit of the Western world, anchored in the US hegemony.

The other problem came with the descent of ruling parties into corruption and authoritarianism. In Algeria, a one-party system and the associated authoritarianism of the National Liberation Front (FLN) led to rising discontent, which took the form of Islamic protest. It resulted in the open rebellion in the beginning of 1990s and led to a decade of bloodshed in the country. In the Islamic world as well in India, the opposition to the order of the day shifted from a secular politics—which, after all, formed the basis of a Third World movement for modern development—to a politics of religion. In the Islamic

world, countries as diverse as Egypt, Iran, Pakistan, Afghanistan, Lebanon, and Sudan became increasingly assertive in Islamic politics. The prominence of religious politics—at the expense of secular politics—also appeared in India, Sri Lanka, and Turkey.

The rise of Newly Industrialized Countries (NICs), also known as the "Asian Tigers" in East Asia—Hong Kong, Taiwan, South Korea, and Singapore—led to demise of dependency principle. These countries showed that although capitalism remained an unequal system, there were economic opportunities for countries that put their efforts in developing certain niche strengths. An example of this improvement is found in the economic fortunes of China, which has become the factory of the world because of its manufacturing capacity; this example has further solidified the case against dependency. To a certain extent, the improvements in India's economic fortune had made it possible to conceive the world economic system as allowing for the mobility of countries in the Third World.

A number of theorists—Andre Gunder Frank, for example—have argued that the center of world power is slowly returning again to Asia. With the deepening of globalization, it is argued that perhaps the best way to conceive international inequality in not by using a geographic-based approach—of which the Third World versus the First World is a prime example—but a social approach. The presence of Third World within the First World and vice versa has led to arguments that the best way of understanding inequality in the world is by following the transnational chain of those connected to international economy and those who are excluded by this economy. But such areas as sub-Saharan Africa—that in the past had been conceptualized as the Fourth World by some—have remained marginalized even under globalization.

AMANDEEP SANDHU

See also Asian Tigers; Bandung Conference (1955); Colonialism: History; Colonialism: Legacies; Eurocentrism; Fanon, Frantz; Globalization: Impact on Development; Group of 77; Modernization; Neocolonialism; Newly Industrialized Economies (NIEs); Nonaligned Movement; Underdevelopment

References and Further Reading

Berger, M., ed. "After the Third World [Special Issue]." *Third World Quarterly* 25, no. 1 (2004).
Chossudovsky, M. *The Globalisation of Poverty: Impacts of IMF and World Bank Reforms.* London: Zed Books, 1997.
Fanon, F. *The Wretched of the Earth.* New York: Grove Press, 1963.
Frank, A. *ReOrient: Global Economy in the Asian Age.* Berkeley, CA: University of California Press, 1998.
Hoogvelt, A. *Globalization and the Postcolonial World: The New Political Economy of Development.* Baltimore, MD: Johns Hopkins University Press, 1997.
Malley, R. *Third Worldism, Revolution and the Turn to Islam.* Berkeley, CA: University of California Press, 1996.
Singham, A., ed. *The Non-Aligned Movement in World Politics.* Westport, CT: Lawrence Hill, 1977.
So, A. *Social Change and Development: Modernization, Dependency, and World-System Theories.* Newbury Park: Sage, 1990.
Stavrianos, L. *Global Rift: The Third World Comes of Age.* New York: William Morrow, 1981.
Worsley, P. *The Three Worlds: Culture and World Development.* Chicago: University of Chicago Press 1984.

THREE GORGES DAM

The Three Gorges Dam, the largest hydroelectric project in the world, is one of the most controversial projects currently under construction in China. The Three Gorges are located in the upper regions of the Yangtze River and are among China's most fantastic tourist attractions. The idea of building the dam was debated and planned for nearly seven decades. The government of the People's Republic of China (PRC) conducted extensive feasibility research and site selections in the 1950s and 1960s. However, due to budget constraints, the project stayed in the planning stage until the 1980s.

When the project was revived in 1992, widespread opposition forced the government to delay the project once more. After a period of heated debate, the project was finally approved by the People's Congress, China's highest decision-making body. The project officially broke ground in 1994. Two phases of construction have already been completed, and the power plant has partially been put into production. The remaining works are scheduled to be completed by 2009.

The project is mammoth in magnitude. Once completed, the dam will create a huge reservoir stretching 350 miles upstream in the Yangtze River. An estimated 1.13 million local residents must be relocated to make way for it. Many urban centers and villages will be partially or completely submerged. The resettlement alone consumes about one-third of the total cost of the project. More than 125 million cubic meters of earth and rocks have to be removed, and 26 million cubic meters of concrete are required for the six hundred-foot-tall dam. A five-level ship lock, the largest in the world, has been built to allow ships to pass through. The total projected cost is over $24 billion (USD).

The dam will power the largest power plant on earth. The initial scope of the project called for twenty-six seven-hundred-thousand-kilowatt turbogenerators. In 2003, an expansion plan was approved to add six

additional generators. The new plant will be located in an underground tunnel inside a mountain adjacent to the dam. If completed, the total power-generating capacity of the dam will reach 22.40 megawatts at peak time.

The benefits of this project to China's development are evident: the electricity produced will feed industrial development in China's coastal and central regions. The clean energy will replace more than 50 million tons of coal burned at plants, currently the chief source of electricity. The reduction in carbon monoxide emission will help reduce acid rain and minimize the greenhouse effect. It is also hoped that the dam will play a major role in controlling floods, enhancing irrigation, and improving navigation. According to the project planners, the dam will greatly diminish the threat of annual flooding and keep the reoccurring flood damage in the downstream areas to the minimum.

Critics believe that the project's environmental and social costs are too great to justify the benefits. Some observers believe that relocating more than 1 million residents will be difficult or even impossible. Other critics fear that 1,300 known historical and cultural sites may be wiped out; that the sediment problem may eventually render the dam useless; that the costs of the project may outweigh the energy production; that the potential damages to the region's ecological systems have been underestimated; that the quality of the construction may compromise the dam's safety; and that the dam is vulnerable to military attack.

The government maintains that the resettlement project will be part of a poverty relief program helping the displaced persons improve their standard of living. The government plans to invest in new cities and infrastructures to support six hundred thousand urban migrants. However, the government acknowledges that the challenge is indeed tremendous. While there was not great resistance to the mandatory relocation, many individuals and families complained of inadequate compensation. Official corruption may complicate the issue even further. Nevertheless, over seven hundred thousand people have already been relocated as of early 2004. Among them, 160,000, mostly from rural areas, have been relocated to eleven provinces and some metro areas such as Shanghai.

To save the historical and cultural relics in the region, the government organized 60% of the country's archeological workforces to save, excavate, and relocate cultural sites. Since 1997, more than 720,000 square meters of cultural sites have been uncovered, and 7 million square meters of cultural sites have been surveyed. More than 1,074 sites will be protected at a cost of 1 billion Chinese Yuan. A new Three Gorges Museum and several Three Gorges Cultural Protection Centers will be built to house all the cultural relics discovered in the area. In order to save the historical city of Dachang, for instance, the entire city was removed and rebuilt in its original state. Nonetheless, the number of cultural sites discovered far exceeded the official estimates. In Badong County alone, the number of sites in need of protection has quickly risen from forty-four to two thousand. Because many of the archeological projects were completed hastily, record keeping and classification may not have been precise, and thus many unknown cultural sites will be submerged by water.

Another criticism is the potential damage to the ecological system of the Yangtze River. Some accused the project planners of failing to conduct adequate scientific studies on environmental hydrology; cumulative impacts; biological, physical, and chemical responses; and potential human use patterns of the Three Gorges Reservoir. Some worry that the water quality will deteriorate; others believe that certain fish species might go extinct because the dam will make seasonal upstream migration impossible. Long-term decline in reservoir fisheries is believed to be inevitable since this result is well documented for many similar river dam projects around the world.

Clearly, the Three Gorges Dam is one of the most comprehensive projects ever undertaken by the Chinese. It comprises numerous and varied smaller projects that involve a great deal of planning. Extensive efforts and studies have been made to address these concerns. To ensure water quality, for instance, the government has initiated several large-scale projects, including a long-term reforestation and soil erosion reduction program in the upper Yangtze River. Wastewater processing plants and garbage-processing facilities are being built along the river bank to stop water pollution. The project is also considered an important part of the Great Western Development Strategy initiated in 1990s to narrow the economic gap between the coastal and inland areas.

BAOGANG GUO

See also China, People's Republic of; Environment: Government Policies; Energy: Impact on Development

References and Further Reading

Albert, Justin, and Jodie Foster. *Three Gorges Biggest Dam in the World.* Produced by Discovery Channel (Film) and Transatlantic Films. Bethesda, MD: Discovery Channel Video, 1999. Videocassette.

Barber, Margaret, and Gráinne Ryder. *Damming the Three Gorg: What Dam Builders Don't Want You to Know: A Critique of the Three Gorges Water Control Project Feasibility Study.* 2nd ed. London: Earthscan, 1993.

Luk, Shiu-hung, and Joseph B. Whitney. *Megaproject: A Case Study of China's Three Gorges Project.* Armonk, NY: M.E. Sharpe, 1993.

Steffen, W. L. *Challenges of a Changing Earth: Proceedings of the Global Change Open Science Conference, Amsterdam, the Netherlands, July 10–13, 2001. Global Change— The Igbp Series.* Berlin, and New York: Springer, 2002.

The River Dragon Has Come! The Three Gorges Dam and the Fate of China's Yangtze River and Its People. Armonk, NY: M.E. Sharpe.

"The Three Gorges Dam in China: Forced Resettlement, Suppression of Dissent and Labor Rights Concerns." *Human Rights Watch/Asia* 7, no. 2, 1995.

TIBET

Any discussion of Tibet is inextricably bound to debates about the governance of Tibetans. The occupation of Tibet by China that began in 1949, followed by the invasion of 1951 and culminating in the Tibetan uprising against the occupying forces in 1959, is the shared experience that links Tibetans in Tibet, the refugee Diaspora communities, and over 1,500 Tibet support groups in Asia, Europe, and North America. Tibet is an occupied country without representation at the United Nations (UN). At the time of China's invasion the Dalai Lama, who ruled Tibet, had asked the UN to intervene, and a dispute was registered between Tibet and China. China is a permanent member of the UN Security Council and uses its veto to prevent discussion of that dispute.

The Tibetan Government in Exile, a constitutional democracy, governed by the *Kashag* (or Cabinet) and led by the *Kalon Tripa* (Head of Cabinet), is based in Dharmsala, India. The vast majority of Tibetans acknowledge the Dalai Lama's leadership, both spiritual and political; but he insisted that his status as the fourteenth Dalai Lama of Tibet should become that of a spiritual—but not political—leader through the development of a new constitution. The first *Kalon Tripa* (or Prime Minister) under that constitution was Samdhong Rinpoche, a Tibetan Lama.

Tibet comprises 2.5 million square kilometers, with an average altitude of thirteen thousand feet (3,962 meters) above sea level. The economy is based largely on intensive agriculture and pastoralism (animal herding). Tibet is the watershed for much of Asia, with the Yarlung Tsangpo River (called the Brahmaputra in India), the Drichu River (called the Yangtze in China), Senge Khabab River (called the Indus in India), Phungchu River (called the Arun in India), Gyalmo Ngulchu River (called the Salween in Burma), and the Zachu River (called the Mekong in Thailand, Vietnam, Cambodia, and Laos). The country's wildlife includes the wild yak, Tibetan gazelle, black-necked crane, giant panda, red panda, golden monkey, wild ass, and Tibetan Argali. Domestic animals include four distinct breeds of Tibetan dog, including the well-known Lhasa Apso.

Prior to occupation, Tibet was divided into three provinces: U-Tsang, Amdo, and Kham. The Tibetan population was about 6 million in 1949. It dropped by about 1.2 million when many perished as the result of Chinese occupation; while reliable information is not available, the population appears to have rebounded to about 6 million. During the 1980s, population transfers, illegal under international law, moved 7.5 million Chinese (mainly Han) into Tibet. While the Chinese still regard moving to Tibet with much the same reserve that citizens of central Russia have about moving to Siberia, many are tempted by the special privileges afforded to Chinese in Tibet. Under Chinese occupation, Tibet's three provinces of U-Tsang, Amdo, and Kham have been divided into new regions: the Tibetan Autonomous Region (consisting in the Tibetan province of U-Tsang and part of Kham; about 1.2 million square kilometers) in Qinghai Province; Tianzu Tibetan Autonomous County and Gannan Tibetan Autonomous Prefecture in Gansu Province; Aba Tibetan-Qiang Autonomous Prefecture, Ganzi Tibetan Autonomous Prefecture, and Mili Tibetan Autonomous County in Sichuan Province; and Dechen Tibetan Autonomous Prefecture in Yunnan Province. When Tibetans in the Tibetan Diaspora refer to Tibet, they invariably mean the three provinces of Kham, U-Tsang, and Amdo because Tibetan refugees come from all parts of all three provinces. When the government of China refers to Tibet, it tends to refer only to the Tibetan Autonomous Region, with a population of about 2 million Tibetans. Most of Tibet, therefore, lies outside of what the Chinese government calls "Tibet."

Almost all Tibetans are Mahayana Buddhists. Tibetan Buddhism, also called Lamaism, is distinct in its emphasis upon finding the Tulkus, or reincarnations of highly realised or enlightened Lamas. The most important reincarnated Lama is the Dalai Lama, who is believed to be a manifestation of *Chenrasigs* (also called *Avalokitesvara*), the Bodhisattva of Compassion. It is difficult to overestimate the symbolic importance of the Dalai Lama himself and the system of Tibetan Buddhism that he represents. The Dalai Lama's personal example and Tibetan Buddhism, with its profound emphasis upon the development of compassion and personal responsibility, compose a central cultural theme for the Tibetan Diaspora community.

Over one hundred thousand Tibetans followed the Dalai Lama, as refugees, to India and neighboring countries after the March 10, 1959 uprising. The Dalai Lama established a government-in-exile in Dharmsala, in northern India, to coordinate efforts to provide for the refugees' needs of and to develop institutions to preserve Tibetan learning and culture

while Tibetans were separated from their country. The occupation of Tibet by China resulted in the destruction of more than six thousand monastic communities, which were the religious, educational, and administrative centers of Tibetan society. China's policies of forced assimilation, exacerbated by massive population transfers from China to Tibet and coupled with human rights violations and the destruction of Tibetan ecology, have caused widespread international concern and do not bode well for Tibet's future development.

The influx of Tibetans to India and other countries continued after the initial exodus, straining resources in India; in 1967, the Dalai Lama appealed to the international community to accept Tibetan refugees. Switzerland was the first nation to offer resettlement, and Canada was the second.

Tibetans inside and outside of Tibet have gained support internationally because of their nonviolent resistance to China's occupation of their country. For his continued commitment to these peaceful means, the Dalai Lama was awarded the Nobel Peace Prize in 1989.

Exiled Tibetans have also developed a parliament-in-exile that includes elected Members of Parliament (MPs) from each region with a population of Tibetan refugees. In 1992, the Canada Tibet Committee established the Canada Tibet Network on the Internet to link the Tibetan-Canadian communities. Subsequently renamed World Tibet Network, the service now serves Tibetans and Tibetan support groups globally.

The human rights situation in Tibet continues to be a serious embarrassment to the government of China; but with the Dalai Lama and the Tibetan Government in Exile asking for negotiations that would lead to Tibetan internal autonomy rather than complete independence, China is being offered a way forward.

BRIAN J. GIVEN

See also Buddhism; China, People's Republic of; East Asia: History and Economic Development; East Asia: International Relations; Ethnic Conflicts: East Asia

References and Further Reading

Goldstein, Melvyn C. *The Snow Lion and the Dragon: China, Tibet, and the Dalai Lama*. Berkeley, CA: University of California Press, 1997.
———, and Matthew T. Kapstein, eds. *Buddhism in Contemporary Tibet: Religious Revival and Cultural Identity*. Berkeley, CA: University of California Press, 1998.
Harrer, Heinrich. *Return to Tibet: Tibet after the Chinese Occupation*. Translated by Ewald Osers. New York: J.P. Tarcher/Putnam, c1998.
Margolis, Eric S. *War at the Top of the World: The Struggle for Afghanistan, Kashmir, and Tibet*. New York: Routledge, 2000.
McKay, Alex, ed. *Tibet and Her Neighbours: A History*. London: Edition Hansjorg Mayer, c2003.
Patt, David. *A Strange Liberation: Tibetan Lives in Chinese Hands*. Ithaca, NY: Snow Lion Publications, c1992.
Smith, Warren W. *Tibetan Nation: A History of Tibetan Nationalism and Sino-Tibetan Relations*. Boulder, CO: Westview Press, 1996.
Tsering, Shakya. *The Dragon in the Land of Snows: A History of Modern Tibet since 1947*. New York: Columbia University Press, 1999.

TIANANMEN SQUARE MASSACRE

China has been ruled by the dictatorial Communist Party since 1949, when Mao Zedong led the party to victory over the Nationalists (who fled to the island of Taiwan). In the tradition of Lenin and Stalin, the party allowed no democracy or popular dissent. Resistance was crushed at the cost of millions of lives, the repression reaching a peak during the period known as the Cultural Revolution (1966–1976).

With the death of Mao Zedong in 1976, China began to moderate its commitment to communism. A power struggle between Mao's successors resulted in the victory of Deng Xiaoping, a relative moderate. Deng believed that China's loyalty to traditional socialism was holding it back from maintaining its status as a world power. He advocated economic modernization and encouraged investment by foreign corporations. By the late 1980s, capitalism was taking root in China, and Deng's policies were resulting in record growth in China's gross national product (GNP).

Deng's support for economic reform, however, did not extend to political reform. He maintained the Communist Party's firm control over all of China's political institutions and opposed introducing Western ideas, such as free speech and democracy. Subordinates, such as Hu Yaobang, who advocated a more liberal society, were dismissed. Despite Deng's opposition to certain reforms, the growing economic freedom in China led many, particularly among younger Chinese intellectuals, to desire political and social freedoms to go along with China's growing economic freedom.

Events in China were also influenced by those in the neighboring Union of Soviet Socialist Republics (USSR). Since its birth in 1917, the Soviet Union had been the driving force behind world communist movements. But in 1985, reformist leader Mikhail Gorbachev had come to power, advocating economic and political reforms. By 1989, the beginnings of democratic institutions that would bring down the Soviet Union had formed. In Eastern Europe, starting with Hungary, communist governments were moving (some voluntary, some forced by events) away from communist one-party rule and toward democracy.

Chinese intellectuals were watching these events closely, particularly so because in 1989 Premier Gorbachev was due to visit China.

The trigger for the Tiananmen Square demonstrations came with the death of the pro-reform leader Hu Yaobang on April 15, 1989. Although no longer in power, Hu had become a symbol for those desiring greater freedom. A few thousand students marched to Tiananmen Square to demonstrate; ostensibly, they were demanding posthumous recognition for Hu; actually, as would quickly become clear, they were demanding a vast change in government policy in favor of greater freedom. The demonstrations escalated during April, with students, often supported by citizens of Beijing, gathering in tens of thousands in the square despite government prohibitions.

These demonstrations were troubling to Deng Xiaoping and his government, not simply because of their size but also because they were taking place in the heart of China. Tiananmen Square is the largest public square in the world (forty-four hectares, or over one hundred acres) and lies in the center of Beijing. With the Great Hall of the People (which houses the People's Congress) on one side and Mao's tomb on another, any demonstrations in Tiananmen could not help but have historic and international repercussions.

By the middle of May 1989, there was a permanent encampment of thousands of student protestors camped in the square. Other protestors began to arrive from elsewhere in China. International journalists flocked to the square and listened to earnest young students talk about freedom and democracy for China. Some of the protestors staged hunger strikes, demanding democracy and press freedoms. With Gorbachev in Beijing and extensive international press coverage, the government was restrained in its dealings with the demonstrators.

However, after Gorbachev's departure, and with the failure to successfully negotiate with the more moderate student leaders, the government's position hardened. On May 20, the government declared martial law, and on May 21 attempted to move troops into the square. The attempts, however, were blocked by students and Beijing residents, who physically placed themselves in front of military vehicles. The demonstrators, taking heart at this success, became bolder in their demands. On May 30, the demonstrators built a "Goddess of Democracy" statue out of plaster; the statue symbolized their demand for greater freedom and was reminiscent of the Statue of Liberty in New York harbor.

On June 3, government troops again moved against Tiananmen Square, but this time in much greater force. Reports of what happened are conflicting, and Chinese government censorship makes an accurate account impossible to achieve. Reports do consistently describe Chinese soldiers firing on civilians. They may not have fired indiscriminately into crowds, as has been reported, but clearly unarmed civilians in and around Tiananmen square were killed. During two days of struggle, there was extensive violence. Some of the violence was caused by crowds of Beijing residents who supported the demonstrators and tried to block the army vehicles moving through Beijing's streets. Many military trucks were destroyed in the fighting, and there were some military casualties. There were also some reports of troops acting sympathetically to the demonstrators being fired on by more hard-line forces. Most casualties, however, were civilian. Estimates range from hundreds (the government's figure) to thousands of casualties. The actual figure cannot be known with any accuracy, but probably more than two thousand people were killed during June 3, 4, and 5, 1989.

International leaders, including President George Bush of the United States, condemned the brutal repression of the Tiananmen Square protests but did little else (the United States, for example, maintained full trade relations with China). Human rights organizations were scathing in their criticism. Some protestors escaped to Western countries like the United States to continue their fight for greater democracy, and many more were arrested by the Chinese government. Fairly quickly the disturbances in Beijing and elsewhere in China died down, and the government was able to continue Deng's policies of economic liberalization without granting any political freedom.

It remains difficult to assess the Tiananmen Square uprising's effects. While there are still prodemocracy activists in China, they seem few and are heavily persecuted by government security services. Most Chinese citizens seem to have accepted the government's Faustian bargain of a growing economy and material prosperity without any political liberalization. Many prosperous Chinese regard the Tiananmen demonstrations as an impractical effort by naive students.

However, Chinese prosperity is not uniform. In the countryside, where poor peasants envy the disproportionate benefits enjoyed by the cities, there may be more sympathy for the memory of Tiananmen and more chance for a revival of a similar movement. For people around the world, the image of individual Chinese citizens putting their bodies in front of tanks in the name of democracy remains as an inspirational symbol for those advocating greater freedom in their own countries.

CARL SKUTSCH

See also China, People's Republic of; Chinese Communist Party; Deng Xiaoping

References and Further Reading

Black, George. *Black Hands of Beijing: Lives of Defiance in China's Democracy Movement*. New York: John Wiley, 1993.

Brook, Timothy. *Quelling the People: The Military Suppression of the Beijing Democracy Movement*. Stanford, CA: Stanford University Press, 1999.

Fewsmith, Joseph. *China Since Tiananmen: The Politics of Transition*. Cambridge; New York: Cambridge University Press, 2001.

Han Minzhu, ed. *Cries for Democracy: Writings and Speeches from the 1989 Chinese Democracy Movement*. Princeton, NJ: Princeton University Press, 1990.

Mills, James R. *The Legacy of Tiananmen: China in Disarray*. Ann Arbor, MI: University of Michigan Press, 1996.

Zhang, Liang Zhang, Andrew J. Nathan, Perry Link, and Zhang Li. *The Tiananmen Papers: The Chinese Leadership's Decision to Use Force Against Their Own People—In Their Own Words*. New York: Public Affairs Press, 2001.

Zhao, Dingxin. *The Power of Tiananmen: State-Society Relations and the 1989 Beijing Student Movement*. Chicago: University of Chicago Press, 2001.

TITO, JOSIP BROZ (MARSHALL TITO)

A revolutionary, president for life, and internationally respected leader, Josip Broz Tito (Tito was a Communist Party name Broz accepted in 1934) ruled former Yugoslavia for more than three decades, from 1945 to the time of his death in 1980. He is remembered as the most important political figure of the former Yugoslavia, a leader who skillfully kept the country's numerous ethnic animosities contained under the policy of brotherhood and unity while building his own and Yugoslavia's international reputation and prestige.

Son of a Croat father and a Slovene mother, Tito (1892–1980) was born in the small Croatian town of Kumrovec (at that time part of the Habsburg Monarchy) into a working class family. He attended primary and secondary schools and was trained as a locksmith. Soon after finishing his education and assuming his first employment in Zagreb, Tito became involved in local politics by joining the Croatian Social-Democrats. His first experience with communism was in Russia during World War I, where he spent several years as a prisoner of war after being drafted and sent to fight the Russian army in Romania. In 1920, Broz formally became a member of the Russian Communist Party, and soon after returned to his homeland and joined the Communist Party of Yugoslavia which, at that time, was rather marginal and not a very influential political party. In the period between the two World Wars, his status climbed rapidly from that of an ordinary party member to eventually becoming its leader in 1938. Despite Tito's personal skills, the communists lacked large public support, mainly because of their revolutionary ideas

and political organizational methods based on Soviet models. Such ideas, although directed against a widely disliked regime, attracted little support in a democracy. On the other hand, when World War II broke out, the Communists were among the first to organize a resistance against German forces and local puppet regimes. This time, revolutionary methods proved to be useful in helping Tito become established as a leader of communist partisans and antifascist fighters. Because of this status, Tito emerged from World War II not only as an undisputed communist leader but also as the leader of a revolution that abolished a kingdom. At the end of the war, Yugoslavia's communists solidified their position as the strongest party, gained legal recognition, and established the regime that lasted for the next forty-five years.

Tito's political role and accomplishments as a leader are still a matter of debate amongst scholars. On one hand, he is portrayed as having been a dictatorial opportunist who used the system for personal promotion and the development of a personality cult, building an international image while ignoring internal problems. Proponents of this theory justify their view with Tito's "President for Life" title, which was given to him in 1974. On the other hand, Tito is considered a great uniter of Southern Slavs who put Yugoslavia on the world map, bravely resisted the Soviet Union in 1948, and stabilized the region previously (and still in the early twenty-first century) considered an ethnic powder keg. Regardless of perspectives, the general consensus is that Tito possessed the characteristics of a skillful politician and charismatic leader. Under his leadership, a predominantly agricultural country, awash in the economic backwaters of Europe, experienced rapid transformation. The Communists' priorities were industrialization, urbanization, and education improvements, which were generally accomplished, although not without negative consequences. One developmental problem was the Communists' inability to comprehend the negativity associated with running the country through strict ideological limits which created many obstacles to economic development.

During the early post–World War II years, Tito consolidated his power by acting as prime-, foreign-, and defense-minister. Finally, in 1953, he was selected as the President of Yugoslavia. He held this position, with some modifications, until his death. Perhaps the most significant contribution of Tito's personality to the Yugoslav people was his rejection of Stalin's attempts to control the country's Communists. Not willing to follow anyone's orders in terms of implementation of communistic ideology, Tito pursued an independent path, which brought Yugoslavia to the brink of war with the Soviet Union in 1948 and expulsion from Cominform (a Moscow-dominated

organization of Communist parties), but Yugoslavia never became its satellite state. Because of his very strong stand against Stalin and the Soviet Union, Tito quickly rose in the eyes of Western leaders, many of whom began providing him with economic support. After Stalin's death in 1953, Khrushchev normalized relations with Tito, and after that Tito used his sensitive position between superpowers to obtain favors from both sides.

On the international scene, Tito's biggest contribution was the 1961 formation of the Non-Alignment Movement (NAM) with cofounders Gamal Abdel Naser of Egypt and India's Jawaharlal Nehru. This was an international organization of countries unwilling to align themselves with either side in the Cold War. In this role, Tito was the leading ambassador. Through his friendships with many leaders in this organization, Yugoslavia benefited economically as many of its companies received lucrative contracts from throughout Asia and Africa.

Domestically, after initial success in modernizing the economy and implementing so-called "market socialism," the country struggled to overcome ideological barriers that were blocking economic reforms and the eventual establishment of a free market economy. Through a series of reforms in the 1950s, state ownership of production was replaced with the workers' management of factories. This arrangement helped reduce the government's ultimate power in the decision-making process and accelerated economic growth. Yet in the 1960s, in order to prevent inflation and rising foreign debt resulting from market socialism, Tito's government began implementing reforms, which, although on a path to success, were soon abandoned for being ideologically unacceptable. Thereafter, under greater government control, the Yugoslav economy continued to weaken.

From the beginning of his rule, Tito always held a tight grip on nationalistic and separatist tendencies that arose among the various ethnic groups residing in Yugoslavia. Although he encouraged coexistence, Tito's methods were vigorously repressive when dealing with unsatisfied sides in the Yugoslav federation. In 1971, for example, Tito arrested hundreds of Croatian protesters who had mounted a spirited challenge to the existing system. Tito died in 1980 in Ljubljana, Slovenia.

ZORAN PAVLOVIĆ

See also Ethnic Conflicts: Central and Eastern Europe; Yugoslavia

References and Further Reading

Dedijer, Vladimir. *Tito Speaks: His Self Portrait and Struggle with Stalin*. London: Weidenfeld and Nicolson, 1953.

Đilas, Milovan. *Tito: The Story From Inside*. New York: Harcourt Brace Jovanovich, 1980.

Ridley, Jasper. *Tito: A Biography*. Philadelphia, PA: Trans-Atlantic Publications, 1994.

Tito, Josip Broz. *The Essential Tito*. Henry M. Christman, ed. New York: St. Martin Press, 1970.

West, Richard. *Tito and the Rise and Fall of Yugoslavia*. New York: Carroll and Graf, 1995.

TOGO

Togo (the official name of the Togolese Republic) was a part of the French occupations in Africa, a then French-administered United Nation (UN) trusteeship. It was called French Togoland, and its name was changed after independence in 1960.

The main ethnic groups in Togo are Ewe, Kabiy, Gurma, and Dagomba. In Togo's population, religious affiliations include Indigenous beliefs of 50%, Christian beliefs of 35%, and Muslim beliefs of 15%. In July 2004, the population of Togo was estimated at 5,556,812, with an approximate growth rate of 2.27%.

French is the official language and the language of commerce, while some African languages are widespread, mainly Ewe and Mina (in the south), Kabye or Kabiye, and Dagomba (in the north). Lomé is the capital and the main city.

The currency of Togo is the franc of the *Communauté Financière d'Afrique*, or the franc of the African Financial Community, called the CFA franc, and it consists of one hundred centimes (490 francs equal one US dollar or USD as of March 2005). The first political party in Togo was formed in 1941: the Committee of Togo Union. From 1969 until 1991, the Togolese People's Assembly was the sole political party. Togo now has a multiparty system, adopted in 1992 via a constitution approved by the High Council of the Republic and by a public referendum, and many political parties are now active.

The legislative body in Togo is unicameral National Assembly (eighty-one seats; members are elected by popular vote to serve five-year terms). General Gnassingbe Eyadema, installed as a military ruler in 1967, is Togo's president and Africa's longest-serving head of state. Officially, presidential elections based on a popular vote are held every five years. Despite the constitution mentioned above, however, Eyadema and his Rally of the Togolese People (RPT) party continue to wield virtually all political power in the country.

Togo's high population growth rate has placed increasing pressure on the country's natural resources. Environmental problems are widespread, and include deforestation, desertification, water pollution, and air pollution. Many wildlife species are endangered. Togo's government has signed a number

of conservation agreements, but basic services such as access to safe drinking water and sanitation services, especially in rural areas, are still lacking.

As a dependent economy, Togo faces many problems, including corruption and widespread poverty. The economy depends on commercial and subsistence agriculture. Though 65% of the population is employed in the agricultural sector, Togo must nevertheless import some of its staple foods. It exports cocoa, coffee, cotton, and phosphate; however, power shortages and mining costs caused phosphate production to drop by about one-fifth in 2002. The Togolese government has made attempts at economic reform, per the International Monetary Fund and World Bank guidelines; but these efforts, as well as attempts to bring in foreign investments, have moved slowly. In addition, most of Togo's international aid has been suspended due to allegations of human rights abuses.

NILLY KAMAL EL-AMIR

References and Further Reading

Arnold, Guy. *A Guide to African Political and Economic Development*. London: Fitzory Dearborn Publishers, 2001.
Boutros, Ghali. "The Marginalization of Africa." *Mediterranean Quarterly* 3, no. 1 (Winter, 1992).
———. "Europe and Democracy in Post Cold War Africa: How Serious is Europe and for What Reason?" *African Affairs* 97 (1998).
Rosenau, James N. "Global Changes and Theoretical Challenges: Toward a Post International Politics for the 1990s." *Global Changes and Theoretical Challenges: Approaches to World Politics for the 1990s*, Ernst-Otto Czempiel and James N. Rosenau, eds. Lexington: D.C. Heath and Company, 1995.

TONGA

The Kingdom of Tonga consists of 171 islands, thirty-six of them inhabited, near the Tropic of Capricorn and just west of the International Dateline in the Pacific Ocean. According to the 1996 census, the population (made up almost entirely of Polynesians) numbered 97,446, with the bulk of them living on the main islands of Tongatapu (68% of the population), Vava'u, Hu'apai, and Niua. The capital, Nukuloafa, is on the island of Tongatapu and is home to approximately one-fifth of the total population. The climate is tropical with an average annual temperature of 70°F (21°C) and rainfall between fifty-nine to seventy-one inches (1500 and 1800 millimeters). The warmer months, when the temperature gets into the thirties, are October to April, and trade winds occur all year round at a constant fourteen to eighteen knots. The islands are a mix of coral and volcanic areas with most being flat. Many look like iconic Pacific islands with coconut palms, white beaches, and lagoons bordered by reefs.

Tonga is unusual in the Pacific in that it has maintained its independence and has never been colonised. Despite being a protectorate of the United Kingdom from 1900 to 1970, Tonga has been continuously ruled by a relatively small group of nobles and the Royal Family without major disruption. The major changes have been the adoption of Christianity and the introduction of limited forms of democratic government and processes. A constitution was granted by King George Tupou I in 1875, a fan of British monarchy (hence the adoption of the name George), and a Constitutional Monarchy was established. Since independence in 1970, the government has been made up of a Cabinet that is appointed by the King, nine nobles elected by thirty-three hereditary nobles, and nine representatives elected by popular vote. The first political party was formed in 1994. The Royal Family and King Taufa'ahau Tupou IV continue to exercise absolute economic and political control over the country, although there have been challenges to this control. In addition to being a Constitutional Monarchy, Tonga is also a very religious country with the main church being the Free Wesleyan Church of Tonga. Christian religious beliefs have been merged with traditional Tongan cultural traditions, and the church is an important focus for community and cultural life. Tongans enjoy a good life expectancy (seventy-one years), high levels of education, and a literacy rate of 90%.

Tonga's economic development has been hampered by a reliance on a small range of exported products and varying demand for these products; regular cyclones (typically a major cyclone occurs every three years); the poor management of the economy, including the resources devoted to a large public service; and a dependence on remittances and foreign aid. Agriculture provides 95% of total exports, and the manufacturing base is small. Exports have been dominated by squash (pumpkin) and fish, with bananas and coconut products becoming less important crops throughout the 1990s. In 2003, exports were valued at $31 million US, with $26 million US going to Japan and the United States. At the same time, imports amounted to $100 million, with $43 million coming from New Zealand, primarily in the form of meat, timber, boats, and dairy products. External indebtedness has continued to rise from $24 million in 1985 to $64 million in 1995 and $73 million in 2003. Tourism and fishing play an important role in contributing to income although what sustains the Tongan economy to a significant extent are aid and

remittances. Aid has declined in recent years ($39 million in 1995 to $19 million in 2000), which has added to an unfavourable balance of trade and reduced local economic development options. Remittances, or the money sent to Tonga citizens from Tongan residents who live overseas, is significant and has been estimated to represent 45% of the gross domestic product (GDP). There is a large diaspora of the Tongan population, especially in New Zealand and the United States, with a level of ongoing emigration that limits population growth in Tonga itself (typically to 0.5% growth per annum). The overall effect of these various factors is indifferent economic performance (real GDP growth in 2002 was −1.1), a substantial trade imbalance, budget deficit, and employment growth considerably less than the rate of increase in the labour force.

International agencies, such as the Asia Development Bank and the World Bank, along with governments who supply aid, notably New Zealand and Australia, have been pressing for economic reform. One issue has been the numbers employed in public service (the government payroll accounted for 57% of expenditure in this line of work for 2001). Prince Lavaka, who was elected Prime Minister in 2000, has made a concerted effort to restrict government activity and employment to the core public services. The Public Finance Act, passed in 2003, has set the agenda for tax reform and the rationalisation of the public service. There is also political pressure for change. The Human Rights and Democracy Movement (formerly the People's Party), led by Member of Parliament (MP) Akilisi Pohiva, have been pushing for more public accountability and democratic participation in the running of Tonga. Part of the government's response has been to restrict debate and to punish opposition, including banning a prodemocracy newspaper, *Taimi o Tonga*, and imprisoning opposition MPs and activists. Social problems add to the issues facing Tonga. The Asia Development Bank Programme for 2005–2006 will focus on improving urban infrastructure, in part because of growing social problems, including youth unemployment, increasing crime rates, prostitution, substance abuse, and teenage pregnancies.

Tonga remains one of the most hierarchical countries in the Pacific with significant political, economic, and social challenges. Power is concentrated in the hands of the nobles and the Royal Family, and while there is considerable respect for these traditional rulers, there are also growing levels of concern and outright opposition. Structural reforms have begun to address the concentration of resources and employment in the public service, but the reliance on a few exports to a small number of countries as well as the imbalance between imports and exports and the role of aid and remittances in supplementing locally generated income will all contribute to a difficult economic future.

PAUL SPOONLEY

See also Oceania: History and Economic Development; Oceania: International Relations

References and Further Reading

Asia Development Bank. 2005. *Tonga*. http://www.adb.org/Tonga.

Brown, R. P. C., and Connell, J. *Entrepreneurs in the Emergent Economy: Migration, Remittances and Informal Markets in the Kingdom of Tonga*. Canberra: National Centre for Development Studies, 1993.

Economist Intelligence Unit. *Country Profile, Pacific Islands*. New York: 2004.

Gailley, C. W. "State Formation, Development, and Social Change in Tonga." *Social Change in the Pacific Islands*, A. Robillard, ed. London: Kegan Paul, 1992.

Hau'ofa, E. *Our Crowded Islands*. Suva: University of the South Pacific, 1977.

TORRIJOS HERRERA, OMAR

In 1968, Lieutenant Colonel Omar Torrijos Herrera (1929–1981) led a successful *coup d'état* against democratically elected President Arnulfo Arias. Although this was the third time that Arias had been forcibly removed from office, the 1968 *coup d'état* was fundamentally different from previous military revolts in Panamanian history. Torrijos, who ruled Panama until his death in a suspicious plane crash in 1981, epitomized the populist-reformist trend of some military governments in Latin America during the 1960s and 1970s. He immediately consolidated his power by dissolving all political parties in Panama. At the head of the Panamanian National Guard of eight thousand well-armed men, Torrijos excluded the traditional elites—known in Panama as the *rabiblancos* (white tails)—from political power, but he allowed them to keep their economic power. Torrijos, who catered to the nationalistic sentiments of the masses to gain support, implemented an authoritarian Socialist dictatorship. Torrijos balanced his populist, leftist rhetoric with strong support of the business sector and maintained a friendly relationship with the United States.

Born in Santiago on February 13, 1929, in the province of Veraguas, Torrijos was the sixth of twelve children. The son of a rural schoolteacher, Torrijos won a scholarship to a military academy in El Salvador. He graduated with a commission as a second lieutenant and joined the Panamanian National Guard in 1952. He was promoted to the rank of captain in 1956 and

continued his military studies at the US Southern Command's School of the Americas in the Canal Zone. By 1966, he had reached the rank of lieutenant colonel. He promoted himself to the rank of brigadier general in 1969. Torrijos unveiled a new constitution in 1972 that granted the executive branch of government exceptional powers. He implemented a series of social and economic reforms collectively referred to as "military socialism."

Torrijos used carrot and stick policies to co-opt the various corporatist sectors of Panamanian society. Although Panama's most fertile land remained in the hands of the oligarchy, Torrijos distributed 5% of the nation's agricultural land to the peasants. Major public housing projects and social welfare programs were especially appealing to the urban poor.

Torrijos also implemented a new labor code in 1972 that significantly improved the bargaining position of the workers. He implemented liberal banking and tax legislation that lured more than one hundred international banks to Panama. The bank secrecy laws, however, made Panama a repository for money laundered from the narcotics trade. The most popular of his populist policies was the 1977–1978 Panama Canal Treaty that provided for Panamanian control of the Canal Zone by 2000.

Although Torrijo stepped down as the head of state in 1978, he continued to be the commander of the Panamanian National Guard until his death. Meanwhile, Torrijos created his own political party, the *Partido Revolucionario Democrático* (PRD). After Torrijos's death, however, Manuel Noriega, who had been Torrijos's chief of intelligence, discarded Torrijos's military socialism and nationalistic economic development programs and implemented a corrupt, brutal regime. Regardless, Torrijos's brand of authoritarian populism is still appealing to many of Panama's people.

MICHAEL R. HALL

See also Panama; Panama Canal Treaties, 1977

References and Further Reading

Greene, Graham. *Getting to Know the General: The Story of an Involvement*. New York: Simon & Schuster, 1984.
Koster, R. M., and Guillermo Sanchez. *In the Time of Tyrants: Panama, 1968–1990*. New York: W.W. Norton, 1990.
Major, John. *Prize Possession: The United States Government and the Panama Canal, 1903–1979*. Cambridge: Cambridge University Press, 2003.
Priestley, George. *Military Government and Popular Participation in Panama: The Torrijos Regime, 1968–1975*. Boulder, CO: Westview, 1986.

TOTALITARIANISM

Totalitarianism is a completely modern phenomenon, something only foreshadowed before the twentieth century. In an age of mass democracy, the "totalitarian concept" has been a useful term to typify a particular genre of contemporary regime in which the population can be controlled by a variety of means, especially terror. Dictatorships, despotisms, and autocratic regimes are akin to totalitarian ones in their elitist rule, arbitrary use of political power, minimization of private individual rights, and their ordered and hierarchical institutions. Police states have similarities in the strong intervention of state power and the arbitrary exercise of police power, often including a secret police.

Totalitarianism depends on manipulating and controlling the masses that make up the object as well as the rationale for the totalitarian dictatorships. In *The Origin of Totalitarianism*, Hanna Arendt points out, "Practically speaking, it will make little difference whether totalitarian movements adopt the pattern of Nazism or Bolshevism, organize the masses in the name of race or class, pretend to follow the laws of life and nature or dialectics and economics" (Arendt 1951). For Arendt, the rise of totalitarianism was preeminently the story of breakdown: of the nation-state, the class system, and the political parties. The root of this breakdown was in the nineteenth century. It was largely accomplished in the twentieth century, and its most terrifying fruits were the totalitarian regimes of Germany and the Soviet Union. The unrestrained working of the Capitalist system before World War I led to what Arendt regarded as the breakdown of the nation-state, with its commitment to a real politics and to the rule of law, in favor of a world of total economic competition. However, how such a development, if it really took place, led to totalitarianism is not at all clear.

Sociologist Philo C. Washburn, after examining Fascist Germany and Stalin's Russia, identified some of the interrelated social conditions that were favorable to the development of totalitarian systems. These include a long tradition of autocratic rule; a pathological distrust of foreigners; hypernationalism and racism; absence of democratic characteristics; mass mobilization; central leadership committed to rapid industrialization; and a single state determined ideology (Washburn 1982).

Many of today's Third World countries, such as North Korea, Iran, and Saudi Arabia, exhibit a number of social conditions mentioned by Washburn. North Korea, Saudi Arabia (under the Saud family), and Iran, especially during the period under Ayatollah Khomeini (1979–1989), do not have totalitarian regimes but do assert substantial control over culture,

religious practices, and social life. Therefore, the tendency toward totalitarian rule has been apparent in these countries in recent decades. At present, only a few countries have totalitarian regimes, but there is no guarantee that totalitarianism will not rear its ugly head again.

In *Totalitarian Dictatorship and Autocracy*, Carl Friedrich and Zbigniew Brzezinski developed the most widely cited analysis of totalitarian regimes. They insisted on the modernity of totalitarianism, giving it a "preliminary characterization as ... an autocracy based on modern technology and mass legitimation." "In this sense," they argued, "totalitarian dictatorship is the adaptation of autocracy to twentieth-century industrial society." According to these authors, a totalitarian political system is composed of a cluster of six traits. A totalitarian dictatorship exists only when all six characteristics are present. Each can exist separately in some constitutional democracies. The six points are summarized by Friedrich and Brzeziniski (1956) as follows:

1. An official ideology covering all aspects of human existence to which every member of the society must adhere, not only by outer forms but also by inner convictions;
2. A single mass party led by one man, the "dictator," and consisting of a relatively small percentage of population;
3. A system of terroristic police controls making full use of modern science and, more especially, modern psychology;
4. Centralized state control of the mass media;
5. Complete control over all means of effective armed combat; and
6. A central control and direction of the entire economy through bureaucratic coordination of all productive enterprises.

Friedrich and Brzezinski note that there may be additional characteristics that often accompany these six. Among the most important of these are administrative control of justice and the courts as well as political expansionism. However, they argue that these are not to be regarded as defining characteristics of totalitarian rule.

The essence of Friedrich and Brzezinski's book was a careful analysis of Nazi and Soviet politics in terms of their six points. They recognize that there may be variations between totalitarian dictatorships. The dictatorships all might not exhibit the key characteristics to the same degree. For example, the ideology of Russia under Stalin was more specifically committed to certain principles than was the ideology of German Fascism—where ideology was formulated by the leader of the party. In Italy, some of these traits were

hardly present at all. They took different periods of time to reach the stage of monopolistic political control in which all opposition, actual or potential, had been eliminated and terror became the dominant element in the system. However, all totalitarian systems share, to some extent, the same six traits. Examples offered by Friedrich and Brzezniski are those of the USSR, pre–World War II Germany under Hitler, Italy under Mussolini, and the post–World War II Communist countries in Europe, China, Cuba, and Ghana.

Totalitarian systems embody not only strong and arbitrary power but also the insistence on conformity of the whole society, mass mobilization, the subjugation of all classes to a dominant political group, and attacks on the enemies of the system and on their ideology. Resting on mass support and mass movements, totalitarian regimes are tutelary in nature, purporting to incarnate the true and necessary values to give meaning to the lives of its citizens. Totalitarianism has meant that no interest falls outside the embrace of the state or the wielders of power; that the purposes of individuals, groups, and society are subordinate to those of state; that the state or ruling group monopolizes decision-making processes; that all opposition is prohibited; that there are no independent expressions of public opinion; that there is no constitutional form of self-government; and that there are few or no limits on the rulers.

Totalitarianism and Modern Science

Many of the basic characteristics of totalitarians listed previously by Friedrich and Brzezinski are possible only in modern society. They point out that although historical dictatorships had characteristics of totalitarian systems, modern technology is required for the ruling dictatorship to control every phase of society, every means of production, and every aspect of human life. The monopoly of communication would be impossible without modern technology. Friedrich and Brzezinski also point out that the centrally directed economy presupposes the reporting, cataloging, and calculating devices provided by modern technology. Technology does not cause totalitarianism, but without its usefulness in providing and categorizing data, "propaganda, the terror, and central planning would be quite impossible" (Friedrich and Brzezinski).

Totalitarianism and the Use of Terror

If there is any single characteristic that differentiates totalitarian systems from others, it is the extreme use

of terror although regimes differ widely in the amount, type, and ways of using terror. As Solzhenitsyn (1973) points out, totalitarian systems, at least in some of their phases, have been characterized by massive coercion–police acting unrestrained by any outside controls, concentration camps and torture, imprisonment and executions without proof of guilt, repressive measures against whole categories of people, the absence of public trial and even an opportunity for defense, and the imposition of penalties completely out of proportion to the actions of the accused, all on a scale without precedence in recent history. Hannah Arendt similarly argues that totalitarianism is a form of government "whose essence is terror and whose principle of action is the logicality of ideological thinking" (Arendt 1951). The terror can be physical or psychological and is used by governments in the deliberate effort to intimidate. Stalin's Russia was the setting for political assassinations, expropriation of personal property, forced labor, the widespread use of terror as a means of political control, and mass executions. Governmental terror seeks to frighten those under its sway into conformity and obedience. It therefore may create a measure of consensus and willing cooperation. The effect of the terror is to generate a pervasive atmosphere of anxiety and a general sense of insecurity.

Although totalitarian regimes were usually developed out of civil wars and one-party dictatorships, Arendt cautions against confusing totalitarian terror with terror associated with civil wars and revolutions. According to him, a one-party dictatorship develops into a full-blown totalitarian state when political liberties and other human rights become nonexistent, dissidents and nonconformity are not tolerated, and almost all of those citizens who do not submit often vanish or are dispatched to the firing squad. Genuinely totalitarian terror sets in when the regime resorts to political assassinations and mass executions as means of total political control (Arendt 1994).

Terror keeps totalitarian society in constant motion. It is a principle radically opposed to the principle of law, which is designed to function as a stabilizing factor for the ever-changing movements of man. By subjugating its population to constant and arbitrary persecution, totalitarian rule destroys the world as a relatively stable order that can be counted on.

Just as significant, if not more, as the scale of the terror in some totalitarian systems has been its use against whole categories of people irrespective of any evidence of guilt or even intention of threatening the political system. The deprivation of human rights, wholesale arrests, and extermination of people who belong to a certain ethnic group (such as Jews and gypsies by the Nazis) or a certain class (such as landlords and clergy in Communist countries) have been unique in modern times. Between 1941 and 1945, the German Fascists systematically killed millions of men, women, and children because they were Jews, Gypsies, or Slavs and were defined by the dominant ideology as threatening to Germany. In those cases, the victims did not need to be personally guilty of any acts against the state or the social order, and their prosecutors did not have to attempt to make a case against them based on any charges, real or imagined.

Another unique feature is the extension of the terror to members of the elite. In fact, the harsher punishment particularly under Stalin of those who had taken part in the revolution with him and those who had positions of responsibility, and whose loss of favor or trust in other systems would lead to their demotion, returned to private life and often to powerlessness. Many of the intellectuals who had played key roles in the Russian Revolution of 1917 were killed off in the Great Purge. Later, Marxist critics of the regime met the same fate.

Mobilization of the Masses

The mobilization of the masses is essential to the modern totalitarian dictatorship. This mobilization is done through a combination of ideology with its promise of security and future utopia, mass propaganda, and mass education. The infusion of ideology becomes an important catalyst to the proper mobilization of society. Manipulating symbols and mobilizing society are important ingredients of totalitarianism. Under Fascist rule, members of the mass public were to devote themselves to the German race and the Fatherland—a combination of undiluted racism and extreme chauvinism. People were to dedicate themselves without question to their nation, for the community was all-important and the individual totally insignificant apart from the nation. They were to give their unquestioning loyalty and obedience to their leader, Adolf Hitler, who was to be considered the infallible representative of the true will of the German people. They were to attend marches, to attend huge mass rallies, and to sing songs that reinforced these prescribed loves and hates. They were to deal with the enemies identified by the regime in a ruthless and often violent manner.

Totalitarian regimes are always dependent on mass support for their survival. According to Hannah Arendt:

> Hitler's rise to power was legal in terms of majority rule and neither he nor Stalin could have maintained the

leadership of large populations, survived many interior and exterior crises, and braved the numerous dangers of the relentless intraparty struggles if they had not had the confidence of the masses. (Arendt 1951)

Ideology and Totalitarianism

There can be no doubt that totalitarian leaders, individuals, or groups, in contrast to other nondemocratic rulers, derive much of their sense of mission, their legitimation, and often very specific policies from their commitment to some holistic conception of man and society. The initial commitment of a ruler or ruling group to an ideology imposes constraints, excluding a greater or smaller number of alternative values, goals, and styles of thinking and sets a framework that limits the range of alternative policies.

Ideologies in totalitarian systems are a source of legitimacy and a source of a leader's or a ruling group's mission. While the ideology imposes some constraints, more or less narrow, on the rulers and their actions, the relationship is not one-sided, and much of the effort in such systems goes into the manipulation, adaptation, and selective interpretation of ideological heritage, particularly in the second generation of rulers. Supposedly based on Marxism-Leninism, the Stalinist era has been explained or defended by the need to create those conditions necessary for the building of a Socialist society. However, it is difficult to ascertain whether the Stalinist practice was in any way related to that need or based on ideological conviction.

The reason why ideology is perceived as so fundamentally important to totalitarian dictatorship stems from the role given to propaganda directed ultimately at the maintenance in power of the party controlling it. Propaganda and educational training are viewed as the means for achieving the total ideological integration of the people.

Totalitarianism has been a valuable term for designating the uniqueness of a limited number of systems at a specific moment in modern history. Their style, organizational devices, and political structures differentiate them from other nondemocratic systems. The relationship between the rulers and the ruled separates them from despotic dictatorships or outright tyrannies, such as those of the Third World countries.

NASSER MOMAYEZI

See also Authoritarianism; Bureaucratic Authoritarianism; Dictatorships; Single-Party States

References and Further Reading

Arendt, Hannah. *The Origins of Totalitarianism*. New York: Harcourt, Brace and World, 1951.
———. *Totalitarianism: Part Three of the Origins of Totalitarianism*, New York; Orlando, FL: Harcourt, 1985.
———. "On the Nature of Totalitarianism." *Essays in Understanding*, ed. Jerome Kohn. New York: Harcourt Brace, 1994.
Brzeziniski, Zbigniew K. *Ideology and Power in Soviet Politics*. New York: Frederick A. Praeger, 1962.
Drucker, Peter F. *The End of Economic Man: The Origins of Totalitarianism*. New Brunswick, NJ: Transaction Publishers, 1995.
Friedrich, Carl J., and Zbigniew K. Brzezinski. *Totalitarian Dictatorship and Autocracy*. New York: Frederick A. Praeger, 1956.
Gleason, Abbott. *Totalitarianism: The Inner History of the Cold War*. New York: Oxford University Press, 1995.
Halberstam, Michael. *Totalitarianism and the Modern Conception of Politics*. New Haven, CT: Yale University Press, 1999.
Howe, Irving. *1984 Revisited: Totalitarianism in Our Century*. New York: Harper & Row Publishers, 1983.
Linz, Juan J. *Totalitarian and Authoritarian Regimes*. Boulder, CO: Lynne Rienner Publishers, 2000.
O'Kane, Rosemary H. T. *Terror, Force and States: The Path from Modernity*. Brookfield, VT: Edward Elgar Publishing Company, 1996.
Solzhenitsyn, Aleksander I. *The Gulag Archipelago 1918–1956: An Experiment in Literary Investigation*. New York: Harper & Row, 1973.
Talmon. J. L. *The Origins of Totalitarian Democracy*. New York: Frederick A. Praeger, 1968.
Vetterli, Richard, and William E. Fort, Jr. *The Essence of Totalitarianism*. New York: University Press of America, 1997.
Wahburn, Philo C. *Political Sociology: Approaches Concepts Hypotheses*. Englewood Cliffs, NJ: Prentice Hall, 1982.

TOURÉ, SÉKOU

Sékou Touré was the first president of the Republic of Guinea, West Africa, and a well-known anticolonial figure throughout Africa and the Third World.

Touré (1922–1984) was born in a poor Muslim *Mandinka* farming village in the colony of French Guinea. He claimed descent from the late-nineteenth-century anticolonial resistance hero, Samori Touré. Sékou Touré was sent to study in Conakry and then held numerous jobs in the capital city, including the post of secretary general of the Post and Telecommunications Workers' Union in the late 1940s, and organized several labor strikes. In 1958, he joined with some other West African Nationalist leaders, such as Felix Houphouet-Boigny of the Ivory Coast (Cote d'Ivoire), to establish the *Rassemblement Democratique Africain*, which was in the forefront of West African opposition to French colonialism.

Touré was twice elected to the French National Assembly, and in 1956, he was elected mayor of Conakry. He belonged to several political and union organizations that sought autonomy for Guinea. With his eloquent, passionate, and direct calls for immediate independence, Touré reached not only the educated elite but also urban workers and rural peasants. In 1958, when President Charles De Gaulle of France offered a choice between membership in a French community or immediate independence, Touré led the fight for severing all ties with the colonial power. Guinea was the only territory to vote for autonomy. France quickly stopped all assistance, repatriated its citizens, who made up the majority of the skilled workers, and dismantled and carted off as much of the infrastructure as possible. Touré, elected shortly after the independence vote, desperately sought help from both the Eastern and Western blocs. The Soviet Union eventually responded, and Touré established warm relations with the Eastern bloc and further antagonized the French and the West. He rapidly transformed Guinea into a Socialist state with agricultural collectivization schemes, state-run industries, and a highly centralized economy and bureaucracy. Despite his draconian efforts, Guinea, which was popularly known as "Guinea Sékou Touré," was one of the poorest and most isolated countries in the world. Touré blamed foreign saboteurs and indigenous resistors to socialism for deteriorating economic conditions. He established a virtual police state, detaining, exiling, or killing anyone, including peasants, he felt resisted his rule and the Socialist state. Thousands died, and more than 1 million fled, particularly into neighboring Senegal and Cote d'Ivoire, both of which had cut all ties to his regime. Only President Kwame Nkrumah of Ghana maintained cordial relations with Sékou Touré.

Touré was an outspoken proponent of pan-Africanism and African liberation. Touré became a hero and sponsor of several militant groups in Africa and overseas. Some African-American dissidents, such as Stokey Carmichael (later Kwame Touré), took refuge in Guinea. Numerous assassination and *coup* attempts against Touré, some French sponsored and others internally motivated, intensified his authoritarian rule and intolerance for any dissent. Touré visited the United States several times, usually to address the United Nations. He died unexpectedly of heart failure in a Cleveland hospital on March 26, 1984, without appointing a successor.

ANDREW F. CLARK

See also Guinea; West Africa: History and Economic Development; West Africa: International Relations

Bibliography

Adamolekun, Lapido. *Sékou Touré's Guinea: An Experiment in Nation Building.* New York: Methuen, 1976.
O'Toole, Thomas, and Ibrahima Bah-Lalya. *Historical Dictionary of Guinea.* Latham, MD: Rowan and Littlefield, 1995.
Sékou Touré. Panaf Great Lives. New York: Panaf, 1978.
Sorry, Charles. *Sékou Touré: L'ange Exterminateur: Un Passé a Dépassé.* Paris: L'Harmattan, 2000.
Touré, Sékou. *Permanent Struggle: Selected Writings of Sékou Touré.* New York: Monthly Review, 1974.

TRADE POLICIES AND DEVELOPMENT

Trade is a highly unusual topic in development in that the strongly polarized dialogue surrounding it seems to have moderated considerably in the twenty-first century. While there are growing protests about international trade, the main thrust of these seems to be more about modifying the ways in which trade is carried out, and, more particularly, how international trade agreements are reached, rather than whether trade is beneficial or harmful for development. These developments can be traced by first examining trade theory from its economic origins, then looking to the historical development of political economy schools of thought on trade and development, and finally taking a brief overview of the most prominent contemporary issues.

Trade is the exchange of goods, and thus trade, like markets, exists in any society. Trade can be considered a natural part of human relations. As the development of a modern nation-state took hold in Europe in the sixteenth century, a doctrine called "mercantilism" laid out some initial thoughts on trade. The basic idea behind mercantilism is that the nation-state should seek to gain benefits, generally unilateral, from trade. Thus, mercantilists saw trade as a zero-sum game in which they could gain by protecting their domestic market while making money from exporting to other countries. Important variants of this thinking have filtered into contemporary trade theories and are discussed in the upcoming paragraphs.

Modern trade theory, however, largely rests upon the classical economic works of the eighteenth century, primarily the work of Adam Smith and David Ricardo. Adam Smith's classic work *The Wealth of Nations* lays out the benefits of trade among nations in what he called "absolute advantage." Smith laid out the most important principle that specialization in production can lead to gains. Thus, if a country, such as England, is better at making a product such as cloth, and Portugal at making wine, then both

would be better off in *concentrating on the goods they produce best* and trading with each other. David Ricardo is the other seminal theorist on trade, and he lays out the principle of "comparative advantage." Ricardo pointed out that even where one country, such as Portugal, could produce goods cheaper than a potential trading partner, such as England, trade would still benefit both. The reason again is *specialization*. If England specialized in the product it produced most cheaply, the overall production of both nations could be increased. The very powerful principle of specialization as a basis for trade is, then, made even more important by the more contemporary concept of "economies of scale." Economies of scale means that the per-unit cost of producing a good, like automobiles, decreases as large production runs are reached. Thus, if a country wants to produce goods with high economies of scale efficiently, which is the case with many manufactured goods, it needs to produce large amounts of them at a time. With the investment of time, resources, and people skilled to work in such factories, it makes even more sense in the present day to trade so that nations can specialize in certain manufactures.

One of the real questions, if the above principles are accepted, is how to determine which nations produce which goods. The principle economic theories behind this include the Heckscher-Ohlin theorem, the Stolper-Samuelson factor price equalization theorem, and a number of other theories, including the new endogenous growth theory that attempts to take technology and "human capital" into account.

The basic idea behind the Heckscher-Ohlin theorem is that countries will have a comparative advantage in the goods for which they have the most abundant resources. Thus, a country that is relatively rich in agricultural land (compared to other nations), such as Argentina, will have a natural comparative advantage in agriculture. Stolper and Samuelson point out that under certain conditions, trade will have important effects on factor prices. Thus, as Argentina begins to produce more agricultural goods for trade, the domestic price of land will go up. The price of land in its trading partners' countries (that produce other goods) should decline as they reduce their agricultural production because they can now import food more cheaply.

The basic idea behind the Stolper-Samuelson theorem contains profound implications for the *distributional* effects of trade. This theorem has led to a whole literature on political coalitions for and against trade policies. Another important component of modern trade theory is a series of writings that concern the role of technology. The Harrod-Domar model of the 1950s pointed out the important role of technology in

the costs of production. Theodore Schultz pointed out that the level of workers' skills also had important effects on the costs of production. These two insights, in particular, have led to a contemporary debate about whether comparative advantage can be changed and developed, known as "strategic trade theory," which is discussed below.

Moving beyond the purely economic issues of trade, one can encounter a much more contentious debate about it. This debate can be characterized as a discussion between three basic schools of thought. The first is the "liberal" perspective, which reflects the Ricardian basis of mainstream international economics. The second is the Marxist school of thought and its more trade-oriented application of dependency. The third is the structuralist school of thought, which seems to reach some middle ground between the first two perspectives. A key variable for understanding these three schools of thought is the role of the state (government) in economic affairs.

The liberal school of thought emphasizes the *absolute* benefits of trade to all parties who engage in it. Because liberals believe in natural factors of comparative advantage, they do not see any need for major state intervention in the economy. More modern liberals are called "neoliberals" because they see the government as playing an important but limited role in making sure markets function smoothly. Thus, a government may be needed to reach free trade agreements and to ensure that "externalities" to markets, such as pollution, are limited. Neoliberals believe that if a government distorts natural comparative advantage, it is simply working against its own citizens' interests. Because competition through trade should lead to lower prices, all consumers benefit the most if governments reduce interventions to a minimum.

The Marxist approach looks at trade in terms of economic classes. Economic classes can be generally understood as natural groups in a society of people who work in similar kinds of professions and of similar levels of income and wealth. In the most basic terms, the upper, middle, and lower classes can be referred to. Marxists would make much finer distinctions and clarify that economic classes depend in good part on how production is organized in a society. Thus, a primarily agriculture-producing country would have a different "mode" of production and thus have different economic classes rather than an industrial manufacture-producing one. The most potent contemporary Marxist application to trade theory is the dependency school, whose adherents are known as *dependistas*, focusing on the relations between developing and developed countries. While some Marxists, such as Lenin, believed that capitalist relations (that is the dominance of the capitalist class

and mode of production) would eventually spread across the world, *dependistas* see both domestic and international economic relations between the developed and developing worlds as inherently exploitative. They point out that these exploitative relationships started out with the way that colonies were set up under mercantilism, as providers of raw materials to the mother countries. Colonizers often took steps to squelch out industries in the developing world, as was the case with England crushing the Indian textile industry.

The modern *dependistas* point out that a form of "neocolonial" relations continues to exist between the developing and developed worlds. Thus, the developing world *depends* on the developed world for export markets for its products, technology, investment, and a host of other factors that allow its economies to function. However, this dependency is one-way because developed nations have no such reliance on developing nations. Thus, trade is seen as another vehicle of exploitation carried out by local *comprador* classes, with more ties to developed countries than the majority of their own. The primary weakness of the dependency theory is the failure to propose a clear solution to these problems. However, Marxist theory in general sees the need for a socioeconomic revolution, in which the state, as an embodiment of the revolting classes, could reorganize economic relations. Moreover, from this point of view, a revolutionary state should cut the exploitative ties to the First World that choke the local economy.

One of the keys to the dependency argument and one that is shared with the structuralist school of thought is the "terms of trade" debate. An important tenet of both schools is that there is a different price trajectory for manufactures versus raw materials and basic goods in the international market. Thus, there is a tendency for the relative price of manufactured goods to increase over time relative to raw materials and agricultural goods. Since the developing world still primarily exports the latter, it faces declining or deteriorating terms of trade over time. That is, even while its economies try to grow, the countries are paying more for imports and receiving less for their exports in international trade over time.

The structuralist school of thought recognizes this problem but rejects the implied solution of dependency to cut exploitative ties and push for self-sufficiency. Structuralist thought has its origins in mercantilism in the sense that it also sees the need for strong state intervention to maximize the *relative* gains of trade. Thus structuralists would fully buy the terms of the trade argument, but the central focus of their thought is that such disadvantages *can be overcome through state action*. Structuralists believe that a comparative

advantage can be molded, modified, and created to some extent. Thus, the developing state could take actions to move from the production of raw materials toward industrialized goods and services. The state's actions might take any number of paths, including tariff protection for domestic "infant" industries to funding basic research that would create new technologies. The contemporary variant of structuralism is called "strategic trade theory." In good part, this wave of the political economy literature came out in response to the highly successful trade policies of East Asia, discussed further below, which seem to embody the relative gains view of trade and which have led to changes in comparative advantage over time.

In terms of development, modern trade theory really comes into play after World War II. Part of the postwar recovery plan set up by the United States and its European allies included the Bretton Woods regime, which set up the basic rules and institutions for international exchange and trade. The Bretton Woods regime really embodies the liberal paradigm of mutual gains in international trade. In terms of trade, the most important treaties are the General Agreement on Tariffs and Trade, signed in 1947, which sought to reduce tariff barriers to trade, and its complement named the General Agreement on Trade in Services, signed in 1994, which includes services. It is fair to say that the rules and institutions of international trade have been dominated by the First World.

The principal international institutions for international trade include the International Monetary Fund (IMF), the World Bank, the World Trade Organization (WTO), and the various meetings of the largest developed economies, including the G-7 (G meaning group of), G-5, and the Triad. In addition, there exist various regional institutions, such as the Inter-American Development Bank and the Asian Development Bank, that promote and study regional trade and development. All of these institutions, as well as the United Nations (UN), rely heavily upon developed countries, particularly the United States, for their funding. Thus, developed countries have a proportionately much higher say in their policies and decisions. Nonetheless, their ability to control developing countries' economic policies should not be overemphasized. Like all international law and agreements, there is no direct enforcement mechanism. Thus, for example, the GATS agreements are riddled with voluntary "exceptions" that countries take to reducing domestic intervention. In terms of development, there is some degree of overlap among the principal institutions, but in practice they seem to generally occupy certain niches of activity. The IMF tends to concentrate on balance-of-payments and

related exchange rates problems. The World Bank's and the UN's various arms focus more on longer term issues of development, but the World Bank is generally more project- and sector-oriented. The regional banks also focus on projects but also have a larger proportion geared toward certain regional objectives, such as basic human needs, which change over time.

It is interesting to note that the role of the international institutions, despite the fact that their true independence of action is quite limited, has become increasingly controversial. After World War II, there was a great expansion of international trade, which gave new prospects to developing countries in the 1960s for growth. At that time, most developing nations were following a structuralist-inspired or Socialist-inspired trade strategy. In Africa, the state became heavily involved in setting up both agricultural and industrial enterprises, sometimes calling for a Socialist transformation. The rapid historical industrialization of Russia seemed to point to the need for heavy state intervention for economic development. Thus, the first generation of independent leaders in Africa, including Nkrumah in Ghana and Nyerere in Tanzania, believed that their new states could achieve rapid growth and egalitarian results through a "big push" from the state.

Developing countries in general adopted policies by which the state was heavily involved in setting up domestic industries, often times owning them, and placing barriers on foreign investment and trade. However, there were important variants of trade policy both within and across regions. Latin American countries generally had proportionately less state dominance of their economies than their African counterparts, with the important exception of Socialist Cuba. Latin American economies were guided by the work of the United Nations' Economic Commission for Latin America to follow a policy called "import substituting industrialization" (ISI). The basic idea behind ISI was that the government would set up or create incentives for new industries to arise to serve the domestic market. The previously imported manufactures would now be made at home. At some point later, when domestic industries had "grown up," they could compete with foreign manufacturers. In practice, ISI ran into a number of practical policy problems. First, there was a problem in terms of the difficulties of setting up whole new industries, which require a substantial amount of technical and managerial expertise as well as skilled labor and financing capital. Second, to solve this problem, Latin American governments taxed their natural resources and agricultural sectors. This naturally led over time to a decline in the productivity and volume of their principal exports of agriculture. Along with the decline in

exports came a need to import equipment and expertise from abroad to set up the factories. The combination of these two major factors led to increasing inflationary and exchange rate crises by the end of the 1960s. Third, though growth rates were relatively high and the industrial base was built, there was an increasing inequality and unevenness of the growth so that the main benefits of ISI tended to accumulate among the "enclaves" of the industrial factories, their managers, and their workers. The increasing inequality fed directly into the blossoming of dependency analysis in Latin America. Fourth, the state-run enterprises and incentives, both in Latin America and Africa, tended to become politicized so that state companies could no longer make budgetary, pricing, and hiring decisions on the basis of economic or financial logic. Many parastatals and state-owned enterprises became patronage machines, with policies and personnel changing on the basis of political whims.

Despite the lack of well-developed proposals, the dependency theory has had practical impacts on trade policies. A number of countries in the developing world expropriated foreign assets, though often with some level of compensation. A number of countries also imposed strong restrictions on multinational companies, such as limiting levels of profit repatriation or requiring a certain level of local hiring and training. Several developing (and developed) countries, including India and Egypt, promoted "cultural" industries, such as filmmaking, to combat dependency on US communications and media. A number of ambitious South-South developing country forums were established to create a list of demands on the developed world for better international economic rules. These demands reached a peak in the mid-1970s with the creation of the New International Economic Order (NIEO) manifesto, including a demand for international buffer stocks to stabilize commodity prices. These proposals, as well as ones in the future for debt relief and South-South integration, have largely come to naught in terms of actual changes in the international economy.

East Asian states, in part because of their *lack* of easy natural resources and in part because of the historical context of Japanese and then United States occupation, followed a different strategy toward industrialization. Their policy can be described as export-oriented industrialization (EOI). EOI has the same analytical base in structuralist thought but with a huge difference. East Asian states industrialized with the idea of producing goods for the US and European markets, not their own domestic markets. Thus, EOI was able to reduce two of the major pitfalls of the ISI: exchange rate crises and increasingly uncompetitive and inefficient enterprises. Because East Asian states

forced their new industries to export, they had to reach international levels of quality. The fact that the companies were exporting meant that the export revenue could be used as a new source of funds to fuel further investments in (new) industries. More importantly, East Asian countries tended to create more competition among their own industries for subsidies and protection. Following the Japanese model, East Asian countries, namely South Korea and Taiwan, created incentives and goals, such as export targets, that domestic and foreign investors had to reach to qualify for favorable treatment. Another interesting contrast between East Asia and other developing regions is that they undertook a major agrarian reform and invested heavily in education and health care, so there was much less tension over distributional issues of growth.

The Socialist and ISI experiments of the 1960s might have come crashing down in the early 1970s were it not for the new development of an international financial market. The breakdown of the original Bretton Woods system, the development of Eurobanks, and the new appearance of "petrodollars" from the newly rich oil-producing countries combined to create a large pool of capital in the 1970s. This international financial capital was used by countries to pay for the imports of both oil and the inputs needed for industrialization. When the United States heavily raised interest rates in 1982 and oil prices began to drop, international liquidity dried up. The result was the debt crisis, which, for the reasons mentioned earlier, hit Africa and Latin America especially hard. "The lost decade" of the 1980s was one in which countries struggled to make their debt payments amidst dealing with the higher interest rates. Because of this continuing financial straightjacket, both Latin American and African countries were forced to make major adjustments to their trade policies, generally in the mid-1980s.

The new set of policies is called "neoliberal" because it reflects the liberal view of trade. Neoliberal trade policies call for reducing state favoritism in the economy, which is seen as distortional and generally ineffective. The idea is that foreign competition should be allowed on an even playing field and that those national competitors who are viable will be able to enter the market regardless. If the state tries to favor national competitors, it will create inefficient enterprises that need continual subsidies. Those subsidies will have to be raised by taxing more productive sectors. Thus, it makes more sense for market forces to make allocative decisions. Moreover, in neoliberal thinking, the ultimate beneficiaries are the developing country consumer and the entrepreneur. Consumers can now choose goods from anywhere according to

their liking and at a natural market price. If domestic producers have an advantage in producing certain goods, this fact should be reflected in the price, and local demand will therefore spur local production in a way that makes sense. Similarly, local entrepreneurs should see the opportunities in both local and international markets for new types of production. They will be more nimble, incentivized, and efficient in this pursuit than governments ever could be because they are using their own resources and not the resources of taxpayers or external lending agencies. The neoliberal record of policy results on trade is still too new for an adequate assessment, but the volume of trade has increased dramatically, along with a growing inequality in the benefits. A second generation of neoliberal policies has moved beyond basic monetary and fiscal tightening toward privatization and deregulation, thus further dismantling the ISI structure.

Part of this "second round" of neoliberal adjustments to trade involves the growth of international and regional free trade agreements. Following the inconsistent but steady progress of free trade in the European Union (EU), the early 1990s saw the development of a number of major new trade pacts and organizations. Among the Southeast Asian countries, the development of the Association of Southeast Asian Nations (ASEAN) trade agreement created a forum for local coordination of economic policies. The Asia-Pacific Economic Cooperation (APEC) organization is working toward free trade between the Pacific states of the Western Hemisphere and those in Asia. The most important agreement outside the EU was the creation of the North American Free Trade Agreement (NAFTA).

The NAFTA agreement between Canada, the United States, and Mexico, created in 1994 has been and continues to be highly controversial. Critics of NAFTA believe that the agreement overlooks labor exploitation, environmental degradation, and generally lax government regulation of Mexican industries. On the other side, US and Canadian companies see Mexico as a necessary part of their strategy to compete in international markets. Since East Asian countries and Japan have been so successful in wracking up consistent trade surpluses and in entering new product lines, North American companies have begun to look for new ways to compete. NAFTA gives them a cheaper source of labor, by which they can lower their production costs and thus lower the price of their goods. NAFTA has been strongly attractive to other Latin American economies, so there are serious explorations of a Free Trade Agreement of the Americas (FTAA) that would include all countries of the Western Hemisphere. However, because of the contentious nature of the NAFTA debate and the

lack of "fast track" authority for the president to negotiate the terms of a new treaty, the FTAA has hardly gotten off the discussion table.

After NAFTA and the EU really consolidated by the late 1990s, there was much concern about the creation of "regional blocs" of international trade for the Western Hemisphere, East Asia, and Europe. Concern rose about a dampening effect on trade among the various blocs from extraregional protectionist measures. Much of this discussion has died down in the twenty-first century for a number of reasons. First, the regional bloc scenario does not make much sense if one recognizes that almost all trade and investment is among the triad of the United States, Japan, and the EU, not between the North and the South. Second, for the reasons mentioned earlier, East Asia could never be considered a viable bloc when most of its trade is oriented outwardly toward EU and US markets. Third, there has been a big push to keep multilateral organizations and negotiations on a parallel track, hence the creation of the APEC and the continued activity in the WTO.

Nonetheless, patterns of North-South trade along regional lines do exist. For example, most Latin American countries almost exclusively trade with the United States. For most African countries, Europe is the main trading partner. Thus, the possibilities for trading between nontraditional partners seem more limited because the preferential treatment given by First World Nations tends to favor countries within the same region. However, even within the same region, there are important differences in terms of access to markets. NAFTA gives Mexico strong advantages over Latin American counterparts. The countries included in the US Caribbean Basin Initiative (CBI) enjoy better terms for some products than others. Similarly, Europe has separate agreements and differential access to its markets, so poorer European states, such as Greece, enjoy multiple advantages over any African competitors.

One particularly interesting experiment is the Southern Cone Common Market (MERCOSUR), which is a free trade agreement between Brazil, Argentina, Uruguay, and Paraguay, with Chile and Bolivia as associate and conditional members. MERCOSUR is the only real case of successful South-South integration thus far. In many ways, it does not make much sense for developing nations to integrate with each other. They tend to compete with each other for the same international markets, and their economies are geared toward export and import ties with the First World. Thus, the level of trade among developing countries, even those who are neighbors, is usually far below than the level of trade between these countries and a developed country.

MERCOSUR was created in 1994 in good part in response to NAFTA, which left other Latin American countries out. Part of the thinking behind MERCOSUR is to create a bloc that can negotiate better terms for an eventual FTAA, but there is also genuine hope that developing countries can find a new source of economic growth through trade with each other. Indeed, MERCOSUR has led to dramatic increases in intraregional trade. The hope is that as local companies learn to compete within MERCOSUR, they will eventually be ready for international-level competition in an FTAA. Despite the gains in trade, the MERCOSUR is still far more limited than either the NAFTA or the EU. There are important exclusions from MERCOSUR for sensitive industries, such as exclusions regarding automobiles and footwear. There is no real regional organization and no clear dispute resolution. In short, MERCOSUR remains very much a limited agreement and one whose progress depends on continual diplomatic negotiations.

The growing levels of relative inequality, the continuing extremely high levels of debt, and the feeling that international trade rules are unfairly biased in favor of First World corporations are the main complaints about the current international trading system in regard to development. Although the neoliberal period has brought growth in trade volumes, the gap between developed and developing nations has continued to increase. The gap between the rich and the poor *within* most nations has also tended to increase. In fairness, the structuralist period of economic policies experienced the same phenomenon. However, as the process of the globalization of production progresses, whereby different parts of the production process are done in different parts of the world, there is a fear that the developing world will be left with only the most labor-intensive, unskilled parts of that process. Unlike Raymond Vernon's seminal work on the product cycle, which expected that products, over time, would be shifted to the Third World, the greatest areas of economic growth have come from high technology and high innovation products. The information technology revolution and the spread of computers are marked by a continual innovation. The developing world has been able to capture only a small part of these new industries.

There is a general sentiment that many developing countries liberalized their trade too easily in the most recent trade rounds (such as those in Uruguay in 1995) without wresting away enough concessions from the First World. In fact, despite its high-flown rhetoric, the First World remains a highly protectionist and interventionist region for developing countries. The high levels of subsidies and protection for agriculture are a particularly sore point as the basic theory of

comparative advantage would seem to point to the gross inefficiency of such measures. On the other side, First World countries would like to gain greater protection for intellectual and artistic property rights and greater access to newly emerging service markets. Thus, one particular bone of contention revolves around First World pharmaceutical companies' ability to control the sale of the medicines that they develop through large research and approval procedures. In a number of developing countries, both artistic material and intellectual property are copied ("pirated") and sold at a much lower cost, with no royalty to the creator. These are the issues at the forefront of the post-Uruguay round of ministerial meetings; they surround the issue of China's accession to the World Trade Organization.

Other issues are also prominent, but these do not seem to have gained the formal attention of the international and national trade negotiators and institutions. The well-publicized protests at the 2000 WTO Ministerial meeting in Seattle included a long list of complaints, such as the need for forgiveness of developing countries' debts; for international environmental and labor protections; and for greater insulation for national priorities, such as a national health care system. Perhaps the most pressing issue is the general lack of public participation in trade fora. This has been a major polemic surrounding the EU free trade agreement and is a galvanizing catalyst for the anti-WTO protesters. They correctly point out that there so far has been only limited consultation and input from the public in trade negotiations, despite the fact that the effects on everyday life are profound. It is interesting to note that there are a number of other issues affecting trade that are not really explored by either the protest movements or the international trading institutions. One of the most prominent of these is the massive movements of illegal immigrants from the developing world to the developed world. Another is the development of increasingly sophisticated narco-trafficking networks. For the most part, even the more mainstream issues of trade and development suffer from a lack of well-developed analysis. The lack of clear evidence makes it extremely difficult to sift through the different views on basic trade issues, such as the positive and/or negative effects of the NAFTA agreement on different groups within Mexican, US, Canadian, and other countries.

ANIL HIRA

See also Asia-Pacific Economic Cooperation (APEC); Association of Southeast Asian Nations (ASEAN); Development History and Theory; Free Trade Area of the Americas (FTAA); General Agreement on Tariffs and Trade (GATT); Globalization: Impact on Development; Import Substitution Industrialization; International Monetary Fund (IMF); Neoliberalism; North American Free Trade Agreement (NAFTA); Southern Cone Common Market (MERCOSUR)

References and Further Reading

Bhagwati, Jagdish N. *Lectures on International Trade.* Cambridge, MA: MIT Press, 1998.
Cohn, Theodore H. *Global Political Economy: Theory and Practice.* New York: Longman, 2000.
Dillman, Bradford. *State and Private Sector in Algeria: The Politics of Rent-Seeking and Failed Development.* Boulder, CO: Westview, 2000.
Dunn, Robert M., and John Mutti. *International Economics.* London: Routledge, 2000.
Evans, Peter. *Dependent Development: The Alliance of Multinational, State, and Local Capital in Brazil.* Princeton, NJ: Princeton University Press, 1979.
Haggard, Stephan. *Pathways from the Periphery: The Politics of Growth in the Newly Industrializing Countries.* Ithaca, NY: Cornell University Press, 1990.
Hocking, Brian, and Steven McGuire, eds. *Trade Politics.* New York: Routledge, 1999.
Krueger, Anne O. *Political Economy of Policy Reform in Developing Countries.* Cambridge, MA: MIT Press, 1993.
Wade, Robert. *Governing the Market: Economic Theory and the Role of Government in East Asian Industrialization.* Princeton, NJ: Princeton University Press, 1990.

TRADING PATTERNS, GLOBAL

Growth in Trade

"Trade" is commonly defined as the exchange of goods and/or services between countries. Aggregate trade among countries has increased significantly since the mid-twentieth century, generating over $5 trillion USD per annum at the beginning of the twenty-first century. Since 1950, the increasing integration of the global economy became apparent due, in part, to the fact that merchandise trade grew faster than merchandise production. Developing world economies have benefited from the increasing volume of global trade, as trade is a key mechanism for technology transfer from developed world economies. Exports from developing world economies prior to 1945 were typically primary products, such as food and raw materials sold to colonial powers, but by 1970 the composition of developing world exports had changed along with the recipient nations, as the value of manufactured product exports exceeded that of primary products. Data on world trade in services only became available from 1980 onward, and the current contribution of such trade is

estimated by the World Trade Organization (WTO) to be at least 20% of total world trade. Global trade in services occurs mostly in the developed world and plays a smaller role for developing market economies.

Spatial Patterns

The geography of trade is very complex due to varying levels of specialization in agricultural, fossil fuel, and industrial production throughout the world. As Knox *et al.* (2003) assert, "advanced industrial economies have long dominated international trade, and in general, the trend has been towards intensification of the long-standing domination of trade within and between developed countries at the expense of trade between developed countries and less-developed countries—with the major exception of trade in oil" (pp. 48–49). Bearing this statement in mind, with the realization that developing economies are no longer just exporters of primary products but are turning increasingly to exports of manufactures and services, it is possible to identify several distinct patterns of trade for developing economies.

In general, disparities among developing world nations' participation and success in global trade have increased. Oil is the most important single commodity in world trade, and oil-exporting countries have seen steady growth in exports, both for the large-volume Middle Eastern oil states and smaller nations such as Nigeria and Cameroon in Africa as well as Venezuela and Ecuador in Latin America. Other non-oil raw material exporting countries, though, have had little participation in international trade. For example, Asia, Bangladesh, Pakistan, Sri Lanka, Nepal, and Afghanistan have remained isolated from the global economy through the implementation of protectionist policies, such as high tariffs (cross-border taxes or duties) or non-tariff barriers, including quotas, subsidies, or licenses. Most countries in sub-Saharan Africa have had declining export volumes in the latter part of the twentieth century due to the reliance on non-oil primary products, the inability to replace export of primary products with manufactures, and worsening terms of trade. "Terms of trade" refers to the ratio of the prices at which exports and imports are exchanged. In the case of these primary product-exporting countries, the price of their exports has fallen relative to the price of imports (manufactures and services) from the developed economies or newly industrialized countries (NICs).

Imports of primary products to the developing world from the developed world include food exports from Australia, Canada, and the United States.

Imports of manufactures to the developing world from the developed world tend to be such things as heavy machinery and transport goods from such countries as the United States, Japan, and Germany.

Approximately three-fourths of the developing world's manufactured exports come from eleven countries: Asian countries include China, Hong Kong, India, Malaysia, Singapore, South Korea, Taiwan, and Thailand; Latin America countries are Brazil, Mexico, and Chile. The first developing world exporters were South Korea, Taiwan, Singapore, and Hong Kong, often labeled the original East Asian Tigers, NICs, or newly industrialized economies (NIEs), and export mostly to Organization for Economic Cooperation and Development (OECD) economies. These developing world exporters are relatively large recipients of foreign direct investment (FDI) and are seen as the most successful developing nations in the global economy. Exports from these NICs are characterized by growing domestic market penetration of developed economies such as those of the United States, United Kingdom, Germany, and Japan. Generally, the East Asian economies are more important as exporters of manufactured goods than they are as producers. Newer NICs, such as Malaysia and Thailand in Southeast Asia as well as Brazil and Mexico in Latin America, are also increasing the volume of exports of manufactured goods. Other emerging markets, such as Argentina, China, Indonesia, and India—usually the largest nations in their respective continents—have also seen increases in export volume of manufactured goods to developed economies.

More than two-thirds of all developing world nonservices exports go to developed world nations, and one of the most controversial nontariff barriers imposed by the developed world is the Multifibre Agreement (MFA) that involves quotas on textile and clothing imports from the developing world. The MFA was took effect in 1970 and has lasted through 2005; the end of this barrier will have significant implications for the geography of trade within the textile and garments industry, probably resulting in an increase in the volume of exports from China, India, and other South Asian nations.

The transitional economies of the former Soviet Union are worthy of consideration because of the dynamic nature of economic restructuring and the potential for trade participation of some of the larger economies, especially the Russian Federation, Poland, Czech Republic, and Hungary. These nations have seen a small but steady increase in the rate of manufactures exports, and the inclusion of all but the Russian Federation in the European Union (EU) in 2004 will likely alter both the economic development and spatial trading patterns in Eastern Europe.

Although global trade in services did not become fully established until the end of the twentieth century, some developing world economies, particularly Hong Kong, China, South Korea, and Singapore, are now top services exporters. Tradable services, such as telecommunications, financial services, management, advertising, as well as professional and technical services (including software), play an increasing role in these countries' gross national products (GNPs).

Impact of Transnational Corporations

Much of the impetus driving the changing patterns of global trade since 1950 can be attributed to the role played by transnational corporations (TNCs), which are sometimes also called multinational corporations (MNCs). According to Dicken (2003), "a TNC is a firm that has the power to coordinate and control operations in more than one country, even if it does not own them" (p. 198). TNCs account for about two-thirds of world exports of goods and services, and much of that is intrafirm trade, which is much more difficult to measure than trade between countries. TNCs have the ability to coordinate and control processes and transactions within and between different countries. They have the ability to take advantages of geographical differences in the distribution of factors of production (labor, resources, and capital) and in trade-related state policies. TNCs also have great geographical flexibility with the ability to switch resources and operations between global locations through the use of subcontracting and subsidiaries. A New International Division of Labor (NIDL), which is defined as a reorganization of spatial divisions of labor and was formerly organized at the national scale and then to a global scale based on international production and marketing systems, is driven primarily by TNCs.

TNCs and Foreign Direct Investment

Most trade in exports from the developing world—albeit in a very uneven geographic pattern—goes to the developed world. Consideration of imports to the developing world has to address the role of foreign direct investment (FDI) done primarily by TNCs. FDI is direct investment in a foreign country by a (usually large) company through firm takeover or creation of new subsidiaries; the goal is to achieve managerial and production control. According to Dicken (2003), for the global economy "the primary mechanism of integration has shifted from trade to FDI. Trends in the growth of FDI, trade and

production are not independent of each other. The common element is the TNC" (p. 52). Historically, FDI was concentrated in the primary (natural resources) sector' until the 1980s, most FDI was directed to the manufacturing sector. By 2000, the services sector saw the greatest relative increase.

Advanced industrial economies still absorb most flows of FDI, but the amount of foreign investment in the developing world is increasing. At the beginning of the twenty-first century, approximately three-quarters of all FDI inflows to the developing world went to just seven NICs: in Asia, the inflows went to Singapore, South Korea, Malaysia, and China (including Hong Kong); in Latin America, they went to Mexico, Brazil and Argentina. A new trend in FDI is seen with the emergence of TNCs from developing countries. The greatest amount of outward FDI from developing countries comes from China (including Hong Kong), Singapore, Taiwan, South Korea, Malaysia, and Brazil and goes to other developing nations as well as developed market economies.

Globalization, Regionalization, and Trade Regulation

It is important to note that another feature of the geography of trade is that the bulk of international trade is based on a few trading blocs with most trade taking place *within* these blocs. A "trading bloc" is defined as a group of countries with formalized systems of trading agreements. "Membership of these trading blocs is principally the result of the effects of (1) distance, (2) the legacy of colonial relationships, (3) geopolitical alliances" and recognizes "the persisten[t] dependence of less developed countries (LDCs) on trade with developed countries that are geographically or geopolitically close (Knox *et al.* 2003: 48, 51). Trade statistics show, for example, that the United States is the chief trading partner of Latin American countries, and Japan is the main trading partner for Asian LDCs.

The first international regulatory mechanism for trade was established after World War II. The General Agreements on Tariffs and Trade (GATT) had, at its inception, a membership of twenty-three countries. In 1995, GATT evolved into the World Trade Organization (WTO) that has more than 130 member nations. During the lifetime of GATT, average tariffs were reduced from 40% in 1940 to 5% in 1994. The basis of GATT (and now WTO) is establishment of nondiscrimination, using the most-favored nation principle (MFN) and the national treatment rule. MFN states that a trade concession negotiated

between two countries must apply to all countries, and the national treatment rule states that imported foreign goods are treated in the same way as domestic goods.

An important caveat to the MFN principle is that an exception to equality can occur if a subset of WTO members forms a regional trading organization, such as a customs union or a free trade area. The least restrictive regional trading institution is a "free trade area" where trade restrictions between member nations are removed, but individual members retain their individual trade policies with nonmembers. A "customs union" is an institution where members belong to a free trade area but also have a common external trade policy toward nonmembers. Further economic integration occurs within a "common market" where trade barriers are removed and where a common external trade policy is adopted, but in addition, free movement of capital and labor between members is permitted. The most integrated regional economic alliance is an "economic union," which adds harmonization of economic policy and limited supranational political and legislative capabilities to the common market characteristics.

The WTO nondiscrimination and equality principles are challenged, therefore, when the sheer number of such regional economic alliances is counted. In the Western Hemisphere for example, the North American Free Trade Agreement (NAFTA) links the economies of the United States, Canada, and Mexico in a free trade area; the Southern Cone Common Market (MERCOSUR) binds Argentina, Brazil, Paraguay, and Uruguay in a common market; and the Caribbean Community (CARICOM) involves fourteen island nations in a common market. In the Asian realm, AFTA—the Association of Southeast Asian Nations (ASEAN) Free Trade Agreement—links ten Southeast Asian economies in a free trade area, and in the European realm, the EU ties twenty-five European nations together in an economic union. In Africa, a new institution—the African Union (AU), formerly the Organization of African Unity or OAU—was created in 1994 and comprises fifty-three member nations that have the goal of establishing a continent-wide African Economic Community (AEC).

SHARON C. COBB

See also Asian Tigers; Multinational Corporations and Development; Trade Policies and Development; World Trade Organization (WTO)

References and Further Reading

Cook, P., and C. Kirkpatrick. "Globalization, Regionalization and Third World Development." *Regional Studies* 31 (1997): 55–66.

Dicken, Peter. *Global Shift: Reshaping the Global Economic Map in the 21st Century.* New York: The Guilford Press, 2003.

Held, David, Anthony McGrew, David Goldblatt, and Jonathon Perraton. *Global Transformations: Politics, Economics and Culture.* Stanford, CA: Stanford University Press, 1999.

Hoekman B., and Kosteki, M. *The Political Economy of the World Trading System: From GATT to WTO.* Oxford: Oxford University Press, 1995.

Knox, Paul, Agnew, John, and Linda McCarthy. *The Geography of the World Economy.* New York: Oxford University Press, 2003.

Powell, A. "Commodity and Developing County Terms of Trade: What does the long run show?" *Economic Journal* 101 (1991): 1485–1496.

Stutz, Frederick P., and Barney Warf. *The World Economy: Resources, Location, Trade and Development.* New York: Prentice Hall, 2005.

United Nations Conference on Trade and Development (UNCTAD). 2005. Home Page. http://www.unctad.org.

World Bank http://www.worldbank.org.

World Trade Organization http://www.wto.org.

TRANSPARENCY

"Transparency" is a term loosely used to signify that political and business decisions and documents are open to public scrutiny. Transparency is a safeguard against corruption and abuse of power. Equated with accountability and democratic values, transparency presupposes a public sphere of robust debate that sustains reasoned consensus. The ensemble of communication channels that is part of the mass media constitutes the public sphere. Thus, a press free of undue governmental coercion and excessive manipulation by private interests would form the bulwark of an ideal transparent society. The utopian goal of the eighteenth-century Enlightenment was that the free reign of reason would render society transparent to itself. "Transparency" is the late twentieth-century truncated expression of that goal.

The idea of transparency has tremendous significance for developing nations seeking aid, investment, and integration into Western economic, political, and security alliances. Industrialized nations use freedom of the press and openness in governmental and business sectors as criteria to gauge the level of corruption and degree of risk factors that condition aid and investment. As World Bank President James D. Wolfensohn once stated that "corruption undermines development" and dries up grassroots Western support for aid to developing countries.

However, with respect to Western aid, investment and trade transparency is a reciprocal concern. Salient issues include how funds intended for public projects are administered and allocated and who is

held accountable for policies and decisions. In addition, the visibility in corporate hiring practices, licensing agreements, joint ventures, and profit margins are all salient issues as well.

Transparency is thought to promote trust and better service. Visibility and accountability are antidotes to mismanagement, inefficiency, waste, and poor service. Uncertainty and suspicion dissipate when constituents and clients are allowed to see the actions taken on their behalf. In the event of a process going awry, public visibility permits intervention and possible salvation before the process reaches closure. Thus, transparency promotes greater efficiency and responsiveness.

Historical Development of the Concept Transparency

In *Discourse on Method* (1637), René Descartes formulated a method for ascertaining the truth using *reason* and provided an embryonic definition of transparency: *clarity* and *distinctness*.

Jean-Jacques Rousseau's writings wielded tremendous influence on modern political theory and the creation of democratic institutions. Rousseau spread the "cultural ideal of transparent and unmediated intellectual exchange among citizens themselves" (Hesse 1994).

Adhering to Descartes' great faith in the power of reason and influenced by Rousseau, Immanuel Kant added the crucial idea of using unfettered reason in the *public sphere*. "The public use of one's reason must always be free, and it alone can bring about enlightenment among men," Kant asserted in the essay *What Is Enlightenment?* (1784).

Transparency in the Information Age

In the eighteenth century of Rousseau and Kant, the channels for *unmediated* or undistorted communication included coffee houses, books, pamphlets, speeches, journals, and newspapers. However, the complexity and size of modern societies requires that public opinion be *mediated*. The global span of communication technologies and the mass media's ubiquity seem to have provided the means of propagating knowledge and realizing the Enlightenment goal of self-determination based on transparency.

However, the philosopher Gianni Vattimo argues that information saturation has not made societies more transparent or enlightened, but rather more complex and chaotic. In a deluge of information, fatigue from overload and separating the important from the trivial, among competing interpretations, become problematic. Jurgen Habermas argues that commercial interests have transformed the public sphere "into a medium of advertising" and public relations. Thus, vested interests have muddied the clear channels of the public sphere, producing distorted information. Indeed, the very term "transparency" has become the mantra of public relations campaigns and election promises.

The volume of entreaties on transparency issuing from corporations, governments, Non-Governmental Organizations (NGOs), the European Union (EU), the World Bank, and the World Trade Organization (WTO) have brought the term to the brink of oversaturation and insipidity. Transparency is not always desirable. Bringing to light a bank's temporary instability may erode public confidence and prevent recovery. Internal bank forecasts about interest rates and inflation expectations may affect public perceptions and cause panic. Opaqueness in patent information and trade secrets is warranted as preventing industrial espionage.

As digital communication penetrates developing countries, so too will the technology enabling breaches in the veil of privacy. The availability of consumer information garnered from credit card purchases, banks, Web site visits, voting records, and scores of governmental data banks may bring unwanted transparency. Such information is sifted, mixed, matched, and recombined to form myriad lists that are sold to direct marketers, special interest groups, and political parties—typically without citizen knowledge or consent. Increasingly, citizens are classified based on income, buying patterns, and voting behavior. The result is information segregation predicated on potential "value": different messages for different segments.

Transparency and Compliance

The degree of compliance with standards and laws is ultimately an impressionistic judgment. For example, an international NGO annually releases a *Corruption Perceptions Index* based on surveys that document the *perceptions* of analysts, academics, and business people. The 2001 profile of ninety-one countries ranks Finland first (9.9)—10 is a perfect "clean" score—and Bangladesh last (0.4).

There are many ways to circumvent the disclosure of information. In spite of legal obligations, compliance is essentially a measure of good faith. Compliance

does not ensure that proffered information is useful. In instances of closed-door policy deliberations, for example, "transparency" simply means that meeting minutes, however vague or incomplete, are posted. Essentially toothless, disclosure policies are no guarantee that information will reach the public. Both the IMF and the World Bank release certain information only to their member governments, never directly to citizens. An agency may choose to disclose pedestrian data or to obfuscate information in lengthy documents couched in tortured language. And there are always exemptions. Both the US Freedom of Information Act (1966) and the NAFTA transparency decision against Canada (2000) permit governments to withhold information *those governments* deem vital to national security.

An idea spawned from a rich philosophical lineage, transparency states a goal, the freedom—actualized by self-governance—and the means for achieving it, open communication in the public sphere. Utopian transparency, which is impossible to fully measure and achieve, is the pithiest expression of the quest for self-determination and self-legislation. Ultimately, the dissemination of useful information will depend more on providing motives and incentives than the threat of sanctions and uncertain enforcement.

TONY OSBORNE

References and Further Reading

Descartes, Rene. *Discourse on Method and Meditations on First Philosophy*. Translated by Donald A. Cress. Indianapolis: Hackett, 1980.

Habermas, Jurgen. *The Structural Transformation of the Public Sphere*. Translated by Thomas Burger. Cambridge: MIT, 1991.

———. *The Theory of Communicative Action, Volume I: Reason and the Rationalization of Society*. Translated by Thomas McCarthy. Boston: Beacon, 1984.

Hesse, Carla. "Kant, Foucault, and Three Women." *Foucault and the Writing of History*, Jan Goldstein, ed. Oxford and Cambridge, MA: Blackwell, 1994.

Heskett, James L., Earl W. Sasser, W. Earl, and Leonard A. Schlesinger. *The Service Profit Chain*. New York: The Free Press, 1997.

Kant, Immanuel. "What Is Enlightenment?" *Kant on History*. Translated by Lewis White Beck. New York: Macmillan, 1963.

Rousseau, Jean-Jacques. *The Basic Political Writings*. Translated by Donald A. Cress. Indianapolis, IN: Hackett, 1987.

Vattimo, Gianni. *The Transparent Society*. Translated by David Webb. Cambridge: Polity Press, 1992.

TRINIDAD AND TOBAGO

Trinidad and Tobago are the southernmost islands in the archipelago of the Caribbean, lying about eleven degrees north of the Equator. While Tobago lies entirely within the Atlantic Ocean, Trinidad itself faces the Atlantic on the east and southeast, the Caribbean in the west and northwest. The larger of the two islands, Trinidad, lies within sight of the coast of Venezuela; the silt and debris from the delta of the Orinoco River reach the southern coast of the island. The silt and debris also travel as far as Tobago, which is twenty-two miles to the northeast of Point Toco on Trinidad. Geologically speaking, Trinidad is part of the South American continent.

The climate is tropical, with a rainy season in the summer and fall. Precipitation, however, is higher to the north, where a tropical rainforest covers the northern slopes and reaches almost one thousand meters above sea level, which is impressive because of the sudden rise of the landmass from the sea. The climate is rather dry toward the southwest. The hurricanes do not reach Trinidad although they occasionally devastate portions of Tobago. Cane fields spread across the southern two-thirds of the island, which is mostly hilly.

The population of Trinidad, estimated at 1,104,000 (in 2003), is quite diverse. Before the "Columbian Exchange," the mix of culture and race that occurred after Christopher Columbus reached the Western Hemisphere, got underway, the island was settled by Carib Native Americans who inhabited much of the coastal areas of northern South America. The Caribs displaced the Arawak, who may have been the first to settle the islands, or miscegenated with them. Some Native Americans survived on the islands as late as the eighteenth century; in fact, there is still a Carib community in Arima, Trinidad.

Although the statistics may be misleading, it is generally accepted that Blacks and East Indians are evenly matched in numbers. The so-called mixed population, recorded at 18.4%, could belong to either ethnic group. There is also a prominent white minority, albeit less than 1%, as well as a Chinese minority involved in commerce. The history of the island of Trinidad explains the presence of both French and Spanish surnames and place-names, beginning with the name Trinidad itself. Port-of-Spain is the capital city, one of the few towns with an Anglicized name, while Tobago has mostly English place-names and a population with English surnames. Nevertheless, English is the language spoken by most citizens although Hindi is spoken also, and there is a smattering of other languages. With regard to religion, there is a Catholic plurality, with a sizable Hindu minority. Fundamentalist Christian denominations and Muslims, especially Black Muslims, are probably the fastest growing religious groups.

Although Trinidad was christened by Columbus during his third transatlantic voyage in 1498 and

colonized on behalf of the rulers of Spain, it remained sparsely populated until the late eighteenth century. Tobago suffered the fate of most islands of the Caribbean, changing colonial masters as a function of European wars. Trinidad, however, was under continuous Spanish jurisdiction until 1797, when it was captured by the British and held briefly by the French. In 1814, the British also took Tobago from the French.

The society and economy of Tobago and Trinidad are rather different. Tobago had a plantation economy with a majority slave population going far back in time, whereas Trinidad had relatively few slaves. Although the latter produced tobacco and cocoa, it was not until near the end of the eighteenth century that sugar became an important commodity; along with sugar, the population, particularly the slaves transported from West Africa, increased rather suddenly. Cocoa remained an important commodity to the end of the nineteenth century. Sugar production remained considerable in Trinidad, roughly on a par with (the much smaller) Barbados and second only to Guyana.

By 1807, when the British parliament abolished the slave trade, the majority of the islanders on both islands were of African, particularly Igbo, descent. While in Tobago there were many generations of slaves, in Trinidad slavery lasted little more than a single generation. West Africans, including Yoruba from what is present-day Nigeria, continued to arrive after emancipation in 1833, leaving an imprint on the syncretic culture of Trinidad in particular. Consequently, race relations, attitudes, and politics in Tobago, with its more homogenous population, also differ from those of Trinidad.

Oil, exploited since 1909, and gas, the production of which has risen considerably in the last few years, are the mainstay of the economy. In fact, Trinidad and Tobago are the most prosperous of the island-nations in the Caribbean, and the gross domestic product (GDP) is once again on the rise, particularly in the twenty-first century.

Although oil prices have their ups and downs on the world market, Trinidad and Tobago have both achieved and maintained the highest per capita income in the region, except for Puerto Rico. The GDP per capita in 1999 was about the same as in 1971, before the boom. Between 1973 and 1980, however, the value of manufacturing increased by about 15%, thanks to the public sector and, more specifically, to the diversification project at Point Lisas, on the Gulf of Pariah, masterminded by Eric Williams. Trinidad and Tobago produce canned goods, beverages, and a large range of other manufactured products, some of which are exported to other Caribbean islands.

While industrial production experienced modest gains since 1970, agriculture has declined steadily, resulting in greater need for imports. Thus, it is possible to describe the country as a "monoculture" because of the reliance on oil for export earnings (mostly to the United States). Thanks to the efforts of the People's National Movement led by Williams, in August 1962 the island-country achieved independence from the United Kingdom. Eventually, in 1976, it achieved republican status.

Civil society is well established. While elections are heavily contested, the transfer of power between the major parties, the People's National Movement (PNM) and the United National Congress (UNC), has been relatively peaceful. The country has experienced two major attempts at a *coup d'état*, one by the "Black Power" movement in 1970—Stokely Carmichael aka Kwame Toure, the founder of the Black Power movement in the United States and elsewhere, was born in Trinidad—and the other by a group of Black Muslims in 1990, who managed to hold Prime Minister Robinson hostage, temporarily.

The legislative is bicameral, with a Senate of thirty-one seats, appointed by the president, and a House of Representatives, with only thirty-six seats. Tobago has a separate legislature, with a House of Assembly of fifteen members. Since 2002, the prime minister is Patrick Manning, who replaced Basdeo Panday.

During the twentieth century, Trinidad and Tobago, along with the rest of the Caribbean, was increasingly drawn into the sphere of influence of the United States. One manifestation of the US influence was the transfer of the naval base at Chaguaramas, immediately west of the Port of Spain capital, from the United Kingdom to the United States at the very beginning of World War II (eventually returned to the jurisdiction of the island-nation). American influence is reinforced by the fact that the West Indian diaspora—the dispersion of West Indians to other lands—gravitates toward the United States, particularly New York, rather than London. Closer cultural and family ties with the United States inevitably result in the loosening of ties with the United Kingdom.

The tourist trade on Tobago accounts to a large extent for the increasing prosperity of that island, but has also occasioned friction and conflicts. Indeed, prior legislation against foreign ownership of land, particularly on Tobago, has now been rendered ineffective; and the growing tourist trade has elicited a backlash, but also has fueled movements for greater autonomy, if not independence.

MARIO D. FENYO

References and Further Reading

Brereton, Bridget. *A History of Modern Trinidad, 1783–1962*. London: Heinemann, 1981.

Hope, Ronald Kempe. *Economic Development in the Caribbean.* New York: Praeger, 1986.

Mandle, Jay R. *Persistent Underdevelopment; Change and Economic Modernization in the West Indies.* Gordon and Breach, 1996.

Murray, Winston. *Politics of the Dispossessed [The History and Economy of Tobago].* Port of Spain: Beacon Publishing, 1976.

Williams, Eric. *History of the People of Trinidad and Tobago.* New York: Praeger, 1964.

TRUJILLO, RAFAEL LEONIDAS

Born in 1891 in San Cristóbal, Dominican Republic, Raphael Leonidas Trujillo Molina worked as telegraph operator and sugar mill security guard before joining the national constabulary force in 1916. He was promoted through the ranks of the national police force before being named general and chief of staff of the Dominican National Army in 1928. Two years later, he joined the revolt against President Horacio Vásquez Lajara and later in 1930 ran unopposed in the presidential elections of 1930. His inauguration marked the beginning of the "Era of Trujillo." For thirty-one years, the "Benefactor of the Fatherland" ruled the Dominican Republic as if it were his fiefdom and as though he had complete control over all aspects of Dominican life.

Trujillo took over a country that was morally, politically, and economically bankrupt, and he transformed it into a debt-free, self-sufficient (in terms of food), and politically stable nation. The Dominicans, however, paid a high price, for the Era of Trujillo was one of the darkest periods in Caribbean history.

Trujillo's philosophy on development was a simple one: political and economic stability through his guidance was foremost, and political freedom and dissent were not to be tolerated. To achieve his objectives, Trujillo depended on two key ingredients: the military and the United States. Trujillo's tight control over the armed forces gave him a most effective vehicle to achieve political stability, while his close ties with the United States provided him with much-needed economic modernization.

Following his staunch support for the Allies during World War II, "El Jefe," as he was known throughout the Dominican Republic, took advantage of the Cold War by becoming the sentinel of anticommunism in the Americas. Lauded by US politicians and business figures, the Trujillo regime was a principal recipient of United States economic and military aid.

The 1950s were Trujillo's glory years. Buildings were constructed in the capital. Electricity was brought to the countryside. The tourism industry saw its rise, and capital investments multiplied. In addition, the Dominicans, for the first time in their history, felt safe from their Haitian neighbors.

The Benefactor of the Fatherland, however, was the main beneficiary of this unprecedented economic growth. It is estimated that at the time of his death in 1961, Trujillo controlled 65% of the Dominican economy, and the Trujillo family private fortune was calculated to be between $800 million and $1 billion.

In 1959, though, cracks began to develop in Trujillo's governmental apparatus. Demand for Dominican commodities dropped in the world market, and the Dominican masses were confronted with unemployment and price increases. Furthermore, the Trujillo family's voracious appetite for corruption and lavish spending fueled public discontent. Moreover, middle-class students, dissatisfied with the stifling political and intellectual climate, longed for individual rights.

In June 1959, Dominican exiles, supported by Venezuelan President Rómulo Betancourt, landed in the Dominican Republic and were crushed mercilessly. Alarmed by Trujillo's repressive tactics, Catholic bishops issued a warning to "El Jefe." On June 24, 1960, Trujillo retaliated against his Venezuelan nemesis when his hired men attempted to assassinate Betancourt. On August 20, 1960, in response to the assassination attempt, the Organization of American States virtually declared the Trujillo government an outcast and imposed strict sanctions.

In 1961, the new administration of John F. Kennedy, tired of Trujillo's antics, began to contact disgruntled officers in Trujillo's vaunted military. On May 30, 1961, as Trujillo was driven to his hometown of San Cristóbal, "El Jefe" was assassinated.

JOSÉ B. FERNÁNDEZ

See also Caribbean: History and Economic Development; Caribbean: International Relations; Dominican Republic; Organization of American States (OAS)

References and Further Reading

Atkins, G. Pope, and Wilson, Larman. *The United States and the Trujillo Regime.* New Brunswick, NJ: Rutgers University Press, 1972.

Gleijeses, Piero. *The Dominican Crisis: The 1965 Constitutionalist Revolt and the American Intervention.* Baltimore, MD: Johns Hopkins University Press, 1978.

Mencía, Lester Rafael. *Trujillo y Su Época.* Miami, FL: Solo Printing, 1996.

Wiarda, Howard. *Dictatorship and Development: The Methods of Control in Trujillo's Dominican Republic.* Gainesville, FL: University of Florida Press, 1970.

Wiarda, Howard, and Kryzanek, Michael. *The Dominican Republic: A Caribbean Crucible.* Boulder, CO: Westview Press, 1982.

TUDJMAN, FRANJO

As the most prominent figure of the Balkans in the late twentieth century, besides Slobodan Milošević, Franjo Tudjman (1922–1999) is credited with the creation of an independent Croatia.

Called the "Father of the Croatian Nation," Tudjman was a brilliant strategist and excellent diplomat. He normalized relations with Serbia in 1998 though he permitted the North Atlantic Treaty Organization (NATO) to use Croatia's airspace against Serbia during the Kosovo campaign. After Croatian independence, he focused his work on the country's admission to the European Union (EU) and NATO. However, Tudjman has been criticized for his nationalism and his authoritarian paternalistic rule, during which civil liberties were curtailed and power was concentrated in the hands of a small group, mostly made up of members with close ties to Tudjman.

Born in northern Croatia/Velko Tragoviste, Tudjman was educated in the Croatian nationalistic spirit. He envisioned Panslavism under Croatian leadership in Yugoslavia but became frustrated because of Serbian hegemony. Persecuted for his views in 1940, Tudjman joined Josip Broz Tito's partisan forces, becoming a carrier soldier after 1945. Despite his appointment as a general in 1960, he left active military service, dedicating himself to the study of geopolitics and earning a doctorate in political science in 1965. Distanced from mainstream politics, he was the leader of the 1971 "Croatian Spring," which was crushed by Tito who perceived it as a threat to Yugoslavia's unity. Tito imprisoned Tudjman, who was released only a year later. Due to his dissident stance and his interviews given to Western media, in which he denounced the failure of the Yugoslavism and the oppression of the Croats, he was imprisoned again in 1982. Tudjman was publicly skeptical of the Serbian nationalistic myth, which was based on the disputed number of victims at the Jasenovac concentration camp, the largest World War II concentration camp in Croatia and possibly the third largest in the world at the time. Serbian Nationalists used these numbers as a moral justification for revenge and creation of a united Serbian Yugoslavia, in fact a Greater Serbia.

In 1990, after the split of the Yugoslav Communist League and founding of his HDZ or Croat Democratic Union party in 1989, Tudjman won Yugoslavia's first presidential elections. In 1991, he declared Croat independence, relying heavily on the sympathy and support of Germany, Austria, Hungary, and the Catholic Church. Serbian forces waged war on the new Croatian state, attacking the major cities and practicing what became known as ethnic cleansing, as many civilians were killed or forced to flee.

In 1993, Tudjman reached a deal with Milošević upon the partition of Bosnia. In 1995, he captured the self-proclaimed Serbian Republic of Krajina, causing a mass exodus of two hundred thousand Serbs. Later that year, however, Tudjman signed the Dayton agreement in 1995 on behalf of the Bosnian Croats, and the war ended. Once the Greater Serbia ideal had been defeated, he agreed to the cautious return of Serbian refugees, cooperated with the UN War Crimes Tribunal, and resolved the conflicts with Bosnian Croat Separatists intent on leaving the confederation and forming their own republic. Although his vision of Great Croatia, which would have included Bosnia, was not realized, Tudjman was successful in keeping all the territories of the Socialist Croat Republic.

Tudjman was elected to three consecutive terms as Croatia's president. In 1999, however, his health declined, and he died on December 10, 1999.

LASZLO KOCSIS

See also Balkan Wars of the 1990s; Croatia; Ethnic Conflicts: Central and Eastern Europe; Milošević, Slobodan; Serbia; Yugoslavia

References and Further Reading

Tanner, M. *Croatia, A Nation Forged in War*. New Haven, CT: Yale University Press, 1997.
James, Minahan. *Miniature Empires: A Historical Dictionary of the New Independent States*. London: Fitzroy Dearborn Publishers, 1998.
Gallagher, T. *The Balkans after the Cold War: From Tyranny to Tragedy*. London: Routledge, 2003.
Gojko, Skoro. *Genocide over the Serbs in the Independent State of Croatia: Be Catholic or Die*. Belgrade: Institute of Contemporary History, 2000.

TUNISIA

The Tunisian Republic (*al Jumhuriyah at Tunisiyah* as translated in Arabic) is a small state located in North Africa, also called the *Maghreb*. It borders Algeria to the west and Libya to the southeast, with shores along the Mediterranean Sea to the north and east. The climate is semiarid, with desert covering the southern and central regions. Northern Tunisia is cooler and incorporates the eastern edge of the Atlas mountain system and the Medjerda Valley, whose river system empties into the Gulf of Tunis. Almost all of Tunisia's fertile soil is located in this region. Tunisia covers a total of 163,610 square kilometers. Its population is estimated at 9,974,722, with a growth rate of approximately 1.01%. Life expectancy is 74.7 years, and the literacy rate is 74%. The gross domestic product (GDP) grew by 5.1% in 2004 to $68.2 billion. Per

capita income is $6,900. Resources include agricultural products, iron, phosphate, natural gas, and petroleum. The population is largely Arab Berber and Sunni Muslim, with small Jewish and Christian minorities. The official language is Arabic, with French widely used in commerce. The capital city is Tunis, located in the northeast on the Lake of Tunis, with a population estimated at 674,100.

After Rome destroyed Carthage in 146 BC, the Medjerda Valley became the Empire's breadbasket. The Vandals and Byzantines ruled Tunisia until the Arab conquest in the seventh century. Tunisia became a part of the Ottoman Empire in 1574. In 1705, Hussein bin Ali founded the Husainid dynasty, which ruled until the monarchy's abolition in 1957. Ahmed Bey's rule from 1837 to 1855 saw the establishment of light weaponry and food processing industries as well as a short-lived ban on slavery. In 1869, European creditors of a bankrupt Tunisian state imposed the International Finance Commission to control the budget, undermining Tunisia's economic sovereignty. France invaded the country in 1881, making it a protectorate in 1883. The authorities promoted migration by transferring land from religious trusts to European settlers, while agricultural production expanded and while phosphate mines opened in the south. Increasing nationalistic sentiment and World Wars I and II led to Tunisian independence in 1956. A year later, the Neo-Destour party leader Habib Bourguiba became president.

At the time of independence, Tunisian industry was largely controlled by foreigners. The technical and managerial positions in 257 of the 290 industries with over fifty employees were almost entirely held by non-Tunisians. The economy was closely linked to France's, with the latter buying 55% of Tunisia's exports and providing 69% of its imports. Economic policy in the early years of statehood was a mix of liberalism and statism. Bourguiba believed that Tunisia's future lay with Europe and the West, while the General Union of Tunisian Workers (UGTT) sought more interventionist policies. The government nationalized infrastructure, including the railways, ports, electricity, and gas utilities. It also expropriated land owned by religious trusts for sale to rural elites in exchange for their support. Between 1956 and 1960, the number of state employees rose from twelve thousand to eighty thousand. There was also extensive social change as polygamy was outlawed, the judiciary was secularized, and a minimum age was set for marriage of women. In 1958, a central bank was created, and in 1959, the Tunisian dinar was adopted as the currency.

The 1961 installation of former UGTT leader Ahmed Ben Salah as Minister of Social Affairs and Economy signaled a shift toward socialism. In 1962, the government adopted central planning and banned the Communist Party, officially installing one-party rule. The state emphasized public sector-driven industrialization and invested heavily in Tunisia's periphery by financing steel mills, fertilizer plants, and other manufacturing activities. The government equated this move from primary to secondary production with decolonization. By the end of the decade, agriculture accounted for 18% of GDP, down from 24% in 1960. By 2004, services made up 54% of GDP, the highest of any North African state. In 1964, a wage increase triggered a fiscal crisis that caused the first-ever devaluation of the dinar, while the Neo-Destour became the Socialist Destour Party. The era of central planning ended in 1969 when Bourguiba dismissed Ben Salah and launched a policy of economic opening, or *infitah*.

Law 72-38, adopted in April 1972, underpinned the new approach. It granted export-oriented industries tax-exempt status, free reign to import their inputs, and guaranteed the right to repatriate profits. The following year, Law 73-19 created the Industrial Promotion Agency (API), whose mandate was to streamline investment rules and attract foreign investors. Exports rose from 12% of GDP in 1969 to 42% in 1981. Manufacturing went from one-fifth in 1970 of exports, to one-third in 1977, to two-thirds in 1988. Textiles also became an important good, rising from 2% of exports in 1971 to 30% in 1986. The Tunisian economy became increasingly tied to Europe's: exports to the European community rose from 50% of the total at the start of the *infitah* to over 80% by the 1990s. The policy's success was mixed: annual growth during the 1970s averaged 7.3%, but an expanding current accounts balance deficit reached over $800 million by 1984. Increasing labor unrest culminated in a general strike on January 28, 1978. Two hundred died in clashes between workers and the military.

Rising inflation, falling oil prices, and declining terms of trade forced the adoption of a stabilization plan, triggering bread riots in 1984 that left up to 120 dead. With foreign reserves virtually exhausted, the government turned to the International Monetary Fund (IMF) in 1986. In 1987, Prime Minister Ben Ali took advantage of the chaotic situation to declare Bourguiba incompetent and take power. Austerity measures included a currency devaluation and the removal of trade barriers. Public debt in 2004 was $14 billion, or 60% of GDP. In 1990, Tunisia joined the General Agreement on Tariffs and Trade. In 1995, it became the first South Mediterranean country to sign an association agreement with the European Union (EU), committing itself to forming a free trade area with the EU by 2008. In 1996, an EU-funded program of technological modernization was

launched. As of April 2003, it had approved 2.4 billion dinars for 1,448 firms.

ADAM ALLOUBA

References and Further Reading

Bechri, Mohamed Z., and Sonia Naccache. May 2003. "The Political Economy of Development Policy in Tunisia." http://www.erf.org.eg/html/grp/GRP_Sep03/Tunisia-Pol_Econ.pdf.
White, Gregory. *A Comparative Political Economy of Tunisia and Morocco: On the Outside of Europe Looking In.* State University of New York Press: Albany, 2001.

TUPAMAROS

The Tupamaros, also known as the *Movimiento de Liberación Nacional* (MLN) or the National Liberation Movement, were an urban guerrilla organization in Uruguay founded in 1965. They caused a fierce but relatively short period of antiestablishment terror in Uruguay in the late 1960s. They named themselves after the Inca Chief Tupac Amaru, who fought the Spanish and was quadrisected by the Spaniards on May 18, 1781, in Cuzco (Peru). This name was reused also by the revolutionary group *Movimiento Revolucionario Tupac Amaru* (MRTA), or the Tupac Amaru Revolutionary Movement, in Peru, notorious for their 126-day siege of the Japanese embassy in Lima in 1996.

Initially located in the countryside, the Tupamaros accepted a Robin Hood style of distributing stolen food and money among the poor in the suburbs. In 1963, a group of young men raided the Swiss Gun Club, an event that marked the birth of Latin America's most famous urban guerrilla group. They engaged in urban terrorism, political kidnappings, and murder, temporarily paralyzing Uruguay's political and economic life. News of their success inspired extremists worldwide, and they served as a role model for European urban guerrillas.

Following the assassination in August 1970 of Dan A. Mitrione, a US security official, and the kidnapping of British Ambassador Geoffrey Jackson in January 1971, both by the Tupamaros, parliament imposed twice suspension of all civil liberties. On September 9, 1971, after the escape from prison of more than one hundred Tupamaros, President Pacheco put the army in charge of all counterguerrilla activity.

In April 1972, after a bloody shooting with the Tupamaros, President Juan María Bordaberry declared a state of "internal war," suspending all civil liberties and adopting a draconian State Security Law. By the year's end, the army had decisively defeated the Tupamaros, whose surviving members were either imprisoned or had fled into exile. Despite this accomplishment, the civilian government relinquished running the country to a military *junta*—the Generals' Council (June 27, 1973)—that led to further repression against the population. Until that date, Uruguay had been the sole country in Latin America with the continuing tradition of a civilian democratic government.

Democracy was restored in 1985, and the Tupamaros became one of the few Latin American examples of successful transition to a legal political force. As a former urban guerrilla organization, with several hundred members, it was politically insignificant. In order to run candidates in the November 1989 elections, the former Tupamaros together with other ultra-leftist forces created the People's Participation Movement (*Movimiento de Participación Popular,* MPP). Since the Spring of 1995, it has been represented in the Parliament by the sixty-two-year-old Pepe Mujica, a founding member of the movement, who was held for thirteen years by the military government in absolute isolation. Later, this faction joined a larger Left reunion, Frente Amplio, further renouncing armed struggle and accepting democratic procedure.

STEPHAN E. NIKOLOV

See also Guerrilla Warfare; Terrorism; Uruguay

References and Further Reading

Bruschera, Oscar. *Las Décadas Infames, 1967–1985.* (*Hoy es Historia* series.) Montevideo: Librería Linardi y Risso, 1986.
Gilio, M. E. *The Tupamaro Guerrillas.* Translated by Anne Edmondson. New York: Saturday Review Press, 1972.
Porzecanski, Arturo C. *Uruguay's Tupamaros: The Urban Guerrilla.* New York: Praeger, 1973.
Weinstein, Martin. *Uruguay: Democracy at the Crossroads.* Boulder, CO: Westview Press, 1988.
Wilson, Carlos. *The Tupamaros: The Unmentionables.* Boston: Branden Press, 1974.

TURKEY

The Republic of Turkey (*Turkiye,* in Turkish) is a Eurasian country that occupies the Anatolian peninsula and a small portion of the Balkans. Turkey borders Greece, Bulgaria, Georgia, Armenia, Azerbaijan, Syria, Iraq, and Iran. In addition, Turkey lies along the Mediterranean Sea, the Aegean Sea, and the Black Sea. Turkey's total land area is approximately 779,452 square kilometers. The country contains sharp contrasts in topography, ranging from the Pontus and Taurus Mountains in the east, the high central plateau, and narrow coastal plains in the west. Turkey often suffers from earthquakes due to tectonic

pressures from the African landmass moving against Eurasia. The climate of Turkey can best be described as Mediterranean with extreme variations; for instance, moderate coastal plains are contrasted by harsh conditions in the interior and east. Rainfall corresponds to this variability as the coastal regions experience a wet rainy season with an average rainfall of 2,500 millimeters. The more prominent lakes and rivers of Turkey are found in the east and include Lake Van and the Tigris, Euphrates, and Araks rivers. Most of Turkey's growing population of 72.3 million (a United Nations estimate) lives in an area ranging from the central plains to the western coast. The capital is Ankara and has a population of more than 3.5 million. Turkey's largest metropolis is its former capital, Istanbul, with a population of more than 15 million. Urbanization has transformed Turkey from an agricultural society to an increasingly urbanized one, with roughly two-thirds of the population residing in cities.

Although the term "Turk" is applied to denote all of its citizens, Turkey has a multiethnic society whose genetic origins link it to the Balkans and the Caucasus as well as the Levant and Central Asia. Modern Turks speak an Altaic language that is part of the larger Ural-Altaic linguistic family (including such disparate members as Mongolian, Finnish, Uzbek, and Hungarian). Turks comprise 78% of the population and include various distinctions, such as Anatolians and Rumelians. There are also a considerable number of Muslims from the Caucasus, including Circassians, Georgians, and the Laz. Turkey's largest ethnic minority are the Kurds, whose numbers range from 10% to as high as 20%. They can, in turn, be broken down into disparate groups who sometimes cannot comprehend each other's dialect. *Kurmanji* is the majority's dialect of the Indo-European Kurdish language in Turkey, while a minority speak the southern *Kurdi* dialect, which is more prominent in neighboring Iraq. *Dimli* is a related Iranian tongue that is often confused for a Kurdish dialect, but it is actually a separate language spoken by close to 1 million people. In addition, a significant number of self-identifying Kurds have abandoned the use of Kurdish and either speak it as a second language or simply speak Turkish. Arabic speakers are concentrated in southern Turkey along the Syrian border and number more than 1 million. Other prominent minorities in Turkey include refugees from Bulgaria, Iran, and Bosnia as well as small numbers of Greeks and Armenians.

Religion in Turkey is tempered by the secular state, but the vast majority of Turks are nominally Muslim. However, the secularism of Turkey is not of the same vein as that found in the European Union (EU). Turkey's government directly regulates religion and even trains religious scholars and *mullahs,* and thus practices a form of governmental regulation of religion rather than a strict separation of church and state as is prominent in the West. Sunni Islam dominates Turkey with 75% to 80% of the population adhering to this sect, while the Alevi, a variant branch of Shia Islam, make up at least 19% of the remainder. Most of the Dimili (or Zaza), for example, distinguish themselves further through their adherence to Shia Islam, as do Azerbaijanis and Turkmen. Sufism is the more philosophical and meditative branch of Islam that is historically responsible for converting large numbers of Greeks and Armenians to Islam. Most of the Christian minority in the country includes Greeks, Armenians, and Assyrians. In addition, a small Jewish community of Ladinos and Ashkenazi is found mainly in Istanbul.

Turkey's diversity is derived from its central location near the world's earliest civilizations as well as a history replete with population movements and invasions. The Hattite culture was prominent during the Bronze Age prior to 2000 BCE, but was replaced by the Indo-European Hittites who conquered Anatolia by the second millennium. Meanwhile, Turkish Thrace came to be dominated by another Indo-European group, the Thracians for whom the region is named. The Hittites and Thracians were swept aside by Greeks who came to dominate the history of western and central Anatolia, while the Armenians and possibly early proto-Kurdish groups may have entered eastern Anatolia by the first millennium BCE. Persians and mainland Greeks contested the region, which culminated in Greek conquest and colonization of the Persian Empire itself by 323 BCE. Subsequently, *hellenization* of the elites transformed Anatolia into a largely Greek-speaking region.

Roman conquest in Anatolia was complete by forty-three CE and morphed into the Byzantine Empire. Christianity became the dominant faith of Anatolia and would remain so until the arrival of Islam. Small bands of Muslim Turks began moving into Anatolia by the early part of the second millennium CE. The pivotal point that began the transformation of Anatolia into a Turkish-speaking Islamic domain was the Battle of Manzikert in 1071, where the Byzantine army was defeated by Seljuk Turkish invaders. The Byzantine Empire would last until 1453 when the Ottoman Turks finally took the city of Constantinople. Like the Byzantine Empire before it, however, the Ottoman Empire began a slow decline even as it reached its apogee, losing the Crimea, Egypt, and most of its Balkan territories during the nineteenth century. World War I witnessed the Ottoman Empire's last gasp as its alliance with Germany and the Austro-Hungarian Empire in 1914 proved to be a fatal gamble.

Even as the Ottoman Empire disintegrated, the Young Turk Movement and its founder, Mustafa Kemal (later dubbed "Ataturk"), spearheaded a Turkish Nationalist revival based on a Turkish ethnic identity rather than a multiethnic empire. Following the disastrous war, the Turks were given harsh terms by the Allies: not only were the lands not populated by Turks divided among imperial powers, but the Turkish majority areas also were to be partitioned by the Allies. Ataturk, who had emerged as a national hero, rallied the Turkish resistance and pressured the Ottoman government to relinquish its authority in 1921. The Nationalists led by Ataturk laid out their own terms that included renouncing claims that lay outside Turkish Muslim territories. France and Italy found the new Turkish military too formidable to challenge in its own homeland and withdrew, leaving only the Greeks to confront the resurgent Turkish forces. The Bolsheviks of the newly formed USSR had no desire to confront Turkey and signed a peace treaty in 1921 following cooperation between the two states in subjugating the newly independent state of Armenia.

The war against the Greek army was equally successful: Turkish Nationalist forces drove out the last of the Greeks by August 1922. Following these developments, the Allies renegotiated, and the Treaty of Lausanne, signed in Switzerland in November 1922, recognized Turkey as a state. The Allies gave in to Turkish demands, including recognition of the new Nationalist government and borders that corresponded to Muslim-Turkish majority areas (and northern Kurdish areas claimed by Turkey) as formed by Turkey's War of Independence. Thus was born the modern secular Republic of Turkey. Ataturk transformed Turkey into a Western and more "Turkish" state by separating religion and state; replacing the Arabic alphabet with a Latin script; ordering name changes from Arabic to ethnic Turkish; and adopting Western clothing, traditions, and laws into both government and society. Turkey aligned itself with the West following World War II, and during the Cold War it was a frontline state confronting the USSR. Despite sporadic conflicts with Greece over the Aegean region and Cyprus, Turkey has been a North Atlantic Treaty Organization (NATO) member and a consistent ally of the West. It is poised to become the first Muslim majority state to join the EU sometime in the first decade of the twenty-first century.

Turkey's political landscape has evolved since its inception. The Republican People's Party (*Cumhuriyet Halk Partisi* [CHP] in Turkish) dominated the early years of the republic. Following elections after World War II, the CHP lost power to the Democrat Party (DP) in 1950, which stayed in power for a decade. The DP began to cement its control, which led to civil unrest and prompted one of the many military *coups d'état* that would take place in modern Turkish history. The DP government was dismantled and replaced by a military council, which held elections in 1961. Thus began an oft-repeated cycle in Turkish politics, with a civilian government devolving into chaos, a military *coup* staged to restore order, and then another round of elections and purges. The Justice Party (*Adalet Partisi* [AP] in Turkish) emerged as the new rival to the CHP. Military intervention again took place in 1971 as the various political parties in Turkey could not form a government, and civilian control was again restored in 1973 following a regime appointed by neutral nonparty intellectuals. During this period, in 1974, conflict with Greece over the Cyprus issue embroiled Turkey in a conflict that persists in the twenty-first century. In addition, Kurdish nationalism came to the forefront during the 1970s and would also persist into the twenty-first century. Fearing Islamic influence in the government of the late 1970s, the military again intervened in 1980 and then restored civilian control in 1982 with the ascension of Turgat Ozal and the Motherland Party, whose administration would remain closely overseen by the military. The True Path Party came to power in a peaceful transition in 1991, and Turkey has maintained peaceful democratic elections since. The Justice and Development Party (*Adalet ve Kalkinma Partisi* [AKP] in Turkish) is the party in power since elections in 2002, which again relegated the CHP to secondary status. Some secularists fear the AKP's moderate Islamic leanings, but it seems unlikely that the legacy of Ataturk's secularism will be altered anytime in the near future, if at all.

Turkey's economy has had a similar tumultuous history, but it has been steadily improving for decades. The transition to a free market economy has helped to improve some aspects of the Turkish economy since the 1980s. Substantial deficits and a large debt (more than $104 billion) have led to high inflation rates and an anemic banking industry. However, under the International Monetary Fund's (IMF's) assistance, which has included substantial loans aimed at helping Turkey's transition toward market-oriented reforms, Turkey has shown significant changes in government policy including restrained fiscal policies and liberalization of previously state-controlled industries, banks, and energy concerns. Turkey has suffered economically as well as politically from the tumultuous crisis in Iraq, and the chaos has heighted Turkish worries about an independent Kurdish state with substantial oil reserves on its doorstep.

In addition, trade with Iran has declined substantially as many EU states now trade with Iran via the

Persian Gulf rather than through Turkey. Turkey has made great strides in manufacturing, which makes up 30% of its economic activity, while agriculture has improved in efficiency. Turkey continues to import far more than it exports, and underemployment has led to a substantial diaspora of Turkish guest workers moving to EU countries, especially to Germany (with more than 1 million living there indefinitely). Unemployment is not substantially higher than most EU countries, but a substantial number of Turks live at or below the poverty line (roughly one-fifth of the population). Foreign Direct Investment (FDI) was high in the 1990s, but it has slowed following fears of slow reforms, continued state control in many sectors of the economy, Turkey's massive debt, and perceived political worries over the possible rise of Islamic parties (which view themselves as more akin to the Christian Democrats in Germany as opposed to the ruling clerics of Iran). Turkey's prospects have greatly improved as a positive timetable has been set for its entry into the EU in the not too distant future but with strict conditions, including recognition of Cyprus. In addition, debate rages over fears of an onslaught of Turkish workers flowing out of Turkey and into more prosperous parts of Europe.

Many Europeans have shown concern over Turkey's large and growing population, Islamic character, and spotty human rights record, including its treatment of the Kurds. However, Turkey's economic improvements and diligent attempts to comply with EU standards have made its entry almost inevitable. Turkey has conducted reforms that allow for the free flow of international capital and protection of intellectual property rights, and this appears to have led to increased interest from foreign investors. With an increasingly educated populace and a per capita income that has reached Eastern European levels ($6,700 in 2003), Turkey's economic prospects continue to improve, barring the destabilizing political issues it faces with Kurdish nationalism, an Iraqi civil conflict, and continued problems with Greece over the Cyprus issue.

ALI AHMED

See also Cyprus

References and Further Reading

Aricanli, Ali Tousun, and Dani Rodrik, eds. *The Political Economy of Turkey: Debt, Adjustment, and Sustainability*. New York: Macmillan, 1990.
Chapman, Helen Metz. *Turkey: A Country Study (Area Handbook Series)*. 5th ed. Baton Rouge, LA: Claitor's Law Books and Publishing Division, 1997.
———. "Country Watch." *Turkey Country Review* (July 2003).
Faroqhi, Suraiya, and Bruce McGowan, Donald Quataert, and Sevket Pamuk. *An Economic and Social History of the Ottoman Empire, Volume 2*. Cambridge: Cambridge University Press, 1997.
Kreyenbroek, Philip G. *The Kurds: A Contemporary Overview*. London: Routledge, 1992.
Shaw, Stanford J., and Ezel Kural Shaw. *History of the Ottoman Empire and Modern Turkey*. (2 vols.) Cambridge: Cambridge University Press, 1976.

TURKMENISTAN

The Republic of Turkmenistan is located in Central Asia, bordering with Iran in the south, with Afghanistan in the southeast, with Uzbekistan in the northeast, and Kazakhstan in the north. The Caspian Sea forms a natural border in the west. The country has a land area of 488,100 square kilometers (188,455 square miles) and is the second largest in the Central Asian region.

The population of Turkmenistan is estimated at 4.86 million, with 55% living in rural areas. The country's capital city, Ashgabad, is home to 580,000 people, or 8% of the population. Turkmenistan has a population growth rate of 1.85%, and it is estimated that its population will double by 2040. Turkmen is spoken by approximately 72% of the population, Russian by 12%, and Uzbek by 9%; other languages make up 7% of the population. The predominant religion is Islam, practiced by 89% of the population, and 9% of the population are Eastern Orthodox Christians.

Until the twentieth century, animal husbandry (horses, sheep, camels, and cattle) was the main source of income, supplemented by trade on the Silk Road. The desert terrain, which occupies almost four-fifths of the country, can support millions of sheep and camels, but there are few arable oases. The economic development of Turkmen land was often interrupted by war, and many cities and oases never recovered after the Mongol invasion in the thirteenth century and decades of internal conflicts in the seventeenth and nineteenth centuries. The Russian Empire established political control after overcoming resistance of the Turkmen tribes in 1881.

Capitalism was brought to the Turkmen society with the arrival of the Russians in the end of the nineteenth century and the building of a major railroad, but this only aggravated social disparity. After the Russian Revolution of 1917, with the help of British forces, Turkmen Nationalists declared independence from the Bolshevik state but eventually were brought back, becoming a part of the Turkistan Soviet Autonomous Republic. On October 27, 1924, Turkmenistan was established within its present borders,

becoming a Soviet Socialist Republic, a constituent part of the USSR. The Communist Party of Turkmenistan (CPT) came to power and remained the republic's single ruling party for the next seventy years.

The Soviet concept of development deeply affected Turkmenistan development from the 1930s until the 1980s, as the state initiated radical political and economic changes, state control of all types of economic activities, and central state planning. Between the 1930s and 1980s, the government forced all farmers to join large-scale farming centered around *kolkhozy*, state-controlled collective farms, and invested huge resources into building the Karakum Canal irrigation system, the largest in the USSR. After World War II, the Soviet government also initiated an industrialization program that brought into the republic the heavy industry, light industries (textile, garment, and carpets), petrochemical industry, and natural resources extraction (gas, oil, iodine, and other such resources). The government also heavily invested into the social sector, improving literacy, developing extended free education, and offering medical and social welfare services to all sectors of the population. At the same time, basic political and religious freedoms, free entrepreneurship, and cultural relations with countries outside the "iron curtain" were suppressed. According to official statistics, the Turkmenistan industrial production grew twelve-fold between 1940 and 1984, at an average annual rate of 8%–10%. By the end of the 1980s, Turkmenistan became the second largest gas producer in the USSR. The extensive economic development, however, led to ecological problems such as salinisation.

In the mid-1980s, the central government led by Mikhail Gorbachev introduced major changes, relinquishing centrally planned economy and introducing limited democratization. These changes were largely peaceful although the Turkmenistani elite silently resisted *perestroika*. The government banned emerging opposition parties, and the CPT easily won majority of 175 seats in the new Parliament and formed the government in January 1990. Its representative, Saparmurad Niyazov, ran unopposed in the October 1990 presidential election.

Further Developments

On October 27, 1991, Turkmenistan declared its independence from the USSR. President Niyazov moved swiftly to introduce a new constitution (May 1992) and some political and economic changes. Gradually, these reforms brought into life one of the most extravagant political regimes in the former USSR, combining extreme forms of statism, egalitarianism, and authoritarianism combined with nationalism and emphasis on traditional values. In December 1999, Mr. Niyazov-Turkmenbashy was elected as the president-for-life.

After independence, the Turkmenistan government rejected radical economic changes. The government believed that the sale of its gas reserves would allow it to achieve prosperity within ten years. It approved small-scale privatisation, limited price liberalization and currency reforms, allowed private entrepreneurship, and liberalized its trade. But at the same time, it retained some form of the centrally planned economy. The national currency—the *manat*—was introduced in November 1993, but it remained unconvertible. In 1992 through 1998, the annual inflation rate was between 600% to 3000% but declined to 9.5% in 2003 (CIA estimate).

However, the economic miracle did not materialise, largely due to nonpayments for the gas by the Commonwealth of Independent States (CIS) partners, absence of pipeline capacities to the non-CIS market, and flaws in the economic development model chosen by Turkmenistan's leaders. According to the World Bank, Turkmenistan's economy declined at an average annual rate of 4.8% between 1990 and 2000 but rebounded in 2001 through 2004. The country increasingly relies on the export of raw materials to the international market, mainly its gas, cotton, and agricultural products. Turkmenistan needs considerable foreign direct investments to modernize existing gas and oil extracting capacities and to build major pipelines.

Agriculture, industries, and services are the three main pillars of post-Soviet Turkmenistan's economy, contributing 27.3%, 50.0%, and 22.6%, respectively, to the gross domestic product (GDP) (World Bank estimate, 2001). The exports are narrowly based on sales of raw materials in international markets. The country's main exports are gas (exported 38.6 billion cubic meters of gas (CIA estimate 2001), textiles, cotton (Turkmenistan is the world's tenth largest producer of cotton), silk, and other agricultural products.

The post-Soviet economic changes led to a steady decline in living standards among all groups of the population, despite the state's supplying water, electricity, and gas for free to all citizens of the country and despite the recent macroeconomic stabilisation. The country remains one of the poorest countries of the former Soviet Union, with 58% of population living below the poverty line (2001 est.) and an average life expectancy of sixty-one years. In 2004, the United Nations Development Programme's (UNDP's) Human Development Index (HDI) put Turkmenistan in 86th place out of 177.

ALFIA ABAZOVA AND RAFIS ABAZOV

See also Commonwealth of Independent States: History and Economic Development; Commonwealth of Independent States: International Relations

References and Further Reading

Abazov Rafis. *Historical Dictionary of Turkmenistan*. Lanham, MD; Oxford: Scarecrow Press, 2004.

International Monetary Fund. *Turkmenistan: Recent Economic Developments*. Series: IMF Staff Country Report No. 99/140. Washington, DC: Author, 1999.

———. *Turkmenistan—The Burden of Current Agricultural Policies*. Series: Working Paper WP/00/98 99/140. Washington, DC: Author, 2000.

Miyamoto, Akira. *Natural Gas in Central Asia: Industries, Markets and Export Options of Kazakhstan, Turkmenistan and Uzbekistan*. London: Royal Institute of International Affairs, 1998.

Pomfret, R. *The Economies of Central Asia*. Princeton, N.J.: Princeton University Press, 1995.

United Nations Development Programme. *Turkmenistan. National HumanDevelopment Report*. Ashgabad: Author, 2000.

World Bank. *Turkmenistan*. Washington, DC: Author, 1994.

TUTU, BISHOP DESMOND

Bishop Desmond Tutu, a black South African Archbishop and a Nobel Peace Prize winner, is best known for his defiant opposition to apartheid. Born in Klerksdorp, South Africa, in 1931, Tutu rose from an impoverished childhood to become the archbishop of Cape Town, the highest position in the South African Anglican Church. When Tutu was twelve, his family moved to Johannesburg, where his father had found a better teaching position and his mother was also fortunate enough to find work as a cook in an Anglican missionary school. Tutu attended the Johannesburg Bantu High School (Madibane) in Western Native Township and went on to earn a teacher's diploma from the Bantu Normal College in Pretoria in 1953 and a BA degree in teaching from the University of South Africa a year later. He received his initial formal training in religion from St. Peter's Theological College in Johannesburg, from 1958 to 1960, and followed it up with a BA (honors) in London and then a master's degree in Theology from King's College in London in 1966.

It was during his childhood in Johannesburg that Tutu met Father Trevor Huddleston, a fearless critic of apartheid, who became Tutu's mentor until his (Huddleston's) death in 1998. Under the guidance of his parents and the spiritual mentorship of Huddleston, Tutu became aware of the damaging impacts of apartheid on Blacks and the need to oppose it, not with violence, but with love, reconciliation, and respect for others; these themes were later woven into Tutu's theology of *ubuntu*. Tutu had an illustrious teaching career—from his appointments as a high school teacher at Madibane (1954–1955) and Munsieville High School in Krugersdor (1955–1958) to his lectureships at the Federal Theological Seminary in Alice, Cape Province (1967–1969), and the University of Lesotho (1970–1971)—before his major leadership roles in the church in South Africa, which included his positions as the Dean of St. Mary's Cathedral in Johannesburg in 1975, Bishop of Lesotho in 1976, General-Secretary of the South African Council of Churches in 1978, and Bishop of Johannesburg in 1985, all of which culminated in his position as the Archbishop of Cape Town, from 1986 to 1996.

Tutu's *Ubuntu* Theology

In a number of sermons, speeches, and books, Tutu advanced an eclectic theology, which combines elements of African spirituality, liberation theology, and Christian teachings, with a dose of South African politics, under the rubric *ubuntu*. The concept of *ubuntu*, often translated as "community" and sometimes as "humanity" or "respect for others," is seen by Tutu as the mysterious quality that makes a person a person. According to Tutu, one is a Christian only to the extent that he or she cares for others and that people are human through their relationships with others—hence, his favorite saying is "*U muntu ngu muntu ngabantu,*" which means "a person is a person through other people." Tutu sees this focus on community and relationships with others as a corrective worldview to the Western salvation theology, which is centered on the individual. *Ubuntu* is also premised on the Christian doctrine that human beings are created by God in his image (*imago Dei*). Implicitly, a race-based discriminatory system like apartheid makes no theological sense from the standpoint of Tutu's *ubuntu*, as it undermines this notion of *imago Dei*. Unlike apartheid, which gives the primacy of human identity to race, Tutu's *ubuntu* gives it to the human spirit or the image of God. *Ubuntu* certainly underpins Tutu's advocacy for nonviolence and reconciliation, even in the face of intense provocation. No documentation of Tutu's theology can be complete without some mention of his delicious humour. Tutu notes in his foreword to Mary Benson's *Nelson Mandela* (1986) that "we laugh only because if we did not, we would cry and cry." According to Tutu, humour is liberating because it helps a person not to take the isolated self as seriously as the self in relation to others.

Tutu's Role in the Political Transformation of South Africa

With the conviction that religion and politics are inseparable, it is hardly surprising that Tutu was constantly embroiled in the South African apartheid politics. To him, Christianity is not a personal matter, as it invariably has public consequences, especially in South Africa where religion was used as a medium of oppression. As he once put it in an interview with *The Australian*, Tutu says that "in a situation of injustice and oppression as we have in South Africa, not to choose to oppose it is in fact to have chosen to side with the . . . oppressor." Not surprisingly, Tutu has been vilified by whites, who brand him as anything from a "theological imposter," "political agitator," to a "communist operative," and by blacks, especially the youth, who criticize him for holding back their liberation struggle with his antiviolence stance. Tutu once admitted in his characteristic straightforwardness that "if I were a young black, I wouldn't listen to Tutu any more."

Tutu, a consummate peace-lover, rejects all forms of violence, either from the erstwhile apartheid system or from those who sought to overthrow it. At the same time, he was realistic enough to warn, as he did in an open letter to Prime Minister John Vorster in May 1976, that "a people made desperate by despair, injustice and oppression will use desperate means." Tragically, just the following month, Tutu's warning came to pass, with the Soweto uprising in which some six hundred black children were killed. Tutu's abhorrence for violence compelled him to favour economic sanctions against South Africa. Working with the international prosanctions lobby, made up of such notables as Rajiv Gandhi, the British Labour Party, and the exiled African National Congress—against equally formidable opposition from the likes of President Reagan, Margaret Thatcher, and Chancellor Helmut Kohl—Tutu's defiant advocacy facilitated the dismantling of apartheid and the ultimate transformation of the South African society; indeed, the only thing that kept Tutu from prison, then, was his international fame.

Tutu's anti-apartheid views have long put him in a collision course with the government. In 1981, the government accused Tutu and the South African Council of Churches, of which he was the General Secretary, of financial mismanagement and subversion and appointed the Eloff Commission to investigate. Tutu was defiant as ever, asserting in his submission to the Commission that "they may remove a Tutu . . . but God's intension to establish His Kingdom of justice, of love, of compassion will not be thwarted." At the end of its long inquiry, the Commission uncovered nothing that could justify any kind of censure for lawbreaking. In 1990, as sanctions intensified and political violence increased, President de Klerk heeded the relentless warning by Tutu and other anti-apartheid advocates and released Nelson Mandela, paving the way for free and democratic South Africa. Mandela spent his first night of freedom in Tutu's house, in appreciation for the latter's outstanding contribution to his release. Tutu was named the Chairman of the Truth and Reconciliation Commission set up by the Mandela government to investigate the abuses of the apartheid government.

Tutu's selfless opposition to apartheid has earned him numerous reputable citations and awards, including the Nobel Peace Prize in 1984. Other notable ones are honorary degrees from Oxford, Harvard, Columbia, Emory, Yale, Kent, Sydney, Cape Town, and Ruhr universities. He also holds the Order for Meritorious Services Award (gold) from President Mandela; the Archbishop of Canterbury's Award for Outstanding Services to the Anglican Communion; the Prix d'Athene (Onassis Foundation); the Mexican Order of the Aztec Medal (Insignia Grade); the Martin Luther King Jr. Humanitarian Award of Annual Black American Heroes and Heroines Day; and the Martin Luther King Jr. Peace Award and many more.

JOSEPH MENSAH

See also Apartheid; Human Rights as a Foreign Policy Issue; Human Rights: Definition and Violations; Mandela, Nelson; South Africa

References and Further Reading

Battle, Michael. *Reconciliation: The Ubuntu Theology of Desmond Tutu.* Cleveland, OH: The Pilgrim Press, 1997.

Bentley, Judith. *Archbishop Tutu of South Africa.* Hillside, NJ: Enslow, 1988.

Du Boulay, Shirley. *Tutu: Voice of the Voiceless.* Grand Rapids, MI: William B. Eerdmans, 1988.

Kunnie, Julian. *Models of Black Theology: Issues in Class, Cultures and Gender.* Valley Forge, PA: Trinity Press International, 1994.

Mungazi, Dickson A. *In the Footsteps of the Masters: Desmond M. Tutu and Able T. Muzorewa.* Westport, CT; London: Praeger, 2000.

Tutu, Desmond (with Douglas Abrams). *God Has a Dream.* New York: Doubleday, 2004.

———. *No Future without Forgiveness.* New York: Doubleday, 1999.

———. *Sermons and Speeches*, John Webster, ed. Compiled by Mothobi Mutloatse. Grand Rapids, MI: W.B. Eerdmans, 1984.

TUVALU

Tuvalu is an independent Pacific microstate. A parliamentary democracy with the British monarch as

nominal head of state, Tuvalu has ties to a number of international organizations, including the British Commonwealth, the Pacific Islands Forum, and the United Nations. It comprises a chain of nine small atolls and coral islands stretching from northwest to southeast in a four-hundred-mile long arc south of the Equator and just west of the International Dateline. Its nearest neighbors are the Republics of Kiribati to the north and Fiji to the south. Tuvalu, as the former Ellice Islands, and Kiribati, as the former Gilbert Islands, constituted a protectorate and then colony under British control from 1892 to 1975, but Fiji is now Tuvalu's most important link to the outside world.

From north to south, the Tuvalu islands are Nanumea, Niutao, Nanumaga, Nui, Vaitupu, Nukufetau, Funafuti, Nukulaelae, and Niulakita (a relatively recent addition purchased by colonial authorities after World War II as a population safety valve for the most crowded island, Niutao). The total land area of the archipelago is only about ten square miles. Loyalty to individual islands is strong and has been recognized with a degree of constitutional decentralization.

The climate is tropical maritime (the average daily maximum temperature is 75°F–86°F or 24°C–30°C) with a stormy season from November through March. A rainfall of 105 to 140 inches per year generally precludes prolonged drought, but storage constraints and saltwater contamination have encouraged systems of communal rationing when required. Soils pose a challenge for agriculture, being 98% calcium or magnesium carbonate and therefore highly alkaline. The most adaptive form of cultivation (primarily of swamp taro, *Cyrtosperma chamissonis*) uses large compost-filled pits dug down into the top layers of freshwater lenses. Other cultigens include varieties of coconut palms, pandanus, bananas, and breadfruit, all suited to atoll conditions, as well as "real" taro (*Colocasia esculenta*), which requires special treatment and soil production. Copra used to be produced for export, but low market prices and transport difficulties mean the industry is now virtually defunct. Inshore and lagoon fishing are still practiced intensively, and some of the catch is now sold locally.

The 2002 census recorded a population of about 9,500, meaning growth had slowed overall, but its uneven spread had intensified. Funafuti, the capital and "urban" center, had almost 4,500 inhabitants; Vaitupu, the location of the main high school, had about 1,500; and the rest had between four hundred and seven hundred, except for Niulakita (thirty-five). Many people on Funafuti are "outer islanders" in search of economic opportunities, education, and medical treatment, or they are visiting relations. About three thousand Tuvaluans have moved to New Zealand, the country mentioned most often as

an environmental refuge in the event of global warming (despite the government there downplaying such commitments). Scientists disagree as to whether Tuvalu is genuinely threatened by rising sea levels, but climate change in the form of more frequent and/or more serious storms may be just as great a threat.

Protestant evangelization began in the 1860s and 1870s, and the Tuvalu Christian Church is still overwhelmingly the main denomination. A significant proportion of household income is diverted into the upkeep of church administration and local pastors. In return, the church has provided primary education and some elite employment opportunities. Since independence in 1978, however, most of the educational system has been run by the government. Primary education is mostly free and universal; secondary and tertiary education levels are restricted to fees-paying or scholarship students. Tuvalu has a relatively high literacy rate, usually cited as well over 90%, though this may mask declining achievement. Young men compete to enter the local maritime institute at Amatuku to train as merchant seamen for international shipping lines. Seamen's wages are an important source of remittances.

Infrastructural development and the development of a cash economy proceeded slowly under the British colonial administration but received a boost from Tuvalu's position as a northerly forward Allied base in World War II. US forces built airfields, including what remains the only international airport on Funafuti, and some locals found employment in construction. Straddling this wartime "boom" was an influx of money from overseas laborers, mainly in the phosphate mining operations of Banaba and Nauru, now closed or near the end of their economic life.

These developments all reinforce the depiction of Tuvalu as a classic MIRAB economy, that is, based on **MI**gration, **R**emittances, **A**id, and **B**ureaucracy. Being small and poor in land-based natural resources, the country has had to survive by managing its political relations with metropolitan aid donors and has done so quite successfully, even though Tuvalu has no natural migration outlet (with no rights of access to Britain, the former colonial power) and despite the prospect of remittance "decay" from those living overseas. Tuvaluan leaders have turned Tuvalu into an internationally recognized symbol of impending environmental disaster from global warming and have garnered rewards through the cultivation of good diplomatic relations with countries like Taiwan, which seeks friends in the Pacific. Another source of income is the Pacific Islands Forum Fisheries Agency, which negotiates licensing agreements with Distant Water Fishing Nations seeking to exploit the valuable Central Pacific tuna fishery. With an Economic

Exclusive Zone of about 600,000 square miles, Tuvalu gains substantial income from this source ($6.5 million Australian in 2002).

The Tuvalu Trust Fund was established by Australia, Britain, and New Zealand with a grant of $27 million Australian in 1987. Its market valuation had more than doubled by 2000, providing substantial income for the running of government services (perhaps as much as 40% by 1998). Government remains the most important area of employment, especially on Funafuti, though the private sector is growing. Other revenue accrues from licensed use of Tuvalu's Internet domain suffix (.tv). Managed by a Canadian company, returns were expected to reach almost $20 million Australian in 2002 and to continue growing. Rental of spare telecommunications capacity also briefly provided some major windfall revenue in the 1990s, but this declined abruptly with the revelation that much of it came from international phone sex lines, prompting opposition from the church hierarchy. Tourism is constantly touted as another avenue of economic development but, given Tuvalu's relative inaccessibility and infrastructural problems, has only a small role to play for the foreseeable future.

In short, Tuvalu is a tiny democratic microstate, lacking natural resources and infrastructure and handicapped by geographical remoteness and fragmentation. Its people survive by generating revenue from a number of fortuitous engagements in the global economy, which supplement the localized pursuit of agriculture and fishing.

MICHAEL GOLDSMITH

See also Ethnic Conflicts: Oceania; Fiji; Kiribati; Oceania: History and Economic Development; Oceania: International Relations; Samoa

References and Further Reading

Chambers, Anne. *Nanumea*. 2d ed. Canberra: Australian National University, Development Studies Centre, 1984. (*Atoll Economy: Social Change in Kiribati and Tuvalu, No. 6.*)

Chambers, Keith, and Anne Chambers. *Unity of Heart: Culture and Change in a Polynesian Atoll Society*. Prospect Heights, IL: Waveland Press, 2001.

Connell, John. "Environmental Change, Economic Development, and Emigration in Tuvalu." *Pacific Studies* 22, no. 1 (1999): 1–20. Reprinted in *Globalization and Culture Change in the Pacific Islands*, Victoria S. Lockwood, ed. Upper Saddle River, NJ: Pearson Education, 2004.

Goldsmith, Michael, and Niko Besnier. "Tuvalu." *Countries and Their Cultures*, Melvin Ember and Carol R. Ember, eds. Vol. IV. New York: Macmillan Reference USA, 2001.

Knapman, Bruce, Malcolm Ponton, and Colin Hunt. *Tuvalu: 2002 Economic and Public Sector Review*. Manila: Asian Development Bank, 2002.

Munro, Doug. "Migration and the Shift to Dependence in Tuvalu: A Historical Perspective." *Migration and Development in the South Pacific*, John Connell, ed. Canberra: National Centre for Development Studies, Research School of Pacific Studies, The Australian National University, 1990a.

———. "Transnational Corporations of Kin and the MIRAB System: The Case of Tuvalu." *Pacific Viewpoint* 31, no. 1 (1990b): 63–66.

Simati, Aunese Makoi, and John Gibson. "Do Remittances Decay? Evidence from Tuvaluan Migrants in New Zealand." *Pacific Economic Bulletin* 16, no. 1 (2001): 55–63.

Taafaki, Tauaasa. *Governance in the Pacific: Politics and Policy in Tuvalu. Economics Division Working Paper 95/9*. Canberra: Australian National University, Research School of Pacific and Asian Studies, 1995.

———. "Polynesia in Review: Tuvalu." *Contemporary Pacific* 10, no. 1 (1998): 240–243.

26TH OF JULY MOVEMENT

The 26th of July Movement was the guerrilla opposition in Cuba led by Fidel Castro and his instrument to gain support of the Cuban people for the overthrow of Cuban dictator Fulgencio Batista y Zaldivar. July 26 commemorates the day in 1953 on which Castro and his comrades attacked the Moncada army barracks at Santiago de Cuba. The date of the attack, July 26, 1953, was deliberately chosen because it was the 100th anniversary of the birth of the Cuban writer and patriot Jose Martí who fought against the Spanish rule over Cuba. This futile but defiant 1953 attack and his long speech of self-defense at his trial made Castro a hero among the Cubans. Six and one-half years later, Castro was able to seize power, and despite all odds and misfortunes, he is still in command.

The attack on Moncada barracks was doomed as an act of despair and poorly designed by a group of visionary and radicalized youngsters. It was a reaction to the March 10, 1952, coup d'état that made the comeback of Fulgensio Batista in the power. Nearly 1,500 people, almost everyone under thirty years of age, were involved in the preparations for the attack, and none of them betrayed. They intended, benefiting of surprise, to seize the barracks, catch the arms they needed, inducing soldiers to join them, and on the radio station nearby to call on the people to rise up against Batista.

On July 26, 1953, with the town busy celebrating a carnival, 125 young men and women gathered to ignite the spark that they were convinced would loose a revolutionary tempest over the entire country. At 5:15 a.m., they rallied by singing the national anthem and reciting the poem "Ya Estamos en Combate" (We Are in the Battle) by soldier-poet Raul Gomez Garcia, and verses by Jose Marti declaimed by Fidel Castro himself. The attack itself went badly

wrong for the young revolutionaries. Half the forces, the better armed, lost their way in the unfamiliar city streets and never made it to the battle. The others who made it there were unable to take the garrison, and the order to withdraw was given. Few lives were lost in the battle itself; 95% of the casualties came from the army's brutality against revolutionaries who were captured alive. Fidel, his brother Raul, and about eighteen others managed to escape. A week later, they decided to come out of hiding in order to save innocent people in Santiago from the terror and reprisals. At the open trial, Castro, a professed lawyer and gifted orator, delivered his famous speech, "History Will Absolve Myself". He was sentenced to fifteen years in prison on the Isle of Pines but received amnesty on May 15, 1955, after serving only eleven months. With few followers, he fled to Mexico, the site of military training for guerrilla warfare. In July 1955, in exile, they founded the Movimiento Revolucionario 26 de Julio (MR-26-7, 26 July Revolutionary Movement), named after their first revolutionary act in 1953. Here, their team was joined by the physician from Argentina Ernesto Guevara, alias "Che."

On November 30, 1956, three hundred men (led by Frank País) wearing red and black armbands with the July 26 emblem attacked police headquarters, the Customs House, and the harbor headquarters in Santiago. This was planned to coincide with the arrival of Granma boat with eighty-two rebels from Mexico, but stormy weather delayed the trip and sent forlorn sailors to a remote place. All but twelve were slain in the first combat with the regular army, but most of the important leaders—Fidel, Raul, Che, Camilo Cienfuegos, and Juan Almeida—made their way into the Sierra Maestra mountains.

Rebel forces relied on the peasants for support. Their first guerrilla unit of the 26 July Movement was combat-ready on December 18, 1956. Batista's ruthless attacks against pro-Castro helpers only stirred up more support for the rebel leader. Batista's troops were unprepared for the fighting conditions in the mountains and the guerilla style of warfare; desertion and surrender were commonplace among the dictator's forces.

On May 24, 1958, Batista launched Operacion Verano. With seventeen battalions, tanks, planes, and gunboat fire from the sea, they intended to easily defeat Castro's rebels. Though greatly outnumbered, rebels repeatedly inflicted heavy casualties on the army and drove them back. Eventually, Batista decided that the situation was hopeless, decided to give up the fight, and on New Year's Eve, he fled to Spain.

Santa Clara was taken by Guevara's army, who then turned toward Havana. Santiago surrendered without a fight. The forts in Havana also relinquished, and Castro's forces triumphantly entered the capital. It was just five years, five months, and five days after the attack on the Moncada barracks.

After the revolution's success, the 26th of July Movement was joined with other groups to form the United Party of the Cuban Socialist Revolution. Castro began to refer to the revolution as "socialist" and Marxist-Leninist—though still in his "History Will Absolve Me" speech, he stated clearly that "the revolutionary government would have assumed all the faculties inherent to it: it would have assumed the legislative, executive, and judicial powers"—only during 1961. On October 3, 1965, the new Communist Party was founded, replacing the party originally established in 1925. The First Congress of the Communist Party met in 1975 and drafted a new constitution.

July 26 remains the most important date in the Cuban revolutionary calendar. The former Batista Presidential Palace is now the Museum of the Revolution and contains "Granma," and countless artifacts and insignia and flags of the 26th of July Movement. This day is the best chance to see *el Commandante* Fidel Castro in one of his most prominent roles of a captivating public speaker—albeit with his progressing age, he lost most of the charisma of his younger days. Commonly, these speeches were delivered in front of a massive gathering of thousands of people and involve a vivid dialogue between the leader and the crowd.

STEPHAN E. NIKOLOV

See also Batista, Fulgencio; Castro, Fidel; Cuba; Cuban Revolution; Guerrilla Warfare; Guevara, Ernesto "Che"; Marxism; Social Revolutions

References and Further Reading

26th of July Movement, "Program Manifesto of the 26th of July Movement," in *Cuba in Revolution*, ed. by R. Bonachea and Nelson Valdes. Garden City, NJ, 1972.

Leonard, Thomas M. *Castro and the Cuban Revolution.* Westport, CT: Greenwood Press, 1999.

Paterson, Thomas. *Contesting Castro: The United States and the Triumph of the Cuban Revolution.* New York, 1994.

Pérez-Stable, Marifeli. *The Cuban Revolution: Origins, Course and Legacy.* New York: Oxford University Press, 1999.

Suchlicki, Jaime. *Cuba: From Columbus to Castro.* Washington, DC: Pergammon, 1985.

Thomas, Hugh. *Cuba: The Pursuit of Freedom.* New York: Harper and Row Publications, 1971.

U

UGANDA

Uganda is located in East Africa. It has the largest freshwater lake in the world—Nalubale, or Lake Victoria. Uganda is bordered to the north by Sudan; to the south by Tanzania, Rwanda, and Burundi; to the east by Kenya; and to the west by the Democratic Republic of the Congo. The climate is tropical but mild, with average daytime temperatures of 75°F–82°F (24°C–28°C). The dry season is from November to March, with July as the coolest month of the year. Near Lake Victoria and in the mountains, average annual rainfall is 60 inches; in the northeast of the country, it is less than 40 inches. The population is estimated at 26,404,543, with an estimated growth rate of 2.97% annually (CIA estimate July 2004). The capital, Kampala, is located in the southeast region of the country on Lake Victoria and has a population of about 1.2 million.

The delimitation of Ugandan territory by European colonial powers brought together an African population composed of about fifteen different ethnic groups, which can be categorized into four main language clusters: Bantu, Nilo-Sudanic, Lwo, and Ateso. Although during the period of its rule over Uganda the British government was committed to developing the country as a single political unit, in practice the colonial government's economic and political policies fostered uneven development between regions. In addition, the sociopolitical policy of ethnic compartmentalization pursued in the colonial period, combined with economic policies, militated against territory-wide social cohesion. Preferential treatment of Buganda and Busoga by the British colonial administration allowed for the first formal political organizations on the national scene to emerge in that region of the country. After World War II, Africans began political agitation, first to demand their rights in the political process and then to challenge the pyramidal racial power structure in the country. In Buganda, the Bataka Party was formed in 1946, and the Uganda African Farmers Union was inaugurated the following year. After the insurrection by Africans in 1949, the British colonial government granted Africans in Buganda the right to elect their representatives to the Colonial National Legislative Council, on which hitherto only Europeans and Asians had sat. The action heralded populist politics against the colonial authorities in Buganda; in the 1950s, it spread to other parts of the country.

The first mass political party, the Uganda National Congress (UNC), was founded in March 1952 and was a lineal descendant of the Bataka Party and the Uganda African Farmers Union. Although the UNC was initially a Buganda-based political party, its leadership identified itself with Africans across the country. As it expanded, its leadership became dominated by Protestants. This caused apprehension among Roman Catholics, and in 1956 they recast nationwide the Democratic Party (DP), which had been launched in Buganda in 1954 by Catholic action to represent their interests.

Although the UNC was arguably the most broad-based Nationalist party in the country, it was, after the formation of the DP, torn by internal division and

personal bickering. A number of splinter parties emerged, one of which was the Uganda Peoples Union (UPU). In March 1960, the UPU and A. Milton Obote's faction of the UNC amalgamated to form the Uganda Peoples Congress (UPC), which adopted a Pan-Africanist posture at the same time that it exhibited antipathy toward Buganda; in fact, two groups were bound together by common fear of domination of the rest of the country in Buganda in a postcolonial Uganda. In October 1958, the first general elections on the basis of qualified franchise were held to elect African representatives to the Legislative Council. However, only eighteen constituencies in Uganda participated; the Buganda Lukiiko (traditional parliament), fearing the erosion of its privileged status and committed to Kiganda nationalism, together with the districts of Ankole and Bugisu, dissociated themselves from the elections.

In March 1961, a second general election, conducted by the British colonial authorities on common rolls and with a broadened qualified franchise-based on income, was held. Although the general election brought a substantial majority of elected African representatives to the Legislative Council and even though about 80% voted throughout Uganda, only 3% turned out in Buganda. The results of the election, favoring the DP over the UPC, pointed to the emergence of an ideological alliance in the country along ethnoregional and religious lines. The results also demonstrated that there were now only two dominant political parties in the country. But because only a minuscule proportion of the population in Buganda participated in the elections, there was the distinct possibility that the Buganda Lukiiko could constitute a third force in Ugandan politics. That possibility became a reality when late in 1961 a political party representing the interests of the Buganda Lukiiko and opposed to the Catholic-based DP, the Kabaka Yekka (KY, known also as "the King Alone"), was formed for the principal purpose of allying itself with the non-Kiganda but predominantly Protestant party, the UPC.

In April 1962, another general election was held to presage the granting of juridical independence to Uganda. The UPC gained forty-three seats and the DP twenty-four in a parliamentary National Assembly of ninety-one seats. The remaining twenty-four seats were claimed, in accordance with a provision in the constitution, by the Buganda Lukiiko for its political party, the KY, which then entered into an alliance with the UPC. Thus, when Britain granted political independence to Uganda on October 9, 1962, it was the UPC–KY alliance that formed the first postcolonial government of the country. By the terms of the UPC–KY coalition, the leader of the UPC, A. Milton Obote, became prime minister and thus executive head of state, but his position was offset by the appointment of the *Kabaka* as president—the titular head of state. The UPC and the KY were opposed on virtually every policy issue, but they were held together by their common resentment of the Catholic-dominated DP.

Within a year of the formation of the coalition, strains in the UPC–KY relationship quickly developed when the UPC began to establish political branches in Buganda. One year later, in 1964, the alliance broke down irretrievably when the UPC, in accordance with a constitutional provision, resolved to settle a territorial issue while the *Kabaka* attempted to secure Baganda's retention of two counties at issue by settling Buganda's ex-servicemen there. The termination of the UPC–KY alliance led to a bloody military confrontation between the *Kabaka's* forces and those of Obote in 1966 and the resultant demise of the Kiganda monarchy.

The use of the military by Obote to settle political differences between the UPC and the KY emboldened the army to intervene directly in politics. This was, among other things, a precondition of the *coup d'état* of January 25, 1971, led by Gerald Idi Amin Dada. Since then, the equation of power has rested on the determination of the military, which in July 1985 overthrew the second government of the UPC and was in turn ousted on January 25, 1986, by another military organization, the National Resistance Army (NRA), led by Yoweri Kaguta Museveni.

P. GODFREY OKOTH

See also East Africa: History and Economic Development; East Africa: International Relations; Ethnic Conflicts: East Africa

References and Further Reading

Byrnes, Rita M., ed. *Uganda: A Country Study*. Washington, DC: Federal Research Division, Library of Congress, 1992.

Karugire, Samwiri R. *A Political History of Uganda*. London: Heinemann, 1980.

Mukherjee, Ramkrishna. *Uganda, An Historical Accident?: Class, Nation, State Formation*. Trenton, NJ: Africa World Press, 1985.

Nabudere, Dan W. *Imperialism and Revolution in Uganda*. London: Onyx, 1980.

Okoth, Godfrey P. *Uganda: A Century of Existence*. Kampala: Fountain Publishers, 1995.

Omara-Otunnu, Amii. *Politics and the Military in Uganda, 1980–1985*. London: Macmillan, 1987.

Thomas P. Ofcansky. *Uganda: Tarnished Pearl of Africa*. Boulder, CO: Westview Press, 1996.

Tumusiime, James, ed. *Uganda 30 Years: 1962–1992*. Kampala: Fountain Publishers, 1992; 1998.

UKRAINE

Ukraine is the second largest country in Europe. The area of the country is 233,090 square miles (603,700 square kilometers), and its population reached 47,732,079 in 2004. Ukraine borders Russia, Belarus, Poland, Hungary, Slovakia, Romania, Moldova, and the Black Sea. The Ukrainian flag consists of two horizontal stripes: blue on top and yellow at the bottom, representing the golden grain fields under blue skies. Trident, another common national symbol of Ukraine, dates to the medieval times of Kievan Rus (a preheraldic symbol visible, for instance, on coins of Vladimir the Great and his successors). The capital of Ukraine is Kiev, one of the oldest cities in Ukraine that dates to the times of the Kievan Rus. It is also the largest Ukrainian city with the population presently exceeding 2.6 million. Although Ukraine was represented in the United Nations (UN) as an autonomous country, it was one of the Soviet Union republics until 1991. Ukrainians celebrate their Independence Day on August 24, a day that commemorates an anniversary of breaking up with the Soviet Union in 1991.

Ukrainian diverse ecosystems consist of lowlands along the Black Sea coast, open areas—steppes in central and southern Ukraine—wetlands, forested uplands in the central and northern parts of the country, and the Carpathian and Crimean Mountains in the south and southwest. The highest point is Hora Hoverla at 6,762 feet (2,061 meters) in the Carpathians, and the second highest mountain is Roman-Kosh in the Crimea, reaching 1,543 meters above sea level. Ample annual rainfalls and snowfalls contribute to numerous rivers and lakes. Several big rivers cut through the country, flowing generally from north to south and southeast. All rivers except for those in the extreme western part of the country contribute to the Black Sea watershed. The biggest among them are Dnepr, Dniestr, Boh, and Donets. Southern Ukraine borders the Black Sea with Crimean Peninsula.

The climate in Ukraine ranges from Mediterranean-like, warm, and humid in southern part of the country, to continental and dry in central and northern Ukraine. Generally, summers are warm or even hot in the central and the southern regions, and winters are mild in the south but cold and snowy in the central, northern, and western parts of the country. Ukraine still suffers from one of the most dramatic environmental disasters of the twentieth century: the Chernobyl Nuclear Power Plant accident of 1986 caused radiation contamination especially in the northeastern Ukraine and also around the world, but especially in Eastern and northeastern Europe.

Ukraine has always been a multicultural country with several significant ethnic groups and many other ethnic minorities. Modern ethnic relations include Ukrainians at 75% and Russians at about 20%; other minority groups are Romanians, Belarussians, Moldovans, Tatars, Bulgarians, Poles, Hungarians, and Jews. Other, less numerous ethnic groups include Slovaks, Germans, Swedes, Greeks, Albanians, Serbs, Karaims, Armenians, and Romas. Several ethnographic cultures are recognizable within Ukrainian territory. Among them, the best known are the Tartars of the Crimea and the Hutsul Highlanders in the Carpathians. Ethnic diversity caused several significant conflicts in the past, namely between Ukrainians and Jews as well as Ukrainians and Poles. Modern Ukraine adopted a policy to solve ethnic conflicts peacefully, and Crimean Tartars, who were displaced under the Soviet ruling from their homeland in the Crimea, were allowed to return to southern Ukraine. The newly elected Ukrainian president Victor Yushchenko promised the Polish minority in Western Ukraine more cultural rights. Languages spoken in Ukraine include Ukrainian, Russian, and Polish, especially in western Ukraine, and Hungarian and Romanian are spoken in the southwestern part of the country. The Ukrainian language belongs to the Indo-European family of languages and is classified as one of the Slavic languages of Eastern Europe. It uses the Cyrillic alphabet. There are several local dialects of the official language that developed in the eighteenth century, like the Boyko or Hutsul dialects in the west or the Volynian dialect in northern part of the country. Most Ukrainians speak the Ukrainian language although some, especially those who live in the eastern, more industrialized part of the country, claim Russian as their native language. After 1991, the use of the Ukrainian language increased. Cultural diversity can also be seen in a variety of religions followed by modern Ukrainians. The dominant religion is Orthodox Christianity, which includes Ukrainian Orthodox, Ukrainian Catholic (Uniate), and Ukrainian Autocephalous Orthodox. Other religions are also present, namely Roman Catholicism, Judaism, Protestantism, and Islam.

In the past, some areas of Ukraine were included into one of the first Eastern Slavic pristine states, the Kievian Rus, which originated in the tenth century. It is not clear who established the state. Historians link its origins with a group of people who probably migrated from the Scandinavian region and settled on the Dneper River, where Kiev is located. Archaeological records confirm the existence of Scandinavian artifacts in the early levels of medieval Kiev. The first ruling dynasty was named the Ruriks; they ruled a wide region occupied by people of Slavic origin. The Kievan kingdom is sometimes called the *Red Rus* in the historic sources. The state persisted for about two hundred

years and declined at the time of Mongolian rides in the beginning of the thirteenth century and during the fourteenth century. By the end of the fourteenth century, Ukraine became a part of the Lithuanian kingdom, and after Polish and Lithuanian unification in 1386, Ukrainian lands became the domain of the Polish kingdom. During the sixteenth and seventeenth centuries, Ukraine was part of one of the most politically and economically significant European state, the Commonwealth composed of Lithuania, Belarus, Ukraine, and Poland. At the same time, in the southern part of Ukraine in Zaporozhian Sich, Cossacks formed a military-like political entity, a sort of a chiefdom run by military chieftains (hetmans).

The Cossacks initiated several uprisings mostly against the Commonwealth dominated by the Polish noblemen. The most memorable was the rebellion led by hetman Bohdan Khmelnytsky, whom historians see as the one who formulated the first concept of the Ukraine as a sovereign state. After 1654, the Cossack military chiefdom was limited in its political activities as an aftermath of the Pereiaslav Agreement, when most of Ukraine was incorporated into the Russian domain, but the final blow to its existence was the Empress Catherine II's Decree of 1775 that extended the Russian ruling over the traditionally free Cossacks lands. Even until the twenty-first century, the Cossacks are seen as the first attempt toward free Ukraine and bearers of Ukrainian national culture and identity. At the time of partition of the Polish kingdom at the end of the eighteenth century by Russia, Austria, and Prussia, the western part of Ukraine was occupied by Austria and the eastern part with Kiev by Russia. Regions under the Russian rules suffered the most as the Russian authorities officially banned the Ukrainian language. After the Russian Revolution of 1917, Eastern and Western Ukraine gained independence, and two separate Ukrainian states briefly existed before unification in 1919.

In 1922, a part of western Ukraine was incorporated to Poland, while the rest of the country became one of the republics of the Soviet Union. The Soviet rules over Ukraine were harsh. Despite a brief revival of Ukrainian culture in the 1920s, the destructive process of eliminating the Ukrainian symbols from culture continued throughout the 1920s and 1930s. The Soviets were also accused of causing a genocidal famine of 1933 when more than 7 million Ukrainians, mostly peasants who preserved the traditional Ukrainian culture, perished. In September 1939, the Polish part of Western Ukraine was taken over by the Soviet Union, when the Nazi Germany invaded Poland from the west and the Soviet Red Army from the east, initiating World War II. During 1941 through 1944, Ukraine was occupied by the Nazi Germany.

Some Ukrainian forces joined the Nazis, while others fought alongside the Red Army to liberate Europe. During the war, old ethnic conflicts erupted, especially in western Ukraine that witnessed ethnic cleansing of Poles, Ukrainians, and Jews. Polish, Ukrainian, and Soviet resistance forces also clashed. Many Ukrainians suffered the hardship of war, and many migrated to other countries, mostly Canada, the United States, and Western Europe. Is has been estimated that the Ukrainian population decreased by about seven million, including more than half a million Jews. After the war, Ukraine remained a part of the Soviet Union, and it gained independence again in 1991.

Ukraine is one of the most industrialized regions in Eastern Europe. The country was traditionally an agricultural state, but, beginning in the mid-1990s, it has turned into a more industrialized economy. The most common natural resources include iron ore, coal, manganese, natural gas, oil, salt, sulfur, graphite, titanium, magnesium, kaolin, nickel, mercury, timber, and arable land. Due to the lack of other significant resources, Ukraine depends on Russia for several critical resources like natural gas. Diversified heavy industry, including steel mills and coal mines, is concentrated in the eastern part of the country, whereas the western part is mostly agricultural. Key industries include those of coal, electric power, ferrous and nonferrous metals, machinery and transport equipment, chemicals, and food processing (especially sugar). Most significant agricultural products are grain, sugar beets, sunflower seeds, and vegetables; beef and milk are also products. Export commodities include ferrous and nonferrous metals, fuel and petroleum products, chemicals, machinery and transport equipment, and food products. Among export partners, the most significant are Russia 17.8%, Germany 5.9%, Italy 5.3%, and China 4.1%. The Ukrainian labor force is presently diversified. Most people work in services (44%), industry (32%), and agriculture (24%). Ukraine imports mostly energy, machinery and equipment, and chemicals. Among the key import partners are Russia 35.9%, Germany 9.4%, and Turkmenistan 7.2%. The Ukrainian currency is known as the hryvnia.

In general, Ukraine is characterized as a parliamentary republic with a president who nominates the prime minister who forms the government. Administrative structure of Ukraine includes twenty-four provinces, one autonomous republic (Crimea), and two municipalities (Sevastopol and Kiev). The new Ukrainian Constitution was adopted June 28, 1996. The Ukrainian political system includes the executive, the legislative, and the judicial branches of the political structure. The legislative branch is composed of a unicameral 450-seat Supreme Council elected for a four-year term. The judicial branch consists

of the Supreme Constitutional Court, and the executive branch of the government consists of the president elected by the popular vote for a five-year term. The head of the government is the prime minister appointed by the president and confirmed by the Supreme Council. The government is appointed by the president and approved by the Supreme Council. The president is a chief of state. In stormy presidential elections of November–December 2004, Victor Yushchenko defeated Viktor Yanukovych and replaced Leonid Kuchma as the president of Ukraine. The event was labeled by journalists as the "Orange Revolution" after the most popular color used by Yushchenko's followers in Ukraine and elsewhere. Hundreds of thousand of Ukrainians, mostly in Kiev and other big cities of western Ukraine, demonstrated against the outcome of the first round of presidential elections when Yanukovych was proclaimed the winner. They accused the authorities of falsifying the results of the election, and international observers confirmed that claim. Yushchenko's followers gathered in the Freedom Square in Kiev, and some of them stayed there for several weeks until the results of the repeated voting were made official, and Yushchenko was announced to be the next Ukrainian president. It is significant to notice that the conflict was solved peacefully although information about a planned *coup d'état* reached the public. Due to involvement of several European politicians in solving the Ukrainian internal conflict, the danger of bloodshed was diffused, and Yushchenko was sworn in as the president of Ukraine on January 26, 2005. He briefly outlined the key points of his politics, emphasizing that he would initiate talks with the European Union about Ukraine becoming its member in the future.

LUDOMIR LOZNY

See also Commonwealth of Independent States: History and Economic Development; Commonwealth of Independent States: International Relations; Ethnic Conflicts: Commonwealth of Independent States

References and Further Reading

Kuzio, Taras, and Andrew Wilson. *Ukraine: Perestroika to Independence*. 2nd ed. New York: St. Martin's Press, 2002.
Reid, Anna. *Borderline: A Journey through the History of Ukraine*. Boulder, CO: Westview Press, 1999.
Robert, Paul Magocsi. *A History of Ukraine*. University of Washington Press, 1996.
Subtelny, Orest. *Ukraine: A History*. 3rd ed. University of Toronto Press, 2000.
Vernadsky, George. *Kievan Russia*. Yale University Press, 1973.
Wilson, Andrew. *The Ukrainians: Unexpected Nation*. 2nd ed. Yale University Press, 2002.

ULMANIS, GUNTIS

Guntis Ulmanis, born September 13, 1939, in Riga, Latvia, spent his early years in extradition by the Soviet authorities with his family in Siberia. He graduated from the Department of Economy of the Riga Latvian University in 1965, and, after completing his service in the Soviet Army, he mingled teaching at the Riga Polytechnics and Riga University with administrative jobs. Later he became an employee of the Riga public utilities' company and rose through positions in the management to become its director. Being a *nomenklatura* position, he was invited to join the Communist Party. He remained member until 1989, when, with the height of the nationalistic movement, he became affiliated with the newly founded Latvian Popular Front.

In 1992, Ulmanis became member of the Board of the Central Bank of Latvia. He was named and soon elected honorary president of the traditional center-right party, the Latvian Farmers Union (*Latvijas Zemnieku Savienība*, LZS), founded in 1917 with his great-uncle Karlis Ulmanis as its leader. LZS scored fourth in the elections to the Saeima (Parliament) in June 1993, and G. Ulmanis became the Minister of Parliament (MP). On July 7, 1993, he was elected by the Saeima to the newly established position with limited jurisdiction, the president of the republic.

President Ulmanis was able to usher his country to an independent position and to secure essential preliminary requirements for a sustainable development. He urged for amending the controversial citizenship law, thus obtaining international approval for Latvia's citizenship policy, and opened doors for Latvian membership in the Council of Europe and European Union (EU). He imposed a cessation for the execution of death penalty beginning in 1996. Another important achievement was the agreement for the withdrawal of the Russian troops from Latvia, which was completed on August 31, 1994.

Thus, a man who would remain an ordinary citizen in other circumstances emerged as the needed national leader in a time of a great transformation for his nation. He was able to bring political foes together to form a government in late 1995 when it looked like the contention and libel would go on forever. Thanks to his intervention, a government coalition far surpassing expectations was finally tailored; he has been instrumental in the formation of other governments since then. On June 18, 1996, Ulmanis was reelected for a second term. Three years later, legally prohibited to seek a third term, Ulmanis was replaced on June 17, 1999, by the independent candidate Vaira Vike-Freiberga. Initially, Ulmanis returned to position of the LZS honorary president; however, on September 6,

2001, Ulmanis retired from the LZS, and later he supported the project of Einars Repse, president of the central bank, to found a new center-right party.

STEPHAN E. NIKOLOV

See also Glasnost and Perestroika; Gorbachev, Mikhail; Latvia; Soviet Bloc

References and Further Reading

Hansen, Birthe, and Bertel Heurlin. *The Baltic States and World Politics*. Surrey: Curzon Press, 1998.

Jubilis, Mark J. "The External Dimension of Democratization in Latvia: The Impact of European Institutions." In: *International Relations* 4 (1996).

Lieven, Anatol. *The Baltic Revolution: Estonia, Latvia, Lithuania and the Path to Independence*. New Haven, Conn.: Yale University Press, 1993.

Smith, Graham. *The Baltic States: The National Self-Determination of Estonia, Latvia, and Lithuania*. New York: St. Martin's Press, 1994.

UM NYOBE, REUBEN

Reuben Um Nyobe (1913–1958) was the first secretary general of Cameroon's *Union des Populations du Cameroun* (UPC). A member of the Bassa tribe, Um Nyobe was born in 1913 in the village of Boumnyebel. He attended the Teachers Training College in Sangmelima. On April 10, 1948, a group of Nationalists, led by Leonard Bouli, met in Douala to form a national liberation movement, which resulted in the founding of the UPC on April 14, 1948. Although Um Nyobe could not attend the meeting because he was hospitalized in Sackbayeme, within six months he had not only joined the movement but had also taken over leadership of the movement.

As the leader of the UPC, Um Nyobe's main goals were the liberation of Cameroon from European colonialism and the unification of the British and French Cameroon. After World War I, the League of Nations gave 80% of German Cameroon to France and 20% of German Cameroon to the United Kingdom. The British sector was subsequently divided into Northern and Southern Cameroon. Given the differences in colonial administration and language, the possibility of unifying the British and French sectors of Cameroon was a daunting proposal. Nevertheless, Um Nyobe argued that unification was essential to Cameroon's political and economic future. After independence, Um Nyobe envisioned a socialist economy and a complete break in political and economic ties with France.

In 1955, the UPC launched a war of national liberation in French Cameroon. Claiming that the UPC had engaged in terrorist activities and was dominated by Communists, the French authorities declared the UPC illegal. Um Nyobe and his supporters fled to the southern section of British Cameroon. Between 1955 and 1958, Um Nyobe frequently met with officials of the United Nations (UN) to discuss the impending independence of Cameroon. Um Nyobe, however, was killed by French forces on September 13, 1958, at Boumnyebel. He was succeeded as general-secretary of the UPC by Felix-Roland Moumie, who was killed by French security agents in Geneva, Switzerland, on October 15, 1960.

On January 1, 1960, French Cameroon became an independent republic. Since independence, contrary to the wishes of Um Nyobe, Cameroon has maintained close ties with France and pursued a Capitalist form of economic development. In 1961, the southern portion of the British colony joined the Federal Republic of Cameroon, while the northern portion of the British colony joined Nigeria. Significant portions of the population in the former southern sector of British Cameroon continue to argue that Um Nyobe's ideas of unification were misguided and that the southern sector of the former British colony should be an independent nation known as Ambazonia.

MICHAEL R. HALL

See also Cameroon; Nigeria

References and Further Reading

Ardener, Edwin, and Shirley Ardener. *Kingdom on Mount Cameroon: Studies in the History of the Cameroon Coast, 1500–1960*. New York: Berghan Books, 2003.

Mbaku, John Mukum, and Joseph Takougang. *The Leadership Challenge in Africa: Cameroon under Paul Biya*. Trenton, NJ: Africa World Press, 2003.

Njeuma, Martin. *Introduction to the History of Cameroon: Nineteenth and Twentieth Centuries*. Gordonville, VA: Palgrave Macmillan, 1990.

UNDERDEVELOPMENT

Origin and Evolution of the Concept of Underdevelopment

On January 20, 1949, Harry S. Truman, in his inaugural address as president of the United States, spoke of embarking on "a bold new program for the growth of 'underdeveloped areas.'" Two years later, the terms "underdevelopment" and "underdeveloped" were used for the first time in a United Nations (UN) report entitled *Measures for the Economic Development of Underdeveloped Countries,* with reference

to nonindustrial societies. Later, to avoid the charge of using a value-laden label, the term "underdeveloped" was replaced by "developing." But this change did not necessarily make the task of spelling out the meaning of the concept any less onerous.

Early in the 1950s, socioeconomic progress in nonindustrial societies was analyzed in terms of economic growth. The so-called underdeveloped countries were characterized, in the main, by a relatively low standard of living. The way out of this predicament was said to consist in a significant increase of the productivity of their economies. Growth was generally regarded as a quantitative process involving expansion of the existing system of production. It was believed that absence of economic growth could be assessed by, among other criteria, stagnation in the amount of goods and services produced and of trade as well as a stationary per capita national income.

Somewhat later, the concept of growth yielded place to "development." If growth was basically a quantitative concept, development was conceived in both quantitative and qualitative terms that included the generation of new structures and institutions. Although some die-hard economists continued to look at these largely in economic terms, it soon became clear that the process of development was also attended by certain noneconomic characteristics, and that, because development implied a total process, it was futile to attempt a separation between the economic and the noneconomic aspects of the phenomenon.

An early thinker to emphasize the inadequacy of the prevailing assumptions of classical economics was the Swedish economist, Gunnar Myrdal. Myrdal argued that one of the central concepts of classical liberal economics, "equilibrium," that is supposed to operate through the self-regulating mechanism of market forces actually presents a distorted picture of the underdeveloped countries. He also stressed the need to conceptualize development as a total process in which economic and noneconomic factors were closely intertwined. Myrdal's lead was followed by several others, among them Dudley Seers (1972) and those that were later instrumental in preparing the United Nations Development Program's (UNDP's) Human Development Index (HDI).

Causes of Underdevelopment

Causes of underdevelopment have been analyzed from a variety of perspectives, frequently related to contrasting theoretical orientations and ideologies. Preoccupied with the notion of evolution, some nineteenth-century thinkers explained uneven development

of various societies with reference to their progression from one stage to another. Such attempts often resulted in the construction of unilinear "grand theories," embracing the entire spectrum of human history and covering different societies of the world (theories of Auguste Comte, Lewis Henry Morgan, and Karl Marx and Friedrich Engels). Other scholars, less ambitious, focused on a central notion that is supposed to highlight the transition from one stage to another. For Henry Maine, this meant the substitution of "status," stressing the social bond, and by "contract," symbolizing the growing importance of individuality in a modern society. The German social scientist Ferdinand Tönnies expressed the process as a passage from *gemeinschaft* ("community") to *gesellschaft* ("association"), while the French sociologist Emile Durkheim offered a comparable idea by referring to "mechanical solidarity" in the traditional society yielding place to "organic solidarity" in the modern industrial world. Max Weber of Germany saw in the march of "rationality" the quintessence of the unfolding of civilization, traditional societies with sluggish development characterized by limited rationality.

Recent attempts to account for underdevelopment, stunted development, and distorted development have been more context specific and grounded in empirical data. In the 1950s and the early 1960s, some leading social scientists, such as S. N. Eisenstadt and Talcott Parsons, offered both a diagnosis of underdevelopment and a prescription for a course of action that would, they claimed, lead to development in general and industrialization in particular. This approach, labeled as the modernization model, suggests that prevailing social institutions accompanied by appropriate values and beliefs account for the backwardness of underdeveloped societies. It argues that the history of socioeconomic development of the West is not to be considered as something unique, but rather as the model to be emulated by non-Western societies (designated as "traditional") whose development is retarded or sluggish. The traditional-modern dichotomy did not find universal acceptance, even among Western social scientists. Some spoke of a "transitional" phase before full modernity is achieved, and others claimed that there are several stages of growth. W.W. Rostow identified five distinctive stages to "economic maturity," the final phase promising to be the age of mass consumption. The takeoff stage, the third step in the sequence, is the "great watershed" when growth becomes a "normal" circumstance. More than implicit in this model is the supposition that entrepreneurship and capital accumulation constitute the single most important factor in the development process. This is what emerges

as crucial from Western experience, and this is what needs to be replicated in the rest of the world for a successful passage from underdevelopment to development.

A contrasting approach takes note of the historical circumstances surrounding imperial expansion of the West, including the establishment of colonies. A leading example of this kind is the Marxist analysis of underdevelopment focusing on the international framework of power sustained by the world capitalist system. A corollary of this is the asymmetrical relationship between the industrial world of the West and developing countries of Africa, Asia, and Latin America. The seminal work expounding this perspective was produced by V. I. Lenin (1916), in which he defined imperialism as the monopoly stage of capitalism. Lenin argued that the export of capital from capitalist countries resulted in the annexation of colonies and the subjugation of their inhabitants. This state of affairs does not only cause underdevelopment in the dependencies, but it also leads to imperialist wars because of renewed demands for a redivision of the world in keeping with the uneven development of individual capitalist countries.

At the end of World War II, the international situation changed dramatically. Starting in the late 1940s, many dependencies in Asia and Africa gained formal independence. However, this did not necessarily alter the division of power worldwide, and it did not end the state of underdevelopment former colonies suffered from. Indeed, some observers, such as the first President of Ghana Kwame Nkrumah (1965), argued that in the changed circumstances, despite formal decolonization, many former dependencies have been subjected to a kind of socioeconomic domination from the outside that is not based on direct political control. Since such a state of affairs contributes to their persistent socioeconomic stagnation and dependence on the outside, neocolonialism, it was argued, has to be considered a prime cause of underdevelopment in the modern period.

The international framework involving the unequal relationship between capitalist countries of the West and the Third World was emphasized additionally by certain Marxist economists such as Paul Baran (1957). Baran conceived of underdevelopment as the undermining of the potential for development and argued that this was caused by the appropriation by capitalist countries of the economic surplus of the Third World. Similar in approach is the "dependency" model of capitalist underdevelopment that enjoyed a certain amount of currency in Latin America (such as those models of André Gunder Frank, F. H. Cardosa, and J. Petras) in the 1960s and the 1970s. According to this perspective, the draining of their resources and surplus to the "metropolitan centers" has caused the industrial backwardness of Third World countries that have, consequently, remained "satellites" on the "periphery of the metropolitan centers." The way out of this predicament is for the satellite countries to dislodge from their position of power the agents of the metropolitan bourgeoisie in their respective countries. According to the dependency theory, this can be achieved through joint action of the peasantry and industrial working class in a satellite as well as the establishment of a self-reliant socialist economy.

Like the dependency theory, the world systems theory, as expounded by Immanuel Wallerstein, also rejects the attempt to study underdeveloped countries in isolation from the international framework. According to this model, the lack of development of the Third World is to be seen as a by-product of capitalist development in the world at large. It holds further that there is a single-world capitalist mode of production with different manifestations of colonial and neocolonial dominance. An international division of labour buttresses this, without being necessarily sustained by a unified structure of power. Critics of the world systems theory point, however, to its implicit tendency to assign a passive role to the Third World—the periphery—and by implications to accept the dominant role of the center in the development process.

Disillusionment with the prevailing orthodoxies regarding the concept of underdevelopment and suggested paths to generate "real" development has given rise to what is sometimes called "alternative development." This phrase stands for a range of ideas that are not necessarily related but that generally agree on the need to reject the simplistic equation between development and the growth of capitalism driven by the thrust for mass production and urban growth.

A populist, and some would say utopian, movement of this nature, aimed at bringing "the capitalist demon" to heel, was spearheaded in the early nineteenth century by Robert Owen in Britain via the establishment of cooperative settlements. Critics argue that this attempt was bound to fail because it was unaccompanied by any effort to squeeze the life out of the demon—capitalism—with the Capitalist production relations remaining virtually the same in the society at large.

On the other hand, an ecological movement challenges the argument that absence or limited use of modern technology causes underdevelopment. It further rejects the conventional idea of development that lays emphasis on the cumulative process of mechanization, industrialization, and urbanization. Starting on a low key, the ecological protest against wanton

destruction of nature has now grown into a powerful movement, with substantial social and even political mobilization, leading to its participation in decision making at different levels in several countries. Side by side, the United Nations Environment Program (UNEP) and the World Resources Institute, supported by several other organizations, have been articulating this position internationally with some success.

A third stream in alternative development counters the idea that underdevelopment is causally related to the application of simple production techniques using local materials and producing for local consumption. This approach, summed up in the notion of "alternative technology," sets considerable store by social egalitarianism. It rejects in no uncertain terms imported high technology that only wealthy elites can afford and that tends in the long run to widen the gap between the rich and poor, thus contributing to the persistence of underdevelopment.

Measuring Underdevelopment

The active engagement of international agencies, such as the World Bank (since the late 1970s) and the UNDP (since 1990), in the lively debate surrounding development issues has added a comparative and global dimension to the field and contributed at the same time to the systematization of the methodology to study the phenomenon of underdevelopment. A spin-off of this dialogue is seen in the many experiments that have been carried out for designing various indicators to capture, singly or collectively, diverse dimensions of underdevelopment. In addition to the HDI, the UNDP itself has applied several other indexes such as the Gender Empowerment Measure, the Gender-Related Development Index, and the Human Poverty Index (HPI) to gauge aspects of social life that impinge on the development process as some of its causes as well as consequences. Additional indexes that have been suggested during the last two or three decades are the Corruption Perception Index (constructed by the Transparency International operating from Berlin), the Economic Freedom Index (constructed by the Fraser Institute of Vancouver), and the World Competitive Index (constructed by the Institute for Management Development of Switzerland).

A major problem with using a variety of indicators to subsume diverse factors that challenge the problem of underdevelopment relates to the task of combining them into a single composite index capturing the quintessence of development and the quality of life. Research by Adelman and Morris (1973) and Dudley

Seers (1972) and a collaborative study carried out by the United Nations Research Institute for Social Development (UNRISD) in Geneva (1969) were some of the early attempts in this field. The UNDP took a significant step in this direction with the construction of the HDI, composed of three indicators: life expectancy at birth, educational attainment, and the standard of living as measured by the gross national product (GNP) per capita. The HDI constitutes the main focus of a succession of annual human development reports being published by the UNDP starting in 1990.

Twenty-First Century State of Underdevelopment

At the beginning of the twenty-first century, all indications point to the markedly skewed nature of world development. The World Bank's *World Development Report 2002* estimated that in 2000 CE, 903 million people of world's population enjoyed a gross average income per capita of $27,450 US dollars (USD) measured in terms of purchasing power parity. These were concentrated overwhelmingly in eighteen countries of Western Europe, together with Australia, Canada, Japan, New Zealand, and the United States. This data can be contrasted with 5,152 million people, drawn almost entirely from Africa, Asia, the Caribbean islands, and Latin America, who belonged to the low and middle income categories, with an average gross per capita income of $3,890 USD, calculated according to purchasing power parity. The global inequality is also seen in measures that are broader in scope. According to the HDI figures of 1999 (UNDP *Human Development Report 2001*), forty-eight countries and areas enjoyed high human development in that year (HDI 0.800 and above). Only ten of them were in Asia and none in Africa. In the same year, thirty-six countries and areas had low human development (HDI below 0.500), of which twenty-nine were in Africa and six in Asia. Haiti was the only other country to be included in this group.

This situation may lead some people to a facile conclusion that underdevelopment is causally associated with race and culture. In the second half of the nineteenth century, such popular misconception was given an "academic" veneer by A. de Gobineau. Gobineau argued that the essential factor contributing to a society's development is the racial composition of its people. This view was introduced into Germany by H.S. Chamberlain toward the end of the nineteenth century. The doctrine was later incorporated in the ideological repertoire of the national socialism of

Germany. In the 1960s, the American psychologist Arthur Jensen, supported by some other academics, aimed to demonstrate a linkage between race and intelligence (leading, on its part, to achievement and development)—an attempt that generated an animated debate. However, no conclusive evidence has been found to prove that certain races are inferior to others in intelligence or cultural and developmental potential due to biological reasons.

Notwithstanding several decades of intensive and coordinated efforts to ensure greater equality worldwide and within countries, a certain degree of stubbornness seems to have characterized the uneven state of development that has been taking place. According to an early world development report of the World Bank of 1984, leaving out the five high-income oil-exporting countries (Kuwait, Libya, Oman, Saudi Arabia, and the United Arab Emirates), nineteen industrial market economies represented by fourteen countries of Western Europe plus Australia, Canada, Japan, New Zealand, and the United States constituted the richest category in 1982 with an average annual GNP per capita of $11,070 USD. In the same year, there were thirty-four low-income economies in the world including China and India with an average annual GNP per capita of only $280 USD. About two decades later in 2001, all the nineteen high-income countries of 1982 were still in the top bracket, while thirty-two of the developing countries of 1982 remained, as before, in the low-income category, although with some changes in their income levels.

Yet things have not proved to be entirely static. According to the *World Development Report 2000/ 2001*, compared to 1984, the ranks of the high-income group increased, in 1999, to fifty. Granted, some of these economies belong to small territories and dependencies of various sorts for which separate statistical reports are available. It is furthermore true that several new states emerged in the intervening period (such as Slovakia and Slovenia), and because of their high income they are included in the top category. But all this cannot obscure the fact that several countries, which were not very prosperous before, rose to the top income bracket between 1984 and 2001. These include the Bahamas, Barbados, Brunei, Cyprus, Greece, Hong Kong, Israel, Portugal, Singapore, Taiwan, and the United Arab Emirates. Some other countries like the Republic of Korea (South Korea) and People's Republic of China, although not forming part of the high-income group, have made significant strides toward fuller development, both in terms of GNP per capita and the HDI.

A consideration of the points delineated in the previous paragraphs suggests that development is better regarded as a process rather than a specific goal to be targeted. This view is further upheld when taking note of the fact that in a *very general sense*, all countries are underdeveloped because no country can claim to be fully developed at any time. The flexibility of the concept, reflected in its sidedness, appropriately underscores the need to capture its essence through different indicators—to which references have been made previously. There are attempts to take the debate to a deeper level and focus on *human* development: its progress, stagnation, or decline. The *2001 Human Development Report*, thus, sums it up:

> Human development is about much more than the rise or fall of national incomes. It is about creating an environment in which people can develop their full potential . . . . Development is thus about expanding the choices people have to lead lives that they value.

In like manner, it can be said that underdevelopment exists when people's choices are constricted.

ANSU DATTA

See also Basic Human Needs; Development History and Theory; Development, Measures of; International Bank for Reconstruction and Development (IBRD) (World Bank); Modernization; Neocolonialism; Nkrumah, Kwame; United Nations Conference on Trade and Development (UNCTAD); United Nations Development Program (UNDP); United Nations Industrial Development Organization (UNIDO)

References and Further Reading

Adelman, I., and C. T. Morris. *Economic Growth and Social Equity in Developing Countries*. Stanford, CA: Stanford University Press, 1973.

Bagchi, Amiya Kumar. *The Political Economy of Underdevelopment*. Cambridge: Cambridge University Press, 1992.

Bernstein, Henry, ed. *Underdevelopment and Development: The Third World Today—Selected Readings*. Harmondsworth: Penguin, 1973.

Frank, A. G. "Sociology of Development and Underdevelopment of Sociology." *Latin America: Underdevelopment or Revolution*, A.G. Frank, ed. New York: Monthly Review Press, 1969.

Kay, Geoffrey. *Development and Underdevelopment: A Marxist Analysis*. Basingstoke: Macmillan, 1975.

Lenin, V. I. *Imperialism—The Highest Stage of Capitalism*. 1916.

Nkrumah, Kwame. *Neo-colonialism: The Last Stage of Imperialism*. London: Nelson, 1965.

Paul Baran. *The Political Economy of Growth*. United States: Monthly Review, 1957.

Seers, Dudley. "What We are Trying to Measure?" *The Journal of development Studies* 8, no. 3 (1972).

United Nations Development Program (UNDP). *Human Development Report 2001*. New Delhi: Oxford University Press, 2001.

United Nations Research Institute for Social Development, Statistics Unit. *Compilation of Development Indicators*. New York: Author, 1969.

UNITED ARAB EMIRATES (UAE)

The United Arab Emirates (UAE) is a small oil-rich country located on the Arabian Peninsula. Within a generation of its formation in 1971, the UAE has transformed from a nomadic tribal structure to one of the most economically developed and technologically advanced societies in the world. Inevitably, this development has been uneven in some areas, and issues in governance, gender equity, and labour rights are among those areas requiring further consideration.

Political Background

The UAE is composed of seven emirates that act together as a single state. The emirates are Abu Dhabi, Dubai, Sharjah, Fujeirah, Ras al-Kheimah, Ajman, and Umm al-Qawein. The capital city is Abu Dhabi although the largest city is Dubai, which also houses most of the commercial and technological centres of the country. Sharjah hosts the bulk of the small manufacturing and processing industries, while the remaining four northern emirates are considered comparatively poor and underdeveloped. Abu Dhabi was selected as the capital at the formation of the country in 1971, when Sheikh Zayed, the emir of Abu Dhabi, was elected as the ruler and remained the ruler until his death at the end of 2004.

The UAE has achieved considerable levels of wealth owing to the presence of oil and hydrocarbons in its territory. Some 60% of total revenue in Abu Dhabi derives from this source, and another significant portion is accounted for by investment mostly related to the industry. Both sources of revenue are volatile and depend on the international political situation and on the perception of locating future reserves. Most of this resource is located in Abu Dhabi and is managed by the Abu Dhabi National Oil Company (ADNOC). Abu Dhabi provides large subsidies to the others. Approximately 40% of all revenues are recycled through the Abu Dhabi Investment Authority (ADIA), which has made investment decisions internationally on a massive scale. It is believed that the ADIA works on the basis that all known oil and gas reserves will be exhausted within approximately 120 years and that returns on investments made will have enabled long before then a continued level of income to all UAE nationals. In other words, as long as the world economy continues within predictable limits, there will be no economic need for any UAE citizen to have to work.

Nevertheless, some within the UAE, especially from Dubai, are seeking to position themselves as leaders of the Arab world economically and culturally. This has manifested in the creation of the Internet and media city office complexes as well as the creation of new airlines and television networks to provide sophisticated and high-technology media content.

The political system is autocratic and lacks transparency. There are neither political parties nor trade union organisations, and political dissidence is not encouraged. The country is strongly linked with the Islamic faith, and although Shariah law is not officially in force, religious beliefs inform many legal practices and decisions, including the nature of marriage and divorce, children's rights, and free speech rights. UAE citizens receive significant personal subsidies in terms of low cost or free telephone services and electricity as well as freedom from other regulations. This has led to abuses in the case of some businesses. No personal income tax is collected on any earnings inside the country. The large personal incomes of many private individuals and religious injunctions to give to charity mean that institutions exist to care for underprivileged individuals in some categories. Charitable giving as also been linked to money laundering in some cases and some high profile—though not openly discussed—incidences of fraud have cast some doubt about the suitability of the business environment for investment.

History

The emirates have historically been small, open trading ports occupying a position of trade routes frequented by Arabs, Persians, and Indians, among others. In a territory with very few natural resources or comparative advantages, most people continued to live nomadic lives, trading with coastal towns and developing complex intertribal relationships. Islamicization occurred very early (by 1000 AD), and the area remained something of a backwater under Arab and subsequently Ottoman rulers. During the period of European expansion, trading posts were created along the coast, and British ships presented a tempting target for the dominant Al Qawasim tribe, but this attracted a fierce response from the British, who enforced treaties that brought the UAE under its effective control, established as the Trucial States. Leadership of the tribes passed to the Bani Yas tribe thatwas based inland at Al Ain and remained there under the rule of Sheikh Zayed.

Independence was finally achieved in 1971 following the withdrawal of British presence from the region. In negotiations, Qatar and Kuwait decided on independence, as did Ras Al Kheimah although it joined

the confederation a few months later. Subsequently, the UAE has remained a strong ally of the West, recognizing the importance of providing a stable oil supply to ensure the development of its own people and acting as a moderate voice in Arab councils concerning Israeli-Palestine relations and other areas of potential conflict. At the time of independence, citizenship was awarded to all people who lived within the borders of the new country, and, henceforth, all discussions of previous ethnicity were strongly discouraged. Many women have been imported to the UAE as wives (as the men are allowed to take four wives according to Islamic tradition) from a range of other Islamic countries, including Egypt and northern Africa. However, statistics relating to these issues are not available, and development is hampered to some extent by the lack of accurate census data. The presence of hydrocarbons has led to rapid economic development, and the main cities of the country are now advanced in technology and services and offer excellent infrastructure. However, smaller villages and traditional tribal areas continue to provide a challenge for the provision of services owing to the difficulties and expense of building in the climate and the terrain. Questions have also been raised about the sustainability of development and the efficiency of resource allocation.

Geography and Climate

The emirates are located along the Persian Gulf and the Gulf of Oman, in the eastern part of the Arabian Peninsula. Saudi Arabia is to the west of the UAE, with Kuwait and Qatar along the coast to the north and Oman to the south. The climate is uniformly hot and dry (although humid) throughout the year. Rainfall is limited to a few days per year. Daily temperatures average 104°F (40°C), making agriculture challenging; dates represent the only agricultural product in any form of abundance. Most forms of meat, vegetables, and fruit are imported from India, Iran, or further afield. However, the sea provides fish and seafood for supplementary protein.

Inland, the traditional centre of Al Ain is based on an oasis, and some agricultural production is possible there. Former UAE president Sheikh Zayed articulated his vision of "greening the desert," and resources are being devoted on a large scale to developing the physical infrastructure. The brightly lit Abu Dhabi-Dubai and Abu Dhabi-Al Ain highways are among the few human-made artifacts now visible from space.

International Relations

The UAE has sought a multilateral course that satisfies the religious sensibilities of its people together with the need for security that its alliances with Western countries represent. Sheikh Zayed himself took the lead in promoting the idea of Islamic and Arabic unity through careful negotiation and the judicious use of financial inducement. Egypt was returned to the fold of Arab states in 1982, while solidarity in the Gulf States through the Gulf Cooperation Council (GCC) helped to prevent further turmoil in the wake of the Iraqi invasion of Kuwait and the subsequent US-led war to overthrow Saddam Hussein. The long-term occupation by Iran of three disputed islands, Greater and Lesser Tumb and Abu Musa, has been contained by similar tactics although the issue has not been resolved.

The UAE has been a willing partner in the fight against money laundering and the spread of terrorism. However, a general lack of transparency in both the government and the private sector has tended to militate against complete success in these areas. Abu Dhabi joined Organization of Petroleum Exporting Countries (OPEC) in 1967 and has played an important although unspectacular part in the cartel subsequently by being the only major player to retain significant excess capacity.

Industry and Economy

The economy of the UAE remains dominated by the extraction of oil and liquid natural gas. Much of the extraction is managed by foreign firms in partnership with the UAE government, and the product is sold in large-scale, long-term contracts to promote economic stability. Foreign firms benefiting from the industry are generally required to offset profits by investing in other sectors of the UAE economy with a view of diversification. In addition, certain strategic business sectors have been identified as being important because of diversification and possible creation of comparative advantage. Taking advantage of free trade zones and subsidized production as well as some manufacturing and assembly work takes place in textiles and consumer goods; however, these industries are fundamentally unsustainable because of a lack of international competitiveness. Capital intensive industries such as banking and financial services offer more sustainable economic development possibilities.

Health Care

Health care facilities rapidly improved during the last decades of the twentieth century, and capital-intensive importing of medical staff and technology has significantly improved life expectancy. This has helped to boost the population of permanent residents as the number of young people continues to increase.

In the population as a whole, the prevalence of men of working age in the country has had an impact on health priorities, while workplace accidents continue to be significant risks. Smoking is a widespread practice, while cultural factors have raised concerns about reproductive health issues, especially among women.

Labour Market and Population

The majority of the population in the UAE is composed of temporary migrant workers. Approximately 60% to 70% of the population comes from South Asia, the Middle East, and Europe, with representatives from most countries of the world. Since most migrants are male, there is a significant gender imbalance in the country. Owing to the strongly conservative Islamic culture of most UAE citizens, women remain at home or otherwise away from public scrutiny, and so public spaces in the country are dominated by men. Many of the expatriate workers are overqualified for the work they do and suffer from low job security and inability to express entrepreneurial skills.

Women's fertility remains high with an average of more than six births per woman. This is possible with the generous support provided to mothers. Nevertheless, UAE women face a number of social issues in entering the labour market and rarely stray from the public sector, where salaries and benefits are very generous for UAE women, and provisions for maternity leave and for sequestered working space are deemed appropriate by most families.

The education system has increased in scope and capacity through the opening of several new universities, including the female-only Zayed University, which has significantly improved the education of women. Large numbers of young men continue to be sent overseas for their higher education. Even so, the Colleges of Higher Education network has helped to inculcate vocational and practical skills in young people of both genders. Literacy levels, however, remain at a comparatively low rate, and few women are able to exercise their education and skills outside of the home. Men, meanwhile, also face significant

disincentives to work and study, and many corporations registered as being under local control are in fact managed by expatriate workers.

JOHN WALSH

See also Islam; Middle East: History and Economic Development; Middle East: International Relations

References and Further Reading

International Monetary Fund (IMF). March, 2003. *United Arab Emirates: Selected Issues and Statistical Appendix, IMF Country Report 03/67*: http://www.imf.org/external/pubs/ft/scr/2003/cr0367.pdf Kechichan, Jospeh A., ed. *A Century in Thirty Years: Shaykh Zayed and the United Arab Emirates*. Middle East Policy Council, 2000.

Salloum, Habeeb. "Women in the United Arab Emirates." *Contemporary Review* no. 283 (August 2003): 101–104.

Walsh, John. "The Competitiveness of the UAE Economy." *Proceedings of the Fifth Annual Conference at College of Business and Economics—UAE University* 4, (March 24–25, 2002): 974–1014.

Zahlan, Rosemarie Said. *The Making of the Modern Gulf States: Kuwait, Bahrain, Qatar, the United Arab Emirates and Oman*. London; Boston: Unwin Hyman, 1989.

UNITED ARAB REPUBLIC (UAR)

The United Arab Republic (UAR) was a union of Egypt and Syria that lasted from 1958 to 1961. Proclaimed in the aftermath of the 1956 Suez war, it underlined the soaring popularity of Egyptian leader Gamal Abdel Nasser in the Arab world; its dissolution marked the collapse of the Nationalist dream of the Arab union.

Syria was under enormous external and internal pressures by 1958. The competition between Nasser, the charismatic Arab Nationalist leader, and the Western powers and their conservative Arab allies was roiling the Middle East. Syria's 1955 arms purchase from Czechoslovakia and subsequent dealings with the Soviet bloc led the United States to fear it was going Communist, while Syria feared the United States was plotting to overthrow its government. Western efforts to form an anti-Soviet defensive pact in the region set in motion the events leading to the 1956 British, French, and Israeli effort to seize the Suez Canal from Egypt; the reversal of this aggression established Nasser as the undisputed champion of Arab Nationalist interests. Nasser's popularity in Syria skyrocketed when Egypt landed troops there in October 1957 to protect it against possible Western aggression. Internally, intense competition between the Ba'ath and Communist parties, which were outbidding one another with ever more fervent calls for Arab union, coupled with a fractious military threatened the foundations of political order.

On January 12, 1958, senior Syrian army officers abruptly flew to Cairo to beg Nasser to save Syria from collapse, and they were closely followed by the Syrian cabinet carrying the same message. Nasser had pushed the idea of Arab unity as opposed to a union, and he was reluctant to agree to an immediate merger. But given Syria's precarious situation and Nasser's desire to maintain his position in the Arab world, Nasser believed he had little choice. Nasser imposed major conditions on the union: he demanded a free hand, a highly centralized state, the dissolution of political parties, and the withdrawal of the army from politics. With virtually no planning or preparation, the United Arab Republic was proclaimed on February 1, 1958.

Frightened by the merger of the two leading Arab Nationalist states, the Hashemite monarchies in Jordan and Iraq quickly proclaimed their own union. But a military *coup d'état* led by Arab Nationalist officer Abdel Karim Qasim overthrew the Iraqi monarchy in July 1958. This precipitated US and British military interventions in Lebanon and Jordan, respectively, to shore up those countries' pro-Western governments. Qasim, though, was not a Nasserite, and with the cooperation of the Communists, he suppressed a bloody revolt by UAR-backed Arab Nationalist and Ba'athist army officers in March 1959. Nasser's rivalry with Qasim pushed Egypt closer to its former foes in Jordan, Saudi Arabia, and the United States. When Qasim laid claim to Kuwait in June 1960, Nasser endorsed the British military intervention to uphold Kuwaiti sovereignty. Nasser's moves to reconcile with the conservative monarchies and the Western powers at the expense of an Arab Nationalist regime in Baghdad caused many in Syria to rethink the union with Egypt.

Domestic factors also undercut Syrian support for the UAR. First, most of the Syrian players had miscalculated and came to repent their precipitous decision for union. The Communists had not been serious about the union, but they had advocated this position to undercut the Ba'ath. Unable to win control of the state through the ballot box, the Ba'ath saw the union as a way to gain power and eliminate its rivals. Despite the ban on political parties, the Ba'ath believed it would play a major role in the UAR as Nasser's ideological guiding force. Both parties thought the union would free them of military interference in politics, while the military thought the union would allow it to rule without the meddling of politicians. Nasser sidelined them all.

The Ba'ath in particular felt betrayed. The party dissolved itself to secure its goal of Arab union, yet the UAR did not fulfill its expectations or expand its ideological influence. Nasser did not turn to the party for guidance, and it did poorly in the July 1959 Syrian elections. The possibility of further gains for the Arab union seemed out of reach given Nasser's opposition to the regime in Iraq; worse still, Nasser was siding with reactionary forces against Baghdad. In protest against Nasser's removal of a Ba'athist minister in September, the other Ba'athists resigned from the cabinet in December 1959. This earned the Ba'ath Nasser's enmity.

Ordinary Syrians chafed under the UAR as their country became "Egyptianized." Egyptian officials were sent to rule Syria, bringing with them the opaque, red tape complexities of Egyptian bureaucracy. Egyptians dominated the Syrian Cabinet, and decisions were made in Cairo without input from Damascus. The Egyptian-controlled intelligence and security services were ruthless. Syria had had an active, almost hyperkinetic, political society prior to union, but it now found itself cut off from effective participation and unable to voice its discontents. Bitter at its subordination to the Egyptians, the army began to plot against the UAR.

On September 28, 1961, the Syrian army proclaimed a national uprising, packed Nasser's men on a plane to Cairo, and seceded from the UAR. Nasser angrily responded that he had not wanted the union to begin but had been forced into it by Syrian popular will. He refused to recognize the new Syrian regime and began to wage a fierce propaganda battle against it. The heated exchanges between Cairo and Damascus nearly brought about the collapse of the Arab League.

In early 1963, the Ba'athists seized control in both Syria and Iraq and clamored for union with Egypt. Nasser was not about to be dragged into another ill-conceived union project, and he used the Cairo talks that spring to humiliate and punish the Ba'athists, especially the Syrians. When the Syrian Ba'athists brutally suppressed a pro-Nasserite *coup* attempt in July, the war of words was renewed between Damascus and Cairo. Pro-Nasserite elements did succeed in ending the Iraqi Ba'ath's bloody rule in November, sparking an all-out propaganda battle between Ba'athist Syria and Iraq's new Arab Nationalist leaders. Far from uniting the Arab world, the United Arab Republic and its aftermath bitterly divided it.

BETH K. DOUGHERTY

See also Arab Nationalism; Ba'ath Party; Baghdad Pact; Central Treaty Organization (CENTO); Nasser, Gamal Abdel

References and Further Reading

Jankowski, James. *Nasser's Egypt, Arab Nationalism, and the United Arab Republic.* Boulder, CO: Lynne Rienner, 2002.

Kerr, Malcolm. *The Arab Cold War 1958–1967: A Study of Ideology in Politics.* New York: Oxford University Press, 1967.

Podeh, Elie. *The Decline of Arab Unity: The Rise and Fall of the United Arab Republic.* Brighton, UK: Sussex Academic Press, 1999.

Seale, Patrick. *The Struggle for Syria.* New Haven, CT: Yale University Press, 1987.

UNITED MALAYS NATIONAL ORGANIZATION (UMNO)

Sixty years after the formation of The United Malays National Organization (UMNO), the organization's main objective of protecting the Malays' interests has not changed. The UMNO, founded in May 1946, has adopted a number of economic policies, including the creation of a Malayan business class. Malayan businesspeople, virtually all of whom had UMNO connections, were given preference in obtaining licenses, credit, and government contracts.

UMNO has been the strongest Malayan political party since its foundation. Its leaders place it preeminently in the history of Malayan nationalism and independence. Historically, the leaders of UMNO were more concerned with safeguarding the rights of Malays (the ethnic group that makes up the majority of the Malaysian society) vis-à-vis the other races of Malaya. UMNO was more likely to collaborate with the British authorities in opposition to radicalism within their own community. Thus, the formation of UMNO was a remarkable event, as it was the first time a Malayan movement emerged to attack British policy. The Malayan union is usually regarded as the colonial challenge that provoked the emergence of a united Malayan Nationalist movement.

UMNO was founded as a communal party concerned exclusively with the protection of Malays' interests. It was by no means a radical Nationalist party. Many of its leaders were employed as civil servants. Only in the 1950s did UMNO begin to campaign for independence from British rule.

UMNO's policies reflected the interests of its leaders, who were largely drawn from the Malayan upper and middle classes. Most of its early leaders were civil servants, often from aristocratic or semiaristocratic family backgrounds. In later years, aristocratic leaders were less prominent than a new class of educated Malays, often from fairly humble backgrounds, who were produced by postindependence education policies. Grassroots leaders were often local officials, teachers in Malayan schools, and rural landowners.

In the late 1970s, as a result of the New Economic Policy (NEP), Malayan businesspeople became more prominent as business opportunities were channeled to party supporters. UMNO came to represent mainly conservative groups that had little interest in social reform for the peasants, small landholders, and fishermen, who made up a large part of the Malayan population.

NILLY KAMAL EL-AMIR

See also Malaysia

References and Further Reading

Abu Bakr, Mohamad. "Islam, Civil Society, and Ethnic Relations in Malaysia." *Islam and Civil Society in Southeast Asia*, Nakamura Mitsuo, Sharon Siddiqueand Omar Bajumd, eds. Singapore: Institute of Southeast Asian Studies, 1998.

Baginda, Abdul Razak. *Malaysia in Transition: Politics and Society.* London: ASEAN Academic Press, 2003.

Crouch, Harold. *Government and Society in Malaysia.* Australia: Talisman, 1996.

Stockwell, A. J. "The Formation and First Years of the United Malays National Organization (UMNO)." *Modern Asian Studies* 11, no. 4 (1977).

UNITED NATIONS CENTER FOR HUMAN SETTLEMENTS (UNCHS)

The United Nations Center for Human Settlements (UNCHS) is the United Nations (UN) agency responsible for sustainable urban development. UNCHS is more commonly known as UN-HABITAT and was created in 1978 after a UN-sponsored meeting, known as Habitat I, held in Vancouver, Canada. Its ultimate goal is to promote socially and environmentally sustainable towns and cities that provide adequate shelter for all people, especially in the developing world. UN-HABITAT is headquartered in Nairobi, Kenya, with regional offices in Fukuoka, Japan and Rio de Janeiro, Brazil. The agency has a full-time staff of two hundred people and an annual budget of $300 million. UN-HABITAT works with governments, nongovernmental organizations (NGOs), and civic action groups in an attempt to reduce urban poverty and promote sustainable development.

When the agency was founded, less than one-third of the world's people lived in urban settlements. During the last quarter of the twentieth century, however, there was a rapid urbanization process throughout the globe, especially in the developing world. During that period, UN-HABITAT was in the forefront of the global movement to prevent and alleviate the problems caused by rapid urbanization, especially in Third World cities. By the end of the twentieth century, half of the world's people lived in urban areas. In 1996, the UN sponsored a second conference, known as Habitat II, in Istanbul, Turkey, to evaluate the

progress of UN-HABITAT and formulate the agency's agenda for the twenty-first century. The result of the conference, known as the Habitat Agenda, was an extensive list of one hundred commitments and six hundred recommendations signed by representatives from 171 nations.

Given the desperate situation of the world's urban poor, especially in the developing world, UN-HABITAT is committed to improving the lives of 100 million slum dwellers by 2020. Although UN-HABITAT's efforts are to be commended, 100 million slum dwellers only represent 10% of the current global slum population, which is increasing by 25 million people each year. Demographers predict that more than two-thirds of the world's population will live in urban areas by 2050. Thus, as cities and towns grow at alarming rates, sustainable urbanization planning by agencies such as UN-HABITAT is essential to ameliorate disease, crime, pollution, and poverty. Slum dwellers have little or no access to shelter, water, and sanitation. To prevent growing social unrest, UN-HABITAT initiates projects that seek to provide slum dwellers with access to safe water and sanitation, safe shelter, and social inclusion, while simultaneously protecting the environment.

UN-HABITAT supports two major global campaigns: the Global Campaign on Urban Governance and the Global Campaign for Secure Tenure. For example, UN-HABITAT participates in a joint UN-HABITAT/World Bank slum upgrading program, known as the Cities Alliance, which promotes effective housing development policies; helps campaign for housing rights; promotes sustainable cities and urban environmental planning and management; and addresses postconflict land management and reconstruction in nations devastated by war or natural disasters. The Safer Cities Program helps fight urban crime, while other programs address solid waste management, urban planning training for local leaders, and urban investment. As of 2005, UN-HABITAT was operating over 150 technical programs in 61 nations, most of which are among the least developed nations of the world. UN-HABITAT currently has projects in postwar societies such as Afghanistan, Somalia, Iraq, Rwanda, and the Democratic Republic of the Congo (the nation formerly known as Zaire). Essential to revitalizing urban areas in these war-torn countries is providing shelter for all, improving urban governance, and reducing urban poverty within the framework of self-reliant and self-sustainable management.

One of UN-HABITAT's most significant programs is the Sustainable Cities Program. A sustainable city, according to UN-HABITAT guidelines, is a city where achievements in economic, physical, and social development are made to last. Sustainable cities have access to natural resources and use them wisely. In addition, sustainable city planners develop strategies to minimize the effect of potentially devastating environmental hazards. For example, development on land prone to flooding should be avoided. Since cites are centers of economic productivity, the success of the Sustainable Cities Program is essential to economic and social development at the national level. Following the economic development strategies first devised by Albert Hirschman, the Sustainable Cities Program devises urban development strategies based on a case-by-case approach. Since all cities, especially in the Third World, have vastly different environmental settings and administration development, a single holistic policy of urban development is not applicable to the Sustainable Cities Program.

The Sustainable Cities Program currently has projects in Accra, Ghana; Amman, Jordan; Asuncion, Paraguay; Concepción, Chile; Dar es Salaam, Tanzania; Dakar, Senegal; Freetown, Sierra Leone; Gaza, Palestine; Guayaquil, Ecuador; Ibadan, Nigeria; Ismailia, Egypt; Katowice, Poland; Lusaka, Zambia; Madras, India; Maputo, Mozambique; Nampula, Mozambique; Shenyang, People's Republic of China; St. Petersburg, Russia; Tunis, Tunisia; and Wuhan, People's Republic of China. Other cities, such as Belo Horizonte, Brazil; Blantyre, Mallawi; Colombo, Sri Lanka; Harare, Zimbabwe; Jinja, Uganda; and Kampala, Uganda, have petitioned for participation in the Sustainable Cities Program. Given the success of the Sustainable Cities Program in Concepción, Ismailia, Ibadan, and Dar es Salaam, secondary cities in Chile, Egypt, Nigeria, and Tanzania, have begun the process of applying to the program.

MICHAEL R. HALL

See also Poverty: Impact on Development; Urbanization: Impact on Development; Urbanization: Impact on Environment

References and Further Reading

Hill, Dilys M. *The Planning and Management of Human Settlements with Special Emphasis on Participation: Report Submitted to Habitat, the United Nations Conference on Human Settlements.* Barcelona: International Union of Local Authorities, 1975.
Keane, Mary T. *Nichols Village to the Global Village: An Interface of the Principles of the United Nations Conference.* Fairfield, CT: Fairfield University, 1978.
Miller, Norman N. *Habitat: The New United Nations Initiative in Human Settlements.* Washington, DC: American Universities Field Staff, 1981.
Moser, Caroline O. N. *Housing Policy and Women: Towards a Gender Aware Approach.* London: University College of London, 1985.

Weiss, Thomas G., David P. Forsythe, and Roger A. Coate. *United Nations and Changing World Politics.* Boulder, CO: Westview Press, 2004.

UNITED NATIONS CHILDREN'S FUND (UNICEF)

The United Nations Children's Fund (UNICEF) is one of the oldest humanitarian assistance agencies formed under the aegis of the United Nations (UN). The UN General Assembly Resolution that gave life to UNICEF was approved on December 11, 1946, in the very first session of the world body. The initially temporary nature of UNICEF was in keeping with the belief that the crisis prevailing at the close of World War II in the numbers of displaced persons, refugees, and war-ravaged populations that disproportionately affected children would eventually abate. Although UNICEF has continued throughout its history to provide emergency assistance for children, eventually it took on activities to promote long-term development assistance for children, and in the decades since its inception, UNICEF has evolved into one of the major international development agencies.

Genesis and Early Years

UNICEF was established in a climate of crisis and concern about the highly vulnerable status of children among the thirty million persons displaced by World War II. The international community had become increasingly aware of the needs of children even as early as the League of Nations, which promoted efforts to eradicate the trafficking of women and children. In 1924, the league adopted the Geneva Declaration that asserted the rights of children. While the League of Nations, and the UN as its successor, believed as most people do now that the protection and nurturing of children properly and primarily rests with the family, circumstances arise, as they did during World War II and its immediate aftermath, that place overwhelming stress on both families and governments to meet the basic needs of children. Increasingly, the international community has acknowledged its duty to offer assistance for the primary institutions of the family so that children are not subjected to unnecessary hardship. Given the large numbers of war-affected refugees after World War II, the displacement of families and the tens of thousands of children who were orphaned, steps by the international community to alleviate the situation were essential. During World War II, the UN Relief and Rehabilitation Administration (UNRAA) addressed the emergency needs of displaced persons in Europe. However, this body ceased to exist in 1946 in Europe and in 1947 in Africa as well as in the Far East, so its assets were inherited by several other UN bodies, including UNICEF.

Given the overwhelming emergency needs of children in the postwar setting, UNICEF provided blankets, food aid, and medicine for children. However, as the emergency situation abated, UNICEF, although still providing material aid, initiated programs designed to provide technical assistance to governments in promotion of child welfare, including the fields of health and nutrition. Thus, although UNICEF, like so many other emergency assistance bodies established after the war by the UN, was initially seen as a temporary and *ad hoc* response to emergency needs, it began to carve out for itself a more permanent position in the constellation of UN development bodies. It assumed the lead role in advocacy for the social welfare needs of children, and in 1953, the name of the organization was changed from the UN International Children's Emergency Fund to the UN Children's Fund although the acronym UNICEF continued to be used. As the UN grew in size with the addition of new member states, mostly from the developing world, UNICEF and other specialized agencies of the UN found themselves shifting attention to the daunting needs of poorer nations.

Structure and Authority

UNICEF is a specialized agency of the UN and reports to the Economic and Social Council (ECOSOC). ECOSOC chooses the thirty-six members of the Executive Board of UNICEF. Board members serve three-year terms. The board oversees the operations of UNICEF and monitors its budgets and programs. In turn, UNICEF is administered by the director of the UNICEF Secretariat. The director administers the budget and operational programs from UNICEF headquarters in New York. UNICEF maintains a Supply Division in Copenhagen, Denmark, where critical supplies, such as measles vaccines, are stored. It also runs a Research Center in Florence, Italy, and maintains regional offices in Geneva, Brussels, Panama City, Bangkok, Nairobi, Amman, Katmandu, and Dakar.

UNICEF is funded entirely by voluntary contributions, two-thirds of which come from governments. The other one-third of the budget is raised from millions of private individuals. Much of this private fund-raising is promoted by thirty-eight National

Committees for UNICEF, which are private nongovernmental bodies established in various countries to support the work of UNICEF. Popular and well-known fundraising efforts include the UNICEF "trick-or-treat" program in which children themselves become diplomats and fundraisers for UNICEF at Halloween time. A portion of UNICEF expenses is met by the sale of holiday cards, which from its earliest years served as a means of both publicizing its work internationally and earning some independent revenue. Measured in terms of its annual budget and expenditures, UNICEF is one of the largest UN assistance agencies. Its work is undertaken in 126 country offices, with programs that reach 157 nations.

Development Activities

Starting in the 1960s, when many former colonies gained their independence and began to join the UN, UNICEF's move into development assistance activities accelerated. Many of these new UN members required not only multilateral aid to meet various needs associated with children but also the technical support to develop national infrastructures and programs. UNICEF, in efforts to prevent childhood diseases and high mortality rates, supplemented its emergency aid and oral rehydration programs with support for the development of potable water supplies and sanitation in areas where waterborne diseases, including diarrhea, were major causes of death for children. UNICEF also sponsored programs for primary health care, especially for pregnant and lactating mothers, childhood immunization programs, and various initiatives to promote basic education and literacy among children. In the 1980s, the appearance of acquired immunodeficiency syndrome (AIDS) among children prompted UNICEF to participate in international efforts to curb the spread of the epidemic. In pursuing its work in areas with high percentages of childhood human immunodeficiency virus (HIV) infection, UNICEF collaborates extensively with other UN development bodies, including the UN Development Program (UNDP) and the World Health Organization (WHO).

Although an increasingly large portion of UNICEF's budget is set aside for development-related programs, UNICEF still responds to disasters and emergencies throughout the developing world, and it collaborates extensively with the UN High Commissioner for Refugees and the World Food Program. UNICEF is a member of the UN's Inter-Agency Standing Committee, whichhelps to coordinate international responses to complex emergencies through the UN Office for the Coordination of Humanitarian Affairs. Much of this emergency aid focuses on provision of clean water, on children's health, and on nutrition.

In more recent decades, UNICEF, as part of its work to implement the UN Convention on the Rights of the Child, has been active in promoting international attention issues affecting children. In 1990, UNICEF was instrumental in the UN World Summit for Children, at which 159 countries produced a World Declaration and Program of Action on the Survival, Protection, and Development of Children. Governments established goals and objectives to reduce rates of infant mortality, maternal mortality, and malnutrition as well as to expand access to safe drinking water, to improve sanitation, and to provide universal basic education. More recently, UNICEF was a major actor in the Special Session on Children of the UN General Assembly, held in May 2002. The program of action emerging from the special session emphasized the theme of creating a "World Fit for Children." The terrible conditions in which many families and children find themselves, especially in war-torn regions, continue to challenge UNICEF and the entire international community. The general development and economic prosperity of families represent the key to the health and vitality of children, and so even in the most difficult emergency situations where the primary task is immediately to save lives, UNICEF and like-minded international agencies and governmental bodies work to maintain a long-term vision that builds to a peaceful society and sustainable economy.

UNICEF's work in highlighting the rights of children, including the most basic rights of good nutrition, health, and education, necessarily has a development focus. Many international agencies, including UNICEF, have undertaken initiatives to promote civil society, especially in those countries most seriously affected by civil strife. For this goal, UNICEF and international agencies must work with and respect the rights of primary institutions, including families and local governments, which are the institutions most directly engaged in and responsible for the promotion of stability and the welfare of children. To promote education and broader awareness of the needs of families and children, UNICEF undertakes an ambitious publications program, which includes the annual *State of the World's Children Report* that provides comprehensive analyses of the conditions facing children in every country throughout the world. UNICEF promotes the full implementation of the UN Convention on the Rights of the Child, which won swift and nearly universal adoption by the nations of the world in the early 1990s.

Conclusion

A sample of UNICEF's recent activities finds its representatives working to involve the international community in the humanitarian crisis in Darfur, Sudan, where ethnic cleansing of local populations has produced hundreds of thousands of refugees and displaced persons. In India, UNICEF programs help locally affected families in Assam to cope with floods that compromised water and sanitation systems and increased the incidence of waterborne diseases. While oral rehydration salts distributed by UNICEF save lives, the agency also restores safe water supplies and sanitation. In Madagascar, UNICEF launched a program for vaccination of ten million children to forestall a potential epidemic in August, 2004. In Iraq, UNICEF worked to provide safe water supplies, while encouraging the massive countrywide return of children to schools, many of which had long served as ammunition warehouses. Carol Bellamy, UNICEF's executive director, in the same month traveled to Liberia, where civil war caused about fifteen thousand children to be conscripted into rebel armies or otherwise separated from their families. UNICEF promoted the reintegration of such child soldiers with their families.

UNICEF sponsors a similar program in Afghanistan, where child soldiers were also common. In the Democratic Republic of the Congo, which has been torn by civil conflict since 1995, UNICEF sponsors a program for children subjected to rape and physical and mental abuse. Elsewhere, UNICEF sponsors programs on AIDS awareness. Much of UNICEF's work still focuses on emergency needs, but other programs, such as those focusing on the availability of water, sanitation, child nutrition, and education, are essential building blocks for the establishment of the foundation of economic and social development.

ROBERT F. GORMAN

See also United Nations Development Program (UNDP); United Nations Economic and Social Council; United Nations High Commissioner for Refugees (UNHCR); World Food Program; World Health Organization (WHO)

References and Further Reading

Black, Maggie. *Children First: The Story of UNICEF, Past and Present*. New York: Oxford University Press, 1996.

Gorman, Robert F. *Great Debates at the United Nations: An Encyclopedia of Fifty Key Issues, 1945–2000* Westport, CT: Greenwood, 2001.

Kent, Randolf. *Anatomy of Disaster Relief: The International Network in Action* London: Pinter Publisheres, 1987.

LeBlanc, Laurence J. *The Convention of the Rights of the Child: United Nations Lawmaking on Human Rights*. Lincoln, NE: University of Nebraska Press, 1995.

Machel, Graça. *The Impact of War on Children: A Review of Progress since the 1966 United Nations Report on the Impact of Armed Conflict on Children*. Hampshire, England: Houndmills, 2001.

Spiegelman, Judith. *We Are the Children: A Celebration of UNICEF's First Forty Years*. New York: Atlantic Monthly Press, 1981.

UNICEF. *State of the World's Children Report. Annual UN Yearbooks, 1946–latest*. New York: UNICEF.

UNITED NATIONS COMMISSION ON CRIME PREVENTION AND CRIMINAL JUSTICE (CCPCJ)

The United Nations Commission on Crime Prevention and Criminal Justice (CCPCJ) is the major body of the United Nations (UN) providing policy guidance in the field of crime prevention and criminal justice. It was established in 1992 by the UN Economic and Social Council (ECOSOC), but international efforts to harmonize criminal justice policy date back to the nineteenth century, when representatives of various European nations met periodically to exchange information and to consider common standards in the treatment of offenders. The CCPCJ consists of forty members elected by ECOSOC on the basis of the principle of equitable geographical distribution, which is described as follows: African States (12), Asian States (9), Latin American and Caribbean States (8), Western European and other States (7), Eastern European States (4).

The CCPCJ's priority themes include organized crime; economic crime, including money laundering; the role of criminal law in the protection of the environment; crime prevention in urban areas, including juvenile and violent criminality; and improving the efficiency and fairness of criminal justice administration systems. Aspects of those themes are selected for consideration at each session of the commission, which meets yearly at its headquarters in Vienna, Austria.

In the broadest sense, the mandate of the CCPCJ covers the management and development of international cooperation in crime prevention and standards of criminal justice. More specifically, it assists the UN in setting policy, monitors progress at the international level, and develops international instruments (agreements) in the area of crime prevention and criminal justice while overseeing the implementation of those already in existence. It also works to improve the management of national justice systems in the interest of efficacy and the humane treatment of offenders, and it coordinates UN technical assistance

to member states, including assistance in formulating or revising laws to bring domestic legislation in line with international standards. Because of overlapping interests, the CCPCJ coordinates its activities with those of the Commission on Narcotic Drugs and the Centre for International Crime Prevention of the Office of Drug Control and Crime Prevention of the UN Secretariat.

The CCPCJ provides policy guidance to member states in the field of crime prevention and criminal justice. It develops, monitors, and reviews the implementation of the UN Crime Prevention Programme. The commission facilitates and helps to coordinate the activities of the interregional and regional institutes on the prevention of crime and the treatment of offenders as well as mobilize the support of member states.

The Centre for International Crime Prevention (CICP) has the role of implementing the decisions of the UN CCPCJ. The UN, through its crime prevention and criminal justice programme, is endeavouring to promote cooperation between its member states in combatting an accelerating crime problems and to bring about common standards of criminal justice in the interests of facilitating adherence and follow-up to international agreements; the UN also ensures the respect for human rights that is necessary for sustainable human development.

CLÉMENTINE OLIVIER

References and Further Reading

Clark, Roger S. *The United Nations Crime Prevention and Criminal Justice Program Formulation of Standards and Efforts at Their Implementation*. Philadelphia: University of Pennsylvania Press, 1994.

United Nations. *The United Nations and Crime Prevention*. New York: Author, 1991.

———. *Basic Facts About the United Nations*. New York: United Nations Department of Public Information, 1995.

UNITED NATIONS CONFERENCE ON TRADE AND DEVELOPMENT (UNCTAD)

The impact of trade on development is one of the issues that has occupied the attention of countries and multilateral bodies ever since the Great Depression and increasingly so in the aftermath of World War II. The United Nations Conference on Trade and Development (UNCTAD) was formed in 1964 as a UN-specialized agency through which the trade and development interests of countries in the developing world could be voiced more effectively.

A consensus existed after World War II that the individual economies of nations and the international economy generally would benefit from a policy of free trade; in addition, the rapid and reciprocal reduction in tariffs and other barriers to trade would be a great economic boon in terms of eliminating artificial barriers to trade, increasing competition, lowering prices on goods, increasing production, and stimulating economic growth. To this end, the General Agreement on Tariffs and Trade (GATT) was instituted in 1947 as a means by which countries could negotiate free trade agreements. However, as many new and poorly developed countries gained their independence, and as the implications of the GATT system of reciprocal reductions in trade barriers on developing country economies became clearer, developing countries began to call for special consideration to be given to the structural difficulties their economies faced in the GATT system. UNCTAD became the forum in which the countries' calls for reform of the GATT system were articulated.

Developing Countries: Terms of Trade Dilemmas

While the GATT system of reciprocal trade reductions promoted an expansion of global trade, the impact of the system on newly independent countries of the developing world was not always positive in light of the terms of trade problem. Industrialized countries benefited from the system owing to the fact that manufactured goods generally held or increased their value on world markets, but developing countries that depended largely on commodity exports often saw commodity prices decline over the long term, relative to manufacturing goods. This led to a net transfer of income in trade from the developing world to the developed world. Moreover, developing countries were in no position to develop nascent industrial sectors because these could not possibly compete with the better established enterprises in the industrialized nations. As long as a reciprocal tariff reduction system along GATT lines persisted, developing countries seemed consigned to a status of permanent dependence with agriculturally or commodity based economies.

The UN was aware of this problem as early as 1954, when the Economic and Social Council (ECOSOC) established a Commission on International Commodity Trade to study the problem of commodity fluctuations. In 1962, this commission reported that a long-term trend of commodity price declines was

well established. In response, ECOSOC called for the convening of a conference on trade and development. After the UN General Assembly's approval and preparatory meetings, UNCTAD met from March to June 1964 in Geneva, Switzerland. One of the chief and controversial recommendations of the UNCTAD meetings concerned the granting of preferential trade rights to developing countries. Under a preferential trade rights system, a country relying on commodities as exports could enjoy low tariff access to developed country economies while imposing tariffs on manufactured goods imported from those countries. This would permit them to protect infant industries from foreign competition and would also give them a fighting chance to establish a manufacturing sector for their domestic economies. The UN General Assembly approved the establishment of UNCTAD as a specialized agency, and like GATT, it continued to meet every four years to discuss the important nexus of trade to development, under the influence of the large majority of developing countries. This majority is known as the Geneva 77, named after the seventy-seven developing countries that attended the original UNCTAD meeting. Although the members' number grew substantially in subsequent years, the term "Geneva 77" continues to be used to describe this influential bloc of developing countries.

Trade Reforms and Controversies

Owing in part to the persistent demands of UNCTAD and the growing number of developing countries that enjoyed majorities in UNCTAD and the UN generally, wealthier countries began revising GATT regulations concerning reciprocal tariff reductions, and eventually a preferential trade rights system was adopted to redress the adverse terms of the trade situation facing developing countries. Known as the General System of Preferences, this system was eventually adopted by the European Economic Community and by the United States in their trade agreements with developing nations.

The Geneva 77 continued to press, both in the UNCTAD forum and in the UN system at large, for other major reforms. UNCTAD became the vehicle through which developing countries pushed for a new international economic order, not only in trade but in regard to such issues as setting minimum transfers of foreign assistance, transferring technology, restructuring the international monetary system, and promoting debt reduction and cancellation. These debates were often quite shrill and controversial and produced little agreement or progress, as important

developed countries refused to accommodate to the wide range of proposed reforms.

Further Developments

With the failure to gain much ground from confrontation, many developing countries began to explore domestic economic reforms rather than attempting to leverage resources through international negotiation. The collapse of the Communist systems in the early 1990s added pressure to the international assistance networks even as the collapse removed some of the ideological heat from international development dialogue. The rapid globalization of international trade was given further impetus in 1995 with the establishment of the World Trade Organization (WTO), which replaced GATT. In the following year, the UN called upon UNCTAD to undertake a thorough review of its role in light of the new global trade system. It has focused much of its work on identifying problems facing the most heavily indebted poor countries.

ROBERT F. GORMAN

See also General Agreement on Tariffs and Trade (GATT); United Nations Economic and Social Council; World Trade Organization (WTO)

References and Further Reading

Hoekman, Bernard, and Michael Kostecki. *The Political Economy of the World Trading System: From GATT to WTO.* Oxford: Oxford University Press, 1995.

Weiss, Thomas G. *Multilateral Development Diplomacy in UNCTAD: The Lessons of Group Negotiations, 1964–1984.* London: Macmillan, 1986.

Williams, Marc. *Third World Cooperation: The Group of 77 in UNCTAD.* New York: St. Martin's, 1991.

UNITED NATIONS DEVELOPMENT PROGRAM (UNDP)

The United Nations Development Program (UNDP) was established by the United Nations (UN) General Assembly in 1965 in the wake of intensified international discussions about how best to address the poverty faced by many newly independent countries that had recently gained membership in the UN. In the constellation of UN agencies, UNDP's role is to offer technical assistance to governments and to coordinate—especially at the country level—the variety of national, bilateral, and multilateral initiatives and programs addressing development. Its function, then, is less operational than consultative and coordinative in nature.

The Genesis of UNDP

Under the League of Nations, a number of technical organizations were established to deal with economic, financial, health, communication, and transportation issues. The league also cooperated with other international organizations, such as the International Institute of Commerce and the International Labor Organization, concerned with national and international development activities. The increasing need for economic and technical cooperation among nations became apparent even before World War II. After the war ended and reconstruction efforts began, governments realized a more pressing need to address international development questions more explicitly at the international level. Thus, the International Bank for Reconstruction and Development (World Bank, IBRD) and the International Monetary Fund (IMF) were created to assist in postwar recovery, and the UN Food and Agriculture Organization (FAO) was initiated to enhance international cooperation in the development of agriculture. The United Nations found itself addressing development-related questions in its own right, even as other specialized agencies, such as the UN Educational, Scientific, and Cultural Organization (UNESCO), the World Health Organization (WHO), and the General Agreement on Tariffs and Trade (GATT) were established to address various components of the international trade and development process. In the late 1940s and early 1950s, the UN itself was directly involved in the creation of various assistance agencies, such as UNICEF, the International Refugee Organization (IRO), the UN Relief and Works Agency for Palestine, and the UN High Commissioner for Refugees, which replaced the IRO.

In 1950, at the initiative of the United States, the UN General Assembly established the Expanded Program of Technical Assistance (EPTA) to supplement and expand the work of the growing number of agencies focused on development. The EPTA funds were accumulated on a strictly voluntary basis, with the United States underwriting as much as 60% of the revenue in the early years. Initially, the EPTA resources stood at about $20 million, but as other countries joined the efforts, the pool of resources reached about $50 million in the early 1960s, and the US government portion of contributions dropped to about 40%. With new revenues to administer, a Technical Assistance Administration was established within the UN Secretariat, and a Technical Assistance Board of member states was established to oversee the process. During the late 1950s and early 1960s, additional international development organizations were established, including the International Finance Corporation (IFC), the International Development Association (IDA), and the World Food Program (WFP). During this period, a sense of greater urgency arose regarding development issues. In 1957, after spirited debate among the developed and developing member states, the Special UN Fund for Economic Development (SUNFED) was established. Its pool of resources was less substantial than poorer countries had hoped for, but it soon attracted considerable voluntary support, substantially more than the EPTA, which continued to operate as a separate, though related, source of development programming technical assistance.

UN membership grew by thirty nations in the first half of the 1960s, and all of them were developing countries that voiced the need for more extensive UN assistance to further their economic development. The need for a single UN agency to coordinate technical assistance became apparent, and the first proposal to establish the UNDP was brought forward in 1962. After three years of study, the UN General Assembly established UNDP and its governing body, composed of roughly equal numbers of developed and developing states. The EPTA and SUNFED programs continued to operate but under UNDP oversight. The initial UNDP budget was $145 million. In subsequent decades, the UNDP budget rose substantially, hitting the $1 billion mark in 1989 and rising even higher in subsequent years. What had begun as a modest experiment in the coordination of technical assistance and development programming blossomed into a substantial and integrated approach in development planning and coordination.

Structure and Authority

The UNDP is governed by a thirty-six member executive board of member states. This body meets three times a year to oversee the budget, programs, and operations of the UNDP Secretariat. The secretariat is led by the administrator, who manages the organization's technical assistance activities in 166 countries. The majority of executive board members represent African, Asian, Pacific Rim, Latin American, and Caribbean nations, with sixteen seats occupied by Eastern European, Western European, and other economically developed countries. The UNDP administrator is the third highest ranking official in the UN system. The administrator is appointed by the UN secretary-general and approved by the UN General Assembly and serves a four-year term. The administrator in turn reports to the executive board.

UNDP works with developing countries to provide technical expertise to assist in their economic development. This process is furthered through the national offices of UNDP resident representatives, who serve as the coordinating authority for all UN assistance in particular countries and as the UN contact point for the host government's development-related ministries. UNDP coordinates the in-country development planning process. This puts UNDP squarely at the center of development planning within the UN system and as the principal actor in consultation with governments. The governments themselves determine program needs and priorities, and UNDP assists in facilitating them and promoting coordination of international and local assistance initiatives and activities.

UNDP Programming Efforts

Given the wide range of activities that fall under the rubric of economic development, UNDP serves as a centralized reservoir of consultative resources to assist governments in promotion of agricultural development, environmental quality, conservation and reforestation, crisis management, disaster prevention, emergency aid, poverty reduction, development of transportation and communication infrastructure, energy supply, health policy, job creation and diversification, financial stability, extension services, protection of human rights, promotion of the role of women in development, promotion of democratic governance, modernization of information systems, and promotion of business enterprise. Various UN agencies that specialize in these areas of international cooperation in turn work with UNDP to coordinate funding and other development-related efforts. In recent years, UNDP has reached out to the wide variety of nongovernmental organizations (NGOs) and multinational corporations that supply an additional reservoir of expertise and resources to direct these resources in support of a country's own development priorities and planning.

The UNDP began approaching development programming as a long-term and regional process in the early 1970s with the emergence of zonal development strategies. Problems and needs were identified and strategies for addressing them mapped out over periods of five and ten years. Even where emergency problems, droughts, or refugee flows interrupted plans, these were to be addressed through attention of the impact of emergency assistance on longer-term development. UNDP involvement in the African drought and refugee crises of the 1980s was critical in the formulation of refugee-related development assistance

programs. At this time, UNDP also began to explore more aggressively the need to interact with NGOs and businesses as partners with national governments in the development programming enterprise.

With the holding of the UN Millennium Summit in 2000, the UNDP has been actively involved in the follow-up program in pursuit of the Millennium Development Goals, which include promoting democratic governance, reducing poverty rates by half by the year 2015, coping more successfully with natural disasters and civil conflicts via early warning systems and conflict resolution mechanisms, enhancing energy resources without degradation of the environment, and managing the impact of HIV/AIDS in developing countries. The UNDP supports national efforts in all of these areas in its current programming.

Promoting democratic governance, for instance, is an important aspect of political development and of stable civic institutions. Cambodia, a country that recently suffered from bloody civil wars, is now embarking on an unprecedented effort at judicial reform by training Cambodian lawyers and judges in democratic principles of justice and in international humanitarian law. The UNDP supports these seminars and programs as a part of its larger effort to promote political stability as a precursor to economic development. To help countries in their efforts to reduce poverty, UNDP works with governments to incorporate Millennium 2000 goals into their national development strategies. UNDP also works to promote the education and empowerment of women as productive agents of development through gender equality programs in a number of countries; for example, in Kyrgyzstan, the UNDP cosponsors gender-related seminars at the university level. In support of the Millennium Development Goal of promoting crisis prevention and recovery, UNDP has supported land mine removal programs in various countries such as Angola, where agricultural activities are inhibited by the danger of mine-littered farms and fields. UNDP is engaged in a study with the International Peace Research Institute to study the impact of mines on development and how best to integrate de-mining programs into national development planning processes. Similarly, UNDP has supported efforts to reintegrate ex-combatants in the Democratic Republic of the Congo, which has been plagued by deadly civil war. Reintegration kits give ex-soldiers an incentive to reintegrate into productive civil life, thus enhancing national recovery efforts. UNDP engages in similar programs in the Ivory Coast (Cote d'Ivoire) and in Liberia, where it is also engaged with the World Bank and the IMF in promoting economic reconstruction.

In promoting Millennium Development Goals in the areas of energy and the environment, the UNDP

emphasizes programs for water usage and conservation measures (especially in the area of combating desertification) to encourage incorporation of environmental awareness into national energy and development planning and conservation of biodiversity. An example of UNDP efforts in a variety of these areas is its Drylands Development Center, which combines research and action programs in nearly twenty countries in Africa, the Arab States, and West Asia. Similarly, UNDP is a cosponsor of the UNAIDS program, which seeks to prevent the spread of AIDS in developing countries through galvanizing governmental agencies at all levels in promoting AIDS awareness and prevention.

Conclusion

UNDP is one of the major actors in the UN system for promotion of economic development, one of the chief goals of the UN Charter. Because of its mandate to coordinate UN specialized agency activities with member governments, it is the most central actor among all the agencies. While the work of the UNDP does not involve the huge outlays of resources characteristic of World Bank activities or bilateral assistance programs of governments, it is nonetheless essential in terms of providing key consultative support and in coordinating the overall development strategy of countries as they seek greater economic stability and prosperity.

ROBERT F. GORMAN

See also United Nations Food and Agricultural Organization (FAO); General Agreement on Tariffs and Trade (GATT); International Bank for Reconstruction and Development (IBRD) (World Bank); International Development Association (IDA); International Monetary Fund (IMF); World Food Program; World Health Organization (WHO)

References and Further Reading

Bennett, A. LeRoy, and James K. Oliver *International Organization: Principles and Issues*. Upper Saddle River, NJ: Prentice-Hall, 2002.

Bird, Graham. *International Financial Policy and Economic Development*. London: Macmillan, 1987.

Gorman, Robert F. *Great Debates at the United Nations: An Encyclopedia of Fifty Key Issues, 1945–2000*. Westport, CT: Greenwood Press, 2001.

Mendez, Ruben P. "United Nations Development Programme." United Nations Studies at Yale; Bruce Russett, Director. www.yale.edu/unsy/UNDPhist.htm

Stoesz, David, Charles Guzzetta, and Mark Lusk. *International Development* New York: Allyn and Bacon, 1998.

UNDP. *Human Development Report 2004: Cultural Liberty in Today's Diverse World*. New York: Author, 2004.
———. *Choices: The Human Development Magazine*. http://www.undp.org/dpa/choices/.

Weiss, Thomas G. *Multilateral Development Diplomacy in UNCTAD: The Lessons of Group Negotiations, 1964–1984*. London: Macmillan, 1986.

UNITED NATIONS ECONOMIC AND SOCIAL COMMISSION FOR ASIA AND THE PACIFIC (ESCAP)

Following World War II, the United Nations (UN) initiated a program to address the specific needs of postwar reconstruction in Europe and Asia. Two regional commissions were established, namely, the Economic Commission for Europe (ECE, established in 1947) and the Economic Commission for Asia and the Far East (ECAFE, established in 1947). ECAFE became the Economic and Social Commission for Asia and the Pacific (ESCAP) in 1974 and, along with the ECE, was joined by the Economic Commission for Africa (1958), the Economic Commission for Latin America and the Caribbean (1948), and the Economic and Social Commission for Western Asia (1974).

Overview of the Commissions

The commissions are regarded as an integral part of the decentralisation of the UN's economic and social development activity, which is a major portion of the UN's work. Each commission has determined its own pattern of organization, with separate committees for areas of particular concern in their region, but they all operate under the auspices of the UN Economic and Social Council (ECOSOC) to which they report annually. The commissions work with other UN agencies, such as the Food and Agricultural Organization (FAO) and the UN Development Program (UNDP), and with other regional organizations, such as the Organization of African Unity (OAU) and the Organization of American States (OAS).

The commissions have had differing degrees of success. According to Bennet (1988), ECLAC has contributed to the establishment of the Latin American Free Trade Association, the Central American Common Market, and the Inter-American Bank. On the other hand, ECA, while involved in the establishment of the African Development Bank, has not been as effective in the region because it has been hampered by internal dissent among member states.

An evaluation of ESCAP reveals both progress and the challenges facing multilateral agencies. It has been involved in major regional projects, such as the Mekong River Development, and in the establishment of institutions, such as the Asian Development Bank. But it has also been criticised as being ineffectual, bureaucratic, and overly centralised and criticised for covering the work of already existing agencies.

History and Functions of ESCAP

ESCAP has fifty-three members (2004), primarily UN member states within the Asia Pacific but including European countries, such as the United Kingdom and France, with interests in the region. There are also nine associate members, such as the island states of Guam, New Caledonia, and Hong Kong (SAR), that are states within the region but are nonmembers of the UN. ESCAP's region of activity stretches from West and Central Asia through South Asia, Southeast Asia, and North and East Asia and also includes economic giants such as Japan and China as well as the small island states of the Pacific such as Fiji. This diversity in itself has presented challenges to the viable functioning of ESCAP because these countries represent vastly different needs and agendas for development.

Based in Bangkok, ESCAP's purpose is to serve as the UN's main economic and social development forum within the Asia Pacific by formulating and coordinating relevant projects, initiating and facilitating technical cooperation, and strengthening economic relations and cooperation within and between the region and countries outside it. In practical terms, these aims are primarily carried out in the conferences and specialist seminars organized by the ESCAP secretariat and in data collection and publications, such as economic and social surveys of the Asia Pacific that fall within its terms of reference. ESCAP can also provide advisory services to governments if requested.

ESCAP is designed to formulate and promote activities and projects in line with the needs and priorities of the region. These needs are determined by the commission, the main legislative body of ESCAP that meets every year at ministerial level to set policy within UN guidelines and resources. Ministerial meetings can also be held on an *ad hoc* basis to address specific issues under the auspices of ESCAP's program committees. The commission is intended as a forum for member states to discuss economic and social issues in the region and to enhance opportunities for cooperation. Liaising between the commission and the secretariat is the Advisory Committee of Permanent Representatives (ACPR) and other representatives designated by members of the commission; they meet every month with the executive secretary to provide advice and input into the commission's work. The ACPR is composed of ESCAP members and associates.

The ESCAP Secretariat, a branch of the UN Secretariat, includes the Office of the Executive Secretary and a series of divisional subcommittees. It coordinates all the activities of ESCAP, prepares for the commission and other meetings, conducts research, and implements and provides coordination for programs in the region. The secretariat and its subcommittees organize and document ESCAP conferences and workshops held throughout the Asia Pacific each year. The secretariat is also responsible for coordinating ESCAP activities with other intergovernmental organizations and UN agencies and departments.

A series of committees and subcommittees guide the commission's work and make recommendations in accordance with program areas. Three thematic committees focus on poverty reduction, globalisation management, and emerging social issues. Each committee has its own objectives and terms of reference and is designed to act as a regional forum for members and associates to promote cooperation, review research and trends, examine best practice development models, evaluate program implementation and effectiveness, and disseminate information on these more specific issues. The focus on poverty reduction ties in with wider UN goals documented in the Millennium Declaration (2000). There are eight subcommittees under the ambit of their relevant thematic committees, with areas of interest corresponding to the subprograms of ESCAP. These subprograms indicate the current priority areas of the commission and include social development (including emerging social issues); environment and sustainable development; information, communication, and space technology; poverty and development; statistics; trade and investment; and transport and tourism. Administrative services and program management committees provide logistical and administrative support. There are also two Special Bodies that focus on the particular issues facing least developed and landlocked countries, such as Laos, and Pacific island developing countries.

One of ESCAP's principle activities is the organization of conferences, forums, and training workshops and the provision of opportunities for technical cooperation. In 2004, more than two hundred various regional meetings, training workshops, and conferences were held. For example, ESCAP convened a meeting of e-commerce law experts from the region to discuss assistance to the governments of less developed

countries in planning their legal and regulatory systems for e-commerce. ESCAP also assists intergovernmental liaison and interdevelopmental consultations prior to international conferences. The commission encourages governments to contribute to the provision of these services.

Some of the challenges ESCAP faces can be discerned from the overview of its functions and structure just described. An early critique was that the organization was overly centralised in Bangkok and neglected the Pacific region. This was addressed by establishing a Pacific Operations Centre in Vanuatu in 1984. There are also an additional four regional institutions: the Asian and Pacific Centre for Transfer of Technology (in India); the Regional Coordination Centre for Research and Development of Coarse Grains, Pulses, Roots, and Tuber Crops in the Humid Tropics (in Indonesia); the Statistical Institute for Asia and the Pacific (in Japan); and the Centre for Agricultural Engineering and Machinery in China.

The multilateral nature of the organization presents challenges to its effectiveness that are familiar to similar bodies; most notably, one of the challenges involves the dependence on cooperation and support of member states that may at times have conflicting agendas. Differences over goals and resources have led to tentative relationships with governments in the region. According to Alley (1998), ESCAP has had to limit its involvement in intergovernmental cooperation, avoiding more contentious matters such as public/private sector links, the harmonisation of trade and nontariff barriers, resource issues (such as water and waste management), and the removal of nontariff barriers. A common issue has been the disagreement over the wording of documents. Attempts to establish regional sustainability plans have met with reluctance on the part of members to fund activity.

Other critics have claimed ESCAP has failed to present empirical indicators to support development goals in the region. This, it could be argued, is an unfair assertion given ESCAP's major focus on research and analysis. It is perhaps the most convenient, least controversial space of operations given the constraints of dealing with diverse member states. Maintaining this level of cooperation with member states can, however, also encourage the development of an aversion to risk taking. The major tool that ESCAP has is persuasion, but as Bennet (1988) has suggested, persuasion is a relatively weak technique for driving cooperation and coordinating states concerned with protecting their sovereignty and the autonomy of their own programs and projects.

ESCAP's lack of authority and diverse channels of operation makes coordination difficult, but this was compounded by a burgeoning of other UN agencies in the region. The commission itself has been critical of this sectoral rather than coordinated approach to regional development, particularly when UN agencies have established their own regional networks and multiplied their offices (Taylor 2000). Avoiding a bureaucratic culture and the duplication of work have become complex issues. Policies such as joint meetings, joint divisions of UN agencies and the commission, and posting of agency staff in commission offices have been implemented. These have been useful steps but not always fully effective according to Taylor (2000), and it can be a costly policy in terms of staff and budgets.

With limited resources and influence, dependent on the cooperation of governments and other agencies, it could be argued that ESCAP has not played a central role in economic and social development in the Asia Pacific. It does not develop economic policy as such, leaving this to bodies such as the International Monetary Fund (IMF) and the Asian Development Bank. There has been a lack of implementation of its own plans, such as the Manila Declaration of 1994 that declared the eradication of poverty by 2010 from the ESCAP region, targeting in particular health care, elderly and education sectors, employment expansion, social integration, and the decline of gender, ethnic, and cultural discrimination.

However, while resisting some measures, ESCAP members have, according to Alley (1998), managed to coordinate joint positions to meet moderate reform objectives, particularly relating to social goals. The secretariat has produced major reports and surveys on the social and economic states of the region, organized wide-ranging conferences and workshops to disseminate information and skills, and in some areas has established working relations with other agencies, such as with the UNEP with regard to environment programs.

An evaluation of ESCAP and its programs began in the 1990s, culminating in an organizational review in 2000 that identified major issues that needed to be addressed in the organization's future role; the review also addressed comparative advantage, budgetary concerns, external image, governance, management culture, human resources and program management, and administrative blockages (*ESCAP Towards 2020* 2004). Several strategies and recommendations were made, including the grouping of programs under the three themes already noted; a shift in focus from microinitiatives to larger, interdisciplinary projects; the continued support for decentralisation with plans for further regional institutions; and a new structure for conferences aligned with the program themes. There were also initiatives to restructure the secretariat in 2003, reorienting the organization toward

"performance" and "results-based" management. Changes in priorities, policies, and structure have been designed to translate into the future effectiveness of ESCAP's programs and activities.

MELISSA BUTCHER

See also Asian Development Bank; United Nations Development Program (UNDP); United Nations Economic and Social Council; United Nations Economic Commission for Latin America and the Caribbean (ECLAC)

References and Further Reading

Alley, R. *The United Nations in South East Asia and the South Pacific.* United Kingdom: Macmillan Press, 1998.

Bennet, A. L. *International Organisations: Principles and Issues.* 4th ed. United States: Prentice Hall, 1988.

ESCAP Towards 2020. New York: The United Nations, 2004.

Krasno, J. E. *The United Nations: Confronting the Challenges of a Global Society.* United Kingdom/Colorado: Lynne Rienner Publishers, 2004.

Taylor, P. "Managing the Economic and Social Activities of the United Nations System: Developing the Role of ECOSOC." *The United Nations at the Millennium: The Principle Organs,* P. Taylor and A. J. R. Groan, eds. London/New York: Continuum, 2000.

United Nations Economic and Social Commission for Asia and the Pacific. 2005. Home Page. www.unescap.org.

UNITED NATIONS ECONOMIC AND SOCIAL COUNCIL (ECOSOC)

One of the six major organs of the United Nations (UN), the Economic and Social Council (ECOSOC) was established with the negotiation of the UN Charter in San Francisco in 1945. The League of Nations prepared the way for the emergence of ECOSOC through the wide range of technical committees that dealt with economic, social, and health concerns. Even before ECOSOC's demise, an evaluation of league activities identified the need for a more effective coordination of these areas of functional cooperation between governments. Thus, under pressure from smaller powers, governments at San Francisco decided to elevate ECOSOC to the status of a UN organ, so that it might serve as the central coordinating body of the economic and social work of the UN and of the UN's work with other international and nongovernmental bodies.

One of the four main purposes of the UN, as stipulated in Article 1 (3), is to "achieve international co-operation in solving international problems of an economic, social, cultural, or humanitarian character, and in promoting and encouraging respect for human rights and fundamental freedoms." Coupled with the UN Security Council, which was established

to prevent and control conflict, ECOSOC was seen as being responsible for addressing a wide range of underlying causes of conflict, which if properly addressed would reduce the frequency of conflict among nations while fostering cooperation in mutual problem solving. To this end, Chapters IX and X of the UN Charter vest in ECOSOC a variety of specific issues for discussion and action, including "a. higher standards of living, full employment, and conditions of economic and social progress and development; b. solutions of international economic, social, health, and related problems; and international cultural and educational co-operation; and c. universal respect for, and observance of, human rights and fundamental freedoms for all." The UN Charter explicitly names ECOSOC as the body responsible for bringing all international bodies working toward these ends into coordination with the UN. It also has the authority to make recommendations regarding these policy areas and to coordinate the work of the various agencies. It may establish commissions, initiate studies, issue reports, call international conferences, recommend the creation of new agencies, and propose treaties dealing with all matters within its competence. It is the focal point of UN consultation with nongovernmental organizations (NGOs). All UN specialized agencies report to ECOSOC, which in turn reports to the UN General Assembly. In short, ECOSOC is a very important coordinating and policy body dealing with international economic- and development-related issues.

Early Initiatives

ECOSOC was active from the very outset of the UN in organizing its work and in establishing ties with other international agencies, such as with UNICEF in 1946, the World Bank in 1947, and the World Health Organization (WHO) in 1948. ECOSOC was swiftly involved in the process of reorganizing international responses to the refugee situation in Europe with the creation of the International Refugee Organization in 1946 and the UN Relief for Palestine Refugees in 1948. In 1946, ECOSOC established the Human Rights Commission, tasking it with the drafting of human rights agreements, including the Universal Declaration of Human Rights and the Genocide Convention, which were eventually adopted by the UN in 1948. Its humanitarian activities continued with the establishment of the UN Relief and Works Agency for Palestine in 1950 and the UN High Commissioner for Refugees in 1951. In 1946, ECOSOC established a Commission for Narcotic Drugs; in 1947, the organization established a Population Commission. In the

meantime, war in Korea necessitated an international response to the economic and humanitarian situation there, precipitating the establishment of the UN Korean Relief and Reconstruction Agency. To focus and rationalize its attention on economic development issues, ECOSOC established two regional economic commissions in 1947, the UN Economic Commission for Europe and the UN Economic and Social Commission for Asia and the Pacific. This was followed in 1948 by the establishment of the UN Economic Commission for Latin America and the Caribbean. Two additional commissions were established for Africa in 1958 and Western Asia in 1973. All of these bodies report directly to ECOSOC.

During its second decade, the UN increasingly began to focus on issues of concern to the growing number of developing countries that had gained membership upon attainment of independence. In 1965, ECOSOC was expanded from eighteen to twenty-seven seats and in 1973 from twenty-seven to fifty-four seats; most of the new seats were occupied by states from the developing world. The voice of developing countries increasingly elevated attention to matters of concern to them, including the problems of underdevelopment, poverty, foreign assistance, transfer of technology, international trade and investment reforms, debt relief, racial discrimination, and resource development. In 1961, the Food and Agriculture Organization (FAO) and the UN initiated the World Food Program (WFP) to cope with emergency food needs. International development planning and cooperation, which had previously been promoted by the Expanded Program of Technical Assistance (EPTA) since 1950, was further emphasized in 1957 with the establishment of the Special UN Fund for Economic Development (SUNFED). These programs were later combined under the UN Development Program (UNDP) in 1965. The World Bank added a special International Development Fund (IDA) in 1960. The UNDP itself was a product of three years of debate that began in ECOSOC in 1962.

At the same time, developing countries met in Geneva in 1964, establishing the UN Conference on Trade and Development (UNCTAD), as an alternative mechanism to voice developing country concerns about the General Agreement on Tariffs and Trade (GATT) system that tended to ignore the adverse terms of the trade situation for many developing countries. In 1967, yet another UN development bureaucracy, the UN Industrial Development Organization, was established. Thus, as ECOSOC and the UN entered their third decade together, much of the work of these bodies was marked by increasing controversy over how best to promote economic development in the Third World. Developing countries lobbied for extensive assistance programs and expanded multilateral activity by UN bodies, while many developed countries resisted these demands and began to call for more careful rationalization of programs and budgets. ECOSOC was in the thick of international debates concerning the establishment of what was called the New International Economic Order (NIEO), which called for substantial restructuring of international aid, trade, and investment policies.

ECOSOC and Conference Diplomacy

ECOSOC has routinely called for international conferences to deal with the growing controversies among developed and developing nations. Such conferences ranged from those dealing with the environment (1972), population (1964, 1974, 1984, 1994), food (1974), women (1975), and human settlements (1976), among many others. These conferences often recommended the establishment of new agencies placed under the coordination of ECOSOC. These included, for instance, the UN Environment Program, the UN Fund for Population Activities, the UN International Research and Training Institute for the Advancement of Women, and the UN Human Settlements Program. The formation of UNCTAD in 1964 drew ECOSOC into the very heart of the controversial debates regarding the NIEO, which were often at the center of disputes at various international conferences as well. The array of UN economic development bodies established by governments reflected a piecemeal approach to problems based on voting majorities in the UN who wished to emphasize development concerns rather than a coherent strategic plan of organization. The result was a large number of often overlapping and competing agencies, together with the inefficiencies that necessarily resulted from this incoherent approach. Countries in the developing world objected to this growing bureaucracy and to what they saw as the increasingly irresponsible budgetary implications of it. Since the wealthier developed countries pay for most of the costs of UN development activity, they began to insist during the 1980s and 1990s that UN specialized agencies show greater budgetary restraint. During the same period of time, the UN undertook substantial reforms, both in its administrative organization and in its spending.

The role of ECOSOC as an initiator of international conferences and debate and as a coordinating body is seen in the progress of these many and wide-ranging disputes. ECOSOC is not, itself, a programmatic body. Rather, it serves as the mechanism through which a wide variety of UN agencies cooperate and

coordinate their activities. The organization is driven by the voices of its member states, along with those of the UN General Assembly, to which the ECOSOC reports. ECOSOC serves as a mechanism for the gathering of information and the articulation of interests by thousands of NGOs that have gained consultative status with it. Thus, ECOSOC, which now sits at the apex of the UN Department of Economic and Social Affairs after the restructuring of the UN's administrative operations, is not a development agency proper but, rather, a political body that serves to coordinate the work of operational agencies. Thus, as the nature of international economic and development debates evolve, ECOSOC is the body in which changing problems are dealt with by changing policy approaches.

For example, the 1970s and early 1980s were dominated by shrill and often unproductive disputes between developed countries and developing ones, the latter demanding and the former resisting international economic reforms of various kinds. Sometimes agreements were reached, as with the establishment of general systems of preference in trade that helped developing countries compete more effectively on international markets; however, as often as not, reform efforts failed, as with the idea of mandatory levels of foreign aid, mandatory transfer of technology, codes of conduct on international investment, mandatory commodity indexation schemes, and the like. Much of the controversy generated in these debates centered on Capitalist, Socialist, and Communist ideological differences. However, with the collapse of communism throughout much of the world in the late 1980s, the tone of international debates on development also changed. ECOSOC and other UN bodies began exploring ways to enhance global trade and investment, promote commerce, reduce barriers to business, encourage the growth of private enterprise, encourage democracy, and promote reductions in inefficient state-owned and state-operated enterprises. A greater degree of realism and a sense of cooperation have thus been reflected in various international initiatives related to trade, giving rise to the World Trade Organization in 1995. Similar realism and serious discussion has evolved in regard to global monetary issues, such as debt rescheduling and cancellation, and in rationalization of international humanitarian responses to complex emergencies.

Future Outlook

The world has moved rapidly since the 1990s toward the globalization of international trade, communication,

and investment. These developments have placed a great deal more power into the hands of individuals, private businesses, and enterprises. This represents a considerable shift from the idea of world organization that prevailed during the 1970s and 1980s. Governments still sit at the center of the discussion about how to structure and manage economic development today, and they will continue to use multilateral bodies such as the UN, ECOSOC, and other multilateral bodies as avenues for discussion and action. In this process, ECOSOC will continue to function as a forum for debate, a mechanism for multilateral cooperation, and a means for coordination of economic, social, cultural, and humanitarian affairs.

ROBERT F. GORMAN

See also United Nations Conference on Trade and Development (UNCTAD); United Nations Development Program (UNDP)

References and Further Reading

Bennett, A. LeRoy, and James K. Oliver. *International Organizations: Principles and Issues.* 7th ed. Upper Saddle River, NJ: Prentice-Hall, 2002.
Culpeper, Roy *et al. Global Development Fifty Years after Bretton Woods.* New York: St. Martin's, 1997.
Diehl, Paul F., ed. *The Politics of Global Governance: International Organizations in an Interdependent World.* 2d ed. Boulder, CO: Lynne Rienner, 2001.
Donnelly, Jack. *International Human Rights.* Boulder, CO: Westview Press, 1998.
Gorman, Robert. *Great Debates at the United Nations: An Encyclopedia of Fifty Key Issues, 1945–2000.* Westport, CT: Greenwood Press, 2001.
Muldoon, James P., Jr. *et al.,* eds. *Multilateral Diplomacy and the United Nations Today.* Boulder, CO: Westview Press, 1999.
Riggs, Robert D., and Jack C. Plano. *The United Nations: International Organization and World Politics.* Belmont, CA: Wadsworth, 1994.
UN Yearbooks. New York: UN Department of Public Information.
Weiss, Thomas G., David P. Forsythe, and Roger A. Coate. *The United Nations and Changing World Politics.* Boulder, CO: Westview Press, 1997.
Williams, Douglas. *The Specialized Agencies and the United Nations.* New York: St. Martin's, 1987.

UNITED NATIONS ECONOMIC COMMISSION FOR LATIN AMERICA AND THE CARIBBEAN (ECLAC)

The United Nations Economic Commission for Latin America, commonly known as the *Comisión Económica para America Latina* (CEPAL), was one of the most influential sources of development ideas in the post-World War II period. CEPAL was founded in

Santiago, Chile, in 1948. CEPAL was a product of the representatives of Latin America, who insisted on some kind of recovery plan similar to the Marshall Plan for the region. While CEPAL originally covered just Latin America, it later expanded to include the developing nations of the Caribbean. In its English translation, the organization became entitled the United Nations Economic Commission for Latin America and the Caribbean (ECLAC). It is interesting to note that although ECLAC has always been a part of the United Nations (UN), it has always had a high degree of independence from the rest of the organization. ECLAC was one of five regional commissions set up for postwar recovery, but it has had little collaboration over the years with its counterparts.

The organization's mission centers on the economic development of Latin America, including its ties to the rest of the world economy. As Santiago is fairly remote, ECLAC has over the years opened subregional headquarters in Mexico City and Trinidad and Tobago. ECLAC also has country offices in Brasilia, Brazil; Buenos Aires, Argentina; Montevideo, Uruguay; and Bogotá, Colombia. In addition, ECLAC has a liaison office in Washington, D.C.

ECLAC is headed by the Office of the Executive Secretariat. The secretariat's office generally sets the policy direction for the organization; sets up meetings of the member states; and otherwise supervises activities. It is important to note that ECLAC is a client of and serves its member states, to which the secretariat must respond. The states have a continual conversation with the organization, but the biannual meetings organized by the secretariat are the main vehicle for assessing and changing the direction of the organization. The member states include the United States and several European countries, including the United Kingdom and France. The main divisions of ECLAC include the field offices already noted; the Office of the Deputy Executive Secretary; the Programme Planning and Operations Division; the Office of the Secretary of the Commission; the Division of Administration; the Latin American and Caribbean Institute for Economic and Social Planning or IL-PES, the Spanish acronym; and the various research divisions.

ECLAC's current programs for Latin America include most prominently work on macroeconomic stability; on improving competitiveness in the international economy; on improving sectoral performance, including the development of infrastructure; on economic integration; on social equity, including a special office on women; on population growth; and on the environment. Historically speaking, ECLAC's prominence, scope, and types of activity have changed dramatically over time.

After ECLAC was founded, it became for the next two decades the most prominent economic development organization around the world and a dominant influence on economic policy decisions in Latin America. It is interesting to note that although the United States has been a long-time principal funding source, ECLAC has always been able to maintain a fairly independent line of analysis on Latin American development. Part of the reason for ECLAC's great influence initially was the absence of any well-developed corps of economists in Latin America at the time as well as a basic lack of economic data. ECLAC continues today to serve as a leading source for regional statistics. ILPES for a time served as the premier training location for economists from around Latin America. In other words, ECLAC was at the center of most conversations concerning Latin American development. Most important, economists from Latin America participated in some way with ECLAC, whether through meetings, training sessions, or policy discussions.

The other important reasons for ECLAC's influence concerned its charismatic leader, Raul Prebisch, and the development of a distinct view of economic development called "structuralism." Prebisch, an Argentine by birth, was a Latin American "caudillo" in the classic sense. He was a natural born leader, with a keen intellect and the ability to command audiences' attention and loyalty. His early work in the Central Bank of Argentina, which experienced frequent problems in paying off external national debts, helped him to begin constructing the basic tenets of structuralist thought, which would spread his and ECLAC's name around the world.

The main tenets of structuralist thought are found in Prebisch's 1948 report to ECLAC called *The Economic Development of Latin America and its Principal Problems.* In the report, Prebisch lays out a number of problems endemic to Latin America and proposes some basic remedies. The first tenet of structuralism is called the Prebisch-Singer hypothesis. The basic idea is that the prices of primary product goods, such as raw materials and basic foodstuffs, that the developing world has traditionally produced, have a *relatively* lower price than the manufactures that the First World produces. Thus, the developing world is stuck making products that are worth less and less as time goes on. The second basic tenet considers inflation. Prebisch considered that there were basic "bottlenecks" in developing economies that prevented or delayed production from increasing in response to increasing demand. Thus, even as consumers in developing economies began to demand more products, such as televisions and automobiles, the local economies were unable to respond with increases in

production. The bottlenecks that slowed down the development of local production could be any number of things, from the inability to obtain credit to a basic lack of infrastructure, such as reliable and cheap energy. The third basic tenet of structuralism was that only the government or "the state" could solve these problems. The state could do so through two basic strategies. The first was to move toward the production of industrialized goods that would not suffer from the deteriorating terms of the trade price problem noted previously. The second was that the state could proactively begin to cut or loosen the bottlenecks also already noted. These ideas were eventually embraced around the developing world. It is important to note that structuralism did not start state intervention into developing economies, but rather it created a logical framework and plan of action around which it could develop.

Like other theoretical perspectives, structuralism was a dynamic analytical framework that was added to and modified as events played out. As several Latin American governments (and many outside of the region), notably Chile, Brazil, and Mexico, began to adopt structuralist policies, several problems started to become apparent. The first related to the policy of "import substituting industrialization." By this policy, Latin American governments taxed agriculture and other primary product exports and protected finished industrial goods to promote their domestic production. In many cases, governments actually created state-owned enterprises to produce these goods. By the mid-1960s, Latin American governments began to experience severe inflationary and balance-of-payments problems. A key source of these problems was that these countries were still importing the equipment, expertise, and capital to produce the final industrial products at the same time as they were taxing their exports. Another problem, which still continues in the twenty-first century, was a basic inability to balance government budgets. The result was a major economic imbalance. At that time, ECLAC began to emphasize the importance of paying attention to agricultural productivity and to suggest that land reform was an important key. The general situation led economist Albert O. Hirschman to come up with the idea of economic "linkages." Hirschman pointed out that developing economies needed to consider production as a whole process, not just as producing the final versions of goods. Thus, part of the problem was importing car parts to assemble cars instead of producing the parts as well.

Another problem was the limited size of the domestic markets of Latin American countries. Industrial products need to be produced in large numbers to reach the lowest per unit cost, or "economies of scale." There were simply not enough consumers to lead to adequate production runs in Latin America, so ECLAC began to promote the importance of exports, and became, and has continued to be, a major promoter of intra-Latin American economic integration. ECLAC also began to propose some cautious steps toward income redistribution, which it felt would further increase the size of the domestic markets. Unfortunately, these reforms were never really embraced. Exports were never seriously promoted. Agricultural reform was tepid at best in most places. The ostentatious signing of integration agreements had nothing to do with the reality that there was a very limited and retreating will to move toward the integration of economies.

By the end of the 1960s, as in the rest of the world, Latin America was wracked by a polarization of leftist groups agitating for major social change, usually in the form of socialism, and rightists who wanted a more moderate, if any, pace of reform. ECLAC itself was internally divided along these lines, and the momentum of structuralist thought and policies was lost. In addition, Prebisch moved on to leadership in the United Nations Conference on Trade and Development in Geneva, and his leadership was missed. One camp of ECLAC moved closer to the newly emerging dependency paradigm, which is much more pessimistic about the prospects for development. Two members of ECLAC, Fernando Henrique Cardoso and Enzo Faletto, wrote the most important book of the dependency school: *Dependency and Development in Latin America*. The book was very much a product of the times, when leftist guerrillas were active throughout the region and socialism seemed like a viable alternative. ECLAC itself was torn apart when Salvador Allende's government was overthrown by General Augusto Pinochet's military government. Many core members of ECLAC who had sympathized with Allende fled Chile during the Pinochet regime, and the organization itself went into a lull of inactivity. By the end of the 1970s, the structuralist policies concerning import substituting industrialization had largely fallen into disrepute, much as socialism and dependency did ten years later.

In retrospect, it really is quite unfair to consider structuralist policies a clear "failure." As Rosemary Thorp points out in *An Economic History of Latin America in the 20th Century*, the period of import substituting industrialization succeeded for the most part in creating a strong industrial base for domestic production, albeit one that was wracked by efficiency, technical, and managerial problems. Moreover, economic growth rates in several Latin American economies, particularly Mexico and Brazil, were quite high during the 1960s. So even though income distribution

worsened, there was substantial progress in improving the absolute living standards of Latin Americans. However, structuralism was never reformed along the lines already noted. The revolutionary leftist groups failed in securing power as the military took over in most of the region. Instead of carrying through the already described needed reforms, Latin American governments began borrowing massive amounts of capital to smooth out balance of payments problems and continuing increasing government spending. This borrowing set the region directly up for the external debt crisis when international interest rates rose dramatically upon the direction of the United States in 1982. The ensuing decade is known as "the lost decade" as Latin America began to sink into ten years of economic contraction. Whether the reforms to structuralism could have "saved" the set of economic policies is one of those historical imponderables that does not seem to receive adequate discussion.

ECLAC itself reorganized in the 1980s around a new set of policies that it called "neostructuralism." Neostructuralist thought was best articulated by Ricardo Ffrench-Davis in the 1980s but has nowhere near the impact of its predecessor. Basically, neostructuralism seeks to implement a softer version of the neoliberal model, one in which a minimal social safety net, environmental preservation, and other concerns are taken into account. While still honoring the memory of Prebisch, ECLAC has also changed in other ways.

ECLAC now has a large contingency of American-trained economists, who have a more mainstream orientation than the Prebisch generation. ECLAC also has lost much of its leadership position in Latin America. There are a number of reasons for this loss, but two primary reasons are that most countries now produce their own economic experts and that they have their own research and statistical databases. It remains to be seen whether ECLAC can regain its importance among Latin American states. The organization continues to serve as an important information portal for Latin American economic statistics and research and as an important place for regional economic studies.

ANIL HIRA

See also Neoliberalism

References and Further Reading

Ffrench-Davis, Ricardo. "An Outline of the Neo-Structuralist Approach." *CEPAL Review* 34 (April 1988): 37–44.
Furtado, Celso. *La Fantasia Organizada*. Buenos Aires: Editorial Universitaria de Buenos Aires, 1988.
Hira, Anil. *Ideas and Economic Policy in Latin America: Regional, National, and Organizational Case Studies*. Westport, CT: Praeger, 1998.
Hodara, Joseph B. *Prebsich y CEPAL: Sustancia, Trayectoria y Contexto Institucional*. Mexico City: Colegio de Mexico, 1987.
Prebisch, Raul. *The Economic Development of Latin America and its Principal Problems*. New York: United Nations, 1950.
Sikkink, Kathryn. *Ideas and Institutions: Developmentalism in Argentina and Brazil*. Ithaca, NY: Cornell University Press, 1991.
Thorp, Rosemary. *Progress, Poverty, and Exclusion: An Economic History of Latin America in the 20th Century*. Washington, DC: Inter-American Development Bank, 1998.
United Nations Economic Commission for Latin America and the Caribbean (ECLAC). 2005. Home Page. http://www.cepal.org.

UNITED NATIONS FOOD AND AGRICULTURE ORGANIZATION (FAO)

The United Nations Food and Agriculture Organization (FAO) was established on October 16, 1945, in Quebec, Canada, with the ultimate goal of defeating world hunger. The FAO attempts to raise levels of nutrition and standards of living, increase agricultural productivity, and improve the condition of rural populations. The FAO seeks to meet the needs of present and future generations by promoting development that does not endanger the environment and is technologically appropriate, economically viable, and socially acceptable. FAO officials contend that making sure people have regular access to sufficient quantities of high-quality food will enable people to lead active, healthy lives and contribute to the growth of the world economy. To bring global awareness to the plight of the world's peoples suffering from hunger, in 1981 the FAO declared that October 16 would henceforth be celebrated as World Food Day. The theme for World Food Day in 2004 was biodiversity for food security, which highlighted biodiversity's role in ensuring that people have sustainable access to enough high-quality food to lead active and healthy lives.

The FAO employs approximately 3,500 staff members. In addition to its headquarters in Rome, the FAO maintains regional offices in Egypt, Thailand, Ghana, and Chile. The FAO also supports over seventy-five country offices, primarily in the developing world. The FAO is composed of eight departments that focus on administration and finance, agriculture, economic and social issues, fisheries, forestry, general affairs and information, sustainable development, and technical cooperation.

The FAO is involved in four major areas of activity: putting information within the reach of people, sharing policy expertise, providing a meeting place

for concerned nations, and bringing knowledge into the field. In an attempt to foster development, the FAO staff (made up of agronomists, foresters, fisheries and livestock specialists, nutritionists, social scientists, economists, statisticians, and other professionals) collects, analyzes, and distributes information to millions of people. In addition to publishing a plethora of reports, books, documents, newsletters, and magazines, the FAO maintains an extensive site on the World Wide Web. As such, the FAO serves as a virtual clearinghouse of information, providing farmers, scientists, traders, and government officials with the knowledge they need to make rational decisions.

In an attempt to achieve rural development and alleviate hunger, the FAO works on a national level to help individual countries devise agricultural policy, draft effective legislation, and create national development strategies. The FAO is a neutral forum where representatives from the developed and developing nations can meet to discuss the major food and agricultural concerns facing the world. The FAO monitors international standards and helps organize international conventions and agreements as well as regularly hosts conferences, technical meetings, and consultations of experts. Since its inception in 1945, the FAO has supported thousands of field projects throughout the world, especially in the developing nations. The FAO is committed to reducing global hunger in half by 2015.

MICHAEL R. HALL

See also Agriculture: Impact of Globalization; Agriculture: Impact of Privatization; Food and Nutrition

References and Further Reading

Abbott, John. *Politics and Poverty: A Critique of the Food and Agriculture Organization of the United Nations.* New York: Routledge, 1992.

Loftas, Tony, and Jane Ross. *Dimensions of Need: An Atlas of Food and Agriculture.* Santa Barbara, CA: ABC-Clio, 1995.

Marchisio, Sergio, and A. Diblase. *The Food and Agriculture Organization.* Leiden, Netherlands: Martinus Nijhoff, 1991.

Nordquist, Myron, and John Norton Moore. *Current Fisheries Issues and the Food and Agriculture Organization of the United Nations.* Leiden, Netherlands: Brill Academic Publishers, 2000.

UNITED NATIONS HIGH COMMMISSIONER FOR REFUGEES (UNHCR)

The United Nations High Commissioner for Refugees (UNHCR) is one of the largest United Nations (UN) assistance agencies. The vast majority of the refugees and other people under its care and protection reside in asylum countries of the developing world. Although the UNHCR is charged first and foremost with the protection of refugees, its assistance activities have a direct bearing on the development situation in countries that host refugees and in countries of origin that receive returnees home from exile.

Origins and Development of UNHCR

The UNHCR was established on January 1, 1951, as the successor to the International Refugee Organization (IRO), which in turn had been established as a temporary body to resolve the circumstances of millions of refugees and others displaced by the events of World War II. With several hundred thousand refugees in displaced persons camps remaining as the IRO drew near the end of its five-year term of existence, governments decided to create the UNHCR as a temporary agency to finish the work of the IRO by repatriating, permanently settling, or resettling refugees. The role of the UNHCR was limited at the time to offering legal protection services to refugees. Other bodies were to provide actual operational assistance. But in time, the UN General Assembly allowed the UNHCR to seek voluntary assistance from its member states for the benefit of refugee populations. The UNHCR's mandate was gradually extended from three to five years and has been routinely reauthorized at five-year intervals ever since its inception; this extension is a result of the growing need for the UNHCR's protection and assistance services, as refugee situations began to arise outside of Europe, such as in Africa, Asia, and Latin America. As both the number of refugee situations and the numbers of refugees began to increase, especially in developing countries unable to cope with the economic and social consequences of large refugee flows, the UNHCR found itself confronted with the need to offer both emergency and long-term care and maintenance assistance as necessary components of the organization's protection activities on behalf of refugees.

Zonal Development Programs

In the early 1960s, UNHCR programs on behalf of Burundian and Rwandan refugees in Central Africa acknowledged that assistance to refugees must take into account the effects of the refugee flows on the local economies of the host countries. One of the

observations made by UNHCR was that the targeting of large amounts of emergency assistance, food aid, medical assistance, housing, and social services on refugees alone could quickly place a refugee population in a privileged position relative to the often poor and underprivileged host population, leading to resentments among the latter toward refugees and to protection problems for refugees. On the other hand, to the extent that aid was aimed at the entire population of a refugee-affected area, both the refugees and the local population benefited, leading to a more harmonious relationship in which protection of refugees was more easily guaranteed. However, the UNHCR labored with the self-understanding that it was a nonoperational agency. It could intercede on behalf of refugees to convince governments that they should offer asylum and protection, and it could issue appeals for assistance on behalf of refugees; however, it was the responsibility of the governments and of other intergovernmental and nongovernmental organizations to actually implement assistance programs on behalf of the refugees. Thus, although the zonal development idea was a promising one, the UNHCR was not equipped to promote it, and other UN bodies with explicit development-related responsibilities did not at the time adopt the idea as one worthy of consistent and wide application; this was especially true since development agencies viewed refugee aid as a temporary and emergency-related activity lasting only a few months or a few years, whereas development horizons encompassed much longer spans of time. There was no sense of urgency in the 1960s to integrate or coordinate short-term humanitarian aid with long-term development assistance (Betts 1984).

The Process of the International Conference on Assistance to Refugees

The zonal development notion waned to the point of extinction during the 1970s, but as refugee situations, especially in Africa, began to proliferate during the late 1970s and into the early 1980s, the notion experienced a renaissance; by the time of the second International Conference on Assistance to Refugees (ICARA II), held in 1984 at Geneva, the idea of refugee-related development assistance gained new currency. At ICARA II, largely at the urging of the UNHCR, governments hosting large numbers of refugees or returnees were encouraged to identify development-related projects related to the economic and social infrastructure of refugee- and returnee-affected areas of their countries. More than 100 projects were submitted for funding in the hope that donor countries

might fund road building, reforestation, education, health care, agricultural programs, food storage, and other development-related programs in refugee-affected regions. Although many of the projects failed to attract funding, the notion that refugee aid and regional development planning were linked had become firmly planted in the outlook of both the UNHCR and gradually among other UN development agencies, such as the UN Development Program (UNDP), which was a cosponsor of ICARA II. In the late 1980s, the Central American Refugee Conference (CIREFCA) also attempted to link the aid for refugees, returnees, and displaced persons to the larger development needs of Central American states seeking to rehabilitate badly degraded infrastructures after a decade of civil discord. International responses the CIREFCA proved more generous than toward ICARA II projects.

UNHCR as the Catalyst for Refugee Aid and Development Linkages

The linkage of refugee aid to the development strategy of a refugee hosting country was to a very large extent advanced by the UNHCR, which over the years developed substantial experience in responding to refugee situations in developing nations. The UNHCR, unlike its sister development agencies in the UN system, had extensive contacts in developing countries directly and through nongovernmental organizations (NGOs) with which it contracted to implement emergency care and maintenance assistance to refugees. This routine presence in the field attuned UNHCR personnel to the effects of its assistance on refugees and on the host populations alike. Often called upon to assist and protect not only refugees but other displaced populations in refugee-like circumstances,

UNHCR became more acutely aware of the ways in which its assistance activities either helped or hurt the livelihood of local populations. Large amounts of refugee food aid imported from foreign sources, for instance, typically had the affect of driving local food prices lower, thereby providing disincentives for local food producers. On the other hand, if cereal grains could be purchased from local stocks, local producers had incentives to produce more. If refugees were given food for work opportunities, resentment among locals tended to increase. Likewise, if refugees were given access to health care clinics, local animosity was likely to grow. When such opportunities and services were extended to local people and the refugees alike, the former tended to look upon the presence of refugees as an asset to the local economy. To the extent that

refugee labor could be directed toward projects aimed at strengthening local infrastructure, the UNHCR could encourage not only a safer environment for refugees but also contribute in modest ways to the eventual development of refugee-affected regions. Thus, the UNHCR for many years had discovered ways in which it could offer refugee aid in a way that was compatible to the development of host countries.

The more difficult step was convincing UN development agencies and the development arms of local and donor governments to take into account in their long-range indicative planning processes the refugees' impact on regional development within receiving countries. By engaging the UNDP at ICARA II and CIREFCA, the UNHCR took a big step in increasing the awareness among UN agencies and governments to the linkages between its humanitarian work on behalf of refugees with the development work of such sister agencies. Large refugee or returnee populations represent a burden on local infrastructures. Refugees foraging for firewood can quickly denude wide areas surrounding refugee settlements, creating potentially long-term and adverse environmental effects. Overland shipments of food aid can degrade local roadways. In arid regions, large refugee populations overtax local water supplies, both by reducing supplies and, where sanitation is poor, by polluting them. Disease in densely crowded refugee settings can easily spread to the local population and overwhelm the capacity of the local health infrastructure. Even when refugees have managed to settle spontaneously, outside of formally established refugee camps and settlements, pressures on local schools, hospitals, clinics, and other social services placed on such infrastructure and services can be severe.

While development agencies of host governments might consider such pressures to be temporary, there are many cases in which refugee populations spend more than a decade in their countries of asylum before opportunities to repatriate to their homeland materialize. It behooves governments, UN agencies, and NGOs alike, then, to anticipate the effects of large-scale refugee populations on the development of the host country. The UNHCR, by persistently and patiently reminding the international community of these realities in a variety of fora during the 1980s, placed these concerns in the mainstream of international policy making.

UN Policy Responses

In 1992 and again in 1997, the UN became increasingly aware that coordination of humanitarian and development assistance in situations involving civil war and complex emergencies would require greater interagency cooperation. During the 1980s, refugee-related development questions gained greater visibility in the development planning processes of various countries. In the preparation of country development strategy plans of refugee-receiving states, in cooperation with in-country roundtable discussions with donors and in the consultative group process of the World Bank, refugee-related issues rose to the fore as matters worthy of discussion in development planning circles. During the early 1990s, the establishment of a Department of Humanitarian Affairs (DHA) to serve as a coordinating body for humanitarian aid in developing country contexts provided a first step toward greater interagency sharing of information and coordination of assistance packages to regions of the world experiencing humanitarian emergencies. The establishment of the UN Office for the Coordination of Humanitarian Affairs further consolidated this effort. The UNHCR is a major player in these interagency contexts.

The fact that the overwhelming majority of refugees throughout the world flee from developing countries into neighboring developing countries means that UN aid-giving bodies, including the UNHCR and a host of UN development agencies, will need to continue coordinating with one another as they pursue their respective mandates. The days when development assistance was provided without regard to refugees and refugee assistance without regard to the wider development situation are long gone. But effective distribution of such assistance continues to put a premium on the effective coordination of UN agencies, governments, and NGOs, as both refugee problems and development needs persist throughout the developing world.

ROBERT F. GORMAN

See also Migration; Refugees

References and Further Reading

Betts, T. F. "Evolution and Promotion of the Integrated Rural Development Approach to Refugee Policy in Africa." *Africa Today* 31, no. 1: 7–24.

Chambers, Robert. "Hidden Losers: The Impact of Rural Refugees and Rural Programs on Poorer Hosts." *International Migration Review* 20, no. 2: 245–263.

Cuenod, Jacques. "Refugees: Development or Relief." *Refugees and International Relations*, Gil Loescher and Laila Monahan, eds. Oxford: Oxford University Press, 1989: 219–253.

Cuny, Frederick. *Disasters and Development*. New York: Oxford University Press, 1983.

Gallagher, Dennis, and Diller, Janelle. *CIREFCA: At the Crossroads Between Uprooted People and Development in*

Central America. Washington, DC: Commission for the Study of International Migration and Cooperative Economic Development, 1990.

Gorman, Robert F. *Historical Dictionary of Refugee and Disaster Relief Organizations*. Lanham, MD: Scarecrow Press, 2000.

———. *Refugee Aid and Development: Theory and Practice*. Westport, CT: Greenwood Press, 1993.

———. *Coping with Africa's Refugee Burden: A Time for Solutions*. Dordrecht: Martinus Nijhof, 1987.

Keller, Stephen. *Uprooting and Social Change: The Role of Refugees in Development*. New Delhi, India: Manohar Book Service, 1975.

Zolberg, Aristide, Astri Suhrke, and Sergio Aguayo. *Escape from Violence: Conflict and the Refugee Crisis in the Developing World*. New York: Oxford University Press, 1989.

UNITED NATIONS INDUSTRIAL DEVELOPMENT ORGANIZATION (UNIDO)

The United Nations Industrial Development Organization, referred to as its acronym UNIDO, was set up in 1966, but it became a specialized agency of the United Nations (UN) in 1985. UNIDO has responsibility for promoting industrialization throughout the developing world, in cooperation with its 171 member states. Its headquarters are in Vienna, Austria, and it is represented in thirty-five developing countries.

The main purpose of the UNIDO is to bridge the gap between the poor and the rich, in other words between the developing and developed states. The importance of the UNIDO's role is increasing in light of the following facts: sub-Saharan Africa's share of the world's manufacturing value-added has fallen from 0.8% in 1975 to 0.3% in 1995; industry accounts for one-third of the world's greenhouse emissions and a large percentage of hazardous materials; for every ton of food produced, developed countries spend $180 on processing it, while developing nations spend $40; between 60% and 70% of the female population is employed in the agriculture sector, while the majority of women employed in industry work as an unskilled labor force; and, finally, one-fourth of the gold sold on the world market comes from artisanal miners who use mercury for extracting gold ore. This method pollutes hundreds of kilometers of rivers. More than two million small-scale gold miners work in Africa, Asia, and Latin America, and seven million people depend on related activities. In this respect, many projects have been implemented by UNIDO to end problems related to pollution resulting from industrial activities.

UNIDO assists the Philippines in substituting for the use of mercury by small-scale miners. A similar programme was successfully completed in Venezuela, where gold miners agreed to change their work methods. They improved their living and working conditions, the source of pollution was eliminated, and their activities were legalized. More than ten countries have solicited the implementation of this UNIDO progrmme. Another project was implemented in Cospa Mica, the Romanian town and the most polluted place in Europe in 1991. People, animals, grass, facades, and virtually everything was black from the soot emitted by the Cabosin chemical plant, while the Sometra smelter factory discharged lead. A UNIDO project was implemented, and it took seven years to clean up Copsa Mica. UNIDO advised the closure of Cabosin, while Sometra improved its production methods and managed to transform the town. UNIDO's concern for environmental protection is translated into numerous programmes. Cleaner production centers—ten in existence worldwide—provide training in the efficient use of raw materials and energy, elimination of toxic raw materials, and reduction of emissions and wastes. UNIDO is one of the four implementing agencies of the Montreal Protocol, which was ratified in 1987, and calls for eliminating the production of ozone-depleting substances. In addition, many women in Africa support their families by selling agricultural products and garments, and the value added to their work increases profits. UNIDO's programme in Tanzania focused on the use of improved technology and development of entrepreneurial skills. Numerous projects in Africa, Asia, and Latin America train small and medium-sized business entrepreneurs in ways to add value to their work, improve production, expand business operations, and generate profits.

The main objectives of UNIDO are (i) to promote sustainable industrial development in countries with developing and transition economies, (ii) to harness the joint forces of government and the private sector to foster competitive industrial production, (iii) develop international industrial partnerships and promote socially equitable and environmentally friendly industrial development, and (iv) to create a better life for people by laying the industrial foundation for long-term prosperity and economic strength.

The United Nations Industrial Development Organization (UNIDO) helps developing countries and countries with economies in transition in implementing their development plans that are facing the challenges of the globalization age. The organization mobilizes knowledge, skills, information, and technology to promote productive employment, a competitive economy, and a sound environment. In its work, UNIDO has eight service modules that are Industrial Governance and Statistics, Investment and Technology Promotion, Industrial Competitiveness and Trade,

Private Sector Development, Agro-industry, Sustainable Energy and Climate Change, the Montreal Protocol (regarding substances that deplete the ozone layer), and Environmental Management.

Recently, UNIDO has launched two initiatives. One is the Market Access Initiative, launched at the International Conference of Financing for Development in Monterrey, Mexico, in March 2002. The second is the Rural Energy for Productive Use Initiative, launched a the World Summit for Sustainable Development in Johannesburg, South Africa, in September 2002.

UNIDO works not only with governments but also with business associations, high-level experts, and individual companies to solve industrial problems. During the 1990s, UNIDO experienced pressure to reform its operations, which were mainly in the administration rather than in its programmes. Despite UNIDO's reform efforts, the United States withdrew from the organization at the end of 1996, citing as the reasons federal cutbacks in foreign aid expenditures and a lack of commitment to the agency from some members of the US Congress. Moreover, in 1996, Britain and Australia also announced plans to withdraw from UNIDO. Critics in the United States and Britain concede that UNIDO has made substantial progress in meeting the reform goals of member nations. The decision of both countries to withdraw from the organization instead reflects domestic political considerations and the desire to send a message to the UN about disagreements concerning the organization's policies. Critics also argue that at least two other UN organizations—the United Nations Development Program (UNDP) and the United Nations Conference on Trade and Development (UNCTAD)—focus on development in impoverished nations. Because the United States and Britain contributed one-third of the organization's budget, their withdrawals have affected the survival of UNIDO.

NILLY KAMAL EL-AMIR

See also Industrialization; United Nations Conference on Trade and Development (UNCTAD); United Nations Development Program (UNDP)

References and Further Reading

Aorere, Manatu. *United Nations Handbook 2001*. New Zealand: New Zealand Ministry of Foreign Affairs and Trade, 2002.

Jacobowicz, Jean-Michel. *The United Nations in Our Daily Lives*. New York: The United Nations Publications, 1998.

United Nations Department of Public Information. *Basic Facts about the United Nations*. New York: The United Nations Publications, 2002.

UNITED NATIONS INTERNATIONAL COURT OF JUSTICE (ICJ)

The International Court of Justice (ICJ) is based in The Hague (Netherlands). It is the principal judicial organ of the United Nations. The ICJ was created in 1945. Its jurisdiction and powers are established by the Statute of the International Court of Justice. The ICJ is at times colloquially referred to as the "World Court" although this is not its official title.

Functions

The ICJ has two principal functions. First, the court must settle legal disputes submitted to it by those states that have accepted its jurisdiction. Second, the court must render advisory opinions on legal questions referred to it by authorized international organizations and agencies. In either case, the ICJ decides the questions before it in accordance with international treaties and conventions, international custom, and the general principles of law, supplementing its analysis with reference to decisions of other courts as well as the writings of well-known publicists [Statute of the International Court of Justice, art. 38(1)]. The ICJ does not have jurisdiction over individuals or entities that are not states [Statute of the International Court of Justice, art. 34(1)]. This differentiates the ICJ from the International Criminal Court which, when it comes into effect, will be able to prosecute individuals who commit genocide, crimes against humanity, and war crimes.

Contentious Disputes Among States

Contentious disputes between consenting states occupy most of the ICJ's attention. States can consent to jurisdiction in a particular dispute in one of three ways. First, the states can make between them a special agreement to submit the dispute to the ICJ. Second, the states can consent by virtue of what international lawyers call a "jurisdictional clause," which is a clause in a treaty that requires disputes arising under that treaty to be brought before the ICJ. When a treaty contains a jurisdictional clause, the ICJ will assume jurisdiction over a dispute among states that are parties to that treaty when the dispute involves the meaning, effect, or application of that treaty [Statute of the International Court of Justice, art. 36(1)]. Many treaties or conventions contain a jurisdictional clause. Third, the states can consent through declarations made by a state under the ICJ

Statute that it accepts ICJ jurisdiction as compulsory in the event the state enters into a dispute with another state that has made the same declaration (Statute of the International Court of Justice, art. 36[2]). That the jurisdiction of the ICJ over a state is based on that state's consent reflects the importance of state sovereignty in the international legal order.

Proceedings begin with a written phase during which disputants file and exchange pleadings. This is followed by an oral phase consisting of public hearings before the judges. Following the oral phase, judges deliberate and thereafter deliver the judgment publicly. Judgments are final and without appeal (Statute of the International Court of Justice, arts. 59–60). Should a state fail to comply with an ICJ judgment, this may constitute a violation of the UN Charter of the United Nations, and the other party may have recourse to the UN Security Council. The two official languages of the ICJ are English and French.

Personnel

The ICJ consists of fifteen judges elected to nine-year terms by the UN General Assembly and Security Council. No two judges can be of the same nationality. Elections are held every three years for one-third of the judge positions. Retiring judges may be reelected. ICJ judges do not represent their governments. The composition of the ICJ reflects the principal legal systems of the world.

Jurisprudential Activity

As of 2001, the ICJ has delivered a total of seventy-two judgments on disputes and twenty-four advisory opinions. The ICJ has been involved in boundary disputes (land and maritime), civil claims, legality of the use of force, noninterference in the internal affairs of states, and diplomatic relations. The ICJ also has addressed violations of humanitarian law. Advisory opinions have concerned a number of issues, including admission to UN membership, reparation for injuries suffered in the service of the UN, and the legality of the threat or use of nuclear weapons.

Of the nearly twenty-five cases pending before the ICJ, half concern disputes between two developing countries or one country from the South and one from the North. This is an important change, given that as recently as the 1970s the ICJ mostly was called upon to settle disputes among developed nations.

The ICJ and Development Issues

Although the ICJ's competence is limited by its statute largely to concern itself with disputes concerning the interpretation of treaties, questions of international law, and breaches of international obligation, in a number of opinions it has discussed development issues. Specifically, the ICJ has considered sustainable development, the alleged right of development, and intergenerational equity. Although discussion of some of these concepts only has been undertaken in separate opinions, the ICJ has been helpful in propounding principles of international law that harmonize economic development with environmental concerns and social justice.

Sustainable development—the notion that economic development is to meet the needs of the present without compromising the ability of future generations to meet their own needs—was discussed by the ICJ in its 1997 decision in the Gabcíkovo-Nagymaros Project (Hungary vs. Slovakia). This dispute arose because Hungary reneged on a treaty commitment it had made that it and Slovakia would construct and operate locks on the Danube River. Hungary suspended work and withdrew from the treaty owing to evidence that the project would damage the environment. Slovakia continued with the project by implementing a modified system that drastically reduced the downstream flow of the Danube into Hungary. The ICJ directed both parties to restructure and revitalize the project and, in so doing, to consider the principle of sustainable development (*Case Concerning the Gabcíkovo-Nagymaros Project* 1997). In a separate opinion, ICJ Vice President Christopher Gregory Weeramantry wrote that sustainable development was a principle with normative value that forms an integral part of modern international law (*Case Concerning the Gabcíkovo-Nagymaros Project* 1997, separate opinion). Interestingly, Weeramantry noted that sustainable development emerged from a need to reconcile the right to development (a right that developing nations strenuously have argued for) with the right to environmental protection. By affirming that the right to development constitutes a juristic base for sustainable development, Weeramantry may have increased the currency of developmental rights. However, for the most part, developed countries have not been supportive of developmental rights.

Intergenerational equity also has caught the eye of Vice President Weeramantry. Intergenerational equity posits that justice and fairness concerns are not only to operate within the present dimension. Instead, economic development and other motivations of present generations should be informed by the needs of

future unborn generations. The majority of the ICJ has not dealt with the concept of intergenerational equity. However, Weeramantry's dissenting opinion in 1995 in the Nuclear Tests Case (New Zealand vs. France), in which he identified the principle of intergenerational equity as an important and rapidly developing principle of contemporary environmental law, may constitute an important bellwether for future cases that specifically may involve the law of development.

MARK A. DRUMBL

References and Further Reading

Damrosch, Lori Fisler, ed. *The International Court of Justice at a Crossroads.* Dobbs Ferry, NY: Transnational Publishers, 1987.

Lowe, Alan, and M. Fitzmaurice, eds. *Fifty Years of the International Court of Justice.* Cambridge: Cambridge University Press, 1996.

Rosenne, Shabtai. *The Law and Practice of the International Court.* Dordrecht: M. Nijhoff, 1985.

Wellens, Karel. *Economic Conflicts and Disputes Before the World Court (1922–1995): A Functional Analysis.* The Hague and Boston: Kluwer Law International, 1996.

UNITED NATIONS INTERNATIONAL DRUG CONTROL PROGRAM (UNDCP)

The United Nations Drug Control Program (UNDCP) was established in 1991. It was renamed the United Nations Office on Drugs and Crime (UNODC) in 2002 and received a broader mandate. It was established in response to an increasing threat to the global security and stability from the growing production and distribution of illicit drugs, which burgeoned to a black-market business of $500 billion US (UNODC est. 2004). In the 1990s and early 2000s, the illicit drugs production and distribution became a particularly serious issue, as the so-called drug dollars were increasingly channeled to finance international terrorism and local and regional conflicts in various parts of the world. The agency was established to govern the international system of treaties on drug control and to coordinate activities of the individual states and international agencies fighting illicit drugs' production and distribution.

The UNODC has the following objectives: to conduct research and analytical work on harmful effects of illicit drugs and drug-related crimes and disseminate the information about development in these areas; to provide all forms of assistance to individual states in developing domestic legislation on drugs, crimes, and terrorism and in implementing international treaties on drug-related issues; and to implement technical cooperation projects to combat illicit drugs trade, trafficking, and terrorism.

The UNODC basis its work on three major international drug control treaties: the Single Convention on Narcotic Drugs (1961), the Convention on Psychotropic Substances (1971), and the Convention against Illicit Trafficking in Narcotic and Psychotropic Substances (1988).

The UNODC sponsors or supports several major actions around the world, including projects in Central Asia aimed at combating narcotics trafficking; projects in Southern and Eastern Africa aimed at in improving judiciary system and training law enforcement officials; and projects in Bolivia, Columbia, and Peru aimed at counter narcotics cooperation and judiciary reforms. The agency also provides support to drug-abuse treatment and rehabilitation centers around the world. In 2003, the UNODC was accused of corruption; in response, the United Nations Office of International Oversight Services (OIOS) conducted an independent assessment and found no evidence of corruption or mismanagement.

The UNODC has its headquarters in Vienna (Austria), a liaison office in New York, and twenty-one field offices in various countries of Africa, the Americas, Asia, and Europe. The agency has about five hundred staff members, and its director is appointed by the UN secretary-general. The agency's budget is formed partly by contributions from the United Nations and partly by voluntary contributions from the member states. As of 2004, the United States was the largest single contributor to the agency's budget as it committed about $140 million USD to various projects, mainly through the Department of State's Bureau of International Narcotics and Law Enforcement Affairs.

RAFIS ABAZOV

See also Black Market/Shadow Economy; Drug Trade; Drug Use

References and Further Reading

Forsythe, David P. *et al. The United Nations and Changing World Politics.* 3d ed. Boulder, CO: Westview Press, 2000.

Knight, Andy, ed. *Adapting the United Nations to a Postmodern Era: Lessons Learned. Global Issues Series.* New York: Macmillan, 1999.

United Nations International Drugs Controlling Program. *World Drug Report 2000: United Nations Office for Drug Control and Crime Prevention (World Drug Report).* New York: Oxford University Press, 2001.

United Nations Office on Drugs and Crime. 2005. Home Page. http://www.unodc.org/unodc/index.html.

UNITED NATIONS INTERNATIONAL FUND FOR AGRICULTURAL DEVELOPMENT (IFAD)

The International Fund for Agricultural Development (IFAD), a specialized agency of the United Nations (UN), was established as an international financial institution in 1977. The IFAD was a direct outcome of the resolutions proclaimed at the 1974 World Food Conference, which was held in response to the food crises of the early 1970s that affected the Sahel region of Africa. The participants at the UN-sponsored conference insisted that an international fund for agricultural development be established to finance agricultural development projects for food production in the developing countries. The delegates to the congress contended that the causes of food insecurity and famine in the Third World were not so much failures in food production in as much as they were structural problems relating to poverty and that a significant number of the Third World's people lived in the rural areas. The IFAD is committed to achieving the UN's Millennium Development Goals, especially the proposal to reduce the proportion of hungry and extremely poor people by 50% before 2015.

Through low-interest loans and grants, the IFAD works with Third World governments to develop and finance projects that enable the rural poor to overcome poverty themselves. Currently, there are about two hundred IFAD-supported rural poverty eradication programs and projects, valued at more than $6 billion, half of which have been funded by the IFAD. The rest of the financing is contributed by partners, such as governments, bilateral donors, and multilateral donors. The IFAD's current projects are expected to benefit 100 million families in the rural regions of the developing world. Since its inception in 1978, the IFAD has invested almost $9 billion in funding for more than 650 programs and projects in the Third World. These programs and projects have benefited more than 250 million families in the developing world. Funding from external donors to IFAD programs and projects has exceeded $16 million.

The IFAD was created to mobilize resources for programs that alleviate rural poverty and improve nutrition. Unlike other international financial institutions that have a broad range of objectives and goals, the IFAD has the specific mandate to combat hunger and rural poverty in developing countries. The IFAD attempts to enable the rural poor in the developing countries to overcome their poverty by fostering social development, gender equity, income generation, improved nutrition, a sustainable environment, and good governance. In addition, IFAD projects and programs focus on country-specific solutions to increase the rural poor peoples' access to financial services, markets, technology, and land.

IFAD projects and programs seek to develop and strengthen the ability of the poor to confront the issues they define as critical, increase access to knowledge so that poor people can overcome obstacles, enhance the bargaining power of the poor in the marketplace, and expand the influence that the poor people exert over public policy. IFAD programs and projects strive to empower the rural poor to take the initiative in their own development. The IFAD insists that the rural poor must be able to develop and strengthen their own organizations so they can advance their own interests and dismantle the obstacles that prevent them from creating better lives for themselves.

MICHAEL R. HALL

See also Agriculture: Impact of Globalization; Poverty: Impact on Development; World Food Program

References and Further Reading

Berthelot, Yves *Unity and Diversity in Development Ideas: Perspectives from the UN Regional Commissions.* Bloomington, IN: Indiana University Press, 2004.

Eicher, Carl, Carl K. Eichler, and John M. Staatz. *International Agricultural Development.* Baltimore, MD: Johns Hopkins University Press, 1998.

Jolly, Richard, Louis Emmerij, Dharam Ghai, and Frederic Lapeyre. *UN Contributions to Development: Thinking and Practice.* Bloomington, IN: Indiana University Press, 2004.

Meisler, Stanley. *United Nations: The First Fifty Years.* London: Atlantic Monthly Press, 1997.

UNITED NATIONS INTERNATIONAL INSTITUTE ON AGING (UNIIA)

The United Nations International Institute on Aging (UNIIA) was established in 1987 as an autonomous body under auspices of the United Nations (UN). It was officially inaugurated in 1988 and established its headquarters in Malta.

The institute was established due to the growing concern over the population aging in many developing and developed countries. According to the United Nations Development Program (UNDP), the number of people over the age of sixty will surpass those under the age of fifteen. It might become a particular problem for developing countries, as it is expected that the number of people over the age of sixty will rise from 8% in 1999 to 19% in 2050 and to 30% in 2150. Some of the issues arising from the aging populations are those concerned with social security and

health care for the elderly as well as opportunities for them to stay active.

A long-term action-oriented program was needed to provide direction for the international community to overcome social and economic problems expected in the aging societies. In 1979, the General Assembly of the United Nations called for a World Assembly on Aging to be held in 1982. The World Assembly on Aging adopted the Vienna International Plan of Action on Aging. This document became the key international document for the worldwide actions on aging. Following this recommendation, the UN Economic and Social Council (ECOSOC) created resolution 1987/41, and the official agreement was signed between the United Nations and the Government of Malta in October 1987. The agreement was officially inaugurated by the UN secretary-general on April 15, 1988.

The UNIIA has the following mandate: to empower the less developed countries to deal with the issue of the aging population and to build their capacity to train their own personnel to formulate and implement their own policies; to help establish regional training centers; to provide continuing support to the network of the training institutions; and to promote interactive partnerships between developing countries and facilitate information transfer on the issue of mass longevity from developed to developing countries.

The main objective of the institute is to provide training to the developing countries and to facilitate implementation of the International Plan of Action on Aging. The UNIIA provides training through regular training programs in Malta and *in-situ* training programs in various developing countries, such as Brazil, China, India, Kuwait, Russia, Singapore, Tunisia, and some other countries. By 2005, the institute had trained more than 1,600 people from 128 countries (INIA est. 2004), and more than 1,100 people were trained through its *in-situ* programs.

In addition to the training activities, the UNIIA collects data, produces publications, promotes research and technical cooperation between various institutions and research groups, and maintains its website. The institute carries its own research projects, hosts meetings for the expert groups, and provides consultancy services. It also cooperates with the University of Malta in running a postgraduate diploma course in gerontology and geriatrics. The UNIIA publishes a quarterly international gerontological journal entitled *BOLD*.

Most activities of the institute are funded by the UN agencies, regional and international organizations, and individual governments through cosharing arrangements. The training programs are financially supported by the UN Population Fund (UNFPA).

The work of the institute is carried out under the supervision of the International Board that consists of nine members. The board's term of office is three years. The secretary-general of the United Nations appoints its Chairman and six members, while the government of Malta appoints the remaining two members.

RAFIS ABAZOV

See also United Nations Development Program (UNDP); United Nations Population Fund (UNFPA)

References and Further Reading

International Institute on Ageing. 2005. Home Page. http://www.inia.org.mt/.

Maddox, George, ed. *The Encyclopedia of Aging: A Comprehensive Resource in Gerontology and Geriatrics.* 3d ed. New York: Springer Publications, 2001.

Makoni, Sinfree, and Koen Stroeken, eds. *Ageing in Africa: Sociolinguistic and Anthropological Approaches.* Aldershot, England; Burlington, VT: Ashgate, 2002.

Phillips, David, ed. *Ageing in the Asia-Pacific Region: Issues, Policies and Future Trends.* London; New York: Routledge, 2000.

Report of the World Assembly on Aging. New York: United Nations, July 26–August 6, 1982.

United Nations Development Program. 2005. Home Page. http://www.undp.org.

UNITED NATIONS INTERNATIONAL RESEARCH AND TRAINING INSTITUTE FOR THE ADVANCEMENT OF WOMEN (INSTRAW)

The United Nations (UN) International Research and Training Institute for the Advancement of Women (INSTRAW) was established by the UN Economic and Social Council (ECOSOC) in 1976. This action was based on a recommendation of the World Conference of the International Women's Year held in Mexico City in 1975 to found a research and training institute devoted to the advancement of women. It is one of the three institutes within the UN system that is dedicated to the advancement of women worldwide and that plays the role of a special adviser to the Secretary-General on Gender Issues and Advancement of Women (OSAGI) and the Inter-Agency Network of Gender Focal Points (IANWGE). Other bodies and programs within the UN system cope with gender issues only within their programs of work.

INSTRAW is autonomous. It is the only UN body commissioned to advance gender equality, particularly in developing countries, through research, training, and the collection and dissemination of information. The institute serves as a vehicle to integrate women as participants and as beneficiaries in the developmental

process, to raise awareness of women's issues worldwide, and to assist women to meet new challenges and directions. To realize these mandates, INSTRAW also plays a catalytic role assisting the efforts of intergovernmental, governmental, and nongovernmental organizations.

In 1979, ECOSOC recommended that INSTRAW locate in the Dominican Republic, a developing country. As a result, the headquarters of INSTRAW were established in the Dominican Republic on premises donated by the host country. In late 2003, former Deputy Minister of Foreign Affairs of Mexico Carmen Moreno was appointed by Secretary-General Kofi Annan as director of INSTRAW.

INSTRAW's activities promote, establish, and undertake research and training projects and programs on gender and women's issues. Thus far, these projects and programs include diversified issues related to women's economic and political empowerment in developing countries. The following topics are addressed by INSTRAW: gender statistics and indicators; measuring and imputing value to the unpaid work of women; women in the informal sector; women and economic development; women and credit; women and rural development; women's studies and curricula development; women and water supply and sanitation; women and new and renewable sources of energy; women and environmental and sustainable development; women and media and communications; women and ageing; women and migration; and women and development planning.

One of the main activities of INSTRAW is establishing and undertaking training projects to raise awareness about gender inequality and its manifestations. INSTRAW holds a number of gender workshops, lectures, discussions, and seminars with collaboration with other institutes worldwide to mainstream gender and women's issues in development and ultimately to bring about a change in consciousness, behavior, and attitudes of policy makers.

In 1995, INSTRAW Acting Director Martha Dueñas-Loza gave an overview of INSTRAW's future role. Basing her comments on recommendations of the Fourth World Conference on Women in Beijing, she identified major issues devoted to the advancement of women. A major issue concerned elderly women in development. Rapid population growth and migration will have an increasing impact on economic and social infrastructure of all countries. INSTRAW published "Ageing in a Gendered World: Women's Issues and Identities" in 1999, which explains that the majority of elderly people are women who live in poverty and maintains that the issues of the elderly women must be addressed as individual components within development plans and programs.

Among other research projects based on the Beijing Conference is the project of Women, Peace, and Security. INSTRAW highlighted gender-based violence as the greatest threat to women's security in times of both conflict and conflict resolution. In collaboration with the United Nations Development Fund for Women (UNFEM), research on this issue has continued.

INSTRAW also perceives significance of the economic and social contributions of women migrants to developing countries and their development strategies although the majority of studies and programs have ignored the issue of remittances by women migrants in spite of the fact that a number of women independently migrate as main economic providers. The institute understands that remittances by women migrants include the movement of money from an immigrant woman to family members in her country of origin as well as a transformation of social and political values in both countries that has been stimulated by women's international transfer of funds. Through the research project, INSTRAW urges the inclusion of a gender perspective in research, programs, and policies of remittances to eliminate gender discrimination on banking and financial policies and to clarify the new economic, social, and political roles of women migrants.

In 1999, INSTRAW obtained a new and additional mandate to perform its activities through the utilization of new information and communication technologies (ICTs). Responding to the new mandate, the institute developed a new operational methodology of the production, management, and dissemination of gender-related knowledge and information: the Gender Awareness Information and Networking System (GAINS). GAINS is a pioneering electronic system that serves as a "virtual workshop" for collaborative research, training, and networking and promotes interactive dialogues between civil society and governments through the virtual places. Using the GAINS methodology, INSTRAW has facilitated two collaborative research programs that aspire to the promotion of a more holistic and cooperative response: Men's Roles and Responsibilities in Ending Gender-Based Violence and Women's Access to Information and Communication Technologies.

INSTRAW carried out two main research projects concerning women in development in the early 2000s. These were Financing for Development and Remittances and Gender. In the former, INSTRAW noted the lack of gender perspectives in three major agreements on financing for development that the international community reached during 2000 to 2002: (i) the Millennium Development Goals in 2000, (ii) the IV Ministerial Conference of the World

Trade Organization, and (iii) the Final Declaration of the International Conference on Financing for Development, known as the Monterrey Consensus (2002). In "Gender Issues and Concerns in Financing for Development" (2004), INSTRAW insists that all stakeholders (such as governments, UN agencies, international financial institutions, and NGOs) consider the harmful influence of development on women's living and consider mainstreaming a gender perspective in financing for development.

Thus, INSTRAW has made efforts to promote gender equality and empower women, particularly in developing countries, through creating as well as sharing knowledge to mainstream the gender perspective in development policy and practice.

YOSHIE KOBAYASHI

See also Women and Development

References and Further Reading

Fraser, Arvonne S., and Irene Tinker, eds. *Developing Power: How Women Transformed International Development*. New York: Feminist Press at the City University of New York, 2004.

Gorman, Robert F. *Great Debates at the United Nations: An Encyclopedia of Fifty Key Issues 1945–2000*. Westport, CT: Greenwood Press, 2001.

INSTRAW. *Gender Concepts in Development Planning: Basic Approach*. Santo Domingo, Dominican Republic: United Nations International Research and Training Institute for the Advancement of Women, 1996.

———. *The Migration of Women: Methodological Issues in the Measurement and Analysis of Internal and International Migration*. Santo Domingo, Dominican Republic: United Nations International Research and Training Institute for the Advancement of Women, 1996.

INSTRAW. 2005. Home Page. http://www.un-instraw.org/en/index.html.

UNITED NATIONS PERMANENT FORUM ON INDIGENOUS PEOPLES

The Permanent Forum on Indigenous Peoples, created in 2000, is the highest-level international body ever empowered to deal with the rights and needs of indigenous populations. It is the first time indigenous voices nominated by indigenous peoples are speaking for indigenous peoples as members of an official United Nations (UN) body. Established by means of a resolution of the UN Economic and Social Council (ECOSOC), the forum consists of sixteen members, eight to be nominated by governments and elected by ECOSOC and eight to be appointed by the president of the council following formal consultation. The forum's mandates are (i) to provide advice and recommendations on indigenous issues to ECOSOC as well as to programs, funds, and agencies of the UN through the council; (ii) raise awareness and promote integration and coordination of activities relating to indigenous issues within the UN system; and (iii) prepare and disseminate information on indigenous issues.

Indigenous peoples, representing five thousand languages and cultures, inhabit more than seventy countries in the world. Historically displaced by powerful expanding states, many indigenous peoples have become minorities within sovereign nations. Although some nation-states have instituted laws guaranteeing original rights to the communal lands held over millennia by aboriginal peoples, many indigenous communities have been expelled from their lands, prohibited from using their languages and practicing their lifestyles. Indigenous peoples are among the most vulnerable and poorest populations in the world (OIT/ILO 2003; AIUSA 2003). In the early twenty-first century, indigenous peoples have become increasingly involved in the shaping of international procedures involving their human and cultural rights.

The establishment of the permanent forum represents an achievement for indigenous peoples that has taken decades of persistent effort from within the UN and outside it. It is the outcome of many accumulated events, principally of the UN Working Group on Indigenous Populations that was established in 1982. According to an Economic and Social Council Resolution and part of the UN Sub-Commission on the Promotion and Protection of Human Rights, the UN Working Group on Indigenous Populations was established to promote and protect indigenous peoples' human rights and fundamental freedoms by developing international standards, measures, and review mechanisms related to indigenous rights. The working group has played an important role in increasing the participation of indigenous people in the formation of international policies. Meeting annually in Geneva since 1982, it has become one of the largest UN forums on human rights, with hundreds of indigenous nongovernmental organizations (NGOs) in attendance. The group contributed to many advancements in indigenous rights and a growing awareness of indigenous issues at the international, governmental, and local levels.

The Permanent Forum on Indigenous Peoples met for the first time in May 2002 at the UN in New York City. Subsequent meetings took place in May 2003 and 2004 and are expected to be held annually. Meetings occur over ten days, allowing discussion of cultural and human rights as well as of environmental, educational, and health concerns. Although only persons who represent the indigenous peoples of the UN's member countries are authorized participants, the

sessions may be attended by any person representing indigenous organizations, indigenous advocacy NGOs, or other interested parties and observers.

JANET M. CHERNELA

References and Further Reading

United Nations Permanent Forum on Indigenous Peoples. 2005. Home Page. http://www.un.org/esa/socdev/unpfii/

UNITED NATIONS POPULATION FUND (UNFPA)

The United Nations Population Fund (UNFPA) is the world's largest source of funding for population and reproductive health programs. It directly controls 25% of the world's population assistance to developing countries. Sub-Saharan Africa receives the largest percentage of UNFPA assistance. Since it began operations in 1969, the UNFPA has provided $6 billion in assistance to developing countries. UNFPA, which currently has about one thousand employees, has worked with governments and nongovernmental organizations (NGOs) in more than 140 countries. Initially established as the United Nations Fund for Population Activities, in 1987 the organization was renamed the United Nations Population Fund, but the acronym of UNFPA remained the same. UNFPA was originally administered by the United Nations Development Program (UNDP). In recognition of the scope of its operations, UNFPA was placed under the UN General Assembly's direct authority in 1972, raising it to the same status as the UNDP.

One of the fundamental goals of UNFPA is to improve reproductive health. The UN has consistently argued that reproductive health is a means to sustainable development and a basic human right. Investments in reproductive health save and improve lives, slow the spread of HIV/AIDS, and encourage gender equality. This, in turn, helps to stabilize population growth and reduce poverty. UNFPA promotes a holistic approach to reproductive health care that includes access to safe and affordable contraceptive methods, counseling, prenatal care, assistance with deliveries, emergency obstetric care, postnatal care, and the prevention of sexually transmitted diseases, including, but not limited to, HIV/AIDS. Since UNFPA began operations in 1969, access to voluntary family planning programs in the developing world has increased, and fertility rates in the Third World have diminished by 50%.

Although all UNFPA programs promote women's equality, many UNFPA programs specifically target gender-based discrimination and violence. UNFPA has specifically sought to develop projects that empower women economically and promote legal reforms. UNFPA also advocates reproductive health and rights, including the right to choose the number and spacing of one's children.

UNFPA works to ensure that adolescents and young people between the ages of fifteen and twenty-four have accurate information, nonjudgmental counseling, and comprehensive and affordable services to prevent unwanted pregnancy and sexually-transmitted infections such as HIV. UNFPA efforts in sub-Saharan Africa, the area of greatest HIV infection, have dramatically increased to confront the spread of HIV, which has a devastating impact on health as well as on the social and economic stability of developing nations. HIV prevention, which is being integrated into reproductive health programs throughout the world, is the main focus of UNFPA's campaign against the disease. Prevention methods include promoting safer sexual relations among young people and making condoms readily available. In many developing nations, condoms are urgently needed to prevent the further spread of the deadly HIV virus.

UNFPA also supports projects that help people who are displaced by human-made and natural disasters. In conflicts, the risk of sexual violence and the spread of sexually transmitted infections, including HIV, increases dramatically. Complications of pregnancy and childbirth are the leading causes of death for displaced women of childbearing age. UNFPA provides supplies and services to protect the reproductive health of displaced peoples, especially those in refugee camps. UNFPA also assists developing nations to collect and analyze population data and integrate population and development strategies into national and regional planning.

The UNFPA contends that people's needs for education and health are a prerequisite of sustainable development. After the International Conference on Population and Development (ICPD) held in Cairo in 1994, UNFPA was charged with implementing the conference's program of action. By 2015, UNFPA hopes to facilitate universal access to reproductive health care services, foster universal primary education, close the gender gap in education, reduce maternal mortality by 75%, reduce infant mortality, and increase life expectancy. Regarding one of the most serious threats to humankind in recent years, UNFPA hopes to reduce HIV infection rates in people fifteen to twenty-four years of age by 25% by 2010.

MICHAEL R. HALL

See also Children and Development; HIV/AIDS; Population Growth: Impact on Development

References and Further Reading

Anderson, Barbara A. *Reproductive Health: Women and Men's Shared Responsibility.* Sudbury, MA: Jones & Bartlett Publishers, 2004.

Ehrlich, Paul R., and Anne H. Ehrlich. *The Population Explosion.* Portland, OR: Touchstone Books, 1991.

Rao, Mohan. *Unheard Scream: Reproductive Health in India.* New Delhi: Kali for Women, 2004.

United Nations Population Fund. *State of the World Population 2004: The Cairo Consensus at Ten Population, Reproductive Health and the Global Effort to End Poverty.* New York: United Nations, 2004.

Vandermeer, John H., and Deborah E. Goldberg. *Population Ecology: First Principles.* Princeton, N.J.: Princeton University Press, 2003.

Weeks, John R. *Population: An Introduction to Concepts and Issues.* Belmont, CA: Wadsworth Publishing, 2001.

UNITED NATIONS RELIEF AND WORKS AGENCY FOR PALESTINE (UNRWA)

The United Nations Relief and Works Agency for Palestine (UNRWA) was established as a temporary agency by the international community in response to the flight of Palestinians from their homes during the first Arab-Israeli war following the creation of Israel by the United Nations in 1948. Initially, the UN turned to the International Refugee Organization (IRO) to offer assistance to Palestinian refugees, but the IRO's mandate was limited to Europe, and so it declined to expand operations to Palestine.

The UN then established the UN Relief for Palestinian Refugees (UNRPR) program to address the needs of the hundreds of thousands of Palestinians displaced by the war. UNRWA succeeded UNRPR in December 1949. It commenced operations in May 1950, and it remained in charge of Palestinian refugee programs even after the establishment of the UN High Commissioner for Refugees (UNHCR) in 1951. The initial focus of UNRWA contained both a relief and development component, with the initial emphasis being on relief. Over time, however, UNRWA got involved in the establishment of education programs and other activities of a more clearly developmental nature, such as health and social services. UNRWA made its headquarters principally in Vienna, Austria, until 1996 when its headquarters were transferred to the Gaza and Amman, Jordan, at a time when progress was being made in resolution of Israeli-Palestinian relations. Though a "temporary" body, its mandate has been repeatedly renewed by the UN General Assembly as the Palestinian refugee situation has persisted. UNRWA's budget primarily focuses on assistance to about 1.3 million Palestinian refugees who continue after generations to reside in refugee camps in Israel, the West Bank, and the Gaza Strip as well as in Lebanon, Syria, and Jordan.

Background

The Arab-Israeli dispute exploded after the creation of the UN partition of the Palestinian Mandate previously administered by the United Kingdom. The partition plan called for the creation of both a Jewish and a Palestinian state. Arab countries, however, refused to acknowledge the existence of Israel and invaded Palestine for the purpose of destroying Israel before it had a chance to establish itself. Confident of victory, Arab countries urged Arab Palestinians to flee, await victory and the destruction of Israel, and return home to a Palestinian state. Events proved otherwise. Israel not only resisted extermination but actually expanded its size to include areas originally slated to be part of the Palestinian state. Neighboring Arab countries seized other parts of what might have become a Palestinian state, and thus Palestinians found themselves under the rule of either Israel or neighboring Arab States, with as many as seven hundred thousand of them qualifying as stateless refugees. Thus was born the Palestinian refugee problem. To address the situation, the UN eventually established UNRWA to offer relief- and development-related assistance to refugees until they were able to return home. Repatriation of Palestinian refugees has been a controversial matter between Israel and Arab countries and remains almost sixty years later an unrealized dream. Thus, although UNRWA was established as a temporary agency, it has actually become a permanent feature of the humanitarian assistance and political landscape of the Middle East.

The fortunes of the Palestinians have been closely tied ever since to the ups and downs of the Arab-Israeli dispute, and the UNRWA, though attempting to navigate an impartial course through the disputes, has had to cope with the reality of the highly politically charged atmosphere in which the staff works. For political reasons, refugee situations and often deprived camp settings that might have been resolved years ago remain festering problems that continue to contribute to the hatred and violence so characteristic of the Arab-Israeli dispute, including the legacy of terrorism, suicide bombings, periodic open rebellion, and Israeli government retaliation against such activities. In wider humanitarian assistance circles, the Palestinian case is regarded as a textbook example of how not to deal with a refugee situation, and long-term refugee

situations are often described as having suffered from a "Palestinization process," that is, a politically prolonged situation.

From Relief Activities to Development

In its first decade, the UNRWA applied the majority of its funds to the immediate needs of Palestinian refugees, including emergency food, medical attention, and eventually housing. A major problem in the early years was the high infant mortality rate owing to malnutrition and dehydration. UNRWA focused on provision of clean water, proper sanitation in camp settings, immunization against common diseases, and oral rehydration programs for infants. Within the first few years, the emergency situation abated, and as with most refugee situations, especially when emergency situations ease, the attention began to focus on education, long-term health, and other development-related activities, including promotion of businesses and development of enterprises. Typically, UNRWA dedicates 60% of its budget to educational activities, including building schools, training teachers, training in the technical and vocational arenas, offering university scholarship programs, providing textbooks, and guaranteeing free primary and preparatory education to Palestinian refugees. UNRWA now operates nearly 650 schools with a staff of almost 17,000 who reach about 490,000 students. By law, UNRWA must use the curriculum of the country in which it operates schools, and these are sadly often highly prejudicial, propagandistic, and ideologically motivated. To counter this, UNRWA attempts to offer programs with supplemental texts and a program emphasizing nonviolent conflict resolution and respect for human rights. It is difficult to assess how well these programs function in light of the periodic and pervasive situation of violence that has marked the politics of the region.

In sixty years, refugee camps might well have been eliminated given the levels of aid provided, but many complicated factors unite to make the camps a persistent feature of the region. Palestinian leaders have seen the camps as convenient symbols of ongoing Israeli oppression. While emergency relief assistance has declined to a mere 11% of the UNRWA budget, every time violence is renewed, the need recurs for emergency assistance, including food, employment aid, and funds for reconstruction of destroyed housing. Thus, UNRWA has repeatedly found itself seeking special emergency assistance from the international community, especially during periods of

intifadah or uprising, when access to both employment and education becomes problematical for refugees living in the occupied territories. Thus, while the lion's share of the UNRWA budget is dedicated to education and health activities, the agency has been in the long-term business of emergency aid depending on where the violence and conflict are most keenly felt. Its emergency work has generally increased after conflicts, such as after the 1967 and 1973 wars.

During the early 1980s, Lebanon was the center of dispute and conflict, when the Palestine Liberation Organization (PLO) took up residence in that country and used southern Lebanon as a launching pad for terrorist activities inside Israel. Israel predictably retaliated against such actions, often targeting refugee camps from which suspected terrorists mounted their assaults. In 1982, Israel intervened in southern Lebanon and forced the PLO to leave Lebanon altogether. This period marked a very delicate time for the UNRWA, especially in attempting to provide humanitarian aid to the innocent Palestinian refugee population. Uprisings in the West Bank and Gaza occurred in 1987 and most recently from the year 2000 to 2005. These situations of generalized violence generally have set back efforts at peace, have promoted higher levels of unemployment among Palestinians, and have disrupted educational activities as well, forcing UNRWA to seek additional international assistance to cope with rising needs. At other times, a glimmer of hope has explicitly focused energies on development activity, such as in the aftermath of the Oslo Peace Accords in the mid-1990s.

Other Development-Related Activities

Coupled with its large educational programs, UNRWA has sponsored small-scale enterprise programs with subsidized loans ranging from $1,000 to $75,000. More than a thousand small businesses have benefited from such loans, which have stimulated small industries; agricultural and manufacturing enterprises; and medical, publishing, and domestic services. A microenterprise credit program funding similar activities has reached forty-three thousand beneficiaries. UNRWA has developed women's solidarity group loan programs that encourage Palestinian women to engage in the local economy. More than twenty thousand such loans, which amount to a few hundred dollars, have been awarded. UNRWA operates more than 120 primary health care facilities in refugee camps and among local populations affected by the presence of refugees, employing several thousand local staff to provide these services.

UNRWA has funded shelter rehabilitation programs since 1993 as part of its Peace Implementation Program that followed the Oslo Peace Accords breakthrough. Subsequent violence in the region and the destruction of additional housing continues to give this program much work. UNRWA has also funded the establishment of women's centers and community rehabilitation centers, where the special needs of the disabled can be addressed training and employment.

Future Prospects

The death of Yasser Arafat in November 2004 holds out the promise under new Palestinian leadership that peace negotiations can be restored and a greater emphasis placed on the long-term development agenda of UNRWA, which now employs Palestinians as the principal managers of its work. Israel in the meantime has embarked on a unilateral program of withdrawal from the vast majority of the occupied territories. At the same time, it has begun construction of a security wall to prevent terrorist attacks in Israel. The wall seems to have succeeded in reducing such attacks, but it has also caused much hardship among Palestinians whose homes lie on one side and whose jobs lie on the other side of the security barrier. The Israeli government has shown some willingness to compromise on resituating the barrier to reduce such hardships but has insisted, in principle, on the necessity of the project for its national safety and security. The general course of the wall follows lines fairly similar to those indicated by the Wye Peace Agreement, which was ultimately rejected by Yasser Arafat but that might find new life in the wake of his death. All of this leaves open the possibility that a new Palestinian leadership might be in a position finally to consolidate authority and begin a more determined road to peaceful statehood. In that event, UNRWA's involvement could be largely devolved to the capable Palestinian management, which to a large extent already performs the bulk of UNRWA program activity. International funding of these activities might well need to be continued; however, UNRWA, which was always conceived as a temporary agency, may at long last complete its work and bequeath its efforts to a full Palestinian administration.

ROBERT F. GORMAN

See also Palestine; Palestinian Diaspora; Refugees; United Nations High Commissioner for Refugees (UNHCR)

References and Further Reading

Adelman, Howard. *Palestinian Refugees and Durable Solutions*. Oxford: Refugee Studies Programme Monograph, 1987.

Besson, Yves. "UNRWA and Its Role in Lebanon." *Journal of Refugee Studies* 10, no. 3 (September 1997): 335–348.

Buehrig, Edward. *The UN and the Palestinian Refugees: A Study in Non-Territorial Administration*. Bloomington, IN: Indiana University Press, 1971.

Morris, Benny. *The Birth of the Palestinian Refugee Problem, 1947–1949*. Cambridge: Cambridge University Press, 1987.

Peretz, Don. *Palestinians, Refugees and the Middle East Peace Process* Arlington, VA: United States Institute of Peace Press, 1993.

Schiff, Benjamin. *Refugees unto the Third Generation: UN Aid to Palestinians*. Syracuse, NY: Syracuse University Press, 1995.

Swann, Robert, ed. "Palestinian Refugees and Non-Refugees in the West Bank and Gaza Strip." Special issue of the *Journal of Refugee Studies* 2, no. 1 (1989): 1–219.

Viorst, Milton. *Reaching for the Olive Branch: UNRWA and Peace in the Middle East*. Washington, DC: Middle East Institute, 1989.

UNITED NATIONS TRUSTEESHIP COUNCIL

With the establishment of the League of Nations in 1919, the principle of self-determination of nations was articulated, along with the idea that non-self-governing territories should be prepared for eventual self-government. This principle was applied in the Mandate System set up to prepare former colonies of the Axis powers for their eventual dependence under the guidance of various victorious powers, which served as the new governing authorities in these territories. Three classes of mandates were established depending on their initial readiness for political and economic dependence. The United Nations (UN) reiterated many of these principles in the UN Charter, especially in its Declaration Regarding Non-Self-Governing Territories and in its establishment of the International Trusteeship System. In 1945, the various League of Nations mandates were placed under the stewardship of the Trusteeship Council, along with various territories detached from Japan and some other territories placed voluntarily under a trust territory system. Economic development was one of the main areas of concern to the Trusteeship Council as it received reports from the trustee nations that exercised administrative responsibility for the territories. The Trusteeship Council successfully completed its work in 1994 when the last of the trust territories achieved independence; as of 2005, the members of the council

consist of the five permanent members of the UN Security Council, and no further work for the body has yet been agreed upon.

The Purposes of the Trusteeship System

The UN Charter conceived of the Trusteeship System as a means of maintaining international peace and security by placing non-self-governing territories under a system of stewardship that would prepare them for eventual independence. To this end, the governments charged with administrative oversight were obliged under Article 76 of the UN Charter "to promote the political, economic, social, and educational advancement of the inhabitants of the trust territories, and their progressive development towards self-government or independence." This also called for a respect for human rights and fundamental freedoms of the inhabitants. Members of the Trusteeship Council included all countries serving as administrators of trust territories, the permanent members of the UN Security Council, and other countries selected by the UN General Assembly to ensure an equal number of administering and nonadministering governments. The Trusteeship Council entered into agreements with the trust authorities, received and considered annual reports from them, received petitions from indigenous populations, and made occasional visits to the territories. The reports made to the Trusteeship Council were based on its authority to seek and receive information from the administrative government concerning the "political, economic, social, and educational advancement of the inhabitants."

The Trusteeship Council was not conceived primarily as a UN agency for economic development. Indeed, the UN Charter (Article 91) called upon it to "avail itself of the assistance of the Economic and Social Council and of the specialized agencies" in regard to economic matters falling outside its own competence. However, inherent in the notion that a trust territory must be prepared for self-government was the necessary principle that the inhabitants should achieve the capacity for political and economic development, and all the trust territories qualified as developing areas.

Outcome of the Trusteeship System

All eleven territories placed under the UN Trusteeship system are now independent states. In Africa, British Togoland became independent as Ghana in 1957, while French Togoland achieved independence in 1960 as Togo. Somaliland gained independence from Italy and joined with the British protectorate of Somaliland to form Somalia in 1960. The French Cameroons attained independence in 1960 as Cameroon, while in 1961 the British Cameroons divided at independence, the northern territory joining Nigeria and the southern Cameroon. Tanganyika (later Tanzania) gained its independence from the British in 1961. Ruanda-Urundi divided at independence from Belgium in 1962 to form the new states of Rwanda and Burundi. In the Pacific, Western Samoa achieved independence as Samoa from New Zealand in 1962, Nauru from Australia in 1968, and New Guinea from Australia in 1975, as Papua New Guinea. The Trust Territory of the Pacific gained independence from the United States as four new countries: Micronesia, the Marshall Islands, and the Northern Mariana Islands, all in 1990, and then Palau in 1994.

All of the trust territories continue to fall under the rubric of developing nations, each with specific challenges and struggling economies. The most severely underdeveloped of the countries, namely Somalia, Rwanda, and Burundi, have also experienced the most intense and prolonged civil unrest, war, and large-scale loss of life. Tanzania is a country lacking substantial natural resources, but it has enjoyed political stability. With the adoption of economic reforms, it has posted strong economic growth in recent years. Ghana, known in colonial times as the "Gold Coast," has achieved significant gains in development in recent years with the restoration of a stable government and new gold discoveries, but it remains heavily indebted. The Cameroon is one of the better resource endowed countries in sub-Saharan Africa, with rich farmland and oil resources, but these resources have not been consistently well managed. The Island States of the Pacific, with the exception of New Guinea, are lightly populated. Nauru, with only thirteen thousand citizens, faces substantial economic challenges with the depletion of its once significant phosphates resources. Papua New Guinea on the other hand has more than five million people and substantial resources although most of its people engage in subsistence activities. Samoa enjoys the greatest per capita wealth of all the former trust territories, but a major share of this wealth takes the form of remittances from its citizens employed overseas. Tourism is another area in which the island nations have made economic gains, notably the Northern Mariana Islands, but many of the former Pacific Island trust territories continue to rely heavily on assistance from the United States. Although the trust territories have experienced variable levels of economic development since independence, each continues to face significant challenges while struggling to achieve greater prosperity.

ROBERT F. GORMAN

See also Burundi; Cameroon; Marshall Islands, Republic of; Micronesia, Federated States of; Papua New Guinea; Samoa; Somalia; Tanzania; Togo

References and Further Reading

Groom, A. J. R. "The Trusteeship Council: A Successful Demise." *The United Nations at the Millennium*, Paul G. Taylor and A. J. R. Groom, eds. New York: Continuum International Publishing Group, 2001.

Parker, Tom. *The Ultimate Intervention: Revitalizing the UN Trusteeship Council for the 21st Century*. Sandvika, Norway: Centre for European and Asian Studies at the Norwegian School of Management, 2003. http://www.bi.no/templates/omSkolested_28642.aspx.

Toussaint, Charmian Edwards. *The Trusteeship System of the United Nations*. Westport, CT: Greenwood, 1976.

UNITED NATIONS UNIVERSITY (UNU)

In 1969, the United Nation's (UN) Secretary-General U. Thant suggested that consideration be given to establishing an international university devoted to world progress and peace. In response, the UN General Assembly voted to establish the United Nations University (UNU) in 1973. The government of Japan pledged $100 million to UNU's endowment fund and offered a headquarters for the university in Tokyo. UNU began activities in 1975 at its Tokyo headquarters, focusing mainly on peace and conflict resolution, development in a changing world, and science and technology in relation to human welfare.

UNU operates under the joint sponsorship of the United Nations and the United Nations Educational, Scientific, and Cultural Organization (UNESCO). Its mission is to find original, forward-looking solutions to the most pressing problems that concern the United Nations and the peoples of its member states. The UNU undertakes research and training on a broad range of issues, including food and nutrition, information technology, land use and climate change, the freshwater crisis, urbanization, and the causes of complex humanitarian emergencies. Experts in the UNU engage in the direct exchange of ideas and research findings with policy makers and practitioners around the world.

The UNU's Peace and Governance Program organizes and supports research that produces policy-oriented recommendations for solving contemporary problems and identifying longer term trends that have implications for peace, security, and governance. Its challenging agenda includes finding solutions to civil and ethnic conflict, interstate war, terrorism, poverty, the threat of weapons of mass destruction, the scourge of small arms, the negative impacts of economic globalization, human rights abuses, and the problems experienced by transitional and democratizing societies.

Administratively, the UNU consists of a council of twenty-four members who serve as the governing board of the university; a rector is responsible for the administration, programming, and coordination of the university, and the University Center assists the rector. The council is appointed jointly by the UN secretary-general and UNESCO's director-general. The rector is appointed by the UN secretary-general and normally serves for five years, with the possibility of reappointment. The center, which is located in Tokyo, promotes exchanges of scholars as well as scientific and technical ideas and information within the world academic community, particularly in developing countries through conferences, workshops, and publications. The UNU operates as an autonomous academic institution under the joint sponsorship of the UN and UNESCO. Its chief source of funding is an endowment fund established by Japan and augmented by the voluntary contributions of other countries and private foundations.

Scholars and institutions from around the world collaborate in the work of the UNU. They represent a wide spectrum of disciplines, ideologies, and cultural backgrounds. The UNU does not have a student body. Instead, it offers postgraduate training to people from developing countries to study at a worldwide network of research and postgraduate training centers. Three of these centers are the Institute of Nutrition of Central America and Panama (located in Guatemala City), Chiang Mai University in Thailand (for the study of agroforestry systems), and the Tropical Agricultural Research and Training Center in Costa Rica.

PAUL J. MAGNARELLA

Further Reading

American Council for The United Nations University. *The United Nations University Today: Introduction and Basic Facts*. McLean, VA: 1984.

Newland, Kathleen. *The UNU in the Mid-Eighties*. Tokyo: United Nations University Press, 1984.

United Nations University. *The United Nations University Annual Reports*. Tokyo: United Nations University Press.

———. *Work in Progress/UNU Newsletter*. Tokyo: United Nations University Press.

———. *UNU Strategic Plan 2000: Advancing Knowledge for Human Security and Development*. Tokyo: United Nations University Press, 2000.

UNITED STATES AGENCY FOR INTERNATIONAL DEVELOPMENT (USAID)

The United States Agency for International Development (USAID) is an independent federal agency that receives its direction from the US Secretary of State. Independent federal agencies are created by the US Congress to deal with complex policy matters that Congress cannot address because it does not have the resources nor the desire to manage these matters. Congress entrusts independent agencies with decision-making powers beyond those granted to other federal agencies. USAID is headed by the administrator, who is appointed by the president and must be confirmed in office by the US Senate. In 2004, the agency's administrator was Andrew S. Natsios; he has held this position since April 2001. USAID is the US government agency responsible for nearly all of the United State's bilateral foreign aid programs. The agency plans and administers the world's largest bilateral aid program. In 2004, USAID administered some $12.65 billion in foreign aid, of which $2.44 billion of this was USAID assistance to Iraq.

As a US government agency, USAID has always shaped its policy and aid programs by the perceived national security and domestic political needs of each US presidential administration and of the US Congress. Hence, during the Cold War, USAID's underlying priorities included a strong dose of anticommunism and, following the September 11, 2001, terrorist attacks on the United States under the George W. Bush administration, antiterrorism. A second concern that conditions how USAID is able to operate is that although the United States. contributes more than any other nation to international development, its contributions have remained stagnant and have even declined slightly over time; they are among the smallest on a percentage basis of any of the major developed nations. Only about 0.5% of the US budget is spent on nonmilitary foreign assistance (Tarnoff and Nowles 2004). Although USAID's assistance programs concentrate on aid to the developing world, it is important to realize that USAID's primary goal is to further the foreign policy goals of the United States.

Assistance provided by USAID largely falls into three categories: Economic Support Funds, Development Assistance, and Food for Peace. Economic Support Funds (ESF) provide about half of all US economic aid. ESF include direct cash transfers, commodity import programs, and individual development programs. ESF, more than any other US aid program, are targeted at assisting politically important countries to advance US political and security objectives (Hoy 1998). Although the legislation authorizing ESF states that ESF should be used to the maximum extent possible for development, two-thirds to three-fourths of ESF are spent on security (Hoy 1998; Burnell 1997). Moreover, historically the majority of the funds, although this proportion is generally decreasing, assist Israel and Egypt.

Development Assistance (DA) is the second category of US foreign assistance. DA consists of grants to support economic development programs (Hoy 1998). Congress specifies specific sectors, such as health, population, agriculture, and rural development. DA funding has been on the decline and during the 1980s and 1990s was the frequent target of cuts. The third category of USAID assistance is Food for Peace. While food aid is welcome during emergencies, the Institute for Food Policy, for example, charges that the United States often uses food aid to dispose of domestic surpluses, to open new markets for commercial sales of US farm products, and to extend the reach of US agribusiness (Hoy 1998). Indeed, US food aid to Somalia was blamed for discouraging local production, making the food crisis even worse.

A Short History of USAID

USAID was created by an executive order from President John F. Kennedy on November 3, 1961. The creation of USAID followed the reorganization of US foreign assistance by the Foreign Assistance Act (FAA) passed by Congress on September 4, 1961. The new law required the creation of a separate agency to administer foreign economic aid programs. Hence, USAID was created as the first US foreign assistance agency to take a long-term approach to economic development separately from military aid. Indeed, prior to the creation of USAID, almost 80% of all US foreign aid was military aid. Following the birth of USAID, more than half of US foreign aid would become economic aid intended to foster long-term economic development in developing countries.

USAID fused into a single agency the functions of several preexisting US agencies. USAID combined the economic and technical assistance operations of the International Cooperation Agency, the foreign loan functions of the Development Loan Fund, the bequests of the Development Grant Fund, the local currency support of the Export-Import Bank, and the Food for Peace program of the Department of Agriculture. Moreover, the 1961 FAA and USAID highlighted the new Kennedy administration's commitment to maintaining and increasing foreign assistance to developing countries. Kennedy championed the creation of USAID and the administration's new

emphasis on foreign assistance on several premises: (i) the fragmented, awkward, inconsistent, and slow foreign aid programs of the time proved largely unsatisfactory and ill suited for the needs of both the United States and developing countries; (ii) the economic collapse of developing countries that "would be disastrous to our national security, . . . and offensive to our conscience;" and (iii) the perception that 1960s presented a historic opportunity for industrialized nations to move less-developed nations into self-sustained economic growth. Kennedy saw US direct foreign aid to developing counties as a moral obligation and "counter to totalitarianism" (About USAID 2004). Furthermore, Kennedy asserted that for the United States to fail in meeting its moral obligations would be a long-term disaster for the nation and the world, threatening the security of the United States.

USAID's most important goal was toward long-term economic and technical assistance on a country-by-country basis with the commitment of aid on a multiyear and programmatic basis. This would mean bilateral as opposed to multilateral aid. The United States would continue to contribute to multilateral aid agencies and organizations, but USAID would concentrate on bilateral aid. In addition, the foci of USAID would be on economic growth, political stability, and democracy in the developing world to prevent the threat of instability arising from poverty and the spread of communism. Furthermore, the birth of USAID also marked a change in strategy for US foreign aid away from major industrial projects to other areas such as agriculture. Data from the mid-1960s show that only 10% of USAID went to industrial and mining projects (Wood 1986).

The early USAID's development program was based on the development theory (also known as modernization theory) of Walt W. Rostow, President Kennedy's Deputy Special Assistant to the President for National Security Affairs and President Lyndon B. Johnson's Special Assistant for National Security Affairs (modern equivalent is National Security Advisor). Rostow's 1960 book, *The Stages of Economic Growth: A Non-Communist Manifesto,* posited that economic development takes place in five stages: traditional society, preconditions for take-off, take-off, drive to maturity, and high mass consumption. Rostow argued that a stimulus, such as foreign assistance in the form of capital, technology, and expertise, is needed to propel the developing world beyond the precondition stage to the take-off stage. Beyond this latter stage, foreign aid would no longer be required because economic growth becomes an automatic process.

According to USAID, one of its crowning achievements under the FAA of 1961 was setting up country-by-country planning and long-term, rather than short-term or crisis, development planning mechanisms. Also among the agency's early benchmarks was the Alliance for Progress. The 1961–1973 Alliance for Progress was intended as a Marshall Plan for Latin America. The United States pledged $20 billion in assistance through grants and loans (Scheman 1988). In comparison, the Marshall Plan dispensed $13 billion mostly to Europe. The Alliance for Progress was the largest US aid program for developing countries up to that point. USAID hoped that the aid program would strengthen capitalism, economic development, and democracy in Latin America and strengthen ties between the United States and Latin America. Even though the Alliance for Progress was a bold step, it did not seem to improve the economic and political situations of Latin America extensively, and the program was abandoned. Yet, in retrospect, the record of the Alliance for Progress is better than perceived at the time.

USAID and the FAA have been subject to change over time as a result of US domestic politics and events in international affairs. For example, in the early 1970s, in part a counter-reaction to the Vietnam War and in part a reaction to perceptions that US foreign aid to developing countries was counterproductive and wasteful, Congress rejected President Richard M. Nixon's foreign assistance spending authorization bills. The result was that Congress amended the FAA to ensure that USAID assistance would be reserved for the poorest sectors of developing countries with the notion that assistance ought to go to directly to the recipient nation's needy population to provide for their basic needs. Under this new "Basic Needs" approach, Congress replaced old categories of technical assistance grants and development loans with new functional categories aimed at specific problems such as agriculture, family planning, and education. The aim of bilateral development aid was to concentrate on sharing American technical expertise and commodities to meet development problems rather than relying on large-scale transfers of money and capital goods. One significant 1973 amendment to the FAA, the Helms Amendment, prohibits the use of US funds for abortion services. The structure of the FAA remains much the way it was following the 1973 amendments. Another change in 1979 divested administrative power from the secretary of state to the administrator of USAID.

In 1984, President Ronald Reagan announced a more stringent US, policy on foreign assistance concerning abortion. Reagan announced a ban on US government financial support for US and foreign family planning agencies that were involved in any way with the provision of abortion in foreign countries. The ban, known as the Mexico City Policy, totally removed all US government funding from

international agencies that provided abortion procedures, provided abortion counseling, or advocated for women's abortion access anywhere in the world. Thus, a family planning agency's funding might have been cut off from its contraceptive/family planning counseling services in one country if it had any abortion-related activity in the same or in another country. President William J. Clinton rescinded this ban in 1993 through an executive order. The ban was reinstated by President George W. Bush in 2001.

Another major change in USAID direction occurred under the George H. W. Bush administration, was renewed with vigor under the William J. Clinton administration, and confirmed again by the George W. Bush administration. In response to the wave of democratic transitions of the late 1980s, USAID issued a new initiative in December 1990, the Democracy Initiative. USAID would focus its resources explicitly to help promote and consolidate democracy. Democracy assistance programs were implemented to be further strengthened in 1995. Moreover, reflecting the revolutionary changes occurring in the world during the late 1980s and 1990s, democracy, economic, and technical assistance programes were expanded to include USAID assistance to Russia and the post-Soviet states from 1993 onward. The promotion of democracy had always been given lip service by the United States and USAID, but during the 1960s, 1970s, and 1980s, the United States tolerated and even assisted authoritarian states as long as they were anti-Communist.

A second major change in direction for USAID was the 1993 Clinton administration's decision to contract out some USAID development programs. By 1998, half of all USAID funds for development assistance were delivered in the form of contracts. This means that although funds still are used in developing countries, the services are provided by US firms, which is where the funds actually go. This change was initiated to appease domestic US critics who claim US foreign aid is wasted money. If the funds go to US firms and create US jobs, critics may be silenced. Nevertheless, the policy has possible shortcomings such as too many large-dollar contracts awarded to too few contractors, recipient needs becoming less important than US domestic economic interests, an emphasis on fulfilling the contract rather than fulfilling the need, noncompetitive contract awards, and very low standards of acceptable contract performance (Berríos 2000). Widely reported examples, but not of aid contracts administered by USAID, of the tenacity and possible validity of some of these criticisms surrounds the 2002 to 2004 condemnation of the contracts awarded to Bechtel Corporation and Halliburton by the Pentagon for the rebuilding of Iraq.

Since September 11, 2001, antiterrorism became a priority of USAID. "Defeating terrorism is our nation's primary and immediate priority," asserted President George W. Bush in the White House press release entitled *National Strategy for Combating Terrorism* of February 14, 2003. USAID has joined the effort to deny terrorists resources and state sponsorship and to work toward amending the conditions of poverty and oppression that terrorists seek to exploit (Natsios 2004). The war on terrorism brought USAID new funding for projects in Afghanistan, Iraq, the Philippines, and Palestine, but the bulk of these have gone to Iraq and are not new developmental assistance projects. Many of the projects that are now labeled as targeted against fostering the conditions of terrorism are the same projects relabeled. Nevertheless, the new urgency of international development, even under the label antiterrorism, is not negative for the developing world. It means that USAID and like programs will be easier to justify to Congress.

President George W. Bush announced in a speech at the Inter-American Development Bank on March 14, 2002, that the United States would increase its core development assistance by 50% during the following three years, resulting in a $5 billion annual increase over current levels. President Bush said that combating poverty is a moral imperative and that he has made it a US foreign policy priority. To meet this challenge, the president has proposed increased accountability for rich and poor nations alike, linking greater contributions by developed nations to greater responsibility by developing nations. Bush's proposal would mark the largest single-year increase in bilateral aid in decades (Brainard *et al.* 2003). Bush's proposal also marks a newfound interest in and emphasis on international development.

USAID priorities and programs since 2004 have included initiatives to build roads in Afghanistan; to train educators in Africa, Latin America, and the Caribbean; to prevent the trafficking and sexual exploitation of people, particularly women and children; to promote clean energy and electrification in developing nations; to promote economic development in Central Africa while conserving the region's forests and wildlife; to expand information and communications technologies in Senegal, Peru, and Indonesia; to empower community and faith-based organizations (under the Bush administration's controversial policy on faith-based initiatives); to address global climate change; to combat the spread of communicable diseases, particularly AIDS, tuberculosis, and malaria, in developing nations; to assist in the development of agricultural technology for families and communities to fight hunger in Africa; to promote economic growth and job creation in Central

America and Africa; and to improve access to clean water throughout the developing world.

JAMES A. NORRIS

See also Canadian International Development Agency (CIDA)

References and Further Reading

Barrett, Deborah, and Amy Ong Tsui. "Policy as Symbolic Statement: International Response to National Population Strategies." *Social Forces* 78, no. 1 (1999).
Berríos, Rubén. *Contracting for Development: The Role of For-Profit Contractors in US Foreign Development Assistance*. Westport, CT; London: Praeger, 2000.
Brainard, Lael, Caril Graham, Nigel Purvis, Steven Radelet, and Gayle E. Smith. *The Other War: Global Poverty and the Millennium Change Account*. Washington, DC: Center for Global Development, Brookings Institution Press, 2003.
Burnell, Peter. *Foreign Aid in a Changing World*. Buckingham; Philadephia, PA: Open University Press, 1997.
Hoy, Paula. *Players and Issues in International Aid*. West Hartford, CT: Kumarian Press, 1998.
Natsios, Andrew. "Fighting Terror with Aid: Underlying Conditions that Foster Terrorism." *Harvard International Review* 26, no. 3 (2004).
Payaslian, Simon. *US Foreign Economic and Military Aid: The Reagan and Bush Administrations*. London; Lanham, MD: University Press of America, 1996.
Revelle, Roger. "Global Partnership: International Agencies and Economic Development." *International Organization* 22, no. 1 (1968).
Rostow, Walt W. *The Stages of Economic Growth: A Non-Communist Manifesto*. New York; Cambridge: Cambridge University Press, 1960.
———. *Security, Democracy, Prosperity: Strategic Plan, Fiscal Years 2004–2009, Aligning Diplomacy and Development Assistance*. Washington, DC: United States Department of State and United State Agency for International Development, 2004.
Scheman, L. Ronald. "The Alliance for Progress: Concept and Creativity." *The Alliance for Progress: A Retrospective*. New York; London: Praeger, 1988.
Tarnoff, Curt, and Larry Nowels. *Foreign Aid: An Introductory Overview of US Programs and Policy*. Washington, DC: Congressional Research Service, 2004.
USAID. 2004. *About USAID*. Washington, DC: United States Agency for International Development. www.USAID.gov
Wood, Robert E. *From Marshall Plan to Debt Crisis: Foreign Aid and Development Choices in the World Economy*. Berkeley, CA; London: University of California Press, 1986.

UNITED STATES–DOMINICAN REPUBLIC–CENTRAL AMERICA FREE TRADE AGREEMENT

For obvious geographical reasons, the United States has always been an influential actor in the evolution of political and economic life in Central America and the Caribbean, starting in the years after the United States's independence in 1776. The Monroe Doctrine from US President James Monroe stated as early as 1823 that European powers could no longer intervene in America's countries, allowing the United States to become the main foreign power in the Western Hemisphere. By the early twentieth century, the doctrine had been extended to justify military intervention in the area and the implantation of semiprotectorates.

Rapidly after independence in 1821, Central America's economies developed as export-led economies. Coffee and banana were the main export products and were central in the process of integrating the region in the world economy. The United States rapidly became the first buyer of the region's goods. As early as 1920, the American market was the destination of between 50% (for Costa Rica) and more than 85% (Honduras) of exports of the different countries of the Central American subcontinent. These two trends are to be kept in mind to understand the evolution of the relations between the United States and Central America.

A major attempt to break the export-led development scheme was envisaged in the 1960s and 1970s with the formation of the Central American Common Market (CACM) that promoted an import substitution model, whereby industrialization was seen as the main solution to solve the problems of underdevelopment. Unfortunately, for some political and economic reasons, this effort to ground economic development on a "closed regionalism," that is on the formation of an economic bloc that protected its internal markets, failed to reach sustainable success, even if the CACM raised the rate of the intraregional trade in relation with foreign trade from less than 7% in 1960 to more than 25% in 1970.

In the 1990s, two events occurred that would have significant importance in the process leading to the signature of the United States–Dominican Republic–Central American Free Trade Agreement (US-DR-CA-FTA). The creation of the World Trade Organization (WTO) in 1995 confirmed a tendency through the multilateralization of trade negotiations. Even if, at the same time, a lot of bilateral and regional trade agreements were signed, the ideological context of these integration treaties moved from a "closed regionalism" to an "open regionalism," where the regional trading blocs were seen as a step to integrate the globalizing economy rather than to isolate them like it was the case in the 1960s and the 1970s. Nevertheless, by 1999, the opposition between different groups of countries having divergent interests concerning the widening of the WTO (such as on the question whether an agreement protecting and promoting foreign investments should be

negotiated) showed all the limits of the multilateral framework.

The second event was the launch of negotiations for the creation of a Free Trade Area of the Americas (FTAA) at the beginning of the 1990s. The objective was to form a free trade zone that would enter into force at the beginning of 2005. The negotiations were much more difficult than anticipated, and by the years 2002 and 2003, it appeared more and more that this goal was impossible to attain.

Facing such difficulties in the multilateral and hemispheric forums, the administration of President George W. Bush, led by Trade Representative Robert Zoellick, launched a succession of bilateral negotiations leading to bilateral or regional free trade agreements. For Central American countries whose economies are historically dependent on the US market, the signature of a free trade agreement then became the sole opportunity to penetrate and consolidate their link to this market.

The negotiations between the United States and Central American countries began in January 2003, and a final agreement was signed in May 2004. Then, in August, the Dominican Republic joined the treaty that became the United States–Dominican Republic–Central American Free Trade Agreement that was yet to be ratified.

The treaty is relatively classical in the sense that it covers the same components shared by other free trade agreements ratified by the United States in the last decade. It provides facilitated access for goods and services, offers better protection for foreign investment (and the possibility for investors to get access to international arbitration in case of dispute with the state receiving their investments), and forces countries to apply rules regarding government procurements and the protection of intellectual property. It includes a chapter on labor and another on the environment that essentially mandate member countries to enforce their own legislation on these two subjects. Possibly the strongest critique of the agreement concerns the issue of agriculture. Central American farmers fear to be unable to compete with the highly subsidized American multinationals that will now have an easier access to their market.

RÉMI BACHAND

See also Central America: History and Economic Development; Central American Common Market (CACM); Costa Rica; Dominican Republic; El Salvador; Free Trade Area of the Americas (FTAA); Guatemala; Honduras; Import Substitution Industrialization; Latin American Integration Association (ALADI); Nicaragua; Panama

References and Further Reading

Axline, W. Andrew. "Free Trade in the Americas and Sub-Regional Integration in Central America and the Caribbean." *Canadian Journal of Development Studies* 21, no. 1 (2000): 31–53.

Bull, Benedict. "'New Regionalism' in Central America.'" *Third World Quarterly* 20, no. 5 (1999): 957–970.

Bulmer-Thomas, Victor. "The Central American Common Market: From Closed to Open Regionalism." *World Development* 26, no. 2 (1998): 313–322.

Larraín, Felipe B., ed. *Economic Development in Central America.* 2 Vols. Cambridge, MA: John F. Kennedy School of Government, Harvard University, 2001.

Phillips, Nicola. "Hemispheric Integration and Subregionalism in the Americas." *International Affairs* 79, no. 2 (2003) 327–349. United States Trade Representative. "Dominican Republic-Central America FTA." http://www.ustr.gov/Trade_Agreements/Bilateral/CAFTA-DR/Section_Index.html.

UNIVERSAL DECLARATION OF HUMAN RIGHTS

In 1948, the United Nations (UN) General Assembly adopted the Universal Declaration of Human Rights as an international commitment to humanity. Although many philosophers, statesmen, and religious leaders had argued throughout the ages for human rights, it took the genocide and crimes against humanity committed during World War II to finally make countries commit themselves to protecting human rights in a unified way.

The Nazi Holocaust of World War II resulted in the enslavement, torture, and murder of millions of people: Jews, Poles, gypsies, Soviet prisoners of war, homosexuals, the mentally and physically handicapped, and Nazi political opponents. Efforts to defeat the Axis powers became synonymous with the struggle to universalize human rights and punish those who violated them. President Franklin D. Roosevelt's Four Freedoms speech before the United States Congress in 1941 propelled the momentum toward universal recognition of inalienable human rights. In his address, Roosevelt proclaimed that all people were entitled to freedom of speech and expression, freedom of worship, freedom from want, and freedom from fear.

On April 25, 1945, as World War II was coming to an end, representatives from forty-six nations gathered in San Francisco, California, to form the United Nations and agree on the UN Charter. That UN Charter gave human rights a new international legal status. Its preamble identifies human rights as one of the four founding purposes of the UN. The UN Charter's first article declares that UN member states must work to "achieve international cooperation . . . in

promoting and encouraging respect for human rights and for fundamental freedoms for all without distinction as to race, sex, language or religion." Article 55 states that the UN will promote "universal respect for, and observance of, human rights and fundamental freedoms," and Article 56 states that members "pledge themselves to take joint and separate action" to achieve that respect. The UN Charter does not, however, define human rights. Instead, its Article 68 mandated that the UN Economic and Social Council (ECOSOC) should create a commission for that purpose.

ECOSOC established the official eighteen-member UN Commission on Human Rights in June 1946. The commission elected US Delegate Eleanor Roosevelt as its chairperson, China's P.C. Chang and France's René Cassin as vice chairmen, and Lebanon's Charles Malik as rapporteur. The UN Secretariat supported the commission's work under the direction of John P. Humphrey, Director of the UN's Human Rights Division. The commission formed a subcommittee to draft a universal human rights document. The subcommittee was composed of Roosevelt, Chang, Malik, and Humphrey as well as representatives from Australia, Chile, France, the Philippines, the Soviet Union, the Ukrainian SSR, the United Kingdom, Uruguay, and Yugoslavia.

The subcommittee completed the *Universal Declaration of Human Rights* on June 18, 1948, and on December 10, 1948, the UN General Assembly voted to adopt it without dissent. Forty-eight member states voted yes, while eight abstained (the Soviet bloc countries, South Africa, and Saudi Arabia). Two countries were absent and did not vote.

The declaration's preamble recognizes that "the inherent dignity and . . . the equal and inalienable rights of all members of the human family [are] the foundation of freedom, justice and peace in the world." It goes on to state that, "Member States have pledged themselves to achieve, in co-operation with the United Nations, the promotion of universal respect for and observance of human rights and fundamental freedoms." Because "a common understanding of these rights and freedoms is of the greatest importance for the full realization of this pledge, . . . the General Assembly proclaims this Universal Declaration of Human Rights as a common standard of achievement for all peoples and all nations."

According to the declaration's thirty articles, universal human rights include the right to life, liberty, and security of a person; freedom from torture and discrimination based on race, religion, ethnicity, or gender; freedom of thought, conscience, religion, opinion, speech, and press; the right to participate in the political system, to own property, to marry and have a family, and to associate with others; freedom from arbitrary arrest and searches; the right to a fair trial, to confront prosecution witnesses, and to put on witnesses and evidence in one's own defense; the right to work and to an education; and the right to maintain one's culture and native language. Article 29 states that every person also has the duty to respect the rights and freedoms of others, and that governments may limit human rights listed in the declaration only for purposes of "meeting the just requirements of morality, public order and the general welfare in a democratic society."

The UN adopted the Universal Declaration of Human Rights as an aspirational rather than as a legally binding document. The UN General Assembly intended the Universal Declaration to become the basis for a single, comprehensive human rights convention that states could formally ratify and thereby legally bind themselves. Unfortunately, the polarization of the Cold War prevented this from happening. The West, especially the United States, favored a convention containing only civil and political rights, while the Communist countries favored social and economic rights. The result was the creation of two separate documents: the Covenant on Civil and Political Rights (CCPR) and the Covenant on Economic, Social, and Cultural Rights (CESCR). Both were adopted by the UN General Assembly in 1966. A decade later, enough countries had ratified both for them to come into force. The United States ratified the CCPR in 1992 but has refused to ratify the CESCR.

Since its adoption in 1948, the Universal Declaration of Human Rights has grown in stature and respect. It has become a basic source for the development of the international law of human rights. Human rights advocates worldwide constantly invoke its principles, and numerous countries have incorporated it into their national constitutions. Consequently, the Universal Declaration has become the basis of domestic law of many states.

PAUL J. MAGNARELLA

See also Human Rights as a Foreign Policy Issue; Human Rights: Definition and Violations

References and Further Reading

Alfredsson, Gudmundur, and Eide, Asbjorn. *The Universal Declaration of Human Rights: A Common Standard of Achievement.* The Hague; Boston: Martinus Nijhoff, 1999.

Johnson, M. Glen. *The Universal Declaration of Human Rights: A History of Its Creation and Implementation, 1948–1998.* Paris: Unesco, 1998.

Glendon, Mary Ann. *A World Made New: Eleanor Roosevelt and the Universal Declaration of Human Rights.* New York: Random House, 2001.

Morsink, Johannes. *Universal Declaration of Human Rights: Origins, Drafting, and Intent.* Philadelphia: University of Pennsylvania Press, 1999.

Power, Samantha, and Allison, Graham, eds. *Realizing Human Rights: Moving from Inspiration to Impact.* New York: St. Martin's Press, 2000.

United Nations. Department of Social Affairs. *The Impact of the Universal Declaration of Human Rights.* New York, 1953.

van der Heijden, Barend, and Tahzib-Lie, Bahia, eds. *Reflections on the Universal Declaration of Human Rights: A Fiftieth Anniversary Anthology.* The Hague; Boston: Martinus Nijhoff, 1998.

UNTOUCHABLES (DALITS)

The Reservation Policy, India's version of Affirmative Action, has brought about great changes in the lives of India's Untouchables, now commonly called Dalits. Quotas in political bodies and educational institutions as well as in government service have created some political power but most importantly a sizable and vocal middle class. However, the development of pride and self respect has also resulted in rural attempts to better conditions that have frequently resulted in violence against Dalits, graphically reported in *Broken People.*

Scheduled Castes, Harijans, Ex-Untouchables, and Dalits

The names used for the lowest castes in the Indian hierarchy of caste indicate the history of change. In 1935, the British government in India placed more than four hundred castes on a list or schedule to receive government benefits. These castes were discriminated against because they worked with leather, human waste, dead animals, or cremation grounds; in addition, they could also have been held to be polluting by birth in spite of work such as basket making and village guard. The benefits have been continued and expanded for ex-Untouchables, so called because the practice of "untouchability" was made illegal in the Indian Constitution in 1950.

"Harijan" was Mahatma Gandhi's term for the Untouchables, developed in 1932 when he campaigned against their depressed conditions, but "people of God" was rejected as a patronizing and useless name by politicized Untouchables. "Dalit" (meaning broken down, oppressed) began to be used proudly in the early 1970s in the context of a militant group of Untouchables in the state of Maharashtra, Dalit Panthers, and the development of protest literature, Dalit Sahitya, a genre of literature that has been translated from the Marathi in *Poisoned Bread.* Dalit has become the standard word for modernizing Untouchables and has been used in the general press. All these words are in use in various contexts.

The Basis of Untouchability

Untouchable castes have been in evidence since about the sixth century CE although the idea of despised and polluting individuals is apparent in the literature that followed the earliest text, the *Rig Veda.* A theory of purity (the Brahmins, the priestly caste) and pollution (the Untouchables), the top and bottom of a graded hierarchy, was the religious justification for denying water and temple rights, a place in the village itself, and even literacy until the modern period. The *varna* system of Brahmin, *Kshatriya* (warrior, ruler), *Vaishya* (merchant), and *Shudra* (workers) did not include the Untouchable, who was outside the hierarchy but in specific castes—these castes included *Chamars* (leather workers); *Pariahs* (drummers), whose name has come into English as "outcaste;" *Bhangis* (waste removers); and *Mahars* (village servants). The majority of Untouchables are and probably were part of landless agricultural labor.

Untouchables are not separate by race from higher caste Hindus, just as the Burakumin of Japan are not separated; these people of Japan are part of a despised leather-working and butcher group and are treated much as are treated Indian Untouchables, even though Japan has no caste system as such. Much of the treatment and progress of the Untouchables in India, however, bears similarities to that of the treatment of the African-Americans in the United States.

Dr. B. R. Ambedkar (1891–1956)

Although India has had reformers and protesters against "untouchability" since the time of the Buddha, the most important was (and is) Bhimrao Ramji Ambedkar, a *Mahar* from Maharashtra who led the Untouchable movement in his day and now has become a symbol of progress and protest in most sections of India. Ambedkar secured an extraordinary education in the United States and England with the help of reformist non-Brahmin princes and used that education to bring legal redress to boycotts, to found

an educational system, to speak to all British parliamentary bodies, and, in a final triumph, to serve as chairman of the Drafting Committee of the Constitution of India and as law minister in independent India's first cabinet. After decades of protest against the caste system, Ambedkar also converted to Buddhism, taking millions of followers with him. His statue today, usually with one hand holding a book that represents the constitution, is seen in most town squares and Untouchable localities as a symbol of achievement. Resentment of Untouchable advances by higher caste Hindus is often shown by attempts to dishonor or destroy the statue. The Bahujan Samaj Party that honors Ambedkar, especially in the North, has superseded Ambedkar's Republican Party in importance.

Progress and Problems

India's commitment to equality may be seen in the current position of a Dalit, K. R. Narayanan, as the very effective president of India, and the late G. M. C. Baliyogi, as speaker of the India Parliament, also a Dalit. Educational advances have resulted in the appointment of Dalits in both the vice chancellor and the registrar positions of the University of Mumbai. Meanwhile, more Dalits than higher caste Hindus are below the poverty line, and literacy rates are a consistent 15% below that of higher caste Hindus, with Dalit women lagging 24% behind. Village atrocities continue, and many Dalits fear that with privatization will come many fewer jobs for the ex-Untouchables.

ELEANOR ZELLIOT

See also Caste Systems; India

References and Further Reading

Bains, Ravinder Ssingh, *Reservation Policy and Anti Reservationists*. Delhi: B.R. Publishing, 1994.

Dangle, Arjun, ed. *Poisoned Bread: Translations from Modern Marathi Dalit Literature*. Hyderabad: Orient Longman, 1992.

Deliege, Robert. *The Untouchables of India, TR from the French by Nora Scott*. Oxford; New York: Berg Publishers, 1999.

Mendelsohn, Oliver, and Marika Vicziany. *The Untouchables, Subordination, Poverty and the State in Modern India*. Cambridge: Cambridge University Press, 1998.

Narula, Smita. *Broken People: Caste Violence Against India's Untouchables*. London; New York: Human Rights Watch, 1999.

Zelliot, Eleanor. *From Untouchable to Dalit: Essays on the Ambedkar Movement*. 3rd ed. New Delhi: Manohar, 1992; 2001.

URBANIZATION: IMPACT ON DEVELOPMENT

It is conventional to measure the level of urbanization as the percentage of a country's population living in areas classified as urban and its level of development by calculating its per capita gross domestic product (PCGDP). Neither measure is perfect. Countries' definitions of what qualifies as "urban" vary, and GDP, the value of all goods and services produced in a specified time period, usually one year, is an estimate subject to frequent revisions. The population divisor is an annual interpolation between censuses, themselves prone to error; in addition, for purposes of comparison, different countries' PCGPDs have to be converted to a common currency, typically US dollars, and adjusted to correct for differences in purchasing power.

Subject to these caveats and qualifications, comparison of the two variables is illuminating. One method is to plot countries as points in a graph that has level of urbanization on the vertical axis and level of development on the horizontal axis. With data for 1950, the graph reveals a close correlation. A narrow band of points rises from countries that have low levels of both urbanization and development to countries that have high levels of the two variables. The band of points is contained within a floor and a ceiling to urbanization, both of which rise with development. The graph for 2000 is different. Whereas there still is a rising floor to urbanization as development increases, the ceiling is gone. Instead of a narrow band of points, there is a scatter throughout the triangle above the floor. Countries at low levels of development now display levels of urbanization that vary from low to the levels achieved in world's most developed regions. The change occurred because the second half of the twentieth century saw the decoupling of the relationship between urbanization and development in significant ways. Only the floor to the level of urbanization now rises with economic development.

1950: Development Drives Urbanization

In 1950, economists believed that simple causal relationships linked urbanization to economic development. On the demand side, Engel's Law was said to hold: because the income elasticity of demand for urban commodities is greater than that for rural commodities, the demand for urban commodities will increase faster than that for rural commodities as incomes rise. Thus, the society in which economic

development is occurring devotes more of its resources to urban activities. Complementing this, on the supply side, unbalanced technical change in which faster progress is made in manufacturing than in agriculture results in faster growth in manufacturing jobs and the attraction of migrant workers from agriculture to find urban employment. Hence, urbanization was said to be a consequence of economic development. The evidence was the pattern in the 1950 graph described in the previous paragraphs.

2000: Massive Overurbanization?

The radical changes that unfolded between 1950 and 2000 suggest that this comfortable argument of Engel's Law may be of declining utility. Between 1950 and 2000, the world's urban population increased from 750 million to 2.86 billion and the urban percentage from 30 to 47. In the developing countries, the urban population increased from 392 million to 2.16 billion and the urban percentage from 20% to 42%. The number of cities in the world with a population of more than 1 million increased from 83 to 387—those in the developing countries increased from 43 to 297, or from 52% to 77% of the total. But much of this increase in developing country urbanization was in areas where the level of economic development, although increasing, remained low, belying the earlier idea that it is development that drives urban growth. Immigration to urban areas came from zones of rapid population increase marked by high fertility and the reduced death rates produced by improved medical services as well as from areas with growing pools of surplus labor caused by technological advance in the agricultural rather than the industrial sector.

In part, the early rush may have been encouraged by urban bias in the policies of newly independent developing country governments. Exchange rates, tariffs, and tax policies penalized rural dwellers and favored the urban elite. The consequence has been "overurbanization," the growth of cities to sizes unsupportable by their traditional economic bases, with much resulting poverty and distress. The problem is most apparent in sub-Saharan Africa, but elsewhere, faced by the same immense challenges, the response has been remarkable. Price distortions have been reduced, often through reforms introduced by structural adjustment programs imposed by the World Bank and International Monetary Fund (IMF). More important, the new urban populations are inventing specializations that are turning the theory of

the 1950s around: instead of development driving urbanization, urbanization now is beginning to drive developing-country growth.

The New Dynamic: Cities Propel Growth

Many features of life in the new cities are creating conditions conducive to growth. There are substantial health advantages to urban living compared with the rural alternative, as evidenced by greater declines in the mortality rate in urban areas. Urban areas offer better infrastructure and easier access to health care services. In some developing countries, chronic and degenerative diseases, accidents, and injuries are becoming more important than infectious diseases as causes of death, a sure sign that the mortality transition that accompanies development is well advanced. Large urban areas also offer marked advantages in the provision of piped water, waste disposal, electricity, and schools. They also influence individual and family perceptions of economic costs, benefits, and uncertainties. New urban opportunities are affecting women's wage rates and, through wages, the opportunity costs of time spent in child care. These opportunity costs have long been identified as important factors in fertility decisions. In many developing countries, the other half of the demographic transition—reduced fertility—is now beginning to take hold. Parents also are becoming aware of the economic returns to schooling and are increasingly willing to forego high fertility to have fewer but better-educated children. Such increased investment in human capital pays off in the creation of a more capable labor force that can attract economic activities from elsewhere, first the factories seeking low money wages and later those that rely on education and skills. This in turn increases urban income growth, which raises government revenue and provides the means to further improve public services.

With improved preconditions for growth, other economic factors begin to play their role: initially, the benefits of increased returns to scale and, subsequently, innovation and agglomeration economies. When production is characterized by increasing returns to scale—a doubling of inputs yielding more than a doubling of output—firms are motivated to concentrate their production spatially. Concentration of production implies concentration of the labor force. Two varieties of concentration are evident. Localization economies arise when the firms of a given industry cluster spatially, permitting the suppliers of inputs tailored to that industry to save on transport

costs and allowing for further specialization in the production of inputs. Urbanization economies arise with the cross-industry clustering of firms and the suppliers of inputs used across a variety of industries. When firms are spatially clustered, workers can search among them more efficiently, expending less time and fewer resources in locating jobs that are well matched to their human capital. Consumers can benefit from the increased array and quality of differentiated goods.

Layered on top of localization and urbanization are new types of agglomeration economies produced by spillovers of ideas and technologies both within and between industries. Such spillovers may be produced when one firm is able to observe the innovations, experiments, production processes, or competitive strategies of another. Workers carry such innovative ideas with them as they circulate among firms. They may also arise from the stimuli provided by diversity so that creative energies in one industry are stimulated by the collision of disparate ideas and facilitated by developments in other industries: creative ferment occurs when entrepreneurs, scientists, artists, and firms find themselves struck by analogies and by the observation of activity in spheres that overlap but do not wholly coincide with their own. These benefits of urban diversity are greatest in the initial stages of product development. Once a production process becomes standardized, some of its elements can be relocated to sites where wages and rents are lower. Services and production in high-technology sectors derive special benefits from economies of diversity, as is evident on the remarkable scale of change in the cities of Asia, particularly those of the Pacific Rim. Initially spurred by multinational corporations' search for cheap productive labor, growth in cities as diverse as Bangalore in India, Shenzhen in southern China, and Kuala Lumpur in Malaysia now is driven by technology and innovation, as it was earlier in Singapore and Hong Kong and throughout South Korea and Taiwan. In such cases, cities have been able to mobilize great quantities of human capital, to attract foreign investment, and to invent new economic specializations in a short period of time, becoming the engines driving their nations' economic growth.

The largest developing country cities now are joining the ranks of the "World Cities" that have pivotal roles in the global economy. Among these, New York, London, and Tokyo occupy the uppermost tier because of their dominance of finance and specialized services, their importance as sites of production and innovation, and their role as markets for new products and services. There are, however, as many as thirty other places, many in the developing world, that now play a central role in the internationalization of capital, production, service, and culture.

BRIAN J. L. BERRY

See also Urbanization: Impact on Environment

References and Further Reading

Berry, B. J. L. *Comparative Urbanization: Divergent Paths in the Twentieth Century*. Basingstoke, United Kingdom: Macmillan, 1982.

Kelly, A. C., and J. G. Williamson. *What Drives Third World City Growth?* Princeton, NJ: Princeton University Press, 1984.

Montgomery, Mark R., Richard Stren, Barney Cohen, and Holly E. Reed, eds. *Cities Transformed. Demographic Change and Its Implications in the Developing World*. Washington, DC: The National Academies Press, 2003.

Sassen, S. *The Global City*. 2nd ed. Princeton, NJ: Princeton University Press, 2001.

Short, J. R., and Kim, Y.-H. *Globalization and the City*. London: Longman, 1999.

Shukla, V. *Urbanization and Economic Growth*. Delhi: Oxford University Press, 1996.

URBANIZATION: IMPACT ON ENVIRONMENT

The world's urban population increased fourfold between 1950 and 2000, with most of the increase occurring in middle- and low-income developing countries (Table 1). A growing share of this increase was in cities with more than one million inhabitants, for which the developing countries accounted for 77% of the world total of 387 in 2000, compared with 52% of a total of 83% in 1950 (Table 2). Megacities with a population of more than five million increased from 8 to 39 in the same time span, with 30 in the developing countries in 2000 compared with only 3 fifty years before (Table 3). The United Nations (UN) predicts that by 2010, more than half the world's population will live in urban areas, growing to two-thirds by 2030 when the developing countries are expected to account for 83% of the world's urban population of some five billion.

What are likely to be the environmental consequences of this massive surge of big-city population concentration in the developing countries? There are no definitive answers because little monitoring and even less analysis has been undertaken in these countries. One must rely on research conducted in high-income nations, recognizing that the consequences may differ because much of the developing world is characterized by lower incomes, different physical environments and cultures, and frequent absence of effective urban planning and environmental

Table 1: World urban population, 1950 and 2000[1]

	Mid-year population (millions)	
Region	1950	2000
World total	751	2862
High-income countries	359	697
Middle- and low-income countries	392	2165

High-income countries have gross national income per capital of $9266 or more.
[1] United Nations (2002); World Bank (2002).

Table 2: Urban areas and their populations by size, 1950 and 2000[1]

	Number of cities		Urban population (in millions)	
City Size	1950	2000	1950	2000
World total				
Ten million or more	1	16	12	225
Five to ten million	7	23	42	169
One to five million	75	348	144	675
High-income countries				
Ten million or more	1	4	12	67
Five to ten million	4	5	26	38
One to five million	38	81	77	183
Middle- and low-income countries				
Ten million or more	0	12	0	158
Five to ten million	3	18	16	132
One to five million	40	267	68	491

[1] United Nations (2002).

Table 3: Urban agglomerations with five million people or more, 1950 and 2000[1]

Region	1950	2000
High-income countries		
Europe	Paris	Paris
	Rhein-Ruhr	Rhein-Ruhr
	London	London
North America	New York	New York
		Los Angeles
		Chicago
Asia	Tokyo	Tokyo
		Osaka
		Hong Kong
Middle- and low-income countries		
Asia	Shanghai	Shangai
		Beijing
		Tianjin
		Seoul
		Bombay
		Calcutta
		Bangalore
		Delhi
		Hyderabad
		Madras
		Wuhan
		Jakarta
		Teheran
		Istanbul
		Bangkok
		Metro Manila
		Karachi
		Lahore
		Dhaka
Africa		Cairo
		Lagos
		Kinshasa
Latin America and the Caribbean	Buenos Aires	Buenos Aires
		Rio de Janeiro
		São Paulo
		Mexico City
		Lima
		Santiago
		Bogota
Europe		Moscow

[1] United Nations (2002).

regulation. Developed-world research reveals that modifications of the physical environment produced by rapid urban growth occur at three geographic scales: local, regional, and global.

At a local scale, urban development alters the nature of the Earth's surface. The natural surface of soil, grass, and trees is replaced by brick, concrete, glass, and metal at different levels above the ground. These artificial materials change the nature of the reflecting and radiating surfaces, the heat exchange near the surface, and the aerodynamic roughness of the surface.

Among the most important local effects are the land-use changes that affect the hydrologic regime (the system of rivers and streams and the patterns of runoff); changes in peak-flow characteristics (the scale and speed of runoff after storms); changes in total runoff; changes in water quality; and changes in hydrologic amenities (the desirability of water bodies for recreation). After urbanization, runoff occurs more rapidly and with a greater peak flow than under nonurban conditions. Urbanization increases the impervious land area, and the urban area may be served by storm sewers. Both increase the peak

Table 4: Effects of large cities on environment[1]

Element	Compared to rural environs	
Contaminants	Condensation nuclei (particles that serve to attract condensation)	10 times more
	Particulates (e.g., soot)	50 times more
	Gaseous admixtures (mixtures of polluting gases)	5–25 times more
Radiation	Total on horizontal surface	0–20% less
	Ultraviolet, winter	30% less
	Ultraviolet, summer	5% less
	Sunshine duration	5–15% less
Cloudiness	Clouds	5–10% more
	Fog, winter	100% more
	Fog, summer	30% more
Precipitation	Amounts	5–15% more
	Days with less than 0.20 inches (5 millimeters)	10% more
	Snowfall, inner city	5–10% more
	Snowfall, lee of city	10% more
	Thunderstorms	10–15% more
Temperature	Annual mean	0.5–3.0°C more
	Winter minimums (average)	1–2°C more
	Summer maximums	1–3°C more
	Heating degree days	10% less
Relative humidity	Annual mean	6% less
	Winter	2% less
	Summer	8% less
Wind speed	Annual mean	20–30% less
	Extreme gusts	10–20% less
	Calm	5–20% more

[1] Landsberg (1981).

discharge: maximum sewerage and imperviousness result in peak discharges that are more than six times greater than those in nonurbanized conditions. In turn, sharper peak discharges increase flood frequencies and the ratio of over-bank flows. Urbanization thus increases the flood volume, the flood peak, and the flood frequency, and the flushing effect of storm water discharge increases turbidity (the mixing of sediments in the water) and pollutant loads. On the other hand, sediment loads may fall. The channel response will therefore shift from aggradation (build-up of sediment deposits) to bank erosion. Water pollution changes the quality of downstream resources, the ecology of the riverine environment, and the amenity value of the river bank or estuary. The effects become pronounced downstream of larger cities, where natural flushing is incapable of preventing long-term damage, and in coastal bays and estuaries, depending upon the city's location.

At the scale of the metropolitan region, by generating large amounts of heat artificially and by altering the composition of the atmosphere via emissions of gaseous and solid pollutants, big cities begin to create their own climates (principal changes are noted in Table 4).

At certain times of the year in midlatitude cities, artificial heat input into the atmosphere by combustion and metabolic processes may approach or even exceed that derived indirectly from the sun. The heat island that results serves as a trap for pollutants. Other things being equal, the temperature difference between the city core and the rural periphery increases with city size; the difference is small and ephemeral in cities of a population of 250,000 or less but is substantial and longer lasting in larger cities. The heat island expands and intensifies as the city grows, and stronger and stronger winds are needed to overcome it. Wind speeds of 5 m/sec^{-1} (12 mi/hr) can eliminate the heat island in a city of 250,000, but speeds of 10 m/sec^{-1} (22 mi/hr) are required for a city with a population of one million, and speeds of 14 m/sec^{-1} (32 mi/hr) are required for a city with a population of ten million. Yet, the surface roughness of the city serves to reduce wind speeds and inhibit this ventilation: average wind speed may be reduced as much as 30% by a big city. In cities with a population of more than ten million, the

mean annual minimum temperature may be as much as 2.5°C higher than that of the surrounding rural periphery. This difference is much greater in summer than in winter.

The causes of changes in climate in cities are two-fold, both of which are seasonally dependent. In summer, the tall buildings, pavement, and concrete of the city absorb and store large amounts of solar radiation, and less of this energy is used for evaporation than in the countryside because of the high runoff. The stored energy is released at night, warming the urban air. In winter, human-made energy used for heat and light produces warming, yet the blanket of emissions reduces incoming solar radiation by as much as 20% (a phenomenon known as heat rejection). When the Boston-Washington megalopolis reaches a population of 50 to 60 million, it will be characterized by heat rejection of 65 cal/cm^2/d. In winter, the rejection is 50% of the heat received by solar radiation on a horizontal surface; in summer, this number decreases to 15%. In Manhattan, the heat produced by combustion alone in winter has been estimated to be 2.5 times the solar energy reaching the ground. This energy is trapped by the blanket of pollutants over the city, including particulates, water vapor, and carbon dioxide, and is reemitted downward to warm the ambient air.

In addition to the heat island, other regional-scale climatic effects—all increasing with city size—include greater cloudiness, fog, dust, and precipitation but lower humidity. When wind dissipates the heat island, a downwind urban heat plume is detectable in the atmosphere. Along this plume, there are increased precipitation, thunderstorm, and hail probabilities, often quite distant from the city.

Beyond such regional-scale consequences, urban activities are a major source of gaseous discharges into the atmosphere that may affect future global climates. Urban contributions to sulfur and carbon dioxide levels in the atmosphere are believed to be contributing to global warming. If warming increases, polar ice sheets will be reduced, leading to rising sea levels. Such changes are likely to be of greatest consequence for major coastal cities. Fluorocarbon emissions have been reduced significantly in the developed world but have already contributed to ozone depletion, producing the southern hemisphere "ozone hole" that has permitted increased ultraviolet radiation to reach the earth's surface, raising skin cancer rates in southern latitudes.

Lack of effective environmental regulations in developing countries means that their cities are replacing those of the developed world as the principal sources of sulfur and carbon dioxide emissions and of fluorocarbons. Thus, it is the rapid urbanization of the developing world that is most likely to propel global environmental change in the years ahead.

BRIAN J. L. BERRY

See also Urbanization: Impact on Development

References and Further Reading

Berry, B. J. L. "Urbanization." *The Earth as Transformed by Human Action: Global and Regional Changes in the Biosphere over the Past 300 Years*, B. L. Turner II, W. C. Clark, R. W. Kates, J. F. Richards, J. T. Mathews, and W. B. Meyer, eds. Cambridge, United Kingdom: Cambridge University Press, 1990.

Landsberg, H. E. *The Urban Climate*. New York: Academic Press, 1981.

Leopold, L. B. "Hydrology for Urban Land Planning." *Geological Survey Circular 554*. Washington, DC: US Government Printing Office, 1968.

Montgomery, Mark R., Richard Stren, Barney Cohen, and Holly E. Reed, eds. *Cities Transformed. Demographic Change and Its Implications in the Developing World*. Washington, DC: National Academies Press, 2003.

United Nations. *World Urbanization Prospects: The 2001 Revision. Data Tables and Highlights*. United Nations, Department of Economic and Social Affairs, Population Division, 2002.

Wolman, M. G. "The Cycle of Sedimentation and Erosion in Urban River Channels." *Geografisker Annaler* 49A (1967): 285–295, 355.

World Bank. *World Development Report 2002. Building Institutions for Markets*. New York: Oxford University Press, 2002.

URUGUAY

With an area of 776,853 square feet (72,172 square meters), Uruguay is the second smallest republic in South America. Its topography is characterized by the *cuchillas* (rolling hills) and the grasslands, which are an extension of the pampas.

With land ideally suited for raising cattle and sheep, Uruguay's economy is almost entirely dependent on livestock products. However, Uruguay's 3.4 million inhabitants are not rural dwellers. More than 75% of its population is considered urban. Uruguay's capital, Montevideo, contains more than half of the country's population.

Uruguay's population is not as racially diverse as that of other Latin American nations. As a result of a large scale European migration in the late nineteenth century, Uruguay's population is 88% caucasian, 8% mestizo, and 4% black. It has one of the highest literacy rates in the world at 98% and one of the highest life expectancy rates in Latin America at 76 years of age. Although its GDP purchasing power parity per capita ($12,600) is high by Latin American standards, 16% of its population is unemployed.

During the Spanish colonial era, Uruguay was just a buffer zone between Spanish-held Argentina and Portuguese-controlled Brazil. When wars for independence spread throughout the Spanish Empire, *gaucho* patriot, José Gervasio Artigas, drove the Spaniards out of Uruguay in 1816, but Portugal annexed it to Brazil. In 1822, when Brazil became independent, it remained part of the Brazilian Empire. In 1828, the Brazilians withdrew, and two years later the *Republica Oriental del Uruguay* was proclaimed.

The Uruguayan Republic, however, was plagued by political instability as the *Colorado* (Red) faction, composed of liberal-minded city dwellers, and the *Blanco* (White) faction, composed of conservative-minded landowners, battled for political control, plunging the country into civil wars.

In the twentieth century, conditions would change in Uruguay with the rise of José Batlle y Ordóñez. President from 1903 until 1907 and from 1911 until 1915, Batlle became the most influential politician in Uruguayan history. His plans for state-sponsored social welfare programs, state participation in key economic sectors, and his system of political proportional representation were crystallized in the constitution of 1919.

The *Batllista* economic program of state involvement benefited Uruguay enormously during the 1920s as demand for Uruguayan commodities rose in the world market. The world depression of the 1930s negatively impacted Uruguay's economy. To deal with the crisis, a new constitution was proclaimed, eliminating the *Colegiado*, a nine-member Uruguayan National Council that limited presidential powers. However, the *Batllista* socioeconomic system was retained.

World War II brought a period of prosperity for Uruguay as Allied dependency on Uruguayan products increased. Postwar Uruguay became the model country in Latin America for both democratic and socioeconomic progress. In 1951, Uruguayans held a plebiscite for a new constitution calling for a nine-member executive Uruguayan National Council with no president. Based on proportional representation, the council's chair rotated on a yearly basis.

During the early 1950s, the Uruguayan economy continued to grow, for Europe was in need of Uruguayan imports, and the Korean War kept its commodities in high demand. While US investments in Uruguay were minimal, diplomatic relations with the United States continued to improve as Uruguay saw the United States as a bulwark against Perónist expansionism in the region.

Juan Domingo Perón's overthrow in 1955 ended the Argentine menace. However, a more serious situation developed. Cheaper synthetic wool substitutes cost Uruguay 50% of its export revenues. In addition, demand for Uruguayan beef plummeted as a result of a hoof-and-mouth disease.

Faced with keeping the welfare state, the National Council turned to inflationary measures. As inflation reached astronomical proportions, a political crisis developed in 1966, and Uruguayans turned to a new constitution thath replaced the National Council with a strong presidency.

In 1967, Uruguay asked the International Monetary Fund (IMF) and the World Bank for help. It received a $500 million loan but had to incorporate a plan containing austerity measures. This action caused labor strikes and civil unrest. By the early 1970s, both Uruguayan democracy and the *Batllista* system were in danger. The *Tupamaros*, an urban guerrilla group, began to destabilize the country through terrorist attacks. Voters showed their dissatisfaction with both the *Colorado* and *Blanco* parties when in the elections of 1971, the newly created *Frente Amplio*, a leftist learning coalition, received 30% of the Montevideo vote and 18% of the nationwide vote.

Shortly after the inauguration of the President Juan María Bordaberry in 1972, the *Tupamaros* launched a new wave of terrorist attacks. They wanted to provoke the military into conflict with hopes that a popular uprising against military intervention would result in the establishment of a Uruguayan Marxist state.

Unable to stop the urban violence, Bordaberry suspended civil liberties, gave the military a free hand to deal with the *Tupamaros*, and virtually became a puppet. In 1976, the military replaced him with Aparicio Méndez, another puppet president.

Scores of *Tupamaros* were imprisoned or killed, but innocent civilians suspected of being guerrilla sympathizers were jailed and tortured. Although the *Tupamaros*'s hope for a popular uprising never materialized, they succeeded in practically destroying Uruguayan democracy. In 1981, Lieutenant General Gregorio Alvarez assumed direct control as president. The military regime, successfully having eradicated the *Tupamaros*, hoped to stay in power until 1987. However, a gargantuan debt, as well as international condemnation, prompted the regime to return power to constitutional government in 1984.

In 1984, *Colorado* candidate Julio María Sanguinetti was elected president. Since 1984, three *Colorado* and one *Blanco* party members have occupied the presidency. Although the state still plays a major role in the economy, both *Blanco* and *Colorado* administrations have conducted a limited privatization policy, and in 1995, Uruguay joined MERCOSUR, the Southern Cone Common Market.

As a result of economic crises faced by its major trading partners, Brazil and Argentina, the Uruguayan economy has been adversely impacted since

2002. However, it is expected to recover as a result of a weakened dollar, low interest international loans, and high prices for Uruguayan products. As the pendulum swings, Battle's dream has not disappeared; rather, it waits for better times.

JOSÉ B. FERNÁNDEZ

See also Southern Cone Common Market (MERCO-SUR); Southern Cone (Latin America): History and Economic Development; Southern Cone (Latin America): International Relations; Tupamaros

References and Further Reading

Blouet, Brian W., and Olwyn M. Blouet. *Latin American and the Caribbean: A Systematic and Regional Survey*. New York: John Wiley & Sons, 1993.

Fitzgibbon, Russell. *Uruguay: Portrait of a Democracy*. New York: Russell and Russell, 1966.

Fynch, Martin H. J. *A Political Economy of Uruguay since 1870*. New York: St. Martin's Press, 1981.

Kaufman, Edy. *Uruguay in Transition: From Civilian to Military Rule*. New Brunswick, NJ: Transaction Brooks, 1979.

Pendle, George. *South America's Welfare State*. London: Royal Institute of International Affairs, 1952.

Porzecanski, Arturo C. *Uruguay's Tupamaros: The Urban Guerrillas*. New York: Preger Special Studies in International Politics and Government, 1973.

Taylor, Philip B. "Uruguay: The Costs of Inept Corporatism." *Latin American Politics and Development*, Howard J. Wiarda and Harvey F. Kline, eds. Boulder, CO: Westview Press, 1985.

Weinstein, Jean. *Uruguay: The Politics of Failure*. London: Greenwood Press, 1975.

UZBEKISTAN

Uzbekistan is situated at the very center of Central Asia. It is the most populous of the former Soviet Central Asian states, holding about twenty-five million people. Roughly the same size as California in area, Uzbekistan lies at about the same latitude as Italy and experiences a continental climate. Much of the country is occupied by the Kyzyl Kum (Red Sand) and Kara Kum (Black Sand) deserts in the west, and most of the remaining land is arid steppe. Few locations receive more than ten inches of precipitation yearly, and agriculture is made possible only by the presence of two great rivers, the Amu Darya and Syr Darya, whose waters supply extensive irrigation works. The southeastern reaches of the country are mountainous, and this region contains the Fergana Valley, the country's most important agricultural area.

Uzbekistan has been part of the Muslim world for more than 1,200 years, but was absorbed into the Russian empire in the mid-nineteenth century. The Tsar's forces captured Tashkent, the largest city, in 1865, and political control of the region remained in Russian (later Soviet) hands for about 125 years. The imprint of Slavic culture remains strong, as Russian is widely spoken and the Muslim prohibition against alcohol is seldom observed. Independent Uzbekistan faces enormous challenges in the wake of Soviet collapse. These include widespread environmental degradation, a rapidly expanding population, a stagnant economy only tenuously connected to the global economy, widespread political instability, and human rights abuses.

In the wake of World War II, Uzbekistan became the Soviet Union's primary source of cotton, which not only satisfied domestic demand but also provided badly needed foreign earnings when sold on the international market. After 1960, a vast amount of new acreage was opened to the production of "white gold," as the lucrative crop came to be called by Central Asians. The water for increased production came from the region's streams, primarily the Amu Darya and its smaller cousin, the Syr Darya. The "monoculture" of cotton had two extremely detrimental effects on Uzbekistan: catastrophic environmental damage and a retardation of economic development, as the agricultural sector was emphasized over the industrial and service sectors for most of the period after 1945.

Environmental degradation took its most obvious form in the demise of the Aral Sea. As recently as 1960, the Aral Sea was the world's fourth largest lake, but overuse of the rivers supplying it (the Amu Darya and Syr Darya) resulted in an unprecedented decline. Satellite images from the late 1990s reveal that the area covered by the Aral Sea is one-half that of the early 1960s, and a host of health and economic problems accompanied this collapse. As the sea shrank, its salinity increased, ultimately killing most of the fish and subsequently destroying the commercial fishing industry, which in turn resulted in the loss of thousands of jobs. The disaster has had a dramatic impact on the health of those around the sea as well, with tens of thousands of people suffering from increased incidence of certain cancers, blood diseases, and respiratory ailments.

After becoming an independent state in 1991, the Uzbek administration remained under the control of the former Uzbek Communist Party First Secretary, Islom Karimov. During Karimov's tenure, full economic integration with the global economy has failed to materialize, and as of 2001, the country's currency unit, the som, remains nonconvertible in international financial markets. Official statistics for poverty levels and unemployment in Uzbekistan are generally low, but probably significantly underreported is the actual magnitude of these problems. The transition from

the Soviet-era command economy to a free market system has followed a policy of "gradualism," and much of the agricultural and industrial sectors remain in government hands.

The potential for economic development in Uzbekistan is high if the disadvantages of distance from international markets can be overcome. Sizeable deposits of gold and natural gas are present and serve as important sources of foreign earnings. The country has a reasonably well-developed infrastructure, highlighted by a recently expanded and remodeled international airport in Tashkent. In addition, about 40% of the population is urbanized, a fairly high percentage in the region, and approximately 10% of the workforce holds a postsecondary degree. However, to date, the amount of foreign investment has fallen short of expectations, and there is little internal investment capital available. Much of the potential for tourism remains undeveloped although Uzbekistan contains many important historical sites and much natural beauty.

Prior to 1991, Uzbekistan had never existed as an independent political entity. Having emerged from the Soviet empire, the new state has not implemented stable traditions of democratic government and has been slow in developing institutions typically associated with civil society. The government is authoritarian, the media is tightly controlled by the administration, the judiciary is not independent of governmental influence, and the few opposition parties that are represented in the *Oliy Majlis*, or parliament, are in fact pawns of the ruling faction. Opposition groups that formed in the late 1980s, such as *Birlik* ("Unity") and *Erk* ("Will") have been driven underground and their leadership forced into exile.

The process of constructing a national identity is ongoing in Uzbekistan. This process involves resurrecting and honoring the deeds of historical figures connected to the country's past, such as Amir Timur (Tamerlane), Babur, and Alisher Navoi; promoting Uzbek as a national tongue; and reconnecting to Islam. The latter movement, however, is tightly controlled by the government, which asserts that a "fundamentalist" threat to the nation's stability has grown during the 1990s, a claim bolstered by mysterious bombings in Tashkent in 1999 and subsequent incursions by Islamic insurgents in the Fergana region. Critics of the Karimov regime argue that the dangers of Islamic radicalism have been dramatically exaggerated by the government to justify a general crackdown on dissent and to silence those who wish to promote a more open, democratic society.

REUEL R. HANKS

See also Commonwealth of Independent States: History and Economic Development; Commonwealth of Independent States: International Relations

References and Further Reading

Allworth, Edward. *The Modern Uzbeks*. Stanford, CA: Hoover Institution Press, 1990.

Critchlow, James. *Nationalism in Uzbekistan*. Boulder, CO: Westview Press, 1991.

Gleason, Gregory. *The Central Asian States*. Boulder, CO: Westview Press, 1997.

Hanks, Reuel. *Uzbekistan*. Oxford; Santa Barbara, CA: Clio Press, 1999.

Manz, Beatrice, ed. *Central Asia in Historical Perspective*. Boulder, CO: Westview Press, 1994.

Melvin, Neil. *Uzbekistan: Transition to Authoritarianism on the Silk Road*. Amsterdam: Harwood Academic Publishers, 2000.

Ruffin, Holt M., and Daniel Waugh, eds. *Civil Society in Central Asia*. Seattle; London: University of Washington Press, 1999.

V

VÄHI, TIIT

Tiit Vähi was born on January 10, 1947, in Valga, Estonia. Vähi received a degree in engineering from Tallinn Technical University in 1970. Upon graduation, Vähi pursued a management career with the Valga Trucking Company. Vähi emerged as one of the leaders of the Estonian Popular Front at the beginning of the national independence movement in 1989. Later in the year, Vähi was appointed Minister for Transport and Communications, where he embarked on a mission of improving transit relations with the Nordic countries and the other Baltic states. Vähi was crucial to the realignment of Estonia's infrastructure, such as seaports, railway hubs, and airports to Estonian control after fifty years of Soviet control.

Vähi became Prime Minister on January 30, 1992. Vähi's priorities included the implementation of policies to steer Estonia towards a Western market economy. The Estonian *Kroon* became the official currency of the nation in June 1992, effectively severing fiscal ties to Russia. Vähi played an essential role in the creation of the Estonian Privatization Agency, responsible for the denationalization of businesses and industries. In accordance with his agreement with the transitional government, Vähi did not seek a parliamentary position in the September 1992 elections.

Amidst public discontent about the harsh, sweeping economic reforms pursued by the conservative reformer Maart Laar and his government from 1992–1994, former communists won the largest number of seats in parliamentary elections in 1995. A coalition government was formed, and President Lennart Meri appointed Vähi as Prime Minister. Vähi's government was comprised of political parties that held diametrically opposed views on major issues such as tariffs. Ultimately, this led to a persistent sense of governmental instability during a critical period in Estonia's economic and political transformation. Despite some public hope for a softening of the economic reforms implemented by the Maar government and renewed relations with Russia, the government continued implementing institutional reforms, thereby strengthening ties with Western Europe. The coalition was unable to deliver on campaign promises to increase social benefits and higher pensions. In October 1995, however, Vähi's government collapsed amidst rumors of illegal surveillance and wiretapping by Interior Minister Edgar Savisaar.

Despite the cabinet scandal, Vähi remained prime minister and created a new cabinet. 1996 proved to be a tumultuous year for the government. The results of local elections in the nation's capital, Tallinn, created great political difficulty. The conservative reformists expanded the local coalition to the national political arena, leaving Vähi governing in a minority position. In late 1996, Vähi introduced his "Ten Commandments," promising a more "socially oriented" market economy in the hopes of rejuvenating public support for his government, which had dwindled to 5%.

Ultimately, Vähi lost political acumen in 1997 amidst allegations of unethical privatization while he was head of Tallinn's City Council from 1993 to 1995. Laar revealed that under Vähi's watch, nearly

two hundred apartments in the city had been sold to prominent individuals for as little as 5% of their market value. Despite claiming innocence, Vähi resigned as prime minister prior to a scheduled vote of no-confidence in February 1997.

JONATHAN H. L'HOMMEDIEU

See also Estonia; Laar, Mart

References and Further Reading

Smith, David J., Artis Pabriks, Aldis Purs, and Thomas Lane. *The Baltic States: Estonia, Latvia, and Lithuania.* New York: Routledge Press, 2002.
Lauristin, Marju and Peeter Vihalemm, ed. *Return to the Western World: Cultural and Political Perspectives on the Estonian Post-Communist Transition.* Tartu: Tartu University Press, 1997.

VANUATU

Location and Description

The Republic of Vanuatu consists of over eighty islands located in the South Pacific with the capital, Port Vila, on Efate. The aggregate landmass is twelve thousand square kilometres, and it claims a territorial coastal zone of twelve nautical miles and a two hundred-mile exclusive economic zone.

Volcanic activity is apparent with frequent minor tremors. A tropical climate is moderated by the southeast trade winds. The area is subject to cyclones, and in recent years they have severely affected the economy.

Colonial Past and Social Development

The former New Hebrides became independent on July 30, 1980. The colony had been jointly ruled by both Britain and France by a administration known as the Condominium, a dual system in which every police post had an officer of both nationalities. There were two education systems, two legal systems, and two official languages. Two national flags flew side by side, and great pains were taken to ensure they were exactly the same height.

Unofficially, there was intense rivalry between Anglo and Gallic functionaries. This extended to the indigenous population, some of whom saw themselves as either black Frenchmen or black Englishmen. These rivalries were evident in secessionist revolts (with covert French support) on Espiritu Santo and Tana at independence.

Colonial rivalry was matched by local rivalries. Language and cultural differences not only separated islands but the islanders themselves. The island of Tana alone has four distinct languages (as well as English, French, and Bislama the *lingua franca*). A sense of national unity was something new that had to be carefully fostered.

Economic Development

One result of the end of World War II on Vanuatu was the John Frum cargo cult. Cargo cults, indigenous to Melanesia with roots dating back to the nineteenth century, believe that the spirits of dead ancestors will return with cargoes of material goods for their descendants. The so-called cargo cults received a boost during the Second World War, when the Allies air-dropped large amounts of cargo onto the South Pacific Islands. At the end of the war, a figure known as Jon (sometimes John) Frum allegedly appeared on the island of Tana. Some people believe that he was a Vanuatu native posing as a god; in any case, his followers believe him to be a messianic figure who lives in a nearby volcano with an army twenty thousand strong. His message was to throw away money, slaughter the animals, and feast, as all needs would be met by the goods that he would provide. The Jon Frum movement survives to the present day, with Jon Frum Day celebrated annually on February 15; the movement even has its own political party.

After independence Vanuatu produced a development plan that aimed at self-reliance in fifteen years. The measure of success was to be Vanuatu's ability to match imports with foreign exchange earnings and fiscal requirements from domestic revenues. The plan identified three areas of concern: domestic savings were inadequate for investment, there was a gap between revenue and expenditure, and the cost of imports was far greater than the country earned in exports.

The plan was to encourage the private sector and the emergence of "national entrepreneurs" (National Planning Office ND). Foreign aid was to be invested in productive infrastructure to increase exports and substitute domestic product for imports. Finally, the government intended to stabilise expenditure through wage restraint, a ceiling on bureaucracy, increased efficiency, and to "stabilise the levels of social infrastructure investment."

However, for most of the 1980s, the economy stagnated and economic growth was minimal. Economic

growth averaged 1.6%, while population grew by 2.9%, leading to a fall in the standard of living. There were good years; 1984 saw a sharp rise in copra prices which, combined with increased tourism, pushed growth up to nearly 7%, giving a sound balance of payments position and allowing a build-up of foreign exchange reserves. However, Vanuatu's vulnerability to fluctuations in world markets was demonstrated from 1985–1987, with zero growth due to the collapse of copra prices and a decline in tourism.

Economic development is hindered by a number of factors. The distance to both export markets and between islands is a handicap. Lack of skilled labour caused a reliance on high cost expatriates. Most importantly there are few exports other than primary produce—copra, kava, beef, timber, coffee—while imports include machinery, equipment, food, and fuel. The dependence on imported fuels and the imbalance between imports of value added goods and export of agricultural products is reflected in the balance of trade. The 1999 estimates had exports at $25.3 million, while imports were $77.2 million.

Current Economic Situation

Subsistence agriculture remains highly important, providing for 65% of the population. Fishing, offshore financial services, tourism, and copra produce much of the foreign exchange. There is a small light industrial sector for the domestic market. The gross domestic product (GDP) comprises agriculture, 20%; industry, 9%; and service industries, 71%. The labour force consists of 65% engaged in agriculture; 32% in the services industry, and only 3% in industry. Industries include food and fish freezing, meat canning, and wood processing. GDP growth averaged less than 3% during the 1990s. The real growth rate in 1999 was –2.5%. Despite several attempts at government reform and implementation of policies, the development plan has failed to meet its objectives.

The assumptions upon which the development plan was based are those of the International Monetary Fund and the World Bank—an open economy based on private sector activity, increasing gross national product (GNP), and exports balancing imports. Many people now question whether this development model is appropriate to a small country like Vanuatu. It is hard to see how exports could ever equal imports in value. Nor does GNP measure many of the subsistence and community activities that make up the greater part of the local economy.

The development plan aimed to balance economic development with social responsibility and the cultural and environmental heritage. Yet the development process lessened the value of cultural produce. Prestige became a key factor with people preferring imported canned fish, canned meat, and rice to what they caught or grew themselves. Similarly, ownership of motor vehicles and outboard motor boats has become an important aspiration for many people in rural areas with demand for these items closely related to their value as prestige items. In effect, local "production" is being replaced by imports with a detrimental effect on both traditional culture and the balance of payments.

Two factors give some hope for Vanuatu's development in the broad sense. First, the colonial experience combined with local differences has made the people adept at evaluating different ways of doing things and selecting the method that best suits their needs. Second, there are organizations such as Jon Frumm, which has evolved from a cargo cult into a strong cultural movement that counters the "prestige" alternatives and values traditional production and custom. Perhaps Vanuatu can find some middle ground between the dictates of a full-blown Western economy and the pragmatic dictates of a very small country.

GRAHAM BARRIGAN

See also Oceania: History and Economic Development; Oceania: International Relations

References and Further Reading

Cole, Rodney V. and Somsak Tambunlertchai. *The Future of Asia-Pacific Economies: Pacific Islands at the Crossroads?* Canberra: National Centre for Development Studies, 1993.
Crocombe, Ron and Ahmed Ali, eds. *Politics in Melanesia*, Fiji: University of the South Pacific, 1982.
MacDonald-Milne, Brian, ed. *Yumi Stanap Leaders & Leadership in a New Nation*, Fiji, University of the South Pacific, 1981.
Shears, Richard. *The Coconut War: The Crises in Espiritu Santo*. New South Wales: Cassell Australia, 1980.
Sturton, Mark and Andrew McGregor. *Vanuatu: Toward Economic Growth*. Economic Report No 2, Hawaii, Pacific Island Development Program, 1991.
National Planning Office. *First National Development Plan 1982–1986*. Port Vila, [N.D.]
Vanuatu: 10 Years of Independence. Rozel, New South Wales: Other People Publications, 1990.

VARGAS, GETÚLIO

Getúlio Dornelles Vargas (1883–1954) was born in São Borja, in the far southern, cattle-raising state of Brazil, Rio Grande do Sul. He would become

the most significant political leader in modern Brazilian history. Although socio-economic change was a crucial means by which he obtained and kept power; of itself it was not his guiding objective. Such change served as but a means to his ultimate end, controlling with consummate skill the forces of political power.

The son of a general, Vargas graduated from law school in 1907. Elected to the state legislature and then the national congress, he achieved the coveted position of minister of finance in 1926. Elected governor of Rio Grande do Sul in 1928, he became a candidate for president in 1930. Defeated by powerful traditional forces, he rejected the results of the election after the assassination of his vice presidential running mate. Leading a coup to overthrow the incumbent president, Vargas became provisional president of Brazil at the end of 1930.

He faced a worldwide economic depression and plummeting prices for Brazil's most important export product, coffee. Vargas moved to consolidate his hold on political power and to manipulate or adapt to the social and economic changes developing in the country. Under a new constitution, he was elected president in 1934. Suppressing political uprisings from the communist left and fascist right, he established a dictatorial regime in 1937, the "New State," and remained in power until 1945.

For fifteen years, he molded the society and economy of Brazil. He organized unions under the federal government. He won new political adherents by authorizing a minimum wage, creating health, vacation, and retirement benefits for workers, and granting the vote to women.

As Europe prepared for war, it sought Brazilian raw materials, particularly iron for armaments and other manufactured products. With the Brazilian economy thus reignited, Vargas acted to diversify it through development of national industry, particularly iron and steel manufacturing. Thereby, further corporate segments of labor and business came to support him.

Vargas emphasized nationalism and development of cultural activities for the political ends they could serve. By projecting Brazil as a united nation under a beneficent federal government, he prepared the country for war and appeared as a defense against subversion and divisiveness. The emerging force of radio became a vehicle to propagate nationalism and the benefits of the Vargas government. In conjunction with the emerging record industry, radio also projected popular Brazilian culture, highlighting samba dance music and Carnival festivities.

The defeat of fascism at the end of World War II in 1945 meant that Vargas could no longer remain in power; and he was removed by a military coup. However, in 1950 he won reelection to the presidency and was inaugurated at the beginning of the following year. Pledging to develop Brazil's petroleum industry as a government-controlled corporation, he provoked the ire of military and civilian political forces on the right. They exposed corruption in his administration, and the army prepared to remove him from office. To prevent that humiliation from occurring once again, he committed suicide on August 24, 1954.

EDWARD A. RIEDINGER

See also Brazil; Kubitschek, Juscelino

References and Further Reading

Baer, Werner. *The Brazilian Economy: Growth and Development*, 5th ed. Westport, CT: Praeger, 2001.

Dulles, John W. F. *Vargas of Brazil*. Austin, TX: University of Texas Press, 1967.

Levine, Robert M. *Father of the Poor? Getúlio Vargas and His Era*. New York: Cambridge University Press, 1998.

Rose, R. S. *One of the Forgotten Things: Getúlio Vargas and Brazilian Social Control, 1930–1954*. Contributions in Latin American Studies, 15. Westport, CT: Greenwood, 2000.

VELVET REVOLUTIONS

On November 16, 1989, students in Bratislava, Czechoslovakia, began a peaceful protest against the communist rulers of their country. One day later, another group of peacefully protesting students—this time in Prague—were beaten by the government's riot police. The treatment of the second group of students triggered a series of peaceful anti-government demonstrations involving hundreds of thousands of Czech and Slovak citizens.

The Czechs and Slovaks had taken to the streets in peaceful protests before—in the famed Prague Spring of 1968. But unlike in 1968, Soviet tanks and troops did not occupy the nation to crush the nascent rebellion. This time, on November 28, 1989, the Czechoslovak communist government announced that it would yield exclusive power, power that it abandoned altogether by the end of December.

Thus, in a nearly bloodless upheaval, the people had thrown off the Soviet shackles that had oppressed them since World War II. By demonstrating solidarity without violence, they had brought a formerly mighty empire to its knees and won.

The Czechoslovak revolution was later called the Velvet Revolution—a term that was, in time, applied to the series of political changes that shredded the Iron Curtain and conceived democratic governments throughout Central and Eastern Europe.

Rust in the Iron Curtain

Czechoslovakia and other countries in Central and Eastern Europe had been locked behind what Winston Churchill called an "Iron Curtain" since the end of World War II. The Iron Curtain was a zone of *de facto* Soviet occupation—self-determination was not tolerated under the Soviets, who had in fact brutally put down a number of "uprisings" in the 1950s, 1960s, and 1970s—in the German Democratic Republic (East Germany) in 1953, Hungary in 1956, Czechoslovakia in 1968, and Poland in 1970 and 1976. The threat of violence helped squelch another strike in Poland in 1980–1981.

But force could only accomplish so much. The Soviet Union was reeling from the effects of a disastrous war that it had brought on itself in Afghanistan. The Soviet economy was in a shambles, especially as the Soviet military machine spent itself into oblivion trying to match American defense spending and technological development during Ronald Reagan's presidency. A new Soviet leader, Mikhail Gorbachev, introduced *glasnost* (openness) and *perestroika* (transformation) of the Soviet system to allow limited democracy and market-based economies.

Gorbachev, who assumed leadership of the Soviet communist party in 1985, was—unlike his predecessors—not inclined to use Soviet arms to put down protests in satellite nations. He rejected the "Brezhnev Doctrine," a longstanding policy of the Soviet Union—first articulated by Soviet Premier Leonid Brezhnev on November 13, 1968, in a speech before the Fifth Congress of the Polish United Workers' Party—to intervene, with force, if necessary, in the affairs of satellite states if those states pursued policies perceived as "antisocialist." Demonstrations for greater autonomy and democracy were, according to the Brezhnev Doctrine, antisocialist.

Gorbachev's rejection of the Brezhnev Doctrine seemed to open the door for Warsaw Pact nations to break away from Soviet hegemony.

Solidarity

The first break came, ironically, in Poland, where the Brezhnev Doctrine was first articulated to the world. Polish workers had for years been restive under Soviet occupation. They first protested in 1956 and won some concessions from the Soviets before the brutal repression of the Hungarian Revolution later that year. Two workers' revolts in Poland in 1970 and 1976 also were brutally put down.

Workers were still restless, however, and another strike began on August 14, 1980, in the Lenin Shipyards in Gdansk. An unemployed electrical engineer, Lech Walesa, who had been fired from a shipyard job in 1976 because of his union activities, climbed over the wall surrounding the shipyard and joined the striking workers. He became their leader, but had ambitions beyond the shipyard. He began organizing a much broader movement that became known as Solidarity. Fears of another round of Soviet repression led to the outlawing of the movement a year later, but Walesa and Solidarity merely went underground.

By 1988, the Polish Communist Party realized it would have to yield some power in order to prevent another wave of civil unrest. The government began two months of negotiations with Walesa and Solidarity in February 1989. The negotiations ended in the legalization of Solidarity, increased power for the Polish Sejm (parliament), and the right of candidates from Solidarity to run for seats in the Sejm. In elections that were held in June of that year, Solidarity won every seat it was allowed to compete for—enough seats for Solidarity to form a government without forming a coalition with the Communists. The Soviets kept to Gorbachev's word and did not intervene to keep the Polish Communist Party in power.

Walesa was elected president of Poland in a landslide in 1990.

A Snip Through the Wire

The next sign of a corroding Iron Curtain appeared in Hungary, where Soviet forces crushed a 1956 revolt and executed its leader, Hungarian Prime Minister Imre Nagy—who tried to take his country out of the Warsaw Pact—two years later.

The wounds from 1956 had not healed, however, and the Hungarian parliament, led by reformist Prime Minister Miklos Nemeth, passed a measure recognizing political parties other than the Communist Party in January 1989. On May 2, Hungarian Foreign Minister Gyula Horn used a set of wire cutters to cut the barbed wire fence between Hungary and Austria.

Hungarian border guards began letting small groups of East Germans cross the border into Austria and freedom. Word spread, and thousands gathered in Hungary waiting for their chance to escape. Hungary was caught in a bind—it was a signatory to two conflicting treaties, an international accord pledging humane treatment of refugees, and another pact with East Germany that promised it would not allow East Germans to pass through its borders to the West. The

Hungarian government announced on September 11, 1989, that it would honor its human rights responsibilities. As the word spread, tens of thousands of East Germans began heading south to Hungary, then west to freedom.

Again, Soviet forces did not intervene. The East German government, destabilized by the mass exodus of its citizens, began to crumble.

Tearing Down the Wall

East Germany possessed one of the most repressive of the Soviet Bloc regimes. In 1961, the Communist government, with the assistance of the Soviets, built one of the most recognizable and hated symbols of twentieth century repression—the Berlin Wall. Communist propagandists called it a barrier to Western imperialism. It was a barrier, but one built to keep the East Berlin residents trapped inside, not to keep foreign aggressors outside.

East German leader Eric Honecker was determined to resist the tide of liberalization. But as his citizens fled through the open gates at the Hungarian border, his power steadily ebbed. The East Germans began to take to the streets to protest the regime. Honecker looked to the Soviet Union for help, but the winds of change were blowing from Moscow.

Honecker had issued orders for his secret police to fire on demonstrators, but his subordinates were not inclined to obey. Honecker, obviously powerless, was ousted and replaced by his former internal security chief, Egon Krenz. Krenz promised change and dialogue, but the protests grew—as many as half-a-million protesters took to the Alexanderplatz in East Berlin on November 4, 1989.

By November 8, East German officials had promised to begin issuing exit visas for East German citizens the next day—at 8 a.m. Crowds gathered at a number of gates along the Wall the next morning, November 9, in anticipation. A nervous East German border guard, fearful that the crowd lining up at his gate would get out of control, opened the way west. Other gates were opened as word spread, and people flooded out of the city that had seemed a prison for almost thirty years.

The East German government soon gave up all pretense of controlling travel. Jubilant crowds on both sides of the wall began tearing the hated symbol apart. West German Chancellor Helmut Kohl openly talked of reuniting the two Germanys. By October 3, 1990, just before East Germany would have reached its forty-first birthday, the nation split apart in the aftermath of World War II was one once more.

From Prague Spring to Velvet Revolution

When Alexander Dubcek assumed the leadership of the Czechoslovak Communist Party on January 5, 1968, he was determined to reform the party and implement "socialism with a human face." On March 4 of that year, he announced the abolition of media censorship and tolerance of non-Communist parties. Prague Spring was thus born, but its life was short, as Soviet tanks rolled into Prague on August 21 to crush the movement. Dubcek was arrested and transported to Moscow, forced to surrender to Soviet demands, and then sent to internal exile in Czechoslovakia. The Soviet troops stayed in Czechoslovakia, where they maintained order—but they could not make the people forget what was lost.

When the Iron Curtain began crumbling in Poland, Hungary, and East Germany, Czechoslovakian citizens sensed the time to again demand their own freedoms had arrived. On November 17, 1989, an anti-Nazi protest by Prague students metamorphosed into an antigovernment rally. Police attacked the protesters. The battle was won by the authorities, but had sown the seeds of their own defeat in the nearly bloodless war that resulted.

A group of students, artists, and other intellectuals met at the Magic Lantern Theatre in Prague and formed the Civic Forum. A leader emerged in those meetings—Vaclav Havel, a writer whose plays helped inspire Prague Spring and who had been imprisoned several times by Communist authorities.

With the help of the organizational and propaganda skills of the member of the Civic Forum, thousands of people filled the streets of Prague and other Czechoslovak cities demanding free elections and other reforms. On November 24, just one week after the students were attacked by Czechoslovak police, Havel and Dubcek spoke to and inspired 350,000 protesters who filled Wenceslas Square.

That night, the Communist government began a catastrophic collapse. The Politburo was replaced en masse overnight. Czechoslovak workers joined a call for a general strike, and Gustav Husak, the longtime leader who reimposed the Brezhnev Doctrine in the aftermath of Prague Spring, stepped down on December 10. By December 29, free elections were held—Havel was elected president, and Dubcek was elected premier.

Death of a Dictator

Romanian strongman Nicolae Ceausescu was determined that he would not be bullied by protesters, but

he made the fatal mistake of ignoring the momentum sweeping through the Soviet Bloc. Ceausescu's initial blunder came on December 10, 1989, when he tried to oust Laszlo Tokes, a minister of a Hungarian Reformed Church in Timisoara, Romania, from the congregation because of comments Tokes had made critical of the Ceausescu administration. Parishioners began to rally in support of their ministers. Others joined the protests, which were peaceful.

Ceausescu ordered his police to fire on the protesters, but initially his orders were ignored. On December 17, he denounced the commanders, and said he wanted a Tiananmen Square-style massacre. That night, Ceausescu got his wish.

Initial reports were that the massacre claimed thousands of casualties—the actual number was about one hundred—but anger toward Ceausescu swept the nation. Fighting broke out in Bucharest. By December 22, Romania's military, in response to rumors that Ceausescu had the defense minister killed for being too soft on protesters, withdrew its support from the dictator. The army gave its support to a coalition of former Ceausescu aides and dissidents called the National Salvation Front. The coalition declared itself the legitimate government of Romania.

By the time Ceausescu realized power no longer rested in his hands, it was too late. He and his wife, Elena, tried to escape in a helicopter, but the pilot betrayed them and they were captured. On December 25, Ceausescu and his wife were tried, found guilty of genocide, and executed by firing squad.

Aftermath

The remaining communist governments in Europe soon fell. Albania and Bulgaria abandoned communism fairly quietly. Yugoslavia, not part of the Soviet Bloc, disintegrated into a series of bloody ethnic conflicts among its former republics. The Czechs and Slovaks, on the other hand, peacefully divorced in 1992, dividing the former Czechoslovakia into two countries, the Czech Republic and Slovakia. Walesa, hero of the Solidarity movement, discovered the joys of democracy when he lost his bid to be reelected president of Poland in 1995.

Several former Soviet Bloc countries have since joined the North Atlantic Treaty Organization (NATO)—the alliance they were aligned against as members of the Warsaw Pact. They are Bulgaria, the Czech Republic, Hungary, Poland, Romania, and Slovakia. The territory of East Germany became part of NATO after its reunification with West Germany.

The Soviet Union even ceased to exist after an August 19, 1991, coup by hard-line Communists failed. Boris Yeltsin, president of the Russian Federation, stood up to the rebels and assumed more power as leader of a rejuvenated Russia. Gorbachev, the engineer of the reforms that led to the dissolution of the Soviet empire, found himself consigned to the dustbin of history.

DAVID M. LAWRENCE

See also Albania; Berlin Wall (1961–1989); Bulgaria; Ceausescu, Nicolae; Civil Disobedience; Civil Rights; Czech Republic; Dictatorships; Dubcek, Alexander; Elections; Glasnost and Perestroika; Gorbachev, Mikhail; Havel, Vaclav; Human Rights as a Foreign Policy Issue; Human Rights: Definition and Violations; Hungarian Crisis of 1956; Hungary; Jaruzelski, Wojciech; Krushchev, Nikita; Marxism; Poland; Prague Spring, 1968; Romania; Russia; Self-Determination; Slovakia; Socialism; Solidarity Union; Soviet Bloc; Totalitarianism; Walesa, Lech

References and Further Reading

Ash, Timothy Garton. 2002. *The Polish Revolution: Solidarity*, 3rd ed. New Haven, CT: Yale University Press.

William Barbour and Carol Wekesser, eds. *The Breakup of the Soviet Union: Opposing Viewpoints*. San Diego: Greenhaven Press, 1994.

Barner-Barry, Carol. *The Politics of Change: The Transformation of the Former Soviet Union*. New York: St. Martin's Press, 1995.

Buckley, William F., Jr. *The Fall of the Berlin Wall*. Hoboken, NJ: John Wiley and Sons, 2004.

Carrere D'Encausse, Helen. *The End of the Soviet Empire: The Triumph of the Nations*. (Translated by Franklin Philip.) New York: Basic Books, 1992.

Coleman, Fred. The Decline and Fall of the Soviet Empire: Forty Years That Shook the World, from Stalin to Yeltsin. New York: St. Martin's Press, 1996.

Kotkin, Stephen. *Armageddon Averted: The Soviet Collapse, 1970–2000*. Oxford: Oxford University Press, 2001.

Lévesque, Jacques. *The Enigma of 1989: The USSR and the Liberation of Eastern Europe*. Berkeley, CA: University of California Press, 1997.

Shepherd, Robin E.H. *Czechoslovakia : The Velvet Revolution and Beyond*. New York: St. Martin's Press, 2000.

Smith, Graham. The Post-Soviet States: Mapping the Politics of Transition. London; New York: Oxford University Press, 1999.

Stokes, Gale. *The Walls Came Tumbling Down: The Collapse of Communism in Eastern Europe*. New York: Oxford University Press, 1992.

Suny, Ronald Grigor. *The Revenge of the Past: Nationalism, Revolution, and the Collapse of the Soviet Union*. Stanford, CA: Stanford University Press, 1993.

Walker, Edward W. *Dissolution: Sovereignty and the Breakup of the Soviet Union*. Lanham, MD: Rowman and Littlefield, 2003.

White, Stephen. Communism and Its Collapse. New York: Routledge, 2001.

VENEZUELA

Venezuela occupies approximately 353,841 square miles of the northwestern part of the continent of South America. Venezuela can be considered a Caribbean nation, because that sea has been its main gateway to the world. It controls several Caribbean Islands, the largest being the famous tourist spot Isla Margarita. Its capital, Caracas, is close to the sea.

Guyana, Colombia, and Brazil are at its borders. There have been ongoing border disputes with both Guyana and Colombia. Venezuela's territory is remarkably diverse and rich in biological and mineral resources. Venezuela has tropical areas near the Caribbean coast; Lake Maracaibo, one of the greatest sources of petroleum in the hemisphere; *llanos* (central plains) and mountains in the interior; and vast sections of Amazonian jungle that are largely undeveloped. Towards the border with Brazil are the fantastic Angel Falls and the impressive mesa region. In this same Amazon area are a number of indigenous tribes as well as largely untapped mineral deposits. Venezuela thus is a highly unevenly developed country, with strong regional inequalities. Venezuela's petroleum wealth, concentrated around Lake Maracaibo, is a major factor in the very high levels of urbanization of the country, with 75% of the population residing in cities.

With a population of just 23,707,000, and incredible petroleum wealth, Venezuela would seem to have great possibilities for a very high standard of living. Unfortunately, Venezuela's wealth is highly skewed, because only a small proportion of its population has reaped most of the benefits from petroleum. Mismanagement, corruption, political instability, and poor institutional development have held back both distributional and developmental progress.

Because of its location, Venezuela was of strategic importance to the Spanish colonizers who arrived in 1498, but it was relatively neglected early on, since it lacked the gold and silver riches of Mexico and Peru. Before petroleum, Venezuela was dominated by agriculture, principally cattle-raising. With its relative isolation in the Spanish Empire, Venezuela was at the forefront of the Independence movement, and the home of its hero, Símon Bólivar.

Early Venezuelan history is marked by a series of personalistic dictatorships based around the agricultural elite and led by military officers. Despite the ongoing political instability, Venezuelan governments developed constitutions, and by the end of the nineteenth century began to develop a more widespread constituency. A long period of stability took hold under Juan Vicente Gómez, who ruled from 1909 to 1935. Gómez ruthlessly developed efficient military and police control of the population during this period, and was able to woo foreign investors into the nascent petroleum industry.

Immigration to Venezuela occurred more recently than in other Latin American countries and was spurred by the development of the oil industry. Large numbers of immigrants from Europe came to Venezuela in the first decades after World War II. Since then, the majority of immigrants, many illegal, have come from other Latin American nations. In conjunction with urbanization, high fertility rates have placed heavy pressures for public services on the Venezuelan government.

"Sowing the oil" is the catchword for Venezuela's avowed economic strategy for the better part of this century. Venezuela was the leader in creating the Organization of Petroleum Exporting Countries (OPEC) in 1960. Venezuela also was instrumental in increasing fourfold the price of petroleum in 1973. Thus, Venezuela has been able to use its petroleum platform and related revenues to conduct an activist foreign policy in the region.

Venezuela is at the forefront of the Group of Three, with Colombia and Mexico, that seeks to promote Caribbean Basin economic cooperation, and was a promoter of many of the Central American peace processes during the 1980s.

In some ways, Venezuela has managed to use its petroleum to support industrialization. First, there has been an expansion into the petrochemical industry, including the development of local refineries. The Venezuelan state oil company Petróleos de Venezuela (PEDEVESA) is a world leader in the petroleum industry, and even owns retail (Citgo) gasoline stations in the United States. Second, revenues from petroleum have been used to develop light and heavy industries, including consumer goods, motor vehicle assembly, iron and steel works, and, most successfully, an internationally competitive aluminum industry. Third, Venezuela has attempted to buttress its agricultural sector through protection and subsidies, although these efforts have not had much success.

Although an industrial base has been built, Venezuela still suffers from an over-dependence on petroleum. Venezuela suffers from the same economic problem as many natural resource producers who experience a boom: the newfound revenue increases inflation, or local prices. The increase in exports also usually leads to an appreciation of the currency, so that local exports become more expensive to overseas buyers. Thus, the boom industry, in this case, petroleum, tends to "crowd out" other sources of livelihood, including both competing industries and agriculture. Of course, the overall result may

not be negative if the industry in question has great employment itself, or has industries that are linked to it that benefit from the boom. Unfortunately, petroleum tends to be a relatively isolated and concentrated capital-intensive enterprise, so that its ability to provide new jobs or demands on local industry are very limited. Thus, the real key for Venezuela would be to use the revenues from petroleum to develop other, unrelated industries. Unfortunately, Venezuelan governments have historically found it difficult to effectively sow the petroleum revenues into product diversification and overall higher standards of living. Despite a history of stable democratic governance, Venezuela's political process has been rife with mismanagement and corruption.

Upon Juan Vicente Gómez's death in 1935, the Venezuelan political system began experimenting with democratic rights. At the same time, Venezuelan governments began their attempts to claim a better deal from their foreign partners in petroleum exploitation. These attempts began with a "revision" announced by President Medina as part of a law in 1943. The Hydrocarbons Act of 1943 is considered by many to be one of the cornerstone pieces to the consolidation of the "petro-state." The key revisions embodied by the law were to shift petroleum taxes from those based upon customs and concessions to those placed on income. More importantly, Medina adopted the "50/50" principle by which the industry's revenues should not exceed those going to the state. In return for accepting these changes, foreign companies were given full concession rights for forty years until 1983. The new revenues allowed the Venezuelan government to begin a continuing tradition of public supports for industry and for public services during this period. Medina's government was overthrown by a then-progressive group of military and civilian activists in 1945.

The new group that took over with a coup was led by Rómulo Betancourt, the leader of Democratic Action (Acción Democrática or AD). AD was widely supported, and passed a new Constitution that reflected several key concerns that had been brewing. Foremost was Venezuela's continuing desire to capture even more of the petroleum wealth for itself. This led to a move towards a 50/50 split of all future profits. Secondly, AD had a strongly supportive labor rights policy. Third, the new government supported increased social spending on housing, health, education, and further agricultural and industrial projects.

Conservative elements of the military reacted strongly, with a military coup in November 1948. General Pérez Jimenez took over as a military dictator. He immediately outlawed political activity and took steps to crush AD support in labour and the universities.

He also abandoned much of the social reform spending begun by AD. Amidst widespread popular protests, a group of military officers overthrew the dictator and reinstalled a transitional military–civilian government for one year, with Betancourt as its head.

Betancourt was reelected in 1959, and remained president until 1964. This administration was a watershed, because it set the political tone for Venezuelan politics for the next forty years. The two major political parties, the AD and the Social Christian Party (Partido Social Cristiano, or COPEI), generally working in cahoots, came to dominate the political landscape with an important agreement of cooperation called the *Pacto de Punto Fijo,* signed in 1958. The idea was to ensure democratic party cooperation and moderation so that the military would not have any reason for future intervention. In this point, the new system succeeded without doubt. They created a unique system of limited democracy, using strong party discipline and patron-client networks to ensure their domination of elections. At the same time, they were able, during most of the period, to develop a consultative political culture, in which disputes were ironed out. The leadership shared a general consensus that oil revenues would be used to fund industrialization. The two leaders, Betancourt and Caldera, served as the hubs of the party patronage networks and served as the focal points of party loyalty.

In 1959, Betancourt softened much of the reform thrust of his 1945 government. The government nonetheless passed an agrarian reform law in 1960, and began a national steel industry in 1962. Despite this progress, the Betancourt government was rocked by economic crisis and a guerrilla war with Communists aided by Fidel Castro. After another AD administration, COPEI's longtime leader, Rafael Caldera, won the Presidential election in 1968. Although the patronage network changed, in practice, COPEI's basic platform was hard to distinguish from AD's. Nonetheless, the Caldera government did take majority ownership of the banking industry, control of the natural gas industry, and declared a moratorium on new oil concessions.

The early 1970s marked an important turning point for Venezuelan history, as new President Carlos Andrés Pérez nationalized the iron ore industry in 1975 and the petroleum industry in 1976. In combination with the OPEC oil price hikes, the Venezuelan government was able to increase its public spending projects and patronage graft through the rest of the decades. As oil prices declined in 1979 and continued the slide in the 1980s, the Venezuelan government found itself in the midst a major economic crisis, including a huge external debt, capital flight, a general slowdown in productivity, and growing unemployment.

The slowdown in oil prices hurt Venezuela's ability to pay back its external debt, which had been based on foreign borrowing with the expectation of future long-term payoffs. More importantly, the patron-client type networks that pervaded and held up the two-party system, were dependent upon the lubricating expenditures of oil revenues. A series of AD and COPEI governments was unable to wrest themselves from the crisis. In 1989, Pérez was reelected, and surprisingly began a neoliberal austerity program. The budget-tightening measures, including the raising of prices of basic goods, led to widespread riots in 1989, which were put down by the military. Pérez survived two coup attempts in 1992, including one led by a previously unknown Hugo Chávez Frías, who was then put in jail. However, Pérez did not survive charges of corruption, and he was forced to leave office in 1993.

After several interim presidents, omnipresent Rafael Caldera was reelected, this time as an independent. Caldera's independence worked in his favor, because the population seemed weary of the AD-COPEI power-sharing arrangement, which was widely seen as both corrupt and inefficient. Caldera inherited a situation of economic chaos, in which both inflation and growing capital flight hamstrung possibilities for recovery. The government at first moved towards increasing monetary liquidity in order to restore growth, but later reinstituted austerity measures, including raising taxes to cover a budget deficit and introducing a fixed exchange rate to restore investor confidence. Caldera's attempts to stabilize the economy failed, not in the least part, because of Congressional opposition to changes in the tax code. The government's plan to raise funds and efficiency through privatization also met with limited success. The privatization process, which began under Pérez, was completed for several key enterprises: the national telephone company, CANTV (a state TV broadcasting channel), and the steel sector. However, the plans for privatization of other sectors was put off, and questions about whether a fair price was received and whom benefited abounded. In 1995, a number of major bank failures and growing labor unrest, including strikes, increased tensions further. The worsening economic crisis set the stage for a revolution in Venezuela's development.

Hugo Chávez, released from prison after leading a coup attempt in 1992, decisively won the 1998 presidential elections with his new Patriotic Pole party. With 80% of the Venezuelan population living in poverty, the previous system of AD-COPEI administration led by the Betancourt–Caldera generation had clearly exhausted any remaining patience. Chávez wasted no time in suggesting a number of wholesale changes to Venezuelan politics, beginning with a new Constituent Assembly, which created a new Constitution, approved by voters in 2000. The new Constitution promises agrarian reform, access to health care, education, housing, and social security for the whole population. On the other hand, his economic policy initiatives in contrast to his rhetoric, are much more mainstream and evolutionary in nature. There has been no significant land reform; no universal access to social services has occurred, and the marginalized majority of Venezuela are no better off, in many ways worse off, than when Chávez started. In fact, his economic policy has been rather conservative, avoiding any major swings in government spending, and avoiding the subject of further privatization or state initiatives. Even though the changes have been piecemeal, a strong minority of Venezuelans have taken to the streets regularly to protest, which has been met by counterprotests. The political and economic chaos led initially to a deterioration in overall support for the president. In 2002, a clash between the two groups led to a military coup by forces linked to conservative elements in society. As support for the coup began to melt away amidst massive demonstrations and international condemnations (with the notable absence of the United States, at least initially), Chávez purged elements of the military and government institutions, seizing upon his triumphant return from the short-lived coup. An effort to create a referendum to recall the President seemed to go nowhere by the summer of 2004.

Particularly key have been Chávez's efforts to take control of Pedevesa, the national oil company, which have been met with resistance by both skilled workers and management. However, up to now, the previously formidable opposition, including AD and COPEI, have shown no ability to act as coalitional vehicles, related to the general repudiation of their years of corrupt rule and economic mismanagement.

ANIL HIRA

References and Further Reading

Coppedge, Michael. "Prospects for democratic governability in Venezuela," *Journal of Interamerican Studies & World Affairs*, Summer 1994, 36(2): 39-51.

Coronil, Fernando. *The Magical State: Nature, Money, and Modernity in Venezuela.* Chicago: The University of Chicago Press, 1997.

Crisp, Brian F. *Democratic Institutional Design: The Powers and Incentives of Venezuelan Politicians and Interest Groups,* Stanford, CA: Stanford University Press, 2000.

Ellner, Steve and Daniel Hellinger, eds. 2003. *Venezuelan Politics in the Chávez Era: Class, Polarization, and Conflict.* L. Rienner Publishers (December 1, 2002).

Karl, Terry Lynn. *The Paradox of Plenty: Oil Booms and Petro-States,* Berkeley, CA: University of California Press, 1997.

McCoy, Jennifer L. *Venezuelan Democracy Under Stress*. New Brunswick, NJ: Transaction, 1995.

Naim, Moises. *Paper Tigers and Minotaurs: The Politics of Venezuela's Economic Reforms*, Washington, DC: Carnegie Endowment for International Peace, 1993.

"The Venezuelan Story: Revisiting the Conventional Wisdom," *Journal of Democracy*, April 2001, 12(2):17–31.

VERWOERD, HENDRIK

An Afrikaner nationalist politician, Hendrik Verwoerd (1907–1966) was born in Holland. His family emigrated to South Africa while he was still an infant. He attended Anglo schools and studied at Stellenbosch University, with further studies in Germany, Holland and the United States. In 1927, he became Professor of Applied Psychology at Stellenbosch. During this time, Verwoerd developed an interest in Afrikaner impoverishment and organized the seminal 1936 National "Poor White Problem" Conference. He became an influential promoter of the notion that charity was no solution, instead advocating state-led ("affirmative action") interventionism to uplift, educate, and create industrial and civil service jobs to end Afrikaner poverty. In 1937, the National Party (NP) established a newspaper, *Die Transvaler*, to promote Afrikaner nationalism in Johannesburg, and appointed Verwoerd as editor. In this capacity, Verwoerd became leader of Transvaal Afrikaners, especially those raised out of poverty by the policies he promoted.

Transvaal nationalists were more ideologically dogmatic and ardently segregationist than Cape nationalists, who, representing more affluent Afrikaners, leaned towards laissez faire economics; by contrast, the Transvaal NP favoured state interventionism and race-based job-reservation in order to promote interests of working and lower middle class Afrikaners. When Malan's NP won the 1948 election, Verwoerd entered Parliament. In 1950, he was appointed Minister of Native Affairs and served in this position until 1958. During his tenure as Minister of Native Affairs, Verwoerd became the chief architect of apartheid (which he called "separate development"). He was regarded as the key intellectual behind apartheid—a socioeconomic policy that he built on the imported Dutch social theory of *verzuiling*.

As a politician, Verwoerd always faced the problem that he was regarded as "too intellectual" and a "social engineer." But over time, fewer and fewer NP politicians were prepared to challenge his views. Becoming Prime Minister in 1958, Verwoerd moved to fully implement his apartheid plan. Native Affairs was split into two departments, Bantu Administration & Development and Bantu Education. The term "native" was dropped. Verwoerd remained in control of Bantu affairs while Prime Minister. He proposed a policy of "internal decolonization" in which separate black states would be created and eventually given independence so that ultimately there would be no black citizens of South Africa. Verwoerd argued that, otherwise, whites would be "culturally swamped" by a black majority. In 1959, legislation was passed creating separate territorial authorities on black tribal land, known as Bantustans, and removed black representation in the "white" Parliament. Ten "homeland" governments and the Bantu Education authorities were charged with promoting the traditions and culture of black ethnic groups. 1959 also saw the creation of new black universities and the Bantu Investment Corporation to promote economic development in the homelands. This was intended to "reverse the flow" of black people from tribal areas to the cities (so these cities could be kept "white"). Within "white areas," blacks were designated as foreign guest labourers—essentially, cheap labour.

Verwoerd's policies sparked urban black resistance beginning with the Sharpeville uprising (1960). Black political movements (ANC and PAC) were banned (1960), and Mandela was jailed (1964). In 1960, Verwoerd shocked Anglo South Africans by calling a referendum over becoming a republic. South Africa became a republic (1961) and withdrew from the British Commonwealth. Afrikaners celebrated severing links with the British monarchy as "independence." Verwoerd was a central player in developing the racial-capitalist framework for industrializing and urbanizing South Africa. He was killed in the South African Parliament House of Assembly in 1966, stabbed to death by a parliamentary messenger. It remains unclear whether the murder was a politically motivated assassination or whether the killer, who suffered from schizophrenia, was motivated entirely by mental delusions.

P. ERIC LOUW

See also Apartheid; Bantustans; South Africa

References and Further Reading

Kenney, H. *Architect of Apartheid: H.F. Verwoerd, an Appraisal*. Johannsburg: Jonathan Ball, 1980.

Kruger, D.W. *The Making of a Nation*. Johannesburg & London: MacMillan, 1969.

Worden, Nigel. *The Making of Modern South Africa*. Oxford & Malden, MA: Blackwell, 2000.

VIET CONG

(*See People's Liberation Armed Forces [PLAF]*)

VIET MINH

The Viet Nam Doc Lap Dong Minh Hoi, commonly known as the Viet Minh (Vietnam Independence League), was founded by Ho Chi Minh and others at the Eighth Plenum of the Indo-Chinese Communist Party (ICP) in May 1941. It served as the organizational hub for the development of a broad, national program. They called on "patriots of all ages and all types" to join a united front to oppose Japanese occupation and French rule. The purpose of the Viet Minh was tactical, never strategic. Its flexibility allowed the ICP to alter its course rapidly in response to each specific military and political situation. The Viet Minh temporarily downplayed Communist class struggle and focused on national liberation. As a result they involved all social and political groups in the "national" struggle. Anticolonialism, patriotism, and nationalism were the only prerequisites for joining this national united front. To this end, the Viet Minh made temporary alliances with several noncommunist organizations in order to achieve its more immediate objectives.

Following the Japanese invasion of 1940 and the collaboration of the Vichy French, there seemed to be no national resistance; however, General Vo Nguyen Giap raised an army for the Viet Minh which, with some US aid, effectively fought the Japanese throughout World War II. On March 9, 1945, the Japanese executed a relatively bloodless coup against French colonial forces, only to surrender to the Allies five months later. With few Allied forces available to occupy Indochina, a political void formed. Being the only well trained force in the region, the Viet Minh fully exploited the situation. In August 1945 (the August Revolution), the Viet Minh marched into Ha Noi and proclaimed Vietnamese independence.

On September 2, 1945, in Ba Dinh Square, with US Office of Special Services (OSS) operatives standing next to him, Ho read an official declaration ending French colonialism, Japanese occupation, and the Nguyen Dynasty. Shortly after Ho's declaration of independence, the ICP announced that it was dissolving, leaving the Viet Minh as the only official party apparatus.

To the chagrin of the Viet Minh and most Vietnamese, postwar Allied treaties allowed the French to return in 1946 as colonial masters of Indochina. This touched off a war between the French and Viet Minh. As they had done during World War II, Ho and Giap withdrew the Viet Minh to mountain strongholds and appealed for broad support by ostensibly disbanding the Communist Party and emphasizing anti-imperialism, even though the communists,

bolstered with aid from the Communist Bloc, never surrendered control of the Viet Minh.

In 1951, Communist established the Vietnamese Workers' Party (VWP) (Dang Lao Dong Viet Nam). According to revolutionary theory, the broad-based front was to be revised whenever historical circumstances shifted. As such, during the war with France, the VWP reconstituted the Viet Minh as the Lien Viet Front (United Viet Nam National Front), and in 1955, shortly after the Geneva Accords, reformed it again as the Viet Nam Fatherland Front. There is some question as to the actual date of the reconstitution of the Viet Minh. Scholars, such as Hoang Van Dao, in *Viet Nam Quoc Ddn Dang,* argue that the Viet Minh became the Lien Viet in April 1946. Others suggest that it was the Viet Minh that fought the French from 1946 to 1954. No matter, the Viet Minh have popularly been associated with the army that defeated the French at the Battle of Dien Bien Phu.

When the French left in 1954, the Communists took power in the north, while in the south, where the Viet Minh were never very strong because of a more pronounced French colonial influence, President Diem's US-supported non-Communist regime held sway. By 1960, southern cadres of the old Viet Minh had reorganized as the National Front for the Liberation of South Viet Nam (NFLSV). Their military arm, the People's Liberation Armed Forces (PLAF) or "Viet Cong," launched the communist-led guerrilla war against Diem's regime in South Viet Nam.

CECIL B. CURREY AND WILLIAM P. HEAD

References and Further Reading

Currey, Cecil B. *Victory at Any Cost: The Genius of Viet Nam's General Vo Nguyen Giap.* Washington, DC: Brassey's, 1997.

Duiker, William J. *The Rise of Nationalism in Vietnam, 1900–1941.* Ithaca, NY: Cornell University Press, 1976.

Fall, Bernard B. *Street Without Joy: Indochina at War, 1946–1954.* Harrisburg, PA: The Stockpole Press, 1961.

———. The *Two Viet-Nams: A Political and Military Analysis.* New York: Frederick A. Praeger Press, 1964.

———. *The Viet Minh Regime: Government and Administration in the Democratic Republic of Vietnam.* Ithaca, NY, Cornell University Press, 1956.

———. *Hell in a Very Small Place: The Siege of Dien Bien Phu.* New York: Vintage Press, 1966.

History of the August Revolution. Ha Noi: Foreign Languages Publishing House, 1972.

Hoang Van Dao. *Viet Nam Quoc Dan Dang.* Sai Gon: Published by the Author, 1970.

Huynh Kim Khanh. "The Vietnamese August Revolution." Translated in *Journal of Asian Studies* Vol. 30, No. 4 (August 1971): pp. 761–782.

Woodside, Alexander B. *Community and Revolution* in *Modern Vietnam.* Boston: Houghton Mifflin, 1976.

VIETNAM

Viet Nam, today known as the Socialist Republic of Vietnam (SRV), is an "S-"shaped country that extends along the eastern coast of mainland Southeast Asia from the border with the People's Republic of China (PRC) to the Gulf of Thailand. It is bordered on the west by Laos and Cambodia. It has a total area of 329,560 square kilometers, about the size of New Mexico. SRV has a tropical climate with dense jungles, lush rice paddies, and even mountains to the north and west.

As of July 2004, the population of the SRV was 82,689,518, the second largest in Southeast Asia after the Republic of Indonesia. The largest city is Ho Chi Minh City, formerly Saigon, 5,894,100, while Hai Phong is the largest port. The median age is 24.9 years, the literacy rate 94%, and the life expectancy is 70.35. A total of 85% of the people are ethnic Vietnamese. Other ethnic groups include Thai, Khmer (Cambodians), Cham (Malayo-Polynesian), Chinese, and nearly sixty tribal groups. Although the vast majority are Buddhist, there are over 2 million Roman Catholics, 2 million in the Cao Dai and the Hoa Hao sects and three hundred thousand Muslims. The primary language is Vietnamese, with many people speaking English, French, Chinese, and Khmer.

The SRV capital is Ha Noi. Under the most recent constitution, the nation is divided into fifty-nine provinces. The minimum voting age is eighteen. There is one legal party—Vietnamese Communist Party (VCP) and the General Secretary is Nong Duc Manh. The Chief of State since September 1997 has been President Tran Duc Luong, and the Head of Government has been Prime Minister Phan Van Khai. The 498-seat National Assembly is a unicameral body.

The historical Vietnamese homeland in the Red River Delta can be traced to the seventh-century BC. From about the third century BC through the eleventh century AD, Chinese rulers dominated the region. For the next six centuries, the Chinese confronted internal rebellions, each resulting in the weakening of its control over Vietnam. In the 1540s, the Portuguese became the first Europeans to arrive in the area, but their staying power quickly dissipated. Finally, in the late 1850s, the French came to stay. By 1884, they imposed a protectorate over Vietnam that lasted until 1954.

The French developed and exported rice, rubber, tea and other tropical fruits, while creating a monopoly for the importation of French manufactured goods. The French also constructed roads and railroads throughout the country to support the export businesses. But the Vietnamese workers did not benefit from the system. The French also introduced Western democratic institutions and education, but greatly restricted Vietnamese participation in both, usually to a handful of wealthy natives. For the Vietnamese, the colonial experience was oppressive and humiliating, a fact that contributed to longstanding resistance to the French presence.

In the early 1900s, self-determination emerged as a factor in local politics, and by the 1920s several local political parties, groups, and organizations emerged to call for the ouster of the French from Indochina. The most significant individual was Nguyen Al Quoc (Nguyen the Patriot), later known as Ho Chi Minh. Ho became a founding member of the French Communist Party in 1920. In 1924, he established a proto-Marxist political organization called the Revolutionary Youth League, and five years later, the league transformed it into the Indochinese Communist Party (ICP).

The onset of World War II ended French authority in Indochina. In the fall of 1940, Vichy French colonial regime permitted the Japanese to use military installations in Indochina. Operating as a multiparty nationalist alliance called the Viet Minh Front, the ICP organized guerrillas under Gen. Vo Nguyen Giap and fought the Japanese from the mountains north of the Red River Delta. After the Japanese surrender in August 1945, the Viet Minh occupied Ha Noi and declared the creation of Democratic Republic of Viet Nam (DRV).

In the south, the British returned power to the French in Sai Gon. Ho and the French commenced negotiations regarding the relationship between Vietnam and France. In the summer of 1946, formal negotiations in France broke down and war erupted in December. Viet Minh forces retreated back to the countryside to wage guerrilla resistance.

During the First Indochina War (1946–1954), the Viet Minh grew in strength emphasizing national independence and land reform, despite French efforts to undercut the DRV by forming a puppet government under former emperor Bao Dai. In October 1949, the Viet Minh also began receiving aid from the newly created People's Republic of China (PRC). Even with US support for the French, the war turned into a stalemate and French public support steadily weakened. In the spring of 1954, France agreed to a peace conference in Geneva. Negotiations opened just after the Viet Minh victory at Dien Bien Phu. In July, the parties agreed to a cease-fire and a division of the nation with the DRV holding the north and the French and Bao Dai controlling the south. A demilitarization zone at the Seventeenth Parallel separated the states. A political declaration drafted at Geneva and approved by all representatives except

Bao Dai and the United States called for national elections in 1956 to create a united Viet Nam.

After Geneva, Ho hoped that elections would re-unify the country under DRV rule, but in Sai Gon, a new anti-communist government led by Ngo Dinh Diem refused to hold elections. President Dwight D. Eisenhower supported Diem, who faced a big challenge since the population in the South was so diverse. Diem, a Roman Catholic, never did gain the support of the 85% of the population that was Buddhist. While he agreed to US requests to form a new constitutional republic, his repression of all opposition alienated intellectuals and many ethnic and religious groups. By 1958, military conflict between the two governments marked the beginning of the Second Indochina War.

In 1960, with guidance from Ha Noi, the National Front for the Liberation of South Vietnam (NFLSV or NLF) was born. Like the Viet Minh, they stressed nationalism over class struggle. At first, party strategists, fearful of US intervention, sought victory through negotiations and later insurgent forces in the South—the People's Liberation Armed Forces (PLAF), popularly known as the Viet Cong (VC). President John F. Kennedy responded by increasing US assistance to the RVN. In the summer of 1963, Buddhists began protests over Diem's favoritism toward Catholics. The White House, frustrated by Diem's refusal to broaden his support base, turned a blind eye to a coup that overthrew Diem in early November. Diem and his brother, Ngo Dinh Nhu, were killed.

In early 1965, as the situation in the South deteriorated, President Lyndon B. Johnson sent US combat troops and began a bombing campaign against the DRV to reduce their support for the insurgency and obtain a negotiated settlement. Concurrently, increasing numbers of People's Army of Viet Nam (PAVN) forces infiltrated into the RVN and the conflict evolved into a more conventional war. The United States eventually committed more than five hundred thousand troops to support the RVN government of President Nguyen Van Thieu. By late 1967, most Americans thought that victory was near. That belief was shattered by the Tet Offensive in January–February 1968 and also marked the beginning of the end of US involvement. The war forced Johnson from the presidency and contributed to the 1968 presidential election of Richard M. Nixon with a promise to withdraw US forces. The war dragged on, however, and Nixon expanded it into Cambodia.

Peace negotiations that began in 1968 culminated in an agreement on January 27, 1973, that required the United States to withdraw all of its troops, but left more than one hundred thousand communist forces in the south. In early 1975, the PAVN began another offensive that ended with the fall of Saigon on April 30, 1975.

One year later, on April 25, 1976, Communist leaders replaced the DRV with the Socialist Republic of Vietnam (SRV), with its capital in Ha Noi. The Party and government leadership remained the same, although some NFLSV leaders were assigned senior positions. While some Southerners complained, unification took place with little violence, although thousands were sent to reeducation camps for indoctrination or punishment.

The SRV had a hard time achieving its goal of building a socialist society. In spite of heavy wartime damage, lack of capital, and the challenge of integrating the South into the socialist North, Party leaders launched an ambitious program of socialist transformation. In early 1978, all industry and commerce above the family level were nationalized, while private farmers were forced into collective farms. Thousands of Vietnamese, many of them ethnic Chinese who believed the new laws were directed at them, fled the country into the PRC. Economic production declined, and unrest broke out among many sectors of society.

The economy continued to downspiral, illustrated by a record inflation rate of 774.7% in 1986. As a result, the VCP Sixth National Congress elected Nguyen Van Linh as Party Chief, and subsequently implemented a policy called "Doi Moi" or "do Maui" (social and economic renovation). SRV leaders initiated a more tolerant attitude toward the private sector that brought about an improvement in the economy.

Vietnam's relations with its neighbors also improved during the 1980s. Relations with neighboring Cambodia and the PRC deteriorated and border clashes began in 1975. The fanatical Khmer Rouge regime of Pol Pot in Phnom Penh refused the SRV's proposal to form an alliance of the three Indochinese countries under Vietnamese guidance. Vietnamese troops occupied Cambodia in December 1978, and the PRC responded with a brief but bloody invasion of northern Viet Nam in February 1979. When Vietnamese forces created a new pro-Viet Nam government in Phnom Penh, the PRC joined other countries, including the United States, in imposing an economic embargo on the SRV. The strain on Vietnamese resources became extreme. Throughout this period, the SRV was conducting a two-front war by defending its northern border against a Chinese invasion, and supporting its sixty thousand-man army in Cambodia. The situation changed after the election of Nguyen Van Linh as party chief in 1986. He directed the withdrawal of Vietnamese troops from Laos and Cambodia in 1988, and by September 1989, virtually all

troops were gone. Viet Nam signed the Cambodian peace agreement in October 1991 and soon after restored diplomatic relations with China.

Beyond Asia, new partnerships were formed. In 1990, the European Economic Union established diplomatic relations with the SRV. This trend continued in 1992, when the SRV established full relations with both the Association of Southeast Asian Nations (ASEAN) and the Republic of Korea (South).

The SRV also improved relations with the US as a result of Vietnamese cooperation in resolving the issue of MIAs. In February 1994, President Bill Clinton ended the economic embargo and on July 11, 1995, the United States normalized relations with the SRV. In April 1997, a pact was signed with the United States designed to repay the $146 million wartime debt incurred by the RVN government. In November 2001, the National Assembly approved a trade agreement that opened US markets to Vietnamese goods and services, with tariffs rates dropping from rates as high as 40%. Viet Nam in return opened its state markets to foreign competition.

Despite the benefits that economic growth has brought to many Vietnamese, performance and structural inadequacies continue to plague the country. Its people continue to experience a substantial divide in terms of income and wealth distribution, and substantial incidences of poverty remain although macro economic successes have taken place. During the 1990–1993 growth period, the country's estimated overall poverty rate was 58% and food poverty affected 25% of the population. By 1998, overall poverty declined to 37% and food poverty dropped to 15%. Despite growth and poverty eradication, poverty plagues many Vietnamese. For example, Vietnam's population of about 82 million means that overall poverty affects some 27 million Vietnamese and 13 million of them go hungry and malnourished.

While poverty eradication tops the "list of things to do," Vietnamese scholars identify structural inadequacies that must be dealt with if growth with poverty eradication is going to be sustained. Policy generating *and* implementing institutions remain weak, regulatory systems are vague and often contradictory and the legal system, while improved, remains seriously underdeveloped. Government lacks the capacity to create sound accounting standards and its adjudication processes are inadequate when it comes to settling disputes on consistently reasonable bases. Bureaucratic red tape, high and growing levels of public corruption and abuse of power, and a haphazard taxation system that is in a constant state of flux, make conducting economic activity in the country an adventure. Banking decisions proceed without sufficient concern for

prudential lending and transparency. Production and consumption patterns contributed to environmental degradation and urban pollution, and resource preservation and human health protection efforts remain inadequate.

Vietnam remains among the lowest 25% of the world's countries measured by per capita income—no more than $400 per year. No single measure can successfully address the causes of poverty, but clearly Vietnam's labor force is a primary contributor to what Vietnam has accomplished, and it stands to make substantial contributions to macroeconomic progress in the future if it is fully developed and used. However, numerous other obstacles stand in the way of doing so: one is high population growth rate; another is a relatively young and rapidly urbanizing population; also, a large segment of the rural work force is unskilled and deprived of sources of information. Urban immigrants tend to be young and unskilled and augmented by refugees, disabled veterans, demobilized soldiers and persons made unemployed due to shifts from State-Owned Enterprises to private-sector firms, they all make up a largely disadvantaged pool of labor.

Poverty-stricken poor Vietnamese make up 25% of all Vietnamese rural households. They live in poverty so pronounced that they could not afford to provide 2,100 calories of food per person *even if* all of their income was spent on food. Poverty in Vietnam continues to have a distinct rural bias: the ratio of urban to rural poverty increased from 1:6 to 1:10 over the 1993–1998 period. The rural poor tend to live in larger families with a larger number of both old and young dependents. They are more likely to be illiterate, have fewer years of schooling, faced limited access to credit and own less property. Ninety percent of all poorer households live in rural areas, and younger members of these family groups immigrate to urban areas where they swell the ranks of the urban poor and tax the country's capacity to generate education opportunities. This is important because while formal education has led to a nationwide basic literacy rate of 94.25% in 1996, in rural areas it was a slightly less 93.43%. Based on their education, 12.31% of the total population was trained with a useful skill, but in rural areas only 7.77% of the population had skills that were useful in a modernizing economy.

The Government of Vietnam attempted to confront poverty and, in 1997, it announced a seven-point poverty eradication strategy centering on improving economic management and competitiveness, strengthening the banking and financial system, and reforming state-owned enterprises. The strategy also involved strengthening physical and social infrastructures,

improving public administration, accelerating rural development, protecting the environment, and investing in people via formal and non-formal education and promoting social equity. In 1998, the government launched a social equity initiative in the form of its Hunger Eradication and Poverty Reduction Program (HEPRP) that targeted 1,715 of the country's poorest communities. The program included a combination of infrastructure improvement, credit expansion, population resettlement, subsidization of fees paid by the poor and training, vocational education, and agricultural extension services.

In 2000, the government sought to coordinate its various poverty eradication and alleviation initiatives via a Poverty Reduction Partnership Agreement (PPA) with the Asian Development Bank. The PPA focused on promoting sustainable development featuring agricultural diversification, social development emphasizing health and education, improving governance by concentrating on public administration reforms ,and geographically targeting the poor for special treatment designed to improve agricultural output in the central regions of the country. The Agreement also concentrated on generating bilateral and multilateral assistance.

In 1998, the SRV began a drive to eliminate bureaucratic inefficiency and corruption and to curtail civilian criminal activity. These efforts reached a high water mark in June 2003, with the conviction of the notorious criminal syndicate boss Truong Van Cam, known as Nam Cam. He was sentenced to death, along with 155 other defendants, and executed in June 2004.

Despite the appointment in April 2001 of progressive Nong Duc Manh to replace Le Kha Phieu as VCP general secretary, change has been slow. There have been no concerted reform and renovation initiatives designed to bring about a more civil society by relaxing restrictions on the media, reducing the harassment of critics and dissidents, eliminating restrictions placed on individual political association, and permitting the formation of competing political parties. VCP leaders fearful of becoming another toppled communist regime continued to oppose political and civil reforms.

ROBERT L. CURRY, JR. AND WILLIAM P. HEAD

See also Ethnic Conflicts: Southeast Asia; Ho Chi Minh; Southeast Asia: History and Economic Development; Southeast Asia: International Relations; Viet Minh; Vietnam War

References and Further Reading

Anderson, Kym. *Vietnam's Transforming Economy and WTO Accession*. Singapore: Institute of Southeast Asian Studies, 1999.

Buttinger, Joseph. *The Dragon Embattled*. 2 Volumes. London: Pall Mall Press, 1967.
———. *Dragon Defiant: A Short History of Vietnam*. New York: Praeger, 1972.
Duiker, William J. *Vietnam: Nation in Revolution*. 2nd ed. Boulder, CO: Westview Press, 1995.
Fforde, Adam. *The Institutions of Transition from Central Planning: The Case of Vietnam*. Canberra: Research School of Pacific and Asia, 1994.
——— and Suzanne H. Paine. *The Limits of National Liberation: Problems of Economic Management in the Democratic Republic of Vietnam*. London: Croom & Holm, 1987.
——— and Stefan de Vylder. *From Plan to Market: The Economic Transition in Vietnam*. Boulder, CO: Westview Press, 1996.
FitzGerald, Frances. *Fire In the Lake: The Vietnamese and Americans in Vietnam*. New York: Random House, 1972.
Hy V. Luang. *Postwar Vietnam: Dynamics of a Transforming Society*. Singapore: Institute of Southeast Asian Studies, 2003.
Lilestrom, Rita, *et al. Profits and Poverty in Rural Vietnam: Winners and Losers of a Mismatched Revolution*. Surrey, England: Curzon Press, 1996.
Natetrop, Eric and Ivan Wolfers. *Health and Health Care in Transition: The Example of Vietnam*. Amersterdam: Vrije University Press, 1996.
Pham, Hoang Mai. *Foreign Direct Investment and Development in Vietnam*. Singapore: Institute of Southeast Asian Studies, 2003.
United Nations. *Catching Up: Capacity Development for Poverty Elimination in Vietnam*. Hanoi: UNDP and UNICEF, 1996.
Van de Walle, Dominique. "Infrastructure and Poverty in Vietnam," *Living Standard Measurement Study Working Paper No. 121*. Washington, DC: World Bank:, 1996.

VIETNAM WAR

It is difficult to determine when this long conflict began. Its initial phases could include the self-exile to which a young Ho Chi Minh (born Nguyen Sinh Cung) dedicated himself when he left Viet Nam in 1911 for decades of world travel preaching the advantages of communism. It could have been when, on May 3, 1940, a dedicated communist history schoolteacher in Ha Noi, Vo Nguyen Giap, fled into China, fearing arrest by the French and internment or death at their hands. It could have been between August 19 and 30, 1945, when the Viet Minh (Ho's communist political party) ascended to power from the Red River to the Mekong Delta, a time known as "the August Revolution." It could have been the next month, September, when the British overseer of the occupation forces in the southern portion of Viet Nam repudiated the Viet Minh there and began a military campaign against them and turned the governance there once more over to the French.

Some might argue that the conflict began when the French government sent troops back into northern Viet Nam in early 1946 in an effort to regain control

of its colony. That sparked the first armed conflict when in December 1946 the French launched an open attack against poorly armed and trained Viet Minh troops at Hai Phong and Ha Noi. Retreating into the hills of the north, Ho's followers carried on desultory but bloody warfare with the French for the next several years. As those days passed, the Viet Minh military became ever stronger and more able to fight French troops.

Perhaps the war started on March 13, 1954, at 5:00 p.m. when Viet Minh artillery shells rained down upon French defensive positions at Dien Bien Phu, the beginning shots of the "set piece" battle, which the French had sought for so long. Or was it on May 7, 1954, at 5:30 p.m. when the beaten French soldiers at Dien Bien Phu finally hoisted a white flag over their ruined bunkers and surrendered? Thereafter, France surrendered all territory north of the seventeenth parallel, retaining a troop presence only in the south.

The Viet Minh soldiers there continued their "war of national liberation" against the French occupiers and a new Vietnamese government was authorized by the Geneva Conference of May 1954 in an attempt to bring peace to Indochina. Its president was Ngo Dinh Diem. Those in the south who opposed and fought against that new government were vilified by President Diem as "Viet Cong," a slang term for "Vietnamese communist." They might have been defeated except that they were aided occasionally by men and supplies sent down from the north. Working all through the following years to keep those allies provided were the two hundred thousand laborers controlled by northern General Vo Nguyen Giap. Those laborers moved enormous quantities of supplies to locations where they were most needed.

Two hostile nations now occupied the narrow strip of land facing along the South China Sea—the Democratic Republic of Viet Nam in the north and the Republic of Viet Nam in the south. With that development, by any standards, the war began.

In the last years of the French efforts against the Viet Minh, the United States had provided men, material, and treasure amounting to 85% of the cost of the war. Now, with the French defeated, the United States moved in to take their place. Advisers arrived in the south to instruct President Diem on how he might establish a longlasting, noncommunist government south of the seventeenth parallel. Americans advised military units, working from the highest to the lowest levels. Civilians were given the benefit of American experience and wisdom. It was never enough. Those from the United States who traveled to Viet Nam did not understand the people or their problems, belittled them, failed to learn to speak their language, and were generally unproductive.

It was not long before a major difference appeared between the nation of the north and that of the south. In Ha Noi throughout the war, for the most part, the same leaders continued to control policies and programs and could thus present a strong approach to problems. It was different in the south. Following the coup of 1963 and the assassination of President Ngo Dinh Diem, there was a rapid succession of governments. They changed so often that American Undersecretary of State George Ball coined the phrase: "The government of the week." And none of them were able to create a winning strategy against the north.

The war went on. It came to be known as a "People's War of National Liberation" by those who favored the efforts of the north. In the south, it was simply an illegal and murderous rebellion that Americans found ever more difficult either to understand or to combat. The Central Intelligence Agency (CIA) described it as "a civil war with dynastic overtones." The US government saw it as a contest between the feared Soviet Union and America, champion of world freedom. By the end of Dwight Eisenhower's presidency, some nine hundred Americans served there. When President Kennedy was assassinated, that number had grown to 16,300. Then under President Lyndon Johnson, American presence in Southeast Asia rose exponentially until it reached 536,100—and still the generals called for more soldiers. Johnson was able to so increase US participation because of supposed attacks on August 2 and possibly again on August 4, 1964, by North Vietnamese patrol torpedo boats against the American destroyers, C. Turner Joy, and the Maddox in Tonkin Bay. At Johnson's request, Congress quickly passed the Tonkin Bay Resolution, giving him full power to do whatever he might wish to protect attacks on American forces. He was quick to act. The Selective Service System fed hundreds of thousands of draftees into the Army.

The American presence became irrevocable when, on March 8, 1965, a little after 9:00 a.m., the ninth Marine Expeditionary Brigade stormed ashore onto the beaches of Da Nang wearing full combat gear. They were met by school girls in brightly colored *au dais* carrying bouquets of flowers, the mayor of the city, and a few army men holding signs saying: "The army welcomes the marines to Viet Nam." They were purportedly sent there to guard American installations, but soon Westmoreland had them operating offensively and spent the remainder of his tenure calling for ever more troops.

In the years thereafter until American withdrawal, US forces fired more small arms rounds, shot more artillery shells, and dropped more bombs than had been used in all theaters by all sides in World War II.

Many of the Americans resented their forced participation in the war. It became common to see soldiers wearing slogans on their helmets such as "Fuck the Army," or "UUUU," which meant "We are the Unwilling, led by the Unqualified, doing the Unnecessary for the Ungrateful." Traditional discipline disappeared and disillusioned soldiers at least once did the unthinkable, as at My Lai, where civilian women, children, and old men were slaughtered.

The intensity of the war grew only slowly. In the years prior to the massive infusion of American troops, the conflict was marked only by raids, murders, and kidnappings. A few years later, American forces faced large units totally dedicated to destroying them at places like "Hamburger Hill" in the Au Shau Valley and Khe Sanh. By 1968, at the time of the Asian Tet New Year's holiday, the Viet Cong (officially known as the People's Liberation Armed Forces) and the North Vietnamese Army were able to field divisions of men to attack throughout the south. They engaged American and south Vietnamese forces in forty-one of the forty-four southern provinces and in five of the six largest cities. Finally beaten back, they held on in Hue for nearly a month, during which time they executed some five thousand civilians and buried them in mass graves.

Troops there were led successively by generals William Childs Westmoreland, Creighton Abrams, and Fred Weyand. Such "tactics" were imposed on US troops as "Search and Destroy," "Free Fire Zones," "Harassing and Interdicting Fires," "Reconnaissance by Fire," and widespread bombings by the Air Force. Meanwhile, increasing numbers of Vietnamese began to sympathize with and fight for the Viet Cong.

It became the "helicopter" war, and thousands of those machines dotted the skies, carrying food and supplies, transporting wounded, taking combat-ready soldiers to attack points (landing zones), and ferrying the dead back to collection points. In the Ca Mau peninsula and the Delta, small well-armed patrol boats conducted riverine warfare, cruising the many rivers searching for enemy soldiers.

Despite the nearly unlimited supply of airplanes and artillery, M-16 rifles and mortars, napalm and night scopes, draft levies and swollen defense budgets, the richest nation on earth failed to impose a military solution on one of the poorest countries of Asia. Thus it was that, following Tet 1968, the American government began to look for ways to disengage from the conflict in Viet Nam. Newly elected President Richard Nixon said that the way to do so was to "Vietnamize" the war, to turn the fighting over to the Vietnamese themselves. Vietnamization would serve as the rationale for withdrawal.

Peace talks began in Paris in 1968 and continued four years, eight months, and seventeen days during which time more than twenty thousand Americans and perhaps three-quarters of a million Vietnamese on both sides were killed. Finally signed on January 27, 1973, its provisions gave the DRV much of what it had sought but did little or nothing to sustain the interests of the ROV. It did, however, allow the United States to escape from Asia. The last military unit was withdrawn from Viet Nam only weeks later, on March 29, 1973.

After the American withdrawal, the North Vietnamese began to launch massive attacks against southern armies. Saigon fell on April 30, 1975. The war had finally ended.

CECIL B. CURREY

See also Ho Chi Minh; People's Liberation Armed Forces (PLAF); Viet Minh; Vietnam

References and Further Reading

Cincinnatus. *Self-Destruction: the Disintegration and Decay of the United States Army During the Vietnam Era.* New York: W. W. Norton, 1982.
Cecil B. Currey. *Edward Lansdale: The Unquiet American.* New York: Houghton Mifflin, 1988.
———. *Victory at Any Cost: The Genius of Viet Nam's General Vo Nguyen Giap.* Washington, DC: Brassey's, Inc., 1997.

VIRGIN ISLANDS (BRITISH)

The Virgin Islands are the collective name for more than 120 small islands, islets, and cays located in the West Indies; twenty have permanent residents. The British Virgin Islands (BVI) consist of four major islands (Tortola, Anegada, Virgin Gorda, and Jost Van Dyke), thirty-two smaller islands, and two dozen islets totaling fifty-nine square miles. The Virgin Islands form a portion of the Leeward Islands, the westernmost part of the Lesser Antilles, situated in the Anegada Passage between the Caribbean Sea and the Atlantic Ocean, forty miles east of Puerto Rico. The British islands lie to the southwest of Anegada and the passage; adjacent American islands are located immediately to the southwest and south. The US Virgin Islands (USVI) and BVI are, at their nearest point, less than one mile apart. The islands are the peaks of submerged mountains that comprise the eastern extension of a submarine plateau in the Greater Antilles. Elevations rise from mean sea level to 225 feet, but isolated peaks, notably Mount Sage on Tortola, have an altitude of 1,780 feet. There is little groundwater; hence, inhabitants rely upon cisterns. Bare rock outcrops are common, and there are substantial areas of coral sand and shallow loam derived from volcanic material. A sparse deciduous forest was

exploited for charcoal production early in the history of the islands; scrub timber and Guinea grass are the current primary vegetation. The islands have a year-round subtropical humid climate (65–90° F range, 78° F average) moderated by easterly trade winds. Rainfall is from forty to sixty inches per annum (average forty-five inches), varying from island to island, with higher elevations receiving the greater amounts. The rainy season is May to November, but there are seasonal and annual variations; hurricanes and tropical storms (July to October) are natural hazards.

Native American hunters and coastal maritime gatherers inhabited the islands as early as 710 BCE. By 100 CE, Taino Indians lived in villages located in sheltered bays, made pottery, and practiced horticulture, but by the 1400s, Carib and Arawak Indians inhabited the islands. During his second voyage to America in 1493, Christopher Columbus arrived at Sugar Bay or Salt River Bay on St. Croix (USVI) and fought with the indigenous Caribs. Naming the islands Las Virgines in memory of St. Ursula, Columbus claimed them for Spain but no Spanish settlements were established because of Carib attacks. Charles I of Spain ordered that these natives be killed; between military attacks and introduced European diseases, the natives died or left by the late 1500s. The islands were temporary havens for Spanish treasure galleons and a favorite haunt of buccaneers. Early economic development was controlled by the Danish West India Company, which established a free port at St. Thomas (USVI). There was a brief incursion by the British during the Napoleonic Wars in 1801; the islands were occupied from 1807 to 1815, and several thousand English naval and army personnel were quartered there. The northeastern islands became the British Virgin Islands in 1672, and fifteen of the sixty islands in the BVI are currently inhabited. Tortola (Spanish for "turtle dove") covers twenty-one square miles and was initially settled by the Dutch in 1648 and was occupied by the English in 1666. African slaves were brought to work on European sugar plantations beginning in 1673. Anegara, or "drowned" island (15 square miles), makes reference to the flat landscape and maximum elevations only a few feet above mean sea level. Virgin Gorda, "fat virgin" (eight square miles), has a maximum elevation at 1,359 feet. Westernmost Jost Van Dyke (2.5 square miles) has only two hundred inhabitants. The Peter, Salt, Beef, Cooper, Ginger, and Norman Islands are among the small islets, many clustered round the Sir Francis Drake Channel; most are uninhabited or privately owned. The major settlement and capital of the BVI is Road Town, located at a harbor on the south side of Tortola Island. The largest towns on Virgin Gorda are The Valley, Spanish Town, and North Sound.

British plantations gave way to small farming and cattle-raising in the 1800s. Current exports include rum, fresh fish, fruits, gravel, and sand. BVI tourism generates nearly half of the national income. An estimated four hundred thousand companies are listed on the offshore registry of incorporated companies established in the mid-1980s. Geographic proximity and an intertwined British-American economy prevail because most BVI inhabitants work in the USVI and, established in 1959, the currency in local use is the US dollar. The BVI joined the West Indies Federation of British Islands in 1958. The BVI are an internal-governing, overseas territory of the United Kingdom. The islands are governed by a government administrator who is subject to the governor (appointed by the British monarch), an executive council composed of ministers appointed from the elected thirteen member legislative council. The population of the BVI, estimated at 22,187 (2004), has a growth rate of 2.1%; 83% is Black, with the remainder Caucasian, Indian, Asian, and mixed ethnic and racial groups. Protestant religions predominate (Methodist 33%, Anglican 17%, Church of God 9%, Seventh-Day Adventists 6%, Baptist 4%, Jehovah's Witnesses 2%, others 15%), Roman Catholic 10%, none 2%, and other 2%. English is the official language, but some Creole is spoken.

CHARLES C. KOLB

See also Caribbean: History and Economic Development; Virgin Islands (United States)

References and Further Reading

Fabbri, Patrizia [English translation, Julia Weiss]. *British Virgin Islands*. Florence, Italy and New York: Casa Editrice Bonechi, 1998.

Mauer, Bill. *Recharting the Caribbean: Land, Law, and Citizenship in the British Virgin Islands*. Ann Arbor, MI: University of Michigan Press, 1997.

Penn, Howard R. *A Personal Account of the Politics and History of the British Virgin Islands in the 20th Century*. Road Town, BVI: Penn, 1991.

Pickering, Vernon W. *Early History of the British Virgin Islands: From Columbus to Emancipation*, 3rd ed. New York: Falcon Publications International, 2000.

VIRGIN ISLANDS (UNITED STATES)

The Virgin Islands is the collective name of more than 120 small islands, islets, and cays located in the West Indies; twenty have permanent residents. The United States Virgin Islands (USVI), officially Virgin Islands of the United States, is an unincorporated territory that is the easternmost United States possession, is composed of three major inhabited islands (St. Thomas, St. John, and St. Croix), plus about sixty-five islets and cays with a land area of 133 square miles. The British

islands and adjacent American islands at their nearest point are less than one mile apart. Elevations rise from mean sea level to 225 feet; isolated peaks rise to 1,556 feet on St. Thomas, 1,277 feet on St. John, and 1,165 feet on St. Croix. There is little ground water, so inhabitants rely upon cisterns. The fresh water supply is now augmented by seawater distillation plants on St. Thomas and St. Croix. St. Croix (Santa Cruz to Spanish speakers), the largest of the islands (eighty-two square miles), lies forty miles south of St. Thomas and has a population concentrated in the cities of Christiansted and Frederiksted. St. John (nineteen square miles) is situated two miles east of St. Thomas and less than a mile from British Tortola. Most inhabitants live in the towns of Cruz Bay and Coral Bay. St. Thomas (twenty-seven square miles) is dominated by the city of Charlotte Amalie, capital of the Virgin Islands and a major seaport. For additional information on the geography and early history, see *British Virgin Islands*.

After Columbus's visit in 1493 and minor Spanish expeditions, English settlers voyaging to establish the colony at Jamestown, Virginia, in 1607 briefly visited the islands. Dutch and English settlers landed on St. Croix in 1625 but were expelled two decades later by Spaniards from Puerto Rico. The islands became temporary havens for Spanish treasure galleons and also were a favorite haunt of buccaneers. Beginning in 1673, African slaves were brought to work on European sugar plantations. The Spanish were supplanted by the French, and the French controlled St. Croix until they sold the island to the Danish government in 1733. A permanent Danish colony was founded on St. Thomas in 1672 and Danes settled St. John in 1717, eventually establishing 109 sugar cane plantations. Economic development was controlled by the Danish West India Company, which established a free port at St. Thomas. A six-month slave uprising and massacre of European residents in 1733 decimated St. Thomas's commercial prospects. There was a brief British incursion during the Napoleonic Wars in 1801, and the islands were occupied from 1807 to 1815 by several thousand English naval and army personnel. A slave rebellion on St. Croix in 1848 led to the abolition of slavery in the Danish islands on July 3, 1848. Renewed Danish commercial enterprises proved unsuccessful because of the decline of the sugar industry because of competition from other Caribbean islands. Between 1835 and 1915, the population dwindled from forty-three thousand to twenty-three thousand.

Denmark and the United States signed a treaty on August 4, 1916, transferring control of the Danish West Indies for $25 million in gold. The treaty, ratified on January 17, formally ceded the Danish islands on March 31, 1917. The islands are situated halfway between New York and Panama, and to protect the newly-constructed Panama Canal, an airbase was constructed on St. Croix and a submarine base in St. Thomas harbor, and the islands were administered by the US Navy from 1917 to 1931. In 1927, US Virgin Islanders became American citizens. A fifteen-member unicameral territorial legislature was established by the Revised Organic Act of 1954; executive power is vested in a governor appointed by the president of the United States. The right to self-elect their governor and legislators was granted in 1968. In 1958, John Merwin was appointed as the first native-born governor, succeeded by Ralph Paiewonsky in 1961–1969, and by Melvin Evans, who became the first native-born black governor. Virgin Islanders have a nonvoting representative in the US Congress but remain under the jurisdiction of the Office of Insular Affairs, US Department of the Interior.

Tourism is the primary economic activity, accounting for 80% of the gross domestic product, and features water recreation as well as cultural tourism. Laurance Rockefeller purchased land on St. John in order to establish the Virgin Islands National Park, created officially by Congress on August 2, 1956. Enlarged in 1962 and in 1978, it occupies nearly three-fourths of St. John and has enhanced ecotourism. In 1976, the United Nations designated the park a biosphere reserve. Major manufacturing includes two rum distilleries, bauxite and petroleum refineries, basalt mining, and textile mill, which contribute to the export economy. One of the world's largest petroleum refineries is located on St. Croix. Scientific instruments, electronics, pharmaceuticals, perfume, jewelry, and watches are other manufactures. Beef, dairy products, and eggs are the primary agricultural products, but most food is imported; commercial fishing is limited. Tourism, manufacturing, construction, and government (the territorial government and US National Park Service) are major employers.

Slavery and migration created a mixed population of more than twenty ethnic groups. The current population is 108,775 (2004); 78% Black, 10% Caucasian, and 12% other. Protestant denominations (primarily Baptist), Roman Catholic, Episcopalian, Jewish, and other faiths are represented. English is the official language, but many islanders speak Virgin Island Creole English and lesser numbers speak Dutch Creole or Spanish, or are bilingual.

CHARLES C. KOLB

See also Caribbean: History and Economic Development; Virgin Islands (British)

References and Further Reading

Creque, Darwin D. *The US Virgins and the Eastern Caribbean.* Philadelphia, Whitmore Publishing Co., 1968.

Ethnologue. "Languages of the Virgin Islands." *Ethnologue: Languages of the World*, 14th ed. Dallas: SIL International. http://www.ethnologue.com/show_country.asp?name=U.S.+Virgin+Islands

Hall, Neville. *Slave Society in the Danish West Indies: St. Thomas, St. John, and St. Croix*. Johns Hopkins Studies in Atlantic History and Culture, Baltimore: Johns Hopkins University Press, 1992.

Lawaetz, Erik J. *St. Croix: 500 Years Pre-Columbus to 1990* Herning, Denmark: P. Kristensen, 1991.

Olwig, Karen F. *Cultural Adaptation and Resistance of St. John: Three Centuries of Afro-Caribbean Life*. Gainesville, FL: University Press of Florida.

VIRTUAL WATER TRADE

"Virtual water" is increasingly being used in the context of discussions on freshwater (hereafter referred to simply as "water") security, particularly in reference to the developing world. It was coined in the mid-1990s by Professor J.A. Allan and refers to the water required in the production of goods and services. For example, it takes on average 1,200 cubic meters of water to produce one metric tonne of wheat (Hoekstra 2003). The water is said to be "virtual" because, once the wheat is grown, the real water used to produce the crop is no longer contained in the grain. "Virtual water trade" refers to the idea that when countries or regions trade goods and certain services, they are generally also trading virtual water. For every tonne of wheat that a country trades, it is said to import or export 1,200 cubic meters of virtual water.

The virtual water trade concept was first envisioned as a solution for semi-arid and arid countries struggling with large water deficits. It is essentially an extension of the comparative advantage theory of international trade; its innovation is that it treats water as a key factor of production. It posits that a water-scarce country should limit its exports of virtual water and, depending on the level of water scarcity, resort to virtual water imports to avoid depleting its own water supplies. Indeed, if a water-scarce country imports one tonne of wheat, it is essentially freeing up 1,200 cubic meters of real indigenous water that can be used for other purposes. Water-short countries can optimize their water resources by limiting their production of water-intensive goods that have a low economic value, keeping their scarce water for highly valued uses as well as uses that yield high economic return per unit of water consumed, and by importing the water-intensive goods no longer produced domestically from water-rich regions.

Policies that encourage water conservation and technologies and practices that optimize or augment supplies, such as desalination and efficient irrigation systems, remain important tools in dealing with water scarcity. However, in the case of severely water short developing countries, water-demand management can only stretch resources so far and technological means may be prohibitively expensive. The comparative advantage of virtual water trade is that, at present, it is generally more economic to obtain grains and certain other water-intensive goods on the international market than to desalinate water or to pump groundwater from great depths in order to grow it domestically.

The virtual water trade concept is based on the observation that the "world water crisis" is not one of total quantity, but one of distribution. While there is enough water on earth to satisfy everyone's needs in a sustainable way, the problem is that where the demand for water is high, the supply of renewable water resources is not always sufficient. Although water is a renewable resource, only a finite amount can be used up before tapping into nonrenewable supplies. At the core of the virtual water trade concept is the premise that water-rich countries—assuming they produce the water-intensive goods and services in a sustainable way—can support to a certain extent water-scarce countries through the trade of water-intensive goods and services.

Allan (2002a) estimates that many countries, such as Egypt, Israel, and Jordan, have now been dependent on virtual water imports for a few decades. Their indigenous water supplies are simply too low to allow these countries to meet all their domestic water demands. Since agriculture accounts for the overwhelming proportion of global water withdrawals (Shiklomanov 2000) and tends to yield low economic returns to water requirements, Allan (1996) observed that it becomes the reducible sector. This means that as demand exceeds supplies, water-scarce countries tend to become increasingly dependent on food imports. Israel and Jordan are two countries that have consciously adopted a virtual water trade strategy—gearing domestic production towards water-efficient goods—to try to manage their water budgets. Other water-scarce countries continue to deplete their water resources to produce low-value, water-intensive goods that they could obtain on the international market (World Water Council 2004; Qadir *et al.* 2003).

The virtual water trade paradigm is very controversial. Proponents argue that "virtual water trade" is a useful metaphor because it forces recognition of the opportunity costs associated with different uses of water. For instance, if water is used to irrigate a field, it is no longer available for domestic uses or to provide environmental services. Moreover, since the production of one tonne of wheat—to expand on our example—requires different amounts of water depending on where in the world it is produced (due mainly to differences in climatic conditions), virtual

water trade can lead to global water savings if wheat is produced in regions where the water requirement is low and exported to regions where the requirement is higher. Finally, the measurement of global virtual water trade flows also alerts us to the fact that increasing demand in water-scarce regions is placing growing stress on water resources elsewhere on the planet.

Critics stress the undesirable implications and difficulties of resorting to virtual water trade to achieve sustainable water resource development and argue that these are magnified in developing countries. They decry the recommendation to reduce the agricultural sector, which is an important source of income and employment for many in the developing world and an important means of stemming the flow of rural-urban migration. Virtual water trade also implies having to generate foreign exchange, another scarce resource in the developing world, in water-efficient, high-return (that is, industrial or service) economic activities. This is no mean feat since industrialisation has proven an elusive goal in many countries, water-scarce or not. Industrialisation also may lead to other environmental problems. Furthermore, food security is an important component of national security, and many states are weary of having to depend on access to the international market to meet domestic needs. Many people also prefer or derive a certain pride from locally grown agricultural products. In certain societies, water, agriculture, and local food have great historical, cultural, and religious value that the virtual water trade concept is said to ignore.

KATHERINE CINQ-MARS

See also Irrigation; Water Resources and Distribution

References and Further Reading

Allan, J.A. *The Middle East Water Question: Hydropolitics and the Global Economy.* London, New York: Tauris Academic Studies, 2002a.
———. "The political economy of water: reasons for optimism but long-term caution," in *Water, Peace, and the Middle East.* J.A. Allan, ed. 75–119, London, New York: Tauris Academic Studies, 1996.
Lofgren, Hans, ed. *Food, Agriculture, and Economic Policy in the Middle East and North Africa.* Washington, DC: JAI, 2003.
Shiklomanov, Igor A. "World fresh water resources," in *Water Crisis: A Guide to the World's Fresh Water Resources.* Peter Gleick, ed. 13–24, New York: Oxford University Press, 1993.
Wichelns, Dennis. "The role of 'virtual water' in efforts to achieve food security and other national goals, with an example from Egypt," *Agricultural Water Management,* Vol. 49 (2001): 131–151.
Yang, Hong and Alexander Zehnder. "Water Scarcity and Food Import: A Case Study for Southern Mediterranean Countries," *World Development,* 30:8 (2002): 1413–1430.
———. "China's regional water scarcity and implications for grain supply and trade," *Environment and Planning,* Vol. 33 (2001): 79–95.
World Water Council. *E-Conference Synthesis: Virtual Water Trade–Conscious Choices,* March 2004. http://www.worldwatercouncil.org/virtual_water/documents/virtual_water_final_synthesis.pdf.

VISEHRAD GROUP

The Visehrad Four is an unofficial name given to the four Central European post-communist countries the Czech Republic, the Republic of Hungary, the Republic of Poland and the Slovak Republic. Originally, the group was called the Visehrad Troika and the Four is the result of the split of the Czech and Slovak Federal Republic in 1993. The name of this grouping was chosen during a meeting of the President of the CSFR, Vaclav Havel; the Prime Minister of Hungary, Jozsef Antall; and the President of Poland, Lech Walesa at an event held at the north Hungarian city of Visehrad on February 15, 1991. At this meeting, the leaders signed a declaration on a close cooperation of these three (today four) countries on their way to European integration.

The Visehrad Group reflects the efforts of the countries of the Central European region to work together in a number of fields of common interest within all-European integration. The Czech Republic, Hungary, Poland, and Slovakia have always shared cultural and intellectual values and common roots of religious traditions that they wish to preserve and further strengthen.

All the V4 countries aspired to become members of the European Union (EU), perceiving their integration in the EU as another step forward in the process of overcoming artificial dividing lines in Europe through mutual support. They reached this aim in May 1, 2004, when they all became members of EU.

The Visehrad Group countries are committed to closely cooperating with their nearest partners in the Central European region. They also are ready to cooperate in specific areas of common interest with countries within the wider region, with other regional groupings in Europe as well as with third countries and international organizations.

The Prime Ministers of the Visehrad Group countries express their deep conviction that further cooperation between their countries, rooted in centuries of interlinked history and based on similar political, economic, and social developments in the past decades, will enrich the community of European nations and contribute to the building of a reunited, democratic, and prosperous Europe.

All the activities of the Visehrad Group are aimed at strengthening stability in the Central European

region. The participating countries perceive their co-operation as a challenge and its success as the best proof of their ability to integrate also into such structures as is, for example, the European Union.

The V4 countries agreed on efforts to preserve contributions from the member countries to the EU 2007–2013 budget at the current level of 1.24% of the gross domestic product of each country. Some EU countries proposed lowering the limit.

The economic issues and cooperation of the V4 are managed within the Central European Free Trade Association (CEFTA). The four countries, counting the Czech Republic and Slovakia as the former Czechoslovakia, were founding members of the CEFTA in 1992.

STEPHAN E. NIKOLOV

See also Central and Eastern Europe: History and Economic Development; Central and Eastern Europe: International Relations; Czech Republic; Havel, Václav; Hungary; Poland; Slovakia; Soviet Bloc; Velvet Revolutions; Walesa, Lech

References and Further Reading

Bakalska, Patrycja. *A New Visehrad Group in the New EU*. Warszaw, Centre for Eastern Studies, 2003.

Bracker, J. "How Would an EU Membership of the Visehrad Countries Affect Europe's Economic Geography?" In: *Annals of Regional Science*, 32 (1998), pp. 91–114.

Fitzmaurice, John. *Politics and Government in the Visegrad Countries: Poland, Hungary, The Czech Republic and Slovakia*. London: Macmillan, 1988.

Latawski, Paul. The security route to Europe: The Visegrad Four. *Whitehall Paper* No. 28. London: Royal United Services Institute for Defense and Security Studies 2004.

Shea, J. and C. Stefes. "EU Integration of the Visegrad Countries." In: *Journal of Public and International Affairs*, 7(1996), pp. 182–207.

WAŁĘSA, LECH

Lech Wałęsa, known to everyone in Poland as Lech or Lechu, a charismatic leader of the 1980s, the 1983 Noble Peace Prize recipient and the president of Poland 1990–1995, was born in September 29, 1943, in Popowo, near Włoclawek in northern Poland. In 1967 he started working as an electrician at the Lenin Shipyard in Gdansk.

Wałęsa's political anti-communist activities date back to December 1970, the time of social upheaval in the coastal Pomerania region in Poland, triggered by the increase in food prices. He participated in the December 1970 strike in the shipyard. The communist government officials did not negotiate with the workers, but instead crushed the strike by force. Many workers died when police and the military opened fire. Wałęsa witnessed the tragedy and his involvement in the political opposition of the late 1970s was inspired by the events of December 1970.

The tragic events of the strike caused a governmental crisis. The new communist party leadership with the first secretary Edward Gierek appointed a new administration. Wałęsa was among those who trusted the new leadership, but the government had no intention of changing the workers' economic situation. In the second half of the 1970s a new opposition movement was formed in the coastal industrial centers—the Free Trade Union of the Coast. Its objective was to inform workers of their situation and their rights. Wałęsa joined the opposition and was arrested several times for his participation in an illegal anti-government organization. As the economic situation declined, workers became more determined. During the summer months of 1980, social upheaval erupted and workers all over Poland protested. The Gdańsk-Gdynia shipyards became the core area of the protest and Wałęsa, who was not employed by the shipyard at the time, joined the strike in the Lenin Shipyard.

Because of his involvement in the 1970 strike and in the Free Trade Unions, he was elected the head of the shipyard's strike committee. The local communist authorities complied with the mostly economic demands of the protestors and the strike was about to end when strikers from other regions of Poland asked the shipyard workers to continue the strike and help them achieve their demands. The shipyard's strike committee agreed out of solidarity with all workers and formed a new strike committee called the Interfactory Strike Committee, representing demands of factories all over Poland. Soon several intellectuals, members of the political opposition, joined the workers and became key advisors to Wałęsa and the Committee. Subsequently, in addition to the economic demands, the Committee also issued unprecedented political demands such as the existence of independent trade unions, free press, the right to strike, abolishment of censorship, freedom of speech, and so forth. The demands were known as "the 21 postulates." This was the beginning of the movement later called "Solidarity," which by the end of 1980 incorporated more than 10 million members. Wałęsa was in the middle of all events, first as a head of the shipyard's strike committee and subsequently as a head of the nation-wide Interfactory Strike Committee.

"Solidarity" became the major political power of the early 1980s in Poland. The government was still controlled by the Communist Party but had to respond to the increasing demands from the movement. Solidarity was officially recognized by the authorities and registered as a trade union in October 1980. Wałęsa became the chairman of the movement, supported by a committee composed of leaders from all regions, some of them with long-standing experience in the opposition movement like Andrzej Gwiazda, Aleksander Hall, Bodgan Borusewicz, and his friends from the Free Trade Unions of the Coast. Solidarity existed until December 13, 1980, when the government imposed martial law in Poland and Solidarity was outlawed and its leaders arrested. Wałęsa was put under house arrest, separated from his advisors and supporters, and detained for almost a year before the authorities allowed him to return home in November 1982. Wałęsa became an ordinary citizen, but remained a leader of underground Solidarity.

In 1983 Wałęsa received the Nobel Peace Prize for his contribution to "universal freedom of organisation in all countries." Fearing that the government would not let him back into Poland if he attended the ceremony in Oslo, he remained in Poland and his wife Danuta went to Oslo to accept the award on his behalf.

Another social upheaval in 1988 brought Solidarity back into official existence. It was a different Solidarity with different leadership. Many previous members emigrated or were forced to leave the country; several leaders left Solidarity and politics. Lech Wałęsa retained his leadership and once again negotiated with the communist government regarding the future of the trade union and the future of the country. The talks are known as the Round Table Agreement of 1989. Solidarity gained a new political status and in effect the first truly free elections in the Soviet Bloc were held in June 1989. Politicians who ran on the Solidarity ticket won the majority of seats in the Polish Parliament (Sejm) and formed the first non-communist Polish government since 1945. Wałęsa refused to become the prime minister of this historic government and instead supported Tadeusz Mazowiecki as the premier.

In 1990, however, he ran against Mazowiecki in the first Polish direct presidential elections and won by a landslide. He became the first democratically elected postwar Polish president. In 1995 he sought reelection but lost to a former member of the communist party, Aleksander Kwaśniewski. As a politician Wałęsa was unpredictable, often infuriating, but he had a natural genius for politics, a matchless ability for sensing popular moods, and great powers of swaying a crowd. More recently, Wałęsa has not been active politically, although in November 2004 he visited Kiev in the Ukraine in support of free presidential elections.

LUDOMIR LOZNY

See also Central and Eastern Europe: History and Economic Development; Poland; Solidarity Union

References and Further Reading

Craig, Mary. *Lech Walesa and His Poland.* New York: Continuum, 1987.
Goodwyn, Lawrence. *Breaking the Barrier: The Rise of Solidarity in Poland.* New York: Oxford University Press, 1991.
Solidarity Friends—The Book of Lech Walesa: A Collective Portrait. New York: Simon & Schuster, 1982.
Wałęsa, Lech. *A Way of Hope: An Autobiography.* New York: Henry Holt, 1987.
———. *The Struggle and the Triumph.* New York: Arcade, 1992.

WAR AND DEVELOPMENT

Two Worlds of Conflict and Development

The recovery of societies from international or civil conflict is a major concern in contemporary world politics. Yet, there are important distinctions between the effects of global versus intrastate violence on sustainable growth and development. While nations such as Germany and Japan that were once devastated by the Second World War eventually returned to their original levels of economic vitality, many developing countries continue to be caught in a cycle of poverty and internal strife. When taken as a whole, the domestic conflict experienced by the nations of Africa and Asia from the mid-twentieth century to the present has produced more destruction and loss of life than both of the world wars combined. States are more seriously damaged by civil wars, as they are fought wholly on the home territory of a country. The diversion of government funds from health and infrastructure to building the military significantly reduces incomes and thus harms the national economic welfare. As vital resources and factors of production are lost or destroyed during conflict, domestic clashes can continue to have a negative impact on the prospects for growth even after a struggle has ended. The emphasis of public spending on maintaining security and police forces needed to preserve peace in the postwar period can also undermine efforts at reconstruction. Moreover, internal wars can have ripple

effects that spread beyond the borders of the affected country, producing global pathologies such as crime, disease, poverty and terrorism that will have their greatest impact in the years to come.

Thus, while the effects of war on national economies may have some general attributes, different conditions hold for the ability of nations to fully achieve prosperity after the experience of catastrophic violence. In the present world climate, international wars have become relatively rare and short-lived, while domestic conflicts are prolonged and often recurring. At the same time, a core of stable and prosperous nations enjoys peace, while civil war continues to affect certain types of developing states. The conflict-resolution issues facing these countries involve more fundamental concerns of political stability and structural viability than typically affects the industrialized nations. Managing the return to prosperous societies and economic systems therefore requires a closer look at the relationship between differing aspects of conflict and a wide range of political and economic variables.

Classical Theories of War and Development

A number of classic studies have sought to determine the roles of labor, capital, and technology in the achievement of economic growth. One such work distinguishes between the impact of short- and long-term growth rates on future economic performance. This is known as the theory of convergence, which maintains that the economies of developing countries will grow faster than those of industrialized nations because of their greater investment and earnings potential. Thus, even in the event of a war or major conflict that destroys a nation's primary resources and industries, the overall social system can be expected to recover rapidly as the government seeks to restore productivity. Because of the greater possibilities for growth, the actual severity of the conflict experienced by a country is therefore positively related to the speed and extent of its eventual economic renewal.

Subsequent analyses that build on these findings have produced a statistically based theory known as the "Phoenix Factor." This theory maintains that although a country that is defeated in a world war may suffer significant losses of national power, it will catch up with and eventually overtake the victor as its postwar growth rates begin to accelerate. Such a conclusion suggests that contrary to conventional wisdom, it is a nation's pattern of domestic economic performance, rather than the provision of foreign aid, that holds the key to its recovery. The accumulated

evidence demonstrates that an advanced society that suffers severe wartime damage in terms of its population and infrastructure can return to its initial level of development within one generation.

However, while such studies may accurately portray the prospects for the great powers, this theory is not easily applicable to the majority of developing countries, which do not exhibit the internal conditions or policies conducive to rapid postwar regeneration. These nations are often faced with unresolved structural problems that foster continued instability. High levels of internal conflict rather than involvement in international wars typify the political histories of many Third World states. Despite the seeming frequency of warfare in developing regions such as Africa, there have been only two recorded African interstate conflicts since the year of independence that resulted in greater than 1,000 casualties: between Somalia and Ethiopia from 1977–1978, and Uganda and Tanzania in 1978.

Where major institutions are weak or do not enjoy broad popular legitimacy, a segment of the national population may continually challenge the government's right to rule. This is especially true of decolonizing and newly independent states. The economies of these countries have often been characterized by long-term periods of stagnation, or programs of state-led development pursued by authoritarian regimes that promote doctrines of socialism or "self-reliance." Some development policies may also produce vast disparities of income between urban elites and rural poor who rely on traditional practices and forms of subsistence, fostering tensions between social classes. These nations thus often become caught in a "poverty trap," in which high rates of fertility and increasing population levels are combined with minimal economic growth. This can slow or prevent the transition from an economy based upon the harvesting of primary goods to one based on industrial production and high technology. Worse still, the lack of effective means of dispute resolution within formal institutions can perpetuate dissatisfaction and conflict.

Conditional Theories of War and Development

Just as there are important distinctions between the effects of conflict on the industrialized versus the developing nations, there are also differences in political and structural factors that may significantly influence the prospects for postwar reconstruction. If problems such as social inequality, weak institutions, and ethnic disputes remain unresolved in the aftermath of civil

war, these will continue to hamper the rebuilding of the society and economy. Additionally, the likelihood that conflict and economic degradation will continue is dependent on the goals and decision-making behavior of political leaders, and whether they pursue policies that benefit the society as a whole, or are designed to maintain their hold on power.

A second class of theories therefore seeks to address the influence of social conditions and domestic politics on the relationship between war and economic progress. The theory of collective goods applied to conflict resolution posits that in the aftermath of war, growth is hindered by the existence of institutional structures that are occupied and controlled by certain privileged groups. These ruling coalitions have a vested interest in maintaining the prewar political order, because it allows them to accumulate wealth for themselves rather than contributing resources to improving the general welfare. Therefore, it becomes a necessary first step to carry out reforms that remove entrenched political forces before significant economic gains can be achieved. The logical conclusion of this premise is that the revolutionary change or collapse that often accompanies a major war can eliminate the dominance of these groups, leading the way to modernization and growth. However, while these conditions may be of significance in producing and maintaining beneficent economic policies, this process has been shown to have little relationship to the actual rate of economic recovery.

Most essential to this issue is the observation that once a country has experienced a major internal conflict, the probability increases that conflict will resume within the near future. Therefore, the immediate postwar period is a critical phase during which the conditions for political stability and economic recovery must be created in order to prevent a recurrence of hostilities. This relates directly to the concept of a "poverty-conflict trap," in which underdevelopment and conflict occur as a cycle. Underdevelopment occurs where there are insufficient resources to sustain growth and improve economic competitiveness. Low economic growth perpetuates the tensions that foster domestic struggles and civil wars, which in turn produce the circumstances that are associated with poverty. These frictions are worsened by the maldistribution of wealth that is common in many Third World countries, in which an elite few enjoy the benefits of modern conveniences, while the majority of the population is deprived of basic necessities. Further, conflicts have often intensified where leaders have resorted to repression by the police and military in order to protect privileged classes and silence social unrest. For example: the resistance movements in Latin American nations such as El Salvador and Nicaragua were fueled by the terror tactics used by the allies of a small group of landowning families and dictatorial governments.

Yet another important element of this equation is the intentions of political leaders in pursuing policies that may either benefit or harm the economic welfare of their countries. Unpopular leaders who seek to remain in power might engage in conflicts such as foreign policy crises or a campaign against insurgents in order to divert public attention from a poor economic performance. By demonstrating their ability to conduct a war or respond to threats, they may satisfy enough of the citizenry to maintain their hold on power, despite an obvious record of malfeasance. This in turn perpetuates the policies that foster low growth and poverty. These conflicts also waste valuable resources and hinder the investment necessary for increased productivity, insuring that these negative conditions endure. Yet again, it is certain countries, or those that suffer from an initially low level of available capital, that are most likely to be caught in the cycle of war and underdevelopment. These cases are especially concentrated in regions of the world such as sub-Saharan Africa.

Another such study of conditional factors seeks to account for both the impact of civil wars on domestic economic growth, and the extent of "spillover effects," or collateral damage on the welfare of neighboring countries. The authors extend the classical growth model by including an input for human capital in order to test for the disruptive effects of conflict on factors related to economic prosperity such as trade and foreign investment, as well as the diversion of resources from domestic investment and savings to military spending. The authors find that civil wars have an indirectly negative effect on short-term rather than long-term growth. Because low-income countries have more rapid growth rates, in the event that economic fundamentals such as labor, human capital, and investment are not directly altered, their economies can be expected to recover fairly quickly from the effects of internal war. At the same time, the degree of impact on neighboring countries is largely equivalent to the actual intensity of the conflict. Altogether, these findings demonstrate that civil wars are not simply an isolated problem that can be ignored by the developed nations.

Greed and Grievance in War and Development

Armed rebellion and guerrilla warfare has long been a prevalent feature of the politics of developing nations. As the frequency of internal conflicts has surpassed

that of interstate warfare in the post–Cold War era, determining their causes has invited the application of different kinds of approaches in the study of war and development. Thus, the most recent crop of research into the causes and consequences of internal violence in the Third World attempts to present economic explanations for domestic conflict and civil wars. While traditional analyses of intrastate conflict seek to identify the political motivations for group violence, contemporary approaches have begun to emphasize the role of resource endowments and profit seeking in the initiation of civil wars, as well as their overall effect on economic prosperity. These studies have produced evidence that armed uprisings in the developing nations are motivated largely by "greed," or the desire to control valuable resources, rather than "grievance," or a protest against inequality of political rights. This is also linked to the finding that the risk of civil war is greatest in countries whose economies are highly dependent on income from natural resource exports, as rebel organizations can capture these industries as a source of finances for military operations. For instance, during the new wave of conflict in the Democratic Republic of Congo that began in 1998, forces led by Laurent Kabila gained control over the diamond mines that produced the income necessary to fund his regime. The results indicate that opportunities for organized rebellion afforded by illegal finances or resource wealth provide a stronger explanation for the outbreak of civil wars across countries than do variables such as inequality, political rights, or ethnic differences. Controlling access to such resources may therefore hold a key to stemming or limiting the likelihood of violent uprisings in these countries.

More problematic for the cause of preserving peace in developing nations have been the significant changes in the form that domestic conflicts commonly take. This is evidenced by a shift from the prevalence of traditional guerilla insurgencies, such as those that took place in China, Cuba, and Vietnam, to a proliferation of new types of internal wars in which the combatants have no clear intent other than to kill their enemies and gain wealth and power. These conflicts most often take place in what are typically labeled as "failed states," in which central government authority has collapsed or is too weak to control large areas of the country. African countries such Liberia, Somalia, and the former Zaire are familiar examples of such states. A main characteristic of these conflicts is that the participant forces do not initiate war in the pursuit of a defined political objective. In classical guerilla warfare, soldiers are motivated by an ideological doctrine, on the basis of which they intend to overthrow the existing government and replace it

with a revolutionary regime. In addition, one of the central strategies of guerilla movements is to garner popular support for their cause by responding to the needs of those most affected by underdevelopment. In contrast, the soldiers in the new internal conflicts do not seek to occupy their society as a foundation for carrying out a prolonged struggle. Rather, their primary goal is to gather weapons and gain control over territory that provides access to valued goods such as minerals or narcotics. These resources generate income upon which warlords can further build their armies and personal fiefdoms. The conditions for a perpetuation of conflict are further intensified where warring populations inhabit the same areas and communities, particularly in the case of ethnic or religious disputes. This situation has been observed in countries such as Bosnia and Rwanda, where displaced refugees are forced to return to neighborhoods co-populated by those who perpetrated ethnic killings. What makes the prospect of resolution of these wars even more difficult is that the task does not simply end with the cessation of conflict. It requires additional efforts toward state building, in which basic administrative functions must be restored before the stability necessary for reconstruction can be achieved. The dilemma of state building is especially evident in centers of international crisis such as Afghanistan.

The Future of Conflict and Development

Overall, the evidence produced by twenty-first century research on war and development indicates that civil wars have become more prevalent than international conflicts, and that they are largely concentrated in a particular group of low-income developing countries. In some cases, the responsibility for the prevention or resolution of civil wars lies with the individual government of the affected country. Yet, the notion that these conflicts do not affect the well-being of wealthy nations is a falsehood. Because the instability generated by domestic conflicts can impact not only neighboring countries but also the world as a whole, the problem demands a global agenda for action.

The two primary difficulties involved in organizing such efforts are the costs to participant governments, and determining which approaches will be effective in a given setting. Experience since the 1990s suggests that the provision of foreign aid to these countries would be problematic or even ineffectual. There is often little incentive to offer aid packages to war-torn or severely impoverished nations, which may have no ability to allocate funds effectively or to repay their debts. Further, the feasibility of introducing

broad institutional or policy reform into a country at the international level is limited. In the case of attempting to impose democratic accountability and constitutional government on unstable societies, it could be potentially destructive. This demands a more careful approach to intervention and the delivery of foreign assistance in the post-conflict period. Rather than the traditional method of providing an immediate infusion of money and peacekeeping forces that are quickly withdrawn after initial stability is achieved, foreign investment and reconstruction aid should be made conditional upon the introduction of necessary preliminary reforms as a foundation upon which to base future institution-building efforts.

In addition to the management of post-conflict environments in developing countries, the preservation of peace calls for the introduction of preventive strategies as well. One possible measure that the international community might pursue to decrease the actual incidence of civil war is to help control the access to natural resources that militant groups rely upon as a source of income. This would involve creating transparency measures that would make public the manner in which revenues from the harvesting of these valuables are used. Another would be to provide resource management assistance to countries whose economies are highly dependent on primary commodities in order to reduce the impact of shocks caused by a rapid decline in world product price levels. These downturns in economic welfare have been shown to create instability that increases the likelihood of violent conflict. Lastly, though regulation of military spending and arms buildups by international monitors is a highly challenging prospect, a possible alternative might lie in a coordinated effort by financial institutions and regional organizations to reduce arms purchases. In general, the degree of success with which international peacekeeping forces can prevent the resumption of internal conflicts is dependent on the level of commitment by the parties involved. Yet, while such efforts at intervention may prove expensive in the short term, the cost of neglect in terms of the overall impact on global peace and prosperity is far greater.

JASON E. STRAKES

See also Military and Development

References and Further Reading

Blomberg, S. Brock, Gregory D. Hess, and Sidharth Thacker. "Is there Evidence of a Poverty-Conflict Trap?" *Wellesley College Working Paper* 2000-06 (2000).

Collier, Paul et al. *Breaking the Conflict Trap: Civil War and Development Policy*. The World Bank and Oxford University Press, 2003.

Collier, Paul. "On the Economic Consequences of Civil War." *Oxford Economic Papers* 51 (1999), pp. 168–183.

Henderson, Errol A. and J. David Singer. "Civil War in the Post-Colonial World, 1946–1992." *Journal of Peace Research*, Vol. 37, No. 3 (2000), pp. 275–299.

Koubi, Vally. "War and Economic Performance." *Working Paper* 9-2002. Swiss Federal Institute of Zurich, Center for International Studies, 2002.

Kugler, Jacek and Marina Arbetman. "Exploring the 'Phoenix Factor' with the Collective Goods Perspective." *The Journal of Conflict Resolution*, Vol. 33, No. 1 (1989), pp. 84–112.

Marshall, Monty G. *Third World War: System, Process and Conflict Dynamics*. Rowman & Littlefield, 1999.

Olson, Mancur. *The Rise and Decline of Nations*. New Haven. CT: Yale University Press, 1982.

Organski, A. F. K. and Jacek Kugler. "The Costs of Major Wars: The Phoenix Factor." *The American Political Science Review*, Vol. 71, No. 4. (1977), pp. 1347–1366.

Snow, Donald. *Distant Thunder: Patterns of Conflict in the Developing World*, 2nd ed. Armonk, NY: M.E. Sharpe, 1997, pp. 21–55.

WASTE MANAGEMENT

Defining Waste Management

Technological and industrial development has led to high volumes of different types of generated waste. Waste management includes all activities that seek to minimize the environmental, health, and aesthetic impacts of disposed waste. In order to reach sufficient results and introduce proper options in waste-management practices, waste is divided into several categories according to different characteristics—origin, physicochemical properties, material, and management options. Dividing it by origin, waste can be domestic, industrial, commercial (institutional), agricultural, and so forth. By physicochemical properties, it is divided into liquid and solid; hazardous (toxic, flammable, radioactive, etc.) and non-hazardous. The material can be paper, metal, glass, wood, food scraps, textile, and so forth. The chosen management option depends on the type of waste (combustible, recyclable, compostable, etc.).

Waste-management approaches have developed over time. In ancient times waste was thrown into the streets and roads, where it was left to accumulate. The first disposal methods were simple and consisted of open pits located out of the residential areas. As population increased, efforts were made to transport waste farther from the residential sides. Demographic and economic developments led to increased volumes of generated waste. This emphasized the importance of the way wastes are managed. The type of the waste

(combustible, recyclable, compostable, etc.) determines the way it is handled, collected, disposed of, and stored.

Waste release, accumulation, and disposal are recognized as posing risks to the environment and public health. In order to minimize adverse effects caused by released wastes, different waste-management practices have been developed. The tasks of collecting, treating, transporting, and disposing of wastes present complex challenges. They vary with regard to the type of waste—solid or hazardous. Waste management will be discussed below in terms of the specifics of solid-waste management and hazardous-waste management.

Solid Waste Management

Solid waste is material that is not in liquid form and has served its purpose or has no value for the person who holds it. Solid waste is accumulated through different activities: residential, commercial, institutional, and industrial. Some types of waste that can pose dangers to human health and environment are defined as hazardous; these will be covered in a separate discussion under the Hazardous-Waste Management section. All non-hazardous solid waste from a community (houses, streets and public places, shops, offices, etc.) is called municipal solid waste (MSW). Although some words such as "garbage," "rubbish," "refuse," and "trash" are used as synonyms for solid waste, they have specific definitions and uses. Refuse comprises garbage and rubbish. Garbage is refuse resulting from the preparation, cooking, and dispensing of food. Rubbish includes heterogeneous household and business wastes that are not classified as garbage or ashes. This involves paper, wood, glass, rags, and metals. Trash is rubbish that includes bulky items, for instance couches, refrigerators, and so forth. Except for municipal solid waste, part of the generated solid wastes are also sewage-treatment solids (biomass sludge, settled solids, etc.); mining wastes; industrial wastes (chemicals, sand, paints, etc.); and agricultural wastes (crop residues, farm animal manure, etc.).

Adequate solid-waste management requires more than just dividing waste into different groups. It is a complex issue that requires technological skills and involves social, legal, financial, and institutional aspects. It demands coordination and management of a large workforce and collaboration among many stakeholders. Good waste management identifies three major points: (1) collection and transportation; (2) solid-waste treatment approaches; and (3) integrated

waste management. The way wastes are managed is crucial to the economy, health, and the environment. When thoughtful approaches are applied, waste management reveals the potential use of waste materials as valuable resources. Waste composition and quantity vary among nations and communities depending on the level of commercialism and institutionalism. In the United States, for instance, nearly 36% of the total MSW generation, which in 2001 comprised 229 million tons, is paper and paperboard. The second-largest component is yard trimmings, followed by food scraps, plastics, metals, rubber, textile, leather, wood, and other miscellaneous materials. In Europe, waste also constitutes a challenge. Annually, the total amount of waste generated is around 2,000 million tons. Paper and organic waste make a significant share of the municipal solid waste, with an increasing share of plastic. Low-income countries score low in terms of waste-generation rates, ranging between 0.4 and 0.9 kg per capita per day. The major part of their waste content is organic. Waste composition rates are important for precise solid-waste management plans.

Waste collection is the first step in the long waste-management chain. It is important for the protection of human health, environmental quality, and safety. It is one of the most expensive parts in the waste-management process and often inadequate financing can lead to poor waste-collection services. Usually the people remaining without waste collection services belong to the low-income population. Collection costs (as percentage of income) vary from country to country. For low-income countries they are between 0.9% and 1.7%. They represent 0.5%–1.1% for middle-income countries and 0.2%–0.4% for industrialized countries. However, financial restrictions are not the only factor that can affect adequate waste-collection services. Operational methods can also influence the efficiency of the solid-waste services. These include organizational structures and procedures, management capacity, and appropriate technologies.

Waste collection should occur at frequent intervals but not less than once per week because of the rapid decomposition of some residues. Waste transportation is an important stage of waste management. It is of crucial importance especially for large and densely populated areas, when an optimal route should be selected. Specially designed trucks are used for waste transportation to the final destination of the refuse. If it is not near the place where waste is generated, then transfer stations might be designed. Waste-transfer stations are facilities where municipal solid waste is unloaded from collection vehicles and held while it is reloaded onto larger, long-distance transport vehicles for shipment to landfills or other treatment or disposal sites.

Solid Waste Treatment

Collected municipal solid waste can be treated in different ways in order to reduce the total volume and weight of the material that will be disposed of. There are three major methods of waste treatment: biological treatment, thermal treatment, and landfilling. The following sections discuss these each in detail.

Biological Treatment

Organic waste does not have to be thrown away. It may be reused and considered as a fertilizer through a process called *composting*. Composting can be defined as a biological decomposition of the organic constituents of wastes under controlled conditions. The process can be presented as follows:

$$\text{organic matter} + O_2 \xrightarrow{\text{aerobic bacteria}} \text{new cells} + CO_2 + NH_3 + H_2O + SO_4$$

The material being composted decomposes as a result of the activity of the bacteria, fungi, actinomycetes, and protozoa present in the waste material. There are also key inorganic nutrients required in the composting. These include nitrogen, phosphorus, sulphur, potassium, magnesium, calcium, and sodium. A broad range of organic matter including manure from plant-eating animals, dead leaves and garden plants, grass clippings, and so forth are used in the composting process. The starting materials are piled up and the pile itself can be either loose on the ground or enclosed using a variety of materials.

The relevant process parameters for composting include temperature, carbon and nitrogen ratio, oxygen, moisture content, and pH. Moisture conditions influence the speed of the decomposition. The appropriate carbon and nitrogen ratio can facilitate optimal decomposition. Preferably it includes 30 parts carbon to 1 part nitrogen. The composition process is exothermic and it goes through temperature variations throughout its development. It can reach 150°F (65°C). The time it takes microorganisms to decompose the starting materials in compost varies. Factors that influence decomposition include the size of the pile, the nature of the starting materials (green materials decompose more rapidly than brown materials), and techniques that are used to manage the compost. The final product of composting consists of minerals and complex organic material. It is called *humus*. It is rich in nutrients and when added to soil it is beneficial to plant growth.

The use of composting is increasing as it yields a number of benefits compared to the other solid-waste treatment methods. It has a positive effect on the quality and longevity of the soil and involves a lower health risk than the other methods. Whereas landfilling and incineration are expensive ways to accomplish waste disposal, composting is the least-cost alternative for waste management.

Thermal Treatment

When composting or recycling is not feasible, incineration of waste with energy recovery is a preferable step according to the waste hierarchy. Incineration of waste is a way of utilizing energy in the waste and decreasing its volume and weight. However, incineration of waste is a subject of considerable public concern. If there are no effective controls, pollutants may be emitted into the air, soil, and water, and these can be harmful for human health and the environment. Moreover, incineration plants are among the most expensive solid-waste management options, requiring careful maintenance. For these reasons, incineration tends to be a good choice only when other simpler and less expensive waste-management options are not available. Considering all of the above, incineration includes both advantages and disadvantages as a waste-management option.

Incineration is an efficient way to reduce the original volume of combustibles by 80% to 95%. Incineration plants can be located close to the waste-generation center and thus reduce the cost of waste transportation. One of the most attractive features of incineration is that the released energy of the combustion process can be recovered for heat or power consumption. Using incinerators as a method of waste management reduces the volumes of landfill disposed wastes. Waste incineration may be advantageous when a landfill cannot be used because of a lack of suitable sites or due to long transportation routes, which result in high costs. All waste-disposal alternatives eventually decompose organic material into simpler carbon molecules such as CO_2 (carbon dioxide) and CH_4 (methane). Incineration provides the best way to eliminate methane gas emissions from waste-management processes. Energy from wastes provides a substitute for fossil fuel combustion. Despite these two ways in which incineration helps reduce greenhouse emissions, air pollution control remains a major problem for incineration of solid waste.

Incineration requires strict controls to prevent adverse environmental impacts and negative influences on human health. One of the main concerns that have been expressed is about the emissions of certain organic compounds from incinerators—dioxins and furans. In many cases, the term dioxin either refers to the

seven toxic dioxins or only to the most toxic dioxin, called 2,3,7,8—TCCD (2,3,7,8-tetrachlorodibenzo-*p*-dioxin). Other pollutants are also released as a result of the incineration process. These include lead, mercury, cadmium, and others. Lead has been associated with a variety of negative effects on human health—slowed nerve conduction, reduced vitamin D metabolism, reduced hemoglobin production, kidney damage, and others. Mercury exposure affects behaviour and can lead to renal damages even at low levels. In addition to emissions of heavy metals, dioxins, and furans, the incineration of waste generates acid gases and particulate matter. Acid gases can cause respiratory problems and can lead to ecosystem damage by acidification. Particulate matter in the atmosphere can also cause adverse effects on human health. Last but not least, incineration plants require much investment and high operating costs. For a plant to be economically feasible, costs must be minimized through sale of energy recovered. Incinerators that convert the heat released from combustion into a stream of hot water are called waste-to-energy plants. Their systems require special equipment and controls and highly skilled technical personnel.

Landfilling

The most traditional method of disposing of municipal solid waste has been landfills. *Open dumps* are a primitive stage of landfill development. Open dumps consist of unselective disposal of waste and limited measures to control operations, including those related to the environmental effects of landfills. As this is not a sustainable method of landfill waste management, the open dump approach will be mentioned, but not discussed further here.

Operated dumps are the first-stage-upgraded landfills, which operate under control measures. Incoming wastes are inspected and recorded and other measures are applied in order to achieve better control mechanisms. However, certain issues are not taken into consideration where operated dumps are used. These include environmental cautionary approaches such as leachate and landfill gas management. Leachate is a water-type liquid that seeps out of a landfill. It results from rain infiltration through the landfill and also from the moisture fraction in the waste. Because of the predominantly anaerobic environment, leachate is contaminated with heavy metals and organics and is highly toxic. It is important that the leachate is not allowed to reach and enter surface water or groundwater. Landfill gas is a result of the anaerobic degradation of biodegradable wastes. The released gas contains around 60% methane and 40% carbon dioxide. Methane is poisonous and potentially explosive and as such it must be controlled. Converting open dumps or operated dumps to engineered landfills and sanitary landfills is a crucial step for introducing sustainable landfill management.

A safer alternative to landfill waste disposal is the use of *sanitary landfills*—solid waste is disposed of at a carefully selected location, constructed and maintained by engineering techniques that minimize the pollution of air, water, and soil, as well as reduce other risks to human health and the environment. Sanitary landfills apply measures to control gas and collect and treat leachate. The construction of a sanitary landfill must consider different technical aspects: siting, design, operation, and environmental impacts. The selection of the landfill site depends on many factors. These include:

Economic and technical criteria: haul distance, available land, etc.

Geology/hydrology of the landfill site: soil should have a very low hydraulic conductivity, $<10^{-9}$ m/s, so as to prevent leachate penetration through the site. If the hydraulic conductivity does not meet the technical requirement, then additional protection material is necessary. Depending on the type of waste to be disposed of and the specifics of the location, it has become a practice to provide a protective lining system. The lining system can be either single- or multilayer and it can be made of naturally *in situ* clay, imported clay, bentonite, or synthetics. For safety reasons, a seismically unsafe zone should be avoided for landfill sites.

Ecological and biological conditions should be also considered when a landfill is designed. These include existing and potential water supply sources, protected areas or species, climate conditions, etc.

Socioeconomic factors also play a role. They involve human settlements, recreational zones, historical and archaeological sites, agricultural regions, etc.

On sanitary landfills waste is spread and compressed in thin layers. Each day the compacted waste is covered with a layer of soil so that it prevents negative impacts such as odour, dust, rodents, birds, and other pests. The final cover for a completed landfill may also be topsoil, which can support vegetative growth.

Worldwide there are different landfill practices. As Johannessen and Boyer (1999) note in *Observations of Solid Waste Landfills in Developing Countries: Africa, Asia, and Latin America,* solid-waste landfills sites range from open dumps to sanitary landfills. At the national level, decisions are made mainly with regard

to the gross national product (GNP), available infrastructure, and investment projects. The European Union has introduced stringent technical requirements for reducing adverse effects of waste and landfills and landfill taxes have been applied in some European countries.

Although each of the three options for solid-waste treatment propose solutions for generated waste, it is becoming more and more difficult to find adequate sites for landfills, since not all waste is proper for composting and incineration also has limits. One of the crucial issues in managing various types of waste is integrated waste management.

Integrated Waste Management

Integrated solid-waste management involves a combination of techniques to manage municipal solid waste. It is based on the fact that the waste stream consists of different materials. The idea behind integrated solid-waste management is that a combination of approaches can be used to handle the miscellaneous content of the waste stream. Source reduction and reuse of materials, recycling, combustion, and landfilling are all methods of waste management. They form the hierarchy of integrated waste management.

Source reduction stays at the top of the hierarchy. It addresses how products are produced, purchased, and used. Source reduction can be achieved through design of the products, packaging with minimum material, increased product lifetime, and decreased consumption, among other methods. Implementation of source-reduction approaches can be done through education, research, financial incentives, technological development, and so forth.

Recycling is the next level in the integrated waste-management hierarchy. It cannot alone solve all waste-management problems, but it can reduce significantly the volumes of waste that are disposed of on landfills or are thermally treated. Recycling requires separation and sorting of waste. Source separation is done at the point where waste is generated (e.g., the households, business, etc.). In many cases, different materials are segregated (e.g., paper, glass, aluminum, etc.). This type of municipal waste collection is more expensive than ordinary refuse collection. An alternative to source separation are drop-off centers, which are usually situated at shopping centers or other convenient locations. Commonly recycled materials include paper (newspapers, corrugated cardboard, high-grade paper), aluminum, glass, ferrous metals (iron and steel), plastics (polyethylene teraphthalate [PTE]), high-density polyethylene (HDPE), mixed plastics, other plastics, and batteries.

The places where recyclables are received and processed are called materials recovery facilities (MRFs). MRFs may be designed to handle all types or certain categories of recyclables.

Recycling programs are one of the first waste-management options because they can divert significant quantities of materials from ultimate disposal. They reduce the overall waste stream that is directed either to landfills or combusting. In addition to this, recycling can have a positive impact on composting. Most recyclable materials such as glass, plastic, and metals are considered contaminants in the compost product and moreover, they are not easily composted. Recycling of toxic-containing products (e.g., batteries) leads to removal of hazardous constituents (lead, cadmium, etc.), which increases the product's quality as waste material. Integrated waste management suggests that waste-management alternatives should be designed to complement each other environmentally and economically. It shows the close link among the different waste-management options, and suggests solutions for mitigating the adverse effects of waste generation.

Hazardous Waste Management

Hazardous waste is any solid, liquid, or gas material that can cause death, illness, or injury to people or environmental destruction if it is improperly stored, treated, transported, or discarded. Wastes are considered hazardous if they are *ignitable* (capable of burning or causing fire), *reactive* (able to explode), *corrosive* (able to harm organisms because of high contents of acidic or alkaline substances), *toxic* (poisonous), *containing heavy metals,* or *radioactive* (emitting ionizing energy that can harm living organisms).

Sources of Hazardous Waste

Hazardous wastes result from different activities. Industries are one of the major producers of hazardous wastes. Agriculture also releases wastes that create hazards to human health and environmental safety (e.g., nitrates, herbicides, pesticides, fluoride wastes, etc.). Household-generated waste can also contain hazardous materials. These include, for instance, toxic paints, drugs, toxic batteries, pesticides, consumer electronic products containing cadmium, mercury, or flame-retardant materials. Waste from hospitals also must be treated with caution. Infected materials such as used bandages, needles, scalpels,

or materials contaminated with blood or tissue must be disposed of carefully.

Radioactive waste, particularly nuclear fission waste, continues to be one of the most dangerous hazardous wastes. It remains radioactive for thousands of years before fully decaying. Because of the complexity of the problem, the management of radioactive waste is usually considered to be a separate engineering task from other forms of hazardous-waste management.

Hazardous waste is generated at a particular site. In order to provide safe storage and further treatment of hazardous wastes, one of the initial hazardous-waste management steps is obtaining a suitable container for the waste. Safety is the primary consideration in container selection. It is also a general requirement that containers be labeled with a description of the waste material and the words "hazardous waste." In addition to safe storage, safe transportation of hazardous waste is also given special attention due to the threats that hazardous waste creates. Transportation vehicles and containers where hazardous waste is stored are designed in a way to avoid adverse impact that hazardous waste might have. Standards for cargo trucks and shipping containers are included in governmental regulations. In case of accidents during transportation, immediate and appropriate actions must be taken so that environmental and public health hazards can be reduced.

Hazardous Waste Management Options

Hazardous-waste management options are similar to those that apply to solid waste.

Hazardous waste reduction is the most desirable stage in hazardous waste management. Although reducing the quantity of generated waste or reusing and recycling waste materials are good options, they do not solve all problems with hazardous waste. There will always be need for their treatment and disposal. Chemical treatment includes oxidation, neutralization, and ion exchange. Physical processes include sedimentation, evaporation, and filtration of hazardous waste. These processes lead to reducing its volume. Biological treatment also suggests ways for handling hazardous waste. Microbes can be used on contaminated sites for stabilizing hazardous waste. This process is called *bioremediation*. In other cases, genetically engineered species that can metabolize the waste are used. Thermal treatment destroys hazardous wastes. However, high-temperature incineration can cause air pollution and this is one of the major problems posed by hazardous waste thermal treatment.

Proper disposal of hazardous waste is important in order to avoid adverse impacts on public health and the environment. A secure hazardous-waste landfill must have impermeable liners and leachate collection systems. An impermeable cover is placed over a finished landfill so as to reduce potential environmental damage. Hazardous waste can pollute the soil, surface and underground water, or the air.

Legislative Framework

Worldwide about 400 million metric tons of hazardous wastes are generated each year. This requires coordinated actions and efforts to minimize hazardous-waste generation and disposal. In response to the concerns regarding toxic waste being dumped from industrialized countries in developing countries and countries in transition, in 1989 the Basel Convention on the Control of Transboundary Movements of Hazardous Wastes and Their Disposal was adopted. The Convention entered into force on May 5, 1992. At the start the main focus of the Basel Convention was the "transboundary" movement of hazardous wastes, which is movement of such wastes across international borders. The Convention's objectives are to ensure environmentally sound management and adequate disposal facilities; to dispose of wastes as close as possible to the point of their generation; to minimize quantity and hazard of wastes generated; and to reduce transboundary movements. The Basel Convention introduces "environmentally sound management," the aim of which is to protect human health and the environment by minimizing hazardous waste production whenever possible. It proposes a set of strategies in order to stimulate and promote efficient activities by the parties involved.

MILENA NOVAKOVA

See also Environment: Government Policies; Pollution, Agricultural; Pollution, Industrial

References and Further Reading

Countreau-Levine, Sandra. *Private Sector Participation in Municipal Solid Waste Services in Developing Countries. Volume 1: The Formal Sector*. Washington, DC: The World Bank, 1994, 1995.

———. *Municipal Solid Waste in the United States: 2001 Facts and Figures*. Available at http: http://www.epa.gov/epaoswer/non-hw/muncpl/pubs/msw2001.pdf (last consulted February 17, 2005).

European Commission. *EU Focus on Waste Management*. Luxemburg: Office for Official Publications on the European Communities, 1999.

Hoornweg, Daniel and Laura Thomas. *What a Waste: Solid Waste Management in Asia*. Washington, DC: The

World Bank, 1999. Available at http://www.wds.world bank.org/ (last consulted on February 17, 2005).

Johannessen, Lars Mikkel and Gabriella Boyer. *Observations of Solid Waste Landfills in Developing Countries: Africa, Asia, and Latin America.* Washington, DC: The World Bank, Urban Development Division, Waste Management Anchor Team, 1999.

Nathonson, Jerry. "Environmental Works" In *Encyclopedia Britannica Deluxe Edition 2004 CD-ROM.*

Rand, T., J. Haukohl, and U. Marxen. *Municipal Solid Waste Incineration. A Decision Maker's Guide.* Washington, DC: The World Bank, 2000.

US Environmental Protection Agency. *Decision-Makers' Guide to Solid Waste Management.* Washington, DC: US Environmental Protection Agency, Office of Solid Waste, 1989.

WATER RESOURCES AND DISTRIBUTION

The Hydrological Cycle

Freshwater is vital to all living organisms. It is the medium in which living processes occur and all organisms require water to complete their life cycle. Humans use water for drinking; irrigating crops; watering livestock; in industry; and as a medium to dilute, assimilate, and remove wastes. Lakes and rivers provide habitat for aquatic species and many of these are used by humans for food (e.g., fish, aquatic plants) and building materials (e.g., reeds for thatching). Aquatic systems provide humans with other ecological services such as flood control and water quality enhancement. Water bodies are also used for transport and recreation, and they give humans aesthetic pleasure. Water resources are unevenly distributed over the earth's surface, largely because of climatic influences on the hydrological or water cycle.

The earth is a watery planet with 75% of its surface covered in oceans. A total of 97.6% of water on earth is stored in the oceans and saltwater lakes that are too saline to provide water for many human uses. Of the remaining 2.4%, most (87%) is frozen as ice, snow, and permafrost; only 13% of freshwater is liquid. Much of this liquid water is stored underground in aquifers and soil. Only 3% is readily accessible in surface water bodies such as rivers, lakes, and wetlands. In other words, surface water bodies contain less than 0.01% of the earth's water and many of these water bodies are in remote areas far from human settlements.

Transfers between the reservoirs of water (oceans, atmosphere, land surface, and underground stores) occur through the hydrological cycle. Water, evaporated from the oceans by heat from the sun, condenses in the atmosphere to form clouds and returns to the earth's surface as precipitation (rain, hail, dew, sleet, and snow). Approximately 80% of all precipitation returns directly to the oceans, while the remainder, an estimated thirty-three thousand to forty-seven thousand cubic kilometers per year, falls on land. Of the water falling on land, some is intercepted by vegetation and evaporates from leaves and stems, some flows down the plants to the ground, and some falls directly on the soil surface. Water that reaches the ground either infiltrates the soil or flows along the surface. Surface runoff and groundwater may flow into streams and rivers, eventually returning the water to the oceans. Some water may replenish groundwater reservoirs. Water stored in the soil may be absorbed by plants and used by them for growth and in photosynthesis. Most water taken up by plants is returned to the atmosphere through *evapotranspiration.*

Groundwater resources consist of either shallow, rechargeable aquifers that are connected to rivers and streams or those that filled many years ago with "fossil water" and are not currently recharged. The former are replenished as rainwater infiltrates the overlying soil and enters the aquifer. Water enters an aquifer through a recharge zone, a porous layer sandwiched between two impermeable layers of rock or clay that form the underground reservoir.

Water resources vary in time and space largely through seasonal and inter-annual variations in climate. In the tropics, radiant heat from the sun is concentrated over a smaller area than in temperate regions. Greater radiant heat input at the equator warms the air and it expands and rises. As it rises, the air cools and since cold air holds less moisture, rain falls. The rising air spreads out and falls in a high pressure zone around 30°N and S. The cool, dry air warms as it falls to earth and deserts tend to occur at these latitudes. This differential heating generates trade winds that meet in an equatorial low pressure trough, the Inter-Tropical Convergence Zone (ITCZ). The convergence zone moves north of the equator during the northern summer (June–August), bringing rain to the underlying regions. At the end of the northern summer, the ICTZ migrates south of the equator, bringing rain to the southern tropics and subtropics between November and February. Equatorial regions have two wet seasons, with rainfall occurring each time the ITCZ crosses the equator. These temporal variations in climate significantly affect the availability of water resources. For example, nearly 80% of all runoff from Asia occurs in six months (May–October), and in arid regions of Africa, about 80% of annual runoff occurs in one to two

months each year. Spatially, the boundaries of lakes and wetlands may change seasonally, expanding during wet seasons and contracting in dry seasons. The discharge of rivers and streams may also vary seasonally and corresponding water levels in floodplain lakes rise and fall with the flood pulse.

Changes in surface water resources also vary inter-annually, with more water stored or discharged during wet years and less during droughts. Much of the inter-annual variation can be related to the strength of El Niño events. In El Niño years, reversal of winds and ocean currents across the Pacific results in droughts in southern Africa, eastern Australia, and Brazil; droughts and forest fires in Indonesia; and storms and wet weather along the American west coast from Alaska to Peru. Computer models that analyze tiny temperature fluctuations in the Pacific Ocean can be used to predict El Niño years, and these models provide an early-warning system that assists in planning relief efforts designed to minimize the effects of drought-induced famines. El Niño events could become more intense with global warming since warmer oceans will increase the potential for El Niño events to develop.

Water Resource Distribution and Human Populations

The human population of the world exceeded 6 billion in 2000. It has been projected that the population will peak by 2050 at between 7.3 billion and 10.7 billion. After that time the population is predicted to stabilize or fall. Per capita freshwater use is increasing in almost all countries and the frequency of critical water shortages is expected to increase. In 2001, 1.2 billion people lacked access to safe drinking water and 2.5 billion have inadequate access to water for sanitation, washing, and food preparation. Globally, between 1950 and 2000, annual per capita water availability decreased from 16,900 cubic meters to 6,800 cubic meters. This is predicted to decline to 5,400 cubic meters by 2025, as human population growth outstrips increases in water supply. A widely accepted threshold for water adequacy is 1,600 cubic meters per capita, per year. 1.7 billion people live in river basins with per capita water availability below 1,000 cubic meters, and the resultant water stress impedes food production and economic development. Most such countries are in the developing world.

The distribution of water resources corresponds poorly with the distribution of human populations. Asia, where 60% of the world's population lives,

has access to only 30% of global runoff. Conversely, South America with approximately 5% of the human population, contributes 26% to global runoff from land to sea, with the Amazon River alone accounting for 15% of global runoff. This uneven distribution, in both time and space, of water and corresponding human populations, is the underlying cause of many water-resource problems. For example, the Amazon River supplies only 0.5% of the world's population and therefore most, perhaps up to 95%, of its runoff is not utilized by humans. Conversely, so much water is diverted from the Ganges River that little, if any, reaches the sea during periods of low flow. The Huang He River in China is so heavily used that in 1997, a drought year, the lower course of the river was without water from February to August. Reducing flows in rivers can seriously impact in-stream communities and water quality, and some countries have established minimum flow regimes (environmental flows) that, when reached, water abstraction must cease.

With the growth in the world's human population, per capita water availability has declined on all continents. Predicting future water need for human use is difficult, and many of the projections produced in the past have over-estimated consumption because they were based simply on extrapolation of existing trends. More recent projections, incorporating sophisticated computer modeling, are more reliable, but these have generally been applied in developed countries and there is a keen need for their application in the developing world. These projections are key as the development of water-resource infrastructure requires planning years in advance of actual need. Increasing water demand by larger human populations may be offset by increased water-use efficiencies. However, by 2025 at least 3 billion people in ninety countries are expected to face severe water stress.

Human Settlements and Surface Water Resources

Water availability is the key factor in the development of flourishing human settlements. Most early settlements were built on the banks of rivers or lakes that not only provided water but also a means for exploring and colonizing new sites. Freshwater supplies can be enhanced by increasing water-storage capacity to store runoff (dams and reservoirs), inter-basin transfers of water, increasing withdrawal of groundwater, conversion of saltwater to freshwater (desalinization), and by improving water use efficiencies.

In order to reduce their dependence on the vagaries of climate that largely control the availability of water resources, humans have managed water resources for millennia. Archaeological remains of water storage dams have been found in Jordan and Egypt that date back to at least 5000 BCE. However, construction of large storage reservoirs only began in the early 1900s and by the end of the twentieth century, there were over 45,000 large (more than 15 meters high) dams in over 150 countries. During the 1990s, an estimated US$32–46 billion was spent annually on large dams, four-fifths of it in developing countries. Of the US$22–31 billion invested in dams each year in developing countries, about four-fifths are financed by the public sector.

Half the world's large dams were built exclusively or primarily for irrigation, and an estimated 30% to 40% of the 271 million hectares of irrigated lands worldwide rely on dams. Reservoirs are estimated to provide irrigation water that results in 12–16% of world food production. About 12% of large reservoirs are designated as domestic water supplies. Through multipurpose use, reservoirs may also provide flood control and hydroelectricity as well as sites for fishing, recreation, and tourism.

Dams can have significant negative social, economic, and environmental impacts. Impoundments reduce downstream flows and this impacts human populations living on the banks of the lower reaches of regulated rivers. Displacement of human populations from the land flooded by new reservoirs has had significant social consequences, and dam development projects often meet with strong resistance and protests from people living nearby. Scheduled for completion in 2009, the Three Gorges dam on the Yangtze River in China will impound the world's largest reservoir and supply hydroelectric power to 150 million people. The reservoir will flood large areas of high-quality farmland, displace almost 2 million people, and the Yangtze River and reservoir could become polluted from wastes from the industries that will develop to use the hydroelectric power generated. The weight of water in the reservoir could trigger landslides and earthquakes.

The Aswan High Dam in Egypt forms a barrier, trapping the rich sediment that previously built up the rich, alluvial soils of the lower Nile valley and delta. The delta has declined in area and agricultural production has had to rely more on expensive, imported fertilizers. The annual sardine harvest in the eastern Mediterranean has declined by over 80%, partially resulting from the reduction in nutrient-rich silt previously carried out to sea through the delta.

Waterways have also been modified to improve navigation, drain wetlands for agriculture and urban developments, construct irrigation systems, and enable inter-basin water transfers. These often massive engineering works have facilitated water transport, contained flood waters, generated hydroelectric power, and provided irrigation water for agriculture and urban areas, but these benefits must be weighed against the environmental and social costs.

Groundwater reserves are particularly important in arid areas where access to surface waters is limited. Approximately 1.5 billion people use groundwater as their sole source of domestic water supply. In many areas, abstraction of water from groundwater reserves exceeds the rate at which they are replenished (groundwater mining). In Asian cities such as Bangkok, Manila, Beijing, and Madras, high rates of groundwater extraction have lowered water tables by over ten meters. Groundwater abstraction may result in land subsidence (sinking or cracking of the hardened soil as water is extracted) or, in coastal regions, significant saltwater intrusion. Saltwater intrusion into the coastal aquifer underlying Madras has been detected ten kilometers inland. Abstraction of water from shallow aquifers also reduces flows in surface waters, which these aquifers supply.

Another significant problem with use of groundwater relates to declining water quality as aquifers are recharged with polluted agricultural runoff, urban drainage, and wastewater. In the small nations of the South Pacific with low-lying islands such as those found in Kiribati, Fiji, and Tonga, groundwater reserves exist as a lens of freshwater overlying saline water tables. These freshwater lenses are very susceptible to pollution with wastewater and to salinization if use exceeds recharge rates. In some densely populated, small-island nations, such as Nauru, water has to be imported.

Basic information on groundwater resources, such as storage capacities, exploitation, and recharge rates and water quality, is lacking in many developing nations. In the 1970s Bangladesh initiated a program to utilize groundwater resources for drinking water, reducing dependence on contaminated and polluted surface waters. This program significantly reduced infant mortality from water-related diseases. Unfortunately, groundwater in the region has high levels of arsenic, derived from naturally occurring minerals. Signs of arsenic poisoning are becoming more apparent in humans drinking well water with high arsenic levels, and the number of people affected may be as high as 18 million.

In arid areas near the sea, desalinization of seawater may provide freshwater to satisfy domestic and some industrial needs. Desalinization is an energy-intensive process and therefore costly, but improved technologies such as multistage flash distillation and

reverse osmosis, have, in certain circumstances, made the process economically feasible. However, production costs prohibit the use of desalinated water in agriculture. Another drawback of this source of freshwater is the disposal of the concentrated brine produced. Disposal of the salt in the sea can seriously impact marine life in nearby areas. Desalinization plants supply freshwater to communities in the Caribbean, Pacific Islands, Middle East, and North Africa.

Human Uses of Water Resources

Human adults require three to five liters of clean drinking water per day just to survive. In addition, minimum requirements for sanitation, bathing, and food preparation have been estimated at, respectively, twenty, fifteen, and ten liters per person per day. This total of approximately fifty liters per person per day is the minimum required to sustain life in a moderate climate and excludes the much larger volumes of water required to grow food. Per capita water use varies considerably between countries and approximately 2.2 billion people live in over sixty countries that report average domestic water use below the fifty liter minimum.

In addition to domestic supply, the main human uses of water are for agriculture, industry, and removal of domestic and industrial wastes. Globally, agriculture accounts for about 68% of withdrawals, industry uses 19%, and municipal and domestic uses account for 9%. Regionally, these use ratios vary significantly. In Africa, agriculture, industrial, and domestic use percentages are 90%, 4%, and 6%, respectively. In India, 93% of water use is directed towards agriculture, whereas in arid Kuwait only 12% of water withdrawals are used for agriculture. A dry climate precludes significant water use for agriculture and Kuwait, through its rich oil resources, is able to import food and water and to supplement water supplies through energy-intensive desalinization of seawater.

Food production is water-intensive. It takes five hundred to one thousand cubic meters of water to grow one tonne of grain. Water required to produce an average human diet varies from 640 cubic meters per capita per year in Africa to 1,830 cubic meters per capita per year in the United States. Most of this variation can be attributed to differences in calorific intake and the proportion of meat in the diet.

Almost one-fifth of the world's agricultural land is irrigated and these lands account for about 40% of the world's agricultural production and almost 70% of the world's water use. Water diverted for irrigation has in many areas significantly altered hydrological regimes. For example, water abstracted from rivers that flow into the Aral Sea (Uzbekistan and Kazakhstan) has reduced, by over 50%, the area of what once was the world's fourth-largest lake and in some areas, the shoreline has retreated by 120 kilometers. Fish production has declined and twenty of the twenty-four fish species previously recorded from the lake are no longer caught.

One of the most serious consequences of irrigation is the increase in the salt content of agricultural soils or salinization. As irrigation water evaporates, it leaves behind the salts dissolved in it. Excessive water application can move salts up the soil profile, exacerbating the problem. It has been estimated that 20% of irrigated lands are salt-impacted; developing countries with significant problems include Argentina, Egypt, Iran, and Pakistan. Very large transfer of water from inflows to the Aral Sea has resulted in the salinization of its waters. The exposed bed of the Aral Sea, twenty thousand square kilometers in area, contains toxins and salts that are spread by the wind to surrounding farmlands. Intensive agriculture that often accompanies irrigation can also lead to soil loss, nutrient depletion, and soil compaction.

Irrigation has played a significant role in maintaining per capita food production in the last three decades of the twentieth century. However, trends indicate that the increase in food production is slowing. Growth in cereal production declined from 2.6% per year between 1967 and 1982 to 1.3% per year in the 1990s. This is partly due to reduction in the rate of expansion of agricultural lands under irrigation. In the 1970s irrigated lands were expanding at more than 2% per year but this rate fell to less that 1.4% per year in 2000. This decline in the growth rate of areas under irrigation is due to higher costs associated with irrigating more marginal land and reduced water availability. Many new high-yielding crop varieties require more water. While these new varieties have higher yields, production gains come at the cost of additional stress on water and soil resources.

Livestock use water directly and also indirectly through the production of the forage and feeds that they consume. Large differences in human per capita water requirements can be attributed to the quantity of meat in human diets. Approximately 40% of grain produced is fed to livestock and this requires a significant quantity of water to produce. Reduced meat consumption will not only increase food availability, it will also reduce water consumed in food production.

Many industrial processes require significant quantities of water, but much of it is returned to the environment, albeit often with reduced quality. Water is very effective at carrying away heat and up to 90% of water used in industry is for cooling; little is

consumed in this process and most is returned to the source. Thermal pollution (disposal of water at elevated temperature) can impact aquatic organisms in the receiving waters directly (many aquatic organisms are very sensitive to small temperature changes) or indirectly by reducing the dissolved oxygen content. Industry also uses water to dissipate wastes and this leads to significant pollution and reduced water quality. This is particularly true in newly industrialized urban areas in developing countries where few pollution controls have been implemented. Water used in industry generates economic returns per unit use of water that are fifty to seventy times greater than those from agriculture. However, due to political and social considerations and the desire for food security, many governments give agriculture a high priority in the allocation of water resources.

Water is used to carry away domestic, industrial, and agricultural wastes. Up to 80% of water withdrawn for domestic use is returned to rivers and groundwater as wastewater. Significant advances have been made in developing techniques for the treatment and recycling of wastewater. Primary treatment of sewage effluent consists of screening the wastewater to remove large particles followed by storage in ponds to allow time for smaller particles to settle. Secondary treatment involves techniques that promote bacterial breakdown of organic matter in the effluent. Tertiary sewage treatment removes certain pollutants that remain. However, in most developing countries, wastewater is either untreated or receives only primary treatment, and significant problems include high incidence of water-borne diseases and *eutrophication* (excess nutrient enrichment/pollution) of receiving water bodies. Economic development provides the opportunity to treat wastewaters and also for the implementation of economic incentives and penalties for polluters ("polluter pays" principle).

In many parts of the world, wastewater is more commonly being viewed as a resource that can be treated and cleaned to a level appropriate for a specific use. Suitably treated, wastewater can be used to irrigate urban parks and golf courses, as industrial cooling water, and for irrigation of certain agricultural crops such as fruit trees and pastures. In arid countries such as Israel, Egypt, Saudi Arabia, and Tunisia, wastewater is used extensively in agriculture and this also reduces the need for fertilizers. Alternative disposal of recycled wastewater may be required during wet seasons when irrigation needs decline. Purification costs are higher if the end-use of wastewater is to be potable water, and few developing countries have made the necessary investment. Namibia has done so and reclaimed water provides up to 30% of the total water supply to the capital city, Windhoek.

Other uses of inland water bodies include flood control, fish production, hydroelectricity generation, transportation, recreation, and tourism. Fisheries based on natural fish stocks have little direct impact on water resources. However, fish culture in ponds is a fast-growing industry and currently provides 20% of total fish production. Aquaculture requires large quantities of water and diverts supplies away from irrigated agriculture. Aquaculture ponds are enriched with fertilizers and livestock wastes and disposal of water from them may lead to eutrophication of receiving waters.

Hydroelectricity generation provides a significant component of energy resources in many developing countries. Hydropower currently provides 19% of the world's total electricity supply, and is used in over 150 countries with twenty-four of these countries depending on it for 90% of their supply.

Water Quality

Safe drinking water and adequate sanitation are essential for human health. In 1977, the United Nations Water Conference declared that all people, regardless of their socioeconomic standing, have a right to clean drinking water and sanitation services that prevent diseases. A goal of the United Nations Millennium Declaration is to halve, by 2015, the proportion of people who are unable to reach or to afford safe drinking water. Contaminated water causes millions of preventable deaths every year, especially among children.

Water quality is declining through pollution, salinization, and enhanced sediment loads from soil erosion. Poor water quality is common in areas with high rates of population growth, poor sanitary conditions, and poverty. Water quality issues are more severe in arid areas where dilution of wastes is minimal. Pollutants include microorganisms that affect human health; excessive nutrients; heavy metals such as lead, mercury, and cadmium; and numerous chemical compounds including persistent and toxic organic pollutants such as PCBs and DDT. Pesticide use in India increased over fifty-fold in the latter half of the twentieth century. Pharmaceutical drugs even in low concentrations can act as carcinogens or endocrine disrupters. Poor land management and deforestation has elevated sediment loads in many tropical rivers. Most developing countries lack the resources and trained personnel to establish and maintain programs

that monitor the quantity and quality of water resources.

Water-Borne Diseases

Between 5 million and 10 million people die each year from water-related diseases stemming from inadequate access to safe drinking water and from poor sanitation. Many disease vectors rely on water for at least part of their life cycle and it has been estimated that 80% of infections in developing countries are related to water. Pathogenic organisms (viruses, bacteria, and protozoans) are found in areas where untreated sewage and effluents from animal husbandry operations enter domestic water supplies. Sewerage systems in many developing countries are inadequate, serving only a small proportion of urban populations. Significant diseases that are either water-borne or spread by vectors requiring free water to complete their life cycle include: diarrhea, schistosomiasis, malaria, dengue fever, poliomyelitis, Bancroftian filariasis, and onchocerciasis.

Water Resources and Global Warming

Global warming will accelerate the hydrological cycle through enhanced rates of evaporation and precipitation. This will alter water resource availability, but exactly how is difficult to predict, particularly in the tropics where most developing countries are situated. The degree of uncertainty in predicting the impacts of climate change further complicates forecasting water resource needs. Water supplies in developing countries are already under stress. Alterations to water supply through climate change can only add to the stresses caused by expanding human populations and pollution. Climate change could also exacerbate economic and political tensions, particularly in the more arid regions where water resources are already scarce.

Several predictive models of global climate suggest that rainfall in the tropics will become more intense, leading to increased runoff and reduced soil infiltration. Freshwater ecosystems will be influenced by elevated water temperatures and altered flow regimes. In some regions the frequency and duration of large floods will increase; in others droughts will be more common and prolonged. These changes will severely stretch provision of government services. Floods affected 65 million people between 1972 and 1996, more than any other type of disaster including war, drought, and famine.

Water Resource Planning

Government policies on water resources have largely been directed toward increasing supply to meet increasing demand and to guarantee food security. Emerging trends indicate that we are approaching a "water crisis" in several regions—most notably the Middle East and North Africa where per capita water availability is presently 1,247 cubic meters per capita, one of the lowest in the world, compared with 18,742 cubic meters per capita in North America and 23,103 cubic meters per capita in Latin America. The main causes of water shortages are a dry climate, periods of low rainfall (drought), poor management of natural resources (deforestation, overgrazing), and water stress brought about through human population growth outstripping the growth in water supply. The main constraint to agricultural production in many areas in the near future will be the availability of water, not land.

As water resources become more limited, long-term planning becomes imperative. This process requires accurate prediction of future water demand and the development of water resources to meet that demand. The planning process should be carried out for whole watersheds and should include the environmental consequences resulting from the construction of water resource infrastructure. Effective planning will require data on precipitation, evaporation, river flows, groundwater depletion and recharge rates, and water quality, as well as information on aquatic resources and habitats.

Governments are beginning to implement water management strategies that emphasize conservation, efficient use, and watershed protection, and to develop mechanisms that encourage wise use of water resources through education, regulation, and economic incentives such as water rights trading. Implementation of these strategies has been accompanied by water resource audits, enhanced monitoring, and pollution abatement programs. The most effective water resource management plans have focused on watersheds or river basins that integrate land and water management issues in a multi-sectoral approach. Whole basin management becomes more challenging where the basin straddles one or more international borders.

Politics and Water Resources

Water disregards political boundaries. One-third of the countries in water-stressed regions of the world are

expected to face severe water shortages this century. Water resource issues (supply, distribution, and quality) have been identified as a potential major cause of political instability. Depletion and degradation of water supplies, population growth, and unequal access to water resources shared between nations all combine to make water issues a threat to human security. Worldwide, demand for water is outstripping supply and water quality is declining. Small conflicts over water have already occurred and evidence suggests that the lack of water can be linked with both poverty and political instability. There are 261 watersheds that cross the political boundaries of two or more countries and 145 nations share water resources. These international basins cover 45% of the land surface of the earth and affect about 40% of the world's human population. Four river basins in developing countries (Congo, Niger, Nile, and Zambezi) are shared by between nine and eleven countries. The Amazon, Ganges-Brahmaputra-Meghna, Mekong, Tigris-Euphrates, and La Plata extend over five to eight countries.

Water has caused political tension between Jordan and Israel, India and Bangladesh, and between the countries drained by the Nile River, particularly Egypt and Sudan. The total human population of the Nile Basin is 145 million (1990 estimate) and the runoff from the Nile is approximately 85 cubic kilometers per year. The average per capita water availability is therefore less than 600 cubic meters per person per year. Actual water availability per capita, through re-use, is higher than this. The Sudanese live upstream from the Egyptians and theoretically have access to 3,150 cubic meters per person per year compared with the 925 cubic meters per person, per year available to the average Egyptian. Sudan has abided by a treaty signed with Egypt and passed on much of the water that flows through its territory. Cooperation has partly come through Sudan's inability to use its water effectively owing to political instability, and tension over water could potentially rise in the future.

Political disputes over water tend to be more prevalent in developing countries because water supply is more closely linked with human survival, opportunities to reduce use are fewer, and resources to supplement supply are meager. States will need to focus more on including principles of water resource sharing in national water legislation, developing policies that address water resource issues, and negotiating treaties with states that share regional water resources.

A number of international organizations promote strategies for the wise and cooperative use of the world's water resources. The United Nations Development Program (UNDP) provides advice, technical support, and capacity building to member nations on policy, legal, and regulatory issues relating to improving sustainable use of water resources. The United Nations Environment Program (UNEP), through its Freshwater Unit, promotes integrated management and use of freshwater and environmentally sustainable development. The Food and Agriculture Organization (FAO) works to raise levels of nutrition and living standards, to improve agricultural productivity, and to improve living conditions of rural populations. With regard to water resources, FAO provides advice and development assistance on water use for agriculture, fisheries, and aquaculture. The Global Water Partnership (GWP), created in 1996 by the World Bank, United Nations Development Program (UNDP), and the Swedish International Development Agency, coordinates activities among government agencies, public institutions, private companies, professional organizations, and multilateral development agencies involved in water management. The GWP promotes Integrated Water Resource Management (IWRM), an approach that seeks to balance human, industrial, agricultural, and environmental needs. The International Commission on Large Dams promotes progress in the establishment of design, construction, operation, and maintenance of large dams. The World Water Commission promotes awareness of critical water issues at all levels and facilitates efficient conservation, protection, development, planning, management, and use of water in all its dimensions on an environmentally sustainable basis.

The rapidly growing human population, movement of humans from rural to urban areas, and effects of economic development are exerting stresses on finite water resources. Water scarcity is exacerbated by declining water quality. In some parts of the world, the rate of increase in demand for water has slowed in recent years and this can be attributed to more efficient use and less waste. This trend needs to accelerate and developing countries need to implement measures to conserve water supplies, reduce leaks in distribution systems, reduce use, and develop techniques that recycle water efficiently.

PATRICK L. OSBORNE

References and Further Reading

Food and Agriculture Organization. *Drops and Crops*. Rome: Author, 2000.

Gleick, Peter H. "Making Every Drop Count." In *Annual Editions: Environment* 2002/2003, pp. 158–162. McGraw-Hill, 2002.

———. *Water in Crisis: A Guide to the World's Fresh Water Resources*. Oxford University Press, New York, 1993.

———. *The World's Water 2000–2001. The Biennial Report on Freshwater Resources.* Washington, DC: Island Press, 2000.

Johnson, N., C. Revenga, and J. Echeverria. "Managing Water for People and Nature." *Science*, 292: 1071–1072, 2001.

Postel, Sandra L. *Pillar of Sand: Can the Irrigation Miracle Last?* New York: Worldwatch Books, Norton, 1999.

———, Gretchen C. Daily, and Paul R. Ehrlich. "Human Appropriation of Renewable Freshwater." *Science*, 271: 785–787, 1996.

Shumway, C. *Forgotten Waters: Freshwater and Marine Ecosystems in Africa.* Biodiversity Support Program, USAID, 1999.

World Commission on Dams, Dams and Development. *A New Framework for Decision-Making.* London: Earthscan, 2000.

World Water Council, World Water Vision. *Commission Report—A Water Secure World. Vision for Water, Life and the Environment.* Author, 2000.

WEST AFRICA: HISTORY AND ECONOMIC DEVELOPMENT

In order to provide the necessary geographic context for a discussion of the development of West Africa, we first need to grapple with the spatial definition of the region. Undoubtedly the region constitutes Africa's "big bulge," but how far north does it go? Where does the Sahara, for instance, begin and end? And, where does West Africa end and East Africa begin?

Basing their regionalization on ethnicity, the physical environment, history, culture, and the colonial frameworks, De Blij and Muller (2000), two influential world regional geographers, take West Africa to "include the countries of the western coast and Sahara margin from Senegal and Mauritania in the west to Nigeria and Niger (and part of Chad) in the east" (p. 357). Basil Davidson, one of the most respected Africanists, for his part, sees West Africa as "a handy term for all the land and the offshore islands between about 20° of latitude north of the equator down to the West African coast, and eastward to about 15° of longitude" (1998, p. 3). For Eugene Mendonsa (2002, p. 17), West Africa extends not right from the equator but from 5° to 25° north latitude and from 17° west to 15° east longitude; fairly similar latitudinal and longitudinal ranges were used by Mabogunje decades earlier. Evidently, like all perceptual or vernacular regions, West Africa has no exact geographical meaning, even though we all know where to point to on a map.

With insight from these authors, and conscious of our present interest in not only the historiography but also the economic development of the region (and, consequently, the need for reliable empirical data),

West Africa is here defined as the formal region embracing all the countries from the southern edge of the Sahara in the north to the Gulf of Guinea in the south, and from Senegal in the west to Niger and Nigeria in the east. This spatial definition includes the following sixteen countries: Benin, Burkina Faso, Cape Verde, Côte d'Ivoire, Gambia, Ghana, Guinea, Guinea-Bissau, Liberia, Mali, Mauritania, Niger, Nigeria, Senegal, Sierra Leone, and Togo. It is important to note that all the countries listed are members of the Economic Community of West African States (ECOWAS). Furthermore, the delimitation adopted here is almost coterminous with those of Davidson (1998) and De Blij and Muller (2000), with the explicit exclusion of Chad and Cameroon, both of which do not self-identify as West African countries, having opted to join the Economic Community of Central African States (ECCAS) instead of ECOWAS. Clearly "West Africa" is a mental construct, the boundaries of which can vary depending on the analysis one seeks to pursue. This should not surprise anyone, for neither the historiography nor the economic development of West Africa is actually separable from that of Africa as a whole.

Physical Environment and Climate

While environmental determinism is now rightly rejected by most geographers and development analysts, there is no denying that more than most parts of the World, the physical environment of West Africa has strongly influenced much of its economic development over the centuries. West Africa is characterized by east–west climatic and vegetation belts, which vary sharply as one moves from the north to the south. Lying astride the equator, West Africa has a relentlessly high temperature for the greater part of the year. While the region's perpetual high temperature means that the growth of plants and animals cannot be retarded for lack of heat and light, it still makes the availability of moisture a serious problem; consequently, the role of air masses becomes the more vital in any analysis of the region's climate and vegetation. West Africa is influenced by two main air masses: the tropical continental air mass (or the harmattan) and the tropical maritime air mass. The harmattan is a warm, dry, dusty air mass that forms over the Sahara Desert and moves southwesterly from December to March. At its maximum extent in January, it covers nearly all parts of West Africa with its desert-like conditions. As the name suggests, the tropical maritime airmass emanates from the ocean—more precisely, the southern Atlantic ocean—and

moves northeasterly across West Africa. It is a warm, humid airmass that peaks around July and August to about latitude 20° north, bringing much of the rainfall in West Africa. These two airmasses are separated by the Inter-tropical Front (ITF) or the Inter-Tropical Convergence Zone (ITCZ). It is along this front that much of the convectional activities that cause rainfall in West Africa take place. From around January to July, the ITCZ moves progressively northwards, bringing rain to large parts of West Africa. However, it retreats to the south from about July to December, extending the spell of dry conditions across most parts of West Africa. The north–south oscillation of the airmasses, the ITCZ, and consequently, rain, undergirds the discernable latitudinal variation in West Africa's environmental conditions and vegetation, which range from the Sahara Desert in the north through the Sahel, to the Savanna, on to the rain forest, and finally to the coastal plains along the Atlantic Ocean.

By world standards, West Africa does not seem to be a densely populated region. With a land area of some 6 million square kilometers (about five-sixths the area of the United States) and a population of 236 million in 2000, the arithmetic density of West Africa is 39 persons per square kilometer, compared to China's 131 persons per square kilometer, and India's 309 persons per square kilometer. In fact the population of all the sixteen countries of West Africa is just about a quarter of China's or India's (World Bank 2002a and 2002b). Travel across West Africa and you would be readily impressed by its vast open spaces, especially in countries such as Mali, Niger, and Mauritania. But a closer look at the soil would quickly reveal the extent of soil infertility that many West Africans have to grapple with. Not surprisingly, the average arable land per capita for West African countries for 1997–1999, for instance, stood at a mere 0.25 hectares, with a range of 0.06 hectares in Liberia to 0.52 in Togo (the comparable figures for China and India are 0.10 hectares and 0.17 hectares, respectively). The soils of West Africa's Sahel and the Savanna zones are loaded with iron and aluminum, with few nutrients. The forest soils, though relatively better, are excessively leached, and highly susceptible to sun baking, erosion, and nutrient depletions, especially following the removal of the forest cover that provides much of the decaying biomass that enriches the soil. West Africa's high temperatures, and to some extent high humidity, create natural breeding grounds for a variety of disease-carrying organisms, including mosquitoes, fleas, flies, worms, and snails, which are implicated in the spread of yellow fever, sleeping sickness, malaria, Bilharzia, and other distressing diseases across West Africa.

History

Until quite recently, the outside world knew very little about the history of West Africa—and, indeed, of Africa, as a whole. The common misconception was that African history has little in its own right beyond the European activities. This is how Trevor Roper, once the Chair of History at Oxford University, put it: "Perhaps in the future there will be some African history to teach. But at present there is none; there is only the history of Europeans in Africa. The rest is darkness . . . and darkness is not the subject of history" (Mendonsa 2002, p. 40). This notion of a "historyless people" has almost disappeared, thanks to the recent upsurge of anti-Eurocentric scholarship. According to Davidson (1998, p. 25), "the written history of England, substantially, can be said to have begun around the same time as the written history of the Western Sudan (now West Africa)." He based this supposition on the fact that the Islamic scholar Abu Ubayd al-Bakri's *Kitab al-Masalic wa'l Mamali* (*The Book of the Routes and Realm*), which dealt with the trans-Saharan trade in West Africa, was completed in Cordoba in AD 1068—just a couple of years after the landmark Norman invasion of England (Davidson 1998, p. 25).

The history of West Africa is invariably a central part of any meaningful attempt to understand humanity's struggles to tame and survive in the vast and difficult continent of Africa, a continent believed to be the original home of the human race. Not only that, as the main source of Black African slaves, upon whose back the so-called New World was developed, West Africa holds a special place in the minds of Westerners, in both Europe and the Americas.

Early States and Empires

West Africa had strong and durable cities, states, and empires prior to the European adventure in the region. The oldest empires include the Ancient Ghana, Mali, and Songhay (or Songhai) empires. Ancient Ghana—whose real name was Wagadu, with *ghana* (or war chief) being the title of one of its kings—was located to the northwest of the modern Republic of Ghana, covering parts of present-day Mali, Mauritania, and Senegal. While the origin of Ancient Ghana remains understandably obscure, scholars place its founding date around the second or third century AD, based on traditions recorded by Islamic scholars such as Es Sadi, al Fazari, al Kwarizmi, and al Bakri. The Soninke people of Ancient Ghana (the descendents of modern Senegal) owed much of their prominence

to the trans-Saharan trade, benefiting from their strategic location at the southern end of the caravan routes from North Africa across the Sahara, and the northern end of the trading routes that emanated from the gold- and ivory-producing regions of the south. Thus, the people of Ancient Ghana traded in gold and ivory procured from the south and salt and other commodities from the north.

For thousands of years, the kings of Ancient Ghana managed to weld various groups of people into a stable state, with the king's capital, which most likely moved from one place to another, complete with markets, religious shrines, foreign merchants, and fortified royal retreats. Available records show that at the height of its prosperity—that is, before the eleventh century AD when Ancient Ghana was invaded by the Almoravids—Kumbi Selah, its capital city, located some 320 kilometers north of present-day Bamako, was indisputably the largest city in West Africa, with more than 15,000 inhabitants. Tolls and levies on traded commodities and taxes from subjugated people were used to maintain an army and to exert law and order in the empire. Berber Muslims from the north mounted a series of invasions against Ancient Ghana around AD 1050, ruining its farmland and disrupting its trading link with the north. These invasions eventually led to the disintegration of the empire by AD 1098.

With the decline of Ancient Ghana came the upsurge and development of the Mali Empire. Originally located just east of Ancient Ghana, the Mali Empire continued to expand eastward along the Niger River, conquering Jenne and Timbuktu, both of which became major centres of the empire—ironically, the latter has somehow become the epitome of geographic isolation in the minds of many Westerners.

Writings of the famous Moroccan-born Islamic traveler and scholar, Ibn Batuta, who visited Mali in the mid-fourteenth century when the empire was at it zenith, indicate that the rulers of the Mali Empire were staunch Muslims who routinely participated in the annual pilgrimage to Mecca. The Mandingoes Muslims who ruled the empire were closely related to the Soninke of Ancient Ghana. Gold continued to be the most important export from the area, and formed the basis of Mali's wealth. In a nutshell, the people of Mali duplicated the achievements of Ancient Ghana, and exceeded them. However, it is important to note that while the active history of Ancient Ghana covered about a thousand years, that of Mali spanned only about two centuries, in which three main periods of succession occurred. The first major one was under Sundianta (1235–1260), who is known to have founded the Mali Empire. The second was under Mansa Sakuru (1298–1308); Ibn Khaldum, the great North African historian, once noted that under Mansa

Sakuru, Mali became so mighty that all the nations of West Africa stood in awe of its success. The third major period was under Mansa Kankan Musa (1312–1337), who again extended the power and influence of the empire (Davidson 1998, p. 41). By the early 1400s, Mali had outgrown its political and military strength and became highly vulnerable to invasion. The Tuareg invaded Timbuktu in 1431, and by the end of the century, Mali's rulers had lost control of the empire.

As the Mali Empire declined, other powers emerged, the noteworthy among which was that of the Songhay people of the Middle Niger, whose empire peaked around the mid-fifteenth century with the city of Goa as its principal centre of trade, wealth, and power. Other notable states and kingdoms that emerged in West Africa, prior to the European skirmish and the eventual colonization of the region, include those of the Mossi, Kanem-Bornu, Hausa, Bamabara, Wolof, Oyo, Yoruba, Benin, Dahomey, Ashanti, Bono, and the Awkamu.

Contacts with Europeans: Trade, Slavery, and Colonization

European involvement in West Africa is generally traced to the early fifteenth century, when Portuguese explorers arrived in that region. The European adventure in West Africa did not merely interrupt the path of West Africans' civilization, it irreversibly changed their entire cultural, social, economic, and political systems. By the early seventeenth century, European trading ships were arriving at all the major West African coasts, from the coast of present-day Senegal in the west to Nigeria in the east. But the Europeans were yet to subdue militarily the West African states they encountered, as the latter was highly capable of repelling the former's threats of violence. And, as the accounts of Davidson and many other historians indicate, added to the perils of the ocean travel, the fevers and malarias of the mosquito-infested interior, and the fierce resistance and ambushes of the natives, were the risk of intense rivalry and fighting between the Europeans themselves. The Portuguese, who held the upper hand over the English and French, during the initial years were overtaken by the Dutch, with the capture of Portugal's Elmina Castle in the Gold Coast (present-day Ghana), which was the most active scene of European trade in West Africa during the sixteenth and seventeenth centuries. Notwithstanding the ensuing intra-European battles and native resistance, the European merchants kept coming to West Africa, due primarily to pressures from powerful political and commercial interests in Europe. With so much at stake—in terms of the procurement of gold,

ivory, and, ultimately, slaves, from West Africa—it did not take much for the Europeans to see the need for peaceful partnerships, a realization that culminated in the infamous Berlin Conference of 1884–1885, by which virtually all of Africa was divided up among the imperial powers of Europe.

The slave trade did not become a regular part of the European trade until after about 1620, when the Europeans got established in the Americas and needed more laborers to work on their budding mines and plantations. It is hard to find anything that more greatly undermined the basic humanity of both West Africans and Europeans during their contact centuries ago—and, indeed, continues to conjure emotional and sometimes vitriolic debate if not confrontation, among these two groups—than the enterprise of slavery. Common, unsophisticated, and racially motivated allegations of Blacks' inferiority, slavish mentality, and lack of self-esteem, and of Whites' hyper-cruelty, hypocrisy, and proclivity toward human exploitation are routinely tied to the trans-Atlantic slave trade. Contrary to what many believe, Europeans were not the first to engage in the trading and exporting of Black African slaves. The work of Chancellor Williams (1987), for instance, shows that Arab imperialism and slave trade in Africa preceded that of Europeans by centuries. Still, there is no denying that the version of slavery perpetrated by the Europeans in (West) Africa surpassed all the others in its sheer volume and brutality. Nobody knows for sure how many Blacks were shipped from Africa, primarily from West Africa, but common estimates range from 10 to 15 million people, with millions perishing not only in their capture and transshipment, but also from hard work and maltreatment in the mines and plantations of the Americas (Rodney 1974).

The key to understanding how the slave trade began and persisted as long as it did, according to the insightful analysis of Davidson (1998), lies in the slave system that existed in West Africa prior to the Europeans. African chiefs and kings, as in other parts of the world then, regularly turned war captives and some lawbreakers into slaves, who were sometimes sold, exchanged, or simply given away as gift to other chiefs, kings, and elites of society. And with time it was not exceedingly difficult for the Europeans to persuade the African chiefs and kings to sell these slaves or barter them in exchange for European goods, especially for firearms upon which the very survival of the African kingdoms and their kings came to depend.

Quite expectedly, European incursions and slave trade faced stiff resistance and battles in many parts of West Africa; perhaps the most notable were those mounted by the Ashanti warriors of the Gold Coast against the British. Yet, the lure of European goods (e.g., alcohol and firearms) was far too strong for many people to resist. The proliferation of firearms across West Africa turned out to be awfully detrimental to the Europeans themselves, and perhaps no one captured the conundrum faced by the Europeans in this regard better than William Bosman, a Dutchman then living in the Elmina Castle in the Gold Coast: "[W]e sell them very great quantities, and in doing this we offer them a knife with which to cut our own throat" (Davidson 1998, p. 191).

As the demand of West African goods and slaves increased over the years, so did inter-tribal wars, slave raids, and invasions across the region. By the early seventeenth century, West Africans were squarely in the midst of the "profitable" triangular trade, which entailed the shipment of goods such as cotton, alcohol, and firearms from European ports for sale in West Africa, from where the Europeans procured slaves for sale in the plantations of the Americas in exchange for sugar, tobacco, rum, and other products, which were then shipped to Europe.

In the second half of the nineteenth century, after more than four hundred years of contact, the Europeans managed to lay claim to nearly all the lands of West Africa, following the Treaty of Berlin in 1885. Only Liberia was a sovereign state in the region at the beginning of the twentieth century. Apart from Guinea-Bissau and Cape Verde, which came under Portuguese control, West Africa, comprised four British colonies—Nigeria, Ghana, Sierra Leone, and Gambia—which lie separated from one another, and nine amorphously contiguous French colonies. In 1957, Ghana became the first independent nation in West Africa, spurring a series of liberation struggles that resulted in the emancipation of the entire region by the early 1970s, under the leadership of such notables as Kwame Nkrumah of Ghana, Ahmed Sékou Touré of Guinea, Nnamdi Azikiwe of Nigeria, and Leopold Sédar Senghor of Senegal.

Economic Development

Despite more than five centuries of contact with Europeans and other societies around the world, through trade and the diffusion of innovations, West Africa (and indeed, Africa), is still one of the most marginalized and least developed regions of the world. West Africa continues to experience a substantial decline in its relative position in terms of world trade, investment, production, consumption, and access to computers and Internet connectivity. The region's exports are still dominated by minerals

and agricultural commodities such as coffee in the cases of Côte d'Ivoire and Guinea; cocoa in Ghana and Côte d'Ivoire; and maize in Benin and Burkina Faso. Despites the primacy of agriculture, West Africa still relies heavily on food imports and sometimes even food aid, as the rate of population growth outstrips that of food production in nearly all parts of the region.

Another striking feature of the West African economy is the relative weakness of the manufacturing sector. By 2000, with the exception of Senegal, Côte d'Ivoire, and Sierra Leone, the contribution of the manufacturing sector to the respective gross domestic products (GDPs) of West African countries was generally below 15% (World Bank 2002b). With both Sierra Leone and the Côte d'Ivoire engrossed in civil wars, this figure is likely to shrink. In 2000, the average gross national income (GNI) per capita for the sixteen countries stood at a mere US$385, and ranged from a low of US$130 in Togo to a high of US$1,330 in Côte d'Ivoire. And, despite some improvements in the education of women and access to healthcare, most West African countries are burdened with high infant mortality rates (IMR). In 2000, the estimated average IMR for the sixteen countries was as high as 98 deaths per 1,000 live births; the worst rates were recorded in Sierra Leone (154), Guinea Bissau (126), and Niger (114). The region's problems are certainly not confined to the economic and social spheres alone; they have inevitably spilled over to its natural and living environments, with acute levels of deforestation, desertification, soil erosion, and serious deterioration of sanitary conditions occurring in nearly all parts of the region. In recent years, however, it is the unfortunate proliferation of civil war in such places as Sierra Leone, Liberia, and Côte d'Ivoire that is posing the greatest hindrance to the economic development of West Africa, as a growing number of people are thrown into precarious refugee situations.

The economic and geopolitical conditions in West Africa reflect and reinforce the region's long-standing dependence on the West in a core-periphery framework, hardened not only through colonialism and neo-colonialism, but also through the Cold War, and, critics have argued, through the World Bank- and International Monetary Fund-sponsored Structural Adjustment Programmes.

The geopolitical boundaries of West Africa are a product of colonialism, with some minor tinkering in the post-colonial period. This made-in-Europe boundary framework paid minimal attention to the West African cultural mosaic at the time, lumping people who had histories of strife together, and elsewhere, such as along the Ghana–Togo border, splitting people of common cultural bonds into different countries.

It is not hard to see how this could undermine the geopolitical stability of these countries. Furthermore, the railroads and high-standard roads in all the coastal countries, from Senegal to Nigeria, still bear the imprint of colonialism. One still finds a situation where these transportation networks are orientated towards the coast, from the interior, to facilitate the shipment of goods to Europe, with minimal intra–West African connectivity. The transportation system of the landlocked countries (that is, Niger, Mali, and Burkina Faso) are even worse, with access to ocean transportation coming only at an exorbitant price, thanks to the massive spatial segmentation wrought by the political boundaries.

Faced with crop failures, lack of agricultural credit, and land shortages, many rural West Africans are migrating to the cities in search of a livelihood. This familiar scene makes West Africa one of the most urbanizing regions of the world. The growing urban population, in the absence of a corresponding increase in housing and other urban facilities, has led to serious overcrowding, high traffic density, intense air and water pollution, and the spread of slums and squatter settlements in major cities such as Lagos in Nigeria, Abidjan in Côte d'Ivoire, Darker in Senegal, and Accra in Ghana.

It would certainly be disingenuous to attribute West Africa's development problems solely to colonialism, neo-colonialism, and other external factors, such as unfair terms of trade and the manipulations of donor countries and international financial institutions. The destructive roles of the nation-states in the region, epitomized by the growing political instability and the lack of institutional capacity; mismanagement and corruption; and disregard for human rights and the value of science and research, are all to be blamed for the economic problems of the region. While corruption is not peculiar to West Africa, nor to Africa, it is without a doubt one of the leading endogenous problems undermining the region's economic development. Given the long-standing David-and-Goliath-like struggles between West Africans (and indeed Africans) and the West in the global capitalist system, it is not surprising that an increasing number of scholars, including Davidson (1994), Manuel Castells (2000), and Bingu Wa Mutharika (1995), are calling for some form of self-reliance in Africa's development. A carefully crafted endogenous development approach—with a reasonable infusion of external scientific know-how—couched in regional cooperation and a diversified economy that blurs the usual dichotomy between agriculture and industry and eschews the detrimental reliance on monocropping and external aid, would help alleviate West Africa's development malaise. The recent strengthening of

democratic governance (albeit among a handful of countries, most notably, Ghana); the increasing regional cooperation through ECOWAS; and ongoing improvements in national and intra-regional infrastructure (for example, the construction of the region's trans-coastal and trans-Saharan highways), point to good development prospects in West Africa.

In the final analysis, though, viewed from the standpoint of "development," measured primarily with economic indicators such as GDP or GNI per capita, economic growth rates, and stock market capitalization, West Africa could not be seen in much positive light. Some would even assert categorically, as did Eugene Mendonsa (2002, p. 473), that "[d]evelopment in West Africa has failed." However, the only way the notion of development can even purport to hold any universal applicability is to move beyond its present individualistic, materialistic, and economistic underpinnings to incorporate the rich complexities of non-economized societies, such as those of West Africa. It is only through such a holistic interpretation of development that the true wealth of West Africa can be appreciated by outside observers.

JOSEPH MENSAH

See also Benin; Burkina Faso; Colonialism: History; Colonialism: Legacies; Cote d'Ivoire; Economic Community of West African States (ECOWAS); Gambia; Ghana; Guinea; Guinea-Bissau; Liberia; Mali; Mauritania; Niger; Nigeria; Nkrumah, Kwame; Senegal; Sénghor, Leopold; Sierra Leone; Structural Adjustment Programmes (SAPs); Touré, Sékou; Togo; West Africa: International Relations; West African Monetary Union (WAMU)

References and Further Reading

Bayart, Jean-François Bayart, ed. *The State in Africa: The Politics of the Belly.* Translated by Mary Harper, Christopher Harrison, and Elizabeth Harrison. London and New York: Longman, 1993.

Castells, Manuel. *End of Millennium.* Oxford, UK: Blackwell, 2000.

Crowder, Michael. *West Africa: An Introduction to its History.* London: Longman, 1977.

Davidson, Basil. *The Black Man's Burden: Africa and the Crisis of the Nation-State.* New York: Times Books, 1994.

———. *West Africa: Before the Colonial Era: A History to 1850.* London and New York: Longman, 1998.

De Blij, H. J. and Peter O. Muller. *Geography: Realms, Regions and Concept, 2000.* New York: Wiley, 2000.

Ghai, Dharam. "African Development in Retrospect and Prospect." In Dharam Ghai, ed., *Renewing Social and Economic Progress in Africa.* London: Macmillan Press; New York: St. Martin's Press, 2000, pp. 1–21.

Mabogunje, Akin L. "The Land and Peoples of West Africa." In J. F. Ajayi and Michael Crowder, eds., *History of West Africa.* London: Longman, 1976, pp. 1–32.

Mendonsa, Eugene L. *West Africa: An Introduction to Its History, Civilization and Contemporary Situation.* Durham, NC: Carolina Academic Press, 2002.

Osae, T. A. and S. N. Nwabara. *A Short History of West Africa.* London: University of London Press, 1968.

Rodney, Walter. *How Europe Underdeveloped Africa.* Washington, DC: Howard University Press, 1974.

Wa Mutharika, Bingu. *One Africa, One Destiny: Towards Democracy, Good Governance and Development.* Harare, Zimbabwe: Sapes, 1995.

William, Chancellor. *The Destruction of Black Civilization: Great Issues of Race from 4500 BC to 2000 AD.* Chicago: Third World Press, 1987.

World Bank. *African Development Indicators—2002.* Washington DC: Author, 2002a.

———*World Development Indicators—2002.* Washington DC: Author, 2002b.

WEST AFRICA: INTERNATIONAL RELATIONS

In order to better understand the international relations of West Africa, it is necessary to underscore some of the most salient characteristics that help give shape to the subregion's interactions with states and non-state actors within the external environment. As with the rest of Africa, West Africa's political balkanization is one of its dominant characteristics. The net result of European colonization, the subregion is made up of seventeen sovereign states that are as diverse as they are similar. They are Benin, Burkina Faso, Cape Verde, Cote d'Ivoire, Gambia, Ghana, Guinea, Guinea-Bissau, Liberia, Mali, Mauritania, Niger, Nigeria, Senegal, Sierra Leone, and Togo—with Cameroon on the margins. There are vast differences not only in the population and territorial sizes of the countries but also in their military and economic powers. For instance, at about 130 million people, Nigeria's population is substantially higher than the combined total of all the rest of the other regional states. There are also huge differences in physical size between some of the larger states of the region such as Mali (461,389 square miles), Mauritania (432,000 square miles), Niger (458,874 square miles), and Nigeria (356,669 square miles) as compared to some of the smaller states such as Cape Verde (1,557 square miles), Gambia (3,977 square miles), and Sierra Leone (27,925 square miles). The overall effect of such disparities in power attributes may be seen in the differential capacity of states to influence international relations and events.

In many ways, the assorted differences in physical characteristics, level of development, and military and political powers of the states tend sometimes to mask many areas of similarities. Modern West African states are all largely the artificial creations of their European colonial powers—the United Kingdom,

France, Portugal, and Spain in the case of the still disputed Western Sahara. As such, they share a legacy of non-natural boundaries and the resulting separation of relatives and communities. Largely underdeveloped, they also share characteristics of dependency to Western (especially European) political economies. While there are huge differences, the combined effects of colonial legacy, natural disasters, and poor governance structures have served to create a subregion that suffers from a high degree of indebtedness, poverty, disease, political instability, and conflict.

Despite their diversity, and differing problems, West African states have sought to overcome the negative effects of their fragmentation by seeking to build more coherent and effective economic and political structures. Weak and inadequately equipped individually to deal equally and effectively with the leading industrial states of Europe and North America, the states of West Africa have sought ways of dealing with the severe challenges posed by a seemingly hostile external environment. As such, they have resolved to work toward developing pertinent institutions and structures that would allow them collectively to address common issues ranging from conflict prevention and resolution initiatives to coordinated approaches in addressing issues of health and the economy. Nevertheless, their general dependence and weakness vis-à-vis the leading states of Europe and North America, as well as their differing priorities and national interests, have also served to impede greater commitments to collaborative activities. The net result has been that they have struggled at times to address some of the critical factors and conditions that shape their external relations. Primarily, those factors have included the need for: economic development; conflict prevention and resolution; and poverty and disease reduction and control. Let us now examine those issues by looking at each of the four separable (albeit cross-cutting) layers of international relationships involving members of the West African subregion.

Subregional Relations in West Africa

As with states in other parts of the world, member states of West Africa have a great need to interact with each other, not only in pursuit of common interests but also to address common problems. During the 1990s, ECOMOG, the regional military arm of the Economic Community of West African States (ECOWAS), became active in several countries within the region, especially in Liberia and Sierra Leone, where it provided decisive military counterbalance to the warring factions, and in Cote d'Ivoire where it has been attempting to negotiate a political solution to the problems.

To alleviate poverty, control diseases, and foment economic growth and development, governments often find it easier and more effective to do so through cooperation mechanisms. This is especially so for weak and dependent states, which not only need infusions of external financial aid, investments, materials, and skilled workforce, but also must secure them from a hostile external environment driven by competing priorities.

Hampered by persistent poverty and underdevelopment, West African states sought to improve their bargaining capacity by pooling ideas and resources and working together. This way, they hope to achieve collectively objectives that may be harder to achieve as separate nations. This was the conceptual basis of the ECOWAS, which was founded in 1975 by its member states to serve as a vehicle for economic cooperation and integration within the subregion. It was expected that with such an integrating structure, the states of West Africa would be able to overcome many of the pervasive problems that serve to retard development, such as their narrowly-based economies, heavy reliance on the export of primary products, inadequate infrastructure, low levels of resource flows from advanced countries, declining terms of trade for their tradable goods, protectionist policies of their Western trading partners, expensive transport systems, lack of sufficient skilled labor, and small domestic markets. By sharing burdens and benefits and combining resources, the states of the subregion sought to enable members not only to promote the prevention and peaceful resolution of conflicts within and between member states, but also to create a bigger and more attractive market for internal and external investment. It would also allow them to have a stronger voice in their relations with external actors and at international forums.

Unfortunately, the colonial historical experiences of the West African subregion have also created tensions and divisions among the member states. Deep suspicions and rivalries, particularly along the Francophone and Anglophone lines, have served as a crucial seam. Not surprisingly, there was a proliferation of overlapping subregional structures, which soon came to flounder due to their relative neglect and weakness. The impact of this colonial legacy, as well as fears about the regional dominance of Nigeria, have combined to weaken collaborative activities within the region. Nevertheless, since the late 1990s, there have been some areas of appreciable progress including health, agriculture, military, and economic policy making. Important frameworks and structures

that have been established include the West African Parliament, a subregional bank (ECOBANK), the West African Chamber of Commerce, the Federation of West African Manufacturers, a regional insurance scheme, and free movement of primary goods and handicrafts throughout the subregion.

Plans for a common West African monetary system have remained in place despite a series of delays due not only to challenges posed by the adopted convergence criteria, but also to the existence of a single monetary zone that groups Guinea Bissau and seven former French colonies—Benin, Burkina Faso, Cote d'Ivoire, Mali, Niger, Senegal and Togo—under the CFA franc. As envisioned in 2005, the currency integration exercise will take place in two phases. In the first phase, the governments of all the six non-CFA countries—Gambia, Sierra Leone, Ghana, Guinea, Liberia, and Nigeria—will adopt a single currency on July 1, 2005. The second phase will involve the integration of the CFA countries into the West African monetary union.

Relations with Other Continental States

In regard to other regional relations, West African states have continued to play important roles within the African continent. Due to residual effects of their colonial experiences and relatively weak economies, many of these relationships have been largely political. Variously, West African states played important roles in the African decolonization processes between the late 1960s and early 1990s. Although much of their roles centered on political and diplomatic support, states such as Nigeria, Ghana, and Guinea were at the forefront of efforts that culminated in the establishment of the Organization of African Unity in 1963 and its successor, the African Union, in 2002. They provided not only academic scholarships and aid to affected Africans but also substantial financial and material support to liberation movements from Angola, Mozambique, Namibia, South Africa, and Zimbabwe. For its part, Nigeria worked very closely with the Front Line States as they battled to dislodge the apartheid system in South Africa.

Very little formal inter-African trade takes place. In 2004, such trade accounted for only about 10% of Africa's total exports and imports. West African trade with other African countries follows similar patterns to those of the rest of Africa. This is with the possible exception of Nigeria, whose light manufactures and petroleum products find their way legally and illegally into other African markets. This is partly due to the nature of West African states'

integration into the global economy as competing producers of raw materials for European markets. Other important reasons for the low level of intra-African trade include weak infrastructure, especially the comparatively feeble transport communications systems, encumbering trade policies, non-convertible currencies, high political instability, poor telecommunications networks, low worker availability and retention, poor governance structures (particularly, the lack of the rule of law, transparency, accountability, and severe corruption); and ethnic, cultural, and linguistic diversity. The introduction of the New Partnership for Africa's Development (NEPAD) has coincided with a growing importance of intra-African trade. Though criticized by some for reflecting similar patterns of global inequality as previous arrangements—particularly in the substitution of real partnership with impunity and dictation by one of the "partners"—NEPAD has remained the single most important instrument available for Africa's economic revitalization and recovery in the short and medium terms.

Relations with Global Powers and Beyond the Continent

As with the rest of Africa, West African states have worked hard to develop and nurture their relations with non-African states, particularly Western Europe, North America, and other members of the OECD and the Commonwealth. For most, however, their flexibility and ability to shape their external relations have been severely delimited by the political and economic strictures inherited by the post-colonial state. With economies, infrastructure, and even politics that were often configured to suit the political and economic interests and policy preferences of their former Western colonizing powers, and a post-colonial international environment dominated by the West, most West African states have labored to stay relevant in the post–Cold War global politics. While some such as Ghana, Guinea, and Nigeria have managed (more or less) to pursue relatively independent foreign policies, most others have struggled to extricate themselves from what appears to be lingering post-colonial influences. Perhaps the most enduring relationship between the states of the subregion and the world beyond Africa has been that of the former French colonies and France. Like many other former French colonies, francophone West African states (with the exception of Guinea) were linked to France in terms of preferential trade arrangements, military defense pacts, and monetary stability arrangements. Not surprisingly,

French influence not only remains palpable in the francophone areas but there is also a growing source of tensions and instability as occurred during 2004 in Cote d'Ivoire.

Although many of the relationships cultivated by West African states have been driven by the need to foment economic development, major global issues such as the Cold War and the latest US concern, the "war against terrorism," have also affected West African states—indeed, so much so that NATO Commander General James Jones described West Africa as "where the action is." Through various security initiatives aimed at conflict prevention and management, US and European political and military leaders have crisscrossed Africa to push collaborative military programs aimed at training and equipping African security forces. Driven by the increasingly vital and fast-emerging oil resources in the Gulf Basin states (anchored by Nigeria)—which include Angola, Cameroon, Equatorial Guinea, Gabon, São Tomé, and Principe—as well as the growing influence of rabid Moslem fundamentalism, the West African subregion has attracted renewed attention from US political and security strategists.

Western governments are particularly concerned about growing political instability and Moslem extremism in an area whose vast oil resources are increasingly important as an alternative to the even more volatile oil-producing Middle East. Nigeria, the principal oil producer and dominant political economy in the area, has been particularly hard-hit by political instability due not only to its deep societal cleavages and growing criminality, but also to interactive effects of rapid economic decline and unprecedented poverty. The ensuing political, communal, and religious violence has imposed huge costs on lost human lives and property. The recourse to the Islamic Sharia legal system in twelve of Nigeria's northern states has served to further worsen domestic tensions at both national and local levels. To some US political and military strategists, much of this has also been exacerbated by Osama bin Laden's designation of Nigeria as one of his top-priority targets. Although the poor human rights record and endemic corruption of the Nigerian government have limited direct assistance to that country, there is strong evidence of increasing prioritisation of both Nigeria and West Africa by the United States and her Western allies. Indeed, since September 11, 2001, African and US security-based partnerships have been growing. An example of these is the Pan-Sahel Initiative (PSI) under which military forces from Chad, Mali, Mauritania, and Niger received specialized antiterrorism training.

Beleaguered by pervasive economic decline and high indebtedness, ethnic tensions and political instability,

new and significant threats from AIDS and narcotics, severe deterioration of infrastructure, and declining or low foreign exchange earnings, West African states have looked to Western Europe and North America for relief and development assistance as well as more balanced partnerships. The New Partnership for Africa's Development (NEPAD) instrument has been touted by some of its supporters as a mechanism for achieving such a relationship. Various other arrangements—such as the African Growth and Opportunity Act (AGOA) offered by the United States, the Commission for Africa by the British government, and the revised Lome Agreement with the European Community—have also been established over the recent past as potentially effective mechanisms for enabling these countries to break the cycle of underdevelopment and poverty. For instance, under the Lome IV Agreement regime, Europe would provide general trade and aid benefits to African, Caribbean, and Pacific (ACP) countries through negotiated differential relationships with these countries. As part of the negotiations in pursuit of the proposed Economic Partnership Agreements (EPAs) with the European Community, West African states adopted a six-point plan in their August 4, 2004, meeting in Accra, which outlines the subregion's medium- and short-term ambitions:

- The progressive establishment, in accordance with WTO rules, of a free trade zone between ECOWAS and the European Community for a period of twelve years, starting January 1, 2008;
- The need to accord priority to development and poverty reduction;
- Cooperation in trade-related matters;
- Deepening of the integration process in West Africa;
- Enhancement of competitiveness: capacity building and upgrading; and
- Improved access for West African exports to the EU market.

Despite these lofty goals, some critics maintain that the new thinking on aid to the poorer regions of the world continues to miss the point on what is actually needed by these states to achieve effective transformative development. As such, they insist that the self-styled Economic Partnership Agreements (EPAs)—reciprocal free-trade agreements due to come into effect by 2008—are unlikely to provide the palliative needed for the transformation of West Africa's weak economies. Indeed, under the current negotiation framework, which split the ACP states into six regional groupings, West Africa is forced to negotiate its own unique relationship with Europe—thereby further weakening the putative collective bargaining strength they had as part of the ACP. There are growing

concerns that the EPAs will actually further open European investment and trade access into African markets in areas that these countries had resisted vigorously during the 2003 World Trade Organization negotiations.

Also important for many West African states are their relations with international financial and trading institutions such as the International Monetary Fund, the World Bank, and the World Trade Organization. In the two decades between 1985 and 2005, virtually all of the states in the subregion have come under the economic reform programs pushed by these institutions.

While West African external economic relations have been dominated by their interactions with Western Europe and North America, the subregion also enjoys important economic relationships with East Asian, Southeast Asian, South Asian, and Latin American states. Indeed, economic relations with countries such as Japan, China, Brazil, and Malaysia have grown in significance over the past two decades. All that notwithstanding, West Africa states have strong and long-standing political or cultural relationships with states of the global South including East Asia, Southeast Asia, South Asia, Latin America, the Middle East, Eastern Europe, and the Caribbean. The collaborative political processes date back not only to the liberation struggles during the colonial era, but also to the early post-colonial period with the Group of 77 and the Nonaligned Movement.

most West African states (including Cote d'Ivoire, Ghana, Guinea, Liberia, Nigeria, and Sierra Leone) actually regressed in terms of their per capita income and quality of life during the last two decades of the twentieth century.

All that notwithstanding, West Africa (through ECOWAS and the embryonic African Union) continues to represent one of Africa's most promising prospects for transformative development. The end of the Cold War ushered in a new era in West African relations with the world beyond the African continent. Although significant and steady economic decline of the late 1970s and 1980s had brought about demands for significant institutional and structural changes through much of the continent, the post–Cold War political climate served not only to intensify the domestic pressures, but also to remove external political support and protection for non-performing governments. The combined net effect was a dramatic shift in the formal, official attitude within the subregion toward conflict management and resolution, economic growth, development, and political liberalization and democracy.

UFO OKEKE UZODIKE

See also Benin; Burkina Faso; Cameroon; Cote d'Ivoire; Economic Community of West African States (ECOWAS); Ethnic Conflicts: West Africa; Gambia, The; Ghana; Guinea; Guinea-Bissau; Liberia; Mali; Mauritania; Niger; Nigeria; Senegal; Sierra Leone; Togo; West Africa: History and Economic Development; West African Monetary Union (WAMU)

West Africa's International Relations: Prospects for the Future

Generally, ECOWAS has failed to live up to expectations. The member states have been fraught with internal problems such as political instability, pervasive mismanagement and corruption, human rights abuses, lack of transparency and accountability, a culture of leadership impunity, and the suffocation of civil society. Weakened by these internal as well as many other external factors, ECOWAS has generally struggled for relevance and effectiveness due to the absence of adequate commitment on the part of the political leadership. Despite a growing appearance of commitment at the turn of the twenty-first century, many of its integration schemes have remained rhetorical and administrative chimeras. The net effect of these problems and failures has been palpable increases in poverty, criminality, prostitution, corruption, waste, disease, environmental decay, and societal ills and conflict. Indeed, it is an objective fact that

References and Further Reading

Adekeye, A. *Liberia Civil War: Nigeria, ECOMOG, and Regional Security in West Africa.* Boulder, CO: Westview Press, 2002.

Adekeye, A. and R. Ismail, eds. *West Africa's Security Challenges: Building Peace in a Troubled Region.* Project of the International Peace Academy, 2004.

Aning, Emmanuel K. *Managing Regional Security in West Africa: ECOWAS, ECOMOG, and Liberia.* Copenhagen, Denmark: Centre for Development Research, 1994.

———. *The International Dimensions of Internal Conflict: The Case of Liberia and West Africa.* Copenhagen, Denmark: Centre for Development Research, 1997.

McGowan, Patrick J. and Philip Nel. *Power, Wealth and Global Equity: An International Relations Textbook for Africa*, 2nd ed. Lansdowne, South Africa: UCT Press, 2002.

Nwokedi, Emeka. *Politics of Democratization: Changing Authoritarian Regimes in Sub-Saharan Africa.* Boulder, CO: Westview Press, 1994.

———. *Regional Integration and Regional Security: ECOMOG, Nigeria and the Liberian Crisis.* Bordeaux, France: Centre d'Etude d'Afrique Noire, 1992.

Obiozor, George A., Adebayo O. Olukoshi, and C. I. Obi. *West African Regional Economic Integration: Nigerian Policy Perspectives for the 1990s.* Lagos, Nigeria: NIIA, 1994.

Schwab, Peter. *Designing West Africa: Prelude to Twenty-First Century Calamity.* New York: Macmillan, 2004.

Sesay, A., ed. *Civil Wars, Child Soldiers and Post Conflict Peace Building in West Africa.* Ibadan, Nigeria: College Press, 2003.

Shaw, Tim and J. Okolo. *The Political Economy of Foreign Policy in ECOWAS.* New York: St. Martin's Press, 1994.

Uche, Chibuike U. *The Politics of Monetary Sector Cooperation Among Economic Community of West African States Members.* Washington, DC: World Bank Institute, 2001.

WEST AFRICAN ECONOMIC AND MONETARY UNION (WAEMU)

(See West African Monetary Union [WAMU])

WEST AFRICAN MONETARY UNION (WAMU)

Origins

The West African Monetary Union (WAMU), now called the West African Economic and Monetary Union (WAEMU), was created by the Dakar Treaty of January 10, 1994, which formally came into effect on August 1, 1994. Comprising eight francophone countries in West Africa—Benin, Burkina Faso, Guinea-Bissau, Ivory Coast, Mali, Niger, Senegal, and Togo—WAEMU has its origins in 1895, when France, the colonial power, decided for administrative purposes to centralize the administration of its colonies in West Africa. The administrative capital chosen was Dakar, Senegal. A more defining characteristic of this consolidation was the introduction in 1945 of a common currency for all the countries in the zone, the *Franc de la Communauté Financière d'Afrique* (The Franc of the African Financial Community or the CFA Franc). The CFA was and still is backed by the French treasury and linked to the French franc at a fixed rate of exchange. Over the years, the CFA has gone through several bouts of devaluation. It was after the last devaluation, on January 10, 1994, that the countries in the group decided to transform what was then essentially a currency area to a monetary union—the West African Economic and Monetary Union (WAEMU).

The objectives as spelled out in the charter are:

1. To reinforce the competitiveness of the economic and financial activities of Member States in the context of an open and rival market and a rationalized and harmonized juridical environment;
2. To ensure the convergence of the macroeconomic performances and policies within the institution of a multilateral control procedure; and
3. To create a common market, based on the free circulation of people, goods and services, and capital.

Members of the union have a common central bank, Central Bank of the West African States (BCEAO), headquartered in Dakar, Senegal, which has the sole right to issue currency for the member states. The administrative structure of the union is as follows:

- The Conference of Heads of States;
- The Council of Ministers;
- The Banking Commission; and
- The Savings and Financial Markets Regional Council.

The Conference of Heads of State

As the name implies, the Conference of Heads of State is the "supreme authority of the Union." It decides on additions to the Union; settles issues referred to it by the Council of Ministers; and as the supreme authority, has the final say on all matters. It meets at least once a year in ordinary sessions and as often as necessary in extraordinary sessions.

The Council of Ministers

The Council of Ministers acts as the executive arm of the Union. Each member country sends two ministers to the Council but only one of them votes. It is responsible for defining "the monetary and credit policy of the Union in order to safeguard the value of the common currency (CFA)." It also provides financing for the activities and development of the states of the Union. It deliberates on all matters affecting the union as outlined in the Treaty establishing the Union.

The Banking Commission

The Banking Commission is at the center of the banking system of the Union. It came into force on October 1, 1990, with the express goal of restructuring

the banking system and providing the conditions for uniformity and good-quality banking in the member states. Among the functions of the Commission are the following:

1. Off- and on-site inspection of banks and financial institutions;
2. Expression of views on the requests for authorization submitted by banks and financial institutions;
3. Taking of administrative measures when applicable provisions are not respected; and
4. Disciplinary sanctions according to the gravity of the infraction committed.

The Commission prepares Annual Reports on the banking conditions of the Union. It has a permanent secretariat comprising the officers of its common central bank, the Central Bank of West African States (BCEAO).

The Savings and Financial Markets Regional Council

The Savings and Financial Markets Regional Council is the second arm in the goal of developing and integrating the economies of the Union through common financial and capital markets. The first arm is The Banking Commission/Central Bank. When in December 1993 the Council of Ministers decided to create the second arm, a Regional Financial Exchange, the task was delegated to the Central Bank (BCEAO), which recommended the creation of two entities under the Regional Financial Exchange structure, namely:

- The Regional Council for (Public) Savings and Financial Markets
- The Securities Exchange (*Bourse Régionale des Valeurs Mobiliers*—BRVM)

The Regional Council for Savings and Financial Markets is a public institution with the goal of overseeing the Securities Exchange and representing the general interest of the public. The Securities Exchange is a private entity but the member states own minority shares.

Successes

There is no doubt that within the context of the African continent, WAEMU and its sister organization, the Central African Economic and Monetary Union (CAEMU), have already succeeded beyond any comparable measure. The harmonization of monetary and fiscal policies among the eight countries that make up the union is very notable. Through its central bank, BCEAO, the WAEMU has been an active participant in reforming insurance, business law, and the mobilization of savings in the region. The use of a common currency has made trade among the countries easier and may thus be responsible for some modest amount of economic growth and integration. The establishment of a common securities exchange to mobilize savings and foster economic development is a laudable goal. The union has also often spoken with one voice in international fora on matters of common interest.

The Future and Its Challenges

Even as the WAEMU has become stronger over the years, there is little disagreement about the fact that this strength came from the special relationship the countries have with France and the fact that the French franc has been the anchor for the CFA franc. With Europe (and France) moving to a common currency, the *euro*, it remains to be seen whether WAEMU can survive in the new environment. Furthermore, as the rest of mostly anglophone West Africa (Ghana, Gambia, Guinea, Liberia, Nigeria, and Sierra Leone) move toward forming their own common currency area, it will be interesting to speculate on what could happen to the older WAEMU. Would the two currency areas merge into a one strong economic and monetary union, or would they compete? If they do compete, how would the smaller WAEMU fare against a more populous, economically bigger opponent? Or perhaps the WAEMU will seek to forge closer ties with its sister, the CAEMU. These are some of the challenges ahead for the WAEMU.

SAMUEL K. ANDOH

See also West Africa: History and Economic Development; West Africa: International Relations

References and Further Reading

Borna, Bertin, Commissaire de la Commission de UEMOA. "West African Economic and Monetary Union." *De La Tribune*, World Food Summit, November 13–17, 1996, Rome, Italy.

Outtara, Alassane D. *The West African Economic and Monetary Union (WAEMU): Facing the Challenges of the Future.* Meeting of the External Relations Branch of the Conseil Economique et Social, France, June 30, 1998. Available: www.imf.org/external/np/speeches/1998/063098.htm

The Savings and Financial Markets Regional Council. http://www.brvm.org/en/presentation/marche.htm

"West African States: All About this Economic and Monetary Community" http://www.wbcc.fsnet.co.uk/af-was.htm

West African Monetary Union (WAMU) http://www.bceao.int/internet/bcweb.nsf/English.htm

WHITE COMMUNITY IN AFRICA

There has been long-standing European contact with Africa's northern coastline but a European presence south of the Sahara only emerged in the fifteenth century when Portugal established a sea trading route to India. The Portuguese transformed the economies of the Atlantic region by initiating the Atlantic slave trade from their trading forts and small colonies of slave traders along the African coast. These colonies of white slave traders along Africa's Atlantic coast used African agents to supply them with human beings who were shipped to Brazil and Portugal as slaves. An Atlantic trading system was built in which Africa was tied to Europe and the Americas. Portuguese penetration of the Indian Ocean had the effect of disrupting the old Muslim trading and slaving system. This precipitated a period of economic decline and decay along the East African coast because the Portuguese failed to rebuild an East African trading system equivalent to the one they had disrupted. Portuguese power was generally limited to gunshot range from their forts and only two small Portuguese colonies were planted in Africa, namely, in Angola and Mozambique. But the Portuguese made a significant cultural impact upon Africa by introducing new crops from South America, including maize, cassava, and groundnuts. These crops altered the African staple diet.

During the seventeenth and eighteenth centuries the Dutch, Danes, French, and British copied the Portuguese slaving model when establishing themselves in Africa. During this slaving period, whites were largely confined to a few forts along the Atlantic coast. The one exception to the rule was the creation by the Dutch of the Cape Colony in 1652. Africa's first significant white community was established at Cape Town to produce food for Dutch ships trading with the Dutch East Indies (Indonesia). An agricultural sector producing wheat, fruit, vegetables, and wine was established in the southwestern Cape, built upon a settlement of Dutch and German "free burgers" and the importation of slaves from Indonesia, Madagascar, and Africa. In the last years of the seventeenth century, French Huguenot refugees joined the Dutch and German settlers in the expanding Cape Colony. During the early eighteenth century these Dutch-French-German settlers began calling themselves "Afrikaners" (Africans) during a rebellion against Dutch rule. In the process of indigenising

themselves to Africa, they developed a new language called Afrikaans. Despite attempts by the Dutch authorities to restrict white colonization to the immediate vicinity of Cape Town, Afrikaners began pushing inland as *trekboers* ("migrating farmers"). The Khoi-San inhabitants of southwestern Africa were conquered and assimilated into the "coloured" group of mixed-race Afrikaans-speaking labourers. The *trekboers* adopted pastoralism (borrowing from African pastoral practices) as white settlements dispersed across the interior and effectively slipped beyond the control of Dutch authorities. By the mid-nineteenth century these Afrikaners had established white communities (and "Boer" states) as far inland as the Limpopo River. This inland white community became substantively cut off from contact with other Europeans and its socioeconomic and political practices became partially Africanized through a process of interaction and conflict with surrounding African tribes. A different sort of white community evolved around Cape Town based upon plantation agriculture (deploying slave labour up until 1833), and remaining connected to the European trading system.

The Three Types of White African Community

During the nineteenth century, Africa was divided up amongst European colonial powers, which led to three different forms of white community evolving in Africa over the next 150 years.

Firstly, small outposts of *white colonial administrators* (British, French, Belgian, Portuguese, and German) proliferated across Africa. The colonial administrators were never settlers. Instead they were transient functionaries of a foreign imperial machine, transferred to Africa as bureaucrats, magistrates, soldiers, and policemen in order to coerce and administer "the natives," or to run the plantations and mines. They returned "home" to Europe at the end of their tours of duty. These colonial administrators were always few in number (in places like Nigeria, Gold Coast, French West Africa, Tanganyika, and Uganda) and always remained culturally aloof and detached from the imperial possessions they administered. White colonial administrators congregated in small colonies in the administrative capitals, but most were dispersed to the rural "district commissioner" offices across rural Africa.

Secondly, *white colonists* settled in some African countries during the nineteenth and twentieth centuries. These colonies never attracted the large numbers of settlers seen in North America and Australasia.

Instead, white colonists tended to be dispatched to quite localized geographical areas deemed suitable for European settlement by the colonial authorities. Within these colonial possessions, white settlers became politically and economically dominant and used their power to force black and Arab populations into subservient relationships. By the mid-twentieth century, five colonial possessions contained white settler communities sizeable enough to offer resistance to the decolonisation process.

Algeria's white community of over 1 million French colons (settlers) emerged during the French colonial period (1830–1962). The first white colons arrived in the 1830s–1840s but the largest wave of settlers migrated between 1870 and 1900, mostly from France. However, large numbers of Italians, Spaniards, Maltese, and Jews were also assimilated into the Algerian white community. The colons reproduced a southern European-type agriculture (producing wheat, olives, and grapes) on fertile coastal land conquered from the Arabs. This colon community saw itself as an integral part of France—an extension of the mother country on the other side of the Mediterranean.

Angola's white community of 250,000 Portuguese grew only toward the end of the colonial period, in the 1960s, when the Salazar government launched settlement schemes to transfer Portuguese peasants and unemployed urban workers to Angola to relieve economic pressures in Portugal and to try and strengthen imperial control of Angola. Under Salazar, an extraction and plantation economy dominated by the white settlers emerged in the western parts of Angola. The white community in Portugal's other major African colony, Mozambique, never grew to the same extent as Angola's, there being only 65,000 whites in Mozambique at independence.

Rhodesia's (Zimbabwe) white community of 250,000 was largely Anglo but with a significant Afrikaner minority. White settlement began with the arrival of Anglo South Africans in the 1890 "Pioneer column." Later, Afrikaners, migrating to escape poverty after their defeat in the Boer War, became farmers in the "white highveld" area. But the largest influx of white settlers arrived from a war-ravaged Britain after World War II. They settled overwhelmingly in urban areas where they built a commercial and industrial economy based upon exploiting cheap black labour.

Kenya's white community of seventy thousand was numerically dominated by British settlers. Kenya's white community was born in 1903 when the British colonial government recruited Anglo South Africans as settlers. They were followed by a wave of post–Boer War Afrikaner migrants. Then after World War I, a government-run soldier resettlement scheme initiated a wave of British settlement during the 1920s.

Kenya's white community created a plantation economy on the "white highlands" west of Nairobi, which was built upon the exploitation of cheap black labour.

South West Africa/SWA's (Namibia) white community of 75,000 are mostly Afrikaners, although some Germans remain from the German colonial period (1884–1914). The largest wave of Afrikaner settlers arrived in the 1920s when the new South African colonial masters of SWA worked with the Portuguese authorities to transfer a community of Afrikaners out of southern Angola and into northern SWA where they established a pastoral industry based on cheap black labour. Between 1949 and 1990 SWA effectively became another South African province and the SWA white community became merely an extension of the wider South African white community—SWA whites elected representatives directly to the South African Parliament and SWA became enmeshed in the wider South African economy.

The third form of white community in Africa was called "colonialism of a special type" or "internal colonialism" by Slovo (1985). This refers to the way an *indigenised white community* emerged in South Africa that had no European "motherland" to which it could retreat in the post-colonial era. This community attempted to segregate itself from black Africans through the policy of apartheid.

The South African white community, numbering over 5 million by 1990, developed a number of characteristics seen in no other white community in Africa. Most significantly, South African whites indigenised themselves—coming to see themselves as Africans rather than as European colonials in Africa. This community developed its own cultural forms, which although derivative of northwest European forms, became autonomous and distinctively "South African." The South African white community also developed some unique internal divisions associated with a conflict between Afrikaans-speaking and English-speaking whites. South Africa's Anglo community was born of British settlement schemes (in the 1820s, 1850s, and after the Boer War) and from major nineteenth-century migrant waves generated by diamond and gold rushes that attracted settlers from Britain, Ireland, the United States, Germany, and Australia. The Witwatersrand gold rush precipitated the Boer War, which generated long-standing animosity between the Anglo and Afrikaner communities. Another unique feature of the South African white community was that, unlike other white African communities, this community included members occupying a wide array of socioeconomic status positions, including a "poor white" *lumpenproletariat,* a working class, a middle class, a professional class, and a business-capitalist

class. Significantly, white South Africans are the only Africans to have produced an indigenous capitalist class—which consequently transformed Johannesburg into an autonomous sub-metropole of capitalism. Further, following the Second World War, white South Africans created Africa's most extensive industrial complex (built upon the exploitation of cheap black labour). In consequence, by the end of the twentieth century, 90% of white South Africans were urbanized. The South African white population is also a highly multicultural community, containing (in addition to Afrikaners and Anglos) large sub-cultures of Portuguese-speakers, Jews, Greeks, Italians, and Germans.

The white South African community has given birth to a number of small offshoot communities in Namibia, Zimbabwe, Botswana, Zambia, and Swaziland.

Africa's White Communities Following Decolonization

The 1950s–1960s saw the British, French, and Belgian Empires dismantled in Africa. The notion of decolonization met with some resistance in those African territories containing sizeable white communities because these communities feared for their fate under governments dominated by black Africans or Arabs. In consequence, armed conflicts broke out in these territories.

Algeria was the first African state to experience the outbreak of a guerrilla war aimed at overthrowing the colonial order. A war waged by Algerian nationalists from 1954 to 1962 saw bombs planted in the cities, colon farms attacked, and French schools burned down. It was a conflict that destabilized not only Algeria, but the French state itself. The colons tried to convince the French government to retain control of Algeria and continue to fight the nationalist guerrillas, but in 1962 France granted independence to Algeria. This precipitated a massive exodus of white colons from Algeria, many of whom moved to Corsica.

In 1951 Kenyan black nationalists launched a guerrilla struggle when white colonials in Kenya blocked an extension of black political influence. Between 1951 and 1960 a struggle aimed at overturning the Kenyan colonial order was led by the Mau Mau. Although the British army eventually triumphed over the Mau Mau guerrillas, the British thereafter opted to negotiate with the black nationalists concerning their demands and in 1963 granted independence to Kenya. As a result, many of Kenya's white community migrated to Britain, South Africa, or Australia.

Portugal refused to participate in the 1960s decolonization process. Consequently, they soon faced guerrilla struggles—beginning in Angola in 1961, followed by Portuguese Guinea in 1963, and Mozambique in 1964. These guerrilla struggles eventually led to a revolution in which the Portuguese armed forces overthrew the Lisbon government in order to end the wars. When Angola and Mozambique were granted their independence in 1975, most of the white population of these countries fled to Portugal or South Africa.

The white community in Rhodesia unilaterally declared itself independent from Britain in 1965 when it became clear the British government was not prepared to accept the continuance of white rule in Rhodesia. From 1967 the Rhodesians faced an escalating guerrilla struggle aimed at ending white rule. By 1980 the Rhodesians were beaten and Zimbabwe gained its independence. Two-thirds of Rhodesia's white community migrated to South Africa, Britain, or Australia.

In 1966 a guerrilla war was launched in Namibia aimed at ending South African control of that territory. The resultant struggle grew into a major South African-Angolan-Cuban-Namibian war during the 1980s, which became very costly for the South Africans. Namibia was granted its independence in 1990 following negotiations to end the Angolan war. No significant exodus of Namibia's white community appears to have taken place.

During the 1980s an intense anti-apartheid struggle was waged within South Africa. This led to a new constitution being negotiated that ended white rule and brought to power the first black-dominated government in 1994. Post-1994 socioeconomic changes triggered an exodus of sections of the South African white community (especially Anglos) to Britain, Australia, the United States, Canada, and New Zealand, and an internal migration of whites to the Western Cape.

P. ERIC LOUW

See also Apartheid; Namibia; South Africa; Southern Africa: History and Economic Development; West Africa: History and Economic Development

References and Further Reading

Abshire, David and Michael Samuels, eds. *Portuguese Africa: A Handbook*. London: Pall Mall Press, 1969.
Bennett, George. *Kenya Political History. The Colonial Period*. London: Oxford University Press, 1963.
Blake, Robert. *A History of Rhodesia*. London: Eyre Methuen, 1977.
Bryer, Lynne and Keith Hunt. *The 1820 Settlers*. Cape Town, South Africa: Don Nelson, 1984.

Collins, Robert. *Europeans in Africa*. New York: Knopf, 1971.

Davenport, T. R. H. and Christopher Saunders. *South Africa: A Modern History*. Basingstoke, UK: MacMillan, 2000.

De Klerk, Willem. *The Puritans of Africa. A Story of Afrikanerdom*. Harmondsworth, UK: Penguin, 1976.

Du Pisani, Andre. *SWA/Namibia. The Politics of Continuity and Change*. Johannesburg, South Africa: Jonathan Ball Publishers, 1986.

Maddox, Gregory. The *Colonial Epoch in Africa. Vol 2*. New York: Garland, 1993.

Pickles, Dorothy. *Algeria and France*. New York: Praeger, 1963.

Slovo, Joe. "Reforms and Revolution in South Africa." *Sechaba*, February 1985.

Thompson, Virginia and Richard Adloff. *French West Africa*. London: Allen & Unwin, 1958.

WILDLIFE PRESERVATION

The future of human civilization will be greatly affected by its capacity to preserve endangered species and their habitats. The variety of life on earth, ranging from mammals, birds, reptiles, and amphibians to insects, has been pushed to the brink of extinction. Conserving living resources and diverse life forms on earth is critical to human well-being not only because of their intrinsic and aesthetic worth but also because of tangible economic values derived from their proper management. In response to a growing recognition of the issue, international initiatives have been taken, since the early 1970s, to develop mechanisms for viable and sustainable conservation and use of wildlife resources and habitat.

Species Extinction

According to various estimates, our planet has been home to as many as 500 million kinds of plants, animals, and microorganisms. Some scientific research suggests that today the world contains 10–80 million species, and approximately 420 to 490 million species are estimated to have been terminated. Careful scientific examination of ecosystem destruction indicates that as many as one hundred species are driven to extinction each day with an astounding annual number of thirty-six thousand species. These species are dying up to one thousand times faster than their natural rate of extinction. This alarming rate of extinction is specifically induced by a variety of human influences.

Destroying or significantly changing just one part of interdependent relationships among species harms the entire ecosystem. The extinction of one species is followed by the elimination of other species that depended on it, since many species have developed complex mutual relationships with each other through their evolutionary processes. The destruction of the rainforests, containing approximately half of the earth's species, illustrates this intricate relationship. Each fallen tree brings down ten to thirty other species with it, including monkeys, sloths, birds, and rare orchids. Also gone are amphibians like poison dart frogs, which dwelled on the microhabitat of moss- and fungi-blanketed branches. The ground-level land is now stripped of vegetation full of microscopic bacteria and fungi, and soil becomes hard and infertile.

The destruction of a vast track of a tropical rain forest is completed after leaving only one small island of rain forest. Some species may manage to survive devastation and flee to the remaining patch of an undisturbed forest. In a tiny refugee patch overcrowded by huge immigration, food and shelter scarcity becomes severe with the increased number of species. The conversion of a large habitat to isolated islands reduces the interior of each forest patch and is inhospitable since many species cannot simply breed in small patches of forest. Species have evolved to avoid competing with one another within the same habitat. When species adapted to different ecosystems are cast together, intense competition in the pursuit of food and other scarce resources can result in species extinction.

Values

Human species are a dependent part of the delicate ecological balance, and our own existence relies on millions of life forms. The loss of species has long-term, cumulative effects for ecosystem stability with consequences that undermine conditions for our survival. The health of larger ecological communities is maintained by a variety of functions performed by all species. Ecosystems recycle the chemical elements that make up soils and atmosphere. Nutrient cycling involves actions of all life forms (plants as the base of the food chain, animals as the consumers of plants, and decomposers such as bacteria). Whereas plants produce protein and sugars in the form of leaves and fruits to be consumed by insects and birds, their clients help their reproduction by pollinating flowers.

Biological resources have been used for supplying food, pharmaceuticals, and other physical needs for humans. The economic benefits provided by our fellow species are astronomical; the origins of hundreds of products used every day are traced back to wild species. A large percentage of the world's medicines are derived directly or indirectly from wild plants and animals. Wild species with millions of years of

evolution can help human society meet the unknown challenges of the present and future generations with scientific information that could be of great practical value. Each vanishing species can mean the loss of an opportunity to expand the breadth of human potential.

In addition, wildlife and their habitat provide a rich aesthetic resource separated from their consumptive uses. Human attitudes toward wildlife have changed with the decline in tribal cultures and religions that respect the ecosystem's own needs, intrinsic values, cycles, and energies. Recognizing other organisms' right to live and preserving endangered plants and animals are ethical issues, especially with human acquisition of the means to destroy the world. Our life is spiritually enriched by the sight of a swan nudging her offspring to swim; the lumbering grizzly bear on a grassy meadow; the graceful dive of the humpback whale; and the power of an elephant.

Causes of Extinction

Many species are vanishing at an unprecedented rate due to habitat destruction, fragmentation or alteration, introduction of alien species, hunting, and deliberate extermination. In particular, habitat loss ranks as the leading cause of extinction and remains as the greatest long-term threat to many endangered species. When tropical rain forests, coral reefs, and wetlands are reduced, the existence of species living in the habitat is seriously challenged. Once forests, wetlands, rivers, islands, or grasslands are rendered inhospitable to the inhabitants, the progression toward species extinction proves difficult to reverse, since this has serious ripple effects with the loss of resources that many species depend on for their survival.

Natural habitats are destroyed by large-scale agriculture, cattle ranching, logging, home building, hydroelectric dams, oil extraction, and mining operations. A large number of landless poor people in Brazil and other developing countries are encouraged to convert natural areas to farms by their governments. Logging demands destroy forest habitats that are home to countless rare wildlife species, and local agriculture sucks watersheds dry. There are also multiple threats to migration with the destruction of summer and winter habitats and the resting spots in between.

Migration routes are either blocked or made difficult by human land use patterns. For example, Caribou in Arctic Canada face loss of their summer grazing tundra lands to oil drilling and pipeline installation; coniferous forests farther south used for their winter home are lost to the lumber industry.

A consistent decline in the population of migratory songbirds is attributed to the transformation of their summer habitats into suburbia, and the conversion of their winter habitat in Central America is lost to plantations. Habitat fragmentation limits availability of nesting sites and reduces food resources.

Massive species extinction can also be attributed to climatic change, water pollution, and atmospheric contamination. The vanishing sea ice in the Arctic marine ecosystem, affected by changes in the global climate patterns, threatens the very survival of the polar bear. The essential habitat of countless birds, marshes, and wetlands for aquatic life will be permanently flooded due to global warming. Unfavorable conditions for the survival of wild species are created by emissions of contaminants affecting air and wild land. Poisoning by DDT and other pesticides has taken a huge toll on the populations of eagles, peregrine falcon, brown pelicans, the California condor, and other types of wildlife.

The introduction of alien species into new territories, intentional or accidental, brings native species into extinction. In particular, islands are vulnerable to foreign species. This is illustrated by the extinction of 90% of all bird species in Hawaii following the influx of domestic animals that came with massive human settlement. In New Zealand, more than half the native birds faced a similar fate.

Increased hunting, fishing, and other natural resource exploitation threaten already stressed ecosystems. The world's fishery stocks have been heavily depleted by commercial fishing equipped with motorized boats and trawl nets. Commercial hunting is systematically putting many currently threatened species at further risk. The Asian medicine trade preys on bears for their gall bladders, tigers for their bones, and rhinos for their horns. The African continent's wild population of northern white rhinoceroses has declined from more than two thousand in the 1980s to a few left in Garamba National Park in the Congo. Many of the rhinoceroses in Africa have been slaughtered by poachers engaged in smuggling the horns to Asia to be sold for coveted medicinal properties.

In Virunga National Park on the eastern border of the Democratic Republic of Congo, the number of hippopotamuses was reduced from 29,000 in the early 1970s to 1,300 in 2003. The alarming number of hippos was killed to meet an increasing demand for hippo canine teeth in the illegal ivory trade. Smuggling rare, protected species generates increased profits, and international illegal wildlife trade becomes a lucrative business with stakes of 10 billion dollars a year. Wildlife trade has resulted, in particular, in a drastic decline in elephants, bears, gorillas, rhinos, tigers, jaguars, and cheetahs.

The elephant is expected to be close to extinction in many parts of Africa in the near future due to poaching and other systematic killings. Five hundred years ago, 10 million elephants populated Africa's forests and savannas. The elephant population dropped drastically, by nearly 50%, from an estimated 1.3 million in 1979 to 625,000 in 1989. The dramatic drop in the elephant population is attributed to the ivory trade, as the demand for ivory encourages the illegal poaching of the African elephant.

Whale hunting is another widely known example. One species after another were hunted town to the brink of extinction before commercial whaling was significantly reduced by the International Whaling Commission's regulations. In order to keep their whaling industry alive, however, Japan, Norway, and Iceland continue to harm whales under the guise of scientific research despite the international ban. Both Japan and Norway plan even to increase the number of whales to be hunted, ignoring international pressure. Japan expects to increase the number of whales killed per year from 260 to 380 in the Northern Pacific Ocean and from 50 to 120 along the Japanese coast on top of 400 whales in the Antarctic Ocean. Norway's parliament has called for a threefold increase in whale hunting. Encouraged by these examples, Iceland restarted its whaling industry in 2003 in a celebratory mood after a fourteen-year hiatus.

The world's current economic system does not value diverse biological resources. Wildlife is not given a high priority on the agendas of many states in the same way that oil or other mineral resources are. Expanding economic demand for more natural resources exposes many species to the spiral toward extinction. Profit-craving corporations and government development projects are responsible for the disappearance of huge natural areas.

Strategies for Preservation

Traditional conservation efforts focus on the species level through devotion of resources to the maintenance of individual species under pressure for the most imminent danger of extinction. Given insufficient knowledge and resources, only a tiny proportion of the world's endangered species can be adequately surveyed, and far less will benefit from the recovery plans. The allocation of scarce resources to the conservation of a small number of high-profile or priority species may not overall prove the most efficient, because this approach does not benefit any other species under threat. Where diversity is unquantifiable with unnamed species, large areas of habitats have to be protected. All of the species will have a better chance of survival if an entire ecological community is left intact.

The goal of conservation must be widened to embrace species everywhere because the maintenance of a complicated web of mutually dependent relationships is important to the survival of many species. Diversity within and between species is critical to the balance of the ecological complexes. Genetic variation is necessary even at the smallest level of the population in order to evolve or to adapt to changes in the environment.

At the same time, the conservation of biodiversity can be considered at different levels (such as the genetic, ecosystem, and landscape) with each level supporting the next. Ecosystem-level conservation action needs to be based on the notion that the web of mutually beneficial interactions between different life forms is woven by species living in a particular ecosystem. Methods of maintaining ecological integrity can be designed to enhance the ability of ecosystems to cope with stress and build their self-organizational capacities.

The stability of a wildlife species population is affected by the extent to which the habitat supplies the needs of that species in the complex natural communities. Dramatic changes in a physical or organic environment can have a long-range impact on species relationships. The least possible degradation for wilderness is to preserve naturalness with a lack of visible human activities. A natural process has to be allowed, to the greatest extent possible, so as to not disturb natural distributions and interactions of indigenous species of wildlife.

The long-term challenge of preventing species from becoming endangered is to protect natural habitat. The Serengeti National Park in Tanzania, the Galapagos Islands in Ecuador, and Manas Wildlife Sanctuary in India, all designated as UN World Heritage Sites, contain significant natural habitats for conserving biodiversity. To maintain representative ecosystems or important habitat types, a network of protected areas can be designated through controls on land use. In some Latin American countries, part of the rain forest was turned over to indigenous people who wanted to maintain sustainable living as common lands. Land management plans have been consolidated to maintain a critical wildlife habitat in the biologically diverse Central Andean region that is under threat from unregulated logging, poorly planned road construction, and infrastructure development. About 10% of Suriname's entire land territory was designated as a Nature Preserve. In Venezuela, a permanent title to a region of the forest, similar in size to Austria, was transferred to a native tribe.

The emerging consensus is that the larger the reserved areas, the better for conserving species. Many species need a vast range for hunting or grazing or migrate to seek their favorite weather patterns outside the borders of reserved areas. In small islands of habitats, populations are reduced below the levels that are critical to successful reproduction. A small population of Asian tigers and African lions in widely separated national parks is vulnerable to infectious disease, as exemplified by the death of one-third of the lions in the Serengeti from a viral infection in 1994.

The traditional strategy for safeguarding tigers, jaguars, cheetahs, and snow leopards in wildlife reserves was not effective for the reason that they hunt their prey over vast stretches of land. For instance, cheetahs in southern Africa traverse across six hundred square miles, and tigers in the Russian Far East reign over four hundred square miles. Even large parks would not be able to contain the fiercely territorial creatures, and they have been increasingly gunned down or poisoned by farmers, loggers, and poachers, especially when these creatures roam outside a wildlife reserve.

Since many preserved areas are too small to support all the species they shelter, establishing buffer zones and connecting corridors are essential for wide-ranging species. Reserved natural habitats can be further protected with the establishment of buffer zones and restriction of such human activity as timber cutting or cattle grazing. A strip of land can be set aside as the wildlife corridor to connect isolated patches of habitat for animals trapped in small habitat fragments by human settlement.

Mixed landscapes allow movements of species from core protected areas through land shared with humans such as tea plantations in India. In collaboration with the Indian and Nepali governments, Save the Tiger, and other groups, the World Wildlife Fund launched the Terai Arc Landscape Program in 2001 in order to turn eleven isolated preserves into one continuous, functioning ecosystem inhabited by tigers, elephants, rhinos, and deer. The World Conservation Society proposed a two thousand-mile-long chain of public and private lands needed to link the disparate populations of jaguars in the Americas. The proposed link extending from Mexico through Central America to northern Argentina would be able to save jaguar populations that lost their habitat to logging and ranching.

Resolving Human/Wildlife Conflict

In many areas of the world with rapidly growing human populations and expanding economies, designing practical solutions to resolve human/wildlife conflict is a top priority. Human/wildlife conflicts create difficulties for protecting a large number of threatened endemic species of wildlife. Wild species are often unfairly blamed for the destruction of agricultural lands and even food shortages as well as loss of human life. Natural habitat loss has been the main reason for the encroachment of zebras and other wild herbivores along with their predators such as lions on pasture lands for domestic livestock.

Wildlife, especially in densely populated parts of the world, is under extreme threat, largely because protected areas have become too small to meet the ecological needs of the animals. Elephant ranges have contracted with the extended use of forests and lands that were designated unsuitable even for agriculture as well as the rapid human population growth. Damage to crops is often caused by the expansion of human activities near or into elephant habitats or migration corridors.

Elephants invariably lose conflicts with the destruction and degradation of large areas of habitats. Hundreds of elephants are killed each year in Sri Lanka because they enter agricultural land. Kenya has been trying to mitigate conflict arising from elephant destruction of agricultural lands by moving four hundred elephants to a more suitable habitat. Although the project is innovative, it faces such challenges as insufficient space in designated reserve areas and costs involved in translocation of these huge creatures. To save elephants would require managing them across landscapes.

Human/wildlife conflict can be managed by the optimal use of land. By realizing the benefit from living harmoniously with their wild neighbors, local residents can become partners. A non-destructive economic role can be fashioned in integrating local people's needs. Saving threatened species from extinction requires collaborative projects with local scientists and educators as well as villagers and the park administration.

In collaboration with local communities in Kenya, the American Wildlife Foundation has been trying to identify key habitats for migratory wildlife and critical zones for human economic activities. Conservation priorities were determined based on the patterns of elephant movements in relation to the location of water and vegetation. This information is used to manage the daily occurrence of wildlife/human conflict with changes in land use patterns.

Trees or tall thatch grass can be used as cover by tigers prior to being harvested. The recovery of forests and grasslands brings back wild pigs, deer, and other tiger prey, reducing disturbance to farmers. In Southern Nepal's Bagmara Forest, locals directly benefit

from the return of tigers, elephants, and rhinos with the growing number of tourists who come to see the wildlife. The success results from a tree nursery set up with the help of the World Wildlife Fund and the King Mahendra Trust for Nature Conservation.

National Parks

Granting reserve status would be more effective before any massive deforestation. National parks and reserves should be large enough to ensure the conservation of important ecosystems on adjacent land. An alarming decline in the number of species is reported in all national parks but the largest ones; this is largely related to insufficient space for all the inhabitants.

Setting aside larger areas for protection in developing countries may not be politically and economically feasible without the financial support of developed countries. The deforestation of the Virunga Volcano ecosystem by Rwandan farmers in the early part of 2004 destroyed mountain gorilla habitats that had been preserved over the past thirty years. Outside support is needed to protect Virunga National Park, which supports over half of the world's seven hundred mountain gorillas.

Some national parks, in particular, with pristine stretches of rain forests, have become one of the fastest growing tourist destinations. The government of Indonesia created a park in West Java to protect the only viable populations of Javan gibbon, leaf monkey, and a host of other endemic plants and animals. Peru's Manu National Park and Biosphere Reserve houses a variety of plant and animal life, including monkeys, reptiles, birds, and insects. As one of the largest, least touched reserves in the world, Manu offers its inhabitants ample room for sustained growth, but some species are still in danger due to human intrusion.

International Conservation Efforts

In protecting wildlife and wild lands, expertise and funds can be poured into conservation projects, including a direct purchase and management of habitat for rare and endangered species. The World Wildlife Fund has worked with partners in the southwestern Amazon to establish protected areas and conserve natural resources, culminating in the official recognition of Manu National Park in 1973. A more recent accomplishment is the approval of a ten-year plan to create a network of protected areas almost twice as large as any US national park with a multi-million dollar Amazon fund established by the World Wildlife Fund in 2004.

The Indonesian government recently established Tesso Nilo National Park on the island of Sumatra (originally slated for logging) in order to preserve the park's unmatched biodiversity. In support of the government's initiatives, the World Wildlife Fund has been negotiating with logging companies to increase the acreage of the new park, which is inhabited by endangered Sumatran tigers and elephants and has a plant diversity twice as high as that of the Amazon. In collaboration with Conservation International and other international and national environmental organizations, the World Wildlife Fund purchased 147,500 acres of biologically rich temperate rain forest in southern Chile's Valdivian Coastal Range. Local communities and the government were invited to develop conservation management plans and sustainable development activities.

The World Conservation Union (IUCN) compiles a Red List of Endangered Species to provide policy guidance for governments and international organizations. Expertise in wildlife research can be developed through collaboration with local academic and research institutions. The Wildlife Trust has been working with the Asian Elephant Research and Conservation Center in Bangalore, India. The activities of the National Wildlife Federation, Sierra Club, Audubon Society, and Wilderness Society are concentrated on lobbying activities in the legislative arena.

Future Actions

Whereas worldwide efforts need to be intensified to set aside old-growth forests and other regions of biodiversity, a high population pressure has placed hundreds of thousands of wildlife species at a great risk, with a demand for further resources. The spread of human populations to natural habitats would not be slowed without control over human population growth rates through family planning services. Financial resources need to be made available to help impoverished or debt-ridden tropical countries, which contain most of the world's diverse ecosystems. Rich countries should share the cost for wildlife preservation since it is an issue of common human heritage. Developed countries can assist in capacity-building and the transfer of technology and finance.

The protection of biodiversity on public and private land needs to be mandated by more stringent environmental laws at a national level. Many programs such as the Endangered Species Act (combined with

biodiversity reserves, buffer zones, and connecting corridors) are certainly helpful for improvement in wildlife management, but they are stopgap measures. Any of these measures alone cannot be adequate enough to keep pace with burgeoning agricultural development, urbanization, and other human demands.

To live with the biological principles of sustainability demands, systematic changes are needed in the way we conduct business. The efficient utilization of resources would greatly reduce habitat destruction caused by timber harvesting and mining. Recycling minimizes our need for the consumption of more natural resources as well as the amount of pollution. Turning to renewable energy resources such as sunlight and wind could be part of the solution to global warming, acid deposition, and oil spills, which have a devastating impact on natural habitats. Long-term conservation depends upon a drastic change in human perceptions of nature.

In practicing sustainability, individual-level actions can become an essential part of the solution. A great many people live too far from ecosystems to develop any understanding of our dependence upon nature. Only a small minority in most parts of the world, such as indigenous people, maintains a sustained way of living. The challenge will remain that any measures to reduce species loss have to be tailored to the ecosystem and the local community.

HO-WON JEONG

See also Biodiversity Conservation; Environment: Government Policies; Environmentalism

References and Further Reading

Groombridge, Brian and M. D. Jenkins. *World Atlas of Biodiversity: Earth's Living Resources in the Twenty-First Century.* Berkeley, CA: University of California Press, 2002.

Higgs, Eric. *Nature by Design: People, Natural Process, and Ecological Restoration.* Boston: MIT Press, 2003.

Kunich, John Charles. *Ark of the Broken Covenant: Protecting the World's Biodiversity Hotspots.* New York: Praeger, 2003.

Melchias, Gabriel. *Biodiversity and Conservation.* Enfield, NH: Science Publishers, 2001.

National Resource Conservation Service. *Wildlife Habitat Basics: A Series of 52 Short Articles on Wildlife Conservation,* 2004.

Trefil, James. *Human Nature: A Blueprint for Managing the Earth—By People, For People.* New York: Times Books/Henry Holt, 2004.

WILLIAMS, ERIC

Dr. Eric Eustace Williams is well-known in a dual capacity: as a noted historian, and as the founding father and first Prime Minister of Trinidad and Tobago, a position he held until his death in 1981. He ranks among the greatest Black intellectuals and statesmen of the twentieth century.

One of twelve children, Eric Williams was born in Trinidad in 1911. From 1922 to 1931 he attended the Queen's Royal College in Port of Spain. Thanks to a scholarship, he attended Oxford University between 1932 and 1939, earning a doctorate in history. His dissertation, revised and published in 1944 in the United States under the title *Capitalism and Slavery,* along with the *Negro in the Caribbean,* published two years earlier, established his reputation as a scholar. These works contained several theses, hotly debated to this day, one of which pertains to slavery and the slave trade as major sources of the capital that enabled, or at least facilitated, the launching of the Industrial Revolution in Great Britain. It interpreted the abolitionist movement in the United Kingdom and the emancipation of slaves in the British West Indies in 1833 as largely due to economic factors. In several of his works he also argued that racism was not the cause of the Transatlantic slave trade, but rather the centuries of chattel slavery were largely responsible for the spread of racial prejudice.

After a teaching appointment as professor of social and political science at Howard University, he returned home and entered the political arena with his founding of the People's National Movement. Between 1957 and 1962 Williams devoted considerable energy to the realization of his vision of a Caribbean Federation, to include at least the English-speaking islands of the West Indies. On its collapse he led Trinidad and Tobago to independence in 1962, retaining membership in the British Commonwealth at first, but eventually achieving status as a republic in 1976. Williams remained at the helm for a quarter of a century. With his emphasis on development, especially industrial development as in the renowned Point Lisas complex, and thanks to the country's oil and gas resources, Trinidad and Tobago is the world's leading exporter of methanol and nitrogenous fertilizers and has thus been able to avoid the vicious cycle of underdevelopment. It ranks among the middle-income nations of the world.

His political activities notwithstanding, Eric Williams never ceased writing and publishing. Among over six hundred articles, speeches, pamphlets, lectures, and books, his major works include a history of the Caribbean, *From Columbus to Castro: a History of the People of Trinidad and Tobago; British Historians and the West Indies; Documents of West Indian History*; and his intellectual autobiography, *Inward Hunger* (1969).

The works and political activities of Eric Williams have been the subject of several international conferences, including those at the Rockefeller Conference

and Study Center, Bellagio, Italy, in 1984; the University of the West Indies in Trinidad and Tobago in 1996; Wellesley College, Massachusetts, in 2000; and the New York Public Library's Schomburg Center in 2002. The books and papers of Dr. Eric Williams, along with memorabilia and dozens of cubic feet of relevant correspondence from a variety of sources, comprise the Eric Williams Memorial Collection at the University of the West Indies, Trinidad and Tobago campus—the very institution he was so instrumental in bringing to fruition.

MARIO D. FENYO

See also Caribbean: History and Economic Development; Trinidad and Tobago

References and Further Reading

Connell, Erica Williams. Eric Williams Memorial Collection; P.O. Box 561631, Miami, FL 33256-1631, USA; Tel: 305-271-7246; Fax: 305-271-4160.
Cudjoe, Selwyn R., ed. *Eric Williams Speaks*. Wellesley, MA: Calaloux Publications, 1993.
www.mainlib.uwi.tt/eric.html
http://palmm.fcla.edu/eew/
Williams, Eric. *Inward Hunger: The Education of a Prime Minister*. London: Deutsch, 1969.

WOJTYŁA, KAROL (JOHN PAUL II)

On October 16, 1979, a cardinal from Kraków, Poland, Karol Józef Wojtyła (1920–2005), a poet, playwright, philosopher, scholar, and priest, was elected the 264th pope.

Karol Józef Wojtyla was born in the small town of Wadowice near Kraków in southern Poland in 1920. His youth years were marked by several deaths in the family: His mother passed away in 1929 and an older brother died when Wojtyła was twelve. After that he lived with his father in Wadowice and in Kraków until his father's death in 1941. After graduating from high school in 1938, he enrolled in the school of drama at Jagiellonian University in Kraków. Official schooling stopped during WWII when Karol Wojtyła worked in a quarry and in the Solvay chemical factory. In 1942 he began his study in the Kraków seminary. At the same time he participated in the clandestine works of the "Rhapsodic Theatre" in Krakow. After the war, Karol Wojtyla continued studies in the Kraków seminary and in the faculty of theology of Jagiellonian University. On November 1, 1946, he was ordained to the priesthood and soon after left for Rome. He obtained his doctorate in theology in 1948. His dissertation was entitled "Love and Responsibility." It laid out the foundation for what George Weigel (2001) calls "a modern Catholic sexual ethic." For a short time after finishing his studies, Wojtyła worked with Polish emigrants in Western Europe, namely France, Belgium, and Holland, and later in 1948 he returned to Poland. In 1951 Wojtyła enrolled in the Catholic University of Lublin to study philosophy and theology and in 1953 defended his second dissertation devoted to Catholic ethics in the ethical system of Max Scheler. Later he became a professor of ethics at his alma mater.

In July 1958 Karol Wojtyla was appointed auxiliary bishop of Kraków and in 1964 an archbishop of Kraków. On June 26, 1967, he became cardinal and in October 1979 was elected the pope and took up the name John Paul II. He participated in Vatican Council II, a sweeping program of modernization of the worldwide Catholic Church, and contributed to the Constitution *Gaudium et spes.* Mehmet Ali Agca, a Turk believed to have been serving the Bulgarian intelligence service, attempted to assassinate the pope in 1981.

Wojtyła, like his mentor Cardinal Stefan Wyszyński, is a skilled politician who dealt with the Communist government in a very pragmatic manner, opposing the secularization of Polish society. His papal years are often characterized as charismatic. He was the most traveled pope in history, having completed 102 visits to foreign countries since 1978. An advocate of interfaith cooperation and reconciliation, Wojtyla was the first pope to visit a synagogue and the first to visit the Holocaust Memorial at Auschwitz; he was also the first pope to visit Egypt. His foreign visits regularly gathered crowds of more than a million people. He was fluent in several languages.

Critics, however, say that John Paul's record is mixed. Although the church has expanded in Africa and Latin America, it has lost followers in the industrialized world. John Paul II's leadership of the Church is grounded in its conservative tradition. His rejection of contraception and abortion has been absolute and rigid.

Though John Paul's first two decades as pope were characterized by his vigor and energy, his health began to deteriorate. He had arthritis in his legs, which made it difficult for him to stand unassisted, and he underwent operations for the removal of a tumor, a hip replacement, and a tracheotomy. In January 2001, one of his doctors publicly acknowledged that the pontiff was suffering from Parkinson's disease. He cut back his hours and decreased his international travel, but made no indication that he would consider stepping down due to concerns for his health. Pope John Paul II finally succumbed to ill health and age on April 5, 2005, after completing the third longest reign in the history of papacy. He was succeeded by Pope Benedict XVI.

Throughout his career, John Paul was a prolific writer on philosophical and ethical issues. Among his best-known philosophy works are *The Acting Person,* a philosophical essay on phenomenology; *Fruitful and Responsible Love*; *Ethics and Morality*; and others. He addressed numerous topics, but was particularly concerned with the meaning of freedom and the dangers of materialism, selfishness, and consumerism. Despite his busy schedule and his frail health, he wrote a number of books, including *Rise, Let Us Be on Our Way,* and *Memory and Identity*. He has also written a number of plays and essays on theatre, and has released a book of poetry. He was a frequent commentator on international politics and an outspoken critic of dictatorial regimes, as well as a supporter of Poland's Solidarity movement. He was an opponent of the US-led 2003 invasion of Iraq.

LUDOMIR LOZNY

See also Christianity; Poland; Religion; Roman Catholic Church; Solidarity Union; Wyszyński, Cardinal Stefan

References and Further Reading

Bernstein, Carl and Marco Politi. *His Holiness: John Paul II and the Hidden History of Our Time*. New York, Doubleday, 1996.
Cornwell, John. *The Pontiff in Winter: Triumph and Conflict in the Reign of John Paul II*. New York: Doubleday, 2004.
Pope John Paul II. *Gift and Mystery: On the Fiftieth Anniversary of My Priestly Ordination*. Image, 1996.
———. *Place Within: The Poetry of Pope John Paul II*. Jerzy Peterkiewicz, trans. Random House, 1994.
Weigel, George. *A Witness to Hope: The Biography of Pope John Paul II*. Harper Collins, 2001.

WOMEN: LEGAL STATUS

An increasing number of legal documents address the status of women in society, at work, and, more recently, within the family. The intention of these legal documents is to formalise and promote equality between men and women in all spheres of life by addressing issues ranging from the reconciliation between maternity and employment, to the right to vote and hold public office, to the prohibition of exploitation in a variety of different industries. In this sense, women's legal status is defined through the recognition of the rights essential for women's existence, but which need to be formally recognised in order to be protected and promoted effectively.

States define and promote women's rights in their constitutions, national laws, acts of parliament, and so forth. While the promotion of the status of women enjoys varying degrees of success worldwide, most national legal instruments do make mention of the situation of women. It is nevertheless at the international level that the process of definition of women's legal status proves the most meaningful: while it would be impossible to describe the specificities of the hundreds of national laws dealing with women's status, the international legal framework is central to defining what are the universally recognised rights of women. The legal status of women will therefore be presented by reference to international human rights instruments at the United Nations' level. The United Nations (UN) has, from the time of its creation in 1945, recognised the need to promote gender equality and to fight against discrimination based on sex. The preamble of the first modern instrument of human rights, the Universal Declaration of Human Rights, makes it clear that "... the peoples of the United Nations have in the Charter reaffirmed their faith in fundamental human rights, in the dignity and worth of the human person and in the equal rights of men and women ...." Article Two guarantees the enjoyment of the rights outlined by the Universal Declaration "without distinction of any kind, such as ... sex ...." From then on, numerous UN treaties would reaffirm the prohibition of discrimination based on sex and promote equality between women and men.

Prior to presenting what constitutes women's legal status within the human rights framework, the challenges linked to addressing women's status within a legal and rights-based framework will be addressed. A short account of the historical evolution toward the official recognition of women's rights will be given before presenting the central instrument of women's legal status today: the Convention on the Elimination of all Forms of Discrimination Against Women.

The Value of a Legal Approach to Women's Status

One popular refrain of the contemporary human rights discourse is that "women's rights are human rights." By proclaiming so, women's groups intend to emphasise the fact that, as human beings, women should enjoy the benefits of the protection offered by human rights in general. Because the two central principles attached to human rights are their indivisibility and universality, women should benefit from the entire apparatus of rights without having to claim it. Nevertheless, the historical and gendered construction of human rights has made obvious the necessity for women to re-characterise and reaffirm their status within the human rights discourse. Historically, women have been excluded from the elaboration, implementation, and monitoring of human rights instruments. There was a widespread failure to recognise the

need to characterise the subordination of women as a human rights violation. Similarly, the fact that women's rights should be a full part of human rights was not self-evident at the time of the creation of modern human rights law and subsequently had to be reaffirmed. The legal framework for the recognition of women's rights is also conditioned by the fact that the development of human rights law has been partial and androcentric. Women's lack of power in both private and public spheres was not taken into account when drafting the first human rights instruments. As a result, the narrow language of rights did not account for women's systemic subordination in society. Another central problem of mainstream human rights law is that it does not integrate the specificities of women's lives and identities. Mainly linked to women's reproductive functions, these specificities call for the recognition of rights linked to reproductive autonomy, motherhood, and care. For all these reasons, women's rights have been reaffirmed, within as well as alongside the human rights discourse.

A legal approach to women's status can also be said to account only partly for women's actual position. The problematic nature of defining women's status is linked to the public and private spheres divide. The latter sphere originally emerged from classical Western liberal thought. Its contemporary application means that women, who are more likely than men to be confined to the privacy of the home—that is, the private sphere—do not benefit from the protection of human rights that apply, in their traditional understanding, specifically to the public sphere. While the right of women to participate politically in their state's structure is broadly accepted, there is hostility towards their right to live free from violence or to decide how to plan their pregnancy and decide on the number of children they will have. One task for women's rights activists and feminists today, therefore, is to challenge the divide and to make human rights more relevant to the reality of women's everyday life. Defining women's legal status is purposeless if it ceases to apply once women have crossed their doorstep.

As a preliminary conclusion, one could say that defining the legal status of women is useful provided that the "rights" they are subsequently given are adapted to women's particular situations and needs.

Toward Recognising Women's Rights: The UN Decade on Women and International Women's Rights Conferences

The determination of women's status in the international framework came to a turning point in 1975 when the UN General Assembly, following the proposition of the Commission on the Advancement of Women, accepted the adoption of a "programme of concerted international action for the advancement of women" to be implemented over the "UN Decade for Women." This decade was the result of an increasing consciousness of the necessity to address women's status worldwide following growing concerns over the issues of the world's food situation and population growth. Because of their reproductive role, women were identified as central actors of this debate and their status was thus brought to the front of the international human rights stage. The first worldwide women's rights conference was held in 1975 in Mexico City and it focused on the three issues of equality, development, and peace. Several women's rights institutions were created in the wake of the Mexico City conference. Five years later, in 1980, a second worldwide women's conference was held in Copenhagen, focusing on issues of equal access to education, employment opportunities, and adequate health care. The third women's conference took place in Nairobi in 1985, entitled "World Conference to Review and Appraise the Achievement of the UN Decade for Women: Equality, Development and Peace." While the obvious conclusion of the conference was that objectives had not been reached, participants and representatives agreed that it had been a success in terms of making the women's movement more visible, in highlighting progress that needed to be made, and in creating the structures necessary for addressing their needs. What has been by far the most important women's rights conference took place in Beijing from September 4–15, 1995. The Beijing conference was important in part because it brought together a very high number of women's organisations from all over the world. The "Beijing Declaration and Platform for Action for Equality, Development and Peace" was adopted at the end of the conference. It sets out clear objectives and identifies twelve critical areas of concern for women: poverty, education and training, health, violence against women, armed conflicts, the economy, power and decision making, institutional mechanisms, human rights, the media, the environment, and the girl-child. The review of the Beijing Platform for action was organised five years later through a special session of the UN General Assembly. At the so-called "Beijing + 5," further areas of concerns were identified. Parallel to these developments, the women's movement in civil society was also gaining significant momentum. The "Beijing + 5" session closed with the adoption of a document entitled "Further Actions and Initiatives to Implement the Beijing Declaration and Platform for Action." The next review process will be "Beijing + 10" in 2005.

The Convention on the Elimination of All Forms of Discrimination Against Women—An Overview

Adoption of CEDAW

The most important international instrument for defining women's legal status is the Convention on the Elimination of Discrimination Against Women (CEDAW). CEDAW was adopted in 1979 and entered into force on September 3, 1981, after twenty countries had ratified it. On March 26, 2004, CEDAW had 98 signatories and 177 ratifications, making it the second most widely ratified UN instrument. It is the first instrument that brings together different categories of rights relevant to women; prior to CEDAW, the only instruments available were topic-oriented conventions adopted by the Commission on the Status of Women. CEDAW is innovative in that it brings together rights already recognised with newly identified ones, such as family planning and reproductive rights (article 12). CEDAW also addresses issues of culture and tradition in order to make clear that such cannot be used as excuses to justify the violation of other recognised rights. Like other UN treaties, the implementation of CEDAW is monitored by the committee it creates.

Content of CEDAW

CEDAW is central to defining women's legal status. It lists the rights specifically to be enjoyed by women and prohibits discrimination between women and men in the enjoyment of all other human rights. In its first article, CEDAW defines discrimination as:

> [A]ny distinction, exclusion or restriction made on the basis of sex which has the effect or purpose of impairing or nullifying the recognition, enjoyment or exercise by women, irrespective of their marital status, on a basis of equality of men and women, of human rights and fundamental freedoms in the political, economic, social, cultural, civil or any other field.

Besides defining discrimination, CEDAW also provides for the necessity for states to engage in a series of positive actions, to the end of implementing the provisions listed. By ratifying CEDAW, states commit "to incorporate the principles of equality of men and women in their legal system, abolish all discriminatory laws and adopt appropriate ones prohibiting discrimination against women; to establish tribunals and other public institutions to ensure the effective protection of women against discrimination; to ensure

elimination of all acts of discrimination against women by persons, organisations or enterprises" (www.un.org/womenwatch/daw/cedaw).

CEDAW comprises a preamble and thirty articles, organised in six parts:

I. Definitions and obligations (articles 1 to 6);
II. Political rights and rights to citizenship (articles 7 to 9);
III. Economic rights (articles 10 to 14);
IV. Civil and political rights (articles 15 and 16);
V. The Committee on the Elimination of All Forms of Discrimination Against Women, and the treaty mechanism (article 17 to 22); and
VI. Implementation, ratification, and entry into force (articles 23 to 30).

Part I is dedicated to defining discrimination and detailing the nature of the obligations created by states' accession to the Convention. The formula used in the text of CEDAW is that "States shall take all appropriate measures" to implement the rights listed. This means that the responsibility for implementing the rights provided for by CEDAW depends upon national states adopting the necessary correlative legislation. These measures ought to be undertaken in order to combat elements potentially prejudicial to the promotion of women's equal status, including culture and stereotypes, in all fields of life. Part II addresses the promotion of the right of women to vote and be elected (articles 7 and 8) as well as the recognition of the fact that women's decisions regarding their nationality should be independent from external factors like marriage (article 9). Part III looks at women's economic and social rights, in particular women's equal right to education (article10), health care (article 12), and rights linked to other areas of economic and social life (article 13). Article 11 promotes women's equal right to work and to enjoy work-related benefits, including equal pay for equal work and access to related social benefits; the second part of the article provides for protective measures related to women's work and maternity. Part IV provides for women's equal status before the law and their equal right to enter into contractual relationships (article 15). Article 16 focuses on women's position with regard to marriage and family matters. More specifically, it emphasises women's autonomous status with regard to entering and leaving a marriage relationship, planning and bringing up children, as well as acquiring property. The article also provides that it is not legally recognized for underage girls to be married. Part V deals with the establishment of CEDAW's committee, outlines its responsibilities and functioning mechanisms, and describes its composition and its relation with other UN agencies. Finally, Part VI

details accession, ratification, reservations, and interpretation of the Convention.

Another tool provided for by CEDAW in the protection of the status of women is the possibility, under article 21, for the Committee to make general recommendations (GR) on substantial or procedural points relating to CEDAW. The most recent general recommendation, the 25th, looks at temporary special measures. Others have dealt with a variety of issues, including circumcision (GR No. 14), AIDS (GR No. 15), and violence against women (GR No. 19). They prove a useful tool in clarifying the content of certain rights and explaining procedures more clearly, as well as increasing international attention and awareness on specific points.

CEDAW formalises a broad range of rights covering most aspects of women's lives. Nevertheless, feminists argue that CEDAW is failing to adequately address women's position in life. It addresses women's status in relation to men's and aims at bringing women to an equal position with men; however, it does not take an independent approach to women's needs and strengths. One suggestion consists of focusing "on powerlessness, exclusion, and disadvantage of women, rather than on sameness and difference" (Cook 1994, p. 156). One further problem is that while women's legal status is clearly defined through the thirty articles of CEDAW, the de facto situation is substantially different, as states do not necessarily fully implement these rights and cannot be compelled to do so. The effectiveness of CEDAW, like any other human rights instrument, rests upon states' willingness to comply; the only sanction that can be imposed is a public denunciation by CEDAW's Committee.

CEDAW's Reporting Procedure and the Committee

CEDAW's Committee (the Committee) is responsible for monitoring the implementation of the Convention. The committee is made up of twenty-three experts sitting in their own personal capacity. While they are nominated by states and elected by state parties for four years, they remain independent from their respective countries. The main procedure involving the Committee is the reporting procedure. Like other treaty bodies, the Committee is given the competence and power to request, examine, and analyse state reports on the situation of women's rights in that country. The reports must account for actions that have been undertaken in order to ensure women's status is in conformity with the standards under CEDAW. States are required to submit reports to the Committee at least every four years. The accuracy of the information detailed in the reports is left to the discretion of the states, but is usually counterbalanced by shadow reports produced by nongovernmental organisations (NGOs). The Committee is responsible for examining the state reports and giving its conclusions. This monitoring procedure is the main tool available with regard to women's legal status, as internationally defined.

The Optional Protocol to CEDAW

On October 6, 1999, the General Assembly of the UN adopted the Optional Protocol to CEDAW; it entered into force on December 22, 2000. It enables individuals—or groups of individuals—from a state party to this Protocol to bring a complaint for violation of rights guaranteed by CEDAW, before the Committee. While the conditions attached to the individual complaint procedure are restrictive, it is believed that the development of this procedure will allow for better protection of women's rights. Another procedure was also created that consists of the possibility for the Committee to enquire into a "situation of grave or systematic violations of women's rights" (rules 82 and 83 of the Protocol).

Conclusion

In conclusion, the legal status of women is thoroughly addressed in international human rights law. Nonetheless, women are still the victims of multiple discriminations and rights violations. High illiteracy rates, malnutrition, discrimination in the workplace, and violation of women's reproductive rights are not recent phenomena and prove that there is still a long way to go in making this formal legal status a reality. Other women's rights violations, such as trafficking in women, are now being uncovered, and although strongly denounced, highlight a need for the rethinking of the current legal apparatus and the mechanisms available to implement it. Cultural exceptions are especially relevant to the status of women, as is shown by the significant number of culture-based reservations made to CEDAW. Even if sensitive in nature, these cultural exceptions need to be addressed in order to guarantee women a more meaningful legal status. As suggested by the Beijing Platform for Action, empowering women to address the problems they face and to suggest alternatives to the present system is the key to improving the value of their present legal status.

AUDREY GUICHON

See also Basic Human Needs; Women: Role in Development

References and Further Reading

Charlesworth, Hilary, Christine Chinkin, and Shelley Wright. "Feminist Approaches to International Law." *American Society of International Law* 85 (1991): 613–645.

Clark, Belinda. "The Vienna Convention Reservations Regime and the Convention on Discrimination Against Women." *American Journal of International Law* 85, no. 2 (1991): 281–321.

Cook, Rebecca J., ed. *Human Rights, Women, National and International Perspectives*, Philadelphia: University of Pennsylvania Press, 1994.

Division for the Advancement of Women. http://www.un.org/womenwatch/daw/

Evatt, Elizabeth. "Finding a Voice for Women's Rights." *George Washington International Law Review* 34 (2002): 515–553.

Felipe Gomez, Isa. "The Optional Protocol for the Convention on the Elimination of All Forms of Discrimination Against Women: Strengthening the Protection Mechanisms of Women's Human Rights." *Arizona Journal of International and Comparative Law* 20, (2002): 291–321.

Mayer, Ann Elizabeth. *Islam and Human Rights, Traditions and Politics*, 3rd ed. Oxford, UK: Westview Press, 1999.

Pietilä, Hilkka. *Engendering the Global Agenda: The Story of Women and the United Nations*. Geneva: United Nations Non-Governmental Liaison Service, 2002.

Thomas, Dorothy Q., and Beasley, Michelle E. "Domestic Violence as a Human Rights Issue." *Human Rights Quarterly* 15 (1993): 37–62.

WOMEN LIVING UNDER MUSLIM LAWS (WLUML)

Women Living Under Muslim Laws (WLUML) is an international network that provides assistance, information, and channels for communication to women whose lives are affected or governed by laws and customs said to derive from Islam. The network aims to develop autonomy and strengthen solidarity among women in Muslim countries and communities. WLUML's goal to document and support women experiencing various forms of discriminations and oppressions connected to Muslim rulings, laws, or various traditions existing in Muslim communities is guided through networking, media alerts, various collective projects, and publications.

WLUML began its formation in 1984 as a result of three pressing cases in which women were being denied rights. Such incidents were symptomatic of a larger challenge facing women of systematic marginalization through reference to laws said to be "Islamic." Thereafter, nine women from eight countries came together to support specific women's struggles. This collaboration evolved into its near-global network of WLUML in 1986. By 2004 WLUML was operating in more than seventy countries.

The network extends to women in countries where Islam is the state religion, where secular states have Muslim majorities, and where political groups are pressing for religious laws; it also extends to women from Muslim communities in which minority religious laws preside, those in Muslim minority communities around the world, and non-Muslim women who may have Muslim laws applied to them. The network serves marginalized women, such as minorities facing discrimination, oppression, or racism, and women who face discrimination because of their assertions of sexuality, including sexual orientation.

As part of its overall strategy, WLUML bridges identities by building a network of individuals and feminist and human rights organizations at local and global levels through which it facilitates communication and information. Women can seek assistance, alliances, information on their legal rights, shelter, mediation, contacts to lawyers, psychological support, and the sharing of experiences. Such a forum enables dialogue among women of various ideologies and stances to break barriers and face common obstacles to their autonomy and self-development. Thereby, individuals' local experiences are connected to the wider context of international injustices perpetrated against women.

WLUML collects, analyses, and circulates information regarding women's diverse experiences and strategies in Muslim contexts using a variety of media. WLUML initiates and circulates "Alerts for Action" and campaigns to an international forum as a strategy of resistance. Through locally initiated information networks, women themselves can articulate their local situation. WLUML then distributes the information to connections that include Amnesty International, UNICEF, and women's organizations. WLUML also initiates letter-writing campaigns.

WLUML organizes "collective projects," which include initiatives that arise out of women's specific needs, interests, and analyses. A project typically involves three to over twenty groups and lasts from a few months to ten years. Collective projects include training sessions, workshops, research for advocacy, meetings, and exchanges around specialized topics.

Previous projects have included an exchange program (1988), Qur'anic interpretations meetings (1990, 2002, 2004), the Women and Law in the Muslim World Programme (1991–2001), a program on feminism in the Muslim World Leadership Institutes (1998 and 1999), gender and displacement in Muslim contexts (1999–2002), and the Initiative for Strengthening Afghan Family Laws (INSAF) (began in 2002). WLUML, moreover, implements capacity-building initiatives of its networks through internships at the coordination offices, as well as exchanges, trainings, and workshops.

WLUML brings awareness of women's situations though publications. It produces a theme-based dossier, an occasional journal that provides information about the lives, struggles, and strategies of women; a quarterly newssheet on women, laws, and society; occasional papers; and other publications on specific issues such as family laws, women's movements, and initiatives.

WLUML focuses on the concrete realities of women's lives. These include bringing awareness to basic human rights abuses against women, relocating women forced to marry against their will, as well as rescuing children kidnapped by their fathers to Muslim countries. However, in principle, WLUML responds to requests for help, as opposed to initiating cases.

WLUML has been successful in mitigating harsh sentences by rallying the international community for support. Highlighting but a few incidents, in 1995 in the United Arab Emirates a sixteen-year-old Filipino girl was pardoned after she was sentenced to death for killing her employer after he brutally raped her. WLUML called for preventing the execution, demanded the UAE government amend rape laws where the onus of truth is on the rape victim. Also in 1995 when a Muslim religious leader in Chad called for the killing of a woman for making a film denouncing female genital mutilation, WLUML alerted women's and human rights groups to her sentence. With a combined effort to petition the government of Chad, the imam was made to withdraw his decree. In 2002, Toujan Al-Faisal, a feminist and anti-corruption campaigner and Jordan's first female MP, was released from jail after WLUML in a combined effort petitioned for her release. After intense letter writing in late 2004 for the release of civil society activist Dr. Mahboobeh Abbasgholizadeh, she was released on bail from the Iranian authorities. However, the network also studies the theoretical underpinnings of women's oppressions. It concentrates on themes such as empowerment, fundamentalisms, state control, militarization, sexuality, health and reproductive rights, and violence. Particular attention is given to the effects of laws and law reform. Aiming to dispel the myth that one homogenous Islamic law exists, the network documents diverse practices and laws classified as Islamic, which have developed from male-dominated interpretations of religious texts and/or the political use of religion, and which are mixed with the differing local customs and practices, formal or informal. Female researchers trace the evolution of laws and identify contradictions between customs and scripts. One of its major activities continues to include reinterpreting "Islamic" sources for Muslim laws from this exhaustive inventory to support women's issues.

At times, cases or problems take years for the network to resolve. WLUML, nonetheless, brings awareness to women's voiced concerns under Muslim laws, and in so doing incrementally effects change within Muslim countries and communities towards greater egalitarianism, justice, and stronger civil societies. It is unique in that it encourages women to pursue and define justice without essentializing women's diverse identities.

WANDA C. KRAUSE

See also Islam; Islamic Fundamentalism; Women: Role in Development; Women: Legal Status

References and Further Reading

Ahmed, Leila. *Women and Gender in Islam*. New Haven, CT: Yale University Press, 1992.
Joseph, Suad. "Gender and Family in the Arab World." In *Arab Women: Between Defiance and Restraint*, edited by Suha Sabbagh. New York: Olive Branch, 1996.
Haddad, Yvonne Yazbeck and John L. Esposito. *Islam, Gender, and Social Change*. New York: Oxford University Press, 1998.
Kandiyoti, Deniz, ed. *Gendering the Middle East: Emerging Perspectives*. London: I.B. Tauris, 1996.
Pepall, Jennifer. "Women Living Under Muslim Laws: A Solidarity, Information, and Research Network." *IDRC Reports: Stories on Research in the Developing World*, 1997, http://idrinfo.idrc.ca/archive/reportsintra/pdfs/1997 e/112193.htm
Mir-Hosseini, Ziba. *Marriage on Trial: A Study of Islamic Law in Iran and Morocco*, 2nd ed. London: I.B. Taurus, 2000.
Shaheed, Farida. "Controlled or Autonomous: Identity and the Experience of the Network, Women Living under Muslim Laws." *Signs* 19, no. 4 (summer 1994): 997–1019.
Women Living Under Muslim Laws, http://www.wluml.org/english/index.shtml
Yamani, Mai., ed. *Feminism and Islam: Legal and Literary Perspectives*. New York: New York University Press, 1996.

WOMEN: ROLE IN DEVELOPMENT

Women

The sociological category "woman" was analytically dismantled in the latter decades of the twentieth century. Feminist scholars recognised that women's experiences and activities were necessarily different due to the specific factors of every woman's social and historical context. While women in many societies share similar experiences and problems, their similarities must be balanced against women's very different experiences worldwide, especially in relation

to how their lives are shaped by race, colonialism, the rise of global capitalism, and the interventions of international development agencies. Women cannot be treated as an homogenous category; there are social differentiations between women according to rank, age, employment, earning capacity, and caste, for example, and women are affected differently in different countries by global capitalist development.

Although women's biology impels many into reproduction and the caregiving duties associated with infant and child socialisation, women's physiology presents different possibilities in different societies. This means that women can engage in the social role of mothering and, depending on the society in which they live, a range of other roles. The possibilities open to women are culturally elaborated, so that even the supposedly natural function of mothering is culturally defined. When focusing on what women do, questions about the sexual division of labour in different societies and about the related divisions of social life into "domestic/female" versus "public/male" domains, are raised. Many scholars argue that although women may be perceived as separate and different from men, in numerous cultures this does not necessarily imply inferiority or subordination to men. Various quality studies have shown that gender relations, that is, social relations between women and men, in many societies have been radically altered due to the impact of colonisation, Westernisation, and global capitalism. A number of studies have noted that development and wage labour make women more dependent on men by undermining local customary systems where women have, in the past, enjoyed a certain amount of control over production and reproduction. Some argue that men take control of women's land, goods, labour, and reproductive capacity by armed force or physical and psychological intimidation. In severe contrast, other studies refer to the "myth of male dominance" in which statements made about women, that is, statements expressing cultural ideologies, often represent women as less powerful than they actually are in their daily lives. They propose that although men have been represented as dominant in many societies, many women possess and wield considerable power and influence. Women may possess power that is complementary to, rather than in overt contestation with, male power. In addition, they argue that cultural valuations of women and men and their respective work in different societies often fail to reflect women's and men's respective access to and control over resources. For example, women may earn significant social respect due to their control over land in matrilineal societies. And women may be the principal food providers for their family due to their agricultural work and their animal-husbandry labours.

Women and Development

While the focus on women across cultures has produced conflicting reports, women and development is an arena of research and practice that has linked questions about gender and gender relations with an analysis of the social and economic role of the state. Women and development focuses on the characteristics and management of state institutions, economic planning, policy formation, decision making, and the exercise of state power. It examines and questions male dominance and male privilege in relation to access to state resources and political power, and it raises issues concerning gender ideologies and how these ideologies inform planning and policy. In the arena of women and development, the issue of the success or failure of state policies designed to benefit women is discussed in terms of what kind of economic and sociopolitical changes are envisaged and implemented in order to bring about development. This field of enquiry overlaps an analysis of how women organise socially and politically, women's responses to development initiatives, and women's reactions to and perceptions of the state and its agents. Studies demonstrate that development is a complex and difficult field, because it blends theory and practice in ways that can drastically affect people's daily lives. Development is also fraught because it raises questions about relations of power: Who actually benefits from development? How do development project designers know what is best for disadvantaged peoples? How much damage are they causing with their interventions? What strategies are in place to enable disadvantaged peoples, particularly women, to contribute to the design, planning, and implementation of development projects? And how can development project designers judge what "disadvantage" actually means for people in cultures that are different from their own?

The deleterious effects of many development projects on women with regard to their access to and control over land, property, technology, training, and decision making are well documented. And although the effects of agricultural change on women have been diverse, nonetheless, a key trend that has emerged from evaluations of development projects to the end of the twentieth century has been the weakening of women's authority and decision-making powers. This has occurred because of changing roles in production, especially within the increasing commercialisation of agriculture, and the exclusion of women from technology, training, and credit schemes. Early writers on women and development demonstrated that many of the negative effects of development programmes on women were due to a neglect and/or

misunderstanding of women's key roles in all areas of subsistence production. And early development programmes mistakenly presumed that men were the most important workers in food and factory production. More innovative and radical policies and programmes aimed specifically at women have been moderately successful. However, improving women's participation in decision making, bureaucratic institutions, and women's political representation generally, has been judged by many to be a spectacular failure.

The key intellectual and social context for discussing women's role in development is to question why inequalities between women and men exist and why they are maintained in the face of discourses about universal human rights. Social structures; institutions; and values such as norms, customs, rights, and laws link with economic institutions such as markets to shape relationships between women and men, to form their socially expected roles, and to influence what resources women and men have access to, what activities they can or cannot undertake, and how they may participate in broader society and the economy.

While the social and economic institutions that shape and structure people's lives in different societies can be slow to change, they are never static. For example, in developing countries households are fundamental to the way that women and men experience their lives from childhood and how gender relations are transmitted between generations. The ways that tasks are allocated between daughters and sons, girls' and women's degree (if any) of autonomy, and what social expectations are promoted within the household all create, reinforce, and form seemingly rigid differences between genders. But such differences must be explored because different behaviours, social expectations, and perceptions of what is womanly or manly change across and within cultures. Studies note, for example, that although gender disparities tend to be less among élite and dominant classes, in some societies with rigid gender divisions (such as Bangladesh, Pakistan, and Saudi Arabia) wealthy families invest far more of their sense of status, dignity, and prestige in female modesty and seclusion, particularly when they enjoy high socioeconomic status. Female modesty thus becomes a key symbol of their status.

Although gender inequalities persist among both the rich and the poor, they are often greatest among the poor, particularly in terms of household financial investments in education and health. Education is considered to be a fundamental and universal human right and a necessity for enhancing social and economic development. But as a result of different financial investments in education, major differences can be observed between boys and girls, particularly in terms of the numbers of girls who attend school and for how long.

Nutritional studies show that receiving little or no formal education creates women with high levels of fertility and mortality, poor nutritional status, low earning potential, and little autonomy within their household. Low investments in female education translate into poorer health and nutritional practices by mothers, so that all children feel the effects, and the flow to the health, well-being, and productivity of the next generation may suffer. Low investments in female education are considered to be instrumental in reinforcing the asymmetry of power relations between men and women and, without women's education, a great deal of a country's talent, skill, and energy remain untapped. Conversely, high numbers of educated females and levels of female education are two of many reasons cited as positively contributing to general economic development, social progress, and gender equality. Nevertheless, school curricula and teachers' attitudes may act to reinforce existing gender biases in society. Some studies critique the ways that schools in many countries reflect the patriarchal cultural ideologies that often prevail among the élite and dominant class. Pupils are schooled to conform, and girls are taught to accept authoritarian structures, relations of male domination, and success on male terms.

Low financial investments in health produce high rates of malnutrition and mortality among girls, and can affect whether girls are allowed to be born. In the latter case, adverse female sex ratios in some states of India and China suggest endemic female foeticide (destruction in the womb by technologies such as ultrasound scanning and amniocentesis), infanticide, and neglect of young girls is occurring in cultures and societies where boys are preferred and girls are considered an unnecessary or expensive addition to a family.

Women, Gender, and Development

Issues about women's power and women's capacity for active human agency in cultures and societies that often create significant structural barriers to women's existence as equal social actors have come to the fore as development studies and practices begin to more fully integrate concepts of gender.

As a consequence, it is impossible to discuss the ways in which the concepts of gender and gender relations have changed development without reflecting on the debates that have surrounded women's role(s) in development. Literature about gender and

development in the twentieth century can be categorized into three waves: women in development (WID); women and development (WAD); and gender and development (GAD). The key strategy of WID theory and practice was to progress women's social condition via broader economic growth. WID was concerned with maximising women's access to the modern sector, and opening the border between the traditional and modern sectors, to allow for an equal proportion of women within the latter. WID assessments of social and economic inequalities between women and men presupposed that a gradual process of reform would eventually produce gender equality. Structures such as male bias that were seen to exclude women from development were not perceived as grave, as science and enlightened reason were perceived as antidotes to the vestiges of prejudiced patriarchal superstition and ignorance that located women outside many cultures' ideas about what it is to be properly "human"—that is, male. The strategy sadly failed because development studies, social planning, and project design remained firmly orientated toward men; the concepts of man and men were deemed by Western development planners to be synonymous with all people; and, prior to 1970 it was thought that the development process affected women and men in the same way. These erroneous notions equated productivity with the cash economy and consequently ignored most women's work, which is based in non-cash agricultural labour, caregiving to family members within households, and provision of unpaid social management and community support.

A move then evolved to critically analyse the ways in which received ideas about women within Western epistemologies created discriminatory practices in Western cultures and societies, which were then imposed on other peoples through the frameworks and processes of development. A common assumption among Western development planners was that the social and economic problems of women in developing countries were attributable to their status; for example, the United Nations devised a Commission on the Status of Women. However, the concept of the status of women ignores the enormous variety of situations in which individual women live their daily experiences, and ignores women's diverse and complex cultures. In many cultures the flexibility of interpretation over status gives women and men sufficient leverage to operate relations of power to the advantage of the "self." This social practice suggests women's concerns as individuals need to be considered in tandem with their concerns as members of familial and social collectives. Certainly men and women in many cultures, such as those of Melanesia in the southwest Pacific, do not represent themselves

as separate autonomous beings. However, women's move in the latter decades of the twentieth century to urban environments has attenuated their ties with family, kin, and broader social collectives to the point that women can and do see themselves as individuals, albeit within a complex network of mutual responsibilities and cooperation.

An alternative vision of development *with* women was proposed. The WAD approach worked to integrate women's participation into development processes. It underscored the idea that the rise of globalisation, with its inequitable gender relations and prioritisation of global capitalism, was also inimical to men in developing countries. WAD also attempted to explain male domination and violence. Theorists contended that it is the structure of capitalism that keeps women at home in the domestic arena, not men, and male frustration with the class system was regarded as the determining factor in male abuse of women. But many theorists did not recognise the ways that men benefit from women's domestic labour, nor the extent to which women may also benefit from men's labour, and the complex economic exchanges that occur in the domestic arena. In consequence, WAD practices in development projects were criticised for privileging class over gender, in terms of remaining located in the processes of global capitalism and ignoring the complex social interactions between women and men at the grassroots level of economic production.

WAD failed in many countries because it did not adequately cater to rural and semi-urban women's needs. Many projects did little to change the distribution of household labour or increase women's access to resources, and surveys revealed that women's projects received dramatically less funding and attention than larger developments that employed male labour. The WAD approach failed due to insufficient awareness and sensitivity of planners, inadequate financial support and staff, unrealistic time frames for the achievement of project goals, and the lack of participation of women as the beneficiaries in project design and decisions. In essence, it remained anchored in dominant, powerful Western male modes of thought.

Although Western gender roles too often are used in support of a male ideology that seeks to exclude women from many important areas of modern life, it is equally important to recognise that conceiving of women solely as subordinate to men may provide little information about prevailing female–male relations, as expressed ideas about gender rarely accurately replicate social relations. In some cases women are represented as far more subordinate than they are in actuality. The WID and WAD approaches were condemned for focusing on "women" as a category and

thereby conflating women's diverse experiences into "otherness" as victim.

The newer theories driving gender and development (GAD) address the fundamental structures of inequality between women and men. A GAD approach makes visible the power relations that exist between men and women in most societies and the subordination to male power structures that many women face in a globalising capitalist world. Ideologically, GAD focuses not just on women but on the social relations that exist between women and men, on all aspects of women's lived experiences, and also centres gender and class relations, arguing that gender relations have to be located within hierarchical relations of domination that operate both at the micro and macro level of analysis in order to see clearly how changes may take place. Gender mainstreaming has become a strategy increasingly associated with GAD, for assessing the potential and actual effects of policies and programmes for women and men.

Such theoretical stress on gendered relations of power in many societies has been helpful, as GAD conceives "empowerment" to be the harnessed, self-generating power of women to act in their own interest. Indeed, more recent studies analysing women's agency suggest women are not passive victims of cultural and socioeconomic relations and structures, but rather they actively strategise and negotiate in order to achieve goals for themselves; their children; and extended family, kin, and clan members.

A number of studies have asked whether the diverse experiences of women across and within cultures and societies can be adequately addressed by development projects conceptualised, designed, and implemented by agencies in Western countries. To combat the disparities between theorisations about women, women's actual lived experiences, and women's roles in development, social anthropologists and comparative sociologists concerned with linking empirical data with perspectives of gender have engaged in rigorous inquiries into gender symbolism within and across cultures. As a consequence, they have critiqued Western notions of gender roles. Non-Western anthropologists, writing from within their own communities, show that variations in folk constructs about ideas of "male" and "female," and the probable relationships that exist or are considered socially appropriate between women and men, do not necessarily correspond to Western universalisations of "sex" and "gender" based on notions of hierarchies and oppositions between culture and nature, public and private. For example, decision making may denote some degree of agency, and hence the ability to form goals, commitments, and values. But to judge someone's success as an agent one must know what decisions the person may, does, or must make; for whom and to what extent her decisions can then be implemented; and by whom the decisions are implemented. Because decisions classified by outsiders as being made exclusively by women may not be considered to be decisions by men, researchers argue that definitions of agency are specific to different cultures, as are concepts of choice and decision making.

Cross-cultural researchers argue that the key element to be drawn from observing how people live with gendered codes about social interactions is to analyse people's active agency in creating, re-creating, and resisting the system from their position within it. They contend that development practitioners need to consider how people, as active cultural agents, negotiate the limitations of their social structures, how different cultural agents experience life, and how they produce and manage various social identities. Development planners may need to rethink their ideas about active cultural agency in relation to the different activities conducted by women and men, because Western definitions of cultural agency are not as important as the social use of the concept in different societies.

The WID, WAD, and GAD debates demonstrate the important theoretical and practical changes that have occurred over time in analysing the topic of women's role in development.

Women's Roles in Development: Current Emphases

Current emphases in theory and research on the topic of women in development recognise the multiple facets of women's activities and therefore pluralise their roles. Classical economic analyses are being radically rethought as their intellectual constraints do not acknowledge most of women's social roles, their work, or the diversity of their work. Globally, women engage in biological reproduction via childbearing and early nurturing of infants, and perform the bulk of childcare and household maintenance. They also engage in social reproduction via the care and maintenance of the household such as housework; food preparation; and care for the sick, children, and the elderly; and in social management in terms of maintaining kinship linkages, developing neighbourhood networks, and carrying out religious or ceremonial duties in the community. Women in most cultures and societies combine household work with market or non-market work to generate income or raise household consumption. Such work has not been captured in classical economic theory or traditional labour force statistics. Women in rural areas are responsible for

subsistence agriculture. Small animals such as chickens and pigs, which can be fed on household scraps, are kept. Because female smallholders often find it difficult to hire men to undertake heavy physical tasks such as land preparation and pesticide application, they may be forced to leave some of their land uncultivated. The impact on women of the modernisation of agriculture is complex and contradictory, varying according to the crops produced, the size of farm and the farming system, the economic position of an individual farm family, and the cultural and political structure of the society. Women have often been excluded from agrarian reform and training programmes in new agricultural methods because Western experts have assumed a pattern of responsibility for agriculture similar to their own societies, in which men are the main decision makers. This lack of insight has resulted in the failure of many agriculturally based development projects.

Women tend to work significantly more hours than men when both market and household work are calculated. As many women undertake household work at the expense of income-generating activities, their bargaining power and decision-making capacity in the home can be limited, having implications for their overall well-being. Local politics and laws may also perceive women as less worthy of credit than men, thus adding to their difficulties.

Women also frequently head households where men have died, moved away due to marital instability, or migrated. Their households are often among the poorest as they contain fewer working adults than male-headed households and women earn lower wages than men. They may become poverty traps in which children become further disadvantaged because they may have to leave school early to seek paid employment or take over household chores to allow the mother to work outside the home. Maternal neglect and lack of paternal discipline may encourage truancy, delinquency, and perpetuate a family pattern of deprivation.

While these are important issues, researchers are also recognising the multifaceted nature of women's lives and work in impoverished and developing countries. In some cases women choose to establish their own household to gain decision-making independence, or to escape male violence and/or economic reliance on an irresponsible man. Such households can have a positive effect on women's autonomy and, despite frequently being socially stigmatised, they may function successfully as socioeconomic units.

A new phase of scholarship about women and development in the global economy has emerged around processes that suggest changes in the gendered nature of women's social roles, in women's psychology and in women's ideas about how they live as members of a nation-state. Research is also focussing on female immigrants, trafficking, and the potential for empowerment of women on the move. Authors argue that migration work is gendered, in the sense that the labour that underlies migration is often unpaid women's work. Women subordinate their own interests to the care of their families, negotiate to obtain resources for the family, link their family to broader society and maintain social networks, give up further education and careers, save money by reducing consumer spending, and rear children.

A key link between issues of migration and women's work in developing countries is the growing presence of women being trafficked across borders. Although cross-border routes are diverse, they share a vital feature, that is, they are profit- or revenue-making routes that are developed from the needs of severely disadvantaged women. Illegal trafficking provides hard currency for individuals and for governments, and provides people for the formal and informal labour markets of nursing, teaching, entertainment, tourism, and prostitution. Women search for work but illegal traffickers and governments contribute to the trafficking of women from developing economies. However, many developing economies can be described more accurately as struggling, stagnant, or failed states that have imposed survival strategies on people living in economies that are enduring the closure of small and medium-sized enterprises, moves to national rather than export markets, and the burden of large government debts.

Quality studies focused on the feminisation of survival in developing countries in terms of planting crops to earn cash and the rise of wage labour in agrarian communities then turned to the feminisation of workers as manufacturing internationalised. A concentration on the price urban women pay for development has been generated by world events. The 1997 Asian financial crisis exposed dangerous weaknesses in regional and global economies, and in development practices, which placed more crisis-induced burdens on women than on men. The impact was not confined to Asian regions but had a global ripple effect. The relative contributions and impediments that globalisation has given to the socioeconomic development of the region, and the extent to which global changes had a different impact on women and men regionally and locally, have created new questions about the impact of development on women. When the perspective of gender is infused into development studies, the existing image of regions such as East Asia as areas of affluence, with strong states, internal homogeneity, cultural cohesion, and a stable social order, must be

reassessed. Studies are showing that the three key processes of development—industrialisation, economic restructuring, and migration—have yielded new forms of women's subordination and inequality in work organisation and in society. Women are now strategising to gain from, and contest the process of, development.

Women's Networks and Development

As women move from rural to urban areas, they often command improvements in urban services as they work to cope with the problems of housing and access to services for themselves and their children. Women's survival strategies habitually depend on building networks within the community. Some women's groups may provide a focus for the politicisation of women's lives around issues of importance such as rising food costs or the disappearance of their children at the hands of political and military repression, as has occurred in Argentina and Chile. Development agencies are also advocating the spread of grassroots women's groups because they are seen to avoid confrontation with established cultural patterns and prevent the subordination of women's interests and leadership to men. Women's groups affiliated with established churches in the southwest Pacific are increasingly being used by development agencies because they are active in townships and rural areas, conduct important group activities, and serve their community's needs. Several studies argue that the church has become so powerful an institution in many developing countries that development agencies and the state cannot afford to ignore it as an important vehicle for implementing development programmes.

Acknowledging the role of women's groups enables an understanding of the complex, multifaceted, and diverse cultures and societies that constitute developing nations, women's pivotal roles in contemporary societies, and differing ideas about and social uses of the concept of women's active cultural agency, and it offers the opportunity to examine modes of being that are established through alternatives to Euro-American experiences of modernity. The drive toward global homogeneity is constantly undermined as local peoples interpret, adapt, and transform external influences just as readily as they might internalise them and make them their own. Recognising the diversity of local people's cultural strategies is mandatory to expand critical perspectives within development studies, to problematise project design, and to enable researchers and development practitioners to acknowledge the importance of involving local women in their discussions and planning processes, particularly from sources such as church groups that Westerners typically do not acknowledge as powerful social and political arenas.

Including the church as a significant social institution, and thinking about women and gender as durable but flexible sociocultural concepts, have the potential to encourage possibilities for women's resistance, subversion of oppressive power relations, and freedom. The significant insights about women, gender, and agency generated from non-Western communities should be more widely used in development planning and practice.

Directions in Theory and Practice

Sad evidence testifies to the fact that development strategies based solely on macroeconomic theories, such as structural adjustment programmes, have failed to solve the problems of poverty in developing countries. Moreover, many have produced the unforeseen consequence of making impoverished women even poorer. This situation has been recognized by some donor agencies including the World Bank, and their policies have broadened to encompass microeconomic aspects of development.

Resources are being channeled to the kinds of organisations that are being initiated and sustained by female workers in the unorganised sector, and by women in organisations where they do not feel threatened by overt male power. Gender planning constitutes one of the ways in which the problems associated with women's roles in development are currently being addressed. The general goal of gender planning is the release of women from social, political, and economic subordination and to achieve gender equity, equality, and empowerment through meeting practical and strategic needs. It includes several critical characteristics: Gender planning is political and technical, assumes there will be conflict in the planning process, involves transformative processes, and characterises planning as debate. Gender planning therefore uses a methodology that emphasises discussion, negotiation, and conflict resolution.

Despite such progressive approaches, structural problems continue to limit women's roles in development. Bilateral technical assistance agencies (from one government to another) and multilateral agencies (from many governments working through the United Nations or global conduits to many other governments) have been instituted and staffed by men as part of established national agencies, foreign policies, and the maintenance of global relations that reinforce

a status quo of powerful male interactions. Women's bureaus, departments, and ministries within these agencies are usually underfunded and understaffed, and operate with limited jurisdiction. Rather than resourcing women for their needs, "gender" can be too easily mainstreamed as a political concession.

Advocates have successfully pressed for incorporating gender into development project design, planning, and implementation, an action that altered the term "women" and symbolised change. However, change has not necessarily been anchored in practice. Gender as a sociological term has been criticised as not translating well into languages other than English. Nonetheless, regardless of the viewpoints of theorists, researchers, and practitioners in relation to development, many are now engaging with the question of whether there can be any development. Should "post-development" be considered as a more progressive mode of working *with* rather than *for* more people, especially women? Authors are addressing the issue and its problems from tentative yet innovative positions and are courageously facing the gaps and silences in existing knowledge.

HELEN JOHNSON

See also Basic Human Needs; Children and Development; Globalization: Impact on Development; Labor; Sex Trade/Trafficking; Women: Legal Status

References and Further Reading

Benería, Lourdes and Savitri Bisnath, eds. *Gender and Development: Theoretical, Empirical and Practical Approaches*, vol. 2. Cheltenham, UK, and Northampton, MA: Edward Elgar, 2001.

Fenster, Tovi, ed. *Gender, Planning, and Human Rights*. London, New York: Routledge, 1999.

Ghorayshi, Parvin and Claire Bélanger, eds. *Women, Work, and Gender Relations in Developing Countries: A Global Perspective*. Westport, London: Greenwood Press, 1996.

Moore, Henrietta. *Feminism and Anthropology*. Cambridge, Oxford: Polity Press, 1988.

Ostergaard, Lise, ed. *Gender and Development: A Practical Guide*. London and New York: Routledge, 1992.

Rowbotham, Sheila and Swasti Mitter, eds. *Dignity and Daily Bread: New Forms of Economic Organising Among Poor Women in the Third World and the First*. London and New York: Routledge, 1994.

Saunders, Kriemild, ed. *Feminist Post-Development Thought: Rethinking Modernity, Postcolonialism and Representation*. London and New York: Zed Books, 2002.

Takunani, Sirivi and Marilyn Taleo Havini, eds. *As Mothers of the Land: The Birth of the Bougainville Women for Peace and Freedom*. Canberra, Australia: Pandanus Books, 2004.

The World Bank. *Engendering Development Through Gender Equality in Rights, Resources, and Voice*. Washington, DC, and New York: World Bank and Oxford University Press, 2001.

WORLD BANK
(See International Bank for Reconstruction and Development [IBRD])

WORLD CONFEDERATION OF LABOUR (WCL)

A congress at The Hague in 1920 established the International Confederation of Christian Trade Unions—usually known by its French initials, CISC—on behalf of 3.5 million workers in ten European nations. Its policies reflected the social teachings of the Roman Catholic and some Protestant churches, emphasising "spiritual" rather than "material" values, rejecting both radical socialism and liberal capitalism, and promoting cooperative relations among workers, employers, and governments. During World War II the CISC was forced into abeyance.

In 1945 the CISC refused to join the World Federation of Trade Unions (WFTU), formed by the trade union movements of the victorious Allied nations in an effort to continue the East–West collaboration of World War II. Again in 1949, after Cold War tensions caused many Western European and North American union affiliates to break from the WFTU to create the International Confederation of Free Trade Unions (ICFTU), the CISC maintained its separation from both the now patently pro-Soviet WFTU and the equally pro-Western IFCTU. This basic three-way division within the international trade union movement was to remain intact for the next five decades.

Given the already high degree of unionisation in Europe and North America, and the growing clamour by non-Western and colonised peoples for political independence and economic development, all three international trade union groupings concluded that real growth for their organisations could only be found in what was becoming known as "The Third World." It was assumed that this task would be most difficult for the Brussels-based CISC, which, in the post-WWII period had been reduced to just four main unions: France's CFDT, Belgium's CSC, and the Netherlands' NKV and CNV.

Nevertheless, at its 1952 congress at The Hague, the CISC counted twenty member organisations: twelve of them European, six Latin American, one Asian, and one Canadian. Contributing to the 1968 congress in Luxemburg were seventy-four affiliates representing sixty-eight countries, including: twenty-nine from Latin America, twenty from Africa, nineteen from Europe, five from Asia, and one from North America. Such growth was impressive, even if many affiliates were workers' associations rather than full trade unions, and the claimed total membership of 12.7

million was obviously inflated. A key factor in CISC's success in the Third World was its decision to divert significant resources there, much of it from an "International Solidarity Fund" supported by wealthier affiliates. Church charities and the Dutch government likewise funneled overseas aid money through this fund.

Also, the CISC chose to support semi-autonomous regional groupings, the first of which was the Latin American Federation of Christian Trade Unions (CLASC), formed in 1954—though this later became the Latin American Workers Central (CLAT). Other regional organisations established by CISC were the Pan-African Workers Congress (PAWC), begun in 1959 but dissolved in 1974 under pressure from African governments; and the Brotherhood of Asian Trade Unionists (BATU), set up in 1963 with headquarters in the Philippines and which since then has established affiliates in many Asian nations. The absence of the word "Christian" from the latter two titles reflected CISC's pragmatic efforts to attract non-Christian members in regions like Africa and Asia. But this shift in turn encouraged a wider secularisation process, leading to the 1968 CISC congress decision to change the organisation's name to World Confederation of Labour (WCL).

At this time the WCL also was going through an ideological transformation that reflected both an overall reorientation from the First World to the Third World, and the growing presence within the upper levels of the organisation of representatives from less developed nations. New constitutional principles reaffirmed the primacy for the organisation at large of spiritual values, condemned both capitalism and communism as incompatible with humane society; somewhat contradictorily, however, they also advocated "class struggle" and worker control of resources and production, and promoted forms of syndicalist democracy.

In the early 1970s the WCL faced major problems with the dissolution of its own African regional organisation, the loss of its Vietnamese affiliates, and growing pressure on its Latin American membership from authoritarian regimes. Nevertheless, "privileged partnerships" were established with the Organization of African Unity's official union body (OATUU), and with the similarly constituted International Confederation of Arab Trade Unions (ICATU). Around the same time, the WCL was accusing the powerful US union grouping, the AFL-CIO, of "neo-colonial brutality" in Latin America, Africa, and Asia, and was describing itself as being in "a positive state of war" with official ICFTU bodies in Latin America.

Critics of the WCL, meanwhile, were charging it with unhealthy links to corrupt Christian Democratic regimes in Latin America, and of lacking a clear view of what its slogan, "Solidarity and Liberation," actually meant. On the other hand, some considered this particular labour international to have a more subtle understanding of Third-World realities than either the First World-oriented ICFTU or the Second World-oriented WFTU, especially regarding linkages with groups like the poor, unemployed, women, peasants, and indigenous peoples. In the 1980s–1990s, too, the WCL was more proactive in networking with the new social movements emerging in response to issues like the environment, human rights, and globalisation.

Over time, some core constituencies inside the WCL became alienated by its leftward lurch and Third World-ist reorientation—and, indeed, by its overall failure to match the two giant internationals. Most significantly, its large French affiliate, the CGT, departed in 1977 to join the opposition ICFTU. Other affiliates, mainly Western, pushed periodically for merger talks with that same international, but for a long time such moves were rejected by the WCL's governing body. Finally, in late 2004, while describing itself as "representing some 27 million workers worldwide," the WCL leadership announced that during the coming year the organisation would formally unite with its long-time "free union" competitor, the ICFTU. Given their relative sizes, it is inevitable that the WCL will surrender most in the merger process.

TOM RYAN

See also Labor

References and Further Reading

Munck, Ronaldo. *The New International Labour Studies: An Introduction*. London: Zed Books, 1988.
Pasture, Patrick. *Christian Trade Unionism in Europe Since 1968*. Aldershot, UK: 1994.
———. *Histoire du Syndicalisme Chrétien International: La Difficile Recherché d'une Troisième Voie*. Paris: L'Harmattan, 1999.
Windmuller, J. P. *Labor Internationals*. Ithaca: New York State School of Industrial and Labor Relations, Cornell University, Bulletin 61, 1969.
———. *The International Trade Union Movement*. Deventer, the Netherlands: Kluwer, 1980.

WORLD COUNCIL OF CHURCHES

History

The founding of the World Council of Churches (WCC) at Amsterdam in 1948 was the result of numerous attempts to bring together an international

fellowship of churches that had left the Roman Catholic Church at the time of the sixteenth-century Protestant Reformation in Europe. Previous steps toward unity, but not union, had included an 1810 call by the English Baptist missionary William Carey for global mission conferences to discuss evangelistic strategies. In 1946 the Evangelical Alliance met in Liverpool to form a united Protestant front against Roman Catholic advances in Britain and North America. A 1910 Edinburgh Conference met at a time when missionaries from Europe, North America, and Australasia were following imperial entrepreneurs and governments into Africa, Asia, and Latin America. In 1920 the Ecumenical Patriarch of Constantinople appealed for cooperation in a "League of Churches" similar to the post–World War I League of Nations. Protestant church leaders echoed this call, but no action occurred.

As Hitler's forces moved into Austria in 1937, two ecumenical bodies formed to implement agreements of the 1910 Edinburgh Conference, a Committee on Life and Work, and one on Faith and Order, and elected a provisional committee that met at Utrecht in 1938. That year the International Missionary Council (IMC) also considered the proposal to join a World Council of Churches, but several missionary groups expressed concern that they could lose their autonomy. In 1961 the IMC finally joined the WCC. In 1971 the World Council on Christian Education that had begun in 1907 as the World's Sunday School Association joined the WCC.

In 1938, American McCrea Cavert suggested a name, "World Council of Churches," and William Temple, Archbishop of York, became chairman of a provisional committee. W. A. Visser't Hooft of the Netherlands became the first general secretary. They invited 196 churches—including a personal invitation to the Vatican—to attend a first WCC General Assembly in August 1941, but World War II broke out before they could convene. From 1940 to 1946 the provisional committee met in the United States, England, and Switzerland. It lent support to chaplain services, released prisoners of war and provided refugee assistance, and prepared for postwar reconciliation of the Protestant churches in Europe.

The first General Assembly of the World Council met on August 22, 1948. A total of 147 churches from forty-four countries represented most Christians outside the Church of Rome. Both the Life and Work and the Faith and Order groups merged with the new Council. As the Cold War began, the Soviet Union was claiming hegemony over most Eastern European states and was constructing a wall between East and West Berlin. The WCC basis for membership declared no political agenda, although the term "godless communism" had already spawned an international ideological war.

The World Council would be a fellowship of national churches that accepted a simple statement of faith in "our Lord Jesus Christ as God and Savior." By 1961 the Third Assembly at Nairobi would revise that formula to acknowledge fidelity to the trinity and scripture. The new statement held that the WCC professed faith in "the Lord Jesus Christ as God and Savior according to the scriptures," and sought to fulfill a "common calling to the glory of the one God, Father, Son and Holy Spirit." Tinkering with the dogmatic basis for ecumenical unity, but not union with an elaborate creed and discipline, continued for the WCC's first fifty years as it tried to be both catholic (universal) and evangelical, with members who often held diametrically opposed views on both faith and order.

As of this writing, the World Council claims 320 churches, denominations, and fellowships, with membership of about 400 million in over 100 countries. The criteria for membership are that churches have a "sustained independent life and organization" and apply for membership without seeking permission of any other body or person. Members must accept the idea that churches are "interdependent" and need to engage in "constructive ecumenical relations" in their nation and region. A church needs to have a membership of at least 25,000.

As conservative nationalists of the McCarthy era of the 1950s were concerned that the United Nations would become a super-state, some denominationalists worried that the World Council of Churches was becoming a super-church, with Geneva as a Protestant Rome and the General Secretary as a Protestant Pope. Would the WCC impose political, theological, or social dogma that member churches would find unacceptable? Would it make alliances with anti-Christian, anti-democratic, anti-free enterprise political regimes or with religious bodies, Christian or non-Christian, that would violate the sensibilities or doctrines of its members? Could member churches veto actions taken by the General Assembly, Central Committee, or Executive Council? Could WCC leaders embarrass member churches by social-political activities that were unacceptable to church members in the nations that supplied the WCC with most of its funding? For a half-century such issues have arisen regularly in WCC meetings and in the press.

Theological Issues

World Council staff member Marlin VanElderen wrote: "Had the church continued to resemble the

portrait of the earliest Christian community given in Acts 2:44–47, the World Council of Churches would not be necessary." Yet he acknowledged that while Jesus' prayer was "that they may all be one . . . so that the world might believe" (John 17:21), and while the early church "had all things in common" in terms of possessions, "greed, lack of commitment, racial exclusiveness, lust for power, theological differences, personality conflicts, opposition from outside" plagued the church from the beginning. Such quarrels would also cause theological, as well as socio-political strife in the WCC from its earliest days.

Charged debates have occurred around such issues as the admission of churches to World Council membership that did not follow basic Christian or Protestant dogmas, such as those who did not practice the traditional sacraments. How would WCC members share the Lord's Supper fellowship when they differed in who administered the sacrament and how it was to be done? What about the Society of Friends and the Salvation Army who saw the sacrament as unnecessary for salvation? This matter was tied to ordination—who were the clergy (priesthood) who could administer sacraments, and what was their relationship to the extra-biblical "laity"? Some churches believed in apostolic succession; only a man who was a properly ordained as a priest by a bishop could administer the sacraments of baptism and communion, whereas congregationally based denominations extended priestly functions to the laity and women in the 1950s, and gays in the 1960s, and held that all believers were ministers and equal in function, even if they held different church offices.

Some Protestant denominations complained that the Council was too aggressive in making peace with the Roman Catholic Church and feared that negotiations would lead to merger under papal authority. In 1960 the Vatican established a Secretariat for Promoting Christian Unity and invited Protestant and Orthodox observers to the Second Vatican Council (1962–1965). As a result of a 1964 Decree on Ecumenism, Rome opened discussions with Protestants and Orthodox Christians. In 1969 Pope Paul VI visited the WCC's Geneva headquarters. The Catholic Church sends observers to WCC Assemblies and has membership on some of its committees. In 1999 John Paul II became the first Pope to visit Orthodox nations, with both warm meetings and chilly receptions in Eastern Europe. Also in 1999 Lutherans and Catholics signed a declaration on the doctrine of justification, the principal theological issue behind Martin Luther's excommunication that largely resolved their differences on that dogma.

Political and Social Issues

Political issues also threatened the World Council of Churches fellowship. During the Cold War some Western denominations, particularly in the United States, found it difficult to fellowship with Eastern Orthodox churches that had close ties to communist (atheistic) governments. Along that same line, fundamentalist denominations found the WCC staff to be too liberal (socialist or even Marxist) when it supported 1960s–1990s Third World liberation movements that were receiving weapons and humanitarian aid from communist states. This was particularly true when the WCC involvement was political, as opposed to purely humanitarian. Why did the WCC send funds directly to Marxist guerrilla groups in southern Africa and aboriginal groups in the West rather than provide grants to social programs sponsored by local churches or church councils? The WCC staff and most mainline denominations found colonialism and apartheid to be anti-Christian abominations that could only be wiped out by strong political as well as social action.

Perhaps the most controversial action by the World Council in the political-social arena was the establishment of the Program to Combat Racism (PCR) in 1969. It had already taken a strong stand against racial-ethnic segregation in 1954 when its Second Assembly at Evanston, Illinois, declared segregation to be "contrary to the gospel and incompatible with the Christian doctrine of man and with the nature of the church of Christ." At the time segregation was commonly practiced in the United States and apartheid was state policy in South Africa. By 1961, when the WCC held its Third Assembly at New Delhi, India, 18 of the 23 new members were from Africa, Asia, and Latin America, and four others were from the Russian, Rumanian, Bulgarian, and Polish Orthodox Churches. At a 1966 World Conference on Church and Society in Geneva, for the first time at a large ecumenical conference Western participants were in the minority. A majority of the 420 delegates were laypersons. The Uppsala, Sweden, Assembly in 1968 witnessed sit-ins, walkouts, pickets, and vigils, with a large number of youth present. Black novelist James Baldwin asked whether the WCC had "the moral energy, the spiritual daring, to atone, to repent, to be born again." The next year the WCC set up the PCR to combat "institutional white racism, entrenched in social, economic and political power structures, with the understanding that the victims of racism must undertake their own liberation and outsiders play only a supportive role" (VanElderen 1992).

As an example of the rift in WCC member churches and national councils, in 1970 the Christian

Council of Rhodesia voted to support the WCC's PCR program with only two dissenting votes. Following the meeting the international Salvation Army withdrew from the Council, and attacked the WCC for abetting violence promulgated by atheistic Marxists. In June 1978, at the apex of Zimbabwe's independence war, Africans killed two Salvationist female missionaries at a school near Bulawayo. Three months later the WCC-PCR gave Zimbabwe's Patriotic Front guerrillas an $85,000 grant. A month later the Salvation Army suspended its WCC membership, making the break final in 1981 from membership that extended back to 1948. Fifteen of twenty-six Army leaders who had addressed a 1979 Toronto conference wanted full membership, while twenty-three favored some form of membership. African Salvationists expressed their anger with General Arnold Brown by marching on the Army's Harare headquarters. Few fundamentalist churches belonged to the WCC, and some conservatives in mainline churches voted with their purses not to support its work.

NORMAN H. MURDOCH

References and Further Reading

Beffa, Pierre and Ans van der Bent, et al., eds. *Index to World Council of Churches' Official Statements and Reports, 1948–1994.*

Murdoch, Norman H. "The World Council of Churches and the Salvation Army: A 1978–1985 Debate over Zimbabwe's Liberation Movement." Conference Proceedings, Association of Third World Studies, 1996, pp. 68–78.

Raiser, Konrad. *To Be the Church: Challenges and Hopes for a New Millennium.* Geneva: WCC Publications, 1997.

Sjollema, Baldwin. *Isolating Apartheid: Western Collaboration with South Africa:* Policy *Decisions by the World Council of Churches and Church Responses.* Geneva: Program to Combat Racism: World Council of Churches, 1982.

Van der Bent, Ans. *Historical Dictionary of Ecumenical Christianity.* Lanham, MD: Scarecrow Press, 1994.

VanElderen, Marlin. *Introducing the World Council of Churches.* Geneva: World Council of Churches, 1992.

Visser't Hooft, W. A. *The Genesis and Formation of the World Council of Churches.* Geneva: World Council of Churches, 1982.

Webb, Pauline, ed. *A Long Struggle: The Involvement of the World Council of Churches in South Africa.* Geneva: WCC Publications, 1994.

WORLD FEDERATION OF TRADE UNIONS (WFTU)

At the outbreak of World War II the existing trade union internationals closed down, though their networks were used by resistance groups in German-occupied Europe. With the 1941 entry into the war of the USSR, the need to coordinate industrial production for the anti-fascist cause led to the All Union Central Council of Trade Unions (AUCCTU) working with the British Trades Union Congress (TUC) to form the Anglo-Soviet Trade Union Council. After the United States joined the Allied cause later the same year, the powerful American Federation of Labour (AFL) agreed to cooperate with the TUC—but not with its own domestic rival, the Congress of Industrial Organisations (CIO), or the communist AUCCTU.

Churchill, Stalin, and Roosevelt strongly supported close cooperation between each government and its national labour movement, and between the trade union centres of their respective countries. During wartime, trade unions were accorded far more status and power than they had enjoyed in peacetime. Then, as the war approached its conclusion, labour movements were considered key players in securing peace, achieving economic reconstruction, and rebuilding civil society. In Britain and throughout Europe, moreover, rank-and-file workers felt a special sense of solidarity with the Soviet people because of their leading role in defeating Nazism.

Consequently, at a Paris conference in October 1945 the World Federation of Trade Unions (WFTU) was born. Its main backers were the TUC, the CIO, and the AUCCTU—with the latter delivering over half the organisation's claimed 65 million members. The main objectives of the WFTU were the eradication of war and fascism; the promotion of democratic institutions; and full employment, decent wages, regulated workplaces, and social security for all citizens. But many British and US union leaders remained suspicious of their Soviet counterparts' ongoing support for "political" trade unionism, especially the spread of "real socialism."

Within the WFTU a major crisis occurred with the announcement of the Marshall Plan in October 1947. This proposal was welcomed by most Western unions as consistent with WFTU policies, but the AUCCTU condemned it as "the weapon of the transatlantic republic of the dollar and the atom bomb to split Europe." A tightening of unity amongst communist elements inside the WFTU followed. This was matched by a consolidation of anticommunist control over most Western national union centres. Finally, in January 1949, the TUC and the CIO led a major walkout from the WFTU; soon after they were joined by numerous other Western union groupings.

The main trade union centres remaining with the WFTU were from countries with Marxist-Leninist governments, but very quickly the organisation began to mirror the political tensions within that bloc. In 1950 the Yugoslav national affiliates were expelled

for, allegedly, letting their country "restore capitalism" and become a base for "imperialist aggression." Then, in 1953 and 1956, the WFTU supported Soviet crackdowns on popular protests in East Germany and Hungary, respectively. China and Albania were ejected in 1966 after accusing the international of supporting Soviet "expansionism" and "revisionism." During the 1968 "Prague Spring" uprising, the WFTU secretariat—based in that city and responding to pleas from Czech unions—briefly condemned the Warsaw Pact invasion, as did its affiliated French and Italian unions. But order was quickly re-imposed within the WFTU, and in 1976 when worker protests in Poland were violently suppressed, the secretariat said nothing. Two years later, the frustrated Italian affiliates totally withdrew, although their French colleagues opted to pursue "internal reform" a few years more.

WFTU views on the Third World reflected current East–West relations and the core tenets of Marxist-Leninist ideology. In practice, "development" was reduced to "the struggle of the workers and of the peoples against imperialism, exploitation by the transnational corporations, and an economic system causing a backwardness of the majority of the peoples." The USSR and its satellites were presented as models of socialist development and proletarian democracy, and Third World labour movements were expected to combine historical materialist analyses and "appropriate" revolutionary strategies to ensure their countries attained similar heights. Especially strong support was given by the WFTU to affiliated unions involved in anticolonial and anticapitalist liberation struggles, such as in Vietnam, South Africa, and Chile.

By 1980 national union centres and affiliates from seventy-five countries, mainly in the Third World, were said to be attached to the WFTU, though the bulk of its claimed 190 million individual members were still in Eastern Europe. The organisation itself was intensely bureaucratic and quite divorced from ordinary workplaces and workers. Unsurprisingly, the collapse of the Soviet Union in 1989–1990 was a disaster for the WFTU. Over the next few years this once-powerful international lost most of its Russian and East European affiliates and members—plus the monies and state support they had long provided. While ostensibly still based in Prague, the WFTU rapidly became a disoriented and decentered organisation.

After a decade of relative inactivity, a World Congress of the WFTU was held in 2000 in New Delhi, funded by Indian unions. It was the first congress in the fifty-five year history of the organisation to be held outside Europe. While the official Web site described attendance by "delegates and observers from seventy-four countries representing a membership of 407 million," such claims are misleading. Most

illustrative is the inclusion of the 135 million members of the ACFTU, China's national trade union centre, even though its representatives were attending only as observers. Actual figures for national union centres, individual unions, and individual members directly connected to the WFTU in the twenty-first century must be considerably less than those for the 1980s.

Key ongoing issues, the WFTU says, are "the struggles to defend jobs, social security, health protection, trade union rights, poverty, environmental degradation, exploitation of child labour, etc." Institutional enemies include "neoliberal capitalist globalisation" and agencies such as the World Bank, the International Monetary Fund, and the World Trade Organisation. Similarly odious are economic sanctions against Third World countries like Cuba, Libya, and Iraq, and military ventures by the United States and its allies. Clearly the WFTU remains committed to "working class solidarity," "international socialism," and "anti-imperialist struggle." The only real changes seem to be that its leadership and agenda are now oriented towards the Third World rather than the (ex-)Second World, and that the "East–West" paradigm of its past has been replaced by the more recent "North–South" debates.

Tom Ryan

See also Labor

References and Further Reading

Munck, Ronaldo. *The New International Labour Studies: An Introduction*. London: Zed Books, 1988.

Waterman Peter, and Jane Wills, eds. *Place, Space and the New Labour Internationals*, Oxford, UK: Blackwell, 2001.

Windmuller, J. P. *Labor Internationals*. Ithaca: New York State School of Industrial and Labor Relations, Cornell University, Bulletin 61, 1969.

———. *The International Trade Union Movement*. Deventer, the Netherlands: Kluwer, 1980.

WORLD FOOD PROGRAM

The United Nations General Assembly established the World Food Program (WFP) in 1961 for the purpose of providing emergency food aid to areas of the world experiencing famine and disaster. It became fully operational in 1963, working closely with its parent organization, the Food and Agricultural Organization (FAO), which was in turn the brainchild of the Allied Conference at Hot Springs, Virginia, in 1943. The FAO commenced operations in October 1945, and with the establishment of the UN came into close association with the United Nations Economic and Social Council as the lead technical agency

for food issues at the UN. The focus of the FAO, however, was on long-term development planning, and the increasing numbers of food emergencies during the early 1960s argued for creation of a sister agency to focus on the emergency food needs of countries afflicted with famines and disasters reducing local food supplies. WFP, like the FAO, maintains its headquarters in Rome.

From Emergency to Development

The WFP was instituted on a trial basis. In 1966, it gained permanent status as the lead UN food logistics agency in emergency settings. The WFP specializes in tracking food supplies and food shipments globally, and in redistributing food supplies when shortages strike various areas of the world. It relies on in-kind contributions of food from food-producing countries and on voluntary cash contributions used for purchasing and shipping food. About sixty countries contribute to the WFP's assets, while around ninety benefit from its assistance. Swift shipping of food to famine-affected areas is essential for saving lives. The WFP has access to aircraft, ships, and hundreds of trucks, often on charter from governments, in order to distribute food supplies. In-country distribution of food aid is done in cooperation with governments and often with non-governmental organizations, such as CARE, that specialize in food-delivery systems and logistics.

Emergency food aid can have the effect of glutting food markets, reducing local food prices and thus inhibiting incentives for local production of food grains. To avoid this, the WFP attempts to free up available surpluses within the countries and regions where drought, famine, or emergency food needs have arisen. The use of local grains and the infusion of cash into local economies and food markets prior to importation of outside assistance is one way the WFP attempts to respect the integrity of development production. In addition, the WFP has developed food-for-work programs, which involve payment in food for work done on various development infrastructure and public works projects, such as road-building and reforestation programs. An example of a WFP food-for-work program during the 1980s was a collaborative effort with the World Bank and the UN High Commissioner for Refugees (UNHCR) in Pakistan, where the influx of large Afghan refugee populations led to degradation of roads. By paying refugees and local Pakistani workers in food to maintain and develop roads, this program helped to enhance Pakistan's road infrastructure while providing food for workers who would otherwise have remained unemployed. Such work by the WFP often extends to technical support to governments attempting to enhance food production, food storage, and food-distribution systems.

Interagency Collaboration

Emergency food-aid policies are related to development policies and programs, so the WFP often interacts with other humanitarian aid bodies such as the UN High Commissioner for Refugees (UNHCR) and the International Committee for the Red Cross, as well as the UN Development Program, the World Bank, UNICEF, and the World Food Program's parent agency, the FAO. The WFP's work requires cooperation with UN specialized agencies in both humanitarian and development programs. In Africa, where the lion's share of WFP programming is implemented, the WFP is heavily engaged in development-related food-for-work programs, refugee assistance, and food aid to various complex emergencies, including the major humanitarian emergencies in the Great Lakes Region of Africa, the Congo, and the Sudan. The WFP is a member of the Interagency Standing Committee of the UN Office for Coordination of Humanitarian Affairs (UNOCHA), where it maintains close ties to the various UN emergency-assistance organizations and contributes to Consolidated Appeals for aid to countries facing emergency situations.

A Legacy of Effective Action

The WFP's aid programs reach tens of millions of people every year, saving many lives and improving nutrition throughout the developing world. In recent years its programs have served more than 100 million people in more than eighty countries. It is directly involved in the world's most difficult humanitarian situations, conflict-torn regions, and disaster-affected areas. Additionally, by focusing on the mitigation of hunger in non-disaster areas, the WFP attempts to prevent malnutrition that stunts the full potential of young people as they mature. The WFP promotes school feeding programs to encourage child education programs. It provides food aid to encourage the development of schools, home shelters, and irrigation systems. It emphasizes disaster mitigation by using food as an incentive to build better roads, food-storage capacity, reforestation, and conservation programs. In all these ways, WFP assistance maintains

a long-term development focus as well as a commitment to rapid humanitarian response.

ROBERT F. GORMAN

See also CARE; United Nations Economic and Social Council

References and Further Reading

Cuny, Frederick. *Famine, Conflict and Response: A Basic Guide.* West Hartford, CT: Kumarian, 1999.

World Food Program. *Annual Reports.* See the WFP Web site for a list of publications available online and for purchase at www.wfp.org

World Food Program/International Food Policy Research Institute. *Food as Aid: Trends, Needs and Challenges in the Twenty-First Century.* Rome: WFP, 2003.

WORLD HEALTH ORGANIZATION (WHO)

Established in 1948, the World Health Organization is one of the four most important specialized institutions among the sixteen agencies officially affiliated with the United Nations, together with the United Nations Educational, Scientific, and Cultural Organization (UNESCO); the Food and Agriculture Organization (FAO); and the International Labor Organization (ILO).

Since the middle of the nineteenth century, concerted efforts had been undertaken in the field of international public health, and several international bodies were created. International Sanitary Conferences had been convened, notably to coordinate quarantine measures in times of cholera and later yellow fever, the first in 1851 in Paris, and the eleventh held in 1903. In 1907, twelve states agreed in Rome on the creation of the International Office of Public Hygiene (OIHP), based in Paris. The League of Nations established its own Health Organization in 1920. The two international health organizations coexisted until after World War II. The United Nations Relief and Rehabilitation Administration (UNRRA), added later, took over OIHP's role. Several regional bodies also dealt with health questions, particularly quarantine. The new idea to create a single international organization in all fields of public health emerged in 1945, at the UN Conference on International Organizations, held in San Francisco, and was recommended in a joint declaration submitted by Brazil and China.

The Constitution of the new World Health Organization (WHO) was signed by sixty-one states on July 22, 1946, and entered into force on April 7, 1948. Amendments to it were adopted in 1959, 1965, 1967, 1973, 1976, 1978, 1986, and 1998, of which five became integral parts without, however, touching on the fundamental principles of the Constitution (Burci and Vignes 2004, p. 18). The principles and functions outlined in the Constitution indicated a clear reorientation from those of the preceding health organizations, created for the "civilized" countries in order to protect them and establish a sanitary belt around the developed nations (Beigbeder 1995, p. 13). While WHO's objective is stated to be "the attainment by all peoples of the highest possible level of health" (Article 1), the preamble of the Constitution is visionary:

> Health is a state of complete physical, mental and social well-being and not merely the absence of disease or infirmity.
>
> The enjoyment of the highest attainable standard of health is one of the fundamental rights of every human being without distinction of race, religion, political belief, economic or social condition.
>
> The health of all peoples is fundamental to the attainment of peace and security and is dependent upon the fullest co-operation of individuals and States.

To achieve its objective, WHO is entrusted with multiple functions—both operational and normative—of cooperation, research, training and information. They include technical assistance to governments in strengthening their health services; actions to eradicate epidemic or endemic diseases; emergency aid, promotion of improved nutrition, housing, sanitation, recreation, economic and working conditions, and environmental hygiene; promotion of maternal and child health and welfare; activities in the field of mental health; and establishing international standards with respect to food, biological, and pharmaceutical products.

Membership and Structure

Membership is based on the principles of universality and statehood. There are now 192 member states and two associate members (Puerto Rico and Tokelau). The structure of the Geneva-based organization is threefold and comprises the World Health Assembly, the Executive Board, and the Secretariat under the responsibility of the Director-General.

The *World Health Assembly* consists of delegates, representatives, and observers. Delegates represent members and their number is limited to three per member state, although they may be accompanied by delegations of varying sizes. Delegates are chosen for their competence in the field of health, and preferably represent health administrations. Associate members are entitled to send representatives. Observers may be invited for a limited period, but there are also "quasi-permanent" observers. The Assembly meets in regular

annual sessions, for about two weeks, while several committees work continuously.

The Assembly's role is to determine the policies of the organization. It elects the Director-General and the members of the Executive Board. Most of the decisions of the Assembly are recommendations to its members, which are not legally binding but nevertheless are important. It has also the normative authority to adopt regulations and binding conventions or agreements on health matters.

The *Executive Board* is composed of thirty-two persons. The selection of board members respects regional criteria, and they serve as government representatives rather than in their personal capacity, as was the case until 1998. The Board meets twice per year and follows an agenda set up by the Director-General. Its role is both technical and political; it prepares the Assembly's work and as such decides on the matters to be discussed (or not discussed); it is responsible for implementing the Assembly's decisions, can decide on emergency matters, and is a determining factor for the choice of the Director-General. The Board also appoints various committees to fulfill its task.

The staff of the *Secretariat* is under the authority of the Director-General and constitutes the third organ of the Organization. Since WHO's creation, five persons have occupied the post of Director-General. The initial five-year appointment can, since 1996, be renewed once only. The Director-Generals have been: Dr. Brock Chrisholm (Canada 1948–1953), Dr. Marcolino Gomes Candau (Brazil 1953–1973), Dr. Halfdan T. Mahler (Denmark 1973–1988), Dr. Hiroshi Nakajima (Japan 1988–1998), and Dr. Gro Harlem Brundtland (Norway 1998–2003). The first mandate of Dr. Jong-Wook Lee (Republic of Korea) started in 2003. The Director-General is "the chief technical and administrative officer of the Organization" (Article 31, Constitution), but the position's responsibilities go far beyond this and the individual's influence is considerable.

Regionalization

From WHO's beginnings, the historical importance of regionalization was recognized and six geographical areas were delineated on the basis of continental groupings but also considering standards of health and the epidemiological situation in the countries to be included. The regions are Africa, the Americas, Southeast Asia, Europe, the Eastern Mediterranean, and the Western Pacific. The six originally determined regions have not been changed fundamentally, although some countries did change their affiliation to

a specific area. Each region has its own organization consisting of a regional committee and office. In some regions, special arrangements had to be made to account for preexisting regional structures and their relationship with WHO, as was the case for the Pan Arab Regional Health Bureau at Alexandria and for the Pan American Health Organization (PAHO).

WHO's Relations with States

Relations with states are structured around obligations deriving from their membership and also from a network of agreements, for example, "host country agreements" with countries hosting the headquarters or regional offices; also "basic agreements" for technical cooperation with member states, notably with developing countries. More than 150 member states have concluded such "basic agreements" with WHO.

WHO's Relations with Intergovernmental Organizations

WHO's primary relationship is of course with the United Nations, since it is one of its specialized agencies, but it also has significant relationships with the international agencies that predated its creation (PAHO, International Office of Public Health). WHO has formal agreements with sixteen organizations, mostly within the United Nations system. Other examples are the African Development Bank and the League of Arab States. There are also less formal, umbrella-type agreements and WHO collaborates on policy issues with the United Nations Economic and Social Council (ECOSOC) (for example, on tobacco control and HIV/AIDS). First with the United Nations Expanded Program of Technical Assistance (EPTA) and later with the United Nations Development Program (UNDP), the relationship has always been characterized by the difficulty to maintain a balance between resisting the United Nation's centralization attempts of technical cooperation by the resident coordinator and the effort to cooperate with the UNDP in order to integrate health programs in development activities (Burci and Vignes 2004, p. 75).

WHO has always had close relations with UNICEF, because of the overlap of the two bodies, particularly UNICEF's emphasis on maternal and child health and nutrition, on immunization, family planning, emergency relief, and so forth. The two bodies also have a Joint Committee on Health Policy (JCHP). First

concentrated on the eradication of a number of diseases, the cooperation became particularly important around the strategy of "Health for All by the Year 2000" and its focus on primary health care (see below). The 1978 Alma Ata Conference on Primary Health Care was indeed organized jointly by UNICEF and WHO. Other examples of close collaboration are the 1979 International Code for the Marketing of Breast-Milk Substitutes and the Children's Vaccine Initiative, at the World Summit for Children, in 1990.

Several long-term programs are co-sponsored by WHO and other United Nations agencies: the Special Program for Research and Training in Tropical Diseases (TDR); the Special Program for Research, Development and Research Training in Human Reproduction (HRP); the FAO-WHO Codex Alimentarius Commission; and the Joint United Nations Program on HIV/AIDS (UNAIDS).

TDR and HRP are based on the recognized necessity to pool international expertise, the political will of the states concerned, and financial resources. Co-sponsored and executed by WHO, they are mostly financed by extra-budgetary contributions. TDR was established in the 1970s, in a period when biomedical progress facilitated research on the prevention and treatment of major tropical diseases. At the same time, there was also awareness that pharmaceutical companies were not interested in developing medicines for the "diseases of the poor."

Before the creation of UNAIDS, the reaction of WHO to the pandemic was to establish, in 1987, the Global Program on AIDS, headed by the widely respected Dr. Jonathan Mann who emphasized the social dimensions of AIDS. There was also a parallel Inter-Agency Advisory Group on AIDS as well as a WHO-UNDP Alliance to Combat AIDS. In the early 1990s, the focus shifted to a biomedical perspective. It became clear, however, that the complexity of the growing pandemic brought challenges in various sectors that needed to be addressed by coordinated action. WHO's Director-General received the mandate, in 1993, to consider developing an inter-agency program in consultation with UNDP, UNICEF, UNFPA, UNESCO, and the World Bank. ECOSOC became involved later and proposed a membership formula. The Health Assembly and the other six co-sponsors agreed to the establishment of UNAIDS in 1995, as a joint and co-sponsored United Nations program on HIV/AIDS. Its secretariat is located in Geneva, headed by an Executive Director who is appointed by the UN Secretary General upon proposal of the six co-sponsors. UNAIDS operates in developing countries through the country-based staff of its co-sponsors. Coordinated action is decided by the UN Theme Group on HIV/AIDS.

International Agency for Research on Cancer (IARC)

Created by Resolution WHA18.44 in 1965, IARC is a non-statutory body of WHO and is open to participation of all WHO Member States (as of February 2005, it had sixteen participating states: Australia, Belgium, Canada, Denmark, Finland, France, Germany, Italy, the Netherlands, Norway, the Russian Federation, Sweden, Switzerland, the UK, and the USA). Its headquarters are in Lyon, France, because of the French origin of the initiative to create such a body and also because of its closeness to Geneva. IARC has a Governing Council, a Scientific Council, and a Secretariat. Its objective is to promote international collaboration in cancer research. Its functions are the collection and dissemination of cancer epidemiology and research information, the support of cancer research projects, and education and training of personnel for cancer research.

WHO's Relations with NGOs

From the beginning of the World Health Organization, its interaction with mostly international NGOs has been one of its most important means to accomplish its mandate. From twenty-six, in 1951, their number increased to over 190 in 2002 (Burci and Vignes 2004, p. 89). The working or official relations, as they are called, between WHO and NGOs reach from cooperation in technical matters to operational activities. Related NGOs have a variety of objectives and range from scientific associations, to advocacy and humanitarian organizations, to youth and women's organizations, to private companies.

Relations with the Private Sector

At the time of WHO's establishment, the private sector and commercial companies were not considered important partners to international health policy. The relationship with private companies developed gradually, and cautiously, as WHO recognized the role particularly of pharmaceutical companies (for collaboration in research and development of new drugs and vaccines) but was also aware its policies may affect the commercial sector, which in turn might try to influence the outcome of WHO activities. Since the 1980s, WHO has adopted a patent policy by which, depending on the circumstances, the results of funded research are not necessarily placed in the public domain, as might be expected of publicly funded

research, but patent rights and any financial or other benefits associated therewith are used to promote the development, production and wide availability of health technology in the public interest. This permits, for example, the organization to support the development of new drugs in the area of tropical diseases. WHO has also sometimes encouraged donations in kind or money by private pharmaceutical companies to developing countries, monitoring the shipping, distribution, and use of donated drugs, and arranging for research and development. This was for example the case in 2001, when Aventis Pharma made a donation for five years of the drugs Pentamidine, Melarsoprol, and Eflorinthine for the treatment of trypanosomiasis (sleeping disease) in endemic African countries (Burci and Vignes 2004, p. 97).

The multiplication of such relations with the private sector has, however, also raised concerns about WHO's image as an impartial and objective policy agency, independent from undue influences, concerns which recently revised guidelines have not completely dissipated. The proliferation in recent years of longer-term "public–private partnerships" (PPPs) has been both criticized and welcomed, particularly when philanthropic foundations, such as the Gates Foundation, support financially the for-profit enterprises.

"Health for All" Strategy

Immediately after its establishment, during the post-war years, emergency measures against malaria, tuberculosis, and sexually transmittable diseases were WHO's priority, as well as maternal and child hygiene and nutrition. Gradually, a conception of health as an essential element to industrial and agricultural development imposed itself. Social dimensions, prevention, and the necessary training of health care workers shifted to the foreground, together with the importance of sanitation and clean water.

During the 1960s, the fight against transmittable diseases, the strengthening of basic health care services, the training of the needed personnel, and nutrition and environmental concerns were still priorities. At the same time, the arrival of many recently independent state members made the interweaving of health and development obvious. Although the strategy against malaria made some points—except in Africa—large parts of the world's population continued to have no access to basic health care.

By the mid-1970s, no real progress had been accomplished; worse, some sectors were declining and the lack of basic health care services remained the most preoccupying problem. The ways to conceive

of health were more and more questioned; the approach appeared to be fragmented and static. In the developing world, expensive urban hospitals drained national health expenditures. Smaller dispensaries and clinics were rare and had little resources. Millions of people had no access to even rudimentary health care. During this period, WHO initiated a series of studies of successful and innovative initiatives in developing countries. Although the experiences were varied, they had in common a "commitment to universal coverage" (Burci and Vignes 2004, p. 161) and to bring basic health care to those most in need. In 1974, the United Nations General Assembly urged WHO to intensify its international action to improve sanitary conditions in developing countries and to concentrate its actions on prevention and access to basic health care services for collectivities. The Assembly insisted that complicated treatments and high technologies add little to sanitary development where it is most needed and drain precious resources. WHO is asked to reorient its resources and activities.

Probably the most important and long-lasting contribution of WHO to international health policy will be the adoption by the World Health Assembly, in 1977, of the concept of *Health for All by the Year 2000*. The International Conference at Alma Ata (USSR) culminated the following year in a Declaration recognizing primary health care as the adequate approach in order to attain this goal. The United Nations General Assembly expressed its support for the *Health for All by the Year 2000* strategy in 1981. The goal "by the year 2000" was, without doubt, too ambitious; but the policy was revised and reaffirmed in 1998, and continues to orient WHO's activities in the twenty-first century. The strategy is built around five principles, based on the primary health care approach as developed at the Alma Ata Conference. The main components are: (1) the equal distribution of resources and the accessibility of essential health care to everyone; (2) the individual and collective right and duty to participate in sanitary development; (3) equal importance of health promotion, disease prevention, and curative care; (4) scientifically sound technology for all, as economically affordable; and finally, (5) the recognition that the attainment of the highest level of health has to be a concerted effort of all domains of human activity. These guiding principles are further detailed in specific fields, such as education and training, nutrition, clean water, mother and child health, vaccination, and improving access to essential and other medicines. WHO's activities in the field of pharmaceuticals merit special mention. In order to assure rational selection of medicines, low prices, financing on the country level, supply, and delivery, WHO encouraged a policy of differential prices for

poor countries. It also raised awareness of how certain provisions of the Agreement on Trade-Related Aspects of Intellectual Property Rights (TRIPS) limit the affordability of medicines. A Declaration on the TRIPS Agreement and Public Health was adopted in 2001.

Challenges

WHO has had its share of criticisms and challenges. Like all inter-governmental organizations, it has to deal with the fundamental contradiction of programs that are international in scope but have to be implemented nationally. Regional differences in WHO's administration have been controversial from its beginnings, as have been administrative problems at the head office. The proliferation of "special programs," each with its own quite independent board, has been considered a factor undermining WHO's central leadership. Competition from other agencies, such as the World Bank, UNDP, or UNICEF, questions its credibility. Both the politicization and the Health Assembly's voting system, where each member has one vote, gave rise to criticism.

Since the World Health Organization's creation, enormous scientific and medical advances have been made while at the same time adverse side effects of certain treatments appeared (e.g., overuse of antibiotics or pesticides). The health gap between the developed and developing world has led to new strategies, but the most serious problems remain and new challenges, such as the deterioration of the environment and the AIDS pandemic, have to be addressed. The "Health for All" strategy with its emphasis on prevention leaves in the dark numerous congenital or accidental afflictions that cannot be prevented. It is also considered by many a "poor man's" approach to health. Finally, the normative function of WHO has often been controversial, most prominently around the International Code of Marketing of Breast-Milk Substitutes.

RUTH MURBACH AND MIKHAEL ELBAZ

See also Basic Human Needs; Children and Development; Doctors Without Borders/Médecins sans Frontières; Health Care; HIV/AIDS; Infectious Diseases; Public Health

References and Further Reading

Beaglehole, R. *Shaping the Future*. Geneva: World Health Organization, 2003.
Beigbeder, Y. *L'Organisation Mondiale de la Santé*. Institut Universitaire des Hautes Études Internationales de Genève. Paris: Presses Universitaires de France, 1995.
Burci, G. L. and C. H. Vignes. *World Health Organization*. The Hague, Netherlands: Kluwer Law International, 2004.
Buse, K. and G. Walt. "The WHO and Global Public-Private Partnership." In M. R. Reich, ed., *Public–Private Partnerships for Public Health*. Cambridge, MA: Harvard University Press, 2002, p. 171.
Deveaud, B. and B. Lemennicier. *L'OMS: Bateau Ivre de la Santé Publique*. Paris: L'Harmattan, 1997.
Shubber, S. *The International Code of Marketing of Breast-Milk Substitutes: An International Measure to Protect and Promote Breastfeeding*. The Hague, Netherlands: Kluwer Law International, 1998.
The World Health Organization. *Primary Health Care— Report of the International Conference on Primary Health Care*. Geneva: Author, 1978.
———. *The World Health Organization. Fifty Years of International Public Health*. Online: www.who.int/archives/who50/
———. *World Health Report* (published annually since 1995). Online: www.who.int/whr/en/

WORLD METEOROLOGICAL ORGANIZATION (WMO)

The World Meteorological Organization (WMO) is an intergovernmental agency composed of more than 180 member states and territories, established by the United Nations to foster international cooperation in the collection, sharing, and analysis of meteorological, hydrological, and associated geophysical data.

The WMO's roots lie in the International Meteorological Organization (IMO), which had been founded in 1873. The successor was established by the "Convention of the World Meteorological Organization," a multilateral treaty that was signed on October 11, 1947, and which went into effect March 23, 1950.

The mission of the WMO is utilitarian—to improve human life and promote human activities by improving understanding of the environmental factors that affect those lives and activities the most. By establishing a coordinated network for the gathering and exchange of meteorological, hydrological, and geophysical data, for example, the WMO has provided benchmarks by which potential environmental threats to human welfare can be assessed.

Throughout its history, the WMO has helped scientists and policy makers understand weather-related climate disasters—such as the Sahel droughts that have caused famines throughout West Africa since the 1960s; or El Niño, a cyclical phenomenon that has the potential to disrupt global climate patterns. WMO programs can provide early warning of impending natural and man-made disasters. Such early warnings are necessary in order to provide citizens of

developing and developed nations adequate time to prepare for environmental changes.

Among the major issues of concern to the WMO are climate change, which may occur abruptly, but which have the potential—despite the rate of change—to cause significant disruptions to human lives and activities over the next century; desertification, whether caused by unwise land use or by natural phenomena; natural disasters such as an increase in the frequency or intensity of tropical storms, or climate effects from major volcanic eruptions; maintaining adequate supplies of clean water for growing human populations; pollution; food production; ozone depletion; and climate effects on the incidence and severity of human diseases.

The WMO's major programs include: (1) the Applications of Meteorology Programme, which focuses on development of meteorological services to agricultural, aeronautical, and marine interests; (2) the Atmospheric Research and Environment Programme, which integrates monitoring and research activities concerning, for example, atmospheric chemistry, ozone depletion, tropical meteorology, and weather prediction; (3) the Education and Training Programme, which ensures that member nations have adequate numbers of trained meteorologists, hydrologists, engineers, and technicians; (4) the Hydrology and Water Resources Programme, which is devoted to the monitoring of water resources and mitigation of water-related hazards; (5) the Regional Programme, which focuses on the problems of specific regions; (6) the Technical Cooperation Programme, which facilitates the sharing of relevant knowledge and technologies among member states; (7) the World Climate Programme, which promotes improved understanding of climatic processes; (8) the Space Programme, which supports the development of space-based weather observation platforms and the sharing and utilization of data from those platforms; and (9) the World Weather Watch Programme, which coordinates the acquisition of meteorological and hydrological data and the sharing of that data among WMO members.

DAVID M. LAWRENCE

See also Acid Precipitation; Deforestation; Desertification; Disaster Relief; Environment: Government Policies; Environmentalism; Erosion, Land; Global Climate Change; Infectious Diseases; Irrigation; Natural Disasters; Pollution, Agricultural; Pollution, Industrial; Rain Forest, Destruction of; United Nations Food and Agriculture Organization (FAO); Urbanization: Impact on Environment; Water Resources and Distribution; Wildlife Preservation; World Health Organization (WHO)

References and Further Reading

Burroughs, William, ed. *Climate: Into the Twenty-First Century*. New York: Cambridge University Press, 2003.
Obasi, G. O. P., ed. *Decade of Progress: The World Meteorological Organization in the 1990s and the New Century*. Geneva, Switzerland: World Meteorological Organization, 2003.
Tank, Albert Klein, ed. *Global Climate System Review: July 1996–December 2001*. Geneva, Switzerland: World Meteorological Organization. World Climate Data and Monitoring Programme: United Nations Environment Programme, 2003. http://www.wmo.ch/web/wcp/wcdmp/review/950rev.htm
World Meteorological Organization. "Convention of the World Meteorological Organization." October 11, 1947. *WMO Basic Documents No. 1* (Publication 15). Geneva, Switzerland: 1995.

WORLD TRADE ORGANIZATION (WTO)

The World Trade Organization is a global, multilateral intergovernmental organization that promotes, monitors, and adjudicates international trade. Together with the regional and bilateral arrangements, the WTO is central to the overall expectations and practices of states with regard to international trade. The WTO is the successor organization to the General Agreement on Tariffs and Trade (GATT), which was created in 1947 to facilitate free trade on a multilateral basis. For most of its existence, the name GATT was the source of considerable confusion because it was both the name of a treaty and the name of the organization headquartered in Geneva, Switzerland. In fact, the GATT was more of a negotiating framework than an administrative institution. It did not actually regulate trade. That confusion has now ended. The GATT treaty was amended to create the World Trade Organization, which superseded the GATT organization as of January 1, 1995. Therefore, references to the organization now use WTO, and the treaty is referred to as the GATT. Although the GATT was a regime with little institutional infrastructure until the mid-1990s, it did have a small secretariat with headquarters in Geneva, Switzerland. In addition to its main role as a negotiating forum, the GATT helped to arbitrate trade disputes, helped to clarify the rules, and assisted states in observing them.

Since 1995 the GATT agreements on manufactured goods have been subsumed into the WTO framework and then extended to include trade in services and intellectual property. The WTO has some powers of enforcement and an international bureaucracy, which monitors trade policies and practices in each member state and adjudicates disputes that members

bring to the WTO. It is unclear how much power the WTO will eventually be able to wield over states in practice.

Over time the membership of GATT/WTO has grown from the original 23 countries to 148 members as of October 2004. Almost all of the world's major trading states are among the WTO's members. Two notable exceptions, however, are Russia and Saudi Arabia. They, along with twenty-one other countries, are seeking admission to the WTO. The United States and other countries demand, as a condition of membership, liberalization of the trading practices of Russia and other would-be members. The trade of the full members accounts for approximately 90% of all world trade. The GATT and the WTO have played an important role in promoting the meteoric expansion of international trade. The organization has sponsored a series of trade negotiations that have greatly reduced tariffs and non-tariff barriers, such as import quotas.

A Brief History of the WTO

Since the Industrial Revolution swept across Europe in the early nineteenth century, industrialization and international trade have been closely interconnected. One of the main effects of the Industrial Revolution was the specialization of labor. In the early 1800s, the British economist David Ricardo developed the theory of comparative advantage. This theory holds that individuals, firms, regions, and nations can gain by specializing in the production of low-cost goods. Nations make further gains by exchanging low-cost goods for goods that they can only produce at high cost and others can produce at low cost. This implies that low-cost goods producers use productive resources more efficiently.

In a world consisting of open economies, comparative advantage is a central organizing principle of international trade. International competition makes it possible for domestic producers having a comparative advantage in a particular good or service to compete effectively in foreign markets and to profit from the export of these goods and services. In turn, a country's export revenues generate the necessary purchasing power to import goods and services produced at a lower cost in another country. The result of free trade is an expansion in both output and consumption in domestic markets. Low-cost domestic consumers gain by having a greater choice of lower-cost products.

Historically, nations have erected barriers such as tariffs and quotas to protect domestic jobs. As the

wave of protectionism raged during the 1930s (which may or may not have played a significant role in the Great Depression), international trade simply collapsed. Trade restrictions such as tariffs and import quotas, however, carry a hefty price for consumers. A tariff is simply a tax against foreign imports. An import quota specifies the quantity or value of a good allowed to be imported into a country for a given year. By creating an artificial ceiling on the amount of a product allowed to be sold in the domestic market, prices for the quota-protected product are higher than they would be if the quotas were removed. From the standpoint of consumers, quotas are more costly than tariffs. Tariffs do not limit the supply of imported goods, but quotas do. Trade quotas are the policy of restricting the quantity of traded goods and services. They may be used as a means of observing a bilateral or multilateral previous agreement, such as when some countries agree to limit their competition in certain products in the markets of partners to enable the partners' producers to maintain a certain level of the share of their domestic markets. Trade quotas are also used for political reasons. Since the 1960s, tariffs have been declining steadily as a result of multilateral trade negotiations among nations subscribing to the General Agreement on Tariffs and Trade (GATT). In spite of five decades of consecutive GATT negotiations, during 1990, twenty-one US industries protected by import barriers cost US consumers about $70 billion paid in higher prices.

The post–World War II era, therefore, brought increasing efforts in developed countries to seek ways to forestall such trade slumps in the future. The United States and Britain, through a series of meetings and conferences, agreed to institutionalize trade policies, which resulted in creating the International Trade Organization (ITO) in 1945. The main purposes of ITO were to lower restrictions on trade and set rules of commerce. Policy planners hoped that this organization could assist in avoiding repetition of the international economic catastrophe that followed World War I. This plan encountered widespread resistance from European nations, developing countries, and domestic US political constituencies concerned with protection of domestic jobs and national sovereignty. Furthermore, its character became so watered down by other countries' demands for exemptions from generalized rules that Congress refused to approve it. In its place, the United States sponsored the General Agreement on Tariffs and Trade (GATT). Although initially designed as a provisional arrangement, the GATT became the cornerstone of the liberalized trading scheme originally embodied in the ITO.

In 1947, the GATT was negotiated by twenty-three countries. Under the aegis of the GATT, states

undertook a series of multilateral trade negotiations, called "rounds," aimed at reducing tariffs and resolving related issues. The eighth and most recent session (as of this writing), the Uruguay Round, completed in 1994, replaced GATT with a new World Trade organization (WTO), thus resurrecting the half-century-old vision of a global trade organization with teeth. The Uruguay Round started in 1986 in Uruguay. Although the rough outlines of a new GATT agreement emerged after a few years, efforts to wrap up the Uruguay Round failed at five successive G7 summit meetings in 1990–1994. It was estimated that a successful conclusion to the round would add hundreds of billions of dollars to the world economy over the remainder of the decade. But that money was a collective good, which would be enjoyed both by states that made concessions in the final negotiations to reach agreement and those that did not.

An agreement was finally reached in late 1994. In this round the United States and the European Union (EU) settled most of their differences on agriculture. In the end the United States got some, but not all, of what it wanted. The Uruguay Round negotiations were not only designed to reduce tariffs but also to confront more ubiquitous and less tractable forms of new protectionism that have become widespread. Non-tariff barriers are among the most ubiquitous of these.

Non-Tariff Barriers

Non-tariff barriers (NTBs) to trade cover a wide range of government regulations that have the effect of reducing or distorting international trade, including health and safety regulations, restrictions on the quality of goods that may be imported, government procurement policies, domestic subsidies, and antidumping regulations. NTBs comprise one of several new protectionist challenges to the principle of free trade often called "neomercantilist" challenges. *Neomercantilism* is "a trade policy whereby a state seeks to maintain a balance-of-trade surplus and to promote domestic production and employment by reducing imports, stimulating home production, and promoting exports" (Walters and Blake 1992). Neomercantilist practices have assumed greater prominence in US foreign economic policy in recent decades. They are also evident in other countries, as witnessed by the concern among US trade partners about the consequences of genetically engineered agricultural products, of which the United States is the leading exporter.

The Principles of the WTO

Since its inception, the GATT was based on four principles: most favored nation (MFN), reciprocity, nondiscrimination, and transparency. Members of the WTO, according to the MFN principle, are supposed to grant tariff or barrier reduction to all other WTO members. For example, if the United States reduced import tariffs for German automobiles by 8%, the US import tariffs for all automobile imports from WTO member countries had to be reduced by 8%. In this way, the WTO does not get rid of barriers to trade altogether but equalizes them in a global framework in order to create a level playing field for all member states. States may also extend MFN status to others that are not WTO members, as the United States did with China. President Clinton at first tried to use MFN status, which must be renewed annually, as a form of leverage to induce China to change its rights practices. When this failed, he unlinked human rights and trade relations with China, granting MFN status unconditionally.

Reciprocity bolsters the MFN principle because it implies that a country's reduction in tariffs, for example, will be reciprocated by other WTO members. In the absence of a reciprocal tariff reduction by other partners, a WTO member is under no obligation to unilaterally reduce import tariffs. The two remaining principles are nondiscrimination and transparency, which means that foreign goods will be treated the same as domestic goods; that is, foreign goods will not be discriminated against. Nondiscrimination holds WTO members accountable for treating imported and domestic products on an equal competitive basis within the national market.

The Structure and Role of the WTO

The WTO is headquartered in Geneva, Switzerland, and as of 2005 is headed by Director-General Supachai Panitchpakdi, a former deputy prime minister of Thailand, who took office in 2002. Countries can file complaints against one another for violation of the GATT. The WTO has the power to enforce the provisions of the GATT and to assess trade penalties against countries that violate the accord. While any country can withdraw from the WTO by giving six months' notice, that country would suffer significant economic perils because its products would no longer be subject to the reciprocal low tariffs and other advantages WTO members accord one another. When one country charges another with a trade

violation, a three-judge panel under the WTO hears the complaint. If the panel finds a violation, the WTO may impose sanctions on the offending country. Each country has one vote in the WTO, and sanctions may be imposed by a two-thirds vote. This means, among other things, that domestic laws may be disallowed by the WTO if they are found to be de facto trade barriers.

The WTO judicial process has been busy. From 1995 through January 2004, the WTO handled 305 cases. The first case in 1995 involved a complaint by Singapore against Malaysia related to its prohibition of imports of polyethylene and polypropylene. Case number 305 filed in early 2004 by the United States charged Egypt with maintaining illegally high tariffs on textiles and apparel products. However, most of the cases brought to the WTO between 1995 and 2004 were settled without the need for arbitration. When the WTO was called upon to adjudicate disputes, no government defied any of its rulings. Even though some countries were short-term losers in particular cases, they still abided by the WTO because of the broader and long-term benefits of WTO membership.

The WTO provides a way to resolve the dispute and avoid the bilateral retaliation, counter-retaliations, and occasional wars that have marked trade disputes in the past. When the George W. Bush administration imposed protective tariffs, some countries took quick retaliation against the United States by restricting their purchase of US goods, but the EU, Japan, and most other countries were satisfied to sue the United States in the WTO and to threaten retaliation if Washington lost the dispute and still refused to give way. In the end, that was not necessary. Most observers believe that the US presidents have wisely chosen not to risk major damage to the relatively free trade system and to the WTO, which the United States has been instrumental in creating.

The WTO and Its Critics

The GATT/WTO has been considered by intellectuals and policy makers in Less Developed Countries (LDCs) as an exclusive club of rich nations. Influential economists have challenged the conventional wisdom of free trade. They contend that as exporters of single commodities or natural resources, developing nations are considered to be highly dependent on unstable world commodity markets, while rich industrial nations enjoy the core benefits of trade as exporters of capital.

Conservationist groups such as the World Wildlife Federation (WWF) argue that trade has a destructive impact on the environment because trade facilitates the over-consumption of natural resources. The WWF believes that strengthening environmental regulations worldwide should take place before seeking greater trade liberalization. Another point made by many environmentalists is that companies will try to evade costly environmental standards in one country by setting up shop in another country where there are lax standards.

The WTO rejects the assumption that there is necessarily a trade-off between the environment and the economy as in the example of low trade barriers to environmental goods and services. In addition, the WTO's secretary general has argued that the real cause of environmental degradation is poverty, not trade.

In 1999, an unusual mix of individuals and organizations went to Seattle to protest a number of issues including environmental degradation, lost jobs, and the lack of accountability of the WTO. Protestors virtually shut down the WTO meeting. One of the common denominators of the protestors was that they were upset about the globalization process. The WTO is the most visible symbol of that process.

More specifically, the two biggest complaints against the WTO were related to environmental and labor issues. Protestors concerned with labor issues focused on the wages of workers in the Third World, where in some places, transnational corporations pay workers a dollar an hour or less, and where working conditions are often inhospitable and even dangerous. Of particular concern to the labor protestors in Seattle was the apparent trend of transnational companies to set up factories in countries with very low wages. Lower wages in the Third World countries, they believe, end up affecting wage levels in the United States. In short, US workers must settle for lower wages in order to keep their jobs from being sent overseas.

Assessment and Future Challenges

From its inception, the GATT/WTO has generally resulted in significant tariff reductions through multilateral agreements. It is agreed that the level of tariffs facing member countries of the WTO are much lower today, in the early twenty-first century, than they have ever been. For LDCs, joining the WTO has enabled them to participate in its various multifarious negotiations, thereby giving them the opportunity to present their multifarious cases to the Developed Countries (DCs). It seems that GATT/WTO has generally been in the interest of LDCs by enabling them to suffer lesser trade barriers than they would have suffered without such a multilateral agreement.

Nevertheless, many of the benefits of GATT/WTO's provision are designed to be more favorable to the DCs than the LDCs. For example, tariff reductions on goods exported by the DCs—industrial goods—far outweigh tariff reductions on goods exported by the LDCs—that is, primary products. Although there exists a GATT principle of preferential treatment of the exports of LDCs, known as the Generalized System of Preferences (GSP), which provides for reduced tariffs on selected manufactured goods exported by LDCs, the countries have not really benefited much from it. This is because many key industrial manufactured products exported from LDCs are exempted from the benefits of the GSP: textiles and apparel, processed raw materials, and a wide range of industrial and labor-intensive products.

Although the WTO has gotten off to a promising start, its future is not clear. The question is: What will happen if one or more member countries, especially powerful ones, refuse to abide by the WTO rules and reject the findings of the judicial process? So far, when Washington and the EU have lost a case, they have quietly given way, as the United States did in 2003 in the face of an adverse WTO ruling on the steel tariffs. What remains to be seen, however, is the reaction when a highly sensitive case is brought before the WTO.

The WTO is facing several major challenges in the future. First and foremost, the WTO must deal with the question of what type of organization it will be. Most observers agree that the WTO will continue to be dominated by governments seeking to hold onto as much national sovereignty as possible. Most of its members are not very interested in granting the WTO too many powers. In addition, there is often no real consensus among WTO member states about how policy problems should be dealt with. One should not get the impression, however, that the WTO is totally hampered by the whims of nation-states. Its members do understand the need for cooperation, and the WTO is heading into an increasingly large number of new areas.

NASSER MOMAYEZI

See also General Agreement on Tariffs and Trade (GATT); International Bank for Reconstruction and Development (IBRD) (World Bank); International Monetary Fund (IMF)

References and Further Reading

Babai, Don. "General Agreement on Tariffs and Trade." In *The Oxford Companion to Politics of the World*, edited by Joel Krieger. Oxford, UK: Oxford University Press, 1993.

Bagwell, Kyle. *The Economics of the World Trading System.* Cambridge, MA: MIT Press, 2002.

Das, Bhagirath Lal. *An Introduction to the WTO Agreements: Trade and Development Issues and the World Trade Organisation.* New York: St. Martin's Press, 1998.

Destler, I. M. and Peter J. Balint. *The New Politics of American Trade: Trade, Labor, and the Environment.* Washington, DC: Institute for International Economics, 1999.

Ford, Jane. *A Social Theory of the WTO: Trading Cultures.* Houndmills, Basingstoke, UK; Hampshire, New York: Palgrave Macmillan, 2003.

Friedman, Thomas L. *The Lexus and the Olive Tree: Understanding Globalization.* New York: Farrar, Straus and Giroux, 1999.

Gilpin, Robert. *The Challenge of the Global Capitalism: The World Economy in the Twenty-First Century.* Princeton, NJ: Princeton University Press, 2000.

Hoekman, Bernard M. *The Political Economy of the World Trading System: WTO and Beyond.* Oxford, UK; New York: Oxford University Press, 2001.

Mansfield, Edward D. and Helen V. Milner, eds. *The Political Economy of Regionalism.* New York: Columbia University Press, 1997.

Rao, P. K. *The World Trade Organization and the Environment.* New York: St. Martin's Press, 2000.

Rothgeb, John M., Jr. *US Trade Policy: Balancing Economic Dreams and Political Realities.* Washington, DC: CQ Press, 2001.

Suzman, Mark. "US Domestic Concerns Sank Seattle." *Financial Times*, December 6, 1999.

Walters, Robert S. and David H. Blake. *The Politics of Global Economic Relations*, 4th ed. Englewood Cliffs, NJ: Prentice Hall, 1992.

Williams, Frances and Vanessa Houlder. "WTO Defends Record on the Environment." *Financial Times*, October 15, 1999.

WYSZYŃSKI, CARDINAL STEFAN

Cardinal Stefan Wyszyński (1901–1981) led the Polish Catholic Church from 1948, when Pope Pius XII made him primate of Poland, until his death in 1981. He was popular among Poles both religious and not and a great proponent of the Vatican II Council. His legacy is rooted in the tradition of the Polish Catholic Church as not just a spiritual, but also a political and social institution.

Wyszyński was born on August 3, 1901, in the small village of Zuzela near Łomża in northeastern Poland. He received his education in a seminary in Włocławek where he studied philosophy and theology and in the Lublin Catholic University from 1924 to 1929 where he obtained a doctorate in canon law. His dissertation was entitled "The Rights of the Family: The Church and the State in Relation to Schools." After his doctorate he received a scholarship and in 1929–1930 he studied the Christian social sciences in Italy, Austria, France, Belgium, Holland, and Germany. In 1931 Wyszyński was appointed to the

faculty of the Włocławek Seminary and served until the German–Polish War of 1939. During WWII he lived and worked near Warsaw and was briefly arrested by the Gestapo in October 1941. In 1946 he was elected the bishop of Lublin and in 1948 he was promoted to the metropolitan see of Gniezno and Warsaw. In May 1953 he was made cardinal and received the title of S. Maria in Trastevere in May 1957.

A skilled administrator and politician, Wyszyński managed to establish the relationship between the Church and the Communist government in post-WWII Poland. As the primate he navigated the Catholic Church in Poland through years of harsh restrictions mixed with short periods of a more liberal approach. He skillfully created a pragmatic approach to deal with the Communist government. His way of approaching the authorities was criticized by those who expected a much harder line from the Church. The proponents of Wyszyński's politics say that his resistance to communism saved the Polish Church and perhaps also the Polish cultural identity. The critics, on the other hand, say that Wyszyński accommodated the Communist government too much. His position toward the Communist government can be characterized by the concept of the limit of concession stated: "Non possumus"—we cannot yield any more—that he formulated around 1953. His nonconformist position resulted in house arrest confinement from September 25, 1953, until October 28, 1956. During the period of martial law in Poland he was featured on stamps issued by the Wrocław "Fighting Solidarity" (underground issue).

Cardinal Wyszyński participated in conclaves in 1958, 1963, and 1978. He attended the Vatican II Council from 1962–1965 and was active in the works of the Council from 1967–1979. He died on May 28, 1981, and is buried in the metropolitan cathedral in Warsaw. His brother Stefan Franczak named one of his summer-flowering Clematis varieties of the Jackmanii species, "Kardynał Wyszyński."

LUDOMIR LOZNY

References and Further Reading

Micewski, Andrzej. *Cardinal Wyszynski: A Biography*. Translated from Polish by William A. Brand and Katarzyna Mroczkowska-Brand. San Diego, CA: Harcourt Brace Jovanovich, 1984.

Wyszyński, Stefan. *A Freedom Within: The Prison Notes of Cardinal Stefan Wyszynski*. Translated by Barbara Krzywicki-Herburt and Walter J. Ziemba; foreword by John Cardinal Krol. San Diego, CA: Harcourt Brace Jovanovich, 1983.

Y

YAHYA KHAN, AGHA MUHAMMAD

Agha Muhammad Yahya Khan (1917–1971), was born at Chakwal in February 1917. His father, Saadat Ali Khan, was from Peshawar. Yahya received primary education from Chakwal and Peshawar and later joined the Punjab University. In 1938, Yahya Khan was commissioned in the Indian Army and joined the Indian Military Academy at Dehra Dun. During World War II, he performed his duties in North Africa, Iraq, and Italy. During the Indo-Pakistan War of 1965, he commanded an infantry division. In 1966, he was appointed Commander-in-Chief of the Pakistan Army, with the rank of General.

When Ayub Khan resigned in March 1969 due to massive agitation against his government, General Yahya Khan took power, declared a second Martial Law, and assumed the title of Chief Martial Law Administrator. He terminated the constitution and dissolved the National and Provincial Assemblies. On March 31, 1969, he became President of Pakistan, and on March 29, 1970, through an Ordinance, Yahya presented an interim constitution: The Legal Framework Order. Under the new constitution, in 1970 he held the first fair and free general elections in the history of Pakistan. Two parties won the elections: Awami League under the leadership of Sheikh Mujeeb-ur-Rahman swept 160 of 165 seats allocated to East Pakistan and Zulfiqar Ali Bhutto's Pakistan People's Party emerged as the single largest party from Punjab and Sind and managed to win eighty-one National Assembly seats. Both parties failed to get even a single seat from any province of the country.

This split mandate resulted in political chaos, where neither Bhutto nor Mujeeb was ready to accept his opponent as the Prime Minister of Pakistan. In the circumstances, Yahya failed to transfer power to the majority party, and the situation became worse. The people of the eastern wing demanded autonomy, a demand that Yahya's government considered a challenge to the country's solidarity. His inability to manage the political situation led to the outbreak of civil war in March 1971. At that time, Yahya facilitated a secret trip of Henry Kissinger to Beijing in July 1971, which strongly disturbed the Soviet Union. As a result, the Soviet Union and India signed the Twenty Years Treaty of Peace, Friendship, and Cooperation on August 9, 1971, and declared war on Pakistan. During the war of 1971, the Soviet Union stood firmly with India and defeated Pakistan's allies, the United States and China together. Yahya, as President as well as the Commander-in-Chief of the Pakistan Army, failed to prevent war and protect the country. This ultimately resulted in the defeat of Pakistan, dismemberment of the country, and imprisonment of more than ninety thousand Pakistanis. The surrender of Pakistani forces without resistance and the fall of Dacca caused a plummet in Yahya Khan's popularity and authority. Thus, he was left with no other option but to hand over power to the leader of the minority party of the remaining part of Pakistan, Zulfiqar Ali Bhutto, on December 20, 1971. Bhutto placed Yahya Khan under house arrest in 1972.

HUSAIN KASSIM

See also Ayub Khan, Mohammed; Bhutto, Benazir; **Central Asia: History and Economic Development; Central Asia: International Relations; Pakistan**

References and Further Reading

Feldman, Herbert. *The End and the Beginning: Pakistan 1969–1972.* London: Oxford University Press, 1976.
Choudhury, G. W. *The Last Days of United Pakistan.* Bloomington, IN: Indiana University Press, 1975.
Cohen, Stephen P. Cohen. *The Pakistan Army.* Berkeley, CA: University of California Press, 1989.
Javed Burki, Shahid. *Pakistan: A Nation in the Making.* Boulder, CO: Westview Press, 1986.

YEMEN

The Republic of Yemen (ROY) was created on May 22, 1990, by voluntary unification of the Yemen Arab Republic (North Yemen, with its capital at San'a) and the People's Democratic Republic of Yemen (South Yemen with its capital at Aden). The merger went poorly and civil war broke out in 1994. Northern armed forces defeated the southern rebels and reunified the country. The political leader at this writing, President Ali Abdullah Saleh (b. 1942) is a cautious authoritarian modernizer.

The ROY occupies approximately two hundred thousand square miles of the strategic southwestern corner of the Arabian peninsula, commanding the narrow strait of Bab al Mandab at the mouth of the Red Sea. Yemen has three main regions: (1) a hot, arid strip along the Red Sea coast; (2) the central highlands, which receive enough rain to grow crops on steep, terraced mountainsides; and (3) the *wadis* (usually dry river canyons) of the eastern region. Temperature and precipitation depend on altitude. The capital, San'a, although only 15° N of the equator, lies at seven thousand feet elevation and so is pleasant even in the summer.

Yemen is isolated, densely populated, and very poor. Its 19 million people (2003 estimate) are Arabs by race, language, and culture, but tribal and religious cleavages generate internal conflict. Yemen faces serious political, social, and economic challenges, the most basic of which is to create a sense of patriotism. Almost all Yemenis are Muslim, but Shi'ites predominate in the north and Sunnis in the south. The Salafist movement, which preaches a return to life as lived by the Prophet in the seventh century, is believed to have a few thousand followers in Yemen.

Yemen's classical history serves as a foundation for modern nationalism. Most famous of the ancient Yemeni kingdoms was Saba (Sheba). Its wealth was based on control of caravan routes that brought frankincense and myrrh from Hadramawt to the Mediterranean world. At various times, Yemen was controlled by Persians, Ethiopians, and Egyptians. Yemenis accepted Islam during the Prophet's lifetime. The Shi'ite Zaydi dynasty ruled San'a from the ninth century until 1962. The Turkish Ottoman empire claimed sovereignty over the whole region, but Yemenis have always given primary allegiance to their own tribal chieftains. Great Britain seized the port of Aden in 1839 but exercised only indirect control over the tribal hinterland.

A republican revolution broke out in North Yemen in 1962. For eight years, the country was wracked by civil war as Egyptian President Gamal Abdel Nasser sent troops to help the republicans while Saudi Arabia backed Yemeni monarchists. In 1977, Lieutenant Colonel Ali Abdullah Saleh, formerly the military governor of Ta'izz, declared himself the new head of state. In May 1983, the National Parliament confirmed Saleh as President for another five years. He won subsequent elections by disqualifying his opponents and remains firmly in power today.

South Yemen won independence from Great Britain in 1967 after a bitter guerrilla war. The Marxist leaders of the People's Democratic Republic of Yemen had constant internal conflict. When the Soviets ceased to subsidize them, they opened negotiations with Saleh for national unification.

President Saleh rules through a five-member Presidential Council with the help of his political party, the General People's Congress. The constitution vests legislative power in a 301-member House of Representatives, but President Saleh allows parliament very little real power. The press is best characterized as semi-free.

Yemen remains economically undeveloped. Only a few roads are paved. More than half the labor force is employed in agriculture—the chief crops being potatoes, wheat, barley, sorghum, cotton, coffee, and a wide variety of fruit. In recent years, much arable land has been given over to cultivation of *qat*, a mildly narcotic plant that is popular in Yemen. Pastureland is grazed by sheep and goats. Only 10% of the labor force is now employed in industry, but there are commercially exploitable deposits of iron ore, copper, gold, and other minerals. Hopes for economic progress center on oil deposits of unproven size. Yemen's considerable potential for tourism has been curbed by widely publicized kidnappings of foreigners and the presence of al-Qaeda operatives.

The central government in San'a is unable to control large areas of the country. Yemen's legal system is

based on a combination of British, Turkish, and Islamic (Shariah) law, and tribal custom. Yemen is awash with an estimated 60 million guns, three for every man, woman, and child. Tribal feuds and skirmishes are constant—some tribes even possess heavy artillery.

Education in Yemen is free through the primary and secondary levels, but the public school system is rudimentary, compared with that in more affluent countries. Only half the children of primary school age attend school and the adult literacy rate, particularly among females, is well under 50%. There are few rural clinics, and many tropical diseases are endemic.

Yemen's foreign policy tends to focus on a perceived threat from the Kingdom of Saudi Arabia. President Saleh leaned toward Iraq in the Persian Gulf War and the Saudis retaliated by summarily expelling all 750,000 Yemeni expatriate workers, whose remittances had made up a large part of Yemen's foreign exchange receipts. Yemen has been burdened with an influx of refugees from wars on the Horn of Africa. Foreign aid will be required for the foreseeable future.

The San'a government's inability to control its own territory has created opportunities for terrorist organizations. Al Qaeda is believed to operate training camps in the mountains near Sa'dah. In October 2000, al-Qaeda terrorists blew up the USS Cole in Aden harbor, killing seventeen Americans. After the World Trade Center attacks of September 11, 2001, President Saleh, who fears political Islamists, promised to cooperate with the United States in its war against terrorism.

ROSS MARLAY

See also Middle East: History and Economic Development; Middle East: International Relations

References and Further Reading

Burrowes, Robert D. *Historical Dictionary of Yemen.* Asian Historical Dictionaries, No. 17, London and Lanham, Md.: Scarecrow Press, 1995.
Dresch, Paul. *A History of Modern Yemen.* Cambridge, UK: Cambridge University Press, 2000.
———. *Tribes, Government and History in Yemen.* Oxford and New York: Oxford University Press, 1989.
Halliday, Fred. *Nationalism and Religion in the Middle East.* Boulder, CO: Lynne Rienner, 2000.
Mackintosh-Smith, Tim. *Yemen: Travels in Dictionary Land.* London: John Murray, 1997.
Stookey, Robert W. *South Yemen: A Marxist Republic in Arabia.* London: Croom Helm, and Boulder, CO: Westview, 1982.
———. *Yemen: The Politics of the Yemen Arab Republic,* Boulder, CO: Westview, 1978.

YUGOSLAVIA

Location

Yugoslavia, "Land of the South Slavs," existed from 1918 to 2003 under three different names and two types of government. The Kingdom of the Serbs, Croats, and Slovenes, named Kingdom of Yugoslavia in 1929, existed from 1918 to 1941. It was followed by the Federal People's Republic of Yugoslavia established in 1946, which became the Socialist Federal Republic of Yugoslavia in 1963. In 1992, when four of its six constituents' republics seceded, the remaining part was renamed Federal Republic of Yugoslavia and lasted until 2003.

Located in southeastern Europe, Yugoslavia extended over half of the Balkan Peninsula. The borders were established in 1921–1925 and barely changed until 2003, except for the years 1941–1945. The total land area was 248,987 square kilometers in 1921 and 255,804 square kilometer in 1991. The country was surrounded by Italy, Austria, Hungary, Rumania, Bulgaria, Greece, and Albania and opened on the Adriatic coast.

The population, 11,984,911 in 1921, increased to 23,528,230 inhabitants, according the last census of 1991. World War II took a heavy toll of about 10% of the population between 1941 and 1945. Yugoslavia was home to a mosaic of people. Serbs, Croats, Bosnians, Slovenes, Montenegrins, Macedonians coexisted with numerous minorities, Albanian, Hungarians, Slovaks, Romanians, and others. Belgrade, the capital city remained the same under the different regimes.

Land and climate

Yugoslavia was a country of contrasts. The Pannonian plain, its most fertile area extended from Hungary into North Central Yugoslavia (Vojvodina, Slavonia). The forests and highlands of the Dinaric Alps run northwest to south east and dominated the center and the west of the country. The Dalmatian coast, rocky narrows stripe stretched along the Adriatic Coast. The limestone ranges and basins of the Balkans Mountains distinguished the southeastern regions.

The main rivers were the Danube and its tributaries, the Sava, the Drina, and the Drava. The Morava and the Vardar valleys bisected South Serbia and Macedonia. Two major lakes, Prespa and Ohrid, are located in Macedonia along the Albanian border. The climate varied from Mediterranean along the Adriatic

coast to continental around Zagreb and Belgrade up to Sarajevo and Skopje with frigid winters and hot, dry summers.

Origins to 1918

For centuries, the Yugoslav's lands had been occupied, divided, and influenced by political and religious outside powers: the Austrian, Ottoman, Russian Empires, and the republic of Venice. The South Slavs people were affected by their respective regime's main character: Strongly centralized under the Ottoman rule for the Serbs, while the Croats retained autonomy in the Habsburg Empire. Part of the South Slavs (Croats) became Catholic, while the majority chose Orthodoxy and the sense of church belonging left its print in the mentalities. Conversions to Islam occurred mainly in Bosnia-Herzegovina. The situation lasted five centuries until the decline of the Ottoman Empire and the development of nationalism after 1848.

The concept of Yugoslavia that is the unification of the South Slavs people into a joint state arose among Croatian intellectuals in Austria-Hungary. Ljudevit Gaj (1809–1872) and later Josip Strossmayer (1815–1905) defended the idea that South Slavs people were ethnically close sharing a similar language, but history has separated and placed them under foreign rule.

The Yugoslav State is born out from World War I. From 1914 to 1918, the Yugoslav cause gained an increasing support in Serbia and Croatia. Leaders in France and Great Britain also supported the union of the South Slavs in order to defeat Austria-Hungary. In 1917, Prime Minister Nicolas Pasic of the Serb government in exile in Corfu signed an agreement with Ante Trumbic of the Yugoslav Committee, defending the interests of the South Slavs in the Habsburg Empire. The text proclaimed the future union under Peter I Karageorgevic of Serbia, but this was more a declaration of intentions than a political program. In November 1918, delegates from the Croatian National Council representing the short-lived Croatian state signed a "memorandum" with Pasic and Trumbic, emphasizing the bonds among the South Slavs in Serbia, Montenegro, and those of the former Austria-Hungary. Finally, the Kingdom of the Serbs, Croats, and Slovenes was proclaimed December 1, 1918, in Belgrade.

The First Yugoslavia 1918–1941

The First Yugoslavia was plagued by an open confrontation between its two main people, the Serbs and the Croats; the former ruled the kingdom highly centralized around the government, while the latter expected the regime to become a federation.

On June 28, 1921, a new constitution was adopted despite the Croatian opposition; the same year, Alexander became King after Peter's death. The text strengthened the power of the royal government. The administration and the army were concentrated into the Serb's hands. The national institutions did not function properly, as the Croats boycotted systematically votes taken in the Parliament. As a result, clashes between Serbs centralists and Croats federalists occurred regularly, and most governments were short-lived. Nicolas Pasic, leader of the Serb Radical Party, dominated the political life until his death in 1926. Yugoslavia joined the "Little Entente" with Romania and Czechoslovakia in 1921–1922. Close to France, the alliance was formed to ensure the borders and to oppose the revision of the Paris peace treaties signed after 1918.

In 1928, the situation deteriorated as a Montenegrin opened fire in the middle of a parliamentary session. He fatally wounded Stepan Radic, head of the Croatian Peasant Party, the main political force against the Serbs party. The incident led to a complete rupture between the Serbs and the Croats. In January 1929, King Alexander established a dictatorship. The kingdom became formally Yugoslavia. In order to solve the national question, Alexander reorganized the country and local administration by breaking up the traditional historical units. A "Yugoslavian" national identity was supposed to replace the ethnic ones.

Opposition to Alexander rose sharply. In 1934, while on a visit to France, he was assassinated by Macedonian agent of the Croatian nationalist movement, the Ustachis ("rebel"). A Regency under Prince Paul tried to hold the country together while under pressure of Germany and Italy. Internal tensions were still more acute as the Croatian issue became untenable. Finally in 1939, only a few weeks before the war started, the government of Milan Stojadinovic agreed with Vlado Macek, leader of the Croatian Peasant Party, to establish an autonomous Croatian province that included part of Bosnia. The regime lasted until 1941.

On March 25, 1941, the Yugoslav government bowed to German pressure and signed an alliance with the Axis powers. Within days, a military coup occurred and the seventeen-year-old Crown Prince Peter was declared king. Less than two weeks later, Hitler's troops occupied Yugoslavia in eleven days. The Yugoslav lands were dismantled between Germany, Italy, Hungary, and Bulgaria. Croatia under the leadership of Ante Pavelic was proclaimed independent but, in fact, remained under the control of the German Reich.

Yugoslavia in World War II

From 1941 to 1945, Yugoslavia was devastated by a double war. Armed resistance against the German occupation started immediately, as monarchists lead by Colonel Draza Mihailovic and communists partisans around Tito (Josip Broz), supported by the USSR, set up two organizations that fought against each other as much as they fought against the Axis troops. A civil war raged with numerous massacres and atrocities on all sides as the Germans turned against the civilian populations.

In 1942, the communists set up the Anti-Fascist Council of National Liberation of Yugoslavia that would, one year later, become and act as a future national government (Congresses of Bihac and Jajce). Mihailovic's Chetnik ("armed bands") were supported by the government of Peter II in exile in London and by the British government. In 1943, the partisans won the support of the British-American forces, and by 1944, the partisans liberated the country from the foreign occupation.

The Second Yugoslavia 1945–1992

In November 1945, national elections were held despite the opposition abstention, and the newly elected constituent assembly proclaimed a Federal People's Republic. The 1946 constitution, modeled after the Soviet constitution of 1936, established six constituent republics: Bosnia-Herzegovina, Croatia, Macedonia, Montenegro, Serbia, and Slovenia and two autonomous provinces within Serbia, Kosovo-Metohidja, and Voijvodina. In 1947, the Italian peace treaty awarded most of Istria, the eastern part of Venezia Gulia, Rijeka, and Zadar to Yugoslavia. However, a conflict over Trieste lasted until 1975 and ended with a partition agreement.

Until 1948–1949, Yugoslavia was a communist state close to the Soviet Union. A policy of agricultural collectivization, central planned economy, and forced industrialization was undertaken, and opposition was suppressed. The headquarters of the Communist Information Bureau (Cominform) that gathered communist parties under the Soviet leadership was established in Belgrade. However, on June 28, 1948, a crucial break-up between Stalin and Tito occurred as the Communist Party of Yugoslavia was accused of deviation from Communism and was ousted from the Cominform. In fact, Stalin had long been suspicious about Tito's loyalty and his growing independent ambitions in Southeastern Europe.

Tito began a new policy based on a balance between capitalism and communism. He received economic and military assistance from the West. In 1954, Yugoslavia signed a military defense pact with Greece and Turkey, both NATO members. Cordial relations resumed with the USSR under Krutchev in 1955. Tito created the Non-Aligned-Movement, gathering new states, mostly former European colonies, that wanted an alternative or a "third way" between the East and West.

In 1963, a new genuinely federal constitution was adopted and Tito became President for life. Communism was abandoned in favor of Socialism. However, a double-contradictory tendency emerged as further decentralization and reforms were granted to the republics, but the actual power remained in the hands of the Communist Party of Yugoslavia. Introducing a new economic policy of "self-management," councils of workers participated in the management of their companies.

Between 1968 and 1971, agitation and national question revived. Unrest appeared first in Kosovo where the large Albanian population demanded national and cultural rights. Then, in 1970–1971, Croatian intellectuals and students launched a series of manifestations asking for more autonomy. Tito crushed the movement called the "Croatian Spring," perceived as a national Croat opposition. However, the trend toward greater autonomy was pursued, and in 1974, the country's last constitution transformed Yugoslavia into an almost confederation. The Muslims became the six constituent people, while the central government continued to retain the political power. At the same time, the economy began to stagnate. After Tito's death in 1980, his successors were unable to maintain national unity or to undertake the drastic reforms as they clashed over the conflicting interests of their republics.

In 1987, a new leader emerged—Slobodan Milosevic—who began an aggressive campaign to reassert Serbian and communist hegemony over a recentralized Yugoslavia. As leader of the Serbian communist party, he limited the autonomy of Kosovo-Metohidja and Vojvodina and sent troops to Kosovo to suppress the protests (1988–1989). One year later, the disintegration process started, as in January 1990, the Slovenian and Croatian delegates walked away from the Congress of the League of Communist of Yugoslavia, one of the pillars of the Yugoslav regime. The conjunction of prosperity and revival of nationalism gave the Croatian and Slovenian leaders the strength to secede from Belgrade. Later that year, multiparty elections were held in each of the six republics. On June 25, 1991, Croatia and Slovenia declared independence, followed by Macedonia and Bosnia-Herzegovina in 1992.

The secession of the four republics was followed by three wars. The first one occurred in Slovenia in June–July 1991. The Slovenes were determined to secure their borders, and the conflict ended with the retreat of the Federal Yugoslav Army. The second one started in July 1991 in Croatia, in the Serbian-populated regions of Slavonia and Kraijna. Since the elections of the nationalist leader Franco Tudjman, the 12% Serb minority's rights have been restricted. Following Milosevic's orders, the federal army helped the Serbian militia fighting the Croats. The intervention of the United Nations in December froze the front, but the Serbs occupied 30% of Croatian territory until 1995. The third war erupted in Bosnia-Herzegovina in 1992, where Serbs fought first against the Croats and later against an "uneasy alliance Croats-Muslims" concluded under the US auspices. The siege of Sarajevo lasted until 1994. The leaders, Tudjman, Milosevic, and Izetbegovic alternatively fought against each other and negotiated the partition the country. Following the failed interventions of the European Union and the United Nations, the war ended with NATO bombing operations in 1995. The Dayton Agreement sponsored by Washington established that Bosnia-Herzegovina will consist of two entities: the Bosnian-Serb Republic (Republika Srpska) and the Croat-Muslims Federation.

The End of Yugoslavia

The Federal Republic of Yugoslavia was born during the war in April 1992. It included Serbia and Montenegro as well as Kosovo and Voivodina. Milosevic, who became president in 1997, pursued his aggressive policy toward the Albanians in Kosovo. Tensions rose and battles erupted between a Kosovar guerilla army (KLA) and the Yugoslav troops. In 1999, NATO bombed Yugoslavia for more than two months. Since then, the province is placed under the administration of the United Nations (Resolution 1244). In September 2000, after his defeat in the presidential elections, Milosevic refused to yield power and massive demonstrations took place in Belgrade. On October 5, the regime collapsed. The opposition candidate, Vojislav Kostunica, became president and Zoran Djindic prime minister. Milosevic was arrested and on June 28, 2001, was extradited to the War Tribunal in La Hague where he was charged with genocide and war crimes.

After long and intense negotiations between Serbian and Montenegrins representatives, both parties agreed to establish a loose federal union of Serbia and Montenegro. After the proclamation of a new constitution, in February 2003, Yugoslavia ceased to exist and the name was erased from the European map.

NADINE AKHUND

See also Bosnia and Herzegovina; Croatia; Milosevic, Slobodan; Montenegro; Serbia; Tito, Josip Broz (Marshall Tito); Tudjman, Franjo

References and Further Reading

Allock, John, B. *Explaining Yugoslavia*. New York, Columbia University Press, 2000.

Crampton, Richard J. *The Balkans Since the Second World War*. London 2002.

Djokic, Dejan. *Yugoslavism: Histories of a Failed Idea, 1918–1992*. Madison, WI: University of Wisconsin Press 2003.

Glenny, Misha. *The Balkans, Nationalism, War, and the Great Powers, 1804–1999*. New York, 1999.

Lampe, John R. *Yugoslavia as History: Twice There Was a Country*. Cambridge, UK: Cambridge University Press 1996.

Naimark, Norman, M. and Holly Case. *Yugoslavia and its Historians: Understanding the Balkans Wars of the 1990s*. Stanford, CA: Stanford University Press, 2003.

Ramet, Sabrina, P. *Nationalism and Federalism in Yugoslavia, 1962–1991*. Bloomington, IN: Indiana University Press, 1992.

Shoup, Paul. *Communism and the Yugoslav National Question*. New York: Columbia University Press, 1968.

Stavrianos, Leften, S. *The Balkans Since 1453*. New York, 2000.

Z

ZAIRE

(*See Congo, Democratic Republic of the*)

ZAMBIA

Geography, Topography, and Climate

Landlocked Zambia is situated on the Central African High Plateau, with an average altitude of between 1,060 and 1,363 metres above sea level, and covers 464,937 square kilometres. The climate is moderate most of the year, though the river valleys are often tropical and very humid. Annual rainfall in the north averages 1,250 millimetres, while in the southwest, where Zambia borders the Kalahari, it averages 500 millimetres. The environment is favorable for growing crops, vegetables, and fruits in many parts of the country.

Historic Past and Current Economic Situation

Zambia has been inhabited by humans for at least one hundred thousand years. The Bantu peoples, who now make up the bulk of the population, entered the country relatively recently. In 1889, the entrepreneur Cecil Rhodes obtained mining concessions from the Barotse people and sent British mining specialists and farmers to the area soon thereafter. The territory was extended with the consent of the British government and ruled by Rhodes' "British South Africa Company" (BSAC). In 1924, the British government took over the administration of the colony, which was then called "Northern Rhodesia." The influx of white settlers, especially after World War II, led to the marginalization of many African peasants, since the white population took possession of the most fertile lands. The BSAC, and later the British government, levied taxes on Africans to force them to seek work in the mines. The development of the mining industry and Zambia's concomitant industrialization led to the transformation and urbanization of what previously had been a rural peasant society. The worsening situation of the African population after World War II led to protest and the formation of African political parties. Protests were furthermore triggered by a white-dominated confederation between Northern Rhodesia, Southern Rhodesia, and Nyasaland. Northern Rhodesia became independent in 1964 and was renamed Zambia. It was ruled by Kenneth Kaunda and his "United National Independence Party" (UNIP), most of the time as a one-party state. A long-lasting economic crisis provoked domestic pressure that eventually forced Kaunda to give way to a multiparty democracy in 1990. Elections in 1991 led to the defeat of Kaunda by Frederick Chiluba, chairman of the "Movement for Multiparty Democracy" (MMD), who was reelected in 1996. In December 2001, Levy Mwanawasa of the incumbent MMD emerged as the new president.

Although Zambia is blessed with mineral resources as well as waterpower and fertile land, it is largely dependent on revenues from its copper exports. However, low prices for copper on the world market, ineffective industrial enterprises, and an inflated public sector make Zambia one of the most heavily indebted countries in Africa. For the past decade, the country has been pursuing economic reform programs under the auspices of the International Monetary Fund (IMF) and the World Bank, which has resulted in the reduction of labour in the public sector and the privatization of statal and parastatal industries like the giant "Zambian Consolidated Copper Mines" (ZCCM) and the "Roan Antelope Mining Corporation of Zambia" (RAMCOZ). Coupled with these policies is Zambia's young labour force, which continues to grow. As a result, the unemployment rate is very high (50% in 2003). There is, however, no national strategy to tackle this problem. Real wages of the employees have continued to fall. The situation of the Zambian worker is aggravated by the rapid devaluation of the national currency against the US dollar and the attendant rise in inflation.

Gross domestic product per capita was estimated at $800 in 2002; the labor force occupation in 2001 comprised agriculture (85%), industry (6%), and services (9%). The infant mortality rate total was estimated at 99.29 deaths/1000 live births in 2003. Life expectancy of the total population amounts to 35.25 years (2003). The country's rates of HIV/AIDS are still great: the prevalence of the disease among adults was 21.5% (1.2 million people in 2001). In 2001, approximately 120,000 Zambians died of AIDS. The CIA factbook (2003) estimates that 80.6% of the total population aged fifteen years and older can read and write English.

Economic and Civil Development Since 1945

In the late 1920s, extensive copper deposits were discovered in the Copperbelt, and by the late 1930s, about four thousand European and some twenty thousand African laborers were employed there. The Africans protested against the discrimination and ill treatment to which they were subjected with strikes in 1935, 1940, and 1956. The British authorities did not allow African trade unions but did organize self-help "welfare" groups, which brought together persons of diverse ethnic backgrounds. In 1946, delegates from these groups met in Lusaka and formed the "Federation of African Welfare Societies." Up to that point, Africans were effectively excluded by the colonial administration from any political power: the Legislative Council,

the central political instrument of the Crown Colony, was left to whites only. In 1946, the British created the "African Representative Council," which was filled by Africans. This council deserved its name, since its members had representative functions only, with no political power. Only from 1948 onwards were a few Africans allowed to sit in the Legislative Council. In the same year, the Federation of African Welfare Societies was transformed into the "Northern Rhodesia African Congress," the first African political party of the colony.

From 1953 to 1963, Northern Rhodesia formed a federation with Southern Rhodesia and Nyasaland in order to create a political and economic British counterpart to the influence of Boer-dominated South Africa, to reduce costs for administration and to feed bankrupt Southern Rhodesia with Northern Rhodesian export revenues. Protests by Northern Rhodesian African leaders against the Federation were fruitless. In 1956, copper revenues, the main source of income for the Federation, dropped dramatically, and many miners lost their jobs. Many Africans stiffened protests against their barring from political and economic power. In 1958, members of the Northern Rhodesian African Congress founded the "Zambian African National Congress" (later UNIP). The new party, led by Kenneth Kaunda, took a much more radical anticolonial line than did the Northern Rhodesian African Congress. On December 31, 1963, the Federation floundered, and in October 1964, Northern Rhodesia gained independence as the Republic of Zambia.

After independence, Zambia's economy was relatively stable and prosperous, since the price of copper rose considerably between 1964 and 1970, and because the government had acquired mineral rights from the BSAC. In 1965, the government concluded projects for social services and education, and slowly the Africans started to dominate the upper ranks of the public sector while the whites dominated the economic sector for a while.

Although Zambia was dependent on railroad tracks and pipelines through neighbouring countries, which were ruled by white minority regimes, Kaunda made Zambia a "frontline state" against these regimes and granted refuge to members of South African resistance movements. As a result, Zambia was cut off from the routes through Rhodesia and Angola. China built a railroad from the Zambian copper belt to Dar es Salaam (Tanzania) instead. This railroad was opened in October 1975.

In 1969, Zambia began to nationalize foreign copper mines. However, in 1970, a harsh economic crisis hit the country, since revenues from the copper export fell, while the price for oil and other import goods increased. Dissatisfaction with Kaunda's government

grew, which led to the fission of the "United Progressive Party" from UNIP under Simon Kapwepwe in 1971. Kaunda reacted by transforming Zambia into a de facto one-party state (in December 1972), intimidating the opposition and greasing opposition leaders with lucrative posts. He established a sophisticated patronage system, created jobs by inflating the bureaucracy, and kept the ailing urban population at bay by subsidizing food prices. This subsidizing program was financed at the expense of heavy debt burdens and squandered relief funds. The International Monetary Fund (IMF), one of Zambia's main donors, in return put pressure on the government to cancel food subsidizing. In 1986, Kaunda agreed to stop it, but reestablished it in 1987, provoking the withdrawal of the IMF from the donor community. Kaunda's second attempt to cancel food subsidizing in 1990 caused major upheavals, particularly in urban areas, which effectively put an end to his regime.

His successor, Chiluba, had promised economic and social reforms as well as a commitment to human rights. However, in terms of "good governance," his status after two terms in office was negative, particularly with regard to economic reforms. Since the government believed that static development policies during the UNIP era were a major factor in creating the economic problems faced by the country and that any recovery would require the financial support of the IMF and the World Bank, they committed themselves to a hasty privatization of state enterprises. In urban areas, the opening of the economy to foreign investors has caused a high level of unemployment and an expansion of the informal sector. Although the government acknowledges that the agricultural sector should play the dominant economic role, its policies do not give it priority.

MMD's governing policies are characterized by corruption and xenophobia. Opposition leaders are threatened with forced exile by denying them their Zambian citizenship. The discontent and aggressions of the growing army of impoverished Zambians are frequently directed towards the Asian minority and the 250,000 refugees in Zambia, mainly from Angola and the D.R. Congo.

REINHARD KLEIN-ARENDT

Further Reading

Baylies, Carolyn and Morris Szeftel. "The Fall and Rise of Multi-Party Politics in Zambia," *Review of African Political Economy*, 54 (1992).

Beveridge, Andrew A. and Anthony R. Oberschall. *African Businessmen and Development in Zambia*. Princeton, NJ: Princeton University Press, 1979.

Chipungu, Samuel N. *Guardians in Their Time: Experiences of Zambians Under Colonial Rule, 1890–1964*. London and Basingstoke: MacMillan Press, 1992.

Craig, John. "Putting Privatisation Into Practice: The Case of Zambia Consolidated Copper Mines Limited," *The Journal of Modern African Studies*, 39:3 (2001).

Donge, Jan Kees van. "Reflections on Donors, Opposition and Popular Will in the 1996 Zambian General Elections," *The Journal of Modern African Studies*. 36:1 (1998).

———. *Zambia*. Oxford: Clio Press, 2000.

Grotpeter, John J. *Historical Dictionary of Zambia*. Metuchen, NJ: Scarecrow Press, 1979; 2nd ed., John J. Grotpeter, Brian V. Siegel, and James R. Pletcher, eds. Lanham, MD: Scarecrow Press, 1998.

Phiri, Bizeck J. "Decolonization and Multi-Racial Liberalism in Northern Rhodesia: A Reassessment," *Zambia Journal of History*. 5 (1992).

ZAPATISTA NATIONAL REVOLUTIONARY ARMY (EZLN)

Background

On January 1, 1994, following years of clandestine work, a well-organised army of mostly Mayan Indians simultaneously occupied four towns in the southern state of Chiapas. The uprising was led by the Zapatista Army for National Liberation (EZLN), named after Emiliano Zapata's famous guerrilla band of the 1910s. The revolt was timed to begin with the institution of the North American Free Trade Agreement (NAFTA), which Zapatista leaders thought would further erode their standards of living. The government overreacted by sending a huge contingent of soldiers into the region to suppress the revolt. Under internal and international pressure, former President Salinas agreed to negotiate, by using Catholic leaders as mediators. Ongoing negotiations have been periodically revived with successive Mexican governments without reaching a satisfactory conclusion.

Causes of the Conflict

Despite being Mexico's resource-richest state, Chiapas had suffered more poverty, government neglect, lack of basic infrastructure, and landowner abuse than did the rest of the country. A large percentage of the population is composed of descendants from Maya Indians who, over the centuries, have suffered from discrimination and whose demands for a fairer distribution of land and recognition of their basic human rights have been ignored. The decision to take up arms was finally prompted by the government's attempts to revoke Article 27 of the Mexican

constitution, which protected communal land holdings administered by Indian communities (*ejidos*) from privatization.

Aims

The Zapatistas have been described by Castañeda as "armed reformists" rather than revolutionaries. Unlike all other armed revolutionary movements, they have not sought to seize state power or become a political party. The armed uprising was part of a larger strategy to promote the struggle for land reform, democracy, and indigenous rights, and to force the government into the negotiating table.

Structure of the Movement

One remarkable trait that distinguishes the Zapatistas from other armed movements is the subordination of the military to civilian leadership. The highest political body is the Clandestine Revolutionary Indigenous Committee (CCRI), composed of elected representatives from all the Zapatista communities. This body represents the collective decision making of the communities, since decisions are taken by consensus following extensive consultations and approval across communities. The same model of direct democracy applies at every level, from the autonomous municipalities to the local Zapatista communities, combining democratic principles with traditional indigenous assemblies.

Achievements

Within the communities, the uprising had major consequences. One was the perceived need to redress traditional discrimination against women, which resulted in the Revolutionary Women's Law. Another major gain was the creation of a partially liberated zone in part of eastern Chiapas, where thousands of Zapatista communities have carried out their own experiment in self-administration by following customary practices. Thus, the uprising instilled a new-found confidence and politicisation among the most marginalised sectors of Mexican society.

In February 1996, the parties signed the San Andres Accord. So far, only the first provision has been completed, recognising the autonomy of Mexico's 10 million Indians and their rights to multilingual education.

Economic issues, such as control of natural resources and land redistribution, remain unresolved. The demand to demilitarise the indigenous areas in Chiapas is still to be met, but incorporative creative politics continues to flourish in the region.

SUSANA A. EISENCHLAS

See also Mexico: History and Economic Development

References and Further Reading

Collier, G. A and E. L. Quaratiello. *Basta!: Land and the Zapatista Rebellion in Chiapas*. Oakland, CA: The Institute for Food and Development Policy, 1999.

Harvey, N. *The Chiapas Rebellion: The Struggle for Land and Democracy*. Durham, NC: Duke University Press, 1998.

Holloway, J. and E. Pelaez, eds. *Zapatista!: Reinventing Revolution in Mexico*. London; Sterling, VA: Pluto Press, 1998.

Weinberg, B. *Homage to Chiapas: The New Indigenous Struggles in Mexico*. London; New York: Verso, 2000.

Weller, W. H. *et al. Conflict in Chiapas: Understanding the Modern Mayan World*. North Manchester, IN: DeWitt Books, 2000.

Womack, J., ed. *Rebellion in Chiapas: An Historical Reader*. New Press: Distributed by W.W. Norton, 1999.

ZHOU ENLAI

Zhou Enlai (1898–1976) was born in Huai'an, Jiangsu, China, on March 5, 1898. Educated in China, Japan, France, Germany, and England, he belonged to the group of urbanised and cosmopolitan intellectual leaders of the Chinese Communist Party (CCP). He joined the Communist Party in France in 1921, returned to China in 1924, and soon became a prominent leader of the Chinese Communist movement.

He participated in the Long March (1934–1935), acted as chief liaison officer between the CCP and the Guomindang during the Sino-Japanese War (1937–1945), and became a follower of Mao's political line in the early 1940s, starting with the Yan'an Rectification Campaign (1942–1945). After 1949, Zhou Enlai increasingly took over the role of handling the every day problems of Communist rule. The many speeches he made in his capacity as premier of the Chinese Communist government and leading member of the CCP reflect his ideas on questions of development in economic, political, and social terms his main concern being the necessity to overcome underdevelopment and poverty in order for China to reclaim its position among the most advanced nations of the world.

In the field of economics, Zhou Enlai first adhered to the Soviet Union model of socialist construction regarding the development of heavy industry as the most important task of the modernising socialist

state. At the same time, private entrepreneurs should be allowed to contribute under the regime of state capitalism to the well-being of society and economy by investing into the light industry. Agricultural production was supposed to gain momentum as a consequence of land reform and cautious collectivisation. He was convinced that China did not need the kind of large-scale state-run agriculture of the Soviet Union, but also believed in the enhancement of agricultural output with the help of a form of collectivisation that would conform with the peasants needs and wishes.

But in 1956 already, Zhou Enlai expressed his doubts about the Soviet model and started to reflect on the rearrangement of priorities in economic development. In this context, he repeatedly underlined the problems of a planned economy, but never lost hope in the possibility to accelerate development by planning on the basis of "seeking truth in facts." As a consequence of severe problems arising during and after the Great Leap Forward, he finally agreed to regarding agriculture as the foundation of development, serving the light industry with the necessary products the production and consumption of which would provide the sector of heavy industries with the necessary capital. By this, he hoped to overcome the central problem of shortage of capital without having to rely on financial aid from the Soviet Union or other countries of the Socialist block. In terms of speed, this new setting of priorities would slow down the process of modernisation, but it would at the same time prevent the country from suffering under the kind of disproportionate growth it had gone through during the enthusiastic years of the Great Leap Forward. On the top of that, the Great Famine from 1959 to 1961 had shown that without focusing on agriculture, the newly founded People's Republic would not even be able to supply its population with the necessary amount of grain.

Politically, Zhou Enlai stressed the necessity to integrate as many members of society as possible under the leadership of the Communist Party. Recurring to his experiences gained as head of the liaison office in Chongqing during the war against Japan (1937–1945), he was aimed at slowly convincing as many members of society, even those from so called "hostile classes," to submit to the leadership of the CCP and contribute to the improvement of livelihood in China. Thus, he emphasized the length of the so-called transitional period and the necessity to allow for different forms of property rights to coexist.

As Zhou Enlai's development strategies were focused on modernising China so as to enable it to catch up with the highly industrialised countries of the world, he was extremely concerned with mobilising the intelligentsia for the cause of enhancing the education of the younger generation. He was convinced that China could join the countries with the highest standards in science and technology and strongly argued against anti-intellectualism. As early as 1956, he gave a speech on the role of intellectuals as well as of science and technology in socialist construction asking the whole nation "to march towards science." After severe persecution and criticism of intellectuals during the Campaign against Rightists (1957–1958), Zhou Enlai used the period of readjustment during the early 1960s to reinforce his policies towards intellectuals, reiterating that the overwhelming majority of intellectuals were patriotic, progressive, and served socialism wholeheartedly, and should therefore be regarded as part of the working class.

It is mainly because of this focus of his modernisation strategy that Zhou Enlai is still acclaimed as a humane socialist without the personal ambitions of many intellectuals in the PRC. Stressing that without him, the economy in mainland China would have collapsed during the tumultuous early years of the Cultural Revolution (1966–1976), many who lived through the chaos of that period commemorate him as the saviour of the country. Zhou Enlai did not submit absolutely to Mao Zedong's will during the years 1966 to 1976. However, while participating in "class struggle," he laid the foundation of the reform policy Deng Xiaoping, his successor as premier of the PRC, would later promote as the "four modernisations." Using his increased influence after the death of designated party leader Lin Biao, Zhou Enlai spent the last years of his life attempting to redefine China's role in international politics and prepare the ground for the modernisation of agriculture, industry, national defence, science, and technology. He died on January 8, 1976.

SUSANNE WEIGELIN-SCHWIEDRZIK

See also Chinese Communist Party; Chinese Revolution; Deng Xiaoping; Mao Zedong; Modernization

References and Further Reading

Chang, David W. *Zhou Enlai and Deng Xiaoping in the Chinese Leadership Succession Crisis.* Lanham, MD: The University Press of America, 1983.
Lee, Chae-Jin. *Zhou Enlai: The Early Years.* Stanford, CA: Stanford University Press, 1996.
MacFarquhar, Roderick, ed. *The Politics of China, 1949–1989.* Cambridge, UK: Cambridge University Press, 1993.
Shao, Kuo-Kang. *Zhou Enlai and the Foundation of Chinese Foreign Policy.* Basingstoke: Palgrave, 1996.
Zhou Enlai. *Selected Works of Zhou Enlai.* Beijing: Foreign Language Press, Vol.1, 1981.

ZIA UL-HAQ, MUHAMMED

Muhammed Zia ul-Haq (1924–1988) was born on August 12, 1924, at Jalundhar. He was the eldest son of Muhammad Akram, a teacher in the British Indian Army. Zia received his early education in the Government High School Simla and obtained a B.A. Honours from St. Stephen's College (Delhi). He joined the British Army in 1943 and served in Burma, Malaya, and Indonesia during the World War II. At the time of independence of Pakistan in 1947, Zia joined the Pakistan army as a major. In 1963–1964, he went to the United States for a training course in the Commander and Staff College. During the Indo-Pakistan war of 1965, he acted as the Assistant Quarter Master of the 101st Infantry Division, which was posted at Kiran sector. Zia was posted to Jordan from 1967–1970, where he was an instructor in the Jordan military academy. In 1975, he was appointed as Core Commander of Multan, and in 1976, Prime Minister Zulfikar Ali Bhutto appointed him Chief of the Army Staff. In July 1977, he overthrew the democratically elected Bhutto government due to the political uncertainty and declared martial law for the third time in the brief history of Pakistan. Bhutto was imprisoned by Zia's government and was charged with conspiring to murder a party colleague; in April 1979, he was hanged by Zia's military regime. Zia promised to hold elections in the next ninety days, but in 1977, he postponed the elections and decided to start an accountability process for politicians. He established a Disqualification Tribunal that disqualified many politicians during the next seven years.

On September 16, 1978, after the retirement of President Fazl Ellahi Chudhary, Zia assumed the office of President and announced a Nizam-e-Mustafa (Islamization) programme. In 1979, Zia joined the Non-Aligned Movement and also joined the US partnership against the Soviet invasion of Afghanistan in December 1979. The Afghan war enabled Zia to continue martial law and legitimised its military regime. His government received $3.2 billion and $4.2 billion in economic and military aid from the United States. The US administration and the Congress waive the Symington amendment and make an exception regarding Islamabad's nuclear programme. Thus, Zia's government's clandestine efforts successfully achieved nuclear weapons capability and produced weapons-grade uranium. In 1980, he introduced a 284-member Majlis-i-Shura (nominated by the president) as an advisory council for the president. In 1985, Zia was declared President through a dubious referendum, amended the constitution, and institutionalised the supremacy of the military in decision-making by the inclusion of the three chiefs of staff in the National Security Council.

In 1985, Zia announced elections on a non-party basis, and the major political parties boycotted them. The results showed that many victors belonged to local, regional, ethnic, and religious parties. Zia nominated Muhammad Khan Junejo as the prime minister from among the members of the assembly. But before handing over the power to the new government, he introduced the eighth amendment under which the president had the right to dissolve the elected assembly. These measures were endorsed by the parliament before Zia lifted the state of emergency in the country in 1986. On May 29, 1988, he dissolved the National Assembly and removed the Prime Minister under article 58(2)B of the amended constitution due to differences on the issue of parliamentarians' freedom and decision to sign the Geneva Accord (April 1988). Zia again promised to hold elections within ninety days, but before any decision, he died in an air crash near Bahawalpur on August 17, 1988. Zia-ul-Haq was buried in the premises of Faisal Mosque (Islamabad), and later the country celebrated the rule of democracy.

HUSAIN KASSIM

References and Further Reading

Craig Baxter. *Zia's Pakistan: Politics and stability in a Frontline State*. Boulder, CO: Westview Press, 1985.

Hassan Gardezi and Jamil Rashid, ed. *Pakistan: The Roots of Dictatorship*. London: Zed Press, 1983.

Karl F. Newman. *Pakistan Under Ayub, Bhutto, and Zia ul-Haq*. Munich: Weltforum Verlag, 1986.

Mohammed Waseem. *Pakistan Under Martial Law 1977–1985*. Lahore: Vanguard, 1987.

Muhammed Munir. *From Jinnah to Zia*. Lahore: Vanguard, 1980.

Robert Wirsing. *Pakistan Security Under Zia 1977–1988: The Policy Imperatives of a Peripheral Asian State*. New York: St. Martin's Press, 1991.

Sayed Serajul Rizvi. "The Paradox of Military Rule in Pakistan," *Asian Survey*, 24:5 (May 1984), pp. 534–55.

ZIMBABWE

Zimbabwe in southern African has a landlocked area if 150,804 square miles, with South Africa, Botswana, Zambia, Malawi, and Mozambique as neighbors. Its 2003 population was 12,890,000 but decreased to an estimated 12,671,860 (CIA) in 2004 due to the HIV/AIDS crisis. By 2050, Zimbabwe's population could fall to 12,658,000 if present trends continue. The United Nations estimates that 34% of the adult population is infected by HIV/AIDS. Another report cites life expectancy as 40.1 years for Zimbabwe

males; 39.7 years for females. But a United Nations (UN) Human Development report places life expectancy at 32 years, compared with 50 years three decades ago, for the Southern African states of Zimbabwe, Zambia, Malawi, Swaziland, Mozambique, Lesotho, and the Central African Republic.

Zimbabwe's largest cities are Harare, the capital, with a population of 1,868,000, and Bulawayo, with 824,000 inhabitants. Approximately 24% of Zimbabwe's workers are employed in service industries. Schooling is compulsory for ages five to 12; literacy is 90.7%. Religion is a syncratic mix of Roman Catholic, Protestant, and traditional African beliefs. African-led churches, often with a mix of charismatic or pentecostal emphases, are increasing.

Nearly two-thirds of Zimbabwe's people live in rural areas, where only 7% of the land is arable. Thus, most rural people are subsistence farmers who depend on irregular rainfall to produce maize, and cotton, tobacco, wheat, coffee, and cotton. Livestock was estimated at 5.70 million in 2002.

South African whites took the arable land from Zimbabwe's Bantu and Ndebele population in 1890. Cecil Rhodes invaded in order to extract mineral resources: gold and diamonds. Zimbabwe also had nickel, copper, chrome, veradium, tin, and platinum.

Eighty-two percent of the natives are of Shona-related ethnic groups; 14% are Ndebele-speakers.

Before Rhodes' British South Africa Company (BSAC) arrived, Shona and Ndebele (a Zulu tribe from the South) ruled Zimbabwe. Portuguese traders and Roman Catholic missionaries had visited from Mozambique long before Rhodes had established his diamond trade in South Africa in 1880. In 1890, Rhodes and his Pioneer Column defeated the Shona and established Fort Salisbury. Rhodes detested African culture and stole African land and minerals after he got Ndebele King Lobengula to sign a phony treaty. Queen Victoria ceded political control of Mashonaland and Matabeleland to the BSAC, which ruled "Rhodesia" from 1890 to the 1920s. Rhodes gave three thousand acres to white pioneers and allowed white farmers and miners to rule.

British and other whites brought capitalism, imperial rule, and Christianity to Zimbabwe. Rhodes awarded grants to missions to impose "Christian" culture in subsidized schools, clinics, and churches. The BSAC granted land and stipends for missionary teachers and doctors. Christian culture included religion, Western dress, marriage customs, English language, and deference to whites. They rechristened the landscape with Christian names. The BSAC and Christian missions married acquisition of wealth to imperialism and faith.

A scramble for African land involved carnal and religious interests that became so intertwined as to be almost indistinguishable. Their interests were to transform African culture and to dominate its people. Africans would become forced laborers in mines and on farms, and they would be transformed into believers with European habits and often Christian names. They would abandon African religious rites for European beliefs.

Professor C. J. M. Zvobgo argues that Christian missions shared two beliefs with Rhodes' BSAC. As a result of early London Missionary Society (LMS) and Jesuit experiences, missionaries believed that success in converting the "heathen" to the Christian ways depended on breaking Ndebele power by force. They argued that the Ndebele were masters of the Shona. The missions were indebted to Rhodes for mission land grants and were willing to support use of force to maintain BSAC rule. By 1925, the BSAC had given missions 325,730 acres, mostly without permission of African chiefs.

Rough white South African miners had little interest in religion. Their interest was in material wealth. Thus, most missions turned to work among Africans when BSAC offered land grants. Few missionaries raised issues of BSAC land confiscation, hut taxes, and forced labor from Africans. And few missions sought African advice on health, education, or church policy. Paternalism held that Africans were incompetent in management matters. On the whole, deaths of whites were seen as "martyrdoms," with no connection to their theft of land or denial of African cultural/political self-determination.

In 1923, white settler government replaced BSAC rule, and in 1965, Ian Smith's settler government unilaterally declared independence from Britain and established a minority white-ruled "republic" to deny the vote to the majority African population. In the early 1960s, Africans had begun to organize guerrilla forces to fight for independence. Warfare lasted until the British negotiated a settlement in 1979. Patriotic Front leaders Robert Mugabe and Joshua Nkomo gained one-person-one-vote democracy and renamed the country Zimbabwe. The new African state was recognized by the United Kingdom, United States, and United Nations. UN sanctions, supported by a World Council of Churches' (WCC) Program to Combat Racism and work of international relief agencies, combined with weapons from Asia and Eastern Europe, helped bring Prime Minister Mugabe's multi-party government to power in 1980.

African and white political parties and white and African churches chose sides in the war. Irish Presbyterians, the Reformed Church, and Salvation Army broke with the WCC over humanitarian grants to the

"Marxist" insurgents. Zimbabwe's war became an extension of cold war politics for American and British conservatives. But when war ended, Mugabe's Shona army engaged in a brutal civil struggle with Nkomo's Ndebele. Later Mugabe sealed an alliance with the Ndebele wing of the Patriotic Front that held to the early twenty-first century in spite of Mugabe's increasingly autocratic rule.

After a period of peace and relative prosperity under President Mugabe, Zimbabwe experienced political instability and economic crises in the 1990s. Joining a civil war in Zaire (Congo) squandered Zimbabwe's capital. Inflation reached 900%. Whites emigrated due to attacks on their property by Mugabe's veterans of the independence war. U.K. and US funds for land redistribution to Africans did not arrive to restore land to Africans. And an HIV/AIDS epidemic broke the spirit of Zimbabweans.

It remains to be seen whether President Mugabe will step aside at the end of his present term and permit a democratically elected government to succeed him. When that occurs, land reform may proceed by legal due process and the international community may offer assistance. In the meantime, Zimbabwe may find a way to heal itself and capitalize on its wealth and cultural heritage.

NORMAN H. MURDOCH

See also Mugabe, Robert

References and Further Reading

Banana, Canaan, ed. *Turmoil & Tenacity: Zimbabwe, 1890–1990*. Harare: College Press, 1989.
Beach, D. N. *The Shona & Zimbabwe, 900–1850*. London: Heinemann, 1980.
———. *War & Politics in Zimbabwe, 1840–1900*. Gweru: Mambo, 1986.
Moyo, Sam. *The Land Question in Zimbabwe*. Harare: Sapes Books, 1995.
Ranger, T. O. *Revolt in Southern Rhodesia, 1896–1897*. Evanston, IL: Northwestern University Press, 1967.
Thompson, Carol B. *Challenge to Imperialism: The Frontline States in the Liberation of Zimbabwe*. Harare: Zimbabwe Publishing House, 1985.
Zvobgo, C. J. M. *A History of Christian Missions in Zimbabwe, 1890–1939*, Gweru: Mambo, 1996.

ZIONISM

Zionism is a much-maligned concept in the developing world. The word is often misunderstood, and in recent years, has taken on meanings that would not likely be embraced by its originators.

Traditional Zionism may best be defined as "Jewish nationalism." In essence, the early Zionist movement's primary goal was to create a Jewish national homeland in Palestine and to reconstitute Jewish sovereignty over what was the biblical Land of Israel.

While the movement successfully achieved its primary goal with the creation of the State of Israel in 1948, it was simultaneously responsible for displacing and disenfranchising the existing residents of the region, namely the Palestinian Arabs. As a result, Zionism remains a controversial movement, particularly, though not solely, in the Arab and Muslim worlds.

The Origins and Evolution of Zionism

The father of the modern Zionist movement, Theodor Herzl (b. 1860), was a secular European Jewish writer, thinker and visionary who, in 1896, wrote the book *Judenstaat* ("The Jewish State"). The book's thesis suggested that the solution to the problem of Jews living as insecure, threatened, and weak minorities in the lands of Europe and elsewhere (the Jewish Diaspora) was the (re)creation of a Jewish homeland in Palestine, with Jerusalem as its political and cultural capital. There, Jews could run their own affairs and determine their own destiny in a safe refuge free of anti-Semitism and other hatreds and dangers.

The First Zionist Conference met a year later, in 1897. Its purpose, and the purpose of succeeding Zionist conferences and meetings throughout the early twentieth century, was to encourage *aliyah*, mass Jewish migration to Palestine. Upon arrival, Jews from throughout the world sought to develop social, economic, and political structures that would facilitate eventual independent statehood. These structures included the creation of mechanisms to acquire and settle the land, to build cities and communal agricultural settlements (*kibbutzim* and *moshavim*), to create a governance structure, and to create and adopt a new common language, *Ivrit*, that is, Modern Hebrew. The Jewish community at this time became known as the *Yishuv*, and its governing structure was known as the World Zionist Organization, later to become the Jewish Agency during the British Mandatory period.

Anti-Zionist Sentiment in the Developing World

From its earliest beginnings, the actions and ideas of the Zionist movement were opposed by the Palestinian Arab residents of the region, by other Arab and Muslim communities, and by other countries and

groups around the world. Many saw Zionism as a form of European colonialism and imperialism under Jewish guise.

The 1917 Balfour Declaration declaring "sympathy with Jewish Zionist aspirations" marked a significant moment in Zionist history, as a major power, the United Kingdom, openly expressed support to the movement's cause. And yet, throughout the British Mandatory period in Palestine (1917–1947), local Arabs used both diplomatic and at times military means in an attempt to discourage Jewish immigration to Palestine. The mid-1930s was an especially notable period of Arab unrest against the Jewish presence in Palestine, which ultimately contributed to the issuance of the British White Paper of 1939 that placed limitations on Jewish immigration to the region.

This was a partial victory for the Palestinians, but it was a short-lived success. The end of World War II and the revelation to the world community that millions of Jews had been slaughtered in Adolf Hitler's concentration camps drew sympathy to the Zionist movement and its goals. This sentiment came to a head when, in late 1947, the United Nations Special Committee on Palestine put forward a partition plan to create a Jewish state alongside an Arab state in post-colonial Palestine.

The Arab community rejected the plan. Soon thereafter, on May 14, 1948, the Jews of Palestine unilaterally declared the creation of the new State of Israel, which was quickly recognized by the United States, the Soviet Union, and other key global powers. Neighboring Arab states did not accept Israel's existence, however, and initiated a war the following day. The war, which Israelis refer to as their "Independence War," was won handily, though there were numerous casualties on both sides. The war only further harmed Palestinian interests, as the Zionist claim to Palestine was formalized and consolidated.

And yet the Arab states, the Palestinians, and others who saw the Zionists and their cause as illegitimate, if not illegal, continued to fight for its eradication from Palestine. After years of activity both within the Middle East and around the world, the anti-Zionist movement achieved a diplomatic victory. In November 1975, the United Nations (UN) General Assembly issued Resolution 3379, a proclamation that effectively condemned Israel's very existence and equated Zionism with racism.

In part, this argument was premised upon the nature of Israel's "Law of Return," a centerpiece of Zionist ideology. The law states that a Diaspora Jew may "return" to Israel as an Israeli national, with the full rights that status offers. Non-Jews, on the other hand, cannot effectively achieve this status (although they may be citizens of the state; nearly 20% of modern Israel's citizens are non-Jews), regardless of their birthplace.

Only in December 1991—sixteen years later—did the UN retract this resolution with Resolution 46/86. Some Arab and Muslim states, as well as Cuba, North Korea, and Vietnam, expressed their opposition to the repeal of the 1975 resolution.

Zionism in the 21st Century

The UN World Conference Against Racism in Durban, South Africa, in September 2001 brought the issue of Zionism to the fore once again. Resolution draft language again equated the movement with racism, suggesting that it is "a new form of apartheid" which is inherently discriminatory and based on racial superiority. Protests against this language from the United States, Israel, and other parties were responsible for its eventual removal, and the final draft document made no mention of Zionism in this context.

That said, Zionism remains a controversial movement throughout the developing world and is typically equated with the imperialistic and racist ideologies that fueled the European colonial enterprise throughout Asia and Africa during the eighteenth and nineteenth centuries. Thus, the word "Zionist" often is used as an epithet against those, Jewish or not, who are seen as acting against the interests of Third World peoples.

STEVEN C. DINERO

See also Balfour Declaration; Israel; Middle East: History and Economic Development; Middle East: International Relations; Palestine; Palestinian Diaspora

References and Further Reading

Edelheit, Hershel and Abraham J. Edelheit. *History of Zionism: A Handbook and Dictionary.* Boulder, CO: Westview Press, 2000.

Halpern, Ben and Jehuda Reinharz. *Zionism and the Creation of a New Society (Studies in Jewish History).* Oxford: Oxford University Press, 1998.

Hertzberg, Arthur, ed. *The Zionist Idea: A Historical Analysis and Reader.* Philadelphia: Jewish Publication Society, 1997.

Herzl, Theodore. *The Jewish State.* Mineola, NY: Dover Publications, 1989.

Laqueur, Walter. *A History of Zionism.* New York: Fine Communications, 1997.

Stanislawski, Michael. *Zionism and the Fin de Siècle: Cosmopolitanism and Nationalism from Nordau to Jabotinsky.* Berkeley, CA, and Los Angeles: University of California Press, 2001.

INDEX

INDEX

INDEX

Topics

Persons

Organizations

THEMATIC LIST OF ENTRIES

Countries and Regions

Afghanistan
Albania
Algeria
Andean South America: History and Economic
    Development
Andean South America: International Relations
Angola
Anguilla
Antigua and Barbuda
Argentina
Armenia
Azerbaijan
Bahamas
Bahrain
Bangladesh
Barbados
Belarus
Belize
Benin
Bhutan
Biafra
Bolivia
Bosnia and Herzegovina
Botswana
Brazil
Brunei
Bulgaria
Burkina Faso
Burundi
Cambodia
Cameroon
Caribbean: History and Economic Development
Caribbean: International Relations
Cayman Islands
Central Africa: History and Economic Development
Central Africa: International Relations
Central African Republic
Central America: History and Economic
    Development
Central America: International Relations

Central and Eastern Europe: History and
    Economic Development
Central and Eastern Europe: International Relations
Central Asia: History and Economic Development
Central Asia: International Relations
Chad
Chile
China, People's Republic of
Colombia
Commonwealth of Independent States: History
    and Economic Development
Commonwealth of Independent States:
    International Relations
Comoros
Congo, Democratic Republic of the
Congo, Republic of the
Costa Rica
Cote d'Ivoire (Republic of the Ivory Coast)
Croatia
Cyprus
Czech Republic
Djibouti
Dominica
Dominican Republic
East Africa: History and Economic Development
East Africa: International Relations
East Asia: History and Economic Development
East Asia: International Relations
East Timor
Ecuador
Egypt
El Salvador
Equatorial Guinea
Eritrea
Estonia
Ethiopia
Fiji
French Guiana
Gabon
Gambia, The
Georgia
Ghana

LIST OF ENTRIES A–Z

A

Acid Precipitation
Afghanistan
African Development Bank (ADB)
African Diaspora
African Monetary Fund (AfMF)
African National Congress (ANC)
Agriculture: Impact of Globalization
Agriculture: Impact of Privatization
Ahidjo, Ahmadou
Albania
Algeria
All-African People's Conference (AAPC)
Allende Gossens, Salvador
Alliance for Progress
All-India Muslim League (AIML)
Amin, Idi
Amnesty International
Andean Community
Andean South America: History and
   Economic Development
Andean South America: International Relations
Anglican Communion
Anglo-Iranian Oil Company (AIOC)
Angola
Anguilla
Antigua and Barbuda
Apartheid
Aprismo
Aquino, Benigno, and Corazón
Arab Economic Unity Council
Arab Maghreb Union (AMU)
Arab Nationalism
Arabian American Oil Company (ARAMCO)
Arab–Israeli Wars (1948, 1956, 1967, 1973)
Arafat, Yasser
Árbenz Guzmán, Jacobo
Argentina
Arias Sanchez, Oscar
Aristide, Jean-Bertrand
Armed Forces of the People
Armenia
Arms and Armaments, International Transfer of
Arms Industry

ASEAN Free Trade Association
ASEAN Mekong Basin Development
   Cooperation (Mekong Group)
Asian Development Bank (ADB)
Asian "Economic Miracle"
Asian Monetary Fund
Asian Tigers
Asia-Pacific Economic Cooperation (APEC)
Association of Caribbean States (ACS)
Association of Southeast Asian Nations (ASEAN)
Aswan High Dam and Development in Egypt
Aung San Suu Kyi
Authoritarianism
Awami League
Ayub Khan, Muhammad
Azerbaijan
Azikiwe, Benjamin Nnamdi

B

Ba'ath Party
Baghdad Pact
Bahamas
Bahrain
Balfour Declaration
Balkan Wars of the 1990s
Bandung Conference (1955)
Bangladesh
Bank for International Settlements (BIS)
Banking
Bantustans
Barbados
Basic Human Needs
Batista y Zaldívar, Fulgencio
Bedouin
Begin, Menachem
Belarus
Belize
Ben Bella, Ahmed
Ben-Gurion, David
Benin
Berbers
Berlin Wall (1961–1989)

TABLE OF CONTENTS

LIST OF CONTRIBUTORS

Susanne Weigelin-Schwiedrzik
University of Heidelberg

Roland J. Wenzlhuemer
Salzburg University

Bruce M. Wilson
University of Central Florida

James E. Winkates
Air War College, Maxwell Air Force Base

Pamela A. Zeiser
University of North Florida

Eleanor Zelliot
Carleton College

Xinjun Zhang
Tsinghua University

Verónica M. Ziliotto
Universidad de Buenos Aires

Evert van der Zweerde
University of Nijmegen

Amandeep Sandhu
University of California at Santa Barbara

L. Natalie Sandomirsky
Southern Connecticut State University

Christopher Saunders
University of Cape Town

Christian P. Scherrer
Ethnic Conflict Research Project

Ulrike Schuerkens
Ecole des Hautes Etudes en Sciences Sociales

Alexander Hugo Schulenburg
Corporation of London

Stephen R. Schwalbe
Air War College

David Schwam-Baird
University of North Florida

James D. Seymour
Columbia University

Rodger Shanahan
University of Sydney

Scott E. Simon
University of Ottawa

Amrita Singh

Udai Bhanu Singh
Institute for Defence Studies

Carl Skutsch
The School of Visual Arts

E. Valerie Smith
Florida Gulf Coast University

Subhash R. Sonnad
Western Michigan University

Radhamany Sooryamoorthy
University of Kwazulu-Natal

Paul Spoonley
Massey University

Jeffrey W. Steagall
University of North Florida

Jason E. Strakes
Claremont Graduate School

Mira Sucharov
Carleton University

Tadeusz Swietochowski
Columbia University

Joseph Takougang
University of Cincinnati

Mary Ann Tétreault
Trinity University

Daniel S. Tevera
University of Zimbabwe

Amos Owen Thomas
Maastricht School of Management

Marius Tita
Bucharest, Romania

Brian Turner
Randolph-Macon College

Ufo Okeke Uzodike
University of KwaZulu-Natal

Cheryl Van Deusen
University of North Florida

John M. VanderLippe
State University of New York at New Paltz

Carlos Velásquez Carrillo
York University

Iain Walker
University of Sydney

John Walsh
Shinawatra International University

Yosay Wangdi
Grand Valley State University

Fredrick O. Wanyama
Maseno University

LIST OF CONTRIBUTORS

James A. Norris
Texas A&M International University

Milena Novakova
National Assembly of Republic of Bulgaria

P. Godfrey Okoth
Maseno University

Clémentine Olivier
National University of Ireland

Jorge Ortiz Sotelo
Peruvian Institute of Economy and Politics

Lazarus F. O'Sako
Ohio University

Patrick L. Osborne
International Center for Tropical Ecology,
University of Missouri at St. Louis

Tony Osborne
American University in Bulgaria

Úrsula Oswald S.
CRIM-UNAM and Diverse Women for Diversity

Charlene T. Overturf
Armstrong Atlantic State University

Steven Paulson
University of North Florida

Zoran Pavlović
Oklahoma State University

William D. Pederson
Louisiana State University in Shreveport

Carlos Pérez
California State University at Fresno

J. E. Peterson
University of Arizona

María Luisa Pfeiffer
Universidad de Buenos Aires

Aaron Z. Pitluck
University of Konstanz

Vincent Kelly Pollard
University of Hawai'i at Manoa

Nancy J. Pollock
Victoria University

Peter R. Prifti
San Diego, California

Lesley J. Pruitt
Arkansas State University

Ilie Rad
Babes-Bolyai University

Edward A. Riedinger
Ohio State University

Leonora Ritter
Charles Sturt University

Benjamin Rivlin
City University Graduate Center

Paul Rivlin
Tel Aviv University

Bruce D. Roberts
Minnesota State University Moorhead

Magaly Rodríguez García
Vrije Universiteit Brussel

David Romano
McGill University

Horacio N. Roque Ramirez
University of California at Santa Barbara

Stéphanie Rousseau
University of North Carolina at
Chapel Hill

Paul S. Rowe
University of Western Ontario

Werner Ruf
University of Kassel

Tom Ryan
University of Waikato

Arvee S. Salazar
San Fernando, Philippines

Steven S. Sallie
Boise State University

Jonathan H. L'Hommedieu
University of Turku

Yianna Liatsos
Rutgers University

Tracy L. R. Lightcap
LaGrange College

Natasha J. Lightfoot
New York University

John Lodewijks
University of New South Wales

Staffan Löfving
Stockholm University

Roger D. Long
Eastern Michigan University

P. Eric Louw
University of Queensland

Ludomir Lozny
Hunter College

Ronald Lukens-Bull
University of North Florida

Christopher Lundry
Arizona State University

Carmela Lutmar
New York University

Paul J. Magnarella
Warren Wilson College

Plamen Makariev
Sofia University

Arman Manukyan
Central European University

Richard R. Marcus
University of Alabama in Huntsville

Ross Marlay
Arkansas State University

Daniel M. Masterson
United States Naval Academy

Dee F. Matreyek
Restorative Justice Center of the Inland Empire

Jean F. Mayer
Concordia University

John Mukum Mbaku
Weber State University

Tamba E. M'bayo
Michigan State University

William McBride
Purdue University

Grant McCall
University of New South Wales

Christopher McDowell
Macquarie University

Elisabeth McMahon
Indiana University

Joseph Mensah
York University

Nasser Momayezi
Texas A&M International University

Waltraud Q. Morales
University of Central Florida

Ishmael Irungu Munene
State University of New York at Albany

Ruth Murbach
Université du Québec à Montréal

Norman H. Murdoch
University of Cincinnati

Diego I. Murguía
Universidad de Buenos Aires

Loretta Napoleoni
London, England

Caryn E. Neumann
Ohio State University

Stephan E. Nikolov
Bulgarian Academy of Sciences

LIST OF CONTRIBUTORS

Frank J. Hoffman
West Chester University

Ha Thi Thu Huong
TMC Academy

Sylvanus Ikhide
University of Namibia

International Commission on Irrigation and Drainage
New Delhi, India

Muhammad Muinul Islam
University of Dhaka

Serguey Ivanov
American University in Bulgaria

M. R. Izady
New York, New York

B. M. Jain
Rajasthan University

Uzma Jamil
McGill University

Ho-Won Jeong
George Mason University

Helen Johnson
The University of Queensland

Rebecca R. Jones
Widener University

Nantang Jua
University of Buea

Lars v. Karstedt
University of Hamburg

Husain Kassim
University of Central Florida

John Keep
Bern, Switzerland

Kembo-Sure
Moi University

Kenneth Keulman
Harvard University

Arne Kislenko
Ryerson University

Reinhard Klein-Arendt
University of Cologne

Wm. Gary Kline
Georgia Southwestern State University

Yoshie Kobayashi
Gunma Prefectural Women's University

Laszlo Kocsis
Covasna, Romania

Charles C. Kolb
National Endowment for the Humanities

Waldemar Koziol
Warsaw University

Alisa Krasnostein
The University of Western Australia

Wanda C. Krause
University of Exeter

Krum Krumov
Sofia University

Chi-Kong Lai
University of Queensland

George M. Lauderbaugh
Jacksonville State University

Robert Lawless
Wichita State University

David M. Lawrence
J. Sargeant Reynolds Community College

Michael C. Lazich
Buffalo State College

Lavina Lee
University of Sydney

Keith A. Leitich
Seattle, Washington

Hal Levine
Victoria University of Wellington

Mark A. Drumbl
University of Arkansas, Little Rock

Whitney D. Durham
Oklahoma State University

Mohammad Ehsan
University of Dhaka

Susana A. Eisenchlas
Griffith University

Nilly Kamal El-Amir
Cairo University

Mikhael Elbaz
Laval University

Nader Entessar
Spring Hill College

Jo-Anne Everingham
The University of Queensland

Mark Everingham
University of Wisconsin

Nicholas Farrelly
Australian National University

Mario D. Fenyo
Bowie State University

José Fernandez
University of Central Florida

Volker Frank
University of North Carolina at Asheville

Doris Fuchs
University of Munich

Mobo C. F. Gao
University of Tasmania

Andy Gibson
Griffith University

Brian J. Given
Carleton University

Arthur Goldschmidt, Jr.
The Pennsylvania State University

Michael Goldsmith
University of Waikato

Robert F. Gorman
Southwest Texas State University

Gustavo Adolfo Guerra Vásquez
University of California at Berkeley

Audrey Guichon
University of Birmingham

Juan-Carlos Gumucio Castellon
University of Uppsala

Alexander Gungov
Emory University

Michael M. Gunter
Tennessee Technological University

Michael M. Gunter, Jr.
Rollins College

Baogang Guo
Dalton State College

Michael R. Hall
Armstrong Atlantic State University

Reuel R. Hanks
Oklahoma State University

W. John Hansen
Ann Arbor, Michigan

Syed Hassan
Claflin University

Jonathan Haughton
Beacon Hill Institute for Public Policy

William P. Head
Warner Robins Air Logistics Center

Joseph Held
South Yarmouth, Massachusetts

Sirkku K. Hellsten
University of Birmingham

Anil Hira
Simon Fraser University

LIST OF CONTRIBUTORS

Ralf Buckley
Griffith University

Melissa Butcher
University of Sydney

Laura M. Calkins
Texas Tech University

David H. Carwell
Eastern Illinois University

James Chalmers
United Nations Development Programme,
Papua New Guinea

Frederick B. Chary
Indiana University Northwest

Dawn Chatty
University of Oxford

Janet M. Chernela
University of Maryland

James Chin
Universiti Malaysia Sarawak

George Cho
University of Canberra

Cristina Cielo
University of California at Berkeley

Katherine Cinq-Mars
McGill University

Andrew F. Clark
University of North Carolina at Wilmington

John F. Clark
Florida International University

Sharon C. Cobb
University of North Florida

Chris Coney
University of Melbourne

Daniele Conversi
London, England

Jose da Cruz
Armstrong Atlantic State University

Cecil B. Currey
Lutz, Florida

Robert L. Curry, Jr.
California State University at Sacramento

Kamran M. Dadkhah
Northeastern University

Kishore C. Dash
Thunderbird, The Garvin School of
International Management

Ansu Datta
Calcutta, India

Kusum Datta
Calcutta, India

Craig Davis
Point of Rocks, Maryland

Alan Dearling
Devon, England

Mahinda Deegalle
Bath Spa University College

Neil Denslow
Poole, Dorset, England

Linus digim'Rina
University of Papua New Guinea

Barbara J. Dilly
Creighton University

Steven C. Dinero
Philadelphia University

Thomas P. Dolan
Columbus State University

Manochehr Dorraj
Texas Christian University

David Dorward
LaTrobe University

Beth K. Dougherty
Beloit College

Emma Dowling
University of Birmingham

LIST OF CONTRIBUTORS

Rafis Abazov
Columbia University

Alfia Abazova
Dag Hammarskjöld Library

Janet Adamski
Southwestern University

Ali Ahmed
University of Birmingham

Nadine Akhund
Columbia University

Adam Allouba
McGill University

Samuel K. Andoh
Southern Connecticut State University

Anne Androuais
CNRS/FORUM/University Paris X

Christien van den Anker
University of Birmingham

Gasser Auda
University of Wales

Louis Augustin-Jean
University of Waseda

Rémi Bachand
Université Paris 1 (Panthéon-Sorbonne)

Josiah R. Baker
University of Central Florida

Mina Baliamoune
University of North Florida

Assefaw Bariagaber
Seton Hall University

John H. Barnhill
Yukon, Oklahoma

Graham Barrigan
La Trobe University

Greg Barton
Deakin University

Bob Beatty
Washburn University

Derek A. Bentley
Armstrong Atlantic State University

Mark T. Berger
University of New South Wales

Brian J. L. Berry
University of Texas at Dallas

Charles Boewe
Pittsboro, North Carolina

Valentin Boss
McGill University

Laura E. Boudon
American University

Lawrence Boudon
Library of Congress

Viviane Brachet-Márquez
El Colegio de México

Jillian Brady
Bayswater, Victoria, Australia

Susan Love Brown
Florida Atlantic University

Jürgen Buchenau
University of North Carolina at Charlotte

BOARD OF ADVISORS

Published in 2006 by
Routledge
Taylor & Francis Group
270 Madison Avenue
New York, NY 10016

Published in Great Britain by
Routledge
Taylor & Francis Group
2 Park Square
Milton Park, Abingdon
Oxon OX14 4RN

Printed in the United States of America on acid-free paper
10 9 8 7 6 5 4 3 2 1

International Standard Book Number-10: 1-57958-388-1 (set) 0-415-97662-6 (Vol 1) 0-415-97663-4 (Vol 2) 0-415-97664-2 (Vol 3)
International Standard Book Number-13: 978-1-57958-388-0 (set) 978-0-415-97662-6 (Vol 1) 978-0-415-97663-3 (Vol 2) 978-0-415-97664-0 (Vol 3)
Library of Congress Card Number 2005049976

Library of Congress Cataloging-in-Publication Data

Encyclopedia of the developing world / Thomas M. Leonard, editor.
    p. cm.
  Includes bibliographical references and index.
    ISBN 1-57958-388-1 (set : alk. paper) -- ISBN 0-415-97662-6 (v. 1 : alk. paper) -- ISBN 0-415-97663-4 (v. 2 : alk. paper) --
ISBN 0-415-97664-2 (v. 3 : alk. paper)
    1. Developing countries--Encyclopedias. I. Leonard, Thomas M., 1937-

HC59.7.E52 2005
909'.09724'03--dc22
    2005049976

Taylor & Francis Group is the Academic Division of T&F Informa plc.

Visit the Taylor & Francis Web site at
http://www.taylorandfrancis.com

and the Routledge Web site at
http://www.routledge-ny.com

ENCYCLOPEDIA OF THE
DEVELOPING WORLD

Volume 3
O–Z
INDEX

THOMAS M. LEONARD
EDITOR

 Routledge
Taylor & Francis Group
New York   London

ENCYCLOPEDIA OF THE
DEVELOPING
WORLD

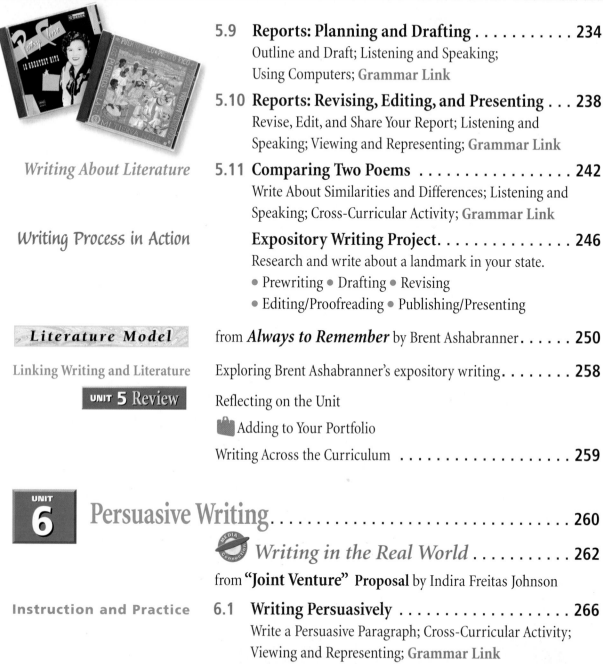

Business and Technical Writing 332

Part 2 Grammar, Usage, and Mechanics

Isn't it time you set your kids straight on tomato frogs?

Visit Brookfield Zoo and your kids can see how reclusive creatures really look, instead of jumping to conclusions. To find out more, call us at 708-485-0263. You're closer than you think.

BROOKFIELD ZOO
Where Imagination Runs Wild

Part 3 | Resources and Skills

LITERATURE MODELS

Composition Models

Each literature selection is an extended example of the mode of writing taught in the unit.

Skill Models

Excerpts from outstanding works of fiction and nonfiction exemplify specific writing skills.

LITERATURE MODELS

Language Models

Each Grammar Review uses excerpts to link grammar, usage, or mechanics to literature.

FINE ART

Fine art—paintings, drawings, photos, and sculpture—is used to teach as well as to stimulate writing ideas.

"*I want to write, but more than that, I want to bring out all kinds of things that lie buried deep in my heart.*"

—Anne Frank, *Anne Frank: The Diary of a Young Girl*

Fernand Leger,
*Fleurs Dans un
Element Mecanique,*
1943

PART 1

Composition

1

"Warm skies and gulf blue
streams are in my blood"

—Margaret Walker

Sorrow Home

2

Personal Writing

The memoir—a recollection of a person's past—is a popular form of personal writing in the media. The following excerpt is from the memoir of Laurence Yep. In it, Yep recalls the grocery store his parents owned during his childhood in San Francisco.

from *The Lost Garden* by Laurence Yep

The one thing that ruled my family's lives was our grocery store. I can still smell it. Even today, if I smell old plaster, I feel almost as if I am back in our old storeroom where the plaster was crumbling off the wooden laths. Or if I smell the coppery odor of liver, I think of washing out the bloody pan in which we used to display that kind of meat. If I smell old dollar bills, I can imagine myself back in the dark, quiet store, helping my mother put away the day's receipts.

A small grocery store is like a big beast that must be continually fed and cared for. Cans, packages, and bottles have to be put on shelves to take the place of things sold, produce like greens and celery have to be nursed along to keep them fresh as long as possible, and there are hundreds of other details that the customers never notice—unless they aren't done. In a small, family-owned store, certain chores must be done at a specific time each day. There is no choice.

Our store had its own daily rhythms just like a farm would have. It began before eight in the morning when my mother would pick her way down the unlit back stairs and along the dark alleyway to the backdoor of the store. Balancing the box with the cash register money in the crook of her arm, she would find the keyhole by feel and let herself in. Then, going through the darkened store, she would put the money in the cash register drawer. There were no neat rolls of coins. Instead, she had them each in a small paper bag, from pennies to fifty-cent pieces, and also dollar bills and bigger denominations in separate sacks.

At about the same time of day, my father stumped down the front steps of the Pearl Apartments. He usually wore thick-soled shoes for his feet, tan work pants, a flannel shirt, and a felt hat. Though a former athlete, his legs were slowly going bad from having to stand on them constantly for twelve hours seven days a week. He obviously was carrying no money, so there would be no temptation to rob him.

Memoir author
Laurence Yep

L aurence Yep, award-winning writer of fantasies, went in a totally new direction when he decided to write *The Lost Garden*. This personal story, or memoir, of growing up in San Francisco challenged him to piece together memories of his past. He began writing the book shortly after his father's death. "In a way, *The Lost Garden* was therapy," Yep explains. "It was my way to go back to these various places I used to go to with my father, and in some cases I tried to do it physically, but most of the time it was in my imagination and in my memory."

A Writer's Process

Prewriting

Gathering Memories

To help him recall memories, Yep used his senses, especially the sense of smell. "The layer of memory that is closest to the brain is not a layer of visual memories; it's the memory of smells. That's why a smell is more evocative than any visual detail," Yep explains.

Yep used memories of scents to help him mentally reconstruct his family's grocery store. The smell of crumbling plaster and wall materials brought back the hot summer afternoons he spent in a place that no longer exists. Smells brought back sights as one memory led to another. "From there I drew a map of the whole store, as best I could, and as I did that, I started remembering certain corners of the store," Yep recalls.

Photographs can also be helpful when gathering memories. During the writing of *The Lost Garden,* Yep kept several photographs of family members in front of him on his desk.

Memories provide rich background material for personal writing. Yet simply recalling past events isn't enough. The writer must understand them as well. What do the past events mean? What impact did they have?

"People think that, because they've lived something, they actually understand it, when that's not true," says Yep. "What they've done is experience it, but understanding is quite another matter—it's the next step."

Yep explains, "What it requires, to understand something, is actually to step away from that experience, so you can look at things more objectively, and that's also one of the steps in writing."

Photos of the the family store in San Francisco helped Yep recall memories of his childhood.

Drafting
Fitting the Pieces Together

Simple memories provide rich details for personal writing. While drafting his memoir, Yep focused on writing about daily life. Yep says, "Really the best writing is bringing out the specialness of ordinary things."

Yep compares the drafting stage to solving a puzzle. The pieces of the puzzle are his collection of memories. While drafting, he has to find a way to fit all those pieces together. Like most puzzle solving, the process can be both fun and frustrating.

To help organize his draft, Yep makes an informal outline, which he uses as a guide. He accepts the fact that he may have to go back and start a scene again.

He says, "You realize that you've got to redesign the puzzle, that an outline is only a scaffolding inside of which you've got to build a ship. And sometimes you get the ship almost built, and you realize that this darned thing isn't going to float, and so you have to tear it down, and

bring it down to the keel, and begin again."

Yep doesn't get discouraged about starting over. He realizes that rewriting is an essential part of the writing process.

Revising
Testing the Fit

A chief quality that Yep looks for in his own work is *authenticity,* the characteristic of being real or true. He revises his drafts to make certain that he has described events as accurately as possible. He makes sure that the feelings behind the scenes have a ring of truth.

By asking friends or relatives for their feedback, a writer can see how well his or her point of view has been communicated. But, finally, the writing is whatever the writer wants it to be. Yep says, "You have to write for yourself."

He tells students, "Writing is a way of exploring other selves and other worlds inside yourself. I think it can be very satisfying, whether you get a good mark on it or not."

Yep's memoir *The Lost Garden* includes many photos from his life.

Personal Writing

Examining Writing in the Real World

Analyzing the Media Connection

Discuss these questions about the article on page 4.

1. What are some sensory details in Yep's excerpt that appeal to the sense of smell?

2. In the second paragraph, to what does Yep compare a small grocery store? What are some details that he uses to support the comparison?

3. What detail does Yep use to help the reader visualize the darkness of the "unlit backstairs" that his mother navigated each morning?

4. What other details does Yep use that appeal to the sense of sight?

5. What details help the reader understand that Yep's parents are hard-working shopkeepers?

Analyzing a Writer's Process

Discuss these questions about Laurence Yep's writing process.

1. How does Yep use various senses to recall locations and personal experiences?

2. What graphic aids does Yep look at or create to help him gather his memories?

3. During drafting, does Yep always follow his outline, or does he tend to try new ideas and approaches? Explain why.

4. What chief criteria does Yep use to evaluate his writing?

5. When revising, how can a writer test whether he or she has succeeded in communicating the intended point of view?

Grammar Link

Use appositives to make your writing clearer and more interesting.

An appositive is a noun or a noun phrase placed next to another noun to identify it or add information about it.

Laurence Yep, **award-winning writer of fantasies,** *went in a totally new direction. . . .*

Write each sentence, adding an appositive to each italicized noun.

1. In this photo are my *cousins.*
2. I clearly remember the *scene.*
3. We used to live in *Burton.*
4. These *items* helped me gather details.
5. The memory sparked two *feelings.*

See Lesson 9.6, pages 391–392.

Writing for Yourself

In personal writing you express your own thoughts and feelings. Sometimes you write to share with others. At other times, you write just for yourself.

You can't wait to tell someone. It's such great news. You grab the phone and call a friend. "I have a brand-new baby sister!" you brag. In a brief note you tell another friend how excited you are about your new sister. These are personal thoughts and feelings, and your note is an example of personal writing.

Get Personal

Notes to yourself or letters to friends and family are personal writing. A private journal—a book for your most personal thoughts and feelings—is one of the best places for personal writing. What you write there is only for you. A classroom journal is another place for personal writing. Classroom journals are a tool for recording ideas and information, and they are often shared with classmates or teachers. Your classroom journals can also be an excellent source of ideas for writing assignments.

You can include more than just your writing in a journal. You might add photographs, magazine clippings, drawings, or even doodles.

Letters are another form of personal writing. Lonnel wrote the following letter to his sister Tamika, and he included the photograph on the right. Read the letter to see what personal experience Lonnel wanted to share.

Dear Tamika,

It's a really nice day here at Bowen Lake. It's almost noon, and the woods and the lake are warm in the sun. I'm sitting on a rock on the top of a kind of hill—as much like a hill as anything they have around here. I haven't seen anyone for over an hour. Earlier two people in a canoe drifted by. They were far away, and I could hardly see them. I could hear their voices, though. It's quiet now. There's a kind of magic in being all alone with nature.

How's the family? Is Jason back from training camp? What's Mom's job like now that she's back at work? Send me news!

Your brother,
Lonnel

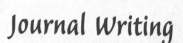

Journal Writing

Jot down the names of friends or family members to whom you might write a letter. Then list ideas of what to tell them. You can include both experiences and thoughts.

Keep a Journal

Writing in a journal can help you explore and remember your private thoughts without worrying about what anyone else thinks. Once you've begun your journal, you'll get more out of it if you write in it regularly. The following journal entry was written by author Louisa May Alcott as a girl.

Her writing here sounds like a conversation with a close friend.

Do you think this writing could appear in a letter to a friend? Why?

Literature Model

I am in the garret with my papers round me, and a pile of apples to eat while I write my journal, plan stories, and enjoy the patter of rain on the roof, in peace and quiet. . . . Being behind-hand, as usual, I'll make note of the main events up to date, for I don't waste ink in poetry and pages of rubbish now. I've begun to *live*, and have no time for sentimental musing. . . .

Norma Johnston, editor, *Louisa May:
The World and Works of Louisa May Alcott*

Below are some journal entries and a postcard. The writer used a private journal to record thoughts and experiences. Some of them were shared in a postcard to a friend. Read both and see how alike and how different they are.

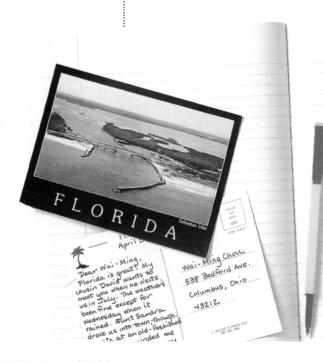

FLORIDA
Sebastian Inlet

Dear Wai-Ming,
Florida is great! My cousin David wants to meet you when he visits us in July. The weather's been fine except for Wednesday when it rained. Aunt Sandra drove us into town though. . . . at an old-fashioned . . . . reminded me . . .

Wai-Ming Chou
538 Bedford Ave.
Columbus, Ohio
43212

April 3
I'm really enjoying our visit to Aunt Sandra's. My cousins have all changed—David is almost as tall as I am.
I didn't think it would be so different down here: palm trees, amazing plants and insects, blue-green ocean—and warm sand everywhere!
It's raining today, so Aunt Sandra drove us into town. We had lunch at an old-fashioned diner.

April 4
The sun's out again, and it's warm. Lee says they practically live on the beach when the weather is this nice. The rest of us have to go to school.
We rented bicycles today and rode up the coast. Along one stretch of beach there's a bike path for cyclists and joggers. Dave said he thought he saw dolphins, but no one else saw them.

April 5
Went back to the beach. David's friend Chris came with us, and we

Write a Letter

You can write to a friend who is distant or to one whom you see often. Write about some experience you have had recently or about anything that's on your mind. Write as though you're talking to your friend.

PURPOSE To write a personal letter
AUDIENCE A good friend
LENGTH 1 page

WRITING RUBRICS To write your letter effectively, you should

- express your thoughts and feelings.
- include a doodle or drawing.

Listening and Speaking

In a small group, discuss your thoughts about sending and receiving personal letters. Have one group member act as a discussion leader, asking questions such as: Do you write many personal letters? Do you receive many? What do you like most about writing or receiving personal letters? Why? What do you like least?

Artist unknown, Pompeii, *Portrait of a Young Woman*, first century A.D.

Summarize your group's discussion for the class.

Cross-Curricular Activity

HISTORY The image on this page is from a wall painting found in the ruins of the ancient city of Pompeii. That city and its people were buried when Mount Vesuvius suddenly erupted in A.D. 79. Look at the young woman in this painting. Write the entry she might have written in her personal journal the day of the catastrophe. Remember, life was going on peacefully. What might she have done on that day?

Grammar Link

Use the possessive pronoun *its* and the contraction *it's* correctly.

The tree lost its leaves.
It's getting colder every week.

Complete each sentence with the correct word: *it's* or *its*.

1. It rained this morning, but _____ a beautiful afternoon.
2. My dog has injured _____ paw.
3. As I look at our house, I see _____ paint is cracking.
4. When _____ my turn to recite, I have to be ready.
5. Do you know _____ title?

See Lesson 11.4, pages 441–442.

LESSON 1.2

Writing to Learn

A learning log is another type of journal. In it you can keep a record of new facts or ideas you have learned in a class, as well as your thoughts and reactions to what you've learned. The example below was written after a science class. Read the entry and notice the clippings the writer included with it.

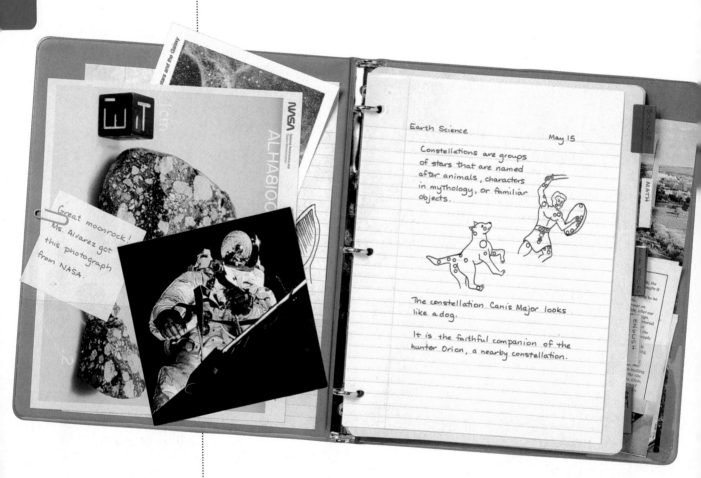

Great moonrock! Ms. Alvarez got this photograph from NASA.

Earth Science   May 15

Constellations are groups of stars that are named after animals, characters in mythology, or familiar objects.

The constellation Canis Major looks like a dog.

It is the faithful companion of the hunter Orion, a nearby constellation.

Record Your Progress

A learning log is a form of personal writing. It's for you. Writing in a log is an opportunity to become more involved in your learning and more aware of the progress you're making. For example, after reading a passage in your textbook, you can record your questions and thoughts in your learning log. Perhaps you'll raise these questions during your next class discussion. The chart below shows the kinds of entries you might put in your log. The goal is to make the information you study make sense to you.

Keeping a Learning Log	
Purpose	**Entry**
Summarize content.	Very hot stars are blue-white; cooler stars are orange or red.
Identify main ideas.	Sunspots are dark areas on the sun's surface that are cooler than surrounding areas.
Define problems, and ask questions.	I'm still not clear why our sun is called an average star.
Evaluate schoolwork.	The information on planets seemed easier than that on stars (because of the unit review?).

Journal Writing

What questions do you have about something you're learning now? Begin a learning log by writing down one or two of these questions.

Write and Think

Below is an example of how a learning log can be used. A student took the notes on the left as she read a textbook chapter on exploration of Mars. Then she wrote in her learning log. After a class discussion of this topic, she reread the textbook passage and looked over her notes. Then she used her learning log to rewrite the passage in her own words.

Text

Scientists are currently developing plans to further explore Mars. Because the distance between Earth and Mars is many millions of kilometers, it could take about three years to get to Mars and back. Because of the long duration of the flight, astronauts would face much more danger than they do in space shuttle missions.

the near-zero gravity in outer space,
Bones might

How does the question help the student focus on things to learn?

Distance to Mars—many millions of kilometers
Length of Mars trip—maybe three years
Danger—lowered calcium in bones due to near-zero gravity; weak bones might break once astronauts land on Mars or return to Earth.

Notes

What are some of the problems astronauts will face in exploring Mars?

One of the main problems is the length of the flight. Mars and Earth are many millions of kilometers apart. Traveling to the planet and back could take about three years. On the flight, astronauts' bones will lose calcium because of zero gravity. Once the crew reaches Mars or returns to Earth, their weak bones might fracture easily.

Learning Log

Write a Learning Log Entry

Choose a difficult paragraph, page, or chapter from a homework assignment for another class. Then choose one of the options in the chart on page 13 and write a learning log entry.

PURPOSE To clarify a difficult section of a book

AUDIENCE Yourself

LENGTH 1 paragraph

WRITING RUBRICS To use your learning log entry effectively, you should

- use the entry you have created to make sense out of the information
- during the next class of the subject for which you wrote the learning log entry, ask any question raised by the assignment.

Using Computers

Try keeping your learning log on the computer. You can underline or boldface key ideas. You can also keep an index or glossary of important words or ideas.

Viewing and Representing

Choose three images you like from magazines. Describe in a paragraph why you find these images interesting or useful. What does a graphic image show that words alone cannot express? Would you use graphics in a learning log? Explain. Share your ideas with the class.

Grammar Link

Use the correct verb form when the subject of a sentence is an indefinite pronoun.

Some indefinite pronouns—*all, any, most, none,* and *some*—can be either singular or plural, depending on the phrase that follows.

What **are some of the problems** astronauts will face? . . .

Complete each sentence with the correct choice of verb.

1. All of the water (is, are) crucial.
2. None of the other planets (is, are) hospitable to human life.
3. Most of the problems (has, have) been anticipated.
4. Some of the constellations (is, are) difficult to spot.
5. Any of this (is, are) suitable.
6. None of it (is, are) complete.
7. Any of these questions (is, are) worthy of further research.
8. All of my notes (is, are) here.
9. Most of the work (requires, require) special skills.
10. Some of the confusion (is, are) due to the difficult terminology.

See Lesson 16.4, pages 547–548.

Writing About Wishes and Dreams

If I had a photograph of myself ten years from now, this is what I'd see. I am a tall, sleepy-eyed medical student in a white coat. I'm studying to be a heart surgeon. My white coat is rumpled because I slept in it on my break. I'm at a patient's bedside listening to his heart. He had heart surgery yesterday, and I was there in the operating room. During the operation I was

*J*ournal writing is a good way to explore and record your wishes or dreams. Can you see yourself ten years from now? What will you look like? How will you have changed? What will you be doing? Where will you be? Read the journal entry at the left to see what one student wrote.

Look at Yourself

To imagine the future, it could be helpful to look at yourself as you are now. One way to do that is to use a cluster diagram like the one below. In your diagram you can record your interests, successes, failures, feelings, and reactions. You can even indicate how they relate to one another. Making connections may help you uncover interests you can combine as you begin to think about your future.

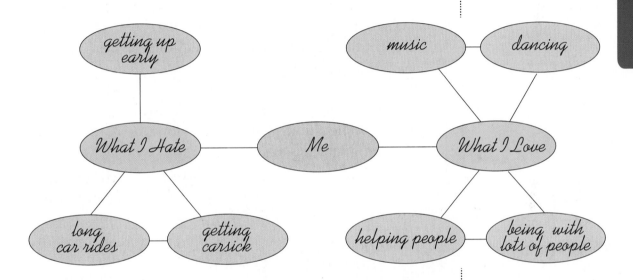

Journal Writing

In your journal make a *me* diagram—a cluster of magazine pictures that illustrates your interests. Below your diagram, write a paragraph entry explaining how the pictures show who you are.

Shape Your Future

You can explore your wishes and dreams in a number of ways. You could write a letter to a friend, relative, or favorite teacher. You could privately explore this topic in your journal. You might draw a picture of yourself as you want to be and include a few sentences describing your picture.

In the diary excerpt below, the poet Sylvia Plath reflects, at seventeen, on the future.

Literature Model

What is the best for me? What do I want? I do not know. I love freedom. I deplore constrictions and limitations. . . . I am not as wise as I have thought. I can see, as from a valley, the roads lying open for me, but I cannot see the end—the consequences. . . .

Oh, I love *now,* with all my fears and forebodings, for now I still am not completely molded. My life is still just beginning. I am strong. I long for a cause to devote my energies to. . . .

Sylvia Plath,
Letters Home

Write a Journal Entry

In your journal describe a childhood dream that has come true.

PURPOSE To describe a childhood dream
AUDIENCE Yourself
LENGTH 2 paragraphs

WRITING RUBRICS To write your journal entry effectively, you should

- give details to make images clear
- tell how you feel now and how you felt before
- explain what the fulfillment of this dream means to you

Cross-Curricular Activity

ART Suppose that someone were to photograph you in the future. Your appearance and an object you are holding will reflect the career dreams you have achieved. Write a paragraph in which you describe the photo and tell how it represents the future you.

Listening and Speaking

Think again about your future photo. Write a dialogue between the you of the photo and the you of today. What would you like to ask the future you? What answers might you get? Present the dialogue to a partner to get feedback on its effectiveness.

Avoid sentence fragments in formal writing.

Sentence fragments are acceptable in your personal journal. When you write for others, however, use complete sentences.

I am a tall sleepy-eyed medical student in a white coat.

Revise each fragment below into a sentence by adding either a subject or a predicate.

1. My career in art.
2. Have enrolled in a pottery class.
3. Jennifer DuBerry, the instructor.
4. The wheel and the kiln.
5. Created an odd-looking vase.

See Lesson 8.2, pages 361–362.

Writing One's Own Story

An autobiography is the story of a person's life written by that person. The passage below is autobiographical. Maya Angelou describes her first meeting with Martin Luther King Jr. Read it and see what her reaction was.

Literature Model

I walked into my office and a man sitting at my desk, with his back turned, spun around, stood up and smiled. Martin King said, "Good afternoon, Miss Angelou. You are right on time."

The surprise was so total that it took me a moment to react to his outstretched hand.

I had worked two months for the SCLC, sent out tens of thousands of letters and invitations signed by Rev. King, made hundreds of statements in his name, but I had never seen him up close. He was shorter than I expected and so young. He had an easy friendliness, which was unsettling. Looking at him in my office, alone, was like seeing a lion sitting down at my dining-room table eating a plate of mustard greens.

Maya Angelou,
The Heart of a Woman

Identify Turning Points

You have had important moments, turning points, in your own life. Some may have even changed the course of your life. The diagram below shows turning-point events in one student's life. Study the diagram and its entries. Make a similar map for yourself. Put the important events in chronological order, the order in which they happened. If you need help recalling either the event or the timing, ask someone in your family. Save your diagram to use as you plan your own autobiographical writing.

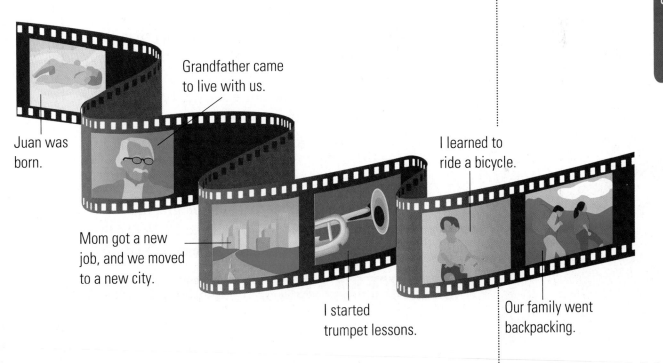

Juan was born.

Grandfather came to live with us.

Mom got a new job, and we moved to a new city.

I started trumpet lessons.

I learned to ride a bicycle.

Our family went backpacking.

Journal Writing

Look at the events in your diagram. Choose the one that is the most meaningful to you. Write about it in your personal journal.

Write About Your Life

Choose a turning point in your life, and think about how you felt before and after that time. Consider which details would bring this event to life for someone else. A student wrote the journal entry below. Read it and notice the details he used to make clear how he felt.

Which details show that Rosenberg's life has changed for the better?

Student Model

During cold, snowy days, I love to cuddle up with Shelly. As she lies against me, I feel as though I had just drunk a cup of hot chocolate. Whenever I walk into the room, her eyes light up brighter than the sun as she recognizes me. Then, she smiles her toothless grin and tries to say, "Barrwie." At those times, I love my little Shellster a lot. Since she was born, nothing has been the same; it's been better.

Barry Rosenberg, Southfield, Michigan
First appeared in *Stone Soup*

The chart below shows the steps in autobiographical writing. It uses a turning point from the map on page 21. Notice the kinds of details the student uses to bring the experience to life.

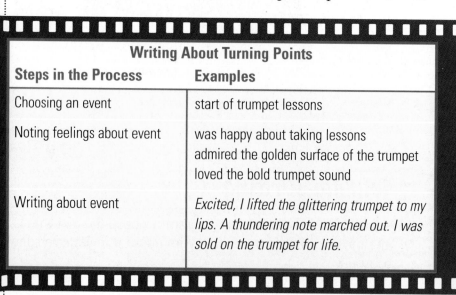

Writing About Turning Points

Steps in the Process	Examples
Choosing an event	start of trumpet lessons
Noting feelings about event	was happy about taking lessons admired the golden surface of the trumpet loved the bold trumpet sound
Writing about event	*Excited, I lifted the glittering trumpet to my lips. A thundering note marched out. I was sold on the trumpet for life.*

Write About an Event

Choose an event from your life, and write an autobiographical composition. To plan and draft your composition, follow the steps outlined on page 22.

PURPOSE To describe a turning point in your life

AUDIENCE Your teacher and classmates

LENGTH 1 page

WRITING RUBRICS To write your autobiographical composition effectively, you should

- tell what happened
- explain how you felt before and after
- use details that make the event come to life for a reader

Viewing and Representing

You have often seen paintings or photographs of people that seemed to capture the subject's personality. What kind of picture would best represent you? Does such a picture exist? Describe a picture of yourself, whether it exists or may someday exist. Write your description. Share it with a partner or small group. If the picture exists, share it also.

Cross-Curricular Activity

HEALTH One way to feel good about yourself is to review events in your life that you feel positive about. In your journal complete the following sentence to help you identify these events: "I felt really proud of myself when. . . ." Write a one-page description of the incident or event.

Grammar Link

Use object pronouns—*me, us, him, her, them*—as the object of a verb or a preposition.

> . . . *I had never seen* **him** *up close.*
> *Looking at* **him** *in my office . . .*
> . . . *at Jane and* **him**.

Write each sentence correctly.

1. The gift from Jem and she is here.
2. Jarmila chose he.
3. The news about Su and I is false.
4. Rodrigo met they at school.
5. The boys were kind to we.
6. Tino walked she to the door.
7. Tara wrote a thank-you letter to he.
8. The storm woke I last night.
9. The test was easy for she.
10. Don't call they too early tomorrow.

See Lesson 11.1, pages 435–436, and Lesson 11.3, pages 439–440.

LESSON 1.5

WRITING ABOUT LITERATURE
Responding in a Journal

Poems are often a form of personal writing, and people's reactions to poetry can be very personal. What is your response to the poem below?

Literature Model

Ray Vinella, *Aspen Grove*, 1960

The Clouds Pass

The clouds pass in a blue sky
Too white to be true
Before winter sets in
The trees are spending all their money

I lie in gold
Above a green valley
Gold falls on my chest
I am a rich man.

Richard Garcia

A journal is a good place for responding to literature. Which images did you see most clearly in the poem? Record these in your journal. Also tell how you liked the poem.

Respond to Literature

The way you react to a poem can take many forms. Your response may be a quiet smile, a hearty laugh, or a flood of memories. Compare the following journal responses to Richard Garcia's poem to your own response.

In the poem "The Clouds Pass," Richard Garcia explains a great gift of nature. In autumn time nature gives the trees' leaves a beautiful golden color. Now these leaves are the money which the trees are dropping—spending.

Sarah Fisher, Solomon Schechter Day School,
Skokie, Illinois

This reader reacts to Garcia's poem with an explanation and with appreciation.

What aspects of the poem does this reader highlight?

An autumn afternoon. The air is crisp and cool, a hint of the frosty weather to come. But the sun is warm on my skin. Like the trees in Garcia's poem, I want to spend my "money" before winter arrives and sends me indoors. The warm, gold days of Indian summer make everyone feel rich. Garcia's poem celebrates Indian summer. It makes me feel lucky to be alive to enjoy this glorious time of year.

This reader responds to Garcia's poem with sensory descriptions.

What feelings does Garcia's poem raise for this reader?

Journal Writing

In your journal jot down the name of a poem that you've enjoyed. Close your eyes, and try to remember what you thought and felt as you read the poem. Record your answers in your journal.

Vary Your Responses

Writing is one way to respond to literature or to explore your reactions to what you've read. You can express your thoughts and feelings in many ways. You could create an illustration, research and write about a topic contained in your reading, or write what one character might say to another. Which way is best for you? Begin by asking questions about the literature and how you felt about it. Look at some of the questions below to help you get started.

Questions to Help You Get Started

1. What did the literature make you think about?

2. How did it make you feel?

3. Which words brought pictures to mind?

4. What would you change about it?

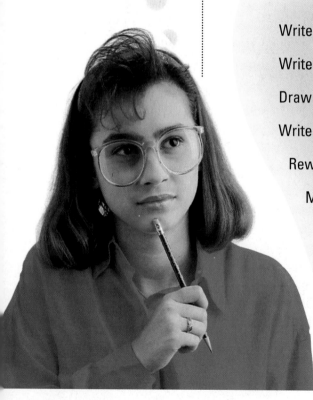

Forms of Response

Write about how the literature makes you feel.

Write a poem expressing your feelings about the work.

Draw a picture of an image from the work.

Write a letter to the author.

Rewrite a passage with your own changes.

Make a cartoon based on the work.

Create a magazine ad for the work.

If the work is a poem, set it to music.

Dramatize a scene from the work.

Write a Response to Literature

Read a poem of your choice, and write an entry about it in your journal.

PURPOSE To respond to a poem
AUDIENCE Yourself
LENGTH 2–3 paragraphs

WRITING RUBRICS To write your response effectively, you should

- explain what you like best about the poem in general: its subject, its sound, its setting, the pictures it created in your mind
- think about whether the poem tells you anything new or says something you haven't heard before

Using Computers

On the computer, write a poem of your own that responds to the one you chose or that is similar to it in form or subject. If you correspond with someone on e-mail, send that person your poem and ask for a response.

Listening and Speaking

Think about the difference between silent and oral reading of poems. With a partner, take turns selecting a poem and reading it aloud. Discuss the meaning of each poem. Then write your own journal response to both poems and to the experience of reading aloud and hearing a poem read aloud.

Grammar Link

Use vivid adjectives in your writing.

Vivid adjectives help crystallize images in your reader's mind and make your meaning very precise.

*The air is **crisp** and **cool**, a hint of the **frosty** weather to come.*

Revise the sentences below, replacing the underlined adjectives with stronger, more vivid ones.

"The Clouds Pass" praises the <u>yellow</u> leaves of fall. The color of the leaves makes the speaker feel <u>rich</u> and <u>happy</u>.

When I read the poem, I shared the speaker's <u>happy</u> emotions. At the same time, the falling leaves make me <u>sad</u>. The poem is a <u>good</u> one.

See Lesson 3.3, pages 122–125.

Personal Writing

Writing Process in Action

Personal Writing

In preceding lessons you've learned how to gather and organize your ideas to describe the events in an important personal experience. You've learned how to describe the feelings you had because of that experience. You've also had the chance to write journal entries about your personal experiences. Now, in this lesson you will write about an experience you shared with someone else.

Assignment

Context	You have decided to contribute to *America, America,* a publication of personal reflections and images from across the United States. Write about an experience you have shared with someone else.
Purpose	To share, in writing, a personal experience
Audience	A general audience of all ages
Length	2 paragraphs

The following pages can help you plan and write your personal experience composition. Read through them, and then refer to them as you need to. But don't be tied down by them. You're in charge of your own writing process.

Prewriting

To come up with possible topics for this assignment, try to recall shared experiences that taught you something about life, another person, or yourself. This may help you focus on the people who are close to you and whom you see every day.

The options graphic below offers ways to tap into memories for ideas. The notebook gives an example of listing to generate ideas.

Drafting

Exploring your ideas thoroughly during prewriting helps drafting go smoothly. As you review your notes, consider details that will help the reader understand what happened. Write down your ideas just as they come to you. You can polish the good ones later.

Your writing may be clearest if you time-order events. Notice how Gary Soto uses time transitions:

Option A
Review journal entries.

Option B
Brainstorm with a friend.

Option C
Freewrite for ideas.

Helped Mrs. Magnino paint lawn furniture; then she painted her kitchen— nothing could stop her. Both of us almost overcome by paint fumes. Opened the window and a bird flew in.

Literature Model

The next day I woke tired and started picking tired. The grapes rained into the pan, slowly filling like a belly, until I had my first tray and started my second. So it went all day, and the next, and all through the following week, so that by the end of the thirteen days the foreman counted out, in tens mostly, my pay of fifty-three dollars.

Gary Soto, *Living up the Street*

Drafting Tip

For more information about putting events in order, see Lesson 1.4, pages 20–23.

Remember to focus on the shared experience and your own feelings. Review your prewriting notes, your journal, some old photos, anything that works. At this stage, don't edit—just write. You may find it helpful to review pages 4–8 and 16–19.

Revising

To begin revising, read over your draft to make sure that what you've written fits your purpose and audience. Then have a **writing conference.** Read your draft to a partner or small group. Use your audience's reactions to help you evaluate your work.

Question A

Have I put events in time order?

Question B

Have I included interesting details?

Question C

Have I shared my feelings about the experience?

Mrs. Magnino lived down the street from us for as many years as I could remember.

Her husband died several years ago. I hardly
~~her husband passed away.~~
~~remember him.~~ She's been alone ever since, and
Now she s
~~has~~ depended on neighbors for favors and help
One day she asked Mom if I
whenever possible. ~~My parents thought it would~~
could help with a few odd jobs around the yard.
~~be a good idea if I offered to help her around~~
Mom thought it was a good idea.
~~the house.~~

We started by painting her lawn furniture.

It hadn't been painted in years, but it was still

in decent shape.

Editing/Proofreading

You must complete one more step before you share your writing with others. In the editing stage carefully look over every sentence and word. Don't make your readers struggle through incorrect grammar or misspellings. **Proofread** for these errors, and use the standard proof-reading symbols.

Use the editing checklist on the right to help you edit your writing. If certain grammar or punctuation rules give you problems, add them to the checklist. Then read through your work several times, looking for only one or two kinds of errors each time.

> *Editing Checklist*
> 1. *Have I corrected any sentence fragments?*
> 2. *Do my verbs agree with their subjects?*
> 3. *Are all personal pronouns in the correct form?*
> 4. *Have I used standard spelling, capitalization, and punctuation?*

Publishing/Presenting

Before you turn in your assignment, think of some suggestions you could give to the editors of *America, America* for the published version of your article. For example, you might suggest some footnotes to help readers with unfamiliar words or names. Maybe you have ideas for illustrations or photographs that could accompany your story. Turn your suggestions in with your writing.

Proofreading

For proofreading symbols, see page 79.

Journal Writing

Reflect on your writing process experience. Answer these questions in your journal: What do you like best about your personal experience writing? What was the hardest part of writing it? What did you learn in your writing conference? What new things have you learned as a writer?

Literature Model

Living up the Street

by Gary Soto

In Living up the Street, *Gary Soto writes about his growing-up years in Fresno, California. In the excerpt below, Soto describes the experience and feelings he had on his first job, picking grapes alongside his mother. As you read, pay special attention to the details Soto uses to make his experiences and feelings clear. Then try the Linking Writing and Literature activities on page 38.*

cut another bunch, then another, fighting the snap and whip of vines. After ten minutes of groping for grapes, my first pan brimmed with bunches. I poured them on the paper tray, which was bordered by a wooden frame that kept the grapes from rolling off, and they spilled like jewels from a pirate's chest. The tray was only half filled, so I hurried to jump under the vines and begin groping, cutting, and tugging at the

Susan Moore, *With No Visible Sign,* 1988

grapes again. I emptied the pan, raked the grapes with my hands to make them look like they filled the tray, and jumped back under the vine on my knees. I tried to cut faster because Mother, in the next row, was slowly moving ahead. I peeked into her row and saw five trays gleaming in the early morning. I cut, pulled hard, and stopped to gather the grapes that missed the pan; already bored, I spat on a few to wash them before tossing them like popcorn into my mouth.

I had to daydream and keep my mind busy because boredom was a terror almost as awful as the work itself.

So it went. Two pans equaled one tray—or six cents. By lunchtime I had a trail of thirty-seven trays behind me while Mother had sixty or more. We met about halfway from our last trays, and I sat down with a grunt, knees wet from kneeling on dropped grapes. I washed my hands with the water from the jug, drying them on the inside of my shirt sleeve before I opened the paper bag for the first sandwich, which I gave to Mother. I dipped my hand in again to unwrap a sandwich without looking at it. I took a first bite and chewed it slowly for the tang of mustard. Eating in silence I looked straight ahead at the vines, and only when we were finished with cookies did we talk.

"Are you tired?" she asked.

"No, but I got a sliver from the frame," I told her. I showed her the web of skin between my thumb and index finger. She wrinkled her forehead but said it was nothing.

"How many trays did you do?"

I looked straight ahead, not answering at first. I recounted in my mind the whole morning of bend, cut, pour again and again, before answering a feeble "thirty-seven." No elaboration,[1] no detail. Without looking at me she told me how she had done field work in Texas and Michigan as a child. But I had a difficult time listening to her stories. I played with my grape knife, stabbing it into the ground, but stopped when Mother reminded me that I had better not lose it. I left the knife sticking up like a small, leafless plant. She then talked about school, the junior high I would be going to that fall, and then about Rick and Debra, how sorry they would be that they hadn't come out to pick grapes because they'd have no new clothes for the school year. She stopped talking when she peeked at her watch, a bandless one she kept in her pocket. She got up with an *"Ay, Dios,"* and told me that we'd work until three,

---

1 **elaboration** (i lab′ ə rā′ sh ə n) giving more details

Anthony Ortega, *Farmworkers de Califas,* 1990

leaving me cutting figures in the sand with my knife and dreading the return to work.

Finally I rose and walked slowly back to where I had left off, again kneeling under the vine and fixing the pan under bunches of grapes. By that time, 11:30, the sun was over my shoulder and made me squint and think of the pool at the Y.M.C.A. where I was a summer member. I saw myself diving face first into the water and loving it. I saw myself gleaming like something new, at the edge of the pool. I had to daydream and keep my mind busy because boredom was a terror almost as awful as the work itself. My mind went dumb with stupid things, and I had to keep it moving with dreams of baseball and would-be girlfriends. I even sang, however softly, to keep my mind moving, my hands moving.

I worked less hurriedly and with less vision. I no longer saw that copper pot sitting squat[2] on our stove or Mother waiting for it to whistle. The wardrobe that I imagined, crisp and bright in the closet, numbered only one pair of jeans and two shirts because, in half a day, six cents times thirty-seven trays was two dollars and twenty-two cents. It became clear to me. If I worked eight hours, I might make four dollars. I'd take this, even gladly, and walk downtown to look into store windows on the mall and long for bright madras[3] shirts from Walter Smith or Coffee's, but settling for two imitation ones from Penney's.

> *If I worked eight hours,*
> *I might make four dollars.*

That first day I laid down seventy-three trays while Mother had a hundred and twenty behind her. On the back of an old envelope, she wrote out our numbers and hours. We washed at the pump behind the farm house and walked slowly back to our car for the drive back to town in the afternoon heat. That evening after dinner I sat in a lawn chair listening to music from a transistor radio while Rick and David King played catch. I joined them in a game of pickle, but there was little joy in trying to avoid their tags because I couldn't get the fields out of my mind: I saw myself dropping on my knees under a vine to tug at a branch that wouldn't come off. In bed, when I closed my eyes, I saw the fields, yellow with kicked up dust, and a crooked trail of trays rotting behind me.

The next day I woke tired and started picking tired. The grapes rained into the pan, slowly filling like a belly, until I had my first tray and started my second. So it went all day, and the next, and all through the following week, so that by the end of thirteen days the foreman counted out, in tens mostly, my pay of fifty-three dollars. Mother earned one hundred and forty-eight dollars. She wrote this on her envelope, with a message I didn't bother to ask her about.

The next day I walked with my friend Scott to the downtown mall where we drooled over the clothes behind fancy windows, bought popcorn, and sat at a tier of outside fountains to talk about

---

2 **squat** (skwot) short and thick; low and broad
3 **madras** (mad′rəs) a fine, striped or plaid cotton cloth

girls. Finally we went into Penney's for more popcorn, which we ate walking around, before we returned home without buying anything. It wasn't until a few days before school that I let my fifty-three dollars slip quietly from my hands, buying a pair of pants, two shirts, and a maroon T-shirt, the kind that was in style. At home I tried them on while Rick looked on enviously; later, the day before school started, I tried them on again wondering not so much if they were worth it as who would see me first in those clothes.

Linking Writing and Literature

Readers Respond to the Model

How do Gary Soto's descriptions give a vivid picture of his experience and his feelings?

Explore Gary Soto's personal writing by answering the following questions. Then read how other students responded to his work.

1. Based on Soto's writing, how would you describe his job of picking grapes?
2. What feelings, interests, habits, and dreams does Soto have that are similar to those of many teenagers?
3. How is Soto's life different, or more difficult, than that of many teenagers?
4. Based on Soto's writing, what adjectives would you use to describe the setting of the grape fields?
5. While picking grapes, what does Soto look forward to buying with the money he will earn? What does he do once he has the money? In your opinion, why?

What Students Say

"Since I am Hispanic (Puerto Rican), I put myself in the boy's place. I even enjoy some of the same things that he does. For example, I really like swimming, and I go to the YMCA pool, too.

I remembered well a number of the scenes from the selection. For example, I can still picture the boy's lunch with his mother and the grape picking. I think that, because the author kept my attention by describing these scenes in detail they stayed in my mind.

I would recommend this literature selection to a friend. I think it helps the reader see how some people have to struggle to make a little money."

Paul Roustan

"I clearly remember the scene in which the boy gives up his dreams. He forgets about what he was going to buy, such as a copper teapot for his mother and stylish clothes for himself. He was hit with the reality of hard work. I liked the details about how tired he felt from working."

Joshua Zapata

Reflecting on the Unit

Summarize what you have learned.

1 What is personal writing?

2 Why is a journal a good place for personal writing?

3 What is a learning log?

4 How can you explore the future through personal writing?

5 What kinds of events might you describe or explore in an autobiography?

6 In what ways can you respond to a piece of literature?

 ## Adding to Your Portfolio

CHOOSE A SELECTION FOR YOUR PORTFOLIO Look over the writing you did for this unit. Select a piece of writing for your portfolio. The writing you choose should show one or more of the following:

- your personal experiences: ideas, thoughts, feelings, activities, and memories

- discoveries you have made about yourself and the world in which you live

- your wishes or dreams for the future

- important events or turning points that have changed the direction of your life

- a personal response to a poem or other piece of literature

REFLECT ON YOUR CHOICE Attach a note to the piece you chose, explaining why you chose it and what you learned from writing it.

SET GOALS How can you improve your writing? What skill will you focus on the next time you write?

Writing Across the Curriculum

MAKE A SCIENCE CONNECTION Select a personal experience that happened in the natural world. To think of ideas, list places where you have contact with nature. Then write a journal entry describing an experience. Use sensory details to create a picture of the setting.

"The night had warmed and the rain had stopped, leaving puddles at the curbs."

—Walter Dean Myers

The Treasure of Lemon Brown

UNIT 2

The Writing Process

Writing in the Real World

MEDIA
TV Script
Connection

The process of producing a documentary involves steps similar to those used in the process of writing: research, drafting a script, and editing the film. The following is a script written for a TV documentary. Bill Kurtis, award-winning journalist, produced the show.

from "Rock 'n' Roll Physics"
produced by Bill Kurtis

VISUALS	SOUND
Fade up on professor and bored kids in classroom	(Bring up Dave's music, then sound of "professor" droning on) (Prof.: Now let's continue with our review of Isaac Newton's theories concerning universal gravitation and we'll begin on the second paragraph of page 252. What property of the earth determines how large 4 or pie square in case sub b of the sun. Now Newton certainly suspected that the inverse square log attraction to light an object, not only to the earth and moon but also to the planets moon. Alright, class, now we're getting to the most important part of our lesson on universal gravitation. What property of a body determines it's gravitational . . .)
Bill on camera in classroom.	(BILL OC[2]: This is no way to teach physics!)
Diz[1] to Bill on camera in roller coaster.	(BILL OC: *This* is the way to teach physics!) Bring up nat sound of rollercoaster, riders, then bring up Davemusic BILL VO[3]: **Two men on an impossible mission: teaching physics you can actually understand.**

```
. . .                    BILL VO: Their names are Chris Cheviarina
                         and Jim Hicks, but to their high school
         . . .           physics classes, they are Mr. C and Uncle
                         Jim and they are leading a teaching revolu-
                         tion.
Underwriter
credits                  (JIM: "You see how the wave kind of gets
                         very narrow?")

                         (CHRIS: "Hang on, Stacey! Here we go!")

Montage Jim &            (JIM: "Now if you were into reading flames,
Chris teaching           you could tell what frequency they
                         were. . .")
```

```
                         (CHRIS: "Keep pushing at 50! Good, good.")


                                        ¹ Diz: dissolve
                                        ² OC: on camera
                                        ³ VO: voice-over
```

A Writer's Process

Bill Kurtis often travels when filming *The New Explorers*. His filming location might be the Amazon or an amusement park.

Prewriting
Gathering Information

One night back in 1987, TV journalist Bill Kurtis was filming a zoologist who was searching for a new species of bird in Peru. Kurtis said that suddenly "a light went on. In a flash I saw a series of stories following scientists into the field."

His idea developed into a television series called *The New Explorers* produced by Kurtis himself. Each program in the series profiles a scientist—a hero to Kurtis. One episode featured Chris Cheviarina and Jim Hicks—Mr. C and Uncle Jim. They're high school science teachers "on a mission to teach physics you can actually understand."

To tell their story, Kurtis wanted to combine graphics, action, and kids. So Kurtis's staff went after

more information. "We may go to the library," Kurtis explained. "We may do interviews. Ultimately, we have to go out and shoot film or video."

In this case, shooting takes place before the script for the show is written. The film visuals guide the writing of the scenes.

The first step in shooting "Rock 'n' Roll Physics" was to catch the teachers in action. Kurtis sent a camera crew to Barrington High School outside Chicago. "I said, just follow the teachers and shoot everything they do," Kurtis explained.

Drafting/Revising
Creating a Rough Cut

Kurtis wanted to show the teachers bringing physics to life. So the producer pulled the best moments from the interviews. Based on these moments, a script was drafted with a clear opener, a beginning, a middle, and an end.

Next the script called for Kurtis to explain the show's subject and to introduce the heroes—the new explorers. "This is my getting-to-know-you section," Kurtis said. "I want viewers to get to know the heroes and their work." High-energy scenes would then take viewers from class to pool to parking lot to roller coaster. "I like to change the pace often to keep the viewer's attention," Kurtis emphasized.

The ending would showcase students discussing the class and their teachers. Who could explain better why Uncle Jim and Mr. C's unusual teaching style works?

Revising/Editing
Fine-Tuning the Show

The draft of the script was revised. The film editor cut fifty hours of video down to four using only the images that best fit the script.

The editor then created a rough cut of the show. A "rough cut" is the first rough cutting together of film or video images. Little details—such as background music or exactly how long a shot lasts—will be decided later, in the final version, or fine cut.

Now it was time for Kurtis and his team to revise. "I'll tell you," he said, "on 'Rock 'n' Roll Physics' we looked at the rough cut and said 'We need to do some work here.' Frankly, I wasn't understanding the science." The team re-edited the video. After nearly eight weeks of work, "Rock 'n' Roll Physics" was ready to go.

Presenting
Broadcasting the Show

Unlike most other kinds of writing, TV writing doesn't end in a written script. Kurtis's final presentation was the documentary itself, which was broadcast on television.

Examining Writing in the Real World

Analyzing the Media Connection

Discuss these questions about the script on pages 42–43.

1. What two things does Kurtis compare and contrast in the script? Why do you think he opens this way?

2. Why do you think Kurtis chose to dissolve from the image of bored kids to a roller coaster? Describe the impact the roller coaster images might have on a viewer.

3. How does Kurtis describe what Mr. C and Uncle Jim are doing? Why did he choose the phrase *impossible mission?*

4. Kurtis presents a strong point of view about his subject. How would the script be more or less effective if Kurtis had used an impartial point of view?

5. Kurtis's purpose is to get viewers excited about a new way of teaching physics. How well does this excerpt fulfill his purpose? Explain.

Analyzing a Writer's Process

Discuss these questions about Bill Kurtis's writing process.

1. What are the steps that Kurtis follows to put a program on the air? Compare and contrast these steps with the ones you use in your writing process.

2. Where did Kurtis get the idea for the series? Do you think it's a good idea? Why or why not?

3. Why do you think Kurtis begins by shooting film rather than by creating script? What problems might arise if the script came first and the shooting second?

4. What is the difference between a rough cut and a fine cut? Why are both stages necessary?

Bill Kurtis uses specific verbs.

*The train **zoomed** along.*

Revise each sentence below by replacing the italicized verb with a more specific verb.

1. The class *looked* at the roller coaster demonstration.
2. Mr. C *said,* "Watch out!"
3. I really *like* this class.
4. Bored kids *sat* at their desks.
5. I *walked* out of the room, ready to make my own video.

See Lesson 3.3, pages 122–125.

Working with the Writing Process

*W*hen the Camera Club members decided to build a
darkroom in the basement of their school, they made
a plan. First they scouted for a location; then they made a
few sketches and lists.

Go Through a Process

Just as building doesn't begin with a hammer, writing doesn't
begin with a pen. Both activities involve several stages—from
the first idea to a finished product.

PREWRITING   The prewriting stage begins with selecting and
exploring a topic. One useful technique is to search your memory for experiences you'd like to share. Begin by looking at old
photos of yourself and your friends, jotting down
ideas as you go. Think about which ideas you'd
enjoy writing about and which might interest others. Decide how to organize these ideas.

DRAFTING   When you draft, you turn your
prewriting notes into sentences and paragraphs.

This writer
made several
prewriting notes
before finding an
idea she wanted
to explore.

Making the soccer team

Working on the science
project

Trying out for the play

Tutoring the third graders

Starting the newcomers
club

Being a new student

I felt nervous
Strangers, but friendly
Ms. Osaka broke the ice

You arrange your ideas in the order you chose in prewriting. New ideas will continue to come. Write them all down. Some will work, and some won't. Your draft may look messy, but don't worry. You can fix it later.

REVISING Step back and look over what you've written. Read it aloud to peer reviewers, and answer questions like the following: Are your ideas clear? Do they fit together? What other details might help your readers understand and enjoy what you've written?

EDITING/PROOFREADING In the editing/proofreading stage, you examine each word, phrase, and sentence in your writing. This is the time to find and correct any errors in grammar, spelling, and punctuation. Your goal is to make a neat, error-free copy for others to read and enjoy.

PUBLISHING/PRESENTING In the publishing/presenting stage, you share your writing. You can read a report aloud in class. You can work with others to publish a class poetry book. You can write a letter to the editor of the school newspaper. What other ways can you think of to share your work?

Drafting

I felt nervous walking in that first morning. The halls were crowded. People seemed happy to ___ new year. They

Revising

to Carver Junior High School
I felt nervous walking in that

first morning. The halls were
Friends greeted each other,
crowded. People seemed happy to
together
be starting a new year. They

didn't seem to need to know a new
especially
person, and one from another
faraway Japan.
country at that.

Journal Writing

Create your own chart to summarize the writing process and to help you remember it. Refer to it as you complete your writing assignments.

Be Flexible

Writing is a messy process. Ideas rarely flow in an orderly way. Novelist James A. Michener once said, "I have never thought of myself as a good writer. Anyone who wants reassurance of that should read one of my first drafts. But I'm one of the world's great rewriters."

At any stage in the writing process, a writer can think of new ideas to include and better ways to say something. Feel free to move backward and forward in the writing process. For example, if you get stuck while writing your draft, go back to prewriting and add to your notes. In editing, if a sentence doesn't say what you mean, return to drafting. If you have a new idea, insert it. One of this writer's best ideas about a small world came during a revision.

Revising

How wrong I was! The first surprise came when I met
icebreaker
Ms. Osaka. ∧the school librarian I couldn't believe that she'd moved here just a year ago from Kushiro, my native city in Japan. Immediately, I understood the meaning of the term "small world."

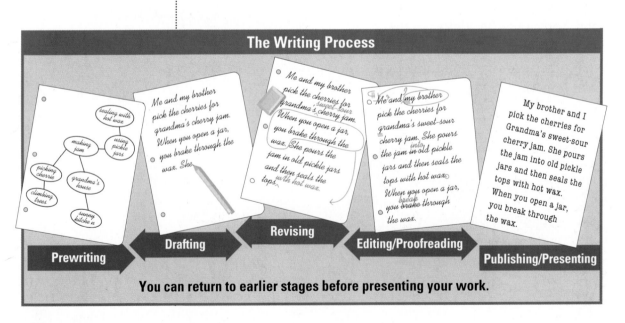

The Writing Process

Prewriting → **Drafting** → **Revising** → **Editing/Proofreading** → **Publishing/Presenting**

My brother and I pick the cherries for Grandma's sweet-sour cherry jam. She pours the jam into old pickle jars and then seals the tops with hot wax. When you open a jar, you break through the wax.

You can return to earlier stages before presenting your work.

Write a Paragraph

Are the stages of creating a sculpture like the stages of creating a piece of writing? Make some notes to yourself about the process Oldenburg may have used to create his toothbrush sculpture. How is it like the writing process? Write a paragraph comparing the two processes.

PURPOSE To compare two creative processes
AUDIENCE Your classmates
LENGTH 1 paragraph

WRITING RUBRICS To write a compare-and-contrast paragraph, you should

- think about each process you are comparing
- list ways they are alike; then list ways they are different
- use your lists to write your comparison

Claes Oldenburg, *Notebook Page: Cross-section of Toothbrush in Glass, 'sun dial,'* 1980

Claes Oldenburg, *Cross-section of a Toothbrush with Paste, in a Cup, on a Sink: Portrait of Coosje's Thinking,* 1983

Viewing and Representing

Imagine you are planning a video presentation. You will show Oldenburg's sculpture to a television audience. What camera angles will you use? Create a storyboard for each view of the sculpture you will show. Write a caption for each storyboard.

Cross-Curricular Activity

MATH The sketches in Oldenburg's notebook lead one to ask whether the toothbrush sculpture might have been planned as a sundial. Could the sculpture have been a sundial? Research to find out how sundials work. Then write a paragraph for or against using the sculpture in a sundial, giving reasons for your views.

Grammar Link

Use subject pronouns—*I, we, she, he, they*—in the subject of a sentence.

*My brother and **I** pick cherries.*

Write each sentence, correcting errors in the use of pronouns.

[1] Me and her take piano lessons. [2] Us often play duets. [3] Me and you can sing this song. [4-5] In fact, me and Maria can play while you and him sing.

See Lesson 11.1, page 435, and Lesson 11.3, page 439.

Prewriting: Determining Audience and Purpose

The tools of a writer are words. The words must be chosen to suit the writer's purpose and audience.

The eighth-graders at Carver Junior High School did many different kinds of writing. For example, they wrote an article about the Foods-of-the-World Festival. They wrote postcards during their class trip to Washington, D.C. They wrote a program for the talent show. They created posters advertising the craft fair. Finally, they made a memory book—a kind of yearbook—about their eighth-grade activities. Jot down one or two possible audiences for each of these pieces of writing.

Write for Your Readers

When writers know who their readers are, they can tailor their writing to their readers. How does the writer of the first article below signal that the audience is young readers?

Literature Model

Hollis Conway has always had long, skinny legs. When he was growing up in Shreveport, Louisiana, his minister called him Linky Legs.

Little did anyone know that those slender legs would one day launch Hollis over a high-jump bar set nearly eight feet off the ground! Hollis, now 24, is one of the best high jumpers in history.

Sports Illustrated for Kids

> What words and ideas make this opening right for young readers?

Literature Model

Low, smoky clouds rolled in off the Wasatch Mountains above Provo, Utah, last Saturday night as high jumper Hollis Conway prepared for his second attempt at an American record $7'\ 9\frac{3}{4}''$.

Merrell Noden, *Sports Illustrated*

> What audience do you think this writer had in mind?

Journal Writing

Find two magazines with similar content, one for children and one for adults. Examine some articles in each. Write notes in your journal about how the words and ideas in each magazine reflect its audience.

Know Your Purpose

The purpose of both passages about high jumping was to inform. The selection below has a different purpose—to narrate, or tell a story. Read this narrative about an exciting event in the writer's life. To consider two more purposes for writing, consult the chart below.

Student Model

Finally, it was my turn. . . . I ran as fast as I could, and approaching the first hurdle, I made it over but bumped my toe slightly. I was embarrassed. I ran on, afraid that I would repeat my error on the next hurdle. Perspiration rolled down my face.

I leaped over the second hurdle with the grace of an antelope; I felt as if my feet had wings. My classmates cheered. I heard comments like "Boy, that kid's good!" and "Wow, look at him go!"

I then flew over the third hurdle like an eagle and raced to the finish line. The gym teacher looked at his stopwatch in disbelief. "You got the highest score in the class, Ken!" he said. I felt good that I had done something better than everybody else.

Ken Priebe, Grosse Pointe Woods, Michigan
First appeared in *Cricket*

What purpose and audience do you think Ken had in mind? How does his writing reflect both?

Purposes for Writing

To describe	Although short and thin, Ken was a fast runner.
To narrate	Finally, Ken leaped over the last hurdle.
To inform	Ken finished in first place because of his great efforts.
To persuade	Your contribution will help support the track team.

Collect Topic Ideas

Choose a topic for the piece you will develop through the stages of the writing process.

PURPOSE To list topic ideas, to identify purpose and audience

AUDIENCE Yourself

LENGTH 1 page

WRITING RUBRICS To plan your writing, you should

- decide on your purpose. Do you want to give information? Tell a story? Describe? Persuade?
- brainstorm for topic ideas
- identify the audience for each of your topic ideas

Listening and Speaking

Brainstorm in a small group for writing ideas. Spin off ideas from the painting on this page. List two ideas for each purpose listed in the chart on page 52. Here are some ideas to get started.

- a story set in the past (narrate)
- what people should eat (persuade)

Viewing and Representing

ANALYZING COLOR What is happening in the scene in *Humble Ménage*? Does the scene show a happy or a serious moment? How can you tell? How do the colors help you understand the painting's meaning? Share your ideas with a partner.

Avoid run-on sentences.

One way to correct a run-on sentence is to use a semicolon between the two main clauses.

I leaped over the second hurdle with the grace of an antelope; I felt as if my feet had wings.

Write five compound sentences that are punctuated with a semicolon.

See Lesson 14.1, page 505.

Elizabeth Nourse, *Humble Ménage*, 1897

LESSON 2.3

Prewriting: Investigating a Topic

Once you have chosen your topic and decided on your purpose and your audience, you need to explore ideas about your topic. What will you include? What will you leave out?

The eighth-graders had decided to make a memory book about their last year at Carver Junior High. Which activities should they include? Miguel said, "Let's brainstorm." In brainstorming, one idea sparked others, so the class listed all of them. Later they decided which ideas to include in their memory book.

Opening football game
Skit for after-school program
Art museum trip

Explore Your Topic

Once you have chosen a topic, you can explore it by brainstorming, freewriting, clustering, or listing. To freewrite, set a time limit—say, ten minutes—and write everything that comes to mind about the topic.

Don't let the pen stop moving. If you can't think of anything, keep writing the same word again and again. Often your best ideas—or at least the seed of them—will pop out.

Clustering and listing are also helpful techniques. Some students used clustering to explore ideas for the memory book. Kelly listed details for the class mural project. No matter which method you use, keep every idea for now.

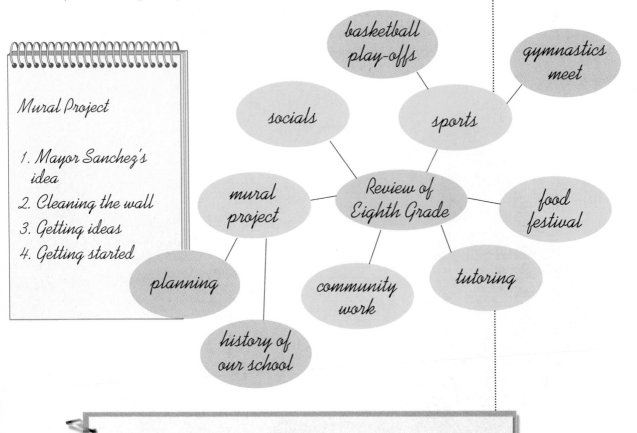

Mural Project

1. Mayor Sanchez's idea
2. Cleaning the wall
3. Getting ideas
4. Getting started

basketball play-offs

gymnastics meet

socials

sports

mural project

Review of Eighth Grade

food festival

planning

community work

tutoring

history of our school

Journal Writing

What stands out as the most important event of the past school year? Set a timer for ten minutes. In your journal freewrite about why the event was important.

Gather Facts and Details

Writers start with what they know, but they often need more information to help them shape their ideas. To find it, they tap a wide range of sources, such as books, magazines, and newspapers. Sometimes the best sources are people with special knowledge of the topic. For example, Ayako wondered, "Why was our class chosen to work on the mural? What do people think of it?" To find out, she interviewed the mayor.

To conduct a successful interview, come prepared with good open-ended questions, such as the ones Ayako listed. Listen well, and take notes carefully. With the interviewee's permission, you can use a tape recorder as well. Don't interrupt or rush ahead to the next question. Allow the person time to answer. Ask follow-up questions: "That's interesting. Can you say more about it?" After the interview reread your notes, and jot down what you learned.

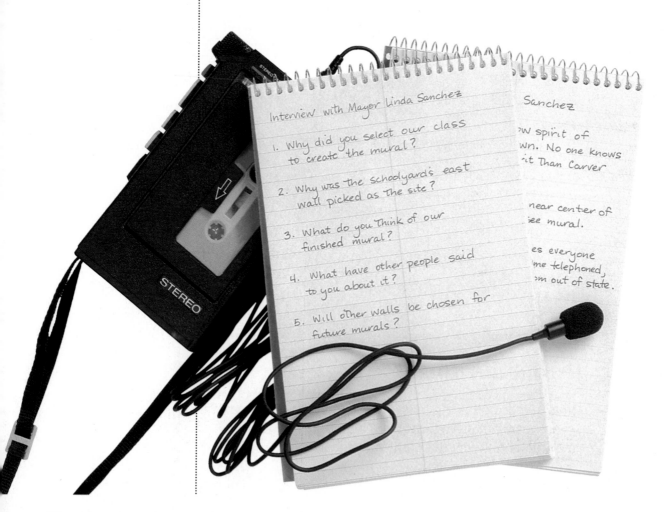

Interview with Mayor Linda Sanchez

1. Why did you select our class to create the mural?

2. Why was the schoolyard's east wall picked as the site?

3. What do you think of our finished mural?

4. What have other people said to you about it?

5. Will other walls be chosen for future murals?

Sanchez

...w spirit of ...wn. No one knows ...it than Carver

...near center of ...ee mural.

...es everyone ...me telephoned, ...m out of state.

2.3 | Writing Activities

Investigate Your Topic

Choose two of your best topic ideas to explore and investigate. For each topic idea, do one of the activities listed under the Writing Rubrics heading.

PURPOSE To create a set of prewriting notes about your topic

AUDIENCE Yourself

LENGTH 1–2 pages

WRITING RUBRICS To explore your topic ideas, you can

- brainstorm for ideas about the topic
- freewrite about the topic
- list ideas about the topic
- cluster to explore the topic
- interview someone about your topic

Using Computers

A computer allows you to do "invisible writing," which is an excellent freewriting technique. Choose a topic and set a timer for ten minutes. Dim the screen and begin to freewrite about your topic. Since you cannot see what you are writing, you will be able to let your ideas flow without interrupting your thoughts to make corrections.

Grammar Link

Use correct verb forms.

Write each sentence, using the past tense or past participle of the verb in parentheses.

1. Dylan had (rise) to his feet.
2. He (take) notes on our ideas.
3. All of us have (draw) on many sources.
4. We (seek) out new sources too.
5. We had (speak) to many people.
6. Books and articles (give) us additional facts.
7. Then we (make) use of all that information.
8. We have (begin) to discover a unifying thread.

See Lesson 10.11, page 421, and Lesson 10.12, page 423.

Viewing and Representing

COOPERATIVE LEARNING In a small group, view a videotape of a TV interview with a famous or newsworthy person. Then read an interview of a similar figure in the newspaper. Do you learn more from watching or from reading an interview? Why? Take notes as you discuss your ideas. Then share ideas with another group.

The Writing Process

Prewriting: Organizing Ideas

*O*rganizing ideas involves several steps—weeding out what doesn't belong, organizing the remaining ideas in a sensible way, and filling in missing details.

Rafael prepared to organize his ideas for the introduction to the class memory book. He gathered his notes and found resources, such as back issues of the school newspaper, to help him fill in missing details.

Weed Out What Doesn't Belong

Not all the ideas you gather on a topic belong in your writing. You have to decide what to keep and what to take out. First, think about what you want to say about your topic, and express that idea in one sentence. Then list the details, and cross out any that don't belong. Rafael asked himself which activities really helped to support his idea about "the activities our class did together." Notice how he weeded out some ideas.

Listing ideas

Topic

The activities our class did together made eighth grade a year to remember.

talent show — April

mural project — October

tutoring ~~~~ not a group activity

craft fair — May

Olympic Day — June

~~parents' night~~ more for the parents

Foods-of-the-World Festival — December

class trip — March

~~visiting author~~ she talked, we listened

Journal Writing

Write a sentence expressing your opinion about a school activity. List details about the activity. Then ask yourself: Which details support my opinion, or main idea? Which do not? Cross out the "weeds."

Organize Your Ideas

Now you need to organize your ideas in a way that makes sense. How you do that depends on your purpose: are you going to describe, narrate, inform, or persuade?

To describe something, you sometimes arrange the details in order of location, or **spatial order.** You might begin with what you see first; then move from left to right or from near to far. To narrate a story, you'd usually arrange the events in the order in which they happened, or **chronological order.** To explain, you could **compare and contrast ideas** or use chronological order to tell when events happened. If you plan to persuade, you might give reasons for an opinion **in order of importance.** You'd begin with your most important reason and then work toward your least important, or you could begin with your least important reason and build up to your most important reason. Which order did Rafael choose?

> Could Rafael have chosen another order for these events? Explain your answer.

Organizing ideas

The activities our class did together made eighth grade a year to remember.

④ talent show—April

① mural project—October

~~tutoring~~

⑤ craft fair—May

⑥ Olympic Day—June

~~parents' night~~

② Foods-of-the-World Festival—December

③ class trip—March

~~visiting author~~

Organize Your Ideas

Look back at your prewriting notes. Now choose the topic you want to write about—you can always change your mind later.

PURPOSE To organize your ideas
AUDIENCE Yourself
LENGTH 1–2 pages

WRITING RUBRICS To organize your ideas, you should

- state your main idea in a topic sentence
- circle supporting ideas in your pre-writing notes
- add any new ideas you have
- plan how you will organize your writing

Listening and Speaking

COOPERATIVE LEARNING In a small group, brainstorm to create a list of jobs you might like to have someday. Each group member should copy the completed list. Individually each member should cross out the jobs that seem less attractive and number the remaining jobs in order of importance, with number one as the favorite. Discuss reasons for your choices.

Grammar Link

Capitalize the names of people, places, institutions, events, months, and days.

Carver Junior High School
Olympic Day

Write the paragraph below, using capital letters correctly.

¹One of my favorite relatives is uncle joe. ²A veteran of the vietnam war, he is now principal of kennedy high school in hawaii. ³I visited him last july. ⁴One saturday and sunday we spent in oahu. ⁵The pacific regatta was being held there. ⁶The crew from the university of hawaii came in first.

See Lesson 19.2, page 585; Lesson 19.3, page 587; and Lesson 19.4, page 589.

Using Computers

Use a word processing program to list all your prewriting notes. Highlight the notes you think you'll use for this writing project, using boldface type. Move any prewriting notes that aren't needed into a new file; you may want to refer to them for another writing project.

Drafting: Writing It Down

*D*rafting is putting your notes into sentences and paragraphs that work together to make an effective piece of
writing.

This mural artist used sketches to help her decide what to
include and how to arrange and rearrange all the mural parts.
Rafael is at a similar point in the writing process. His next step
is drafting. He'll turn his prewriting notes into the sentences
and paragraphs that will work together to introduce the class
memory book.

Start Your Draft

One place to
begin drafting is at
the beginning, with
an introduction.
Leads, or openings,
are important. A
writer must create
interest and make
readers want to
keep reading. Try
out some tech-
niques that profes-
sionals use in writ-
ing leads. You
could ask a ques-
tion, present an
unusual detail, or use a dramatic quotation. Be sure to state the
main idea clearly and explain what will follow. Here's a first
draft that Rafael wrote as an introduction to the memory book.

Was it worth the wait? Turn the pages to see for yourself. Remember how hard it was to decide what to include in our memory book? We finally picked the great activities our eighth-grade class did together. Join us as we relive the mural project, the Foods-of-the-World Festival, the D.C. trip, the talent show, the craft fair, and the Olympic Day.

What does Rafael accomplish in his first and last sentences?

Not all writers begin at the beginning. Some start in the middle, on a part that seems easier to write. Others tackle their conclusion first. Drafting means trying options and taking chances. You may get stuck. To get unstuck, try one of these strategies.

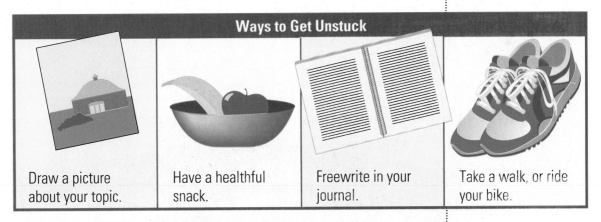

Ways to Get Unstuck

Draw a picture about your topic.	Have a healthful snack.	Freewrite in your journal.	Take a walk, or ride your bike.

Journal Writing

What strategies have helped you start drafting or get unstuck? What new strategies could you try? In your journal make a list to refer to when you're stuck.

Let It Flow

As you draft, use your prewriting notes. They'll remind you of your purpose, audience, and plan of organization. Let your ideas flow freely. Don't interrupt the flow of ideas by thinking about grammar or spelling or even about writing in paragraphs. You'll have a chance to make changes later.

How can we forget The mural project began the year. The idea was to capture the spirit of our school and community in paint strokes. Barb and Deji led us in forming comitees, and then we all got into the act. Four paint-soaked months later our beautiful mural was done, ready for all to see.

Later, the writer will correct spelling errors in this line. When the ideas are flowing, keep going!

Write a Draft

Use your prewriting notes to help you draft your piece. Skip every other line to leave room for changes. Don't worry about correctness. At this stage, you are still exploring what you want to say.

PURPOSE To create a draft
AUDIENCE Yourself
LENGTH 1–2 pages

WRITING RUBRICS To create a draft, you should

- decide where to start—with the lead or in the middle
- let your ideas flow

Diego Rivera, *Allegory of California*, 1931

Cross-Curricular Activity

MUSIC Draft song lyrics to go with the mural on this page. Begin with notes about what your purpose is and what parts of the mural you want to write about.

Grammar Link

Use various kinds of sentences: declarative, interrogative, imperative, and exclamatory.

Write a paragraph, following the directions below.

1. Write an imperative sentence. Tell readers to create a committee.
2. Write a declarative sentence. Explain the committee's job.
3. Write an exclamatory sentence. Warn the committee of what's ahead.
4. Write an interrogative sentence. Ask about an event.

See Lesson 8.1, page 359.

Viewing and Representing

The mural on this page is about California. What would you show on a mural of your state? Work in a small group. Research to learn about your state. List the ideas to include on a state mural. Then sketch and create the mural on poster board.

Revising: Taking a Fresh Look

*W*hen you revise, *you take a fresh look at your writing and refine it. After you've finished your first draft, put it aside for a time—at least a day, if possible. When you read your draft again, you'll have a better idea about how your writing will sound to readers.*

Revise for Clarity and Sense

Begin by reading aloud. Ask yourself, Is this clear? Does it make sense? Have I chosen the right words? The revising stage is a good time to consider whether you've used the best words. You might use a thesaurus to help you find words that say exactly what you mean. Examine the suggested revisions on the facing page. Then study the chart to help you revise.

Revising Tip

Elaboration

As you revise, consider whether you have provided enough supporting details and information. Elaborate where necessary.

After some recipe revisions suggested by his family, Ben's contribution to the Foods-of-the-World Festival was just right.

Eighth-grade eating habits may have been changed forever by this event. Foods from places like Puerto Rico, India, and China expanded our taste experiences. ~~Food,~~ *Spicy dishes* such as tacos and curries made peanut butter sandwiches seem like kids' stuff. Who can forget the parade of taste sensations that marched across our tongues at the Foods-of-the-World Festival? ~~Jenny Diaz covered the tables with blue and white tablecoths and put a colorful bouquet on each one.~~

How did the writer improve the paragraph by changing "food" to "spicy dishes"?

Moving this topic sentence to the beginning will help the writer focus on the main idea.

Questions for Revising

1. Is my writing clear? Does it make sense?
2. What is my purpose, and do I accomplish it?
3. Do I consider my audience?
4. Have I chosen the best, most precise words?
5. Do I say enough about my idea?
6. Could I elaborate more?

Journal Writing

Review your journal for entries about recent events in your life. Choose one entry that interests you. To strengthen it, make at least two major revisions. Refer to the list above for ideas.

Ask a Peer to Review Your Work

One way to identify trouble spots in your work is to read it to others and ask for their comments. These peer reviewers will help you see your writing from the point of view of your audience. You can return the favor by listening to their work. As a peer reviewer, comment first on what is successful about the piece—in other words, say what works well for you. Then suggest any changes you think would help readers understand better. Read the paragraph below, comparing the peer reviewer's comments with the writer's revisions.

You made the food festival sound like fun.

Maybe you should list the ingredients.

Does the sentence about learning to cook belong?

I am confused by the last sentence.

We sampled delicious treats from several ~~countries, but~~ among the highlights *of the festival* were the pot stickers from the kitchen of Ms. Yu, our teacher. Ms. Yu used *an old family recipe* ~~a way~~ that had been passed down to her from her mother. ~~Her mother taught her how to cook.~~ Ms. Yu offered everyone a fortune cookie. Reading our fortunes aloud added a touch of humor to the event. Our greatest fortune came *when Ms. Yu gave us* ~~with~~ the recipe for those yummy pot stickers.

You can follow all or some or none of your peer reviewer's suggestions. Notice that the writer of the paragraph above made two of the three suggested changes. A peer reviewer's comments can help you decide what changes to make, but the final decisions are up to you. As the writer, you're in charge.

Revise Your Draft

Look again at the draft you have written. Make sure some time has gone by—at least a day—before you begin to revise it.

PURPOSE To revise your draft, to have a writing conference
AUDIENCE Yourself, your peer reviewers
LENGTH 1 page of comments

WRITING RUBRICS To revise your draft, you should

- put yourself in the place of your audience and read over your draft, using the questions on page 67
- have a writing conference
- make changes to your paper

Listening and Speaking

COOPERATIVE LEARNING In a small group, discuss the ways peer reviewers can help writers improve their writing. (For example, peer reviewers may suggest new ideas about the topic.) Discuss the kinds of comments from peer reviewers that are most helpful.

Using Computers

Revising on a computer allows you to move text around and to try out different words and phrases. Save versions of your drafts and go back to a previous version if you think you've lost track of your original ideas.

Grammar Link

Use specific nouns in your writing.

*Spicy **dishes**, such as **tacos** and **curries**, made peanut butter **sandwiches** seem like **kids' stuff**.*

Rewrite the sentences below, replacing each italicized noun with a more specific noun.

1. Other *people* and I went shopping yesterday.
2. All of us found just what we needed at the *store.*
3. Jenny bought a *tool* for her father's birthday.
4. George bought a *book* and immediately sat down to read it.
5. A lovely little *plant* charmed Kathleen.
6. The twins were drawn to a display of *clothes.*
7. The *pets* in the window snagged Jemal's attention.
8. As for me, I bought *footwear.*
9. The *employees* rang up our purchases.
10. After shopping, we treated ourselves to *food.*

See Lesson 3.3, page 122.

Revising: Writing Unified Paragraphs

As a writer, you want to make sure that each paragraph has a single, clear focus and that the sentences work together.

Alicia wanted to write about the class visit to the Washington Monument. When she looked at photos of the class trip, she found two of the monument. Which do you think she chose? Why?

Check for Unity

A paragraph is unified if all its sentences work together to express one main idea. That main idea is usually expressed in a topic sentence, which may appear at the beginning or the end or even in the middle of the paragraph. In revising, decide whether the main idea would be clearer if you added or revised a topic sentence. Make sure that all the details support the main idea. What unifies the paragraphs below?

Literature Model

There are two levels on which to enjoy a tour through black history in the nation's capital: Visit those neighborhoods that stand now and those monuments erected in memory of past struggles and accomplishments. Then, as you drive or walk around the city, try to imagine what once was.

Since 1790, when Congress ordered that a federal city be built on the Potomac River, blacks have made rich and varied contributions. Benjamin Banneker, a black surveyor, assisted Pierre L'Enfant, the city's designer, in laying out the new capital. When the temperamental L'Enfant was dismissed, taking his design notes with him, Banneker's memory was invaluable.

Patrice Gaines-Carter,
"Washington as a Mecca of Black History"

> The details explain the "two levels" introduced in the topic sentence.

> Why does the writer begin a new paragraph here?

Journal Writing

List ten or more ideas about what you think is special about your town or city. Review your list, and write topic sentences for paragraphs that could include two or more of the ideas.

Connect Ideas

The ideas in a paragraph must relate in clearly understandable ways. Writers connect their ideas, using words and phrases called *transitions*. Notice the transitions in the following passage.

Transitions

Time

after	before	finally
first	next	at once

Place

above	across	beside
below	next to	near

Cause and Effect

as a result	because
since	therefore

Using Transition Words

After our long bus ride, we were glad to reach our hotel in downtown Washington, D.C. The next morning found us revived and ready for our tour. The first stop was the Washington Monument. After waiting in line for an hour, we took the minute-long elevator ride to the top. When we got there, we looked out across the city. How awesome it was!

Our next stop was the Lincoln Memorial. Since Lincoln is one of my heroes, I took some photos of the seated statue. The statue's huge size reminded me of what a great president Lincoln was.

You don't think about transitions as you draft. When you revise, however, be sure that you've made smooth connections between ideas. In descriptive writing you may use spatial transitions, such as *nearby* and *on one side*. In narrative writing you may arrange ideas chronologically and use time transitions, such as *first* and *then*. When writing to explain, you can use cause-and-effect transitions, such as *therefore* and *as a result*.

Check for Unified Paragraphs

Take another look at your draft. Are there ways you can make it even clearer for your audience?

PURPOSE To revise your draft for unity
AUDIENCE Yourself
LENGTH Necessary changes on your draft

WRITING RUBRICS To revise your draft for unity, check that

- each paragraph focuses on one main idea
- all the sentences in each paragraph support the main idea
- you have used transition words to link ideas

Monika Steinhoff, *La Plazuela, La Fonda (Hotel)—Santa Fe, New Mexico*, 1984

Viewing and Representing

Examine the painting on this page. Is the artist inviting you into the scene or closing it off from you? Write a paragraph giving your interpretation. Use examples from the painting to support your ideas.

Cross-Curricular Activity

ART Notice the patterns surrounding the doors in Steinhoff's painting. As a group project, create similar designs. Together, experiment with placing the designs in an order that will create a unified look. Discuss reasons for moving and rearranging the designs.

Grammar Link

Use commas to set off introductory elements and word groups that interrupt the sentence.

Write each sentence, adding commas where necessary.

1. Rudely awakened by the alarm clock I slowly opened my eyes.
2. Mario you see had set it an hour early.
3. With a sudden burst of energy I jumped out of bed.

See Lesson 20.2, page 601, and Lesson 20.3, page 603.

The Writing Process

Revising: Writing Varied Sentences

A good writer tries to produce a pleasing rhythm in his or her sentences. Varying the length and structure of your sentences gives your writing this rhythm.

Kim and Emily arranged the acts for a class talent show. Rather than opening with three vocal solos in a row, they inserted a comedy act and a dance routine between two singers' solos. The variety gave a pleasing rhythm to the show.

In much the same way, a writer strives to produce a pleasing rhythm in his or her sentences. When you revise, read your sentences aloud, and listen to them. What will they sound like to your readers? Do they seem to plod along like three vocal solos in a row? Or do they flow smoothly, with the rhythm of a well-planned talent show?

Vary Sentence Structure

One way to give your writing a pleasing rhythm is to vary your sentence structure. Instead of always beginning with a subject, start some sentences with an adverb, a prepositional phrase, a participial phrase, or a subordinate clause. Rafael realized that he'd used the same basic pattern—a subject followed by a predicate—over and over again. Notice how he achieved a better rhythm by varying his sentence beginnings.

The Writing Process

To open the show,
~~The opening act was~~ Maria. ~~She~~ sang the song "Memory" from the musical Cats. Everyone was surprised at the emotion Maria put into her song. Since She's usually so quiet, Raoul performed next. His comedy act drew peals of laughter from the audience. We weren't surprised by that. Raoul is funny even when he's not on stage.
and Kim
For the next act Shanti performed a dance routine to rap music. ~~Kim danced with her.~~

How did Rafael change his first sentence?

What else did Rafael do to vary his sentences?

Journal Writing

Read several paragraphs of your writing aloud. How do the paragraphs sound? Examine the sentence patterns. Look especially at your sentence beginnings. If necessary, revise your work to vary the structure and patterns of sentences.

Vary Sentence Length

Good writers avoid monotony. They do not string long sentences together. They avoid the choppiness of too many short sentences. The narrator of the selection below is a young boy traveling by train from Mexico to California. Notice the sentence rhythm. Then study the graphic to see how you can "cut and paste" to revise your sentences for length.

> **Which sentences vary widely in length? How does this variety affect the writing?**

Literature Model

During the afternoon dark clouds had piled up over us, rolling over the desert from the mountains. At sunset the first drops fell on our canvas roof. The rain picked up and the train slowed down. It was pouring when we began to pass the adobe huts of a town. We passed another train standing on a siding, the deck of our flatcar flooded and the awnings above us sagging with rainwater and leaking. It was night.

Ernesto Galarza, *Barrio Boy*

Changing Sentence Length

The lights in the theater dimmed. | A hush fell over the audience. | The curtains slowly slid apart.

▼

As the lights in the theater dimmed, a hush fell over the audience, and the curtains slowly slid apart.

As Linh displayed the hat for the audience to inspect, it was obvious that the rabbit had disappeared.

▼

Linh displayed the hat for the audience to inspect. | The rabbit had obviously disappeared.

Revise for Variety

Now look at your sentences. Are there ways you can make them more varied?

PURPOSE To revise for sentence variety
AUDIENCE Yourself
LENGTH Changes on the draft

WRITING RUBRICS To revise your draft for sentence variety, check for

- a mixture of long and short sentences
- variety in the order of words and phrases
- sentences that can be combined to express ideas more clearly

Listening and Speaking

Tape-record yourself as you read your draft. Then listen to the recording. Is there a pleasing rhythm to your work, or does it drone on? Are your sentences too much alike? How can you change them? Take notes as you listen and use your notes to revise.

Using Computers

Word processing programs include an editing feature that allows you to cut and paste easily. This is especially useful when combining two or three short sentences into one long one or when breaking a long sentence into two or three shorter ones.

Grammar Link

Use adverb clauses to achieve sentence variety.

You can often combine the ideas in two simple sentences into one sentence. One effective method is to state the idea in one of the sentences in an adverb clause.

Even when he's not on stage, Raoul is funny.

When the adverb clause comes first in a sentence, use a comma after it.

Combine each of the pairs of sentences below by turning one of the sentences into an adverb clause. Use commas where necessary.

1. Sophia called. I went to meet her.
2. There was a sale. We walked to the mall.
3. It was raining. We took our umbrellas.
4. The prices were low. We did not buy anything.
5. We spotted the bus at the bus stop. We climbed aboard.

See Lesson 14.5, page 513; Lesson 20.3, page 603; and Lesson 21.4, page 635.

LESSON 2.9

Editing/Proofreading: Fine-tuning Your Work

During the editing stage, the goal is to get your writing ready to share with others. You want your finished product to be as nearly perfect as possible.

After all that hard work on the memory book, the first thing people see shouldn't be a misspelled word on the cover. Correcting spelling may seem like a little thing, but it's important to do before the book reaches its audience. To begin the editing process, ask a peer reviewer to look over your piece of writing. A fresh pair of eyes will often catch mistakes you have overlooked.

Check Your Sentences

Your first step is editing your sentences. Read them over carefully to check word choice and to identify any sentence fragments or run-on sentences. Examine the following edited paragraph. The writer has identified errors and marked them with proofreading symbols.

Proofreading			
Symbol	**Meaning**	**Symbol**	**Meaning**
∧	Insert	⊙	Period
⌿	Delete	⌄	Comma
⟳	Reverse	≡	Capital letter
⁋	New paragraph	/	Lower-case letter

Lydia displayed
At the craft fair ∧ Several items of jewelry made from ordinary office supplies. One of the most beautiful pieces was a pin in the shape of a skyscraper ⊙ ∧ it ≡ was made out of neon-colored paper clips, gold staples, and the cap from a portable pencil sharpener.

The writer has broken the sentence into two shorter ones. Is there another way to correct this run-on sentence?

Journal Writing

In your journal freewrite for five minutes about any topic that interests you. Let your work sit for a few hours. When you return to it, fix the errors that you find.

Proofread for Mechanics and Grammar

After editing for sentence structure, proofread for errors in mechanics—spelling, capitalization, and punctuation—and in grammar. Once you've proofread your draft, prepare a clean, legible final copy. Read your work over one more time. If you find a small mistake, correct it neatly.

Why did the writer circle "staggerd" and "principle"?

What is the meaning of each proofreading mark used in this paragraph?

¶ After the minimarathon had ended and the last few runners had (staggerd) into the schoolyard, the closing ceremonies for Olympic Day began. Justin, our star musician, had composed a song just for this day. The words reflected the spirit of the events. With the winning athletes leading the parade, we marched into the School auditorium, singing Justin's song. Ms. tsao, our (principle) handed out ribbons as we all cheered.

"Mind if we check the ears?"

Some writers proofread as they draft and revise. Most writers, however, concentrate on getting their ideas down during these stages and leave proof-reading for a later stage.

Edit Your Writing

After revising the draft of your paper, you should be satisfied that your draft says what you want it to in the best possible way. Now you are ready for the editing stage of the writing process. During this stage, you will proofread your paper, checking carefully for errors.

PURPOSE To edit for corrections
AUDIENCE Yourself
LENGTH Changes on the draft

WRITING RUBRICS To edit your paper, you should

- check your paper word-by-word for errors
- look for one kind of error at a time
- use proofreading symbols to mark your paper

Using Computers

The ability of your word processing program to check spelling can be useful, but do not leave all the proofreading up to the computer. Your program probably won't alert you if you've written *form* instead of *from* or *their* instead of *there*. After using your computer to find obvious misspellings, proofread your work again.

Grammar Link

Use proofreading symbols to edit your writing.

As you edit, correct run-on sentences and sentence fragments. Fix errors in capitalization and punctuation. Add missing words and delete extra words.

Ms. tsao, our principle, handed out ribbons as we all cheered.

First, copy the passage below just as it is written. Then use proofreading symbols to edit it.

[1]Sean took also a booth at the craft fair, this was a chance for him to display his pottery. [2]Including several vases. [3]He was thrilled when he sold three Pieces, a vase a pot with a lid and a bowl bowl. [4]Sean been practicing with irish designs in his work. [5]The bowl he sold is a copy of an ancient Ceremonial piece.

See Lessons 7.1–7.9, pages 308–331.

Viewing and Representing

You may wish to include a visual with your work. Create an illustration, draw a cartoon, sketch a diagram, or find another way to represent an idea in your paper.

The Writing Process

Publishing/Presenting: Sharing Your Writing

Now that you've invested so much time, energy, and talent in your writing, you'll want to share it. Who will want to read it? What is the best way to present it to them?

These pages of pictures are from the eighth-grade memory book, *This Unforgettable Year.* Who in Carver Junior High School will probably want a copy? What audience might the memory book have outside the school?

This Unforgettable Year in Pictures

Everybody helped us with the Foods-of-the-World Festival. The result was a feast fit for a king or queen of any nation.

Mrs. Talerico waited with us patiently to visit the United States Capitol.

The talent show gave everyone a chance to perform. Sylvia Lin practiced her solo for hours before going on stage.

Present Your Writing at School

Some of the best audiences you'll ever find are at school. Here are ways to share your writing. Submit a piece to the school newspaper. Write the text for a bulletin-board display, or create a poster to promote an activity. Some classes exchange letters with students in other countries. Others publish an anthology of poems and stories, a memory book, or a yearbook.

This is the final revision of a page from *This Unforgettable Year.*

Who can forget the parade of taste sensations that marched across our tongues at the Foods-of-the-World Festival? This event may have changed eighth-grade eating habits forever. Foods from places such as Puerto Rico, India, and China expanded our taste experiences. Spicy dishes, such as tacos and curries, made peanut butter sandwiches seem like kids' stuff.

Among the highlights of the festival were the pot stickers from the kitchen of Ms. Yu, our teacher. Ms. Yu used an old family recipe passed down to her from her mother. These traditional treats tickled our taste buds and made us all want to travel to China. To add to our pleasure, Ms. Yu offered everyone a fortune cookie. Reading our fortunes aloud added a touch of humor. Our greatest fortune came when Ms. Yu gave us the recipe for those yummy pot stickers.

Journal Writing

In your journal list opportunities for presenting your writing in your school. Choose two you would like to try. Find out where and how to submit your work.

Present Your Writing to Others

How can you "publish" your writing outside school? One of the best ways is to write letters to friends and family members. If you have ideas about a local problem, write a letter to the editor. If you are interested in a hobby or sport, find a specialty magazine, and exchange ideas with fellow enthusiasts. Two excellent magazines, *Merlyn's Pen* and *Stone Soup,* publish stories, poems, and other writing by students your age.

Contests offer still another opportunity for presenting your writing. The National Council of Teachers of English and other local and national organizations sponsor writing contests for young people. Your teacher or librarian may know about local groups, such as civic and veterans organizations, that sponsor essay contests. You can find other ideas in the collage below.

Present Your Writing

You have taken your writing through prewriting, drafting, revising, and editing, and now it's time for the payoff—presenting, publishing, or sharing your writing!

PURPOSE To present your finished work

AUDIENCE Your chosen audience

LENGTH Whatever is appropriate for your purpose

WRITING RUBRICS To present your finished work, you should

- prepare your work in the format that is best for your audience and purpose
- make your paper as neat and attractive as you can

Viewing and Representing

COOPERATIVE LEARNING In a small group, plan a class newsletter. Brainstorm for ideas for articles and stories related to school activities and events. Have one member of the group record your ideas. Once the group has decided what activities and events to include, each member should choose a writing assignment. When all members have completed their writing, come together to revise and edit each piece. Then work together to lay out the newsletter. If possible, duplicate a copy for each class member or present your completed newsletter as part of a classroom bulletin-board display.

Grammar Link

Make subjects and verbs agree.

Occasionally the subject of a sentence comes after the verb, but subject and verb must still agree.

*Among the highlights of the festival were the **pot stickers** from the kitchen of Ms. Yu, our teacher.*

Write each sentence, underlining the subject and using the correct form of the verb in parentheses.

1. There (is, are) many unusual sights on this camping trip—too many for Soraya.
2. Outside our tent (sits, sit) two fat raccoons, begging for a handout.
3. At the crossroads (stands, stand) a huge bull moose, watching us unconcernedly.
4. Here (comes, come) three baby porcupines and their mother.

See Lesson 16.2, page 543.

Using Computers

Write an e-mail to a friend. Describe the writing process you just finished. Share the problems you solved and tell what you are most proud of about your work.

The Writing Process

Writing Process in Action

WRITING Online

Visit the *Writer's Choice* Web site at **writerschoice. glencoe.com** for additional writing prompts.

The Writing Process

The Writing Process

In preceding lessons you've learned about the stages of the writing process and how writers go back and forth between stages before they present their writing in final form. You've also practiced what you've learned about the writing stages. In this lesson you're invited to relive an exciting event you've experienced by writing about it.

Assignment

Context	This year the theme of your school newspaper's annual writing contest is "And You Were There." Entries must portray an exciting event experienced by the writer.
Purpose	To involve readers with your account of an exciting event
Audience	Readers of your school newspaper
Length	2 paragraphs

The following pages can help you plan and write an account of an experience. Read through them, and then refer to them as you need to. But don't be tied down by them. You're in charge of your own writing process.

Prewriting

What have you done recently that was exciting? Did you compete in a race or a chess match? Did you attend a concert or a pep rally? Did you have your artwork shown at an exhibit?

Use one of the options below, or an idea of your own, to begin thinking about a topic. Once you've decided on a topic, develop your ideas by listing, brainstorming, or interviewing.

Drafting

You can make an account of an event exciting by creating suspense. One way to create suspense is to emphasize time pressures. For example, in the brainstorming example on the right, the writer focused on guests fighting the snow to get to a wedding on time. In the example below, the author uses time pressures to create suspense throughout his account of a basketball game.

Option A

Look at old programs and photos.

Option B

Read through your journal.

Option C

Brainstorm ideas.

Prewriting Tip

Look at pages 54–57 for suggestions on using brainstorming to develop a topic.

Prewriting Tip

Pages 58–61 tell you how to use lists to make sure your supporting details fit your main idea.

Person skiing through very heavy snow. Brother Michael's wedding. Big snowstorm night before. Cars snowed in, buses late. People got to Village Hall any way they could.

Literature Model

We came out in the second half and played it pretty cool. Once we came within one point, but then they ran it up to five again. We kept looking over to Mr. Reese to see what he wanted us to do and he would just put his palms down and nod his head for us to play cool. There were six minutes to go when Mr. Reese put me and another guy named Turk in.

Walter Dean Myers, *"The Game"*

Writing Process in Action

Drafting Tip

For more information about using transitions to show the passage of time, see Lesson 2.7, page 70.

Revising Tip

Read your writing aloud to check its rhythm. For more help with sentence variety, see Lesson 2.8, pages 74–77.

Question A

Is my account clear?

Question B

Have I varied my sentences?

Question C

Have I written unified paragraphs?

As you write your draft, think about ways to emphasize the time element to create suspense. For example, in a movie, a hero needs to defuse a bomb. Suspense is created by repeatedly showing the bomb's timer ticking away the seconds.

Remember, in the drafting stage you need to let your writing flow to get your ideas down. You can make changes later. See pages 62–65 for more help with drafting.

Revising

To begin revising, read over your draft to make sure that what you have written fits your purpose and your audience. Then have a writing conference. Read your draft to a partner or small group. Use your audience's reactions to help you evaluate your work so far. The following questions can help you and your listeners.

"I can't imagine where she is," Michael said into
counted the eighth ring of his call to Anika's.
~~the receiver as he paced back and forth.~~
and the wedding was scheduled for noon.
It was eleven thirty. I wanted to ask if they'd had
, knowing that she was probably stuck in the snow,
a fight, but I kept my mouth shut.
from the front door of the Village Hall,
Just then I heard Kenny yell, "Hey, everyone,
As I reached the door,
you've got to see this!" I couldn't believe my eyes.

It was Anika in her wedding dress, skiing down the street to the hall. It was 11:45. The guests who had made it to the hall applauded when Anika came inside, shaking the snow from her dress.

Editing/Proofreading

A careful editing job shows your readers that you care about your work and that you don't want errors to distract them from your ideas. The Editing/ Proofreading Checklist will help you catch errors. Usually writers **proofread** for only one kind of error at a time. If you do the same, you will probably do a better job of finding your mistakes. Use a dictionary and the Grammar, Usage, and Mechanics part of this book to help you with your editing.

Editing/Proofreading Checklist

1. Have I used the correct form of each pronoun?
2. Have I used irregular verbs correctly?
3. Have I capitalized all proper nouns?
4. Have I used commas and semicolons correctly?
5. Is every word spelled correctly?

Publishing/Presenting

Make sure your account of an exciting event is neatly written or typed on clean white paper before you submit it to "And You Were There."

As an alternative way of presenting your writing, you might like to give an oral presentation. Let the excitement of the event come through in your voice, facial expressions, and gestures. You might want to include recorded background noise or music for your presentation. For example, you might want to record the sound of a crowd cheering or booing if your account is of a sports event.

Proofreading Tip

For proofreading symbols, see page 79. If you composed on the computer, use the spelling- and grammar-checking features.

Journal Writing

Reflect on your writing process experience. Answer these questions in your journal: What do I like best about my article? What was the hardest part of writing it? What did I learn in my writing conference? What new things have I learned as a writer?

Literature Model

THE GAME

by Walter Dean Myers

With New York City's 116th Street as the setting, Walter Dean Myers's narrator, Stuff, reports the play-by-play action at the year's most important neighborhood basketball game in this chapter from Fast Sam, Cool Clyde, and Stuff. *As you read, pay special attention to how the author gets you interested in the story. Then try the activities in Linking Writing and Literature on page 95.*

We had practiced and practiced until it ran out of our ears. Every guy on the team knew every play. We were ready. It meant the championship. Everybody was there. I never saw so many people at the center at one time. We had never seen the other team play but Sam said that he knew some of the players and that they were good. Mr. Reese told us to go out and play as hard as we could every moment we were on the floor. We all shook hands in the locker room and then went out. Mostly we tried to ignore them warming up at the other end of the court but we couldn't help but look a few times. They were doing exactly what we were doing, just shooting a few lay-ups and waiting for the game to begin.

They got the first tap and started passing the ball around. I mean they really started passing the ball around faster than anything I had ever seen. Zip! Zip! Zip! Two points! I didn't even know how they could see the ball, let alone get it inside to their big man. We brought the ball down and one of their players stole the ball from Sam. We got back on defense but they weren't in a hurry. The same old thing. Zip! Zip! Zip! Two points! They could pass the ball better than anybody I ever saw. Then we brought the ball down again and Chalky missed a jump shot. He missed the backboard, the rim, everything. One of their players caught the ball and then brought it down and a few seconds later the score was 6–0. We couldn't even get close enough to foul them. Chalky brought the ball down again, passed to Sam cutting across the lane, and then walked. They brought the ball down and it was 8–0.

They were really enjoying the game. You could see. Every time they scored they'd slap hands and carry on. Also, they had some cheerleaders. They had about five girls with little pink skirts on and white sweaters cheering for them.

Clyde brought the ball down this time, passed into our center, a guy named Leon, and Leon turned and missed a hook. They got the rebound and came down, and Chalky missed a steal and fouled his man. That's when Mr. Reese called time out.

"Okay, now, just trade basket for basket. They make a basket, you take your time and you make a basket— don't rush it." Mr. Reese looked at his starting five. "Okay, now, every once in a while take a look over at me and I'll let you know when I want you to make your move. If I put my hands palm down, just keep on playing cool. If I stand up and put my

Red Grooms, *Fast Break*, 1983–1984

hands up like this"—he put both hands up near his face—"that means to make your move. You understand that?"

Everyone said that they understood. When the ball was back in play Chalky and Sam and Leon started setting picks from the outside and then passed to Clyde for our first two points. They got the ball and started passing around again. Zip! Zip! Zip! But this time we were just waiting for that pass underneath and they knew it. Finally they tried a shot from outside and Chalky slapped it away to Sam on the break. We came down real quick and scored. On the way back Mr. Reese showed everybody that his palms were down. To keep playing cool.

They missed their next shot and fouled Chalky. They called time out and, much to my surprise, Mr. Reese put me in. My heart was beating so fast I thought I was going to have a heart attack. Chalky missed the foul shot but Leon slapped the ball out to Clyde, who passed it to me. I dribbled about two steps and threw it back to Leon in the bucket. Then I didn't know what to do so I did what Mr. Reese always told us. If you don't know what to do then, just move around. I started moving toward the corner and then I ran quickly toward the basket. I saw Sam coming at me from the other direction and it was a play. Two guards cutting past and one of the defensive men gets picked off. I ran as close as I could to Sam, and his man got picked off. Chalky threw the ball into him for an easy lay-up. They came down and missed again but one of their men got the rebound in. We brought the ball down and Sam went along the base line for a jump shot, but their center knocked the ball away. I caught it just before it went out at the corner and shot the ball. I remembered what Mr. Reese had said about following your shot in, and I started in after the ball but it went right in. It didn't touch the rim or anything. Swish!

One of their players said to watch out for 17—that was me. I played about two minutes more, then Mr. Reese took me out. But I had scored another basket on a lay-up. We were coming back. Chalky and Sam were knocking away just about anything their guards were throwing up, and Leon, Chalky, and Sam controlled the defensive backboard. Mr. Reese brought in Cap, and Cap got fouled two times in two plays. At the end of the half, when I thought we were doing pretty well, I found out the score was 36–29. They were beating us by seven points. Mr. Reese didn't seem worried, though.

"Okay, everybody, stay cool. No sweat. Just keep it nice and easy."

We came out in the second half and played it pretty cool. Once we came within one point, but then they ran it up to five again. We kept looking over to Mr. Reese to see what he wanted us to do and he would just put his palms down and nod his head for us to play cool. There were six minutes to go when Mr. Reese put me and another guy named Turk in. Now I didn't really understand why he did this because I know I'm not the best basketball player in the world, although I'm not bad, and I know Turk is worse than me. Also, he took out both Sam and Chalky, our two best players. We were still losing by five points, too. And they weren't doing anything wrong. There was a jump ball between Leon and their center when all of a sudden this big cheer goes up and everybody looks over to the sidelines. Well, there was Gloria, BB, Maria, Sharon, Kitty, and about four other girls, all dressed in white blouses and black skirts and with big T's on their blouses and they were our cheerleaders. One of their players said something stupid about them but I liked them. They looked real good to me. We controlled the jump and Turk drove right down the lane and made a lay-up. Turk actually made the lay-up. Turk once missed seven lay-ups in a row in practice and no one was even guarding him. But this one he made. Then one of their men double-dribbled and we got the ball and I passed it to Leon, who threw up a shot and got fouled. The shot went in and when he made the foul shot it added up to a three-point play. They started down court and Mr. Reese started yelling for us to give a foul.

"Foul him! Foul him!" he yelled from the sidelines.

Now this was something we had worked on in practice and that Mr. Reese had told us would only work once in a game. Anybody who plays basketball knows that if you're fouled while shooting the ball you get two foul shots and if you're fouled while not shooting the ball you only get one. So when a guy knows you're going to foul him he'll try to get off a quick shot. At least that's what we hoped. When their guard came across the mid-court line, I ran at him as if I was going to foul him. Then, just as I was going to touch him, I stopped short and moved around him without touching him. Sure enough, he threw the ball wildly toward the basket. It went over the base line and it was our ball. Mr. Reese took me out and Turk and put Sam and Chalky back in. And the game was just about over.

We hadn't realized it but in the two minutes that me and Turk played the score had been tied. When Sam and Chalky came back in they outscored the other team by four points in the last four minutes. We were the champs. We got the first-place trophies and we were so happy we were all jumping around and slapping each other on the back. Gloria and the other girls were just as happy as we were, and when we found that we had an extra trophy we gave it to them. Then Mr. Reese took us all in the locker room and shook each guy's hand and then went out and invited the parents and the girls in. He made a little speech about how he was proud of us and all, and not just because we won tonight but because we had worked so hard to win. When he finished everybody started clapping for us and, as usual, I started boo-hooing. But it wasn't so bad this time because Leon starting boo-hooing worse than me.

You know what high is? We felt so good the next couple of days that it was ridiculous. We'd see someone in the street and we'd just walk up and be happy. Really.

Linking Writing and Literature

Readers Respond to the Model

How does Walter Dean Myers interest you in the story?

Explore how Walter Dean Myers interests readers by answering these questions. Then read what other students liked about his story.

1. Walter Dean Myers tells the story through the words of one of the players, Stuff. Why do you think Myers does this?

2. What details about the other team create interest and suspense at the beginning of the story?

3. What details about the players on Stuff's team add to the suspense of the game?

4. Which character in the story do you like the best? Why?

What Students Say

"My favorite character was Mr. Reese, the coach. He trusted his players, and he didn't show favoritism. I remember the scene in which he let some less able players get on the court. I was surprised because the team was behind, but their coach had confidence in them. The writer made Mr. Reese seem real by showing how happy he was and how proud he was of his players. It was his spirit that the players drew upon. "

Keianna Chatman

"The story made me feel as if I was part of the game. The coach, Mr. Reese, was my favorite character. When the team was losing by several points, he told them to keep cool, and he kept them steady. He also kept them together. Without teamwork, a team would have nothing. "

Benjamin Rodriguez

UNIT 2 Review

Reflecting on the Unit

Summarize.

1 What are the stages of the writing process?

2 Why should the writing process be flexible?

3 What is involved in the prewriting stage?

4 What does drafting mean?

5 What does revising a piece of writing involve?

6 What kinds of errors are corrected in the editing stage?

7 What does presenting mean?

 ## Adding to Your Portfolio

CHOOSE A SELECTION FOR YOUR PORTFOLIO Look over the writing you did for this unit. Choose a piece of writing to put into your portfolio. The piece you choose should show one or more of the following:

- connections to ideas found and explored in prewriting
- words and ideas that reflect a specific audience and purpose
- an opening that interests readers and explains what will follow
- revisions that you made after you and a peer had reviewed it
- a pleasing sentence rhythm
- editing for sentence structure, grammar, and mechanics

REFLECT ON YOUR CHOICE Attach a note to the piece you have chosen, explaining briefly why you chose it and what you learned from writing it.

SET GOALS How can you improve your writing? What skill will you focus on the next time you write?

Writing Across the Curriculum

MAKE A SCIENCE CONNECTION Think about an important scientific invention or discovery that interests you. Write a paragraph about the event as if you had been there working with the scientists. Try to help readers sense your scientific team's excitement about the event or discovery.

TIME

Facing the Blank Page

Inside the writing process with TIME writers and editors

Writing for TIME

The stories published each week in TIME are the work of experienced professionals who research, write, and edit for a living. The writing is clear; the facts are accurate; and the grammar, spelling, and punctuation are as error-free as possible.

Behind the scenes, however, another story emerges. TIME staffers face many of the same challenges that students do in the messy, trial-and-error process that is writing. Just like you, they must find a topic, conduct research, get organized, write a draft, and then revise, revise, and revise again. In these pages, they tell you how they do it.

What is the secret to the quality of writing in TIME? Beyond experience and hard work, the key is collaboration. As the chart below illustrates, TIME stories are created through a form of "group journalism" that has become the magazine's hallmark. The writers and editors teach and learn from each other every week. You can do the same. Try out the writing and collaboration strategies in "Facing the Blank Page" to discover what works for you.

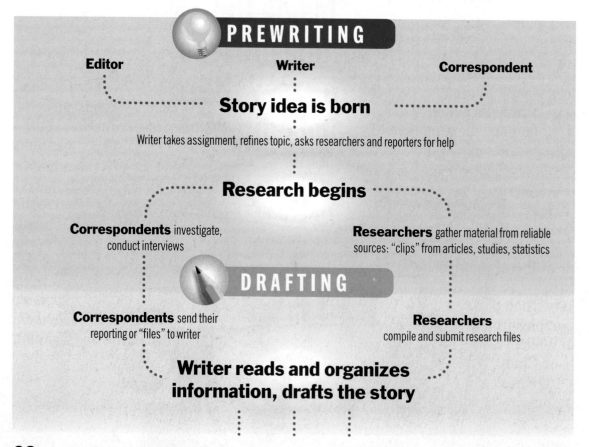

PREWRITING

Editor   Writer   Correspondent

Story idea is born

Writer takes assignment, refines topic, asks researchers and reporters for help

Research begins

Correspondents investigate, conduct interviews

Researchers gather material from reliable sources: "clips" from articles, studies, statistics

DRAFTING

Correspondents send their reporting or "files" to writer

Researchers compile and submit research files

Writer reads and organizes information, drafts the story

REVISING

Editor reads draft, suggests revisions

Correspondents
check interpretation,
make suggestions

 Writer revises, sends draft to members of the team for comments

Researchers
check accuracy,
details

Writer and editor revise again, "green" (edit for length)

EDITING AND PROOFREADING

Checks for conformity to TIME
style and conventions

Copy Desk

Checks and corrects grammar,
mechanics, spelling

PUBLISHING AND PRESENTING

**Managing Editor chooses to
print, hold, or "kill" (omit) story**

Circulation of TIME
rises or falls

**Readers respond
to published story**

E-mail and letters
to the editor

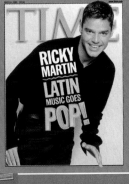

Prewriting

Reading to Write

TIME writers know that the most important preparation for writing is reading. They read extensively to gather background material. Reading also helps generate story ideas.

Assistant Managing Editor Howard Chua-Eoan explains how the process works at TIME:

❝ Before a TIME writer begins drafting, he or she has to read through and organize the information that has been gathered by correspondents and researchers. If you have the luxury of time, you should read all the material;

Howard Chua-Eoan: Reading paves the way for writing.

JAY COLTON FOR TIME

at the least, you should skim everything. That will help you decide what's important. What is the story you have to tell? What's the best way to tell it? Is the best way to open the story with a discussion of the issue, or to start with an anecdote, or to begin with a quote? You'll have all the material you need at hand, and you'll figure out what the best way is to deploy it throughout the story. ❞

TIME staffers need to read to have a general background for their writing, too. Andrea Sachs writes about books, authors, and book trends for TIME. Like all journalists, she has to stay on top of the news.

Senior Reporter Andrea Sachs:

❝ I'm a big newspaper reader. If you want to be a news reporter, you have to do a lot of reading. I read a couple of newspapers a day, and I read a lot of magazines. I'm not a big reader online, however. I much prefer paper. But I do monitor TV news in my office. I have to know every 15 minutes what is going on! I can't get enough news. ❞

LEARNING FROM THE WRITERS

DISCUSSION

1. What role does reading play for Howard Chua-Eoan and Andrea Sachs? How does reading help them do their jobs better?

2. Recall a piece of writing you completed that required you to read extensively first. What did you need to read? How did the reading shape or influence what you wrote?

3. What are the sources you find most useful in preparing to write a report? Read "Get the Facts" in Lesson 5.7 for a list of sources as well as tips for taking notes effectively. Lesson 24.1, "Using Book Features," and Lesson 24.2, "Skimming, Scanning, and Careful Reading," also provide strategies for getting the most out of your sources.

Background Reading: Using the Web

Andrea Sachs covers the publishing industry for TIME. Though she prefers not to read newspapers online, she knows the value of the Internet in researching her stories. As a TIME reporter, she has access to special Internet periodical search services, but she also uses websites to lead her to the information she needs.

Senior Reporter Andrea Sachs:

❝We have some fancy bells and whistles here to pull clips, or articles, on any subject, but there are periodical search services on the Web, too. To learn what's new in publishing, I visit booksellers' websites. They have all the book listings; that's free to anyone with a computer. When I'm looking for a particular company, that's how I locate it. There are a lot of small publishing companies with their own websites that I couldn't find otherwise.**❞**

TIME has its own website, located at *www.time.com*

Some of the resources TIME's writers and researchers gather to write articles for the magazine become material for the website. A special section called "Newsfiles" serves as an excellent resource for information related to current stories, including timelines, references to other articles, and background material.

LEARNING FROM THE WRITER

DISCUSSION
Do you read any magazines, newspapers, or other periodicals on the Web? In print? As a class, brainstorm a list of what you read regularly, online or off. How can reading these publications help you as a writer?

TRY IT OUT
1. Explore a website.
Visit a news website and read the top stories. Pick a story that interests you and read more about it by following links on the site.

2. Search the Web.
For your next paper, try typing the topic into the "search" feature of a newspaper or magazine website. Are the results useful? Surprising?

Drafting

Writing as Thinking

Writing freely, whether in a journal, diary, or as a first step in drafting, can help you discover what you want to say and enable you to say it better. Writing gives shape to your thoughts; by writing on a daily basis, you can develop the discipline required for clear thinking. Early, exploratory drafts help you shape your ideas.

Editor Barrett Seaman reflects on the value of keeping a journal:

❝Anytime you sit down to gather your thoughts, whatever the subject, there is a crystallizing effect. Some things that you allow to be mushy in your mind as you mull them over cannot be mushy when you put them down on paper.

That was one of the first things I learned in keeping a daily diary. First of all, there is discipline in doing so, and second, that crystallizing effect takes place when you have to say, 'All right, this is what I think. No more messing around here.' If you have a debate that you can't resolve in your mind, then you crystallize the points of the debate, identifying what exactly are the areas of dispute. That is a terrific discipline for anyone to go through. ❞

KEITH BEDFORD

**Lance Morrow:
Thinking on paper.**

Staff Writer James Poniewozik has also found that writing clarifies his thinking:

❝In the process of writing, you really learn more about what you think about your subject. Writing itself is an exercise through which you are setting ideas in opposition to each other, exploring tangents, and teasing out the implications of what you've already learned. The process of writing can stimulate you to go down different alleys.

Some people argue that before you begin to write, you should know exactly what you're going to say, and I think the opposite is true. There's a famous quote from the writer E.M. Forster: 'How do I know what I think until I see what I say?' Writing is not just getting down a completely formed thought that you have in your head. Writing is actually a process of thinking in itself. ❞

Essayist Lance Morrow agrees:

❝Writing is a way of thinking on paper. I can't think unless I do it on paper or on a computer. I have to test my ideas with language and with an architecture of language and propositions: 'If this, then what about this?' My thinking then becomes coherent. ❞

In its January 1, 2000, issue, TIME published an essay by Roger Rosenblatt. Written as a letter to America in the future, it is an informal and reflective piece in which the reader can hear the writer "thinking on paper."

A Letter to the Year 2100

Dear America,

    Are you wearing pajamas? I do not mean to begin this letter by getting personal. I was just wondering if you people leave the house anymore—something that seems to be increasingly unnecessary these days, a hundred years ago. Not that leaving the house is always a good idea. Outside lies the wide and brittle world of wars, scandal, disease, superstition, willful ignorance, envy, and pettiness. In your perfected age, all such things undoubtedly have been eradicated. (How I wish I could hear your laughter.) Are you six-feet-six? Are you fly-fishing on Mars? Are you talking on a cell phone? We are, usually.

    As lovers leaving lovers say, By the time you read this, I'll be gone. Or possibly I won't. Given the way life is being prolonged these days, I could write this letter in my century and pick it up in yours. No thanks. It is enough to be able to send these words across the years to tell something of who we are. We are members of a storytelling species, you and I—two eras connected by a story that changes just enough to keep it interesting.

    As long as I am on the subject of language, do the following have any meaning for you: "like"; "you know"; "what's up with that?"; "like, you know, what's up with that?"? You have no idea what I am talking about? Good. How about "yada yada yada": "fuhgeddaboutit"; "pumped"; "zine"; "you're history"? (*We're* history.)

—Roger Rosenblatt

LEARNING FROM THE WRITER

DISCUSSION
1. Explain, in your own words, what Barrett Seaman means by "crystallizing process."
2. Do you agree with James Poniewozik and Lance Morrow that "writing is thinking"? Have you had the experience they describe of discovering more about a topic through writing?
3. Read the excerpt above by essayist Roger Rosenblatt. Do you think he knew what he was going to say before he wrote this piece? Where can you see him "testing his ideas" on paper?

TRY IT OUT
1. Reread entries from your daily journal or diary to identify passages in which a "crystallizing process" or moment of discovery has taken place.
2. Compose the first draft of your next writing assignment in the form of a letter. Talk through your ideas on paper as if you were writing to a friend. Refer to the letter as you write your next draft.

HOW I WRITE
Do you keep a daily journal or learning log? What kinds of things do you write about? If you keep a journal for school as well as one at home, describe how they are alike or different. What are the benefits of writing daily?

Revising

The Role of the Editor

At TIME, writers submit their completed drafts to editors who read them and suggest changes. The process is remarkably similar to the one used in student writing conferences. TIME's writers agree that in the end, editors help them refine their thoughts and convey their ideas in clear, concise, and convincing language.

Staff Writer James Poniewozik:

❝You need to have someone look over your piece and give you the devil's advocate argument, to test your piece and make it stronger. I think it can be collaborative, too. I've often had editors rewrite or reorganize sections of my stuff, and I'll think, 'Wow, they just said what I was trying to say better and in half the space and more coherently than I did.' If you're a good writer, you probably have some sort of natural resistance to having your work tampered with. But it's necessary and good to have another set of eyes going over your work.❞

Assistant Managing Editor Howard Chua-Eoan explains how a good editor can help writers revise:

❝Even the best writers need an editor. For example, sometimes you think you've figured everything out, but you've slid over an essential step in reasoning a story. An editor will say: 'I know what you're trying to do and I agree with you, but you missed a step explaining how you got from this point to that point.'❞

WRITING TIP

Listening to Editors

"Editors are helpful; they serve as the first reader of the story. They might find something confusing and want it clarified, or they might want one more example. When the editor is good, it can be so useful. But it's scary, too. People are sensitive about having their writing changed." **—Andrea Sachs**

LEARNING FROM THE WRITERS

DISCUSSION

1. In what specific ways do Poniewozik and Chua-Eoan feel an editor can help improve a piece of writing? What do they cite as the difficult aspects of being edited?
2. What does Poniewozik mean by the "devil's advocate argument"?
3. Who edits your work? Are you sensitive to criticism of your writing?

TRY IT OUT

The value of revision.
"Writers don't revise enough," argues James Poniewozik. Is he right? Select a piece you've written and see if you can revise it more. Work on your own, then have friends or family members help. Do you agree with their advice?

HOW I WRITE

1. As a writer, how do you feel about being edited? Have you helped anyone edit his or her work before? If so, describe the process. Was it anything like the process at TIME? Was it a collaborative effort?
2. If you haven't edited anyone's work but your own, trade papers with a classmate and edit each other's work. Read Lesson 2.6 for tips on successful peer review.

Tightening: Editing for Space

Writers' drafts are typically too long. It is the editor's job to "green" or shorten the piece to fit the allotted space, making sure that each printed word carries its weight.

Read these two drafts of "Kinder Grind" by TIME columnist Amy Dickinson:

FIRST DRAFT

Today's typical kindergartner is a kid anywhere between 4 to 6 years old, with an increasing number of parents (especially affluent ones) deciding to delay the start of school to give their children (usually boys) an extra year of pre-school. This trend—known as "redshirting," after the practice of holding back freshman college athletes—is widening the developmental and age gaps among the students chronologically and developmentally. Younger students generally go to kindergarten with little or no pre-schooling, while older children may have been in nursery school for up to three years. Add to that the naturally wide variation in the developmental range of young children, and a "typical" kindergarten class now contains some students who barely know their letters, while others may be fairly fluent readers. Sue Bredekamp, editor of "Developmentally Appropriate Practice in Early Childhood Programs," a guide for teachers published by the National Association for the Education of Young Children, says she wonders how more rigid instruction will serve children well. "What teachers tell us is that expectations for kindergartners have become more standardized, while the pool of kids in kindergarten has become more diverse."

FINAL DRAFT

More parents (especially affluent ones) are delaying the start of school to give their children an extra year of pre-school. This trend—known as "redshirting," after the practice of holding back freshman college athletes—is widening the developmental and age gaps among students. A "typical" kindergarten class contains kids ages 4 to 6 whose level of development varies widely. Some barely know their letters, while others are fairly fluent readers. Sue Bredekamp, editor of a widely used guide for teachers of young children, says, "What teachers tell us is that expectations for kindergartners have become more standardized, while the pool of kids in kindergarten has become more diverse."

DISCUSSION

1. What is the difference in line count between the unedited and final versions of this excerpt about kindergarten from TIME?

2. Identify one passage that the editor cut or "greened." If you were the writer, would you object to this revision?

3. What tips for tightening a piece of writing can you draw from this example? List them as a class.

TRY IT OUT

Striving for conciseness. Take a sample paragraph from a recent piece of writing and count its lines. Rewrite the paragraph to fit in a space or line count 25% smaller. What can you cut? What can you rephrase, rewrite, and tighten?

Editing and Proofreading

Clichés: No Laughing Matter

Copy editors at TIME work to ensure that every article, caption, and headline in the magazine is correct. They catch and change errors in grammar, usage, and spelling. Copy editors also strive to make every story as clean and readable as possible. Sometimes this means spotting and getting rid of clichés, expressions that were once original but have been so overused that they've lost their impact. See "As Stale as Day-old Bread" on page 670 for more on clichés.

Henry Muller, a former Managing Editor at TIME, sent this memo to the TIME staff:

" In our ongoing search-and-destroy mission to ferret out journalistic clichés in all ways, shapes and forms, I have resolved with grim determination to compile a list of these offenses, which are anathema to all true believers in our craft. I invite you to hold your feet to the fire, keep your nose to the grindstone and go through your copy with a fine-tooth comb, excising badly splintered parties, stunning upsets, stern warnings, yawning deficits, rumbling tanks, rattling machine guns and other frequent offenders. **"**

Below are a few of the words and phrases that made Muller's list. This compilation is but the tip of the iceberg (to use yet another tired expression!). Some of these are certified clichés, while others threaten to become so. All of them need a rest:

at the end of the day
awesome ■ big break
brief stint ■ fast lane
force to be reckoned with
lifestyle ■ no easy answers
no laughing matter
not to worry ■ stay tuned
running on empty
up for grabs

LEARNING FROM THE EDITORS

DISCUSSION
1. What is a cliché? Think of a common example. Why do writers try to avoid them?
2. Analyze the memo from Henry Muller. List the clichés he uses. What do you think he was trying to impress upon his staff, and why did he choose this way to do it?

TRY IT OUT
The campaign against clichés. Write a memo modeled on Muller's, using a variety of clichés to dissuade classmates from using these worn-out terms in their own writing. Then rewrite the paragraph without using a single cliché.

HOW I WRITE
Look through your writing portfolio, your journal, or old papers. List any clichés you've used, and contribute them to a class cliché list. Do you see a pattern of repeated expressions? What phrases could you use as a substitute? Choose three sentences to rewrite.

Publishing and Presenting

Why I Write

Journalism is not just a job for TIME writers and editors. For many, it is a calling, the expression of their lifelong love of language and storytelling. Assistant Managing Editor Howard Chua-Eoan calls writing his passion; Senior Reporter Andrea Sachs describes journalism as "the best profession there is."

Howard Chua-Eoan:

❝The thing that I'm passionate about, and what I have always been passionate about, is writing. I love working with words. I like seeing what words can do and what words can convey. The journalism part is something that I fell in love with as I worked more and more with it. Journalism is about conveying what's out there in as vibrant, powerful, and yet as accurate a way as possible. The other side of writing, of course, is fiction and poetry and everything else. But in newswriting, you have the most powerful sort of structure of all: the truth. How do you convey that, how do you perceive that, and how do you make other people see that?❞

Andrea Sachs recalls why, working as a lawyer in Washington, D.C., she changed paths to become a journalist:

❝The day President Reagan was shot, I went down the street to George Washington University Hospital, and I watched the reporters work. There must have been 1000 people out there, and I got interviewed as a 'person on the street.' I watched television reporter Sam Donaldson do his report. My heart was pounding: 'This is what I want to do!' I knew it. I never questioned that, and I went back to journalism school. That's why I became a writer. It's the best profession there is. It's so exciting to be tapped into the news and to get paid for learning things. I've never been disappointed. I've been doing this for 15 years now, and I love it.❞

LEARNING FROM THE WRITERS

DISCUSSION

1. Do you agree with Chua-Eoan's definition of journalism? How would you define it? What does Andrea Sachs see as the benefits of being a journalist?

2. Chua-Eoan makes a distinction between journalism and "the other side of writing, fiction and poetry and everything else"—in other words, forms of imaginative writing. He claims journalists use the most powerful structure of all: the truth. Do you agree with his statement? Do you think novelists and poets would agree? Can novels, short stories, and poems be based on the truth or tell the truth?

TRY IT OUT

1. Identify a passion. Write a paragraph of your own using Howard Chua-Eoan's opening line: "The thing that I'm passionate about is…"

2. Recall a defining moment. Have you had an experience like that of Andrea Sachs in which you discovered "this is what I want to do"? Write about it. Is what you want to do linked to what you're passionate about?

"*A drowsy, dreamy influence seems to hang over the land.*"

—Washington Irving

The Legend of Sleepy Hollow

108

UNIT 3

Descriptive Writing

Writing in the Real World

In the following passage from *How the García Girls Lost Their Accents,* Alvarez describes the mother through the eyes of her young daughter Sandi.

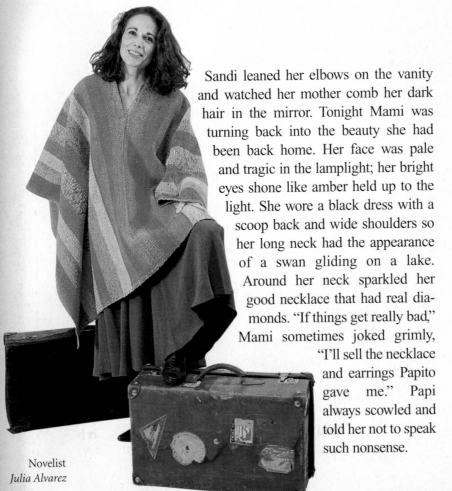

**From *How the García Girls Lost Their Accents*
by Julia Alvarez**

Sandi leaned her elbows on the vanity and watched her mother comb her dark hair in the mirror. Tonight Mami was turning back into the beauty she had been back home. Her face was pale and tragic in the lamplight; her bright eyes shone like amber held up to the light. She wore a black dress with a scoop back and wide shoulders so her long neck had the appearance of a swan gliding on a lake. Around her neck sparkled her good necklace that had real diamonds. "If things get really bad," Mami sometimes joked grimly, "I'll sell the necklace and earrings Papito gave me." Papi always scowled and told her not to speak such nonsense.

Novelist
Julia Alvarez

A Writer's Process

> *Entering the world of the imagination, that's a portable homeland. . . . I can take out my pad of paper in the Dominican Republic, here in Vermont, in California, in Turkey—and it's the same blank page. It's the same sense of creating a world, of making meaning, wherever you go.*
>
> —Julia Alvarez

Prewriting
Playing with Words

"Much of writing is playfulness with words. It's trying things out," Alvarez says. "You're not probably going to get it right the first time. So just let yourself get *some* of it right."

Learning to create vivid description takes time and practice for every writer. The writer must learn to notice the things of the world and to describe those things in fresh ways. To help herself do this, Alvarez plays a word game. In her journal she'll describe what she sees in daily life. She might look at the sheep grazing near her house and think of different images to describe them, such as powder puffs and cumulus clouds.

She explains the benefits of this practice: "What's great is that maybe two weeks down the line—maybe two years down the line—wouldn't you know it, but I'll have a character looking at a sheep farm!"

Drafting
Discovering Details

People often say that something important is "beyond words." Yet Julia Alvarez finds the words to describe complicated experiences and feelings. She does so by keeping things simple. "I think when somebody says that they can't describe something, they're trying for the big thing, instead of the little details that, of course, they can describe," she says.

Alvarez creates large effects with small details. She notices the intimate details that bring a reader close to a character or experience. The detail might be the feel of sun shining on top of a character's head. Or it might be the look of Mrs. García's neck while she is combing her hair. When writing the description of Mrs. García shown in the excerpt on page 110, Alvarez wanted to give a picture of what the mother looked like. Alvarez says, "I was trying to get a sense of the glamour and beauty of the mother, as seen from a little girl's eyes. I wanted to show that there was something beautiful and mysterious about the mother."

Revising
Seeing What Works

As Alvarez writes a draft, she often discovers new images and ideas. "That's part of the fun—when it all falls into place," she says. "You know I'll discover something, and then all of a sudden, I'll have to go back and redo the beginning."

Alvarez sometimes reads her work out loud after she writes a few sentences. If it doesn't sound right, she makes the necessary changes. In this way she does some revising as she goes along.

When she finishes a draft, she does more revising. She may add details to a description to make it more clear, precise, or interesting. Alvarez says, "As you revise and

revise, you happen upon things that you see are working. Then you polish them, or bring in new things to enhance them."

Sometimes Alvarez invites others to read her descriptions aloud. That makes it easier for her to hear what needs revising. "What you write gets coated with your voice," Alvarez explains. "Having somebody else read out loud to you, you hear all the places that it's really off, in a way you can't hear it when you're writing."

The revision process requires writers to think from their readers' point of view. Will readers understand what a character is feeling? Will they pick up on the mood or tone of a description? Alvarez revises her work until she is confident that her ideas have been communicated clearly to the readers. Sometimes, communicating ideas clearly requires many rewrites. Alvarez says, "I know it's a process! And that certain things that get you started in a description later have to go."

Examining Writing in the Real World

Analyzing the Media Connection

Discuss these questions about the excerpt on page 110.

1. Who is described in the passage? From whose point of view is the description narrated?

2. Is the mood of this description quiet and nostalgic or lively and spirited? What words and images help establish the mood?

3. A simile is a comparison using the word *like* or *as*. What simile does Alvarez use to describe Mami's eyes? Why is this image effective?

4. Why do you think Alvarez uses the image of a swan to describe Mami's appearance?

5. How can you tell that the diamond necklace is worth more to Mami and Papi than the jewels inside it?

Analyzing A Writer's Process

Discuss these questions about Julia Alvarez's writing process.

1. How does Alvarez's journal contribute to her descriptive writing?

2. What would Alvarez advise you to do if you were struggling with describing a breathtaking scene?

3. When does Alvarez read her work out loud? Why does she do this?

4. Why does she sometimes ask others to read her work aloud?

5. Do you agree with Alvarez that the process of revision can be fun? Why or why not?

Use adjective clauses to describe a noun or a pronoun.

An adjective clause often begins with a relative pronoun—*who, whom, whose, which,* or *that.*

> Around her neck sparkled her good necklace **that had real diamonds.**

Incorporate each adjective clause below into a sentence. Start by thinking of a noun or a pronoun for each to modify.

1. who was shouting
2. which had been lost
3. whose hands were like ice
4. that won the game
5. that they liked the best

See Lesson 14.3, page 509, and Lesson 21.3, page 633.

Writing Descriptions

A good description re-creates sights, sounds, and other impressions. Read the passage below, and share a hot summer night with Lorraine Hansberry.

Lorraine Hansberry recalls the sights, sounds, smells, and feelings from her Chicago childhood. The reader can hear doors slamming and can sniff freshly cut lemons in the steamy night air.

Literature Model

Evenings were spent mainly on the back porches where screen doors slammed in the darkness with those really very special summertime sounds. And, sometimes, when Chicago nights got too steamy, the whole family got into the car and went to the park and slept out in the open on blankets. Those were, of course, the best times of all because the grownups were invariably reminded of having been children in rural parts of the country and told the best stories then. And it was also cool and sweet to be on the grass and there was usually the scent of freshly cut lemons or melons in the air. And Daddy would lie on his back, as fathers must, and explain about how men thought the stars above us came to be and how far away they were.

Lorraine Hansberry, "On Summer"

Descriptive Writing

Observe Details

Descriptive writing often starts with a memory or an observation—something that catches your attention. The details that make someone or something stay in your mind become the raw material for creating a description. Notice how writer Nicholasa Mohr brings to life details about Puerto Rico through the observation of one of her characters.

Literature Model

She saw the morning mist settling like puffs of smoke scattered over the range of mountains that surrounded the entire countryside. Sharp mountainous peaks and curves covered with many shades of green foliage that changed constantly from light to dark, intense or soft tones, depending on the time of day and the direction of the rays of the brilliant tropical sun. Ah, the path, she smiled, following the road that led to her village. Lali inhaled the sweet and spicy fragrance of the flower gardens that sprinkled the countryside in abundance.

Nicholasa Mohr, *In Nueva York*

> What words does the writer use to help you see the changing mountains?

> Mohr draws you into her memories with a walk along the path.

Journal Writing

Think about how Nicholasa Mohr brings her village to life. List at least five words that the author uses to describe it. Then choose a memory of your own. Write at least five specific details.

Notice Descriptive Writing

Good descriptive writing involves using your senses to observe, selecting precise details, and organizing your ideas. You probably read descriptions more often than you realize. The chart below shows some examples of descriptive writing. In the model that follows the chart, Michael Lim describes an unusual fish.

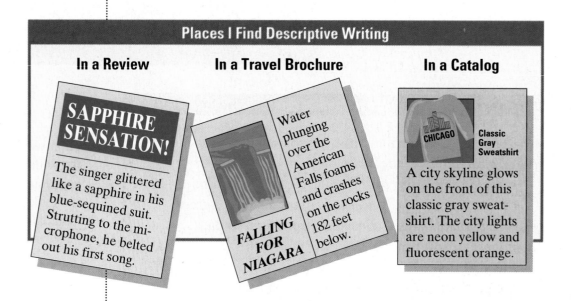

Places I Find Descriptive Writing

In a Review

SAPPHIRE SENSATION!

The singer glittered like a sapphire in his blue-sequined suit. Strutting to the microphone, he belted out his first song.

In a Travel Brochure

Water plunging over the American Falls foams and crashes on the rocks 182 feet below.

FALLING FOR NIAGARA

In a Catalog

CHICAGO   Classic Gray Sweatshirt

A city skyline glows on the front of this classic gray sweat-shirt. The city lights are neon yellow and fluorescent orange.

Student Model

The writer includes details such as the color and shape of the fish to help the reader see it.

At the bottom of the pool, in the very center, was a fish, lying quietly. . . . The fish was a blazing yellow with streaks of almost metallic blue running down its sides, resembling a slender torpedo in shape. It was at least several feet long, streamlined, its head and tail tapered down from its thicker body. The fish's fins and tail were the same blue as its streaks, only translucent.

Michael Lim
The American International School, Vienna, Austria
First appeared in *Merlyn's Pen*

Describe a Person

Picture in your mind a person with whom you enjoy spending time. List words or phrases that capture the person's appearance and personality. Use these details in a written description.

PURPOSE To describe a person by using details
AUDIENCE Yourself
LENGTH 1–2 paragraphs

WRITING RUBRICS To describe by using details, you should

- choose details that will bring life to your description
- use your senses to help you choose details

Artist unknown, Mughal, *Fantastic Birds*, c. 1590

Cross-Curricular Activity

ART Imagine you saw one of the birds in the painting on your way to school. Write to a friend and describe what you saw. Include as many precise details as possible about the bird to help your friend picture it.

Listening and Speaking

COOPERATIVE LEARNING Describe to a small group a favorite memory or special place. Make notes on what you will say and include several precise details. As you speak, change the loudness and tone of your voice to fit what you are saying. Use your voice to help bring your description to life for your listeners.

Grammar Link

Use vivid adjectives to describe people, places, and things.

Sharp mountainous peaks . . .

Complete each sentence below with one or two vivid adjectives.

1. They enjoyed the _____ dinner.
2. The _____ players left the arena.
3. It was late on a _____ summer evening.
4. She smiled when she heard the _____ music.
5. We neared the _____ mountains.

See Lesson 3.3, page 122, and Lesson 12.1, page 457.

Collecting Sensory Details

We use our sight, hearing, smell, touch, and taste to experience the world. These sensory details help bring a description to life.

Imagine that you've stepped into the painting below. What do you see, hear, feel, smell, and taste?

Thomas Hart Benton, *Cradling Wheat,* 1938

Use Sensory Detail

Artists use color, shape, and pattern to pull you into a painting. Writers do the same thing with sensory language—language that appeals to the senses. Sensory language describes how something looks, sounds, feels, smells, or tastes. In the following passage, Beverly Cleary takes us with her by engaging our senses.

These walks, with the sound of cowbells tinkling in the woods by the river, and bobwhites, like fat little hens, calling their names, filled me with joy as I searched for flowers whose names Mother taught me: shy kitten's ears with grayish white, soft-haired pointed petals which grew flat to the ground and which I stroked, pretending they really were kitten's ears; buttercups and Johnny-jump-ups to be gathered by the handful; stalks of fox-gloves with pink bell-shaped flowers which I picked and fitted over my fingers, pretending I was a fox wearing gloves; robin's eggs, speckled and shaped like a broken eggshell, which had such a strong odor Mother tactfully placed my bouquet in a mason jar on the back porch "so they will look pretty when Daddy comes in."

Beverly Cleary, *A Girl from Yamhill*

Before you take notes for a description, close your eyes and concentrate on the senses of taste, touch, hearing, and smell.

What words does Cleary use to appeal to different senses?

Descriptive Writing

Cleary, like all good writers, tries to engage her reader's senses when she writes a description. You can hear the tinkling cowbells and see grayish white kitten's ears. You can feel the velvet touch of petals and smell the nasty odor of robin's-eggs flowers. The writer takes you with her by telling exactly what she experienced.

Journal Writing

In your journal, list words and phrases describing a meal you remember: the food you ate and the people you were with. Use words and phrases from all five senses.

Use Observations to Write Descriptions

Writing a good description begins with careful observation. This first step may be difficult if you are not used to looking at things closely. The chart shows how you can move from observing details to writing descriptions. In the model Jessica Griffiths uses details she observed to describe a familiar day.

From Observing to Writing	
Impressions	**Description**
Relaxed smile **New (short) haircut**	Mr. Marshall greets students with a relaxed smile. His thick black hair, which was rather long last year, is clipped neatly above his ears.
Slamming lockers **Squeaky new shoes**	As the hallways fill with students, locker doors slam with a staccato beat. New shoes squeak as they skid across the freshly polished floor.
Shiny pencil sharpener **Smelly pencil shavings**	On the first day of school, the shiny pencil sharpener doesn't get a rest. It grinds pencils to a sharp point. The strong smell of shavings fills the air.

Student Model

What sounds of the first day of school does the writer describe?

The writer combines sounds and scents to create this description.

The first day of school is always exciting and a bit scary. Students greet old friends, and teachers chat in the hallways. The squeak of new shoes and the scuffling of sneakers on the linoleum floor mingle with the girls' giggling. Slamming lockers echo in the long corridors. The scent of bubble gum contrasts with the sharp smell of erasers and lead shavings. Pencil sharpeners grinding are a reminder that class has started. Late students hurry to their classrooms. A new school year has begun.

Jessica Griffiths, Springman Junior High School
Glenview, Illinois

Write a Description of a Walk

Think of a walk you take often. It could be down the hall of your school or through a park. List sensory details from your walk.

Use the details to write a paragraph describing your walk. Have a friend read and comment on your description. Take into account your friend's comments as you revise your writing.

PURPOSE To describe a familiar walk using sensory details

AUDIENCE A friend

LENGTH 1 paragraph

WRITING RUBRICS To use sensory details in a description, you should

- observe or recall the details of your experience
- take notes on what you see, hear, smell, touch, and taste
- use your notes to write your description

Listening and Speaking

COOPERATIVE LEARNING In a group, list names of characters from television or books. Select characters familiar to everyone in the group. List details that describe each character. Then choose a character to describe. Share your description and challenge the group to identify the character you described.

Viewing and Representing

Choose an advertisement from a magazine. The advertisement should picture an item that appeals to the senses, such as a pile of dried leaves or a freshly baked pizza. Write a one-para-graph description to go with the picture. Be sure to use sensory details. Share your description with a partner.

Grammar Link

Use apostrophes correctly in possessive nouns.

Use an apostrophe plus *s* to form the possessive of a singular noun and of a plural noun that does not end in *s*. Use an apostrophe alone to form the possessive of a plural noun that ends in *s*.

Some examples are *a **kitten's** paws, the **mice's** tails, the **girls'** friends.*

Write each sentence, using apostrophes where necessary.

1. The childrens tears were salty on their tongues.
2. The suns rays warmed my skin.
3. When Al opened the carton, both boys noses wrinkled in disgust.
4. Not a ripple disturbed the lakes placid surface.

See Lesson 20.7, page 611.

Using Precise Language

Precise language is exact language; it says what the writer means and creates an image in the reader's mind. On a poster for a lost dog, precise language gets results.

LOST
During Storm

Small dog, smooth coat.
Some black marks.
Funny-looking tail.
Please call 555-3454
if you see our dog.

Harry the beagle is
LOST

Mixed brown, black,
and white coat.
Pink nose
with small black marks.
All-black ears.
Tail bent slightly.
Please call 555-3454.

Choose Precise Nouns and Adjectives

A good description includes specific nouns and exact adjectives. A precise noun, *beagle* or *Harry*, is more informative than a general noun, *dog*. The adjectives *brown, black*, and *white* describe the dog's coat more precisely than the vague adjective *smooth*. The difference between a general and a precise description is like the difference between the dogs in the pictures on the next page. Notice the precise words that Sarah Burch used in the next model.

From General to Specific

Dog

Golden Retriever

Jake

Literature Model

As the sound of thunder rumbles through the foggy November rain, you sit next to the roaring fire in your cozy living room. Waiting patiently for the wicked storm to pass, you notice clouds of varying shapes and textures highlighted by zig-zags of lightning. Branches plunge to the ground as winds gust violently. Rain forms muddy puddles along the rutty driveway. The crackling birch in the fireplace and the constant glow of the embers comfort you throughout the ferocious storm.

Sarah Burch, Springman Junior High School
Glenview, Illinois

What adjectives does the writer use to contrast the scenes inside and outside the house?

Journal Writing

Imagine that you have lost an object that is important to you. Make a list of precise words that describe the lost object. Then use the words to write a notice asking for help in locating the object.

Before reading your finished writing aloud, use a dictionary to check the pronunciation of any words you are not sure how to pronounce.

Choose Precise Verbs and Adverbs

Just as precise nouns and adjectives help create a vivid description, precise verbs and adverbs energize descriptive writing. Your choice of words will depend on the impression you want to make. For example, you might decide on the verb *devour* or *gobble*, rather than *eat*, to describe the action of eating hungrily.

Notice how the writer concentrated on finding more precise verbs and more vivid adverbs as she revised her description of her guinea pig.

Find examples of precise, well-chosen adverbs.

Why does "whirls" create a clearer picture of Attila than "circles"?

"Stalks" is more exact than "walks."

Attila is a guinea pig with an attitude. From his tiny white ears to his short black legs, Attila wages war mercilessly. Mealtime is his battlefield. At dinnertime he fixes his beady eyes on me as he ~~eats~~ *devours* his well-prepared guinea pig salad. Then his plump, black-and-white body tenses. He waits impatiently for the main course. Attila ~~scratches angrily~~ *claws fiercely* at the cage. He ~~circles~~ *whirls* around the cage. All night long Attila ~~walks~~ *stalks* restlessly near his plate. The next morning the battle begins again.

Describe from an Animal's Point of View

Using precise words, write a description of an object from an animal's point of view. Choose your own topic or one of these: a canoe as it might seem to a whale; a pizza slice as it appears to an ant; a ball of yarn from the point of view of a cat playing with it.

PURPOSE To use precise words to create vivid and energetic descriptions

AUDIENCE Your classmates

LENGTH 1–2 paragraphs

WRITING RUBRICS To write a vivid description, you should

- use specific nouns and adjectives
- use precise verbs and adverbs

Listening and Speaking

COOPERATIVE LEARNING In a small group, revise a piece of writing found in a newspaper or magazine. One person in the group should list precise nouns. The second should list vivid adjectives. The third should list strong verbs. The fourth should list intense adverbs. The group should work together to complete the revision. Finally, one member of the group should make a final copy that includes all the changes and read the revised article aloud to the group.

Viewing and Representing

Make up a sales brochure—for clothing, hobbies, music, or another kind of product. Draw illustrations of your product or clip them from magazines. Arrange the pictures on paper that has been folded in thirds, like a letter. Then write two or three sentences of vivid, precise description beneath each illustration.

Grammar Link

Use vivid adverbs to describe verbs, adjectives, and other adverbs.

*Attila wages war **mercilessly**.*
*Attila claws **fiercely** at the cage.*

For each sentence below, list three different adverbs that could be used to complete it.

1. The horse trotted _____ around the paddock.
2. Jamila approached the foul line _____ tentatively.
3. Quentin searched _____ for his lost notebook.
4. The _____ graceful dancers moved to the beat of the music.
5. The car traveled _____ down the street.

See Lesson 3.3, page 122, and 12.5, page 465.

Using Spatial Order

A painter arranges details so that the viewer sees an ordered picture. A writer describes details so that the reader imagines a scene clearly.

The Flemish painter Jan Vermeer arranged the details in this image so that the viewer's eye moves from behind the artist to the scene he is painting. Writers, like painters, arrange the details of a scene in a certain order and for a particular reason.

Jan Vermeer, *Allegory of the Art of Painting*, c. 1665–1670

Order Details Logically

Writers can order details in several ways, depending on the point in space that seems a logical starting place. Details can be ordered from top to bottom, from near to far, or from left to right. When looking at a building, for example, you might first see a nearby detail such as a decorative door frame. Then, farther up the front of the building, you notice decorative stone faces above the windows. To describe this building, you could order these details from near to far.

Three Kinds of Spatial Order

Top to Bottom	Near to Far	Left to Right

Sometimes a scene lends itself to a particular kind of spatial order. Notice how Laurence Yep uses top-to-bottom spatial order to describe a Chinese playground.

Literature Model

In those days, it consisted of levels. The first level near the alley that became known as Hang Ah Alley was a volleyball and a tennis court. Down the steps was the next level with a sandbox (which was usually full of fleas), a small director's building, a Ping-Pong table, an area covered by tan bark that housed a slide, a set of bars, and a set of swings and other simple equipment.

Laurence Yep, *The Lost Garden*

Which words in the description identify the spatial order as top to bottom?

Journal Writing

Imagine that you are at a place you remember well. Choose one type of spatial order to describe the details of the place. In your journal write your description in that order.

Editing Tip

As you edit, punctuate prepositional phrases correctly. For more information see Lesson 20.2, page 601.

Link the Details

When you use spatial order, you must give your audience a way to picture the scene as you move from one detail to the next. Transition words, such as *under, to the right,* and *behind,* help to link details so that readers can follow the path you've created. Notice how transition words act as directional signposts in Sarah Fisher's description of a room and in the diagram based on her description.

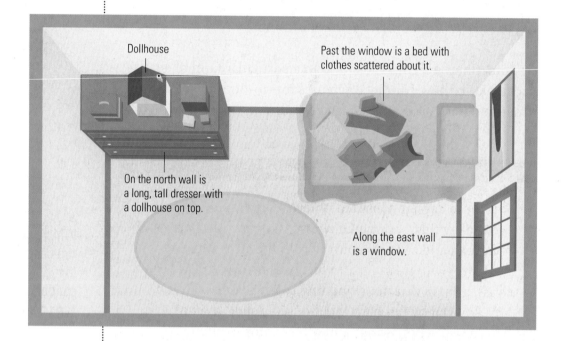

Dollhouse

Past the window is a bed with clothes scattered about it.

On the north wall is a long, tall dresser with a dollhouse on top.

Along the east wall is a window.

Student Model

Along the east wall is a window. Past the window is a bed with clothes scattered about it. On the north wall is a long, tall dresser with a dollhouse on top. To the right of the dollhouse are three jewelry boxes, one big and two small. To the left of the dollhouse is a purple box with a pink handle. This box holds my hair accessories and small gift boxes.

Sarah Fisher, Solomon Schechter Day School
Skokie, Illinois

Notice how Sarah uses phrases like "on the north wall" to help you find your way around the room.

Use Spatial Order

Use spatial order to write a one-paragraph description. Choose your own topic or one of these: a person's face from top to bottom or a ballpark from home plate to left field.

PURPOSE To describe, using spatial order
AUDIENCE Your teacher
LENGTH 1 paragraph

WRITING RUBRICS To describe using spatial order, you should

- decide how you will describe—from top to bottom, near to far, or left to right
- use transition words to help readers follow your spatial description

Carolyn Brady, *Sky Blue and Peach,* 1989

Cross-Curricular Activity

ART Write a one-paragraph description of Carolyn Brady's painting, using one kind of spatial order. Show your description to a friend, and ask if he or she can identify the type of order you've used.

Grammar Link

Use prepositional phrases in spatial descriptions.

> ***Down the steps*** *was the next level . . .*

Incorporate each prepositional phrase below into a sentence of spatial description.

1. through the swinging doors
2. across the street
3. between the two paintings
4. on top of the crates
5. against the opposite wall

See Lesson 13.1, page 481, and Lesson 21.1, page 629.

Listening and Speaking

Write a one-paragraph spatial description of a real or imagined place. Read your description to a partner. Your partner should sketch the place according to the details you have provided. Use the drawing to evaluate whether your description was precise. Then trade roles.

Describing a Thing

Describing a thing involves creating a clear image of that particular thing in the reader's mind. The reader can picture the object's size and shape; more importantly, the reader knows what makes it special.

A packed suitcase bulges before you. You're in a new place, about to unpack and start a new life. Your thoughts turn to the things you couldn't bring with you. You picture some of the treasures you left behind. How can you describe something that is important to you? In the student model below, notice how Amanda Morgan describes a well-loved bear.

Student Model

Teddy is no placid-looking bear. He is stubborn looking. He is very well loved (as bears often get), and he is beginning to come apart at the seams. Mom tried to fix this tragic problem by sewing him up with bright red-and-blue yarn. The yarn is faded and looking a bit tattered itself, for the surgery was done about nine years ago.

Amanda Morgan, Neskowin, Oregon
First appeared in *Treasures: Stories and Art by Students in Oregon*

Choose the Details

The process of writing a good description begins with choosing an object that has meaning for you. It may be right in front of your eyes, or it may be stored in your memory. Once you decide on your subject, note details that will help you describe it. If you're looking at the object, jot down the details you observe. If you're remembering something, list details that make it memorable for you.

Asking yourself questions can help you choose details. For example, you might ask how something appears at different times of the day, what senses you use to observe it, or to what you might compare it. The questions below, although linked to a specific object, may help you think of other questions you can ask yourself to remember descriptive details.

1. *How old is my bike?*
   My brother bought it new three years ago.
2. *What condition is it in?*
   worn but well cared for; cracked seat
3. *What color is my bike?*
   mostly metallic blue with gray tires
4. *What memories about my bike come to mind?*
   the first time I rode it down our street after moving here; riding in the rain with Chris

Journal Writing

Write three or four questions about the appearance of something that is important to you. Answer your questions in your journal, making sure to record specific details.

Organize the Details

As you list the important details that describe a thing, consider ways to group these details. The thing itself may suggest a certain kind of grouping. The chart below shows three principles you can use to group details.

Grouping Details by Different Principles	
Principle	**Examples**
Shape/Color	Baggy blue-gray sweater, ankle-length denim skirt
Appearance/Function	Porch chair, rusted and bent, but still comfortable
Whole/Parts	Broken checkerboard, a bag of dominoes

As you draft your description, use sensory details to bring your subject to life. Remember to use precise language, follow spatial order, and include transitions. Notice how Leslie Marmon Silko describes sandstone. She uses a *simile*—a comparison between two dissimilar things linked by the word *like* or *as*—while grouping her details around the color of sandstone.

Literature Model

But this time there was something about the colors of the sandstone. The reddish pink and orange yellow looked as if they had been taken from the center of the sky as the sun went down. She had never seen such intense color in sandstone. She had always remembered it being shades of pale yellow or peppered white—colors for walls and fences. But these rocks looked as if rain had just fallen on them.

Leslie Marmon Silko, "Private Property"

What precise adjectives does the writer use?

Write a Description of a Childhood Treasure

Think of something that was important to you in your childhood, such as a book or a stuffed animal. Write a description of it to share with a friend.

PURPOSE To write an effective description of an object
AUDIENCE A friend
LENGTH 1–2 paragraphs

WRITING RUBRICS To write an effective description, you should

- list details
- group the details in a logical order, such as by shape/color, appearance/function, or whole/parts

Cross-Curricular Activity

SOCIAL STUDIES One common childhood treasure is the teddy bear. How did teddy bears come to be? What president is the bear named after, and why? Find out the history of teddy bears. Write a paragraph and share your findings with the class.

Using Computers

Create two computer vocabulary files, one listing words that describe or name sensory details, the other listing transition words. In your file of sensory details, you might list adjectives that describe colors, shapes, textures, smells, and sizes. Refer to the lists as you draft a description.

Grammar Link

Be sure that each pronoun clearly refers to its antecedent.

The antecedent is the word or group of words to which a pronoun refers. A pronoun must agree with its antecedent in number and gender.

*But these **rocks** looked as if rain had just fallen on **them**.*

Complete the sentences below with appropriate pronouns.

1. When Sam's mother asked to see his report, ____ showed ____ to ____.

2. The principal posted the announcements so that we could read ____.

3. The students weren't expecting the fire drill buzzer, so ____ were startled when ____ heard ____.

4. Since my younger sister knows I'm good in math, ____ asked ____ to help ____ with the word problems.

5. Sarah said that ____ does not know who will be at the party.

See Lesson 11.1, page 435, and Lesson 11.2, page 437.

WRITING ABOUT LITERATURE

Describing the Subject of a Biography

In a biography a writer, or biographer, tells the true story of a person's life. In the following passage, Lisa Aldred creates a verbal snapshot of the young boy who would later become Supreme Court Justice Thurgood Marshall.

Literature Model

He "was a jolly boy who always had something to say." But, she added, Thurgood showed a serious side as well. "I can still see him coming down Division Street every Sunday afternoon about one o'clock," she said. "He'd be wearing knee pants with both hands dug way into his pockets and be kicking a stone in front of him as he crossed over to Dolphin Street to visit his grandparents at their big grocery store on the corner. He was in a deep study, that boy, and it was plain something was going on inside him."

Lisa Aldred, *Thurgood Marshall*

A biographer's purpose is to make the subject of the biography come to life on the page. In this model biographer Lisa Aldred uses the words of a family friend, Odell Payne, to give us a vivid glimpse of the serious side of young Thurgood Marshall—future Supreme Court Justice.

Form Strong Impressions

By telling what a person did and said, a biographer can bring the person to life on the pages. Descriptions of the subject's physical appearance and personality help the reader form impressions of the person. Here are some students' reactions to young Thurgood Marshall.

> The description of the boy reminds me of my cousin Wilma. She used to spend hours skipping stones at the pond. I once crept up behind her. She didn't even notice me. Like Thurgood, Wilma was always "in a deep study." Sometimes that annoyed me, though!

How is Thurgood like this student's cousin Wilma?

> I just read a book my grandfather should read. It tells about the early life of Thurgood Marshall, who was a Supreme Court justice. Grandfather's always telling me to pay attention. If he reads the book, he'll know I'm just "in a deep study."

This student has a good impression of Thurgood because he sees some of his own traits in the famous man.

Journal Writing

Describe someone you know well doing something he or she does often. Concentrate on using this action to illustrate your subject's personality.

Editing Tip

As you edit, be sure that you have correct subject-verb agreement in your sentences. For more information, see Lessons 16.1–16.5, pages 541–550.

Focus on the Subject

A good biography paints a portrait of the subject, including his or her appearance, personality, and attitudes. With precise language, sensory details, clear organization, and strong transitions, the subject of a biography comes into sharp focus. After reading Jean Fritz's *The Great Little Madison*, Andrea Gaines wrote the imaginary letter below. Notice how she uses details that paint a portrait of the young Madison.

Student Model

October 16, 1769

Dear Aunt Winnefred,

How are you?

Sorry I haven't written you lately, but I've been busy here at Princeton. This is only my first year here, but I feel as though I have a number of friends already. One of them is a quiet sophomore, James Madison. He's kind of short and thin, and has a very low voice. His handsome face glows with energy. He throws himself into everything he does, whether it's reading books, protesting British taxes, or joining student fun.

I must run to class. I'll write to you later about my other friends.

Your loving niece,
Susan

Andrea Gaines,
Martha M. Ruggles
Elementary School,
Chicago, Illinois

What details of Madison's appearance does Andrea provide?

What details of Madison's personality does Andrea point out?

Eighteenth-century Princeton University

Write a Descriptive Response

Respond to a biography about a political figure. You may use the excerpt from *Thurgood Marshall* or choose another biography that interests you. Think of creative ways to respond, as Andrea Gaines does on the previous page. Include your own description of the subject, as you see him or her.

PURPOSE To write a descriptive response
AUDIENCE Your teacher and classmates
LENGTH 2 paragraphs

WRITING RUBRICS To write a descriptive response, you should

- use vivid details and precise language to describe your impressions
- make sure your description brings the subject to life

Viewing and Representing

Locate images of the subject you have chosen for your response. View photographs, portraits, political cartoons, and even film footage, if available. What does each image show of the personality of your subject? List your reactions and discuss them with a partner.

Use quotation marks and other punctuation correctly in direct quotations.

"A painting, as well as a book, can be a biography," said the art teacher.

Write each sentence, adding quotation marks and other punctuation where necessary.

1. The student asked Did Joan Brown really swim to Alcatraz?
2. She tried said the teacher but she did not make it to the island.
3. A ship passed by her and the wake nearly caused her to drown explained the teacher.
4. The teacher explained She created a painting after she attempted to swim to the island.

See Lesson 20.6, page 609.

Using Computers

Using a software drawing program, create a graphic organizer, such as a web. Organize details about your subject in the graphic organizer. Add precise words that will help you describe. Then use your web to develop your descriptive response.

Writing Process in Action

WRITING Online

Visit the *Writer's Choice* Web site at **writerschoice. glencoe.com** for additional writing prompts.

Descriptive Writing

In preceding lessons you've learned about using memories and observations in descriptive writing. You've learned about sensory details, precise language, and order of details. You've written a variety of descriptions. Now, in this lesson, you'll have a chance to describe the people, places, and things that are part of something you enjoy doing.

Assignment

Context	You are writing an article for the magazine *Popular Hobbies.* This magazine contains descriptions of the people, places, and things associated with various student hobbies.
Purpose	To describe people, places, and things related to your favorite hobby
Audience	Student readers of *Popular Hobbies*
Length	1 page

The following pages can help you plan and write your descriptions. Read through them, and then refer to them as you need to. But don't be tied down by them. You're in charge of your own writing process.

Prewriting

Start by thinking about the people, places, and things that go with your favorite hobby. To explore your answers, you might use one or all the options at the right. Perhaps you'll observe and take notes, use your journal to recall details, or freewrite.

Option A

Observe and take notes on details.

Option B

Review your journal.

Option C

Explore your ideas through freewriting.

I zoom along the smooth path by the park. People picnic, play radios, and eat things like fried chicken. I remember my bike rides by the songs I hear and food that I smell.

Drafting

Look over your prewriting, and think about ways of organizing your material into clear images. You might start with the most important details or with the details closest to you. Just use the order that makes the most sense to you, and let the writing flow. Notice how David Weitzman sets the scene at an old-time

---

Literature Model

It was like the Fourth of July. Kids clambered up and slid down the hay stacks, played tag and skip-to-my-lou. Some of the men were pitching horseshoes and you could hear the thump of shoes fallen too short and the solid clank of a ringer. The women looked after all the little kids and put out lunches on big tables—heaps of potato salad, sandwiches, cakes and cookies, and frosty pitchers of iced tea.

David Weitzman, *Thrashin' Time*

Drafting Tip

For more information about using sensory details, see Lessons 3.1 and 3.2, pages 114–121.

harvest. A description rich in detail and sensory language can give your readers a clear picture of the world of your hobby.

Writing Process in Action

Revising Tip

Check that your description uses specific nouns and verbs and vivid modifiers. For more information, see Lesson 3.3, pages 122–125.

Revising

Begin by rereading the assignment. Have you written what's been asked for? As soon as you're satisfied that you have, you can move on.

Now it's time to look at your draft and make it better. But first put your draft aside for a day, if possible. During this time, you might go back and review pages 66–77.

To begin revising, read over your draft to make sure that what you have written fits your purpose and your audience. Then have a writing conference. Read your draft to a partner or small group. Use your audience's reactions to help you evaluate your work.

Look at the revision below and use questions like the ones shown to guide your own revisions. Remember, revising is where many great writers do their best work, so work with care.

Question A

Have I used all my senses?

Question B

Are my images crisp and clear?

Question C

Are my details specific and linked with transitions?

Biking by the park is a great hobby because of
all the picnics you *wiz* past. On weekends you
zoom *blasting* and smell the barbecues
can go by and hear radios. You pass by all the
on soft blankets
people sitting or throwing Frisbees. And
see
sometimes when you *sea* people you know, you
can stop and talk to them or share a glass of
sweet pink
lemonade. Alongside you all the sights, sounds,
and smells blur together.

Editing/Proofreading

Edit your description to correct any mistakes. Read it several times, using the questions in this checklist. Ask a different question each time through. For example, you might **proofread** for capitalization and punctuation on your first pass and spelling on your second pass. Afterward, have someone else review your work. Other people can often see your mistakes better than you can.

Publishing/Presenting

Make a clean copy of your description. If possible, use a computer or word processor to give your work a professional look. Now you are ready to send your work to *Popular Hobbies*. You may want to include a drawing or photograph to illustrate your description. Do not feel that you have to include an illustration, though. Even without a picture, your description should be detailed enough so that your readers should be able to imagine the people, places, and things related to the hobby you have chosen.

Editing/Proofreading Checklist

1. Have I correctly used apostrophes in possessive nouns?
2. Do my pronouns have clear antecedents?
3. Have I correctly punctuated quotations?
4. Have I spelled every word correctly?

Proofreading Tip

For proofreading symbols, see page 79. If you have composed on the computer, use the spelling and grammar checkers to help with proofreading.

Journal Writing

Reflect on your writing process experience. Answer these questions in your journal: What did you like best about your description? What was the hardest part of writing it? What did you learn in your writing conference? What new things have you learned as a writer?

Literature Model

Descriptive Writing

Thrashin' Time

by David Weitzman

In Thrashin' Time: Harvest Days in the Dakotas, *David Weitzman describes farm life in 1912 North Dakota through the eyes of young Peter Anders. As you read the following passage, pay special attention to the way Peter describes an autumn day when the whole neighborhood gathers to see a steam traction engine for the first time. Then try the activities in Linking Writing and Literature on page 148.*

Anna and I began pestering Pa to take us over to see the new engine. But it didn't take much doing. I could tell he wanted to go as much as we did. Pa glanced again at the smoke billowing into the sky. "Ya, sure, we can go. I'll finish up a bit here. Peter, you go hitch the horses up to the wagon. Maggie, if you and Anna put up a picnic, we'll go have us a look at that steam engine."

We got there to find that a lot of folks had come in wagons and buggies to gather 'round and watch the thrashin'.[1] Steam engines were still

---

1 **thrashin'** (thrash' ən) [or threshing (thresh'ing)] separating grain or seeds from a plant

new in these parts. And there it was, the engine with its dark blue boiler, shiny brass whistle, red wheels all decorated with yellow stripes, gears spinning and rods going back and forth, rocking gently in time to the puffs of smoke from the stack—*tucka-tucka-tucka-tucka-tucka.* The sounds, that's what I liked. *Tucka-tucka-tucka-tucka* and the little steam engine going *ss—ss—ss—ss—ss—ss—ss.* The engine was quieter than I thought it would be. It was almost alive like the horses working everywhere 'round it. And the horses. Why, I'll betcha there were sixty head, big horses—Belgians and Percherons[2]—coming and going that afternoon. Teams pulled bundle wagons heaped tall with sheaves of wheat in from the fields, pulled wagons of yellow grain away from the separator to the silo. Another team hauled the water wagon, and another wagon brought loads of cord wood to keep the engine running sunup to sundown.

It was like the Fourth of July. Kids clambered up and slid down the hay stacks, played tag and skip-to-my-lou. Some of the men were pitching horseshoes and you could hear the thump of shoes

David Weitzman, from *Thrashin' Time,* 1991

---

2 **Belgians** (Bel' jənz) **and Percherons** (Pur' chə ronz') large, powerful horses used to drag heavy loads

fallen too short and the solid clank of a ringer. The women looked after all the little kids and put out lunches on big tables—heaps of potato salad, sandwiches, cakes and cookies and frosty pitchers of iced tea. Dogs napped in the dark cool under the wagons, not paying any mind to the puppies tumbling all over them. The older boys stood around together, pretending they were chewing plugs of tobacco, hawking and spitting, like the thrashermen, only theirs wouldn't come brown. The men stood around the engine and the separator, puffing on their pipes, thumbs hooked under their suspenders. They inspected every part of that machine, pointing to this and that, looked up and down the belt stretching between the engine and the separator in a long figure eight. Most of them had never seen a steam traction engine before.

> **"** *You know, Peter, that's a wonderful thing, the steam engine. You're witnessin' the beginnin's of real scientific farmin'.* **"**

Some of the older folks didn't like the new machine. "The old ways is the best ways," one of them said, tug-

ging on his whiskers. "All this talk about steam engines is just a bunch of gibble-gabble," agreed another, "I'll stick to my oxen and horses." Others told of hearing all about engines exploding, killing and maiming[3] the thrashin' crews, of careless engineers starting fires that burned up the farmer's whole crop and his barn besides. "Horses live off the land," Mr. Bauer said, "and don't need wood or coal. No, nothin' but some hay and oats and we don't have to buy that! What's more they give you foals." He reached over and rubbed his hand down the neck of a stout gray Percheron mare hitched to a grain wagon. "All you get from steam engines is debt." Mr. Bjork agreed, "and what would we do for fertilizer? Steam engines don't make much manure, you know." Everyone laughed. "More trouble than they're worth. Why, last year Silas McGregor had to come borrow my oxen to pull his engine out of the mud. Wouldn't have one of those smoke-snortin' strawburners on my place," old Mr. Erstad scoffed, turning and waving away the scene.

---

3 **maiming** (mām' ing) causing an injury so as to cripple or cause the loss of some part of the body

Thomas Hart Benton, *July Hay,* 1943

But Mr. Torgrimson, now I could tell he was enjoying it. We were looking at the steam engine there up on the boiler, the connecting rod whizzing back and forth and the flywheel spinning so that the spokes were just a red blur. He was smiling and his eyes just twinkled. Then he pointed the stem of his pipe at the engine, squinted in a thoughtful way and rocked back and forth on his heels. "You know, Peter, that's a wonderful thing, the steam engine. You're witnessin' the beginnin's of real scientific farmin'." He couldn't take his eyes off that engine. "I read about a steam outfit—over Casselton way it was—that thrashed more than six thousand bushels in one day! Imagine that, six thousand bushels in just one day! Why you and your Ma and Pa all workin' together couldn't do more'n twenty or thirty in the same time."

Mr. Torgrimson was the one who told me all about bonanza farming, where a bunch of engines would start out together, side-by-side, before daybreak, each pulling a fourteen-bottom plow almost as wide as our house. "They go all day, Peter, breakin' up thousands of acres of prairie grasslands before they rest at night—some even have head lamps so they can just keep going all night. The holdin's are so big, young fellow,

that they go on 'n on for days like that 'fore they reach their line and turn 'round and plow back to where they started. Day after day, week after week they go up and back. Then they sowed all that land to wheat and thrashed one hundred and sixty-two thousand—here, I'll just write that number in the dust so you can see how big it is—162,000 bushels of wheat that season."

> ❝ *They go all day, Peter, breakin' up thousands of acres of prairie grasslands before they rest at night* ❞

I could tell Pa liked the engine too. He got up on the wagon and pitched bundles for a while, and then stood on the engine platform talking to the engineer, Mr. Parker. When he got down, he came over and put his hand on my shoulder, all the time looking at the engine, shaking his head like he couldn't believe his eyes. "Parker's got some machine there, by jippers, quite an outfit. What do you think about all this, Peter, steam power instead of horse power?"

I wasn't sure. "If the engine took the place of the horses, I think I'd miss Annie and Lulu and Quinn. Wouldn't you, Pa?"

"I would, but, you know, horse-power thrashin' is awful hard on them, son. Sure, I'd miss them, but we work them hard all year plowin' and diskin',[4] and seedin' and mowin'.

> *If the engine took the place of the horses, I think I'd miss Annie and Lulu and Quinn. Wouldn't you, Pa?*

Then just when they're so tuckered out, about to drop and needin' a good rest, we put them to thrashin'.

You and I both have seen too many good horses broken, seen them drop, die of the heat and tiredness right there in the traces. And for all their work we might get a hundred bushels, maybe two in a day. I don't know, Peter, maybe steam power is a better thing. I just don't know." Pa chuckled and his eyes got all crinkled and wrinkled with laugh lines the way they do. "I do know one thing though. If you asked the horses, I betcha they wouldn't be against this new steam power the way some folks 'round here are."

---

4 **diskin'** (disk´ən) breaking up soil with a disk-shaped tool

Linking Writing and Literature

Readers Respond to the Model

How does David Weitzman use descriptive writing to bring a different time to life?

Think about David Weitzman's descriptions as you answer these questions. Then read what other students liked about his descriptions.

1. What surprised you most about the steam engine that David Weitzman described? How does Weitzman's use of details add to your new image of the steam engine?

2. Did any details of his descriptions of the setting and the people who had come to see the steam engine stand out for you? Which ones?

3. How are the details organized in these descriptions? Can you think of another way they could have been organized?

What Students Say

❝I liked the scene in which the older people argued about the steam engine. They talked about the disadvantages of modern technology. Mr. Torgrimson was different, though. The invention thrilled him, and he thought about all the advantages of the invention.

I remember most clearly Mr. Torgrimson's talking with Peter about bonanza farming. He went on and on about how all that work could be done. He was my favorite character because he seemed more thoughtful.

I would end the story differently. I would have the father choose whether he wanted the steam engine or horses. ❞

Marinel A. Marty

❝The author gave a good, detailed look at the steam engine. I enjoyed reading different points of view about the steam engine. I also liked reading the thoughts and feelings of the narrator. ❞

Nitida Wongthipkongka

Reflecting on the Unit

Summarize what you have learned in this unit by answering the following questions.

1. How does descriptive writing begin?
2. How do sensory details improve descriptive writing?
3. What does describing an object involve?
4. What kind of language improves a description?
5. Why is clear spatial order important to descriptive writing?
6. How can a biographer bring a person to life?

 ## Adding to Your Portfolio

CHOOSE A SELECTION FOR YOUR PORTFOLIO Look over the writing you did for this unit. Choose a piece of writing for your portfolio. The writing you choose should show one or more of the following:

- personal memories or observations
- vivid word pictures
- sensory details that appeal to more than one of the five senses
- precise language
- details in a clear spatial order
- an effective choice of details

REFLECT ON YOUR CHOICE Attach a note to the piece you chose, explaining briefly why you chose it and what you learned from writing it.

SET GOALS How can you improve your writing? What skill will you focus on the next time you write?

Writing Across the Curriculum

MAKE A HISTORY CONNECTION Think about your favorite hobby, and imagine that you are living before electricity was used in homes. How would living then affect the people, places, or things that are part of your hobby? Would your hobby exist? If not, what hobby might you have instead? Write a paragraph explaining how you might have spent your time.

"You are the prettiest girl here,
will you dance . . .
and we are dancing. . . ."

Sandra Cisneros

Chanclas

Narrative Writing

Writing in the Real World

MEDIA
Monologue
Connection

A narrative is writing or speech that tells a story. Since history abounds with compelling stories about real people, it is fertile ground for narrative writing. Arthur Johnson is an interpreter of African American history for Colonial Williamsburg, a "village" that recreates life in the 1700s. Johnson attempts to take on the personality, mannerisms, and character of the historical figure he portrays—Matthew Ashby.

Matthew Ashby of Colonial Williamsburg, Monologue performed by Arthur Johnson

"I'll never forget when I got married. For me it was a great, great day. You see, that night the preacher had come around. His name was Gowan. It seemed like all of my friends were around, such as Adam, who gave me a bucket.

"Gowan said a few words to Ann and me. And it seemed like when he told us to jump over that broom—and we jumped—Ann let me jump the farthest, to let me know that she would be with me no matter what."

History interpreter
Arthur Johnson

A Writer's Process

Prewriting
Researching Matthew Ashby

Many narrative writers invent the characters in their stories, so they need only consult their imaginations before beginning to write. Arthur Johnson, however, was writing about a historical figure. Before he could write his narrative, he needed to unearth facts and events of Matthew Ashby's life.

Johnson learned that Matthew Ashby was one of the African Americans who made up half of Williamsburg's population in the 1700s. He was a carter by trade, which meant he transported goods by cart or wagon. "Ashby was born free sometime in the 1720s," Johnson says. "As a teenager, he worked with a slave by the name of Joe, who took care of horses and carted his master's property. Ashby learned his work from Joe."

Johnson also learned that Matthew Ashby met his wife, Ann, when she was a slave. The couple married in 1762. The marriage ceremony involved the tradition of jumping over a broom (see the opening excerpt). After his marriage, Ashby worked hard as a carter, earned a good reputation in Williamsburg, and won freedom for Ann and his two children in 1769.

How did Johnson uncover these facts about Matthew Ashby? Johnson studied historical records that had survived the Revolutionary War. Ashby's will, for example, listed his belongings, including carpenter's tools, a harness for two horses, and a cart. As Johnson read these documents, he took careful notes that would become part of his presentation.

Drafting
Creating the Character

While more was known about Matthew Ashby than about most free African Americans of the 1700s, the historical records were far from complete. How did Johnson flesh out Matthew Ashby's character? He built on the information he found. For example, historians know that a free-black community once existed outside Williamsburg, so Johnson felt safe assuming that Matthew Ashby and his family had lived there. "With a skeleton of facts, we can add meat to a character, based on what we know about the period," Johnson explains.

Like any narrative writer, Johnson needed to find ways

Arthur Johnson prepares for his role as Matthew Ashby. ▼

Narrative Writing

to make his character believable. Johnson realized that one of Ashby's strengths was perseverance. "I feel I can relate to Matthew Ashby because Ashby would be a survivor whether he was in the eighteenth century or the twentieth century," Johnson says.

Day by day, Johnson developed his narrative. Since he would be enacting the role of Ashby for an audience, a lot of his preparation involved speaking practice. Working in front of a mirror, Johnson practiced speaking with words and mannerisms that he thought Matthew Ashby might have used. Later, Johnson rehearsed the narrative in front of his wife. She listened, commented, and encouraged Johnson. Finally, Johnson was confident that he had developed an accurate, realistic monologue for his character.

In character as Ashby, Johnson performs Ashby's daily tasks as a carter. ▼

Revising/Editing
Keeping in Character

Narrative writers need to maintain their characters' point of view. Johnson reviewed his monologue to make sure he was staying "in character." During a performance, Johnson always thinks of what Ashby would do or say. "Matthew wouldn't say a word like *cool*," for example, Johnson explains. Nor would Ashby recognize modern electronic items. What does Johnson do if a visitor asks to take his picture? "In the eighteenth century there were no cameras," Johnson explains. "So Matthew would say, 'Sir, I don't know what you're talking about. And whatever that is you're holding up to your eye, please, you might want to take it down.'"

Publishing/Presenting
The Narrative Is Shared

As carriages slowly creak past old brick buildings at Colonial Williamsburg, visitors come upon Johnson spinning the story of Matthew Ashby. To draw an audience, the six-foot, five-inch bearded giant in colonial work clothes calls to visitors strolling by. "Good day! . . .We need some help on the wagon. . . ."

He might also say, "I'm getting some runners and putting them up and getting these barrels on the cart here. You see, Mr. Prentis has given me some credit for taking these barrels and boxes down to Queen Anne's Port. That's what I do. I'm a carter, a carter by trade. I take anything, anywhere, anytime."

When his work is done, the character of Ashby relaxes and takes questions from the audience. Johnson answers as completely as he can. He uses his narrative to give visitors to Colonial Williamsburg a valuable glimpse into one facet of America's past.

Examining Writing in the Real World

Analyzing the Media Connection

Discuss these questions about the excerpt on page 152.

1. What is the main impression Johnson wants visitors to take away from his narrative? Do you think he accomplishes his aim? Why or why not?
2. What historical details does Johnson use to make his narrative authentic?
3. How does Arthur Johnson help visitors become engaged with Matthew Ashby's life?
4. Why do you think Johnson mentions specific names, such as "Gowan," "Adam," and "Ann"?
5. Why do you think Arthur Johnson selected Matthew Ashby as the subject of his narrative?

Analyzing a Writer's Process

Discuss these questions about Arthur Johnson's writing process.

1. What historical documents did Johnson research as he was interpreting Matthew Ashby's life and character?
2. After researching historical documents, how did Johnson further round out Ashby's character?

3. Who helped Johnson refine his narrative and performance? Why might it be helpful to have someone edit your writing?
4. Why is it so important for Johnson to stay in the character of Ashby when performing for visitors to Colonial Williamsburg?
5. What lessons does Johnson teach as he presents his narrative?

Grammar Link

Use an appositive to identify a noun. Use commas to set off an appositive that adds nonessential information to a sentence.

Arthur Johnson, **an interpreter of African American history at Colonial Williamsburg,** *makes the past come alive.*

Use an appositive to combine the following pairs of sentences.

1. Matthew Ashby was a free African American. He worked in Colonial Williamsburg.
2. Ashby learned his trade from Joe. Joe was a local carter.
3. Ashby was employed at Prentis & Company. It was a Williamsburg business.
4. He married his wife in 1762. Her name was Ann.

See Lesson 9.6, pages 391-392.

Writing the Stories of History

Jacob Lawrence, *Frederick Douglass Series, No. 21, The Fugitive,* 1938–1939

A narrative is a story or account of an event. A historical narrative is a story about people and events in history.

In any time period you can find exciting stories of real people who changed the world. The 1800s, for example, gave us the great antislavery fighter Frederick Douglass. Like a story, Jacob Lawrence's painting presents one event in Douglass's life. A person, a place, an event—the basic elements of a story are all here.

Find Your Inspiration

Some writers get their ideas for historical narrative from an event; others, from a person. Writer Victoria Ortiz was inspired by a woman from the 1800s. Ortiz was a civil rights worker in Mississippi when she became interested in Sojourner Truth. In the biography she wrote, Ortiz tells how Sojourner spoke strongly for the abolition of slavery and for women's rights. An uneducated former slave, Sojourner lectured with wit and power. On the next page is a paragraph from Victoria Ortiz's book. Read it to see how she showed the character of Sojourner Truth.

Literature Model

One of the first times Sojourner was present at a Woman's Rights Convention was in October, 1850, in Worcester, Massachusetts. As she later retold the experience to Harriet Beecher Stowe, Sojourner sat for a long time listening to Frederick Douglass, Lucy Stone, Wendell Phillips, William Lloyd Garrison, and Ernestine Rose speak about women's rights. She soon became intrigued, and when called upon to speak she presented her position quite concisely: "Sisters, I aren't clear what you be after. If women want any rights more than they got, why don't they just take them and not be talking about it?" For Sojourner, it was obvious that action was more effective than words.

Victoria Ortiz, *Sojourner Truth: A Self-Made Woman*

Note that Sojourner Truth was a real person involved in a real event in history.

Why do you think some of the same people were advocates of both abolition and women's rights?

To find a topic for a historical narrative, think about people, places, times, and events in history that interest you. A person, a setting, an event—any one of these can spark an idea for a historical narrative.

Once you have an idea, explore and narrow it. Focusing on one point allows you to explore a topic in depth. For example, if you decide to write about a person, you may need to narrow your topic to a single event in his or her life. It is the details, such as Sojourner's statement on women's rights, that bring history to life.

Activist Sojourner Truth

Journal Writing

Create a chart entitled Story Ideas from History. Make three columns, headed Person, Event, and Setting. Skim your history textbook for ideas for historical narratives. List each idea under the appropriate heading.

Hook Your Readers

Realistic details are especially important in writing about a historical event. Often writers uncover valuable details through research. Sometimes, however, a writer also needs to make up likely details to keep a narrative realistic and exciting. When you're ready to draft your historical narrative, you can use realistic details in your introduction to interest your reader immediately.

A good introduction often presents a person, a setting, and an event. One writer chose the persons and event below for a historical narrative. Read the paragraph that introduces the narrative, and think about the question in the box.

What question does this introduction raise? How does this question make readers want to keep on reading?

It's a bright August morning in 1962. Many of the major grape growers of southern California have come to Delano City Hall to hear a man named Cesar Chávez. He has come to talk with the people who have the power to improve the lives of his followers. The outcome will have a serious effect on the farm workers' future.

Introducing a Historical Narrative	
Persons	Cesar Chávez, the grape growers
Event	A meeting to discuss the problems of farm workers
Setting	A bright August morning in 1962 at the City Hall in Delano, California

Write an Introduction

Consult the Story Ideas from History chart in your journal, and plan a historical narrative for younger students to read.

PURPOSE To introduce a historical narrative
AUDIENCE Fifth-grade students
LENGTH 1–2 paragraphs

WRITING RUBRICS To write an effective introduction for a historical narrative, you should

- make prewriting notes based on your chart
- use specific details about the person or setting to get your readers' attention
- write legibly in cursive or print for your young readers

Cross-Curricular Activity

HISTORY In a group, brainstorm historical periods that have exciting stories. Pick a historical period, and brainstorm story ideas. Each member should list persons, settings, and events, including problems the persons faced. Each member should then write a narrative introduction to the event, trying to create interest and excitement.

Listening and Speaking

COOPERATIVE LEARNING In your group, read your introduction aloud, using your voice to make your introduction dramatic. Compare and contrast the introductions written by group members. Use feedback from the group to make your introduction more effective.

Use complete sentences for clarity.

Your notes for a historical piece will often be in the form of sentence fragments, but use complete sentences in your narrative.

For Sojourner, it was obvious that action was more effective than words.

Revise the fragments below into paragraphs about scientist Robert Goddard. Use complete sentences.

1. As boy, read H. G. Wells, dreamed of space flight.
2. Wrote article on rocketry in 1919—largely ignored.
3. Launched first liquid propellant rocket in 1926—tiny.
4. Flight of two and a half seconds.
5. Vision of lunar landing ridiculed.
6. When real lunar landing—gained wider recognition.
7. Also predicted orbiting space station and probe to Mars.
8. Goddard ahead of time.
9. Speculated about journeys to distant solar systems.
10. Some day true?

See Lesson 8.2, page 361.

Using Chronological Order

Any story makes better sense if the writer thinks about time order, or chronology. A story is in chronological order when the events are presented in the time order in which they occurred.

Movies, television, and videotapes allow us to tell stories in words and images. Suppose you use pictures alone or pictures with words to tell a story—in a comic strip, a slide series, a videotape, or even a photo album. In what order would you arrange your pictures to tell a story?

Choose a Time Frame

When you write a narrative, you have to decide on a time frame—when your story will begin and end. The chart on the next page shows that time spans for narratives vary widely. Some narratives cover decades, even centuries. A short narrative may cover days, hours, or even minutes.

In *Homesick: My Own Story,* Jean Fritz tells about her childhood in China and her teen years in the United States. Fritz presents realistic pictures of life in China and America in the early 1900s. The following excerpt tells about a time just before Fritz began eighth grade in her first American school. As you read it, notice how she relates some of one day's events in chronological order. What details suggest that the setting is long ago?

Literature Model

The next day Aunt Margaret took me to Caldwell's store on Main Street and bought me a red-and-black-plaid gingham [cotton] dress with a white collar and narrow black patent leather belt that went around my hips. She took me to a beauty parlor and I had my hair shingled [a close-cut style].

When I got home, I tried on my dress. "How do I look?" I asked my grandmother.

"As if you'd just stepped out of a bandbox [a box for hats and collars; means 'perfectly groomed']."

I wasn't sure that was the look I was aiming for. "But do I look like a regular eighth grader?"

"As regular as they come," she assured me.

Jean Fritz, *Homesick: My Own Story*

> What words used here would not be used today in describing a well-dressed eighth grader?

Time Spans for Historical Narratives

A Day

One Lifetime

Two Centuries

Journal Writing

Freewrite about two time periods, one that covers one recent day and one that covers two days. Include details and events that you would include in a narrative.

Make Time Order Clear

Ben Aylesworth researched the history of Wheaton, Illinois, a city near his home. He visited the Wheaton History Center and the Wheaton Public Library, where he read about his topic. He also interviewed his grandmother. Finally, Ben decided to focus on one event in the city's history and to relate the stages of that event in chronological order.

As he drafted, Ben used good transitions, such as *later* and *afterward,* to clarify the order of events. In writing a narrative, vary your transitions. If you always use *first, next,* and *finally,* your writing may sound dull. Find the transitions in the model below.

Lester Schrader, *Theft of the Records,* mid- to late-nineteenth century

Student Model

How would you feel if citizens of a rival town stole your town's records, forever changing its history? In 1838 Naperville held the county records of the new DuPage County. Naperville and nearby Wheaton were fierce rivals. Both wanted the county seat. In an 1867 referendum Wheaton narrowly won the county seat, but the records stayed in Naperville.

Late one night that year, some young Wheaton men broke into the Naperville courthouse and stole the county records. An alarm sounded, and they dropped some of the papers. Later, fearing another raid, Naperville officials moved the remaining records to Chicago for safekeeping. But these were destroyed in the Great Chicago Fire of 1871. Wheaton has been the county seat ever since that famous midnight raid.

Ben Aylesworth, Hadley Junior High School,
Glen Ellyn, Illinois

What transitions does Ben use to make the chronological order clear?

Write a Narrative

A future historian will want to know about special events in your school and community. Plan and write a narrative about one annual event, such as a concert, a game or tournament, or a holiday parade and picnic.

PURPOSE To narrate the story of a school or community event

AUDIENCE Future historians

LENGTH 1–2 paragraphs

WRITING RUBRICS To write an effective narrative, you should

- choose an event, and list its stages
- arrange the stages in chronological order
- in drafting and revising, use appropriate transitions
- use appropriate verb forms

Cross-Curricular Activity

HISTORY In a small group, brainstorm to discover what you all know about the history of your town or city. Choose one important event from that history and work together to write a narrative of that event. Arrange the details, or stages, of that event in chronological order. Include transitions to make the order of the events clear.

Grammar Link

Use the correct verb—singular or plural—when the subject is an indefinite pronoun.

Some indefinite pronouns (like *one* and *each*) are singular and require a singular verb. Some (like *both* and *many*) are plural and take a plural verb.

   Both want the county seat.

Choose the correct verb to complete each sentence.

1. Many of the families (has, have) lived in Park Cities for several generations.
2. Everyone in the community (knows, know) the brilliantly lit pecan tree on Armstrong Parkway.
3. Each of the other old pecan trees in Park Cities (was, were) damaged or destroyed by an ice storm in 1965.
4. Only one of the trees (was, were) left standing.
5. Ever since, few in the town of Park Cities (has, have) taken pecan trees for granted.

See Lesson 16.4, page 547.

Viewing and Representing

CREATING A COMMUNITY COLLAGE Use your town library and other local sources to find pictures of the historical event you wrote about. Arrange copies of the pictures into a collage.

Establishing Point of View

In narratives the point of view is important. Some stories are told by a main character in the first person—using "I" or "we." Others are told by an observer in the third person—using "he," "she," or "they."

In the story below, Justin Hoest speaks in the voice of a fictional grandfather in the early 2000s, telling his grandson about the 1960s civil rights movement.

Student Model

Let me start in the beginning. I was born in Birmingham, Alabama, in 1952. Back then, in southern states, it was segregated. There were separate water fountains, waiting rooms, stores, schools. Everywhere, some people were trying to keep segregation, and others were trying to stop it. The times were troubled.

Martin Luther King Jr. came to Birmingham when I was ten. I met him some years later during the Selma marches. He helped organize demonstrations. There were sit-ins like in Nashville, and adults would picket up and down the streets. We'd go to the meeting house in the evening. We would sing all night, or so it seemed. Everyone would dress in nice clothes, and the church smelled so good with the fresh candles burning.

> Note that although the story is fictional, it is set in a real time and place.

Song filled the place:

> I'm so glad; I'm fightin' for my rights;
> I'm so glad; I'm fightin' for my rights;
> Glory, Hallelujah!

Finally my day came. We were clapping and singing. Some of us were carrying signs. The day was bright, but there was a menacing dark cloud lingering in the sky. We weren't scared, only nervous. Our feet on the hard pavement made a sound that represented the whole movement.

Justin Hoest, Maplewood Middle School,
Menasha, Wisconsin

Why do you think Justin chose to have the grandfather tell his own story?

Presenting Tip

When you present your narrative, you can accompany your writing with photos or recordings.

Use the First Person

In telling his story, Justin has chosen a first-person point of view. That is, he lets the grandfather tell the story using the pronouns *I* and *me*. First-person narratives describe just what the narrator witnesses and thinks. The reader sees all the events through the narrator's eyes and views them as the narrator views them.

A reporter is getting a first-person account of the game.

Journal Writing

Make column headings that name three important events in American history. In ten minutes create as many fictional characters as you can think of under each heading. They may be participants, like the grandfather, or just observers.

Grammar Editing Tip

In editing your narrative, check to make sure you've used subject and object pronouns correctly. For more on using pronouns, see page 439.

Try the Third Person

Many short stories and other narratives are told from the third-person point of view. That is, the author uses the pronouns *he, she, it,* and *they*. In the following narrative poem, the poet uses the pronoun *she* because the main characters are the Island Queen and her daughter. From what you know about the history of the American Revolution, you may be able to figure out who these characters are.

Literature Model

There was an old lady lived over the sea
And she was an Island Queen.
Her daughter lived off in a new country,
With an ocean of water between;
The old lady's pockets were full of gold
But never contented was she,
So she called on her daughter to pay her a tax
Of three pence a pound on her tea.

The tea was conveyed to the daughter's door,
All down by the ocean's side;
And the bouncing girl pour'd out every pound
In the dark and boiling tide;
And then she called out to the Island Queen,
"O mother, dear mother," quoth she,
"Your tea you may have when 'tis steep'd enough
But never a tax from me."

Traditional

What point of view would you choose for a narrative? You may write a short story, an imaginary journal or letter, a song, or a narrative poem from the first-person point of view. The main character is then the *I* of the story. Or you may write it from the third person point of view. The main character will be *he* or *she*. Most writers decide on their point of view in prewriting. Then they use their imaginations to bring their narratives to life.

Formats

Journal

Ballad

Letters

Write a Narrative Paragraph

Choose one of the fictional characters you created in your journal entry for this lesson. Write a narrative paragraph from the point of view of that character. Describe the historical event the character observed or took part in. Don't identify yourself specifically in the writing. See if your classmates can tell exactly what event you are describing and how your character related to the event.

PURPOSE   To use the first-person point of view
AUDIENCE   Classmates
LENGTH   1 paragraph

WRITING RUBRICS   To write an effective first-person narrative paragraph, you should

- use first-person pronouns correctly
- make clear your character's relationship to the event
- use specific details from the event
- proofread to make sure pronouns and verb tenses are consistent and correct

Viewing and Representing

ILLUSTRATING HISTORY   Create a poster to illustrate the historical event you have written about. The poster should project the viewpoint of the character you have created. In a small group, share your posters and see whether you can connect the posters with the written narratives.

Using Computers

To enhance your understanding of the historical event you have chosen, use the Internet to learn more about the event. In addition to general facts and information, look for details that your character might use in his or her narrative—details about the event that are not common knowledge.

Grammar Link

Make subjects and verbs agree in sentences beginning with *there*.

*There **was** an old lady. . . .*
*There **were** sit-ins. . . .*

Complete each sentence below with the correct verb: *was* or *were*.

[1]There _____ more than four thousand people killed in a 1995 earthquake in Kobe, Japan. [2]There _____ also massive property damage. [3]There _____ little looting, though goods lay everywhere. [4]There _____ many people who helped care for others.

See Lesson 16.1, page 541.

Writing Realistic Dialogue

Dialogue can make a story come to life—or fall flat on its face.

Study the picture below. What do you think the two figures might be saying? How do you think they might be saying it? Jot down your ideas.

Anthony Ortega, *Two Little Old Men*, 1984

Now read two openers that were written for a story. Which one would be more likely to catch your interest? Why?

Jenny said she saw Joseph walking home.

Jenny burst in shouting, "Hey, everybody, Joseph's come home!"

Let Characters Speak for Themselves

Dialogue—direct quotations of spoken words or conversations—is a way of revealing character. What does the following conversation reveal about Hideyo and his mother?

Literature Model

Mother opened her mouth and could not close it for several seconds.

"Most of my classmates have enlisted," said Hideyo, serious for once. "I have decided to go to help our country."

"You cannot go, Hideyo!" Mother told him. "You must talk with Father. You just cannot make such a decision alone."

"Mother, I have already sent in my application," said Hideyo. "I will take the written and physical examinations!"

"How could you?" Mother moaned. "Why didn't you tell me?"

"I am eighteen. Big enough to make my own decision."

Yoko Kawashima Watkins, *So Far from the Bamboo Grove*

> The mother's words tell you she loves her son and fears for his life.

> What does the dialogue reveal about Hideyo?

Letting characters speak for themselves is easy when you write about someone you know well. Ask yourself, "What would this person say here?" After you draft some dialogue, it helps to put it aside for a day or so. Then, when you reread it, you can ask yourself if it sounds authentic. If it does not, see how to improve it.

Grammar Editing Tip

As you edit your dialogue, check your punctuation, capitalization, and paragraphing. For more about writing dialogue, see Lesson 20.6, page 609.

Journal Writing

Listen to the speech of others, and jot down bits of conversation you hear. Next to each quotation identify the speaker—a bus driver, for instance, or a relative.

Make Conversation

Your dialogue will sound natural if your characters talk the way real people do. Below is a natural-sounding dialogue between a brother and sister. What did the writer do to make this conversation sound realistic?

> "I can too run!" Antonio glared at her, arms locked stubbornly over his chest.
>
> "I didn't say you can't run, 'Tonio," Gina retorted. "I just said I can run faster than you!"
>
> "Yeah, well, I can run farther!"
>
> Gina rolled her eyes. "In your dreams, <u>fratello</u>!" she crowed. "You can't even run without tripping on something!"
>
> "Can too!"
>
> "Think about it, 'Tonio! Remember last year's Fourth of July picnic? Who wanted to run barefoot and then stepped on a wasp four seconds into the race? Not me!" Gina roared.

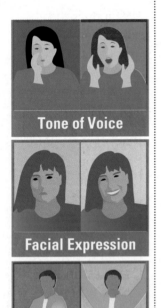

Tone of Voice

Facial Expression

Body Language

Did you notice the slang, sentence fragments, contractions, and descriptions of facial expressions and body language? Without these, the conversation would sound stiff and unnatural. Suppose the writer had Gina say this: "I am sorry, but you are badly mistaken, brother. You cannot run without falling down." Even Gina's use of the Italian term *fratello*, which means "brother," adds interest.

Write a Dialogue

What's happening in the painting on this page? Where is the man? What is he doing there? Write a dialogue between two students trying to make sense of the picture.

PURPOSE To create a realistic dialogue
AUDIENCE Your teacher and classmates
LENGTH 1–2 short paragraphs

WRITING RUBRICS To write an effective dialogue, you should

- list some words or phrases you might use to react to the painting
- make your dialogue sound natural
- punctuate and indent correctly

Hughie Lee-Smith, *Man Standing on His Head*, 1969

Using Computers

Use a computer to prepare scripts. Your word-processing program allows you to indent actors' parts so that each character's name is clearly visible in the left margin.

Listening and Speaking

COOPERATIVE LEARNING In a small group, present oral readings of your dialogue. Discuss the similarities and differences in the opinions and interpretations of the characters you and your group members created.

Grammar Link

In dialogue, use quotation marks and other punctuation correctly.

"Most of my classmates are going," said Hideyo. . . .

"You cannot go, Hideyo!" Mother told him.

Write each sentence below, using quotation marks and other punctuation where necessary.

1. You're not leaving this house in that outfit Mrs. Curphy announced.
2. But Mom! All the kids are wearing pants like these Patty whined.
3. I don't care what the other kids are doing, Mrs. Curphy declared.
4. Mom! Patty moaned.
5. No daughter of mine is leaving my house looking that way, said Mrs. Curphy, and that's final.

See Lesson 20.6, page 609.

LESSON 4.5

Relating a Historical Event

Andō Hiroshige, *The Wave*, c. 1850

Hannah Wilson read as much as she could find about Japanese immigrants of the 1920s. Then she created a character, gave her a problem, and let her tell her story.

Read this excerpt from Wilson's story. See what the point of view tells you about the character.

Student Model

Mamma—I wish she were here now. I still miss her so much. I wish with all my heart she could be here to see this baby born. I remember how comforting she always was. I need that comfort now. Every day seems the same to me. Up at dawn, fix breakfast for Seiji and myself, off to work in the fields all day while Seiji goes fishing, hardly stopping to eat. The lonely nights when Seiji must stay on the fishing boats all night.

I love America and Seiji, and I want a baby so much, but I miss Mamma and Papa and Sachiko and Akiko.

Hannah Wilson, Newton Elementary School,
Strafford, Vermont

> What can you tell about the person whose voice you hear in this narrative?

Create a Character

If you, like Hannah Wilson, chose immigration as the subject for your narrative, your next step would be investigation. You might begin by reading immigration stories, jotting down details about ordinary people's lives. Then you might think of a character and imagine problems the character could face.

Can you see the germ of one or more story ideas in these prewriting notes?

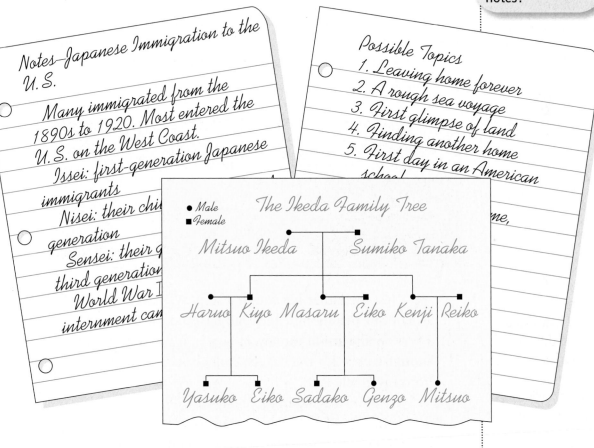

Notes—Japanese Immigration to the U.S.

Many immigrated from the 1890s to 1920. Most entered the U.S. on the West Coast.
Issei: first-generation Japanese immigrants
Nisei: their chi[ldren] generation
Sensei: their g[rand] third generation
World War I[I] internment ca[mps]

Possible Topics
1. Leaving home forever
2. A rough sea voyage
3. First glimpse of land
4. Finding another home
5. First day in an American school

The Ikeda Family Tree
● Male
■ Female

Mitsuo Ikeda   Sumiko Tanaka

Haruo Kiyo Masaru Eiko Kenji Reiko

Yasuko Eiko Sadako Genzo Mitsuo

Journal Writing

Talk to a friend or family member about an immigration experience. Create a fictional character in the same time and place, and freewrite about problems your character might face.

Prewriting Tip

In prewriting look for details about the setting. You can use them to enrich your narrative with strong, colorful descriptions.

Choose Your Approach

After giving the character a problem or conflict, decide on an approach. You could write a short story, a series of journal entries, or some letters home. Formats such as these allow you to show a character's feelings and actions.

Like Hannah, Philip Garran wrote an immigration story. In his prewriting investigation, he researched the Irish potato crop failures, which led to famine and caused many to leave their homeland. Unlike Hannah, Philip focused on the early part of the experience, before his main character left home. He, too, made up the details, but they were based on his research. Read the model, and see why a journal entry was a logical approach for Philip to use.

Contract Ticket No. ....

INSPECTION CARD.

(Immigrants and Steerage Passengers.)

Port of Departure, LIVERPOOL.   Date of Departure,

Name of Ship ... MEGANTIC, ... Jan. 8th. 1921.

Name of Immigrant .... *Delany Lillie*

Last Residence ....   *Ireland*

Student Model

Using sensory language, Philip paints a vivid word picture of the Irish countryside and conveys the narrator's feelings for his homeland.

What possible conflict is the writer setting up in these sentences?

At last my father has found a ship. We have packed all of our belongings, and Dad has sold the cottage for a very small sum of money. However, it was almost enough to pay for the tickets, and we borrowed the rest from my Uncle Paul.

We will be leaving in three days. I will miss the green fields, the blue sky, and the sparkly rivers and lakes. But I will not miss the misery that has descended on us like fog. I hear that America is a land of amazing wealth, and the land there is incredibly cheap. I can't wait to see America.

Philip Garran, Newton Elementary School,
Strafford, Vermont

4.5 | Writing Activities

Write a Narrative Journal Entry

Invent a character who is fleeing by boat or ship from a country that has become dangerous to live in. Write an entry he or she would add to a personal journal while on board.

PURPOSE To reflect a historical event
AUDIENCE Yourself
LENGTH 1–2 paragraphs

WRITING RUBRICS To write an effective narrative journal entry, you should

- focus on the flight from home, the voyage itself, or hopes for the future
- convey feelings as well as facts
- capitalize proper nouns and adjectives

Cross-Curricular Activity

HISTORY Use a library or the Internet to do some additional research about the time and place of the immigration experience you wrote about in your journal entry for this lesson. Write a letter home from the fictional character you created. Include historical details and problems your character might have faced.

Viewing and Representing

PICTURING HISTORY To illustrate your letter, use photographs or other pictures from the period of your character's immigration experience. Try to find images that reflect your character's experiences. With a small group, exchange letters and see if group members can match your letter with your pictures.

Grammar Link

Capitalize nouns and adjectives denoting nationalities and languages.

first-generation Japanese immigrants

Write each sentence below, using capital letters where necessary.

1. My uncle, a guatemalan by birth, speaks english, spanish, portuguese, and french.
2. In my neighborhood I hear more vietnamese than english.
3. Many italians who immigrated between 1899 and 1924 chose to return to their native land.
4. By 1910 the labor force in the West included native-born white americans, mexican americans, african americans, chinese americans, and tens of thousands of new mexican and japanese immigrants.
5. In later years many haitians and cubans settled in Florida.

See Lesson 19.4, page 589.

Writing a News Story

News stories, which record history as it happens, can become a resource for future historians. Strong news stories, such as the one below, answer these questions: What happened? When? Where? Who was involved? How did it happen? Why was the event important?

Collaborating on Computers

Computer Museum consults Martin Luther King Jr. Middle School students in developing new exhibit

By Teresa A. Martin
SPECIAL TO THE GLOBE

When the Computer Museum designed its new 3,600-square-foot, $1 million personal computer exhibit, it looked for inspiration in many places, including an eighth-grade class at the Martin Luther King Jr. Middle School in Dorchester, Massachusetts.

The collaboration was so successful that the museum is making such arrangements part of the development of all future exhibits.

"One of the things you often see is lip service to consulting with schools," said Greg Welch, director of exhibits at the museum. "But for us this was a concerted effort to find out their needs."

The exhibit in question, which opened last month and will be permanent, is called "Tools and Toys: The Amazing Personal Computer."

Tell the Five Ws and an H

News writers try to answer all or most of these questions—*who? what? when? where? why?* and *how?*—in their lead, or opening. How many of the basic questions—five Ws and an H—are answered in each lead below?

FLORIDA BRACES FOR HURRICANE ANDREW
Associated Press

MIAMI–Hurricane Andrew surged relentlessly toward southern Florida Sunday, and forecasters warned it would be the most powerful storm to hit the United States in decades. More than 1 million residents were told to flee.

A SUMMER SEARCH
BY MARK FERENCHIK
Repository staff writer

LAKE TWP.–What did teacher Pete Esterle do for his summer vacation? He went slogging through a south Florida swamp, in search of an airplane wreck apparently undisturbed for about 50 years. Esterle, an art teacher at Lake High School, and his brother found it earlier this month.

RUNAWAY CHIMP FINDS UNWILLING PLAYMATE
New York Times News Service

INMAN, S.C.–A 78-year-old woman hanging sheets on a clothesline Monday became the unsuspecting playmate of a rambunctious chimpanzee that, along with two companions, escaped from nearby Hollywild Animal Park.

Some leads present only the basic facts; the details come later in the story. Other leads open with a question or an intriguing detail designed to get readers' attention. Which of the leads above opens with an attention grabber?

Grammar Revising Tip

When you revise, use possessive pronouns where appropriate. For more information about possessive pronouns, see Lesson 11.4, page 441.

Journal Writing

Many things happen in a school day. Think about what happened yesterday, and choose one newsworthy event. Write answers to the five Ws and an H.

Go into Detail

In investigating a topic for a story, news reporters gather all the information they can. Then, after writing the lead, they bring their story to life with details they have gathered. Read the opening section of this news story.

Literature Model

The national anthems played most often four years ago in Seoul—those of the USSR and the German Democratic Republic (GDR)—will be noticeably missing during the 25th Olympic Games that begin today. Now, the USSR and GDR no longer exist, and neither does the intense East-West rivalry that has marked the Games during the Cold War era.

This will be the first Olympics in decades with no "good guys" or "bad guys," and that could make these Games the most refreshing in recent memory—approaching the Olympic ideal of spectators cheering for the best athletes regardless of the country they represent.

Bud Greenspan, *Parade*

According to Bud Greenspan, why are there no "good guys" or "bad guys" in this Olympics?

Be sure to include details in your news story. Cover all sides of the story. Save your opinions for a letter to the editor. Finally, check the accuracy of your facts and the spelling of names.

If you were in this audience, how could you exemplify the "Olympic ideal"?

Write a News Story

Write a news story about a recent event at your school. Cover the five Ws and an H in a lively lead. Write two paragraphs for the story. Include important details about the event.

PURPOSE To create a lead and details for a news story
AUDIENCE Readers of your school newspaper
LENGTH 2–3 paragraphs

WRITING RUBRICS To write an effective news story, you should

- use vivid language and sharp details
- cover all aspects of the event
- base your story on fact, not opinion
- leave your readers well informed

Using Computers

Most word-processing software allows you to print text in parallel columns as in a newspaper. Find out how to set up the format line for this option, and print out your story in newspaper format.

Viewing and Representing

MAKE AN ILLUSTRATION Draw a cartoon (funny or serious) that captures a key moment in the event you have written about. In a small group, critique each other's news articles and illustrations.

Grammar Link

Avoid double comparisons.

To form the comparative and superlative degrees of modifiers that have one syllable and of some that have two syllables, add the suffixes *-er* and *-est*. For most modifiers of two or more syllables, use the words *more* and *most*. Never use both a suffix and *more* or *most*.

> Esterle . . . and his brother found it **earlier** this month.

> . . . forecasters warned it would be the **most powerful** storm. . . .

Write each sentence below, eliminating double comparisons.

1. Charlie Spradley was the most fastest sprinter in school.
2. He captured a more greater number of all-state titles than his brother.
3. Kate Shoemaker played more better tennis than ever before.
4. Nonetheless, she lost the match in straight sets to Shalewa Bigham, the most youngest player on the other team.
5. The audience applauded Kate's performance more longer than Shalewa's.

See Lesson 12.3, page 461, and Lesson 12.6, page 467.

Responding to a Historical Narrative

*T*he excerpt below is a young Jewish girl's firsthand account of Nazi Germany.

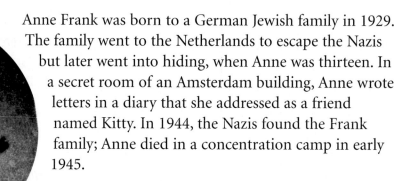

Anne Frank was born to a German Jewish family in 1929. The family went to the Netherlands to escape the Nazis but later went into hiding, when Anne was thirteen. In a secret room of an Amsterdam building, Anne wrote letters in a diary that she addressed as a friend named Kitty. In 1944, the Nazis found the Frank family; Anne died in a concentration camp in early 1945.

Literature Model

Wednesday, 29 March, 1944

Dear Kitty,

Bolkestein, an M.P. [Member of Parliament], was speaking on the Dutch News from London, and he said that they ought to make a collection of diaries and letters after the war. Of course, they all [Anne's family and the others in hiding with them] made a rush at my diary immediately. Just imagine how interesting it would be if I were to publish a romance of the "Secret Annexe." The title alone would be enough to make people think it was a detective story.

But, seriously, it would seem quite funny ten years after the war if we Jews were to tell how we lived and what we ate and talked about here. Although I tell you a lot, still, even so, you only know very little of our lives.

Anne Frank, *The Diary of a Young Girl*

Respond to Historical Events

Anne Frank's diary offers stark glimpses into wartime reality. Johanna Yngvason responded to Anne's diary by describing the terror of living in hiding. She focused on how historic events affected ordinary people, such as Anne Frank and her family.

Narrative Writing

Student Model

Hide! Hide! The Nazis are invading!" This was a terrifying sound heard by many Jews, many times, and caused them to go into hiding. A small closet became a bedroom, an attic became a home. . . . The Jews were rounded up like cattle and shipped off to concentration camps such as Auschwitz and Bergen-Belsen, where the majority of them died.

Such a fate befell young Anne Frank. . . . The only surviving member of the party, Anne's beloved father, returned to the dusty attic after the war. There in the rubble was the diary, which he later published. . . . Although Anne didn't survive the Holocaust, her thoughts and memories live on.

Johanna Yngvason, Canyon Park Junior High School, Bothell, Washington

---

> Johanna reflects Anne's dread when she uses the word *terrifying*.

> What does this sentence reveal about Johanna's feelings?

Follow Johanna's example when you respond in writing to a nonfiction narrative. Tell what happened, but add your own thoughts and feelings.

Journal Writing

Take a few moments to think about a narrative story that moved you. How did it make you feel? Write some words and phrases that best express your feelings.

Vocabulary Revising Tip

As you revise, a thesaurus can help you locate just the right words to express your thoughts and feelings about a non-fiction historical narrative.

Respond to People Behind the Events

Amy Groat read, and wrote about, *Farewell to Manzanar*. This nonfiction narrative tells the story of Jeanne Wakatsuki, interned with her family in a wartime relocation camp for Asian Americans. Read it and see how Amy sympathizes with Jeanne.

Amy shows how important the book was to her by suggesting that all eighth-graders in the district should read it.

Which words and expressions reveal Amy's sympathy for Jeanne Wakatsuki?

Student Model

Farewell to Manzanar deals with a mixture of problems that bombarded the internees in the camp Manzanar. The minorities of today deal with the same discrimination but in a subtler form. By reading and discussing this book, eighth-graders in our district will have a better understanding of the events and traumas that rocked Japanese Americans during World War II. . . .

When the Wakatsuki family reentered the "real world," Jeanne faced a cultural gap between herself and her classmates. She wanted desperately to fit in but was discriminated against because of her ethnic background. She eventually was able to blend in with her classmates by joining after-school activities, but she was never able to deal with the generation gap in her family.

Amy Groat, Oak Creek Ranch School,
Cornville, Arizona

One way of responding to a historical narrative—fiction or nonfiction—is to show how a character is like you. In reading *Farewell to Manzanar*, Amy discovered how the people from another time and place were like her.

Responding to a Spoken Narrative

One type of narration is storytelling. Talk to a person who has survived a war. Have him or her describe fears, thoughts, and emotions of that time.

Write a one-page response. Tell how the survival story made you feel.

PURPOSE To respond to a spoken narrative
AUDIENCE Your teacher and classmates
LENGTH 1 page

WRITING RUBRICS To write an effective response to a spoken narrative, you should

- use precise language to describe your feelings about the story
- provide enough detail to suggest a basis for your feelings
- show how the event affected the narrator's life

Cross-Curricular Activity

HISTORY After you have heard the story of the war survivor, find out more about the war that affected the survivor. Use the library and the Internet to obtain more facts and information. Compile lists or create graphs and charts that reflect the general scope and impact of the war.

Narrative Writing

Grammar Link

Use commas to set off nonessential adjective clauses but not clauses that are essential to the meaning of the sentence.

There in the rubble was the diary, **which he later published**. . . .

. . . the problems **that bombarded the internees in the camp Manzanar.**

Write the paragraph, using commas as needed.

In *The Road from Home* David Kherdian tells the story of his mother who grew up in the Armenian quarter of a Turkish town. Conflict raged in Turkey which was part of the Ottoman Empire. The Armenians who were often targeted by the Turks suffered terribly. Kherdian re-creates the tension that mounted in 1914 and 1915.

See Lesson 20.3, page 603.

Listening and Speaking

COOPERATIVE LEARNING In a small group, take turns reporting on the research you have done on the specific war. Then take turns summarizing the responses you wrote to the survivor's story. Discuss how the personal accounts reinforced, expanded, or contradicted what you learned about the war from the print and electronic sources.

Writing Process in Action

WRITING
Online

Visit the *Writer's Choice* Web site at **writerschoice. glencoe.com** for additional writing prompts.

Narrative Writing

In preceding lessons you've learned how time order, point of view, realistic details, and dialogue can make a historical narrative come to life. You've also had a chance to write narratives about people, places, and events in history. Now, in this lesson, you're invited to write a historical narrative about one of your ancestors or someone else whose life interests you.

Assignment

Context	You are going to write a historical narrative about an ancestor or someone else whose life is important to you. Although you may find facts about this person, you'll have to invent some likely—and lively—details about speech, actions, and attitudes.
Purpose	To make the past come alive in a historical narrative
Audience	Your family or friends
Length	4–5 paragraphs

The following pages can help you plan and write your historical narrative. Read through the pages, and then refer to them as you need to. Don't be tied down by them, however. You're in charge of your own writing process.

Prewriting

Is there a person in history whose life fascinates you? Would you like to know more about how an ancestor came to this country?

- Begin exploring ideas about an ancestor's life by interviewing relatives.
- Refer to old photo albums for pictures of where people lived, played, and worked in those days and to letters, diaries, and family records. Jot down notes and ideas in your journal. Begin thinking about where you might begin and end your narrative. Make a list of events, or simply begin writing where it feels right.

Option A
Interview people, look at photos, read letters.

Option B
Read about the period.

Option C
Jot down notes about a turning point in the story.

Krista given money on her eighteenth birthday. Not much—the farm in Denmark was too poor. Older children used money to move to the city to find work. Krista wanted to go to America.

Drafting

As you draft your historical narrative, include details to make the life of your subject real. Notice the details Katherine Paterson uses to portray a nineteenth-century factory.

Literature Model

Within five minutes, her head felt like a log being split to splinters. She kept shaking it, as though she could rid it of the noise, or at least the pain, but both only seemed to grow more intense. If that weren't trial enough, a few hours of standing in her proud new boots and her feet had swollen so that the laces cut into her flesh.

Katherine Paterson, *Lyddie*

Writing Process in Action

Narrative Writing

Drafting Tip

For a reminder about chronological order, review pages 160–163.

When drafting your historical narrative, use details that put your readers in the subject's shoes by making them feel part of the events and surroundings. Instead of simply saying, "the factory was noisy," or "Lyddie's feet hurt," Paterson takes her readers back to the mill to see her character and to feel her pain.

If you get stuck while drafting, look again at your prewriting notes for fresh ideas.

Revising

To begin revising, read over your draft to make sure that what you've written fits your purpose and audience. Then have a writing conference. Read your draft to a partner or small group. Use your audience's reactions to help you evaluate your work so far. The following questions can help you and your listeners.

Question A

Does every sentence contribute to my narrative?

Question B

Have I used specific details?

Question C

Have I established a clear point of view?

Krista's feet were bleeding by the time she walked the nine miles from the station to the farm where she was to work. She wished she had heavy boots, instead of her Sunday ~~brought old shoes instead of her best shoes, with~~ to America. her. This farm was bigger than the one she had left behind in Denmark. As she thought of the scrubbing, mending, and cooking hours of hard work that faced her, ~~she became~~ her heart sank. ~~sad.~~

Editing

You've worked hard to figure out what you want to say and how to say it well. Since you'll be sharing this with your family or friends, you'll want them to pay attention to the story, not to any errors you might have made. During the editing stage, you'll want to **proofread** your work and eliminate mistakes that might detract from the ideas and feelings you want to share.

This checklist will help you catch errors you might otherwise overlook.

Presenting

You may wish to include a photograph or a drawing of your subject in your historical narrative. Pictures of a house or the city your subject lived in and of clothing or vehicles from your subject's era will also add interest to your narrative. If your computer software prints some old-fashioned type styles, they can also add a feeling of historical accuracy to your narrative.

Editing Checklist

1. Have I correctly punctuated appositives and adjective clauses?

2. Have I eliminated any double comparisons?

3. Do my verbs agree with their subjects?

4. Have I used standard spelling and capitalization?

5. Is my cursive or printed handwriting clear?

Proofreading Tip

For proofreading symbols, see page 331.

Journal Writing

Reflect on your writing experience. Answer these questions in your journal: What do you like best about your narrative writing? What was the hardest part of writing it? What did you learn in your writing conference? What new things have you learned as a writer?

LYDDIE

by Katherine Paterson

In the mid-1800s the hope for a better life prompted many to join the ranks of factory laborers. Katherine Paterson's historical narrative relates how thirteen-year-old Lydia Worthen travels to Lowell, Massachusetts, seeking mill work and the chance for a new life. As you read, pay special attention to how Paterson tells Lydia's story. Then try the activities in Linking Writing and Literature on page 194.

The four-thirty bell clanged the house awake. From every direction, Lyddie could hear the shrill voices of girls calling to one another, even singing. Someone on another floor was imitating a rooster. From the other side of the bed Betsy groaned and turned over, but Lyddie was up, dressing quickly in the dark as she had always done in the windowless attic of the inn.

Her stomach rumbled, but she ignored it. There would be no breakfast until seven, and that was two and a half hours away. By five the girls had crowded through the main gate, jostled their way up the outside staircase on the far end of the mill, cleaned their machines, and stood waiting for the workday to begin.

"Not too tired this morning?" Diana asked by way of greeting.

Constantin Meunier, *In the Black Country,* c. 1860–80

Lyddie shook her head. Her feet were sore, but she'd felt tireder after a day behind the plow.

"Good. Today will be something more strenuous, I fear. We'll work all three looms together, all right? Until you feel quite sure of everything."

Lyddie felt a bit as though the older girls were whispering in church. It seemed almost that quiet in the great loom room. The only real noise was the creaking from the ceiling of the leather belts that connected the wheels in the weaving room to the gigantic waterwheel in the basement.

The overseer came in, nodded good morning, and pushed a low wooden stool under a cord dangling from the assembly of wheels and belts above his head. His little red mouth pursed, he stepped up on the stool and pulled out his pocket watch. At the same moment, the bell in the tower above the roof began to ring. He yanked the cord, the wide leather belt above him shifted from a loose to a tight pulley, and suddenly all the hundred or so silent looms, in raucous[1] concert, shuddered and groaned into fearsome life. Lyddie's first full day as a factory girl had begun.

Within five minutes, her head felt like a log being split to splinters. She kept shaking it, as though she could rid it of the noise, or at least the pain, but both only seemed to grow more intense. If that weren't trial enough, a few hours of standing in her proud new boots and her feet had swollen so that the laces cut into her flesh. She bent down quickly to loosen them, and when she found the right lace was knotted, she nearly burst into tears. Or perhaps the tears were caused by the swirling dust and lint.

Now that she thought of it, she could hardly breathe, the air was so laden with moisture and debris.[2] She snatched a moment to run to the window. She had to get air, but the window was nailed shut against the April morning. She leaned her forehead against it; even the glass seemed hot. Her apron brushed the pots of red geraniums crowding the wide sill. They were flourishing in this hot house. She coughed, trying to free her throat and lungs for breath.

Then she felt, rather than saw, Diana. "Mr. Marsden has his eye on you," the older girl said gently, and put her arm on Lyddie's shoulder to turn her back toward the looms. She pointed to the stalled loom and the broken warp[3] thread that must be tied. Even though Diana had stopped the loom, Lyddie stood rubbing the powder into her fingertips, hesitating to plunge her hands into the bowels of the machine. Diana urged her with a light touch.

I stared down a black bear, Lyddie reminded herself. She took a deep breath, fished out the broken ends, and began to tie the weaver's knot that Diana had shown her over and over again the afternoon before. Finally, Lyddie managed to make a clumsy knot, and Diana pulled the lever, and the loom shuddered to life once more.

How could she ever get accustomed to this inferno?[4] Even when the girls were set free at 7:00, it was to push and shove their way across the bridge and down the street to their boardinghouses, bolt down their hearty breakfast, and rush back, stomachs still churning, for "ring in" at 7:35. Nearly half the mealtime was spent simply going up and down the staircase, across the mill yard and bridge, down the row of houses—just getting to and from the meal. And

---

1 **raucous** (rô′kəs) hoarse; rough-sounding
2 **debris** (də brē′) bits of rubbish; litter
3 **warp** (wôrp) threads running lengthwise in a loom
4 **inferno** (in fur′nō) hell or any place suggesting hell

Eyre Crowe, *The Dinner Hour, Wigan*, 1874

the din[5] in the dining room was nearly as loud as the racket in the mill—thirty young women chewing and calling at the same time, reaching for the platters of flapjacks and pitchers of syrup, ignoring cries from the other end of the table to pass anything.

Her quiet meals in the corner of the kitchen with Triphena, even her meager bowls of bark soup in the cabin with the seldom talkative Charlie, seemed like feasts compared to the huge, rushed, noisy affairs in Mrs. Bedlow's house. The

half hour at noonday dinner with more food than she had ever had set before her at one time was worse than breakfast.

At last the evening bell rang, and Mr. Marsden pulled the cord to end the day. Diana walked with her to the place by the door where the girls hung their bonnets and shawls, and handed Lyddie hers. "Let's forget about studying those regulations tonight," she said. "It's been too long a day already."

Lyddie nodded. Yesterday seemed years in the past. She couldn't even remember why she'd thought the regulations important enough to bother with.

---

5 din (din) a loud, continuous noise

She had lost all appetite. The very smell of supper made her nauseous[6]—beans heavy with pork fat and brown injun bread with orange cheese, fried potatoes, of course, and flapjacks with apple sauce, baked Indian pudding with cream and plum cake for dessert. Lyddie nibbled at the brown bread and washed it down with a little scalding tea. How could the others eat so heartily and with such a clatter of dishes and shrieks of conversation? She longed only to get to the room, take off her boots, massage her abused feet, and lay down her aching head. While the other girls pulled their chairs from the table and scraped them about to form little circles in the parlor area, Lyddie dragged herself from the table and up the stairs.

Betsy was already there before her, her current novel in her hand. She laughed at the sight of Lyddie. "The first full day! And up to now you thought yourself a strapping country farm girl who could do anything, didn't you?"

Lyddie did not try to answer back. She simply sank to her side of the double bed and took off the offending shoes and began to rub her swollen feet.

"If you've got an older pair"—Betsy's voice was almost gentle—"more stretched and softer . . ."

Lyddie nodded. Tomorrow she'd wear Triphena's without the stuffing. They were still stiff from the trip and she'd be awkward rushing back and forth to meals, but at least there'd be room for her feet to swell.

She undressed, slipped on her shabby night shift, and slid under the quilt. Betsy glanced over at her. "To bed so soon?"

Lyddie could only nod again. It was as though she could not possibly squeeze a word through her lips. Betsy smiled again. She ain't laughing at me, Lyddie realized. She's remembering how it was.

"Shall I read to you?" Betsy asked.

Lyddie nodded gratefully and closed her eyes and turned her back against the candlelight.

Betsy did not give any explanation of the novel she was reading, simply commenced to read aloud where she had broken off reading to herself. Even though Lyddie's head was still choked with lint and battered with noise, she struggled to get the sense of the story.

The child was in some kind of poorhouse, it seemed, and he was hungry. Lyddie knew about hungry children. Rachel, Agnes, Charlie—they had all been hungry that winter of the bear. The hungry little boy in the story had held up his bowl to the poorhouse overseer and said:

"Please sir, I want some more."

And for this the overseer—she could see his little rosebud mouth rounded in

---

6 nauseous (nô'shəs) feeling sickness in the stomach

horror—for this the overseer had screamed out at the child. In her mind's eye little Oliver Twist looked exactly like a younger Charlie. The cruel overseer had screamed and hauled the boy before a sort of agent. And for what crime? For the monstrous crime of wanting more to eat.

"That boy will be hung," the agent had prophesied. "I know that boy will be hung."

She fought sleep, ravenous[7] for every word. She had not had any appetite for the bountiful meal downstairs, but now she was feeling a hunger she knew nothing about. She had to know what would happen to little Oliver. Would he indeed be hanged just because he wanted more gruel?

She opened her eyes and turned to watch Betsy, who was absorbed in her reading. Then Betsy sensed her watching, and looked up from the book. "It's a marvelous story, isn't it? I saw the author once—Mr. Charles Dickens. He visited our factory. Let me see—I was already in the spinning room—it must have been in—"

But Lyddie cared nothing for authors or dates. "Don't stop reading the story, please," she croaked out.

"Never fear, little Lyddie. No more interruptions," Betsy promised, and read on, though her voice grew raspy with fatigue, until the bell rang for curfew. She stuck a hair ribbon in the place. "Till tomorrow night," she whispered as the feet of an army of girls could be heard thundering up the staircase.

---

7 ravenous (rav'ə nəs) greedy

Linking Writing and Literature

Readers Respond to the Model

What makes Katherine Paterson's narrative come to life?

Explore Katherine Paterson's historical narrative by answering these questions. Then read what other students liked about her narrative.

1. Katherine Paterson's narrative tells the story of a young girl's experience in a factory during the nineteenth century. How does the opening paragraph draw the reader into the story?

2. From anywhere in the selection, choose a paragraph that is particularly realistic in creating the setting.

What specific details make this setting realistic?

3. *I stared down a black bear, Lyddie reminded herself.* What does this line reveal about Lyddie's character? How does the line help the reader to identify with Lyddie?

What Students Say

"This story is about a thirteen-year-old girl, Lyddie, who lived the life of an adult. After her first full day working in the mill, she was so exhausted that she didn't have enough energy to speak. She was my favorite character because of her courage to work in a mill at her age. "

Eliza Ali

"Lyddie was my favorite character because what she did was adventurous and courageous at the same time. It was adventurous because Lyddie was living and working on her own. It was courageous because her job in the mill was hard. I liked the fact that Lyddie got to feel what it was like to be an adult. "

Trina Cbu

Reflecting on the Unit

Summarize what you learned in this unit by answering the following questions.

1. What is a narrative?
2. Where can you get ideas for historical narratives?
3. Why is the use of chronological order helpful?
4. From what points of view can a narrative be told?
5. How does dialogue help to enrich a narrative?
6. On what facts do news stories focus?

Adding to Your Portfolio

CHOOSE A SELECTION FOR YOUR PORTFOLIO Look over the narrative writing you did for this unit. Choose a piece of writing for your portfolio. The writing you choose should show one or more of the following:

- a realistic portrayal of a person, event, or setting from history
- an opening that introduces a person, event, or setting and that draws readers into the story
- lively dialogue that shows what the characters are like
- fictional but true-to-life characters to portray a historical era or event
- a lead that tells most or all of the five *W*s and an *H*

REFLECT ON YOUR CHOICE Attach a note to the piece you chose, explaining briefly why you chose it and what you learned from writing it.

SET GOALS How can you improve your writing? What skill will you focus on the next time you write?

Writing Across the Curriculum

MAKE A HISTORY CONNECTION Think of a historical event that took place during the lifetime of the character about whom you wrote your narrative. Write a paragraph telling some of the effects that event had on your character's life.

"All the pages had let loose at the seams and were flapping free into the gutters..."

—Naomi Shihab Nye

Thank You in Arabic

Writing in the Real World

MEDIA Travel Connection

Expository writing invites readers to enter real worlds and meet actual people. Gary McLain, Choctaw-Irish author and artist, wanted to invite non-Indian travelers into his world. So he wrote a guide called *Indian America*, a traveler's guide to Native American peoples in the continental United States. Part of the guide, such as the following excerpt, provides basic facts to help readers locate and identify individual groups.

from *Indian America*
by Gary McLain
"Eagle/Walking Turtle"

Nett Lake Reservation Business Committee
(Bois Fort)
Nett Lake, MN 55772
(218) 757-3261

Ojibwa (to roast till puckered up)

Location: The location of the powwow grounds can be obtained by calling the tribal office.

Public Ceremony or Powwow Dates: The first weekend in June is powwow time with traditional dancing and drum groups. Call the tribal office for dates and times.

Art Forms: Arts and crafts are sold at the powwow. The work will include paintings, feather work, leather work, and beadwork.

Visitor Information: The Bois Fort Wild Rice Company is doing well. For interesting information on wild rice, see the general history of the Ojibwa at the beginning of this section.

Ni-Mi-Win
Spirit Mountain Sky Facility
Duluth, MN
(218) 897-1251

Ojibwa (to roast till puckered up)

Location: Call the number above for the location of the powwow.

Public Ceremony or Powwow Dates: The third weekend in August is the Ni-Mi-Win celebration. It is the greatest joint Ojibwa celebration, and its goal is to bring everyone together. Traditional and intertribal dances are performed.

Art Forms: You will find black ash basket making along with leather work, beadwork, birch bark baskets, and all kinds of arts and crafts.

Visitor Information: If you like to powwow, don't miss this one.

A Writer's Process

Prewriting
Collecting and Organizing the Facts

When McLain decided to write *Indian America,* he already knew a great deal about many Native American groups. Even so, he needed to gather more information.

Using his knowledge and a list from the Bureau of Indian Affairs, McLain mailed five hundred letters to tribal offices around the country. Three hundred tribal offices responded with information that would be helpful to travelers. Information included the group's name, address, and tribal office phone number and location, as well as its public ceremonies and art forms. Some groups even responded with histories written by tribal historians. Before long McLain had a stack of material three feet high.

With the facts in hand, McLain next decided on the parts and organization of his guide. He says, "I divided the country into nine regions based mostly on how Indian people live."

McLain planned to open the guidebook with information on Indian beliefs. The guide to the tribes would follow, organized by region. To help travelers picture locations, McLain decided to include regional maps.

Drafting
Writing the Book

With his book plan in mind, McLain started writing, a job that would take him three months. For days at a time, he wrote from sunup to midmorning, from mid-afternoon until 10:00 P.M.

As McLain worked with his material, he found that he needed two writing styles to present the different types of information. In the introduction to each region, he wrote in con-versational prose. For example, in his introduction to the Great Plains, McLain explained how people were bound together in a great sacred hoop.

McLain used a much different writing style for his guide to each group. Here he wrote in short, pertinent sentences for travelers on the go. He organized the copy for this part of the guide under a

The Great Plains

The Great Plains

set of heads that were easy to scan: tribal name, location, ceremony or powwow dates, art forms, and visitor information.

In the visitor-information section, McLain provided travelers with useful and intriguing facts. For the Taos Pueblo in New Mexico, he focused on photography rules for visitors. For the Cherokee in North Carolina, he described a restored Cherokee village, a museum, and various tourist activities. By contrast, his section on the Comanche in Oklahoma discussed the tribe's history, not its modern life. The

reason? "There are no more reservations in Oklahoma," McLain explains. "The Comanche live in white frame houses that don't look much different from those in Ohio or Indiana. Yet the Comanche were hunters who lived up and down the central plains. They were great horsemen and great warriors and had much ceremony in their lives. I thought a little more attention to the history of the tribe could help visitors feel connected to these people."

Revising
Making the Story Complete

Once McLain had his book on paper, he revised sections to make them clearer and more engaging. His editor suggested some of the changes. For example, McLain's editor asked him to expand his section on sweetgrass and sage, healing plants used by Medicine People in Plains ceremonies. In his first draft, McLain had done little more than mention the plants. He revised his brief comment to read: "The Medicine People use sage, cedar, and sweetgrass, and the sweet smell carries the healing forward from the past into the future . . . in the sacred dances of our people across the land."

8 / Great Plains

buckskins. And dances and songs and chants developed entertainment and spiritual appreciation of the creation ing things.

Medicines for the body and spirit evolved with time a cedar, and sweetgrass were used in the sacred ceremonies of ple. The Creator provided the knowledge of how to medicines through the Medicine P

Examining Writing in the Real World

Analyzing the Media Connection

Discuss these questions about the model on page 198.

1. When might you use the information in Gary McLain's guide?

2. What key words do you notice in the excerpt? What calls your attention to them?

3. McLain uses typographical features, such as italics. What other kinds of typographical features and formatting can help clarify information in your expository reports?

4. What information would be helpful to you if you were shopping for Indian jewelry? What information would help you find the dates for tribal ceremonies?

5. If you were traveling to Nett Lake Reservation, what information from the excerpt might you jot down in your personal travel journal?

Analyzing a Writer's Process

Discuss these questions about Gary McLain's writing process.

1. What audience did McLain choose for his book *Indian America?*

2. Why do you think McLain chose the topic for his book? What made him well qualified to write the book?

3. What sources of information did McLain use to collect his material?

4. How did he organize the material? Why was it important for McLain to choose a pattern of organization before he began to write?

5. Explain the two different writing styles McLain used in his guidebook. How did each style match a specific kind of information?

Grammar Link

When proofreading, professional writers make sure that their verbs agree with their subjects.

*The first **weekend** in June **is** pow-wow time.*

On your own paper, write the correct verb for each sentence.

1. The Bois Fort Wild Rice Company are doing well.
2. If you likes to powwow, don't miss this one.
3. The Comanches lives in white frame houses.
4. They was great horsemen.
5. We says that America is the great melting pot of the world.

See Lesson 16.1, pages 541–542.

Conveying Information

Expository writing informs and explains. In the model below, the writer uses expository writing to convey information about a traditional Inuit game, the blanket toss.

Literature Model

Members of the community grabbed hold of the edge of an animal skin. When everyone pulled at once, the center snapped up, propelling the person who sat or stood in the center of the skin into the air, just as if he or she were on a trampoline. The leader of the most successful whaling crew was often rewarded with the place on the skin; it was then a matter of pride to remain standing throughout the vigorous tossing.

Kevin Osborn, *The Peoples of the Arctic*

Write to Inform

The most familiar form of expository writing is the essay. An essay consists of an introduction, a body, and a conclusion. The introduction usually contains a thesis statement—a sentence that states the main idea of the essay. The body is made up of one or more paragraphs that include details supporting the thesis statement. The conclusion draws the essay to a close. It may restate what has been said or suggest a different way of looking at the material. Notice in the model below how Michele Casey begins her essay on sharks.

Student Model

Although shark attacks do occur, they are not so frequent that swimmers must arm themselves with shark repellents. Survivors of airplane or ship disasters, though, need an effective shark repellent, since they have practically no defenses. The most promising advances are sound/electronic barriers. All other methods have major drawbacks.

Michele Casey, Glen Crest Junior High School,
Glen Ellyn, Illinois

> What is the thesis statement in Michele's essay?

The body of Michele's essay goes on to discuss various shark repellents. Her conclusion states, "Shark repellents of today and the future will help prevent further disaster for survivors at sea."

Journal Writing

Imagine that a friend has asked you how to play a game you know well. Write a thesis statement explaining the main goal of the game.

Expository Writing

Choose an Approach

The goal of expository writing is to explain or inform. The model on page 215 explains by describing the steps of a process. Expository writing can take other forms. The chart below explains four approaches to expository writing. These approaches can be used alone or combined in any expository piece. To explain about dolphins, the writer of the sample below chose the cause-and-effect approach.

Approaches to Expository Writing	
Approach	**Sample Writing**
Definition	Sivuquad, a name for St. Lawrence Island, means squeezed dry. The islanders believed that a giant had made the island from dried mud.
Compare-Contrast	The boats in a coastal fishing fleet often stay at sea for days or weeks. Long-range fishing fleet vessels can remain at sea for months.
Process	To breathe, a whale surfaces in a forward rolling motion. For two seconds, it blows out and breathes in as much as 2,100 quarts of air.
Cause-Effect	The discovery of oil and gas in Alaska in 1968 led to widespread development in that region of the world.

According to the writer, why has the dolphin been protected?

For centuries dolphins have fascinated people. Stories about dolphins that guided ships and rescued swimmers have led some people to idealize these creatures. Further, traditional respect and increasing public concern have resulted in measures intended to protect the dolphin.

Write an Informative Essay

A television program called *What in the World?* challenges viewers to send in answers to questions, such as "What is a solar eclipse?" or "How are a whale and a dolphin alike?" Choose one of these two questions, do some research, and write a brief essay that answers it.

PURPOSE To convey information
AUDIENCE Television viewers (your classmates)
LENGTH 2–3 paragraphs

WRITING RUBRICS To write an informative essay, you should

- choose an appropriate approach from the chart on the previous page
- elaborate, giving sufficient details and examples to support your answer
- include an introduction, a body, and a conclusion

Listening and Speaking

AS SEEN ON TV Work in a small group to prepare your essay as a presentation on *What in the World?* All group members should be prepared to both give feedback about each person's presentation and to receive feedback about their own. If possible, videotape your presentation and review the tape to make sure you speak clearly.

Grammar Link

Avoid using pronouns without clear antecedents.

To avoid confusion when using pronouns, you must be sure that the noun or group of words to which the pronoun refers—the antecedent—is clear.

> *Stories about dolphins that guided ships and rescued swimmers have led some people to idealize* **these creatures.**

If this sentence ended "to idealize *them,*" readers would not know if *them* referred to *dolphins, ships,* or *swimmers.*

Revise the paragraph below to eliminate confusing pronouns.

[1]Heather is helping Jen in the garden; Chad, Mike, and she are planting tomatoes. [2]They are proud of the garden. [3]Then Chad and Mike will weed his garden and the Wongs' garden.

See Lesson 11.2, pages 437–438.

Viewing and Representing

USING IMAGES TO EXPLAIN Assemble photos, drawings, and other visual aids to help make your TV talk more lively and interesting. Use the aids at appropriate times to illustrate your talk.

Structuring an Explanation

Choosing and arranging details to support a statement are the foundations of expository writing. Notice how the writer of the model below uses supporting details to explain how computers tackle mountains of information in a flash.

Literature Model

Printed circuit boards are the heart of the computer. On them are mounted the transistors, capacitors, chips, and other electrical marvels that create a computer. Their undersides have ribbons of solder, through which electricity flows. It is not necessary for you to have the foggiest idea how all this works. But do consider how small, lightweight, and portable the printed circuit boards are. Each board has a special function: some provide memory for the computer; others provide the processing and arithmetic logic functions; still others convert the power supply to and from the required voltages.

Carol W. Brown, *The Minicomputer Simplified*

Elaborate with Details

Supporting details are the heart of expository writing. They support the thesis statement in the introduction of your essay. The details you select for an essay will depend on the approach to expository writing you're using. If you're writing a cause-and-effect essay, you might use reasons as supporting details. In the model Carol W. Brown uses facts to define circuit boards. You can also use statistics, examples, or incidents to support what you say. Note the examples of the types of details listed in the chart below.

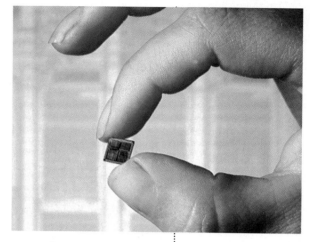

Details in Expository Writing	
Type	**Example**
Facts	Momenta International of California introduced a computer that can recognize and interpret printed handwriting.
Statistics	The processor inside a typical computer can carry out one million additions in only a second.
Examples/ Incidents	The optical processor is an example of a computer that uses light beams to process information.
Reasons	Computer manufacturers are developing smaller computers because businesspeople demand them for use when they travel.

Journal Writing

Think about something you would like to explain to a friend. Write your thesis statement, and list the details you would include, trying to use all four types of details.

Grammar Tip

When editing an essay that uses time order, be sure the verb tenses reflect the order. For more on tenses, refer to Lessons 10.5–10.9, pages 409–417.

Arrange the Details

Once you've selected supporting details for your explanation, you're ready to organize them. Ask yourself what you're trying to do in your essay. For example, are you going to show the cause and effect of a tidal wave? Are you going to use a comparison-contrast essay to point out the similarities and differences between two comedians? Questions such as these can help you organize your ideas—the supporting details—logically.

You might choose a number of ways to arrange information and supporting details. If you're defining something, you might arrange features from most to least significant. If you're writing about a process, then chronological order, or time order, might be more logical. In the model below, notice the kinds of details that Emilie Baltz uses and how she arranges them.

Student Model

What types of details are in the writing?

What kind of organization does the writer use?

Thomas Edison's invention of the electric light bulb in 1879 came about only after a long, hard process. Finding the right material for the tiny filament inside the light bulb had been difficult. Edison tested 1,600 materials before finally using a piece of burned thread. Because it contained no air, the thread did not burn quickly inside the bulb. This invention would eventually bring light into the world.

Emilie Baltz, Hufford Junior High School,
Joliet, Illinois

Write an Explanation

Imagine that a person from the 1800s has come to visit you. He is curious about some modern invention, such as a computer or a blender. Write a simple explanation of how the device works and what it can be used for.

PURPOSE To use supporting details to explain how a device works and what it can be used for

AUDIENCE A person from the 1800s

LENGTH 2–3 paragraphs

WRITING RUBRICS To explain the purpose and features of a device, you should

- describe the major purposes of the device
- make clear how the device is used
- arrange the details in an organized, logical way
- make the explanation clear and legible for the audience.

Using Computers

You can use a computer to illustrate your explanation with pictures, graphs, charts, and diagrams. Some word processing programs have graphic functions. Clip art—pictures you can copy and paste into your document—is also available.

Grammar Link

Form the plurals of compound nouns correctly.

Add -*s* or -*es* to the end of one-word compound nouns and to the most important part of other compound nouns.

undersides

printed circuit boards

Use the plural form of each compound noun below in a sentence.

1. bookend
2. halfback
3. father-in-law
4. showcase
5. great-aunt
6. runner-up
7. storybook
8. basketball
9. pot of gold
10. paper plate
11. vice president
12. editor in chief
13. suitcase
14. brother-in-law
15. windowsill
16. nosebleed
17. groundhog
18. toothpaste
19. sunbeam
20. ice rink

See Lesson 9.2, pages 383–384.

Listening and Speaking

COOPERATIVE LEARNING In a small group, read your explanation aloud. Have group members pay special attention to word choices, making sure that any technical terms are explained or defined. Edit your explanation on the basis of the feedback you get.

Writing to Compare and Contrast

*W*hen you compare two things, you explain how they're similar. When you contrast two things, you explain how they're different. Comparing and contrasting two items can be a useful way of explaining them.

Tanya enjoys country and western music. Classmate Ben prefers Latin American music. These two kinds of music are different in some ways and alike in others. Think about two types of music. Jot down two or three things about them that are similar and two or three things that are different.

Identify Similarities and Differences

By looking carefully at two things, you see their similarities and differences. This close look often helps you understand each thing better. Comparing and contrasting requires an analytical approach.

Before you write a compare-and-contrast essay, you need to identify similarities and differences in your subjects. A Venn diagram, such as the one below, may help you. Be sure that your subjects are related, as two kinds of music are. Also, compare and contrast the same set of features, such as cultural sources and sound, that relate to the subjects.

Vocabulary Tip

When drafting an opening sentence for a compare-and-contrast essay, choose words that will grab your reader's attention.

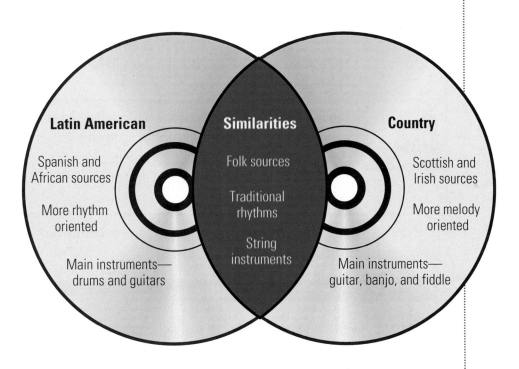

Latin American

Spanish and African sources

More rhythm oriented

Main instruments— drums and guitars

Similarities

Folk sources

Traditional rhythms

String instruments

Country

Scottish and Irish sources

More melody oriented

Main instruments— guitar, banjo, and fiddle

Journal Writing

Think of two musical artists or groups that are related in some way. In your journal make a Venn diagram. Use the diagram to compare and contrast the musicians in terms of the same features.

Organize by Subject or by Feature

You can organize compare-and-contrast writing either by subject or by feature. In organizing by subject, you discuss all the features of one subject and then the features of the other. For example, you might explain the sources and sound of Latin music and then discuss the contrasting sources and sound of country music. When organizing by feature, you discuss one feature at a time for both subjects. See the chart below.

Organizing by Subject or Feature	
Subject	Latin American music sources are Spanish and African. The beat of the music is strong and rhythmic. The main instruments used in Latin American music are drums and guitars. Country music, on the other hand, is influenced by Scottish and Irish sources. It is more melody oriented than Latin American music.
Feature	Latin American music sources are Spanish and African, while country music is influenced by Scottish and Irish sources. The sound of the two kinds of music is also different. Latin American music is rhythmic and country music is melodic.

How did Michael Shapiro organize the paragraph below on classical musicians Yo-Yo Ma and Emanuel Ax?

Literature Model

Does the writer organize his contrast by feature or by subject?

How are Yo-Yo Ma and Emanuel Ax different?

They seem, on the surface, an unlikely pair, as is often the case with friends who never seem to lose the rhythm of their relationship. Ma was the child wonder who came of age musically in the warm embrace of such mentors as Isaac Stern and Leonard Rose. Ax grew up never knowing whether he would be able to become a concert pianist. For Ma playing the cello has always come easily. For Ax the musician's life is one for which he feels forever grateful.

Michael Shapiro, *"Yo-Yo and Manny"*

Write a Compare-and-Contrast Essay

Write an essay about two people, places, or things that you are studying in school, such as two characters from a book or two cities.

PURPOSE To compare and contrast items
AUDIENCE Your teacher or classmates
LENGTH 2–4 paragraphs

WRITING RUBRICS To write an effective compare-and-contrast essay, you should

- use a Venn diagram to identify similarities and differences
- organize by subject or by feature

Cross-Curricular Activity

HEALTH AND PHYSICAL EDUCATION
Choose two sports that are popular in your school. In a brief essay, compare and contrast the two by explaining how they are alike or different in terms of factors such as cost, health benefits, danger, and strategy. Conclude by expressing an opinion about which of the two you believe is more deserving of school and community support. Base your opinion on the details you used in your essay.

Grammar Link

Make the verb agree with the closer subject when the parts of a compound subject are joined by or or nor.

Compound subjects are common in compare-and-contrast writing:

Neither Ma nor Ax hides his talent.

Write the correct verb for each sentence.

1. Neither Mozart nor Haydn are very popular at my house.
2. Either the Beatles or the Grateful Dead were Mom's favorite.
3. Neither Jethro Tull nor Cat Stevens appeal to my parents.
4. Either my uncles or my dad rave about the Rolling Stones.

See Lesson 16.5, pages 549–550.

Listening and Speaking

ADDRESSING THE ISSUE In a small group, deliver your sports paper as if you were presenting it to a meeting of the school board. Adjust your tone, volume, and vocabulary for that audience. Ask the "school board" to respond to your presentation. As a group, compare and contrast the various opinions about sports that are presented.

Writing About a Process

Everyday life is full of step-by-step processes. In this lesson you will learn to explain an everyday process so that others can understand how to complete it.

Making pizza dough may look difficult, but it isn't. There are, however, some basic steps that you need to follow. You also need a recipe, of course. In the photos below, the basic steps in making dough are broken down.

Making Pizza Dough in Four Steps

| Mix Ingredients | Knead Dough | Let Dough Rise | Shape Dough |

Have a Clear Purpose

Knowing how to do something does not guarantee that you can easily share that knowledge with others. Some people find it more difficult to explain a step-by-step process than to actually do it. The instructions in the model on the next page use clear and simple language to explain a rather complicated process: handling hot chilies.

Wearing rubber gloves is a wise precaution, especially when you are handling fresh hot chilies. Be careful not to touch your face or eyes while working with them.

To prepare chilies, first rinse them clean in cold water. (Hot water may make fumes rise from dried chilies, and even the fumes might irritate your nose and eyes.) Working under cold running water, pull out the stem of each chili and break or cut the chilies in half. Brush out the seeds with your fingers. In most cases the ribs inside are tiny, and can be left intact, but if they seem fleshy, cut them out with a small, sharp knife. Dried chilies should be torn into small pieces, covered with boiling water and soaked for at least 30 minutes before they are used. Fresh chilies may be used at once, or soaked in cold, salted water for an hour to remove some of the hotness.

Recipes: Latin American Cooking

The word "first" helps identify what step to begin with.

What are the steps in preparing fresh chilies?

Grammar Tip

As you edit your essay, notice that some of your transitions can appear in adverb clauses. For information see Lesson 14.5, pages 513–514.

Expository Writing

To explain a process, choose a topic that you understand well or can research if necessary. Then identify your audience and what they may already know. Locate terms they'll understand and those you'll have to explain. Be clear about your purpose. You may be helping readers make or do something themselves, such as making tacos. On the other hand, you may be explaining how something works or happens, such as how a Mexican chef makes tacos.

Journal Writing

In your journal use a cluster map to explore topics for a process explanation. You might choose a hobby or another activity you enjoy. Circle your three best ideas.

Make the Order Clear

Before you write about a process, gather information through research, observation, or interviews. List the steps of the process in chronological order. Then write your draft. Use transition words, such as *first, next,* and *later,* to connect the steps. The chart shows a plan one student followed to write the explanation that appears below.

Relating a Process	
Organizing Your Writing	**Example**
Topic	How to make a pizza
Audience	Friends
What the audience needs to know	The steps in making the pizza
Gathering information	Watch the video I taped. Read a pizza cookbook.
Listing steps	1. Spread dough. 2. Spread cheese. 3. Add vegetables. 4. Top with fresh tomatoes.

Student Model

The writer lists the four steps in chronological order.

First, spread the dough so that you have an inch-wide rim around the sides. The rim keeps the filling from leaking out while the pizza's cooking. Now it's time to put in the fillings. Place the cheese on the dough to keep it from getting soggy. Then add peppers, onions, or other vegetables that could burn if they were on top. Place fresh chopped tomatoes over the vegetables. Your pizza's oven-ready.

What transition words does the writer use in the explanation?

Luke Lapenta Proskine, Wilmette Junior High School, Wilmette, Illinois

Write a Step-by-Step Guide

Select an ordinary task, such as how to tie your shoes or how to find a library book. Write a step-by-step explanation for someone who knows little or nothing about the task.

PURPOSE To explain how to perform a simple task

AUDIENCE Someone who does not know how to perform the task

LENGTH 1/2 page

WRITING RUBRICS To write an effective step-by-step explanation, you should

- explain terms the reader may not know
- write the steps in chronological order
- use appropriate transition words
- use precise verbs to make your explanation clear

Listening and Speaking

COOPERATIVE LEARNING In a small group, brainstorm different kinds of foods that you know how to cook. Choose a food from the list, and draft a brief but clear step-by-step explanation of how to cook the food. If you need to do any research, individual students can take responsibility. Read your draft explanation in the group, and discuss how to revise the steps to make them clearer or more informative. Assemble your final explanation into a cookbook with other groups.

Use precise verbs to clarify explanations.

Precise verbs tell your readers exactly what you mean.

. . . *pull* out the stem of each chili and *break* or *cut* the chilies in half.

Revise each sentence below, replacing general verbs with more specific ones.

1. To make sugar cookies, first put oil on a shiny cookie sheet.
2. After making the dough, get it to cool down for several hours in the refrigerator.
3. Cook the cookies at 350° for 10 minutes.
4. Enjoy the cookies with a glass of milk, but do not eat all of them at one time.
5. Be sure to clean up the counters afterward.

See Lesson 3.3, page 122, and Lesson 10.1, page 401.

Viewing and Representing

CREATING VISUAL AIDS Create a series of four or five drawings that illustrate your step-by-step explanation. In your small group, be sure group members can connect your drawings with your essay. Attach the drawings to the essays for a "How to. . ." booklet.

LESSON 5.5

Explaining Connections Between Events

Sometimes events are connected—one event or situation causes another, and so on. The cause always comes before the effect, or result.

The skyscraper reflects billowing clouds. You ask yourself, What would cause an architect to use reflective glass in a skyscraper's windows? James Cross Giblin answers this question.

Literature Model

The energy crisis of the 1970s presented yet another threat to the windows in homes, schools, and office buildings. The all-glass architectural styles of the post-war years had depended on a steady supply of inexpensive fuel for heating and air-conditioning. Now there was a danger that that supply might be cut off, or drastically reduced.

To conserve energy and meet the demand for even better climate control in buildings, manufacturers developed an improved window covering—reflective glass. Reflective glass was coated with a thin, transparent metallic film. This mirrorlike coating reflected the sun's rays away from the glass and lowered heat gain within the building much more than mere tinted glass could.

James Cross Giblin, *Let There Be Light*

Be Clear About Cause and Effect

Giblin uses cause and effect to explain the origins of mirror-like skyscraper windows. The cause (the energy crisis) led to an effect (the development of reflective-glass windows). A cause-and-effect explanation may show one cause and one effect. Or it may explain a series of effects resulting from a single cause. It can also present multiple causes and multiple effects.

Make sure that your topic describes true cause and effect. Because one event follows another doesn't mean that the first caused the second. Suppose you close a window, and then the phone rings. Shutting the window didn't make the phone ring. Nick Poole linked cause and effect correctly in the paragraph below.

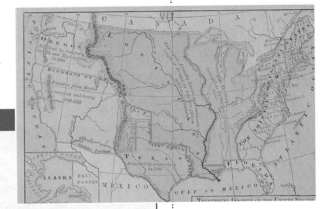

Student Model

During the nineteenth century, Americans were part of a tremendous expansion westward. These pioneering Americans left their homes back east for at least three reasons. Some were seeking fertile soil for farming. Many were looking for economic development. Trade was one way of making money. The pioneers traded with Native Americans, especially for furs. Various goods were also available from Mexicans. Finally, other Americans just went west for the adventure.

Nick Poole, Wilmette Junior High School,
Wilmette, Illinois

What three causes of westward expansion does Nick identify?

Journal Writing

Select a recent event that held some particular meaning for you. Identify the causes or effects of the event. In your journal list each cause or effect.

Choose an Organizational Pattern

The chart below shows steps you can take to organize a cause-and-effect essay. First, select a topic, and ask yourself if a clear cause-and-effect relationship exists. Next, explore the types of cause-and-effect relationships present. Is there one cause for several effects? Are there several causes leading to a single effect? Or are there multiple causes with multiple effects?

Finally, choose a pattern of organization for your writing. You can organize your cause-and-effect draft in one of two ways. One method involves identifying a cause and then explaining its effects. The other method involves stating an effect and then discussing its cause or causes. After you've completed your draft, review it to be sure the cause-and-effect relationships are clear.

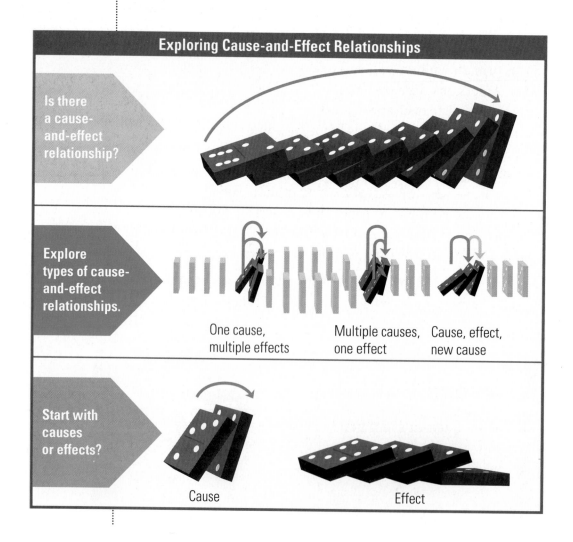

Exploring Cause-and-Effect Relationships

Is there a cause-and-effect relationship?

Explore types of cause-and-effect relationships.

One cause, multiple effects

Multiple causes, one effect

Cause, effect, new cause

Start with causes or effects?

Cause

Effect

Write a Cause-and-Effect Letter

You are concerned about the poor condition of the town's swimming pool and basketball courts. Write a letter to a town government official. Explain what could be the result if no action is taken. Present some solutions.

PURPOSE To present a cause-and-effect explanation

AUDIENCE Town government official

LENGTH 3–4 paragraphs

WRITING RUBRICS To write an effective cause-and-effect letter, you should

- establish a cause-and-effect connection between the conditions and possible outcomes
- explain possible multiple effects
- include facts and examples to support your case

Cross-Curricular Activity

SCIENCE Think of a natural process that involves a cause-and-effect relationship, such as the way a plant or a storm develops. Use your science book or other resources, including the Internet, to find information on the process. Then write a brief essay, aimed at fourth graders, designed to explain the cause-and-effect process. Be sure to explain or define any technical terms you use.

Grammar Link

Watch out for confusing word pairs.

Be sure to choose the correct word in pairs like *than* and *then*.

> . . . lowered heat gain . . . much more **than** mere tinted glass could.

Complete each sentence with the correct word.

I was [1](laying, lying) down; [2](than, then) my sister's friends arrived for her party. I had to [3](raise, rise)—no more [4](quiet, quite) for me. I could [5](accept, except) that because Ann would [6](leave, let) me join the party. To help out, I [7](sat, set) the table; [8](all together, altogether) there were ten of us. Each would [9](choose, chose) food from a buffet. [10](Beside, Besides) sandwiches, we were offering Chinese dishes.

See Lessons 17.1–17.3, pages 559–564.

Listening and Speaking

COOPERATIVE LEARNING In a small group, deliver your science essay as an oral presentation. Ask for feedback to help you make your presentation more suitable for younger students. If possible, arrange to present your science essay to a fourth-grade class.

Answering an Essay Question

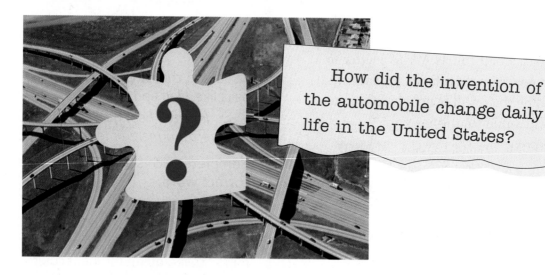

How did the invention of the automobile change daily life in the United States?

Essay questions on tests call for explanations. Understanding what the question calls for will help you improve your answers.

Writing a good answer to an essay question takes some planning. First, read the question carefully. Then decide roughly how many minutes you'll spend on each of the following tasks: (1) underlining key words and jotting down key ideas to include in the answer; (2) developing a thesis statement and a brief outline; (3) drafting your answer; and (4) revising and editing as time permits.

Begin planning your answer. Look at the question for clue words that can help you compose your answer. Then identify key ideas you'll want to discuss. You might explore them by using a cluster diagram or organize them by renumbering. The facing page shows how a student organized some key ideas to answer the test question at the top of this page. The chart below the student model gives examples of clue words.

Revising Tip

When you revise your answer, cross out any unnecessary details. Insert details that will make your answer more complete.

People ~~Farmers~~ are no longer isolated.   *Places*

Places like motels, drive-ins, and large shopping malls are a part of daily life.

People within cities can travel to jobs many miles from their homes.

People can drive many miles on short or long vacations.

The items in the list have been grouped as they will be discussed in the draft.

Clue Words in Essay Questions		
Clue Word	**Action to take**	**Example**
Describe	Use precise details to paint a picture of something.	Describe the appearance of the first Model T Ford.
Explain	Use facts, examples, or reasons to tell why or how.	Explain how the car was developed.
Compare	Tell how two or more subjects are alike.	Compare the steam car and the electric car.
Contrast	Tell how two or more subjects are different.	Contrast the Model T with a car of today.
Summarize	State main points in brief form.	Summarize how a four-cycle engine works.

Journal Writing

Use one clue word from the chart to write a question. Choose a topic that intrigues you. Take the notes you would need to answer the question.

Write Your Answer

Your answer should be a well-organized essay. The introduction to your essay should contain a statement of the main ideas in your answer. One effective way to begin is by restating the question.

Follow your introductory statement with the body of your answer. Include information from your notes as you write your supporting details. Then write a conclusion that restates your beginning statement and summarizes your answer. When you've finished your draft, see whether your content words match the content words of the question. Content words are the key words that relate to the subject matter. Finally, revise and edit your draft. Notice how one writer drafted an answer to the question on page 222.

The first sentence of the answer restates the question.

What details does the writer use in the body to show the change in Americans' daily life?

The conclusion restates the introductory statement.

> The invention of the automobile has changed daily life in the United States in two important ways. First, Americans are constantly on the move. City people can drive to jobs far from their homes. Farmers can travel to stores and offices miles away. Vacationers can drive to faraway places. Second, American businesses now provide services to go. Motels, drive-ins, and malls suit the needs of Americans on the run. Automobiles have changed America into a nation on wheels.

Write a Question and Its Answer

Write an essay question and answer dealing with the issue of energy use and conservation in your community. The question should enable you to use facts and information that are generally known.

PURPOSE To answer an essay question
AUDIENCE Your history teacher
LENGTH 2 paragraphs

WRITING RUBRICS To write an effective essay question and answer, you should

- develop a question that is challenging but realistic
- plan an answer that connects to the key words of the question
- organize your answer with an introduction, a body, and a conclusion

Listening and Speaking

COOPERATIVE LEARNING With a small group look through another textbook for a single essay question for everyone to answer. Take twenty minutes to answer the question. Then share your answers. Talk about the best parts of the organization and content of each essay. Discuss possible improvements.

Grammar Link

Use commas to separate items in a series.

Motels, drive-ins, and malls. . . .

Write each sentence, adding commas where necessary.

1. Sound heat and light are all forms of energy.
2. Water wind and geothermal energy are used to generate electricity.
3. Environmentalists policymakers and consumers do not always agree on energy issues.
4. Ski resorts office buildings and airplanes all require large amounts of energy to operate.

See Lesson 20.2, pages 601–602.

Cross-Curricular Activity

ART In a small group, select an interesting piece of artwork from this book. Together, develop an essay question that requires the writer to interpret and explain the meaning of the artwork. Individually, write answers to the group's question. Compare and contrast answers to see how much agreement or disagreement there was about the meaning of the artwork.

Expository Writing

Reports: Researching a Topic

*F*inding and narrowing a topic are the first tasks in preparing a research report.

On television you see a man flying an airplane, leading a flock of Canada geese. The man has raised these orphaned geese. Because they have not been able to learn to fly on their own, the pilot is teaching them. Why do the geese follow the airplane? When were they ready to learn to fly? Where will they go in the winter?

Find a Research Topic

When you prepare to write a research report, think about things you'd like to know more about. Read your journal for thoughts, questions, and possible topics. Think of a list of questions that you'd like to explore.

How and when do birds learn to fly?
Do geese use all their feathers to help them fly?
Why do birds migrate?
How do they find their way? Do they use landmarks or the position of the sun, moon, and stars?

Sometimes it's difficult to know whether your questions pertain to one topic or to several. You can decide by considering the length of your report. Are you writing a two-page report or a twelve-page report? The length of your report will determine what you can tell your readers.

The list of questions on page 226 is about birds, but the general topic of birds is too large for one report. The topic of Canada goose feathers is probably too narrow. The topic of Canada goose migration is probably just the right size for a two-page report.

Next, consider your purpose and your audience. What do you want to explain? What information do you want to share? Decide who your readers will be and how much they already know about your topic. Can you provide all the necessary background information and facts?

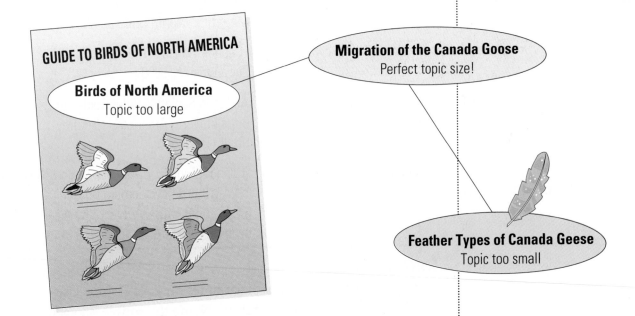

Journal Writing

Pick a news or sports event and jot down some questions about it. Is there a report topic here? If so, summarize what kinds of information you might include in the report.

Research Tip

Unit 22, pages 640–662, explains how to use the library's resources to find the information you need for your report.

Get the Facts

Now it's time to gather the facts you'll need to draft your report. Begin by looking for sources of information on your topic. At the library, for example, you might find books, articles, Web sites, CD-ROMs, or videocassettes about your topic. The chart below includes examples of the kinds of sources you might use. It also illustrates the format you should use in the bibliography at the end of your report.

Source Types and Bibliography Models		
Sources	**Example**	**Bibliography Listing**
Books	*Field Guide to Birds*	Mead, Chris. Bird Migration. New York: Facts on File, 1983.
Magazines & Newspapers	*Audubon*	Warden, J.W. "Migration! The Great Spring Event." Petersen's Photographic Magazine /April/ 1992: 22–25.
Encyclopedias	*The World Book Encyclopedia*	"Canada Goose." The World Book Encyclopedia. 1999
Video materials	*Audubon Society's Video-Guides to Birds of North America: Volume 1*	Audubon Society's VideoGuides to Birds of North America: 1. Godfrey-Stadin Productions, 1985.
Online information database	*Britannica Online*	"Canada Goose." Britannica Online. Vers. 99.1. 1994–1999. Encyclopædia Britannica. 8 Dec. 1999 <http://www.britannica.com/bcom/eb/article/212.html>.

Take Notes

As you read your sources, take notes on index cards. Use one card for each piece of information. Name the source on each card so that you can give proper credit when you use the information in your report. You must always tell readers when you use someone else's words or ideas. For example, you might write, "As Chris Mead wrote on page 35 of Bird Migration, . . ."

In your notes, you may write a paraphrase, a summary, or a direct quotation. A paraphrase is a restatement of a passage in your words, capturing the details. A summary is a restatement of the main idea of a passage. When you write a quotation, you copy the passage word for word, including the punctuation. Always put quotation marks around the quotations.

Expository Writing

Choose a Topic and Begin Your Research

Write down three or four topics that you would like to research. Think about which topic you would most enjoy researching and writing about. Write your topic at the top of a piece of paper. Write the headings Books, Magazines and Newspapers, People, Other Sources. Beside each one, note specific research sources. Use the library to get more ideas for sources and begin taking notes.

PURPOSE To gather information for a report
AUDIENCE Yourself
LENGTH 1 page of source ideas; at least 15 note cards

WRITING RUBRICS To choose a topic and begin your research, you should

- choose a topic you would enjoy learning more about
- narrow the topic so you can cover it thoroughly
- ask questions about your topic and use your sources to find answers
- write notes from your research on note cards, carefully naming your sources

Listening and Speaking

COOPERATIVE LEARNING Work with a small group of classmates to narrow your topics and add sources. Ask someone who knows about your subject for more ideas for sources.

Grammar Link

Punctuate and capitalize titles correctly.

"Migration! The Great Spring Event"
The World Book Encyclopedia

Write each title, adding capital letters, quotation marks, and italics (underlining) as needed.

1. following in sherman's footsteps (magazine article)
2. minneapolis star tribune (newspaper)
3. robert m. stuart's guide to civil war battlegrounds (video)
4. the red badge of courage (book)
5. the journal of the civil war (magazine)
6. gettysburg as theme park? (newspaper article)
7. the battle hymn of the republic (song)
8. the battle of bull run (book chapter)

See Lesson 19.4, pages 589–590, and Lesson 20.6, pages 609–610.

Using Computers

Check to see if your library has its card catalog on the computer. If so, ask a librarian to show you how to search for books and magazine articles about your topic.

Reports: Writing a Business Letter to Request Information

*W*riting a business letter can help you get answers to questions that other sources can't answer. As the model below shows, you can write a business letter to request information or to ask someone for an interview.

> 1565 Shadyside Road
> Dover, DE 19809
> January 10, 20--
>
> Ms. Maria Washington, Director
> Sellar's Island
> National Wildlife Refuge
> Route 3
> Tyler, DE 19968
>
> Dear Ms. Washington:
>
> I am an eighth-grade student at Dover Junior High School in Dover, Delaware, and I am working on a report on the migration of the Canada goose. I am writing to you to ask for information on the Canada geese that spend the winter at Sellar's Island. I'd appreciate it very much if you would answer these questions for me.
>
> 1. What features at Sellar's Island attract the large flock of geese?
>
> 2. What is the estimate for the actual number of geese that pass through each winter?
>
> 3. Have you done any leg banding to try to find out whether the same geese return each year?
>
> The answers to these questions, and any other information that you can provide, will be very helpful to me in my report. I live only about thirty miles from Sellar's Island. Would it be convenient for me to visit you for a brief interview and a tour of the refuge? I could arrange to come any weekday after school in the next two weeks. Thank you for your help. I look forward to hearing from you and learning more about the Canada goose.
>
> Yours truly,
>
> *Roberto Estevado*
>
> Roberto Estevado

Know Why You're Writing a Business Letter

When you write a business letter, you should have a clear reason for writing. If you're writing a business letter to request information, state your questions clearly. Make your request specific and reasonable and make sure you're asking for information you can't get anywhere else. If you're requesting an interview, explain what you want to discuss. Suggest some dates and times. Business letters have other uses, such as placing an order or lodging a complaint. A letter to the editor is a business letter written to express an opinion.

Grammar Tip

When editing, check your use of pronouns and antecedents. For more information see Lessons 11.1–11.7, pages 435–448.

Expository Writing

Guidelines for Writing Business Letters

1. Use correct business-letter form. Some dictionaries and typing manuals outline different forms of business letters.
2. Be courteous and use standard English.
3. Be brief and to the point. Explain why you need the information.
4. Use clean white or off-white paper. Make a neat presentation.
5. Be considerate. Request only information you can't get another way. If unsure where to find information, ask your librarian.
6. When requesting an interview, suggest a few dates so that the interviewee may be able to arrange a meeting with you.

Don't hesitate to write business letters to request information. Many people will be happy to tell what they know.

Journal Writing

Look in your journal for a possible report topic. Make a list of possible sources for information on this topic, other than the library, and think about how to contact those sources.

Get Down to Business

Readers expect business letters to be clear and to follow certain rules. At the beginning of your letter, introduce yourself and your purpose for writing. Use the paragraphs that follow to support your purpose with details. Conclude by stating clearly exactly what you want from the reader. Are you requesting an interview? Are you asking for answers to specific questions? Show your draft to a peer reviewer and ask whether your message is clear. When readers notice the care you took in writing to them, they will be more likely to respond to you.

The heading gives the writer's address and the date on separate lines.

The inside address gives the name, title, and address of the person to whom the letter is being sent.

The introductory paragraph states the purpose for writing.

The body presents supporting details—reasons and facts.

Use Sincerely or Yours truly, followed by a comma, for the closing.

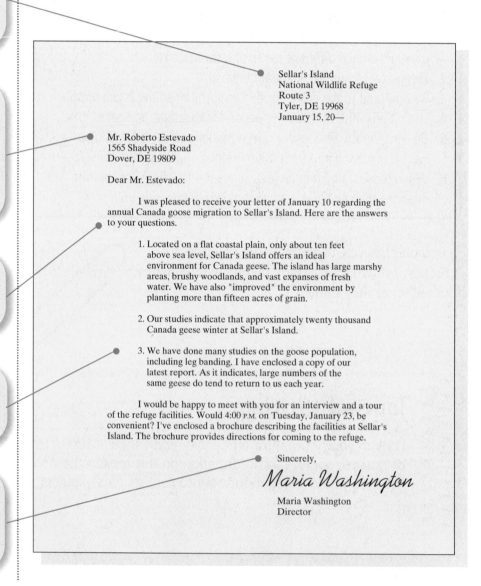

Sellar's Island
National Wildlife Refuge
Route 3
Tyler, DE 19968
January 15, 20—

Mr. Roberto Estevado
1565 Shadyside Road
Dover, DE 19809

Dear Mr. Estevado:

I was pleased to receive your letter of January 10 regarding the annual Canada goose migration to Sellar's Island. Here are the answers to your questions.

1. Located on a flat coastal plain, only about ten feet above sea level, Sellar's Island offers an ideal environment for Canada geese. The island has large marshy areas, brushy woodlands, and vast expanses of fresh water. We have also "improved" the environment by planting more than fifteen acres of grain.

2. Our studies indicate that approximately twenty thousand Canada geese winter at Sellar's Island.

3. We have done many studies on the goose population, including leg banding. I have enclosed a copy of our latest report. As it indicates, large numbers of the same geese do tend to return to us each year.

I would be happy to meet with you for an interview and a tour of the refuge facilities. Would 4:00 P.M. on Tuesday, January 23, be convenient? I've enclosed a brochure describing the facilities at Sellar's Island. The brochure provides directions for coming to the refuge.

Sincerely,

Maria Washington

Maria Washington
Director

Write a Business Letter

Look again at the topic you chose in the Journal Writing activity on page 231. Somewhere there is an expert on that subject who can give you information you can use in a report. Ask your local librarian to help you locate an expert. If the person lives in your area, use a letter to request an interview. Then prepare and carry out the interview. If your expert does not live near you, use a letter to ask the questions you would ask in an interview.

PURPOSE To gain expert information for a report

AUDIENCE Your interviewer; yourself

LENGTH 1-page letter; 1–2 pages of notes from the interview

WRITING RUBRICS To write an effective business letter, you should

- be clear about what you want
- be brief and considerate
- use correct form
- proofread to correct mechanical errors

Listening and Speaking

COOPERATIVE LEARNING In a small group, read your letters aloud to one another. Be prepared to both give and receive feedback about ways to improve the letters.

Grammar Link

Use correct punctuation in a business letter.

Write the business letter below, using the sample letter on page 232 as a guide.

> 4464 Rheims Place
> Dallas TX 75205
> January 20 20–

Dr. Cheryl Anne White
33 Parker Street
Cambridge MA 02138

Dear Dr. White

I heard you speak in Austin Texas on November 10 20– and was impressed with your advice on feeding birds. Please send me information about how I can order copies of your brochure "Winter Feeding Stations."

Thank you for your assistance.

Yours truly

Aaron Jacobs

See Lesson 20.4, pages 605–606, and Lesson 20.5, pages 607–608.

Using Computers

Proofread your business letter carefully—even after your computer checks for spelling errors. Most programs can't find errors caused by homophones, such as *to, too,* and *two.*

Reports: Planning and Drafting

*I*n this lesson, as you use research notes to begin planning and drafting, you will pull together all you've learned about reports.

© Watterson 1992. Universal Press Syndicate

Like Calvin, you've decided on a topic for your report. Unlike Calvin, however, you've done your research. Now that you've collected a lot of valuable information, it's time to learn a few strategies to help you begin your report.

Develop a Plan of Action

Before you begin planning and drafting a report, make sure you have a clear idea of your purpose for writing and of your audience. Knowing this information will help you focus your planning and drafting.

Review your notes, looking for a focus or a main idea that you can express in a sentence or two. Draft a thesis statement based on this main idea. Although your thesis statement may change as you continue researching or begin drafting, it can guide you as you write your outline.

After determining your thesis statement, you need to decide what main ideas you will cover in your report and draft an outline. Begin by looking through your note cards and grouping them according to topics. Each group of note cards can then become a main heading in your outline. The facts and details on the cards can become subtopics. The beginning of Roberto's outline appears below.

The Canada goose's migration pattern has dramatically changed in recent years.

I. Characteristics of the Canada goose
   A. What the Canada goose looks and sounds like as it flies overhead
   B. What its traditional migration pattern used to be
   C. How the pattern has changed

II. Basic needs of the Canada goose, and how they relate to migration
   A. Food
   B. Water
   C. Protection

III. Why and where the Canada goose used to migrate

The thesis statement identifies the topic and the main idea of the report.

The major outline heads state the main ideas of the paragraphs. Subheads note supporting facts and details.

Like all wildlife, Canada geese have a few basic requirements for
____ and their

Source: John Terborgh, Where Have All the Birds Gone?
____ Princeton

____rld War I, corn harvested by
____r harvested by machine—leaves up
____nt of crop in field. This will feed
____ birds. Therefore "the winter
____pacity for Canada geese
____ly been raised many fold."

Journal Writing

Read a newspaper or magazine article. In your journal, jot down the headline or title and the article's main idea or thesis. Then, on the basis of the article, create an outline of the article's main ideas and subtopics.

Put the Plan into Action

After you get your ideas organized, use your notes and outline to draft the three main parts of your report. The **introduction** presents your topic and thesis statement. It offers a chance to engage your readers and should grab their attention. Consider including a thought-provoking quotation, fact, statement, eyewitness account, or anecdote. The **body** supports your thesis statement with reasons and facts. The **conclusion** may reflect your thesis statement by summarizing main points. It should bring the report to a logical and graceful end. If your paper raises any new issues or questions, try including them in the conclusion.

Follow the process shown below in drafting a report from notes and an outline. Grammar and spelling errors will be corrected later.

Diet: grains, such as corn and wheat
—insects and water plants

Migration: families of Canada geese have flown as far south as northern Florida and northern Mexico

The Canada goose's migration pattern has dramatically changed in recent years.

I. Characteristics of the Canada goose
   A. What the Canada goose looks and

...erhead

...migration

...changed

...a goose

Drafting

Like all wildlife, Canada geese have a few basic requirements for survival. They need food, and their favorite foods is grains. They need water. They migrate in order to find areas that will provide a rich supply of there basic requirments. They need safety. The main enemy of the Canada goose is the human.

The Canada geese always used to fly to warm, southern areas in the fall. However scientists who study

Outline and Draft

You have done your research and made your note cards. You are now ready to develop a plan of action and then write the draft of your report. Now is the time to finalize the focus of your report. Be sure your main ideas all relate to your thesis statement. Group the notes you have taken into similar topics and then create an outline from the notes. Use your notes and outline to draft the three main parts of your report. Do not worry about spelling and grammar; you will correct errors in these later.

PURPOSE To outline and draft a report
AUDIENCE Peer reviewers
LENGTH 2–3 pages

WRITING RUBRICS To plan and begin your draft, you should

- write a clear thesis statement
- use your note cards to create an outline
- use your outline to help you develop your draft

Listening and Speaking

COOPERATIVE LEARNING Work in a small group and share your outlines with each other. Check to make sure the main ideas make sense and relate clearly to the thesis of the paper. Use the feedback to revise your outlines before beginning your draft.

Grammar Link

Use an apostrophe to form possessive nouns.

The Canada **goose's** migration pattern. . . .

To make the singular noun goose possessive, add '*s*. To make the plural noun *geese* possessive, also add '*s*: *geese's*. If a plural noun already ends in -*s*, add just an apostrophe: *birds'*.

Write each possessive phrase below, adding apostrophes where necessary.

1. the childrens playground
2. their parents voices
3. mices eating habits
4. a dogs life cycle
5. several students reports
6. the womens decision
7. my bosss orders
8. the planets orbits
9. universities research grants
10. peoples attitudes

See Lesson 20.7, pages 611–612.

Using Computers

Check to see whether your word-processing program has an Outlining feature to help you create an outline. Use it to organize your report.

Reports: Revising, Editing, and Presenting

Revising and editing are crucial steps in presenting your topic clearly and effectively.

Sometimes you become so involved in researching and writing your report that you are too close to evaluate your work objectively. You need to read your report as if you were reading the information for the first time.

Read Between the Lines

After you've finished the first draft of your report, put the draft aside for a while so you can return to it with a fresh eye. Then you can begin revising. Start by reading for sense. Are your main ideas clear? Have you supported your ideas with strong facts, statistics, examples, incidents, and reasons? Have you used transitions to help your readers move from one main idea to the next? Put yourself in your readers' place. If they know little or nothing about the topic, imagine that you don't either. Read carefully. The hints in the following chart may help you.

Revising Checklist

Question	Example
Do the main ideas in the paper support the thesis statement?	Summarize the main idea of each paragraph in the paper's body. Be sure that each main idea supports the thesis statement.
Do the main ideas appear in a logical sequence that builds to the conclusion?	List the main ideas in the order they appear. Can you think of a better order?
Does the conclusion sum up the main ideas and reflect the report's purpose?	Summarize the conclusion and compare it with the thesis statement. The thesis statement should lead logically to the conclusion.

Like all wildlife, Canada geese have a few basic requirements for survival. They need food, *an ample supply of* and their favorite foods is grains. They need water. They migrate to find areas that will provide a rich suply of there basic requirments. *also protection from their predators.* They need safety. The main enemy of the Canada goose is the human. *predator*

The Canada geese always used to fly to warm, Southern areas in the fall. However scientists who study these birds have discovered a change.

Moving this sentence connects two important thoughts.

Journal Writing

Review some of your earliest journal writing. How would you revise your writing now? Jot down some notes or revise a passage. Notice the difference a fresh eye can make.

Cross the t's and Dot the i's

When you edit your report, you proofread for any errors in grammar, spelling, punctuation, and word use. For more information, review pages 78–81. For help with a particular problem, see the **Troubleshooter** Table of Contents on page 309. You may find it easier to proofread for one type of error at a time. Some word processing programs will help you check for spelling errors. Remember, however, to read your draft for missing words and words that are easily confused, such as *their* and *there*. If you add a bibliography—a listing of your sources—follow the examples on page 228. Attach a clean cover sheet to your report, giving your name, the title of your report, and the date.

Spelling errors are corrected.

Errors in subject-verb agreement are corrected.

Like all wildlife, Canada geese have a few basic requirements for survival. They migrate to find areas that will provide a rich suply of there basic requirments. They need an ample supply of food. Their favorite foods is grains. They need water. They also need protection from their predators. The main predator of the Canada goose is the human.

Canada geese always used to fly to warm, Southern areas in the fall. However scientists who study these birds have discovered a change. Over the past few years, more and more Canada geese have remained in northern areas during the winter.

Migration Habits of Canada Geese
Roberto Estevado
February 28, 20–

Revise, Edit, and Share Your Report

Now revise and edit your report, making sure that it says what you want it to say. Does it support your thesis statement? Will it interest your readers?

PURPOSE To finish and share a research report
AUDIENCE Classmates, teacher, family
LENGTH 2–3 pages

WRITING RUBRICS To refine and present your report, you should

- revise your report to make it clear, organized, and interesting
- proofread to correct errors in grammar, usage, or spelling
- make a neat, legible final copy for others to read and study

Listening and Speaking

COOPERATIVE LEARNING In a small group, take turns reading your drafts aloud. Then exchange papers with a partner in the group. Write revision suggestions for each other and discuss each other's suggested changes. Make only the changes that you agree with. Exchange papers again and edit for errors in spelling and sentence structure.

Viewing and Representing

CREATING COVER ART Find or create a picture or drawing that would prepare a reader for your report. Reproduce or draw the image to use as a cover for your report.

Grammar Link

Use a comma after introductory words or phrases.

However, scientists who study these birds discovered a change.
Like all wildlife, Canada geese have a few basic requirements. . . .

Write each sentence, adding commas where necessary.

1. Indeed a family that adopts a dog takes on new responsibilities.
2. Unlike wild dogs domestic dogs depend on people to provide food and shelter.
3. Because of their long relationship with humans domestic dogs require human contact to thrive.
4. Originally bred to work most domestic dogs today are nonworking dogs and thus need regular exercise.
5. In return for all this care domestic dogs give their owners companionship and fun.

See Lesson 20.2, pages 601–602.

WRITING ABOUT LITERATURE
Comparing Two Poems

Expository writing can be used to describe a piece of literature, answer an essay question about it, or compare and contrast two selections.

These two poems describe one part of fall—migration. As you read the poems, jot down some of your reactions.

Literature Model

Fall

The geese flying south
In a row long and V-shaped
Pulling in winter.

                                    Sally Andresen

Something Told the Wild Geese

Something told the wild geese
    It was time to go.
Though the fields lay golden
    Something whispered,—"Snow."
Leaves were green and stirring,
    Berries luster-glossed,
But beneath warm feathers
    Something cautioned,—"Frost."
All the sagging orchards
    Steamed with amber spice,
But each wild breast stiffened
    At remembered ice.
Something told the wild geese
    It was time to fly,—
Summer sun was on their wings,
    Winter in their cry.

                                    Rachel Field

Write a Personal Reaction

Reading a poem is like listening to a song. It may create a picture in your mind, stir up feelings, or bring back a memory. Think about the pictures that come to your mind as you read the two poems on the previous page. Then jot down your responses to the following questions.

Grammar Tip

When editing your comparison-contrast essay, be sure you have used comparative and superlative adjectives correctly. For more information see Lesson 12.3, pages 461–462.

Questions About the Poems

1. In which poem do you see the geese from a distance? In which close up? Compare and contrast these views.

2. What sensory details does each poet use to describe the change of seasons from fall to winter?

3. How would you summarize the poems?

4. How would you compare their forms?

One student's answer to the second question appears below.

In "Fall" I look at a _V_ of geese straining in the sky. They seem to be pulling in winter. In "Something Told the Wild Geese" I see the geese with summer sun on their wings. Below them I notice golden fields, shiny, sparkling berries, and orchards full of ripened fruit.

Journal Writing

Find two poems about the same topic. In your journal, note any details that interest you. Which poem do you like better? Why? Write your impressions.

Drafting Tip

For more information about compare and contrast writing, review Lesson 5.3, pages 210–213.

Compare and Contrast

To compare or contrast two poems in an essay, you might like to begin with a Venn diagram such as the one below. Decide how to arrange your essay. You can write about the features of one poem and then write about the same kind of features in another. Or you can compare and contrast the poems one feature at a time.

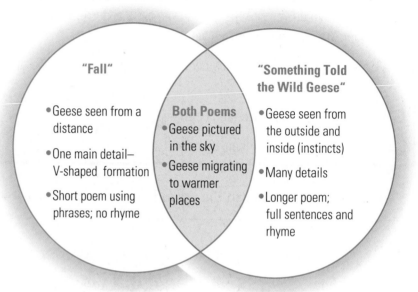

"Fall"
- Geese seen from a distance
- One main detail— V-shaped formation
- Short poem using phrases; no rhyme

Both Poems
- Geese pictured in the sky
- Geese migrating to warmer places

"Something Told the Wild Geese"
- Geese seen from the outside and inside (instincts)
- Many details
- Longer poem; full sentences and rhyme

Student Model

The introduction identifies the two poems and states the thesis.

What method of organization did this student use to compare and contrast the two poems?

"Fall" and "Something Told the Wild Geese" are two very different poems about geese. "Something Told the Wild Geese" is a sixteen-line poem that rhymes. Using descriptive words, the poet paints pictures of geese, fields, and orchards. "Fall," however, is a haiku, which does not rhyme. This poem shows geese flying, pulling in a different season. Reading the two poems is like looking at two different snapshots of geese.

John Moore, Wilmette Junior High School, Wilmette, Illinois

Writing About Similarities and Differences

Create a Venn diagram to compare and contrast the following poem with another poem about the sun. Then write an essay telling how the two poems are alike and different.

Sunset

The sun spun like
a tossed coin.
It whirled on the azure sky,
it clattered into the horizon,
it clicked in the slot,
and neon-lights popped
and blinked "Time expired,"
as on a parking meter.

Oswald Mbuyiseni Mtshali

PURPOSE Compare two poems
AUDIENCE Yourself
LENGTH 3–4 paragraphs

WRITING RUBRICS To write an effective compare-and-contrast essay, you should

- use a Venn diagram to organize your ideas
- choose a way to arrange your essay—selection-by-selection or feature-by-feature
- include similarities and differences

Listening and Speaking

READING POETRY In a small group, take turns reading the poems you found about the sun. Rehearse your presentation so that your reading will help listeners

Use participial phrases to modify nouns or pronouns.

In "Fall" I look at a V of geese straining in the sky.

Use each participial phrase below as an adjective in a sentence.

1. compared to our old house
2. staring at the ground
3. recommended by my brother
4. hidden in the grass

See Lesson 15.1, pages 527–528.

understand the poem. After each person reads his or her poem, the group should read or listen to that person's compare-and-contrast essay. Group members should discuss their interpretations and opinions of the poems and essays.

Cross-Curricular Activity

ART Find copies of two paintings of dogs, horses, or other animals. In one or two paragraphs, compare and contrast the two paintings. Do the artists share the same view of the animal? Do the settings help suggest the artists' views? Are the moods alike or different?

Writing Process in Action

WRITING Online

Visit the *Writer's Choice* Web site at **writerschoice. glencoe.com** for additional writing prompts.

Expository Writing

In preceding lessons, you've learned about writing essays and about using details to support various purposes, such as writing reports or answering test questions. You've also had the chance to write about a topic of interest to you. In this lesson, you're invited to apply what you know to research and write information for a guidebook for travelers in your state.

Assignment

Context	You have been asked to write about how a certain statue, memorial, or commemorative building came to be built in your neighborhood, city, or state. Your writing will be published in a guidebook for travelers.
Purpose	To inform travelers about the development and construction of a landmark
Audience	Visitors to your neighborhood, city, or state
Length	1 page

The following pages can help you plan and write your essay. Read through the pages. Refer to them as you need to, but don't be tied down by them. You're in charge of your own writing process.

Prewriting

You might begin prewriting by listing your own first impressions of landmarks in your neighborhood, city, or state or by thinking about where you'd take friends or relatives from out of town. What places and details would most fascinate them?

Use the options at the right to help you. If you need more facts, do research at a library, historical society, or travel agency.

Option A

Make a cluster diagram of local places of interest.

Option B

List five or six of your favorite places.

Option C

Do some small-group brain-storming.

Freedom House, on Hamilton Pike— historic home, Underground Railroad, museum about slavery in America. Just celebrated its twentieth anniversary as official landmark. Others in area: Strauss Hall?

Drafting

Once you've gathered all your facts, begin drafting. First, decide which facts would be the most interest-ing and useful to your audience. Next, decide how to organize your writing. In the passage below, notice how the author organizes his writing around the steps for choos-ing a design for the Vietnam War Memorial in Washington, D.C.

Literature Model

A total of 2,573 individuals and teams registered for the competition. They were sent photographs of the memorial site, maps of the area around the site and of the entire Mall, and other technical design information. The competitors had three months to prepare their designs, which had to be received by March 31, 1981.

Of the 2,573 registrants, 1,421 submitted designs, a record number for such a design competition. When the designs were spread out for jury selection, they filled a large airplane hangar.

Brent Ashabranner, *Always to Remember*

Drafting Tip

For more information about handling the details in an essay, see Lesson 5.2, pages 206–209.

Writing Process in Action

The purpose of the drafting stage is to get your thoughts and ideas on paper. If your writing contains many statistics, wait to check your facts later as part of the revising process. Do not worry about spelling, grammar, or punctuation at this point—just let the words flow. You will correct your errors in the revising and editing stages.

Revising

To begin revising, read over your draft to make sure that what you've written fits your purpose and audience. Then have a **writing conference.** Read your draft to a partner or small group. Use your audience's reactions to help you evaluate your work.

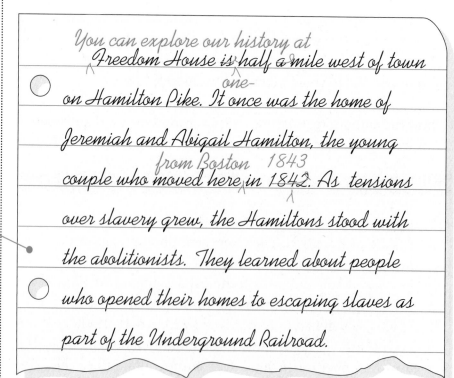

Question A

Will my introduction command attention?

Question B

Are details clear and accurate?

Question C

Does my conclusion reflect the main idea?

Editing

At this point you've put a lot of time and effort into the assignment. Don't let a few editing mistakes spoil the effect of an otherwise good piece of writing. When you **proofread** your revised draft, ask yourself questions like those listed on the right. If any part of the draft doesn't sound quite right, you may want to get additional advice from a teacher or friend.

Presenting

Before you present your finished work, con-

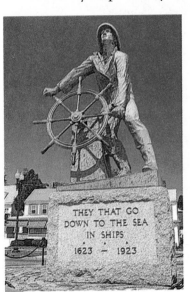

sider having someone at your chamber of commerce or local historical society read your report. That person might be able to give you some little-known details that you could add to the paper. Also, you might consider attaching copies of authentic photographs such as of people who inspired the memorial, a building being renovated, or a statue being installed.

Editing/Proofreading Checklist

1. Do all my subjects and verbs agree?
2. Do all my pronouns have clear antecedents?
3. Have I used commas correctly?
4. Have I used apostrophes correctly in possessive nouns?
5. Have I spelled every word correctly?

Proofreading Tip

For proofreading symbols, see page 331.

Journal Writing

Reflect on your writing process experience. Answer these questions in your journal: What do you like best about your expository writing? What was the hardest part of writing it? What did you learn in your writing conference? What new things have you learned as a writer?

Literature Model

Always to Remember

by Brent Ashabranner

In 1980 Vietnam War veteran Jan Scruggs and lawyers Roberet Doubeck and John Wheeler persuaded Congress to approve the building of a Vietnam War memorial in Washington, D.C. They hoped that the memorial would help to heal the bitter feelings that still existed because of this country's involvement in that war, even though it had ended in 1973. Brent Ashabranner tells the story of the national competition to design the war memorial. As you read his essay, notice what he does to capture and hold your attention. Then try the activities in Linking Writing and Literature on page 258.

The memorial had been authorized by Congress "in honor and recognition of the men and women of the Armed Forces of the United States who served in the Vietnam War." The law, however, said not a word about what the memorial should be or what it should look like. That was left up to the Vietnam Veterans Memorial Fund, but the law did state that the memorial design and plans would

A section of the Vietnam Veterans Memorial

have to be approved by the Secretary of the Interior, the Commission of Fine Arts, and the National Capital Planning Commission.

What would the memorial be? What should it look like? Who would design it? Scruggs, Doubek, and Wheeler didn't know, but they were determined that the memorial should help bring closer together a nation still bitterly divided by the Vietnam War. It couldn't be something like the Marine Corps Memorial showing American troops planting a flag on enemy soil at Iwo Jima. It couldn't be a giant dove with an olive branch of peace in its beak. It had to soothe passions, not stir them up. But there was one thing Jan Scruggs insisted on: the memorial,

Literature Model **251**

whatever it turned out to be, would have to show the name of every man and woman killed or missing in the war.

But there was one thing Jan Scruggs insisted on: the memorial, whatever it turned out to be, would have to show the name of every man and woman killed or missing in the war.

The answer, they decided, was to hold a national design competition open to all Americans. The winning design would receive a prize of $20,000, but the real prize would be the winner's knowledge that the memorial would become a part of American history on the Mall in Washington, D.C. Although fund raising was only well started at this point, the choosing of a memorial design could not be delayed if the memorial was to be built by Veteran's Day, 1982. H. Ross Perot contributed the $160,000 necessary to hold the competition, and a panel of distinguished architects, landscape architects, sculptors, and design specialists was chosen to decide the winner.

Announcement of the competition in October, 1980, brought an astonishing response. The Vietnam Veterans Memorial Fund received over five thousand inquiries. They came from every state in the nation and from every field of design; as expected, architects and sculptors were particularly interested. Everyone who inquired received a booklet explaining the criteria.[1] Among the most important: the memorial could not make a political statement about the war; it must contain the names of all persons killed or missing in action in the war; it must be in harmony with its location on the Mall.

A total of 2,573 individuals and teams registered for the competition. They were sent photographs of the memorial site, maps of the area around the site and of the entire Mall, and other technical design information. The competitors had three months to prepare their designs, which had to be received by March 31, 1981.

---

1 **criteria** (krī tir′ē ə) standards, rules, or tests by which something is judged

Of the 2,573 registrants, 1,421 submitted designs, a record number for such a design competition. When the designs were spread out for jury selection, they filled a large airplane hangar.[2] The jury's task was to select the design which, in their judgment, was the best in meeting these criteria:

- a design that honored the memory of those Americans who served and died in the Vietnam War.
- a design of high artistic merit.
- a design which would be harmonious with its site, including visual harmony with the Lincoln Memorial and the Washington Monument.

All who come here can find it a place of healing. This will be a quiet memorial . . .

- a design that could take its place in the "historic continuity" of America's national art.
- a design that would be buildable, durable, and not too hard to maintain.

The designs were displayed without any indication of the designer's name so that they could be judged anonymously, on their design merits alone. The jury spent one week reviewing all the designs in the airplane hangar. On May 1 it made its report to the Vietnam Veterans Memorial Fund; the experts declared Entry Number 1,026 the winner. The report called it "the finest and most appropriate" of all submitted and said it was "superbly harmonious" with the site on the Mall. Remarking upon the "simple and forthright" materials needed to build the winning entry, the report concludes:

This memorial, with its wall of names, becomes a place of quiet reflection, and a tribute to those who served their nation in difficult times.

All who come here can find it a place of healing. This will be a quiet memorial, one that achieves an excellent relationship with both the Lincoln Memorial or Washington Monument, and relates the visitor to them. It is uniquely horizontal, entering the earth rather than piercing the sky.

This is very much a memorial of our own times, one that could not

---

2 **hangar** (hang′ ər) a building or shed to store airplanes in

have been achieved in another time and place. The designer has created an eloquent[3] place where the simple meeting of earth, sky and remembered names contain messages for all who will know this place.

The eight jurors signed their names to the report, a unanimous decision.

> *How could this be? How could an undergraduate student win one of the most important design competitions ever held?*

When the name of the winner was revealed, the art and architecture worlds were stunned. It was not the name of a nationally famous architect or sculptor, as most people had been sure it would be. The creator of Entry Number 1,026 was a twenty-one-year-old student at Yale University. Her name—unknown as yet in any field of art or architecture—was Maya Ying Lin.

How could this be? How could an undergraduate student win one of the most important design competitions ever held? How could she beat out some of the top names in American art and architecture? Who was Maya Ying Lin?

The answer to that question provided some of the other answers, at least in part. Maya Lin, reporters soon discovered, was a Chinese-American girl who had been born and raised in the small midwestern city of Athens, Ohio. Her father, Henry Huan Lin, was a ceramicist[4] of considerable reputation and dean of fine arts at Ohio University in Athens. Her mother, Julia C. Lin, was a poet and professor of Oriental and English literature. Maya Lin's parents were born to culturally prominent families in China. When the Communists came to power in China in the 1940s, Henry and Julia Lin left the country and in time made their way to the United States.

Maya Lin grew up in an environment of art and literature. She was interested in sculpture and made both small and large sculptural figures, one cast in bronze. She learned silversmithing and made jewelry. She was surrounded by books and read a great deal, especially fantasies such as *The Hobbit* and *Lord of the Rings*.

---

3 **eloquent** (el′ ə kwənt) having a strong effect on people's ideas and feelings
4 **ceramicist** (sə ram′ ə sist) an expert in making pottery

The Vietnam Veterans Memorial in Constitution Gardens, Washington, D.C.

But she also found time to work at McDonald's. "It was about the only way to make money in the summer," she said.

A covaledictorian[5] at high school graduation, Maya Lin went to Yale without a clear notion of what she wanted to study and eventually decided to major in Yale's undergraduate program in architecture. During her junior year she studied in Europe and found herself increasingly interested in cemetery architecture. "In Europe there's very little space, so graveyards are used as parks," she said. "Cemeteries are cities of the dead in European countries, but they are also living gardens."

---

5 **covaledictorian** (cō′ val ə dik tôr′ ē ən) one who shares the position of the highest-ranking student in a class, who delivers the farewell address at graduation

In France, Maya Lin was deeply moved by the war memorial to those who died in the Somme offensive in 1916 during World War I. The great arch by architect Sir Edwin Lutyens is considered one of the world's most outstanding war memorials.

Back at Yale for her senior year, Maya Lin enrolled in Professor Andrus Burr's course in funerary (burial) architecture. The Vietnam Veterans Memorial competition had recently been announced, and although the memorial would be a cenotaph—a monument in honor of persons buried someplace else—Professor Burr thought that having his students prepare a design of the memorial would be a worthwhile course assignment.

Surely, no classroom exercise ever had such spectacular results.

After receiving the assignment, Maya Lin and two of her classmates decided to make the day's journey from New Haven, Connecticut, to Washington to look at the site where the memorial would be built. On the day of their visit, Maya Lin remembers, Constitution Gardens was awash with a late November sun; the park was full of light, alive with joggers and people walking beside the lake.

It just popped into my head. . . . It was a beautiful park. I didn't want to destroy a living park.

"It was while I was at the site that I designed it," Maya Lin said later in an interview about the memorial with *Washington Post* writer Phil McCombs. "I just sort of visualized it. It just popped into my head. Some people were playing Frisbee. It was a beautiful park. I didn't want to destroy a living park. You use the landscape. You don't fight with it. You absorb the landscape . . . When I looked at the site I just knew I wanted something horizontal that took you in, that made you feel safe within the park, yet at the same time reminding you of the dead. So I just imagined opening up the earth. . . ."

When Maya Lin returned to Yale, she made a clay model of the vision that had come to her in Constitution Gardens. She showed it to Professor Burr; he liked her conception and encouraged her to enter the memorial competition. She put her design on paper, a task that took six weeks, and mailed it to Washington barely in time to meet the March 31 deadline.

A month and a day later, Maya Lin was attending class. Her roommate slipped into the classroom and handed her a note. Washington was calling and would call back in fifteen minutes. Maya Lin hurried to her room. The call came. She had won the memorial competition.

Linking Writing and Literature

Readers Respond to the Model

How does Brent Ashabranner make his essay a thought-provoking and meaningful story for his readers?

Explore Brent Ashabranner's writing by answering these questions. Then read what other students liked about his essay.

1. The first thing a writer must do is choose an appropriate topic for a particular audience. What makes the subject of Ashabranner's essay right on target for readers of your age?

2. What kind of order does Ashabranner use to present the facts and details in his essay? Why is this the best order for the information he is presenting?

3. The author has space for only a limited number of facts about Maya Ying Lin. Reread the facts about her background and tell why you think the author chose to include them.

4. In the essay, find two places where the author interrupts the events to ask a series of questions. In each case, what effect does this technique have on you as a reader?

What Students Say

❝I enjoyed reading about the competition to choose the memorial for the soldiers who served in Vietnam. I had never heard about it before. I was very surprised when I read that a student attending Yale won. I had predicted that one of the architects would win.

If I had written this selection, I would provide more details about the competition. I would write some background information about Maya Ying Lin.

I would recommend this selection to a friend. I think that they too would be surprised to hear who won the competition. ❞

Faris Karadsheh

❝Always to Remember" was a good selection. I was so surprised when I found out that a twenty-one-year-old unknown artist from Yale won an important competition.

I enjoyed reading everything about the memorial wall and what it took to make it.

I would recommend this selection, especially to friends who like history. ❞

Shanna Breckenfeld

Reflecting on the Unit

Summarize what you have learned in this unit by answering the following questions.

1 What are the parts of an essay?
2 Name four types of expository writing.
3 How can you get your message across clearly?
4 How should you answer an essay question?
5 What are the stages in writing a report?
6 What is one way to respond to poetry?

Adding to Your Portfolio

CHOOSE A SELECTION FOR YOUR PORTFOLIO Look over the expository writing you did for this unit. Choose a piece of writing for your portfolio. The writing you choose should show one or more of the following:

- an introduction, body, and conclusion
- facts, statistics, examples, or reasons
- a strong organization and smooth transitions

REFLECT ON YOUR CHOICE Attach a note to the piece you chose, explaining briefly why you chose it and what you learned from writing it.

SET GOALS How can you improve your writing? What skill will you focus on the next time you write?

Writing Across the Curriculum

MAKE A MUSIC CONNECTION Choose two songs or other compositions by musicians with whom you are familiar. Write a one-page essay to compare and contrast the two compositions. Include information about the lyrics, rhythm, and melody, as well as your personal response to the two pieces. To review ways to organize information in comparison-contrast essays, see Lesson 5.3, pages 210–213, and Lesson 5.11, pages 242–245.

"Now *is* the time to make real the promises of democracy. . ."

—Martin Luther King, Jr.

I Have a Dream

Persuasive Writing

Writing in the Real World

Not-for-profit groups sometimes give money to support worthwhile projects. In order to receive funding support, interested people need to submit proposals. By definition, every proposal is an example of persuasive writing. Besides explaining their projects, the writers must convince the funding group that their projects are worth being supported. Many artists, like Indira Freitas Johnson, write proposals to get funding. This effort casts them in the dual role of artist and writer. The excerpt that follows is from Johnson's proposal.

**From "Joint Venture"
by Indira Freitas Johnson**

Joint Venture

Working title for a collaborative exhibition between SHARE (Support the Handicapped Rehabilitation Effort) and Indira Freitas Johnson.

Cloth and fiber arts have linked women all over the world for thousands of years. "Joint Venture" will be one more link, as it proposes to combine the drawings of an Indian-born American woman, Indira Freitas Johnson, and the hand work of SHARE, a Bombay-based group of women and handicapped persons.

A true collaboration means equal sharing. As such, while the drawings are done by Indira, they are interpreted totally by the various workers at SHARE. Hence, we see a unique blend of the trained and the untrained eye, the simple flow of a line drawing translated into the complexity of a pieced surface using miles upon miles of stitches.

Indira's work documents the feelings she experiences living between two vastly different cultures. She uses the philosophy and imagery of India to illustrate her experience of living in contemporary America. There is a surreal quality to much of her work, and the random choices of color, texture, and pattern used by SHARE employees sometimes enhance this surreal quality. . . .

A Writer's Process

Prewriting
Getting Started

For some writers, getting started is the hardest part. Indira Johnson agrees. Johnson says, "I sometimes think that getting started is very difficult. You have all these ideas. I think that's when you just need to start [writing]."

At this early stage, when she is trying to describe her ideas for a project, Johnson uses a form of freewriting: she simply gets words down onto paper. She tries to explain her project ideas as clearly as possible. But she doesn't worry that her prose isn't perfect or that her ideas aren't yet totally coherent. "I think from that initial writing you can say, 'This part is good' or 'This part needs reworking' or 'Juggle it around.'"

Johnson also does research during the prewriting stage, not just to gather information but also to help develop ideas. "Very often," she says, "I'll go to the library and just read up on various aspects of a particular project that I want to do. For example, I'll ask myself, 'Has it been done before?'"

Drafting
Writing to the Audience

A successful proposal addresses the concerns and interests of a specific audience. Johnson carefully considers her audience as she writes. "Who am I asking for support?" she asks herself. If her readers are professionals in the art world, she stresses the artistic advantages of her project. If the audience is interested in social service or cultural issues, Johnson emphasizes those points in the proposal. Adapting a proposal to an audience

The ideas that Johnson generates in her drawings eventually appear in details of the quilts made by SHARE.

may also influence a writer's point of view. In her "Joint Venture" proposal, Johnson wrote about herself in the third person instead of using the pronoun *I*. She wanted to stress that she was a member of a group effort and that this was not just her personal project.

Revising/Editing
Getting Feedback

Johnson knows the stage of revising well. "When I was writing in school, my father always said that there was no way to write a good paper the first time. You have to rewrite," she recalls.

For Johnson rewriting sometimes means "reseeing". As Johnson explains, "What happens very often is you become too close to a particular subject. You may have the sense that you're explaining it very clearly. But,

because you know all the details, you could be skipping over important facts." Johnson likes to ask someone outside the project, often her son or the owner of the gallery that shows her work, to read her proposal in order to see if it makes sense.

Response from a reader helps Johnson bring clarity to her writing. "I have a tendency to write something that has beautiful words and sounds really nice, but is it really pinpointing the meaning?" After getting reader response, Johnson revises one more time, incorporating the feedback into her finished piece.

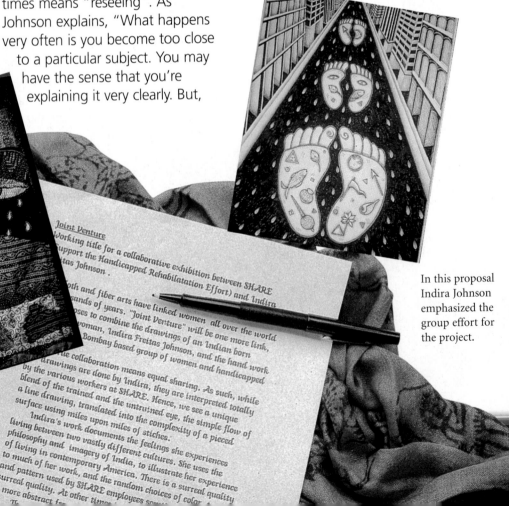

In this proposal Indira Johnson emphasized the group effort for the project.

Joint Venture
Working title for a collaborative exhibition between SHARE [to] support the Handicapped Rehabilatation Effort) and Indira Freitas Johnson .

[...]oth and fiber arts have linked women all over the world [...thou]sands of years. "Joint Venture" will be one more link, [...propo]ses to combine the drawings of an Indian born [...w]oman, Indira Freitas Johnson, and the hand work [...a] Bombay based group of women and handicapped [...]

[...the] collaboration means equal sharing. As such, while [...] drawings are done by Indira, they are interpreted totally by the various workers at SHARE. Hence, we see a unique blend of the trained and the untrained eye, the simple flow of a line drawing, translated into the complexity of a pieced surface using miles upon miles of stiches.

Indira's work documents the feelings she experiences living between two vastly different cultures. She uses the philosophy and imagery of India, to illustrate her experience of living in contemporary America. There is a surreal quality to much of her work, and the random choices of color and pattern used by SHARE employees somes [...] surreal quality. At other times [...] a more abstract f[...]

Examining Writing in the Real World

Analyzing the Media Connection

Discuss these questions about the proposal excerpt on page 262.

1. Why did Indira Johnson write the proposal "Joint Venture"?
2. What do you think Johnson is emphasizing in this particular excerpt?
3. Is Johnson writing to an audience who is more interested in the fine arts or in the social benefits of collaborating with an Indian group? How can you tell?
4. What support does Johnson provide to show that her project is one of "true collaboration"?
5. Why does Johnson speak of herself in the third person throughout the excerpt?

Analyzing A Writer's Process

Discuss these questions about Indira Johnson's writing process.

1. What does Johnson say is the best thing to do when you have difficulty getting your writing started? When and how could you adapt her methods in getting started to your own writing process?

2. What kinds of research does Johnson conduct?
3. How does researching contribute to Johnson's writing?
4. What key question does Johnson ask herself to keep her persuasive writing on target?
5. How and why does Johnson use feedback from readers during revision?

Capitalize proper nouns and proper adjectives.

Indira Freitas Johnson is an Indian-born American woman.

Write each sentence, using capital letters where necessary.

1. A new exhibit is opening at the garcia gallery on friday.
2. It will feature native american, european, hispanic, and asian art.
3. This area was first settled by the navajo, then by germans, then by mexicans and laotians.
4. Gallery owner jose garcia calls the show "visions of home."
5. It will truly be an all-american exhibit.

See Lessons 19.2–19.4, pages 585–590.

Writing Persuasively

*W*hen you write to persuade, you try to convince your audience to think or act in a particular way. Often an image can be a powerful form of persuasion. This poster helped convince many Americans to enlist during World War I.

State Your Case

In most persuasive writing, the writer states an opinion or urges an action and then offers reasons why readers should accept the opinion or support the action. Reasons are often supported by facts, examples, or stories. What kinds of support does the writer of the model on the next page use to back up her opinion?

Student Model

One of the most disturbing trends I see is the draining of wetlands. Thousand-year-old swamps are being destroyed in just days to build skyscrapers and shopping malls or to plant crops. Where are ducks, geese, and other wildfowl going to raise their families or find food and rest when migrating? The answer is simple: each species will slowly die. These animals' habitats are being taken from *all* of us. It is sad, it truly is, to know the birds I love are moving closer to extinction.

April Barnes, Decatur, Alabama
First appeared in *Merlyn's Pen*

April wants her readers to take the problem personally, as she does. How does she appeal to their emotions?

Your world is full of topics for persuasive writing. What changes would you like to see in your school and community and in the larger world? By exploring the following sources, you can discover some issues you care about.

Look for Issues in Your Reading

Look for Issues in Other Media

Look for Issues in Conversation

Journal Writing

List some changes you'd like to see, using the sources above for ideas. As you study this unit, add to your list, and use the ideas in your persuasive writing.

Revising Tip

Even as you draft and revise, continue to look for information on your topic. Strengthen your case by adding any additional proof.

Back It Up

Research is an important step in persuasive writing. Your opinions will carry weight only if you can back them up. To gather support, investigate your topic by reading, observing, and discussing, and sometimes by interviewing experts—those with special knowledge about the issue. Patrick MacRoy felt strongly about a local issue: an electric company's plan to run wires along a nature trail. He wrote the following article for his school paper.

Student Model

The Prairie Path is one of the last areas around here in which to enjoy nature. It is used by cyclists, hikers, horseback riders, and even schools as a site for nature classes. It was even recognized by the U.S. government as a national recreation trail. Groups like Friends of the Illinois Prairie Path are working hard [to save] the trail by circulating petitions and holding public meetings. Citizen groups say there are alternate routes for the power lines, if [the electric company] is willing to find them.

If you want to help save the path, there will be a petition to sign in the lunchroom for the next few days. Thanks for your help.

Patrick MacRoy, Glen Ellyn, Illinois
First appeared in *Call of the Wildcat*

What information does Patrick include to show the usefulness of the path?

Notice that Patrick supports his opinion by referring to expert sources.

Write a Persuasive Paragraph

Think of an environmental issue that affects your school or community. You might see an appropriate issue on the list you created for this lesson's Journal Writing activity. Research the issue and discuss it with others. Make prewriting notes.

PURPOSE To state and support a position
AUDIENCE Classmates; city council
LENGTH 1–2 paragraphs

WRITING RUBRICS To write an effective persuasive paragraph, you should

- state your position clearly
- use facts to back up your position

Cross-Curricular Activity

ART Your city council intends to install the sculpture shown on this page in a park near your home. State your opinion in writing. Offer reasons that will persuade the city council to install or not to install the art.

Mariam Schapiro, *Anna and David*, 1987

Viewing and Representing

MAKE A POSTER In a magazine, find a picture of a sculpture, painting, or other work of art. Cut the picture out and paste it to a piece of poster board or cardboard. Surround the picture with persuasive comments—both favorable and unfavorable—about the art.

Make sure the verb agrees with the subject, not with a word in an intervening phrase.

One of the most disturbing trends I see is the draining of wetlands.

Complete each sentence with the correct choice of verb.

1. The home of my ancestors (is, are) not for sale.
2. A classroom for small children (require, requires) toys.
3. Boys of my father's generation (was, were) routinely drafted at age eighteen.
4. A path through the woods (offers, offer) many small pleasures.

See Lesson 16.2, page 543.

LESSON 6.2

Determining a Position

If you've visited a zoo, you've seen people of all ages looking at and learning about animals from around the world. Some people, however, claim that animals belong only in the wild, not in captivity. Other people defend zoos as humane, well-designed environments that preserve endangered species and educate visitors.

Take a Stand

Once you take a stand on an issue, you must find support for it. At the same time, you should also consider arguments your opponents might make against your position. During the prewriting step, list both *pros* (points that can be used to support your argument) and *cons* (points that might be used against it). Look at the example on page 271.

Pro

1. Zoos protect endangered species.
2. Modern zoo environments resemble habitats.
3. Zoos educate public about conservation.
4. Zoos are run by professionals.

Con

1. Zoos are animal prisons.
2. Captivity changes animals' behavior.
3. Animals should not be entertainment.
4. Capture/confinement can hurt animals.

Student Model

Zoos today are important to the survival of many species. They do not abuse the animals, but instead they offer a safe and healthy environment. At the same time they provide an enjoyable viewing experience for people of all ages. This gives us an opportunity to better appreciate animals and learn more about their preservation. As stated in the *Utne Reader* [a general-interest magazine about ideas and issues], zoos are "institutions we should see not as abusers of the world's animals, but as vital forces saving animals from extinction."

Jacqueline Parks, Springman Junior High School
Glenview, Illinois

According to Jacqueline, how do zoos benefit both animals and people?

Grammar Tip

In editing, check for a comma before a coordinating conjunction, such as *and, but, or,* or *nor,* when it joins the two main clauses of a compound sentence. For more on compound sentences, see Lesson 14.1, page 505, and Lesson 20.3, page 603.

Journal Writing

Think of an issue on which someone disagrees with you. Create pro and con lists like the ones above. Try to include strong points on both sides.

Consider Your Audience

Your audience is important in persuasive writing. When your goal is to influence opinions, you need to know who your readers are and how they think. Study the models below. The first, from the foreword of a book for children, is written to their parents. The second speaks to educators.

Literature Model

What criticism of video games is Berry answering?

It isn't that video games in and of themselves are harmful. Problems arise instead when the attitudes, priorities, or habits of their users are out of line. That's why children must be encouraged to view video games in a balanced, reasonable way and to take responsibility for their proper use.

Who will do this encouraging?

Joy Wilt Berry, *What to Do When Your Mom or Dad Says . . ."Don't Overdo with Video Games!"*

Literature Model

What criticism of video games is Turkle answering?

There is nothing mindless about mastering a video game. The game demands skills that are complex and differentiated . . . and when one game is mastered, there is thinking about how to generalize strategies to other games. There is learning how to learn.

Why would this appeal to teachers?

Dr. Sherry Turkle
The Second Self: Computers and Human Spirit

Both writers defend video games but for different readers. Berry reassures worried parents and explains that attitudes and not video games are the problem. Turkle addresses educators and speaks about thinking skills.

Write a Position Paper

Think of a controversial issue on which you have not yet formed an opinion. Develop an argument for each side. Decide which side is stronger and defend it in a persuasive piece directed at others who are still undecided.

PURPOSE To defend a position

AUDIENCE Your classmates, readers of a newspaper

LENGTH 1 page

WRITING RUBRICS To write an effective position paper, you should

- state your position clearly

- use facts and language that are targeted to your audience

Cross-Curricular Activity

HEALTH You've traveled back in time to the nineteenth century. You're aboard an English sailing ship docked in a Caribbean harbor. The sailors tell you that for months they've eaten nothing but hard biscuits and salt pork, with no fresh fruits or vegetables. Now their gums are bleeding. They've heard from other sailors that oranges will help the condition, but on this island, there are only limes. Write a conversation between yourself and a sailor, trying to persuade him to eat the limes.

Use a comma before a conjunction that links two main clauses.

*They do not abuse the animals, **but** instead they offer a safe and healthy environment.*

Write each sentence, adding commas where necessary.

1. Young people like the challenge of video games and that challenge can stimulate learning.

2. Some games are designed to be educational but even purely recreational games can spark the imagination.

3. Both young people and their parents should exercise good judgment for not all video games are appropriate for all ages.

See Lesson 14.1, page 505, and Lesson 20.3, page 603.

Listening and Speaking

PRESENT A DRAMATIC DIALOGUE With a partner, present your persuasive conversation from the Cross-Curricular Activity on this page as a dramatic dialogue for your classmates. As you rehearse, consider your audience and the setting, taking care to use effective rate, volume, pitch, and tone. Ask the class to evaluate your dialogue for content and presentation.

Evaluating Evidence

Advertisers and others who want to sell you products or services also use the techniques of persuasion. Even a cereal box can be a persuasive tool.

Nutrition information per one-ounce serving:

Calories	90
Protein	4 g
Carbohydrates	20 g
Fat	0 g
Cholesterol	0 mg
Sodium	0 mg
Potassium	105 mg

YOUR GOOD-HEALTH GAME PLAN

SUPER BOWL

"DELICIOUS"

FITNESS FLAKES

Your grocery list says "healthful cereal," so you hurry past Sugary Chunks and Sweet Treats. You spot an unfamiliar brand, Super Bowl Fitness Flakes. Read the labels on the box. What is the real difference between Fitness Flakes and Sweet Treats? When it's time to make your choice, will the box front or the labels be more helpful? Why?

Support Opinions with Evidence

The information on the cereal box illustrates two kinds of evidence—facts and opinions. Facts can be proved—the cereal could be tested for the number of calories per one-ounce serving. Opinions, such as "delicious," are personal judgments. They can't be proved. When you state an opinion, back it up with evidence: facts, statistics, and examples.

Read the following paragraph, and notice the facts, opinions, and other kinds of evidence it contains. Then study the chart that follows.

Many Americans hate their bodies. "We have declared war on our bodies," charges Andrew Kimbrell, the author of The Human Body Shop. This war includes 34 percent of all men and 38 percent of all women. They spent $33 billion on diets in 1990. A preteen boy guzzles protein drinks, hoping to increase his size and strength, while a fifty-five-year-old woman gets a face-lift. Technology and social pressure are causing us to make extreme changes.

The opinion is stated first.

The writer supports the opinion with evidence.

The writer draws a conclusion.

Evidence in Persuasive Writing	
Kinds	**Examples**
Fact	Americans spent $33 billion on diet products in 1990.
Statistic	Thirty-four percent of men and 38 percent of women spent $33 billion on diets in 1990.
Example	A fifty-five-year-old woman gets a face-lift.

Journal Writing

Jot down the evidence that persuaded you to change your mind about something or someone. Label each piece of evidence as one or more of the three kinds shown above.

Select Strong Evidence

Not all pieces of evidence are equally strong. Some "facts" are really opinions in disguise. When you write persuasively, check your facts, and make sure that they back up your point. In the model below, nutritionist Jane Brody says that choosing soft drinks over water "presents a . . . serious threat to good nutritional health." Does she persuade you? Why or why not?

Literature Model

No beverage in America gives water greater competition than flavored soft drinks. And probably no other choice presents a more serious threat to good nutritional health. Soft drinks are the epitome [ideal example] of empty calories. They contain water (with or without carbon dioxide), artificial colorings and flavorings, and sugar—as many as *6 teaspoons of sugar in one 8-ounce serving!* Nothing else. Some noncarbonated drinks add vitamin C, and "fruit" or "fruit-flavored" drinks may even contain some real fruit juice. But for the most part, they are just wet, sweet calories.

Jane Brody, *Jane Brody's Nutrition Book*

What kind of evidence does this sentence contain, facts or opinions?

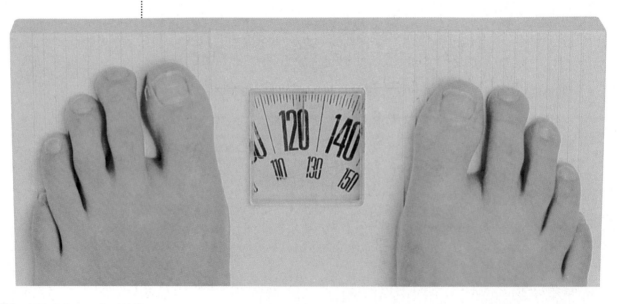

Write a Persuasive Essay

Usually you look for evidence supporting a position you already hold. Sometimes, however, the reverse happens. A fact "grabs" you, and you want to learn enough to develop a position on the issue. Find a piece of evidence, such as the fact that some fast-food chains use polystyrene containers rather than paper.

Try to connect this piece of evidence with what you already know. Develop a one page persuasive essay for an audience of your choice.

PURPOSE To persuade someone about an issue
AUDIENCE Your choice
LENGTH 1 page

WRITING RUBRICS To write an effective persuasive essay, you should

- include facts, statistics, examples, and reasons as evidence
- examine your evidence critically to be sure that facts are correct and that they support your argument

Learning and Speaking

PANEL DISCUSSION Has the world become warmer because of excess carbon dioxide and other gases? Are recent extreme temperatures simply normal climatic variations?

With two or three classmates, research the existence and possible causes of the greenhouse effect. Prepare and present a short panel discussion for the class. Afterwards, discuss the presentation's strengths and weaknesses.

Grammar Link

Use a plural verb with a compound subject joined by *and*.

Technology and social pressure are causing us to make extreme changes.

Write each sentence, correcting errors in subject-verb agreement.

1. At the end of this hilarious book, Perry's dog and his luggage ends up in China.
2. A sensible diet and an exercise program contributes to good health.
3. Three facts and one example supports the writer's opinion.
4. A sincere apology and a full refund has been sent to each angry customer.
5. Strong evidence and good organization makes your case more convincing.

See Lesson 16.5, page 549.

Viewing and Representing

In a science magazine or on the Internet, find some pictures relating to recent environmental changes due to temperature variations. Use the pictures to support the evidence you present in your panel discussion.

LESSON 6.4

Developing a Strategy

As Calvin demonstrates in the cartoon below, even a reluctant audience can be reached with the right attention-grabbing strategy. The first step in persuasion is to get the attention of your reader. Newspapers, magazines, television, and radio all compete for attention. You must find ways to make your message stand out from all the rest.

© Watterson 1992. Universal Press Syndicate

Get Attention

How can you capture your readers' attention? As many writers have discovered, a playful imagination can work wonders. The following student model brings an everyday object to life in a humorous, imaginative way; her serious purpose, however, is to draw attention to an important issue.

As one of the many cheap, unreliable, plastic department store bags, I'd like to speak out. Even though humans think of us as worthless, I wish they wouldn't throw us out their car windows, leaving us to fight for our lives on busy, treacherous highways. Wind gusts from cars going sixty miles an hour blow our flimsy bodies everywhere. Sometimes we land on windshields and cause accidents. Even worse, humans often leave us to baby-sit their small children. Don't get me wrong— we like kids, but not when they put us over their heads or in their mouths and begin to choke, turn blue, and die. . . .

So please, be careful when you dispose of us. Don't throw us out car windows or give us to babies. We like humans and definitely would not want to have them angry at us for wrecking their cars and killing their kids.

Dina Morrison, Pittsburgh, Pennsylvania
First appeared in *Merlyn's Pen*

The surprise of a talking plastic bag attracts the reader's attention and arouses interest.

What problems does the writer identify, and how does she suggest that people solve them?

Persuasive Writing

Some lively formats for persuasive writing include real-life stories, fables, parables, ballads, and letters to people from the past or future. You might also use visuals, such as pictures, charts, and graphs, to call attention to the issue.

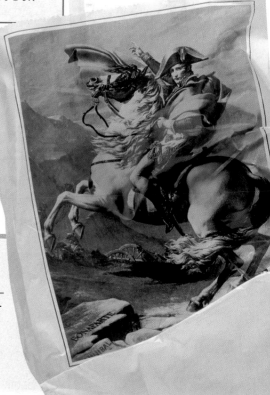

Journal Writing

Poet Robert Frost said that if there is no surprise for the writer, there will be no surprise for the reader. List some elements that have drawn your attention to persuasive messages. Analyze why they caught your attention.

Organize Your Argument

Your case, or argument, consists of a statement of your position and supporting evidence arranged in an orderly manner. Notice how this writer includes an answer to an opposing idea.

> This is the topic sentence, since it expresses the main idea. What is the main idea?

> The writer says this idea is the most important. Do you agree? Why might the writer have saved it for last?

On quiet nights the sound of a distant train reminds me of a time when railroads provided our most reliable passenger transportation. Rail passenger service, vital to America's past, can be even more important to its future. But, you say, trains are slow. True, but with today's crowded airports and new "bullet-train" technology, rail service can compete with the airlines in speed as well as cost. Trains use less fuel per passenger-mile than planes, cars, or buses do. Most important, trains' fuel efficiency conserves oil and decreases air pollution.

Grammar Tip

In editing make sure you use past and present tense correctly. For more information on verb tense, see Lesson 10.5, page 409.

First, the paragraph grabs attention with a nostalgic image involving trains. Then it presents its main point, answers opposition, and provides additional supporting evidence. The following chart summarizes what you should include in most arguments.

How to Build Your Case
1. State your position clearly.
2. Present sound, relevant evidence.
3. Anticipate and answer the opposition.
4. Begin or end with your strongest point.

Write a Presentation

Your school district is considering ending athletic contests between schools. Supporters of this view argue that the athletic program wastes money and takes time away from education. Write a presentation to your school board supporting your view of interscholastic athletics.

PURPOSE To persuade readers about school athletic contests

AUDIENCE Your school board

LENGTH 2–3 paragraphs

WRITING RUBRICS To write an effective persuasive presentation, you should

- choose a strategy to gain attention and interest
- grab your readers' attention
- state your position and evidence
- begin or end with your strongest point
- answer the opposition

Learning and Speaking

ORGANIZE A FUND RAISER With a group of classmates, make a list of charitable projects you might support (for example, meals for homeless families). Debate the merits of each project and choose one. Meet with the class to consider other groups' ideas. Then decide on a fund raiser, such as a car wash, special athletic event, or bake sale. Create a flyer to urge families to support the project. Decide on the content of the flyer, and divide the tasks necessary to prepare it.

Grammar Link

Use commas to set off words that interrupt the flow of the sentence.

*But, **you say**, trains are slow.*

Rewrite the following, adding commas where necessary.

1. One way to reduce trash obviously is to reduce usage. Buying fewer objects you know means fewer discards.

2. Another way of course is to recycle materials. Organic materials even kitchen garbage can go to a compost heap. Some materials like glass and aluminum are easily reused.

3. Plastics and old tires on the other hand pose a challenge. Recycled plastic for example may be used in rugs.

4. Unrecycled materials for the most part end up in landfills or incinerators.

See Lesson 20.2, page 601.

Using Computers

To add a picture to a document, open the document, pull down the Insert menu, and select Picture. Browse through the picture file and select the one you want. Insert by clicking on the Insert button.

Strengthening Your Argument

*W*riting persuasively is a challenge. You can strengthen your argument by revising your work and filling in the gaps.

Just as the acrobats at the left must have sturdy equipment, your position must have strong support. And just as the acrobats have to synchronize their movements, you must organize your ideas so that they all work together to make your point.

Take Another Look

The word *revising* means "seeing again." To revise persuasive writing, set it aside for a time, and return to it later. You often have assignments that are due on a certain date, so you can't wait days or weeks to finish a piece of writing. However, if you begin your assignment several days before it is due, you will allow time for revision. Professional writers agree that setting your work aside, even if only for a day, will give you a fresh, new perspective. You may find that your best ideas will come during revision.

Peer reviewing is another helpful technique. Before you revise, ask a classmate to listen to your draft to help you identify any problems. To see how peer reviewing works, read the following draft. Then read the peer reviewer's comments, and decide whether you agree with them.

Paragraph 1:
I like your opening paragraph. It grabs my attention. Are the slang words OK here?

Paragraph 2:
Good ideas, but you provide little evidence. Do you have any facts and examples?

Paragraph 3:
Is summer employment a reason why you don't want year-round school? Can you make this paragraph clearer?

I have something to say to those adults who want to keep schools open all year long. Give me a break! Please don't do anything so drastic!

Eliminating summer vacation will cause enormous stress for everyone. Teachers will burn out faster. Nobody will pay attention in class in the middle of July, and the air-conditioning bills will be enormous. Also, additional salaries for teachers and janitors will be astronomical!

Year-round school will not help education, but it may reduce learning because many students take summer jobs to save for college tuition.

Notice that this peer review contains questions and suggestions—not commands. After peer review, it's up to you to read over the comments, decide which ones you agree with, and make those changes.

Journal Writing

Describe one good and one unsatisfactory experience you've had with a peer reviewer. In your opinion what are the characteristics of a good peer reviewer?

Fill in the Gaps

Holes, or gaps, in the argument weaken a persuasive appeal. The questions that follow will help you check your argument for adequate support.

Revising Persuasive Writing

1. Do I make my position clear?

2. Do I present enough evidence?

3. Is the evidence strong? Is it relevant?

4. Do I keep my audience in mind?

5. Are my ideas organized effectively?

Revision is far more than simply changing a word here and there. You may need to add, delete, or move whole sentences and paragraphs. During the revising stage, you must read, ask yourself questions, experiment, and revise some more. You may even need to do more research. The paragraph below works well because David Levine supports his point with strong evidence.

Literature Model

What position does Levine state in the first sentence?

Staying in school and graduating extends the range of options of what you can do with your life. It's also a fact that the consequences of dropping out are severe and the prospects for dropouts are bleak. According to the National Dropout Prevention Center, less than 50 percent of dropouts find jobs when they leave school. When they do, they earn 60 percent less than high school graduates (over a lifetime that adds up to $250,000).

Levine's evidence is powerful, solid, and relevant to his audience.

David Levine, "I'm Outta Here"
First appeared in *Seventeen*

Revise a Persuasive Piece

Take another look at a writing assignment that you completed earlier in this unit. Consider the five questions on the chart on the preceding page. Then revise the piece.

PURPOSE To review and revise an earlier piece of persuasive writing

AUDIENCE Yourself

LENGTH 3–4 paragraphs

WRITING RUBRICS To effectively revise a persuasive piece, you should

- look at your piece with a new perspective
- ask yourself the five questions on the chart on page 284
- make sure there are no gaps in your argument
- add or change words and sentences as necessary

Using Computers

Sometimes writers prefer to revise at their computer terminals. Having a revision checklist right on the screen, along with the piece of writing you want to revise, is helpful. Develop a list of ten or twelve items for the checklist, and use a split screen to keep the list available as you revise.

Grammar Link

Use subject pronouns as the subject of a sentence and object pronouns as the object of a verb or preposition.

I have something to say. . . .
Give me a break!

Be especially careful with compound elements: *Sue and I saw Joe and him.*

Write each sentence, correcting errors in pronoun usage.

1. Rachel and me support the proposed art curriculum.
2. However, Rachel can better explain it to you and he.
3. Ginny was always available to help Ralph and she.
4. Here is a gift from Trudy and I.
5. Tell Martin and she the news.

See Lesson 11.1, page 435, and Lesson 11.3, page 439.

Listening and Speaking

EVALUATE YOUR REVISION With a small group, take turns reading aloud your original persuasive pieces and your revisions. After each presentation, discuss the ways in which each revision improved the original work.

Persuasive Writing

Creating an Ad

*Y*ou find advertising almost everywhere you look. Ads *try* to sell products, places, candidates, and ideas. *Advertising agencies use many approaches in their efforts to persuade.*

At what audience is this ad aimed? Does the ad make you want to visit Brookfield Zoo? Jot down your reaction and some reasons for it. Consider why the ad works or doesn't work for you.

Isn't it time you set your kids straight on tomato frogs?

Visit Brookfield Zoo, and your kids can see how nature's creatures *really* look, instead of jumping to conclusions. To find out more, call us at 708-485-0263. We're closer than you think.

BROOKFIELD ZOO
Where Imagination Runs Wild

Write to Sell

All those catchy commercial slogans that pop up in ads—and in your memory—come from the minds of ad writers. Persuasive writing is their business.

In advertising audience is of the utmost importance. Ads are not aimed at the world in general but rather at particular groups. Market research provides ad writers with information about a group of potential buyers—their needs, their desires, and how they will probably spend their money.

Once the audience is defined, or targeted, the writing begins. Ad writing demands a lively imagination and a good feel for language. Getting the point across in as few words as possible is essential.

Writers in advertising are constantly reminded that ads should attract Attention, arouse Interest, create Desire, and cause Action (AIDA). How well does the "tomato frogs" ad meet these standards?

Vocabulary Tip

You can create memorable ads by playing with words. For example, use figures of speech, such as personification ("Make your carpet happy").

AIDA in Action	
Attention	"Tomato frogs! What an unusual name for an animal!"
Interest	"*Where imagination runs wild.* I certainly want to help my kids develop their imaginations."
Desire	"I want my kids to learn about many things, including tomato frogs. Let's visit the zoo."
Action	"I'll call this number to find out what the zoo's hours are, what the cost is, and what's the best way to get there."

Journal Writing

Find a magazine or newspaper ad that you consider persuasive. Copy or paste it into your journal. Identify its audience, and analyze it with an AIDA chart.

The slogan appeals to the consumer's desire for athletic and personal confidence.

How do the words and images in this ad work to persuade consumers to buy Power Pumps?

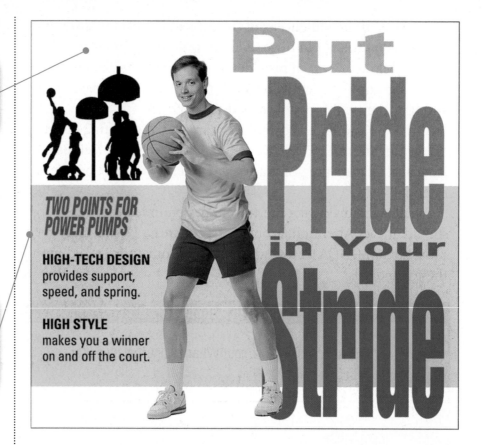

TWO POINTS FOR POWER PUMPS

HIGH-TECH DESIGN provides support, speed, and spring.

HIGH STYLE makes you a winner on and off the court.

Put Pride in Your Stride

Distinguish the Truthful from the Tricky

Advertising is tricky. As the AIDA chart shows, an ad can turn facts into feelings. It is a fact that children can see tomato frogs at the zoo, but the ad appeals to feelings of curiosity and parental concern. Ad writers know that consumers base decisions about what to buy on feelings more than on facts. Ads may appeal to either positive feelings (hope, love, duty) or negative feelings (guilt, fear, envy).

Sometimes ads use language more for the way it sounds than for what it means. Words may sound scientific, for example, but actually say nothing except "buy this product." What does "high-tech design" mean? Advertisers must maintain certain standards of truth, but measuring "truth" is a complicated task.

Now look at the Power Pumps ad again. What evidence does it use to persuade you to buy? What feelings does it appeal to? Do you think this ad would work?

Write an Ad

An exhibit of works by artist Faith Ringgold will be shown at a local community center. Write a half-page newspaper ad to announce this exhibition. What can you say about the artist on the basis of the story quilt below? Notice how Ringgold combines quilting and painting, figures and words. What can you say to persuade people to come to this exhibit?

PURPOSE To persuade people to visit an exhibit

AUDIENCE Your choice

LENGTH 1/2 page

WRITING RUBRICS To write an effective ad, you should

- select your audience
- check that your ad draws attention, arouses interest, creates desire, and causes action
- appeal to people's feelings, but be truthful

Faith Ringgold, *Dream Two: King and the Sisterhood*, 1988

Grammar Link

Do not use apostrophes in possessive pronouns.

Put Pride in Your Stride!

Write each sentence, correcting any errors in possessive pronouns.

1. Notice it's quality.
2. If she takes our advice, the world is her's!
3. Travel with us—our's is a better way to go.
4. Compare and see—we can match theirs' any day, for less!
5. Remember, you're wish is our command.

See Lesson 11.4, page 441.

Listening and Speaking

CREATE A RADIO AD Working with a small group, create a radio ad for a particular product or event. Use literary devices (such as suspense, dialogue, or figurative language) as a way to persuade. Perform your ad aloud for the group or for the whole class.

Cross-Curricular Activity

SCIENCE Your class is having a science fair. Create a poster to promote the event. Be sure your text and visuals are attractive and interesting. Be persuasive.

Writing a Letter to the Editor

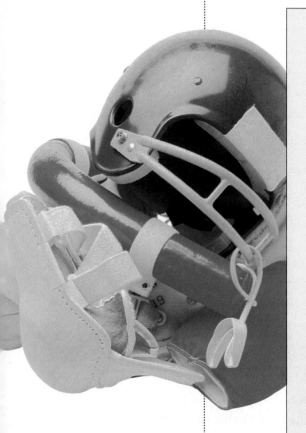

You may not be old enough to vote, but you can have a voice in public decision making. One of the most influential public arenas is the editorial page, and it's open to everyone.

Most newspapers and magazines invite letters from their readers. The following letter appeared in a popular magazine for young readers. Often in persuasive writing, the main idea comes at or near the beginning. This letter writer, however, has saved his main idea for the end. Why do you think he did that?

Dear Editor:

In the fall of 1989, I fractured one of my vertebrae playing football. I remained inactive for several months, wearing a full-body plastic jacket. The injury means no more football, no more soccer, no more baseball, or anything! As you may have noticed, my injury has a big effect on my life. Now I just go and watch my friends play.

I am not telling everybody to stop playing football. I'm just telling them to wear the right equipment.

Jon Good, Summit, New Jersey

First appeared in Sports Illustrated for Kids

Make and Support Your Point

A letter to the editor is really a letter to the readers of the newspaper or magazine. Like other persuasive writing, letters to the editor state a position and offer support for it. In the letter on the preceding page, Jon uses his own experience to support his argument that football players should use the right equipment. In the letter below, what does the writer want readers to think? What support does he offer?

Dear Editor:

I would like to tell readers that gymnastics is not only a sport for girls, but that it's also a sport for boys! Many people make fun of boys in this sport, but gymnastics is hard work, and all that hard work pays off when you get older. If you look at the men in the Olympics, you will see that they are fairly strong. So all you boys out there, don't tease us. Try gymnastics and see for yourselves: It's fun!

Philip Trevino, Gilroy, California
First appeared in Sports Illustrated for Kids

What is the writer's opinion, and what evidence does he use to support it?

Journal Writing

In a newspaper or magazine find a letter to the editor that persuades you to think or act as the writer wishes. Paste it in your journal. Make notes about what persuades you.

Presenting Tip

When you write a letter to the editor, you are far more likely to see it in print if you use the correct business-letter form. For an example see Lesson 5.8, pages 230–233.

Think About Your Tone

Frustration and anger have inspired many a letter to the editor. To make your letter persuasive, however, you need to keep uncontrolled emotion from weakening your message. Editors reject angry outbursts. The following letter expresses strong emotions but supports the writer's point in a calm, controlled way. Remember that there are usually at least two sides to an issue. You should express *your* viewpoint reasonably; if you do, your letter will be much more persuasive.

How might referring to the magazine's purpose make Kelinda's letter more persuasive?

Student Model

Dear Editor,

 I am a thirteen-year-old native St. Louisan who lives in North County. I was extremely hurt when an article appeared in your April issue about plush and desirable places to live. To my surprise North County never appeared in the article. Why? North County is a beautiful place to live, filled with friendly faces. This to me, and probably many people, is extremely desirable.

 The homes and subdivisions of this area are just as nice as the [ones] in the counties you featured. If you are *St. Louis Magazine*, then you should make a conscientious effort to represent *all* of the Metropolitan St. Louis area.

Kelinda Peaples, Florissant, Missouri
First appeared in *St. Louis Magazine*

Write a Letter to the Editor

Select an organization in your community that serves an important role or offers fine service but rarely receives public attention. Write a letter to the editor of the local newspaper in which you praise this organization and its service. Persuade the public to pay more attention to the organization and to support it.

PURPOSE Support a worthwhile organization
AUDIENCE Your community, especially adults
LENGTH 3–5 paragraphs

WRITING RUBRICS To write an effective letter to the editor, you should

* state your main idea at the beginning or end—wherever it will be most effective
* support your views
* keep your tone reasonable

Cooperative Learning

LISTENING AND SPEAKING In a small group, brainstorm about issues appropriate for letters to the editor of your school newspaper. As a group, choose one of the issues that you have differing opinions about. Divide the group so members can write on the side of the issue with which they agree. Write letters to the editor. Read each other's letters aloud, and constructively evaluate

Grammar Link

Avoid double negatives.

*The injury means **no** more football, **no** more soccer, **no** more baseball, **or anything**!*

Revise each sentence below to eliminate double negatives.

1. Sometimes football players don't have no protective equipment.
2. How people dress isn't none of your business.
3. He didn't have no reason to be so negative about everything.
4. Hardly nobody knows nothing about that.
5. I won't say nothing to him.
See Lesson 12.8, page 471.

them. Consider how well each letter succeeded in presenting a strong argument in a calm, reasonable manner.

Viewing and Representing

MAKE AN EDITORIAL DISPLAY Look in local newspapers for letters to the editor or for editorial columns written from a variety of ethnic and community perspectives. Clip the pieces and arrange them on the bulletin board. Identify and discuss the issues that concern and affect people across cultural and geographic boundaries.

WRITING ABOUT LITERATURE
Writing a Book Review

Book reviews—you have probably written dozens. Book reviews can be persuasive. They help you decide what to read.

Literature Model

My own grandma, AnadaAki, was born in a tipi during the eighteen eighties. She has come a long way to her present place in life, which includes being the family elder as well as being a devoted fan of the TV serial "As the World Turns." If you heard her British-accented voice calling out for someone to turn on the TV, you would not imagine that she was raised in the household of one of the last great medicine men among the Bloods.

Beverly Hungry Wolf, *The Ways of My Grandmothers*

Beverly Hungry Wolf's grandmother has something to give you—stories of a past you may know nothing about. She speaks in the pages of the book *The Ways of My Grandmothers*. But how will readers find out about her and hear her wonderful stories? Sometimes people tell others about a book they liked, and the word spreads. Often, though, the best way to learn about new books is through book reviews.

Know Your Audience

Book reviews can help readers in two ways. The reviews summarize a book's contents and in that way answer every reader's first question: What's it about? Reviews also evaluate the book, telling whether, in the reviewer's opinion, the book is worth reading:

Literature Model

It is a compilation of history, social life and customs. . . . There are stories . . . about the lives of her mother and grandmother, and others of her Elders, as well as accounts of some of her own experiences in learning how to live in the traditional [Blackfoot] manner. . . . Apart from its content, which is extremely valuable, one special quality of this work is its depiction of Native [American] people living a happy, normal and fulfilling existence—here are *anybody's* grandmothers, yours, mine, human beings. . . .

Beverly Hungry Wolf is a very good writer. Her book is interesting, moving, and, here and there, pretty funny.

Doris Seale, review of *The Ways of My Grandmothers*
First appeared in *Interracial Books for Children Bulletin*

Here the reviewer summarizes the book's contents, explaining what it is about.

Here she evaluates the book. What does she consider its strengths?

Different people look for different qualities in books. Some enjoy drama and suspense, while others read mainly for information. Some respond to the quality of the writing itself. Many look for new books by their favorite authors. When you review a book you've liked, you may have too much to say about it. Knowing your audience and their interests can help you decide what to include and what to leave out.

Journal Writing

Think of a book that you feel strongly about. List reasons why you like it or don't like it. Then list some people you could try to persuade to read—or not read—this book. Explain how you would persuade your audience.

Grammar Tip

When editing a book review, be sure to underscore the book title. Use italics if your word-processing program allows you to. See Lesson 20.6, page 609.

Personalize Your Review

Some reviewers respond to books in a personal way. For example, *The China Year* tells of experiences similar to the reviewer's, so Melinda Eldridge also tells readers something about herself. Notice how Melinda's use of the first-person point of view makes her review all the more personal.

What particular part of the main character's experience interested Melinda? Why?

Student Model

The best parts of the book . . . are the friendships that evolved during Henrietta's year in China. I know first-hand how much fun it is to have friends from another culture, but I also know how much more painful it is to leave them because you don't know if you'll ever see them again.

The *China Year* is an excellent book for people of all types and from all walks of life. It stands as great testimony to the wonderful adventures one can have by living outside one's own culture.

Melinda Eldridge,
Arlington, Texas
First published in
Stone Soup

As a book reviewer, you have a wide range of options. You can compare the book to others by the same author or to others of the same type. You can comment on whether the book holds your interest. You can suggest certain types of readers who would enjoy the book. You can relate the book to events in your own experience, as Melinda did. The choice is yours.

Write a Book Review

Think of a book you've read in the past that meant something special to you. Think especially of books in which you were able to identify with a character whose experiences were something like yours. Write a review, recommending the book to other readers your own age.

PURPOSE To review your favorite book
AUDIENCE Your classmates
LENGTH 1 page

WRITING RUBRICS To write an effective book review, you should

- tell what the story is about
- explain whether the book is worth reading
- keep your audience in mind

Carol Soatikee, *Students,* 1969

Grammar Link

Use the correct forms of the adjectives *good* and *bad.*

Rewrite each sentence below, correcting errors in the use of adjectives.

1. Of the two stories, the writing in LeGuin's is more good.
2. The plot is totally unbelievable, the worstest I've ever read.
3. The dialogue is most good when it's most natural.
4. The descriptions are badder than the action scenes.

See Lesson 12.3, page 461.

Cross-Curricular Activity

ART Study the painting on this page. Do the figures seem to be together or apart? How do colors and shapes create a mood? Write a review for a student art forum. Describe the painting's content and give your opinion. Include your reasons.

Listening and Speaking

PRESENT A REVIEW Taking turns with a partner, read aloud your book reviews from the writing activity on this page. Act as peer reviewers for one another's work. Evaluate the reviews, based on an adequate plot summary and a well-supported argument.

Writing Process in Action

WRITING Online

Visit the *Writer's Choice* Web site at **writerschoice. glencoe.com** for additional writing prompts.

Persuasive Writing

In the preceding lessons you've learned how to state and support your opinions. You have had the opportunity to write a letter and a book review. Now, in this lesson, you're invited to write persuasively about how an important current issue might affect the future.

Assignment

Context	Your class has decided to publish *Our Future,* a magazine that deals exclusively with how what people do today may affect the future.
Purpose	To persuade people to behave today in ways that will improve the future
Audience	Your classmates and the readers of your magazine
Length	1 page

The following pages can help you plan and write your persuasive article. Read through them, and then refer to them as you need to. But don't be tied down by them. You're in charge of your own writing process.

Prewriting

One of the best ways to find a topic about the future is to look around you today. What if pollution continues at the current rate? Ask yourself *what if* questions until you hit on a topic. The chart below suggests more ways to find a topic.

Your next task is to research your topic to learn exactly how it might influence the future.

Consider your audience; would it be best to write a letter, a short essay, or perhaps a short story?

Option A
Explore your journal.

Option B
Brainstorm with a friend.

Option C
Freewrite for ideas.

Watching the cars and trucks pour in all day carrying their bottles, papers, and cans for recycling—You can't convince me that this doesn't help people and the environment. We just need to keep it up!

Drafting

Once you have gathered facts concerning your topic, you will need to organize them in a way that has a strong impact on the reader. Your goal is to change people's behavior. In order to do this, you must use specific, vivid language.

Notice how Rachel Carson focuses on the negative events that have happened, using words such as *misfortunes* and *disasters*. These present realities influenced her fictional description of the world of tomorrow.

Drafting Tip

For more information about effectively making your case, see Lesson 6.4, pages 278–281.

Literature Model

I know of no community that has experienced all the misfortunes I describe. Yet every one of these disasters has actually happened somewhere, and many real communities have already suffered a substantial number of them.

Rachel Carson, *Silent Spring*

Once you have all you need in order to write, think about the order in which you will present your ideas, facts, and examples. Then, using your notes, begin writing. At this stage just write steadily, and let your ideas flow.

Revising

To begin revising, read over your draft to make sure that what you have written fits your purpose and your audience. Then have a **writing conference.** Read your draft to a partner or a small group. Use your audience's reactions to help you evaluate your work so far. The questions below can help you and your listeners.

Question A

What is my purpose?

Question B

Do I consider my audience?

Question C

Have I captured my readers' attention?

Nuclear man probably recycled some materials. Scholars have not determined, however, if Nuclear man had any system for *organized* recycling. It may be that recycling was a *is likely* haphazard occurrence in the life of Nuclear man. The fact that Nuclear man seemed obsessed with the word garbage suggests that Nuclear man had only the slightest notion of resource management and allocation. *a complex term with many meanings but thought to refer to unrecycled material*

Editing/Proofreading

Careful editing is essential to persuasive writing. Why? Some readers will dismiss your argument because of a misspelling or a grammatical error. Use your dictionary. Check your sentences and **proofread** for mechanics. Be sure you write legibly and in cursive if you aren't using a word processor. Check for only one kind of error at a time.

Publishing/Presenting

Once you've edited your composition, you are ready to submit your work to *Our Future.* Think about and discuss with your class what the cover of your magazine should look like.

Editing/Proofreading Checklist

1. Do my verbs agree with their subjects?
2. Have I used subject and object pronouns correctly?
3. Have I used possessive pronouns correctly?
4. Have I eliminated any double negatives?
5. Have I checked spelling and capitalization?

Proofreading Tip

For proofreading symbols, see page 79.

Journal Writing

Reflect on your writing process experience. Answer these questions in your journal: What do you like best about your persuasive writing? What was the hardest part? What did you learn in your writing conference? What new things have you learned as a writer?

Literature Model

Silent Spring

by Rachel Carson

Written more than thirty years ago by scientist Rachel Carson, Silent Spring *begins with this fable that shows humanity's carelessness and irresponsibility. As you read, think about how the fable affects your view of current environmental problems. Then try the activities in Linking Writing and Literature on page 306.*

There was once a town in the heart of America where all life seemed to live in harmony with its surroundings. The town lay in the midst of a checkerboard of prosperous farms, with fields of grain and hillsides of orchards where, in spring, white clouds of bloom drifted above the green fields. In autumn, oak and maple and birch set up a blaze of color that flamed and flickered across a backdrop of pines. Then foxes barked in the hills and deer silently crossed the fields, half hidden in the mists of the fall mornings.

> *Even in winter the roadsides were places of beauty.*

Along the roads, laurel, viburnum and alder, great ferns and wildflowers delighted the traveler's eye through much of the year. Even in winter the roadsides were places of beauty, where countless birds came to feed on the berries and on the seed heads of the dried weeds rising above the snow. The countryside was, in fact, famous for the abundance and variety of its bird life, and

Leonard Koscianski, *Whirlwind*, 1992

when the flood of migrants was pouring through in spring and fall people traveled from great distances to observe them. Others came to fish the streams, which flowed clear and cold out of the hills and contained shady pools where trout lay. So it had been from the days many years ago when the first settlers raised their houses, sank their wells, and built their barns.

> *On the mornings that had once throbbed with the dawn chorus of robins, catbirds, doves, jays, wrens, and scores of other bird voices there was now no sound . . .*

Then a strange blight crept over the area and everything began to change. Some evil spell had settled on the community: mysterious maladies swept the flocks of chickens; the cattle and sheep sickened and died. Everywhere was a shadow of death. The farmers spoke of much illness among their families. In the town the doctors had become more and more puzzled by new kinds of sickness appearing among their patients. There had been several sudden and unexplained deaths, not only among adults but even among children, who would be stricken suddenly while at play and die within a few hours.

There was a strange stillness. The birds, for example—where had they gone? Many people spoke of them, puzzled and disturbed. The feeding stations in the backyards were deserted. The few birds seen anywhere were moribund; they trembled violently and could not fly. It was a spring without voices. On the mornings that had once throbbed with the dawn chorus of robins, catbirds, doves, jays, wrens, and scores of other bird voices there was now no sound; only silence lay over the fields and woods and marsh.

On the farms the hens brooded, but no chicks hatched. The farmers complained that they were unable to raise any pigs—the litters were small and the young survived only a few days. The apple trees were coming into bloom but no bees droned among the blossoms, so there was no pollination and there would be no fruit.

The roadsides, once so attractive, were now lined with browned and withered vegetation as though swept by fire. These, too, were silent, deserted by all living things. Even the streams were now lifeless. Anglers no longer visited them, for all the fish had died.

The roadsides, once so attractive, were now lined with browned and withered vegetation as though swept by fire.

In the gutters under the eaves and between the shingles of the roofs, a white granular powder still showed a few patches; some weeks before it had fallen like snow upon the roofs and the lawns, the fields and streams.

No witchcraft, no enemy action had silenced the rebirth of new life in this stricken world. The people had done it themselves.

This town does not actually exist, but it might easily have a thousand counterparts in America or elsewhere in the world. I know of no community that has experienced all the misfortunes I describe. Yet every one of these disasters has actually happened somewhere, and many real communities have already suffered a substantial number of them. A grim specter has crept upon us almost unnoticed, and this imagined tragedy may easily become a stark reality we all shall know.

Linking Writing and Literature

Readers Respond to the Model

What makes Rachel Carson's fable persuasive?

Explore Rachel Carson's persuasive writing by answering these questions. Then read what other students liked about her writing.

1. Carson could have started her book by citing dramatic examples of the misuse of chemicals. Why do you think she chose to start with a fable instead?

2. What effect do the descriptions in the fable have on you?

3. From the selection choose one particular passage that you find especially persuasive. What specific words or phrases make this passage persuasive?

What Students Say

"The fable from *Silent Spring* is a story about a beautiful town with peaceful surroundings. It seemed as if an evil plague crept over the town, for bad things started happening. The writer's point is that even though the story is fiction, many things like that are happening in America, and people are the cause of them.

I liked the descriptions the best. They were so vivid you could almost see what was happening. I would recommend this story to friends, because it gives them something to ponder. "

Alina Braica

"This story held my attention throughout. I think Rachel Carson wrote it as she did to let her readers know that everything beautiful doesn't have to stay that way and that we should take nothing for granted in this lifetime. I would recommend this story because I would want my friends to enjoy it as much as I have. "

Tashaunda Jackson

Reflecting on the Unit

Summarize what you have learned in this unit by answering the following questions.

1 How does persuasive writing effect change?

2 What kinds of evidence can you use to support your position?

3 What do you need to keep in mind in order to write persuasively?

4 What kinds of activities go into developing a strategy?

5 What should you focus on when revising your persuasive writing?

Adding to Your Portfolio

CHOOSE A SELECTION FOR YOUR PORTFOLIO Look over the writing you did for this unit. Choose a piece of writing for your portfolio. The writing you choose should show one or more of the following:

- an unusual or a surprising way of addressing a problem or an issue
- an opinion about a change you consider especially important
- words and ideas appropriate to a specific audience
- strong evidence gathered from at least two sources

REFLECT ON YOUR CHOICE Attach a note to the piece you chose, explaining briefly why you chose it and what you learned from writing it.

SET GOALS How can you improve your writing? What skill will you focus on the next time you write?

Writing Across the Curriculum

MAKE A SCIENCE CONNECTION Think of a current environmental problem, such as ozone deterioration or destruction of the rain forest, that you have learned about in science class. Write a persuasive composition that states and supports your opinion about what we should do to remedy the problem.

" 'You know, honey, we gotta figure a way'…"

—Gary Soto

Mother and Daughter

308

Troubleshooter

*U*se Troubleshooter to help you correct common errors in your writing.

Problem 1

Fragment that lacks a subject

> *frag* Sol went to the airport. *Wanted to leave today.*
>
> *frag* Dora jogged to school. *Was late for class.*
>
> *frag* My car broke down today. *Couldn't start it.*

SOLUTION Add a subject to the fragment to make a complete sentence.

Sol went to the airport. He wanted to leave today.

Dora jogged to school. She was late for class.

My car broke down today. I couldn't start it.

Problem 2

Fragment that lacks a predicate

> *frag* Jo caught a plane yesterday. *The plane at noon.*
>
> *frag* Colin baked a cake today. *The cake in the oven.*
>
> *frag* Tatiana likes that court. *The tennis court in the park.*

SOLUTION   Add a predicate to make the sentence complete.

Jo caught a plane yesterday. The plane left at noon.

Colin baked a cake today. The cake is in the oven.

**Tatiana likes that court. The tennis court in the park
is the one she likes.**

Problem 3

Fragment that lacks both a subject and a predicate

frag   Sylvia played the violin. ⟮In the symphony
orchestra.⟯

frag   My cousin rode his bike. ⟮To the store today.⟯

frag   Alex bought new skis. ⟮From the sports store.⟯

SOLUTION   Combine the fragment with another sentence.

Sylvia played the violin in the symphony orchestra.

My cousin rode his bike to the store today.

Alex bought new skis from the sports store.

   *If you need more help avoiding sentence fragments, turn to
Lesson 8.2, pages 361–362.*

7.2 Run-on Sentence

Two main clauses separated by only a comma

run-on *Barb went water-skiing, she skied behind the boat.*

run-on *I stopped reading, my eyes were tired.*

run-on *I worked hard on this chapter, I did well on my test.*

SOLUTION A Replace the comma with a period or another end mark, and begin the new sentence with a capital letter.

Barb went water-skiing. She skied behind the boat.

SOLUTION B Replace the comma between the main clauses with a semicolon.

I stopped reading; my eyes were tired.

SOLUTION C Insert a coordinating conjunction after the comma.

I worked hard on this chapter, and I did well on my test.

Two main clauses with no punctuation between them

run-on *My dog has fleas he scratches behind his ears.*

run-on *Husam bought that book he read it last week.*

SOLUTION A   Separate the main clauses with a period or another end mark, and begin the second sentence with a capital letter.

My dog has fleas. He scratches behind his ears.

SOLUTION B   Insert a comma and a coordinating conjunction between the main clauses.

Husam bought that book, and he read it last week.

Problem 3

Two main clauses with no comma before the coordinating conjunction

run-on Samantha went home and she went to bed early.

run-on I can go to Roberta's party but I can't stay long.

SOLUTION   Insert a comma before the coordinating conjunction.

Samantha went home, and she went to bed early.

I can go to Roberta's party, but I can't stay long.

If you need more help in avoiding run-on sentences, turn to Lesson 8.6, pages 369–370.

7.3 Lack of Subject-Verb Agreement

Problem 1

A subject that is separated from the verb by an intervening prepositional phrase

> *agr*   One of the radios *are* broken.
>
> *agr*   The boys in the class *is* singing.

SOLUTION   Ignore a prepositional phrase that comes between a subject and a verb. Make sure that the verb agrees with the subject of the sentence. The subject is never the object of the preposition.

One of the radios is broken.

The boys in the class are singing.

Problem 2

A sentence that begins with *here* or *there*

> *agr*   There *go* the local train.
>
> *agr*   Here *is* the students who will write the report.
>
> *agr*   There *is* oil paintings in the art gallery.

SOLUTION   The subject is never *here* or *there*. In sentences that begin with *here* or *there*, look for the subject *after* the verb. The verb must agree with the subject.

There goes the local train.

Here are the students who will write the report.

There are oil paintings in the art gallery.

Problem 3

An indefinite pronoun as the subject

agr   Neither of the girls (have) their umbrella.

agr   Many of the books (is) old.

agr   All of my pleading (were) in vain.

Some indefinite pronouns are singular, some are plural, and some can be either singular or plural, depending upon the noun they refer to.

SOLUTION   Determine whether the indefinite pronoun is singular or plural and make the verb agree.

Neither of the girls has her umbrella.

Many of the books are old.

All of my pleading was in vain.

Problem 4

A compound subject that is joined by *and*

agr   Posters and balloons (was) strewn around the gym.

agr   The star and team leader (are) Rico.

SOLUTION A   If the parts of the compound subject do not belong to one unit or if they refer to different persons or things, use a plural verb.

Posters and balloons were strewn around the gym.

SOLUTION B   If the parts of the compound subject belong to one unit or if both parts refer to the same person or thing, use a singular verb.

The star and team leader is Rico.

Problem 5

A compound subject that is joined by *or* or *nor*

agr   Either the actor or the actress (appear) onstage.

agr   Neither the tomato nor the bananas (looks) ripe.

agr   Either Mom or Dad (are) driving us to the movie.

agr   Neither my brother nor my uncles (likes) trains.

SOLUTION Make the verb agree with the subject that is closer to it.

Either the actor or the actress appears onstage.

Neither the tomato nor the bananas look ripe.

Either Mom or Dad is driving us to the movie.

Neither my brother nor my uncles like trains.

Problem 6

A compound subject that is preceded by *many a, every,* or *each*

> *agr* Every nook and cranny (were) searched.
>
> *agr* Each boy and girl (smile) brightly.

SOLUTION Use a singular verb when *many a, each,* or *every* precedes a compound subject.

Every nook and cranny was searched.

Each boy and girl smiles brightly.

 If you need more help with subject-verb agreement, turn to Lessons 16.1–16.5, pages 541–550.

7.4 Incorrect Verb Tense or Form

Problem 1

An incorrect or missing verb ending

tense   Have you reach all your goals?

tense   Last month we visit Yosemite National Park.

tense   The train depart an hour ago.

SOLUTION   Add *-ed* to a regular verb to form the past tense and the past participle.

Have you reached all your goals?

Last month we visited Yosemite National Park.

The train departed an hour ago.

Problem 2

An improperly formed irregular verb

tense   The wind blowed the rain from the roof.

tense   The loud thunder shaked the house.

tense   Sophia bringed the horse back to the barn.

The past and past participle forms of irregular verbs vary. Memorize these forms, or look them up.

> **SOLUTION**   Use the correct past or past participle form of an irregular verb.
>
> **The wind blew the rain from the roof.**
>
> **The loud thunder shook the house.**
>
> **Sophia brought the horse back to the barn.**

Problem 3

Confusion between the past form and the past participle

tense Mimi has rode *the horse home from school.*

> **SOLUTION**   Use the past participle form of an irregular verb, not the past form, when you use the auxiliary verb *have*.
>
> **Mimi has ridden the horse home from school.**

If you need more help with correct verb forms, turn to Lessons 10.1–10.12, pages 401–424.

7.5 Incorrect Use of Pronouns

Problem 1

A pronoun that could refer to more than one antecedent

pro   *Sonia jogs with Yma, but (she) is more athletic.*

pro   *After the dogs barked at the cats, (they) ran away.*

pro   *When Sal called out to Joe, (he) didn't smile.*

SOLUTION   Rewrite the sentence, substituting a noun for the pronoun.

Sonia jogs with Yma, but Yma is more athletic.

After the dogs barked at the cats, the cats ran away.

When Sal called out to Joe, Joe didn't smile.

Problem 2

Personal pronouns as subjects

pro   *Vanessa and (me) like to camp in the mountains.*

pro   *Georgianne and (them) drove to the beach.*

pro   *(Her) and Mark flew to London.*

SOLUTION Use a subject pronoun as the subject of a sentence.

Vanessa and I like to camp in the mountains.

Georgianne and they drove to the beach.

She and Mark flew to London.

Problem 3

Personal pronouns as objects

pro Joel is coming with Manny and she.

pro Please drive Rose and I to the store.

pro The dog brought the stick to Chandra and I.

SOLUTION Use an object pronoun as the object of a verb or a preposition.

Joel is coming with Manny and her.

Please drive Rose and me to the store.

The dog brought the stick to Chandra and me.

 If you need more help with the correct use of pronouns, turn to Lessons 11.1–11.7, pages 435–448.

7.6 Incorrect Use of Adjectives

Problem 1

Incorrect use of *good, better, best*

> adj   Is mountain air more good than ocean air?
>
> adj   Marla is the most good babysitter I know.

SOLUTION The comparative and superlative forms of *good* are *better* and *best*. Do not use *more* or *most* before irregular forms of comparative and superlative adjectives.

Is mountain air better than ocean air?

Marla is the best babysitter I know.

Problem 2

Incorrect use of *bad, worse, worst*

> adj   Mandy's cold is the baddest cold I've ever seen.

SOLUTION The comparative and superlative forms of *bad* are *worse* and *worst*. Do not use *-er* or *-est* for irregular forms of comparative and superlative adjectives.

Mandy's cold is the worst cold I've ever seen.

Problem 3

Incorrect use of comparative adjectives

adj   *Twine is (more stronger) than thread.*

SOLUTION   Do not use both *-er* and *more* at the same time.

Twine is stronger than thread.

Problem 4

Incorrect use of superlative adjectives

adj   *This is the (most hardest) test I've ever taken.*

SOLUTION   Do not use both *-est* and *most* at the same time.

This is the hardest test I've ever taken.

If you need more help with the incorrect use of adjectives, turn to Lesson 12.3, pages 461–462.

Incorrect Use of Commas

Problem 1

Missing commas in a series of three or more items

com   We had fish·vegetables·and bread for dinner.

com   Help me make the beds·sweep the floor·and wash the windows.

SOLUTION   When there are three or more items in a series, use a comma after each one, including the item that precedes the conjunction.

We had fish, vegetables, and bread for dinner.

Help me make the beds, sweep the floor, and wash the windows.

Problem 2

Missing commas with direct quotations

com   "The concert·" said Dora·"was loud and boring."

com   "Tomorrow·" said Burton·"I will read that book."

SOLUTION The first part of an interrupted quotation ends with a comma followed by quotation marks. The interrupting words are also followed by a comma.

"The concert," said Dora, "was loud and boring."

"Tomorrow," said Burton, "I will read that book."

Problem 3

Missing commas with nonessential appositives

com *Mr. Unser ₒour English teacher ₒwas born in England.*

com *Ms. Charo ₒmy mother's supervisor ₒis taking us to dinner.*

SOLUTION Determine whether the appositive is truly not essential to the meaning of the sentence. If it is not essential, set off the appositive with commas.

Mr. Unser, our English teacher, was born in England.

Ms. Charo, my mother's supervisor, is taking us to dinner.

Problem 4

Missing commas with nonessential adjective clauses

com   *Devin₀who arose early₀smelled the eggs and bacon.*

SOLUTION   Determine whether the clause is truly essential to the meaning of the sentence. If it is not essential, set off the clause with commas.

Devin, who arose early, smelled the eggs and bacon.

Problem 5

Missing commas with introductory adverb clauses

com   *When the whistle blows₀the workday is over.*

SOLUTION   Place a comma after an introductory adverbial clause.

When the whistle blows, the workday is over.

If you need more help with commas, turn to Lessons 20.2–20.4, pages 601–606.

Problem 1

Singular possesive nouns

apos ⟨Beths⟩ dress is from France.

apos My ⟨boss⟩ report is on ⟨Angelas⟩ desk.

apos ⟨My gerbils⟩ fur is brown and white.

SOLUTION Use an apostrophe and an -*s* to form the possessive of a singular noun, even one that ends in -*s*.

Beth's dress is from France.

My boss's report is on Angela's desk.

My gerbil's fur is brown and white.

Problem 2

Plural possessive nouns ending in -*s*.

apos The ⟨boys⟩ shirts are too big for them.

apos My ⟨horses⟩ manes are long and thick.

apos My ⟨parents⟩ friends joined them for dinner.

SOLUTION Use an apostrophe alone to form the possessive of a plural noun that ends in *-s.*

The boys' shirts are too big for them.

My horses' manes are long and thick.

My parents' friends joined them for dinner.

Problem 3

Plural possessive nouns not ending in *-s*

apos The (childrens) books are in the library.

apos The (womens) meetings are in this building.

SOLUTION Use an apostrophe and an *-s* to form the possessive of a plural noun that does not end in *-s.*

The children's books are in the library.

The women's meetings are in this building.

Problem 4

Possessive personal pronouns

apos This new tape is (her's) but the CD is (their's)

SOLUTION   Do not use an apostrophe with any of the possessive personal pronouns.

This new tape is hers, but the CD is theirs.

Confusion between *its* and *it's*

apos   The bird built it's nest in the oak tree.

apos   I want to know if its going to be sunny today.

SOLUTION   Do not use an apostrophe to form the possessive of *it*. Use an apostrophe to form the contraction of *it is*.

The bird built its nest in the oak tree.

I want to know if it's going to be sunny today.

If you need more help with apostrophes and possessives, turn to Lesson 20.7, pages 611–612.

7.9 Incorrect Capitalization

Problem 1

Words referring to ethnic groups, nationalities, and languages

cap   *Many (canadian) citizens speak (french.)*

SOLUTION   Capitalize proper nouns and adjectives that refer to ethnic groups, nationalities, and languages.

Many Canadian citizens speak French.

Problem 2

The first word of a direct quotation

cap   *Devon said, "(the) new highway will run through town."*

SOLUTION   Capitalize the first word in a direct quotation that is a complete sentence. A direct quotation gives the speaker's exact words.

Devon said, "The new highway will run through town."

If you need more help in capitalizing, turn to Lessons 19.1–19.4, pages 583–590.

Problem 3

Words that show family relationships

cap *Dennis asked* (aunt) *Silvie to drive him to school.*

cap *Yesterday* (dad) *cooked dinner.*

SOLUTION Capitalize words that show family relationships when such words are used as titles or as substitutes for people's names.

Dennis asked Aunt Silvie to drive him to school.
Yesterday Dad cooked dinner.

Proofreading Symbols		
⊙	Lieut Brown	Insert a period.
∧	No one came to the party.	Insert a letter or a word.
∧̣	The bell rang the students left for home.	Insert a semicolon.
≡	I enjoyed paris.	Capitalize a letter.
/	The Class ran a bake sale.	Make a capital letter lowercase.
‿	The campers are home sick.	Close up a space.
(sp)	They visited N.Y. (sp)	Spell out.
∧	Sue please help.	Insert a comma.
∩	He enjoyed feild day.	Transpose the position of letters or words.
#	alltogether	Insert a space.
ꝺ	We went to to Boston.	Delete letters or words.
⌄ ⌄	She asked, Who's coming?	Insert quotation marks.
/=/	mid January	Insert a hyphen.
¶	"Where?" asked Karl. "Over there," said Ray.	Begin a new paragraph.
⌄	She liked Sarah's glasses.	Insert an apostrophe.

Business and Technical Writing

Contents

Business Letters

Abusiness letter is a formal letter written to a person who can grant a request, satisfy a complaint, or give information.

The following business letter is written to express a complaint. Note how the writer follows the tips suggested in the chart on the following page.

440 Mountain Rd.
Pickett, Idaho 67098
August 15, 2001

The letter is addressed to a specific person.

Mr. David Payne, Manager
The Sport Shop
2786 Aspen Avenue
Pickett, Idaho 67098

Dear Mr. Payne:

On August 13, I purchased a pair of in-line skates at the Sport Shop. That same day, I discovered that one of the wheels on the left skate is permanently stuck and won't roll.

The writer explains her complaint in the first paragraph.

On August 14, I took the skates back, and a customer service representative, Mr. Greely, said the skates couldn't be returned because they were bought on sale. Then he showed me a sign that said, "No Returns or Exchanges on Sale Items." I explained that the skates were unusable because of a defect, but Mr. Greely just pointed at the sign and helped the next person.

The writer tells the story of what happened.

I understand that the skates were on sale and are not returnable, but I feel that your store should either replace the defective skate or refund my money. I am enclosing a copy of my receipt.

The writer tells how she thinks the complaint should be resolved.

I also feel that it was wrong of Mr. Greely to ignore my complaint. My family has been shopping at the Sport Shop for years, and nothing like this has happened before. Thank you for taking care of this problem.

Sincerely yours,

Rachel Goldstein

The writer gives additional information.

Types of Business Letters

Business letters are a direct and effective way to communicate on many different topics.

Use a business letter when you want to inquire, make a request, state an opinion, or voice a complaint. Keep the tone of your business letter formal and polite. Don't use slang or clichés (worn out expressions). Keep language simple. "Thank you for taking care of this problem," is better than "I would appreciate it if you would look into this situation at your earliest convenience and take appropriate action."

When you write a business letter, remember that the person receiving it is probably very busy, so a short letter is more likely to be read than a long wordy one. Keep business letters to one page or less. Include only necessary information in a logical sequence.

When you write a business letter, use persuasive writing. If you are writing to complain about a problem with a product or service, you want to convince the person to correct the problem. When you write a letter of opinion, you want to persuade someone to agree with you and take action. Use a letter of application to convince someone to hire you for a job or consider you for membership or an award. Use a letter of inquiry when you want someone to give you information.

Knowing how to write an effective business letter is a skill you will use often.

TYPES OF BUSINESS LETTERS			
COMPLAINT LETTER	**REQUEST LETTER**	**OPINION LETTER**	**APPLICATION LETTER**
Identify the product or service clearly.	Be brief.	State your opinion in the first sentence or two.	Write to a specific person.
Describe the problem accurately.	State your request clearly.	Support your opinion with reasons, facts, and examples.	Describe the job or program for which you're applying.
Request a specific solution.	Include all necessary information.		List your qualifications.
Be polite.	Make your request specific and reasonable.	Summarize your main points and offer a solution if possible.	Tell why you're the best person for the job or award.
Keep a copy of your letter until your complaint has been resolved.	Include your phone number or a stamped self-addressed envelope.		Request an application form or an interview.

Style

Business letters are usually written in one of two forms: block style or modified block style.

Block Style In the block style, all lines begin at the left margin. Paragraphs are not indented; they are separated by a line space. The letter on page 333 is typed in the block style.

Modified Block Style In the modified block style, the heading, the closing, your signature, and your typed name begin in the center of the line. The paragraphs may be indented—five spaces on a typewriter or half an inch on a computer—or not indented. The letter below is in the modified block style with paragraphs indented.

Heading

455 Pleasant Street
Moran, California 78987
May 3, 2001

Mr. Kevin Kulakowski, Manager
Moran Movie Theater
304 South Main Street   **Inside Address**
Moran, California 78987

Dear Mr. Kulakowski: **Salutation**

    On Saturday, May 1, I went to a movie at your theater. During the movie, I stood up to go to the concession stand and almost fell over because my feet had stuck to the floor! I know you can't clean up every single spill after every movie, but the sticky mess was so thick that it must have been there for a long time. When I moved to sit in a different part of the theater, the floor there was just as sticky.

    The men's restroom was very messy. Paper towels were strewn all over, and there were bugs around the floor drain.   **Body**

    Please let me know when these problems have been corrected, so that my friends and I can come back to your theater and enjoy the movies again.

Closing   Sincerely,

Name and signature   Kurt Brady

The Parts of a Business Letter

A business letter has six parts.

The Heading There are three lines in the heading.
- your street address
- your city, state, and ZIP code
- the date

The Inside Address The inside address has four or more lines.
- the name of the person to whom you're writing (with or without a courtesy title such as *Ms., Mr.,* or *Dr.*)
- the title of the person to whom you're writing (Place a short title on the same line with the person's name. A long title requires a separate line.)
- the name of the business or organization
- the street address of the business or organization
- the city, state, and ZIP code

The Salutation or Greeting The salutation should include a courtesy title, such as *Dear Mrs. Biedermeyer* or *Dear Mr. Bogden.* If you don't know the name of the person, begin with Dear and the person's title: *Dear Customer Service Representative* or *Dear Manager.* The salutation of a business letter is followed by a colon.

The Body The body tells your message.

The Closing The closing is a final word or phrase, such as *Sincerely* or *Yours truly.* The closing is followed by a comma.

Name and Signature Type your name four lines below the closing. Then sign your name in the space between the closing and your typed name.

Neatness Counts

Your reader will pay more attention to your opinion if your letter is neat.
- Type your letter or use a computer.
- Use unlined white paper.
- Leave a two-inch margin at the top and at least a one-inch margin at the left, right, and bottom of the page.
- Single-space the heading. Allow one or more blank lines between the heading and the inside address, depending on the length of your letter.
- Single-space the remaining parts of the letter, leaving an extra line between the parts and between the paragraphs in the body.

Friendly Letters

A personal, or friendly, letter differs from a business letter in purpose, tone, and length. The tone of a letter depends on the closeness of your relationship with the receiver. A friendly letter may be short (a thank-you note) or long (a detailed account of an interesting experience). Contrast the following friendly thank-you letter with the business letters on pages 333 and 335.

The familiar greeting is followed by a comma.

24 Hardcastle Lane
Pickett, Idaho 67098
August 10, 2001

Dear Aunt Elsie,

Thank you for the beautiful card and the generous birthday check. You never forget my special day!

Now I'll be able to buy the in-line skates I've had my eye on for months. Whenever I go skating, I promise I'll think of you.

Mom and Dad send their best. We're looking forward to seeing you for Thanksgiving. Thanks again for remembering me.

Your loving niece,

Rachel

The tone is informal and friendly. The letter may be typed or handwritten.

The closing is informal. Even if the letter is typed, the signature is handwritten.

Activity

Imagine that your family traveled a long way to get to a vacation spot where you had reservations at a motel. When you arrived, your rooms had been given to someone else and the motel was full. Write a letter of complaint to the motel manager. Use either the block or the modified block format.

PURPOSE   To write a letter of complaint

AUDIENCE   Classmates

LENGTH   One page

WRITING RUBRICS To write an effective letter of complaint, you should

- state your complaint in the first paragraph of your letter
- tell what you think is a fair solution and why

Technology Tip

You can set up a template for one or both of the business letter formats. Select **Page Setup** in the **File** menu to set the margins. Next, use the ruler to set any tabs or paragraph indentations you need. Then type in a made-up letter, format it with the size and style of type you want, and save the letter as a template. When you need to write a business letter, open the template, rename it (so that the original remains unchanged), and replace the made-up copy with your new letter. Some word processing programs have built-in templates or offer free downloads of templates at their Web sites.

Memos

A memo is a brief business note that gives the reader important information on a topic. Memos are written in formal language but have a friendly tone. Memos are usually written to people you know or work with.

TO: All Students

FROM: Mrs. Montoyez, School Cafeteria Manager

SUBJECT: Cafeteria Will be Closed on Monday, March 5

DATE: March 3, 2001

On Monday, March 5, the school cafeteria will be closed while the ceiling is being repaired and repainted. Please bring a sack lunch that day and take it to the gymnasium during your lunch period. Tables and chairs will be set up there. The cafeteria will be open again on Tuesday, March 6. Thanks for everyone's cooperation.

> The writer tells whom the memo is for.

> The writer identifies herself.

> The writer states the subject briefly.

> The writer includes all important information.

> The writer thanks people for their cooperation.

Types of Memos

Memos can be used to convey many kinds of important messages. You can write a memo to make an announcement, ask or answer a question, or make an assignment. A grocery store manager might write a memo to all cashiers about how to redeem a new store coupon. A church pastor might write a memo to the ushers, thanking them for volunteering and inviting them to a special dinner.

When you write a memo to make an announcement, include the most important details in one or two paragraphs. If you are using a memo to make a request, tell your reader exactly what you want him or her to do. For example, you might say, "Please see me on Tuesday at 1:30 P.M. to discuss this." Use a memo when you want to remind people of an upcoming event they may have known about but forgotten or to remind them to do something. When you write a memo to assign a task, describe the task and include the date when it must be finished.

Always keep memos brief—one page or less. Don't include any extra information. Use formal language, but keep the tone friendly.

TYPES OF MEMOS

ANNOUNCEMENT	REQUEST	REMINDER	ASSIGN A TASK
Headline your announcement in a few words on the subject line.	State your request briefly on the subject line.	Begin the message with words such as, "I'd like to remind you to . . ."	Name the task in the subject line.
Make the announcement in one or two short sentences in the first paragraph.	Make your request clear in the first sentence.	Give the most important information in the first sentence.	In the first sentence, use language such as, "Your job is to . . ." or "This assignment includes . . ."
Give details in a second paragraph.	Tell how people can respond to your request.	Include necessary details like dates, times, and phone numbers.	Give a brief description of the task.
Include dates and times.	Thank the readers for their help.		Give a date by which the task must be completed.

Style

Memos are written in the block style. Each heading and paragraph starts at the left margin. Memo headings are printed in capital letters and followed by a colon. The words following the colon are capitalized like a title. Memos can include simple charts or a bulleted list if needed.

Words after headings align at the left.

Headings

TO: All Members of the Student Photography Club

FROM: Mr. Lee

SUBJECT: Pinhole Camera Project

DATE: September 9, 2001   Date

Message The activity during our September 20 meeting will be to make a pinhole camera. You will need the following supplies:
- cereal box
- sewing needle
- 1 sheet of wax paper   Bulleted list
- rubber band
- pair of scissors

Please bring all materials to the meeting with you.

Memos

The Parts of a Memo

Headings A memo heading is a title word in capital letters followed by a colon. Most memos have four headings: TO, FROM, SUBJECT, and DATE, followed by the corresponding information.

Message The message is written in one or more paragraphs. Sentences are usually short—not longer than about twenty words. Some memos may include a bulleted or numbered list.

Neatness Counts

Create memos on a typewriter or computer. If you must handwrite a memo, neatly print in black ink.

- Use unlined white paper.
- Leave a two-inch margin at the top and one-inch margins at the sides and bottom of the page.
- Double-space each heading line.
- Use a double space between the headings and the message and between paragraphs.
- Single-space the lines of each paragraph.

 Activity

Write a memo to your classmates about an upcoming school or classroom event. Create your memo on a computer and revise it to make sure it is concise and flows logically. Proofread your memo for grammar and usage, spelling, and word choice. Make a clean copy and post it in your classroom.

PURPOSE	To create a memo
AUDIENCE	Classmates
LENGTH	One page or less

WRITING RUBRICS To write an effective memo, you should

- state the topic clearly in the subject heading
- include all important information
- be brief

 **Technology Tip**

Use a computer's word processing functions to help create a neat memo. Your software may contain one or more templates for memos. You can also create your own memo design. Experiment with typefaces and styles and sizes of type, but don't get too fancy. A memo's appearance, like its message, should be simple and to the point.

Work Plans

Work plans are written documents that describe the details of a project and show the progression of the work. The following work plan shows the tasks assigned to individuals and the dates they will be completed.

> The writer identifies the plan in a title.

> The writer organizes information into columns.

Cady School Newsletter Work Plan
March 2001 Issue

Student	Assignment	Due Date
Ali Ziad	writing article on school election distributing newsletter to all classrooms	2/5 3/3
Matt Abrams	writing school calendar column	2/9
Tracy Everett	compiling sports schedule	2/9
Eiko Sanjo	editing election articles editing school calendar & sports schedule editing newsletter draft	2/9 2/15 2/28
Enrique Salinas	taking photos developing film	2/15 2/20
Greta Anderson	typing all articles into computer layout taking final copy to printer picking up copies from printer	2/23 3/3 3/5
Reema Johnson	adding graphics and scanning in photos	2/25

> The writer lists each assignment and its due date.

Types of Work Plans

Work plans can be written to describe a project, list dates and times when work will be completed, show who is assigned to each task, and note how the project is to be paid for.

When you describe a project, start by listing its objectives (goals). Then make a list of all tasks to be completed. Describe in detail how each one is to be done.

Create a schedule to show when each task must be completed. You can do this by making a table like the one in the model on page 343. List each task under its deadline date.

You can write a schedule that shows the responsibilities of each person working on the project. You could organize this schedule in three columns, showing the person's name, his or her tasks, and the due date of each assignment, as in the model on page 341.

Some work plans need a budget column that shows the expected costs of a project. To make a simple budget, list all the materials and other expenses involved.

Then, next to each item, list the estimated cost. Leave a blank column to show the actual cost as money is spent.

Work plans make clear to everyone involved what his or her responsibilities are and when the work must be finished. A well thought out work plan can keep people working smoothly together to finish a project on time.

TYPES OF WORK PLANS			
PROJECT SCHEDULE	**ASSIGNMENT SCHEDULE**	**PROCESS OUTLINE**	**BUDGET**
Use a title to show what the schedule is for.	Name tasks briefly.	Use an outline or a series of numbered steps to explain a process (how a task should be done).	Include a list of all of the costs involved in the project.
List every task to be done.	Make a graphic organizer to show who does what and when it is due.	List the steps of a process in the order in which they must be completed.	Estimate each cost.
Give the date each task is to be completed.	Include every person involved and every task that must get done.		Record actual expenses as they are paid.
Organize the information in a table or columns so that it will be easy to understand.	Include a due date for each task.	Be brief.	
		Include only necessary steps.	

Style

Work plans may include some sections written in paragraph form. Do not indent paragraphs. Instead, leave a line of space between paragraphs. Begin each line at the left margin.

If your work plan includes an outline, use Roman numerals for each item and capital letters to list details under each item.

Tables should be centered on the page if they are narrower than the width of your type block.

The Parts of a Work Plan

Title Work plans are titled to show the project or job they are for.

Objectives Work plans begin by stating the goals of the project.

Body The body can but does not need to include task descriptions and assignments, dates, schedules, an outline, and a budget.

Organization Counts

A badly organized work plan will confuse people and delay the completion of the project. Before writing a work plan, make lists of pertinent information; then experiment with the organization of your plan. Use a computer to create and revise your plan.

Business & Technical Writing

Title

Goals

School Garden Project Work Plan

Objectives
* To plan and plant a butterfly garden in the central courtyard
* To beautify the school grounds
* To provide a habitat for butterflies
* To teach students gardening skills
* To teach students about butterflies

Dates

Project Dates
The project will begin on February 1, 2001, and will be completed by June 15, 2001.

Work schedule

Task Listing

Work Schedule

Tasks	February	March	April	May	June
	Research flowers and shrubs	Draw landscape plan	Lay out garden	Plant trees and flowering shrubs	Transfer seedlings to garden
	Make final plant and tree selection	Order Seeds	Dig beds	Install birdbath	Purchase annuals and plant them
	Study seed catalogues		Start seeds in trays indoors		Make mulch beds

Activity

Brainstorm a list of projects you might describe in a work plan. Choose one and create a work plan to show the progression of the project. Use the models on pages 341 and 343 to help you organize your plan.

Trade plans with a partner and discuss how the plans could be made clearer.

After you have finished revising your plan, make a final clean copy to display in the classroom.

PURPOSE To write a work plan
AUDIENCE Classmates
LENGTH One page

WRITING RUBRICS In order to write an effective work plan, you should
● write clear objectives
● list each task separately
● set realistic due dates
● organize the information in a clear, easy-to-read format

Public Service Announcements

A public service announcement or ad carries a message for a good cause. These ads are created by advertising agencies free of charge at the request of government agencies and nonprofit organizations. The ads are often published at no charge by media such as radio, TV, newspapers, and magazines. The model below is a script for a thirty-second radio spot created for the state police.

State Police ●——— [The ad was created for a specific group.]

"Click to Start" ●——— [Ad title]

:30 Radio ●——— [Tells the length in seconds and the type of script]

SFX:	2 car doors slamming
Alex:	Let's see. First the seatbelt . . .
SFX:	metallic click
SFX	Silence
Mom:	Start the car, Alex.
Alex:	Can't.
Mom:	You passed driver ed. Don't be scared.
Alex:	I'm not scared.
Mom:	Then, what? I've got to get the grocery shopping done.
Alex:	When I was little you always told me the car wouldn't start until everyone had their seat belts buckled.
Mom:	Oh, for Pete's sake!
SFX:	Silence
Mom:	Alex?
Alex:	Mom?
SFX:	metallic click
SFX:	engine starting
SFX:	loud rock music
ANNCR:	If they don't buckle up, don't rev it up. Seat belts save lives!

[Sound effect]

[Characters' dialogue]

[Announcer's lines]

Types of Public Service Announcements

Public service announcements are written for a wide range of causes. Writers of these announcements use persuasive writing to make their messages convincing. The following are examples of public service messages: adopt a pet from the humane society; exercise for good health; stop smoking; don't do drugs.

There are three types of public service ads.

Broadcast ads include TV and radio commercials and announcements. TV ads rely on sights (visuals) and sounds. TV commercials are made up of action scenes to catch and hold the viewer's attention. Radio commercials rely on spoken dialogue and sound effects.

Outdoor ads are created for billboards, posters, and the sides of buildings. Billboards are only seen at a glance as people drive past, so the message uses large, eye-catching visuals and few words.

Print ads are found in magazines and newspapers. A headline catches the viewer's attention and a visual holds it. Print ads include a few lines of copy (text) to explain the message and to give other information the audience may need such as a phone number or location.

When you create a public service ad, you should always limit it to a single idea. Make that idea clear at first glance. Make your ad tell a story, as in the radio spot on page 344. Use persuasive writing to convince your audience to change an opinion or take action. You can persuade by example, as in the model radio script, or by including reasons to do something, as in the model print ad on page 346. Sometimes public service announcements are factual and serious in tone. For example, an announcement might show the effects of a car accident caused by a drunk driver. Other public service announcements use humor to deliver the message.

TYPES OF PUBLIC SERVICE ANNOUNCEMENTS		
BROADCAST (TV AND RADIO)	**OUTDOOR (BILLBOARDS AND POSTERS)**	**PRINT (NEWSPAPERS AND MAGAZINES)**
Limit ad to fifteen or thirty seconds for TV, thirty or sixty seconds for radio.	Use colorful visuals.	Use a clever headline to get the audience's attention.
Check the timing of an ad by reading it aloud several times.	Let the picture tell the story at a glance.	Include pictures and copy.
Use persuasive writing to support a cause.	Keep the copy to a very few words.	Keep the copy brief and persuasive.
		Include information on how people can take action.

Style

TV and radio commercials are written in script form, as shown in the model on page 344. Billboards, posters, and print ads are created as art to fit the size of the finished ad. Print ads are published in standard sizes, such as a full page, half page, and quarter page. The space you have for an ad will help you determine how many details and how much copy you can include.

Cold feet? Get a bed warmer from the Humane Society **Headline**

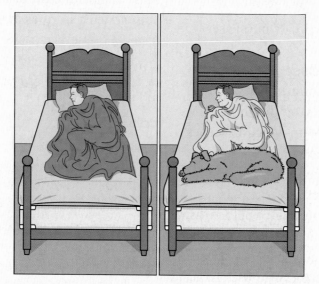

Visual

You know your normal body temperature is 98.6°, but did you know that a dog's body temperature is 101.5°? Those extra three degrees are the reason the Inuits brought a dog or two into the igloo on frigid arctic nights. **Copy**

Now you can get your own personal igloo warmer (OOPS!) bed warmer from the Humane Society. The best friend bit is a bonus.

The Humane Society has three locations in Rock Creek. **Information on where to go and what to do**

Call 1-800-DOG-GONE

Business & Technical Writing

The Parts of a Public Service Ad

Public service ads have some or many of the following parts, depending on the medium used.

Headline A headline is a short, catchy statement designed to get attention. Both print and outdoor ads use headlines, but headlines on outdoor ads are even shorter than those on print ads.

Message The purpose of an ad is to carry a message to an audience. Each of the following parts helps to convey the message of an ad:

- headline
- copy (the written text in a print ad)
- visuals (any part of an ad that appeals to sight, such as pictures, artwork, movies, or animation)
- sound effects (in radio and TV ads)
- contact information (where to send a donation, what phone number to call, travel directions to a place)

Presentation Counts

In an ad, presentation is everything. If you are writing a TV or radio commercial, your story must unfold in a logical sequence to keep your audience watching or listening. In outdoor ads, your billboards must be eye-catching and deliver the message at a glance. In print advertising, your ad must first catch the audience's eye and then keep its interest with clever copy.

Activity

Work in a small group to choose a good cause for which you will create a public service announcement. Your ad may be a print ad, a poster, or a radio or television commercial. Decide which form is best for your announcement.

If you choose to create a print ad or a poster, you will want to start by making a sketch that shows the location of the headline, visual, and copy. When your ad is ready for publication, display it in the classroom.

If you choose to create a radio or television commercial, first write a script and read it aloud while timing it. It should fit a thirty- or sixty-second time slot. When your commercial is ready to be aired, play the final recording for the class.

PURPOSE	To create a public service ad
AUDIENCE	Teachers and students
LENGTH	Thirty- or sixty-second commercial, one-page print ad, or one poster

WRITING RUBRICS To create an effective public service announcement, you should

- keep your copy short and to the point
- include contact information
- use visuals that work well with your copy
- use precise wording
- proofread carefully

Newsletters

A newsletter is a publication that reports on topics of interest to a specific group. Newsletters are collections of articles and are often formatted in columns. The model below is from a newsletter sent to residents of a particular neighborhood.

> The newsletter is for a specific group.

> The articles report on items of interest to the group.

Walnut Acres Newsletter

A Newsletter for Residents of Walnut Acres

Volume 1, No. 3   October 2001

Board Meeting Schedule

Following is the schedule for board meetings for the last three months of 2001. All meetings will be held at the community room in the public library from 7 P.M. to 10 P.M. Every homeowner is welcome to attend.

Monday, October 8
Tuesday, November 6
Monday, December 3

Snow Plow Contract Awarded

The board of directors has awarded a contract to Snowbusters, Inc., to plow our streets after each snowfall throughout the winter.

Walnut Acres Teenager to the Rescue!

Thirteen-year-old Demetra Koufalis of Hazelnut Street was walking by the north Walnut Acres entrance when a truck, eastbound on Hickory Road, veered out of control and demolished the entrance sign. The driver was not hurt, but he backed up over the sign and drove away.

Demetra memorized the license number of the truck and later identified the driver to the police.

Because of Demetra's great memory and quick thinking, the board was able to collect $534.98 from the driver to replace the sign. Thanks, Demetra!

President's Message

At the September meeting, the board of directors set the following goals for 2002:

- Establishing a garden committee to develop and maintain flowerbeds for the south and west entrances to Walnut Acres. Anyone who is interested in serving on this committee should call Janelle Whitmore at 987-0876.

- Purchasing and installing new playground equipment in the west park. To help with this project, call Josh Bernard at 987-4356.

- Hiring a lawn-cutting service for the park areas. Neighborhood teens are welcome to bid for this job. Call Steve Harms at 987-6545 for a complete job description and information on how to submit a bid.

> The writer gives specific information, such as times and dates.

> The writer includes contact information.

Types of Newsletters

Newsletters can be used to communicate information of interest to different audiences. Newsletters are published at regular intervals, such as weekly, monthly, or quarterly. How often a newsletter is published and how it is distributed depends on its purpose. A newsletter to keep employees aware of work progress might be published weekly and distributed by putting out a pile of copies in the room where workers take their breaks. A newsletter for stamp collectors might be published once a month and mailed to members' homes. A newsletter whose purpose is to give information on an annual event, such as an art fair, might only be published once a year and mailed to people who attended previous fairs.

You might regularly receive more than one newsletter, depending on what your interests and hobbies are.

When you create a newsletter, include factual information such as dates, times, and locations of meetings and events. Also include articles on topics of interest to your audience. Keep newsletter articles short and to the point. You can include graphics to illustrate articles.

TYPES OF NEWSLETTERS

CLUB OR SPECIAL INTEREST GROUP	EMPLOYEE	CUSTOMER
Give the newsletter a name that reflects the purpose of the group, such as *Bits and Bytes* for a computer group.	Include dates, times, and details on events for employees, such as the company picnic.	Publish as a form of advertising for a business.
Publish the newsletter on a regular schedule.	Report news about employees, such as promotions, awards earned, retirement dinners, and new people in the company.	Send to customers or potential customers.
Include a calendar of club meetings and special events of interest to members.	Include photographs if possible.	Include information about special sales or store events.
Include a summary of the last group meeting.	Employees may be encouraged to produce the newsletter themselves.	Include a column of information useful to customers, such as household hints or safety tips.

Style

Newsletters are written as a series of articles. The articles can be laid out in columns, like a newspaper, or in a single column the width of the page. Headings are used to separate articles. Some newsletters are more formal than others. A newsletter published by a large corporation might be printed on glossy white paper, written in formal language, and be several pages long. A club newsletter might have a catchy name, be printed on brightly colored paper, and be written in a conversational tone.

A newsletter keeps the same style and organization of articles from issue to issue. For example, the masthead (box with the newsletter name) is always printed in the same style so that readers will recognize the newsletter on sight. The main column on the front page might always be a message from the club president, and the lower right corner of the front page might always be used for the meeting schedule.

Masthead

Trail Talk

The Newsletter of the Fresh Air Hiking Club for Teens

Volume and issue numbers

Volume 3, No. 4

Date of this issue   *April 2001*

On the Trail

Articles

by Byron Brock

Last month five members of the Coventry Chapter walked the five-day route of the Painted Rock Trail through the Coventry Wilderness Area. The first day was very slow going because the trail was muddy from recent rains. On the second day, as we climbed higher, the trail became dry and views of the canyon below were spectacular. On the third day, we saw two black bears and a moose. In spite of the mud, I recommend this trail to experienced hikers.

Upcoming Club Hikes

The following backpack trips are open to all members. For more information or to sign up, call Tanya Smith at (877) 876-3939.

Trail	Dates
Redmond	April 6-8
Cling Peak	April 20-21
Black Creek	May 11-13

May Meeting Features Slide Show

Our May meeting will be held at 5:00 P.M. on May 27 in the Grange Hall at 594 Forest Street in Coventry. Andrew Lim, who hiked part of the Appalachian Trail last summer, will present a slide show entitled "Scenes of Appalachia." This meeting includes a potluck dinner. Bring your favorite trail dish and copies of the recipe.

Classified

Coleman Dual Fuel Backpack Lantern for sale. Good condition. Call Jeff at (734) 555-7477.

Lightweight tent for sale. Two-person dome with fly. Only used once. Best offer. Call Murph at (734) 555-8897.

The Parts of a Newsletter

The Masthead The masthead includes the following information:

- title of the newsletter
- volume number (The volume number represents a period of publication, such as one year. All newsletters published in the first year would be Volume 1. All newsletters published the next year would be Volume 2, and so on. A school newsletter might start a new volume when the school year begins in September.)
- issue number (Issues are numbered in order throughout a volume. The first issue of each volume would be number 1.)
- date

Articles Newsletters are divided into articles on different topics. Some topics appear regularly, such as a meeting schedule or a classified ad section.

Organization Counts

Your newsletter is more likely to be read if it looks interesting and is well organized. Some tips:

- Create your newsletter on a computer.
- Give each article a title.
- Use graphics or illustrations to add interest.
- For a one- or two-page newsletter, use a single sheet of 8½-by-11-inch paper.
- Jazz up your newsletter with colored paper.

Activity

Class Project: Create and publish a class or school newsletter.

- Divide the following jobs among teams and individuals: design a masthead, decide on a title, brainstorm for article ideas, interview subjects, write articles, edit articles, design graphics and illustrations, lay out the newsletter on a computer.
- Some things you might include in your newsletter are coming events, school news, cafeteria menus, lost and found items, and student essays.
- Edit and proofread your newsletter, publish it, and distribute it to students, parents, and teachers.

PURPOSE To create and publish a newsletter

AUDIENCE People interested in your school

LENGTH One page

WRITING RUBRICS In order to create an effective newsletter, you should

- give your newsletter an appropriate title
- create a layout that is both attractive and easy to read
- use visuals to enhance the messages of articles and features

Multimedia Presentations

In multimedia presentations multiple kinds of media are used to present a topic. A television commercial might be described as multimedia because it has both sights and sounds.

Types of Media

In a multimedia presentation, you use multiple sight and sound media to give your audience information on your topic. You can use such media as photos, slides, posters, diagrams, charts, videos, handouts, CDs, and audio cassettes. If presentation software is available, you can combine text, various graphics, and sounds on a computer "slide show."

Multimedia presentations can be used for many kinds of reports. You can make a multimedia presentation to inform your audience about a subject, to persuade an audience to take some action, or even to sell a product. The chart below gives examples of different kinds of media you might use. Begin by thinking of possible subjects. Think about each subject and how it could be presented with different types of media. What facts could be made into graphic organizers? What sounds are associated with the subject? Do research at the library or on the Internet to learn more about each possible subject. Search for facts, statistics, and expert opinions.

Once you choose a topic, you can contact experts on the subject by fax or e-mail. Experts can answer your questions and also give you quotations you can use to make your presentation stronger.

When making a sales presentation, you want to make your product as appealing as possible. For example, if you are trying

TYPES OF MEDIA		
VISUALS (SIGHTS)	**SOUND**	**OTHER OPTIONS**
Use a photograph or slide to make your subject clear.	Play a cassette or CD—of a bird's song or sounds of the ocean, for example—to help your audience hear your subject.	Appeal to your audience's sense of touch by having individuals handle an object such as a seashell or a snake's shed skin.
Give a demonstration of how something works.	Use background music to help create a mood.	If you are selling a food product, pass out samples to taste.
Make a video to show action and appeal to your audience's sense of hearing.	Add sound effects to a slide show.	
Use a series of slides to show a process.		
Make handouts of information you want your audience to have.		

to promote your new lawn-mowing service, you might make a series of slides that tell why your mowing service is better than your competitors' services. You could even add the sound of a lawn mower as a sound effect every time you change slides. You could conclude your presentation by giving the audience a handout showing your rates and information on how to contact you.

Style

- Keep each visual simple.
- Use large type for visuals. Experiment with type sizes in the room where you will present. See which type sizes would be visible from the back of the room.
- Do not crowd your visuals. Two type-faces and three colors are sufficient.
- Use the same border and background color on all your visuals to tie them together.

The Parts of a Multimedia Presentation

All multimedia presentations have three parts.

Introduction   Introduce your topic in a way that will attract your audience's attention by using sound or a visual, or both.

- Introduce yourself by saying something like, "I'm Mario, and my presentation will show you why you should use my mowing service to keep your yard looking its best."

- Use a transparency or a slide to show your thesis in headline form while you introduce yourself orally.
- Use music to set the mood; then introduce yourself and your thesis.
- Give a demonstration of a product while explaining who you are and what you are doing.

The Body   The body is the longest and most important part of your presentation. You explain your topic and support it with facts gathered from reliable sources, such as experts on the subject and encyclopedias and other reference books. Use media to present your facts and arguments in interesting ways. You can make sure your audience gets your message by allowing time for questions. You should try to think of possible questions in advance so that you can have extra facts and statistics ready to answer them.

Conclusion   Use the final few moments of your presentation to restate your thesis and sum up the most important points. Keep your conclusion brief. Thank your audience for their attention.

Multimedia Presentations

Presentation Counts

If you were Mario, you could begin by playing a short recording of a lawn mower and then saying, "That's the sound of your grass being mowed down to size by Mario's Mowing Service." Or you could present a video commercial showing your service in action.

Experiment with the order of your presentation on your family and friends until you find the most successful combination. Use humor when possible.

When it comes time to give your presentation, be enthusiastic, and your audience will be enthusiastic too.

The presenter uses favorite songs that the audience associates with summertime to add sound to his presentation.

The tee shirt is a visual and introduces the subject to the audience at first glance.

The presenter uses a slide to visually show the main points of his topic.

Why Mario's?

- No lawn too big or too small
- Lawns cut weekly
- A free extra mowing when your lawn is growing fast
- All workers thorough and polite
- Shrubs, trees, and flowerbeds trimmed
- Clippings picked up and removed
- Driveway edging available at a small extra charge

Activity

As a class, use a video camera to make a multimedia commercial to sell a product or a service. Present your finished commercial to another class.

- Divide the class into working groups. Researchers can identify a product or a service, writers can write the script, and actors can star in the commercial. Other specialty jobs include set designers, prop persons, camera operators, and director.

- Include a description of all scenes in the script. You can find screenplay scripts in a library to show you how to do this. Specify how your commercial will include visuals and sounds.

- You may want to do a storyboard of your presentation. A storyboard includes rough sketches that show each shot of your movie as the shot should look on camera. You can combine storyboard and script into a single document that will vividly summarize your commercial.

- Before filming the commercial, review the script with your classmates. Discuss ways to rearrange the material to make the commercial more effective.

PURPOSE   To make a multimedia video commercial

AUDIENCE   Another class

LENGTH   Three minutes

WRITING RUBRICS In order to create an effective multimedia commercial, you should

- write an engaging script that will persuade the audience
- create and use visuals that will strengthen the message
- use reference materials as needed

Technology Tip

Presentation software allows you to combine text with sounds and graphics into a single production that can be shown on a computer monitor. Programs include a Help function that will help you create a presentation.

"During the day the glass sun shimmered a beautiful yellow, the blue a much better color than the sky outside: deeper, like night."

—Alma Luz Villanueva, *Golden Glass*

Hamish MacEwan,
The Park #3,
date unknown

357

UNIT 8

Subjects, Predicates, and Sentences

Kinds of Sentences

■ A **sentence** is a group of words that expresses a complete thought.

Different kinds of sentences have different purposes. A sentence can make a statement, ask a question, give a command, or express strong feeling. All sentences begin with a capital letter and end with a punctuation mark. The punctuation mark at the end of the sentence is determined by the purpose of that sentence.

> Our class is reading "The Raven" by Edgar Allan Poe.

■ A **declarative sentence** makes a statement. It ends with a period.

Edgar Allan Poe wrote suspenseful short stories.

> Was it fun?

■ An **interrogative sentence** asks a question. It ends with a question mark.

Did Poe also write poetry?

> It surely scared me!

■ An **exclamatory sentence** expresses strong feeling. It ends with an exclamation point.

What a great writer Poe was!

> Read some of his other poems.

■ An **imperative sentence** gives a command or makes a request. It ends with a period.

Read "The Pit and the Pendulum."

Édouard Manet, Illustration to Poe's "The Raven," c. 1875

Exercise 1   Identifying Kinds of Sentences

Write whether each sentence is *declarative, interrogative, exclamatory,* or *imperative.*

1. Edgar Allan Poe was born in Boston in 1809.
2. Did you know that Poe lost his parents at a very early age?
3. How awful that must have been!
4. The boy lived with his foster parents.
5. Wasn't his foster father a wealthy merchant?
6. Poe was raised in Richmond, Virginia.
7. He attended college briefly.
8. Did he enlist in the army?
9. I can't believe that he went to West Point!
10. Read a biography of Poe.
11. Didn't he also edit magazines?
12. What impressive writing Poe produced!
13. Poe was a master of the short story.
14. How greatly he influenced other writers!
15. Tell me what you think about his writing.
16. Poe died at the age of forty.
17. Isn't that very young?
18. How sad that his life was so short!
19. What a tragedy!
20. Find out more about Poe.

Exercise 2   Capitalizing and Punctuating Sentences

Write each sentence, adding capital letters and punctuation marks where needed.

1. is it true that Edgar Allan Poe wrote the first detective story
2. is private detective C. Auguste Dupin in one of Poe's tales
3. tell me if you have read Poe's famous poem about the raven
4. what a harrowing ending this poem has
5. Poe's writings are very popular in Europe
6. Did the young man go to college in Virginia
7. poe is also highly regarded for his literary criticism
8. he lived in Philadelphia during a part of his career
9. His writing includes mystery, suspense, fantasy, and humor
10. What a great adventure story "The Narrative of A. Gordon Pym" is

8.2 Sentences and Sentence Fragments

Every sentence has two parts: a subject and a predicate.

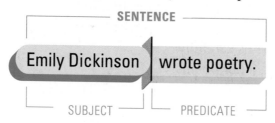

- The **subject part** of a sentence names whom or what the sentence is about.
- The **predicate part** of the sentence tells what the subject does or has. It can also describe what the subject is or is like.

A sentence must have both a subject and a predicate. It must also express a complete thought.

- A **sentence fragment** does not express a complete thought. It may also be missing a subject, a predicate, or both.

You often use fragments when talking with friends or writing personal letters. Some writers use sentence fragments to produce special effects. You should use complete sentences, however, in anything you write for school or business.

Correcting Sentence Fragments		
Fragment	**Problem**	**Sentence**
Her sister.	The fragment lacks a predicate. *What did her sister do?*	Her sister discovered the poems in her bureau.
Wrote about her emotions.	The fragment lacks a subject. *Who wrote about her emotions?*	This gifted poet wrote about her emotions.
Of meaning.	The fragment lacks both a subject and a predicate.	Her poems contain many layers of meaning.

Exercise 3   Identifying Sentences and Sentence Fragments

Write each sentence, underlining the subject part once and the predicate part twice. If it is a fragment, write *fragment* and explain why it is a fragment.

1. Emily Dickinson lived in Amherst, Massachusetts.
2. At her parents' home.
3. Few of her poems were published during her lifetime.
4. Considered one of the greatest American poets.
5. You should study her poems carefully.
6. Dickinson's sister collected her poems.
7. This famous poet.
8. Insisted on complete privacy.
9. Her poems reflect her intensely emotional nature.
10. Many readers are attracted to her highly original style.
11. Dickinson's poetry comments on all matters of life.
12. Wrote about love and beauty.
13. Dickinson analyzes her emotions poetically.
14. So much fine work.
15. Found a world of her own.
16. With clear, precise observation.
17. Her writing style gives every word weight.
18. Her poetry uses sharp phrases and rich imagery.
19. Most of her poems include original insights.
20. To every possible human concern.

Exercise 4   Correcting Sentence Fragments

Rewrite each sentence fragment to make it a complete sentence. Add a subject or a predicate or both.

1. Emily Dickinson author.
2. Lived from 1830 to 1886.
3. With clarity and style.
4. Began to retreat into herself at the age of twenty-three.
5. Moved quietly about the house.
6. Caught only glimpses of her.
7. In the nineteenth century.
8. Biographies of Dickinson.
9. Dickinson's poetry.
10. Observed the world and wrote about it.

8.3 Subjects and Predicates

A sentence consists of a subject and a predicate that together express a complete thought. Both a subject and a predicate may consist of more than one word.

Complete Subject	Complete Predicate
Dickens's **novels**	**are** still popular today.
My English **teacher**	**wrote** an article on Dickens.

- The **complete subject** includes all of the words in the subject of a sentence.

- The **complete predicate** includes all of the words in the predicate of a sentence.

Not all of the words in the subject or the predicate are of equal importance.

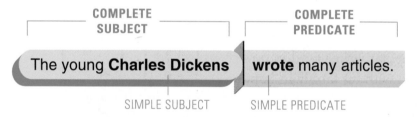

- The **simple subject** is the main or most important word or group of words in the complete subject.

The simple subject is usually a noun or a pronoun. A **noun** is a word that names a person, a place, a thing, or an idea. A **pronoun** is a word that takes the place of one or more nouns.

- The **simple predicate** is the main word or group of words in the complete predicate.

The simple predicate is always a verb. A **verb** is a word that expresses an action or a state of being.

Sometimes the simple subject is also the complete subject. Similarly, the simple predicate may also be the complete predicate.

Exercise 5   Identifying Subjects and Predicates

Write each sentence. Draw a line between the complete subject and the complete predicate.

1. Charles Dickens's first works consisted of articles about life in London.
2. These early works appeared under the name of Boz.
3. Their popularity led to publication of *Pickwick Papers.*
4. That first novel was highly successful.
5. Dickens wrote for the rest of his life.
6. Dickens's early experiences influenced much of his writing.
7. His only historical novel is *A Tale of Two Cities.*
8. *David Copperfield* is one of his most popular books.
9. The novel *Martin Chuzzlewit* reflects Dickens's trip to America.
10. The author gave dramatic readings of his works.

Exercise 6   Identifying Subjects and Predicates

Write each item. Draw a vertical line between the complete subject and complete predicate. Underline the simple subject once and the simple predicate twice.

1. Charles Dickens wrote many great novels during his lifetime.
2. The English novelist remains a very popular writer.
3. He created memorable characters.
4. This very popular writer lived in poverty as a child.
5. Dickens lived with his family in London.
6. The youngster labored in a shoe polish factory at an early age.
7. The English courts sent Dickens's father to debtors' prison.
8. His family needed money then.
9. The young Dickens found work for a short while as a court stenographer.
10. He took notes at court for two years.
11. Dickens reported news for a local newspaper too.
12. He published short articles on life in London.
13. His writing appeared first under a different name.
14. The best early articles appeared in *Sketches by Boz.*
15. His first novel was *Pickwick Papers.*
16. Most Dickens novels appeared in installments in periodicals.
17. People waited eagerly for each new chapter.
18. Dickens edited two periodicals.
19. My favorite Dickens novel is *Hard Times.*
20. Dickens's own favorite novel was *David Copperfield.*

8.4 Identifying Subjects and Predicates

In most sentences, the subject comes before the predicate.

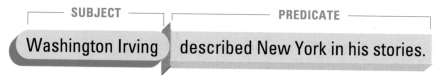

SUBJECT — Washington Irving | PREDICATE — described New York in his stories.

Other kinds of sentences, such as questions, begin with part or all of the predicate. The subject comes next, followed by the rest of the predicate.

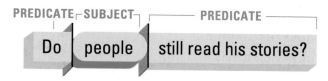

PREDICATE Do | SUBJECT people | PREDICATE still read his stories?

To locate the subject of a question, rearrange the words to form a statement.

Predicate	Subject	Predicate
Did	Irving	write many funny stories?
	Irving	did write many funny stories.

The predicate also precedes the subject in sentences with inverted word order and in declarative sentences that begin with *Here is, Here are, There is,* or *There are.*

PREDICATE There is | SUBJECT Irving's original manuscript.

In requests and commands, the subject is usually not stated. The predicate is the entire sentence. The word *you* is understood to be the subject.

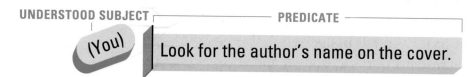

UNDERSTOOD SUBJECT (You) | PREDICATE Look for the author's name on the cover.

Exercise 7 — Identifying the Subject in Sentences

Write the complete subject in each sentence. If the sentence is a command, write *(You)*.

1. Did Washington Irving achieve international fame?
2. Name two stories about Irving's childhood in New York.
3. There is a Washington Irving story with roots in German folklore.
4. Did Washington Irving live from 1783 to 1859?
5. Does Irving use a particular writing style in this tale?
6. Read Irving's satire on New York.
7. Examine Irving's humorous sketches of New York society first.
8. Did he write during his stay in England?
9. Did Irving devote himself completely to literature?
10. Has the class discussed his short story "The Legend of Sleepy Hollow"?
11. Here are Irving's two books on Columbus.
12. There are four books about his travels in Spain.
13. Study his style of writing.
14. Did Irving's *The Sketch Book* bring new importance to the short story?
15. Here is *The Sketch Book of Geoffrey Crayon.*
16. Do critics regard his short stories as his best achievement?
17. Discuss Irving's influence on other writers.
18. Here is a collection of his short stories.
19. There lies Irving's biography.
20. Did you read all of Irving's stories?

Exercise 8 — Identifying the Subjects and Predicates in Sentences

Write each sentence. If the sentence is a command, write *(You)* before it. In each sentence, underline the complete subject once and the complete predicate twice.

1. Learn more about Washington Irving.
2. Was his life interesting?
3. Did Irving use the pen name Diedrich Knickerbocker?
4. There was *A History of New York* published under that name.
5. Find out the origin of his pen name.
6. Irving lived in Spain twice.
7. Was he interested in Spanish culture?
8. Did Irving represent the U.S. in Spain?
9. Tell about Irving's travels in the West.
10. Did Irving read his works to frontier audiences?

8.5 Compound Subjects and Compound Predicates

A sentence may have more than one simple subject or simple predicate.

■ A **compound subject** is two or more simple subjects that have the same predicate. The subjects are joined by *and, both . . . and, or, either . . . or, neither . . . nor,* or *but.*

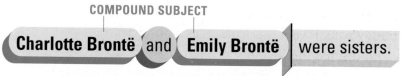

COMPOUND SUBJECT

Charlotte Brontë and **Emily Brontë** were sisters.

When the two simple subjects are joined by *and* or by *both . . . and,* the compound subject is plural. Use the plural form of the verb to agree with this plural compound subject.

When the two simple subjects are joined by *or, either . . . or,* or *neither . . . nor,* however, the compound subject may be singular or plural. The verb must agree with the nearer simple subject.

> Either **Charlotte** or **Emily is** my favorite author.
> Neither **Charlotte** nor her **sisters were** outgoing.

In the first sentence, *Emily* is the nearer subject, and so the singular form of the verb is used. In the second sentence, *sisters* is the nearer subject, and so the plural form is used.

■ A **compound predicate** is two or more simple predicates, or verbs, that have the same subject. The verbs are connected by *and, both . . . and, or, either . . . or, neither . . . nor,* or *but.*

COMPOUND PREDICATE

Many students **read** the novel *Jane Eyre* and **enjoy** it.

The compound predicate in this sentence consists of *read* and *enjoy.* Both verbs agree with the plural subject. Notice the balanced, parallel structure of the verbs *read* and *enjoy.*

Write whether each sentence has a *compound subject* or a *compound predicate*.

1. Either Charlotte or Emily Brontë will be the subject of my research paper entitled "A Great Nineteenth-century Novelist."
2. Neither Anne nor Emily is as well known as Charlotte.
3. Many readers have read and enjoyed their books.
4. Some scholars buy or sell rare editions of their books.
5. Neither the Brontë sisters nor their brother was long-lived.
6. The Brontë sisters lived and wrote in Yorkshire, England.
7. Charlotte's mother and sisters died early.
8. Anne Brontë both wrote novels and worked as a governess.
9. Scholars study and discuss the Brontës' novels.
10. Either *Wuthering Heights* or *Jane Eyre* is my favorite Brontë novel.

Exercise 10   Making Subjects and Verbs Agree

Write the correct form of the verb in parentheses.

1. Neither Emily Brontë's poems nor her one novel (deserve, deserves) to be forgotten.
2. Either *Wuthering Heights* or her poetic works (draw, draws) praise from critics everywhere.
3. Her writing (show, shows) an understanding of people and (reveal, reveals) her love of England.
4. Critics and other readers (discuss, discusses) and (praise, praises) her single novel.
5. Critics or other readers (pay, pays) more attention to Charlotte Brontë's works.
6. Charlotte's novel *Shirley* (paint, paints) a portrait of Emily and (show, shows) her feelings for her sister.
7. Charlotte's novels (reflect, reflects) her life experiences and (reveal, reveals) her dreams.
8. Both Anne Brontë's novel *Agnes Grey* and Charlotte's *The Professor* (tell, tells) love stories.
9. Charlotte's novels *Shirley* and *Villette* (receive, receives) less attention today.
10. Neither Anne's *The Tenant of Wildfell Hall* nor Charlotte's *Shirley* (attract, attracts) many readers today.

Simple and Compound
Sentences

■ A **simple sentence** has one subject and one predicate.

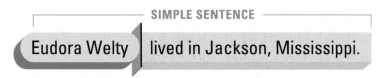

A simple sentence may have a compound subject, a compound
predicate, or both, as in the following example.

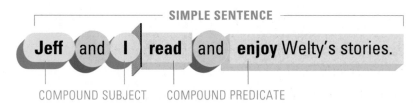

■ A **compound sentence** is a sentence that contains two or more
simple sentences joined by a comma and a coordinating conjunction or by a semicolon.

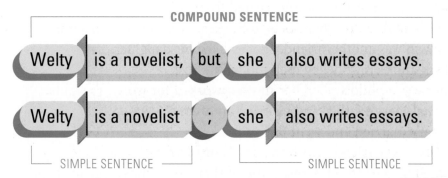

A run-on sentence is two or more sentences incorrectly
written as one sentence. To correct a run-on, write separate
sentences or combine the sentences as shown below.

Correcting Run-on Sentences	
Run-on	**Correct**
Welty wrote novels she wrote essays. Welty wrote novels, she wrote essays.	Welty wrote novels. **S**he wrote essays. Welty wrote novels, **and** she wrote essays. Welty wrote novels**;** she wrote essays.

| Exercise 11 | Identifying Simple and Compound Sentences |

Write whether each sentence is *simple* or *compound*.

1. Elizabeth Barrett Browning and Robert Browning were poets.
2. They were famous for their poetry and their love.
3. Browning liked Elizabeth Barrett's poetry, and he wrote to her.
4. Elizabeth and Robert wrote hundreds of letters to each other.
5. Scholars and other people read and study these letters.
6. Elizabeth wanted to marry Robert, but her father forbade this.
7. The couple got married anyway, and they moved to Italy.
8. Her father never forgave her; he returned her letters unopened.
9. Elizabeth wrote love poems, and Robert wrote dramatic poems.
10. People still read and enjoy the couple's poems and letters.

| Exercise 12 | Identifying Simple, Compound, and Run-on Sentences |

Write whether each sentence is *simple, compound,* or *run-on.* If it is a run-on sentence, rewrite it correctly.

1. Percy Bysshe Shelley lived and wrote in the nineteenth century.
2. He was a Romantic poet his wife, Mary Shelley, was a novelist.
3. Three of his poems are "Ozymandias," "Ode to a Skylark," and "Adonais."
4. *Frankenstein* was Mary Shelley's most famous novel.
5. Percy Shelley traveled in Europe and visited friends.
6. Shelley made friends with other poets; John Keats was Shelley's friend.
7. William Godwin was another friend, Shelley liked his daughter.
8. Mary Godwin and Percy Shelley met and fell in love.
9. Mary's father was a philosopher, her mother worked for women's rights.
10. Percy respected Mary's father and visited him often.
11. Percy and Mary married and went to Europe.
12. Mary and Percy were friendly with the poet Lord Byron.
13. Byron wrote long, beautiful poems; some of them are almost epic in scope.
14. Byron was one of the greatest Romantic poets students still study his work.
15. Byron, Keats, and Shelley were ranked together as great Romantic poets.
16. Poetry lovers and scholars read and discuss the men's poems.
17. I love Byron's lyrical poems, but some people prefer his satirical work.
18. *Childe Harold's Pilgrimage* and *Don Juan* are Byron's masterpieces.
19. Byron loved Greece, he traveled there.
20. He fell ill in Greece, and he died there.

Grammar Review

SUBJECTS, PREDICATES, AND SENTENCES

Russell Baker wrote about his early life in the memoir *Growing Up*. In this excerpt, he describes his reaction to having his work read publicly for the first time. The passage has been annotated to show some examples of the kinds of subjects, predicates, and sentences covered in this unit. Notice how he uses fragments for special effect.

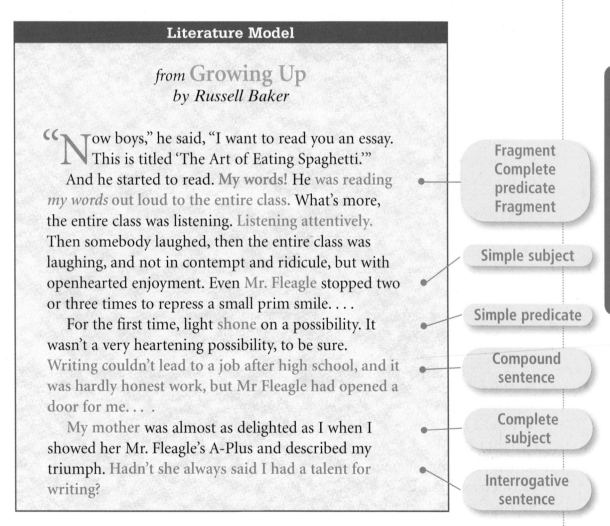

Literature Model

from Growing Up
by Russell Baker

"Now boys," he said, "I want to read you an essay. This is titled 'The Art of Eating Spaghetti.'"
And he started to read. **My words!** He was reading *my words* out loud to the entire class. What's more, the entire class was listening. Listening attentively. Then somebody laughed, then the entire class was laughing, and not in contempt and ridicule, but with openhearted enjoyment. Even Mr. Fleagle stopped two or three times to repress a small prim smile. . . .

For the first time, light shone on a possibility. It wasn't a very heartening possibility, to be sure. Writing couldn't lead to a job after high school, and it was hardly honest work, but Mr Fleagle had opened a door for me. . . .

My mother was almost as delighted as I when I showed her Mr. Fleagle's A-Plus and described my triumph. Hadn't she always said I had a talent for writing?

- Fragment
- Complete predicate
- Fragment
- Simple subject
- Simple predicate
- Compound sentence
- Complete subject
- Interrogative sentence

Grammar Review

Review: Exercise 1   Identifying Sentences and Sentence Fragments

Write each sentence and draw a line between the complete subject and the complete predicate. If it is a fragment, write *fragment*, and explain why it is a fragment.

SAMPLE   Said he could write.
ANSWER   fragment; no subject

1. Baker wrote an essay about eating spaghetti.
2. Mr. Fleagle read the essay out loud.
3. The entire class.
4. Laughed with genuine and honest good humor.
5. The author ranked Mr. Fleagle as one of the finest teachers.
6. He showed his mother the A-Plus on his paper.
7. Baker's proud mother.
8. Didn't think writing would lead to a job after high school.
9. This experience opened a door for him.
10. Baker's newspaper column is read by millions of people.

Review: Exercise 2   Identifying Complete Subjects and Complete Predicates

Write each sentence. Underline the complete subject once and the complete predicate twice.

SAMPLE   The class studied English with Mr. Fleagle.
ANSWER   <u>The class</u> <u>studied English with Mr. Fleagle.</u>

1. Mr. Fleagle assigned the class an informal essay.
2. This form of writing seemed dull to Russell Baker.
3. A homework sheet listed a choice of topics.
4. Russell Baker chose "The Art of Eating Spaghetti."
5. That title brought up memories.
6. The young boy remembered a spaghetti dinner.
7. Not many people ate spaghetti in those days.
8. The family talked about this exotic dish.
9. Everyone had a good time that night.
10. Russell wrote about their funny arguments.

Review: Exercise 3   Identifying Simple Subjects and Simple Predicates

Write the simple subject and the simple predicate for each sentence.

SAMPLE   Russell Baker wanted a career in newspapers.
ANSWER   Russell Baker wanted

1. The author began his career in journalism in 1947.
2. The *Baltimore Sun* hired the young journalist.
3. He joined the *New York Times* in 1954.
4. The new *Times* reporter covered the White House and Congress.
5. Baker started his "Observer" column in 1962.
6. The award winner received the Pulitzer Prize in 1979.
7. His columns appear in several collections.
8. Baker's humor entertains millions of people.
9. The writer became a television host.
10. Watchers of *Masterpiece Theater* enjoy Baker's introductions to the show.

Review: Exercise 4   Identifying Subjects and Predicates in Questions

Rewrite each question to form a statement. Then underline each complete subject once and each complete predicate twice.

SAMPLE   Was the story about spaghetti?
ANSWER   <u>The story</u> <u>was about spaghetti.</u>

1. Had Baker's mother encouraged his writing skills?
2. Did Baker's teacher like his essay?
3. Did the class enjoy the essay?
4. Was the class laughing at Baker's story?
5. Did everyone like the essay?
6. Did Baker get an A-Plus on his paper?
7. Did this experience give Baker ideas about a career?
8. Had Mr. Fleagle opened a door for Baker?
9. Was Mr. Fleagle one of the finest teachers in Baker's school?
10. Was Baker's mother pleased with her son?

Subjects, Predicates, and Sentences

Grammar Review

Review: Exercise 5   Identifying Subjects and Predicates

Write the simple subject and the simple predicate in each sentence. If the sentence is a command, write *(You)*.

SAMPLE   Was Russell Baker born in Virginia?
ANSWER   Russell Baker   was born

 1. Find out about Baker's early life.
 2. Was Baker's father a stonemason?
 3. Did his mother teach school?
 4. Was Baker's sister named Doris?
 5. Here is a picture of Baker's family.
 6. Point to Baker in the picture.
 7. Did Baker win a college scholarship?
 8. Tell the name of his college.
 9. There are many books by Russell Baker.
10. Read *Growing Up*.

Review: Exercise 6   Identifying Compound Subjects and Compound Predicates

Write whether the sentence has a *compound subject* or a *compound predicate*.

SAMPLE   The cook boils spaghetti and adds sauce.
ANSWER   compound predicate

 1. Russell Baker and his family ate spaghetti one night.
 2. They enjoyed the food and argued about technique.
 3. Both children and adults like spaghetti.
 4. People all over the world prepare and eat pasta.
 5. The Italians created and named dozens of different types of pasta.
 6. The Chinese and the Japanese use noodles in many dishes.
 7. My family and I eat ziti often.
 8. Mom boils the ziti and covers it with sauce.
 9. She adds cheese and bakes the ziti.
10. My sister and I wait with our forks ready!

Review: Exercise 7   Making Compound Subjects and Verbs Agree

Write the correct form of the verb in parentheses.

1. Russell Baker's wisdom or his humor (attract, attracts) readers.
2. Critics and other readers (praise, praises) his autobiography.
3. *Growing Up* or his other books (earn, earns) him fame.
4. Baker's childhood memories and stories (create, creates) a picture of his family.
5. His family and his life (interest, interests) readers.
6. His words and his voice (affect, affects) and (delight, delights) people.
7. His newspaper columns or his television appearances (win, wins) praise.
8. Critics or other viewers (enjoy, enjoys) his commentaries.
9. His columns and poems (appear, appears) regularly and (sell, sells) well.
10. The George Polk Award or the Pulitzer Prize (prove, proves) his worth.

Review: Exercise 8   Identifying Simple and Compound Sentences

Write whether each sentence is *simple* or *compound*.

1. Russell Baker began his journalism career at the age of eight; his mother got him a job.
2. He and his mother met and talked to a man from Curtis Publishing Company.
3. The man liked Russell, and he hired the boy.
4. Russell began his career at the bottom; he sold the *Saturday Evening Post*.
5. Russell placed the magazines in a bag and walked to a busy intersection.
6. He stood on a corner and waited for customers.
7. Russell waited for hours, but no one bought a single magazine.
8. Russell's mother was upset by this, and she taught Russell about salesmanship.
9. Russell's uncle felt sorry for the boy and bought a magazine.
10. Russell handed him a magazine, and Uncle Allen paid Russell a nickel.

Review: Exercise 9   Identifying Compound Sentences and Run-on Sentences

Write whether each sentence is *compound* or *run-on*. If it is a run-on sentence, rewrite it correctly.

1. Russell Baker's mother wanted him to do well, and she encouraged him to study.
2. She didn't have much money, but she bought books and literary magazines for Russell.
3. Russell wasn't interested in literature he never read the books.
4. The magazines didn't appeal to him, he didn't read them either.
5. Russell's friend Charlie applied to Johns Hopkins University; he encouraged Russell to apply also.
6. Russell's family couldn't afford college, but Charlie told him about scholarships.
7. Russell applied for a scholarship to Johns Hopkins he didn't expect to get it.
8. Many students wanted scholarships they had to pass an exam.
9. The exam lasted four hours, and Russell worried about passing it.
10. Two weeks later a letter came from Johns Hopkins, Russell had won the scholarship.

Review: Exercise 10   Writing Compound Sentences

Combine each pair of simple sentences to form a compound sentence. Use the coordinating conjunction *and, but,* or *or.*

1. Russell Baker grew up in Baltimore. His first job was with a Baltimore newspaper.
2. Baker dreaded Mr. Fleagle's reaction. Mr. Fleagle liked Baker's story very much.
3. Mr. Fleagle read Baker's story to the class. The class enjoyed it.
4. Baker could have covered his ears. He could have left the room.
5. Baker needed a real job. He loved to write anyway.

Review: Exercise 11

Proofreading

The following passage is about American artist Joseph Raffael, whose work appears below. Rewrite the passage, correcting the errors in spelling, capitalization, grammar, and usage. Add any missing punctuation. There are ten errors.

Joseph Raffael, *Joseph and Reuben,* 1984

Joseph Raffael

[1]Joseph Raffael is an american artist known for his brightly colored paintings of landscapes, fish, flowers, and birds. [2]In the painting on the previous page, however, Raffael has took a different approach. [3]Its a portrait of the artist and his son, who appear as if they were posing. [4]For a photograph

[5]The strong contrast between light and dark in the painting add to the effect and give it the accidental quality of a snapshot. [6]Raffael is experimanting with the different qualities of light and color. [7]The colors—from the warm yellow to the deep purple—are as much the subject of the painting as the artist and his' son. [8]What a dramatic portrait this is

Review: Exercise 12

Mixed Review

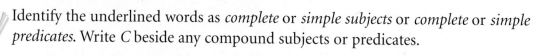

Identify the underlined words as *complete* or *simple subjects* or *complete* or *simple predicates*. Write *C* beside any compound subjects or predicates.

1. Russell Baker <u>showed his talent in high school.</u>
2. His English <u>teacher</u> assigned the class an essay.
3. <u>Baker and the other students</u> had a choice of topics.
4. Baker <u>chose and wrote about the topic "The Art of Eating Spaghetti."</u>
5. <u>Another title for Baker's essay</u> might have been "How Not to Eat Spaghetti."
6. Baker's <u>teacher</u> returned everyone's paper but Baker's.
7. Mr. Fleagle <u>read</u> Baker's essay to the class.
8. <u>Mr. Fleagle's encouragement and support</u> gave Baker food for thought.
9. <u>The young writer</u> liked to make people laugh.
10. He <u>thought</u> about journalism as a career.
11. Journalism <u>couldn't lead to a job and wasn't honest work.</u>
12. Many people <u>write for a career.</u>
13. <u>Both magazines and newspapers</u> use many writers.
14. Newspaper reporters <u>gather information and write articles.</u>
15. <u>Columnists such as Russell Baker</u> present their opinions and ideas to the readers.
16. <u>Writers</u> for magazines write articles on a wide variety of topics.
17. Other writers <u>create</u> books of fiction and nonfiction.
18. Some writers <u>combine words with photography and create photo essays.</u>
19. <u>All these possibilities</u> are open to a young writer.
20. Russell Baker <u>finally realized his luck.</u>

Writing Application

TIME

For more about the writing process, see **TIME Facing the Blank Page,** pp. 97-107.

Sentence Patterns in Writing

Maya Angelou varies both the length and the organization of her sentences in this passage from *The Heart of a Woman*. Pay particular attention to the sentence structure.

> I had worked two months for the SCLC, sent out tens of thousands of letters and invitations signed by Rev. King, made hundreds of statements in his name, but I had never seen him up close. He was shorter than I expected and so young. He had an easy friendliness, which was unsettling. Looking at him in my office, alone, was like seeing a lion sitting down at my dining-room table. . . .

Techniques with Sentence Patterns

Try to apply some of Maya Angelou's techniques when you write and revise your own work.

① Mix short and long sentences to create variety. Compare the following:

REPETITIVE SENTENCE PATTERN
He had an easy friendliness. It was unsettling. I looked at him in my office. It was like seeing a lion sitting down at my dining-room table.

IMPROVED VERSION He had an easy friendliness, which was unsettling. Looking at him in my office, alone, was like seeing a lion sitting down at my dining-room table. . . .

② Combine two simple sentences into one compound sentence to communicate related ideas:

CHOPPY VERSION I had made hundreds of statements in his name. I had never seen him up close.

IMPROVED VERSION I had made hundreds of statements in his name, but I had never seen him up close.

Practice Revise the following passage on a separate sheet of paper. Pay particular attention to the underlined words.

Last year my dad made some shelves for my rock collection. <u>I watched as he cut the wood. Then he sanded it.</u> Perched on top of some old boxes, <u>I could feel the vibrations of the saw. I watched it slice through each length of wood.</u> Buzzing filled the room. Sawdust piled up like blonde snow. <u>The sawdust was under the workbench. I wanted to help. Dad said why didn't I just keep him company.</u> So I told him stories about my rocks. <u>I described</u> where they came from. It was a special time together.

UNIT 9

Nouns

9.1 Kinds of Nouns

Look at the incomplete sentence below. Decide which of the words in the box that follows can complete the sentence.

The historian wrote about many famous  .

women	colorful	places	events
ago	ideas	did	pretty

The words *women, ideas, places,* and *events* can complete the sentence. These words are called nouns.

■ A **noun** is a word that names a person, place, thing, or idea.

There are two basic kinds of nouns: proper nouns and common nouns.

■ A **proper noun** names a *specific* person, place, thing, or idea.

■ A **common noun** names *any* person, place, thing, or idea.

The first word and all other important words in proper nouns are capitalized.

Common nouns can be either concrete or abstract.

■ **Concrete nouns** name things that you can see or touch.

■ **Abstract nouns** name ideas, qualities, or feelings that cannot be seen or touched.

Kinds of Nouns		
Proper	**Common**	
	Concrete	**Abstract**
Supreme Court	document	truth
Queen Victoria	crown	courage
December	snow	time
Museum of Anthropology	museum	history
Native American	buffalo	heritage

Exercise 1   Identifying Common and Proper Nouns

Write each noun that appears in the following sentences. Indicate whether each is a *common noun* or a *proper noun*. Remember to capitalize each proper noun.

1. A baby named isabella began life in slavery in the united states.
2. Slavery was allowed in the united states before the civil war.
3. Isabella worked very hard as a child.
4. The slaveholder chose a husband for isabella.
5. Isabella had thirteen children.
6. Isabella later became a free person.
7. Then isabella took the name sojourner truth.
8. This brave crusader worked for the freedom of women and african americans.
9. Sojourner truth traveled around the country.
10. Sojourner talked about the evils of slavery.
11. The brave woman spoke to large numbers of people in many states.
12. The speaker faced danger on many occasions.
13. Sojourner truth became famous as a result of her many speeches.
14. Sojourner met with president abraham lincoln at the white house.
15. After her visit with the president, sojourner stayed in washington, d.c.
16. She worked to improve conditions for african americans in the city.
17. She helped find work for other people who had once been enslaved and had come to washington.
18. Like sojouner truth, harriet tubman was also born in slavery in maryland.
19. Harriet tubman led her people to freedom on the underground railroad.
20. Sojourner truth and harriet tubman were important women in history.

Exercise 2   Identifying Concrete and Abstract Nouns

Write *abstract* or *concrete* for each underlined noun.

1. Born in <u>slavery</u>, Frederick Douglass escaped and fled to Massachusetts.
2. In 1841 he addressed a meeting and talked about <u>freedom</u>.
3. After he spoke, he was hired to talk to other <u>groups</u>.
4. It took <u>courage</u> for him to speak out as he did.
5. After his <u>autobiography</u> was published in 1845, he went to England.
6. When he returned, he continued to talk about his <u>beliefs</u>.
7. He helped <u>men</u>, <u>women</u>, and <u>children</u> flee to Canada.
8. Frederick Douglass is honored by many <u>people</u> in this <u>country</u>.
9. Douglass's books are appreciated for their <u>honesty</u>.
10. He was an important <u>person</u> in the <u>history</u> of the United States.

9.2 Compound Nouns

The noun *storybook* is made up of two words: *story* and *book*. Such a noun is called a compound noun.

■ **Compound nouns** are nouns made of two or more words.

A compound noun can be one word, like *storybook;* more than one word, like *ice cream;* or joined by hyphens, like *runner-up.*

Compound Nouns	
One word	housekeeper, showcase, bookmark, football, storybook
Hyphenated	mother-in-law, runner-up, great-grandmother, kilowatt-hour
More than one word	dining room, ice cream, maid of honor, music box

To form the plural of compound nouns written as one word, add *-s* or *-es.* To form the plural of compound nouns that are hyphenated or written as more than one word, make the most important part of the compound noun plural.

Forming Plural Compound Nouns	Singular	Plural
One word	Add **-s** to most words. Add **-es** to words that end in *ch, sh, s,* or *x.* Exception:	football**s**, headlight**s** strongbox**es**, rosebush**es** passer**s**by
Hyphenated	Make the most important part of the compound noun plural.	great-grandmother**s**, runner**s**-up, mother**s**-in-law
More than one word	Make the most important part of the compound noun plural.	maid**s** of honor, music box**es**

Whether the compound noun is singular or plural, the verb must agree with it.

My sister-in-law **writes** books. My sisters-in-law **write** books.

| Exercise 3 | Making Compound Nouns Plural |

Write the plural form of each compound noun below.

1. lifeguard	6. father-in-law	11. textbook	16. music box
2. vice-principal	7. sheepskin	12. police station	17. flight deck
3. golf club	8. window sash	13. passerby	18. great-grandson
4. master-at-arms	9. president-elect	14. roller skate	19. driving range
5. sweet potato	10. clubhouse	15. headache	20. drugstore

| Exercise 4 | Using Plural Compound Nouns |

Write each sentence, using the plural form of the compound noun in parentheses.

1. Voters go to (ballot box) to determine who is president.
2. The White House is the residence for each of our (commander in chief).
3. All (vice president) have had another residence.
4. Many (sergeant-at-arms) guard the White House.
5. John Adams was the first of the (chief executive) to live there.
6. (Sightseer) flock to the White House.
7. (Editor in chief) of newspapers must show passes to enter the White House.
8. President Franklin D. Roosevelt had small (swimming pool) added to the residence.
9. Under President John F. Kennedy, (guidebook) to the building's history were published.
10. Presidents can have daily (workout) in the gymnasium.
11. (Grandparent) sometimes visit the White House.
12. Overnight visitors sleep in (guest room) on the second floor.
13. In 1908 a meeting on the conservation of (natural resource) was held in the White House.
14. Many of the visitors to the White House are (jobholder).
15. In the West Wing are (workplace) for the president's staff.
16. Once a week the Cabinet, a group of (policymaker), gathers for a meeting.
17. Some presidents asked their daughters or (daughter-in-law) to serve as hostesses.
18. A meeting of (map maker) was held in the map room, a private area.
19. At the White House, no (shortcut) are taken where security is concerned.
20. (Political scientist) study how the White House operates.

9.3 Possessive Nouns

A noun can be singular, naming only one person, place, thing, or idea; or it can be plural, naming two or more. A noun can also show ownership or possession of things or qualities. This kind of noun is called a possessive noun.

■ A **possessive noun** names who or what owns or has something.

Possessive nouns can be common nouns or proper nouns. They can also be singular or plural. Notice the possessive nouns in the following sentences:

> **Rita** has a book on history.
> **Rita's** book is new.

> Read the **books**.
> Note the **books'** major themes.

Possessive nouns are formed in one of two ways. To form the possessive of most nouns, you add an apostrophe and *-s ('s)*. This is true for all singular nouns and for plural nouns not ending in *-s*. To form the possessive of plural nouns already ending in *-s*, you add only an apostrophe. These rules are summarized in the chart below.

Forming Possessive Nouns		
Nouns	**To Form Possessive**	**Examples**
Most singular nouns	Add an apostrophe and **-s** (**'s**).	a girl—a girl**'s** name a country—a country**'s** products
Singular nouns ending in **-s**	Add an apostrophe and **-s** (**'s**).	Lewis—Lewis **'s** explorations Chris—Chris**'s** homework
Plural nouns ending in **-s**	Add an apostrophe (**'**).	animals—animals**'** habits the Joneses—the Joneses**'** car
Plural nouns not ending in **-s**	Add an apostrophe and **-s** (**'s**).	women—women **'s** history children—children**'s** history

Forming Possessive Nouns

Write the possessive form of each underlined word or group of words.

1. Queen Elizabeth reign
2. documents pages
3. Arizona landscape
4. citizens rights
5. Dickens work
6. people choice
7. King Charles laws
8. women rights
9. city law
10. children books

11. artists works
12. birds nests
13. car engine
14. New England weather
15. democracy benefits
16. whales bones
17. Cape Cod bicycle trails
18. song refrain
19. book theme
20. Andy Warhol soup cans

Exercise 6   **Using Possessive Nouns**

For each sentence, write the correct possessive form of the noun in parentheses.

1. Meriwether Lewis was one of (Virginia) famous people.
2. He shared many (children) love of exploring.
3. Lewis served as President (Jefferson) personal secretary.
4. Jefferson guided (Lewis) preparations for an expedition.
5. Lewis and William Clark explored the (nation) uncharted territory.
6. Lewis depended on (Clark) skill at map making.
7. The (expedition) route ran through the Louisiana Territory and the Oregon region.
8. With the (Native Americans) help, they were able to cross the Rocky Mountains.
9. The team spent more than two (years) time in the Northwest.
10. They followed the Columbia (River) waters to the Pacific Ocean.
11. The (explorers) friends in St. Louis thought they had died on their trek.
12. The (men) bravery won great praise.
13. Later John Charles Frémont followed in Lewis and (Clark) footsteps.
14. (Frémont) explorations took him to Oregon, Nevada, and California.
15. He inspired Americans to oppose (Mexico) control of California.
16. He served as (California) U.S. Senator from 1850–1851.
17. In 1856 he became the Republican (Party) first candidate for president.
18. In the Civil War, he commanded one of the Union (Army) departments.
19. Strongly antislavery, he took over (slaveholders) lands in Missouri.
20. Frémont was married to (Thomas Hart Benton) daughter.

9.4 Distinguishing Plurals, Possessives, and Contractions

Most plural nouns, most possessive nouns, and certain contractions end with the letter -s. As a result, they sound alike and can be easily confused. Their spellings and meanings are different, however.

Noun Forms and Contraction		
	Example	**Meaning**
Plural Noun	The **students** wrote a play.	more than one student
Plural Possessive Noun	The **students'** play is good.	the play of the students
Singular Possessive Noun	I saw the **student's** play.	the play of one student
Contraction	The **student's** the author.	The student is the author.

■ A **contraction** is a word made by combining two words into one and leaving out one or more letters. An apostrophe shows where the letters have been omitted.

In the sentence *Naomi's participating in the science fair,* the word *Naomi's* is a contraction. It is made by combining the singular proper noun *Naomi* and the verb *is.* The apostrophe takes the place of the letter *i.* The contraction *Naomi's* sounds the same and is spelled the same as the singular possessive form of the proper noun *Naomi.*

Possessive Nouns and Contractions		
	Example	**Meaning**
Possessive	**Naomi's** exhibit is about bone fractures.	the exhibit prepared by Naomi
Contraction	**Naomi's** participating in the science fair.	Naomi is participating.

Forming Possessives and Contractions

Write each sentence, adding apostrophes to the possessive nouns and the contractions.

1. Woodrow Wilson was Americas twenty-eighth president.
2. As a student at Princeton, he joined the schools debating society.
3. Before becoming president, he served as Princeton Universitys president.
4. Wilsons regarded today as an educational and political reformer.
5. He was elected New Jerseys governor in 1910.
6. His success in New Jersey brought him to the Democrats attention.
7. Wilsons first term of office as president began in 1913.
8. The wars outbreak in Europe kept his attention on foreign affairs.
9. During his second term, he helped make the peace among Europes powers.
10. He had a stroke and was not able to fight for the peace treatys acceptance.

Exercise 8   Using Plurals, Possessives, and Contractions

Write the word in parentheses that correctly completes each sentence.

1. Herman (Melville's, Melvilles) a great American writer.
2. Herman (Melville's, Melvilles) life was full of adventure.
3. Melville traveled on sailing (ships, ship's) as a young man.
4. The (sailor's, sailors') lives were full of challenges.
5. Did Melville keep a record of his (experience's, experiences)?
6. Melville began his (adventures', adventures) as a cabin boy in 1837.
7. The young (man's, mans') destination was Liverpool.
8. (Liverpool's, Liverpools') an important city in Great Britain.
9. Special ships hunted (whales', whales) at this time.
10. These whaling (ships', ships) crews searched the world for whales.
11. (Whales, Whales') blubber provided many products.
12. (Nantucket's, Nantuckets) wealth depended on trade in whale products.
13. You can still visit the whaling (captains, captains') beautiful homes there.
14. Melville joined a whaling (ships, ship's) crew in 1841.
15. He visited the beautiful (islands, islands') of the Pacific Ocean.
16. Melville wrote (books', books) about his experience.
17. The public enjoyed this (writers', writer's) work.
18. In his masterpiece, *Moby Dick,* (sailors, sailors') hunt a great white whale.
19. The book describes the (dangers, dangers') of life aboard a whaling ship.
20. At the time, few people appreciated the (books, book's) power.

9.5 Collective Nouns

■ A **collective noun** names a group that is made up of individuals.

Collective Nouns			
committee	audience	swarm	club
family	team	crowd	orchestra
flock	class	jury	herd

Nouns and verbs always must show agreement in sentences. Collective nouns, however, present special agreement problems. Every collective noun can have either a singular meaning or a plural meaning. If you speak about the group as a unit, then the noun has a singular meaning. If you want to refer to the individual members of the group, then the noun has a plural meaning.

The **crowd cheers** the passing parade. [refers to group as a unit, singular]

The **crowd move** to their favorite spots along the parade route. [individual members, plural]

When you are thinking of the group as a unit, use a collective noun and the form of the verb that agrees with a singular noun. When you want to refer to the individual members of the group, use the collective noun and the form of the verb that agrees with a plural noun.

To help you determine whether a collective noun in a sentence is singular or plural, substitute the word *it* for the collective noun and any words used to describe it. If the sentence still makes sense, the collective noun is singular. If you can substitute they, the collective noun is plural.

The **team** works on its project. [it, singular]

The **team** work on their separate projects. [they, plural]

The **crowd move** to their favorite spots.

The **crowd cheers.**

Identifying Singular and Plural Collective Nouns

For each sentence, write the collective noun. Write *singular* or *plural* to describe it.

1. The group received first place in the competition.
2. The crowd in the club danced the entire night.
3. The gaggle of geese made a tremendous racket.
4. The students were given a range of choices on the test.
5. After the program, the band played an encore.
6. The family received a memento of the event.
7. The jury returned to their seats.
8. Company came to dinner last night.
9. A majority of the players voted to cancel the game.
10. The infantry fought from a dangerous position.

Exercise 10   **Using Collective Nouns**

For each sentence, write the collective noun. Then write the correct form of the verb in parentheses.

1. The class of seventh-graders (describes, describe) their vacations.
2. The entire class (meets, meet) at 2:00 p.m. every day.
3. The family (takes/take) their biggest towels with them to the beach.
4. The film club (devours/devour) its popcorn in the darkened theater.
5. Girl Scout Troop 39 (presents, present) a tribute to athletes.
6. The committee (argues, argue) among themselves over the suggestion.
7. The audience (cheers, cheer) its favorite contestants.
8. The orchestra (performs, perform) my favorite symphony.
9. The football team (eats/eat) its pregame meal in silence.
10. The herd (returns, return) to the same meadow each year.
11. The crowd of students (claps, clap) their hands to the music.
12. The public (supports, support) its local basketball team.
13. The whole wolf pack (roams, roam) the countryside.
14. The audience (shows/show) its approval by clapping and whistling.
15. The jury (reaches, reach) its verdict.
16. The battalion (marches, march) five miles each day.
17. The majority of stockholders (demands/demand) their ballots.
18. That family (takes, take) their responsibilities very seriously.
19. The whole litter (is, are) being given away to another family.
20. The flock of geese (grooms/groom) their feathers after the rain.

9.6 Appositives

- An **appositive** is a noun that is placed next to another noun to identify it or add information about it.

    James Madison's wife **Dolley** was a famous first lady.

The noun *Dolley* adds information about the noun *wife* by giving the wife's name. *Dolley* in this sentence is an appositive.

- An **appositive phrase** is a group of words that includes an appositive and other words that describe the appositive.

    Madison, **our fourth president**, held many other offices.

The words *our fourth* describe the appositive *president*. The phrase *our fourth president* is an appositive phrase. It adds information about the noun *Madison*.

An appositive or appositive phrase must appear next to the noun that it identifies.

    Our fourth president, Madison held many other offices.

    Many historians have studied the life of Madison, **our fourth president**.

An appositive phrase is usually set off from the rest of the sentence with one or more commas. If, however, the appositive is needed to identify the noun or if it is a single word, you do not use commas.

    Madison's friend **Thomas Jefferson** was president before him.

    Madison's father, **James Madison**, was a plantation owner.

Since Madison had more than one friend, the name *Thomas Jefferson* is needed to identify this particular friend. No commas are needed. Since Madison had only one father, however, the father's name is not needed to identify him. Then commas are used.

Identifying Appositive Phrases

Write each sentence. Underline each appositive noun or phrase and draw an arrow to the noun it identifies. Add commas where they are needed.

1. Madison and his friend Jefferson formed a new political party.
2. This party the Democratic-Republican party was the forerunner of the present Democratic party.
3. Thomas Jefferson the author of the Declaration of Independence was the third president.
4. Jefferson appointed his friend James Madison as secretary of state.
5. The Louisiana Purchase one of Madison's most significant achievements took place in 1803.
6. Madison and his vice president George Clinton were elected in 1809.
7. Dolley Madison a vivacious and very pleasant hostess was known for her extravagant parties.
8. Britain and France two major powers were engaged in a trade war.
9. In 1812 the United States declared war on Great Britain a much stronger nation.
10. American forces tried to take Canada a British territory but they were unsuccessful.

Exercise 12   **Using Appositives**

Write each sentence, using commas around appositives where needed.

1. James Madison grew up on Montpelier a plantation.
2. He attended Princeton a college in New Jersey.
3. Madison a dedicated student completed college in two years.
4. He first held office in his home colony Virginia.
5. In 1776 Thomas Jefferson another young politician served in the first state assembly with Madison.
6. Madison a devoted patriot served in the Continental Congress.
7. He also represented his home state Virginia at the Constitutional Convention of 1787.
8. Madison a believer in strong government played an active role at the convention.
9. He wrote *The Federalist* with his colleagues Hamilton and Jay.
10. A series of letters to newspapers *The Federalist* still offers the best explanation of the Constitution.

Grammar Review

NOUNS

Barbara Jordan, by James Haskins, is a biography of the first African American woman from Texas to serve in the United States Congress. The following passage contains an excerpt from Jordan's keynote speech at the 1976 Democratic National Convention. The passage has been annotated to show some of the kinds of nouns covered in this unit.

Literature Model

from Barbara Jordan
by James Haskins

"One hundred and forty-four years ago, members of the Democratic Party first met in convention to select a presidential candidate. Since that time Democrats have continued to convene once every four years and draft a party platform and nominate a presidential candidate. . . .

"But there is something different about tonight. There is something special about tonight. What is different? What is special? I, Barbara Jordan, am a keynote speaker."

She was interrupted by wild applause and cheering, and she would be interrupted again and again as she spoke of the problems of the country and her hopes for America. . . . The overwhelming response was one of pride, not just from women because she was a woman, not just from blacks because she was black, not just from Democrats or from Texans, but from all segments of the population, because she was an American.

- Common noun
- Concrete noun
- Appositive
- Singular noun
- Plural noun
- Proper noun
- Abstract noun

Nouns

Grammar Review

Review: Exercise 1	Identifying Kinds of Nouns

Write each noun that appears in the following sentences. Indicate whether each is a *common noun* or a *proper noun*. (Remember to capitalize each proper noun.)

SAMPLE As keynote speaker, barbara jordan had an important role.
ANSWER speaker, common; Barbara Jordan, proper; role, common

1. Texas is the birthplace of barbara jordan.
2. It gained independence from mexico in the last century.
3. It is bordered by the states of oklahoma, arkansas, and louisiana.
4. The rio grande forms the southern border.
5. Texas has many artificial lakes formed from dams on rivers.
6. The weather is usually very hot.
7. Some places average 48 inches of precipitation a year.
8. Oil fields produce many gallons of petroleum.
9. The arkansas national wildlife refuge is home to some rare birds.
10. Major cities include dallas, houston, and san antonio.

Review: Exercise 2	Using Possessive Nouns

For each sentence, write the correct possessive form of the singular or plural noun in parentheses.

SAMPLE Washington, D.C., is our (nation) capital.
ANSWER nation's

1. It is the (committee) decision to report out the bill.
2. Here is the minority (party) report on the bill.
3. Hearings will be held in a (month) time.
4. This new law will affect the (nation) postal system.
5. Senator (Jones) bill goes to the floor of the Senate tomorrow.
6. Not everyone agrees with the (bill) provisions.
7. Both (sides) opinions have to be taken into consideration.
8. The (members) votes were tallied by computer.
9. The House will now debate the (Senate) version of the bill.
10. The bill still requires the (president) signature.

Review: Exercise 3   Using Plurals, Possessives, and Contractions

The following sentences are based on the passage from *Barbara Jordan*. Write the word in parentheses that correctly completes the sentence.

SAMPLE   The audience cheered (Jordans, Jordan's) speech.
ANSWER   Jordan's

1. Barbara Jordan described the Democratic (Parties, Party's) first meeting.
2. She was welcomed by listeners at the (Democrats, Democrats') convention.
3. There is something special about being the (conventions, convention's) keynote speaker.
4. A (conventions, convention's) an important part of choosing a presidential candidate.
5. (Styles, Style's) an important aspect of public speaking.
6. The applause and cheers expressed the (Democrats, Democrats') pride in the congresswoman from Texas.
7. A better (Americas, America's) everyone's hope for the future, including Jordan's.
8. Jordan also talked about (womens, women's) rights.
9. This country's (populations, population's) impressed by speeches like Jordan's.
10. (Jordans, Jordan's) remembered as a notable force in American politics.

Review: Exercise 4   Using Collective Nouns

Each sentence contains a collective noun. Write the form of the verb in parentheses that agrees with the noun.

SAMPLE   The audience (roars, roar) its approval during the keynote speech.
ANSWER   roars

1. A committee (chooses, choose) the convention city.
2. The group (meets, meet) to draft its party's policies.
3. Then the committee (states, state) their opinions.
4. During the convention, the party (nominates, nominate) its candidates for president and vice president.
5. After both candidates have been nominated, the team (delivers, deliver) their speeches.

Grammar Review

Review: Exercise 5   **Using Appositives**

The following sentences are about Barbara Jordan. Write each sentence, adding the appositive or appositive phrase. Add a comma or commas where needed. In some cases, more than one answer may be possible.

SAMPLE   Barbara Jordan received her law degree from Boston University. (a lawyer)

ANSWER   Barbara Jordan, a lawyer, received her law degree from Boston University. **OR**
A lawyer, Barbara Jordan received her law degree from Boston University.

1. When Jordan was born, Texas was segregated by race. (her home state)
2. In high school, Jordan did well in debating. (the art of formal discussion)
3. Her university had only African American teachers and students. (Texas Southern)
4. Jordan studied law at an integrated school. (Boston University)
5. After returning to Houston, Jordan became involved in local politics. (a lawyer with her own practice)
6. In 1960 Jordan campaigned for John F. Kennedy. (the Democratic nominee)
7. Kennedy's running mate was a Texan like Jordan. (Lyndon Johnson)
8. Jordan was asked to run for office in Texas. (a strong organizer and speaker)
9. Jordan was elected to the Texas State Senate in 1966. (a good campaigner)
10. The senate awarded her the Outstanding Senator Award her first year. (a body of thirty-one members)
11. Lyndon Johnson invited Jordan to a conference. (the vice president)
12. The participants discussed fair-housing proposals. (civil rights leaders)
13. Jordan served in the House of Representatives. (a Texas Democrat)
14. She sat on the House Judiciary Committee. (a very important assignment)
15. Jordan took a firm stand to impeach Richard Nixon. (the president)
16. She said no one should lie to the American people. (freedom's champion)
17. Jordan worked to promote the good of the country. (a role model)
18. She worked to pass legislation banning discrimination and dealing with another important issue. (the environment)
19. Jordan was also asked to address the Democratic National Convention in 1992. (a powerful speaker)
20. The audience's response to Jordan's speech was a tribute to a notable American. (a standing ovation)

Proofreading

The following passage is about the artist Henri Matisse, whose work appears below. Rewrite the passage, correcting the errors in spelling, grammar, and usage. Add any missing punctuation. There are ten errors.

Henri Matisse

¹Henri Matisse a French artist, was the leader of the Fauves. ²This group of painters began one of the twentieth centurys important art movements. ³These painter's bright colors and simple designs was one of their trademarks.

⁴Matisse made no atempt to represent reality in his colorful paintings or in the compositions he made from paper cutouts. ⁵Many of Matisses cutouts represents dancers. ⁶In one cutout, for example, the vivid colors and bold shape's suggest an enormous energy. ⁷A dancer stands proud and tall among the birds' and flowers. ⁸Shes full of strength and dignity.

Henri Matisse, *La Négresse,* 1952

Nouns

Grammar Review

Review: Exercise 7

Mixed Review

Identify the underlined nouns as *common, proper, collective,* or *possessive.* More than one label may apply to a single noun.

Franklin Delano Roosevelt

¹Franklin Delano Roosevelt inspired ²Americans with his speeches, as well as with his actions. He became ³president in 1933, when the country was in the depths of the ⁴Great Depression. The ⁵public was suffering, and many people were starving. His inaugural ⁶address's words gave Americans ⁷courage and confidence. His ⁸words "The only thing we have to fear is fear itself" called for faith in our ⁹country.

Born into a wealthy ¹⁰family, he believed in public service. At the age of thirty-nine, Roosevelt was stricken with polio. His ¹¹legs were paralyzed, and he was unable to stand without help. Eleven years later he was elected president of the United States, following ¹²President Herbert Hoover.

In ¹³"The Hundred Days" after he first took office, Roosevelt launched his ¹⁴New Deal. The laws that he introduced and that Congress passed helped farmers, ¹⁵industry, the unemployed, and the common worker.

Though the Great Depression continued, Roosevelt won ordinary ¹⁶citizens' admiration and affection. He was elected president four times—a ¹⁷record unmatched by any other president.

Roosevelt knew how to reach voters. He used the radio effectively to speak to the American ¹⁸people. He often addressed the ¹⁹nation in radio talks that were called "fireside chats." The public liked the sound of his ²⁰voice and gained ²¹confidence in him and in the ²²ideals that he represented.

At the time of ²³Japan's attack on Pearl Harbor, Roosevelt, in his address before Congress, called December 7 "a date that will live in infamy." ²⁴Roosevelt's ringing words inspired Americans and helped prepare them for the long and very difficult ²⁵war that lay ahead. Roosevelt met many times during the war with Winston Churchill, the prime minister of ²⁶England, and with ²⁷Joseph Stalin, the premier of Russia.

Roosevelt died in April 1945, just before the end of the war. A huge ²⁸crowd gathered at the ²⁹White House as word of his death spread. He was deeply mourned by millions of people all over the ³⁰world.

Writing Application

TIME

For more about the writing process, see **TIME Facing the Blank Page**, pp. 97-107.

Nouns in Writing

In this passage from *Thrashin' Time*, David Weiztman uses nouns to capture the excitement and details of an early twentieth-century farming event. Read the passage carefully, noting the italicized nouns.

> The *engine* was quieter than I thought it would be. It was almost alive like the horses working everywhere round it. And the horses. Why, I'll betcha there were sixty *head*, big *horses—Belgians* and *Percherons*—coming and going that *afternoon. Teams* pulled *bundle wagons* heaped tall with *sheaves* of *wheat* from the *fields,* pulled *wagons* of yellow *grain* away from the *separator* to the *silo.* Another team hauled the water *wagon,* and another *wagon* brought loads of cord *wood* to keep the *engine* running sunup to sundown.

Techniques with Nouns

Try to apply some of David Weiztman's techniques when you write and revise your own work.

❶ When appropriate, use proper nouns to make your writing more exact:

COMMON NOUNS there were sixty head, big horses coming and going

WEIZTMAN'S VERSION there were sixty head, big horses—*Belgians* and *Percherons*—coming and going

❷ Make your writing more vivid by replacing general or abstract words with concrete specific nouns. Compare the following:

GENERAL WORDS heaped tall with *crops*

WEIZTMAN'S VERSION heaped tall with *sheaves* of *wheat* in from the *fields*

Nouns

Practice Practice these techniques as you revise the following passage on a separate piece of paper. Instead of the underlined words, use proper nouns and more specific nouns to make the passage more vivid.

Today I saw <u>an ocean</u> for the first time. <u>Birds</u> dove and soared above the hills lining the <u>coast of the land</u>. Waves curled and crashed onto the beaches below. Out on the water, <u>pieces</u> of white <u>wave</u> spread like lace across a huge blue <u>piece of fabric</u>. Amongst the people gathered at the edge of the road, I could see people wearing <u>city</u> T-shirts, <u>people</u> struggling to read the <u>signs in another language</u>, and <u>people</u> holding eager children away from the <u>side</u>.

UNIT 10 Verbs

10.1 Action Verbs

You may have heard of the movie director's call for "lights, camera, *action!*" The actions in movies and plays can be named by verbs. If a word expresses action and tells what a subject does, it is an action verb.

■ An **action verb** is a word that names an action. An action verb may contain more than one word.

ACTION VERB

Notice the action verbs in the following sentences.

The director **shouts** at the members of the cast.
The lights **are flashing** above the stage.
The audience **arrives** in time for the performance.
Several singers **have memorized** the lyrics of a song.

Action verbs can express physical actions, such as *shout* and *arrive.* They can also express mental activities, such as *memorize* and *forget.*

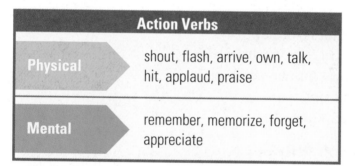

Action Verbs	
Physical	shout, flash, arrive, own, talk, hit, applaud, praise
Mental	remember, memorize, forget, appreciate

Have, has, and *had* are action verbs too when they name what the subject owns or holds.

The actors in this play already **have** their uniforms.
The director **has** a script in her back pocket.
The theater **has** a trapdoor.
Rosa **had** a theater program from 1959.

She **acted** as if . . .

. . . she **remembered** her lines.

Identifying Action Verbs

Write each action verb and then write whether it expresses a *physical* or a *mental* action.

1. Eugene O'Neill's father, an actor, toured the country.
2. O'Neill learned about the theater from his father.
3. O'Neill's father sent him to Princeton University.
4. Soon O'Neill developed an interest in the sea.
5. He left home for two years of travel.
6. Later, a drama teacher at Harvard University inspired O'Neill.
7. O'Neill knew the value of his own work.
8. He journeyed to Cape Cod for the summer.
9. A group of friends admired this new playwright.
10. They used a stage in their town for theatrical productions.
11. O'Neill also wrote many plays while in Connecticut.
12. He joined a group of performers and writers.
13. The young O'Neill worked long hours.
14. On some days, O'Neill walked along the wharves.
15. Sometimes he met friends along the way.
16. The playwright considered ideas for new plays.
17. In 1936 he received the Nobel Prize for literature.
18. Many theater groups perform his plays each year.
19. Audiences like the dramatic situations.
20. Most of the plays express dark moods.

Exercise 2 **Using Action Verbs**

Write an appropriate action verb for each sentence. Answers will vary.

1. Our drama and history teachers _____ a joint project for our class.
2. First, our history teacher _____ us into four small groups.
3. Then he _____ the new assignment in detail.
4. The whole class _____ to the library every day for a week.
5. In our small groups, we _____ everyday life in colonial times.
6. Then the drama coach _____ us the next part of the assignment.
7. Each group _____ a one-act play set in the colonial period.
8. The coach _____ our plays for an acting workshop.
9. All of us _____ our lines and movements over the weekend.
10. Finally, we _____ our plays for the class and in a competition.

Verbs

10.2 Transitive and Intransitive Verbs

In some sentences, the predicate consists of only a verb.

The actor **remembered.**

Usually sentences provide more information. The predicate often names who or what received the action of the verb.

The actor remembered **lines** from the play.

DIRECT OBJECT

In the sentence above, *lines* tells what was remembered. It is the direct object.

■ A **direct object** receives the action of a verb. It answers the question *whom?* or *what?* after an action verb.

Some sentences have a compound direct object. That is, a sentence may have more than one direct object.

We saw **Maurice** and **Inez** in the audience.

When an action verb transfers action to a direct object, it is transitive. When an action verb has no direct object, it is intransitive.

■ A **transitive verb** has a direct object.

■ An **intransitive verb** does not have a direct object.

Many action verbs can be transitive or intransitive. Such verbs can be labeled transitive or intransitive only by examining their use in a particular sentence.

The audience **applauds** the actors. [transitive]
The audience **applauds** loudly. [intransitive]

Exercise 3   Identifying Transitive Verbs

For each sentence, write the action verb. If the verb is transitive, write the direct object.

1. Japanese kabuki theaters present popular scenes from dramas and dances.
2. Kabuki performers often wear very elaborate costumes.
3. Male actors perform all the female roles.
4. Characters make entrances and exits along the "flower way" aisle.
5. Instrumentalists behind a screen on stage provide the music.

Exercise 4   Distinguishing Transitive and Intransitive Verbs

For each sentence, write the action verb. If the verb has a direct object, write T. If it does not, write I.

1. The director remembered this fine old theater from past performances.
2. He loved its air of history and elegance.
3. Day after day, week after week, the cast rehearsed.
4. Finally, the day of the first performance arrived.
5. The director inspected the scenery, costumes, and lights.
6. Many people bought tickets to the new play.
7. The almost-silent audience watched.
8. Nearly all the people liked the music and the drama.
9. At the end of the play, everyone clapped wildly.
10. Some enthusiastic spectators even cheered.
11. The majority of the critics enjoyed the performance.
12. They wrote favorable reviews.
13. The musical show succeeded.
14. In fact, the director won an award for it from a theater guild.
15. At the awards ceremony, the director spoke.
16. The cast and their guests listened carefully.
17. The director thanked the producers.
18. A newspaper reporter asked some questions.
19. The director complimented the stage crew for the scenery.
20. He praised the actors for their performances.

10.3 Verbs with Indirect Objects

Words that answer the question *whom?* or *what?* after an action verb are called direct objects.

> Amalia wears a **costume.**

Sometimes both a direct object and an indirect object follow an action verb.

■ An **indirect object** answers the question *to whom?* or *for whom?* an action is done.

Friends sent the **actors** flowers.

to whom?

INDIRECT OBJECT

The direct object in the sentence above is *flowers.* The indirect object is *actors. Actors* answers the question *to whom?* after the action verb *sent.*

Some sentences have a compound indirect object.

> The audience gave the **cast** and the **orchestra** an ovation.

An indirect object appears only in a sentence that has a direct object. Two easy clues can help you recognize an indirect object. First, an indirect object always comes before a direct object. Second, you can add the preposition *to* or *for* before the indirect object and change its position. The sentence will still make sense, although there will no longer be an indirect object.

> Friends sent the **actors flowers.**
> [*Actors* is an indirect object.]
> Friends sent flowers **to the actors.**
> [*Actors* is not an indirect object.]

You know that in the first sentence *actors* is the indirect object because it comes before the direct object and because it can be placed after the preposition *to,* as in the second sentence.

Exercise 5   Distinguishing Direct and Indirect Objects

For each sentence, write the direct object. If the sentence contains an indirect object, write it and underline it.

1. None of the musicians know the composition.
2. The orchestra leader brings the musicians the music.
3. For several days, the orchestra leader teaches the orchestra a song.
4. The sopranos learn their part first.
5. The audience loves the musical comedy.
6. That famous director frequently gives performers drama lessons.
7. She also gives children lessons in the afternoon.
8. She wrote plays and operas for many years.
9. Now she shows her students her special techniques.
10. The theater offers young people many opportunities.
11. Students ask actors and directors questions about different roles.
12. The expert director and producers bring the show success.
13. The director offers her students advice about their careers.
14. The actors memorize scripts.
15. One young writer sold a producer and a director his screenplay.
16. The theater club offers subscribers a discount.
17. The theater also sends subscribers performance information.
18. Subscribers often buy extra tickets for their friends.
19. Generous patrons give the theater large donations.
20. The theater usually gives generous patrons free tickets.

Exercise 6   Using Indirect Objects

Rewrite each sentence, changing each prepositional phrase into an indirect object.

SAMPLE   The cast members gave interviews to the press.
ANSWER   The cast members gave the press interviews.

1. The playwright gave a special tribute to her mother.
2. The youngest cast member handed a dozen roses to the star.
3. Cast members made a comical top hat for the director.
4. The audience offered thunderous applause to the entire cast.
5. The play's producer sent fifteen photographs of the event to the local newspaper.

10.4 Linking Verbs and Predicate Words

LINKING VERB

■ A **linking verb** connects the subject of a sentence with a noun or adjective in the predicate.

Bess Powell **was** the director.

LINKING VERB

The verb *was* is a form of the verb *be*. It links the word *director* to the subject, telling what the subject is.

■ A **predicate noun** is a noun that follows a linking verb. It defines the subject by telling what it is.

■ A **predicate adjective** is an adjective that follows a linking verb. It describes the subject by telling what it is like.

A sentence may contain a compound predicate noun or a compound predicate adjective.

> The set designer was a **carpenter** and **electrician.** [compound predicate noun]
> He is **stern** but **kind.** [compound predicate adjective]

Some of the more common linking verbs are listed below.

Common Linking Verbs			
be	appear	turn	smell
become	look	taste	sound
seem	grow	feel	

Many of these verbs can be used as action verbs also.

> The director grew angry. [linking verb]
> The director grew a beard. [action verb]

Identifying Action and Linking Verbs

Write each verb. Then write whether it is an *action* verb or a *linking* verb.

1. Lorraine Hansberry became the first African American woman with a play on Broadway.
2. *A Raisin in the Sun* is the title of that play.
3. Hansberry used a line from a Langston Hughes poem for the title.
4. The play tells the story of an African American Chicago family and the dreams of the different family members.
5. In the course of the play, the family grows stronger and closer.

Exercise 8 Identifying Linking Verbs and Predicate Nouns and Adjectives

Write each verb and label it *action* or *linking*. If it is a linking verb, write the predicate word or words and add the label *predicate noun* or *predicate adjective*.

1. William Shakespeare was a great playwright and poet.
2. In fact, he is a giant in world literature.
3. Characters in Shakespeare's plays seem universal.
4. Some of the characters were actually historical figures.
5. Some costumes in Shakespeare's plays look odd.
6. The styles of earlier times appear strange today.
7. Shakespeare's language puzzles some modern listeners.
8. In time, however, that language becomes very clear and understandable.
9. Many of Shakespeare's plots sound exaggerated.
10. His stories thrill audiences all over the world with their power, beauty, and truth.
11. Some of the characters are more popular than others.
12. In *Romeo and Juliet* a character drinks poison.
13. In *Othello* the main character grows jealous.
14. In *The Merchant of Venice* a clever young woman teaches other characters about justice and mercy.
15. Some members of Shakespeare's original casts were children.
16. The children played women's roles.
17. Films of Shakespeare's plays are plentiful and popular.
18. Great actors and actresses perform complex roles.
19. Laurence Olivier and John Barrymore were great Hamlets.
20. More recently Mel Gibson and Kenneth Branagh have played Hamlet.

10.5 Present and Past Tenses

The verb in a sentence tells what action takes place. It also tells when the action takes place. The form of a verb that shows the time of the action is called the **tense** of the verb.

■ The **present tense** of a verb names an action that occurs regularly. It can also express a general truth.

A great actor **wins** awards.

In the present tense, the base form of a verb is used with all subjects except singular nouns and the words *he, she,* and *it*. When the subject is a singular noun or *he, she,* or *it, -s* is usually added to the verb. Remember that a verb in a sentence must agree in number with its subject.

Present Tense Forms	
Singular	**Plural**
I **walk.**	We **walk.**
You **walk.**	You **walk.**
He, she, *or* it **walks.**	They **walk.**

■ The **past tense** of a verb names an action that already happened.

The past tense of many verbs is formed by adding *-ed* to the verb.

The actors **practiced** their lines.

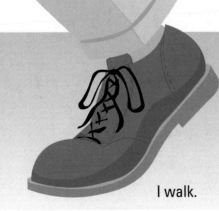

I walk.

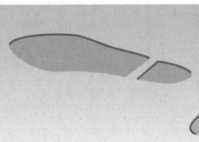

I walk**ed.**

Exercise 9   Distinguishing Present and Past

Write the correct form of the verb that is in parentheses. Then write whether it is in the *present tense* or *past tense.*

1. A month ago, our music teacher (introduce) my sister and me to opera.
2. Opera is a form that (combine) music and drama into one production.
3. That combination (suit) my sister and me perfectly.
4. Last week we (attend) a light opera by Gilbert and Sullivan.
5. Every day that week, the show (start) precisely on time.
6. However, we (arrive) late because of bus delays.
7. After the show, we always (purchase) tickets for tomorrow's opera.
8. Yesterday a reviewer (compare) the lead performer with Caruso.
9. Enrico Caruso (live) at the beginning of the twentieth century.
10. In his lifetime, he (appear) in many operas throughout the world.
11. Caruso (arrive) in America in 1903.
12. Sometimes he (pass) out free tickets to poor people.
13. Caruso (earn) more money than any other singer at the time.
14. He always (maintain) a warm affection for his many fans.
15. Caruso often (play) tricks on his fellow performers.
16. He (possess) a dynamic personality.
17. Today singers still (talk) about his wonderful voice.
18. Now some people (listen) to his original recordings.
19. Some modern singers (copy) the great singer's style and technique.
20. That great Italian tenor (inspire) singers even today.

Exercise 10   Using Past Tense

For each sentence, write the present tense verb. Then write its past tense form.

1. People in the audience chat with one another before the performance.
2. Several classes of students almost fill the second balcony.
3. The lights blink on and off—once, twice, three times.
4. Members of the audience settle into their seats.
5. Darkness descends on the theater except for the glow of safety lights.
6. Not a sound disturbs the silence.
7. Then a spotlight focuses on the heavy red curtain across the stage.
8. The curtains part and reveal a city street.
9. Suddenly actors and actresses appear on the stage.
10. The magic of theater captivates the audience.

10.6 Main Verbs and Helping Verbs

Verbs have four principal parts that are used to form all tenses. Notice how the principal parts of a verb are formed.

Principal Parts of Verbs			
Base Form	**Present Participle**	**Past Form**	**Past Participle**
act	acting	acted	acted

You can use the base form itself and the past form alone to form the present and past tenses. The present and past participles can be combined with helping verbs to form other tenses.

■ A **helping verb** helps the main verb tell about an action or make a statement.

■ A **verb phrase** consists of one or more helping verbs followed by a main verb.

They **are acting** in another play right now.

In the sentence above, the word *are* is the helping verb, and the present participle *acting* is the main verb. Together they form a verb phrase.

The most common helping verbs are *be, have,* and *do.* Forms of the helping verb *be* include *am, is,* and *are* in the present and *was* and *were* in the past. They combine with the present participle of the main verb.

Forms of the helping verb *have* include *has* in the present and *had* in the past. They combine with the past participle form of a verb.

Have, Has, Had, and the Past Participle			
Singular	**Plural**	**Singular**	**Plural**
I **have** acted.	We **have** acted.	I **had** acted.	We **had** acted.
You **have** acted.	You **have** acted.	You **had** acted.	You **had** acted.
She **has** acted.	They **have** acted.	She **had** acted.	They **had** acted.

Identifying Helping Verbs and Participles in Verb Phrases

For each sentence, write each verb phrase. Then circle the helping verbs.

1. Stagehands are preparing the scenery.
2. They had started their work before dawn.
3. One young woman is checking on the correct placement of all the props.
4. Earlier she had inspected all the backstage props and equipment.
5. The director had joined the crew later in the day, and now he is conducting his own last-minute check.
6. The star of the show has earned her fame by a number of huge successes.
7. The press and the public are expecting an excellent performance from this famous cast.
8. Theater has remained a popular form of entertainment.
9. People are buying tickets to many different shows.
10. Theater companies are staging plays, musicals, and revivals of older shows.

Exercise 12   **Using Helping Verbs and Present and Past Participles**

For each sentence, choose and write the correct helping verb that is in parentheses. Then write the participle and label it *present participle* or *past participle*.

1. Now groups (are, have) performing dramas on television.
2. As a result, people (are, have) developing a taste for theater.
3. Television audiences (are, had) watching great performances, both comedies and tragedies.
4. Many of these productions (are, have) attracted huge numbers of viewers from all over the country.
5. The best of them (are, have) achieved very high ratings and rave reviews from critics and viewers alike.
6. Emmy awards (are, have) announced each year in the category for drama-comedy specials.
7. The number and success of these productions (are, have) awakened substantial interest in drama.
8. Producers and advertisers (are, have) responding to people's interest in high-quality television programs.
9. Live theater (is, has) experienced a surge in interest.
10. Both professional companies and community theater groups (are, have) welcoming a new generation of theatergoers.

Verbs

10.7 | Progressive Forms

You know that the present tense of a verb names an action that occurs repeatedly. To describe an action that is taking place at the present time, you use the present progressive form of the verb.

■ The **present progressive** form of a verb names an action or condition that is continuing in the present.

Althea **is finishing** her song.

The present progressive form of a verb consists of the present participle of the main verb and a form of *be*, such as *am, are,* or *is*.

Present Progressive Form	
Singular	**Plural**
I **am leaving**.	We **are leaving**.
You **are leaving**.	You **are leaving**.
He, she, *or* it **is leaving**.	They **are leaving**.

The past progressive form names an action that was continuing at some point in the past.

■ The **past progressive** form of a verb names an action or condition that continued for some time in the past.

The plot **was becoming** scary.

The past progressive form of a verb consists of the present participle and the helping verb *was* or *were*.

Past Progressive Form	
Singular	**Plural**
I **was following**.	We **were following**.
You **were following**.	You **were following**.
He, she, *or* it **was following**.	They **were following**.

For each sentence, write the present progressive or past progressive form of the verb that is in parentheses.

1. This next semester my music class (go) to an opera production every week.
2. We (examine) the difference between nineteenth- and twentieth-century operas.
3. We (compare) German, French, Italian, and American operas.
4. The schedule (tire) for some students.
5. They (fall) behind in their schoolwork.
6. Our teacher (plan) a big party for us later.
7. She (praise) us yesterday for our patience and diligence.
8. At the end of this semester, we (expect) a period of relaxation.
9. Last month we (attend) two productions a week.
10. Together with our other responsibilities, that schedule (overwhelm).
11. Our parents said they (worry) about our lack of time for anything else.
12. Last year we (study) the comic operas of Gilbert and Sullivan.
13. From 1875 to 1895, the two men (collaborate) on a number of light operas.
14. William Gilbert (work) as a lawyer and a journalist.
15. Arthur Sullivan (write) music for various productions of Shakespeare.
16. Even today many theater groups (present) Gilbert and Sullivan.
17. Time and again, new audiences (discover) the joys of these lively comedies.
18. Last year the city (prepare) a plan for a Gilbert and Sullivan festival.
19. As part of that festival, next spring we (stage) *The Pirates of Penzance.*
20. Many of us in the music class (hope) for good roles in that production.

Exercise 14   Using Progressive Forms

In each sentence, if the verb is in the present tense, change it to the present progressive form. If the verb is in the past tense, change it to the past progressive form.

1. The new theater season begins soon.
2. Local playwrights submitted their entries over a two-week period.
3. A committee reads the scripts.
4. Committee members hoped for a play with a large cast.
5. Last season this company attracted large audiences to its productions.
6. This year the members dream of an equally successful season.
7. One new play caused much excitement among the entries.
8. In this play, a brother and sister investigate the story of a treasure.
9. Meanwhile, the children's parents organize a search for them.
10. Near the end of the play, everyone rushes to the same hilltop.

Verbs

10.8 Perfect Tenses

- The **present perfect tense** of a verb names an action that happened at an indefinite time in the past. It also tells about an action that happened in the past and is still happening now.

> The actor **has rehearsed** for many hours.
>
> Nick and Maria **have seen** *Guys and Dolls* five times.
>
> He **has played** in the band for three years.

The present perfect tense consists of the helping verb *have* or *has* and the past participle of the main verb.

Present Perfect Tense	
Singular	**Plural**
I **have performed**. You **have performed**. He, she, *or* it **has performed**.	We **have performed**. You **have performed**. They **have performed**.

- The **past perfect tense** of a verb names an action that took place before another action or event in the past.

The past perfect tense is often used in sentences that contain a past tense verb in another part of the sentence.

> We **had** just **arrived** when the play **began**.
>
> The play **had been rewritten** several times before it **opened.**

The past perfect tense of a verb consists of the helping verb *had* and the past participle of the main verb.

Past Perfect Tense	
Singular	**Plural**
I **had started**. You **had started**. He, she, *or* it **had started**.	We **had started**. You **had started**. They **had started**.

Exercise 15   Identifying Present Perfect and Past Perfect Tenses

For each sentence, write the verb phrase. Then write whether it is in the *present perfect* or the *past perfect* tense.

1. My favorite television show has earned six Emmy nominations this year.
2. Before this year, it had collected three major Emmies: for best drama, best actor, and best actress.
3. The actress had appeared in several other shows before this one.
4. All of her shows have challenged the boundaries of television.
5. This new one, however, has proved itself the best of all.

Exercise 16   Using Present Perfect Tense

For each sentence, write the present perfect tense of the verb that is in parentheses.

1. That actress (perform) in several award-winning plays.
2. Her drama coach (help) her a great deal.
3. The cast (learn) discipline and craft.
4. Our drama club (wait) for the opening of the opera season.
5. The members (plan) weekly theater parties.
6. Some new students (join) the club this year.
7. The club (elect) Tanya president.
8. She (appear) in most of our club's productions.
9. She (contribute) time and energy to every one of them.
10. All of us (benefit) from her work and good nature.

Exercise 17   Using the Past Perfect Tense

For each sentence, write the past perfect tense of the verb that is in parentheses.

1. Before the show began, the cast (rehearse) for weeks.
2. Artists (create) the scenery before the opening.
3. The costume designers (locate) boxes and boxes of Roaring Twenties clothes.
4. Before the first rehearsal, our teacher (talk) to us.
5. She (warn) us of the hard work ahead.
6. Also, however, she (predict) an enjoyable, worthwhile activity for us.
7. Before opening night, the cast (suffer) from stage fright.
8. We (present) only one show before last year.
9. Until last week, every member of the cast (attend) every rehearsal.
10. The director (demonstrate) many valuable techniques.

Expressing Future Time

The future tense of a verb is formed by using the helping verb *will* before the main verb. The helping verb *shall* is sometimes used when the subject is *I* or *we* (or with *you* or *they* to express determination).

There are other ways to show that an action will happen in the future. *Tomorrow, next year,* and *later* are all words that express a future time. These words are called **time words,** and they are used with the present tense to express future time. Read the sentences below.

> Our show **opens next week.**
>
> **Tomorrow** we **design** scenery and rehearse.

The present progressive form can also be used with time words to express future actions.

> **Next Friday** our show **is opening.**
>
> **Soon** we **are ending** rehearsals.

Another way to talk about the future is with the future perfect tense.

■ The **future perfect tense** of a verb names an action that will be completed before another future event begins.

The future perfect tense is formed by adding *will have* or *shall have* before the past participle of the verb.

> Thursday I **shall have performed** six times.
>
> By next week the production **will have closed.**

Exercise 18   Using the Perfect Tense

For each sentence, change the underlined verb to the future perfect tense.

1. Until the show, we <u>shall practice</u> every day.
2. Tomorrow I <u>will learn</u> my part by heart.
3. I <u>give</u> my first performance next Saturday.
4. By the time the show closes, I <u>shall perform</u> "Some Enchanted Evening" fifteen times.
5. My presence on stage <u>will startle</u> many skeptical people.

Exercise 19   Identifying Verb Tenses

For each sentence, write the verb or verb phrase, and write whether it is in the *present, future, present progressive,* or *future perfect* tense.

1. All the dancers are practicing tomorrow morning.
2. That afternoon we will have our final dress rehearsal.
3. Tomorrow evening we are giving our first benefit performance for senior citizens.
4. By then Adam will have organized the ticket booth.
5. The O'Leary twins go today for another make-up lesson.
6. Tomorrow they demonstrate their techniques on the rest of us.
7. The day after tomorrow, my new costume arrives.
8. Until then I am wearing a costume from last year's production.
9. Our official first night will come on Saturday.
10. By then we will have ironed out all the problems.
11. In the next few weeks, we will stage six performances of our show.
12. Then, next month, we are going to the state drama competition.
13. At the state competition, we present our play in front of a panel of expert judges.
14. They will have observed four other clubs before us.
15. Judges will score us on the basis of action, dialogue, and pace.
16. On the last day, we shall learn the names of the winners.
17. We will cross our fingers very tightly.
18. After the competition, we are changing our schedule completely.
19. Next year we are focusing on musical theater.
20. We will have gained considerable stage experience by then.

Active and Passive Voice

■ A sentence is in the **active voice** when the subject performs the action of the verb.

> George Bernard Shaw **wrote** that play.

■ A sentence is in the **passive voice** when the subject receives the action of the verb.

> That play **was written** by George Bernard Shaw.

In the first sentence above, the author, George Bernard Shaw, seems more important because *George Bernard Shaw* is the subject of the sentence. In the second sentence, *play* seems more important than the name of the author because *play* is the subject of the sentence.

Notice that the verbs in passive voice consist of a form of *be* with the past participle. Often a phrase beginning with *by* follows the verb in passive voice construction.

> Plays are performed **by actors.**

The active voice is usually a stronger, more direct way of expressing ideas. Use the passive voice only if you want to emphasize the receiver of the action or to de-emphasize the performer of the action or if you do not know who the performer is.

The curtain **was drawn** to reveal an empty stage.

> *The Tempest* **was performed.** [You may want to emphasize the play.]
>
> The curtain **was drawn.** [You may not want to say who did it.]
>
> The theater **was burned.** [You may not know who did it.]

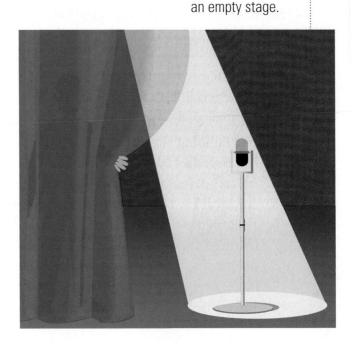

| **Exercise 20** | **Distinguishing Active and Passive Voice** |

For each sentence, write whether the sentence is in the *active* or *passive voice*. For passive voice sentences, write the word that names the receiver of the action.

1. *Pygmalion* was written by George Bernard Shaw.
2. Shaw's play is based on an ancient Greek myth.
3. Many people saw the play at the theater.
4. A show at the playhouse was criticized by many in the audience.
5. Critics gave it poor reviews in the newspapers.
6. The script was written by a brilliant playwright.
7. She created strange and unusual characters.
8. The director did his very best with the material.
9. The director was praised by several critics.
10. The scenery was designed by the playwright's relatives.
11. Costumes were created by the cast members.
12. The show was produced by members of a local drama club.
13. Most people predicted a short run for the show.
14. The public was surprised by the show's long run.
15. The cast used the criticism as a source for improvement.
16. Many people liked the show.
17. They told their friends about it.
18. Critics reconsidered their reviews.
19. The show was awarded a prize.
20. Now it is performed everywhere.

| **Exercise 21** | **Using Active Voice** |

Rewrite each sentence, changing the verb from the passive to the active voice. Some modifiers can be placed in more than one position.

1. In 1861 a church in Washington, D.C., was leased by John T. Ford.
2. The building was managed by Ford as a music hall.
3. It was destroyed by fire in 1862.
4. An architectural gem was built on the site by Ford.
5. On April 14, 1865, the theater was attended by President Abraham Lincoln.
6. That night *Our American Cousin* was performed by the theater company.
7. During the performance, Lincoln was assassinated by John Wilkes Booth.
8. In 1866 the building was bought by the federal government for office space.
9. It was restored to its original function by the government in 1968.
10. Today Ford's Theater and its museum are visited by many tourists.

10.11 Irregular Verbs

Irregular Verbs			
Pattern	**Base Form**	**Past Form**	**Past Participle (have, had)**
One vowel changes to form the past and the past participle.	begin	began	begun
	drink	drank	drunk
	ring	rang	rung
	shrink	shrank *or* shrunk	shrunk *or* shrunken
	sing	sang	sung
	spring	sprang *or* sprung	sprung
	swim	swam	swum
The past form and past participle are the same.	bring	brought	brought
	buy	bought	bought
	catch	caught	caught
	creep	crept	crept
	feel	felt	felt
	get	got	got *or* gotten
	keep	kept	kept
	lay	laid	laid
	lead	led	led
	leave	left	left
	lend	lent	lent
	lie	lay	lain
	lose	lost	lost
	make	made	made
	pay	paid	paid
	say	said	said
	seek	sought	sought
	sell	sold	sold
	sit	sat	sat
	sleep	slept	slept
	swing	swung	swung
	teach	taught	taught
	think	thought	thought
	win	won	won

Verbs

Identifying the Past and Past Participle of Irregular
                      Verbs

For each sentence, write the verb or verb phrase. Then write whether it uses
the *past form* or the *past participle*.

1. We had thought the old theater a good home for our production.
2. However, problems began with our first rehearsal there.
3. We had paid good money for renovation of the curtains.
4. Somehow, in the process, they shrank.
5. A number of us caught the habit of carelessness too.
6. Before, we had kept our props and costumes in a member's barn.
7. A week after our arrival at the old theater, however, someone lost them.
8. We had made an examination of the electrical system some time ago.
9. We had sought out every possible problem.
10. Then bells in the sound system rang at odd moments.

Exercise 23   Using the Past and Past Participle of Irregular Verbs

Write the correct form (either *past form* or *past participle*) of the verb that is
in parentheses.

1. Earlier the first performance had (begin).
2. I had (lose) my way to the new theater.
3. The star had (sing) two songs before my arrival.
4. I already had (pay), but I could not find the ticket.
5. I have (sit) in the theater for a long time.
6. Unfortunately the manager (leave) for a few minutes.
7. He has (keep) me waiting for ten minutes.
8. Luckily I (bring) a book with me.
9. I finally have (catch) my breath by sitting quietly.
10. One of my friends (bring) me a copy of the program.
11. Finally I (get) in.
12. I (think) the show was superb.
13. A famous teacher had (teach) the performers well.
14. At the show's end, the members of the audience (spring) to their feet.
15. The leading actor had (win) our hearts.
16. I (feel) happy and sad at the same time.
17. After the performance, we (seek) autographs.
18. The shy star (shrink) from the crowd.
19. At last she (creep) away.
20. She (say) she wanted to rest.

Verbs

10.12 More Irregular Verbs

Irregular Verbs			
Pattern	**Base Form**	**Past Form**	**Past Participle**
The base form and the past participle forms are the same.	become come run	became came ran	become come run
The past form ends in *-ew*, and the past participle ends in *-wn*.	blow draw fly grow know throw	blew drew flew grew knew threw	blown drawn flown grown known thrown
The past participle ends in *-en*.	bite break choose drive eat fall give ride rise see speak steal take write	bit broke chose drove ate fell gave rode rose saw spoke stole took wrote	bitten broken chosen driven eaten fallen given ridden risen seen spoken stolen taken written
The past form and the past participle do not follow any pattern.	am, are, is do go tear wear	was, were did went tore wore	been done gone torn worn
The base form, past form, and past participle are the same.	cut let put	cut let put	cut let put

Verbs

Identifying the Past and Past Participles of Irregular Verbs

For each sentence, write the verb or verb phrase. Then write whether it uses the *past* form or the *past participle.*

1. Our class went on a field trip to Broadway in New York City.
2. For a long time, Broadway has been a symbol of American theater.
3. The name came from the Dutch *Brede Weg,* broad way.
4. The midtown section of the street is known as the Great White Way.
5. The many theaters in the area have run thousands of productions over the years.
6. The winds of fortune blew one way and then another over these theaters.
7. Over the years, some have fallen into disrepair.
8. Others rose to glory, elegance, and prominence.
9. Through Broadway's influence, the theater bug has bitten many young people.
10. Broadway has done a great deal for theater professionals and audiences.

Exercise 25   Using the Past and Past Participle of Irregular Verbs

Write the correct form (*past* or *past participle*) of the verb in parentheses.

1. A prominent actress has (write) about her experiences with stage fright.
2. One night onstage she (become) immobile.
3. Before her appearance on stage, she had (know) her lines by heart.
4. She (take) several slow, deep breaths.
5. She regained her confidence and (throw) herself into the part.
6. Her drama coach had (give) her good advice about stage fright.
7. The actress eventually (come) through with a fine performance.
8. She (draw) on her knowledge of the character's personality.
9. The actress (grow) into the part.
10. She (see) through her character's eyes.
11. She even (wear) similar clothes.
12. By the end of the play, the actress (speak) her lines flawlessly.
13. A majority of theater critics have (choose) her for an award.
14. They say she has (steal) the show.
15. She has (grow) more confident.
16. Awareness of her experiences has (drive) me to try again.
17. I have (let) the director assign me to a speaking role.
18. Before that I had (draw) away from any public performance.
19. I had (run) away from opportunities for personal growth.
20. Now with this new determination, I have (break) away from the old me.

Verbs

VERBS

The play *Our Town* by Thornton Wilder focuses on the fictional New England town of Grover's Corners, New Hampshire. The play consists of three acts, each with a single theme. These themes are a typical day in the town, love and marriage, and death. Each act is introduced by the stage manager, who also breaks into the action now and then to explain something about the town or its inhabitants. In the excerpt presented here, the stage manager sets the stage for the second act. The passage has been annotated to show examples of the kinds of verbs covered in this unit.

Literature Model

from Our Town
by Thornton Wilder

STAGE MANAGER: Three years **have gone** by. Yes, the sun's come up over a thousand times. Summers and winters **have cracked** the **mountains** a little bit more and the rains have brought down some of the dirt. Some babies that weren't even born before have begun talking regular sentences already; and a number of people who thought they were right young and spry have noticed that they can't bound up a flight of stairs like they used to, without their heart fluttering a little. All that can happen in a thousand days. Nature's been pushing and contriving in other ways, too: a number of young people **fell** in love and got married. Yes, the mountain got bit away a few fractions of an inch; millions of gallons of water **went** by the mill; and here and there a new home **was set up** under one roof.

> Present perfect tense of an irregular verb

> Action verb followed by a direct object

> Past tense of an irregular verb

> Passive voice

Verbs

Grammar Review

Review: Exercise 1   Identifying Action Verbs and Direct Objects

For each sentence, write the action verb. Then write and circle each direct object.

SAMPLE   This semester we read Thornton Wilder's play.
ANSWER   read (play)

1. Thornton Wilder used unconventional forms in his plays.
2. For example, any production of *Our Town* requires very few props.
3. Wilder's words and the audience's imagination provide the scenery.
4. This technique emphasizes the characters in the play.
5. The Henry Miller Theater hosted the first New York performance in 1938.
6. Thornton Wilder won the Pulitzer Prize for drama that year.
7. He wrote other successful plays and novels, too.
8. In 1965 he received the first National Medal for literature.
9. Both critics and ordinary people enjoy his books.
10. Thornton Wilder truly deserves his high position in American literature.

Review: Exercise 2   Distinguishing Transitive and Intransitive Verbs

For each sentence, write the action verb. Then write any direct objects. Write whether the verb is *transitive* or *intransitive*.

SAMPLE   This edition of the play gives stage directions in italics.
ANSWER   gives, directions — transitive

1. Thornton Wilder includes few stage directions in the script of *Our Town*.
2. The audience arrives to a stage with nothing on it.
3. The stage manager brings tables, chairs, and a bench on stage.
4. Then he leans against a pillar on the left of the stage.
5. At that moment the theater darkens.
6. Now the stage manager speaks into the darkness.
7. He provides a verbal map of Grover's Corners.
8. He also introduces the major characters to the audience.
9. The tables and chairs remain on stage for act 2.
10. In this act the stage manager talks about the passage of time.

Verbs

Review: Exercise 3   Distinguishing Direct and Indirect Objects

For each sentence, write the direct object. If the sentence contains an indirect object, write it and then underline it.

1. In the first scene of *Our Town,* the audience sees morning activities.
2. Young Joe Crowell hands Dr. Gibbs a newspaper.
3. The stage manager shows the audience Joe's future.
4. Mrs. Webb serves her family a hearty breakfast.
5. Mrs. Webb and Mrs. Gibbs both scold their children for their misbehavior.
6. George Gibbs asks his mother for a larger allowance.
7. Mrs. Gibbs sends Rebecca's teacher her congratulations.
8. Mrs. Gibbs and Mrs. Webb discuss antiques and beans.
9. The stage manager tells the audience the history of Grover's Corners.
10. A woman in the balcony asks Mr. Webb a question.

Review: Exercise 4   Identifying Action Verbs and Linking Verbs

For each sentence, write each verb and write whether it is an *action verb* or a *linking verb.* Then write whether each underlined word is a *predicate noun, predicate adjective, direct object,* or *indirect object.*

SAMPLE   Organist Simon Stimson directs the church <u>choir.</u>
ANSWER   directs, action verb; direct object

1. Joe Crowell's knee predicts the day's <u>weather.</u>
2. Howie Newsome delivers <u>milk</u> to local families.
3. Banker Cartwright is very <u>wealthy.</u>
4. Rebecca Gibbs loves <u>money</u> most of all.
5. A second-hand furniture man offers <u>Mrs. Gibbs</u> money for her highboy.
6. Long ago Mrs. Gibbs promised <u>herself</u> a trip to Paris, France.
7. Professor Willard became an <u>expert</u> on the history of Grover's Corners.
8. Charles Webb edits the local <u>newspaper,</u> the *Sentinel.*
9. In Mr. Webb's opinion, Grover's Corners seems very <u>ordinary.</u>
10. Emily Webb and George Gibbs are very good <u>friends.</u>

Grammar Review

Review: Exercise 5   Distinguishing Past and Present Tenses

Write the correct form of the verb in parentheses. Then write whether it is in the *present* or *past tense.*

SAMPLE   For eight years in childhood, Thornton Wilder (live) in China.
ANSWER   lived, past

1. Thornton Wilder was born in 1897 and (die) in 1975.
2. At the announcement of a new Wilder novel, buyers (line) up at bookstores.
3. Critics today still (applaud) Wilder's emphasis on ordinary people.
4. That emphasis (make) his work very appealing to us today.
5. Many new readers (comment) on Wilder's compassion.
6. Probably his most famous novel (remain) *The Bridge of San Luis Rey.*
7. He (publish) this book in 1927.
8. This story (explore) the lives of five people who die in a bridge collapse.
9. In 1944 Hollywood (release) a film version of *The Bridge of San Luis Rey.*
10. This movie (fail) at the box office.

Review: Exercise 6   Using Present and Past Progressive Forms

For each sentence, write the verb form indicated in italics.

SAMPLE   I (join) the community theater. *present progressive*
ANSWER   am joining

1. Our theater (consider) a production of *Our Town. present progressive*
2. Committee members (debate) between that play and *The Glass Menagerie* by Tennessee Williams. *present progressive*
3. At first they (lean) toward a musical production. *past progressive*
4. Then they (worry) about the cost of a musical. *past progressive*
5. Now they (look) for a regular drama. *present progressive*
6. I (hope) that they choose *Our Town. present progressive*
7. If so, I (try) out for the role of Emily. *present progressive*
8. My sister (tell) me about her experiences with the play. *past progressive*
9. Last year she and her friends (aim) for a production. *past progressive*
10. That project, however, (interfere) with other plans. *past progressive*

Review: Exercise 7   Identifying Future Tenses

For each sentence, write the verb and whether it is in the *future* or *future perfect* tense.

SAMPLE   By act 2, we will have met the important characters.
ANSWER   will have met, future perfect

1. Mr. Cartwright will buy the first automobile in Grover's Corners in 1906.
2. By 6:00 A.M., Shorty Hawkins will have flagged the train to Boston.
3. Folks in town will wake up shortly.
4. Miss Foster will marry a man from Concord sometime soon.
5. According to the stage manager, Joe Crowell will earn a scholarship.
6. By the time of his college graduation, a world war will have broken out.
7. By ten o'clock, Wally will have his head full of information about Canada.
8. Because of her sore throat, Mrs. Webb will skip choir this evening.
9. Mrs. Webb will have canned forty quarts of beans over the next few weeks.
10. In her dreams, Mrs. Gibbs will travel to Paris, France, someday.

Review: Exercise 8   Using Active Voice

Rewrite each sentence, changing the sentence from the passive voice to the active voice.

SAMPLE   The factory is owned by Banker Cartwright.
ANSWER   Banker Cartwright owns the factory.

1. *Our Town* was written by Thornton Wilder.
2. Each act is introduced by the stage manager.
3. The baby was delivered by Doc Gibbs.
4. The newspaper is published by Charles Webb.
5. The choir is directed by Simon Stimson.
6. The dead are remembered by the living.
7. The kitchen stove is filled with wood by Mrs. Webb.
8. Part of her allowance was saved by Rebecca Gibbs.
9. Fossils were found by archaeologists in Silas Peckham's cow pasture.
10. A hundred years ago, the area of Grover's Corners was settled by the English.

Verbs

Grammar Review

Review: Exercise 9 **Using the Past and Past Participle of Irregular Verbs**

For each sentence, write the appropriate form of the verb in parentheses.

1. Grover's Corners has (see) the comings and goings of many generations.
2. Not many young people (leave) Grover's Corners after graduation.
3. The stage manager has not (know) any remarkable people to come out of Grover's Corners.
4. Dr. Gibbs (bring) the Goruslawksi twins into the world—and most of the other babies in town too.
5. The folks in town (sleep) later in the morning than those out on the farms.
6. The residents of Grover's Corners had (begin) their morning routine.
7. Rebecca Gibbs (wear) her blue gingham dress to school.
8. George Gibbs (eat) his breakfast with his geography book on the table.
9. Before her marriage, Miss Foster (teach) Joe Crowell's grade-school class.
10. Mrs. Webb has (grow) enough beans to feed her family for the winter.
11. She (bite) into one to see whether it was sweet and ripe.
12. That day Emily had (spoke) to her class about the Louisiana Purchase.
13. Despite criticism, George has again (throw) his ball into the air.
14. George had (break) one of his father's rules.
15. Dr. Gibbs had (take) his biannual trip to the Civil War battlefields.
16. By now he has (seek) out almost all of them.
17. The church bell (ring) out over the town of Grover's Corners.
18. Despite her poor voice, Mrs. Gibbs (sing) in the church choir.
19. According to the ladies in the choir, Mr. Stimson had (drink) too much before practice.
20. Dr. Gibbs worried that Mrs. Gibbs had (catch) cold on her way home from choir practice.
21. The Cartwright family has just (lay) the foundation for a new bank in Grover's Corners.
22. From her window, Emily (give) George hints about his algebra homework.
23. Professor Willard had (come) over from the university for his lecture on the history of Grover's Corners.
24. As editor of the town newspaper, Mr. Webb had (become) the town's unofficial spokesperson.
25. A woman in the balcony had (rise) to her feet to ask Mr. Webb a question.

Verbs

Proofreading

The following passage is about artist Roger Brown, whose work appears below. Rewrite the passage, correcting the errors in spelling, grammar, and usage. Add any missing punctuation. There are ten errors.

Roger Brown

¹The painting below was did by Chicago artist Roger Brown. ²This work show a row of houses backed by sand dunes and palm trees. ³The ocean and the setting sun lies beyond the dunes and trees. ⁴The dunes rigid mounds of sand, seem to be carved out of stone.

⁵The characters in this work have shrank to silhouettes. ⁶They are either sitting seperately in their homes or walking alone along the sidewalk. ⁷The walkers are moving fast; perhaps they will think they are late. ⁸They are the only things moveing in the picture. ⁹The ocean looks as if no one has ever swam there. ¹⁰Even the sun, cutted in half by the horizon, looks motionless.

Roger Brown, *Coast of California*, 1987

Verbs

Grammar Review

Mixed Review

For each numbered item, write the appropriate form of the word requested. Be sure that your completed sentences make sense.

The title of the play *Our Town* ¹(*action verb, present tense*) a strong clue to the story's theme. Even though the action ²(*keep—present tense, passive voice*) in one small New Hampshire town, author Thornton Wilder is really giving ³(*indirect object*) the whole world. Other clues ⁴(*linking verb, present tense*) obvious too. In act 1, Rebecca notices that the same moon ⁵(*intransitive verb, present tense*) down on other countries. Later in the act, she ⁶(*tell—future tense*) her brother the story of a letter addressed to Jane Crofut, Grover's Corners, the Universe.

Wilder once wrote that he deliberately ⁷(*emphasize—past tense*) big numbers such as *thousands* and *millions.* By doing so he ⁸(*suggest—present progressive tense*) that the big and the small ⁹(*linking verb, present tense*) one. The stage manager is one ¹⁰(*predicate noun*) who comments on the big picture and the small.

Many universal events ¹¹(*intransitive verb, present tense*). In act 1, twin babies ¹²(*deliver—present tense, passive voice*) by Dr. Webb. In act 2, Emily Webb and George Gibbs ¹³(*get—present progressive tense*) married, just as millions of people ¹⁴(*do—present perfect tense*) in the past and millions ¹⁵(*do—future tense*) in the future. Some characters in the play ¹⁶(*intransitive verb, present tense*) and are buried in the town cemetery.

Many scenes in the play emphasize ordinary ¹⁷(*direct object*). Families ¹⁸(*transitive verb, present tense*) meals together in every act. Children ¹⁹(*intransitive verb, present tense*) to school, and adults do chores. Wilder also stresses small daily ²⁰(*direct object*), such as the sound of birds, the scent of flowers, the smell of food, or the feel of newly ironed clothes. These joys, he suggests, are the real ²¹(*predicate noun*) of life. In act 3, Emily ²²(*learn—present tense*) anew to appreciate such joys. Dead people in the cemetery give ²³(*indirect object*) advice about achieving peace and harmony. She ²⁴(*learn—present perfect tense*) not to take life for granted.

By the end of the play, the audience ²⁵(*catch—future perfect tense*) a glimpse of their own lives.

Verbs

Writing Application

TIME

For more about the writing process, see **TIME Facing the Blank Page,** pp. 97-107.

Verbs in Writing

As you read this passage from *Lyddie,* notice Katherine Paterson's precise verbs and how verb forms convey the sounds and actions of Lyddie's first day in the factory. Study the passage, focusing on the italicized words.

> His little red mouth *pursed,* he *stepped* up on a stool and *pulled* out his pocket watch. At the same moment, the bell in the tower above the roof *began* to *ring.* He *yanked* the cord, the wide leather belt above *shifted* from a loose to a tight pulley, and suddenly all the hundred or so silent looms, in raucous concert, *shuddered* and *groaned* into fearsome life. Lyddie's first full day as a factory girl *had begun.*

Techniques with Verbs

Try to apply some of Katherine Paterson's writing techniques when you write and revise your own work.

❶ Whenever possible, replace vague and common verbs with vivid and specific verbs. Compare the following:

VAGUE COMMON VERBS *moved* into fearsome life

PATERSON'S VERSION *shuddered* and *groaned* into fearsome life

❷ Keep the timing of your characters' actions clear by correctly forming the tenses of irregular verbs:

INCORRECT VERB TENSE Lyddie's first full day as a factory girl *had began.*

PATERSON'S VERSION Lyddie's first full day as a factory girl *had begun.*

Verbs

Practice Practice these techniques by revising the following passage, using a separate sheet of paper. Pay particular attention to the underlined words.

Park and Noah <u>walked</u> slowly along the sidewalk, deep in conversation. They took no notice of their surroundings, <u>not noticing</u> the hustle and bustle of busy commuters and the noise of cars <u>driving</u> by on the street. An occasional pedestrian <u>made</u> a glance at the two friends, but neither boy <u>noticed.</u> After several blocks, Park finally <u>touched</u> Noah's shoulder and <u>turned</u> him towards a small coffee shop. "Let's <u>take</u> a bite. I haven't eaten since breakfast!" Then they <u>started</u> their conversation <u>again,</u> heads close together.

UNIT 11

Pronouns

11.1 Personal Pronouns

- A **pronoun** is a word that takes the place of one or more nouns and the words that describe those nouns.

- Pronouns that are used to refer to people or things are called **personal pronouns**.

Personal pronouns are singular or plural. Some personal pronouns are used as the subjects of sentences. Others are used as the objects of verbs or prepositions.

- A **subject pronoun** is a pronoun in the nominative case used as the subject of a sentence.

  Rita likes books. **She** particularly likes novels.

In the example above, the pronoun *She* replaces the noun *Rita* as the subject of the sentence.

- An **object pronoun** is a pronoun in the objective case used as the object of a verb or a preposition.

  The novel amuses Rita. The novel amuses her. [direct object of the verb *amuses*]

  For Raul's birthday Rita gave him a novel. [indirect object of the verb *gave*]

  Rita presented a biography of Mark Twain to us. [object of the preposition *to*]

Personal Pronouns		
	Singular	**Plural**
Used as Subjects	I you he, she, it	we you they
Used as Objects	me you him, her, it	us you them

Write each pronoun and identify it as a *subject* pronoun in the nominative case or an *object* pronoun in the objective case.

1. Gwendolyn Brooks writes poems; they are about everyday life.
2. Slang and the rhythms of jazz and the blues are important to her.
3. She was born in Topeka, Kansas, but grew up in Chicago.
4. The poet Langston Hughes gave her literary advice.
5. Brooks always loved poetry; she wrote it from the age of seven.
6. Brooks taught poetry to students; she was a role model for them.
7. In 1949 she wrote a poetry collection called *Annie Allen*.
8. It made Brooks the first black poet to receive a Pulitzer Prize.
9. I have read the book, and the poems fascinate me.
10. The combination of street talk and American verse will amuse you.

Exercise 2   **Using Personal Pronouns**

Write the pronoun you could use in place of each underlined word or words.

1. Sarah Orne Jewett was an American writer of the nineteenth century.
2. The *Atlantic Monthly* first published Jewett.
3. This author wrote the stories at age nineteen.
4. These stories are about history and tradition.
5. The Jewetts lived amid Maine's many villages.
6. Sarah's father was a doctor with an interest in books and people.
7. Sarah studied books and people with her father.
8. Young Sarah observed people's ways of life.
9. She described the people in her stories.
10. She wrote stories about her experiences.
11. Readers learned about life in New England.
12. Bob wrote a research report on Sarah Jewett.
13. "A White Heron" is Sarah Jewett's best-known story.
14. The heron catches a young girl's attention.
15. The young girl approaches the nest.
16. The wild bird avoids the young girl.
17. "A White Heron" appeals to Robert.
18. Our class had difficulty with the story.
19. Luisa pointed out the theme to our class.
20. Rosa said, "Let Rosa help you."

11.2 Pronouns and Antecedents

Read the following sentences. Can you tell to whom the pronoun *She* refers?

> Louisa May Alcott wrote a novel about a young woman. **She** has three sisters.

The sentence is not clear because *She* could refer either to the *young woman* or to *Louisa May Alcott*. Sometimes you must repeat a noun or rewrite a sentence to avoid confusion.

> Louisa May Alcott wrote a novel about a young woman. **The young woman** has three sisters.

■ The noun or group of words that a pronoun refers to is called its **antecedent.**

When you use a pronoun, you should be sure that it refers to its antecedent clearly. Be especially careful when you use the pronoun *they*. Notice this pronoun in the following sentence.

> WRONG: **They** have two books by Alcott at the school library.

To whom does *They* refer? Its meaning is unclear. The sentence might be corrected in the following way.

> RIGHT: The school library has two books by Alcott.

Be sure every pronoun agrees with its antecedent in number (singular or plural) and gender. The gender of a noun or pronoun may be masculine, feminine, or neuter (referring to things). Notice the pronoun-antecedent agreement below.

> The Marches must face a death in their family. **They** face **it** with courage.

Write the correct pronoun for the second sentence in each pair. Then write the antecedent the pronoun refers to.

1. Louisa May Alcott lived near Boston, Massachusetts. _____ had many famous neighbors.
2. Alcott came from a poor family. _____ wanted to help earn money.
3. Alcott worked as a teacher. Students learned history from _____.
4. But that job was not enough. _____ did not pay well.
5. Alcott also made dresses. Women paid Alcott money for _____.
6. The writer also tried housekeeping. That job didn't suit _____.
7. Alcott then tried writing. Finally _____ had found a career!
8. Alcott's first book contained stories for young children. _____ was called *Flower Fables*.
9. Two more books by Alcott appeared quickly. _____ describe her hospital work and her teaching days.
10. An editor asked Alcott to write a book for girls. The editor finally persuaded _____.
11. In 1868 Alcott published the first part of *Little Women*. _____ was a success.
12. The full-length edition of *Little Women* was very popular. _____ changed people's ideas about women's role in society.
13. In the novel, Jo March is the main character. _____ eventually becomes a writer.
14. The father is a chaplain in the Civil War. _____ is away.
15. The girls and mother have little money. Life is hard for _____.
16. The March sisters attend school. _____ also earn money for their family.
17. Women had difficulty finding suitable work. _____ were not paid well.
18. Jo has an independent spirit. _____ is the most independent girl.
19. Jo turns down marriage to the boy next door. Jo says no to _____.
20. She tells her sisters. _____ are shocked.
21. Then Jo meets Fritz Bhaer. She ultimately falls in love with _____.
22. Beth is a musician. _____ dies of a terrible illness.
23. Alcott relied on incidents from her own childhood. _____ seem realistic.
24. At the library, I found Alcott's *An Old-Fashioned Girl*. _____ was published in 1870.
25. We have *Little Men* and *Jo's Boys*. I have read _____.

Pronouns

11.3 Using Pronouns Correctly

Subject pronouns in the nominative case are used in compound subjects, and object pronouns in the objective case are used in compound objects.

> Tina and Sam recently read *Heidi*. **She** and **he** recently read *Heidi*. [*She* and *he* form the compound subject.]
>
> *Heidi* appealed to Sam and Tina. *Heidi* appealed to **him** and **her**. [*Him* and *her* form the compound object.]

Whenever the subject pronoun *I* or the object pronoun *me* is part of the compound subject or object, *I* or *me* should come last.

> Tina and **I** liked the book. [not *I and Tina*]

Sometimes a pronoun and a noun are used together for emphasis. The form of the pronoun depends on its function in the sentence.

> **We** students read the book. [*We* is the subject.]
> The book delighted **us** readers. [*Us* is the direct object.]

Some sentences make incomplete comparisons. The form of the pronoun can affect the meaning of such sentences. In any incomplete comparison, use the pronoun that would be correct if the comparison were complete.

> Heidi liked Peter more than **she** [did]. [Heidi and Klara liked Peter, but Heidi liked him more than Klara did.]
>
> Heidi liked Peter more than [she liked] **her**. [Heidi liked Peter and Klara, but Heidi liked Peter more than she liked Klara.]

In formal writing, use a subject pronoun after a linking verb.

> Heidi's closest friend is **he.**

SUBJECT

Tina and Sam

read
about

Peter and Heidi.

OBJECT

Pronouns

Exercise 4 **Identifying Pronouns in the Nominative and Objective Cases**

Write the correct pronoun for each underlined noun. Then write whether each one is a *subject* pronoun in the nominative case or an *object* pronoun in the objective case.

1. Eudora Welty and <u>William Faulkner</u> are famous writers from Mississippi.
2. Works by <u>Welty</u> and Faulkner are intimately connected to the atmosphere of the South.
3. Faulkner wrote in a more serious tone than <u>Welty</u>.
4. <u>Faulkner</u> demands much of us readers.
5. Important prizes were awarded to both Welty and <u>Faulkner</u>.

Exercise 5 **Using Pronouns in the Nominative and Objective Cases Correctly**

Write the correct word or words in parentheses. Then write whether each pronoun is a *subject* pronoun in the nominative case or an *object* pronoun in the objective case.

1. *Heidi* entertained (we, us) readers.
2. Steffi and (me, I) read the story last weekend.
3. Heidi is an orphan; Grandfather takes care of (she, her).
4. (She, Her) and Grandfather live in the Swiss Alps.
5. Heidi and (he, him) tend goats together.
6. Peter and (her, she) love the mountains.
7. Peter becomes a friend to Heidi's grandfather and (she, her).
8. Grandfather is stern, although no one is kinder than (he, him).
9. (We, Us) readers grow fond of Grandfather.
10. My favorite character is (he, him).
11. Grandfather became almost real to (Juan and I, Juan and me).
12. (She, Her) and Peter tend goats.
13. Heidi says good-bye to (Peter and he, Peter and him).
14. (We, Us) readers feel very sympathetic toward Heidi.
15. In fact, I felt almost as sad as (she, her).
16. Between Peter and (she, her), they help Klara toward recovery.
17. Klara and (she, her) become friends in the city.
18. Heidi's dearest friends are Grandfather and (he, him).
19. Klara cannot walk, so Heidi aids the family and (she, her).
20. (Tom and I, Me and Tom) guessed the ending.

11.4 Possessive Pronouns

You often use pronouns to replace nouns that are subjects and nouns that are objects in sentences. You can use pronouns in place of possessive nouns too.

■ A **possessive pronoun** is a pronoun in the possessive case. It shows who or what has something. A possessive pronoun may take the place of a possessive noun.

Read the following sentences. Notice the possessive nouns and the possessive pronouns that replace them.

> Lisa's class put on a play. **Her** class put on a play.
> The idea was Lisa's. The idea was **hers.**

Possessive pronouns have two forms. One form is used before a noun. The other form is used alone. The chart below shows the two forms of possessive pronouns.

Possessive Pronouns		
	Singular	**Plural**
Used Before Nouns	my your her, his, its	our your their
Used Alone	mine yours hers, his, its	ours yours theirs

Unlike possessive nouns, such as *Mei's* or *cats'*, possessive pronouns do not contain an apostrophe.

Do not confuse the possessive pronoun *its* with the word *it's. It's* is a contraction, or shortened form, of the words *it is*.

> **Its** subject is William Shakespeare. [possessive pronoun]
> **It's** a famous play by Shakespeare. [contraction of *it is*]

Exercise 6   **Identifying Possessive Pronouns**

Write each possessive pronoun. Then write *N* if the pronoun *comes before a noun* or *A* if it *stands alone*.

1. Our class is putting on a play by Shakespeare.
2. He wrote centuries ago, but his plays still thrill audiences.
3. *Hamlet* is Lian's favorite, but *Romeo and Juliet* is mine.
4. Have you seen your favorite play yet?
5. Gina was in *Hamlet*, but it's not a favorite of hers.
6. I know my part in the play, but some students have trouble with theirs.
7. The language of Shakespeare sounds strange to their ears.
8. To Shakespeare our English would seem like a foreign language.
9. Some of his words look odd in print; the spellings are unfamiliar.
10. The spoken words of Shakespeare are more eloquent than mine.

Exercise 7   **Using Pronouns in the Possessive Case**

Write the correct possessive pronoun for each underlined word or group of words.

1. The play's setting is the city of Verona.
2. Romeo was an uninvited guest at the feast of Romeo's enemy.
3. When Romeo and Juliet meet, Romeo and Juliet's love story begins.
4. Later Romeo sees Juliet and hears Juliet's confession of love for him.
5. A friar performs Romeo and Juliet's secret marriage the next day.
6. Mercutio, a friend of the bridegroom's, meets Tybalt, an enemy of Mercutio's.
7. Mercutio and Tybalt fight; Romeo stops Mercutio and Tybalt's fight.
8. Romeo draws his sword and kills Romeo's friend's murderer.
9. Romeo's sentence is banishment.
10. Romeo visits Juliet secretly; the meeting was Romeo and Juliet's alone.
11. Juliet refuses to marry Count Paris, but Juliet's father insists.
12. The night before the wedding, Juliet drinks a sleeping potion of Juliet's.
13. The potion's effects will render her apparently lifeless for forty hours.
14. The friar's message to Romeo is, "Rescue Romeo's wife; she is awake."
15. The friar's message gets mixed up; Romeo hears that Juliet is dead.
16. Romeo buys poison, goes to Juliet, and says, "Death is Romeo and Juliet's."
17. Thinking that Juliet is dead, Romeo drinks Romeo's poison and dies.
18. Juliet awakes and finds Romeo's body and the cup by her side.
19. Juliet guesses what has happened; she stabs Juliet's chest.
20. This story is a favorite of our class's.

11.5 Indefinite Pronouns

■ An **indefinite pronoun** is a pronoun that does not refer to a particular person, place, or thing.

> **Each** thinks about the plot.

Most indefinite pronouns are either singular or plural.

Some Indefinite Pronouns			
Singular			**Plural**
another	everybody	no one	both
anybody	everyone	nothing	few
anyone	everything	one	many
anything	much	somebody	others
each	neither	someone	several
either	nobody	something	

In addition, the indefinite pronouns *all, any, most, none,* and *some* are singular or plural, depending on the phrase that follows.

When an indefinite pronoun is used as the subject of a sentence, the verb must agree with it in number.

> **Everyone reads** part of the novel. [singular]
> **Several enjoy** it very much. [plural]
> **Most** of the story **takes** place in England. [singular]
> **Most** of the characters **are** memorable. [plural]

Possessive pronouns often have indefinite pronouns as their antecedents. In such cases, the pronouns must agree in number. Note that the intervening prepositional phrase does not affect the agreement.

> **Several** are presenting **their** interpretations of the novel.
> **Each** of the students has **his** or **her** ideas about its meaning.

Choosing Indefinite Pronouns

Write the indefinite pronoun that agrees with the verb or possessive pronoun.

1. (Neither, All) of Robert Frost's poems are enjoyed by their readers.
2. (One, Many) of the poems have New England as their setting.
3. (Much, Many) of their narrators are people living close to nature.
4. (Much, Others) of the poetry has rhythm, and its lines rhyme.
5. (Both, Each) of these poems has its own rhyme.
6. (Somebody, Several) in this poem narrates his or her own tale.
7. (Most, Everyone) have their own interpretations of Frost's metaphors.
8. (All, One) of the guests have read their poems at the bookstore.
9. (Both, One) of the guests has read her own poem about Frost.
10. (Each, Several) of the readers of Frost's poems has his or her favorite.

Exercise 9   Using Indefinite Pronouns

Write each sentence, using the correct verb or possessive pronoun in parentheses. Then underline the indefinite pronoun and write whether the pronoun is *singular* or *plural*.

1. Everyone studies (his or her, their) *Alice's Adventures in Wonderland*.
2. Most of the characters (is, are) animals.
3. Some of them (attends, attend) a comical tea party.
4. Nothing (makes, make) sense in Wonderland.
5. Everything in Wonderland (confuses, confuse) Alice.
6. No one (answers, answer) her questions.
7. Many of the characters (talks, talk) peculiarly.
8. Some of them even (speaks, speak) in riddles.
9. The Cheshire cat disappears; nothing (is, are) left but its smile.
10. Few really (believes, believe) in disappearing cats.
11. None of the characters (looks, look) more bizarre than the Mock Turtle.
12. Several offer Alice (his or her, their) advice.
13. Each has (their, his or her) point of view.
14. Nothing predictable (happens, happen) in Wonderland.
15. Most of the story (occurs, occur) down a rabbit hole.
16. Everyone (know, knows) the story's author—British writer Lewis Carroll.
17. Much (has, have) been written about *Alice's Adventures in Wonderland*.
18. All of the critics (praises, praise) it.
19. None of them (gives, give) a bad review.
20. Everyone in class enjoys (his or her, their) reading the book.

Pronouns

11.6 Reflexive and Intensive Pronouns

Reflexive and intensive pronouns are formed by adding *-self* or *-selves* to certain personal and possessive pronouns.

Reflexive and Intensive Pronouns	
Singular	**Plural**
myself	ourselves
yourself	yourselves
himself, herself, itself	themselves

REFLEXIVE PRONOUN

Sometimes *hisself* is mistakenly used for *himself* and *theirselves* for *themselves.* Avoid using *hisself* and *theirselves.*

■ A **reflexive pronoun** refers to a noun or another pronoun and indicates that the same person or thing is involved.

The woman bought **herself** a book by Horatio Alger.

REFLEXIVE PRONOUN

■ An **intensive pronoun** is a pronoun that adds emphasis to a noun or pronoun already named.

Horatio Alger **himself** wrote more than one hundred books.

I **myself** have never read his books.

Reflexive and intensive pronouns have special uses. They should never be used as the subject of a sentence or as the object of a verb or preposition.

Yolanda and **I** read *Sink or Swim*. [not *Yolanda and myself*]

It pleased Yolanda and **me.** [not *Yolanda and myself*]

Pronouns

Identifying Reflexive and Intensive Pronouns

Write each reflexive and intensive pronoun and identify it as a *reflexive pronoun* or an *intensive pronoun*.

1. You should occupy yourselves by reading one of Edgar Allan Poe's tales.
2. His first three books of poetry were themselves not successful.
3. Poe did not think himself a writer of inferior material.
4. Poe himself had a high opinion of his abilities.
5. One of his first tales was superb; the tale itself won a $100 prize.
6. One of the contest judges himself got Poe a job as a magazine editor.
7. Edgar Allan Poe has endeared himself to readers of the macabre.
8. I myself would not read any of his short stories at night.
9. Poe may not be the author for you; only you yourself can decide.
10. You can get yourself a book of his stories and poems from the library.

Exercise 11   **Using Reflexive and Intensive Pronouns**

Write the correct pronoun in parentheses. Write whether the pronoun is a *reflexive, intensive, subject,* or *object* pronoun.

1. I (me, myself) wrote a review of a book by Horatio Alger.
2. I found (me, myself) inspired by the characters' adventures.
3. Read a story (yours, yourself) about making hard work into a fortune.
4. Alger's life (it, itself) seems like one of his success stories.
5. Harvard Divinity School was near his home; Alger attended (it, itself).
6. His church congregation thought (themselves, theirselves) lucky.
7. Alger thought (hisself, himself) ambitious and moved to New York.
8. He helped the homeless; (they, themself) became characters in his stories.
9. The characters improve (them, themselves) through work and luck.
10. Yusuf and Tony (themselves, theirselves) were impressed by Alger's books.
11. Horatio Alger (he, himself) lived from 1832 to 1899.
12. Alger's birthplace (it, itself) attracts visitors.
13. We enjoyed (us, ourselves) during a visit to his home.
14. Alger's stories (them, themselves) usually take place in large cities.
15. A friend and (I, myself) have read ten of Alger's books.
16. Alger's style seems warm and light to (me, myself).
17. For Alger, ambition (it, itself) can bring about success.
18. According to (him, himself), any child could become a success.
19. (He or she, Themselves) just has to be intelligent, hard-working, and honest.
20. Alger's books became symbols of success (theirselves, themselves).

11.7 Interrogative and Demonstrative Pronouns

■ An **interrogative pronoun** is a pronoun used to introduce an interrogative sentence.

The interrogative pronouns *who* and *whom* both refer to people. *Who* is used when the interrogative pronoun is the subject of the sentence. *Whom* is used when the interrogative pronoun is the object of a verb or a preposition.

> **Who** borrowed the book? [subject]
>
> **Whom** did the librarian call? [direct object]
>
> For **whom** did you borrow the book? [object of preposition]

Which and *what* are used to refer to things and ideas.

> **What** interests you?   **Which** is it?

Whose shows that someone possesses something.

> I found a copy of *Great Expectations*. **Whose** is it?

When writing, be careful not to confuse *whose* with *who's*. *Who's* is the contraction of *who is*.

■ A **demonstrative pronoun** is a pronoun that points out something.

The demonstrative pronouns are *this, that, these,* and *those. This* (singular) and *these* (plural) refer to something nearby. *That* (singular) and *those* (plural) refer to something at a distance.

> **This** is an interesting book. [singular, nearby]
>
> **These** are interesting books. [plural, nearby]
>
> **That** is a long book. [singular, at a distance]
>
> **Those** are long books. [plural, at a distance]

that

this

Using Interrogative and Demonstrative Pronouns

Write the correct word given in parentheses.

1. (These, This) is Arturo's favorite book.
2. From (who, whom) did you get that copy?
3. (That, Those) is the small orphan named Pip.
4. (That, Those) are Pip's books.
5. (Who, Whom) taught Pip about books?
6. With (who, whom) does Pip live?
7. (This, These) are Pip's sister and her husband.
8. (Who, Whom) does Pip meet?
9. (What, Who) does the stranger want?
10. (This, These) is food for the stranger.

Exercise 13   **Distinguishing Between Pronouns and Contractions**

Write the correct word given in parentheses. Then write *I* if your choice is an *interrogative* pronoun, *D* if it is a *demonstrative* pronoun, or *C* if it is a *contraction*.

1. (Whose, Who's) Joe?
2. To (who, whom) was Joe married?
3. (Who's, Whose) Miss Havisham?
4. (This, These) is the mansion of Miss Havisham.
5. (That, These) was the time on the clocks.
6. (This, Those) are her bridal robes.
7. (Who, Whom) did Miss Havisham see?
8. (This, These) was the girl at Miss Havisham's home.
9. To (who, whom) did Estella get married?
10. (This, What) are Pip's great expectations?
11. (Who, Whom) becomes Pip's guardian?
12. (That, These) is a mystery.
13. (Who's, Which) of the schools does Pip attend?
14. To (who, whom) does Pip turn for help?
15. (What, Who) did Lawyer Jaggers give Pip?
16. (Who, Whom) paid Lawyer Jaggers?
17. (This, These) are the payments from the stranger.
18. (What, Who) became of the stranger?
19. (What, Who's) helping Pip now?
20. (Whose, Who's) the author of this novel?

Grammar Review

PRONOUNS

The following passage is from a biography of Emily Dickinson by Bonita Thayer. In addition to writing nearly eighteen hundred poems, Dickinson wrote many letters to friends. These letters reveal much about her thinking at different periods of her life. In the passage below, Thayer quotes from Dickinson's letters to Colonel Higginson, a writer and abolitionist (someone who opposed slavery). The passage has been annotated to show examples of the kinds of pronouns covered in this unit.

Literature Model

from Emily Dickinson
by Bonita E. Thayer

Some of Emily's letters to Higginson reveal her feelings about the public in general. "Truth is such a rare thing, it is delightful to tell it," she says in one note. Later she asks him, "How do most people live without any thoughts? There are many people in the world—you must have noticed them in the street—how do they live? How do they get strength to put on their clothes in the morning?"

She seemed satisfied with her life as she was living it. Her own thoughts filled her mind and were joined with the thoughts of others whose writings she studied.

"There is no frigate like a book to take us lands away," she wrote. She felt that she could travel the world and meet all the people she wanted to through books. She never had to leave her own home, which she considered to be the best and safest place for her.

> **Indefinite Pronoun**

> **Subject Pronoun agrees with its antecedent,** *Emily*

> **Object pronoun agrees with its antecedent,** *many people*

> **Possessive Pronoun**

Pronouns

Grammar Review

Review: Exercise 1   Using Subject, Object, and Possessive Pronouns

Write each sentence, replacing the underlined word or words with the correct pronoun. Write whether the pronoun you used is a *subject* pronoun, an *object* pronoun, or a *possessive* pronoun.

1. <u>Emily Dickinson</u> avoided having <u>Dickinson's</u> picture taken.
2. <u>Dickinson</u> had <u>one photograph</u> taken at about age sixteen.
3. <u>The author</u> craved biographies and portraits about <u>literary favorites.</u>
4. Dickinson started writing poetry in <u>Dickinson's</u> early twenties.
5. <u>The thought of publishing her poems</u> was abhorrent to <u>Dickinson</u>.

Review: Exercise 2   Using Pronouns and Antecedents

Write the second sentence in each of the following pairs, using the correct pronoun in each blank. Then write the antecedent of the pronoun with its number (singular or plural) and gender (masculine, feminine, or neuter).

SAMPLE   After their mother's death, Emily and her sister, Lavinia, became recluses. Emily and _____ never left home.

ANSWER   Emily and she never left home. Lavinia, singular, feminine

1. Emily Dickinson was born in Amherst, Massachusetts, in 1830. _____ was the daughter of Edward and Emily.
2. Dickinson's father was a Renaissance man. _____ was a lawyer, a politician, and a college treasurer.
3. The poet's brother, named William Austin, was always called Austin. _____ was the oldest child and only son.
4. The mother's job was care of the family. _____ was an important task.
5. Austin became treasurer at the same college as the father. Eventually Austin succeeded _____ father.
6. Austin married Susan Gilbert. The father built _____ a house next door.
7. Dickinson and her sister, Lavinia, never married. _____ lived at home all their lives.
8. After the father died, the mother became paralyzed. _____ was confined to bed.
9. Emily and Lavinia shared the task of caring for the mother. Both took good care of _____.
10. The three children were close in age. _____ were devoted to one another.

Review: Exercise 3   Using Subject and Object Pronouns Correctly

Write the correct pronoun in parentheses. Then write whether each pronoun is a *subject* pronoun or an *object* pronoun.

1. Emily and (she, her) were sisters and friends.
2. (She, Her) and Charles Wadsworth were friends and correspondents.
3. Dickinson and (he, him) were friends and companions.
4. The poet and a friend corresponded with Thomas Higginson and (he, him).
5. (She, Her) and other poets wrote poems and letters.
6. (They, Them) and others are published in English and other languages.
7. Emily's poems and letters amused those students and (we, us).
8. An editor and (her, she) gave the poems numbers but no titles.
9. (Me and Surya, Surya and I) read poem 812 and poem 1017 today.
10. Poem 173 and poem 188 made Akim and (me, I) smile.

Review: Exercise 4   Using Indefinite Pronouns

Write each sentence, using the correct verb in parentheses. Then underline the indefinite pronoun and write whether it is *singular* or *plural*.

SAMPLE   Some of her poetry (is, are) deceptively simple.
ANSWER   <u>Some</u> of her poetry is deceptively simple. *Singular*

1. Many (consider, considers) Dickinson one of the best American poets of the nineteenth century.
2. Few of her poems (was, were) published during her lifetime, perhaps only seven.
3. Most of her poems (is, are) very brief.
4. All of her work (is, are) interesting.
5. Some of her poems (was, were) circulated among her close friends.
6. Everything in her poems (reveal, reveals) her love of nature.
7. Everyone (like, likes) the spoofing fun of her valentines.
8. Much (has, have) been written about how she never left home.
9. Several of us (enjoy, enjoys) her work.
10. Something about her poetry (capture, captures) the reader's imagination.

Pronouns

Grammar Review

Review: Exercise 5   **Using Subject, Object, Reflexive, and Intensive Pronouns**

Write the correct pronoun given in parentheses. Write whether the pronoun is a *reflexive, intensive, subject,* or *object* pronoun.

1. Dickinson (she, herself) knew that her words could attract readers.
2. But she did not want the readers (theirselves, themselves) at her door.
3. In midlife she rarely left the Dickinson property (it, itself).
4. Within the homestead, (she, herself) had an active life.
5. The poet had many friends and wrote many letters to (them, themselves).
6. Friends and neighbors brought the outside world to (her, herself).
7. The garden needed tending in summer; she did that (itself, herself).
8. The cause of her reclusiveness (it, itself) is not fully understood.
9. She may have made the choice (her, herself) to remain in seclusion.
10. Emily Dickinson was devoted to her parents and took care of (them, themselves) until they died.

Review: Exercise 6   **Using Interrogative and Demonstrative Pronouns**

Write the correct word given in parentheses.

SAMPLE   (Who, Whom) was the most important influence on her poetry?
ANSWER   Who

1. To (who, whom) did Dickinson send the first samples of her poetry?
2. (This, These) are the first four poems she showed him.
3. (What, Whose) was his opinion of the poems?
4. (This, What) were the questions he asked of the poet?
5. (Which, Whom) are the three poems she sent in reply?
6. (What, Which) did writer Helen Hunt Jackson think of the poetry?
7. (Who's, Whose) poetry did Jackson praise?
8. (This, These) is the poetry Dickinson's niece brought to the publisher.
9. (Whose, Who's) idea was it to publish only some of them?
10. (That, Those) were the last of her poems to be published.

Proofreading

The following passage is about the artist Paul Sierra, whose work appears below. Rewrite the passage, correcting the errors in spelling, grammar, and usage. Add any missing punctuation. There are ten errors.

Paul Sierra

¹Paul Sierra was born in Havana the capital of Cuba. ²His parents wanted himself to become a doctor, but he wanted to be a painter. ³When Sierra was sixteen, him and his family immigrated to the United States and settled in Chicago.

⁴Sierra began his formal training as a painter in 1963 and he later went to work as a commercial layout artist. ⁵He still works in advertizing as a creative director. ⁶Because he does not have to rely on sales of paintings for his' livelihood, he is free to paint whatever he wants.

Paul Sierra, *Degas' Studio,* 1990

Pronouns

⁷Sierra's unusual use of color is saw in the painting on the previous page. ⁸The images theirselves, however, are drawn from the paintings of Edgar Degas. ⁹The woman's head, for instance, is taken from a famous portrait done by he. ¹⁰The horse and jockey reflects Degas's fascination with the sport of racing.

Review: Exercise 8

Mixed Review

After each sentence number, list in order the pronouns that appear in the sentence. Identify each pronoun as *personal, possessive, indefinite, reflexive, intensive, interrogative,* or *demonstrative.*

¹Emily Dickinson drew her last breath on May 15, 1886. ²She left a legacy of nearly eighteen hundred poems and a thousand remarkable letters. ³These were not published in their entirety until 1958.

⁴In the late 1850s, Dickinson herself had copied dozens of finished poems into booklets. ⁵Dickinson had made them by sewing folded notepaper into sheaves. ⁶This was a way to organize the bits of scrap paper containing the drafts. ⁷What became of the booklets? ⁸Who found them?

⁹After Dickinson's death, Lavinia discovered the booklets; she persuaded Higginson and one of Austin's friends to edit a volume of the poetry. ¹⁰Reviews of the book were discouraging, but the public demand for it was heartening. ¹¹In 1945 the last of Dickinson's poetry was published, and virtually all of Dickinson's poems were finally in print, sixty years after her death!

¹²Dickinson's poetry itself is concise and intense. ¹³Most of the poems are brief. ¹⁴They usually are about nature and the themes of love, death, and immortality. ¹⁵She introduced new rhymes and rhythms, often within a single poem. ¹⁶Both give her poems originality and add richness. ¹⁷The phrases are themselves quite simple. ¹⁸Her diction is stripped to the fewest words. ¹⁹She delighted herself with paradox; the concrete and the abstract, the serious and the funny, the usual and the unusual exist side by side in Dickinson's work. ²⁰The style is easily recognized as hers.

Writing Application

TIME

For more about the writing process, see **TIME Facing the Blank Page**, pp. 97-107.

Pronouns in Writing

This passage from *The Game* includes references to many characters. Writer Walter Dean Myers uses different pronouns to lend variety to his prose and make the references to his characters clear. Review the passage below, noticing the italicized pronouns.

> *We* controlled the jump and Turk drove right down the lane and made a lay-up. Turk actually made the lay-up. Turk once missed seven lay-ups in a row in practice and *no one* was even guarding *him.* But this one *he* made. Then one of *their* men double-dribbled and *we* got the ball and *I* passed *it* to Leon, *who* threw up a shot and got fouled. The shot went in and when *he* made the foul shot *it* added up to a three-point play.

Techniques with Pronouns

Try to apply some of Walter Dean Myers's writing techniques when you write and revise your own work.

❶ When appropriate, use possessive pronouns to make your writing more concise. Compare the following:

WORDY VERSION Then one of *the men on the other team* double-dribbled

MYERS'S VERSION Then one of *their* men double-dribbled

❷ Avoid confusing your readers. Be sure to choose correctly between subject and object pronouns.

INCORRECT PRONOUN CHOICE But this one *him* made.

MYERS'S VERSION But this one *he* made.

Practice Apply these techniques as you revise the following passage. On a separate sheet of paper, complete the sentences by adding appropriate pronouns.

When the phone rang, Kay jumped up quickly to answer it. "It's for _____," _____ yelled. Just then Mrs. Oliver entered the room, carrying Willy, the baby, on _____ left hip and _____ briefcase in _____ right hand.

"Good thing _____ were here to answer the phone, Kay. _____ might have dropped _____ trying to reach _____ ," _____ said.

As _____ mother spoke, Kay waved _____ away and quickly finished the phone call.

Pronouns

UNIT 12

Adjectives and Adverbs

12.1 Adjectives

An adjective describes a person, place, thing, or idea. An adjective provides information about the size, shape, color, texture, feeling, sound, smell, number, or condition of a noun or a pronoun.

The **eager, large** crowd of visitors examines the

huge painting.

In the sentence above, the adjectives *eager* and *large* describe the noun *crowd*, and the adjective *huge* describes the noun *painting*.

■ An **adjective** is a word that modifies, or describes, a noun or a pronoun.

Most adjectives come before the nouns they modify. However, an adjective can be in the predicate and modify the noun or pronoun that is the subject of the sentence.

The painting is **realistic** and **timeless.**

In the sentence above, the adjectives *realistic* and *timeless* follow the linking verb *is* and modify the subject, *painting*. They are called predicate adjectives.

■ A **predicate adjective** follows a linking verb and modifies the subject of the sentence.

The present participle and past participle forms of verbs may be used as adjectives and predicate adjectives.

Christina's World is a **haunting** painting. [present participle]

Christina's World is **inspired.** [past participle]

For each sentence below, write each adjective and the noun or pronoun it modifies. If any adjective is a participle form, circle it.

1. Georgia O'Keeffe is a major artist.
2. Her permanent residence was in the Southwest.
3. O'Keeffe's works hang in numerous museums.
4. The dry desert provided her with interesting material.
5. Georgia O'Keeffe spent several years in Wisconsin.
6. She studied art at a large school in Chicago in the early 1900s.
7. She lived for a short time in bustling New York City.
8. As a young woman, O'Keeffe had not yet found the right subjects.
9. In 1912 she became aware of the interesting scenery in Texas.
10. She made an enlightening journey to Amarillo, Texas.
11. The bright flowers and whitened bones of the desert inspired her.
12. The endless landscape seemed filled with strange objects and ghostly figures.
13. Her unique style combined abstract design with realistic scenery.
14. O'Keeffe's best paintings were based on nature.
15. She might pick up an interesting shell on a sandy beach.
16. At first she made realistic paintings of what she found.
17. She would paint the white shape of the shell alongside a gray shingle.
18. Perhaps she would add two large green leaves to the objects.
19. She kept a large collection of shells under a glass tabletop.
20. O'Keeffe was recognized by leading museums as a major artist.

Exercise 2 Identifying Predicate Adjectives

Write each predicate adjective. Then write the noun or pronoun it modifies in parentheses.

1. The day was young.
2. The beach was deserted except for one lone walker.
3. The others were still asleep.
4. Even the waves were distant and respectful.
5. That silent woman was aware of everything around her.
6. She was curious about all she saw.
7. Everything around her was radiant in the morning light.
8. The colors were true and clear.
9. A piece of red coral was especially eye-catching.
10. Such a simple thing was wonderful to her.

12.2 Articles and Proper Adjectives

The words *a, an,* and *the* make up a special group of adjectives called **articles.** *A* and *an* are called **indefinite articles** because they refer to one of a general group of people, places, things, or ideas. *A* is used before words beginning with a consonant sound, and *an* before words beginning with a vowel sound. Don't confuse sounds with spellings. When speaking, you would say *a university* but *an uncle.*

a unit   **a** painting   **an** etching   **an** hour

The is called a **definite article** because it identifies specific people, places, things, or ideas.

The valuable statue is **the** only one of its kind.

■ **Proper adjectives** are formed from proper nouns. A proper adjective always begins with a capital letter.

The **Italian** statue is on exhibit in the **Houston** museum.
The **February** exhibit follows a show of **French** paintings.

Although most proper adjectives are formed from proper nouns by adding one of the endings listed below, some are formed differently. Check the spellings in a dictionary.

Common Endings for Proper Adjectives				
-an	Mexico Mexic**an**	Morocco Morocc**an**	Alaska Alask**an**	Guatemala Guatemal**an**
-ese	China Chin**ese**	Bali Balin**ese**	Sudan Sudan**ese**	Japan Japan**ese**
-ian	Canada Canad**ian**	Italy Ital**ian**	Nigeria Niger**ian**	Asia As**ian**
-ish	Spain Span**ish**	Ireland Ir**ish**	Turkey Turk**ish**	England Engl**ish**

Adjectives and Adverbs

| Exercise 3 | Using *A* and *An* |

Write the correct indefinite article that would come before each word or group of words.

1.	satellite	11.	unknown rock
2.	electrical storm	12.	typical day
3.	transmitter	13.	masterpiece
4.	vehicle	14.	awkward age
5.	howling wind	15.	instrument
6.	expedition	16.	high-wire act
7.	unicorn	17.	explanation
8.	unique event	18.	hourly report
9.	anonymous writer	19.	honest effort
10.	unexplored part	20.	activity

| Exercise 4 | Forming Proper Adjectives |

Rewrite each sentence, changing the proper noun into a proper adjective. You may have to change the article and eliminate other words.

1. The first exhibit included a drum from Africa.
2. One of my classmates was wearing a bracelet from Mexico.
3. Our class included an exchange student from China.
4. We braved a snowstorm in January to come to the show.
5. An artist from Poland was listening to an audio tape.
6. One painting represented a wedding in April.
7. A class favorite featured a bobsled from Alaska.
8. One parent arrived late in a car from Japan.
9. A snowy scene reminded the teacher of a winter in Minnesota.
10. A writer from Ireland introduced himself to the tour guide.
11. The furniture display included a clock from Taiwan.
12. Some of us chatted with a visitor from Italy.
13. Two people were copying a portrait of a dancer from Mexico.
14. I heard an art critic from Germany talking about the exhibit.
15. What he said puzzled a sailor from France.
16. A tourist from Egypt listened to her with interest.
17. At the museum restaurant, the waitress offered us a tea from Australia.
18. A flag from Nigeria was displayed in the museum gift shop.
19. One postcard there showed a celebration in July.
20. The jewelry counter had a copy of a ring from Bolivia.

12.3 Comparative and Superlative Adjectives

- The **comparative form** of an adjective compares two things or people.
- The **superlative form** of an adjective compares more than two things or people.

For most adjectives of one syllable and some of two syllables, -er and -est are added to form the comparative and superlative.

Comparative and Superlative Forms	
Comparative	She is **younger** than the other painter.
Superlative	She is the **youngest** painter in the entire group.

For most adjectives with two or more syllables, the comparative or superlative is formed by adding *more* or *most* before the adjective.

Comparative and Superlative Forms of Longer Adjectives	
Comparative	The one next to it is **more colorful.**
Superlative	The painting in the next room is the **most colorful.**

Never use *more* or *most* with adjectives that already end with -er or -est. This is called a double comparison.

Some adjectives have irregular comparative and superlative forms.

Irregular Comparative and Superlative Forms		
Adjective	**Comparative**	**Superlative**
good, well	better	best
bad	worse	worst
many, much	more	most
little	less	least

Identifying Correct Comparative and Superlative Forms

Rewrite each sentence, correcting the comparative or superlative form of the adjective.

1. You can't really say that my taste is worser than yours.
2. If someone has good taste in art, how can there be gooder taste?
3. You just don't like my favoritest painter.
4. Does that mean that the one you like is more good?
5. First of all, my favorite is more young than your favorite.
6. As she gets more older, her work improves.
7. Her bestest work has been done in the last ten years.
8. I know that critics have attacked her most early works.
9. The more large her paintings get, the more exciting they are.
10. The later paintings all sell for much more high prices.

Using Comparative and Superlative Adjectives

Write the correct comparative or superlative form of the adjective in parentheses.

1. Michelangelo was one of the (great) artists of all time.
2. He was also the (famous) artist of his own time.
3. Are his statues (good) than his paintings?
4. Which is the (fine) statue, *David* or the *Pietà?*
5. Michelangelo's figures were (large) than life.
6. Few paintings are (beautiful) than the one on the ceiling of the Sistine Chapel.
7. His buildings may be (famous) than his renowned statues and paintings.
8. Pablo Picasso may be the (great) painter of our century.
9. His early paintings are (realistic) than his later work.
10. His (early) works were really quite traditional.
11. The work of Picasso's Blue Period included some of his (dark) views of life.
12. Picasso's (bleak) mood of all came during World War II.
13. During his Rose Period, though, his paintings were much (cheerful).
14. For Picasso painting was the (important) thing in his life.
15. His cubist works are probably the (famous) of all.
16. Cubism may have been the (original) of Picasso's many styles.
17. Critics argue over the question of his (good) style of all.
18. They also disagree on his (bad) style.
19. Few artists completed (many) paintings than he did.
20. Of all artists, he showed the (quick) response to change.

12.4   Demonstratives

The words *this, that, these,* and *those* are called demonstratives. They "demonstrate," or point out, people, places, or things. *This* and *these* point out people or things near to you, and *that* and *those* point out people or things at a distance from you. *This* and *that* describe singular nouns, and *these* and *those* describe plural nouns.

This, that, these, and *those* are called demonstrative adjectives when they describe nouns.

■ **Demonstrative adjectives** point out something and describe nouns by answering the questions *which one?* or *which ones?*

The words *this, that, these,* and *those* can also be used as demonstrative pronouns. They take the place of nouns and call attention to, or demonstrate, something that is not named.

Notice the demonstratives in the following sentences.

That gallery has modern art.

This gallery contains Impressionist works.

Demonstrative Words	
Demonstrative Adjectives	**Demonstrative Pronouns**
This painting is my favorite.	**This** is my favorite painting.
I like **these** kinds of paintings.	**These** are the paintings I like.
That portrait is well known.	**That** was the first stage.
He draws **those** sorts of pictures.	**Those** are from his Cubist phase.

The words *here* and *there* should not be used with demonstrative adjectives. The words *this, these, that,* and *those* already point out the locations *here* and *there.*

> **This** painting is by Matisse. [not *This here painting*]

The object pronoun *them* should not be used in place of the demonstrative adjective *those.*

> I saw **those** pictures. [not *them pictures*]

Exercise 7   Identifying Demonstrative Adjectives and Pronouns

Write the demonstrative from each sentence. Then write *adjective* or *pronoun* to tell what kind it is.

1. You can tell that this artist admired Cézanne's work.
2. All of these pictures show, in some way, Cézanne's influence.
3. This doesn't mean that the artist copied Cézanne's work.
4. Can you see how he uses these colors the same way?
5. Doesn't it remind you of those paintings of Cézanne's we just saw?
6. On the other hand, this one reminds me more of Van Gogh's work.
7. Now, this is a painting I could look at every day.
8. All of those paintings by the Impressionists appeal to me.
9. I'm also interested in those abstract paintings in the next room.
10. This was a good day for seeing a wide variety of styles.

Exercise 8   Using Demonstratives

Write the correct word or words from the parentheses.

1. The artist saw (that, those) things in a new way.
2. (This, This here) painting shows her imaginative style.
3. This (kinds of, kind of) painting has become famous.
4. (This, That) painting over there shows an acrobat.
5. Usually (those, them) colors together would clash.
6. (This, These) are her brushes and palette.
7. (That there, That) painting by Paul Cézanne is influential.
8. (This, This here) is an early work.
9. Cézanne breaks up the dimensions of (this, these) objects.
10. Then he rearranges (these, these here) fragments.
11. This (kind of, kinds of) painting shows his technique.
12. (These, These here) are explorations of space.
13. The angles in (this, this here) picture seem to overlap.
14. These (kinds of, kind of) angles do form solids.
15. The *Pietà* is not (that, that there) kind of sculpture.
16. (This, These) is a fine example of abstract art.
17. Many are familiar with (that, that there) artist.
18. One artist produced all (this, these) works.
19. (Those, Them) paintings are older than his.
20. (These, These here) pieces are by an unknown artist.

■ An **adverb** is a word that modifies, or describes, a verb, an adjective, or another adverb.

What Adverbs Modify	
Verbs	People handle old violins **carefully.**
Adjectives	**Very** old violins are valuable.
Adverbs	Some violins are played **extremely** rarely.

Some adverbs tell *to what extent* a quality exists. These adverbs are sometimes called **intensifiers.** *Very, quite,* and *almost* are intensifiers.

An adverb may tell *when, where,* or *how* about a verb. The adverbs in the sentences below all modify the verb *play.*

Ways Adverbs Modify Verbs	
How?	Many pianists play **well** with a large orchestra.
When?	Pianists **sometimes** play duets.
Where?	Some pianists play **everywhere** in the country.

When modifying an adjective or another adverb, an adverb usually comes before the word. However, when modifying a verb, an adverb can occupy different positions in a sentence.

Many adverbs are formed by adding -*ly* to adjectives. However, not all words that end in -*ly* are adverbs. The words *friendly, lively, kindly,* and *lonely* are usually adjectives. Similarly, not all adverbs end in -*ly.*

Adverbs Not Ending in -*ly*			
afterward	often	there	hard
sometimes	soon	everywhere	long
later	here	fast	straight

Identifying the Purpose of Adverbs

Write each adverb, and write whether it tells *how, when,* or *where.*

1. Our chorus finally has enough basses.
2. Unlike in previous years, our conductor can comfortably assign the parts.
3. Becky sometimes had to find choral arrangements with three parts.
4. Now she heads straight for the four-part works.
5. We've moved to another room because we have more space there.
6. She's arranged the seating differently, too.
7. Now each part sits in a wedge-shaped section.
8. That will give us better balance anywhere we sing.
9. She conducts us well, so we are happy.
10. We sing enthusiastically.

Exercise 10 **Identifying Adverbs**

Write each adverb and write the word it describes in parentheses.

1. The early Greeks studied music thoroughly.
2. To the Greeks, music and mathematics were very similar.
3. Pythagoras strongly believed in the enormous power of music.
4. His ideas about music were certainly important.
5. People sang choral music often at ancient ceremonies.
6. The notes of each singer were exactly alike.
7. These choruses almost surely sang without accompaniment.
8. Composers later wrote separate parts for different voices.
9. Musicians of the Middle Ages developed part singing rather quickly.
10. Some unusually beautiful music resulted.
11. The parts were highly complex.
12. Modern choruses are very professional groups of singers.
13. These choruses perform everywhere.
14. Many choral singers are totally dedicated to their work.
15. People often overlook this kind of music.
16. Some people await major choral concerts eagerly.
17. Chorus singers are sometimes called choristers.
18. They generally sing pieces for four parts, or voices.
19. Tenors are sometimes female singers.
20. Some conductors always insist on male tenors.

12.6 Comparative and Superlative Adverbs

- The **comparative form** of an adverb compares two actions.
- The **superlative form** of an adverb compares more than two actions.

Long adverbs require the use of *more* or *most*.

Comparing Adverbs of More than One Syllable	
Comparative	The audience listened **more attentively** last night than tonight.
Superlative	Last Sunday's audience responded **most enthusiastically** of all.

Shorter adverbs need *-er* or *-est* as an ending.

Comparing One-Syllable Adverbs	
Comparative	Did the pianist play **louder** than the cellist?
Superlative	Did the drummer play the **loudest** of all?

Here are some irregular adverbs.

Irregular Comparative and Superlative Forms		
Adverb	**Comparative**	**Superlative**
well	better	best
badly	worse	worst
little (amount)	less	least

The words *less* and *least* are used before some short and long adverbs to form the negative comparative and the negative superlative.

I play **less well.** I play **least accurately.**

Exercise 11   Forming the Comparative and Superlative

Write the comparative and superlative forms of each of the following
adverbs.

1. tenderly
2. fast
3. little
4. easily
5. violently
6. rapidly
7. close
8. gently
9. awkwardly
10. loud
11. soon
12. well
13. harshly
14. eerily
15. hard
16. effectively
17. late
18. openly
19. negatively
20. often
21. gracefully
22. slow
23. frequently
24. effortlessly
25. long

Exercise 12   Using Comparative and Superlative Adverb Forms

For each sentence, write the correct comparative or superlative form of the
adverb in parentheses.

1. The performance began (late) tonight than last night.
2. My sister sat (far) from the stage than we did.
3. Several backup singers rehearsed (long) than the piano player.
4. The lead singer sang (badly) last year than this year.
5. The guitarists sang (little) during this concert than during their last one.
6. The drummer played (forcefully) during her solo than before.
7. We heard the first song (clearly) of all the songs.
8. The band played (energetically) of all at the end.
9. I clapped (loudly) during the second half than during the first.
10. I understand the band played (badly) at rehearsals than they ever had before.
11. (Often) than not, Miss Elly had to say, "Now, James, now!"
12. She expected (good) of him but couldn't be sure of it.
13. The night of the dress rehearsal came (quickly) than seemed possible.
14. There sat James in the percussion section as the music grew (fast).
15. He was staring even (blankly) into space than before.
16. "Now, James, now!" Miss Elly cried (desperately) than ever.
17. The entire band turned around and shouted even (loudly)than Miss Elly,
    "Now, James, now!"
18. The actual performance, however, went (well) than anyone expected.
19. James hit that triangle the (hard) he ever had, right on time.
20. The evening ended (soon) than expected.

12.7   Using Adverbs and Adjectives

Adverbs and adjectives are often confused, especially when they appear after verbs. A predicate adjective follows a linking verb.

> The musicians are **professional.**

In the sentence above, the predicate adjective *professional* describes *musicians.*

In the sentence below, the adverb *professionally* describes the action verb *behaved.*

> The musicians behaved **professionally.**

People also sometimes confuse the words *bad, badly, good,* and *well. Bad* and *good* are both adjectives. They are used after linking verbs. *Badly* is an adverb. It is used after an action verb. *Well* can be either. When used to describe an adjective or verb, *well* is an adverb. When used after a linking verb to describe a person's health or appearance, *well* is an adjective.

Louis Armstrong was a **real** innovator in jazz.

His music was **really** popular.

Distinguishing Adjective from Adverb	
Adjective	**Adverb**
The sound is **bad**. The band sounds **good**. The soloist seems **well**.	The actor sang **badly**. The band played **well**.

People also confuse *real, really; sure, surely;* and *most, almost. Real, sure,* and *most* are adjectives. *Really, surely,* and *almost* are adverbs.

Distinguishing Adjective from Adverb	
Adjective	**Adverb**
Music is a **real** art. A pianist needs **sure** hands. **Most** pianos have eighty-eight keys.	Music is **really** popular. Piano music is **surely** popular. Piano strings **almost** never break.

Exercise 13   Using *bad, badly, good,* and *well*

For each sentence, write the correct adjective or adverb given in parentheses.

1. The big bands did very (good, well) during the 1930s and 1940s.
2. As (good, well) as they were, they needed national radio to succeed.
3. Even (bad, badly) bands took advantage of the interest in this music.
4. The big bands' era is over, but their records still sell (good, well).
5. If you listen really (good, well), you'll still hear bands with that sound.

Exercise 14   Identifying Adjectives and Adverbs

Write each sentence, and underline each verb. Circle the adverb or adjective that follows it, and draw an arrow to the word it modifies. Label each adjective or adverb.

1. Louis Armstrong was famous as a jazz trumpeter.
2. Armstrong began his music career early in the 1900s.
3. He played the trumpet well during his teens in New Orleans.
4. Armstrong listened carefully to other musicians' styles.
5. He seemed enthusiastic about a new singing style called "scat."
6. Scat was rhythmic in its use of syllables instead of words.
7. He seemed ready for a new career as an actor in motion pictures.
8. Big bands played everywhere.
9. They were popular in the 1930s.
10. Louis Armstrong traveled widely and made a number of hit records.
11. Both the soloists and the conductors of the big bands became widely known.
12. The Dorsey brothers were extremely successful as popular musicians.
13. They worked steadily throughout the 1940s.
14. Dinah Shore sang often with big bands.
15. Dinah became very popular as a solo artist.
16. The Spike Jones band is still popular with some people.
17. Spike's versions of some well-known songs were hilarious.
18. In some songs a fire whistle screamed wildly.
19. Meanwhile, the poor tenor sang unconcernedly in the background.
20. The Spike Jones band played well but sounded bad.

12.8 | Avoiding Double Negatives

The adverb *not* is a **negative word,** expressing the idea of "no." *Not* often appears in a shortened form as part of a contraction. Study the words and contracted forms below.

Contractions with *Not*		
is not = isn't	cannot = can't	have not = haven't
was not = wasn't	could not = couldn't	had not = hadn't
were not = weren't	do not = don't	would not = wouldn't
will not = won't	did not = didn't	should not = shouldn't

The apostrophe replaces the *o* in *not* in all but two words. In *can't* both the letter *n* and the letter *o* are dropped. *Will not* becomes *won't.*

Other negative words are listed below. Each negative word has several opposites. These are **affirmative words,** or words that show the idea of "yes."

Negative and Affirmative Words	
Negative	**Affirmative**
never	ever, always
nobody	anybody, somebody
none	one, all, some, any
no one	everyone, someone, anyone
nothing	something, anything
nowhere	somewhere, anywhere

Be careful to avoid using two negative words in the same sentence. This is called a **double negative.** You can correct a double negative by removing one of the negative words or by replacing one with an affirmative word.

Incorrect:	The clarinet **isn't no** new instrument.
Correct:	The clarinet **isn't a** new instrument.
Correct:	The clarinet is **no** new instrument.

Exercise 15   Correcting Double Negatives

Rewrite each sentence, avoiding any double negatives.

1. My older brother doesn't take no piano lessons.
2. He plays the piano, but he can't hardly read music.
3. He plays by ear, but I haven't never been able to do that.
4. If we both want to play, we don't never agree who'll get the piano.
5. Sometimes I get there first, and he can't never stand it.
6. He hangs around, as though he doesn't have nothing to do.
7. Then he acts like he hasn't never wanted to play, just to sing.
8. But he starts singing so badly, I can't stand it no more.
9. I start laughing, and there isn't nothing can stop me.
10. Anyone laughing that hard can't hardly play the piano very well.

Exercise 16   Using Negative Words

Write the correct word or words given in parentheses.

1. Didn't (anyone, no one) play pipe organs before Roman times?
2. We (would, wouldn't) hardly recognize the Roman pipe organ today.
3. Aren't there (no, any) old Roman pipe organs still in existence?
4. The pipe organ (was, wasn't) scarcely used outside of churches.
5. Scarcely (no, any) ancient civilizations were without musical instruments.
6. The Egyptians (weren't, were) no exception.
7. Hardly (any, none) of their paintings leave out cymbals and drums.
8. The harp and flute weren't seen (nowhere, anywhere) until centuries later.
9. The zither (was, wasn't) heard nowhere before it was developed in China.
10. Hardly (no, any) ancient lyres are on public display.
11. If you haven't (ever, never) seen a lyre, try an art museum.
12. Some museums have instruments that are rarely played (anymore, no more).
13. They have instruments that can't be seen (nowhere, anywhere) else.
14. No one (should, shouldn't) have trouble understanding how music is made.
15. Didn't you (never, ever) learn that sounds come from making the air move?
16. Early stringed instruments weren't (ever, never) rubbed, only plucked.
17. Only later did (nobody, somebody) think of striking a string with a hammer.
18. Not all woodwind instruments (aren't, are) made of wood.
19. The brass instruments don't have (no, any) reeds at all.
20. Older percussion instruments aren't too different from ours (either, neither).

Grammar Review

ADJECTIVES AND ADVERBS

During the 1600s, Juan de Pareja became enslaved to the great Spanish painter Diego Velázquez. *I, Juan de Pareja,* by Elizabeth Borton de Treviño, tells how Juan became the artist's friend and assistant. In this passage, de Pareja explains his duties. The passage has been annotated to show some of the types of adjectives and adverbs covered in this unit.

Literature Model

from I, Juan de Pareja
by Elizabeth Borton de Treviño

One by one, he taught me my duties. First, I had to learn to grind the colors. There were many mortars for this work, and pestles in varying sizes. I soon learned that the lumps of earth and metallic compounds had to be softly and continuously worked until there remained a powder as fine as the ground rice ladies used on their cheeks and foreheads. It took hours, and sometimes when I was sure the stuff was as fine as satin, Master would pinch and move it between his sensitive fingers and shake his head, and then I had to grind some more. Later the ground powder had to be incorporated into the oils, and well-mixed, and much later still, I arranged Master's palette for him, the little mounds of color each in its fixed place, and he had his preferences about how much of any one should be set out. And, of course, brushes were to be washed daily, in plenty of good Castile soap and water. Master's brushes all had to be clean and fresh every morning when he began to work.

Demonstrative adjective

Adverb

Adjective

Article

Past participle used as an adjective

Proper adjective

Adjectives and Adverbs

Grammar Review

Review: Exercise 1 Identifying Adjectives

Write each adjective. Then write in parentheses the noun or pronoun it modifies. Do not include articles *a*, *an*, and *the*.

1. Velázquez painted in a large room on the second floor of the house.
2. A huge window let in a pure light from the north.
3. Juan learned to stretch the cotton canvas for the painter.
4. The artist never wrote down the secret formulas for preparing the canvas.
5. He called them professional secrets, and Juan had to memorize them.
6. Juan was a trustworthy assistant.
7. Velázquez liked the early light and would paint until late afternoon.
8. The painter's wife was a merry person and a thrifty housekeeper.
9. Juan had to arrange colorful backgrounds for Velázquez.
10. Juan always wore a gold earring.

Review: Exercise 2 Using Comparative and Superlative Adjectives

Write the correct comparative or superlative form of the adjective in parentheses.

SAMPLE De Pareja was (young) than Velázquez.
ANSWER younger

1. Juan de Pareja ground the colors into the (fine) powder.
2. The artist's fingers were (sensitive) than Juan's.
3. He used the mounds of color on his palette to create some of the (beautiful) paintings of all.
4. Every day Juan de Pareja made sure the artist's brushes were (clean) and (fresh) than Velázquez had left them.
5. Velázquez used the (good) materials he could.
6. The painter often sat staring at his subject for the (long) time.
7. When asked why, the artist explained that this was the (good) way to feel the object's shape.
8. The (exciting) moment came when the king asked Velázquez to paint his portrait.
9. That meant the family would move in the (high) circles of society.
10. The king turned out to be (tall) and (pale) than Juan had expected.

Review: Exercise 3   **Identifying Adverbs**

Write each sentence. Underline each adverb, and draw an arrow to the word it modifies.

1. The compounds had to be worked continuously.
2. Sometimes the painter would ask for more grinding.
3. Brushes had to be washed daily in soap and water.
4. Juan worked clumsily with his carpentry.
5. He could soon cut and fit the pieces.
6. Occasionally he posed so that the painter could draw or paint him.
7. The painter usually started work early in the morning.
8. Velázquez drew silently, making many drawings.
9. Juan earnestly asked the artist if he could learn to paint.
10. But Velázquez answered simply, "I cannot teach you."

Review: Exercise 4   **Using Comparative and Superlative Adverbs**

Write the correct comparative or superlative form of the adverb in parentheses.

SAMPLE   He painted (boldly) than before.
ANSWER   more boldly

1. Velázquez represented his subjects (realistically) than had many earlier artists.
2. Of all the techniques, the artist's use of rich colors, light, and shadow (clearly) characterized his style.
3. Velázquez painted portraits (frequently) of all.
4. Although many artists have imitated his style, Velázquez (heavily) influenced modern painters.
5. He traveled (far) than many other artists of his day to study the art of ancient Rome.
6. Velázquez faced an upcoming trip to Italy (calmly) than did his family.
7. His wife stayed behind in Spain the (reluctantly) of all.
8. Velázquez found that the light shone (softly) in Italy than in Spain.
9. Juan moved around (freely) in Italy than in Spain.
10. He could buy paint supplies (easily) in Italy, too.

Grammar Review

Review: Exercise 5 Using Comparatives and Superlatives

Write the correct comparative or superlative form of the adverb or adjective in parentheses.

1. Fictional biography presents (interesting) problems than even straight fiction does.
2. Events must be evaluated (deliberately) than in straight fiction.
3. Biographers are (dependent) on written records than are writers of straight fiction.
4. Suppose that the main figure was one of the (famous) painters who ever lived.
5. Painters write (few) letters and diaries than do authors.
6. Velázquez wrote only a handful of letters, which makes things even (hard).
7. What is (difficult) than imagining conversations he might have had?
8. The (helpful) clues are in the artist's paintings.
9. The subjects of the paintings and how they are presented offer the (good) clues to the artist's interests and attitudes.
10. For de Pareja the clues are even (available) because he was less well known than his teacher.

Review: Exercise 6 Distinguishing Between Adjectives and Adverbs

Write the correct adjective or adverb in parentheses.

1. Velázquez and de Pareja became (good, well) friends.
2. Velázquez recognized his assistant's (real, really) love for art.
3. The two worked (easy, easily) together.
4. Velázquez was never (harsh, harshly) with his assistant.
5. Juan was (frank, frankly) about his admiration of Velázquez.
6. He worked (eager, eagerly) to further Velázquez's career.
7. The portrait of de Pareja shows how (high, highly) he was regarded by Velázquez.
8. De Pareja had a (sure, surely) talent for painting.
9. Juan de Pareja served Velázquez (loyal, loyally) until the artist died.
10. De Pareja became a (true, truly) artist himself.

Review: Exercise 7

Proofreading

The following passage is about Spanish artist Diego Velázquez, whose work appears on the next page. Rewrite the passage, correcting the errors in spelling, capitalization, grammar, and usage. Add any missing punctuation. There are ten errors.

Diego Rodriguez de Silva y Velázquez

¹Diego Rodriguez de Silva y Velázquez (1599–1660) was born in the Spain city of Seville. ²He studied a italian artist Caravaggio, whose realistic figures were painted in contrasting light and dark tones. ³Velázquez become the official painter for Spain's King Philip IV in 1623. ⁴However, the artist's portraits of the royal family looked most like pictures from a personal album than paintings advertising the greatly power of Spain.

⁵Velázquez skillful captures the personalities of his subjects. ⁶When he painted his friend, Juan de Pareja, Velázquez omit neither his intelligence nor his dignity.

Review: Exercise 8

Mixed Review

On your paper, write the twenty adjectives and adverbs that appear in the following paragraph. Do not include articles. Identify each word as an *adjective* or *adverb*.

Portraits

¹Why do many painters do portraits? ²There are commissioned portraits and noncommissioned portraits. ³When an artist does a commissioned portrait, he or she has been asked directly to do so by someone who will pay for the finished work. ⁴Sometimes it is the patrons, or buyers, who will sit for the portrait. ⁵Other times they want a painted record of someone dear to them. ⁶Or it may be an official portrait of an important person. ⁷If artists do a noncommissioned portrait, it is usually because they have seen a face that they feel they have to capture. ⁸That kind of portrait has a distinct advantage to sincere artists. ⁹They can paint exactly what they see and do it honestly. ¹⁰When artists are paid, the patron may be concerned with appearances rather than honesty.

Adjectives and Adverbs

Diego Velázquez, *Juan de Pareja*, 1650

Writing Application

TIME

For more about the writing process, see **TIME Facing the Blank Page**, pp. 97-107.

Adjectives and Adverbs in Writing

In this passage from "On Summer," Lorraine Hansberry uses adjectives and adverbs to convey the mood of summer nights in Chicago. As you read the passage, notice the italicized adjectives and adverbs.

> Evenings were spent *mainly* on the *back* porches where screen doors slammed in the darkness with *those really very special summertime* sounds. And, *sometimes*, when *Chicago* nights got too *steamy*, the *whole* family got into the car and went to the park and slept out in the open on blankets. Those were, of course, the *best* times of all because the grownups were *invariably* reminded of having been children in *rural* parts of the country and told the *best* stories then.

Techniques with Adjectives and Adverbs

Try to apply some of Lorraine Hansberry's writing techniques when you write and revise your own work.

1. Add detail and interest to your descriptions by combining several adjectives and adverbs in a group of descriptive words. Compare the following:

   GENERAL DESCRIPTION special sounds

   HANSBERRY'S VERSION *those really very special summertime* sounds

2. When appropriate, use a proper adjective to make your descriptions more precise.

   GENERAL DESCRIPTION when nights in *our city*

   HANSBERRY'S VERSION when *Chicago* nights

Practice   Practice these techniques as you revise the following passage on a separate piece of paper. Experiment with adding one or more adjectives and adverbs in the blanks provided.

Every morning Jason _____ crossed off a day on his _____ calendar. _____ five more until his _____ trip to Gona's house. Gona was _____ special,_____ for a grown-up! Jason could reveal his _____ worries, and she'd understand them _____. She never laughed or teased. Plus, just _____ to Gona's _____ house was the world's _____ restaurant. After his mom's _____ sausage, Jason was _____ for hot _____ food.

UNIT
13

Prepositions, Conjunctions, and Interjections

Prepositions and Prepositional Phrases

■ A **preposition** is a word that relates a noun or a pronoun to some other word in a sentence.

The boy **by** the window is French.

The word *by* in the sentence above is a preposition. *By* shows relationship of the word *boy* to the noun *window*.

Commonly Used Prepositions				
about	before	during	off	to
above	behind	for	on	toward
across	below	from	onto	under
after	beneath	in	out	until
against	beside	inside	outside	up
along	between	into	over	upon
among	beyond	like	since	with
around	by	near	through	within
at	down	of	throughout	without
as				

A preposition can consist of more than one word.

Yasmin will visit Trinidad **instead of** Jamaica.

Compound Prepositions			
according to	aside from	in front of	instead of
across from	because of	in place of	on account of
along with	far from	in spite of	on top of

■ A **prepositional phrase** is a group of words that begins with a preposition and ends with a noun or pronoun, which is called the **object of the preposition.** The sentence below has two prepositional phrases.

The painting **near you** is **by a Brazilian artist.**

Exercise 1   Identifying Prepositional Phrases and Objects of Prepositions

Write each prepositional phrase. Draw a line under the preposition, and circle the object of the preposition.

1. The Louvre is a famous museum in Paris.
2. Do you know the history of this stately building?
3. The Louvre was once a residence for royalty.
4. Then the royal family moved to Versailles.
5. The galleries throughout the Louvre contain paintings and sculpture.
6. Paris, the French capital, is in northern France.
7. Vineyards stretch across the French countryside.
8. Picturesque old churches are scattered about the landscape.
9. Many harbors lie along the Mediterranean coast.
10. The largest French port, Marseilles, is on the Mediterranean Sea.
11. The high-speed Train à Grande Vitesse travels throughout France very quickly.
12. Ferries travel across the English Channel.
13. Cars and trains can also use a tunnel under the Channel.
14. The English held Calais for more than two centuries.
15. Many people enjoy winter sports in the French Alps.
16. Several resort cities cluster along the southern coast.
17. Most of the French kings were crowned at the cathedral in Reims.
18. Travelers to Europe will find many museums in Paris.
19. Each of these museums offers opportunity.
20. Visitors can also view many spacious and elegant gardens in European cities.

Exercise 2   Identifying Compound Prepositions

Write each prepositional phrase, and circle any compound prepositions.

1. According to our history book, a major change recently impacted Germany.
2. In place of two nations, West Germany and East Germany, Germany became one unified nation.
3. In spite of the challenges, most Germans celebrated becoming one nation again.
4. Visitors in front of the Brandenburg Gate can imagine the wall that once divided the city.
5. In eastern Berlin, visitors will find old buildings instead of the modern additions of the western city.

13.2 Pronouns as Objects of Prepositions

When the object of a preposition is a pronoun, it should be an object pronoun and not a subject pronoun.

Dan handed the tickets to Natalie.
Dan handed the tickets to **her.**

In the example above, the object pronoun *her* is the object of the preposition *to.*

Sometimes a preposition will have a compound object: two nouns or a noun and a pronoun. The pronoun in a compound object must be an object pronoun.

I borrowed the suitcase from **Ivan and Vera.**
I borrowed the suitcase from **Ivan and her.**

Natalie traveled with **Ivan and me.**

In the second sentence above, *Ivan and her* is the compound object of the preposition *from.* In the third sentence, *Ivan and me* is the compound object of the preposition *with.*

If you are unsure about whether to use a subject pronoun or an object pronoun, try saying the sentence aloud with only the object pronoun.

I borrowed the suitcase from **her.**
Natalie traveled with **me.**

The pronoun *whom* is an object pronoun. *Who* is never an object.

The man of **whom** I spoke is from Colombia.
To **whom** did you lend the guidebook?

Write the correct form of the pronoun in parentheses. Be sure each pronoun you choose makes sense in the sentence.

1. Carmen's aunt in Spain sent a postcard to David and (her, she).
2. This is the aunt about (who, whom) Carmen and David have told.
3. According to Carmen and (he, him), Spain is a great place to visit.
4. Carmen showed photographs of the Costa del Sol to Hector and (him, he).
5. There was one of David and (her, she) in front of the Alhambra in Granada.
6. The castle's magnificent gardens can be seen behind (them, they).
7. It was hard to distinguish between Carmen's cousin and (he, him); they look alike.
8. Because they look so much alike, Carmen's aunt could be mother to either of (them, they).
9. Aside from David, Carmen, and (he, him), no one in our class has been to Spain.
10. The Moors, who occupied Spain for eight hundred years, left architecture that impressed all of (us, we).
11. The description of the Alcázar given by Carmen and (her, she) was impressive.
12. Most of (us, we) thought the Alcázar was the Moors' best gift to Spain.
13. The Spanish lived alongside (them, they) for centuries.
14. The strong North African influences were described by David and (she, her).
15. Since only eight miles separate Spain from Africa at the narrowest point, this influence made perfect sense to (us, we).
16. Carmen explained to (me, I) that the Strait of Gibraltar is very narrow.
17. David showed the class how the Atlantic Ocean waters flow far beneath the surface while Mediterranean waters flow above (they, them).
18. Then Sheila asked why there were no pictures of (him, he) next to the water.
19. David pointed out to (her, she) that he had spent most of his trip inland.
20. Referring to the class map above (him, he), David located Barcelona.
21. Reaching across (I, me), Carmen gave Sheila a picture of a cathedral designed by Antonio Gaudí.
22. Carmen is standing between David and (him, he) in the first photograph.
23. The cathedral absolutely towers above (them, they) as they smile and point.
24. We were amazed to hear the history recounted by David and (her, she) of this never-finished wonder.
25. Some of (us, we) thought Gaudí's building looked a little like a sand castle.

■ A prepositional phrase is an **adjective phrase** when it modifies, or describes, a noun or pronoun.

A temple **of great size** stands here.

I noticed some men **with heavy suitcases.**

In the first sentence above, the prepositional phrase *of great size* modifies the subject of the sentence, *temple*. In the second sentence, the prepositional phrase *with heavy suitcases* describes a noun in the predicate, *men*.

Notice that, unlike most adjectives, an adjective phrase usually comes after the word it modifies.

■ A prepositional phrase is an **adverb phrase** when it modifies, or describes, a verb, an adjective, or another adverb.

Adverb Phrases Modifying a Verb, an Adjective, and an Adverb	
Describes a verb	The tourists travel **in a group**.
Describes an adjective	The temple is impressive **from this view.**
Describes an adverb	It has held up well **for its age**.

An adverb phrase tells *when, where,* or *how* an action occurs.

How Adverb Phrases Function	
When?	They left the hotel **in the morning**.
Where?	The curious visitors went **to Japan**.
How?	The large group traveled **by airplane**.

Prepositions, Conjunctions, and Interjections

Exercise 4   Identifying Adjective and Adverb Phrases

Write each prepositional phrase, and write whether it is an *adjective phrase* or an *adverb phrase*.

1. Most people in Japan follow the traditional customs of their country.
2. The Japanese traditionally bow on certain occasions.
3. They show great respect for their elders.
4. Throughout their history, the Japanese have also loved beauty.
5. Their gardens are models of grace and delicacy.
6. Japanese gardens are exceptional in their harmony.
7. Artificial and natural elements blend together in their gardens.
8. Soft woven mats cover the floors of many Japanese homes.
9. People customarily wear comfortable slippers inside their homes.
10. The guests of a family receive much kindness and consideration.
11. People sometimes cook on small charcoal stoves.
12. They often prepare bowls of noodles.
13. Diners frequently sit around very low tables.
14. Many Japanese people eat with chopsticks.
15. Hosts serve small cups of fragrant tea.
16. The Japanese tea ceremony has remained popular over the centuries.
17. We can enjoy our memories of Japan more fully with photos.
18. A guide translates the language with care.
19. Many people feel that Japanese is a language of great beauty.
20. When written, its letters are formed with graceful strokes.

Exercise 5   Writing Sentences with Prepositional Phrases

Rewrite each group of sentences, making a single sentence with adjective or adverb phrases.

1. Japan experienced little influence. The influence was from the outside.
2. Japan became an industrial nation. It became an industrial nation within fifty years.
3. We recently visited Nara. A Buddhist temple of historical significance can be seen at Nara.
4. Brightly colored plants dot the hills. The hills are below Kyushu's mountainous slopes.
5. The volcano Mount Aso stands. It stands at the island's highest point.

13.4 Conjunctions

■ A **coordinating conjunction** is a word used to connect parts of a sentence, such as words, clauses, or phrases. *And, but, or, for, so, yet,* and *nor* are coordinating conjunctions.

Using Coordinating Conjunctions	
Compound Subject	Allison **and** Rosita have lived in Mexico City.
Compound Predicate	Tourists shop **or** relax on the beaches.
Compound Object of a Preposition	Amiri went to Brazil **and** Peru.
Compound Sentence	Tom shopped every day, **but** we toured.

To make the relationship between words or groups of words especially strong, use a correlative conjunction.

■ **Correlative conjunctions** are pairs of words used to connect words or phrases in a sentence. Correlative conjunctions include *both . . . and, either . . . or, neither . . . nor,* and *not only . . . but also.*

> Examples of great architecture exist in **both** New York **and** Paris. **Neither** Carlo **nor** I have visited those cities.

When a compound subject is joined by the conjunction *and,* it is usually plural. The verb must agree with the plural subject.

When a compound subject is joined by *or* or *nor,* the verb must agree with the nearest part of the subject.

> Winema **and** Tanya **are** in Madrid this week.
> Neither the twins **nor** Ann **is** studying Spanish.

Exercise 6   Identifying Conjunctions

Write each conjunction. Write whether it forms a *compound subject*, a *compound predicate*, a *compound object of a preposition*, or a *compound sentence*.

1. Our teacher traveled to France and toured Paris.
2. The tour took a long time, but it was fascinating.
3. A cathedral or a museum in France may be very old.
4. Visitors spend hours in the bookstores and galleries.
5. After Paris, our teacher went to Normandy, which is between Paris and the English Channel.
6. This picturesque farming region is famous for delicious apples and cheeses.
7. Mr. King told us that he sampled some of the cheeses, but he enjoyed the fresh apple cider the most.
8. The leader and most of the participants voted for seeing the Loire Valley, a region known for its magnificent castles.
9. Our teacher agreed with us, but he requested that the group return to Dunkirk at the end of the tour.
10. Since Mr. King's trip, the tour company offers separate trips to one or the other of these regions.

Exercise 7   Making Compound Subjects and Verbs Agree

Write each sentence, using the correct verb form. Underline each coordinating or correlative conjunction.

1. An auto or a train (is, are) the best transportation for tourists.
2. Neither our teacher nor her companions (speaks, speak) French.
3. Both a subway and a bus system (serves, serve) Paris.
4. Either a taxi or a subway train (is, are) quick.
5. Two buses and a train (goes, go) to the Eiffel Tower.
6. Sometimes musicians and jugglers (performs, perform) in the subway stations in Paris.
7. Neither the Royal Palace nor the Louvre (is, are) open.
8. Still, Parisians and visitors alike (gathers, gather) outside these architectural points of interest.
9. Both the Left and the Right banks of the Seine (is, are) parts of Paris.
10. Either a tour boat or a stroll down the river banks (affords, afford) an intimate view of the city.

13.5 Conjunctive Adverbs

You can use a special kind of adverb instead of a coordinating or correlative conjunction to join the simple sentences in a compound sentence.

Many Asians use chopsticks, but some use forks.

Many Asians use chopsticks; **however,** some use forks.

Conjunctive adverbs, such as *however* in the sentence above, are usually stronger and more precise than coordinating conjunctions.

Using Conjunctive Adverbs	
To replace *and*	also, besides, furthermore, moreover
To replace *but*	however, nevertheless, still
To state a result	consequently, therefore, so, thus
To state equality	equally, likewise, similarly

■ A **conjunctive adverb** may be used to join the simple sentences in a compound sentence.

When two simple sentences are joined with a conjunctive adverb, a semicolon always appears before the second sentence. The conjunctive adverb can appear at the beginning, at the end, or in the middle of the second sentence. When it comes at the beginning or end, it is set off with a comma. When it appears in the middle, one comma precedes it, and one follows it.

Chinese cooks often stir-fry their food; **therefore**, they must cut it into very small pieces.

Stir-frying should be done quickly; the wok must be very hot, **therefore.**

Vegetables cook more quickly than meat; they must, **therefore,** be added to the wok last.

Exercise 8   **Identifying Conjunctive Adverbs**

Write each sentence. Underline each conjunctive adverb and add any needed punctuation.

1. People in different lands often have different eating styles moreover they may use different utensils.
2. Many people in India use bread as a scoop some however use a fork.
3. Chinese cooks cut meat into bite-size pieces similarly they chop or slice most vegetables.
4. Food is bite-size thus a knife isn't needed.
5. Soup may be served without spoons it must however be sipped carefully.
6. In the United States, Chinese restaurants may offer diners chopsticks still forks are usually found at each place.
7. Europeans may push their food onto the fork consequently they hold both the knife and the fork while eating.
8. Each of these utensils has its own unique history consequently a complete understanding of the topic requires time and effort.
9. The fork was once used as a fishing tool likewise ancient people took their forks to battle as weapons.
10. The first known table fork in England was made of fragile glass thus it was kept with great care.

Exercise 9   **Using Conjunctive Adverbs**

Write a conjunctive adverb that makes sense in completing the sentence.

1. Cuisines differ from country to country; _____, they often feature similar dishes.
2. A crepe is a thin pancake around a filling; _____, an enchilada may feature cheese inside a pancake.
3. Each nation has its specialities; _____, these are the best foods to sample.
4. You can enjoy these foods in restaurants; _____, cookbooks offer recipes.
5. You could spend a week trying Asian foods; _____, you could spend a week on other international foods.
6. France is rich in dairy products; _____, French cooks use cream and cheese.
7. Indian food is sometimes vegetarian; _____, it is often spicy.
8. Rice is a staple of Chinese cooking; _____, it is a staple of Japanese cooking.
9. Italian cuisines vary from region to region; _____, each type is delicious.
10. Our school serves international foods; _____, American favorites appear on the menu.

13.6 Interjections

You can express very strong feelings in a short exclamation that may not be a complete sentence. These exclamations are called interjections.

■ An **interjection** is a word or group of words that expresses strong feeling. It has no grammatical connection to any other words in the sentence.

Interjections are used to express emotions, such as surprise or disbelief. They are also used to attract attention.

Any part of speech can be used as an interjection. Some of the more common interjections are listed below.

Common Interjections			
aha	good grief	oh	well
alas	ha	oh no	what
awesome	hey	oops	whoops
come on	hooray	ouch	wow
gee	look	phew	yes

An interjection that expresses very strong feeling may stand alone either before or after a sentence. Such interjections are followed by an exclamation mark.

We are taking a boat ride around Venice. **Hooray!**

When an interjection expresses a milder feeling, it can appear as part of a sentence. In that case, the interjection is separated from the rest of the sentence by a comma.

Wow, that view of the skyline is spectacular.

You use interjections frequently when you speak. You should use them sparingly, however, when you write. Overusing interjections will spoil their effectiveness.

Exercise 10   Identifying Interjections

Write each sentence, adding punctuation where needed. Underline the interjection in each sentence.

1. Wow Doesn't Venice, Italy, have a lot of canals!
2. Imagine There are hardly any cars in Venice.
3. The city is built upon nearly 120 islands. Phew.
4. Alas we won't have time to visit every island.
5. There's a candy-striped pole up ahead. Oh, no
6. My goodness that was close.
7. Oops Look out for that gondola on your left.
8. Psst what is that bridge?
9. It is the famous Rialto Bridge. Yippee
10. No kidding Shall we visit it after lunch?
11. Good grief I can't believe I lost my camera.
12. Did you visit the Galleria dell'Accademia? Awesome
13. Come on There's a great outdoor restaurant very near the museum.
14. Hey Did you notice how the narrow, winding streets usually lead to a large, airy plaza?
15. Gee did you realize that the Grand Canal is so long?
16. Is rain in the forecast? Ugh
17. Hey the water is rough in this canal.
18. Eek Don't tip us over.
19. Oh, no Don't stand up in the gondola.
20. Whee Let's spend the whole day on this gondola.

Exercise 11   Identifying Interjections

Write an interjection that could complete each sentence. Make sure the sentence makes sense. Answers will vary.

1. _____! Our next stop in Italy will be the ancient city of Rome.
2. The city was first built during the great Roman Empire, more than 2,500 years ago. _____!
3. _____! Today's Romans live surrounded by remnants of an entirely different civilization.
4. _____! The Colosseum isn't one of the stops on today's tour.
5. _____! We are planning instead to lunch on some of Italy's more than two hundred kinds of pasta.

13.7 Finding All the Parts of Speech

Each separate word in a sentence performs a particular job. Each word belongs to a category called a **part of speech.** A word's part of speech depends on the job it performs in the sentence. You have learned all eight parts of speech. The sentence below contains an example of each category.

Gee, Venice is astonishingly beautiful, and it has classic architecture in every quarter.

Prepositions, Conjunctions, and Interjections

Parts of Speech		
Word	**Part of Speech**	**Function**
Gee	Interjection	Expresses strong feeling
Venice	Proper noun	Names a specific place
is	Linking verb	Links *Venice* with the adjective *beautiful*
astonishingly	Adverb	Describes the adjective *beautiful*
beautiful	Adjective	Describes the subject, *Venice*
and	Conjunction	Joins two simple sentences
it	Pronoun	Takes the place of a noun
has	Action verb	Names an action
classic	Adjective	Describes the object, *architecture*
architecture	Common noun	Names a thing
in	Preposition	Relates *architecture* and *quarter*
every	Adjective	Describes the noun *quarter*
quarter	Common noun	Names a thing

Exercise 12   **Identifying Parts of Speech**

Write each underlined word and its part of speech.

1. Moira often <u>travels</u> to <u>foreign</u> countries.
2. <u>In</u> June <u>she</u> will go to Chile.
3. She <u>is</u> <u>especially</u> fond of Greece.
4. <u>Spain</u> is also close to her <u>heart</u>.
5. Next year she <u>plans</u> to visit Japan <u>and</u> Taiwan.

Exercise 13   **Using Parts of Speech**

Complete each sentence below by supplying a word whose part of speech is indicated in parentheses. Be sure your finished sentences make sense.

1. Tony (conjunction) Sadie have been to more (common noun) than any other people I know.
2. (Pronoun) visited (proper noun) last year.
3. (Preposition) January they will (action verb) to Israel and Egypt.
4. Tony thought Portugal (linking verb) (adjective).
5. Tony went to (correlative conjunction) Peru (correlative conjunction) Chile.
6. He was (negative adverb) in Asia; Sadie, (conjunctive adverb), went to China.
7. She found (proper noun) amazing, and she (action verb) to go there again.
8. Africa reflects a patchwork of cultures; (conjunctive adverb), its climate varies from desert (preposition) tropical rain forest.
9. (Interjection)! How do so many climates exist in a (adjective) continent?
10. Kyle (adverb) visited Scandinavia, stopping in Norway (conjunction) Sweden.
11. It (linking verb) July, when days are long and the (common noun) is warm.
12. (Pronoun) flew to Lithuania, where he (action verb) this newly open nation.
13. (Correlative conjunction) Kyle (correlative conjunction) Sadie had studied Vilnius in detail.
14. (Interjection), their timetables allowed only two days to see this (adjective) city.
15. Tony, (time adverb), was in Brazil visiting the glorious (conjunction) vanishing rain forest.
16. He (linking verb) amazed by São Paulo, South America's largest (common noun).
17. This (adjective) city's factories produce (indefinite pronoun) from fabrics to electrical equipment.
18. (Preposition) Mexico City, these globe-trotters will (adverb) go home.
19. Good grief! I bet they'll be (adjective) to touch (proper adjective) soil again.
20. (Pronoun) is amazing how often they travel; (conjunctive adverb), they learn.

PREPOSITIONS, CONJUNCTIONS, AND INTERJECTIONS

On a Caribbean island, a young girl discovers Christopher Columbus's boat. The passage is annotated to show some of the parts of speech covered in this unit.

Literature Model

from Morning Girl
by Michael Dorris

I forgot I was still beneath the surface until I needed air. But when I broke into the sunlight, the water sparkling all around me, the noise turned out to be nothing! Only a canoe! The breathing was the dip of many paddles! It was only *people* coming to visit, and since I could see they hadn't painted themselves to appear fierce, they must be friendly or lost.

I swam closer to get a better look and had to stop myself from laughing. The strangers had wrapped every part of their bodies with colorful leaves and cotton. Some had decorated their faces with fur and wore shiny rocks on their heads. Compared to us, they were very round. Their canoe was short and square, and, in spite of all their dipping and pulling, it moved so slowly. What a backward, distant island they must have come from. But really, to laugh at guests, no matter how odd, would be impolite, especially since I was the first to meet them. If I was foolish, they would think they had arrived at a foolish place.

Preposition

Prepositional phrase (adverb phrase)

Coordinating conjunction

Prepositional phrase (adjective phrase)

Compound preposition

Noun as object of preposition

Grammar Review

| Review: Exercise 1 | Identifying Prepositional Phrases and Objects of Prepositions |

Write each prepositional phrase. Draw a line under the preposition, and circle the object.

1. She swam beneath the blue waters.
2. Morning Girl saw an unusual canoe on its way toward her.
3. Its many paddles cut crisply through the clear water.
4. Until this day, Morning Girl had not known people could be so round.
5. The strangers did not look dangerous and wore no paint on their faces.
6. Morning Girl was curious about the new arrivals.
7. The strangers wore fur over their skin.
8. Torn between laughter and courtesy, Morning Girl chose courtesy and greeted the oddly dressed strangers warmly.
9. She wished her mother were beside her.
10. She would help Morning Girl behave correctly and would remind her of island customs.
11. Morning Girl could have called Star Boy from his work.
12. Since the storm, Star Boy had spent many days on his shell collection.
13. Morning Girl could not know how the boat and its occupants would change the lives of the island people.
14. Morning Girl wondered why the strangers were covered by those colorful leaves and cotton.
15. Perhaps they would tell her the meaning of these odd items.
16. The sun shone behind the canoe as the current gently cradled it.
17. Suddenly, Morning Girl saw her island through strangers' eyes.
18. How different the sparkling water and lush trees looked for the first time.
19. Morning Girl waved, as she had seen older people on her island do.
20. One stranger met Morning Girl's wave with a loud shout.
21. She explained who she was and gave her name and the names of her family members.
22. Morning Girl struggled for the correct words and invited the strangers ashore.
23. Although Morning Girl couldn't understand the strangers, she was sure they would all be friends before midday.
24. A meal shared among people usually created friendships.
25. As she turned up the path, Morning Girl observed the strangers in an argument.

Review: Exercise 2 Using Pronouns as Objects of Prepositions

Write the correct form of the pronoun in parentheses. Be sure each pronoun you choose makes sense in the sentence.

1. Morning Girl's visitors brought gifts to Star Boy and (her, she).
2. Morning Girl's story is based on the Native American people about (who, whom) Christopher Columbus wrote.
3. Columbus set sail from Spain in 1492 on a mission long cherished by (him, he).
4. Although Columbus believed in his journey, Queen Isabella was initially skeptical of the voyage planned by (him, he).
5. Columbus convinced the queen that his travels would bring riches and glory to (her, she).
6. Columbus thought that sailing west would bring India and its riches to (he, him).
7. As for the other explorers, most of (they, them) believed that India was to the east.
8. Columbus's men were discouraged, but they believed in (him, he).
9. At last the Caribbean Islands lay before (they, them).
10. The explorers met Native Americans who offered greetings to (they, them).

Review: Exercise 3 Writing Sentences with Pronouns as Objects of Prepositions

Write a pronoun form that would correctly complete the sentence.

1. He thought that these people occupied India, so "Indians" was the name Columbus gave to _____.
2. The Taino is the name they have given to _____.
3. The story could be based on Morning Girl and how change washed around _____ one day.
4. The Taino lived on the bounty of the land and sea around _____.
5. They caught giant turtles from the waters below _____.
6. Some Taino groups made hammocks from twisted cotton and slept in _____.
7. Each village had a chief, and its people looked to _____ for advice.
8. Because the chief was special, a special house was built for _____.
9. Therefore, when meeting Columbus, they gave ready welcome to _____.
10. Columbus started a colony among _____ before he left.

Review: Exercise 4   Identifying Adjective and Adverb Phrases

Write each prepositional phrase, and write *adjective phrase* or *adverb phrase* to tell how it is being used.

SAMPLE   She splashed through the surf.
ANSWER   through the surf (adverb phrase)

1. Morning Girl dove into the water.
2. In the distance, she heard an unfamiliar sound.
3. The strangers were wrapped in leaves and cotton.
4. Some wore shiny rocks on their heads.
5. Morning Girl swam boldly toward the exotic visitors.
6. She hid her laughter and momentarily plunged beneath the waves.
7. Inside her mind, Morning Girl silently addressed the sister she'd named She Listens.
8. She Wins the Race, Morning Girl's mother, had said a new sister would soon add her smiles to the family.
9. Morning Girl had awaited her baby sister with great curiosity.
10. When her mother asked, Morning Girl had a name for the baby sister.
11. Her mother said, "A person isn't real without a name."
12. Morning Girl wondered what was happening when her mother made an unexpected visit to Grandmother's house.
13. She'd known that Father was worried by Mother's absence.
14. Morning Girl was disappointed when only her mother returned from Grandmother's house.
15. Throughout all the months, she had imagined her sister as a companion.
16. There would always be a perfect understanding between them.
17. This sister wouldn't complain about carrying heavy fruit.
18. If Morning Girl misbehaved, her sister would forgive her without hesitation.
19. Surely this friendly sister would always listen to Morning Girl.
20. Morning Girl felt almost as if this sister were really standing beside her.
21. She paused suddenly under the morning sky.
22. She Listens would be the name of her new sister.
23. As Morning Girl approached the strangers, she shared her thoughts with She Listens.
24. She chose her words with great care so she would make no mistakes.
25. Morning Girl kicked through the water.

Review: Exercise 5 Using Pronouns as Objects of Prepositions

Write each conjunction, and write *compound subject*, *compound predicate*, *compound object of a preposition*, or *compound sentence* to tell what it forms.

SAMPLE   Their canoe was square, and it was shorter than any other canoes she had ever seen.

ANSWER   and (compound sentence)

1. She wanted to laugh, but she knew that would be impolite.
2. Morning Girl approached the strangers and called out a greeting.
3. The strangers either had come to visit or were lost.
4. In spite of all their dipping and pulling, the canoe moved very slowly.
5. Morning Girl and her brother Star Boy often played together.

Review: Exercise 6 Making Compound Subjects and Verbs Agree

Write each sentence, using the correct verb form from the parentheses. Then underline each coordinating or correlative conjunction.

SAMPLE   Neither Michael Dorris nor any other anthropologist (know, knows) all about the Taino people.

ANSWER   Neither Michael Dorris nor any other anthropologist knows all about the Taino people.

1. Christopher Columbus and the Taino people (was, were) real people.
2. Both Morning Girl and Star Boy (is, are) fictional characters.
3. Michael Dorris's Native American heritage and his anthropology training (give, gives) him strong ties to Morning Girl's story.
4. Neither history teachers nor history books (focus, focuses) often on the people who first met Christopher Columbus.
5. Both Native Americans and their experiences (is, are) overlooked.
6. *Morning Girl* and other works by Michael Dorris (remedy, remedies) this shortage of information.
7. Both Dorris's interests and background (influence, influences) his writing.
8. Sometimes both awards and high sales (greet, greets) Dorris's work.
9. He and Louise Erdrich (were, was) coauthors of *The Crown of Columbus.*
10. Neither the history nor the descriptions (fail, fails) to capture our interest.

Review: Exercise 7 Using Conjunctive Adverbs

Substitute the conjunctive adverb in parentheses for each of the underlined conjunctions. Then write each compound sentence. Be sure to punctuate the resulting sentences correctly.

SAMPLE Morning Girl swam near the ship, <u>but</u> the crew members didn't see her. (however)

ANSWER Morning Girl swam near the ship; however, the crew didn't see her.

1. She had never seen people dressed as they were, <u>and</u> she didn't know what to make of them. (furthermore)
2. Star Boy collected shells, <u>but</u> he lost them all in a storm. (however)
3. Morning Girl was hot <u>and</u> she swam. (so)
4. The strangers were oddly dressed, <u>and</u> she thought they must have come from a backward island. (therefore)
5. Morning Girl knew it was impolite to laugh at strangers, <u>and</u> Morning Girl didn't want them to think she was foolish. (besides)

Review: Exercise 8 Using Interjections

SAMPLE "_____!" cried Mother and Father when they discovered the necklaces I had carefully placed in their doorway.

ANSWER Look

1. "_____!" thought Star Boy's mother as she realized the storm was worsening and her son still had not come home.
2. "_____! It's not like Star Boy to disappear like this. Where can he be?" asked She Wins the Race for the hundredth time that day.
3. "_____! I hear footsteps coming up the trail," said the villager who was watching for Star Boy with us.
4. "_____! We found him. We found him," shouted my father when he saw Star Boy stride into the village.
5. "_____!" said Morning Girl to herself, not realizing how worried she had been about her brother.

Proofreading

The following passage is about the American artist Nereyda García-Ferraz, whose work appears below. Rewrite the passage, correcting the errors in spelling, grammar, and usage. Add any missing punctuation. There are ten errors.

Nereyda García-Ferraz

¹Nereyda García-Ferraz is born in Havana, Cuba, in 1954. ²She left Cuba behind she and immigrated to the United States when she was seventeen.

(continued)

Nereyda García-Ferraz, *Without Hearing—Without Seeing,* 1991

³García-Ferraz draws on her experence of living in Cuba for many of her works. ⁴Her images have specific meanings moreover they often tell a story.

⁵García-Ferraz titled this painting *Without Hearing—Without Seeing*, which in spanish is *Sin Oir—Sin Ver*. ⁶The word in the middle of the painting, *nadabas*, refer to swimming. ⁷Words and bright colors is often part of García-Ferraz's work. ⁸Both emotion and intellect is blended by she in her finished works of art.

Review: Exercise 10

Mixed Review

Write a preposition, conjunction, or interjection that would make sense in each sentence. Use the clue in parentheses as a guide in choosing the appropriate word or words.

1. Morning Girl's people called themselves the Taino; _____ , (conjunctive adverb) they are members of a larger group known as the Arawak people.
2. The Arawak lived on islands _____ (preposition) the Caribbean Sea.
3. These islands included three groups now called the Bahama Islands, the Greater Antilles, _____ (coordinating conjunction) the Lesser Antilles.
4. Since Christopher Columbus was searching for India when he sailed among _____ (object pronoun), he named these islands the West Indies.
5. Although Columbus is often considered the first European to reach America, current research suggests that he may have been _____ (compound preposition) the first.
6. Historians believe that Columbus first landed _____ (adverb phrase) in the Bahama Group.
7. Both Watling Island and Samana Cay _____ (present-tense linking verb) among the possible first landing sites.
8. _____! (interjection) There are no longer any Arawaks living in the Caribbean Islands.
9. Many died from European diseases; _____, (conjunctive adverb) the poor living conditions under Spanish enslavement killed many more.
10. The Arawak were primarily a _____ (adjective) people and went to battle only when necessary.

Writing Application

TIME

For more about the writing process, see **TIME Facing the Blank Page,** pp. 97-107.

Conjunctions and Prepositions in Writing

Sometimes the small words make a big difference. Notice how Gary Soto uses conjunctions and prepositions to link his ideas. As you read the passage below from *Living up the Street,* pay particular attention to the italicized words.

> I played *with* my grape knife, stabbing it into the ground, *but* stopped when Mother reminded me that I had better not lose it. I left the knife sticking up like a small, leafless plant. She then talked *about* school, the junior high I would be going to next fall, *and* then about Rick *and* Debra. . . . She stopped talking when she peeked *at* her watch, a bandless one she kept *in* her pocket.

Techniques with Conjunctions and Prepositions

Try to apply some of Gary Soto's writing techniques when you write and revise your own work.

❶ Stress the relationship between ideas or events with appropriate use of conjunctions, such as and, but, and or. Study the following:

EVENTS LINKED I played with my grape knife . . . I stopped when Mother reminded me.

SOTO'S VERSION I played with my grape knife, . . . *but* stopped when Mother reminded me.

❷ Use prepositions to add information to a sentence.

BLAND VERSION She talked.

SOTO'S VERSION She talked about school . . . .

Prepositions, Conjunctions, and Interjections

Practice Apply some of Soto's techniques by revising the following passage, using a separate sheet of paper. Add conjunctions or prepositions in the places indicated by carets (∧). Answers will vary.

Ethan suggested the latest horror film, ∧ Doreen said she was sure to get nightmares. They then discussed every film ∧ town until Doreen finally burst out, " ∧ I don't care which film we see. Let's just go!" ∧ the theater, the two friends still couldn't agree on anything. "Come on, Dorrie," insisted Ethan, "I'll sit ∧ the back, ∧ I can't see up close." The disputes began again the minute Doreen ∧ Ethan emerged ∧ the theater. "That was the most awful movie," pronounced Doreen.

Clauses and Complex Sentences

14.1 Sentences and Clauses

A **sentence** is a group of words that has a subject and a predicate and expresses a complete thought.

■ A **simple sentence** has one complete subject and one complete predicate.

The **complete subject** names whom or what the sentence is about. The **complete predicate** tells what the subject does or has. Sometimes it tells what the subject is or is like.

Complete Subject	Complete Predicate
The Cincinnati Reds	played their first baseball game in 1869.
This Ohio team	was the first professional baseball team.
The American League	played its first games in 1901.

■ A **compound sentence** contains two or more simple sentences. Each simple sentence is called a main clause.

■ A **main clause** has a subject and a predicate and can stand alone as a sentence.

Main clauses can be connected by a comma plus a conjunction, a semicolon, or a semicolon plus a conjunctive adverb. The conjunctive adverb is followed by a comma. In the compound sentences below, each main clause is in black; the connecting elements are highlighted in red.

Abner Doubleday supposedly invented baseball**, but** some reject this claim. (comma plus coordinating conjunction)

Alexander Joy Cartwright established rules**;** he was a good organizer. (semicolon)

Cartwright improved the game**; moreover,** many now regard him as the inventor of modern baseball. (semicolon plus conjunctive adverb)

Exercise 1   **Identifying Simple and Compound Sentences**

Identify each sentence as *simple* or *compound*.

1. Abner Doubleday or Alexander Cartwright invented baseball.
2. Cartwright wrote rules for the Knickerbocker Baseball Club.
3. The first modern baseball game took place in 1846.
4. One team brought the ball, and the other team provided the field.
5. Pitchers threw underhand, but their pitches were slow.
6. The first team with twenty-one runs would win the game.
7. Both teams played hard; however, only one team could win.
8. The game ended; two men were on third base.
9. The winners were the New York Nines.
10. The first teams were amateur; the players did not earn any money.
11. Baseball players were not paid until the end of the 1860s.
12. Today, North American baseball teams are divided into two leagues.
13. One league is the National League, and the other is the American League.
14. The National League was organized in 1876; it had ten teams at that time.
15. The American League was founded in 1900; its first season began in 1901.
16. The Montreal Expos became the first Canadian team in the National League.
17. Some teams change cities, but they usually keep their names.
18. The Boston Braves moved to Milwaukee and became the Milwaukee Braves.
19. Later, the Braves moved south to Atlanta.
20. The St. Louis Browns moved to Baltimore; they became the Orioles.

Exercise 2   **Punctuating Compound Sentences**

Write each sentence, and underline each main clause. Add a comma or a semicolon as needed. If it is a simple sentence, write *simple*.

1. There are many theories about baseball's origin but the truth remains a mystery.
2. Ancient people played bat-and-ball games therefore these games could be ancestors of baseball.
3. Did baseball begin as rounders or did it come from cricket?
4. The British played rounders in the early nineteenth century.
5. Baseball resembles cricket however the rules of the game are very different.
6. Cartwright established the rules but Henry Chadwick improved them.
7. Baseball has many serious and devoted fans.
8. Some fans attend baseball games some listen to the games on the radio.
9. You can watch a game on television or you can read about it in the newspaper.
10. More than fifty million fans attend major league baseball games each year.

A **main clause** has a subject and a predicate and can stand alone as a sentence.

Sometimes sentences have a main clause and a subordinate clause.

■ A **subordinate clause** is a group of words that has a subject and a predicate but does not express a complete thought and cannot stand alone as a sentence. It is always combined with a main clause.

■ A **complex sentence** has a main clause and one or more subordinate clauses.

In each complex sentence below, the main clause is in light type, and the subordinate clause is in dark type.

> Many basketball fans visit Springfield, Massachusetts, **which was the birthplace of basketball.**
>
> Basketball has increased in popularity **since it began in Springfield.**
>
> Many people know **that basketball is played by men and women.**

Subordinate clauses can function in three ways: as adjectives, as adverbs, or as nouns. In the examples above, the first sentence has an adjective clause that modifies the noun *Springfield,* the second has an adverb clause that modifies the verb *has increased,* and the third has a noun clause that is the direct object of the verb *know.* Such clauses can be used in the same ways that single-word adjectives, adverbs, and nouns are used.

The team waits on the sidelines, **while the substitute warms the bench.**

MAIN CLAUSE   SUBORDINATE CLAUSE

Identify the main clause in each sentence. Then label each sentence complex or simple.

1. Professional basketball is played during the winter, which was once a dull season for sports.
2. James Naismith developed the game when he saw a need for an indoor sport.
3. He was an instructor for the YMCA in Massachusetts.
4. A soccer ball was the ball that was first used.
5. The first baskets were two half-bushel peach baskets that were hung from balconies.
6. Naismith planned a game with little physical contact because he did not envision basketball as a rough sport.
7. The rules of the game were drafted in 1891.
8. There were thirteen rules that penalized players for rough conduct.
9. Before the first official game was played in 1892, probably no one outside of Naismith's YMCA had heard of basketball.
10. Basketball still follows most of Naismith's original thirteen rules.
11. Although originally nine players were on each team, now each team has five players on the court at one time.
12. In the early 1900s, the first women's teams were formed.
13. Do the rules of the game change when men and women play basketball together?
14. Although the rules for men's and women's basketball are similar, the ball is different.
15. The referee tosses the ball into the air.
16. After the referee tosses the ball, one player from each team jumps within the center circle.
17. Each player tries for the ball.
18. When a team scores, the opposing team takes the ball out of bounds from behind the base line.
19. The team then takes the ball to the basket that is at the other end of the court.
20. A team scores points when it gets the ball into its own basket.
21. The baskets at the top of ten-foot poles are usually called goals.
22. Behind each goal is a backboard, which can guide the ball down into the basket.
23. A special excitement belongs to basketball, which is a fast-moving game.
24. Basketball has won many fans who are dedicated basketball enthusiasts.
25. Many players who are popular have fan clubs.

14.3 Adjective Clauses

■ An **adjective clause** is a subordinate clause that modifies, or describes, a noun or pronoun in the main clause of a complex sentence.

> The Aqua-Lung, **which divers strap on,** holds oxygen.
> The divers breathe through a tube **that attaches to the tank.**

Each subordinate clause in dark type in these sentences is an adjective clause. An adjective clause adds information about a noun or pronoun in the main clause.

An adjective clause is usually introduced by a relative pronoun. Relative pronouns signal a subordinate clause, which cannot stand alone.

Relative Pronouns			
that	who	whose	what
which	whom	whoever	

An adjective clause can also begin with *where* or *when.*

> Divers search for reefs **where much sea life exists.**

A relative pronoun that begins an adjective clause can be the subject of the clause.

> Some divers prefer equipment **that is lightweight.**
> Willa is a new diver **who is taking lessons.**

In the first sentence above, *that* is the subject of the adjective clause. In the second sentence, *who* is the subject.

Identifying Adjective Clauses

Write each adjective clause and underline each relative pronoun. Write the noun or pronoun that each adjective clause modifies.

1. Scuba equipment, which is used for deep diving, gets its name from the phrase *self-contained underwater breathing apparatus.*
2. Jacques Cousteau, who is famous for underwater exploration, designed the Aqua-Lung.
3. Divers sometimes wear weights that they strap on.
4. Divers often wear wet suits, which are basic diving equipment.
5. Diving methods, which are now advanced, allow close observation of sea life.
6. Alexander the Great, who lived in the fourth century B.C., used a barrel for diving.
7. Leonardo da Vinci, who was a famous artist and inventor, designed a piece of diving equipment.
8. The equipment that da Vinci designed was a leather diving helmet.
9. The helmet, which had spikes on it for protection from monsters, had a long breathing tube.
10. At the end of the tube was a cork that kept the tube afloat.
11. Divers needed an apparatus that would protect them from high water pressure.
12. Diving bells were the earliest containers that were reliable.
13. The diving bells that were used in the 1500s were quite large.
14. Edmund Halley, who was an astronomer and mathematician, designed the first real diving bell in 1716.
15. Halley, whose most famous discovery was Halley's Comet, actually designed two very different diving bells.
16. One bell, which was made of wood, looked like an upside-down bucket.
17. Halley's other diving bell, which stood eight feet tall, could carry several divers.
18. It was the larger one that was made of lead.
19. Halley and four other divers could dive to a depth of ten fathoms, which is equal to sixty feet.
20. The five men, who were very brave, stayed at that depth for over an hour.
21. The only problem that they reported was a pain in their ears.
22. The pain that they felt was due to an increased pressure at that depth.
23. Auguste Piccard designed the bathyscaphe, which is a diving vehicle.
24. Jacques Piccard, who is Auguste's son, wanted to explore the Gulf Stream.
25. The Gulf Stream is a warm undersea current that flows through the Atlantic.

Essential and Nonessential Clauses

Read the sentence below. Is the adjective clause in dark type needed to make the meaning of the sentence clear?

The woman **who is near the pool** is a good swimmer.

The adjective clause here is essential, or necessary, to the meaning of the sentence. The clause identifies which woman is a good swimmer.

The swimmer **who is in lane six** won last time.

Our team, **which is undefeated,** is favored to win the championship.

■ An **essential clause** is an adjective clause that is necessary to make the meaning of the sentence clear. Do not use commas to set off an essential clause from the rest of the sentence.

Notice, however, the adjective clauses in the sentences below.

Swimmers enjoy the pool, **which is extremely clean.**

The pool, **which is open all week,** is never crowded.

In the sentences above, the adjective clauses are set off by commas. The clauses are nonessential, or not necessary, to identify which pool the writer means. The clauses give only additional information about the noun that they modify.

■ A nonessential clause is an adjective clause that is not necessary to make the meaning of the sentence clear. Use commas to set off a nonessential clause from the rest of the sentence.

Did you see the meet **that** our team won yesterday? (essential)

The meet, **which** began late, ended well after dark. (nonessential)

Exercise 5   Identifying Essential and Nonessential Clauses

Write each adjective clause. Identify the adjective clause as *essential* or *nonessential.*

1. The athletes whom I most admire are swimmers.
2. Swimming, which requires strength and stamina, is a challenging sport.
3. A swimmer who wishes to participate in serious swimming competitions must practice constantly.
4. Some swimmers are nervous before competitions, which are usually referred to as swim meets.
5. Our women's team, whose record stands, enters the pool area.
6. The team members, who hope for a win today, listen to the coach's advice.
7. Each race that the team members swim is called a heat.
8. The contestants, who are wearing special racing suits, will swim eight lengths of the pool in the first heat.
9. The racers stand on the starting blocks that are at the far end of the pool.
10. The signal that starts each race is a gunshot.

Exercise 6   Punctuating Essential and Nonessential Clauses

Write each sentence and underline each adjective clause. Identify each as *essential* or *nonessential,* and add commas as needed.

1. In the 1800s, the Australian crawl which replaced the breast stroke in popularity came into use.
2. In the 1920s, Johnny Weissmuller whose other career was acting in movies perfected the front crawl.
3. The skillful athlete who portrayed Tarzan in twelve movies was known to many people as a swimmer rather than an actor.
4. Weissmuller whose swimming ability was quickly recognized began swimming at a young age.
5. He worked hard for the three gold medals that he won at the 1924 Olympics.
6. The two additional gold medals that Weissmuller won at the 1928 Olympic Games probably made all his long hours of practice seem worthwhile.
7. Weissmuller was the athlete who set sixty-five United States and world records.
8. In 1927 he swam to a new record which was 100 yards in 51 seconds.
9. In 1968 Jim Counsilman studied techniques that swimmers were using.
10. Counsilman whose observations were later published became a world-famous coach.

14.5 Adverb Clauses

■ An **adverb clause** is a subordinate clause that often modifies, or describes, the verb in the main clause of a complex sentence.

An adverb clause tells *how, when, where, why,* or *under what conditions* the action occurs.

After she bought safe equipment, Lee explored the undersea world.

Scuba divers wear tanks **because they cannot breathe underwater.**

In the first sentence above, the adverb clause *After she bought safe equipment* modifies the verb explored. The adverb clause tells when Lee explored the undersea world. In the second sentence, the adverb clause *because they cannot breathe underwater* modifies the verb wear. The adverb clause tells why scuba divers wear tanks.

An adverb clause is introduced by a subordinating conjunction. Subordinating conjunctions signal a subordinate clause, which cannot stand alone.

Subordinating Conjunctions			
after	before	though	whenever
although	if	unless	where
as	since	until	whereas
because	than	when	wherever

You usually do not use a comma before an adverb clause that comes at the end of a sentence. However, you do use a comma after an adverb clause that introduces a sentence.

Exercise 7   Identifying Adverb Clauses

Write each sentence. Underline each adverb clause and circle each subordi-nating conjunction. Draw an arrow to the verb that each adverb clause modifies.

1. Divers wear wet suits and rubber fins when they swim.
2. They wear wet suits because the water might be cold.
3. Divers wear masks since they need them for underwater vision.
4. After you dive for the first time, you will have more confidence.
5. Divers wear weighted belts when they want to stay underwater for a long time.
6. When they return to the surface, divers should rise slowly and carefully.
7. Divers can suffer the bends if they rise to the surface too quickly.
8. Because this condition can occur, divers must learn how to control the ascent.
9. Although they sometimes are in a hurry, divers must rise slowly.
10. Divers should work with partners whenever they dive in unfamiliar waters.
11. Unless she has a buddy with her, a diver should not make a dive.
12. Because it is so mysterious, the deep sea fascinates people.
13. Interest in the deep seas began before Alexander the Great first went diving.
14. He sat inside a glass barrel as sailors lowered it into the sea.
15. Undersea quests progressed after Alexander the Great made his barrel dives.
16. Auguste Piccard flew in a balloon before he invented the bathyscaphe.
17. After he designed this craft, Piccard and his son Jacques descended in it.
18. Jacques used the bathyscaphe when he explored the Gulf of Mexico.
19. Until Jacques Costeau invented the Aqua-Lung, deep-sea diving was difficult.
20. Study of the oceans became much easier after scuba gear was invented.

Exercise 8   Punctuating Adverb Clauses

Write each sentence. Underline each adverb clause, and add a comma as needed.

1. Although it may not seem easy diving is not difficult for most people.
2. Hopeful divers can enroll in diving school when they are ready to learn.
3. Before they learn scuba diving students should learn snorkeling.
4. Trainers teach about the bends since this condition can be life-threatening.
5. The bends can occur when a diver surfaces too quickly.
6. If they surface slowly divers can avoid this problem.
7. After they complete long training and many practice dives divers are certified.
8. Can certified divers dive wherever they like?
9. New divers should dive only 130 feet since deeper dives can be dangerous.
10. If you dive in Belize you will have the ultimate diving experience.

14.6 Noun Clauses

■ A **noun clause** is a subordinate clause used as a noun.

Notice how the noun in dark type in the sentence below can be replaced by a clause.

> **Players** must skate extremely well.
>
> **Whoever plays ice hockey** must skate extremely well.

The clause in dark type, like the noun it replaces, is the subject of the sentence. Since this kind of clause acts as a noun, it is called a noun clause.

You can use a noun clause in the same ways that you can use any noun—as a subject, a direct object, an object of a preposition, or a predicate noun. With most sentences containing noun clauses, you could replace the noun clause with the word it, and the sentence would still make sense.

How Noun Clauses Are Used	
Subject	**What makes ice hockey exciting** is the speed.
Direct Object	Players know **that the game can be dangerous.**
Object of a Preposition	Victory goes to **whoever makes more goals.**
Predicate Noun	This rink is **where the teams will play.**

Following are some words that can introduce noun clauses.

Words That Introduce Noun Clauses		
how, however	where, whether	whom, whomever
that	which, whichever	whose
what, whatever	who, whoever	why, when

Exercise 9   Identifying Noun Clauses

Write each noun clause.

1. That ice hockey began in Canada is not surprising.
2. Where the sport began is not easily verified.
3. Three different cities claim that they hosted the first hockey game.
4. Most people believe that the game was played in Jamaica as early as 1830.
5. The fact is that the first recorded game occurred in Montreal around 1875.
6. You could argue that Canadians are still among the best hockey players.
7. There have been some changes in how ice hockey is played.
8. Whoever plays hockey today must wear protective equipment.
9. Do you know which sport is most dangerous?
10. Some people question whether hockey has to be so dangerous.

Exercise 10   Identifying Noun Clauses and Their Use

Write each noun clause, and label it *subject, direct object, object of a preposition,* or *predicate noun.*

1. Most people realize that ice hockey is a game of action.
2. Did you know that hockey is the fastest of all team sports?
3. Fast starts, stops, and turns are what the game demands.
4. What the players pursue is the puck.
5. Where they want to put the puck is inside the other team's goal.
6. That the puck often moves over one hundred miles an hour may surprise you.
7. The puck's speed is why hockey players must react so quickly.
8. The goalies know that their role is critical.
9. The goalie is who must block the other team's slap shots.
10. What is important to the team is a goalie's dependability.
11. Chris will demonstrate how a goalie drops to the ice and blocks shots.
12. Whoever stands and blocks shots is called a stand-up goalie.
13. The Vezina Trophy is awarded to whoever is the best goalie of the year.
14. Whoever asks can learn for whom the trophy was named.
15. The answer is that the trophy is awarded in honor of George Vezina.
16. Each year the Stanley Cup Playoffs determine which team is best.
17. That no team won the Stanley Cup in 1919 baffled me.
18. The truth is that a flu epidemic prematurely ended the finals.
19. How players respond can be crucial to the game.
20. Players must respond quickly to whatever happens.

Grammar Review

CLAUSES AND COMPLEX SENTENCES

In this passage, Mickey Mantle tells of his weaknesses in playing the field. The annotations show some of the types of clauses and sentences covered in this unit.

Literature Model

from The Education of a Baseball Player
by Mickey Mantle

My fielding, I knew, was often sorry. I had learned to charge a ground ball well and if I could get an angle on a ball, I could field it cleanly and get off a fast throw. My arm was unusually strong, and my throws would really hum across the diamond. But when a ball came straight at me, I was often undone. Somehow it was almost impossible for me to judge the speed or the bounce of a ground ball like that. I might back off foolishly, letting the ball play me, and then lose it altogether. Or I would turn my head as it reached me, and the ball would skip by or bounce right into my face. I carried around uncounted fat lips in that day from stopping ground balls with my mouth. And the more often I got hit, the more I would shy at such a ball. Even the balls I fielded cleanly did not always mean an out, for I had a habit of rejoicing so in the strength of my arm that I would not take the time to get a sure eye on the target. I would just let fly with my full strength, and often the ball would sail untouched into the stands.

> Main clause

> Complex sentence

> Adverb clause

> Adjective clause

> Compound sentence

Clauses and Complex Sentences

Grammar Review

Write whether each sentence is *simple* or *compound*. If it is compound, write it and add commas where needed.

SAMPLE Mickey Mantle's father loved baseball and he shared this love with his son.

ANSWER Mickey Mantle's father loved baseball, and he shared this love with his son. (compound)

1. As a young boy, Mantle frequently played ball from morning to night.
2. His father gave him a professional-model baseball glove for Christmas one year and he cared for it devotedly.
3. Mantle considered himself the worst player on his team.
4. His fielding was erratic and other boys hit better than he did.
5. Mantle was known for not only his powerful hitting but also his fast running.
6. Mickey Mantle was a superb base runner but he stole few bases.
7. Base running and base stealing are two different skills.
8. A player may be a good base stealer but he may not be a good base runner.
9. Players like Ty Cobb were good at both.
10. Lou Brock was a great base stealer and he was an excellent base runner.

Review: Exercise 2 — Punctuating Simple and Compound Sentences

Write each sentence, and underline each main clause. Add a comma or a semicolon as needed.

SAMPLE He stole fewer bases than Mantle each season but he was considered an excellent base runner.

ANSWER He stole fewer bases than Mantle each season, but he was considered an excellent base runner.

1. Joe DiMaggio's father was a fisherman in San Francisco.
2. Joe did not like the smell of fish he chose baseball as a career.
3. His father wasn't thrilled but he wished his son luck.
4. Another DiMaggio son also played baseball.
5. Vince DiMaggio earned his living as a baseball player and he introduced Joe to the game.

Clauses and Complex Sentences

Review: Exercise 3 Distinguishing Between Simple and Complex Sentences

Label each sentence as *simple* or *complex*. If it is complex, write the subordinate clause.

SAMPLE   When Willie Mays joined the New York Giants, Mickey Mantle was playing center field for the American League Yankees.

ANSWER   (complex) When Willie Mays joined the New York Giants,

1. In the 1950s, the Giants were the National League team from New York.
2. Willie Mays was twenty when he became a Giants player in 1951.
3. Mays played center field, which requires a powerful arm.
4. The arrival of Mays caused a controversy among baseball fans.
5. Fans argued all the time about who was the better player.
6. Some said that Mantle, with his speed and power, was the better of the two.
7. Mays, however, may have been the greatest player of all time.
8. Since Mays was a terrific all-around player, many agree with that opinion.
9. Injuries hindered Mickey Mantle's performance throughout his career.
10. Although he was often in pain, Mantle played well.

Review: Exercise 4 Distinguishing Between Compound and Complex Sentences

Label each sentence as *compound* or *complex*. If it is complex, write the subordinate clause.

1. New York State has a long baseball history, and it has had many teams.
2. The teams that played for New York include the Yankees, Dodgers, and Giants.
3. When the Dodgers and the Giants moved to California, New York had no National League team.
4. The Mets, which is a National League team, was formed in 1962.
5. Fans agree that some of baseball's best teams have come from New York.
6. Did you know that from 1936 to 1964 the Yankees won sixteen World Series?
7. The Yankees had great teams then, but perhaps the best was the 1961 team.
8. That team had incredibly talented players; Mickey Mantle was one of them.
9. Roger Maris, who came to the Yankees in 1959, also starred on that team.
10. Maris and Mantle both hit more than fifty home runs that season, and they soon became known as the M & M boys.

Grammar Review

Review: Exercise 5   **Identifying Adjective Clauses**

Write each sentence. Underline each adjective clause once and each relative pronoun twice. Circle the noun that each adjective clause modifies.

SAMPLE   In 1955 New York State had another team that is considered one of baseball's best.

ANSWER   In 1955 New York State had another (team) that is considered one of baseball's best.

1. You must mean the 1955 Brooklyn Dodgers, who later moved to Los Angeles.
2. Branch Rickey, whose courage and foresight brought amazing talent to the Dodgers' organization, was the manager of the team then.
3. It was one particularly courageous act that brought fame to Branch Rickey.
4. Branch Rickey signed Jackie Robinson, who was African American.
5. The major league color line, which had restricted African American players to the Negro League, was broken by Jackie Robinson in 1947.
6. Robinson soon proved his worth in the face of the jeers that surrounded him.
7. Insults that came from fans and opposing players surely must have hurt.
8. Jackie responded with the quiet dignity that marked his life and career.
9. Pee Wee Reese, who was a teammate, openly supported Jackie on the field.
10. In 1955 Robinson and the Dodgers won the World Series against the Yankees, whose roster included the young slugger Mickey Mantle.

Review: Exercise 6   **Identifying Essential and Nonessential Clauses**

Write each adjective clause. Label the clause *essential* or *nonessential,* and add commas as needed.

1. Mickey was named after the catcher Mickey Cochrane who made it into the Hall of Fame.
2. Mantle's father who worked in the lead mines had played semi-pro ball.
3. The baseball glove that his father gave him one year cost twenty-two dollars.
4. Mantle who was named the Most Valuable Player three times also played in sixteen All-Star games.
5. Mantle hit 536 home runs during the years that he played with the Yankees.

Review: Exercise 7   Identifying Adverb Clauses

Write each sentence. Underline the adverb clause, and circle the word that the clause modifies. Add commas where needed.

SAMPLE   When Mantle joined the Yankees Casey Stengel was the manager.
ANSWER   <u>When Mantle joined the Yankees,</u> Casey Stengel (was) the manager.

1. When Mantle was just an infant his father Mutt put baseballs in his crib.
2. Mutt talked baseball to his infant son whenever he got the chance.
3. Mantle considered himself lucky because his father pushed and encouraged him.
4. Mantle was only nineteen years old when the Yankees signed him.
5. Mantle hit poorly because he was confused by major league pitchers.
6. Since he was struggling the Yankees sent him down to the minor leagues.
7. Although he was now a professional Mantle still needed his father's advice.
8. Mantle quickly improved after his father gave him good advice.
9. While he played for the Yankees they were the dominant team in baseball.
10. Mantle was elected to the Hall of Fame as soon as he became eligible.

Review: Exercise 8   Identifying Noun Clauses

Write each noun clause, and label it *subject, direct object, object of a preposition,* or *predicate noun.*

SAMPLE   Mantle's father knew that baseball could provide a future for his son.
ANSWER   that baseball could provide a future for his son; direct object

1. What made the young Mickey Mantle so extraordinary was his speed.
2. His coaches were amazed at how quickly he sped around the bases.
3. Opposing players knew that Mantle's speed was practically unbeatable.
4. What made Mantle consult a doctor at age fifteen was an injured ankle.
5. Mickey's doctor discovered that Mickey had a serious bone infection.
6. The doctor's conclusion was that Mickey would never play baseball again.
7. Mickey could hardly believe what he had heard.
8. Time and history proved how wrong the doctor was.
9. Whoever knows about Mantle's illustrious career knows the truth.
10. Courage and determination were what kept Mantle's career hopes alive.

Grammar Review

Review: Exercise 9	Writing Complex Sentences

Combine each pair of sentences below, using the relative pronoun or subordinating conjunction in parentheses. Put the subordinate clause where it makes sense, and add commas where they are needed.

1. I saw some films about baseball. I was home sick last week. (while)
2. One film was *Eight Men Out*. It was about the 1919 "Black Sox" scandal. (which)
3. Allegedly, eight players took money to lose the World Series. They were members of the Chicago White Sox. (who)
4. The eighth man never admitted guilt in the scheme. The scheme remained a black mark on the history of baseball. (which)
5. The movie was good. I didn't like it as much as others. (although)
6. *Field of Dreams* was my favorite. It starred Kevin Costner. (which)
7. Costner is an Iowa farmer. His character's name is Ray Kinsella. (whose)
8. Ray hears a voice. It says "If you build it, he will come." (that)
9. Ray ponders the mysterious message. He makes a discovery. (as)
10. The "he" in the message refers to Shoeless Joe Jackson. Jackson was one of the eight men in the Chicago "Black Sox" scandal. (who)
11. All the acquitted Chicago players come out of Ray's cornfield. Ray builds the baseball diamond. (when)
12. These men play baseball. These men have been dead for years. (who)
13. Another good film is *A League of Their Own*. You should see it. (that)
14. This story is about a special time in baseball during World War II. Women played professional baseball then. (when)
15. Many of the male players had been drafted into the armed forces. A women's professional baseball league was formed. (because)
16. The All-American Girls Professional Baseball League enlisted top female athletes. It was in existence from 1943 to 1954. (which)
17. Women had played baseball in school and at the amateur level. They had never played professional ball. (although)
18. The film's producer, Penny Marshall, interviewed some of the actual players at a ceremony in Cooperstown. She made the movie. (after)
19. The women must have enjoyed seeing the movie. Their story is also told in a book by Sue Macy titled *A Whole New Ball Game*. (whose)
20. These women put up with taunts and jeers from men. The women loved baseball and were excellent players. (who)

Review: Exercise 10

Proofreading

The following passage is about the American artist Morris Kantor, whose work appears below. Rewrite the passage, correcting the errors in spelling, capitalization, grammar, and usage. Add any missing punctuation. There are ten errors.

Morris Kantor

[1]Morris Kantor was an american painter who lived during the early part of this century. [2]Although Kantor received formal art training his style seems primitive.

[3]*Baseball at Night,* which apears below shows a group of people enjoying a game of semiprofessional baseball. [4]Mutt Mantle, who was Mickey Mantle's father was playing baseball at about the same time and he probably played under similiar conditions.

[5]Mickey Mantle who became an American hero came from the world of small towns and sandlot baseball that Kantor depicts in *Baseball at Night.* [6]Although Spavinaw, Oklahoma, may not have had night baseball it did produce at least one outstanding major league player.

Morris Kantor, *Baseball at Night,* 1934

Clauses and Complex Sentences

Grammar Review

Review: Exercise 11

Mixed Review

Write whether each sentence is *simple, compound,* or *complex.* If a sentence is complex, write the subordinate clause. Then indicate whether the clause is an *adverb clause,* an *adjective clause,* or a *noun clause.*

¹While three-year-old Mickey Mantle was learning about baseball in Oklahoma, another future baseball star was born. ²He was Roberto Clemente from Carolina, Puerto Rico. ³Roberto, who had six older brothers and sisters, was shy as a young boy. ⁴In spite of this, Roberto eagerly helped others whenever he could. ⁵Roberto also had strong leadership qualities, which helped him enlist the aid of others. ⁶Young Roberto learned about baseball from his older brothers. ⁷They shared with him what they knew about the game. ⁸Roberto had very large hands; he could easily catch a ball. ⁹As his love for baseball grew, his talent also grew. ¹⁰The manager of a softball team for which sixteen-year-old Roberto played recognized this talent. ¹¹The manager believed that Roberto could be a professional. ¹²When major league scouts saw Roberto, they agreed. ¹³The boy had a powerful and accurate throwing arm; he also hit well. ¹⁴Clemente, whose major league career began with the Brooklyn Dodgers, ended up with the Pittsburgh Pirates. ¹⁵He played there until he died on Christmas Eve in 1972. ¹⁶At the time he was thirty-eight. ¹⁷The plane in which he was traveling crashed. ¹⁸He and others were on their way to Nicaragua, where there had been a terrible earthquake. ¹⁹The plane was carrying relief supplies. ²⁰Roberto Clemente had reached out to others all his life; this was true even at the time of his death.

Writing Application

TIME

For more about the writing process, see **TIME Facing the Blank Page**, pp. 97-107.

Clauses in Writing

In *Silent Spring* Rachel Carson uses clauses to expand on her description of the natural world. Examine the passage, focusing on the italicized clauses.

The countryside was, in fact, famous for the abundance and variety of its bird life, and *when the flood of migrants was pouring through in spring and fall* people traveled from great distances to observe them. Others came to fish the streams, *which flowed clear and cold out of the hills and contained shady pools where trout lay*. So it had been from the days many years ago *when the first settlers raised their houses, sank their wells, and built their barns.*

Techniques with Clauses

Try to apply some of Rachel Carson's writing techniques when you write.

❶ Notice Carson's use of elaboration with the addition of an adjective clause.

WITHOUT EXTRA DETAIL Others came to fish the streams.

CARSON'S VERSION Others came to fish the streams, *which flowed clear and cold out of the hills* . . .

❷ Emphasize the relationship between events and ideas in your writing by combining related sentences into compound sentences. Compare the following:

WEAKER CONNECTION The countryside was, in fact, famous for the abundance . . . and variety of its bird life. People traveled to observe them.

CARSON'S VERSION The countryside was, in fact, famous for the abundance . . . of its bird life, *and when the flood of migrants was pouring through in spring and fall* people traveled . . .

Clauses and Complex Sentences

Practice Apply some of these techniques as you revise the following passage, using a separate sheet of paper. Reorganize or reword the sentences, combining clauses as appropriate to show the relationships among your ideas.

Ben had never used a bank account before. Today he made his first deposit. The Bank It! program was new at Ben's school. The students were learning all about deposits and withdrawals. Ben was eager to learn banking. He hoped to save enough money to buy a new bike. He'd been keeping his savings at home. They were stashed in a shoe box under the bed. The box was getting full. Ben knew that his money would be safer in the school bank.

Participles and Participial Phrases

A present participle is formed by adding *-ing* to the verb. A past participle is usually formed by adding *-ed* to the verb. A participle can act as the main verb in a verb phrase or as an adjective to describe, or modify, nouns or pronouns.

> The player has **kicked** the ball. [main verb in a verb phrase]
> The **kicked** ball soared. [adjective modifying *ball*]

Sometimes a participle that is used as an adjective is part of a phrase. This kind of phrase is called a participial phrase.

> **Cheering for the home team,** the fans were on their feet.
>
> The ball **kicked by Donnell** soared into the goal.

■ A **participial phrase** is a group of words that includes a participle and other words that complete its meaning.

A participial phrase that is placed at the beginning of a sentence is always set off with a comma.

The **kicked** ball soared . . .

> **Running for the ball,** a player slipped in the mud.

Other participial phrases may or may not need commas. If the phrase is necessary to identify the modified word, do not set it off with commas. If the phrase simply gives additional information about the modified word, set it off with commas.

. . . into the goal.

> The player **kicking the ball** is Donnell.
> Donnell, **kicking the ball,** scored the final point.

A participial phrase can appear before or after the word it describes. Place the phrase as close as possible to the modified word; otherwise, the meaning of the sentence may be unclear.

Exercise 1   Identifying Participles

Write each participle. Write whether it is used as a *verb* or as an *adjective.*

1. Soccer can be a challenging game.
2. Many young people are participating in the sport.
3. The size of the playing field for soccer may vary.
4. Have rules for the sport changed over the years?
5. A player on our team has scored the winning goal.

Exercise 2   Using Participial Phrases

Write each sentence. Underline each participial phrase. Then draw two lines under the word that the phrase describes. Add commas if needed to set off the phrase.

1. Attracting huge crowds soccer is a popular sport.
2. The game consists of two teams competing for goals.
3. Playing within certain areas the goalkeepers can touch the ball with their hands.
4. For other players, the only contact permitted by the rules is with their feet, heads, or bodies.
5. The two teams playing the game kick off.
6. The teams moving almost constantly during play kick the ball back and forth.
7. Varying their formations players move about the field.
8. By the 1800s, English schools playing a similar game had drawn up the first set of rules.
9. Spreading throughout the world soccer became especially popular in Europe and Latin America in the late 1800s.
10. Spectators standing on the sidelines cheered the teams.
11. Representing two rival towns the teams took their places on the field.
12. Last year's champions defending their title played energetically.
13. Blowing a whistle the referee started the game.
14. The team dressed in blue tried to advance the ball toward the goal.
15. Kicking the ball out of bounds the blue team lost its advantage.
16. The team's star player dribbling the ball toward the goal suddenly tripped.
17. An opponent rushing toward the ball prevented a goal.
18. Passing the ball from player to player the team traveled down the field.
19. The goalkeeper jumping as high as possible was unable to catch the ball.
20. Kicking the ball high into the air a player on the blue team finally scored a goal.

15.2 Gerunds and Gerund Phrases

The previous lesson explains that the present participle may be used as a verb or as an adjective. It may also be used as a noun, in which case it is called a *gerund*.

The **playing** field is one hundred yards long. [adjective]

Playing is our favorite activity. [gerund]

■ A **gerund** is a verb form that ends in *-ing* and is used as a noun.

Like other nouns a gerund can serve as the simple subject of a sentence. It can also be a direct object or the object of a preposition.

Blocking requires strength. [subject]

The athletes enjoy **exercising.** [direct object]

They maintain endurance by **running.** [object of a preposition]

■ A **gerund phrase** is a group of words that includes a gerund and other words that complete its meaning.

Kicking the ball takes skill.

A team tries **scoring a touchdown.**

A touchdown results from **moving the ball across the goal.**

You can identify the three functions of *-ing* verb forms if you remember that a present participle can serve as a verb, as an adjective, or as a noun, in which case it is called a gerund.

The Giants are **winning** the game. [main verb]

The **winning** team scores the most points. [adjective]

Winning is always exciting. [gerund]

Identifying Verbals

Copy each underlined word, and write *main verb, adjective,* or *gerund* to show how it is used in the sentence.

1. The coach or the captain chooses <u>playing</u> strategies.
2. The quarterback does not like <u>guessing</u> the next play.
3. The team members are <u>hoping</u> for a victory.
4. <u>Scoring</u> in football can occur in four different ways.
5. A team earns six points by <u>crossing</u> the opponent's goal line.

Exercise 4 **Identifying Gerunds**

Write each gerund or gerund phrase. Then write *subject, direct object,* or *object of a preposition* to show how it is used in the sentence.

1. A win requires earning more points than the opponent.
2. Kicking earns points in two different ways in this sport.
3. A team earns three points by kicking a field goal.
4. Teams also try converting for one point after a touchdown.
5. Defending the team's own goal is crucial.
6. A team's defense features tackling.
7. Blocking is another important element of a good defense.
8. Passing makes football exciting.
9. Testing your skills is an important part of football.
10. Skilled players increase spectators' enjoyment by adding dramatic action to the game.
11. Watching football on television is a favorite pastime for many people.
12. The defense tries to keep its opponents from scoring a touchdown.
13. Enforcing the rules is the referee's job.
14. The home team advanced by passing the ball toward the goal line.
15. Playing well involves speed and teamwork.
16. Shoes with cleats prevent slipping.
17. Players can improve their skills with good coaching.
18. A coach's work involves deciding which positions team members will play and what plays will be used.
19. After preparing the game plan, a coach sometimes discusses ideas with the team's quarterback.
20. Kicking off is decided by flipping a coin.

15.3 Infinitives and Infinitive Phrases

Another verb form that may function as a noun is an infinitive.

To referee requires training.

Trainees learn **to referee.**

■ An infinitive is formed from the word *to* together with the base form of a verb. It is often used as a noun in a sentence.

How can you tell whether the word *to* is a preposition or part of an infinitive? If the word *to* comes immediately before a verb, it is part of the infinitive.

Those young players want **to win.** [infinitive]

The coach is pointing **to the pitcher.** [prepositional phrase]

INFINITIVE

The player starts **to run.**

She runs
to home base.

PREPOSITIONAL
PHRASE

In the first sentence, the words in dark type work together as a noun to name what the players want. In the second sentence, the words in dark type are a prepositional phrase used as an adverb that tells *where* the coach is pointing.

Since infinitives function as nouns, they can be subjects and direct objects.

To referee demands patience. [subject]

Athletes often try **to argue.** [direct object]

■ An **infinitive phrase** is a group of words that includes an infinitive and other words that complete its meaning.

A player may try **to influence the call.**

To go to every game of the season is my dream.

Exercise 5 Identifying Infinitives

Write each underlined group of words and label it *infinitive* or *prepositional phrase.*

1. <u>To win</u> is the dream of every World Series player.
2. The top team in each division goes <u>to the play-offs.</u>
3. The two winners are invited <u>to the World Series.</u>
4. <u>To excel</u> is each team's goal at these games.
5. Millions of people plan <u>to watch</u> the World Series on television.
6. We went <u>to a baseball game</u> last Saturday.
7. Would you like <u>to become</u> a professional player?
8. <u>To begin</u> by playing Little League is good.
9. As players improve, they move from the rookie <u>to the minor leagues.</u>
10. <u>To sponsor</u> Little League teams, local organizations pay for uniforms.

Exercise 6 Identifying Infinitive Phrases

Write each infinitive or infinitive phrase. Label it *subject* or *direct object.*

1. To play in the American or National League is an accomplishment.
2. Most players prefer to play home games.
3. To leave means losing the support of all the home town fans.
4. To understand baseball requires knowledge of the structure of the game.
5. The players want to improve their strategies.
6. We've decided to root for the American League team in the World Series.
7. To attend a World Series game is one of my goals.
8. I want to go to Dodger Stadium.
9. Have you learned to pitch a fastball?
10. People began to play baseball in the 1800s.
11. Players learn to hit the ball.
12. To catch the ball is also very difficult.
13. The catcher needs to wear a mask, a chest protector, and shin guards.
14. To throw a variety of pitches is the goal of every pitcher.
15. Players need to check the batting order.
16. When the ball is hit, the player tries to run.
17. When the bases are loaded, the runner hopes to advance.
18. Try to tag the base!
19. To reach home plate is a wonderful feeling.
20. Would you like to join our team?

Grammar Review

VERBALS

In 1960 Wilma Rudolph became the first American woman to win three gold medals in track and field at the Olympic games. Shortly before she competed in her first Olympics, however, Rudolph was defeated at a regional high school track meet in Tuskegee, Alabama. In the following passage from "Wilma," an autobiographical essay, Rudolph describes how the defeat at Tuskegee motivated her to win in the future. The passage has been annotated to show some of the types of verbals covered in this unit.

Literature Model

from **Wilma**
by Wilma Rudolph

I ran and ran and ran every day, and I acquired this sense of determination, this sense of spirit that I would never, never give up, no matter what else happened. That day at Tuskegee had a tremendous effect on me inside. That's all I ever thought about. Some days I just wanted to go out and die. I just moped around and felt sorry for myself. Other days I'd go out to the track with fire in my eyes and imagine myself back at Tuskegee, **beating them all**. Losing as badly as I did had an impact on my personality. **Winning all the time in track** had given me confidence; I felt like a winner. But I didn't feel like a winner any more after Tuskegee. My confidence was shattered, and I was thinking the only way I could put it all together was **to get back the next year and wipe them all out**.

> **Participial phrase used as adjective**

> **Gerund phrase used as subject**

> **Infinitive phrase**

Grammar Review

Review: Exercise 1   Identifying Participial Phrases

Write each sentence. Underline each participial phrase. Then draw two lines under the word that the phrase describes. Add commas as needed.

SAMPLE   The runner refusing to let her defeat stop her continued to train.
ANSWER   The <u>runner,</u> <u>refusing to let her defeat stop her</u>, continued to train.

1. Rudolph having won two gold medals tried for a third in the 400-meter relay.
2. Crouched at the starting line the runners waited for the signal to start.
3. Leading the field the first runner streaked over the track.
4. Taking the baton the second runner raced away.
5. One runner reaching for the baton nearly let it drop.
6. The spectators watched Rudolph pulling ahead.
7. The runner taking one final stride lunged through the tape.
8. Trying to break a record the runner felt exhilarated.
9. Roaring wildly the crowd rose from their seats.
10. Gasping for breath she knew she could win.

Review: Exercise 2   Using Participles and Participial Phrases

Rewrite each sentence, inserting the participle or participial phrase in parentheses. Use commas as needed.

SAMPLE   Rudolph gained confidence. (running hard)
ANSWER   Running hard, Rudolph gained confidence.

1. The track meet at Tuskegee shocked the runner. (defeated)
2. Rudolph felt like quitting. (shattered by her defeat)
3. She briefly thought she might give up the sport. (discouraged at her failure)
4. She dreamed of winning the meet. (imagining herself back at Tuskegee)
5. The athlete never gave up. (fiercely determined)
6. She realized that a champion can try again, even after a defeat. (crushing)
7. Rudolph helped the 1956 Olympic relay team win a bronze medal. (having trained for just a year)
8. The young woman gained the respect of her coaches. (a talented athlete)
9. Rudolph won a trophy. (honoring her achievements)
10. Rudolph was pursued by reporters. (hoping for an interview)

Review: Exercise 3   Identifying Gerund Phrases

Write each gerund phrase. Then write *subject, direct object,* or *object of a preposition* to tell how it is being used.

1. Having polio when she was young left Rudolph unable to walk without a special shoe.
2. Rudolph proved her determination by learning to walk after her illness.
3. Her Olympic running seemed like a miracle.
4. She had also tried playing basketball.
5. Before setting a world record at the Olympics, Rudolph ran many practice races.
6. After winning her third gold medal in the 1960 Olympics, Rudolph returned home a hero.
7. She anticipated helping other women become runners.
8. Winning a gold medal is not all that matters in the Olympics.
9. Taking part is a great honor.
10. Participating in the Olympics is the high point of an athlete's career.

Review: Exercise 4   Using Gerunds and Gerund Phrases

Write a sentence that answers each question, using the word or words in parentheses.

SAMPLE   What is Wilma Rudolph best known for? (winning three gold medals at the Olympics)

ANSWER   Wilma Rudolph is best known for winning three gold medals at the Olympics.

1. By what means did Rudolph first achieve fame? (competing in the 1956 Olympic games)
2. What is another of Rudolph's achievements? (setting world records in the 100-meter and 200-meter races)
3. What might have prevented Rudolph from pursuing a career in track? (having polio as a young girl)
4. By what means did Rudolph strengthen her muscles after her illness? (running)
5. What was Rudolph's most recent challenge? (working with young people in sports and educational programs)

Verbals

Review: Exercise 5   Identifying Infinitive Phrases

Write each infinitive phrase. Then write *subject* or *direct object* to tell how it is being used.

1. To run a marathon tests the endurance and courage of even the most dedicated runners.
2. In the high jump, an athlete needs to leap over a high bar.
3. Jumpers learn to kick their legs out at the end of their jump.
4. Pole vaulters need to thrust themselves into the air with a pole.
5. As the pole straightens, they try to twist their bodies.
6. Some athletes prefer to jump over hurdles.
7. To win a hurdle race requires speed, strength, and skill.
8. Broad jumpers like to land in a soft sand pit.
9. To throw the discus requires tremendous strength.
10. To measure jumps and throws accurately demands the skill of experienced and well-trained judges.

Review: Exercise 6   Using Infinitives and Infinitive Phrases

Write a sentence that answers each question, using the infinitive phrase in parentheses. Use the phrase as the part of speech indicated.

SAMPLE   What must a race walker learn?
(to maintain proper technique—direct object)
ANSWER   A race walker must learn to maintain proper technique.

1. What is the purpose of the hurdle race?
(to run and jump over obstacles placed on the track—subject)
2. What must relay racers learn?
(to pass the baton smoothly and quickly—direct object)
3. What does a high jumper attempt to do?
(to leap over an upraised bar—direct object)
4. What is an important skill in throwing events?
(to propel an object as far as possible—subject)
5. What requires years of training?
(to throw a discus—subject)

Review: Exercise 7

Proofreading

The following passage is about Jacob Lawrence, an African American artist whose work appears on the next page. Rewrite the passage, correcting the errors in spelling, grammar, and usage. Add any missing punctuation. There are ten errors.

Jacob Lawrence

¹Jacob Lawrence was born in New Jersey in 1917 but growed up in Harlem. ²Studying art in after-school programs he acheived success at an early age. ³Gaining popularity in his twenties Lawrence becomed the first African American artist to have a one-person show at the Museum of Modern Art in New York. ⁴Vivid primary colors and highly stylized figures make Lawrences' work unique. ⁵In the poster shown on the next page, for example, the relay racers visibly strains to cross the finish line. ⁶Imitating Wilma Rudolph's determination each runner wants to win. ⁷The artist using gestures and facial expressions, conveys his figure's emotions.

Review: Exercise 8

Mixed Review

Write *participial phrase, gerund phrase,* or *infinitive phrase* to tell how each underlined phrase is used.

The Olympics, held first in Olympia, Greece, began 3,500 years ago. Greek competitors underwent training for the Games. Reviving the Games was the idea of Pierre de Coubertin. In 1896 thirteen nations decided to send athletes. Each country desiring participation needs to organize a committee. The city holding the Games spends years preparing. As the Games begin, spectators love watching a runner with the Olympic flame. The athletes, carrying their national flag, enter the stadium. Dressed in their uniforms, they watch the release of pigeons. As the birds begin to fly away, the Games

(continued)

officially open. In summertime athletes, <u>running around the track</u>, demonstrate great speed. <u>Diving off a high board</u> is another event. In winter people like <u>to watch skiers</u>. Athletes <u>talented in their sport</u> want <u>to bring home a medal</u>, but few expect <u>to win the gold</u>. Even fewer are like Wilma Rudolph, <u>receiving three gold medals</u>. <u>Participating in the Games</u> is a dream come true.

Jacob Lawrence, *Study for the Munich Olympic Games Poster*, 1971

Writing Application

TIME

For more about the writing process, see **TIME Facing the Blank Page**, pp. 97-107.

Verbals in Writing

Brent Ashabranner uses participles and gerunds to bring a sense of action to his essay about the Vietnam War Memorial. As you read this passage from *Always to Remember*, pay special attention to the italicized verbals.

> The answer, they decided, was to hold a national design competition open to all Americans. The *winning* design would receive a prize of $20,000, but the real prize would be the winner's knowledge that the memorial would become a part of American history on the Mall in Washington, D.C. Although fund *raising* was only well started at this point, the *choosing* of a memorial design could not be delayed if the memorial was to be built by Veteran's Day, 1982.

Techniques with Verbals

Try to apply some of Brent Ashabranner's writing techniques when you write and revise your work.

❶ Use participle verb forms as adjectives to make your descriptions more lively and engaging. Compare the following:

FLAT VERSION The design *that won* would receive a prize.

ASHABRANNER'S VERSION The *winning* design would receive a prize. . . .

❷ When appropriate, add a sense of action to your sentences by using gerunds.

LESS ACTIVE WORDS They had only just started to raise funds.

ASHABRANNER'S VERSION Although fund *raising* was only well started. . . .

Practice Revise the following passage on a separate sheet of paper. Focusing on the underlined words, add gerunds and participles to make it more active.

"It will be <u>a real challenge</u> <u>to work</u> on my science project without electricity," said Sam to his teacher. "I know," Ms. Clayton replied. "The extra effort will expand <u>what you learn</u> from the experience." She flashed Sam a grin <u>that tried to encourage</u> him. "Oh well," he thought. "It's not my style <u>to quit</u>. It's <u>of interest to invent</u> new methods." He started <u>to gather</u> what he needed to mix chemicals and headed for home.

Verbals

UNIT 16

Subject-Verb Agreement

Making Subjects and Verbs Agree

The basic idea of subject-verb agreement is a simple one—a singular noun subject calls for a singular form of the verb, and a plural noun calls for a plural form of the verb. The subject and its verb are said to *agree in number.* Read the sentences below. You can see that the subjects and verbs agree.

Note that in the present tense, the singular form of the verb usually ends in *-s* or *-es.*

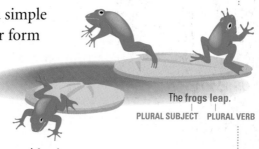

The frogs leap.
PLURAL SUBJECT   PLURAL VERB

A frog leaps.
SINGULAR   SINGULAR
SUBJECT   VERB

Subject and Verb Agreement	
Singular Subject	**Plural Subject**
An **ecologist studies** nature.	**Ecologists study** nature.
The **boy learns** about ecology.	The **boys learn** about ecology.
Judy plants seedlings.	**Judy** and **Kim plant** seedlings.

The verb must also agree with a subject pronoun. Look at the chart below. Notice how the verb changes. In the present tense, the *-s* ending is used with the subject pronouns *it, he,* and *she.*

Subject Pronoun and Verb Agreement	
Singular	**Plural**
I **hike**.	We **hike**.
You **hike**.	You **hike**.
He, she, *or* it **hikes**.	They **hike**.

The irregular verbs *be, do,* and *have* can be main verbs or helping verbs. They must agree with the subject, regardless of whether they are main verbs or helping verbs.

I **am** a ranger. They **are** tagging a bear. He **is** digging.

She **does** well. She **does** climb cliffs. They **do** garden.

He **has** gear. He **has** saved birds. They **have** traveled.

Exercise 1   Making Subjects and Verbs Agree

Rewrite each sentence, changing singular subjects to plural and plural subjects to singular. Make the verbs agree with the subjects. Remember that other parts of the sentences might have to change when the subject changes.

1. The student plans a hike to the bog.
2. Bogs contain an interesting variety of organisms.
3. The state park is fun for everyone.
4. A leaflet explains the plants and animals in the park.
5. We are interested in learning more about the park's plants.
6. A ranger speaks to visitors every day at noon.
7. She identifies the various plants growing in the bog.
8. Guidebooks provide good information about the types of plants.
9. A bog offers opportunities for people hunting for fossils.
10. Bogs develop in former glacial lakes.

Exercise 2   Using Correct Subject and Verb Agreement

Write the correct form of the verb in parentheses.

1. The day (is, are) perfect for a visit to the bog.
2. The students always (enjoy, enjoys) field trips.
3. Bogs (contain, contains) acidic soil and many mosses.
4. Swamps (is, are) similar to bogs in many ways.
5. The acidity (tell, tells) you about the type of bog.
6. A bog (is, are) usually smaller than a swamp.
7. Ecosystems (is, are) communities of living and nonliving factors.
8. An ecosystem (include, includes) the surrounding air.
9. An ecosystem (has, have) distinct cycles.
10. Water (is, are) an important part of all ecosystems.
11. An ecologist (do, does) a great deal of fieldwork.
12. Bogs often (provide, provides) interesting ecosystems.
13. This bog (have, has) supported a rare ecosystem.
14. A unique fungus (grow, grows) in this bog.
15. Many creatures (live, lives) in bogs.
16. Ecosystems (consist, consists) of many different plants and animals.
17. Our survival (do, does) depend upon the painstaking work of the ecologists.
18. Their research often (have, has) a great impact on our view of our planet.
19. We (rely, relies) on the research of ecologists.
20. They (has, have) changed our understanding of our planet.

16.2　Problems with Locating the Subject

Making a subject and its verb agree is easy when the verb directly follows the subject. Sometimes, however, a phrase containing another noun comes between the subject and the verb.

In the sentence below, the phrase *except in the polar regions* contains a plural noun. The verb *becomes* must agree with the singular subject of the sentence, *desert,* not with the plural noun *regions,* which is the object of the preposition in the phrase.

The **desert,** except in the polar regions, **becomes** very hot.

In inverted sentences, the subject follows the verb. Inverted sentences often begin with a prepositional phrase. Do not mistake the object of the preposition for the subject of the sentence.

In the desert **roam herds** of camels.

In inverted sentences beginning with *Here* or *There,* look for the subject after the verb. *Here* or *There* is never the subject.

There is a high **mountain** near the desert.

Here at the top **are** many damp **rocks.**

By rearranging each sentence so that the subject comes first, you see the subject and verb in their usual order.

A high **mountain** there **is** near the desert.

Many damp **rocks are** here at the top.

In some interrogative sentences, an auxiliary verb comes before the subject. Look for the subject between the auxiliary verb and the main verb.

Do any **deserts contain** large animals?

Exercise 3   Making Subjects and Verbs Agree

Write each sentence. Underline the simple subject once and its verb twice. If they agree, write *correct.* If they do not agree, correct the verb.

1. The savanna, with its waving grasses, lie next to the desert.
2. It is on the margin of the trade-wind belts.
3. In the savanna lives many large animals.
4. The savanna, except in its rainy summers, are dry.
5. In Africa are the largest savannas.
6. Do savannas exist everywhere in the world?
7. There is many giraffes in the grassland.
8. Names for a savanna includes prairie, scrub, and veld.
9. Do much rain fall each year in a savanna?
10. The balance between grasses and woody plants is delicate.

Exercise 4   Using the Correct Verb Form

Write the correct form of the verb in parentheses.

1. The plains near the North Pole (is, are) very cold.
2. The temperature in these zones (is, are) usually below zero.
3. In this area (live, lives) many animals.
4. During the brief summers (grow, grows) a rare moss.
5. In the moss (nest, nests) many birds.
6. There (is, are) little rainfall during the summer.
7. (Does, Do) snow provide the needed moisture?
8. Some areas of the Arctic (is, are) drier than the world's deserts.
9. There (is, are) several hundred species of plants in the Arctic.
10. Summer melting of icy areas (create, creates) nesting sites for birds.
11. Smog (accumulate, accumulates) over some Arctic areas.
12. Fish, such as cod and salmon, (live, lives) under the ice cap.
13. There (is, are) a reason for the white color of many Arctic animals.
14. (Does, Do) the absence of reptiles affect the ecosystem?
15. Along a well-traveled route (roam, roams) herds of caribou.
16. Here the threat to their habitat (is, are) from oil pipeline construction.
17. The dense, woolly coat of musk oxen (is, are) called *quivet.*
18. There (is, are) many uses for quivet, a valuable raw fiber.
19. In summer (appear, appears) many types of grasses.
20. (Does, Do) lichens help create new soil?

Collective Nouns and Other Special Subjects

It is sometimes difficult to tell whether certain special subjects are singular or plural. For example, collective nouns follow special agreement rules. A **collective noun** names a group. The noun has a singular meaning when it names a group that acts as a single unit. The noun has a plural meaning when it refers to each member of the group acting as individuals. The meaning of the noun determines whether you use the singular or plural form of the verb.

The **team agrees** to save papers. [one unit, singular]

The **team agree** to store them in their homes. [individuals, plural]

Certain nouns, such as *mathematics* and *news*, end in -s but take a singular verb. Other nouns that end in -s and name one thing, such as *trousers* and *pliers*, take a plural verb.

Mumps is a disease that is spread through the air. [singular]

Scissors are not practical for shredding paper. [plural]

When the subject refers to an amount as a single unit, it is singular. When it refers to a number of individual units, it is plural.

Ten years seems a long time. [single unit]

Ten years have passed since you left. [individual units]

Five cents is the deposit on one bottle. [single unit]

Five cents are in my hand. [individual units]

A title of a book or work of art is considered singular even if a noun within the title is plural.

***Recycling Successes* is** now a best-selling book. [one book]

The team . . .

. . . **collect** cans and bottles at the shore.

The team . . .

. . . **collects** cans and bottles for recycling.

| **Exercise 5** | **Identifying Verbs for Collective Nouns** |

Write each sentence. Underline the collective noun subject once and the verb twice. If they agree, write *correct*. If they do not agree, correct the verb.

1. *Recycling Tips* are a pamphlet of helpful ideas on ways to recycle.
2. Fifteen is the average number of refillings for a returnable bottle.
3. News about the town's recycling efforts are hopeful.
4. After lunch, the class empty their trays in the recycling bins.
5. Each week, the committee award a prize for the best recycling tip.
6. Two tons were the weight of last month's scrap metal collection.
7. Simple mathematics show the value of turning old paper into newsprint.
8. The cafeteria staff show their support by helping students recycle.
9. Scissors is in the desk drawer.
10. The parents' group have donated more recycling bins.

| **Exercise 6** | **Using the Correct Verb Form with Collective Nouns** |

Write the correct form of the verb in parentheses.

1. The committee (decide, decides) to recycle paper.
2. The committee (decide, decides) among themselves.
3. The audience (leave, leaves) when they are bored.
4. The audience (applaud, applauds) in unison.
5. News (is, are) being made at this town meeting.
6. Even eyeglasses (is, are) recyclable.
7. *Seven Ways to Recycle Newspapers* (is, are) the book we need.
8. The class (discuss, discusses) their different opinions about pollutants.
9. The group (discuss, discusses) the problem of landfills.
10. The herd of goats (graze, grazes) at the landfill.
11. The herd (is, are) all healthy.
12. One million gallons (is, are) a large amount of pollutants.
13. *Energy Alternatives* (is, are) an important book.
14. Five hundred dollars (is, are) available for a recycling program.
15. *Fragile Lands* (do, does) seem a significant film.
16. The class (is, are) working on a group project.
17. The group (see, sees) a movie about landfills.
18. Two years (seem, seems) a long time for recovery.
19. Trousers (is, are) recycled with other forms of clothing.
20. The class (draws, draw) posters showing their household recycling efforts.

16.4 Indefinite Pronouns as Subjects

■ An **indefinite pronoun** is a pronoun that does not refer to a specific person, place, or thing.

Some indefinite pronouns are singular. Others are plural. When an indefinite pronoun is used as a subject, the verb must agree in number. Study the indefinite pronouns in the chart below.

Indefinite Pronouns			
Singular			**Plural**
another	everybody	no one	both
anybody	everyone	nothing	few
anyone	everything	one	many
anything	much	somebody	others
each	neither	someone	several
either	nobody	something	

A few indefinite pronouns take a singular or plural verb, depending on the phrase that follows. These pronouns include *all, any, most, none,* and *some.*

Notice how these indefinite pronouns are used below.

Most of the forest **lies** to the east. [singular]

Most of those scientists **study** the process of respiration. [plural]

Some of her lawn **is** brown. [singular]

Some of the ferns **are** large. [plural]

The prepositional phrases include nouns that are singular or plural. To determine whether the verb should be singular or plural, look at the object of the preposition. For example, in the third sentence above, *some* refers to *lawn.* Because *lawn* is singular, the verb is singular. In the fourth sentence, *some* refers to *ferns.* Because *ferns* is plural, the verb is plural.

Identifying Indefinite Pronouns

Write the indefinite pronoun from each sentence. Then write *singular* or *plural* to tell what verb form it takes.

1. All of the students are working in the science laboratory.
2. All of the needed information is printed in the lab manual.
3. Most of the steps are easy to carry out.
4. None of the laboratory equipment is dangerous to use.
5. Some of the results need to be explained to the class.
6. Most of the experiment concerns respiration.
7. Any of the lab stations have the needed equipment.
8. Some of the underlying theory is written on the chalkboard.
9. None of the lab reports have been written yet.
10. All of the oxygen is used up as the candle burns.

Exercise 8 **Using the Correct Verb Form with Indefinite Pronouns**

Write the correct form of the verb in parentheses.

1. Much of the process of respiration (is, are) complex.
2. Few completely (understand, understands) it.
3. Many (study, studies) the two types of oxygen exchange.
4. Much (happen, happens) during the two processes.
5. Someone (explain, explains) the respiratory system.
6. Another of our problems (is, are) water pollution.
7. One (need, needs) understanding of the solutions.
8. Some of them (improve, improves) the water supply immediately.
9. Many (provide, provides) sensible approaches.
10. Either of the processes (clean, cleans) the water equally well.
11. Both of them (call, calls) for further study.
12. Neither (is, are) apparently preferable.
13. Most of the higher animals (have, has) lungs.
14. All of the oxygen exchange (occur, occurs) there.
15. Most of the processes (is, are) clearly written.
16. Nobody (deny, denies) the value of the project.
17. Many of the volunteers (work, works) diligently.
18. Any of the projects (need, needs) extra volunteers.
19. Most of the people (support, supports) conservation.
20. Several of the volunteers (suggest, suggests) ideas.

Agreement with Compound Subjects

A compound subject contains two or more simple subjects for the same verb. Compound subjects take either a singular or a plural verb, depending on how the parts of the subject are joined. When the simple subjects are joined by the coordinating conjunction *and* or by the correlative conjunction *both . . . and,* the verb is plural.

In all of the sentences below, the reference is to more than one place, thing, or idea.

> New York, Denver, **and** London **have** smog.
>
> **Both** automobiles **and** factories **create** smog.
>
> Air inversion **and** the absence of wind **aid** the conditions.

Occasionally *and* is used to join two words that are part of one unit or refer to a single person or thing. In these cases, the subject is considered to be singular. In the sentence below, notice that *captain* and *leader* refer to the same person. Therefore, the singular form of the verb is used.

> The captain **and** leader of the air-testing team **is** Joan.

When two or more subjects are joined by the conjunctions *or* or *nor, either . . . or,* or *neither . . . nor,* the verb agrees with the subject that is closer to it.

> The city **or** the state **responds** to pollution complaints.
>
> **Either** smoke **or** gases **cause** the smog.

In the first sentence, *responds* agrees with *state,* which is the subject noun closer to the verb. The verb is singular because the subject is singular. In the second sentence, *cause* agrees with *gases,* which is closer. The verb is plural because *gases* is plural.

Exercise 9   Using the Correct Verb Form with Compound Subjects

Write the correct form of the verb in parentheses.

1. A savanna and a desert (is, are) next to each other.
2. Rain forests and deserts (make, makes) good study sites.
3. Jungles, forests, and bogs (has, have) different characteristics.
4. Both Caldwell and the girls (want, wants) to study swamps.
5. The researcher and author (is, are) the opening speaker at the conference.
6. Food, water, and air (is, are) essential to life.
7. Both food and oxygen (come, comes) from plants.
8. Plants and animals in a community (is, are) interdependent.
9. Both days and seasons (change, changes) natural systems.
10. The wind, the sun, and the tides (is, are) sources of energy.
11. Oil and natural gas (forms, form) today's major energy supply.
12. The group's teacher and leader (is, are) an expert on ecological issues.
13. Too much rain and snow (do, does) affect the area.
14. States, cities, and towns (have, has) responsibilities.
15. Air pollution and water pollution (responds, respond) to clean-up actions.
16. The engineer and head of the hiking club (is, are) the pollution inspector.
17. Trout and salmon (need, needs) clean water to survive.
18. Both temperature and acidity (is, are) measured every day.
19. Environmental club members and their leader (helps, help) measure temperature.
20. Both club members and their families (participates, participate) in the program.

Exercise 10   Identifying Compound Subjects

Write the compound subjects for each sentence. Then write *singular* or *plural* to tell what verb form they take.

1. Neither rain nor snow is predicted for the weekend's weather.
2. Television bulletins or radio announcements warn people to evacuate.
3. Either high winds or heavy rains pose a danger of flooding.
4. The town or the state assists in the evacuation efforts.
5. Either a fire fighter or a rescue worker knocks on each resident's door.
6. Either a state helicopter or local boats are used to rescue the stranded.
7. The school gym or the town hall offers a refuge from the storm.
8. Hot chocolate or coffee warms those chilled by the weather.
9. Either soup or sandwiches are provided for the rescue workers.
10. Neither levees nor a dam has been built for flood control.

Grammar Review

SUBJECT-VERB AGREEMENT

To learn about bats, journalist Diane Ackerman accompanied a world authority on the subject to a cave in Texas. In the following excerpt from her essay "Bats," the writer observes an emergence of Mexican free-tailed bats. The passage has been annotated to show some examples of subject-verb agreement covered in this unit.

Literature Model

from Bats
by Diane Ackerman

In the early evening, I take my seat in a natural amphitheater of limestone boulders, in the Texas hill country; at the bottom of the slope is a wide, dark cave mouth. Nothing stirs yet in its depths. But I have been promised one of the wonders of our age. Deep inside the cavern, twenty million Mexican free-tailed bats are hanging up by their toes. They are the largest known concentration of warm-blooded animals in the world. Soon, at dusk, all twenty million of them will fly out to feed, in a living volcano that scientists call an "emergence. . . ."

A hawk appears, swoops, grabs a stray bat out of the sky, and disappears with it. In a moment, the hawk returns, but hearing his wings coming, the bats in the column all shift sidewise to confuse him, and he misses. As wave upon wave of bats pours out of the cave, their collective wings begin to sound like drizzle on autumn leaves.

> Agreement between a singular subject and verb in an inverted sentence

> Agreement between a plural pronoun subject and a plural verb

> Agreement between a plural subject and a verb that have a prepositional phrase between them

Grammar Review

| Review: Exercise 1 | Making Verbs Agree with Noun and Pronoun Subjects |

Write the correct form of the verb in parentheses.

1. Snakes (prowls, prowl) by the cave mouth, hunting for fallen bats.
2. A researcher (puts, put) on protective clothing before entering the cave.
3. Free-tailed bats (cruises, cruise) at thirty-five miles an hour.
4. The cave (stretches, stretch) 1,000 feet into the limestone hill.
5. It (averages, average) sixty feet in diameter.
6. Many researchers (comes, come) to see the emergence of the bats.
7. They (finds, find) the sight of the bats awe-inspiring.
8. A hawk (grabs, grab) a stray bat out of the sky.
9. The bats' wings (sounds, sound) like drizzle on autumn leaves.
10. Diane Ackerman (compares, compare) the emergence to a volcano.

| Review: Exercise 2 | Making Forms of *Be*, *Do*, and *Have* Agree with Subjects |

SAMPLE   Diane Ackerman (is, are) interested in the behavior of bats.
ANSWER   is

1. Bats (is, are) warm-blooded animals.
2. Ackerman (does, do) seem interested in the study of bats.
3. This cave (is, are) a nursery full of mothers and their babies.
4. The cave mouth (is, are) at the bottom of the slope.
5. The spectators (has, have) a splendid view of the emerging bats.
6. Researchers (has, have) carried out many studies of this bat population.
7. Bats (does, do) sleep upside down.
8. A bat (is, are) the only mammal with the ability to fly.
9. A bat (do, does) have a good sense of smell.
10. Some people (has, have) a fear of bats.

Review: Exercise 3 Locating Subjects and Making Verbs Agree

Write each sentence, choosing the correct form of the verb in parentheses. Underline the simple subject once and the verb twice.

SAMPLE The bats inside the dark cave (hangs, hang) upside down.
ANSWER The <u>bats</u> inside the dark cave <u>hang</u> upside down.

1. In the cave (is, are) twenty million bats.
2. The hawk, a predator with keen eyes, (swoop, swoops) down upon a bat.
3. Here (is, are) a vivid example of a predator-prey relationship.
4. The bats, reacting to the hawk, (shifts, shift) their position sidewise.
5. (Does, Do) the bats rely on echolocation to know the hawk's position?
6. The scientific name for bats (is, are) *Chiroptera,* meaning "hand wing."
7. There (is, are) forty different kinds of bats in North America.
8. (Is, Are) there a law protecting colonies of bats?
9. The reproductive rate of bats (is, are) quite low.
10. Here (is, are) an important reason to protect bat colonies.

Review: Exercise 4 Making Verbs Agree with Collective Nouns and Other Special Subjects

Write the correct form of the verb in parentheses.

1. Binoculars (gives, give) the researchers a clear view of the bats.
2. The research team (takes, take) their seats on the boulders.
3. The bat colony (raises, raise) the temperature inside the cave.
4. Twenty million (is, are) an estimate of the cave's bat population.
5. For those watching the bats, the hours (passes, pass) quickly.
6. "Bats" (is, are) an entertaining and informative essay.
7. The colony (clings, cling) to their roosts on the cave ceiling.
8. *National Geographic* (has, have) published several good articles on bats.
9. News (travels, travel) quickly among the individuals in a bat colony.
10. This colony (represents, represent) the world's largest concentration of warm-blooded animals.

Review: Exercise 5   Making Verbs Agree with Indefinite Pronoun Subjects

Write the correct form of the verb in parentheses.

1. Everyone (has, have) an opinion about bats.
2. Many (fears, fear) the animals.
3. Few (knows, know) very much about them.
4. Most of the folklore (is, are) untrue.
5. Few (lives, live) in belfries.
6. Everyone (thinks, think) that bats get in people's hair.
7. Nobody (recognizes, recognize) how helpful bats are.
8. Much (remains, remain) to be learned about bats.
9. Some of the species (uses, use) high-frequency sounds to navigate in the dark.
10. Most of these sounds (extends, extend) beyond the range of human hearing.

Review: Exercise 6   Making Verbs Agree with Compound Subjects

Write the correct form of the verb in parentheses.

1. Both snakes and hawks (preys, prey) on bats.
2. Neither the flying fox nor the vampire bat (hibernates, hibernate) in winter.
3. Fruit or insects (provides, provide) food for bats.
4. Either fear or ignorance (accounts, account) for the way many people react to seeing bats.
5. Caves and hollow trees (provides, provide) roosts for bats.
6. Both migration and hibernation (is, are) ways of coping with cold winter weather.
7. Either migration or hibernation (protects, protect) bats from the cold.
8. Both the sense of sight and the sense of smell (is, are) well developed in bats.
9. Either plant nectar or plant pollen (is, are) consumed by some bats.
10. The head scientist and leader of the bat research team (is, are) Dr. Tuttle.

Review: Exercise 7

Proofreading

This passage is about the artist Leonard Koscianski, whose work appears on the following page. Rewrite the passage, correcting the errors in spelling, capitalization, grammar, and usage. Add any missing punctuation. There are ten errors.

Leonard Koscianski

[1]Many of Leonard Koscianski's paintings reflects his concern with issues affecting the earth's future, such as environmental pollution. [2]The painter believes that human society impose an artificial order on the world, the result of such interference are a disruption of the balance of nature.

[3]In *Forest Spirit,* for example, the artist represents the natural order in the forest, where a hawk swoops down to attack hiden prey. [4]Like the mexican free-tailed bats in "Bats," the prey is seized and killed. [5]Koscianski suggest that such activities are neccesary to maintain the natural balance. [6]Besides, many animals fights back. [7]Most of the bats in Ackerman's essay is able to protect themselves and escape.

Review: Exercise 8

Mixed Review

Write the correct verbs in parentheses.

Diane Ackerman, the author of "Bats," [1](has, have) also written essays about other animals. "White Lanterns" [2](is, are) the title of her essay about young penguins being raised at Sea World in California. Scientists and volunteers [3](care, cares) for the young animals by feeding and holding them.

A baby penguin exhibits thigmotaxis, the drive to press up hard against a parent. In the wild, either the mother or the father [4](respond, responds) to the youngster. A colony of penguins [5](is, are) filled with

(continued)

the whistles of the young birds. Parents, in the midst of this noise, ⁶(distinguish, distinguishes) the whistles of their own offspring. Everybody ⁷(identify, identifies) with penguins. Why ⁸(does, do) we have this reaction? There ⁹(is, are) many possible explanations. Most of these explanations ¹⁰(revolve, revolves) around the similarities between penguins and people. As Ackerman says, we see penguins "as little humanoids."

Leonard Koscianski, *Forest Spirit*, 1991

Subject-Verb Agreement

Writing Application

TIME

For more about the writing process, see **TIME Facing the Blank Page,** pp. 97-107.

Subject-Verb Agreement in Writing

Lack of subject-verb agreement will distract readers from the information you wish to convey. Examine the passage below from *Always to Remember,* noting how Brent Ashabranner keeps his subjects and verbs in agreement. Focus especially on the italicized words.

> *Maya Lin,* reporters soon discovered, was a Chinese-American girl who had been born and raised in the small midwestern city of Athens, Ohio. Her *father,* Henry Huan Lin, was a ceramicist of considerable reputation and dean of fine arts at Ohio University in Athens. *Her mother,* Julia C. Lin, was a poet and professor of Oriental and English literature. Maya Lin's parents were born to culturally prominent families in China.

Techniques with Subject-Verb Agreement

Check carefully for agreement when you write your work.

❶ When checking for subject-verb agreement, remember to bypass phrases that come between a subject and its verb. Compare the following:

HARDER TO CHECK *Maya Lin,* reporters soon discovered, *was* a Chinese American girl.

EASIER TO CHECK *Maya Lin was* a Chinese American girl.

❷ Be careful about suject-verb agreement when subjects include more than one word. Identify the most important words before checking for agreement:

INCORRECT AGREEMENT Maya Lin's parents *was* born to . . .

CORRECT AGREEMENT Maya Lin's *parents were* born to . . .

Practice Complete the following passage on a separate sheet of paper. In each blank, write a present-tense verb that agrees with the subject noun or pronoun.

My family _____ local sports. Both my parents _____ most of the football, baseball, and soccer games that _____ played here. My brother Ken and I sometimes even _____ with the team to road games. Citizens, especially those whose children participate in sports, _____ their support most effectively by being present. Burnsville's athletes _____ better when their friends and family _____ around them. We, the cheering squad for your local sports teams, _____ you to join us at the next game!

Glossary of Special Usage Problems

Using Troublesome Words I

Like all languages, English contains a number of confusing expressions. The following glossary will help you understand some of the more troublesome ones.

Word	Meaning	Example
accept **except**	"to receive" "other than"	We do not readily **accept** new ideas. Few **except** scientists understand them.
all ready **already**	"completely prepared" "before" or "by this time"	They are **all ready** for new ideas. Ideas have **already** changed.

all together
 	
altogether
	"in a group"
	
	"completely"
		The planets **all together** weigh less
		    than the Sun.
		Most stars are **altogether** too distant to
		    study.

a lot	"very much" *A lot* is two
	    words. Its meaning is
	    vague; avoid using it.
		A lot of stars can't be seen. [vague]
		Thousands of stars can't be seen.
		    [more precise]

beside **besides**	"next to" "in addition to"	In May the moon appeared **beside** Mars. **Besides** Saturn, Jupiter and Uranus have rings.

between
 	
among
	Use *between* for two
	    people or things.
	Use *among* when talking about
	    groups of three or more.
		Mercury is **between** Venus and the Sun.
		
		Meteor trails are seen **among** the stars.

bring
 	
take
	"to carry from a distant
	    place to a closer one"
	"to carry from a nearby
	    place to a more distant one"
		Astronomers **bring** exhibits to schools.
		
		Students will **take** the model planets
		    home.

can **may**	indicates ability expresses permission or possibility	We **can** see Pluto with a telescope. **May** we see the charts?
choose **chose**	"to select" "selected"	**Choose** a planet to study. Last year we **chose** Mars.

Exercise 1 — Choosing the Correct Word

For each sentence, write the correct word or words in parentheses.

1. Our galaxy is one (among, between) many.
2. There may be more galaxies (beside, besides) the ones we know.
3. Many people (accept, except) the idea that space is endless.
4. (Can, May) we use that telescope?
5. (Bring, Take) a compass to the lab when you go.
6. Galaxies are (all together, altogether) too numerous.
7. The students were outdoors (all ready, already) to study the night sky.
8. The instructor (choose, chose) a hill away from the glare of city lights.
9. "Stand (beside, besides) me," he told the class.
10. We stood (all together, altogether), looking at the stars.

Exercise 2 — Using the Correct Word

For each sentence, write the correct word or words from the lesson. Use the clues in parentheses to help you.

1. We _____ see Pluto through this telescope. (have the ability)
2. Before today we'd observed every planet _____ Pluto. (other than)
3. Scientists have _____ learned a great deal about comets. (by this time)
4. They will _____ our class a meteorite. (carry to a closer place)
5. We will _____ the meteorite home. (carry to a farther place)
6. The instructor told us to _____ a partner. (select)
7. I _____ Marjorie Hall for my partner. (selected)
8. The partners were to share observations _____ themselves. (two people)
9. If you look over there, you _____ see the Big Dipper. (are able to)
10. There was a murmur of agreement _____ the students. (three or more people)
11. We learned the ancient Greeks named forty-eight constellations _____. (in all)
12. We _____ knew that the constellations have Latin names. (by this time)
13. The Big Dipper stars are _____ those of Ursa Major. (three or more things)
14. The instructor said, "You _____ use my telescope." (expresses permission)
15. I will gladly _____ his offer. (receive)
16. _____ the Big Dipper is the Little Dipper. (Next to)
17. There are two ways you might _____ to locate the North Star. (select)
18. Follow a line _____ the stars in the front of the Big Dipper's cup. (two things)
19. You _____ also see it as the end of the Little Dipper's handle. (are able to)
20. The students will _____ many ideas away with them. (carry to a farther place)

Word	Meaning	Example
fewer	Use in comparisons with nouns that can be counted.	There are **fewer** sunspots this year than last year.
less	Use in comparisons with nouns that cannot be counted.	Mars has **less** gravitational force than Earth.
formally	the adverb form of *formal*	A sun is **formally** a star.
formerly	"in times past"	Pluto was **formerly** thought to be a moon of another planet.
in	"inside"	Our Sun is **in** the Milky Way.
into	indicates movement from outside to a point within	Meteorites fall **into** the atmosphere.
its	the possessive form of *it*	A comet wobbles in **its** orbit.
it's	the contraction of *it is*	**It's** difficult to see Neptune.
lay	"to put" or "to place"	**Lay** the charts on the table.
lie	"to recline" or "to be positioned"	Layers of dust **lie** on the moon.
learn	"to receive knowledge"	Astronauts **learn** astronomy as part of their training.
teach	"to give knowledge"	Many astronomers **teach** at colleges.
leave	"to go away"	We will **leave** after the eclipse.
let	"to allow"	The school **let** us use the telescope.
loose	"not firmly attached"	Scientists gather **loose** particles in space and bring them back to study.
lose	"to misplace" or "to fail to win"	Comets **lose** particles.
many	Use with nouns that can be counted.	We know the weight of **many** stars.
much	Use with nouns that cannot be counted.	**Much** of the weight is gas.
precede	"to go or come before"	Typewriters **preceded** computers.
proceed	"to continue"	*Voyager 2* will **proceed** to Neptune.

Glossary of Special Usage Problems

Exercise 3 Choosing the Correct Word

For each sentence, write the correct word in parentheses.

1. There are (many, much) kinds of telescopes.
2. Astronomers were (formally, formerly) limited by crude optics.
3. *Voyager 2* is traveling deep (in, into) space.
4. A telescope's power is determined by the size of (its, it's) lens.
5. Our astronomy club is (formally, formerly) organized.
6. Our astronomy club has (fewer, less) than five telescopes.
7. I write my astronomy notes (in, into) a notebook.
8. I (lay, lie) the notebook on the ground beside me while I use a telescope.
9. My young brother wants me to (learn, teach) him about the stars.
10. Tonight I will (precede, proceed) to give him his first lesson.

Exercise 4 Using the Correct Word

For each sentence, write the correct word from the lesson. Use the clues in parentheses to help you.

1. Volcanoes _____ erupted on the moon. (in times past)
2. I can _____ on the ground for hours, looking at the sky. (recline)
3. _____ that telescope stay where it is! (allow)
4. A _____ lens will make a telescope inoperable. (not firmly attached)
5. Astronomers _____ from space probes. (receive knowledge)
6. Astronomy involves _____ study. (amount that cannot be counted)
7. That study must _____ the field work. (go before)
8. Those not willing to study should _____ the class. (go away from)
9. More observation and _____ memory is needed. (amount that cannot be counted)
10. Like the stars, Earth was _____ a glowing sphere. (in times past)
11. Some planets have _____ moons. (amount that can be counted)
12. Our Sun can be _____ defined as a giant ball of hot gases. (in a formal manner)
13. Planets are dark, solid bodies _____ space. (inside)
14. _____ than three are closer than Earth to the Sun. (countable comparison)
15. Over time, stars _____ their heat and light. (misplace)
16. At night stars and planets look _____ alike. (amount that cannot be counted)
17. I can _____ you how to tell a star from a planet. (give knowledge)
18. A planet may glow, but _____ light is not like a star's. (possessive of *it*)
19. Relative to stars, planets do not always _____ in the same place. (be positioned)
20. You will _____ that our galaxy has 100 billion stars. (receive knowledge)

Word	Meaning	Example
quiet	"silent" or "motionless"	It is very **quiet** in outer space.
quite	"completely" or "entirely"	It is **quite** dark in outer space.
raise	"to cause to move upward"	**Raise** heavy binoculars with a tripod.
rise	"to move upward"	The stars **rise** into view.
set	"to place" or "to put"	She **set** the camera down carefully.
sit	"to place oneself in a seated position"	Let's **sit** and watch the sky.
than	introduces the second part of a comparison	The sun is denser **than** the earth.
then	"at that time"	Choose a planet, and **then** locate it.
their	the possessive form of *they*	Ask **their** advice about lenses.
they're	the contraction of *they are*	**They're** using special night lenses.
theirs	"that or those belonging to them"	**Theirs** is a reflecting telescope.
there's	the contraction of *there is*	**There's** also a refracting telescope in our observatory.
to	"in the direction of"	Let's go **to** the observatory.
too	"also" or "excessively"	Why don't you come **too**?
two	the number after one	We have only **two** telescopes in our observatory.
where at	Do not use *at* after *where* to indicate what place.	**Where** is the Milky Way? [not *Where is the Milky Way at?*]
who's	the contraction of *who is*	**Who's** a famous astronomer?
whose	the possessive form of *who*	**Whose** discoveries are the most significant?
your	the possessive form of *you*	I liked **your** essay about Mars.
you're	the contraction of *you are*	**You're** looking at the North Star.

Glossary of Special Usage Problems

Exercise 5   Choosing the Correct Word

For each sentence, write the correct word in parentheses.

1. Jupiter's moons look stationary, but (they're, their) always in orbit.
2. Pluto is smaller (than, then) the other planets.
3. (Who's, Whose) bringing the camera to the site?
4. (Set, Sit) the tripod over there.
5. Each of the planets is (quite, quiet) different in color.
6. (Your, You're) sure to see Venus tonight.
7. (Who's, Whose) count of Saturn's rings is correct?
8. Most observers (sit, set) in deck chairs.
9. (Theirs, There's) Venus now!
10. You can see it if you look (to, too, two) your right.

Exercise 6   Using the Correct Word

For each sentence, write the correct word from the lesson. Use the clues in parentheses to help you.

1. Our friends will bring _____ compass and camera. (possessive form of *they*)
2. The telescope is _____. (that belonging to them)
3. The observation site is on a _____ hill. (calm)
4. The night sky can be _____ stunning. (completely)
5. Venus will _____ soon. (move upward)
6. We will _____ our eyes and our spirits. (cause to move upward)
7. _____ our watch will begin. (at that time)
8. I hope it's not _____ cold. (excessively)
9. Mercury and Venus are _____ planets between Earth and the Sun. (a number)
10. I wonder _____ turn it is to use the new telescope. (possessive of *who*)
11. You must _____ your telescope a few degrees to see Mars. (move upward)
12. It is very _____ here, away from the noise of the city. (silent)
13. Find the closest planets, and _____ find the farthest ones. (at that time)
14. _____ going to make a model of the inner planets? (contraction of *who is*)
15. Outer planets are hard to model because _____ distant. (contraction of *they are*)
16. Which planets are _____ far away to see without a telescope? (excessively)
17. It looks as though _____ a white streak in the sky. (contraction of *there is*)
18. I think _____ referring to the Milky Way galaxy. (contraction of *you are*)
19. That's the galaxy _____ we live. (in what place)
20. It's bigger _____ it looks and contains billions of stars. (part of a comparison)

Grammar Review

GLOSSARY OF SPECIAL USAGE PROBLEMS

In her essay "Star Fever," Judith Herbst discusses people's age-old fascination with stars. In the following passage, Herbst considers the worlds that may lie beyond our vision. She also explains the usefulness of the stars. The passage has been annotated to show some troublesome words covered in this unit.

Literature Model

from Star Fever
by Judith Herbst

I love the stars. Sometimes I **lie** awake at night and think about them. I imagine that they all have planets with strange forms of life. I see red, rugged landscapes bathed in the glare of two suns, one swollen and scarlet, the other a cold steel blue. I see steamy tropical planets covered with silver vines that snake in and out of silver trees. I see planets with methane oceans and iron mountains. **It's** not so crazy. They could be out there, you know. . . .

The stars not only mark the seasons, they also tell you where north, south, east, and west are. Stars "**rise**" in the east and "set" in the west, so all you have to do is look for the appearance of a new constellation. If you see one that wasn't there an hour before, **you're** facing east. Once you know east it's a snap to find the other three directions. Just look behind you for west, to the right side for south, and to the left for north.

As you can imagine, without the compass the early sailors absolutely relied on the stars to find their way around. There are no landmarks on the high seas.

> Lie, meaning "to recline"

> It's, contraction of *it is*

> Rise, meaning "to move upward"

> You're, contraction of you are

Grammar Review

Review: Exercise 1 Making Usage Choices

For each sentence write the correct word in parentheses.

SAMPLE (Beside, Besides) marking the seasons, stars can also be used to tell directions.

ANSWER Besides

1. The stars (can, may) be used as a means to navigate only when the sky is clear.
2. On an overcast night, (fewer, less) stars are visible in the sky.
3. Chinese navigators were (all ready, already) using magnetic compasses to guide their ships by the 1100s.
4. Some of the objects we see (between, among) the stars are planets.
5. Do you (accept, except) the idea that there may be life on other planets?
6. (Many, Much) stars formed more than ten billion years ago.
7. The color of a star's light depends on (its, it's) surface temperature.
8. As a star dies, it slowly begins to (loose, lose) material and shrink.
9. About one hundred ball-like clusters of stars (lay, lie) around the center of the Milky Way galaxy.
10. People can (learn, teach) about stars at a planetarium.
11. The Sun is nearer to Earth (than, then) any other star is.
12. Scientists have learned (quiet, quite) a bit about other stars by studying the Sun.
13. (Theirs, There's) a solar telescope in Tucson, Arizona, that helps astronomers study the Sun's light.
14. (Who's, Whose) studies in the early 1500s challenged earlier scientists' findings?
15. Polish astronomer Nicolaus Copernicus challenged (their, they're) beliefs about the Sun.
16. Today, scientists continue to (raise, rise) questions about the Sun and its impact on people.
17. There are more than 200 billion billion stars (altogether, all together) in the universe.
18. A powerful telescope can (take, bring) distant stars close enough to view.
19. Stars eventually run out of hydrogen gas and (than, then) stop shining.
20. New stars form from (loose, lose) masses of gas and dust in space.

Proofreading

The following passage is about Fernand Léger, whose work appears below. Rewrite the passage, correcting the errors in spelling, grammar, and usage. Add any missing punctuation. There are ten errors.

Fernand Léger

¹Fernand Léger a French painter born in 1881, used an abstract stile of art. ²An artist using this style choses many fragmented aspects of an object and combines them within a single picture. ³Léger frequently chose cubes and other forms too create mechanical figures that represented the new machines developed in the early 1900s. ⁴The artist used his talent two explore the relationship among a person and the industrial world.

⁵Léger present his vision of a world produced by machines in *The Creation of the World.* ⁶As it lays beneath a moon and a handful of stars, Léger's world recalls the planets that Judith Herbst imagined in "Star Fever." ⁷Perhaps much of the strange images in the painting all ready exist under some distant star.

Fernand Léger, *The Creation of the World,* c. 1925

Review: Exercise 3

Mixed Review

For each sentence, write the correct word or words in parentheses.

1. Migration is an important concept (between, among) the world's creatures.
2. Migration, (formally, formerly) defined, is movement from place to place.
3. Migration (in, into) the past was a way for people and animals to find better living conditions.
4. Today (a lot, millions) of people still migrate.
5. Animals also migrate so that they (can, may) find better living conditions.
6. (Many, Much) different kinds of animals migrate, including birds, whales, fish, frogs, and toads.
7. In the autumn, many birds gather in flocks (all ready, already) to migrate to warmer climates.
8. Although they may enjoy warm weather, (its, it's) plentiful food they seek.
9. Seasonal migrations of animals take place (to, too, two) times a year.
10. The distance that animals migrate (between, among) two habitats varies.
11. Some animals migrate (fewer, less) than a mile.
12. On the other hand, Arctic terns travel up to 22,000 miles each year between (their, they're) summer and winter residences.
13. Salmon migrate from small streams (to, too, two) the vast ocean.
14. They stay where (theirs, there's) a plentiful supply of food.
15. (Than, Then) they reverse the process and return to their home stream.
16. There the female will (lay, lie) her eggs, and the male will fertilize them.
17. The adult salmon may die after spawning, but their offspring (precede, proceed) to develop within the eggs.
18. Without parents to (learn, teach) them, the young salmon repeat the pattern.
19. We must (accept, except) the mystery of animal migration.
20. What sense (brings, takes) animals away to another home?
21. What sense (brings, takes) them back to the exact spot where they once lived?
22. Humans can (choose, chose) the instruments that guide them.
23. They can (leave, let) the stars or a compass be their guide.
24. Electronic equipment will pinpoint (where at, where) they are sailing or flying.
25. Although humans have a great deal of knowledge, we still have much to (learn, teach) about animal migrations.

Writing Application

TIME

For more about the writing process, see **TIME Facing the Blank Page,** pp. 97-107.

Usage in Writing

Katherine Paterson chose her words carefully for this passage from *Lyddie* that uses troublesome words correctly. Read the passage, focusing especially on the italicized words.

Her stomach rumbled, but she ignored it. There would be no breakfast until seven, and that was *two* and a half hours away. By five the girls had crowded through the main gate, jostled their way up the outside staircase on the far end of the mill, cleaned their machines, and stood waiting for the workday *to* begin.

"Not *too* tired this morning?" Diana asked by way of greeting.

Techniques with Usage

Try to apply some of Katherine Paterson's writing techniques when you write and revise your own work.

① Remember that some word pairs have related meanings, although their spellings and usages differ. Check each word against its context carefully before making your final choice:

INCORRECT USAGE that was *too* and a half hours

PATERSON'S VERSION that was *two* and a half hours

② Homophones, or words with the same sound but different spellings and meanings, are easily confused. Be sure to choose the correct word and spelling for your intended meaning.

INCORRECT USAGE Not *to* tired this morning?

PATERSON'S VERSION Not *too* tired this morning?

Practice Try out these techniques on the following passage, revising it on a separate sheet of paper. Pay particular attention to the underlined words.

"Edna and Tamara asked me to come to <u>they're</u> house to help paint their treehouse. <u>Can</u> I go, Dad?" asked Mari.

"If you <u>may</u> finish <u>you're</u> chores before lunch, <u>its</u> fine with me," replied her father. "The only question is, <u>whose</u> going to bring you home?"

"<u>Among</u> Edna's mom and Tamara's dad, I'm sure someone <u>may</u> do it. They asked me to bring a paintbrush. Will you help me <u>chose</u> one? We have so <u>much</u>," said Mari.

"No problem. Let's get started," answered her father.

Glossary of Special Usage Problems

UNIT 18 Diagraming Sentences

Diagraming Simple Subjects and Simple Predicates

The basic parts of a sentence are the subject and the predicate. To diagram a sentence, first draw a horizontal line called a baseline. Then draw a vertical line that crosses and extends below the baseline.

To the left of the vertical line, write the simple subject. To the right of the vertical line, write the simple predicate. Capitalize any words that are capitalized in the sentence. Do not include punctuation, however.

People are working.   People | are working

The positions of the subject and the predicate in a diagram always remain the same.

Operators sat by the machines.   Operators | sat

By the machines **sat operators.**   operators | sat

Exercise 1   **Diagraming Simple Subjects and Simple Predicates**

Diagram each simple subject and simple predicate.

1. People arrived early.
2. They started the machines.
3. Other people were standing around.
4. Four women have arrived late.
5. Most factories are busy.
6. Finally lunchtime arrived.
7. The workers ate lunch.
8. Men took walks.
9. People are watching a show.
10. People played games.
11. Then the workers returned.
12. They restarted the machines.
13. They liked their tasks.
14. The supervisor praises them.
15. The workers show loyalty.
16. They have worked for decades.
17. The factory resembles a home.
18. People care about one another.
19. They work together.
20. The workers help one another.

Diagraming the Four Kinds of Sentences

The simple subject and the simple predicate of the four kinds of sentences are diagramed below. Recall that in an interrogative sentence, the subject often comes between the two parts of a verb phrase. In an imperative sentence, the word *you* is understood to be the simple subject.

Note that the positions of the simple subject and the simple predicate in a sentence diagram are always the same, regardless of their positions in the original sentence.

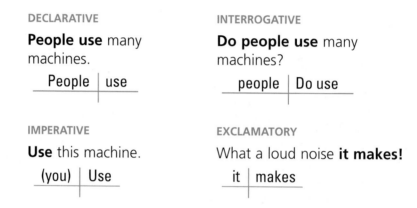

DECLARATIVE

People use many machines.

People	use

INTERROGATIVE

Do people use many machines?

people	Do use

IMPERATIVE

Use this machine.

(you)	Use

EXCLAMATORY

What a loud noise **it makes!**

it	makes

Exercise 2   Diagraming Simple Subjects and Predicates

Diagram the simple subject and the simple predicate of each sentence.

1. Where do people use machines?
2. Machines exist in homes, office buildings, and hospitals.
3. What amazing things machines can do!
4. Listen to the radio.
5. Some machines perform several tasks.
6. Do you use a computer?
7. Try this program.
8. What a fast printer you have!
9. How long does it take?
10. This printer works beautifully.

Diagraming Direct and Indirect Objects

A direct object is part of the predicate. In a sentence diagram, place the direct object to the right of the verb. The vertical line between the verb and the direct object should not extend below the baseline.

Computers solve **problems.** | Computers | solve | problems

Computers process **data.** | Computers | process | data

An indirect object is also part of the predicate. It usually tells to whom or for whom the action of a verb is done. An indirect object always comes before a direct object in a sentence. In a sentence diagram, place the indirect object on a line below and to the right of the verb. Then join it to the verb with a slanted line.

Operators feed
computers data. | Operators | feed | data
                          \ computers

Exercise 3   **Diagraming Direct and Indirect Objects**

Diagram the simple subject, the simple predicate, and the direct object of each sentence. Diagram any indirect objects as well.

1. People solve problems every day.
2. A computer will provide answers.
3. An idea enters your mind.
4. You collect the information.
5. The method gives you the answer.
6. You offer someone the results.
7. The operator gives the computer a problem.
8. The computer gives you an answer.
9. You may check it again.
10. The computer saves us time.

Diagraming Adjectives, Adverbs, and Prepositional Phrases

In a diagram, place adjectives and adverbs on slanted lines beneath the words they modify.

Efficient software sells.

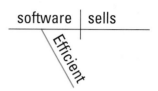

Very efficient software sells **very quickly.**

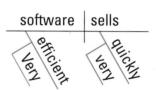

A prepositional phrase can function as either an adjective or an adverb. In the sentence below, the prepositional phrase *by the hundreds* modifies the verb *appear*. Study the diagram.

Programs appear **by the hundreds.**

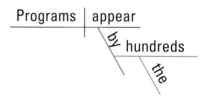

Exercise 4   Diagraming Sentences

Diagram each sentence.

1. Many people use computers regularly.
2. An extremely efficient computer works very quickly.
3. Businesses of all kinds need computers constantly.
4. Computers have changed our way of life.
5. People often play complicated games on personal computers.

Diagraming Sentences

18.5 Diagraming Predicate Nouns and Predicate Adjectives

You have learned that in a sentence diagram the direct object is placed after the action verb.

People use telephones.

| People | use | telephones |

To diagram a sentence with a predicate noun, place the predicate noun after the linking verb. Use a slanted line to separate the predicate noun from the verb.

Telephones are useful **instruments.**

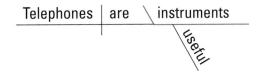

Diagram a predicate adjective in the same way.

Telephones are **useful.**

| Telephones | are \ useful |

Exercise 5　Diagraming Sentences

Diagram each sentence.

1. The telephone is a recent invention.
2. Alexander Graham Bell was the inventor.
3. Telephones have become common.
4. Many calls are international.
5. Early telephones looked odd.
6. The first big change was the dial.
7. A much later improvement was the undersea cable.
8. The cable was a real benefit.
9. The world grew much smaller.
10. Some modern telephones look sleek.

18.6 Diagraming Compound Sentence Parts

Coordinating conjunctions such as *and, but,* and *or* are used to join compound parts: words, phrases, or sentences. To diagram sentences with compound parts, place the second part of the compound below the first. Write the coordinating conjunction on a dotted line connecting the two parts.

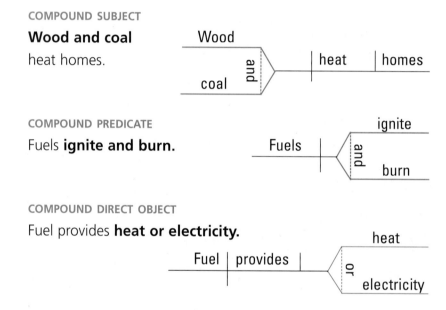

COMPOUND SUBJECT

Wood and coal heat homes.

COMPOUND PREDICATE

Fuels **ignite and burn.**

COMPOUND DIRECT OBJECT

Fuel provides **heat or electricity.**

Exercise 6   Diagraming Sentences

Diagram each sentence.

1. Oil or electricity heats most buildings.
2. Prices for fuels rise and fall.
3. Some families use windmills or solar energy.
4. Stoves and furnaces provide heat.
5. Heated air or heated water circulates through the house.

Diagraming Compound Sentences

To diagram compound sentences, diagram each clause separately. If the main clauses are connected by a semicolon, use a vertical dotted line to connect the verbs of each clause. If the main clauses are connected by a conjunction such as *and, but,* or *or,* write the conjunction on a solid horizontal line and connect it to the verbs of each clause by dotted lines.

An electric typewriter once was the essential office tool, **but** today it has been replaced by the desktop computer.

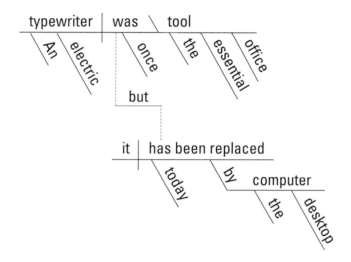

Diagraming Sentences

Diagram each sentence.

1. C. L. Sholes experimented with typewriters in 1867, and he patented a typewriter in 1868.
2. E. Remington marketed the machine in 1874, and soon other firms manufactured typewriters.
3. Businesses used the larger typewriters, but students definitely preferred portables.
4. Word processors have extensive capabilities, but most have rather small display screens.
5. Word processors are efficient, but computers can perform more tasks.

Diagraming Complex Sentences with Adjective and Adverb Clauses

To diagram a sentence with an adjective clause, diagram the main clause in one diagram and the adjective clause beneath it in another diagram. Draw a dotted line between the adjective clause and the word it modifies in the main clause. In the adjective clause, diagram the relative pronoun according to its function in its own clause. In the sentence below, *who* is the subject of the verb *cooked.*

ADJECTIVE CLAUSE

People **who cooked** used enormous stoves.

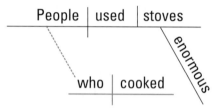

To diagram a sentence with an adverb clause, follow the same process. Then write the subordinating conjunction on the dotted line connecting the verb of each clause.

ADVERB CLAUSE

When people cooked, they used enormous stoves.

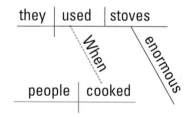

| Exercise 8 | **Diagraming Sentences** |

Diagram each sentence.

1. People once used only stoves that burned wood.
2. Such stoves required attention while they were hot.
3. People who cooked on those stoves worked hard.
4. Families inserted the wood that these stoves required.
5. As the wood burned, ashes and dirt accumulated.

Diagraming Noun Clauses

Noun clauses can be used in sentences as subjects, direct objects, objects of prepositions, or predicate nouns. In the sentence below, the noun clause is a direct object.

I know **what a refrigerator costs.**

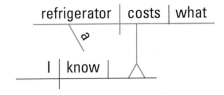

Notice that the clause is placed above the baseline on a "stilt" where the direct object usually appears. The word that introduces a noun clause is diagramed according to its function within the clause. In the noun clause above, the word *what* is the direct object. If the word that introduces the noun clause is not part of either the noun clause or the main clause, place the word on its own line above the verb of the clause it introduces.

You know **that refrigerators are beneficial.**

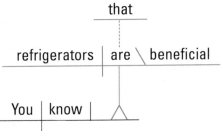

Exercise 9   Diagraming Sentences

Diagram each sentence.

1. Whoever uses a refrigerator should be appreciative.
2. That iceboxes were helpful is undeniable.
3. People eagerly awaited what the ice wagon delivered.
4. When refrigeration began may surprise you.
5. People in the last century knew how it worked.

18.10 Diagraming Verbals I

When diagraming a participle or a participial phrase, make a line that descends diagonally from the word the participle modifies and then extends to the right horizontally. Write the participle along that angled line, as shown below.

The machine, **humming loudly,** cooled the air rapidly.

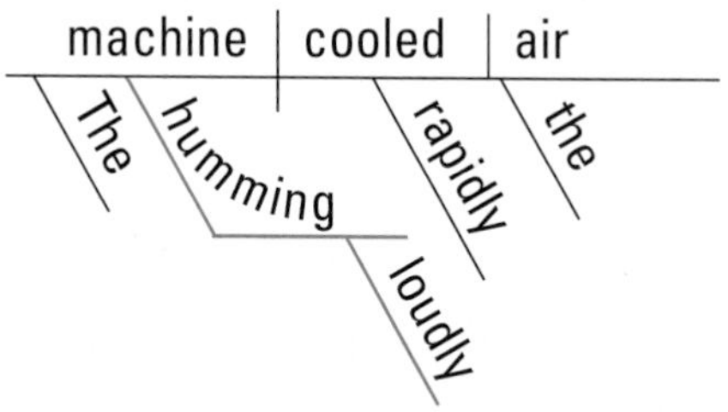

When diagraming a gerund or a gerund phrase, make a "stilt" located according to the role of the gerund. (A gerund can be a subject, an object of a verb or a preposition, or an appositive.) Then write the gerund on a "step" above the stilt.

Cleaning the air is another job of the machine.

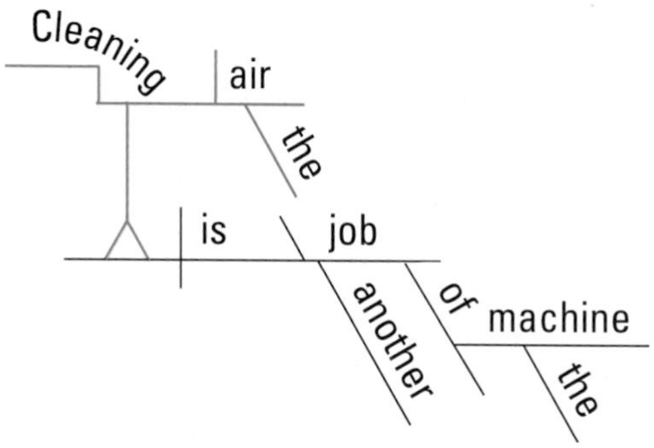

Exercise 10 Diagraming Sentences

Diagram each sentence.

1. Cooling the air was the subject of much research.
2. The machines cool the heated air.
3. Controlling the temperature is not an easy task.
4. The circulating air cools everyone.
5. Working people appreciate this modern invention.

18.11 Diagraming Verbals II

When diagraming an infinitive or an infinitive phrase that is used as either an adjective or an adverb, diagram it like a prepositional phrase.

The microscope **to choose** depends upon your needs.

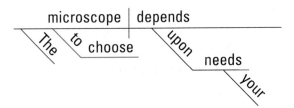

When diagraming an infinitive or an infinitive phrase that is used as a noun, make a "stilt" in the subject or complement position. Then diagram the phrase as you would a prepositional phrase.

The function of the microscope is **to magnify objects.**

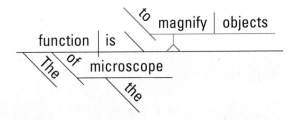

| Exercise 11 | **Diagraming Sentences** |

Diagram each sentence.

1. The Romans may have used glass crystal to magnify objects.
2. To invent the compound microscope was Janssen's mission.
3. It is important to use microscopes carefully.
4. Sloan's job is to prepare the microscope for use.
5. The work to do governs the preparation.

UNIT 19 Capitalization

19.1 Capitalizing Sentences, Quotations, and Salutations

A capital letter appears at the beginning of a sentence. A capital letter also marks the beginning of a direct quotation and the salutation and closing of a letter.

RULE 1: Capitalize the first word of every sentence.

Many people helped our country gain independence.

Among them were George Washington, Thomas Jefferson, and Benjamin Franklin.

RULE 2: Capitalize the first word of a direct quotation that is a complete sentence. A direct quotation gives a speaker's exact words.

Travis said, "Another one of those people was Paul Revere."

RULE 3: When a quoted sentence is interrupted by explanatory words, such as *she said*, do not begin the second part of the sentence with a capital letter.

"I read a famous poem," said Kim, "about Paul Revere."

When the second part of a quotation is a new sentence, put a period after the explanatory words, and begin the second part of the quotation with a capital letter.

"I know that poem," said Sarah. "My class read it last week."

RULE 4: Do not capitalize an indirect quotation. Because an indirect quotation does not repeat a person's exact words, it does not appear in quotation marks. It is often preceded by the word *that*.

The teacher said **the** poem was written by Longfellow.

Travis said **that** another man rode with Paul Revere.

RULE 5: Capitalize the first word in the salutation and closing of a letter. Capitalize the title and name of the person addressed.

Dear Mrs. Adams,   Yours truly,

Capitalization

Write each word that needs to be capitalized. If a sentence contains no error, write correct.

1. our class was learning about heroes of the American Revolution.
2. we wanted to learn more about Paul Revere.
3. he came from Boston and lived in a house that is now open to the public.
4. "let's go to the library," said Lisa, "and see what we can find."
5. one book about Paul Revere says, "he designed the first issue of Continental money."
6. Hasan said that Paul Revere was a silversmith and an engraver.
7. "my aunt," said Hasan, "visited a Boston museum that had a Revere teapot."
8. "he designed the colonies' first official seal," said Hasan. "then he engraved it."
9. "did you know that he took part in the Boston Tea Party?" asked Lisa.
10. about fifty other American patriots went to the harbor in December 1773.
11. "he is best known," said Hasan, "for warning the people that the British were coming."
12. on April 18, 1775, he rode through Lexington toward Concord shouting, "the British are coming! the British are coming!"
13. lanterns were used as signals in the steeple of the Old North Church.
14. we read that on his famous ride Paul Revere was assisted by William Dawes.
15. "isn't it funny," said Hasan, "that Dawes is not known for this deed?"
16. "yes, it is," Lisa agreed. "the famous poem about the ride mentions only Paul Revere."
17. "did you know," asked Hasan, "that the poem was written by Henry Wadsworth Longfellow, who lived in Cambridge?"
18. we also learned that the poem was written more than eighty years after that important ride happened.
19. "because of Paul Revere's ride," said Lisa, "the Minutemen were prepared."
20. we thought we had discovered many interesting facts about this famous hero.
21. we decided to submit our report to a magazine.
22. Hasan began the letter, "dear sir or madam."
23. "we have written a report on Paul Revere," he wrote. "we would like to submit it to you."
24. a few weeks later we received a reply from the magazine.
25. they said that they would publish it.

19.2 Capitalizing Names and Titles of People

A common noun is the general name of a person, place, or thing. A common noun is not capitalized. A proper noun names a particular person, place, or thing and is capitalized.

RULE 1: Capitalize the names of people and the initials that stand for their names.

Lucretia Mott   E. C. Stanton

RULE 2: Capitalize a title or an abbreviation of a title when it comes before a person's name or when it is used in direct address.

In 1918 President Wilson planned the League of Nations.
"Has peace been declared, General?"

Do not capitalize a title that follows or is a substitute for a person's name.

Dwight D. Eisenhower was a general during World War II.

RULE 3: Capitalize the names and abbreviations of academic degrees that follow a person's name. Capitalize *Jr.* and *Sr.*

Martin Greer, Ph.D.   Eve Tanaka, M.D.   Carl Healy Sr.

RULE 4: Capitalize words that show family relationships when used as titles or as substitutes for a person's name.

We have pictures of Aunt Meg marching for women's rights.
In 1902 Grandmother was a suffragist.

Do not capitalize words that show family relationships when they follow a possessive noun or pronoun.

Maria's cousin wrote about women's suffrage.
My aunt has told me about the women's movement.

RULE 5: Always capitalize the pronoun *I*.

History is the subject I like best.

Exercise 2 — Capitalizing Proper Names and Titles

Write each item, using capital letters where needed.

1. miss lucy stone
2. benjamin davis jr.
3. sonia fox, d.d.s.
4. edward r. murrow
5. beth parker, ph.d.
6. peter ashike, m.a.
7. dr. michael thomas
8. general robert e. lee
9. sir walter raleigh
10. j. p. slaughter
11. aunt martha
12. ben casey, m.d.
13. mayor riley
14. private bailey
15. gerald r. ford
16. uncle dexter
17. hillary r. clinton
18. pablo cruz sr.
19. mr. ted dover
20. king george

Exercise 3 — Using Capital Letters for Names, Titles, and Abbreviations

Write each item from the following sentences that needs a capital letter. If a sentence is correct, write correct.

1. Without susan b. anthony, women might not have the vote today.
2. Unfortunately, miss anthony died before women were allowed to vote.
3. With elizabeth cady stanton and m. j. gage, anthony wrote *History of Woman Suffrage.*
4. miss anthony met elizabeth cady stanton in New York.
5. esther p. newton, my great-grandmother, was a suffragist.
6. My great-grandmother once met miss anthony.
7. At the time, most people knew about miss anthony.
8. Later she met president wilson.
9. "Should women vote, mr. wilson?" she asked.
10. A shy man, woodrow wilson did not care to comment.
11. warren g. harding was the first president elected after women could vote.
12. Because harding died in office, calvin coolidge became president in 1923.
13. My great-grandmother knew the importance of the right to vote.
14. My grandmother, beverly newton walsh, says that her mother always voted.
15. She served in the army under general dwight d. eisenhower.
16. A colonel in the army, aunt helen owes a debt of gratitude to the women's movement.
17. In the army, she also met charles lindbergh and general george c. patton.
18. aunt helen smiled and replied, "Yes, sir!"
19. My uncle and i often tease, "Do you think women belong in the military?"
20. I'm sure esther p. newton would have been proud of aunt helen.

Capitalizing Names of Places

The names of specific places are proper nouns and are capitalized. Do not capitalize articles and prepositions that are part of geographical names, however.

RULE 1: Capitalize the names of cities, counties, states, countries, and continents.

    Chicago   Dade County   Hawaii

RULE 2: Capitalize the names of bodies of water and other geographical features.

    Dead Sea   Gulf of Mexico   Rocky Mountains

RULE 3: Capitalize the names of sections of a country.

    New England   Midwest   the South

RULE 4: Capitalize compass points when they refer to a specific section of a country.

    the West Coast   the West   the Northwest

Do not capitalize compass points when they indicate direction.

    Milwaukee is north of Chicago.

Do not capitalize adjectives derived from words indicating direction.

                   southerly wind   northern Texas

RULE 5: Capitalize the names of streets and highways.

    River Road   West Side Highway

RULE 6: Capitalize the names of buildings, bridges, monuments, and other structures.

    Golden Gate Bridge

    Lincoln Memorial

You are now entering North Dakota.

Great West Highway

This way north

Capitalizing Place Names

Write each item, using capital letters where needed.

1. northern illinois	8. carlsbad caverns	15. ford's theater
2. world trade center	9. nebraska	16. bryce canyon
3. spain	10. atlantic ocean	17. caspian sea
4. arabian desert	11. yellowstone river	18. dallas
5. northern california	12. yankee stadium	19. great britain
6. front street	13. fifth avenue	20. lake erie
7. national boulevard	14. mediterranean sea	

Exercise 5   **Using Capital Letters for Place Names**

Write each geographical name, using capital letters where needed. Write *correct* if none are needed.

1. The louisiana purchase covered 827,987 square miles.
2. The united states bought the land from france.
3. At that time, Napoleon Bonaparte was the leader of france, and Thomas Jefferson was our president.
4. It extended from canada to mexico.
5. Some of the states that were once part of this territory are arkansas, kansas, nebraska, and oklahoma.
6. The land was bordered by the mississippi river on the east and by the rocky mountains on the west.
7. The platte river and the missouri river are also in this region.
8. new orleans was an important city.
9. It is located on the gulf of mexico.
10. The purchase of the land doubled the size of the united states of america.
11. It also ended French control of the mississippi valley.
12. spain still owned parts of florida and texas.
13. General Andrew Jackson defeated the British in new orleans in 1815.
14. The United States had wanted only a small piece of land that allowed access to the west.
15. Leaving from st. louis, missouri, Lewis and Clark explored this region.
16. They traveled to what is now bismarck, north dakota.
17. Meanwhile, people in washington, d.c., were thinking of these men.
18. Lewis and Clark reached the pacific ocean by traveling down the columbia river.
19. Now Americans could move farther westward.
20. Someday the country might extend to the west coast.

Capitalization

19.4 Capitalizing Other Proper Nouns and Adjectives

Many nouns besides the names of people and places are proper nouns. Adjectives that are formed from proper nouns are called proper adjectives. For example, the proper adjective *Cuban* is formed from the proper noun *Cuba*.

RULE 1:　Capitalize the names of clubs, organizations, businesses, institutions, government bodies, and political parties.

　　American Bar Association　　Farragut Middle School　　the Senate

RULE 2:　Capitalize brand names but not the nouns following them.

　　Smoothies lotion　　　　　　　　Neato sneakers

RULE 3:　Capitalize the names of important historical events, periods of time, and documents.

　　Vietnam War　　　　　Renaissance　　　　Gettysburg Address

RULE 4:　Capitalize the names of days of the week, months of the year, and holidays. Do not capitalize names of the seasons.

　　Friday　　　　July　　　　Thanksgiving Day　　　　winter

RULE 5:　Capitalize the first word, the last word, and all important words in the title of a book, play, short story, poem, essay, article, film, television series, song, magazine, newspaper, and chapter of a book.

　　Profiles in Courage　　"The Necklace"　　*Newsweek*

RULE 6:　Capitalize the names of ethnic groups, nationalities, and languages.

　　Vietnamese　　　　　　Chilean　　　　　　German

RULE 7:　Capitalize proper adjectives that are formed from the names of ethnic groups and nationalities.

　　Chinese cooking　　　　　　Japanese flag

Capitalizing Proper Nouns and Adjectives

Write the following items, using capital letters where needed.

1. sunnyvale school
2. *reader's digest*
3. english
4. magna carta
5. "yankee doodle"
6. egyptian history
7. american red cross
8. girl scouts
9. wheatola cereal
10. *boston globe*
11. boston tea party
12. memorial day
13. general motors corp.
14. lipton tea
15. mexican food
16. *the red pony*
17. world war II
18. colby college
19. treaty of paris
20. russian literature

Exercise 7   **Using Capital Letters**

Write each proper noun and adjective needing capitalization. Write *correct* if the sentence has no errors.

1. The emancipation proclamation ended slavery in the South.
2. President Abraham Lincoln wrote this document in the summer of 1862.
3. Lincoln issued it during the civil war.
4. It became official in the winter of 1863.
5. It is as well known as the declaration of independence and the bill of rights.
6. These three writings are vital documents of american history.
7. Lincoln is also famous for the gettysburg address, a short speech he delivered in november 1863.
8. The french, the english, and other peoples around the world have read them.
9. In march 1861 the russians freed their serfs.
10. The Thirteenth Amendment, ratified in december 1865, ended slavery in the United States.
11. *uncle tom's cabin,* a book by Harriet Beecher Stowe, helped end slavery.
12. She wrote the novel while her husband taught at bowdoin college.
13. The book was printed in *national era,* a popular magazine before the civil war.
14. The book was an american best seller.
15. The Fourteenth Amendment to the constitution was also ratified soon after the war.
16. Before each amendment became law, congress had to pass it.
17. The *new york times* printed articles about these amendments.
18. The fourteenth amendment gave african americans the right to vote.
19. The civil war was well documented in *harper's weekly.*
20. Today we can read about the civil war in books like *the blue and the gray.*

Grammar Review

CAPITALIZATION

Morning Star, Black Sun by Brent Ashabranner details the efforts of the Northern Cheyenne to preserve their cherished homeland. In the following passage from the book, Joe Little Coyote, a young Northern Cheyenne man, relates the story of how his people had obtained their reservation. The passage has been annotated to show some of the rules of capitalization covered in this unit.

Literature Model

from Morning Star, Black Sun
by Brent Ashabranner

"When General Miles—the Indians called him Bear Coat—decided to help my ancestors get a reservation," Joe Little Coyote said, "he picked a group of Cheyenne under Chief Two Moons and a troop of soldiers and told them to ride through the country until they found good land for a reservation. The Cheyenne rode straight to the Tongue River, and they said that was the land they wanted. The soldiers wanted them to look further, to be sure they had found the best place. They were afraid General Miles might think they hadn't done their job right. But the Cheyenne said, 'No. This will be our land.'"

Then Joe Little Coyote said, "Our spiritual history is here, in this land, and in Bear Butte where Sweet Medicine received the Sacred Arrows. This is more than a reservation. This is our homeland." And he added, "You don't sell your homeland."

> Title coming before a person's name

> Name of a person

> Name of a body of water

> First word of a direct quotation that is a complete sentence

> Place name

Grammar Review

Review: Exercise 1   Capitalizing Sentences and Quotations

Write each sentence, correcting any errors in capitalization.

SAMPLE   Joe Little Coyote said, "our spiritual history is in this land."
ANSWER   Joe Little Coyote said, "Our spiritual history is in this land."

1. "My ancestors got the reservation," he explained, "With the help of General Miles."
2. general Miles said that we should look for reservation land.
3. "soon a group of Cheyenne headed for a good place to live," Joe said.
4. Chief Two Moons said That they wanted the land along the Tongue River.
5. the Cheyenne were interested in living on this land.
6. the soldiers asked the Cheyenne, "do you want to look further?"
7. "my ancestors were afraid they hadn't looked carefully enough," said Joe.
8. the Cheyenne said that the land near the Tongue River would be their home.
9. "our spiritual history is here," said Joe. "the land is sacred to us."
10. Joe Little Coyote said, "you don't sell your homeland."

Review: Exercise 2   Capitalizing Direct Quotations

Write each sentence, correcting any errors in capitalization.

1. Brendan said, "many Navajo who live in places like Monument Valley and Canyon de Chelly still live as their ancestors did."
2. "some make jewelry," said Jason. "they use silver, turquoise, and coral."
3. "did you know," asked Jennifer, "that they are also weavers?"
4. "yes," said Brendan. "they raise their own sheep and spin the wool."
5. "when they weave," said Jason, "their designs are based on ancient patterns."
6. Jennifer said, "once I saw a sand painting that was made by a Navajo."
7. "did you know," she added, "that there are more than five hundred designs?"
8. "no, I didn't," said Brendan. "how big are they?"
9. "some are small and take only an hour or two to make," said Jennifer. "others are so large that several people work for hours."
10. "these pictures are not made from paint at all," added Jason.

Review: Exercise 3   Capitalizing Names and Titles of People

Write only names and titles of people, using capital letters as needed.

SAMPLE   sitting bull isn't the only famous Native American.
ANSWER   Sitting Bull

1. According to howard w. hill, ph.d., pocahontas was always well known.
2. Legend says that she saved the life of captain john smith.
3. Later, she married john rolfe and was baptized under the name rebecca.
4. She is the main character in an old play by j. n. barker and is also the star of the walt disney animated movie called *pocahontas*.
5. squanto, who helped the Pilgrims, was captured by sir ferdinando gorges.
6. william bradford was surprised to find that squanto spoke English.
7. He helped settlers like captain miles standish and governor john carver.
8. Much later, sacajawea helped meriwether lewis and william clark.
9. president thomas jefferson wanted them to find a way to the Pacific Ocean.
10. Artist john white depicted scenes of Native American life.

Review: Exercise 4   Capitalizing Names of Places

Write any place names that need capital letters.

SAMPLE   People first came to north america by crossing over from asia.
ANSWER   North America; Asia

1. During the Ice Age, there was a land bridge between russia and alaska.
2. People settled in the southwest, the east, and other areas of the united states.
3. The first people to see the columbia river were Native Americans.
4. At plymouth rock, the Wampanoag greeted the Pilgrims.
5. narragansett bay, a Native American name, is part of the atlantic ocean.
6. In those days, there was no route 6 winding through cape cod.
7. Many years later, the colonists in boston built Faneuil hall.
8. Soon settlers headed west, traveling along the santa fe trail.
9. Monument valley in utah and arizona was sacred to the Native Americans.
10. Other Native American nations include the cree and the sioux.

Capitalization

Grammar Review

Review: Exercise 5   Capitalizing Other Proper Nouns

Write each item, using capital letters where needed.

SAMPLE   girl scouts of america
ANSWER   Girl Scouts of America

1. speed king sneakers
2. monday, september 6
3. *reader's digest*
4. korean war
5. memorial day
6. american medical association
7. general motors
8. "the open window"
9. *the red badge of courage*
10. middle ages

11. kennedy middle school
12. treaty of paris
13. irish
14. republicans and democrats
15. *the lion king*
16. victorian age
17. cadillac sedan
18. fourth of july
19. new york historical society
20. declaration of independence

Review: Exercise 6   Capitalizing Proper Adjectives

Write the proper noun from each item correctly. Then write each group of words, changing the proper noun to a proper adjective.

SAMPLE   the language of spain
ANSWER   Spain, the Spanish language

1. a poodle from france
2. the capital of egypt
3. music of germany
4. cars from japan
5. clothes from india
6. antiques from england
7. a bank in korea
8. a lantern from china
9. wood from south america
10. elephants from africa

11. food from brazil
12. the language of norway
13. a beach in hawaii
14. a glacier in alaska
15. a boomerang from australia
16. the mountains of switzerland
17. a doll from russia
18. a song from greece
19. a book from nigeria
20. a palm tree in samoa

Review: Exercise 7

Proofreading

The following passage is about artist Robert Henri, whose work appears on the next page. Rewrite the passage, correcting the errors in spelling, capitalization, grammar, and usage. Add any missing punctuation. There are ten errors.

Robert Henri

[1]Robert Henri (1865–1929) was an american portrait and cityscape painter whose subjects sparkle with life. [2]The Artist painted ordinary and exotic people rather than the rich and famous. [3]His paintings of urban life helped portray a newer, more modern Era.

[4]Henri's aim in painting were to capture feeling sensation, and character. [5]*Portrait of Po Tse (Water Eagle)* conveys this spirit thru the subject's expressive, dignified face. [6]The subject who is dressed in traditional clothes, shows pride in his Native American heritage. [7]like joe Little Coyote in *morning Star, Black Sun,* the subject in the portrait cherishes his homeland.

Review: Exercise 8

Mixed Review

Write each sentence, correcting any errors in capitalization.

SAMPLE there have been many famous native americans in our history

ANSWER There; Native Americans

1. massasoit signed a treaty in 1621 with governor john carver of plymouth colony.
2. crazy horse defeated lt. col. george a. custer in the battle of little bighorn on june 25, 1876.
3. geronimo, an apache, once fled to the sierra madre in mexico.
4. He later returned to the united states.
5. he lived on the san carlos indian reservation.
6. sitting bull, a sioux, was born near the grand river in south dakota.
7. "jim thorpe won gold medals in the 1912 olympic games," said jill.
8. he played baseball for the cincinnati reds, a national league baseball team.

(continued)

9. an excellent football player, too, he is enshrined in the football hall of fame in canton, ohio.

10. william cody presented "buffalo bill's wild west show" in the east.

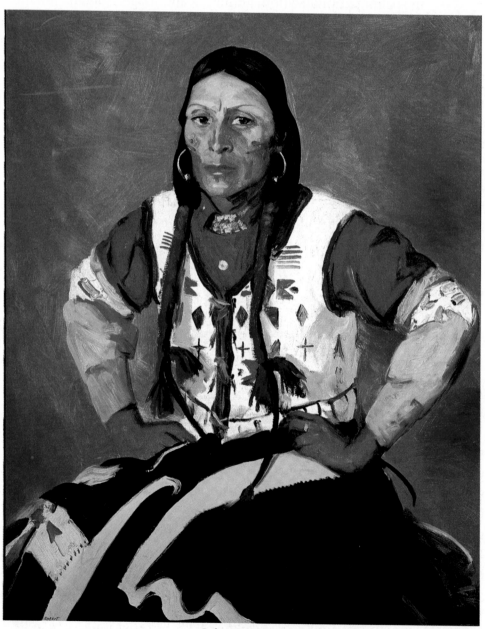

Robert Henri, *Portrait of Po Tse (Water Eagle)*, c. 1916–1925

Writing Application

TIME

For more about the writing process, see **TIME Facing the Blank Page,** pp. 97-107.

Capitalization in Writing

Examine the following passage from *So Far from the Bamboo Grove,* noting how Yoko Kawashima Watkins uses capitalization to identify characters. Pay particular attention to the italicized words.

"Most of my classmates have enlisted," said *Hideyo,* serious for once. "*I* have decided to go to help our country."

"*You* cannot go, *Hideyo!*" *Mother* told him. "*You* must talk with *Father. You* just cannot make such a decision alone."

"*Mother,* I have already sent in my application," said *Hideyo.* "*I* will take the written and physical examinations!"

"How could *you*?" *Mother* moaned. "Why didn't *you* tell me?"

"*I* am eighteen. Big enough to make my own decision."

Capitalization Techniques

Try to apply some of Yoko Kwashima Watkins's writing techniques when you write and revise your own work.

❶ Capitalize people's names, and names describing family relationships when they replace a name:

INCORRECT "How could you?" *his Mother* moaned.

WATKINS'S VERSION "How could you?" *Mother* moaned.

❷ Always capitalize the pronoun *I.* Capitalize other pronouns only when they begin a sentence:

INCORRECT "Why didn't *You* tell me?" "*i* am eighteen."

WATKINS'S VERSION "Why didn't you tell me?" "*I* am eighteen."

Practice Practice these capitalization techniques as you revise the following passage, using a separate sheet of paper. Focus especially on the underlined words.

"<u>i</u> have never been to New Haven," said <u>eve</u>.

"Of course <u>You</u> have," replied <u>aunt petra</u>. "Don't <u>You</u> remember the cranes we saw while crossing the bridge?"

"<u>father</u> told me about them, but <u>i</u> can't recall what they look like," insisted <u>eve</u>. "How about <u>You, marty</u>? Can <u>You</u> describe them?" asked <u>eve</u>, turning toward her <u>Cousin marty</u>.

"Yes," said <u>marty</u>. "<u>i</u> think they were painted bright red. <u>you</u> always said they looked like giant grasshopper legs, only red."

"Oh, yeah!" exploded <u>eve</u>. "Now <u>i</u> remember."

Capitalization

UNIT 20 Punctuation

Using the Period and Other End Marks

Three punctuation marks signal the end of sentences. The period is used for declarative and mild imperative sentences. The question mark is used for interrogative sentences. The exclamation point is used for exclamatory sentences, strong imperatives, and interjections.

RULE 1: Use a period at the end of a declarative sentence. A declarative sentence makes a statement.

> Tractors perform many jobs on a farm.
> I worked on a farm last summer.

RULE 2: Use a period at the end of an imperative sentence that does not express strong feeling. An imperative sentence gives a command or makes a request.

> Turn the key. [command]
> Please start the motor. [request]

RULE 3: Use a question mark at the end of an interrogative sentence. An interrogative sentence asks a question.

> When was the first tractor built?
> Were you aware of that?
> Do modern tractors have both speed and power?

RULE 4: Use an exclamation point at the end of an exclamatory sentence or a strong imperative. An exclamatory sentence expresses strong feeling.

> What a powerful tractor that is!
> Get out of the way!

RULE 5: Use an exclamation point at the end of an interjection. An interjection is a word or group of words that expresses strong emotion.

> Wow!   My goodness!   Hi!   Hey!
> Hooray!   Oh, boy!   Oops!   Phew!

Write the last word of each sentence, and add the correct end mark. Then write whether each sentence is *declarative, imperative, interrogative,* or *exclamatory.*

1. Please tell me about the history of tractors
2. Read about tractors in your book
3. The first tractor was used in the 1870s
4. This tractor was driven by steam and required a licensed steam engineer to operate and repair it
5. Was this machine very large
6. Could it haul and pull heavy loads
7. Can you believe that this tractor could pull as many as forty plows at one time
8. What an amazing sight it must have been
9. Internal combustion tractors were built in the 1890s but did not become practical until about 1920
10. Both early tractors and tractors today are used to move or operate other equipment, such as combines, threshers, or posthole diggers
11. Do some research to find out what else these kinds of equipment do
12. Please tell me about the early days of farming
13. Open your history book
14. Read about the fascinating techniques used by ancient farmers
15. Did you know that the first cultivated crops were probably grasses grown from wild seed
16. The early Egyptians developed the first large-scale irrigation system, which allowed them to distribute water efficiently over a large area
17. What a tremendous advancement this was
18. Each year the Nile River overflowed its banks
19. Farmers discovered they could grow crops by using this water
20. Did farmers prosper when the Nile overflowed
21. In 3000 B.C., Egyptian farmers invented the ox-drawn plow
22. This plow helped Egyptian farmers produce a great deal of food
23. Did your history teacher tell you that they not only fed their own people but also exported huge quantities to other countries
24. Can you imagine the work involved to grow, harvest, and ship twenty million bushels of grain to Rome each year
25. Look at the stylized pictures on Egyptian pottery to see how they raised poultry and cared for their sheep

20.2 Using Commas I

Commas signal a pause between parts of a sentence.

and clog city streets.

RULE 1: Use commas to separate three or more items in a series.

Cars, buses, and trucks clog city streets.

RULE 2: Use commas to show a pause after an introductory word and to set off names used in direct address.

Yes, most cities have few parking garages.

Tony, are you going downtown?

RULE 3: Use a comma after two or more introductory prepositional phrases, when the prepositional phrase is very long, or when the comma is needed to make the meaning clear. A comma is not needed after a single, short prepositional phrase, but it is acceptable to use one.

In the fall of 1991, Frank M. Jordan was elected mayor.

RULE 4: Use a comma after an introductory participle and an introductory participial phrase.

Plagued by deficits, many cities need state aid.

RULE 5: Use commas to set off words that interrupt the flow of thought in a sentence.

A large city, as you can see, employs many police officers.

RULE 6: Use a comma after conjunctive adverbs such as *however, moreover, furthermore, nevertheless,* and *therefore.*

The city is growing; therefore, the city payroll must grow.

RULE 7: Use commas to set off an appositive if it is not essential to the meaning of a sentence.

Alpine Inc., this city's oldest company, joined a large cartel.

Exercise 2   **Using Commas**

Write each sentence, adding a comma or commas where needed. If the sentence needs no changes, write *correct*.

1. Yes cities offer many different places to live.
2. People can live in apartment buildings private homes town houses residential hotels or rooming houses.
3. In the middle of the city you can see skyscrapers.
4. Some buildings are neat clean and attractive.
5. Other buildings are dirty and neglected.
6. The city has a large population.
7. In the tiny yards behind some city buildings the residents have created charming "pocket gardens."
8. Yolanda did you know that San Diego is one of the nation's fastest-growing cities?
9. A big city in my opinion is the best place to live.
10. No I do not mind the crowding; the hustle and bustle in my opinion are part of a city's appeal.
11. Norm do you prefer the city or the country?
12. Does Jo your new friend enjoy living in the city?
13. Pausing a moment to consider my answer I responded that she likes the city.
14. Moreover she has never lived in the country.
15. Eva dislikes the city; nevertheless she refuses to move.
16. Traveling away from the center of the city you can find less crowded living conditions.
17. Country houses you might imagine have more land.
18. I hope Maya that you can find a big house in the country.
19. The suburbs I suppose would be a good alternative Maya.
20. The town of Ridgemont a northern suburb offers some of the advantages of both city and country.
21. From the top of the ridge in the town cemetery you can see the lights and towers of the city.
22. The center of town the commercial district offers convenient services.
23. Around the square at the very center you can find a drug store a bakery a restaurant a hardware store a clothing shop and a shoe store.
24. In most areas outside the city's center grass and trees dominate the landscape.
25. The residents are inspired by this landscape; consequently many take up gardening as a hobby.

20.3 Using Commas II

Commas clarify meaning in sentences with more than one clause. A clause is a group of words that has a subject and a predicate and is used as part of a sentence.

RULE 8: Use a comma before *and, or,* or *but* when it joins main clauses.

Farming is a business, and farmers need to make a profit.
Farmers must sell their crops, or they cannot afford to replant.
Farming can be rewarding, but it is hard work.

RULE 9 Use a comma after an introductory adverb clause. Adverb clauses begin with subordinating conjunctions, such as *after, although, as, because, before, considering (that), if, in order that, since, so that, though, unless, until, when, whenever, where, wherever, whether,* or *while.*

When the weather is too dry, farmers have problems.
If there is no rain, crops can be ruined.

In most cases, do not use a comma with an adverb clause that comes at the end of a sentence.

Farmers have problems when the weather is too dry.
Crops can be ruined if there is no rain.

RULE 10: Use a comma or a pair of commas to set off an adjective clause that is not essential to the meaning of a sentence. This means that the clause merely gives additional information. Adjective clauses often begin with the relative pronouns *who, whom, whose, which,* or *that.*

Dairy cows, which are common on farms, are raised for their milk.

Do not use a comma or pair of commas to set off an essential clause from the rest of the sentence. An adjective clause is essential when it is necessary to the meaning of the sentence.

An animal that is raised for milk is the dairy cow.

Exercise 3   Using Commas with Main Clauses

Write each sentence. Find the main clauses and the conjunction. Add commas where necessary. If the sentence needs no commas, write *correct*.

1. Farmers prepare the soil and then they plant crops in the fields.
2. Sometimes they plant a cover crop and plow it into the soil in spring.
3. They sometimes add organic material, which helps build the soil.
4. They maintain a compost pile from which they add finished compost to the soil.
5. Some seeds are planted directly in the ground but others are started indoors.
6. Some seeds are started in a greenhouse and they are planted outdoors when it's warm.
7. The farmers can buy the seeds fresh or they can save them from a previous crop.
8. Even when the plants are in the ground, the farmers' work is not done.
9. Weeds of all kinds suddenly appear and the farmers must act quickly.
10. They must remove the weeds carefully or they will disturb the young plants.

Exercise 4   Using Commas with Subordinate Clauses

Write the subordinate clause in each sentence, adding commas where needed.

1. Whenever farmers grow crops insects move in for the feast.
2. IPM which stands for Integrated Pest Management helps control insects.
3. Because insects flourish in debris farmers try to keep their fields clean.
4. They make sure that seedlings are insect-free before they plant them.
5. They rotate crops so that soil insects don't have a chance to multiply.
6. They choose varieties that can hold their own against insects.
7. Breeders whose job it is to develop such varieties watch for resistant plants.
8. They isolate these plants which are then used to produce seed.
9. When insects are large another effective control is handpicking them.
10. Physical barriers that keep insects away are also helpful.
11. An example is a row cover which discourages maggots and beetles.
12. If an insect responds to visual or chemical cues it can be caught in a trap.
13. A bright red plastic apple lures apple maggots which stick to its surface.
14. Electronic lures that zap bugs are not very effective.
15. Strong pesticides are avoided because they kill beneficial insects.
16. These insects which include lady bugs and praying mantises eat other insects.
17. Although many people fear wasps some wasps help control harmful insects.
18. If all else fails farmers must rely on pesticides.
19. When they do they limit application to the exact problem area.
20. The safest kind is insecticidal soap which doesn't linger in the soil.

20.4 Using Commas III

Several rules for using commas—among those the rules for punctuating dates and addresses—are a matter of standard usage.

> **RULE 11:** Use commas before and after the year when it is used with both the month and the day. If only the month and the year are given, do not use a comma.
>
> The antipollution project began on May 25, 1992, and lasted a year.
> The first meeting was held in July 1992 and made headlines.
>
> **RULE 12:** Use commas before and after the name of a state or a country when it is used with the name of a city. Do not use a comma after the state if it is used with a ZIP code.
>
> Speakers came from Palo Alto, California, to speak at the meeting.
> The address on the envelope was as follows: 123 Ridge Road, Orange, CT 06477.
>
> **RULE 13:** Use a comma or pair of commas to set off an abbreviated title or degree following a person's name.
>
> One expert on pollution and health is Jay Carr, M.D.
> Peter Fujita, Ph.D., wrote a book on pollution.
>
> **RULE 14:** Use a comma or commas to set off *too* in the middle of a sentence, when *too* means "also."
>
> Air pollution, too, creates problems. The courts, too, are involved.
>
> **RULE 15:** Use a comma or commas to set off a direct quotation.
>
> Dr. Flores said, "Pollution causes serious problems in our cities."
> "We will try," said Joan, "to fight pollution."
>
> **RULE 16:** Use a comma after the salutation of a friendly letter and after the closing of both a friendly and a business letter.
>
> Dear Sharon,   Your friend,   Yours truly,
>
> **RULE 17:** Use a comma for clarity in reading a sentence.
>
> Instead of three, four panelists discussed pollution.

Exercise 5   Using Commas with Names, Titles, Dates, and Quotations

Write each sentence below, adding commas where necessary, or write *correct* if the sentence needs no changes.

1. Larry said "Our conference on pollution is sure to be successful."
2. A letter from Austin Texas arrived today.
3. It said that Jean Loubet Ph.D. will be attending.
4. "Is Dr. Jean Loubet" asked Evan "a physician?"
5. His most famous book appeared in June 1995.
6. His letter told us that dozens of boxes of materials will be sent ahead by train.
7. We must prepare them for distribution at the conference.
8. Dr. Loubet will arrive at the conference on November 5 2001 and depart a week later.
9. He and Sarah McInerney M.D. will be our featured speakers.
10. Dr. McInerney too has written many books and articles.
11. She does research in Ann Arbor Michigan at the university.
12. Dr. McInerney asked "Should I send materials ahead too?"
13. She doesn't have a Ph.D. but is as famous as Dr. Loubet.
14. Larry told both speakers "We're delighted to have you here."
15. Both Dr. McInerney and Jean Loubet, Ph.D. agreed to attend the 2002 conference to deliver speeches.

Exercise 6   Using Commas in Letters

Write each numbered item below, adding commas where necessary.

[1]109 National Boulevard

[2]Los Angeles California 90034

[3]September 30 2001

[4]Dear Aunt Patricia

[5]Last week my teacher said "We can all do more to stop pollution." [6]I think that students too can help. [7]I said to Yoko "Let's make posters for the Stop Pollution Fair." [8]The fair will be like the one that was held on January 5 2000 in Denver Colorado. [9]Alex Gafar M.A. will speak on recycling.

[10]Much love

Antonia

20.5 Using Semicolons and Colons

RULE 1: Use a semicolon to join the parts of a compound sentence when a coordinating conjunction, such as *and, or, nor,* or *but,* is not used.

Many people in Africa farm small pieces of land; these farmers raise food for their families.

RULE 2: Use a semicolon to join parts of a compound sentence when the main clauses are long and are subdivided by commas. Use a semicolon even if these clauses are already joined by a coordinating conjunction.

Herding is an important job for the Dinka, Masai, and Turkana; but plowing, planting, and harvesting are also crucial tasks.

RULE 3: Use a semicolon to separate main clauses joined by a conjunctive adverb, such as *consequently, furthermore, however, moreover, nevertheless,* or *therefore.* Be sure to use a comma after a conjunctive adverb.

Many African farmers grow crops on family-owned farms; however, in some areas, farmers work on land owned by the government.

RULE 4: Use a colon to introduce a list of items that ends a sentence. Use a phrase such as *these, the following,* or *as follows* to signal that a list is coming.

African farmers grow the following: corn, millet, and sorghum.

Do not use a colon immediately after a verb or a preposition.

Some farmers work with hoes, knives, and digging sticks.

RULE 5: Use a colon to separate the hour and the minute when you write the time of day.

Many farmers start working at 5:15 in the morning.

RULE 6: Use a colon after the salutation of a business letter.

Dear Sir or Madam: Dear Ms. Ngai:

Exercise 7   Using Semicolons and Colons

Write each sentence. Add a semicolon or a colon where needed. Remember to use a comma after a conjunctive adverb.

1. I was bored at 330 in the afternoon then the mail arrived.
2. It included these items two bills, three ads, and a letter from my cousin.
3. Jill wrote about her work in Africa she is teaching English in Tanzania.
4. Africa contains these regions deserts, jungles, grasslands, and farmlands.
5. The equator cuts through Africa however most land lies north of it.
6. Some areas are not very hospitable nevertheless most are inhabited.
7. There is fertile land in North Africa however the desert predominates.
8. The southern edge of the desert merges into grassland further south the grassland merges into a tropical rain forest.
9. Southern Africa lies in the temperate zone snow falls there occasionally.
10. Africa is rich in resources thus it supports a variety of life styles.
11. Rubber trees flourish in the rain forest olive trees grow near the sea.
12. In the grasslands, farmers grow wheat and barley they also raise sheep.
13. South Africa is a major wool producer its main crops are corn and sugar.
14. Spectacular rivers flowing through Africa include the following the mighty Nile in the east, the Congo in Central Africa, and the Niger in the west.
15. Agriculture dominates the economy mining is another important activity.
16. Jill mentioned the following Tanzanian products cotton, coffee, and sugar.
17. Some areas are quite poor consequently farmers must struggle to survive.
18. Subsistence farmers depend on corn they may also raise cattle or goats.
19. Jill finds life in Africa fascinating nevertheless she misses home.
20. Now at 345 I am no longer bored Jill's letter has sparked my imagination.

Exercise 8   Using Semicolons and Colons in Letters

Write the numbered items, adding a semicolon or a colon where needed.

[1]Dear Mr. Bishop

[2]I am buying a farm for my venture, I will need farming equipment. [3]I will have to buy plows, tractors, and spreaders. [4]In the near future, I will also need the following seed, fertilizer, and more machinery. [5]I am currently pricing equipment therefore, please send me a list of your prices.

Sincerely yours,

Eleni Ruiz

20.6 Using Quotation Marks and Italics

Quotation marks enclose a person's exact words, as well as the titles of some works. Italic type—a special slanted type that is used in printing—identifies titles of other works. In handwriting, use underlining to show italic type.

RULE 1: Use quotation marks before and after a direct quotation.

"A nomad is a person who wanders," May said.

RULE 2: Use quotation marks with both parts of a divided quotation.

"Most nomads," said Ali, "travel by animal or on foot."

RULE 3: Use a comma or commas to separate a phrase such as *he said* from the quotation itself. Place the comma inside closing quotation marks.

"Most nomads," Betsy explained, "raise animals."

RULE 4: Place a period inside closing quotation marks.

José said, "Some nomads move their animals through deserts."

RULE 5: Place a question mark or an exclamation point inside the quotation marks when it is part of the quotation.

Bo asked, "Do nomads travel to find water for their herds?"

RULE 6: Place a question mark or an exclamation point outside the quotation marks when it is part of the entire sentence.

Did Ms. McCall say, "Write an essay on nomads"?

RULE 7: Use quotation marks for the title of a short story, essay, short poem, song, magazine or newspaper article, or book chapter.

"Dusk" [short story]   "Mending Wall" [poem]   "Skylark" [song]

RULE 8: Use italics (underlining) for the title of a book, play, long poem, film, television series, magazine, newspaper, or work of art.

The Sea Wolf [book]   *Julius Caesar* [play]   *Newsweek* [magazine]

Exercise 9   **Punctuating Titles**

Write each item below, adding quotation marks or underlining for italics where needed.

1. Nanook of the North (film)
2. New York Times (newspaper)
3. The Eternal Nomad (short poem)
4. The Old Man and the Sea (book)
5. Dream-Children (essay)
6. Star Trek (television series)
7. The Skin of Our Teeth (play)
8. Scientific American (magazine)
9. The Coldest Land (magazine article)
10. To Build a Fire (short story)

Exercise 10   **Using Quotation Marks and Italics**

Write the following sentences, adding quotation marks and other punctuation marks and underlining for italics where needed.

1. Frieda asked Have you read the assignment in our textbook
2. Bonnie shouted What an interesting article on nomads that was
3. I didn't know said Barry that some nomads live in northern Europe
4. Yes said Ms. Ito Lapland lies in Russia, Finland, Sweden, and Norway
5. Did Ms. Ito say The people of Lapland are called Lapps
6. Barry asked Have you read the article on Lapps in National Geographic
7. No I answered but I read about them in another magazine
8. The Lapps have two seasons said Frieda day and night
9. Does the night season really last nine months asked Barry
10. The book The Far North says Lapland has only six weeks of warm weather a year
11. Did the book say Only mosses and a few trees grow in Lapland
12. Why are the Lapps considered nomads asked George
13. Bonnie answered The people live by hunting and fishing
14. During the summer season I said they lay in supplies for the winter
15. Reindeer and dogs added Frieda are their only domestic animals
16. Do the people follow the reindeer all summer asked George
17. Bonnie replied The herds must keep moving to find enough to eat
18. Tim asked What do the Lapps do with the reindeer
19. The article The Land of the Lapps says they use the milk, meat, and hides
20. Did you know asked Ms. Ito that both male and female reindeer have antlers

20.7 Using Apostrophes

An apostrophe shows possession as well as the missing letters in a contraction. It can also signal the plural of letters, numbers, or words.

You **are**

You **'re**
a

You ' re

RULE 1: Use an apostrophe and an *s* (*'s*) to form the possessive of a singular noun.

girl + **'s** = girl**'s**   Francis + **'s** = Francis**'s**

RULE 2: Use an apostrophe and an *s* (*'s*) to form the possessive of a plural noun that does not end in *s*.

women + **'s** = women**'s**   mice + **'s** = mice**'s**

RULE 3: Use an apostrophe alone to form the possessive of a plural noun that ends in *s*.

girls + **'** = girl**s'**   Johnsons + **'** = Johnson**s'**

RULE 4: Use an apostrophe and an *s* (*'s*) to form the possessive of an indefinite pronoun.

anyone + **'s** = anyone**'s**   somebody + **'s** = somebody**'s**

Do not use an apostrophe in a possessive pronoun.

That map is **theirs**.   Is this mark **mine**?

The books on the table are **hers**.   The bird flapped **its** wings.

RULE 5: Use an apostrophe to replace letters that have been omitted in a contraction.

it + is = it**'s**   you + are = you**'re**

there + is = there**'s**   did + not = didn**'t**

RULE 6: Use an apostrophe to form the plural of letters, figures, and words when they are used as themselves.

three *t* **'s**   five 6 **'s**   no *and* **'s,** *if* **'s,** or *but* **'s**

RULE 7: Use an apostrophe to show missing numbers in a date.

the class of **'**87

Exercise 11   Using Apostrophes in Possessives

Write the possessive form of each of the words below.

1. cities
2. nation
3. everybody
4. children
5. Mr. Schultz
6. dogs
7. man
8. Sharice
9. woman
10. geese
11. classes
12. teacher
13. Alex
14. someone
15. oxen
16. Jim
17. the Gilsons
18. landowners
19. managers
20. people
21. rooster
22. family
23. nobody
24. Ms. Tremon
25. clowns

Exercise 12   Using Apostrophes

Write each plural, possessive, or contraction. Use apostrophes where needed.
Write *correct* if the sentence needs no changes.

1. This citys outlook is uncertain.
2. Ours is an uncertain future.
3. Today cities arent built beneath the earth.
4. Its strange to think of underground cities.
5. Perhaps well see cities floating on the water.
6. Many city planners ideas are unusual.
7. Their reports usually are filled with too many *if*s.
8. Tomorrows cities are a mystery to us.
9. No city can plan its future exactly.
10. All of our visions are full of *maybe*s.
11. What will actually happen to cities is anybodys guess.
12. These authors new book predicts the end of cities.
13. The Murrays idea is that we wont need cities.
14. In their view, computers will let us live anywhere.
15. I can do my job at my house, you can do yours at your house, and other people can work out of their houses too.
16. Ill believe that when I see it.
17. Other peoples dreams take them to space.
18. One of Arthur C. Clarkes books is about a city in a space station.
19. The residents lives would be very different from ours.
20. Someone elses book predicts that cities will expand outward.

20.8 Using Hyphens, Dashes, and Parentheses

RULE 1 Use a hyphen to show the division of a word at the end of a line. Always divide the word between its syllables.

Forests and their products are of the greatest importance to people.

RULE 2 Use a hyphen in compound numbers.

eighty-seven   thirty-nine

RULE 3 Use a hyphen in a fraction that is spelled out.

Forest rangers receive **one-half** pay upon retirement. [modifier]

One-half of all tree diseases are caused by fungi. [noun]

RULE 4 Use a hyphen or hyphens in certain compound nouns.

great-grandfather   brother-in-law   attorney-at-law

RULE 5 Hyphenate a compound modifier only when it precedes the word it modifies.

It's a **well-maintained** park.   It is **well maintained.**

RULE 6 Use a hyphen after the prefixes *all-*, *ex-*, and *self-*. Use a hyphen to separate any prefix from a word that begins with a capital letter.

all-powerful   ex-wife   self-educated   pre-Columbian

RULE 7 Use a dash or dashes to show a sudden break or change in thought or speech.

Mrs. Poulos—she lives nearby—helps the park attendants.

RULE 8 Use parentheses to set off words that define or helpfully explain a word in the sentence.

In tropical rain forests, dozens of species of plants may grow in one square mile (2.6 square kilometers) of land.

Exercise 13   Using Hyphens

Write each item. Use a hyphen where needed. Write *correct* if the item needs no hyphens.

1. two thirds majority
2. one-half of the pie
3. exchampion
4. self knowledge
5. well loved author
6. all inclusive
7. Great aunt Katie
8. sixty five
9. mid American
10. postwar
11. one quarter finished
12. father in law
13. well known author
14. seventy three
15. pro Irish

Exercise 14   Using Hyphens, Dashes, and Parentheses

Write the following sentences, adding any needed hyphens, dashes, or parentheses. Write *correct* if the sentence needs no changes.

1. Before people began to clear the forest for farms and cities, forests covered about one half of the earth.
2. Dr. Orzeck he is an expert on ecology spoke about deforestation.
3. His presentation was well documented.
4. People have used wood products since the beginning of time but more about that later.
5. One tree may have as many as forty two uses.
6. In pre Columbian America vast all pine forests were common.
7. Some pines were huge, up to 240 feet tall and 2 feet in diameter.
8. British law see text on page 311 reserved these huge trees for the Crown.
9. The super straight trunks were perfect for the masts of sailing ships.
10. In 1947 a month long fire in a Maine forest provided a forest laboratory.
11. At first sun loving flowers and shrubs grew up to fill the new clearings.
12. Now, evergreen trees that don't shed their leaves are shading out the birches.
13. These shade tolerant trees will again dominate the forest.
14. About 748 species of trees are native in the continental United States.
15. The National Register of Big Trees page 221 lists champion trees.
16. A sequoia truly a giant at eighty-three feet in circumference is the largest tree.
17. Some sequoias in California have been growing for three thousand years.
18. Others want to protect the remaining old growth forests in the country.
19. Forests grow only where there is at least fifteen inches thirty-eight centimeters of rainfall per year.
20. Forests also require a frost free growing period of at least three months.

20.9 Using Abbreviations

RULE 1: Abbreviate the titles *Mr., Mrs., Ms.,* and *Dr.* before a person's name. Also abbreviate any professional or academic degree that follows a name, along with the titles *Jr.* and *Sr.*

Mr. Roy Sims **Jr.**   Rita Mendez, **M.D.**   Hugo Allen **Sr.**

RULE 2: Use capital letters and no periods with abbreviations that are pronounced letter by letter or as words. Exceptions are *U.S.* and *Washington, D.C.,* which do use periods.

WHO World Health Organization   **JV** junior varsity

ROTC Reserve Officers' Training Corps

RULE 3: With exact times, use A.M. (*ante meridiem,* "before noon") and P.M. (*post meridiem,* "after noon"). For years use B.C. (before Christ) and, sometimes, A.D. (*anno Domini,* "in the year of the Lord," after Christ).

7:15 A.M.   9:30 P.M.   40 B.C.   A.D. 476

RULE 4: Abbreviate days and months only in charts and lists.

Sun.   Tues.   Wed.   Feb.   Jul.   Aug.   Sept.

RULE 5: In scientific writing abbreviate units of measure. Use periods with English units but not with metric units.

inch(es) **in.**   pound(s) **lb.**   gallon(s) **gal.**

kilometer(s) **km**   liter(s) **l**   milliliter(s) **ml**

RULE 6: On envelopes only, abbreviate street names and state names. In general text, spell out street names and state names.

Street **St.**   Avenue **Ave.**   Road **Rd.**   Drive **Dr.**
Boulevard **Blvd.**   Parkway **Pkwy.**   Place **Pl.**
Arizona **AZ**   Colorado **CO**   Hawaii **HI**   Oklahoma **OK**
Kentucky **KY**   Utah **UT**   Virginia **VA**   Missouri **MO**
[on an envelope]   Mrs. Emily Anderson
                      3117 Chelsea **Ave.**
                      Norfolk, **VA** 23503

but   We still live on Chelsea **Avenue** in Norfolk, **Virginia.**

National
Aeronautics and
Space
Administration

Punctuation

Exercise 15   Using Abbreviations

Write the correct abbreviation for each underlined item.

1. _anno Domini_ 2000
2. David Parker <u>Junior</u>
3. 153 <u>kilometers</u>
4. <u>February</u> 23
5. <u>Wednesday</u>
6. 1066 <u>before Christ</u>
7. <u>Young Women's Christian Association</u>
8. <u>Mister</u> Al Moreno
9. ninety-eight <u>pounds</u>
10. Saratoga <u>Road</u>
11. 67 Ryer <u>Avenue</u>
12. Sam Blie <u>Senior</u>
13. Phoenix, <u>Arizona</u>
14. Lewis Wright, <u>Medical Doctor</u>
15. <u>Students Against Driving Drunk</u>
16. _post meridiem_
17. Ann Carey, <u>Doctor of Philosophy</u>
18. Cato <u>Boulevard</u>
19. Denver, <u>Colorado</u>
20. <u>Columbia Broadcasting System</u>

Exercise 16   Using Abbreviations in Sentences

Write the correct abbreviation for each underlined item in the following sentences. Write _correct_ if there are no changes.

1. The address on the envelope read 48 Bolton <u>Street</u>, Madison, <u>Wisconsin</u>.
2. It contained information from <u>Doctor</u> Rita Tapahonso.
3. <u>Mister</u> Ed Jones is teaching ecology.
4. Last year, classes met from 9:30 <u>in the morning</u> until 3:30 <u>in the afternoon</u>.
5. Scheduled speakers included <u>Doctor</u> Robin Oren.
6. Also present will be a representative of the <u>Environmental Protection Agency.</u>
7. Classes begin in <u>September.</u>
8. My adviser will see me on <u>Tuesday</u>.
9. Do you know the purpose of most <u>United Nations</u> agencies?
10. I know <u>United Nations International Children's Emergency Fund</u> helps children and mothers in developing nations.
11. Also, the <u>International Labor Organization</u> promotes employment and fair labor conditions.
12. The President lives at 1600 Pennsylvania <u>Avenue</u>, Washington, <u>District of Columbia.</u>
13. I was born on <u>February</u> 29, 1980, at 6:50 _ante meridiem._
14. Madeline Jefferson, <u>Master of Arts</u>, is our English teacher.
15. Mix 3 <u>gallons</u> of Substance A with 2 <u>pounds</u> of Substance B.
16. Salt Lake City, <u>Utah</u>, and Tulsa, <u>Oklahoma</u>, are often compared.
17. Kim Yang, <u>Doctor of Dental Surgery</u>, has been my dentist for three years.
18. His office address is 412 Mullins <u>Road</u>, Kalamazoo, <u>Michigan</u>.
19. Mexico, <u>Missouri</u>, and Paris, <u>Kentucky</u>, are both <u>United States</u> cities.
20. What is the sum of 12 <u>liters</u> and 48 <u>milliliters</u>?

20.10 Writing Numbers

In charts and tables, numbers are always written as figures. However, in an ordinary sentence some numbers are spelled out and others are written as numerals.

RULE 1: Spell out all numbers up to ninety-nine.

My dad had not visited his hometown for **twenty-five** years.

RULE 2: Use numerals for numbers of more than two words.

Approximately **250** people used to live in his hometown.

RULE 3: Spell out any number that begins a sentence, or reword the sentence so that it does not begin with a number.

Nine thousand two hundred people now live in Dad's hometown.

RULE 4: Write very large numbers as a numeral followed by the word *million* or *billion*.

The population of the United States is about **263 million**.

RULE 5: If related numbers appear in the same sentence, use all numerals.

Of the **435** graduates, **30** have received a scholarship to college.

RULE 6: Spell out ordinal numbers (*first, second,* and so forth).

Jan is the **sixth** person to use the new library.

RULE 7: Use words to express the time of day unless you are writing the exact time or using the abbreviation A.M. or P.M.

Classes begin at **nine o'clock**.
They end at **2:45** P.M.

RULE 8: Use numerals to express dates, house and street numbers, apartment and room numbers, telephone numbers, page numbers, amounts of money of more than two words, and percentages. Write out the word *percent.*

May **24, 1887**   **62** Oak Drive   Room **307**   **98** percent

---

Exercise 17   **Writing Numbers**

Write the sentences below, using the correct form for writing numbers. Write *correct* if a sentence needs no changes.

1. My father graduated from Red Bank Regional High School with the class of nineteen hundred sixty-one.
2. His class recently had a reunion after thirty years.
3. The reunion was scheduled for April ninth.
4. The party began at seven-thirty P.M.
5. Dad was the 13th person to arrive that evening.
6. The reunion was held in room forty-two, the old cafeteria.
7. 220 people came to the reunion.
8. Of these, 180 guests were graduates and forty were spouses.
9. More than 50% of the graduates attended.
10. There were three hundred thirty-four students in his graduating class.
11. Dad was happy to see his old best friend, whom he had not seen in 27 years.
12. He learned that Mr. Elton has moved back to town, to One Eighteen Jay Road.
13. Dad, Mr. Elton, and 2 other old friends agreed to get together in the coming year.
14. They figure three hundred sixty-five days gives them enough time to plan something.
15. Each alumnus contributed twenty dollars.
16. The committee collected 4 thousand 4 hundred dollars.
17. The party lasted until one o'clock.
18. My father graduated 5th in his class.
19. 75% of the class went on to college.
20. Of these students, 41 did not complete college.

Exercise 18   **Writing Numbers**

In the following paragraph, use the correct form for writing numbers.

[1]In nineteen hundred ninety-one the population of the United States was approximately 248 million. [2]The estimated population of North America was three hundred ninety million. [3]North America has the 3rd largest population of the world's continents. [4]Asia has the largest, with fifty-nine percent. [5]More than three billion people live in Asia. [6]Africa ranks 2nd in the world's population. [7]Close to seven hundred million people live there. [8]Australia and New Zealand account for only 20,000,000 people. [9]Antarctica has no permanent population, and fewer than 1,000 scientists stay the winter. [10]Overall, more than five point three billion people inhabit the earth.

Grammar Review

PUNCTUATION

Tourists see a place differently from the way local inhabitants do. In *A Small Place,* Jamaica Kincaid writes about her homeland, the small Caribbean island of Antigua. In the following passage from the book, Kincaid looks at the island through the eyes of a tourist. She describes the island's beauty and discusses its history. She also expresses her hopes for the future of Antigua. The passage has been annotated to show some of the rules of punctuation covered in this unit.

Literature Model

from A Small Place

by Jamaica Kincaid

Oh, but by now you are tired of all this looking, and you want to reach your destination—your hotel, your room. You long to refresh yourself; you long to eat some nice lobster, some nice local food. You take a bath, you brush your teeth. You get dressed again; as you get dressed, you look out the window. That water—have you ever seen anything like it? Far out, to the horizon, the color of the water is navy-blue; nearer, the water is the color of the North American sky. From there to the shore, the water is pale, silvery, clear, so clear that you can see its pinkish-white sand bottom. Oh, what beauty! Oh, what beauty! You have never seen anything like this. You are so excited. You breathe shallow. You breathe deep.

Comma before *and* used to join main clauses

Semicolon to join parts of a compound sentence without a conjunction

Dash to show an interrupted thought

Comma after two introductory prepositional phrases

Punctuation

Grammar Review **619**

Grammar Review

Review: Exercise 1   Using Commas

Write each sentence, adding commas where needed.

1. Tourists come for the white sand beaches colorful reefs and balmy climate.
2. Antigua unlike other islands of the Lesser Antilles is not mountainous.
3. Most of the island is flat; however there are hills in the Southwest.
4. These hills the remnants of ancient volcanoes bear patches of rain forest.
5. Did you know Catherine that Antigua was once covered by rain forest?
6. It was deforested by its original inhabitants British planters and modern developers.
7. Antigua does not have much rainfall; therefore rain seldom interferes with tourists' plans.
8. Mangroves tidal flats salt ponds and freshwater pools are found near the shore.
9. These watery habitats as you can imagine host a great variety of wildlife.
10. Magnificent frigate birds black seabirds with long wings soar the cliffs.

Review: Exercise 2   Using Commas with Introductory Words and Phrases

Write each sentence, adding commas where needed.

SAMPLE   Lying among the Leeward Islands Antigua is a Caribbean jewel.
ANSWER   Lying among the Leeward Islands, Antigua is a Caribbean jewel.

1. Blessed with low humidity and year-round trade winds Antigua has an ideal climate for tourists.
2. Fringed by coral reefs the island is a snorkeler's paradise.
3. With its miles of undulating coastline it appeals to beach lovers from all over the world.
4. Shimmering in the tropical sun the turquoise waters are very inviting.
5. Indeed all kinds of water sports are popular with both natives and tourists.
6. In the sheltered water of English Harbor sailboats find safe haven.
7. From old military installations on Shirley Heights Antiguans and visitors can view fabulous sunsets.
8. No the capital is not at English Harbor.
9. Situated on the northwest coast St. John's Harbor welcomes cruise ships.
10. Yes that irregular coastline also provides many smaller bays for swimming.

Review: Exercise 3 **Using Commas with Adverb Clauses**

Write each sentence, adding commas where needed. Write *correct* if the sentence is correct.

SAMPLE   If you want to see mahogany trees stroll through Walling Woodlands.
ANSWER   If you want to see mahogany trees, stroll through Walling Woodlands.

1. Because McKinnon's Salt Pond is very shallow it appeals to sandpipers.
2. Where Indian Creek flows into the sea brown pelicans dive for tarpon.
3. You won't find a tropical rain forest unless you drive up Boggy Peak.
4. Before you drive back down you should look for scarlet tanagers.
5. Visit the lovely beaches of Carlisle Bay after you leave Boggy Peak.
6. Since Farley Bay is accessible only by foot or by water it is very peaceful.
7. Look for unusual shells when you go to Rendezvous Bay.
8. Although blue herons are everywhere Potswork Reservoir attracts the most.
9. If you want to see a mature stand of evergreens visit Weatheralls Hill.
10. In hotel gardens, you will see hummingbirds because they want the nectar in the resort's tropical flowers and fruit trees.

Review: Exercise 4 **Using Commas with Adjective Clauses**

Write each sentence, adding commas where needed. Write *correct* if the sentence is correct.

SAMPLE   Christopher Columbus who arrived in 1943 named Antigua.
ANSWER   Christopher Columbus, who arrived in 1493, named Antigua.

1. Tourists who like to explore have many options on Antigua.
2. Paradise Reef which offers a mile of coral is popular with snorkelers.
3. Glass-bottomed boats which let nonswimmers see the reef are also popular.
4. You may see the hawksbill whose shell is used for tortoiseshell jewelry.
5. The hawksbill which is named for its beaky upper jawbone is a sea turtle.
6. On Green Castle Hill are rock formations that may date to ancient times.
7. Fig Tree Drive which is named for the Antiguan fig is lush with trees.
8. Devil's Bridge is a natural formation that was created by pounding waves.
9. Captain Horatio Nelson who later became a famous British admiral served for a time in Antigua and gave his name to Nelson's Dockyard.
10. A strenuous hike leads to Monk Hill which overlooks two harbors.

Grammar Review

Review: Exercise 5   Using Commas

Write each sentence, adding commas where needed.

1. Leona's home is at 1147 Schyler Street Gary Indiana.
2. Her aunt Jo lives in Falmouth Antigua.
3. Josephine Susannah Hardy M.D. is her aunt's full name.
4. Leona arrived for a visit on July 15 2000.
5. Leona's brother Conrad came too.
6. "It's great to be here" said Leona "because I love to swim."
7. "You'll have lots of beaches to choose from" said Aunt Jo.
8. Among these three are especially recommended.
9. Leona and Conrad swam every day and studied Antiguan birdlife too.
10. On August 2 2000 they regretfully waved goodbye to Antigua.

Review: Exercise 6   Using Commas, Semicolons, and Colons

Write each sentence, adding commas, semicolons, and colons where needed.

SAMPLE   Old towns can be revived the story of English Harbor proves it.
ANSWER   Old towns can be revived; the story of English Harbor proves it.

1. English Harbor bustled for two centuries but then its glory faded.
2. The English navy sailed for home and traders found different ports.
3. Nelson's Dockyard itself was badly decayed old buildings had fallen in.
4. In 1951 the governor founded the Society of the Friends of English Harbor its purpose was to restore the harbor.
5. The group unearthed original plans consequently their restoration is historically accurate.
6. They tried to get these details right hand-hewn beams, pegged wood, and old glass.
7. Interest among natives, sailors, and business people grew and soon old-timers, visitors, and new residents made the streets bustle again.
8. Now Nelson's Dockyard is full of shops the Galley, the Saw Pit, the Cooper and Lumber Store, and more.
9. Tourists flock to these shops therefore the economy has steadily grown.
10. Charter boats and private boats crowd the harbor it once again welcomes travelers from the sea.

Review: Exercise 7 **Using Commas and End Marks in Direct Quotations**

Write each sentence, adding commas and end marks where needed.

SAMPLE   "Let's visit an Arawak dig" suggested Ann.
ANSWER   "Let's visit an Arawak dig," suggested Ann.

1. "The Caribbean Islands are just like stepping stones from Venezuela to Florida" said Ron
2. Keisha added "Most of the first inhabitants came from South America"
3. "Among those who settled Antigua" said Mr. Hays "were the Arawaks"
4. Did you say "The Arawaks lived in wooden houses"
5. "Yes" said Mr. Hays "the houses were wood with thatched roofs"
6. "Didn't the Arawaks play an early kind of soccer" asked Ron
7. "The object of the game" said Keisha "was to keep the ball in the air"
8. "And you couldn't use your hands" exclaimed Ann
9. Ron asked "How were the points scored"
10. "If you let the ball touch ground, the other side scored a point" said Ann

Review: Exercise 8 **Punctuating Direct Quotations**

Write each sentence, adding quotation marks and underlining for italics, commas, and end marks where needed.

SAMPLE   Who were the first people on Antigua asked Tony.
ANSWER   "Who were the first people on Antigua?" asked Tony.

1. I have been reading about the Arawaks and Caribs in a beautiful book called Lost Empires
2. In it there is a chapter about the Caribbean called Crossroads Cultures
3. I told the class The Arawaks used sophisticated farming methods
4. They knew how to control erosion and irrigate their fields explained Tim
5. Manioc was their chief crop I said but they also grew other foods
6. Tony asked What's manioc
7. It's a starchy, edible root like cassava answered Mr. Hays
8. The sea I said provided the Arawaks with fish and turtles
9. Tim asked Weren't the Arawaks eventually conquered by the Caribs
10. The Caribs were cannibals I exclaimed

Punctuation

Grammar Review

| **Review: Exercise 9** | Using Apostrophes, Hyphens, Dashes, and Parentheses |

Write each sentence, inserting apostrophes, hyphens, dashes, and parentheses where needed.

SAMPLE   Antigua has a well developed educational system.
ANSWER   Antigua has a well-developed educational system.

1. The country of Antigua and Barbuda has a total land area of 171 square miles 442 square kilometers.
2. Barbuda is a game preserve, and its anyones guess how many species of birds live there.
3. Redonda an uninhabited island is also part of the island country.
4. The country has been a self governing nation since 1981.
5. The three islands terrain is mostly flat.
6. Most of the countrys population live on the island of Antigua.
7. The majority of the people descendants of Africans speak English.
8. The peoples main foods include beans, fish, lobsters, and sweet potatoes.
9. On their jobs, theyre bankers, shopkeepers, hotel workers, taxi drivers, farmers, and manufacturers.
10. Drought often harms farmers crops of sugar cane and cotton.

| **Review: Exercise 10** | Using Abbreviations and Numbers |

Write each sentence, correcting the errors in abbreviations and numbers.

1. Mister Vere Cornwall was the prime minister of Antigua and Barbuda.
2. About two percent of the people live on Barbuda, the smaller island.
3. The islands receive about 45 in. of rain annually.
4. 2 deaths and 80 million dollars in property damage resulted when Hurricane Hugo struck in 1989.
5. The island's hospitals need qualified Drs.
6. Slavery was abolished on Antigua in eighteen thirty-four.
7. Forests cover 15.9% of Antigua, and 59.1% of the land is agricultural.
8. When it's 2 o'clock in VA, it's 3 o'clock in Antigua.
9. Tourists can choose from among three hundred sixty-five beaches on Antigua.
10. Summer Carnival is celebrated in late Jul. and early Aug.

Review: Exercise 11

Proofreading

Rewrite the following passage, correcting the errors in spelling, grammar, and usage. Add any missing punctuation. There are ten errors.

Interior at Nice

¹The young woman in the picture on the next page sit in front of a window on a hotel balcony in France. ²With her back to the sea she gazes at the observer. ³The sun reflects off the sea and bathe the room in silvery light. ⁴Intense pinks blues, and grays help convey the atmosphere of warmth.

⁵Like Jamaica Kincaid in the passage from *A Small Place* Henri Matisse has captured a momant by the sea. ⁶The picture on the hotel wall—a picture within the picture duplicate the figure of the woman on the balcony. ⁷The observer's attention is drawed to the woman. ⁸What differences can you find between *A Small Place* and *Interior at Nice*

Review: Exercise 12

Mixed Review

Write each sentence, correcting all errors in punctuation, quotation marks, italics, and numbers.

¹Born on May 25, 1949 young Jamaica Kincaid loved to read, one of her favorite books was Jane Eyre. ²Although she had a happy childhood Kincaid realized that her family her mother father and three brothers underestimated her abilities she also felt stifled by the island. ³By 16 she was a very self directed young woman and she left Antigua for a job in New York. ⁴She attended several colleges but she never earned a degree. ⁵After she had written articles for teenagers magazines she became a staff writer for The New Yorker magazine. ⁶She wrote gardening articles however now her interest in fiction motivated her to write Girl, a short story. ⁷Most of the 10 stories in At the Bottom of the River, which was published in 1983 deal with mothers and daughters. ⁸Among the stories are the following Girl My Mother and In the Night. ⁹Kincaid's 2nd book

(continued)

Annie John, is about a young Antiguan girl who grows from childhood to adolescence. [10] Kincaid also wrote A Small Place which criticizes British colonialism and the government of Antigua.

Henri Matisee, *Interior at Nice*, 1921

Writing Application

TIME

For more about the writing process, see **TIME Facing the Blank Page,** pp. 97-107.

Apostrophes in Writing

David Weitzman uses apostrophes in this passage from *Thrashin' Time* to make his farming characters' dialogue sound realistic. Study the passage, paying close attention to the italicized words.

> "What do you think about all this, Peter, steam power instead of horse power?"
>
> I *wasn't* sure. "If the engine took the place of the horses, I think I'd miss Annie and Lulu and Quinn. *Wouldn't* you, Pa?"
>
> "I would, but, you know, horsepower *thrashin'* is awful hard on them, son. Sure, I'd miss them, but we work them hard all year *plowin'* and *diskin',* and *seedin'* and *mowin'.* Then just when *they're* so tuckered out, about to drop and *needin'* a good rest, we put them to *thrashin'.*"

Techniques with Apostrophes

Try to apply some of David Weitzman's writing techniques when you write.

❶ Use apostrophes to create contractions and help your writing flow more smoothly.

AWKWARD VERSION I *was not* sure.

WEITZMAN'S VERSION I *wasn't* sure.

❷ Dialogue conveys information about a character. Replacing missing letters with apostrophes shows a character's natural speech patterns. The first version, although correct, is not how Pa really speaks.

LESS INFORMATION we work them hard all year *plowing* and *disking,* and *seeding* and *mowing*

WEITZMAN'S VERSION we work them hard all year *plowin'* and *diskin',* and *seedin'* and *mowin'*

Practice Rewrite the following passage, adding apostrophes to the underlined words to make the dialogue sound more natural.

"<u>Nothing doing</u>, Fred," said Mr. Felters. "I <u>cannot</u> accept this wood. <u>It is</u> not cut short enough."

"Come on, Felters, <u>we have</u> been <u>working</u> together for <u>going</u> on ten years. Trust me. <u>I will</u> come tomorrow and cut it shorter for you," implored Fred.

"Nope! <u>Before</u> I take it, <u>it has</u> got to be right. Cut <u>them</u> down to two-foot lengths and <u>I will</u> be a happy man," insisted Mr. Felters.

"If I must," sighed Fred, "I guess I may as well get <u>going</u> on it."

Punctuation

Sentence Combining

Prepositional phrases are effective tools for sentence combining. They describe nouns and verbs, just as single-word adjectives and adverbs do. Furthermore, because they show relationships between words, prepositional phrases can express complicated ideas.

EXAMPLE   **a.** The landscape has undergone a change.

b. This change is **for the worse.**

c. This is **according to Rachel Carson.**

According to Rachel Carson, the landscape has undergone a change **for the worse.**

The new information from sentences *b* and *c* is added to sentence *a* in the form of prepositional phrases. In the new sentence, the prepositional phrase *According to Rachel Carson* modifies the verb *has undergone*, and the prepositional phrase *for the worse* modifies the noun *change*. Prepositional phrases follow the nouns they modify. Prepositional phrases that modify verbs can precede or follow the verbs they modify. (For a list of common prepositions, see page 481.)

■ A **prepositional phrase** is a group of words that begins with a preposition and ends with a noun or pronoun. Prepositional phrases modify nouns, verbs, and pronouns.

Exercise 1   **Combining Sentences with Prepositional Phrases**

The following sentences are based on an excerpt from *Silent Spring* by Rachel Carson, which you can find on pages 302–305. Combine each group of sentences so that the new information is turned into a prepositional phrase. In the first few items the new information is in dark type.

1. **a.** Carson describes a mythical town.
   b. The town was one **of great natural beauty.**
2. **a.** Prosperous farms surrounded the town.
   b. The farms were dotted **with rich productive fields.**
3. **a.** Birds filled the trees and bushes.
   b. The birds were **of many different kinds.**

(continued)

Sentence Combining

4. **a.** People visited this town.
   b. They came from miles away.
   c. They came on account of the romantic beauty of this special place.
5. **a.** A blight covered the land.
   b. The blight was one of unknown origin.
6. **a.** A powdery chemical snow fell.
   b. It fell on buildings and land alike.
7. **a.** Strange sicknesses were in the human and animal communities.
   b. Doctors studied the strange sicknesses.
   c. The doctors studied with the latest medical tools.
8. **a.** The vegetation was dead or dying.
   b. The dying vegetation was beside the roads.
   c. The dying vegetation was in the orchards.
9. **a.** Silence now reigned in the springtime.
   b. It reigned after the disappearance of the birds.
10. **a.** The countryside changed dramatically.
    b. It turned into a scene of mysterious mourning.

Exercise 2   Combining Sentences

Rewrite the following paragraphs. Use prepositional phrases to combine sentences. Make any other changes in wording that you feel are necessary.

Rachel Carson describes some tragedies caused by people. She describes them in her book *Silent Spring*. These tragedies were not caused by any alien or mysterious agent. Her mythical town faced a bright and hopeful future. Then people destroyed the land. They destroyed it with their thoughtless actions. Now the land was dying. Everything on it was dying. There were no new young plants and animals to replace those that had died. Therefore, the only prospect was despair.

No one place has suffered all the tragedies described by Carson. However, each blight has occurred somewhere. The blights are upon the environment. Each one might have occurred in this country, or it might have been in other parts of the world. Many communities have undergone several of these misfortunes. This fact is without exaggeration. Carson writes of a "grim specter." This specter is upon our landscape. Carson writes in her book *Silent Spring*. The tragedy might become a reality. The tragedy is that of the mythical town. The reality is for all of us. This is according to Rachel Carson.

21.2 Appositives

Appositives allow you to combine sentences in a compact and informative way. Appositives and appositive phrases identify or reveal something new about a noun or pronoun.

EXAMPLE
   a. Maya Lin designed the Vietnam Veterans Memorial.

   b. Maya Lin was **an architecture student.**

Maya Lin, **an architecture student,** designed the Vietnam Veterans Memorial.

The appositive phrase *an architecture student* tells us more about *Maya Lin.* The appositive is set off with commas because it gives additional information. If an appositive supplies essential information, it is not set off with commas. (For more information about appositives, see pages 391–392.)

■ An **appositive** is a noun placed next to another noun to identify it or give additional information about it. An **appositive phrase** includes an appositive and other words that describe it.

Exercise 3   Combining Sentences with Appositives

The following sentences are based on "Always to Remember" by Brent Ashabranner, which you can find on pages 250–257. Combine each group of sentences so that the new information is turned into an appositive or appositive phrase. In the first few items, the new information is in dark type. Add commas when necessary to your new sentences.

1. **a.** Congress had authorized the Vietnam Veterans Memorial.
   b. The memorial was to be **a monument to the war's dead and missing soldiers.**
2. **a.** Over one thousand contestants submitted plans.
   b. This number of contestants was **a record number for a design competition.**
3. **a.** The winner was Maya Lin.
   b. She was **the daughter of the dean of fine arts at Ohio University.**
   c. The dean was **Henry Huan Lin.**
4. **a.** She was the child of cultured and educated parents.
   b. Maya Lin felt that art and literature were always beside her.
   c. Art and literature were her childhood friends.

Sentence Combining

5. **a.** Maya Lin studied architecture at Yale University.
   b. She was valedictorian in high school.
6. **a.** Lin was a student in Europe.
   b. There she became interested in the architecture of cemeteries.
   c. Cemeteries are also called "cities of the dead."
7. **a.** In France she was impressed by a memorial.
   b. The memorial was the work of the architect.
   c. The architect was Sir Edwin Lutyens.
8. **a.** Maya learned of the Memorial Competition from Andrus Burr.
   b. She was a Yale student.
   c. He was a professor of funerary (burial) architecture.
9. **a.** During a visit to the site, Maya Lin envisioned the winning design.
   b. The site was in Constitution Gardens.
   c. Maya Lin was an architecture student.
10. **a.** The winner described her feelings to a *Washington Post* writer.
    b. Maya Lin was the winner.
    c. The writer was Phil McCombs.

Exercise 4   Combining Sentences

Rewrite the paragraph below. Use appositives and appositive phrases to combine sentences. Make any changes in wording you feel necessary.

Before making her design, Maya Lin visited the monument's proposed site. The site was Constitution Gardens in Washington, D.C. During her visit, the park was being enjoyed by many people. These people were Washington, D.C., residents and tourists. Lin did not want to destroy a living, beautiful park with a grim monument. That monument would be a structure out of harmony with its surroundings. Upon returning to Yale, Lin made a clay model of her vision. The vision she had in Constitution Gardens. Professor Burr had been the catalyst to Lin's involvement. He liked her ideas. She plunged onward, and finally her design was ready to submit. It took her six weeks of work to complete. Lin's design fits in with the park's landscape. Her final design was a long wall of polished black stone.

21.3 Adjective Clauses

Adjective clauses are useful in combining sentences. When two sentences share information, one of them can be made into an adjective clause that modifies a word or phrase in the other.

EXAMPLE
    a. Lyddie began her working day long before breakfast.

    b. Lyddie **labored in a cloth factory.**
       [, who . . . ,]

Lyddie, **who labored in a cloth factory,** began her working day long before breakfast.

The new information from sentence b, *labored in a cloth factory,* becomes an adjective clause modifying *Lyddie* in sentence a. The pronoun *who* now connects the clauses. Notice the commas in the new sentence. Adjective clauses that add nonessential information require commas. Adjective clauses that add essential information do not require commas. (For more information about adjective clauses, see pages 509–510.)

■ An **adjective clause** is a subordinate clause that modifies a noun or pronoun in the main clause. The relative pronouns *who, whom, whose, which, that,* and *what* tie the adjective clause to the main clause.

Exercise 5   **Combining Sentences with Adjective Clauses**

The following sentences are based on an excerpt from *Lyddie* by Katherine Paterson, which you can find on pages 188–193. Combine each group of sentences so that the new information is turned into an adjective clause. In the first three items, the new information is in dark type. The information in brackets indicates the relative pronoun to use and whether a comma or commas are needed.

1. **a.** The girls began their working day long before breakfast.
   b. The girls **labored in the cloth factory.** [who]
2. **a.** Lyddie found a job in a cloth factory.
   b. Lyddie **had come from the country.** [, who . . . ,]
3. **a.** The overseer pulled the cord to the leather belt.
   b. The belt **set the factory machinery into motion.** [that]

(continued)

4. **a.** The girls had to rush back at seven-thirty.
   b. The girls were released at seven for breakfast.
5. **a.** Lyddie examined her boots.
   b. Her boots had knotted laces.
6. **a.** Lyddie ran to the window for a breath of fresh air.
   b. Lyddie's eyes were filled with tears.
   c. She needed the breath of fresh air so desperately.
7. **a.** The window was nailed shut.
   b. It was the window Lyddie reached first.
8. **a.** Diana gently guided Lyddie back to the loom.
   b. Diana had already been a great friend to Lyddie.
9. **a.** The day now seemed an endless nightmare.
   b. The day had begun with so much hope.
10. **a.** By the end of the day, Lyddie was too tired to think about the regulations.
    b. These were the rules that all the girls had to learn.

Exercise 6   Combining Sentences

Rewrite the paragraphs below, using adjective clauses to combine sentences. Make any other changes in wording or punctuation you think necessary.

The bountiful supper table made Lyddie nauseated tonight. It might otherwise appeal to Lyddie. Finally, after sitting listlessly through the meal, Lyddie reached her bed. There she began to undress. She struggled with her clothes. She had donned the clothes so quickly and deftly just that morning. The boots were now a sore burden to her. The boots had been her special pride. Triphena's old boots sat on the floor near Lyddie's bed. She had left them there the night before. Maybe these old boots would give Lyddie's swollen feet some breathing space. These boots were stiff and awkward.

Betsy felt Lyddie's pain. She was a fellow sufferer. She remembered the horrors of her own first day. Maybe reading would make Lyddie feel better as well. It always helped Betsy to escape. With this thought in mind, Betsy picked up a book. She hoped Lyddie would enjoy this book.

Betsy read out loud from the novel *Oliver Twist*. *Oliver Twist* was written by Charles Dickens. The novel tells the story of a hungry boy. The boy is punished for asking for more food at a poorhouse. Lyddie heard the description of Oliver's punishment. The man reminded her of the factory overseer. The man scolded Oliver. The overseer had frightened her that very day. Lyddie now wanted to hear the whole story of Oliver. Lyddie had before been too tired to speak. Betsy read on until the curfew bell. Betsy's voice grew hoarse with fatigue.

21.4 Adverb Clauses

Adverb clauses are a frequently used and highly effective way to combine sentences. Adverb clauses help you establish clear relationships between two or more ideas or actions. For example, you can use adverb clauses to show that one action causes another or results from another.

EXAMPLE **a.** Mr. Reese drilled the team thoroughly.

b. They would soon be playing for the championship. **[since]**

Mr. Reese drilled the team thoroughly **since they would soon be playing for the championship.**

In the new sentence, the adverb clause *since they would soon be playing for the championship* explains why Mr. Reese drilled the team so thoroughly. Note that the subordinating conjunction *since* makes the cause-effect relationship very clear. An adverb clause can occupy several positions within a sentence. If it begins the sentence, it is followed by a comma. (For more information about adverb clauses, see pages 513–514.)

■ An **adverb clause** is a subordinate clause that often modifies or describes the verb in the main clause. Adverb clauses are introduced by subordinating conjunctions such as *after, although, as, before, if, since, when, whenever, wherever,* and *while.*

Exercise 7   **Combining Sentences with Adverb Clauses**

The following sentences are based on "The Game" by Walter Dean Myers, which you can find on pages 90–94. Use adverb clauses to combine each group of sentences. In the first few items, the information in brackets signals the subordinating conjunction and the punctuation you should use.

1. **a.** The narrator's team was warming up for the championship game. **[As ...,]**
   b. They tried not to look at their opponents at the other end of the court.
2. **a.** The other team dominated the game's opening minutes.
   b. They passed and shot the ball extremely well. **[because]**
3. **a.** The narrator's team made a few mistakes. **[When ...,]**
   b. Mr. Reese, the coach, called timeout to give the players a rest.

(continued)

4. **a.** Mr. Reese seemed as calm and reassuring as he usually was.

   b. His team was not playing well. [**although**]

5. **a.** The team returned to the floor [**When . . . ,**]

   b. They began to play much better.

6. **a.** The other team took the ball and immediately tried a slick move.

   b. The narrator's team was ready and handily outmaneuvered them.

7. **a.** The narrator was in the right place at just the right time.

   b. He made his first basket.

8. **a.** Mr. Reese urged the team to stay cool.

   b. They were losing by seven points.

9. **a.** A basketball player is fouled in the process of making a shot.

   b. He gets two foul shots, not one.

10. **a.** The narrator's teammates were happy and proud.

    b. They had beaten a very rough team.

Exercise 8   Combining Sentences

Rewrite the following paragraphs. Use adverb clauses to combine sentences. Make any other changes in punctuation or wording that you feel are necessary to improve the flow of the paragraph.

The opposing side was tricked by the "Foul him!" strategy. The narrator's team got the ball. The score was tied. The narrator did not realize it at the time. There were just four minutes left in the game. Sam and Chalky, two good players, came back in. They outscored the other team by four points. The narrator's team won the championship.

    The narrator's teammates were given their first-place trophies. They began to jump up and down and slap each other on the back. They had an extra trophy. They gave it to their cheerleaders. The coach shook each player's hand. Then he invited the players' parents and the cheerleaders into the locker room. Mr. Reese made a little speech to the group. He said he was proud of the team. They had worked so hard to win. Mr. Reese finished speaking. The parents and cheerleaders gave the team a round of applause. The narrator started to cry. He often did this. However, this time he was not embarrassed. Leon was crying even more. For the next few days, the narrator and his friends were walking on air. They saw someone in the street. They would just "walk up and be happy."

Mixed Review

The following sentences are based on *Living up the Street* by Gary Soto, which you can find on pages 32–37. Combine each group of sentences using a phrase or clause, as indicated in brackets. The bracketed directions also indicate any pronouns or punctuation that is needed.

1. **a.** Gary Soto describes the experience.
    b. The experience is that of his first day picking grapes. [**prepositional phrase**]
    c. This information appears in his autobiography. [**prepositional phrase; +,**]
2. **a.** Gary had trouble keeping up.
    b. It is with his mother that he had this trouble. [**prepositional phrase**]
    c. She is the person with whom he was picking. [**prepositional phrase; ,+,**]
3. **a.** Mother worried that Gary would get tired.
    b. She is an experienced picker. [**appositive phrase; ,+,**]
    c. He may feel that way before the day is over. [**prepositional phrase**]
4. **a.** Gary ate the sandwich.
    b. He had brought the sandwich for lunch. [**adjective clause; that . . .**]
5. **a.** Mother remembered long ago days.
    b. Those days she worked in the fields. [**adverb clause; when . . .**]
    c. These were the fields of Texas and Michigan. [**prepositional phrase**]
6. **a.** Gary played with his knife.
    b. It was the tool necessary to his job. [**adverb clause; because . . .**]
    c. He was careful not to lose it. [**adjective clause; which . . .**]
7. **a.** Gary thought longingly of the swimming pool.
    b. It was the swimming pool at the YMCA. [**appositive**]
    c. He felt the hot sun. [**adverb clause; when . . .**]
8. **a.** Mother glanced gratefully at Gary.
    b. It was his singing that entertained them. [**adjective clause; , whose . . .**]
    c. They worked at this time. [**adverb clause; as . . .**]
9. **a.** Gary saw the new jeans.
    b. He saw them whenever he closed his eyes. [**adverb clause; Whenever . . . ,**]
    c. These were the jeans that his earnings would buy. [**adjective clause; that . . .**]
10. **a.** He and Scott made several shopping trips. [**adverb clause; After . . . ,**]
    b. Gary finally chose a pair.
    c. It was a pair of pants. [**prepositional phrase**]

Sentence Combining

"Herald what your mother said/Read the books your father read/Try to solve the puzzle in your own sweet time."

—Des'ree and A. Ingram, *You Gotta Be*

Francis Picabia,
Physical Culture,
1913

PART 3

Resources and Skills

639

22.1 The Sections of a Library

Learning how a library is organized can help you unlock a wealth of information. Although no two libraries are exactly alike, all libraries group like things together. Books for adults are in one section. Children's books are in another. Novels and stories are usually separate from information books. Magazines and newspapers have their own section. So do videos and audiotapes. Look at the photo below. What familiar parts of a library do you recognize? Turn the page to see how a typical library is organized.

No two libraries are alike, but most of them share the same characteristics and have similar resources.

Librarian   A librarian can be the most important resource of all. He or she can help you use the library wisely by directing you to different resources, showing you how to use them, and giving you advice when needed. You might want to prepare your questions for the librarian ahead of time. Remember to ask your questions clearly and quietly. Do not disturb other library users.

Young Adult and Children's Section   Young readers can find books written for them in a separate area of the library. Sometimes reference materials for students are also shelved here, along with periodicals and audiovisual materials.

Stacks   The stacks are the bookshelves that hold most of the library's books. Stacks for fiction books are usually in an area separate from the nonfiction stacks.

Circulation   At the circulation desk, you can use your library card to check out materials you want to take home.

Reference The reference area holds dictionaries, encyclopedias, atlases, and other reference works. Usually, you are not allowed to check out these materials. They are kept in the library so everyone has access to them. Computer databases are also part of the reference area. These systems allow you to search for facts or articles from periodicals. For example, *InfoTrac* provides complete articles and article summaries from over one thousand newspapers and magazines. Some computer databases allow you to search for particular types of information, such as history or art. Computers in the reference section, or in a media center, provide access to the Internet.

Periodicals You can find current issues of periodicals—newspapers, magazines, and journals—in a general reading area. Periodicals are arranged alphabetically and by date. Older issues may be available in the stacks or on microfilm or microfiche. Use the computer catalog to locate them or ask a librarian to help you.

Audio Visual Materials Audiocassettes, compact discs (CDs), videotapes, digital videotapes (DVDs), and computer software are in the audiovisual section. In this section, you can check out a movie, a CD of your favorite music, or a book on tape. Some libraries have listening and viewing areas with audiocassette players, videocassette players, and computers to allow you to review the materials while at the library.

Computer or Card Catalog The computer or card catalog describes each book in the library and tells you where to find it.

Exercise 1

In which section of the library might you find these items?

1. A compact disc of the musical *Cats*
2. The magazine *American Heritage*
3. *To Kill a Mockingbird* (a novel)
4. The *Dictionary of American Biography*
5. The video of *The Call of the Wild*

22.2   Call Number Systems

If you walk through the stacks in the library, you will see that the books are labeled with numbers and letters. These numbers and letters are part of the system the library uses to organize its collection.

Many libraries use the Dewey decimal system. Under this system, a library uses numbers to group books into ten categories of knowledge. Other libraries use the Library of Congress system. The Library of Congress system uses letters, then numbers, to group books.

Ask your librarian which system your library uses. You don't have to memorize the letters and numbers for these systems. It's best, however, to know how each system works. You also should know where your library has posted the chart that identifies and explains the system it uses. Both systems are shown in the chart below. When doing library research, you will have to begin by deciding which major category or categories your topic falls into.

Library Classification Systems

Dewey Decimal System		Library of Congress System	
Numbers	**Major Categories**	**Letters**	**Major Categories**
000–099	General works	A, Z	General works
100–199 200–299	Philosophy Religion	B	Philosophy, religion
300–399	Social sciences	H, J, K, L	Social sciences, political science, law, education
400–499	Language	P	Language
500–599	Science	Q	Science
600–699	Technology	R, S, T, U, V	Medicine, agriculture, technology, military and naval sciences
700–799	The arts, recreation	M, N	Music, fine arts
800–899	Literature	P	Literature
900–999	History, geography	C–G	History, geography, recreation

Each general category contains subcategories. The first number or letter always indicates the main category and will be followed by other numbers or letters. The diagram below shows how each system works.

How the Two Systems Work		
Dewey Decimal	**Description**	**Library of Congress**
700	A book about art	N
750	A book about painting (a subcategory of art)	ND
759	A book about Spanish painting (a subcategory of painting)	ND800
759.609	*The Story of Spanish Painting*	ND804

Exercise 2

1. Suppose a library used the Dewey decimal system. What number (in the hundreds) would it use to show the category of each of the following books?

   a. *A History of Colonial America*
   b. *Science for the Nonscientist*
   c. *Language Made Easy*
   d. *World Religions*
   e. *The Novels of Charles Dickens*

2. At your school or neighborhood library, find an interesting book in each section listed below. Write down the book's title, topic, and full Dewey decimal or Library of Congress call number.

   a. 200–299 or B   c. 400–499 or P   e. 900–999 or C
   b. 300–399 or H   d. 500–599 or Q

Library Catalogs

So many books, so little time! Maybe you've had this thought since you began your research at the library. The library catalog makes searching for books easier and saves you time.

Using a Computer Catalog

The computer catalog lists all the books, periodicals, and audiovisual materials in the library. You can search for these materials by title, author, subject, or keyword. A *keyword* is a word or phrase that describes your topic. If you type an author's name, you can view a list of all the books written by that author. By typing a subject, you can view all the books about that particular topic. The computer catalog tells you the title, author, and call number of each book, and whether it is available for check out.

For example, suppose you are looking for books by the writer Milton Meltzer. Your computer search might proceed as follows:

1. Type in the author's name, *Meltzer, Milton.*

2. The computer will show a list of all the books in the library by this author. Each item will have a call number.

3. Type the call number of the book you are interested in to get more information about it.

4. Information about the book will appear, including the book's location and availability.

The way the computer catalog works may differ slightly from library to library. Follow the on-screen directions to use any computer catalog. If you have trouble with your search, ask a librarian for help.

To search enter one of the following commands:

A/Author-name   to find items by author name
T/Title   to find items by title
S/Subject   to find items by subject
KW   to find items by WORD or
                NAME or to COMBINE
                WORDS
AY   to see your reserves/
                checkouts/fines

1. Title: All Times, All Peoples: A World
                History of Slavery
   Author: Meltzer, Milton
   Published: 1980
   Media: Book   Call No: 326 M528a

2. Title: American Politics: How It
                Really Works
   Author: Meltzer, Milton
   Published: 1989
   Media: Book   Call No: 320.473 M528a

3. Title: American Politics: How It
                Really Works
   Author: Berger, Melvin
   Published: 1989
   Media: Book
                Call No: 320.473 M528a

The Library owns 2 copies of this book. It is
shown as available at:
   Main Branch   Juvenile
   East Branch   Juvenile

Using a Card Catalog

Some libraries use an older method of organizing books called a
card catalog. A card catalog is a cabinet of long narrow drawers that
holds cards arranged alphabetically. Each card contains the description of a book and has that book's call number in the upper left-hand
corner. Fiction books have an author card and a title card. Nonfiction
books have a subject card as well. Because each book has two or three
cards, a book can be found by searching under its title, its author, or
sometimes its subject.

Finding a Book

When you have located a book you want in the catalog, write down the call number shown on the card or computer screen. Note the area in the library where the book is shelved. You will use this information to locate the book.

In the stacks, signs on the shelves tell which call numbers are included in each row. Books with the same call number are alphabetized by the author's last name or by the first author's last name when there is more than one author.

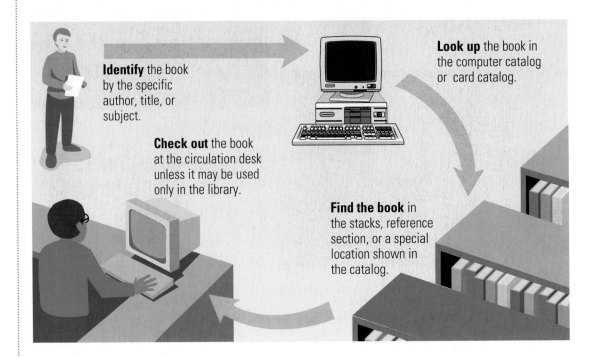

Identify the book by the specific author, title, or subject.

Look up the book in the computer catalog or card catalog.

Check out the book at the circulation desk unless it may be used only in the library.

Find the book in the stacks, reference section, or a special location shown in the catalog.

Exercise 3

Use the card catalog or computer catalog to find a book about any five of the following topics. List the author, title, and call number of each book you find.

1. The brain
2. The development of television
3. Poetry by X. J. Kennedy
4. Marsupials
5. The Spanish language
6. Professional football
7. Mountains
8. The mind

22.4 Types of Reference Works

When you look up the answer to a question or read a book to find information for social studies class, you are doing research. When you check with friends who know more than you do about your bike, you are doing research. For research you need experts. You'll find the opinions and discoveries of many experts in the reference materials in your library.

Reference works are designed to help you locate specific information quickly. You may be doing research for a class project, looking for a single fact, or just feeling curious about a topic. Whatever your purpose, the reference area offers many interesting resources.

The chart below describes some general types of reference sources found in most libraries. Find out where each of these kinds of references is kept in your public library. Locate those references that are available in your school library or classroom as well. You can also access many reference sources on your computer—both on CD-ROM and online.

Using General Reference Works to Answer Questions		
Questions	**Where to Look for an Answer**	**Examples of Sources**
When did Henry Ford introduce the Model T?	**Encyclopedias** include general information on a variety of topics.	• *World Book Encyclopedia* • *Grolier Encyclopedia* • *Encyclopaedia Britannica*
What major cities are on the Ohio River?	**Atlases** are collections of maps. They often include special maps on climate, population, and other topics.	• *Hammond Contemporary World Atlas* • *The Rand McNally Atlas of World Exploration*
Who received the Nobel Peace Prize in 1999?	**Almanacs** provide lists, statistics, and other information on recent and historical topics.	• *Information Please Almanac* • *Guinness Book of World Records*
Where was Mark Twain born?	**Biographical reference works** include biographies of notable persons, both past and present.	• *Dictionary of American Biography* • *Webster's Biographical Dictionary*

Encyclopedias

You will find one-volume encyclopedias and sets made up of many volumes. Encyclopedias may be either general or specialized. General encyclopedias contain articles about all branches of knowledge. Specialized encyclopedias present articles in a specific area of knowledge, such as history, science, or the arts. Two examples of specialized encyclopedias are the *McGraw-Hill Encyclopedia of Science and Technology* and *The New York Times Encyclopedia of Film.*

Most encyclopedias are organized alphabetically. To find all of the articles with information on your topic, look up the topic in the index. The index is usually the last volume of a multi-volume encyclopedia. It contains an alphabetical listing of topics. After each topic, you will find the subjects related to the topic you are investigating. The index tells you the volume and page number of the article where you will find the information. Sometimes the index refers you to a different topic heading for a list of articles.

Many encyclopedia entries end with a list of books that contain additional information. These books may be available at your library. The entry may also list other related articles in the encyclopedia.

Atlases

Atlases are collections of maps. General atlases contain maps of all parts of the world. In a general atlas, you can find map information about population, industry, farming, and other topics for all parts of the world. These atlases may also contain graphs, charts, and pictures. For example, the *National Geographic Atlas of the World* includes satellite images of the earth's major regions.

Some atlases are specialized. They may cover one part of the world, such as a single country. Others have maps on a special topic, such as population, the environment, or animals. Travelers often rely on atlases that show highways, national parks, and places of interest to tourists. Historical atlases contain maps for different periods in history and various parts of the world.

Almanacs and Yearbooks

If you're looking for very current information or statistics, consult almanacs and yearbooks. These references contain the most recent available information on a variety of topics. A new edition is published every year.

Two widely used almanacs are the *Information Please Almanac* and the *World Almanac and Book of Facts*. Both cover a wide range of information, from baseball statistics to the latest scientific discoveries. Much of the information is presented in the form of lists or tables.

A yearbook is a book issued each year by some encyclopedia publishers to update their regular encyclopedia volumes. It contains articles about events and developments of that year. The yearbooks for an encyclopedia generally follow the *Z* volume or the Index volume on the reference shelf.

Biographical Dictionaries

Biographical dictionaries contain information on important people. Some of these dictionaries include living persons as well as persons from history. These references may have many volumes or may be contained in a single book.

In the larger, multivolume dictionaries, such as the *Dictionary of American Biography*, entries are lengthy and give a detailed life history. An example of a shorter reference is *Webster's Biographical Dictionary*. In this work, the entries are much briefer, sometimes only a few lines long. An example is shown below. Biographical dictionaries are useful when you need information about particular people.

> **Cassatt** (kə sat´), Mary Stevenson. 1844–1926. American painter, b. Allegheny City, Pa. To Paris (1866); first exhibited at Salon (1872); associated with Impressionists, esp. Degas and Courbet; exhibited with Impressionists (1879, 1880, 1881, 1886); first solo exhibit (1891); produced oils, pastels, prints, etchings; known esp. for figure studies and portrayals of mothers and children.

Exercise 4

1. Name the type of reference work in which you would expect to find answers to the following:

   a. Who was the Olympic champion in the women's long jump in 1988?
   b. Of what country is Jakarta the capital?
   c. What occupations did Samuel Clemens follow before becoming a writer?
   d. In what state is the Painted Desert located?
   e. What was *Sputnik,* and why was it important?

2. Use a library reference to write the answers to any two of the above questions.

Until the early 1990s, most periodical searches were done with printed indexes, which then led the searcher to periodicals or microforms (copies of magazines and newspapers stored on film). Today, you can search periodicals electronically on the Internet and on various databases. A database is a collection of electronic files that are easily retrieved by a computer. Most libraries have magazine and newspaper databases, such as *InfoTrac*, that contain full articles or article summaries from hundreds of magazines and newspapers.

If you are searching for older materials, however, such as a magazine from around 1980 or before, you still need to search the old way. Scan for your topic in a bound copy of the *Readers' Guide to Periodical Literature* and then follow your citation to the correct issue of the magazine in the periodical section.

However, often you will search online. Most libraries provide two types of electronic databases for periodicals: general databases and databases specific to a subject. *Electric Library*, which searches newspapers, general magazines, maps, and TV and radio transcripts, is an example of a general periodical database. *Social Issues Resource* is an example of a database that is focused on one main subject area, sociology and current social problems.

All databases share common features. Most offer the option to do a basic search or a more advanced search. Each has a query screen. On it you key in your search term(s)—either one word or a search phrase. Many databases allow you to use natural language. In other words, you ask the question the way you would ask a friend.

Sample Periodical Search

This search was done on the database called *Electric Library*, which searches current magazines and newspapers. The student was investigating some ideas for a term paper on roller coasters. The following are some of the references that appeared.

Click on a <u>TITLE</u> to view a full text document.

Relevancy: 100;
Date: 06-18-1999
Reading Level: 6.

<u>Variations on a Theme Park</u>; The Washington Post
Alexa Steele; 06-18-1999 Size: 23K

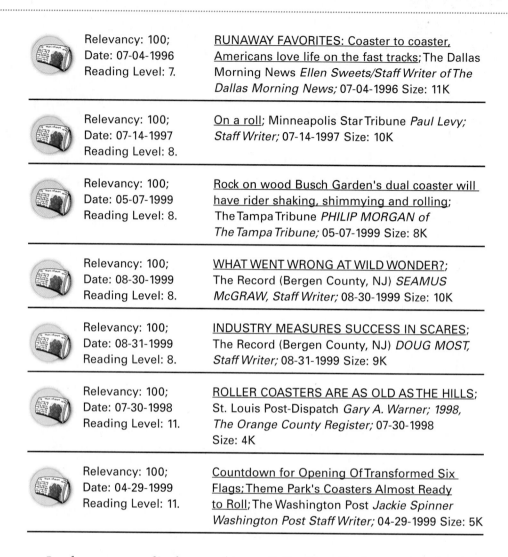

Relevancy: 100; Date: 07-04-1996 Reading Level: 7.	RUNAWAY FAVORITES: Coaster to coaster, Americans love life on the fast tracks; The Dallas Morning News *Ellen Sweets/Staff Writer of The* *Dallas Morning News;* 07-04-1996 Size: 11K
Relevancy: 100; Date: 07-14-1997 Reading Level: 8.	On a roll; Minneapolis Star Tribune *Paul Levy;* *Staff Writer;* 07-14-1997 Size: 10K
Relevancy: 100; Date: 05-07-1999 Reading Level: 8.	Rock on wood Busch Garden's dual coaster will have rider shaking, shimmying and rolling; The Tampa Tribune *PHILIP MORGAN of* *The Tampa Tribune;* 05-07-1999 Size: 8K
Relevancy: 100; Date: 08-30-1999 Reading Level: 8.	WHAT WENT WRONG AT WILD WONDER?; The Record (Bergen County, NJ) *SEAMUS* *McGRAW, Staff Writer;* 08-30-1999 Size: 10K
Relevancy: 100; Date: 08-31-1999 Reading Level: 8.	INDUSTRY MEASURES SUCCESS IN SCARES; The Record (Bergen County, NJ) *DOUG MOST,* *Staff Writer;* 08-31-1999 Size: 9K
Relevancy: 100; Date: 07-30-1998 Reading Level: 11.	ROLLER COASTERS ARE AS OLD AS THE HILLS; St. Louis Post-Dispatch *Gary A. Warner; 1998,* *The Orange County Register;* 07-30-1998 Size: 4K
Relevancy: 100; Date: 04-29-1999 Reading Level: 11.	Countdown for Opening Of Transformed Six Flags; Theme Park's Coasters Almost Ready to Roll; The Washington Post *Jackie Spinner* *Washington Post Staff Writer;* 04-29-1999 Size: 5K

Look over your display results carefully. The display screen gives you important information about each article. It includes the title, the author, the source, and the date of the article. It also provides the article's reading level and *relevancy*—an estimate of how closely this article is related to your search item.

Exercise 5

Look at the sample screen and answer these questions.

1. Which of these articles might be difficult reading for an eighth grader?
2. Which are the two most current articles?
3. In your opinion, what term paper topics about roller coasters might these articles suggest?
4. What do you need to do to read the full text of one of these articles?

22.6 Using the Internet and Other Media

Libraries offer several kinds of media. The word *media* (singular *medium*) means methods of communication, such as newspapers, magazines, movies, and television. During the 1990s, a new medium rose to prominence—the Internet.

The Internet

Computers at your public library will also provide access to the Internet, a valuable source of information. The World Wide Web is the part of the Internet that provides information in various formats, including print, sound, graphics, and video.

Because there are so many Internet sites, the best way to find worthwhile information on the Net is by using a *search engine.* If you do not get any useful results with one search engine, try several others. They each search the Internet differently.

All Internet sources are not equally reliable, however. Always check any site for accuracy and timeliness. Check to see when it was last updated. Check for errors and omissions. Check to see what agency sponsors the site. Many libraries now provide a collection of recommended Web sites.

Online libraries Online libraries on the Internet are important reference sources. You can connect from home if you have access to a computer and a modem. Examples of excellent online reference sites include: *The Internet Public Library,* sponsored by the School of Information at the University of Michigan, and *Thor: The Virtual Reference Desk +,* the online resource site of Purdue University Library.

Some Additional Internet Search Terms	
Term	**Definition**
Abstract	a summary of an article or information source.
Discussion Groups	a virtual place where you can discuss problems and current events.
Hit	a successful result after you have searched online.
Full Text	term indicating that all of an article is present online. However, sometimes full-text articles do not include charts and graphics.
Search Engine	computer software that browses the Internet for places where your search words appear. Examples are Yahoo, Goober, Lycos, and Ask Jeeves.
URL	stands for Universal Resource Locator. This is an address for a Web site.

Tapes and Discs

Most libraries and media centers offer videotapes of movies, travelogues, and instructional (how-to) films. Audiotapes and compact discs (CDs) contain sound recordings of music, drama, language lessons and readings of literature. Compact discs also store printed information such as periodical indexes and encyclopedias. These CDs are read by a computer, which provides very fast searches for information.

Using Nonprint Media		
Type of Media	**Information Available**	**Equipment Needed**
Microforms	Back issues of newspapers and magazines	Microform viewer or viewer/printer (at the library)
Videotapes	Movies, documentaries, travel and instructional films	VCR and television set
Digital Video Discs	Movies, documentaries, travel and instructional films	DVD player and television set
Audiotapes	Music, readings, dramas, language lessons	Audiocassette player
Compact discs	Same as audiotapes Information sources	CD player and stereo system CD-ROM drive and computer

Exercise 6

In which medium would you expect to find each of the following items? More than one answer may be appropriate in some cases.

1. An article describing a new type of computer
2. Recorded Russian lessons for travelers
3. A documentary about the canal era in Ohio
4. An article about a student from your school who just won a national award
5. *The Grolier Encyclopedia* on computer

22.7 The Dictionary

You can enrich your knowledge of English by frequent use of the dictionary—an essential tool for a writer. A dictionary is an alphabetical listing of words with definitions and often with word origins and other information. Today you can find dictionaries in print, on CD-ROM, and on the Internet. Most dictionaries fall into one of several categories.

Types of Dictionaries

Dictionaries differ according to their purposes. Some have more entries than others and provide detailed word histories. The three main categories are described below.

Type	Characteristics	Examples
Unabridged Dictionaries	• 250,000 or more entries • Detailed word histories • Detailed definitions • Found mostly in libraries	• *Random House Unabridged Dictionary* • *Webster's Third New International Dictionary*
College Dictionaries	• About 150,000 entries • Detailed enough to answer most questions on spelling or definitions • Widely used in schools, homes, and businesses	• *Random House Webster's College Dictionary* • *American Heritage Dictionary of the English Language* • *Webster's New World Dictionary*
School Dictionaries	• 90,000 or fewer entries • Definitions suitable for students' abilities • Emphasizes common words	• *The Scribner's Dictionary* • *Webster's School Dictionary*

The illustrations show how to use two helpful dictionary features. Guide words help you locate words quickly. The pronunciation key can help you sound out a word.

Guide words show the first and last entry on the page. Use them to zero in on the word you are seeking.

foot soldier, a soldier trained or equipped to fight on foot; infantryman.

foot·sore (fŏŏt´sôr´) *adj.* having sore or tired feet, as from much walking.

foot·step (fŏŏt´step´) *n.* **1.** a step or tread of the foot: *a baby's first awkward footsteps.* **2.** the sound made by this: *I heard his footsteps in the hall.* **3.** the distance covered in a step.

    to follow in someone's footsteps. to imitate or follow the same course as someone: *Dan followed in his father's footsteps and became a teacher.*

foot soldier / fore-and-aft

for·bid·ding (fĕr bid´ing) *adj.* looking unfriendly or dangerous; frightening; grim: *The old house was dark and forbidding.* —**for·bid´ding·ly,** *adv.*

for·bore (fôr bôr´) the past tense of **forbear** .

for·borne (fôr bôrn´) the past participle of **forbear** .

force (fôrs) *n.* **1.** power, strength, or energy: *The batter struck the ball with great force. The force of the explosion broke windows in the nearby buildings.* **2.** the use of such power, strength, or energy; violence: *The sheriff dragged the outlaw off by force.* **3.** the power to convince, or control: *The force of her argument won*

The pronunciation key uses well-known words to interpret the pronunciation symbols.

oneself from (doing something): refrain from: *Tom could not forbear smiling at his embarrassed friend.* [Old English *forberan* to hold back.]

for·bear² (fôr´ber) another spelling of **forebear.**

for·bear·ance (fôr berŏns) *n.* **1.** the act of forbearing. **2.** self-control or patience: *Jim showed great forbearance during his long illness.*

for·bid (fôr bid´) *v.t.,* **for·bade** or **for·bad, for·bid·den** or *(archaic)* **for·bid, for·bid·ding.** to order not to do something; refuse to allow; prohibit: *I forbid you to go out. The school forbids eating in the classrooms.*

fore-and-aft (fôr´en aft´) *adj.* from bow to stern of a ship: *a fore-and-aft sail.*

at; āpe; cär; end; mē; it; īce; hot; ōld; fôrk; wood; fōōl; oil; out; up; turn; sing; thin; this; hw in white; zh in treasure. The symbol ə stands for the sound of a in about, e in taken, i in pencil, o in lemon, and u in circus.

Other useful features are located in the front and back pages of the dictionary. In the front, you can find a complete pronunciation key, a list of abbreviations used in entries, and information about punctuation and capitalization. Some dictionaries include a short history of the English language. In the back of the dictionary you may find sections with biographical and geographical entries. Some dictionaries include such information with the regular word listings.

Entry Word

A dictionary entry packs a great deal of information into a small space. By becoming familiar with the basic elements of an entry, you'll find it easier to explore new words.

The entry word is the first element in each entry. It is printed in bold type, which makes it easy to find the beginning of an entry. The entry word shows how to divide a word of more than one syllable. Notice how *flourish* is divided by the dot. Not every dictionary entry is a single word. Some entries are two words, such as *cuckoo clock,* and some, such as *T-shirt,* are hyphenated.

> **flour** (flour, flouʹər) *n.* **1.** soft, powdery substance obtained by grinding and sifting grain, esp. wheat, used chiefly as a basic ingredient in baked goods and other foods. **2.** any soft powdery substance. —*v.t.* to cover or sprinkle with flour. [Form of FLOWER in the sense of "finest part" (of the grain).]
>
> **flour·ish** (flurʹish) *v.i.* **1.** to grow or develop vigorously or prosperously; thrive: *Crops flourish in rich soil. His business is flourishing.* **2.** to reach or be at the peak of development or achievement: *a civilization that flourished thousands of years ago.* —*v.t.* **1.** to wave about with bold or sweeping gestures; brandish: *to flourish a sword; to flourish a baton.* **2.** to display ostentatiously; flaunt. —*n.* **1.** a brandishing: *He bowed to her with a flourish of his hat.* **2.** ostentatious or dramatic display or gesture: *She entered the room with a flourish.* **3.** decorative stroke or embellishment in writing. **4.** elaborate, ornamental passage or series of notes, as a trill or fanfare, added to a musical work. [Old French *floriss-,* a stem of *florir* to flower, bloom, going back to Latin *flōrēre* to flower, bloom] —**Syn.** *v.i.* see **prosper.**

Entry word

Definition

Pronunciation

Part of speech

Word origin

Synonym reference. You can find a list of synonyms for *flourish* in the entry for *prosper.*

Pronunciation

The pronunciation of a word follows the entry word. It is written in special symbols that allow you to sound out the word. If you are not sure how to pronounce a syllable, check the pronunciation key, which is usually at the bottom of the page. The simple words in the key show the sounds of the most common symbols. To see a complete pronunciation key, turn to the front pages of the dictionary. Some words have more than one pronunciation; the most common is generally shown first.

Part of Speech

Every dictionary entry indicates a word's part or parts of speech. For example, in the entry for *flourish, v.i.* stands for *intransitive verb* and *v.t.* for *transitive verb.* The letter *n.* stands for noun. What would you expect the abbreviations for adjective and adverb to be? A list of the abbreviations is located in the front of the dictionary.

Definition

The definition, or meaning, of the word is the heart of the entry. Many words have more than one meaning. These meanings are usually numbered from most common to least common. Some unabridged and college dictionaries, however, use a different method. They give definitions from the earliest-known meaning to the most recent meaning. Look at the sample entries on page 659 to see how the definitions of *flourish* are numbered.

Word Origins

The word origin is a brief account of how the word entered the English language. Many words, like *flourish*, were used in more than one language before entering English. For example, look at the *flourish* entry. The source of the word is Latin. The word then moved into Old French. English speakers borrowed it from Old French. Many dictionaries use abbreviations for the language from which a word comes, such as *L.* for Latin. A list of these abbreviations is located at the front of the dictionary.

Exercise 7

Use the dictionary entries in this lesson to answer the following questions:

1. How many definitions does this dictionary include for the verb form of the word f*lourish?*
2. Which meaning of *flourish* is implied in the following sentence? *The students flourished their hand-made signs at the rally.*
3. Does the first syllable of *flourish* rhyme with the first syllable of *flower, flurry,* or *Florence?*
4. Which of the meanings shown for *flour* do you find in the following sentence? *I floured the chicken before putting it into the oven.*
5. What was the meaning of the Latin word that was the original source of *flourish?*

22.8 The Thesaurus

More than 150 years ago a British doctor, Peter Mark Roget [rō zhā ´], developed a thesaurus. A thesaurus is a dictionary of synonyms—words with similar meanings. Since that time, the thesaurus has grown and changed. Print, CD-ROM, and on-line thesauruses are all available today. In fact, if you do word processing on your computer, you probably have a thesaurus as part of your software.

Using a Thesaurus

Roget organized his thesaurus by categories. Then he listed the categories in an index. When you use this type of thesaurus, you find the category you want in the index. The index will refer you to the lists of synonyms you want.

The excerpt below is from another kind of thesaurus, one in which the words are arranged like those in a dictionary. In a dictionary-style thesaurus the word entries are in alphabetical order.

Clever   *adjective*
1. Mentally quick and original: *The child is clever but not brilliant.*
    Syns: alert, bright, intelligent, keen, quick-witted, sharp, sharp-witted, smart.
    —*Idiom* smart as a tack (*or* whip).
2. Amusing or pleasing because of wit or originality: *made the audience laugh with a few clever, offbeat comparisons.*
    Syns: scintillating, smart, sparkling, sprightly, witty.
3. DEXTEROUS.
4. SHARP.
clew   *noun*   SEE **clue.**
cliché   *noun*
A trite expression or idea: *a short story marred by clichés.*
    Syns: banality, bromide, commonplace, platitude, stereotype, truism.
cliché   *adjective*   TRITE.
click   *noun*   SNAP.
    click   *verb*
    1. RELATE.
    2. SNAP.
    3. SUCCEED.

Part of speech is indicated.

Synonyms are grouped by definition.

Usage examples are given.

In this thesaurus capital letters indicate a cross-reference to another entry. More synonyms are found under the cross-reference entry.

Library and Reference Resources

Finding Synonyms

Knowing how the thesaurus is arranged can help you find the exact word you need. You can see from the samples on the previous page that each definition is followed by several synonyms or by a cross-reference to another entry. Synonyms, you recall, are words that have *similar* meanings. The thesaurus can help you distinguish among many synonyms to find the most exact one.

The words in capital letters lead you to further synonyms. If you look up a word shown in capital letters, you will find a definition and many additional synonyms. *Dexterous,* for example, means *clever,* but in a specific way: exhibiting or possessing skill or ease in performance. Your expert handling of a bike might be called dexterous. Conversation on a talk show may be clever, but it is not necessarily dexterous.

Most libraries will have more than one type of thesaurus available. A similar resource, a dictionary of synonyms, is also available to help you locate the most precise word. Two examples are *Webster's New Dictionary of Synonyms* and *Webster's New World Dictionary of Synonyms.*

Many thesauruses list antonyms—words with opposite meanings—as well as synonyms. Your library may have *Webster's Collegiate Thesaurus,* which includes antonyms. For more information on synonyms and antonyms, see pages 676–678.

Exercise 8

Use a thesaurus to find two synonyms for each word below. Then write an original sentence to illustrate the meaning of each synonym. Check the exact meaning of each word in a dictionary before you use it in a sentence.

1. speak (verb)
2. run (verb)
3. thin (adjective)
4. foam (noun)
5. shiny (adjective)

UNIT 23

Vocabulary and Spelling

23.1   Words from American English

People all over the world use the word *okay*. It began, however, as an American-English word. How did *okay* become so widespread?

Citizens of many nations borrowed this word from American travelers. Speakers of one language will often borrow words from speakers of another language. As contact between peoples around the world increases, so will borrowed words.

Kayak

Words from Native Americans

English colonists began settling in North America in the early 1600s. They often borrowed Native American words to name foods, plants, and animals new to them. Some examples are the words *pecan, hickory, squash, moose, chipmunk,* and *skunk*.

Europeans also borrowed Native American words to name natural features and places. The Mississippi River's name, for example, comes from Algonquian words meaning "great water." More than half the states and many cities and counties in the United States have names with Native American origins. Hawaii's name came from its original Polynesian settlers.

Raccoon

States with Native American Names		
Alabama	Kansas	Ohio
Alaska	Kentucky	Oklahoma
Arizona	Massachusetts	Oregon
Arkansas	Michigan	South Dakota
Connecticut	Minnesota	Tennessee
Idaho	Mississippi	Texas
Illinois	Missouri	Utah
Indiana	Nebraska	Wisconsin
Iowa	North Dakota	Wyoming

Other Early Borrowed Words

Europeans from France and Spain were in America even before the English. English speakers had already borrowed many words from the French in Europe. As American English developed, its speakers borrowed more French words in North America. Other new English words came from the Spanish and from Spanish-speaking Mexicans in the Southwest. Some examples of these words of French and Spanish origin are included in the chart below.

Some American-English Borrowed Words	
Sources	**Words**
French	toboggan, pumpkin, bayou, prairie, dime, chowder
Spanish	mustang, ranch, rodeo, stampede, cafeteria, canyon
Dutch	sleigh, cole slaw, Santa Claus, cookie, boss, waffle
African	gumbo, voodoo, juke, jazz, tote
German	hamburger, noodle, pretzel, kindergarten, semester
Yiddish	kosher, bagel, klutz, kibitzer, schmaltz
Italian	macaroni, spaghetti, pizza, ravioli

Americans are often called Yankees or Yanks. The word came from Dutch colonists in America in the 1600s. The Dutch called New Englanders Yankees. (The name was considered an insult at the time.) The Dutch colony of New Netherland and its port city, New Amsterdam, were taken over by the British. The British renamed the colony and the city New York. The Dutch lost their American colony, but they left a number of their words in American English.

Rodeo

Most of the Africans in colonial America were brought here as slaves. Their contribution to the English language included such words as *gumbo, voodoo,* and *juke* (as in *jukebox*). The origin of the word *jazz* is uncertain, but it, too, may have come from an African language. These and some other words that became part of American English are shown in the chart above.

Words from Immigrants

Over the centuries millions of immigrants—Italians, Poles, Czechs, Greeks, Chinese, Filipinos, Haitians, Cubans, and many more—came to America. They passed on some of their customs and some of their words to Americans. These words became part of American English. Often the use of the words spread from the United States throughout the English-speaking world. Some examples are included in the chart on the previous page.

Words Made in America

Jukebox

Americans have also contributed new words that did not originate in another language. *Okay* is an example of a word that was "made in the U.S.A." Inventions and customs that started in America often led to new words. Some examples are *refrigerator, telephone, jeep, inner city, flow chart, zipper, laser,* and *airline.* Like *okay,* these words are now used throughout the world. Can you think of any other words that were probably made in America?

Exercise 1

Work with a small group. Develop a list of more English words that originated in America. The words can have come from Native American languages or from the languages of immigrants to America. They might be words invented by Americans.

Begin by looking at the place names in your area. Where did the names of mountains, rivers, counties, or cities come from? Look in your library for books or articles on the origins of place names. Think about the names of foods you eat that originated in other countries. If family members or friends are recent immigrants, ask them if they know of any American English words that came from their language. Use your dictionary to check the origins of words on your list.

Wordworks

TECHNO-TALK

What do the words *nylon*, *silo*, and *gearshift* have in common? All these words—and countless others—entered the English language as a result of developing technology. New machines, products, and processes required a new vocabulary.

Technical words enter the language by different routes. Some words are coined. A coined word is simply created—none of its parts have any meaning by themselves. For instance, in 1938 scientists developed synthetic fiber, and the word *nylon* was coined as a name for it.

Another route into English is through borrowing. The word *silo* was borrowed into English in 1881 as a name for an airtight container for fodder, or food for livestock. The word is Spanish in origin and carries the same meaning in that language.

Another way languages gain new technical words is by compounding. The word parts *gear* and *shift* have existed in English for a long time. It was only because of developing technology that they were combined to name a part of an automobile transmission. Other examples of combining include *transmission* (from Latin word parts) and *telephone* (from Greek word parts). Some words for new inventions originated as names of people; *Ferris wheel* is an example.

Tele—
far off
or distant
television
telephone
telescope
telecast
telephoto

> ### CHALLENGE
>
> *What new technology uses the word* silo? *Think of another technology that named a product a* tweeter. *How do the original meanings of these words fit the new ways in which they are used?*

ACTIVITY

Name That Invention

Create several names for the imaginary inventions listed below. Use any of the sources for word formation.

1. a car for air, water, and all surfaces
2. a thermal container that will biodegrade within twelve hours
3. earphones that don't "leak" noise and that allow for loud music without damage to hearing

Vocabulary and Spelling

23.2　Context Clues

Do you check your dictionary every time you read or hear a new word? Probably not—most people don't. The best way to build your vocabulary is to be an avid reader and an active listener. You also can learn the meaning of a new word by looking for context clues. The words and sentences around the word are its context.

Using Specific Context Clues

Context clues help you unlock the meaning of an unfamiliar word. Sometimes the context actually tells you what the word means. The following chart shows three types of specific context clues. It also gives examples of words that help you identify the type of context clue.

Using Specific Context Clues		
Type of Context Clue	**Clue Words**	**Example**
Comparison The thing or idea named by the unfamiliar word is compared with some-thing more familiar.	also same likewise similarly identical	A *rampant* growth of weeds and vines surrounded the old house. The barn was <u>likewise</u> covered with uncontrolled and wild growth.
Contrast The thing or idea named by the unfamiliar word is contrasted with some-thing more familiar.	but on the other hand on the contrary unlike however	Thank goodness Martin didn't *bungle* the arrangements for the party; <u>on the contrary</u>, he handled everything very smoothly and efficiently.
Cause and effect The unfamiliar word is explained as a part of a cause-and-effect relationship.	because since therefore as a result	<u>Because</u> this rubber raft is so *buoyant*, it will float easily, and we won't have to worry about its sinking.

Using the General Context

How do you figure out an unfamiliar word if there are no specific context clues? With a little extra detective work you often can find general clues in the context. Look at the two sentences below. What context clues help you understand the meaning of the word *liaison*?

> Joel is a liaison from one group (the students) to another (the faculty).

Joel was chosen student <u>liaison</u> to the faculty. Everyone hoped his appointment would improve communication between the students and the teachers.

> Note that the word *communication* helps you figure out that being a liaison means acting as a line of communication between two groups.

Exercise 2

Divide the words below between you and a partner. Use a dictionary if necessary to find the meanings of your words. Then write a sentence using each one. Your sentences should contain context clues to help a reader figure out the meanings of the words. Try to use different types of context clues in the sentences.

Next, exchange papers with your partner and read his or her sentences. Try to use your partner's context clues to understand the words from the list. Discuss how your context clues helped you and your partner understand the meanings of each other's words.

1. depreciate
2. collaborate
3. fathom (noun)
4. adobe
5. crucial

6. olfactory
7. refulgence
8. fathom (verb)
9. omnipotent
10. brinkmanship

Wordworks

A S STALE AS
D AY - OLD B READ

If you listen to a cassette tape over and over, most likely you'll get tired of listening to it. Hearing a cliché is something like listening to that cassette tape.

Clichés are expressions you have heard many times before. All clichés, though, were once fresh and original. Some clichés have been in use for centuries. For example, the phrase *I'm all ears* originated in 1634. That's when John Milton (1608–1674) wrote in *Comus,* "I was all ear."

As you can see, sometimes clichés develop through alteration of the writer's or speaker's original words. If you've ever told someone a secret, you may have said, "This is between you and me." That expression comes from a novel by Charles Dickens (1812–1870) called *Nicholas Nickleby* (1838). Dickens's phrase in the book, however, was "between you, me, and the lamppost." This form of the cliché is still in use, although it is much less popular now than in previous generations. Another cliché, *cool as a cucumber,* can be traced to the playwrights Francis Beaumont and John Fletcher. Their phrase in the seventeenth-century play *Cupid's Revenge* was "cold as cucumbers."

CHALLENGE

Rewrite the following without the clichés:

Beyond a shadow of a doubt, too many clichés will put you in hot water. Sad but true, a cliché sticks out like a sore thumb. Avoid clichés like the plague.

ACTIVITY

Do these Clichés Ring a Bell?
Look up the following clichés in *Bartlett's Familiar Quotations* or another reference book, and record the sources.

1. as old as the hills
2. vanish into thin air
3. busy as a bee
4. few and far between
5. Variety is the spice of life.

23.3 Prefixes and Suffixes

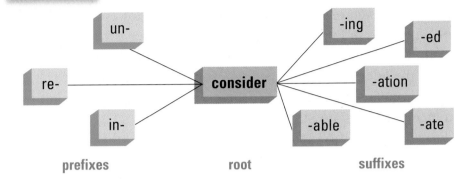

prefixes   root   suffixes

The illustration above shows how word parts can be put together to form many different words. These word parts are called roots, prefixes, and suffixes.

Roots

The **root** of a word carries the main meaning. Some roots (like the word *consider* above) can stand alone. Others (like *lect*, shown in the chart below) make little or no sense without a prefix or suffix. Knowing the meanings of roots can help you figure out the meanings of unfamiliar words.

Word Roots		
Roots	**Words**	**Meanings**
bio means "life"	biography biosphere	the story of a person's life part of the atmosphere where living things exist
dent means "tooth"	dentist trident	person who treats diseases of the teeth spear with three prongs, or teeth
flex or *flec* means "to bend"	flexible reflect	easily bent to bend back (light)
lect means "speech"	lecture dialect	a speech form of a language spoken in a certain region
tele means "distant"	television telescope	device for receiving pictures from a distance device for viewing distant things

Vocabulary and Spelling

Prefixes

A **prefix** is a syllable used in front of a word root. Adding a prefix can change, or even reverse, the meaning of a root (for example, *belief—disbelief*). In English, a number of prefixes have the same, or nearly the same, meaning. For example, *dis-, un-,* and *in-* all can mean "not" or "the opposite of." On the other hand, some prefixes have more than one meaning. The prefix *in-* can also mean "into," as in the word *incise* ("to cut into").

The chart below shows some common prefixes and their meanings. Notice in the example words how the prefixes change the word root's meanings. Learning these prefixes can help you figure out unfamiliar words.

Prefixes			
Categories	**Prefixes**	**Words**	**Meanings**
Prefixes that reverse meaning	*un-* means "not" or "the opposite of"	unnatural unhappy	not natural not happy
	in- means "not" or "the opposite of"	inconsiderate intolerant	not considerate not tolerant
	il- means "not" or "the opposite of"	illegal illogical	not legal not logical
	im- means "not" or "the opposite of"	immoderate imbalance	not moderate lacking balance
	ir- means "not" or "the opposite of"	irregular irreplaceable	not regular not able to be replaced
Prefixes that show relations	*pre-* means "before"	prepay prearrange	to pay in advance to arrange beforehand
	post- means "after"	postdate postpone	to assign a later date to delay until a later time
	sub- means "below" or "beneath"	submarine subway	an underwater boat an underground way or passage
	co- means "with" or "partner"	copilot cooperate	relief or second pilot to work with others

Vocabulary and Spelling

Suffixes

Suffixes are syllables added to the end of a word root. Like prefixes, suffixes change the meanings of roots. Like prefixes, they can have more than one meaning. They can have the same meaning as one or more other suffixes. Unlike prefixes, however, suffixes can also change the part of speech of a word root. For example, adding the suffix -*ness* to *quick* (an adjective) makes it into *quickness* (a noun). Adding -*ly* to *quick* makes *quickly* (an adverb).

Learning suffixes and how they change a root can help build your vocabulary. The following chart shows a sample of common suffixes. As you look at it, try to think of other words to which each suffix might be added.

Suffixes			
Categories	**Suffixes**	**Words**	**Meanings**
Suffixes that mean "one who does [something]"	-er, -or	worker sailor	one who works one who sails
	-ee, -eer	employee profiteer	one who is employed one who profits
	-ist	pianist chemist	one who plays the piano one who works at chemistry
	-ian	physician	one who practices medicine (once called "physic")
Suffixes that mean "full of"	-ful	joyful wonderful	full of joy full of wonder
	-ous	furious courageous	full of fury (anger) full of courage
Suffixes that mean "in the manner of" or "having to do with"	-ly	happily secretly	in the manner of being happy in the manner of a secret
	-y	windy icy	having to do with wind having to do with ice
	-al	musical formal	having to do with music having to do with form

When suffixes are added to words, the spelling of the word may change. For example, when -*ous* is added to *fury,* the *y* in *fury* is changed to *i* to make the word *furious.* See pages 684–686 to learn more about the spelling of words that have suffixes added to them.

Exercise 3

Write a word containing each root listed below. Try to use a word that is not used in the word roots chart. Then write a definition of each word. Check your dictionary if necessary.

1. bio
2. dent
3. flec or flex
4. tele

Exercise 4

Write a word to fit each of the definitions below. Each word should have a prefix or a suffix or both. Underline the suffixes and prefixes in the words. Use the charts in this lesson and a dictionary for help.

1. full of beauty
2. to behave badly
3. to fail to function correctly
4. below the earth
5. one who is a specialist in mathematics
6. a note written at the end of a letter, after the main part of the letter is complete (often abbreviated)
7. not able to be measured
8. in the manner of being not perfect
9. to live or exist together at the same time and in the same place
10. in the manner of being not happy

Wordworks

WEIRD OLD WORDS

If someone called you a popinjay, would you be pleased? Do you like to show off a little when you know you look good? A popinjay is a vain, strutting person. The word is old-fashioned and not used much today, but the type of personality it describes isn't old-fashioned at all.

Words come and go in any language. If a word has disappeared from use, some dictionaries label it obsolete. An example of an obsolete word is an older definition of *popinjay*: a "parrot." No one today uses *popinjay* instead of *parrot*. So this meaning for the word is obsolete.

Many words have disappeared from English. Some vanish completely: *egal* once

meant "equal," and a *prest* was money one person was forced to lend another. Neither word is used now. Other obsolete words leave traces. For example, a horse that could be hired out for riding was called a hackney or hack. This meaning of *hack* is now obsolete, but modern English does have a related word. Taxis are often called hacks. It's easy to trace this connection, since people hire taxis today, not riding horses, when they want to get around town.

The next time you pick up your dictionary, keep in mind that it's a work in progress.

> ### CHALLENGE
>
> *Words vanish, and one reason may be that they aren't really needed to do the job. List a synonym for each of these obsolete words:* joyance, impressure, argument *(meaning an outward sign).*

ACTIVITY Gone but Not Forgotten

Think of a modern word related to each of the old words below. The definitions in parentheses should give you a clue or two. A college dictionary will also help.

1. grue (to shiver)
2. gruel (to exhaust)
3. lorn (forsaken, abandoned)
4. yelk (yellow)

Vocabulary and Spelling

Synonyms and Antonyms

You want your writing to be as clear as you can make it. How can you be sure you have written just the right word to express exactly what you mean? Becoming familiar with synonyms and antonyms—and knowing how to locate them—can help you in your writing. At the same time, you can increase your vocabulary.

Synonyms

Partly because of the borrowings from other languages, English speakers can choose from many words to express the same idea. These words that have the same, or nearly the same, meanings are called **synonyms.**

fast
rapid
quick
fleet
speedy
swift

The important thing to remember is that synonyms rarely mean *exactly* the same thing. When searching for just the right word, the best place to find synonyms is in a thesaurus. (See pages 661–662 for information on how to use a thesaurus.) To use the right word, not *almost* the right word, check your dictionary for the definitions of synonyms, and notice the usage examples given, or refer to a book of usage.

For example, suppose you're writing about someone who spoke before a group. You look up synonyms for the word *speech* and find *address* and *oration. Speech* is a more general choice than *address* and *oration.* A speech may or may not be formal. An address is a prepared formal speech. An oration is even more formal and is always given at a special occasion. For example, you may have read Abraham Lincoln's Gettysburg Address. Before Lincoln gave that famous address, another speaker gave a two-hour oration.

Knowing synonyms also helps make your writing more interesting. Writing that uses tired, colorless clichés—no matter how precise—is almost always boring. Use your knowledge of synonyms to substitute lively verbs and adjectives for lifeless, dried-out words.

Antonyms

Antonyms are words with opposite or nearly opposite meanings. The easiest way to form antonyms is by adding a prefix meaning "not." *Un-, il-, dis-, in-,* and *non-* are all prefixes that reverse the meaning of a root. They form antonyms, such as *untrue, illegible, disbelief, insufficient,* and *nonfat.* Sometimes an antonym can be made by changing the suffix. For example, *cheerful* and *cheerless* are antonyms.

fast

slow

As with synonyms, the important thing to keep in mind when choosing an antonym is finding exactly the right word. You need to check your dictionary to make sure you are using the right word for your context. When making an antonym by adding a prefix, make sure you check the dictionary. Be sure you are using the right prefix.

Exercise 5

For each of the following words, write two synonyms. Then write a sentence using one of the synonyms in each group. Use your dictionary and thesaurus as needed.

1. difficulty
2. nice
3. confusion
4. idea
5. slow (adjective)

Exercise 6

Replace the underlined word or words in each of the following sentences with an antonym. Use a thesaurus and a dictionary if you wish.

1. Jeremy's <u>good health</u> seems to be changing.
2. Andrea looks especially <u>pale</u> tonight.
3. That was the <u>most difficult</u> test I've ever taken.
4. Jake <u>closed</u> his eyes and saw the man who had been chasing him for so many days.
5. This fruit is so <u>dried out</u> I can't eat it.

Wordworks

EATING YOUR WORDS— A GREAT DIET?

Can you ever gain weight from eating your words? As a matter of fact, people don't generally sit down to a meal of their words. That's because they know that the expression *eat your words* really means "to take back something you've said." It's an idiom.

Let's look at some idioms and pull them apart. If you have decided *to put up with* something, where do you put it? If you *go back on* a promise, where have you gone? The point is, you can't understand an idiom just by putting together the meanings of the parts.

Idioms are a pretty big part of everybody's vocabulary. Some idioms are so ordinary that we hardly give them a thought—such as *to put over (a trick* or a *joke)*, or *to come down with (a sickness)*. Others add color to language. For example, you might keep a secret *up your sleeve* or *under your hat.*

Idioms arise in various ways. Some are translations from other languages. Many more probably started out having a word-for-word meaning. Later, people changed the meaning to include other situations. For example, at one time *to break the ice* only meant "to cut through river ice in the winter to make a path for ships and boats." Later the phrase's meaning extended to the process of starting a conversation.

CHALLENGE

English has many idioms that contain the names of animals. How many idioms can you think of that use the names of the following animals?

cat duck crow bird

ACTIVITY

Idio-Matic

How many idioms do you know? Test your idiom vocabulary. Match the following idioms with their meanings.

1. in the pink   **a.** gloomy
2. draw the line   **b.** get angry
3. in the dumps   **c.** healthy
4. a good egg   **d.** set a limit
5. hit the ceiling   **e.** nice person

Vocabulary and Spelling

23.5 Homographs and Homophones

If you're like most people, you may have to think for a minute about whether to write *principal* or *principle* when you're talking about the head of your school. Or you might write *there* in your essay when you mean *their*. When someone points out your mistake, you think, "I knew that!" Some words sound alike but are spelled differently. Others are spelled the same but have different meanings.

Homographs

Words that are spelled alike but have different meanings and sometimes different pronunciations are called homographs. The root *homo* means "same," and *graph* means "write" or "writing." *Homograph,* therefore, means "written the same" (in other words, spelled alike).

Fly and *fly* are homographs. You can swat a fly or fly a plane. Although the two words are spelled alike, they have different meanings. The following chart shows some common homographs used in sample sentences. See if you can tell how the homographs in each group differ in meaning.

Homographs
Ed finished the test with one *minute* left before the bell.   To build very small model airplanes, one must enjoy *minute* details.
It's difficult to *row* a canoe upstream.   We sat in the third *row* of seats in the balcony.   We had a terrific *row* yesterday, but today we're getting along fine.
I hope I pick the winning *number*.   This snow is making my feet *number* by the minute.
Abby tried to *console* her little sister when their cat died.   The television *console* has speakers built into it.
Don't let that *wound* on your arm get infected.   Jim *wound* the rope around the tree branch.

Homophones

Homophones are words that sound alike but are spelled differently and have different meanings. Write and right are homophones. The chart below shows some common homophones with their spellings and meanings.

Homophones			
Words	**Meanings**	**Words**	**Meanings**
sight site cite	act of seeing or ability to see a location to quote an authority	scent cent sent	an odor one one-hundredth of a dollar past tense of *send*
read reed	the act of reading the stalk of a tall grass	bore boar	to tire out with dullness a male pig
four fore	the number following three located at the front	main mane	most important long hair on an animal's neck
mail male	items delivered by lettercarrier the sex opposite the female	blue blew	the color of a clear sky past tense of *blow*
real reel	actual, not artificial spool on which something is wound	would wood	past tense of *will* hard material that makes up a tree

Exercise 7

Write the homophone from the parentheses that best completes each of the following sentences. Use a dictionary for help if necessary.

1. Jackie tried to (real, reel) in the fish.
2. The lion is the (main, mane) attraction at the zoo.
3. Chiyo thought that the speech was a (boar, bore).
4. This is the (cite, sight, site) on which the museum will be built.
5. What is that strange (scent, cent, sent) in the air?
6. A wild (bore, boar) can be dangerous if it attacks.
7. Sol (sighted, sited, cited) a thesaurus as his source.
8. I (scent, cent, sent) the letter on Tuesday.

Wordworks

WHEN IS A NOUN NOT A NOUN?

The labels on the figure below are nouns that name body parts. English lets you put these same words into action as verbs. Here's how—from head to toe.

You can *head* a committee, *eye* a bargain, or *nose* a car into a parking space. You can *shoulder* a burden, *elbow* your way through a crowd, *hand* over the key, *knuckle* down to work, *thumb* a ride, *back* into a room, *foot* the bill, and *toe* the mark.

For hundreds of years, speakers of English have used these nouns and many others as verbs. Some words shifted in the other direction, from verb to noun. Today you can *walk* on a *walk, park* in a *park,* and *pitch* a wild *pitch.* Some shifts involve pronunciation. Notice which syllable you accent:

Will you *perMIT* me to drive?
Yes, when you get a *PERmit.*

Does your garden *proDUCE* carrots?
No, I buy *PROduce* at the market.

Still another shift involves nouns that became adjectives, as in the following: Sara unlocked the *steel* door. Tom wore a *straw* hat. Marty made *onion* soup.

So, when is a noun not a noun? When it's used as a verb or an adjective. The only way to identify a word's part of speech is to see it in a sentence.

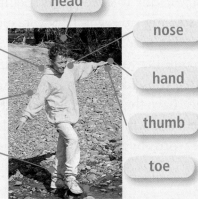

head
nose
shoulder
hand
elbow
thumb
foot
toe

ACTIVITY

Double Duty

Use these clues to identify some words that have two functions.

1. *noun:* a very young person
   verb: to pamper
2. *verb:* to walk with regular steps
   noun: music with a steady beat
3. *verb:* throw pictures onto a screen
   noun: special work in science class

CHALLENGE

Suppose you got this written message: Ship sails today. *What does it mean? Put* the *before* ship; *then put* the *before* sails. *Why can this sentence have two different meanings?*

You may not know it, but you may have something in common with Noah Webster (of dictionary fame). He wanted to simplify the spelling of American English. He convinced people that the British *gaol* should be spelled *jail* in American English. He also got rid of the *k* in the British *musick* and *publick*. Webster especially disliked silent letters. He tried to get people to accept *frend* (*friend*), *hed* (*head*), and *bilt* (*built*), among other spellings.

However, most people didn't like Webster's spelling reforms, so today we have a system of spelling filled with rules and exceptions and words spelled nothing like the way they are pronounced. Using a dictionary to check spelling is the best way to avoid mistakes.

Common Spelling Rules

You won't always have a dictionary handy to check your spelling. Memorizing some of the following spelling rules will help you spell most words correctly even when you don't have a dictionary.

Spelling *ie* and *ei*   The letter combinations *ie* and *ei* are found in many English words, and they often cause confusion in spelling. The problem is that two words might have the same vowel sound— long *e*— but one word might be spelled *ie* while the other is spelled *ei*. You can master the spelling of these words by memorizing the rhyme below.

Rule	Examples
Put *i* before *e*	achieve, retrieve, grieve
except after *c*	deceive, receipt, ceiling
or when sounded like *a*, as in *neighbor* and *weigh*.	eighty, veil, freight
Exceptions: species, weird, either, neither, seize, leisure, protein, height	

Spelling Unstressed Vowels   The unstressed vowel sound in many English words can cause spelling problems. Dictionary pronunciation guides represent this unstressed vowel sound by a special symbol called a schwa (ə). Listen to the unstressed vowel sound in the word *about*. This vowel sound can be spelled in more than a dozen ways—with any vowel letter and with several combinations of vowel letters—but it always sounds the same. Here are a few examples. Pronounce each word, and listen for the sound represented by the underlined letter or letters:

> canv<u>a</u>s, ang<u>e</u>l, penc<u>i</u>l, rid<u>i</u>cule, cart<u>o</u>n, medi<u>u</u>m, enorm<u>ou</u>s, anci<u>e</u>nt, pig<u>eo</u>n, courag<u>eou</u>s.

Notice that you hear the schwa sound only in unstressed syllables.

As always, the best way to make sure of your spelling is to check a dictionary. When you can't use a dictionary, you might be able to figure out the spelling of the unstressed vowel sound. Think of a related word in which the vowel is stressed. The word *informative*, for example, has an unstressed vowel, which happens to be spelled *a*. If you don't know that, you might think of the related word *information*, in which the vowel is stressed and sounds like an *a*. The chart below shows some additional examples of how to use this strategy.

Spelling Unstressed Vowels		
Unknown Word	**Related Word**	**Word Spelled Correctly**
popul_rize	popul**a**rity	popularize
plur_l	plur**a**lity	plural
aut_mation	aut**o**	automation
influ_nce	influ**e**ntial	influence
not_ble	not**a**tion	notable
form_l	form**a**lity	formal
practic_l	practic**a**lity	practical
pol_r	pol**a**rity	polar
inhabit_nt	habit**a**tion	inhabitant
hospit_l	hospit**a**lity	hospital

Adding Prefixes   Adding prefixes to words usually doesn't present any spelling problems. Keep the spelling of the word, and attach the prefix. If the prefix ends in the same letter as the first letter of the word, keep both letters. Some common examples include the following:

co- + pilot = copilot   dis- + service = disservice

il- + legal = illegal   co- + operate = cooperate

Suffixes and the Final _y_   Adding suffixes to words that end in _y_ can often cause spelling problems. The following rules will help you:

- When a word ends in a consonant + _y_, change the _y_ to _i_.

imply + -es = implies   reply + -ed = replied

pry + -ed = pried   apply + -es = applies

- If the suffix begins with an _i_, keep the _y_.

supply + -ing = supplying   fly + -ing = flying

- When a word ends in a vowel + _y_, keep the _y_.

toy + -ing = toying   stay + -ing = staying

delay + -ed = delayed   prey + -ed = preyed

Doubling the Final Consonant   When adding suffixes to words that end in a consonant, you sometimes double the final consonant. In other cases you simply add the suffix without doubling the consonant.

Double the final consonant when a word ends in a single consonant following one vowel and

- the word is one syllable

strip + -ed = stripped   sad + -er = sadder

shop + -ing = shopping   ship + -ed = shipped

war + -ing = warring   tap + -ed = tapped

- the word has an accent on the last syllable, and the accent remains there after the suffix is added

occur + -ence = occurrence   repel + -ing = repelling

forget + -able = forgettable   commit + -ed = committed

upset + -ing = upsetting   refer + -ed = referred

Do not double the final consonant when
- the accent is not on the last syllable

  flavor + -ing = flavoring

  envelop + -ment = envelopment

  remember + -ing = remembering

- the accent moves when the suffix is added

  refer + -ence = reference

  fatal + -ity = fatality

- two vowels come before the final consonant

  remain + -ed = remained   floor + -ing = flooring

  lead + -ing = leading   train + -ed = trained

- the suffix begins with a consonant

  master + -ful = masterful   dark + -ness = darkness

  tear + -less = tearless   leader + -ship = leadership

  loyal + -ty = loyalty   flat + -ly = flatly

  great + -ness = greatness

- the word ends in two consonants

  bring + -ing = bringing   stick + -ing = sticking

  inspect + -or = inspector   hunt + -ed = hunted

  attach + -ment = attachment

SPECIAL CASE: When a word ends in *ll*, and the suffix *-ly* is added, drop one *l*.

  dull + -ly = dully   full + -ly = fully

Suffixes and the Silent *e*   Noah Webster did his best to get rid of the silent letter *e* in American-English spelling. He succeeded in changing *axe* to *ax*. However, he lost the battle to change *give* to *giv*, and *medicine* to *medicin*. He also failed to change the spellings of other words ending in silent *e*. The public was not willing to give up spellings with which they were familiar.

The silent *e* can still cause spelling problems, especially when you add a suffix to a word that ends in a silent *e*. Sometimes the silent *e* is dropped when adding a suffix, and sometimes it is kept. The following chart shows the rules for adding suffixes to words that end in silent *e*.

Adding Suffixes to Words That End in Silent *e*

Rule	Examples
When adding a suffix that begins with a consonant to a word that ends in silent *e*, keep the *e*.	state + -ment = statement complete + -ly = completely
Common exceptions	awe + -ful = awful judge + -ment = judgment
When adding *-ly* to a word that ends in *l* plus a silent *e*, always drop the *e*.	able + -ly = ably sensible + -ly = sensibly remarkable + -ly = remarkably
When adding *y* or a suffix that begins with a vowel to a word that ends in a silent *e*, usually drop the *e*.	state + -ing = stating nose + -y = nosy
Common exceptions	lime + -ade = limeade mile + -age = mileage
When adding a suffix that begins with *a* or *o* to a word that ends in *ce* or *ge*, keep the *e* so the word will retain the soft *c* or *g* sound.	exchange + -able = exchangeable courage + -ous = courageous
When adding a suffix that begins with a vowel to a word that ends in *ee* or *oe*, keep the *e*.	disagree + -able = disagreeable shoe + -ing = shoeing flee + -ing = fleeing

Forming Compound Words   The rule for spelling compound words is very simple. In most cases, just put the two words together. Seeing two consonants together, such as *hh, kk,* or *kb,* may seem odd. The English language does not have many words with these combinations. However, the rule is to keep the original spelling of both words, no matter how the words begin or end.

foot + lights = footlights   fish + hook = fishhook
busy + body = busybody   book + keeper = bookkeeper
book + bag = bookbag   light + house = lighthouse

Some compound words, such as *hand-me-down* and *forty-niners,* are hyphenated. Others, like *honey bear* (but not *honeybee*), are spelled as two words. Use a dictionary when in doubt.

Forming Plurals   The way plurals are formed in English is generally simple, and the rules are fairly easy to remember. The most common way to form plurals is to add *-s* or *-es*. The following chart shows the basic rules, their exceptions, and example words.

Rules for Plurals		
If the Noun Ends in	**Then Generally**	**Examples**
ch, *s,* *sh,* *x,* or *z*	add *-es*	witch → witches toss → tosses flash → flashes ax → axes buzz → buzzes
a consonant + *y*	change *y* to *i* and add *-es*	story → stories folly → follies
a vowel + *y*	add *-s*	play → plays jockey → jockeys
a vowel + *o*	add *-s*	studio → studios rodeo → rodeos
a consonant + *o*	generally add *-s* **Common exceptions** but sometimes add *-es*	piano → pianos photo → photos hero → heroes veto → vetoes echo → echoes
f or *ff*	add *-s* **Common exceptions** change *f* to *v* and add *-es*	staff → staffs chief → chiefs thief → thieves leaf → leaves
lf	change *f* to *v* and add *-es*	self → selves half → halves
fe	change *f* to *v* and add *-s*	life → lives knife → knives

A few nouns form plurals in a special way. Most of these special cases should not give you any problems in spelling. If you do not already know the irregular forms, such as *goose—geese,* you can memorize them. The following chart lists the special rules for plurals and gives some examples.

Special Rules for Plurals	
Special Case	**Examples**
To form the plural of proper names, add either *-s* or *-es,* following the general rules for plurals.	Smith → Smiths Jones → Joneses Perez → Perezes
To form the plural of one-word compound nouns, follow the general rules for plurals.	homemaker → homemakers blackberry → blackberries latchkey → latchkeys
To form the plural of hyphenated compound nouns or compound nouns of more than one word, generally make the most important word plural.	father-in-law → fathers-in-law lunch box → lunch boxes chief of state → chiefs of state
Some nouns have irregular plural forms and do not follow any rules.	goose → geese mouse → mice tooth → teeth child → children
Some nouns have the same singular and plural forms.	deer → deer sheep → sheep fish → fish

Improving Spelling Skills

Learning spelling rules will help you spell new words correctly. You can further improve your spelling skills by developing a method for learning these words.

Keep a notebook of unfamiliar words or words that are hard to spell. When you write, take note of any words you have trouble spelling, and add them to your notebook. As you come across new words, add them to your list. When you master the spelling of a word, cross the word off your list. Follow the steps on the next page to learn to spell those difficult words.

Say It	**Visualize It**	**Write It**	**Check It**
Look at the printed word or the word as it is written in your notebook. Say it out loud. Say it a second time, pronouncing each syllable clearly.	Close your eyes, and imagine seeing the word printed or written. Picture how the word is spelled.	Look at the printed word again, and write it two or three times. Then write it again without looking at the printed word.	Check what you have written against the printed word. Did you spell it correctly? If not, go through the process again until you can spell it correctly.

Exercise 8

Find the misspelled word in each sentence and write its correct spelling.

1. Mr. Harrison, the bookkeeper, has applyed for a government grant to buy new computers.
2. The book describes the lifes of famous artists.
3. Hector is fullly aware that we have to proceed with the polar expedition.
4. Stefanie spends her leisure time with the Walshs.
5. Kevin should be in the barnyard shoeing one of the remainning horses.
6. The zookeeper believes he will succeed in transfering the monkeys from the old cages without any problems.
7. The librarian has suggested two referrence books that should contain photos of wolves.
8. The summer weather has been so changeable that everyone is completly convinced we will have an unusually bad winter.
9. The puffs of clouds in the springtime sky reminded me of sheeps in a meadow.
10. The recent recurrence of fighting between the two warring nations is upseting to everyone who hopes for a peaceful settlement.

Wordworks

VOWEL SWITCH

Spelling in English can be a real mystery. Why should the first vowel sounds in *pleasant* and *please* be spelled the same even though they are pronounced differently? Why not spell the sound in *pleasant* with just an *e*, as in *pen* and *red*?

Here's the scoop: Sometime between 1400 and 1600 the pronunciation of certain vowels underwent a change. The vowel in *please* was pronounced like the e in *pen,* only it was longer. This sound gradually shifted to a long ā sound as in *pane.* Meanwhile, the long vowel ā had begun to take on the long ē sound as in *feed,* while the long vowel ē had begun to take on the long ī sound as in *ride.* Similar changes occurred in the other long vowels. These pronunciation changes are called the Great Vowel Shift.

Meanwhile, the short vowels (as in *pleasant*) did not change. Because spelling didn't always keep up with pronunciation changes, the words *please* and *pleasant* were still spelled with the same vowel even though *please* was now pronounced like *plays.* Later, some words like *please* changed again. By about 1700 most people pronounced *please* the way you pronounce it today.

So the next time you're puzzled by English spelling, remember that the way a word is spelled sometimes holds a clue to its history.

	Before 1400	After 1600	After 1700
please	plez	plāz	plēz
pleasant	plezant		

ACTIVITY

Shifty Vowels

Which of the following word pairs demonstrate the Great Vowel Shift?

1. crime, criminal
2. mouse, mice
3. breathe, breath
4. serene, serenity
5. die, death

23.7 Becoming a Better Speller

Spelling the *really* difficult words—such as *pusillanimous* (meaning "cowardly")—is usually not too much of a problem. The reason is that when you use such words (which is not often), you will probably look them up in the dictionary.

What about the less difficult but more common words that you use often? Following is a list of such words. See if any of them are words you have had trouble spelling. What words would you add to the list?

Words Often Misspelled			
absence	curiosity	incidentally	pneumonia
accidentally	develop	incredibly	privilege
accommodate	definite	jewelry	pronunciation
achievement	descend	laboratory	receipt
adviser	discipline	leisure	recognize
alcohol	disease	library	recommend
all right	dissatisfied	license	restaurant
analyze	eligible	maintenance	rhythm
answer	embarrass	mischievous	ridiculous
attendant	environment	misspell	schedule
ballet	essential	molasses	separate
beautiful	February	muscle	sincerely
beginning	fulfill	necessary	souvenir
beneficial	foreign	neighborhood	succeed
business	forty	niece	technology
cafeteria	funeral	noticeable	theory
canceled	genius	nuisance	tomorrow
canoe	government	occasion	traffic
cemetery	grammar	original	truly
changeable	guarantee	pageant	unanimous
choir	height	parallel	usually
colonel	humorous	permanent	vacuum
commercial	hygiene	physical	variety
convenient	imaginary	physician	various
courageous	immediate	picnic	Wednesday

Spelling and Misspelling

Do you have trouble remembering the spellings of common words? How many *c*'s and *m*'s are in *recommend* and *accommodate*? Is it *separate* or *seperate*? Words like these cause many people problems. The following techniques will help you learn to spell troublesome words.

- Use rhymes (such as "*i* before *e* except after *c* . . .") and memory tricks (such as "there's *a rat* in *separate*").
- Pay special attention to words likely to be confused with other words. Below are some examples. You can find more in the list of homophones on page 680.

Words Often Confused	
accept except	Marianne will not *accept* the nomination for class president. All the students *except* Barry were on time.
affect effect	This cold weather can *affect* my sinuses. The space program could have an *effect* on future generations.
formally formerly	The new president was *formally* introduced to the student body. Ananda *formerly* lived in southern California.
its it's	Since *its* walls collapsed, the mine entrance has been closed. *It's* been a long time since I saw Winston so happy.
stationary stationery	The radio transmitting station is mobile, not *stationary*. Her *stationery* is decorated with tiny blue flowers.
thorough through	They completed a *thorough* revision of the student handbook. *Through* the window we could see them coming up the path.
than then	The final draft of my story is much better *than* the first draft. What happened *then*?
their there they're	What was the outcome of *their* first game? The address you are looking for is over *there*. The team members say *they're* happy with the new gym.
weather whether	I hope the *weather* stays nice for the picnic. I'm not sure *whether* it was luck or skill, but I made the team.

Exercise 9

Work with one or two other students. Choose three words from the list of Words Often Misspelled on page 691 of this lesson. Develop a memory aid that will help you spell each word. Share your completed memory aids with the class.

Exercise 10

Write the word in the parentheses that correctly completes each sentence.

1. The school decided to change the name of (its, it's) football team.
2. One of the test questions asked for an (effect, affect) of the Civil War.
3. Pete (formerly, formally) played on a soccer team at his old school.
4. If you leave your books (their, there, they're), they may get lost.
5. The cat pushed (its, it's) way through the swinging door.
6. Use your best (stationery, stationary) for the thank-you notes.
7. Have you decided what dress (your, you're) going to wear to the party?
8. The detective was very (thorough, through) in his investigation of the crime.
9. We would like to know (whether, weather) it will rain or be sunny on the day of our field trip.
10. The two dogs need to have (their, there, they're) coats brushed after being out all day.
11. I've never been (formerly, formally) introduced to the new counselor.
12. The three girls said that (their, there, they're) going to go swimming.

UNIT 24 Study Skills

24.1 Using Book Features

Imagine you're writing a research paper on the Civil War. You've narrowed your topic to the Battle of Gettysburg, focusing on Pickett's Charge, a key event in the three-day battle. You find that the library has many books on the Battle of Gettysburg—but you certainly can't read them all.

How do you decide which books will be the most useful? Looking at certain pages in the front or back of a book will help you narrow your choice.

You can use the pages shown below—title page, table of contents, and index—to help you find the information you need. The title page and table of contents appear in the front, before the main text of the book. You'll find the index in the back.

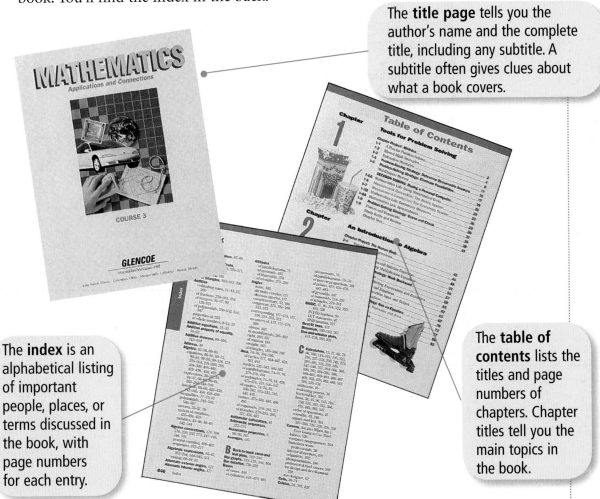

The **title page** tells you the author's name and the complete title, including any subtitle. A subtitle often gives clues about what a book covers.

The **index** is an alphabetical listing of important people, places, or terms discussed in the book, with page numbers for each entry.

The **table of contents** lists the titles and page numbers of chapters. Chapter titles tell you the main topics in the book.

Study Skills

Many books include other informative sections separate from the main text. The copyright page follows the title page. It tells you the year in which the book was published. Also in the front of a book, you may find a foreword, a preface, or an introduction. In the back of some books are glossaries for definitions and pronunciations of unusual words. The chart below shows you how to use some of these parts of a book.

Using a Book Effectively	
Questions	**Where to Look for the Answer**
Who is the author of this book?	The title page contains the author's name and the complete title.
Will this book contain information about my topic?	The table of contents identifies the main topics.
Will this book contain recent information about my topic?	The copyright page tells when a book was published or updated.
Will I find the people, places, and events I'm researching in this book?	The index is an alphabetical listing of people, places, events, and other topics covered in the book.

Exercise 1

Use this textbook to answer all but the first of the following questions:

1. Suppose you were studying how the human heart functions and wanted to find a definition of atrium. In what part of a science book would you look?
2. On what page or pages of this book are synonyms discussed?
3. In what year was this book published?
4. What is the title of Unit 10?
5. Does this book discuss homographs and, if so, on what page(s)?

Skimming, Scanning, and Careful Reading

What if you needed information about the structure of the human heart? You would probably read a book about your topic. You can use a number of strategies as you read for information. Using the right reading strategy for a particular purpose can save valuable time.

Skimming

When you want to know if a book covers the information you need, skimming is a good technique. Skimming can be very helpful in your research or when previewing or reviewing texts. To skim a text, you glance over the text to find the main ideas. You look at the chapter titles, words in italic or boldface type, and at the topic sentence of each paragraph. Without taking too much time, you can grasp the most important ideas in a given chapter. For instance, the notes below were made while a reader was skimming a detailed chapter on the makeup of the human heart.

> Heart has four chambers—right and left atria, right and
>   left ventricles.
> Right ventricle pumps blood from body through lungs.
> Left ventricle pumps blood from lungs through body.
> Blood from the body enters right *atrium*, through two
>   veins, called *superior vena cava* and *inferior vena cava*.
> Blood carrying oxygen flows from lungs to left *atrium*
>   through *pulmonary veins*.

Scanning

When you are searching for specific information, you can use a strategy called scanning. Scanning is glancing from point to point quickly but thoroughly. While scanning, you move your eyes over a page, looking for key words. When you locate the information you want, you read carefully for specific details.

Careful Reading

Careful reading allows you to understand material thoroughly and to monitor your comprehension. When you use this technique, you read the text slowly. You pay close attention to all details to make sure you clearly understand the information presented. Read carefully when learning material for the first time, such as when studying a new chapter in a science textbook. Pay attention to how well you have understood what you've read. Reread, if a passage is unclear, and jot down questions or comments for later review.

You also practice careful reading when preparing to explain material to someone else. Suppose you were going to present an oral report on the human circulatory system. Any book you find explaining the circulatory system would probably include medical information unfamiliar to you. The only way to fully understand the content is to read slowly and carefully. Read a passage several times until you fully understand it. If you understand what you will be speaking or writing about, you will be able to explain it better to your audience. Keep a dictionary nearby so that you can look up any unfamiliar words.

Exercise 2

Decide which reading strategy—skimming, scanning, or careful reading—should be used in each of the following situations. Explain each decision.

1. You find a library book on a topic that interests you. You wonder whether the book is worth reading.
2. You've been asked to read the first half of a chapter in your science textbook before tomorrow's class.
3. You need information about the causes of the American Revolution for a report you are writing. You need to decide which of the ten books on the American Revolution you've found would best fit your needs.

24.3 Summarizing

Explaining the main ideas of something in your own words is called summarizing. Every time you tell a friend about a movie you saw or a book you read, you are summarizing. You might summarize yesterday's science lesson to a friend who was sick that day. You also might find that explaining or summarizing something for someone else helps you understand it better.

When to Summarize

Though you often make informal summaries, there are also times when you need to make formal ones. When researching material for a report, for instance, you need to summarize important ideas. You also might summarize information you hear in a lecture, speech, or film presented in class. After you take notes on what you read or hear, you can summarize the main ideas for reference or review.

You can also use summarizing as a study tool when reading or reviewing material in your text. Writing passages from a textbook in your own words can help you better understand and remember the material. The following chart shows when and why you might summarize material.

When to Summarize	
Situation	**Purpose**
Preparing a written or oral research report	To include important ideas from your reading in your report
Reading textbook material	To better understand and remember ideas from the textbook
Listening to lectures or speeches	To write a report or prepare for a test on ideas from the lecture or speech
Viewing a film or video documentary	To write a report or prepare for a test on ideas from the film

Study Skills

How to Summarize

When you write a summary, put the ideas in your own words. Concentrate on the main ideas, leaving out examples and supporting details. Look below at the example of an original text and one student's summary of it. Notice what details are left out and how the student's language differs from the original.

Abraham Lincoln (1809–1865), considered one of our greatest presidents, preserved the Union at a time of unrest during the Civil War. With the United States facing disintegration, he showed that a democratic form of government can endure.

One of Lincoln's most important qualities was his understanding. Lincoln realized that the Union and democracy had to be preserved. Lincoln was also a remarkable communicator, able to clearly and persuasively express ideas and beliefs in speech and writing. His most famous speech was the brief but powerful Gettysburg Address. His first and second inaugural addresses were also very significant.

Abraham Lincoln, one of our greatest presidents, is remembered for holding the Union together through the Civil War. He is noted for his understanding and his ability to communicate effectively and persuasively

Exercise 3

With a partner, choose a film or television documentary, a lesson or chapter from a book, or an encyclopedia article about a subject that interests you. Read or discuss the material, and then work together to write a summary. Identify the main ideas, and put them in your own words. Decide whether to use any direct quotes. Share your completed summary with the class.

Making Study Plans

If you think about ways to study effectively and then take some time to learn good study skills, you can improve your school performance and increase your free-time. Think about studying well, not just about spending time studying.

Setting Goals

A good study plan begins with goal setting. Review your assignments, and then set your goals for each class. Break down your assignments into short-term and long-term goals. Short-term goals can be completed in one study session; long-term goals, of course, will take more time. Break down your long-term goals into smaller tasks. Be realistic about what you can get done in each study session.

The chart below shows some short-term and long-term goals and how long-term goals can be broken down.

Setting Goals	
Short-Term Goals	1. learning a short list of spelling or vocabulary words 2. reading several pages in your textbook 3. completing a math exercise for homework
Long-Term Goals	1. completing a research report *short-term tasks* • find library materials • do prewriting • write rough draft • revise draft • prepare final report 2. preparing for a unit test *short-term tasks* • read Chapter 22 • read Chapter 23 • review key terms

Effective Study Time

Once you've determined your goals, set a reasonable deadline for reaching each goal. Write the deadline in a study-plan calendar that includes your regular activities and assignments. When you schedule your study time, keep your deadlines and your other activities in mind. Don't schedule too many deadlines for the same day. Look at the following studying tips. What other tips could you add?

Tips on Studying

1. Study at the same time and in the same place each day. Also, keep your study tools, such as pencils, pens, notepads, and dictionaries, in the same place.

2. Take a short break after reaching each goal.

3. Begin study time with your most difficult assignment.

4. Focus on one assignment at a time.

5. Try a variety of study methods, such as reading, summarizing what you have read, developing your own graphic aids (like clusters), or discussing material with a study partner.

Exercise 4

Keep a "study log" for two weeks. Record the beginning and ending time of each study session, even if it's only fifteen minutes at lunch. Write down what you study each day, and comment on how effective your studying is. You may want to include observations on circumstances that affect your ability to study on a particular day. (For example: It was raining, so I was glad to be inside studying; I had a headache, so I had trouble concentrating.) At the end of the two weeks, take a good look at your study log. Identify the factors that contributed to your most effective use of study time.

24.5 The SQ3R Method

The SQ3R method can help make your study time more productive. SQ3R is an effective method for improving your ability to read and remember written information. SQ3R stands for the steps in the process: **s**urvey, **q**uestion, **r**ead, **r**ecord, and **r**eview. Using this method can help you study more efficiently and remember more of what you read. The diagram shows how the SQ3R method works.

Survey	**Question**	**Read**	**Record**	**Review**
Preview the material by skimming. Read heads, highlighted terms, and the first sentence of each paragraph. Look at all pictures and graphs.	Ask questions about the material. Your questions might begin with *who, what, when, where, why,* and *how.*	Read the selection carefully. Identify the main idea of each section. Take notes and add questions to your list.	Write answers to your questions without looking at the text. Make brief notes about additional main ideas and facts.	Check your answers in the text. Continue to study the text until you can answer all questions correctly.

The SQ3R method works with any subject. Practice the method, and make it a habit. Once you thoroughly learn the SQ3R method and use it regularly, you will

- remember more of what you read,
- better understand the material by developing specific questions about it, and
- be better prepared to participate in class.

Survey

The purpose of surveying, or previewing, written material is to get a general idea of what it is about. The main ideas are sometimes contained in section headings or subheadings. Read each heading and subheading, and skim all the material. (See page 697 for hints on skimming.) If the material does not include headings, skim each paragraph to find its topic sentence. It will often be the first sentence of the paragraph.

Sometimes important ideas in the text are shown in bold or italic print. Make sure you take note of these ideas. When previewing, also take note of all pictures, charts, graphs, and maps. Examine them to see how the graphic aids fit in with the text. Read the title and caption for each one.

Question

After you survey and before you read, prepare a list of questions you want to be able to answer after reading the material. Having a list of questions before you begin helps you focus on the important ideas. Use questions that begin with *who, what, when, where, why,* and *how.* For example, suppose you're reading a chapter on the Battle of Gettysburg for your history class. You might write questions such as these: Who were the opposing generals in the battle? When did the battle take place? What was the outcome? You might also look at any review questions at the end of each chapter or lesson and add those to your list.

Read

Once you have prepared your list of questions, you are ready to read the material carefully. (See page 698 for tips on careful reading.) As you read, look for answers to the questions on your list. Take brief notes about the main ideas. (See pages 706–707 for more information on taking notes.) For example, your notes might include "Battle of Gettysburg fought July 1–3, 1863. Confederate General Robert E. Lee; Union General George G. Meade. Turning point of Civil War." Add more questions to your list as they arise during your reading. Make sure you thoroughly understand all the ideas. If the ideas are complicated and you are having difficulty, reread the material slowly to help clarify your understanding of important vocabulary concepts.

Record

When you complete your reading, write the answers to your questions without looking at the book or article. If there is a large amount of material, you may wish to stop and answer your questions after you finish reading each section. Answering the questions from your memory will test whether you have thoroughly learned the material. If you have difficulty answering the questions, reread the material. Then try to answer the questions again without looking at the text. Make sure your questions apply to the material. If the material you're studying does not thoroughly answer the questions, revise your questions to fit the text.

Review

Check the answers to your questions against the material you've read. Did you answer them all correctly? If not, review the material to find the answers. Try rewriting some of the questions you missed, or write several new questions that cover the same material. Review the material again, and then answer the new questions. Check your answers against the material. If you miss some of these questions, go through the process again, rewriting questions and reviewing the material until you are able to correctly answer all questions. Save your review questions and answers. You can use them later to study or review for tests.

Exercise 5

Work with a small group of classmates. Each member should choose an event from American history, then find an encyclopedia article or a passage from a book about that event. Study your material using the SQ3R method. Allow each member to give a brief oral report to the group on the material studied. Group members may evaluate one another's reports and discuss how the SQ3R method helped them.

24.6 | Gathering and Organizing Information

Can you remember the important ideas from a discussion you heard two weeks ago? Unless you took notes, you've probably forgotten what was said. Taking notes and organizing them helps clarify what you hear or read. It also helps you remember information. Well-written notes also come in handy when you're studying for a test or writing a report.

Taking Notes

Taking notes can be challenging, whether you are working from a lecture, a film or video shown in class, or from research material. You may find you are either trying to write down too much or not enough. Taking notes requires special skill.

The notes you take while listening are important for your later review. They'll help you understand and remember what you hear. The notes you take while reading will allow you to review the important ideas from a source. With good notes, you may not have to go back to a source to reread it.

Tips for Taking Notes

While Listening
1. Take down only main ideas and key details.
2. Listen for transitions and signal words.
3. Use numerals, abbreviations, and symbols for speed, making sure that later you can understand what you have written.

While Doing Research
1. Take notes only on material that applies directly to your topic.
2. Use a card for each piece of information, and record the source of the information at the top of the card.
3. Summarize as much as possible.
4. Use direct quotations only for colorful language or something that's particularly well-phrased.

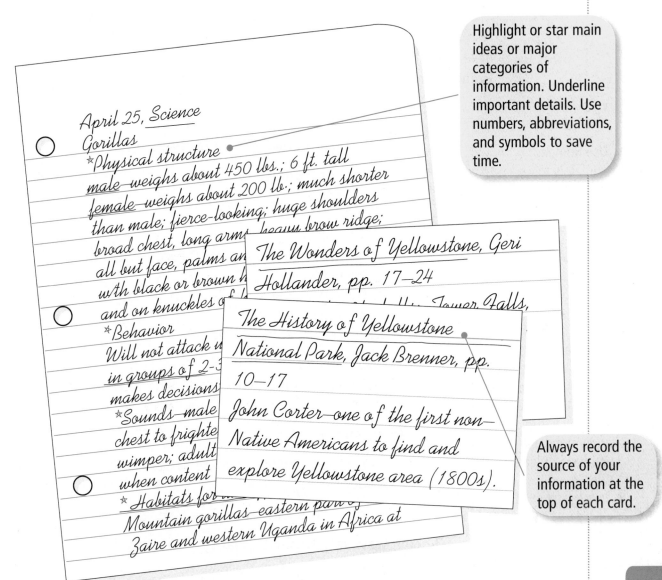

April 25, Science
Gorillas
*Physical structure
male—weighs about 450 lbs.; 6 ft. tall
female—weighs about 200 lb.; much shorter
than male; fierce-looking; huge shoulders
broad chest, long arms, heavy brow ridge;
all but face, palms an...
with black or brown h...
and on knuckles of l...
*Behavior
Will not attack u...
in groups of 2-3...
makes decisions...
*Sounds—male...
chest to frighte...
wimper; adult...
when content...
*Habitats for...
Mountain gorillas—eastern part of
Zaire and western Uganda in Africa at

The Wonders of Yellowstone, Geri
Hollander, pp. 17–24

The History of Yellowstone
National Park, Jack Brenner, pp.
10–17

John Corter—one of the first non—
Native Americans to find and
explore Yellowstone area (1800s).

> Highlight or star main ideas or major categories of information. Underline important details. Use numbers, abbreviations, and symbols to save time.

> Always record the source of your information at the top of each card.

Outlining

Once you complete your research, put your note cards in order and prepare an outline. The order you use depends on the kind of paper you are writing. If you're writing a paper on historical events, you might use chronological order, or the order in which events happen. A science paper might be ordered by cause and effect.

Group together your note cards that cover similar topics. Each group will become a main topic. Within each group put similar cards into subgroups. These will become your subtopics.

As your outline develops, you may find that you need to do more research. You may also find that you do not need all the notes you have taken. Set aside any note cards that don't apply to your outline. Examine the sample outline below.

Use Roman numerals to number the main topics, or important ideas, of your paper.

Indent and use letters and numbers for subtopics and their divisions. Do not use subtopics or divisions unless you have at least two.

Yellowstone National Park

I. The History of Yellowstone

   A. Earliest Explorers

      1. John Colter
         a. member of the earlier Lewis and Clark expedition
         b. first non-Native American to see Yellowstone
         c. visited in early 1800s

      2. Jim Bridger
         a. famous "mountain man" and explorer
         b. visited the region about 1830

   B. Washburn Expedition

      1. confirmed earlier reports of natural wonders

      2. worked to make area a national park

II. Yellowstone's Natural Beauty

Exercise 6

Working with a small group of classmates, look through a number of educational magazines. Choose an article that interests all of you. Have each member of the group read the article, take notes on it, and write a detailed outline. Then compare notes and outlines, discussing the differences.

24.7 Graphic Information

Imagine trying to use words alone to explain how a car engine works. A simple written description of a process may seem confusing or incomplete. However, a picture or diagram can make it much easier for people to understand how something works.

Tables and Graphs

Many books use graphic aids such as tables and graphs to present figures or other data that are hard to explain with words alone. Tables and graphs organize information and make it more understandable.

Tables Tables allow you to group facts or numbers into categories so that you can compare information easily. The left-hand column of a table lists a set of related items. Across the top of the table are column headings that describe the items in each column. With this arrangement, you can read a table horizontally or vertically, and you don't have to read all the information to find the piece you need. For example, in the table below, you can easily find the population growth of the five largest U.S. cities. Looking across the rows, you can see how a particular city's population increased or decreased over the years. Looking down the columns, you can compare the populations in the different years listed.

Population of Largest U.S. Cities							
Rank	City	1950	1960	1970	1980	1990	1998
1	New York City	7,891,984	7,781,984	7,895,563	7,071,639	7,322,564	7,420,166
2	Los Angeles	1,970,358	2,479,015	2,811,801	2,966,850	3,485,537	3,597,556
3	Chicago	3,620,962	3,550,404	3,369,357	3,005,072	2,783,726	2,802,079
4	Houston	596,163	938,219	1,233,535	1,595,138	1,654,348	1,786,691
5	Philadelphia	2,071,605	2,002,512	1,949,996	1,688,210	1,585,577	1,436,287

Source: U.S. Bureau of the Census

Study Skills

Bar Graphs   In bar graphs, each quantity is shown as a bar. The length of the bar indicates the amount, making it easy to visually compare the amounts. Bar graphs can have horizontal bars or vertical bars. Look at the bar graph below. Use the graph to compare the sales figures for different types of athletic shoes sold in the United States.

Each bar represents a different type of athletic shoe. The height of each bar shows the total sales for one type of shoe.

By comparing the lengths of the bars, you see that walking shoes outsold all other types of athletic shoes in 1994.

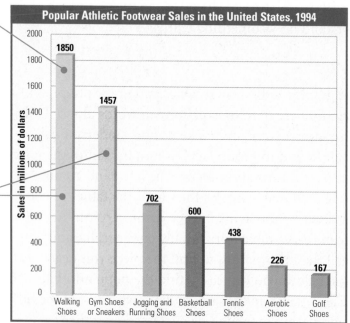

Popular Athletic Footwear Sales in the United States, 1994

Line Graphs   Line graphs help the reader see at a glance changes in certain numbers or statistics. They also show the period of time in which these changes take place. The line graph at the left shows the amount of solid waste thrown away between 1960 and 1994.

Amounts are shown along the vertical axis. Horizontal lines make it easy to locate the amount for a given year.

Years are shown along the horizontal axis. Vertical lines on the graph make it easy to see where the year intersects the graph line.

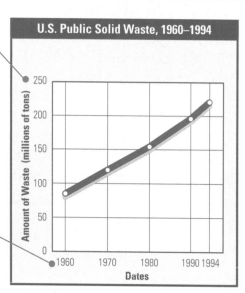

The amount of garbage, in millions of tons, is listed along the left-hand side, or vertical axis. The years are shown along the bottom, or horizontal axis. By following the line, you can quickly see that the amount of garbage thrown away in the United States rose over the years given.

Circle Graphs   Circle graphs, or pie charts, begin with a circle representing the whole of something. The parts are shown as slices of a pie, with each slice representing part of the whole. Because a circle graph shows parts of a whole, information is often presented as percentages. For instance, instead of representing the population of North America in numbers of people, a circle graph might show it as a percentage of the total world population.

The circle graph on this page uses the same information as the bar graph on the opposite page. The whole circle represents the total of athletic shoes sold in the United States in 1994. The graph is then divided into the different types of athletic shoes. The sizes of the slices allow you to easily compare the portions of total sales for each type of shoe.

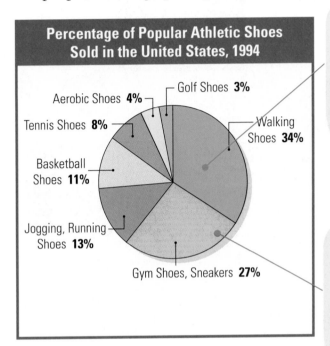

Percentage of Popular Athletic Shoes Sold in the United States, 1994

Golf Shoes **3%**
Aerobic Shoes **4%**
Tennis Shoes **8%**
Basketball Shoes **11%**
Jogging, Running Shoes **13%**
Gym Shoes, Sneakers **27%**
Walking Shoes **34%**

Walking shoes are represented by a slice that represents 34 percent of all athletic shoes sold in 1994.

The next largest slice, representing gym shoes and sneakers, accounts for 27 percent of all athletic shoes sold in 1994.

Diagrams

Diagrams may illustrate the steps in a process or show how the parts of an object work together. You might find it difficult to learn about a complex process by reading about it or by listening to someone give an explanation. You might not be able to follow all the stages or understand all the parts without the help of a diagram.

In a diagram, each part of the object or process is labeled, sometimes with an explanation of its function. The diagram on the next page, for example, shows how heat energy is turned into electricity. Notice how each important part is labeled. Note also how the arrows show the movement of water and energy.

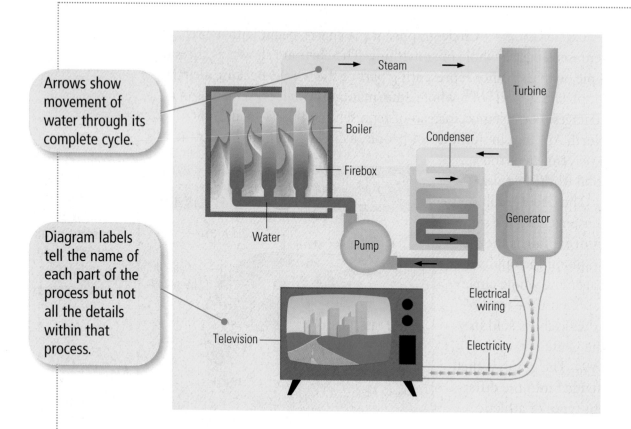

Arrows show movement of water through its complete cycle.

Diagram labels tell the name of each part of the process but not all the details within that process.

Steam

Turbine

Boiler

Condenser

Firebox

Generator

Water

Pump

Electrical wiring

Television

Electricity

Exercise 7

Work with a classmate on one of the following projects. Display your completed project in class.

1. Find out the high temperature in a chosen city for each day of a particular week. Draw the appropriate graph showing the week's temperatures. Then write a brief paragraph explaining the graph.

2. Find the total number of games won by five competing athletic teams this season. Develop an appropriate graphic showing the number of games won by each of the five teams. Then write a brief paragraph explaining your graphic.

24.8 Memorizing

Do you ever call your best friend on the phone? Of course you do. Do you look up your friend's number in the phone book every time you call? You don't if you have it memorized. Memorizing phone numbers is easy, but what about things you need to know in school? What you memorize for school can be as helpful as learning a friend's phone number.

How to Memorize

Different people have different learning styles. A system may work for one person but not for someone else. The following are two techniques for memorizing. Try them and see which works better for you.

The most common technique for memorizing is repetition. If you combine writing with rereading, you may memorize important information even more quickly. If you learn better by hearing, tape record as you read aloud. Play back the tape as many times as necessary until you have memorized what you need to remember.

Visualizing is another method of memorizing. Use it to memorize small pieces of information, such as phone numbers, formulas, or the spelling of words. Look at the information. Then close your eyes and "see" the number or word in your mind. Visualize it in an interesting or humorous way. If you can get a unique picture in your mind, you're more likely to be able to visualize it again.

Tricks for Memorizing

Using memory games or tricks is another way to remember information. There are many different tricks or games you can use. Try making a sentence out of words that start with the first letter of each item in a list you want to memorize. Or make up a name using those same letters. You could also try writing a rhyme. Look at the chart on page 714. When you need to memorize something, try some of these memory tricks.

Tricks for Remembering	
Purpose	**Memory Aid**
To remember the number of days in each month of the year	Thirty days has September, April, June, and November. All the rest have thirty-one, Except February alone, Which has twenty-eight. In leap year, coming once in four, February then has one day more.
To remember the year Columbus sailed to the Americas	In fourteen hundred and ninety-two, Columbus sailed the ocean blue.
To remember the order of the planets from the sun: **M**ercury, **V**enus, **E**arth, **M**ars, **J**upiter, **S**aturn, **U**ranus, **N**eptune, and **P**luto	**M**y **v**ery **e**xcellent **m**other **j**ust **s**erved **u**s **n**ine **p**izzas.
To remember that the person who runs a school is a *principal,* not a *principle*	The princi<u>pal</u> is my <u>pal</u>.

Exercise 8

Develop a memory trick to remember the parts of the sun: core, photo-sphere, chromosphere, corona. Work on your own or with a classmate or two.

Exercise 9

With a partner choose at least two words from the list of Words Often Confused on page 692 in Lesson 23.7. Develop ways to memorize each word.

Study Skills

UNIT 25 Taking Tests

715

Strategies

Think of a skilled athlete, an accomplished musician, or an inspiring public speaker. Each of these people prepares thoroughly to ensure the success of his or her performance. Being prepared and knowing good test-taking strategies will help you be relaxed and more confident in a test-taking situation.

Preparing for a Test

Preparing for a test begins well before the day of the test. Before you study, try to find out what information will be on the test. Then make a study schedule. Include time for reviewing your class notes, homework, quizzes, and textbook. As you review, jot down questions that you think might be on the test. Try to answer these questions as you go through material. If some questions are difficult to answer, spend some extra time looking up the answers.

When you think you know the material, work with another student or a group of students. Test these students with your study questions. Explaining the answers to someone else will help you learn the information. In addition, ask the students in your group to test you with questions they wrote. They may have come up with some you hadn't thought of yourself.

Taking a Test

You need to make careful use of your time during a test. First, make sure you understand all the test directions. Then estimate how much time each test section will take. Begin with the sections that will take less time, and don't spend too much time on one section. Planning your test time wisely may help you answer all of the questions. The chart on the following page offers suggestions for budgeting your time.

Tips for Budgeting Time During a Test
1. Read the directions carefully. Be sure you understand them before you begin the test.
2. Begin with the section of the test that will take the least amount of time.
3. Answer easier items first. Skip the ones you can't answer.
4. Return to the more difficult items when you have answered everything else.
5. Use any time left over to check your answers. Check the numbers to be sure you didn't write an answer in the wrong place.

Exercise 1

Write the letter of the response that best answers each of these questions.

1. Which of these strategies is a good way to prepare for a test?
   a. Save all studying until the night before you take the test.
   b. Allow plenty of time to review the material.
   c. Sleep with your book under your pillow.
   d. none of the above
2. Which items should you answer first on a test?
   a. the last ones
   b. the first ones
   c. the easy ones
   d. the difficult ones
3. Which of these is *not* a good test-taking strategy?
   a. Skip the items you know.
   b. Read the directions carefully.
   c. Begin with a section that won't take much time.
   d. Check your answers.

25.2 Classroom Tests

You have just found out that your upcoming exam in science will include true-false, multiple-choice, matching, fill-in, short-answer, and essay questions. You can feel confident about taking your exam by learning a few simple strategies for answering these types of questions.

True-False Items

True-false items can be tricky. A single item may include both true and untrue information. You must read the whole statement carefully before answering. If any part of the statement is not true, the answer to the item should be false. Look at the statement below.

> California does have more people than any other state. However, Alaska is the largest state in area. The statement is false.

California has more people and more land than any other state in the United States.

Multiple-Choice Items

Multiple-choice items include either an incomplete sentence or a question and three or four responses. You need to pick the response that best completes the sentence or answers the question. Read the tips below for answering multiple-choice items. Then answer the question that follows.

- Read each item carefully to know what information you are looking for.
- Read all responses before answering. Sometimes an answer may seem correct, but a response that follows it may be better.
- Eliminate answers you know are incorrect.
- Be careful about choosing responses that contain absolute words, such as *always, never, all,* or *none.* Since most statements have exceptions, absolute statements are often incorrect.

Taking Tests

Who was the first woman nominated by a major political party to be vice president of the United States?

a. Sandra Day O'Connor

b. Shirley Chisholm

c. Geraldine Ferraro

d. Barbara Jordan

> All these women were first in some way. Geraldine Ferraro, however, was the first woman nominated for vice president by a major party.

Matching Items

To complete a matching item, you must match items found in one group to items in another. For example, you might have to match terms with definitions, cities with countries, or causes with effects. Compare the groups. Do they contain the same number of items? Will every item be used only once? Complete easier items first.

If each item will be used only once and if you are allowed to write on your test copy, cross out each item after you use it. When you get to the harder items, you will have fewer choices left.

> The number of items in each column is not the same. One item in column 2 will not be used.

Read the following example. Match the events or documents in the first column with the dates in the second. Use each date only once.

___ 1. U.S. Civil War begins   a. 1950

___ 2. Korean War begins   b. 1945

___ 3. U.S. Constitution   c. 1861

___ 4. Emancipation Proclamation   d. 1789

            e. 1863

> The answers to the matching items: 1. c; 2. a; 3. d; 4. e

Fill-in Items

To complete a fill-in item, you need to fill in one or more blanks in a sentence. Your answer must make the sentence true as well as grammatically correct. Rereading the sentence with your answer included will help you determine whether you have made the correct choice. Look at the fill-in test item below.

The blank is preceded by the word an, so the answer must be singular and begin with a vowel. The answer is *amphibian*.

Note that three responses are called for and that their order is not important. The correct answers are *solid*, *liquid*, and *gas*.

> 1. A cold-blooded vertebrate that has gills early in life and then develops lungs later in life is an _____.
>
> 2. The three states in which matter exists are _____, _____, and _____.

Short-Answer Items

In responding to short-answer items, you must provide specific information. Your answer should be clearly and simply stated and should be written in complete sentences. For example, look at the question and answer below.

The question asks for an explanation. In your answer you must tell why the amendments are called the Bill of Rights.

> Why are the first ten amendments to the United States Constitution known as the Bill of Rights?

Note that the answer is written in a complete sentence.

> The first ten amendments are called the Bill of Rights because they preserve and protect specific rights of the people.

Taking Tests

Essay Questions

Essay questions usually require an answer that is at least one paragraph long. To answer an essay question, take time to think about your main idea and the details that will support it. Also allow yourself time to write and revise your answer.

Exercise 2

Read the passage below, and answer the questions that follow.

Most of the paper we use today comes from trees. After the bark has been removed, the wood is ground up and mixed with water. This mixture is called wood pulp. The wet pulp is pressed into layers by machines, which dry the pulp on a series of screens and large rollers. The dried paper is then wound onto rolls.

Different types of paper are made from a variety of materials that are mixed with the pulp. These include wax, plastic, rags, and wastepaper. Making wastepaper into usable paper products is called recycling. Recycling is an important way to save trees.

1. Is the following statement true or false?

   Paper comes from paper plants.

2. Which of the following is not normally used in the making of paper?
   a. wax   **b.** plastic   **c.** wood pulp   **d.** bark

3. Fill in the correct response: Before paper is made, the _____ of a tree must be removed.

4. Correctly match the items in the first column with those in the second.
   1. wood pulp   **a.** added to wood pulp
   2. screens   **b.** saves trees
   3. wax, plastic, rags   **c** ground wood plus water
                                 d. what the pulp is dried on

5. What is an important reason you should use recycled paper?

25.3 Standardized Tests

Standardized tests are exams given to groups of students around the country. Educators evaluate scores in order to arrive at a certain national "yardstick" for measuring student performance. Knowing what kinds of questions might be on the tests can help you relax and concentrate on doing well.

Reading Comprehension

Reading-comprehension items measure how well you understand what you read. Each reading-comprehension section includes a written passage and questions about the passage. Some questions will ask you to identify the main idea. Others will ask you to draw conclusions from information in the passage. Practice your skills by reading the passage below and answering the questions.

The paragraph focuses on describing a sushi bar. The best title is *b*.

If you reread the paragraph's second sentence carefully, you will see that *d* is the correct choice.

> If you have ever been to a sushi bar, you have had an experience that is new to most Americans. Sushi is a Japanese delicacy created from raw fish, seasoned rice, pickles, seaweed, and horseradish. At a sushi bar customers sit at long counters and watch expert chefs prepare sushi by hand. The chefs shape some pieces one at a time. They slice other pieces from a long roll of rice, fish, and seaweed.
>
> 1. What is the best title for this paragraph?
>   a. Japanese Traditions
>   b. What Is a Sushi Bar?
>   c. Raw Fish Is Good for You
>   d. Japanese Cooking
>
> 2. What is sushi made of?
>   a. horseradish
>   b. raw fish and rice
>   c. seaweed and pickles
>   d. all of the above

Vocabulary

Vocabulary items are usually multiple-choice. Some items ask you to choose the correct meaning of a word used in a sentence. Others may ask you to choose the word that best completes a sentence or a definition. If you are unfamiliar with the word, look for context clues to help you with the meaning. Also, look for prefixes, suffixes, and roots that may be familiar. For example, you may not know what the word *dentifrice* means. If you recognize the root *dent*, you might guess that it is related to *denture* and *dentist*. If you were asked to choose *boardwalk, can opener, toothpaste,* or *sherbet,* which definition would you choose?

Now try these sample test items.

> The correct answer would be *toothpaste*.

Choose the letter of the correct definition of or the synonym for each underlined word.

1. Jeremy could not make up his mind whether to go to the circus or to the baseball game. He was <u>ambivalent</u>.

   a. carefree
   b. feeling angry
   c. having two conflicting wishes
   d. having no energy

2. "Please be <u>rational</u>!" insisted Mae Ling. It annoyed her when her brother made no sense at all.

   a. sensible   b. confused   c. eager   d. polite

3. Samuel planned to perform tricks with his <u>biplane</u> in the county fair competition.

   a. a plane with three sets of wings
   b. a plane with two sets of wings
   c. a glider
   d. a car with two sets of wheels

> Context clues can help you guess the meaning of *ambivalent*. Jeremy can't decide between two things. The answer is *c*.

> Note that Mae Ling wants her brother to make sense. *Rational* probably means "sensible." Choice *a* is correct.

> The word *biplane* contains two parts: the prefix *bi-*, meaning "two," and the word root. Choice *b* makes the most sense.

Analogies

Analogy items test your understanding of the relationships between things or ideas. On a standardized test you may see an analogy written as *animal* : *whale* :: *tool* : *hammer*. The single colon stands for "is to"; the double colon reads "as." The relationship between the words in the example above is that the category *animal* includes the whale and the category *tool* includes the hammer.

This chart shows some word relationships you might find in analogy tests.

Word Relationships in Analogy Tests		
Type	**Definition**	**Example**
Synonyms	Two words have the same general meaning.	vivid : bright :: dark : dim
Antonyms	Two words have opposite meanings.	night : day :: tall : short
Use	Words name a user and something used.	writer : pen :: chef : spoon
Cause and Effect	Words name a cause and its effect.	heat : boil :: cold : freeze
Category	Words name a category and an item in it.	fruit : pear :: flower : rose
Description	Words name an item and a characteristic of it.	baby : young :: sky : blue

Try to complete these sample analogies.

Identify the relationship. A violin is a part of an orchestra. A clown is a part of a ___. The correct answer is *circus*, or *d.*

Although *a* may seem like the right choice, it is not a feeling, as is *sadness*. The correct answer is *b.*

1. violin : orchestra :: clown : ___

   a. saxophone b. juggler c. make-up   d. circus

2. weeping : sadness :: laughter : ___

   a. comedian b. joy   c. yelling d. discomfort

Grammar, Usage, and Mechanics

Standardized tests measure your understanding of correct grammar, usage, and mechanics by asking you to identify errors. You may be given a sentence with portions underlined and lettered; or you may be given a sentence with numbered sections. In either case, you will be asked to identify the section that contains an error. Most tests include one choice to indicate that the sentence has no errors.

Before you complete the sample items, study this list of common errors included in standardized grammar tests:

- errors in grammar
- incorrect use of pronouns
- subject-verb agreement
- wrong verb tenses
- misspelled words
- incorrect capitalization
- punctuation mistakes

Now choose the section in each item that contains an error.

> In section *c* the preposition *on* is incorrect.

> Section *b* includes a double negative, *there wasn't … nothing.*

1. <u>Both he and I</u> <u>will be foreign exchange students</u>
       a   b
   <u>on Mexico City</u> <u>in the fall</u>. no error
       c   d   e

2. <u>Ernie always said</u> <u>there wasn't really nothing like</u>
           a   b
   <u>jumping into an icy cold lake</u> <u>in Colorado</u>. no error
           c   d   e

3. <u>Mr. Anglim said enthusiastically,</u> <u>"our school has just</u>
             a   b
   <u>bought a new computer</u>." no error
         c   d

> The first word of a quoted sentence is always capitalized. Section *b* contains the error.

The word *scenes* is misspelled in the third section. Therefore, choice *c* is the answer.

4. Frida Kahlo was a Mexican artist who painted
   a
   beautiful, dreamlike senes of her life. no error
   b   c   d

5. When John Henry was a little baby, he sat on his
   a   b
   father's knee and plays with a hammer. no error
                     c   d

6. We really should ought to thank Grandma for the
   a   b
   presents she sent to us. no error
   c   d

The phrase *should ought* to is incorrect. Either *should* or *ought to* could be used, but not both. So *a* is the answer.

The action in this sentence is taking place in the past. The verb should be *played*, not *plays*. Choice *c* contains the error.

Taking a Standardized Test

Standardized tests are different from classroom tests. Instead of writing your answers on the test itself, you will be provided with a separate answer sheet. Since answer sheets are usually graded electronically, you should be careful to avoid stray marks that might be misread.

Some standardized tests do not subtract points for incorrect answers. If this is true for the test you are taking, try to give an answer for every item. You might improve your test score by guessing correctly. But don't just guess wildly. Eliminate options that you know are wrong before making a guess.

If you can't answer a question, don't waste time thinking about it. Go on to the next item. You can come back to any unanswered items, if time permits.

Exercise 3

Reading-Comprehension Items   Read the passage below and answer the questions that follow it.

Medical Research Secretary. Two years' experience in related field required. Must type 50 words per minute. Please send résumé and salary requirements to Tulane University.

1. Where would you most likely find the above paragraph?
   a. the help-wanted page of a newspaper
   b. a teen diary
   c. a science textbook
   d. the front page of a newspaper

2. What experience would be most acceptable?
   a. a typist in a bank
   b. a chemist at a laboratory
   c. a cashier at a supermarket
   d. all of the above

(continued)

(continued)

Vocabulary Item   Find the best synonym for the under-lined word.

3. We have to make a <u>unified</u> effort, or we will never win the election.
   a. shared   **b.** difficult   **c.** untried   **d.** mighty

Analogy Item   Complete the analogy.

4. flock : geese :: _____ : wolves
   a. herd   **b.** pack   **c.** collection   **d.** sheep

Grammar, Usage, and Mechanics Item   Identify the section that contains an error.

5. <u>The entire side of the mountain</u> <u>exploded into the</u>
                 a   b
   <u>air</u> <u>when Mt. St. Helens was erupted.</u> no error
                     c   d

INTRODUCTION

The following pages of exercises have been designed to familiarize you with the standardized writing tests that you may take during the school year. These exercises are very similar to the actual tests in how they look and what they ask you to do. Completing these exercises will not only provide you with practice, but also will make you aware of areas you might need to work on.

These writing exercises—just like the actual standardized writing tests—are divided into three sections.

Sentence Structure In this section, pages 730 to 737, you will be given a short passage in which some of the sentences are underlined. Each underlined sentence is numbered. After you finish reading the passage, you will be asked questions about the underlined sections. The underlined sections will be either incomplete sentences, run-on sentences, correctly written sentences that should be combined, or correctly written sentences that do not need to be rewritten. You will need to select which is best from the four choices provided.

Usage In this section, pages 738 to 745, you will also be asked to read a short passage. However, in these exercises, a word or words in the passage will be omitted and a numbered blank space will be in their place. After reading the passage, you will need to determine which of the four provided words or groups of words best belongs in each numbered space.

Mechanics Finally, in the third section, pages 746 to 753, the short passages will have parts that are underlined. You will need to determine if, in the underlined sections, there is a spelling error, capitalization error, punctuation error, or no error at all.

Writing well is a skill that you will use the rest of your life. You will be able to write more accurate letters to your friends and family, better papers in school, and more interesting stories. You will be able to express yourself and your ideas more clearly and in a way that is interesting and engaging. These exercises should help to improve your writing and to make you comfortable with the format and types of questions you will see on standardized writing tests.

Standardized Test Practice

Read each passage. Some sections are underlined. The underlined sections may be one of the following:

- Incomplete sentences
- Run-on sentences
- Correctly written sentences that should be combined
- Correctly written sentences that do not need to be rewritten

Choose the best way to write each underlined section and mark the letter for your answer. If the underlined section needs no change, mark the choice "Correct as is" on your paper.

> A company that supplies lunches to schools has started providing organic lunch options in select elementary schools. <u>Some people consider organic foods to be healthier than non-organic foods. Organic foods are not sprayed with pesticides or herbicides during farming.</u> (1) It is best to wash organic foods thoroughly because of the way that they are grown.
>
> <u>Apart from the usual options of macaroni and cheese and hamburgers. Kids can make their own salads from a salad bar or order a veggie burger from among the hot entrees.</u> (2) The company buys their produce from local farmers.

1 A Some people consider organic foods to be healthier than non-organic produce when organic foods are not sprayed with pesticides or herbicides during farming.

B Some people consider organic foods to be healthier than non-organic foods organic foods are not sprayed. With pesticides or herbicides during farming.

C Some people, who consider organic foods to be healthier than non-organic produce, are not sprayed with pesticides or herbicides during farming.

D Some people consider organic foods to be healthier than non-organic produce because organic foods are not sprayed with pesticides or herbicides during farming.

2 F Apart the usual options of macaroni and cheese and hamburgers, then kids can make their own salads from a salad bar or order a veggie burger from among the hot entrees.

G Apart from the usual options of macaroni and cheese and hamburgers, kids can make their own salads from a salad bar or order a veggie burger from among the hot entrees.

H Apart from the usual options of macaroni and cheese and hamburgers are the usual options but they can make their own salads from a salad bar or order a veggie burger from among the hot entrees.

J Correct as is

Go on

The sea horse is one of the strangest looking creatures in nature. <u>The sea horse swims very poorly it</u>
<u>seems to be going in the wrong direction.</u>
(1)
It would be much more streamlined if it did not swim belly-
forward. <u>It moves very slowly. It waves a fin on its back.</u> Perhaps the most unusual thing about sea horses,
(2)
however, is the way that they give birth. <u>The female deposits her eggs. In a special pouch on the male's belly.</u>
(3)
After one to two weeks, the eggs hatch and the males "give birth" to the young.

1 **A** The sea horse swims very poorly and
seems to be going in the wrong
direction.
   B The sea horse swims very poorly. And it
seems to be going in the wrong
direction.
   C The sea horse very poorly. It seems to be
going in the wrong direction.
   D Correct as is

2 **F** It moves and waves a fin on its back
very slowly.
   G It moves very slowly, and it moves by
waving a fin on its back.
   H It moves very slowly by waving a fin on
its back.
   J It moves very slowly that waves a fin on
its back to move.

3 **A** The female deposits her eggs in a special
pouch being on the male's belly.
   B The female depositing her eggs it is a special pouch on the male's belly.
   C The female deposits her eggs in a special
pouch on the male's belly.
   D Correct as is

STOP

Standardized Test Practice

Read each passage. Some sections are underlined. The underlined sections may be one of the following:

- Incomplete sentences
- Run-on sentences
- Correctly written sentences that should be combined
- Correctly written sentences that do not need to be rewritten

Choose the best way to write each underlined section and mark the letter for your answer. If the underlined section needs no change, mark the choice "Correct as is" on your paper.

Donna adored science fiction books. <u>She would take them with her. When she went anywhere.</u> Donna
(1)
had packed a large bag full of science fiction books to take with her on vacation to a lake house. Summer was a perfect time to read numerous books. <u>When Donna and her parents arrived at the lake house. Donna</u>
(2)
<u>realized that she had forgotten the bag of books at home.</u> Fortunately, there was a library in the town that had a large selection of science fiction books. <u>Every other day Donna biked to the library she borrowed a</u>
(3)
<u>new book.</u>

---

1 A She was taking them with her when she went anywhere.
B She would take them with her and she went anywhere.
C She would take them with her when she went anywhere.
D Correct as is

2 F When Donna and her parents arrived. At the lake house Donna realized that she had forgotten the bag of books at home.
G When Donna and her parents arrived at the lake house, Donna realized that she had forgotten the bag of books at home.
H When Donna and her parents arrived at the lake house and Donna realized that she had forgotten the bag of books at home.
J Correct as is

3 A Every other day Donna biked to the library and borrowed a new book.
B Every other day Donna biked to the library. And borrowed a new book.
C Biking to the library every other day. She borrowed a new book.
D Correct as is

Go on

We all know Thomas Edison. He was the inventor of the light bulb. It seems Edison was a person who
                                    (1)
took many risks. When he was a boy, Edison saved a man's life by pulling him off the train tracks. After the
                                                                        (2)
train had passed and the man was safe, the stationmaster came over to him. The stationmaster thought
Edison had done something wrong, he firmly boxed his ears. Because of this, Thomas Edison was almost
                                    (3)
entirely deaf in one ear for the rest of his life.

1 **A** We all know Thomas Edison as the inventor of the light bulb.
  B We all know Thomas Edison when it was the inventor of the light bulb.
  C We all know Thomas Edison, and we know he was the inventor of the light bulb.
  D We all know the inventor of the light bulb and it was Thomas Edison.

2 **F** When he was a boy, Edison saving a man's life by pulling him off the train tracks.
  G When he was a boy. Edison saved a man's life by pulling him off the train tracks.
  H When he was a boy, it is Edison saved a man's life by pulling him off the train tracks.
  J Correct as is

3 **A** The stationmaster, thinking Edison had done something wrong. He firmly boxed his ears.
  B The stationmaster thought Edison had done something wrong. And firmly boxed his ears.
  C The stationmaster thought Edison had done something wrong and firmly boxed his ears.
  D Correct as is

STOP

Standardized Test Practice

Read each passage. Some sections are underlined. The underlined sections may be one of the following:

- Incomplete sentences
- Run-on sentences
- Correctly written sentences that should be combined
- Correctly written sentences that do not need to be rewritten

Choose the best way to write each underlined section and mark the letter for your answer. If the underlined section needs no change, mark the choice "Correct as is" on your paper.

Jose was teaching Spanish at a high school in Connecticut. Where he lived in an old Victorian house. At
(1)
night, he heard the sound of flapping wings and high-pitched chirping over his head. Jose thought he was
just imagining the noises. Because he was so tired. Then, he realized that there was something flying around
(2)
in the attic. One night, Jose went up to the attic and saw a big bat flying around. Since the bat wasn't hurt-
(3)
ing anything, Jose decided to leave him alone. He did buy earplugs though to keep out the noise at night!

1 **A** Jose teaching Spanish at a high school in Connecticut and living in an old Victorian house.
   B Jose was teaching Spanish at a high school in Connecticut, where he lived in an old Victorian house.
   C Jose was teaching Spanish at a high school in Connecticut, then he lived in an old Victorian house.
   D Correct as is

2 **F** Jose thought he was just imagining the noises because he was so tired.
   G Jose thought he was just imagining the noises this is because he was so tired.
   H Jose being so tired, and just imagining the noises.
   J Correct as is

3 **A** One night, Jose went up to the attic and sees a big bat flying around.
   B One night, Jose went up to the attic. And saw a big bat flying around.
   C One night, Jose went up to the attic, saw a big bat flying around.
   D Correct as is

Go on

Celia was born in Odessa. <u>Celia had lived in New York for more than five years. She took the citizenship</u>
<u>exam.</u> The interviewer asked her many questions. For example, he asked her, "Who was the first President of
the United States?" and "When did the American Revolution take place?" <u>By correctly answering these ques-</u>
<u>tions, Celia proved a sufficient knowledge of the English language. She also proved a sufficient knowledge of</u>
<u>American history.</u> The interviewer complimented her on her good work. <u>Celia was happy it was because she</u>
<u>passed the test.</u> She was proud to be an American citizen.

1 A Celia had lived in New York for more
than five years, and she took the citizenship exam.

   B Celia had lived in New York for more
than five years when it was she took the
citizenship exam.

   C Celia had lived in New York and she
took the citizenship exam and it was
more than five years.

   D Celia had lived in New York for more
than five years before she took the citizenship exam.

2 F By answering these questions correctly,
which proved a sufficient knowledge of
American history, Celia proved a sufficient knowledge of the English language.

   G By answering these questions correctly,
Celia proved a sufficient knowledge of
the English language and American
history.

   H By answering these questions correctly,
Celia proved a sufficient knowledge of
the English language and she also
proved a sufficient knowledge of
American history.

   J By answering these questions correctly,
Celia proved a sufficient knowledge of
the English language and American history, sufficiently.

3 A Celia was happy. Because she passed the
test.

   B Celia being happy. She passed the test.

   C Celia was happy because she passed the
test.

   D Correct as is

Standardized Test Practice

Read each passage. Some sections are underlined. The underlined sections may be one of the following:

- Incomplete sentences
- Run-on sentences
- Correctly written sentences that should be combined
- Correctly written sentences that do not need to be rewritten

Choose the best way to write each underlined section and mark the letter for your answer. If the underlined section needs no change, mark the choice "Correct as is" on your paper.

Mrs. Carlos took her class on a field trip to the Hartsfield Atlanta International Airport she took them to see the arrival of two giant pandas from China. **(1)** Everyone was excited to witness the welcoming ceremony for the two-year-old pandas who had traveled seventeen hours from Beijing.

It was in the early afternoon. Mrs. Carlos's class and many other interested people waited. **(2)** Mrs. Carlos told her students to watch for the plane that would be arriving shortly. "The pandas traveled from China in special crates," she said.

Moments after she said this, the plane landed. Carrying the two new visitors to the United States. **(3)** Mrs. Carlos promised her class that the next field trip they would make would be to the zoo to see the pandas in their new home.

---

1 A Mrs. Carlos. She took her class on a field trip to the Hartsfield Atlanta International Airport to see the arrival of two giant pandas from China.
  B Mrs. Carlos took her class on a field trip to the Hartsfield Atlanta International Airport. To see the arrival of two giant pandas from China.
  C Mrs. Carlos took her class on a field trip to the Hartsfield Atlanta International Airport to see the arrival of two giant pandas from China.
  D Correct as is

2 F It was in the early afternoon therefore Mrs. Carlos's class and many other interested people waited.
  G In the early afternoon Mrs. Carlos's class waited many other interested people.
  H It was in the early afternoon, and Mrs. Carlos's class waited and many other interested people waited.
  J In the early afternoon, Mrs. Carlos's class and many other interested people waited.

3 A Moments after she said this, the plane landed carrying the two new visitors to the United States.
  B Moments after she said this, the plane landed it was carrying the two new visitors to the United States.
  C Moments after she said this, the plane landed carrying the two new visitors. To the United States.
  D Correct as is

Go on →

NASA, the United States' space program, created a spacecraft called the Mars Orbiter. <u>It was launched into space in January 1999. It was on a mission to study the atmosphere of Mars.</u> About 9 months later, the spacecraft reached its destination. <u>The Orbiter, however, came too close to the Martian atmosphere, it (1) burned up.</u> Scientists on Earth were puzzled over why this happened. Later, they realized that the accident had been caused by a simple miscommunication. <u>One team of scientists used the English system of inches and feet. The other team used the metric system for their calculations.</u> This mistake caused the Orbiter to (3) stray from its course.

1 **A** It was launched into space in January 1999, and it was on a mission to study the atmosphere of Mars.
   B It was launched into space in January 1999 on a mission to study the atmosphere of Mars.
   C It was launched into space in January 1999 when it was on a mission to study the atmosphere of Mars.
   D It was launched on a mission to study the atmosphere of Mars into space in January 1999.

2 **F** The Orbiter, however, too close to the Martian atmosphere. It burned up.
   G The Orbiter, however, came too close to the Martian atmosphere, causing it to burn up.
   H The Orbiter, however, came too close to the Martian atmosphere. Causing it to burn up.
   J Correct as is

3 **A** One team of scientists used the English system of inches and feet, while the other team used the metric system for their calculations.
   B One team of scientists used the English system of inches and feet, or the other team used the metric system for their calculations.
   C One team of scientists used the English system of inches and feet since the other team of scientists used the metric system for their calculations.
   D For their calculations, one team of scientists used the English system of inches and feet and the other team used the metric system for their calculations.

Standardized Test Practice

Read each passage and choose the word or group of words that belongs in each space. Mark the letter for your answer on your paper.

> Mei had a conference with Mr. Cellan, her junior high school advisor, about _____(1)_____ to a specialized summer camp. "What are your favorite hobbies?" asked Mr. Cellan.
>
> "I _____(2)_____," said Mei. "Except sleeping."
>
> "Sleeping? Is that all? There must be something else you enjoy doing outside of school," Mr. Cellan _____(3)_____.
>
> "After I sleep," Mei explained, "I transcribe my dreams and then I draw pictures of _____(4)_____."
>
> "That's intriguing," commented Mr. Cellan. He suggested that Mei might enjoy converting her hobby into an actual career path.
>
> Now Mei is applying to several art camps. That is, after she takes a nap, of course.

1 **A** apply
   B application
   C applying
   D applied

2 **F** have never hardly any
   G have never any
   H have barely any
   J have not none

3 **A** persisting
   B persist
   C persistence
   D persisted

4 **F** their
   G them
   H they
   J theirs

Go on

When Marisol was eighteen years old, her father _____(1)_____ a new car and gave her his old station wagon. Marisol drove the car to a garage to get it _____(2)_____. The mechanic said the car was fine and put a new inspection sticker on the windshield.

On the way home, Marisol heard a strange sound and _____(3)_____ pulled into the breakdown lane. She had a flat tire! Luckily, her father _____(4)_____ her how to change a tire and there was a spare in the trunk.

1 A is buying
   B bought
   C has bought
   D was bought

2 F inspect
   G inspected
   H inspection
   J inspecting

3 A slow
   B more slow
   C more slowly
   D slowly

4 F was teaching
   G had taught
   H teach
   J is teaching

STOP

Standardized Test Practice

Read each passage and choose the word or group of words that belongs in each space. Mark the letter for your answer on your paper.

There are two photographers living in big cities on opposite sides of the world. Marta lives in New York and Wei lives in Hong Kong. Both of _____(1)_____ have personal Web sites where they display their photographs of the cities they live in. Last year, Marta found Wei's Web site. She was very inspired by what she _____(2)_____. She wrote Wei an e-mail message asking if he would like to _____(3)_____ .

"Yes," Wei wrote back.

Now Marta takes photos of New York and sends her rolls of film to Wei in Hong Kong. Wei puts Marta's roll of film into his camera and _____(4)_____ photos of Hong Kong. The double exposures they get merge the two cities into one.

---

1 **A** us
   B it
   C you
   D them

2 **F** had seen
   G see
   H is seeing
   J saw

3 **A** collaboration
   B collaborate
   C collaborated
   D collaborating

4 **F** was taking
   G took
   H has taken
   J takes

Go on ➡

Max knows trains well: He is a train conductor. He works on the Vermonter train which runs from Grand Central Station in New York City to Montpellier, Vermont. Max lives in Middletown, Connecticut, which is just about the middle of the train's route. It _____(1)_____ Max a long time to get to New York, so the train picks him up in Connecticut.

On the train, Max collects tickets and punches holes in the _____(2)_____ spaces. He _____(3)_____ as a conductor on this train for many years. With time and experience, Max has come to know the route like the back of his hand. He even knows many of the regular travelers by name. On the long stretches between stations, Max likes to converse with the customers about where they _____(4)_____ and where they came from.

1 **A** will have taken
   B will take
   C would take
   D took

2 **F** most rightly
   G rightness
   H right
   J more right

3 **A** has worked
   B will be working
   C works
   D was working

4 **F** is going
   G goes
   H are going
   J was gone

STOP

Standardized Test Practice

Read each passage and choose the word or group of words that belongs in each space. Mark the letter for your answer on your paper.

Bonsai trees are miniature trees that _____(1)_____ and pruned into a particular shape. These dwarf trees _____(2)_____ resemble old and gnarled trees.

Bonsai means "tray-planted" in Japanese and _____(3)_____ to the small trays or pots that are most often used for planting bonsai trees. The tradition of making bonsai originated in China, but _____(4)_____ a trademark of Japanese culture. A bonsai tree can live a hundred years or more, but the art of bonsai has been around for roughly a thousand years.

1 **A** has been cut
  B is cut
  C are cut
  D were cut

2 **F** close
  G closely
  H more closer
  J closest

3 **A** is referring
  B refers
  C referred
  D has been referring

4 **F** will become
  G has become
  H was becoming
  J have become

Go on

It seems that everybody _____(1)_____ pizza. The Neapolitans first created pizza out of the ingredients _____(2)_____. Because pizza was relatively easy to make and could be baked quickly, it became popular throughout Italy. Each region added its own _____(3)_____ touch. Many other cultures have their own versions of the pizza idea. In Greece and the Middle East, for example, they make a spicy pizza without tomato sauce.

The first pizzeria in America opened in 1905, in New York City. The pizza industry skyrocketed after World War II, when American soldiers came back from Italy. The soldiers missed the taste of _____(4)_____ favorite Italian specialty. Now there are scarcely any towns in America without a pizzeria.

1 **A** eat
   B ate
   C is eating
   D has eaten

2 **F** most available
   G available
   H more available
   J availablest

3 **A** specialty
   B specialist
   C specialness
   D special

4 **F** its
   G their
   H his
   J your

STOP

Standardized Test Practice

Read each passage and choose the word or group of words that belongs in each space. Mark the letter for your answer on your paper.

In 1963, Duke Ellington ____(1)____ his band on a tour of the Middle East, India, and Ceylon. The journey was a musical discovery for both the band and their audiences. The musicians ____(2)____ by music lovers in every city they visited. When they returned home, Ellington and his co-writer, Billy Strayhorn, were inspired to write a series of musical compositions called the *Far East Suite.*

Throughout their travels, Ellington's band had encountered many different musical traditions that influenced the *Far East Suite.* One of the compositions, called *The Bluebird of Delhi,* was particularly influenced by the songs of the exotic birds in India, the likes of which the band ____(3)____ before. In ____(4)____ you can hear the clarinet playing the part of the bird's sweet song.

---

1 A took
   B taken
   C is taking
   D has taken

2 F was welcomed
   G is welcomed
   H were welcomed
   J has been welcomed

3 A hadn't hardly witnessed
   B had never witnessed
   C hadn't never witnessed
   D had barely never witnessed

4 F them
   G you
   H it
   J him

Go on

Mr. Calder taught an introduction to architecture class at the high school. On the first day of class, he entered with an immense stack of newspapers. He told the students that he would _____(1)_____ for an hour while they each built something out of the newspaper.

An hour later he returned to find intricate newspaper castles, airplanes, sailing ships, and many creative objects made from newspaper. The students watched him expectantly, waiting for their teacher to praise the _____(2)_____ work.

Mr. Calder picked up a piece of newspaper folded in two like a little triangular tent.

"This," he said, "is a great work of architecture." The students were _____(3)_____. The architect explained, "Paper is light and fragile. It is not good for airplanes, boats, and castle walls, but it is easy to fold and _____(4)_____ thin edges can bear weight. Therefore, the 'tent' is the perfect object for this particular building material—newspaper."

1 A have left
   B leave
   C leaving
   D left

2 F best
   G most best
   H bestest
   J more best

3 A confuse
   B confusing
   C confused
   D confusion

4 F their
   G our
   H its
   J your

STOP

THE
PRINCETON
REVIEW

Standardized Test Practice

Read each passage and decide which type of error, if any, appears in each underlined section. Mark the letter for your answer on the paper.

<u>It's hard to imagine, but, movies have been around</u> now for a hundred years. In the beginning, they were
(1)
very different from what we see at the theaters today. <u>Two frenchmen, Louis and Auguste Lumiere, invented</u>
(2)
the "cinematographe" in 1895. This machine could record and project moving images from film.

<u>The first nickelodeon, or old-fashioned movie theater, was built in Philadelphia</u> in 1896, the year after
(3)
the invention of the cinematographe. <u>Nowadays, cinemas can have up to twenty diffrent theaters</u> with
(4)
twenty different movies playing at the same time.

<u>Today some filmakers make their movies on video cameras and computers</u> are used for editing.
(5)
Although you can watch <u>movies at home on videotape or even on your computer people</u> still enjoy going to
(6)
the movies and seeing films projected from something very much like the first cinematographe.

1 A Spelling error
   B Capitalization error
   C Punctuation error
   D No error

2 F Spelling error
   G Capitalization error
   H Punctuation error
   J No error

3 A Spelling error
   B Capitalization error
   C Punctuation error
   D No error

4 F Spelling error
   G Capitalization error
   H Punctuation error
   J No error

5 A Spelling error
   B Capitalization error
   C Punctuation error
   D No error

6 F Spelling error
   G Capitalization error
   H Punctuation error
   J No error

Go on

Maine is called <u>"vacationland" for a good reeson. Nature lovers visit Maine</u> because there are many
(1)
national and state forests and parks. The Appalachian Trail, which runs <u>from Maine to Georgia, begins at</u>
(2)
<u>Mount katahdin.</u> Maine is also home for much wildlife, including bears, moose and beautiful water birds.

   <u>There are many senic towns along Maine's seacoast</u> and all of them have a rich history. Wiscasset is con-
(3)
sidered Maine's prettiest village. It is located on <u>the Sheepscot river, in the southwestern region</u> of the state.
(4)
Wiscasset used to be Maine's most important port city in the 18th century.

   <u>Like many things in Maine, that has changed.</u> Now it is a tourist attraction. People also come <u>to see Fort</u>
(5)
<u>Edgecombe, a wooden fort</u> built in preparation for the War of 1812 between America and England.
(6)

1   **A**   Spelling error
      B   Capitalization error
      C   Punctuation error
      D   No error

2   **F**   Spelling error
      G   Capitalization error
      H   Punctuation error
      J   No error

3   **A**   Spelling error
      B   Capitalization error
      C   Punctuation error
      D   No error

4   **F**   Spelling error
      G   Capitalization error
      H   Punctuation error
      J   No error

5   **A**   Spelling error
      B   Capitalization error
      C   Punctuation error
      D   No error

6   **F**   Spelling error
      G   Capitalization error
      H   Punctuation error
      J   No error

STOP

Standardized Test Practice

Read each passage and decide which type of error, if any, appears in each underlined section. Mark the letter for your answer on your paper.

Alfred Nobel is the <u>Swedish chemist who invented dynamite.</u> Nobel's discoveries made him a very rich
(1)
man. <u>Alfred Nobel had many intrests outside of chemistry.</u> When he died in 1896, he left behind a substan-
(2)
tial fortune that was to be used for annual prizes for achievements in physics, chemistry, medicine, litera-

ture, and peace.

When Alfred Nobel was a <u>young man, he had a fondness for english literature.</u> Throughout his busy life
(3)
as a scientist, Nobel also wrote his own poetry and drama. Although he did not achieve fame as a writer, the

Nobel Prize for Literature <u>has become the worlds most prestigious literary award.</u>
(4)
The last Nobel Prize for Literature of the <u>20th century went to Günter Grass, a famous German Writer.</u>
(5)
Günter Grass became well known for <u>his novel *The Tin Drum* which is about a boy who decides not to grow up.</u>
(6)

1 A Spelling error
   B Capitalization error
   C Punctuation error
   D No error

2 F Spelling error
   G Capitalization error
   H Punctuation error
   J No error

3 A Spelling error
   B Capitalization error
   C Punctuation error
   D No error

4 F Spelling error
   G Capitalization error
   H Punctuation error
   J No error

5 A Spelling error
   B Capitalization error
   C Punctuation error
   D No error

6 F Spelling error
   G Capitalization error
   H Punctuation error
   J No error

Go on ➡

Chantal asked her father if he could help her with her math homework. "Of course," he said. Let's get to work." Chantal showed her father the asignment, which involved calculating averages.
(1)
(2)

After studying the math lesson Chantal's father said he had an idea. He took a stack of papers from a
(3)

drawer. "Let's calculate the avarage we spent per month on electricity this year," said her father. Chantal was
(4)

ambivalent about the project. However, once they started working, she could see the value in applying the
(5)   (6)

Knowledge she learned in math class to a situation in real life.

1 **A** Spelling error
   B Capitalization error
   C Punctuation error
   D No error

2 **F** Spelling error
   G Capitalization error
   H Punctuation error
   J No error

3 **A** Spelling error
   B Capitalization error
   C Punctuation error
   D No error

4 **F** Spelling error
   G Capitalization error
   H Punctuation error
   J No error

5 **A** Spelling error
   B Capitalization error
   C Punctuation error
   D No error

6 **F** Spelling error
   G Capitalization error
   H Punctuation error
   J No error

STOP

Standardized Test Practice

Read each passage and decide which type of error, if any, appears in each underlined section. Mark the letter for your answer on your paper.

Scientists have had <u>a hard time studying the sloth, a reclusive, tree-dwelling mammel.</u> Sloths are found
(1)
<u>in tropical south and central America. It is hard to</u> photograph sloths because they are mostly active at night
(2)
and get scared by the light from camera flashes.

One way to get <u>around this is to use a special infrared film which does not require</u> artificial lighting. The
(3)
infrared film <u>picks up heat signal's from the</u> moving animals. Sometimes <u>the photographs are blury because</u>
(4)   (5)
<u>of</u> the movement of the tree sloths. <u>Still, these pictures reveal that the sloth hangs upside down most of the</u>
(6)
<u>time: nearly three-fifths of each day!</u>

1 A Spelling error
   B Capitalization error
   C Punctuation error
   D No error

2 F Spelling error
   G Capitalization error
   H Punctuation error
   J No error

3 A Spelling error
   B Capitalization error
   C Punctuation error
   D No error

4 F Spelling error
   G Capitalization error
   H Punctuation error
   J No error

5 A Spelling error
   B Capitalization error
   C Punctuation error
   D No error

6 F Spelling error
   G Capitalization error
   H Punctuation error
   J No error

Go on

Michael is a <u>screenwriter living in Ottawa Canada.</u> <u>Every year</u> he writes a screenplay that is turned into a
(1)
two-hour movie. <u>His agent in Los Angeles, Sam,</u> represents Michael at the film studios and keeps contact
(2)
with producers and directors <u>who might be interested in buying Michaels scripts.</u>
(3)

Last year, <u>Michael struck his bigest deal.</u> He wrote a <u>script about a gangster</u> who figures out that he is a
(4)
character in the movies and wants to get out into real life. Sam sold the idea <u>to Paramount pictures for half</u>
(5)
<u>a million</u> dollars.

The film did very well at the box office, so now Michael is taking a break from screenwriting to do a
documentary film. The film is about his hometown and the <u>stories of Greek imigrant families, like his own,</u>
(6)
who came to live there.

1 **A** Spelling error
    B Capitalization error
    C Punctuation error
    D No error

2 **F** Spelling error
    G Capitalization error
    H Punctuation error
    J No error

3 **A** Spelling error
    B Capitalization error
    C Punctuation error
    D No error

4 **F** Spelling error
    G Capitalization error
    H Punctuation error
    J No error

5 **A** Spelling error
    B Capitalization error
    C Punctuation error
    D No error

6 **F** Spelling error
    G Capitalization error
    H Punctuation error
    J No error

STOP

Standardized Test Practice

Read each passage and decide which type of error, if any, appears in each underlined section. Mark the letter for your answer on your paper.

Wolfgang Amadeus Mozart was a child prodigy. <u>At an early age he impresed everyone with his</u> amazing
(1)
talent for playing the piano. <u>He was even able to impress the austrian queen</u>.
(2)

Legend has it <u>that on a visit to the palace the young Mozart played</u> a piece of music perfectly that he had
(3)
just heard performed for the first time by the royal court pianist. The Queen challenged him <u>to play the</u>

<u>piece again, this time with a long piece of felt</u> over the <u>keys. Mozart accomplished the task beautifully</u>.
(4)   (5)

This child prodigy would go on to write some of the most cherished classical <u>music in the world, includ-</u>

<u>ing operas like *The Magic Flute*, *Figaro* and *Don Giovanni.*</u>
(6)

---

1 A Spelling error
   B Capitalization error
   C Punctuation error
   D No error

2 F Spelling error
   G Capitalization error
   H Punctuation error
   J No error

3 A Spelling error
   B Capitalization error
   C Punctuation error
   D No error

4 F Spelling error
   G Capitalization error
   H Punctuation error
   J No error

5 A Spelling error
   B Capitalization error
   C Punctuation error
   D No error

6 F Spelling error
   G Capitalization error
   H Punctuation error
   J No error

Go on

We all know that the cavity is the healthy <u>tooth's greatest enemy, but where do cavities come from?</u> The
(1)
enamel coating of your teeth <u>is very strong. Certain foods, however create an acidity level</u> in your mouth
(2)
that deteriorates the tooth's surface. <u>Then bacteria from foods can get into the little holes, and that is how</u>
(3)
<u>cavities begin.</u>

The average number of cavities per person has increased. Hundreds of years ago, people did not have
<u>toothbrushes, but they also did not eat candy bars and drink Soda.</u> The modern sugary diet <u>greatly increeses</u>
(4)
<u>the likelihood of cavities. That is why</u> fluoride is added to the public water supply in many cities. Fluoride
(5)
helps to strengthen the teeth and can even stop small cavities from growing bigger.

Most dentists recommend brushing <u>your teeth three times a day. Chosing the right</u> food can also help
(6)
guard against cavities.

1   **A** Spelling error
    B Capitalization error
    C Punctuation error
    D No error

2   **F** Spelling error
    G Capitalization error
    H Punctuation error
    J No error

3   **A** Spelling error
    B Capitalization error
    C Punctuation error
    D No error

4   **F** Spelling error
    G Capitalization error
    H Punctuation error
    J No error

5   **A** Spelling error
    B Capitalization error
    C Punctuation error
    D No error

6   **F** Spelling error
    G Capitalization error
    H Punctuation error
    J No error

STOP

UNIT 26

Listening and Speaking

Effective Listening

Understanding what you hear begins with good listening skills. It's often hard to listen when people are talking and moving around or when other noises attract your attention. But you can learn how to tune out distractions and tune in to what is being said. You can improve your listening skills and increase your ability to understand.

Listening in Class

What happens when you don't understand how to do your homework assignment? It's difficult to do a good job when you don't understand what's expected of you. Learning how to listen better will make tasks that depend on understanding directions much simpler. The following tips will help you improve your listening skills to better understand what you hear.

Tips for Effective Listening

1. First, eliminate any distractions that may make it difficult to concentrate; turn off the phone, the TV, or the radio.

2. Determine the type of information you are hearing. Are you listening to a story, or is someone giving you directions? Knowing what you are listening for makes understanding easier.

3. Take notes. Identify the main ideas as you hear them, and write them in your own words.

4. Take a note if you hear a statement that tells when you will need the information you are listening to.

5. If you don't understand something, ask a question. Asking questions right away helps avoid confusion later on.

6. Review your notes as soon as possible after the listening experience. Reviewing them soon afterward will allow you to fill in any gaps in your notes.

Listening and Speaking

Listening to Persuasive Speech

What type of argument most easily persuades you? Is it one that includes facts and logical conclusions or one that appeals to your emotions? Speakers who want to persuade you may concentrate on emotional appeals. They may even use faulty thinking to persuade you to accept their opinions.

Faulty Thinking   Faulty thinking may be intentional or unintentional. That is, the speaker may be trying to deceive you or simply may not be thinking clearly. It's up to you, the listener, to analyze the speaker's statements and arguments. Are they well thought out, or are they flawed? Following are some examples of statements you might hear from a political candidate. However, you can find examples of faulty thinking in other kinds of persuasive speeches as well.

Questioning What You Hear	
Statements	**Questions**
Every child in America will have food on the table if I'm elected.	This is a broad statement. Do you think any one candidate can keep such a promise?
Don't vote for my opponent. His brother was investigated by the IRS two years ago.	What was the nature of the investigation? What were its results? Should a candidate be judged by someone else's activities?
I have the support of the great governor of our state in my campaign for senator.	Does the support of the governor prove a person is qualified to be senator? Is the governor a political ally of the candidate?
Voters in three states claim health care is important. I listen to America.	Might voters in some other states have different needs?

Speaker's Bias   Speakers may try to persuade audiences to agree with them by presenting only one side of an issue. Such speeches are biased, or slanted, in favor of one opinion. Always listen with a questioning attitude. Ask yourself if the speaker is dealing with all sides of the issue. Maybe the speaker is giving only the facts that support one opinion.

Be alert for speeches that show bias, such as the first example below. The other example is more objective. As you read, notice the facts each speaker uses.

BIASED SPEAKER: You should vote in favor of the proposed tax increase on gasoline. This tax will give the government enough revenue to rebuild the nation's crumbling highway system. It will provide many thousands of new jobs in the construction industry. It also will help us reduce the national debt. Our country needs this tax increase.

UNBIASED SPEAKER: This tax increase has faults as well as benefits. True, it will help rebuild highways and provide more jobs in highway construction. But it will also place a burden on those who must drive to make a living. The added cost of gas may drive many independent truckers and drivers out of work. People who take buses may find themselves paying higher fares.

The biased speaker gives only arguments in favor of the tax increase. The unbiased speaker admits that the arguments of the biased speaker are valid. However, this speaker points out that the increase will also have some negative effects.

Listening to Radio and Television News

Do you ask questions when you listen to the news? You might be surprised at how much there is to question. It's important to sort out facts from opinions in print, radio, and television news coverage. Doing so will help you evaluate the news coverage for truthfulness and accuracy. It will help you form your own unbiased opinion about what's being said.

Journalists are supposed to be objective. This means that they should not let their own opinions affect what they report and how they report it. This is sometimes a difficult thing to do. For example, a news commentator may call someone an "influential senator." Is the senator really influential, or is the commentator only expressing an opinion? The answer will help you evaluate anything the senator says. It will also help you evaluate what the commentator says about the senator.

Journalists are taught to provide sources for their information. Often it's important to know where the information in a news item came from. For example, suppose you heard the following two items on a newscast. Which would you be more likely to believe?

- Certain unnamed sources reported today that the President would not seek a second term of office.
- The President's chief of staff announced this afternoon that the President plans to seek a second term.

Journalists also try to present information that is complete. In their reports they usually try to answer the questions *what, who, when, where, how,* and *why.* If you carefully read or listen to almost any news story, you will see that it answers questions such as these:

- *What* happened?
- *Who* was involved?
- *When* did it happen?
- *Where* did it happen?
- *How* did it happen?
- *Why* did it happen? (or *Why* is it important?)

The questions may not always follow the above order, but they will all be answered. They'll usually be answered in the first paragraph of a newspaper story or the first minute or so of a radio or television newscast.

When you listen to a news broadcast, you can evaluate the quality of the reporting. Ask yourself some questions, such as the following:

- Was the report complete?
- Is all the information provable, or are some statements only opinions?
- Is any of the report based on faulty thinking?
- If an opinion is expressed, does the reporter tell whose opinion it is?
- Did the reporter identify the sources of the information?

Following are some other examples of how asking questions will help you evaluate a news broadcast.

Evaluating News Statements

Sample Statements	Questions to Ask
The candidate has a liberal voting record on defense spending.	What is a liberal voting record? Who defines *liberal?* Does the candidate's record match the definition?
A reliable source stated that the company has been dumping toxic waste into the river.	Who is the source? How reliable is he or she? Did the source actually see the dumping?
One eyewitness stated that the defendant fired three shots.	Who is this witness? Where was the witness at the time? Does the witness know the defendant?
An expert claims we are in a recession.	Who is the expert? In what field is he or she an expert? Was any proof provided? Do other experts agree?
The tobacco company denies any proven relationship between smoking and illness.	Doesn't the company have an interest in denying the relationship? On what facts does the company base its statement?
Last winter's frost is driving the price of fruit upward.	Is there a proven relationship between the frost and rising fruit costs? Are there other possible reasons for the rising costs?

Exercise 1

Divide into small groups. Each group will form a news broadcast team. Select one person to be the news anchor. Other members of the group can be reporters on special assignments.

Decide which current events in your school or neighborhood to cover. Assign a story to each person. Students should research their stories and write short reports to deliver during a news broadcast of no more than ten minutes. Rehearse your newscast within the group, then present it to the class. Other members of the class should evaluate each broadcast according to criteria the class has generated.

26.2 Interviewing Skills

If you wanted answers to three or four questions on the topic of fly fishing, what would be an efficient way to get them? Would you read about the topic in an encyclopedia or interview a neighbor who is a fly fisher? In an encyclopedia you'd have to sift through much information to get to the facts you want. In an interview your questions could be answered directly as you asked them. An interview with an expert can often provide you with exactly the right amount of information on exactly the right topic.

Whom to Interview

Who is an expert? An expert usually is someone who has very precise, in-depth, and up-to-date information. More importantly, the expert probably has first-hand knowledge about a topic. Look at the topics and the list of people in the chart. People like these might have interesting information you could use in an oral report.

People to Interview	
Topic	**Source**
Local government	mayor, city council member, governor, state legislator
Scuba diving	local diving expert or instructor, equipment shop owner
Automobile engines	auto mechanic, auto designer, school shop teacher
The circulatory system	doctor, nurse, medical student, science teacher
Portrait photography	fashion photographer, portrait studio photographer
Caring for infants	parent, day-care worker, nurse, pediatrician

When you have determined that interviewing an expert will add to your report, you must decide on the kind of interview you want to set up. If the person lives far from you, you might arrange a telephone, letter, or e-mail interview. If the subject is nearby, consider an in-person interview. Whichever form you choose, be sure to keep the following things in mind during the early contacts with your subject.

Setting Up the Interview
1. Make sure you clearly state who you are and why you are seeking the interview.
2. Tell the person if you have a deadline, but respect the fact that your interviewee may be very busy.
3. Ask the subject to suggest times for an interview.
4. Give the person the option of an in-person, letter, telephone, or e-mail interview. You can state your preference, but leave the decision to the subject of the interview.

Preparing to Interview

Before you meet with your subject, research your topic thoroughly. Try to learn all you can about the topic before the interview. This preparation will help you to think on your feet during the questioning. You will be able to ask more intelligent questions if you are familiar with the topic. You also will be able to take advantage of interesting information that your subject might reveal. If you know how a new fact fits into the whole picture, you'll be better able to use it or to discard it as irrelevant.

Also try to learn as much as you can about the person you will interview. If the person is a public figure or is in business, you might ask his or her office for biographical information. Or you might request it from the person before the interview. You should know about the person to whom you are talking. This information will help you formulate good questions. It also saves you the trouble of asking questions that can be answered in a biographical handout.

Before you conduct the interview, write out the questions you plan to ask. It helps if you have a purpose for listening in mind. Are you trying to gather specific or general information about a topic? Are you trying to solve a problem? Regardless of your purpose, try to make your questions open-ended. Don't ask questions that have a yes or no answer. Instead, encourage your subject to talk freely. A *Why?* may bring out important and interesting information. Look at these questions you might ask a marathon runner:

1. How many marathons have you run? Where did you place?
2. How do you prepare for a marathon?
3. What is your weekly running schedule?
4. What types of terrain do you run on when you are in training?
5. What kind of special equipment do you wear?
6. What kind of diet do you eat?
7. What are the three most important aspects of your training?

Conducting the Interview

Your manner during an interview should be serious and respectful, but relaxed. You will put the person you are interviewing at ease if you appear comfortable and confident. This attitude will make the interview flow smoothly. It's much more pleasant to talk in a relaxed atmosphere.

Study the journalist's questions covered in the last lesson. Remember how you used them to evaluate how well a reporter covered a story? See how many *what, who, when, where, how,* and *why* questions you can use in your interview. You'll find that *how* and *why* questions are particularly good for probing deeply into a topic.

Sometimes a person being interviewed will get side-tracked onto something that really doesn't apply to your topic. In this case, it's your job to politely but firmly lead the discussion back to the topic at hand.

Talk as little as possible yourself. Your job as an interviewer is to ask questions clearly and briefly. Then listen to the response and take notes. If the interviewee mentions something interesting that you hadn't thought about, ask some follow-up questions. You might bring out an unexpected piece of information—something that might not have been revealed otherwise. That's when an interview can get exciting.

During the interview you have two jobs to perform. You need to keep track of the questions you've prepared, so you don't forget something important. At the same time, you need to listen carefully to what the person is telling you. Be open to new information you didn't think about and that may raise new questions. You can develop this "thinking on your feet" skill by following some tips.

Tips for Interviewing

1. State your topic and the general scope of the discussion you'd like to have. This will give the person you are interviewing an idea of the boundaries that can be expected during the questioning.

2. Look at the person you're interviewing. Nothing cuts the connection between reporter and subject more quickly than the loss of eye contact. If you're conducting a telephone interview, comment briefly after each point the subject makes.

3. Be courteous at all times, even if your subject wanders away from the topic.

4. If you are unclear about anything the person says, ask a question right away. Then you can build on information you understand.

5. Follow up interesting statements quickly by asking another question. Don't wait, or you might forget the importance of the statement.

6. *Take notes.* At the end of the interview, glance over them. *If something is unclear, ask a question.*

7. Thank the person for the interview. Ask if you can call back if you have a follow-up question or if something is not clear. Review your notes thoroughly when you are alone. If you need to call the person back, do so as soon as you can.

Exercise 2

Work in pairs, and take turns playing the roles of expert and interviewer. Each interviewer should choose a topic. The interviewer's job is to ask good questions and to lead the expert back gently and politely if he or she wanders from the topic. Use one of the following topics or one of your own choosing:

- Why it's important to do well in mathematics

- How to have a great vacation in your own backyard

- The most important person in your life

26.3   Informal Speech

Someone stops you on the street and asks directions to the nearest grocery store. You talk with your friends on the way to school. You respond to a question the teacher asks in class. All of these situations call for informal speech. They are spontaneous and unrehearsed. They are among the most common speech situations.

There are other kinds of informal speech—discussions and announcements, for example. Four types of informal speech are included on the chart below. The chart describes each type and includes some hints that will help you be an effective participant in that type of speaking.

Tips on Informal Speaking		
Type	**Description**	**Hint**
Conversations	Conversations can occur at almost any time and in almost any place. Each person involved contributes and responds to the others.	Be courteous to the person speaking. Taking turns enables everyone to air his or her thoughts.
Discussions	Discussions can occur in many settings, including classrooms. Usually one person leads the discussion, and all are asked to share their thoughts in an orderly manner.	Stick closely to the topic and follow the directions of the discussion leader. Following these rules will ensure an interesting and productive discussion.
Announcements	Announcements summarize the most important information about an activity or event.	List the information you want to include before you make your announcement. Double-check it for accuracy and completeness.
Demonstrations	Demonstrations explain and show a process—how something works, for example. They are useful in many settings, including classrooms.	Number the steps in the process you will demonstrate to make sure the sequence is clear.

The purpose of all speech should be to communicate clearly. To take part in a discussion, you must be prepared and familiar with the topic the group is going to discuss. For example, to answer a question, you must have the information being asked for. In a conversation, on the other hand, you do not need to prepare in advance. You may cover many topics. Your answer to a question may very well be, "I don't know."

Another factor is attitude. Which of the following words describes how you feel when you talk to friends, family, and teachers?

shy enthusiastic confident eager uninterested

Once you've identified your attitude, you can build on your strengths. You can change whatever gets in the way of good communication. It may take practice, but it will benefit you in the end.

Making Introductions

Everyone is a newcomer at one time or another. Entering into a new situation is much easier if someone in the group knows how to make correct introductions. With practice, that someone can be you.

Keep the following points in mind when introducing two people: First, be sure you look at each person. Don't let either party feel left out. You may be introducing one person to a group of people. In this case, make eye contact with the new person and with members of the group. Also, gesture from one person to another as you make the introduction. This will help point out which person you are referring to.

State each person's full name. You might say, "Evan, I'd like to introduce you to Miguel Hernandez. Miguel, this is Evan Schmit." If there are several people in the group, you might mention first names only for people your own age. First and last names are more appropriate when introducing adults. First and last names are also best used when introducing an adult and a younger person.

Tell each person something interesting about the other. If they have something in common, share that. It will become a natural conversation starter.

Participating in a Discussion

Rules of the game exist for discussions as well. A discussion usually has a leader, whose job it is to guide the discussion and keep it on track. The leader may be appointed for the group or chosen by the group. Sometimes a group member just takes over as leader.

As a discussion becomes lively and members of the discussion group get excited about what they are saying, the discussion becomes more difficult to organize. For this reason, it's important that you help the leader by managing your own comments. Be sure they contribute to the topic.

Discussions can focus on any topic. The idea is to come together in an organized group to share ideas and draw conclusions about the subject. A discussion depends totally on the comments of those involved. Before you enter a discussion, have a thorough knowledge of your subject. That way you can be a valuable participant. The following chart has a few more tips about how to act responsibly in a discussion.

Tips for Taking Part in a Discussion

1. Come prepared. Review important information, and bring visual aids or research you can use to illustrate the points you want to make.

2. Be polite. Take turns speaking and listening. You're there to learn as well as to contribute.

3. Go into the discussion willing to modify your opinion. That's the best way to learn.

4. Let the discussion leader take the lead. Concentrate on your part in the discussion—expressing yourself and listening to others.

5. Make your comments brief and concise. People will pay attention to your ideas if they are well thought out and clearly presented.

6. When you state your opinions, back them up with reasons or examples. You'll be much more convincing if you do this.

7. If a member of the group says something you don't understand, ask about it. It's likely that you aren't the only one confused.

Listening and Speaking

Explaining a Process

If you want to explain how to bake a cake, you must do several things. First, you should tell the type of cake the recipe is for. Next, you need to list the ingredients. Then you'll explain the steps to follow.

An explanation of almost any process has the same parts: materials needed, steps to follow, and the result. If the process is long or complicated, you may need to number the steps. Or you might simply use words such as *before, next,* and *finally* to make the sequence of steps clear.

Correct order is all-important. For example, if the steps for building a model airplane are out of sequence, the plane may be incorrectly assembled. To be sure you don't leave out a part of the process, take time to prepare well. Write your explanation in the proper order. Review your instructions to make sure you haven't left out a step or put one in the wrong place.

Making Announcements

When you're asked to make an announcement, think first about what information your listeners need. If you're planning an announcement for an activity, the important facts include the date, the time, the place, and the price of a ticket.

Next, try to determine the briefest way to deliver your information. Announcements should always be short and to-the-point. They are no-fuss pieces of information. You'll want to include just enough information to interest the audience and convey the important facts.

Below are two examples of how the same information might be conveyed. Which is the better announcement?

Example 1

Tryouts for cheerleaders are coming soon. Get in shape now! Don't miss this once-in-a-school-year opportunity!

Example 2

Tryouts for cheerleaders will be this Wednesday afternoon in the gym right after school. Wear loose clothing and plan to stay a few hours. No need to sign up—just show up Wednesday for this once-in-a-school-year opportunity!

Finally, don't forget your audience! Speak so everyone can understand you. That means you must think about who is listening. You might word an announcement one way for preschoolers and another way for their parents.

Exercise 3

Divide into small groups. Let each member of the group select one of the events listed below. Jot down information about the event, including the date, time, and place. Fold the papers and mix them together. Each group member will select a topic at random, then write a short announcement based on the information on the paper. If you need additional pieces of information, invent them. Read your announcements to the group. Discuss how helpful and effective each announcement is.

- Band tryouts
- Countries of the World Festival
- Square-dancing lessons
- Debate Club meeting

26.4 Oral Reports

What image comes to mind when you think about giving an oral report? For some students the image might be exciting; for others, a little scary. However you feel, you can make the experience more enjoyable by preparing well.

You can prepare to give an oral report in three ways. First, you must prepare the content of your report. Make sure you understand everything you will be saying about your topic. Second, you need to prepare your presentation. Practice is the key here. Finally, you need to prepare yourself mentally so that you feel good about your presentation.

Preparing the Report

Think for a few moments about the purpose of your report. Is it to inform, persuade, explain, narrate, or entertain? Perhaps you have more than one purpose. An oral report can inform, persuade, and entertain, but one purpose should be the main one.

Another important consideration is your audience. To whom will you be speaking? Students your own age? Younger people? Older people? A mixed audience? What is the best way to reach your particular audience?

When you've thought about your purpose and audience, think a little further about your topic. Is it sufficiently narrowed down? If not, can you narrow it further? A precisely defined topic is easier to research than one that is unfocused. It is also easier to write about.

Now begin your research. Read articles in newspapers, magazines, encyclopedias, and other sources. You may also want to interview an expert in the field. Take notes. Develop an outline. Check the relationship of your main ideas and supporting details.

When you feel comfortable with the amount of information you've gathered, prepare your notes for the report. You may want to write out the entire report as you'd like to deliver it. Or you may write the key ideas and phrases on note cards. You might want to note the transitions you'll use to get from one main idea to the next. The transitions will jog your memory as you speak and help you move through your report smoothly.

Listening and Speaking

Practicing the Report

Practicing your report is important. Practice will help you understand and remember your main ideas and supporting details. In addition, practice will give you confidence about your presentation. You will know how you want to speak the words, make the gestures, and display any visual materials you've decided to use.

Begin practicing alone. Speak in front of a mirror. Use the voice and gestures you would use if you were in front of a live audience. Time your report as you practice so that you can adjust the length if necessary.

The more you practice, the more natural the report will sound. Practice glancing from your note cards to the audience. You don't want to read your report word for word, but you'll probably want to memorize parts of it.

When you feel comfortable with your report, ask a friend or family member to listen to your delivery. Then try giving it before more than one person.

Ask your practice audience to listen *and* watch you. You'll want feedback about both the content of the report and your presentation. If the audience thinks the content or delivery needs work, make the changes you think are necessary. Then begin your practice sessions over again. If you need work on the delivery of your report, try using the following tips.

Tips on Delivering an Oral Report

1. Make eye contact with the audience. This helps people feel involved in what you are saying.

2. Use your voice to emphasize main points. You can raise or lower it, depending upon the effect you want to achieve.

3. Stop a moment after you've made an important point. This stresses the point and allows people to think about what you've said.

4. Use gestures if you've practiced them.

5. If they relate to your topic, use visual aids to help your audience understand your ideas.

Presenting the Report

When it's time to deliver your report, relax. (You'll find some tips for relaxing on page 774.) Deliver your report just as you've prac-

ticed it. Speak in a clear, natural voice, and use gestures when they are appropriate.

As you speak, show that you find your information interesting. Be enthusiastic. Think of your audience as people who are there because they're interested in what you have to say. Speak to them as if they were friends. They'll respond to your positive attitude.

When you conclude your report, ask for questions. Remain in front of the audience until you have answered everyone's questions.

Exercise 4

Select a topic from the following list, or use one of your own choosing. Write how you would narrow the topic. Then write your ideas for researching it.

Share the ideas you've developed with a partner. Ask for comments and suggestions. Then look at your partner's work, and make constructive comments about how he or she narrowed the topic and planned to research it.

- The migration of the monarch butterfly
- How our Constitution provides for the election of a president
- How to navigate by compass
- Kente cloth from Ghana

26.5 Formal Speeches

Delivering a formal speech in front of a live audience is the last stage of a five-stage process. You can think of it as the reward for successfully completing the earlier steps in the process. Once you've prepared thoroughly, delivering the speech can be fun and rewarding.

Preparing a Speech

You are familiar with the stages of writing a report: prewriting, drafting, revising, editing, and presenting. Formal speaking depends on a similar five-stage process. In preparing a speech, however, the editing stage becomes practicing. In effect, you edit your speech as you practice giving it. You are preparing for an audience of listeners rather than of readers.

Each step builds on the work done in the previous step. However, you may find it necessary to move back and forth during the drafting, revising, and practicing stages. For example, you might find during the practicing stage that your speech is too short or too long. To shorten it, you can back up to the revising stage or even the drafting stage to prepare a shorter version. The chart shows the process in detail.

Before you move to the practicing stage you'll want to have a speech you feel confident about. Word it in a way that will be easy to deliver.

TIME

For more about the writing process, see **TIME Facing the Blank Page,** pp. 97-107.

Prewrite
- Define and narrow your topic.
- Remember your purpose and your audience.
- Complete your research.

Draft	**Revise**	**Practice**
• Make an outline, using main ideas and supporting details. • Write your speech, or jot down the main points on note cards.	• Make sure your ideas are in order. • Mark transitions on cards. • Change wording until it is the way you want it.	• Give the speech in front of a mirror. • Time your speech. • Deliver it to a practice audience. • Use the suggestions you receive.

Present
- Relax, and deliver your speech just as you've practiced it.

Listening and Speaking

You don't want words you'll stumble over or phrases that sound awkward. If you aren't sure how to pronounce a term, look it up. If you still aren't comfortable with it, find another term that means the same thing.

Practicing a Speech

Practicing also involves several steps. When you practice your speech out loud, you want to make sure it sounds natural. The first time you practice it, just listen to the words as you speak. Listening to yourself on a tape recorder can be helpful. The rhythm of the speech should feel comfortable to you. If you don't like a phrase, rework it out loud until you come up with another way to express the idea.

The next time through, try looking in a mirror and using a few hand gestures to emphasize main points. Don't force the gestures. Try to think about what you're saying, and let your gestures develop spontaneously. Once you see where you need emphasis, make a point of practicing the gestures while speaking until they feel comfortable to you.

Finally, ask friends or relatives to listen to your delivery. Use their responses to fine-tune your speech. Below are a few more tips for practicing your speech.

Tips for Practicing a Speech

1. Each time you deliver your speech in practice, act just as if you were giving it before a live audience. Try to imagine the audience in front of you. This will help cut down on nervousness when you actually present the speech before a real audience.

2. Practice making eye contact with your imaginary audience. Let your eyes sweep slowly across the room from one side to the other, making contact with each member of the audience. Focus on talking to them, rather than on practicing your speech.

3. Make sure your gestures feel comfortable and fit with the points in the speech. Emphasize main points, or direct attention to visual aids, using gestures that are natural to you.

Delivering a Speech

Formal speaking is like conversation. Although you are the only one talking, your audience is communicating with you. Your success depends in part on how well you can interpret and use the signals they are sending you.

Keep your mind on your speech, and read the audience's response at the same time. A good speaker does both. The best speakers add a third element: They can change what they're doing to accommodate the needs of the audience.

Tips for Relaxing
1. Take a few deep, slow breaths before you begin speaking. When you pause at important points in your speech, you can repeat the process to keep yourself relaxed.
2. When you deliver your speech, talk to people in the audience as individuals rather than to the group as a whole. This will help personalize your message and make you feel comfortable. Some speakers like to pick out and concentrate on a few friendly faces in the audience.
3. Speak in a tone that is normal for you. Speak loudly enough to be heard throughout the room, but don't shout.
4. Let your voice rise and fall naturally at key points in your speech. The idea is to sound comfortable and natural.
5. Keep alert. Don't let your thoughts wander. Focus on the content of your speech and on sharing it with your audience.

Focusing on the audience can help you feel less nervous. The charts on this page can give you some help. The one above contains some tips for relaxing. The chart below offers some suggestions for communicating with your audience.

Communicating with Your Audience

Audience Signals	Speaker Response
People are yawning, stretching, or moving restlessly. They seem not to be paying attention to you.	You may have lost the attention of your audience. Try adding some enthusiasm to what you are saying.
People look confused or seem to want to ask a question.	You may have confused your audience. Try asking if there are questions.
People are sitting forward in their chairs, trying to hear you.	People may be having trouble hearing you. Speak more loudly, and note whether or not that eliminates this audience response.
People look pleased with what you are saying. They nod in agreement.	You are doing a great job. Finish your speech in the same manner.

Exercise 5

With a small group, brainstorm ways to become better listeners and create a list of common listening problems. Then agree on one or two hours of television or radio programming that all of you will watch or listen to in the next few days. Include several types of programming.

Listen to the programs your group selected. After each program write comments telling why you found the listening easy or difficult. When you meet again as a group, compare notes, and discuss kinds of programming that are easy to listen to and those that are more challenging. Discuss distractions and ways to eliminate them in order to listen more carefully to programming with which you had difficulties.

Exercise 6

1. Prepare a two-minute speech on a topic of your choice. Go through each of the steps outlined in this lesson. Then take turns delivering your speeches within small groups. Discuss and evaluate each speech. Share ideas you can all use to improve the presentation and content of your speeches. Then make revisions, and deliver the revised speeches to the class.

2. Exchange copies of speeches with someone in your group. If you have notes instead of a complete written speech, exchange note cards. Alter the speech to suit your manner of speaking, but keep the content the same. Practice delivering the new speech. Join your group, and take turns delivering your new speeches. Discuss how and why they differ from the originals.

26.6 Storytelling

For thousands of years, people from many different cultures have used storytelling as a way to pass on their history, to teach their young, to explain why things happen in nature, and to entertain. Alex Haley, a U.S. novelist and journalist, said, "I acknowledge immense debt to the griots [tribal poets] of Africa—where today it is rightly said that when a griot dies, it is as if a library has burned to the ground."

Today, in the United States, storytelling has become an art and is mostly used to entertain and delight audiences of all ages. Good storytellers rely on their voices and words to create pictures in the minds of their listeners. Use the guidelines that follow to help you better understand the art of storytelling and then prepare a story to tell to your own audience.

Choose a story that you like and feel comfortable with. Obviously, it would be difficult to do a good job telling a story you don't like. If you choose a story that is from a culture different from your own, you should do some research about that culture to get a feeling for the people in the story. Try to find a story that is short but still interesting—one that will capture the audience's imagination.

Get to know the story. After first reading the story for pleasure, read it over and over again to familiarize yourself with the story's sentence structure, unusual phrases, action, setting, beginning and ending, and other elements. Study the story's characters. Note the way in which each one talks, acts, and thinks. Think about what particular aspect of this story you responded to and how you can relate this aspect to your readers. For example, did the story's humor appeal to you? Did a certain character touch you? Was there a particular lesson taught that is important to you?

Commit the story to memory. You don't have to memorize the whole story word for word. Rather, study the story until you think you can tell it to someone else, using some of your own words. Be sure to preserve the spirit of the story. Memorize exact words and phrases that are central to the story's meaning and that help the audience create a mental picture and put themselves in the place of the story's characters.

Practice, practice, practice. Practice telling your story to anyone who will listen. Use the following tips to help you as you practice your story.

Tips for Practicing Storytelling

❶ Adapt your story to your audience. If you know that you will be telling your story mainly to young children, make sure you adapt the vocabulary you use. You might also wish to introduce the story to an audience that is unfamiliar with it, explaining the story's origin and its relevance to your own culture today.

❷ Correct pacing of the story is very important. Some stories are meant to be told at a brisk pace, whereas others should be told in a slow, leisurely drawl. In many stories, the pace changes throughout. The story's action, sentence structure, and style of writing will give you clues to how to pace your story. In general, action sequences should be told fairly quickly, while poetic, creative passages should be told more slowly.

❸ Practice using your voice to make your story as entertaining as possible. For example, when a girl pushes open the door to an old, abandoned house, you might pause to add suspense before you continue. You might also lower the volume of your voice to a whisper and slow the pace. Decide on an appropriate voice for each character and use the same voice for each one consistently.

❹ Stay connected with the audience. To keep your listeners involved in your story, make eye contact with them frequently.

❺ Use gestures and facial expressions that you would use in everyday conversation. Don't try to dramatize every scene. Remember that you are *telling* a story, not acting it out.

Keep distractions to a minimum. In order for your listeners to get the most out of your story, neither they nor you should be bothered by distractions. Close the door, turn off the radio, and close the windows so that you have the undivided attention of your listeners.

Exercise 7

Use the guidelines in this section to help you select a story and prepare to tell it. Once you think you are ready to tell the story, find a partner and tell the story to him or her. Ask your partner to evaluate your storytelling and to make suggestions for improvement. You may then tell the story to the class or another group of people.

Viewing and Representing

27.1 Interpreting Visual Messages

A recent report by the American Academy of Pediatrics stated that most young people in the United States spend more of their non-school time watching television than performing any other activity except sleeping. A study by the United States Department of Education shows that students who watch television more than ten hours a week generally get lower grades than those who watch less television.

Mass Media   Young people, far more than their parents and grandparents, are greatly influenced by **mass media**, a term that means "a form of communication that is widely available to many people." Along with television, mass media includes newspapers, magazines, radio, movies, videos, and the Internet.

Most forms of mass media contain advertisements or commercials—messages that have one purpose: to persuade people to buy a certain product. By the time of high school graduation, the typical student will have probably seen an estimated 360,000 television commercials.

The various forms of mass media will have a great influence on your life. Some forms of the media will have positive influences, enabling you to learn new skills and explore new ideas and opportunities or allowing you to relax and enjoy inspiring dramas and music. However, some forms of the media can have negative effects. If you are not careful, the media can mislead you, confuse you, and even endanger you.

As you face such challenges, the best solution is to learn how to make responsible, educated decisions about which media messages are valuable, uplifting, and truthful and which messages are harmful, unfair, or just plain silly. This unit will help you learn how to interpret, analyze, and evaluate the various forms of mass media. With these skills comes the power to enjoy the media's benefits and to protect yourself against possible negative influences.

Media and Values   All media productions—text, pictures, and even music—contain points of view about the world. No media product is neutral or value-free. Each is designed carefully to attract and appeal to a particular audience and to create specific reactions. Every form of media except radio contains visual art. Like all forms of media, each piece of visual art, whether it is a photograph, painting, cartoon, drawing, advertisement, or computer graphic, is created carefully to send a distinct visual message. If you understand how artists and photographers craft visual art to send messages, you will be able to "read" each message and evaluate its value and truthfulness.

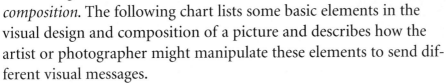

Understanding Visual Design

The use of colors, shapes, and various types of lines makes up the *visual design* of a piece of art. The arrangement of such visual elements is called *composition*. The following chart lists some basic elements in the visual design and composition of a picture and describes how the artist or photographer might manipulate these elements to send different visual messages.

Study the photograph above. Note that the mountain is positioned at the top and is emphasized by sunlight. The viewer's eye is immediately drawn to this dominant feature. Then the eye is attracted to the curved, bright line of the waterfall, which flows into the darkened forest. The visual message of this photograph is the power of the wilderness, as represented by the dominant rocky mountain and the rushing stream.

Exercise 1

Choose a photograph in this textbook other than the two on this page. Use the Elements of Visual Design and Composition chart on the next page to interpret the visual message contained in the photograph you chose. Explain how positioning—as well as colors, light, and shadows—and the use of straight and curved lines work together to send the message.

Elements of Visual Design and Composition

Element	Possible Significance
Lines	
Heavy, thick lines	Emphasize an object, person, or space; can suggest boldness or power
Thin lines	Can give a sense of sharpness; create a feeling of lightness and grace
Straight lines	Point in a direction or lead the eye to something else
Curved lines	Suggest motion
Gentle, wavy lines	Create calming, soothing effect
Sharp, zigzag lines	Suggest tension or energy
Vertical lines	Suggest power, status
Horizontal lines	Suggest peace, stillness
Diagonal lines	Suggest tension, action, energy
Repeating lines	Create patterns
Light	
Brightly lit areas	Draw the eye to a specific area; create a cheerful mood
Dimly lit areas or shadows	Give a sense of mystery or sadness; show a lack of emphasis
Colors	
Cool colors (blue, green, gray)	Convey a sense of calm and coolness
Warm colors (orange, yellow, red)	Convey a sense of energy and vibrancy
Bright Colors	Create a sense of warmth and joyfulness
Subdued or pastel colors	Suggest innocence or softness
Repetition of color	Can suggest a pattern or assign a value to what is portrayed
Position of subjects	
Center of picture	Suggests strength, dominance; draws attention to the subject
Top of picture	Suggests power, importance
Bottom of picture	Suggests weakness; adds contrast to images positioned in the middle or top of the picture
Space	
Large space around object	Draws attention to subject; can suggest loneliness, vastness
Small amount of space around subject	Makes subject seem very powerful

Viewing and Representing

Reading a Political Cartoon

Tom Toles, the *Buffalo News* political cartoonist, drew this cartoon
in 1999 as a comment on the growing world population.
Note Toles's use of position and size—"Phone Booth
Earth" surely dominates the page, and the curved lines
emphasize that the phone booth is about to burst. What
message might Toles have wanted to send by making the
inside of the phone booth the most brightly lit part of the
cartoon? Then note the dialogue, both in the bubble and
at the bottom of the cartoon. What message might Toles
have wanted to send with those words? What thoughts
and feelings do the jam-packed phone booth bring to
your mind? What do you think the cartoonist suggests
might happen to an overcrowded planet Earth?

Exercise 2

Study the cartoon below by the *Boston Globe* political cartoonist Paul
Szep, entitled "Happy New Year." Identify the visual message that he
intends the cartoon to send. Then explain how his use of lines, position,
repetition, space, and facial expressions extend or emphasize that
message.

Understanding Film Techniques

Like a short story or novel, every motion picture and television
drama or comedy tells a story. Also like written literature, films use
dialogue to tell much of the story. However, films also use a variety of
other narrative elements that go beyond what can be done on the
written page. Directors of movies and television shows employ many
of the techniques listed in the Elements of Visual
Design and Composition chart on page 782 to extend
or emphasize the mood or message of the film.
Additionally, filmmakers can employ the following
special visual techniques.

In many of his early films, movie actor Humphrey
Bogart played a tough, savvy, wise-guy villain.
Directors generally thought that he was neither tall
enough nor handsome enough to be cast as a leading

man. The public disagreed. Therefore, as Bogart's stardom increased, directors began to cast him as a tough, savvy, wise-guy *hero*. Some of his most famous roles included Sam Spade, a private detective, and Rick, the lonely but gallant hero of *Casablanca*.

Study the movie still to the left. It is from the 1942 movie *Across the Pacific*, in which Bogart plays a clever detective who must track down enemy spies. In this scene, director John Huston has Bogart use his characteristic tough stance as he protects the character played by Mary Astor.

Note that the camera angle is low, shooting up at Bogart from the ground. Why might director John Huston have chosen this angle? Note also that Bogart is shown with full, head-on light, making him seem strong and dominant. However, his eyes are shaded by his hat, giving him a mysterious, sly look. Note which elements from the Elements of Visual Design and Composition chart are used by Huston. He has probably instructed Bogart to stand as straight as possible so that the vertical line of that stance would emphasize the character's power. Note the pattern Huston creates with lines. Contrast the parallel lines of the gun and the line painted on the ship with the suggested diagonal lines of vision of both actors. Why might Huston have carefully set up such a diagonal pattern?

What dialogue might the characters be speaking in this shot? How does Huston's visual image extend or emphasize that message? If you were on the creative staff of this movie, what type of background music would you choose for this scene in order to manipulate the audience's emotional response?

Film Techniques for Sending Visual Messages

Technique	Possible Significance
Camera angle	
High (looking down on subjects)	Often makes subject seem smaller, less important, or more at risk
Low (looking up on subjects)	Emphasizes the subject's importance or power
Straight-on (eye level)	Puts viewer on equal level with subject; can make viewer identify with subject
Camera shots	
Close-up (picture of subject's face)	Emphasizes character's facial expressions; leads viewer to identify with him or her
Long shot (wide view, showing character within larger setting)	Shows relationship between character and setting
Lighting	
High, bright lighting	Creates cheerful, optimistic tone
Low, shadowy lighting	Creates gloomy, mysterious tone
Light from above	Makes subject seem to glow with power or strength
Light from below	Increases audience tension
Editing	
Quick transitions between frames	Quickens pace; increases suspense or excitement
Slow dissolve or fade out	Indicates change in perspective or time; may introduce a flashback or dream sequence
Special effects	
Slow motion	Emphasizes movement and heightens drama
Blurred motion	Suggests speed, confusion, or a dream-like state
Background music	Manipulates audience's emotional response

Exercise 3

Study the color still, or movie photo, on page 784. Identify the visual message that the filmmakers intend to send to viewers. Then, using the Elements of Visual Design and Composition chart on page 782 and the Film Techniques for Sending Visual Messages chart on this page, explain what techniques the filmmakers use to extend and emphasize the message.

27.2 Analyzing Media Messages

Photographs, movies, and television programs often seem realistic; they show scenes, characters, actions, and conflicts that could easily happen in real life. Some media presentations *are* realistic. However, all media messages are constructed carefully, to emphasize a particular point of view. Even a factual film documentary or a public service message on a topic such as health care or environmental protection uses carefully chosen colors, lines, and camera angles to persuade the viewer to accept and agree with a certain point of view.

The artist, photographer, or director makes many decisions about what pictures and information to include, what camera angles will prove most effective, and what information should *not* be included. Follow three steps to unravel the sometimes confusing messages sent by the media.

1. Identify the visual message that an artist, photographer, cartoonist, or film director is sending.
2. Spot the techniques of design, composition, and film that were used to extend and emphasize that message.
3. Decide whether you agree or disagree with that message.

Key Questions for Analyzing Media

To analyze a media message, ask yourself these Key Questions:

- What message is this photo (or drawing, cartoon, movie, television show, music video) trying to send me?

- How did the artist or photographer use elements of visual design and composition and/or film techniques to emphasize the message and to persuade the audience to accept and agree with the message?

- What do I already know about this subject?

- How can I use what I already know to judge whether this message is
  - ❏ fair or unfair
  - ❏ based on reality or fantasy
  - ❏ based on facts or opinions

- What sources might I use to find other viewpoints on this subject that I can trust?
  - ❏ parent, teacher, or other trusted adult
  - ❏ reliable books or other reference sources
  - ❏ other _____.

Then, on the basis of your answers to the questions and other trusted viewpoints, make a decision about the visual message. Make sure that in your own mind you can support that decision with well-thought-out reasons.
  - ❏ I agree with the visual message because _____.
  - ❏ I disagree with the visual message because _____.

Exercise 4

Practice the Key Questions by analyzing one of the political cartoons shown on page 783. Write answers to the questions. Compare your findings, and your ultimate decision, with those of your teacher and classmates.

Exercise 5

Watch carefully as your teacher plays a scene or two from a popular movie or television show and then shows a popular music video. Use the Key Questions for Analyzing Media to have a class discussion analyzing and evaluating the visual messages you received from each segment or video you saw.

Exercise 6

Choose a favorite movie, television show, or music video. Use the Key Questions to analyze and evaluate the visual messages. Write a brief report on your findings and conclusions.

Analyzing Advertisements and Commercials

You can also use the Key Questions to analyze and evaluate the media messages contained in advertisements appearing in newspapers, magazines, and Web sites, as well as on television commercials.

More than any other form of media, advertisements and commercials have one goal: *to persuade the viewer to buy the product or service being advertised.* To accomplish that goal, advertisers often use techniques listed in the Elements of Visual Design and Composition chart on page 782, and the Film Techniques for Sending Visual Messages chart on page 785. Additionally, they often use one or more of the following advertising techniques.

Common Advertising Techniques		
Element	**Description**	**Example**
"Jump on the **bandwagon** and join in the fun!"	using visual images or carefully chosen words to show that "all popular, attractive, well-liked people" use this product	An advertisement for a certain brand of clothing shows attractive, smiling people enjoying each other's company as they wear that brand of clothing.
"Be like your favorite **celebrity!"**	showing a popular star of movies or television, a famous athlete, or a leading musical performer using the product	An advertisement for a certain shampoo or other cosmetic shows a popular television or movie star who claims that he or she uses that product.
"Use this for **incredible results!"**	using oils, dyes, special lighting, or other "tricks" to make the product results "too good to be true"	An advertisement for jeans uses make-up, special lighting, air-brush photography, or other special effects to make a model look excessively slim and gorgeous while wearing that brand of jeans.
"Leading experts are convinced that you should use this product."	using actors to pretend that they are doctors, dentists, and other experts	In an advertisement for a headache medicine, an actor portrays a doctor who recommends using the product.
"Feel guilty or foolish if you don't buy this important product."	manipulating scientific terms, statistics, or other data to convince viewers that using another product would be foolish or wasteful	An advertisement for a certain brand of computer suggests that using any other brand will make you less efficient and successful.
Be smart, rich, and successful!	using persuasive language and visual images to make people feel that the "elite" (rich, powerful, and successful people) already use this product	An advertisement for a certain car shows stylish, successful people driving to an exclusive restaurant or golf club.
Enjoy romance!	using persuasive language and visual images to make people feel that using this product will bring them excitement or romance	A fragrance advertisement shows two people looking fondly at each other.

Viewing and Representing

Although commercials and advertisements often contain a few convincing facts, those facts are surrounded by persuasive words and often unrealistic claims. Don't be fooled by the glossy images and exuberant proclamations of advertisements. Use a version of the Key Questions to "cut through" the glitter and make informed, wise decisions about which products to buy. As an example, examine the model of an advertisement on this page.

In time, he may forget whether it rained or not that magic night.
In time, he may forget what song the band was playing when he caught your eye. What he'll never forget will be the dazzle in your eyes, the lightness in your step.

Dazzle.
Shine.
Be unforgettable.
Choose clothes by L'Essence.

Exercise 7

Use the Key Questions for Analyzing Media to analyze and evaluate the above advertisement. Discuss your findings with classmates.

Exercise 8

Work with a group to make a collage of advertisements that appear in popular magazines. Use labels and captions to point out the "tricks" that the advertisers used to persuade people to buy the products. Display your poster in class. Discuss your findings with classmates.

Exercise 9

Watch carefully as your teacher plays a video clip of one or more television commercials. Then work as a class to use the Key Questions for Analyzing Media Messages to identify, analyze, and evaluate the message or messages you have just seen.

27.3 Producing Media Messages

Another way to increase your understanding of media messages is to produce your own media messages, applying the techniques that artists, filmmakers, and advertisers use. This section will help you to create two types of media messages: a political cartoon and a scene from a television program.

Creating a Political Cartoon

Political cartoonists often use one or more of the following techniques to send a visual message about a current issue or event. Although political cartoons use humor to get their points across, there is virtually always a serious issue behind the cartoon.

Elements of Humor Often Used by Cartoonists

- **Exaggeration:** Drawing something bigger or greater than it would normally be, causing it to have larger-than-life effects on other objects or people

  Example: Tom Toles shows an enormous "Phone Booth Earth" filled with very tiny people.

- **Irony:** Providing an outcome that is completely unexpected or unusual

  Example: Instead of continuing the celebration, Paul Szep's New Year's celebrant went right back to his dull, disinterested pose as soon as midnight passed.

- **Satire:** Poking fun at a person, event, or situation

  Example: A cartoon about a politician who voted against an environmental proposal might show the politician snarling as he frantically chops down a forest of trees.

Satire is perhaps the most common humorous element in political cartoons. Each day political cartoonists poke fun at politicians, news events, or situations that they find amusing. This type of cartoon often carries the strongest visual message because the purpose is not only to create humor but to send a message of criticism about a person, event, or situation.

Tips for Creating a Cartoon

1. **Brainstorm.** Think about issues, events, and situations at school and in the local and national news, as well as global issues such as the environment or world peace. Concentrate on topics that you would enjoy poking fun at through exaggeration, irony, and satire. You might select a rule or a law that you disagree with, a politician or other public figure whose opinions are contrary to your own, or a serious issue or situation on which you'd like to make a strong statement. Jot down several ideas and then pick one idea to develop into a political cartoon.

2. **Identify your purpose and message.** What underlying message do you want your cartoon to express? What point of view do you intend to get across through humor? Summarize your point of view in a sentence or two. Keep your point of view in mind as you draw.

3. **Identify your audience.** To what specific group do you want to focus your message—classmates, all students at your school, members of a particular team or club, neighbors, or family members? Think about what your specific audience already knows and thinks about your topic. What other information might your audience need to know in order to understand your humorous message? Make sure that you somehow include that information in your cartoon.

4. **Decide whether to use words.** Often the best cartoons use the picture to show, rather than words to tell, the message to the viewer. Will your message be clear from your picture alone, or do you need a caption to make your message precisely clear? Should the characters be labeled so that their identity is clear? Should they speak through speech balloons in order to make the meaning clear? Experiment using words and omitting words until you are satisfied that your message is clear.

5. **Make layout sketches.** On scrap paper, draw several versions of the cartoon. Refer to the Elements of Visual Design and Composition chart on page 782 for ideas about such elements as lines, colors, positions, and space.

(continued)

6 Make your final copy. When you are satisfied with your sketches and your decision of whether to include words in your cartoon, make a final copy. If possible, use black felt markers of various thicknesses to give your political cartoon a professional, crisp "newspaper" look.

7 Publish your cartoon. Share your cartoon with your selected audience. You might publish it in the school newspaper or display it where it will catch the attention of your intended audience. Ask for feedback. Find out if your viewers understood and agreed with your message.

Exercise 10

Use the Tips for Creating a Cartoon to send an effective, humorous media message by creating a political cartoon.

Creating a Scene from a Television Drama

The production of a television program requires the skills and cooperation of a group of people. Group members take on one or more roles, based on their skills and interests. By pooling talents, group members can create a production that one member of the team could not manage alone. Follow these tips to create an effective scene from a television drama. On film, your scene should run for about ten minutes.

Tips for Creating a Television Drama

1 Build a production team. Have each member of your group commit to one or more of the following roles:

- **Director** – leads the group, overseeing the work of all team members and supervising the filming

- **Source Advisor** – works with the scriptwriter to adapt a published book or short story into a television format

- **Scriptwriter** – writes and revises the script on the basis of input and suggestions from the Source Advisor and Director

- **Organizer and layout expert** – creates a "storyboard," a series of simple sketches that shows each step in the scene. The storyboard outlines the format of the scene from beginning to end. The director, actors, camera operator, and music arranger follow this plan during the filming

- **Set and Props Captain** – works with the director, scriptwriter, and layout expert to gather or make all elements of the scenery and props; has all sets and props in place prior to the filming

- **Actors** – follow the director's guidance to speak the dialogue and act out the scene

- **Lighting expert** – follows the director's plan for creating the proper lighting during the filming

- **Video operator** – videotapes the show

- **Music arranger** – works with the director to choose any background music that may be used; follows the director's cue to start the music at the appropriate time during the filming

2 **Find your source.** Work together with your group to discuss books and short stories that might provide the source for your television scene. Keep in mind your time limitations. You have only ten minutes of film in which to portray one scene. Keep in mind your set limitations. Avoid scenes that will require extensive scenery or props—or extensive imagination on the part of your viewers!

3 **Work cooperatively to plan the scene.** Hold a team meeting to begin the planning process. Make suggestions to the director regarding the elements of visual design and film techniques he or she might use. Then work independently to plan and prepare your assigned part of the production. Come together to go over and revise ideas until everyone is satisfied.

4 **Rehearse.** Do several run-throughs of the scene before actually taping it. At this point, the director should be in charge, planning the camera shots and angles, the lighting, the movements and positions of the actors, and the voice and music cues.

(continued)

⑤ **Shoot!** Tape the scene, following the plan that you perfected during rehearsals. Don't get upset if mistakes occur—they happen in real television and movie studios too! Reshoot if necessary.

⑥ **Present your scene.** Hold a film festival at which your group joins other groups in presenting your films. After each performance, pause for feedback and discussion. Which camera angles, lighting, dialogue, and visual details seemed most effective in sending media messages? Why?

Exercise 11

With a group, use the Tips for Creating a Television Drama to create a dramatic television scene.

Electronic Resources

28.1 Computers and the Internet

For students whose schools boast computer labs or classroom computers, or for those whose families compete for time on a personal computer at home, the beginnings of the computer age may seem like ancient history. It wasn't all that long ago, and we've come a long way since then. The first operational computers—named Eniac and Univac—were developed in the 1940s and occupied enormous amounts of space. Eniac was more than six feet high and twenty-six yards long! Users required training in a special computer language to access the databases of these machines.

Today's computers are so compact that they are portable and so simple to operate that they can be used by young children. Even computers that respond to the sound of the human voice are now on the

Electronic Resources

market. One of the most helpful resources made available through computers is the Internet. The **Internet** is an electronic connection to a huge fund of information and general data. It uses telephone lines, cable lines, and satellites to link computers all over the world. Among the computer terms that have become a permanent part of our vocabulary are *cyberspace, information superhighway,* and *surfing the Web.*

What we generally refer to as the "Internet" is the part of the Internet called the **World Wide Web**. The World Wide Web is one of the best ways to explore the Internet. The Web, as it is often called, was designed to make it easy to allow millions of computers to exchange data that include text, video, graphics, animation, and sound. You can consult experts in specialized fields, find information in a variety of encyclopedias, listen to radio programs, and find late-breaking news from all over the world on the Web. You can use the Web to communicate with students in other cities, other states, and even other countries. If you don't own a computer, you can access the Internet at a school computer lab or a public library. Many public libraries now have Internet terminals available to their patrons.

Exercise 1

Working in a small group, list the different ways in which you and your family use computers. Then predict how you will use the Internet in your daily life in the next year and what uses the Internet will have in ten years. Finally, predict how your children will use the Internet when they are your age. Compare your predictions with those of others in your class.

28.2 Getting on the Internet

The three basic things you need to access the Internet are a computer, a modem, and an Internet service provider. A **modem** is a device that allows a computer to communicate and share information with other computers over telephone or cable lines. An **Internet service provider**, or ISP, provides a service (for a fee) that allows your computer to dial into the Internet. You can also get onto the Internet by using an online service, such as America Online or Microsoft Networks. Such a service lets you access the Internet as well as its own private services. For example, America Online users can use private chat rooms and other exclusive features.

Browsers

To display the contents of a Web site, your computer must have a browser. A **browser** is a software program that displays Web pages as text, graphics, pictures, and video on your computer. The most popular browsers are Netscape Navigator and Microsoft Internet Explorer. If your computer does not already have a browser installed, your service provider should be able to provide you with one.

Once you have a browser, software programs called plug-ins will allow you to use your browser to play sounds or display movies from a Web site. Examples of plug-ins include RealAudio, which allows you to listen to recorded music and radio broadcasts, and RealVideo, Quicktime, and Shockwave, which show movies.

Net Addresses

The World Wide Web is made up of millions of Web sites. A **Web site** is a page, or collection of pages, that have been put together by a person, a company, or an organization such as a university. A Web site may include photos, artwork, sound, and movies in addition to text. A **Webmaster** is the person in charge of building and maintaining a Web site.

To get to a particular Web site, you need to know its address. Every Web site on the Internet has a unique address, or **URL**. URL stands for Uniform Resource Locator. No two Web sites can have the same URL.

As an Internet user, you may want to keep track of some Web sites that you visit. URLs can often be long and difficult to remember. You can keep an easy record of these URLs by using your browser's **bookmark** or **favorites** option. (Bookmark is the term used in Navigator; Internet Explorer calls them favorites.) This function lets you keep a list of the URLs of your favorite sites so that you don't have to remember them. To access a site, just pull down the bookmark or favorites menu and click on the site's name.

As you add to your list of bookmarks/favorites, you may want to organize them into folders for categories such as search engines, reference sources, and news. Some browsers allow you to save your bookmarks to a diskette. You can share your bookmarks with other students or access the bookmarks you have selected from another computer.

Hyperlinks

You may notice as you begin to investigate various Web sites that some words or phrases are underlined or are in a different color from the rest of the text. These words are called hyper-

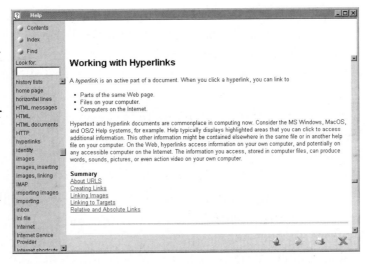

text links, or hyperlinks. A **hyperlink** is text or a graphic that, when clicked on, takes you to a related Web site or a new page in the site you are on. Sometimes it may be difficult to find a hyperlink on a Web page, especially if it is a photo. If you are not sure whether the text or graphic is a hyperlink, drag the arrow over it. If the arrow changes to a pointing finger, you've found a hyperlink.

Using a Search Engine

One way to find information on the Web is to type in the URL for a specific site. But often you do not know exactly where on the Web you might find the information. How do you find Web sites that will give you the specific information you are looking for? The fastest way is to start with a search engine. A **search engine** lets you look for information on the Web by searching for keywords. A **keyword** is a word or phrase that describes your topic. For example, if you wanted information about the early years of the National Football League, you might try *NFL* and *history* as keywords.

Choosing keywords carefully can help you get better results. Use phrases in quotation marks and combine terms (using a + sign) to narrow your search. If your keyword is too general, try adding additional terms that will help find the information you are looking for. For example, if the keyword *dog* is too general, try searching for *dog* + *"golden retriever"* + *training* to help you find information about training a golden retriever.

Using the commands AND, OR, and NOT can also help narrow your searches. These three words are the basis of **Boolean logic**. If you are searching for Web pages that contain information about three types of birds—cardinals, blue jays, and parrots—you would use the Boolean command AND to link those keywords (cardinals AND "blue jays" AND parrots). The search engine will then suggest only sites that use all three terms. Note the use of quotation marks around the two-word name.

When searching for terms with different spellings, like *theater* and *theatre*, link them with the Boolean command OR (theater OR theatre). Using OR between the words will lead you to Web sites with either spelling. To find Web sites that feature information about dogs other than golden retrievers, you would use NOT in combination with AND to narrow the search (dogs AND NOT "golden retriever").

Metasearch engines, such as Dogpile and Metafind, allow you to submit a keyword to several search engines at the same time. You will not get as many results as you would if you were using a specific search engine. However, you are likely to get the most relevant and useful information from each engine that the metasearch engine searches—provided your keywords were well chosen.

If you haven't narrowed your search to a specific topic, you can start with a subject directory. A **subject directory** lists general topics, such as arts and humanities, science, education, entertainment, sports, and health. After you select a broad topic, the directory will offer a list of possible subtopics from which to choose. Click on a subtopic and you'll get a group of more specific topics. Most subject directories also offer a search function.

As you use search engines, remember that you should always "surf the Web" with a purpose. Spending time exploring search engines and Web sites will give you an idea of the kinds of things available on the Internet. When you find something that could be of value later, print a page from the Web site as a reminder of what is there. File the sheet in a binder that you can refer back to or share with other students when you are looking for specific information.

The chart that follows lists some search engines and subject directories that will help you get around the Internet more quickly and efficiently.

Search Engines and Subject Directories		
Name	**Type**	**URL**
Alta Vista	search engine	http://www.altavista.com
The Argus Clearinghouse	subject directory	http://www.clearinghouse.net
Excite	search engine	http://www.excite.com
Galaxy	subject directory	http://www.galaxy.com
HotBot	search engine	http://www.hotbot.com
Infoseek	search engine	http://www.infoseek.com
Lycos	search engine	http://www.lycos.com
The Mining Company	subject directory	http://www.miningco.com
Yahoo!	subject directory	http://www.yahoo.com

Exercise 2

Using a search engine or a subject directory to locate appropriate Web sites, find the answers to the following questions.

1. Where is Richard Nixon's dog, Checkers, buried?
2. What role did actress Suzy Amis play in the movie *Titanic*?
3. What year was the Beatles' album *Abbey Road* released?
4. Where is the National Inventors Hall of Fame located?
5. How many people attended the first World Series game in 1903?
6. What was Lewis Carroll's given name?
7. Where was Jesse Hilton Stuart born?
8. Name two books written by Japanese author Yoko Kawashima Watkins.
9. What is the Statue of Liberty's complete name?
10. What is the medical name for Lou Gehrig's disease?

Exercise 3

Search for a subject with a single search engine. Then search for the same subject on a metasearch engine. Which engine provided the most results? Which provided the most helpful links?

Exercise 4

As a class, create five subject folders under the bookmark or favorites option of your browser. Bookmark at least five sites in each of the folders. Then create a directory for the classroom that lists the subject headings and the Web site addresses that provide useful information for those headings.

28.3 Evaluating Internet Sources

As you search the Internet and discover new Web sites, remember that anyone can create a Web site. What that means is that you cannot always be sure that the Web site information is correct. Newspapers, magazines, and books are reviewed by editors, but the Internet is a free-for-all. People and organizations who post information on the Internet are not required to follow any specific guidelines or rules. Therefore, it is your responsibility to determine what information is useful to you, whether that information is accurate, and how current the information is.

You'll want to make sure the sources you use in a presentation or research paper are reliable. How can you be sure? One way is to find out who owns the Web site or who created it. For instance, if you are looking for the batting average of a baseball player on the New York Yankees, you could probably rely on the official Yankees Web site to be accurate. However, if you find the data on a personal Web site created by a baseball fan, you may want to find a second source to back up the information.

When evaluating a Web site, ask these questions:

- What person, organization, or company is responsible for the Web site?
- When was the site last updated?
- Can the information presented there be verified?
- Does the site refer to other reliable sources for similar or related information?
- Does the site's text contain spelling mistakes, incorrect grammar, and typographical errors that make you suspicious about the reliability of the information?

Citing Sources

Just as you are expected to document the print sources you use when writing a report or giving a presentation, you are also expected to document information from the Internet. Sometimes Web sites disappear or change location, so if you do pull information from the Internet, you should always provide the URL, the title, and information about the author. You should also include the date that the material was available at that Web site and provide a printout of the information.

Works Cited

"Titanic Diary." <u>Encyclopedia Titanica</u>. 14 Oct. 1999

<http://atschool.eduweb.co.uk/phind/>.

"Titanic." <u>Encyclopaedia Britannica Online</u>. 15 Oct. 1999

<http://www.eb.com/boltopic?eu=745428sctn=1>.

Exercise 5

Working with a small group of classmates, create a checklist to use for evaluating Web sites. Include the basic information in your checklist (name of site, URL, etc.).

- Develop a scale by which to rank Web sites.

- Make copies of your checklist to pass out to other students in the class.

- Choose five different Web sites, and ask students to use your checklist to evaluate each of them.

- Use the results to present a brief summary of the five Web sites.

Troubleshooting Guide

As you work on the Web, you may need help in dealing with possible problems.

Here are some error messages that you might see as you spend time on the Web. They are followed by their possible causes and some suggestions for eliminating the errors.

Message: Unable to connect to server. The server may be down. Try connecting again later.

Possible Causes: The server is having technical problems. The site is being updated or is not communicating properly with your browser.

Suggestion: It usually helps if you try again in a few minutes; however, it could be a few days before the server is working properly.

Message: Unable to locate the server: www.server.com. The server does not have a DNS (Domain Name System) entry. Check the server name in the URL and try again.

Possible Causes: You have typed in the URL incorrectly, or the site no longer exists.

Suggestion: Be sure you have entered the URL correctly—check for proper capitalization and punctuation. If you have entered it correctly, try using a search engine to find the site. Keep in mind, though, the possibility that the site may have been abandoned.

Message: File Not Found: The requested URL was not found on this server.

Possible Causes: You have reached the server, but that particular file no longer exists or you have entered the path or filename incorrectly.

Suggestion: Check the URL again. If you have entered it correctly, try searching for the page from the server's home page.

Message: Network connection refused by the server. There was no response.

Possible Causes: You have reached the server, but it is too busy (too many other people are trying to access it) or temporarily shut down.

Suggestion: Try to access the site later.

Message: Connection timed out.

Possible Causes: Your browser attempted to contact the host, but the host took too long to reply.

Suggestion: Try to access the site later.

Message: Access denied. You do not have permission to open this item.

Possible Causes: The URL has moved, the Webmaster no longer allows public access to the site, or you have been denied access to the site.

Suggestion: Contact the Webmaster to verify the URL or try the site again in a few days. Sometimes there is nothing you can do if access has been denied. Many colleges, for example, allow access to parts of their sites only to faculty and registered students.

28.4 Using Other Internet Features: E-Mail

A popular feature of the Internet is electronic mail, or **e-mail.** E-mail programs allow you to receive, send, and forward e-mail messages. Millions of Americans send or receive e-mail every day. With the click of a button, you can send a message to anyone in the world. A feature called attachments, available with most e-mail software, lets you attach other files to the e-mail. You can send someone pictures of yourself, send a sound clip of a piece of music to a friend, or send a story you have written to a Web site that accepts and publishes submissions from young writers.

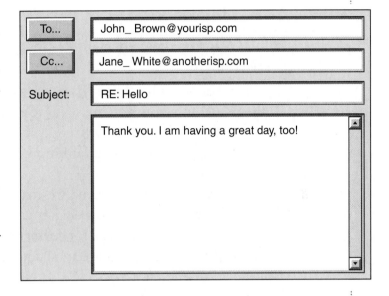

To send e-mail, you need an e-mail address. Like Web site addresses, e-mail addresses are unique. No two people can have the same e-mail address. Your Internet service provider will provide you with an e-mail address. You can also use another service, such as Yahoo!, to provide you with an e-mail account.

On many e-mail programs, you can store frequently used e-mail addresses in an address book. Then, when you want to send a message to a person whose address is in your address book, all you have to do is double-click on his or her name. You can also store additional information, such as the person's street address, birthday, and phone number, in your address book.

Just as you can send an e-mail message to anyone in the world, anyone in the world can send an e-mail message to you. Sometimes you will receive junk e-mail, or **spam.** It is similar to the junk mail your family receives at home. Advertisements are the main form of spam, and sometimes this kind of e-mail can be offensive. If you receive an e-mail from someone whose e-mail address you do not recognize, show it to an adult and do not write back unless the adult gives you permission. Some people send links to Web sites through e-mail. If you receive a message with a link to a Web site, show it to an adult before clicking on the link.

E-Mail Etiquette

When sending e-mail, follow the Internet rules of etiquette, called **Netiquette.**

- Use the subject line wisely. Be as brief as you can, but let the person to whom you are sending e-mail know what your message is about.
- Use appropriate capitalization. Using all capital letters is considered SHOUTING.
- Avoid sending unfriendly e-mail. Sending an unfriendly e-mail message is called "flaming."
- Check your message for correct spelling.
- Always include your e-mail address at the bottom of any message you send.
- Be careful when using humor or sarcasm. It can be difficult to indicate emotion in print. Use "smileys" if you want to show emotion. Smileys are also called emoticons, a term made up of the words *emotion* and *icons.* They are little faces made by the characters on a keyboard—for example:

:-) (a smile)		;-) (a wink)
:-((a frown)		:-D (laughing)

- Keep messages short and to the point.
- Remember that good behavior on the Internet is no different from good behavior in face-to-face situations. Treat others as you would like them to treat you.

Viruses and Security

A **virus** is a computer program that invades your computer by means of a normal program or message and may damage your system. A virus may be spread by e-mail, but more often it occurs when you download a software program and run it on your computer. All computers that are connected to the Internet should have virus-protection software. You can obtain such software from your service provider or your local computer store, or you can even download a program from the Internet.

A **hacker** is a computer criminal who may steal valuable data from your computer. A hacker may "tap" into your computer from another location and read through all of your program files. That is why it is important to choose your password carefully. A password for e-mail or other accounts should be random and meaningless, yet easy to remember. Don't tell anyone your password. If you must write it down to remember it, don't leave it near a computer. Most programs that require a password will allow you to change your password if you think somebody might know it. If you do think somebody has your password, let an adult know.

Message Boards and Mailing Lists

A **message board**, also known as a bulletin board, is a place on a Web site where people with similar interests can post and read messages on a specific topic. Message boards are found on certain Web sites and commercial online services, such as America Online. Anyone can post messages on a message board, but the Web site generally asks a user to register first with a full name and an e-mail address. As you surf the Web, look for Web sites that have message boards. If you have a comment or question about a Web site, post your message on its message board. You can use message boards on certain Web sites to post reviews of books, CDs, and movies.

If there is a particular subject that you need to research, you might want to consider subscribing to a **mailing list** concerned with your topic. A mailing list is like a bulletin board on which you exchange information through e-mail. Since there are more than 25,000 mailing lists, there's a good chance that there's one on a topic that might interest you. Use a search engine to find a mailing list that discusses your topic of interest. Use *listserv* as a keyword. Once you find and join a mailing list, you will receive e-mail messages from people discussing your subject of interest. Before you post your own messages on the mailing list, read the list's rules and FAQ (frequently asked questions) file and study the postings until you are familiar with the type of discussion the group is having. You can cancel your subscription to a mailing list at any time.

Exercise 6

Find a Web site that allows you to post reviews of books, movies, or CDs. Choose a book, movie, or CD that you have a strong opinion about and review it. Print the Web page that lists your review and share it with the rest of the class.

Exercise 7

With the help of your teacher, select a class at an elementary school to trade e-mail with. Ask the younger students to send you any questions they might have about the Internet or e-mail. Work together, doing research if necessary, to answer the questions and send them back to the students. As a class, discuss the responses to the questions.

28.5 Other Electronic Resources

In your search for information, you may use other sources of electronic information besides the Internet. CD-ROMs and DVDs store information electronically and can be borrowed from or used at a library. They can also be purchased. As with other electronic data, you must have a computer to access their stored information.

CD-ROMs

A **CD-ROM**, or Compact Disc–Read-Only Memory, looks like an audio compact disc, but it stores more than just audio information. **Read-only memory** is computer memory on which data has been prerecorded. Once data has been written onto a CD-ROM, it cannot be removed or changed; it can only be read by the computer. A CD-ROM can store text, graphics, and video files.

Because CD-ROMs can store large amounts of information, many dictionaries, encyclopedias, and other reference works are stored on them. In fact, one CD-ROM can store as much information as hundreds of diskettes. You can use CD-ROMs to read text and look at pictures. You can also use them to view video and audio files of historic events. To use a CD-ROM, your computer must have a CD-ROM drive. Such drives are standard on most new computers.

DVDs

A **DVD**, or Digital VideoDisc, can store up to six times the data of a CD-ROM on the same surface area. Similar in size and shape to a CD-ROM, a DVD can hold enough information for a full-length movie. Like a VCR, a DVD player can be used to watch movies, and like a CD-ROM, a DVD requires a special drive on the computer. Some computers now come equipped with DVD drives, which may eventually replace CD-ROM drives. Although a DVD drive can play CD-ROMs, a CD-ROM drive cannot play DVDs.

Removable Storage

Your computer uses a built-in hard drive that stores information. All computers also include a drive for removable discs that can increase your storage capacity. You can insert a removable disc into another computer and transfer files to it. These removable discs can also be used to send information to someone else or to store files as a backup in case your hard drive crashes and you lose the information there.

Diskettes, also called floppy disks, have been commonly used for years to store text documents. The average computer user still uses diskettes to store information, although most software is now being distributed on a CD-ROM. The use of diskettes, however, may be coming to an end. Many computers now come with Zip drives, and some have abandoned diskette drives altogether. A Zip disc can hold as much information as about seventy diskettes. As more people get more involved in multimedia, they need storage devices that can hold the larger multimedia files.

Digital Magnetic tape for a computer is similar to tape for an audiocassette player. The tape stores information on a magnetically coated strip of plastic. The tape can store large amounts of information, but it is not as convenient to use as a CD-ROM or a diskette. It is more difficult to access information from a magnetic tape. If you need to view information that is at the end of a tape, you must sort through all of the information on the tape until you find it. CD-ROMs and diskettes let you choose the information you wish to view with the click of a button. Magnetic tape is used mostly for backing up information or storing large quantities of information that do not have to be accessed quickly.

Exercise 8

A CD-ROM incorporates many different elements (text, audio, graphics, video). Work in a small group to select a subject that could be presented on a CD-ROM. Use a library, the Internet, or other resources to find information that you could include on your CD-ROM.

For the audio portion of your CD-ROM, find audiocassettes or CDs that could provide music or spoken word segments. For the visual portion, make drawings of what you would include. If possible, use a video camera to record images to illustrate your subject. After you have compiled all the elements, prepare an audio and visual presentation similar to one that you would find on a CD-ROM and present it to the class.

WRITING AND LANGUAGE
GLOSSARY

This glossary will help you quickly find definitions used in writing and grammar.

A

Adjective. A word that modifies, or describes, a noun or a pronoun. An adjective may tell *what kind, which one, how many, or how much.*

The **comparative degree** of an adjective compares two people, places, things, or ideas. (*worse, sadder*)

The **superlative degree** of an adjective compares more than two people, places, things, or ideas. (*worst, saddest*)

A **possessive adjective** is a possessive noun or pronoun used before a noun. (*John's, my*)

A **predicate adjective** always follows a linking verb. It modifies the subject of the sentence.

A **proper adjective** is formed from a proper noun. It always begins with a capital letter.

A **demonstrative adjective** is the word *this, that, these,* or *those* used before a noun.

Adjective clause. A dependent clause that modifies a noun or pronoun.

Adverb. A word that modifies a verb, an adjective, or another adverb. Adverbs may tell *how, when, where, in what manner,* and *how often.*

Some adverbs have different forms to indicate **comparative** and **superlative degrees.** (*loud, louder, loudest; sweetly, more sweetly, most sweetly*)

Adverb clause. A dependent clause that modifies a verb, an adjective, or an adverb.

Allusion. A reference in a piece of writing to a well-known character, place, or situation from a work of literature, music, or art or from history.

Analysis. The act of breaking down a subject into separate parts to determine its meaning.

Anecdote. A short story or incident usually presented as part of a longer narrative.

Antecedent. *See* Pronoun.

Appositive. A noun placed next to another noun to identify it or add information about it. (My basketball coach, *Ms. Lopes,* called for a time out.)

Argument. A statement, reason, or fact for or against a point; a piece of writing intended to persuade.

Article. The adjectives *a, an,* and *the.* *A* and *an* are **indefinite articles.** They refer to any one item of a group. *The* is a **definite article.** It indicates that the noun it precedes is a specific person, place, or thing.

Audience. The person(s) who reads or listens to what the writer or speaker says.

B

Base form. *See* Verb tense.

Bias. A tendency to think a certain way. Bias may affect the way a writer or speaker presents his or her ideas.

Bibliography. A list of the books, articles, and other sources used as reference sources in a research paper.

Body. The central part of a composition that communicates and explains the main idea identified in the introduction.

Bookmarks/favorites. The feature on many Web browsers that allows the user to save addresses of Internet sites so that the sites can be accessed quickly.

Brainstorming. A group activity in which people generate as many ideas as possible without stopping to judge them.

C

Case. The form of a noun or pronoun that is determined by its use in a sentence. A noun or pronoun is in the **nominative** case when it is used as a subject, in the **objective** case when it is used as an object, and in the **possessive** case when it is used to show possession.

Cause-and-effect chain. A series of events in which one cause leads to an effect that in turn leads to another effect, and so on.

Characterization. The methods a writer uses to develop the personality of the character. A writer may make direct statements about a character's personality or reveal it through the character's words and actions or through what other characters think and say about the character.

Chronological order. The arrangement of details according to when events or actions take place.

Clarity. The quality of a piece of writing that makes it easy to understand.

Clause. A group of words that has a subject and a predicate and that is used as part of a sentence.

An **independent clause,** also called a **main clause,** has a subject and a predicate and can stand alone as a sentence.

A **dependent clause,** also called a **subordinate clause,** has a subject and a predicate, but it makes sense only when attached to a main clause.

Cliché. An overused expression. (*white as snow*)

Clustering. The grouping together of related items as a way of organizing information.

Coherence. A quality of logical connection between the parts of a paragraph or composition.

Cohesive writing. A type of writing in which sentences and paragraphs are logically connected to one another.

Collaboration. The process of working with others on writing or other projects.

Colloquialism. A casual, colorful expression used in everyday conversation.

Comparative degree. *See* Adjective; Adverb.

Comparison-and-contrast organization. A way of organizing ideas by illustrating their similarities and differences.

Complement. A word or phrase that completes the meaning of a verb. Three kinds of complements are **direct objects, indirect objects,** and **subject complements.**

Conceptual map. A graphic device that develops a central concept by surrounding it with examples or related ideas in a weblike arrangement.

Conclusion. A restatement or summing up of the ideas in a composition that brings it to a definite close.

Conflict. The struggle between two opposing forces that lies at the center of the plot in a story or drama.

Conjunction. A word that joins single words or groups of words.

A **coordinating conjunction** (*and, but, or, nor, for, yet*) joins words or groups of words that are equal in grammatical importance. **Correlative conjunctions** (*both . . . and, just as. . . so, not only. . . but also, either. . . or, neither. . . nor*) are pairs of words used to connect words or phrases in a sentence.

Connotation. The thoughts and feelings associated with a word, rather than its dictionary definition.

Constructive criticism. Comments on another person's writing made with the intention of helping the writer improve a particular draft.

Context. The words and sentences that come before and after a specific word and help to explain its meaning.

Coordinating conjunction. *See* Conjunction.

Correlative conjunction. *See* Conjunction.

Credibility. The quality of a speaker or writer that makes that person's words believable.

Declarative sentence. A sentence that makes a statement.

Deductive reasoning. A way of thinking or explaining that begins with a general statement or principle and applies that principle to specific instances.

Definite article. *See* Article.

Demonstrative adjective. *See* Adjective.

Denotation. The dictionary definition of a word.

Dependent clause. *See* Clause.

Descriptive writing. Writing that uses sensory detail to convey a dominant impression of, for example, a setting, a person, an animal, and so on.

Desktop publishing. The use of computer programs to format and produce a document that may include written text, graphics, and/or images.

Dialect. A variation of a language spoken by a particular group of people. A dialect may be regional (based on location) or ethnic (based on cultural heritage).

Dialogue. The conversation between characters in a written work.

Diction. A writer's choice of words and the arrangement of those words in phrases, sentences, or lines of a poem.

Direct object. *See* Complement.

Documentation. Identification of the sources used in writing research or other informative papers; usually in the form of endnotes or footnotes, or using parenthetical documentation.

Drafting. One of the steps in the writing process; the transforming of thoughts, words, and phrases into sentences and paragraphs.

Editing. One of the steps in the writing process in which a revised draft is checked for standard usage, varied sentence structure, and appropriate word choice.

Editorial. An article in a newspaper or other form of media that expresses an opinion about a topic of general interest.

Elaboration. The support or development of a main idea with facts, statistics, sensory details, incidents, anecdotes, examples, or quotations.

Ellipsis. A mark of punctuation, consisting of three spaced periods, that shows the omission of a word or words.

E-mail. Short for electronic mail. Messages, usually text, sent from one person to another by way of computer.

Evaluating. Making a judgment about the strengths and weaknesses of a draft in content, organization, and style.

Evidence. Facts or examples from reliable sources that can be used to support statements made in speaking or writing.

Exclamatory sentence. A sentence that expresses strong or sudden emotion.

Explanatory writing. *See* Expository writing.

Expository writing. A kind of writing that aims at informing and explaining. Examples of expository writing are news articles, how-to instructions, and research papers.

Expressive writing. Writing that emphasizes and conveys the writer's feelings.

Fact. A piece of information that can be verified.

Feedback. The response a listener or reader gives to a speaker or writer about his or her work.

Figurative language. Words used for descriptive effect that express some truth beyond the literal level. Figures of speech such as similes, metaphors, or personification are examples of figurative language.

Formal language. Language that uses correct grammar and omits slang expressions and contractions. It is especially common in nonfiction writing that is not personal.

Fragment. An incomplete sentence punctuated as if it were complete.

Freewriting. A way of finding ideas by writing freely, without stopping or limiting the flow of ideas, often for a specific length of time.

Future tense. *See* Verb tense.

Generalization. A statement that presents a conclusion about a subject without going into details or specifics.

Genre. A division of literature. The main literary genres are prose, poetry, and drama. Each of these is further divided into subgenres.

Gerund. A verb form ending in *–ing* that is used as a noun.

Graphic organizer. A visual way of organizing information; types of graphic organizers are charts, graphs, clusters, and idea trees.

Home page. The location on a Web site by which a user normally enters the site. A typical home page may explain the site, summarize the content, and provide links to other sites.

Hyperlink. Highlighted or underlined phrases or words on a Web page that, when clicked, move the user to another part of the page or to another Web page.

Hypertext. Links in some electronic text that take the user to another document or to a different section in the same document.

Idiom. A word or phrase that has a special meaning different from its standard or dictionary meaning. (*Burning the midnight oil* is an idiom that means "staying up late.")

Imagery. Language that emphasizes sensory impressions that can help the reader of a literary work to see, hear, feel, smell, and taste the scenes described in the work.

Imperative sentence. A sentence that makes a request or gives a command.

Indefinite article. *See* Article.

Indefinite pronoun. *See* Pronoun.

Independent clause. *See* Clause.

Inductive reasoning. A way of thinking or explaining that begins with a series of examples and uses them to arrive at a general statement.

Infinitive. A verbal made up of the word *to* and the base form of a word. An infinitive often functions as a noun in a sentence.

Informative writing. A kind of writing that explains something, such as a process or an idea. *See also* Expository writing.

Intensifier. An adverb that emphasizes an adjective or another adverb. (*very* important; *quite* easily)

Interjection. A word or phrase that expresses strong feeling. An interjection has no grammatical connection to other words in the sentence.

Internet. A worldwide computer network that allows users to link to any computer on the network electronically for social, commercial, research, and other purposes.

Interpretation. An explanation of the meaning of a piece of writing, a visual representation, or any other type of communication.

Interview. A question-and-answer dialogue that has the specific purpose of gathering up-to-date or expert information.

Intransitive verb. *See* Verb.

Introduction. The beginning part of a piece of writing, in which a writer identifies the subject and gives a general idea of what the body of the composition will contain.

Inverted order. The placement of a predicate before the subject in a sentence. In most sentences in English, the subject comes before the predicate.

Irregular verb. *See* Verb tense.

J

Jargon. Special words and phrases used by a particular trade, profession, or other group of people.

Journal. A personal notebook in which a person can freewrite, collect ideas, and record thoughts and experiences.

L–M

Learning log. A journal used for clarifying ideas about concepts covered in various classes.

Lexicon. A wordbook or dictionary.

Listing. A technique for finding ideas for writing.

Literary analysis. The act of examining the different elements of a piece of literature in order to evaluate it.

Logical fallacy. An error in reasoning often found in advertising or persuasive writing. Either-or reasoning and glittering generalities are types of logical fallacies.

Main clause. *See* Clause.

Main idea. *See* Thesis statement.

Main verb. The most important word in a verb phrase.

Media. The forms of communication used to reach an audience; forms such as newspapers, radio, TV, and the Internet reach large audiences and so are known as mass media.

Memoir. A type of narrative nonfiction that presents an account of an event or period in history, emphasizing the narrator's personal experience.

Metaphor. A figure of speech that compares seemingly unlike things without using words such as *like* or *as*. (*He is a rock.*)

Mood. The feeling or atmosphere of a piece of writing.

Multimedia presentation. The use of a variety of media, such as video, sound, written text, and visual art to present ideas or information.

N

Narrative writing. A type of writing that tells about events or actions as they change over a period of time and often includes story elements such as character, setting, and plot.

Nonfiction. Prose writing about real people, places, and events.

Noun. A word that names a person, a place, a thing, an idea, a quality, or a characteristic.

Noun clause. A dependent clause used as a noun.

Number. The form of a noun, pronoun, or verb that indicates whether it refers to one (**singular**) or more than one (**plural**).

O

Object. *See* Complement.

Onomatopoeia. The use of a word or phrase that imitates or suggests the sound of what it describes. (*rattle, boom*)

Opinion. A belief or attitude that cannot be proven true or false.

Oral tradition. Literature that passes by word of mouth from one generation to the next. The oral tradition of a culture may reflect the cultural values of the people.

Order of importance. A way of arranging details in a paragraph or other piece of writing according to their importance.

Organization. A system of ordering ideas.

Outline. A systematic arrangement of main and supporting ideas, using Roman numerals, letters, and numbers, for a written or an oral presentation.

P

Paragraph. A unit of writing that consists of related sentences.

Parallel construction. The use of a series of words, phrases, or sentences that have similar grammatical form.

Paraphrase. A restatement of someone's ideas in words that are different from the original passage but retain its ideas, tone, and general length.

Parenthetical documentation. A specific reference to the source of a piece of information, placed in parenthesis directly after the information appears in a piece of writing.

Participle. A verb form that can function as an adjective. Present participles always end in -*ing*. Although past participles often end in -*ed,* they can take other forms as well.

Peer response. The suggestions and comments provided by peers, or classmates, about a piece of writing or another type of presentation.

Personal pronoun. *See* Pronoun.

Personal writing. Writing that expresses the writer's own thoughts and feelings.

Personification. A figure of speech that gives human qualities to an animal, object, or idea.

Perspective. *See* Point of view.

Persuasion. A type of writing that aims at convincing people to think or act in a certain way.

Phrase. A group of words that acts in a sentence as a single part of speech.

A **prepositional phrase** begins with a preposition and ends with a noun or a pronoun. A **verb phrase** consists of one or more auxiliary verbs followed by a main verb.

Plagiarism. The dishonest presentation of another's words or ideas as one's own.

Plot. The series of events that follow one another in a story, novel, or play.

Plural. *See* Number.

Poetry. A form of literary expression that emphasizes the line as the unit of composition. Traditional poetry contains emotional, imaginative language and a regular rhythm.

Point of view. The angle, or perspective, from which a story is told, such as first- or third-person.

Portfolio. A collection of various pieces of writing, which may include finished pieces and works in progress.

Predicate. The verb or verb phrase and any of its modifiers that make an essential statement about the subject of a sentence.

Predicate adjective. *See* Adjective.

Preposition. A word that shows the relationship of a noun or pronoun to some other word in the sentence.

Prepositional phrase. *See* Phrase.

Presenting. The last step in the writing process; involves sharing the final writing product with others in some way.

Present tense. *See* Verb tense.

Prewriting. The first stage in the writing process; includes deciding what to write about, collecting ideas and details, and making an outline or a plan. Prewriting strategies include brainstorming and using graphic organizers, notes, and logs.

Prior knowledge. The facts, ideas, and experiences that a writer, reader, or viewer brings to a new activity.

Progressive form. *See* Verb tense.

Pronoun. A word that takes the place of a noun, a group of words acting as a noun, or another pronoun. The word or group of words that a pronoun refers to is called its **antecedent.**
A **personal pronoun** refers to a specific person or thing.

Pronoun case. *See* Case.

Proofreading. The final part of the editing process that involves checking work to discover typographical and other errors.

Propaganda. Information aimed at influencing thoughts and actions; it is usually of a political nature and may contain distortions of truth.

Proper adjective. *See* Adjective.

Prose. Writing that is similar to everyday speech and written language, as opposed to poetry and drama.

Publishing. The preparation of a finished piece of writing often involving available technology, so that it can be presented to a larger audience.

Purpose. The aim of writing, which may be to express, discover, record, develop, reflect on ideas, problem solve, entertain, influence, inform, or describe.

 R

Regular verb. *See* Verb tense.

Representation. A way in which information or ideas are presented to an audience.

Research. The search for information on a topic.

Review. The analysis and interpretation of a subject, often presented through the mass media.

Revising. The stage of the writing process in

which a writer goes over a draft, making changes in its content, organization, and style in order to improve it. Revision techniques include adding, elaborating, deleting, combining, and rearranging text.

Root. The part of a word that carries the main meaning.

Run-on sentence. Two or more sentences or clauses run together without appropriate punctuation.

Sensory details. Language that appeals to the senses; sensory details are important elements of descriptive writing, especially of poetry.

Sentence. A group of words expressing a complete thought. Every sentence has a **subject** and a **predicate.** *See also* Subject; Predicate; Clause.

A **simple sentence** has only one main clause and no subordinate clauses.

A **compound sentence** has two or more main clauses. Each main clause of a compound sentence has its own subject and predicate, and these main clauses are usually joined by a comma and a coordinating conjunction. A semicolon can also be used to join the main clauses in a compound sentence.

A **complex sentence** has one main clause and one or more subordinate clauses.

Sentence variety. The use of different types of sentences to add interest to writing.

Setting. The time and place in which the events of a story, novel, or play takes place.

Simile. A figure of speech that compares two basically unlike things, using words such as *like* or *as.*

Simple sentence. *See* Sentence.

Spatial order. A way of presenting the details of a setting according to their location—for example, from left to right or from top to bottom.

Standard English. The most widely used and accepted form of the English language

Style. The writer's choice and arrangement of words and sentences.

Subject. The noun or pronoun that tells who or what the sentence is about.

Subordinate clause. *See* Clause.

Summary. A brief statement of the main idea of a composition.

Supporting evidence. *See* Evidence.

Suspense. A literary device that creates growing interest and excitement leading up to the climax and resolution of a story. A writer creates suspense by providing clues to the resolution without revealing too much information.

Symbol. An object, a person, a place, or an experience that represents something else, usually something abstract.

Tense. *See* Verb tense.

Theme. The main idea or message of a piece of writing.

Thesis statement. A one- or two-sentence statement of the main idea or purpose of a piece of writing.

Time order. The arrangement of details in a piece of writing based on when they occurred.

Tone. A reflection of a writer's or speaker's attitude toward a subject.

Topic sentence. A sentence that expresses the main idea of a paragraph.

Transition. A connecting word or phrase that clarifies relationships between details, sentences, or paragraphs.

Unity. A quality of oneness in a paragraph or composition that exists when all the sentences or paragraphs work together to express or support one main idea.

URL. The standard form of an Internet address; stands for Uniform Resource Locator.

Venn diagram. A graphic organizer consisting of two overlapping circles; used to compare two items that have both similar and different traits.

Verb. A word that expresses an action or a state of being and is necessary to make a statement.

Verbal. A verb form that functions in a sentence as a noun, an adjective, or an adverb. The three kinds of verbals are participles, gerunds, and infinitives. *See also* Gerund; Infinitive; Participle.

Verb phrase. *See* Phrase.

Verb tense. The form a verb takes to show when an action takes place. The **present tense** names an action that happens regularly. The **past tense** names an action that has happened, and the **future tense** names an action that will take place in the future. All the verb tenses are formed from the four principal parts of a verb: a **base form** (*freeze*), a **present participle** (*freezing*), a **simple past** form (*froze*) and a **past participle** (*frozen*). A **regular verb** forms its simple past and past participle by adding *-ed* to the base form. Verbs that form their past and past participle in some other way are called **irregular verbs**.

In addition to present, past, and future tense, there are three perfect tenses—present perfect, past perfect, and future perfect. Each of the six tenses has a **progressive** form that expresses a continuing action.

Voice. The distinctive use of language that conveys the writer's or narrator's personality to the reader. Sentence structure, word choice, and tone are elements that communicate voice.

Web site. A location on the World Wide Web that can be reached through links or by accessing a Web address, or URL. *See* URL.

Word Processing. The use of a computer for the writing and editing of written text.

World Wide Web. A global system that uses the Internet and allows users to create, link, and access fields of information. *See* Internet.

Writing process. The series of stages or steps that a writer goes through to develop ideas and to communicate them.

GLOSARIO
DE ESCRITURA Y LENGUAJE

Este glosario permite encontrar fácilmente definiciones de gramática inglesa y términos que usan los escritores.

Adjective/Adjetivo. Palabra que modifica, o describe, un nombre (*noun*) o pronombre (*pronoun*). Un adjetivo *indica qué tipo, cuál, cuántos o cuánto.*

> **Comparative degree/Grado comparativo.** Adjetivo que compara a dos personas, lugares, cosas o ideas (*worse, sadder;* en español: *peor, más triste*).

> **Superlative degree/Grado superlativo.** Adjetivo que compara más de dos personas, lugares, cosas o ideas (*worst, saddest;* en español: *el peor, la más triste*).

> **Possessive adjective/Adjetivo posesivo.** Pronombre posesivo que va antes del nombre.

> **Predicative adjective/Adjetivo predicativo.** Siempre va después de un verbo copulativo y modifica al sujeto de la oración.

> **Proper adjective/Adjetivo propio*.** Adjetivo que se deriva de un nombre propio; en inglés siempre se escribe con mayúscula.

> **Demonstrative adjective/Adjetivo demostrativo.** Se usa antes del nombre: *this, that, these, those (este, ese, aquel, estos, esos, aquellos).*

Adjective clause/Proposición adjetiva. Proposición dependiente que modifica un nombre o un pronombre.

Adverb/Adverbio. Palabra que modifica a un verbo, adjetivo u otro adverbio. Los adverbios indican *cómo, cuándo, dónde, de qué manera* y *qué tan seguido* sucede algo. Algunos adverbios tienen diferentes formas para indicar los grados **comparativo** (*comparative*) y **superlativo** (*superlative*) (*loud, louder, loudest; sweetly, more sweetly, most sweetly;* en español: *fuerte, más fuerte, lo más fuerte; dulcemente, más dulcemente, lo más dulcemente*).

Adverb clause/Proposición adverbial. Proposición dependiente que modifica un verbo, un adjetivo o un adverbio.

Allusion/Alusión. Referencia en un texto escrito a un personaje, lugar o situación muy conocidos de una obra literaria, musical, artística o histórica.

Analysis/Análisis. Acción de descomponer un tema o escrito en distintas partes para encontrar su significado.

Anecdote/Anécdota. Narración breve o incidente que se presenta como parte de una narrativa más larga.

Antecedent/Antecedente. *Ver Pronoun.*

Appositive/Apositivo. Nombre colocado junto a otro para identificarlo o agregar información sobre él. (Mi entrenadora de baloncesto, *Ms. Lopes*, pidió tiempo fuera.)

Argument/Argumento. Afirmación, razón o hecho en favor o en contra de algún comentario; texto escrito que trata de persuadir.

Article/Artículo. Nombre dado a las palabras *a*, *an* y *the* (en español: *un, uno/a, el, la*). *A* y *an* son artículos **indefinidos** (*indefinite articles*), que se refieren a cualquier cosa de un grupo. *The* es un artículo **definido** (*definite article*); indica que el nombre al que precede es una persona, lugar o cosa específicos.

Audience/Público. Persona (o personas) que lee o escucha lo que dicen un escritor o un hablante.

B

Base form/Base derivativa. *Ver Verb tense.*

Bias/Tendencia. Inclinación a pensar de cierta manera. La tendencia influye en la manera en que un escritor o hablante presenta sus ideas.

Bibliography/Bibliografía. Lista de los libros, artículos y otras fuentes que se utilizan como referencia en una investigación.

Body/Cuerpo. Parte central de una composición que comunica la idea principal identificada en la introducción.

Bookmarks/favorites/Marcadores/favoritos. Característica de muchos buscadores de red que permiten guardar direcciones de Internet para entrar a ellas rápidamente.

Brainstorming/Lluvia de ideas. Actividad de grupo en que se generan tantas ideas como sea posible sin detenerse a analizarlas.

C

Case/Caso. Forma de un nombre o pronombre que está determinado por su uso en la oración. El nombre o pronombre está en caso **nominativo** (*nominative case*) cuando se utiliza como sujeto; en caso **acusativo** y **dativo** (*objective case*) cuando recibe la acción del verbo, y en caso **posesivo*** (*possessive case*)

cuando se utiliza para indicar posesión o propiedad.

Cause-and-effect chain/Cadena de causa y efecto. Serie de acontecimientos en que una causa lleva a un efecto que, a su vez, lleva a otro efecto, y así sucesivamente.

Characterization/Caracterización. Métodos que utiliza un escritor para crear sus personajes. Puede ser describiendo directamente su personalidad, o revelándola con sus palabras y acciones, o bien a partir de lo que otros personajes piensan y dicen de él.

Chronological order/Orden cronológico. Organización de detalles de acuerdo con el tiempo en que sucedieron los acontecimientos o acciones.

Clarity/Claridad. Cualidad de un escrito que lo hace fácil de entender.

Clause/Proposición. Grupo de palabras que consta de sujeto y predicado, y que se usa como parte de una oración compuesta.

> **Independent clause/Proposición independiente.** También llamada **proposición principal** (*main clause*); tiene sujeto y predicado y hace sentido por sí misma.
> **Dependent clause/Proposición dependiente.** También llamada **proposición subordinada** (*subordinate clause*); tiene sujeto y predicado pero depende de la proposición principal.

Cliché/Cliché. Expresión usada con demasiada frecuencia (*blanco como la nieve*).

Clustering/Agrupamiento. Reunión de temas relacionados para organizar la información.

Coherence/Coherencia. Relación lógica entre las partes de un párrafo o composición.

Cohesive writing/Escritura coherente. Tipo de escritura en que las oraciones y párrafos están lógicamente relacionados entre sí.

Collaboration/Colaboración. Proceso de trabajar en equipo para escribir un texto o realizar un proyecto.

Colloquialism/Expresión coloquial. Expresión informal y pintoresca que se utiliza en la conversación diaria.

Comparative degree/Grado comparativo. *Ver Adjective; Adverb.*

Comparison-and-contrast/Comparación y contraste. Manera de organizar ideas, señalando sus similitudes y diferencias.

Complement/Complemento (u objeto). Palabra o frase que complementa el significado de un verbo. Tres complementos son: **directo** (*direct object*), **indirecto** (*indirect object*) y **predicativo (atributo)** (*subject complement*).

Conceptual map/Mapa conceptual. Recurso gráfico que desarrolla un concepto central rodeándolo con ejemplos o ideas relacionadas a manera de red.

Conclusion/Conclusión. Afirmación que resume las ideas de una composición, antes de ponerle punto final.

Conflict/Conflicto. Lucha entre dos fuerzas opuestas que constituye el elemento central de la trama en un cuento u obra de teatro.

Conjunction/Conjunción. Palabra que une palabras o grupos de palabras.

> **Coordinating conjunction/Conjunción coordinante.** Las palabras *and, but, or, nor, for, yet* (*y, pero, o, no, para, aun*) unen palabras o grupos de palabras que tienen igual importancia gramatical.
>
> **Correlative conjunction/Conjunción correlativa*.** Las palabras *both . . . and, just as . . . so, not only . . . but also, either . . . or, neither . . . nor* (*tanto . . . como, así como, no sólo . . . sino, o . . . o*) son palabras en pares que vinculan palabras o frases en una oración.

Connotation/Connotación. Pensamientos y sentimientos relacionados con una palabra, más que con su definición de diccionario.

Constructive criticism/Crítica constructiva. Comentario sobre lo que escribe otra persona, con la intención de ayudar a que mejore el borrador.

Context/Contexto. Palabras y oraciones que vienen antes y después de una palabra y ayudan a explicar su significado.

Coordinating conjunction/Conjunción coordinante. *Ver Conjunction.*

Correlative conjunction/Conjunción correlativa*. *Ver Conjunction.*

Credibility/Credibilidad. Cualidad de un hablante o escritor que hace creer sus palabras.

D

Declarative sentence/Oración afirmativa. Oración que declara algo.

Deductive reasoning/Razonamiento deductivo. Pensamiento o explicación que parte de una afirmación o principio generales y los aplica a casos específicos.

Definite article/Artículo definido. *Ver Article.*

Demonstrative adjective/Adjetivo demostrativo. *Ver Adjective.*

Denotation/Denotación. Definición de una palabra que da el diccionario.

Dependent clause/Proposición dependiente. *Ver Clause.*

Descriptive writing/Escritura descriptiva. Tipo de escritura que ofrece detalles sensoriales para comunicar la impresión de un escenario, persona, animal, etcétera.

Desktop publishing/Edición por computadora. Uso de programas de computadora para formar un documento con texto escrito, gráficas y/o imágenes.

Dialect/Dialecto. Variedad de lenguaje hablado que usa un grupo particular. Un dialecto puede ser regional (de un lugar) o étnico (de un grupo cultural).

Dialogue/Diálogo. Conversación entre personajes en un escrito.

Diction/Dicción. Palabras que escoge un escritor y cómo las utiliza en frases, oraciones o versos.

Direct object/Complemento directo. *Ver Complement.*

Documentation/Documentación. Identificación de las fuentes que se emplean para escribir un artículo u otros textos informativos; generalmente se ponen como notas al pie, al final del texto o entre paréntesis.

Drafting/Borrador. Paso del proceso de escritura; transformación de ideas, palabras y frases a oraciones y párrafos.

E

Editing/Edición. Paso del proceso de escritura en que se revisa que el borrador corregido tenga un lenguaje estándar, una estructura sintáctica variada y la elección adecuada de palabras.

Editorial/Editorial. Artículo en un periódico u otro medio que expresa una opinión sobre un tema de interés general.

Elaboration/Elaboración. Sustento o desarrollo de una idea principal con hechos, estadísticas, detalles sensoriales, incidentes, anécdotas, ejemplos o citas.

Ellipsis/Puntos suspensivos. Signo de puntuación que consiste en dejar tres puntos para indicar que se están suprimiendo una o varias palabras.

E-mail/Correo electrónico. Mensajes, generalmente textos, que se envían por computadora.

Evaluating/Evaluación. Juicio sobre las fallas y aciertos de un borrador en cuanto a contenido, organización y estilo.

Evidence/Evidencia. Datos o ejemplos de fuentes confiables que sirven para sustentar afirmaciones escritas o habladas.

Exclamatory sentence/Oración exclamativa. Oración que expresa una emoción fuerte o repentina.

Explanatory writing/Texto explicativo. *Ver Descriptive text.*

Expository writing/Texto descriptivo. Tipo de escritura que informa o explica, como artículos periodísticos, instrucciones y artículos de investigación.

Expressive writing/Texto expresivo. Texto que realza y transmite los sentimientos del escritor.

F

Fact/Hecho. Información que puede comprobarse.

Feedback/Retroalimentación. Respuesta del escucha o lector al mensaje de un hablante o escritor.

Figurative language/Lenguaje figurado. Palabras usadas con un efecto descriptivo que expresa una verdad más allá del nivel literal. Los tropos, como el símil, la metáfora y la personificación, son ejemplos de lenguaje figurado.

Formal language/Lenguaje formal. Lenguaje que utiliza una gramática correcta y omite contracciones y expresiones coloquiales. Es común en textos de no ficción, que no son de carácter personal.

Fragment/Fragmento. Oración incompleta con puntuación de oración completa.

Freewriting/Escritura libre. Búsqueda de ideas escribiendo durante un tiempo determinado, sin detenerse ni limitar el flujo de ideas.

Future tense/Tiempo futuro. *Ver Verb tense.*

G-H

Generalization/Generalización. Afirmación que presenta una conclusión sobre un tema sin dar detalles específicos.

Genre/Género. Clasificación literaria o de otro medio. Los principales géneros literarios son la prosa, la poesía y el drama. Cada uno se divide en subgéneros.

Gerund/Gerundio. Verboide que termina en –*ing* y se usa como nombre (en inglés).

Graphic organizer/Organizador gráfico. Manera visual de organizar la información, como las tablas, las gráficas, las redes y los árboles de ideas.

Home page/Página principal. Página por medio de la cual un usuario entra normalmente a un sitio de Web. Por lo general, explica el sitio, resume el contenido y proporciona vínculos con otros sitios.

Hyperlink/Hipervínculo. Oraciones o palabras sombreadas o subrayadas en una página en red que al activarse con un clic conectan con otra parte de la página o con otra página de la red.

Hypertext/Hipertexto. Vínculos en textos electrónicos que llevan a otro documento o a una sección distinta del mismo documento.

I-J

Idiom/Modismo. Palabra o frase cuyo significado es diferente del significado estándar o de diccionario. (*Se le pegaron las sábanas* es un modismo que significa "se levantó muy tarde").

Imagery/Imaginería. Lenguaje que describe impresiones sensoriales para que el lector de un texto literario pueda ver, oír, sentir, oler y gustar las escenas descritas.

Imperative sentence/Oración imperativa. Oración que exige u ordena algo.

Indefinite article/Artículo indefinido. *Ver Article.*

Indefinite pronoun/Pronombre indefinido. *Ver Pronoun.*

Independent clause/Proposición independiente. *Ver Clause.*

Inductive reasoning/Razonamiento inductivo. Pensamiento o explicación que parte de varios ejemplos para llegar a una afirmación general.

Infinitive/Infinitivo. Verboide que consta de la palabra *to* y la base del verbo (en español terminan en -*ar*, -*er* o -*ir*). Se usa como sustantivo en la oración.

Informative writing/Texto informativo. Texto que explica un proceso o una idea. *Ver también Descriptive text.*

Intensifier/Intensificador. Adverbio que refuerza un adjetivo u otro adverbio (*very* important, *quite* easily; *muy* importante, *bastante* fácil).

Interjection/Interjección. Palabra o frase que expresa un sentimiento muy fuerte. La interjección no tiene relación gramatical con las demás palabras de la oración.

Internet/Internet. Red mundial computarizada que permite comunicarse electrónicamente con cualquier computadora de la red para buscar información social, comercial, de investigación y de otro tipo.

Interpretation/Interpretación. Explicación del significado de un texto, de una representación visual o de cualquier otro tipo de comunicación.

Interview/Entrevista. Diálogo a base de preguntas y respuestas cuyo propósito es obtener información actualizada o de expertos.

Intransitive Verb/Verbo intransitivo. *Ver Verb.*

Introduction/Introducción. Sección inicial de un texto en la que el escritor identifica el tema y da la idea general de lo que contendrá el cuerpo del mismo.

Inverted order/Orden invertido. Colocación del predicado antes del sujeto. En la mayoría de las oraciones en inglés, el sujeto va antes del predicado.

Irregular verb/Verbo irregular. *Ver Verb tense.*

Jargon/Jerga. Palabras y frases que usa un determinado grupo.

Journal/Diario. Libreta personal en la que con toda libertad se anotan ideas, pensamientos y experiencias.

Learning log/Registro de aprendizaje. Diario para aclarar ideas sobre conceptos tratados en varias clases.

Lexicon/Léxico. Diccionario.

Listing/Lista. Técnica para generar ideas a partir de las cuales se escribe un texto.

Literary analysis/Análisis literario. Examen de las diferentes partes de una obra literaria a fin de evaluarla.

Logical fallacy/Falacia lógica. Error de razonamiento que se encuentra con frecuencia en publicidad o en escritos persuasivos, como razonamientos con dos alternativas opuestas o generalidades muy llamativas.

Main clause/Proposición principal. *Ver Clause.*

Main idea/Idea principal. *Ver Thesis statement.*

Main verb/Verbo principal. La palabra más importante de una frase verbal.

Media/Medios. Formas de comunicación usadas para llegar a un público. Los periódicos, la radio, la televisión y la Internet llegan a públicos muy grandes, por lo que se conocen como medios de comunicación masiva.

Memoir/Memoria. Tipo de narrativa de no ficción que presenta el relato de un hecho o período de la historia, resaltando la experiencia personal del narrador.

Metaphor/Metáfora. Tropo que compara dos cosas aparentemente distintas sin usar las palabra *like* o *as (como)*. *(Él es una roca.)*

Mood/Atmósfera. Sentimiento o ambiente de un texto escrito.

Multimedia presentation/Presentación multimedia. Uso de una variedad de medios como video, sonido, texto escrito y artes visuales para presentar ideas e información.

Narrative writing/Narrativa. Tipo de escritura que narra sucesos o acciones que cambian con el paso del tiempo; por lo general tiene personajes, escenario y trama.

Nonfiction/No ficción. Texto en prosa acerca de personas, lugares y sucesos reales.

Noun/Nombre (o sustantivo). Palabra que nombra a una persona, lugar, cosa, o a una idea, cualidad o característica.

Noun clause/Proposición nominal. Proposición dependiente que se usa como nombre.

Number/Número. Forma del nombre, pronombre o verbo que indica si se refiere a uno (**singular**) o a más de uno (**plural**).

Object/Objeto. *Ver Complement.*

Onomatopoeia/Onomatopeya. Palabra o frase que imita o sugiere el sonido que describe (*rattle, boom;* en español: *pum, zas*).

Opinion/Opinión. Creencia o actitud; no puede comprobarse si es falsa o verdadera.

Oral tradition/Tradición oral. Literatura que se transmite de boca en boca de una generación a otra. Puede representar los valores culturales de un pueblo.

Order of importance/Orden de importancia. Forma de acomodar los detalles en un párrafo o en otro texto escrito según su importancia.

Organization/Organización. Sistema para ordenar las ideas.

Outline/Esquema. Organización sistemática de ideas principales y secundarias con números romanos, letras y números arábigos para una presentación oral o escrita.

Paragraph/Párrafo. Una unidad de un texto que consta de oraciones relacionadas.

Parallel construction/Construcción paralela. Serie de palabras, frases y oraciones que tienen una forma gramatical similar.

Paraphrase/Parafrasear. Repetir las ideas de otro con palabras diferentes del original pero conservando las ideas, el tono y la longitud general.

Parenthetical documentation/Documentación parentética. Referencia específica a la fuente de la información que se pone entre paréntesis directamente después de ésta.

Participle/Participio. Verboide que se usa como adjetivo. El participio presente siempre termina en *–ing* y el participio pasado por lo general termina en *–ed*.

Peer response/Respuesta de compañeros. Sugerencias y comentarios que dan los compañeros de clase sobre un texto escrito u otro tipo de presentación.

Personal pronoun/Pronombre personal. *Ver Pronoun.*

Personal writing/Escritura personal. Texto que expresa los pensamientos y sentimientos del autor.

Personification/Personificación. Tropo que da cualidades humanas a un animal, objeto o idea.

Perspective/Perspectiva. *Ver Point of view.*

Persuasion/Persuasión. Tipo de escritura encaminado a convencer a pensar o actuar de cierta manera.

Phrase/Frase. Grupo de palabras que forma una unidad en una oración.

> **Prepositional phrase/Frase preposicional.** Comienza con una preposición y termina con un nombre o un pronombre.
> **Verb phrase/Frase verbal.** Consta de uno o más **verbos auxiliares** (*auxiliary verbs*) seguidos del verbo principal.

Plagiarism/Plagio. Presentación deshonesta de palabras o ideas ajenas como si fueran propias.

Plot/Trama. Serie de sucesos en secuencia en un cuento, novela u obra de teatro.

Plural/Plural. *Ver Number.*

Poetry/Poesía. Forma de expresión literaria compuesta por versos. La poesía tradicional contiene un lenguaje emotivo e imaginativo y un ritmo regular.

Point of view/Punto de vista. Ángulo o perspectiva desde el cual se cuenta una historia; por ejemplo, primera o tercera persona.

Portfolio/Portafolio. Colección de varias obras escritas de un estudiante, que puede tener obras terminadas y otras en proceso.

Predicate/Predicado. Verbo o frase verbal y sus modificadores que hacen una afirmación esencial sobre el sujeto de la oración.

Predicate adjective/Adjetivo predicativo. *Ver Adjective.*

Preposition/Preposición. Palabra que muestra la relación de un nombre o pronombre con otra palabra en la oración.

Prepositional phrase/Frase preposicional. *Ver Phrase.*

Presenting/Presentación. Último paso del proceso de escritura que implica compartir con otros lo que se ha escrito.

Present tense/Tiempo presente. *Ver Verb tense.*

Prewriting/Preescritura. Primer paso del proceso de escritura: decidir sobre qué se va a escribir, reunir ideas y detalles, y elaborar un plan para presentar las ideas; usa estrategias como lluvia de ideas, organizadores gráficos, notas y registros.

Prior knowledge/Conocimiento previo. Hechos, ideas y experiencias que un escritor, lector u observador lleva a una nueva actividad.

Progressive form/Durativo. *Ver Verb tense.*

Pronoun/Pronombre. Palabra que va en lugar del nombre; grupo de palabras que funcionan como un nombre u otro pronombre. La palabra o grupo de palabras a que se refiere un pronombre se llama **antecedente** (*antecedent*).
　　Personal pronoun/Pronombre personal. Se refiere a una persona o cosa específica.

Pronoun case/Caso del pronombre. *Ver Case.*

Proofreading/Corrección de pruebas. Último paso del proceso editorial en que se revisa el texto en busca de errores tipográficos y de otra naturaleza.

Propaganda/Propaganda. Información encaminada a influir en los pensamientos o acciones; en general es de naturaleza política y puede distorsionar la verdad.

Proper adjective/Adjetivo propio*. *Ver Adjective.*

Prose/Prosa. Escritura similar al lenguaje cotidiano tanto oral como escrito, a diferencia de la poesía y el teatro.

Publishing/Publicación. Presentación de una obra escrita terminada mediante el uso de la tecnología, para darla a conocer a un público amplio.

Purpose/Finalidad. Objetivo de la escritura: expresar, descubrir, registrar, desarrollar o reflexionar sobre ideas, resolver problemas, entretener, influir, informar o describir.

Regular verb/Verbo regular. *Ver Verb tense.*

Representation/Representación. Forma en que se presenta información o ideas al público.

Research/Investigación. Proceso de localizar información sobre un tema.

Review/Reseña. Análisis e interpretación de un tema presentado por lo general a través de los medios de comunicación masiva.

Revising/Revisión. Paso del proceso de escritura en que el autor repasa el borrador, cambia el contenido, la organización y el estilo para mejorar el texto. Las técnicas de revisión son agregar, elaborar, eliminar, combinar y reacomodar el texto.

Root/Raíz. Parte de una palabra que contiene el significado principal.

Run-on sentence/Oración mal puntuada. Dos o más oraciones o proposiciones seguidas, cuyo significado es confuso debido a su inadecuada puntuación.

S

Sensory details/Detalles sensoriales. Lenguaje que apela a los sentidos; los detalles sensoriales son elementos importantes de la escritura descriptiva, sobre todo en la poesía.

Sentence/Oración. Grupo de palabras que expresa un pensamiento completo. Cada oración tiene **sujeto** (*subject*) y **predicado** (*predicate*). *Ver también Subject; Predicate; Clause.*

> **Simple sentence/Oración simple.** Consta de una proposición principal y no tiene proposiciones subordinadas.
>
> **Compound sentence/Oración compuesta.** Tiene dos o más proposiciones principales, cada una con su propio sujeto y predicado; por lo general van unidas por una coma y una conjunción coordinante, o por un punto y coma.
>
> **Complex sentence/Oración compleja.** Tiene una proposición principal y una o más proposiciones subordinadas.

Sentence variety/Variedad de oraciones. Uso de diferentes tipos de oraciones para agregar interés al texto.

Setting/Escenario. Tiempo y lugar en que ocurren los sucesos de un cuento, novela u obra de teatro.

Simile/Símil. Tropo que compara dos cosas esencialmente distintas, usando las palabras *like* o *as* (como). *(Su pelo era como hilo de seda.)*

Simple predicate/Predicado simple. *Ver Predicate; Sentence; Subject.*

Simple sentence/Oración simple. *Ver Sentence.*

Spatial order/Orden espacial. Forma de presentar los detalles de un escenario según su ubicación: de izquierda a derecha o de arriba hacia abajo.

Standard English/Inglés estándar. La forma más ampliamente usada y aceptada del idioma inglés.

Style/Estilo. Forma en que un escritor elige y organiza las palabras y oraciones.

Subject/Sujeto. Nombre o pronombre principal que informa sobre quién o sobre qué trata la oración.

Subordinate clause/Proposición subordinada. *Ver Clause.*

Summary/Resumen. Breve explicación de la idea principal de una composición.

Supporting evidence/Sustento. *Ver Evidence.*

Suspense/Suspenso. Recurso literario que genera interés y emoción para llegar al clímax o desenlace de una historia. Un escritor crea suspenso al proporcionar pistas sobre el desenlace pero sin revelar demasiada información.

Symbol/Símbolo. Objeto, persona, lugar o experiencia que representa algo más, por lo general, abstracto.

Tense/Tiempo. *Ver Verb tense.*

Theme/Tema. Idea o mensaje principal de una obra escrita.

Thesis statement/Exposición de tesis. Exposición de la **idea principal** o finalidad de una obra en una o dos oraciones.

Time order/Orden temporal. Organización de detalles en un texto escrito según el momento en que ocurrieron.

Tone/Tono. Reflejo de la actitud del escritor o hablante hacia un sujeto.

Topic sentence/Oración temática. Oración que expresa la idea principal de un párrafo.

Transition/Transición. Palabra o frase de enlace que aclara las relaciones entre los detalles, oraciones o párrafos.

U-V

Unity/Unidad. Integridad de un párrafo o composición; coherencia entre todas las oraciones o párrafos para expresar o sustentar una idea principal.

URL/URL. Forma estándar de una dirección de Internet. (Son iniciales de *Uniform Resource Locator.*)

Venn diagram/Diagrama de Venn. Organizador gráfico que consta de dos círculos que se traslapan, usado para comparar dos cosas con características comunes y diferentes.

Verb/Verbo. Palabra que expresa acción o estado y que es necesaria para hacer una afirmación.

Verbal/Verboide. Forma del verbo que funciona como nombre, adjetivo o adverbio en la oración. Los verboides son: participio *(participles)*, gerundio *(gerunds)* e infinitivo *(infinitives)*.

Verb phrase/Frase verbal. *Ver Phrase.*

Verb tense/Tiempo verbal. El tiempo de un verbo indica cuándo ocurre la acción.

Present tense/Presente. Indica una acción que sucede regularmente.

Past tense/Pasado. Indica una acción que ya sucedió.

Future tense/Futuro. Indica una acción que va a suceder.

En inglés todos los tiempos verbales están formados por las cuatro partes principales del verbo: **base derivativa** *(base form)* *(freeze, congelar)*, **participio presente** *(present participle)* *(freezing, congelando)*, **pretérito simple** *(simple past form)* *(froze, congeló)* y **participio pasado** *(past participle)* *(frozen, congelado)*.

Un **verbo regular** *(regular verb)* forma su pretérito simple y su participio pasado agregando la terminación *ed* al infinitivo. Los verbos que forman su pretérito y participio pasado de otra forma se llaman **verbos irregulares** *(irregular verbs)*.

Además de los tiempos presente, pasado y futuro hay tres tiempos perfectos: **presente perfecto** *(present perfect)*, **pretérito perfecto** *(past perfect)* y **futuro perfecto** *(future perfect)*.

Cada uno de los seis tiempos tiene una forma **durativa** *(progressive form)* que expresa acción continua.

Voice/Voz. Uso del lenguaje que transmite al lector la personalidad del escritor o narrador. La estructura de la oración, la elección de las palabras y el tono son elementos que comunican la voz.

Web site/Sitio Web. Sitio de World Wide Web que puede ser alcanzado mediante vínculos o una dirección Web o URL. *Ver también URL; World Wide Web.*

Word processing/Procesador de palabras. Programa de computadora para escribir y editar un texto.

World Wide Web/World Wide Web. Sistema global que usa Internet y permite a los usuarios crear, vincularse y entrar a campos de información. *Ver también Internet.*

Writing process/Proceso de escritura. Serie de pasos o etapas por los que atraviesa un escritor para desarrollar sus ideas y comunicarlas.

*Este término o explicación solamente se aplica a la gramática inglesa.

INDEX

U

Underlining. *See* Italics
Understood subject, 572
Unity, 71, 821
URL, 655, 791, 821
Usage, special problems in, 559, 561, 563
Usage items, on standardized tests, 725–726
Using Computers
  bold typeface feature, 15
  column option, 179
  creating vocabulary fields, 133
  cut and paste options, 77
  e-mail collaboration on, 85
  drawing on, 137
  graphic function, 209
  inserting pictures, 281
  invisible writing on, 57
  library catalog on, 229
  organizing prewriting notes on, 61
  outlining feature on, 237
  researching the Internet, 167
  revising on, 69, 285
  spell checking on, 81, 233
  underlining on, 15
  word processing program, 171
  writing poetry on, 27

V

Variety, in sentences, 74–76, 820
Venn diagrams, 211, 213, 244, 821.
  See also Graphic organizers
Verb phrases, 411, 527, 529, 531, 818–819
Verb tense, 821
  base form, 821
  consistency in, 116, 280
  future, 417, 821
  future perfect, 417
  past, 409, 821
  past perfect, 415
  present, 409, 821
  present perfect, 415
  Troubleshooter for, 318–319
Verbals, 821
  diagraming, 580–581
  gerunds and gerund phrases, 529, 580

infinitives and infinitive phrases, 531, 581
participles and participial phrases, 527, 601
Verbs
  action, 401, 403, 405
  active voice of, 419
  agreement with subject, 314–317, 541, 543, 549
  choosing precise, 124
  and complement, 407
  conjugating, 409, 411, 413, 415, 541
  definition of, 363, 821
  with indirect objects, 405
  helping, 411
  intransitive, 403
  irregular, 421, 423, 821
  linking, 407
  main, 411, 817
  passive voice of, 419
  past progressive form of, 413
  present progressive form of, 413
  principal parts of, 411
  regular, 411, 821
  simple predicate, 363
  transitive, 403
Videotapes, 656
Viewing and Representing, 15, 23, 49, 53, 57, 65, 81, 85, 121, 125, 137, 163, 167, 175, 179, 205, 217, 241, 269, 277, 293, 778–787
Visual messages, 778–783
  composition, 779–782
  film, 781
  mass media, 778
  motion pictures, 781
  political cartoons, 781
  values, 778
  visual design, 779–782
Vocabulary
  borrowed words in, 664–666
  context clues in, 668–669
  prefixes in, 672
  roots in, 671
  slang in, 283
  on standardized tests, 723
  suffixes in, 673–674
  See also Words
Voice
  active, 419
  passive, 419
  tone in, 821

W

Weather, whether, 692
Web site, 791–792, 796, 797, 821
Webbing. *See* Clustering
Webmaster, 791
Where at, 563
Whether, weather, 695
Who, whom, 414
Who's, whose, 563
Wood, would, 680
Word parts
  prefixes, 672
  roots, 671
  suffixes, 673
Word processing, 821
Words
  apostrophes to form plural of, 611
  borrowed, 664–666, 667
  clichés, 670
  coined, 667
  compound, 667, 686
  double duty, 681
  idioms, 678
  obsolete, 675
  often confused, 559, 561, 563, 680, 692
  often misspelled, 691
  prefixes for, 672
  pronunciation, 659, 690
  roots, 671
  suffixes for, 673–674
  See also Vocabulary
Work plans, 341–344
  appearance, 341, 343
  parts, 344
  purpose, 341
  style, 343
  types, 341–342
World Wide Web, 655, 790–797, 804–805, 821
  for prewriting, 101
Writing about art, 19, 49, 65, 73, 117, 129, 175, 245, 269, 297
Writing about literature
  book review, 294–297
  comparing two poems, 242–245
  describing subject of biography, 134–137
  narrative, 180–183
  responding in journal, 24–27
Writing across the curriculum. *See* Cross-curricular writing

Y

ACKNOWLEDGMENTS

Text

UNIT ONE Reprinted by permission of Simon & Schuster, from *The Lost Garden* by Laurence Yep. Copyright © 1991 by Laurence Yep.

"Jukebox Showdown" by Victor Hernandez Cruz. Copyright © 1976 by Victor Hernandez Cruz. Reprinted by permission of Random House, Inc.

From *Living Up the Street: Narrative Reflections* by Gary Soto. Copyright © 1985 by Gary Soto. Reprinted by permission of the author.

UNIT TWO "The Game" from *Fast Sam, Cool Clyde, and Stuff* by Walter Dean Myers. Copyright © 1975 by Walter Dean Myers. Reprinted by permission of Viking Penguin, a division of the Penguin Putnam.

UNIT THREE From *How the García Girls Lost Their Accents*. Copyright © 1991 by Julia Alvarez. Published by Plume, an imprint of Dutton Signet, a division of Penguin USA, Inc., and originally in hardcover by Algonquin Books of Chapel Hill. Reprinted by permission of Susan Bergholz Literary Services, New York. All rights reserved.

From *Thrashin' Time* by David Weitzman. Copyright © 1991 by David Weitzman. Reprinted by permission of David R. Godine, Publisher, Inc.

UNIT FOUR From *Lyddie* by Katherine Paterson. Copyright © 1991 by Katherine Paterson. Reprinted by permission of Penguin Putnam, Inc.

UNIT FIVE "Fall" by Sally Andersen from *A New Treasury of Children's Poetry: Old Favorites and New Discoveries* edited by Joanna Cole. Copyright © 1984 by Joanna Cole. Published by Doubleday & Company.

"The Vision of Maya Ying Lin" from *Always to Remember* by Brent Ashabranner. Copyright © 1988. Reprinted by permission of Penguin Putnam.

UNIT SIX From *Silent Spring* by Rachel Carson. Copyright © 1978. Reprinted by permission of Houghton Mifflin Company. All rights reserved.

Photo

Cover KS Studios; **vi** Art Wise; **vii viii** PhotoDisc, Inc; **ix** (t)PhotoDisc, Inc., (b)Allan Landau; **x** Hampton University Museum; **xi** Greg Probst/Allstock; **xii** (t)Art Wise, (b)Cathlyn Mellon/Tony Stone Images; **xiii** (t)Historical Pictures/Stock Montage, (b)PhotoDisc, Inc; **xiv** Tom McCarthy/PhotoEdit; **xv** (1)courtesy Brookfield Zoo, (r)file photo; **xvi** (t)Art Wise, (b)PhotoDisc, Inc; **xvii** (t)PhotoDisc, Inc., (b)Phillip Evergood. *Lily and the Sparrow*, 1939. Oil on composition board, 30 x 24 in. (72.6cm x 61cm). Collection of the Whitney Museum of American Art. Purchase 41.42; **xviii** (t)courtesy Nereyda Garcia-Ferraz, (b)Artville; **xx** Faith Ringgold; **xxi** PhotoDisc, Inc; **xxii** (t)Art Wise, (b)Digital Stock; **xxiii** (t)PhotoDisc, Inc., (b)courtesy Anthony Ortega; **xxiv** file photo; **xxv** courtesy Bernice Steinbaum Gallery; **xxvi** R. Fukuhara/Westlight; **xxii-1** Christie's Images/SuperStock; **2-3** Michael A. Keller/The Stock Market; **5 6** Laurence Yep; **8 9 10** Allan Landau; **11** Leonard Von Matt/Buochs Switzerland; **12** Allan Landau; **16 18** Art Wise; **20** CORBIS; **24** Courtesy Ray Vinella; **26** Allan Landau; **28** Tony Freeman/PhotoEdit; **32** Agricultural Research Service, USDA; **33** Courtesy Susan Moore; **35** Courtesy Anthony Ortega; **36** Agricultural Research Service, USDA **39** Michael A. Keller/The Stock Market; **40-41** Mark Douet/Tony Stone Images; **43** Courtesy Kurtis Productions, Ltd; **46** Art Wise **49** Courtesy Claes Oldenberg Studio; **50** Art Wise; **53** Collection of the Grand Rapids Art Museum. Gift of Mrs. Cyrus E. Perkins; **54 56 58** Art Wise; **62** Jeff Dunn/Stock Boston; **64** Larry Kolvoord/The Image Works; **65** Located in San Francisco at the Pacific Stock Exchange; **66** Art Wise; **70** (l)Barbara Alper/Stock Boston, (r)Charles Fell/Stock Boston; **73** The Jamison Galleries, Santa Fe NM; **74 78** Art Wise; **80** THE FAR SIDE, FARWORKS, INC. Used by permission. All Rights Reserved; **82 84** Art Wise; **86** Tom McCarthy/PhotoEdit; **89** Glennon Donohue/Tony Stone Images; **90 91** file photo; **92** Red Grooms/ARS; **96** Mark Douet/Tony Stone Images; **108-109** Jack Dykinga/Tony Stone Images; **110** Tad Merrick; **111 112** Ralph J. Brunke; **114** Larry Kolvoord/The Image Works; **115** Robert Frerck/Odyssey Productions, Chicago; **117** Courtesy American Federation of the Arts; **118** St. Louis Art Museum; **119 122** Allan Landau; **123** (l)Cindy Brodie, (r)Alex Murdoch; **126** Erich Lessing/Art Resource, NY; **129** Courtesy Nancy Hoffman Gallery; **130** Allan Landau; **134** Bettmann/CORBIS; **136** Princeton University Library; **138** Bob Daemmrich/The Image Works; **143** From *Thrashin' Time: Harvest Days in the Dakotas* ©1991 by David Weitzman. Reprinted by permission of David R. Godine, Publisher, Inc; **145** The Metropolitan Museum of Art, George A. Hearn Fund, 1943; **149** Jack Dykinga/ Tony Stone Images; **150-151** The Purcell Team/CORBIS; **152 153 154** Tom Green; **156** Hampton University Museum; **157** CORBIS; **160** Art Wise; **162** Naper Settlement Village Museum; **164** Vernon Merritt/Black Star; **165** Focus on Sports; **168** Robert Miller Gallery, New York; **171** Courtesy Hughie Lee-Smith; **172** Courtesy June Kelly Gallery, New York, photo by Manu Sassoonian; **174** Giraudon/ Art Resource, NY; **176** Neal Hamburg; **178** Focus on Sports; **180** (t)CORBIS, (b)Joe Viesti/Viesti and Associates; **182** David Young-Wolff/PhotoEdit; **184** Tom Prettyman/PhotoEdit; **189** Erich Lessing/Art Resource, NY; **191** Manchester City Art Galleries; **195** The Purcell Team/CORBIS; **196-197** Owen Franken/CORBIS; **198** Courtesy Gary McLain; **199** Greg Probst/Allstock; **200** (l)Courtesy Cherokee Historical Association, (c)Stephen Trimble, (r)Art Wise; **202** Clark Mishler/Alaska Stock Images; **206** Art Wise; **207** The Museum of Fine Arts, Houston. Museum purchase with funds provided by Panhandle Eastern Corporation; **208** CORBIS; **210 214** Art Wise; **218** Edith G. Haun/Stock Boston; **219** Culver Pictures; **222 224** Jim Pickerell/The Image Works; **226** William Lishman & Associates **230** Art Wise; **234** CALVIN AND HOBBES ©1990 Watterson. Reprinted with permission of Universal Press Syndicate. All rights reserved; **238** Sharon Hoogstraten; **242** Jack Wilburn/ Animals Animals; **246** Holt Confer/The Image Works; **249** Tom Wurl/Stock Boston; **251** Bill Barley/SuperStock; **255** David M. Doody/Uniphoto; **259** Owen Franken/CORBIS; **260-261** W. Perry Conway/CORBIS; **262** Art Wise; **263** Courtesy Indira Freitas Johnson; **264** (t)Courtesy Indira Freitas Johnson, (b)Ralph Brunke; **266** Historical Pictures/Stock Montage; **268** David Young-Wolff/PhotoEdit; **269** Courtesy Bernice Steinbaum Gallery; **270** (t)Leonard Lee Rue III/Stock Boston, (b)Herb Snitzer/Stock

Boston; **276** Art Wise; **278** CALVIN AND HOBBES ©1986 Watterson. Reprinted with permission of United Press Syndicate. All rights reserved; **279** Art Wise; **282** R. Fukuhara/Corbis Los Angeles; **286** Courtesy Brookfield Zoo; **288** Art Wise; **289** Faith Ringgold; **290** Art Wise; **291** Mitchell B. Reibel/Sports Photo Masters, Inc; **292 294** Art Wise; **296** Alain Le Garsmeur/Tony Stone Images; **297** U.S. Department of The Interior/Indian Arts and Crafts Board/Southern Plains Indian Museum and Crafts Center; **298** Peter Menzel/Stock Boston; **301** Dean Abramson/Stock Boston; **303** Phyllis Kind Gallery, New York/Chicago; **307** W. Perry Conway/CORBIS; **308-309** Charles E. Rotkin/CORBIS; **356 357** Hamish MacEwan/SuperStock; **359** Courtesy Museum of Fine Arts, Boston. Gift of W.G. Russell Allen; **377** Courtesy Nancy Hoffman Gallery, New York; **389** Myrleen Ferguson/PhotoEdit; **397** Henri Matisse, *La Negresse*, Ailsa Mellon Bruce Fund, © 1992 National Gallery of Art, Washington, 1952. Collage on canvas/paper collage on canvas, 4.539" x 6.233"; **401** Rhonda Sidney/Stock Boston; **431 453** Phyllis Kind Gallery, New York/Chicago; **469** Dennis Stock/Magnum; **478** The Metropolitan Museum of Art, Fletcher Fund, Rogers Fund, and Bequest of Miss Adelaide Milton de Groot (1876-1967) by exchange, supplemented by gifts from Friends of the Museum, 1971. **491** Joan Messerschmidt/Leo de Wys; **493** Julie Houck/Tony Stone Images; **501** Courtesy the artist and Deson Saunders Gallery, Chicago; **511** Focus on Sports; **523** National Museum of American Art, Washington D.C./Art Resource, NY; **538** Paul Macapia/Seattle Art Museum; **545** (t)Jon Riley/Tony Stone Images, (b)David Young-Wolff/PhotoEdit; **556** Phyliss Kind Gallery, New York/Chicago; **567** Giraudon/Art Resource, NY; **596** Robert Henri, *Portrait of Po Tse (Water Eagle)* Oil on Canvas, 40 x 32 inches. Courtesy Gerald Peters Gallery, Santa Fe NM; **626** Henri Matisse, French, 1869-1954, *Interior at Nice*, oil on canvas, 1921, 132.1 x 88.9 cm, Charles H. and Mary F.S. Worcester Collection; **638–639** Philadelphia Museum of Art/CORBIS; **641** Allan Landau; **642** Cathy Ferris; **651 653** Allan Landau; **658 659 661** file photo; **664** Frank Oberle/Photo Resource; **665** Bob Daemmrich/Stock Boston; **666** Richard Pasley/Stock Boston; **667 through 690** (gears)VCG/FPG; **675** Steve Bentsen/Natural Selection; **676** Lori Adamski Peek/Tony Stone Images; **677** (t)George Chan/Tony Stone Images, (b)Pete Seaward/Tony Stone Images; **681** David Young-Wolff/PhotoEdit; **695** Ralph Brunke; **771** Billy E. Barnes/Stock Boston; **778** Geoff Butler; **781** (t)Rosemary Calvert/Tony Stone Images, (b)Art Wolfe/Tony Stone Images; **783** Toles ©1999 The Buffalo News. Reprinted with permission of Universal Press Syndicate. All rights reserved. (b)Paul Szep/Boston Globe; **784** Movie Still Archives; **787** SuperStock; **789** (l)file photo, (r)Doug Martin; **799** file photo.